BRADFORD'S
CROSSWORD
SOLVER'S
DICTIONARY

BRADFORD'S CROSSWORD SOLVER'S DICTIONARY

Collins

HarperCollins Publishers
Westerhill Road
Bishopbriggs
Glasgow
G64 2QT
Great Britain

Seventh Edition 2007

First edition published by
Longman; second, third and fourth
editions published by Peter Collin
Publishing Ltd

ISBN 978-0-00-725359-3

Collins® is a registered trademark of
HarperCollins Publishers Limited

www.collins.co.uk

A catalogue record for this book is
available from the British Library

Technical support and typesetting
by Thomas Callan

Printed and bound in Germany by
Bercker

Contents

Author's Preface

It is hard to believe that 50 years have flown by since I started reversing the standard dictionary in order to have easier access to crossword solutions. This has truly been my life's work yet the fascination is as strong as ever. What a delight when reading a dictionary definition to come across a totally unexpected meaning tucked in there – the equivalent, I feel sure, to the thrill a treasure seeker must get when the metal detector changes tone.

This 7th edition includes further sections listed by word-length, and hopefully will encourage confidence in users to attempt ever more complicated puzzles. You have my word for it!

My thanks, as ever, to my supporters at Collins, and beyond.

Anne R. Bradford *2007*

Solving Crossword Clues

Crossword puzzles tend to be basically 'quick' or 'cryptic'. A 'quick' crossword usually relies on a one- or two-word clue which is a simple definition of the answer required. Many words have different meanings, so that the clue 'ball' could equally well lead to the answer 'sphere', 'orb', or 'dance'. The way to solve 'quick' crosswords is to press on until probable answers begin to interlink, which is a good sign that you are on the right track.

'Cryptic' crosswords are another matter. Here the clue usually consists of a basic definition, given at either the beginning or end of the clue, together with one or more definitions of parts of the answer. Here are some examples taken from all-time favourites recorded over the years:

1. *'Tradesman who bursts into tears'* (**Stationer**)

    Tradesman is a definition of stationer. *Bursts* is cleverly used as an indication of an anagram, which *into tears* is of stationer.

2. *'Sunday school tune'* (**Strain**)

    Here *Sunday* is used to define its abbreviation S, *school* is a synonym for train, and put together they give strain, which is a synonym of *tune*.

3. *'Result for everyone when head gets at bottom'* (**Ache**)
   (used as a 'down' clue)

    This is what is known as an '& lit' clue, meaning that the setter has hit on a happy composition which could literally be true. *Everyone* here is a synonym for each, move the *head* (first letter) of the word to the *bottom*, and the answer is revealed, the whole clue being the definition of the answer in this case.

4. *'Tin out East'* (**Sen**)

    In this example, *tin*, implying 'money', requires its chemical symbol Sn to go *out*(side) *East*, or its abbreviation, E, the whole clue being a definition of a currency (sen) used in the East.

5. *'Information given to communist in return for sex'* (**Gender**)

   Information can be defined as gen; *communist* is almost always red, *in return* indicates 'reversed', leading to gen-der, a synonym for *sex*.

6. *'Row about no enclosure of this with sardines'* (**Tin-opener**)

   Row is a synonym for tier, *about* indicates 'surrounding', *no enclosure* can be no pen, leading to ti-no pen-er, and another '& lit' clue.

7. *'Cake-sandwiches-meat, at Uncle Sam's party'* (**Clambake**)

   Meat here is lamb, *sandwiches* is used as a verb, so we have C-lamb-ake, which is a kind of party in America. *Uncle Sam* or US is often used to indicate America.

8. *'Initially passionate meeting of boy and girl could result in it'* (**Pregnancy**)

   Initially is usually a sign of a first letter, in this case 'p' for *passionate* + Reg (a *boy*) and Nancy (a *girl*), and another clever '& lit'.

With 'cryptic' clues the solver needs to try to analyse the parts to see what he or she is looking for – which word or words can be the straight definition, and which refer to the parts or hint at anagrams or other subterfuges. Whilst it would be unrealistic to claim total infallibility, practice has shown that in most crosswords some 90% of the answers are to be found in this work.

Anne R. Bradford

How to use the Dictionary

This dictionary is the result of over fifty years' analysis of some 300,000 crossword clues, ranging from plain 'quick' crosswords requiring only synonyms to the different level of cryptic puzzles. Therefore the words listed at each entry may be connected to the keyword in various ways, such as:

- a straightforward synonym

- a commonly-associated adjective

- an associated or proper noun

- a pun or other devious play on words

Keywords are listed alphabetically; in cases where the heading consists of more than one word, the first of these words is taken to be the keyword, and in cases where the end of a word is bracketed, the material up to the opening bracket is taken to be the keyword. Keywords marked with the symbol ▶ refer the user to other entries where additional information may be found. Keywords marked with the symbol ▷ give leads to anagrams and other ploys used by crossword setters. If the keywords found in the clue do not lead directly to the required answer, the solver should look under words given as cross-references to other entries. These are indicated by the symbol →, with the cross-referenced word shown in capitals.

Some additional entries have been divided into two parts – a general entry similar to the standard entries which appear elsewhere, and a panel entry which contains a list of more specific or encyclopedic material. So, for example, the entry 'Artist(ic)' includes not only a list of general words connected with 'Artist' or 'Artistic' in some way, such as 'Bohemian', 'Cubist', 'Fine' and 'Virtuoso', but also a panel with the heading 'Artists' containing a list of the names of specific artists, such as 'Bellini', 'Constable', and 'Rembrandt'. For added help, the words in these panels are arranged by length, with all three-letter words grouped together in alphabetical order, then all four-letter words, then all five-letter words, and so on.

About the Author

Anne Bradford's love of words began to make itself evident even in her schooldays, when, as Head Girl of her school, she instituted a novel punishment – instead of making rulebreakers write lines, she had them write out pages from a dictionary, on the grounds that this was a more useful exercise. Little did she know this was soon to be her own daily routine!

In time, crosswords became a magnificent obsession for Anne. All lovers of crosswords can understand the irresistible lure of solving them, but Anne's interest went much deeper than most people's, and when she stopped work in 1957 to have her first child, she found herself starting to note down answers to particularly tricky clues as an aid to memory, in case she should come across them again in another puzzle. It was from this simple beginning that this crossword dictionary evolved.

Over the space of 25 years, Anne continued to build on her collection of solutions, analysing every crossword clue as she solved it and adding it to her steadily growing bank of entries. This unique body of material eventually reached such proportions that she had the idea of offering it to her fellow crossword-solvers as a reference book, and since then, the book has gone from strength to strength, providing valuable help to countless cruciverbalists over a number of editions.

Anne Bradford continues to devote time each day to solving crosswords, averaging some 20 a week – both quick and cryptic – and still avidly collects new solutions for her *Crossword Solver's Dictionary* at a rate of around 150 a week, compiling each solution by hand (without the use of a computer!). This latest edition therefore includes much new material, gleaned by a true crossword lover who not only solves crosswords but, as an active member of the Crossword Club, can offer the user an insight into the mind of a cunning crossword compiler.

The Crossword Club

If you are interested in crosswords, you might like to consider joining the Crossword Club. Membership is open to all who enjoy tackling challenging crosswords and who appreciate the finer points of clue-writing and grid-construction. The Club's magazine, Crossword, contains two prize puzzles each month. A sample issue and full details are available on request.

The Crossword Club
Coombe Farm
Awbridge
Romsey, Hants.
SO51 0HN
UK

email: bh@thecrosswordclub.co.uk
website address: www.thecrosswordclub.co.uk

Aa

A, An Ack, Adult, Ae, Alpha, Angstrom, Are, Argon, D, Ein, Her, If, L, One, Per, They
A1 Tiptop
AA Milne
Aardvark Ant-bear, Ant-eater, Earth-hog, Ground-hog
Aaron's Rod Hagtaper
Aba, Abba Patriarch
Abacus Counter, Soroban
Abaft Astern, Sternson
Abalone Ormer, Paua, Perlemoen
Abandon(ed), Abandonment Abdicate, Abnegate, Abort, Adrift, Amoral,
   Apostasy, Back down, Cade, Cancel, Castaway, Corrupt, Decommission, Defect,
   Derelict, → **DESERT**, Desuetude, Discard, Disown, Dissolute, Ditch, Drop, Dump,
   Elan, Evacuate, Expose, Flagrant, Forhoo(ie), Forhow, Forlend, Forsake, Gomorra,
   Immoral, Jack(-in), Jettison, Jilt, Leave, Loose, Louche, Maroon, Old, Orgiastic,
   Profligate, Quit, Rakish, Rat, Relinquish, Renounce, Reprobate, Scrap, Shed, Sink,
   Strand, Vacate, Waive, Wanton, Yield
Abase Degrade, Demean, Disgrace, Grovel, → **HUMBLE**, Kowtow, Lessen
Abash Daunt, Discountenance, Mortify
Abate(ment) Allay, Appal, Decrescent, Defervescence, Diminish, Let up, Lyse, Lysis,
   Moderate, Reduce, Remit, → **SUBSIDE**
▷ **Abate** *may indicate* a contention
Abattoir Knackery, Slaughterhouse
Abbey Abbacy, Bath, Buckfast, Cloister, Downside, Fonthill, Fountains, Glastonbury,
   Györ, Je(r)vaulx, Medmenham, Melrose, Minster, Nightmare, Northanger, Priory,
   Rievaulx, Tintern, Westminster, Whitby, Woburn
Abbot Aelfric, Archimandrite, Brother, Friar
Abbreviate, Abbreviation Abridge, Ampersand, Compendium, Condense, Curtail,
   → **SHORTEN**, Sigla
ABC Absey
Abdicate, Abdication Cede, Demission, Disclaim, Disown, Resign
Abdomen Belly, C(o)eliac, Epigastrium, Gaster, Hypochondrium, Opisthosoma,
   Paunch, Pleon, → **STOMACH**, Tummy, Venter
Abduct(ed), Abduction Enlèvement, Kidnap, Rapt, Ravish, Shanghai, Steal
Aberdeen Granite City
Aberrant, Aberration Abnormal, Aye-aye, Deviant, Idolon, Perverse
Abet(tor) Aid, Back, Candle-holder, Second
Abeyance, Abeyant Dormant, Shelved, Sleeping, Store
Abhor(rent) → **DETEST**, Execrable, → **HATE**, Loathe, Odious, Shun
Abide Adhere, Dwell, Inhere, → **LAST**, Lie, Live, Observe, Remain, Stand, Tarry
Abigail Maid, Masham
Ability Aptitude, Calibre, Capacity, Cocum, → **COMPETENCE**, Efficacy, ESP, Facility,

Faculty, Ingine, Initiative, Instinct, Lights, Potential, Power, Prowess, Savey, Savoir-faire, Savv(e)y, Skill, Talent

Abject Base, Craven, Grovel, Humble, Servile, Slave

Abjure Eschew, Forswear, Recant, Renege, Reny

Ablaze Afire, Ardent

Able Ablins, Accomplished, → **ADEPT**, Aiblins, Apt, Capable, → **COMPETENT**, Fere, Literate, Proficient, Seaman, Yibbles

Abnormal(ity) Anomalous, Atypical, → **DEVIANT**, Dysfunction, Ectopic, Erratic, Etypical, Freakish, Malocclusion, Odd, Peloria, Preternatural, → **QUEER**, Sport, Teras, Trisome, Unnatural, Varus

Aboard On

Abode Domicile, Dwelling, Habitat, → **HOME**, Lain, Libken, Limbo, Midgard, Remain, Seat

Abolish, Abolition(ist) Annihilate, Annul, Axe, → **BAN**, D, Delete, Destroy, Eradicate, Erase, Extirpate, John Brown, Nullify, Repeal, Rescind, Wilberforce

Abomasum Read

Abominable, Abominate, Abomination Bane, Cursed, → **HATE**, Nefandous, Nefast, Revolting, Snowman, Vile, Yeti

Aboriginal, Aborigine Adivasi, Ainu, Aranda, Autochthon, Binghi, Boong, Buck, Bushmen, Carib, Evolué, Fringe-dweller, Gin, Gurindji, Indigenous, Jacky(-Jacky), Kamilaroi, Kipper, Koori, Lubra, Maori, Mary, Motu, Myall, Pintubi, Pitjant(jat)jara, Pre-Dravidian, Sakai, San, Sican, Siwash, Truganini, Vedda(h), Warlpiri, Yupik

Abort(ion), Abortive Apiol, Cancel, Ecbolic, Miscarry, Moon-calf, Slip, Sooterkin, Teras, Termination

Abound(ing) Bristle, Copious, Enorm, Overflow, Rife, Swarm, Teem

About A, Almost, Anent, Around, C, Ca, Circa, Circiter, Concerning, Encompass, Environs, Going, Near, Of, On, Over, Re, Regarding, Soon at

▷ **About** *may indicate* one word around another

Above Abune, Aforementioned, Aloft, Over, Overhead, Overtop, Owre, Sopra, Superior, Supra-, Suspicion, Upon

Abracadabra Cantrip, Heypass

Abrade, Abrasive Carbanado, Carborundum®, Chafe, Emery, Erode, File, Garnet paper, → **GRATE**, Rub, Sand, Scrape, Scrat, Scuff

Abraham Lincoln, Patriarch, Urite

Abreast Alongside, Au courant, Au fait, Beside, Level, Up

Abridge(ment) Audley, Compress, Condense, Cut, Digest, Dock, Epitome, Pot, Shorten, Trim

Abroad Afield, Away, Distant, Forth, Offshore, Out, Overseas

▷ **Abroad** *may indicate* an anagram

Abrogate Abolish, Repeal, Replace

▷ **Abrupt** *may indicate* a shortened word

Abrupt(ly) Bold, Brusque, Curt, Gruff, Offhand, Premorse, Prerupt, Short, Staccato, Terse

Abscess Gumboil, Impost(h)ume, Ulcer, Warble

Abscond Absquatulate, Decamp, Desert, Elope, Flee, Leg-bail, Levant, Skase, Welch

Abseil(ing) Dulfer, Rappel, Roping-down

Absence, Absent(ee), Absent-minded(ness) Abs, Abstracted, Away, Distant, Distracted, Distrait, Exeat, Exile, Hookey, Malingerer, Missing, Mitch, Sabbatical, Scatty, Skip, Truant, Vacuity, Void, Wanting, Wool-gathering

Absinthe Wormwood

Absolute(ly) Bang, Complete, Dead, Deep-dyed, Downright, Fairly, Implicit,

Ipso facto, Just, Meer, Mere, Mondo, Nominative, Plenary, Plumb, Quite, Real, Sheer, Total, Truly, Unconditional, Unmitigated, Unqualified, Utter, Veritable, Very

Absolve, Absolution Acquit, Assoil, Assoilzie, Clear, Exculpate, Excuse, Pardon, Shrive

Absorb(ed), Absorbent, Absorbing, Absorption Assimilate, Autism, Blot, Consume, Desiccant, Devour, Digest, Dope, Drink, → ᴇɴɢʀᴏss, Enrapt, Imbibe, Ingest, Intent, Merge(r), Occlude, Occupy, Osmosis, Porous, Preoccupation, Preoccupied, Rapt, Sorbefacient, Spongy, Unputdownable

Absquatulate Skedaddle

Abstain(er), Abstemious, Abstinence, Abstinent Band of Hope, Celibacy, Chastity, Continent, Desist, Eschew, Forbear, Forgo, Maigre, Nazarite, Nephalism, Pioneer, Rechab(ite), Refrain, Resist, Sober, Temperate, TT

Abstract(ed), Abstraction Abrege, Abridge, Academic, Appropriate, Brief, Deduct, Digest, Discrete, Distrait, Epitome, Essence, Metaphysical, Musing, Notional, Précis, Preoccupied, Prepossessed, Prescind, Remove, Resumé, Reverie, Stable, Steal, Summary, Syllabus, Tachism

Abstruse Arcane, Deep, Esoteric, Obscure, Recondite

Absurd(ity) Alician, Apagoge, Fantastic, Farcical, Folly, Inept, Irrational, Laputan, Ludicrous, Madness, Nonsense, Paradox, Preposterous, Ridiculous, Silly, Solecism, Stupid, Toshy, Whim-wham

Abundance, Abundant A-gogo, Ample, Aplenty, Bounty, Copious, Excess, Flood, Flush, Fouth, Fowth, Fruitful, Galore, Lashings, Lavish, Mickle, Mine, Mint, Muckle, Oodles, Oodlins, Opulent, Over, Plenitude, Plenteous, → ᴘʟᴇɴᴛɪғᴜʟ, Plenty, Pleroma, Plethora, Plurisie, Profusion, Prolific, Relative, Replete, Rich, Rife, Routh, Rowth, Sonce, Sonse, Store, Stouth and routh, Surfeit, Tallents, Teeming, Tons, Uberous

Abuse, Abusive Assail, Becall, Billingsgate, Blackguard, Chemical, Cruelty, Flak, Fustilarian, Fustil(l)irian, Hail, Ill-treat, Insult, Invective, Jobbery, Limehouse, Malpractice, Maltreat, Miscall, → ᴍɪsᴛʀᴇᴀᴛ, Misuse, Mofo, Obloquy, Opprobrium, Philippic, Rail, Rampallian, Rate, Rayle, Revile, Ritual, Satanic, Satire, Scarab(ee), Scurrilous, Serve, Sexual, Slang, Slate, Sledging, Snash, Solvent, Strap, Substance, Thersitical, Tirade, Vilify, Violate, Vituperation

Abut Adjoin, Border, Touch

Abysm(al), Abyss Avernus, Barathrum, Barranca, Chasm, Deep, Gulf, Swallet, Tartarean, Tartarus

AC Current, Erk

Acacia Bablah, Boree, Brigalow, Eumong, Eumung, Gidgee, Gidjee, Koa, Mimosa, Mulga, Myall, Sallee, Shittim, Wattle

Academic(ian) A, Acca, Acker, Della-Cruscan, Don, Erudite, Fellow, Hypothetic(al), Immortals, Literati, Master, Pedantic, PRA, Prof(essor), RA, Reader, Rector

Academy, Academic Athenaeum, Dollar, Donnish, French, Loretto, Lyceum, Military, Naval, Royal, St Cyr, Sandhurst, School, Seminary, The Shop, West Point

Acanthus Blankursine, Ruellia

Accelerate, Acceleration, Accelerator Antedate, Betatron, Bevatron, Collider, Cosmotron, Cyclotron, Festinate, G, Gal, Grav, Gun, Hasten, Increase, Linac, Linear, Rev, Signatron, Speed, Stringendo, Synchrotron

Accent(ed), Accentuate Acute, Beat, Breve, Brogue, Bur(r), Circumflex, Cut-glass, Doric, Drawl, Enclitic, Enhance, Gammat, Grave, Hacek, Intonation, Kelvinside, Long, Macron, Marcato, Martelé, Mockney, Morningside, Mummerset, Nasal, Orthotone, Oxford, Oxytone, Paroxytone, Perispomenon, Pitch, Primary, Proparoxytone, Rhythm, Secondary, Stress, Tittle, Tone, Tonic, Twang

Accentor Dunnock

Accept(able), Acceptance, Accepted A, Accede, Admit, Adopt, Agree, Allow, Approbate, Bar, Believe, Buy, Can-do, Common, Consent, Cool, Cosher, Decent, Done, Embrace, Grant, Idee recue, Kosher, Meet, Obey, On, Pocket, Putative, Resipiscence, Settle, Stand, Suppose, Swallow, Take, Tolerate, U, Valid, Wear, Widespread

Access(ible) Avenue, Blue-jacking, Card, Come-at-able, Conditional, Credit, Direct, Door, Entrée, → **ENTRY**, Fit, Get-at-able, Hack, Ingo, Key, Log in, Log on, Passe-partout, Password, Phreaking, Random, Recourse, Remote, Sequential, Spasm, Wayleave

Accessory, Accessories Abettor, Addition, Aide, Ally, Ancillary, Appendage, Appurtenance, Attribute, Bandanna, Bells and whistles, Cribellum, Cuff-links, Findings, Fitment, Staffage, Trappings, Trimming

Accident(al) Adventitious, Bechance, Blowdown, Blunder, Calamity, → **CHANCE**, Circumstance, Contingency, Contretemps, Crash, Dent, Disaster, Fall, Fluke, Fortuitous, Hap, Hit and run, Mischance, Mishap, Promiscuous, Rear-ender, Shunt, Smash, Smash-up, Spill, Stramash, Unmeant, Wreck

Accidie Acedia, Sloth, Torpor

Acclaim Accolade, Applaud, Brava, Bravo, Cheer, Eclat, Fame, Fanfare, Hail, Kudos, Ovation, Praise, Salute

Accolade Award, Brace, Honour, Palm, Token, Tribute

Accommodate, Accommodation Adapt, Almshouse, B and B, Bedsit, Berth, Billet, Board, Botel, Bunkhouse, Camp, Chalet, Compromise, Crashpad, Digs, Flotel, Gaff, Gite, Grace and favour, Homestay, Hostel, Hotel, House, Lend, Loan, Lodge, Lodgement, Minshuku, Motel, → **OBLIGE**, Parador, Pension, Quarters, Rapprochement, Recurve, Room, Sheltered, Single-end, Sorehon, Stabling, Stateroom, Steerage, Storage, Wharepuni, Xenodochium

▷ **Accommodating** *may indicate* one word inside another

Accompany(ing), Accompanied (by), Accompaniment, Accompanist Accessory, Alberti, And, Attend, Backing, Chaperone, Chum, Concomitant, Consort, Continuo, Descant, → **ESCORT**, Fixings, Harmonise, Herewith, Obbligato, Obligate, Obligato, Repetiteur, Soundtrack, Trimmings, Vamp

Accomplice Abettor, Aide, → **ALLY**, Collaborator, Confederate, Federarie, Partner, Shill, Stale, Swagsman

Accomplish(ed), Accomplishment Able, → **ACHIEVE**, Arch, Attain, Clever, Complete, Consummate, Done, Effect, Master, Over, Perform, Polished, Prowess, Realise, Ripe, Savant, Success, Tour de force

Accord(ingly), According to After, Agree, Ala, Allow, As per, Attune, Chime, Consensus, Give, Grant, Harmony, Jibe, Meech Lake, Meet, Sort, Thus

According to nature SN

Accordion Button, Concertina, Flutina, Piano, Squeeze-box

Accost Abord, Approach, Greet, Hail, Importune, Molest, Solicit, Tackle

Account(s) AC, Anecdote, Appropriation, Audit, Battels, Behalf, Bill, Budget, Cause, Charge, Checking, Chequing, Chronicle, Control, Current, Deposit, Discretionary, Drawing, Enarration, Expense, Explain, Exposition, ISA, Joint, Lawin, Ledger, Log, Long, Memoir, Narration, Nominal, Nostro, Numbered, Procès-verbal, Real, Reason, Recital, Regest, Register, → **REPORT**, Repute, Resumé, Sake, Short, Suspense, Swindlesheet, Tab, Tale, Thesis, Trust, Version, Vostro

Accountable Responsible

Accountant Auditor, Bean counter, CA, Cost, Forensic, Hyde, Liquidator, Reckoner, Vestry-clerk

Accredit Attribute

Accumulate, Accumulation Accrue, Adsorb, Aggregate, → AMASS, Augment, Backlog, Build, Collect, Gather, Hoard, Lodg(e)ment, Pile, Rack up, Run up, Stockpile, Uplay

Accuracy, Accurate(ly) Bang-on, Cocker, → CORRECT, Dead-on, Fair, Fidelity, Minute, Precise, Right, Spot-on, True, Veracious, Word-perfect

Accursed Argued, Blest, Blist, Sacred

Accusation, Accuse(d) Allege, Arraign, Attaint, Bill, Blame, Censure, Challenge, Charge, Criminate, Denounce, Dite, Gravamen, Impeach, Incriminate, Panel, Plaint, Suspect, Tax, Threap, Threep, Traduce, Wight, Wite, Wyte

Accustom(ed) Acquaint, Attune, Enure, General, Habituate, Harden, Inure, Teach, Wont, Woon

Ace(s) Basto, Blackjack, Crabs, Dinger, → EXPERT, Jot, Master, Mournival, One, Quatorze, Spadille, Spadill(i)o, Spot, Tib, Virtuoso, Wonderful

Acerbate Intensify

Ache, Aching Aitch, Die, Long, Mulligrubs, Nag, Otalgia, Pain, Stitch, Work, Yearn, Yen

Achieve(ment) Accomplish, Acquisition, Attain, Come, Compass, Cum laude, → EFFECT, Exploit, Feat, Fulfil, Gain, Hatchment, Masterpiece, Realise, Res gestae, Satisfice, Satisfy, Stroke, Succeed, Threepeat, Triumph, Trock, Troke, Truck

Acid(ity) Acrimony, Corrosive, Drop, EPA, Etchant, Hydroxy, Reaction, Ribosomal, Ribozyme, Solvent, Sour, Tart, Vinegar, Vitriol

---

ACIDS

2 letters:	Iodic	Marine	Chloric
pH	L-dopa	Niacin	Chromic
	Lewis	Nitric	Creatin
3 letters:	Malic	Oxalic	Cystine
DNA	Mucic	Oxygen	Ellagic
HCL	Oleic	Pectic	Eugenic
LSD	Orcin	Phenol	Ferulic
Oxo	Osmic	Picric	Folacin
RNA	Trona	Quinic	Fumaric
		Serine	Fusidic
4 letters:	*6 letters:*	Sialic	Glycine
Acyl	Adipic	Sorbic	Guanine
Dopa	Bromic	Tannic	Leucine
Pyro	Capric	Tiglic	Malonic
Uric	Cholic	Toluic	Meconic
Wood	Citric	Valine	Melanic
	Cyanic		Muramic
5 letters:	Erucic	*7 letters:*	Nitrous
Algin	Formic	Abietic	Nucleic
Amide	Gallic	Acrylic	Orcinol
Amino	Lactic	Alanine	Peracid
Auric	Lauric	Alginic	Proline
Boric	Leucin	Benzoic	Prussic
Caro's	Lipoic	Butyric	Pteroic
Fatty	Lysine	Caproic	Pyruvic
Folic	Maleic	Cerotic	Racemic

Sebacic
Selenic
Silicic
Stannic
Stearic
Suberic
Terebic
Titanic
Valeric
Vanadic
Xanthic
Xylonic

8 letters:
Abscisic
Adenylic
Arginine
Ascorbic
Aspartic
Butanoic
Caprylic
Carbamic
Carbolic
Carbonic
Chlorous
Cinnamic
Creatine
Cresylic
Crotonic
Cyclamic
Cysteine
Decanoic
Ethanoic
Fulminic
Glutamic
Glyceric
Glycolic
Guanylic
Hippuric
Iopanoic
Itaconic
Linoleic
Lysergic
Manganic

Margaric
Muriatic
Myristic
Nonanoic
Palmitic
Periodic
Phthalic
Retinoic
Rhodanic
Succinic
Sulfonic
Tantalic
Tartaric
Telluric
Tungstic
Tyrosine
Uridylic
Valproic

9 letters:
Aqua-regia
Cevitamic
Citydylic
Dichromic
Histidine
Hydrazoic
Hydriodic
Isocyanic
Linolenic
Methanoic
Nalidixic
Nicotinic
Ornithine
Panthenic
Pentanoic
Polybasic
Propanoic
Propenoic
Saccharic
Salicylic
Sassolite
Selenious
Sulphonic
Sulphuric

Tellurous
Threonine

10 letters:
Aquafortis
Asparagine
Barbituric
Carboxylic
Citrulline
Dithionous
Dodecanoic
Glucoronic
Glutamatic
Glutaminic
Hyaluronic
Isoleucine
Margaritic
Methionine
Neuraminic
Orthoboric
Pelargonic
Perchloric
Phosphonic
Phosphoric
Proprionic
Pyrogallic
Ricinoleic
Thiocyanic
Thymidylic
Trans-fatty
Tryptophan

11 letters:
Arachidonic
Butanedioic
Decanedioic
Ethanedioic
Ferricyanic
Ferrocyanic
Gibberellic
Hydnocarpic
Hydrobromic
Hydrocyanic
Hyponitrous

Methacrylic
Octanedioic
Pantothenic
Permanganic
Phosphorous
Ribonucleic
Sarcolactic
Taurocholic

12 letters:
Dicraboxylic
Hydrochloric
Hydrofluoric
Hypochlorous
Indoleacetic
Orthosilicic
Persulphuric
Phenylalanin
Polyadenalic
Propanedioic
Prostacyclin
Pyroligneous
Terephthalic

13 letters:
Galactosamine
Heptadecanoic
Indolebutyric
Phenylalanine
Prostaglandin
Pyrosulphuric
Thiosulphuric

14 letters:
Metaphosphoric
Pyrophosphoric

15 letters:
Orthophosphoric
Pteroylglutamic

16 letters:
Deoxyribonucleic

Acknowledge(ment) Accept, Admit, Allow, Answer, Avow, Confess, Credit, Grant, Mea culpa, Nod, Own, Receipt, Recognise, Resipiscence, Respect, Righto, Roger, Salute, Ta, Touché, Wilco, Yo

Acme Apex, Apogee, Climax, Comble, Crest, Peak, Summit, Top, Zenith

Acolyte Nethinim, Novice, Server, Thurifer

Acorn(s), Acorn-shell Balanus, Glans, Mast, Rac(c)ahout, Valonia

Acoustic(s) Harmonics, Phonics, Sonics

Acquaint(ance), Acquainted Advise, Cognisant, Enlighten, Familiar, → INFORM, Knowledge, Nodding, Notify, Tell, Versed

Acquiesce(nce), Acquiescent Accept, Bow, Conform, Resigned, Righto, Roger, Wilco, Yield

Acquire, Acquisition Acquest, Cop, Earn, Ern, Gain, → GET, Glom, Irredentist, Land, Obtain, Procure, Purchase, Steal, Take-over, Target, Usucap(t)ion

Acquit(tal) Assoil, Cleanse, Clear, Exonerate, Free, Loose, Loste, Pardon

Acre(s) A, Area, Bigha, Hide, Rival, Rood

Acrid, Acrimony Bitter(ness), Empyreuma, Pungent, Rough, Sour, Surly

Acrobat(s), Acrobatics Equilibrist, Gymnast, Hot dog, Jerry-come-tumble, Ropedancer, Speeler, Splits, Trampoline, Tumbler, Wing-walker

Acropolis Citadel, Parthenon

Across A, Ac, Athwart, Opposite, Over, Through

Act(ing), Action, Acts A, Actus reus, Affirmative, Antic, Assist, Assumpsit, Auto, Barnstorm, Barrier, Behave, Bit, Business, Camp, Campaign, Case, Caster, Cause, Charade, Class, Come, Conduct, Consolation, Coup, Daff, Deal, → DEED, Delaying, Deputise, Detinue, Direct, Do, DORA, Double, Enabling, Enclosure, Epitasis, Excitement, Exert, Exploit, Factory, Feat, Feign, Forth-putting, Function, Furthcoming, Habeas corpus, Histrionic, Homestead, Identic, Impersonate, Improbation, Incident, Industrial, Juristic, Lance-jack, Litigate, Locutionary, Measure, Method, Movement, Mum, Mutiny, Navigation, Overt, Partypiece, Pas, Perform(ance), Perlocutionary, Personate, Play, Positive, Pp, Practice, Pretence, Private, Procedure, Process, Public, Qua, Qui tam, Reflex, Replevin, Represent, Riot, Rising, Roleplay, Routine, Sasine, Scenery, Secondary, Septennial, Serve, Showdown, Shtick, Sick-out, Simulate, Speech, Stamp, Stanislavski, Statute, Steps, Suit, Synergy, Terminer, Test, Theatricise, Thellusson, Thing, Transitory, Treat, Trover, Truck, Turn, Twig, Uniformity, Union, Vicegerent, War, Windlass

Actinium Ac

Actinon An

Activate Arm, Engage, Goad, Spark, Spur, Stur, Styre, Trigger

Active, Activist, Activity A, Agile, Alert, At, Athletic, Brisk, Busy, Cadre, Deedy, DIY, Do(ing), Dynamited, Dynamo, Ecowarrior, Effectual, Energetic, Energic, Erupting, Exercise, Extra-curricular, Floruit, Fluster, Game, Go-go, Goings-on, Hum, Hyper, Leish, Licht, Live, Mobile, Motile, Nimble, Ongo, On the go, Op, Operant, Optical, Play, Rambunctious, Residual, Sideline, Sprightly, Springe, Spry, Sthenic, Stir, Surge, Third house, Vacuum, Voice, Wick, Wimble, Ya(u)ld

Actor(s), Actor-like Agent, Alleyn, Artist, Ashe, Barnstormer, Benson, Betterton, Bit player, Burbage, Cast, Character, Company, Diseur, Donat, Equity, Gable, Garrick, Gielgud, Guiser, Ham, Hamfatter, Heavy, Histrio(n), Jay, Juve(nile), Kean, Luvvie, MacReady, Mime, Mummer, Olivier, Performer, Player, Playfair, Protagonist, Roscian, Roscius, Savoyard, Sim, Stager, Strolling, Super, Thespian, Tragedian, Tree, Tritagonist, Trouper, Understudy, Utility man, Wolfit

Actress Bankhead, Duse, Ingenue, Loren, Pierrette, Siddons, Soubrette, Terry, West

Actual(ity), Actually De facto, Entelechy, Literal, Live, Material, Real, Real-life, Tangible, True, Very

Acumen Insight, Sense

Acupressure Jin shin do, Shiatsu

Acupuncture Stylostixis

Acute Astute, Dire, Fitché, Incisive, → INTENSE, Keen, Quick-witted, Sharp

Adage Aphorism, Gnome, Maxim, Motto, Paroemia, Proverb, Saw, Saying, Truism

Adam Bede, Delved

Adamant Firm, Inexorable, Insistent, Obdurate, Rigid, Unbending

Adapt(er), Adaptable, Adaptations, Adaptor Bushing, Ecad, Flexible, Persona, Pliant, Reorient, Resilient, Tailor, Timeserver, Transform, Versatile

Add(ed), Addendum, Adder Accrue, Adscititious, → **APPENDIX**, Attach, Cast, Coopt, Dub, Ech(e), Eik, Eke, Elaborate, Embroider, Enhance, Fortify, Insert, Lace, Puff, Reckon, Score, Spike, Sum, Summate, Tack on, Tot(e), Total, Viper

Addict(ion), Addicted Abuser, Acidhead, Base head, Blunthead, Buff, Couch potato, Dependency, Devotee, Dope-fiend, Etheromaniac, Fan, Fiend, Freak, Hophead, Hype, Jones, Joypopper, Junkie, Lover, Mainliner, Mania, Need, Pillhead, Pillpopper, Pothead, Shithead, Slave, Space-cadet, Speedfreak, User, Vinolent, Wino

Addison Spectator

Addition(al) Accession, Addend, Additive, Adscititious, Adulterant, Advene, Also, And, Annexure, (As an) in, Bolt-on, Braata, Codicil, Corollary, Eik, Eke, Encore, Epithesis, Etc, Extender, Extension, → **EXTRA**, Extramural, Footnote, → **IN ADDITION**, Increment, Makeweight, Monkey, New, Odd, On, On top, Other, Padding, Paragog(u)e, Parergon, Plus, PS, Rider, Ripieno, Spare, Suffect, Suffix, Supplementary, Surcharge, Thereto, Top-up, Verandah

Address, Address system Accommodation, Accost, Adroit, Allocution, Apostrophe, Apostrophise, Appellation, Art, → **ATLAS**, Ave, Bub, Buster, Call, Compellation, Dedication, Delivery, Den, Diatribe, Direction, Discourse, Election, Epilogue, Epirrhema, Esquire, Gettysburg, Gospodin, Hail, Home, Homily, IP, Lala, Lecture, Mester, Mister, Mush, Mynheer, Nkosi, Ode, Orate, Parabasis, Pastoral, Poste-restante, Prelection, Rig, Salute, Sermon, Sir(ree), Speech, Stance, Tact, Tannoy®, → **TITLE**, Towkay, Tuan, Valedictory, Wambenger, Web, Wus, Y'all

Adduce Cite

Adelphic Adam

Adept Able, Adroit, Buff, Dab, Deacon, Don, → **EXPERT**, Fit, Handy, Mahatma

Adequate Condign, Does, Due, Egal, Equal, Ere-now, Passable, Proper, → **SUFFICIENT**, Tolerable, Valid

Adhere(nt), Adherence, Adhesive Allegiance, Ally, Araldite®, Bond, Burr, Child, Cling, Conform, Cow Gum®, Dextrin, Disciple, Emplastic, Epoxy, Fidelity, Follower, Glue, Goldsize, Guebre, Gum, Hot-melt, Impact, Jain(a), Loyalist, Mucilage, Nomism, Partisan, Resin, Sectator, Servitor, Stand pat, Sticker, Supporter, Synechia, Votary, Waterglass

Adjacent, Adjoining Bordering, Conterminous, Contiguous, Handy, Nigh

Adjective Adnoun, Epithet, Gerundive

Adjourn(ment) Abeyance, Defer, Delay, → **POSTPONE**, Prorogate, Recess, Rise, Suspend

Adjudicate, Adjudicator Arbiter, Judge, Jury, Referee, Try, Umpire

Adjunct Addition, Aid, Ancillary, Rider

Adjust(able), Adjustment, Adjuster Accommodate, Adapt, Attune, Coapt, Dress, Ease, Fine-tune, Fit, Focus, Gang, Gauge, Gerrymander, J'adoube, Modify, Modulate, Orientate, Prepare, Reduce, Regulate, Reorientate, Reset, Scantle, Scotopia, Sliding, Suit, Temper, Toe-in, Tram, Trim, True, Tune, Tweak, Vernier

▷ **Adjust** *may indicate* an anagram

Adjutant Aide, Argala, Officer, Stork

Adler Irene

Ad-lib Wing it

Administer, Administration, Administrator Adhibit, Anele, Apply,

Arrondissement, Bairiki, Bureaucrat, Control, Corridors of power, → **DIRECT**, Dispence, Dispense, Executive, Intendant, Intinction, → **MANAGE**, Raj, Regime, Registrar, Run, Secretariat, Soke, Steward

Admirable, Admiration, Admire(d), Admirer Clinker, Clipper, Conquest, Crichton, Esteem, Estimable, → **EXCELLENT**, Flame, Fureur, Gaze, Ho, Iconise, Idolater, Laudable, Partisan, Regard, Ripping, Splendid, Toast, Tribute, Venerate, Wonder, Wow

Admiral Adm, AF, Anson, Beatty, Beaufort, Benbow, Blake, Bligh, Boscawen, Butterfly, Byng, Byrd, Capitan, Drake, Effingham, Fisher, Hood, Hornblower, Howard, Jellicoe, Keyes, Marrowfat, Navarch, Nelson, Raeder, Red, Rodney, Spee, Sturdee, Togo, Vanessa, Van Nieman, Van Tromp, White

Admission, Admit(ting), Admittance Accept, Access, Agree, Allow, Avow, Concede, → **CONFESS**, Enter, Entrée, Entry, Estoppel, Grant, Induct, Ingress, Initiate, Intromit, Ordain, Ordination, Owe, Own, Recognise, Shrift, Take, Tho(ugh), Yield

Admonish, Admonition Caution, Chide, Lecture, Moralise, Pi-jaw, Rebuke, Reprimand, → **SCOLD**, Tip, Warn

Ado Bother, Bustle, Fuss

Adolescent Developer, Grower, Halflin, Immature, Juvenile, Neanic, Teenager, Veal, Youth

Adonais Keats

Adonis Pheasant's Eye

Adopt(ed) Accept, Affect, Affiliate, Assume, Dalt, Embrace, Espouse, Father, Foster, Mother

Adoration, Adore Doat, Dote, Homage, Idolise, Latria, Love, Pooja(h), Puja, Revere, Venerate, Worship

Adorn(ed), Adornment Aplustre, Attrap, Banderol, Bedeck, Bedight, Bejewel, Caparison, Clinquant, Deck, Dight, Drape, Embellish, Emblaze, Emblazon, Embroider, Enchase, Equip, Festoon, Flourish, Furnish, Garnish, Grace, Graste, Ornament, Riband, Tattoo, Tatu, Tinsel, Trappings

Adrenaline Epinephrin(e)

Adroit Adept, Clever, Dextrous, Expert, Skilful

Adulate, Adulation Flatter(y), Praise, → **WORSHIP**

Adullam Cave

Adult Amadoda, Consenting, Grown-up, Man, Mature, Upgrown, X

Adulterant, Adulterate Cut, Debase, Impurify, Lime, Mix, Multum, → **POLLUTE**, Sophisticate, Weaken

Adulterer, Adultery Avoutery, Cuckold, Fornication, Francesca, Lenocinium

Advance(d) A, Abord, Accelerate, Anabasis, Ante, Approach, Ascend, Assert, Better(ment), Charge, Develop, Extreme, Far, Fore, Forge, Forward, Further, Gain, Get on, Grubstake, Haut(e), Hi-tec(h), Impress, Imprest, Incede, Late, Lend, → **LOAN**, March, Mortgage, On(ward), Overture, Pass, Piaffe, Posit, Postulate, Precocious, Prefer, Prest, Process, Progress, → **PROMOTE**, Propose, Propound, Retainer, Ripe, Rise, Scoop, Sub, Submit, Tiptoe, Upfront, Voorskot

Advantage(ous) Accrual, Aid, → **ASSET**, Avail, Batten, Benefit, Bisque, Boot, Edge, Emolument, Expedient, Exploit, Favour, Fruit, Gain, Grouter, Handicap, Handle, Head-start, Help, Interess, Interest, Lever(age), Nonmonetary, Odds, One-up, Oyster, Pecuniary, Percentage, Plus, Privilege, Prize, Pro, Purchase, Salutary, Stead, Strength, Toe-hold, Upper-hand, Upside, Use, Van, Whiphand, Whipsaw

Advent(ist) Coming, Shaker

Adventure(r), Adventuress, Adventurous Argonaut, Assay, Aunter, Buccaneer,

Casanova, Conquistador, Dareful, Daring, Emprise, Enterprise, Escapade,
→ **EXPLOIT**, Filibuster, Gest, Lark, Mata Hari, Mercenary, Merchant, Picaresque,
Picaro, Picaroon, Risk, Routier, Rutter, Swashbuckler, Vamp, Voyage

Adversary Antagonist, Cope(s)mate, Enemy, Foe

Adverse, Adversity Calamity, Cross, Down, Harrow, Misery, Reversal, Setback,
Untoward, Woe

Advert(ise), Advertisement, Advertising Ad, Air, Allude, Attack, Bark, Bill,
Blipvert, Circular, Classified, Coign(e), Coin, Commercial, Copy, Display, Dodger,
Flier, Flyer, Flyposting, Flysheet, Hard sell, Hype, Infomercial, Jingle, Madison
Avenue, Mailshot, Niche, Noise, → **NOTICE**, Out, Packshot, Parade, Personnel,
Placard, Plug, → **POSTER**, Promo, Promote, Promulgate, Prospectus, Puff,
Quoin, Refer, Semisolus, Sky-write, Splash, Spot, Stunt, Subliminal, Teaser, Tele-,
Throwaway, Tout, Trailer, Trawl, Want(s) (ad)

Advice Conseil, Counsel, → **GUIDANCE**, Guideline, Information, Invoice, Opinion,
Read, Recommendation, Reed, Re(e)de

Advise(d), Adviser, Advisable Acquaint, Avise(ment), CAB, Cabal, Camarilla,
Counsel, Egeria, Enlighten, Expedient, Genro, Induna, Inform, Instruct, Mentor,
Oracle, Peritus, Politic, Prudent, Ralph, → **RECOMMEND**, Tutor, Urge, Wise

Advocate(d) Agent, Argue, Attorney, Back, Counsel, Devil's, Endorse, Exponent,
Gospel, Intercede, Lawyer, Move, Paraclete, Peat, Peddle, Pleader, Pragmatist,
Preach, Proponent, Silk, Syndic, Urge

Aerial Aeolian, Aery, Antenna, Beam, Clover, Clover leaf, Communal, Dipole, Dish,
Ethereal, Ferrite-rod, Folded dipole, Frame, Ground-plane, Long-wire, Loop,
Minidish, Parabolic, Rhombic, Satellite dish, Slot, Yagi

Aerobatics Stunt

Aerobics Pilates, Step

Aerodrome → **AIRPORT**, Rotor-station

Aerofoil Spoiler

▶ **Aeroplane** *see* **AIRCRAFT**

Aerosol Atomiser, Mace®

Aesir Loki

Aesthetic Arty, Tasteful

Affable Amiable, Avuncular, Benign, Gracious, Suave, Urbane

Affair(s) Amour, Business, Concern, Current, Effeir, Effere, Event, External, Fight,
Fling, Foreign, Go, Indaba, Internal, Intrigue, Matter, Pash, Pi(d)geon, Pidgin, Ploy,
Relationship, Res, Romance, Shebang, Subject, Thing

Affect(ed), Affectation, Affection(ate) Air, Airtsy-mairtsy, Alter, Arty, Breast,
Camp, Chi-chi, Concern, Crachach, Crazy, Endearment, Euphuism, Foppery, Grip,
Hit, Impress, Ladida, Lovey-dovey, Mimmick, Minauderie, Mincing, Minnick,
Minnock, Mouth-made, Phoney, → **POSE**, Poseur, Precieuse, Preciosity, Pretence,
Prick-me-dainty, Smitten, Spoilt, Stag(e)y, Storge, Susceptible, Sway, Sympathetic,
Tender, Topophilia, Touched, Touchy-feely, Twee, Unction, Unnatural, Upend

Affiliate, Affiliation Adopt, Associate, Merge, Unite

Affinity Bro, Kin(ship), Penchant, Rapport, Tie

Affirm(ative), Affirmation Assert, Attest, Maintain, Predicate, Profess,
Protestation, Uh-huh, → **VERIFY**, Yebo

Affix(ed) Append, Ascribe, → **ATTACH**, Connect, Fasten, On

Afflict(ed), Affliction Aggrieve, Ail, Asthma, Cross, Cup, Curse, Disease,
Furnace, Harass, Hurt, Lumbago, Molest, Nosology, Palsy, Persecute, Pester,
Plague, Scourge, Smit, Sore, → **SORROW**, Stricken, Teen, Tene, Tic, Tribulation,
→ **TROUBLE**, Try, Unweal, Visitation, Woe

Affluence, Affluent Abundance, Dinky, Fortune, Grey panther, Opulence, Wealth

Afford Allow, Bear, Give, Manage, Offer, Provide, Spare, Yield

Affray Brawl, Fight, Mêlée, Scuffle, Skirmish

Affront Assault, Defy, Facer, → INSULT, → OFFEND, Outrage, Scandal, Slight, Slur

Afghan(istan) Bactria, Dard, Hound, Kaf(f)ir, Pakhto, Pakhtu, Pashto, Pashtu, Pathan, Pushto(o), Pushtu

Afloat Aboard, Abroach, Adrift, Natant

Afoot Astir, Up

Aforesaid Above, Same

Afraid Adrad, Alarmed, Chicken, Fearful, Funk, Rad, Regretful, Scared, Timorous, Windy, Yellow

Africa(n) Abyssinian, Adamawa, Akan, Algerian, Amakwerekwere, Angolan, Ashanti, Baganda, Bambara, Bantu, Barbary, Barotse, Basotho, Basuto, Bechuana, Beento, Bemba, Beninese, Berber, Biafran, Bintu, Black, Boer, Botswana, Bushman, Caffre, Cairene, Carthaginian, Chewa, Chichewa, Ciskei, Congo(l)ese, Cushitic, Damara, Dinka, Duala, Dyula, Efik, Eritrean, Ethiopian, Eve, Fang, Fanti, Fingo, Flytaal, Fula(h), Gabonese, Galla, Gambian, Ganda, Gazankulu, Grikwa, Griqua, Guinean, Gullah, Hamite, Hausa, Herero, Hottentot, Hutu, Ibibi, Ibo, Igbo, Impi, Kabyle, Kaffer, Kaf(f)ir, Kenyan, Khoikhoi, Kikuyu, Kongo, Lango, Lesotho, Liberian, Libyan, Lowveld, Lozi, Luba, Luo, Maghreb, Maghrib, Malawi, Malian, Malinke, Mande, Mandingo, Masai, Mashona, Matabele, Mende, Moor, Moroccan, Mossi, Mozambican, Mswahili, Munt(u), Mzee, Nama, Nama(qua), Namibian, Negrillo, → NEGRO, Ngoni, Nguni, Nilot(e), Nubian, Nuer, Numidian, Nyanja, Oromo, Ovambo, Pedi, Pied noir, Pondo, Rastafarian, Rhodesian, Rwandan, San, Senegalese, Shilluk, Shluh, Shona, Somali, Songhai, Sotho, Soweto, Sudanese, Susu, Swahili, Swazi, Temne, Tiv, Togolese, Tonga, Transkei, Transvaal, Tshi, Tsonga, Tswana, Tuareg, Tutsi, Twi, Ugandan, Venda, Voltaic, Waswahili, Watu(t)si, Wolof, X(h)osa, Yoruban, Zairean, Zulu

Afrikaan(s), Afrikaner Cape Dutch, Crunchie, Hairyback, Mynheer, Taal, Volk, Voortrekker

After(wards) About, A la, At, Behind, Beyond, Eft, Epi-, → LATER, On, Once, Past, Rear, Since, Sine, Subsequent, Syne

Afterbirth Secundines, Sooterkin

Afterimage Photogene

▷ **After injury** *may indicate* an anagram

Aftermath Consequence, Fall out, Legacy, Mow(ing), Rawing, Rawn, Rowan, Rowen, Rowing, Sequel(a)

Afternoon A, Arvo, PM, Postmeridian, Undern

Afterpiece, Afterthought Addendum, Codicil, Epimetheus, Exode, Footnote, Note, PS, Supplement

Again Afresh, Agen, Anew, Back, Bis, De novo, Ditto, Do, Eft, Eftsoons, Encore, Iterum, More, Moreover, O(v)er, Re-, Recurrence, Reprise, Than, Then

Against A, Anti, Beside, Con, Counter, Gainsayer, Into, Nigh, On, Opposing, To, V, Versus

Agape Feast, Hiant, Ringent, Yawning

Agate Chalcedonyx, Moss, Murr(h)a, Onyx, Ruin

Agave Century plant, Henequen, Lily, Maenad, Maguey

Age(d), Ages, Aging Absolute, Achievement, Ae, Aeon, Aet, Alcheringa, Anno domini, Antique, Archaise, Atomic, Augustan, Azilian, Bronze, Calpa, Century, Chellean, Coon's, Copper, Cycle, Dark, Date, Day, Doddery, Eld, Elizabethan, Eon, Epact, Epoch(a), Era, Eternity, Generation, Gerontic, Golden, Grey, Heroic,

Hoar, Hore, Ice, Information, Iron, Jazz, Jurassic, Kaliyuga, Kalpa, La Tene, Lias, Magdalenian, Maglemosian, Mature, Mental, Mesolithic, Middle, Millennium, Neolithic, New, New Stone, Of, Old, Oligocene, Paleolithic, Passé, Periclean, Period, Phanerozoic, Progeria, Reindeer, S(a)eculum, Saros, Senescence, Silver, Solera, Space, Stone, Third, Villanovan, Yellow, Yonks, Yug(a)

Agency, Agent Agitator, Alkylating, Ambassador, Antistatic, Art, Autolysin, Bailiff, Bargaining, Barm, Bond, Broker, BSI, Bureau, Catalyst, Cat's paw, Cause, Chelating, Child support, Commis, Complexone, Comprador(e), Confidential, Consul, Consular, Countryside, Crown, Customs, Dating, Del credere, Developing, Disclosing, Distributor, Doer, Double, Emissary, Environment, Envoy, Enzyme, Escort, Estate, Exciseman, Executant, Executor, Factor, Fed, Finger, Flack, Forwarding, Free, Galactagogue, G-man, Go-between, Hand, Hirudin, House, Implement, Indian, Influence, Institorial, Instrument, Intermediary, Kinase, Law, Legate, Literary, Magic bullet, Man, Means, Medium, Mercantile, Mitogen, Mole, Moral, Mutagen, Narc, Narco, Nerve, Ninja, Nucleating, OO, -or, Order paper, Oxidizing, Parliamentaire, Parliamentary, Patent, Pathogen, Peace corps, Penetration, Pinkerton, Press, Procurator, Proxy, Realtor, Reducing, Rep(resentative), Resident, Reuters, Riot, Road, Runner, Salesman, Secret (service), Setter, Shipping, SIS, Sleeper, Solvent, Soman, Spook, Spy, Stock, Surfactant, Syndic, Tass, Teratogen, Third party, Ticket, Training, Travel, UNESCO, Vakeel, Vakil, Virino, Voice, Welfare, Wetting, Wire service

Agenda Business, Hidden, Programme, Remit, Schedule

Aggie Agnes, Ines, Nessa, Nesta

Aggravate Annoy, Exasperate, Inflame, Irk, Needle, Nettle, Provoke, Try, Vex

Aggregate, Aggregation Ballast, Congeries, Detritus, Etaerio, Granulite, Gravel, Omnium, Ore, Sum, Total

Aggression, Aggressive, Aggressor Arsey, Attack, Bare-knuckle, Bellicose, Belligerent, Biffo, Bullish, Butch, Defiant, Enemy, Feisty, Foe, Gungho, Hard-hitting, Hawk, Invader, In-your-face, Militant, On-setter, Pushing, Rambo, Rampant, Road rage, Shirty, Truculent, Wild

Agile Acrobatic, Deft, Lissom(e), Nifty, Nimble, Quick, Spry, Supple, Swank, Twinkletoes

Agitate(d), Agitation, Agitator Activist, Ado, Agitprop, Betoss, Boil, Bolshie, Bother, Chartist, Churn, Commotion, Commove, Convulse, Demagogue, Discompose, Distraught, → **DISTURB**, Doodah, Ebullient, Emotion, Excite, Extremist, Fan, Fantad, Fanteeg, Fantigue, Fantod, Ferment, Firebrand, Flurry, Fluster, Flutter, Fraught, Frenzy, Fuss, Goad, Heat, Hectic, Jabble, Lather, Militant, Overwrought, Panicky, Pedetic, Perturb, Poss, Pother, Rattle, Restless, Rouse, Ruffle, Seethed, Shake, Sod, Stir(-up), Swivet, Tailspin, Taking, Tempest, Tew, Thermal, Tizzy, Toss, Tremor, Trepidation, Trouble, Turmoil, Tweak, Twitchy, Unrest, Upset, Welter, Whisk, Wrought up, Ytost

▷ **Agitate** *may indicate* an anagram

Agley Awry, Unevenly

Aglow Alight, Tipsy

▶ **Agnes** *see* **AGGIE**

Agnostic Laodicean

Ago Lang syne, → **SINCE**

Agog Astir, Athirst, Eager, Keen, Pop-eyed

Agonise, Agony Ache, Anguish, Brood, Dread, Ecstasy, Heartache, → **PAIN**, Throe(s), Torment, Torture

Agree(ing), Agreed, Agreement Accede, Accept, Accord, Acquiescence, Agt,

Allow, Amen, Analog(ue), Analogy, Apply, As one, Assent, Assort, Atone, Ausgleich, Aye, Bilateral, Bipartite, Bond, Camp David, Cartel, Champerty, Charterparty, Chime, Closing, Coincide, Collective, Comart, Community, Compact, Comply, Comport, Concert, Concord(at), Concur, Conform, Congree, Congruent, Consension, Consensus, → **CONSENT**, Consonant, Contract, Contrahent, Convention, Correspond, Cotton, Covenant, Cushty, Dayton Accords, Deal, Deffo, Deign, Done, Entente, Equate, Escrow, Fadge, Gatt, Gentleman's, Handfast, Harmony, Homologous, Indenture, Jibe, Knock-for-knock, League, Like-minded, Mercosur, Munich, National, Net Book, Nod, Nudum pactum, Okay, Pact, Pair, Placet, Plant, Plea bargaining, Prenuptial, Procedural, Productivity, Rabat(te), Repo, Repurchase, Right(o), Right on, Roger, Sanction, Schengen, Service, Settlement, Side, Sort(ance), Specialty, Sponsion, Square, Standstill, Substantive, Suit, Sweetheart, Sympathy, Synchronise, Synesis, Syntony, Tally, Technology, Threshold, Trade, Treaty, Uh-huh, Union, Unison, Unspoken, Wilco, Wukkas, Yea, Yea-say, Yes

Agreeable Amene, Harmonious, Pleasant, Sapid, Sweet, Well-disposed, Willing, Winsome

Agriculture, Agricultural(ist) Arval, Geoponic, Georgic, Inari, Permaculture, Slash and burn, Smallholding, Tull

Aground Ashore, Beached, Sew, Stranded

Ague Dumb

▷ **Ague(ish)** *may indicate* an anagram

Ah Ach, Ay

Ahead Anterior, Before, Foreship, Forward, Frontwards, In store, Onward, Precocious, Up

Aiblins Perhap, Perhaps, Yibbles

Aid(s), Aide Accessory, Adjutant, Artificial, Assist, Decca, → **DEPUTY**, First, Foreign, Galloper, Gift, Grant, Hearing, Help, Key, Legal, Lend-lease, Monitor, Optophone, Orthosis, PA, Realia, Relief, Serve, Sex, Subsidy, Subvention, Succour, Support, Teaching, Visual, Yeoman('s) service, Zimmer®

AIDS Slim

Ail(ment) Affect, Afflict(ion), Complaint, Croup, Disease, Malady, Narks, Occupational, Pink-eye, Pip, Sickness

Aim Approach, Aspire, Bead, Bend, End, Ettle, Eye, Goal, Hub, Intent, Level, Mark, Mint, Mission, Object, Peg, Plan, Plank, Point, Point blank, Purpose, Reason, Sake, Seek, Sight(s), Target, Tee, Telos, Train, View, Visie, Vizy, Vizzie, Zero-in

Aimless Adrift, Drifting, Erratic, Haphazard, Random, Unmotivated

Air(s), Airer, Airy Aerate, Aerial, Aero, Affectation, Allure, Ambiance, Ambience, Aquarius, Arietta, Atmosphere, Attitude, Aura, Bearing, Breath, Calypso, Canzona, Canzone, Cavatina, Compressed, Dead, Demaine, Descant, Ditty, Draught, Dry, Emphysema, Ether(eal), Expose, Fan, Filmy, Front, Gemini, Heat-island, Heaven, Horse, Inflate, Libra, Lift, Light, Liquid, Look, Lullaby, Madrigal, Manner, Melody, Microburst, Mien, Night, Nitre, Oat, Open, Ozone, Parade, Periptery, Pneumatic, Radio, Screen, Scuba, Serenade, Serenata, Serene, Shanty, Side, Sky, Slipstream, Solo, Song, Strain, Swank, Thin, Trigon, → **TUNE**, Vent, Ventilate, Vital, Wake, Wind

Airborne Ab

Air-conditioning Plenum system

Aircraft, Airship Aerodyne, Aerostat, Angels, AST, Auster, Autoflare, Autogiro, Autogyro, Aviette, Avion, Biplane, Blimp, Brabazon, Bronco, Camel, Canard, Canberra, Chaser, Chopper, Coleopter, Comet, Concorde, Convertiplane, Corsair,

Crate, Cropduster, Cyclogiro, Delta-wing, Dirigible, Doodlebug, Drone, Eagle, F, Ferret, Fixed-wing, Flivver, Flying wing, Fokker, Freedom-fighter, Freighter, Galaxy, Glider, Gotha, Gyrodyne, Gyroplane, Hang-glider, Harrier, Hawkeeze, Heinkel, Helicopter, Hercules, Hunter, Hurricane, Interceptor, Intruder, Jet star, Jumbo, Jump-jet, Kite, Lancaster, Liberator, Lifting-body, Messerschmitt, Microjet, Microlight, Microlite, MIG, Mirage, Monoplane, Mosquito, Moth, Multiplane, Nightfighter, Nightfinder, Oerlikon, Orion, Ornithopter, Orthopter, Parasol, Penguin, Phantom, → **PLANE**, Provider, Prowler, Pusher, Ramjet, Rigid, Rotaplane, Runabout, Scramjet, Semi-rigid, Skiplane, Skyhawk, Sopwith, Sopwith Camel, Spitfire, SST, Starfighter, Starlifter, Stealth bomber, STOL, Stratocruiser, Stratotanker, Stuka, Super Sabre, Sweptwing, Swing-wing, Tankbuster, Taube, Taxiplane, Thunderbolt, Thunderchief, Tomcat, Tornado, Tracker, Trident, Tri-jet, Triplane, Tube, Turbofan, Turbo-jet, Turbo-prop, Turboramjet, Vigilante, Viking, Viscount, Vomit comet, Voodoo, VTOL, Wild weasel, Zeppelin

Aircraftsman, Airman AC, Aeronaut, Erk, Fokker, Kiwi, LAC, RAF
Aircraftswoman Penguin, Pinguin
▸ **Airfield** *see* **AIRPORT**
Air force Luftwaffe
Airlift Thermal
Airline, Airway Aeroflot, Anthem, BAC, BEA, Duct, Larynx, Lot, Lyric, Purple, Qantas, SAS, S(ch)norkel, TWA, Weasand(-pipe), Windpipe
▸ **Airman** *see* **AIRCRAFTSMAN, FLIER**
Airport Drome, Entebbe, Faro, Gander, Gatwick, Heliport, Idlewild, Kennedy, La Guardia, Landing strip, Lod, Luton, Lydda, Lympne, Orly, Prestwick, Runway, Shannon, Stansted, Stolport, Terminal, Vertiport, Wick
Air-raid Blitz, Mission
Air-tight Hermetic, Indisputable, Sealed
Aisle Gangway
Aitch Ache, Aspirate, H
Ajax Loo
Aka Alias
Akin Alike, Cognate, Congener, Kindred
Alabaster Oriental
Alarm Alert, Arouse, Bell, Bleep, Caution, Concern, Dismay, Eek, False, Fire, Fricht, Fright, Ghast, Hairy, Larum, Panic, Perturb, Rock, Rouse, Siren, Smoke, Startle, Tirrit, Tocsin, Warn, Yike(s)
Alas Ah, Alack, Ay, Eheu, Ha, Haro, Harrow, Io, Lackadaisy, Lackaday, O, Oh, Ohone, O me, Ou, Sadly, Waesucks, Waly, Well-a-day, Wellanear, Wel(l)away, Woe
Alaskan AK, Sourdough, Yupik
Alban Berg
Albanian Arna(o)ut
Albatross Alcatras, Golf, Gooney(-bird), Millstone, Omen, Onus, Wandering
Albeit Tho(ugh)
Albert Chain, Chevalier, Consort, Hall, Herring, Slang
Album Autograph, Looseleaf, Photo, Record, Stamp
Albumen, Albumin Chalaza, Glair, Leucosin, Mucin, Myogen, Protein, Ricin, Serum, White
Alchemic, Alchemist, Alchemy Adept, Brimstone, Faust(us), Hermetic(s), Multiplier, Orpiment, Paracelsus, Quicksilver, Sal ammoniac, Sorcery, Spagyric, Spagyrist, Witchcraft
Alcides Hercules

Alcohol(ic) Absolute, Acrolein, Aldehyde, Amyl, Bibulous, Booze, Borneol, Catechol, Cetyl, Chaptalise, Cholesterol, Choline, Citronellol, Cresol, Denatured, Diol, Dipsomaniac, Drinker, Ethal, Ethanol, Ethyl, Farnesol, Feni, Fenny, Firewater, Fusel-oil, Geraniol, Glycerin(e), Grain, Grog, Gut-rot, Hard, Hard stuff, Inebriate, Inositol, Isopropyl, Jakey, Jungle juice, Lauryl, Linalool, Lush, Mahua, Mahwa, Mannite, Mannitol, Mercaptan, Mescal, Methanol, Meths, Methyl, Mow(r)a, Nerol, Phytol, Plonko, Propyl, Rotgut, Rubbing, Rubby, Scrumpy, Secondary, Snake juice, Sorbitol, Sphingosine, Spirits, Spirits of wine, Spirituous, Sterol, Taplash, Terpineol, Tincture, Tocopherol, Triol, Wash, Wino, Wood, Xylitol

Alcove Apse, Bay, Bole, Carrel(l), Dinette, Inglenook, Lunette, Niche, Nook, Recess, Tokonoma

Alcyonarian Sea-feather

Aldehyde Acrolein, Aldol, Vanillin

Alder Fothergilla

Alderman Bail(l)ie, CA

Alderney CI, Cow

Ale, Alehouse Audit, Barleybree, Barley-broo, Barley-broth, Barley wine, Beer, Brown, CAMRA, Church, Four, Heather, Humming, Humpty-dumpty, Lamb's wool, Light, Mild, Morocco, Nappy, Nog, Nogg, October, Pale, Plain, Porter, Purl, Real, Small, Stout, Swats, Tiddleywink, Tipper, White, Whitsun, Wort, Yard, Yill, Yorkshire stingo

Alert Amber, Arrect, Astir, Attentive, Aware, Conscious, Gleg, Gogo, Intelligent, Open-eyed, Qui vive, Red, Scramble, Sharp, Sprack, Sprag, Stand-to, Tentie, Up and coming, Vigilant, Volable, Wary, Watchful, Wide-awake

Alewife Barkeeper, Gaspereau

Alexander, Alexandrine Alex, Arius, Macedonian, Pope, Sandy, Sasha, Sawn(e)y, Selkirk, Senarius

Alfalfa Lucern(e), Luzern

Alfred Dreyfus, Garnet, Jingle

Alfresco Barbecue, Plein-air

Alga(e) Anabaena, Blanketweed, Chlorella, Conferva, Desmid, Diatom, Dulse, Heterocontae, Isokont, Jelly, Nostoc, Periphyton, Phycology, Pleuston, Pond scum, Prokaryon, Protococcus, Red, Seaweed, Spirogyra, Star-jelly, Stonewort, Ulothrix, Ulotrichales, Valonia, Volvox, Witches' butter, Zooxanthella

Algebra Boolean, Linear, Quadratics

Algerian Kabyle, Nimidian

Algonquin Innu

Alias Aka, Byname, Epithet, Moni(c)ker, Nick(name), Pen-name, Pseudonym

Alibi Excuse, Watertight

Alien(ate), Alienation A-effect, Amortise, Disaffect, Ecstasy, Erotic, Estrange, ET, Exotic, External, Foreign, Forinsecal, Fremd, Hostile, Martian, Metic, Outlandish, Outsider, Philistine, Repugnant, Strange(r)

Alight Alowe, Availe, Detrain, Disembark, Dismount, In, Lambent, Land, Lit, Perch, Pitch, Rest, Settle

Align Arrange, Associate, Collimate, Dress, Juxtapose, Marshal, Orient, Straighten

▶ **Alike** *see* LIKE

Alimentary Oesophagus, Pharynx

Aliquot Submultiple

Alive Alert, Animated, Breathing, Extant, Quick

Alkali(ne), Alkaloid Antacid, Apomorphine, Atropine, Base, Bebeerine, Berberine, Betane, Borax, Brucine, Caffein(e), Capsaicin, Chaconine, Choline, Cinchon(id)ine,

Codeine, Colchicine, Corydaline, Curarine, Emetin(e), Ephedrine, Ergotamine, Gelsemin(in)e, Guanidine, Harmalin(e), Harmin(e), Hydrastine, Hyoscine, Hyoscyamine, Ibogaine, Lixivium, Lobeline, Lye, Mescalin, Narceen, Narceine, Nicotine, Papaverine, Physostigmine, Pilocarpin(e), Piperine, Potash, Potass, Quinine, Reserpine, Rhoeadine, Scopaline, Scopolamine, Soda, Solanine, Sparteine, Thebaine, Theine, Theobromine, Theophylline, Totaquine, Tropine, Veratridine, Veratrin(e), Vinblastine, Vinca, Vincristine, Volatile, Yohimbine

Alkane Hexane

All A, → ENTIRE, Entity, Finis, Omni, Pan, Quite, Sum, → TOTAL, Toto, Tutti, Whole

Allah Bismillah, God

All at once Holus-bolus, Suddenly

Allay Alleviate, Calm, Disarm, Lessen, Quieten, Soothe

Allegation, Allege Accuse, Assert, Aver, Claim, Obtend, Plead, Purport, Represent, Smear

Allegiance Faith, Foy, Loyalty

Allegory, Allegorical Apologue, Fable, Mystic, Myth, Parable

Allergy Atopy, Aversion, Bagassosis, Hay fever, Hives

Alleviate Allay, Alleg(g)e, Calm, Mitigate, Mollify, Palliate, → RELIEVE, Temper

Alley Aisle, Blind, Bonce, Bowling, Corridor, Ennog, Ginnel, Lane, Laura, Marble, Passage, Rope-walk, Silicon, Tin Pan, Twitten, Vennel, Walk, Wynd

Alliance Agnation, Axis, Bloc, Cartel, Coalition, Combine, Compact, Confederation, Dreibund, Dual, Federacy, → LEAGUE, Marriage, NATO, Quadruple, Syndicate, Triple, Union

Alligator Al(l)igarta, Avocado, Caiman, Cayman

Alliteration Cynghanedd, Head-rhyme

Allocate, Allocation Allot, Apportion(ment), Assign, Designate, Distribute, Earmark, Placement, Priorate, Ration, Share, Zone

Allot(ment), Allow(ance), Allowed, Allowing Admit, Affect, Alimony, Allocation, Although, Aret(t), Assign, Attendance, Award, Batta, Beteem(e), Brook, Budget, Charter, Cloff, Confess, Cor(r)ody, Diet, Discount, Dole, Draft, Enable, Entitle, Excuse, Expenses, Feod, Give, Grant, House-bote, Husbandage, Indulge, Jobseekers', Latitude, Legit(imate), Let, Licit, Luit(en), Machining, Mag, Mobility, Okay, Palimony, Parcel, Pension, Percentage, → PERMIT, Personal, Pittance, Plot, Portion, Quarterage, Quota, Ratio, Ration, Rebate, Rood, Salt-money, Sanction, Separation, Sequel, Share(-out), Shrinkage, Sizings, Stint, Stipend, Subsistence, Suffer, Tare, Tax, Teene, Though, Tolerance, Tolerate, Tret, Viaticum, Weighting, Yield

Allotment-holder Cleruch

▸ **Allow** *see* ALLOT

Alloy Albata, Alnico®, Amalgam, Babbitt, Bell-metal, Billon, Brass, Britannia metal, Bronze, Cermet, Chrome(l), Compound, Constantan, Cupronickel, Duralumin®, Electron, Electrum, Eutectoid, Ferrochrome, Gunmetal, Invar®, Iridosmine, Kamacite, Latten, Magnalium, Magnox, Manganin®, Marmem, Mischmetal, Mix, Monel®, Nichrome®, Nickel-silver, Nicrosilal, Nimonic, Nitinol, Occamy, Oreide, Orichalc, Ormolu, Oroide, Osmiridium, Paktong, Pewter, Pinchbeck, Platinoid, Porous, Potin, Pot metal, Prince's metal, Shakudo, Shibuichi, Similor, Solder, Speculum, Spelter, Steel, Stellite®, Tambac, Terne, Tombac, Tombak, Tutenag, Zircal(l)oy, Zircoloy

▷ **Alloy** *may indicate* an anagram

Allright A1, Assuredly, Fit, Hale, Hunky(-dory), Jake, OK, Safe, Tickety-boo, Well

All-round Overhead, Versatile

All-seeing Panoptic

Allspice Jamaica pepper, Pimiento

All the same Nath(e)less, Nevertheless

Allude, Allusion Hint, Imply, Innuendo, Mention, Refer, Reference, Suggest

Allure, Alluring Agaçant(e), Charm, Circe, Decoy, Entice, Femme fatale, Glam, Glamour, Inviting, It, Magnet(ic), SA, Seduce, Seductive, Tempt, Trap, Trepan, Vamp

Alluvium Carse

Ally, Allied Accomplice, Agnate, Aide, Alley, Alliance, Backer, Belamy, Cognate, Colleague, Dual, Foederatus, German(e), Holy, Marble, Marmoreal, Partner, Plonker, Related, Taw, Unholy

Almanac Calendar, Clog, Ephemeris, Nautical, Nostradamus, Whitaker's, Wisden, Zadkiel

Almighty Creator, Dollar, God, Jehovah, Omnipotent

Almond Amygdal, Emulsion, Jordan, Marchpane, Marzipan, Orgeat, Praline, Ratafia, Sugared, Valencia

Almost Anear, Anigh, Close on, Most, Near, Nigh(ly), Practically, Ripe, Une(a)th, Virtually, Well-nigh, Welly

Alms Awmous, Charity, Dole, Handout, Zakat

Aloe Agave, Pita

Alone Hat, Jack, Lee-lane, Onely, Pat, Secco, Separate, Single, Singly, Sola, Solo, Solus, Tod, Unaccompanied, Unaided, Unattended, Unholpen

Along, Alongside Abeam, Aboard, Abreast, Apposed, Beside, By, Parallel

Aloof Abeigh, Apart, Asocial, Cool, Detached, Distant, Hou inch, Indrawn, Mugwump, Offish, Remote, Reserved, Reticent, Skeigh, Snooty, Stand-offish, Toffee-nosed, Unapproachable

Alpaca Paco

Alphabet ABC, Absey, Augmented Roman, Black-out, Brahmi, Braille, Chalcidian, Christcross, Cyrillic, Deaf, Devanagari, Estrang(h)elo, Futhark, Futhorc, Futhork, Glagol, Glagolitic, Glossic, Grantha, Hangul, Horn-book, International, IPA, ITA, Kana, Kanji, Katakana, Kufic, Latin, Manual, Nagari, Og(h)am, Pangram, Phonetic, Pinyin, Romaji, Roman, Runic, Signary, Syllabary

Alpine, Alps Australian, Bernese, Cottian, Dinaric, Gentian, Graian, Julian, Laburnum, Lepontine, Maritime, Matterhorn, Ortles, Pennine, Rhaetian, Savoy, Southern, Transylvanian, Tyrol, Western

Also Add, And, Eke, Item, Likewise, Moreover, Plus, Too, Und

Altar, Altar-cloth, Altarpiece Butsudan, Diptych, Dossal, Dossel, High, Polyptych, Retable, Shrine, Tabula, Triptych

Alter, Alteration Adapt, Adjust, Bushel, Change, Changeover, Cook, Correct, Customise, Distort, Evolve, Falsify, Lib, Modify, Modulate, Mutate, Recast, Revise, Transpose, Up-end, → **VARY**

▷ **Alter(native)** *may indicate* an anagram

Altercation Barney, Brawl, Fracas, Row, Words, Wrangle

Alternate, Alternating, Alternation, Alternative Boustrophedon, Bypass, Exchange, Instead, Metagenesis, → **OPTION**, Ossia, Other, Rotate, Second string, Solidus, Staggered, Systaltic, Tertian, Variant, Vicissitude

▷ **Alternately** *may indicate* every other letter

Althaea Mallow, Malva

Although Admitting, Albe(e), All-be, But, Even, Howsoever, Howsomever, Whereas, While

Altitude Elevation, Height, Meridian, Rated

Alto Countertenor

Altogether Algate(s), All-to-one, Completely, Entirely, Holus-bolus, Idea, In all, Nude, Nudity, Purely, Slick, Tout, Uncut, Wholly

▷ **Altogether** *may indicate* words to be joined

Altruistic Heroic, Humane, Philanthropic, Selfless, Unselfish

Alum Potash

Aluminium, Alumino-silicate Al, Bauxite, Gibbsite, Sillimanite, Stilbite, Tinfoil

Alumnus Graduate, OB

Always Algate(s), Ay(e), Constant, E'er, Eternal, Ever(more), Forever, I, Immer, Semper, Sempre, Still

Amalgamate Coalesce, Consolidate, Fuse, Merge, Unite

Amalthea Cornucopia

Amarylli(d)s Leocojum, Lily, Polianthes

Amass Accumulate, Assemble, Collect, Gather, Heap, Hoard, Pile, Upheap

Amateur(s) A, AA, Armchair, Beginner, Corinthian, Dilettante, DIY, Enthusiast, Ham, Inexpert, L, Laic, Lay, Neophyte, Novice, Prosumer, Sunday painter, Tiro, Tyro

Amatory Eros, Erotic, Fervent

Amaze(d), Amazement, Amazing Astonish, Astound, Awe, Awhape, Bewilder, Cor, Criv(v)ens, Dumbfound, Far out, Flabbergast, Gee-whiz, Gobsmack, Goodnow, Grace, Incredible, Jesus wept, Magical, Monumental, O, Open-eyed, Open-mouthed, Perplex, Poleaxe, Pop-eyed, Prodigious, Stagger, Stupefaction, Stupendous, Thunderstruck, Unreal

Amazon(ian) Ant, ATS, Brimstone, Britannia, Dragon, Hippolyta, Hoyden, Jivaro, Orellana, Penthesilea, Shield-maid, Shield-may, Thalestris, Tupi, Virago

Ambassador At-large, Diplomat, Elchee, Elchi, Eltchi, Envoy, Extraordinary, HE, Internuncio, Leaguer, Ledger, Legate, Leiger, Minister, Nuncio, Plenipo, Plenipotentiary

Amber Colophony, Lammer, Ligure, Resin, Retinite, Succinum

Ambience Aura, Milieu, Setting

Ambiguous, Ambiguity Amphibology, Cryptic, Delphic, Double, Double entendre, Enigmatic, Epicene, Equivocal, Loophole, Oracular, Weasel words

Ambit Scope

Ambition, Ambitious Aim, Arrivisme, Aspiring, Careerism, Drive, Emulate, Go-ahead, Goal, Go-getter, High-flier, Keen, Office-hunter, Purpose, Pushy, Rome-runner, Thrusting

Amble Meander, Mosey, Pace, Poddle, Saunter, Single-foot, Stroll

Ambrose Emrys

Ambrosia(l) Amreeta, Amrita, Beebread, Fragrant, Odorant, Ragweed, Savoury

Ambulance, Ambulanceman Badger, Blood-wagon, Field, Meat wagon, Pannier, Paramedic, Van, Yellow-flag, Zambu(c)k

Ambulatory Stoa

Ambush(ed) Ambuscade, Belay, Bushwhack, Embusque, Latitant, Lurch, Perdu(e), Trap, Watch, Waylay

Amelia Bloomer

Ameliorate Amend, Ease, Improve, Remedy

Amen Ammon, Approval, Inshallah, Verify

Amenable Putty

Amend(ment) Alter, Change, Correct, Expiate, Expurgate, Fifth, Protocol, Redress, Reform, Repair, Restore, → **REVISE**, Satisfy

▷ **Amend** *may indicate* an anagram

Ament Catkin, Idiot

America(n) A, Algonki(a)n, Algonqu(i)an, Am, Angeleno, Basket Maker, Caddo, Cajun, Carib, Chicano, Chickasaw, Chinook, Copperskin, Digger, Doughface, Down-easter, Federalist, Flathead, Fox, Gringo, Huron, Interior, Joe, Jonathan, Latino, Miskito, Mistec, Mixtec, Native, New World, Norteno, Olmec, Paisano, Salish, Stateside, Statesman, Statist, Tar-heel, Tico, Tupi, Uncle Sam, US(A), WASP, Yankee, Yanqui

Americium Am

Amethyst Oriental

Amiable Friendly, Genial, Gentle, Inquiline, Mungo, Sweet, Warm

Amid(st) Among, Atween, Between, Inter, Twixt

Amide Asparagine

Amine Putrescine, Spermine

Amino-acid Dopa, Tyrosine, Valine

Amiss Awry, Ill, Up, Wrong

Ammonia(c) Amide, Amine, Choline, Ethylamine, Hartshorn, Oshac

Ammonite Serpent-stone

Ammunition Ammo, Bandoleer, Bandolier, Buckshot, Bullets, Chain-shot, Dum-dum, Grape(shot), Grenade, Round, Shot, Slug, Tracer

Amnesia Anterograde, Fugal, Fugue, Lethe, Retrograde

Amnesty Oblivion, Pardon

Amoeba Melboean

Amok Rampaging

Among Amid(st), In, Inter al, Within

Amorous(ly) Casanova, Erotic, Fervent, Lustful, Smickly, Spoony, Warm

Amorphous Formless, Shapeless, Vague

Amount Come, Dose, Element, Figure, Handful, Lashings, Levy, Lot, Number, Ocean, Pot(s), Premium, Price, Quantity, Quantum, Span, Stint, Sum, Throughput, Volume, Whale, Wheel

Amour Affair(e), Intrigue, Love

Ampersand Tironian sign

Amphetamine Benny, Benzedrine, Speed

Amphibian, Amphibious Amb(l)ystoma, Amtrack, Anura, Axolotl, Batrachian, Caecilia, Caecilian, Desman, Eft, Frog, Guana, Hassar, Labyrinthodont, Mermaid, Mudpuppy, Newt, Olm, Proteus, Rana, Salamander, Salientia, Seal, Tadpole, Toad, Urodela(n), Urodele, Weasel

Amphipod Sand-screw, Shrimp

Amphitheatre Bowl, Circus Maximus, Coliseum, Colosseum, Ring, Stage

Ample, Amplitude Bellyful, Copious, Enough, Generous, Good, Large, Opulent, Profuse, Rich, Roomy, Round, Sawtooth, Uberous, Voluminous

Amplifier, Amplify Booster, Double, Eke, Enlarge, Hailer, Laser, Loud hailer, Maser, Megaphone, Push-pull, Solion, Tannoy®, Transistor, Treble

Amulet Abraxas, Charm, Churinga, Fetish, Greegree, Grigri, Grisgris, Haemon, Pentacle, Periapt, Phylactery, Sea-bean, Talisman, Tiki, Toadstone, Token

Amuse(ment), Amusing(ly) Caution, Cottabus, Disport, Diversion, Divert, Divertimento, Divertissement, Drole, Droll, Game, Gas, Giocoso, Glee, Hoot, Killing, Levity, Light, Occupy, Pleasure, Popjoy, Priceless, Regale, Rich, Scream, Slay, Solace, → **SPORT**, Tickle, Titillate, Wacky

Amy Johnson, Robsart

▶ **An** *see* **A**

Ana(s) Story, Teal

Anabaptist Abecedarian, Dipper, Dopper, Hutterite, Knipperdolling
Anableps Four-eyes
Anachronism Archaism, Solecism
Anaconda Water boa
Anacreon Te(i)an
Anaemia Aplastic, Cooley's, Fanconi's, Favism, Haemolytic, Megaloblastic,
  Pernicious, Sickle-cell, Thalassaemia
Anaesthetic, Anaesthetise, Anaesthetist Analgesic, Avertin®, Benzocaine,
  Bupivacaine, Caudal, Chloralose, Chloroform, Cocaine, Endotracheal, Epidural,
  Ether, Eucain(e), Freeze, Gas, General, Halothane, Infiltrate, Intravenous, Jabber,
  Ketamine, Lidocaine, Lignocaine, Local, Metopryl, Morphia, Novocaine, Number,
  Opium, Orthocaine, Pentothal, Phenacaine, Procaine, Rhigolene, Special K, Spinal,
  Stovaine, Topical, Trike, Urethan(e)
Anagram Jumble
Anal, Anus Poepol, Proctal, Tewel
Analgesic Aspirin, Bute, Codeine, Diclofenac, Disprin, Fentanyl, Ketamine,
  Menthol, Methadone, Morphia, Moxa, Opium, Painkiller, Paracetamol, Pethidine,
  Phencyclidine, Quina, Salicin(e), Sedative
Analogous, Analogy Akin, Corresponding, Like, Parallel, Similar
Analyse(r), Analysis Alligate, Anagoge, Anatomy, Assess, Blot, Breakdown,
  Combinatorial, Conformational, Construe, Diagnosis, Emic, Eudiometer, Examine,
  Explication, Factor, Force-field, Fourier, Gravimetric, Harmonic, Input-output, Job,
  Kicksorter, Lexical, Linguistic, Logical, Miscue, Numerical, Parse, Pollen, Process,
  Psych out, Qualitative, Quantative, Quantitative, Risk, Rundown, Sabermetrics,
  Scan(sion), Semantics, Sift, Spectral, Spectroscopic, Spectrum, Systems, Test,
  Transactional, Volumetric
▷ **Analysis** *may indicate* an anagram
Analyst Alienist, Investment, Jung, Lay, Psychiatrist, Shrink, Trick cyclist
Anarchist, Anarchy Black Bloc(k), Black Hand, Bolshevist, Chaos, Kropotkin,
  Nihilism, Provo, Rebel, Revolutionary, Trotskyite
Anathema Ban, Curse, Execration, Oath, Warling
Anatole, Anatolian France, Hittite, Turk
Anatomy, Anatomist Bones, Framework, Herophilus, Histology, Malpighi, Morbid,
  Prosector, Schneider, Spiegel, Worm
Ancestor, Ancestral, Ancestry Adam, Avital, Descent, Extraction, For(e)bear,
  Forefather, Gastraea, Humanoid, Lin(e)age, Parent, Predecessor, Proband,
  Profectitious, Progenitor, Propositus, Roots, Sire, Tipuna, Tree, Tupina
Anchor(age) Atrip, Berth, Bower, Cell, Deadman, Drag, Drift, Drogue, Eremite,
  Grapnel, Hawse, Hermit, Kedge, Kedger, Killick, Killock, Laura, Moor, Mud-hook,
  Mushroom, Nail, Ride, Roads(tead), Rode, Root, Scapa Flow, Sea, Sheet, Spithead,
  Stock, Stream, Toehold, Waist, Weather
Anchorite Recluse
Anchovy Fish, Pear
Ancient Antediluvian, Archaic, Auld-warld, Bygone, Early, Gonfanoner, Historic,
  Hoary, Iago, Immemorial, Lights, Neolithic, Ogygian, → **OLD(ER)**, Old-world,
  Primeval, Primitive, Pristine, Ur, Veteran
Ancient city Carthage, Ur
Ancillary Adjunct, Secondary, Subservient
And Als(o), Ampassy, Ampersand, Amperzand, Ampussyand, Besides, Et,
  Furthermore, Item, 'n', Plus, Tironian sign, Und
Andalusite Macle

Andiron Chenet, Dog, Firedog
Andrew(es) Aguecheek, Lancelot, Merry
Androgynous Epicene
Android Automaton, Golem, Robot
Anecdote(s) Ana, Exemplum, Story, Tale, Yarn
Anemometer Wind-sleeve, Windsock
Anemone Actinia, Pasque-flower, Windflower
Anew De integro, De novo
Angel(s) Abdiel, Adramelech, Apollyon, Archangel, Ariel, Arioch, Asmadai, Azrael, Backer, Banker, Beelzebub, Belial, Benefactor, Cake, Cherub, Clare, Destroying, Deva, Dominion, Dust, Eblis, Falls, Fuzzy-wuzzy, Gabriel, Guardian, Heavenly host, Hierarchy, Host, Iblis, Investor, Israfel, Ithuriel, Lucifer, Michael, Nurse, Power, Principality, Raphael, Recording, Rimmon, St, Seraph, Spirit, Throne, Uriel, Uzziel, Virtue, Watcher, Zadkiel, Zephiel
Angela Brazil
Angelica Archangel
Angel's wings Begonia
Anger, Angry → ANNOY, Bate, Bile, Black, Bristle, Choler(ic), Conniption, Cross, Dander, Displeased, Dudgeon, Enrage, Exasperation, Face, Fury, Gram, Heat, Het up, Horn-mad, Huff, Incense, Inflame, Infuriate, Iracund, Irascible, Ire, Kippage, Livid, Mad, Monkey, Moody, Nettle, Pique, Provoke, Radge, Rage, Rampant, Ratty, Renfierst, Rile, Roil, Rouse, Sore, Spleen, Steam, Stroppy, Tamping, Tantrum, Tarnation, Teen(e), Temper, Tene, Tooshie, Vex, Vies, Warm, Waspish, Waxy, Wound up, Wrath, Wroth, Yond
Angina Sternalgia, Vincent's
Angle(d), Angler, Angular, Angles, Angling Acute, Argument, Aspect, Attitude, Axil, Azimuthal, Canthus, Cast, Catch, Chiliagon, Coign, Complementary, Conjugate, Contrapposto, Corner, Cos, Critical, Diedral, Diedre, Dihedral, Elbow, Elevation, Ell, Exterior, Facial, Fish, Fish-hook, Fork, Geometry, Gonion, Hade, Hip, Hour, Hyzer, In, Incidence, Interior, L, Laggen, Laggin, Loft, Mitre, Mung, Negative, Oblique, Obtuse, Parallax, Pediculate, Perigon, Peterman, Piend, Piscator, Pitch, Pitch-cone, Plane, Polyhedral, Position, Positive, Quoin, Radian, Rake, Re-entrant, Reflex, Right, Rodster, Round, Sally, Saltchucker, Sine, Sinical, Slip, Solid, Spherical, Stalling, Steeve, Steradian, Straight, Supplementary, Sweepback, The gentle craft, Trotline, Vertical, Viewpoint, Visual, Walton, Washin, Weather, Wide-gab
Anglesey Mona
Anglican(s) CE-men, Conformist, Episcopal
Anglo-Catholic High-church
Anglo-Indian Qui-hi, Qui-hye, Topi-wallah
Angora Goat, Mohair, Rabbit
Angst Dread
Anguish(ed) Agony, Distress, Gip, Grief, Gyp, Hag-ridden, Heartache, Misery, → PAIN, Pang, Sorrow, Throes, → TORMENT, Torture, Woe
Angus Aberdeen
Animal(s) Acrita, Anoa, Armadillo, Atoc, Bag, Bandog, Barbastel, Beast, Bestial, Brute, Cariacou, Carnal, Chalicothere, Cleanskin, Coati, Creature, Criollo, Critter, Ethology, Fauna, Felis, Gerbil, Herd, Ichneumon, Jacchus, Jerboa, Kinkajou, Klipdas, Mammal, Marmoset, Marmot, Menagerie, Moose, Noctule, Oribi, Pack, Parazoon, Pet, Political, Protozoa, Pudu, Quagga, Rac(c)oon, Rhesus, Sensual, Sloth, Stud, Symphile, Tarsier, Teledu, Urson, Waler, Xenurus, Yale, Yapock, Zerda, Zoo

Animal-catcher Utricularia
Animate(d), Animation Activate, Actuate, Arouse, Biophor, Ensoul, Excite, Fire, Hortatory, Hot, Inspire, Live, Morph, Mosso, Perky, Pixil(l)ation, Rouse, Spiritoso, Spritely, Suspended, Verve, Vivacity, Vivify
Animosity Enmity, Friction, Hostility, Ill-will, Malice, Pique, Rancour
Ankle Coot, Cuit, Cute, Hock, Hucklebone, Knee, Malleolus, Talus
Ankle(t), Ankle covering Cootikin, Cuitikin, Cutikin, Gaiter, Jess
Anna, Anne, Annie Boleyn, Hathaway, Laurie, Oakley, Page, Pavlova, Pice, Sewell, Sister
Annal(s) Acta, Archives, Chronicles, Register
Annatto Roucou
Annex(e) Acquire, Add, Affiliate, Attach, Codicil, Extension, Subjoin
Annihilate Destroy, Erase, Exterminate, Obliterate, Slay
Anniversary Birthday, Feast, Jubilee, Obit, Triennial, Wedding, Yahrzeit
Annotate, Annotator Comment, Interpret, Note, Postil, Scholiast
Announce(r), Announcement Banns, Bellman, Biil(ing), Blazon, Bulletin, Communiqué, Declare, Decree, Divulgate, Gazette, Herald, Hermes, Inform, Intimate, Meld, Newsflash, Noise, Post, Preconise, Proclaim, Profess, Promulgate, Pronunciamente, Publish, Release, → REPORT, Rescript, Speaker(ine), State, Toastmaster, Town crier, Trumpet
Annoy(ance), Annoyed, Annoying Aggravate, Aggrieve, Anger, Antagonise, Badger, Blight, Bother, Bug, Bugbear, Chagrin, Choleric, Cross, Deuce(d), Disturb, Doggone, Doh, Drat, Fash, Fleabite, Frab, Fumed, Gall, Gatvol, Hack off, Hang, Harass, Hatter, Hector, Hip, Huff, Hump, Humph, Incense, Irk, → IRRITATE, Mickey-taking, Miff, Mischief, Molest, Moryah, Nag, Nark, Nettle, Noisome, Noy(ance), Peeve, Pesky, Pester, Pipsqueak, Pique, Plague, Provoke, Rankle, Rats, Ratty, Resentful, Ride, Rile, Roil, Rub, Shirty, Tiresome, Tracasserie, Try, Vex, Wazzock
Annual, Annuity Book, Contingent, Deferred, Etesian, → FLOWER, Half-hardy, Hardy, Immediate, Life, Pension, Perpetuity, Rente, Tontine, Yearbook, Yearly
Annul(ment) Abolish, Abrogate, Cashier, Cassation, Dissolution, Invalidate, Irritate, Negate, Recision, Repeal, Rescind, Reversal, Revoke, Vacatur, → VOID
Annular Toric
Anodyne Balm, Narcotic, Paregoric, Sedative
Anoint(ing) Anele, Cerate, Chris(o)m, Embrocate, Grease, Hallow, Nard, Smear
Anomaly Eccentric, Gravity, Magnetic, Mean, True
▷ **Anomaly** *may indicate* an anagram
Anon Again, Anew, Later, Soon
Anonymous Adespota, Anon, A.N.Other, Faceless, Grey, Impersonal, Somebody, Unnamed
Anorak Nerd, Wonk
Another Extra
Answer(ing), Answer(s) Account, Acknowledge, Amoebaean, Ans, Antiphon, Because, Comeback, Crib (sheet), Defence, Dusty, Echo, Key, Lemon, Light, No, Oracle, Rebuttal, Rebutter, Rein, Rejoin(der), Repartee, Reply, Rescript, Respond, Response, Responsum, Retort, Return, Riposte, Serve, Sol, Solution, Solve, Verdict, Yes
Ant(s), Anthill Amazon, Army, Bull(dog), Carpenter, Colony, Driver, Dulosis, Emmet, Ergataner, Ergates, Ergatomorph, Fire, Formic, Formicary, Leafcutter, Legionary, Myrmecoid, Myrmidon, Nasute, Neuter, Pharaoh, Pismire, Sauba, Slave, Soldier, Termite, Thief, Umbrella, Velvet, White, Wood

Antacid Magnesia, Peptic
Antagonist(ic), Antagonise Adverse, Estrange, Hostile, Oppugnant, Peare, Peer
Antarctica Adelie Land, Byrd Land, Graham Land, Wilkes Land
Ant-bear Tamanoir
Ante Bet, Punt, Stake
Ant-eater Aardvark, Banded, Echidna, Edental, Giant, Manis, Numbat, Pangolin, Scaly, S(e)ladang, Spiny, Tamandu, Tamandua, Tapir
Antelope Addax, Antilope, Blackbuck, Blaubok, Blesbok, Bloubok, Bluebuck, Bongo, Bontebok, Bubal(is), Bushbuck, Cabric, Chamois, Chikara, Chiru, Dikdik, Duiker, Duyker, Dzeren, Eland, Elk, Gazelle, Gemsbok, Gerenuk, Gnu, Goa, Goral, Grysbok, Harnessed, Hartbees, Hartebeest, Impala, Inyala, Kaama, Kid, Klipspringer, Kob, Kongoni, Koodoo, Kudu, Lechwe, Madoqua, Marshbuck, Mhorr, Mohr, Nagor, Nilgai, Nilgau, Nyala, Nylghau, Oribi, Oryx, Ourebi, Ox, Pale-buck, Pallah, Prongbuck, Pronghorn, Pronk, Puku, Pygarg, Reebok, Reedbuck, Rhebok, Sable, Saiga, Sasin, Sassaby, Serow, Sitatunga, Situtunga, Springbok, Steenbok, Steinbock, Stemback, Stembok, Suni, Takin, Thar, Topi, Tragelaph, Tsessebe, Waterbuck, Wildebeest
Antenna Aerial, Dipole, Dish, Feeler, Horn, Sensillum, TVRO
Anterior Anticous, Earlier, Front, Prior
Anthelmintic Worm
Anthem Chant, Die Stem, Hymn, Introit, Isodica, Marseillaise, Motet(t), National, Psalm, Red Flag, Responsory, Song, Star Spangled Banner, Stem, Theme, Tract, Troparion
Anthology Album, Ana, Chrestomathy, Digest, Divan, Florilegium, Garland, Pick, Spicilege
Anthony Absolute, Adverse, Trollope
Anthracite Blind-coal
Anthrax Sang
Anthropo(i)d Peripatus, Sivapithecus
Anthropologist Heyerdahl, Mead
Anti Against, Agin, Con, Hostile
Anti-aircraft AA
Anti-bacterial, Antibiotic Actinomycin, Amoxicillin, Ampicillin, Aureomycin®, Avoparcin, Bacitracin, Bacteriostat, Cecropin, Cephalosporin, Cipro®, Ciprofloxacin, Cloxacillin, Colistin, Cortisone, Co-trimoxazole, Doxorubicin, Doxycycline, Drug, Erythromycin, Gentamicin, Gramicidin, Griseofulvin, Interferon, Interleukin, Kanamycin, Lincomycin, Lineomycin, Magainin, Methicillin, Mitomycin, Neomycin, Nystatin, Opsonin, Oxacillin, Oxytetracycline, Penicillin, Polymixin, Quinolone, Rifampicin, Rifamycin, Spectinomycin, Streptomycin, Streptothricin, Terramycin®, Tetracycline, Tyrocidine, Tyrothricin, Vancomycin, Virginiamycin, Wide-spectrum
Antibody Agglutinin, Amboceptor, Antitoxin, Blocker, H(a)emolysin, Hybroid, Isoagglutinin, Lysin, Monoclonal, Opsonin, Precipitin, Reagin
Antic(s) Caper, Dido, Frolic, Gambado, Hay, Prank, Shenanigan, Stunt
Anti-carlist Queenite
Anticipate, Anticipation Antedate, Augur, Await, Drool, → EXPECT, Forecast, Foresee, Foresight, Forestall, Foretaste, Forethought, Hope, Intuition, Preparation, Prevenancy, Prolepsis, Prospect, Second-guess, Type
Anticlimax Bathos, Damp squib, Deflation, Letdown
Anticline Upwrap
Anticlockwise Dextrorse, Laevorotatory, Widdershins, Withershins

Anticoagulant C(o)umarin, Heparin, Hirudin, Prostacyclin, Warfarin
Anticommunist McCarthyism
Anticyclone High
Antidote Adder's wort, Alexipharmic, Angelica, Antivenin, Arrowroot, Bezoar, Contrayerva, Cure, Dimercaprol, Emetic, Guaco, Interleukin, Mithridate, Nostrum, Orvietan, Remedy, Ribavirin, Senega, Theriac(a), (Venice-)Treacle
Anti-freeze Glycerol, Lagging
Antigen Agglutinogen, Hapten(e)
Antihistamine Dimenhydrinate
Anti-imperialist Guelf, Guelph
Antimacassar Tidy
Antimonopoly Trust buster
Antimony Kohl, Sb, Stibium, Tartar emetic
Antioxidant Lycopene
Anti-parliamentarian Poujadist
Antipasto Caponata
Antipathy Allergy, Aversion, Detest, → DISLIKE, Enmity, Intolerance, Repugnance
Anti-perfectionist Cobden
Antiphon The Reproaches
Antipodean Abo, Antarctic, Antichthon, Enzed, Underworld
Antipope Novatian(us)
Anti-protectionist Cobden
Antiquated, Antique, Antiquarian Ancient, Archaic, A(u)stringer, Bibelot, Curio, Dryasdust, FAS, Fog(e)y, Fogram(ite), Fossil, Old-fangled, Ostreger, Relic
Anti-reformer Obscurant
Anti-revolutionary White
Anti-Roman Ghibel(l)ine
Anti-royalist Whig
Anti-Semitic Pamyat
Antiseptic Acriflavine, Carbolic, Cassareep, Creosote, Disinfectant, Eupad, Eusol, Formaldehyde, Formalin, Formol, Germicide, Guaiacol, Iodine, Lister, Lysol®, Phenol, Sterile, Tar, Thymol, Tutty
Anti-slavery Free-soil, Wilberforce
Anti-smoker ASH, Misocapnic
Antisocial Hostile, Ishmaelitish, Misanthropic, Oik
Antithesis Contrary, Converse, Opposite
Anti-three Noetian
Antitoxin Antibody, Antivenin, Guaco, Serum, Vaccine
Anti-union Secesher
Antivitamin Pyrithiamine
Antler(s) Bosset, Crown, Horn, Palm, Rights, Staghorn, Surroyal, Tine
Ant-proof Bilian
▶ **Anus** see ANAL
Anvil Bick-iron, Block, Incus, Stiddie, Stithy
Anxiety, Anxious Angst, Brood, Care(ful), Cark, Concern, Disquiet, Dysthymia, Fanteeg, Fantigue, Fantod, Fraught, Grave, Heebie-jeebies, Hypochondria, Inquietude, Itching, Jimjams, Jumpy, Keen, Nerviness, Reck, Restless, Scruple, Separation, Solicitous, Stress, Suspense, Sweat, Tension, Toey, Trepidation, Twitchy, Unease, Unquiet, Upset, Uptight, White-knuckle, Worriment
Any Arrow, Ary, Some

Anybody, Anyone Everyman, One, Whoso, You

Anyhow, Anyway Anyroad(s), However, Leastways, Regardless

Anything Aught, Diddly-squat, Oucht, Owt, Whatnot

▷ **Anyway** *may indicate* an anagram

Apache Arizona, AZ

Apart Aloof, Aside, Asunder, Atwain, Beside, Separate

Apartheid Racism, Verkrampte

Apartment Atrium, Ben, Condominium, Digs, Duplex, Efficiency, Flat, Insula, Mansion, Pad, Paradise, Penthouse, Pied-a-terre, Quarters, Room, Simplex, Solitude, Suite, Tenement, Unit, Walk-up

Apathetic, Apathy Accidie, Acedia, Incurious, Indifferent, Languid, Lethargic, Listless, Lobotomized, Pococurante, Stoical, Torpid

Ape(-like), Apeman Anthropoid, Barbary, Big-foot, Bonobo, Catarrhine, Copy, Dryopithecine, Gelada, Gibbon, Gorilla, → IMITATE, Magot, Mimic, → MONKEY, Orang, Paranthropus, Parrot, Pithecoid, Pongo, → PRIMATE, Proconsul, Sacred, Simian, Simulate, Yowie

Aperient Cascara, Laxative, Senna

Aperitif → DRINK, Pernod®

Aperture Balistraria, Chink, Fenestella, Hole, Keyhole, Opening, Orifice, Osculum, Peephole, Pinhole, Porta, Relative, Spiracle, Swallow, Window

Apex Acme, Culmen, Gonion, Keystone, Knoll, Knowe, Solar, Summit, Vortex

Aphid Ant-cow, Phylloxera

Aphorism Adage, Epigram, Gnome, Pensée, Proverb, Sutra

Aphrodisiac, Aphrodite Cytherean, Erotic, Idalian, Paphian, Philter, Philtre, Spanish fly, Urania, Yohimbine

Aplomb Assurance, Cool, Equanimity, Poise, Sangfroid, Serenity

Apocryphal Spurious, Tobit

Apograph Roneo®

Apollo Belvedere, Pythian, Sun

Apology Excuse, Justifier, Mockery, Oops, Pardon, Scuse, Sir-reverence

Apostate Citer, → HERETIC, Pervert, Rat, Recreant, Renegade, Runagate, Turncoat

Apostle, Apostolic Cuthbert, → DISCIPLE, Evangelist, Johannine, Jude, Matthew, Pauline, Spoon, Thad(d)eus, Twelve

Apostrophe, Apostrophise Elision, O(h), Soliloquy, Tuism

Apothegm Dictum, Maxim, Motto

Appal(ling) Abysmal, Affear(e), Aghast, Dire, Dismay, Egregious, Frighten, Horrify, Piacular, Shock, Tragic

▷ **Appallingly** *may indicate* an anagram

Apparatus Alembic, Alkalimeter, Appliance, Aspirator, Autoclave, Caisson, Calorimeter, Chemostat, Churn, Clinostat, Coherer, Colorimeter, Commutator, Condenser, Cosmotron, Critical, Cryostat, Davis, Defibrillator, → DEVICE, Digester, Ebullioscope, Effusiometer, Electrograph, Electrophorus, Electroscope, Eprouvette, Equipment, Eudiometer, Exciter, Fixings, Gadget, Gasogene, Gazogene, Golgi, Graith, Gyroscope, Heliograph, Helioscope, Hemocytometer, Hodoscope, Holophote, Hydrophone, Hygrostat, Incubator, Injector, Inspirator, Installation, Instrument, Jacquard, Kipp's, Kymograph, Lease-rod, Life-preserver, Loom, Masora(h), Microreader, Mimeograph, Multi-gym, Nephoscope, Nitrometer, Oscillograph, Oxygenator, Pasteuriser, Percolator, Phonometer, Photophone, Photostat®, Phytotron, Plate-warmer, Plethysmograph, Plumber's snake, Potometer, Projector, Proto®, Pulmotor®, Radiosonde, Replenisher, Resistor, Respirator, Respirometer, Resuscitator, Retort, Rotisserie, Rounce, Scintiscanner,

Scrubber, Scuba, Semaphore, Set, Skimmer, Slide rest, Snorkel, Soundboard, Sphygmograph, Spirophore, Stellarator, Steriliser, Still, Substage, Switchgear, Tackle, Tackling, Talk-you-down, Telecine, Teleprinter, Teleseme, Tellurian, Thermopile, Tokamak, Transformer, Transmitter, Tromp(e), Tuner, Ventouse, Wheatstone's bridge, Whip-and-derry, ZETA

Apparel Attire, Besee, → **COSTUME**, Garb, Raiment, Wardrobe, Wardrop

Apparent(ly) Ap, Clear, Detectable, Manifest, Ostensible, Outward, Overt, Plain, Prima facie, Seeming, Semblance, Visible

▷ **Apparent** *may indicate* a hidden word

Apparition Dream, Eidolon, Fetch, Ghost, → **ILLUSION**, Phantom, Shade, Spectre, Visitant, Wraith

Appeal(ing) Ad, Beg, Cachet, Catchpenny, Charisma, Charm, Cri de coeur, Cry, Entreat, Entreaty, Epirrhema, Fetching, Invocation, It, Miserere, O, Oomph, Plead, SA, Screeve, Sex(iness), Solicit, SOS, Suit

Appear(ance) Advent, Air, Apport, Arrival, Aspect, Broo, Brow, Burst, Cast, Compear, Debut, Emerge, Enter, Exterior, Eye, Facade, Facies, Far(r)and, Farrant, Fa(s)cia, Feature, Format, Garb, Guise, Habitus, Hue, Image, Kithe, Kythe, Looks, Loom, → **MANNER**, Mien, Occur, Ostensibly, Ostent, Outward, Person, Phase, Phenomenon, Physiognomy, Presence, Prosopon, Represent, Rig, Rise, Seem, Semblance, Show, Spring, Superficies, Theophany, View, Visitation, Wraith

Appease(ment) Allay, Alleviate, Calm, Conciliation, Danegeld, Mitigate, → **MOLLIFY**, Munichism, Pacify, Placate, Propitiate, Satisfy, Soothe, Sop

Append(age) Adjunct, Affix, Aglet, Allantois, Annex, Antennule, Aril, Arista, Cercus, Chelicera, Codpiece, Ctene, Fang, Flagellum, Hanger-on, Lobe, Lug, Palp(us), Paraglossa, Parapodium, Pedipalp, Postfix, Stipel, Stipule, Suffix, Swimmeret, Tail, Tailpiece, Tentacle, Ugly, Uropod, Uvula

Appendix Addendum, Apocrypha, Codicil, Grumbling, Label, Pendant, Pendent, Rider, Schedule, Vermiform

Appetite, Appetitive, Appetise(r) Amuse-bouche, Antepast, Antipasto, Aperitif, Appestat, Bhagee, Bhajee, Bulimia, Bulimy, Canapé, Concupiscence, Concupy, Crudités, Desire, Dim-sum, Entremes(se), Entremets, Flesh, Hunger, Limosis, Malacia, Meze, Mezze, Nacho, Orectic, Orexis, Passion, Pica, Polyphagia, Relish, Tapa(s), Titillate, Twist, Ventripotent, Yerd-hunger, Yird-hunger

Applaud, Applause Acclaim, Bravo, → **CHEER**, Clap, Claque, Eclat, Encore, Extol, Hum, Kentish fire, Olé, Ovation, Praise, Root, Ruff, Tribute

Apple Adam's, Alligator, Bad, Baldwin, Balsam, Biffin, Blenheim orange, Braeburn, Bramley, Cashew, Charlotte, Codlin(g), Cooker, Costard, Crab, Custard, Dead Sea, Discord, Eater, Granny Smith, Greening, Jenneting, John, Jonathan, Leather-coat, Love, Mammee, May, McIntosh (red), Medlar, Nonpareil, Oak, Pacific Rose, Pearmain, Pippin, Pomace, Pome(roy), Pom(e)water, Pomroy, Potato, Punic, Pupil, Pyrus, Quarantine, Quarenden, Quar(r)ender, Quarrington, Quodlin, Redstreak, Reinette, Rennet, Ribston(e), Ripstone, Rotten, Ruddock, Russet, Seek-no-further, Snow, Sops-in-wine, Sorb, Sturmer, Sturmer (Pippin), Sugar, Sweeting, Thorn, Toffee, Windfall, Winesap

Apple juice Malic

Apple-picker Atalanta

Applicant Ordinand, Postulant

Application, Apply, Appliance(s) Address, Adhibit, Appeal, Appose, Assiduity, Barrage, Blender, Devote, Diligence, Dressing, Exercise, Foment, Give, Implement, Inlay, Juicer, Lay, Liquidiser, Lotion, Mixer, Ointment, Opodeldoc, Petition, Plaster,

Poultice, Put, Request, Resort, Respirator, Rub, Sinapism, Stupe, Toggle, Truss, → **USE**, Vice, White goods

Appliqué Hawaiian

Appoint(ee), Appointment Advowson, Assign, Berth, Date, Delegate, Depute, Designate, Dew, Due, Executor, Induction, Installation, Make, Name, → **NOMINATE**, Nominee, Office, Ordain, Position, Post, Posting, Rendezvous, Room, Set, Tryst

▷ **Appointed** *may indicate* an anagram

Apportion(ment) Allocate, Allot, Mete, Parcel, Ration, Share, Weigh

Apposite Apt, Cogent, Germane, Pat, Pertinent, Relevant, Suitable

Appraise, Appraisal Analyse, → **EVALUATE**, Gauge, Guesstimate, Judge, Once-over, Tape, → **VALUE**, Vet

Appreciate, Appreciation Acknowledgement, Cherish, Clap, Dig, Endear, Esteem, Gratefulness, Increase, Phwoar, Prize, Realise, Recognise, Regard, Relish, Rise, Sense, Stock, Taste, Thank you, Treasure, → **VALUE**

Apprehend, Apprehension Afears, Alarm, Arrest, → **CATCH**, Collar, Fear, Grasp, Insight, Intuit, Perceive, Quailing, See, Suspense, Take, Toey, Trepidation, Uh-oh, Unease, Uptake

Apprehensive Jumpy, Nervous, Uneasy

Apprentice(ship) Article, Commis, Cub, Devil, Garzone, Improver, Indent(ure), Jockey, L, Learner, Lehrjahre, Novice, Noviciate, Novitiate, Printer's devil, Pupillage, Snob, Tiro, Trainee, Turnover, Tyro(ne)

Approach(ing), Approachable Abord, Access, Accost, Advance, Affable, Anear, Appropinquate, Appulse, Avenue, Close, Come, Converge, Cost(e), Draw nigh, Drive, Driveway, Fairway, Feeler, Gate, Imminent, Line, Near, Nie, Overture, Pitch, Procedure, Road, Run-up, Towards, Verge

Appropriate Abduct, Abstract, Annex, Apposite, Apt, Asport, Assign, Bag, Borrow, Collar, Commandeer, Commensurate, Confiscate, Convenient, Due, Embezzle, Expedient, Fit, Germane, Good, Happy, Hijack, Hog, Impound, Jump, Just, Meet, Nick, Pertinent, Pilfer, Plagiarise, Pocket, Pre-empt, Proper, Purloin, Right, Seise, Seize, Sequester, Sink, Snaffle, Steal, Suit, Swipe, Take, Timely, Trouser, Usurp

Approval, Approve(d), Approbation Adopt, Allow, Amen, Applaud, Attaboy, Aye, Blessing, Bravo, Brownie points, Change, → **COUNTENANCE**, Credit, Cushty, Dig, Endorse, Favour, Hear hear, Homologate, Hubba-hubba, Imprimatur, Initial, Kitemark, Know, Laud, Nod, Okay, Olé, Orthodox, Plaudit, Rah, Ratify, Rubber-stamp, Sanction, Stotter, Thumbs-up, Tick, Tribute, Yay, Yes, Zindabad

Approximate(ly), Approximation Almost, Circa, Close, Coarse, Estimate, Guess, Imprecise, Near, Roughly

Apricot Mebos

April, April fool Apr, Huntiegowk, Hunt-the-gowk

Apron Barm-cloth, Bib, Blacktop, Brat, Bunt, Canvas, Dick(e)y, Ephod, Fig-leaf, Gremial, Ice, Napron, Pinafore, Pinner, Pinny, Placket, Stage, Tablier, Tier, Waist

Apse Concha, Exedra, Niche, Recess, Tribune

Apt(ly) Apposite, Appropriate, Apropos, Ben trovato, Capable, Evincive, Fit, Gleg, Happy, Liable, Pat, Prone, Suitable, Tends

Aptitude Ability, Bent, Faculty, Flair, Gift, Knack, Skill, Talent, Tendency

Aqua(tic) Euglena, Flustra, Lentic, Lotic, Regia, Zizania

Aqualung Rebreather, Scuba

Aquamarine Madagascar

Aqueduct Canal, Channel, Conduit, Hadrome, Xylem

Arab(ian), Arabia, Arabic Abdul, Adeni, Algorism, Ali, Baathist, Bahraini, Bahrein, Bedouin, Druse, Druz(e), Effendi, Fedayee(n), Gamin, Geber, Hashemite, Himyarite, Horse, Iraqi, Jawi, Lawrence, Moor, Mudlark, Nabat(a)ean, Nas(s)eem, Nes(h)ki, Omani, Omar, PLO, Qatari, Rag(head), Saba, Sab(a)ean, Saracen, Saudi, Semitic, Sheikh, Street, Syrian, UAR, Urchin, Yemen

Arabis Cress

Arachnid Podogona, Ricinulei, → **SPIDER**

Arbiter, Arbitrator ACAS, Censor, Daysman, Judge, Negotiator, Ombudsman, Prud'homme, Ref(eree), Umpire

Arbitrary Despotic, Haphazard, Peculiar, Random, Wanton

Arboreal, Arbour Bower, Dendroid, Pergola, Trellis

Arc Azimuth, Bow, Carbon, → **CURVE**, Flashover, Fogbow, Halo, Island, Limb, Mercury, Octant, Quadrant, Rainbow, Reflex, Seadog, Trajectory, White rainbow

Arcade Amusement, Burlington, Cloister, Gallery, Loggia, Mall, Penny, Triforium

Arcadia(n) Idyllic, Nemoral, Sylvan

Arcane Esoteric, Obscure, Occult, Orphism, Recherché, Rune, Secret

Arch(ed), Arching Acute, Admiralty, Arblaster, Arcade, Arcature, Archivolt, Arcuate, Camber, Chief, Coom, Counterfort, Crafty, Cross-rib, Crown-green, Ctesiphon, → **CUNNING**, Curve, Elfin, Embow, Espiegle, Fallen, Flying buttress, Fog-bow, Fornicate, Fornix, Gill, Gothic, Hance, Haunch, Hog, Horseshoe, Instep, Intrados, Keel, Keystone, Lancet, Leery, Lierne, Limb-girdle, Marble, Neural, Norman, Ogee, Ogive, Opistholomos, Order, Parthian, Pectoral, Pelvic, Pointed, Portal, Proscenium, Recessed, Relieving, Roach, Roguish, Roman, Safety, Saucy, Segmental, Shouldered, Skew, Soffit, Span, Squinch, Stilted, Trajan, Triumphal, Vault, Zygoma

Archaeological, Archaeologist Carter, Dater, Dig, Evans, Industrial, Layard, Leakey, Mycenae, Petrie, Pothunter, Sutton Hoo, Wheeler, Woolley

Archangel Azrael, Gabriel, Israfeel, Israfel, Israfil, Jerahmeel, Michael, Raguel, Raphael, Sariel, Satan, Uriel, Yellow

Arch-binder Voussoir

Archbishop Anselm, Augustine, Cosmo, Cranmer, Davidson, Dunstan, Ebor, Elector, Hatto, Lanfranc, Lang, Langton, Laud, Metropolitan, Primate, Temple, Trench, Tutu, Whitgift

Archdeacon Ven

Archduke Trio

Archer Acestes, Bow-boy, → **BOWMAN**, Cupid, Eros, Hood, Philoctetes, Sagittary, Tell, Toxophilite

Archetype Avatar, Form, Model, Pattern

Archibald, Archie, Archy Ack-ack, Cockroach, Oerlikon, Rice, Roach

Archilochian Epode

Archipelago Alexander, Antarctic, Azores, Bismarck, Camaguey, East Indian, Fiji, Franz Josef Land, Gulag, Japan, Kerguelen, Malay, Maldives, Marquesas, Mergui, Novaya Zemlya, Palmer, Paumotu, St Pierre and Miquelon, Severnaya Zemlya, Spitsbergen, Sulu, Svalbard, Tierra del Fuego, Tonga, Tuamoto, West Indies

Architect(ure), Architectural Arcology, Baroque, Bauhaus, Bricolage, Brutalism, Byzantine, Churrigueresque, Composite, Computer, Corinthian, Creator, Data-flow, Decorated, Designer, Domestic, Doric, Early English, Elizabethan, Entablature, Federation, Flamboyant, Georgian, Gothic, Greek Revival, Ionic, Italian, Jacobean, Landscape, Lombard, Mission, Moderne, Moorish, Moresque, Mudejar, Naval, Neoclassical, Neo-gothic, Norman, Palladian, Pelasgian, Perpendicular, Planner, Plateresque, Prostyle, Queen Anne, Romanesque,

Saracenic, Saxon, Spandrel, Spandril, Tectonic, Tudor, Tudorbethan, Tuscan, Vitruvian

ARCHITECTS

4 letters:
Adam
Kent
Loos
Nash
Shaw
Webb
Wood
Wren

5 letters:
Gaudi
Inigo
Nervi
Pugin
Scott
Soane

Utzon
Wyatt

6 letters:
Casson
Foster
Nissen
Repton
Spence
Street
Wright

7 letters:
Behrens
Bernini
Columbo
Gropius

Lutyens
Venturi
Vignola

8 letters:
Bramante
Palladio
Piranesi
Saarinen
Vanbrugh

9 letters:
Hawksmoor
Macquarie
Vitruvius

10 letters:
Inigo Jones
Mackintosh
Trophonius
Van der Rohe

11 letters:
Abercrombie
Butterfield
Le Corbusier

12 letters:
Brunelleschi

14 letters:
Vitruvius Pollo

Architrave Epistyle, Platband
Archive(s) Backfile, Muniment, PRO, Records, Register
Archon Draco
Arch-villain Ringleader
Arctic Estotiland, Frigid, Hyperborean, In(n)uit, Inupiat, Polar, Tundra
Ardent, Ardour Aflame, Aglow, Boil, Broiling, Burning, Fervent, Fervid, Fiery, Fire, Flagrant, Heat, Het, → **HOT**, Hot-brained, In, Mettled, Mettlesome, Passion(ate), Perfervid, Rage, Spiritous, Vehement, Warm-blooded, Zealous, Zeloso
Arduous Laborious, Uphill
Are A, Exist, 're
Area Acre, Aleolar, Apron, Arctogaea, Are, Bailiwick, Belt, Bovate, Broca's, Built-up, Carucate, Catchment, Centare, Centiare, Centre, Conurbation, Craton, Curtilage, Dec(i)are, Dedans, Depressed, Dessiatine, Development, Disaster, District, Domain, Endemic, Eruv, Extent, Farthingland, Gau, Goal, Grey, Growth, Heartland, Hectare, Henge, Hide, Husbandland, Imperium, Input, Karst, Landmass, Lathe, Latitude, Lek, Locality, Lodg(e)ment, Manor, Metroplex, Milieu, Morgen, Mush, Neogaea, No-go, Notogaea, Orb, Oxgang, Oxgate, Oxland, Parish, Patch, Penalty, Place, Pleasance, Plot, Precinct, Province, Purlieu, Quad, Quadrat, Quarter, Range, Redevelopment, Refugium, → **REGION**, Renosterveld, Rest, Restricted, Retrochoir, Rood, Sector, Service, Shire, Site, Slurb, Special, Staging, Sterling, Subtopia, Support, Target, Technical, Terrain, Territory, Theatre, Tie, Tract, Tundra, Tye, Urban, Ure, White, Work station, Yard, Zone
Arena Circus, Cockpit, Dohyo, Field, Lists, Maidan, Olympia, → **RING**, Rink, Stadium, Tiltyard, Velodrome, Venue
Argal Ergo
Argent Ag, Silver
Argentina RA
Argon Ar

Argonaut Acastus, Jason, Lynceus, Meleager, Nautilus

Argot Flash, Idiom, Jargon, Lingo, Scamto, Shelta

Argue, Argument(ative) Altercation, Antistrophon, Argie-bargie, Argle-bargle, Argy-bargy, Bandy, Beef, Blue, Brush, Case, Casuism, Choplogic, Conflict, Contend, Contest, Cosmological, Debate, Deprecate, Diallage, Difference, Dilemma, Dispute, Dissent, Elenchus, Elenctic, Enthymeme, Eristic, Exchange, Expostulate, Forensic, Free-for-all, Generalisation, Hysteron proteron, Logic, Logomachy, Moot, Ob and soller, Object, Ontological, Paralogism, Patter, Pettifog, Plead, Polemic, Polylemma, Premiss, Propound, Quarrel, Quibble, Quodlibet, Rammy, Ratiocinate, → **REASON**, Remonstrate, Row, Run-in, Sophism, Sophistry, Sorites, Spar, Stickle, Straw man, Stroppy, Summation, Syllogism, Teleological, Theme, Thetic, Third man, Tiff, Transcendental, Trilemma, Wrangle, Yike

Argyle Argathelian

Aria Ballad, Cabaletta, Melody, Song

Arid Dry, Parched

Ariel Pen

Arise Appear, Be, Develop, Emanate, Emerge, Upgo, Wax

Aristocracy, Aristocrat(ic) Blood, Boyar, Buckeen, Classy, Debrett, Duc, Elite, Eupatrid, Gentle, Gentry, Grandee, High-hat, Junker, Nob, Noble, Optimate, Passage, Patrician, Thane, Tony, U-men, Upper-crust, Well-born

Aristotle Peripatetic, Stagirite, Stagyrite

Arithmetic(ian) Algorism, Algorith, Arsmetrick, Cocker, Euclid, Logistic, Modular, Sums

Ark(wright) Chest, Noah

Arly Thicket

Arm(ed), Arms Akimbo, Arsenal, Bearing, Brachial, Branch, Bundooks, Canting, Cove, Crest, Cross bow, Embattle, Equip, Escutcheon, Fin, Firth, Frith, Gnomon, Halbert, Hatchment, Heel, Heraldic, Inlet, Jib, Krupp, Limb, Loch, Long, Member, Olecranon, Pick-up, Quillon, Radius, Ramous, Rocker, Rotor, SAA, Secular, Shield, Shotgun, Side, Small, Smooth-bore, Spiral, Tappet, Tentacle, Timer, Tone, Tooled-up, Transept, Tremolo, Ulnar, → **WEAPON**, Whip

▷ **Arm** *may indicate* an army regiment, etc.

Armada Spanish

Armadillo Dasypod, Dasypus, Fairy, Giant, Pangolin, Peba, Pichiciago, Tatou(ay), Xenurus

Armature Keeper, Shuttle

Armenian Haikh, Yezedi

Armistice Truce

Armour(ed) Ailette, Armature, Armet, Barbette, Beaver, Besagew, Bevor, Brasset, Breastplate, Brigandine, Buckler, Byrnie, Camail, Cannon, Casspir, Cataphract, Chaffron, Chain, Chamfrain, Chamfron, Character, Chausses, Corium, Cors(e)let, Couter, Cuirass, Cuish, Cuisse, Culet, Curat, Curiet, Cush, Defence, Fauld, Garniture, Gear, Genouillère, Gere, Gorget, Greave, Habergeon, Hauberk, Hoplology, Jack, Jambeau, Jazerant, Jesserant, Lamboys, Loricate, Mail, Male, Mentonnière, Nasal, Nosepiece, Palette, Panoply, Panzer, Pauldron, Petta, Placcat, Placket, Plastron, Plate, Poitrel, Poleyn, Pouldron, Rerebrace, Sabaton, Scale, Secret, → **SHIELD**, Solleret, Spaudler, Splint, Stand, Tace, Tank, Taslet, Tasse(t), Thorax, Tonlet, Tuille, Vambrace, Vantbrass, Ventail, Visor, Voider, Weed

Armpit Axilla, Oxter

Armstrong Louis, Satchmo

Army Arrière-ban, BEF, Blue Ribbon, Church, Colours, Confederate, Crowd, Federal,

Field, Fyrd, Golden (Horde), Horde, Host, IRA, Junior Service, Land, Landwehr, Lashkar, Legion, Line, Military, Militia, Mobile Command, Multitude, New Model, Para-military, Red, SA, Sabaoth, Salvation, SAS, Sena, Service, Soldiers, Standing, Swarm, TA, Territorial, Thin red line, Volunteer, War, Wehrmacht

▷ **Army** *may indicate* having arms

Aroma(tic) Allspice, Aniseed, Aryl, Balmy, Coriander, Fenugreek, Fragrant, Odorous, Pomander, Spicy, Stilbene, Vanillin, Wintergreen

Around About, Ambient, Circa, Near, Peri-, Skirt, Tour

▷ **Around** *may indicate* one word around another

Arouse, Arousal Alarm, → EXCITE, Fan, Fire, Incite, Inflame, Must(h), Needle, Provoke, Stimulate, Stole, Suscitate, Touch up, Urolagnia, Waken

Arrange(r), Arrangement Adjust, Array, Attune, Bandobast, Bank, Bundobust, Concert, Concinnity, Configuration, Design, Display, Dispose, Do, Edit, Engineer, Finger, Fix, Foreordain, Format, Formation, Formwork, Grade, Ikebana, Layout, Marshal, Modus vivendi, Orchestrate, Orchestration, Ordain, → ORDER, Ordnance, Organise, Pack, Pattern, Perm, Permutation, Plan, Position, Prepare, Prepense, Quincunx, Redactor, Regulate, Run, Schedule, Schema, Scheme, Score, Set, Settle, Sort, Spacing, Stack, Stage-manage, Stereoisomerism, Stow, Straighten, Style, System, Tabulate, Tactic, Taxis, Tidy, Transcribe, Vertical

▷ **Arrange** *may indicate* an anagram

Arras Tapestry

Array(ed) Attire, Bedight, Deck, Herse, Logic, Marshal, Muster, Panoply, Phased, Seismic

Arrear(s) Aft, Ahint, Backlog, Behind, Debt, Owing

Arrest(ed), Arresting Abort, Alguacil, Alguazil, Ament, Apprehend, Attach, Attract, Blin, Book, Bust, Caption, Capture, Cardiac, Catch, Check, Citizen's, Collar, Detain, False, Furthcoming, Hold, House, Knock, Lift, Lightning, Nab, Nail, Nick, Nip, Nobble, Pinch, Pull, Restrain, Retard, Riveting, Round-up, Run-in, Salient, Sease, Seize, Snaffle, Stasis, Stop, Sus(s)

Arris Groin

Arrival, Arrive, Arriving Accede, Advent, Attain, Come, Get, Happen, Hit, Inbound, Influx, Johnny-come-lately, Land, Latecomer, Natal, Nativity, Pitch up, Reach, Show, Strike

Arrogance, Arrogant Assumption, Bold, Bravado, Cavalier, Cocksure, Contemptuous, Disdain, Dogmatic, Effrontery, Haughty, Haut(eur), High, High-hat, Hogen-mogen, Hoity-toity, Hubris, Imperious, Jumped up, Lordly, Morgue, Overweening, Presumption, Proud, Side, Snobbish, Stuck-up, Surquedry, Toploftical, Turkeycock, Uppish, Uppity, Upstart

Arrogate Appropriate, Assume, Claim, Impute, Usurp

Arrow, Arrow-head Acestes, Any, Ary, Blunt, Bolt, Broad(head), Cloth-yard shaft, Dart, Dogbolt, Filter, Flechette, Flight, Missile, Pheon, Pointer, Quarrel, Reed, Sagittate, Shaft, Sheaf, Straight

Arrowroot Kuzu, Maranta, Pia

Arsenal Ammo, Armo(u)ry, Depot, Magazine, Side, Toulon

Arsenate, Arsenic(al), Arsenide As, Erythrite, Realgar, Resalgar, Rosaker, Salvarsan, Scorodite, Skutterudite, Smaltite, Speiss, Zarnich

Arson(ist) Firebug, Pyromania

Art(s), Arty, Art school, Art style Abstract, Alla prima, Applied, Ars, Arte Povera, Bauhaus, Bloomsbury, Bonsai, Britart, Brut, Chiaroscuro, Clair-obscure, Clare-obscure, Clip, Cobra, Commercial, Conceptual, Constructivism, Contrapposto, Craft, Cubism, Culture vulture, Cunning, Curious, Dada, Daedal(e), Deco, Decorative,

Dedal, De Stijl, Die Brucke, Diptych, Divisionism, Earth, Ekphrasis, Environmental, Es, Expressionism, Fauvism, Feat, Fine, Finesse, Flemish, Folk, Fugue, Futurism, Genre, Graphic, Guile, Impressionist, Jugendstil, Kakemono, Kano, Ka pai, Kinetic, Kirigami, Kitsch, Knack, Liberal, Mandorla, Mannerism, Martial, Mehindi, Minimal, Modern(e), Montage, Motivated, Music, Mystery, Nabis, Nazarene, Neoclassical, Neo-impressionism, New Wave, Noli-me-tangere, Norwich, Nouveau, Optical, Origami, Orphic Cubism, Orphism, Outsider, Pastiche, Performance, Performing, Perigordian, Plastic, Pointillism, Pop, Postimpressionism, Postmodern, Practical, Pre-Raphaelite, Primitive, Psychedelic, Public, Quadratura, Quadrivium, Relievo, Sienese, → SKILL, Still-life, Suprematism, Surrealism, Synchronism, Tachism(e), Tatum, Tenebrism, Toreutics, Trecento, Triptych, Trivium, Trompe l'oeil, Trouvé, Tsutsumu, Useful, Verism, Virtu, Visual, Vorticism

▷ **Art** *may indicate* an -est ending

Artefact(s) Neolith, Tartanalia, Tartanry, Xoanon

▷ **Artefact** *may indicate* an anagram

Artemis Selene

Artemus Ward

Artery Aorta, Carotid, Coronary, Duct, Femoral, Frontal, Iliac, Innominate, M1, Maxillary, Phrenic, Pulmonary, Radial, Route, Spermatic, Temporal

Artful Cute, Dodger, Foxy, Ingenious, Quirky, Shifty, Sly, Subtle, Tactician

Arthropod Limulus, Peripatus, Prototracheata, Tardigrade, Trilobite, Water-bear

Artichoke Cardoon, Jerusalem

Article(s) A, An, Apprentice, Column, Commodity, Cutting, Definite, Feature, Five, Indefinite, Indenture, Item, Leader, Leading, Paper, Piece, Pot-boiler, Shipping, Sidebar, Specify, The, Thing, Thinkpiece, Thirty-nine, Treatise, Ware

Articulation, Articulate(d) Clear, Coherent, Coudé, Diarthrosis, Distinct, Eloquent, Enounce, Express, Fluent, Fortis, Gimmal, Gomphosis, Hinged, Intonate, Jointed, Jymold, Lenis, Limbed, Lisp, Pretty-spoken, Pronounce, Schindylesis, Trapezial, Utter, Vertebrae, Voice

Artifice(r), Artificial Bogus, Chouse, Contrived, Dodge, Ersatz, Factitious, Finesse, Guile, Hoax, In vitro, Logodaedaly, Man-made, Mannered, Opificer, Postiche, Pretence, Prosthetic, Pseudo, Reach, Ruse, Sell, Set, Sham, Spurious, Stratagem, → STRATEGY, Synthetic, Theatric, → TRICK, Unnatural, Wile, Wright

Artificial respiration Kiss of life, Schafer's method

Artillery Battery, Cannon, Field, Fougade, Fougasse, Guns, Mortar, Ordnance, Pyroballogy, RA, Rafale, Ramose, Ramus, Train

Artiodactyl Camel, Chevrotain, Deerlet

Artisan Craftsman, Decorator, Joiner, Journeyman, Mechanic, Peon, Pioner, Pyoner, Shipwright, Workman

Artist(ic) Barbizan, Blaue Reiter, Bohemian, Cartoonist, Colourist, Cubist, Dadaist, Daedal(e), Deccie, Decorator, Die Brucke, Etcher, Fauve, Fine, Foley, Gentle, Gilder, ICA, Impressionist, Left Bank, Limner, Linear, Maestro, Master, Mime, Miniaturist, → MUSICIAN, Nabis, Nazarene, Oeuvre, Orphism, → PAINTER, Pavement, Paysagist, Piss, Plein-airist, Pre-Raphaelite, Primitive, Quick-change, RA, Romantic, Screever, → SCULPTOR, Sien(n)ese, Tachisme, Trapeze, Trecentist, Virtuose, Virtuoso

---

ARTISTS

3 letters:		4 letters:	
Arp	Cox	Cuyp	Dali
	Rap	Dadd	Doré
			Dufy

Etty
Goya
Hals
John
Klee
Lely
Miró
Opie
Phiz

5 letters:
Aiken
Appel
Bacon
Bakst
Bosch
Corot
Crome
Degas
Dulac
Dürer
Ensor
Ernst
Hoare
Hooch
Klimt
Leech
Léger
Lippi
Lotto
Lowry
Makar
Manet
Monet
Munch
Orpen
Redon
Riley
Rodin
Seago
Steen
Steer
Tatum
Watts

6 letters:
Boudin
Braque
Brucke

Calder
Callot
Derain
D'Orsay
Escher
Fuseli
Giotto
Greuze
Guardi
Haydon
Ingres
Knight
Le Nain
Millet
Moreau
Renoir
Ribera
Rivera
Romney
Rothko
Rubens
Seurat
Signac
Sisley
Stubbs
Tissot
Titian
Turner
Warhol
Zeuxis

7 letters:
Apelles
Audubon
Bellini
Bernini
Bonnard
Cézanne
Chagall
Chardin
Cimabue
Collier
Courbet
Cranach
Da Vinci
Duchamp
El Greco
Epstein
Gauguin

Hobbema
Hockney
Hogarth
Hokusai
Holbein
Hoppner
Kneller
Matisse
Millais
Morisot
Morland
Murillo
Nattier
Picasso
Pissaro
Poussin
Prudhon
Raeburn
Raphael
Rouault
Sargent
Sickert
Spencer
Tiepolo
Uccello
Utamaro
Utrillo
Van Dyke
Van Eyck
Van Gogh
Vermeer
Watteau
Zeuxian
Zoffany

8 letters:
Daubigny
Eastlake
Kirchner
Landseer
Leonardo
Magritte
Mantegna
Masaccio
Mondrian
Nevinson
Perugino
Piranesi
Reynolds

Rousseau
Topolski
Veronese
Whistler

9 letters:
Beardsley
Bonington
Canaletto
Carpaccio
Constable
Correggio
Delacroix
Donatello
Fragonard
Gericault
Giorgione
Grunewald
Hiroshige
Kandinsky
Rembrandt
Velasquez

10 letters:
Alma-Tadema
Botticelli
Burne-Jones
Guillaumin
Madox Brown
Modigliani
Rowlandson
Signorelli
Sutherland
Tintoretto
Van der Goes

12 letters:
Gainsborough
Lichtenstein
Michelangelo
Winterhalter

14 letters:
Jackson Pollock

15 letters:
Hieronymus Bosch
Toulouse-Lautrec

Artless Candid, Ingenuous, Innocent, Naive, Open, Seely, Simple

Art nouveau Jugendstil
Arturo Toscanini
Arum Acorus, Green-dragon, Lily, Taro
As Aesir, Als, Arsenic, Coin, Eg, Forasmuch, Kame, Qua, Ridge, 's, Since, So, Thus, Ut, While
As above US, Ut supra
Asafoetida Hing
As before Anew, Ditto, Do, Stet
Asbestos Amiant(h)us, Amosite, Chrysolite, Crocidolite, Earthflax, Fireproof, Rockwood
Ascend(ant), Ascent, Ascension Anabasis, Climb, Dominant, Escalate, Gradient, Lift, Pull, Ramp, Right, Rise, Sclim, Sklim, Slope, Up, Upgang, Uphill, Uprise, Zoom
Ascertain Determine, Discover, → **ESTABLISH**, Prove
Ascetic Agapetae, Anchor(et), Anchorite, Ancress, Ashramite, Austere, Dervish, Diogenes, Encratite, Eremital, Essene, Fakir, Faquir, Gymnosophist, Hermit, Jain(ite), Monk, Nazarite, Nazirite, Nun's flesh, Sad(d)hu, Simeon Stylites, Stylite, Sufic, Therapeutae, Yogi(n)
Ascidian Chordate, Urochordate
Asclepiad Stapelia
Ascribe Assign, → **ATTRIBUTE**, Blame, Imply, Impute
Asdic Sonar
As far as Quoad
As good as Equal, Tantamount
Ash(es), Ashy Aesc, Aizle, Bone, Breeze, Cinders, Cinereal, Clinker(s), Easle, Embers, Fly, Kali, Lahar, Pallor, Pearl, Pozz(u)olana, Prickly, Rowan, Ruins, Soda, Sorb, Spodo-, Tephra, Urn, Varec, Wednesday, Weeping, White, Witchen, Yg(g)drasil(l)
Ashamed Abashed, Embarrassed, Hangdog, Mortified, Repentant, Shent
Ashore Aland, Beached, Grounded, Stranded
Ash-pan Backet
Asia(n), Asiatic Altaic, Azari, Balinese, Bangladeshi, Bengali, Cambodian, Cantonese, E, Evenki, Ewenki, Gook, Hun, Hyksos, Indian, Karen(ni), Kashmir, Kirghiz, Korean, Kurd, Kyrgyz, Lao, Malay, Mongol, Naga, Negrito, Nepalese, Phrygian, Pushtu, Samo(y)ed, Shan, Siamese, Sogdian, Tamil, Tartar, Tibetan, Tocharian, Tokharian, Turanian, Turk(o)man
Asia Minor Anatolia, Ionic
Aside Apart, By, Despite, Private, Separate, Shelved, Sotto voce
Asinine Crass, Dull, Idiotic, Puerile, Stupid
Ask Bed, Beg, Beseech, Bid, Cadge, Demand, Desire, Enquire, Entreat, Evet, Implore, Intreat, Invite, Newt, Petition, Prithee, Pump, Quiz, Request, Require, Rogation, Seek, Solicit, Speer, Speir, Touch
Askance Asconce, Askew, Oblique, Sideways
Askew Agee, Aglee, Agley, Ajee, Aslant, Awry, Crooked, Skivie
Asleep Dormant, Inactive, Napping
Asparagus Asperge, Sparrow-grass, Spear, Sprew, Sprue
Aspect Angle, Bearing, Brow, Face, Facet, Facies, Feature, Look, Mien, Nature, Outlook, Perfective, Perspective, Side, → **VIEW**, Visage, Vista
Aspersion Calumny, Innuendo, Libel, Slander, Slur, Smear
Asphalt Bitumen, Blacktop, Gilsonite®, Jew's pitch, Pitch, Pitch Lake, Uinta(h)ite
Aspirant, Aspirate, Aspiration, Aspire Ambition, Breath, Buckeen, Challenger,

Desire, Dream, Endeavour, Ettle, Goal, H, Hope(ful), Pretend, Pursue, Rough, Spiritus, Wannabe(e), Would be, Yearn

Ass Buridan's, Burnell, Burro, Cardophagus, Chigetai, Clot, Couscous, Cuddie, Dick(e)y, Donkey, Dziggetai, Funnel, Golden, Hemione, Hemionus, Hinny, Jack, Jenny, Jerusalem pony, Kiang, K(o)ulan, Kourbash, Kourmiss, Kouskous, Kumiss, Kurbash, Kyang, Liripipe, Liripoop, Moke, Neddy, Nitwit, Onager, Quagga, Sesterce, Simp, → **STUPID PERSON**

Assail(ant) Assault, Attack, Batter, Bego, Belabour, Bepelt, Beset, Bombard, Harry, Impugn, Onsetter, Oppugn, Pillory, Ply, Revile

Assassin(ate), Assassination Booth, Brave, Bravo, Brutus, Casca, Character, Frag, Gunman, Highbinder, Hitman, Killer, Ninja, Sword, Sworder, Thuggee, Tyrannicide

Assault ABH, Assail, Assay, Attack, Battery, Bombard, GBH, Hamesucken, Head-butt, Indecent, Invasion, Maul, Mug, → **RAID**, Scalade, Stoor, Storm, Stour, Stowre

Assay Cupel, Examine, Proof, Test, Wet

Assemble, Assembly Agora, Audience, Ball, Bottom-hole, Bundestag, Chapter, Chatuaqua, Cho(u)ltry, Church, Co, Collation, → **COLLECTION**, Comitia, Company, Conclave, Concourse, Congeries, Congress, Consistory, Constituent, Convene, Conventicle, Convention, Convocation, Convoke, Corroboree, Cortes, Council, Court, Curia, Dail Eireann, Dewain, Diet, Divan, Donnybrook, Ecclesia, Eisteddfod, Erect, Feis(anna), Folkmoot, Folkmote, Force, Forgather, Gather(ing), Gemot(e), General, Gorsedd, Group, Headstock, Hoi polloi, Jirga, Kgotla, Knesset, Landtag, Legislative, Lekgotla, Levee, Loya jirga, Majlis, Make, Mass, → **MEETING**, Mejlis, Moot, Muster, National, Panegyry, Panoply, Parishad, Parliament, Patron, Pattern, Plenum, Pnyx, Powwow, Prefabrication, Presence, Primary, Quorum, Rally, Rechate, Recheate, Reichstag, Repair, Resort, Riksdag, Roll up, Sanghat, Sanhedrin, Sanhedron, Sejm, Senate, Skupshtina, Sobranje, Soc, Society, Stort(h)ing, Synagogue, Synedrion, Synod, T(h)ing, Tribunal, Troop, Unlawful, Vidhan Sabha, Volksraad, Wapens(c)haw, Wapins(c)haw, Wappens(c)haw, Wardmote, Weapon-s(c)haw, Witan, Witenagemot, Zemstvo

Assent Accede, Acquiesce, Agree, Amen, Aye, Comply, Concur, Jokol, Nod, Placet, Royal, Sanction, Viceregal, Yea, Yield

Assert(ing), Assertion Affirm, Allege, Bumptious, Constate, Contend, → **DECLARE**, Ipse-dixit, → **MAINTAIN**, Pose, Predicate, Proclaim, Pronounce, Protest, Rumour, Swear (blind), Thetical

Assess(ment) Affeer, Appraise, Audition, Cense, Estimate, Evaluate, Gauge, Guesstimate, → **JUDGE**, Levy, Means test, Measure, Perspective, Rating, Referee, Risk, Scot and lot, Size up, Special, Stent, Summative, Tax, Value, Weigh

Asset(s) Advantage, Capital, Chargeable, Chattel, Current, Fixed, Floating, Goodwill, Intangible, Inventory, Liquid, Net, Plant, Property, Resource, Talent, Virtue, Wasting

Assiduous Attentive, Busy, Constant, Diligent, Studious, Thorough

Assign(ation), Assignment Allocate, → **ALLOT**, Apply, Appoint, Aret, Ascribe, Attribute, Award, Date, Dedicate, Duty, Entrust, Errand, Fix, Give, Grant, Impute, Point, Quota, Refer, Transfer, Tryst

Assimilate(d) Absorb, Blend, Digest, Esculent, Fuse, Imbibe, Incorporate, Merge

Assist(ance), Assistant Acolyte, Adjunct, Aid(e), Aide-de-camp, Ally, Alms, Attaché, Au pair, Best boy, Busboy, Cad, Chainman, Collaborate, Counterhand, Counter-jumper, Dresser, Ex parte, Facilitate, Factotum, Famulus, Feldschar, Felds(c)her, Gofer, → **HAND**, Handlanger, Help, Henchman, Legal aid, Matross, Mentor, National, Offsider, Omnibus, Proproctor, Public, Reinforce, Relief, Second,

Server, Servitor, Shill, Sidesman, Smallboy, Social, Stead, Subsidiary, Subsidy, Suffragan, Supernumerary, → **SUPPORT**, Usher

Assize Botley, Circuit, Court, Maiden, Oyer

Associate, Association Accomplice, Affiliate, Alliance, Amphictyony, Ass, Attach, Bedfellow, Brotherhood, Cartel, Chapel, Chum, Clang, Club, Cohort, Combine, Comecon, Community, Compeer, Complice, Comrade, Concomitant, Confrère, → **CONNECT**, Consort(ium), Co-partner, Correlate, Crony, Enclisis, Fellow, Fraternise, Free, Gesellschaft, Guild, Hobnob, Housing, Inquiline, Intime, Join, Kabele, Kebele, League, Liaison, Lloyds, Mell, Member, Mess, Mix, Moshav, Oddfellows, Pal, Parent teacher, Partner, Phoresy, Press, Probus, Professional, Relate, Residents', Ring, Round Table, Samit(h)i, Sangh(at), Sidekick, Sodality, Stablemate, Staff, Symbiosis, Syndicate, Tenant's, Toc H, Toenadering, Trade, UN(A), Union, Verein, Whiteboy, Word, Yoke-mate

Assort(ed), Assortment Paraphernalia, Pick-'n'-mix, Various

▷ **Assorted** *may indicate* an anagram

Assuage Allay, Appease, Beet, Calm, Ease, Mease, Mitigate, Mollify, Slake, Soften, Soothe

As such Qua

Assume, Assuming, Assumption Adopt, Affect, Arrogate, Attire, Axiom, Believe, Don, Donné(e), Feign, Hypothesis, Lemma, Occam's Razor, Posit, Postulate, Preconception, Premise, Premiss, Presuppose, Pretentious, Principle, Putative, Saltus, Suppose, Surmise, Take

▷ **Assumption** *may indicate* 'attire'

Assure(d), Assurance Aplomb, Aver, Avouch, Belief, Calm, → **CERTAIN**, Comfort, Confidence, Confirm, Earnest, Gall, Guarantee, Life, Pledge, Poise, Warranty

Assuredly Indeed, Perdie, Verily, Yea

Astatine At

Astern Abaft, Apoop, Rear

Asteroid Ceres, Eros, Eros 433, Hermes, Hygiea, Juno, Pallas, Phaethon, Pholus, Star, Starfish, Trojan, Vesta

Astir Afoot, Agate, Agog

Astonish(ed), Astonishing, Astonishment, Astound Abash, Admiraunce, Amaze, Banjax, Bewilder, Confound, Corker, Crikey, Daze, Donnert, Dum(b)found, Dumbstruck, Eye-popping, Flabbergast, Gobsmack, Heavens, Mind-boggling, Open-eyed, Open-mouthed, Phew, Pop-eyed, Prodigious, Rouse, Singular, Stagger, Startle, Stun, Stupefaction, Stupefy, Stupendous, Surprise, Thunderstruck, Wow

Astray Abord, Amiss, Errant, Lost, Will, Wull

Astride Athwart, Spanning, Straddle-back

Astringent Acerbic, Alum, Catechu, Dhak, Gambi(e)r, Harsh, Kino, Krameria, Myrobalan, Rhatany, Sept-foil, Severe, Sour, Styptic, Tormentil, Witch-hazel

Astrologer, Astrology, Astrological Archgenethliac, Chaldean, Culpeper, Faust, Figure-caster, Genethliac, Judicial, Lilly, Midheaven, Moore, Nostradamus, Soothsayer, Starmonger, Zadkiel

Astronaut Cosmonaut, Gagarin, Glenn, Lunarnaut, Spaceman, Spacer, Talkonaut

Astronomer, Astronomy, Astronomical Almagest, Aristarchus, Barnard, Bessel, Bradley, Brahe, Callipic, Cassini, Celsius, Copernicus, Eddington, Encke, Eratosthenes, Eudoxus, Flamsteed, Galileo, Gamma-ray, Hale, Halley, Herschel, Hertzsprung, Hewish, Hipparchus, Hoyle, Hubble, Huggins, Infra red, Jeans, Kepler, Lagrange, Laplace, Leverrier, Lockyer, Lovell, Meton, Neutrino, Omar Khayyam, Oort, Physical, Planetology, Ptolemy, Radar, Radio, Reber, Roche, Roemer, Russell, Ryle, Schwarzschild, Selenography, Selenology, Sosigenes,

Stargazer, Star read, Telescopy, Tycho Brahe, Ultraviolet, Urania, Uranic, Uranography, X-ray, Zwicky

Astrophel Penthia

Astrophysicist Seifert

Astute Acute, Canny, Crafty, Cunning, Downy, Perspicacious, Shrewd, Subtle, Wide, Wily

As usual Solito

As well Additionally, Also, Both, Even, Forby, Too

Asylum Bedlam, Bin, Bughouse, Frithsoken, Funny-farm, Girth, Grith, Haven, Institution, Loony bin, Lunatic, Madhouse, Magdalene, Nuthouse, Political, Rathouse, Refuge, Retreat, Sanctuary, Shelter, Snake-pit

Asymmetric(al) Contrapposto, Lopsided, Skew

At Astatine, In, Kip, To, Up-bye

Atahualpa Inca

At all Ava, Ever, Oughtlings

At all events Algate

Atavistic Reversion, Throw-back

Atheist Doubter, Godless, Infidel, Sceptic

Athenian, Athene Attic, Cleruch, Pallas, Pericles, Solon, Timon

Athlete, Athletic(s) Agile, Agonist, Blue, Coe, Discobolus, Field, Gymnast, Hurdler, Jock, Leish, Miler, Milo, Nurmi, Olympian, Pacemaker, Quarter-miler, Runner, Sexual, Sportsman, Sprinter, Track

Athodyd Ram-jet

Athwart Across, Awry, Oblique, Traverse

Atlantic Millpond, Pond

Atlas Dialect, Linguistic, Maps, Range, Silk

▷ **At last** *may indicate* a cobbler

Atmosphere Aeropause, Afterdamp, Air, Ambience, Aura, Chemosphere, Elements, Epedaphic, Ether, F-layer, Geocorona, Ionosphere, Lid, Magnetosphere, Mesosphere, Meteorology, Miasma, Ozone, Standard, Thermosphere, Tropopause, Troposphere, Upper, Vibe(s), Vibrations

At most Al piu

Atoll Bikini, Eniwetok, Kwajalein, Male, Motu, Tarawa

Atom(ic), Atoms, Atomism Boson, Electron, Excimer, Free, Gram, Ion, Iota, Isobare, Isotone, Isotope, Labelled, Ligand, Logical, Molecule, Monad, Monovalent, Muonic, Nematic, Nuclide, Odoriphore, Particle, Pile, Primeval, Radionuclide, Recoil, Sellafield, Side-chain, Steric, Stripped, Substituent, Tagged, Windscale, Xylyl

Atomiser Airbrush

At once Ek dum, Holus-bolus, Immediate, Instanter, Presto, Statim, Straight away, Swith, Tight, Tit(e), Titely, Tout de suite, Tyte

Atone(ment) Aby(e), Acceptilation, Appease, Assoil, Expiate, Penance, Redeem, Redemption, Yom Kippur

Atop Upon

▷ **At random** *may indicate* an anagram

Atrocious, Atrocity Abominable, Brutal, Diabolical, Flagitious, Heinous, Horrible, Monstrous, Outrage, Vile

Atrophy Degeneration, Marasmus, Sudeck's, Sweeny, Wasting

▷ **At sea** *may indicate* an anagram

Attach(ed), Attachment Accessory, Accrete, Adhesion, Adhibition, Adnate, Adnation, Adscript, Affix, Allonge, Annexe, Bolt, Bro, Byssus, Cleat, Covermount,

Devotement, Devotion, Distrain, Dobby, Feller, Garnish, Glom, Glue, → **JOIN**, Netsuke, Obconic, Pin, Reticle, Snell, Stick, Tie, Weld

Attack(ing), Attacker Access, Affect, Airstrike, Alert, Anti, Apoplexy, Asperse, Assail, Assault, At, Banzai, Batten, Bego, Belabour, Beset, Bestorm, Blitz(krieg), Bodrag(ing), Bombard, Bordraging, Bout, Broadside, Bushwhack, Camisade, Camisado, Campaign, Cannonade, Charge, Clobber, Club, Counteroffensive, Coup de main, Denounce, Descent, Diatribe, Feint, Fit, Flèche, Foray, Gas, Get, Handbag, Heart, Iconoclast, Ictus, Impingement, Impugn, Incursion, Inroad, Invade, Inveigh, Lampoon, Lese-majesty, Let fly, Maraud, Molest, Mug, Offensive, Onding, Onfall, Onrush, Onset, Onslaught, Oppugn, Panic, Pillage, Polemic, Predacious, Pre-emptive, Push, Quart(e), Raid, Rough, Sail, Sandbag, Savage, Seizure, Sic(k), Siege, Skitch, Snipe, Sortie, Storm, Strafe, Strike, Swoop, Thrust, Tilt, Vilify, Vituperate, Wage, Warison, Wolf-pack, Zap

Attain(ment) Accomplish, Arrive, Earn, Fruition, Get, Land, Reach

Attempt Bash, Bid, Burl, Crack, Debut, Effort, Egma, Endeavour, Essay, Go, Mint, Nisus, Seek, Shot, Show, Shy, Stab, Strive, → **TRY**, Venture, Whack, Whirl

Attend(ance), Attendant Accompany, Aide, Apple-squire, Await, Batman, Bearer, Be at, Behold, Bulldog, Caddy, Cavass, Chaperone, Chasseur, Checker, Corybant, Courtier, Cuadrilla, Cupbearer, Custrel, Doula, Entourage, Equerry, Escort, Esquire, Famulus, Footman, Gate, Gillie, Hand-maiden, Harken, Hear, → **HEED**, Hello, Holla, Iras, Kavass, Led captain, → **LISTEN**, Loblolly-boy, Maenad, Marshal, Mute, Note, Orderly, Outrider, Outrunner, Page, Panisc, Panisk, Paranymph, People, Pew-opener, Presence, Pursuivant, Respect, Roll-up, S(a)ice, Satellite, Second, Server, Sowar, Steward, Syce, Trainbearer, Trolleydolly, Turn-out, Up at, Valet, Varlet, Visit, Wait, Watch, Whiffler, Zambuck

Attention, Attentive Achtung, Alert, Assiduity, Court, Coverage, Dutiful, Ear, Gallant, Gaum, Gorm, Heed, Interest, Mind, Notice, Present, Psst, Punctilious, Qui vive, → **REGARD**, Selective, Solicitous, Spellbound, Tenty, Thought

Attenuate, Attenuation Lessen, Neper, Rarefy, Thin, Weaken

Attest Affirm, Certify, Depose, Guarantee, Notarise, Swear, → **WITNESS**

Attic Bee-bird, Cockloft, Garret, Greek, Koine, Loft, Mansard, Muse, Salt, Sky parlour, Solar, Soler, Sollar, Soller, Tallat, Tallet, Tallot

Attila Etzel, Hun

Attire Accoutre, Adorn, Apparel, Clobber, → **DRESS**, Garb, Habit

Attitude Air, Aspect, Behaviour, Demeanour, Light, → **MANNER**, Mindset, Nimby, Outlook, Pose, Posture, Propositional, Sense, Song, Stance, Tone, Uppity, Viewpoint

Attorney Advocate, Counsellor, DA, District, Lawyer, Private, Proctor, Prosecutor, Public

Attract(ion), Attractive, Attractor Attrahent, Bait, Barrie, Becoming, Bewitch, Bonny, Bootylicious, Catchy, Charisma, → **CHARM**, Cheesecake, Clou, Comely, Crowd puller, Cute, Cynosure, Dinky, Dipolar, Dish(y), Draught, → **DRAW**, Dreamboat, Duende, Engaging, Entice, Epigamic, Eye candy, Eye-catching, Eyeful, Fanciable, Fascinate, Feature, Fetching, Fox(y), Goodly, Gravity, Great, Groovy, Heartthrob, Himbo, Hot stuff, Hunky, Inducement, Inviting, It, Loadstone, Lodestone, Looker, Lovable, Lovely, Lure, Luscious, Magnes, Magnet(ism), Mecca, Mediagenic, Meretricious, Nubile, Personable, Photogenic, Picturesque, Pull, Sematic, Sexpot, Shagtastic, Sideshow, Sightly, Slick, Snazzy, Soote, Speciosity, Spunk, Stotter, Striking, Studmuffin, Stunner, Taking, Taky, Tasteful, Tempt, Theme-park, Weber, Winning, Winsome, Zaftig, Zoftig

Attribute, Attribution Accredit, Allot, Ap(p)anage, Ascribe, Asset, By, Credit, Gift,

Impute, Lay, Metonym, Owe, Proprium, Quality, Refer, Shtick, Strength
Attune Accord, Adapt, Temper
Atypical Aberrant
Aubergine Brinjal, Brown jolly, Egg-plant, Mad-apple
Aubrey Beardsley
Auburn Abram, Chestnut, Copper, Titian, Vill(age)
Auction(eer) Barter, Bridge, Cant, Dutch, Hammer, Knock out, Outcry, Outro(o)per, Roup, Sale, Subhastation, Tattersall, Vendue
Audacious, Audacity Bald-headed, Bold, Brash, Cheek, Chutspah, Cool, Der-doing, Devil-may-care, Effrontery, Face, Hardihood, Indiscreet, Insolence, Intrepid, Neck, Nerve, Rash, Sauce
Audience, Auditorium Assembly, Court, Durbar, Gate, Hearing, House, Interview, Pit, Sphendone, Theatre, Tribunal
Audiovisual AV
Audit(or) Accountant, Check, Ear, Environmental, Examine, Green, Inspect, Listener, Medical, Position
Audition Cattle-call, Screen-test
Auditory Acoustic, Oral
Audrey Hoyden
Auger Miser
Augment(ed) Boost, Eche, Eke, Ich, Increase, Supplement, Swell, Tritone
Augury Ornithoscopy
August Awe-inspiring, Grand, Imperial, Imposing, Lammas, Majestic, Noble, Royal, Solemn, Stately, Stern
Augustine, Augustus Austin, Hippo, John
Auk Guillemot, Ice-bird, Puffin, Roch, Rotch(e)
Aunt(ie) Agony, Augusta, Beeb, Giddy, Maiden, Naunt, Sainted, Tia
Aura Aroma, Emanation, Halo, Mystique, Nimbus, Odour, Vibe(s), Vibrations
Aureole Coronary, Halo, Nimbus
Auricle Ear, Otic
Aurora Eos, Leigh, Matutinal, Merry dancers, Northern lights
Auspice(s) Aegis, Patronage
Auster S-wind
Austere, Austerity Ascetic, Astringent, Bleak, Dantean, Hard, → **HARSH**, Moral, Plain, Rigour, Severe, Spartan, Stern, Stoic, Stoor, Strict, Vaudois, Waldensian
Austin Friar
Australia(n) Alf, Antichthone, Antipodean, Aussie, Balt, Banana-bender, Bananalander, Billjim, Canecutter, Cobber, Coon, Currency, Current, Darwinian, Digger, Gin, Godzone, Gumsucker, Gurindji, Jackie, Jacky, Koori, Larrikin, Lucky Country, Murree, Murri, Myall, Norm, Ocker, Ossie, Oz, Pintupi, Roy, Sandgroper, Strine, Wallaby, Yarra-yabbies
Austrian Cisleithan, Tyrolean
Authentic(ate) Certify, Des(h)i, Echt, Genuine, Honest, Notarise, Official, Real, Sign, Simon-pure, Test, True, Validate
Author(ess) Anarch, Auctorial, Inventor, Me, Parent, Volumist, Wordsmith, → **WRITER**
▷ **Author** *may refer to* author of puzzle
Authorise(d), Authorisation Accredit, Clearance, Countersign, Delegate, Empower, Enable, Exequatur, Imprimatur, Legal, Legit, → **LICENCE**, Official, OK, Passport, → **PERMIT**, Plenipotentiary, Retainer, Sanction, Sign, Stamp, Warrant
Authority, Authoritarian, Authoritative Canon, Charter, Circar, Cocker,

Commission, Commune, Crisp, Definitive, Domineering, Dominion, Establishment, Ex cathedra, Expert, Fascist, Free hand, Gravitas, Hegemony, Inquirendo, Jackboot, Leadership, Licence, Local, Magisterial, Mandate, Mantle, Mastery, Name, Oracle, Permit, Potency, → **POWER**, Prefect, Prestige, Pundit, Remit, Right, Rod, Say-so, Sceptre, Sircar, Sirkar, Source, Supremacy, Unitary, Warrant

Autobiography Memoir

Autocrat(ic) Absolute, Caesar, Cham, Despot, Khan, Neronian, Tsar, Tyrant

Autograph Signature

Autolycus Scrapman

Automatic, Automaton Android, Aut, Browning, Deskill, Instinctive, Machine, Mechanical, Pistol, Quarter-boy, Quarter-jack, Reflex, Robot, RUR, Zombi

Auto-pilot George

Autopsy Necropsy

Auto-suggestion Coueism

Autumn(al) Fall, Filemot, Leaf-fall, Libra, Philamot

Auxiliary Adjunct, Adjuvant, Adminicle, Aide, Be, Feldsher, Foederatus, Have, Helper, Ido, Subsidiary

Avail(able) Benefit, Dow, Eligible, Going, Handy, Off-the-shelf, On call, On tap, Open, Out, Pickings, → **READY**, Serve, Use, Utilise

Avalanche Bergfall, Deluge, Landfall, Landslide, Landslip, Lauwine, Slide, Slip, Snowdrop

Avant-garde Modernistic, Spearhead

Avarice, Avaricious Cupidity, Golddigger, Greed, Money-grubbing, Pleonexia, Sordid

Avatar Epiphany, Incarnation, Rama

Avaunt Away, Go

Avenge(r) Eriny(e)s, Eumenides, Goel, Kurdaitcha, Nightrider, Punish, Redress, Requite, → **REVENGE**, Steed, Wreak

Avenue Alley, Arcade, Boulevard, Channel, Corso, Cradle-walk, Hall, Madison, Mall, Midway, Passage, Vista, Way, Xyst(us)

Aver Affirm, Assert, Asseverate, Depose, Swear, Vouch

Average Adjustment, Av, Batting, Dow Jones, Mean, Mediocre, Middle-brow, Middling, Moderate, Moving, Norm, Par, Particular, Run, Run-of-the-mill, Soso, Standard, Weighted

Averse, Aversion, Avert Against, Antipathy, Apositia, Disgust, Dislike, Distaste, Hatred, Horror, Opposed, Pet, Phobic, Risk, Scunner, Stave off

Avert Avoid, → **DEFLECT**, Forfend, Parry, Ward

Aviary Volary, Volery

Aviator Airman, Alcock, Bleriot, Brown, Byrd, Earhart, Flier, Hinkler, Icarus, Johnson, Lindbergh, Pilot, Red Baron, Richthofen

Avid Agog, → **EAGER**, Greedy, Keen

Avifauna Ornis

Avignon Pont

Avocado Aguacate, Guac(h)amole, Pear

Avocet Scooper

Avoid(er), Avoidance Abstain, Ba(u)lk, Boycott, Bypass, Cop-out, Cut, Dodge, Duck, Elude, Escape, Eschew, Evade, Evitate, Evite, Fly, Forbear, Gallio, Hedge, Miss, Obviate, Parry, Prevaricate, Scutage, Secede, Shelve, Shun, Sidestep, Skirt, Spare, Spurn, Waive

Avoirdupois Size, Weight

Avow(ed) Acknowledged, Affirm, Declare, Own, Swear

Await Abide, Bide, Expect, Tarry

Awake(ning) Aware, Conscious, Conversion, Fly, Rouse, Vigilant

Award Academy, Accolade, Acquisitive, Addeem, Addoom, Allot, Alpha, Arbitrament, Aret(t), Bafta, Bar, Bestow, Bursary, Cap, Clasp, Clio, Crown, Emmy, Exhibition, Genie, Golden Raspberry, Golden Starfish, Grammy, Grant, Honours, Juno, Logie, Lourie, Medal, Meed, Mete, MOBO, Oscar, Padma Shri, Palatinate, Palme d'Or, Premium, Present(ation), Prix Goncourt, → **PRIZE**, Queen's, Razzie, Scholarship, Tony, Trophy, Vir Chakra, Yuko

Aware(ness) Alert, C(o)enesthesis, Cognisant, Conscious, Conversant, ESP, Est, Hep, Hip, Informed, Knowing, Liminal, Mindshare, Onto, Panaesthesia, Prajna, Presentiment, Samadhi, Scienter, Sensible, Sensile, Sensitive, Sentience, Streetwise, Switched on, Vigilant, Weet, Wit, Wot

Away Abaxial, Absent, Afield, Apage, Avaunt, By, For-, Fro(m), Go, Hence, Off, Out, Past

▷ **Away** *may indicate* a word to be omitted

Awe(d) D(o)ulia, Dread, Fear, Intimidate, Loch, Overcome, Popeyed, Regard, Respect, Reverent, Scare, Solemn, Wonderment

Awe-inspiring Numinous

Awful(ly) Alas, Deare, Dere, Dire, Fearful, Horrendous, O so, Piacular, Rotten, Terrible

▷ **Awfully** *may indicate* an anagram

Awkward Angular, Bolshy, Bumpkin, Clumsy, Complicated, Corner, Crabby, Cubbish, Cumbersome, Cussed, Dub, Embarrassing, Farouche, Fiddly, Fix, Gangly, Gauche, Gawky, Handless, Howdy-do, Inconvenient, Inept, Kittle-cattle, Lanky, Loutish, Lurdan(e), Lurden, Maladdress, Mauther, Mawr, Naff, Nasty, Nonconformist, Ornery, Perverse, Refractory, Slummock, So-and-so, Spot, Sticky, Stiff, Stroppy, Stumblebum, Swainish, Uneasy, Ungainly, Unwieldy, Wry

Awl(-shaped) Brog, Els(h)in, Nail, Stob, Subulate

Awn(ing) Barb, Beard, Canopy, Ear, Shade, Velarium

Awry Agley, Amiss, Askent, Askew, Cam, Haywire, Kam(me), Pear-shaped, Wonky

Axe Abolish, Adz(e), Bardiche, Bill, Celt, Chop(per), Cleaver, Curtal, Eatche, Gisarme, Gurlet, Halberd, Halbert, Hatchet, Holing, Ice, Jeddart staff, Jethart-staff, Labrys, Lochaber, Mattock, Palstaff, Palstave, Partisan, Piolet, Retrench, Sax, Slate, Sparth(e), Sperthe, Spontoon, Stone, Thunderbolt, Tomahawk, Twibill

Axeman Bassist, Guitarist

Axe-shaped Securiform

Axiom Adage, Motto, Peano's, Proverb, Saw, Saying

Axis Alliance, Anorthic, Anticous, Axle, Caulome, Chital, Cob, Columella, Epaxial, Henge, Hinge, Major, Minor, Modiolus, Myelon, Neutral, Optic, Pivot, Polar, Principal, Rachis, Radical, Spindle, Sympodium, Visual, X, Y, Z

Axle, Axle-shoulder Arbor, Axis, Driving, Fulcrum, Hurter, Journal, Live, Mandrel, Mandril, Pivot, Spindle, Stub

Ay I, Indeed

Aye Always, Eer, Ever, Yea, Yes

Ayesha She

Azo-dye Para-red

Aztec Nahuatl

Bb

B Bachelor, Black, Book, Born, Boron, Bowled, Bravo, Flipside

Babble(r) Blather, Brook, Chatter, Gibber, Haver, Lallation, Lurry, Prate, Prattle, Runnel, Tonguester, Twattle, Waffle

Babel Charivari, Confusion, Din, Dovercourt, Medley

Baboon Ape, Bobbejaan, Chacma, Cynocephalus, Dog-ape, Drill, Gelada, Hamadryas, Mandrill, Sphinx

Baby Bairn, Band-Aid®, Blue, Bub, Bunting, Changeling, Coddle, Designer, Duck, Grand, Infant, Jelly, Neonate, Nursling, Pamper, Papoose, Plunket, Preverbal, Rhesus, Sis, Small, Sook, Suckling, Tar, Test tube, Thalidomide, Tot, War, Wean

Babylonian Mandaean, Semiramis, Sumerian

Bacchanalian, Bacchus Ivied, Upsee, Ups(e)y

Bacchantes Maenads

Bachelor BA, Bach, Benedict, Budge, Celibate, En garçon, Knight, Pantagamy, Parti, Seal, Single, Stag, Wifeless

Bacillus Comma, Germ, Klebs-Loffler, Micrococcus, Tubercle, Virus

Back(ing), Back up, Backward Abet, Accompany, Addorse, Again, Ago, Anticlockwise, Antimacassar, Arear, Arrear, Arrière, Assist, Baccare, Backare, Bankroll, Buckram, Champion, Chorus, Consent, Defender, Dorsal, Dorse, Dorsum, Dos, Ebb, Empatron, Encourage, Endorse, Finance, Frae, Fro, Full, Fund, Gaff, Half, Help, Hind, Historic, Incremental, La-la, Late, Notaeum, Notal, Notum, On, Patronise, Pendu, Poop, Pronotum, Punt, Rear(most), Retral, Retro(grade), Retrogress, Retrorse, Retrospective, Return, Rev, Reverse, Ridge, Root, Running, Shy, Spinal, Sponsor, Stern, Sternboard, → **SUPPORT**, Sweeper, Tail, Telson, Tergum, Third, Thrae, Three-quarter, Tonneau, Ulu, Uphold, Verso, Vie, Vo, Wager, Watteau

▷ **Back(ing)** *may indicate* a word spelt backwards

Back and forth Boustrophedon

Backbiter, Backbiting Catty, Defame, Detract, Libel, Molar, Slander

Backbone Chine, Grit, Guts, Mettle, Spina, Spine

Backchat Lip, Mouth, Sass

Backer Angel, Benefactor, Patron, Punter, Seconder, Sponsor

Backfire Boomerang

Backgammon Acey-deucy, Blot, Lurch, Tick-tack, Trick-track, Tric-trac, Verquere

Background Antecedence, Chromakey, Cyclorama, Field, Fond, History, Horizon, Microwave, Muzak, Setting, Ulterior

Backhander Bribe, Payola, Reverso, Sweetener

Backroom Boffin, Boy, Moor

Backslide(r), Backsliding Apostate, Lapse, Regress, Relapse, Revert

Backwash Rift

Backwater Bogan, Ebb, Logan, Retreat, Slough, Wake

Backwoods Boondocks, Boonies, Hinterland

Backyard Court, Patio

Bacon Bard, Canadian, Collar, Danish, Essayist, Flitch, Francis, Gammon, Lardo(o)n, Pancetta, Pig, Pork, Rasher, Roger, Spec(k), Streaky, Verulam

Bacteria, Bacterium Acidophilus, Actinomycete, Aerobe, Amphitricha, Bacilli, Bacteriological, Botulinum, → **BUG**, Campylobacter, Chlamydia, Clostridia, Cocci, Coliform, Culture, Detritivore, Diplococcus, Escherichia, → **GERM**, Gonococcus, Gram-negative, Gram-positive, Intestinal flora, Klebsiella, Legionella, Listeria, Lysogen, Meningococcus, Microbe, Micrococcus, Microphyte, Mother, MRSA, Mycoplasma, Nitrous, Nostoc, Packet, Pasteurella, Pathogen, Pneumococcus, Probiotic, Prokaryote, Proteus, Pseudomonas, Pus, Ray-fungus, Rhizobium, Rickettsia, Salmonella, Schizomycete, Septic, Serotype, Serum, Shigella, Spirilla, Spirochaete, Spore, Staph, Staphylococcus, Strep(tococcus), Streptobacillus, Streptomyces, Sulphur, Superbug, Thermophil(e), Treponemata, Vibrio, Vinegar-plant, Yersinia, Zoogloea

Bad, Badness Addled, Chronic, Crook, Defective, Diabolic, Dud, Duff, Dystopia, Egregious, Execrable, Faulty, God-awful, Half-pie, Heinous, Ill, Immoral, Inferior, Injurious, Lither, Mal, Naughty, Nefandrous, Nefarious, Nice, Off, Ominous, Oncus, Onkus, Piacular, Poor, Rancid, Rank, Ropy, Scampish, Scoundrel, Sinful, Spoiled, Turpitude, Undesirable, Unspeakable, Useless, Wack, Wick, → **WICKED**

▷ **Bad(ly)** *may indicate* an anagram

Badge Brassard, Brooch, Button, Chevron, Cockade, Cockleshell, Comm, Cordon, Crest, Emblem, Ensign, Epaulet, Episemon, Fáinne, Film, Flash, Garter, Gorget, ID, Insigne, Insignia, Kikumon, Mark, Mon, Numerals, Pilgrim's sign, Rosette, Scallop, Shield, Shouldermark, → **SIGN**, Symbol, Tiger, Token, Vernicle, Vine branch, Vine-rod, Wings

Badger → **ANNOY**, Bait, Bedevil, Beset, Brock, Browbeat, Bug, Bullyrag, Cete, Dassi(e), Ferret, Gray, Grey, → **HARASS**, Hassle, Heckle, Hog, Honey, Hound, Nag, Pester, Plague, Provoke, Ratel, Ride, Roil, Sand, Sow, Stinking, Teledu, Wisconsin

Bad habit Cacoethes, Vice

Badinage Banter, Chaff, Raillery

Bad luck Ambs-ace, Ames-ace, Deuce-ace, Hard cheese, Hard lines, Hoodoo, Jinx, Jonah, Shame, Voodoo

Bad-tempered Carnaptious, Curmudgeon, Curnaptious, Curst, Grouchy, Grum(py), Irritable, Moody, Nowty, Patch, Shirty, Splenetic, Stroppy

Bad woman Harridan, Loose, Mort

Baffle(d), Baffling Anan, Balk, Bemuse, Bewilder, Confound, Confuse, Elude, Evade, Floor, Flummox, Foil, Fox, Get, Hush-kit, Mate, Muse, Mystify, Nark, Nonplus, Perplex, Pose, Puzzle, Stump, Throw, Thwart

Bag(gage), Bags Acquire, Air, Alforja, Allantois, Amaut, Amowt, Ascus, Ballonet, Besom, Bladder, Blue, Body, Bounty, Bulse, Bum, Buoyancy, Caba(s), Caecum, Callet, Capture, Carpet, Carrier, Carryall, Case, Cecum, Clutch, Cly, Cod, Colostomy, Cool, Corduroy, Crone, Crumenal, Cyst, Daypack, Dilli, Dilly, Dime, Diplomatic, Ditty, Doggy, Dorothy, Douche, Duffel, Dunnage, → **EFFECTS**, Emery, Excess, Flannels, Flotation, Follicle, Galligaskins, Game, → **GEAR**, Gladstone, Grab, Grip, Gripsack, Grow, Holdall, Ice, Impedimenta, Jelly, Jiffy®, Kill, Knapsack, Ladies' companion, Lavender, Lithocyst, Marsupium, Materiel, Meal-poke, Minx, Mixed, Money, Monkey, Moon, Mummy, Musette, Musk, Muzzle, Mystery, Nap, Net, Nunny, Organiser, Overnight, Oxford, Packsack, Pantaloons, Plastic, Plus fours, Pochette, Pock(et), Pocketbook, Pockmanky, Pockmantie, Poke, Politzer's, Poly(thene), Port(manteau), Portmantle, Portmantua, Post, Pot, Pouch, Pounce, Pudding, Punch, Purse, Rake, Red, Reticule, Ridicule, Rucksack, Sabretache,

Sac(cule), Sachet, Sack, Saddle, Sag, Satchel, Scent, School, Scrip, Scrotum, Sea, Shopper, Sick, Slattern, Sleeping, Sponge, Sporran, Stacks, Strossers, Sugar, Survival, Tea, Tote, → **TRAP**, Trews, Trollop, Trouse(r), Tucker (box), Udder, Unmentionables, Utricle, Valise, Vanity, Viaticals, Waist, Wallet, Water, Weekend, Win, Woolpack, Work, Wrap, Ziplock

Bagatelle Bauble, Fico, Trifle, Trinket

Bagpipe Biniou, Chorus, Cornemuse, Drone, Gaita, Musette, Pibroch, Piffero, Skirl, Sourdeline, Uillean, Zampogna

Bahama(s), Bahamian BS, Conch

Bail(er), Bailment Bond, Ladle, Mainpernor, Mainprise, Mutuum, Replevin, Replevy, Scoop

Bailey Bridge, Castle wall, Ward

Bailiff Adam, Bandog, Beagle, Bum, Factor, Foud, Grieve, Huissier, Hundreder, Hundredor, Land-agent, Nuthook, Philistine, Reeve, Shoulder-clapper, Shoulder-knot, Steward, Tipstaff, Water

Bairn Baby, → **CHILD**, Infant, Wean

Bait Badger, Berley, Brandling, Burley, Capelin, Chum, Dap, Decoy, Entice, Gentle, Gudgeon, Harass, Hellgram(m)ite, Incentive, Lobworm, Lug(worm), Lure, Mawk, → **RAG**, Ragworm, Sledge, Teagle, Tease, Tempt

Bake(r), Baked, Baking Alaska, Batch, Baxter, → **COOK**, Fire, Kiln-dry, Pieman, Roast, Scorch, Shirr

Baker's daughter Own

Baker Street Irregular

Balance(d) Account, Beam, Compensation, Counterpoise, Counterweight, Equate, Equilibrium, Equipoise, Equiponderate, Even, Fixed, Funambulate, Gyroscope, Gyrostat, Hydrostatic, Invisible, Isostasy, Launce, Libra, Librate, Meet, Otolith, Peise, Perch, Peyse, Poise, → **REMAINDER**, Remnant, Residual, Rest, Running, Scale, Sea-legs, Spring, Stand, Steelyard, Symmetry, Torsion, → **TOTAL**, Trial, Trim, Tron(e), Visible

Balcony Circle, Gallery, Loggia, Mirador, Moucharaby, Porch, Quarter-gallery, Sundeck, Tarras, Terrace, Veranda(h)

Bald, Baldness Alopecia, Apterium, Awnless, Barren, Calvities, Coot, Crude, Egghead, Fox-evil, Glabrous, Hairless, Madarosis, Open, Peelgarlic, Pilgarlic(k), Pollard, Psilosis, Slaphead, Smoothpate, Stark, Tonsured

Balderdash Drivel, Flapdoodle, Nonsense, Rot

Baldmoney Emeu, Meu, Spignel

Bale Bl, Bundle, Evil, Lave, Pack, Sero(o)n, Truss

Baleful Evil, Malefic, Malignant

▶ **Balk** *see* **BAULK**

Balkan Albanian, Bosnian, Bulgarian, Macedon, Rumanian, Serb, Vlach

Ball(s) Aelopile, Aelopyle, Aeolipile, Aeolipyle, Agglomerate, Alley, Ally, Ammo, Aniseed, Apple, Beach, Bead, Beamer, Birthing, Bobble, Boll, Bolus, Bosey, Bouncer, Break, Buckshot, Buzzer, Caltrap, Caltrop, Camphor, Cap, Cherry, Chin, Chinaman, Chopper, Clew, Clue, Condyle, Cotill(i)on, Cramp, Creeper, Croquette, Crystal, Cue, Curve, Daisy-cutter, → **DANCE**, Delivery, Dink, Dodge, Dollydrop, Dot, Dribbler, Eight, Ensphere, Eolipile, Eolipyle, Eolopile, Eolopyle, Falafel, Felafel, Fungo, Gazunder, → **GLOBE**, Glomerate, Gobstopper, Googly, Gool(e)ys, Goolies, Grub, Gutta, Gutter, Hank, Hop, Hummer, Inswinger, Ivory, Jinglet, Jump, Knob, Knur(r), Leather, Leg-break, Leg-cutter, Lob, Long-hop, Marble, Masked, Masque(rade), Matzo, Medicine, Minié, Mirror, Moth, Nur(r), O, Object, Off-break, Off-cutter, Off-spin, Orb, Outswinger, Over, Overarm, Pakora, Pea, Pellet, Pill, Poi, Pomander,

Pompom, Pompon, Prom, Puck, Punch, Quenelle, Rabbit, Rissole, Root, Round, Rover, Rundle, Seamer, Shooter, Shot, Sliotar, Sneak, Sphere, Spinner, Stress, Strike, Swinger, Taw, Testes, Thenar, Three, Tice, Time, Track(er), Witches, Wood, Yorker, Zorb®

Ballad Bab, Bothy, Broadside, Bush, Calypso, Carol, Fanzone, Folk-song, Lay, Lillibullero, Lilliburlero, Mento, Singsong, → **SONG**, Torch-song

Ballast Kentledge, Makeweight, Stabiliser, Trim, Weight

Ball-boy Dry-bob

Ballerina Coryphee, Dancer, Pavlova, Prima

Ballet, Ballet movement, Ballet-system Battement, Bharat Natyam, Bolshoi, Cambré, Chainé, Changement, Checkmate, Daphnis and Chloe, Développé, Don Pasquale, Écarté, Echappé, Enchainement, Entrechat, Firebird, Fouette, Giselle, Jeté, Kirov, Laban, Labanotation, Leg business, Pas de basque, Pas de bourrée, Pas de chat, Petit battement, Pirouette, Plie, Pointe, Pointer, Port de bras, Relevé, Saut, Swan Lake

Ballet-interlude Divertimento

Ballistic Wildfire

Balloon(ist) Aeronaut, Aerostat, Airship, Bag, Barrage, Billow, Blimp, Bloat, Dirigible, Dumont, Fumetto, Hot air, Lead, Montgolfier, Pilot, Rawinsonde, Sonde, Trial, Weather, Zeppelin

Ballot Butterfly, Election, → **POLL**, Referendum, Second, Suffrage, Ticket, Vote

Ballot-box Urn

Ballpoint Bic®, Biro®

Balm(y) Anetic, Arnica, Balsam, Calamint, Fragrant, Garjan, Gilead, Gurjun, Lemon, Lenitive, Lotion, → **MILD**, Mirbane, Myrbane, Nard, Oil, Opobalsam, Ottar, Redolent, Remedy, Soothe, Spikenard, Tiger, Tolu, Unguent

Balmoral Bonnet

Baloney Bunk, Hooey, Nonsense

Balsam Canada, Copaiba, Copaiva, Friar's, Nard, Noli-me-tangere, Peruvian, Resin, Spikenard, Tamanu, Tolu(ic), Touch-me-not, Tous-les-mois, Turpentine

Balt Esth, Lett

Baltic Estonian, Lettic

Bamboo Kendo, Split cane, Tabasheer, Whangee

Bamboozle(d) Cheat, Dupe, Flummox, Hoodwink, Mystify, Nose-led, Perplex, Trick

Ban Abolish, Accurse, Anathema, Black(ing), Censor, Debar, D-notice, Embargo, Estop, Excommunicate, Forbid, For(e)say, For(e)speak, Gate, Green, Moratorium, No, Outlaw, Prohibit, Proscribe, Suppress, Taboo, Tabu, Test, Veto

Banal Corny, Dreary, Flat, Hackneyed, Jejune, Mundane, Platitudinous, → **TRITE**, Trivial

Banana(s) Abaca, Hand, → **MAD**, Matoke, Musa, Plantain, Scitamineae, Split, Strelitzia, Top

Band(s) Absorption, Alice, Ambulacrum, Anadem, Anklet, Armlet, Barrulet, Belt, Border, Braid, Brake, Brass, Brassard, Brassart, Caravan, CB, Channel, Chinstrap, Chromosome, Cingulum, Circlet, Citizens', Clarain, Cohort, Collar, Collet, Combo, Company, Conduction, Corslet, Coterie, Crape, Crew, Deely boppers, Elastic, Endorse, Energy, Enomoty, Facia, Falling, Fascia, Fasciole, Ferret, Ferrule, Fess, Filament, Fillet, Frequency, Frieze, Frog, Frontlet, Galloon, Gamelan, → **GANG**, Garage, Garland, Garter, Gasket, Gaskin, Geneva, German, Gird, Girth, Guard, → **HOOP**, Hope, Iron, Jazz, Jug, Kitchen, Label, Laticlave, Lytta, Maniple, Mariachi, Massed, Military, Mourning, Myrmidon, Noise, One-man, Orchestra, Orchestrina, Pack, Parral, Parrel, Parsal, Parsel, Pass, Patte, Pipe, Plinth, Property, Purfle,

Puttee, Retinaculum, Rib, Ribbon, Rigwiddie, Rigwoodie, Rim, Ring, Robbers, Rubber, Rymme, Sash, Scarf, Screed, Scrunchie, Scrunchy, Sect, Shadow, Shallal, Shash, Sheet, Shoe, Snood, Steel, Strake, Strap, Stratum, String, Stripe, Swath(e), Sweat, Tambu-bambu, Tape, Tendon, Thoroughbrace, Throat-latch, Tie, Tippet, Torques, Tourniquet, Train, Tribute, Troop, Troupe, Tumpline, Turm, Tyre, Unite, Valence, Vinculum, Virl, Vitrain, Vitta, Wanty, Wedding, Weed, Weeper, Welt, With(e), Wristlet, Zona, Zone, Zonule

Bandage Bind, Blindfold, Capeline, Dressing, Fillet, Ligature, Lint, Living, Pledget, Roller, Scapular, Sling, Spica, Suspensor, Swaddle, Swathe, T, Tape, Truss, Tubigrip®, Wadding

Bandicoot Bilby, Pig-rat

Bandit Apache, Bravo, Brigand, Desperado, Fruit-machine, Gunslinger, Klepht, Moss-trooper, Outlaw, Pirate, Rapparee, → **ROBBER**, Squeegee, Turpin

Bandsman, Band-leader Alexander, Bugler, Conductor, Maestro, Miller, Wait

Bandy Bow, Exchange, Revie, Toss, Vie

Bane Curse, Evil, Harm, Poison

Bang(er) Amorce, Big, Cap, Chipolata, Clap, Cracker, Crock, Explode, Flivver, Fringe, Haircut, Heap, Implode, Jalopy, Maroon, Rattletrap, Report, Sausage, Sizzler, Slam, Sonic, Thrill, Wurst

Bangle Anklet, Armlet, Bracelet, Kara

Banish(ment) Ban, Deport, Depose, Exile, Expatriate, Expel, Extradition, Forsay, Maroon, Ostracise, → **OUTLAW**, Relegate, Rusticate

Banjo Ukulele

Bank(ing) An(n)icut, Asar, Backs, Bar, Bay, Bk, Blood, Bluff, Bottle, Brae, Brim, Bund, Camber, Cay, Central, Chesil, Clearing, Cloud, Commercial, Cooperative, Data, Depend, Deposit, Dogger, Down, Dune, Dyke, Earthwork, Escarp, Fog, Gene, Giro, Glacis, Gradient, Gradin(e), Hele, Hill, Home, Incline, Jodrell, Land, Left, Lender, Levee, Link, Lombard Street, Memory, Merchant, Mound, Nap, National, Needle, Nore, Overslaugh, Oyster, Parapet, Penny, Piggy, Pot, Private, Rake, Ramp, Rampart, Reef, → **RELY**, Reserve, Retail, Rivage, Riverside, Rodham, Row, Sandbar, Savings, Seed, Shallow, Shelf, Side, Slope, Soil, Sperm, Staithe, State, Sunk, Telephone, Terrace, Terreplein, Tier, Vault, West, World

Banker Agent, Financial, Fugger, Gnome, Lombard, Medici, → **RIVER**, Rothschild, Shroff, Teller

▷ **Banker** *may indicate* a river

Banknote(s) Flimsy, Greenback, Snuff-paper

Bankrupt(cy) Break, Broke, Bung, Bust, Cadaver, Carey Street, Crash, Debtor, Deplete, Duck, Dyvour, Fail, Fold, Insolvent, Lame duck, Notour, Penniless, Receivership, Ruin, Rump, Scat, Sequestration, Skatt, Smash

▷ **Bankrupt** *may indicate* 'red' around another word

Bank system Giro

Bann(s) Out-ask

Banner Banderol(e), Bandrol, Bannerol, → **FLAG**, Gumphion, Labarum, Oriflamme, Sign, Streamer

Banquet Beanfeast, Dine, Feast, Junket, Spread

Banquette Firestep

Bant Diet, Reduce

Banter Backchat, Badinage, Borak, Chaff, Dicacity, Dieter, Jest, → **JOKE**, Persiflage, Picong, Rag, → **RAILLERY**, Rally, Ribaldry, Roast, Tease

Bantu Bosotho, Gazankulu, Herero, Lebowa, Qwaqwa, Shangaan, Sotho, Transkei, Tutsi, X(h)osa

Bap Bread, Roll, Tommy

Baptise(d), Baptism, Baptist Affusion, Amrit, Christen, Dip, Dipper, Dopper, Dunker, Illuminati, Immersion, John, Mersion, Sabbatarian, Sprinkle, Tinker

Bar(s) Address, Angle-iron, Anti-roll, Astragal, Asymmetric, Axletree, Bail, Ban, Barrelhouse, Baulk, Beam, Bierkeller, Bilboes, Billet, Bistro, Blackball, Blacklist, Block(ade), Bloom, Bolt, Boom, Bottega, Brasserie, Buffet, Bull, Bumper, But, Buvette, Café(-chantant), Café-concert, → **CAGE**, Came, Cantina, Capo, Capstan, Channel, Cocktail, Coffee, Colour, Counter, Cramp(on), Cross(head), Crow, Crush, Currency, Dive, Double-tree, Draw, Drift, Dumbbell, Efficiency, Espresso, Estop(pel), Except, Exclude, Fen, Fid, Flinders, Fonda, Forbid, Foreclose, Forestall, Fret, Gad, Gemel, Glazing, Grate, Grid, Grog-shop, Hame, Handspike, Heck, → **HINDRANCE**, Horizontal, Hound, Hyphen, Impediment, Ingoes, Ingot, Ingowes, Inn, Inner, Judder, Juice, Karaoke, Keeper, Kickstand, Knuckleduster, Latch, Let, Lever, Limbo, Line, Local, Lounge, Macron, Mandrel, Mandril, Measure, Menu, Milk, Mousing, Muesli, Mullion, Nail, Nanaimo, Navigation, No-go, Norman, Obstacle, Onely, Orgue, Outer, Overslaugh, Oxygen, Parallel, Perch, Pile, Pinch, Pole, Posada, Prescription, Private, Prohibit, Pub, Public, Putlog, Rabble, Rack, Rail, Ramrod, Rance, Randle-balk, Randle-perch, Randle-tree, Raw, Reach, Restrict, Rib, Risp, Rod, Roll, Roo, Rung, Saddle, Salad, Saloon, Sans, Save, Saving, Scroll, Semantron, Shaft, Shanty, Shet, Shut, Singles, Skewer, Slice, Slot, Snack, Snug, Spacer, Spar, Speakeasy, Sperre, Spina, Spit, Splinter, Sprag, Stancher, Stanchion, Status, Stave, Sternson, Stick, Stirre, Stretcher, Stripe, Strut, Sway, Swee, T, Tael, Tap(-room), Tapas, Taphouse, Tavern(a), Temple, Toll, Tombolo, Tommy, Tool, Torsion, Tow, Trace, Trangle, Transom, Trapeze, Triblet, Trundle, Type, Vinculum, Wall, Ward, Wet, Whisker, Window, Wine, Wire, Wrecking, Z, Zed, Zygon

Barabbas Robber

Barb(ed) Bur(r), Fluke, Harl, Herl, → **HOOK**, Jag(g), Jibe, Pheon, Prickle, Ramus, Tang, Thorn, Vexillum

Barbados, Barbadian Bajan, Bim(m)

Barbara Allen, Major

Barbarian, Barbaric Boor, Crude, Fifteen, Foreigner, Goth, Heathen, Hottentot, Hun, Inhuman, Lowbrow, Outlandish, Philistine, Rude, Savage, Tartar, Tatar(ic)

Barbary Ape, Roan

Barbecue Braai(vleis), Cook-out, Flame-grill, Grill, Hangi, Hibachi, Roast, Spit

Barbel Beard

Barber Epilate, Figaro, Scrape(r), Shaver, Strap, Todd, Tonsor, Trimmer

Barbiturate Goofball

Bard(ic) Ariosto, Gorsedd, Griot, Heine, Meat, Minstrel, Muse, Ossian, Scald, Scop, Skald, Taliesin

Bare, Bare-headed Adamic, Aphyllous, Bald, Barren, Blank, Bodkin, Cere, Décolleté, Denude, Hush, Lewd, Marginal, Moon, → **NAKED**, Open, Plain, Scablands, Scant, Sear, Stark, Topless, Uncase, Uncover, Unveil

Barefoot Discalced, Unshod

Barely At a pinch, At a stretch, Hand-to-mouth, Hardly, Just, Merely, Scarcely, Scrimp

Bargain(ing) Bargoon, Barter, Braata, Chaffer, Champerty, → **CHEAP**, Collective, Contract, Coup, Deal, Dicker, Distributive, Effort, Find, Go, Haggle, Higgle, Horse-trade, Huckster, Integrative, Option, → **PACT**, Plea, Productivity, Scoop, Snip, Steal, Supersaver, Time, Trade, Trock, Troke, Truck, Wanworth, Wheeler-dealing

Barge Birlinn, Bucentaur, Budgero(w), Butty, Gabbard, Gabbart, Galley-foist, Hopper, Intrude, Jostle, Keel, Lighter, Nudge, Obtrude, Pra(a)m, Ram, Scow, → **SHIP**, Trow, Wherry
▷ **Barge** *may indicate* an anagram
Bargee, Bargeman Keeler, Keelman, Legger, Lighterman, Ram, Trow
Barium Ba, Witherite
Bark Angostura, Ayelp, Azedarach, Bass, Bast, Bay, Bowwow, Calisaya, Cambium, Canella, Caribbee, Cascara, Cascara sagrada, Cascarilla, Cassia, China, Cinchona, Cinnamon, Cork, Cortex, Cusparia, Honduras, Jamaica, Jesuit's, Kina, Kinakina, Latration, Liber, Mezereum, Myrica, Parchment, Peel, Pereira, Peruvian, Phloem, Quebracho, Quest, Quill, Quillai, Quina, Quinquina, Red, Rind, Sagrada, Salian, Sassafras, Scrape, Scurf, Shag, → **SHIP**, Skin, Slippery elm, Tan, Tap(p)a, Totaquine, Waff, Waugh, Winter's, Woof, Wow, Yaff, → **YAP**, Yellow, Yelp, Yip
Bar-keep(er), Barmaid, Barman Advocate, Ale-wife, Bencher, Curate, Hebe, Luckie, Lucky, Tapster, Underskinker
Barley (water) Awn, Bear, Bere, Bigg, Hordeum, Malt, Orgeat, Pearl, Pot, Scotch, Truce, Tsamba
Barm(y) Yeast
Barmecide, Barmecidal Imaginary
Barn Bank, Byre, Cowshed, Dutch, Farm, Grange, Mow, Perchery, Skipper, Tithe
Barnaby Rudge
Barnacle Acorn, Cypris, Goose(neck), Limpet
Barometer Aneroid, Glass, Orometer, Statoscope, Sympiesometer, Torricellian tube, Weatherglass
Baron B, Corvo, Drug, Munchausen, Noble, Thyssen, Tycoon
Baronet Bart
Baronne Dudevant Sand
Baroque Fancy, Gothic, Ornate, Rococo
▷ **Baroque** *may indicate* an anagram
Barrack(s), Barracking Asteism, Boo, Cantonment, Casern(e), Cat-call, Garrison, Heckle, Irony, Jeer, Quarters
Barrage Balloon, Fusillade, Heat, Salvo
Barred Banned, Edh, Trabeculated
Barrel Bl, Butt, Cade, Capstan, Cascabel, Cask, Clavie, Cylinder, Drum, Hogshead, Keg, Kibble, Morris-tube, Oildrum, Organ, Pièce, Pork, Run(d)let, Tan-vat, Thrall, Tierce, Tun, Vat, Water, Wood
Barrel-organ Apollonicum, Hurdy-gurdy, Street piano
Barren Addle, Arid, Badlands, Blind, Blunt, Clear, Dry, Eild, → **EMPTY**, Farrow, Hardscrabble, Hirstie, Jejune, Sterile, Unbearing, Waste, Wasteland, Wilderness, Yeld, Yell
Barrier Bail, Barrage, Bayle, Block, Breakwater, Cauld, Checkrail, Cheval de frise, Chicane, Cordon (sanitaire), Crash, Crush, → **DAM**, Defence, Drawgate, Dyke, Fence, Fraise, Gate, Heat, Hedge, Hurdle, Mach, Obstruct, Pain, Potential, Rail(-fence), Rampart, Restraint, Revetment, Roadblock, Rope, Screen, Skreen, Sonic, Sound, Spina, Stockade, Thermal, Tollgate, Trade, Transsonic, Turnpike, Turnstile, → **WALL**
Barrister Advocate, Attorney, Counsel, Devil, Lawyer, Revising, Rumpole, Sergeant (at law), Serjeant(-at-law), Silk, Templar, Utter
Barrow Dolly, Handcart, Henge, How, Hurley, Kurgan, Molehill, Mound, Pushcart, Tram, Trolley, Truck, Tumulus
Barrow-boy Coster, Trader

Bar-tail Scamel, Staniel, Stannel

Barter Chaffer, Chop, Coup, Dicker, → EXCHANGE, Haggle, Hawk, Niffer, Sco(u)rse, Swap, → TRADE, Traffic, Truck

Basalt Diabase, Melaphyre, Tachylite, Tephrite, Toadstone, Trap(pean), Traprock, Wacke

Base Adenine, Air, Alkali, Bed, Beggarly, Billon, Bottom, Caitiff, Camp, Choline, Codon, Cytosine, Degenerate, Degraded, Dog, Down, E, Erinite, → ESTABLISH, First, Floor, Foot, Foothold, Footstall, Found, Foundation, Fundus, Guanine, Harlot, Histamine, Hydroxide, Ignoble, Indamine, Infamous, Install, Knowledge, Leuco, Lewis, → LOW, → MEAN, Nefarious, Nook, Oasis®, Parasaniline, Partite, Patten, Platform, Plinth, Podium, Premise, Ptomaine, Purin(e), Pyrimidine, Pyrrolidine, Raca, Radix, Rascally, Ratty, Rests, Ribald, Root, Rosaniline, Schiff, Servile, Shameful, Shand, Sheeny, Socle, Soda, Spaceport, Staddle, → STAND, Station, Substrate, Ten, Thymine, Torus, Triacid, Turpitude, Unworthy, Uracil, Vile

Baseball Apple, Nine

Baseless Idle, Unfounded, Ungrounded

Base-line Datum

Basement Bargain, Below stairs

Bash Belt, Bonk, Clout, Go, Hit, Rave, Shot, Slog, Strike, Swat, Swipe

Bashful Awed, Blate, Coy, Modest, Retiring, Shamefast, Sheep-faced, Sheepish, → SHY

Basic(s), Basically, Basis ABC, Abcee, Alkaline, Aquamanale, Aquamanile, Crude, Elemental, → ESSENTIAL, Fiducial, Fond, Fundamental, Ground(work), Gut, In essence, Integral, Intrinsic, Logic, Meat and potatoes, Nitty-gritty, No-frills, No-nonsense, Pou sto, Presumption, Primordial, Principle, Radical, Rudimentary, Spit-and-sawdust, Staple, Substance, Underlying, Uracil

Basilica St Peter's

Basilisk Cannon, Lizard

Basin Aquamanale, Aquamanile, Artesian, Aspergillum, Aspersorium, Benitier, Bidet, Bowl, Canning, Catch, Catchment, Cirque, Corrie, Cwm, Dish, Dock, Doline, Donets, Drainage, Foxe, Geosyncline, Great, Impluvium, Kuzbass, Kuznetsk, Lavabo, Laver, Minas, Monteith, Ocean, Okavango, Pan, Park, Piscina, Playa, Porringer, Pudding, Reservoir, River, Scapa Flow, Sink, Slop, Stoop, Stoup, Sugar, Tank, Tarim, Tidal, Washhand

Bask Apricate, Revel, Sun, Sunbathe, → WALLOW

Basket, Basket-work Baalam, Bass, Bassinet, Bread, Buck, Cabas, Calathus, Canephorus, Car, Cesta, Chip, Cob, Coop, Corbeil(le), Corbicula, Corf, Creel, Cresset, Dosser, Fan, Flasket, Flax kit, Frail, Gabian, Hamper, Hask, Junket, Kago, Kajawah, Kipe, Kit, Kite, Leap, Litter, Maund, Mocock, Mocuck, Moses, Murlain, Murlan, Murlin, Osiery, Pannier, Ped, Petara, Pitara(h), Plate, Pollen, Pottle, Punnet, Rip, Round file, Scull, Scuttle, Seed-lip, Skep, Skull, Trolley, Trout, Trug, Van, Wagger-pagger(-bagger), Waste(-paper), Wattlework, Whisket, Wicker(-work), Will(e), Wisket, Work

Basketball Tip-off

Basket-bearer Canephor(a), Canephore, Canephorus

Basket-maker Alfa, Cane, Halfa, Wicker

Basque Euskarian

Bass Alberti, Ale, Alfie, B, Black, Continuo, Deep, Double, El-a-mi, Figured, Fish, Ground, Largemouth, Low, Ostinato, Serran, Smallmouth, String, Thorough, Walking

Bast Liber

Bastard, Bastard-wing Alula, Base, By-blow, Filius nullius, Git, Haram(za)da, Illegitimate, Mamzer, Momzer, Mongrel, Sassaby, Side-slip, Slink, Spuriae, Spurious, Whoreson

▷ **Bastard** *may indicate* an anagram

Baste Enlard, Sew, Stitch, Tack

Bastion Citadel, Lunette, Moineau

Bat(sman), Bat's wing, Batter, Batting, Batty Aliped, Ames, Assail, Barbastelle, Baton, Belfry, Blink, Chiroptera, Close, Club, Cosh, Crackers, Cudgel, Dad, Die Fledermaus, Eyelid, False vampire, Flittermouse, Flying fox, Fruit, Grace, Hammerhead, Hatter, Haywire, Hit, Hobbs, Hook, Horseshoe, In, Ink mouse, Insectivorous, Kalong, Language, Leisler, Man, Mastiff, Maul, May, Mormops, Mouse-eared, Myopic, Nictate, Nictitate, Night, Nightwatchman, Noctilio, Nora, Nurdle, Opener, Patagium, Pinch-hit, Pipistrel(le), Poke, Pummel, Racket, Racquet, Ram, Rearmouse, Reremice, Reremouse, Roussette, Ruin, Sauch, Saugh, Scotch hand, Serotine, Sledge, Spectre, Stick, Stonewall, Straight, Striker, Swat, Switch hitter, Trap-stick, Vampire, Vespertilionid, Viv, Whacky, Willow, Wood

Batch Bake, Bunch, Clutch

Bath(room) Aerotone, Aeson's, Bagnio, Bain-marie, Balneotherapy, Bed, Blanket, Blood, Bubble, Caldarium, Cor, Dip, En suite, Epha, Foam, Hammam, Hip, Hummaum, Hummum, Jacuzzi®, Laver, Mik vah, Mud, Mustard, Oil, Piscina, Plunge, Salt, Sauna, Shower, Sitz, Slipper, Soak, Spa, Sponge, Steam, Stew, Stop, Tepidarium, Therm, Tub, Turkish, Tye, Vapour, Whirlpool, Wife

Bathe, Bathing Balneal, Balneation, Balneology, Balneotherapy, Bay(e), Beath, Bogey, Bogie, Dip, Dook, Douk, Embay, Foment, Immerse, Lave, Lip, Skinny-dip, Souse, Splash, Stupe, → **SWIM**, Tub, → **WASH**

Batman Valet

Baton Mace, Rod, Sceptre, Staff, Truncheon

Batrachian Frog, Toad

▷ **Bats, Batting** *may indicate* an anagram

Battalion Bn, Corps, Troop

Batten Dropper, Fasten, Tie

Batter(ed) Bombard, Bruise, Buffet, Decrepit, Pound

Battery Accumulator, Artillery, Drycell, Field, Galvanic, Heliac, Henhouse, Li(thium)-ion, Nicad, Penlight, Pra(a)m, Primary, Solar, Storage, Troop, Voltaic, Waffle, Water

Battle(s), Battleground Action, Affair, Ben, Clash, Cockpit, Combat, → **CONFLICT**, Encounter, Engagement, Field, → **FIGHT**, Fray, Front, Hosting, Joust, Pitched, Royal, Running, Sarah, Sciamachy, Skiamachy, Spurs, Stoor, Stour, Stowre, Theatre, Wage, → **WAR**

BATTLES

3 letters:	Laon	Allia	Marne
Kut	Loos	Arcot	Parma
Ulm	Mons	Arras	Pydna
	Nile	Boyne	Sedan
4 letters:	Zama	Bulge	Somme
Alma		Crecy	Tours
Chad	*5 letters:*	Ipsus	Valmy
Ivry	Accra	Issus	Ypres
Jena	Alamo	Lewes	

6 letters:
Actium
Arbela
Argyle
Arnhem
Barnet
Camlan
Cannae
Cressy
Crimea
Lutzen
Maldon
Midway
Naseby
Sadowa
Senlac
Shiloh
Tobruk
Varese
Verdun
Vigrid
Wagram
Wipers

7 letters:
Aboukir
Alamein
Argonne
Bautzen
Beaches
Britain
Bull Run
Cambrai
Chalons
Colenso
Coronel
Corunna
Dunkirk
Evesham

Flodden
Flowers
Glencoe
Jericho
Jutland
Lepanto
Magenta
Marengo
Nations
Newbury
Orleans
Picardy
Plassey
Poltava
Pultowa
Salamis
Vitoria
Warburg

8 letters:
Antietam
Ardennes
Ayacucho
Blenheim
Borodino
Bosworth
Clontarf
Culloden
Edgehill
Erzurium
Flanders
Fontenay
Hastings
Inkerman
Jemappes
Le Cateau
Manassas
Marathon
Metaurus

Naumachy
Navarino
Omdurman
Palo Alto
Philippi
Poitiers
Ragnarok
Saratoga
Syracuse
Talavera
Waterloo

9 letters:
Agincourt
Balaclava
Caporetto
El Alamein
Gallipoli
Ladysmith
Otterburn
Oudenarde
Pharsalus
Princeton
Ramillies
Sedgemoor
Solferino
St Vincent
Theomachy
Trafalgar
Worcester

10 letters:
Armageddon
Austerlitz
Bennington
Bunker Hill
Camperdown
Gettysburg
Lundy's Lane

Petersburg
Quatre Bras
Shipka Pass
Stalingrad
Steenkerke

11 letters:
Armentières
Bannockburn
Belleau Wood
Chattanooga
Hohenlinden
Marston Moor
Prestonpans
Thermopylae
Wounded Knee

12 letters:
Flodden Field
Monte Cassino
Roncesvalles

13 letters:
Bosworth Field
Little Bighorn
Passchendaele
Spanish Armada

14 letters:
Castlebar Races
Stamford Bridge

15 letters:
Missionary Ridge
Plains of Abraham
Teutoberger Wald

Battle-axe Amazon, Bill, Gorgon, Halberd, Ogress, Sparth(e), Termagant, Termagent, Turmagant, Turmagent
Battlement Barmkin, Crenellate, Merlon, Rampart
Battle-order Phalanx
Battleship Carrier, Destroyer, Dreadnought, Gunboat, Man-o'-war, Pocket, Potemkin
Bauble Bagatelle, Gaud, Gewgaw, Trifle
Bauhaus Gropius
Baulk Demur, Gib, Hen, Impede, Jib, Reest, Reist, Shy, Thwart
Bavardage Fadaise

Bawd(y) Hare, Raunchy, Sculdudd(e)ry, Skulduddery

Bawl Bellow, Gollar, Howl, Weep

Bay Ab(o)ukir, Aere, Arm, Baffin, Bantry, Bark, Bell, Bengal, Bight, Biscay, Bonny, Botany, Broken, Byron, Cape Cod, Cardigan, Chesapeake, Cienfuegos, Cleveland, Colwyn, Corpus Christi, Cove, Covelet, Creek, Daphne, Delagoa, Delaware, Discovery, Dublin, Dundalk, Dvina, False, Famagusta, Fleet, Frobisher, Fundy, Galway, Gdansk, Georgian, Gibraltar, Glace, Golden, Great Australian Bight, Green, Guanabara, Guantanamo, Gulf, Hangzhou, Harbour, Hawke's, Herne, Horse, → **HOWL**, Hudson, Inhambane, Inlet, Ise, James, Jervis, Jiazhou, Kavalla, Kuskokwim, Laura, Laurel, Layby, Loading, Lobito, Loblolly, Lutzow-Holm, MA, Magdalena, Manila, Massachusetts, Montego, Morton, Narragansett, New York, Niche, Oleander, Omaha, Oriel, Passamaquoddy, Pegasus, Pigs, Plenty, Plymouth, Port Phillip, Poverty, Recess, Red, Roan, St Austell, St Michel, San Pedro, Scene, San Francisco, Santiago, Setubal, Shark, Sick, Sligo, Suvla, Swansea, Table, Tampa, Tasman, Thunder, Tor, Toyama, Tralee, Trincomalee, Ungava, Vae, Vigo, Vlore, Voe, Vyborg, Waff, Walfish, Walvis, Wash, Whitley, Wick, Yowl

Bayonet Jab, Skewer, Stab, Sword

Bazaar Alcaiceria, Emporium, Fair, Fete, Market, Pantechnicon, Sale, Sook, Souk

BBC Auntie

Be Exist, Live, Occur

Beach Bondi, Chesil, Coast, Daytona, Ground, Hard, Lido, Littoral, Machair, Miami, Omaha, Palm, Plage, Raised, Sand, Seaside, Shingle, Shore, Storm, Strand, Waikiki

Beachcomber Arenaria

Beacon Belisha, Fanal, Landing, Lightship, Need-fire, Pharos, Racon, Radar, Radio, Robot, Signal

Bead(s), Beaded Adderstone, Aggri, Aggry, Astragal, Baily's, Ballotini, Bauble, Blob, Bugle, Cabling, Chaplet, Crab-stones, Dewdrop, Drop, Droplet, Gadroon, Gaud, Job's tears, Kumbaloi, Mala, Moniliform, Ojime, Passament, Passement, Paternoster, Poppet, Poppit, Prayer, Rosary, St Cuthbert's, Se(a)wan, Subha, Sweat, Tear, Wampum(peag), Worry

Beadle Apparitor, Bederal, Bedral, Bumble, Herald, Paritor, Shammes, Verger

Beagle Spy

Beak AMA, Bailie, Bill, Cad, Cere, Coronoid, Egg-tooth, Gar, JP, Kip(p), Magistrate, Master, Metagnathous, Mittimus, Nasute, Neb, Nose, Pecker, Prow, Ram, Rostellum, Rostrum, Shovel

Beaker Bell, Cup, Goblet

Beakless Erostrate

Beak-shaped Coracoid

Beam(ing) Arbor, Balance, Bar, Ba(u)lk, Binder, Boom, Bowstring, Box, Breastsummer, Bressummer, Broadcast, Bum(p)kin, Cantilever, Carline, Carling, Cathead, Collar, Crossbar, Crosshead, Crosspiece, Deck, Electron, Girder, Grin, Hammer, Hatch, Herisson, Holophote, I, Irradiate, Joist, Ke(e)lson, Landing, Laser, Lentel, Lintel, Manteltree, Molecular, Needle, Outrigger, Particle, Pencil, Principal, Purlin, Putlock, Putlog, Radio, → **RAFTER**, → **RAY**, Rayon, Refulgent, Rident, Ridgepole, Rood, Roof-tree, Sandwich, Scale, Scantling, Searchlight, Shaft, Shine, Shore, Sleeper, Smile, Soffit, Solive, Stanchion, Stemson, Sternpost, Straining, Streamer, Stringer, Stringpiece, Summer, Support, Tailing, Tie, Timber, Trabeate, Trabecula, Transom, Trave, Trimmer, Truss, Universal, Viga, Walking, Weigh-bauk, Yard, Yardarm

Beamish Galumphing, Nephew

Bean Abrus, Adsuki, Aduki, Adzuki, Arabica, Asparagus pea, Baked, Berry, Black,

Black-eye, Borlotti, Broad, Bush, Butter, Cacao, Calabar, Castor, Cluster, Cocoa, Coffee, Cow-pea, Dwarf, Fabaceous, Fava, Flageolet, French, Frijol(e), Garbanzo, Goa, Gram, Green, Haricot, Harmala, Head, Horse, Jack, Jelly, Jumping, Kachang putch, Kidney, Lablab, Lentil, Lima, Locust, Molucca, Moong, Moth, Mung, Nelumbo, Nib, Noddle, Ordeal, Pichurim, Pinto, Runner, St Ignatius's, Scarlet, Scarlet runner, Shell, Snap, Soy(a), String, Sugar, Sword, Tonga, Tonka, Tonquin, Urd, Wax, Winged, Yard-long

Beanfeast → **PARTY**, Spree, Wayzgoose

Bear(er), Bear lover Abide, Abrooke, Andean, Arctic, Arctophile, Baloo, Balu, Beer, Bigg, Breed, Brook, Brown, Bruin, Brunt, → **CARRY**, Cave, Churl, Cinnamon, Coati-mondi, Coati-mundi, Cub, Demean, Dree, Ean, → **ENDURE**, Engender, Exert, Fur-seal, Gonfalonier, Great, Grizzly, Hack, Ham(m)al, Harbinger, Have, Hold, Honey, Humf, Hump(h), Jampani, Keb, Kinkajou, Koala, Kodiak, Koolah, Lioncel(le), Lionel, Lug, Mother, Nandi, Nanook, Owe, Paddington, Panda, Polar, Pooh, Rac(c)oon, Roller, Rupert, Russia, Sackerson, Seller, Shoulder, Sit, Sloth, Spectacled, Stand, Stay, Stomach, → **SUFFER**, Sunbear, Sustain, Targeteer, Teddy, Teem, Thole, Throw, Tolerate, Tote, Transport, Undergo, Upstay, Ursine, Water, Whelp, White, Wield, Woolly, Yield

Bearberry Manzanita, Uva-ursi

Beard(ed) Aaron, Alfalfa, Anchor, Arista, Assyrian, Aureole, Awn, Balaclava, Barb, Barbiche, Beaver, Belgrave, Cadiz, Cathedral, Charley, Charlie, Confront, Defy, Ducktail, Face, Five o'clock shadow, Forked, Fungus, Goatee, Hair(ie), Hairy, Hear(ie), Imperial, Jewish, Kesh, Lincolnesque, Mephistopheles, Old Dutch, Olympian, Outface, Peak, Pencil, Raleigh, Rivet, Roman T, Screw, Shenandoah, Spade, Stibble, Stiletto, Stubble, Swallowtail, Tile, Trojan, Tuft, Uncle Sam, Vandyke, Whiskerando, Whiskery, Ziff

Beardless Callow, Clean, Tahr, Tehr

▷ **Bearhug** *may indicate* Teddy or similar around a word

Bearing(s) Air, Allure, Amenaunce, Armorial, Aspect, Azimuth, Babbitt, Ball, Behaviour, Bush, Carriage, Deportment, Direction, E, Endurance, Gait, Hatchment, Haviour, Heading, → **HERALDIC**, Hugger-mugger, Lioncel(le), Lionel, Manner, Martlet, Mascle, Middy, Mien, N, Needle, Nor, Pheon, Port, Presence, Reference, Relevant, Roller, S, Subordinary, Teeming, Tenue, Thrust, W, Yielding

▷ **Bearing** *may indicate* compass points

Beast → **ANIMAL**, Arna, Behemoth, Brute, Caliban, Caribou, Chimera, → **CREATURE**, Dieb, Dragon, Dzeren, Gargoyle, Gayal, Genet, Grampus, Hippogriff, Hodog, Hog, Hy(a)ena, Hydra, Jumart, Kinkajou, Lion, Mammoth, Marmot, Mastodon, Mhorr, Monoceros, Oliphant, Opinicus, Oryx, Panda, Potto, Quagga, Rac(c)oon, Rhytina, Rother, Rumptifusel, Sassaby, Steer, Sumpter, Tarand, Teg, Theroid, Triceratops, Triton, Wart-hog, Whangam, Yahoo, Yak, Yale, Zizel

Beat(ing), Beaten, Beater Anoint, Arsis, Athrob, Bandy, Bang, Baste, Bastinado, Batter, Battue, Belabour, Belt, Bepat, Best, Blatter, Bless, Bo Diddley, Bubble, Cadence, Cane, Cat, Chastise, Clobber, Club, Clump, Cob, Conquer, Cream, Cudgel, Cuff, Curry, Debel, → **DEFEAT**, Ding, Donder, Dress, Drub, Duff up, Excel, Fatigue, Faze, Feague, Feeze, Fibbed, Firk, Flagellate, Flail, Flam, Float, Flog, Floor, Flush, Fly, Fustigate, Hipster, Hollow, Horsewhip, Ictus, Inteneration, Jole, Joll, Joule, Jowl, Knock, Knubble, Lace, Laidie, Laidy, Lambast(e), Larrup, Lash, Lather, Laveer, Lay, Lick, Lilt, Lounder, Mall, Malleate, Mersey, Nubble, Outclass, Outdo, Outflank, Outstrip, Paik, Palpitate, Pandy, Paradiddle, Pash, Paste, Ploat, Pommel, Pound, Prat, Pug, Pulsate, Pulsatile, Pulse, Pulsedge, Pummel, Pun, Quop, Raddle, Ram, Ratten, Resolve, Retreat, Rhythm, Ribroast, Rope's end, Round, Rowstow, Ruff(le),

Scourge, Scutch, Slat, Smight, Smite, Soak, Sock, Strap, Strap-oil, Strike, Swinge, Swingle, Systole, Taber, Tabor, Tabrere, Tachycardia, Tact, Tala, Tattoo, Thesis, Thrash, Thresh, Throb, Thud, Thump, Thwack, Tick, Tired, Top, Torture, Tricrotic, Trounce, Tuck, Tund, Verberate, Vibrate, Wallop, Wappend, Weary, Welt, Wham, Whip, Whisk, Whitewash, Wraught, Ybet, Yerk, Yirk

▷ **Beaten-up** *may indicate* an anagram

Beat it Skedaddle, Vamo(o)se

Beatitude Macarism

Beau Admirer, Blade, Brummel, Cat, Damoiseau, Dandy, Flame, Geste, Lair, Lover, Masher, Nash, Spark, Tibbs

Beaufort Scale, Windscale

Beaut(y) Advantage, Bathing, Belle, Bellibone, Bombshell, Camberwell, Charmer, Colleen, Comeliness, Corker, Dish, Doll, Glory, Houri, Hyperion, Lana, Monism, Picture, Pride, Pulchritude, Purler, Sheen, Smasher, Stunner

Beautiful, Beautify Astrid, Bonny, Bright, Embellish, Enhance, Exquisite, Fair, Fine, Gorgeous, Junoesque, Ornament, Pink, Radiant, Smicker, Specious, To kalon

Beauty spot Patch, Tempe, Tika

Beaver Beard, Castor, Eager, Grind, Mountain, Oregon, Rodent, Sewellel

Because (of) As, Forasmuch, Forwhy, Hence, In, Inasmuch, Sens, Since

Beckon Gesture, Nod, Summons, Waft, Wave

Become, Becoming Apt, Besort, Decent, Decorous, Enter, Fall, Fit, Flatter, Get, Go, Grow, Happen, Occur, Seemly, Suit, Wax, Worth

Bed(s), Bedding, Bedstead Air, Allotment, Amenity, Apple-pie, Arroyo, Bacteria, Base, Bassinet, → **BEDCOVER**, Berth, Bottom, Bottomset, Box, Bundle, Bunk, Caliche, Camp, Carrycot, Channel, Charpoy, Cill, Cot(t), Couch(ette), Counterpane, Couvade, Coverlet, Cradle, Crib, Cross, Cul(t)ch, Day, Divan, Doona, Doss, Duvet, Erf, False, Feather, Filter, Fluidized, Flying, Four-poster, Futon, Gault, Greensand, Hammock, Inlay, Kago, Kang, Kip, Knot, Knot garden, Layer, Lazy, Lilo®, Litter, Marriage, Mat, Matrix, Mattress, Murphy, Nap, Nest, Nookie, Oyster, Pad, Paillasse, Pallet, Palliasse, Pan, Parterre, Passage, Patch, Pavement, Pay, Pig, Plank, Plant, Plot, Procrustean, Puff, Quilt, Retire, River, Rollaway, Roost, Rota, Sack, Scalp, Settle, Shakedown, Sill, Sitter, Sleep, Sofa, Standing, Stratum, Stretcher, Sun, Tanning, T(h)alweg, Test, Thill, Trough, Truckle, Trundle, Twin, Wadi, Wady, Ware, Water, Wealden, Wedding

Bedaub Cake, Deck, Smear

Bed-bug B, B flat, Chinch, Flea, Louse, Vermin

Bedchamber, Bedroom Boudoir, Bower, Chamber, Cubicle, Dorm(itory), Dormer, Dorter, Ruelle, Ward

Bedcover Palampore, Palempore

Bedeck Adonise, Adorn, Array, Festoon

▷ **Bedevilled** *may indicate* an anagram

Bedjacket Nightingale

Bedlam Chaos, Furore, Madness, Nuthouse, Tumult, Uproar

Bed-rest Dutch-wife

Bedwetting Enuresis

Bee Athenia, Bumble, Carpenter, Cuckoo, Deborah, Debra, Deseret, Dog, Drone, Drumbledor, Dumbledore, Group, Hiver, Honey, Humble, Killer, King, Lapidary, Leaf-cutter, Mason, Melissa, Mining, Nurse, Queen, Quilting, Raising, Solitary, Spell, Spell-down, Spelling, Swarm, Worker, Working

Beech Antarctic, Copper, Fagus, Hornbeam, Mast, Taw(h)ai, Tree

Bee-eater Merops, Rainbow-bird

Beef(y) Baron, Bleat, Brawny, Bresaola, Bull(y), Bullock, Carpaccio, Charqui, Chateaubriand, Chuck, Clod, Complain, Corned, Filet mignon, Groan, Grouse, Hough, Jerk, Kobe, Liebig, Mart, Mice, Moan, Mousepiece, Muscle, Neat, Ox, Pastrami, Peeve, Plate, Porterhouse, Rother, Salt-junk, Sauerbraten, Sey, Silverside, Sirloin, Stolid, Stroganoff, Topside, Tournedos, Tranche, Undercut, Vaccine, Wellington

Beefeater Billman, Exon, Gin, Oxpecker, Warder, Yeoman

Bee-glue Propolis

Beehive Alveary, Apiary, Ball, Gum, Skep

Beelzebub Devil

Beer Ale, Alegar, Amber fluid, Amber liquid, Bantu, Barley sandwich, Bitter, Black, Bock, Chaser, Draught, Drink, Dry, Entire, Export, Gill, Ginger, Granny, Grog, Guest, Heavy, Herb, Home-brew, Kaffir, Keg, Kvass, Lager, Lambic, Lite, Lush, Malt, March, Middy, Mild, Mum, Near, Nog, October, Pils(e)ner, Pint, Pony, Porter, Real, Real ale, Rice, Root, Saki, Scoobs, Sherbet, Skeechan, Small, Spruce, Stingo, Stout, Swanky, Swats, Swipes, Switchel, Table, Taplash, Tinnie, Tipper, Tshwala, Tube, Wallop, Wheat, Zythum

Beer garden Brasserie

Bee's nest Bink

Beet Blite, Chard, Fat-hen, Goosefoot, Mangel(wurzel), Seakale, Silver, Spinach, Sugar

Beetle Ambrosia, Anobiid, Argos tortoise, Asiatic, Bacon, Bark, Batler, Bee, Blister, Bloody-nosed, Boll weevil, Bombardier, Bruchid, Bug, Bum-clock, Buprestidae, Buprestus, Burying, Bustle, Buzzard-clock, Cabinet, Cadelle, Cane, Cantharis, Carabid, Cardinal, Carpet, Carrion, Chafer, Christmas, Churchyard, Cicindela, Click, Clock, Cockchafer, Cockroach, Coleoptera, Coleopterous, Colorado, Coprophagan, Curculio, Darkling, Deathwatch, Dermestid, Devil's coach-horse, Diamond, Diving, Dor(r), Dor-fly, Dumbledore, Dung, Dyticus, Dytiscus, Elater, Elytron, Elytrum, Firefly, Flea, Furniture, Glow-worm, Gold(smith), Goliath, Gregor, Ground, Hammer, Hangover, Hercules, Hop-flea, Hornbug, Huhu, Humbuzz, Impend, Japanese, Jewel, June, Khapra, Ladybird, Ladybug, Lamellicorn, Larder, Leaf, Leather, Longhorn, Longicorn, Mall(et), Maul, May-bug, Meloid, Minotaur, Museum, Musk, Oakpruner, Oil, Overhang, Pill, Pinchbuck, Pine, Pine-chafer, Potato, Project, Protrude, Race(-bug), Rhinoceros, Rhynchophora, Roach, Rosechafer, Rove, Sacred, Saw palmetto, Scamper, Scarab(ee), Scavenger, Scolytus, Scurry, Sexton, Shard, Skelter, Sledge(-hammer), Snapping, Snout, Soldier, Spanish fly, Spider, Spring, Stag, Tenebrio, Tiger, Toktokkie, Tortoise, Tumble-bug, Tumble-dung, Turnip-flea, Typographer, Vedalia, VW, Water, Weevil, Whirligig, Wireworm, Woodborer, Wood-engraver

Beetle-crushers Cops

Befall Happen, Occur

Before(hand) A, Advance, Ante, Avant, By, Coram, Earlier, Early, Ere, Erst(while), → **FORMER**, Or, Pre, Previously, Prior, Pro, Sooner, Till, To, Until, Van, Zeroth

Before food Ac

Befriend Assist, Cotton, Fraternise, Support

Befuddle(ment) Bemuse, Dwaal, Inebriate, Stupefy

Beg(gar), Beggarly, Begging Abr(ah)am-man, Ask, Badgeman, Beseech, Besognio, Bey, Bezonian, Blighter, Blue-gown, Cadge, Calendar, Clapper-dudgeon, Crave, → **ENTREAT**, Exoration, Flagitate, Fleech, Gaberlunzie, Gangrel, Hallan-shaker, Implore, Impoverish, Irus, Jarkman, Lackall, Lazar(us), Lazzarone, Lumpenproletariat, Maund, Mendicant, Mooch, Mouch, Mump, Niggardly, Obtest,

Palliard, Panhandle, Pauper, Penelophon, Penniless, → **PLEAD**, Pled, Pray, Prig, Prog, Ptochocracy, Rag, Randie, Randy, Ruffler, Ruin(ate), Sadhu, Schnorr(er), Screeve, Scrounge, Shool(e), Skelder, Skell, Solicit, Sue, Supplicate, Thig(ger), Toe-rag, Touch, Undo, Uprightman, Whipjack

Beget Gender, Kind

Beggar rule Ptochocracy

Begging bowl Clackdish, Clapdish

Begin(ner), Beginning Ab ovo, Alpha, Author, B, Babyhood, Black, Cause, Clapdash, Commence, Daw, Dawn, Deb, Debut, Embryo, Enter, Exordium, Fall-to, Fledgling, Genesis, Germ, Go, Greenhorn, Inaugural, Inception, Inchoate, Incipient, Incipit, Initial, Initiate, Intro, Johnny-raw, L, Lead, Learn, Learner, Logos, Nascent, Neophyte, → **NOVICE**, Oncome, Onset, Ope(n), Ord, → **ORIGIN**, Outbreak, Pose, Prelim(inary), Presidium, Primer, Rookie, Seed, Set, → **START**, Startup, Takeoff, Tenderfoot, Tiro, To-fall, Tyro(ne), Yearn

Begone Aroint, Aroynt, Avaunt, Scram, Shoo, Vamo(o)se

Begonia Elephant's-ear(s)

Begorrah Bedad, Musha

Begrudge Envy, Resent

Beguile(r) Bewitch, Charm, Coax, Distract, Divert, Enchant, Ensnare, Entice, Flatter, Gull, Intrigue, Jack-a-lantern, Tice, Wile

Behalf Ex parte, For, Part, Sake

Behave, Behaviour, Behaving Acquired, Act, Conduct, Consummatory, Convenance, Decorum, Demean, Deportment, Do, Epimeletic, Etepimeletic, Ethics, Form, Goings-on, Guise, Horme, → **MANNER**, Meme, Nature, Netiquette, Noblesse oblige, Obey, Orientation, Praxeology, Quit, React, Response, Satisficing, Strong meat, Tribalism, Unreasonable

Behead Decapitate, Decollate, Guillotine

Behind(hand) Abaft, Aft(er), Ahind, Ahint, Apoop, Arear, Arere, Arrear, Arse, Astern, Beneath, Bottom, Bum, Buttocks, Croup, Derrière, Fud, Late, Overdue, Post, Prat, → **REAR**, Slow, Tushie

Behold(en) Affine, Ecce, Eye, Here's, Indebted, La, Lo, Look, Observe, See, View, Voilà

Beige Greige, Tan

Being Cratur, Creature, Ens, Entia, Entity, Esse, Essence, Existence, Human, Man, Metaphysics, Mode, Nature, Omneity, Ontology, → **PERSON**, Saul, Soul, Subsistent, Substance, Supreme, Ubiety, Wight

Bejabers Arrah

Belch Boak, Boke, Brash, Burp, Emit, Eruct, Erupt, Rift, Spew, Yex

Belcher Foulard, Handkerchief, Hanky, Toby

Beldam(e) Crone, Hag, Harridan, Scold

Belfry Campanile, Tower

Belgian Flemish, Walloon

Belief, Believe, Believed, Believer, Believing Accredit, Anata, Ativism, Bigot, Buy, Christian, Conviction, Creationism, Credence, Credit, Creed, Cult, Culture, Deem, Deist, Doctrine, Doxastic, Doxy, Dukkha, Faith, Formulism, Gnostic, Heresy, Heterodoxy, Hold, Holist, Idea, Ideology, Islam, Ism, Ludism, Manichaeism, Meme, Messianist, Methink, Mysticism, Notion, → **OPINION**, Orthopraxy, Ovist, Pacifism, Pantheism, Persuasion, Physicism, Pluralism, Presumption, Religion, Reputed, Seeing, S(h)aivism, Shema, Solfidian, Superstition, Suspect, Swallow, Tenet, Thanatism, Theist, Theosophy, Think, Threap, Threep, Traducianism, Transcendentalism, Trinitarian, Triphysite, Trow, Trust, Ubiquitarianism,

Umma(h), Unitarian, Universalism, Wear, Ween, Wis(t)

Belittle Cheapen, Cry down, Decry, Depreciate, Derogate, Detract, Diminish, Discredit, Disparage, Downgrade, Humble, Pooh-pooh, Slight

Bell(s) Acton, Angelus, Ben, Big Ben, Bob, Bow, Bronte, Cachecope, Canterbury, Carillon, Chime, Chinese pavilion, Crotal, Curfew, Currer, Daisy, Diving, Division, Ellis, Gong, Grandsire, Jar, Low, Lutine, Market, Mass, Minute, Mort, Muffin, Pancake, Passing, Pavilion, Peal, Peter, Pinger, Pudding, Ring, Roar, Sacring, Sanctus, Shark, Sleigh, Tailor, Tantony, Tenor, Tent, Tintinnabulum, Tocsin, Toll, Tom, Triple, Tubular, Vair, Vaire, Verry, Vesper

Bell-bird Arapunga, Campanero

Belle Beauty, Starr, Toast, Venus

Bell-founder Belleter

Bellicose, Belligerent Chippy, Combatant, Gung-ho, Hostile, Jingoist, Martial, Militant, Truculent, Warmonger

Bellow(s) Buller, Holla, Holler, Moo, Rant, Rave, Roar, Rout, Saul, Thunder, Troat, Tromp(e), Trumpet, Windbag

Bell-ringer, Bell-ringing Bob, Campanology, Changes, Clapper, Course, Grandsire, Handstroke, Hunting, Maximus, Quasimodo, Rope, Sally, Tocsin, Toller

Belly Abdomen, Alvine, Bag, Beer, Beer-gut, Boep, Bunt, Calipee, Celiac, Coeliac, Gut, Kite, Kyte, Pod, → **STOMACH**, Swell, Tum(my), Venter, Wame, Weamb, Wem(b), Womb

Belong, Belonging(s) Apply, Appurtenant, Chattels, Effects, Incident, Inhere, Intrinsic, Paraphernalia, Pertain, → **PROPERTY**, Relate, Traps

Beloved Acushla, Alder-lief, Amy, Boyfriend, David, Dear, Doy, Esme, Inamorata, Joy, Lief, Morna, Pet, Popular, Precious

Below Beneath, Inf(erior), Infra, Nether, Sub, Subjacent, Under, Unneath

Belt(ed) Baldric(k), Band, Bandoleer, Bandolier, Baudric(k), Bible, Black, Cartridge, Chastity, Cholera, Clitellum, Clobber, Clock, Commuter, Conveyor, Copper, Cotton, Crios, Demolition, Equator, Fan, Flog, Fold and thrust, Galvanic, Garter, Gird(le), Girt, Great, Green, Hip, Hydraulic, Inertial, Judoka, Kuiper, Lap, Larrup, Life, Lonsdale, Mitre, Money, Muesli, Orion's, Orogenic, Polt, Pound, Radiation, Roller, Rust, Safety, Sam Browne, Sanitary, Sash, Seat, Speed, Stockbroker, Storm, Strap, Stratosphere, Sun, Surcingle, Suspender, Swipe, Sword, Taiga, Tear, Thump, Tore, Tract, Van Allen, Wampum, Wanty, Webbing, Wing, Zodiac, Zone, Zoster

Belt up Sh

Belvedere Gazebo, Mirador

Bemoan → **LAMENT**, Mourn, Sigh, Wail

Bemuse Infatuate, Stonn(e), Stun, Stupefy, Throw

Ben Battle, Hur, Jonson, Mountain, Nevis, Spence

Bench Banc, Banker, Bink, Bleachers, Counter, Court, Cross, Exedra, Form, Front, King's, Knifeboard, Magistrates, Optical, Pew, Queen's, Rout seat, Rusbank, → **SEAT**, Settle, Siege, Stillage, Thoft, Thwart, Treasury, Trestle, Widow's

Benchmark Criteria, Yardstick

Bend(er), Bending, Bends Angle, Arc, Arch, Articular, Becket, Bight, Binge, Bow, Buck(le), Bust, Camber, Carrick, Chicane, Circumflect, Corner, Crank(le), Cringe, → **CROOK**, Curl, Curve, Diffraction, Dog-leg, Double up, Elbow, Engouled, Epinasty, Es(s), Expansion, Falcate, Fawn, Flex(ural), Flexion, Flexure, Fold, Geller, Geniculate, Genu, Genuflect, Grecian, Hairpin, Hinge, Hook, Horseshoe, Hunch, Incline, Inflect, Kink, Knee(cap), Kneel, Knot, Kowtow, Meander, Mould, Nutant, Ox-bow, Pitch, Plash, Plié, Ply, Recline, Reflex, Retorsion, Retortion, Retroflex, Riband, S, Scarp, Sheet, Souse, Spree, Spring, Stave, Stoop, Swan-neck, Trend,

Twist, U, Ups(e)y, Uri, Wale, Warp, → **YIELD**, Z
▷ **Bendy** *may indicate* an anagram
Beneath Below, Sub, Under, Unworthy
Benedict(ine) Black Monk, Cluniac, Cluny, Dom, Eggs, Maurist, Olivetan, OSB, Tironensian, Tyronensian
Benediction Blessing, God-speed
Benefactor Angel, Backer, Barmecide, Carnegie, Donor, Maecenas, → **PATRON**, Philanthropist, Promoter
Beneficial, Beneficiary, Benefit, Benefice Advantage, → **AID**, Alms, Ameliorate, Asset, Avail, Behalf, Behoof, Behove, Bonus, Boon, Boot, Charity, Collature, Commendam, Commensal, Devisee, Disablement, Dole, Donee, Endorsee, Enure, FIS, Fringe, Housing, Incapacity, Incumbent, Inheritor, Injury, Inure, Invalidity, Legal aid, Living, Manna, Maternity, Ménage, Neckverse, Pay, Perk, Perquisite, Plus, Portioner, Postulate, Prebend, Profit, Sake, Salutary, Sanative, Sickness, Sinecure, Spin-off, Stipend, Supplementary, Symbiotic, Unemployment, Use, Usufruct
Benevolence, Benevolent Charitable, Clement, Dobbie, Dobby, Humanitarian, Kind, Liberal, Pecksniffian, Philanthropy, Sprite
Benighted Ignorant
Benign Affable, Altruistic, Gracious, Kindly, Trinal
Benin DY
Benito Duce, Mussolini
Benjamin Franklin
Bennett Alan, Phil
Bent Akimbo, Bowed, Brae, Coudé, Courb, Crooked, Curb, Determined, Dorsiflex, Falcate, Fiorin, Flair, Geniculate, Habit, Heath, Inclination, Ingenium, Intent, Inverted, Leant, Peccant, Penchant, Ply, Predisposition, Reclinate, Redtop, Round-shouldered, Scoliotic, Stooped, Talent, Taste, Twisted
▷ **Bent** *may indicate* an anagram
Bent grass Fiorin, Redtop
Bentham Utilitarian
Benzine Kinone, Phene, Toluene, Toluol
Bequeath, Bequest Bestow, Chantr(e)y, Demise, Endow, Heirloom, → **LEAVE**, Legacy, Mortification, Pass down, Pittance, Transmit, Will
Berate(d) Censure, Chide, Jaw, Reproach, Scold, Shent, Slate, Vilify
Berber Almoravide, Kabyle, Moor, Rif(i), Riff, Shluh, Tuareg
Bereave(d), Bereavement Deprive, Loss, Mourning, Orb, Sorrow, Strip, Widow
Beret Green
Berg Alban, Floe
Bermuda Shorts
Bernard Levin, Shaw
Bernini Baroque
Berry Acai, Allspice, Bacca, Blackcurrant, Cubeb, Fruit, Goosegog, Haw, Konini, Miracle, Pepo, Peppercorn, Persian, Pigeon, Pimento, Poke, Pottage, Rhein, Rhine, Sal(l)al, Slae, Sloe, Sop, Tomatillo
Berserk Amok, Ape-shit, Baresark, Frenzy, Gungho, Rage
Berth Anchorage, Bunk, Cabin, Couchette, Dock, Moor, Seat, Space
Beryl Aquamarine, Emerald, Heliodor, Morganite, Silica
Beryllium Be
Beseech Beg, Crave, Entreat, Implore, Invoke, Obsecrate
Beset Amidst, Assail, Assiege, Badger, Bego, Environ, Harry, Perplex, Scabrid, Siege
Beside(s) Adjacent, Alone, And, At, Au reste, Else, Forby(e), Further(more),

Moreover, Next, On, Withal, Yet

Besiege(d) Beset, Best(ed), Blockade, Gherao, Girt, Invest, Obsess, Plague, Surround

▷ **Besiege** *may indicate* one word around another

Besmirch(ed) Bloody, Bludie, Smear, Soil, Sully

Besom Cow, Kow

Besot(ted) Dotard, Infatuate, Intoxicate, Lovesick, Stupefy

Bespangle Adorn, Gem

Bespeak, Bespoken Address, Bee, Beta, Engage, Hint

Best A1, Ace, Aristocrat, Beat, Choice, Conquer, Cream, Creme, Damnedest, Deluxe, Elite, Eximious, Finest, Flagship, Flower, Foremost, Greatest, Ideal, Optima, Outdo, Outwit, Overcome, Peak, Peerless, Pick, Pièce de résistance, Pink, Plum, Purler, Quintessence, Ream, Sunday, Super, The, The tops, Tiptop, Top, Topper, Transcend, Vanquish, Wale

Bestiality Zoophalia

Bestiary Physiologus

Best man Paranymph

Bestow(al) Accord, Bequeath, Donate, Endow, → **GIVE**, Impart, Investiture, Present

Bestride Cross

Bet(ting), Betting System A cheval, Ante, Antepost, Back, Banco, Chance, Daily double, Double, Each way, Flutter, Gaff, Gamble, Go, Hedge, Impone, Lay, Long shot, Martingale, Mise, Note, Pari-mutuel, Parlay, Perfecta, Pip, Pot, Punt, Quadrella, Quinella, Ring, Risk, Roll up, Saver, Set, Spec, Sport, Spread, Stake, Superfecta, Tattersalls, Tatts, Totalisator, Totalise, Tote, Treble, Treble chance, Triella, Trifecta, → **WAGER**, Yankee

Betel Catechu, Paan, Pan, Pawn, Siri(h)

Betimes Anon, Early, Soon

Betise Solecism

Betray(al), Betrayer Abandon, Abuse, Belewe, Bewray, Cornuto, Desert, Divulge, Dob, Dobbin, Double-cross, Gethsemane, Giveaway, Grass, Judas, Renegade, Renege, Rumble, Sell, Sellout, Shop, Sing, Sinon, Stab, Traditor, Traitor, Treachery, Treason, Turncoat

Betroth(ed), Betrothal Assure, Engage, Ensure, Espouse, Fiancé(e), Handfasting, Pledge, Promise, Subarr(h)ation

Better Abler, Amend, Apter, Bigger, Buck, Cap, Convalescent, Fairer, Finer, Gambler, Gamester, Imponent, Improve, Meliorate, Mend, Outdo, Outpoint, Outshine, Outsmart, Outstrip, Outwit, Preponderate, Punter, Race-goer, Reform, Superior, Surpass, Throw, Top, Turfite, Worst

Between Amid, Bet, Betwixt, Inter, Interjacent, Linking, Mesne, Twixt

Bevel Angle, Cant, Oblique, Slope, Splay

Beverage Ale, Cocoa, Coffee, Cordial, Cup, → **DRINK**, Hydromel, Nectar, Tea

Bevy Flock, Group, Herd, Host

Beware Cave, Fore, Heed, Mind, Mistrust, Pas op

Bewilder(ed), Bewildering, Bewilderment Amaze, At sea, Baffle, Buffalo, Confuse, Consternation, Daze, Flummox, Mate, Maze, Mind-boggling, Mystify, Perplex, Stun, Taivert, Wander, Will, Wull

Bewitch(ed), Bewitching Charm, Delight, Elf-shot, Enchant, Ensorcell, Glam(orous), Hex, Hoodoo, Jinx, Obeah, Obiah, Strike

Beyond Above, Ayont, Besides, Farther, Outwith, Over, Past, Thule, Trans, Ulterior

Bias(ed) Angle, Aslant, Bent, Chauvinism, Discriminatory, Grid, Imbalance, Loaded, One-sided, Partial, Parti pris, Partisan, Penchant, Preconception, Predilection, → **PREJUDICE**, Prepossess, Set, Sexism, Skew, Slope, Tendency, Unjust, Warp

Bib, Bibulous Apron, Beery, Feeder, Pout, Tope, Tucker

Bibelot Objet d'art

Bible Adulterous, Alcoran, Alkoran, Antilegomena, Apocrypha, ASV, Authority, AV, Avesta, Bamberg, Book, Breeches, Bug, Coverdale, Cranmer, Cromwell, Douai, Douay, Family, Ferrara, Fool, Forgotten sins, Gemara, Geneva, Gideon, Good book, Goose, Gospel, Gutenberg, Hagiographa, Heptateuch, Hexapla, Hexateuch, Holy, Idle, Isagogic, Itala, Italic, King James (version), Leda, Matthew Parker, Mazarin(e), Midrash, Missal, Murderer, New English, NT, Omasum, Ostrog, OT, Pentateuch, Peshito, Peshitta, Peshitto, Polyglot, Psalter, Revised Version, RSV, RV, Scriptures, Septuagint, Stomach, Talmud, Tanach, Tantra, Targum, Taverner, Taverners, Thirty-six-line, Treacle, Tyndale, Unrighteous, Vinegar, Vulgate, Whig, Wicked, Wife-hater, Wyclif(fe), Zurich

Biblical scholar Rechabite, USPG, Wycliffe

Bibliophagist, Bibliophile Bookworm

Bicarb Saleratus

Bicker Argue, Bowl, Brawl, Coggie, Dispute, Tiff, Wrangle

Bicycle, Bike(r) Bambi, Bone-shaker, Chopper, Coaster, Crog(gy), Dandy-horse, Dirt, Draisene, Draisine, Exercise, Fixed-wheel, Hobby, Hobbyhorse, Mixte, Moped, Mount, Mountain, Multicycle, Ordinary, Pedal, Penny-farthing, Quad, Raleigh®, Recumbent, Roadster, Safety, Scooter, Spin, Stationary, Tandem, Trail, Tree, Velocipede

Bid(der), Bidding (system) Acol, Apply, Blackwood, Call, Canape, Command, Contract, Cue, Declare, Double, Forcing, Gone, Hostile, Invite, Jump, Misère, Nod, NT, → **OFFER**, Order, Pass, Pre-empt, Proposal, Psychic, Puffer, Redouble, Shut-out, Summon, Take-over, Tell, Tender, Vied, White bonnet

Biddy Gammer, Hen

Biennial Trieteric

Bier Hearse, Litter

Big Beamy, Bulky, Bumper, Burly, Cob, Enormous, Fat, Ginormous, Gross, → **LARGE**, Loud, Mansize, Massive, Mighty, Obese, Skookum, Slockdoliger, Slockdologer, Soc(k)dologer, Sogdolager, Sogdoliger, Stonker, Strapping, Swopper, Thumping, Tidy, Vast, Whacker, Whopper

Bigamy, Bigamist, Bigamous Bluebeard, Diandrous

Bighead Ego

Bight Canterbury, Great Australian, Heligoland

Bigot(ed) Chauvinist, Dogmatist, Fanatic, Hide-bound, Intolerant, Narrow-minded, Racialist, Racist, Sexist, Wowser, Zealot

Bigshot, Bigwig Cheese, Law lord, Nib, Nob, Oner, Oneyer, Oneyre, Swell, → **VIP**

Bijou Doll-like

▶ **Bike** *see* **BICYCLE**

Bikini Atoll, Tanga

Bile, Bilious(ness) Cholaemia, Choler, Gall, Icteric, Melancholy, Scholaemia, Venom, Yellow

Bilge Leak, Pump, Rhubarb, Rot, Waste

Bilingual Diglot

Bilk Default

Bill(ed), Billy Ac(c), Accommodation, Accompt, Account, Act, Ad, Addition, Appropriation, Barnacle, Beak, Becke, Budd, Buffalo, Can, Caress, Carte, Chit(ty), Cody, Coo, Coronoid, Demand, Dixy, Docket, Double, Due, Exactment, Fin, Finance, Foreign, Gates, Goat, Hybrid, Inland, Invoice, Kaiser, → **LAW**, Lawin(g), Legislation, Liam, Liar, List, Measure, Menu, Neb, Ness, Nib, → **NOTE**, Notice,

Platypus, Pork barrel, Portland, Poster, Private, Programme, Pruning, Public, Puffing, Reckoning, Reform, Remanet, Rhamphotheca, Rostral, Rostrum, Score, Short, Shot, Show, Sickle, Silly, Sparth(e), Sperthe, Spoon, Sticker, Tab, Tomium, Trade, Treasury, True, Twin, Victualling, Willy

Billet Berth, Casern, Cess, Chit, Coupon, Note, Quarter

Billet doux Capon, Valentine

Billiards, Billiards player, Billiards stroke Bar, Cannon-game, Cueist, Jenny, Lagging, Long jenny, Massé, Pocket, Pool, Potter, Pyramids, Short jenny, Snooker, String, Whitechapel

Billion Gillion, Milliard, Tera

Bill of sale Bs

Billow Roil, Roller, Rule, Surge, Swell, Wave

▶ **Billy** *see* BILL

Bin Bing, Box, Chilly, Container, Crib, Dump, Hell, Litter, Loony, Receptacle, Sin, Snake-pit, Stall, Wagger-pagger, Wheelie, Wheely

Binary ASCII, Semidetached

Bind(er), Binding Adherent, Adhesive, Akedah, Alligate, Apprentice, Astrict, Astringent, Bale, Bandage, Bandeau, Bandster, Bias, Bibliopegist, Brail, Burst, Calf, Cerlox®, Chain, Cinch, Circuit, Clamp, Colligate, Complain, Cord, Cummerbund, Deligation, Drag, Edge, Embale, Enchain, Engage, Enslave, Enwind, → FASTEN, Fetter, Galloon, Gird, Girdle, Grolier, Half-leather, Hay-wire, Hold, Incumbent, Indenture, Iron, Keckle, Lash(er), Law-calf, Leash, Ligament, Ligature, Mail, Marl, Morocco, Muslin, Obi, Obligate, Oblige, Oop, Organdie, Oup, Parpen, Perfect, Pinion, Raffia, Restrict, Ring, → ROPE, Roxburghe, Seize, Sheaf, Spiral, Strap, Stringent, Stygian, Swathe, Syndesis, Tape, Tether, Thirl, Thong, Three-quarter, Tie, Tree-calf, Truss, Twine, Valid, Whip, Withe, Yapp, Yerk, Yoke

Bindweed Bearbine, Convolvulus, With(y)wind

Bing Crosby, Go, Heap

Binge Bat, Beano, Bend(er), Blind, Carouse, → DRINK, Drinking-bout, Party, Riot, Soak, Souse, Splore, Spree, Toot, Tout

Bingo Beano, Housey-housey, Keno, Lotto, Tombola

Binocular(s) Glasses, Jumelle, OO, Stereoscope

Biochemical, Biochemist(ry) Ames, DNA, Proteomics

Biographer, Biography Boswell, CV, Hagiography, History, Life, Memoir, Plutarch, Potted, Prosopography, Suetonius, Vita

Biology, Biologist Algology, Cladistics, Genetics, Mendel, Morphology, Phenetics, Photodynamics, Somatology, Stoechiology, Stoich(e)iology, Taxonomy, Teratology, Transgenics

Bioscope Kinema

Birch Birk, Cane, Cow, Flog, Hazel, Kow, Larch, Reis, Rice, Rod, Silver, Swish, Twig, Weeping, Whip, White, Withe

Bird(s) Al(l)erion, Altricial, Aves, Avian, Bertram, Brood, Damsel, Doll, Early, Flier, Fowl, Gal, → GIRL, Grip, Hen, Jail, Left, Limicoline, Ornis, Ornithology, Pecker, Pen, Perching, Poultry, Praecoces, Prison, Quod, Raptor, Roaster, Sentence, Sis, Skirt, Time

BIRDS

2 letters:	3 letters:	Boo	Fum
Ka	Ani	Cob	Jay
Oi	Auk	Emu	Kae

Kea
Maw
Mew
Moa
Nun
Owl
Pea
Pie
Ree
Roc
Ruc
Tit
Tui

4 letters:
Barb
Chat
Cirl
Cobb
Coly
Coot
Crax
Crow
Dodo
Dove
→ **DUCK**
Emeu
Erne
Eyas
Fung
Gled
Gnow
Guan
Guga
Gull
Hawk
Hern
Huia
Huma
Ibis
Iynx
Jynx
Kagu
Kaka
Kite
Kiwi
Knot
Koel
Kora
Lark
Loom

Loon
Lory
Mina
Monk
Myna
Nene
Otis
Pavo
Pawn
Pern
Piet
Pink
Pown
Pyot
Rail
Rhea
Roch
Rook
Ruff
Ruru
Rype
Shag
Smee
Sora
Swan
Taha
Tara
Teal
Tern
Tick
Tody
Tuli
Weka
Wren
Xema
Yale
Yite

5 letters:
Agami
Ardea
Ariel
Bennu
Booby
Bosun
Capon
Colin
Colly
Crake
Crane
Diver

Egret
Finch
Fleet
Galah
Glede
Goose
Goura
Grebe
Heron
Hobby
Homer
Isaac
Junco
Kawau
Kight
Liver
Lowan
Macaw
Madge
Manch
Mavis
Merle
Mimus
Mohua
Monal
Murre
Mynah
Nandu
Nelly
Noddy
Ousel
Ox-eye
Peggy
Pekan
Pewit
Picus
Pilot
Piper
Pipit
Pitta
Poaka
Poker
Potoo
Prion
Quail
Quest
Quist
Raven
Reeve
Robin
Rotch

Ryper
Saker
Scape
Scart
Scaup
Scops
Scray
Scrub
Serin
Shama
Sitta
Skart
Snipe
Solan
Soree
Spink
Sprug
Squab
Stare
Stilt
Stint
Stork
Swift
Sylph
Terek
Tewit
Topaz
Twite
Umber
Umbre
Urubu
Veery
Vireo
Wader
Whaup
Widow
Wonga
Yaffa

6 letters:
Aquila
Avocet
Avoset
Bantam
Barbet
Bishop
Bittor
Bittur
Bonxie
Boubou
Brolga

Bulbul	Lourie	Seapie	Bluecap
Canary	Lungie	Shrike	Blue-eye
Chough	Magpie	Simara	Blue jay
Chukar	Martin	Simorg	Bluetit
Condor	Matata	Simurg	Boobook
Corbie	Menura	Siskin	Bullbat
Coucal	Merlin	Skarth	Bunting
Cuckoo	Merops	Smeath	Buphaga
Curlew	Missel	Soland	Bush-tit
Cushat	Mistle	Sorage	Bustard
Darter	Monaul	Strich	Buzzard
Dikkop	Mopoke	Sultan	Cacique
Dipper	Mossie	Sylvia	Cariama
Drongo	Motmot	Tailor	Cheeper
Duiker	Musket	Takahe	Chewink
Dunlin	Mutton	Tarcel	Chicken
Duyker	Nandoo	Tassel	Coal-tit
Elanet	Oriole	Tewhit	Cole-tit
Evejar	Oscine	Thrush	Colibri
Falcon	Osprey	Tom-tit	Corella
Fulmar	Oxbird	Toucan	Cotinga
Gambet	Parrot	Towhee	Courlan
Gander	Parson	Trogon	Courser
Gannet	Pavone	Turaco	Cow-bird
Garuda	Peahen	Turbit	Creeper
Gentle	Peeper	Turkey	Crombec
Gentoo	Peewee	Tyrant	Cropper
Go-away	Peewit	Tystie	Diamond
Godwit	Pernis	Verdin	Dinorus
Gooney	Petrel	Walker	Dottrel
Goslet	Phoebe	Waxeye	Dovekie
Grakle	Pigeon	Whidah	Dunnock
Grouse	Piopio	Whydah	Emu-wren
Hagden	Plover	Willet	Fantail
Hagdon	Pouter	Woosel	Fern-owl
Haglet	Progne	Yaffle	Figbird
Hermit	Puffin	Ynambu	Finfoot
Hoopoe	Pukeko	Yucker	Flicker
Houdan	Pullet	Zoozoo	Frigate
Jabiru	Queest		Gleerie
Jacana	Quelea	***7 letters:***	Gobbler
Jaeger	Quoist	Amokura	Goburra
Kakapo	Redcap	Anhinga	Gorcrow
Kotare	Reeler	Antbird	Goshawk
Kotuku	Roller	Apteryx	Grackle
Lanner	Scamel	Axebird	Grallae
Leipoa	Scarth	Babbler	Hacklet
Linnet	Scaury	Bécasse	Hadedah
Lintie	Scraye	Bee-kite	Hagbolt
Loerie	Sea-cob	Bittern	Hagdown
Loriot	Sea-mew	Bittour	Halcyon

Harrier
Hemipod
Hoatzin
Humming
Ice-bird
Jacamar
Jackdaw
Kahawai
Kamichi
Kestrel
Killdee
Kinglet
Koekoea
Lapwing
Leghorn
Limpkin
Manakin
Maribou
Martlet
Mesites
Minivet
Mudlark
Oilbird
Ortolan
Oscines
Ostrich
Pandion
Peacock
Peafowl
Pelican
Penguin
Phoenix
Pickmaw
Piculet
Pinnock
Pintado
Pintail
Pochard
Pockard
Poe-bird
Poy-bird
Quetzal
Rainbow
Rasores
Ratitae
Redpoll
Redwing
Regulus
Rooster
Rosella
Rotchie

Ruddock
Sakeret
Sawbill
Scooper
Scourie
Sea-mell
Simurgh
Sirgang
Sitella
Skimmer
Skylark
Snow-cap
Spadger
Sparrow
Squacco
Staniel
Stinker
Sturnus
Sunbird
Swallow
Tanager
Tanagra
Tarrock
Tattler
Teacher
Teuchat
Tiercel
Tinamou
Titanis
Titlark
Titling
Tokahea
Totanus
Touraco
Tumbler
Tweeter
Vulture
Vulturn
Wagtail
Warbler
Waxbill
Waxwing
Whooper
Widgeon
Wimbrel
Witwall
Woosell
Wren-tit
Wrybill
Wryneck
Yang-win

8 letters:
Aasvogel
Accentor
Adjutant
Aigrette
Alcatras
Altrices
Amadavat
Aquiline
Arapunga
Arenaria
Avadavat
Barnacle
Bellbird
Blackcap
Bluebird
Blue-wing
Boatbill
Boattail
Bobolink
Bob-white
Buln-buln
Caracara
Cardinal
Cargoose
Cheewink
Chirn-owl
Cockatoo
Cockerel
Coquette
Curassow
Dabchick
Didapper
Dip-chick
Dobchick
Dotterel
Estridge
Fauvette
Fernbird
Fish-hawk
Flamingo
Gambetta
Gang-gang
Garefowl
Garganey
Greenlet
Grosbeak
Guacharo
Hackbolt
Hangbird
Hangnest

Hawfinch
Hazelhen
Hemipode
Hernshaw
Hickymal
Hoactzin
Hornbill
Killdeer
Kingbird
Kiskadee
Landrail
Lanneret
Laverock
Longspur
Lorikeet
Lyrebird
Magotpie
Megapode
Mire-drum
Miromiro
Morepork
Murrelet
Nightjar
Notornis
Nuthatch
Ovenbird
Oxpecker
Paradise
Parakeet
Peetweet
Percolin
Petchary
Pheasant
Philomel
Pihoihoi
Podargus
Poorwill
Prunella
Puffbird
Quarrian
Quarrion
Rainbird
Rallidae
Redshank
Redstart
Reedling
Reed-wren
Rice-bird
Ringtail
Riroriro
Sandpeep

Scolopar
Screamer
Sea-eagle
Shake-bag
Shoebill
Silktail
Sittella
Skua-gull
Snowbird
Stanniel
Struthio
Surfbird
Swiftlet
Tantalus
Tapacolo
Tapaculo
Teru-tero
Thrasher
Thresher
Throstle
Ticklace
Titmouse
Tom-noddy
Toucanet
Tragopan
Trembler
Troopial
Troupial
Tubenose
Umbrella
Umbrette
Water-hen
Wheatear
Whimbrel
Whinchat
Whipbird
Whitecap
White-eye
Wildfowl
Wirebird
Woodchat
Woodcock
Woodlark
Woodwale
Yoldring

9 letters:
Accipiter
Aepyornis
Albatross
Aylesbury

Baldicoot
Baltimore
Beccaccia
Beccafico
Beefeater
Bergander
Blackbird
Blackhead
Blackpoll
Blood bird
Bower-bird
Brambling
Broadbill
Bullfinch
Campanero
Cassowary
Chaffinch
Chatterer
Chickadee
Coachwhip
Cockatiel
Cormorant
Corncrake
Crocodile
Cross-bill
Currawong
Dove prion
Dowitcher
Estreldid
Fieldfare
Fig-pecker
Fire-crest
Fledgling
Francolin
Friarbird
Frogmouth
Gallinule
Gerfalcon
Gier-eagle
Goldcrest
Goldfinch
Goosander
Grassquit
Grenadier
Guillemot
Happy Jack
Helldiver
Heronshaw
Hornywink
Icteridae
Impundulu

Jack-snipe
Kittiwake
Lintwhite
Mallemuck
Merganser
Mistletoe
Mollymawk
Mousebird
Night-hawk
Nutjobber
Nutpecker
Olive-back
Ossifraga
Ossifrage
Pardalote
Partridge
Peaseweep
Peregrine
Phalarope
Pictarnie
Pine finch
Porphyrio
Ptarmigan
Razorbill
Riflebird
Rosy-finch
Sabrewing
Salangane
Sandpiper
Sapsucker
Satinbird
Scansores
Sea-turtle
Secretary
Seedeater
Sheldrake
Shoveller
Silver eye
Skunk-bird
Solitaire
Spoonbill
Standgale
Stonechat
Stormbird
Storm-cock
Sugarbird
Swart-back
Sword-bill
Talegalla
Thickhead
Thick-knee

Thornbill
Trochilus
Trumpeter
Turnstone
Volucrine
Water cock
Water-rail
Wind-hover
Woodspite
Xanthoura

10 letters:
Aberdevine
Bearded tit
Bluebreast
Bluethroat
Brain-fever
Bubbly-jock
Budgerigar
Butter-bump
Chiff-chaff
Crested tit
Demoiselle
Dickcissel
Didunculus
Dive-dapper
Dollarbird
Ember-goose
Eyas-musket
Fallow-chat
Fly-catcher
Four o'clock
Fringillid
Goatsucker
Gobemouche
Grassfinch
Greenfinch
Greenshank
Hen-harrier
Honey-eater
Honey guide
Kingfisher
Kookaburra
Locust-bird
Mallee fowl
Marsh-robin
Meadowlark
Night-churr
Noisy miner
Nutcracker
Peckerwood

Pettichaps
Pettychaps
Pick-cheese
Pine-marten
Pratincole
Quaker-bird
Racket-tail
Rafter-bird
Rain-plover
Ramphastos
Regent-bird
Rhinoceros
Roadrunner
Ruby-throat
Saddleback
Saddlebill
Sanderling
Sandgrouse
Sea swallow
Shearwater
Sheathbill
Sicklebill
Silverbill
Snowy egret
Spatchcock
Stone-snipe
Tanagridae
Tropicbird
Wattlebird
Weaver bird
Whisky-jack
Whisky-john
Wonga-wonga
Woodpecker

Woodpigeon
Yaffingale
Yellowbird
Yellowhead
Yellowlegs
Yellowyite

11 letters:
Apostlebird
Bokmakierie
Bristlebird
Butcherbird
Cape sparrow
Fallow-finch
Fringilline
Gnatcatcher
Grallatores
Happy-family
Honey-sucker
House martin
Humming-bird
Ichthyornis
Java sparrow
Leatherhead
Mockingbird
Moss-bluiter
Moss-cheeper
Nightingale
Pied wagtail
Plantcutter
Pyrrhuloxia
Reed-warbler
Scissortail
Snowbunting

Sparrow-hawk
Stilt-plover
Stone-curlew
Storm petrel
Stymphalian
Thunderbird
Tree-creeper
Wall creeper
Whitethroat
Woodcreeper
Woodswallow
Woodwarbler
Yellow-ammer

12 letters:
Bronze-pigeon
Drongo-cuckoo
Drongo-shrike
Flowerpecker
Hedge-warbler
Honey creeper
Peppershrike
Ring-dotterel
Sage-thrasher
Sedge-warbler
Serpent-eater
Standard-wing
Stonechatter
Stormy petrel
Throstle-cock
Whippoorwill
Willy wagtail
Yellow-hammer
Yellow-yowley

13 letters:
Archaeopteryx
Cetti's warbler
Cock-of-the-rock
Mocking thrush
Oyster-catcher
Pipiwharauroa
Plantain-eater
Willow-wagtail
Willow warbler
Wilson's petrel

14 letters:
Manx shearwater
Tawny frogmouth
Woodchat shrike

15 letters:
Montagu's harrier

16 letters:
Tyrant flycatcher
White-fronted tern

17 letters:
Pectoral sandpiper
Spotted flycatcher

18 letters:
Paradise flycatcher

▷ **Bird** *may indicate* a prison sentence
Bird-catcher Avicularia, Fowler, Papageno
Bird-like Hirundine, Sturnine
Bird's nest(ing) Caliology, Monotropa, Soup
Bird-watcher Augur, Twitcher
Birkenhead F.E.Smith
Birmingham Brum(magem)
Birth Burden, Congenital, Delivery, Drop, Extraction, Genesis, Happy event, Jataka, Lineage, Multiple, Nativity, Natural, Origin, Parage, Parity, Parturition, Virgin
Birthday Anniversary, Genethliac
Birthmark Blemish, Mole, Mother-spot, Naevus, Port wine stain, Stigmata, Strawberry
Birthright Heritage, Mess, Patrimony
Birthwort Aristolochia
Biscuit Abernethy, Bath-oliver, Biscotto, Bourbon, Brandysnap, Brown George, Butterbake, Captain's, Charcoal, Cookie, Cracker, Cracknel, Crispbread,

Dandyfunk, Digestive, Dog, Dunderfunk, Fairing, Flapjack, Florentine, Fortune cookie, Four-by-two, Garibaldi, Ginger nut, Gingersnap, Hardtack, Kiss, Langue de chat, Lebkuchen, Macaroon, Marie, Mattress, Matza(h), Matzo(h), Nut, Oatcake, Oliver, Osborne, Parkin, Perkin, Petit four, Petticoat tail, Pig's ear, Pilot, Poppadom, Poppadum, Pretzel, Ratafia, Rice, Rusk, Rye-roll, Sea, Ship's, Shortbread, Snap, Soda, Sweetmeal, Tack, Tararua, Tea, Wafer, Water, Wine, Zwieback

Bisexual AC/DC, Freemartin, Switch-hitter

Bishop(ric) Aaronic, Abba, Aidan, Ambrose, Bench, Berkeley, Bp, Cambrensis, Cantuar, Chad, Coadjutor, Coverdale, Diocesan, Dunelm, Ebor, Ely, Eparch, Episcopate, Eusebian, Exarch, Exon, Golias, Hatto, Henson, Latimer, Lord, Magpie, Metropolitan, Norvic, Odo, Ordainer, Patriarch, Peter, Petriburg, Piece, Polycarp, Pontiff, Prelate, Priest, Primate, Primus, Proudie, Roffen, RR, Sarum, Sleeve, Suffragan, The purple, Titular, Tulchan, Weaver, Weed, Winton, Wrexham

Bismarck Otto

Bismuth Bi

Bison Bonas(s)us, Buffalo, Ox, Wisent

Bit Baud, Cantle(t), Centre, Chad, Cheesecake, Chip, Coin, Crumb, Curb, Curn, Drib, Excerpt, Flibbert, Fraction, Gag, Haet, Hate, Ion, Jaw, Jot, Mite, Modicum, Morsel, Mote, Mu, Nit, Ort, Ounce, Pelham, Peni, Penny, → **PIECE**, Port, Rap, Rare, Ratherish, Scintilla, Scrap, Section, Shaving, Shiver, Shred, Smidgen, Smidgeon, Smidgin, Snaffle, Snatch, Snippet, Some, Soupcon, Spale, Speck, Splinter, Spot, Spudding, Suspicion, Tad, Tait, Tate, Threepenny, Trace, Unce, Vestige, What, Whit

Bite(r), Biting, Bitten Canapé, Caustic, Chelicera, Chew, Eat, Engouled, Erose, Etch, Gnash, Gnat, Hickey, Hickie, Incisor, Knap, Masticate, Midge, Molar, Mordacious, Mordant, Morsel, Morsure, Nibble, Nip(py), Occlude, Peck, Pium, Premorse, Rabid, Sarcastic, Sharp, Shrewd, Snap, Sound, Spammie, Tart

Bitter(ness) Absinth, Acerb, Acid, Acrid, Acrimonious, Ale, Aloe, Angostura, Bile, Cassareep, Caustic, Eager, Edge, Ers, Fell, Gall, Keen, Marah, Maror, Myrrh, Pique, Rancorous, Rankle, Resentful, Sarcastic, Sardonic, Snell, Sore, Spleen, Tart(aric), Venom, Verjuice, Virulent, Vitriolic, Wersh, Wormwood, Wry

Bittern Boomer, Bull-of-the-bog, Butterbump, Heron, Sedge, Siege

Bittersweet Dulcamara, Staff-tree

Bitumen Albertite, Asphalt, Blacktop, Elaterite, Gilsonite®, Maltha, Mineral tar, Pissasphalt, Pitch, Tar, Tarseal, Uintaite

Bivalve Clam, Cockle, Lamellibranch, Mollusc, Muscle, Mussel, Oyster, Pelecypod, Piddock, Razorshell, Scallop, Tuatua, Whelk

Bivouac Camp

Bizarre Antic, Curious, Eccentric, Exotic, Fantastic, Far-out, Freaky, Gonzo, Grotesque, Odd, Off-the-wall, Outlandish, Outré, Pythonesque, Queer, Strange, Surreal, Weird

▷ **Bizarre** *may indicate* an anagram

Blab Babble, Gossip, Prate, Squeal

Black(en), Blackness, Black-out Amadoda, Atramental, B, BB, Bess, Blae, Boong, Cape Coloured, Carbon, Char, Charcoal, Cilla, Coloured, Coon, Cypress, Darkie, Darky, Death, Denigrate, Dinge, Dwale, Ebon(y), Eclipse, Ethiop, Fuzzy-wuzzy, Geechee, Gladwellise, Graphite, Grime, Heben, Hole, Ink(y), Ivory, Japan, Jeat, Jet, Jim Crow, Kohl, Lepidomelane, Malign, Market, Melanic, Melano, Moke, Moor, Muntu, Myall, Negritude, Negro, Niello, Niger, Nigrescent, Nigritude, Obliterate,

Obscure, Outage, Oxford, Piceous, Pitch, Platinum, Pongo, Prince, Pudding, Puke, Quashee, Quashie, Raven, Sable, Sambo, Scab, School, Sericon, Sheep, Slae, Sloe, Snowball, Sodium, Solvent, Sombre, Soot, Sooterkin, Spode, Spook, Stygian, Swart(y), Swarth(y), Tar, Uncle Tom, Weeds

Black art Necromancy, Nigromancy

Blackball Ban, Exclude, Pill, Pip, Reject

Blackberry Acini, Bramble, Mooch, Mouch

Blackbird Collybird, Crow, Jackdaw, Ousel, Raven, Woosel

Blackcurrant Quinsy-berry

Black eye(d) Half-mourning, Mouse, Shiner, Susan

Blackguard Leg, Nithing, Raff, Revile, Rotter, Scoundrel, Sweep

Blackhead Comedo

Black hole Collapsar

Blackjack Billie, Billy, Cosh, Flag, Sphalerite, Tankard, Truncheon, Vingt(-et)-un

Blackleg Fink, Rat, Scab, Snob

Black-letter Gothic

Black magic Goety

Blackmail(er) Bleed, Chantage, Chout, Exact, Extort, Ransom, Shakedown, Strike, Vampire

Blackout ARP, Eclipse, Faint, Swoon

Black Sea Pontic, Pontus Euxinus

Black sheep Neer-do-well, Reprobate

Blacksmith Brontes, Burn-the-wind, Farrier, Forger, Harmonious, Plater, Shoer, Vulcan

Blackthorn Sloe

Bladder(wort) Air, Balloon, Blister, Cholecyst, Cyst, Gall, Hydatid, Isinglass, Popweed, Sac, Sound, Swim, Urinary, Utricle, Varec(h), Vesica, Vesicle

Blade(s) Acrospire, Bilbo, Brand, Brown Bill, Cleaver, Co(u)lter, Cutlass, Dandy, Espada, Faible, Foible, Forte, Gleave, Gouge, Guillotine, Hydrofoil, Knife, Lance, Lawnmower, Leaf, Man, Mouldboard, Oar, Omoplate, Palmetto, Peel, Propeller, Rachilla, Rapier, Razor, Rip, Rotor, Scimitar, Scull, Scythe, Skate, Spade-, Spatula, Spatule, Spear, Spoon, Stiletto, Stock, Strigil, Sweep, → **SWORD**, Symitar, Toledo, Turbine, Vane, Vorpal, Web

Blair Eric, Lionel, Tony

Blame(worthy) Accuse, Censure, Condemn, Confound, Decry, Dirdam, Dirdum, Dispraise, Fault, Guilt, Inculpate, Odium, Rap, Reprehensible, Reproach, Reprove, Stick, Thank, Twit, Wight, Wite, Wyte

Blameless Innocent, Irreproachable, Lily-white, Unimpeachable

Blanch Bleach, Etiolate, Scaud, Whiten

Blancmange Carrageen, Flummery, Mould, Shape, Timbale

Bland Anodyne, Glop, Mild, Pigling, Sleek, Smooth, Spammy, Suave, Tame, Unctuous

Blandish(ment) Agremens, Agrement, Cajole, → **COAX**, Flatter, Treacle, Wheedle

Blank Burr, Cartridge, Empty, Erase, Flan, Ignore, Lacuna, Mistigris, Planchet, Shot, Space, Tabula rasa, → **VACANT**

Blanket Afghan, Bluey, Chilkat, Counterpane, Cover, Electric, Fire, General, Hudson's Bay, Kaross, Mackinaw, Manta, Obscure, Overall, Poncho, Quilt, Rug, Saddle, Sarape, Security, Serape, Shabrack, Smog, Space, Stroud, Wagga, Wet, Whittle

Blare Horn, Trumpet

Blarney Cajolery, Flattery, Nonsense, Sawder, Taffy

Blasé Worldly

Blaspheme, Blasphemous Abuse, → **CURSE**, Defame, Profanity, Revile

Blast(ed) Blight, Blore, Blow, Bombard, Dang, Darn, Dee, Drat, Dynamite, Explode, Fanfare, Flaming, Flurry, Fo(e)hn, Gale, Gust, Noser, Oath, Parp, Pryse, Rats, Scarth, Scath(e), Sere, Shot, Sideration, Skarth, Stormer, Tantara, Toot, Tromp(e), Trump(et), Volley

Blatant Flagrant, Hard-core, Noticeable, Open, Strident, Vulgar

Blather Baloney, Gabble

Blaze(r) Beacon, Bonfire, Burn, Cannel, Conflagration, Firestorm, → **FLAME**, Flare, Glare, Jacket, Low(e), Lunt, Palatinate, Race, Ratch, Sati, Star, Sun, Tead(e)

Bleach Agene, Blanch, Chemic, Chloride, Decolorate, Etiolate, Janola®, Keir, Kier, Peroxide, Whiten, Whitster

Bleak Ablet, Bare, Blay, Bley, Cheerless, Dour, Dreary, Dreich, Gaunt, Raw, Wintry

Bleary Blurred, Smudged

Bleat Baa, Blat, Bluster, Maa

Bleed(er), Bleeding Cup, Ecchymosis, Epistaxis, Extravasate, Fleam, Haemorrhage, Leech, Menorrhagia, Menorrh(o)ea, Metrorrhagia, Milk, Purpura, Root-pressure

Bleep Earcon, Pager

Blefuscudian Big-endian, Little-endian

Blemish Birthmark, Blot, Blotch, Blur, Botch, Defect, Flaw, Mackle, Mark, Milium, Mote, Naevus, Scar, Smirch, Spot, Stain, Sully, Taint, Tash, Vice, Wart, Wen

Blench Flinch, Recoil, Wince

Blend(ing) Amalgam, Coalesce, Commix, Contemper, Contrapuntal, Counterpoint, Electrum, Fuse, Go, Harmonize, Hydrate, Interfuse, Interlace, Liquidise, Meld, Melt, → **MERGE**, Mingle, Mix, Osmose, Portmanteau, Scumble, Sfumato, Synalepha

▷ **Blend** *may indicate* an anagram

Blenny Eel-pout, Gunnel, Shanny

Bless(ing), Blessed(ness) Amen, Approval, Asset, Beatitude, Benedicite, Benediction, Benison, Benitier, Bensh, Bismillah, Boon, Brachah, Brocho, Charmed, Consecrate, Cup, Damosel, Darshan, Elysium, Ethereal, Felicity, Gesundheit, Godsend, Grace, Gwyneth, Holy (dam), Kiddush, Luck, Macarise, Mercy, Mixed, Sain, Saint, Sanctify, Sanctity, Sheva Brachoth, Sheva Brochos, Toronto, Urbi et orbi, Xenium

Bless me Lawk(s)

Blight Afflict, Ague, American, Apple, Bespot, Blast, Destroy, Eyesore, Fire, Planning, Potato, Rot, → **RUIN**, Rust, Sandy, Shadow, Viticide, Waldersterben, Wither

Blighter Cuss, Perisher, Varment, Varmint

Blimey Coo, Cor, Crimini, O'Riley, Strewth

Blimp Airship, Colonel

Blind(ness), Blind spot Amaurosis, Amblyopia, Artifice, Austrian, Beesome, Bisson, Blend, Blotto, Carousal, Cecity, Chi(c)k, Cog, Concealed, Dazzle, Drop serene, Eyeless, Feint, Festoon, Gravel, Hemeralopia, Homer, Hood, Jalousie, Legless, Meropia, Mole, Night, Nyctalopia, Onchocerciasis, Persian, Persiennes, Pew, Prestriction, Rash, Roller, Roman, Scotoma, Seel, Shade, Shutter, Snow, Stimie, Stimy, Stymie, Sun, Teichopsia, Typhlology, Venetian, Window, Word, Yblent

Blindfish Amblyopsis

Blindfold Bandage, Hoodwink, Muffle, Seal, Wimple

Blindworm Anguis

Blink, Blinker(s), Blinkered, Blinking Bat, Blepharism, Blinders, Bluff, Broken, Eye-flap, Flash, Haw, Idiot, Insular, Nictate, Owl-eyed, Owly, Twink, Wapper, Wink

Bliss(ful) Beatitude, Bouyan, Composer, Delight, → ECSTASY, Eden, Elysium, Happy, Idyll, Ignorance, Married, Millenium, Nirvana, Paradise, Rapture, Sion, Tir-na-nog, Valhalla, Walhalla, Wedded

Blister(ed), Blistering Blab, Blain, Bleb, Bubble, Bullate, Cold sore, Epispastic, Fever, Herpes, Overgall, Pemphigus, Phlyct(a)ena, Scorching, Tetter, Vesicant, Vesicle, Visicate, Water

Blitz Attack, Bombard, Onslaught, Raid

Blizzard Buran, Gale, Snowstorm, Whiteout

Bloat(er) Buckling, Puff, Strout, Swell, Tumefy, Two-eyed steak

Blob Bead, Bioblast, Drop, Globule, O, Pick, Spot, Tear

Bloc Alliance, Cabal, Cartel, Party

Block(er), Blockage, Blocked, Blocking Altar, Anvil, Ashlar, Atresia, → BAR, Barricade, Barrier, Battle-axe, Brake, Breeze, Brick, Briquet(te), Building, Bung, Bunt, Catasta, Cavity, Chinese, Choke, Chunk, Cinder, Cleat, Clint, Clog, Clot, Cloy, Compass, Congest, Constipated, Cut-off, Cyclopean, Cylinder, Dado, → DAM, Dead-eye, Debar, Dentel, Dentil, Die, Dit, Domino, Electrotint, Embolism, Emphractic, Encompass, Euphroe, Fipple, Hack-log, Heart, High-rise, Hunk, Ice, Ileus, Impasse, Impede, Impost, Ingot, Insula, Interclude, Interrupt, Investment, Jam, Licence, Lifestyle, Line, Lingot, Lodgment, Log-jam, Lump, Mental, Ministroke, Mitre, Monkey, Mounting, Mutule, Nerve, Nifedipine, Nog, Notepad, Oasis®, Obstacle, → OBSTRUCT, Occlude, Office, Opossum, Oppilate, Pad, Page, Parry, Perched, Pile-cap, Pile-up, Pillow, Plinth, Plummer, Power, Pre-empt, Prevent, Process, Psychological, Quad, Ram, Saddle, Scotch, Sett, Siege, Snatch, Stalemate, Stap, Starting, Stenosis, Stimie, Stimy, Stone, Stonewall, Stop, Stumbling, Stymie, Sun, Swage, Tamp, Thwart, Tint, Tower, Tranche, Trig, Triglyph, Truck, Uphroe, Upping-stock, Vibropac®, Wig, Wood(cut), Wrest, Writer's, Zinco, Zugzwang

Blockbuster Epic

Blockhead Jolterhead, Mome, Nitwit, Noodle, Pig sconce, Stupid

Bloke Beggar, Chap, Cove, Fellow, Gent, Man, Oik

Blond(e) Ash, Cendré, Fair, Flaxen, Goldilocks, Peroxide, Platinised, Platinum, Strawberry, Tallent, Tow-haired, Towhead

Blood(y), Blood letting A, Ancestry, B, Bad, Bally, Blue, Blut, Claret, Clot, Cold, Cruor, Cup, Ecchymosis, Ensanguine, Epigons, Factor, First, Full, → GORE, Haemal, Haemorrhage, Ichor, Internecine, Introduce, Kin, Kinship, Knut, Menses, Microcyte, New, Nut, O, Opsonin, Parentage, Persue, Pigeon's, Plasma, Platelet, Plurry, Properdin, Pup, Race, Rare, Red, Rh negative, Rh positive, Ruby, Sang, Schistosoma, Serum, Show, Stroma, Toff, Venisection, Welter, Whole, Young

Blood disease, Blood disorder, Blood-poisoning Hypinosis, Isch(a)emia, Leukemia, Lipaemia, Oligaemia, Purpura, Pyaemia, Sapraemia, Septicemia, Spanaemia, Thalassemia, Thrombocytopenia, Toxaemia, Uraemia

Bloodhound Lime, Lyam, Rach(e), Ratch, Sleuth, Spartan

Bloodless Anaemic, Isch(a)emic, Wan, White

Blood-letter Leech, Phlebotomist, Sangrado

Blood money Eric

▶ **Blood-poisoning** see BLOOD DISEASE

Blood-pressure Hypertension, Hypotension

Bloodshot Red-eyed

Blood-sport Hunting, Shooting, Venery

Blood-sucker Asp, Dracula, Flea, Gnat, Ked, Leech, Louse, Mosquito, Parasite, Reduviid, Sponger, Tick, Vampire(-bat)

Bloom(er), Blooming Anthesis, Bally, Blossom, Blow, Blush, Boner, Cobalt, Dew, Effloresce, Error, Film, Florence, Florescent, Flowery, Flush, Gaffe, Glaucous, Heyday, Knickers, Loaf, Miscalculation, Nickel, Out, Pruina, Rationals, Reh, Remontant, Rosy, Ruddy, Thrive, Underwear

▷ **Bloomer** *may indicate* a flower

Blossom Blow, Burgeon, Catkin, Festoon, Flourish, Flower, May, Orange, Pip

Blot Atomy, Blob, Cartel, Delete, Disgrace, Dry, Eyesore, Obscure, Smear, Smudge, Southern, Splodge, Splotch

Blotch(y) Blemish, Giraffe, Monk, Mottle(d), Spot, Stain

Blotto Legless

Blouse Choli, Garibaldi, Gimp, Guimpe, Kerbaya, Middy, Pneumonia, Sailor, Shirtwaist, Smock, Tunic, Waist(er), Windjammer

Blow(er) Appel, Bang, Bash, Bat, Bellows, Biff, Billow, Blip, Bloom, Brag, Breeze, Buckhorse, Buffet, Bump, Burst, Calamity, Clap, Clat, Claut, Clip, Clout, Clump, Conk, Coup, Cuff, Dad, Daud, Dawd, Dev(v)el, Dinnyhayser, Dint, Dod, Douse, Dowse, Estramacon, Etesian, Facer, Fan, Fillip, Gale, Grampus, Gust, Hammer, Haymaker, Hit, Hook, Ictus, Impact, Insufflate, Karate, Kibosh, Knuckle sandwich, KO, Lame, Lander, Left-hander, Lick, Lounder, Muff, Neck-herring, Northerly, Noser, Oner, One-two, Paddywhack, Paik, Pash, Phone, Piledriver, Plague, Plug, Plump(er), Polt, Pow, Puff, Punch, Purler, Rats, Rattler, Rib-roaster, Roundhouse, Sas(s)arara, Scat, Settler, Short, Sideswipe, Side-winder, Sis(s)erary, Skiff, Skite, Skyte, Slat, Slog, Slug, Snell, Snot, Sock, Sockdolager, Sockdologer, Southwester, Spanking, Spat, Spout, Squall, Squander, Stripe, Stroke, Strooke, Stunning, Sufflate, Supercharger, Swash, Swat, Swinger, Telephone, Thump, Thwack, Tingler, Tootle, Trump(et), Tuck, Undercut, Upper-cut, Waft, Wallop, Wap, Waste, Welt, Whammy, Whample, Whang, Whap, Wheeze, Wherret, Whiffle, Whirret, Whistle, → **WIND**, Winder, Wipe, Wuther

Blown-up Elated, Enlarged, Exploded

Blow-out Binge, Bloat, Exhale, Feast, Feed, Flat, Fulminate, Lava, Nosh-up, Snuff, Spiracle, → **SPREAD**

Blowpipe Hod, Peashooter, Sarbacane, Sumpit(an)

Blub(ber) Cry, Fat, Snotter, Sob, Speck, → **WEEP**, Whimper

Bludge Sinecure

Bludgeon Bully, Club, Cosh, Cudgel, Sap

Blue(s) Abattu, Accablé, Adult, Anil, Aquamarine, Azure, Azurn, Beard, Berlin, Bice, Bleuâtre, Blow, Bottle, Butterfly, C, Caesious, Cafard, Cambridge, Cantab, Celeste, Cerulean, City, Clair de lune, Classic, Cobalt, Coomassie, Copenhagen, Cornflower, Country, Coventry, Cyan, Danish, Danube, Dejected, Dirty, Disconsolate, Doldrums, → **DOWN**, Duck-egg, Eatanswill, Eggshell, Electric, Facetiae, Firmament, Fritter, Gentian, Germander, Glaucous, Glum, Hauyne, Heliotrope, Hump, Indecent, Indigo, Indol(e), Iron, Isatin(e), Lapis lazuli, Lavender, Lewd, Lionel, Low, Mazarine, Methylene, Midnight, Monastral®, Mope, Morose, Murder, Nattier, Naughty, Navy, Nile, Obscene, Ocean, Off-colour, Oxford, Peacock, Periwinkle, Perse, Petrol, Phycocyan, Porn, Powder, Prussian, Rabbi, Ribald, Riband, Right, Ripe, Robin's egg, Royal, Sad, Sapphire, Saxe, Saxon(y), Scurrilous, → **SEA**, Shocking, Sky, Slate, Smalt(o), Smutty, Sordid, Spirit, Splurge, Squander, Stafford, Steel, Stocking, Teal, Thenard's, Tony, Tory, Trist, True, Trypan, Turnbull's, Turquoise, Ultramarine, Unhappy, Urban, Verditer, Washing,

Watchet, Wedgwood®, Welkin, Woad, Zaffer, Zaffre
▷ **Blue** *may indicate* an anagram
Bluebell Blawort, Blewart, Campanula, Harebell
Bluebottle Blawort, Blewart, Blowfly, Blowie, Brommer, Brummer, Cop, Cornflower, Fly, Policeman
▸ **Blue-legged** *see* **BLUESTOCKING**
Blueprint Cyanotype, Draft, Drawing, Plan, Recipe
Bluestocking, Blue-legged Basbleu, Carter, Erudite, Femme savante, Hamburg(h), Mrs Montagu, Précieuse, Sheba
Bluff(ing) Blunt, Cle(e)ve, Cliff, Clift, Crag, Fake, Flannel, Four-flush, Frank, Hal, Headland, Height, Hoodwink, Kidology, Pose, Precipice, Steep, Trick
Blunder(er), Blundering Barry (Crocker), Betise, Bévue, Bish, Bloomer, Blooper, Boob, Break, Bull, Bumble, Clanger, Clinker, Cock-up, Err, Faux pas, Floater, Flub, Fluff, Gaff(e), Goof, Howler, Inexactitude, Irish, Josser, Malapropism, → **MISTAKE**, Muddle, Mumpsimus, Slip, Solecism, Stumble, Trip
Blunt(ed), Bluntly Abrupt, Alleviate, Bald, Bate, Bayt, Brash, Brusque, Candid, Deaden, Disedge, Downright, Forthright, Frank, Hebetate, Mole, Morned, Obtund, Obtuse, Outspoken, Pointblank, Rebate, Retund, Retuse, Roundly, Snub, Straight-out, Stubby
Blur(red), Blurring Cloud, Confuse, Fog, Fuzz, Halation, Mackle, Macule, Muzzy, Pixilation, → **SMUDGE**, Stump, Tortillon
Blurb Ad, Puff
Blush(ing) Colour, Cramoisy, Crimson, Erubescent, Erythema, Incarnadine, Mantle, → **REDDEN**, Rouge, Rubescent, Ruby, Rufescent, Rutilant
Bluster(ing), Blusterer, Blustery Arrogance, Bellow, Blore, Brag, Hector, Rage, Rant, Rodomontade, Roister, Sabre-rattler, Squash, Swagger, Vapour, Windbag, Wuthering
Boar Barrow, Calydonian, Erymanthian, Hog, Pentheus, Sanglier, Sounder, Tusker, Wild
Board(s), Boarding Abat-voix, Admiralty, Aquaplane, Baffle, Banker, Barge, Beaver, Billet, Bristol, Bulletin, Catchment, Centre, Cheese, Chevron, Circuit, Collegium, Committee, Contignation, Counter, Cribbage, Dagger, Dart, Daughter, Deal, Directors, Diving, Draft, Draining, Drawing, Embark, Embus, Emery, Enter, Entrain, Fare, Fascia, Featheredge, Fibro, Fibrolite®, Flannelgraph, Full, Gib(raltar), Gutter, Hack, Half, Half-royal, Hawk, Hoarding, Idiot, Instrument, Insulating, Ironing, Kip, Lag, Leader, Ledger, Lodge, Magnetic, Malibu, Masonite®, Match, Message, Mill, Monkey, Mortar, Moulding, Notice, Otter, Ouija, Palette, Pallet, Panel, Parochial, Particle, Patch, Pedal, Peg(board), Pension, Planch(ette), Plank, Plug, Ply(wood), Punch, Quango, Ribbon-strip, Roof, Running, Sandwich, Sarking, Scale, Scaleboard, School, Score, Screed, Sheathing, Shelf, Shifting, Shingle, Shooting, Side-table, Sign, Skim, Skirting, Sleeve, Snow, Sounding, Splasher, Spring, Stage, Strickle, Stringboard, Supervisory, Surf, Switch, → **TABLE**, Telegraph, Thatch, Theatre, Trencher, Verge, Wainscot, Wobble, Wokka, Wood chip
▷ **Board** *may refer to* chess or draughts
Boarder Interne, Pensioner, PG, Roomer
Boarding house Digs, Kip, Lodgings, Pension
Boast(er), Boastful, Boasting Big-note, Blew, Blow, Blowhard, Bluster, Bobadil, Bounce, Brag, Braggadocio, Breeze, Bull, Cock-a-hoop, Crake, Crow, Fanfaronade, Gas, Gascon(nade), Glory, Hot air, Jact(it)ation, Line, Ostent(atious), Prate, Rodomontade, Scaramouch, Skite, Swagger, Swank, Tall, Thrasonic, Vainglory, Vapour, Vaunt, Yelp

Boat Ark, Barge, Bark, Bawley, Billyboy, Black skipjack, Canal, Cat, Clinker-built, Coaster, Cock, Codder, Corvette, Cott, Cruiser, Curragh, Cutter, Double scull, Dragon, Eight, Flagship, Flatboat, Fly(ing), Fore-and-after, Four, Foyboat, Goldie, Gravy, Gulet, Hatch, Hooker, Hydroplane, Isis, Jolly, Keel, Kit, Lapstrake, Lap streak, Launch, Liberty, Long, Lymphad, Mackinaw, Monkey, Monohull, Mosquito, Motor, Narrow, Outrigger, Pair-oar, Pedalo, Pont, Privateer, PT, Pucan, Puffer, Pulwar, Q, Revenue cutter, Sailer, Sauce, Scooter, Sculler, Sea Dog®, Shallop, She, → SHIP, Sidewheeler, Skiff, Slogger, Smack, Stake, Sternwheeler, Swing, Tangle-netter, Tanker, Tender, Tilt, Torpid, Trek-ox, Vaporetto, Vedette, → VESSEL, Vidette, Wager, Weekender, Whiff

Boater → HAT, Punter, Straw

Boatman Bargee, Charon, Cockswain, Coxswain, George, Gondolier, Harris, Hoveller, Phaon, Voyageur, Waterman, Wet-bob

Boat population Tank(i)a

Boat-shaped Carina, Scaphoid

Boatswain Bosun, Serang, Smee

Bob Acres, Beck, Curtsey, Deaner, Dip, Dock, Dop, Duck, Float, Hod, Hog, Jerk, Major, Maximus, Minor, Page-boy, Peal, Plain, Plumb, Plummet, Popple, Rob, Royal, S, Shingle, Skip, Sled(ge), Sleigh

Bobbin Quill, Reel, Shuttle, Spindle, Spool

Bobble Pompom

Bobby Bluebottle, Busy, Copper, Flatfoot, Patrolman, Peeler, Pig, → POLICEMAN

Bobby-dazzler Dinger, Stunner

Bock Stein

Bode Augur

Bodice Basque, Bolero, Bustier, Chemise, Chemisette, Choli, Corsage, Gilet, Halter, Jirkinet, Liberty, Plastron, Polonie, Polony, Spencer, Tucker, Watteau

Bodkin Eyeleteer, Needle, Poniard, Stilet(to)

Body, Bodies, Bodily Administration, Amount, Anatomic, Astral, Barr, Board, Bouk, Buik, Buke, Bulk, Cadaver, Cadre, Carcase, Carcass, Carnal, Caucas, Centrosome, Chapel, Chapter, Chassis, Chondriosome, Ciliary, Clay, Coachwork, Coccolite, Cohort, Column, Comet, Committee, Contingent, Cormus, Corpor(e)al, Corps, Corpse, Corpus, Corse, Cytode, Detail, Earth, Elaiosome, Flesh, Food, Frame, Fuselage, Gazo(o)n, Golgi, Goner, Grey, → GROUP, Heavenly, Hull, Immune, Incarnate, Inclusion, Kenning, Ketone, Lewy, Lich, Lifting, Like, Lithites, Malpighian, → MASS, Militia, Mitochondrion, Moit, Mote, Mummy, Nacelle, Nucleole, Nucleolus, Olivary, Ore, Pack, Personal, Phalanx, Pineal, Plant, Platelet, Platoon, Polar, Politic, Posse, Purview, Quango, Relic(t), Remains, Review, Ruck, Satellite, Senate, Solid, Soma, Soredium, Sound-box, Soyle, Spinar, Spore, Squadron, Square, Staff, Statoblast, Stiff, Syndicate, Tagma, Testis, Thallus, Torse, Torso, Trunk, Turm, Ulema, Vitreous, Wolffian, X

▷ **Body** *may indicate* an anagram

Body builder Steroid

Bodyguard Amulet, → ESCORT, Gentleman-at-arms, House-carl, Minder, Praetorian, Protector, Retinue, Schutzstaffel, → SHIELD, SS, Triggerman, Varangian, Yeomen

Body segment Arthromere, Genome, Metamere

Boer Afrikaner, Kruger, Van der Merwe

Boffin Brain

Bog(gy) Allen, Blanket, Can, Carr, Clabber, Fen, Gents, Glaur, Hag, Lair, Latrine, Letch, Loo, Machair, Marish, Marsh, Merse, Mire, Moory, Morass, Moss(-flow),

Mud, Muskeg, Peat, Petary, Quag, Raised, Serbonian, Slack, Slade, Slough, Spew, Spouty, Stodge, Sump, Vlei, Washroom, WC, Yarfa, Yarpha

Bog(e)y Boggart, Bug(aboo), Bugbear, Chimera, Colonel, Eagle, Mumbo jumbo, Nis(se), Par, Poker, Rawhead, Scarer, Spectre, Troll

Boggle Astonish, Bungle, Demur, Hesitate, Perplex, Shy

Bog-trotter Tory

Bogus Assumed, Counterfeit, Fake, False, Histrionic, Phoney, → **SHAM**, Snide, Snobbish, Spoof, Spurious

Bohemian Arty, Beatnik, Demi-monde, Gypsy, Hippy, Hussite, Mimi, Offbeat, Taborite, Trustafarian

Boil(er), Boiled, Boiling (point) Angry, Anthrax, Blain, Botch, Brew, Bubble, C, Carbuncle, Coction, Cook, Cree, Dartre, Decoct, Ebullient, Foam, Furuncle, Gathering, Hen, Herpes, Kettle, Leep, Ligroin, Pimple, Pinswell, Poach, Poule, Rage, Reflux, Samovar, Seethe, Simmer, Sod, Sore, Steam, Stew, Stye, Tea-kettle, Water tube

Boisterous Gilp(e)y, Goustrous, Gusty, Hoo, Knockabout, Noisy, Rambunctious, Randy, Riotous, Rorty, Rough, Stormy, Strepitoso, Termagant, Turbulent, Wild

Bold(ly), Boldness Assumptive, Brash, Brass, Bravado, Bravery, Bravura, Brazen, Brussen, Caleb, Crust, Daredevil, Defiant, Derring-do, Diastaltic, Familiar, Free, Gallus, Hardihood, Heroics, High-spirited, Impudent, Intrepid, Malapert, Mature, Outspoken, Parrhesia, Pert, Plucky, Presumptive, Rash, Risoluto, Sassy, Temerity, Unshrinking

Bole Stem, Trunk

Bolivar Liberator

Bollard Cone, Kevel

Bolshevik, Bolshie Communist, Maximalist, Rebel, Soviet

Bolster Cushion, Dutch wife, Pillow, → **PROP**

Bolt Arrow, Captive, Carriage, Coach, Cuphead, Dash, Dead, Eat, Elope, Expansion, Explosive, Fish, Flee, Gobble, Gollop, Gorge, Gulp, Latch, Levant, Levin, Lightning, Lock, Machine, Missile, Panic, Pig, Pintle, Ragbolt, Rivet, Roll, Scoff, Slot, Snib, Sperre, Stud, Tap, Through, Thunder, Toggle, U, Wing, Wolf, Wring

Bolus Ball

Bomb(ed), Bomber, Bombing Atom, Attack, B, Blitz, Blockbuster, Borer, Buzz, Candle, Car, Carpet, Cluster, Cobalt, Daisycutter, Depth charge, Deterrent, Dirty, Doodlebug, Drogue, Egg, Fission, Flop, Flying, Fragmentation, Fusion, Glide, Greek fire, Grenade, H, Harris, Homicide, Hydrogen, Lancaster, Land-mine, Letter, Liberator, Loft, Logic, Mail, Megaton, Millennium, Mills, Minnie, Mint, Molotov cocktail, Mortar, Nail, Napalm, Necklace, Neutron, Nuclear, Nuke, Packet, Parcel, Petar, Petard, Petrol, Pineapple, Pipe, Plaster, Plastic, Prang, Precision, Radium, Ransom, Robot, Sex, Shell, Skip, Smart, Smoke, Sneak-raid, Stealth, Stick, Stink, Stratofortress, Stuka, Suicide, Tactical, Terrorist, Thermonuclear, Time, Torpedo, Turkey, V1, Volcanic, Walleye

Bombard(ment) Attack, Battery, Blitz, Cannonade, Drum-fire, Mortar, Pelt, Shell, Stone, Stonk, Strafe, Straff

Bombardon Tuba

Bombast(ic) Euphuism, Fustian, Grandiose, Hot air, Magniloquence, Orotund, Pomp, Rant, Timid, Tumid, Turgent

Bombay Nasik

Bombay duck Bum(m)alo

▶ **Bomber** *see* **BOMB**

Bona fide Echt, Genuine

Bonanza Luck, Windfall
Bonaparte Boney, → NAPOLEON, Plon-plon
Bond(s), Bondage, Bondsman Adhesive, Affinity, Agent, Assignat, Baby, Bail, Bearer, Cedula, Cement, Chain, Chemical, Compact, Connect, Consols, Coordinate, Copula, Corporate, Covalent, Covenant, Daimyo, Dative, Debenture, Deep-discount, Double, Duty, Electrovalent, English, Ernie, Escrow, Esne, Fetter, Fleming, Flemish, Geasa, Gilt, Grammy, Granny, Heart, Herringbone, Hydrogen, Hyphen, Income, Investment, Ionic, James, Junk, Knot, Liaise, Ligament, Link(age), Long, Manacle, Managed, Metallic, Mortar, Municipal, Nexus, Noose, Pair, Peptide, Performance, → PLEDGE, Post-obit, Premium, Property, Rapport, Recognisance, Relationship, Revenue, Running, Samurai, Security, Semipolar, Serf, Servitude, Shackle, Shogun, Single, Singlet, Slave, Solder, Stacked, Starr, Superglue, Surety, Thete, Thral(l)dom, Three-per-cent, → TIE, Treasury, Triple, Valence, Valency, Vassal, Vinculum, Yearling, Yoke, Zebra
Bone(s), Bony Acromion, Anableps, Angular, Apatite, Astragalus, Atlas, Axis, Baculum, Calcaneus, Caluarium, Cannon, Capitate, Capitellum, Carina, Carpel, Carpus, Cartilage, Catacomb, Centrum, Chine, Clavicle, Cly, Coccyx, Coffin, Columella, Concha, Condyle, Coracoid, Coral, Costa, Coxa, Crane, Cranium, Cuboid, Cuneiform, Cuttlefish, Dentary, Diaphysis, Dib, Dice, Diploe, Dolos, Endosteal, Ethmoid, Femur, Fetter, Fibula, Fillet, Frontal, Funny, Ganoid, Gaunt, Hamate, Haunch, Hause-bane, Horn, Humerus, Hyoid, Ilium, Incus, Innominate, Interclavicle, Involucrum, Ischium, Ivory, Jugal, Kneecap, Knuckle, Lacrimal, Lamella, Luez, Lunate, Luz, Malar, Malleolus, Malleus, Mandible, Manubrium, Marrow, Mastoid, Maxilla, Medulla, Membrane, Metacarpal, Metatarsal, Napier's, Nasal, Navicular, Occipital, Olecranon, Omoplate, Orthopaedics, Os, Ossicle, Palatine, Parasphenoid, Parietal, Patella, Pecten, Pectoral, Pedal, Pelvis, Pen, Percoid, Perone, Petrous, Phalanx, Pisiform, Ploughshare, Premaxilla, Pubis, Pygostyle, Quadrate, Rachial, Rack, Radialia, Radius, Relic, Rib, Rump-post, Sacrum, Scaphoid, Scapula, Sclere, Sepium, Sequestrum, Sesamoid, Share, Skeleton, Skull, Sphenoid, Splint, Splinter, Spur, Squamosal, Stapes, → STEAL, Sternebra, Sternum, Stifle, Stirrup, Suboperculum, T, Talus, Tarsus, Temporal, Tibia, Tibiotarsus, Tot, Trapezium, Triquetral, Trochanter, Trochlea, True-rib, Tympanic, Ulna, Vertebrae, Vomer, Whirl, Wish, Wormian, Zygomatic
Bone-head Capitellum, Capitulum
Bonehouse Ossuary
Boneshaker Dandy-horse, Draisene, Draisine
Bonfire Bale-fire, Beltane, Blaze, Chumping, Clavie, Feu de joie, Pyre
Boniface Inn-keeper, Landlord, Taverner
Bonne-bouche Cate
Bonnet Balmoral, Bongrace, Cap, Cornette, Cowl, Easter, Glengarry, Hood, Hummel, Hummle, Kiss-me, Mobcap, Mutch, Poke, Scotch, Sun, Toorie, War
Bonny Blithe, Gay, Merry, Sonsy, Weelfar'd
Bonsai Saikei
Bonus Bisque, Bounty, Braata, Bye, Christmas box, Danger money, Dividend, Escalator, Extra, Hand-out, Lagniappe, No-claim, → PREMIUM, Reversionary, Reward, Scrip, Spin-off, Windfall
Boob Gaffe, Nork, Simpleton, Stumer
Booby Dunce, Hick, Patch, Patchcocke, Patchoke, → STUPID
Boojum Snark
Book(s), Bookish, Bookwork Academic, Album, Antilegomena, Antiphonary, Appointment, Audio, B, Backlist, Bedside, Bestiary, Bestseller, Black, Block, Blotter,

Blue, Cash, Chrestomathy, Classic, Closed, Coffee-table, Diary, Digest, Directory, Diurnal, Ench(e)iridion, Engage, Enter, Erudite, Exercise, Facetiae, Folio, Good, Gradual, Gradus, Guide, Hardback, Hymnal, Imprint, Issue, Lectionary, Ledger, Lib, Liber, Literary, Manual, Memorandum, Missal, Monograph, Muster, Octavo, Octodecimo, Office, Open, Order, Page-turner, Paperback, Pass, Pedantic, Phrase, Pica, Plug, Polyglot, Potboiler, Pseudepigrapha, Publication, Quair, Quarto, Quire, → **RESERVE**, Road, Script, Sext, Sexto, Sextodecimo, Sixmo, Sixteenmo, Sketch, Softback, Spelling, Spine-chiller, Statute, Studious, Study, Style, Swatch, Symbolical, Table, Tablet, Talking, Text(ual), Thriller, Title, Titule, Tome, Trade, Transfer, Twelvemo, Unputdownable, Visiting, Visitor's, Vol(ume), Waste, White, Work, Year

BOOKS

2 letters:
NT
OT

3 letters:
Dan
Eph
Gal
Hab
Hag
Jud
Lam
Log
Rag
Red
Rom
Sir
Sus

4 letters:
Acts
Amos
Edda
Ezek
Ezra
Joel
John
Jude
Luke
Macc
Mark
Mook
Obad
Veda

5 letters:
Atlas

Bible
Chron
Hosea
Kells
Kings
Manga
Micah
Nahum
Pop-up
Snobs
Sutra
To-bit

6 letters:
Aeneid
Baruch
Caxton
Course
Daniel
Eccles
Esdras
Esther
Exeter
Exodus
Haggai
Herbal
I Ching
Isaiah
Jashar
Jasher
Joshua
Judges
Prayer
Primer
Prompt
Psalms
Ration

Reader
Romans
Scroll
Tanach

7 letters:
Chumash
Cookery
Ezekiel
Genesis
Grolier
Malachi
Martyrs
Matthew
Numbers
Obadiah
Octapla
Omnibus
Orarium
Ordinal
Psalter
Susanna
Timothy

8 letters:
Breviary
Clarissa
Domesday
Doomsday
Georgics
Grimoire
Habakkuk
Haggadah
Haggadoh
Hermetic
Libretto
Megillah

Ordinary
Philemon
Porteous
Portesse
Prophets
Proverbs
Triodion
Vercelli
Vesperal

9 letters:
Apocrypha
Ephesians
Formulary
Galatians
Gazetteer
Kama Sutra
Leviticus
Maccabees
Portolano
Reference
Remainder
Satyricon
Sibylline
Sybilline
Telephone
Tripitaka
Vade-mecum
Zephadiah

10 letters:
Apocalypse
Chronicles
Compendium
Cyclopedia
Dictionary
Heptameron

Heptateuch
Hitopadesa
Incunabula
Passionary
Persuasion
Teratology

11 *letters:*
Commonplace

Concordance
Corinthians
Deuteronomy
Evangeliary
Hagiographa
Nomenclator
Philippians
Revelations

12 *letters:*
Bodice-ripper
Ecclesiastes
Encyclopedia
Lamentations
Panchatantra
Paralipomena
Processional
Responsorial

Twelve Tables

13 *letters:*
Penny dreadful
Pharmacopoeia
Thessalonians

Bookbinder, Bookbinding Fanfare, Grolier, Mutton-thumper, Organdie
Book-case Credenza, Press, Satchel
Bookie(s), Bookmaker Binder, John, Layer, Librettist, Luke, Mark, Matthew, Printer, Ringman, To-bit
Booking Reservation
Bookkeeper, Bookkeeping Clerk, Double entry, Librarian, Posting, Recorder, Satchel, Single-entry
Booklet B, Brochure, Folder
Book-like Solander
Book-lover Incunabulist
Bookmark Flag, Tassel
Book-scorpion Chelifer
Bookseller Bibliopole, Colporteur, Conger, Sibyl, Stallman
Bookworm Sap, Scholar
Boom(ing) Baby, Beam, Boost, Bowsprit, Bump, Fishpole, Increase, Jib, Orotund, Prosper, Resound, Roar, Sonic, Spar, Supersonic, Swinging, Thrive, Torpedo, Wishbone
Boomer Bittern, Bull-of the-bog, Butter-bump, Kangaroo, Mire-drum
Boomerang Backfire, Kiley, Kyley, Kylie, Recoil, Ricochet, Throwstick, Woomera
Boon Bene, Benefit, Blessing, Bounty, Cumshaw, Gift, Godsend, Mills, Mitzvah, Prayer, Windfall
Boor(ish) Borel, Bosthoon, Chuffy, Churl, Clodhopper, Crass, Goth, Grobian, Hog, Ill-bred, Jack, Keelie, Kern(e), Kernish, Kill-courtesy, Lob, Lout, Lumpen, Ocker, Peasant, Philistine, Trog, Uncouth, Yahoo, Yob, Yokel
Boost(er) Adrenalin, Afterburner, Bolster, Ego, Encourage, Fillip, Help, Hoist, Impetus, Increase, Injection, Lift, Promote, Raise, Rap, Reheat, Reinforce, Reinvigorate, Spike, Step up, Supercharge, Tonic, Wrap
Boot(s) Addition, Adelaide, Ankle-jack, Avail, Balmoral, Beetle-crushers, Benefit, Blucher, Bottine, Bovver, Brogan, Brogue, Buskin, Cerne, Chukka, Cockers, Cold, Combat, Concern, Cothurn(us), Cowboy, Cracowe, Crowboot, Denver, Derby, Desert, Dismiss, Field, Finn(e)sko, Finsko, Fire, Football, Galage, Galosh, Gambado, Go-go, Granny, Gum, Heave-ho, Hessian, High shoe, Hip, Jack, Jemima, Jodhpur, Kamik, Kletterschuh, Lace-up, Larrigan, Last, Mitten, Moon, Muchie, Muc(k)luc(k), Mukluk, Pac, Para, Profit, Riding, Rock, Russian, Sabot, → sᴀᴄᴋ, Seven league, → sʜᴏᴇ, Surgical, Thigh, Toe, Tonneau, Tops, Trunk, Ugh, Vibram®, Vibs, Wader, Warm, Weller, Wellie, Wellington, Welly
Booth Assassin, Crame, Kiosk, Polling, Stall, Stand, Telephone, Voting
Bootlegger Cooper, Coper, Runner
Bootless Futile, Idle, Unprofitable, Vain
Booty Creach, Creagh, Haul, Loot, Prey, Prize, Spoil(s), Spolia optima, Swag
Booze(r) → ᴅʀɪɴᴋ, Liquor, Pub, Spree, Tipple

Borage Bugloss, Comfrey, Gromwell, Myosote
Borax Tincal
Border(s), Borderland, Borderline Abut, Adjoin, Apron, Bed, Bind, Bound, Boundary, Braid, Checkpoint, Coast, Cot(t)ise, Dado, Dentelle, → **EDGE**, Engrail, Fimbria, Frieze, Fringe, Frontier, Furbelow, Guilloche, Head-rig, Hedgerow, Hem, Herbaceous, Impale, Kerb, Lambrequin, Limb, Limbate, Limbo, Limen, Limes, Limit, Limitrophe, Lip, List, March, Marchland, → **MARGIN**, Mat, Mattoid, Meith, Mete, Mount, Neighbour, Orle, Pand, Pelmet, Penumbra, Perimeter, Purfle, Purlieu, Rand, Rim, Roadside, Roon, Royne, Rubicon, Rund, Rymme, Scottish, Selvage, Selvedge, Side, Skirt, Skirting, Strand, Strip, Surround, Swage, The Marches, Trench, Tressure, Valance, Valence, → **VERGE**
▷ **Borders** *may indicate* first and last letters
Bore(d), Boredom, Borer, Boring Aiguille, Airshaft, Anobium, Anorak, Apathy, Aspergillum, Aspergillus, Aspersoir, Auger, Awl, Beetle, Bind, Bit, Broach, Brog, Bromide, Calibre, Chokebore, Deadly, Drag, → **DRILL**, Dry, Dusty, Dweeb, Eagre, Eat, Eger, Elshin, Elsin, Endured, Ennui, Ennuye, Foozle, Gim(b)let, Gouge, Gribble, Grind, Had, Heigh-ho, Ho-hum, Irk, Jumper, Land, Listless, Longicorn, Longueur, Miser, Mole, Nerd, Noyance, Nudni(c)k, Nuisance, Nyaff, Operose, Pain, Pall, Penetrate, Perforate, Pest, Pholas, Pierce, Pill, Platitude, Probe, Prosaic, Prosy, Punch, Ream(ingbit), Rime, Saddo, Sat, Schmoe, Scolytus, Screw, Severn, Shothole, Snooze, Snore, Sondage, Spleen, Spod, Spudding-un, Sting, Stob, Stupid, Tediosity, Tedious, Tedisome, Tedium, Tedy, Terebra, Teredo, Termes, Termite, Thirl, Tire, Trepan, Trocar, Tunnel, Turn-off, → **WEARY**, Well, Wimble, Windbag, Wonk, Woodworm, Workaday, Worldweary, Xylophaga, Yawn
Borgia Cesare, Lucretia
Boric Sassolin, Sassolite
Born B, Free, Great, Nascent, Nat(us), Né(e)
Borneo Kalimantan
Boron B
Borough Borgo, Close, Pocket, Port, Quarter, Rotten, Township, Wick
Borrow(ed), Borrowing Adopt, Appropriate, Cadge, Copy, Derivative, Eclectic, George, Hum, Leverage, Scunge, Straunge, → **TAKE**, Touch
Bosh Humbug, Nonsense, Rot
Bosom Abraham's, Breast, Bristols, Close, Gremial, Inarm, Intimate, Poitrine
Boson Gauge, Squark
Boss(ed), Bossy Big White Chief, Blooper, Burr, Cacique, Director, Dominate, Domineer, Gadroon, Governor, Headman, Honcho, Hump, Inian, Inion, Jewel, Knob, Knop, Knot, Leader, Maestro, → **MANAGER**, Massa, → **MISTAKE**, Mistress, Netsuke, Noop, Nose-led, Omphalos, Oubaas, Overlord, Overseer, Owner, Pannikin, Pellet, Protuberance, Ruler, Run, Sherang, Straw, Stud, Superintendent, Supremo, Taskmaster, Umbo(nate)
Boston Hub
Bot Oestrus
Botany, Botanist Banks, Bryology, Candolle, Carpology, Cockayne, Dendrologist, Frees, Garden, Godet, Graminology, Herbist, Linnaeus, Mendel, Phytogenesis, Phytology, Pteridology, Tradescant, Weigel
Botch(ed) Bungle, Clamper, Cock-up, Flub, Fudge, Mismanage, Pig's ear, Spoil, Tink
Both Together, Two
Bother(some) Ado, Aggro, Brush, Care, Deave, Deeve, Disturb, Drat, Fash, Fluster, Fuss, Get, Hassle, Hector, Incommode, Irk, Irritate, Moither, Nark, Nuisance,

Perturb, Pesky, Pest(er), Pickle, Reke, Todo, → **TROUBLE**

Bottle(s) Ampul(la), Bacbuc, Balthasar, Balthazar, Belshazzar, Borachio, Bundle, Carafe, Carboy, Chapine, Cock, Cork, Costrel, Courage, Cruet, Cruse, Cucurbital, Cutter, Dead-man, Decanter, Demijohn, Fearlessness, Feeding, Fiasco, Filette, Flacket, Flacon, Flagon, Flask, Glass can, Goatskin, Gourd, Guts, Half-jack, Hen, Imperial, Jeroboam, Junk, Klein, Lachrymal, Lagena, Magnetic, Magnum, Marie-Jeanne, Matrass, Medicine, Melchior, Methuselah, Mettle, Mickey, Middy, Nansen, Nebuchadnezzar, → **NERVE**, Nursing, Phial, Pig, Pilgrim, Pitcher, Pooter, Pycnometer, Rehoboam, Resource, Retort, Salmanaser, Salmanazar, Scent, Screwtop, Siphon, Smelling, Split, Squeeze, Squeezy, Sucking, Tear, Tube, Twenty-sixer, Vial, Vinaigret(te), Wad, Water, Water bouget, Weighing, Winchester, Wine, Woulfe

▷ **Bottle(d)** *may indicate* an anagram or a hidden word

Bottom Anus, Aris, Arse, Ass, Base, Batty, Beauty, Bed, Benthos, Bilge, Booty, Breech, Bum, Butt, Buttocks, Croup(e), Croupon, Demersal, Derrière, Doup, Dowp, End, Fanny, Floor, Foot, Foundation, Fud, Fundus, Haunches, Hunkers, Hurdies, Keel(son), Kick, Lumbar, Nadir, Nates, Planning, Podex, Posterior, Pottle-deep, Prat, Pyramus, Rear, Rock, Root, Rump, Seat, Ship, Sill, Sole, Staddle, Tail, Tush, Weaver

Bottom drawer Glory box

Bottomless Subjacent

Botulism Limberneck

Boudoir Bower, Room

Bouffant Pouf

Bough Branch, Limb

Bought Coft

Boulder Erratic, Gibber, Niggerhead, Rock, → **STONE**

Boule Senate

Bounce(r), Bouncing, Bouncy Bang, Blague, Bound, Caper, Dandle, Dap, Dead-cat, Doorman, Dop, Dud, Eject, Evict, Fib, Jounce, Keepy-uppy, Kite, Lie, Lilt, Resilient, Ricochet, Spiccato, Spring, Stot, Tale, Tamp, Valve, Verve, Vitality, Yorker, Yump

▷ **Bouncing** *may indicate* an anagram

Bound(er), Boundary Adipose, Apprenticed, Articled, Bad, Barrier, Beholden, Border, Bourn(e), Bubalis, Cad, Cavort, Certain, Circumference, Curvet, Decreed, Demarcation, Demarkation, Dool, Dule, Duty, End, Engirt, Entrechat, Erub, Eruv, Event horizon, Exciton, Fence, Four, Frape, Frontier, Galumph, Gambado, Gambol, Girt, Harestane, Hedge, Heel, Held, Hoarstone, Hops, Hourstone, Ibex, Interface, Izard, Jump, Kangaroo, K/T, → **LEAP**, Limes, Limit, Linch, Lollop, Lope, March-stone, Meare, Meer, Meith, Mere, Merestone, Mete, Moho, Muscle, Obliged, Ourebi, Outward, Pale, Parameter, Perimeter, Periphery, Plate, Prance, Precinct, Prometheus, Purlieu, Redound, Ring-fence, Roller, Roo, Roped, Rubicon, Scoup, Scowp, Serf, Side, Sideline, Six(er), Skelp, Skip, Spang, Spring, Sten(d), Stoit, Stylolite, Terminator, T(h)alweg, Tied, Touchline, Upstart, Vault, Verge, Wallaby

▷ **Bounds** *may indicate* outside letters

Bounty, Bountiful Aid, Bligh, Boon, Christian, Generosity, → **GIFT**, Goodness, Grant, Head money, Honorarium, Largess(e), Lavish, Queen Anne's, Queen's

Bouquet Aroma, Attar, Aura, Compliment, Corsage, Fragrancy, Garni, Nose, Nosegay, Perfume, Plaudit, Posy, Scent, Spiritual, Spray

Bourbon Alfonso

Bourgeois(ie) Biedermeier, Common, Middle class, Pleb(eian), Pooter(ish)

Bout Bender, Bust, Contest, Dose, Go, Jag, Match, Spell, Spree, Turn, Venery, Venewe, Venue

Boutique Shop

Bovine Stolid

Bow(ing), Bower, Bowman Alcove, Arbour, Arc, Arch, → ARCHER, Arco, Arson, Bandy, Beck, Bend, Boudoir, Butterfly, Clara, Congé(e), Crescent, Crook, Cupid, → CURVE, Defer, Dicky, Drail, Droop, Duck, Echelles, Eros, Eugh, Eyes, Fiddle(r), Fiddlestick, Foredeck, Halse, Hawse, Honour, Jook, Jouk, Kneel, Kotow, Laval(l)ière, Lean, Long, Loof, Lout, Lowt, Luff, Martellato, Moulinet, Namaste, Nameste, Nod, Nutate, Obeisance, Obtemper, Paganini, Pergola, Prore, Quarrel, Reverence, Salaam, Seamer, Shelter, Slope, Sound, Spiccato, Stick, → SUBMIT, Tie, Torrent, Yew, Yield

Bowdler(ize) Edit(or), Water

Bowels Entrails, Guts, Innards, Viscera

▷ **Bower** *may indicate* using a bow

Bowl(ing), Bowler, Bowl over, Bowls B, Basin, Begging, Bicker, Bocce, Bocci(a), Boccie, Bodyline, Bool, Bosey, Bouncer, Cage-cup, Calabash, Candlepins, Cap, Carpet, Caup, Chalice, Cheese, Chinaman, Christie, Christy, Cog(g)ie, Concave, Coolamon, Crater, Cup, Deliver, Derby, → DISH, Dismiss, Dome, Drake, Dumbfound, Dust, Ecuelle, End, Finger, Fivepin, Goldfish, Googly, Grub, Hog, Hoop, Jack, Jeroboam, Jorum, Kegler, Krater, Lavabo, Laver, Leg-spin, Lightweight, Lob, Locke, Mazer, Monteith, Night, Offbreak, Old, Over-arm, Overpitch, Pace, Pan, Pétanque, Piggin, Pitch, Porringer, Pot-hat, Pottinger, Punch, Raku, Rice, Rink, Roll, Roundarm, Seam(er), Skip, Skittle(s), Spare, Speed, Spinner, Spofforth, Stadium, Stagger, Stummel, Sucrier, Super, Ten-pin, Tom, Underarm, Underhand, Underwood, Voce, Wassail, Wood, York(er)

Box(ing) Baignoire, Ballot, Bandbox, Bareknuckle, Bento, Bijou, Bimble, Binnacle, Black, Blue, Bonk, Booth, Buist, Bunk, Bush, Caddy, Call, Camera, Canister, Case, Cash, Casket, Cassolette, Chest, Chinese, Christmas, Ciborium, Clog, Coach, Coffer, Coffin, Coffret, Coin, Confessional, Cool, Crate, Cuff, Dabba, Deed, Dialog(ue), Dispatch, Ditty, Dog, Drawer, Encase, Enclose, → FIGHT, File, Fist, Fund, Fuse, Fuzz, Glory, Glove, Go-kart, Grass, Hat, Hay, Hedge, Honesty, Horse, Humidor, Hutch, Ice, Idiot, Inherce, Inro, Inter, Jewel, Journal, Junction, Jury, Keister, Kick, Kiosk, Kite, Knevell, Ladle, Letter, Light, Live, Locker, Lodge, Loge, Loose, Lunch, Match, Message, Mill, Mitre, Mocock, Mocuck, Money, Musical, Nest(ing), Omnibus, Orgone, Package, Packing, Paint, Pandora's, Papeterie, Patch, Pattress, Peepshow, Peg, Penalty, Petara, Pew, Phylactery, Pill, Pillar, Pitara, Pix, Poor, Post, Pounce(t), Powder, Press, Prompt, Protector, Puff, Pugilism, Pyxis, Register, Resonance, Ring, Rope-a-dope, Royal, Saggar(d), Sagger, Sand, Savate, Scent, Scrap, Seggar, Sentry, Set-top, Shadow, Shoe, Shooting, Side, Signal, Skinner, Skip(pet), Slipcase, Smudge, Sneeze, Soap, Solander, Sound, Sound body, → SPAR, Spice, Spit, Spring, Squawk, Squeeze, Strong, Stuffing, Swell, Tabernacle, Tee, Tefillin, Telephone, Telly, Thai, Tick, Tin, Tinder, Tool, Touch, Trunk, Tube, Tuck, TV, Urn, Vanity, Vasculum, Vinaigrette, Voice, Weather, Window, Wine, Witness, Yakhdan

Boxer Ali, Amycus, Babyweight, Bantamweight, Bruiser, Bruno, Canine, Carnera, Carpentier, Carthorse, Chinaman, Cooper, Crater, Cruiserweight, Dog, Eryx, Farr, Featherweight, Flyweight, Ham, Heavyweight, Lightweight, McCoy, Middleweight, Mosquito-weight, Pandora, Pollux, Pug, Pugil(ist), Rebellion, Rocky, Shadow, Southpaw, Strawweight, Welterweight, Wilde

Boxing-glove Hurlbat, Muffle, Whirlbat, Whorlbat

Boy(s) Amoretto, Apprentice, Ball, Bevin, Blue-eyed, Breeches, Bub(by), Cabin, Callant, Catamite, Champagne, Chiel(d), → **CHILD**, Chokra, Chummy, Cub, Cupid, Dandiprat, Errant, Galopin, Garçon, Gorsoon, Gossoon, Green Mountain, Groom, Grummet, Ha, Hansel, Jack, Kid, Klonkie, Knave, Knave-bairn, Kwedien, Lackbeard, → **LAD**, Loblolly, Loon(ie), Minstrel, Nibs, Nipper, Office, Page, Poster, Pot, Prentice, Principal, Putto, Rent, Roaring, Rude, Shaver, Ship's, Son, Spalpeen, Sprig, Stripling, Tad, Tar, Ted(dy), Tiger, Toy, Urchin, Whipping, Wide, → **YOUTH**
▷ **Boy** *may indicate* an abbreviated name
Boycott Avoid, Ban, Bat, Black, Blacklist, Exclude, Hartal, Isolate, Ostracise, Shun, Swadeshi
Boyfriend Beau, Date, Fella, Fellow, Steady
Boyle Juno
Bp Bishop, DD, RR
Brace(s), Bracing Accolade, Couple, Crosstree, Fortify, Gallace, Gallows, Gallus(es), Gird, Hound, Invigorate, Ozone, Pair, Pr, Rear-arch, Rere-arch, Sea air, Skeg, Spider, Splint, Steady, Stiffener, Strut, → **SUPPORT**, Suspenders, Tauten, Thorough, Tone, Tonic, Two
Bracelet Armil(la), Armlet, Bangle, Cuff, Darbies, Handcuff, Identity, Manacle, Manilla
Brachiopod Ecardines, Lamp-shell, Spirifer
Bracken Brake, Fern, Pteridium, Tara
Bracket Ancon, Angle-iron, Bibb, Brace, Cantilever, Console, Corbel, Couple, Cripple, Lance rest, Misericord(e), Modillion, Mutule, Parenthesis, Potence, Pylon, Rigger, Sconce, Square, Straddle, Strata, → **STRUT**, Trivet, Truss
Bract Glume(lla), Involucel, Involucre, Leaf, Lemma, Palea, Palet, Phyllary, Spathe
Brad Nail, Pin, Rivet, Sprig
Brag(gart), Bragging Basilisco, Birkie, Bluster, Boast, Bobadil, Boister, Braggadocio, Bull, Cockalorum, Crow, Falstaff, Fanfaronade, Gab, Gascon, Hot-air, Loudmouth, Parolles, Puckfist, Puff, Rodomontader, Skite, Slam, Swagger, Thrason, Thrasonic, Tongue-doubtie, Tongue-doughty, Vainglorious, Vapour, Vaunt
Brahma(n) San(n)yasi(n)
Braid A(i)glet, Aiguillette, Fishbone, French, Frog, Galloon, Lacet, Plait, Plat, Rickrack, Ricrac, Scrambled eggs, Seaming-lace, Sennet, Sennit, Sinnet, Soutache, Tress, Trim, Twist, Weave
Braille (system) Moon
Brain(box), Brains, Brainstorm, Brainy, Brain disease, Brain-power Amygdala, Appestat, Bean, Boffin, Bright, Cerebellum, Cerebrum, Cortex, Diencephalon, Dura mater, Encephalon, Epencephalon, Fornix, Genius, Gyrus, Harn(s), Head, Hippocampus, Hydrocephalus, Hypothalamus, Inspiration, Insula, Intelligence, IQ, Kuru, Left, Limbic, Loaf, Lobe, Mastermind, Mater, Medulla, Medulla oblongata, Metencephalon, Mind, Noddle, Noesis, Nous, Peduncle, Pericranium, Pia mater, Pons, Pontile, Prosencephalon, Rhinencephalon, Rhombencephalon, Sconce, Sense, Sensorium, Striatum, Subcortex, Tapagnosia, Tectum, Telencephalon, Thalamencephalon, Thalamus, Upper stor(e)y, Vermis, Wetware
▷ **Brain(s)** *may indicate* an anagram
Brainless Anencephaly, Bimbo, Stupid, Thick
Brainwash(ing) Indoctrinate, Menticide, Propaganda
Brake, Braking ABS, Adiantum, Aerodynamic, Air, Anchors, Antilock, Bracken, Centrifugal, Curb, Disc, Dive, Drag, Drum, Estate car, Fern, Fly, Foot, Grove, Hand,

Hydraulic, Nemoral, Overrun, Ratchet, Rein, Shoe, Shooting, → **SLOW**, Spinney, Sprag, Tara, Thicket, Vacuum, Westinghouse

Bramble, Brambly Batology, Blackberry, Boysenberry, Brier, Cloudberry, Rubus, Thorn, Wait-a-bit, Youngberry

Bran Cereal, Chesil, Chisel, Oats, Pollard

Branch(ed), Branches, Branching, Branch office Affiliate, Antler, Arm, BO, Bough, Cladode, Cow, Dendron, Dept, Diversify, Diverticulum, Divide, Filiate, Fork, Grain, Jump, Kow, Lateral, Leaf-trace, Limb, Lobe, Loop, Lye, Lylum, Offshoot, Olive, Patulous, Raguly, Ramate, Ramulus, Reis, Rice, Shroud, Special, Spray(ey), Sprig, Spur, Tributary, Turning, Turn-off, Twig, Wattle, Yard

Branch-rib Lierne

Brand Broadsword, Buist, Burn, Cauterise, Chop, Class, Dealer, Denounce, Earmark, Ember, Excalibur, Falchion, Faulchin, Faulchion, Flambeau, Home, Idiograph, Inust, Iron, Label, Line, → **MARK**, Marque, Name, Own, Power, Sear, Sere, Stigma, Sweard, Sword, Torch, Wipe

Brandish Bless, Flaunt, Flourish, Hurtle, Waffle, Wampish, Wave

Brandy Aguardiente, Applejack, Apricot, Aqua vitae, Armagnac, Bingo, Calvados, Cape smoke, Cold without, Dop, Eau de vie, Fine, Framboise, Grappa, Mampoer, Marc, Mobbie, Mobby, Nantes, Nantz, Napoleon, Palinka, Peach, Quetsch, Slivovic(a), Slivovitz, Smoke

Bras Arms

Brash Cocky, Flashy, Impudent, Jack-the-lad, Jumped-up, Pushy, Rain, Rash

Brass(y), Brassware Alpha-beta, Benares, Brazen, Cheek, Club, Corinthian, Cornet, Dinanderie, Face, Front, Harsh, High, Horn, Horse, Latten, Lip, Loot, Lota(h), Loud, Matrix, → **MONEY**, Moola(h), Oof, Oricalche, Orichalc, Pyrites, Sass, Snash, Sopranino, Talus, Top, Trombone, Wood

Brassard Armlet

Brass hat Brig

Brassica Brussels (sprout), → **CABBAGE**, Colza, Turnip

Brassière Gay deceiver

Brat Bairn, Bra(t)chet, Enfant terrible, Gait(t), Gamin, Geit, Get, Git, Gyte, Imp, Lad, Terror, Urchin

Brave(ry) Amerind, Apache, Bold, Conan, Corragio, Courage, Creek, Dare, → **DEFY**, Doughty, Dress, Face, Fearless, Gallant, Game, Gamy, Gutsy, Hardy, Heroism, Indian, Injun, Intrepid, Lion, Lion-hearted, Manful, Manly, → **MEXICAN**, Nannup, → **NORTH AMERICAN**, Plucky, Prow(ess), Sannup, Skookum, → **SOUTH AMERICAN**, Spunk, Stout, Uncas, Valiant, Valour, Wight

Bravo Acclaim, B, Bandit, Bully, Desperado, Euge, Murderer, Olé, Shabash, Spadassin, Villain

Brawl(er) Affray, Bagarre, Bicker, Brabble, Donnybrook, Dust, Fight, Flite, Flyte, Fracas, Fratch, Fray, Melee, Prawl, Rammy, Roarer, Roughhouse, Row, Scuffle, Set-to, Shindig, Stoush, Tar, Wrangle

Brawn Beef, Burliness, Headcheese, He-man, Might, Muscle, Power, Rillettes, Sinew

Bray Cry, Heehaw, Stamp, Vicar, Whinny

Brazen Bold, Brassy, Flagrant, Impudent, Shameless, Unabashed

Brazier Brasero, Fire, Hibachi, Mangal, Scaldino

Brazil(ian) Caboclo, Carioca, Para, Yanomami, Yanomamo

Breach Assault, Break, Chasm, Cleft, Gap(e), Great schism, Infraction, Redan, Rupture, Saltus, Schism, Solecism, Solution, Trespass, Violate

Bread, Bread crumbs Afrikomen, Azym(e), Bagel, Baguette, Bannock, Bap,

Barmbrack, Barm cake, Batch, Baton, Brewis, Brioche, Brownie, Bun, Cash, Chal(l)ah, Chametz, Chapati, Cheat, Ciabatta, Cob, Coburg, Corn, Corsned, Croissant, Crostini, Croute, Crouton, Crumpet, Crust, Currency, Damper, Dibs, Dika, Doorstep, Elephant's-foot, Eulogia, Fancy, Flatbread, Focaccia, French, Garlic, Gluten, Graham, Granary, Grissini, Guarana, Hallah, Hametz, Hometz, Horse, Host, Indian, Injera, Jannock, Johnny-cake, Kaffir, Laver, Lavish, Leavened, Loaf, Long tin, Manchet, Maori, Milk-sop, → **MONEY**, Monkey, Na(a)n, Pain, Panada, Panary, Pane, Paneity, Paratha, Pikelet, Pit(t)a, Pone, Poori, Poppadom, Poultice, Prozymite, Pumpernickel, Puree, Puri, Raspings, Ravel, Roll, Rooty, Roti, Round, Rusk, Rye, Sally Lunn, Schnecken, Shewbread, Shive, Simnel, Sippet, Smor(re)brod, Soda, Soft-tommy, Sop, Sourdough, Staff of life, Standard, Stollen, Stottie, Sugar, Sweet, Tartine, Tea, Tommy, Tortoise-plant, Twist, Wastel, Wrap, Zakuski, Zwieback

Breadfruit Ja(c)k

Breadwinner Earner, Pa

Break, Break-down, Break-in, Break-up, Broken Adjourn, Apn(o)ea, Aposiopesis, Bait, Breach, Breather, Caesura, Caesure, Cantle, Cark, Cesure, Chinaman, Chip, Cleave, Coffee, Comb, Comma, Commercial, Comminute, Compost, Conk, Crack, Crock, Crumble, Deave, Debacle, Deeve, Demob, Destroy, Diffract, Disband, Disintegrate, Disperse, Disrupt, Erupt, Exeat, Fast, Fault, Four, → **FRACTURE**, Fragment, Fritter, Frush, Gaffe, Give, Greenstick, Half-term, Half-time, Hernia, Hiatus, Holiday, Infringe, Interim, Interlude, Intermission, Interrupt, → **INTERVAL**, Irrupt, Kark, Knap, Knickpoint, Lacuna, Lapse, Leave, Lysis, Moratorium, Nickpoint, Nooner, Outage, Part, Pause, Phreak, Playtime, Poach, Polarise, Price, Reave, Recess, Recrudescent, Relief, Rend, Resorption, Respite, Rest, Rift, Ruin, Rupture, Saltus, Schism(a), Secede, Service, Shatter, Shiver, Smash, Smokeho, Smoko, Snap, Split, Stave, Stop, Stop-over, Stove, Sunder, Take five, Take ten, Tame, Tea-ho, Tear, Time-out, Torn, Transgress, Truce, Twist, Vacation, Violate

Breakable Brittle, Delicate, Fissile, Frail, Friable

Breakdown Analyse, Autolysis, Cataclasm, Collapse, Conk, Crack-up, Glitch, Glycolosis, Glycolysis, Histolysis, Hydrolysis, Lyse, Lysis, Nervous, Ruin

Breaker Billow, Circuit, Comber, Ice, Roller, Smasher, Surf

Breakfast B, Brunch, Chota-hazri, Continental, Deskfast, Disjune, English, Kipper, Petit déjeuner, Power, Wedding

Breakneck Headlong

Breakwater Groyne, Jetty, Mole, Pier, Tetrapod

Bream Fish, Porgy, Sar(gus), Sea, Silver, Tai, White

Breast(s), Breastbone, Breastwork Bazuma, Blob, Bosom, Brave, Brisket, Bristols, Bust, Chimney, Counter, Diddy, Duddy, Dug, Falsies, Garbonza, Gazunga, Heart-spoon, Jubbies, Jugs, Knockers, Norg, Nork, Pigeon, Rampart, Redan, Sangar, Stem, Sternum, Sungar, Supreme, Tit, Xiphisternum

Breastplate Armour, Byrnie, Curat, Curiet, Pectoral, Plastron, Rational, Rest, Shield, Thorax, Xiphiplastron

Breath(e), Breathing, Breather Aerobe, Apneusis, Aqualung, Aspirate, Bated, Branchia, Caesural, Cheyne-Stokes, Circular, Cypress-knee, Eupnoea, Exhalation, Expiration, Flatus, Gasp, Gill, H, Halitosis, Hauriant, Haurient, Hobday, Hypernoea, Hyperventilation, Hypopnoea, Inhale, Inspiration, Knee, Lung, Nares, Nostril, Orthopnoea, Oxygenator, Pant, Plosion, Pneuma, Prana, Pulmo, Rale, Respire, Respite, Rest, Rhonchus, Rough, Scuba, Smooth, Snore, Snorkel, Snortmast, Snotter, Snuffle, Spiracle, Spirit, Spiritus, Stertor, Stridor, Tachypnoea,

Vent, Wheeze, Whiff, Whift, Whisper, Whist, Wind, Windpipe

Breathless(ness) Anhelation, Apnoea, Asthma, Dyspnoea, Emphysema, Orthopnoea, Puffed-out, Tachypnoea, Wheezing

Breathtaking Amazing, Asphyxia

Breech(es) Bible, Buckskin, Chaps, Flog, Galligaskins, Hose, Jodhpurs, Kneecords, Knickerbockers, Petticoat, Plushes, Riding, Smallclothes, Smalls, Trews, Trouse(rs), Trunk hose, Trusses

Breed(er), Breeding(-place) Bear, Beget, Cleck, Endogamous, Engender, Engend(r)ure, Eugenics, Fast, Generation, Gentilesse, Gentrice, Hetero, Hotbed, In-and-in, Lineage, → MANNERS, Origin, Panmixia, Procreate, Propagate, Pullulate, Race, Raise, Rear, Seminary, Sire, Species, Stock, Strain, Stud, Telegony, Thremmatology, Tribe, Voltinism

Breeze, Breezy Air, Breath, Brisk, Cakewalk, Catspaw, Chipper, Doctor, Draught, Fresh, Gentle, Gust, Land, Light, Mackerel, Moderate, Sea, Slant, Sniffler, Strong, Tiff, Zephyr

Brethren Bohemian, Darbyite, Elder, Exclusive, Herrnhuter, Kin, Open, Plymouth, Trinity

Breton Armoric, Brezonek

Breve Minim, Note, O

Breviary Portesse, Portous

▶ **Brevity** see **BRIEF**

Brew(ery), Brewer, Brewing Ale, Billycan, Brose, Browst, Bummock, → CONCOCT, Contrive, Dictionary, Distillery, Ferment, Infusion, Liquor, Malt, Percolate, Perk, Potion, Steep, Witches', Yeast, Yill, Zymurgy

Briar Bramble, Canker, Lawyer

Bribe(ry) Backhander, Barratry, Barretry, Bonus, Boodle, Bung, Carrot, Dash, Embracery, Get at, Graft, Grease, Hamper, Hush-money, Insult, Kickback, Oil, Palm, Palm-grease, Palm-oil, Payola, Schmear, Slush, Soap, Sop, Square, Straightener, Suborn, Sweeten(er), Tamper, Tempt, Tenderloin, Vail, Vales

Bric-a-brac Bibelot, Curio, Rattle-trap, Smytrie, Tatt, Virtu

Brick(s), Brickwork Adobe, Air, Bat, Bath, Bonder, Bondstone, Boob, Breeze, Bullnose, Bur(r), Clanger, Clinker, Closer, Course, Dutch clinker, Fletton, Gaffe, Gault, Gold, Hard stocks, Header, Ingot, Klinker, Lateritious, Lego®, Malm, Nogging, Red, Rubber, Soldier, Sport, Stalwart, Stretcher, Terra-cotta, Testaceous, Tile, Trojan, Trump

Brickbat Missile

Bricklayer Churchill

Bride(s) Bartered, Danaides, Ellen, Hen, Spouse, War, Wife, Ximena

Bridesmaid Paranymph

Bridge(head), Bridge player Acol, Air, Al Sirat, Aqueduct, Auction, Avignon, Bailey, Balance, Barre, Bascule, Bestride, Bifrost, Biritch, Board, Bridle-chord, Brig, Brooklyn, Cable-stayed, Cantilever, Capo, Capodastro, Capotasto, Catwalk, Chevalet, Chicago, Chicane, Clapper, Clifton, Contract, Counterpoise, Cross, Cut-throat, Deck, Declarer, Drawbridge, Duplicate, Flying, Flyover, Foot, Four-deal, Gangplank, Gangway, Gantry, Girder, Golden Gate, Hog's back, Humber, Humpback, Humpbacked, Ice, Irish, Jigger, Land, Lattice, Leaf, Lifting, Ligger, Link, London, Menai, Millau, Millennium, Nasion, Overpass, Pivot, Plafond, Ponceau, Ponticello, Pontifice, Pont levis, Pontoon, Raft, Rainbow, Rialto, Rubber, Sighs, Sinvat, Skew, Snow, → SPAN, Spanner, Stamford, Straddle, Suspension, Swing, Tay, Temper, Tête-de-pont, Through, Transporter, Traversing, Trestle, Truss, Turn, Vertical lift, Viaduct, Vint, Waterloo, Weigh, Wheatstone, Wire

Bridge pair EW, NS, SN, WE
Bridge protector Ice-apron
Bridge system Acol
Bridle Bit, Branks, Bridoon, Bristle, Browband, Crownpiece, Curb, Double, Hackamore, Halter, Headstall, Musrol, Noseband, Rein, Scold's
Bridle path Orbit, Track
Brief(s), Briefing, Briefly, Brevity Acquaint, Awhile, Barristerial, Bluette, Brachyology, Breviate, Cape, Compact, → **CONCISE**, Conspectus, Crisp, Curt, Dossier, Fill in, Fleeting, Instruct, Laconic, Nearly, Pants, Pennorth, Pithy, Prime, Scant, → **SHORT(EN)**, Short-term, Short-winded, Sitrep, Sparse, Succinct, Summing, Tanga, Terse, Transient, Undies, Update, Watching
Brig Br, Hermaphrodite, Jail, Nancy Bell, → **SHIP**, Snow
Brigade Boys', Corps, Fire, Fur, Girls', Green-ink, International, Naval, Red, Troop
Brigand Bandit, Bandolero, Cateran, Haidu(c)k, Heiduc, Heyduck, Klepht, Pillager, Pirate, → **ROBBER**, Rob Roy, Trailbaston
Bright, Brightness Afterglow, Alert, Ashine, Bertha, Brainy, Breezy, Brilliant, Brisk, Cheery, Chiarezza, Cla(i)re, Clara, Clear, Clever, Cuthbert, Effulgent, Elaine, Facula, Fair, Floodlit, Florid, Garish, Gay, Glad, Glow, Helen, Hono(u)r, Hubert, Light, Lit, Loud, Lucid, Luculent, Lustre, Net(t), Nit, Nitid, Radiant, Ro(a)ry, Rorie, Rosy, Scintillating, Sematic, Sharp, Sheeny, Sheer, Shere, Skyre, Smart, Spark(y), Stilb, Sunlit, Sunny, Vive, Vivid, White
Bright spot Facula
Brilliant, Brilliance Ace, Aine, Blaze, Brainy, Bravura, Def, Effulgent, Eurian, Flashy, Galaxy, Gay, Gemmy, Gifted, Glossy, High flyer, Inspired, Lambent, Leam, Lucent, Lustre, Mega-, Meteoric, Nitid, Pear, → **RADIANT**, Refulgent, Resplendent, Shiny, Spangle, Splendour, Star, Virtuoso, → **VIVID**, Water
Brim Edge, Lip, Rim, Ugly
Brimstone Hellfire, S, Sulphur
Brindisi Skolion, Toast
Brindled Piebald, Tabby, Tawny
Brine Muriatic, Ozone, Pickle, Saline, Salt
Bring Afferent, Bear, Carry, Cause, Conduct, Convey, Earn, Evoke, Fet, Fetch, Foist, Hatch, Induce, Land, Precipitate, Produce, Wreak
Bring up Breed, Educate, Exhume, Foster, Nurture, Raise, → **REAR**
Brink → **EDGE**, Lip, Rim, Shore, → **VERGE**
Brio Elan
Brisk(ly), Briskness Active, Alacrity, Alert, Allegro, Breezy, Busy, Chipper, Con moto, Crank, Crisp, Crouse, Fresh, Gaillard, Galliard, Jaunty, Kedge, Kedgy, Kidge, Lively, Nippy, Peart, Perk, Pert, Rattling, Roaring, Scherzo, Sharp, Smart, Snappy, Spanking, Spirited, Sprightly, Vivace, Yare, Zippy
Bristle, Bristling, Bristly Aciculum, Arista, Awn, Barb, Bewhiskered, Birse, Bridle, Campodeiform, Chaeta, Flurry, Fraught, Frenulum, Glochidium, Gooseflesh, Hackles, Hair, Hérissé, Hispid, Horrent, Horripilation, Nereid, Polychaete, Seta, Setose, Striga, Strigose, Stubble, Styloid, Vibraculum, Villus, Whisker
Bristle-tail Campodea
Brit Silt
Brit(ish), Briton(s) All-red, Anglo, Herring, Iceni, Insular, Isles, Kipper, Limey, Pict, Pom, Rooinek, Saxon, Silurian, UK
Britain Alban(y), Albion, GB, Old Dart
Britannia, Britannia metal Tutania
Brittany Armorica

Brittle Bruckle, Crackly, Crimp, Crisp, Delicate, → **FRAGILE**, Frush, Hot-short, Redsear, Red-share, Red-shire, Redshort, Shivery, Spall, Spalt

▷ **Brittle** *may indicate* an anagram

Broach Approach, Open, Raise, Spit, Suggest, Tap, Widen

Broad(ly) Crumpet, Dame, Doll, Doxy, Drab, General, Generic, Hippy, Largo, Latitudinous, Loose, Outspoken, Ovate, Pro, Roomy, Spatulate, Tart, Thick, Tolerant, Wide, Woman

Broad-beaked Latirostrate

Broadcast(er), Broadcasting Ad(vertise), Air, Announce, Beam, Breaker, CB, Disperse, Disseminate, Downlink, Emission, Ham, IBA, Monophonic, Multicast, Network, Newscast, OB, On, Outside, Pirate, Programme, Promulgate, Put out, Radiate, Radio, Relay, RTE, Run, Satellite, → **SCATTER**, Scattershot, Screen(ed), SECAM, Seed, Simulcast, Sky, Sow, Sperse, Spread, Sprinkle, Stereophonic, Transmission, Ventilate, Wavelength

Broad-nosed Platyrrhine

Broadside Barrage, Criticism, Salvo, Tire

Broadway Boulevard, Esplanade, Great White Way, Motorway

Brocade Arrasene, Baldachin, Baldaquin, Baudekin, Bawdkin, Kincob, Zari

Brochure Leaflet, Pamphlet, Programme, Tract

Brogue Accent, → **SHOE**

Broke(n) Bankrupt, Bust(ed), Duff, Evans, Fritz, Impoverished, Insolvent, Kaput, On the rocks, Puckeroo, Shattered, Skint, Stony, Stove, Strapped

▷ **Broken** *may indicate* an anagram

Broken off Prerupt

Broker Agent, Banian, Banyan, Go-between, Jobber, Mediator, → **MERCHANT**, Power, Shadchan, Uncle

Bromide Halide, Haloid, Truism

Bromine Br

Bronchitis, Bronchitic Chesty, Husk

Bronte(s) Bell, Cyclops

Brontosaurus Apatosaurus

Bronze, Bronze age Bell, Bras(s), Brown, Eugubine, Gunmetal, Hallstatt(ian), Helladic, Kamakura, Manganese, Minoan, Mycenean, Ormolu, Phosphor, Schillerspar, Sextans, Talos, Tan, Third

Brooch Breastpin, Cameo, Clasp, Fibula, Luckenbooth, Ouch, Owche, Pin, Preen, Prop, Spang, Sunburst

Brood(y) Clock, Clucky, Clutch, Cogitate, Cour, Cover, Covey, Eye, Eyrie, Hatch, Hover, Incubate, Introspect, Kindle, Litter, Meditate, Mill, Mull, Nest, Nid, Perch, Pet, → **PONDER**, Repine, Roost, Sit, Sulk, Team

Brook Abide, Babbling, Becher's, Beck, Branch, Burn, Countenance, Creek, Endure, Ghyll, Gill, Kerith, Kill, Pirl, Purl, Rill(et), River, Rivulet, Runlet, Runnel, Springlet, Stand, Stomach, Stream, Suffer, Tolerate

Broom Besom, Brush, Butcher's, Cow, Cytisus, Genista, Gorse, Greenweed, Knee-holly, Kow, New, Orobranche, Retama, Spart, Sweeper, Whisk

Brose Atholl, Pease

Broth Bouillon, Bree, Brew(is), Cullis, Dashi, Kail, Kale, Muslin-kale, Pot liquor, Pottage, Scotch, Skilly, → **SOUP**, Stock

Brothel Bagnio, Bordel(lo), Cathouse, Corinth, Crib, Den, Flash-house, Honkytonk, Hothouse, Kip, Knocking shop, Red-light, Seraglio, Sporting house, Stew, Vaulting-house

Brother(hood) Ally, Bhai, Billie, Billy, Blood, Boet, Brethren, Bro, Bud, Comrade,

Félibre, Fellow, Fra, Freemason, Lay, → MONK, Moose, Plymouth, Pre-Raphaelite, Sib(ling), Theatine, Trappist, Worker

Brow Crest, Forehead, Glabella, Ridge, Sinciput, Superciliary, Tump-line

Browbeat Badger, Bully, Butt, Cow, Hector, Nut

Brown(ed) Abram, Adust, Amber, Apricate, Auburn, Au gratin, Bay, Biscuit, Bisque, Bister, Bistre, Bole, Br, Braise, Brindle, Bronzed, Brunette, Bruno, Burnet, Burnt umber, Camel, Capability, Caramel, Caromel, Chamois, Cinnamon, Cook, Coromandel, Drab, Dun, Duncan, Fallow, Filemot, Fulvous, Fusc(ous), Grill, Hazel, Infuscate, Ivor, John, Khaki, Liver, March, Meadow, Mocha, Mousy, Mulatto, Mushroom, Nut, Ochre, Olive, Oxblood, Philamot, Rufous, Rugbeian, Russet, Rust, Scorch, Seal, Sepia, Sienna, Snuff, Soare, Sore, Sorrel, Spadiceous, Tan, Tawny, Tenné, Testaceous, Toast, Tom, Umber, Vandyke, Wallflower, Wholemeal, Windsor

Browne Sam

Brownie Dobbie, Dobby, Dobie, Goblin, Hob, Kobold, Leprechaun, Nis(se), Rosebud, Sprite

Browse(r) Graze, Netscape®, Pasture, Read, Scan, Stall-read, Surf

Bruce Robert

Bruise Contund, Contuse, Crush, Damage, Ding, Ecchymosis, Frush, Golp(e), Hurt, Intuse, Livedo, Lividity, Mark, Mouse, Pound, Purpure, Rainbow, Shiner, Ston(n), Stun, Surbate, Vibex

Brummagem Tatty

Brunette Dark, Latin

Brush (off), Brushwood Bavin, Bottle, Brake, Broom, Carbon, Chaparral, Clash, Clothes, Dandy, Dismiss, Dust, Encounter, Fan, Filbert, Filecard, Firth, Fitch, Frith, Grainer, Hag, Hagg, Hair-pencil, Hog, Kiss, Liner, Loofah, Mop, Paint, Pallet, Pig, Pope's head, Putois, Rebuff, Rice, Rigger, Sable, Scrap, Scrub, Scuff, Shaving, Skim, Striper, Thicket, Touch, Whisk, Wire

Brusque Abrupt, Blunt, Brief, Curt, Downright, Pithy, Short

Brussels Carpet, Lace

Brutal, Brute Animal, Barbaric, Beast, Bête, Caesar, Caliban, Cruel, Hun, Iguanodon, Inhuman, Nazi, Nero, Ostrogoth, Pitiless, Quagga, Rambo, Roughshod, Ruffian, Thresher-whale, Yahoo

Brutus Wig

Bryophyte Moss, Tree-moss

Bubble(s), Bubbly Air-bell, Air-lock, Barmy, Bead(ed), Bell, Bleb, Blister, Boil, Buller, Cavitate, Champagne, Cissing, Ebullition, Effervesce, Embolus, Enthuse, Espumoso, Foam, → FROTH, Gassy, Globule, Gurgle, Head, Magnetic, Mantle, Mississippi, Popple, Rale, Reputation, Roundel, Rowndell, Seed, Seethe, Simmer, Soap, South Sea, Vesicle, Widow

Bubble and squeak Colcannon

Buccaneer Corsair, Dampier, Drake, Freebooter, Morgan, Picaroon, Pirate

Buck (up) Bongo, Brace, Cheer, Dandy, Deer, Dollar, Elate, Encheer, Hart, Jerk, Leash, Male, Ourebi, Pitch, Pricket, Ram, Rusa, Sore, Sorel(l), Sorrel, Spade, Spay(a)d, → STAG, Staggard, Stud, Water, Wheel

Buckaroo Cowboy, Cowpoke

Bucket(s) Bail, Bale, Clamshell, Ice, Jacob's ladder, Kibble, Ladle, Noria, Pail, Piggin, Rust, Scuttle, Situla, Slop, Stoop(e), Stope, Stoup, Tub

Buckeye Ohio

Buckle Artois, Clasp, Contort, Crumple, Deform, Dent, Fasten, Warp

▷ **Buckle** *may indicate* an anagram

Buckle-beggar Patrico
Buckler Ancile, Rondache, → SHIELD, Targe
▷ **Bucks** *may indicate* an anagram
Buckshee Free
Buckthorn Cascara, Wahoo
Buckwheat Brank, Sarrasin, Sarrazin
Bucolic Aeglogue, Eglogue, Idyllic, Pastoral, Rural, Rustic
Bud(ding), Buddy Botoné, Bottony, Bulbil, Burgeon, Cacotopia, Clove, Cobber, Deb, Eye, Gem(ma), Germinate, Hibernaculum, Holly, Knop, Knosp, Knot, Nascent, Pal, Scion, Serial, Shoot, Sprout, Statoblast, Taste, Turion
Buddha, Buddhism, Buddhist Abhidhamma, Ahimsa, Amitabha, Anata, Anatta, Anicca, Arhat, Asoka, Bodhisattva, Dalai Lama, Dukkha, Esoteric, Foism, Gautama, Hinayana, Jain, Jataka, Jodo, Kagyu, Mahatma, Mahayana, Maitreya, Maya, Nichiren, Pali, Pitaka, Pure Land, Rinzai, Ryobu, Sakya-muni, Sangha, Shinto, Siddhartha Gautama, Sila, Soka Gakkai, Soto, Sutra, Tantric, Theravada, Tripitaka, Triratna, Vajrayana, Zen(o)
Budge Jee, Move, Stir, Submit
Budget Allocation, Estimate, Operating, Plan, Programme, Save, Shoestring
Buff Beige, Birthday suit, Eatanswill, Fan, Fawn, Nankeen, Natural, Nude, Nut, Polish, → RUB, Streak
Buffalo African, Anoa, Arna, Asiatic, Bison, Bonasus, Bugle, Cap, Cape, Carabao, Ox, Perplex, Takin, Tamarao, Tamarau, Timarau, Water, Zamouse
Buffer Bootblack, Cofferdam, Cutwater, Fender, Sleek-stone
Buffet Bang, Blow, Box, Carvery, Counter, Cuff, Finger-food, Fork luncheon, Fork-supper, Hit, Lam, Maltreat, Perpendicular, Shove, Sideboard, Smorgasborg, Strike, Strook(e)
Buffoon(ery) Antic, Clown, Droll, Goliard, Harlequin, Horseplay, Iniquity, Jester, Mime(r), Mome, Mountebank, Mummer, Nutter, Pantagruel, Pantaloon(ery), Pickle-herring, Pierrot, Punchinello, Scaramouch, Scogan, Scoggin, Scurrile, Slouch, Tomfool, Vice, Wag, Zany
Bug(s) Anoplura, Antagonise, Arthropod, Assassin, Bacteria, Bedevil, Beetle, Berry, Bishop's mitre, Cabbage, Capsid, Chinch, Cimex, Coccidae, Cockchafer, Corixid, Creepy-crawly, Croton, Damsel, Debris, Dictograph®, Eavesdrop, E-coli, Error, Germ, Ground, Harlequin, Hassle, Hemiptera, → INSECT, Jitter, June, Kissing, Lace, Lightning, Listeria, Maori, May, Mealy, Micrococcus, Mike, Millennium, Mite, Nettle, Pill, Reduviid, Rhododendron, Rile, Shield, Skeeter, Sow, Squash, Tap, Vex, Water-measurer, Wheel, Wiretap
Bugbear Anathema, Bête noire, Bogey, Bogle, Bogy, Eten, Ettin, Poker, Rawhead
Buggy Beach, Car, Cart, Pushchair, Shay, Tipcart, Trap
Bughouse Fleapit, Loco
Bugle, Bugle call Boots and saddles, Chamade, Clarion, Cornet, Flugelhorn, Hallali, Last post, Ox, Reveille, Taps, → TRUMPET, Urus
Build, Building(s), Building site Accrue, Anabolism, Ar(a)eostyle, Assemble, Bhavan, Big, Bricks and mortar, Capitol, Chapterhouse, Colosseum, Commons, Construction, Containment, Corncrib, Cot, → CREATE, Cruck, Curia, Develop, Dipteros, Drystone, Duplex, Edifice, Edify, Erect, Fabric, Heapstead, High-rise, Hut, Infill, Insula, Kaaba, Ken, Linhay, Listed, Low-rise, Lyceum, Minaret, Monopteron, Mould, Observatory, Odeon, Odeum, Outhouse, Palazzo, Pataka, Phalanstery, Phalanx, Pile, Portakabin®, Premises, Prytaneum, Quonset®, Raise, Ribbon, Rotunda, Skyscraper, Stance, Statehouse, Structure, Suspension, Synthesis, System, Tectonic, Telecottage, Temple, Tenement, Tholos, Tower,

Town hall, Triplex®, Whata

Builder Brick, Constructor, Engineer, Mason, Millwright, Stonemason, Waller

▷ **Building** *may indicate* an anagram

Bulb Camas(h), Camass, Chive, Cive, Corm, Flash, Globe, Lamp, Light, Olfactory, Pearl, Rupert's drop, Scallion, Set, Shallot, Squill

Bulge, Bulging Astrut, Bag, Bias, Biconvex, Bug, Bulbous, Bunchy, Cockle, Entasis, Expand, Exsert, Inion, Prolate, Protrude, Protuberant, Relievo, Rotund, Strout, Strut, → **SWELL**, Tumid

Bulk(y) Aggregate, Ample, Big, Body, Corpulent, Density, Extent, Gross, Hull, Immensity, Massive, Preponderance, Roughage, Scalar, → **SIZE**, Stout, Vol(ume), Weight

Bull(s), Bullock, Bully Anoa, Apis, Bakha, Beef, Blarney, Bludgeon, Bluster, Bouncer, Bovine, Brag, Brave, Browbeat, Buchis, Bucko, Centre, Cuttle, Despot, Dragoon, Drawcansir, Encierro, Englishman, Eretrian, Fancyman, Farnese, Flashman, Flatter, Gold, Gosh, Hapi, Harass, Hawcubite, Haze(r), Hector, Hoodlum, Huff, Intimidate, Investor, Iricism, Irish(ism), John, Killcow, Lambast, Maltreat, Merwer, Mick(e)(y), Mistake, Mithraism, Mohock, Nandi, Neat, Pamplona, Papal, Piker, Pistol, Placet, Poler, Rhodian, Roarer, Rot, Ruffian, Sitting, Souteneur, Stag, Stale, Strong-arm, Swash-buckler, Taurine, Taurus, Toitoi, Tommy-rot, Tosh, Trash, Tripe, Twaddle, Tyran(ne), Tyrannise, Tyrant, Unigenitus, Victimise, Winged, Zo(bo)

Bulldog Marshal, Tenacious

Bulldoze(r) Angledozer, Coerce, Earthmover, Leveller, Overturn

Bullet Ammo, Balata, Ball, Baton round, Biscayan, Blank, Dumdum, Fusillade, Lead towel, Magic, Minié, Minié ball, Missile, Pellet, Percussio, Plastic, Round, Rubber, Shot, Slug, Soft-nosed, Tracer

Bulletin All points, Memo, Message, Newscast, Newsletter, Report, Summary

Bull-fight(er) Banderillero, Banderillo, Corrida, Cuadrilla, Escamillo, Matador, Picador, Rejoneador, Tauromachy, Toreador, Torero

Bull-head Cottoid, Father-lasher, Pogge, Sea-poacher

Bull-rider Europa

Bull-roarer Rhombos, Tu(r)ndun

Bull's eye Carton, God, Humbug, Target

▶ **Bully** *see* **BULL**

Bulrush Pandanaceous, Raupo, Reed, Reed-mace, Tule

Bulwark Bastion, Defence, Rampart, Resistor

Bum Ass, Beg, Deadbeat, Prat, Sponge, Thumb, Tramp, Vagabond

Bumble Beadle, Bedel(l)

▷ **Bumble** *may indicate* an anagram

Bumboat woman Buttercup

Bumf Spam

Bump(er), Bumps Big, Blow, Bradyseism, Bucket, Clour, Collide, Dunch, Encephalocele, Fender, Hillock, Immense, Inian, Inion, Joll, Jo(u)le, Jowl, Keltie, Kelty, Knar, Knock, Mamilla, Mogul, Organ, Overrider®, Phrenology, Reveille, Rouse, Speed, Thump

Bumph Loo-roll

Bumpkin Bucolic, Bushwhacker, Clodhopper, Hawbuck, Hayseed, Hick, Jock, Lout, Oaf, Put(t), Rube, Rustic, Yokel, Zany

Bumptious Arrogant, Brash, Randie, Randy, Uppity

Bun Barmbrack, Bath, Black, Chelsea, Chignon, Chou, Currant, Devonshire split, Hot-cross, Huffkin, Mosbolletjie, Roll, Teacake, Toorie, Wad

Bunch Acinus, Anthology, Bob, Botryoid, Bouquet, Byndle, Cluster, Fascicle, Finial, Flock, → **GROUP**, Hand, Handful, Lot, Lump, Nosegay, Panicle, Raceme, Spray, Staphyline, Tassel, Tee, Truss, Tuft

Bundle Axoneme, Bale, Bavin, Bluey, Bottle, Byssus, Desmoid, Dorlach, Drum, Fag(g)ot, Fascicle, Fascine, Fibre, Fibrovascular, Kemple, Knitch, Lemniscus, Matilda, → **PACK(AGE)**, Parcel, Sack, Sheaf, Shiralee, Shock, Shook, Stook, Swag, Tie, Top, Trousseau, Truss, Vascular, Wad, Wadge, Wap

Bung Cork, Dook, Obturate, Plug, Stopgap, Stopper

Bungalow Dak

Bungle(r) Blunder, Blunk, Bodge, Boob, Botch, Bumble, Bummle, Dub, Duff, Fluff, Foozle, Foul, Foul up, Goof, Gum up, Mash, Mess, Mis(h)guggle, Muddle, Muff, Mull, Prat, Screw, Spoil

Bunk(er), Bunkum Abscond, Absquatulate, Balderdash, Baloney, Berth, Blah, Bolt, Casemate, Claptrap, Clio, Entrap, Guy, Hazard, History, Hokum, Humbug, Malarky, Nonsense, Rot, Sandtrap, Scuttle, Stokehold, Tosh, Trap, Tripe

Bunter Billy, Owl

Bunthorne Aesthete, Poet

Bunting Bird, Cirl, Flag, Fringilline, Ortolan, Snow, Streamer, Yellow-hammer, Yowley

Buoy (up) Bell, Breeches, Can, Dan, Daymark, Dolphin, Float, Life, Marker, Nun, Raft, Reassure, Ring, Seamark, Sonar, Sonobuoy, Spar, Sustain, Wreck

Buoyant Afloat, Blithe, Floaty, Resilient

Burble Blat, Gibber

Burden Albatross, Beare, Bob, Cargo, Cark, Chant, Chorus, Cross, Cumber, Deadweight, Drone, Droore, Encumber, Encumbrance, Fa-la, Fardel, Folderol, Fraught, Freight, Gist, Handicap, Hum, Lade, → **LOAD**, Lumber, Millstone, Monkey, Oercome, Onus, Oppress, Put-upon, Refrain, Rumbelow, Saddle, Servitude, Shanty, Substance, Tax, Tenor, Torch, Trouble, Weight, White man's, Woe, Yoke

Burdensome Irksome, Onerous, Oppressive, Weighty

Burdock Clote(-bar), Clothur, Cockle-bar, Hardoke, Weed

Bureau Agency, Agitprop, Breakfront, Cominform, Davenport, Desk, Interpol, Kominform, Marriage, → **OFFICE**, Volunteer

Bureaucracy, Bureaucrat(ic) CS, Impersonal, Jack-in-office, Mandarin, Red tape, Tapist, Wallah

Burgeon(ing) Asprout, Blossom, Bud, Grow, Sprout

Burgess, Burgher Citizen, Freeman

Burgh Parliamentary, Police, Royal

Burglar, Burgle Area-sneak, Cat, Crack(sman), House-breaker, Intruder, Peterman, Picklock, Raffles, Robber, Screw, Thief, Yegg

Burgundy Macon, Vin

Burial(place) Catacomb, Charnel, Committal, Crypt, Cubiculum, Darga, Funeral, God's acre, Golgotha, Grave, Interment, Kurgan, Lair, Last rites, Sepulchre, Sepulture, Tomb, Tumulus, Vault, Zoothapsis

Burin Graver

Burlesque Caricatura, Caricature, Comedy, Farce, Heroicomical, Hudibrastic(s), Hurlo-thrumbo, Lampoon, Macaronic, Parody, Satire, Skimmington, Skit, Spoof, Travesty

Burlington RA

Burly Bluff, Stout, Strapping

Burmese Karen(ni), Mon(-Khmer), Naga, Shan

Burn(er), Burning, Burnt Adust, Afire, Alow(e), Ardent, Argand, Arson, Ash,

Auto-da-fé, Bats-wing, Beck, Bishop, Blaze, Blister, Blowtorch, Brand, Bren(ne), Brent, Brook, Bunsen, Causalgia, Caustic, Cauterise, Char, Chark, Chinese, Cinder, Coal, Coke, Combust, Conflagration, Cremate, Crozzled, Crucial, Deflagrate, Destruct, Eilding, Ember, Emboil, Empyreuma, Fervid, Fircone, → **FIRE**, Fishtail, Flagrant, Flare, Flash, Fresh(et), Gleed, Gut, Holocaust, Ignite, In, Incendiary, Incense, Incinerate, Inure, Inust(ion), Itch, Kill, Live, Lunt, Offering, On, Oxidise, Oxyacetylene, Pilot, Plo(a)t, Powder, Pyric, Pyromania, Rill, Sati, Scald, Scorch, Scouther, Scowder, Scowther, Sear, Sienna, Sike, Singe, Sizzle, Smart, Smoulder, Suttee, Swale, Third-degree, Thurible, Torch, Umber, Urent, Ustion, Ustulation, Weeke, Welsbach, Wick

Burp Belch

Burr(ing) Brei, Brey, Clote, Croup, Dialect, Knob, Rhotacism

Burrow(er), Burrowing Dig, Earth, Fossorial, Gopher, Groundhog, Hole, How, Howk, Mole, Nuzzle, Root, Sett, Terricole, Tunnel, Viscacha, Warren, Wombat, Worm

Bursar(y) Camerlengo, Camerlingo, Coffers, Grant, Purser, Scholarship, Tertiary, Treasurer

Bursitis Beat

Burst(ing) Blowout, Brast, Break, Dehisce, Disrupt, Dissilient, Ebullient, Erumpent, Erupt, → **EXPLODE**, Flare-up, Fly, Implode, Pop, Sforzato, Shatter, Spasm, Spirt, Split, Sprint, Spurt, Stave, Tetterous

Bury Cover, Eard, Earth, Embowel, Engrave, Enhearse, Graff, Graft, Imbed, Inearth, Inhearse, Inherce, Inhume, Inter, Inurn, Landfill, Repress, Sepulture, Sink, Ye(a)rd, Yird

Bus Aero, Bandwagon, Car, Charabanc, Coach, Crew, Double-decker, Greyhound, Hondey, Hopper, ISA, Jitney, Mammy-wagon, Purdah, Rattletrap, Single-decker, Tramcar, Trolley, Walking

Bus conductor Cad, Clippy

Bush(y), Bush-man Bitou, Bramble, Brier, Bullace, Busket, Calico, Clump, Cotton, Dumose, Firethorn, Hawthorn, Hibiscus, Ivy-tod, Kapok, Kiekie, Mallee, Matagouri, Mulberry, Outback, Poinsettia, Poly-poly, President, Prostanthera, Sallee, San, Shepherd, Shrub, Sloe, Sugar, Thicket, Tire, Tod(de), Tumatakuru

Bush-baby Durukuli, Galago, Nagapie, Night-ape

Bushel Ardeb, Bu, Co(o)mb, Cor, Ephah, Fou, Homer, Peck, Weight, Wey

Bushwalker Hoon

Business Affair, Agency, Biz, Bricks and clicks, Brokerage, Bus, Cartel, Cerne, Chaebol(s), Co, Commerce, Company, Concern, Conglomerate, Craft, Duty, Enterprise, Ergon, Establishment, Exchange, Fasti, Firm, Funny, Game, Gear, Hong, Industry, Lifestyle, Line, Métier, Monkey, Office, Palaver, Pi(d)geon, Pidgin, Practice, Professional, Racket, Shebang, Shop, Show, To-do, Trade, Traffic, Transaction, Tread, Turnover, Unincorporated, Vocation, Zaibatsu, Zaikai

Businessman Babbitt, Capitalist, City, Entrepreneur, Financier, Realtor, Taipan, Trader, Tycoon

Busk(er) Bodice, Corset, Entertainer, German-band

Buskin(s) Brod(e)kin, Cothurn(us), Shoe

Buss Kiss, Osculate, Smack

Bussu Troelie, Troely, Troolie

Bust Beano, Boob, Brast, Break, Chest, Falsies, Figurehead, Herm(a), Insolvent, Mamma, Rupture, Sculp, Shatter(ed), Spree, Statue, Term(inus), To-tear, To-torne, Ups(e)y

▷ **Bust** *may indicate* an anagram

Bustard Bird, Otis, Turkey

Buster Keaton

Bustle Ado, Beetle, Do, Dress-improver, Flap, Pad, Scurry, → **STIR**, Swarm, Tournure, Whew

Busy Active, At (it), Deedy, → **DETECTIVE**, Dick, Eident, Employ, Engaged, Ergate, Eye, Goer, Hectic, Hive, Humming, Occupied, Ornate, Prodnose, Stir, Stirabout, Tec, Throng, Worksome

Busybody Bustler, Meddler, Noser, Pragmatic, Snooper, Trout, Yenta

But Aber, Algates, Bar, Except, However, Keg, Merely, Nay, Only, Save, Sed, Simply, Tun, Without

Butch He-man, Macho

Butcher(y) Cumberland, Decko, Dekko, Flesher, Ice, Kill, Killcow, Look, Massacre, Ovicide, Sever, Shambles, Shochet, Shufti, Slaughter, Slay, Slink

Butler Bedivere, Bread-chipper, Jeeves, Khansama(h), Major-domo, RAB, Rhett, Samuel, Servant, Sewer, Sommelier, Steward

Butt (in) Aris, Barrel, Bumper, Bunt, Clara, Dimp, Dunch, Enter, Geck, Glasgow kiss, Goat, Header, Horn, Jesting-stock, Laughing-stock, Mark, Nut, Outspeckle, Pantaloon, Pipe, Push, Ram, Roach, Scapegoat, Snipe, Stompie, → **STOOGE**, Straight man, Stump, Target, Tun, Ups

Butter Adulation, Apple, Billy, Brandy, Butyric, Cacao, Cocoa, Coconut, Drawn, Flatter, Galam, Garcinia, Ghee, Ghi, Goa, Goat, Illipi, Illupi, Kokum, Mahua, Mahwa, Maitre d'hotel, Mow(r)a, Nut, Nutter, Palm, Pat, Peanut, Print, Ram, Rum, Scrape, Shea, Spread, Vegetable

▷ **Butter** *may indicate* a goat or such

Buttercup Bumboat woman, Crow-foot, Crow-toe, Goldilocks, Ranunculus, Reate, Thalictrum

Butterfingers Muff

Butterfish Nine-eyes

Butterfly Apollo, Argus, Birdwing, Blue, Brimstone, Brown, Cabbage white, Camberwell beauty, Cardinal, Chequered skipper, Cleopatra, Clouded yellow, Comma, Common blue, Copper, Dilettante, Eclosion, Emperor, Fritillary, Gate-keeper, Grayling, Hair-streak, Heath, Hesperid, Imaginal, Kallima, Large copper, Large white, Leaf, Lycaena, Marbled-white, Meadow brown, Milk-weed, Monarch, Morpho, Mourning-cloak, Nerves, Nymphalid, Nymphean, Orange-tip, Owl, Painted lady, Papilionidae, Peacock, Pieris, Psyche, Purple emperor, Red admiral, Rhopalocera, Ringlet, Satyr(idae), Satyrinae, Scotch argus, Silverspot, Skipper, Small white, Speckled wood, Stamper, Sulphur, Swallow-tail, Thecla, Thistle, Tiger swallowtail, Tortoiseshell, Two-tailed pasha, Vanessa, Wall brown, White admiral

Buttermilk Bland, Lassi

Butternut Souari

Butter-tree Mahua, Mahwa, Mow(r)a

Buttocks Aristotle, Arse, Ass, Bahookie, Booty, Bottom, Can, Coit, Derrière, Doup, Duff, Fanny, Fundament, Gluteus maximus, Heinie, Hinder-end, Hinderlan(d)s, Hurdies, Jacksie, Jacksy, Keester, Keister, Mooning, Nache, Nates, Posterior, Prat, Quoit, Seat, Tush

Button(s) Barrel, Bellboy, Fastener, Frog, Hot, Knob, Mute, Netsuke, Olivet, Page(boy), Panic, Pearl, Press, Push, Snooze, Stud, Switch, Toggle, Toolbar

Buttonhole Accost, Boutonniere, Detain, Doorstep, Eye, Flower

Buttress Brace, Counterfort, Flying, Hanging, Pier, Prop, Stay, Support, Tambour

Butty Chum, Oppo

Buxom Bonnie, Busty, Plump, Sonsy, Well-endowed
Buy(ing), Buyer Believe, Bribe, Coemption, Coff, Corner, Customer, Emption, Engross, Impulse, Monopsonist, Oligopsony, Panic, Purchase, Redeem, Regrate, Shop, Shout, Spend, Take, Trade, Vendee
▷ **Buyer** *may indicate* money
Buzz(er) Bee, Birr, Bombilate, Bombinate, Button, Fly, Hum, Rumour, Scram, Whirr, Whisper, Zed, Zing, Zoom
Buzzard Bee-kite, Bird, Buteo, Hawk, Honey, Pern, Puttock, Turkey, Vulture
By Alongside, At, Gin, Gone, In, Near, Neighbouring, Nigh, Of, On, Past, Per, Through, With, X
Bye Extra
Bye-bye Adieu, Farewell, Tata
Bygone B.C., Dead, Departed, Past, Yore
By Jove Egad
Bypass Avoid, Circuit, Coronary, → **DETOUR**, Evade, Ignore, Omit, Shunt, Skirt
By-product Epiphenomenon, Spill-over, Spin-off
Byre Cowshed, Manger, Stable, Trough
By so much The
Byte Nybble
By the way Apropos, Incidentally, Obiter
Byway Alley, Lane, Path
Byword Ayword, Nayword, Phrase, Proverb, Slogan
Byzantine Catapan, Comnenus, Complicated, Exarch, Intricate, Intrince, Theme

Cc

C Around, Caught, Celsius, Cent, Centigrade, Charlie, Conservative, San

Cab Boneshaker, Crawler, Drosky, Fiacre, Four-wheeler, Growler, Gurney, Hackney, Hansom, Mini, Noddy, Taxi, Vettura

Cabal(ler) Arlington, Ashley, Buckingham, Clifford, Clique, Conspiracy, Coterie, Faction, Junto, Lauderdale, Party, Plot

Cab(b)alistic Abraxis, Mystic, Notarikon, Occult

Cabaret Burlesque, Floorshow

Cabbage(-head), Cabbage soup Bok choy, Borecole, Brassica, Castock, Cauliflower, Cavalo nero, Chinese, Choucroute, Cole, Collard, Crout, Custock, Drumhead, Gobi, Kerguelen, Kohlrabi, Kraut, Loaf, Loave, Pak-choi, Pamphrey, Pe-tsai, Sauerkraut, Savoy, Shchi, Shtchi, Skunk, Thieve, Turnip, Wild, Wort

Caber Fir, Janker, Log, Sting

Cabin Berth, Bibby, Bothy, Box, Cabana, Caboose, Camboose, Coach, Cottage, Crannog, Crib, Cuddy, Den, Gondola, Hovel, Hut, Izba, Lodge, Loghouse, Long-house, Pod, Pressure, Room, Roundhouse, Saloon, Shanty, Stateroom, Trunk

Cabin-boy Grummet

Cabinet Armoire, Bahut, Cabale, Case, Cellaret, Chiffonier, Closet, Commode, Console, Cupboard, Filing, Kitchen, Ministry, Secretaire, Shadow, Shrinal, Unit, Vitrine

Cabinet maker Chippendale, Ebeniste, Hepplewhite, Joiner, PM

Cable(way), Cable-car Chain, Coax(ial), Extension, Flex, Halser, Hawser, Jumper, Jump leads, Junk, Landline, Lead, Lead-in, Lifeline, Null-modern, Oil-filled, Outhaul, Outhauler, Rope, Shroud, Slatch, Snake, Téléférique, → **TELEGRAM**, Telegraph, Telepherique, Telpher(age), Topping lift, Trunking, Wire, Yoke

Cache Deposit, Hidlin(g)s, → **HOARD**, Inter, Stash, Store, Treasure

Cachet Prestige

Cackle Cluck, Gaggle, Gas, Haw, Snicker, Titter

Cacography Scrawl

Cacophony Babel, Caterwaul, Charivari, Discord, Jangle

Cactus, Cactus-like Alhagi, Barel, Cereus, Cholla, Christmas, Dildo, Easter, Echino-, Hedgehog, Jointed, Jojoba, Maguey, Mescal, Mistletoe, Nopal, Ocotillo, Opuntia, Organ-pipe, Peyote, Pitahaya, Prickly pear, Retama, Saguaro, Stapelia, Star, Strawberry, Torch-thistle, Tuna, Xerophytic

Cad Base, Boor, Bounder, Churl, Cocoa, Heel, Oik, Rascal, Rotter, Skunk, Varlet

Cadaver(ous) Body, Corpse, Deathly, Ghastly, Goner, Haggard, Stiff

Caddy Porter, Tea, Teapoy

Cadence Beat, Close, Euouae, Evovae, Fa-do, Flow, Lilt, Meter, Perfect, Plagal, Rhythm

Cadenza Fireworks

Cadet(s) Junior, OTC, Plebe, Recruit, Rookie, Scion, Snooker, Space, Syen, Trainee, Younger

Cadge(r) Bludge, Bot, Bum, Impose, Mutch, → SCROUNGE, Sponge
Cadmium Cd
Caesar Nero
Caesium Cs
Café(teria) Automat, Bistro, Brasserie, Buvette, Canteen, Commissary, Cybercafe, Diner, Dinette, Donko, Eatery, Estaminet, Filtré, Greasy spoon, Hashhouse, Internet, Juke joint, Netcafé, Pizzeria, Pull-in, Snackbar, Tearoom, Transport, Truckstop
Cage Bar, Battery, Box, Cavie, Confine, Coop, Corf, Dray, Drey, Enmew, Faraday, Fold, Frame, Grate, Hutch, Keavie, Mew, Mortsafe, Pen, → PRISON, Safety, Squirrel, Trave
Cahoots Hugger-mugger
Cairn Barp, Clearance, Dog, Horned, Man, Mound, Raise
Caisson Bends
Caitiff Meanie
Cajole(ry) Beflum, Beguile, Blandish, Blarney, Carn(e)y, → COAX, Cuittle, Humbug, Inveigle, Jolly, Persuade, Wheedle, Whilly, Wiles
Cake Agnus dei, Angel, Baba, Babka, Baklava, Banbury, Bannock, Bara brith, Barmbrack, Battenberg, Birthday, Brioche, Brownie, Buckwheat, Bun, Carcake, Cattle, Chapat(t)i, Chillada, Chupati, Chupattie, Chupatty, Clapbread, Clot, Coburg, Cookie, Corn dodger, Cotton, Croquante, Croquette, Cruller, Crumpet, Currant, Dainty, Devil's food, Drizzle, Dundee, Eccles, Eclair, Fancy, Farl(e), Filter, Fish, Flapjack, Frangipane, Frangipani, Fritter, Galette, Genoa, Gingerbread, Girdle, → HARDEN, Hockey, Hoe, Idli, Jannock, Johnny, Jumbal, Jumbles, Koeksister, Kruller, Kuchen, Kueh, Lamington, Lardy, Latke, Layer, Linseed, Macaroon, Madeira, Madeleine, Maid of honour, Marble, Meringue, Millefeuille, Mud, Muffin, Napoleon, Nut, Oatmeal, Oil, Pan, Panettone, Paratha, Parkin, Parliament, Pastry, Pat, Patty, Pavlova, Pepper, Petit four, Pikelet, → PLASTER, Pomfret, Pone, Pontefract, Poori, Popover, Pound, Profiterole, Puff, Puftaloon(a), Puri, Queencake, Ratafia, Ready-mix, Religieuse, Rice, Rock, Rosti, Roti, Rout, Rum baba, Rusk, Sachertorte, Saffron, Sally Lunn, Salt, Sandwich, Savarin, Scone, Seed, Set, Simnel, Singing-hinny, Slab, Slapjack, Soul, Spawn, Spice, Sponge, Stollen, Stottie, Sushi, Swiss roll, Tablet, Tansy, Tea(bread), Tipsy, Torte, Tortilla, Twelfth, Upside down, Vetkoek, Wad, Wafer, Waffle, Wedding, Wonder, Yeast, Yule log
▷ **Cake** *may indicate* an anagram
Cake-shaped Placentiform
Cakestand Curate
Cakewalk Doddle
Calaboose Jail, Loghouse
Calamitous, Calamity Blow, Catastrophe, Dire, → DISASTER, Distress, Fatal, Ill, Jane, Ruth, Storm, Tragic, Unlucky, Visitation, Woe
Calcareous Ganoin, Lithite
Calcium Ca, Colemanite, Dogger, Dripstone, Otolith, Quicklime, Scawtite, Whewellite
Calculate(d), Calculation, Calculator Abacus, Actuary, Comptometer, Compute(r), Cost, Design, Estimate, Extrapolate, Log, Napier's bones, Number-crunch, Prorate, Quip(p)u, Rate, → RECKON, Slide-rule, Sofar, Soroban, Tactical, Tell
Calculus Cholelith, Differential, Functional, Infinitesimal, Integral, Lambda, Lith, Lithiasis, Predicate, Propositional, Science, Sentential, Sialolith, Stone, Tartar, Urolith
Caledonian Kanak

Calendar Advent, Agenda, Almanac, Chinese, Diary, Fasti, Gregorian, Hebrew, Intercalary, Jewish, Journal, Julian, Luach, Lunisolar, Menology, Newgate, New Style, Ordo, Perpetual, Revolutionary, Roman, Sothic

Calender(ing) Dervish, Mangle, Swissing

Calf Ass, Bobby, Box, Cf, Deacon, Divinity, Dogie, Dogy, Freemartin, Golden, Law, Leg, Maverick, Mottled, Poddy, Sleeper, Slink, Smooth, Stirk, Sural, Tollie, Tolly, Tree, Veal, Vitular

Caliban Moon-calf

Calibrate, Calibre Bore, Capacity, Graduate, Mark, → QUALITY, Text

Californium Cf

Caliph Abbasid(e), Omar, Vathek

Call(ed), Calling, Call on, Call up Adhan, Appeal, Arraign, Art, Awaken, Azan, Banco, Bawl, Beck, Behote, Bevy, Bid, Boots and saddles, Business, Buzz, Career, Chamade, Cite, Claim, Clang, Clarion, Cleep, Clepe, Close, Cold, Conference, Conscript, Convene, Convoke, Cooee, Cry, Curtain, Dial, Drift, Dub, Evoke, Gam, Go, Hail, Hallali, Haro, Heads, Heave-ho, Hech, Hete, Hey, Hight, Ho, Hot(e), Howzat, Huddup, Hurra(h), Invocation, Job, Junk, Last (post), Line, Local, Margin, Métier, Misère, Mobilise, Mot, Name, Nap, Need, Nemn, Nempt, Nominate, No trumps, Olé, Page, Peter, Phone, Photo, Post, Proo, Pruh, Pursuit, Rechate, Recheat, Retreat, Reveille, Ring, Roll, Rort, Rouse, Route, Sa-sa, See, Sennet, → SHOUT, Shut-out, Slam, Slander, Slogan, Soho, Sola, SOS, STD, Style, Subpoena, Summon(s), Tails, Tantivy, Taps, Telephone, Term, Toho, Toll, Trumpet, Trunk, Visit, Vocation, Waken, Wake-up, Whoa-ho-ho, Wo ha ho, Yell, Yo, Yodel, Yodle, Yo-ho(-ho), Yoicks, Yoo-hoo

Calla(s) Aroid, Lily, Maria

Caller Fresh, Guest, Herring, Inspector, Muezzin, Rep, Traveller, → VISITOR

Calligraphy Kakemono

Callipers Odd legs

Callisthenics T'ai chi (ch'uan)

Callosity, Call(o)us Bunion, Cold, Corn, Hard, Horny, Obtuse, Ringbone, Seg, Thylose, Tough, Tylosis, Unfeeling

Callow Crude, Green, Immature, Jejune

Calm Abate, Alegge, Aleye, Allay, Allege, Appease, Ataraxy, Composed, Cool, Doldrums, Easy, Easy-osy, Eevn, Equable, Equanimity, Even, Eye, Flat, Glassy, Halcyon, Loun(d), Lown(d), Lull, Mellow, Mild, Milden, Millpond, Nonchalant, Pacify, Peaceable, Peaceful, Philosophical, Phlegmatic, Placate, Placid, Quell, Quiet, Relax(ed), Repose, Restrained, Seraphic, Serena, Serene, Settle, Simmer down, Sleek, → SOOTHE, Sopite, Steady, Still, Stilly, Subside, Tranquil(lise), Unturbid, Windless

Calorie Gram, Kilogram

Calumniate, Calumny Aspersion, Backbite, Defame, Libel, Malign, Sclaunder, Slander, Slur

Calvary Golgotha

Calvin(ist) Accusative, Coolidge, Genevan, Hopkins, Huguenot, Infralapsarian, Predestination, Sublapsarian, Supralapsarian

Calydonian Boar

Calypso Ogygia, Siren, Soca, Sokah, → SONG

Cam Cog, River, Snail, Tappet

Camaraderie Fellowship, Rapport, Team spirit

Camber Hog, Slope

Cambium Phellogen

Cambodian Khmer (Rouge), Montagnard
Cambria(n) Menevian, Wales
Cambridge Cantab, Squat, Uni
Came Arrived
Camel, Camel train Aeroplane, Arabian, Artiodactyla, Bactrian, Caisson, Colt, Dromedary, Kafila, Llama, Oont, Sopwith, Tulu
Cameo Anaglyph, Camaieu, Carving
Camera, Camera man All-round, Box, Brownie®, Camcorder, Candid, Chambers, Cine, Compact, Digital, Disc, Electron, Flash, Gamma, Gatso®, Grip(s), Iconoscope, Instant, Kodak®, Lucida, Miniature, Minicam, Movie, Nannycam, Obscura, Orthicon, Palmcorder, Panoramic, Pantoscope, Periphery, Phone-cam, Pinhole, Polaroid®, Process, Programmed, Reflex, Retina, Schmidt, SLR, Somascope, Speed, Spycam, Steadicam®, Stop-frame, Subminiature, Video, Vidicon, Viewfinder, Webcam
Camouflage Conceal, → DISGUISE, Mark, Maskirovka, War-dress
▷ **Camouflaged** *may indicate an anagram*
Camp(er) Affectation, Aldershot, Auschwitz, Banal, Base, Belsen, Bivouac, Boma, Boot, Buchenwald, Caerleon, Cantonment, Castral, Colditz, Concentration, Dachau, David, Death, Depot, D(o)uar, Dumdum, Epicene, Faction, Fat, Flaunt, Gulag, Happy, Health, High, Holiday, L(a)ager, Labour, Lashkar, Leaguer, Low, Manyat(t)a, Motor, Oflag, Outlie, Peace, Prison, Side, Siwash, Stagey, Stalag, Stative, Swagman, Tent, Theatrical, Transit, Treblinka, Valley Forge, Work, Zare(e)ba, Zariba, Zereba, Zeriba
Campaign(er) Barnstorm, Battle, Blitz, Blitzkrieg, Canvass, Crusade, Doorknock, Drive, Field, Jihad, Lobby, Mission, Offensive, Pankhurst, Promotion, Roadshow, Run, Satyagraha, Smear, Stint, Strategist, The stump, Tree-hugger, Venture, Veteran, War, Warray, Warrey, Whispering, Whistle-stop, Witchhunt
Campanula Rampion
Campeador Chief, Cid
Camp-follower Lascar, Leaguer-lady, Leaguer-lass, Sutler
Camphor Menthol
Campion Knap-bottle, Lychnis, Ragged robin, Silene
▷ **Camptown** *may indicate* de-
Can(s) Able, Billy, Bog, Capable, Churn, Cooler, Dow, Gaol, Garbage, Gents, Headphones, Is able, Jerry, Jug, Karsy, Loo, May, Nick, Pail, Pot, Preserve, → PRISON, Privy, Six-pack, Stir, Tank, Tin, Trash, Watering
Canada, Canadian Abenaki, Acadian, Bella Bella, Bella Coola, Beothuk, Bois-brûlé, Canuck, Comox, Dene, Dogrib, Hare, Heiltsuk, Herring choker, Inuit, Johnny Canuck, Joual, Maliseet, Metis, Montagnais, Naskapi, Nuxalk, Péquiste, Quebeccer, Quebecker, Québecois, Salishan, Salteaux, Saulteaux, Slavey, Stoney, Tsimshian, Ungava, Yukon
Canal Alimentary, Ampul, Anal, Birth, Caledonian, Channel, Conduit, Corinth, Cruiseway, Da Yunhe, Duct, Duodenum, Ea, Enteron, Erie, Foss(e), Gota, Grand (Trunk), Grande Terre, Grand Union, Groove, Gut, Haversian, Houston Ship, Kiel, Klong, Labyrinth, Lode, Manchester Ship, Meatus, Midi, Mittelland, Moscow, Navigation, New York State Barge, Oesophagus, Panama, Pharynx, Pipe, Pound, Regent's, Resin, Rhine-Herne, Ring, Root, Sault Sainte Marie, Scala, Schlemm's, Semi-circular, Ship, Shipway, Soo, Spinal, Stone, Suez, Suo, Urethra, Vagina, Waterway, Welland, Zanja
Canal-boat Barge, Fly-boat, Gondola, Vaporetto
Canapé Cate, Snack, Titbit

Canary Bird, Grass, Roller, Serin, Singer, Yellow

Cancel(led) Abrogate, Adeem, Annul, Counteract, Countermand, Cross, Delete, Destroy, Erase, Kill, Negate, Nullify, Obliterate, Override, Rained off, Red line, Remit, Repeal, Rescind, Retrait, Revoke, Scrub, Undo, Unmake, Void, Wipe, Write off

Cancer(ian), Cancerous Big C, Carcinoma, Crab, Curse, Kaposi's sarcoma, Leukaemia, Lymphoma, Moon child, Oat-cell, Oncogenic, Tropic, Tumour, Wolf

Candela Cd

▶ **Candelabra** see **CANDLE(STICK)**

Candid, Candour Albedo, Blunt, Camera, Franchise, Frank, Honesty, Open, Outspoken, Plain(-spoken), Round, Upfront

Candida Fungus

Candidate(s) Agrege, Applicant, Aspirant, Contestant, Entrant, Field, Nomenklatura, Nominee, Office-seeker, Ordinand, Postulant, Running mate, Stalking horse, Testee

Candied, Candy Angelica, Caramel, Cotton, Eryngo, Eye, Glace, Maple, Rock, Snow, Succade, Sugar, → **SWEET**

Candle(stick), Candelabra Amandine, Bougie, Chanukiah, C(i)erge, Dip, Fetch, Girandole, Hanukiah, International, Jesse, Lampadary, Light, Long-sixes, Menorah, Mould, New, Padella, Paschal, Pricket, Roman, Rushlight, Sconce, Serge, Shammash, Shammes, Shortsix, Slut, Sperm, Standard, Tace, Tallow, Tallow-dip, Taper, Tea-light, Torchère, Tricerion, Vigil light, Wax, Waxlight

Candlefish Eulachon, Oolakon, Oulachon, Oulakon, Ulic(h)an, Ulic(h)on, Ulikon

▶ **Candy** see **CANDIED**

Cane Arrow, Baculine, Bamboo, Baste, Beat, Birk, Crabstick, Dari, Dhurra, Doura, Dur(r)a, Ferula, Ferule, Goor, Gur, Jambee, Malacca, Narthex, Penang-lawyer, Pointer, Raspberry, Rat(t)an, Rod, Split, Stick, Sugar, Swagger-stick, Swish, Switch, Swordstick, Tan, Tickler, Vare, Wand, Whangee, Wicker(-work)

Canine Biter, C, Dhole, Dog, Eye-tooth

Canker Corrosion, Curse, Lesion, Ulcer

Cannabis Benj, Bhang, Bifter, Blow, Boneset, Durban poison, Ganja, Ganny, Grass, Hash, Hemp, Henry, Louie, Number, Pot, Skunk, Zol

Cannibal Anthropophagus, Heathen, Long pig, Man-eater, Ogre, Thyestean, Wendigo

Cannon Amusette, Barrage, Basilisk, Bombard, Breechloader, Carom, Carronade, Chaser, Collide, Criterion, Culverin, Drake, Drop, Falcon, Gun, Howitzer, Kiss, Long-tom, Loose, Monkey, Mons Meg, Nursery, Oerlikon, Saker, Stern-chaser, Water, Zamboorak, Zomboruk, Zumbooru(c)k

Cannot Canna, Cant, Downa(e), Downay

Canny Careful, Frugal, Prudent, Scot, Shrewd, Slee, Sly, Thrifty, Wice, Wily, Wise

Canoe(ist) Bidarka, Bidarkee, Canader, Canadian, Dugout, Faltboat, Kayak, Log, Mokoro, Monoxylon, Montaria, Oomiack, Paddler, Peterborough, Piragua, Pirogue, Rob Roy, Surf, Waka, Woodskin

Canon(ise) Austin, Besaint, Brocard, Camera, Cancrizens, Chapter, Chasuble, Code, Crab, Infinite, Isidorian, → **LAW**, Line, Mathurin(e), Minor, Nocturn, Norbertine, Nursery, Pitaka, Polyphony, Prebendary, Precept, Premonstrant, Premonstratensian, Retrograde, Rota, Round, Rule, Square, Squier, Squire, Standard, Tenet, Unity, White

Canopy Awning, Baldachin, Baldaquin, Chuppah, Ciborium, Clamshell, Dais, He(a)rse, Huppah, Majesty, Marquee, Marquise, Pavilion, Shamiana(h), State, Tabernacle, Tent, Tester, Veranda(h)

Cant Argot, Bevel, Heel, Incline, Jargon, Mummery, Patois, Patter, Rogue's Latin, Shelta, Slang, Slope, Snivel, Snuffle, Tip

Cantankerous Cussed, Fire-eater, Ornery, Querulous, Testy, Tetchy

Cantata Kinderspiel, Motet, Tobacco

Canteen Chuck-wagon, Mess, Munga, Naafi

Canter Amble, Hypocrite, Jog, Lope, Run, Tit(t)up, Tripple

Canto Air, Fit(te), Fitt, Fytte, Melody, Verse

Canton Aargau, Appenzell, Basle, District, Eyalet, Fribourg, Glarus, Graubunden, Jura, Lucerne, Neuchatel, Quarter, St Gall, Schaffhausen, Schwyz, Solothurn, Thurgau, Ticino, Unterwalden, Uri, Valais, Vaud, Zug, Zurich

Cantor Haz(z)an

Cantred Commot(e)

Canvas Awning, Binca®, Burlap, Dra(b)bler, Fly-sheet, Lug-sail, Mainsail, Marquee, Oil-cloth, Paint, Raven's-duck, Reef, → **SAIL**, Staysail, Stuns(ai)l, Tent, Trysail, Wigan, Woolpack

Canvass(er), Canvassing Agent, Doorstep, Drum, Mainstreeting, Poll, Solicit

▷ **Canvasser** *may indicate* a painter or a camper

Canyon Box, Canada, Defile, Grand, Grand Coulee, Nal(l)a, Nallah, Submarine

Cap(ped) Abacot, Amorce, Balaclava, Balmoral, Barret, Baseball, Bathing, Bellhop, Bendigo, Ber(r)et, Biggin, Biretta, Black, Blakey, Blue, Blue-bonnet, Bonnet-rouge, Bycoket, Call, Calotte, Calpac(k), Calyptrate, Capeline, Caul, Chaco, Chape, Chapeau, Chaperon, Chapka, Chechia, Cheese-cutter, Cloth, Cockernony, Coif, College, Coonskin, Cope, Cornet, Cowl, Cradle, Crest, → **CROWN**, Czapka, Davy Crockett, Deerstalker, Dunce's, Dutch, Fatigue, Ferrule, Filler, Flat, Fool's, Forage, Gandhi, Garrison, Gimme, Glengarry, Grannie, Granny, → **HAT**, Havelock, Hummel bonnet, Iceberg, International, Jockey, Juliet, Kalpak, Kepi, Kilmarnock, Kippa, Kippoth, Kipput, Kiss-me(-quick), Knee, Legal, Liberty, Lid, Mob, Monmouth, Monteer, Montero, Mor(r)ion, Mortar-board, Muffin, Mutch, Newsboy, Night, Outdo, Pagri, Patellar, Percussion, Perplex, Phrygian, Pile, Pileus, Pinner, Polar, Puggaree, Quoif, Root, Schapska, Shako, Skullcap, Square, Squirrel-tail, Statute, Stocking, Summit, → **SURPASS**, Taj, Tam(-o'-shanter), Thimble, Thinking, Thrum, Toe, Toorie, Top, Toque, Toy, Trenchard, Trencher, Truck, Tuque, Turk's, Watch, Wishing, Yarmulka, Yarmulke, Zuchetto

Capable, Capability Able, Brown, Capacity, Competent, Deft, Effectual, Efficient, Firepower, Qualified, Skilled, Susceptible, Up to

Capacitance, Capacity Ability, Aptitude, C, Cab, Carrying, Competence, Content, Cor, Cubic, Endowment, Function, Gift, Legal, Limit, Log, Potency, Potential, Power, Qua, Rated, Receipt, Scope, Size, Skinful, Tankage, Thermal, Tonnage, Valence, Vital, Volume

Caparison Robe, Trap(pings)

Cape Agulhas, Almuce, Blanc(o), Bon, Burnouse, Byron, Calimere Point, Canaveral, Canso, Cardinal, Chelyuskin, Cloak, Cod, Comorin, Delgado, Dezhnev, Domino, Dungeness, East(ern), Fairweather, Faldetta, Fanion, Fanon, Farewell, Fear, Fichu, Finisterre, Flattery, Gallinas Point, Good Hope, Guardafui, Harp, Hatteras, Head(land), Helles, Hoe, Hogh, Hook of Holland, Horn, Inverness, Kennedy, Leeuwin, Lindesnes, Lizard, Manteel, Mant(e)let, Mantilla, Mantle, Matapan, May, Miseno, Mo(z)zetta, Muleta, Naze, Ness, Nordkyn, North, Northern, Ortegal, Palatine, Parry, Pelerine, Peninsula, Point, Poncho, Promontory, Race, Ras, Ray, Reinga, Roca, Ruana, Runaway, Sable, St Vincent, Sandy, Scaw, Skagen, Skaw, Sontag, Southwest, Talma, Tippet, Trafalgar, Ushant, Verde, Waterproof, Western, Wrath, York

Caper(ing) Antic, Bean, Boer, Capparis, Capriole, Cavort, Dance, Dido, Flisk, Frisk, Frolic, Gambado, Gambol, Harmala, Harmalin(e), Harmel, Harmin(e), Prance, Prank, Saltant, Scoup, Scowp, Skip, Tit(t)up

Capet Marie Antoinette

Cape Town SA

Capital(s) A1, Assets, Block, Boodle, Bravo, Bully, Cap, Chapiter, Chaptrel, Doric, Equity, Euge, Excellent, Fixed, Flight, Float, Floating, Fonds, Great, Helix, Human, Initial, Ionic, Lethal, Lulu, Metropolis, Principal, Refugee, Risk, Rustic, Seat, Seed, Share, Social, Splendid, Sport, Stellar, Stock, Super, Topping, UC, Upper case, Working

---

CAPITALS

3 letters:	Kiel	Batum	Korov
Fes	Kiev	Belém	Kyoto
Fez	Kobe	Berne	Lagos
Gap	Laon	Bisho	Lassa
Jos	Laos	Boise	Laval
Ray	Leon	Bourg	Le Puy
Rio	Lima	Braga	Lhasa
Ude	Lomé	Cairo	Liege
Ufa	Male	Cuzco	Lille
Zug	Metz	Cuzev	Lyons
	Nara	Dacca	Macao
4 letters:	Nuuk	Dakar	Melun
Acra	Oslo	Delhi	Meroe
Aden	Pegu	Dhaka	Minsk
Albi	Pune	Dijon	Monza
Apia	Riga	Dilli	Namur
Auch	Rome	Dover	Nancy
Baki	San'a	Dutse	Natal
Baku	Sian	Emisa	Nimes
Bari	Sion	Enugu	Nukus
Bern	Susa	Goias	Oskub
Bida	Suva	Gotha	Palma
Boac	Vila	Guaco	Paris
Bonn	Xian	Hanoi	Parma
Brno		Harar	Patna
Caen	*5 letters:*	Hefei	Pella
Cali	Aarau	Hofei	Perth
Chur	Abiya	Hsian	Petra
Cluj	Abuja	Ikeja	Pinsk
Cork	Accra	Jammu	Poona
Dili	Adana	Jinan	Praha
Doha	Agana	Kabul	Praia
Faro	Aijal	Kandy	Quito
Graz	Akure	Karor	Rabat
Homs	Amman	Kazan	Rouen
Hums	Aosta	Kizyl	Salem
Ipoh	Arlon	Konia	Sanaa
Jolo	Assen	Konya	Scone

Seoul
Simla
Sofia
Stans
Sucré
Tepic
Tokyo
Trier
Tunis
Turin
Uxmal
Vadso
Vaduz
Yanan
Yenan
Zomba

6 letters:
Abakan
Albany
Almaty
Andros
Ankara
Annecy
Anyang
Asmara
Astana
Athens
Austin
Bagdad
Baguio
Bamako
Bangui
Banjui
Bassau
Bastia
Batumi
Bauchi
Beirut
Berlin
Bhopal
Bogota
Bruges
Brunei
Cahors
Canton
Colima
Colmar
Cracow
Darwin
Denver

Dessau
Dispur
Dodoma
Dublin
Edessa
Erfurt
Fuchou
Geneva
Giyani
Gondar
Habana
Harare
Havana
Helena
Hobart
Hohhot
Ibadan
Ilorin
Imphal
Jaipur
Jalapa
Johore
Kaduna
Kaunas
Kigali
Kohima
Kuwait
Lahore
Lisbon
Loanda
Lokoja
London
Luanda
Lusaka
Macapá
Maceió
Madrid
Maikop
Majuro
Malabo
Manama
Manaus
Manila
Maputo
Marsan
Maseru
Mekele
Merano
Merida
Moroni
Moscow

Munich
Murcia
Muscat
Nagpur
Nassau
Nevers
Niamey
Nouméa
Ottawa
Oviedo
Owerri
Palmas
Panaji
Panjim
Peking
Pierre
Prague
Puebla
Punaka
Quebec
Ranchi
Recife
Regina
Rennes
Riyadh
Roseau
Ryazan
Saigon
Sardes
Sardis
Sarnen
Sendai
Skopje
Sokoto
Sparta
St Gall
St Paul
Taipei
Tallin
Tarawa
Tarbes
Tarsus
Tehran
Tetuan
Thebes
Thimbu
Tirana
Tobruk
Toledo
Toluca
Topeka

Ulundi
Umtata
Vesoul
Vienna
Warsaw
Xining
Yangon
Yaunde
Zagreb
Zurich
Zwolle

7 letters:
Abidjan
Ajaccio
Alençon
Algiers
Altdorf
Antioch
Atlanta
Auxerre
Baghdad
Bangkok
Barnaul
Begawan
Beijing
Belfast
Belfort
Bien Hoa
Bijapur
Bikaner
Bishkek
Bobigny
Bologna
Calabar
Caracas
Cardiff
Cayenne
Cetinje
Coblenz
Coimbra
Colombo
Conakry
Concord
Cordoba
Cuttack
Douglas
Durango
Foochow
Funchal
Gangtok

Goiania
Guiyang
Haarlem
Halifax
Hanover
Hassett
Herisau
Honiara
Huhehot
Iqaluit
Isfahan
Izhevsk
Jackson
Jakarta
Kaesong
Kaifeng
Kampala
Karachi
Kashmir
Kharkov
Khartum
Koblenz
Konakri
Kuching
Kunming
Lanchow
Lansing
Lanzhou
Lashkar
Liestal
Limoges
Lincoln
Louvain
Lucerne
Lucknow
Madison
Malacca
Managua
Masbate
Mathura
Mbabane
Memphis
Messene
Morelia
Munster
Nairobi
Nalchik
Nanjing
Nanking
Nicosia
Nineveh

Novi Sad
Olomouc
Oshogbo
Pachuca
Palermo
Palikit
Papeete
Phoenix
Pishpek
Plovdiv
Potenza
Potsdam
Punakha
Quimper
Raleigh
Rangoon
San José
San Juan
Santa Re
Sao Tomé
Sapporo
Saransk
Stanley
St John's
Taiyuan
Tallinn
Tangier
Tbilisi
Teheran
Tel Aviv
Thimphu
Tiemcen
Toronto
Trenton
Trieste
Tripoli
Umuahia
Urumshi
Valetta
Venture
Vilnius
Vilnyus
Xanthus
Yaounde
Yerevan

8 letters:
Abeokuta
Abu Dhabi
Adelaide
Agartala

Ashgabet
Asuncion
Auckland
Bar-le-Duc
Belgrade
Belmopan
Beyrouth
Boa Vista
Brasilia
Brisbane
Brussels
Budapest
Cagliari
Calcutta
Campeche
Canberra
Cape Town
Castries
Chambéry
Chaumont
Cheyenne
Chisinau
Coahuila
Columbia
Columbus
Culiacan
Curitiba
Damascus
Dehra Dun
Djibouti
Dushanbe
Ecbatana
Edmonton
Eraklion
Florence
Freetown
Fribourg
Funafuti
Gaborone
Godthaab
Golconda
Hannover
Hargeisa
Hartford
Helsinki
Honolulu
Istanbul
Jayapura
Kandahar
Katmandu
Khartoum

Kilkenny
Kingston
Kinshasa
Kirkwall
Kishinev
Lausanne
Liaoyand
Lilongwe
Luneburg
Mandalay
Mechelen
Mexicali
Monrovia
Monterey
Nanchang
Nanching
Nanterre
Narbonne
Ndjamena
Pamplona
Pergamum
Peshawar
Pnom-Penh
Port Said
Port-Vila
Pretoria
Pristina
Roskilde
Saltillo
Salvador
Salzburg
Santiago
Sao Paulo
Sarajevo
Seremban
Shah Alam
Shanghai
Shenyang
Shillong
Silvassa
Srinigar
St Helier
Tashkent
The Hague
Thonburi
Torshavn
Toulouse
Usumbura
Valletta
Victoria
Vladimir

Warangai
Windhoek
Winnipeg
Yinchuan

9 letters:
Amsterdam
Annapolis
Ashkhabad
Ayutthaya
Banda Aceh
Bandar Ser
Bangalore
Benin City
Birobijan
Bucharest
Bujumbura
Cartagena
Changchun
Changshar
Chengchow
Cherkessk
Chihuahua
Darmstadt
Des Moines
Edinburgh
Fongafale
Fortaleza
Frankfort
Grand Turk
Heraklion
Hyderabad
Innsbruck
Islamabad
Jalalabad
Jerusalem
Karlsruhe
Kathmandu
Kingstown
Knoxville
Kuch Bihar
Leningrad
Ljubljana
Magdeburg
Maiduguri
Marrakesh
Melbourne
Mogadishu
Montauban
Monterrey
Nashville

Nelspriut
Nuku'alofa
Perigueux
Perpignan
Phnom Penh
Podgorica
Polokwane
Port Blair
Port Louis
Porto Novo
Port Royal
Putrajaya
Pyongyang
Reykjavik
Rio Branco
Samarkand
San Merino
Singapore
Solothurn
St George's
Stockholm
Stuttgart
Thorshavn
Trebizond
Ulan Bator
Vientiane
Zhengzhou

10 letters:
Addis Ababa
Basse-terre
Baton Rouge
Bellinzona
Birobidzan
Bratislava
Bridgetown
Campobosso
Carson City
Chandigarh
Charleston
Cooch Behar
Copenhagen
Eisenstadt
Frauenfeld
Georgetown
Harrisburg
Heidelberg
Hermosillo
Joao Pessoa
Klagenfurt
Kragujevac

Launceston
Leeuwarden
Libreville
Little Rock
Maastricht
Mexico City
Middelburg
Mogadiscio
Montevideo
Montgomery
Montpelier
Nouakchott
Panama City
Paramaribo
Persepolis
Podgoritsa
Porto Velho
Providence
Rawalpindi
Sacramento
Trivandrum
Tskhinvali
Valladolid
Washington
Wellington
Whitehorse
Willemstad
Winchester
Yashkar-Ola

11 letters:
Bhubaneswar
Brazzaville
Buenos Aires
Campo Grande
Charlestown
Dares Salaam
Fredericton
Gandhinagar
Guadalajara
Hermoupolis
Johore Bahru
Kuala Lumpur
Montbeliard
Nakhichevan
Ouagadougou
Pandemonium
Pondicherry
Port Moresby
Porto Alegre
Port of Spain

Rio Gallegas
Saarbrucken
San Salvador
Springfield
St Peter Port
Tallahassee
Tegucigalpa
Thohoyandou
Ulaanbaatar
Vatican City
Vladikavkaz
Yellowknife

12 letters:
Antananarivo
Anuradhapura
Bloemfontein
Chilpancingo
Fort-de-France
Indianapolis
Johannesburg
Kota Kinabalu
Mont-de-Marsan
Muzzafarabad
Pandaemonium
Petrozavodsk
Port-au-Prince
Port Harcourt
Rio de Janeiro
Salt Lake City
Santo Domingo
Schaffhausen
Schoemansdal
Seringapatam
Tenochtitian
Villahermosa
Williamsburg
Yamoussoukro

13 letters:
Belo Horizonte
Charlottetown
Florianopolis
Funafuti Atoll
Guatemala City
Hertogenbosch
Jefferson City
Yaren District

14 letters:
Andorra la Vella

Constantinople	Puerto Princesa	*15 letters:*	*16 letters:*
Kuala Trengganu	's Hertogenbosch	Chalons-sur-Marne	Pietermaritzburg
Oaxaca de Juarez		Charlotte Amalie	Trixtia Gutiérrez
		Clermont-Ferrand	

Capitalise Carpe diem
Capitalist Financier, Moneyer, Sloane
▷ **Capitalist** *may indicate* a citizen of a capital
Capitulate Acquiesce, Comply, → SURRENDER
Capless Bare
▷ **Capless** *may indicate* first letter missing
Capone Al, Scarface
▷ **Capriccioso** *may indicate* an anagram
Caprice, Capricious Arbitrary, Boutade, Capernoitie, Cap(p)ernoity, Conceit, Desultory, Erratic, Fancy, Fickle, Fitful, Freak, Humoresk, Humoresque, Irony, Megrim, Mood, Perverse, Quirk, Vagary, Wayward, Whim(sy)
Capsize Crank, Overbalance, Purl, Tip, Turn turtle, Upset, Whemmle, Whomble
▷ **Capsized** *may indicate* a word upside down
Capstan Sprocket, Windlass
Capsule Amp(o)ule, Bowman's, Cachet, Habitat, Internal, Ootheca, Orbiter, Ovisac, Pill, Space, Spacecraft, Spansule, Spermatophore, Suppository, Time, Urn
Captain Ahab, Bligh, Bobadil, Bones, Brassbound, Capt, Channel, Chief, Cid, Commander, Condottiere, Cook, Copper, Cuttle, Flint, Group, Hornblower, Kettle, Kidd, Leader, Macheath, Master, Nemo, Old man, Owner, Patron, Patroon, Post, Privateer, Protospatharius, Skip(per), Standish, Subah(dar), Subedar, Swing, Trierarch
Caption Cutline, Heading, Headline, Inscription, Masthead, Roller, Sub-title, Title
Captious Critical, Peevish
Captivate(d), Captivating Beguile, Bewitch, Charm, Enamour, Enthrall, Epris(e), Take, Winsome
Captive, Captivity Bonds, Duress, POW, Prisoner, Slave
Capture Abduct, Annex, Bag, Catch, Collar, Cop, Electron, Enchain, Enthral(l), Grab, Land, Motion, Net, Prize, Rush, Seize, Snabble, Snaffle, Snare, → TAKE
Capuchin Cebus, Monkey, Sajou
Car Alvis, Astra, Audi, Austin, Auto, Banger, Beetle, Berlin, Biza, BL, Bluebird, Bomb, Boneshaker, Brake, Bubble, Buffet, Bugatti, Buick, Bumper, Bus, Cab(riolet), Cadillac, Catafalco, Catafalque, Chariot, Chorrie, Classic, Clunker, Coach, Company, Concept, Convertible, Cortina, Coupé, Courtesy, Crate, Daimler, Diner, Dodgem®, Drag(ster), Drophead, Dunger, Elf, Estate, E-type, Fastback, Fiat, Flivver, Ford, Formula, Freight, Friday, Gas guzzler, Ghost, Gondola, Griddle, GT, Hardtop, Hatchback, Heap, Hearse, Hillman, Hot hatch, Hot-rod, Irish, Jaguar, Jalop(p)y, Jamjar, Jammy, Jam sandwich, Jaunting, Jim Crow, Kart, Kit, Knockabout, Lada, Lagonda, Lancia, Landaulet, Landrover, Lift-back, Limo, Limousine, Merc(edes), MG, Mini, Model T, Morgan, Morris, Nacelle, Notchback, Observation, Opel, Pace, Palace, Panda, Parlo(u)r, Patrol, Popemobile, Production, Prowl, Pullman, Racer, Ragtop, Railroad, Rattletrap, Restaurant, Roadster, Roller, Rolls (Royce), Rover, RR, Runabout, Runaround, Rust bucket, Saloon, Scout, Sedan, Service, Shooting-brake, Skoda, Sleeper, Sleeping, Soft-top, Speedster, Sports, Squad, Station wagon, Steam, Stock, Stretch-limo, Subcompact, Sunbeam, Supermini, SUV, Tank, Telepherique, Telpher, Three-wheeler, Tin Lizzie, Tonneau, Tourer, Tram, Triumph, Trolley, Tumble, Turbo, Two-seater, Vehicle, Veteran,

Vintage, Voiture, VW, Wheeler, Wheels

Caramel Brûlé

Carat Point

Caravan Caf(f)ila, Convoy, Fleet, Kafila, Motor home, Safari, Trailer

Caravanserai Choltry, Choutry, Inn, Khan

Caraway Aj(o)wan, Carvy, Seed

Car-back Boot, Dick(e)y, Tonneau

Carbamide Urea

Carbide Silicon

Carbine Gun, Musket

Carbohydrate Agar, Agarose, Callose, Carrageenan, Cellulose, Chitin, Dextran, Disaccharide, Glycogen, Heptose, Hexose, Inulin, Ketose, Laminarin, Mannan, Mucilage, Pectin, Pectose, Pentosan(e), Pentose, Saccharide, Sorbitol, Starch, Sucrose, Sugar

Carbolic Orcin

Carbon(ate) Activated, Ankerite, Austenite, Buckminsterfullerene, Buckyball, C, Charcoal, Coke, Dialogite, Diamond, Drice, Dry ice, Flame, Flimsy, Fullerene, Gas black, Graphite, Lampblack, Martensite, Natron, Petroleum coke, Scawtite, Soot, Spode, Spodium, Urao, Witherite, Zaratite

Carbon deficiency Acapnia

Carboy Demijohn

Carbuncle Anthrax, Ruby

Carcase, Carcass Body, Cadaver, Carrion, Corpse, Cutter, Krang, Kreng, Morkin, Mor(t)ling

Card(s), Cardboard Ace, Affinity, Amex®, Arcana, Baccarat, Basto, Bill, Birthday, Bower, Business, Calling, Canasta, Cartes, Cash, Caution, Charge, Cheque, Chicane, Cigarette, Club, Comb, Communion, Community, Compass, Court(esy), Credit, Cue, Curse of Scotland, Dance, Debit, Deck, Deuce, Devil's (picture) books, Diamond, Donor, Drawing, Ecarté, Eccentric, Euchre, Expansion, Face, False, Flash, Flaught, Flush, → **GAME**, Gold, Green, Hand, Hard, Health, Heart, Hole, Honour, ID, Identification, Identity, Intelligent, Jack, Jambone, Jamboree, Joker, Kanban, Key, King, Laser, Leading, Letter, Loo, Loyalty, Magnetic, Manille, Master, Matador, Maximum, Meishi, Meld, Memory, Mise, Mistigris, Mogul, Mournival, Notelet, Oddity, Ombre, Pack, Past, Pasteboard, Payment, PC, Phone, Picture, Placard, Place, Plastic, Playing, Postal, Proximity, Punch(ed), Quatorze, Quatre, Queen, Queer, Quiz, Race, Rail, Ration, Red, Rippler, Rove, Royal marriage, Score, Scraperboard, Scratch, Screwball, Scribble, Shade, Show, SIM, Singleton, Smart, Soda, Solo, Sound, Spade, Spadille, Squeezer, Stiffener, Store, Strawboard, Swab, Swipe, Swish, Switch, Swob, Swot, Talon, Tarok, Tarot, Tease(r), Tenace, Test, Thaumatrope, Ticket, Tiddy, Time, Top-up, Tose, Toze, Trading, Trey, Trump, Two-spot, Union, Valentine, Visa, Visiting, Wag, Warrant, Weirdie, Whitechapel, Wild, Yellow, Zener

Cardigan Ballet-wrap, Jacket, Wam(m)us, Wampus, Woolly

Cardinal Camerlingo, Chief, College, Eight, Eminence, Eminent, Grosbeak, Hat, HE, Hume, Legate, Manning, Mazarin, Medici, Newman, Number, Pivotal, Polar, Prefect, Prelate, Radical, Red, Red-hat, Richelieu, Sacred college, Seven, Sin, Spellman, Ten, Virtue, Vital, Wolsey, Ximenes

Card-player Dealer, Pone

Care(r), Caring Attention, Burden, Cark, Caution, Cerne, Cherish, Community, → **CONCERN**, Cosset, Grief, Heed, Intensive, Kaugh, Keep, Kiaugh, Maternal, Mind, Pains, Palliative, Parabolanus, Primary, Providence, Reck(e), Reke, Residential,

Respite, Retch, Shared, Solicitude, → **TEND**, Tenty, Worry

Careen(ing) Parliament-heel

Career Course, Hurtle, Life, Line, Run, Rush, Speed, Start, Tear, Vocation

▷ **Career** *may indicate* an anagram

Carefree → **CARELESS(LY)**, Dozy, Happy-go-lucky, Irresponsible, → **NEGLIGENT**, Oops, Perfunctory, Rollicking, Thoughtless

Careful(ly) Canny, Chary, Discreet, Gentle, Hooly, Leery, Meticulous, Mindful, Painstaking, Penny-pinching, Penny-wise, Pernickety, Provident, Prudent, Scrimp, Studious, Tentie, Tenty, Thorough, Vigilant, Ware, Wary

Careless(ly) Casual, Cheery, Debonair, Easy, Free-minded, Gallio, Improvident, Imprudent, Inadvertent, Insouciance, Irresponsible, Lax, Lighthearted, Négligé, → **NEGLIGENT**, Nonchalant, Oops, Oversight, Perfunctory, Raffish, Rash, Remiss, Resigned, Riley, Rollicking, Slam-bang, Slapdash, Slaphappy, Slipshod, Sloven(ly), Slubber, Taupie, Tawpie, Thoughtless, Unguarded, Unmindful, Untenty, Unwary

▷ **Carelessly** *may indicate* an anagram

Caress Bill, Coy, Embrace, Fondle, Kiss, Lallygag, Lollygag, Noursle, Nursle, Pet, Straik, Stroke, Touch

Caretaker Concierge, Curator, Custodian, Dvornik, Granthi, Guardian, Interim, Janitor, Nightwatchman, Sexton, Shammash, Shammes, Superintendent, Verger, Warden

Careworn Haggard, Lined, Tired, Weary

Cargo Boatload, Bulk, Burden, Fraught, Freight, Lading, Last, → **LOAD**, Payload, Shipload, Shipment

Caribbean Belonger, Puerto Rican, Soca, Sokah, Taino, WI

Caribou Tuktoo, Tuktu

Caricature, Caricaturist Ape, Beerbohm, Burlesque, Caran d'Ache, Cartoon, Cruikshank, Doyle, Farce, Gillray, Rowlandson, Skit, Spy, Tenniel, Toon, Travesty

Carlin Pug

Carmelite Barefoot, White (Friar)

Carmen AA, BL, Chai, RAC

Carnage Bloodshed, Butchery, Massacre, Slaughter

Carnal Bestial, Lewd, Sensual, Sexual, Worldly

Carnation Clove pink, Dianthus, Gillyflower, Malmaison, Picotee, Pink

Carnival Fair, Fasching, Festival, Fete, Mas, Moomba, Revelry

Carnivore Cacomistle, Cacomixl, Coati, Creodont, Fo(u)ssa, Genet, Glutton, Grison, Meerkat, Ratel, Stoat, Suricate, Viverridae, Wolverine

Carob Algarroba, Locust, St John's bread

Carol(ler) Noel, Sing, Song, Wait, Wassail, Yodel

Carousal, Carouse Bend, Birl(e), Bouse, Bride-ale, Compotation, Drink, Mallemaroking, Mollie, Orge, Orgy, → **REVEL**, Roist, Screed, Spree, Upsee, Upsey, Upsy, Wassail

Carp(er) Beef, Cavil, Censure, Complain, Crab, Critic, Crucian, Crusian, Gibel, Goldfish, Id(e), Koi, Kvetch, Mirror, Mome, Nag, Nibble, Nitpick, Roach, Roundfish, Scold, Twitch, Whine, Yerk, Yirk

Carpenter Beveller, Bush, Cabinet-maker, Carfindo, Chips, Fitter, Joiner, Joseph, Menuisier, Quince, Tenoner, Woodworker, Wright

▷ **Carpenter** *may indicate* an anagram

Carpet Aubusson, Axminster, Beetle, Berate, Bessarabian, Broadloom, Brussels, Castigate, Chide, Dhurrie, Drugget, Durrie, Dutch, Kali, Kelim, Khilim, Kidderminster, Kilim, Kirman, Lecture, Lino, Magic, Mat, Moquette, Persian, Rate, Red, Reprimand, Reproach, Rug, Runner, Shagpile, Shark, Shiraz, Stair, Turkey,

Wall-to-wall, Wig, Wilton
Carrageen Sea-moss
Carriage Air, Ar(a)ba, Aroba, Bandy, Barouche, Bearing, Berlin(e), Bier, Brake, Brit(sch)ka, Britska, Britzka, Brougham, Buckboard, Buggy, Cab, Calash, Calèche, Car, Cariole, Caroche, Carriole, Carryall, Cartage, Chaise, Charabanc, Charet, Chariot, Chassis, Chay, Clarence, Coach, Coch, Composite, Conveyance, Coupé, Curricle, Demeanour, Dennet, Deportment, Désobligeante, Diner, Dormeuse, Dos-a-dos, Do-si-do, Drag, Dros(h)ky, Ekka, Equipage, Fiacre, Fly, Four-in-hand, Gait, Gig, Gladstone, Go-cart, Growler, Gun, Haulage, Herdic, Horseless, Hurly-hacket, Landau(let), Landing, Limber, Mien, Non-smoker, Norimon, Observation-car, Phaeton, Pick-a-back, Pochaise, Pochay, Poise, Port(age), Portance, Postchaise, Posture, Poyse, Pram, Pullman, Purdah, Railcar, Railway, Randem, Rath(a), Remise, Rickshaw, Rockaway, Shay, Sled, Sleeper, Smoker, Sociable, Spider, Spider phaeton, Stanhope, Sulky, Surrey, Tarantas(s), Taxi, T-cart, Tender, Tenue, Tilbury, Tim-whiskey, Tonga, Trail, Trap, Vetture, Victoria, Voiture, Wagonette, Waterage, Whirligig, Whisk(e)y
Carrier Aircraft, Airline, Arm, Baldric, Barkis, Barrow, Bomb-ketch, Bulk, Caddy, Cadge, Camel, Coaster, Common, Conveyor, Escort, Fomes, Fomites, Frog, Grid, Hamper, Haversack, Hod, Janker, Jill, Majority, Minority, Nosebag, Noyade, Obo, Packhorse, Personnel, Pigeon, Porter, Rucksack, Satchel, Schistosoma, Semantide, Sling, Straddle, Stretcher, → **TRAY**, Vector, Wave
Carrion Cadaver, Carcase, Carcass, Flesh, Ket, Stapelia
Carrots Seseli, Titian
Carry(ing) Asport, Bear, Chair, Convey, Enlevé, Escort, Ferry, Frogmarch, Hawk, Hent, Humf, Hump, Humph, Kurvey, Land, Pack, Pickaback, Port, Stock, Sustain, Tide over, Tote, → **TRANSPORT**, Trant, Wage, With, Yank
Carry on Continue, Create, Wage
Carry out Execute, Mastermind, Pursue
Cart Bandy, Barrow, Bogey, Buck, Cape, Car(r)iole, Chapel, Democrat, Democrat wagon, Dog, Dolly, Dray, Furphy, Gambo, Gill, Golf, Governess, Gurney, Hackery, Jag, Jill, Lead, Mail, Pie, Rickshaw, Scot, Scotch, Shandry, T, Tax(ed), Telega, Trolley, Tumbrel, Tumbril, Village, Wag(g)on, Wain, Whitechapel
Cartel Duopoly, Ring, Syndicate
Carthaginian Punic
Carthorse Aver, Shire
Carthusian Bruno
Cartilage Antitragus, Arytenoid, Chondral, Chondrin, Chondrus, Cricoid, Darwin's tubercle, Disc, Epiglottis, Gristle, Hyaline, Lytta, Meniscus, Semilunar, Tendron, Thyroid, Tragus, Worm, Xiphoid
Cartload Seam
Cartographer Cabot, Chartist, Kremer, Mercator, OS, Speed
Carton Box, Case, Crate, Sydney, Tub
Cartoon(ist) Animated, Bairnsfather, Caricature, Comic, Disney, Drawn, Emmet, Fougasse, Fumetto, Garland, Goldberg, Leech, Low, Manga, Mel, Partridge, Popeye, Robinson, Short, Spy, Strip, Tenniel, Thurber, Tidy, Tintin, Trog
Cartridge Ball, Blank, Bullet, Cartouche, Cassette, Crystal, Doppie, Live, Magazine, Magnetic, QIC, Rim-free, Shell, Spent
Cart-track Rut
Cartwheel Handspring
Caruncle Aril, Carnosity
Carve(d), Carver, Carving Abated, Alcimedon, Armchair, Bas relief, Camaieu,

Cameo, Chisel, Cilery, Crocket, Cut, Dismember, Doone, Enchase, Engrave, Entail, Entayle, Fiddlehead, Gibbons, Glyptic, Hew, Incise, Inscribe, Insculp, Intaglio, Knotwork, Netsuke, Nick, Petroglyph, Scrimshaw, Sculp(t), Slice, Tondo, Trophy, Truncheon, Tympanum, Whakairo, Whittle

Caryatid Column, Telamon

Casanova Heartbreaker, Leman

Cascade Cataract, Fall, Lin(n), Stream, Waterfall

Cascara Buckthorn, Honduras bark, Rhamnus, Wahoo

Case(s), Casing Abessive, Ablative, Accusative, Action, Adessive, Allative, Altered, Appeal, Aril, Ascus, Assumpsit, Attaché, Basket, Beer, Bere, Bittacle, Blimp, Box, Brief, Bundwall, Burse, C, Ca, Cabinet, Calyx, Canister, Canterbury, Capsule, Cartouch(e), Cartridge, Cause celebre, Cellaret, Chase, Chitin, Chrysalis, Cocoon, Compact, Crate, Croustade, Crust, Dative, Declension, Detinue, Dispatch, Dossier, Dressing, Elative, Elytron, Enallage, Ensheath, Essive, Etui, Etwee, Example, Flan, Flapjack, Frame, Genitive, Grip, Hanaper, Hard, Hatbox, Hold-all, Housewife, Hull, Humidor, Husk, Imperial, → IN CASE, Index, Indusium, Inessive, Instance, Kalamdan, Keister, Locative, Locket, Lorica, Manche, Matter, Mezuzah, Music, Nacelle, Nominative, Non-suit, Nutshell, Objective, Oblique, Ochrea, Ocrea, Outpatient, Packing, Pair, Papeterie, Patient, Pencil, Penner, Phylactery, Plight, Plummer-block, Pod, Port, Possessive, Prima facie, Puparium, Quiver, Recce, Reconnoitre, Sabretache, Sad, Scabbard, Sheath(e), Shell, Situation, Six-pack, Sporran, Stead, Sted, Subjective, Suit, Tantalus, Tea-chest, Telium, Test, Theca, Tichborne, Trial, Trunk, Valise, Vasculum, Vocative, Volva, Walise, Walking, Wallet, Wardian, Wing, Worst, Writing

Case-harden Nitrode

Casein Curd

Casement Frame, Roger, Sash, Window

Cash Blunt, Bonus, Bounty, Change, Coin, Dosh, Dot, Float, Hard, Idle money, Imprest, Lolly, → MONEY, Needful, Ochre, Oscar, Pence, Petty, Ready, Realise, Redeem, Rhino, Spondulicks, Spot, Stumpy, Tender, Tin, Wampum, Wherewithal

Cashier Annul, Break, Depose, Disbar, Dismiss, Oust, Teller, Treasurer

Cashmere Circassienne

Casino Monte Carlo

Cask(et) Armet, Barrel, Barrico, Bas(i)net, Box, Breaker, Butt, Cade, Casque, Cassette, Drum, Firkin, Galeate, Harness, Heaume, Hogshead, Keg, Leaguer, Octave, Pin, Pipe, Puncheon, Pyxis, Run(d)let, Salade, Sallet, Sarcophagus, Scuttlebutt, Shrine, Solera, Tierce, Tun, Wine

Cask-stand Stillion

Cassava Manioc, Tapioca, Yucca

Casserole Diable, Osso bucco, Pot, Salmi, Terrine, Tzimmes

Cassette Cartridge, Tape, Video

Cassia Cleanser, Senna

Cassio Lieutenant

Cassiterite Needle-tin, Tinstone

Cassock Gown, Soutane, Subucula

Cast (down, off, out), Casting Abattu, Actors, Add, Angle, Appearance, Bung, Cire perdue, Die, Discard, Ecdysis, Ectype, Eject, Endocranial, Exorcise, Exuviae, Exuvial, Fling, Found, Fusil, Grape, Heave, Hob, Hue, Hurl, Impression, Ingo(w)es, Keb, Look, Lose, Mew, Molt, Moulage, Mould, Pick, Plaster(stone), Players, Put, Reject, Shed, Shoot, Sling, Slive, Slough, Spoil, Stookie, Tailstock, → THROW, Toss, Tot, Warp, Wax, Ytost

▷ **Cast** *may indicate* an anagram or a piece of a word missing
Castanet Crotal(um), Knackers
Castaway Adrift, Crusoe, Gunn, Left, Outcast, Selkirk, Stranded, Weft
▷ **Cast by** *may indicate* surrounded by
Caste Brahmin, Burakumin, Class, Dalit, Group, Harijan, Hova, Kshatriya, Rajpoot,
  Rajpout, Rank, Scheduled, Sect, Sudra, Untouchable, Vaisya, Varna
Caster Truckle
Castigate Berate, Chastise, Criticise, Denounce, Keelhaul, Lash, Punish, Rate
Cast-iron Spiegeleisen
Castle(d) Bouncy, Broch, C, Chateau, Citadel, Fastness, Fort, Kasba(h), Maiden,
  Man, Mot(t)e, Move, Rook, Stronghold, Villa

CASTLES

4 letters:	Belvoir	Doubting	Trausnitz
Sand	Braemar	Egremont	
Trim	Calzean	Elephant	*10 letters:*
	Canossa	Elsinore	Caerphilly
5 letters:	Chillon	Inverary	Kenilworth
Blois	Colditz	Kronberg	Pontefract
Conwy	Culzean	Malperdy	
Corfe	Despair	Pembroke	*11 letters:*
Hever	Harlech	Perilous	Carisbrooke
Leeds	Lincoln	Rackrent	Chateauroux
Spain	Otranto	Richmond	Eilean Donan
	Schloss	Stirling	Gormenghast
6 letters:	Skipton	Stokesay	
Casbah	Warwick	Stormont	*12 letters:*
Forfar	Windsor	Tintagel	Fotheringhay
Glamis		Urquhart	Herstmonceux
Howard	*8 letters:*	Wartburg	Sissinghurst
Ludlow	Balmoral		
Raglan	Bamburgh	*9 letters:*	*13 letters:*
	Bastille	Dangerous	Carrickfergus
7 letters:	Berkeley	Dunsinane	
Adamant	Carbonek	Edinburgh	*14 letters:*
Amboise	Chepstow	Lancaster	Motte and bailey
Arundel	Crotchet	Sherborne	

Castor-oil Ricinus
Castrate(d), Castrato Alter, Cut, Doctor, Emasculate, Eunuch, Evirate, Farinelli,
  Geld, Glib, Lib, Manzuoli, Moreschi, Mutilate, Neuter, Senesino, Spado, Spay, Swig
Castro Fidel
Casual Accidental, Adventitious, Airy, Blasé, Chance, Chav(ette), Flippant, Grass,
  Haphazard, Idle, Incidental, Informal, Jaunty, Lackadaisical, Nonchalant,
  Odd(ment), Offhand, Off-the-cuff, Orra, Passing, Promiscuous, Random, Scratch,
  Sporadic, Stray, Temp, Throwaway
Casualty Caduac, Chance-medley, → VICTIM
Casuist Jesuit
Cat Catamount, Dandy, Domestic, Fat, Felid, Feline, Flog, Gossip, Hipster, Jazzer,
  Lair, Mewer, Mog, Native, Neuter, Nib, Oriental, Painter, Palm, Pardal, Practical,

Puss, Sacred, Scourge, Serval, Sick, Singed, Spew, Spue, Swinger, Top, Vomit

CATS

3 letters:
Gib
Gus
Kit
Rex
Tom

4 letters:
Eyra
Lash
Lion
Lynx
Manx
Musk
Pard
Puma

5 letters:
Alley
Civet
Felix
Fossa
Genet
Hodge
Korat
Manul
Ounce
Quoll
Rasse
Rumpy
Tabby
Tiger
Tigon
Zibet

6 letters:
Angora
Birman
Bobcat
Cougar
Foussa
Jaguar
La Perm
Malkin
Margay
Mouser
Musang
Ocelot
Ocicat
Somali
Sphynx
Tibert
Tybalt
Weasel
Zibeth

7 letters:
Burmese
Caracal
Cheetah
Clowder
Dasyure
Foumart
Genette
Leopard
Linsang
Maltese
Nandine
Pallas's
Panther
Persian
Pharaoh
Polecat
Ragdoll
Siamese
Tiffany

Tigress
Viverra

8 letters:
Balinese
Baudrons
Cacomixl
Cheshire
Devon Rex
Kilkenny
Long-hair
Mountain
Munchkin
Ringtail
Snowshoe
Tiffanie

9 letters:
Asparagus
Binturong
Bluepoint
Chantilly
Chartreux
Delundung
Grimalkin
Himalayan
Maine Coon
Marmalade
Mehitabel
Niebelung
Sealpoint
Shorthair
Tobermory
Tonkinese

10 letters:
Abyssinian
Cacomistle

Cornish Rex
Jaguarondi
Jaguarundi
Selkirk Rex
Turkish Van

11 letters:
Colourpoint
Egyptian Mau
Havana Brown
Russian Blue
Tongkingese

12 letters:
American Curl
Scottish Fold

13 letters:
Tortoise-shell
Turkish Angora

14 letters:
Asian Shorthair
Australian Mist
Siberian Forest

15 letters:
Norwegian Forest

16 letters:
American Wirehair

19 letters:
Californian
  Spangled

Catacomb Cemetery, Crypt, Hypogeum, Vault
Catalepsy Catatony, Trance
Catalogue Cattle dog, Dewey, Dictionary, Index, Inventory, List, Litany, Magalog, Messier, Ragman, Ragment, Raisonné, Record, Register, Specialogue, Star, Subject, Table, Tabulate, Thematic, Union
Catalyst Accelerator, Agent, Influence, Kryptonite, Stereospecific, Unicase, Ziegler
Catamite Gunsel, Ingle, Pathic
Catapult Ballista, Ging, Launch, Mangon(el), Perrier, Petrary, Propel, Scorpion,

Shanghai, Sling, Slingshot, Stone-bow, Tormentum, Trebuchet, Wye, Y

Cataract Cascade, Film, Pearl, Pearl-eye, Torrent, Waterfall, Web and pin

Catarrh Coryza, Rheum

Catastrophe Apocalypse, Calamity, → **DISASTER**, Doom, Epitasis, Fiasco, Meltdown

Catatonia Stupor

Cat-call Boo, Jeer, Mew, Miaow, Miaul, Razz, Wawl, Whistle, Wrawl

Catch(y), Caught Air, Apprehend, Attract, Bag, Benet, Bone, C, Capture, Chape, Clasp, Cog, Collar, Contract, Cop, Corner, Cotton on, Ct, Deprehend, Detent, Dolly, Engage, Enmesh, Ensnare, Entoil, Entrap, Fang, Field, Fumble, Gaper, Get, Glee(some), Grasp, Had, Hank, Haud, Haul, Hear, Hitch, Hold, Hook, Inmesh, Keddah, Keight, Kep(pit), Kheda, Kill, Land, Lapse, Lasso, Latch, Lime, Lock, Morse, Nab, Nail, Net, Nick, Nim, Nobble, Noose, Overhear, Overhent, Overtake, Parti, Pawl, Rap, Release, Rope, Round, Rub, Safety, Sean, Sear, See(n), Seize, → **SNAG**, Snap, Snare, Snib, Snig, → **SONG**, Surprise, Swindle, Tack, Take, Tickle, Trammel, Trap, Trawl, Trick, Tripwire, Troll, Twenty two, Twig, Understand, Wrestle

Catchword Motto, Shibboleth, Slogan, Tag

Catechism Carritch, Shorter, Test

Categorise, Category → **CLASS**, Etic, Genre, Genus, Label, Order, Pigeonhole, Range, Stereotype, Taxon, Triage

Cater(er) Acatour, Cellarer, Feed, Manciple, → **PROVIDE**, Purveyor, Serve, Steward, Supply, Victualler, Vivandière

Caterpillar Army worm, Aweto, Boll worm, Cabbageworm, Cotton-worm, Cutworm, Eruciform, Geometer, Gooseberry, Hop-dog, Hornworm, Inchworm, Larva, Looper, Osmeterium, Palmer, Tent, Webworm, Woolly-bear

Catfish Hassar, Woof

Cathartic Turbeth

Cathedral Amiens, Basilica, Birmingham, Burgos, Chartres, Chester, → **CHURCH**, Cologne, Cortona, Dome, Duomo, Durham, Ely, Evreux, Gloucester, Guildford, Hereford, Hertford, Huesca, Kirkwall, Lateran, Lichfield, Lincoln, Lugo, Minster, Mullingar, Notre Dame, Rheims, Ripon, St Albans, St Davids, St Paul's, Salisbury, Santiago de Compostela, Sens, Teruel, Up(p)sala, Viseu, Wakefield, Wells, Westminster, Winchester, Worcester, York

Catherine Braganza, Parr

Catherine-wheel Girandole

Cathode Electrode, Filament, Ray

Catholic Assumptionist, Broad, Defenders, Doolan, Eclectic, Ecumenical, Fenian, General, Irvingism, Jebusite, Latin, Lazarist, Left-footer, Liberal, Marian, Opus Dei, Ostiary, Papalist, Papaprelatist, Papist, Passionist, Recusant, Redemptionist, Roman, Salesian, Spike, Taig, Te(a)gue, Teigue, Theatine, Thomist, Tike, Tory, Tridentine, Tyke, Universal, Ursuline, Waldenses, Wide

Catkin Amentum, Chat, Lamb's tail, Pussy-willow, Salicaceous

Cat-lover Ailurophile

Catmint Nep, Nepeta

Cato Porcian, Uticensis

Cats-eye Chatoyant, Cymophane

Catsmeat Lights

Catspaw Pawn, Tool

Cat's tail Reed-mace, Typha

Cat's whiskers Vibrissa

Cattle(pen) Aberdeen Angus, Africander, Ankole, Aver, Ayrshire, Beefalo, Belgian Blue, Bestial, Black, Brahman, British White, Buffalo, Carabao, Charbray, Charolais, Chillingham, Dexter, Drove, Durham, Fee, Friesland, Galloway, Gaur, Gayal, Guernsey, Gyal, Heard, Herd, Hereford, Highland, Holstein (Friesian), Illawarra, Jersey, Kerry, Kine, Kouprey, Kraal, Ky(e), Kyloe, Lairage, Limousin, Lincoln, Longhorn, Luing, Neat, Nout, Nowt, Owsen, Oxen, Piemontese, Rabble, Redpoll, Rother, Santa Gertrudis, Shorthorn, Simment(h)al, Soum, South Devon, Sowm, Steer, Stock, Store, Stot, Sussex, Tamarao, Tamarau, Teeswater, Welsh Black

Cattle disease Actinobacillosis, Actinomycosis, Anthrax, Black water, Dry-bible, Footrot, Gallsickness, Heart-water, Hoove, Johne's, Listeriosis, Lumpy jaw, Mange, Mastitis, Milk lameness, Moorill, New Forest, Quarter-ill, Red-water, Rinderpest, Scours, Scrapie, Texas fever, Wire-heel, Woody-tongue

Cattle food Fodder

Cattleman Cowboy, Herder, Maverick, Rancher, Ringer, Stock-rider

Catty Kin, Spiteful

Caucasian Aryan, Azabaijani, Azeri, Cherkess, European, Georgian, Iberian, Kabardian, Melanochroi, Paleface, Semite, Shemite, White, Yezdi, Yezidee, Zezidee

Caucus Assembly, Cell, Gathering, Race

▸ **Caught** *see* CATCH

Caul Baby-hood, Kell, Membrane, Sillyhow

Cauldron Kettle, Pot

Cauliflower Curd, Ear, Floret

Caulk Fill, Pay, Pitch, Snooze

Causation, Cause(d), Causes Aetiology, Agent, Beget, Breed, Bring, Compel, Create, Crusade, Determinant, Due, Effect, Efficient, Encheason, Engender, Factor, Final, First, Flag-day, Formal, Gar(re), Generate, Ideal, Induce, Lead, Lost, Make, Material, Motive, Movement, Natural, → OCCASION, Parent, Probable, Provoke, Proximate, Reason, Root, Sake, Secondary, Source, Teleology, Topic, Ultimate, Wreak

Causeway Giant's, Tombolo

Caustic Acid, Acrimonious, Alkaline, Burning, Common, Erodent, Escharotic, Lime, Lunar, Moxa, Pungent, Sarcastic, Scathing, Seare, Soda, Tart, Vitriol, Waspish, Withering

Cauterise, Cauterisation Brand, Burn, Disinfect, Inustion, Moxibustion, Sear

Caution, Cautious (person) Achitophel, Admonish, Ahithophel, Alert, Amber, Awarn, Beware, Cagey, Card, Care, Cave, Caveat, Chary, Circumspect, Credence, Cure, Defensive, Deliberate, Discretion, Fabian, Gingerly, Guard(ed), Heedful, Leery, Prudent, Rum, Scream, Skite, Tentative, Timorous, Vigilant, Ware, → WARN, Wary, Yellow card

Cavalcade Pageant, Parade, Procession, Sowarree, Sowarry

Cavalier Brusque, Cicisbeo, Devil-may-care, Gallant, Lively, Malignant, Offhand, Peart, Rider, Royalist

Cavalry(man) Blues, Car(a)bineer, Car(a)binier, Cornet, Cossack, Dragoon, Equites, Heavies, Horse, Horse Guards, Household, Hussar, Ironsides, Knights, Lancers, Life Guards, Light-horse, Plunger, Ressaldar, Risaldar, Rough-rider, Rutter, Sabres, Silladar, Spahi, Uhlan, Yeomanry

Cave(rn), Caves, Cave-dwelling Acherusia, Aladdin's, Alert, Altamira, Antar, Antre, Beware, Cellar, Collapse, Corycian, Den, Domdaniel, Erebus, Fingal's, Fore, Grot(to), Hollow, Jenolan, Lascaux, Look-out, Lupercal, Mammoth, Nix, Pot-hole, Proteus, Sepulchre, Snow, Spel(a)ean, Speleology, Spelunker, Speos, Tassili, Trophonian, Vault, Waitomo, Ware, Weem, Wookey Hole

Cave-dweller Troglodyte

Caveman Adullam, Aladdin, Fingal, Neanderthal, Primitive, Troglodyte, Troll

Caviare Beluga, Osietra, Roe, Sevruga, Sturgeon

Cavil Carp, Haggle, Quibble

Cavity Acetabulum, Amygdale, Amygdule, Androclinium, Archenteron, Atrial, Body, Camera, Camouflet, Celom, Chamber, Clinandrium, Coelenteron, Coelom(e), Concepticle, Concha, Countermark, Crater, Crypt, Dent, Domatium, Druse, Enteron, Follicle, Foss, Gap, Geode, Glenoid, Hold, Hole, Lacuna, Locule, Mediastinum, Mialoritic, Orbita, Orifice, Pocket, Pulp, Resonant, Segmentation, Sinus, Stomod(a)eum, Tear, Thunderegg, Tympanum, Vacuole, Vein, Ventricle, Vesicle, Vitta, Vomica, Vug, Vugg, Vugh, Well

Cavort(ing) Jag

Cavy Agouti, Capybara, Hograt, Paca

Cease(fire) Abate, Blin, Cut, Desist, Die, Disappear, Halt, Intermit, Lin, Lose, Pass, Refrain, Remit, Sessa, → **STOP**, Truce

Ceaseless Eternal, Incessant

Cecil Rhodes

Cedar(wood) Arolla, Atlas, Deodar, Incense, Jamaica, Japanese, Toon

Cede Grant, Yield

Ceiling Absolute, Barrel, Coffered, Cove, Cupola, Dome, Glass, Lacunar, Laquearia, Limit, Plafond, Roof, Service, Soffit, Stained glass

Celebrate(d), Celebration, Celebrity Ale, Beanfeast, Besung, Bigwig, Binge, Carnival, Cel, Chant, Commemorate, Distinguished, Do, Emblazon, Encaenia, Epithalamion, Epithalamium, Fame, Feast, Fest, Festivity, Fete, Fiesta, Gala, Gaudeamus, Gaudy, Glorify, Grog-up, Harvest home, Hold, Holiday, Honour, Jamboree, Jol, Jollifications, Jollities, Jubilee, Keep, Large it, Laud, Legend, Lion, Loosing, Lowsening, Maffick, Mardi Gras, Mass, Mawlid al-Nabi, Megastar, Monstre sacre, Name, Noted, Nuptials, Observe, Occasion, Orgy, Panathenaea, Pinata, Praise, Randan, Rejoice, Renown, Repute, Revel, Rite, Roister, Saturnalia, Sing, Spree, Star, Storied, Sung, Superstar, Treat, Triumph, Wassail, Wet

Celerity Dispatch, Haste, Speed, Velocity

Celery Alexanders, Smallage, Stick

Celestial Chinese, Divine, Ethereal, Heavenly, Supernal, Uranic

Celibate, Celibacy Bachelor, Chaste, Paterin(e), Rappist, Rappite, Shakers, Single, Spinster

Cell(s), Cellular Battery, Bullpen, Cadre, Chamber, Chapel, Condemned, Crypt, Cubicle, Death, Dungeon, Group, Laura, Padded, Peter, → **PRISON**, Safety, Strip, Tank, Unit

---

CELLS

1 letter:	4 letters:		
T	Axon	Oxum	Flame
	Comb	Soma	Giant
3 letters:	Cone	Stem	Gland
Dry	Cyte	Zeta	Guard
Pec	Fuel		Islet
Sex	Germ	5 letters:	Linin
Wet	Hair	Ascus	Lymph
	HeLa	Basal	Nerve
	Mast	Canal	Nicad
		Clark	Solar

Sperm
Spore
Stone
Swarm
Water
White
X-body

6 letters:
Button
Censor
Collar
Cybrid
Cytoid
Diaxon
Gamete
Goblet
Hadley
Killer
Morula
Mother
Neuron
Oocyte
Plasma
Sensor
Sickle
Somite
Target
Thread
Zygote

7 letters:
Bimorph
Cadmium
Cambium
Cathode
Daniell
Energid
Gemmule
Gravity
Helper T
Initial
Lithite
Myotome
Myotube
Neurite
Neurone
Neutron
Plastid
Primary
Schwann

Sertoli
Somatic
Spireme
Sporule
Storage
Tapetum
Vesicle
Voltaic

8 letters:
Akaryote
Auxocyte
Basidium
Basophil
Blasteme
Blastula
Congenic
Cytology
Daughter
Defensin
Ectomere
Endoderm
Endosarc
Ependyma
Epiblast
Eukaryon
Galvanic
Gonidium
Gonocyte
Hapteron
Hemocyte
Meiocyte
Meristem
Monocyte
Myoblast
Neoblast
Palisade
Parietal
Platelet
Purkinje
Receptor
Retinula
Schizont
Selenium
Seredium
Squamous
Standard
Sweatbox
Symplast
Synergid
Tracheid

Unipolar
Zoosperm
Zoospore

9 letters:
Adipocyte
Antipodal
Astrocyte
Athrocyte
Auxospore
Basophile
Coenocyte
Companion
Corpuscle
Desmosome
Ectoplasm
Embryo-sac
Fibrocyte
Haemocyte
Hybridoma
Idioblast
Internode
Iridocyte
Karyology
Laticifer
Leclanché
Leucocyte
Leukocyte
Merozoite
Microcyte
Micromere
Myelocyte
Myofibril
Organelle
Periplasm
Periplast
Phagocyte
Phellogen
Proembryo
Secondary
Spermatid
Sporocyte
Suspensor
Syncytium
Synkaryon
Thymocyte
Trabecula
Tracheide

10 letters:
Ameloblast

Archespore
Blastoderm
Blastomere
Centrosome
Choanocyte
Chromaffin
Chromosome
Cnidoblast
Eosinophil
Epithelium
Fibroblast
Gametocyte
Histiocyte
Leucoblast
Leukoblast
Lymphocyte
Macrophage
Melanocyte
Mesenchyme
Myeloblast
Neuroblast
Neutrophil
Normoblast
Osteoblast
Osteoclast
Perikaryon
Phelloderm
Protoplast
Spermatium
Spherocyte
Suppressor
Totipotent
White-blood

11 letters:
Aplanospore
Arthrospore
Endothelium
Erythrocyte
Granulocyte
Interneuron
Kinetoplast
Lymphoblast
Megaloblast
Melanoblast
Microgamete
Microvillus
Motor neuron
Odontoblast
Poikilocyte
Propoceptor

Schistocyte
Spheroplast
Suppressor T
Trophoblast

12 letters:
Aplanogamete
Chondroblast

Electrolytic
Gametrangium
Haematoblast
Interstitial
Paraphysisis
Photovoltaic
Reticulocyte
Spermatocyte

Spermatozoid
Spermatozoon
Spongioblast

13 letters:
Chromatophore
Mitochondroin
Photoelectric

Photoreceptor

14 letters:
Spermatogonium
Weston standard

Cellar Basement, Bodega, Coalhole, Dunny, Hypogeum, Ratskeller, Storm, Vault, Vaut, Wine

Cell division Amitosis

Cellist, Cello Casals, Du Pré, Hermit, Prisoner, Tortelier

Celluloid, Cellulose Acetate, Cel, Viscose, Xylonite

Celt(ic) Belgic, Breton, Brython, Cornish, Druid, Gadhel, Gael, Goidel, Helvetii, Kelt, La Tène, P, Q, Taffy, Welsh

Cement Araldite®, Blast-furnace, Compo, Concrete, Fix, Flaunch, Glue, Grout, Gunite, High-alumina, Hydraulic, Lute, Maltha, Mastic, Mortar, Paste, Pointing, Porcelain, Portland, Putty, Rice-glue, Roman, Rubber, Slurry, → STICK, Trass, Water

Cemetery Aceldama, Arenarium, Arlington, Boneyard, Boot Hill, Campo santo, Catacomb, Churchyard, God's Acre, Golgotha, Graveyard, Musall, Necropolis, Père Lachaise, Potter's field, Saqqara, Urnfield

Censer Cassolette, Navicula, Thurible

Censor(ious), Censure Accuse, Admonition, Animadvert, Appeach, Ban, Banner, Berate, Blame, Blue-pencil, Bowdler, Braid, Cato, Comstockery, → CONDEMN, Critical, Criticise, Damn, Dang, Decry, Dispraise, Edit, Excommunicate, Excoriate, Expurgate, Gag, Obloquy, Opprobrium, Rap, Repress, Reprimand, Reproach, Reprobate, Reprove, Satirise, Scold, Scrub, Slam, Slate, Stricture, Suppress, Tax, Tirade, Traduce, Wig

Census, Census taker Count, Numerator, Poll

Cent Bean, Coin, Ct, Penny, Red

Centaur Ch(e)iron, Horseman, Nessus, Sagittary, Therianthropic

Centenary, Centennial Anniversary, Colorado

Centipede Chilopoda, Earwig, Polypod, Scolopendra, Scutiger

Central, Centre Active, Amid, Assessment, Attendance, Axis, Broca's, Bunt, Call, Cardinal, Chakra, Civic, Community, Contact, Core, Cost, Day, Daycare, Dead, Detention, Detoxification, Deuteron, Deuton, Downtown, Drop-in, Epergne, Eye, Field, Focus, Frontal, Garden, Health, Heart, Heritage, Hotbed, Hothouse, Hub, Incident, Inmost, Internal, Interpretive, Kernel, Kingpin, Law, Leisure, Lincoln, Live, Main, Mecca, Median, Medulla, Mid(st), Mission, Music, Nave, Nerve, Nucleus, Omphalus, Pompidou, Profit, Property, Reception, Rehabilitation, Remand, Respiratory, Shopping, Social Education, Storm, Teachers', Trauma, Visitor, Waist, Weather

Central heating Cen, CH

▷ **Centre** *may indicate* middle letters

Centrepiece Epergne

Century Age, C, Era, Magdeburg, Period, Siècle, Ton

Cephalopod Ammonite, Calamary, Cuttle, Loligo, Nautilus, Octopus, Sepia, Squid

Ceramic(s) Agateware, Arcanist, China, Earthen, Ferrite, Porcelain, Pottery, Sialon, Tiles

Cereal Amelcorn, Barley, Blé, Bran, Buckwheat, Bulgar, Bulg(h)ur, Cassava, Corn, Cornflakes, Couscous, Emmer, Farina, Gnocchi, Grain, Granola, Groats, Hominy, Maize, Mandioc(a), Mandiocca, Mani(h)oc, Manihot, Mealie, Millet, Muesli, Oats, Paddy, Popcorn, Rye(corn), Sago, Samp, Sarassin, Seed, Semolina, Sorghum, Spelt, Tapioca, Tef(f), Triticale, Triticum, Wheat, Zea

Cerebrate, Cerebration Pore, Thought

Ceremonial, Ceremony Aarti, Amrit, Baptism, Barmitzvah, Chado, Chanoyu, Common Riding, Coronation, Doseh, Durbar, Encaenia, Enthronement, Etiquette, Eucharist, Flypast, Form(al), Formality, Gongyo, Habdalah, Havdalah, Havdoloh, Heraldry, Investiture, Matsuri, Maundy, Mummery, Observance, Occasion, Ordination, Pageantry, Parade, Pomp, Powwow, Protocol, Rite, Ritual, Sacrament, Sado, Seder, Service, State, Tea, Topping-out, Trooping (the Colour), Unveiling, Usage

Cerium Ce

Cert(ain), Certainty Absolute, Actual, Assured, Banker, Bound, Cast-iron, Cinch, Cocksure, Confident, Convinced, Decided, Exact, Fact, Fate, Indubitable, Inevitable, Infallible, Keen, Monte, Moral, Nap, Needly, One, Positive, Poz, Precise, Racing, Shoo-in, Siccar, Sicker, Snip, Some, → **SURE**, Sure-fire, Truth, Yes

Certainly Agreed, Ay, Certes, Fegs, Forsooth, Indeed, Iwis, Jokol, OK, Oke, Pardi(e), Pardy, Perdie, Siccar, Sicker, → **SURE**, Truly, Verily, Yea, Yes, Yokul, Ywis

Certificate, Certified, Certify Affirm, Assure, Attest, Bene decessit, Birth, Bond, Chit, Cocket, Confirm, Credential, Death, Debenture, Depose, Diploma, Docket, Document, Enseal, Gold, Guarantee, Landscrip, Licence, Lines, Medical, MOT, Notarise, Paper, Patent, Proven, Savings, School, Scrip, Scripophily, Security, Share, Stamp note, Stock, Sworn, Talon, Testamur, Testimonial, Treasury, U, Unruly, Voucher, Warrant

Cesspit Bog, Dungmere, Sinkhole, Slurry

Cetacean Dolphin, Porpoise, Whale

Ceylon(ese) Serendip, Vedda(h)

Chafe(r), Chafing Chunter, Fray, Fret, Harass, Intertrigo, Irritate, Pan, → **RUB**, Seethe, Worry

Chaff(y) Badinage, Banter, Bran, Chip, Cornhusk, Dross, Hay, Husk, Rag, Raillery, Rally, Ramentum, Refuse, Roast, Rot, Tease, Twit

Chaffer(ing) Bandy, Bargain, Haggle, Higgle, Hucksterage, Traffic

Chaffinch Whitewing

Chagrin Envy, Mortify, Spite, Vexation

Chain(s), Chained Acre's-breadth, Albert, Anklet, Band, Bicycle, Bind, Bond, Bracelet, Branched, Bucket, Cable, Catena, Chatelaine, Choke, Cistron, Closed, Cordillera, Cyclic, Daisy, Decca, Dixie, Drive, Duplex, Dynasty, Engineer's, Esses, Fanfarona, Fetter, Fob, Food, Furlong, Gleipnir, Golden, Grand, Gunter's, Gyve, Heavy, Human, Learner's, Lockaway, Markov, Mayor, Micella(r), Micelle, → **MOUNTAIN**, Noria, Open, Pennine, Pitch, Range, Rockies, Rode, Roller, Safety, Seal, → **SERIES**, Shackle, Side, Slang, Snigging, Snow, Sprocket, Straight, String, Strobila, Supply, Surveyor's, Suspensor, Team, Tug, Voluntary, Watch

Chain-gang Coffle

Chair Basket, Bath, Bench, Bentwood, Berbice, Bergère, Birthing, Bosun's, Butterfly, Camp, Cane, Captain's, Carver, Club, Curule, Deck, Dining, Director's, Easy, Electric, Emeritus, Estate, Fauteuil, Fiddle-back, Folding, Frithstool, Garden, Gestatorial, Guérite, High, Jampan, Jampanee, Jampani, Ladder-back, Lounger, Love-seat, Lug, Merlin, Morris, Musical, Nursing, Personal, Pew, Preside, Recliner, Rocker, Rush-bottomed, → **SEAT**, Sedan, Steamer, Stool, Straight, Sugan, Swivel,

Throne, Wainscot, Wheel, Windsor, Wing

Chair-back Ladder, Splat

Chairman Convener, Emeritus, Landammann, Mao, MC, Pr(a)eses, Prof, Prolocutor, Sheraton, Speaker

Chalaza Albumen, Treadle, Treddle

Chaldean Babylonian, Ur

Chalet Cabana, Cot, Skio

Chalice Poisoned

Chalk(y) Calcareous, Cauk, Cawk, Crayon, Credit, Cretaceous, Dentin, French, Senonian, Soapstone, Spanish, Steatite, Tailor's, White(n), Whit(en)ing

Challenge(r), Challenging Acock, Assay, Call, Cartel, Champion, Charge, Confront, Contest, Dare, Defy, Gage, Gauntlet, Glove, Hazard, Hen(ner), Iconoclasm, Impugn, Insubordinate, Oppugn, Provoke, Query, Question, Recuse, Sconce, Shuttle, Tackle, Taker, Tall order, Tank, Threat, Vie, Wero, Whynot

Chamber(s) Airlock, Atrium, Auricle, Bladder, Bubble, Camarilla, Camera, Casemate, Cavern, Cavitation, Cavity, Cell(a), Chanty, Close-stool, Cloud, Cofferdam, Combustion, Cubicle, Decompression, Dene-hole, Dolmen, Echo, Float, Fumatorium, Fume, Gas, Gazunder, Gilded, Hall, Horrors, Hypogea, Inspection, Ionization, Jerry, Jordan, Kiva, Lethal, Locule, Lok Sabha, Lower, Magma, Manhole, Mattamore, Mesoscaphe, Plenum, Po(t), Presence, Priest('s)-hole, Privy, Reaction, Resonance-box, Roum, Second, Serdab, Silo, Spark, Star, Steam-chest, Swell-box, Synod, Thalamus, Undercroft, Upper, Utricle, Vault, Ventricle, Wilson cloud, Zeta

Chamberlain Camerlengo, Camerlingo, Censor

Chameleon American, Anole, Ethiopian, Lizard, Tarand

Chamfer Bevel, Groove

Chamois Ibex, Izard, Shammy

Champ Bite, Chafe, Chew, Chomp, Eat, Gnash, Gnaw, Hero, Mash, Morsure, Munch

Champagne Boy, Bubbly, Charlie, Fizz, Gigglewater, Pop, Sillery, Simkin, Simpkin, Stillery, Troyes, Widow

Champion(s) Ace, Adopt, Ali, Apostle, Belt, Campeador, Cid, Cock, Crusader, Cupholder, Defend, Don Quixote, Doucepere, Douzeper, Dymoke, Enoch, Espouse, Gladiator, Gun, Harry, → **HERO**, Horse, Kemp, Kemper(yman), King, Knight, Maintain, Matchless, Messiah, Messias, Neil, Paladin, Palmerin, Peerless, Perseus, Promachos, Proponent, Protagonist, Roland, St Anthony, St David, St Denis, St George, St James, St Patrick, Seven, Spiffing, Spokesman, Star, Support, Tribune, Upholder, Victor, Wardog, → **WINNER**, Yokozuna

Championship Five Nations, Open, Seven, Six Nations, Super Bowl, Title, Tri-nations

Chance (upon), Chancy Accident, Aleatory, Aunter, Bet, Break, Buckley's, Cast, Casual, Cavel, Coincidence, Contingent, Dice, Earthly, Even, Fat, → **FATE**, Fighting, First refusal, Fluke, Fortuitous, Fortuity, Fortune, → **GAMBLE**, Game, Hap, Happenstance, Hobnob, Iffy, Kevel, Light, Loaves and fishes, Look-in, Lot, → **LOTTERY**, Luck, Main, Meet, Mercy, Occur, Odds, Odds-on, Opening, Opportunity, Outside, Peradventure, Posse, Potluck, Probability, Prospect, Random, Rise, Risk, Run into, Russian roulette, Serendipity, Slant, Spec, Sporting, Stake, Stochastic, Sweep, Toss-up, Treble, Turn, Tychism, Ventre, Venture, Wager

Chancel Adytum, Bema, Nave

Chancellor Adolf, Bismarck, Dollfuss, Kohl, Logothete, Minister, More, Wolsey

Chancery Court, Hanaper

Chandelier Candlestick, Corona, Drop, Electrolier, Gasolier, Girandole, Lustre, Pendant

Chandler Acater, Acatour, Raymond
Chaney Lon
Change(able), Changes, Changing Adapt, Adjust, Agio, Aleatoric, → **ALTER**, Amendment, Attorn, Backtrack, Barter, Become, Bob-major, Capricious, Cash, Catalysis, Chameleon, Channel-hop, Chop, Cline, Commute, Convert, Coppers, Cut, Denature, Departure, Development, Dichrony, Edit, Enallage, Esterify, Eustatic, Evolve, Exchange, Fickle, Find, Flighty, Float, Fluctuate, Flux, Guard, Gybe, Inflect, Innovate, Kembla, Killcrop, Labile, Loose, Make-over, Menopause, Metabolic, Metabolise, Metamorphose, Metamorphosis, Mew, Mobile, Modify, Morph, Mutable, Mutalis mutandis, Mutanda, Mutation, Ontogeny, Parallax, Peal, Pejoration, Peripet(e)ia, Permute, Port, Prisere, Prophase, Protean, Quantum leap, Realise, Recant, Rectify, Reform, Refraction, Regime, Rejig, Reshuffle, Resipiscence, Rest, Reverse, Revise, Revolutionise, Rework, Sandhi, Scourse, Sd, Sea, Seesaw, Sere, Sex, Shake-out, Shake-up, Shift, Silver, Small, Sublimation, Substitute, Swap, Swing, Switch, Tempolabile, Tolsel, Tolsey, Tolzey, Transfer, Transfiguration, Transform, Transition, Transmogrify, Transmute, Transpose, Transubstantial, Turn, Uncertain, Upheaval, U-turn, Vagary, Variant, Variation, Vary, Veer, Versatile, Vicissitude, Volatile, Volte-face, Wankle, Washers, Waver, Weathercock, Wheel, Wow
▷ **Change(d)** *may indicate* an anagram
Changeling Auf, Killcrop, Oaf, Turncoat
Channel Access, Aflaj, Aqueduct, Artery, Beagle, Bed, Billabong, Bristol, Canal, Canaliculus, Chimb, Chime, Chine, Chute, Conduit, Culvert, Cut, Cutting, Distribution, Ditch, Drain, Duct, Dyke, Ea, English, Estuary, Euripus, Fairway, Falaj, Feeder, Floodway, Flume, Foss, Funnel, Furrow, Gat, Gate, Geo, Gio, Glyph, Grough, Gully, Gut, Gutter, Head-race, Ingate, Katabothron, Katavothron, Khor, Kill, Kos, Lane, Latch, Leat, Leet, Limber, Major, Meatus, Medium, Minch, Moat, Mozambique, Multiplex, Narrows, North, Penstock, Pentland Firth, Pescadores, Pipeline, Qanat, Race, Raceway, Rebate, Rigol(l), Rigolets, Rivulet, Run, St George's, Sea-gate, Seaway, Sewer, Shunt, Sinus, Sky, Sloot, Sluice, Sluit, Sny(e), Solent, Solway Firth, Sound, Sow, Spillway, Sprue, Strait, Suez, Sure, Swash, Tailrace, Tideway, Tracheole, Trough, Ureter, Vallecula, Vein, Wasteweir, Watercourse, Waterspout, Wireway, Yucatan
Chant Anthem, Antiphon, Canticle, Cantillate, Cantus, Chaunt, Daimoku, Decantate, Euouae, Evovae, Gregorian, Haka, Harambee, Hymn, Intone, Introit, Mantra(m), Motet, Pennillion-singing, Plainsong, Proper, Psalm, Sing, Slogan, Te Deum, The Reproaches, Yell
Chantilly Cream, Lace
Chaos, Chaotic Abyss, Anarchy, Confusion, Disorder, Fitna, Fractal, Hun-tun, Jumble, Mess, Mixter-maxter, Muss, Shambles, Shambolic, Snafu, Tohu bohu
▷ **Chaotic** *may indicate* an anagram
Chap(s) Beezer, Bloke, Bo, Bod, Bor, Cat, Chafe, Cheek, Chilblain, Chop, Cleft, Cod, Codger, Cove, Crack, Customer, Dog, Fella, Fellow, Flews, Genal, Gent, Gink, Guy, Hack, Joll, Jowl, Kibe, Lad, → **MAN**, Mouth, Mum, Ocker, Rent, Rime, Spray, Spreathe, Spreaze, Spreethe, Spreeze, Wang
Chapel Bethel, Bethesda, Beulah, Cha(u)ntry, Chevet, Ebenezer, Feretory, Galilee, Lady, Oratory, Parabema, Prothesis, Sacellum, Sistine
Chaperon(e) Beard, Cap, Duenna, Escort, Gooseberry, Griffin, Griffon, Gryphon, Muffin
Chaplain CF, Ordinary, Padre, Priest, Skypilot, Slope
Chaplet Anadem, Coronet, Fillet, Garland, Wreath

▷ **Chaps** *may indicate* an anagram

Chapter Accidents, C, Canon, Cap, Capitular, Ch, Chap, Cr, Division, Episode, Lodge, Phase, Section, Social, Sura(h), Verse

Char(woman) Adust, Burn, Cleaner, Coal, Daily, Duster, Mop(p), Mrs Mop(p), Scorch, Sear, Singe, Smoulder, Toast, Togue, Torgoch

Charabanc Bus, Chara, Coach

Character(s) Aesc, Alphabet, Ampersand, Ampussyand, Atmosphere, Aura, Backslash, Brand, Calibre, Case, Cipher, Clef, Cliff, Climate, Coloration, Complexion, Contour, Credit, Delimiter, Deuteragonist, Devanagari, Digamma, Digit, Dramatis personae, Emoticon, Ess, Essence, Eta, Ethos, → FEATURE, Fish, Fist, Form, Grain, Graphics, Grass, Grit, Hieroglyphic, Homophone, Ideogram, Ideograph, Italic, Kanji, Kern, Kind, La(m)bda, Letter, Logogram, Make-up, Mark, Mu, Nagari, → NATURE, Non-person, Nu, Ogam, Ogham, Pahlavi, Pantaloon, Part, Pehlevi, Person(a), Personage, → PERSONALITY, Phonogram, Physiognomy, Pi, Polyphone, Protagonist, Psi, Raisonneur, Reference, Reference-mark, Repute, Rho, Role, Rune, Runic, Sampi, San, Self, Sirvente, Slash, Sonancy, Space, Sphenogram, Stamp, Subscript, Superscript(ion), Swung dash, Syllabary, Symbol, Tab, Testimonial, Ton(e), Trait, Uncial, Unit, Vav, Vee, Waw, Wen, Wild card, Wyn(n), Yogh, Zeta

Characterise(d), Characterism, Characteristic(s) Acquired, Attribute, Aura, Cast, Colour, Distinctive, Earmark, Ethos, Facies, Feature, Hair, Hallmark, Has, Headmark, Idiomatic, Idiosyncrasy, Jizz, Lineament, Mien, Nature, Notate, Peculiar, Persona, Phenotype, Point, Property, Quality, Signature, Stigma, Strangeness, Streak, Style, → TRAIT, Transfer, Typical, Vein, Way

Characterless Anon, Inane, Wet

Charade Enigma, Pretence, Riddle

Charcoal Activated, Carbon, Coke, Fusain, Sugar

Charge(s), Charged, Charger Access, Accusal, Accuse, Aerate, Agist, Allege, Annulet, Arraign, Ascribe, Assault, Baton, Bear, Behest, Blame, Brassage, Brush, Buckshot, Bum rap, Care, Carrying, Cathexis, Commission, Community, Complaint, Congestion, Cost, Count, Cover, Criminate, Damage, Debit, Delate, Delf, Delph, Demurrage, Depth, Depute, Directive, Dittay, Dockage, Due, Duty, Electric, Electron, Entrust, Entry, Exit, Expense, Fare, Fee, Fill, Fixed, Flag fall, Fleur-de-lis, Floating, Flock, Freight, Fullage, Fuse, Fusil, Fuze, Gazump, Giron, Gravamen, Gyron, → HERALDIC, Hot, Hypothec, Impeach, Impute, Indict, Inescutcheon, Inform, Instinct, Ion, Isoelectric, Last, Lien, Lioncel(le), Lionel, Live, Load, Mandate, Mine, Mount, Nuclear, Objure, Obtest, Onrush, Onslaught, Onus, Ordinary, Orle, Overhead, Pastoral, Pervade, Pew-rent, Plaint, Positive, Premium, Prime, Prix fixe, Q, Quayage, Rack-rent, Rap, Rate, Red-dog, Rent, Report, Reprise, Reverse, Roundel, Run, → RUSH, Saddle, Service, Specific, Stampede, Steed, Tariff, Tax, Tear, Terms, Tilt, Toll, → TRAY, Tressure, Trickle, Trust, Tutorage, Upfill, Vaire, Vairy, Verdoy, Vigorish, Ward, Warhead, Wharfage

Chariot(eer) Auriga, Automedon, Biga, Cart, Charet, Curricle, Hur, Phaethon, Quadriga, Vimana, Wagon, Wain

Charisma Oomph, Personality

Charitable, Charity Alms, Alms-deed, Awmous, Benign, Breadline, Caritas, Cause, Chugger, Dole, Dorcas, Eleemosynary, Kiwanis, Largesse, Leniency, Liberal, Lion, Love, Mercy, Oddfellow, Openhanded, Oxfam, Pelican, Zakat

Charivari Rough music, Uproar

Charlatan Cheat, Crocus, Empiric, Escroc, Faker, Imposter, Katerfelto,

Mountebank, Poseur, Quack(salver), Saltimbanco

Charlemagne Carlovingian

Charles, Charley, Charlie Beard, Car, Champagne, Chan, Chaplin, Checkpoint, Elia, Lamb, (Old) Rowley, Pretender, Rug-gown, Sap, Tail-end, Watchman

Charles de Gaulle Airport

Charlock Runch

Charlotte Bronte, Russe, Yonge

Charm(er), Charming Abracadabra, Abrasax, Abraxas, Allure, Amulet, Appeal, Aroma, Attraction, Beguile, Bewitch, Captivate, Charisma, Circe, Comether, Cute, Cutie, Delectable, Emerods, Enamour, Enchant, Engaging, → **ENTRANCE**, Fascinate, Fay, Fetish, Grace, Greegree, Gri(s)gris, Hand of glory, Houri, Juju, Magnetic, Mascot, Mojo, Obeah, Obi(a), Periapt, Phylactery, Porte-bonheur, Pretty, Prince, Quaint, Quark, Ravish, Siren, Smoothie, Spellbind, Suave, Sweetness, Taking, Talisman, Tefillah, Telesm, Tephillah, Tiki, Trinket, Unction, Voodoo, Winning, Winsome

▷ **Charming** *may indicate* an anagram

Chart(ed), Charting Abac, Bar, Breakeven, Card, Control, Diagram, Eye, Flip, Flow, Gantt, Graph, Histogram, Horoscope, Hydrography, Isogram, Isopleth, List, Magna Carta, → **MAP**, Mappemond, Movement, Nomogram, Organisation, Pie, Plane, Plot, Portolano, Ringelmann, Run, Social, Sociogram, Table, Test, Timetable, Waggoner, Weather, Z

Charta, Charter Atlantic, Book, Citizen's, Covenant, Hire, Lease, Let, Novodamus, Rent, Social (Chapter), Tenants', Time, Voyage

Chary Cagey, Careful, Cautious, Frugal, Shy, Wary

Charybdis Maelstrom, Whirlpool

Chase(r), Chasing Cannock, Chace, Chevy, Chivy, Ciseleur, Ciselure, Course, Cranbome, Decorate, Drink, Game, Harass, Hound, → **HUNT**, Jumper, Oxo, Pursuit, Race, Scorse, Sic(k), Steeple, Sue, Suit, Wild-goose

Chasm Abyss, Crevasse, Fissure, Gap, Gorge, Gulf, Schism, Yawn

Chaste, Chastity Agnes, Attic, Celibate, Classic, Clean, Continent, Fatima, Florimell, Ines, Innocent, Modesty, Nessa, → **PURE**, Vestal, Virginal, Virtue

Chasten, Chastise(d), Chastisement Beat, Correct, Discipline, Disple, Lash, Rib-roast, Rollicking, Scold, Scourge, Shame-faced, Spank, Strap, Whip

Chat, Chatter(box) Babble, Bavardage, Blab(ber), Blether, Campanero, Causerie, Chelp, Chinwag, Clack, Clishmaclaver, Confab(ulate), Converse, Cosher, Coze, Crack, Dialogue, Froth, Gab(ble), Gas, Gossip, Gup, Hobnob, Jabber, Jargon, Jaw, Kilfud, Madge, Mag(pie), Natter, Patter, Pie, Pourparler, Prate, Prattle, Rabbit, Rabble, Rap, Rattle, Scuttlebutt, Shmoose, Shoot the breeze, Stone, Talk, Talkee-talkee, Tattle, Tongue-work, Twattle, Waffle, Whin, Windbag, Witter, Wongi, Yacketyyak, Yad(d)a-yad(d)a-yad(d)a, Yak, Yap, Yarn, Yatter, Yellow-breasted, Yoking

Chateau Castle, Cru, Malmaison, Schloss

Chateaubriand René

Chattel Asset, Chose, Deodand

Chaucer(ian) Dan, OE

Chauffeur Cabby, Coachy, Driver, Sice, Syce

Chauvinist Alf, Bigot, Jingo, MCP, Partisan, Patriot, Sexist

Cheap A bon marché, Bargain, Base, Catchpenny, Cheesy, Chintzy, Cut-price, Downmarket, Giveaway, Ignoble, Knockdown, Low, Off-peak, Poor, Sacrifice, Shoddy, Stingy, Tatty, Tawdry, Ticky-tacky, Tinhorn, Tinpot, Tinselly, Trivial, Tuppenny, Two-bit, Twopenny, Undear, Vile

▷ **Cheap** *may indicate* a d- or p- start to a word

Cheapside Bow

Cheat(ers), Cheating Bam, Bamboozle, Beguile, Bilk, Bite(r), Bob, Bonnet, Bucket, Bullock, Burn, Cardsharp(er), Charlatan, Chiaus, Chicane(ry), Chisel, Chouse, Clip, Cod, Cog(ger), Colt, Con, Cozen, Crib, Cross, Cross-bite(r), Cuckold, Cully, Defraud, Delude, Diddle, Dingo, Dish, Do, Doublecross, Duckshove, Dupe, Escroc, Faitor, Fiddle, Finagle, Flam, Fleece, Fob, Foister, Fox, Fraud, Gaff, Gip, Glasses, Gull-catcher, Gum, Gyp, Hoax, Hocus, Hoodwink, Hornswoggle, Horse, Intake, Jockey, Leg, Magsman, Mulct, Mump, Nick, Pasteboard, Picaro(on), Poop, Queer, Rib, Rig, Rogue, Rook, Rush, Scam, Screw, Screw over, Shaft, Sharper, Short-change, Slur, Smouch, Snap, Stack, Stiff, Sting, Swindle, Thimble-rigging, Trepan, Trim, Two-time, Welch, Welsh, Wheedle

Check Arrest, Audit, Bauk, Ba(u)lk, Bill, Bridle, Collate, Compesce, Control, Count, Cramp, Cross-index, Curb, Dam, Damp, Detain, Detent, Discovered, Dogs-tooth, Examine, Foil, Frustrate, Halt, Hamper, Hobble, Houndstooth, Inhibit, Inspect, Jerk, Jerque, Let, Limit, Mate, Monitor, Observe, Overhaul, Parity, Perpetual, Prevent, Rain, Reality, Rebuff, Rebuke, Rein, Repress, Reprime, Repulse, Reread, → **RESTRAIN**, Revoke, Saccade, Screen, Service, Setback, Shepherd's, Shorten, Sit-upon, Sneap, Sneb, Snib, Snub, Sound, Spot, → **STEM**, Stent, Stint, Stop, Stunt, Tab, Tally, Tartan, Tattersall, Test, Thwart, Tick, Trash, Verify, Vet

Checkers Chinese, Piece

Check-out Till

Cheddar Cheese, Gorge

Cheek(y) Alforja, Audacity, Brass-neck, Buccal, Chap, Chollers, Chutzpah, Cool, Crust, Flippant, Fresh, Gena(l), Gum, Hard-faced, Hussy, Impertinent, Impudent, Joll, Jowl, Lip, Malapert, Malar, Masseter, Neck, Nerve, Noma, Pert, Presumption, Quean, Sass, Sauce, Sideburns, Wang, Yankie, Zygoma

Cheep Chirp, Chirrup, Peep

Cheer(s), Cheerful(ness), Cheering Acclaim, Agrin, Applaud, Banzai, Barrack, Blithe, Bonnie, Bravo, Bright, Bronx, Bubbly, Buck, Buoy, Cadgy, Canty, Carefree, Cherry, Chin-chin, Chipper, Chirpy, → **COMFORT**, Crouse, Debonair, Drink, Ease, Elate, Elevate, Enliven, Exhilarate, Festive, Genial, Gladden, Happy-go-lucky, Hearten, Hilarity, Holiday, Hooch, Hoorah, Hurra(h), Huzzah, Insouciance, Jocund, Jovial, Kia-ora, L'allegro, Light-hearted, Lightsome, Lively, Meal, Olé, Ovate, Peart, Perky, Please, Praise, Prosit, Rah, Riant, Rivo, Root, Rumbustious, Shout, Sko(a)l, Slainte, Sonsie, Sunny, Ta, Tata, Thanks, Three, Tiger, Tiggerish, Toodle-oo, Upbeat, Warm, Winsome, Yell

Cheerless Dismal, Drab, Drear, Gloomy, Glum, Wint(e)ry

Cheese, Cheesy American, Amsterdam, Appenzell, Asiago, Bel Paese, Blue, Blue vein, Boc(c)oncini, Boursin, Brie, Caboc, Caerphilly, Cambazola, Camembert, Cantal, Casein, Caseous, Cheddar, Cheshire, Chessel, Chèvre, Colby, Cottage, Coulommiers, Cream, Crowdie, Curd, Damson, Danish blue, Derby, Dolcelatte, Double Gloucester, Dunlop, Edam, Emmental(er), Emmenthal(er), Ermite, Esrom, Ewe, Fet(a), Fontina, Fromage frais, Fynbo, Gloucester, Goat, Gorgonzola, Gouda, Grana Padano, Grand Panjandrum, Green, Gruyère, Halloumi, Hard, Havarti, Huntsman, Ilchester, Islay, Jarlsberg®, Junket, Kebbock, Kebbuck, Kenno, Killarney, Lancashire, Leicester, Limburg(er), Lymeswold®, Macaroni, Mascarpone, Mousetrap, Mozzarella, Mu(e)nster, Mycella, Neufchatel, Oka, Orkney, Paneer, Parmesan, Pecorino, Pont l'Eveque, Port Salut, Pot, Provolone, Quark, Raclette, Rarebit, Reblochon, Red Leicester, Rennet, Ricotta, Romano, Roquefort, Sage Derby, Samso, Sapsago, Skyr, Stilton®, Stone, Stracchino, Swiss,

Taleggio, Tilsit, Tofu, Truckle, Vacherin, VIP, Wensleydale
Cheesecake Pin-up, Talmouse
Cheese-scoop Pale
Chef Commis, Escoffier
Chekhov Anton
Chemical Acanthin, Acid, Acrolein, Adrenalin®, Agent Orange, Alar, Aldehyde,
   Alkali, Allomone, Alum, Amide, Anabolic, Barilla, Bradykinin, Bute, Camphene,
   Camphor, Carbide, Carnallite, Caseose, Catalyst, Cephalin, Cerebroside, Depside,
   Developer, Dopamine, Encephalin, Enkephalin(e), Enol, Ethanal, Fixer, Fluoride,
   Formyl, Freon, Fungicide, Gamone, Glutamine, Glycol, Halon, Harmin, Heavy,
   Hecogenin, Heptane, Hexylene, Hexylresorcinol, Histamine, Hypo, ICI, Imine,
   Imipramine, Indican, Interleukin, Larvicide, Lewisite, Morphactin, Naioxone,
   Natron, Neurotransmitter, Nitre, Nonylphenol, Oestrogen, Olefin, Olein, Oxide,
   Oxysalt, Pentane, Pentene, Pentyl, Peptide, Periclase, Phenol, Phenyl, Pheromone,
   Potash, Potassa, Psoralen, Ptomaine, Reagent, Resorcin, Resorcinol, Restrainer,
   Serotonin, Soman, Soup, Stearate, Strontia, Styrene, Sulphide, Terpene, Thio-salt,
   Toluol, Toner, Trimer, Weedicide, Weedkiller
Chemise Cymar, Sark, Serk, Shift, Shirt, Simar(re), Smock, Symar
Chemist(ry) Adams, Alchemy, Alchymy, Analyst, Apothecary, Bunsen, Butenandt,
   Cavendish, Charles, Cleve, Dalton, Davy, Debye, Dewar, Dispenser, Druggist,
   Drugstore, FCS, Gahn, Hevesy, Inorganic, Lavoisier, Liebig, LSA, Macadam, MPS,
   Nernst, Newlands, Nobel, Nuclear, Organic, Paracelsus, Pasteur, Pharmacist,
   Physical, Pothecary, Pottingar, Proust, Prout, Redwood, RIC, Sabatier, Sanger,
   Schiff, Spageric, Spagiric, Spagyric, Spicer, Stinks, Stoechiometry, Stoich(e)iometry,
   Technical, Urey, Von Babo, Welsbach, Zymurgy
Cheops Khufu
Cheque Blank, Bouncer, Giro, Gregory, Open, Rubber, Stumer, Tab, Traveller's
Chequer Dice
Cherish(ed) Dear, Dote, Enshrine, Entertain, Esteem, Foment, Foster, Harbour,
   Inshrine, Nestle, Nurse, Pamper, Pet, Precious, Treasure
Cheroot Cigar, Manil(l)a
Cherry (tree) Amarelle, Amazon, Ball, Barbados, Bigaroon, Bigarreau, Bird,
   Blackheart, Cerise, Choke, Cornelian, Gean, Ground, Heart, Jerusalem, Kearton,
   Kermes, Kermesite, Malpighia, Marasca, Maraschino, May-duke, Maz(z)ard, Merry,
   Morel(lo), Prunus, Red, Sweet, Whiteheart
Cherry-pie Heliotrope
Cherub Angel, Putto, Seraph
Chervil Cow-parsley
Chess (move), Chess player, Chess term Black, Blindfold, Endgame, Euwe,
   Fianchetto, FIDE, J'adoube, Karpov, Kasparov, Lightning, Miranda, Patzer, Plank,
   Rapid transit, Shogi, Speed, White, Zugzwang, Zwischenzug
Chessman Bishop, Black, Castle, Horse, King, Knight, Pawn, Pin, Queen, Rook,
   White
Chest(y) Ark, Bahut, Bosom, Box, Breast, Buist, Bunker, Bureau, Bust, Caisson,
   Cap-case, Case, Cassone, Chapel, Charter, Chiffonier, Coffer, Coffin, Coffret,
   Commode, Community, Cub, Dresser, Girnel, Hope, Inro, Kist, Larnax, Locker,
   Lowboy, Meal-ark, Medicine, Ottoman, Pectoral, Pereion, Pigeon, Pleural, Safe,
   Scrine, Scryne, Sea, Shrine, Slop, Steam, Sternum, Tallboy, Tea, Thorax, Toolbox,
   Treasure, Trunk, Wangan, Wangun, Wanigan, War, Wind
Chester Deva
Chestnut Auburn, Badious, Ch, Chincapin, Chinese, Chinkapin, Chinquapin, Cliché,

Conker, Dwarf, Favel(l), Hoary, Horse, Marron, Marron glacé, Moreton Bay, Roan, Russet, Saligot, Soare, Sorrel, Spanish, Sweet, Water

Chest protector → ARMOUR, Bib

Chevalier Bayard, Knight, Pretender

Chevron Dancette, Stripe

Chew(ing) Bite, Champ, Chaw, Cud, Eat, Fletcherism, Gnaw, Gum, Manducate, Masticate, Maul, Meditate, Moop, Mou(p), Munch, Ruminate, Siri(h), Spearmint

Chewink Ground-robin

Chiastolite Macle

Chic Dapper, Debonair, Elegant, Heroin, In, Kick, Modish, Posh, Radical, Smart, Soigné, Stylish, Swish, Tonish, Trim

Chicago Windy City

Chicane(ry) Artifice, Deception, Fraud, Wile

Chichester Yachtsman

Chichi Precious

Chick(en) Australorp, Battery, Biddy, Boiler, Broiler, Capon, Cheeper, Chittagong, Chuckie, Clutch, Cochin, Coronation, Coward, Cowherd, Eirack, Gutless, Hen, Howtowdie, Kiev, Layer, Marengo, Minorca, Mother Carey's, Niderling, Pavid, Poltroon, Poot, Pope's nose, Poult, Pout, Prairie, Precocial, Pullus, Quitter, Roaster, Spatchcock, Spring, Squab, Supreme, Timorous, Unheroic, Windy, Wyandotte, Yellow

Chickenfeed Maize, Peanuts

Chickenpox Varicella

Chickpea Chana, Garbanzo

Chickweed Snow-in-summer

Chicory Endive, Radiccio, Succory, Witloof

Chide Admonish, Berate, Dress, Objurgate, Rate, Rebuke, Reprove, Row, Scold, Tick off, Twit, Upbraid

Chief(tain) Arch, Ardrigh, Ariki, Boss, Caboceer, Cacique, Calif, Caliph, Capital, Capitan, Capitayn, Capo, Caradoc, Cazique, Ch, Chagan, Dat(t)o, DG, Dominant, Emir, Finn (MacCool), First, Foremost, Geronimo, Grand, Haggis, → HEAD, Hereward, Jarl, Kaid, King, Leader, → MAIN, Mass, Mugwump, Nawab, Nizam, Nkosi, Oba, Overlord, Paramount, Pendragon, Premier, Primal, Prime, Principal, Quanah, Raja(h), Rajpramukh, Rangatira, Rangatiratanga, Ratoo, Ratu, Sachem, Sagamore, Sarpanch, Sudder, Supreme, Tanist, Tank, Top

Chiffonier Cabinet, Commode

Chilblain Kibe

Child(ish), Childhood, Children Aerie, Alannah, Ankle biter, Babe, Baby, Bach(ch)a, Badger, Bairn, Bambino, Bantling, Boy, Brat, Brood, Butter-print, Ch, Changeling, Cherub, Chick, Chickabiddy, Chit, Collop, Cub, Dream, Elfin, Eyas, Feral, Foster, Foundling, Gait, Gangrel, Ge(i)t, Girl, Gyte, Heir, Hellion, Hurcheon, Imp, Infancy, Infant, Inner, Issue, It, Jailbait, Jejune, Juvenile, Kid, Kiddie(wink), Kiddy, Kinder, Lad, Latchkey, Limb, Litter, Littlie, Littling, Love, Mamzer, Mardy, Minion, Minor, Mite, Munchkin, Naive, Nipper, Nursling, Offspring, Pantywaist, Papoose, Piccaninny, Pickin, Problem, Progeny, Puerile, Puss, Putto, Ragamuffin, Rip, Romper, Rug rat, Scion, Second, Seed, Small fry, Smout, Smowt, Sprog, Street arab, Subteen, Tacker, Ted, Teeny-bopper, Tike, Toddle(r), Tot(tie), Totty, Trot, Tweenager, Tweenie, Tyke, Urchin, Waif, Wean, Weanel, Weanling, Weeny-bopper, Whelp, Younker, Youth

Childbearing, Childbirth Couvade, Dystocia, Intrapartum, Lamaze, Obstetrics, Parity, Puerperal, Tocology, Tokology

Child-killer Herod

Childless Atocous, Atokous, Barren, Nullipara, Sp

Chill(er), Chilly Bleak, Cauldrife, → **COLD**, Frappé, Freeze, Freon®, Frigid, Frosty, Gelid, Ice, Iciness, Mimi, Oorie, Ourie, Owrie, Parky, Raw, Refrigerate, Rigor, Scare

Chilli Bird's eye, → **PEPPER**, Pimentón

Chime(s) Bell, Cymar, Jingle, Peal, Semantron, Tink, → **TOLL**, Wind

Chimera Graft

Chimney (pot), Chimney corner Can, Cow(l), Femerall, Flare stack, Flue, Funnel, Lamp, Lug, Lum, Smokestack, Stack, Stalk, Steeplejack, Tallboy, Tunnel

Chimp(anzee) Ape, Bonobo, Jocko, Pygmy

Chin, Chinwag Chitchat, Double, Genial, Jaw, Jowl, Mentum

China(man), Chinese Ami, Amoy, Boxer, Cameoware, Cantonese, Cathay, Celestial, Ch, Chelsea, Chink(y), Chow, Coalport, Cochin, Cock, Communist, Confucius, Crackle, Crockery, Delft, Derby, Dresden, Eggshell, Etrurian, Flowery land, Friend, Fukien, Google, Googly, Goss, Hakka, Han, Hizen, Hmong, Imari, Ironstone, Kanji, Kaolin, Kuo-yu, Limoges, Manchu, Manchurian, Mandarin, Mangi, Maoist, Mate, Meissen, Min, Ming, Minton, National, Oppo, Pal, Pareoean, Pekingese, Pe-tsai, Pinyin, Porcelain, → **POTTERY**, Putonghua, Queensware, Red, Rockingham, Royal Worcester, Semiporcelain, Seric, Sèvres, Shanghai, Sinaean, Sinic, Sino-, Spode®, Sun Yat-sen, Tai-ping, Taoist, Teng, Tocharian, Tungus, Uigur, Wal(l)y, Ware, Wedgwood®, Whiteware, Willowware, Worcester, Wu, Yellow peril

Chine Chink, Chynd, Ridge

Chink Chinaman, Chop, Cleft, Clink, Cloff, Crack, Cranny, Crevice, Gap, Rent, Rift, Rima, Sinic, Window

Chintz Kalamkari

Chip(s) Blue, Bo(a)st, Carpenter, Counter, Cut, Deep-fried, EPROM, EROM, Fish, Flake, Fragment, Game, Hack, Knap, Log, Nacho(s), Neural, Nick, Pin, Potato, Shaving, Silicon, Spale, Spall, Span, Teraflop, Tortilla, Transputer, Virus

▷ **Chip** *may indicate* an anagram

Chipmunk Gopher, Hackee, Suslik, Zizel

Chipper Jaunty, Spry, Wedge

Chiron Centaur

Chiropody Podiatry

Chiropractic McTimoney

Chirp(y), Chirrup Cheep, Cherup, Chirm, Chirr, Cicada, Peep, Pip, Pipe, Pitter, Stridulate, Trill, Tweet, Twitter

Chisel(ler), Chisel-like Bam, Boaster, Bolster, Bur, Burin, Carve, Cheat, Clip, Drove, Firmer, Gad, → **GOUGE**, Half-round, Mason, Paring, Scalpriform, Scauper, Scorper, Sculpt, Slick, Socket, Sting

Chit Docket, Girl, Note, Voucher

Chivalry, Chivalrous Brave, Bushido, Courtly, Gallant, Grandisonian, Quixotic

Chivvy Badger, Harass, Pursue

Chloride, Chlorine Calomel

Chlorophyll Leaf-green

Chock Trig

Chocolate Aero, Brown, Cacao, Carob, Cocoa, Dragee, Ganache, Milk, Neapolitan, Noisette, Pinole, Plain, Theobroma, Truffle, Vegelate, Vermicelli

Choice, Choose, Choosy, Chosen Adopt, Anthology, Appoint, Aryan, Cherry-pick, Cull, Dainty, Decide, Druthers, Eclectic, Elect, Elite, Esnecy, Fine, Fork, Free will, Hercules, Hobson's, Leet, Leve, Lief, List, Multiple, Opt, Option, Or, Ossian, Peach, Peculiar, → **PICK**, Picking, Plum(p), Precious, Predilect, Prefer, Proairesis, Rare,

Recherché, → SELECT, Superb, Try(e), Via media, Volition, Wale

Choiceless Beggar

Choir, Choral, Chorister, Chorus Antiphony, Antistrophe, Anvil, Apse, Burden, Choragus, Choregus, Chorister, Dawn, Decani, Faburden, Fauxbourdon, Group, Hallelujah, Harmony, Hymeneal, Motet, Ninth, Parabasis, Precentor, Quirister, → REFRAIN, Ritual, Singing, Stop, Strophe, Treble, Triad, → UNISON

Choir-master Choragus, Choregus, Precentor

Choke(r) Block, Clog, Gag, Garotte, Glut, Silence, Smoor, Smore, Smother, Stap, Stifle, Stop, Strangle(hold), Strangulate, → THROTTLE

Choky Can, Prison

Choler Yellow bile

Cholera Hog

Cholesterol Spinacene, Squalene

Choliamb Scazon

▶ **Choose** *see* CHOICE

Chop, Chops, Chopper(s), Choppy Adze, Ax(e), Celt, Charge, Cheek, Chump, Cleave, Côtelette, Cuff, Cutlet, Dice, Fell(er), Flew, Hack, Helicopter, Hew, Ivory, Karate, Lop, Mince, Mouth, Rotaplane, Rough, Standing, Suey, Teeth, To-rend, Underhand, Wang

Chopin Pantoufle, Shoe

Chopstick(s) Waribashi

Chord(s) Altered, Arpeggio, Barré, Broken, Common, Diameter, Eleventh, Harmony, Intonator, Latus rectum, Neapolitan sixth, Nerve, Ninth, Picardy third, Riff, Seventh, Sixth, Submediant, Thirteenth, Triad, Vocal

Chore Darg, Duty, Fag, Task

Chorea Sydenham's

Choreographer Arranger, Ashton, Balanchine, Cecchetti, Cranko, Fokine, Laban, Massine

Chorus Antistrophe, Dawn, Ninth, Stop, Strophe

Chosen Korea

Chough Chewet

Chowder Bouillabaisse, Skink, Soup

Christ Ecce homo, Messiah, Pantocrator, Paschal Lamb, Prince of Peace, Saviour, The Good Shepherd, The Redeemer, X, Xt

Christen(ing) Baptise, Launch, Name-day

Christian(ity) Abcee, Abecedarian, Absey, Adventist, Albigenses, Anabaptist, Beghard, Believer, Cathar(ist), Charismatic, Colossian, Coptic, Dior, Donatist, D(o)ukhobor, Ebionite, Galilean, Giaour, Gilbertine, Gnostic, Godsquad, Goy, Heteroousian, Holy roller, Homo(i)ousian, Hutterite, Jehovah's Witness, Lutheran, Maronite, Marrano, Melchite, Melkite, Methodist, Monarchian, Monophysite, Moral, Mozarab, Muscular, Mutineer, Nazarene, Nestorian, Phalange, Pilgrim, Presbyterian, Protestant, Quaker, Quartodeciman, RC, Sabotier, Scientist, SCM, Shambe, Solifidian, Traditor, Uniat(e), Unitarian, Valdenses, Waldensian, Wesleyan, Xian, Zwinglian

Christian Scientist Eddy

Christmas(time) C(h)rimbo, Chrissie, Dec, Island, Nativity, Noel, Nowel(l), Yuletide

Christopher Kit, Robin, Sly, Wren

Chromatin Karyotin

Chromium Cr

Chromosome Aneuploid, Autosome, Centromere, Cistron, Euchromatin, Genome, Haploid, Homologous, Id(ant), Karyotype, Lampbrush, Operon, Philadelphia,

Ploid(y), Polytene, Prophage, Telomere, Trisomy, X, Y

Chronicle(r) Anglo-Saxon, Annal, Brut, Calendar, Diary, Froissart, Hall, History, Holinshed, Logographer, Moblog, Paralipomena, Parian, Paris, → **RECORD**, Register, Stow

Chrysalis Nymph, Pupa

Chrysanthemum Corn-marigold, Feverfew, Korean

Chrysolite Olivine, Peridot

Chub Cheven, Chevin, Fish

Chubby Butterball, Plump

Chuck (out) Berry, Buzz, Chook(ie), Discard, Eject, Food, Four-jaw, Grub, Independent-jaw, Pat, Pitch, Scroll, Shy, Sling, Three-jaw, Toss, Turf

Chuckle Chortle, Giggle, Gurgle

Chukka Polo

Chum(my) Ally, Boet, Buddy, Cobber, Cock, Companion, Comrade, Crony, Mate, Pal, Sociable, Sodality

Chump Fool, Mug(gins), Noddle, Sap, → **STUPID PERSON**

Chunk(y) Boxy, Chubby, Gob, Piece, Slab, Squat, Wad

Church Abbey, Armenian, Autocephalous, Basilica, Bethel, Bethesda, Broad, Brood, Byzantine, → **CATHEDRAL**, CE, Ch, Chapel, Chevet, Clergy, Collegiate, Congregational, Coptic, Delubrum, Easter (Orthodox), Eastern, EC, Ecumenical, Episcopal, Episcopalian, Established, Faith, Fold, Free, Greek, High, House, Institutional, Kirk, Lateran, Latin, Low, Lutheran, Maronite, Melchite, Methodist, Minster, Moonie, Moravian, Mormon, Mother, National, New, New Jerusalem, Old Light, Oratory, Orthodox, Parish, Peculiar, Pentecostal, Preaching-house, Prebendal, Presbyterian, Ratana, RC, Reformed, Relief, Rome, Russian Orthodox, Shrine, Smyrna, Station, Stave, Steeple, Steeplehouse, Temple, Triumphant, Unification, Unitarian, United Free, United Reformed, Visible, Wee Free, Western, Wool

Churchgoer, Churchman, Churchwarden Antiburgher, Azymite, Baptist, Believer, Cameronian, Classis, Clay, Cleric, Clerk, Congregation, Deacon, Dom, Dopper, Elder, Evangelist, Hatto, Ignorantine, Incumbent, Invisible, Knox, Lector, Lutheran, Methodist, Militant, Moderator, Moonie, Mormon, MU, Newman, Oncer, Parson, PE, Pew-opener, Pipe, Pontiff, Prebendary, Precentor, Predicant, Predikant, Prelate, Presbyterian, Priest, Protestant, Puritan, Racovian, Rector, Romanist, Ruridecanal, Sacristan, Sidesman, Sim, Simeonite, Socinian, Subdeacon, Succentor, Swedenborgian, Tantivy, Triumphant, Ubiquitarian, Unitarian, Verger, Visible, Wesleyan, Worshipper, Wren

Church house Deanery, Manse, Parsonage, Presbytery, Rectory, Vicarage

Churchill Tank, Winston

Churchyard God's acre

Churl(ish) Attercop, Boor, Crabby, Curmudgeonly, Cynical, Ethercap, Ettercap, Gruff, Ill-natured, Nabal, Peasant, Rustic, Serf, Surly

Churn Bubble, Kirn, Seethe

Chute Flume, Runway

CIC Shogun, Sirdar

Cicada Greengrocer, Locust, Periodical, Tettix

Cicatrix Scar

Cicely Myrrh, Sweet

Cicero Cic, Orator, Tully

Cid Campeador, Chief, Hero

Cider Drink, Hard, Perry, Scrumpy, Sweet

Ci-devant Ex

Cigar(ette), Cigarette cards Beedi(e), Bidi, Bifter, Bumper, Burn, Camberwell carrot, Cancer stick, Caporal, Cartophily, Cheroot, Cigarillo, Claro, Coffin nail, Conch, Concha, Corona, Dog-end, Doob, Durry, Fag, Filter-tip, Gasper, Giggle(-stick), Havana, Joint, Locofoco, Long-nine, Loosies, Maduro, Manilla, Number, Panatella, Paper-cigar, Perfecto, Puritano, Reefer, Regalia, Roach, Roll-up, Segar, Smoke, Snout, Splif(f), Stogie, Stog(e)y, Stompie, Twist, Weed, Whiff, Woodbine, Zol

Cinch Belt, Certainty, Duck soup, Easy, Girth, Stroll

Cinchona Kina, Quina

Cinder(s) Ash, Breeze, Clinker, Dander, Embers, Slag

Cinderella Drudge, Stepdaughter

Cinema(s) Art house, Big screen, Biograph, Bioscope, Circuit, Drive-in, Films, Fleapit, Flicks, Grindhouse, Megaplex, Movies, Multiplex, Multiscreen, Mutoscope, New Wave, Nickelodeon, Nouvelle Vague, Odeon, Pictures, Plaza, Theatre, Tivoli

Cinnabar Vermilion

Cinnamon, Cinnamon stone Canella, Cassia(bark), Essonite, Hessonite, Saigon, Spice

Cipher Chi-rho, Code, Cryptogram, Nihil, Nobody, → **NOTHING**, Number, O, Steganogram, Zero

Circle Almacantar, Almucantar, Annulet, Antarctic, Arctic, Circassian, Co, Colure, Company, Compass, Corn, Corolla, Coterie, Cromlech, Crop, Cycloid, Cyclolith, Dip, Disc, Dress, Druidical, Eccentric, Ecliptic, Embail, Enclose, Engird, Epicyclic, Equant, Equator, Equinoctial, Euler's, Family, Fraternity, Full, Galactic, Girdle, Gloriole, Great, Gyre, Halo, Henge, Hoop, Horizon, Hour, Hut, Inner, Inorb, Lap, Longitude, Loop, Magic, Malebolge, Mandala, Meridian, Mohr's, Mural, Nimbus, O, Orb, Orbit, Parhelic, Parquet, Parterre, Penannular, Peristalith, Pitch, Polar, Quality, Rigol, → **RING**, Rondure, Rotate, Roundlet, Seahenge, Sentencing, Set, Setting, Small, Sphere, Stemme, Stone, Stonehenge, Striking, Surround, Tinchel, Traffic, Transit, Tropic, Turning, Umbel, Upper, Vertical, Vicious, Vienna, Virtuous, Volt, Wheel

Circuit(ous) Ambit, AND, Autodyne, Bridge, Bypass, Chipset, Closed, Comparator, Daughterboard, Diocese, Discriminator, Dolby®, Equivalent, Eyre, Gate, Gyrator, IC, Integrated, Interface, Lap, Limiter, Live, Logic, Loop, Microprocessor, Motherboard, NAND, NOR, NOT, Open, OR, Perimeter, Phantom, Phase, Printed, Quadripole, Reactance, Ring, Round, Scaler, Series, Short, Smoothing, Squelch, Stage, Three-phase, Tour, Windlass

Circuit-breaker Fuse

Circular Annular, Court, Flysheet, Folder, Leaflet, Mailshot, Orby, Round, Spiral, Unending, Wheely

Circulate, Circulation Astir, Bloodstream, Cyclosis, Disseminate, Flow, Gyre, Issue, Mingle, Mix, Orbit, Pass, Publish, Report, Revolve, Rotate, Scope, Send round, Spread, Stir, Troll, Utter

▷ **Circulating** *may indicate* an anagram

Circumcise(r), Circumcision Bris, Brith, Brit milah, Infibulate, Milah, Mohel, Pharaonic, Sandek

Circumference Boundary, Girth, Perimeter, Size

Circumflex Perispomenon

Circumlocution Bafflegab, Periphrasis, Tautology

Circumnavigation Periplus

Circumscribe(d) Define, Demarcate, Enclose, Eruv, Restrain

Circumspect Chary, Guarded, Prudential, Wary
Circumstance(s), Circumstantial Case, Detail, Event, Fact, Formal, → INCIDENT, Mitigating, Precise, Shebang, Situation, Stede
Circumvent Bypass, Dish, Evade, Outflank, Outwit, Usurp
Circus, Circus boy Arena, Big top, Eros, Flea, Flying, Harrier, Hippodrome, Marquee, Maximus, Media, Monty Python, Ring, Sanger, Slang, Three-ring
Cissy Nelly
Cistercian Trappist
Cistern Feed-head, Flush-box, Sump, Tank, Tub, Vat
Citadel Acropolis, Alhambra, Castle, Fort(ress), Keep, Kremlin, Sea-girt
Citation, Cite Adduce, Allegation, Instance, Mention, Name, Quote, Recall, Reference, Repeat, Sist, Summon
Citizen(s), Citizenship Burgess, Burgher, Civism, Cleruch, Denizen, Dicast, Ephebe, Franchise, Freeman, Jus sanguinis, Jus soli, Kane, National, Oppidan, Patrial, People, Propr(a)etor, Quirites, Resident, Roman, Second-class, Senior, Snob, Subject, Trainband, Trierarch, Venireman, Vigilante, Voter
Citroen DS
Citron, Citrous Bergamot
Citrus Acid, Calamondin, Cedrate, Lemon, Lime, Mandarin, Min(n)eola, Orange, Pomelo, Tangerine, Ugli
City Agra, Athens, Atlantis, Babylon, Burgh, Cardboard, Carthage, Cosmopolis, Ctesiphon, Dodge, EC, Empire, Eternal, Forbidden, Free, Garden, Gath, Heavenly, Hilversum, Holy, Imperial, Inner, LA, Leonine, Medina, Megalopolis, Metropolis, Micropolis, Municipal, Mycenae, Ninevah, NY, Persepolis, Petra, Pompeii, Rhodes, Salem, Smoke, Sparta, Tech, Teheran, Town, Ur, Vatican, Weltstadt, Wen
Civet Binturong, Cat, Fo(u)ssa, Genet(te), Herpestes, Linsang, Musang, Nandine, Palm, Paradoxine, Paradoxure, Rasse, Suricate, Toddy-cat, Viverra, Zibet
Civil(ian), Civilisation, Civilised, Civility Amenity, Christian, Cit, Citizen, Civ(vy), Comity, Courtesy, Culture, Fertile crescent, Humane, Indus Valley, Kultur, Maya, Municipal, Nok, Non-combatant, Polite, Politesse, Push-button, Secular, Temporal, Urbane
Civil Service CS
Clad(ding) Sarking, Weatherboard
Clag(gy) Stickjaw
Claim(s) Appeal, Arrogate, Assert, Asseverate, Bag, Challenge, Charge, Darraign(e), Darrain(e), Darrayn, Demand, Deraign, Droit, Encumbrance, Haro, Harrow, Lien, List, Maintain, Nochel, Plea, Pose, Posit, Postulate, Pretence, Pretend, Profess, Pulture, Purport, Puture, Revendicate, Right, Set-off, Small, Sue, Title
Claimant Irredentist, Petitioner, Pot-waller, Pretender, Prospector, Tichborne, Usurper
Clairvoyance, Clairvoyancy ESP, Fey, Insight, Lucidity, Psiphenomena, Taisch, Taish, Tel(a)esthesia, Telegnosis
Clam Bivalve, Chowder, Cohog, Geoduck, Giant, Gweduc, Hardshell, Littleneck, Mollusc, Mya, Quahang, Quahog, Round, Soft-shell, Steamer, Tridacna, Venus
Clamant Vociferous
Clamber Climb, Crawl, Scramble, Spra(i)ckle, Sprauchle
Clammy Algid, Damp, Dank, Moist, Sticky, Sweaty
Clamour(ing), Clamorous Blatant, Brouhaha, Din, Hubbub, Hue, Outcry, Racket, Raird, Reird, Rout, Shout, Strepitant, Uproar, Utis, Vociferate
Clamp Beartrap, Clinch, Coupler, Denver boot, Fasten, Grip, Holdfast, Jumar, Pinchcock, Potato-pit, Serrefine, Stirrup, Tread, Vice, Wheel

Clan(sman) Cameron, Clique, Gens, Gentile, Group, Horde, Kiltie, Kindred, Name, Ngati, Phratry, Phyle, Sect, Sept, Society, Stewart, Stuart, Tribe

Clandestine Covert, Furtive, Secret, Underhand

Clang(er), Clanging, Clank Bell, Belleter, Boob, Boo-boo, Clash, Gong, Jangle, Plangent, Ring

Clap(per), Clapping Applaud, Blow, Castanet, Chop, Crotal, Dose, Jinglet, Peal, Plaudite, Thunder, Tonant

Claptrap Bilge, Blab, Bombast, Bunkum, Eyewash, Hokum, Rot, Tripe

Claque(ur) Fans, Hat, Laudator, Sycophant

Clara Bow, Butt

Claret Blood, Loll-shraub, Loll-shrob, Vin

Clarify, Clarifier Clear, Despumate, Dilucidate, Explain, Explicate, Fine, Finings, Purge, Refine, Render, Simplify

Clarinet Reed

Clarion Brassy, Clear, Trumpet

Clary Orval, Sage

Clash(ing) Bang, Clangour, Clank, Claver, Coincide, Collide, Conflict, Friction, Gossip, → **IMPACT**, Incident, Irreconcilable, Jar, Loud, Missuit, Riot, Shock, Showdown, Strike, Swash

Clasp(ing) Adpress, Agraffe, Amplexus, Barrette, Brooch, Button, Catch, Chape, Clip, Embrace, Fibula, Grasp, Hasp, Hesp, Hook, Hug, Inarm, Interdigitate, Link, Morse, Ochreate, Ouch, Slide, Tach(e), Tie, Unite

Class(ification), Classify, Classified, Classy Acorn, Arrange, Assort, Bourgeois(ie), Bracket, Brand, Breed, Business, Cabin, Canaille, Caste, → **CATEGORY**, Chattering, Cheder, Cl, Clan, Clerisy, Clinic, Club, Composite, Course, Criminal, Dalit, Dewey, Digest, Division, Economy, Estate, Evening, Faction, First, Form, Genera, Gentry, Genus, → **GRADE**, Group, Harvard, Haryan, Heder, Hubble, Ilk, Keep-fit, Kohanga Reo, League, Life, Linn(a)ean, List, Lower, Mammal, Master, Meritocracy, Middle, Night, Number, Nursery, Order, Phenetics, Phylum, Pigeon-hole, Pleb(eian), Proper, Race, Range, Rank, Rate, Rating, Raypoot, Raypout, Reception, Remove, Salariat, Second, Secret, Seminar, Shell, Siege, Social, Sort(ation), Spectral, Steerage, Stratum, Stream, Syntax, Taxonomy, Teach-in, Third, Tony, Tourist, Tribe, Tutorial, → **TYPE**, U, Universal, Upper, Varna, Water, Working, World, Year

Classic(al), Classics, Classicist Ageless, Ancient, Basic, Derby, Elzevir, Grecian, Greek, Humane, Leger, Literature, Pliny, Purist, Roman, Standard, Traditional, Vintage

Clatch Blunk, Smear, Spoil

Clatter Bicker, Charivari, Clack, Din, Noise, Rattle

Clause Adjunct, Apodosis, Article, Basket, Complement, Condition, Conscience, Coordinate, Dependent, Disability, Endorsement, Escalator, Escape, Exclusion, Exemption, Filioque, Four, Golden parachute, Grandfather, Independent, Main, Member, Noun, Object, Omnibus, Option, Poison-pill, Predicator, Principal, Protasis, Proviso, Reddendum, Reported, Reservation, Rider, Salvo, Saving, Sentence, Subject, Subordinate, Sunset, Tenendum, Testatum, Testing, Warrandice

Claw Chela, Claut, Crab, Dewclaw, Edate, Falcula, Grapple, Griff(e), Hook, Nail, Nipper, Pounce, Scrab, Scramb, Sere, Talent, → **TALON**, Tear, Telson, Tokay, Unguis

Clay Allophane, Argil, Argillite, Barbotine, B(e)auxite, Bentonite, Blaes, Blaise, Blaize, Bole, Boulder, Calm, Cam, Caum, Ceramic, Charoset(h), China, Cimolite, Cloam, Clunch, Cob, Cornish, Earth, Engobe, Fango, Figuline, Fire, Fuller's earth,

Gault, Glei, Gley, Gumbotil, Hardpan, Haroset(h), Illite, Kaolin, Kokowai, Laterite, Lithomarge, Loam, London, Lute, Malm, Marl, Meerschaum, Mire, Mortal, Mud, Oxford, Papa, Pipeclay, Pipestone, Pise, Plastic, Plastilina, Porcelain, Potter's, Pottery, Puddle, Pug, Saggar(d), Sagger, Scroddle(d), Seggar, Sepiolite, Slip, Slurry, Smectite, Terra sigillata, Thill, Till(ite), Tumphy, Varve, Warrant, Warren, Wax

Clean(er), Cleaning Absterge, Bathbrick, Besom, Bleach, Bream, Broom, Careen, Catharise, Catharsis, Char(e), Chaste, Clear, Daily, Debride, Decontaminate, Dentifrice, Depurate, Deterge(nt), Dhobi, Dialysis, Dicht, Do, Douche, Dredge, Dust(er), Eluant, Emunge, Enema, Erase, Ethnic, Evacuant, Evacuate, Expurgate, Fay, Fettle, Fey, Floss, Flush, Full, Grave, Groom, Gut, Heels, Hoover®, Hygienic, Immaculate, Innocent, Launder, Lave, Lustrum, Lye, Mouthwash, Mrs Mop(p), Mundify, Net, Overhaul, Porge, Pull-through, Pumice, Pure, Purgative, Purge, Ramrod, Rebite, Rub, Rump, Sandblast, Scaffie, Scavenge, Scour, Scrub, Shampoo, Shot-blast, Snow-white, Soap, Soogee, Soogie, Soojey, Sponge, Spotless, Squeaky, Squeegee, Sterile, Sujee, Swab, Sweep, Tidy, Toothpick, Ultrasonic, Vac(uum), Valet, → **WASH**, Whistle, Wipe

Clear(ance), Clearly Absolve, Acquit, Aloof, Apparent, Bell, Berth, Bold, Bore, Brighten, Bus, Categorical, Clarify, Crystal, Decode, Definite, Delouse, Diaphanous, Dispel, Distinct, Downright, Earn, Eidetic, Evacuate, Evident, Exculpate, Exonerate, Explicit, Fair, Five-by-five, Gain, Headroom, Hyaline, Intelligible, Iron, Laund, Leap, Legible, Limpid, Lucid, Luculent, Manifest, Mop, Neat, Negotiate, Net(t), → **NOT CLEAR**, Observable, Obvious, Ope(n), Overleap, Palpable, Patent, Pellucid, Perspicuous, Plain, Play, Pratique, Predy, Pure, Quit, Rack, Realise, Remble, Rid, Ripple, Serene, Sheer, Shere, Slum, Stark, Sweep, Thro(ugh), Thwaite, Transire, Translucent, Transparent, Unblock, Unclog, Uncork(ed), Unequivocal, Vault, Vivid, Void, Well, Windage, Wipe

Clearing Assart, Glade, Opening, Shire, Slash

Cleat Bitt, Wedge

Cleave, Cleavage, Cleft Adhere, Bisulcate, Chimney, Chine, Chink, Cling, Cloff, Cohere, Cut, Divide, Division, Divorce(ment), Fissure, Gap, Ghaut, Goose-grass, Grike, Gryke, Harelip, Pharynx, Rift, Riva, Scissure, Severance, Slack, Space, Spathose, Split, Sulcus

Clef Soprano, Treble

Clematis Montana, Old man's beard, Traveller's joy, Virgin's-bower

Clemenceau Tiger

Clemency, Clement Ahimsa, Grace, Lenience, Lenity, Mercy, Mildness, Quarter, Temperate

Cleopatra Needle

Clergy(man), Cleric(al) Abbé, Canon, Cantor, Cardinal, Chancellor, Chaplain, Cleric, Clerk, Cloth, Curate, Curé, Deacon, Dean, Ecclesiast(ic), Goliard, Incumbent, Josser, Levite, Ministerial, Ministry, Minor canon, Non-juror, Non-usager, Notarial, Paperwork, Parson, Pastor, Pontifex, Pontiff, Preacher, Prebendary, Precentor, Prelate, Presbyter, Presenter, Priest, Primate, Prior, Proctor, Rabbi, Rector, Red-hat, Reverend, Rome-runner, Scribal, Secretarial, Shaveling, Shepherd, Sky pilot, Slope, Spin-text, Spirituality, Squarson, Subdeacon, Theologian, Vartabed, Vicar

Clergy-hater Misoclere

Clerk(s) Actuary, Baboo, Babu, Basoche, Circar, Cleric, Cratchit, Cursitor, Enumerator, Filing, Heep, Lay, Limb, Notary, Paper-pusher, Parish, Pen-driver, Penman, Penpusher, Petty Bag, Poster, Prot(h)onotary, Protocolist, Recorder, Salaryman, Scribe, Secretariat, Shipping, Sircar, Sirkar, Tally, Vicar, Writer

Clever(ness) Able, Adroit, Astute, Brainy, Bright, Canny, Cool, Cute, Daedal(e), Deep-browed, Deft, Genius, Gleg, Ingenious, Intellectual, Jackeen, Know-all, Natty, Nimblewit, Sage(ness), Shrewd, Skilful, Smart(y), Smarty-pants, Souple, Subtle

Clevis Becket

Cliché Banality, Boilerplate, Commonplace, Corn, Journalese, Platitude, Saying, Tag

Click(er), Clicking Castanet, Catch, Forge, Pawl, Rale, Ratch(et), Snick, Succeed, Tchick, Ticktack

Client Customer, Fat, Gonk, John, Patron, Thin, Trick

Cliff(s) Beachy Head, Bluff, Cleve, Corniche, Crag, Craig, Escarp, Palisade(s), Precipice, Sca(u)r

Cliffhanger Samphire, Serial, Thriller

Climate Ambience, Atmosphere, Attitude, Continental, Mood, Sun, Temperament, Temperature, Weather

Climax Apex, Apogee, Catastasis, Come, Crescendo, Crest, Crisis, Culminate, Edaphic, End, Head, Height, Heyday, Orgasm, Payoff, Top, Zenith

Climb(er), Climbing Aid, Alpinist, Aralia, Aristolochia, Artificial, Ascend, Bignonian, Breast, Briony, Bryony, Clamber, Clematis, Clusia, Cowage, Cowhage, Cowitch, Crampon, Creeper, Cucumber, Dodder, Heart-pea, Hedera, Ivy, Jamming, Kie-kie, Kudzu, Lawyer, Layback, Liana, Liane, → **MOUNT**, Munro-bagger, Pareira, Parvenu, Pea, Peg, Prusik, Rat(t)an, Rise, Root, Scale, Scan, Scandent, Scansores, Sclim, Scramble, Shin, Shinny, Sklim, Smilax, Social, Speel, Steeplejack, Sty(e), Swarm, Timbo, Tuft-hunter, Udo, Up(hill), Uprun, Vine, Wistaria, With(y)wind, Woodbine, Zoom

Clinch Attach, Carriwitchet, Determine, Ensure, Fix, Quibble, Rivet, Secure, Settle

Cling(er), Clinging Adhere, Bur(r), Cherish, Cleave, Embrace, Hold, Hug, Ring, Tendril

Clinic Antenatal, Dental, Dispensary, Hospital, Hospitium, Mayo, Well-woman

Clink Gingle, Jail, Jingle, Lock up, Prison, Stir, Ting, Tinkle

Clinker Ash, Slag

Clint Limestone

Clip(ped), Clipper, Clipping Alberta, Banana, Barrette, Bicycle, Brash, Bulldog, Butterfly, Cartridge, Chelsea, Clasp, Crocodile, Crop-ear, Crutch, Curt, Curtail, Cut, Cutty Sark, Dag, Dock, Dod, Excerpt, Fleece, Jubilee, Jumar, Krab, Lop, Money, Outtake, Pace, Paper, Pare, Peg, Prerupt, Prune, Roach, Scissel, Secateur, Shear, Ship, Shore, Shorn, Snip, Spring, Staccato, Tie, Tie-tack, Tinsnips, Topiarist, Trim

Clippy Cad, Conductor

Clique Cabal, Clan, Club, Coterie, Faction, Four Hundred, Gang, Junta, Ring, Set

Clive Arcot

Cloak(room), Cloaks Aba, Abaya, Abba, Abolla, Amice, Bathroom, Buffalo-robe, Burnous, Capa, Cape, Capote, Caracalla, Cardinal, Cassock, Chasuble, Chimer(e), Chlamydes, Chlamys, Chuddah, Chuddar, Conceal, Cope, Cover, Disguise, Dissemble, Djellaba(h), Domino, Gabardine, Gaberdine, Gal(l)abea(h), Gal(l)abi(y)a(h), Gal(l)abi(y)eh, Gentlemen, Gents, Grego, Hall-robe, Heal, Hele, Himation, Hood, Inverness, Jelab, Jellaba, Joseph, Kaross, Korowai, Manta, Manteau, Manteel, Mant(e)let, Mantle, → **MASK**, Mourning, Mousquetaire, Mozetta, Opera, Paenula, Paletot, Pallium, Paludamentum, Pelisse, Pilch, Poncho, Powder-room, Rail, Revestry, Rocklay, Rokelay, Roquelaure, Sagum, Sarafan, Scapular, → **SCREEN**, Shroud, Swathe, Talma, Toga, Vestiary, Vestry, Visite

Clobber Anoint, Apparel, Dress, Garb, Habiliments, Lam, Tack

Clock Alarm, Ammonia, Analogue, Astronomical, Atomic, Beetle, Big Ben, Biological, Blowball, Body, Bracket, Bundy, Caesium, Carriage, Cartel, Clepsydra,

Cuckoo, Dandelion, Digital, Doomsday, Dutch, Floral, Grandfather, Grandmother, Hit, Knock, Long case, Meter, Paenula, Parliament, Quartz, Repeater, Sandglass, Solarium, Speaking, Speedo, Strike, Sundial, Taximeter, Tell-tale, Time(r), Turret, Wag at the wa', Water

Clockmaker Fromanteel, Graham, Harrison, Knibb, Mudge, Tompion

Clockwise Deasil, Deasiul, Deasoil, Deiseal, Deisheal

Clockwork Precision, Regular

Clod Clumsy, Divot, Glebe, Lump, Mool, Mould, Put(t), Scraw, Sod, Stupid, Turf

Clog Accloy, Ball, Block, Clam, Crowd, Dance, Fur, Galosh, Golosh, Hamper, Jam, Lump, Mire, Obstruct, Overshoe, Patten, Sabot

Cloisonné Shippo

Cloister Arcade, Confine, Cortile, Immure, Monastery, Mure, Refuge, Seclude

Clone, Cloning Ramet, Replicant, Reproduce, Therapeutic

Cloots Worricow

Close(d), Closing, Closure Airless, Alongside, Atresia, Block, Boon, By, Cadence, Clammy, Clap, Clench, Complete, Cone off, Court, Dear, Debar, Dense, → END, Epilogue, Ewest, Finale, Forby, Gare, Grapple, Handy, Hard, Hard by, Humid, Imminent, Inbye, Infibulate, Intent, Intimate, Lock, Lucken, Marginal, Mean, Miserly, Muggy, Mure, Narre, Narrow, Near, Nearhand, Neist, Nie, Niggardly, Nigh, Nip and tuck, Obturate, Occlude, Occlusion, Oppressive, Parochial, Penny-pinching, Placket, Precinct, Reserved, Reticent, Seal, Secret, Serre, Serried, Serry, Shet, Shut(ter), Shutdown, Silly, Slam, Snug, Stap, Sticky, Stuffy, Sultry, Tailgate, Temenos, Tight, Uproll, Wafer, Warm, Yard

Close-cropped Crewcut, Not-pated

Close-fitting Skintight, Slinky, Tight

Closet Cabinet, Confine, Cubicle, Cupboard, Dooket, Earth, Locker, Safe, Wardrobe, WC, Zeta

Close-up Detail, Fill, Shut, Stop, Zoom

Closing-time Eleven, End

Clot(ting) Agglutinate, Ass, Clag, Clump, Coagulate, Congeal, Crassamentum, Cruor, Curdle, Dag, Embolism, Embolus, Gel, Globule, Gob, Gout, Grume, Incrassate, Incrust, Jell, Lapper, Lopper, → LUMP, Mass, Prothrombin, Splatch, Stupid, Thicken, Thrombosis, Thrombus

Cloth Aba, Abaya, Abba, Antependium, Bribe, Carmelite, Clergy, Cloot, Clout, Communion, Dishrag, Duster, → FABRIC, → FELT, Frocking, Frontal, Gremial, G-string, Jharan, Loin, Lungi, Manta, → MATERIAL, Nap, Napery, Napje, Nappie, Neckerchief, Needlework, Netting, Pack, Painted, Pall, Pane, Pilch, Priesthood, Print(er), Pull-through, Purificator, Puttee, Putty, Rag, Raiment, Roll, Roon, Runner, Sashing, Scarlet, Serviette, Sheet, Sheeting, Shoddy, Stripe, Stuff, Stupe, Sudarium, Supper, Sweatband, T, Tapestry, Tea, → TEXTILE, Throw, Tissue, Toilet, Vernicle, Veronica, Washrag, Whole

---

CLOTH

1 letter:	Web	Ciré	Haik
J®		Doek	Harn
	4 letters:	Drab	Hyke
3 letters:	Aida	Duck	Ikat
Abb	Amis	Fent	Kelt
Rep	Baft	Flax	Knit
Say	Bark	Gair	Lamé

Lawn
Leno
Line
Mull
Nude
Pina
Puke
Repp
Rund
Shag
Slop
Sulu
Wire
Wool

5 letters:
Atlas
Baize
Beige
Binca
Budge
Chino
Crape
Crash
Crepe
Denim
Dobby
Drill
Duroy
Fanon
Foulé
Frisé
Gauze
Gazar
Grass
Gunny
Haick
Honan
Jaspe
Kanga
Kente
Khadi
Khaki
Kikoi
Linen
Llama
Loden
Lurex®
Lycra®
Moiré
Mongo

Monk's
Mummy
Mungo
Ninon
Nylon
Orlon®
Panel
Panne
Perse
Pilot
Piqué
Plaid
Plush
Poult
Rayon
Satin
Scrim
Serge
Slops
Surah
Surat
Surge
Tabby
Tamin
Tammy
Terry
Tibet
Toile
Towel
Tulle
Tweed
Tweel
Twill
Union
Voile
Wigan

6 letters:
Aertex®
Alpaca
Angora
Armure
Barège
Beaver
Bouclé
Broche
Burlap
Burnet
Burrel
Byssus
Caddis

Calico
Camlet
Camlot
Canvas
Chintz
Cilice
Cloqué
Coburg
Coutil
Covert
Crepon
Cubica
Cyprus
Damask
Devoré
Dimity
Domett
Dossal
Dossel
Dowlas
Dralon®
Duffel
Duffle
Dupion
Durrie
Etamin
Faille
Fannel
Frieze
Gloria
Greige
Gurrah
Haique
Harden
Herden
Hodden
Hoddin
Humhum
Hurden
Jersey
Kersey
Khanga
Kincob
Lampas
Madras
Medley
Melton
Merino
Mohair
Mongoe
Moreen

Muleta
Muslin
Mutton
Nankin
Oxford
Pongee
Rateen
Ratine
Russel
Samite
Satara
Sateen
Saxony
Sendal
Shalli
Sherpa
Sindon
Soneri
Stroud
Tactel®
Tamine
Tartan
Tencel®
Thibet
Tricot
Velour
Velure
Velvet
Vicuna
Wadmal
Wincey
Winsey

7 letters:
Abattre
Alamode
Alepine
Baracan
Batiste
Brocade
Cabbage
Cambric
Camelot
Challie
Challis
Cheviot
Chiffon
Crombie
Cypress
Delaine
Dhurrie

Doeskin
Dorneck
Dornick
Drabbet
Drapery
Droguet
Drugget
Duvetyn
Etamine
Faconné
Fannell
Fishnet
Flannel
Foulard
Fustian
Galatea
Genappe
Gingham
Gore-tex®
Grogram
Hessian
Holland
Hopsack
Jaconet
Jamdani
Khaddar
Kitenge
Lockram
Mockado
Nankeen
Oilskin
Organza
Orleans
Ottoman
Paisley
Percale
Rabanna
Raploch
Raschel
Ratteen
Rattine
Ripstop
Sacking
Sagathy
Schappe
Silesia
Sinamay
Spandex®
Stammel
Supplex®
Tabaret

Tabinet
Taffeta
Tiffany
Tussore
Viyella®
Wadmaal
Webbing
Woolsey
Worsted
Zanella

8 letters:
Aircraft
Algerine
American
Armozeen
Armozine
Arresine
Bagheera
Barathea
Barracan
Bayadere
Bearskin
Bobbinet
Brocatel
Cameline
Cashmere
Casimere
Celanese
Chambray
Chamelot
Chenille
Ciclaton
Corduroy
Corporal
Coteline
Coutille
Cretonne
Drabette
Duchesse
Dungaree
Duvetine
Duvetyne
Eolienne
Gambroon
Gossamer
Homespun
Jacquard
Jeanette
Lava-lava
Lustring

Mackinaw
Mantling
Marcella
Marocain
Mazarine
Moleskin
Moquette
Nainsook
Organdie
Osnaburg
Pashmina
Pleather
Prunella
Rodevore
Sarcenet
Sarsenet
Sealskin
Shabrack
Shalloon
Shantung
Sicilian
Swanskin
Tabbinet
Tarlatan
Toilinet
Whipcord
Wild silk
Zibeline

9 letters:
Aeroplane
Alcantara
Balzarine
Bengaline
Bombasine
Calamanco
Cassimere
Cerecloth
Charmeuse®
Ciclatoun
Corporale
Cottonade
Courtelle®
Crepoline
Crimplene®
Crinoline
Evenweave
Fabrikoid®
Farandine
Filoselle
Folk-weave

Gaberdine
Georgette
Grenadine
Grosgrain
Haircloth
Horsehair
Indiennes
Levantine
Longcloth
Mandilion
Mandylion
Marseille
Matelassé
Messaline
Moygashel
Open-weave
Overcheck
Paramatta
Penistone
Percaline
Persienne
Pinstripe
Polyester
Ravenduck
Sailcloth
Sharkskin
Silkalene
Silkaline
Stockinet
Swansdown
Tarpaulin
Tricotine
Velveteen
Wire gauze
Worcester
Zibelline

10 letters:
Balbriggan
Baldachino
Broadcloth
Brocatelle
Candlewick
Farrandine
Fearnought
Ferrandine
Florentine
Geotextile
Kerseymere
Lutestring
Mousseline

Needlecord	Tuftaffeta	Dreadnought	*12 letters:*
Parramatta	Winceyette	Hammercloth	Brilliantine
Polycotton		Interfacing	Cavalry twill
Ravensduck	*11 letters:*	Kendal green	Crepe de chine
Russel-cord	Abercrombie	Marquisette	Leather-cloth
Seersucker	Bedford cord	Nun's veiling	
Shabracque	Canton crepe	Sempiternum	*13 letters:*
Shiveshive	Cheesecloth	Stockinette	Gros de Londres
Sicilienne	Cloth of gold	Stretch knit	Linsey-woolsey
Tattersall	Dotted Swiss	Swiss muslin	
Toilinette	Drap-de-berry		

Cloth-designing Batik

Clothe(s), Clothing, Clothed Accoutrements, Apparel, Array, Attire, Baggies, Besee, Bib and tucker, Cape, Casuals, Chasuble, Choli, Cits, Clad, Clericals, Clobber, Coat, Combinations, Coordinates, Costume, Cour, Cover, Croptop, Dicht, Dight, Don, Drag, → **DRESS**, Duds, Emboss, Endue, Finery, Frippery, Garb, Garments, Gear, Gere, Get-up, Glad rags, Grave, Gymslip, Habit, Haute couture, Hejab, Innerwear, Judogi, Jumps, Kimono, Layette, Lederhosen, Long-togs, Matumba, Mocker, Muff, Outfit, Pannicle, Plain, Playsuit, Raggery, Rag trade, Raiment, Rami, Rigout, Robes, Samfoo, Samfu, Schmutter, Scungies, Shirtwaister, Shmatte, Shroud, Slops, Sunday best, Swaddling, Swathe, Swothling, Tackle, Togs, Tracksuit, Trappings, Trews, Trousseau, Tweeds, Two-piece, Vernicle, Vestiary, Vestiture, Vestment, Wardrobe, Watteau, Weeds, Widow's weeds, Workwear, Yclad, Ycled

Clothes basket, Clothes horse Airer, Petara, Winterhedge

Cloud(ing), Clouded, Cloudiness, Cloudy Altocumulus, Altostratus, Banner, Benight, C, Cataract, Cirrocumulus, Cirrostratus, Cirrus, Coalsack, Coma, Contrail, Crab Nebula, Cumulonimbus, Cumulus, Dim, Dull, Emission nebula, Fog, Fractocumulus, Fractostratus, Funnel, Goat's hair, Haze, Horsehead Nebula, Infuscate, Magellanic, Mare's tail, Milky, Mist, Molecular, Mushroom, Nacreous, Nephele, Nephelometer, Nepho-, Nimbostratus, Nimbus, Nubecula, Nubilous, Nuée ardente, Obnubilation, Obscure, Octa, Okta, Oort, Overcast, Pall, Pother, Protostar, Rack, Roily, Stain, Storm, Stratocumulus, Strat(o)us, Thunder(head), Turbid, Virga, War, Water-dog, Woolpack, Zero-zero

Cloudberry Mountain bramble

Cloudless Serene

Clough Dale, Gorge, Ravine

Clout Belt, Cloth, Hit, Influence, Lap(pie), Lapje, Pull, Raddle

Clove Chive, Eugenia, Rose-apple, Split

Clover Alfalfa, Alsike, Berseem, Calvary, Cinque, Cow-grass, Four-leaf, Hare's foot, Hop, Japan, Ladino, Lespedeza, Medic(k), Melilot, Owl's, Pin, Rabbit-foot, Red, Serradella, Serradilla, Shamrock, Souple, Sucklers, Sweet, Trefoil, Trilobe, White

Clown(ish) Airhead, Antic, Antick, August(e), Boor, Bor(r)el, Buffoon, Carl, Chough, Chuff, Clout-shoe, Coco, → **COMEDIAN**, Comic, Costard, Daff, Feste, Froth, Girner, Gobbo, Goon, Gracioso, Grimaldi, Harlequin, Hob, Idiot, Jack-pudding, Jester, Joey, Joker, Joskin, Leno, Merry Andrew, Mountebank, Nedda, Nervo, Peasant, Pickle-herring, Pierrot, Put, Rustic, Slouch, Thalian, Touchstone, Trinculo, Wag, Zany

Cloy(ing) Choke, Clog, Glut, Pall, Satiate, Surfeit, Sweet

Club(s), Club-like Adelphi, Airn, Almack's, Alpeen, Apex, Army and Navy, Arsenal, Artel, Association, Athen(a)aeum, Baffy, Band(y), Basto, Bat, Bath, Beefsteak, Blackjack, Blaster, Bludgeon, Boodles, Bourdon, Brassie, Breakfast, Brook's, Bulger, C, Card, Carlton, Caterpillar, Cavalry, Chartered, Chigiriki, Clavate, Cleek, Clip-joint, Combine, Compassion, Conservative, Constitutional, Cordeliers, Cosh, Cotton, Country, Crockford's, Cudgel, Devonshire, Disco(theque), Driver, Driving iron, Drones, Fan, Fascio, Feuillant, Fustigate, Garrick, Glee, Golf, Guards, Guild, Hampden, Hell-fire, Hercules', Honky-tonk, Indian, Investment, Iron, Jacobin, Jigger, Jockey, Junior Carlton, Kennel, Kierie, Kiri, Kitcat, Kiwanis, Knobkerrie, Landsdowne, Lathi, Laughter, League, Leander, Lions, Lofter, Luncheon, Mace, Mallet, Mashie, Maul, Mell, Mere, Meri, Mess, Midiron, Monday, National Liberal, Niblick, Night(stick), Nightspot, Nitery, Nulla(-nulla), Oddfellows, Paris, Patu, Pitching wedge, Polt, Pregnant, Priest, Provident, Pudding, Putter, Quarterstaff, RAC, R & A, Reform, Ring, Rota, Rotarian, Rotary, Round Table, Sand wedge, Savage, Savile, Shillelagh, Slate, Society, Soroptimist, Sorosis, Spoon, Spot, Spurs, Strike, Strip, Supper, Texas wedge, Thatched House, Tong, Travellers, Trefoil, Truncheon, Trunnion, Union, United Services, Variety, Waddy, Wedge, White's, Wood, Yacht, Youth

Club-foot Kyllosis, Po(u)lt-foot, Talipes, Varus

Clubman Member

Club-rush Deer-hair, Scirpus, Sedge

Cluck Chirrup, Dent

Clue Across, Anagram, Ball, Charade, Clavis, Dabs, Down, → **HINT**, Inkling, Key, Lead, Light, Rebus, Scent, Scooby(doo), Signpost, Thread, Tip

Clueless Ignorant

Clump Cluster, Finial, Knot, Mass, Mot(te), Patch, Plump, Tread, Tuft, Tump, Tussock

▷ **Clumsily** *may indicate* an anagram

Clumsy Artless, Awkward, Bauchle, Bungling, Butterfingers, Cack-handed, Calf, Chuckle, Clatch, Clodhopper, Cumbersome, Dub, Dutch, Galoot, Gauche, Gimp, Ham(-fisted), Heavy-handed, Horse-godmother, Inapt, Inelegant, Inept, Inexpert, Klutz, Lob, Loutish, Lubbard, Lubber, Lummox, Lumpish, Maladdress, Maladroit, Mauther, Mawr, Mawther, Messy, Mor, Nerd, Nurd, Oafish, Off-ox, Palooka, Plonking, Rough, S(c)hlemiel, Schlemihl, Spastic, Spaz(zy), Squab, Stot, Swab, Swob, Taupie, Tawpie, Two-fisted, Unco, Ungain, Unskilful, Unsubtle, Unwieldy

Cluster Acervate, Assemble, Asterism, Bunch, Clump, Collection, Concentre, Constellate, Conurbation, Corymb, Cyme, Gather, Gear, Globular, Glomeration, Knot, Oakleaf, Packet, Plump, Raceme, Sheaf, Sorus, Strap, Thyrse, Tone, Truss, Tuffe, Tuft, Umbel, Verticillaster

Clutch Battery, Brood, Chickens, Clasp, Cling, Eggs, Friction, Glaum, Grab, → **GRASP**, Gripe, Nest, Seize, Sitting, Squeeze

Clutter Confusion, Litter, Mess, Rummage

Coach Battlebus, Berlin, Bogie, Bus, Car, Carriage, Chara, Clerestory, Crammer, Diligence, Dilly, Double-decker, Drag, Edifier, Fly, Four-in-hand, Gig, Hackney, Handler, Landau(let), Life, Microbus, Mourning, Phaeton, Post chaise, Pullman, Railcar, Rattler, Repetiteur, Saloon, Shay, Sleeper, Slip, Sobriety, Stage, Surrey, Tally(-ho), Teach(er), Thoroughbrace, Train(er), Tutor, Voiture

Coach-horse Rove-beetle

Coachman Automedon, Bunene, Coachy, Dragsman, Jarvey, Jehu, John

Coagulant, Coagulate, Coagulation Cautery, Clot, Congeal, Curds, Jell, Rennet, Run, Runnet, Set, Solidify, Thicken

Coal Anthracite, Bituminous, Black diamonds, Block, Brown, Burgee, Cannel, Cherry, Clinker, Coking, Coom, Crow, Culm, Dice, Edge, Eldin, Ember, Fusain, Gas, Gathering, Hard, Jud, Knob, Lignite, Maceral, Mineral, Nut, Open-cast, Paper, Parrot, Purse, Sapropelite, Score, Sea, Slack, Soft, Splint, Steam, Stone, Vitrain, Wallsend, White, Wood

Coalesce(nce) Amalgamate, Concrete, Fuse, Merge, Sintery, Synaloepha, Unite

Coalfish Saith

Coalition Alliance, Bloc, Janata, Merger, Rainbow, Tie

Coal-tar Cresol, Indene

Coal-tub Corf, Dan, Scuttle

Coarse(ness) Base, Bawdy, Blowzy, Bran, Broad, Common, Crude, Dowlas, Earthy, Fisherman, Foul, Gneissose, Grained, Grobian, Gross, Grossièreté, Haggery, Ham, Illbred, Indelicate, Low-bred, Plebeian, Rabelaisian, Rank, Rappee, Raunchy, Ribald, Rough, Rudas, Rude, Sackcloth, Schlub, Semple, Slob, Sotadic, Unrefined, Vulgar

Coast(al) Barbary, Beach, Bight, Caird, Causeway, Coromandel, Costa, Drift, Freewheel, Glide, Gold, Hard, Ivory, Littoral, Longshore, Malabar, Maritime, Murman(sk), Orarian, Riviera, Seaboard, Seafront, Seaside, → **SHORE**, Slave, Sledge, Strand, Toboggan, Trucial

Coaster Beermat, Drog(h)er, Mat, Roller, Ship

Coastguard CG, Gobby

Coastline Watermark

Coast-road Corniche

Coat(ed), Coating Abaya, Ab(b)a, Achkan, Acton, Admiral, Afghan, Anarak, Anodise, Anorak, Balmacaan, Barathea, Basan, Bathrobe, Belton, Benjamin, Blazer, Bloomed, Box, British warm, Buff, Buff-jerkin, Calcimine, Car, Chesterfield, Cladding, Claw-hammer, Clearcole, Cloak, Clutch, Cocoon, Coolie, Cover, Covert, Creosote, Crust(a), Cutaway, Dip, Doggett's, Drape, Dress, Duffel, Duster, Electroplate, Enamel, Encrust, Envelope, Ermelin, Ermine, Exine, Extine, Fearnought, Film, Fleece, Frock, Fur, Gabardine, Galvanise, Gambeson, Ganoin, Glaze, Grego, Ground, Ha(c)queton, Hair, Happi, Impasto, Integument, Inverness, Iridise, Jack(et), Jemmy, Jerkin, Jodhpuri, Joseph, Jump, Jupon, Lacquer, Lammie, Lammy, Lanugo, Layer, Laying, Loden, Lounge, Mac, Mackinaw, Matinee, Metallise, Morning, Newmarket, → **OVERCOAT**, Paint, Paletot, Palla, Parka, Parkee, Passivate, Patinate, Pebbledash, Pelage, Pelisse, Perfuse, Peridium, Petersham, Plate, Polo, Pos(h)teen, Primer, Primine, Prince Albert, Raglan, Redingote, Resin, Resist, Riding, Roquelaure, Sack, Saque, Sclera, Scratch, Seal, Sheepskin, Shellac, Sherardise, Sherwani, Silver, Skinwork, Spencer, Sports, Stadium, Surtout, Swagger, Swallowtail(ed), Tabard, Taglioni, Tail, Tar, Teflon, Tent, Top, Trench, Truss, Trusty, Tunic, Tuxedo, Ulster(ette), Underseal, Veneer, Verdigris, Warm, Wash, Windjammer, Wool, Wrap-rascal, Zamarra, Zamarro, Zinc

Coat of arms Crest, Hatchment

Coat-tail Flap

Coax Blandish, Blarney, Cajole, Carn(e)y, Cuittle, Entice, Flatter, Lure, Persuade, Wheedle, Whillywha(w)

Cob Hazel(nut), Horse

Cobalt Co, Zaffer, Zaffre

Cobble(s), Cobbled, Cobbler(s) Bunkum, Claptrap, Cosier, Cozier, Mend, Patch, Pie, Rot, Snob, Soutar, Souter, Sowter, Stone, Sutor, Twaddle, Vamp

Cobra King

Cobweb(by) Arachnoid, Araneous, Gossamer, Snare, Trap

Cocaine Basuco, C, Charlie, Coke, Crystal, Freebase, Moonrock, Nose candy, Number, Ready-wash, Snow

Coccid Wax-insect

Cochlear Scala

Cock(y) Alectryon, Ball, Capon, Chanticleer, Chaparral, Erect, Escape, Fighting, Flip, Fowl, France, Fugie, Half, Hay, Heath, Jack-the-lad, Jaunty, Midden, Penis, Roadrunner, Robin, Rooster, Shake-bag, Snook, Strut, Swaggering, Tap, Tilt, Turkey, Vain, Valve, Vane

Cock-a-hoop Crowing, Elated

Cockatoo Bird, Corella, Galah, Leadbeater's, Major Mitchell, Parrot

Cockboat Cog

Cockchafer Humbuzz, Maybug

Cock crow Skreigh of the day

Cocker Blenheim, Cuiter, Spaniel

Cockeyed Agee, Askew, Skewwhiff

Cockfight Main

Cockle Bulge, Crease, Wrinkle

▷ **Cockle(s)** *may indicate* an anagram

Cockney 'Arriet, 'Arry, Bow, Eastender, Londoner, Londonese

▷ **Cockney** *may indicate* a missing h

Cockpit Greenhouse, Well

Cockroach Archy, Beetle, Black beetle, Croton bug, German, Oriental, Orthoptera

▶ **Cockscomb** *see* **COXCOMB**

Cocktail Alexander, Aperitif, Atomic, Bellini, Between the sheets, Black Russian, Bloody Mary, Brandy Alexander, Buck's fizz, Bumbo, Caipirinha, Cobbler, Cold duck, Crusta, Daiquiri, → **DRINK**, Egg-flip, Fruit, Fustian, Gibson, Gimlet, Grasshopper, Harvey Wallbanger, Highball, → **HORSE**, Horse's neck, Julep, Mai-Tai, Manhattan, Margarita, Martini®, Melange, Mix, Molotov, Moscow mule, Old-fashioned, Piña colada, Pink lady, Planter's punch, Prawn, Punch, Rickey, Rusty nail, Sangaree, Sangria, Sazerac®, Screwdriver, Sherry cobbler, Side-car, Singapore sling, Slammer, Snakebite, Snowball, Spritzer, Stengah, Stinger, Swizzle, Tom Collins, Twist, White-lady

Cocoa Criollo, Nib(s)

Coconut Coco-de-mer, Coir, Copra, Head, Madafu, Poonac, Toddy-palm

Cocoon Dupion, Mother, Pod, Swathe, Trehala

Cod Bag, Cape, Coalfish, Fish, Gade, Gadus, Haberdine, Keeling, Kid, Lob, Man, Morrhua, Murray, Red, Saith, Saltfish, Stockfish, Torsk, Tusk, Whiting

Coda End(ing), Epilogue, Rondo, Tail

Coddle Cosset, Molly, Nancy, Pamper, Pet, Poach

Code, Coding, Codification Access, Alphanumeric, Amalfitan, Area, Bar, Barred, Binary, Bushido, Canon, Character, Cipher, City, Civil, Clarendon, Codex, Colour, Computing, Condition, Country, Cryptogram, Cryptograph, Dialling, Disciplinary, Dogma, Dress, DX, EBCDIC, Enigma, Error, Escape, Ethics, Fuero, Genetic, Gray, Green Cross, Hammurabic, Highway, Hollerith, Iddy-umpty, Justinian, MAC, Machine, Morse, Napoleon(ic), National, Object, Omerta, Opcode, Penal, PGP, Pindaric, Postal, Price, Rulebook, Scytale, Sharia, Shulchan Aruch, Signal, Sort, Source, STD, Talmud, Time, Twelve Tables, Zip

Code-breaker, Code-breaking Bletchley Park, Malpractitioner

Codger Buffer, Fellow

Codicil Addition, Label, PS, Rider

Codon Initiator

Coefficient Absorption, Correlation, Differential, Diffusion, Distribution, Modulus, Partition, Pearson's correlation, Permeability, Saturation, Spearman's rank-order, Transmission, Young modulus

Coelacanth Latimeria

Coerce, Coercion Big stick, Bully, Compel, Dragoon, Gherao, Pressure, Railroad, Restrain, Threaten

Coffee, Coffee beans, Coffee pot Americano, Arabica, Brazil, Cafetiere, Cappuccino, Decaff, Demi-tasse, Espresso, Expresso, Filter, Gaelic, Gloria, Granules, Instant, Irish, Java, Latte, Macchiato, Mocha, Peaberry, Percolator, Robusta, Rye, Skinny latte, Tan, Triage, Turkish

Coffee-house Lloyd's

Coffer Ark, Box, Casket, Cassone, Chest, Lacunar, Locker

Coffin Bier, Box, Casket, Hearse, Kist, Larnax, Sarcophagus, Shell, Wooden kimono, Wooden overcoat

Cog(ged) Contrate, Mitre-wheel, Nog, Pinion, Tooth

Cogent Compelling, Forceful, Good, Sound, Telling

Cogitate Deliberate, Mull, Muse, Ponder

Cognate Paronym

Cohabit Bed, Indwell, Share

Co-heir Parcener

Cohere(nt) Agglutinate, Clear, Cleave, Cling, Logical, Stick

Cohort Colleague, Crony, Soldier

Coif Calotte, Cap, Hood

Coiffure Hairdo, Pompadour, Tête

Coil(s), Coiled Armature, Bight, Bought, Choke, Circinate, Clew, Clue, Convolute(d), Convolve, Curl, Current, Fake, Fank, Furl, Hank, Helix, Ignition, Induction, Loading, Mortal, Moving, Primary, Resistance, Rouleau, Scorpioid, Solenoid, Spark, Spiral, Spiraster, Spire, Tesla, Tickler, Toroid, Twine, Twirl, → **WIND**, Wound, Wreath, Writhe, Yoke

Coin Base, Bean, Bit, Broad(piece), Cash, Change, Coign(e), Contomiate, Copper, Create, Doctor, Dosh, Double-header, Dump(s), Fiver, Han(d)sel, Imperial, Invent, Make, Mill, Mint, → **MONEY**, Neoterise, Numismatic, Nummary, Piece, Plate, Pocket-piece, Proof, Shiner, Slip, Smelt, Specie, Stamp, Sterling, Strike, Subsidiary, Sum, Tenner, Thin'un, Token, Touchpiece, Unity

COINS

1 letter:	Bar	Lei	Sol
D	Bob	Lek	Som
	Cob	Leu	Sou
2 letters:	Dam	Lev	Won
As	Ecu	Lew	Yen
DM	Fen	Mil	Zuz
Kr	Fil	Mna	
Rd	Fin	Moy	*4 letters:*
Xu	Flu	Ore	Anna
	Hao	Pul	Baht
3 letters:	Jun	Pya	Bani
Avo	Kip	Red	Birr
Ban	Lat	Sen	Buck

Cedi
Cent
Chon
Dibs
Dime
Doit
Dong
Dram
Duro
Euro
Fiat
Fils
Inti
Jack
Jane
Jiao
Kina
Kobo
Kuna
Kyat
Lari
Lion
Lipa
Lira
Loti
Luma
Maik
Mark
Merk
Mina
Mite
Mule
Obol
Para
Paul
Peag
Peni
Peso
Pice
Pula
Puli
Punt
Rand
Real
Reis
Rial
Riel
Rock
Ryal
Sene
Sent

Slog
Tael
Taka
Tala
Tein
Toea
Tray
Trey
Vatu
Yuan
Zack

5 letters:
Agora
Angel
Asper
Aurar
Baiza
Bekah
Belga
Bodle
Brown
Butat
Butut
Chiao
Colon
Conto
Crore
Crown
Daric
Dibbs
Dinar
Diram
Dobra
Ducat
Eagle
Eyrir
Franc
Fugio
Gazet
Gerah
Gopik
Groat
Grosz
Haler
Krona
Krone
Kroon
Kurus
Laari
Laree

Leone
Liard
Litai
Litas
Livre
Louis
Lyart
Maile
Manat
Maneh
Mohur
Mongo
Mopus
Naira
Nakfa
Ngwee
Noble
Obang
Oscar
Paisa
Paolo
Pence
Pengo
Penie
Penni
Penny
Plack
Pound
Razoo
Rider
Royal
Ruble
Rupee
Sceat
Scudo
Scute
Semis
Sente
Shand
Soldo
Souon
Sucre
Sycee
Tenge
Thebe
Tical
Ticky
Tiyin
Tolar
Toman
Tyiyn

Unite
Zaire
Zimbi
Zloty

6 letters:
Agorol
Aureus
Balboa
Bawbee
Bender
Bezant
Boddle
Byzant
Canary
Centas
Colone
Copeck
Couter
Dalasi
Danace
Deaner
Décime
Denier
Derham
Dirham
Dirhem
Dodkin
Dollar
Double
Drachm
Ekuele
Escudo
Filler
Florin
Forint
Gilder
Gourde
Guinea
Gulden
Halala
Heller
Hryvna
Jitney
Kobang
Koruna
Kroner
Kroona
Kruger
Kwacha
Kwanza

Lepton
Likuta
Loonie
Makuta
Mancus
Markka
Mawpus
Mongoe
Pa'anga
Paduan
Pagoda
Pataca
Pennia
Peseta
Pesewa
Qintar
Rappen
Rouble
Rupiah
Santum
Satang
Sceatt
Seniti
Sequin
Shekel
Sickle
Siglos
Somoni
Stater
Stiver
Stotin
Talent
Tanner
Tester
Teston
Thaler
Tickey
Toonie
Tugrik
Turner
Vellon
Wakiki

7 letters:
Afghani
Austral

Bolivar
Cardecu
Carolus
Centavo
Chetrum
Cordoba
Crusado
Drachma
Ekpwele
Guarani
Guilder
Hryvnya
Jacobus
Joannes
Kopiyka
Kreuzer
Lemoira
Lisente
Metical
Millime
Milreis
Moidore
Ostmark
Ouguiya
Patrick
Piastre
Piefort
Pistole
Pollard
Quarter
Quetzal
Ringgit
Ruddock
Rufiyaa
Sextans
Solidus
Spanker
Tambala
Testoon
Testril
Thick'un
Thrimsa
Thrymsa
Tughrik
Unicorn
Xerafin

8 letters:
Brockage
Cardecue
Cruzeiro
Denarius
Doubloon
Ducatoon
Emalengi
Farthing
Groschen
Johannes
Kreutzer
Llangeni
Louis d'or
Maravedi
Millieme
Napoleon
Ngultrum
Picayune
Pistolet
Planchet
Portague
Portigue
Quadrans
Rigmarie
Semuncia
Sesterce
Shilling
Skilling
Solidare
Spur-rial
Spur-ryal
Stotinka
Twopence
Xeraphin
Zecchino

9 letters:
Boliviano
Britannia
Centesimo
Dandiprat
Dandyprat
Didrachma
Dupondius
Fourpence

Half-eagle
Half-tiger
Luckpenny
Maple leaf
Ninepence
Pistareen
Rennminbi
Rix-dollar
Rose noble
Schilling
Sou marque
Sovereign
Spur-royal
Yellowboy
Zwanziger

10 letters:
Chervonets
Krugerrand
Portcullis
Reichsmark
Siege-piece

11 letters:
Bonnet-piece
Deutschmark
Double eagle
Sword-dollar
Tetradrachm

12 letters:
Antoninianus

13 letters:
Half-sovereign
Rennminbi yuan

14 letters:
Three-farthings

18 letters:
Maria Theresa
 dollar

Coinage Currency, Invention, Nonce-word
Coincide(nt), Coincidence Accident, Chance, Consilience, Conterminous, Fit,
 Fluke, Homotaxis, Overlap, Rabat(to), Simultaneous, Synastry, Synchronise, Tally
Coke Chark, Coal, Cocaine, Kola

Col Pass, Poort, Saddle

Cold(-blooded) Ague, Algid, Aloof, Arctic, Austere, Biting, Bitter, Bleak, C, Catarrh, Cauld(rife), Charity, Chill(y), Colubrine, Common, Coryza, Ectotherm, Emotionless, Frappé, Frem(d), Fremit, Frigid, Frost(y), Gelid, Glacial, Hiemal, Icy, Impersonal, Jeel, Nippy, Nirlit, Parky, Passionless, Perishing, Piercing, Poikilotherm(ic), Polar, Psychro-, Remote, Rheumy, Rigor, Rume, Snap, Snell, Sniffles, Sour, Standoffish, Starving, Streamer, Subzero, Taters, Weed, Wintry

Cold sore Herpes, Shiver

Coldstream Borderer, Guard

Cole Colza, King, Nat, Porter

Colic Batts, Bots, Botts, Gripe, Lead, Painter's, Sand, Upset, Zinc

Collaborate, Collaborator, Collaboration Assist, Combine, → **COOPERATE**, Keiretsu, Quisling, Synergy, Vichy, Vichyite

Collage Paste up

Collapse Apoplexy, Breakdown, Buckle, Cave, Conk, Crash, Crumble, Crumple, Debacle, Downfall, Fail(ure), Fall, Flake out, Fold, Founder, Give, Implode, Inburst, Landslide, Meltdown, Phut, Purler, Rack, Rot, Ruin, Scat(ter), Sink, Slump, Stroke, Subside, Sunstroke, Swoon, Telescope, Tumble, Wilt, Wrack, Zonk

▷ **Collapsing** *may indicate* an anagram

Collar(ed) Arrest, Astrakhan, Bermuda, Bertha, Berthe, Bib, Bishop, Blue, Brecham, Buster, Butterfly, Button-down, Buttonhole, Capture, Carcanet, Chevesaile, Choke(r), Clerical, Collet, Dog, Esses, Eton, Falling-band, Flea, Gorget, Grandad, Hame, Head(stall), Holderbat, Horse, Jabot, Jampot, Karenni, Mandarin, Moran, Mousquetaire, Nab, Nail, Neckband, Necklet, Ox-bow, Peter Pan, Piccadell, Piccadillo, Piccadilly, Pikadell, Pink, Polo, Puritan, Rabaline, Rabato, Rebater, Rebato, Revers, Rollneck, Roman, Ruff, Sailor, Seize, Shawl, Steel, Storm, Tackle, Tappet, Tie-neck, Torque, Turndown, Turtleneck, Vandyke, Whisk, White, Wing, Yoke

Collation Comparison, Meal, Repast

Colleague(s) Ally, Associate, Bedfellow, Confrère, Mate, Oppo, Partner, Team

Collect(ion), Collective(ly), Collector Accrue, Agglomerate, Aggregate, Album, Alms, Amass, Amildar, Ana, Anthology, Arcana, Assemble, Aumil, Bank, Bow, Budget, Bunch, Bundle, Burrell, Caboodle, Calm, Cap, Cete, Clowder, Compendium, Compile, Congeries, Conglomerate, Covey, Cull, Dossier, Dustman, Earn, Egger, Exaltation, Exordial, Fest, (Fest)schrift, Fetch, Florilegium, Gaggle, Garbo, Garner, Gather, Get, Gilbert, Glean, Glossary, Grice, Heap, Herd, Hive, Idant, In all, Jingbang, Job lot, Kit, Kitty, Levy, Loan, Magpie, Meal, Meet, Meinie, Mein(e)y, Menagerie, Menyie, Miscellany, Mish-mash, Montem, Murmuration, Museum, Muster, Nide, Offertory, Omnibus, Omnium-gatherum, Paddling, Pile, Plate, Pod, Post, Prayer, Quest, Raft, Raise, Rammle, Recheat, Rhapsody, Scramble, Sedge, Serene, Set, Shoe, Siege, Skein, Smytrie, Sord, Sottisier, Sounder, Spring, Stand, Tahsildar, Team, Troop, Unkindness, Uplift, Watch, Wernher, Whipround, Wisp

▷ **Collection** *may indicate* an anagram

Collection-box Brod, Ladle, Rammle

Collectorate Taluk

College(s) Academy, All Souls, Alma mater, Ampleforth, Balliol, Brasenose, Business, C, Caius, Campus, CAT, Cheltenham, Clare, Classical, Coed, Commercial, Community, Corpus, Cow, Cranwell, Downing, Dulwich, Electoral, Emmanuel, Eton, Exeter, Foundation, Freshwater, Girton, Hall, Heralds', Jail, Junior, Keble, King's, Lancing, Linacre, Lincoln, LSE, Lycée, Lyceum, Madras(s)a(h), Madressah, Magdalen(e), Marlborough, Medrese, Medresseh, Merton, Newnham, Nuffield,

Open, Oriel, Pembroke, Poly, Polytechnic, Pontifical, Protonotariat, Queen's, Ruskin, Sacred, St Johns, Saliens, Sandhurst, Selwyn, Seminary, Sixth-form, Somerville, Sorbonne, Staff, Tech(nical), Technikon, Tertiary, Theologate, Training, Trinity, Tug, UMIST, Up, Village, Wadham, Winchester, Yeshwa(h)

Collide, Collision Afoul, Barge, Bird-strike, Bump, Cannon, Carom(bole), Clash, Dash, Elastic, Fender-bender, Foul, Head-on, Hurtle, Impact, Inelastic, Into, Kiss, Meet, Pile-up, Prang, Rencounter, Smash-up, Strike, Thwack

Collie Bearded, Border, Dog, Kelpie, Kelpy, Rough, Sheepdog

Collier Geordie, Hoastman, Miner, Necklace, Patience, Ship

Colloid Aerogel, Gel, Lyophil(e), Sol

Collude, Collusive Abet, Cahoots, Conspire, Deceive

Colon Aspinwall, Sigmoid, Spastic, Transverse

Colonel Blimp, Bogey, Chinstrap, Col, Everard, Goldstick, Newcome, Nissen, Pride

Colonial(ist), Colonist Ant, Antenatal, Boer, Creole, Emigré, Oecist, Oikist, Overseas, Phoenician, Pioneer, Planter, Polyp(e), Settler, Sicel(iot), Sikel(ian), Sikeliot, Stuyvesant, Swarm, Territorial, Voter

Colonnade Eustyle, File, Gallery, Peristyle, Porch, Portico, Stoa

Colony Aden, Cape, Charter, Cleruchy, Crown, Dependency, Halicarnassian, Hive, Hongkong, Kaffraria, Nudist, Penal, Plymouth, Presidio, Proprietary, Rookery, Settlement, Swarm, Termitarium, Warren, Zambia, Zimbabwe

Colophony Rosin

Colossal → ENORMOUS, Epochal, Gigantic, Huge, Vast

Colosseum Amphitheatre

Colour(ed), Colouring, Colours Achromatic, Bedye, Blee, Blush, C, Cap, Chromatic, Chrome, Complementary, Complexion, Crayon, Criant, Cross, Distort, Dye, False, Film, Flag, Florid, Flying, Gouache, Haem, → HUE, Ink, Irised, Kalamkari, Leer, Local, Lutein, Metif, Nankeen, Orpiment, Palette, Pantone®, Pastel, Pied, Pigment, Pochoir, Polychrome, Primary, Prism, Prismatic, Process, Puke, Queen's, Raddle, Reddle, Regimental, Rinse, Riot, Ruddle, Secondary, Sematic, Shade, Solid, Spectrum, Startle, Tertiary, Tie-dye, Tinctorial, Tinc(ture), Tinge, Tint, Tone, Uvea, Wash

COLOURS

2 letters:	Gold	Camel	Rouge
Or	Grey	Chica	Sepia
	Jade	Coral	Taupe
3 letters:	Lake	Cream	Tenné
Bay	Lime	Eosin	Tenny
Jet	Navy	Green	Umber
Red	Pink	Gules	
Tan	Plum	Ivory	6 letters:
	Puce	Khaki	Anatta
4 letters:	Rose	Lemon	Anatto
Anil	Ruby	Lilac	Auburn
Bice	Sand	Lovat	Bisque
Blue	Teal	Mauve	Bister
Buff	Vert	Ochre	Bistre
Cyan		Olive	Cerise
Ecru	5 letters:	Peach	Day-Glo®
Fawn	Beige	Pearl	Isabel

Maroon
Orange
Reseda
Roucou
Sienna
Titian

7 letters:
Annatta
Annatto
Apricot
Arnotto
Caramel
Crimson
Emerald

Filemot
Gamboge
Magenta
Oatmeal
Old gold
Old rose
Saffron
Scarlet
Umbrage

8 letters:
Alizarin
Burgundy
Cardinal
Chestnut

Cinnamon
Lavender
Off-white
Pea-green
Philamot
Philomot

9 letters:
Alizarine
Anthocyan
Chocolate
Royal blue
Solferino
Turquoise
Vermilion

10 letters:
Aquamarine
French navy
Tartrazine
Vermillion

11 letters:
Ultramarine

12 letters:
Cappagh-brown

Colour blindness Daltonism, Deuteranopia, Dichrom(at)ism, Monochromatic, Protanomaly, Protanopia, Protanopic, Tritanopia
▷ **Coloured** *may indicate* an anagram
Colourful Abloom, Brave, Flamboyant, Flowery, Iridescent, Kaleidoscope, Opalescent, Splashy, Vivid
Colourless Albino, Bleak, Drab, Dull, Hyalite, Pallid, Pallor, Wan, White
Colt Cade, Foal, Gun, Hogget, Sta(i)g, Teenager, Two-year-old
Columbine Aquilegia
Column(s), Column foot Agony, Anta, Atlantes, Clustered, Commentary, Control, Corinthian, Correspondence, Cylinder, Decastyle, Diastyle, Doric, Editorial, Eustyle, Fifth, File, Fractionating, Geological, Gossip, Hypostyle, Impost, Lat, Lonelyhearts, Monolith, Nelson's, Newel, Obelisk, Pericycle, Peripteral, Peristyle, Persian, Personal, Pilaster, → **PILLAR**, Pilotis, Prostyle, Pycnostyle, Rouleau, Row, Short, Spina, Spinal, Spine, Stalactite, Stalagmite, Steering, Stylobate, Systyle, Tabulate, Telamone, Third, Tige, Tore, Torus, Trajan's, Vertebral
Columnist Advertiser, Caryatid, Newsman, Stylite, Telamon, Writer
Coma(tose) Apoplexy, Crown, Sedated, Sleep, Torpor, Trance
Comb(er), Combed, Combing Afro, Alveolate, Beehive, Breaker, Card, Copple, Crest, Curry, Dredge, Fine-tooth, Hackle, Heckle, Hot, Kaim, Kame, Kangha, Kemb, Noils, Pecten, Rake, Red(d), Ripple(r), Rose, Scribble, Search, Side, Small tooth, Smooth, Tease(l), Toaze, Tooth, Tose, Toze, Trawl, Tuft, Wave
Combat(ant), Combative Argument, → **BATTLE**, Competitor, Conflict, Contest, Dispute, Duel, → **FIGHT**, Gladiator, Joust, Judicial, Jujitsu, Just, Karate, Kendo, List, Mêlée, Militant, Oppose, Paintball, Protagonist, Spear-running, Unarmed, War
Combination, Combine(d), Combining Accrete, Alligate, Ally, Amalgam, Associate, Axis, Bloc, Cartel, Cleave, Clique, Coalesce, Coalition, Composite, Concoction, Conflated, Conglomerate, Consortium, Coordinate, Crasis, Fuse, Group, Harvester, Incorporate, Integration, Interfile, Join, Junta, Kartell, League, Meld, Merge(r), Mingle, Mixture, Perm(utation), Piece, Pool, Quill, Ring, Solvate, Splice, Syncretize, Synthesis, Terrace, Trivalent, Trona, Unite, Valency, Wed, Zaibatsu
Comb-like Ctenoid, Pecten
Combustible, Combustion Ardent, Fiery, Inflammable, Phlogistic, Phlogiston, Spontaneous, Wildfire
▷ **Combustible** *may indicate* an anagram

Come, Coming (back), Coming out Advent, Anear, Anon, Appear, Approach, Ar(r), Arise, Arrive, Attend, Debouch, Derive, Emerge, Future, Happen, Iceman, Issue, Millenarian, Orgasm, Parousia, Pass, Pop, Respond, Second, Via

Come again Eh

Comeback Boomerang, Bounce, Echo, Homer, Quip, Rally, Rearise, Rebound, Recovery, Repartee, Reply, Retort, Retour, Return, Reversion, Riposte

Comedian Benny, Buffoon, Chaplin, → CLOWN, Comic, Durante, Emery, Goon, Groucho, Hope, Joker, Karno, Keaton, Leno, Quipster, Robey, Scream, Screwball, Stand-up, Tate, Tati, Tummler, Wag, Wise, Yell

Comedo Blackhead

Comedown Avale, Bathetic, Bathos, Disappointment, Drop, Letdown, Shower

Comedy Alternative, Black, Com, Drama, Ealing, Errors, Farce, High, Humour, Keystone, Knockabout, Lazzo, Low, Millamant, Musical, Romcom, Situation, Slapstick, Stand-up, Thalia, Travesty

Comely Beseen, Bonny, Fair, Goodly, Graceful, Jolly, Likely, Pleasing, Pretty, Proper

Comestible(s) Cate, Eats, Fare

Comet Chiron, Geminid, Halley's, Kohoutek, Meteor, Oort cloud, Reindeer, Shoemaker-Levy 9, Vomet, Xiphias

Come through Weather

Comfort(able), Comforter, Comforting, Comfy Amenity, Analeptic, Armchair, Balm, Bein, Bildad, Calm, Canny, Cheer, Cherish, Clover, Cold, Consolation, Console, Convenience, Cose, Cosh, Cosy, Couthie, Couthy, Creature, Crumb, Cushy, Dummy, Dutch, Ease, Easy, Eliphaz, Featherbed, Gemutlich, Heeled, Homely, Job's, Mumsy, Noah, Plum, Plushy, Reassure, Relaxed, Relief, Relieve, Rug, Scarf, Sinecure, Snug, Solace, Soothe, Succour, There, Tosh, Trig, Warm, Wealthy, Well, Well-to-do, Zophar

Comic(al) Beano, Buff, Buffo(on), Bumpkin, Buster, Chaplin, Clown, → COMEDIAN, Dandy, Droll, Eagle, Facetious, Fields, → FUNNY, Gagster, Hardy, Horror, Jester, Knock-about, Laurel, Leno, Mag, Manga, Quizzical, Rich, Robey, Strip, Tati, Trial, Zany

Comma Inverted, Oxford

Command(eer), Commanding, Commandment(s) Behest, Bid, Categorical imperative, Charge, Coerce, Control, Decalogue, Direct, Direction, Dominate, Domineer, Easy, Edict, Fiat, Fiaunt, Fighter, Firman, Haw, Hest, High, Imperious, Impress, Injunction, Instruction, Jussive, Mandate, Maritime, Mastery, Mitzvah, Mobile, → ORDER, Precept, Press, Query language, Requisition, Rule, Seize, Ukase, Warn, Warrant, Will, Wish, Writ

Commander Admiral, Ag(h)a, Ameer, Barleycorn, Bey, Bloke, Blucher, Boss, Brennus, Brig, Caliph, Centurion, Cid, Decurion, Dreyfus, Emir, Emperor, Field cornet, Generalissimo, Hetman, Hipparch, Imperator, Killadar, Leader, Manager, Marshal, Master, Meer, Mir, Moore, Officer, Overlord, Pendragon, Polemarch, Pr(a)efect, Raglan, Seraskier, Shogun, Sirdar, Taxiarch, Trierarch, Turcopolier, Vaivode, Voivode, Waivode, Warlord, Wing

Commando Chindit(s), Fedayee(n), Green Beret, Raider, Ranger, SAS

Commemorate, Commemoration Encaenia, Epitaph, Eulogy, Keep, Memorial, Monument, Plaque, Remember

Commence Begin, Initiate, Open, Start

Commend(ation) Belaud, Bestow, Encomium, Entrust, Laud, Panegyric, → PRAISE, Roose, Tribute

Commensal Epizoon, Messmate

Commensurate Adequate, Enough, Equivalent, Relevant

Comment(ary), Commentator Analyst, Animadvert, Annotate, Apercu, Comm, Coryphaeus, Coverage, Critic, Critique, Descant, Discuss, Editorial, Essay, Exegete, Explain, Exposition, Expound, Footnote, Gemara, Gloss(ographer), Glosser, Hakam, Kibitz, Margin, Marginalia, Midrashim, Note, Obiter dictum, Observation, Par, Platitude, Play-by-play, Postil, Remark, Running, Scholiast, Scholion, Scholium, Voice-over, Zohar

Commerce, Commercial Ad, Barter, Cabotage, Jingle, Marketable, Mercantile, Mercenary, Merchant, Shoppy, Simony, Trade, Traffic

Commercial traveller Drummer, Rep

Commiserate, Commiseration Compassion, Pity, Sympathise

Commissar People's, Political

Commission(er), Commissioned Authorise, Boundary, Brevet, Brokage, Brokerage, Charge, Charity, Countryside, Delegation, Depute, ECE, Employ, Engage, Envoy, Errand, European, Factor, Gosplan, High, Husbandage, Job, Kickback, Law, Magistrate, Mandate, Office(r), Official, Ombudsman, Order, Percentage, Perpetration, Place, Poundage, Price, Rake-off, Resident, Roskill, Roving, Royal, Task, Task force, Trust, Wreck

Commit(tal), Commitment Aret(t), Consign, Contract, Decision, Dedication, Delegate, Devotion, Do, Engage, Entrust, Enure, Impeachment, Perpetrate, Pledge, Rubicon

Committee ACRE, Board, Body, Commission, Commune, Council, Delegacy, Group, Hanging, Joint, Junta, Politburo, Presidium, Propaganda, Review body, Riding, Samiti, School, Select, Standing, Steering, Syndicate, Table, Vigilance, Watch, Works

Commode, Commodious Ample, Closestool, Roomy, Spacious

Commodities, Commodity Article, Futures, Gapeseed, Item, Physicals, Soft, Staple, Ware

Common(ly), Commoner, Commons As per usual, Average, Cad, Conventional, Diet, Dirt, Doctor's, Ealing, Eatables, Enclosure, Endemic, Epicene, Everyday, Familiar, Fare, Folk, General, Green, Greenham, House, Law, Lay, Low, Lower House, Mark, Mere, MP, Mutual, Naff, Non-U, Normal, People, Pleb, Prevalent, Prole, Public, Related, Rife, Roturier, Ryfe, Scran, Sense, Shared, Stray, Tie, Tiers d'état, Trite, Tritical, Tuft, Tye, Use, → USUAL, Vile, Vul(gar), Vulgo, Vulgus, Widespread, Wimbledon

Commonplace Banal, Copybook, Hackneyed, Homely, Humdrum, Idée reçue, Mot, Ordinary, Philistine, Plain, Platitude, Prosaic, Quotidian, Trite, Workaday

Commonsense Gumption, Nous, Savoir-faire, Smeddum, Wit

Commonwealth Protectorate, Puerto Rico, Res publica

Commotion Bluster, Bustle, Carfuffle, Clangour, Clatter, Curfuffle, Dirdam, Dirdum, Do, Dust, Ferment, Flap, Flurry, Fraise, Fuss, Hell, Hoo-ha(h), Hurly-burly, Hurry, Pother, Pudder, Racket, Romage, Rort, Ruckus, Ruction, Rumpus, Shemozzle, Shindig, Shindy, Shivaree, Steery, Stir, Stirabout, Storm, Stushie, Tirrivee, Tirrivie, To-do, Toss, Tumult, Turmoil, Upheaval, Uproar, Whirl, Wroth

Communal, Commune Agapemone, Collective, Com, Meditate, Mir, Paris, Phalanstery, Public, Talk, Township

Communicate, Communication Ampex, Announce, Baud, Bluetooth, Boyau, Cable, Channelling, Conversation, Convey, Cybernetic, E-mail, Expansive, Impart, Infobahn, Inform, Intelpost, Intelsat, Internet, Message, Nonverbal, Note, Oracy, Prestel®, Proxemics, Put across, Reach, Road, Semiotics, Signal, Tannoy®, Telepathy, Teletex, Telex, Telstar, Tieline, Transmit, Utraquist, Viewdata

Communion Creed, Fellowship, Host, Housel, Intinction, Lord's Supper, Species, Viaticum

Communiqué Announcement, Statement

Communism, Communist Apparat(chik), Aspheterism, Bolshevist, Brook Farm, Com, Comecon, Cominform, Comintern, Commo, Comsomol, Deviationist, Engels, Essene, Fourier, Khmer Rouge, Komsomol, Leninite, Maoist, Marxist, Nomenklatura, Perfectionist, Pinko, Politburo, Populist, Red, Revisionism, Soviet, Spartacist, Stalinism, Tanky, Titoist, Trot, Vietcong, Vietminh

Communities, Community Agapemone, Alterne, Ashram, Biome, Body, Brook Farm, Brotherhood, Clachan, Climax, Closed, Coenobitism, Coenobium, Colonia, Colony, Consocies, District, EC, Ecosystem, EEC, Enclave, European, Faith, Frat(e)ry, Global, Kahal, Kibbutz, Mesarch, Neighbourhood, Pantosocracy, People, Phalanx, Phyle, Preceptory, Public, Pueblo, Republic, Seral, Sere, Settlement, Shtetl, Sisterhood, Society, Speech, Street, Toon, Town, Tribe, Ujamaa, Village, Virtual, Volost, Zupa

Commute(r) Change, Convert, Reduce, Straphanger, Travel

Como Lake, Perry

Compact Agreement, Cement, Concise, Conglobe, Covenant, Covin, Coyne, Dense, Entente, Fast, Firm, Flapjack, Hard, Knit, League, Match, Neat, Pledge, Powder, Solid, Tamp, Terse, Tight, Treaty, Well-knit

Companion(able) Achates, Arm candy, Associate, Attender, Barnacle, Bedfellow, Bonhomie, Bud(dy), Butty, CH, China, Comate, Compeer, Comrade, Consort, Contubernal, Crony, Cupman, Duenna, Ephesian, Escort, Feare, Felibre, → **FELLOW**, Fere, Franion, Furked, Handbook, Helpmate, Mate, Native, Pal, Pard, Pheer(e), Playmate, Pot, Sidekick, Skaines mate, Stable, Thane, Thegn, Trojan, Vade-mecum

Company, Companies Actors, Artel, Ass, Assembly, Band, Bank, Battalion, Bevy, → **BUSINESS**, Bv, Cahoot, Cartel, Cast, Cavalcade, Chartered, CIA, Circle, City, Close, Club, Co, Conger, Consort, Cordwainers, Core, Corporation, Corps, Coy, Crew, Crowd, Decury, Dotcom, East India, Enterprise, Entourage, Faction, Finance, Fire, → **FIRM**, Flock, Free, Gang, Garrison, Ging, Guild, Haberdashers, Heap, Holding, Hudson's Bay, ICI, Inc, Indie, In-house, Intercourse, Investment, Jingbang, Joint-stock, Limited, Listed, Livery, Management, Maniple, Muster, Order, Organisation, Parent, Plc, Pride, Private, Public, Public limited, Quoted, Rep(ertory), Room, SA, Sedge, Set, Set out, Shell, Siege, Sort, SpA, Stationers', Stock, Subsidiary, Syndicate, Table, Team, Thiasus, Touring, Troop, Troupe, Trust, Twa, Two(some), Visitor, White

Compare(d), Comparison Analogy, Balance, Beside, Bracket, Collate, Confront, Contrast, Correspond, Cp, Equate, Liken, Match, Odious, Parallel, Relation, Simile, Weigh

Compartment Ballonet, Bay, Booth, Box, Carriage, Casemate, Cell, Chamber, Cofferdam, Cubbyhole, Cubicle, Dog box, Locellate, Locker, Loculament, Loculus, Panel, Partition, Pigeonhole, Pocket, Pod, Room, Room(ette), Severy, Smoker, Stall, Till, Trunk, Watertight

Compass Ambit, Area, Beam, Binnacle, Bounds, Bow, Dividers, Extent, Gamut, Goniometer, Gyro, Gyromagnetic, Gyroscope, Infold, Magnetic, Mariner's, Needle, Orbit, Pelorus, Pencil, Perimeter, Prismatic, Radio, → **RANGE**, Reach, Rhumb, Room, Scale, Sweep, Tessitura, Trammel, Width

Compassion(ate) Aroha, Bleed(ing), Clemency, Commiseration, Empathy, Heart, Humane, Kuan Yin, Kwan Yin, Mercy, Pity, Samaritan, Sympathy, Ubuntu

Compatible Consistent, Fit, Harmonious

Compatriot National

Compel(ling), Compelled, Compulsion, Compulsive, Compulsory Addiction,

Coact, Coerce, Cogent, Command, Constrain, Dragoon, Duress, Enforce, Extort, Fain, → **FORCE**, Force majeure, Gar, Make, Mandatory, Oblige, Pathological, Steamroller, Strongarm, Tyrannise

Compendium Breviate

Compensate, Compensation Amend(s), Balance, Boot, Comp, Counterbalance, Counterpoise, Damages, Demurrage, Guerdon, Indemnity, Offset, Payment, Recoup, Redress, Reparation, Reprisal, Requital, Restitution, Restore, Retaliation, Salvage, Satisfaction, Solatium, Wergild, X-factor

Compère Emcee, Host, MC, Presenter

Compete Contend, Emulate, Enter, Match, Outvie, Play, Rival, Vie

Competence, Competent Ability, Able, Adequate, Can, Capacity, Dab, Dow, Efficient, Fit, Responsible, Sui juris, Worthy

Competition, Competitive, Competitor Agonist, Backmarker, Battle, Bee, Biathlon, Buckjumping, Candidate, Comper, Concours, Contention, Contest, Cup, Drive, Entrant, Event, Field, Finals, Freestyle, Gamesman, Gymkhana, Head-to-head, Heptathlon, Imperfect, Judoka, Jump off, Karateka, Knockout, Match, Match-play, Monopolistic, Open, Opponent, Outsider, Pairs, Panellist, Pentathlon, Perfect, Player, Premiership, Pro-am, Puissance, Race, Rally, Regatta, Repechage, Rival(ise), Rodeo, Runner-up, Show-jumping, Stableford, Super G, Tenson, Test, Tiger, Tournament, Tourney, Trial, Triallist, Wap(p)enshaw, Wild card

Compile(r), Compilation Anthology, Arrange, Collect, Edit, Prepare, Segue, Synthesis, Zadkiel

Complacent Babbitt, Fatuous, Joco, Pleasant, Self-satisfied, Smug

Complain(t), Complainer Adenoids, Affection, Affliction, Alas, Alastrim, Alopecia, Anaemia, Angashore, Angina, Asthma, Barrack, Beef, Bellyache, Bitch, Bleat, BSE, Carp, Cavil, Charge, Chorea, Colic, Crab, Cramp, Criticise, Diatribe, Disorder, Dropsy, Epidemic, Ergot, Exanthema, Girn, Gout, Gravamen, Groan, Grouch, Grouse, Growl, Grudge, Grumble, Grutch, Harangue, Hives, Hone, Hypochondria, Ileitis, → **ILLNESS**, Jeremiad, Kvetch, Lupus, Malady, Mange, Mean(e), Mein, Mene, Moan, Morphew, Mumps, Murmur, Nag, Natter, Neuralgia, Ologoan, Pertussis, Plica, Poor-mouth, Protest, Pule, Pyelitis, Querimony, Rail, Remonstrate, Repine, Report, Rickets, Sapego, Sciatica, Scold, Sigh, Silicosis, Squawk, Staggers, Thrush, Tic, Tinea, Upset, Wheenge, Whimper, Whine, Whinge, Yammer, Yawp

Complaisant Agreeable, Flexible, Suave, Supple

Complement Alexin, Amount, Balance, Finish, Gang, Lot, Reciprocate

▷ **Complement** *may indicate* a hidden word

Complete(ly), Completion Absolute, Accomplish, Achieve, All, Arrant, Attain, Clean, Congenital, Consummate, Crown, Do, End, Entire, Finalise, Finish, Flat, Follow through, Fruition, Fulfil, Full, Full-blown, Hollow, Incept, Integral, In toto, One, Ouroboros, Out, Out and out, Perfect, Plenary, Quite, Ready, Root and branch, Rounded, Self-contained, Sew-up, Sheer, Spang, Sum, Teetotal, Thorough, Total, Unanimous, Unbroken, Uncut, Unequivocal, Unmitigated, Utter, Whole (hog), Wrap

Complex(ity) Abstruse, Advanced, Arcane, Castration, Compound, Difficult, Electra, Golgi, Hard, Heath Robinson, Immune, Inferiority, Intricate, Intrince, Involute, Knot, Manifold, MHC, Military-industrial, Mixed, Multinucleate, Nest, Network, Obsession, Oedipus, Paranoid, Persecution, Phaedra, Plexiform, Superiority, Syndrome, Tangle, Web

Complexion Aspect, Blee, Hue, Leer, Temper, Tint, View

Compliance, Compliant, Comply Agree, Amenable, Assent, Conform, Deference, Docile, Follow, Hand-in-glove, Obey, Observe, Obtemper, Sequacious, Surrender, Wilco, Yield

Complicate(d), Complication Bewilder, Complex, Deep, Elaborate, Embroil, Implex, Intricate, Involution, Involve, Inweave, Node, Nodus, Perplex, Ramification, Rigmarole, Sequela, Snarl, Tangle, Tirlie-wirlie

▷ **Complicated** *may indicate* an anagram

Compliment(s) Baisemain, Bouquet, Congratulate, Devoirs, Douceur, Encomium, Flatter, Flummery, Greetings, Praise, Soap, Trade-last, Tribute

Component(s) Base, Coherer, Constituent, Contact, CRT, Daisy-wheel, Element, Factor, Formant, Guidance, Impedor, Inductor, Ingredient, Longeron, → **PART**, Pre-amp, Profile, Reactance, Resistor, Subunit, Tensor

Compose(d), Composure Aplomb, Arrange, Calm, Choreograph, Consist, Cool, → **CREATE**, Equanimity, Even, Face, Improvise, Indite, Lull, Notate, Orchestrate, Placid, Poise, Produce, Reconcile, Sangfroid, Sedate, Serenity, Settle, Soothe, Tranquil, Unruffled, Write

Composer Contrapunt(al)ist, Hymnist, Inditer, Inventor, Maker, Melodist, Musician, → **POET**, Serialist, Six, Songsmith, Songwriter, Symphonist, Triadist, Tunesmith, Writer

---

COMPOSERS

3 letters:
Bax

4 letters:
Adam
Arne
Bach
Berg
Blow
Brel
Bull
Byrd
Cage
Dima
Graf
Ives
Kern
Lalo
Monk
Nono
Orff
Peri
Raff
Wolf

5 letters:
Auber
Auric
Balfe
Berio
Bizet
Bliss
Bloch
Boito
Boyce
Brian
Bruch
Crumb
D'Indy
Dukas
Elgar
Falla
Fauré
Field
Finzi
Glass
Gluck
Grieg
Harty
Haydn
Henze
Holst
Ibert
Lasso
Lehar
Liszt
Loewe
Lully
Parry
Prout
Ravel
Reger
Rossi
Satie
Sousa
Spohr
Suppe
Tosti
Verdi
Watts
Weber
Weill
Zappa

6 letters:
Alfven
Arnold
Azione
Barber
Bartók
Bennet
Berlin
Boulez
Brahms
Bridge
Burney
Busoni
Chopin
Coates
Delius
Duparc
Dvorák
Flotow
Franck
German
Glière
Glinka
Gounod
Handel
Hummel
Joplin
Kodaly
Lassus
Ligeti
Mahler
Mingus
Morley
Mozart
Ogolon
Pierne
Rameau
Rubbra
Schutz
Tallis
Varese
Wagner

Walton
Webern

7 letters:
Albeniz
Alberti
Allegri
Amadeus
Bantock
Bellini
Berlioz
Berners
Borodin
Britten
Brubeck
Copland
Corelli
Debussy
De Falla
Delibes
Dohnany
Dowland
Gibbons
Ireland
Janácek
Lambert
Mancini
Martinu
Menotti
Milhaud
Nielsen
Novello
Ormandy
Poulenc
Puccini
Purcell
Purnell
Quilter

Rodgers
Rodrigo
Romberg
Rossini
Roussel
Salieri
Smetana
Stainer
Strauss
Tartini
Tippett
Vivaldi
Warlock
Xenakis
Youmans

8 letters:
Alaleona
Albinoni
Boughton
Bruckner
Chabrier
Chausson
Couperin
Gershwin
Gesualdo
Glazunov
Grainger
Granados
Honegger
Kreutzer
Marcello
Mascagni
Massenet
Messager
Messiaen
Paganini
Respighi

Schubert
Schumann
Scriabin
Sessions
Sibelius
Sondheim
Sullivan
Taverner
Telemann
Vangelis

9 letters:
Bacharach
Balakirev
Beethoven
Bernstein
Boulanger
Broughton
Buxtehude
Chaminade
Cherubini
Donizetti
Dunstable
Hindemith
Meyerbeer
Offenbach
Pachelbel
Pergolesi
Prokofiev
Scarlatti
Schnittke
Zemlinsky

10 letters:
Birtwistle
Boccherini
Carmichael
Cole Porter

Monteverdi
Mussorgsky
Palestrina
Ponchielli
Rawsthorne
Saint-Saëns
Schoenberg
Stravinsky
Villa-Lobos
Williamson

11 letters:
Charpentier
Frescobaldi
Humperdinck
Leoncavallo
Mendelssohn
Stockhausen
Tchaikovsky
Wolf Ferrari

12 letters:
Khachaturian
Rachmaninoff
Shostakovich

13 letters:
Havergal Brian
Maxwell Davies

14 letters:
Rimsky-Korsakov

15 letters:
Vaughan Williams

▷ **Composing** *may indicate* an anagram

Composite Aster, Costmary, Foalfoot, Gerbera, Groundsel, Hawkweed, Hybrid, Integral, Motley, Opinicus, Rag(weed), Sphinx, Synthesized, Thistle

Composition, Compositor Albumblatt, Aleatory, Azione, Bagatelle, Beaumontage, Beaumontague, Canon, Capriccio, Caprice, Cob, Concerto, Concertstuck, Creation, Dite, Essay, Etude, Exaration, Fantasia, Inditement, Ingredient, Line, Loam, Met, Montage, Morceau, Nonet(te), Nonetto, Opus, Oratorio, Part-writing, Pastiche, Piece, Pieta, Poem, Polyphony, Polyrhythm, Printer, Quartette, Raga, Rhapsody, Round, Setting, Ship, Sing, Smoot, Sonata, Sonatina, Structure, Suite, Symphony, Synthesis, Terracotta, Texture, Toccata, Treatise, Trio, Typesetter, Verismo, Voluntary, Work

Compost Dressing, Fertilizer, Humus, Vraic, Zoo doo

Compound, Compound stop Addition, Admixture, Amalgam, Anti-inflammatory, Anti-knock, Bahuvrihi, Blend, → CAMP, Composite, Constitute, Coordination, Cpd, Cutting, Derivative, Ethiops, Mix, Mixture, Multiply, Racemate, Rooting, Tatpurusha, Type

COMPOUNDS

3 letters:
Azo

4 letters:
Alum
Clay
EDTA
Enol
Haem
Heme
TEPP
Urea

5 letters:
Algin
Allyl
Aloin
Amide
Amino
Azide
Azine
Azole
Diazo
Diene
Dimer
Diode
Erbia
Ester
Furan
Halon
Imide
Imine
Lipid
Nitro
Olein
Oxide
Oxime
Potin
Pyran
Salol
Sarin
Soman
Tabun
Thiol

Trona
Vinyl

6 letters:
Acetal
Alkane
Alkene
Ammine
Arsine
Baryta
Borane
Calque
Cetane
Chrome
Cresol
Epimer
Fluate
Glycol
Halide
Haloid
Hexene
Isatin
Isomer
Ketone
Kinone
Lithia
Niello
Octane
Phenol
Pinene
Potash
Purine
Pyrone
Retene
Silane
Speiss
Tannin
Tartar
Tetryl
Thymol
Triene
Trimer
Uranyl

7 letters:
Acetone
Acridin
Aglycon
Ammonia
Argyrol®
Aspirin
Barilla
Benzene
Betaine
Borazon
Bromide
Caliche
Calomel
Camphor
Carbide
Chelate
Choline
Cinerin
Creatin
Cumarin
Cyanide
Diamine
Diazine
Diazole
Dioxide
Dvandva
Epoxide
Erinite
Ethanol
Eugenol
Fenuron
Ferrite
Flavone
Hormone
Hydrate
Hydride
Indican
Indoxyl
Lactate
Lactone
Menthol
Metamer
Monomer

Niobite
Nitride
Nitrile
Nitrite
Oxazine
Oxonium
Pentane
Peptide
Peptone
Polyene
Polymer
Prodrug
Protein
Quassia
Quinoid
Quinone
Realgar
Skatole
Steroid
Sulfide
Syncarp
Taurine
Terpene
Toluene
Tritide
Uridine
Wolfram
Zymogen

8 letters:
Acridine
Aglycone
Aldehyde
Alizarin
Arginine
Asbestos
Astatide
Butyrate
Caffeine
Carbaryl
Catenane
Cephalin
Ceramide
Chloride

Chromene
Coenzyme
Coumarin
Creatine
Cyanogen
Datolite
Dieldrin
Dopamine
Ethoxide
Farnesol
Fluoride
Furfuran
Glycogen
Hydroxyl
Indoform
Isologue
Ketoxime
Lecithin
Luteolin
Massicot
Melamine
Monoxide
Oligomer
Pentosan
Peroxide
Phthalin
Piperine
Ptomaine
Purpurin
Pyrazole
Rock-alum
Rotenone
Selenate
Silicide
Siloxane
Sodamide
Stilbene
Sulphide
Sulphone
Tautomer
Tetroxid
Thiazide
Thiazine
Thiazole
Thiophen
Thiotepa
Thiourea
Titanate
Tolidine
Triazine
Triazole

Trilling
Trioxide
Tyramine
Urethane
Xanthate
Xanthine
Zirconia

9 letters:
Aflatoxin
Alicyclic
Aliphatic
Anhydride
Biguanide
Carbazole
Carnitine
Celloidin
Cellulose
Cementite
Cetrimide
Chromogen
Copolymer
Cortisone
Deuteride
Dibromide
Dipeptide
Disulfram
Endorshin
Ferrocene
Flavanone
Fool's gold
Fulleride
Glycoside
Greek fire
Guanosine
Haematein
Histamine
Hydantoin
Hydrazide
Hydroxide
Imidazole
Impsonite
Ionophore
Jasmonate
Limestone
Menadione
Mepacrine
Merbromin
Methoxide
Monoamine
Organotin

Pentoxide
Phenazine
Phenoxide
Pheromone
Phosphide
Piperonal
Polyamine
Porphyrin
Qinghaosu
Quercetus
Quinoline
Saltpetre
Sapogenin
Serotonin
Telluride
Tetroxide
Thiophene
Veratrine

10 letters:
Adrenaline
Amphoteric
Argyrodite
Azobenzene
Bradykinin
Cellosolve®
Cytochroma
Dichloride
Dimethoate
Disulphide
Enkephalin
Ethambutol
Indophenon
Isocyanate
Lumisterol
Mercaptide
Nitrazepam
Nucleoside
Nucleotide
Phenformin
Phenocaine
Picrotoxin
Piperazine
Piperidine
Propionate
Putrescine
Pyrethroid
Pyrimidine
Sildenafil
Sulphonium
Thimerosal

Tocopherol

11 letters:
Acetanilide
Amphetamine
Coprosterol
Dimercaprol
Electrolyte
Fluorescein
Galantamina
Ghitathione
Haliocarbon
Hydrocarbon
Neostigmine
Nitrosamine
Resveratrol
Sesquioxide
Sphingosine
Tributyltin

12 letters:
Carbohydrate
Formaldehyde
Haematoxylin
Hydroquinone
Permanganate
Phenanthrine
Polyurethane
Sulphonamide
Testosterone
Thiosinamine
Triglyceride
Trimethadine

13 letters:
Catecholamine
Cycloheximide
Isoproterenol
Mercurochrome
Metronidazole
Nitroglycerin
Nortriptyline
Phenothiazine
Physostigmine
Sulphonylurea
Trinucleotide

14 letters:
Cyanocobalamin
Oxyhaemoglobin
Phenolphthalin

		15 letters:	*17 letters:*
Polycarboxylic	Sulphonmethane	Perfluorocarbon	Pentachlorophenol
Polyunsaturate	Trohalomethane	Succinylcholine	

▷ **Compound(ed)** *may indicate* an anagram

Comprehend, Comprehensive All-in, Catch-all, Catholic, Compass, Compendious, Contain, Exhaustive, Fathom, Follow, Full-scale, General, Global, Grasp, Include, Indepth, Ken, Large, Omnibus, Panoramic, Perceive, School, Sweeping, Thoroughgoing, Tumble, → UNDERSTAND, Wide

Compress(ed), Compression, Compressor Astrict, Astringe, Axial-flow, Bale, Coarctate, Contract, Pack, Pump, Solidify, Squeeze, Stupe, Thlipsis, Turbocharger

Comprise Contain, Embody, Embrace, Include

Compromise, Compromising Avoision, Brule, Commit, Concession, Endanger, Give and take, Happy medium, Honeytrap, Involve, Middleground, Modus vivendi, Settlement, Time-server, Trade off, Via media

▶ **Compulsion** *see* COMPEL

Compunction Hesitation, Regret, Remorse, Scruple, Sorrow

Computer(s) Analog(ue), Apple (Mac)®, Desknote, Desktop, Digital, Eniac, Front-end, Host, Laptop, Mainframe, Micro, Notebook, Number-cruncher, Palmtop, PC, Personal, Proxy server, TALISMAN, Turing machine

Computer hardware, Computer memory Busbar, Chip, Dataglove®, DRAM, EAROM, EPROM, Floptical, IDE, Modem, Neurochip, Pentium®, Plug'n'play, Processor, PROM, RAM, ROM, Router, Tower, Track(er)ball

Computer language ADA, ALGOL, ASCII, AWK, Basic, C, COBOL, COL, CORAL, Fortran, ICL, Java®, LISP, LOGO, OCCAM, PASCAL, Perl, PROLOG, Scratchpad, Small-talk, SNOBOL, SQL, Weblish

Computer network, Computer systems Arpa, ARPANET, BIOS, Cambridge ring, ERNIE, Ethernet, Evernet, Executive, Extranet, Fileserver, Freenet, HOLMES, Hypermedia, Internet, Intranet, JANET, LAN, Linux, MARC, MIDI, Neural, Peer-to-peer, Stand-alone, Tally, TAURUS, Telnet, Token ring, Unix, Usenet, WAN, Web, Wide-area, WIMP

Computer programs, Computer software Abandonware, Acrobat, ActiveX, Agent, Antivirus, Applet, Application, Assembler, Autotune, Bloatware, Bootstrap, Bot, CADMAT, Cancelbot, Careware, Chatbot, Checksum, Client, Columbus, Crippleware, CU See Me, Debugger, Diagnostic, Dictionary, Emacs, Est, E-wallet, Extreme, Facemail, Firewall, Firmware, Flash, Freeware, Groupware, HAL, Hypermedia, iTunes®, Linker, Loader, Macro, Malware, Middleware, Mmorpg, Object, OCR, Parser, Payware, Plug-in, Relocator, RISC, Servlet, Shareware, Shovelware, Spellchecker, Spyware, Stiffware, Systems, Translator, Trialware, Utility, Vaporware, Warez, Web browser, Webcast, Web crawler, Windows®, Word processor, Worm

Computer terms Address bus, Algorism, Authoring, Autosave, Backslash, Bitmap, Bookmark, Boot, Bot army, Breakpoint, Calculate, Calculus, Chatroom, Clickstream, Clipboard, Coder, Counter, Cybercafe, Cyber(netics), Domain name, Earcon, Estimate, FAT, Figure, GIGO, Gopher, High-end, Hybrid, Hypertext, Inbox, Inputter, Integrator, Interface, IT, Kludge, Linear, Logic, Mail merge, Measure, Morphing, Mouseover, Mung, Network, Neural, Numlock, Nybble, Object, On-line, Outbox, Package, Packet sniffer, Pageview, Patch, Pel, Phishing, Pixel, Platform, Public-key, Pushdown, README file, Read-out, Realtime, Reboot, Reckoner, Rogue dialler, Rootserver, Screensaver, Search engine, Server, Shell, Smart, Smurfing, Soft return, Source, Spim, Spreadsheet, Sprite, String, Subroutine,

Superserver, Systems, Tape streamer, Thick client, Thin client, Time slice, Toggle, Unicode, Username, Vaccine, Voice response, Voxel, Webbie, WebBoard, Webfarm, Wiki, WORM, Wysiwyg, Yottabyte, Zettabyte

Computer user(s) Alpha geek, Anorak, Brain, Browser, Cast(er), Chiphead, Cyberpunk, Cybersurfer, Digerati, Hacker, Liveware, Luser, Mouse potato, Nerd, Nethead, Netizen, Nettie, Otaku, Pumpking, Troll, White hat

Comrade Achates, Ally, Buddy, Bully-rook, Butty, China, Fellow, Friend, Kamerad, Mate, Oliver, Pal, Pard, Roland, Tovarich, Tovaris(c)h

Con(man) Against, Anti, Bunco, Diddle, Dupe, Fleece, Hornswoggle, Jacob, Lag, Learn, Peruse, Read, Scam, Scan, Steer, Sucker, Swindle, Tweedler

Concave Dished, Invexed

Conceal(ed), Concealment Blanket, Blind, Closet, Clothe, Cover, Curtain, Disguise, Dissemble, Doggo, Drown, Feal, Heal, Heel, Hele, → **HIDE**, Latent, Misprision, Occult, Palm, Perdu(e), Recondite, Screen, Scriene, Secrete, Shroud, Sleeve, Smother, Snow job, Stash, Subreption, Ulterior, Whitewash, Wrap

Concede, Concession Acknowledge, Admit, Allow, Budge, Carta, Charter, Compromise, Confess, Favour, Forfeit, Franchise, Grant, Munich, Ou, Ow, Owe, Own, Privilege, Ship, Sop, Synchoresis

Conceit(ed) Bumptious, Caprice, Carriwitchet, Cat-witted, Concetto, Crank, Crotchet, Device, Dicty, Egoist, Egomania, Fancy, Fastuous, Figjam, Flory, Fop, Fume, Hauteur, Idea, Mugwump, Notion, Podsnappery, Prig, Princock, Princox, Puppyism, Quiblin, Self-assumption, Side, Snotty, Stuck-up, Swellhead, Toffee-nose, Vain(glory), Wind

Conceive, Conceivable Beget, Create, Credible, Imagine, Possible, Surmise

Concentrate(d), Concentration Aim, Application, Attend, Bunch, Cathexis, Centre, Collect, Condense, Dephlegmate, Distil, Elliptical, Essence, Extract, Focalise, Focus, Intense, Kurtosis, Listen, Major, Mantra, Mass, Molality, Molarity, Navel-gazing, Potted, Reduce, Rivet, Samadhi, Titrate, Titre, Undivided

Concept(ion) Alethic, Brain, Hent, Ideal, Ideation, Image, Immaculate, Myth, Notion, Sortal, Stereotype

Concern(ed), Concerning About, After, Ail, Altruism, Anent, As to, Bother, Business, Care, Cerne, Company, Disturb, Firm, Going, Heed, In re, Intéressé, Interest, Into, Lookout, → **MATTER**, Mell, Misease, Over, Part, Pidgin, Pigeon, Re, Reck, Regard, Reke, Respect, Retch, Solicitude, Touch, Trouble, Versant, Worry

▷ **Concerned** *may indicate* an anagram

Concert (place) Agreement, Benefit, Chamber, Charivari, Cooperation, Device, Dutch, Gig, Hootanannie, Hootananny, Hootenanny, Hootnannie, Hootnanny, Odeon, Odeum, Pop, Prom(enade), Recital, Singsong, Smoker, Subscription, Symphony, Together, Unison, Unity, Wit

Concertina Bandoneon, Pleat, Squeezebox, Squiffer

Concerto Brandenburg, Emperor, Grosso

▸ **Concession** *see* **CONCEDE**

Conch Shell, Strombus

Conchie CO

Conciliate, Conciliator Allay, Calm, Disarm, Dove, Ease, Mollify, Placate, Reconcile

Concise Compact, Curt, Encapsulated, Laconic, Short, Succinct, Terse, Tight

Conclave Assembly, Caucus, Confab, Meeting

Conclude(d), Conclusion, Conclusive Achieve, A fortiori, Afterword, Amen, Binding, Button-up, Cease, Clinch, Close, Complete, Dead, Decide, Deduce, → **END**, Envoi, Explicit, Finding, Fine, Finis, → **FINISH**, Foregone, Gather, Illation, Infer, Lastly, Limit, Non sequitur, Omega, Over, Peroration, Point, Postlude, Punchline,

Reason, Resolve, Settle, Showdown, Summary, Terminate, Upshot, Uptie
Conclusive Cogent, Convincing, Estoppel, Final
Concoct(ion) Brew, Compound, Creation, Plan, Trump (up)
Concord Concent, Consonance, Harmony, Peace, Plane, Sympathy, Treaty, Unity
Concorde SST
Concourse Assembly, Confluence, Esplanade, Throng
Concrete, Concretion Actual, Aggregate, Beton, Bezoar, Breeze, Cake, Calculus, Caprolite, Clot, Dogger, Gunite, Hard, Lean, Mass, Minkstone, No-fines, Pile-cap, Positive, Prestressed, Reify, Reinforced, Siporex, Solid, Tangible, Tremie
Concubine Apple-squire, Campaspe, Harem, Hetaria, Madam, Mistress, Odalisk, Sultana
Concur Accord, Agree, Coincide, Comply, → CONSENT, Gree
Concurrent(ly) Meantime
Concuss(ion) Clash, Shock, Stun
Condemn(ation) Accuse, Blame, Blast, Cast, Censor, Censure, Convict, Damn, Decry, Denounce, Deprecate, Doom, Judge, Kest, Obelise, Proscribe, Revile, Sentence, Theta, Upbraid
Condense(d), Condenser Abbe, Abbreviate, Abridge, Brief, Capacitator, Compress, Contract, Distil, Encapsulate, Epitomise, Jet, Liebig, Précis, Rectifier, Reduce, Shorten, Shrink, Summarise, Surface, Vernier, Vinificator
Condescend Deign, Patronise, Stoop, Vouchsafe
Condiment Caraway, Catsup, Cayenne, Chutney, Cum(m)in, Flavour, Horse radish, Kava, Ketchup, Mustard, Pepper, Relish, Salt, Sambal, Sambol, Sauce, Spice, Tracklement, Turmeric, Vinegar, Zedoary
Condition(al), Conditioning Autism, Circ(s), Circumstance, Classical, Congenital, Connote, Contingent, Dropsy, Experimental, Fettle, Going, Hammertoe, Hood, If, → IN GOOD CONDITION, Kelter, Kernicterus, Kilter, Latah, Necessary, Nick, Order, Pass, Pavlovian, Plight, Pliskie, Ply, Point, Position, Predicament, Prepare, Prerequisite, Presupposition, Protasis, Proviso, Provisory, Repair, Reservation, Reserve, Rider, Ropes, Sine qua non, Sis, Spina bifida, Standing, State, Sted, Stipulation, String, Sufficient, Term, Tid, Tox(a)emia, Trim, Trisomy, Unless, Vir(a)emia, White finger
Condom(s) Blob, Cap, Franger, French letter, Gumboot, Johnny, Letter, Prophylactic, Rubber, Rubber goods, Safe, Scumbag, Sheath
Condone Absolve, Excuse, Forgive, Overlook
Conduct(or), Conductress Accompany, Administer, Anode, Arm, Arrester, Barbirolli, Bearing, Beecham, Behaviour, Bulow, Bus-bar, Cad, Chobdar, Clippie, Coil, Comport, Demean(our), Deportment, Direct, Disorderly, Drive, Editor, Electrode, Escort, Feedthrough, Fetch, Goings-on, Haitink, Hallé, Ignitron, Karajan, Kempe, Klemperer, Lark, Lead, Liber, Lightning, Maestro, Mantovani, Mho, Microchip, Nerve, N-type, Officiate, Ormandy, Outer, Parts, Photodiode, → PILOT, Previn, Probe, Prosecute, Protocol, Psychagogue, Psychopomp, P-type, Rattle, Safe, Sargent, Scudaller, Scudler, Shunt, Skudler, Solicit, Solti, Stokowski, Tao, Thermal, Thermistor, Toscanini, Transact, → USHER, Varactor, Varistor, Wave guide, Wire, Wood, Zener diode
▷ **Conducting** *may indicate* an '-ic' ending
Conduit Aqueduct, Canal, Carrier, Duct, Main, Penstock, Pipe, Tube, Utilidor
Cone(s), Conical, Cone-shaped Alluvial, Cappie, Circular, Conoidal, Egmont, Ellipse, Female, Fir, Fusion, Moxa, Nose, Pastille, Peeoy, Pineal, Pingo, Pioy(e), Pottle, Puy, Pyramid, Retinal, Seger, Spire, Storm, Strobilus, Taper, Tee, Traffic, Volcanic, Wind, Windsock

Coney Daman, Doe, Hyrax

Confection(er) Candy, Candyfloss, Caramel, Chocolate, Concoction, Conserve, Countline, Ice, Kiss, Marzipan, Noisette, Nougat, Quiddery, Rock, Sweet, Sweetmeat, Tablet

Confederal, Confederacy, Confederate, Confederation Accessory, Alliance, Ally, Association, Body, Bund, Bunkosteerer, Cover, F(o)edarie, Gueux, Illinois, League, Partner, Senegambia, Union

Confer(ence) Bestow, Bretton Woods, Cf, Collogue, Colloqium, Colloquy, Congress, Council, Diet, Do, Dub, Fest, Forum, Grant, Huddle, Hui, Imparlance, Imperial, Indaba, Intercommune, Lambeth, Meeting, Munich, Negotiate, News, Palaver, Parley, Pawaw, Pear, Potsdam, Pourparler, Powwow, Press, Pugwash, Quadrant, Seminar, Settle, Summit, Symposium, Synod, → **TALK**, Teach-in, Video, Vouchsafe, Yalta

Confess(ion), Confessor Acknowledge, Admit, Agnise, Avowal, Concede, Declare, Disclose, Edward, Own, Peccavi, Recant, Shrift, Shriver, Sing, Tetrapolitan, Whittle

Confide(nce), Confident(ial), Confidant Aplomb, Aside, Assertive, Assured, Bedpost, Belief, Bottle, Can do, Certitude, Cocksure, Cocky, Cred, Crouse, Entre nous, Entrust, Extravert, Extrovert, Faith, Feisty, Gatepost, Hardy, Hope, Hush-hush, Intimate, Morale, Nerve, Pack, Private, Privy, Sanguine, Secret, Secure, Self-assured, Self-possessed, Sub rosa, Sure, Tell, Trust, Unbosom, Under the rose, Vaulting

Confine(d), Confines, Confinement Ambit, Bail, Bale, Cage, CB, Chain, Constrain, Contain, Coop, Cramp, Crib, Detain, Emmew, Encase, Enclose, Endemic, Enmew, Ensheath, Gaol, Gate, Gender-moon, House arrest, Immanacle, Immew, Immure, Impound, → **IMPRISON**, Incage, Incarcerate, Incommunicado, Inertial, Inhoop, Intern, Local, Mail, March, Mew, Mure, Narrow, Pen, Pent, Pinion, Poky, Restrict, Rule 43, Rules, Section, Solitary, Tether, Thirl, Trammel

Confirm(ed), Confirmation Addict, Ascertain, Assure, Attest, Bear, Certify, Chris(o)m, Christen, Chronic, Clinch, Corroborate, Dyed-in-the-wool, Endorse, Homologate, Obsign, OK, Ratify, Sacrament, Sanction, Seal, Strengthen, Ten-four, Tie, Validate, Vouch

Confiscate, Confiscation Attainder, Deprive, Dispossess, Distrain, Escheat, Garnishee, Impound, Infangenethef, Raupatu, Seize, Sequestrate

Conflagration Blaze, Holocaust, Inferno, Wildfire

Conflict(ing) Agon, Armageddon, At odds, Battle, Boilover, Camp, Casus belli, Clash, Close, Contend, Contravene, Controversy, Disharmony, Diverge, Encounter, Feud, Fray, Inconsistent, Jar, Lists, Mêlée, Muss, Off-key, Oppose, Psychomachia, Rift, Scrape, Strife, → **STRUGGLE**, Tergiversate, War

Conform(ist), Conformity Accord, Adjust, Comply, Conservative, Consistence, Correspond, Normalise, Obey, Observe, Propriety, Standardize, Stereotype(d), Suit, Trimmer, Yield

Confound(ed) Abash, Amaze, Astound, Awhape, Baffle, Bewilder, Blamed, Blasted, Blest, Blinking, Bumbaze, Contradict, Darn, Dismay, Drat, Dumbfound, Elude, Floor, Jigger, Mate, Murrain, Nonplus, Perishing, Perplex, Rabbit, Spif(f)licate, Stump, Throw

▷ **Confound** *may indicate* an anagram

Confrère Ally

Confront(ation) Appose, Beard, Breast, Eyeball, Face, Face down, Head-to-head, Incident, Loggerheads, Mau-Mau, Meet, Militance, Nose, Oppose, Outface, Showdown, Tackle, Toe-to-toe

Confuse(d), Confusedly, Confusion Addle, Anarchy, Astonishment, At sea,

Babel, Baffle, Bazodee, Bedevil, Befog, Befuddle, Bemuse, Bewilder, Blur,
Bobby-die, Burble, Bustle, Chaos, Cloud, Clutter, Complicate, Debacle, Didder,
Discombobulate, Disconcert, Disorient, Distract, Dither, Dizzy, Dudder, Dust,
Dwaal, Egarement, Embrangle, Embroglio, Embroil, Farrago, Flap, Flat spin,
Flummox, Flurry, Fluster, Fog, Fox, Fuddle, Gaggle, Galley-west, Hash, Havoc,
Hazy, Helter-skelter, Hubble-bubble, Huddle, Hugger-mugger, Hurly-burly,
Hurry-scurry, Hurry-skurry, Imbrangle, Imbroglio, → IN CONFUSION, Indistinct,
Litter, Lost, Lurry, Maelstrom, Maffled, Mayhem, Maze, Melange, Melee, Mess,
Mingle, Mish-mash, Mither, Mixter-maxter, Mixtie-maxtie, Mix-up, Mizzle,
Mizzy maze, Moider, Moither, Moonstruck, Morass, → MUDDLE, Mudge, Muss(e),
Muzzy, Obfuscate, Overset, Pellmell, Perplex, Pi(e), Pose, Ravel, Razzle-dazzle,
Razzmatazz, Rout, Rummage, S(c)hemozzle, Scramble, Skimble-skamble, Snafu,
Spin, Stump, Stupefy, Swivet, Synchysis, Tangle, Throw, Tizzy, Topsy-turvy,
Turbulence, Tzimmes, Welter, Whemmle, Whomble, Whummle, Woolly, Woozy
▷ **Confuse(d)** *may indicate* an anagram
Confute Confound, Contradict, Deny, Disprove, Infringe, Redargue, Refel
Congeal Coagulate, Freeze, Gel, Gunge, Set, Solidify
Congenial Agreeable, Amiable, Compatible, Connate, Couthie, Couthy, Happy,
Kindred, Simpatico, Sympathique
Congenital Connate, Inborn, Innate, Inveterate
Congest(ed), Congestion Coryza, Cram, Crowd, Engorge, Impact, Jam, Logjam,
Turgid
Conglomerate, Conglomeration Aggregate, Banket, Empire, Gather, Heap, Mass
Congo(u) Shaba, Tea
Congratulate, Congratulation Applaud, Felicitate, Laud, Mazeltov, Preen, Salute
Congregate, Congregation(alist) Assembly, Barnabite, Body, Brownist, Class,
Community, Conclave, Ecclesia, Flock, Fold, Gathering, Host, Laity, Oratory,
Propaganda, Synagogue
Congress(man) ANC, Assembly, Conclave, Continental, Council, Eisteddfod,
Intercourse, Legislature, Pan-Africanist, Rally, Senator, Solon, Synod, Vienna
Conifer(ous) Araucaria, Cedar, Cypress, Cyrus, Evergreen, Larch, Macrocarpo,
Picea, Pine, Spruce, Taiga, Taxus, Thuja, Yew
Conject(ure) Fancy, Goldbach's, Guess, Guesswork, Speculate, Surmise, Theory,
View
Conjoin Alligate, Ally, Connect, Knit
Conjugate, Conjugation Couple, Hermitian, Join, Nuptial, Synopsis, Typto,
Zygosis
Conjunction Alligation, Ampersand, And, Combination, Consort, Coordinating,
Nor, Polysyndeton, Subordinating, Superior, Synod, Syzygy, Together, Union,
Unition, Unless
Conjure(r), Conjuror Angekkok, Charm, Contrive, Heypass, Heypresto,
Hocus-pocus, Illusionist, Imagine, Invoke, Mage, Magic, Mystery-man, Palmer,
Prestidigitator, Prestigiator, Thaumaturgus
Conk Nose
Connect(ed), Connection, Connector About, Accolade, Adaptor, Affinity, Agnate,
Anastomosis, And, Associate, Attach, Band, Bind, Bridge, Bridle, Cable, Clientele,
Coherent, Colligate, Conjugate, Couple, Cross-link, Delta, Dovetail, Downlink,
Drawbar, Fishplate, Fistula, Hook-up, → IN CONNECTION WITH, Interlink,
Interlock, Join, Jumper, Kinship, Liaison, Lifeline, Link, Linkup, Marry, Merge,
Mesh, Nexus, On, Online, Patch, Pons, Raphe, Rapport, Relate, Relative, Respect,
Sentence, Shuttle, Splice, S-R, Synapse, Syntenosis, Syssarcosis, Tendon, Through,

Tie, Tie-in, Union, Y, Yoke, Zygon
Connecticut Ct
Connive, Connivance Abet, Cahoots, Collude, Condone, Conspire, Plot
Connoisseur Aesthete, Cognoscente, Epicure, Expert, Fancier, Gourmet, Judge, Maven, Mavin, Oenophil
Connotate, Connotation Imply, Infer, Intent, Meaning
Conquer(or), Conquering, Conquest Alexander, Beat, Conquistador, Cortes, Crush, Debel, Genghis Khan, Hereward, → **MASTER**, Moor, Norman, Ostrogoth, Overcome, Overpower, Overrun, Pizarro, Saladin, Subjugate, Tame, Tamerlane, Vanquish, Victor, Vincent
Conquistador Cortes, Cortez
Conscience, Conscientious Casuistic, Duteous, Heart, Inwit, Morals, Painstaking, Pang, Remorse, Scruple(s), Sense, Superego, Syneidesis, Synteresis, Thorough, Twinge
Conscious(ness) Awake, Aware, Chit, Limen, Mindful, On to, Persona, Sensible, Sentient, Witting
Conscript(ion) Blood-tax, Choco, Commandeer, Draft(ee), Impress, Inductee, Landsturm, Levy, Nasho, → **RECRUIT**, Register
Consecrate(d), Consecration Bless, Enoch, Hallow, Noint, Oint, Sacring, Sanctify, Venerate
Consecutive Sequential, Successive
Consensus Agreement, Harmony, Unanimity
Consent Accord, Acquiesce, Affo(o)rd, Agree, Approbate, Comply, Concur, Grant, Informed, Permit, Ratify, Volens, Yes-but, Yield
Consequence, Consequent(ial), Consequently Aftermath, Consectaneous, Corollary, Effect, End, Importance, Issue, Karma, Knock-on, Logical, Moment, Outcome, Ramification, Repercussion, → **RESULT**, Sequel, Thence, Thereat, Thus, Upshot
Conservative Blimpish, Blue, C, Cautious, Diehard, Disraeli, Fabian, Hard-hat, Hidebound, Hunker, Neanderthal, Old guard, Old-line, Preppy, Progressive, Rearguard, Redneck, Right(-wing), Safe, Square, Thrifty, Tory, True blue, Unionist, Verkramp, Young Fogey
Conservatory Hothouse, Orangery, Solarium
Conserve, Conservation(ist) Can, Comfiture, Husband(ry), Jam, Jelly, Maintain, Maintenance, Noah, NT, Protect, Save
Consider(able), Considerate, Consideration Animadvert, Attention, Avizandum, By-end, Case, Cerebrate, Chew over, Cogitate, Contemplate, Count, Courtesy, Debate, Deem, Deliberate, Entertain, Envisage, Factor, Fair, Feel, Forethought, Gay, Gey, Heed, Importance, Inasmuch, Judge, Many, Materially, Meditate, Muse, Pay, Perpend, Poise, Ponder, Premeditate, Pretty, Rate, Reck, Reckon, Reflect, Regard, Respect, Scruple, See, Sensitive, Several, Shortlist, Solicitous, Song, Speculate, Steem, Study, Substantial, Think, Tidy, Vast, View, Ween, Weigh
Consign(ment) Allot, Award, Batch, Bequeath, Delegate, Deliver, Drop shipment, Entrust, Lading, Ship, Transfer
Consist(ent), Consistency Agree, Coherent, Comprise, Enduring, Even, Liaison, Rely, Sound, Steady, Texture
Consolation, Console Ancon, Appease, Balm, Comfort, Games, Relief, Solace, Sop
Consolidate Coalesce, Combine, Compact, Gel, Merge, Pun, Unify
Consommé Julienne, Soup
Consonant(s) Affricate, Agma, Agreeing, Cacuminal, Cerebral, Explosive, Fortis, Fricative, Harmonious, Implosive, Labial, Lateral, Lenis, Media, Mouillé, Plosive,

Sonorant, Spirant, Surd, Tenuis, Velar

Consort Ally, Associate, Maik, Mate, Moop, Moup, Partner, Spouse

Consortium Coalition, Combine, Ring

Conspicuous Arresting, Blatant, Clear, Eminent, Glaring, Kenspeck(le), Landmark, Light, Manifest, Patent, Salient, Shining, Showy, Signal, Striking

Conspiracy, Conspirator, Conspire, Conspiring Brutus, Cabal, Casca, Cassius, Catiline, Cato St, Champerty, Cinna, Collaborate, Colleague, Collogue, Collude, Complot, Connive, Covin, Covyne, Guy, Highbinder, In cahoots, Intrigue, Oates, Omerta, → **PLOT**, Ring, Scheme

Constable Beck, Catchpole, Cop, Dogberry, Dull, Elbow, Harman(-beck), Headborough, High, John, Officer, Painter, Petty, Pointsman, → **POLICEMAN**, Posse, Special, Thirdborough, Tipstaff, Verges

Constancy, Constant Abiding, Boltzmann, C, Changeless, Chronic, Coefficient, Cosmological, Devotion, Dielectric, Diffusion, Dilys, Dirac, Eccentricity, Eternal, Faith, Firm, Fixed, Fundamental, G, Gas, Gravitational, H, Honesty, Hubble's, K, Lambert, Leal(ty), Logical, Loyal, Magnetic, Often, Parameter, → **PERPETUAL**, Planck's, Pole star, Resolute, Sad, Solar, Staunch, Steadfast, Steady, Time, True, Unfailing, Uniform, Usual

Constellation Andromeda, Antlia, Apus, Aquarius, Aquila, Ara, Argo, Aries, Auriga, Bootes, Caelum, Camelopardalis, Camelopardus, Canes Venatici, Canis Major, Canis Minor, Carina, Cassiopeia, Centaurus, Cepheus, Cetus, Cham(a)eleon, Circinus, Columba, Coma Berenices, Coma Cluster, Corvus, Crater, Cygnus, Cynosure, Delphinus, Delta, Dolphin, Dorado, Draco, Equuleus, Eridanus, Fornax, Galaxy, Gemini, Great Bear, Gru(i)s, Hercules, Horologium, Hydra, Hydrus, Indus, Lacerta, Leo, Leo Minor, Lepus, Libra, Little Bear, Little Dipper, Lupus, Lynx, Lyra, Mensa, Monoceros, Musca, Norma, Octans, Ophiuchus, Orion, Pavo, Pegasus, Perseus, Phoenix, Pictor, Piscis Austrinus, → **PLANET**, Puppis, Pyxis, Reticulum, Sagitta, Sagittarius, Scorpius, Sculptor, Scutum, Serpens, Sextans, Southern Cross, Spica, → **STAR**, Telescopium, The Rule, Triangulum (Australe), Tucana, Twins, Unicorn, Vela, Virgin, Virgo, Volans, Vulpecula, Wag(g)oner, Whale, Zodiacal

Consternation Alarm, Dismay, Doodah, Fear, Horror

Constipate(d), Constipation Astrict, Bind, Block, Costive, Stegnotic, Stenosis

Constituency, Constituent Borough, Component, Element, Immediate, Part, Principle, Seat, Ultimate, Voter

▷ **Constituents** *may indicate* an anagram

Constitute, Constitution(al) Appoint, Charter, Clarendon, Compose, Comprise, Congenital, Creature, Establishment, Form, Fuero, Health, Physique, Policy, Polity, Seat, State, Synthesis, Upmake, Walk

Constrain(ed), Constraint Bind, Bondage, Boundary, Coerce, Confine, Coop, Curb, Duress(e), Force, Hard, Oblige, Pressure, Repress, Stenosis, Taboo, Trammel

Constrict(ed), Constriction Bottleneck, Choke, Coarctate, Contract, Cramp, Hour-glass, Impede, Limit, Narrow, Phimosis, Squeeze, Stegnosis, Stenosis, Strangle, Strangulate, Thlipsis, Tighten, Venturi

Construct(ion), Constructor, Constructive Build, Compile, Engineer, Erect, Fabricate, Facture, Fashion, Form, Frame, Idolum, Make, Manufacture, Partners, Seabee, Stressed-skin, Tectonic, Weave

Construe Deduce, Explain, Expound, Infer

Consul Ambassador, Attaché, Horse, Lucullus, Praetor

Consult(ant), Consultation Avisement, Confer, Deliberate, Discuss, Emparl, Imparl, Joint, Peritus, See, Sexpert, Shark watcher, Surgery, Vide

Consume(r), Consumption, Consumptive Bolt, Burn, Caterpillar®, Conspicuous,

Decay, Devour, Diner, Eat, Engross, Exhaust, Expend, Feed, Glutton, Hectic, Mainline, Scoff, Spend, Swallow, TB, Use, Waste, Wear

Consummate, Consummation Achieve, Crown, Keystone, Seal

Contact Abut, Adpress, Contingence, Fax, Hook-up, Lens, Liaise, Liaison, Meet, Radio, Reach, Shoe, Taction, → **TOUCH**, Touchy-feely, Wiper

Contagious, Contagion Infection, Noxious, Poison, Taint, Variola, Viral

Contain(er) Amphora, Ampulla, Aquafer, Aquifer, Barrel, Bass, Bidon, Bin, Boat, Bottle, Box, Buddle, Cachepot, Can, Canakin, Canikin, Canister, Cannikin, Cantharus, Capsule, Carafe, Carboy, Carry, Carton, Case, Cask, Cassette, Chase, Chest, Churn, Coffer, Comprise, Coolamon, Crate, Crater, Crucible, Cup, Cupel, Decanter, Dracone, Dredger, Enclose, Encompass, Enseam, Esky®, Feretory, Flagon, Flask, Flat, Gabion, Gourd, Growler, → **HOLD**, House, Igloo, Include, Incubator, Intray, Jar, Jeroboam, Jerrican, Jerrycan, Jug, Keg, Kirbeh, Leaguer, Lekythos, Monkey, Monstrance, Mould, Olpe, Out-tray, Pail, Pinata, Piscina, Pitcher, Pithos, Pod, Pottle, Punnet, Reliquary, Repository, Restrain, Sac(k), Saggar, Scyphus, Shaker, Situla, Skin, Skip, Snaptin, Spittoon, Stamnos, Stillage, Tank, Tantalus, Terrarium, Tinaja, Trough, Tub, Tun, Tupperware®, Urn, Vase, Vessel, Vinaigrette, Wardian case, Wineskin, Woolpack, Workbag

Contaminate(d) Adulterate, Corrupt, Defile, Denature, Flyblown, Impure, Infect, Pollute, Soil, Stain, Tarnish

Contemplate, Contemplation Consider, Ecce, Envisage, Hesychasm, Meditate, Muse, Ponder, Reflect, Retrospection, Rue, Samadhi, Spell, Study, Think, Watch

Contemporary AD, Coetaneous, Current, Equal, Fellow, Modern, Modish, Present, Verism

Contempt(ible), Contemptuous Abject, Ageism, Aha, Arsehole, Bah, BEF, Cheap, Contumely, Crud, Crumb, Crummy, Cullion, Cynical, Derision, Despisal, Dis(s), Disparaging, Disrespect, Dog-bolt, Fig, Hangdog, Ignominious, Insect, Low, Mean, Measly, Misprision, Och, Odious, Paltry, Phooey, Pish, Poof, Poxy, Pshaw, Ratfink, Rats, Razoo, Scabby, Scarab, Schlub, Scofflaw, → **SCORN**, Scumbag, Scurvy, Sexism, Shabby, Shithead, Slimeball, Sneeze, Sniffy, Snooty, Snot, Snotty, Soldier, Sorry, Squirt, Squit, Supercilious, Toad, Toerag, Tossy, Vilipend, Weed, Whipster, Wretched

Contend(er) Argue, Candidate, Claim, Clash, Compete, Cope, Debate, Dispute, Fight, Grapple, Oppose, Rival, Stickle, → **STRIVE**, Struggle, Submit, → **VIE**, Wrestle

Content Apaid, Apay, Appay, Blissful, Happy, Inside, Please, Satisfy, Volume

▷ **Content** *may indicate* a hidden word

Contention, Contentious Argument, Bellicose, Cantankerous, Case, Combat, Competitive, Logomachy, Perverse, Polemical, Rivalry, Strife, Struggle, Sturt

Contest(ant) Agon, Battle, Beauty, Biathlon, Bout, Catchweight, Challenge, Championship, Combat, Competition, Concours, Darraign, Decathlon, Defend, Deraign, Dogfight, Duathlon, Duel(lo), Entrant, Eurovision, Event, Examinee, Finalist, Free-for-all, Fronde, Handicap, Heptathlon, Kemp, Kriegspiel, Lampadephoria, Match, Matchplay, Olympiad, Pancratium, Paralympics, Pentathlon, Pingle, Play-off, Prizer, Race, Rival, Roadeo, Rodeo, Scrap, Set-to, Skirmish, Slam, Slugfest, Strife, Struggle, Tenson, Tetrathlon, Tournament, Triathlon, Tug-of-war, Vie, War, With

Context Intentional, Opaque, Transparent

Continent(al) Abstinent, Asia, Atlantis, Austere, Chaste, Dark, Epeirogeny, Euro, European, Gallic, Gondwanaland, Laurasia, Lemuria, Mainland, Moderate, Pang(a)ea, Shelf, Teetotal, Temperate, Walloon

Contingency, Contingent Accident, Arm, Casual, Chance, Conditional, Dependent,

Event, Fluke, Group, Prospect

Continual(ly), Continuous Adjoining, Away, Chronic, Connected, Eer, Endlong, Eternal, Ever, Frequent, Incessant, Non-stop, On(going), Unbroken, Unceasing

Continue, Continuation, Continuing, Continuity Abye, Duration, Dure, During, Enduring, Enjamb(e)ment, Follow-on, Go on, Hold, Keep, Last, Link, Ongoing, Onward, Persevere, Persist, Proceed, Prolong, Remain, Resume, Sequence, Stand, Subsist, Survive, Sustain, Synaphe(i)a, Tenor

▷ **Continuously** *may indicate* previous words to be linked

Contort(ion) Deform, Gnarl, Jib, Twist, Warp, Wreathe, Wry

Contour Curve, Graph, Isallobar, Isobase, Isocheim, Isochime, Isogeothermal, Line, Profile, Silhouette, Streamline, Tournure

Contraband Hot, Illicit, Prohibited, Smuggled

Contraception, Contraceptive Billings method, Cap, Coil, Condom, Diaphragm, Dutch cap, Etonogestrol, IU(C)D, Lippes loop, Loop, Minipill, Oral, Pessary, Pill, Precautions, Prophylactic, Rubber(s), Sheath, Vimule®

Contract(ion), Contractor Abbreviate, Abridge, Affreightment, Agreement, Appalto, Astringency, Bargain, Biceps, Bottomry, Braxton-Hicks, Bridge, Builder, Catch, Champerty, Charter, Clonus, Condense, Consensual, Constringe, Contrahent, Convulsion, Covenant, Cramp, Crasis, Curtail, Debt, Diastalsis, Dupuytren's, Dwindle, Engage, Entrepreneur, Escrow, Fitzgerald-Lorentz, Flex, Gainsay, Gooseflesh, Guarantee, Hand-promise, Hire, Incur, Indenture, Jerk, Ketubah, Knit, Lease, Levator, Lorentz-Fitzgerald, Make, Miosis, Myosis, Narrow, Obligee, Outsource, Party, Peristalsis, Privilege, Promise, Pucker, Purse, Restriction, Risus (sardonicus), Service, Shrink, Shrivel, Sign, Slam, Social, Spasm, Specialty, Squinch, Steelbow, Stenosis, Stipulation, Straddle, Supplier, Sweetheart, Synaloepha, Syngraph, Systole, Telescope, Tetanise, Tetanus, Tic, Tighten, Time bargain, Tonicity, Tontine, Treaty, Triceps, Trismus cynicus, Wrinkle, Yellow-dog, Z

Contradict(ion), Contradictory Ambivalent, Antilogy, Antinomy, Belie, Bull, Contrary, Counter, Dementi, Deny, Disaffirm, Disprove, Dissent, → **GAINSAY**, Negate, Oxymoron, Paradox, Sot, Stultify, Sublate, Threap, Threep, Traverse

Contraption Contrivance

Contrarily, Contrary Adverse, A rebours, Arsy-versy, But, Captious, Converse, Counter, Counterfleury, Crosscurrent, Cross-grained, Cross-purpose, Froward, Hostile, Inverse, Mary, Opposite, Oppugnant, Ornery, Perverse, Rebuttal, Retrograde, Wayward, Withershins

Contrast Chiaroscuro, Clash, Colour, Compare, Differ, Foil, Relief

Contravene Infringe, Oppose, Thwart, Violate

Contribute, Contribution Abet, Add, Assist, Chip in, Conduce, Donate, Dub, Furnish, Go, Help, Input, Kick in, Mite, Offering, Share, Sub, Subscribe, Whack, Widow's mite

▷ **Contributing to** *may indicate* a hidden word

Contrite, Contrition Penance, Penitent, Remorse, Repentant, Rue, → **SORRY**

Contrivance, Contrive(r) Art, Chicaner, Contraption, Cook, Deckle, Deus ex machina, Device, Devise, Dodge, Engine, Engineer, Finesse, Frame, Gadget, Gimmick, Gin, Hatch, Hokey, Intrigue, Invention, Machinate, Manage, Manoeuvre, Page, Plan, Plot, Procure, Rest, Rowlock, Scheme, Secure, Stage, Trump, Wangle, Weave

Control(ler), Controllable Ada, Appestat, Autopilot, Big Brother, Birth, Boss, Bridle, Cabotage, Chair, Check, Chokehold, Christmas tree, Corner, Corset, Curb, Cybernetics, Descendeur, Dirigible, Dirigism(e), Dominate, Dominion, Dynamic,

Elevon, Etatiste, Fast-forward, Fet(ch), Finger, Flood, Fly-by-wire, Gain, Gar, George, Gerent, Govern, Ground, Gubernation, Harness, Have, Heck, Helm, Influence, Influx, Joystick, Keypad, Knee-swell, Lead, Lever, → **MANAGE**, Martinet, Mastery, Moderate, Mouse, Nipple, Noise, Numerical, Operate, Override, Pilot, Placebo, Police, Population, Possess, Power, Preside, Price, Process, Puppeteer, Quality, Radio, Regulate, Regulo®, Rein, Remote, Rent, Repress, Restrain, Rheostat, Ride, Ripple, Rule, Run, School, Servo, Snail, Solion, Steady, Steer, Stop, Stranglehold, Stringent, Subdue, Subject, Subjugate, Supervise, Suzerain, Svengali, Sway, Takeover, Tame, Thermostat, Throttle, Tiller, Tone, Traction, Valve, Weld, Wield, Zapper

Controversial, Controversy Argument, Contention, Debate, Dispute, Eristic(al), Furore, Hot potato, Polemic(al), Tendentious

Conundrum Acrostic, Egma, Enigma, Puzzle, Riddle, Teaser

Convalesce(nt), Convalescence Anastatic, Mend, Rally, Recover, Recuperate, Rest-cure

▸ **Convene** see **CONVOKE**

Convenience, Convenient Behoof, Commode, Eft, Expedient, Facility, Gain, Gents, Handsome, → **HANDY**, Hend, Lav, Leisure, Near, Opportune, Pat, Privy, Public, Suitable, Toilet, Use, Well

Convent Abbatial, Cloister, Fratry, Friary, House, → **MONASTERY**, Motherhouse, Nunnery, Port-royal, Priory, Retreat

Convention(al) Academic, Accepted, Babbitt, Blackwood, Bourgeois, Caucus, Conclave, Conformity, → **CUSTOMARY**, Diet, Done, Formal, Geneva, Habitude, Iconic, Lame, Lingua franca, Mainstream, Meeting, Middlebrow, Middle-of-the-road, More, National, Nomic, Orthodox, Pompier, Proper, Readymade, Schengen, Staid, Starchy, Stereotyped, Stock, Straight, Synod, Uptight, Usage, Warsaw

Converge(nce) Approach, Focus, Meet, Toe-in

Conversation(alist), Converse, Conversant Abreast, Antithesis, Board, Buck, Cackle, Causerie, Chat, Chitchat, Colloquy, Commune, Confab, Crosstalk, Deipnosophist, Dialogue, Discourse, Eutrapelia, Eutrapely, Hobnob, Interlocution, Jaw-jaw, Natter, Opposite, Palaver, Parley, Persiflage, Rap, Rhubarb, Shop, Shoptalk, Socialise, → **TALK**, Transpose, Trialogue, Wongi, Word

Conversion, Converter, Convert(ible) Adapt, Alter, Assimilate, Azotobacter, Bessemer, Cash, Catalytic, Catechumen, Change, Commute, Cyanise, Diagenesis, Disciple, Encash, Etherify, Evangelize, Exchange, Expropriate, Fixation, Gummosis, Hodja, Kho(d)ja, Landau, L-D, Liquid, Marrano, Metanoia, Neophyte, Noviciate, Novitiate, Persuade, Prill, Proselyte, Put, Ragtop, Realise, Rebirth, Reclamation, Recycle, Revamp, Sheik(h), Souper, Tablet, Taw, Torque, Transduce, Transform, Transmute, Try

▷ **Conversion, Converted** may indicate an anagram

Convex(ity) Arched, Bowed, Camber, Curved, Entasis, Extrados, Gibbous, Lenticle, Nowy

Convey(ance) Assign, BS, Carousel, Carriage, Carry, Charter, Coach, Conduct, Cycle, Deed, Deliver, Eloi(g)n, Enfeoffment, Giggit, Grant, Guide, Lease, Litter, Lorry, Mailcar(t), Pirogue, Pneumatic, Re-lease, Sac, Screw, Soc, Tip, Title deed, Tote, Tram, Transfer, Transit, Transmit, Transport, Vehicle

Convict(ion) Attaint, Belief, Bushranger, Certitude, Cockatoo, Cogence, Crawler, Credo, Creed, Criminal, Demon, Dogma, Faith, Felon, Forçat, Government man, Lag, Magwitch, Old chum, → **PERSUASION**, Plerophory, Ring, Trusty, Vehemence, Yardbird

Convince(d), Convincing Assure, Cogent, Doubtless, Luculent, Persuade, Plausible, Satisfy, Sold, Sure

Convivial(ity) Boon, Bowl, Festive, Gay, Genial, Jovial, Social

Convoke Assemble, Call, Convene, Summon

Convolute(d), Convolution Coiled, Gyrus, Helical, Intricate, Spiral, Tortuous, Twisty, Whorl, Writhen

Convolvulus Bindweed, Dodder

Convoy Caravan, Column, Conduct, Escort, Fur brigade, Pilot, Train, Wagon-train

Convulse, Convulsion(s), Convulsive Agitate, Clonic, Clonus, Commotion, Disturb, DT, Eclampsia, → **FIT**, Galvanic, Paroxysm, Spasm, Throe, Tic

Cook(s), Cooker(y), Cooking Aga®, Babbler, Babbling brook, Bake, Balti, Beeton, Benghazi, Bhindi, Bouche, Braise, Broil, Cacciatore, Calabash, Captain, Charbroil, Chargrill, Chef, Coddle, Concoct, Cordon bleu, Cuisine, Deep-fry, Delia, Devil, Do, Doctor, Dumple, Easy over, Edit, Escoffier, Fake, Falsify, Fiddle, Fireless, Flambé, Forge, Fricassee, Fry, Fudge, Gastronomy, Greasy, Grill, Haute cuisine, Haybox, Hibachi, Lyonnaise, Marengo, Marinière, Meunière, Microwave, Nouvelle cuisine, Poach, Prepare, Pressure, Provencale, Ribroast, Rig, Ring, Roast, Roger, Sauté, Sous-chef, Spit, Steam, Stew, Stir-fry, Stove, Tandoori, Tikka, Tire

▷ **Cook** *may indicate* an anagram

Cool(er), Cooling, Coolness Aloof, Aplomb, Calm, Can, Chill, Collected, Composed, Cryogen, Cryostat, Defervescence, Desert, Dispassionate, Distant, Esky®, Fan, Frappé, Fridge, Frigid, Frosty, Gaol, Goglet, Hip, Ice(box), Jail, Jug, Keel, La Nina, Maraging, Phlegm, Prison, Quad, Quod, Reefer, Refresh, Regenerative, Reserved, Sangfroid, Serene, Skeigh, Splat, Stir, Sweat, Temperate, Thou(sand), Trendy, Unruffled, Wint(e)ry

Coop Cage, Cavie, Confine, Gaol, Hutch, Mew, Pen, Rip

Cooper Gary, Henry, Tubman

Cooperate, Cooperation, Cooperative Collaborate, Combine, Conspire, Contribute, Coop, Give and take, Liaise, Play, Synergy, Teamwork, Together, Worker's

Coordinate(s), Coordinated, Coordination Abscissa, Abscisse, Agile, Arrange, Cartesian, Ensemble, Harmony, Nabla, Orchestrate, Ordonnance, Peer, Polar, Right ascension, Spherical, Synergy, Teamwork, Twistor, Waypoint, X, Y, Z

Coot Stupid, Sultan

Cop(s) Bag, Bull, Catch, Dick, Keystone, Peeler, Peon, → **POLICEMAN**, Silent

Copal Dammar, Resin

Cope Chlamys, Deal, Face, Handle, Make do, → **MANAGE**, Mantle, Meet, Negotiate, Pallium, Poncho

Coping (stone) Balustrade, Capstone, Skew

Copious Abundant, Affluent, Ample, Fecund, Fluent, Fruitful, Fulsome, Plentiful, Profuse

Copper As, Atacamite, Blister, Bluebottle, Bobby, Bornite, Busy, Cash, Cent, Chessylite, → **COIN**, Cu, D, Dam, Double, Erinite, Flatfoot, Lawman, Lota(h), Malachite, Mountain-blue, Ormolu, Peacock, Pence, Penny, Pfennig, Pie, Pig, Plack, Policeman, Red, Rosser, Rozzer, S, Sen(s), Slop, Special, Traybit, Venus, Verdet, Washer, Washtub, Wire bar

Copse Thicket

Copulate Boff, Intercourse, Line, Mate, Roger, Tup

Copy(ing), Copier, Copyist, Copywriter Adman, Aemule, Ape, Apograph, Autotype, Calk, Calque, Camera-ready, Carbon, Clerk, Clone, Counterpart, Crib, Cyclostyle, Diazo, Ditto, Download, Dyeline, Echo, Echopraxia, Ectype, Edition,

Eidograph, Electro, Emulate, Engross, Estreat, Example, Facsimile, Fair, Fax, Flimsy, Forge, Hard, Hectograph, → **IMITATE**, Issue, Jellygraph, Knocking, Manifold, Manuscript, Match, Me-tooer, Microdot, Milline, Mimeograph®, Mimic, Mirror, MS, Offprint, Parrot, Photostat®, Plagiarism, Polygraph, Read-out, Repeat, Replica, Repro, Reproduce, Review, Rip, Roneo®, Scribe, Script, Scrivener, Sedulous, Show, Simulate, Skim, Soft, Spit, Stencil, Stuff, Tall, Telautograph®, Telefax, Tenor, Tenure, Trace, Transcribe, Transume, Vidimus, Xerox®

Copyright C, Landgrab

Coquette Agacerie, Flirt, Rosina, Tease, Vamp

Cor Bath, Crumbs, Ephah, Homer

Coracle Currach, Curragh

Coral (reef) Alcyonaria, Aldabra, Atoll, Brain, Cup, Deadmen's fingers, Gorgonia(n), Laccadives, Madrepore, Millepore, Pink, Precious, Red, Reef, Sea fan, Sea ginger, Sea-pen, Sea whip, Seed, Staghorn, Stony, Zoothome

Cord, Cord-like Aiguillette, Band, Bedford, Bind, Boondoggle, Cat-gut, Chenille, Communication, Creance, Drawstring, Elephant, Flex, Fourragère, Funicle, Gasket, Heddle, Lace, Laniard, Lanyard, Ligature, Line, Moreen, Myelon, Nerve, Net, Ocnus, Picture, Piping, Quipo, Quipu, Rep(s), Restiform, Rip, Rope, Sash, Sennit, Service, Shroudline, Sinnet, Spermatic, Spinal, → **STRING**, Tendon, Tie, Tieback, Torsade, Twine, Twitch, Umbilical, Vocal, Wick

Cordial Anise(ed), Anisette, Benedictine, Cassis, Drink, Elderflower, Gracious, Grenadine, Hearty, Hippocras, Kind, Neighbourly, Oporice, Orangeade, Persico(t), Pleasant, Ratafia, Rosa-solis, Roso(g)lio, Shrub, Tar-water, Warm

Cordon Band, Beltcourse, Picket, Ring, Sanitaire, Surround

Corduroy Rep(p)

Cordyline Ti-tree

Core Barysphere, Calandria, Campana, Centre, Chog, Essence, Filament, Hard, Heart, Hub, Kernel, Nife, Nitty-gritty, Plerome, Quintessence, Slug

Co-religionist Brother

Coriander Cilantro

Corinthian(s) Casuals, Caulis, Epistolaters

Cork(ed), Corker Balsa, Bouché, Bung, Float(er), Humdinger, Mountain, Oner, Phellem, Phellogen, Plug, Seal, Shive, Stopper, Suber(ate)

Corkscrew Bore, Opening, Spiral

Cormorant Duiker, Duyker, Scart(h), Skart(h)

Corn(y) Bajr(a), Banal, Blé, Cereal, Cob, Dolly, Durra, Emmer, Epha, Flint, Gait, Graddan, Grain, Green, Grist, Guinea, Icker, Indian, Kaffir, Kanga pirau, Mabela, Maize, Mealie, Muid, Negro, Nubbin, Pickle, Pinole, Posho, Rabi, Rye, Seed, Shock, Stitch, Straw, Sugar, Sweet, Thrave, Trite, Zea

Corncrake Landrail

Cornel Dogberry, Tree

Corner Amen, Angle, Bend, Canthus, Cantle, Canton, Cranny, Dangerous, Diêdre, Elbow, Entrap, Hog, Hole, Hospital, Long, Lug, Monopoly, NE, Niche, Nook, NW, Penalty, Predicament, Quoin, SE, Short, Speakers', Spot, SW, Tack, Tight, Trap, Tree, Vertex

Cornerstone Coi(g)n, Encoignure, Skew-corbel, Skew-put, Skew-table

Cornet Cone, Cornopean, Field, Horn

Cornice Surbase

Cornish(man) Cousin Jack

Cornstalks Strammel, Straw, Strummel, Stubble

Cornucopia Amalthea, Horn

Cornwall SW
Corollary Conclusion, Dogma, Porism, Rider, Theory, Truism
Corona Aureole, Cigar, Larmier, Nimbus, Wreath
Coronation Enthronement
Coroner Procurator fiscal
Corporal Bardolph, Bodily, Bombardier, Brig(adier), Lance-pesade, Lance-prisade, Lance-prisado, Lance-speisade, Master, Naik, NCO, Nym, Pall, Physical, Trim
Corporation Belly, Body, Closed, Commune, Company, Conglomerate, Guild, Kite, Kyte, Paunch, Public, Public service, Stomach, Swag-belly, Tum, Wame, Wem
Corps Body, C, Crew, Diplomatic, Peace, RAC, REME, Unit
Corpse Blob, Body, Cadaver, Carcass, Carrion, Dust, Goner, Like, Mort, Relic, Remains, Stiff, Zombi(e)
Corpulence, Corpulent Adipose, Fat, Fleshy, Gross, Obese, Poddy, Stout, Thickset, Tubby
Corpuscle Cell, Erythrocyte, Malpighian, Meissner's, Microcyte, Neutrophil, Pacinian, Phagocyte, Porkilocyte
Correct(ive), Correcting, Correctly, Correctness, Correction, Corrector Accurate, Alexander, Align, Amend, Aright, Blue-pencil, Bodkin, Castigate, Chasten, Chastise, Check, Decorous, Diorthortic, Emend, Ethical, Exact, Fair, Fix, Grammatical, Legit, Mend, Politically, Preterition, Probity, Proofread, Proper, Propriety, Punctilious, Punish, Purism, Rebuke, Rectify, Rectitude, Redress, Remedial, Reprove, Revise, Right(en), Scold, Spot-on, Sumpsimus, Tickety-boo, Trew, True, Twink, U
▷ **Corrected** *may indicate* an anagram
Correspond(ence), Correspondent, Corresponding Accord, Agree, Analogy, Assonance, Coincident, Communicate, Congruence, Counterpart, Epistolist, Equate, Equivalence, Eye-rhyme, Fit, Foreign, Hate mail, Homolog(ue), Identical, Lobby, Match, On all fours, One to one, Par, Parallel, Parity, Relate, Snail mail, Symmetry, Tally, Veridical, War, Write
Corridor Air, Aisle, Berlin, Entry, Gallery, Greenway, Lobby, Passage, Polish, Re-entry
Corroborate Confirm, Support, Verify
Corrode(d), Corrosion, Corrosive Acid, Acid rain, Brinelling, Burn, Canker, Decay, Eat, Erode, Etch, Fret, Gnaw, Hydrazine, Mordant, → **ROT**, Rubiginous, Rust, Waste
Corrugate Gimp
Corrupt(er), Corrupting, Corruption Abuse, Adulterate, Bastardise, Bent, Bobol, Bribable, Canker, Cesspit, Debase, Debauch, Debosh, Decadent, Defile, Degenerate, Depravity, Dissolute, Dry rot, Emancipate, Embrace(o)r, Embrasor, Empoison, Etch, Evil, Fester, Gangrene, Graft(er), Immoral, Impaired, Impure, Infect, Inquinate, Jobbery, Leprosy, Malversation, Nefarious, Obelus, Payola, Perverse, Poison, Pollute, Power, Putrid, Rakery, Ret(t), Rigged, Rot, Scrofulous, Seduce, Sepsis, Septic, Sleaze, Sodom, Sophisticate, Spoil, Suborn, Tammany, Twist, Venal, Vice, Vitiate
Corsage Buttonhole, Pompadour, Posy, Spray
Corsair Barbary, Picaroon, Pirate, Privateer, Robber, Rover
Corset, Corslet Belt, Bodice, Busk, Girdle, Lorica, Roll-on, Stays, Thorax, Waspie
Corsican Napoleon
Cortege Parade, Retinue, Train
Cortex Cerebral, Renal
Cortisone Hecogenin
Corundum Emery, Sapphire

Corvo Rolfe

Corybant Roisterer

Cosh Sap

Cosmetic Beautifier, Blusher, Bronzer, Chapstick, Conditioner, Eye-black, Eyeliner, Eye-shadow, Face-pack, Foundation, Fucus, Highlighter, Kohl, Liner, Lip gloss, Lip liner, Lipstick, Lotion, Maquillage, Mascara, Mousse, Mudpack, Paint, Pearl-powder, Powder, Reface, Rouge, Talcum, Toner

▶ **Cosmic** *see* **COSMOS**

Cosmonaut Gagarin, Spaceman, Tereshkova

Cosmopolitan International, Urban

Cosmos, Cosmic Globe, Heaven, Infinite, Mundane, Nature, Universe, World

Cossack Ataman, Hetman, Mazeppa, Russian, Tartar, Zaporogian

Cosset Caress, Coddle, Fondle, Pamper

Cost(s), Costly Bomb, Carriage, Charge, Current, Damage, Direct, Earth, Escuage, Estimate, Exes, → **EXPENSE**, Factor, Fixed, Hire, Historic(al), Indirect, Loss, Marginal, Opportunity, Outlay, Overhead, Precious, Price, Prime, Quotation, Rate, Running, Sacrifice, Sumptuous, Toll, Unit, Upkeep, Usurious, Variable

Costa Rica(n) Tico

Costermonger Barrow-boy, Kerb-merchant, Pearly

Costume(s) Apparel, Attire, Camagnole, Cossie, Dress, Ensemble, Get-up, Gi(e), Guise, Judogi, Livery, Maillot, Motley, Nebris, Polonaise, Rig, Ruana, Surcoat, Tanga, Togs, Uniform, Wardrobe, Wear

Cosy Cosh, Gemutlich, Intime, Snug

Cot Moses basket

Coterie Cell, Cenacle, Circle, Clan, Clique, Club, Ring, Set, Society

Cottage(r) Bach, Batch, Bordar, Bothie, Bothy, Bower, Box, Bungalow, Cabin, Cape Cod, Chalet, Cot, Crib, Dacha, Home-croft, Hut, Lodge, Mailer

Cotton Absorbent, Agree, AL, Alabama, Balbriggan, Batiste, Batting, Bengal, Calico, Candlewick, Ceiba, Chambray, Chino, Chintz, Collodion, Coutil(le), Cretonne, Denim, Dho(o)ti, Dimity, Ducks, Fustian, Galatea, Gossypine, Gossypium, Humhum, Ihram, Jaconet, Lavender, Lawn, Lea, Lille, Lint, Lisle, Longcloth, Manchester, Marcella, Muslin, Nainsook, Nankeen, Nankin, Osnaburg, Pongee, Sea-island, Seersucker, Silesia, Stranded, Surat, T-cloth, Thread, Twig, Upland, Velveteen

Cotton soil Regar, Regur

Cotyledon Seed-leaf

Couch Bed, Casting, Davenport, Daybed, → **DIVAN**, Express, Grass, Lurk, Palanquin, Palkee, Palki, Quick, Recamier, Sedan, Settee, Sofa, Studio, Triclinium, Vis-à-vis, Winnipeg, Word

Coué Auto-suggestion

Cougar Cat, Painter, Puma

Cough(ing) Bark, Chin, Croup, Expectorate, Hack, Harrumph, Hawk, Hem, Hoast, Hooping, Kink, Pertussis, Phthisis, Rale, Tisick, Tussis, Ugh, Whooping

Could Couth

Council (meeting), Councillor, Counsel(lor) Achitophel, Admonish, Admonitor, Advice, Advocate, Ahithophel, Alfred, Amphictryon, Anziani, Aread, A(r)re(e)de, Assembly, Attorney, Aulic, Aunt, Ayuntamiento, Board, Body, Boule, Bundesrat, Burgess, Cabinet, Casemate, Committee, Consistory, Corporation, County, Cr, Decurion, Dergue, Devil, Dietine, Divan, Douma, Duma, Ecumenical, Egeria, Europe, European, Executive, Exhort, General, Great, Greenbag, Hebdomadal, Indaba, Induna, Industrial, Info, Islands, Jirga, Junta, Kabele, Kebele, King's, Kite,

Landst(h)ing, Lateran, Leader, Legislative, Loan, Majlis, Mentor, Nestor, Nicaean, Nicene, Panchayat, Paraclete, Parish, Powwow, Press, Privy, Provincial, Queen's, Rede, Regional, Reichsrat, Robber, Runanga, Samaritan, Sanhedrim, Sanhedrin, Security, Senate, Shoora, Shura, Sobranje, Sobranye, Soviet, States, Syndicate, Synedrion, Synod, Thing, Town, Tradeboard, Trades, Trent, Tridentine, Trullan, Vatican, Volost, Wages, Whitley, Witan, Witenagemot, Works, Zemstvo, Zila, Zila parishad, Zillah

Count(ed), Counter(balance), Counting Abacus, Add, Algoriam, Anti, Balance, Bar, Basie, Blood, Buck, Buffet, Calculate, Cavour, Census, Chip, Compute, Coost, Crystal, Desk, Dracula, Dump, Earl, Enumerate, Fish, Geiger, Geiger-Muller, Graf(in), Grave, Itemise, Jet(t)on, Landgrave, Margrave, Marker, Matter, Merel(l), Meril, Milton work, Nobleman, Number, Numerate, Obviate, Olivia, Oppose, Palatine, Palsgrave, Paris, Pollen, Presume, Proportional, Rebut, → **RECKON**, Refute, Rejoinder, Rely, Retaliate, Retort, Rhinegrave, Scaler, Scintillation, Score, Sperm, Squail, Statistician, Stop, Sum, Table, Tally, Tell, Tiddleywink, Ugolino, Weigh, Zeppelin

Countenance Approve, Brow, Endorse, Face, Favour, Mug, Sanction, Support, Visage

Counteract(ing) Ant-, Antidote, Cancel, Correct, Frustrate, Offset, Talion

Counterbalance Bascule, Offset, Undo, Weigh

Counter-charge Recrimination

Counterclockwise L(a)evorotatory

Counterfeit(er) Bastard, Belie, Bogus, Boodle, Brum, Coiner, Duffer, Dummy, Fantasm, Flash, Forge, Imitant, Paperhanger, Phantasm, Phoney, Pinchbeck, Postiche, Pseudo, Queer, Rap, Schlenter, Sham, Shan(d), Simulate, Slang, Slip, Smasher, Snide, Spurious, Stumer

Counterfoil Stub

Counterglow Gegenschein

Counter-irritant Seton

Countermand Abrogate, Annul, Cancel, Override, Rescind, Retract, Revoke

Counterpart Copy, Double, Obverse, Oppo, Parallel, Shadow, Similar, Spit(ting), Tally, Twin

Counterpoint Contrapuntal, Descant

Countersign Endorse, Password

Counterthrust Riposte

Counties, County Co, Comital, District, Metropolitan, Palatine, Parish, Seat, Shire, Six

---

COUNTIES

2 letters:	Cork	Clwyd	Meath
NI	Down	Derry	Moray
Sy	Fife	Dyfed	Notts
	Kent	Essex	Omagh
3 letters:	Mayo	Flint	Perth
Ely	Ross	Gwent	Powys
Som		Herts	Sligo
	5 letters:	Hunts	Wilts
4 letters:	Angus	Kerry	Worcs
Avon	Cavan	Laois	
Beds	Clare	Louth	

6 letters:
Antrim
Armagh
Barset
Carlow
Dorset
Dublin
Durham
Galway
Offaly
Surrey
Sussex
Tyrone

7 letters:
Cumbria
Donegal
Gwynedd
Kildare
Leitrim
Norfolk
Rutland
Suffolk
Torfaen
Wexford
Wicklow

8 letters:
Cheshire
Cornwall
Finnmark
Kesteven
Kilkenny
Limerick

Longford
Lothians
Monaghan
Somerset

9 letters:
Berkshire
Buteshire
Caithness
Champagne
Cleveland
Fermanagh
Hampshire
Loamshire
Roscommon
The Mearns
Tipperary
Waterford
Westmeath
Yorkshire

10 letters:
Banffshire
Ceredigion
Derbyshire
Devonshire
Humberside
Lancashire
Merseyside
Midlothian
Nairnshire
Perthshire
Shropshire
Sutherland

West Sussex

11 letters:
Breconshire
East Lothian
Lanarkshire
Londonderry
Oxfordshire
Radnorshire
Tyne and Wear
West Lothian

12 letters:
Berwickshire
Denbighshire
Kinrossshire
Lincolnshire
Mid-Glamorgan
Peeblesshire
Renfrewshire
Selkirkshire
Warwickshire
West Midlands
Westmoreland
Wigtownshire

13 letters:
Dumfriesshire
Herefordshire
Monmouthshire
Pembrokeshire
Roxburghshire
Staffordshire
Stirlingshire

West Glamorgan
West Yorkshire

14 letters:
Brecknockshire
Dumbartonshire
Glamorganshire
Invernessshire
Leicestershire
Merionithshire
Northumberland
North Yorkshire
South Glamorgan
South Yorkshire

15 letters:
Caernarvonshire
Carmarthenshire
Gloucestershire
Kincardineshire
Montgomeryshire
Neath Port Talbot
Ross and Cromarty
Vale of Glamorgan

16 letters:
Clackmannanshire
Northamptonshire

17 letters:
Kircudbrightshire

Countless Infinite, Innumerable, Myriad, Umpteen, Untold

Country(side), Countrified Annam, Bangladesh, Bolivia, Boondocks, Bucolic, Champaign, Clime, Colchis, Edom, Enchorial, Farmland, Fatherland, Greenwood, High, Karoo, Karroo, → **LAND**, Lea, Lee, Low, Mongolia, Motherland, Nation, Parish, Paysage, People, Province, Realm, Region, Republic, Rural, Satellite, Scenery, Soil, State, Sultanate, The sticks, Thrace, Tundra, Tweedy, Venezuela, Weald, Wold, Yemen

Country girl Amaryllis

Country house Hall, Manor, Quinta

Countryman Arcadian, Bacon, Boor, Culchie, Hick, Hillbilly, Hodge, National, Native, Peasant, Ruralist, Un, Yokel

Coup Blow, Deal, KO, Move, Putsch, Scoop, Stroke, Treason

Coupé Cabriolet, Landaulet

Couple(r), Coupling Acoustic, Ally, Band, Brace, Bracket, Connect, Direct, Duet, Duo, Dyad, Fishplate, Flange, Galvanic, Gemini, Geminy, Hitch, Interlock, Item, → **JOIN**, Marrow, Marry, Mate, Meng(e), Ment, Ming, Octave, Pair, Pr, Relate,

Shackle, Tenace, Tie, Tirasse, Turnbuckle, Tway, Union, Universal, Voltaic, Wed, Yoke

Couple of ducks Spectacles

Couplet Distich, Heroic

Coupon(s) Ration, Ticket, Voucher

Courage(ous) Balls, Ballsy, Bottle, Bravado, Bravery, Bulldog, Cojones, Dutch, Fortitude, Gallantry, Game, Gimp, Grit, Gumption, Guts, Hardihood, Heart, Heroism, Lion-heart, Macho, Manful, Mettle, Moral, Moxie, Nerve, Pluck, Prowess, Rum, Spirit, Spunk, Stalwart, Steel, Stomach, Valiant, Valour, Wight

Courgette Zucchini

Courier Estafette, Guide, Harbinger, Herald, → **MESSENGER**, Postillion, Postman

Course(s) Access, Afters, Aim, Aintree, Antipasto, Appetiser, Arroyo, Ascot, Assault, Atlantic, Back straight, Barge, Bearing, Beat, Belt, Canal, Career, Chantilly, Chase, Circuit, Civics, Collision, Consommé, Conversion, Correspondence, Crash, Current, Curriculum, Cursus, Daltonism, Damp(-proof), Dessert, Diadrom, Dish, Dromic, Easting, Entrée, Epsom, Fish, Food, Foundation, Going, Golf, Goodwood, Greats, Heat, Induction, Isodomon, Lane, Lap, Layer, Leat, Leet, Line, Lingfield, Links, Longchamp, Magnetic, Main, Meal, Meat, Mess, Newbury, Newmarket, Nine-hole, Northing, Nulla, → **OF COURSE**, Orbit, Orthodromic, Period, Policy, PPE, Practicum, Procedure, Process, Programme, Progress, Pursue, Quadrivium, Race, Raik, Refresher, Regimen, Rhumb, Ride, Ring, Rink, Road, Rota, Route, Routine, Run, Rut, Sandown, Sandwich, Semester, Seminar, Series, Slalom, Sorbet, Soup, Southing, Stadium, Starter, Stearage, Steerage, Step(s), Stratum, Streak, Stretch, Stretching, String, Syllabus, Tack, Tanride, Tenor, Track, Trade, Trend, Troon, Vector, Via media, Water table, Way, Wearing, Wentworth, Westing

Court(ship), Courtier Address, Admiralty, Appellate, Arbitration, Arches, Areopagus, Atrium, Attention, Audience, Audiencia, Aula, Banc, Bar, Basecourt, Bench, Beth Din, Bishop's, Boondock, Caerleon, Camelot, Canoodle, Caravanserai, Cassation, Centre, Chancery, Chase, Clay, Commercial, Commissary, Commission, Conscience, Conservancy, Consistory, County, Criminal, Crown, CS, Ct, Curia, Curia Regis, Curtilage, Cutcher(r)y, Date, Dedans, Deuce, Dicastery, Diplock, District, Doctor's Commons, Domestic, Duchy, Durbar, Dusty Feet, En tout cas, Evora, Eyre, Federal, Fehm(gericht), Fehmgerichte, Fiars, Forensic, Forest, Forum, Fronton, Galleria, Garth, Go steady, Grass, Guildenstern, Halimot(e), Hampton, Hard, High, Hof, Holy See, Hustings, Hypaethron, Inferior, Intermediate, Invite, Jack, Justice, Juvenile, Kachahri, Kacheri, Kangaroo, Keys, King, King's Bench, Kirk Session, Knave, Law, Leet, Lobby, Lyon, Magistrate's, Majlis, Marshalsea, Mash, Moot, Old Bailey, Open, Parvis, Patio, Peristyle, Petty Sessions, Philander, Piepowder, Police, Porte, Praetorium, Prerogative, Presbytery, Prize, Probate, Provincial, Provost, Quad, Quarter Sessions, Queen, Queen's Bench, Racket, Request, Retinue, Romance, Rosenkrantz, Royal, St James's, Sanhedrim, Sanhedrin, See, Service, Session, Sheriff, Shire-moot, Spoon, Stannary, Star Chamber, Sudder, Sue, Superior, Supreme, Swanimote, Sweetheart, Thane, Thegn, Traffic, Trial, Tribunal, Vehm, Vehmgericht(e), Vestibulum, Walk out, Ward, Wench, Woo, World, Wow, Yard, Youth

Courteous, Courtesy Affable, Agrement, Bow, Chivalry, Civil, Comity, Devoir, Etiquette, Fair, Genteel, Gracious, Hend, Polite, Politesse, Refined, Urbanity, Well-mannered

Courtesan Aspasia, Bianca, Bona-roba, Delilah, Demi-monde, Demi-rep, Geisha, Hetaera, Lais, Lampadion, Lorette, Madam, Phryne, Plover, Pornocracy, Prostitute, Stallion, Thais

Courtly Chivalrous, Cringing, Dignified, Flattering, Refined

Court-martial Drumhead

Courtyard Area, Close, Cortile, Enceinte, Garth, Marae, Patio, Quad

Cousin(s) Bette, Cater, Country, Coz, Cross, German, Kin, Kissing, Parallel, Robin, Second, Skater

Couturier Dior, Dressmaker

Cove Abraham's, Arm, Bay, Bight, Buffer, Creek, Cure, Gink, Grot, Guy, Hithe, Hythe, Inlet, Lulworth, Nook

Covenant(er) Abrahamic, Alliance, Appurtenant, Bond, Contract, Hillmen, Pledge, Restrictive, Warranty, Whiggamore

Coventry Isolation

Cover(ed), Covering Adventitia, Air, A l'abri, Amnion, Antependium, Antimacassar, Apron, Aril, Attire, Awning, Barb, Bard(s), Bark, Bedspread, Bestrew, Bind, Blanket, Bodice, Brood, Bubblewrap, Bury, Camouflage, Canopy, Cap, Caparison, Cape, Capsule, Casing, Casque, Catch-all, Caul, Ceil, Ciborium, Cladding, Clapboard, Cleithral, Clithral, Coat, Cocoon, Coleorhiza, Conceal, Cope, Copyright, Cosy, Counterpane, Cour, Covert, Cowl, Crust, Curtain, Deadlight, Debruised, Deck, Deputise, Dividend, Dome, Drape(t), Dripstone, Duchesse, Dust-sheet, Duvet, Eiderdown, Encase, Endue, Enguard, Enlace, Enshroud, Envelop(e), Enwrap, Exoderm(is), Exoskeleton, Extra, Face, Falx, Fanfare, Felting, Fielder, Figleaf, Fingerstall, First-day, Flashing, Fother, Front, Gaiter, Gambado, Gobo, Grolier, Ground, Groundsheet, Hap, Harl, Hat, Hatch, Havelock, Heal, Heel, Hejab, Hele, Hell, Helmet, Hijab, Hood, Housing, Hubcap, Immerse, Incase, Indument, Indusium, Inmask, Insulate, Insurance, Insure, Jacket, Lag, Lambrequin, Lay, Leap, Leep, Legging, Legwarmer, Lid, Liner, Loose, Manche, Mantle, Mask, Metal, Mount, Muffle, Mulch, Notum, Numnah, Obscure, OC, Occlude, On, Operculum, Orillion, Orlop, Overlap, Overlay, Palampore, Palempore, Pall, Pand, Parcel, Pasties, Patch, Pebbledash, Pelmet, Periderm, Perigone, Pillow sham, Plaster, Plate, Pleura, Point, Pseudonym, Pullover, Quilt, Radome, Regolith, Robe, Roof, Roughcast, Rug, Sally, Screen, Serviette, Setting, Sheath, Sheet, Shell, Shelter, Shield, Shower, Shrink-wrap, Shroud, Shuck, Skin, Smokescreen, Solleret, Span, Spat, Splashback, Stand-by, Stifle, Superimpose, Swathe, Tampian, Tampion, Tapadera, Tapis, Tarpaulin, Teacosy, Tectorial, Tegmen, Tegument, Tent, Test(a), Tester, Thatch, Thimble, Thumbstall, Tick(ing), Tidy, Tile, Tilt, Tonneau, Top, Trapper, Trench, Trip, Turtleback, Twill, Twilt, Umbrella, Upholster, Valance, Veil, Vele, Veneer, Ventail, Vesperal, Vest, Visor, Volva, Wainscot, Warrant, Waterdeck, Whelm, Whitewash, Wrap, Wrappage, Wrapper, Yapp, Yashmak

Covert(ly) Clandestine, Copse, Privy, → SECRET, Shy, Sidelong, Sub rosa, Surreptitious, Tectrix, Ulterior

Covet(ed), Covetous Avaricious, Crave, Desiderata, Desire, Eager, Envy, Greedy, Hanker, Yearn

Cow Adaw, Alderney, Amate, Appal, Awe, Ayrshire, Boss(y), Bovine, Brahmin, Browbeat, Cash, Charolais, Colly, Crummy, Danton, Daunt, Dexter, Dsomo, Dun, Galloway, Gally, Goujal, Guernsey, Hawkey, Hawkie, Heifer, Hereford, Intimidate, Jersey, Kouprey, Kyloe, Lea(h), Mart, Milch, Mog(gie), Moggy, Mooly, Muley, Mulley, Neat, Overawe, Redpoll, Red Sindhi, Rother(-beast), Sacred, Santa Gertrudis, Scare, Simmental, Slattern, Springing, Stirk, Subact, Teeswater, Threaten, Unnerve, Vaccine, Zebu, Z(h)o

Coward(ice), Cowardly Bessus, Cat, Chicken, Cocoa, Craven, Cuthbert, Dastard, Dingo, Dunghill, Fraidy-cat, Fugie, Funk, Gutless, Hen, Hilding, Jessie, Lily-livered, Meacock, Milk-livered, Niddering, Nidderling, Nidering, Niderling, Niding,

Nithing, Noel, Panty-waist, Poltroon, Pusillanimous, Recreant, Scaramouch, Scaredy cat, Sganarelle, Slag, Sook, Squib, Viliaco, Viliago, Villagio, Villiago, White feather, Yellow, Yellow-belly

Cowboy, Cowgirl Broncobuster, Buckaroo, Cowpoke, Cowpuncher, Gaucho, Inexpert, Io, Jerrybuilder, Leger, Llanero, Puncher, Ranchero, Ritter, Roper, Vaquero, Waddie, Waddy, Wrangler

Cow-catcher Fender, Reata

Cower Croodle, Crouch, Fawn, Quail, Ruck, Skulk, Wince

Cowl Bonnet, Capuchin, Granny, Hood, Kilmarnock

Cowpat Dung, Tath

Cowpox Vaccinia

Cowshed, Cowstall Byre, Crib, Shippen, Shippon, Stable, Stall, Staw

Cowslip Culver-key, Pa(i)gle

Cox Steerer

Coxcomb Aril, Caruncle, Copple, Crest, Dandy, Dude, Fop, Jackanapes, Popinjay, Yellow-rattle

Coy Arch, Coquettish, Demure, Laithfu', Mim, Nice, Shamefast, → **SHY**, Skeigh, Skittish

Coyote SD

CPRS Think tank

Crab(by), Crablike Apple, Attercop, Blue swimmer, Boston, Calling, Cancer, Cancroid, Cantankerous, Capernoity, Cock, Coconut, Daddy, Decapoda, Diogenes, Ethercap, Ettercap, Fiddler, Ghost, Grouch, Hard-shell, Hermit, Horseman, Horseshoe, King, Land, Limulus, Mantis, Mitten, Mud, Nebula, Ochidore, Oyster, Pagurian, Partan, Pea, Perverse, Podite, Roast, Robber, Rock, Sand, Saucepan-fish, Scrawl, Sentinel, Sidle, Soft-shell, Soldier, Spectre, Spider, Velvet, Velvet-fiddler, Woolly-hand, Xiphosura, Zoea

▷ **Crab** *may indicate* an anagram

Crab-apple Scrog-bush, Scrog-buss

Crab-eater Urva

Crabs-eye Abrus

Crack(ed), Cracker(s), Cracking Ad-lib, Admirable, Bananas, Biscuit, Bonbon, Break, Cat, Catalytic, Chap, Chasm, Chat, Chink, Chip, Chop, Clap, Cleave, Cleft, Cloff, Confab, Cranny, Craquelure, Craqueture, Craze, Cream, Crepitate, Crevasse, Crevice, Crispbread, Dawn, Decipher, Decode, Doom, Dunt, Elite, Expert, Fatiscent, Fent, Firework, First-rate, Fisgig, Fissure, Fizgig, Flaw, Flip-flop, Fracture, Go, Graham, Grike, Gryke, Gully, Hairline, Hit, Jibe, Joint, Knacker, Leak, Liar, Little-endian, Matzo, Moulin, Oner, Peterman, Pleasantry, Pore, Praise, Prawn, Quarter, Quip, Rap, Report, Rhagades, Rictus, Rift, Rille, Rima, Rime, Rimous, Rive, Rock, Saltine, Sand, Seam, Shake, Snap, Soda, Solve, Split, Squib, Sulcus, Toe, Top, Try, Waterloo, Wind shake, Yegg

Crackerjack Ace, Nailer, Trump

Crackle, Crackling Craze, Crepitation, Crepitus, Crinkle, Decrepitate, Fizz, Glaze, Rale, Skin, Static

Crackpot Nutter

Cracksman Burglar, Peterman, Raffles

Cradle Bassinet, Berceau, Book rest, Cat's, Cot, Crib, Cunabula, Hammock, Knife, Nestle, Newton's, Rocker

Craft(y) Arch, Art, Aviette, Barbola, Boat, Canal boat, Cautel, Cunning, Disingenuous, Finesse, Fly, Guile, Hydroplane, Ice-breaker, Insidious, Kontiki, Landing, Machiavellian, Mister, Mystery, Oomiack, Reynard, Saic, Shallop, Ship,

Shuttle, → **SKILL**, Slee, Sleeveen, Slim, Slippy, Sly, Slyboots, State, Subdolous, Subtil(e), Subtle, Suttle, Trade, Triphibian, Umiak, Underhand, Versute, → **VESSEL**, Wile, Workmanship

▷ **Craft** *may indicate* an anagram

Craftsman AB, Artificer, Artisan, Artist, Chippy, Cutler, Ebonist, Fabergé, Finisher, Gondolier, Guild, Hand, Joiner, Journeyman, Mason, Mechanic, Morris, Opificer, Wainwright, Wright

Crag(gy) Coralline, Eyrie, Height, Heuch, Heugh, Krantz, Noup, Rock

Cram(mer) Bag, Candle-waster, Cluster, Craig, Fill, Gag, Gavage, Neck, Pang, Prime, Revise, Rugged, Scar(p), Shoehorn, Spur, Stap, Stodge, Stow, Swat, Tuck

Cramp(ed) Agraffe, Charleyhorse, Confine, Constrict, Crick, Hamper, Hamstring, Incommodious, Musician's, Myalgia, Pinch, Poky, Potbound, Restrict, Rigor, Squeeze, Stunt, Tetany, Writer's

Crane, Crane-driver Brolga, Cherry picker, Container, Davit, Deck, Demoiselle, Derrick, Dogman, Dragline, Gantry, Gooseneck, Grabbing, Herd, Heron, Hooper, Ichabod, Jenny, Jib, Jigger, Kenworthy, Luffing-jib, Numidian, Rail, Sarus, Sedge, Shears, Sheer, Siege, Stork, Stretch, Tower, Tulip, Whooper, Whooping, Winch

Crane-fly Leatherjacket, Tipulidae

Cranium Harnpan

Crank(y) Bell, Eccentric, Grouch, Handle, Lever, Mot, Perverse, Whim, Wince, Winch, Wind

Crash Bingle, Collapse, Disk, Ditch, Dush, Fail, Fall, Fragor, Intrude, Linen, Nosedive, Pile up, Prang, Rack, Ram, Rote, Shunt, Slam, Smash, South Sea Bubble, Thunderclap, Topple

▷ **Crashes** *may indicate* an anagram

Crass Coarse, Crude, Rough, Rude

Crate Biplane, Box, Case, Ceroon, Crib, Hamper, Sero(o)n, Soapbox, Tube

Crater Alphonsus, Aniakchak, Aristarchus, Aristotle, Askja, Autolycus, Bail(l)y, Blowhole, Caldera, Cavity, Cissing, Clavius, Copernicus, Fra Mauro, Grimaldi, Hipparchus, Hole, Hollow, Kepler, Kilauea, Maar, Meteor, Newton, Pit, Plato, Ptolemaeus, Pythagoras, Schickard, Sinus iridium, Theophilus, Tycho

Cravat Ascot, Neckatee, Neck-cloth, Oerlay, Overlay, Scarf, Soubise, Steenkirk, Tie

Crave, Craving Appetite, Aspire, Beg, Beseech, Covet, Desire, Entreat, Gasp, Greed, Hanker, Hunger, Itch, Libido, Long, Lust, Malacia, Methomania, Munchies, Opsomania, Orexis, Pica, Polyphagia, Sitomania, The munchies, Thirst, Yearn, Yen

Craven Abject, Coward, Dastard, Hen, Recreant

Crawl(er) All fours, Australian, Back, Clamber, Creep, Cringe, Drag, Front, Grovel, Lag, Lickspittle, Pub, Reptile, Scramble, Scrome, Side, Skulk, Snail, Swim, Sycophant, Tantony, Trail, Trudgen, Yes-man

Crayfish Astacology, Gilgie, Jilgie, Marron, Yabbie, Yabby

Crayon Chalk, Colour, Conté®, Pastel, Pencil, Sauce

Craze(d), Crazy Absurd, Ape, Apeshit, Barmy, Bats, Batty, Berserk, Bonkers, Break, Cornflake, Crack(ers), Crackpot, Cult, Daffy, Dement, Derange, Dingbats, Dippy, Distraught, Doiled, Doilt, Doolally, Doolally tap, Dottle, Dotty, Fad, Flake, Flaw, Folie, Frantic, Furious, Furore, Furshlugginer, Gaga, Geld, Gonzo, Gyte, Haywire, Headbanger, Insane, Loco, Loony, Loopy, Lunatic, Madden, Maenad(ic), Mania, Manic, Mattoid, Melomania, Meshug(g)a, Moonstruck, Nuts, Porangi, Potty, Psycho(path), Rage, Rave, Scatty, Screwball, Skivie, Slatey, Stunt, Typomania, Unhinge, Wacko, Wacky, Wet, W(h)acky, Whim, Wowf, Zany

▷ **Crazy** *may indicate* an anagram

Creak(y) Cry, Grate, Grind, Rheumatic, Scraich, Scraigh, Scroop, Seam, Squeak

Cream(y) Barrier, Bavarian, Best, Chantilly, Cherry-pick, Clotted, Cold, Cornish, Crème fraîche, Devonshire, Double, Elite, Foundation, Frangipane, Glacier, Heavy, Ivory, Jollop, Lanolin, Liniment, Lotion, Mousse, Off-white, Ointment, Opal, Paragon, Pastry, Pick, Ream, Rich, Salad, Salve, Sillabub, Single, Skim, Smitane, Sour, Sun(screen), Syllabub, Vanishing, Whipped, Whipping

Crease Bowling, Crumple, → **FOLD**, Goal, Lirk, Pitch, Pleat, Popping, Return, Ridge, Ruck(le), Ruga, Rugose, Wrinkle

Create, Creation, Creative Arty, Brainstorm, Build, Coin, Compose, Continuous, Devise, Dreamtime, Engender, Establish, Fabricate, Forgetive, Form, Found, Generate, Genesis, Godhead, Hexa(h)emeron, Ideate, Imaginative, → **INVENT**, Omnific, Oratorio, Originate, Produce, Shape, Synthesis, Universe

Creator Ahura Mazda, Author, Demiurge, God, Inventor, Maker, Ormazd, Ormuzd

Creature Animal, Ankole, Basilisk, Beast, Being, Bigfoot, Chevrotain, Cratur, Critter, Crittur, Man, Nekton, Saprobe, Sasquatch, Sphinx, Whiskey, Wight

Credence, Credential(s) Certificate, Document, Papers, Qualifications, Shelf, Testimonial

Credibility Street

Credible, Credit(s), Creditor Ascribe, Attribute, Belief, Billboard, Byline, Carbon, Crawl, Esteem, Extended, Family, Honour, HP, Kite, Kudos, LC, Lender, Mense, Post-war, Probable, Reliable, Renown, Revolving, Shylock, Social, Strap, Street, Tally, Tax, Tick, Title, Trust, Weight, Youth

Credulous Charlie, Gullible, Naive, Simple, Trusting

Creed Apostle's, Athanasian, Belief, Doctrine, Faith, Ism, Nicene, Ophism, Outworn, Sect, Tenet

Creek Antietam, Bay, Breaches, Cooper, Cove, Crick, Dawson, Estuary, Fleet, Geo, Gio, Goe, Indian, Inlet, Kill, Pow, Slough, Vae, Voe, Wick

Creel Basket, Hask, Scull, Skull

Creep(er), Creeping, Creeps Ai, Ampelopsis, Arbutus, Aseismic, Boston ivy, Cleavers, Crawl, Function, Grew, Grovel, Grue, Heebie-jeebies, Heeby-jeebies, Herpetic, Honey, Inch, Insect, Ivy, Mission, Nerd, Nuthatch, Pussyfoot, Repent, Reptant, Sarmentous, Sidle, Sittine, Skulk, Slink, Snake, Sneak(sby), Sobole(s), Soil, Steal, Toad, Tropaeolum, Truckle, Vinca, Vine, Virginia, Wickthing, Willies

Creeping Jenny Moneywort

Cremate, Cremation, Crematorium Burn, Char, Cinerarium, Ghat, Ghaut, Incinerate, Pyre, Sati, Suttee, Ustrinium

Creole Gullah, Haitian, Kriol, Papiamento, Tok Pisin

Crepe Blini, Blintz(e), Canton, Pancake

Crescent Barchan(e), Bark(h)an, Fertile, Growing, Lune(tte), Lunulate, Lunule, Meniscus, Moon, Red, Sickle, Waxing

Cress Cardamine, Garden, Hoary, Isatis, Pepperwort, Swine's, Thale, Wart, Water, Yellow

Crest(ed) Acme, Chine, Cimier, Cockscomb, Comb, Copple, Crista, Height, Kirimon, Knap, Mon, Peak, Pileate, Pinnacle, Plume, Ridge, Summit, Tappit, Tee, → **TOP**, Tufty

Cretaceous Chalky, Senonian

Cretan Candiot(e), Minoan, Teucer

Crevasse Bergschrund, Chasm, Gorge, Rimaye

Crevice Chine, Cranny, Fissure, Interstice, Ravine, Vallecula

Crew Boasted, Company, Complement, Core, Deckhand, Eight, Equipage, Four, Lot, Manners, Men, Oars, Prize, Sailors, Salts, Seamen, Ship men, Team, Teme, Torpid

Crew-cut Not(t)

Crib Cheat, Cot, Cowhouse, Cratch, Filch, Horse, → KEY, Manger, Pony, Purloin, Putz, Shack, Stall, Steal, Trot

Crick Cramp, Kink, Spasm

Cricket(er) Balm, Bat, Botham, Bowler, Bradman, CC, Cicada, Dry-bob, French, Grade, Grasshopper, Grig, Hopper, Jerusalem, Katydid, Keeper, Knott, Leg, Long-leg, Long-off, Long-on, Longstop, March, May, Mid-on, Mole, Muggleton, Nightwatchman, Opener, Packer, Point, Pyjama, Shield, Single-wicket, Slip, Sobers, Stool, Stridulate, Tate, Test, Tettix, Tip and run, Vigoro, Warner, Wart-biter, Windball, Windies, Wisden, XI(gent)

Crier Bellman, Herald, Muezzin, Niobe, Outrooper

Crime Attentat, Barratry, Caper, Chantage, Chaud-mellé, Computer, Corpus delicti, Ecocide, Fact, Felony, Fraud, Graft, Hate, Heist, Iniquity, Inside job, Malefaction, Mayhem, Misdeed, Misdemeanour, → OFFENCE, Organised, Ovicide, Peccadillo, Perjury, Pilferage, Ram raid, Rap, Rape, Rebellion, → SIN, Tort, Transgression, Treason, Victimless, Villa(i)ny, War, White-collar, Wrong

Crimea Balaclava

Criminal Bandit, Bent, Bushranger, Chummy, Con, Cosa Nostra, Counterfeiter, Crack-rope, → CROOK, Culpable, Culprit, Delinquent, Escroc, Fagin, Felon, Flagitious, Forensic, Gangster, Heavy, Heinous, Highbinder, Hitman, Hood(lum), Jailbird, Ladrone, Lag, Larcener, Lifer, Looter, Lowlife, Maf(f)ia, Malefactor, Maleficent, Malfeasant, Mens rea, Mob(ster), Molester, Ndrangheta, Nefarious, Nefast, Offender, Outlaw, Perp(etrator), Peterman, Racketeer, Receiver, Recidivist, Reprehensible, Rustler, Sinner, Snakehead, Thug, Triad, Triggerman, Underworld, Villain, Wicked, Wire, Yakuza, Yardie, Yegg

▷ **Criminal** *may indicate* an anagram

Criminologist Lombroso

Crimp Pleat

Crimson Carmine, Incarnadine, Modena, Red, Scarlet

Cringe, Cringing Cower, Creep, Crouch, Fawn, Grovel, Shrink, Sneaksby, Truckle

Crinkle, Crinkly Rugate, Rugose

Crinoline Farthingale, Hoop

Cripple(d) Damage, Debilitate, Disable, Game, Hamstring, Handicap, Injure, → LAME, Lameter, Lamiter, Maim, Paralyse, Polio, Scotch, Spoil

Crisis Acme, Crunch, Drama, Emergency, Exigency, Fastigium, Fit, Flap, Head, Identity, Make or break, Midlife, Panic, Pass, Quarterlife, Shake-out, Solution, Test

Crisp Brisk, Clear, Crimp, Crunchy, Fresh, Potato, Sharp, Short, Succinct, Terse

Crispin Sutor(ial)

Criss-cross Alternate, Fret, Interchange, Vein

Criteria, Criterion Benchmark, Gauge, Koch's postulates, Measure, Precedent, Proof, Rayleigh, Rule, Shibboleth, → STANDARD, Test, Touchstone

Critic(al), Criticise, Criticism Acute, Agate, Animadversion, Archer, Aristarch, Armchair, Arnold, Attack, Badmouth, Bagehot, Barrack, Bellettrist, Berate, Bird, Blame, Boileau, Boo, Bucket, Captious, Carp, Castigate, Cavil, Censor(ious), → CENSURE, Climacteric, Clobber, Comment, Condemn, Connoisseur, Crab, Criticaster, → CRUCIAL, Crunch, Dangle, Decisive, Denigrate, Denounce, Deprecate, Desperate, Diatribe, Do down, Dutch uncle, Earful, Etain, Exacting, Excoriate, Fastidious, Fateful, Feuilleton, Flak, Flay, Fulminous, Gosse, Harrumph, Higher, Important, Impugn, Inge, Inveigh, Judge, Judgemental, Knife-edge, Knock(er), Lash, Leavis, Life and death, Literary, Masora(h), Mas(s)orete, Mordacious, Nag, Nasute, Nibble, Nice, Niggle, Overseer, Pan, Pater, Puff, Pundit, Quibble, Rap, Rebuke, Reprehend, Review(er), Rip, Roast, Ruskin,

Scalp, Scarify, Scathe, Scorn, Second guess, Serious, Severe, Shaw, Sideswipe, Slag, Slam, Slashing, Slate, Sneer, Snipe, Stick, Stricture, Strop, Tense, Textual, Thersitic, Threap, Touch and go, Ultracrepidate, Urgent, Vet, Vitriol, Vituperation, Watershed, Zoilism

Croak Creak, Crow, Die, Grumble, Gutturalise

Croatian Cravates, Glagolitic, Serb

Crochet Lace, Weave

Crock Chorrie, Crate, Jar, Mug, Pig, Pitcher, Pot, Potshard, Potshare, Potsherd, Stean(e)

Crockery Ceramics, China, Dishes, Earthenware, Oddment, Sunbeam, Ware

▷ **Crocks** *may indicate* an anagram

Crocodile Cayman, File, Flat dog, Garial, Gavial, Gharial, Gotcha lizard, Line, Mud gecko, Mugger, River-dragon, Saltie, Saltwater, Sebek, Teleosaur(ian)

Crocus Autumn, Naked lady, Prairie, Saffron

Croesus Lydia

Croft Pightle

Cromwell Ironside, Lord Protector, Noll, Oliver, Protector, Richard, Roundhead

Crone(s) Beldam(e), Ewe, Graeae, Hag, Mawkin, Ribibe, Rudas, Sibyl, Sybil, Trot, Trout, → **WITCH**

Crony Anile, Chum, Intimate, Mate, Pal, Sidekick

Crook(ed) Adunc, Ajee, Aslant, Asymmetric, Awry, Bad, Bend, Bow, Cam, Camsheugh, Camsho(ch), Criminal, Cromb, Crome, Crosier, Crummack, Crummock, Crump, Curve, Dishonest, Elbow, Fraud, Heister, Hook, Indirect, Kam(me), Kebbie, Lituus, Malpractitioner, Operator, Shank, Shyster, Sick, Skew(whiff), Slick(er), Squint, Staff, Swindler, Thraward, Thrawart, Thrawn, Twister, Wonky, Yeggman

▷ **Crooked** *may indicate* an anagram

Croon(er), Crooning Bing, Como, Lament, Lull, Monody, Murmur, Sing

Crop(s), Cropped, Cropping Basset, Browse, Cash, Catch, Clip, Cover, Craw, Cut, Distress, Dock, Emblements, Energy, Epilate, Eton, Foison, Forage, Harvest, Hog, Ingluvies, Kharif, Ladino, Milo, Not(t), Plant, Poll, Produce, Rabi, Riding, Rod, Root, Shingle, Silage, Standing, Stow, Strip, Subsistence, Succession, Top, Truncate, White

Cropper Downfall, Header, Purler

Croquet (term) Peel, Rover, Wire

Croquette Kromesky, Quenelle, Rissole

Cross(ing), Crossbred Angry, Ankh, Ansate, Archiepiscopal, Banbury, Basta(a)rd, Beefalo, Bestride, Bois-brule, Boton(n)e, Buddhist, Burden, Calvary, Cantankerous, Canterbury, Capital, Cattalo, Celtic, Channel, Chi, Chiasm(a), Choleric, Cleche, Clover-leaf, Compital, Constantine, Crosslet, Crosswalk, Crotchety, Crucifix, Crux, Decussate, Demi-wolf, Dihybrid, Double, Dso(mo), Dzobo, Eleanor, Encolpion, Faun, Fiery, Fitché, Fleury, Foil, Footbridge, Ford, Frabbit, Fractious, Frampold, Franzy, Funnel, Fylfot, Geneva, George, Grade, Greek, Holy rood, Humette, Hybrid, Ill, Imp, Indignant, Interbreed, Intersect, Intervein, Iona, Iracund, Irate, Irked, Iron, Jerusalem, Jomo, Jumart, Kiss, Krest, Ladino, Latin, Level, Liger, Lorraine, Lurcher, Maltese, Mameluco, Market, Mermaid, Military, Misfortune, Mix, Moline, Mongrel, Mule, Narky, Nattery, Node, Norman, Northern, Nuisance, Oblique, Obverse, Ordinary, Orthodox, Overpass, Overthwart, Papal, Patonce, Patriarchal, Pattée, Pectoral, Pedestrian, Pelican, Plumcot, Plus, Pommé, Potence, Potent, Preaching, Puffin, Quadrate, Railway, Ratty, Reciprocal, Red, Roman, Rood, Rose, Rosy, Rouen, Rouge, Rubicon, Ruthwell, Sain, St Andrew's, St Anthony's, St George's, St

Patrick's, St Peter's, Saltier, Saltire, Sambo, Satyr, Shirty, Sign, Snappy, Southern, Splenetic, Strid, Svastika, Swastika, T, Tangelo, Tau, Tayberry, Ten, Testy, Thraw, Thwart, Tiglon, Tigon, Times, Toucan, Transit, Transom, Transverse, Traverse, Tree, Unknown, Urdé, Vexed, Vext, Victoria, → **VOTE**, Weeping, Whippet, Wry, X, Yakow, Zambo, Zebra(ss), Zebrinny, Zebroid, Zebrula, Zebrule, Zedonk, Z(h)o, Zobu

▷ **Cross** *may indicate* an anagram
▶ **Cross-bar** *see* **CROSSPIECE**
▶ **Crossbeam** *see* **CROSSPIECE**
Cross-bearer Crucifer
Cross-bill Metagnathous
Cross-bones Marrowbones
Cross-bow Arbalest, Bal(l)ista
Cross-country Langlauf, Overland
Cross-dressing Eonism
Cross-examine Grill, Interrogate, Question, Targe
Cross-eyed Skelly(-eyed), Squint
Crossfertilisation Allogamy, Heterosis, Hybrid vigour, Xenogamy
Cross-grained Ill-haired, Mashlam, Mashlim, Mas(h)lin, Mashlock, Mashlum, Stubborn
Crosspiece, Cross-bar, Cross-beam, Cross-timber Bar, Cancelli, Footrail, Inter-tie, Lierne, Phillipsite, Putlock, Putlog, Quillon, Serif, Seriph, Stempel, Stemple, Stretcher, Stull, Swingle-tree, Toggle, Transom, Trave, Whiffle-tree, Whipple-tree, Yoke
Crossroads Carfax, Carfox, Carrefour, Compital, Soap
Crossword Cryptic, Grid, Puzzle, Quickie
Crotchet(y) Eccentric, Fad, Fancy, Grouch, Kink, Quarter-note, Toy
Crouch Bend, Cringe, Falcade, Fancy, Lordosis, Ruck, Set, Squat, Squinch
Croup Angina, Cough, Kink, Rump
Crow Boast, Brag, Carrion, Chewet, Chough, Corbie, Corvus, Crake, Currawong, Daw, Flute-bird, Gorcrow, Hooded, Hoodie, Huia, Jackdaw, Jim(my), Murder, Piping, Raven, Rook, Saddleback, Scald, Skite, Squawk, Swagger, Vaunt
Crowbar Gavelock, James, Jemmy, Lever
Crowd(ed) Abound, Army, Bike, Boodle, Bumper, Bunch, Byke, Caboodle, Clutter, Concourse, Congest(ed), Cram, Crush, Crwth, Dedans, Doughnut, Drove, Fill, Flock, Galere, Gang, Gate, Gathering, Herd, Horde, → **HOST**, Huddle, Hustle, Jam, Lot, Meinie, Mein(e)y, Menyie, Mob, Mong, Multitude, Ochlo-, Pack, Pang, Populace, Press, Rabble, Raft, Ram, Ratpack, Ring, Ruck, Scrooge, Scrouge, Scrowdge, Scrum, Serr(é), Shoal, Shove, Slew, Slue, Squash, Squeeze, Stuff, Swarm, Swell, Three, Throng, Trinity, Varletry
Crowfoot Gilcup, Reate
Crown Acme, Bays, Bull, Camp, Cantle, Cap, Capernoity, Cidaris, Civic, Coma, Corona, Cr, Diadem, Ecu, Engarland, Enthrone, Fillet, Garland, Gloria, Haku, Head, Headdress, Instal, Iron, Ivy, Krantz, Laurel, Monarch, Mural, Naval, Nole, Noll, Noul(e), Nowl, Olive, Optical, Ore, Ovation, Pate, Peak, Pschent, Sconce, Stephen's, Taj, Thick'un, Tiara, → **TOP**, Triple, Triumphal, Trophy, Vallary, Vertex
Crucial Acute, Critical, Essential, Key, Pivotal, Quintessential, Vital, Watershed
Crucible Cruset, Melting-pot, Vessel
Crucifix(ion), Crucify Calvary, Cross, Golgotha, Mortify, Rood, Torment, Torture
Crude(ness) Bald, Brash, Brute, Coarse, Earthy, Halfbaked, Immature, Incondite, Primitive, Raunch, Raw, Rough, Rough and ready, Rough-hewn, Rough-wrought, Tutty, Uncouth, Vulgar, Yahoo

Cruel(ty) Barbarous, Bloody, Brutal, Dastardly, De Sade, Draconian, Fell, Fiendish, Flinty, Hard, Heartless, Immane, Inhuman, Machiavellian, Mental, Neronic, Pitiless, Raw, Remorseless, Sadistic, Stern, Tiger, Tormentor, Vicious

▷ **Cruel** *may indicate* an anagram

Cruet Ampulla, Condiments, Decanter

Cruise(r) Booze, Busk, Cabin, Nuke, Prowl, Rove, Sail, Ship, Tom, Travel, Trip, Voyager

Crumb(le), Crumbly, Crumbs Coo, Decay, Disintegrate, Ee, Fragment, Friable, Law, Leavings, Moulder, Mull, Murl, Nesh, Nirl, Ort, Panko, Particle, Ped, Raspings, Rot, Rotter

Crumpet Dish, Girl, Muffin, Nooky, Pash, Pikelet

Crumple Collapse, Crunkle, Crush, Raffle, Scrunch, Wrinkle

Crunch(y) Abdominal, Chew, Craunch, Crisp, Gnash, Graunch, Grind, Munch, Occlude, Scranch

Crusade(r) Baldwin, Campaign, Cause, Pilgrim, Tancred, Templar

Crush(ed), Crusher Acis, Anaconda, Annihilate, Bow, Champ, Comminute, Conquer, Contuse, Cranch, Crunch, Defeat, Destroy, Graunch, Grind, Hug, Jam, Knapper, Levigate, Mangle, Mash, Mill, Molar, Mortify, Oppress, Overcome, Overwhelm, Pash, Policeman, Pound, Press, Pulp, Pulverise, Quash, Quell, Ruin, Schwarmerei, Scotch, Scrum, Scrumple, Smash, Squabash, Squash, Squeeze, Squelch, Squish, Stamp, Stave, Steam-roll, Stove, Suppress, Telescope, Trample, Tread

Crust(y) Argol, Beeswing, Cake, Coating, Coffin, Continental, Cover, Crabby, Craton, Fur, Gratin, Heel, Horst, Kissing, Kraton, Lithosphere, Oceanic, Orogen, Osteocolla, Pie, Reh, Rind, Rine, Sal, Salband, Scab, Shell, Sial, Sima, Sinter, Sordes, Surly, Tartar, Teachie, Terrane, Tetchy, Upper, Wine-stone

Crustacea(n) Amphipod, Barnacle, Brachyuran, Branchiopoda, Camaron, Cirriped, Cirripede, Cirripid, Cladoceran, Copepod, Crab, Crayfish, Cumacean, Cyclops, Cyprid, Cypris, Daphnia, Decapod(a), Entomostraca, Euphausia, Fishlouse, Foot-jaw, Gribble, Isopod, Krill, Langoustine, Lobster, Macrura, Malacostracan, Marine borer, Maron, Nauplius, Ostracoda, Pagurian, Phyllopod, Prawn, Rhizocephalan, Sand-hopper, Sand-skipper, Scampi, Scampo, Schizopod, Sea slater, Shellfish, Shrimp, Slater, Squilla, Stomatopod, Woodlouse, Yabbie, Yabby

Crutch Morton's, Potent

Crux Essence, Nub

Cry(ing) Aha, Alalagmus, Alew, Banzai, Bark, Battle, Bawl, Bell, Bill, Blat, Bleat, Bleb, Blub(ber), Boo, Boohoo, Boom, Bray, Bump, Caramba, Caw, Cheer, Chevy, Chirm, Chivy, Clang, Crake, Croak, Crow, Dire, Euoi, Eureka, Evoe, Exclaim, Fall, Field-holler, Gardyloo, Gathering, Geronimo, Gowl, Greet, Halloo, Harambee, Haro, Harrow, Havoc, Heigh, Hemitrope, Herald, Hinny, Hoicks, Holler, Honk, Hoo, Hoop, Hosanna, Hout(s)-tout(s), Howl, Humph, Io, Kaw, Low, Mewl, Miaou, Miau(l), Miserere, Mourn, Night-shriek, O(c)hone, Oi, Olé, Ow, Pugh, Rabbito(h), Rallying, Rivo, Sab, Scape, Scream, Screech, Sell, Sese(y), Sessa, → **SHOUT**, Shriek, Slogan, Snivel, Snotter, Sob, Soho, Sola, Squall, Squawk, Street, Sursum corda, Tally-ho, Tantivy, Umph, Vagitus, View-halloo, Vivat, Vociferate, Wail, War, Watchword, Waterworks, Waul, Wawl, Weep, Westward ho, Whee(ple), Whimper, Whine, Whinny, Whoa, Whoop, Winge, Wolf, Yammer, Yelp, Yicker, Yikker, Yip, Yippee, Yodel, Yo-heave-ho, Yo-ho-ho, Yoick, Yoop, Yowl

Crypt(ic) Catacomb, Cavern, Chamber, Crowde, Encoded, Favissa, Grotto, Hidden, Obscure, Occult, Secret, Sepulchre, Short, Steganographic, Tomb, Unclear, Undercroft, Vault

Cryptaesthesia ESP
Cryptogam Acotyledon, Acrogen, Fern(-ally), Moss, Pteridophyte
Cryptographer Decoder, Ventris
Crystal(s), Crystal-gazer, Crystalline, Crystallise Allotriomorphic, Axinite,
  Baccara(t), Beryl, Candy, Citrine, Clathrate, Clear, Cleveite, Copperas, Coumarin,
  Cumarin, Dendrite, Druse, Effloresce, Elaterin, Enantiomorph, Epitaxy, Erionite,
  Fuchsin(e), Geode, Glass, Hemihedron, Hemimorphic, Hemitrope, Ice-stone,
  Ideal, Imazadole, Jarosite, Lead, Liquid, Lithium, Love-arrow, Macle, Macro-axis,
  Melamine, Mixed, Nicol, Orthogonal, Orthorhombic, Pellucid, Penninite, Pericline,
  Phenocryst, Piezo, Piezoelectric, Pinacoid, Pinakoid, Prism, Pseudomorph,
  Purin(e), Quartz, R(h)aphide, R(h)aphis, Rhinestone, Rock, Rotenone, Rubicelle,
  Scryer, Shoot, Skatole, Skryer, Smectic, Snowflake, Sorbitol, Spar, Spherulite,
  Spicule, Table, Tolan(e), Trichite, Trilling, Twin(ned), Wafer, Watch-glass,
  Xanthene, Xenocryst, Yag
Cub Baby, Kit, Novice, Pup, Whelp, Wolf
Cube, Cubic, Cubist Bath, Braque, Cu, Die, Magic, Necker, Nosean, Quadrate,
  Rubik's®, Serac, Smalto, Snub, Solid, Stere, Stock, Tesseract
Cubicle Alcove, Booth, Carrel(l), Stall
Cuckold Actaeon, Cornute, Graft, Homer, Lenocinium, Vulcan's badge, Wittol
Cuckoo Ament, Ani, April fool, Bird, Brain-fever bird, Gouk, Gowk, Inquiline,
  Insane, Koekoea, Koel, → **MAD**, Mental, Piet-my-vrou, Stupid
▷ **Cuckoo** *may indicate* an anagram
Cuckoopint Arum
Cucumber Bitter-apple, Choko, Colocynth, Coloquintida, Dill, Elaterium, Gherkin,
  Pickle, Sea-slug, Squirting, Trepang, Wolly
Cuddle Canoodle, Caress, Clinch, Embrace, Fondle, Hug, Nooky, Smooch, Smuggle,
  Snog, Snuggle
Cudgel Alpeen, Ballow, Bludgeon, Brain, Club, Cosh, Drub, Fustigate, Oaken towel,
  Plant, Rack, Rung, Shillelagh, Souple, Stick, Swipple, Tan, Towel, Truncheon
Cue Cannonade, Catchword, Feed, Feed-line, Half-butt, Hint, Mace, → **PROMPT**,
  Reminder, Rod, Sign, Signal, Wink
Cuff Box, Buffet, Clout, French, Iron, Muffettee, Rotator, Strike, Swat
Cuirass Armour, Corselet, Lorica
Cuisine Bourgeoise, Cookery, Food, Lean, Menu, Minceur, Nouvelle
Cul-de-sac Blind, Dead-end, Impasse, Loke
Cull Gather, Pick, Select, Thin, Weed
Culminate, Culmination Apogean, Apogee, Climax, Conclusion, Crest, End, Head
Culpable Blameworthy, Guilty
Cult Aum Shinrikyo, Cabiri, Candomble, Cargo, Creed, Fertility, Macumba, New Age,
  Personality, Rastafarian, Sect, Shango, Shinto, Snake, Voodoo, Wicca, Worship
Cultivate(d), Cultivation Agronomy, Arty, Civilise, Dig, Dress, Ear, Ere, Farm,
  Genteel, Grow, Hoe, Hydroponics, Improve, Labour, Pursue, Raise, Reclaim,
  Refine, Sative, Sophisticated, Tame, Tasteful, Till, Tilth
Culture(d), Cultural Acheulean, Acheulian, Agar, Art(y), Aurignacian, Azilian,
  Bel esprit, Brahmin, Canteen, Capsian, Civil(isation), Clactonian, Club,
  Compensation, Corporate, Enterprise, Ethnic, Experiment, Explant, Gel,
  Gravettian, Grecian, Halafian, Hallstatt, Hip-hop, Humanism, Kultur(kreis), La
  Tène, Learning, Levallois, Magdalenian, Maglemosean, Maglemosian, Meristem,
  Minoan, Mousterian, Organisational, Perigordian, Polish, Pure, Refinement,
  Solutrean, Sophisticated, Starter, Strepyan, Suspension, Tardenoisian, Tissue,
  Villanovan, Water

Cumbersome Clumsy, Heavy, Lumbering, → UNWIELDY
Cunctator Dilatory
Cuneiform Wedge(d)
Cunning Arch, Art, Artifice, Astute, Cautel, Craft(y), Deceit, Deep, Devious, Down, Finesse, Foxy, Insidious, Leery, Machiavellian, Quaint, Skill, Slee(kit), Sleight, Slim, Sly(boots), Smart, Sneaky, Subtle, Vulpine, Wile
Cup(s), Cupped Aecidium, America's, Beaker, Bledisloe, Calcutta, Calix, Calyculus, Cantharus, Chalice, Claret, Communion, Cotyle, Cruse, Cupule, Cyathus, Cylix, Davis, Demitasse, Deoch-an-doruis, Deuch-an-doris, Dish, Doch-an-dorach, Dop, Egg, European, FA, Fairs, Final, Fingan, Finjan, Fruit, Gemma, Glenoid, Goblet, Grace, Grease, Hanap, Horn, Kylix, Loving, Melbourne, Merry, Monstrance, Moustache, Mug, Noggin, Nut, Pannikin, Parting, Planchet, Plate, Poley, Posset, Pot, Procoelous, Quaff, Quaich, Quaigh, Rhyton, Rider, Ryder, Sangrado, Scyphus, Sippy, Stem, Stirrup, Tantalus, Tass(ie), Tastevin, Tazza, Tea-dish, Tig, Tot, → TROPHY, Tyg, UEFA, Volva, Waterloo, World
Cup-bearer Ganymede, Hebe
Cupboard Airing, Almery, Almirah, A(u)mbry, Beauf(f)et, Cabinet, Chiffonier, Chiff(o)robe, Closet, Coolgardie safe, Court, Credenza, Dresser, Fume, Livery, Locker, Meat-safe, Press, Walk-in
Cup-holder Hanaper, Hebe, Plinth, Saucer, Zarf, Zurf
Cupid Amoretto, Amorino, Archer, Blind, Cherub, Dan, Eros, Love, Putto
Cupola Belfry, Dome, Tholos
Cup-shaped Poculiform
Cur Dog, Messan, Mongrel, Mutt, Pi-dog, Scab, Scoundrel, Whelp, Wretch, Yap
Curare, Curari Ourali, Poison, Wourali
Curassow Crax
Curate Barman, Minister, Nathaniel, Padré, Perpetual, Priest
Curator Aquarist
Curb Bit, Brake, Bridle, Check, Clamp, Coaming, Dam, Edge, Puteal, Rein, Restrain, Rim, Snub, Well
Curd(s) Bean, Cheese, Junket, Lapper(ed)-milk, Lemon, Skyr, Tofu
Curdle Clot, Congeal, Earn, Erne, Lopper, Posset, Ren, Rennet, Run, Set, Sour, → TURN, Whig, Yearn
Cure(d), Curative Ameliorate, Amend, Antidote, Antirachitic, Bloater, Cold turkey, Dry-salt, Dun, Euphrasy, Fix, Ginseng, Heal, Hobday, Hydropathy, Jadeite, Jerk, Kipper, Laetrile, Medicinal, Nature, Nostrum, Panacea, Park-leaves, Prairie oyster, → PRESERVE, Reast, Recover, Recower, Reest, Re(i)st, Relief, Remede, Remedy, Restore, Salt, Salve, Serum, Smoke, Smoke-dry, Tan, → TREATMENT, Tutsan, Water
▷ **Cure** *may indicate an anagram*
Curfew Bell, Gate, Prohibit, Proscribe
Curie Ci
Curio, Curiosity, Curious Agog, Bibelot, Freak, Inquisitive, Into, Meddlesome, Nos(e)y, Objet d'art, Objet de vertu, Odd, Peculiar, Prurience, Rarity, Rum, → STRANGE, Wondering
▷ **Curious(ly)** *may indicate an anagram*
Curium Cm
Curl(s), Curler, Curling, Curly Bev, Bonspiel, Cirrus, Coil, Crimp, Crimple, Crinkle, Crisp, Crocket, Dildo, Earlock, Frisette, Friz(z), Frizzle, Heart-breaker, Hog, Inwick, Kiss, Leaf, Loop, Love-lock, Outwick, Perm, Pin, Quiff, Repenter, Ringlet, Roll, Roulette, Scroll, Shaving, Spiral, Spit, Tong, Trunk, Twiddle, → TWIST,

Ulotrichous, Undée, Wave, Wind

Curlew Bird, Whaup, Whimbrel

Curmudgeon Boor, Churl, Grouch, Route, Runt

Currant Berry, Flowering, Raisin, Rizard, Rizzar(t), Rizzer

Currency Cash, Circulation, → **COIN**, Coinage, Decimal, Euro, Finance, Fractional, Jiao, Kip, Koruna, Monetary, → **MONEY**, Prevalence, Reserve, Soft

▷ **Currency** *may indicate* a river

Current Abroad, AC, Actual, Alternating, Amp(ere), Amperage, California, Canary, Contemporaneous, Cromwell, Dark, DC, Direct, Draught, Drift, Dynamo, Ebbtide, Eddy, Electric, El Nino, Emission, Equatorial, Euripus, Existent, Flow, Foucault, Galvanic(al), Going, Gyre, Headstream, Humboldt, Hummock, I, Immediate, Inst, Intermittent, Japan, Kuroshio, Labrador, Maelstrom, Millrace, Modern, Newsy, North Atlantic, Now, Ongoing, Output, Peru, Present, Prevalent, Pulsating, Race, Rapid, Rife, Rip, Roost, Running, Stream, Thames, Thermal, Thermionic, Tide, Tideway, Topical, Torrent, Turbidity, Underset, Undertow, Updraught

Curriculum Core, Cursal, National, Programme

Curry Bhuna, Brush, Comb, Cuittle, Dhansak, Fawn, Groom, Ingratiate, Korma, Madras, Spice, Tan, Tandoori, Turmeric, Vindaloo

Curse Abuse, Anathema, Badmouth, Ban, Bane, Beshrew, → **BLASPHEME**, Blast, Chide, Dam(me), Damn, Dee, Drat, Ecod, Egad, Excommunicate, Execrate, Heck, Hex, Hoodoo, Imprecate, Jinx, Malgre, Malison, Maranatha, Mau(l)gré, Mockers, Moz(z), Mozzle, Nine (of diamonds), Oath, Paterson's, Pize, Plague, Rant, Rats, Scourge, 'Snails, Spell, Swear, Upbraid, Weary, Winze, Wo(e)

Cursive Estrang(h)elo, Run

Cursor Mouse, Turtle

Cursorily, Cursory Casual, Hasty, Lax, Obiter, Passing, Perfunctory, Sketchy, Speedy, Superficial

Curt Abrupt, Blunt, Crusty, Laconic, Offhand, Short, Snappy

Curtail(ment) Abate, Apocope, Crop, Cut, Reduce, Shorten

Curtain(s), Curtain raiser, Curtain-rod Air, Arras, Backdrop, Bamboo, Canopy, Casement, Caudle, Cloth, Cyclorama, Death, Demise, Drape, Drop, Dropcloth, Dropscene, Fatal, Hanging, Iron, Lever de rideau, Louvre, Net, Pall, Portière, Purdah, Safety, Scene, Screen, Scrim, Shower, Tab, Tableau, Tormentor, Tringle, Upholstery, Vail, Valance, Veil, Vitrage, Window

Curtsey Bob, Bow, Dip, Dop, Honour

Curve(d), Curvaceous, Curvature, Curving, Curvy Adiabatic, Aduncate, Anticlastic, Apophyge, Arc, Arch, Archivolt, Assurgent, Axoid, Bend, Bezier, Bight, Bow, Brachistochrone, Camber, Cardioid, Catacaustic, Catenary, Caustic, Characteristic, Chordee, Cissoid, Conchoid, Contrapposto, Crescent, Cycloid, Demand, Diacaustic, Dogleg, Entasis, Epicycloid, Epinastic, Epitrochoid, Ess, Evolute, Exponential, Extrados, Felloe, Felly, Folium, French, Gaussian, Geodesic, Gooseneck, Growth, Hance, Harmonogram, Helix, Hodograph, Hollow-back, Hook, Hyperbola, Hypocycloid, Inswing, Intrados, Isochor, J, Jordan, Kyphosis, Laffer, Learning, Lemniscate, Limacon, Liquidus, Lituus, Lordosis, Loxodrome, Normal, Nowy, Ogee, Parabola, Phillips, Pothook, Pott's disease, Pulvinate, Reclinate, Record, Rhumb, RIAA, Roach, Rondure, Rotundate, Scoliosis, Sheer, Sigmoid flexure, Sinuate, Sinusoid, Slice, Spiral, Spiric, Strophoid, Supply, Survival, Swayback, Synclastic, Tautochrone, Tie, Tractrix, Trajectory, Trochoid, Tumble-home, Twist, Undulose, U-turn, Volute, Witch (of Agnesi)

Cushion(s) Air, Allege, Bolster, Buffer, Bustle, Frog, Ham, Hassock, Kneeler, → **PAD**, Pillow, Pin, Pouf(fe), Pulvillus, Scatter, Soften, Squab, Upholster, Whoopee

Cusp Horn, Spinode, Tine

Custard (apple) Crème caramel, Flam(m), Flan, Flaune, Flawn, Flummery, Pastry, Pa(w)paw, Zabaglione

Custodian, Custody Care, Claviger, Guard, Hold, Janitor, Keeping, Protective, Sacrist, Steward, Trust, Ward

Custom(ised), Customs (officer), Customary Agriology, Coast-waiters, Consuetude, Conventional, Couvade, Dedicated, De règle, Dhamma, Dharma, Douane, Exciseman, Familiar, Fashion, Folklore, → HABIT, Land-waiter, Lore, Manner, Montem, Mores, Nomic, Octroi, Ordinary, Practice, Praxis, Relic, Rite, Routine, Rule, Sororate, Spanish, Sunna, Tax, Thew, Tidesman, Tide-waiter, Tikanga, Time-honoured, Tradition, Unwritten, Usance, Used, Usual, Won, Wont, Woon, Zollverein

Customer Client, Cove, Patron, Prospect, Purchaser, Shillaber, Shopper, Smooth, Stiff, Trade, Trick, Ugly

Cut(ter), Cutting Abate, Abjoint, Ablate, Abridge, Abscission, Abscond, Acute, Adeem, Adze, Aftermath, Ali Baba, Amputate, Apocope, Axe, Bang, Bisect, Bit, Bite, Bowdlerise, Boycott, Brilliant, Broach, Caesarean, Caique, Canal, Cantle, Caper, Carver, Castrate, Caustic, Censor, Chap, Cheese, Chisel, Chopper, Chynd, Circumscribe, Cleaver, Clinker-built, Clip, Colter, Commission, Concise, Coppice, Coulter, Coupé, Crew, Crop, Cruel, Cube, Culebra, Curtail, Deadhead, Decrease, Dedekind, Dicer, Die, Director's, Discide, Disengage, Dismember, Dissect, Division, Divorce, Dock, Dod, Edge, Edit, Emarginate, Embankment, Engraver, Entail, Entayle, Epistolary, Epitomise, Eschew, Estrepe, Excalibur, Excide, Excise, Exscind, Exsect, Exude, Fashion, Fell, Filet mignon, Fillet, Flench, Flense, Flinch, Form, Froe, Frow, Gaillard, Garb, Gash, Go-down, Grater, Graven, Gride, Gryde, Hack, Handsaw, Hew(er), Ignore, Incision, Incisor, Indent, Intersect, Jigsaw, Joint, Junk, Kerf, Kern, Kirn, Lacerate, Lance, Leat, Lesion, Lin, Lop, Math, Medaillon, Microtome, Milling, Minimise, Mohel, Mortice, Mortise, Mower, Nache, Nick, Not, Notch, Nott, Occlude, Omit, Open, Operate, Osteotome, Oxyacetylene, Padsaw, Pare, Pink, Plant, Pliers, Ploughshare, Poll, Pollard, Pone, Power, Precisive, Press, Proin, Quota, Race, Rake off, Rase, Razor, Reap, Rebate, Reduction, Re-enter, Resect, Retrench, Revenue, Ring, Ripsaw, Roach, Rose, Rout, Saddle, Sarcastic, Sarky, Saw(n), Scarf, Scathing, Scion, Scission, Scissor, Score, Scrap, Sculpt, Scye, Scythe, Secant, Secateurs, Sect, Section, Sever, Sey, Share(out), Shaver, Shears, Shingle, Ship, Shive, Shorn, Short, Shred, Shun, Sickle, Side, Sirloin, Skin, Skip, Slane, Slash, Slicer, Slip, Slit, Sloop, Sned, Snee, Snib, Snick, Snip, Snub, Spade, Speedy, Spin, Spud, Steak, Stencil, Stereotomy, Stir, Stramac, Stramazon, Strimmer®, Style, Surgeon, Swath(e), Tailor(ess), Tap, Tart, Tenderloin, Tenotomy, Tomial, Tomium, Tonsure, Tooth, Topside, Transect, Trash, Trench, Trenchant, Trepan, Trim, Truant, Truncate, Urchin, Whang, Whittle, Winey

▷ **Cut** *may indicate* an anagram
▷ **Cutback** *may indicate* a reversed word

Cute Ankle, Pert, Pretty, Taking

Cuticle Epidermis, Eponychium, Periplast, Pleuron, Skin

Cut in Interpose, Interrupt

Cutlass Machete, Sword

Cutlery Canteen, Flatware, Fork, Knife, Setting, Silver, Spoon, Sunbeam, Tableware, Trifid

Cutlet Schnitzel

Cut off Elide, Enisle, Estrange, Inisle, Insulate, Intercept, → ISOLATE, Lop, Prune

Cut-throat Razor, Ruinous

Cuttlebone, Cuttlefish Octopus, Pen, Polyp(e)s, Polypus, Sea-sleeve, Sepia, Sepiost(aire), Sepium, Squid

CV Biodata

Cyanide Acrylonitrile, Nitrile, Potassium, Prussiate

Cycad Coontie, Coonty

Cyclamen Sow-bread

Cycle, Cyclist, Cycling Anicca, Arthurian, Bike, Biorhythm, Business, Cal(l)ippic, Calvin, Carbon, Carnot, Cell, Circadian, Citric acid, Closed, Daisy, Diesel, Eon, Era, Fairy, Four-stroke, Freewheel, Frequency, Geological, Gigahertz, Heterogony, Hydrologic, Indiction, Keirin, Ko, Krebs, Life, Light-year, Lunar, Madison, Metonic, Moped, Nitrogen, Oestrus, Orb, Otto, Pedal, Peloton, Period, Product life, Rankine, Repulp, Revolution, Ride, Roadster, Rock, Rota, Round, Samsara, Saros, Scorch, Series, Sheng, Solar, Song, Sonnet, Sothic, Spin, Sunspot, TCA, Trade, Trick, Trike, Turn, UCI, Urea, Vicious, Water, Wheeler, Wheelman, Wu

Cyclone Cockeye(d) bob, Storm, Tornado, Typhoon, Willy-willy

Cyclops Arges, Arimasp(i), Brontes, Polyphemus, Steropes

Cylinder, Cylindrical Air, Clave, Column, Drum, Licker-in, Magic, Master, Pipe, Pitch, Roll, Rotor, Slave, Spool, Steal, Stele, Swift, Terete, Torose, Treadmill, Tube, Vascular

Cymbal(s) High-hat, Hi-hat, Zel

Cynic(al) Crab, Diogenes, Doubter, Hard-bitten, Hard-boiled, Menippus, Pessimist, Sardonic, Sceptic, Thersites, Timon

Cynosure Centre, Focus

Cynthia Artemis, Moon

Cypress Bald, Lawson's, Leyland(ii), Monterey, Retinospora, Swamp, Tree

Cypriot Enosis, Eoka

Cyst Atheroma, Bag, Blister, Chalazion, Dermoid, Hydatid, Impost(h)ume, Meibomian, Ranula, Sac, Sebaceous, Vesicle, Wen

Czechoslovakia(n) CZ, Moravian, Sudetenland

Dd

D Daughter, Delta, Died, Edh, Eth, Penny

Dab(s) Bit, Daub, Fish, Flounder, Pat, Print, Ringer, Smear, Spot, Stupe, Whorl

Dabble(r) Amateur, Clatch, Dally, Dilettante, Plouter, Plowter, Potter, Smatter, Splash, Stipple, Trifle

Dachshund Teckel

Dactyl Anapaest

Dad(dy) Blow, Dev(v)el, Father, Generator, Hit, Male, Pa(pa), Pater, Polt, Pop, Slam, Sugar, Thump

Daddy-longlegs Crane-fly, Jennyspinner, Leather-jacket, Spinning-jenny, Tipula

Daffodil Asphodel, Jonquil, Lent-lily, Narcissus

Daft Absurd, Crazy, Potty, Ridiculous, Silly, Simple, Stupid

Dag Jag, Pierce, Pistol, Prick, Stab, Tag, Wool

Dagger(s) An(e)lace, Ataghan, Baselard, Bayonet, Bodkin, Crease, Creese, Da(h), Diesis, Dirk, Double, Dudgeon, Han(d)jar, Hanger, Jambiya(h), Katar, Khanjar, Kindjahl, Kirpan, Kreese, Kris, Lath, Misericord(e), Obelisk, Obelus, Poi(g)nado, Poniard, Pugio, Puncheon, Pusser's, Quillon, Rondel, Sgian-dubh, Skean, Skene(-occle), Spanish, Stiletto, Swordbreaker, Whiniard, Whinyard, W(h)inger, Yatag(h)an

Dahlia Cosmea

Daily Adays, Char, Circadian, Cleaner, Diurnal, Domestic, Guardian, Help, Journal, Mail, Mirror, Mrs Mopp, Paper, Per diem, Quotidian, Rag, Regular, Scotsman, Sun, Tabloid

Dainty Cate(s), Cute, Delicacy, Elegant, Elfin, Entremesse, Entremets, Exquisite, Genty, Junket, Lickerish, Liquorish, Mignon(ne), Minikin, → **MORSEL**, Neat, Nice, Particular, Petite, Pussy, Sunket, Twee

Dairy Creamery, Loan, Parlour

Dairymaid Dey, Patience

Dais Estate, Machan, Platform, Podium, Pulpit, Stage, Tribune

Daisy African, Barberton, Bell, Felicia, Gerbera, Gowan, Hen and chickens, Livingstone, Marguerite, Marigold, Michaelmas, Moon, Ox-eye, Ragweed, Shasta, Transvaal, Vegetable sheep

Dale(s) Dell, Dene, Dingle, Glen, Nidder, Ribbles, Swale, Vale, Valley, Wensley, Wharfe, Yorkshire

Dally Coquet(te), Dawdle, Finger, Flirt, Play, Spoon, Sport, Toy, Trifle, Wait

Dam An(n)icut, Arch, Aswan, Aswan High, Bar, Barrage, Barrier, Block, Boulder, Bund, Cabora Bassa, Cauld, Check, Gravity, Hoover, Kariba, Kielder, Ma, Mangla, Mater, Obstacle, Obstruct, Pen, Sennar, Stank, → **STEM**, Sudd, Tank, Three Gorges, Turkey nest, Volta River, Weir, Yangtze

Damage(d), Damages, Damaging Appair, Bane, Banjax, Bruise, Buckle, Charge, Chip, Collateral, Contuse, Cost, Cripple, Dent, Desecrate, Detriment, Devastate, Devastavit, Distress, Estrepe, Exemplary, Fault, Flea-bite, Foobar, Fubar,

Fuck up, Harm, Havoc, Hedonic, Hit, Hole, Hurt, Impair, Injury, Insidious, Loss, Mar, Mayhem, Moth-eaten, Mutilate, Nobble, Opgefok, Pair(e), Prang, Price, Punitive, Ratten, Ravage, Retree, Sabotage, Scaith, Scath(e), Scotch, Scratch, Skaith, Smirch, Solatium, → **SPOIL**, Tangle, Tear, Tigger, Toll, Value, Vandalise, Violate, Wear and tear, Wing, Wound, Wreak, Wreck, Write off

▷ **Damage(d)** *may indicate* an anagram

Dambuster Ondatra

Dame Crone, Dowager, Edna, Gammer, Lady, Matron, Nature, Naunt, Partlet, Peacherino, Sis, Title(d), Trot, Woman

Damn(ation), Damned Accurst, Attack, Blame, Condemn, Curse, Cuss, D, Darn, Dee, Execrate, Faust, Hell, Hoot, Jigger, Malgre, Perdition, Predoom, Sink, Swear, Tarnal, Tarnation, Tinker's, Very

Damp(en), Damping Aslake, Black, Blight, Check, Clam(my), Dank, Dewy, Fousty, Fusty, Humid, Moist, Muggy, Raw, Rheumy, Rising, Roric, Soggy, Sordo, Sultry, Unaired, Viscous, → **WET**, White

Damper Barrier, Check, Dashpot, Killjoy, Mute, Sordino, Sourdine

Damsel Girl, Lass, Maiden, Wench

Damson Plumdamas

Dan Box, Cupid, Leno, Olivetan, Scuttle, Tribe

Dance(r), Dancing Astaire, Baladin(e), Ballabile, Ballant, Ballerina, Ballroom, Bayadère, Bob, Body-popping, Caper, Chorus-girl, Cinderella, Comprimario, Contredanse, Corybant, Coryphee, Dervish, Diaghilev, Dinner, Dolin, Exotic, Figurant, Foot, Gandy, Gigolo, Hetaera, Hetaira, Hoofer, Kick-up, Knees-up, Leap, Maenad, Modern, Nautch-girl, Night, Nijinsky, Nod, Nureyev, Oberek, Old-time, Partner, Pavlova, Petipa, Pierette, Prom(enade), Raver, Ring, St Vitus, Salome, Saltatorious, Skipper, Spring, Step, Strut, Table, Tea, Terpsichore, Thé dansant, Tread, Trip(pant), Vogue(ing), Whirl

DANCES

3 letters:	Clog	Polo	Ceroc®
Bop	Dump	Rain	Conga
Fan	Fado	Reel	Disco
Gig	Folk	Rope	Fling
Hay	Frug	Sand	Furry
Hey	Giga	Shag	Galop
Hop	Go-go	Slam	Ghost
Ice	Haka	Spin	Gigue
Jig	Hora	Spot	Glide
Lap	Hula	Stag	Gopak
Pas	Jive	Taxi	Horah
Poi	Jota	Wire	Limbo
Sun	Juba		Loure
Tap	Juke	*5 letters:*	Mambo
Toe	Kolo	Bamba	Mooch
War	Line	B and S	Natch
	Lion	Belly	Paspy
	Loup	Bogle	Pavan
4 letters:	Mosh	Brawl	Paven
Alma	Nach	Break	Pavin
Ball	Pogo	Carol	Polka
Barn			

Ragga
Robot
Round
Rueda
Rumba
Salsa
Samba
Shake
Skank
Skirt
Snake
Stomp
Sword
Tango
Torch
Truck
Twist
Valse
Volta
Waltz

6 letters:
Almain
Apache
Ballet
Bolero
Boogie
Boston
Branle
Bubble
Canary
Can-can
Cha-cha
Fading
Floral
German
Hustle
Jump-up
Kathak
Lavolt
Maxixe
Minuet
Morris
Pavane
Redowa
Shimmy
Smooch
Square
Trophe
Valeta
Veleta

Waggle

7 letters:
Bambuca
Beguine
Bourrée
Bransle
Brantle
Cantico
Capuera
Carioca
Coranto
Cossack
Country
Courant
Csardas
Farruca
Forlana
Foxtrot
Furlana
Gavotte
Halling
Hoe-down
Lambada
Lancers
Landler
Lavolta
Macabre
Mazurka
Measure
Moresco
Morisco
Morrice
Moshing
One-step
Pericon
Planxty
Polacca
Pyrrhic
Ridotto
Ringlet
Romaika
Roundel
Roundle
Routine
Sardana
Sashaya
Shuffle
Tanagra
Tordion
Toyi-toy

Trenise
Two-step
Ziganka

8 letters:
Alegrias
Boogaloo
Bunnyhop
Bunnyhug
Cachucha
Cakewalk
Canticoy
Capoeira
Chaconne
Cotillon
Courante
Egg-dance
Excuse-me
Fandango
Flamenco
Flip-flop
Galliard
Habanera
Hay-de-guy
Haymaker
Headbang
Hey-de-guy
Heythrop
Hoolican
Hornpipe
Hula-hula
Irish jig
Joncanoe
Junkanoo
Kantikoy
Kapa haka
Kazachok
Kazatzka
Lindy hop
Macarena
Marinera
Matachin
Medicine
Merengue
Murciana
Orchesis
Reindeer
Rigadoon
Robotics
Ronggeng
Saraband

Snowball
Soft-shoe
Taglioni
Trucking

9 letters:
Allemande
Bergamask
Bergomask
Bossanova
Caballero
Cha-cha-cha
Chipaneca
Cotillion
Ecossaise
Eightsome
Farandole
Formation
Gallopade
Hoolachan
Jitterbug
Kathakali
Malaguena
Pas de deux
Paso doble
Passepied
Paul Jones
Polonaise
Poussette
Quadrille
Quickstep
Ring-shout
Roundelay
Siciliana
Siciliano
Sink-a-pace
Tambourin
Tripudium
Variation
Zapateado

10 letters:
Antimasque
Breakdance
Carmagnole
Charleston
Cinderella
Cinque-pace
Corroboree
Gay Gordon's
Hay-de-guise

Hay-de-guyes
Hey-de-guise
Hey-de-guyes
Hokey-cokey
Passamezzo
Petronella
Rug-cutting
Saltarello
Seguidilla
Sicilienne
Sinke-a-pace
Strathspey
Tarantella
Tripudiate
Turkey trot

Tyrolienne
Walk-around

11 letters:
Antistrophe
Black bottom
Buck and wing
Cracovienne
Eurhythmics
Lambeth walk
Palais glide
Passacaglia
Pastourelle
Progressive
Schottische

Shimmy-shake
Varsovienne

12 letters:
Bharat Natyam
Labanotation
Passemeasure
Passy-measure
Virginia reel

13 letters:
Highland fling
Virginian reel

14 letters:
Divertissement
Jack-in-the-green

15 letters:
Soft shoe shuffle

16 letters:
Circassian circle

18 letters:
Sir Roger de
Coverley

Dance hall Disco, Palais

Dance movement Arabesque, Balancé, Battement, Batterie, Brisé, Chassé, Dos-à-dos, Dosido, Entrechat, Fishtail, Fouetté, Glissade, Jeté, Lassu, Pantalon, Pas de basque, Pas de chat, Pas seul, Pigeonwing, Pirouette, Plié, Poule, Poussette, Routine, Sauté, Step

Dance tune Toy

▷ **Dancing** *may indicate* an anagram

Dancing party Ball, Ridotto

Dandelion Kok-saghyz, Piss-a-bed, Scorzonera, Taraxacum

Dander Anger, Gee, Passion, Saunter, Temper

Dandle Dance, Doodle, Fondle, Pet

Dandruff Furfur, Scurf

Dandy Adonis, Beau, Blood, Boulevardier, Buck(een), Cat, Coxcomb, Dapper, → **DUDE**, Exquisite, Fantastico, Fop, Gem, Jay, Jessamy, Johnny, Kiddy, Knut, Lair, Macaroni, Masher, Modist, Monarcho, Muscadin, Nash, Nut, Posh, Puss -gentleman, Roy, Smart, Spark, Spiff, Swell, Ted, Toff, U, Yankee-doodle

Dandy-horse Draisene, Draisine

Dane(s) Clemence, Dansker, Ogier, Ostmen

Danger(ous) Apperil, Breakneck, Chancy, Crisis, Dic(e)y, Dire, Dodgy, Emprise, Fear, Hairy, Hazard, Hearie, High-risk, Hot, Insecure, Jeopardy, Lethal, Menace, Mine, Nettle, Nocuous, Objective, Parlous, Periculous, → **PERIL**, Pitfall, Plight, Precarious, Quicksand, Risk, Serious, Severe, Snag, Snare, Tight, Tight spot, Trap, Wonchancy

Dangle A(i)glet, Aiguillette, Critic, Flourish, Hang, Loll, Swing

Daniel Dan, Defoe, Deronda, Lion-tamer, Portia, Quilp

Dank Clammy, Damp, Humid, Moist, Wet, Wormy

Daphne Agalloch, Agila, Eaglewood, Lace-bark, Laura, Laurel, Mezereon

Dapper Dressy, Natty, Neat, Smart, Spiff, Spruce, Sprush, Spry, → **TRIM**

Darbies Cuffs, Irons, Snaps

Dare, Dare-devil, Daring Adventure, Audacious, Bold, Brave, Challenge, Courage, Dan, Da(u)nton, Defy, Durst, Emprise, Face, Gallant, Gallus, Hardihood, Hazard, Hen, Intrepid, Moxie, Neck, Prowess, Racy, Stuntman, Swashbuckler, Taunt, Venture

Dark(en), Darkie, Darkness Aphelia, Aphotic, Apophis, Black, Blind, Byronic, Cimmerian, Cloud, Colly, Depth, Dim, Dingy, Dirk(e), Dusky, Eclipse, Erebus, Evil, Gloom, Glum, Inky, Inumbrate, Jet, Kieran, Mare, Maria, Melanous, Mulatto,

Murk(y), Negro, Night, Obfuscate, Obscure, Ominous, Ousel, Ouzel, Pall, Phaeic, Pitch-black, Pit-mirk, Rooky, Sable, Sad, Secret, Shades, Shady, Shuttered, Sinister, Solein, Sombre, Sooty, Sphacelate, Stygian, Sullen, Swarthy, Tar, Tenebr(i)ous, Tenebrose, Unfair, Unlit, Wog, Woosel, Yellowboy, Yellowgirl

Darling Acushla, Alannah, Asthore, Beloved, Charlie, Cher, Chéri(e), Chick-a-biddy, Chick-a-diddle, Chuck-a-diddle, Dear, Dilling, Do(a)ting-piece, Duck(s), Favourite, Grace, Honey, Idol, Jarta, Jo(e), Lal, Love, Luv, Mavourneen, Mavournin, Minikin, Minion, Oarswoman, Own, Peat, Pet, Poppet, Precious, Sugar, Sweetheart, Yarta, Yarto

Darn Begorra, Blow, Doggone, Hang, Mend, Repair, Sew

Dart(s), Darter Abaris, Arrow, Banderilla, Dace, Dash, Deadener, Dodge, Fleat, Fléchette, Flirt, Flit, Harpoon, Javelin, Launch, Leap, Scoot, Shanghai, Skrim, Speck, Spiculum, Sprint, Strike, Thrust, Wheech

Dash(ing), Dashed Backhander, Bally, Blade, Blight, Blow, Buck, Charge, Collide, Cut, Dad, Dah, Damn, Dapper, Dart(le), Daud, Dawd, Debonair, Ding, Dod, Elan, En, Fa(s)cia, Flair, Fly, Go-ahead, Hang, Hurl, → **HURRY**, Hustle, Hyphen, Impetuous, Jabble, Jaw, Jigger, Lace, Line, Minus, Modicum, Morse, Natty, Nip, Panache, Pebble, Race, Rakish, Ramp, Rash, Rule, Run, Rush, Sally, Scamp(er), Scapa, Scarper, Scart, Scoot, Scrattle, Scurry, Scuttle, Shatter, Showy, Soupçon, Souse, Spang, Speed, Splash, Splatter, Sprint, Strack, Streak, Stroke, → **STYLE**, Swung, Throw, Touch, Viretot

Dashboard Fascia

Dashwood Hell-fire club

Dastard(ly) Base, Coward, Craven, Nid(d)erling, Poltroon

Data(base), Datum Archie, Cyberspace, Donne(e), Evidence, Facts, Fiche, File, Floating-point, Gen, HOLMES, Info, Input, Material, Matrix, Newlyn, News, Ordnance, Read-out, Soft copy, Triple

Date(d), Dates, Dating AD, Age, AH, Almanac, Appointment, Blind, Boyfriend, Calendar, Carbon, Carbon-14, Computer, Court, Deadline, Engagement, Epoch, Equinox, Era, Escort, Exergue, Expiry, Fission-track, Fixture, Girlfriend, Ides, Julian, Meet, Outmoded, → **OUT OF DATE**, Passé, Past, Radioactive, Radio-carbon, Radiometric, Rubidium-strontium, See, System, → **TRYST**, Ult(imo), Value

Daub Begrime, Blob, Dab, Gaum, Mess, Moil, Noint, Plaister, Plaster, → **SMEAR**, Smudge, Splodge, Teer, Wattle

Daughter (in law) Child, D, Elect, Girl, Jephthah's, Niece, Offspring, Skevington's

Daunt Adaw, Amate, Awe, Deter, Dishearten, Intimidate, Overawe, Quail, Stun, Stupefy, Subdue

Dauphin Delphin

David Dai, Psalmist

Davit Crane, Derrick, Hoist

Davy Crockett, Jones

Daw Bird, Magpie, Margery

Dawdle(r) Dally, Draggle, Drawl, Idle, Lag(gard), → **LOITER**, Potter, Shirk, Slowcoach, Tarry, Troke, Truck

Dawn(ing) Aurora, Cockcrow, Daw, Daybreak, Daylight, Day-peep, Dayspring, Enlightenment, Eoan, Eos, False, Light, Morrow, Occur, Prime, Roxane, Sparrowfart, Start, Sunrise, Ushas

Day(s) Account, Ahemeral, All Fools', All Hallows', All Saints', All Souls', Anniversary, Annunciation, Anzac, April Fool's, Armistice, Ascension, Australia, Bad hair, Baker, Banian, Barnaby, Bastille, Borrowing, Boxing, Broad, Calendar, Calends, Calpa, Canada, Canicular, Civil, Columbus, Commonwealth, Contango,

Continental, D, Daft, Date, Decoration, Degree, Distaff, Dog, Dominion, Double, Duvet, Early, Ember, Empire, Epact, Fast, Fasti, Father's, Feast, Ferial, Field, Flag, Fri, Gang, Gaudy, Groundhog, Guy Fawkes', Halcyon, High, Hogmanay, Holy, Holy Innocents', Holy-rood, Hundred, Ides, Inauguration, Independence, Intercalary, Judgment, Juridical, Kalends, Kalpa, Labo(u)r, Lady, Laetare, Lammas, Last, Law(ful), Lay, Leap, Mardi, Market, May, Memorial, Michaelmas, Midsummer, Mon, Morrow, Mother's, Muck-up, Mufti, Mumping, Name, Ne'erday, New Year's, Nones, Nychthemeron, Oak-apple, Octave, Open, Orangeman's, Pancake, Paper, Pay, Poppy, Post, Pound, Present, Press(ed), Primrose, Pulvering, Quarter, Rag, Rainy, Red-letter, Remembrance, Rent, Rest, Robin, Rock, Rogation, Rood(-mas), Rosh Chodesh, Sabbath, Saint's, St Swithin's, St Thomas's, St Valentine's, Salad, Sat, Scambling, Settling, Shick-shack, Show, Sidereal, Snow, Solar, Solstice, Speech, Sports, Station, Sun, Supply, Tag, Term, Thanksgiving, Thurs, Ticket, Time, Transfer, Trial, Triduum, Tues, Twelfth, Utas, Valentine's, Varnishing, VE, Veterans', Victoria, Visiting, VJ, Waitangi, Wed, Wedding, Working

Daybreak Cockcrow, Cockleert

Daydream(er), Daydreaming Brown study, Castle(s) in the air, Dwam, Dwaum, Fancy, Imagine, Muse, Reverie, Rêveur, Walter Mitty, Woolgathering

Daylight Artificial, Dawn, Space, Sun

Daze(d) Amaze, Bemuse, Confuse, Dwaal, Gally, Muddle, Muzzy, Petrify, Punch drunk, Reeling, Spaced out, → STUN, Stupefy, Stupor, Trance

Dazzle(d), Dazzling Bewilder, Blend, Blind, Eclipse, Foudroyant, Glare, Meteoric, Outshine, Radiance, Resplendent, Splendour, Yblent

Deacon Cleric, Doctor, Minister

Deactivate Unarm

Dead(en) Abrupt, Accurate, Alamort, Asgard, Asleep, Blunt, Brown bread, Bung, Cert, Cold, Complete, D, Deceased, Defunct, Doggo, Expired, Extinct, Gone(r), Inert, Infarct, Late, Lifeless, Morkin, Muffle, Mute, Napoo, Niflheim, Numb, Obsolete, Obtund, Ringer, She'ol, Slain, Smother, Stillborn, True, Utter, Waned

Dead end, Deadlock Blind alley, Cut-off, Dilemma, Impasse, Logjam, Stalemate, Stoppage

Dead-leaf colour Filemot, Philamot, Philomot

Deadline Date, Epitaph, Limit

Deadlock Stand-off, Sticking-point

Deadly Baleful, Dull, Fell, Funest, Internecine, → LETHAL, Malign, Mortal, Mortific, Pestilent, Thanatoid, Unerring, Venomous

Deadly nightshade Belladonna, Dwale

Deadpan Expressionless

Dead reckoning Dr

Dead tree Rampick, Rampike

Deaf(en), Deafness Adder, Asonia, Deave, Deeve, Dunny, Heedless, Paracusis, Presbyc(o)usis, Surd(ity)

Deal(er), Dealing(s), Deal with Address, Agent, Agreement, Allot(ment), Arb, Arbitrageur, Bargain, Breadhead, Brinjarry, Broker, Business, Cambist, Chandler, Chapman, Commerce, Cope, Coup, Cover, Croupier, Dispense, Distributor, Do, Dole, Eggler, Exchange, Fripper, Goulash, Hand(le), Help, Inflict, Insider, Interbroker, Jiggery-pokery, Jobber, Lashing, Lay on, Lay out, Lot, Manage, Mercer, Merchant, Mickle, Middleman, Monger, Mort, Negotiate, New, Operator, Package, Pine, Plain, Productivity, Pusher, Raft, Raw, Red, Sale, Serve, Side, Sort, Spicer, Square, Stockist, Stockjobber, Takeover, Tape, Timber, Totter, Tout(er), → TRADE, Traffic, Transaction, Treat, Truck, Wheeler, White, Wholesaler,

Wield, Woolstapler, Yardie

Dean Acheson, Arabin, Colet, Decani, Doyen, Forest, Head, Inge, Nellie, Provost, RD, Rural, Rusk, Slade, Spooner, Swift, Vale, Vicar-forane, V rev

Dear(er), Dearest, Dear me Ay, Bach, Beloved, Cara, Caro, Cher(e), Cherie, Chou, Chuckie, Darling, Duck(s), Expensive, High, Honey(bun), Lamb, Leve, Lief, Lieve, Loor, Love, Machree, Mouse, My, Pet, Pigsney, Pigsnie, Pigsny, Steep, Sweet, Sweetie, Toots(ie), Up

Dearth Famine, Lack, Paucity, Scantity, Scarcity, → SHORTAGE

Deaspiration Psilosis

Death(ly) Auto-da-fe, Bane, Bargaist, Barg(h)est, Biolysis, Black, Cataplexis, Charnel, Clinical, Cot, Curtains, Cypress, Demise, Departure, Dormition, End, Eschatology, Euthanasia, Exit, Extinction, Fatality, Funeral, Fusillation, Gangrene, Grim Reaper, Hallal, Heat, Infarction, Jordan, Karoshi, Lead colic, Lethee, Leveller, Living, Loss, Mors, Napoo, Necrosis, Nemesis, Night, Obit, Quietus, Reaper, Sati, Sergeant, SIDS, Small-back, Strae, Sudden, Suttee, Terminal, Thanatism, Thanatology, Thanatopsis, Thanatos

Death-flood Styx

Deathless(ness) Athanasy, Eternal, Eterne, Immortal, Struldberg, Timeless, Undying

Debacle Cataclysm, Collapse, Disaster, Fiasco

Debag Dack

Debar Deny, Exclude, Forbid, → PREVENT, Prohibit

Debase(d) Adulterate, Allay, Bemean, Cheapen, Corrupt, Demean, Depreciate, Dialectician, Dirty, Grotesque, Hedge, Lower, Pervert, Traduce, Vitiate

Debate Argue, Combat, Contention, Contest, Deliberate, Dialectic, Discept, Discourse, Discuss(ion), → DISPUTE, Flyte, Forensics, Full-dress, Moot, Paving, Polemics, Powwow, Reason, Teach-in, Warsle, Wrangle, Wrestle

Debauch(ed), Debauchee, Debauchery Corrupt, Decadent, Defile, Degenerate, Dissipate, Dissolute, Heliogabalus, Libertine, Licence, Orgy, Profligate, Raddled, Rake-hell, Riot, Roist, Royst, Seduce, Spree, Stuprate, Wet, Whore

Debenture Bond, Security

Debilitate(d), Debility Asthenia, Atonic, Cachexia, Feeble, Languid, Weak

Debit Charge, Debt, Direct

Debonair Cavalier, Gay, Gracious, Jaunty

Debris Bahada, Bajada, Detritus, Eluvium, Moraine, Moslings, Refuse, → RUBBLE, Ruins, Shrapnel, Tel, Tephra, Waste, Wreckage

▷ **Debris** *may indicate* an anagram

Debt(or) Abbey-laird, Alsatia, Arrears, Arrestee, Bonded, Dr, Due, Floating, Funded, Insolvent, IOU, Liability, Moratoria, National, Obligation, Oxygen, Poultice, Public, Queer Street, Score, Subordinated, Tie, Unfunded

Debt-collector Bailiff, Forfaiter, Remembrancer

Debut Launch, Opening, Outset, Presentation

Debutante Bud, Deb

Decade Rosary, Ten

Decadence, Decadent Babylonian, Decaying, Degeneration, Dissolute, Effete, Fin-de-siècle, Libertine

Decamp Abscond, Absquatulate, Bolt, Bunk, Depart, Flee, Guy, Levant, Mizzle, Slide, Slope, Vamoose

Decant Pour, Unload

Decapitate, Decapitation Aphesis, → BEHEAD, Guillotine

▷ **Decapitated** *may indicate* first letter removed

Decay(ed), Decaying Alpha, Appair, Beta, Biodegrade, Blet, Canker, Caries, Caseation, Consenescence, Crumble, Decadent, Declension, Decline, Decompose, Decrepit, Dieback, Disintegrate, Dissolution, Doat, Doddard, Doddered, Dote, Dricksie, Druxy, Dry rot, Fail, F(o)etid, Forfair, Gangrene, Heart-rot, Impair, Moulder, Pair(e), Perish, Plaque, Putrefy, Radioactive, Ret, Rot, Saprogenic, Sap-rot, Seedy, Sepsis, Spoil, Tabes, Thoron, Wet-rot

Decease(d) Death, Decedent, Demise, Die, Stiff

Deceit(ful), Deceive(r) Abuse, Artifice, Bamboozle, Barrat, Befool, Bitten, Blind, Bluff, Braide, → **CHEAT**, Chicane, Chouse, Con, Cozen, Cuckold, Defraud, Deke (out), Delude, Diddle, Dissemble, Do brown, Double-cross, Double-tongued, Dupe, Duplicity, False(r), Fastie, Fast-talk, Fiddle, Flam, Fool, Four-flusher, Fox, Fraud, Gag, Gerrymander, Gloze, Guile, Gull, Hoax, Hoodwink, Hornswoggle, Humbug, Hype, Illusion, Imposition, Inveigle, Invention, Jiggery-pokery, Kid, Liar, Malengine, Mamaguy, Mata Hari, Mendacious, Mislead, Mislippen, Phenakism, Poop, Poupe, Pretence, Prevaricate, Punic, Rig, Ruse, Sell, Sham, Sinon, Sleekit, Snow job, Spruce, Stratagem, Subreption, Swindle, Swizzle, Tregetour, Trick, Trump, Two-faced, Two-time, Weasel, Wile

Decency, Decent Chaste, Decorum, Fitting, Healsome, Honest, Kind, Modest, Moral, Passable, Seemly, Sporting, Wholesome

Decentralise Disperse

Deception, Deceptive Artifice, Bluff, Catchpenny, Catchy, Cheat, Chicanery, Codology, → **DECEIT**, Disguise, Dupe, Duplicity, Eyewash, Fallacious, False, Flam, Fraud, Gag, Gammon, Guile, Gullery, Have-on, Hocus-pocus, Hokey-pokey, Hum, Hunt-the-gowks, Hype, Ignes-fatui, Ignis-fatuus, Illusion, Insidious, Kidology, Lie, Moodies, Phantasmal, Runaround, Ruse, Sell, Sleight, Smoke and mirrors, Specious, Sting, The moodies, → **TRICK**, Trompe l'oeil, Two-timing, Underhand

Decide(r), Decided, Decision, Decisive Addeem, Adjudge, Agree, A(r)re(e)de, Ballot, Barrage, Bottom-line, Cast, Clinch, Conclude, Conclusive, → **DECISION**, Deem, Definite, Determine, Distinct, Engrenage, Firm, Fix, Jump-off, Mediate, Opt, Parti, Predestination, Pronounced, Rescript, → **RESOLVE**, Result, Rule, Run-off, See, Settle, Split, Sudden death, Tiebreaker, Try

Decimal Mantissa, Recurring, Repeating, Terminating

Decimate Destroy, Lessen, Weaken

Decipher(ing) Cryptanalysis, Decode, Decrypt, Descramble, Discover, Interpret

▷ **Decipher(ed)** *may indicate* an 'o' removed

Decision Arbitrium, Arrêt, Crossroads, Crunch, Decree, Engrenage, Fatwa, Fetwa, Firman, Judg(e)ment, Placit(um), Referendum, Resolution, Resolve, Responsa, Ruling, Sentence, Sudden death, Verdict

Decisive Climactic, Clincher, Critical, Crux, Definite, Final, Pivotal

Deck Adorn, Array, Attrap, Bejewel, Boat, Cards, Clad, Daiker, Daub, Decorate, Dizen, Embellish, Equip, Flight, Focsle, Forecastle, Garland, Hang, Helideck, Hurricane, Lower, Main, Mess, Monkey poop, Orlop, Ornament, Pack, Pedestrian, Platform, Poop, Prim, Promenade, Quarter, Saloon, Spar, Sun, Tape, Upper, Void, Well

Declare, Declaration, Declaim, Decree Absolute, Affidavit, Affirm, Air, Allege, Announce, Annunciate, Aread, A(r)re(e)de, Assert, Asseverate, Aver, Avow, Balfour, Bann(s), Bayyan, Breda, Dictum, Diktat, Doom, Edict, Elocute, Enact, Fatwa(h), Fiat, Firman, Go, Grace, Harangue, Hatti-sherif, Independence, Indulgence, Insist, Interlocutory, Irade, Law, Mandate, Manifesto, Mecklenburg, Meld, Motu proprio, Mou(th), Nisi, Noncupate, Novel(la), Nullity, Nuncupate, Orate, Ordain, Order, Ordinance, Parlando, Pontificate, Predicate, Proclaim, Profess, Promulgate,

Pronounce, Protest, Psephism, Publish, Rant, Recite, Rescript, Resolve, Rights, Rule, Ruling, SC, Sed, Senatus consultum, Senecan, Shahada, Signify, Speak, Spout, State, Statutory, Testify, Testimony, UDI, Ultimatum, Unilateral, Vie, Voice, Vouch, Word

▷ **Declaring** *may indicate* a word beginning 'Im'

Decline, Declining Age, Ail, Atrophy, Catabasis, Comedown, Decadent, Degeneration, Degringoler, Deny, Descend, Deteriorate, Devall, Die, Diminish, Dip, Dissent, Downhill, Downtrend, Downturn, Droop, Dwindle, Ebb, Fade, Fall, Flag, Forbear, Paracme, Peter, Quail, Recede, Recession, Refuse, Retrogression, Rot, Rust, Sag, Senile, Set, Sink, Slide, Slump, Stoop, Twilight, Wane, Welke, → **WILT**, Withdraw, Wither

Decoct(ion) Apozem, Cook, Devise, Ptisan, Tisane

Decode(d) En clair

Decolleté Low, Neckline

Decompose, Decomposition Biodegradable, Crumble, Decay, Disintegrate, Hydrolysis, Mor, Pyrolysis, Rot, Wither

Decompression Bends

Decor Background, Scenery

Decorate(d), Decoration, Decorative Adorn, Angelica, Aogai, Arpillera, Attrap, Award, Bargeboard, Baroque, Beaux-arts, Bedizen, Biedermeier, Bordure, Braid, Brattishing, Braze, Brooch, Cartouche, Centrepiece, Chambranle, Champlevé, Chinoiserie, Christingle, Cinquefoil, Cloissoné, Coffer, Cresting, Crocket, Cul-de-lampe, Daiker, Decoupage, Dentelle, Diamante, Doodad, Dragée, Dragging, Emblazon, Emboss, Embrave, Engrail, Enrich, Epergne, Etch, Fancy, Festoon, Filigree, Finery, Finial, Fleuret(te), Fleuron, Floriated, Flushwork, Fluting, Fourragère, Frieze, Frill, Frog, Frost, Furbish, Gammadion, Garniture, Gaud, Gild, Glitter, Goffer, Gradino, Grecque key, Grotesque, Guilloche, Historiated, Ice, Illuminate, Impearl, Inlay, Intarsia, Intarsio, Interior, Knotwork, Leglet, Linen-fold, Linen-scroll, Marquetry, MC, Medal(lion), Mola, Motif, Moulding, Oath, OBE, Order, → **ORNAMENT**, Ornate, Orphrey, Overglaze, Ovolo, Paint, Paper, Parament, Pâté-sur-pâté, Photomural, Pinata, Pipe, Pokerwork, Polychromy, Pompom, Prettify, Prink, Purfle, Purple heart, Quilling, Rag-rolling, Rangoli, Repoussé, Rich, Rosemaling, Ruche, Scallop, Schwarzlot, Scrimshander, Scrimshaw, Serif, Set-off, Sgraffito, Skeuomorph, Soutache, Spangle, Staffage, Stomacher, Storiated, Strapwork, Studwork, Tailpiece, Tattoo, TD, Titivate, Tool, Topiary, Trim, Veneer, Vergeboard, Wallpaper, Well-dressing, Wirework

Decorous, Decorum Becoming, Demure, Etiquette, Fitness, Parliamentary, Prim, → **PROPER**, Propriety, Sedate, Seemlihe(a)d, → **SEEMLY**, Staid

Decoy Allure, Bait, Bonnet, Button, Call-bird, Coach, Crimp, Entice, Lure, Piper, Roper, Ruse, Shill, Stale, Stalking-horse, Stool-pigeon, Tice, Tole, Toll, Trap, Trepan

Decrease Decrew, Diminish, Dwindle, Iron, Lessen, Press, Ramp down, Reduce, Rollback, Slim, Step-down, Subside, Wane, Wanze

Decree → **DECLAIM**, Saw

Decrepit Dilapidated, Doddery, Failing, Feeble, Frail, Moth-eaten, Time-worn, Tumbledown, Warby, Weak

Decry Condemn, Crab, Denounce, Derogate, Detract, Downgrade

Dedicate(d), Dedication Corban, Devote, Dinah, Endoss, Hallow, Inscribe, Oblate, Pious, Sacred, Single-minded, Votive

Deduce, Deduction, Deductive A priori, Assume, Conclude, Consectary, Corollary, Derive, Discount, Dockage, Gather, Illation, Infer(ence), Natural, Obvert,

Off-reckoning, Reason, Rebate, Recoup, Reprise, Stoppage, Surmise, Syllogism

Deed(s) Achievement, Act(ion), Atweel, Backbond, Back letter, Charta, Charter, Derring-do, Disposition, Escrol(l), Escrow, Exploit, Fact(um), Feat, Indeed, Indenture, Manoeuvre, Mitzvah, Muniments, Premises, Settlement, Specialty, Starr, → **TITLE**, Trust

Deem Consider, Judge, Opine, Ordain, Proclaim, Repute, Think

Deep(en), Deeply Abstruse, Bass(o), Brine, Briny, Enhance, Excavate, Grum, Gulf, Hadal, Intense, Low, Mindanao, Mysterious, → **OCEAN**, Profound, Re-enter, Rich, Sea, Sonorous, Throaty, Upsee, Ups(e)y

Deep-rooted Inveterate

Deer(-like) Axis, Bambi, Barasing(h)a, Barking, Blacktail, Brocket, Buck, Cariacou, Caribou, Carjacou, Cervine, Chevrotain, Chital, Doe, Elaphine, Elk, Fallow, Gazelle, Hart, Hog, Jumping, Moose, Mouse, Mule, Muntjac, Muntjak, Musk, Père David's, Pricket, Pudu, Pygarg, Red, Rein, Roe, Rusa, Sambar, Sambur, Selenodont, Sika, Sorel(l), Spade, Spay(d), Spayad, Spitter, Spottie, Stag(gard), Tragule, Ungulate, Virginia, Wapiti, Water, White-tailed

Deer-hunter Tinchel

Deface Disfigure, Spoil

▷ **Defaced** *may indicate* first letter missing

Defame, Defamatory, Defamation Abase, Bad mouth, Blacken, Calumny, Cloud, Denigrate, Detract, Dishonour, Impugn, Libel, Malign, Mud, Mudslinging, Obloquy, Sclaunder, Scurrilous, Slander, Smear, Stigmatise, Traduce, Vilify

Default(er) Absentee, Bilk, Dando, Delinquent, Flit, Levant, Neglect, Omission, Waddle, Welsh

Defeat(ed), Defeatist Beat, Best, Caning, Capot, Codille, Conquer, Counteract, Debel, Defeasance, Demolish, Discomfit, Dish, Ditch, Donkey-lick, Fatalist, Floor, Foil, Foyle, Hammer, Hiding, Kippered, Laipse, Lick, Loss, Lurch, Marmelize, Master, Mate, Moral, Negative, Out, Outclass, Outdo, Outplay, Outvote, Outwit, → **OVERCOME**, Overpower, Overreach, Overthrow, Overwhelm, Pip, Plaster, Quitter, Reverse, Rout, Rubicon, Scupper, Set, Shellacking, Sisera, Skunk, Squabash, Stump, Tank, Thrash, Thwart, Tonk, Trounce, Vanquish, War, Waterloo, Whap, Whip, Whitewash, Whop, Whup, Wipe-out, Worst

Defecate, Defecation Horse, Mute, Poop, Scumber, Shit, Skummer, Tenesmus

Defect(ion), Defective, Defector Abandon, Amateur, Apostasy, Bug, Coma, Crack, Crawling, Deficient, Failing, Faulty, Flaw, → **FORSAKE**, Frenkel, Halt, Hamartia, Kink, Low, Manky, Mass, Mote, Natural, Paralexia, Point, Psellism, Rachischisis, Renegade, Renegate, Ridgel, Ridgil, Rig, Rogue, Runagate, Schottky, Shortcoming, Spina bifida, Terrace, Treason, Trick, Want, Weakness, Wreath

Defence, Defend(er), Defensible, Defensive Abat(t)is, Alexander, Alibi, Antibody, Antidote, Antihistamine, Apologia, Back, Back four, Bailey, Barbican, Barmkin, Barricade, Bastion, Battery, Battlement, Berm, Bestride, Bridgehead, Bulwark, Calt(h)rop, Catenaccio, CD, Champion, Chapparal, Civil, Curtain, Demibastion, Ditch, Embrasure, Goalie, Hedgehog, Herisson, Hold, J(i)u-jitsu, Justify, Kaim, Keeper, Laager, Laer, Last-ditch, Libero, Linebacker, Maginot-minded, Maintain, Martello tower, MIDAS, Moat, Motte and bailey, Muniment, Outwork, Palisade, Parapet, Pentagon, Perceptual, Propugnation, Protect, Rampart, Redan, Redoubt, Resist, Ringwall, → **SHELTER**, Shield, Stonewall, Strategic, Support, Sweeper, Tenable, Tenail(le), Testudo, Tower, Trench, Trou-de-loup, Uphold, Vallation, Vallum, Vindicate, Wall, Warran(t), Zonal

Defenceless Helpless, Inerm, Naked, Sitting duck, Vulnerable

Defendant Accused, Apologist, Respondent, Richard Roe

Defer(ence), Deferential, Deferring Bow, Complaisance, Delay, Dutiful, Homage, Moratory, Morigerous, Obeisant, Pace, Polite, Postpone, Procrastinate, Protocol, Respect, Shelve, Submit, Suspend, Waive, Yield

Defiance, Defiant, Defy Acock, Bold, Brave, Contumacy, Dare, Daring, Disregard, Do or die, Outbrave, Outdare, Rebellion, Recusant, Resist, Stubborn, Titanism, Truculent, Unruly

Deficiency, Deficient Absence, Acapnia, Anaemia, Beriberi, Defect, Inadequate, Incomplete, Kwashiorkor, Lack, Osteomalacia, Scant, Scarcity, SCID, Shortage, Shortfall, Spanaemia, Want

▷ **Deficient** *may indicate* an anagram

Deficit Anaplerotic, Arrears, Defective, Ischemia, Loss, Poor, Shortfall

Defile(ment) Abuse, Array, Barranca, Barranco, Besmear, Col, Conspurcation, Desecrate, Dishonour, Donga, Enseam, → **FOUL**, Gate, Gorge, Gully, Inquinate, Inseem, Kloof, Moil, Pass, Pollute, Poort, Ravine, Ray, Roncesvalles, Smear, Spoil, → **SULLY**

Define(d), Definition, Definitive Decide, Demarcate, Determine, Diorism, Distinct, Explain, Fix, Limit, Parameter, Set, Tangible, Term

Definite(ly) Classic, Clear, Deffo, Emphatic, Firm, Hard, Indeed, Pos, Positive, Precise, Specific, Sure, Yes

Deflate Burst, Collapse, Flatten, Lower, Prick, Puncture

Deflect(or), Deflection Avert, Bend, Detour, Diverge, Divert, Glance, Holophote, Otter, Paravane, Refract, Snick, Swerve, Throw, Trochotron, Veer, Windage

Deform(ed), Deformity Anamorphosis, Blemish, Crooked, Disfigure, Distort, Gammy, Hammer-toe, Harelip, Misborn, Mishapt, Mooncalf, Mutilate, Phocomelia, Phocomely, Polt-foot, Saddle-nose, Stenosed, Talipes, Valgus, Varus, Warp

▷ **Deformed** *may indicate* an anagram

Defraud Bilk, Cheat, Cozen, Gull, Gyp, Mulct, Shoulder, Sting, Swindle, Trick

Defray Bear, Cover, Meet

Defrost Thaw

Deft Adept, Agile, Dab, Dexterous, Elegant, Handy, Nimble

Defunct Deceased, Extinct, Obsolete

▸ **Defy** *see* **DEFIANCE**

Degenerate, Degeneration, Degenerative Acorn-shell, Ascidian, Atrophy, Balanus, Base, Cirrhipedea, Cirrhipedia, Cirrhopod(a), Cirripedea, Cirripedia, Decadent, Deprave, Descend, Deteriorate, Eburnation, Effete, Fatty, Kaliyuga, Necrobiosis, Pejorate, Pervert, Rakehell, Relapse, Retrogress, Salp, Tunicate

Degrade, Degradation Abase, Cheapen, Culvertage, Debase, Demission, Demote, Depose, Diminish, Disennoble, Embase, Humble, Imbase, Imbrute, Lessen, Lower, → **SHAME**, Waterloo

Degree(s) Aegrotat, As, Attila (the Hun), Azimuthal, BA, Baccalaureate, BCom, BD, B es S, C, Class, D, Desmond (Tutu), Doctoral, Double first, Douglas (Hurd), Engler, Extent, External, F, First, Geoff (Hurst), German, Gradation, Grade, Grece, Gree(s), Greece, Gre(e)se, Grice, Griece, Grize, → **IN A HIGH DEGREE**, Incidence, K, Lambeth, Latitude, Letters, Level, Levitical, Licentiate, Longitude, MA, Measure, Mediant, Nth, Nuance, Order, Ordinary, Pass, Peg, PhD, Pin, Poll, Rate, Remove, Second, Stage, Status, Step, Submediant, Subtonic, Supertonic, Third, Trevor (Nunn), Water

Dehiscence Suture

Dehydrate(d) Exsiccate, Thirsty

Deification, Deify Apotheosis

Deign Condescend, Stoop

Deity Avatar, Cabiri, Demogorgon, Divine, Faun, → **GOD**, → **GODDESS**, Idolise, Immortalise, Krishna, Numen, Pan, Satyr, Zombi(e)

Deject(ed), Dejection Abase, Abattu, Alamort, Amort, Blue, Chap-fallen, Crab, Crestfallen, Despondent, Dismay, Dispirited, Down, Downcast, Gloomy, Hangdog, Humble, Melancholy

Delay(ed) Adjourn(ment), Ambage, Avizandum, Behindhand, Check, Cunctator, Defer, Demurrage, Detention, Fabian, Filibuster, For(e)slow, Forsloe, Frist, Hesitate, Hinder, Hitch, Hold up, Hysteresis, Impede, Laches, Lag, Late, Laten, Let, Linger, Loiter, Mora(torium), Obstruct, Pause, Procrastinate, Prolong, Prorogue, Remanet, Reprieve, Respite, Retard, Setback, Slippage, Sloth, Slow, → **STALL**, Stand-over, Stay, Stonewall, Suspend, Temporise, Wait

Delectable Delicious, Luscious, Tasty

Delegate, Delegation Agent, Amphictyon, Apostolic, Appoint, Assign, Decentralise, Depute, Devolution, Mission, Nuncio, Offload, Representative, Secondary, Transfer, Vicarial, Walking

Delete Cancel, Cut, Erase, Excise, Expunge, Purge, Rase, Scratch, Scrub, Strike, Twink out

Deliberate(ly) Adagio, Consider, Debate, Intentional, Meditate, Moderate, Muse, Overt, Ponder, Prepensely, Ruminate, Studied, Voulu, Weigh, Witting

Delicacy, Delicate Airy-fairy, Beccafico, Blini, Canape, Cate, Caviare, Dainty, Difficult, Discreet, Ectomorph, Eggshell, Elfin, Ethereal, Fastidious, Filigree, Fine, Finespun, Finesse, Flimsy, Fragile, → **FRAIL**, Friand, Gossamer, Guga, Hothouse, Inconie, Incony, Kickshaw, Kidglove, Ladylike, Light, Lobster, Morbidezza, Nesh, Nicety, Niminy-piminy, Ortolan, Oyster, Pastel, Reedy, Roe, Sensitive, Soft, Subtle(ty), Sunket, Sweetmeat, Taste, Tender, Tenuous, Ticklish, Tidbit, Titbit, Truffle

Delicious Ambrosia, Delectable, Exquisite, Fragrant, Goloptious, Goluptious, Gorgeous, Lekker, Lip-smacking, Mor(e)ish, Mouthwatering, Scrummy, Scrumptious, Tasty, Toothsome, Yummo, Yummy, Yum-yum

▷ **Delight** *may indicate* 'darken'

Delight(ed), Delightful Bewitch, Bliss, Charm, Chuff, Delice, Dreamy, Edna, Elated, Elysian, Enamour, Enjoyable, Enrapture, Exuberant, Felicity, Fetching, Frabjous, Gas, Glad, Glee, Gratify, Honey, Joy, Nice, Overjoy, Over the moon, Please, Pleasure, Precious, → **RAPTURE**, Regale, Revel, Scrummy, Super, Taking, Tickle, Turkish, Whacko, Whee, Whoopee, Wizard, Yippee, Yum-yum

Delineate Draft, Sketch, Trace

Delinquent Bodgie, Criminal, Halbstarker, Juvenile, Negligent, Offender, Ted

Delirious, Delirium Deranged, DT, Fever, Frenetic, Frenzy, Insanity, Mania, Phrenetic, Phrenitis, Spaced out, Spazz, Wild

Deliver(ance), Deliverer, Delivery(man) Accouchement, Ball, Birth, Bowl, Breech, Caesarean, Consign, Convey, Courier, Deal, Doosra, Drop, Elocution, Escape, Express, Extradition, Give, Jail, Lead, Liberate, Lob, Orate, Over, Pronounce, Receipt, Recorded, Redeem, Release, Relieve, Render, Rendition, → **RESCUE**, Rid, Round(sman), Salvation, Save, Say, Seamer, Sell, Shipment, Speak, Special, Tice, Transfer, Underarm, Underhand, Utter, Wide, Yorker

Dell Dale, Dargle, Dene, Dimble, Dingle, Dingl(e)y, Glen, Valley

Delphic Pythian

Delphinium Larkspur

Delta Camargue, D, Del, Flood-plain, Kronecker, Nabla, Nile, Oil Rivers, Triangle

Delude, Delusion Bilk, Cheat, Deceive, Fallacy, Fool, Hoax, Megalomania,

→ **MISLEAD**, Paranoia, Schizothymia, Trick, Zoanthropy

Deluge Avalanche, Flood, Ogygian, Saturate, Submerge, → **SWAMP**

De luxe Extra, Plush, Special

Delve Burrow, Dig, Excavate, Exhume, Explore, Probe, Search

Demagogue Agitator, Fanariot, Leader, Mobsman, Phanariot, Speaker, Tribune

Demand(ing) Appetite, Call, Claim, Cry, Dun, Exact, Excess, Exigent, Fastidious, Final, Hest, → **INSIST**, Mandate, Market, Need, Order, Postulate, Pressure, Request, Requisition, Rush, Sale, Stern, Stipulate, Stringent, Summon, Ultimatum, Want

Demean(ing) Belittle, Comport, Debase, Degrade, Humble, Infra dig, Lower, Maltreat

Demeanour Air, Bearing, Conduct, Expression, Front, Gravitas, Mien, Port, Presence

Dement(ed) Crazy, Hysterical, Insane, Mad, Wacko

Demi-god Aitu, Daemon, Garuda, Hero

Demi-mondaine Cocotte, → **LOOSE WOMAN**, Prostitute

Demise Death, Decease, Finish

Demo March, Parade, Protest, Rally, Sit-in

Democracy, Democrat, Democratic D, Hunker, Industrial, Liberal, Locofoco, Menshevik, Montagnard, People's, Popular, Republic, Sansculotte, Social, Tammany

Demoiselle Crane, Damselfish

Demolish, Demolition Bulldoze, Devastate, Devour, Dismantle, Floor, KO, Level, Rack, → **RAZE**, Smash, Tear down, Wreck

▶ **Demon** *see* **DEVIL**

Demoness Lilith

Demonstrate, Demonstration, Demonstrator Agitate, Barrack, Display, Endeictic, Evénement, Evince, Explain, Hunger march, Maffick, Manifest, March, Morcha, Ostensive, Peterloo, Portray, Protest, Prove, Provo, Send-off, → **SHOW**, Sit-in, Touchy-feely, Vigil

Demoralize Bewilder, Corrupt, Destroy, Shatter, Unman, Weaken

Demote, Demotion Comedown, Degrade, Disbench, Disrate, Embace, Embase, Reduce, Relegate, Stellenbosch

Demur Hesitate, Jib, Object

Demure Coy, Mim, Modest, Prenzie, Primsie, Sedate, Shy

Den Dive, Domdaniel, Earth, Hell, Hide-away, Holt, Home, Lair, Lie, Lodge, Opium, Room, Shebeen, Study, Sty, Wurley

Denial, Deny, Denier Abnegate, Antinomian, Aspheterism, Bar, Contradict, Controvert, Démenti, Disavow, Disenfranchise, Disown, Forswear, → **GAINSAY**, Nay, Negate, Nick, Nihilism, Protest, Refuse, Refute, Renague, Renay, Reneg(e), Renegue, Reney, Renig, Renounce, Reny, Repudiate, Sublate, Traverse, Withhold

Denigrate Besmirch, Blacken, Defame, Tar

Denim Jeans

Denizen Diehard, Inhabitant, Resident

Denomination Category, Cult, Sect, Variety

Denote Import, Indicate, Mean, Signify

Denouement Anagnorisis, Catastrophe, Climax, Coda, Exposure, Outcome, Showdown

Denounce, Denunciation Ban, Commination, Condemn, Criticise, Decry, Delate, Diatribe, Fulminate, Hatchet job, Hereticate, Proclaim, Proscribe, Shop, Stigmatise, Thunder, Upbraid

Denry Card

Dense, Density Charge, Compact, Critical, Current, D, Double, Firm, Flux, Intense, Neutral, Opaque, Optical, Packing, Reflection, Relative, Single, Solid, Spissitude, Tesla, Thick, Transmission, Vapour, Woofy

Dent(ed) Batter, Concave, Dancette, Depress, Dimple, Dinge, Dint, Nock, V

Dental, Dentist(ry) DDS, Entodontics, Extractor, Kindhart, LDS, Odontic, Periodontic, Toothy

Dentures Biteplate, Bridge, Bridgework, False teeth, Plate, Prosthodontia, Store teeth, Wallies

▶ **Deny** see **DENIAL**

Deodorant Anti-perspirant, Roll-on

Deoxidise Outgas, Reduce

Depart(ed), Departing, Departure Abscond, Absquatulate, Bunk, D, Dead, Decession, Defunct, Die, Digress, Divergence, Exit, Exodus, Flight, → **GO**, Leave, Lucky, Outbound, Rack off, Remue, Send-off, Vacate, Vade, Vamoose, Walkout

Department Achaea, Ain, Aisne, Allier, Alpes de Provence, Alpes-Maritimes, Angers, Arcadia, Ardeche, Ardennes, Argo, Argolis, Ariege, Arrondissement, Arta, Attica, Aube, Aude, Aveyron, Bas-Rhin, Belfort, Beziers, Bouches-du-Rhône, Branch, Bureau, Calvados, Cantal, Charente, Charente-Maritime, Cher, Commissariat, Corrèze, Cote d'Or, Cotes d'Armor, Cotes du Nord, Creuse, DEFRA, Deme, Deux-Sevres, Division, Dordogne, Doubs, Drôme, El(e)ia, Essonne, Eure, Eure-et-Loir, Faculty, Finistere, Fire, FO, Gard, Gers, Gironde, Greencloth, Guadeloupe, Gulag, Hanaper, Haute-Garonne, Haute-Loire, Haute-Marne, Haute-Normandie, Hautes-Alpes, Haute-Saône, Haute Savoie, Hautes-Pyrenees, Haute-Vienne, Haut-Rhin, Hauts-de-Seine, Herault, Home, Ille-et-Vilaine, Indre, Indre-et-Loire, Isere, Jura, Landes, Loire, Loiret, Loir-et-Cher, Lot, Lot-et-Garonne, Lozere, Maine-et-Loire, Manche, Marne, Mayenne, Meurthe-et-Moselle, Meuse, Ministry, Morbihan, Moselle, Nièvre, Nome, Nomos, Nord, Office, Oise, Orne, Pas-de-Calais, Province, Puy de Dôme, Pyrénées(-Atlantique), Pyrénées-Orientales, Region, Rehabilitation, Rhône, Sanjak, Saône-et-Loire, Sarthe, Savoie, Secretariat(e), Section, Seine-et-Marne, Seine Maritime, Seine St Denis, Somme, Sphere, State, Tarn(-et-Garonne), Treasury, Tuscany, Val de Marne, Val d'Oise, Var, Vaucluse, Vendée, Vienne, Voiotia, War, Wardrobe, Yonne, Yvelines

Depend(ant), Dependence, Dependency, Dependent Addicted, Child, Client, Colony, Conditional, Contingent, Count, Dangle, E, Fief, Habit, Hang, Hinge, Icicle, Lean, Minion, Pensioner, Relier, Rely, Retainer, Ross, Sponge, Statistical, Subject, Subordinate, Trust, Turn on, Vassal

Dependable Reliable, Reliant, Secure, Sheet-anchor, Solid, Sound, Staunch, Sure, → **TRUSTWORTHY**

Depict Delineate, Display, Draw, Limn, Paint, Portray, Present, Represent

Depilate, Depilatory Grain, Rusma, Slate

Deplete Diminish, Drain, Exhaust, Reduce

Deplorable, Deplore Base, Bemoan, Chronic, Complain, Deprecate, Dolorous, Grieve, Lament, Mourn, Piteous, Regret, Rue

Deploy(ment) Extend, Herse, Unfold, Use

▷ **Deploy(ment)** *may indicate* an anagram

Depopulate Deracinate

Deport(ation), Deportment Address, Air, Banish, → **BEARING**, Carriage, Demeanour, Mien, Renvoi, Renvoy, Repatriation

Depose, Deposition Affirm, Banish, Dethrone, Displace, Dispossess, Overthrow, Pieta, Testify

Deposit(s), Depository Aeolian, Alluvial, Alluvium, Aquifer, Arcus, Argol, Arles, Atheroma, Bank, Bathybius, Bergmehl, Calc-sinter, Calc-tuff, Caliche, Cave-earth, Coral, Crag, Delta, Depone, Diatomite, Diluvium, Drift, Evaporite, Fan, File, Firn, Fort Knox, Fur, Gyttja, Illuvium, Kieselguhr, Land, Laterite, Lay, Lay-by, Limescale, Lodge(ment), Loess, Löss, Measure, Moraine, Natron, Outwatch, Park, Pay dirt, Placer, Plank, Plaque, Precipitate, Put, Repose, Residuum, Saburra, Salamander, Saprolite, → **SEDIMENT**, Silt, Sinter, Sludge, Stockwork, Stratum, Surety, Tartar, Terramara, Terramare, Till, Time, Tophus, Tripoli, Turbidite

Depot Barracoon, Base, Camp, Depository, Station, Terminus, Treasure-city, Warehouse

Deprav(ed), Depravity Bestial, Cachexia, Cachexy, Caligulism, → **CORRUPT**, Dissolute, Evil, Immoral, Low, Reprobate, Rotten, Sodom, Total, Turpitude, Ugly, Vice, Vicious, Vile

Deprecate Censure, Deplore, Expostulate, Reproach

Depreciate Abase, Belittle, Derogate, Detract, Discount

Depredate, Depredation Pillage, Plunder, Rob

Depress(ed), Depressing, Depression Accablé, Agitated, Alamort, Alveolus, Amort, Astrobleme, Attrist, Black dog, Blight, Blue devils, Blues, Cafard, Caldron, Canada, Canyon, Chill, Col, Combe, Couch, Crab, Crush, Cyclone, Dampen, Deject, Dell, Demission, Dene, Dent, Despair, → **DIMPLE**, Dip, Dismal, Dispirit, Dolina, Doline, Doomy, Downlifting, Drear, Drere, Dumpish, Endogenous, Exanimate, Flatten, Fonticulus, Foss(ula), Fossa, Fovea, Frog, Geosyncline, Ghilgai, Gilgai, Gilgie, Glen, Gloom, Graben, Grinch, Ha-ha, Hammer, Heart-spoon, Hilar, Hilum, Hilus, Hollow, Howe, Hyp, Hypothymia, Joes, Kettle, Kick(-up), Lacuna, Leaden, Low(ness), Low-spirited, Megrims, Moping, Morose, Neck, Ocean basin, Pan, Pit, Polje, Postnatal, Prostrate, Qattara, Recession, Re-entrant, Retuse, Sad, Saddle, Sag, Salt-cellar, Salt-pan, Scrobicule, Sink, Sinkhole, Sinus, Sitzmark, Slot, → **SLUMP**, Slumpflation, Soakaway, Spiritless, Stomodaeum, Sump, Swag, Swale, Swallowhole, Trench, Trough, Umbilication, Vale, Vallecula, Valley, Wallow, Weigh down, Wet blanket

Deprivation, Deprive(d) Amerce, Bereft, Deny, Disenfranchise, Disfrock, Disseise, Disseize, Expropriate, Famine, Foreclose, Geld, Have-not, Hunger, Reduce, Remove, Rob, Sensory, Withhold

Depth Draught, Draw, F, Fathom, Gravity, Intensity, Isobath, Pit, Profundity

Deputise, Deputy Act, Agent, Aide, Assistant, Commis(sary), Delegate, Legate, Lieutenant, Locum, Loot, Mate, Number two, Prior, Proxy, Represent, Secondary, Sidekick, Standby, Sub, Subchanter, Substitute, Succentor, Surrogate, Vicar, Vice, Viceregent, Vidame

Derange(d) Craze, Détraqué, Disturb, Insane, Manic, Troppo, Unhinge, Unsettle

Derby Boot, Demolition, Donkey, Eponym, Hat, Kentucky, Kiplingcotes, Race, Roller

Derek Bo

Derelict Abandoned, → **DECREPIT**, Deserted, Negligent, Outcast, Ramshackle

Deride, Derision, Derisive Contempt, Gup, Guy, Hiss, Hoot, Jeer, Mock, Nominal, Pigs, Raspberry, → **RIDICULE**, Sardonic, Scoff, Scorn, Snifty, Snort, Yah, Ya(h)boo

Derive, Derivation, Derivative Amine, Ancestry, Creosote, Deduce, Descend, Extract, Get, Kinone, Of, Offshoot, Origin, Pedigree, Picoline, Secondary, Tyramine

▸ **Dermatitis** *see* **SKIN DISEASE**

Derogate, Derogatory Belittle, Decry, Defamatory, Demeaning, Detract, Discredit, Pejorative, Personal, Slighting, Snide

Deronda Daniel

Derrick Crane, Davit, Hoist, Jib, Spar, Steeve

Dervish Calender, Doseh, Mawlawi, Mevlevi, Revolver, Santon, Whirling
Descant Comment, Discourse, Faburden, Melody, Song
Descartes René
Descend(ant), Descent Ancestry, Avail, Avale, Bathos, Blood, Cadency, Catabasis, Chute, Cion, Decline, Degenerate, Derive, Dismount, Dive, Drop, Epigon, Extraction, Heir, Heraclid, → LINEAGE, Offspring, Pedigree, Posterity, Progeny, Prone, Rappel, Said, Say(y)id, Scarp, Scion, Seed, Shelve, Sien(t), Sink, Stock, Syen, Vest, Volplane
Describe, Description, Descriptive Blurb, Define, Delineate, Depict, Designate, Draw, Epithet, Exposition, Expound, Graphic, Job, Narrate, Outline, Paint, Portray, Rapportage, Recount, Relate, Report, Sea-letter, Signalment, Sketch, Specification, Synopsis, Term, Trace, Vignette, Write-up
▷ **Describing** *may indicate* 'around'
Descry Behold, Discern, Get, Notice, Perceive
Desecrate, Desecration Abuse, Defile, Dishallow, Profane, Sacrilege, Unhallow
▷ **Desecrated** *may indicate* an anagram
Desert(er), Deserted, Deserts Abandon, Absquatulate, Apostasy, Arabian, Arid, Ar Rimal, Arunta, Atacama, AWOL, Badland, Barren, Bledowska, Bug, Bunk, Colorado, Come-uppance, D, Dahna, Defect, Desolate, Dissident, Due, Empty, Eremic, Etosha Pan, Factious, Fail, Fezzan, Foresay, Forhoo, Forhow, Forlorn, Forsake, Forsay, Frondeur, Garagum, Gibson, Gila, Gobi, Great Basin, Great Indian, Great Sandy, Great Victoria, Heterodox, Indian, Jump ship, Kalahari, Kara Kum, Kavir, Kyzyl Kum, Libyan, Lurch, Meeds, Merit, Mohave, Mojave, Nafud, Namib, Negev, Nubian, Ogaden, Painted, Pategonian, Pindan, Rat, Refus(e)nik, Reg, → RENEGADE, Reward, Rub'al-Khali, Run, Runaway, Sahara, Sahel, Sands, Secede, Shamo, Simpson, Sinai, Sonoran, Sturt, Syrian, Tacna-Arica, Tergiversate, Thar, Turncoat, Ust(y)urt, Victoria, Void, Wadi, Waste, Western Sahara, Wilderness, Worthiness
Deserve(d) Condign, Earn, → MERIT, Rate, Well-earned, Worthy
Desiccate(d) Dry, Sere
Design(er) Adam, Aim, Arabesque, Architect, Armani, Ashley, Batik, Between-subjects, Broider, Calligram(me), Cardin, Cartoon, Castrametation, Chop, Cloisonné, Create, Cul de lampe, Damascene, Decal(comania), Decor, Deep, Depict, Devise, Dévoré, Dior, Draft, Embroidery, End, Engender, Engine(r), Engineer, Erté, Etch, Fashion, Feng-shui, Former, Hepplewhite, Hitech, Iconic, Impresa, Imprese, Industrial, Intend(ment), Intent(ion), Interior, Issigonis, Layout, Limit-state, Linocut, Logo, Marquetry, Mascle, Matched pairs, Mean, Meander, Mehndi, Millefleurs, Modiste, Monogram, Morris, Mosaic, Motif, Multifoil, Paisley, Pattern, → PLAN, Plot, Propose, Pyrography, Quant, Retro, Ruse, Schema, Scheme, Seal, Sheraton, Sketch, Specification, Stencil, Stubble, Stylist, Sunburst, Tatow, Tattoo, Tattow, Tatu, Think, Tooling, Trigram, Versace, Vignette, Watermark, Weiner, Werkstalte, Whittle, Within-subjects
Designate Earmark, Note, Style, Title
Desirable, Desire, Desirous Ambition, Appetite, Aspire, Avid, Best, Cama, Conation, Concupiscence, Covet, Crave, Cupidity, Dreamboat, Earn, Eligible, Epithymetic, Fancy, Gasp, Hanker, Hope, Hots, Hunger, Itch, Kama(deva), Le(t)ch, Libido, List, Long, Luscious, Lust, Mania, Nymphomania, Orectic, Owlcar, Pica, Plum, Reck, Request, Residence, Salt, Slaver, Streetcar, Thirst, Velleity, Vote, Wanderlust, Want, Whim, Will, Wish, Yearn, Yen
Desist Abandon, Cease, Curb, Pretermit, Quit, Stop
Desk Almemar, Ambo, Bonheur-du-jour, Bureau, Carrel(l), Cash, Check-in,

Cheveret, City, Copy, Davenport, Desse, Devonport, Enquiry, E(s)critoire, Faldstool, Lectern, Lettern, Litany, Pay, Pedestal, Prie-dieu, Pulpit, Reading, Roll-top, Scrutoire, Secretaire, Vargueno, Writing

Desman Pyrenean

Desolate, Desolation Bare, Barren, Desert, Devastate, Disconsolate, Forlorn, Gaunt, Godforsaken, Gousty, Moonscape, Waste, Woebegone

Despair, Desperate, Desperation Acharne, Anomy, De profundis, Despond, Dire, Dismay, Extreme, Frantic, Gagging, Giant, Gloom, Hairless, Headlong, Last-ditch, Last-gasp, Life and death, Reckless, Unhopeful, Urgent, Wanhope

▸ **Despatch** *see* **DISPATCH**

Desperado Bandit, Bravo, Ruffian, Terrorist

Despicable Abject, Base, Bleeder, Caitiff, Cheap, Churl, Contemptible, Heinous, Ignoble, Ignominious, Low-down, Mean, Moer, Poep(ol), Puke, Ratbag, Ratfink, Scumbag, Shabby, Toerag, Wretched

Despise Condemn, Contemn, Forhow, Hate, Ignore, Scorn, Spurn, Vilify, Vilipend

Despite For, Malgré, Notwithstanding, Pace, Though, Venom

Despoil Mar, Ravage, Vandalise

Despondent Dejected, Downcast, Forlorn, Gloomy, Sad

Despot(ism) Autarchy, Autocrat, Bonaparte, Caesar, Darius, Dictator, Napoleon, Nero, Satrap, Stratocrat, Tsar, Tyrant, Tzar

Dessert Afters, Baked Alaska, Baklava, Bavarian cream, Bavarois, Bombe, Charlotte, Charlotte russe, Clafoutis, Cobbler, Compote, Coupe, Crème brulée, Crème caramel, Dulce de leche, Entremets, Flummery, Fool, Granita, Junket, Kissel, Knickerbocker glory, Kulfi, Marquise, Mousse, Mud pie, Nesselrode, Pannacotta, Parfait, Pashka, Pavlova, Peach Melba, → **PUDDING**, Rasmalai, Sabayon, Sawine, Semifreddo, Shoofly pie, Split, Strudel, Sundae, Syllabub, Tartufo, Tiramisu, Tortoni, Trifle, Vacherin, Whip, Zabaglione

Destine(d), Destination Design, End, Fate, Foredoom, Goal, Home, Intend, Joss, Meant, Port, Purpose, Vector, Weird

Destiny Doom, → **FATE**, Karma, Kismet, Lot, Manifest, Moira, Yang, Yin

Destitute Bankrupt, Bare, Broke, Devoid, Dirt-poor, Helpless, Impoverished, Indigent, Needy, Penniless, Poor, Sterile, Void

Destroy(er) Annihilate, Antineutrino, Antineutron, Antiparticle, Apollyon, Atomise, Blight, Can, D, Decimate, Deep-six, Deface, Delete, Demolish, Denature, Destruct, Dish, Dismember, Dissolve, Eat, Efface, End, Eradicate, Erase, Estrepe, Exterminate, Extirpate, Flivver, Fordo, Graunch, Harry, Iconoclast, Incinerate, → **KILL**, KO, Murder, Obliterate, Overkill, Perish, Predator, Ravage, Raze, Ruin, Saboteur, Sack, Scuttle, Slash, Smash, Spif(f)licate, Spoil, Sterilize, Stew-can, Stonker, Stultify, Subvert, Trash, Undo, Uproot, Vandal, Vitiate, Waste, Whelm, Wreck, Zap

Destruction, Destructive Adverse, Autolysis, Bane, Can, Collapse, Deathblow, Deleterious, Devastation, Doom, Downfall, Ecocide, End, Götterdämmerung, Grave, Havoc, Holocaust, Insidious, Internecine, Kali, Lethal, Loss, Maleficent, Pernicious, Pogrom, Quelea, Rack, Ragnarok, Ravage, Sabotage, Speciocide, Stroy, Wrack

Desultory Aimless, Cursory, Fitful, Idle

Detach(ed), Detachment Abstract, Alienate, Aloof, Body, Calve, Clinical, Cut, Detail, Discrete, Insular, Isle, Isolate, Loose, Outlying, Outpost, Patrol, Picket, Picquet, Separate, Sever, Staccato, Stoic, Unfasten, Unhinge

Detached work Ravelin

Detail(s), Detailed Annotate, Dock, Elaborate, Embroider, Expatiate, Explicit,

Expound, Instance, → **ITEM**, Itemise, Minutiae, Nicety, Particular(ise), Pedantry, Point, Recite, Relate, Respect, Send, Spec, Special, Specification, Technicality
▷ **Detailed** *may indicate* last letter missing
Detain(ee), Detention Arrest, Buttonhole, Collar, Custody, Delay, Detinue, Gate, Glasshouse, Hinder, Intern, Keep, POW, Preventive, Retard, Stay, → **WITHHOLD**
Detect(or), Detective Agent, Arsène, Asdic, Bloodhound, Brown, Bucket, Busy, Catch, Chan, CID, Cuff, Dick, Discover, Divine, Doodlebug, Dupin, Espy, Eye, Fed, Find, Flambeau, Flic, Fortune, French, Geigercounter, Geophone, Gumshoe, Hanaud, Hercule, Holmes, Interpol, Investigator, Jack, Lecoq, Lupin, Maigret, Metal, Microwave, Mine, Minitrack®, Nail, Nose, Peeper, PI, Pinkerton, Plant, Poirot, Private, Private eye, Prodnose, Radar, Reagent, Rumble, Scent, Scerne, Sense, Sensor, Shadow, Shamus, Sherlock, → **SLEUTH**, Sleuth-hound, Sofar, Sonar, Sonobuoy, Spot, Tabaret, Take, Tec, Thorndyke, Toff, Trace, Trent, Vance, Wimsey, Yard
Detent Pawl, Trigger
Deter(rent) Block, Check, Daunt, Dehort, Delay, Dissuade, Prevent, Restrain, Turn-off
Detergent Cationic, Cleaner, Non-ionizing, Solvent, Surfactant, Syndet, Tepol, Whitener
Deteriorate, Deterioration Decadence, Degenerate, Derogate, Entropy, Pejoration, Rust, Worsen
▷ **Deterioration** *may indicate* an anagram
▷ **Determination** *may indicate* 'last letter'
Determine(d), Determination Arbitrament, Ardent, Ascertain, Assign, Assoil, Bent, Condition, Dead-set, → **DECIDE**, Define, Doctrinaire, Dogged, Do-or-die, Dour, Drive, Earnest, Fix, Govern, Grit(ty), Headstrong, Hell-bent, Indomitable, Influence, Intent, Judgement, Law, Liquidate, Out, Point, Pre-ordain, Purpose, Quantify, → **RESOLUTE**, Resolve, Rigwiddie, Rigwoodie, Self-will, Set, Settle, Shape, Stalwart, Steely, Type, Weigh
Detest(able) Abhor, Despise, Execrable, Execrate, Hate, Loathsome, Pestful, Vile
Detonate, Detonator Blast, Explode, Fire, Fuse, Fuze, Ignite, Kindle, Plunger, Primer, Saucisse, Saucisson, Tetryl, Trip-wire
Detour Bypass, Deviate, Divert
Detract Belittle, Decry, Diminish, Discount, Disparage
Detriment(al) Adverse, Damage, Harm, Injury, Loss, Mischief
Deuce Dickens, Old Harry, Twoer
Deuteron Diplon
Devalue Debase, Impair, Reduce, Undermine
Devastate Demolish, Destroy, Gut, Lay waste, Overwhelm, Ravage, Ruin, Sack, Traumatise, Waste, Wreck
Develop(er), Developed, Developing, Development Advance, Amidol®, Aplasia, Breakthrough, Breed, Bud, Build, Burgeon, Catechol, Creep, Educe, Elaborate, Enlarge, Epigenetic, Escalate, Evolve, Expand, Expatriate, Foetus, Full-fledged, Fulminant, Genesis, Germinate, Gestate, Grow, Hatch, Hothouse, Hydroquinone, Hypo, Imago, Improve, Incipient, Incubate, Lamarckism, Larva, Mature, Metamorphose, Metol, Morphogenesis, Morphosis, Mushroom, Nurture, Oidium, Ontogenesis, Pathogeny, Pullulate, Pupa, Pyro, Pyrogallol, Quinol, Ribbon, Ripe(n), Sarvodaya, Sensorimeter, Separate, Shape, Soup, Speciation, Sprawl, Subtopia, Technography, Teens, Tone, Unfold, Upgrow
▷ **Develop** *may indicate* an anagram
Deviant, Deviate, Deviation Aberrance, Abnormal, Anomaly, Average, Brisure,

Deflect, Depart, Derogate, Digress, Diverge, Divert, Error, Kinky, Kurtosis, List, Mean, Pervert, Quartile, Sheer, Solecism, Sport, Standard, Stray, Swerve, Transvestite, → **TURN**, Valgus, Varus, Veer, Wander, Wend

Device Allegory, → **APPARATUS**, Appliance, Artifice, Contraption, Contrivance, Deus ex machina, Dodge, Emblem, Expedient, Gadget, Gimmick, Gubbins, Instrument, Logo, Mnemonic, Motto, Pattern, Plan, Safeguard, → **STRATAGEM**, Subterfuge, Tactic, Tag, Thing, Trademark, Trick

DEVICES

3 letters:	Maser	Buzzer	Swivel
Bug	Meter	Charge	Temple
FET	Mixer	Chouri	Tipple
LED	Modem	Choury	Tracer
Mux	Mouse	Cotter	Tremie
Pad	Optic®	Cut-out	Triode
POP	Otter	Dasher	Trompe
Zip	Pager	Deckle	Turtle
	Petar	De-icer	Tympan
4 letters:	Prism	Detent	Viewer
Capo	Probe	Dimmer	Wafter
Drag	Quipu	Dongle	Walker
Fret	Relay	Elevon	Widget
Fuse	Rotor	Engine	Zapper
Gobo	Saser	Etalon	
Grab	Scale	Faller	*7 letters:*
Orle	Scart	Feeder	Bearing
Plug	Servo	Filter	Bendlet
Rest	Shear	Friend®	Bleeper
Shoe	Sieve	Imager	Chopper
Spur	Siren	Jigger	Cleaver
Stop	Snare	Joypad	Clicker
Tram	Sonde	Keeper	Compass
Trap	Spool	Kludge	Counter
	Sprag	Nanite	Coupler
5 letters:	SQUID	Petard	Dashpot
Audio	Stent	Pick-up	Digibox®
Balun	Timer	Pinger®	Divider
Chaff	Tromp	Possum	Doubler
Choke	Truss	Preset	Fuzzbox
Chuck	Valve	Quippu	Gas mask
Clamp	V-chip	Rabble	Genlock
Cleat	Waldo	Reverb	Gimbals
Cramp		Rocker	Grapnel
Crank	*6 letters:*	Roller	Hushkit
Diode	Analog	Router	Imprese
E-nose	Atlatl	Selsyn	Inhaler
Frame	Beeper	Sensor	Isotron
Gizmo	Biodot	Shaker	Jetpack
Gland	Blower	Stoner	Krytron
Input	Bungee	Switch	Lighter

Machine
Minicom
Monitor
Pelorus
Pessary
Pickoff
Plunger
Ratchet
Reactor
Roll-bar
Rotator
Rowlock
Scanner
Shut-off
Shutter
Shuttle
Sniffer
Snorkel
Snuffer
Sounder
Spoiler
Starter
Stinger
Storage
Sundial
Swatter
Synchro
Toaster
Tokamak
Tonepad
Vernier
Vocoder

8 letters:
Airscoop
Alcolock
Analogue
Anti-icer
Atomiser
Autodial
Ballcock
Barostat
Betatron
Bootjack
Calutron
Commutor
Conveyor
Coupling
Demister
Detector
Diagraph

Diestock
Ecraseur
Eggtimer
Enlarger
Episcope
Episemon
Expander
Geophone
Heat pump
Hotplate
Ignitron
Launcher
Monogram
Nailhead
Occluder
Odograph
Odometer
Orthosis
Paravane
Playback
Pulsator
Push-pull
Pyrostat
Radiator
Resister
Shoehorn
Shredder
Silencer
Slip ring
Snow-eyes
Snowshoe
Solenoid
Spray gun
Spreader
Squeegee
Sweatbox
Swellbox
Terminal
Thin-film
Trembler
Varactor
Varistor
Vibrator

9 letters:
Aspirator
Autometer
Capacitor
Compasses
Convector
Converter

Corkscrew
Decoherer
Defroster
Delayline
Detonator
Dispenser
Dynamotor
Eccentric
Excelsior
Exerciser
Generator
Gyroscope
Headstock
Hendiadys
Hodoscope
Hydrofoil
Hydrostat
Hygrostat
Insulator
Keylogger
Konimeter
Kymograph
Megaphone
Mekometer
Metronome
Milometer
Nebuliser
Octophone
Optophone
Overdrive
Pacemaker
Parachute
Pedometer
Periscope
Photocell
Pitchbend
Polariser
Polygraph
Powerpack
Propeller
Rectifier
Regulator
Remontoir
Resonator
Responsor
Rheotrope
Rotachute
Rotameter®
Satellite
Scrambler
Separator

Sequencer
Simulator
Smokejack
Sonograph
Spaceband
Spindryer
Sprinkler
Stairlift
Steadicam
Stretcher
Tabulator
Tape drive
Tasimeter
Telegraph
Telemeter
Telepoint
Thermette
Thyristor
Tonometer
Trackball
Tremulant
Well sweep

10 letters:
Acetometer
Anemoscope
Applicator
Attenuator
Autowinder
Blackberry®
Calculator
Ceilometer
Centrifuge
Chronotron
Clapometer
Commutator
Comparator
Compressor
Copyholder
Cyclometer
Cyclostyle
Daisy-wheel
Databogger
Derailleur
Descendeur
Eprouvette
Groundprox
Humidistat
Hygroscope
Jawbreaker
Jaws of Life

Jellygraph
Kicksorter
Metrostyle
Microphone
Microprobe
Microscope
Mileometer
Noisemaker
Otter-board
Peripheral
Phonoscope
Phonospore
Remontoire
Respirator
Self-feeder
Siderostat
Snowplough
Spirograph
Stabiliser
Stimpmeter
Suppressor
Switchgear
Tachograph
Tachometer
Telewriter
Thermistor
Thermopile
Thermostat
Tourniquet

Transducer
Transistor
Turnbuckle
Ventilator
Vertoscope®
Videophone
Viewfinder
Viscometer
Zener diode

11 letters:
Afterburner
Annunciator
Autochanger
Baffle-plate
Carburettor
Distributor
Epidiascope
Floor turtle
Fluoroscope
Insufflator
Intoximeter
Lie detector
Microfitter
Microreader
Microwriter
Multiplexer
Recuperator
Self-starter

Smokerlyzer
Snickometer
Solarimeter
Space heater
Spectograph
Speedometer
Swingometer
Telestrator
Thermoscope
Trackerball
Transceiver
Transformer
Transmitter
Transponder

12 letters:
Breathalyser
Concentrator
Desert cooler
Ebulliometer
Intrauterine
Lithotripter
Object finder
Oscillograph
Picturephone
Sensitometer
Snooperscope
Spectroscope
Supercharger

Telautograph
Teleprompter
Thermocouple
Turbidimeter
Viscosimeter

13 letters:
Baton-sinister
Dead man's pedal
Metal detector
Phonendoscope
Rack and pinion
Shock-absorber
Smoke detector

14 letters:
Anamorphoscope
Dead man's handle
Interferometer
Intervalometer
Peltier element
Plethysmograph
Scintillometer
Spinthariscope

15 letters:
Radiogoniometer

Devil(ish), Demon Abaddon, Afree, Afrit, Ahriman, Amaimon, Apollyon, Asmodeus, Atua, Auld Hornie, Azazel, Barbason, Beelzebub, Belial, Buckra, Cartesian, Clootie, Cloots, Dasyure, Davy Jones, Deev, Deil, Demogorgon, Demon, Deuce, Devling, Diable, Diabolic, Dickens, Div, Drudge, Dust, Eblis, Falin, Familiar, Fend, Fiend, Fient, Ghoul, Goodman, Goodyear, Grill, Hangie, Hornie, Iblis, Imp, Incubus, Infernal, Lamia, Legion, Lilith, Lord of the Flies, Lori, Lucifer, Mahoun(d), Man of Sin, Manta, Mara, Maxwell's, Mazikeen, Mephisto(pheles), Mischief, Nick, Nickie-ben, Old Bendy, Old Nick, Old One, Old Pandemonium, Old Poker, Old Roger, Old Split-foot, Old Toast, Printer's, Ragamuffin, Rahu, Ralph, Satan, Sathanas, Satyr, Scour, Scratch, Screwtape, Season, Setebos, Shaitan, Shedeem, Snow, Sorra, Succubine, Succubus, Tailard, Tasmanian, Tempter, Titivil, Tutivillus, Wendigo, Wicked, Wicked One, Wirricow, Worricow, Worrycow, Zernebock

Devious Braide, Cunning, Deep, Eel(y), Erroneous, Evasive, Implex, Indirect, Scheming, Shifty, Stealthy, Subtle, Tortuous, Tricky

Devise(d) Arrange, Concoct, Contrive, Decoct, Hatch, Hit-on, Imagine, Invenit, Invent, Plot, Thermette

Devitrified Ambitty

Devoid Barren, Destitute, Empty, Vacant, Wanting

Devolve Occur, Result, Transmit

Devote(e), Devotion(al), Devoted Addiction, Aficionado, Angelus, Attached, Bhakti, Buff, Bunny, Consecrate, Corban, Dedicate, Employ, Fan, Fervid, Fetishism,

Fiend, Holy, Hound, Loyalty, Novena, Ophism, Passion, Pious, Puja, Religioso, Saivite, Sea-green incorruptible, S(h)akta, Sivaite, Solemn, True, Zealous

Devour(ing) Consume, Eat, Engorge, Engulf, Manducate, Moth-eat, Scarf, Scoff, Snarf, → SWALLOW, Vorant

▷ **Devour** *may indicate* one word inside another

Devout Holy, Pia, Pious, Reverent, Sant, Sincere, Solemn

Dew(y) Bloom, Moist, Mountain, Rime, Roral, Roric, Rorid, Roscid, Serein, Serene, Tranter

Dexterity, Dexterous Adept, Adroit, Aptitude, Cleverness, Craft, Deft, Feat(e)ous, Featuous, → HANDY, Knack, Shrewd, Sleight, Slick

Diabolic Cruel, → DEVILISH, Infernal

Diacritic (mark) Acute, Angstrom, Cedilla, Circumflex, Diaresis, Eth, Grave, Háček, Thorn, Tilde, Umlaut

Diadem Coronet, Fillet, Garland, Tiara

Diagnose, Diagnosis, Diagnostic Amniocentesis, Fetal, Findings, Identify, Iridology, Pulse, Scan, Scintigraphy

Diagonal(ly) Bend(wise), Bias, Cater(-corner), Catty-cornered, Counter, Oblique, Slant, Solidus, Twill

Diagram Argand, Block, Butterfly, Chart, Chromaticity, Compass rose, Decision tree, Dendogram, Drawing, Fault-tree, Feynman, Figure, Flow, Graph, Graphics, Grid, Hertzsprung-Russell, Indicator, Logic, Map, Plan, Plat, Run-chart, Scintigram, Scatter, Schema, Stem-and-leaf, Stemma, Stereogram, Tephigram, Topo, Venn, Wind rose

Dial(ling) Card, Face, Mug, Phiz, Phone, Pulse, Ring, STD, Visage

Dialect Accent, Aeolic, Alemannic, Arcadic, Attic, Basuto, Burr, Castilian, Doric, Eldin, Eolic, Erse, Eye, Franconian, Friulian, Gallo-Romance, Gascon, Geechee, Geordie, Greenlander, Hegelian, Idiom, Ionic, Isogloss, Jargon, Jockney, Joual, Khalka, Koine, Konkani, Ladin, Lallans, Landsmaal, Langobardic, Langue d'oc, Langue d'oil, Langue d'oui, Lingo, Low German, Mackem, Min, Norman, Norn, Old Icelandic, Old North French, Parsee, Patois, Pedi, Prakrit, Rhotic, Riffian, Romans(c)h, Salish, Savoyard, Scouse, Sesotho, Syriac, Taal, Talkee-talkee, Talky-talky, Tongue, Tshi, Tuscan, Twi, Vernacular, Wu, Yealdon, Yenglish, Yinglish

Dialogue Colloquy, Conversation, Critias, Discussion, Exchange, Interlocution, Lazzo, Pastourelle, Speech, Stichomythia, Talk, Upspeak

Dialysis Kidney, Peritoneal

Diameter Breadth, Calibre, Gauge, Systyle, Tactical, Width

Diamond(s), Diamond-shaped Adamant, Black, Boart, Brilliant, Bristol, Carbonado, Cullinan, D, DE, Delaware, Eustace, False, Florentine, Hope, Ice, Industrial, Isomer, Jim, Koh-i-Noor, Lasque, Lattice, Lozenge, Paragon, Pick, Pitch, Pitt, Quarry, Rhinestone, Rhomb, Rock, Rose-cut, Rosser, Rough, Rustre, Sancy, Solitaire, Spark, Sparklers, Squarial, Suit

Diana Artemis, Di

Diapason Normal, Open, Ottava, Stopped

Diaphanous Clear, Sheer, Translucent

Diaphoretic Sweater

Diaphragm Cap, Iris, Mid-riff, Phrenic, Stop

Diaresis Trema

▶ **Diarist** *see* DIARY

Diarrhoea Collywobbles, Delhi belly, Gippy tummy, Lientery, Montezuma's revenge, Runs, Scours, Squitters, The shits, Trots, Verbal, Weaning-brash, Wood-evil

Diary, Diarist Chronicle, Dale, Day-book, Evelyn, Hickey, Journal, Kilvert, Log, Nobody, Pepys, Pooter, Record, Video

Diaspora Exodus, Galuth

Diatribe Harangue, Invective, Philippic, Tirade

Dice(r), Dicey Aleatory, Astragals, Bale, Bones, Chop, Craps, Cube, Doctor, Dodgy, Fulham, Fullams, Fullans, Gourd(s), Highman, Jeff, Mandoline, Novum, Poker, Shoot, Snake-eyes, Tallmen

Dichotomy Split

Dick(y), Dickey Clever, Deadeye, Front, Ill, Moby, OED, Policeman, Rumble, Shaky, Shirt, Spotted, Tec, Tonneau, Tucker, Tumbledown, Unstable, Wankle, Weak, Whittington

▷ **Dick** *may indicate* a dictionary

Dickens Boz, Deuce, Devil, Mephistopheles

Dicker Bargain, Barter, Haggle, Trade

▷ **Dicky** *may indicate* an anagram

Dictate, Dictator(ial) Amin, Authoritarian, Autocrat, Big Brother, Caesar, Castro, Cham, Command, Czar, Decree, Demagogue, Despot, Duce, Franco, Fu(e)hrer, Gauleiter, Hitler, Impose, Lenin, Ordain, Overbearing, Peremptory, Peron, Salazar, Shogun, Stalin, Tell, Tito, Totalitarian, Tsar, Tyrant, Tzar

Diction Language, Lexis, Palavinity, Speech, Style

Dictionary Alveary, Calepin, Chambers, Data, Etymologicon, Fowler, Gazetteer, Glossary, Gradus, Hobson-Jobson, Idioticon, Johnson's, Larousse, Lexicon, Lexis, OED, Onomasticon, Thesaurus, Vocabulary, Webster, Wordbook

Dictum Obiter, Say-so

Did Began, Couth, Fec(it), Gan

Didactic Sermonical

Diddle Cheat, Con, Hoax

Dido Antic, Caper, Carthaginian, Elissa

Die(d), Dying Ache, Cark, Choke, Crater, Croak, Cube, D, Decadent, Desire, End, Evanish, Exit, Expire, Fade, Fail, Flatline, Forfair, Fulham, Fulhan, Fullam, Go, Go west, Hallmark, Highman, Hop, Kark, Long, Morendo, Moribund, Ob(iit), Orb, Pass, Peg out, Perdendosi, Perish, Peter, Slip the cable, Snuff, Snuff it, Solidum, Sphacelation, Stamp, Sterve, Succumb, Suffer, Swage, Swelt, Terminal, Tine, Touch, Wane

Diehard Blimp, Fanatic, Intransigent, Reactionary, Standpatter, Zealot

Diesel Red

Diet(er) Assembly, Augsburg, Bant(ing), Cacatrophy, Council, Dail, Eat, Fare, Hay, Intake, Kashrut(h), Ketogenic, Landtag, Lent, Macrobiotic, Parliament, Pleading, Reduce, Regimen, Reichstag, Slim, Solid, Sprat, Staple, Strict, Tynwald, Vegan, Vegetarian, Weightwatcher, Worms

Dietetics Sit(i)ology

Differ(ence), Differing, Different(ly) Allo, Barney, Change, Cline, Contrast, Contretemps, Deviant, Diesis, Disagree, Discord, Discrepant, Disparate, Dispute, Dissent, Dissimilitude, Distinct, Diverge, Diverse, Else, Elsewise, Epact, Nuance, Omnifarious, Other, Othergates, Otherguess, Otherness, Otherwise, Potential, Separate, Several, Symmetric, Tiff, Unlike, Variform, Various, Vary

Differential, Differentiate, Differentiation Calculus, Del, Distinguish, Nabla, Product, Secern, Taxeme, Wage

Difficult(y) Abstruseness, Ado, Aporia, Arduous, Augean, Badass, Balky, Ballbuster, Bitter, Block, Bolshie, Bother, Catch, Choosy, Complication, Corner, Crotchety, Deep, Depth, Dysphagia, Extreme, Fiddly, Formidable, Gordian, → **HARD**, Hassle,

Hazard, Hiccough, Hiccup, Hobble, Hole, Hoor, Ill, Impasse, Indocile, Intractable, Intransigent, Jam, Kink, Knot, Lob's pound, Lurch, Mulish, Net, Nodus, Obstacle, Parlous, Pig, Pitfall, Plight, Predicament, Quandary, Queer St, Recalcitrant, Rough, Rub, Scabrous, Scrape, Scrub, Setaceous, Shlep, Snag, Soup, Steep, Stey, Stick, Sticky, Stiff, Strait, Stubborn, Stymie, Thorny, Ticklish, Tight spot, Trial, Tricky, Troublous, Une(a)th, Uphill, Via dolorosa

Diffident Bashful, Meek, Modest, Reserved, Shy

Diffuse, Diffusion Barophoresis, Disperse, Disseminate, Endosmosis, Exude, Osmosis, Pervade, Radiate, Spread, Thermal

Dig(s), Digger, Digging, Dig up Antipodean, Australian, Backhoe, Beadle, Bed(e)ral, Bedsit, Billet, Bot, Burrow, Costean, Delve, Enjoy, Excavate, Flea-bag, Fossorial, Gaulter, Gibe, Gird, Graip, Grub, Howk, Jab, Kip, Lair, Like, Lodgings, Mine, Navvy, Nervy, Nudge, Pad, Pioneer, Probe, Prod, Raddleman, Resurrect, Root, Ruddleman, Sap, See, Spade, Spit, Spud, Star-nose, Taunt, Till, Tonnell, Trench, Tunnel, Undermine, Unearth

Digest(ible), Digestion, Digestive Abridgement, Absorb, Abstract, Aperçu, Archenteron, Assimilate, Codify, Concoct, Endue, Epitome, Eupepsia, Eupepsy, Fletcherism, Gastric, Indew, Indue, Light, Pandect, Pem(m)ican, Pepsin(e), Peptic, Précis, Salt-cat, Steatolysis, → **SUMMARY**

Digit(s) Binary, Bit, Byte, Check, Dactyl, Figure, Finger, Hallux, Mantissa, Number, Pollex, Prehallux, Thumb, Toe

Dignified, Dignify August, Elevate, Exalt, Handsome, Honour, Lordly, Majestic, Manly, Proud, Solemn, Stately

Dignitary Bigwig, Dean, Name, Personage, Provost, → **VIP**

Dignity Aplomb, Bearing, Cathedra, Decorum, Face, Glory, Grandeur, High horse, Maestoso, Majesty, Nobility, Poise, Pontificate, Presence, Scarf, Tiara

Digraph Ash, Eng, Ng

Digress(ion) Apostrophe, Deviate, Diverge, Ecbole, Episode, Excurse, Excursus, Maunder, Veer, Wander

Dike Bank, Channel, Cludgie, Dam, Ditch, → **DYKE**, Embank(ment), Estacade, Lav(atory), Levee, Wall

Dilapidated, Dilapidation Clapped out, Clunker, Decrepit, Desolate, Disrepair, Eroded, Rickle, Ruined, Rust bucket, Tumbledown

Dilate, Dilation, Dilatation Amplify, Develop, Diastole, Ecstasis, Enlarge, Expand, Increase, Mydriasis, Sinus, Swell, Telangiectasia, Tent, Varix

Dilatory Protracting, Slow, Sluggish, Tardy

Dilemma Casuistry, Choice, Cleft, Dulcarnon, Fix, Horn, Predicament, Quandary, Why-not

Dilettante Aesthete, Amateur, Butterfly, Dabbler, Playboy

Diligence, Diligent Active, Application, Assiduous, Coach, Conscience, Eident, Industry, Intent, Painstaking, Sedulous, Studious

Dill Anise, Pickle

Dilute, Dilution Adulterate, Deglaze, Delay, Diluent, Lavage, Qualify, Simpson, Thin, Water, Weaken

Dim(ness), Dimming, Dimwit Becloud, Blear, Blur, Brownout, Caligo, Clueless, Crepuscular, Dense, Dusk, Eclipse, Fade, Faint, Feint, Gormless, Ill-lit, Indistinct, Mist, Nebulous, Ninny, Obscure, Overcast, Owl, Pale, Shadow, Unsmart

Dimension(s) Area, Breadth, Extent, Fourth, Height, Length, Measure, New, Scantling, Size, Third, Volume, Width

Diminish(ed), Diminishing, Diminuendo, Diminution, Diminutive
Abatement, Assuage, Baby, Bate, Calando, Contract, Cot(t)ise, Deactivate, Decline,

Decrease, Détente, Detract, Disparage, Dissipate, Dwarf, Dwindle, Erode, Fourth, Hypocorism(a), Lessen, Lilliputian, Minify, Minus, Mitigate, Petite, Pigmy, Ritardando, Scarp, Small, Stultify, Subside, Toy, Trangle, Wane, Whittle

Dimple(d) Dent, Depression, Hollow, Orange-peel

Din Babel, Charivary, Chirm, Commotion, Deen, Discord, Gunga, Hubbub, → **NOISE**, Racket, Raird, Randan, Reel, Reird, Uproar, Utis

Dine(r), Dining Aristology, Café, Eat, Feast, Mess, Refect, Sup, Trat(toria)

Dingbat Doodad, Weirdo

Dinghy Pram, Shallop, Ship, Skiff

Dingo Warrigal

Dingy Crummy, Dark, Dirty, Drear, Dun, Fusc(ous), Grimy, Isabel(la), Isabelline, Lurid, Oorie, Ourie, Owrie, Shabby, Smoky

Dining-room Cafeteria, Cenacle, Commons, Frater, Hall, Langar, Mess hall, Refectory, Restaurant, Triclinium

Dinner Banquet, Collation, Feast, Hall, Kail, Kale, Meal, Prandial, Progressive, Repast, Spread

Dinosaur Allosaurus, Ankylosaur, Apatosaurus, Atlantosaurus, Baryonyx, Brachiosaurus, Brontosaurus, Ceratopsian, Ceratosaurus, Ceteosaurus, Chalicothere, Coelurosaur, Compsognathus, Cotylosaur, Cynodont, Dinothere, Diplodocus, Dolichosaurus, Duck-billed, Elasmosaur, Galeopithecus, Glyptodon, Hadrosaur, Ichthyosaur(us), Iguanodon, Megalosaur, Mosasaur, Ornithosaur, Ornithischian, Ornithopod, Oviraptor, Pelycosaur, Perissodactyl, Placoderm, Plesiosaur, Prehistoric, Prosauropod, Pteranodon, Pterodactyl, Pterosaur, Rhynchocephalian, Saurischian, Sauropod, Smilodon, Stegadon(t), Stegosaur, Teleosaurus, Theropod, Titanosaurus, Titanothere, Triceratops, Tyrannosaurus, Uintothere, Velociraptor

Dint Brunt, Dent, Depression, Force, Means, Power

Diocese Bishopric, District, Eparchate, See

Diode Esaki, Tunnel, Zener

Diogenes Cynic

Dioxide Cassiterite, Needle-tin

Dip(per) Bagna cauda, Baptise, Basin, Bathe, Bob, Brantub, Dabble, Dap, Dean, Dib, Diver, Dop, Double, Duck, Dunk, Foveola, Geosyncline, Guacomole, H(o)ummus, Houmous, Hum(m)us, Immerge, Immerse, Intinction, Ladle, Lucky, Magnetic, Ouzel, Paddle, Rinse, Rollercoaster, Sag, Salute, Sheep-wash, Star, Submerge, Tapenade, Taramasalata, Tzatziki, Ursa

Diphthong Synaeresis, Synizesis

Diploma Bac, Charter, Parchment, Qualification, Scroll, Sheepskin

Diplomacy, Diplomat(ic) Alternat, Ambassador, Attaché, CD, Chargé d'affaires, Chateaubriand, Cheque-book, Consul, DA, Dean, Dollar, Doyen, El(t)chi, Envoy, Fanariot, Fetial, Finesse, Gunboat, Legation, Lei(d)ger, Megaphone, Phanariot, Plenipotentiary, Shuttle, Suave, → **TACT**

▷ **Dippy** *may indicate* a bather

Dipsomania Oenomania

Dire Dreadful, Fatal, Fell, Hateful, Ominous, Urgent

Direct(or), Directly Administer, Advert, Aim, Airt, Auteur, Aventre, Board, Boss, Cann, Cast, Chairperson, Channel, Charge, Command, Compere, Con(n), Conduct, Control, Cox, Dead, Due, Dunstable road, Eisenstein, Enjoin, Executive, Explicit, Fast-track, Fellini, First-hand, Forthright, Frontal, Guide, Helm, Hitchcock, Huston, Immediate, Impresario, Instruct, Intendant, Kapellmeister, Lead, Lean, Manager, Mastermind, Navigate, Nonexecutive, Orson (Welles), Outright, Pagnol, Pilot, Play,

Point-blank, Ready, Reed, Refer, Régisseur, Rudder, Send, Set, Signpost, Stear,
→ **STEER**, Straight, Tati, Teach, Tell, Truffaut, Unvarnished, Vector, Welles

Direction Aim, Airt, Arrow, Astern, Bearings, Course, Cross-reference, E, End-on,
Guidance, Guide, Heading, Keblah, L, Line, N, Orders, Passim, R, Route, Rubric,
S, Sanction, Send, Sense, Side, Slap, Tack, Tenor, Thataway, Tre corde, Trend, W,
Way, Wedelns

Direction-finder Asdic, Compass, Decca, Quadrant, Radar, Sextant, Sonar

Directory Crockford, Data, Debrett, Encyclop(a)edia, French, Kelly, List, Red book,
Register, Root, Web, Yellow Pages®

Dirge Ballant, Coronach, Dirige, Epicedium, Knell, Monody, Requiem, Song,
Threnody

Dirigible Airship, Balloon, Blimp, Zeppelin

Dirk Anelace, Dagger, Skean, Whinger, Whiniard, Whinyard

Dirt(y) Augean, Bed(r)aggled, Begrime, Bemoil, Cacky, Chatty, Clag, Clarty, Colly,
Contaminate, Coom, Crock, Crud, Draggle, Dung, Dust, Earth, Festy, Filth, Foul,
Gore, Grime, Grufted, Grungy, Impure, Manky, Moit, Mote, Muck, Obscene,
Ordure, Pay, Pollute, Ray, Scody, Sculdudd(e)ry, Scum, Scungy, Scuzzy, Skanky,
Skulduddery, Smirch, Smut(ch), Soil, Sooty, Sordes, Sordor, Squalid, Stain, Trash,
Unclean, Unsatisfactory, Unwashed, Warb, Yucky, Yukky

Dis Hades, Hell

Disability, Disable(d) Cripple, Gimp, Handicapped, Incapacitate, Kayo, Lame,
Maim, Paralyse, Scissor-leg, Scotch, Wreck

Disadvantage Detriment, Downside, Drawback, Handicap, Mischief, Out, Penalise,
Penalty, Supercherie, Upstage, Wrongfoot, Zugswang

Disagree(ing), Disagreeable, Disagreement Argue, Argy-bargy, Bad, Clash,
Conflict, Contest, Debate, Differ, Discrepant, Dispute, Dissent, Dissonant, Evil,
Fiddlesticks, Friction, Heterodoxy, Pace, Plagu(e)y, Rift, Troll, Unpleasing

Disallow Forbid, Overrule

Disappear(ing) Cook, Dispel, Evanesce, Evanish, Evaporate, Fade, Kook, Latescent,
Melt, Occult, Pass, Skedaddle, Slope, → **VANISH**

Disappoint(ment), Disappointed Anticlimax, Balk, Baulk, Bombshell, Bummer,
Chagrin, Comedown, Crestfallen, Delude, Disgruntle, Frustrate, Gutted, Heartsick,
Lemon, Letdown, Regret, Sell, Setback, Shucks, Sick, Suck-in, Sucks, Swiz(zle),
Thwart, Underwhelm

Disapproval, Disapprove Ach, Animadvert, Boo, Catcall, Censure, Deplore,
Deprecate, Discountenance, Expostulate, Fie, Frown, Harrumph, Hiss, Napoo,
Object, Pejorative, Po-faced, Raspberry, Razz, Reject, Reproach, Reprobate, Squint,
Tush, Tut, Tut-tut, Umph, Veto, Whiss

Disarm(ament), Disarming Bluff, Defuse, Demobilise, Nuclear, Winsome

Disarrange Disturb, Muddle, Ruffle, Tousle, Unsettle

Disarray Disorder, Mess, Rifle, Tash, Undress

Disaster, Disastrous Adversity, Apocalypse, Bale, Calamity, Cataclysm(ic),
Catastrophe, Debacle, Dire, Doom, Evil, Fatal, Fiasco, Flop, Impostor, Meltdown,
Mishap, Pitfall, Rout, Ruin, Screw-up, Seism, Shipwreck, Titanic, Tragedy, Wipeout

Disavow Abjure, Deny, Disclaim, Recant, Retract

Disbelief, Disbelieve(r) Acosmism, Anythingarian, Atheism, Doubt, Gawp,
Incredulity, Mistrust, Nothingarianism, Occamist, Phew, Phooey, Puh-lease,
Puh-leeze, Question, Sceptic, Shoot, Voetsak

Disburse Distribute, Expend, Outlay, Spend

Disc, Disk Bursting, Button, CD, Cheese, Compact, Coulter, Counter, Diaphragm,
Dogtag, EP, Epiphragm, Flexible, Floppy, Frisbee®, Gold, Gong, Hard, Hard card,

Harrow, Impeller, Intervertebral, Laser, LP, Magnetic, Mono, O, Optic(al), Parking, Paten, Patin, Planchet, Plate, Platinum, Puck, RAM, Rayleigh, Record, Reflector, Rosette, Roundel, Roundlet, Rowel, Rundle, Sealed unit, Silver, Slipped, Slug, Stereo, Stylopodium, Sun, Swash plate, System, Tax, Token, Video, Wafer, Wharve, Whorl, Winchester, Wink, WORM, Zip®

Discard(ed) Abandon, Burn, Crib, Defy, Dele, Jettison, Kill, Leave, Obsolete, Off, Offload, Oust, → **REJECT**, Scrap, Shed, Shuck, Slough, Sluff, Supersede, Throw over, Trash

Discern(ing), Discernment Acumen, Acute, Clear-eyed, Descry, Detect, Discrimination, Eagle-eyed, Flair, Insight, Perceive, Percipient, Perspicacity, Realise, Sapient, Scry, See, Skry, → **TASTE**, Tell, Wate

Discharge Absolve, Acquit, Arc, Assoil, Blennorrhoea, Blow off, Brush, Cashier, Catamenia, Catarrh, Conditional, Corona, Dejecta, Deliver, Demob, Disembogue, Disgorge, Dismiss, Disruptive, Dump, Efflux, Effusion, Egest, Ejaculate, Eject, Embogue, Emission, Emit, Encopresis, Enfilade, Evacuate, Excrete, Execute, Exemption, Expulsion, Exude, Fire, Flashover, Flower, Flux, Frass, Free, Gleet, Glow, Lava, Lay off, Leak, Let off, Leucorrhoea, Lochia, Loose, Maturate, Menses, Mitimus, Mute, Offload, Otorrhoea, Oust, Ozaena, Pay, Perform, Period, Planuria, Purulence, Pus, Pyorrhoea, Quietus, Rheum, Rhinorrhoeal, Sack, Salvo, Sanies, Secretion, Show, Shrive, Snarler, Spark, Suppurate, Teem, Unload, Vent, Void, Water, Whites

Disciple(s) Adherent, Apostle, Babi, Baruch, Catechumen, Chela, Follower, John, Judas, Luke, Mark, Matthew, Peter, Simon, Son, Student, The Seventy, Thomist, Votary

Disciplinarian, Discipline Apollonian, Ascesis, Chasten, Chastise, Correct, Despot, Drill, Exercise, Feng shui, Inure, Martinet, Mathesis, Punish, Regimentation, Regulate, Sadhana, School, Science, Spartan, Stickler, Subject, Taskmaster, Train, Tutor

▸ **Disc jockey** *see* **DJ**

Disclaim(er) Deny, Disown, No(t)chel, Recant, Renounce, → **REPUDIATE**, Voetstoots

Disclose, Disclosure Apocalypse, Confess, Divulge, Expose, Impart, Leak, Manifest, Propale, → **PUBLISH**, Report, Reveal, Spill, Tell, Unheal, Unhele, Unrip, Unveil

Discoloration, Discolour(ed) Bloodstain, Bruise, Cyanosis, Dyschroa, Ecchymosis, Fox, Livedo, Livid, Livor, Stain, Streak, Tarnish, Tinge, Weather

Discomfit(ure) Abash, Confuse, Disconcert, Disturb, Frustrate, Lurch, Shend

Discomfort(ed) Ache, All-overish, Angst, Dysphoria, Gyp, Heartburn, Pain, Unease

Disconcert(ing) Abash, Astound, Confuse, Disturb, Embarrass, Faze, Feeze, Flurry, Fluster, Nonplus, Off-putting, Phase, Pheese, Pheeze, Phese, → **RATTLE**, Shatter, Tease, Throw, Upset, Wrong-foot

▷ **Disconcert(ed)** *may indicate* an anagram

Disconnect(ed) Asynartete, Detach, Disjointed, Off-line, Sever, Staccato, Uncouple, Undo, Unplug

Disconsolate Desolate, Doleful, Downcast, → **GLOOMY**

Discontent(ed) Disquiet, Dissatisfied, Humph, Repined, Sour, Umph

Discontinue, Discontinuance, Discontinuity Abandon, Cease, Desist, Desuetude, Drop, Moho, Prorogue, Stop, Terminate

Discord(ant) Absonant, Ajar, Charivari, Conflict, Din, Dispute, Eris, Faction, Hoarse, Jangle, Jar, Raucous, Ruction, Strife

▷ **Discord(ant)** *may indicate* an anagram

Discount Agio, Cashback, Deduct, Disregard, Forfaiting, Invalidate, Quantity, → REBATE, Trade

Discountenance Disfavour, Efface, Embarrass

Discourage(ment) Caution, Chill, Dampen, Dash, Daunt, Deject, Demoralise, Deter, Dishearten, Disincentive, Dismay, Dissuade, Enervate, Frustrate, Intimidate, Opposition, Stifle, Unman

Discourse Address, Argument, Conversation, Descant, Diatribe, Dissertate, Eulogy, Expound, Homily, Lecture, Lucubrate, Orate, Philippic, Preach, Relate, Rigmarole, Sermon, Wash

Discourteous, Discourtesy Impolite, Insult, Rude, Slight, Uncivil, Unmannerly

Discover(y), Discoverer Amundsen, Anagnorisis, Ascertain, Betray, Breakthrough, Columbus, Cook, Descry, Detect, Discern, Discure, Eureka, → FIND, Heureka, Heuristic, Learn, Locate, Manifest, Moresby, Protegé, Rumble, Serendip, Serendipity, Spy, Tasman, Trace, Treasure trove, Unearth, Unhale, Unmask, Unveil

▷ **Discovered in** *may indicate* an anagram or a hidden word

Discredit(able) Debunk, Decry, Disgrace, Explode, Infamy, Scandal, Smear, Unworthy

Discreet, Discretion Cautious, Circumspect, Freedom, Judicious, Option, Polite, Politic, Prudence, Prudent, Trait, Wise

Discrepancy Difference, Gap, Lack, Shortfall, Variance

Discrete Distinct, Separate, Unrelated

Discriminate, Discriminating, Discrimination Ag(e)ism, Colour bar, Diacritic, Differentiate, Discern, Distinguish, Elitism, Handism, Invidious, Lookism, Nasute, Racism, Rankism, Reverse, Secern, Segregate, Select, Sexism, Siz(e)ism, Speciesism, Subtle, Taste

Discursive Roving

Discuss(ed), Discussion Agitate, Air, Canvass, Commune, Conf(erence), Consult, Debate, Dialectic, Dialogue, Dicker, Disquisition, En l'air, Examine, Excursus, Expatiate, Handle, Hob and nob, Interlocution, Korero, Moot, Negotiation, Over, Palaver, Parley, Pourparler, Prolegomenon, Quodlibet, Rap, Re, Symposium, Talk, Tapis, Treatment, Ventilate, Vex

Disdain(ful) Belittle, Contempt, Coy, Deride, Despise, Geck, Poof, Pooh-pooh, Puh, Rats, Sassy, → SCORN, Scout, Sdei(g)n, Sniffy, Spurn, Supercilious, Ugh

Disease(d) Affection, Ailment, Communicable, Complaint, Deficiency, Epidemic, Fever, Functional, Industrial, Infection, Malady, Noso-, Nosocomial, Notifiable, Occupational, Organic, Pest(ilence), Rot, Scourge, Sickness

---

DISEASES

2 letters:	Haw	Clap	*5 letters:*
CD	Pip	Conk	Bang's
MD	Pox	Gout	Black
ME	Sod	Keel	Borna
MS	→ STD	Kuru	Brand
TB	TSE	Loco	Dread
VD	Wog	Lues	Dutch
		Lyme	Ebola
3 letters:		Roup	Edema
ALS	*4 letters:*	Wind	Ergot
BSE	Aids	Yaws	Favus
Flu	Boba		Fifth
	Bunt		

Gapes	Oedema	Purples	Nosology
Hoove	Paget's	Redfoot	Pandemic
Kwok's	Parrot	Rickets	Pathogen
Lupus	Rabies	Ring rot	Pellagra
Lurgi	Sapego	Rosette	Phthisis
Lurgy	Scurvy	Scabies	Phytosis
Mesel	Social	Scrapie	Porrigro
Mumps	Still's	Sequela	Progeria
Ngana	Thrush	Serpigo	Pullorum
Palsy	Tunnel	Tetanus	Rachitis
Pinta	Typhus	Tetters	Raynaud's
Polio	Ulitis	Typhoid	Rose-rash
Pott's	Urosis	Variola	Scaly leg
Rabid	Yuppie	Wilson's	Scrofula
Scall	Zoster	Zymosis	Shingles
Sprue			Smallpox
Surra	**7 letters:**	**8 letters:**	Soft sore
Tinea	Ascites	Addison's	Suppeago
Virus	Batten's	Alastrim	Swayback
Weil's	Bright's	Aujesky's	Swinepox
Worms	British	Beri-beri	Syphilis
	Caisson	Blackleg	Tay-Sachs
	Cholera	Bornholm	The bends
6 letters:	Coeliac	Club root	Trembles
Anbury	Crewels	Crown rot	Venereal
Aphtha	Dieback	Cushing's	Vincent's
Blight	Dourine	Cynanche	Zoonosis
Blotch	Endemic	Diabetes	
Border	English	Dutch elm	**9 letters:**
Cancer	Frounce	Economo's	Bilharzia
Canker	Hansen's	Fishskin	Blackhead
Chagas'	Hardpad	Fowl pest	Black knot
Chorea	Hydatid	Gaucher's	Brown lung
Cowpox	Icterus	Glanders	Chancroid
Crohn's	Kissing	Glaucoma	Chlorosis
Cruels	Leprosy	Gummosis	Christmas
Dartre	Lockjaw	Hodgkin's	Cirrhosis
Dengue	Maidism	Hookworm	Contagion
Eczema	Malaria	Impetigo	Diathesis
Farcin	Marburg	Jaundice	Distemper
Graves'	Miller's	Kala-azar	Dysentery
Herpes	Mimesis	Leaf-roll	Enteritis
Income	Mooneye	Leaf-spot	Exanthema
Johne's	Moor-ill	Liver-rot	Filanders
Mad cow	Murrain	Loose-cut	Gonorrhea
Marck's	Mycosis	Menière's	Idiopathy
Meazel	Myiasis	Minamata	Ixodiasis
Mildew	Pébrine	Mycetoma	Kawasaki's
Morbus	Podagra	Myopathy	Lathyrism
Mosaic	Porrigo	Myxedema	Leucaemia
Nagana			

Leukaemia
Loose smut
Myxoedema
Navicular
Nephritis
Nephrosis
Newcastle
New Forest
Pellagrin
Pemphigus
Phossy-jaw
Porphyria
Seborrhea
Siderosis
Silicosis
Toxicosis
Trichosis
Tularemia
Yuppie flu

10 letters:
Acromegaly
Alzheimer's
Amoebiasis
Asbestosis
Autoimmune
Babesiosis
Bagassosis
Bluetongue
Byssinosis
Chickenpox
Dandy-fever
Diphtheria
Erysipelas
Filariasis

Framboesia
Gonorrhoea
Heartwater
Hemophilia
Iatrogenic
Ichthyosis
Impaludism
Leuchaemia
Limber-neck
Lou Gehrig's
Louping ill
Moniliasis
Muscardine
Neuropathy
Nosography
Ornithosis
Parkinson's
Scarlatina
Seborrhoea
Topagnosia
Tularaemia

11 letters:
Anthracosis
Brittle-bone
Cardiopathy
Consumption
Green monkey
Haemophilia
Hebephrenia
Huntington's
Isle of Wight
Kwashiorkor
Listeriosis
Myxomatosis

Parasitosis
Paratyphoid
Psittacosis
Rickettsial
Scleroderma
Septicaemia
Thalassemia
Trench mouth
Trichinosis
Woolsorter's
Yellow-fever

12 letters:
Avitaminosis
Enterobiasis
Fascioliasis
Finger and toe
Foot and mouth
Furunculosis
Hoof and mouth
Legionnaires'
Molybdenosis
Motor neurone
Osteomalacia
Osteoporosis
Scheuermann's
Shaking palsy
Slapped cheek
Thalassaemia
Tuberculosis
Uncinariasis

13 letters:
Elephantiasis
Leichmaniasis

Leptospirosis
Osteomyelitis
Poliomyelitis
Sclerodermata
Syringomyelia
Toxoplasmosis
Tsutsugamushi

14 letters:
Cystic fibrosis
Histoplasmosis
Leucodystrophy
Onchocerciasis
Pasteurellosis
Pneumoconiosis
Psillid yellows
River blindness
Sporotrichosis
Trichomoniasis
Trichophytosis
Vincent's angina

15 letters:
Schistosomiasis
Trypanosomiasis

16 letters:
Pneumonoconiosis
Sleeping sickness
Sweating sickness

17 letters:
Friedreich's ataxia
Multiple sclerosis

⊳ **Diseased** *may indicate* an anagram
Disembark Alight, Detrain, Land
Disembarrass Extricate, Rid, Unthread
Disembowel Eviscerate, Exenterate, Gralloch, Gut, Viscerate
Disenchant Disabuse, Dismay, Embitter
Disencumber Free, Rid, Unburden
Disengage(d), Disengagement Clear, Detach, Divorce, Liberate, Loosen, Release, Untie
Disentangle Debarrass, Extricate, Red(d), Solve, Unravel, Unsnarl
Disestablishmentarian Cosmist
Disfavour Doghouse, Maugre
Disfigure(ment), Disfigured Agrise, Agryze, Camsho, Deface, Deform, Goitre, Mutilate, Scar, Spoil, Tash, Ugly
⊳ **Disfigured** *may indicate* an anagram
Disgorge Discharge, Spew, Spill, Vent, Void

Disgrace Atimy, Attaint, Baffle, Blot, Contempt, Contumely, Degrade, Discredit, Dishonour, Dog-house, Ignominy, Indignity, Infamy, Obloquy, Opprobrium, Scandal, Shame, Shend, Slur, Soil, Stain, Stigma, Yshend

Disgraceful Diabolical, Fie, Ignoble, Ignominious, Indign, Infamous, Mean, Notorious, Shameful, Turpitude

Disgruntled Brassed off, Malcontent, Resentful, Sore

▷ **Disgruntled** *may indicate* an anagram

Disguise(d) Alias, Blessing, Camouflage, Cloak, Colour, Conceal, Cover, Covert, Dissemble, Hide, Hood, Incog(nito), Mantle, Mask, Masquerade, Obscure, Peruke, Pretence, Pseudonym, Ring, Shades, Travesty, Veil, Vele, Veneer, Visagiste, Visor, Vizard

▷ **Disguised** *may indicate* an anagram

Disgust(ing) Ach-y-fi, Ad nauseam, Aversion, Aw, Bah, Cloy, Discomfort, Execrable, Faugh, Fie, Foh, Fulsome, Grisly, Grody, Irk, Loathsome, Manky, Mawkish, Minging, Nauseous, Noisome, Obscene, Odium, Oughly, Ouglie, Pah, Pho(h), Pish, Pshaw, Pugh, Repel, Repugnant, Repulse, → **REVOLT**, Revulsion, Scomfish, Scumfish, Scunner, Scuzz, → **SICKEN**, Si(e)s, Sir-reverence, Slimeball, Squalid, Tush, Ugh, Ugsome, Vile, Yech, Yu(c)k, Yucko, Yukky

Dish(y) Adonis, Allot, Apollo, Ashet, Basin, Belle, Bowl, Chafing, Charger, Cocotte, Cook-up, Cutie, Dent, Diable, Dole, Dreamboat, Epergne, Flasket, Grail, Kitchen, Laggen, Laggin, Lanx, Luggie, Muffineer, Ovenware, Pan, Pannikin, Paten, Patera, Patin(e), Petri, Plate, Platter, Porringer, Ramekin, Ramequin, Receptacle, Rechauffé, Remove, Sangraal, Sangrail, Sangreal, Satellite, Saucer, Scallop, Scorifier, Scupper, Serve, Service, Side, Smasher, Special, Toll, Watchglass

DISHES

3 letters:	Dolma	Bharta	Roesti
Poi	Gomer	Bhoona	Salmis
	Kasha	Bridie	Sowans
4 letters:	Kibbe	Chilli	Sowens
Fool	Kofta	Cou-cou	Subgum
Kiev	Korma	Cuscus	Surimi
Mess	Laksa	Entrée	Tamale
Olla	Maror	Fondue	Tsamba
Puri	Perog	Haggis	
Sate	Pilau	Hotpot	*7 letters:*
Soss	Pilow	Kimchi	Biriani
Taco	Poori	Kishke	Bobotie
Tian	Raita	Masale	Burrito
	Ramen	Mornay	Calzone
5 letters:	Rosti	Mousse	Cassava
Adobo	Salmi	Muesli	Ceviche
Balti	Satay	Nachos	Comport
Bhaji	Sushi	Paella	Compote
Bhuna	Tamal	Pakora	Crowdie
Bitok	Tikka	Panada	Crubeen
Boxty	Tripe	Pirogi	Crumble
Brose		Quiche	Custard
Champ	*6 letters:*	Ragout	Cuvette
Curry	Bhagee	Regale	Dariole

Dhansak
Dopiaza
Egg roll
Fajitas
Fal-a-fel
Fel-a-fel
Foo yung
Friture
Grav lax
Marengo
Mousaka
Padella
Pierogi
Poutine
Rarebit
Ravioli
Sasatie
Sashimi
Seviche
Soufflé
Stir-fry
Stovies
Tempura
Terrine
Timbale
Tostada

8 letters:
Brandade
Caponata
Chop suey
Chow mein
Coolamon
Coq au vin
Coquille
Couscous
Crostini
Dog's-body
Entremes
Feijoada
Flummery
Frittata
Gado-gado

Halloumi
Handroll
Jalfrezi
Kedgeree
Keftedes
Kickshaw
Kouskous
Kreplach
Linguini
Matelote
Mazarine
McCallum
Meunière
Moussaka
Pandowdy
Pastrami
Porridge
Pot-au-feu
Pot-roast
Raclette
Shashlik
Sillabub
Souvlaki
Squarial
Sukiyaki
Syllabub
Teriyaki
Tzatziki
Vindaloo
White-pot
Yakimono
Yakitori

9 letters:
Carbonara
Carpaccio
Cevapcici
Compotier
Egg-fo-yang
Enchilada
Entremets
Fricassee
Galantine

Gravad lax
Guacamole
Howtowdie
Jambalaya
Manicotti
Marinière
Matelotte
Pastitsio
Pepper-pot
Reistafel
Rijstafel
Rogan josh
Shashlick
Souvlakia
Succotash
Surf n'turf

10 letters:
Blanquette
Bombay duck
Cacciatore
Coulibiaca
Couscousou
Doner kebab
Egg-foo-yung
Jugged hare
Koulibiaca
Mousseline
Nasi goreng
Parmigiana
Plat du jour
Provençale
Quesadilla
Rijsttafel
Salmagundi
Sauerkraut
Scallopine
Shish kebab
Spitchcock
Spring roll
Stroganoff
Teppan-yaki

11 letters:
Buck-rarebit
Fritto misto
Saltimbocca
Sauerbraten
Smorgasbord
Spanakopita
Surf and turf
Welsh rabbit

12 letters:
Eggs Benedict
Shepherd's pie
Solomon Gundy
Steak tartare
Sweet and sour
Taramasalata
Welsh rarebit

13 letters:
Fish and brewis
Rumbledethump
Skirl in the pan
Toad-in-the-hole

14 letters:
Beef stroganoff
Chilli con carne
Rumbledethumps
Scotch woodcock

15 letters:
Bubble and squeak
Eggs in moonshine

16 letters:
Potatoes and point

17 letters:
Cauliflower cheese

Dishabille Disarray, Négligé, Undress
Dishearten Appal, Core(r), Cow, Daunt, Depress, Discourage, Dispirit
Dishevel(led) Blowsy, Blowzy, Daggy, Mess, Rumpled, Touse, Tousle, Touzle, Tumble, Uncombed, Unkempt, Windswept
Dishonest(y) Bent, Crooked, Cross, Dodgy, False, Fraud, Graft, Hooky, Hot, Improbity, Jiggery-pokery, Knavery, Malpractice, Malversation, Shonky, Snide, Stink, Twister, Underhand, Venal, Wrong'un

Dishonour Abatement, Defile, Disgrace, Disparage, Ignominy, Seduce, → SHAME, Violate, Wrong

Disillusion Disenchant, Sour

Disincline(d), Disinclination Apathy, Averse, Loth, Off, Reluctant

Disinfect(ant) Acriflavin(e), Carbolic, Cineol(e), Cleanse, Dip, Eucalyptole, Formalin, Formol, Fuchsine, Fumigate, Lysol®, Phenol, Purify, Sheep-dip, Sheep-wash, TCP, Terebene

Disingenuous Insincere, Mask, Oblique, Two-faced

Disinherit Deprive, Dispossess

Disintegrate, Disintegration Break, Collapse, Crumble, Decay, Erode, Fragment, Lyse, Lysis, Osteoclasis, Rd, Rutherford

Disinter Exhume, Unearth

Disinterested Apathetic, Impartial, Incurious, Mugwump, Unbiased

Disjoint(ed) Bitty, Dismember, Incoherent, Rambling, Scrappy

▸ **Disk** *see* DISC

Dislike Abhor, Allergy, Animosity, Animus, Antipathy, Aversion, Derry, Disesteem, Displeasure, Distaste, Gross out, Hate, Lump, Mind, Needle, Scunner, Warling

Dislocate, Dislocation Break, Diastasis, Displace, Fault, Luxate, Slip, Subluxate

Dislodge Budge, Displace, Expel, Luxate, Oust, Rear, Tuft, Unship, Uproot

Disloyal(ty) False, Treason, Unfaithful, Untrue

Dismal Black, Bleak, Cheerless, Dark, Dowie, Dowly, Drack, Dreary, Funereal, → GLOOMY, Grey, Long-faced, Morne, Obital, Sepulchral, Sombre, Sullen, Trist(e), Wae, Woebegone, Wormy

Dismantle(d), Dismantling Decommission, Derig, Divest, Get-out, Sheer-hulk, Strike, Strip, Unrig

Dismast Unstep

Dismay Amate, Appal, Confound, Consternation, Coo, Daunt, Fie, Ha, Horrify, Lordy, Lumme, Qualms, Strewth

Dismiss(al), Dismissive Airy, Annul, Ax, Boot, Bounce, Bowl(er), Bum's rush, Cancel, Cashier, Catch, Chuck, Congé, Constructive, Daff, Discard, Discharge, Dooced, Expulsion, Fire, Heave-ho, Kiss-off, Lay off, Marching orders, Mitten, Och, Prorogue, Push, Recall, Reform, Reject, Remove, R.O., Road, Sack, Scout, Send, Shoo, Shrug off, Skittle out, Spit, Spurn, Stump, Suka wena, Via, Voetsak, Voetsek, Walking papers, York

Dismount Alight, Hecht

Disobedience, Disobedient, Disobey Contumacy, Defy, Flout, Insubordination, Rebel, Sit-in, Wayward

Disorder(ly), Disordered Affective, Ague, Ailment, Anarchy, Ariot, Asthma, Ataxia, Catatonia, Chaos, Chlorosis, Clutter, Confuse, Consumption, Contracture, Conversion, Defuse, Derange, Deray, Diabetes, Dishevel, Dissociative, Dysthymic, Dystrophy, Echolalia, Entropy, Epilepsy, Farrago, Greensickness, Grippe, Haemophilia, Hallucinosis, Heartburn, Huntingdon's chorea, Hypallage, Inordinate, Irregular, Mange, Mare's nest, ME, Mental, Mess, Misrule, Mistemper, → MUDDLE, Muss(y), Neurosis, Oncus, Onkus, Pandemonium, Panic, Para-, Pell-mell, Personality, Phenylketonuria, Porphyria, Psychomatic, Psychopathic, Psychosis, Ragmatical, Rile, Roughhouse, Rowdy, SAD, St Vitus' Dance, Schizophrenia, Seborrh(o)ea, Shell-shock, Slovenly, Sydenham's chorea, Tarantism, Thalass(a)emia, Thought, Tousle, Turbulence, Unhinge, Unruly, Upheaval, Upset, Virilism

▷ **Disorder(ed)** *may indicate* an anagram

Disorganised At sea, Deranged, Haywire, Scatterbrain, Shambolic, Structureless

Disown Deny, Disclaim, Disinherit, Renounce, Repudiate, Unget

Disparage, Disparaging Abuse, Belittle, Decry, Defame, Denigrate, Depreciate, Detract, Discredit, Lessen, Pejorative, Poor mouth, Racist, → **SLANDER**, Slur, Snide, Traduce, Vilify

Dispassionate Calm, Clinical, Composed, Cool, Impartial, Objective, Serene

Dispatch Bowl, Celerity, Consign, Destroy, Dismiss, Expede, Expedite, Express, Gazette, Kibosh, Kill, Missive, Post, Pronto, Remit, Report, → **SEND**, Ship, Slaughter, Slay, Special

Dispel Disperse, Scatter

Dispensation, Dispense(r), Dispense with Absolve, Administer, Aerosol, Apothecary, Automat, Ax(e), Cashpoint, Chemist, Container, Distribute, Dose, Dropper, Exempt, Handout, Indult, Scrap, Spinneret, Vendor, Visitation

Dispersable, Disperse, Dispersion Deflocculate, Diaspora, Diffract, Diffuse, Disband, Dissolve, Lyophil(e), Scail, Scale, → **SCATTER**, Skail, Sow, Strew

Dispirit(ed), Dispiriting Chapfallen, Crestfallen, Dampen, Dash, Daunt, Discourage, Dishearten, Exorcism, Gloomy, Listless, Sackless

Displace(ment), Displaced Antevert, Blueshift, Depose, Disturb, Ectopia, Ectopy, Fault, Heterotopia, Lateroversion, Load, Luxate, Move, Oust, Proptosis, Ptosis, Reffo, Shift, Stir, Subluxation, Unseat, Unsettle, Uproot, Valgus, Varus, Volumetric

Display, Display ground Air, Array, Blaze, Blazon, Brandish, Bravura, Depict, Eclat, Epideictic, Etalage, Evidence, Evince, Exhibition, Exposition, Express, Extend, Extravaganza, Exude, Fireworks, Flash, Flaunt, Float, Gondola, Hang, Head-down, Head-up, Heroics, Lay out, LCD, LED, Lek, Liquid crystal, Manifest, Mount, Muster, Ostentation, Outlay, Overdress, Pageant, Parade, Paraf(f)le, Peepshow, Pixel, Pomp, Propale, Pyrotechnics, Rode, Rodeo, Roll-out, Scene, Shaw, → **SHOW**, Sight, Spectacle, Splash, Splurge, Sport, Spree, State, Stunt, Tableau, Tattoo, Tournament, Up, Vaunt, Wear

Displease(d), Displeasure Anger, Dischuffed, Humph, Irritate, Provoke, Umbrage

Disport Amuse, Divert, Play

Dispose(d), Disposal, Disposition Apt, Arrange, Bestow, Cast, Despatch, Dump, Eighty-six, Kibosh, Lay(-out), Ordonnance, Prone, Sale, Sell, Service, Settle, Stagger

▷ **Disposed, Disposition** *may indicate* an anagram

Disposition Affectation, Attitude, Bent, Bias, Humour, Inclination, Kidney, Lie, Nature, Penchant, Propensity, Talent, Temper(ament), Trim

Dispossess(ed) Abate, Attaint, Bereft, Depose, Deprive, Evict, Oust

Disproportion(ate) Asymmetric, Extreme, Imbalance, Unequal

Disprove, Disproof, Disproval Debunk, Discredit, Negate, Rebut, Rebuttal, Redargue, Reductio ad absurdum, Refel, Refute

Dispute(d), Disputant Argue, Barney, Brangle, Cangle, Case, Chaffer, Challenge, Chorizont(ist), Contend, Contest, Contravene, Contretemps, Controversy, Debate, Demarcation, Deny, Differ, Discept, Discuss, Eristic, Fracas, Fray, Haggle, Kilfud-yoking, Lock-out, Militate, Ob and soller, Odds, Oppugn, Plea, Polemic, Pro-and-con, Quarrel, → **QUESTION**, Quibble, Rag, Resist, Spar, Stickle, Threap(it), Threep(it), Tiff, Tissue, Tug-of-love, Variance, Wrangle

Disqualify Debar, Incapacitate, Recuse, Reject, Unfit

Disquiet(ed) Agitate, Concern, Discomboberate, Discombobulate, → **DISTURB**, Pain, Perturb(ation), Solicit, Turmoil, Uneasy, Unnerve, Unrest, Vex

Disraeli Dizzy, Tancred

Disregard(ed) Anomie, Anomy, Contempt, Defy, Disfavour, Flout, Forget, Ignore, Oblivion, Omit, Overlook, Oversee, Pass, Pretermit, Slight, Spare, Violate, Waive

Disrepair Dilapidation, Fritz, Ruin

Disreputable, Disrepute Base, Disgrace, Grubby, Louche, Low, Lowlife, Notorious, Raffish, Ragamuffin, Reprobate, Rip, Scuzz(ball), Seamy, Seamy side, Shady, Shameful, Shy, Sleazy

Disrespect(ful) Contempt, Derogatory, Discourtesy, Flip(pant), Impiety, Impolite, Irreverent, Profane, Slight, Uncivil

Disrupt(ion) Breach, Cataclasm, Dislocate, Disorder, Distract, Hamper, Interrupt, Jetlag, Mayhem, Perturb, Quonk, Screw, Upheaval

▷ **Disruption** *may indicate* an anagram

Dissatisfaction Displeasure, Distaste, Humph, Umph

Dissect(ion) Analyse, Dismember, Examine, Necrotomy, Zootomy

Dissemble(r) Conceal, Feign, Fox, Hypocrite, Impostor

Dissent(er), Dissension, Dissenting Contend, Differ, Disagree, Discord, Dissident, Faction, Flak, Heretic, Jain, Leveller, Lollard, Noes, Non-CE, Non-con(formist), Occasional conformist, Old Believer, Pantile, Protest, Raskolnik, Recusant, Sectary, Separat(ion)ist, Splinter group, → **STRIFE**, Vary

Dissertation Essay, Excursus, Lecture, Thesis, Treatise

▶ **Dissident** *see* **DESERTER**

Dissimilar Different, Diverse, Heterogeneous, Unlike

Dissipate(d) Debauch, Diffuse, Disperse, Dissolute, Gay, Revel, Scatter, Shatter, Squander, Waste

▷ **Dissipated** *may indicate* an anagram

Dissociate Separate, Sever, Withdraw

Dissolute Degenerate, Demirep, Falstaffian, Hell, Lax, Libertine, Licentious, Loose, Rake-helly, Rakish, Rip, Roué, Wanton

▷ **Dissolute** *may indicate* an anagram

Dissolution Dismissal, Divorce, End, Repeal, Separation

Dissolve Deliquesce, Digest, Disband, Disunite, Lap, Liquesce, Melt, Repeal, Terminate, Thaw

Dissonance Wolf

Dissuade Dehort, Deter, Discourage

Distaff Clotho, Female, Lady, Rock, Stick

Distance Absciss(a), Afield, Apothem, Breadth, Coss, Declination, Eloi(g)n, Farness, Focal, Foot, Headreach, Height, Hyperfocal, Intercalumniation, Interval, Klick, Kos(s), Latitude, League, Length, Mean, Mean free path, Middle, Mileage, Northing, Outland, Parasang, Parsec, Range, Reserve, Rod, Skip, Span, Spitting, Stade, Striking, Way, Yojan, Zenith

Distant Aloof, Cold, Far, Frosty, Hyperfocal, Icy, Long, Northing, Offish, Outland, Polar, Remote, Tele-, Timbuctoo, Yonder

Distaste(ful) Gross-out, Repugnant, Ropy, Scunner, Unpalatable, Unpleasant, Unsavoury

Distemper Ailment, Colourwash, Equine, Hard-pad, Paint, Panleucopenia, Tempera

Distend(ed), Distension Bloat, Dilate, Ectasia, Emphysema, Expand, Hoove, Inflate, Meteorism, → **STRETCH**, Swell, Turgid, Tympanites, Varicocele, Varicose

Distil(late), Distillation, Distiller, Distilling Alcohol, Alembic, Anthracine, Azeotrope, Brew, Condense, Destructive, Drip, Fractional, Naphtha, Pelican, Pyrene, Pyroligneous, Rosin, Turps, Vacuum, Vapour

▷ **Distillation** *may indicate* an anagram

Distinct(ive) Apparent, Characteristic, Clear, Determinate, Different, Discrete, Evident, Grand, Individual, Peculiar, Plain, Separate, Several, Signal, → **SPECIAL**, Stylistic, Trenchant, Vivid

Distinction Beaut(y), Blue, Cachet, Credit, Diacritic, Difference, Dignity, Diorism, Disparity, Division, Eclat, Eminence, Honour, Lustre, Mark, Mystique, Nicety, Note, Nuance, OM, Prominence, Quiddity, Rank, Renown, Speciality, Style, Title

Distinguish(ed), Distinguishing Classify, Contrast, Demarcate, Denote, Diacritic, Different(iate), Discern, Discriminate, Divide, Elevate, Eximious, Mark, Notable, Perceive, Prestigious, Prominent, Secern, Signal, Stamp, Tell

Distort(ion), Distorted Anamorphosis, Bend, Colour, Contort, Deface, Deform, Dent, Fudge, Garble, Helium speech, Jaundiced, Mangle, Misshapen, Pervert, Rubato, Thraw, Time-warp, Travesty, Twist, → **WARP**, Wow, Wrest, Wring, Wry

▷ **Distort(ed)** *may indicate* an anagram

Distract(ed), Distraction Absent, Agitate, Amuse, Avocation, Bewilder, Divert, Embroil, Éperdu, Forhaile, Frenetic, Lost, Madden, Mental, Nepenthe, Perplex, Scatty, Sidetrack, Sledge, Upstage

▷ **Distract(ed)** *may indicate* an anagram

Distrain(t) Na(a)m, Poind, Sequestrate, Stress

Distraught Deranged, Elfish, Elvan, Frantic, Mad, Troubled

Distress(ed), Distressing Afflict, Ail, Alack, Anger, Anguish, Antique, Distraint, Dolour, Exigence, Extremity, Grieve, Harass, Harrow, Heartbreak, Hurt, Ill, → **IN DISTRESS**, Irk, Misease, Misfortune, Need, Oppress, Pain, Poignant, Prey, Sad, Shorn, Sore, SOS, Straits, Traumatic, Tribulation, → **TROUBLE**, Une(a)th, Unstrung

Distribute(d), Distribution, Distributor Allocate, Allot, Binomial, Busbar, Carve, Chi-square, Colportage, Deal, Deliver(y), Deploy, Dish, Dispense, Dispose, Exponential, F, Frequency, Gamma, Gaussian, Geometric, Issue, Lie, Lot, Mete, Normal, Out, Pattern, Poisson, Prorate, Renter, Repartition, Serve, Share

▷ **Distributed** *may indicate* an anagram

District Alsatia, Amhara, Arcadia, Ards, Area, Arrondissement, Bail(l)iwick, Banat, Banate, Bannat, Barrio, Belt, Canton, Cantred, Circar, Classis, Community, Congressional, Diocese, End, Exurb, Federal, Fitzrovia, Gau, Ghetto, Hundred, Lathe, Liberty, Locality, Loin, Manor, Metropolitan, → **NEIGHBOURHOOD**, Oblast, Pachalic, Pale, Pargana, Parish(en), Paroch, Pashalik, Patch, Peak, Pergunnah, Phocis, Precinct, Province, Quarter, Quartier, Rape, → **REGION**, Ride, Riding, Ruhr, Rural, Sanjak, Section, Sheading, Sircar, Sirkar, Soc, Soke(n), Stake, Stannary, Suburb, Sucken, Talooka, Taluk, Tenderloin, Township, Urban, Venue, Vicinage, Walk, Wapentake, Way, Wealden, Zila, Zillah, Zone

Distrust(ful) Caution, Doubt, Misanthropic, Suspect, Wariness

Disturb(ance), Disturbed Ado, Aerate, Affray, Agitate, Atmospherics, Autism, Betoss, Brabble, Brainstorm, Brash, Brawl, Broil, Carfuffle, Collieshangie, Concuss, Delirium, Dementia, Derange, Desecrate, Disquiet, Dust, Dysfunction, Feeze, Firestorm, Fracas, Fray, Fret, Harass, Hoopla, Incident, Incommode, Infest, Interrupt, Jee, Kerfuffle, Kick-up, Kurfuffle, Muss, Outbreak, Perturb(ation), Prabble, Rammy, Ramp, Riot, Ripple, Romage, Rook, Roughhouse, Rouse, Ruckus, Ruction, Ruffle, Rumpus, Shake, Shellshock, Shindy, Shook-up, Stashie, Static, Steer, Stir, Sturt, Tremor, Trouble, Turbulent, Unquiet, Unrest, Unsettle, Upheaval, Uproot, → **UPSET**, Vex

▷ **Disturb(ed)** *may indicate* an anagram

Disunite Alienate, Dissever, Divide, Divorce, Split

Disuse Abandon, Abeyance, Desuetude, Discard, Lapse

Ditch Barathron, Barathrum, Channel, Crash-land, Cunette, Delf, Delph, Dike, Discard, Donga, Drainage, Drop, Dyke, Euripus, Foss(e), Graft, Grip, Gully, Ha(w)-ha(w), Jettison, Khor, Level, Lode, Moat, Na(l)la(h), Nulla(h), Rean, Reen, Rhine, Rid, Sea, Sheuch, Sheugh, Sike, Sloot, Sluit, Spruit, Stank, Syke, Trench

Dither(ing) Agitato, Bother, Dicker, Faff, Hesitate, Indecisive, Pussyfoot, Twitter
Dittany Gas-plant
Ditty, Ditties Air, Arietta, Canzonet, Departmental, Jingle, Lay, Song
Diuretic Frusemide, Furosemide, Spironolactone
Diva Callas, Patti, Singer
Divan Compilement, Congress, Couch, Council, Settee, Sofa
Dive(r), Diving Armstand, Backflip, Belly-flop, Crash, Dart, Den, Duck, File,
  Full-gainer, Half-gainer, Header, Honkytonk, Jackknife, Joint, Ken, Nitery, Nose,
  Pass, Pickpocket, Pike, Plummet, Plunge, Plutocrat, Power, Saturation, Scoter,
  Skin, Sound, Stage, Stoop, Submerge, Swallow, Swan, Swoop, Tailspin, Urinant
Diver(s) Didapper, Duck, Embergoose, Flop, Frogman, Gainer, Grebe, Guillemot,
  Loom, Loon, Lungie, Many, Merganser, Pearl, Pike, Plong(e), Pochard, Poker,
  Puffin, Sawbill, Scuba, Snake-bird, Speakeasy, Sundry, Urinator, Various, Zoom
Diverge(nce) Branch, Deviate, Divaricate, Spread, Swerve, Variant, Veer
Divers Miscellaneous, Some
Diverse, Diversify Alter, Chequer, Dapple, Different, Eclectic, Interlard,
  Intersperse, Manifold, Motley, Multifarious, Separate, Variegate, Various, Vary
Diversion, Divert(ing) Amuse, Avocation, Beguile, Deflect, Detour, Disport,
  Dissuade, Distract, Entertain, Game, Hare, Hobby, Interlude, Pastime, Pleasure,
  Prolepsis, Ramp, Red-herring, Refract, Reroute, Ruse, Shunt, Sideshow, Sidetrack,
  Siphon, Smokescreen, Sport, Stalking-horse, Steer, Stratagem, Sublimation, Sway,
  Switch, Tickle, Upstage, Yaw
▷ **Diverting** *may indicate* an anagram
Divest Denude, Rid, Strip, Undeck, Undress
Divide(d), Division Abkhazia, Adzharia, Apportion, Balk, Band, Bipartite,
  Bisect, Branch, Cantle, Chancery, Cleft, Comminute, Commot(e), Continental,
  Counter-pale, Cut, Deal, Demerge, Digital, Dimidiate, Dissever, Estrange, Fork,
  Great, Indent, Parcel, Part, Partitive, Party wall, Pentomic, Plebs, Polarise, Ramify,
  Rend, Rift, Separate, Sever, Share, → **SPLIT**, Stanza, Sunder, Tribalism, Trisect,
  Utgard, Watershed, Zone
Dividend Bonus, Div, Interim, Into, Peace, Share
Divination, Diviner Anthroposcopy, Arithmancy, Augury, Auspices, Axinomancy,
  Belomancy, Bibliomancy, Botanomancy, Capnomancy, Cartomancy, Ceromancy,
  Chiromancy, Cleromancy, Coscinomancy, Crithomancy, Crystal-gazing,
  Crystallomancy, Doodlebug, Dowser, Empyromancy, Geloscopy, Geomancy,
  Gyromancy, Hariolation, Haruspex, Hepatoscopy, Hieromancy, Hieroscopy,
  Hydromancy, I Ching, Intuition, Lampadomancy, Leconomancy, Lithomancy,
  Magic, Mantic, Myomancy, Omphalomancy, Oneiromancy, Onychomancy,
  Ornithomancy, Ornithoscopy, Osteomancy, Palmistry, Pegomancy, Pessomancy,
  Pyromancy, Radiesthesia, Rhabdomancy, Scapulimancy, Sciomancy, Seer, Sibyl,
  Sideromancy, Sortes, Sortilege, Spae(man), Spodomancy, Taghairm, Tais(c)h,
  Theomancy, Tripudiary, Vaticanator, Xylomancy, Zoomancy
Divine, Divine presence, Divinity Acoemeti, Ambrose, Atman, Avatar,
  Beatific, Celestial, Clergyman, Conjecture, Curate, DD, Deduce, Deity, Douse,
  Dowse, Ecclesiastic, Forecast, Foretell, Fuller, → **GOD**, → **GODDESS**, Godhead,
  Guess, Hariolate, Heavenly, Holy, Hulse, Immortal, Inge, Isiac, Kami, Mantic,
  Numen, Numinous, Olympian, Pontiff, Predestinate, Predict, Presage, Priest,
  Prophesy, RE, Rector, RI, Rimmon, Scry, Sense, Seraphic, Shechinah, Shekinah,
  Spae, Superhuman, Supernal, Theandric, Theanthropic, Theologise, Theology,
  Triune
Division, Divisible Amitosis, Angiosperm, Arcana, Arm, Arrondissement,

Bajocian, Banat(e), Bannet, Bar, Bizone, Branch, Brome, Caesura, Canton, Cantred, Cantref, Cassini's, Caste, Category, Cell, Champart, Chapter, Classification, Cleft, Cloison, Clove, Comitatus, Commot(e), Commune, Compartment, Coralline Crag, Corps, County, Crevasse, Curia, Department, Dichotomy, Disagreement, Disunity, Duan, Eyalet, Family, Farren, Fissile, Fork, Grisons, Guberniya, Gulf, Gulph, Hedge, Hide, Hundred, Inning, Isogloss, Keuper, Kim(m)eridgian, Lathe, Leet, Legion, Lindsey, List, Lobe, Long, M(e)iosis, Mitosis, Mofussil, Nome, Pachytene, Pargana, Part, Partition, Passus, Pergunnah, Period, Phratry, Phyle, Phylum, Pipe, Pitaka, Platoon, Polarisation, Presidency, Queen's Bench, Quotition, Rape, Red Crag, Reduction, Region, Replum, Reservation, Riding, Sanjak, Schism, Section, Sector, Segment, Semeion, Sept(ate), Sever, Share, Sheading, Shed, Shire, Short, Stage, Subheading, Tahsil, Tanach, Taxis, Telophase, Tepal, Thanet, Trichotomy, Trio, Trivium, Troop, Tuath, Unit, Vilayet, Volost, Wapentake, Ward, Watershed

Divisor Aliquant, Aliquot

Divorce(d) Alienate, Diffarreation, Disaffiliate, Dissolve, Disunion, Div, Estrange, Get(t), Part, Separate, Sequester, → **SUNDER**, Talak, Talaq

Divot Clod, Sod, Turf

Divulge Confess, Disclose, Expose, Publish, Reveal, Split, Tell, Unveil, Utter

DIY Flatpack

Dizziness, Dizzy Beaconsfield, Ben, Capricious, Dinic, Disraeli, Giddy, Giglot, Lightheaded, Mazey, Mirligoes, Scotodinia, Swimming, Vertiginous, → **VERTIGO**, Woozy

DJ Deejay, Mixmaster, Monkey-suit, Presenter, Selecta, Shockjock, Tuxedo, Veejay

DNA Antisense, Centromere, Chromatin, Cistron, Codon, Complementary, Cytosine, Exon, Gene, Heteroduplex, Homopolymer, Intron, Junk, Microsatellite, Mitochondrial, Muton, Nucleosome, Operator, Papovavirus, Plasmid, Poxvirus, Procaryote, Profiling, Prokaryote, Purine, Recombinant, Replication fork, Replicon, RNA, Satellite, Selfish, Southern blot, Synthetic, Telomere, Thymidine, Transposon, Vector, Watson-Crick model

Do(es), Doing Accomplish, Achieve, Act, Anent, Banquet, Beano, Begin, Blow-out, Char, Cheat, Chisel, Cod, Con, Cozen, Deed, Dich, Dish, Div, Doth, Dupe, Effectuate, Enact, Execute, Fare, Function, Gull, Handiwork, Hoax, Mill, Perform, Provide, Same, Serve, Settle, Shindig, Spif(f)licate, Suffice, Thrash, Thrive, Ut

▷ **Do** *may indicate* an anagram

Do away Abolish, Banish, Demolish, Kill

Docile Agreeable, Amenable, Biddable, Dutiful, Facile, Meek, Submissive, Tame, Tractable, Yielding

Dock(er), Docked, Docks Abridge, Barber, Basin, Bistort, Bob, Camber, Canaigre, Clip, Crop, Curta(i)l, Cut, Deduct, De-tail, Dry, Floating, Grapetree, Graving, Knotweed, Longshoreman, Lop, Marina, Moor, Off-end, Pare, Patience, Pen, Pier, Quay, Rhubarb, Rumex, Rump, Scene, Seagull, Shorten, Snakeweed, Sorrel, Sourock, Stevedore, Tilbury, Watersider, Wet, Wharf, Wharfie, Yard

Docket Invoice, Label, Tag

Dockyard Arsenal, Rosyth

Doctor(s) Allopath, Alter, Arnold, Asclepiad, Barefoot, Barnardo, Bleeder, BMA, Bones, Breeze, Bright, Brighton, Brown, Caius, Castrate, Chapitalize, Clinician, Cook, Cup(per), Cure(r), Dale, Diagnose, Dr, Dryasdust, Erasmus, Extern(e), Fake, Falsify, Family, Faustus, Feldsher, Fell, Fiddle, Finlay, Flying, Foster, Fundholder, Galen, Geriatrician, Geropiga, GP, Hakeem, Hakim, Healer, Homeopath, Houseman, Hyde, Imhotep, Intern, Internist, Jekyll, Jenner, Johnson, Kildare, Lace, Leach, Leech, Linacre, Load, Locum, Luke, Manette, Massage, MB, MD, Medicate,

Medico, Middleton, Mindererus, Minister, Misrepresent, MO, MOH, Molla(h), Moreau, Mulla(h), Neuter, No, Ollamh, Ollav, Paean, Panel, Pangloss, Paracelsus, Paramedic, Pedro, PhD, Physician, Pill(s), Practitioner, Quack, Quacksalver, Rabbi, RAMC, Registrar, Resident, Rig, Rorschach, Salk, Sangrado, Saw, Sawbones, School, Script, Seraphic, Seuss, Shaman, Slammer, Slop, Spin, Stum, Surgeon, Syn, Syntax, Thorne, Treat, Vaidya, Vet, Water, Watson, Who, Witch

▷ **Doctor(ed)** *may indicate* an anagram

Doctrine Adoptianism, Adoptionism, Antinomian, Apollinarian, Archology, Arianism, Averr(h)oism, Bonism, Brezhnev, Cab(b)ala, Calvanism, Catastrophism, Chiliasm, Consubstantiation, Credo, Creed, Determinism, Ditheletism, Docetism, Dogma, Doxie, Doxy, Dualism, Esotery, Federalism, Fideism, Finalism, Functionalism, Gnosticism, Gospel, Henotheism, Holism, Idealism, Immaterialism, Immersionism, Indeterminism, Infralapsarianism, Islam, Ism, Jansenism, Krypsis, Laches, Lore, Malthusian, Manich(a)eism, Materialism, Metempsychosis, Molinism, Monadism, Monergism, Monism, Monothel(et)ism, Monroe, Neomonianism, Nestorianism, Neutral monism, Nihilism, Panentheism, Pantheism, Pelagianism, Physiocracy, Pluralism, Pragmatism, Predestination, Premillennialism, Preterition, Probabilism, Psilanthropism, Pythagorean(ism), Real presence, Reformism, Satyagrahi, Scotism, Secularism, Sharia, Sheria, Shibboleth, Solidism, Strong meat, Subjectivism, Sublapsarianism, Subpanation, Substantialism, Swedenborgianism, Syndicalism, Synergism, System, Teleology, → **TENET**, Terminism, Theory, Theravada, Thomism, Transubstantiation, Trialism, Tridentine, Tutiorism, Universalism, Utilitarianism, Voluntarism, Wasm, Weismannism, Whiteboyism, Zoism, Zwinglian

Document(s), Documentary Brevet, Bumf, Bumph, Carta, Certificate, Charge sheet, Charter, Contract, Conveyance, Covenant, Daftar, Deed, Diploma, Docket, Doco, Dompass, Dossier, Fiat, Form, Grand Remonstrance, Holograph, Latitat, Logbook, Mandamus, Offer, Papers, Policy, Precept, Production, Pro forma, Public, Ragman, Ragment, Record, Resort, Roll, Roul(e), Screed, Source, Stamp note, Voucher, Warrant, Waybill, Writ, Write up

Dod Pet, Poll

Dodder(y) Old, Shake, Stagger, Strangleweed, Totter, Tremble

Doddle Easy

Dodge, Dodgy Artful, Avoid, Bell-ringing, Column, Elude, Evade, Evasion, Iffy, Jink, Jook, Jouk, Racket, Ruse, Shirk, Sidestep, Skip, Slalom, Slinter, Tip, Trick, Twist, Urchin, Weave, Welsh, Wheeze, Wire, Wrinkle

Doe(s) Deer, Faun, Hind

Doff Avail(e), Avale, Remove, Rouse, Shed, Tip

Dog(s) Assistance, Bowwow, Canes, Canidae, Canine, Feet, Fire, Fog, Heading, Hot, Hunter, Kennel, Leading, Native, Nodding, Pursue, Ratter, Sea, Search, Seeing-eye, Shadow, Sleeve, Sleuthhound, Spotted, Stalk, Strong-eye, Sun, Tag, Tail, Top, Tracker, Trail, Truffle, Tumbler, Wammul, Water, Water dog, Working, Yellow

---

DOGS

3 letters:	Pug	Bird	Dane
Cur	Rab	Brak	Fido
Eye	Yap	Bran	Heel
Gun		Bush	Iron
Pig	4 letters:	Cant	Kuri
Pom	Barb	Chow	Kuta

Kuti
Leam
Lyam
Mutt
Oath
Peke
Puli
Rach
Sled
Stag
Tike
Toby
Tosa
Tray
Tyke
Wolf

5 letters:
Akita
Alans
Apsos
Argos
Boots
Boxer
Brach
Cairn
Coach
Dhole
Dingo
Guard
Guide
Haunt
Hound
Husky
Hyena
Kurre
Laika
Lorel
Luath
Merle
Moera
Pidog
Pluto
Pooch
Rache
Ratch
Rover
Shock
Spitz
Spoor
Whelp

Zorro

6 letters:
Afghan
Bandog
Barbet
Barker
Basset
Beagle
Bitser
Blanch
Borzoi
Bounce
Bowler
Briard
Caesar
Canaan
Chenet
Cocker
Collie
Dangle
Eskimo
Gelert
Goorie
Heeler
Jackal
Katmir
Kelpie
Kennet
Ketmir
Kratim
Lassie
Mauthe
Messan
Moppet
Pariah
Piedog
Police
Poodle
Pye-dog
Ranger
Saluki
Setter
Shaggy
Shough
Sirius
Sothic
Talbot
Teckel
Touser
Towser

Vizsla
Westie
Yapper
Yorkie

7 letters:
Andiron
Basenji
Bobbery
Boerbul
Bouvier
Brachet
Bulldog
Courser
Griffon
Harrier
Hearing
Iceland
Lowchen
Lurcher
Maltese
Maremma
Mastiff
Mongrel
Orthrus
Pointer
Prairie
Raccoon
Reynard
Samoyed
Sapling
Sausage
Shar-Pei
Sheltie
Shih tzu
Showghe
Sloughi
Sniffer
Spaniel
Starter
→ **TERRIER**
Volpino
Whiffet
Whippet
Yapster

8 letters:
Aardwolf
Aberdeen
Airedale
Alsatian

Blenheim
Bouvrier
Bratchet
Brittany
Carriage
Cerberus
Chow-chow
Doberman
Elkhound
Hovawart
Huntaway
Kangaroo
Keeshond
Komondor
Labrador
Landseer
Malamute
Malemute
Papillon
Pekinese
Pembroke
Pinscher
Samoyede
Sealyham
Sheepdog
Springer
Turnspit
Warragal
Warrigal

9 letters:
Buckhound
Chihuahua
Coonhound
Dachshund
Dalmatian
Deerhound
Dobermann
Draghound
Gazehound
Great Dane
Greyhound
Harlequin
Kerry blue
Lhasa apso
Molossian
Pekingese
Retriever
Schnauzer
Staghound
Wolfhound

10 letters:
Bedlington
Bloodhound
Blueheeler
Fox terrier
Otterhound
Pomeranian
Rottweiler
Schipperke
Shin-barker
Tripehound
Weimaraner

11 letters:
Bichon frise
Irish setter
Jack Russell
Labradoodle
Montmorency
Skye terrier
Tibetan apso
Trendle-tail

Trindle-tail
Trundle-tail
Wishtonwish

12 letters:
Border collie
Gazelle hound
Japanese chin
Newfoundland
Saint Bernard
Welsh terrier
West Highland

13 letters:
Affenpinscher
Dandie Dinmont
Scotch terrier
Sussex spaniel

14 letters:
Italian spinone
Norwich terrier

Tibetan mastiff
Tibetan spaniel
Tibetan terrier

15 letters:
Bernese mountain
Estreia mountain
Hamilton stovare
Mexican hairless
Norwegian buhund
Portuguese water
Swedish vallhund

16 letters:
Australian cattle
Doberman-pinscher
Lancashire heeler
Pyrenean mountain
Russian wolfhound
Shetland sheepdog

17 letters:
Anatolian Shepherd
Dobermann-
  pinscher

18 letters:
Large
  Munsterlander
Old English
  sheepdog
Rhodesian
  ridgeback

20 letters:
Landseer
  Newfoundland

21 letters:
Polish Lowland
  sheepdog

Dog-bane Apocynum
Doge Dandolo
Dogfish Huss, Rigg
Dogged Determined, Die-hard, Dour, Indefatigable, Pertinacious, Stubborn, Sullen
Doggerel Crambo, Jingle, Laisse, Rat-rhyme
Dog letter R
Dogma(tic) Assertive, Belief, Conviction, Creed, Doctrinal, En tête, Ideology, Ipse
  dixit, Opinionative, Pedagogic, Peremptory, Pontifical, Positive, → TENET
Do-gooder Piarist, Reformer, Salvationist, Samaritan, Scout
Dogsbody Bottle-washer, Gofer, Skivvy
Dog star Canicula, Lassie, Sirius, Sothic
Do it Dich
Dolce Stop, Sweet
Dole Alms, Batta, B(u)roo, Give, Grief, Maundy, Payment, Pittance, Pog(e)y, Ration,
  → SHARE, Tichborne, Vail, Vales
Doll(y) Barbie®, Bimbo, Common, Corn, Creeper, Crumpet, Dress, Dutch, Golliwog,
  Kachina, Kewpie®, Maiden, Marionette, Matryoshka, Maumet, Mommet,
  Mummet, Ookpik®, Ornament, Paris, Parton, Peggy, Poppet, Puppet, Ragdoll,
  Russian, Sis(ter), Sitter, Tearsheet, Toy, Trolley, Varden, Washboard, Wax
Dollar(s) Balboa, Boliviano, Buck, Cob, Cob money, Euro, Fin, Greenback, Iron man,
  Peso, Petrol, Piastre, Pink, S, Sand, Sawbuck, Sawhorse, Scrip, Smacker, Spin,
  Sword, Top, Wheel
Dollop Glob, Helping, Share
▷ **Dolly** *may indicate* an anagram
Dolly-bird Dish
Dolour Grief, Pain, Sorrow
Dolphin Amazon, Arion, Beluga, Bottlenose, Cetacean, Coryphene, Delphinus,
  Grampus, Lampuka, Lampuki, Mahi-mahi, Meer-swine, Porpess(e), Risso's,

River, Sea-pig

Dolt Ass, Blockhead, Clodhopper, Noodle, Oaf, Ouph(e), Owl, → **STUPID**

Domain Archaea, Bacteria, Bourn(e), Demain, Demesne, Eminent, Emirate, Empire, Estate, Eukarya, Manor, Predicant, Public, Rain, Realm, Region, Reign

Dome(-shaped) Al-Aqsa, Cap, Cupola, Cupula, Dagoba, Geodesic, Head, Imperial, Louvre, Millennium, Onion, Periclinal, Rotunda, Salt, Stupa, Tee, Tholos, Tholus, Tope, Vault, Xanadu

Domestic(ate) Char, Cleaner, Dom, Esne, Familiar, Home-keeping, Homely, House, Housetrain, Humanise, Interior, Internal, Intestine, Maid, Menial, → **SERVANT**, Swadeshi, Tame, Woman

Domicile Abode, Dwelling, Hearth, Home, Ménage

Dominate, Dominance, Dominant, Domination Ascendancy, Baasskap, Ballbreaker, Bethrall, Clou, Coerce, Control, Enslave, Hegemony, Henpeck, Maisterdome, Mesmerise, Momism, Monopolise, O(v)ergang, Override, Overshadow, Power, Preponderant, Preside, Rule, Soh, → **SUBDUE**, Subjugate, Tower

Domineer(ing) Authoritarian, Boss, Henpeck, Lord, Ride, Swagger, Tyrannize

Dominica(n) Jacobite, Monk, OP, Preaching friar, Predicant, Savonarola, WD

Dominie Maister, Master, Pastor, Sampson, Schoolmaster

Dominion Dom, Empire, Khanate, NZ, Realm, Reame, Reign, → **RULE**, Supremacy, Sway, Territory

Domino(es) Card, Fats, Mask, Matador

Don Academic, Address, Assume, Caballero, Camorrist, Endue, Fellow, Garb, Giovanni, Indew, Juan, Lecturer, Mafia, Prof, Quixote, Reader, Señor, Spaniard, Tutor, Wear

Dona(h) Duckie, Love

Donate, Donation Aid, Bestow, Contribution, Gift, Give, Peter's pence, Present, Wakf, Waqf

Done Achieved, Complete, Crisp, Ended, Executed, Had, Over, Spitcher, Tired, Weary

Donjon Dungeon, Keep

Donkey Ass, Burro, Cardophagus, Cuddie, Cuddy, Dapple, Dick(e)y, Dunce, Eeyore, Fussock, Genet(te), Jackass, Jennet, Jenny, Jerusalem pony, Kulan, Modestine, Moke, Mule, Neddy, Nodding, Onager, Stupid, Years

Donor Benefactor, Bestower, Settlor, Universal

Doo Dove

Doodle(r) Scribble, Yankee

Doodlebug Antlion, Larva, V1

Doofer Thingumabob

Doom(ed) Condemned, Damnation, Date, Destine, Destiny, → **FATE**, Fay, Fey, Fie, Goner, Ill-starred, Lot, Predestine, Preordain, Ragnarok, Ruined, Sentence, Spitcher, Star-crossed, Weird

Doone Carver, Lorna

Door(s), Doorstep, Doorway Aperture, Communicating, Damnation, Drecksill, Dutch, Elephant, Entry, Exit, Fire, Folding, Front, Gull-wing, Haik, Hake, Hatch, Heck, Ingress, Jib, Lintel, Louver, Louvre, Muntin, Oak, Open, Overhead, Patio, Portal, Postern, Revolving, Rory, Screen, Sliding, Stable, Stage, Storm, Street, Swing, Tailgate, Trap, Up and over, Vomitory, Wicket, Yett

Doorkeeper, Doorman Bouncer, Commissionaire, Guardian, Janitor, Ostiary, Porter, Tiler, Tyler, Usher

Doormat Subservient, Weakling

Doorpost Architrave, Dern, Durn, Jamb, Yate, Yett
Dope Acid, Amulet, Bang, Coke, Crack, → **DRUG**, Gen, Goose, Info, Lowdown, Narcotic, Nobble, Rutin, Sedate, Soup, → **STUPID PERSON**, Tea
Doppelganger Double, Ringer
Dorcas Gazelle, Needle, Shepherdess
Dorian, Doric Metope, Mutule
Doris Day, Lessing, Mollusc
Dormant Abed, Comatose, Hibernating, Inactive, Inert, Joist, Latent, Quiescent, Resting, → **SLEEPING**, Torpescent
Dormer Luthern
Dormitory Barrack, Bunkhouse, Dorter, Dortour, Hall, Hostel, Quarters
Dormouse Loir
Dorothy Bag, Dot, Sayers
Dorsal Back, Neural, Notal
Dory Fish, John
Dosage, Dose Absorbed, Acute, Administer, Aperient, Booster, Cascara, Cumulative, Drachm, Draught, Drench, Drug, Hit, Kilogray, Lethal, → **MEASURE**, Permissible, Physic, Posology, Potion, Powder, Rem, Threshold, Tolerance
Doss (house) Dharmsala, Dharmshala, Kip, Padding-ken, Spike
Dossier File, Record
Dot(s), Dotted, Dotty Absurd, Bind(h)i, Bullet, Centred, Criblé, Dieresis, Dit, Dower, Dowry, Ellipsis, Engrailed, Leader, Lentiginose, Limp, Micro, Morse, Occult, Or, Particle, Pinpoint, Pixel, → **POINT**, Polka, Precise, Punctuate, Punctulate, Punctum, Schwa, Semé(e), Set, Speck, Spot, Sprinkle, Stigme, Stipple, Stud, Tap, Tittle, Trema, Umlaut
Dote, Dotage, Doting, Dotard Adore, Anile, Anility, Cocker, Dobbie, Idolise, Imbecile, Pet, Prize, Senile, Spoon(e)y, Tendre, Twichild
Double(s) Amphibious, Ancipital, Bi-, Bifold, Binate, Clone, Counterpart, Crease, Dimeric, Doppel-ganger, Doppio, Dual, Duo, Duple(x), Duplicate, Equivocal, Fetch, Fold, Foursome, Geminate, Gimp, Image, Ingeminate, Ka, Look-alike, Loop, Martingale, Pair, Parlay, Polyseme, Reflex, Replica, Ringer, Run, Similitude, Spit, Trot, Turnback, Twae, → **TWIN**, Two(fold)
Double-barrelled Tautonym
Double-cross, Double dealing Ambidext(e)rous, Two-time
Double-entendre Polyseme, Polysemy
Doublet Peascod, Pourpoint, TT
Doubt(s), Doubter, Doubtful Agnostic, Ambiguous, Aporia, Askance, But, Debatable, Discredit, Distrust, Dubiety, Dubitate, Hesitate, Hum, Iffy, Incertitude, Misgiving, Mistrust, → **NO DOUBT**, Precarious, Qualm, Query, → **QUESTION**, Rack, Scepsis, Sceptic, Scruple, Second thoughts, Shady, Shy, Sic, Skepsis, Sus, Suspect, Suspicious, Suss, Thomas, Thos, Umph, Uncertain, Unsure, Waver
Doubtless Certain, Iwis, Probably, Sure, Truly, Ywis
Douceur Bonus, Sop, Sweetener
Douche Bath, Gush, Rinse, Shower, Wash
Dough(y) Boodle, Cake, Calzone, Cash, Duff, Gnocchi, Hush-puppy, Knish, Loot, Magma, Masa, Money, Paste, Pop(p)adum, Ready, Sad, Sour, Spondulicks, Strudel
Doughboy Dumpling, Soldier
Doughnut Beavertail®, Cruller, Knish, Koeksister, Olycook, Olykoek, Sinker, Torus
Doughty Brave, Intrepid, Resolute, Stalwart, Valiant
Dour Glum, Hard, Mirthless, Morose, Reest, Reist, Sinister, Sullen, Taciturn
Douse Dip, Drench, Extinguish, Snuff, Splash

Dove Collared, Columbine, Culver, Cushat, Diamond, Doo, Ground, Ice-bird, Mourning, Pacifist, → PIGEON, Queest, Quoist, Ring, Rock, Stock, Turtle
Dove-cot(e) Columbarium, Columbary, Louver, Louvre, Lover
Dovetail Fit, Lewis(son), Mortise, Tally, Tenon
Dowager Elder, Widow
Dowdy Frumpish, Mopsy, Mums(e)y, Shabby, Sloppy, Slovenly
Dowel Peg, Pin
Down(s), Downbeat, Downsize, Downward, Downy A bas, Abase, Abattu, Alow, Amort, Bank, Below, Berkshire, Blue, Cast, Catabasis, Chapfallen, Comous, Cottony, Crouch, Darling, Dejected, Dowl(e), Drink, Epsom, Feather, Fledge, Floccus, Flue, Fluff, Fly, Fuzz, Goonhilly, Ground, Hair, Hill, Humble, Humiliate, Jeff, Kennet, Lanugo, Losing, Low, Lower, Nap, Neck, Oose, Ooze, Owing, Pappus, Pennae, Pile, Plumage, Powder, Quash, Repress, Sebum, Slim, Thesis, Thistle, Tomentum, Under, Unserviceable, Urinant, Vail, Wold, Wretched
Downcast Abject, Chapfallen, Despondent, Disconsolate, Dumpish, Hangdog, Hopeless, Melancholy, Woebegone
Downfall, Downpour Cataract, Collapse, Deluge, Fate, Flood, Hail, Onding, Overthrow, Rain, Ruin, Shower, Thunder-plump, Torrent, Undoing, Waterspout
Downgrade(d) Déclassé, Disrate
Downright Absolute, Arrant, Bluff, Candid, Clear, Complete, Flat, Plumb, Plump, Pure, Rank, Sheer, Stark, Utter
Downstairs Below
Downturn Slump
Downwind Leeward
Dowry Dot, Dower, Lobola, Lobolo, Merchet, Portion, Settlement, Tocher
Dowse(r), Dowsing Divine, Enew, Fireman, Radionics, Rhabdomancy, Water-witch
Doxology Gloria, Glory
Doxy Harlot, Loose woman, Wench
Doyen Dean, Senior
Doze Catnap, Ca(u)lk, Dove(r), Nap, Nod, Semi-coma, Sleep, Slip, Slumber
Dozen(s) Baker's, Long, Round, Thr(e)ave, Twal, Twelve
Dr Debtor, Doctor, Dram
Drab Ash-grey, Cloth, Dell, Dingy, Dull, Dun, Ecru, Isabel(line), Lifeless, Livor, Mumsy, Olive, Prosaic, Pussel, Quaker-colour, Rig, Road, Scarlet woman, Slattern, Sloven, Subfusc, Tart, Trull, Wanton, Whore
Drabble Bemoil, Draggle
Dracula Bat, Count, Vampire
Draft Cheque, Draw, Ebauche, Essay, Landsturm, Minute, MS, Outline, Plan, Press, Project, Rough, Scheme, Scroll, Scrowle, → SKETCH
Drag Car, Drail, Dredge, Drogue, Elicit, Eonism, Epicene, Extort, Fiscal, Form, Hale, Harl, → HAUL, Induced, Keelhaul, La Rue, Lug, Nuisance, Parasite, Pressure, Profile, Puff, Pull, Rash, Sag, Schlep, Shockstall, Shoe, Skidpan, Sled, Snig, Sweep, Toke, Tote, Tow, Trail, Trailing vortex, Train, Travail, Travois, Trawl, Treck, Trek, Tug, Tump, Vortex
Draggle Drail, Lag, Straggle
Dragon Aroid, Basilisk, Bel, Bellemère, Chaperon(e), Chindit, Draco, Drake, Fafnir, Fire-drake, Gargouille, Komodo, Kung-kung, Ladon, Lindworm, Opinicus, Peist, Puk, Python, Rouge, Safat, Shrew, Typhoeus, Wantley, Wivern, Worm, Wyvern
Dragonfly Aeschna, Demoiselle, Devil's darning needle, Nymph, Odonata
Dragon's teeth Cadmus, Spartae, Sparti
Dragoon Coerce, Force, Press, Trooper

Drain(ed), Drainage, Draining, Drainpipe Bleed, Brain, Buzz, Catchment, Catchwater, Channel, Cloaca, Condie, Cundy, Delf, Delph, Dewater, Ditch, Dry, Ea(u), → **EMPTY**, Emulge(nt), Exhaust, Field, Fleet, Grating, Grip, Gully, Gutter, Ketavothron, Kotabothron, Lade, Leach, Leech, Limber, Lose, Lymphatic, Milk, Mole, Nala, Nalla(h), Nulla(h), Penrose, Pump, Rack, Rone, Sap, Scupper, Seton, Sew(er), Sheuch, Sheugh, Shore, Silver, Sink, Siver, Sluice, Sluse, Soakaway, Sough, Spend, Stank, Storm, Sump, Sure, Syver, Tile, Trench, Trocar, Unwater, Ureter, U-trap, Weary, Well

Dram Drink, Drop, Nipperkin, Nobbler, Portion, Snifter, Tickler, Tiff, Tot, Wet

Drama(tic), Drama school Auto, Azione, Catastasis, Charade, Closet, Comedy, Costume, Drastic, Epic, ER, Farce, Heroic, Histrionic, Kabuki, Kathakali, Kitchen sink, Legit, Legitimate, Mask, Masque, Mime, Moralities, No, Nogaku, Noh, Piece, Play, RADA, Scenic, Sensational, Singspiel, Stagy, Striking, Tetralogy, Theatric, Thespian, Tragedy, Unities, Wagnerian, Wild

Dramatist Adamov, Aeschylus, Albee, Aristophanes, Beaumarchais, Beaumont, Brecht, Bridie, Calderon, Congreve, Corneille, Coward, Drinkwater, Eumenides, Euripides, Fletcher, Frisch, Fry, Gay, Genet, Gogol, Goldoni, Havel, Ibsen, Ionesco, Jarry, Kyd, Lyly, Massinger, Menander, Middleton, Molière, Odets, O'Neill, Osborne, Otway, Pinero, Pirandello, Plautus, → **PLAYWRIGHT**, Racine, Rostand, Rowe, Rowley, Schiller, Seneca, Shadwell, Shaffer, Sherriff, Sophocles, Stoppard, Strindberg, Synge, Terence, Udall, Vanbrugh, Voltaire, Webster, Wedekind, Wesker, Wilde, Wilder, Will, → **WRITER**, Yeats

Dram-shop Bar, Boozingken, Bousingken

Drape(ry) Adorn, Coverlet, Coverlid, Curtain, Festoon, Fold, Hang, Mantling, Swathe, Valance, Veil, Vest

Draper Clothier, Gilpin, Haberdasher, Hosier, Mercer, Outfitter, Ruth, Scotch cuddy, Tailor

Drastic Dire, Dramatic, Extreme, Harsh, Purge, Senna, → **SEVERE**, Violent

Drat Bother, Dang, Darn

Draught(s), Draughtsman(ship) Aloetic, Aver, Breeze, Dam, Design, Drench, Drink, Fish, Gulp, Gust, Haal, Hippocrene, King, Line, Men, Nightcap, Outline, Plan, Potation, Potion, Pull, Quaff, Sketch, Sleeping, Slug, Swig, Tracer, Up-current, Veronal, Waucht, Waught, Williewaught

▷ **Draught** *may refer to* fishing

Draught-board Dam-board, Dambrod

Dravidian Tamil

Draw (off), Drawer(s), Drawing, Drawn Adduct, Allure, Attract, Bleed, Blueprint, Bottom, Cartoon, Charcoal, Cock, Crayon, Dead-heat, Delineate, Dentistry, Derivation, Describe, Detail, Diagram, Dis(em)bowel, Doodle, Dr, Draft, Drag, Dress, Educe, Elevation, Elongate, Entice, Equalise, Evaginate, Extract, Fet(ch), Freehand, Fusain, Gather, Gaunt, Glorybox, Graphics, Gut, Haggard, Hale, Halve, Haul, Indraft, Induce, Indue, Inhale, Isometric, Lead, Lengthen, Limn, Line, Longbow, Lottery, Mechanical, Monotint, No-score, Orthograph, Pantalet(te)s, Panty, Pastel, Perpetual check, Petroglyph, Profile, Protract, Pull, Rack, Raffle, Remark, Scenography, Scent, Score, Seductive, Sepia, Sesquipedalian, Shottle, Shuttle, Silverpoint, Siphon, Sketch, Slub, Snig, Spin, Stalemate, Stretch, Study, Stumps, Sweepstake, Syphon, Tap, Taut, Technical, Tempt, Tenniel, Tie, Till, Toke, Tole, Tombola, Top, Tose, Tow(age), Toze, Traction, Trice, Troll, Tug, Unsheathe, Uplift, Wash, Working

▷ **Draw** *may indicate* something to smoke

Drawback Catch, Downside, Ebb, Handicap, Impediment, → **OBSTACLE**, Rebate,

Retraction, Shrink, Snag
Drawbridge Bascule, Pontlevis
Drawl Dra(u)nt, Haw, Slur, Twang
▷ **Drawn** *may indicate* an anagram
Drawn up Atrip, Drafted
Dray Cart, Lorry, Wagon
Dread(ed) Angst, Anxiety, Awe, Fear, → **HORROR**, Rasta, Redoubt, Thing
Dreadful Awful, Chronic, Dearn, Dern, Dire, Formidable, Funk, Ghastly,
   Horrendous, Penny, Sorry, Terrible, Willies
Dream(er), Dream home, Dream state, Dreamy Alchera, Alcheringa, Aspire,
   Castle, Desire, Drowsy, Dwalm, Dwa(u)m, Fantast, Fantasy, Faraway, Gerontius,
   Idealise, Illusion, Imagine, Languor, Long, Mare, Mirth, Moon, Morpheus, Muse,
   Nightmare, On(e)iric, Pensive, Phantasmagoria, Phantom, Pipe, → **REVERIE**,
   Rêveur, Romantic, Somniate, Spac(e)y, Stargazer, Surreal, Sweven, Trance, Trauma,
   Vague, Vision, Walter Mitty, Wet
Dreary Bleak, Desolate, Dismal, Doleful, Dreich, Dull, Gloom, Gousty, Gray, Grey,
   Oorie, Ourie, Owrie, Sad
Dredge(r) Caster, Scoop
Dreg(s) Bottom, Draff, Dunder, F(a)eces, Fecula, Gr(e)aves, Grounds, Lag(s), Lees,
   Legge, Mother, Mud, Riffraff, Scaff, Sediment, Settlings, Silt, Snuff, Ullage
Dreikanter Ventifact
Drench Dowse, Sluice, Sluse, Soak, Souse, Steep, Submerge
Dress(ing), Dressed Academic, Accoutre, Adjust, Adorn, Aguise, Align, Ao dai,
   Array, Attire, Attrap, Bandage, Bandoline, Bedizen, Black-tie, Bloomer, Blouson,
   Boast, Bodice, Boun, Bowne, Brilliantine, Busk, Caftan, Cataplasm, Charpie,
   Cheongsam, Chimer, Cimar, Clad, Clericals, → **CLOTHING**, Coat, Cocktail, Comb,
   Compost, Compress, Corsage, Corset, Costume, Court, Curry, Cymar, Dandify,
   Dashiki, Deck, Deshabille, Dight, Dink, Dirndl, Dizen, Doll, Dolly Varden, Dolman,
   Don, Drag, Dub, Dubbin, Elastoplast®, Empire, Endue, Enrobe, Evening, Fancy,
   Far(r)andine, Farthingale, Fatigues, Ferrandine, Fertiliser, Fig, Finery, Flamenco,
   French, Frock, Full, Gamgee tissue, Garb, Garnish, Gauze, Girt, Gown, Graith,
   Granny, Guise, Gymslip, → **HABIT**, Highland, Ihram, Italian, Jaconet, Kabuki,
   Ketchup, K(h)anga, Kimono, Kirtle, Kitenge, Line, Lint, Lounger, Marie Rose,
   Maxi, Mayonnaise, Merveilleuse, Midi, Mineral, Mob, Morning, Mother Hubbard,
   Mufti, Mulch, Muu-muu, National, Oil, Ore, Patch, Peplos, Pinafore, Plaster,
   Pledget, Plumage, Polonaise, Pomade, Potash, Poultice, Power, Prank, Preen,
   Prepare, Princess (line), Rag, Raiment, Rainbow, Ranch, Rational, Ray, Rehearsal,
   Rémoulade, Rig, Robe, Russet, Russian, Rybat, Sack, Sacque, Salad, Salad cream,
   Samfoo, Samfu, Sari, Sarong, Sartorial, Sauce, Scutch, Seloso, Separates, Sheath,
   Shift, Shirt, Shirtwaist(er), Simar(re), Smock, Sterile, Stole, Stupe, Subfusc,
   Subfusk, Suit, Sundress, Symar, Tartan, Tasar, Taw, Tent, Tenue, Tew, Thousand
   Island, Tiff, Tire, Tog, Toga, Toilet, Tonic, Top, Treat, Trick, Trim, Trollopee,
   Tunic, Tusser, Tussore, Tuxedo, Uniform, Vest, Vinaigrette, Wear, Wedding, Well,
   White-tie, Wig, Window, Yclad, Ycled
Dressage Demivolt(e), Manège, Passade, Passage, Pesade, Piaffe
▷ **Dressed up, Dressing** *may indicate* an anagram
Dresser Adze, Almery, Bureau, Chest, Couturier, Deuddarn, Dior, Lair, Lowboy,
   Sideboard, Transvestite, Tridarn, Welsh
Dressing-gown Bathrobe, Negligée, Peignoir
Dressing-room Apodyterium, Vestiary, Vestry
Dressmaker Costumier, Dorcas, Modiste, Seamstress, Tailor

Drew Steeld, Stelled
Dribble Drip, Drivel, Drop, Seep, Slaver, Slobber, Slop, Trickle
Dried fish Bum(m)alo, Bummaloti, Haberdine, Speld(r)in(g), Stockfish
▶ **Dried fruit** *see* **DRY FRUIT**
Drift(ing), Drifter Becalmed, Continental, Cruise, Current, Digress, Diluvium, Drumlin, Float, Genetic, Heap, Impulse, Longshore, Maunder, Natant, North Atlantic, Plankton, Purport, Rorke, Slide, Tendence, Tendency, → **TENOR**, Waft, Wander, Zooplankton
Drill(ing) Appraisal, Archimedean, Auger, Bore, Burr, Close order, Directional, Educate, Exercise, Fire, Form, Hammer, Jackhammer, Jerks, Kerb, Monkey, Pack, PE, Pierce, Pneumatic, Power, PT, Radial, Reamer, Ridge, Rimer, Rock, Seeder, Sow, Square-bashing, Teach, Train, Twill, Twist, Usage, Wildcat
Drink(er), Drunk(enness) AA, Absorb, Adrian Quist, Alkie, Alky, Babalas, Bacchian, Barfly, Bender, Beverage, Bev(v)y, Bezzle, Bib(ite), Bibber, Binge, Birl(e), Bladdered, Bland, Blatted, Blind, Blitzed, Bloat, Blootered, Blotto, Bombed, Boose, Booze, Borachio, Bosky, Bottled, Bouse, Bowl, Bowsey, Bowsie, Bracer, Brandy, Bumper, Burst, Capernoitie, Cap(p)ernoity, Carafe, Carousal, Cat-lap, Chaser, Chota peg, Compotation, → **CORDIAL**, Corked, Cot case, Crapulent, Crapulous, Cratur, Crocked, Cuppa, Cut, Demitasse, Digestif, Dipsomaniac, Double, Down, Drain, Draught, Drop, Ebriate, Ebriose, Elixir, Energy, Entire, Eye-opener, Finger, Fleein', Flush, Flying, Fou, Fuddle-cap, Fuddled, Full, Glug, Half-seas-over, Heart-starter, Heavy wet, High, Hobnob, Hogshead, Honkers, Hooker, Hophead, Imbibe, Indulge, Inhaust, Intemperate, Irrigate, Ivresse, Jag, Jakey, Jar, Juice, Juicehead, Kaylied, Knock back, Lager lout, Langered, Lap, Legless, Lethean, Libation, → **LIQUOR**, Lit, Loaded, Lord, Lower, Lush(y), Maggoty, Maltworm, Maudlin, Merry, Methomania, Methysis, Mixer, Moony, Mortal, Mug, Mullered, Neck, Nog(gin), Obfuscated, Oenomania, Oiled, One, Oppignorate, Overshot, Paid, Paint, Partake, Particular, Peg, Pickled, Pick-me-up, Pie-eyed, Pint(a), Piss-artist, Pissed, Pisshead, Pisspot, Piss-up, Pixil(l)ated, Pledge, Plonk(o), Plottie, Potation, Poteen, Potion, Primed, Quaff, Rat-arsed, Ratted, Roaring, Rolling, Rotten, Round, Rouse, Rumfustian, Rummer, St Martin's evil, Screamer, Screwed, Sea, Shebeen, Shicker, Shotover, Silenus, Sip(ple), Skinned, Slake, Slewed, Sloshed, Slued, Slug, Slurp, Smashed, Smoothie, Snort, Soak, Soused, Sozzled, Sponge, Spongy, Spunge, Squiffy, Steaming, Stewed, Stimulant, Stinko, Stocious, Stoned, Stonkered, Stotious, Stukkend, Stuporous, Suiplap, Sup, Swacked, Swallow, Swig, Swill, Tank, Tanked up, Temulence, Tiddl(e)y, Tiff, Tift, Tight, Tincture, Tipper, Tipple, Tipsy, Tope, Toss, Tossicated, Tost, Two-pot, Two-pot screamer, Usual, Wash, Wat, Wauch, Waught, Well-oiled, Wet, Whiffled, Williewaught, Winebag, Wine bibber, Wino, Wrecked, Zonked

DRINKS

2 letters:	Dop	Rye	Bock
It	Fap	Tea	Bull
	G&T	Tot	Coke®
3 letters:	Hom	Vin	Flip
Ale	Kir		Grog
Ava	L&P	*4 letters:*	Homa
Bub	Mum	Arak	Kava
Cha	Pop	Asti	Kola
Cup	Rum	Beer	Malt

Marc
Mead
Nipa
Ouzo
Port
Purl
Raki
Sack
Sake
Saki
Soda
Soft
Soma
Sour
Sura
Tape
Tass
Tent
Yill

5 letters:
Assai
Bingo
Bombo
Bumbo
Cider
Cocoa
Copus
Crush
Doris
Float
Glogg
Haoma
Hogan
Hooch
Joram
Jorum
Julep
Kefir
Kelty
Kvass
Lassi
Mâcon
Malwa
Mauby
Meath
Medoc
Meths
Mobby
Morat
Mulse

Nappy
Negus
Pekoe
Pepsi®
Perry
Pimms
Polly
Pombe
Punch
Rakee
Rumbo
Rummy
Sarsa
Sarza
Shake
Short
Shrub
Skink
Sling
Smile
Stout
Toddy
Tonic
Totty
Vodka
Xeres

6 letters:
Amrita
Apozem
Arrack
Bishop
Burton
Busera
Cassis
Caudle
Cauker
Chasse
Claret
Coffee
Cognac
Cooler
Cooper
Doctor
Eggnog
Enzian
Geneva
Gimlet
Grappa
Graves
Gutrot

Hootch
Kalied
Keltie
Kephir
Kirsch
Kumiss
Kümmel
Maotai
Meathe
Mescal
Mickey
Mobbie
Nectar
Obarni
Old Tom
Oolong
Orgeat
Oulong
Oxymel
Pastis
Pernod®
Plotty
Porter
Posset
Pulque
Rickey
Rotgut
Saloop
Samshu
Shandy
Sherry
Smiler
Squash
Stingo
Strega
Strunt
Taffia
Tisane
Waragi
Whisky
Yaqona
Zythum

7 letters:
Absinth
Akvavit
Alcopop
Amoroso
Aquavit
Bacardi®
Bitters

Campari®
Caribou
Chablis
Chianti
Cobbler
Curaçao
Curaçoa
Daquiri
Eggflip
Fairish
Fustian
Guarana
Italian
Koumiss
Limeade
Madeira
Malmsey
Mineral
Nobbler
Oenomel
Oloroso
Persico
Philter
Philtre
Pilsner
Pink gin
Quickie
Ratafia
Reviver
Rosiner
Rosolio
Sangria
Sazerac
Screech
Scrumpy
Sherbet
Sherris
Sloe gin
Snifter
Soda pop
Stengah
Swizzle
Tequila
Tio Pepe®
Wassail
Whiskey

8 letters:
Absinthe
Aleberry
Ambrosia

Anisette
Aperitif
Armagnac
Babbelas
Bordeaux
Brown cow
Burgundy
Calvados
Champers
Charneco
Ciderkin
Coca-cola®
Cocktail
Cold duck
Daiquiri
Dog's nose
Dubonnet®
Eau de vie
Geropiga
Gin sling
Gluhwein
Highball
Hollands
Homebrew
Hydromel
Lemonade
Light ale
Mahogany
Nepenthe
Nightcap
Persicot
Pilsener
Ragmaker
Red biddy
Regmaker
Resinata

Resinate
Rice beer
Riesling
Root beer
Rosoglio
Sangaree
Schnapps
Skokiaan
Snowball
Spritzer
Switchel
Tequilla
Vermouth
Witblits

9 letters:
Applejack
Aqua vitae
Ayahuasco
Badminton
Buck's fizz
Burnt sack
Calabogus
Champagne
Chocolate
Claret cup
Cream soda
Cuba libre
Eccoccino
Febrifuge
Firewater
Gingerade
Grenadine
Hippocras
Lambswool
Manhattan

Metheglin
Milk punch
Milkshake
Mint julep
Moonshine
Moose milk
Nipperkin
Orangeade
Refresher
Sauternes
Slivovica
Slivovitz
Snakebite
Soda water
Stiffener
Sundowner
The cratur
Whisky mac

10 letters:
Blackstone
Bloody Mary
Buttermilk
Chartreuse®
Hippomanes
Lolly water
Maraschino
Mickey Finn
Piña colada
Pousse-café
Shandygaff
Tom Collins

11 letters:
Aguardiente
Amontillado

Athole Brose
Benedictine
Black and tan
Black velvet
Boiler-maker
Doch-an-doris
Half-and-half
Niersteiner
Screwdriver
Soapolallie
Tom and Jerry
Whiskey sour

12 letters:
Bloody Caesar
Deoch-an-doris
Doch-an-dorach
Doch-an-doruis
Humpty-dumpty
Jimmy Woodser
Marcobrunner
Old-fashioned
Sarsaparilla

13 letters:
Cobbler's punch
Deoch-an-doruis
Mild and bitter
Mops and brooms
Prairie oyster

14 letters:
John Barleycorn

Drink store Cellar

Drip Bore, Dew-drop, Dribble, Drop, Gutter, IV, Leak, Post-nasal, Saline, Seep, Splatter, Stillicide, Trickle, Wimp

Dripstone Label, Larmier

Drive(r), Driving, Drive out AA, Acquired, Actuate, Amber gambler, Ambition, Automatic, Backseat, Banish, Beetle, Belt, Bullocky, Ca', Cabby, Campaign, Carman, Chain, Charioteer, Chauffeur, Coachee, Coact, Crankshaft, Crew, Crowd, Designated, Disk, Dislodge, Dr, Drover, Drum, Economy, Eject, Emboss, Energy, Enew, Enforce, Engine, Expatriate, Faze, Feeze, Ferret, Fire, Firk, Flexible, Fluid, Force, Four-stroke, Four-wheel, Front-wheel, Fuel, Gadsman, Goad, Hack, Hammer, Haste, Heard, Helmsman, Herd, Hie, Hoon, Hoosh, Hot-rod, Hoy, Hunt, Hurl, Impact, Impel, Impetus, Impinge, Impulse, Jarvey, Jehu, Jockey, Juggernaut, Key(ring), Lash, Libido, Locoman, Lunge, Mahout, Make, Mall, Miz(z)en, Motor, Motorman, Offensive, Overland, Peg, Penetrate, Phase, Piston, Pocket, Power,

Powertrain, Propel, Puncher, Put, Quill, RAC, Rack, Ram, Rear-wheel, Rebut, Reinsman, Ride, Road, Roadhog, Run, Sales, Scorch, Screw, Scud, Senna, Sex, Shepherd, Shoo, Spank, Spin, Spur, Start, Steer, Stroke, Sumpter-horse, Sunday, Sweep, Swift, Tape, Task-master, Teamster, Tee, Test, Thrust, Thumb, Toad, Tool, Tootle, Torrential, Trot, Truckie, Tup, Twoccer, Two-stroke, Urge, Urgence, USB, Vetturino, Wagoner, Warp, Whist, Wood, Wreak

Drivel Balderdash, Blether(skate), Drip, Drool, Humbug, Maunder, Nonsense, Pabulum, Pap, Rot, Salivate, Slabber, Slaver

Driving club AA, Iron, RAC

Drizzle Drow, Haze, Mist, Mizzle, Roke, Scotch mist, Scouther, Scowther, Serein, Skiffle, Smir(r), Smur, Spit

Droll Bizarre, Comic, Funny, Jocular, Queer, Waggish

Drone Bee, Buzz, Dog-bee, Doodle, Dor(r), Drant, Draunt, Drawl, Grind, Hanger-on, Hum, Idler, Parasite, Tamboura, Thrum, Windbag

Drool Drivel, Gibber, Salivate, Slaver

Droop(y), Drooping Cernuous, Decline, Flaccid, Flag, Languish, Lill, Limp, Lob, Loll, Lop, Nutate, Oorie, Ourie, Owrie, Peak, Pendulous, Ptosis, → **SAG**, Slink, Slouch, Slump, Weeping, Welk(e), Wilt, Wither

Drop(s), Dropping Acid, Airlift, Apraxia, Bag, Bead, Beres, Blob, Cadence, Calve, Cascade, Cast, Chocolate, Cowpat, Dap, Delayed, Descent, Deselect, Dink, Dip, Downturn, Drappie, Drib(let), Ease, Ebb, Escarp(ment), Fall, Floor, Flop, Fruit, Fumet, Gallows, Glob(ule), Gout(te), Guano, Gutta, Guttate, Instil, Knockout, Land, Minim, Modicum, Muff, Mute, Omit, Pilot, Plonk, Plummet, Plump, Plunge, Plunk, Precepit, Precipice, (Prince) Rupert's, Rain, Scat, Scrap, Shed, Sip, Skat, Spraint, Stilliform, Tass, Taste, Tear, Turd, Virga, Wrist

Drop-out Beatnik, Hippie, Hippy

Drop-shot Dink

Dropsy Anasarca, Ascites, Edema, Oedema

Dross Chaff, Dregs, Recrement, Scoria, Scorious, Scum, Sinter, Slack, Slag, Waste

Drought Dearth, Drouth, Lack, Thirst

Drove(r) Band, Crowd, Flock, Herd, Host, Masses, Mob, Overlander, Puncher

Drown(ed), Drowning Drench, Drent, Drook, Drouk, Engulf, Inundate, Noyade, Overcome, Sorrows, Submerge

Drowse, Drowsiness, Drowsy Blet, Comatose, Doze, Hypnagogic, Hypnopompic, Lethargic, Nap, Narcolepsy, Narcosis, Nod, Snooze

Drub Anoint, Thrash

Drudge(ry) Devil, Dogsbody, Donkey-work, Fag, Grind, Hack, Jackal, Johnson, Plod, Scrub, Slave(y), Snake, Sweat, Swink, Thraldom, Toil, Trauchle, Treadmill

Drug(ged) Acaricide, ACE inhibitor, Antabuse®, Anti-depressant, Antimetabolite, Antipyrine, Bag, Barbiturate, Base, Blow, Bolus, Bomber, Boo, Botanical, Chalybeate, Cholagogue, Clofibrate, Clot buster, Dadah, Deck, Depot, Depressant, Designer, DET, Diuretic, Dope, Downer, E, Ecbolic, Ecphractic, Elixir, Emmenagogue, Errhine, Euphoriant, Fantasy, Fertility, Fig, Galenical, Gateway, Gear, Hallucinogen, Hard, High, Homeopathy, Immunosuppressant, Knockout drops, Largactic, Lifestyle, Line, Load, Mainline, Medicine, Mind-expanding, Miracle, Modified release, Monged, Nervine, Nobble, Obstruent, OD, Opiate, Orlistat, Painkiller, Paregoric, Parenteral, Peace, Pharmaceutics, Pharmacology, Pharmacopoeia, Poison, Popper, Prophylactic, Psychedelic, Psychoactive, Psychodelic, Recreational, Scag, Sedate, Shit, Sialogogue, Smart, Snort, Soft, Soporific, Sorbefacient, Speedball, Spermicide, Spike, Stimulant, Stone(d), Stupefacient, Stupefy, Styptic, Substance, Sudorific, Synthetic, Tout, Tranquiliser,

Truth, Upper, Vasoconstrictor, Vermicide, Weed, White stuff, Wonder, Wrap, Zeolitic

---

DRUGS

1 letter:
Q

3 letters:
AZT
Eve
Hop
Ice
INH
LSD
PCP®
STP
Tab
Tea

4 letters:
Acid
Adam
Bang
Bute
Dopa
Hemp
Junk
Sida
Soma
SSRI
Toot

5 letters:
Aloes
Benny
Bhang
Candy
Crank
Dagga
Ganja
Grass
Hocus
Intal®
L-dopa
Mummy
Opium
Quina
Rutin
Salep
Salop

Senna
Speed
Sugar
Sulfa
Taxol
Zyban®

6 letters:
Amulet
Amytal®
Ativan®
Charas
Curare
Dragée
Heroin
Inulin
Joypop
Lariam®
Mescla
Mummia
Nubain®
Peyote
Pituri
Prozac®
Saloop
Statin
Sulpha
Valium®
Viagra®
Zantac®

7 letters:
Aricept®
Atabrin
Atebrin®
Botanic
Cascara
Charlie
Churrus
Codeine
Damiana
Dapsone
Diconal®
Ecstasy
Eserine
Eucaine

Guarana
Hashish
Henbane
Hypnone
Insulin
Jellies
Librium®
Metopon
Miltown®
Mogadon®
Morphia
Nurofen®
Patulin
Quinine
Relenza®
Ritalin®
Seconal®
Septrin®
Seroxat®
Steroid
Suramin
Tacrine
Trional
Turpeth
Veronal®
Xenical®

8 letters:
Adjuvant
Ataraxic
Banthine
Benadryl®
Curarine
Diazepam
Fentanyl
Goofball
Hyoscine
Ketamine
Laetrile
Laudanum
Mersalyl
Mescalin
Methadon
Miticide
Moonrock
Morphine

Naloxone
Narcotic
Nembutal
Nepenthe
Nystatin
Oxytocic
Psilocin
Quaalude®
Retrovir®
Rifampin
Roborant
Rohypnol®
Scopolia
Serevent®
Snowball
Special K
Tetronal
Thiazide
Varidase®
Veratrin
Viricide
Zerumbet

9 letters:
Acyclovir
Analeptic
Angel-dust
Anovulant
Antrycide
Augmentin
Barbitone
Biguanide
Busulphan
Captopril
Carbachol
Cisplatin
Clozapine
Compound Q
Corticoid
Cyclizine
Digitalis
Dramamine®
Electuary
Ephedrine
Foscarnet
Frusemide

Ibuprofen
Indinavir
Iprindole
Isoniazid
Jaborandi
Lidocaine
Lorazepam
Meloxicam
Mepacrine
Methadone
Minoxidil
Mydriasis
Naltrexol
Novocaine
Nux vomica
Oxycontin®
Paludrine®
Pethidine
Phenytoin
Practolol
Quinidine
Quinquina
Reserpine
Ritonavir
Synergist
Tamoxifen
Temazepam
Teniacide
Totaquine
Trinitrum
Verapamil
Veratrine
Vermifuge
Wobbly egg
Zanamivir

10 letters:
Amantadine
Ampicillin
Antagonist
Anxiolytic
Atracurium
Belladonna
Benzedrine
Bufotenine
Cimetidine
Clomiphene
Clonazepam
Colestipol
Disulfiram
Ergotamine

Ethambutol
Fluoxetine
Formestane
Gabapentim
Imipramine
Indapamide
Isoaminide
Isoniazide
Ivermectin
Mefloquine
Methyldopa
Mickey Finn
Nalbuphine
Nifedipine
Nitrazepam
Papaverine
Paroxetine
Penicillin
Pentaquine
Phenacetin
Prednisone
Primaquine
Probenecid
Psilocybin
Quinacrine
Raloxifine
Rifampicin
Salbutamol
Saquinavir
Selegiline
Stramonium
Sucralfate
Tacrolimus
Taeniacide
Taeniafuge
Ziduvudine

11 letters:
Alendronate
Allopurinol
Aminobutene
Amoxycillin
Amphetamine
Anastrozole
Beta-blocker
Carbimazole
Carminative
Chloroquine
Ciclosporin
Cinnarizine
Clenbuterol

Clindamycin
Cyclosporin
Deserpidine
Distalgesic
Finasteride
Fluconazole
Fluvoxamine
Galantamine
Gemfibrozil
Haloperidol
Idoxuridine
Ipratropium
Isoxsuprine
Magic bullet
Meprobamate
Neostigmine
Nikethamide
Ondansetron
Paracetamol
Pentamidine
Pentazocine
Phentermine
Pravastatin
Propranolol
Purple heart
Risperidone
Succedaneum
Sulfadoxine
Terfenadine
Thalidomide
Theobromine
Tolbutamide
Tous-les-mois
Tropomyosin
Varicomycin
Vinblastine
Vincristine

12 letters:
Alpha-blocker
Anthelmintic
Antiperiodic
Arsphenamine
Azathioprine
Chlorambucil
Eflornithine
Fenfluramine
Fluphenazine
Glanciclover
Gonadotropin
Guanethidine

Indomethacin
Isoprenaline
Isotretinoin
Mecamylamine
Methaqualone
Methotrexate
Mifepristone
Perphenazine
Physotigmine
Promethazine
Salicylamide
Streptomycin
Sulfadiazine
Trimethoprim

13 letters:
Amitriptyline
Anthelminthic
Antihistamine
Carbamazepine
Depressometer
Flunitrazepam
Materia medica
Nitroglycerin
Penicillamine
Phencyclidine
Pyrimethamine
Spectinomycin
Sulfadimidine
Sulfathiazole
Sulphadiazine
Thiabendazole
Triamcinolone

14 letters:
Bendrofluozide
Bisphosphonate
Butyrhophenone
Combretastatin
Cyclobarbitone
Discodermolide
Flucloxacillin
Norethisterone
Pentobarbitone
Phenacyclidine
Phenobarbitone
Phenylbutazone
Spironolactone
Sulphanilamide

Druid Gorsedd

Drum(mer), Drumming, Drumbeat Arête, Atabal, Barrel, Beatbox, Bodhran, Bongo, Brake, Carousel, Chamade, Conga, Cymograph, Daiko, Dash-wheel, Devil's tattoo, Dhol, Djembe, Dr, Drub, Ear, Flam, Gran cassa, Kettle, Kymograph, Lambeg, Mridamgam, Mridang(a), Mridangam, Myringa, Naker, Ngoma, Oil, Pan, Paradiddle, Percussion, Rappel, Rataplan, Reel, Rep, Ridge, Rigger, Roll, Ruff, Ruffle, Salesman, Side, Skin, Snare, Steel, Tabla, Tabour, Tabret, Taiko, Tambourine, Tam-tam, Tap, Tattoo, Thrum, Timbal, Timp(ano), Tom-tom, Touk, Traps, Traveller, Tuck, Tymbal, Tympanist, Tympano, Whim, Winding, Work

Drum-belly Hoven

Drumstick Attorney, Leg, Rute

▶ **Drunk(ard)** *see* **DRINK**

▷ **Drunken** *may indicate* an anagram

Drupe(l) Etaerio, Tryma

Druse Crystal

Dry(ing), Drier, Dryness Air, Anhydrous, Arefaction, Arefy, Arid, Blot, Bone, Brut, Corpse, Crine, Dehydrate, Desiccate, Detox, Drain, Dull, Ensear, Evaporate, Exsiccator, Firlot, Fork, Harmattan, Hasky, Hi(r)stie, Humidor, Hydrate, Jejune, Jerk, Khor, Kiln, Mummify, Oast, → **PARCH**, Prosaic, Reast, Reist, Rizzar, Rizzer, Rizzor, Scarious, Sciroc, Scorch, Sear, Season, Sec(co), Seco, Sere, Shrivel, Siccative, Siroc(co), Sober, Sponge, Steme, Stove, Ted, Thirsty, Thristy, Toasted, Torrefy, Torrid, Towel, Tribble, Trocken, TT, Unwatery, Watertight, Welt, Wilt, Win(n), Windrow, Wipe, Wither, Wizened, Wry, Xeransis, Xerasia, Xero(sis), Xeroderma, Xerophthalmia, Xerostomia

Dryad Eurydice, Nymph

Dry fruit, Dried fruit Achene, Akene, Currant, Mebos, Prune, Raisin, Samara, Silicula, Siliqua, Silique, Sultana

Dry mouth Xerostoma

DT's Dingbats, Hallucinations, Zooscopic

Dual Double, Twin, Twofold

Dub Array, → **CALL**, Entitle, Hete, Knight, Name

Dubious Doubtful, Equivocal, Fishy, Fly-by-night, Hesitant, Iffy, Improbable, Questionable, Scepsis, Sceptical, Sesey, Sessa, → **SHADY**, Shonky, Suspect, Touch and go, Unlikely

▷ **Dubious** *may indicate* an anagram

Dubliner Jackeen

Duce Leader, Musso(lini)

Duchess Anastasia, Malfi, Peeress, Titled

Duchy Anhalt, Brabant, Brunswick, Cornwall, Dukedom, Franconia, Grand, Holstein, Limburg, Luxembourg, Nassu, Omnium, Realm, Savoy, Swabia, Valois, Westphalian

Duck(ling), Ducked Amphibian, Avoid, Aylesbury, Bald-pate, Bargander, Bergander, Blob, Blue, Bluebill, Bob, Bombay, Broadbill, Bufflehead, Bum(m)alo, Butterball, Canard, Canvasback, → **COUPLE OF DUCKS**, Dead, Dearie, Decoy, Dip, Diving, Dodge, Dodo, Douse, Drook, Drouk, Dunk(er), Eider, Enew, Escape, Evade, Ferruginous, Flapper, Gadwall, Garganey, Garrot, Golden-eye, Goosander, Greenhead, Hareld, Harlequin, Heads, Herald, Immerse, Indian runner, Jook, Jouk, Lame, Long-tailed, Mallard, Mandarin, Muscovy, Musk, Nil, Nodding, Nun, O, Oldsquaw, Old Tom, Orpington, Paddling, Pair of spectacles, Palmated, Paradise, Pekin(g), Pintail, Plunge, Pochard, Poker, Putangitangi, Redhead, Ruddy, Runner, Rush, St Cuthbert's, Scaup, Scoter, Sheld(d)uck, Shieldrake, Shovel(l)er, Shun,

Sitting, Smeath, Smee(th), Smew, Sord, Souse, Sowse, Spatula, Spirit, Sprigtail, Steamer, Surf(scoter), Teal, Team, Tufted, Tunker, Ugly, Velvet scoter, Whio, Whistling, Widgeon, Wigeon, Wood, Zero

Duckbill Ornithorhynchus, Platypus

Duckwalk Waddle

Duckweed Lemna

Ducky Sweet, Twee

Duct Bile, Canal(iculus), Channel, Conduit, Diffuser, Diffusor, Emunctory, Epididymus, Fistula, Gland, Lachrymal, Lacrimal, Laticifer, Lumen, Parotid, Pipe, Tear, Thoracic, Tube, Ureter, Vas deferens, Wolffian

Dud Bouncer, Failure, Flop, Shan(d), Stumer

Dude Cat, Coxcomb, Dandy, Fop, Lair, Macaroni, Popinjay, Roy

Dudgeon Anger, Hilt, Huff, Pique

Due(s) Adequate, Arrearage, Claim, Debt, Deserts, Forinsec, Geld, Heriot, Just, Lot, Mature, Needful, Owing, Reddendo, Rent, Right, → SUITABLE, Thereanent, Toll, Tribute, Worthy

Duel(list) Mensur, Monomachy, Principal, Tilt

Duenna Chaperone, Dragon

Duff Bungle, Dough, Nelly, NG, Plum, Pudding, Rustle

Duffer Bungler, Rabbit, Useless

Dug Ploughed, Teat, Titty, Udder

Dugong Halicore, Sea-cow, Sea-pig, Sirenian

Dug-out Abri, Canoe, Piragua, Pirogue, Shelter, Trench, Trough

Duke(dom) Alva, Clarence, D, Ellington, Fist, Iron, Milan, Orsino, Peer, Prospero, Rohan, Wellington

Dulcimer Cembalo, Citole, Cymbalo, Santir, Sant(o)ur

Dull(ard), Dullness Anodyne, Anorak, Bald, Banal, Barren, Besot, Bland, Blear, Blunt, Boeotian, Boring, Cloudy, Commonplace, Dead (and alive), Deadhead, Dense, Dim, Dinge, Dingy, Ditchwater, Doldrums, Dowf, Dowie, Drab, Drear, Dreich, Dry, Dunce, Faded, Flat, Fozy, Grey, Heavy, Hebetate, Ho-hum, Humdrum, Illustrious, Insipid, Jejune, Lacklustre, Lifeless, Log(y), Lowlight, Mat(t), Matte, Monotonous, Mopish, Mull, Obtund, Obtuse, Opacity, Opiate, Ordinary, Overcast, Owlish, Pall, Pedestrian, Perstringe, Podunk, Prosaic, Prose, Prosy, Rebate, Rust, Slow, Solein, Sopite, Staid, Stick, Stodger, Stodgy, Stolid, Stuffy, Stultify, → STUPID, Sunless, Tame, Tarnish, Tedious, Ticky-tacky, Toneless, Torpor, Treadmill, Tubby, Unimaginative, Vapid, Wonk, Wooden, Zoid

Dumb(ness) Alalia, Aphonic, Crambo, Hobbididance, Inarticulate, Mute, Silent, Stupid

Dumbfound(ed) Amaze, Astound, Flabbergast, Stun, Stupefy, Stupent

Dumb ox Aquinas

Dummy Comforter, Copy, Effigy, Fathead, Flathead, Mannequin, Mannikin, Mock-up, Model, Pacifier, Quintain, Soother, Table, Teat, Waxwork

Dump(ing), Dumps Abandon, Blue, Core, Dejection, Dispirited, Doldrums, Empty, Eyesore, Fly-tipping, Hole, Jettison, Jilt, Junk, Mine, Scrap, Screen, Shoot, Store(house), Tip, Toom, Unlade, Unload

Dumpling Dim sum, Dough(boy), Gnocchi, Gyoza, Knaidel, Knaidloch, Kneidlach, Knish, Kreplach, Matzoball, Norfolk, Quenelle, Ribaude, Suet, Won ton

Dumpy Pudgy, Squat

Dun Annoy, Cow, Importune, Pester, → SUE, Tan

Duncan Isadora

Dunce Analphabet, Booby, Dolt, Donkey, Dullard, Fathead, Schmo, Schmuck, Schnook, Stupid

Dune Areg, Bar, Barchan(e), Bark(h)an, Erg, Sandbank, Seif, Star, Whaleback

Dung(hill) Argol, Buttons, Chip, Cock, Coprolite, Cowpat, Droppings, Fewmet, Fumet, Fumiculous, Guano, Hing, Manure, Midden, Mixen, Mute, Night soil, Ordure, Puer, Pure, Scat, Scumber, Shairn, Shard, Sharn, Siege, Skat, Skummer, Sombrerite, Sombrero, Spawn brick, Spraint, Stercoraceous, Tath

Dungarees Overalls

Dung-eating Merdiverous

Dungeon Bastille, Cell, Confine, Donjon, Durance, Oubliette, Souterrain

Dunk Immerse, Sop, Steep

Dunnock Accentor

Duo Couple, Pair, Twosome

Dupe Catspaw, Chiaus, Chouse, Cony, Cull(y), Delude, Geck, Gull, Hoax, Hoodwink, Mug, Pawn, Pigeon, Plover, Sitter, Soft mark, Sucker, Swindle, → **TRICK**, Victim

Duplex Twofold

Duplicate, Duplicator Clone, Copy, Counterpart, Cyclostyle, Double, Facsimile, Match, Ozalid®, Replica, Reproduce, Roneo®, Spare

Durable Enduring, Eternal, Eterne, Hardy, Lasting, Permanent, Stout, Tough

Duralumin® Y-alloy

Duration Extent, Period, Span

Duress Coercion, Pressure, Restraint

Durham Palatine

During Amid, Dia-, For, In, Over, Throughout, While, Whilst

Dusk(y) Dark, Dewfall, Dun, Eve, Gloaming, Gloom, Owl-light, Phaeic, Twilight, Umbrose

Dust(y) Arid, Ash, Bo(a)rt, Calima, Clean, Coom, Cosmic, Culm, Derris, Devil, Duff, Earth, Fuss, Gold, Khak(i), Lemel, Limail, Lo(e)ss, Miller, Nebula, Pellum, Pollen, Pother, Pouder, Poudre, Powder, Pozz(u)olana, Pudder, Rouge, Seed, Shaitan, Slack, Stour, Talc, Volcanic, Wipe

▷ **Dusted** *may indicate* an anagram

Duster Cloth, Feather, Red, Talcum, Torchon

Dustman Doolittle, Garbo(logist), Scaffie

Dust measure Konimeter, Koniscope

Dutch(man), Dutchwoman Batavian, Boor, Butterbox, Cape, Courage, D(u), Double, Elm, Erasmus, Flying, Frow, Kitchen, Knickerbocker, Middle, Missis, Missus, Mynheer, Parnell shout, Patron, Pennsylvania, Sooterkin, Taal, Wife

Dutiful, Duty Active, Ahimsa, Allegiance, Average, Blench, Bond, Charge, Corvee, Countervailing, Customs, Death, Debt, Deontology, Detail, Devoir, Docile, Drow, Due, Duplicand, End, Estate, Excise, Fatigue, Feu, Function, Heriot, Homage, Imposition, Impost, Incumbent, Lastage, Likin, Mission, Mistery, Mystery, Obedient, Obligation, Octroi, Office, Onus, Pia, Picket, Pious, Point, Preferential, Prisage, Probate, Rota, Sentry-go, Shift, Stamp, Stillicide, Stint, Succession, Tariff, → **TASK**, Tax, Toll, Transit, Trow, Watch, Zabeta

Duvet Doona, Quilt

Dwarf(ism) Achondroplasia, Agate, Alberich, Andvari, Ateleiosis, Bashful, Belittle, Bes, Black, Bonsai, Brown, Doc, Dopey, Droich, Drow, Durgan, Elf, Gnome, Grumpy, Happy, Hobbit, Homuncule, Hop o' my thumb, Knurl, Laurin, Little man, Man(n)ikin, → **MIDGET**, Mime, Minikin, Minim, Nanism, Nectabanus, Ni(e)belung, Nurl, Overshadow, Pacolet, Pigmy, Pygmy, Red, Regin, Ront, Rumpelstiltskin, Runt, Skrimp, Sleepy, Sneezy, → **STUNT**, Tiddler, Titch, Tokoloshe, Tom Thumb,

Toy, Troll, Trow, White

Dwell(er), Dwelling Abide, Be, Bungalow, Cabin, Cell, Cot(tage), Descant, Discourse, Domicile, Habitation, Harp, Heteroscian, Hogan, House, Hut, Laura, Lavra, Live, Lodge, Longhouse, Maison(n)ette, Mansion, Messuage, Midgard, Midgarth, Mithgarthr, Palafitte, Pied-à-terre, Pueblo, Reside, Roof, Sty, Tenement, Tepee, Terramara, Tipi, Weem, Wigwam, Won(ing), Wonning, Woon

Dwindle Decline, Diminish, Fade, Lessen, Peter, Shrink, Wane

Dye(ing), Dyestuff, Dye-seller Acid, Alkanet, Amaranth, Anil, Anthracene, Anthraquinone, Archil, Azo(benzine), Azurine, Bat(t)ik, Benzidine, Brazil(e)in, Burnt umber, Camwood, Canthaxanthin, Carthamine, Catechin, Chay(a), Chica, Chicha, Chico, Choy, Cinnabar, Cobalt, Cochineal, Colour, Congo, Coomassie blue, Corkir, Crocein, Crotal, Crottle, Cudbear, Dinitrobenzene, Direct, Embrue, Engrain, Envermeil, Eosin, Flavin(e), Fluoxene, Fuchsin(e), Fustic, Fustoc, Gambi(e)r, Gentian violet, Grain, Haematoxylin, Henna, Hue, Ikat, Imbrue, Imbue, Incardine, Indamine, Indican, Indigo, Indigocarmine, Indigotin, Indirubin, Indoxyl, Indulin(e), Ingrain, Kalamkari, Kamala, Kermes, Kohl, Korkir, Madder, Magenta, Mauvein(e), Mauvin(e), Methyl violet, Murex, Myrobalan, Nigrosin(e), Orcein, Orchel(la), Orchil, Para-red, Phenolphthalein, Phthalein, → **PIGMENT**, Ponceau, Primuline, Puccoon, Purple, Purpurin, Pyronine, Quercitron, Quinoline, Raddle, Resorcinol, Rhodamine, Rosanilin(e), Safranin(e), Salter, Shaya, → **STAIN**, Stone-rag, Stone-raw, Sumac(h), Sunfast, Tannin, Tartrazine, Tie-dye, Tinct, Tint, Tropaeolin, Turmeric, Turnsole, Valonia, Vat, Wald, Weld, Woad, Woald, Wold, Xanthium, Xylidine

▶ **Dying** *see* **DIE**

Dyke Aboideau, Aboiteau, Bund, Devil's, → **DIKE**, Gall, Offa's, Ring

Dynamic(s) Ballistics, Energetic, Forceful, Gogo, High-powered, Kinetics, Potent

Dynamite Blast, Explode, Gelignite, Giant powder, TNT, Trotyl

Dynamo Alternator, Armature

Dynasty Angevin, Bourbon, Capetian, Carolingian, Chin(g), Ch'ing, Chou, Era, Frankish, Gupta, Habsburg, Han, Hapsburg, Holkar, Honan, House(hold), Hyksos, Khan, Manchu, Maurya, Merovingian, Ming, Omayyad, Osman, Pahlavi, Ptolemy, Qajar, Q'ing, Rameses, Romanov, Rule, Safavid, Saga, Sassanid, Seleucid, Seljuk, Shang, Song, Sui, Sung, Tai-ping, Tang, Tudor, Umayyad, Wei, Yi, Yuan, Zhou

Dysentery Amoebic, Bloody flux, Slugellosis

Dyslexia Strephosymbolia

Dyspeptic Cacogastric

Dysprosium Dy

Dystrophy Duchenne's, Muscular

Ee

E Boat, East, Echo, Energy, English, Spain

Each All, Apiece, Ea, → **EVERY**, Ilka, Per, Severally

Eager(ly) Agog, Antsy, Ardent, Avid, Beaver, Bore, Bright-eyed, Dying, Earnest, Enthusiastic, Fain, Fervent, Fervid, Frack, Game, Gung-ho, Hot, Intent, → **KEEN**, Perfervid, Prone, Race, Raring, Rath(e), Ready, Roost, Sharp-set, Sore, Spoiling, Thirsty, Toey, Wishing, Yare

Eagle Al(l)erion, Altair, American, Aquila, Bald, Bateleur, Berghaan, Bird, Double, Erne, Ethon, Fish, Gier, Golden, Harpy, Hawk, Legal, Lettern, Nisus, Ossifrage, Sea, Spread, Tawny, Wedge-tailed

Ear(drum), Ear trouble Ant(i)helix, Attention, Audience, Auricle, Barotitis, Cauliflower, Cochlea, Concha, Conchitis, Deafness, Dionysius, Dolichotus, External, Glue, Hearing, Helix, Icker, Incus, Inner, Internal, Jenkins, Kieselguhr, Labyrinth, Labyrinthitis, Listen, Locusta, Lop, Lug, Malleus, Middle, Modiolus, Myringa, Myringitis, Nubbin, Otalgia, Otalgy, Otic, Paracusis, Paramastoid, Parotic, Pavilion, Periotic, Petrosal, Phonic, Pinna, Presby(a)c(o)usis, Prootic, Spike, Stapes, Thick, Tin, Tragus, Tympanitis, Utricle

Earl(dom) Belted, Mar, Peer, Sandwich

Earlier, Early Above, Ago, Ahead, Alsoon, AM, Antelucan, Auld, Betimes, Cockcrow, Daybreak, Ere-now, Ex, Germinal, Incipient, Or, Precocious, Precursor, Prehistoric, Premature, Prevernal, Previous, Primeur, Primeval, Primordial, Prior, Rath(e), Rath(e)ripe, Rear, Rudimentary, Soon, Timely, Tim(e)ous

▷ **Early** *may indicate* belonging to an earl

Early man Eoanthropus, Flat-earther

▷ **Early stages of** *may indicate* first one or two letters of the word(s) following

Earmark Allocate, Bag, Book, Characteristic, Flag, → **RESERVE**, Tag, Target, Ticket

Earn(er), Earning(s) Achieve, Addle, Breadwinner, Curdle, Deserve, Digerati, Ern, Gain, Income, Invisible, Make, Merit, O.T.E., Rennet, Runnet, Win, Yearn

Earnest(ly) Ardent, Arle(s)(-penny), Deposit, Fervent, Imprest, Intent, Promise, Serious, Token, Wistly, Zealous

Earring Drop, Hoop, Keeper, Pendant, Sleeper, Snap, Stud

Earshot Hail, Hearing

Earth(y) Alkaline, Antichthon, Art, Asthenosphere, Barbados, Brown, Capricorn, Clay, Cloam, Clod, Cologne, Craton, Diatomite, Dirt, Drey, Dust, E, Eard, Edaphic, Epigene, Foxhole, Friable, Fuller's, Gaea, Gaia, Gault, Ge, Globe, Green, Ground, Heavy, Horst, Infusiorial, Kadi, Lair, Leaf-mould, Lemnian, Lithosphere, Loam, Malm, Mankind, Mantle, Mools, Mould, Mouls, Papa, Pise, Planet, Rabelaisian, Racy, Rare, Red, Samian, Seat, Sett, Sod, → **SOIL**, Subsoil, Taurus, Telluric, Tellus, Terra, Terrain, Terramara, Terrene, Topsoil, Tripoli, Virgo, Wad, Ye(a)rd, Yellow, Yird

Earth-bound Chthonian

Earthenware Arretine, Biscuit, Ceramic, Creamware, Crock(ery), Delf(t),

Della-robbia, Delph, Faience, Figuline, Maiolica, Majolica, Pig, Pot, Queen's ware, Raku, Samian, Sanitary, Terracotta

Earthquake Aftershock, Aseismic, Bradyseism, Foreshock, Mercalli, Richter, Seism, Shake, Shock, Temblor, Trembler, Tremor

Earth's surface Sal, Sial

Earthwork Agger, Bank, Cursus, Gazon, Parados, Rampart, Remblai, Vallum

Earthworm Angledug, Angletwitch, Angleworm, Annelid, Bait, Night-crawler

Earwig Clipshear(s), Eavesdrop, Forkit-tail, Forky-tail

Ease, Easing, Easygoing Alleviate, Carefree, Clear, Clover, Comfort, Content, Defuse, Deregulate, Détente, Easy-osy, Facility, Genial, Hands down, Informal, Lax, Mellow, Mid(dy), Mitigate, Otiosity, Palliate, Peace, Pococurante, Quiet, Relieve, Reposal, Repose, Soothe

East(erly), Eastward Anglia, Asia, Chevet, E, Eassel, Eassil, Eothen, Eurus, Far, Levant, Middle, Near, Orient, Ost, Sunrise

Easter Festival, Island, Pace, Pasch, Pasque

Eastern(er), Eastern language Asian, Kolarian, Oriental, Virginian

East European Lettic, Slovene

Easy, Easily ABC, Breeze, Cakewalk, Carefree, Child's play, Cinch, Cushy, Degage, Doddle, Duck soup, Eath(e), Ethe, Facile, Free, Gift, Glib, Hands down, Independent, Jammy, Kid's stuff, Lax, Light, Midshipman, Natural, Nimps, No-brainer, Oldster, Picnic, Pie, Pushover, Romp, Simple, Sitter, Snotty, Soft, Tolerant, Turkey shoot, User-friendly, Walk-over, Well, Yare

▷ **Easy** *may indicate* an anagram

Eat(able), Eater, Eating Bite, Bolt, Champ, Chop, Commensal, Consume, Corrode, Edible, Edite, Endew, Endue, Erode, Esculent, Etch, Fare, Feast, → **FEED**, Fret, Gastronome, Gnaw, Go, Gobble, Graze, Grub, Have, Hoe into, Hog, Hyperorexia, Hyperphagia, Ingest, Manducate, Muckamuck, Munch, Nosh, Nutritive, Omnivore, Partake, Phagomania, Phagophobia, Predate, Refect, Scoff, Stuff, Sup, Swallow, Syssitia, Take, Taste, Trencherman, Trophesy, Tuck away, Tuck into, Whale

Eavesdrop(per) Cowan, Earwig, Icicle, Listen, Overhear, Pry, Snoop, Stillicide, Tab-hang, Tap, Wiretap

Ebb(ing) Abate, Decline, Recede, Refluent, Sink, → **WANE**

Ebony Black, Cocus-wood, Coromandel, Hebenon, Jamaican

Ebullient Brash, Effervescent, Exuberant, Fervid

Eccentric Abnormal, Antic, Cam, Card, Character, Crank, Curious, Daffy, Dag, Deviant, Dingbat, Ditsy, Ditzy, E, Farouche, Fay, Fey, Fie, Freak, Fruitcake, Geek, Gonzo, Iffish, Irregular, Kinky, Kook(y), Mattoid, Nutcase, Nutter, Odd(ball), Offbeat, Off-centre, Off the wall, Original, Outré, → **PECULIAR**, Phantasime, Pixil(l)ated, Queer, Quirky, Quiz, Rake, Raky, Recondite, Rum, Scatty, Screwball, Screwy, Squirrelly, Wack(y), Way-out, Weird(o), W(h)acko

▷ **Eccentric** *may indicate* an anagram

Ecclesiastic(es), Ecclesiasticus Abbé, Clergyman, Clerical, Lector, Secular, Sir(ach), Theologian, The Preacher

Echelon Formation

Echinoderm Asteroidea, Basket-star, Brittle-star, Comatulid, Crinoid, Heart-urchin, Sea-egg, Sea-lily, Sea-urchin, Starfish

Echo, Echo-sounder Angel, Answer, Ditto, E, Fathometer®, Imitate, Iterate, Rebound, Repeat, Repercussion, Reply, Resonant, → **RESOUND**, Respeak, Reverb(erate), Revoice, Ring, Rote, Tape

Eclat Flourish, Glory, Prestige, Renown

Eclectic Babist, Broad, Complex, Diverse, Liberal

Eclipse Annular, Block, Cloud, Deliquium, Excel, Hide, Lunar, Obscure, Occultation, Outmatch, Outweigh, Overshadow, Partial, Penumbra, Rahu, Solar, Total, Transcend, Upstage

Eclogue Bucolic, Idyll, Pastoral

Eco-community Seral

Ecology Bionomics

Economic(s), Economise Budget, Conserve, Dismal science, Eke, Entrench, Finance, Home, Husband, Intrench, Pinch, Retrench, Scrimp, Skimp, Spare, Sparing, Stagflation, → STINT, Supply-side, Welfare

Economist Angell, Bentham, Chrematist, Cole, Friedman, Keynes, Malthus, Marginalist, Meade, Mill, Pareto, Physiocrat, Ricardo, Tinbergen, Tobin, Toynbee, Veblen, Webb

Economy, Economic(al), Economics Agronomy, Black, Careful, Cliometrics, Command, Conversation, Frugal, Hidden, Knowledge, Market, Mitumba, Mixed, Neat, New, Parsimony, Planned, Political, Pusser's logic, Retrenchment, Shoestring, Siege, Stakeholder, Stumpflation, Thrift, Tiger, Token

Ecstasy, Ecstatic Bliss, Delight, Delirious, Dove, E, Exultant, Joy, Liquid, Lyrical, Nympholepsy, Pythic, Rapture, Rhapsodic, Sent, Trance, Transport

Ecumenical Catholic, Lateran

Eczema Pompholyx, Tetter

Edda Elder, Prose, Younger

Eddy Backset, Curl, Duane, Gurge, Maelstrom, Nelson, Pirl, Purl, Rotor, Sousehole, Swelchie, Swirl, Vortex, Weel, Well, Whirlpool, Wiel

Eden Bliss, Fall, Heaven, Paradise, PM, Utopia

Edentate Ant-eater, Armadillo, Sloth, Tatou, Xenarthra

Edge, Edging, Edgy Advantage, Arris, Bleeding, Border, Bordure, Brim, Brink, Brittle, Brown, Burr, Chamfer, Chimb, Chime, Chine, Coaming, Costa, Cutting, Dag, Deckle, End, Flange, Flounce, Frill, Fringe, Frontier, Furbelow, Gunnel, Gunwale, Hem, Hone, Inch, Inside, Kerb, Knife, Leading, Leech, Limb(ate), Limbus, Limit, Lip, List, Lute, Marge(nt), Margin, Nosing, Orle, Outside, Parapet, Periphery, Picot, Pikadell, Piping, Rand, Rim, Rund, Rymme, Selvage, Selvedge, Sidle, Skirt, Strand, Trailing, Trim, Tyre, Verge, Wear, Whet

▶ **Edible** *see* EAT(ABLE)

Edict(s) Ban, Bull, Clementines, Decree, Decretal, Extravagantes, Fatwa, Firman, Interim, Irade, Nantes, Notice, Pragmatic, Proclamation, Pronunciamento, Rescript, Sext, Ukase

Edifice Booth, Building, Structure, Stupa, Superstructure

Edify Instruct, Teach

Edinburgh Auld Reekie

Edit(or), Editorial Abridge, Article, City, Copy (read), Cut, Dele, Dramaturg(e), Ed, Emend, Expurgate, Footsteps, Garble, Leader, Nantes, Prepare, Recense, Redact, Revise, Seaman

▷ **Edited** *may indicate* an anagram

Edith Sitwell

Edition Aldine, Bulldog, Bullpup, Ed, Extra, Ghost, Hexapla(r), Impression, Issue, Library, Limited, Number, Omnibus, Trade, Variorum, Version

Edmond, Edmund Burke, Gosse, Ironside(s), Rostand, Spenser

Educate(d) Baboo, Babu, Enlighten, Evolué, Informed, Instruct, Learned, Noursle, Nousell, Nousle, Nurture, Nuzzle, Polymath, Preppy, Scholarly, School, → TEACH, Train, Yuppie

Education(alist) Adult, Basic, B.Ed, Classical, Conductive, Didactics, Further,

Heurism, Learning, Literate, Mainstream, Montessori, Paedotrophy, Pedagogue, Pestalozzi, Physical, Piarist, Primary, Schooling, Special, Steiner, Teacher, Tertiary, Upbringing

Educe Elicit, Evoke, Extract, Infer

Edward Confessor, Ed, Elder, Lear, Martyr, Ned, Ted

Eel Conger, Congo, Electric, Elver, Glass, Grig, Gulper, Gunnel, Hagfish, Kingklip, Lamper, Lamprey, Lant, Launce, Leptocephalus, Moray, Murray, Murr(e)y, Olm, Paste, Salt, Sand(ling), Silver belly, Snake, Snig, Spitchcock, Tuna, Vinegar, Wheat, Wolf

Eerie Spooky, Uncanny, Unked, Weird

Efface Cancel, Delete, Dislimn, → **ERASE**, Expunge, Obliterate

Effect(s), Effective(ness), Effectual Able, Achieve, Acting, Auger, Babinski, Bags, Barkhausen, Belongings, Bit, Bohr, Border, Bricolage, Butterfly, Causal, C(h)erenkov, Chromakey, Coanda, Coastline, Competent, Compton, Consequence, Coriolis, Do, Domino, Doppler, Dr(y)ice, Eclat, Edge, Efficacious, Enact, End, Estate, Execute, Experimenter, Fet, Foley, Fringe, Functional, Fungibles, Gear, Goods, Greenhouse, Ground, Gunn, Hall, Halo, Hawthorne, Home, Horns and halo, Impact, Implement(al), Impression, Introgenic, Josephson, Joule(-Thomson), Kerr, Keystone, Knock-on, Magnus, Meissner, Militate, Moire, Mossbauer, Mutual, Neat, Nisi, Notch, Operant, Optical, Outcome, Ovshinsky, Oxygen, Parallax, Peltier, Perficient, Personal, Phi, Photoelectric, Photovoltaic, Piezoelectric, Piezomagnetic, Pinch, Placebo, Pogo, Position, Potent, Practical, Primary, Promulgate, Raman, Ratchet, Recency, Redound, Repercussion, → **RESULT**, Ripple, Schottky, Seebeck, Shadow, Shore, Side, Skin, Slash-dot, Sound, Sovereign, Special, Spectrum, Spin-off, Stage, Stark, Striking, Stroop, Submarine, Tableau, Teeth, Telling, Thermoelectric, Thomson, Toxic, Tunnel, Tyndall, Upshot, Valid, Viable, Virtual, Win, Withdrawal, Work, Zeeman

Effeminate Airtsy-mairtsy, Camp, Carpet-knight, Carpet-monger, Cissy, Cookie-pusher, Dildo, Epicene, Female, Gussie, Jessie, Milksop, (Miss) Nancy, Molly(coddle), Nellie, Nelly, Panty-waist, Poovy, Pretty, Prissy, Punce, Sissy, Swish, Tender, Tenderling, Tonk, Unman, Wuss(y)

Effervescence, Effervescent Bubbling, Ebullient, Fizz, Frizzante, Pétillant, Soda

▷ **Effervescent** *may indicate* an anagram

Effete Camp, Epigon(e)

Efficacious, Efficacy Effective, Operative, Potent, Sovereign, Value

Efficiency, Efficient Able, Businesslike, Capable, Competent, Current, Despatch, Electrode, Ergonomics, Luminous, Productivity, Quantum, Smart, Spectral luminous, Streamlined, Strong, Thermal, Volumetric

Effigy Figure, Guy, Idol, Image, Statua, Statue

Efflorescence Bloom, Blossom, Reh

Effluence, Effluent, Effluvia Air, Aura, Billabong, Discharge, Fume, Gas, Halitus, Miasma, Odour, Outflow, Outrush

Effort Achievement, Attempt, Best, Conatus, Concerted, Drive, Endeavour, Essay, Exertion, Fit, Frame, Hardscrabble, Herculean, Labour, Molimen, Nisus, Pains, Rally, Spurt, Stab, Strain, Struggle, Team, → **TRY**, Work, Yo

Effortless Lenis

Effrontery Audacity, Brass, Cheek, Face, Gall, Neck, Nerve, Temerity

Effulgent Bright, Radiant, Shining

Effuse, Effusion, Effusive Emanate, Exuberant, Exude, Gush, Lyric, Ode, Outburst, Prattle, Rhapsody, Sanies, Screed, Spill

Eft After

Eg As, Example

Egest Eliminate, Evacuate, Excrete, Void

Egg(s) Abet, Benedict, Berry, Blow, Bomb, Caviar(e), Cavier, Chalaza, Cheer, Cleidoic, Clutch, Cockney, Collop, Coral, Curate's, Darning, Easter, Edge, Fabergé, Fetus, Flyblow, Foetus, Free-range, Glair(e), Goad, Goog, Graine, Hoy, Incite, Instigate, Layings, Mine, Nest, Nidamentum, Nit, Oocyte, Oophoron, Ostrich, Ova, Ovum, Pace, Pasch, Plover's, Prairie oyster, Press, Raun, Roe, Rumble-tumble, Scotch, Scrambled, Seed, Setting, Spat, Spawn, Spur(ne), Tar(re), Thunder, Tooth, Tread(le), Urge, Whore's, Wind, Yelk, Yolk, Zygote

Egghead Don, Highbrow, Intellectual, Mensa, Pedant

Egg-plant Aubergine, Brinjal

Egg-producer Gametophyte, Hen, Ovipositor

Egg-shaped Obovate, Oval, Ovate

Egg-white Albumen, Glair

Ego(ism), Egoist Che, Conceit, I, Narcissism, Not-I, Pride, Self, Solipsism, Ubu, Vanity

Egocentric Solipsistic

Egregious Eminent, Flagrant, Glaring, Shocking

Egypt(ian), Egyptologist Arab, Cairene, Carter, Cheops, Chephren, Cleopatra, Copt(ic), ET, Gippo, Goshen, Gyppo, Imhotep, Nasser, Nefertiti, Nilote, Nitrian, Osiris, Ptolemy, Rameses, Syene, UAR, Wafd, Wog

Eiderdown Bedspread, Duvet, Quilt

Eight(h), Eighth day Acht, Byte, Crew, Cube, Middle, Nundine, Octa, Octad, Octal, Octastrophic, Octave, Octet, Ogdoad, Okta, Ottava, Ure, Utas

Eighteen Majority

Eighty Fourscore, R

Einsteinium Es

Either Also, Both, O(u)ther, Such

Ejaculate Blurt, Discharge, Emit, Exclaim

Eject Bounce, Disgorge, Dismiss, Emit, Erupt, Expel, Oust, Propel, Spew, Spit, Spue, Vent

Eke Augment, Eche, Enlarge, Husband, Supplement

Elaborate Detail, Develop, Dressy, Enlarge, Evolve, Florid, Imago, Improve, Intricate, Ornate, Rich, Stretch

Elan Dash, Drive, Esprit, → **FLAIR**, Gusto, Lotus, Panache, Spirit, Vigour

Elapse Glide, Intervene, Pass

Elastic(ity) Adaptable, Bungee, Buoyant, Dopplerite, Elater, Flexible, Give, Resilient, Rubber, Spandex®, Springy, Stretchy, Tone, Tonus

Elastomer Adiprene®

Elate(d), Elation Cheer, Euphoric, Exalt, Exhilarate, Gladden, Hault, High, Ruff(e), Uplift

Elbow, Elbow tip Akimbo, Ancon, Angle, Bender, Cubital, Hustle, Joint, Jostle, Justle, Kimbo, Noop, Nudge, Olecranon, Tennis

Elder(ly), Eldest Ainé(e), Ancestor, Ancient, Bourtree, Chief, Classis, Eigne, Geriatric, Guru, Kaumatua, Kuia, OAP, Presbyter, → **SENIOR**, Sire, Susanna, Wallwort

Eldorado Ophir

Eleanor(a) Bron, Duse, Nora(h)

Elect(ed), Election(eer), Electoral Choice, Choose, Chosen, Co-opt, Eatanswill, Elite, General, Gerrymander, Hustings, In, Israelite, Khaki, Off-year, Opt, Pick, PR, Primary, Psephology, Rectorial, Return, Select, Stump

Electrical discharge Corposant, Ion, Zwitterion
Electrical instrument Battery, Charger, Galvaniser, Mains, Resistor, Rheostat, Shoe
Electrical unit Amp(ere), Coulomb, Farad, Kilowatt, Ohm, Volt, Watt
Electric eye Pec
Electrician Gaffer, Lineman, Ohm, Siemens, Sparks, Tesla
Electricity Galvanism, HT, Juice, Mains, Negative, Positive, Power, Static, Utility,
  Vitreous
Electrify Astonish, Galvanise, Startle, Stir, Thrill
Electrode Anode, Cathode, Dynode, Element, Photocathode
Electrolyte Ampholyte
Electromagnet(ic) Abampere, Armature, Oersted, Solenoid, Weber
Electron(ic), Electronics, Electronic device Cooper pairs, Exciton, FET,
  Fly-by-wire, Linac, Lone pair, Martenot, Polaron, Possum®, Quantum,
  Thermionics, Valence, Valency
Elegance, Elegant Artistic, Bijou, Chic, Classy, Dainty, Daynt, Debonair, Fancy,
  Feat, Finesse, Gainly, Galant, Grace, Jimp, Luxurious, Polished, Recherché, Refined,
  Ritzy, → SMART, Soigné(e), Suave, Swish, Tall, Urbane
Elegy Dirge, Lament, Poem
Element(s), Elementary Abcee, Abecedarian, Absey, Barebones, → COMPONENT,
  Detail, → ESSENCE, Essential, Factor, Feature, Fuel, Heating, Ideal, Identity,
  Insertion, Milieu, Peltier, Pixel, Primary, Principle, Rare earth, Rudimental, Simple,
  Strand, Trace, Tramp, Transition, Weather

ELEMENTS

3 letters:
Air
Tin (Sn)

4 letters:
Atom
Fire
Gold (Au)
Iron (Fe)
Lead (Pb)
Neon (Ne)
Ylem
Zinc (Zn)

5 letters:
Alloy
Argon (Ar)
Boron (B)
Earth
Morph(eme)
Niton
Radon (Rn)
Terra
Water
Xenon (Xe)

6 letters:
Barium (Ba)
Carbon (C)
Cerium (Ce)
Cesium (Cs)
Cobalt (Co)
Copper (Cu)
Curium (Cm)
Erbium (Er)
Helium (He)
Indium (In)
Iodine (I)
Nickel (Ni)
Osmium (Os)
Oxygen (O)
Radium (Ra)
Silver (Ag)
Sodium (Na)

7 letters:
Arsenic (As)
Bismuth (Bi)
Bromine (Br)
Cadmium (Cd)
Caesium (Cs)
Calcium (Ca)

Dubnium (Db)
Fermium (Fm)
Gallium (Ga)
Hafnium (Hf)
Hahnium (Hn)
Halogen
Hassium (Hs)
Holmium (Ho)
Iridium (Ir)
Isotope
Krypton (Kr)
Lithium (Li)
Mercury (Hg)
Niobium (Nb)
Rhenium (Re)
Rhodium (Rh)
Silicon (Si)
Sulphur (S)
Terbium (Tb)
Thorium (Th)
Thulium (Tm)
Uranide
Uranium (U)
Wolfram
Yttrium (Y)

8 letters:
Actinide
Actinium (Ac)
Antimony (Sb)
Astatine (At)
Chlorine (Cl)
Chromium (Cr)
Didymium
Europium (Eu)
Fluorine (F)
Francium (Fr)
Hydrogen (H)
Illinium
Inchoate
Lutetium (Lu)
Masurium
Nebulium
Nitrogen (N)
Nobelium (No)
Platinum (Pt)
Polonium (Po)
Rubidium (Rb)
Samarium (Sm)
Scandium (Sc)
Selenium (Se)
Tantalum (Ta)

Thallium (Tl)
Titanium (Ti)
Tungsten (W)
Vanadium (V)

9 letters:
Alabamine
Aluminium (Al)
Americium (Am)
Berkelium (Bk)
Beryllium (Be)
Brimstone
Columbium
Germanium (Ge)
Joliotium
Lanthanum (La)
Magnesium (Mg)

Manganese (Mn)
Metalloid
Neodymium (Nd)
Neptunium (Np)
Palladium (Pd)
Plutonium (Pu)
Potassium (K)
Ruthenium (Ru)
Strontium (Sr)
Tellurium (Te)
Virginium
Ytterbium (Yb)
Zirconium (Zr)

10 letters:
Dysprosium (D)
Gadolinium (Gd)

Lanthanide
Lawrencium (Lr)
Meitnerium (Mt)
Molybdenum (Mo)
Phlogiston
Phosphorus (P)
Promethium (Pm)
Seaborgium (Sg)
Technetium (Tc)

11 letters:
Californium (Cf)
Einsteinium (Es)
Mendelevium (Md)
Transuranic
Unnilennium (Une)
Unnilhexium (Unh)

Unniloctium (Uno)
Ununquadium
(Uuq)

12 letters:
Kurchatovium
Nielsbohrium
Praseodymium (Pr)
Protactinium (Pa)
Unnilpentium (Unp)
Unnilseptium (Uns)

13 letters:
Rutherfordium
Transactinide
Unniliquadium
(Unq)

Elephant(ine) African, Babar, Hathi, Indian, Jumbo, Kheda, Mammoth, Mastodon, Oliphant, Pachyderm, Pad, Pink, Proboscidean, Rogue, Subungulata, Trumpeter, Tusker, White

Elephant-headed Ganesa

Elephant's ears Begonia

Elevate(d), Elevation, Elevator Agger, Attitude, Cheer, Colliculus, El, Eminence, Ennoble, Foothill, Glabella, Grain, Heighten, Hoist, Jack, Lift, Machan, Montic(u)le, Monticulus, Promote, → **RAISE**, Random, Relievo, Ridge, Rise, Steeve, Sublimate, Up(lift), Uplying, Upraise, Wallclimber

Eleven Elf, Hendeca-, Legs, Side, Tail-ender, Team, XI

Elf, Elves Alfar, Chiricaune, Fairy, Goblin, Imp, Kobold, Ouph, Pigwiggen, Pixie, Ribhus, Sprite

Elicit Evoke, Extract, Toase, Toaze, Tose, Toze

Eligible Available, Catch, Fit, Nubile, Parti, Qualified, Worthy

Eliminate, Elimination Cull, Delete, Discard, Exclude, Execute, Extirpate, Heat, Liquidate, Omit, Preclude, Purge, Red-line, Rid, Separate, Slay, Void, Zap

Elision Synal(o)epha, Syncope

Elite Best, Choice, Crack, → **CREAM**, Elect, Flower, Liberal, Meritocracy, Ton, Top drawer, Twelve pitch, U, Zaibatsu

Elixir Amrita, Arcanum, Bufo, Cordial, Daffy, Essence, Medicine, Panacea, Quintessence, Tinct

Elizabeth Bess(ie), Gloriana, Oriano

Elk Deer, Gang, Irish, Moose

Elkoshite Nahum

Ellipse, Elliptic Conic, Oblong, Oval

Elm Dutch, Slippery, Wahoo, Weeping, Wich, Winged, Wych

Elmer Gantry

Elongate Extend, Lengthen, Protract, Stretch

Elope Abscond, Decamp

Eloquence, Eloquent Articulate, Demosthenic, Facundity, Fluent, Honey-tongued, Oracy, Rhetoric, Speaking, Vocal

Else(where) Absent, Alibi, Aliunde, Other

Elucidate Explain, Expose, Interpret

Elude, Elusive Avoid, Dodge, Escape, → **EVADE**, Evasive, Foil, Intangible, Jink, Slippy, Subt(i)le, Will o' the wisp

▶ **Elves** *see* **ELF**

Elysium Tir-nan-Og

Em Mut(ton), Pica

Emaciated, Emaciation Atrophy, Erasmus, Gaunt, Haggard, Lean, Skinny, Sweeny, Tabid, Thin, Wanthriven, Wasted

Email Flame, Spam

Emanate, Emanation Arise, Aura, Discharge, Exude, Issue, Miasma, Radiate, Spring

Emancipate, Emancipation Deliver, Forisfamiliate, Free, → **LIBERATE**, Manumission, Uhuru

Emasculate Bobbitt, Castrate, Debilitate, Evirate, Geld, Unsex

Embalm Anoint, Mummify, Preserve

Embankment Berm, Bund, Causeway, Dam, Dyke, Earthwork, Levee, Mattress, Mound, Rampart, Remblai, Sconce, Staith(e), Stopbank, Terreplein

Embargo → **BAN**, Blockade, Edict, Restraint

Embark Begin, Board, Enter, Inship, Launch, Sail

Embarrass(ed), Embarrassing, Embarrassment Abash, Ablush, Awkward, Barro, Besti, Buttock-clenching, Chagrin, Cheap, Disconcert, Gêne, Haw, Mess, Mortify, Pose, Predicament, Scundered, Scunnered, Shame, Sheepish, Squirming, Straitened, Toe-curling, Tongue-tied, Upset, Whoopsie, Writhing

▷ **Embarrassed** *may indicate* an anagram

Embassy Consulate, Embassade, Legation, Mission

Embed(ded) Fix, Immerse, Inlaid, Set

Embellish(ed), Embellishment Adorn, Beautify, Bedeck, Deck, Decorate, Dress, Embroider, Enrich, Frill, Garnish, Garniture, Mordent, → **ORNAMENT**, Ornate, Prettify, Rel(l)ish, Roulade, Turn

Ember(s) Ash, Cinder, Clinker, Gleed

Embezzle(ment) Defalcate, Malversation, Peculate, Purloin, Shoulder, → **STEAL**

Embitter(ed) Acerbate, Aggravate, Enfested, Rankle, Sour

Emblem(atic) Badge, Bear, Colophon, Daffodil, Device, Figure, Ichthys, Impresa, Insignia, Kikumon, Leek, Lis, Maple leaf, Oak, Pip, Rose, Roundel, Shamrock, Sign, Spear-thistle, → **SYMBOL**, Tau-cross, Thistle, Token, Totem(ic), Triskelion, Wheel

Embody, Embodied, Embodiment Epitome, Fuse, Impanation, Incarnation, Incorporate, Personify, Quintessence

Embolism Clot, Infarct

Emboss(ed) Adorn, Chase, Cloqué, Engrave, Matelassé, Pounce, Raise, Repoussé, Toreutic

Embrace(d) Abrazo, Accolade, Arm, Canoodle, Clasp, Clinch, Clip, Coll, Complect, Comprise, Cuddle, Embosom, Encircle, Enclasp, Enclose, Enfold, Enlacement, Envelop, Espouse, Fold, Grab, Halse, Haulst, Hause, Hesp, Hug, Imbrast, Inarm, Inclasp, Inclip, Include, Inlace, Kiss, Lasso, Neck, Press, Stemme, Twine, Welcome, Wrap

▷ **Embraces, Embracing** *may indicate* a hidden word

Embrocate, Embrocation Anoint, Arnica, Liniment

Embroider(y) Appliqué, Arrasene, Assisi, Battalia-pie, Braid, Brede, Couching, Crewellery, Crewel-work, Cross-stitch, Cutwork, Drawn threadwork, Embellish, Exaggerate, Eyelet, Fag(g)oting, Fancywork, Featherstitch, Filet, Framework, Gros point, Handiwork, Knotting, Lace(t), Laid work, Mola, Needlepoint, Needlework, Open-work, Opus anglicanum, Orfray, Ornament, Orphrey, Orris, Petit point,

Pinwork, Pulled threadwork, Purl, Sampler, Sew, Smocking, Stitch, Stitchery, Stumpwork, Tambour, Tent, Wrap

Embroideress Mimi

Embroil Confuse, Entangle, Involve, Trouble

Embryo(nic) Blastocyst, Blastospore, Blastula, Conceptus, Epicotyl, Fo(e)tus, Gastrula, Germ, Mesoblast, Morula, Nepionic, Neurula, Origin, Rudiment, Undeveloped

Emend Adjust, Alter, Edit, Reform

Emerald Beryl, Gem, Green, Oriental, Smaragd, Uralian

Emerge(ncy), Emerging Anadyomene, Arise, Craunch, Crise, Crisis, Crunch, Debouch, Eclose, Emanate, Enation, Erupt, Exigency, Hard-shoulder, Issue, Lash-up, Last-ditch, Loom, Need, Outcrop, Pinch, SOS, Spring, Stand-by, Stand-in, Strait, Surface

▷ **Emerge from** *may indicate* an anagram or a hidden word

Emerson Waldo

Emetic Apomorphine, Cacoon, Epicac, Evacuant, Ipecacuanha, Puke, Sanguinaria, Stavesacre, Tartar, Vomitory

Emigrant, Emigration Chozrim, Colonist, Italiot, Jordim, Redemptioner, Settler, When-we, Yordim

Emile Zola

Emily Ellis

Eminence, Eminent Alp, Altitude, Cardinal, Distinguished, Eximious, Grand, Height, Hill, Hywel, Inselberg, Knoll, Light, Lion, Lofty, Luminary, Noble, → **NOTABLE**, Note, Palatine, Prominence, Renown, Repute, Stature, Tor, Trochanter, → **VIP**, Wallah

Emirate Dubai

Emissary Agent, Envoy, Legate, Marco Polo

Emission, Emit Discharge, Emanate, Field, Give, Issue, Spallation, Thermionic, Utter, Vent

Emmer Amelcorn, Wheat

Emollient Paregoric

Emolument Income, Perk, Remuneration, Salary, Stipend, Tip, Wages

Emotion(s), Emotional Affection, Anger, Anoesis, Atmosphere, Breast, Chord, Ecstasy, Empathy, Excitable, Feeling, Flare up, Freak-out, Gusty, Hate, Heartstrings, Hoo, Hysteria, Intense, Joy, Limbic, Nympholepsy, Passion, Reins, Roar, Sensibility, Sensitive, Sentiment, Spirit, Theopathy, Torrid, Transport, Weepy

Emotionless Deadpan, Glassy

Empathy Identifying, Rapport, Rapprochement, Sympathy

Emperor Agramant(e), Akbar, Akihito, Antoninus, Augustus, Babur, Barbarossa, Bonaparte, Caesar, Caligula, Caracalla, Charlemagne, Claudius, Commodus, Concerto, Constantine, Diocletian, Domitian, Ferdinand, Gaius, Genghis Khan, Gratian, Great Mogul, Hadrian, Haile Selassie, Heraclius, Hirohito, Imp, Imperator, Inca, Jimmu, Justinian, Kaiser, Keasar, Kesar, King, Maximilian, Menelik, Mikado, Ming, Mogul, Montezuma, Mpret, Napoleon, Negus, Nero, Nerva, Otho, Otto, Penguin, Peter the Great, Purple, Pu-yi, Rex, Rosco, Ruler, Severus, Shah Jahan, Shang, Sovereign, Sultan, Tenno, Theodore, Theodosius, Tiberius, Titus, Trajan, Tsar, Valens, Valentinian, Valerian, Vespasian, Vitellius, Wenceslaus

Emphasis, Emphasize, Emphatic Accent, Birr, Bold, Dramatise, Ek se, Forcible, Foreground, Forzando, Hendiadys, Italic, Marcato, Positive, Resounding, Sforzando, → **STRESS**, Underline, Underscore, Vehement

Empire Assyria, British, Byzantine, Celestial, Chain, Chinese, Domain, Empery,

First, French, Georgia, Holy Roman, Indian, Kingdom, Latin, NY, Ottoman, Parthia, Persian, Principate, Realm, Reich, Roman, Russian, Second, Turkish, Western

Empiricism Positivism

Emplacement Battery, Platform

Employ(ment) Business, Calling, Designated, Engage, Exercitation, Hire, Occupy, Pay, Place, Portfolio, Practice, Pursuit, Service, Shiftwork, Trade, Use, Using, Utilise, Vocation

Employee(s) Barista, Clock-watcher, Factotum, Hand, Help, Hireling, Intrapreneur, Minion, Munchkin, Networker, Payroll, Pennyboy, Personnel, Rainmaker, Servant, Staff, Staffer, Valet, Walla(h), Worker, Workforce, Workpeople

Employer Baas, Boss, Malik, Master, Melik, Padrone, User

▷ **Employs** *may indicate* an anagram

Emporium Bazaar, Shop, Store

Empower Authorise, Enable, Entitle, Permit

Empress Eugenie, Josephine, Messalina, Queen, Sultana, Tsarina, VIR

Empty Addle, Bare, Barren, Blank, Boss, Buzz, Claptrap, Clear, Deplete, Deserted, Devoid, Disembowel, Drain, Exhaust, Expel, Forsaken, Futile, Gousty, Gut, Hent, Hollow, Inane, Jejune, Lade, Lave, Null, Phrasy, Pump, Shallow, Teem, Toom, Tume, Unfurnished, Unoccupied, Unpeople, Vacant, Vacate, Vacuous, Vain, Viduous, → **VOID**

▷ **Empty** *may indicate* an 'o' in the word or an anagram

Emulate Ape, Copy, Envy, Equal, Imitate, Match

Emulsion Pseudosolution, Tempera

Enable Authorise, Empower, Potentiate, Qualify, Sanction

Enact Adopt, Effect, Ordain, Personate, Portray

Enamel(led), Enamel work Aumail, Champlevé, Cloisonné, Della-robbia, Dentine, Fabergé, Ganion, Lacquer, Nail, Polish, Porcelain, Schwarzlot, Shippo, Smalto, Stoved, Vitreous

Encampment Bivouac, Douar, Dowar, Duar, Laager, Laer, Settlement

Encase(d), Encasement Box, Crate, Emboîtement, Encapsulate, Enclose, Obtect

Enchant(ing), Enchanted, Enchantment Bewitch, Captivate, Charm, Delight, Gramary(e), Incantation, Magic, Necromancy, Orphean, Rapt, Sorcery, Spellbind, Thrill

Enchanter, Enchantress Archimage, Archimago, Armida, Circe, Comus, Fairy, Lorelei, Magician, Medea, Mermaid, Prospero, Reim-kennar, Sorcerer, Vivien, Witch

Encircle(d) Belt, Enclose, Encompass, Enlace, Entrold, Gird, Hoop, Inorb, Introld, Orbit, Pale, Ring, Stemme, → **SURROUND**, Wreathe

Enclave Cabinda, Ceuta, → **ENCLOSURE**, Melilla, Pocket, San Marino

Enclose(d), Enclosing, Enclosure Bawn, Beset, Boma, Box, Cage, Carol, Carrel, Case, Circumscribe, Common, Compound, Corral, Court, Embale, Embowel, Embower, Enceinte, Enchase, Encircle, Enclave, Enhearse, Enlock, Enshrine, Fence, Fold, Forecourt, Garth, Haggard, Haw, Hem, Henge, Hope, Impound, In, Incapsulate, Inchase, Infibulate, Inlock, Insert, Interclude, Lairage, Pale, Peel, Pele, Pen(t), Petavius, Pightle, Pin, Pinfold, Pit, Playpen, Plenum, Rail, Rath, Recluse, Ree(d), Ring, Run, Saddling, Saleyard, Seal, Sekos, Sept, Seraglio, Serail, Several, Sin bin, Steeld, Stell, Stive, Stockade, Sty, → **SURROUND**, Tine, Unsaddling, Vibarium, Ward, Winner's, Wrap, Yard

Encode Cipher, Scramble

Encomium Eulogy, Praise, Sanction, Tribute

Encompass Bathe, Begird, Beset, Environ, Include, Surround

Encore Again, Agen, Ancora, Bis, Ditto, Do, Iterum, Leitmotiv, Recall, Repeat, Reprise

Encounter Battle, Brush, Combat, Contend, Cope, Dogfight, Face, Hit, Incur, Intersect, Interview, → **MEET**, One-one, Rencontre, Ruffle, Skirmish, Tilt

Encourage(ment), Encouraging Abet, Acco(u)rage, Alley-oop, Animate, Attaboy, Bolster, Boost, Brighten, Buck, Cheer, Cohortative, Comfort, Commend, Dangle, Egg, Elate, Embolden, Empatron, Exhort, Fillip, Fire, Fortify, Foster, Fuel, Gee, Hearten, Heigh, Help, Hope, Hortatory, Incite, Inspirit, Nourish, Nurture, Pat, Patronise, Proceleusmatic, Prod, Protreptic, Push, Reassure, Root, Stimulate, Support, Tally-ho, Train, Upcheer, Uplift, Urge, Wean, Yay, Yo

Encroach(ment) Impinge, Infringe, Inroad, Intrude, Invade, Overlap, Overstep, Poach, Purpresture, Trespass, Usurp

Encrypt(ion) Coding, Public key

Encumber, Encumbrance Burden, Charge, Clog, Dead weight, Deadwood, Dependent, → **HANDICAP**, Impede, Load, Obstruct, Saddle

Encyclopaedic Comprehensive, Diderot, Extensive, Universal, Vast

End(ing) Abolish, Abut, Aim, Ambition, Amen, Anus, Arse, Big, Bitter, Bourn(e), Butt, Cease, Climax, Close, Closure, Cloture, Coda, Conclude, Crust, Culminate, Curtain, Curtains, Cut off, Dead, Death, Decease, Denouement, Desinence, Desistance, Destroy, Determine, Dissolve, Domino, Effect, Envoi, Envoy, Epilogue, Exigent, Expire, Explicit, Extremity, Fatal, Fattrels, Feminine, Final(e), Fine, Finis, → **FINISH**, Finite, Gable, Grave, Heel, Ish, Izzard, Izzet, Kill, Kybosh, Last, Let up, Little, Loose, Masculine, Mill, Nirvana, No side, Ort, Outro, Period, Peter, Pine, Point, Purpose, Quench, Receiving, Remnant, Rescind, Result, Roach, Round off, Runback, Scotch, Scrag, Shank, Slaughter, Sopite, Split, Sticky, Stub, Supernaculum, Surcease, Swansong, Tag, Tail, Tailpiece, Telesis, Telic, Telos, Term, Terminal, Terminate, Terminus, Thrum, Tip, Toe, Top, Ultimate, Up, Upshot, West, Z

Endanger Hazard, Imperil, Periclitate, Risk, Threaten

Endear(ing), Endearment Adorable, Affection, Asthore, Caress, Cariad, Ducks, Ducky, Enamour, Hinny, Honey(-bunch), Honey-chile, Ingratiate, Jarta, Luv, Machree, Mavourneen, Peat, Pet, Sweet nothings

Endeavour Aim, Effort, Enterprise, Essay, Morse, Strain, Strive, Struggle, Try, Venture

Endemic Local, Prevalent

Endive Escarole

Endless Continuous, Ecaudate, Eternal, Eterne, Infinite, Interminable, Perpetual, Undated

▷ **Endlessly** *may indicate* a last letter missing

End of the world Ragnarok

Endorse(ment) Adopt, Affirm, Allonge, Approve, Assurance, Back, Certify, Confirmation, Docket, Initial, Okay, Oke, Ratify, Rubber stamp, Sanction, Second, Sign, Subscript, → **SUPPORT**, Underwrite, Visa

Endow(ment) Assign, Bequeath, Bestow, Bless, Cha(u)ntry, Dot, Dotation, Enrich, Foundation, Gift, Leave, Patrimony, State, Vest, Wakf, Waqf

Endurance, Endure(d), Enduring Abought, Aby(e), Bear, Bide, Brook, Dree, Dure, Face, Fortitude, Have, Hold, → **LAST**, Livelong, Lump, Patience, Perseverance, Pluck, Ride, Stamina, Stand, Stay, Stomach, Stout, Support, Sustain, Swallow, Tether, Thole, Timeless, Tolerance, Undergo, Wear, Weather

Endymion Bluebell

Enema Barium, Catharsis, Clyster, Purge

Enemy Adversary, Antagonist, Boer, Devil, Fifth column, Foe(n), Fone, Opponent, Public, Time

Energetic, Energise, Energy Active, Alternative, Amp, Animation, Arduous, Atomic, Bond, Cathexis, Chakra, Chi, Dash, Doer, Drive, Dynamic, Dynamo, E, Enthalpy, Entropy, EV, Fermi, Fireball, Firebrand, Firecracker, Force, Fossil, Free, Fructan, Fusion, Geothermal, Gism, Go, Graviton, Hartree, H.D.R., Horme, Input, Instress, Internal, → **JET**, Jism, Jissom, Joie de vivre, Joule, Karma, Kinetic, Kundalini, Lattice, Libido, Lossy, Luminous, Magnon, Moxie, Nuclear, Orgone, Pep, Phonon, Potency, Potential, → **POWER**, Powerhouse, Prana, QI, Quantum, Quasar, Rad, Radiant, Radiatory, Renewable, Roton, Rydberg, Sappy, Second-wind, Solar, Stamina, Steam, Sthenic, Stingo, Tidal, Trans-uranic, Vehement, Verve, Vibrational, Vigour, Vim, Vital, Wave, Whammo, Wind(-farm), Zappy, Zing, Zip

Enervate Exhaust

Enfold Clasp, Embrace, Envelop, Hug, Stemme, Swathe, Wrap

Enforce(ment) Administer, Coerce, Control, Exact, Implement, Impose

Eng Agma

Engage(d), Engagement, Engaging Absorb, Accept, Appointment, At, Attach, Bespoken, Betrothal, Bind, Book, Busy, Contract, Date, Embark, Employ, Engross, Enlist, Enmesh, Enter, Fascinate, Gear, Gig, Hire, Hold, Interest, Interlock, Lock, Mesh, Met, Occupy, Pledge, Promise, Prosecute, Reserve, Residency, Skirmish, Sponsal, Sponsion, Spousal, Sprocket, Trip, Wage, Winsome

▷ **Engagement** *may indicate* a battle

Engender Beget, Breed, Cause, Occasion, Produce

Engine, Engine part Air, Analytical, Athodyd, Beam, Booster, Bricole, Bypass, Carburettor, Catapult, Compound, Diesel, Donkey, Dynamo, Fan-jet, Fire, Four-cycle, Four-stroke, Gas, Gin, Heat, Humdinger, Internal combustion, Ion, Iron horse, Jet, Lean-burn, Light, Little-end, Locomotive, Machine, Mangonel, → **MOTOR**, Nacelle, Oil, Onager, Orbital, Otto, Outboard, Overhead valve, Petard, Petrary, Petrol, Petter, Pilot, Plasma, Podded, Pony, Pug, Pulp, Pulsejet, Push-pull, Put-put, Radial, Ramjet, Reaction, Reciprocating, Retrorocket, Rocket, Rose, Rotary, Scorpion, Scramjet, Search, Side-valve, Sleeve valve, Stationary, Steam, Stirling, Sustainer, Tank, Terebra, Testudo, Thermometer, Top-end, Traction, Trompe, Turbine, Turbofan, Turbojet, Turboprop, Two-handed, Two-stroke, V, Vernier, V-type, Wankel, Warwolf, Water, Wildcat, Winch, Winding

Engineer(ing), Engineers Aeronautical, AEU, Armstrong, Arrange, Baird, Barnes Wallis, Bazalgette, BE, Bessemer, Brindley, Brinell, Brunel, CE, Chartered, Concurrent, Contrive, De Lessops, Diesel, Fokker, Genetic, Greaser, Ground, Heinkel, Interactive, Junkers, Kennelly, Knowledge, Liability, Manhattan District, Manoeuvre, Marconi, Marine, Mastermind, McAdam, Mechanical, Mechatronics, Military, Mime, Operator, Organise, Otto, Planner, Porsche, Process, RE, Repairman, Reverse, Rig, Rogallo, Sales, Sanitary, Sapper, Savery, Scheme, Siemens, Smeaton, Social, Software, Sound, Stage, Stephenson, Strauss, Systems, Telford, Tesla, Traffic, Trevithick, Wangle, Wankel, Watt, Whittle, Whitworth

England Albany, Albion, Blighty, Demi-paradise, Eden, John Bull, Merrie, Merry, Middle, The Old Dart

English(man) Anglican, Anglice, Baboo, Babu, Basic, Brit, Bro talk, Canajan, Choom, E, Ebonics, Eng, Estuary, Gringo, Hawaiian, Hong Kong, Indian, Irish, Jackeroo, John Bull, King's, Kipper, Limey, Middle, Mister, Modern, Newspeak, Norman, Officialese, Old, Oxford, Philippine, Pidgin, Plain, Pom(my), Pommie, Pongo, Pork-pudding, Queen's, Qui-hi, Qui-hye, Rock, Rooinek, Rosbif, Sassenach,

Saxon, Scotic, Seaspeak, Shopkeeper, Side, Singapore, Singlish, South African, South Asian, Southron, Spanglish, Standard, Strine, Wardour Street, Woodbine, Yanqui, Yinglish

Engorge Devour, Glut, Swallow

Engraft Inset

Engrave(r), Engraving Aquatint, Blake, Carve, Cerography, Cerotype, Chalcography, Character, Chase, Cut, Die-sinker, Dry-point, Durer, Enchase, Eng, Etch, Glyptic, Glyptograph, Hogarth, Impress, Inchase, Inciser, Inscribe, Insculp, Intagliate, Inter, Lapidary, Line, Mezzotint, Niello, Photoglyphic, Photogravure, Plate, Scalp, Scrimshander, Scrimshandy, Scrimshaw, Steel, Stillet, Stipple, Stylet, Stylography, Turn, Wood, Xylographer

Engross(ed) Absorb, Engage, Enwrap, Immerse, Monopolise, → **OCCUPY**, Preoccupy, Prepossess, Rapt, Sink, Writ large

Engulf Overwhelm, Swamp, Whelm

Enhance Add, Augment, Better, Elevate, Embellish, Exalt, Heighten, Intensify

Enigma(tic) Charade, Conundrum, Dilemma, Gioconda, Gnomic, Mystery, Oracle, Poser, Problem, → **PUZZLE**, Quandary, Question, Rebus, Riddle, Secret, Sphinxlike, Teaser

Enjoin Command, Direct, Impose, Prohibit, Require

Enjoy(able), Enjoyment Apolaustic, Appreciate, Ball, Brook, Delectation, Fruition, Glee, Groove, Gusto, Have, High jinks, Lekker, Like, Own, Possess, Relish, Ripping, Savour, Taste, Wallow

Enlarge(ment), Enlarger Accrue, Acromegaly, Add, Aneurism, Aneurysm, Augment, Blow-up, Diagraph, Dilate, Exostosis, Expand, Expatiate, Explain, Increase, → **MAGNIFY**, Piece, Ream, Rebore, Sensationalize, Swell, Telescope, Tumefy, Upbuild, Varicosity

Enlighten(ed), Enlightenment Awareness, Bodhisattva, Dewali, Divali, Edify, Educate, Explain, Haskalah, Illumine, Instruct, Liberal, Nirvana, Revelation, Satori, Verlig(te)

Enlist Attest, Conscript, Draft, Engage, Enrol, Induct, Join, Levy, Muster, Prest, Recruit, Rope in, Roster, Volunteer

Enliven(ed) Animate, Arouse, Brighten, Cheer, Comfort, Exhilarate, Ginger, Invigorate, Merry, Pep, Refresh, Warm

Enmity Animosity, Aversion, Bad blood, Hatred, Malice, Nee(d)le, Rancour, Spite

Ennoble(ment) Dub, Elevate, Ermine, Exalt, Honour, Raise

Ennui Boredom, Tedium

Enormous Colossal, Exorbitant, Googol, Huge, Humongous, Humungous, → **IMMENSE**, Jumbo, Mammoth, Mega, Plonking, Vast, Walloper, Walloping

Enough Adequate, → **AMPLE**, Anow, Basta, Belay, Enow, Fill, Geyan, Nuff, Pax, Plenty, Qs, Sate, Satis, Suffice, Sufficient, Via, When

Enounce Affirm, Declare, State

Enquire, Enquiring, Enquiry Ask, Case, Check, Curious, Eh, Examine, Inquest, Inquire, Organon, Public, Request, Research, Scan, See, Steward's, Trial

Enrage(d) Bemad, Emboss, Enfelon, Imboss, → **INCENSE**, Inflame, Infuriate, Livid, Madden, Wild

Enrapture(d) Enchant, Ravish, Sent, Transport

Enrich Adorn, Endow, Enhance, Fortify, Fructify, Oxygenate

Enrol(ment) Attest, Empanel, Enlist, Enter, Incept, → **JOIN**, List, Matriculate, Muster, Register

Ensconce(d) Establish, Settle, Shelter, Snug

Ensemble Band, Octet(te), Orchestra, Outfit, Ripieno, Set, Tout, Whole

Enshrine Cherish, Sanctify

Ensign Ancient, Badge, Banner, Duster, → **FLAG**, Gonfalon, Officer, Pennon, Red, White

Enslave(ment) Addiction, Bondage, Captivate, Chain, Enthral, Thrall, Yoke

Ensue Follow, Result, Succeed, Supervene, Transpire

Entail Involve, Necessitate, Require

Entangle(ment) Ball, Cot, Elf, Embrangle, Embroil, Encumber, Ensnarl, Entrail, Fankle, Implicate, → **KNOT**, Mat, Ravel, Retiarius, Taigle, Trammel

Enter, Entry Admit, Board, Broach, Come, Enrol, Field, Infiltrate, Ingo, Inscribe, Insert, Intromit, Invade, Lodge, Log, Penetrate, Pierce, Record, Run, Submit, Table, Wild card

Enterprise, Enterprising Adventure, Ambition, Aunter, Cash cow, Dash, Emprise, Free, Go ahead, Goey, Go-getter, Gumption, Industry, Minefield, Plan, Private, Public, Push, Spirit, Starship, Stunt, Up and coming, Venture

Entertain(er), Entertaining, Entertainment Accourt, Acrobat, Afterpiece, All-dayer, All-nighter, Amphitryon, Amuse, Balladeer, Ballet, Beguile, Burlesque, Busk, Cabaret, Carnival, Cater, Charade, Cheer, Chout, Circus, Comedian, Comic, Concert, Conjure, Consider, Cottabus, Crack, Craic, Cuddy, Diseur, Diseuse, Distract, Divert, Divertissement, ENSA, Extravaganza, Fete, Fleshpots, Floorshow, Foy, Fun, Gaff, Gala, Gas, Gaudy, Gig, Harbour, Harlequin, Have, Hospitality, Host(ess), Impressionist, Infotainment, Interest, Interlude, Intermezzo, Jester, Juggler, Karaoke, Kidult, Kursaal, Lauder, Levee, Light, Masque, Melodrama, Minstrel, Movieoke, Musical, Music hall, Olio, Opera, Palladium, Panto, Pap, Party, Peepshow, Performer, Piece, Pierrot, Play, Raree-show, Reception, Regale, Review, Revue, Ridotto, Roadshow, Rodeo, Serenade, Showbiz, Sideshow, Singer, Snake-charmer, Soirée, Son et lumière, Striptease, Table, Tamasha, Tattoo, Treat, Variety, Vaudeville, Ventriloquist, Wattle

Enthral(l) Charm, Enchant, Enslave, Spellbind

Enthuse, Enthusiasm, Enthusiast(ic) Acclamatory, Amateur, Ardent, Ardour, Buff, Bug, Buzz, Cat, Cheerleader, Crazy, Crusader, Delirium, Demon, Devotee, Ebullience, Ecstatic, Estro, Fandom, Fiend, Fire, Flame, Freak, Furor(e), Geek, Get-up-and-go, Gung-ho, Gusto, Hacker, Hearty, Hype, Into, Keen, Lyrical, Mad, Mane, Mania, Muso, Nethead, Nympholept, Oomph, Outpour, Overboard, Passion, Perfervid, Preoccupation, Rah-rah, Raring, Rave, Relish, Rhapsodise, Schwärmerei, Sold, Spirit, Teeny-bopper, Verve, Warmth, Whole-hearted, Wonk, Zealot, Zest

Entice(ment), Enticing Allure, Angle, Cajole, Carrot, Decoy, Lure, Persuade, Seductive, → **TEMPT**, Tole, Toll, Trepan

Entire(ly), Entirety Absolute, All, Bag and baggage, Clean, Complete, Full Monty, Genuine, Inly, Intact, Integral, In toto, Livelong, Lot, Purely, Root and branch, Systemic, Thorough, Total, Tout, → **WHOLE**

Entitle(ment) Empower, Enable, Legitim, Name, Right

Entity Being, Body, Existence, Holon, Monad, Tao, Tensor, Thing, Virino

Entomologist Fabré

Entourage Cortège

Entrail(s) Bowels, Chawdron, Giblets, Gralloch, Guts, Ha(r)slet, Humbles, Lights, Numbles, Offal, Quarry, Tripe, Umbles, Viscera

Entrance(d), Entrant, Entry Access, Adit, Admission, Anteroom, Arch, Atrium, Attract, Avernus, Bewitch, Charm, Closehead, Contestant, Door, Doorstop, Double, Dromos, Eye, Fascinate, Foyer, Gate, Ghat, Hypnotise, In-door, Infare, Inflow, Ingate, Ingress, Inlet, Introitus, Jawhole, Jaws, Jib-door, Mesmerise, Mouth, Narthex, Pend, Porch, Portal, Porte-cochère, Postern, Propylaeum, Propylon,

Ravish, Reception, Record, Regest, Registration, Single, Spellbound, Starter, Stem, Stoa, Stoma, Stulm, Torii

Entreat(y) Appeal, Ask, Beg, Beseech, Flagitate, Impetrate, → IMPLORE, Orison, Petition, Plead, Pray, Precatory, Prevail, Prig, Rogation, Solicit, Sue, Supplicate

Entrée Access, Dish, Entry, Ingate

Entrench(ment) Coupure, Encroach, Fortify, Trespass

Entrepreneur Businessman, E-tailer, Executor, Impresario, Wheeler-dealer

Entrust Aret(t), Confide, Consign, Delegate, Give

▶ **Entry** *see* ENTRANCE

Entwine Complect, Impleach, Intervolve, Lace, Twist, Weave

Enumerate, Enumeration Catalogue, Count, Detail, Fansi, List, Tell

Enunciate, Enunciation Articulate, Declare, Deliver, Diction, Elocution, Proclaim

Envelop(e) Arachnoid, Bangtail, Chorion, Corolla, Corona, Cover(ing), Cuma, Enclose, Entire, First day cover, Floral, Invest, Involucre, Jiffy(bag)®, Muffle, Mulready, Perianth, Sachet, Sae, Serosa, Shroud, Smother, Surround, Swathe, Window

Environment(s), Environmental(ist) ACRE, Ambience, Ecofreak, Econut, Eco-warrior, Element, Entourage, Ergonomics, Green, Greenpeace, Habitat, Milieu, Realo, SEPA, Setting, Sphere, Surroundings, Umwelt, Vicinity

Envisage Contemplate, Imagine, Suppose

Envoi Farewell, RIP

Envoy Agent, Diplomat, Elchee, El(t)chi, Hermes, Legate, Plenipotentiary

Envy, Enviable, Envious Begrudge, Covet, Jaundiced, Jealousy, Penis, Plum

Enzyme ACE, Aldolase, Allosteric, Allozyme, Amylase, Amylopsin, Apyrase, Arginase, Asparaginase, Autolysin, Bromel(a)in, Carbohydrase, Carbonic anhydrase, Carboxylase, Casease, Catalase, Cathepsin, Cellulase, Cholinesterase, Chymopapain, Chymotrypsin, Coagulase, Collagenase, Constitutive, Cyclase, Cytase, Deaminase, Decarboxylase, Dehydrogenase, Diastase, Dipeptidase, Elastase, ELISA, Enolase, Enterokinase, Erepsin, Esterase, Fibrinolysin, Flavoprotein, Guanase, Histaminase, Hyaluronidase, Hydrase, Hydrolase, Inducible, Inulase, Invertase, Isomerase, Kallikrein, Kinase, Lactase, Lecithinase, Ligase, Lipase, Luciferase, Lyase, Lysin, Lysozyme, Maltase, Mutase, Neuraminidase, Nuclease, Oxdoreductase, Oxidase, Oxygenase, Papain, Pectase, Pectinesterase, Penicillinase, Pepsin(e), Peptidase, Permease, Peroxidase, Phosphatase, Phosphorylase, Plasmin, Polymerase, Protease, Proteinase, PSA, Ptyalin, Reductase, Ren(n)in, Restriction, Ribonuclease, Saccharase, Steapsin, Streptodornase, Streptokinase, Subtilisin, Sulfatase, Sulphatase, Telomerase, Thrombin, Thrombokinase, Thromboplastin, Transaminase, Transcriptase, Transferase, Trehalase, Trypsin, Tyrosinase, Urease, Urokinase, Zymase

Eon Arch(a)ean, Epoch

Epaminondas Theban

Ephemera(l) Brief, Day, Drake, Fungous, Mayfly, Momentary, Passing, Transient, Transitory, Trappings

Epic Aeneid, Ben Hur, Beowulf, Calliope, Colossal, Dunciad, Edda, Epopee, Epyllion, Gilgamesh, Heroic, Homeric, Iliad, Kalevala, Lusiad(s), Mahabharata, Nibelungenlied, Odyssey, Ramayana, Rhapsody, Saga

Epicene Hermaphrodite

Epicure(an) Apicius, Apolaustic, Connoisseur, Friand, Gastronome, Gastrosopher, Glutton, → GOURMAND, Gourmet, Hedonist, Sybarite

Epidemic Pandemic, Pestilence, Plague, Prevalent, Rampant, Rash

Epigram Adage, Apophthegm, Gnomic, Mot, Proverb

Epigraph Citation, Inscription, RIP
Epilepsy, Epileptic Clonic, Eclampsia, Falling evil, Falling sickness, Fit, Grand mal, Petit mal, Turn
Epilogue Appendix, Coda, Postscript
Epiphany Twelfthtide
Epiphenomenon ESP
Epiphyte Air-plant
Episcopalian PE, Prelatic
Episode, Episodic Chapter, Incident, Page, Picaresque, Scene
Epistle(s) Catholic, General, Lesson, Letter, Missive, Pastoral, Titus
Epitaph Ci-git, Hic jacet, Inscription, RIP
Epithet Adj(ective), Antonomasia, Apathaton, Byword, Curse, Expletive, Panomphaean, → **TERM**, Title
Epitome, Epitomise Abridge, Abstract, Digest, Image, Model, Summary, Typify
Epoch Age, Eocene, Era, Holocene, Magnetic, Miocene, Neogene, Oligocene, Palaeocene, Palaeolithic, Perigordian, Period, Pl(e)iocene, Pleistocene
Epsom salts Kieserite
Equable, Equably Calm, Just, Pari passu, Placid, Smooth, Tranquil
Equal(ly), Equality, Equal quantities Alike, All square, A(n)a, As, Balanced, Commensurate, Compeer, Egal(ity), Emulate, Equinox, Equiparate, Equity, Even, Even-steven, Ex aequo, Fe(a)re, Feer, Fiere, Fifty-fifty, For, Identical, Identity, Is, Iso-, Isocracy, Isonomy, Level, Level-pegging, Maik, Make, Match, Mate, Owelty, Par, Parametric, Pari passu, → **PEER**, Peregal, Pheer(e), Rise, Rival, → **SO**, Square, Upsides, Wyoming, Ylike
Equanimity Aplomb, Balance, Poise, Serenity
Equate, Equation(s) Balance, Chemical, Cubic, Defective, Differential, Diophantine, Dirac, Exponential, Gas, Identity, Linear, Logistic, Maxwell, Parametric, Personal, Polar, Quadratic, Reduce, Relate, Rhizic, Schrödinger, Simultaneous, Van der Waals', Wave
Equator(ial) Celestial, Galactic, Line, Magnetic, Thermal, Tropical
Equerry Courtier, Officer, Page
Equilibrium Balance, Composure, Homeostasis, Isostasy, Poise, Punctuated, Stable, Stasis, Steady state, Tautomerism, Thermodynamic
Equinox Autumnal, Vernal
Equip(ment), Equipage Accoutrement, Adorn, Aguise, Aguize, Apparatus, Apparel, Appliance, Armament, Array, Attire, Carriage, Clobber, Codec, Deadstock, Deck, Dight, Expertise, → **FURNISH**, Gear, Gere, Get-up, Graith, Habilitate, Hand-me-up, Kit, Material, Matériel, Mechanise, Muniments, Outfit, Paraphernalia, Plant, Receiver, Retinue, Rig, Sonar, Spikes, Stereo, Stock, Stuff, Tack(le), Tool, Trampet(te), Trampoline, Turn-out
Equity Actors, Equality, Justice, Law, Negative, Owner's, Union
Equivalence, Equivalent Akin, Amounting to, Correspondent, Dose, Equal, Equipollent, Ewe, Formal, In-kind, Same, Tantamount
Equivocal Ambiguous, Dubious, Evasive, Fishy, Oracular, Vague
Equivocate Flannel, Lie, Palter, Prevaricate, Quibble, Tergiversate, Waffle, Weasel
Er Um
Era Age, Archaean, C(a)enozoic, Christian, Common, Cretaceous, Cryptozoic, Decade, Dynasty, Ediocaron, Eozoic, Epoch, Hadean, Hegira, Hej(i)ra, Hijra, Jurassic, Lias, Mesozoic, Palaeozoic, Period, Precambrian, Proterozoic, Republican, Vulgar
Eradicate, Erase Abolish, Delete, Demolish, Destroy, Dislimn, Efface, Expunge,

Extirp, Obliterate, Purge, Root, Scrat, Scratch, Stamp-out, Strike off, Uproot, Uptear

Erasmus Humanist

Eratosthenes Sieve

Erbium Er

Erect(ion), Erector Attolent, Boner, Build, Construct(ion), Elevate, Hard-on, Henge, Horn, Perpendicular, Priapism, Prick, Rear, Rigger, Stiffy, Straight-pight, Tentigo, Upright, Vertical

Ergo Argal, Hence, Therefore

Erica Heather, Ling

Ermine Fur, Minever, Miniver, Stoat

Ernie Bondsman

Erode, Erosion Abrade, Corrasion, Denude, Destroy, Deteriorate, Detrition, Etch, Fret, Hush, Planation, Spark, Wash, Wear, Yardang

Eros, Erotic(a) Amatory, Amorino, Amorous, Aphrodisiac, Carnal, Cupid, Curiosa, Lascivious, Philtre, Prurient, Salacious, Steamy

Err(or) Aliasing, Anachronism, Bish, Blip, Blooper, Blunder, Boner, Bug, Clanger, Comedy, Corrigendum, EE, Execution, Fat-finger, Fault, Fluff, Glaring, Heresy, Human, Inaccuracy, Inherited, Jeofail, K'thibh, Lapse, Lapsus, Literal, Mackle, Mesprise, Mesprize, Misgo, Misprint, Misprise, Misprize, Misstep, → **MISTAKE**, Mumpsimus, Out, Parachronism, Probable, Rounding, Rove, Runtime, Sampling, Semantic, Sin, Slip, Slip-up, Solecism, Standard, Stray, Trip, Truncation, Typo, Typographical, Unforced, Wander

Errand Chore, Commission, Fool's, Message, Mission, Sleeveless, Task

Errand-boy Cad, Galopin, Page

Erratic Haywire, Temperamental, Unstable, Vagary, Vagrant, Wayward

Erroneous False, Inaccurate, Mistaken, Non-sequitur

Ersatz Artificial, Synthetic

Erudite, Erudition Academic, Didactic, Learned, Savant, Scholar, Well-read, Wisdom

Erupt(ion), Erupture Belch, Brash, Burst, Ecthyma, Eject, Emit, Emphlysis, Exanthem(a), Exanthemata, → **EXPLODE**, Fissure, Flare, Fumarole, Hives, Hornito, Lichen, Mal(l)ander, Mallender, Morphew, Outbreak, Outburst, Papilla, Paroxysm, Plinian, Pompholyx, Pustule, Rash, Rose-drop, Scissure

Escalate, Escalator Accrescence, Expand, Granary, Grow, Lift, Travolator

Escape(e), Escapade, Escapist Abscond, Atride, Avoid, Bale out, Bolt, Bolthole, Breakout, Caper, Close call, Eject, Elope, Elude, Elusion, Esc, Eschewal, Evade, Exit, Fire, Flee, Flight, Frolic, Fugacity, Gaolbreak, Hole, Hoot, Houdini, Houdini act, Hout, Lam, Leakage, Leg-it, Let-off, Levant, Loop(-hole), Meuse, Mews, Muse, Narrow, Near thing, Outlet, Prank, Refuge, Rollick, Runaway, Sauve qui peut, Scapa, Scarper, Seep(age), Shave, Slip, Vent, Walter Mitty, Wilding, Wriggle

Escapement Anchor, Foliot, Recoil

Eschew Abandon, Avoid, For(e)go, Ignore, → **SHUN**

Escort Accompany, Attend, Bodyguard, Chaperone, Comitatus, Conduct, Convoy, Cortège, Corvette, Date, Destroyer, Entourage, Frigate, Gallant, Gigolo, Guide, Lead, Outrider, Protector, Retinue, See, Send, Set, Squire, Take, Tend, Usher, Walker

Escutcheon Achievement, Crest, Shield

Esker OS

Eskimo Aleut, Caribou, Husky, In(n)uit, Inuk, Inukitut, Thule, Yupik

Esoteric Abstruse, Acroamatic, Arcane, Inner, Mystic, Occult, Orphic, Private,

Rarefied, Recondite, Secret

ESP Psi

Especial(ly) Chiefly, Esp, Espec, Outstanding, Particular

Esperanto Ido, Zamenhof

Espionage Industrial, Spying, Surveillance

Esplanade Promenade, Walk

Esprit Insight, Spirit, Understanding, Wit

Esquire Armiger(o), Esq, Gent

Essay(s) Article, Attempt, Causerie, Critique, Dabble, Disquisition, Dissertation, Endeavour, Festschrift, Go, Paper, Prolusion, Stab, Theme, Thesis, Tractate, Treatise, Try

Essayist Addison, Bacon, Carlyle, Columnist, Elia, Ellis, Emerson, Hazlitt, Holmes, Hunt, Huxley, Lamb, Locke, Montaigne, Pater, Prolusion, Ruskin, Scribe, Steele, → **WRITER**

Essence Alma, Atman, Attar, Aura, Being, Core, Element, Entia, Esse, Extract, Fizzen, Flavouring, Foison, Gist, Heart, Hom(e)ousian, Inbeing, Inscape, Kernel, Marrow, Mauri, Mirbane, Myrbane, Nub, Nutshell, Oil, Ottar, Otto, Perfume, Per-se, Pith, Quiddity, Ratafia, Soul, Ylang-ylang

Essential(ly) Basic, Central, Crucial, Entia, Formal, Fundamental, Imperative, In, Indispensable, Inherent, Integral, Intrinsic, Kernel, Key, Lifeblood, Linch-pin, Marrow, Material, Must, Necessary, Need, Nitty-gritty, Nuts and bolts, Part-parcel, Per-se, Prana, Prerequisite, Quintessence, Radical, Requisite, Sine qua non, Soul, Vital, Whatness

Establish(ed) Abide, Anchor, Ascertain, Base, Build, Chronic, Create, Deploy, Embed, Enact, Endemic, Engrain, Ensconce, Entrench, Erect, Evince, Fix, → **FOUND**, Haft, Imbed, Ingrain, Instal(l), Instate, Instil, Institute, Inveterate, Ordain, Pitch, Pre-set, Prove, Raise, Root(ed), Set, Stable, Standing, Stell, Substantiate, Trad, Trite, Valorise, Verify

Establishment Building, Business, CE, Church, Co, Concern, Creation, Hacienda, Household, Institution, Lodge, Proving ground, Salon, School, Seat, Succursal, System, Traditional

Estate, Estate-holder Allod(ium), Alod, Assets, Commons, Demesne, Domain, Dominant, Dowry, Fazenda, Fee-simple, Fee-tail, Fen, First, Fourth, General, Hacienda, Hagh, Haugh, Having, Hay, Housing, Industrial, Land-living, Latifundium, Legitim, Life, Manor, Messuage, Odal, Personal(ity), Plantation, Press, → **PROPERTY**, Real, Runrig, Second, Situation, Spiritual, Standing, Talooka, Taluk(a), Temporal, Termer, Termor, Thanage, Third, Trading, Trust, Udal, Zamindari, Zemindari

Estate agent Realtor

Esteem(ed), Estimable Account, Admiration, Appreciation, Count, Have, Honour, Izzat, Los, Precious, Prestige, Price, Pride, Prize, Rate, → **REGARD**, Reputation, Respect, Store, Value, Venerate, Wonder, Worthy

Ester Benzocaine, C(o)umarin, Depside, Glyceride, Olein, Palmitin, Phthalate, Psilocybin, Triglyceride, Urethan(e)

▸ **Estimable** *see* **ESTEEM**

Estimate, Estimation Appraise, Assess, Calculate, Carat, Conceit, Cost, Esteem, Extrapolation, Forecast, Gauge, Guess(timate), Inexact, Interval, Opinion, Point, Projection, Quotation, Rate, Rating, Reckon, Regard, Sight, Value, Weigh

Estrange Alienate, Disunite, Wean

Estuary Bay, Clyde, Creek, Dee, Delta, Firth, Gironde, Humber, Inlet, Mouth, Orwell, Ostial, Para, Rio de la Plata

Esurient Arid, Insatiable
Etc(etera) Et al(ia), So on
Etch(ing) Aquafortis, Aquatint(a), Bite, → ENGRAVE, Incise, Inscribe
Eternal, Eternity Aeonian, Ageless, Endless, Everlasting, Eviternal, Ewigkeit,
  Forever, Immortal, Infinity, Never-ending, Perdurable, Perpetual, Sempiternal,
  Tarnal, Timeless
Ether Atmosphere, Ch'i, Crown, Gas, Petroleum, Sky, Yang, Yin
Ethereal Airy, Delicate, Fragile, Heavenly, Nymph
Ethic(al), Ethics Deontics, Ideals, Marcionite, Moral, Principles, Work
Ethiopia(n) African, Amharic, Asmara, Cushitic, Falasha, Galla, Geez, Kabele,
  Kebele, Ogaden
Ethnic Racial, Roots
Ethyl ET
Etiquette Code, Conduct, Kawa, → MANNERS, Politesse, Propriety, Protocol, Ps and
  Qs, Punctilio
Etna Empedocles, Vessel, Volcano
Etonian Oppidan, Victim
Etruscan Tyrrhenian
Etymologist, Etymology Hobson-Jobson, Isodore
Eucalyptus Blackbutt, Bloodwood, Cadaga, Cadagi, Coolabah, Gum-tree, Ironbark,
  Jarrah, Mallee, Marri, Morrell, Sallee, Sally, Stringybark, Sugar gum, Tallow wood,
  Tewart, Tooart, Tuart, Wandoo, Woolly butt, Yate
Eucharist Communion, Housel, Mass, Supper, Viaticum
Eugene Aram, Onegin
Eugenia Jambal, Jambolan(a), Jambu(l)
Eulogy Encomium, Laudatory, Panegyric, Praise, Tribute
Euphausia Krill, Shrimp
Euphemism Fib, Gosh, Gracious, Heck, Hypocorism
Euphoria, Euphoric Cock-a-hoop, Ecstasy, Elation, High, Jubilation, Mindfuck,
  Nirvana, Rapture, Rush
Euphrasia Eyebright
Eurasian Chee-chee, Chi-chi
Europe(an) Balt, Bohunk, Catalan, Community, Continent, Croat, E, Esth, Faringee,
  Faringhi, Feringhee, Fleming, Hungarian, Hunky, Japhetic, Lapp, Lithuanian,
  Palagi, Polack, Ruthene, Ruthenian, Serb, Slavonian, Slovene, Topi-wallah,
  Transleithan, Tyrolean, Vlach, Yugoslav
Europium Eu
Eustace Diamonds
Euthanasia Exit
Evacuate, Evacuation Excrete, Expel, Getter, Medevac, Planuria, Planury,
  Scramble, Stercorate, Stool, Vent, Void, Withdraw
Evadc, Evasion, Evasive Ambages, Avoid, Circumvent, Cop-out, Coy, Dodge, Duck,
  Elude, Equivocate, Escape, Fence, Fudge, Hedge, Loophole, Mealymouthed, Parry,
  Prevaricate, Quibble, Quillet, Salvo, Scrimshank, Shack, Shifty, Shirk, Shuffling,
  Sidestep, Skive, Skrimshank, Slippy, Stall, Subterfuge, Tergiversate, Waive, Weasel,
  Weasel out, Whiffler
Evaluate, Evaluation Appraise, Assess, Estimate, Gauge, Job, Ponder, Rate,
  Review, Waid(e), Weigh
Evanescent Cursory, Fleeting, Fugacious
Evangelical, Evangelist(ical) Buchman, Clappy-doo, Converter, Crusader, Fisher,
  Godsquad, Gospeller, Happy-clappy, Jansen, Jesus freak, John, Luke, Marist,

Mark, Matthew, Missioner, Moody, Morisonian, Peculiar, Preacher, Revivalist, Salvationist, Sankey, Sim(eonite), Stundist, Wild

Evaporate, Evaporation Condense, Dehydrate, Desorb, Dry, Exhale, Steam, Steme, Ullage, Vaporise

Eve(ning) All Hallow's, Nightfall, St Agnes's, Soirée, Subfusk, Sunset, Tib(b)s, Twilight, Vesperal, Vespertinal, Vigil, Yester

Evelyn Diarist, Hope

Even(ly), Evenness Aid, Albe(e), Albeit, All, Average, Balanced, Clean, Drawn, Dusk, Een, Ene, Equable, Equal, Erev, Fair, Fair play, Flush, Forenight, Iron, J'ouvert, Level, Level-pegging, Meet, Pair, Par, Plain, Plane, Plateau, Quits, Rib, Smooth, Square, Standardise, Toss-up, Yet

Evening flight Ro(a)ding

Evensong Vespers

Event Bash, Case, Circumstance, Contingency, Discus, Encaenia, Episode, Fest, Field, Gymkhana, Happening, Happy, Heat, Incident, Iron man, Landmark, Leg, Liquidity, Media, Milestone, Occasion, Occurrence, Ongoing, Outcome, Pass, Regatta, Result, Stick-on, Three-day, Three-ring circus, Track, Triple

Even-toed Artiodactyl

Eventual(ity), Eventually Case, Contingent, Finally, Future, In time, Nd, Sooner or later

Ever Always, Ay(e), Constantly, Eternal, Eviternity

Everglade Vlei

Evergreen Abies, Ageless, Arbutus, Cembra, Cypress, Gaultheria, Golden lie, Ivy, Myrtle, Olearia, Periwinkle, Pinaster, Privet, Thuja, Thuya, Washington, Winterberry, Yacca

Everlasting Cat's ear, Changeless, Enduring, Eternal, Immortal, Immortelle, Perdurable, Recurrent, Tarnal

Every(one), Everything All, Complete, Each, Et al, Existence, Full Monty, Ilk(a), In toto, Monty, Sub chiz, Sum, The works, To a man, Tout, Tout le monde, Universal, Varsal

Everyday Banal, Informal, Mundane, Natural, Ordinary, Plain, Routine

Everywhere Omnipresent, Passim, Rife, Throughout, Ubique, Ubiquity

Evict(or) Disnest, Disseisor, Eject, Expel, Oust

Evidence, Evident Adminicle, Apparent, Argument, Axiomatic, Circumstantial, Clear, Confessed, Credentials, Direct, Distinct, Document, Empirical, Exemplar, Flagrant, Hearsay, Indicate, Internal, King's, Manifest, Marked, Naked, Obvious, Overt, → **PATENT**, Plain, Premise, Prima facie, Probable, Proof, Queen's, Record, Sign, Smoking gun, State's, Surrebuttal, Testimony, Understandable

Evil Ahriman, Alastor, Amiss, Bad, Badmash, Bale, Beelzebub, Budmash, Corrupt, Depraved, Eale, Falling, Guilty, Harm, Heinous, Hydra, Ill, Immoral, Iniquity, King's, Malefic, Malign, Mare, Mischief, Monstrous, Necessary, Night, Perfidious, Rakshas(a), Shrewd, Sin, → **SINISTER**, Theodicy, Turpitude, Vice, Wicked

Evil eye Jettatura

Evince Disclose, Exhibit, Indicate, → **MANIFEST**, Show

Eviscerate(d) Debilitate, Disembowel, Drawn, Gralloch

Evoke Arouse, Awaken, Elicit, Move, Stir

Evolution(ary) Convergent, Countermarch, Development, Emergent, Growth, Holism, Lamarck, Lysenkoism, Moner(on), Neo-Lamarckism, Orthogenesis, Phylogeny, Social, Spencerman, Stellar, Transformism, Turning

▷ **Evolution** *may indicate* an anagram

Evolve Speciate

Ewe Crone, Gimmer, Keb, Rachel, Sheep, Teg, Theave
Ewer Aquamanale, Aquamanile, → JUG
Ex Former, Late, Quondam, Ten
Exacerbate Aggravate, Embitter, Exasperate, Irritate, Needle
Exact(ing), Exactitude, Exactly Accurate, Authentic, Careful, Dead, Definite, Due, Elicit, Estreat, Even, Exigent, Extort, Fine, Formal, It, Jump, Literal, Literatim, Mathematical, Meticulous, Nice(ty), Pat, Point-device, → PRECISE, Require, Slap-bang, Spang, Specific, Spot-on, Strict, Stringent, T, To a 't', Verbatim
Exaction Blackmail, Extortion, Impost, Montem, Sorelion, Tax
Exaggerate(d), Exaggeration Agonistic, Amplify, Ballyhoo, Boast, Brag, Camp, Colour, Distend, Dramatise, → EMBROIDER, Goliathise, Hoke, Hyperbole, Inflate, Lie, Line-shoot, Magnify, Munch(h)ausen, Mythomania, Overdo, Overdraw, Overegg, Overpaint, Overplay, Overrate, Overstate, Overstretch, Over-the-top, Romance, Shoot a line, Steep, Stretch, Tall, Theatrical
Exalt(ed), Exaltation Attitudes, Deify, Dignify, Elation, Enhance, Ennoble, Erect, Extol, Glorify, High, Jubilance, Larks, Lofty, Magnific, → PRAISE, Raise, Rapture, Ruff(e), Sama, Sublime, Supernal, Throne
Exam(ination), Examine, Examinee, Examiner Agrégé, A-level, Analyse, Analyst, Appose, Assess, Audit, Auscultation, Autopsy, Baccalauréat, Biopsy, Case, Check-out, Check-up, Cognosce, Collate, Comb, Common Entrance, Consideration, Cross-question, CSE, Deposal, Depose, Disquisition, Dissect, Docimasy, Eleven plus, Endoscopy, Entrance, Expiscate, Explore, Eyeball, Finals, GCE, GCSE, Going-over, Grade(s), Great-go, Greats, Gulf, Haruspex, Hearing, Inspect, Inter, Interrogate, Interview, Introspection, Jerque, Jury, Little-go, Local, Mark, Matriculation, Medical, Mocks, Moderator, Mods, Mug, O-level, Once-over, Oral, Ordalian, Ordeal, Overhaul, Palp(ate), Paper, Peruse, Physical, Post-mortem, Prelims, Probe, Pry, Psychoanalyse, Pump, → QUESTION, Quiz, Ransack, Recce, Reconnaissance, Resit, Responsions, Review, Sayer, Scan, Schools, Scrutator, Scrutineer, Scrutinise, Search, Seek, Shroff, Sift, Sit, Smalls, Survey, Sus(s), Test, Trial, Tripos, Try, Unseen, Vet, Viva, Voir dire
Example Apotheosis, Assay-piece, Byword, Epitome, Erotema, Foretaste, → FOR EXAMPLE, Illustration, Instance, Lead, Lesson, Model, Paradigm, Paragon, → PATTERN, Praxis, Precedent, Prototype, Role model, Say, Shining, Showpiece, Specimen, Standard, Stormer, Such as, Touchstone, Type, Typify
Exasperate, Exasperating, Exasperation Anger, Embitter, Galling, Irk, Irritate, Nettle, Provoke
Excavate, Excavation, Excavator Armadillo, Burrow, Catacomb, Crater, Cutting, Delf, Delph, → DIG, Dike, Disinter, Ditch, Dragline, Dredge, Drive, Earthwork, Gaulter, Graft, Heuch, Heush, Hollow, JCB, Mine, Pichiciago, Pioneer, Pioner, Pyoner, Quarry, Shaft, Sink, Sondage, Steam-shovel, Stope, Well
Exceed, Exceeding(ly) Amain, Not half, Outdo, Overstep, Surpass, Transcend, Very
Excel(lence), Excellency, Excellent A1, Ace, Admirable, A-per-se, Assay-piece, Awesome, Bangin(g), Bang on, Beat, Beaut, Better, Bitchin', Blinder, Bodacious, Boffo, Bonzer, Booshit, Boss, Bottler, Bravo, Brill, Bully, Capital, Castor, Champion, Cheese, Choice, Class(y), Classical, Copacetic, Copesettic, Copybook, Corking, Crack, Crackerjack, Crucial, Daisy, Def, Dic(k)ty, Dilly, Dominate, Doozy, Elegant, Excelsior, Exemplary, Eximious, Exo, Extraordinaire, Fab, Fantastic, First rate, Five-star, Goodness, Great, Grit, Grouse, HE, High, Humdinger, Hunky(-dory), Inimitable, Jake, Jammy, Jim-dandy, Kiff, Knockout, Lalapalooza, Laudable, Lollapalooza, Lummy, Matchless, Mean, Mega-, Merit, Neat, Noble, Out and outer, Outbrag, Outdo, Outstanding, Outtop, Overdo, Overtop, Paragon, Peachy, Peerless,

Phat, Prime, Pure, Quality, Rad, Rare, Rattling, Ring, Rinsin', Ripping, Ripsnorter, Say-piece, Shagtastic, → **SHINE**, Shit-hot, Sick-dog, Sik, Socko, Spanking, Spiffing, Stellar, Stonking, Stupendous, Sublime, Superb, Super-duper, Superior, Supreme, Swell, Terrific, Tip-top, Top flight, Top-hole, Topnotch, Topping, Transcend, Transcendent, Triff, Virtue, Wal(l)y, War, Way-out, Wicked, Worth

Except(ion) Bar, But, Else, Exc, Nobbut, Omit, Save, Than, Then, Unless

Exceptional Abnormal, Anomaly, Cracker, Egregious, Especial, Extraordinary, Gas, Rare, Ripsnorter, Select, Singular, Special, Uncommon, Zinger

Excerpt(s) Digest, Extract, Passage, Scrap

Excess(ive), Excessively All-fired, Basinful, Exaggeration, Exorbitant, Extortionate, Extravagant, Flood, Fulsome, Glut, Hard, Inordinate, → **LAVISH**, Mountain, Needless, Nimiety, OD, Old, OTT, Outrage, Over, Overage, Overblown, Overcome, Overdose, Overkill, Overmuch, Overspill, Over-the-top, Owercome, Plethora, Preponderance, Profuse, Salt, Satiety, Spate, Spilth, Steep, Superabundant, Superfluity, Surfeit, Surplus, Terrific, Thundering, Too, Troppo, Ultra, Undue, Unequal, Woundily

Exchange Baltic, Bandy, Barter, Bourse, Cambist, Catallactic, Change, Chop, Commute, Contango, Convert, Cope, Corn, Ding-dong, Employment, Enallage, Excambion, Foreign, Inosculate, Interplay, Ion, Labour, Logroll, → **MARKET**, Mart, Needle, Niffer, Paraphrase, PBX, Post, Quid pro quo, Rally, Rate, Recourse, Redeem, Rialto, Royal, Scorse, Scourse, Sister-chromated, Stock, Swap, Switch, Swop, Telephone, Tolsel, Tolsey, Tolzey, → **TRADE**, Traffic, Transfusion, Trophallaxis, Truck

Exchequer Remembrancer

Excise(man), Excise district Ablate, Bobbitt, Crop, Expunge, Gauger, Resect, Ride, Tax

Excite(ment), Excited, Exciting, Excitability Ablaze, Aboil, Abuzz, Aerate, Agitate, Agog, Amove, Animate, Aphrodisiac, Arouse, Athrill, Atwitter, Awaken, Brouhaha, Buck-fever, Climatic, Combustible, Commotion, Delirium, Electrify, Emove, Enthuse, Erethism, Eventful, Feisty, Fever, Fire, Flap, Flat spin, Frantic, Frenzy, Frisson, Furore, Fuss, Galvanise, Gas, Grip, Headiness, Heat, Hectic, Het, Hey-go-mad, Hilarity, Hobson-Jobson, Hoopla, Hothead, Hyped, Hyper, Hypomania, Hysterical, Impel, Incite, Inebriate, Inflame, Intoxicate, Jimjams, Kick, Kindle, Liven, Metastable, Must, Neurotic, Oestrus, Orgasm, Overheat, Overwrought, Panic, Passion, Pride, Prime, Provoke, Racy, Radge, Red-hot, Rile, Roil, → **ROUSE**, Rousement, Ruff(e), Rut, Send, Sexy, Spin, Splash, Spur, Startle, Stimulate, Stir(e), Suscitate, Temperamental, Tetanoid, Tetany, Tew, Thrill, Titillate, Trickle, Turn-on, Twitter, Upraise, Va-va-voom, Waken, Whee, Whet, Whoopee, Work up, Yahoo, Yerk, Yippee, Yoicks

▷ **Excite(d)** *may indicate* an anagram

Exclaim, Exclamation (mark) Ahem, Aue, Begorra, Bliksem, Blurt, Bo, Ceas(e), Crikey, Criv(v)ens, Dammit, Ecphonesis, Eina, Eish, Ejaculate, Epiphonema, Eureka, Expletive, Fen(s), Good-now, Hadaway, Haith, Halleluiah, Hallelujah, Heigh-ho, Hem, Hip, Hookey Walker, Hosanna, Inshallah, Interjection, Moryah, Omigod, Oops, Phew, Pling, Pow, Protest, Pshaw, Sasa, Screamer, Sese(y), Sessa, Unberufen, Vociferate, Walker, Whau, Whoops, Wirra, Wow, Yay, Yippee, Yo-ho-ho, Yummy, Zounds

Exclave Cabinda

Exclude, Excluding, Exclusion Ban, Bar, Block, Competitive, Debar, Deforcement, Disbar, Drop, Eliminate, Ex, Except, Excommunicate, Freeze out, Omit, Ostracise, Outbar, Outwith, Pauli, Shut out, Social

Exclusive Cliquish, Closed-shop, Complete, Debarment, Elect, Monopoly, Particular, Pure, Rare, Scoop, Select, Single, Sole

Excommunicate Curse

Excoriate Flay, Slam

Excrement, Excretion, Excretory Dirt, Doo-doo, Dung, Emunctory, Faeces, Flyspeck, Frass, Jobbie, Keech, Meconium, Oliguria, Ordure, Poo(p), Poo-poo, Puer, Pure, Refuse, Scatology, Shit(e), Sir-reverence, Stercoraceous, Strangury, Turd, Urea, Waste, Whoopsie

Excrescence Aril, Carnosity, Caruncle, Enate, Gall, Growth, Knob, Knurl, Lump, Nurl, Pimple, Pin, Spavin(e), Strophiole, Talpa, Twitter(-bone), Wart

Excruciate, Excruciating Agonising, Rack, Torment, Torture

Exculpate Acquit, Clear, Forgive

Excursion Airing, Cruise, Dart, Digression, Jaunt, Junket, Outing, Road, Sally, Sashay, Sortie, Tour, Trip

Excuse, Excusable Absolve, Alibi, Amnesty, Bunbury, Condone, Essoin, Essoyne, Evasion, Exempt, Exonerate, Faik, Forgive, Let off, Mitigate, Occasion, Off come, Out, Overlook, Palliate, → **PARDON**, Pretext, Release, Salvo, Venial, Viable, Whitewash

Execrate Abhor, Ban, Boo, Curse

Execute(d), Executioner, Executive, Executor Abhorson, Accomplish, Account, Administrate, Behead, Carnifex, Deathsman, Despatch, Discharge, Dispatch, Exor, Finish, Fry, Gan, Gar(r)otte, Gin, Guardian, Hang, Headsman, Implement, Ketch, Kill, Koko, Literary, Lynch, Management, Martyr, Noyade, Official, Perform, Perpetrate, Pierrepoint, Politburo, Scamp, Top, Trustee, Tyburn

Exemplar(y) Byword, Impeccable, Laudable, Model, Paragon, Perfect, St, Warning

Exemplify Cite, Epitomise, Illustrate, Instantiate, Satisfy

Exempt(ion) Dispensation, Exclude, Exeem, Fainites, Fains, Free, Immune, Impunity, Indemnity, Overslaugh, Quarter, Spare, Tyburn ticket, Vains

Exercise(s) Aerobics, Air, Antic, Apply, Bench press, Burpee, Cal(l)isthenics, Callanetics®, Chi kung, Cloze, Constitutional, Drill, Employ, Enure, Eurhythmics, Exert, Falun dafa, Falun gong, Floor, Gradus, Inure, Isometrics, Kata, Keepy-uppy, Kegel, Krav Maga, Lesson, Limber, Manual, Medau, Op, Operation, PE, Physical jerks, Pilates, Ply, Plyometrics, Popmobility, Practice, Practise, Preacher curl, Press-up, Prolusion, PT, Pull-up, Pump iron, Push-up, Qigong, Sadhana, Shintaido, Sit-up, Solfeggi(o), Step (aerobics), Stretch, Tai chi (ch'uan), Thema, Theme, Thesis, Train, Trampoline, Trunk curl, Use, Vocalise, Warm-down, Warm-up, Wield, Work, Work-out, Xyst(us), Yomp

▷ **Exercise(d)** *may indicate* an anagram

Exert(ion) Conatus, → **EFFORT**, Exercise, Labour, Operate, Strain, Strive, Struggle, Trouble, Wield

Ex-European Japhetic

Exhalation, Exhale Breath, Fume, Miasma, Reek, Sigh, Steam, Transpire, Vapour

Exhaust(ed), Exhausting, Exhaustion, Exhaustive All-in, Backbreaking, Beaten, Beggar, Bugger(ed), Burn, Burn-out, Bushed, Clapped out, Consume, Deadbeat, Debility, Deplete, Detailed, Dissipate, Do, Done, Drain, Eduction, Effete, Emission, Empty, End, Enervate, Fatigue, Fordo, Forfeuchen, Forfochen, Forfoughen, Forfoughten, Forjaskit, Forjeskit, Forspent, Forswink, Frazzle, Gruelling, Heat, Heatstroke, Inanition, Jet-lagged, Jet-stream, Jiggered, Knacker, Mate, Milk, Out, Outwear, Play out, Poop, Powfagged, Puckerood, Puggled, Rag, Ramfeezle, Rundown, Sap, Shatter, Shot, Shotten, Spend, Spent, Stonkered, Tailpipe, Tire, Trauchled, Use, Used up, Wabbit, Wappend, Warby, Washed-up, Wasted,

Waygone, → **WEARY**, Wind, Worn, Zonked

Exhibit(ion), Exhibitioner, Exhibitionist Aquashow, Bench, Circus, Concours, Demo, Demonstrate, Demy, Diorama, Discover, Display, Evince, Expo, Expose, Fair, Hang, Indicate, → **MANIFEST**, Olympia, Pageant, Panopticon, Parade, Present, Retrospective, Salon, Scene, Set forth, Show(piece), Showcase, Show-off, Showplace, Viewing

Exhilarate(d) Bubble, Cheer, Elate, Enliven

Exhort(ation) Admonish, Allocution, Caution, Counsel, Incite, Lecture, Par(a)enesis, Persuade, Protreptic, Urge

Exhume Delve, Disinter, Resurrect, Unearth

Exigency, Exigent Demanding, Emergency, Pressing, Taxing, Urgent, Vital

Exile Adam, Babylon, Banish, Deport, Emigré, Eve, Expatriate, Exul, Galut(h), Ostracise, Outlaw, Relegate, Tax, Wretch

Exist(ence), Existing Be(ing), Corporeity, Dwell, Enhypostasia, Entelechy, Esse, Extant, Identity, Inbeing, In esse, Inherent, Life, Live, Ontology, Perseity, Solipsism, Status quo, Substantial, Ubiety

Existentialist Camus, Sartre

Exit Débouché, Door, Egress, Gate, Leave, Log off, Log out, Outlet

Exodus Book, Departure, Flight, Hegira, Hejira

Ex-official Outler

Exogamous Outbred

Exonerate(d) Absolve, Acquit, Clear, Excuse, Exempt, Shriven

Exorbitant Excessive, Expensive, Slug, Steep, Tall, Undue

Exorcise, Exorcist Benet, Lay

Exordium Opening, Preface, Prelude

Exotic Alien, Chinoiserie, Ethnic, Fancy, Foreign, Free, Outlandish, Strange

Expand, Expanse, Expansion Amplify, Boom, Branch out, Bulking, Develop, Diastole, Dilate, Distend, Ectasis, Elaborate, → **ENLARGE**, Escalate, Flesh out, Grow, Increase, Magnify, Ocean, Outspread, Snowball, Spread, Stretch, Swell, Vastitude, Wax, Wire-draw

Expatiate Amplify, Descant, Dwell, Enlarge, Perorate

Expatriate Banish, Colonial, Emigrate, Émigré, Exile, Outcast

Expect(ant), Expectation, Expected, Expecting Agog, Anticipate, Ask, Await, Due, Foresee, Gravid, Hope, Lippen, Look, Natural, Par, Pip, Predict, Pregnant, Presume, Prim, Prospect, Require, → **SUPPOSE**, Tendance, Think, Thought, Usual, Ween

Expectorant, Expectorate Expel, Guaiacol, Hawk, Spit

Expedient Advisable, Artifice, Contrivance, Fend, Make-do, Makeshift, Measure, Politic, Resort, Resource, Shift, Stopgap, Suitable, Wise

Expedite, Expedition, Expeditious Advance, Alacrity, Anabasis, Celerity, Crusade, Dispatch, Excursion, Fastness, Field trip, Hasten, Hurry, Kon-Tiki, Pilgrimage, Post-haste, Quest, Safari, Short cut, Speed, Trek, Trip, Voyage

Expel Amove, Dispossess, Drum out, Egest, Evacuate, Evict, Exile, Exorcize, Hoof, Oust, Out(cast), Read out, Void

Expend(iture) Budget, Consume, Cost, Dues, Gavel, Goings-out, Mise, Occupy, Oncost, Outgo(ing), Outlay, Poll, Squander, Tithe, Toll, Use, Waste

Expendable Cannon-fodder

Expense(s) Charge, Cost, Current, Exes, Fee, Law, Oncost, Outgoing, Outlay, Overhead, Price, Sumptuary

Expensive Chargeful, Costly, Dear, Executive, High, Salt, Steep, Upmarket, Valuable

Experience(d) Accomplished, A posteriori, Assay, Blasé, Come up, Discovery,

Empiric, Encounter, Expert, → **FEEL**, Felt, Find, Foretaste, Freak-out, Gust, Hands-on, Have, Incur, Know, Learn, Live, Mature, Meet, Mneme, Near-death, Old hand, Old-stager, Ordeal, Out-of-body, Pass, Plumb, Seasoned, See, Senior, Sense, Sensory, Spin, Stager, Stand, Street-smart, Streetwise, Taste, Transference, Trial, Trip, Trocinium, Try, Undergo, Versed, Veteran, Work, Worldly wise

Experiment(al) Attempt, Avant-garde, Ballon d'assai, Control, Empirical, Essay, Michelson-Morley, Peirastic, Pilot, Sample, Shy, Single-blind, Taste, Tentative, → **TRIAL**, Trial balloon, Try, Venture, Vivisection

Expert(ise) Accomplished, Ace, Adept, Adroit, Arch, Authority, Boffin, Buff, Cambist, Cocker, Cognoscente, Competent, Connoisseur, Crack, Craft, Dab(ster), Dan, Deft, Demon, Don, Egghead, Finesse, Fundi, Gourmet, Gun, Hotshot, Karateka, Know-all, Know-how, Luminary, Maestro, Masterly, Mastery, Maven, Mavin, Meister, Nark, Old hand, Oner, Oneyer, Oneyre, Peritus, Practised, Pro, Proficient, Pundit, Ringer, Savvy, Science, Shroff, Skill(y), Sly, Specialist, Technique, Technocrat, Troubleshooter, Ulema, Used, W(h)iz

Expiate, Expiation, Expiatory Amends, Atone, Penance, Piacular

Expire(d), Expiry Blow, Collapse, Croak, → **DIE**, End, Exhale, Invalid, Ish, Lapse, Neese, Pant, Sneeze, Terminate

Explain(able), Explanation Account, Annotate, Appendix, Aread, Arede, Arreede, Clarify, Conster, Construe, Decline, Define, Describe, Eclaircissement, Elucidate, Explicate, Exponible, Expose, Expound, Extenuate, Gloss, Glossary, Gloze, Justify, Parabolize, Salve, Solve, Upknit

Explanation, Explanatory Apology, Commentary, Exegesis, Exegetic, Exposition, Farse, Gloss, Gloze, Hypothesis, Key, Note, Preface, Reading, Rigmarole, Solution, Theory

Expletive Arrah, Darn, Exclamation, Oath, Ruddy, Sapperment

Explicit Clean-cut, Clear, Definite, Express, Frank, Full-on, Outspoken, → **PRECISE**, Specific

Explode, Explosion, Explosive Agene, Airburst, Amatol, Ammonal, ANFO, Antimatter, Aquafortis, Backfire, Bang, Bangalore torpedo, Big bang, Blast, Booby-trap, Burst, C4, Cap, Cheddite, Chug, Controlled, Cordite, Cramp, Crump, Cyclonite, Debunk, Demolitions, Detonate, Dualin, Dunnite, Dust, Egg, Erupt, Euchloric, Euchlorine, Fireball, Firecracker, Firedamp, Firework, Fulminant, Fulminate, Gasohol, Gelatine, Gelignite, Grenade, Guncotton, Gunpaper, Gunpowder, HE, High, Iracund, Jelly, Landmine, Low, Lyddite, Megaton, Melinite, Mine, Nail-bomb, Napalm, Nitre, Nitro(glycerine), Outburst, Ozonide, Paravane, Payload, Petar(d), Petre, Phut, Plastic, Plastique, Pluff, Pop, Population, Pow, Priming, Propellant, Ptarmic, Pustular, Report, Roburite, SAM, Semtex®, Sheet, Shrapnel, Snake, Sneeze, Soup, Squib, Supernova, Tetryl, Thunderflash, Tinderbox, TNT, Tonite, Trinitrobenzene, Trotyl, Volatile, Volcanic, Warhead, Xyloidin(e)

Exploit(s), Exploiter, Exploitation Act, Adventure, Coup, Coyote, Deed, Develop, Escapade, Feat, Gest, Harness, Ill-use, Impose, Kulak, Manoeuvre, Milk, Mission, Parlay, Play on, Rachmanism, Ramp, Res gestae, Stunt, Sweat, Tap, Use, Utilise

Explore(r), Exploration Amerigo, Amundsen, Baffin, Balboa, Bandeirante, Banks, Barents, Bellingshausen, Bering, Boone, Burton, Cabot, Cartier, Chart, Columbus, Cook, Cordoba, Cortes, Da Gama, Dampier, Darwin, De Soto, Dias, Diaz, Discover, Dredge, Eric, Eriksson, Examine, Feel, Field trip, Flinders, Frobisher, Fuchs, Humboldt, Investigate, Livingstone, Magellan, Map, Marco Polo, Mungo Park, Nansen, Navigator, Park, Pathfinder, Peary, Pioneer, Potholer, Probe, Przewalski, Rale(i)gh, Research, Rhodes, Ross, Scott, Scout, Search, Shackleton, Spaceship, Speke, Stanley, Sturt, Tasman, Vancouver, Vasco da Gama, Vespucci, Voyageur

▷ **Explosive** *may indicate* an anagram

Exponent Advocate, Example, Index, Interpreter, Logarithm

Export(s) Despatch, Invisible, Klondike, Klondyke, Ship, Visible

Expose(d), Exposure Air, Anagogic, Bare, Bleak, Blot, Blow, Burn, Crucify, Debag, Debunk, Denude, Desert, Disclose, Double, Endanger, En prisé, Exhibit, Flashing, Glareal, Indecent, Insolate, Moon, Nude, Object, Open, Out, Over, Paramo, Propale, Reveal, Showdown, Snapshot, Streak, Strip, Subject, Sun, Time, Uncover, Unmask, Windswept

Exposition Aperçu

Expostulate, Expostulation Argue, Arrah, Protest, Remonstrate

Expound(er) Discourse, Discuss, Exegete, Explain, Open, Prelict, Red, Scribe, Ulema

Express(ed), Expression, Expressive Air, APT, Aspect, Breathe, Cacophemism, Circumbendimus, Cliché, Colloquialism, Conceive, Concetto, Couch, Countenance, Declare, Denote, Eloquent, Embodiment, Epithet, Estafette, Explicit, Face, Fargo, Formulate, Godspeed, Good-luck, Gup, Hang-dog, Hell's bells, Idiom, Isit, Limited, Locution, Lyrical, Manifest, Metonym, Mien, Mot (juste), Neologism, Non-stop, Orient, Paraphrase, Phrase, Pleonasm, Pony, Precise, Pronouncement, Pronto, Put, Quep, Register, Say(ne), Show, Soulful, → SPEAK, State, Strain, Succus, Term, Token, Tone, Topos, Trope, Utterance, Vent, → VOICE

Expressionless Aphasia, Blank, Boot-faced, Deadpan, Impassive, Inscrutable, Po(ker)-faced, Vacant, Wooden

Expressman Fargo

Expropriate Dispossess, Pirate, Seize, Usurp

Expulsion Discharge, Eccrisis, Ejection, Eviction, Exile, Pride's Purge, Sacking, Synaeresis

Expunge Cancel, Delete, Erase, Obliterate

Expurgate Bowdlerize, Castrate, Censor, Purge

Exquisite Beautiful, Choice, Ethereal, Fine, Intense, Lair, Macaroni, Pink, Princox, Refined, Soigné(e), Too-too

Ex-serviceman Vet

Extemporise Ad lib, Improvise, Pong

Extend(ed), Extension Add, Aspread, Augment, Conservative, Cremaster, Draw, Eke, Elapse, Ell, Elongate, Enlarge, Escalate, Expand, Exsert, Extrapolation, Fermata, Grow, Increase, Jumboise, Length, Long, Long-range, Long-stay, Long-term, Offer, Outgrowth, Overbite, Overlap, Pong, Porrect, Proffer, Prolong, Propagate, Protract, Reach, Retrochoir, Span, Spread, Steso, → STRETCH, Substantial, Widen

Extensive, Extent Ambit, Area, Capacious, Catch-all, Compass, Comprehensive, Degree, Distance, Duration, Large, Latitude, Length, Limit, → MAGNITUDE, Panoramic, Range, Reach, Scale, Size, Spacious, Span, Spread-eagle, Sweeping, Wholesale, Wide, Widespread

Extenuate Diminish, Lessen, Mitigate, Palliate

Exterior Aspect, Crust, Derm, Exoteric, Facade, Outer, → OUTSIDE, Shell, Surface, Veneer

Exterminate, Extermination Abolish, Annihilate, Destroy, Holocaust, Uproot

External Exoteric, Exterior, Extraneous, Foreign, Outer

Extinct(ion) Archaeopteryx, Bygone, Chalicothere, Creodont, Dead, Death, Defunct, D(e)inothere, Dodo, Obsolete, Quagga, Quietus, Rasure, Saururae, Theodont

Extinguish Douse, Dout, Dowse, Dowt, Extirpate, Obscure, Quash, Quell, Quench, Slake, Slo(c)ken, Smother, Snuff, Stamp out, Stifle, Suppress

Extirpate End, Erase, Excise, Obliterate, Root, Uproot

Extol Commend, Enhance, Eulogise, Exalt, Laud, Puff

Extort(ion), Extortionate, Extortioner Barathrum, Blackmail, Bleed, Bloodsucker, Chantage, Chout, Churn, Compel, Exact, Force, Gombeen, Montem, Outwrest, Rachman, Rack, Racketeer, Ransom, Rapacious, Screw, Shank, Squeeze, Sweat, Urge, Vampire, Wrest, Wring

Extra Accessory, Additament, Addition(al), Additive, Adjunct, And, Annexe, Attachment, Bisque, Bonus, By(e), Debauchery, Encore, Etcetera, Frill, Further, Gash, Lagniappe, Left-over, Leg bye, Make-weight, More, Nimiety, No ball, Odd, Optional, Out, Over, Overtime, Perk, Plus, Plusage, Reserve, Ripieno, → SPARE, Spilth, Staffage, Sundry, Super, Supernumerary, Supplementary, Suppletive, Surplus, Trop, Undue, Walking-gentleman, Walking-lady, Wide, Woundy

Extract(ion), Extractor Apozem, Bleed, Breeding, Catechu, Clip, Corkscrew, Decoction, Descent, Distil, Draw, Educe, Elicit, Emulsin, Enucleate, Essence, Estreat, Excerpt, Exodontics, Extort, Gist, Gobbet, Insulin, Kino, Liver, Malta, Milk, Mine, Oust, Parentage, Passage, Pericope, Pick, Piece, Pituitary, Pry, Pyrene, Pyrethrin, Quintessence, Render, Retour, Smelt, Snippet, Soundbite, Squeeze, Stope, Suck, Summary, Tap, Tincture, Trie, Try, Vanilla, Vegemite®, Ventouse, Winkle, Worm, Wring, Yohimbine

Extradition Renvoi

Extraneous Extrinsic, Foreign, Irrelevant, Outlying, Spurious

Extraordinary Amazing, By-ordinar, Case, Curious, Humdinger, Important, Phenomenal, Preternatural, Rare, Singular, Startling, Strange, Unusual

Extravagance, Extravagant, Extravaganza Bombastic, Excessive, Fancy, Feerie, Flamboyant, Glitzy, Heroic, High-flown, High roller, Hyperbole, Lavish, Luxury, Outré, Prodigal, Profligate, Profuse, Rampant, Reckless, Riotise, Romantic, Splash, Splurge, Squander, Sumptuous, Superfluous, Waste

Extreme(ly), Extremist Acute, All-fired, Almighty, Butt, Deep-dyed, Desperate, Die-hard, Drastic, Edge, Exceptional, Farthermost, Gross, In spades, → INTENSE, Jacobin, Mega-, Militant, Mondo, National Front, Nazi, Opposite, OTT, Parlous, Pretty, Radical, Root and branch, Steep, Tendency, Terminal, Thule, Too, Tremendous, Ultimate, Ultima thule, Ultra, Unco, Utmost, Utter, → VERY, Vitally, Wing

▷ **Extreme** *may indicate* a first or last letter

Extremity Bourn(e), Crisis, Digit, Ending, Finger(-tip), Limb, Limit, Outrance, Pole, Tip, Toe, Utterance

Extricate Liberate, Loose, Outwind, Rescue, Untangle

Extrinsic Aliunde, External, Irrelevant, Outward

Extrovert Lad, Outgoing

Extrude Debar, Eject, Project

Exuberance, Exuberant Brio, Copious, Ebullient, Effusive, Gusto, Hearty, Lavish, Mad, Overflowing, Profuse, Rambunctious, Rumbustious, Skippy, Streamered

Exudation, Exude Bleed, Ectoplasm, Emit, Extravasate, Guttate, Ooze, Secrete, Still, Sweat, Swelter, Ulmin, Weep

Exult(ant) Crow, Elated, → GLOAT, Glorify, Jubilant, Paeonic, Rejoice, Tripudiate, Triumphant, Whoop

Eye(s), Eye-ball, Eyeful, Eye movement, Eyepiece Aperture, Beady, Canthus, Compound, Cringle, Eagle, Ee, Eine, Electric, Emmetropia, Evil, Glad, Glass, Glim, Glom, Goggles, Hurricane, Huygen's, Iris, Jack, Keek, Klieg, Lamp, Lazy, Lens, London, Magic, Mincepie, Mind's, Mongoloid, Naked, → OBSERVE, Ocellar, Ocular, Ogle, Ommateum, Ommatidium, Optic, Orb, Pedicel, Peeper, PI, Pigsnie,

Pigsn(e)y, Pineal, Private, Pupil, Regard, Retina, Rhabdom, Roving, Saccade, Sclera, Screw, Seeing, Sheep's, Shufti, Shufty, Sight, Spy, Stemma, Storm-centre, Tec, Third, Uvea, Watch, Water-pump, Weather, Whally, Windows, Winker

Eyebright Euphrasy

Eyebrow Bree, Brent-hill, Glib, Penthouse, Superciliary

Eyeglass Loupe

Eyelash Cilium, Winker

Eyelet Cringle, Grommet, Hole

Eyelid Canthus, Ectropion, Haw, Palpebral, Winker

Eye-rod Rhabdom

Eye-shadow Kohl

Eyesore Blot, Disfigurement, Sty(e)

Eye-stalk Ommatophore, Stipes

Eye trouble Amblyopia, Ametropia, Aniseikonia, Anisomatropia, Aphakia, Asthenopia, Astigmatism, Caligo, Cataract, Ceratitis, Coloboma, Cycloplegia, Diplopia, Entropion, Erythropsia, Exophthalmus, Glaucoma, Gravel-blind, Hemeralopia, Hemi(an)op(s)ia, Hypermetropia, Hyperopia, Iritis, Keratitis, Leucoma, Lippitude, Micropsia, Miosis, Monoblepsis, Muscae volitantes, Myosis, Nebula, Nyctalopia, Nystagmus, Ommateum, Palinop(s)ia, Photophobia, Photopsia, Pin and web, Pink-eye, Presbyopia, Retinitis, Retinoblastoma, Sandy blight, Scotoma(ta), Shiner, Stigmatism, Strabismus, Strephosymbolia, Strong, Stye, Synechia, Teichopsia, Thylose, Thylosis, Trachoma, Trichiasis, Tritanopia, Tylosis, Wall-eye, Xeroma, Xerophthalmia

Eye-wash Collyrium

Eyrie Nest

Ezra Pound

Ff

F Fahrenheit, Fellow, Feminine, Fluorine, Following, Force, Foxtrot

Fab Super

Fabian, Fabius Dilatory, Washington

Fable(s) Aesop, Allegory, Apologue, Exemplum, Fiction, Hitopadesa, La Fontaine, Legend, Marchen, Milesian, Myth, Panchatantra, Parable, Romance, Tale, Tarand

Fabric Acetate, → CLOTH, Contexture, Framework, Interfacing, Interlining, Orlon®, Plissé

Fabricate, Fabrication Artefact, Concoct, Construct, Contrive, Cook, Fake, Fangle, Figment, Forge, → INVENT, Lie, Porky, Trump, Weave, Web

Fabulous (beast), Fabulous place Apocryphal, Apologue, Chichevache, Chimera, Cockatrice, Eldorado, Fictitious, Fung, Gear, Griffin, Hippogriff, Hippogryph, Huma, Incredible, Jabberwock(y), Kylin, Legendary, Magic, Manticora, Manticore, Merman, Monoceros, Mythical, Opinicus, Orc, Phoenix, Roc, Romantic, Simorg, Simurg(h), Snark, Sphinx, Tarand, Tragelaph, Unicorn, Unreal, Utopia, Wivern, Wyvern, Yale

Facade Front(age), Frontal, Mask, Pretence

Face, Facing Abide, Affront, Ashlar, Ashler, Aspect, Audacity, Bold, Brave, Brazen, Caboched, Caboshed, Cheek, Chiv(v)y, Coal, Confront, Countenance, Culet, Dalle, Dare, Dartle, Deadpan, Dial, Eek, Elevation, Encounter, Facade, Fat, Favour, Features, Fineer, Fortune, → FRONT, Gardant, Girn, Gonium, Grid, Groof, Groue, Grouf, Gurn, Hatchet, Head-on, Jib, Kisser, Light, Lining, Look, Lore, Mascaron, Meet, Metope, Moe, Mug, Mush, Obverse, Opposite, Outstare, Outward, Pan, Paper tiger, Pavilion, Phisnomy, Phiz(og), Physiognomy, Poker, Puss, Revet, Revetment, Roughcast, Rud, Rybat, Side, Snoot, Socle, Straight, Stucco, Three-quarter, Type, Veneer, Vis(age), Visnomy, Withstand, Zocco(lo)

Face-ache Noli-me-tangere

Face-lift Rhytidectomy

Face-saving Redeeming, Salvo

Facet(ed) Angle, Aspect, Bezel, Culet, Face, Pavilion, Polyhedron

Facetious Frivolous, Jocular, Waggish, Witty

Facile Able, Adept, Complaisant, Ductile, Easy, Fluent, Glib

Facilitate, Facility Amenity, Assist, Benefit, Capability, Committed, → EASE, Expedite, Fluency, Gift, ISO, Knack, Skill

Facsimile Copy, Photostat®, Replica, Repro

Fact(s), Factual Actual, Brass tacks, Case, Corpus delicti, Correct, Data, Datum, Detail, French, Gospel, Griff, Info, Literal, Mainor, Material, Nay, Poop, Really, Statistics, Truism, Truth, Veridical, Yes

Faction Bloc, Cabal, Camp, Caucus, Clique, Contingent, Ghibelline, Guelph, Junto, Red Army, Schism, Sect, Tendency, Wing

Factor Agent, Aliquot, Broker, Cause, Chill, Clotting, Coagulation, Co-efficient, Common, → COMPONENT, Divisor, Edaphic, Element, F, Feel-good, Growth,

House, Intrinsic, Load, Modulus, Multiple, Power, Q, Quality, Reflection, Representative, Rh, Rhesus, Risk, Safety, Steward, Unit, Utilization, Wind chill, X

Factory Cannery, Etruria, Gasworks, Glassworks, Hacienda, Maquiladora, Mill, Plant, Refinery, Sawmill, Steelworks, Sweatshop, Tinworks, Wireworks, Works, Workshop

Factotum Circar, Handyman, Servant, Sircar, Sirkar

Faculty Aptitude, Arts, Capacity, Department, Ear, Ease, Indult, Knack, Moral, Power, School, Sense, Speech, → TALENT, Teachers, Wits

Fad(dish) Crank, Craze, Cult, Fashion, Foible, Ismy, Thing, Vogue, Whim

Fade(d), Fading Blanch, Die, Diminuendo, Dinge, Elapsion, Etiolate, Evanescent, Fall, Filemot, Lessen, Mancando, Pale, Passé, Perdendo(si), Peter, Smorzando, Smorzato, Stonewashed, Vade, Vanish, Wallow, Wilt, Wither

Faeces Cesspit, Dingleberry, Dung, Kak, Meconium, Motion, Mute, Number two, Scybalum, Skatole, Stercoraceous, Stools

Fag-end Ash, Butt, Dout, Lag, Snipe, Stub

Fag(ging) Chore, Cigarette, Drag, Drudge, Fatigue, Gasper, Homosexual, Menial, Pennalism, Quean, Reefer, Snout, Tire, Toil, Weary

Fag(g)ot(s) Bavin, Bundle, Fascine, Firewood, Homosexual, Kid, Knitch, Twigs

Fail(ing), Failure Achalasia, Ademption, Anile, Anuria, Awry, Backfire, Blemish, Blow, Bomb, Bummer, Cark, Chicken, → COLLAPSE, Conk, Crack up, Crash, Cropper, Debacle, Decline, Defalcation, Default, Defect, Demerit, Demise, Die, Dog, Dry, Dud, Fault, Feal, Fiasco, Fink out, Flame out, Flivver, Flop, Flow, Flunk, Fold, Founder, Frost, Glitch, Gutser, Infraction, Lapse, Lemon, Lose, Malfunction, Manqué, Mis-, Miscarry, Misfire, Misprision, Miss, Muff, Nerd, No-hoper, No-no, Omit, Outage, Oversight, Pip, Plough, Plow, Pluck, Pratfall, Reciprocity, Refer, Refusal, Respiratory, Shambles, Short(coming), Short circuit, Shortfall, Slippage, Smash, Spin, Stumer, Tank, Turkey, Vice, Wash-out, Weakness, White elephant, Wipeout

Fain Lief

Faineant Gallio

Faint(ness) Black-out, Conk, Darkle, Dim, Dizzy, Dwalm, Fade, Lassitude, Pale, Stanck, Swarf, Swarve, Swelt, Swerf, Swerve, Swoon, Swound, Syncope, Unclear, Wan, Whitish

Faint-heart Boneless, Coward, Craven, Eery, Timid, Wet

Fair Adequate, Aefauld, Aefwld, A(e)fald, Barnet, Bartholomew, Bazaar, Beauteous, Beautiful, Belle, Blond, Bon(n)ie, Bonny, Brigg, Decent, Dishy, Donnybrook, Equal, Equitable, Evenhanded, Exhibition, Expo(sition), Feeing-market, → FESTIVAL, Fête, Fine, Fiona, Funfair, Gaff, Gala, Gey, Goose, Gwyn, Hiring, Honest, Hopping, Isle, → JUST, Kermess, Kermis, Kirmess, Market, Mart, Mediocre, Mela, Mop, Nundinal, Objective, OK, Paddington, Passable, Play, Pro rata, Rosamond, Sabrina, Sporting, Square, Statute, Steeple, Straight, Tavistock, Tidy, Tolerable, Tow-headed, Trade, Tryst, Unbias(s)ed, Vanity, Wake, Widdicombe, Xanthe

Fair-buttocked Callipygean

Fairing Ornament, Spat

Fairly Clearly, Enough, Evenly, Midway, Moderately, Pari passu, Pretty, Properly, Quite, Ratherish

Fairway Dog-leg, Pretty

Fairy, Fairies Banshee, Befana, Cobweb, Dobbie, Dobby, Elf(in), Fay, Gloriana, Good people, Hob, Hop o' my thumb, Leprechaun, Lilian, Little people, Mab, Morgane(tta), Morgan le Fay, Moth, Nis, Peri, Pigwidgin, Pigwiggen, Pisky, Pixie, Pouf, Puck, Punce, Queen Mab, Sandman, Seelie, Sidhe, Spirit, Sprite, Sugar-plum,

Tink(erbell), Titania, Tooth, Unseelie, Urchin-shows

Faith(ful) Accurate, Achates, Belief, Constant, Creed, Devoted, Doctrine, Faix, Fay, Feal, Fegs, Fideism, Fiducial, Haith, Implicit, Islam, Lay, Loyal, Plerophory, Punic, Puritanism, Quaker, Religion, Shahada, Shema, Solifidian, Staunch, Strict, Troth, → **TRUE**, True-blue, Trust, Truth, Umma(h)

Faithless Atheist, Disloyal, False, Giaour, Hollow, Infidel, Nullifidian, Perfidious, Punic

Fake(r), Faking Bodgie, Bogus, Copy, Counterfeit, Duff(er), Ersatz, False, Fold, Forgery, Fraud, Fudge, Imitation, Imposter, Impostor, Paste, Phoney, Pirate(d), Postiche, Pretend, Pseudo, Sham, Spurious, Toy, Trucage, Truquage, Truqueur, Unreal

Falcon Cast, Gentle, Hawk, Hobby, Iceland, Kestrel, Lanner(et), Merlin, Nyas, Peregrine, Prairie, Saker, Sakeret, Spar-hawk, Sparrow-hawk, Stallion, Staniel, Stannel, Stanyel, Stone, Tassel-gentle, Tassell-gent, Tercel-gentle, Tercel-jerkin

Falklander Kelper

Fall(s), Fallen, Falling Abate, Accrue, Angel, Arches, Astart, Autumn, Boyoma, Cadence, Cascade, Cataract, Churchill, Chute, Collapse, Crash, Cropper, Cross press, Declension, Decrease, Degenerate, Descent, Dip, Domino effect, Douse, Downswing, Dowse, → **DROP**, Ebb, Firn, Flag, Flop, Flump, Folding press, Free, Grabble, Grand, Gutser, Gutzer, Horseshoe, Idaho, Iguaçu, Incidence, Kabalega, Kaieteur, Lag, Landslide, Lapse, Lin(n), Niagara, Oct(ober), Onding, Owen, Perish, Plonk, Plummet, Plump, Plunge, Prolapse, Ptosis, Purl(er), Rain, Reaction, Relapse, Ruin, Sheet, Sin, Sleet, Snow, Soss, Spill, Stanley, Sutherland, Tailor, Takakkau, Topple, Toss, Trip, Tugela, Tumble, Victoria, Voluntary, Wipeout, Yellowstone, Yosemite

Fallacious, Fallacy Elench(us), Error, Gamblers', Idolon, Idolum, Ignoratio elenchi, Illogical, Illusion, Material, Naturalistic, Pathetic, Sophism, Specious, Unsound

Fallible Human, Imperfect

▷ **Falling** *may indicate* an anagram or a word backwards

Fallow Barren, Lea, Tan, Uncared, Uncultivated, Untilled

False, Falsify, Falsification, Falsehood Adulterate, Assumed, Bastard, Bodgie, Bogus, Braide, Bricking, Calumny, Canard, Cavil, Charlatan, Cook, Deceitful, Disloyal, Dissemble, Doctor, Fake, Feigned, Fiddle, Forge, Illusory, Knave, Lying, Meretricious, Mock, Obreption, Perjury, Pinchbeck, Postiche, Pretence, Pseudo, Rap, Refute, Roorback, Sham, Specious, Spoof, Spurious, Treacherous, Trumped-up, Two-faced, Untrue, Veneer

False notions Idola

Falter Hesitate, Limp, Stoiter, Totter, Waver

Fame, Famous Bruit, Cause célèbre, Celebrity, Distinguished, Eminent, Glitterati, Gloire, Glory, Greatness, History, Humour, Illustrious, Kudos, Legendary, Luminous, Megastar, Mononym, Name, Noted, Notorious, Prestige, Reclamé, Renown, Repute, Robert, Rumour, Splendent, Spur, Stardom, Word

Familiar(ise), Familiarity Accustom, Acquaint, Assuefaction, Au fait, Auld, Chummy, Comrade, Conversant, Couth, Crony, Dear, Demon, Easy, Free, Friend, Habitual, Homely, Homey, Incubus, Intimate, Known, Liberty, Maty, Old, Old-hat, Privy, Python, Used, Versed, Warhorse

Family Ainga, Ancestry, Bairn-team, Blood, Breed, Brood, Clan, Class, Close-knit, Cognate, Consanguine, County, Descent, Dynasty, Extended, Eye, House(hold), Issue, Kin, Kind, Kindred, Line, Mafia, Medici, Name, Nuclear, One-parent, Orange, People, Phratry, Progeny, Quiverful, Race, Sept, Sib(b), Sibship, Stem, Stirps, Strain, Taffy, Talbot, Tribe, Whanau

Family tree Pedigree, Stemma
Famine Dearth, Lack, Scarcity
Famish(ed) Esurient, Hungry, Ravenous, Starving
▷ **Famished** *may indicate* an 'o' in the middle of a word
Fan(s), Fan-like Adherent, Admirer, Aficionado, Alligator, Alluvial, Arouse, Bajada, Barmy-army, B-boy, Blow, Cat, Clapper, Claque, Colmar, Cone, Cool, Cuscus, Devotee, Diadrom, Dryer, Enthusiast, Extractor, Fiend, Flabellum, Following, Goth, Grebo, Groupie, Headbanger, Hepcat, Khuskhus, Muso, Nut, Outspread, Partisan, Popette, Punka(h), Rhipidate, Ringsider, Sail, Spectator, Spread, Supporter, Tail, Tifosi, Ventilate, Votary, Voteen, Washingtonia, Wind machine, Wing, Winnow, Zealot, Zelant
▷ **Fan** *may indicate* an anagram
Fanatic(al) Bigot, Devotee, Energumen, Enthusiastic, Extremist, Fiend, Frenetic, Glutton, Mad, Maniac, Nut, Partisan, Phrenetic, Picard, Rabid, Santon, Ultra, Wowser, Zealot
Fancy, Fanciful Caprice, Chim(a)era, Conceit, Concetto, Crotchet, Daydream, Dream, Dudish, Elaborate, Fangle, Fantasy, Fit, Flam, Florid, Frothy, Guess, Hallo, Idea(te), Idolon, → IMAGINE, Inclination, Lacy, Liking, Maya, Mind, My, Nap, Notion, Opine, Ornamental, Ornate, Picture, Pipe dream, Predilection, Reverie, Rococo, Suppose, Thought, Unreal, Urge, Vagary, Visionary, Ween, Whigmaleerie, Whigmaleery, Whim(sy), Woolgather
▷ **Fancy** *may indicate* an anagram
Fane Banner, Pronaos
Fanfare Flourish, Sennet, Show, Tantara, Trump, Tucket
Fang Tooth, Tusk
Fanny Adams, Bottom, Gas-lit, Price
Fantasist, Fantasy, Fantastic Absurd, Antic, Bizarre, Caprice, Chimera, Cloud-cuckoo land, Cockaigne, Cockayne, Escapism, Fab, Fanciful, Grotesque, Hallucination, Idol, Illusion, Kickshaw(s), Lucio, Mega, Myth, Outré, Phantasmagoria, Pipe-dream, Queer, Reverie, Romance, Schizoid, Unreal, Untrue, Walter Mitty, Wannabe(e), → WHIM, Whimsical, Wild, Wishful thinking
Far Apogean, Away, Distal, Distant, Eloi(g)n, Extreme, Outlying, Remote, Thether, Thither
Farce(ur) Burletta, Charade, Comedy, Exode, Feydeau, Lazzo, Mime, Mockery, Pantomime, Rex, Screaming, Sham, Travesty
Fare Apex, Charge, Cheer, Commons, Do, Eat, Excess, Excursion, → FOOD, Go, Passage, Passage money, Passenger, Rate, Table, Traveller
Farewell Adieu, Adios, Aloha, Apopemptic, Bye, Cheerio, Departure, Godspeed, → GOODBYE, Leave, Prosper, Sayonara, Send off, So long, Toodle-oo, Toodle-pip, Totsiens, Vale, Valediction
Far-fetched Fanciful, Improbable, Recherché
Farm(ing), Farmhouse Agronomy, Arable, Bocage, Bowery, City, Cold Comfort, Collective, Cooperative, Croft, Cultivate, Dairy, Deep-litter, Dry, Emmerdale, Estancia, Extensive, Factory, Fat, Fish(ery), Funny, Geoponical, Grange, Hacienda, Health, Home, Homestead, Husbandry, Intensive, Kibbutz, Kolkhoz, Land, Ley, Loaf, Location, Mailing, Mains, Mas, Mixed, No-tillage, Onstead, Orley, Oyster, Pen, Plaas, Plough, Poultry, Ranch, Rent, Set-aside, Sewage, Shamba, Sheep station, Smallholding, Sovkhoz, Station, Stead(ing), Sted(d), Stedde, Steed, Stock, Store, Stump, Subsistence, Tank, Till, Toon, Toun, Town, Trash, Tree, Trout, Truck, Wick, Wind
Farmer Blockie, Boer, Campesino, Carl, Cockatoo, Cocklaird, Cocky, Collins Street,

Colon, Cow cocky, Crofter, Estanciero, Gebur, Gentleman, George, Giles, Hick, Hobby, Macdonald, Metayer, Nester, NFU, Peasant, Pitt Street, Queen St, Ryot, Share-cropper, Smallholder, Sodbuster, Squatter, Stubble-jumper, Tax, Tenant, Tiller, Whiteboy, Yeoman, Zeminda(r)

Farmhand Cadet, Churl, Cottar, Cotter, Cottier, Cowman, Ditcher, Hand, He(a)rdsman, Hind, Ploughman, Redneck, Rouseabout, Roustabout, Shearer, Stockman

▶ **Farmhouse** *see* FARM

Farmyard Barton, Homestall, Villatic

Farouche Awkward, Shy, Sullen

Farrago Hotch-potch, Jumble, Medley, Mélange

Farrier Marshal, Smith

Farrow Litter, Mia, Sow

Far-sighted Presbyte

Fart Poep, Trump

Farthing Brass, F, Fadge, Har(r)ington, Mite, Q, Quadragesimal, Rag

Fascia Band, Fillet, Platband

Fascinate, Fascinating Allure, Attract, Bewitch, → CHARM, Dare, Enchant, Engross, Enthral(l), Fetching, Inthral, Intrigue, Kill, Mesmeric, Rivet, Siren, Witch

Fascist Blackshirt, Blue shirt, Brownshirt, Dictator, Falange, Falangist, Iron Guard, Lictor, Nazi, Neo-Nazi, NF, Phalangist, Rexist, Sinarchist, Sinarquist

Fashion(able), Fashioned Aguise, À la (mode), Bristol, Build, Chic, Construct, Convention, Cool, Corinthian, Craze, Create, Cult, Custom, Cut, Dernier cri, Design, Directoire, Du jour, Elegant, Entail, Fad, Feat, Feign, Forge, Form, Genteel, Go, Hew, High, Hip, Hot, In, Invent, Kitsch, Look, → MAKE, Man-about-town, Manière, Manners, Mode, Mondain(e), Mould, Newgate, Pink, Preppy, Rage, Rag trade, Rate, Roy, Sc, Shape, Smart, Smith, Snappy, Snazzy, Stile, Stylar, Style, Swish, Tailor, Ton, Ton(e)y, Tonish, → TREND(Y), Turn, Twig, Vogue, Way, Wear, With-it, Work, Wrought

Fast(ing), Faster Abstain, Apace, Ashura, Breakneck, Citigrade, Clem, Clinging, Cracking, Daring, Dharna, Dhurna, Double-quick, Elaphine, Express, Fizzer, Fleet, Immobile, Lent, Lightning, Loyal, Maigre, Meteoric, Moharram, Muharram, Muharrem, Pac(e)y, Posthaste, Presto, Pronto, Quadragesimal, Quick, Raffish, Raking, Ramadan, Ramadhan, Rash, Rathe, Relay, Siyam, Spanking, Speedy, Stretta, Stretto, Stuck, Supersonic, Sure, Swift, Tachyon, Thick, Tight, Tisha b'Av, TishaBov, Tishah-Baav, Tishah-b(e)Ab, Tishah-b(e)Av, Whistle-stop, Yarer, Yom Kippur

Fast and loose Fickle, Prick-the-garter, Strap-game

Fasten(er), Fastening Anchor, Attach, Bar, Belay, Bind, Bolt, Buckle, Button, Chain, Clamp, Clasp, Click, Clinch, Clip, Cramp, Cufflink, Dead-eye, Diamond-hitch, Dome, Espagnolette, Eye-bolt, Frog, Gammon, Hasp, Hesp, Hook, Lace, Latch, Lock, Moor, Morse, Nail, Netsuke, Nip, Nut, Padlock, Parral, Patent, Pectoral, Pin, Preen, Press stud, Reeve, Rivet, Rope, Rove, Seal, → SECURE, Sew up, Shut, Spar, Sprig, Staple, Stitch, Suspender, Swift(er), Tach(e), Tag, Tape, Tassel, Tether, Thong, Tintack, Toggle, U-bolt, Velcro®, Wedge, Zip

Fastidious Chary, Critical, Dainty, Fusspot, Fussy, Neat, Nice, Particular, Precieuse, Precious, Purism, Queasy, Squeamish

Fat(s), Fatten, Fatty Adipic, Adipocere, Adipose, Aldermanly, Aliphatic, Arcus, Atheroma, Bard, Batten, Battle, Blubber, Brown, Butter, Calipash, Calipee, Cellulite, Cholesterol, Chubbed, Chubby, Corpulent, Creesh, Degras, Dika-oil, Dosh, Dripping, Embonpoint, Enarm, Endomorph, Ester, Flab, Flesh, Flick, Fozy, Fubsy,

Galam-butter, Grease, Gross, Keech, Kitchen-fee, Lanolin, Lard, Leaf, Lipaemia, Lipid, Lipoma, Love handles, Margarine, Marge, Marrow, Moti, Motu, Obese, Oil, Oleomargarine, OS, Palmitin, Pinguid, Plump, Poddy, Podgy, Polyunsaturated, Portly, Puppy, Pursy, Rich, Rolypoly, Rotund, Saddlebags, Saginate, Saim, Saturated, Schmal(t)z, Seam(e), Sebacic, Sebum, Shortening, Soil, Spare tyre, Spe(c)k, Squab, Stearic, Steatopygia, Steatorrhea, Suberin, Suet, Tallow, Tin, Tomalley, Triglyceride, Tub, Unsaturated, Vanaspati, Waller, Well-padded, Wool

Fatal(ism), Fate(s), Fated, Fateful Apnoea, Atropos, Cavel, Chance, Clotho, Deadly, Death, Decuma, Destiny, Doom, End, Fay, Fell, Joss, Karma, Kismet, Lachesis, Lethal, Lot, Meant, Moera, Moira, Mortal, Mortiferous, Nemesis, Norn(a), Parca, Pernicious, Portion, Predestination, Skuld, Urd, Verdande, Waterloo, Weird, Weird sisters

Father(ly) Abba, Abbot, Abuna, Adopt, Apostolic, Bapu, Begetter, Breadwinner, Brown, City, Conscript, Curé, Dad, Engender, Foster, Founding, Fr, Generator, Genitor, Getter, Gov, Governor, Guv, Male, NASCAR dad, Pa, Padre, Papa, Pappy, Parent, Pater(nal), Paterfamilias, Patriarch, Père, Pilgrim, Pop(pa), Popper, Priest, Rev, Seraphic, Sire, Stud, Thames, Tiber, William

Father-lasher Sea-scorpion

Fathom Delve, Depth, Dig, F, Plumb, Plummet, Understand

Fatigue Battle, Combat, Compassion, Exhaust, Fag, Jade, Jet lag, ME, Metal, Neurasthenia, Overdo, Overwatch, Tire, Weariness, Weary

Fatuous Gaga, Idiotic, Silly, Stupid

Faucet Cock, Spigot, Tap

Fault(y) Arraign, Bad, Beam, Blame(worthy), Blunder, Bug, Cacology, Carp, Compound, Culpa, Culpable, Defect, Demerit, Dip, Dip-slip, Drop-out, Duff, → **ERROR**, Failing, Flaw, Frailty, Gall, Glitch, Gravity, Henpeck, Hitch, Imperfect, Literal, Massif, → **MISTAKE**, Nag, Nibble, Niggle, Nit-pick, Oblique, Oblique-slip, Out, Outcrop, Overthrust, Para, Peccadillo, Pre-echo, Rate, Reprehend, Rift, Rupes Recta, San Andreas, Sclaff, Set-off, Short, Slip, Snag, Step, Strike, Strike-slip, Technical, Thrust, Trap, Trough, Underthrust, Upbraid, Vice

Faultless Immaculate, Impeccable, Lily-white, Perfect

Fauna Mesobenthos, Wild life

Fauvist Matisse

Faux pas Blunder, Boner, Gaffe, Leglen-girth, Solecism

Favour(able), Favoured, Favourite Advance, Advantage(ous), Aggrace, Agraste, Alder-liefest, Approval, Auspicious, Back, Befriend, Behalf, Benign, Bless, Boon, Bribe, Cert, Chosen, Cockade, Curry, Darling, Ex gratia, Fancy, Favonian, Form horse, Good turn, Grace, Graste, Gratify, Gree, Hackle, Hot, In, Indulge, Kickback, Minion, Nod, Odour, Particular, Peat, Persona grata, Pet, Pettle, Popular, → **PREFER**, Promising, Propitious, Resemble, Rib(b)and, Roseate, Rose-knot, Rosette, Side, Smile, Toast, Token, Win-win

Fawn(er), Fawning Adulate, Bambi, Beige, Blandish, Brown-nose, Camel, Crawl, Creep, Cringe, Deer, Ecru, Flatter, Fleech, Grovel, Ko(w)tow, Lickspittle, Obsequious, Servile, Slavish, Smarm, Smoo(d)ge, Subservient, Sycophant, Tasar, Toady, Truckle, Tussah, Tusseh, Tusser, Tussore

Fay Fairy, Korrigan, Peri

FBI G-men

Fear Aichmophobia, Angst, Apprehension, Astra(po)phobia, Awe, Bathophobia, Bête noire, Bugbear, Claustrophobia, Cold sweat, Crap, Creeps, Cyberphobia, Dismay, Doubt, Drad, Dread, Dromophobia, Foreboding, → **FOR FEAR**, Fright, Funk, Hang-up, Horror, Kenophobia, Mysophobia, Nyctophobia, Ochlophobia, Panic,

→ **PHOBIA**, Photophobia, Redoubt, Revere, Taphephobia, Taphophobia, Terror, Thalassophobia, Trepidation, Willies

Fearful Afraid, Cowardly, Dire, Horrific, Nervous, Pavid, Rad, Redoubtable, Timorous, Tremulous, Windy

Fearless Bold, Brave, Courageous, Daring, Gallant, Impavid, Intrepid

Fearsome Dire, Formidable

Feasible Goer, Likely, On, Possible, Practical, Probable, Viable

Feast Adonia, Agape, Assumption, Banquet, Barmecide, Beano, Belshazzar's, Blow-out, Candlemas, Carousal, Celebration, Dine, Do, Double, Eat, Encaenia, Epiphany, Epulation, Festival, Fleshpots, Fool's, Gaudeamus, Gaudy, Hakari, Halloween, Hallowmas, Hockey, Hogmanay, Holy Innocents, Id-al-Adha, Id-al-Fitr, Immaculate Conception, Isodia, Junket, Kai-kai, Lady Day, Lamb-ale, Lammas, Love, Luau, Lucullus, Martinmas, Michaelmas, Midnight, Movable, Noel, Passover, Pentecost, Pig, Potlatch, Purim, Regale, Revel, Roodmas, Seder, Shindig, Spread, Succoth, Sukkot(h), Tabernacles, Tuck-in, Wake, Wayzgoose, Weeks, Yule, Zagmuk

Feast-day Mass

Feat Achievement, Deed, Effort, Exploit, Gambado, Handspring, Stunt, Trick

Feather(ed), Feathers Aigrette, Alula, Barbicel, Boa, Braccate, Cock, Contour, Covert, Crissum, Down, Duster, Filoplume, Flags, Fledged, Fletch, Flight, Gemmule, Hackle, Harl, Hatchel, Herl, Lei, Lure, Macaroni, Manual, Oar, Ostrich, Pen(na), Pin, Pinna, Pith, Plumage, Plume, Plumule, Prince's, Pteryla, Ptilosis, → **QUILL**, Rectrix, Remex, Remiges, Rocket-tail, Saddle-hackle, Scapular, Scapus, Secondary, Semiplume, Shaft, Shag, Sickle, Standard, Stipa, Swansdown, Tectrix, Tertial, Vibrissa, White, Wing covert

Feather-worker Plumassier

Feature(s) Acoustic, Amenity, Appurtenance, Article, Aspect, Attribute, Brow, Character, Chin, Depict, Double, Eye, Eyebrow, Face, Facet, Figure, Hallmark, Highlight, Item, Jizz, Landmark, Lineament, Neotery, Nose, Nucleus, Overfold, Phiz(og), Physiognomy, Signature, Snoot, Spandrel, Star, Temple, Trait, Underlip

Featureless Flat

Febrifuge Atabrin, Atebrin®, Mepacrine, Quina

February Fill-dyke

Fecund(ity) Fertile, Fruitful, Prolific, Uberty

Fed Agent, G-man

Federal, Federation Alliance, Axis, Bund, Commonwealth, Interstate, League, Russian, Statal, Union

Fee Base, Capitation, Charge, Chummage, Commitment, Common, Conditional, Contingency, Corkage, Drop-dead, Dues, Duty, Faldage, Fine, Great, Groundage, Hire, Honorarium, Interchange, Mortuary, Mouter, Multure, Obvention, Pay, Pierage, Premium, Refresher, Retainer, Sub, Subscription, Transfer, Tribute

Feeble Banal, Characterless, Daidling, Debile, Decrepit, Droob, Effete, Feckless, Fizzenless, Flaccid, Foisonless, Footling, Fragile, Fus(h)ionless, Geld, Ineffective, Infirm, Jessie, Limp, Mimsy, Namby-pamby, Pale, Puny, Sassy, Sickly, Slender, Slight, Soppy, Tailor, Tame, Thin, Tootle, Wallydrag, Wallydraigle, Washy, Wastrel, Weak, Weak-kneed, Weak-minded, Weed, Weedy, Wersh, Wet, Wimpish, Worn

Feed(er), Feeding Battle, Bib, Break, Browse, Cake, Cater, Cibation, Clover, Cowfeteria, Cram, Cue, Demand, Dine, Dressing, Drip, → **EAT**, Fatten, Filter, Fire, Fishmeal, Flushing, Fodder, Food, Force, Gavage, Graze, Hay, Line, Lunch, Meal, Nourish, Nurse, Paid, Pecten, Provender, Refect, Repast, Sate, Soil, Stoke, Stooge, Stover, Suckle, Sustain, Tire, Tractor, Wean, Wet nurse

Feedback Negative, Positive

Feel, Feeling(s) Aesthesia, Affetuoso, Animus, Artificial, Atmosphere, Ballottement, Compassion, Darshan, Déja vu, → **EMOTION**, Empathy, Empfindung, Euphoria, → **EXPERIENCE**, Fellow, Finger, Flaw, Frisk, Grope, Groundswell, Handle, Hard, Heart, Heartstrings, Hunch, Intuit, Knock, Know, Palp, Passible, Passion, Phatic, Pity, Premonition, Presentiment, Probe, Realise, Sensate, Sensation, → **SENSE**, Sensitive, Sentiment, Somesthesis, Spirit, Sprachgefühl, Tactual, Touch, Turn, Undercurrent, Vehemence, Vibes, Vibrations, Zeal

Feeler Antenna, Barbel, Exploratory, Overture, Palp, Sensillum, Tentacle

▸ **Feet** *see* **FOOT**

Feign Act, Affect, Colour, Fake, Malinger, Mime, Mock, → **PRETEND**, Sham, Simulate

Feint Deke, Disguise, Dodge, Faint, Fake, Spoof, Trick

Fel(d)spar Adularia, Albite, Anorthite, Gneiss, Hyalophane, Moonstone, Orthoclase, Petuntse, Petuntze, Plagioclase, Sanidine, Saussurite, Sun-stone

Felicity Bliss, Happiness, Joy, Relevance

▸ **Feline** *see* **CAT**

Fell Axe, Chop, Cruel, Deadly, Dire, Dread, Fierce, Heath, Hew, Hide, Hill, Inhuman, Knock-down, KO, Lit, Log, Malign, Moor, Pelt, Poleaxe, Ruthless, Sca, Shap, Skittle

Fellow(s), Fellowship Academic, Associate, Bawcock, Birkie, Bloke, Bo, Bro, Bucko, Buffer, Callan(t), Carlot, Cat, Chal, Chap, Chi, China, Chum, Co, Cock, Cod(ger), Collaborator, Co-mate, Communion, Companion, Comrade, Confrère, Cove, Cully, Cuss, Dandy, Dean, Dog, Don, Dude, Equal, F, Fogey, Fop, Gadgie, Gadje, Gaudgie, Gauje, Gink, Guy, Joe, Joker, Josser, Kerel, Lad, Like, M, Mall, Man, Mate, Member, Mister, Mun, Partner, Peer, Professor, Rival, Seniority, Sister, Skate, Sociate, Society, Sodality, Swab, Teaching, Twin, Waghalter, Wallah

Felon(y) Bandit, Convict, Crime, Gangster, Offence, Villain

Felt Bat(t), Drugget, Knew, Met, Numdah, Numnah, Pannose, Roofing, Sensed, Tactile, Underlay, Velour

Female (bodies), Feminine, Feminist Anima, Bint, Bit, Dame, Distaff, Doe, F, Fair sex, Filly, Girl, Harem, Hen, Her, Kermes, Lady, Libber, Maiden, Muliebrity, Pen, Petticoated, Riot girl, Sakti, Shakti, She, Sheila, Shidder, Soft, Spindle, Thelytoky, -trix, → **WOMAN**, Yin

▹ **Female, Feminine** *may indicate* an -ess ending

Fen Bog, Carr, Ea, Jiao, Marsh, Morass, Silicon, Wash

Fence(r), Fencing (position) Appel, Balestra, Bar, Barrier, Botte, Carte, Croisé, Cyclone®, Derobement, Dogleg, Electric, Enclose, Épée, Feint, Flanconade, Flèche, Foils, Fraise, Froissement, Haha, Hay, Hedge, Hot, Hurdle, Iaido, Imbrocate, Inquartata, Kendo, Line, Link, Mensur, Molinello, Montant, Netting, Obstacle, Ox, Oxer, Pale, Paling, Palisade, Palisado, Parry, Passado, Pen, Picket, Post and rail, Quart(e), Quinte, Rabbit-fence, Rabbit-proof, Raddle, Rail, Rasper, Receiver, Reset, Ring, Scrimure, Seconde, Sepiment, Sept(um), Septime, Singlestick, Sixte, Snake, Snow, Stacket, Stockade, Stramac, Stramazon, Sunk, Swordplay, Tac-au-tac, Tierce, Touché, Trellis, Virginia, Wattle, Wear, Weir, Weldmesh®, Wire, Worm

Fend(er) Buffer, Bumper, Cowcatcher, Curb, Mudguard, Parry, Provide, Resist, Skid, Ward, Wing

Fennel Finnochio, Finoc(c)hio, Florence, Herb, Love-in-a-mist, Narthex, Ragged lady

Fent Offcut, Remnant, Slit

Feral Brutal, Fierce, Savage, Wild

Ferdinand Archduke, Bull

Ferment(ation) Barm, Enzym(e), Leaven, Mowburn, Protease, Ptyalin, Seethe, Solera, Storm, Stum, Trypsin, Turn, Vinify, Working, Ye(a)st, Zyme, Zymo-, Zymology, Zymosis, Zymotic, Zymurgy

Fermium Fm

Fern Acrogenous, Adder's-tongue, Adiantum, Archegonial, Asparagus, Aspidium, Asplenium, Azolla, Barometz, Beech, Bird's nest, Bladder, Bracken, Brake, Bristle, Buckler, Bungwall, Ceterach, Cinnamon, Coral, Cryptogam, Cyathea, Cycad, Dicksonia, Door, Elkhorn, Fairy moss, Filicales, Filices, Filmy, Fishbone, Grape, Hard, Hart's-tongue, Ice, Isoetes, Lady, Maidenhair, Male, Man, Mangemange, Marattia, Marsh, Marsilea, Marsilia, Meadow, Miha, Moonwort, Mosquito, Mulewort, Nardoo, Nephrolepis, Northern, Oak, Ophioglossum, Osmunda, Para, Parsley, Peppergrass, Pepperwort, Pig, Pillwort, Polypody, Polystichum, Ponga, Pteridology, Pteris, Punga, Rachilla, Rhizocarp, Rockbrake, Royal, Rusty-back, Salvinia, Scale, Schizaea, Scolopendrium, Seed, Shield, Silver, Snowbrake, Soft tree, Spleenwort, Staghorn, Sweet, Sword, Tara, Tree, Venus's hair, Walking, Wall rue, Water, Woodsia

Ferocious Brutal, Cruel, Fell, Predatory, Rambunctious, Tiger, Wild

Ferret Albin, Black-footed, Business, Fesnyng, Gill, Hob, Jill, Nose, Polecat, Ribbon, Rootle, Snoop, Trace, Unearth

Ferry(man) Charon, Convey, Harper's, Hovercraft, Passage, Plier, Pont, Roll-on, RORO, Sealink, Shuttle, Soyuz, Train, Traject, Tranect

Fertile, Fertility (symbol), Fertilisation Arable, Ashtoreth, Battle, Cleistogamy, Fat, Fecund, Fruitful, Green, Linga, Priapus, Productive, Prolific, Rhiannon, Rich, Uberous

Fertilise(r), Fertilisation Ammonia, Auxin, Bee, Bone-ash, Bone-earth, Bone-meal, Caliche, Caprify, Compost, Cross, Fishmeal, Guano, Heterosis, Humogen, Humus, In-vitro, IVF, Kainite, Manure, Marl, Nitrate, Nitre, Nitro-chalk, Pearl-ash, Phosphate, Pollen, Pollinator, Potash, Potassa, Self, Sham, Stamen, Superphosphate, Top dressing

Fervent, Fervid, Fervour Ardent, Burning, Earnest, Heartfelt, Heat, Hwyl, Intense, Keen, Passionate, White-hot, Zeal, Zeloso

Fester Beal, Putrefy, Rankle, Rot, Suppurate

Festival, Festive, Festivity Adonia, Agon, Aldeburgh, Ale, Al Hijra(h), All Saints' Day, Ambarvalia, Anniversary, Anthesteria, Ashura, Bairam, Baisak(h)i, Bayreuth, Beano, Beltane, Biennale, Bon, Candlemas, Carnival, Celebration, Cerealia, Chanuk(k)ah, Childermas, Church-ale, Circumcision, Commemoration, Convivial, Corpus Christi, Corroboree, Crouchmas, Dassehra, Dewali, Dionysia, Divali, Diwali, Doseh, Druid, Easter, Eisteddfod, Encaenia, En fête, Epiphany, → **FAIR**, Feast, Feis, Fête, Fête-champêtre, Fête-Dieu, Fête-galante, Fiesta, Fleadh, Fringe, Gaff, → **GALA**, Gaudy, Glastonbury, Glyndebourne, Gregory, Hallowmas, Hanukkah, Harvest, Harvest home, High day, Hock-tide, Hogmanay, Holi, → **HOLIDAY**, Holy-ale, Hosay, Hosein, Id-al-fitr, Imbolc, Imbolg, J'ouvert, Kermess, Kermiss, Kirmess, Kumbh Mela, Kwanzaa, Lady-Day, Lailat-ul-Qadr, Lammas, Laylat-al-Miraj, Lemural, Lemuria, Lesser Bairam, Let-off, Lughnasadh, Lupercalia, Matsuri, Mayday, Mela, Merry-night, Michaelmas, Miraj, Mod, Moomba, Navaratra, Navaratri, Noel, Obon, Palilia, Panathenaean, Panegyry, Pardon, Pasch, Passover, Pentecost, Pesa(c)h, Play, Pongal, Pooja(h), Pop, Potlach, Puja, Purim, Quirinalia, Revel, Rosh Hashanah, Rush-bearing, Samhain, Saturnalia, Seder, Semi-double, Shabuath, Shavuath, Shemini Atseres, Shrove(tide), Simchas Torah, Simchat(h) Torah, Simchat Torah, Slugfest, Terminalia, Tet, Thargelia, Thesmophoria, Tide, Transfiguration, Up-Helly-Aa, Utas, Vesak, Vinalia, Visitation, Vulcanalia, Wake,

Wesak, Woodstock, Yom Tob, Yomtov, Yuan Tan, Yule(tide)

Festoon Deck, Decorate, Encarpus, Garland, Swag, Wreathe

Fetch(ing) Arrive, Attract, Bring, Charming, Fet(t), Get, Gofer, Realise

Fête Bazaar, Champêtre, Entertain, → **FESTIVITY**, Gala, Honour, Tattoo

Fetish(ist) Charm, Compulsion, Gimp, Idol, Ju-ju, Obeah, Obi(a), Talisman, Totem, Voodoo

Fetter Basil, Bilboes, Chain, Gyve, Hamshackle, Hopple, Iron, Leg-iron, Manacle, Shackle

Fettle Arrange, Condition, Frig, Potter, Repair

Feu Tenure

Feud Affray, Blood, Clash, Feoff, Fief, Quarrel, Strife, → **VENDETTA**

Feudal (service), Feudalism Arriage, Auld-farrant, Fief, Forinsec, Old, Vassalage

Fever(ish) African coast, Ague, Beaver, Blackwater, Brain, Breakbone, Buck, Cabin, Calenture, Camp, Cat-scratch, Cerebrospinal, Childbed, Dengue, East coast, Enteric, Ferment, Fog, Frenetic, Gastric, Gate, Glandular, Haemorrhagic, Hay, Heatstroke, Hectic, Hyperpyretic, Insolation, Intense, Intermittent, Jail, Japanese river, Jungle, Kala-azar, Lassa, Malaria, Malta, Marsh, Mediterranean, Miliary, Milk, Mono, Mud, Paratyphoid, Parrot, Parturient, Passion, Puerperal, Putrid, Pyretic, Pyrexia, Pyrogenic, Q, Quartan, Quintan, Quotidian, Rabbit, Ratbite, Recurrent, Relapsing, Remittent, Rheumatic, Rift Valley, Rock, Rocky Mountain spotted, Roseola, Sandfly, Scarlatina, Scarlet, Sextan, Ship, Splenic, Spotted, Spring, Stage, Sunstroke, Swamp, Swine, Tap, Temperature, Tertian, Texas, Tick, Trench, Typhoid, Typhus, Undulant, Valley, Verruga, Vomito, West Nile, Whot, Worm, Yellow(jack)

Few(er) Handful, Infrequent, → **LESS**, Limited, Scarce, Some, Wheen

Fey Clairvoyant, Eccentric, Elfin, Weird

Fez Tarboosh, Tarboush, Tarbush

Fiancé(e) Betrothed, Intended, Promised

Fiasco Bomb, Debacle, Disaster, Failure, Flask, Flop, Lash-up, Wash-out

Fiat Command, Decree, Edict, Order, Ukase

Fib Gag, → **LIE**, Prevaricate, Story, Taradiddle, Untruth

Fibre, Fibrous Abaca, Acrilan®, Acrylic, Aramid, Arghan, Backbone, Bass, Bast, Beta, Buaze, Bwazi, Cantala, Carbon, Coir, Constitution, Cotton, Courtelle®, Cuscus, Dietary, Dralon®, Elastane, Elastin, Filament, Filasse, Flax, Funicle, Gore-Tex®, Graded-index, Hair, Hemp, Henequen, Henequin, Herl, Hypha, Ispaghula, Istle, Ixtle, Jipyapa, Jute, Kapok, Kenaf, Kevlar®, Kittul, Lemniscus, Manilla, Monkey-grass, Monofil, Monomode, Moorva, Moral, Multimode, Mungo, Murva, Muscle, Myotube, Nap, Natural, Nerve, Noil(s), Nylon, Oakum, Olefin(e), Optic(al), Orlon®, Peduncle, Piassaba, Piassava, Pina, Pita, Polyarch, Pons, Pontine, Pulu, Raffia, Ramee, Rami, Ramie, Rayon, Rhea, Rock-cork, Roughage, Rove, Shoddy, Sida, Silk, Sisal, Slagwool, Sleave, Slub(b), Spandex, Splenium, Staple, Stepped-index, Sterculia, Strand, Strick, Sunn-hemp, Tampico, Tencel®, Toquilla, Tow, Uralite, Viver, Vulcanized, Wallboard, Watap, Whisker, Wood pulp

Fibula Bone, Brooch, Perone

Fickle(ness) Capricious, Change, False, Inconstant, Light, Mutable, Protean, Shifty, Varying, Volage, Volatile

Fiction(al), Fictitious Bogus, Chick-lit, Cyberpunk, Fable, Fabrication, Legal, Myth, Pap, Phoney, Picaresque, Romance, Science, Slash, Speculative, Splatterpunk, → **STORY**

Fiddle(r), Fiddling Amati, Bow, Calling-crab, Cello, Cheat, Crab, Cremona, Croud, Crouth, Crowd, Crwth, Do, Fidget, Fix, Gju, Ground, Gu(e), Jerrymander, Kit,

Launder, Nero, Peculate, Petty, Potter, Racket, Rebec(k), Rig, Rote, Sarangi, Saw, Sawah, Scam, Scotch, Scrape, Scrapegut, Second, Spiel, Strad, Sultana, → TAMPER, Tinker, Toy, Trifle, Tweedle(-dee), Twiddle, Viola, → VIOLIN, Wangle

Fidelity Accuracy, Faith, Fealty, Loyalty, Troth

Fidget(y) Fantad, Fanteeg, Fantigue, Fantod, Fike, Fuss, Fyke, Hirsle, Hotch, Jimjams, Jittery, Niggle, Restive, Trifle, Twiddle, Twitch, Uneasy

Fiduciary Trustee

Fief Benefice, Fee

Field(er), Fielding, Fields(man) Aalu, Aaru, Abroad, Aceldama, Aerodrome, Area, Arena, Arish, Arpent, Arrish, Campestral, Campestrian, Catch, Champ(s), Close, Coulomb, Cover, Domain, Electric, Electromagnetic, Electrostatic, Elysian, Entry, Fid, Fine leg, Flodden, Flying, Forte, Fylde, Glebe, Gracie, Gravitational, Grid(iron), Gull(e)y, Hop-yard, Ice, Keep wicket, Killing, Land, Landing, Lare, Lay, Lea(-rig), Leg slip, Ley, Line, Long leg, Long-off, Long-on, Longstop, Lords, Magnetic, Mead(ow), Mid-off, Mid-on, Mid-wicket, Mine, Oil, Padang, Paddock, Paddy, Parrock, Pasture, Peloton, Pitch, Playing, Point, Potter's, Province, Realm, Runners, Salting, Sawah, Scarecrow, Scope, Scout, Shamba, Short leg, Short stop, Silly, Slip, Sphere, Square leg, Stage, Stray, Stubble, Territory, Third man, Tract, Unified, Vector, Visual, W.C., World

▷ **Field** *may indicate* cricket

Field marshal Allenby, Bulow, French, Haig, Ironside, Kesselring, Kitchener, Montgomery, Roberts, Robertson, Rommel, Slim, Wavell

Fieldwork Lunette, Ravelin, Redan, Redoubt, Tenaillon

Fiend Barbason, Demon, → DEVIL, Enthusiast, Flibbertigibbet, Frateretto, Hellhound, Hobbididance, Mahn, Modo, Obidicut, Smulkin, Succubus

Fierce(ly) Amain, Billyo, Breem, Breme, Cruel, Draconic, Dragon, Grim, Hard-fought, Intense, Ogreish, Rampant, Renfierst, → SAVAGE, Severe, Tigerish, Tigrish, Violent, Wild, Wood, Wud

Fiery Ardent, Argand, Aries, Con fuoco, Dry, Fervent, Hot, Hotspur, Idris, Igneous, Impassioned, Leo, Mettlesome, Phlogiston, Sagittarius, Salamander, Zealous

Fiesta Festival, Fête, Gala, Holiday

Fife Piffero

Fifth Column, Diapente, Hemiol(i)a, Nones, Perfect, Quint, Sesquialtera, Sextans

Fifty Bull, Demi-c, Jubilee, L

Fig Bania, Benjamin-tree, Caprifig, Fico, Figo, Footra, Fouter, Foutra, Foutre, Hottentot, Indian, Moreton Bay, Mouldy, Sycamore, Sycomium, Sycomore, Trifle

Fight(er), Fighting Action, Affray, Agonistics, Aikido, Alpino, Altercate, Arms, Bandy, Bare-knuckle, Barney, → BATTLE, Bicker, Biffo, Blue, Bout, Box, Brave, Brawl, Bruiser, Bundeswehr, Bush-whack, Campaign, Chaud-mellé, Chindit, Combat, Compete, Conflict, Contest, Crusader, Cuirassier, Defender, Dog, Donnybrook, Duel, Encounter, Engagement, Extremes, Faction, Fecht, Fence, Fisticuffs, Flyting, Fray, Freedom, Free-for-all, Fund, Ghazi, Gladiator, Grap(p)le, Grudge, Gunslinger, Gurkha, Hurricane, Kite, Kumite, Lapith, Marine, Med(d)le, Medley, Mêlée, Mercenary, MIG, Militate, Mill, Mujahed(d)in, Mujahidin, Naumachy, Night, Partisan, Pellmell, Pillow, PLO, Prawle, Press, Pugilist, Pugnacity, Punch up, Rammy, Rapparee, Repugn, Resist, Ring, Ruck, Ruction, Rumble, Running, Savate, Sciamachy, Scold, Scrap, Scrimmage, Scuffle, Shadow, Shine, Skiamachy, Skirmish, Slam, Soldier, Spar, Spat, Spitfire, Squabble, Stealth, Stoush, Straight, Strife, Struggle, Sumo, Swordsman, Tar, Tatar, Thersites, Toreador, Tuilyie, Tuilzie, Tussle, Umbrella, War(-dog), War-horse, War-man, Warrior, Wraxle, Wrestle, Yike, Zero

Figment Delusion, Fiction, Invention

Figure(s), Figurine, Figurative Action, Arabic, Aumail, Bas-relief, Body, Build, Caganer, Canephorus, Caryatid, Cast, Chladni, Cinque, Cipher, Cone, Cube, Cypher, Decahedron, Digit, Ecorché, Effigy, Eight, Ellipse, Enneagon, Enneahedron, Epanadiplosis, Escher, → **FORM**, Fret, Fusil, Gammadion, Girth, Gnomon, Graph, Heptagon, Hexagon, Hour-glass, Icon, Icosahedron, Idol, Ikon, Image, Impossible, Insect, Intaglio, Integer, Interference, Lay, Lissajous, Magot, Manaia, Mandala, Matchstick, Moai, Monogram, Motif, Nonagon, Number, Numeral, Numeric, Octagon, Octahedron, Orant, Outline, Parallelepiped, Parallelogram, Pentacle, Pentalpha, Plane, Polygon, Polyhedron, Poussette, Prism, Puppet, Pyramid, Reckon, Repetend, Repoussoir, Rhomboid, See, → **SHAPE**, Sheela-na-gig, Significant, Simplex, Solid, Sonorous, Statistics, Statue(tte), String, Tanagra, Telamon, Tetragon, Tetrahedron, Torus, Triangle, Trigon, Trihedron, Triskele, Triskelion, Trisoctahedron, Tropology, Ushabti, Waxwork

Figure of speech Allegory, Alliteration, Analogy, Antimask, Antimasque, Antimetabole, Antithesis, Asyndeton, Catachresis, Chiasmus, Deixis, Diallage, Ellipsis, Euphemism, Hendiadys, Hypallage, Hyperbaton, Hyperbole, Hysteron proteron, Irony, Litotes, Meiosis, Metalepsis, Metaphor, Metonymy, Onomatopoeia, Oxymoron, Paral(e)ipsis, Prosopopoeia, Siddhuism, Simile, Solecism, Syllepsis, Synecdoche, Taxeme, Tmesis, Trope, Tropology, Zeugma

Figure study Arithmetic, Mathematics, Numeration

Figure-weaver Draw-boy

Filament Barbule, Byssus, Cirrus, Fibre, Fimbria, Floss, Gossamer, Hair, Hypha, Mycor(r)hiza, Myofibril, Paraphysis, Protonema, → **THREAD**, Whisker, Wreath

Filch Appropriate, Drib, Pilfer, Pinch, Prig, Purloin, Smouch, → **STEAL**

File, Filing(s) Abrade, Archive, Back up, Bastard, Batch, Binary, Box, Burr, Circular, Clyfaker, Coffle, Croc(odile), Crosscut, Database, Data set, Dead-smooth, Disc, Disk, Dossier, Enter, Floatcut, Folder, Generation, Half-round, Index, Indian, Lever-arch, Limation, Line, Lodge, Nail, Pickpocket, Pigeon-hole, Podcast, Pollute, Quannet, Rank, Rasp, Rat-tail, README, Riffler, Risp, Rolodex®, Row, Scalprum, Scratch, Single, Single-cut, String, Swap, Swarf, Text, Tickler, TIF(F)

Filial generation F1

Filibuster Freebooter, Hinder, Obstruct, Pirate, Run on, Stonewall

Filigree Delicate, Fretwork, Sheer

Filipino Igorot, Moro, → **PHILIPPINE(S)**

Fill(ing), Filler Anaplerosis, Balaam, Banoffee, Banoffi, Beaumontag(u)e, Beaumontique, Billow, Bishop, Bloat, Brick-nog, Brim, Bump, Centre, Charge, Cram, Fat-lute, Ganache, Gather, Gorge, Heart, Imbue, Implete, Impregn(ate), Inlay, Instill, Jampack, Line, Mastic, Occupy, Pabulous, Packing, Permeate, Plug, Replenish, Repletive, Salpicon, Sate, Satisfy, Sealant, Shim, Slush, Stack, Stock, Stocking, Stopping, → **STUFF**, Tales, Tank-up, Teem, Top up, Ullage

Fillet(s) Anadem, Annulet, Band, Bandeau, Bandelet, Bone, Cloisonné, Flaunching, Fret, Goujons, Grenadine, Headband, Infula, Label, Lemniscus, List(el), Mitre, Moulding, Reglet, Regula, Ribbon, Rollmop, Slice, Snood, Sphendone, Stria, Striga, Taeniate, Tape, Teniate, Tilting, Tournedos, Vitta

Fillip Boost, Kick, Snap, Stimulus

Filly Colt, Foal, She

Film(s), Filmmaker, Filmy, Filming Acetate, Actioner, Amnion, Animatronics, Anime, Biopic, Blaxploitation, Blockbuster, Bollywood, Buddy, Carry On, Cartoon, Casablanca, Caul, Cel, Chick-flick, Chiller, Chopsocky, Cine, Cinema vérité, Cinerama®, Circlorama®, Cliffhanger, Cling, Clip, Coat, Compilation,

Creature feature, Deepie, Dew, Diorama, Docudrama, Documentary, Dogme, Dust, Epic, ET, Exposure, Fantasia, Feature, Fiche, Flick, Floaty, Footage, Gigi, Gossamer, Hammer, Haze, Hollywood, Horror, Horse opera, Infomercial, Kell, Kidult, Lacquer, Layer, Loid, Mask, Membrane, Microfiche, Mist, Molecular, Monochrome, Montage, Movie, Neo-noir, Newsreel, Noddy, Noir, Non-flam, Oater, Omnimax®, Outtake, Panchromatic, Patina, Pellicle, Photo, Pilot, Plaque, Prequel, Psycho, Quickie, Quota-quickie, Reel, Release, Reversal, Roll, Romcom, Rush, Safety, Scale, Scent-scale, Screen, Scum, Sepmag, Sheet, Shoot-'em-up, Short, Shot, Silent, Skin, Skin flick, Slasher-movie, Slashfest, Slick, Slo-mo, Snuff, Spaghetti western, Splatter, Star Wars, Studio, Super 8, Suspensor, Talkie, Tear-jerker, Technicolor, Titanic, Toon, Trailer, Travelogue, Trippy, Two-shot, Ultrafiche, Varnish, Vicenzi, Video, Video-nasty, Vitaphone®, Web, Weepie, Weepy, Weft, Western, Wuxia

Film star Extra, Vedette

Filter(ing) Band-pass, Clarify, Colour, Dialysis, Dichroic, High-pass, Leach, Low-pass, Percolate, Perk, Polarizing, Seep, Sieve, → **SIFT**, Sile, Skylight, Strain

Filth(y) Addle, Augean, Bilge, Bogging, Colluvies, Crock, Crud, Defile, Dirt, Dung, Feculent, Foul, Grime, Lucre, Mire, Muck, Obscene, Pythogenic, Refuse, Slime, Smut(ch), Soil, Squalor, Stercoral, Sullage, Yuck

Fin Adipose, Anal, Caudal, Ctene, Dollars, Dorsal, Fiver, Fluke, Pectoral, Pelvic, Pinna, Pinnule, Rib, Skeg, Skegg, Stabiliser, Ventral

Final(e), Finalise Absolute, Closing, Coda, Conclusive, Cup, Decider, End, End-all, Eventual, Exam, Extreme, Grand, Last, Net(t), Peremptory, Sew up, Swansong, Terminal, Ultimate, Utter

Finance, Financial, Financier Ad crumenam, Angel, Back, Banian, Banker, Bankroll, Banyan, Bottomry, Cambism, Chrematistic, Equity, Exchequer, Fiscal, Gnome, Grubstake, Mezzanine, Monetary, Revenue, Sponsor, Subsidise, Treasurer, Underwrite

Finch Bird, Brambling, Bunting, Canary, Charm, Chewink, Crossbill, Darwin's, Fringillid, Gouldian, Grosbeak, Linnet, Marsh-robin, Peter, Redpoll, Rosy, Serin, Siskin, Spink, Twite, Zebra

Find(er), Finding Ascertain, Come across, Detect, Direction, Discover(y), Get, Hit, Inquest, → **LOCATE**, Meet, Provide, Rumble, Trace, Track down, Trouvaille, Unearth, Verdict

Fine, Fine words Amende, Amerce, Amerciament, Arts, Assess, Beau(t), Bender, Blood-wit(e), Bonny, Boshta, Boshter, Boss, Brandy, Brave, Braw, Bully, Buttock-mail, Champion, Dainty, Dandy, Dick, End, Eriach, Eric(k), Estreat, F, Fair, Famous, Forfeit, Gate, Godly, Good(ly), Gossamer, Gradely, Graithly, Grand, Grassum, Hair, Hairline, Handsome, Heriot, Hunkydory, Immense, Impalpable, Inconie, Incony, Infangthief, Issue, Keen, Leirwite, Log, Maritage, Merchet, Mooi, Mulct, Nifty, Niminy-piminy, Noble, OK, Oke, Okey-doke(y), Outfangthief, → **PENALTY**, Phat, Precise, Pretty, Pure, Relief, Righto, Safe, Sconce, Sheer, Sicker, Slender, Smart, Spanking, Subtle, Summery, Super, Tax, Thin, Ticket(t)y-boo, Tiptop, Topping, Transmission, Unlaw, Wally, Waly, Well, Wer(e)gild

Fine-collector Cheater

Finery Braws, Fallal, Frills, Frippery, Gaudery, Ornament, Trinket, Wally, Warpaint

Finesse Artifice, Artistry, Delicacy, Skill, Strategy

Fine-weather All-hallond, All-hallow(e)n, All-hollown

Finger(s), Fingernail Annular, Dactyl, Digit, Fork, Green, Handle, Index, Lunula, Medius, Name, Nip, Piggy, Pinky, Pointer, Potato, Prepollex, Pusher, Ring(man), Shop, Sponge, Talaunt, Talon, Tot, Trigger, White

Finger-hole Lill, Ring

Fingerprint(ing) Arch, Dabs, Dactylogram, DNA, Genetic, Loop, Whorl
Fingerstall Hutkin
Finial Bunch, Knob, Ornament, Tee
Finical, Finicky Faddy, Fastidious, Fussy, Particular, Pernickety, Precise
Finish, Finished, Finishing touch Arch, Blanket, Calendar, Close, Coating, Coda,
   Complete, → CONCLUDE, Crown, Die, Dish, Do, Dope, Dress, → END, Epilog(ue),
   Epiphenomena, Exact, Full, Gloss, Grandstand, Kibosh, Lacquer, Log off, Mat(t),
   Mirror, Neat, Outgo, Outwork, Pebbledash, Peg out, Perfect, Photo, Polish off,
   Refine, Ripe, Round, Satin, Settle, Shot, Spitcher, Surface, Terminate, Through, Top
   out, Up (tie), Veneer, Wau(l)k, Wind-up
Finite Bounded, Limited
Finn(ish) Esth, Huck(leberry), Karelian, Lapp, Mickey, Mordvin, Suomic, Udmurt,
   Votyak
Fiord Bay, Hardanger, Inlet, Oslo, Randers, Trondheim
Fir Abies, Balsam, Douglas, Larch, Oregon, Scotch, Scots, Silver, Spruce, Umbrella
Fire(side) Accend, Agni, Aidan, Aiden, Animate, Ardour, Arouse, Arson, Atar,
   Axe, Bake, Bale, Barbecue, Barrage, Beacon, Behram, Blaze, Boot, Brand, Brazier,
   Brush, Burn, Bush, Central, Chassé, Conflagration, Corposant, Covering, Delope,
   Discharge, Dismiss, Élan, Electric, Element, Embolden, Ena, Energy, Enfilade,
   Enkindle, Enthuse, Flak, Flame, Friendly, Furnace, Greek, Gun, Hearth, Hob, Ignite,
   Inferno, Ingle, Inspire, Kentish, Kiln, Kindle, Launch, Let off, Light, Liquid, Lowe,
   Pop, Prime, Prometheus, Pull, Pyre, Quick, Radiator, Rake, Rapid, Red, Red cock,
   Sack, St Anthony's, St Elmo's, Scorch, Shell, Shoot, Smudge, Spark, Spirit, Spunk,
   Stoke, Stove, Strafe, Tracer, Trial, Wake, Watch, Wisp, Zeal, Zip
▶ **Firearm** *see* GUN
Fireback Reredos
Fireball Bolide
Firebird Phoenix
Fire-break Epaulement, Greenstrip
Firedamp Blower
Fire-dog Andiron
Fire engine Green Goddess
Fire-extinguisher Halon, Hell-bender, Salamander
Firefly Glow-worm, Lightning-bug, Luciferin, Pyrophorus
Fire-guard Fender
Fireman Abednego, Brigade, Deputy, Prometheus, Stoker, Visiting
Fire-opal Girasol
Fireplace Camboose, Chimney, Grate, Hearth, Hob, Ingle, Loop-hole, Range
Fireplug H, Hydrant
Fireproof Abednego, Asbestos, Incombustible, Inflammable, Meshach, Salamander,
   Shadrach, Uralite
Firewalker Salamander
Firewood Billet, Faggot, Knitch, Tinder
Firework(s) Banger, Bengal-light, Bunger, Catherine wheel, Cherry bomb, Cracker,
   Devil, Feu d'artifice, Fisgig, Fizgig, Flip-flop, Fountain, Gerbe, Girandole, Golden
   rain, Iron sand, Jumping jack, Maroon, Pastille, Peeoy, Petard, Pharaoh's serpent,
   Pinwheel, Pioy(e), Pyrotechnics, Realgar, Rocket, Roman candle, Serpent,
   Skyrocket, Slap-bang, Sparkler, Squib, Tantrum, Throwdown, Tourbill(i)on,
   Volcano, Waterloo cracker, Wheel, Whizzbang
Fire-worshipper Parsee
Firing Baking, Fusillade, Mitten, Salvo, Touchpaper

Firm, Firmness Adamant, Agency, Binding, Business, Collected, Compact, Company, Concern, Concrete, Conglomerate, Consistency, Constant, Crisp, Decided, Determined, Duro, Faithful, Fast, Fixed, Hard, Inc, Insistent, Marginal, Oaky, Obdurate, Obstinate, → **RESOLUTE**, Sclerotal, Secure, Set, Siccar, Sicker, → **SOLID**, Sound, Stable, Stalwart, Staunch, Steady, Ste(a)dfast, Steely, Steeve, Stern, Stieve, Stiff, Strict, Sturdy, Sure, Tight, Tough, Unshakeable, Well-knit

Firmament Canopy, Empyrean, Heaven, Sky

First Ab initio, Alpha, Arch, Archetype, Best, Calends, Champion, Chief, Earliest, E(a)rst, Eldest, Foremost, Former, Front, Head, I, Ideal, Imprimis, Initial, 1st, Kalends, Led, Maiden, No 1, One, Opener, Or, Original, Pioneer, Pole, Pole position, Premier, Première, Prima, Primal, Prime, Primo, Principal, Prototype, Rudimentary, Senior, Starters, Top, Uppermost, Victor, Yama

First-aid(ers) Zambu(c)k

First born Ariki, Eigne, Eldest, Heir, Major, Senior

First class, First rate A1, Crack, Prime, Pukka, Supreme, Tiptop, Top(notch)

First day Calends

First fruits Annat, Arles, Primitiae, Windfalls

First man Adam, Ask, Gayomart, Premier, President, Yama, Ymer, Ymir

First offender Eve, Probationer

▶ **First rate** *see* **FIRST CLASS**

First woman Embla, Eve, Pandora, Premier

Firth Estuary, Forth, Inlet, Moray, Pentland, Solway, Tay

Fish(ing) Angle, Bob, Bottom, Cast, Catch, Chowder, Coarse, Cran, Creel, Deep-sea, Dib, Dredge, Dry, Dry-fly, Episcate, Fly, Flying, Frozen, Fry, Game, Gefilte, Gefulte, Goujons, Guddle, Halieutics, Haul, Hen, Inshore, Ledger, Mess, Net, Otterboard, Overnet, Piscine, Queer, Roe, Rough, Runner, Sacred, Sashimi, Shoal, Skitter, Sleeper, Small mouth, Snigger, Sniggle, Spin, Spot, Surimi, Trawl, Troll, Tub, Walking, Wet, White ·

FISH

2 letters:	Koi	Chad	Huso
Ai	Lax	Char	Huss
Id	Lob	Chub	Ikan
	Par	Chum	Jack
3 letters:	Pod	Coho	Kelt
Aua	Ray	Cray	Keta
Ayu	Rig	Cusk	Lant
Bar	Sar	Dace	Leaf
Bib	Tai	Dare	Ling
But	Top	Dart	Luce
Cat		Dory	Lump
Cod	4 letters:	Drum	Maid
Cow	Barb	Fugu	Maze
Dab	Bass	Gade	Moki
Dog	Blay	Goby	Mola
Eel	Bley	Gump	Mort
Gar	Brit	Hake	Opah
Ged	Butt	Harl	Orfe
Hag	Carp	Hoka	Parr
Ide	Cero	Hoki	Peal

Peel
Pike
Pope
Pout
Raun
Rawn
Rigg
Rudd
Ruff
Scad
Scar
Scat
Scup
Seer
Seir
Shad
Sild
Slip
Snig
Sole
Star
Tope
Trot
Tuna
Tusk
Woof

5 letters:
Ablet
Ahuru
Allis
Angel
Apode
Aspro-
Basse
Belta
Blain
Bleak
Bream
Brill
Bully
Capon
Charr
Cisco
Clown
Cobia
Cohoe
Coley
Cuddy
Danio
Dorad

Doras
Doree
Dorse
Elops
Elver
Fluke
Gadus
Gibel
Grunt
Jewie
Jurel
Koura
Laker
Lance
Loach
Lythe
Maise
Maize
Manta
Masus
Mease
Molly
Murre
Murry
Nerka
Padle
Perai
Perca
Perch
Pilot
Piper
Pirai
Platy
Pogge
Powan
Prawn
Roach
Roker
Royal
Ruffe
Saith
Sargo
Saury
Scrod
Sewen
Sewin
Shark
Sheat
Skate
Slope
Smelt

Snoek
Snook
Solen
Speck
Sprat
Sprod
Tench
Tetra
Togue
Torsk
Trout
Tunny
Umber
Wahoo
Whiff
Wirra
Witch
Yabby
Zebra

6 letters:
Alevin
Allice
Anabas
Angler
Archer
Ballan
Barbel
Belone
Beluga
Bichir
Big-eye
Blenny
Bonito
Bounce
Bowfin
Braise
Braize
Bumalo
Burbot
Callop
Caplin
Caranx
Caribe
Cheven
Clupea
Cockle
Comber
Conger
Conner
Cottus

Cudden
Cuddie
Cuddin
Cunner
Cuttle
Darter
Dentex
Diodon
Dipnoi
Discus
Doctor
Dorado
Dun-cow
Ellops
Espada
Finnac
Finnan
Fogash
Fumado
Gadoid
Garvie
Gilgie
Goboid
Goramy
Grilse
Groper
Gulper
Gunnel
Gurami
Gurnet
Haddie
Hapuka
Hassar
Inanga
Jerker
Jilgie
Kipper
Kokiri
Labrus
Lancet
Launce
Lizard
Louvar
Lunker
Mad Tom
Mahsir
Maigre
Marari
Marlin
Meagre
Medaka

Medusa	Tinker	Escolar	Moon-eye
Megrim	Toitoi	Fantail	Morwong
Milter	Tomcod	Findram	Muraena
Minnow	Trygon	Finnack	Oarfish
Morgay	Turbot	Finnock	Old-wife
Mudcat	Twaite	Flattie	Oolakan
Mullet	Ulicon	Garfish	Opaleye
Murena	Ulikon	Garoupa	Osseter
Nerite	Vendis	Garpike	Oulakan
Oyster	Weever	Garvock	Oulicon
Paddle	Wirrah	Geelbek	Panchax
Paidle	Wrasse	Gemfish	Pandora
Pakoko	Yabbie	Goldeye	Peacock
Parore	Zander	Gourami	Pegasus
Parrot	Zingel	Grouper	Pigfish
Patiki		Growler	Pinfish
Pholas	*7 letters:*	Grunion	Piranha
Piraya	Ale-wife	Gudgeon	Pollack
Plaice	Anchovy	Gurnard	Pomfret
Podley	Anemone	Gwiniad	Pompano
Pollan	Asterid	Gwyniad	Pupfish
Porgie	Azurine	Haddock	Ragfish
Puffer	Batfish	Hagdown	Rasbora
Redfin	Bellows	Hagfish	Ratfish
Remora	Bergylt	Halibut	Rat-tail
Rewaru	Birchir	Herling	Redfish
Robalo	Bloater	Herring	Rorqual
Roughy	Bluecap	Hirling	Roughie
Saithe	Boxfish	Hogfish	Sand dab
Salmon	Brassie	Homelyn	Sand-eel
Samlet	Buffalo	Houting	Sardine
Sander	Bumallo	Ichthys	Scalare
Sardel	Bummalo	Inconnu	Scallop
Sargus	Cabezon	Jewfish	Sculpin
Sauger	Capelin	Kahawai	Sea-bass
Saurel	Cavalla	Keeling	Sea-cock
Scampi	Cavally	Koi carp	Sea-dace
Sea-bat	Ceviche	Kokanee	Sea-moth
Sea-owl	Cichlid	Lampern	Sea-pike
Seeder	Codfish	Lamprey	Sea-star
Serran	Copepod	Lampuki	Sea-wife
Shanny	Corvina	Lantern	Sevruga
Sheath	Cottoid	Lingcod	Sillock
Shiner	Crappie	Lobster	Silurid
Skelly	Croaker	Lubfish	Skegger
Sparid	Crucian	Lyomeri	Skipper
Splake	Crusian	Mahseer	Snapper
Sucker	Cutlass	Matelot	Sock-eye
Tailor	Dogfish	Medacca	Sparoid
Tarpon	Eelfare	Merling	Speldin
Tautog	Eel-pout	Mojarra	Sterlet

Sunfish
Sunstar
Surgeon
Teleost
Tiddler
Tilapia
Titling
Torgoch
Torpedo
Tubfish
Ulichon
Vendace
Vendiss
Wall-eye
Whipray
Whistle
Whiting
Wide-gab

8 letters:
Albacore
Albicore
Anableps
Arapaima
Asteroid
Atherine
Billfish
Blennius
Bloodfin
Blowfish
Blueback
Bluefish
Bluegill
Boarfish
Brisling
Bullhead
Bullhorn
Bummallo
Cabezone
Cabrilla
Carangid
Cardinal
Cavefish
Characid
Characin
Chimaera
Coalfish
Corkwing
Cow-pilot
Cucumber
Cyprinid

Dealfish
Dragonet
Drumfish
Eagle-ray
Elephant
Escallop
Eulachon
Fallfish
Fighting
Filefish
Flathead
Flounder
Four-eyes
Frogfish
Gambusia
Ganoidei
Gillaroo
Gilthead
Goatfish
Gobiidae
Graining
Grayling
Hackbolt
Hair-tail
Half-beak
Hard-head
Holostei
Hornbeak
Hornpout
Kabeljou
Killfish
Kingfish
Kingklip
Kukukuma
Lionfish
Luderick
Lumpfish
Lungfish
Mackerel
Mahi-mahi
Mata Hari
Menhaden
Milkfish
Monkfish
Moonfish
Moray eel
Mosquito
Mulloway
Nannygai
Nennigai
Nine-eyes

Oulachon
Paradise
Patutuki
Pickerel
Pilchard
Pipefish
Pirarucu
Redbelly
Red roman
Reperepe
Rock-cook
Rockfish
Rockling
Roncador
Rosefish
Saibling
Sailfish
Saltfish
Sardelle
Scabbard
Scaridae
Sciaenid
Scorpion
Scuppaug
Sea-bream
Sea-devil
Seahorse
Sea-lemon
Sea-raven
Sea-robin
Sergeant
Serranus
Skipjack
Smear-dab
Snake-eel
Sparidae
Sparling
Spelding
Speldrin
Stenlock
Sting-ray
Stonecat
Sturgeon
Tarakihi
Tarwhine
Teraglin
Terakihi
Tile-fish
Toadfish
Trevally
Tropical

Tubenose
Tullibee
Weakfish
Whitling
Wolffish

9 letters:
Ahuruhuru
Amberjack
Anabantid
Anchoveta
Barracuda
Blackfish
Butterfly
Carangoid
Cascadura
Ceratodus
Chaetodon
Chavender
Clingfish
Clupeidae
Coregonus
Coryphene
Cyprinoid
Devilfish
Gaspereau
Glassfish
Globefish
Goldfinny
Goldsinny
Golomynka
Goosefish
Greenbone
Greenling
Grenadier
Haberdine
Hornyhead
Hottentot
Houndfish
Ichthyoid
Jacksmelt
Jewelfish
Kabeljouw
Killifish
Labyrinth
Latimeria
Matelotte
Menominee
Mudhopper
Neon tetra
Pikeperch

Porbeagle
Porcupine
Queenfish
Quillback
Roussette
Scaldfish
Scalefish
Schnapper
Scorpaena
Selachian
Shubunkin
Siluridae
Slickhead
Snailfish
Snakehead
Snipefish
Solenette
Spadefish
Spearfish
Speldring
Stargazer
Steenbras
Stingaree
Stockfish
Stonefish
Surfperch
Surmullet
Swellfish
Swordfish
Sword-tail
Thornback
Threadfin
Tittlebat
Topminnow
Trachinus
Troutfish
Trunkfish

Whitebait
White-bass
Wreckfish
Yellowfin

10 letters:
Amblyopsis
Barracoota
Barracouta
Barramundi
Bitterling
Bombay duck
Bottlehead
Butterfish
Candlefish
Cockabully
Cofferfish
Cornetfish
Cyclostome
Damselfish
Demoiselle
Dollarfish
Etheostoma
Fingerling
Flutemouth
Groundling
Horned pout
Lake-lawyer
Largemouth
Lumpsucker
Maskalonge
Maskanonge
Maskinonge
Midshipman
Mossbunker
Mudskipper
Needlefish

Nurse-hound
Paddlefish
Pakirikiri
Rabbitfish
Red emperor
Red-snapper
Ribbonfish
Rudderfish
Scopelidae
Sea-poacher
Sea-surgeon
Serrasalmo
Sheepshead
Ship-holder
Shovelnose
Silverside
Springfish
Squeteague
Teleostome
Titarakura
Tripletail
Yellowtail

11 letters:
Chondrostei
Cyprinodont
Dolly Varden
Istiophorus
Lapidosteus
Lepidosiren
Lophobranch
Maskallonge
Moorish idol
Muskellunge
Ostracoderm
Oxyrhynchus
Plagiostome

Plectognath
Pumpkinseed
Scolopendra
Seventy-four
Snail darter
Soldierfish
Stickleback
Stoneroller
Surgeonfish
Triggerfish
Trumpetfish
Water souchy
Yellowbelly

12 letters:
Ballan-wrasse
Elasmobranch
Father-lasher
Heterosomata
Histiophorus
Mangrove Jack
Miller's thumb
Mouthbreeder
Mouthbrooder
Orange roughy
Plectognathi
Rainbow-trout
Squirrelfish

13 letters:
Leatherjacket
Musselcracker
Sailor's choice
Sergeant Baker

15 letters:
Crossopterygian

Fish and chips Greasies
Fish-basket Creel, Hask, Kipe
Fish disease Argulus
Fisher(man) Ahab, Andrew, Angler, Black cat, Caper, Codder, Dragman, High-liner, Liner, Pedro, Peter, Piscator, Rodster, Sharesman, Walton
▶ **Fisherwoman** *see* FISHSELLER
Fish-hawk Osprey
Fishing-ground Haaf
Fishing-line G(u)imp, Gymp, Paternoster
Fishpond Ocean, Stew, Vivarium
Fishseller, Fisherwoman Fishwife, Molly Malone, Ripp(i)er, Shawley, Shawlie
Fishy Botargo, Suspicious, Vacant
Fission Multiple, Nuclear

Fissure Chasm, Cleft, Crack, Crevasse, Crevice, Gap, Grike, Gryke, Lode, Rent, Rift, Rolando, Sand-crack, Scam, Sylvian, Sylvius, Vallecula, Vein, Zygon

Fist Clench, Dukes, Hand, Iron, Join-hand, Mailed, Neaf(f)e, Neif, Neive, Nief, Nieve, Pud, Punch, Thump, Writing

Fit(s), Fitful, Fitting(s), Fitness Able, Access, Adapt, Ague, Align, Aline, Apoplexy, Appointment, Appropriate, Apropos, Apt, Babbitt, Bayonet, Beseemly, Bout, Canto, Capable, Cataleptic, Cataplexy, Click, Concinnous, Condign, Congruous, Conniption, Convulsion, Culver-tail, Darwinian, Decent, Decorous, Desultory, Dod, Dove-tail, Due, Eclampsia, Egal, Eligible, Ensconce, Epilepsy, Equip, Exies, Expedient, Fairing, Fay, Fiddle, Form, Furniment, Furnishing, Fytte, Gee, Germane, Gusty, Habile, Hale, Hang, Health, Hinge, Huff, Hysterics, Ictus, Inclusive, In-form, Interference, Intermittent, In trim, Just, Kashrut(h), Like, Lune, Marry, Mate, Meet, Mood, Nest, Opportune, Paroxysm, Passus, Pertinent, Prepared, Press, → **PROPER**, Queme, Ready, Rig, Rind, Ripe, Rynd, Seemly, Seizure, Set, Shrink, Sit, Sliding, Snotter, Sort, Sound, Spasm, Spell, Start, Suit(able), Syncope, Tailor, Tantrum, Throe, To prepon, Turn, Up to, Well, Wobbler, Wobbly, Worthy, Wrath

▷ **Fit(ting)** *may indicate* a 't'

Fitment Adaptor, Unit

Fitzgerald Edward, Ella, Scott

Five(s), Fiver Cinque, Flim, Mashie, Pallone, Pedro, Pentad, Quinary, Quintet, Sextan, Towns, V

Five years Lustre, Lustrum

Fix(ed), Fixer, Fixative Affeer, Anchor, Appoint, Appraise, → **ARRANGE**, Assess, Assign, Attach, Bind, Brand, Cement, Clamp, Clew, Clue, Constant, Corking-pin, Cure, Decide, Destinate, Destine, Determine, Do, Embed, Empight, Encastré, Engrain, Establish, Fast, Fasten, Firm, Fit, Freeze, Gammon, Hold, Hypo(sulphite), Immutable, Impaction, Imprint, Inculcate, Ingrain, Jag, Jam, Locate, Lodge, Mend, Nail, Name, Narcotic, Nobble, Orientate, Peg, Persistent, Pin, Place, Point, Quantify, Repair, Resolute, Rig, Rigid, Rivet, Rove, Rut, Scrape, Screw, Seat, Seize, Set, Settle, Ship, Shoo, Skatole, Skewer, Splice, Stage, Staple, Static, Stell, Step, Stew, Stuck, Tie, Toe, Valorize, Weld

Fixture Attachment, Event, Match, Permanence, Rawlplug®, Unit

Fizz(ed), Fizzy Buck's, Effervesce, Gas, Hiss, Pop, Sherbet, Sod, Soda

Fizzle Failure, Flop, Hiss, Washout

▶ **Fjord** *see* **FIORD**

Flabbergast(ed) Amaze, Astound, Floor, Thunderstruck

Flabby Flaccid, Lank, Lax, Limp, Pendulous, Saggy

Flaccid Flabby, Lank, Limp, Soft

Flag(gy), Flags Acorus, Ancient, Ashlar, Banderol, Banner, Black, Blackjack, Blue (Ensign), Blue Peter, Bunting, Burgee, Calamus, Chequered, Colour(s), Dan(n)ebrog, Decline, Droop, Duster, Ensign, Fail, Faint, Falter, Fane, Fanion, Field colours, Gladdon, Gonfalon, Green, Guidon, Hail, Hoist, Irideal, Iris, Jack, Jade, Jolly Roger, Kerbstone, Languish, Lis, Old Glory, Orris, Pave(ment), Pavilion, Pencel, Pennant, Pennon, Penoncel(le), Pensel, Pensil, Peter, Pilot, Pin, Prayer, Quarantine, Rag, Rainbow, Red, Red Duster, Red Ensign, Repeater, Sag, Sedge, Semaphore, Sick, Sink, Slab(stone), Slack, Stand, Standard, Stars and Bars, Stars and Stripes, Streamer, Substitute, Sweet, Tire, Tricolour, Union (Jack), Vane, Vexillology, Waft, Whift, White (Ensign), Wilt, Wither, Yellow (Jack)

Flagday Tagday

Flagellate Beat, Mastigophora, Scourge, Trypanosome, Whip

Flagon Bottle, Carafe, Ewer, Jug, Pitcher, Stoop, Stoup, Vessel

Flagpole Pin, Staff
Flagrant Egregious, Glaring, Heinous, Patent, Wanton
Flagship Admiral, Barge, Victory
Flail Beat, Drub, Swingle, Swip(p)le, Threshel
Flair Art, Bent, Élan, Gift, Knack, Nose, Panache, Style, → TALENT
Flak AA, Attack, Criticism
Flake Chip, Flame, Flaught, Flaw, Floccule, Flocculus, Fragment, Peel, Scale, Smut, Snow
Flam Impose
Flamboyant Baroque, Brilliant, Florid, Garish, Grandiose, Ornate, Ostentatious, Paz(z)azz, Piz(z)azz, Swash-buckler
Flame, Flaming Ardent, Blaze, Fire, Flake, Flambé, Flammule, Glow, Kindle, Leman, Lover, Lowe, Musical, Olympic, Oxyacetylene, Reducing, Sensitive, Sweetheart
Flan Pastry, Quiche, Tart
Flanders Mare, Moll
Flange Border, Collar, Collet, Lip, Rim
Flank(s) Accompany, Anta, Flange, Flitch, Ilia, Lisk, Loin, Side, Spur
Flannel Blather, Canton, Cloth, Cotton, Face, Flatter, Outing, Soft-soap, Waffle, Washrag, Zephyr
Flap(ped), Flapper, Flapping Ado, Agnail, Aileron, Alar, Alarm(ist), Aventail(e), Bate, Beat, Bird, Bobbysoxer, Bustle, Chit, Dither, Elevon, Epiglottis, Fipple, Flacker, Flaff, Flag, Flaught, Flutter, Fly, Fuss, Giglet, Giglot, Hover, → IN A FLAP, Labium, Labrum, Lapel, Loma, Louvre, Luff, Lug, Operculum, Panic, Spin, Spoiler, Tab, Tag, Tailboard, Tailgate, Tiswas, To-do, Tongue, TRAM, Volucrine, Wave, Whisk
Flare(d), Flares, Flare up Bell, Bell-bottoms, Fishtail, Flame, Flanch, Flaunch, Godet, Magnesium, Scene, Signal, Skymarker, Solar, Spread, Spunk, Ver(e)y, Widen
Flash(y), Flasher, Flashpoint Brash, Coruscate, Cursor, Electronic, Emicant, Essex Man, Fire-flag, Flare, Flaught, Fulgid, Fulgural, Garish, Gaudy, Glaik, Gleam, Glint, Glisten, Glitzy, Green, Green ray, Helium, Indicate, Instant, Jay, Lairy, Levin, Lightning, Loud, Magnesium, Meretricious, Mo, Ostentatious, Photopsy, Raffish, Ribbon, Ring, Roary, Scintillation, Second, Sequin, Showy, Sluice, Snazzy, Spark, Sparkle, Sport, Streak, Strobe, Swank(e)y, Tick, Tigrish, Trice, Twinkle, Vivid, Wire
▷ **Flashing** *may indicate* an anagram
Flask(-shaped) Ampulla, Aryballos, Bottle, Canteen, Carafe, Cask, Coffin, Conceptacle, Costrel, Cucurbit, Dewar, Erlenmeyer, Fiasco, Flacket, Flacon, Florence, Goatskin, Hip, Lekythos, Matrass, Mick(e)(y), Moon, Pocket-pistol, Powder, Reform, Retort, Thermos®, Vacuum, Vial
Flat(s), Flatten(ed), Flattener Adobe, Alkali, Amaze, Ancipital, Apartment, Bachelor, Bald, Banal, Beat, Bed-sit, Blow-out, Bulldoze, Callow, Cape, Complanate, Compress, Condominium, Corymb(ose), Cottage, Coulisse, Dead, Demolish, Dorsiventral, Double, Dress, Dull, Even, Feeble, Flew, Floor, Flue, Fool, Gaff, Garden, Granny, Guyot, Haugh, High-rise, Homaloid, Home-unit, Horizontal, Insipid, Ironed, Jacent, Key, KO, Law, Lay, Level, Lifeless, Llano, Maderised, Marsh, Monotonous, Mud, Nitwit, Norfolk, Oblate, Ownership, Pad, Pancake, Pedestrian, Peneplain, Peneplane, Penthouse, Pentice, Pied-à-terre, Plain, Planar, Plane, Planish, Plat, Plateau, Press, Prone, Prostrate, Recumbent, Rooms, Salt, Scenery, Service, Smooth, Splayfoot, Spread-edged, Squash, Studio, Tableland, Tabular, Tame, Tasteless, Tenement, True, Unsensational, Vapid, Walk-up
Flat-chested Cithara
Flat-faced Socle

Flat-foot(ed) Policeman, Splay
Flat-nosed Camus
Flatter(ing), Flatterer, Flattery Adulate, Becoming, Beslaver, Blandish, Blarney, Bootlick, Butter, Cajole, Candied, Carn(e)y, Claw(back), Complimentary, Comprabatio, Earwiggy, En beau, Eyewash, Fawn, Fillibrush, Flannel, Flannen, Fleech, Flummery, Fulsome, Gloze, Gnathonic(al), Honey, Imitation, Lip-salve, Moody, Palp, Phrase, Poodle-faker, Proneur, Puffery, Sawder, Smarm, Snow job, Soap, Soft soap, Soother, Souk, Spaniel, Stroke, Sugar, Sweet talk, Sycophant, Taffy, Toady, Treacle, Unction, Wheedle, Word
Flatulence Belch, Borborygmus, Burp, Carminative, Colic, Gas, Wind
Flaunt Brandish, Flourish, Gibe, Parade, Skyre, Sport, Strout, Strut, Wave
Flavour(ed), Flavouring Absinth(e), Alecost, Anethole, Angostura, Anise, Aniseed, Aroma, Benne, Bergamot, Bold, Borage, Bouquet garni, Clove, Coriander, Cumin, Dill, Essence, Eucalyptol, Fenugreek, Flor, Garlic, Garni, Gingili, Marinate, Mint, Orgeat, Piperonal, Quark, Race, Ratafia, Relish, Rocambole, Sair, Sassafras, Sesame, Tack, Tang, Tarragon, → **TASTE**, Til, Tincture, Twang, Vanilla
Flaw Blemish, Brack, Bug, Chip, Crack, Defect, Fallacy, → **FAULT**, Gall, Hamartia, Imperfection, Infirmity, Kink, Knothole, Lophole, Red-eye, Rima, Spot, Taint, Tear, Thief, Tragic, Windshake
Flawless Impeccable, Intact
Flax(en) Aleseed, Blonde, Codilla, Harakeke, Harden, Hards, Herden, Herl, Hurden, Line, Linseed, Lint, Lint-white, Linum, Mill-mountain, Poi, Tow
Flay Excoriate, Fleece, Flense, Scourge, Skin, Strip, Uncase, Whip
Flea Aphaniptera, Chigger, Chigoe, Chigre, Daphnid, Hopper, Itch-mite, Lop, Pulex, Sand, Turnip, Water
Flea-bane Erigeron
Fleabite Denier
Fleck Dash, Freak, Spot, Streak
Fledgling Aerie, Eyas, Sorage
Flee(ing) Abscond, Bolt, Decamp, Escape, Eschew, Fly, Fugacity, Lam, Loup, Run, Scapa, Scarper, Scram
Fleece, Fleecy Bleed, Coat, Despoil, Flocculent, Golden, Jib, Lambskin, Lanose, Pash(i)m, Pashmina, Plot, Pluck, Rifte, Ring, Rob, Rook, Shave, Shear, Sheepskin, Skin, Skirtings, → **SWINDLE**, Toison
Fleer Ogle
Fleet(ing) Armada, Brief, Camilla, Convoy, Ephemeral, Evanescent, Fast, First, Flit, Flota, Flotilla, Fugacious, Fugitive, Hasty, Hollow, Lightfoot, Navy, Pacy, Passing, Prison, Spry, Street, Transient, Velocipede
Flesh(y) Beefy, Body, Carneous, Carrion, Corporeal, Corpulent, Creatic, Dead-meat, Digastric, Finish, Goose, Gum, Hypersarcoma, Joint, Jowl, Ket, Longpig, Lush, Meat, Mole, Mons, Mummy, Muscle, Mutton, Proud, Pulp, Quick, Sarcous, Spare tyre, Tissue
Flesh-eating Cannibalism, Carnassial, Creophagus, Omophagic
Fleshless Dry, Maigre, Pem(m)ican
Flex(ible), Flexibility Adaptable, Bend(y), Compliant, Double-jointed, Elastic, Genu, Limber, Lissom(e), Lithe, Pliant, → **RESILIENT**, Rubato, Rubbery, Squeezy, Supple, Tensile, Tonus, Wieldy, Willing, Wiry
▷ **Flexible, Flexuous** *may indicate* an anagram
Flick(er), Flicks Bioscope, Cinema, Fillip, Film, Flip, Flirt, Flutter, Glimmer, Gutter, Movie, Movy, Snap, Snow, Spang-cockle, Switch, Talkie, Twinkle, Waver, Wink, Zap

Flickertail ND
Flier Aerostat, Airman, Alcock, Amy, Aviator, → **BIRD**, Bleriot, Blimp, Brown, Crow, Daedalus, Erk, Fur, George, Gotha, Handout, Icarus, Leaflet, Lindbergh, Montgolfier, Pilot, RAF, Scotsman, Spec, Speedy
Flight(y) Backfisch, Birdbrain, Bolt, Bubble-headed, Capricious, Charter, Contact, Dart, Departure, Escalier, Escape, Exaltation, Exodus, Fast, Fickle, Flaught, Flibbertigibbet, Flip, Flock, Flyby, Fly-past, Free, Fugue, Giddy, Grece, Grese, Gris(e), Guy, Hegira, Hejira, Hejra, Hellicat, Hijra, Lam, Loup-the-dyke, Mercy, Milk-run, Mission, Open-jaw, Pair, R(a)iser, Redeye, Ro(a)ding, Rode, Rout, Skein, Sortie, Stairs, → **STAMPEDE**, Stayre, Steps, Swarm, Test, Top, Tower, Trap, Vol(age), Volatile, Volley, Whisky-frisky, Wing
Flightless Kakapo, Nandoo, Ostrich, Rhea, Struthious
▷ **Flighty** *may indicate* an anagram
Flimsy Finespun, Gimcrack, Gossamer, Jimcrack, Lacy, Sleazy, Sleezy, Tenuous, Thin, Weak, Wispy
Flinch Blench, Cringe, Funk, Quail, Recoil, Shrink, Shudder, Start, Wince
Fling Dance, Flounce, Highland, Hurl, Lance, Pitch, Shy, Slat, Slug, Slump, Spanghew, Spree, Throw, → **TOSS**
Flint Chert, Firestone, Granite, Hag-stone, Hornstone, Microlith, Mischmetal, Optical, Pirate, Rock, Silex, Silica, Stone, Touchstone
Flip(pant), Flipping Airy, Bally, Brash, Cocky, Flick, Frivolous, Impudent, Jerk, Nog, Pert, Purl, Sassy, Saucy, Toss, Turn
Flipper(s) Fin-toed, Paddle, Pinniped(e)
Flirt(ation), Flirting, Flirtatious Bill, Buaya, Carve, Chippy, Cockteaser, Come-hither, Come-on, Coquet(te), Dalliance, Demivierge, Footsie, Gallivant, Heart-breaker, Lumber, Mash, Minx, Neck, Philander(er), Prick-teaser, Rig, Toy, Trifle, Vamp, Wow
Flit Dart, Decamp, Flicker, Flutter, Moonlight, Scoot
Float(er), Floating, Flotation Balsa, Bob, Bubble, Buoy, Caisson, Camel, Carley, Clanger, Drift, Fleet, Flotsam, Flutterboard, Froth, Fucus, Jetsam, Jetson, Levitate, Lifebuoy, Milk, Natant, Neuston, Oropesa, Outrigger, Paddle, Planula, Pontoon, Pram, Quill, Raft, Ride, Sail, Skim, Sponson, Stick, Trimmer, Vacillate, Waft, Waggler, Waterwings
Floating garden Chinampa
Flock(s) Assemble, Bevy, Charm, Chirm, Company, Congregation, Dopping, Drove, Flight, Fold, Forgather, Gaggle, Gather, Gregatim, Herd, Mob, Rally, Sedge, Sord, Spring, Trip, Troop, Tuft, Vulgar, Wing, Wisp, Wool
Flog(ger), Flogging Beat, Birch, Breech, Cane, Cat, Exert, Flay, Hawk, Hide, Knout, Lace, Lambast, Larrup, Lash, Lather, Lick, Orbilius, Rope's end, Scourge, Sell, Strap, Tat, → **THRASH**, Thwack, Tout, Vapulate, Welt, Whip
Flood(ed) Awash, Bore, Cataclysm, Deluge, Deucalion's, Diffuse, Diluvium, Drown, Dump, Eger, Flash, Freshet, Gush, Inundate, Irrigate, Noachic, Overflow, Overswell, Overwhelm, Pour, Rage, Smurf, Spate, Speat, Suffuse, Swamp, Tide, → **TORRENT**, Undam, Washland
Floodgate St(a)unch
Floodlight Ashcan, Blond(e), One-key
Floor(ing) Area, Astound, Baffle, Barbecue, Beat, Benthos, Chess, Deck, Dev(v)el, Down, Entresol, Étage, Fell, Flags(tone), Flatten, Flight, Gravel, Ground, Kayo, KO, Mezzanine, Mould loft, Paralimnion, Parquet, Pelvic, Piano nobile, Pit, Planch, Platform, Puncheon, Screed, Shop, Stage, Story, Stump, Terrazzo, Tessella, Tessera, Thill, Trading, Woodblock

Flop Belly-landing, Bomb, Collapse, Dud, Failure, Fizzer, Fosbury, Lollop, Mare's-nest, Misgo, Phut, Plump, Purler, Washout, Whap, Whitewash

Flora Benthos, Biota, Cybele, Flowers, Intestinal

Florence, Florentine Tuscan

Florid Coloratura, Cultism, Flamboyant, Fresh, Gongorism, High, Red, Rococo, Rubicund, Ruddy, Taffeta

Florida Fa

Floss(y) Dental, Flashy, Florence, Ornate, Silk

▶ **Flotation** *see* FLOAT

Flotilla Armada, Escadrille

Flotsam Detritus, Driftwood, Flotage, Waift, Waveson, Weft

Flounce Falbala, Frill, Furbelow, Huff, Prance, Ruffle, Sashay, Toss

Flounder Blunder, Fluke, Reel, Slosh, Struggle, Stumble, Tolter, Toss, Wallow

Flour Cassava, Couscous(ou), Cribble, Crible, Farina, Graham, Gram, Kouskous, Meal, Middlings, Pinole, Plain, Powder, Red-dog, Rice, Rock, Rye, Self-raising, Soy(a), Strong, Wheatmeal, White, Wholegrain, Wholemeal, Wholewheat, Wood

Flourish(ed), Flourishing Blague, Bless, Bloom, Blossom, Boast, Brandish, Bravura, Burgeon, Cadenza, Epiphonema, Fanfare, Fiorita, Fl, Flare, Floreat, Florescent, Grow, Kicking, Lick, Melisma, Mort, Omar, Palmy, Paraph, Prosper, Rubric, Scroll, Swash, Tantara, Thrive, Tucket, Veronica, Vigorous, Wampish, Wave, Welfare

Flout Disdain, Disobey, Insult, Malign, Mock, Profane, Scorn, Scout

Flow(ing) Abound, Afflux, Cantabile, Cash, Current, Cursive, Cusec, Data, Distil, Ebb, Emanate, Estrang(h)elo, Fleet, Fluent, Fluid, Flush, Flux, Freeform, Gene, Gush, Knickpoint, Lahar, Laminar, Liquid, Loose-bodied, Nappe, Nickpoint, Obsequent, Onrush, Ooze, Popple, Pour, Purl, Rail(e), Rayle, Rill, Rin, Run, Scapa, Seamless, Seep, Seton, Setter, Slip, Slur, Spate, Spurt, Stream, Streamline, Teem, Tidal, Torrent, Trickle, Turbulent, Viscous

Flower (part), Flowering, Flowers, Flower bed Best, Bloom, Bloosme, Blossom, Cream, Develop, Efflorescence, Elite, Fiori, Inflorescence, Parterre, Passion, Plant, Pre-vernal, Prime, Quatrefeuille, Quatrefoil, Remontant, → RIVER, Rogation, Serotine, Spray, Square, Stalked, Stream, Trumpet, Verdoy, Vernal, Wreath

---

FLOWERS

4 letters:	*5 letters:*	Toran	Madder
Arum	Agave	Tulip	Maguey
Cyme	Aster	Umbel	Mimosa
Disa	Brook	Yulan	Nuphar
Flag	Bugle		Onagra
Gold	Camas	*6 letters:*	Orchid
Gool	Daisy	Adonis	Oxslip
Gule	Enemy	Arabis	Paeony
Irid	Hosta	Camash	Pompom
Iris	Oxlip	Camass	Pompon
Knot	Padma	Corymb	Protea
Lily	Pansy	Cosmos	Scilla
Pink	Phlox	Crants	Sesame
Rose	Poppy	Dahlia	Silene
Wald	Spink	Gollan	Smilax
Weld	Tansy	Henbit	Spadix

Tassel
Torana
Wasabi
Yarrow

7 letters:
Aconite
Alyssum
Amarant
Anemone
Astilbe
Bugloss
Campion
Cowslip
Freesia
Fumaria
Gentian
Gilt-cup
Glacier
Gladdon
Godetia
Golland
Gowland
Ipomoea
Kikumon
Lobelia
Melilot
Mimulus
Nosegay
Petunia
Picotee
Primula
Quamash

Rampion
Sulphur
Verbena

8 letters:
Abutilon
Amaranth
Argemone
Asphodel
Bindi-eye
Bluebell
Carolina
Clematis
Cyclamen
Daffodil
Floscule
Foxglove
Gardenia
Geranium
Gillyvor
Gladioli
Glory-pea
Hepatica
Hesperis
Hibiscus
Kok-sagyz
Larkspur
Leucojum
Magnolia
Marigold
Myosotis
Oleander
Primrose

Scabious
Stapelia
Trollius
Tuberose
Turnsole
Valerian

9 letters:
Bald-money
Belamoure
Buttercup
Cineraria
Columbine
Edelweiss
Eglantine
Galingale
Gessamine
Hellebore
Hydrangea
Jessamine
Melampode
Pimpernel
Pyrethrum
Rudbeckia
Santonica
Saxifrage
Speedwell
Strobilus

10 letters:
Bellamoure
Buttonhole
Coronation

Granadilla
Heliotrope
Immortelle
Nasturtium
Pentstemon
Poached egg
Poinsettia
Polyanthus
Pulsatilla
Snapdragon
Stavesacre
Tibouchine
Touch-me-not

11 letters:
Boutonniere
Bur-marigold
Gillyflower
Loose-strife
Meadow-sweet
Saintpaulia

12 letters:
Hortus siccus
None-so-pretty
Pheasant's eye
Tradescantia

13 letters:
Flannelflower

▷ **Flower** *may indicate* a river
Flower arrangement, Flower work Barbola, Ikebana, Lei
Flowery Anthea, Anthemia, Damassin, Orchideous, → **ORNATE**, Pseudocarp,
  Verbose
▶ **Flu** *see* **INFLUENZA**
Fluctuate(r), Fluctuation Ambivalence, Balance, Seiche, Trimmer, Unsteady,
  Vacillate, Vary, Waver
Flue Chimney, Duct, Funnel, Pipe, Recuperator, Tewel, Uptake, Vent
Fluent(ly) Eloquent, Facile, Flowing, Glib, Liquid, Oracy, Verbose, Voluble
Fluff(y) Bungle, Dowl(e), Down, Dust, Dust bunny, Feathery, Flocculent, Floss, Flue,
  Fug, Fuzz, Girl, Lint, Mess-up, Muff, Noil, Oose, Ooze, Thistledown
Fluid Aldehyde, Amniotic, Anasarca, Ascites, Broo, Chyle, Cisterna, Colostrum,
  Condy's, Coolant, Dewdrop, Edema, Enema, Erf, Fixative, Fl, Humour, Joint-oil,
  Juice, Latex, → **LIQUID**, Lymph, Movable, Mucus, Oedema, Perfect, Perilymph,
  Plasma, Sap, Seminal, Serous, Serum, Shifting, Spermatic, Spittle, Succus, Synovia,
  Vitreum, Vril, Water
▷ **Fluid** *may indicate* an anagram

Fluke Accident, Anchor, Chance, Fan, Flounder, Ga(u)nch, Grapnel, Killock, Liver, Lobe, Redia, Schistosome, Scratch, Upcast

Flummery BS, Pudding

Flummox Baffle, Bamboozle, Floor, Nonplus

Flunk Fail

Flunkey Chasseur, Clawback, Haiduck, Heyduck, Jeames, Lackey, Servant, Toady

Fluorescence, Fluorescent Bloom, Day-glo, Epipolism, Glow, Phosphorescence

Fluorine F

Flurry Bustle, Fluster, Haste, Hoo-ha, Shower

Flush(ed) Affluent, Beat, Busted, Even, Ferret, Florid, Flow, Gild, Hectic, Heyday, Hot, Level, Red, Rolling, Rose, Royal, Rud, Scour, Sluice, Spaniel, Start, Straight, Sypher, Thrill, Tierce, Vigour, Wash

Fluster(ed) Befuddle, Confuse, Disconcert, Faze, Flap, Jittery, Pother, Pudder, Rattle, Shake

Flute (player) Bellows-maker, Bohm, Channel, Claribel(la), Crimp, English, Fife, Fipple, Flageolet, German, Glass, Glyph, Groove, Marsyas, Nose, Ocarina, Piccolo, Pipe, Poogye(e), Quena, Shakuhachi, Sulcus, Thisbe, Tibia, Toot, Transverse, Whistle

Flutter Bat, Bet, Fan, Fibrillate, Flacker, Flaffer, Flaught, Flichter, Flicker, Flitter, Fly, → **GAMBLE**, Hover, Palpitate, Play, Pulse, Sensation, Twitter, Waft, Winnow

Flux D, Electric, Flow, Fusion, Luminous, Magnetic, Maxwell, Melt, Neutron, Panta rhei, Radiant, Tesla, Weber

Fly(ing), Flies Abscond, Agaric, Airborne, Alder, Alert, Antlion, Assassin, Astute, Aviation, Awake, Aware, A-wing, Baker, Bedstead, Bee, Black, Blister, Blowfly, Blue-arsed, Bluebottle, Bolt, Bot, Breese, Breeze, Brize, Brommer, Bulb, Bush, Cab, Caddis, Canny, Carriage, Carrot, Cecidomyia, Chalcid, Cheesehopper, Cheese skipper, Cleg, Cluster, Cock-a-bondy, Crane, Cuckoo, → **CUNNING**, Decamp, Deer, Diptera, Dobson, Doctor, Dolphin, Doodlebug, Dragon, Drake, Drone, Drosophila, Dry, Dung, Dutchman, Escape, Face, Fiacre, Flee, Flesh, Flit, Fox, Frit, Fruit, Glide, Glossina, Gnat, Grannom, Greenbottle, Greenhead, Hackle, Hairy Mary, Harl, Harvest, Hedge-hop, Herl, Hessian, Homoptera, Hop, Horn, Horse, Hover, Hurtle, Ichneumon, Instrument, Jenny-spinner, Jock Scott, Lace-wing, Lamp, Lantern, Laputan, March brown, Mosquito, Mossie, Moth, Motuca, Murragh, Musca, Mutuca, Namu, Needle, New Forest, Nymph, Onion, Opening, Ox-warble, Palmer, Para, Pilot, Pium, Plecopteran, Pomace, Rapid, Robber, Saucer, Sciaridae, Scorpion, Scotsman, Screwworm, Scud, Sedge, Silverhorn, Simulium, Smart, Smother, Snake, Snipe, Soar, Spanish, Speed, Spinner, Stable, Stream, Syrphidae, Tabanid, Tachina, Tail, Tear, Thrips, Tipula, Trichopteran, Tsetse, Tube, Turkey brown, Vamoose, Vinegar, Volatic, Volitate, Warble, Watchet, Water, Welshman's button, Wet, Wheat, Wide-awake, Willow, Wily, Wing, Yellow Sally, Yogic, Zebub, Zimb, Zipper

Fly-catcher Attercop, Clamatorial, Cobweb, Darlingtonia, Dionaea, King-bird, Phoebe, Spider, Tanrec, Tyrant

Flying-fox Fruit-bat, Kalong

Flying saucer UFO

Fly-killer Chowri, Chowry, DDT, Swat

Flyover Overpass

Foam(ing) Aerogel, Barm, Bubble, Froth, Lather, Mousse, Oasis®, Polystyrene, Ream, Scum, Seethe, Spindrift, Spooming, Spume, Sud(s), Surf, Wake, Wild water, Yeast, Yest

Fob Chain, Defer, Fub, Pocket, Slang

Focal, Focus Centre, Centrepiece, Converge, Fix, Hinge, Hub, Narrow, Nub, Pinpoint, Point, Prime, Principal, Spotlight, Train

Fodder Alfalfa, Browsing, Buckwheat, Cannon, Clover, Eatage, Emmer, Ensilage, Foon, Forage, Gama-grass, Grama, Guar, Hay, Lucerne, Oats, Oilcake, Pasture, Provender, Rye-grass, Sainfoin, Silage, Soilage, Stover, Straw

Foe Arch, Contender, → ENEMY, Opponent, Rival

Foetus Embryo

Fog Aerosol, Brume, Cloud, Damp, Fret, Haar, (London) Particular, Miasm(a), Mist, Murk, Obscure, Pea-soup(er), Roke, Sea-fret, Sea-haar, Smog, Smoke, Soup, Thick, Vapour, Yorkshire

Fogey Die-hard

Fogg Phileas, Solicitor

Foible Failing, Flaw, Idiosyncrasy, Quirk, Weakness

Foil(ed) Ba(u)lk, Chaff, Cross, Dupe, Epée, Fleurette, Frustrate, Gold, Gold leaf, Lametta, Leaf, Offset, Paillon, Pip, Scotch, Scupper, Silver, Stooge, Stump, Tain, Thwart, Touché

Foist Fob, Insert, Insinuate, Suborn, Wish

Fold(er), Folding, Folded, Folds Anticline, Bend, Binder, Close, Collapse, Concertina, Convolution, Corrugate, Cote, Crash, Crease, Crimp, Crinkle, Crunkle, Diapir, Diptych, Dog-ear, Double, Duo-tang®, Epicanthus, Epiploon, Fake, Fan, File, Fourchette, Fr(a)enum, Frill, Furl, Gather, Groin, Gyrus, Intussuscept, Jack-knife, Lap, Lapel, Lap(p)et, Lirk, Mesentery, Mitre, Monocline, Nappe, Nympha, Obvolute, Octuple, Omentum, Origami, Pastigium, Pen, Pericline, Pintuck, Pleach, → PLEAT, Plica, Plunging, Ply, Prancke, Pran(c)k, Ptyxis, Recumbent, Ruck(le), Ruga, Sheep-pen, Syncline, Triptych, Tuck, Vocal, Wrap

Foliage Coma, Finial, Frond, Frondescence, Greenery, Leafage, Leaves

Folio(s) Crown, Elephant, F(f), File, Foolscap, Imperial, Percy, Royal

Folk(sy) Beaker, Homespun, Kin, People, Public

Follicle Graafian

Follow(er), Following Acolyte, Acolyth, Adhere, Admirer, After, Agree, Amoret, And, Anthony, Attend(ant), Believer, Clientele, Consequence, Copy, Dangle, Disciple, Dog, Echo, Ensew, Ensue, Entourage, Epigon(e), Equipage, F, Fan, Groupie, Heel(er), Henchman, Hereon, Hunt, Jacob, Man, Merry men, Minion, Muggletonian, Myrmidon, Neist, Next, Obey, Pan, Post, Pursue, Rake, Road, Run, Satellite, School, Secundum, Seewing, Segue, Sequel, Seriation, Servitor, Shadow, Sheep, S(h)ivaite, Sidekick, Stag, Stalk, Stear, Steer, Subsequent, Succeed, Sue, Suivez, Supervene, Tag, Tail, Tantony, Trace, Track, Trail, Train, Use, Vocation, Votary

▷ **Follower** 'a follower' *may indicate* B

Folly Antic, Bêtise, Idiocy, Idiotcy, Imprudence, Lunacy, Mistake, Moria, Unwisdom, Vanity

Foment(ation) Arouse, Brew, Embrocation, Excite, Poultice, Stupe

Fond(ness) Amatory, Ardour, Dote, Keen, Loving, Partial, Penchant, Tender, Tendre

Fondant Ice, Sweet

Fondle Canoodle, Caress, Dandle, Grope, Hug, Nurse, Pet, Snuggle

Font Aspersorium, Bénitier, Bitmap, Delubrum, Ennage, Outline, Proportional, Source, True-type, Vector

Food Aliment, Ambrosia, Bakemeat, Balti, Batten, Battill, Battle, Bellytimber, Board, Bolus, Bord, Broth, Browse, Bully, Burger, Cate, Cereal, Chametz, Cheer, Cheese, Chop, Chow, Chuck, Chyme, Cocoyam, Collation, Comestible, Comfort, Commons, Convenience, Course, Curd, Deutoplasm, Dietetics, → DISH, Dodger, Dog's body,

Dunderfunk, Eats, Esculents, Eutrophy, Falafel, Fare, Fast, Fast casual, Felafel, Fodder, Forage, Frankenstein, Freedom, Fuel, Functional, Giffengood, Grub, Hangi, Hometz, Incaparina, Ingesta, Jootha, Jorts, Junk, Kai, Keep, Langar, Leben, Lerp, Long-pig, Maigre, Maki, Manna, Mato(o)ke, Matzoon, Meal, Meat, Muckamuck, Nacho, Nardoo, Nosebag, Nosh, Nourishment, Nourriture, Opsonium, Ort, Oven-ready, Pabulum, Pannage, Pap, Parev(e), Parve, Pasta, Pasture, Peck, Pemmican, Pizza, Prog, Provand, Provender, Provision, Pu(l)ture, Ration(s), Real, Rysttafel, Sambal, Samosa, Sap, Sashimi, Scaff, Scoff, Scran, Sitology, Sizings, Skin, Skran, Slow, Snack, Soil, Soul, Staple, Stodge, Sushi, Table, Tack, Takeaway, Tamale, Taro, Tempeh, Tempura, Teriyake, Tofu, Trimmings, Trophallaxis, Tuck(er), Vegeburger, Veggie-burger, Viand, Victuals, Vivers, Waffle, Yantia, Yittles, Yog(h)urt

Food-plant Laser, Silphium

Foodstore Delicatessen, Grocery, Larder, Pantry, Silo

Fool(hardy), Foolish(ness) Air-head, Anserine, April, Asinico, Assot, Berk, BF, Bob, Booby, Brainless, Brash, Buffoon, Cake, Capocchia, Chump, Clot, Clown, Cockeyed, Coof, Coxcomb, Cuif, Cully, Daft, Dagonet, Daw, Delude, Dessert, Divvy, Doat, Dote, Dummy, Dunce, Empty, Etourdi, Fatuous, Feste, Flannel(led), Folly, Fon, Fond, Fox, Gaby, Gaga, Galah, Git, Glaikit, Goat, Gobbo, Goon, Goose, Gooseberry, Groserts, Gubbins, Gull, Gullible, Halfwit, Hanky-panky, Hare-brained, Haverel, Highland, Huntiegowk, Hunt-the-gowk, Idiotic, Imbecile, Inane, Ineptitude, Injudicious, Jest, Joke, Kid, Kissel, Lark, Loon, Madcap, Mamba, Misguide, Mislead, Mome, Moron, Muggins, Niaiserie, Nignog, Ni(n)compoop, Ninny, Nong, Noodle, Nose-led, Oanshagh, Omadhaun, Patch, Pea-brained, Poop, Poupe, Punk, Rash, Sawney, Scogan, Scoggin, Senseless, Shallow, Shmo, Simpleton, Snipe, Soft, Sot, Spoony, Stultify, → **STUPID**, Sucker, Tom (noddy), Trifle, Unwitty, Vice, Wantwit, Yorick, Yoyo, Zany

Foolproof Fail-safe

Foot(ing), Footwork, Feet Amphibrach, Amphimacer, Anap(a)est, Antibacchius, Antispast, Athlete's, Bacchius, Ball, Base, Board, Choliamb, Choree, Choriamb, Club, Cold, Cretic, Dactyl, Dance, Dipody, Dochmii, Dochmius, Epitrite, F, Hephthemimer, Hoof, Hoppus, Iamb(us), Immersion, Infantry, Ionic, Molossus, Ockodols, Pad, Paeon, Palama, Pastern, Paw, Pay, Pedate, Pedicure, Penthemimer, Pes, Plates, Podiatry, Podium, Proceleusmatic, Pyrrhic, Roothold, Scazon, Semeia, Serif, Shanks's mare, Shanks's pony, Spade, Splay, Spondee, Standing, Syzygy, Tarsus, Terms, Tootsie, Tootsy, Tootsy-wootsy, Tread, Trench, Tribrach, Trilbies, Triseme, Trochee, Trotter, Tube, Ungula, Verse, Wrong

Football(er) Aerial pingpong, American, Association, Australian Rules, Back, Banyana-banyana, Barbarian, Ba'spiel, Camp, Canadian, Centre, Fantasy, FIFA, Five-a-side, Flanker(back), Fly-half, Futsal, Gaelic, Goalie, Gridder, Half, Hooker, Keeper, Kicker, League, Libero, Lineman, Lock, Midfield, Pack, Pele, Pigskin, RU, Rugby, Rugger, Rules, Safety, Seven-a-side, Sevens, Soccer(oos), Sport, Stand-off, Striker, Subbuteo®, Sweeper, Table, Tight-end, Togger, Total, Touch(back), Wallgame, Wing, Wingman

Footboard Stretcher

Foot-fault Bunion, Corn, Hammer-toe, Verruca

Foothold Lodgement, Purchase, Stirrup

Footlights Floats

Footling Trivial

Footloose Peripatetic

Footman Attendant, Flunkey, Lackey, Pedestrian, Pompey, Yellowplush

Footnote Addendum, PS

Footpad Land-rat, Mugger, Robber

Footpath, Footway Banquette, Catwalk, Clapper, Track

Footplate Horseshoe

Footprint Ecological, Electronic, Ichnite, Ichnolite, Pad, Prick, Pug, Seal, Slot, Trace, Track, Tread, Vestige

Footrest, Footstool Coaster, Cricket, Hassock, Pouffe, Stirrup, Stool, Tramp

Footrot, Footsore Blister, Bunion, Corn, Halt, Surbate, Surbet, Weary, Wire-heel

Footslogger Infantryman

Footwashing Maundy, Nipter

Footwear Gumboot, Jackboot, → **SHOE**, Slipper, Sock, Spats, Stocking

Fop(pish) Apery, Barbermonger, Beau, Buck, Cat, Coxcomb, Dandy, Dude, Exquisite, Fallal, Fangled, Fantastico, Finical, La-di-da, Macaroni, Monarcho, Muscadin, Popinjay, Skipjack, Toff

For Ayes, Because, Concerning, Cos, Pro, Since, To

Forage Alfalfa, Fodder, Graze, Greenfeed, Ladino, Lucern(e), Pickeer, Prog, Raid, Rummage, Sainfoin, Search

Foray Attack, Creach, Creagh, Raid, Sortie, Spreagh

Forbear(ance), Forbearing Abstain, Clement, Endure, Indulgent, Lenience, Lineage, Longanimity, Mercy, Overgo, Pardon, Parent, Patient, Quarter, → **REFRAIN**, Suffer, Tolerant, Withhold

Forbid(den), Forbidding Ban, Bar, City, Denied, Don't, Dour, Enjoin, For(e)speak, Gaunt, Grim, Haram, Hostile, Loury, NL, Prohibit, Stern, Taboo, Tabu, Tapu, Tref(a), Verboten, Veto

Force(d), Forceful, Forces, Forcible Activist, Agency, Air-arm, Army, Back emf, Bathmism, Bind, Birr, Bludgeon, Body, Bounce, Brigade, Bring, Brunt, Bulldoze, Cadre, Capillary, Cascade, Centrifugal, Centripetal, Chi, Coerce, Coercive, Cogency, Commando, Compel, Constrain, Coriolis, Cram, Delta, Detachment, Dint, Domineer, Downflow, Dragoon, Drive, Duress(e), Dynamic, Dyne, E, Edge, Electromotive, Emphatic, Energetic, Equilibrant, Erdgeist, Erg, Exchange, Expeditionary, Extort, Extrude, F, Farci, Fifth, Fire brigade, Frogmarch, G, Gar, Gendarmerie, Gilbert, Gism, Gouge, Gravitational, Hale, Host, Hurricane, Impetus, Impose, Impress, Inertial, Instress, Intense, Irgun, Irrupt, Jism, Juggernaut, Kinetic, Kundalini, Labour, Land, Lashkar, Legion, Leverage, Life, Lift, Linn, Lorentz, Magnetomotive, Magnus, Make, Mana, Manpower, Market, Militia, Moment, Momentum, Muscle, Nature-god, Navy, Newton, Numen, Oblige, Od, Odyl(e), OGPU, Old Contemptibles, Orgone, Orotund, Personnel, Phrenism, Physical, Pigs, Pion, Pithy, Plastic, Police, Posse, Potent, Pound, Poundal, Prana, Press(gang), Pressure, Prise, Procrustean, Psyche, Psychic, Pull, Pushy, Put, Qi, Railroad, Rape, Ravish, Reave, Red Army, Regular, Require, Restem, Route, Rush, SAS, Sforzando, Shear, Snorting, Spent, Spetsnaz, Squad, Squirt, Steam(roller), Stick, Stiction, Strained, → **STRESS**, Strong-arm, Subject, Sword, TA, Task, Telergy, Telling, Territorial, The Bill, Thrust, Torque, Tractive, Troops, Van der Waals', Vehement, Vigorous, Vim, Violence, Vires, Vis, Vis visa, Vital, Vively, Vociferous, Vril, Weak, Wedge, Wrench, Wrest, Wring, Zap

▷ **Force(d)** *may indicate* an anagram

Forced labour Begar

Force-feeding Gavage

Forceps Bulldog, Capsule, Crow(s)bill, Hemostatic, Mosquito, Obstetrical, Pedicellaria, Pincers, Rongeur, Tenaculum, Thumb, Vulsella

Ford Anglia, Capri, Car, Crossing, Drift, Escort, Irish bridge, Sierra, Strid, Tin Lizzy, Wade

Forearm Cubital, Radius, Ulna

▸ **Forebear** *see* **FORBEAR**

Foreboding Anxiety, Augury, Cloudage, Croak, Feeling, Freet, Hoodoo, → **OMEN**, Ominous, Premonition, Presage, Presentiment, Sinister, Zoomantic

Forecast(er), Forecasting Augury, Auspice, Divine, Extrapolation, Horoscope, Long-range, Metcast, Metman, Numerical, Perm, Portend, Precurse, Predict, Presage, Prescience, Prevision, Prognosis, Prognosticate, Prophesy, Quant, Rainbird, Scry, Shipping, Skry, Soothsay, Spae, Tip, Weather

Foreclose Bar, Block, Obstruct, Preclude

Forefather(s) Ancestor, Elder, Forebear, Parent, Rude

Forefront Van, Vaward

Forehead Brow, Front(let), Frontal, Glabella(r), Sincipitum, Temple

Foreign(er) Alien, Amakwerekwere, Arab, Auslander, Barbarian, Easterling, Ecdemic, Eleanor, Ethnic, Étranger, Exclave, Exotic, External, Extraneous, Extrinsic, Forane, Forinsecal, Forren, Fraim, Fremit, Gaijin, German, Gringo, Gweilo, Malihini, Metic, Moit, Mote, Outlander, Outside, Oversea, Peregrine, Remote, → **STRANGE**, Stranger, Taipan, Tramontane, Uitlander, Unfamiliar, Wog

Foreknowledge Prescience

Foreman Baas, Boss, Bosun, Chancellor, Clicker, Gaffer, Ganger, Manager, Overseer, Steward, Superintendent, Tool pusher, Topsman, Walla(h)

Foremost First, Front, Leading, Primary, Prime, Supreme, Upfront, Van

▹ **Foremost** *may indicate* first letters of words following

Forenoon Undern

Forepart Cutwater, Front

Forerunner Augury, Harbinger, Herald, Messenger, Omen, Pioneer, Precursor, Prequel, Trailer, Vaunt-courier

Foresee Anticipate, Divine, Preview, Prophesy, Scry

Foreshadow Adumbrate, Augur, Bode, Forebode, Hint, Portend, Pre-echo, Prefigure, Presage, Type

Foreshow Betoken, Bode, Signify

Foresight Ganesa, Prescience, Prophecy, Prospect, Providence, Prudence, Taish, Vision

Foreskin Prepuce

Forest(ry) Arden, Ashdown, Black, Bohemian, Bracknell, Bush, Caatinga, Charnwood, Chase, Cloud, Dean, Elfin, Epping, Fontainebleau, Gallery, Gapo, Glade, Greenwood, Igapo, Jungle, Managed, Monte, Nandi, Nemoral, New, Petrified, Rain, Savernake, Selva, Sherwood, Silviculture, Taiga, Thuringian, Urman, Virgin, Waltham, → **WOOD**, Woodcraft

Forestall Anticipate, Head-off, Obviate, Pip, Pre-empt, Prevent, Queer, Scoop

Forester Foster, Lumberjack, Verderer, Walker, Woodman, Woodward

Foretaste Antepast, Antipasto, Appetiser, Pregustation, Prelibation, Preview, Sample, Trailer

Foretell(ing), Forewarn Augur, Bode, Caution, Divine, Fatidic, Forecast, Portend, Predict, Premonish, Presage, Previse, Prognosticate, Prophecy, Soothsay, Spae

Forethought Anticipation, Caution, Prometheus, Provision, Prudence

Forever Always, Amber, Ay(e), Eternal, Evermore, Keeps

▸ **Forewarn** *see* **FORETELL**

Foreword Introduction, Preamble, Preface, Proem, Prologue

For example Eg, Say, Vg, ZB

For fear Lest

Forfeit Deodand, Fine, Forgo, → **PENALTY**, Relinquish, Rue-bargain, Sconce

Forge(d), Forger(y) Blacksmith, Copy, Counterfeit, Drop, Dud, Fabricate, Fashion, Foundry, Hammer, Heater, Horseshoe, Ireland, Ironsmith, Lauder, Mint, Paper-hanger, Pigott, Progress, Rivet head, Rivet-hearth, Smith(y), Smithery, Spurious, Stiddie, Stiff, Stithy, Stumer, Tilt, Trucage, Truquage, Utter, Valley, Vermeer, Vulcan, Weld

Forget(ful), Forget-me-not Amnesia, Dry, Fluff, Lethe, Myosotis, Neglect, Oblivious, Omit, Overlook, Wipe

Forgive(ness), Forgiving Absolution, Amnesty, Clement, Condone, Divine, Lenity, Merciful, Overlook, Pardon, Placable, Remission, Remittal, Tolerant

Forgo(ne) Abstain, Expected, Refrain, Renounce, Waive

Forgotten Bygone, Lost, Missed, Sad

Forjeskit Overscutched

Fork(ed), Fork out Bifurcate, Biramous, Branch, Caudine, Cleft, Crotch, Crutch, Divaricate, Forficate, Fourchette, Grain, Graip, Morton's, Osmeterium, Pay, Prong, Replication, Runcible, Slave, Sucket, Tine, Toaster, Toasting, Tormenter, Tormentor, Trident, Trifid, Tuner, Tuning, Y

Forlorn(ness) Abject, Aidless, Desolate, Destitute, Drearisome, Miserable, Nightingale, Sad, Woebegone

▷ **Form** *may indicate* a hare's bed

Form(s) Alumni, Bench, Bumf, Cast, Ceremonial, Charterparty, Class, Clipped, Constitute, Coupon, Create, Document, Dress, Experience, Fashion, Feature, Fig, → **FIGURE**, Formula, Free, Game, Gestalt, Hare, Idea, Image, Inscape, Keto, Lexicalise, Life, Logical, Mode, Mood, Morph(ic), Morphology, Mould, Order, Originate, → **OUT OF FORM**, P45, Penitent, Physique, Protocol, Questionnaire, Redia, Remove, Rite, Ritual, Schedule, Shape, Shell, Sonata, Song, Stage, Stamp, State, Stem, Stereotype, Structure, Style, Symmetry, Talon, Ternary, Version

Formal Ceremonious, Conventional, Dry, Exact, Fit, Literal, Methodic, Official, Pedantic, Perfunctory, Precise, Prim, Routine, Set, Solemn, Starched, Stiff, Stodgy, Tails

Formality Amylum, Ceremony, Ice, Pedantry, Protocol, Punctilio, Starch

Formation Battalion, Brown, Configuration, Diapyesis, Echelon, Eocene, Fours, Growth, Line, Manufacture, Origin, Pattern, Phalanx, Prophase, Reaction, Riss, Serried, Wedge

▷ **Former** *may indicate* something that forms

Former(ly) Ance, Auld, Before, Ci-devant, Earlier, Ere-now, Erst(while), Ex, Late, Maker, Matrix, Old, Once, One-time, Past, Previous, Prior, Pristine, Quondam, Sometime, Then, Umquhile, Whilom, Yesterday

Formidable Alarming, Armipotent, Battleaxe, Fearful, Forbidding, Gorgon, Powerful, Redoubtable, Shrewd, Stoor, Stour, Stowre, Sture, Tiger

Formless Amorphous, Invertebrate, Nebulous, Shapeless

▷ **Form of, Forming** *may indicate* an anagram

Formosan Tai

Formula(te) Define, Devise, Doctrine, Empirical, Equation, Frame, Graphic, Incantation, Invent, Kekule, Lurry, Molecular, Paternoster, Prescription, Protocol, Prunes and prisms, → **RECIPE**, Reduction, Rite, Ritual, Stirling's, Structural

Forsake Abandon, Desert, Quit, Renounce

Forsooth Certes, Certy, Even, Marry, Quotha

For sure Pukka

Forswear Abandon, Abjure, Disavow, Renounce, Reny

Forsyte Fleur, Saga, Soames

Fort(ification), Fortress Acropolis, Alamo, Alhambra, Balclutha, Bastille, Bastion,

Battlement, Bawn, Blockhouse, Bonnet, Breastwork, Bridgehead, Burg, Casbah, Castellated, Castellum, Castle, Citadel, Contravallation, Counterscarp, Crémaillère, Demilune, Deva, Dun, Earthwork, Edinburgh, Enceinte, Epaule, Escarpment, Fastness, Fieldwork, Flanker, Flèche, Fortalice, Fortilage, Fortlet, Fraise, Ft, Gabion(ade), Garrison, Gatehouse, Golconda, Haven, Hedgehog, Hill, Hornwork, Kaim, Kame, Kasba(h), Keep, Knox, La(a)ger, Lauderdale, Louisbourg, Maiden, Malakoff, Martello tower, Masada, Merlon, Mile-castle, Moineau, Motte and bailey, Orillion, Pa(h), Peel, Pele, Pentagon, Place, Przernysl, Rampart, Rath, Ravelin, Redoubt, Reduit, Ring, Salient, Sallyport, Sangar, Sconce, Stavropol, Stronghold, Sumter, Talus, Tenaille, Terreplein, Tête-du-pont, Ticonderoga, Tower, Tower of London, Trench, Vallation, Vitrified, William, Worth

Forte F, Métier, Specialty, Strength

Forth Away, From, Hence, Out

Forthright(ness) Blunt, Candid, Direct, Four-square, Frank, Glasnost, Prompt

Forthwith Anon, Directly, Eft(soons), Immediately

Fortify Arm, Augment, Brace, Casemate, Embattle, Lace, Munify, Soup up, Steel, → STRENGTHEN

Fortitude Endurance, Grit, Mettle, Patience, Pluck, → STAMINA

Fortune, Fortunate, Fortuitous Auspicious, Blessed, Blest, Coincident, Godsend, Happy, → LUCKY, Madoc, Opportune, Providential, Well

Fortune teller, Fortune-telling Auspicious, Bonanza, Bumby, Cartomancy, Chaldee, Cha(u)nce, Destiny, Dukkeripen, Fame, Fate, Felicity, Genethliac, Geomancy, Hap, Hydromancy, I Ching, Lot, Luck, Mint, Motser, Motza, Oracle, Packet, Palmist, Peripety, Pile, Prescience, Pyromancy, Sibyl, Soothsayer, Sortilege, Spaewife, Success, Taroc, Tarok, Tarot, Tyche, Wealth, Windfall

Forty, Forties Capot, F, Hungry, Kemple, Roaring

Forty-ninth Parallel

Forum Arena, Assembly, Debate, Platform, Tribunal

Forward(s) Accede, Advanced, Ahead, Along, Anterior, Arch, Assertive, Assuming, Bright, Early, Flanker, Forrad, Forrit, Forth, Fresh, Future, Hasten, Hooker, Immodest, Impudent, Insolent, Lock, Malapert, On(wards), Pack, Pert, Petulant, Porrect, Precocious, → PROGRESS, Promote, Prop, Readdress, Redirect, Scrum, Send, Stem, To(ward), Van, Wing

Fossil(ised), Fossils Amber, Ammonite, Baculite, Belemnite, Blastoid(ea), Calamite, Ceratodus, Chondrite, Conodont, Corallian, Cordaites, Creodont, Crinite, Derived, Encrinite, Eohippus, Eozoon, Eurypterus, Exuviae, Fairy stone, Florula, Florule, Fogy, Goniatite, Graptolite, Hipparion, Hominid, Ichnite, Ichnolite, Ichnology, Ichthyodurolite, Ichthyolite, Index, Jew's stone, Kenyapithecus, Lepidostrobus, Lingulella, Living, Mosasauros, Nummulite, Odontolite, Olenus, Oligocene, Orthoceras, Osteolepis, Ostracoderm, Oxfordian, Pal(a)eo-, Pentacrinus, Petrifaction, Phytolite, Plesiosaur, Pliohippus, Pliosaur, Psilophyton, Pteridosperm, Pterodactyl(e), Pterygotus, Pythonomorph, Relics, Reliquiae, Remanié, Reworked, Sigillaria, Sinanthropus, Sivatherium, Snakestone, Stigmaria, Stromatolite, Taphonomy, Teleosaurus, Tentaculite, Titanotherium, Trace, Trilobite, Uintatherium, Wood-opal, Zinganthropus, Zone, Zoolite

Foster (child, mother), Fostering Adopt, Cherish, Da(u)lt, Develop, Farm out, Feed, Fornent, Further, Harbour, Incubation, Metapelet, Metaplot, Nourish, Nourse(l), Noursle, Nousell, Nurse, Nurture, Nuzzle, → REAR

Foul, Foul-smelling Base, Beray, Besmirch, Besmutch, Bewray, Bungle, → DEFILE, Dreggy, Drevill, Enseam, Evil, Feculent, Funky, Gross, Hassle, Hing, Mephitic, Mud, Noisome, Olid, Osmeterium, Paw(paw), Professional, Putid, Putrid, → RANK,

Reekie, Rotten, Sewage, Soiled, Squalid, Stagnant, Stain, Stapelia, Technical, Unclean, Unfair, Vile, Violation, Virose

▷ **Foul** *may indicate* an anagram

Found (in) Among, Base, Bed, Bottom, Build, Cast, Caught, Emong, Endow, → **ESTABLISH**, Eureka, Institute, Introduce, Met, Occur, Plant, Recovered, Rest, Start, Table

Foundation(s) Base, Bedrock, Corset, Cribwork, Establishment, Footing, Girdle, Grillage, Ground, Groundwork, Hard-core, Hypostasis, Infrastructure, Institution, Matrix, Panty girdle, Pile, Pitching, Roadbed, Rockefeller, Root, Scholarship, Stays, Stereobate, Subjacent, Substrata, Substructure, Trackbed, Underlie, Underlinen

▷ **Foundations** *may indicate* last letters

Founder Author, Bell, Collapse, Crumple, Fail, Inventor, Iron-master, Miscarry, Oecist, Oekist, Patriarch, Perish, Settle, Sink, Steelman, Stumble

Fount Aonian, Digital, Source, Springlet, Wrong

Fountain Acadine, Aganippe, Arethusa, Bubbler, Castalian, Cause, Conduit, Drinking, Fauwara, Forts, Gerbe, Head, Hippocrene, Jet, Pant, Pirene, Salmacis, Scuttlebutt, Soda, Spring, Trevi, Well-spring, Youth

Fountain basin Laver

Four(times), Foursome, Four-yearly Cater, Georges, Horsemen, IV, Mess, Penteteric, Qid, Quartet, Quaternary, Quaternion, Reel, Tessara, Tessera, Tetrad, Tetralogy, Tiddy, Warp

Fourpence Groat

Fourteenth Bastille, Trecento, Valentine

Fourth Deltaic, Estate, Fardel, Farl(e), Firlot, Forpet, Forpit, July, Martlet, Perfect, Quarter, Quartet, Quaternary, Quintan, Sesquitertia, Tritone

Fowl Barnyard, Biddy, Boiler, Brahma, Brissle-cock, Burrow-duck, Capon, Chicken, Chittagong, Cob, Cock, Coot, Domestic, Dorking, Duck, Ember, Gallinaceous, Gallinule, Game, Gleenie, Guinea, Hamburg(h), Heather-bleat(er), → **HEN**, Houdan, Jungle, Kora, Leghorn, Mallee, Moorhen, Orpington, Papageno, Partridge, Pheasant, Pintado, Plymouth Rock, Poultry, Quail, Rooster, Rumkin, Rumpy, Scrub, Solan, Spanish, Spatchcock, Spitchcock, Sultan, Sussex, Teal, Turkey, Wyandotte

Fox(y) Alopecoid, Arctic, Baffle, Blue, Charley, Charlie, Corsac, Cunning, Desert, Fennec, Floor, Flying, Fool, Friend, Fur, Grey, Kit, Lowrie(-tod), Outwit, Pug, Puzzle, Quaker, Red, Reynard, Rommel, Russel, Silver, Skulk, → **SLY**, Swift, Tod, Uffa, Uneatable, Vixen, White, Zerda, Zoril(le), Zorro

Foxglove Cowflop, Deadmen's bells, Digitalis, Witches'-thimble

Foxhole Earth

Foyer Hall, Lobby

Fracas Brawl, Dispute, Mêlée, Prawle, Riot, Rumpus, Scrum, Shindig, Uproar

Fraction Common, Complex, Compound, Continued, Decimal, Improper, Ligroin, Mantissa, Mixed, Packing, Part, Partial, Piece, Proper, Scrap, Simple, Some, Vulgar

Fracture Break, Colles, Comminuted, Complicated, Compound, Crack, Fatigue, Fault, Fissure, Greenstick, Hairline, Impacted, Pathological, Platy, Pott's, Rupture, Shear, Simple, Split, Stress

Fragile Brittle, Crisp, Delicate, Frail, Frangible, Nesh, Slender, Tender, Vulnerable, Weak

Fragment(s) Atom, Bit, Bla(u)d, Brash, Breccia, Brockram, Cantlet, Clastic, Crumb, End, Flinder, Fritter, Frust, Graile, Lapilli, Mammock, Mite, Morceau, Morsel, Ort, → **PARTICLE**, Piece, Piecemeal, Potshard, Potsherd, Relic, Restriction, Rubble, Scrap, Segment, Shard, Shatter, Sheave, Shiver, Shrapnel, Shred, Skerrick, Sliver,

Smithereens, Smithers, Snatch, Splinter

▷ **Fragment of** *may indicate* a hidden word

Fragrance, Fragrant Aromatic, Attar, Bouquet, Conima, Nosy, Odour, Olent, → **PERFUME**, Pot-pourri, Redolent, → **SCENT**, Sent, Spicy, Suaveolent

Frail Brittle, Creaky, Delicate, Feeble, Flimsy, → **FRAGILE**, Puny, Slight, Slimsy, Tottery, Weak

Framboesia Morula, Yaws

Frame(work) Adjust, Airer, Angle, Armature, Bail, Bayle, Body, Bow, Brickbat, Build, Cadge, Cadre, Cage, Case, Casement, Casing, Cent(e)ring, Centreing, Chase, Chassis, Clamper, Climbing, Coaming, Cold, Compages, Companion, Cowcatcher, Cradle, Cratch, Cribwork, Deckel, Deckle, Draw, Dutchwife, Entablature, Everest pack, Fabric, Fender, Fiddley, Fit-up, Flake, Form, Frisket, Gallows, Gambrel, Gantry, Garden, Gate, Gauntry, Grid-iron, Haik, Hake, Heck, Horse, Hull, Jungle gym, Lattice, Limit, Louvre, Mantel, Mixter, Mood, Mount, Mullion, Muntin(g), Newsreel, Ossature, Outrigger, Oxford, Pack, Pannier, Pantograph, Parameter, Partners, Passe-partout, Pergola, Physique, Pillory, Plant, Plot, Plummer-block, Poppet head, Portal, Puncheon, Quilting, Rack, Rave, Redact, Retable, Rib(bing), Rim, Sampling, Sash, Scaffold, Scuncheon, Sect(ion), Set, Setting, Skeleton, Spring-box, Stanchion, Stand, Stern, Still(age), Stitch up, Stocking, Stocks, Straddle, Stretcher, Stretching, Stroma, → **STRUCTURE**, Studwork, Surround, Swift, Tabernacle, Taboret, Tambour, Tent(er), Tepee, Time, Timeline, Trave, Trellis, Tress, Tressel, Trestle, Tribble, Trussing, Vacuum, Victimize, Walking, Wattle, Ways, Window, Yoke, Zarf, Zimmer®

Framley Parsonage

Franc Fr, Leu, Lev, Lew

France Anatole, Marianne, RF, Thibault

Franchise Charter, Contract, Liberty, Pot-wall(op)er, Privilege, Right, Suffrage, Vote, Warrant

Franciscan Custos, Minorite, Observant, Salesian, Scotist, Tertiaries

Francium Fr

Franck Cesar

Frank(ish) Artless, Austrasia, Blunt, → **CANDID**, Direct, Easy, Free, Free-spoken, Honest, Ingenuous, Man-to-man, Merovingian, Natural, Open, Outspoken, Overt, Postage, Postmark, Raw, Ripuarian, Salian, Sincere, Squareshooter, Stamp, Straight, Straightforward, Sty, Upfront

Frankincense Laser, Olibanum, Thus

Frans, Franz Hals, Lehar

Frantic Demoniac, Deranged, Distraught, Frenzied, Hectic, Mad, Overwrought, Phrenetic, Rabid, Violent, Whirl(ing)

▷ **Frantic** *may indicate* an anagram

Frappé Iced

Fraternise, Fraternity Affiliate, Brotherhood, Burschenschaft, Consort, Elk, Fellowship, Lodge, Mingle, Moose, Order, Shrine, Sodality

Fratricide Cain

Fraud(ulent) Barratry, Bobol, Bubble, Charlatan, Cheat, Chisel, Collusion, Covin, Cronk, Deceit, Diddle, Do, Fineer, Gyp, Humbug, Hypocrite, → **IMPOSTOR**, Imposture, Jiggery-pokery, Jobbery, Knavery, Liar, Peculator, Piltdown, Pious, Pseud(o), Put-up, Ringer, Rip-off, Roguery, Rort, Salami technique, Scam, Shoulder surfing, South Sea Bubble, Stellionate, Supercherie, Swindle, Swiz(z), Swizzle, Tartuffe, Trick

Fraught Perilous

Fray(ed) Bagarre, Brawl, Contest, Feaze, Frazzle, Fret, Fridge, Ravel, Riot, Scrimmage, Wigs on the green

Freak Cantrip, Caprice, Chimera, Control, Deviant, Geek, Jesus, Lusus naturae, Mooncalf, Sport, Teras, Whim, Whimsy

Freckle Ephelis, Fern(i)tickle, Fern(i)ticle, Heatspot, Lentigines, Lentigo, Spot, Sunspot

Frederick Barbarossa, Carno, Great

Free(d), Freely Acquit, Assoil, At large, Buckshee, Candid, Canny, Church, Clear, Complimentary, Cuffo, Dead-head, Deliver, Deregulate, Devoid, Disburden, Disburthen, Disengage, Disentangle, Eleutherian, Emancipate, Enfranchise, Enlarge, Excuse, Exeem, Exeme, Exempt, Exonerate, Extricate, Familiar, Footloose, Frank, French, Gratis, House, Idle, Immune, Indemnify, Independent, Kick, Large, Lavish, Lax, Leisure, Let, Liberate, Loose, Manumit, Open, Parole, Pro bono, Quit(e), Range, Ransom, Redeem, → **RELEASE**, Relieve, Rescue, Reskew, Rick, Rid, Sciolto, Scot, Solute, Spare, Spring, Stald, Stall, Trade, Unbowed, Unlock, Unloosen, Unmew, Unmuzzle, Unshackle, Unsnarl, Untangle, Untie, Untwist, Vacant, Verse, Voluntary

▷ **Free** *may indicate* an anagram

Freebooter Cateran, Corsair, Franklin, Marauder, Moss-trooper, Pad, Pindaree, Pindari, Pirate, Rapparee, Snapha(u)nce, Snaphaunch, Thief, Viking

Freedom Abandon, Autonomy, Breadth, Carte blanche, Eleutherian, Exemption, Fear, Fling, Four, Immunity, Impunity, Independence, Laisser aller, Laisser faire, Laissez aller, Laissez faire, Latitude, Liberty, Licence, Moksha, Play, Range, Releasement, Speech, Uhuru, UNITA, Want, Worship

Free gift Bonus, Charism, Perk

Freehold(er) Enfeoff, Franklin, Frank tenement, Odal(l)er, Seisin, Udal(ler), Yeoman

Freelance Eclectic, Independent, Mercenary, Stringer

Freeloader Sponge

▷ **Freely** *may indicate* an anagram

Freeman Burgess, Ceorl, Churl, Franklin, Liveryman, Thegn, Thete, Villein

Freemason(ry), Freemason's son Craft, Lewis, Lodge, Moose, Templar

Free-range Eggs, Outler

Free State Orange

Freethinker Agnostic, Bradlaugh, Cynic, Libertine, Sceptic

Free-trade(r) Cobdenism, Wright

Free-wheel Coast

Freeze(s), Freezer, Freezing Alcarrazo, Arctic, Benumb, Congeal, Cool, Cryogenic, Cryonics, Eutectic, Freon®, Frost, Geal, Harden, Ice, Lyophilize, Moratoria, Nip, Numb, Paralyse, Regelate, Riss, Stiffen, Wage

Freight Cargo, Carriage, Fraught, Goods, Load

French(man), Frenchwoman Alsatian, Anton, Aristo, Basque, Breton, Cajun, Crapaud, Creole, Dawn, Dreyfus, Emil(e), Frog, Gallic(e), Gaston, Gaul, Gombo, Grisette, Gumbo, Huguenot, Joual, Jules, M, Mamselle, Marianne, Midi, Monsieur, Mounseer, Neo-Latin, Norman, Parleyvoo, Pierre, René, Rhemish, Savoyard, Yves

Frenetic Deranged, Frantic, Overwrought

Frenzied, Frenzy Amok, Berserk, Corybantic, Deliration, Delirium, Demoniac, Enrage, Enrapt, Euhoe, Euoi, Evoe, Feeding, Fit, Fury, Hectic, Hysteric, Lune, Maenad, Mania, Must, Nympholepsy, Oestrus, Phrenetic, Rage

Frequency, Frequent(er), Frequently Angular, Attend, Audio, Bandwidth, Channel, Common, Constant, Expected, Familiar, Forcing, Formant, FR, Fresnel, Gene, Habitué, Hang-out, Haunt, Hertz, High, Incidence, Intermediate, Low,

Medium, Megahertz, Natural, Often, Penetrance, Pulsatance, Radio, Recurrent, Regular, Relative, Resort, Spatial, Spectrum, Superhigh, Thick, Ultrahigh, Video

Fresco Intonaco, Sinopia, Tempera

Fresh(en), Freshness Airy, Anew, Aurorean, Brash, Caller, Chilly, Clean, Crisp, Dewy, Entire, Forward, Green, Hot, Insolent, Lively, Maiden, Nas(s)eem, New, Novel, Quick, Rebite, Recent, Roral, Roric, Rorid, Smart, Span-new, Spick, Sweet, Tangy, Uncured, Verdure, Vernal, Virent, Virescent

Freshman Bajan, Bejan(t), Fresher, Frosh, Pennal, Plebe, Recruit, Student

Fret(ful) Chafe, Filigree, Fray, Grate, Grecque, Haze, Impatient, Irritate, Ornament, Peevish, Repine, Rile, Ripple, Roil, Rub, Stop, Tetchy, Tracery, Whittle, Worry

Friable Crisp, Crumbling, Powdery

Friar(s) Augustinian, Austin, Bacon, Barefoot, Black, Brother, Bungay, Capuchin, Carmelite, Conventual, Cordelier, Crutched, Curtal, Dervish, Dominican, Fra(ter), Franciscan, Frate, Grey, Jacobin, Laurence, Limiter, Lymiter, Minim, Minor, Minorite, → MONK, Observant, Observantine, Preaching, Predicant, Recollect, Recollet, Redemptionist, Rush, Tuck, White

Friction Attrition, Conflict, Dissent, Drag, Rift, Rub, Skin, Sliding, Stiction, Stridulation, Tribology, Tripsis, Wear, Xerotripsis

Friday Black, Casual, Girl, Golden, Good, Holy, Man, Person, Savage

Fridge Esky®, Freezer, Icebox, Rub

Fried cake Croquette, Cruller

Friend(ly), Friends Achates, Affable, Ally, Alter ego, Ami(cable), Amigo, Approachable, Associate, Avuncular, Belamy, Benign, Boet(ie), Bosom, Bra, Bro, Bru, Bud(dy), Buster, Butty, Cackermander, Cater-cousin, China, Choma, Chommie, Chum, Circle, Cobber, Cock, Cohort, Compadre, Companion, Companionable, Comrade, Confidant, Cordial, Couthie, Couthy, Crony, Cully, Damon, Downhome, Edwin, Ehoa, En ami, Fairweather, False, Familiar, Feare, Feathered, Feer, Fere, Fiere, Folksy, Gemütlich, Gossib, Gossip, Gregarious, Hail-fellow-well-met, Homeboy, Ingle, Intimate, Inward, Jong, Kith, Litigation, Marrow, Mate, McKenzie, Mentor, Mucker, Near, Next, Oppo, Outgoing, Paisano, Pal, Paranymph, Pen, Penn, Pheere, Privado, Prochain ami, Prochein ami, Pythias, Quaker, Sidekick, Sociable, Societal, Sport, Steady, Tillicum, Tonga, Tosh, Wack(er), Warm, Well-wisher, Wus(s), Yaar

Friendliness, Friendship Amity, Bonhomie, Camaraderie, Contesseration, Entente, Platonic, Rapprochement, Sodality

Frieze Dado, Metope, Penistone, Zoophorus

Fright(en), Frightened, Frightful Afear, Affear(e), Agrise, Agrize, Agryze, Alarm, Aroint, Aroynt, Ashake, Chilling, Cow, Dare, Da(u)nt, Deter, Eek, Eerie, Faceache, Fear(some), Flay, Fleg, Fleme, Fley, Flush, Gallow, Gally, Ghast, Gliff, Glift, Grim, Grisly, Hairy, Horrid, Horrific, Intimidate, Ordeal, Panic, Scar, → SCARE, Scarre, Scaur, Schrecklich, Shocking, Sight, Skear, Skeer, Skrik, Spine-chilling, Spook, Stage, Startle, Terrible, Terrify, Terror, Tirrit, Unco, White-knuckle, Windy, Yitten

Frigid Bleak, Cold, Dry, Frory, Frosty, Ice, Indifferent, Serac, Stiff

Frill Armil, Armilla, Bavolet, Falbala, Furbelow, Jabot, Newgate, Oriental, Ornament, Papillote, Ruche, Ruff(le), Tucker, Valance

▷ **Frilly** *may indicate* an anagram

Fringe(s), Fringed Bang, Border, Bullion, Celtic, Ciliated, Ciliolate, Edge, Fall, Fimbria, Frisette, Interference, Laciniate, Loma, Lunatic, Macramé, Macrami, Newgate, Pelmet, Peripheral, Robin, Ruff, Run, Thrum, Toupee, Toupit, Tsitsith,

Tzitzit(h), Valance, Verge, Zizith
Frisian Holstein
Frisk(y) Caper, Cavort, Curvet, Fisk, Flimp, Frolic, Gambol, Search, Skip, Wanton
Fritillary Snake's-head
Fritter Batter, Beignet, Dribble, Dwindle, Fragment, Fribble, Pakora, Piddle, Potter, Puf(f)taloon, Squander, Waste, Wonder
Frivolous, Frivolity Butterfly, Empty(-headed), Etourdi(e), Facetious, Featherbrain, Flighty, Flippant, Frothy, Futile, Giddy, Idle, Inane, Levity, Light, Light-minded, Lightweight, Playboy, Skittish, Trifling, Trivial
Frizz(le), Frizzly Afro, Crape, Crimp, Crinkle, Curly, Fry, Fuzz, Hiss
Frock Dress, Gown, Ordain, Robe, Smock
Frog Anoura, Anura, Batrachia(n), Braid, Bullfrog, Cape nightingale, Crapaud, Depression, Flying, Fourchette, Frenchman, Frush, Goliath, Hairy, Hyla, Marsupial, Mounseer, Nic, Nototrema, Paddock, Paradoxical, Peeper, Pelobatid, Platanna, Puddock, Puttock, Rana, Ranidae, Tree, Wood, Xenopus
Frogman Diver
Frogmouth Mo(re)poke, Podargus
Frog spawn Redd, Tadpole
Frolic(some) Bender, Bust(er), Cabriole, Caper, Cavort, Curvet, Disport, Escapade, → FRISK(Y), Fun, Galravage, Galravitch, Gambol, Gammock, Gil(l)ravage, How's your father, Jink, Kittenish, Lark, Play, Pollick, Prank, Rag, Rand, Rig, Romp, Scamper, Skylark, Splore, Sport, Spree, Stooshie, Tittup, Wanton
From A, Against, Ex, For, Frae, Off, Thrae
Frond Fern, Leaf, Tendril
Front(al), Frontman Antependium, Anterior, Bow, Brass, Brow, Cold, Cover, Dead, Dickey, Dicky, Esplanade, Facade, Face, Fore(head), Forecourt, Foreground, Groof, Grouf, Grufe, Head, Home, Metope, National, Newscaster, Occluded, Paravant, People's, Plastron, Polar, Popular, Pose, Preface, Presenter, Pro, Prom, Prow, Rhodesian, Sector, Sinciput, Stationary, Tabula, Temerity, Van, Vaward, Ventral, Warm, Western
Frontier(sman) Afghan, Barrier, Border, Boundary, Checkpoint, Limit, Limitrophe, List, March, North-west, Outpost, Pathan, Wild West
Front page P1
Front-ranker Pawn
Frost(ing), Frosty, Frostbite Air, Alcorza, Black, Chill, Cranreuch, Cryo-, Freon®, Frigid, Frore(n), Frorne, Glacé, Ground, Hoar, Hore, Ice, Icing, Jack, Mat, Nip, Rime, Silver, Trench foot, White
Froth(y) Barm, Bubble, Cuckoospit, Cuckoospit(tle), Despumate, Foam, Frogspit, Gas, Head, Lather, Mantle, Nappy, Off-scum, Ream, Saponin, Scum, Seethe, Shallow, Spoom, Spoon, Spume, Sud, Yeasty, Yest, Zephir
Frown Glower, Knit, Lour, Lower, Scowl
Frozen Froren, Frorn(e), Frory, Gelid, Glacé, Graupel, Ice-bound, Spellbound, Static, Tundra
Fructification, Fructify, Fructose Aeci(di)um, Basidium, Fertilise, Flower, Fruit, Inulin
Frugal Meagre, Parsimonious, Provident, Prudent, Scant, Skimpy, Spare, Spartan, Thrifty
Fruit(ing), Fruit tree, Fruity Accessory, Achene, Acinus, Akene, Allocarpy, Apothecium, Autocarp, Bacciform, Cedrate, Coccus, Compot(e), Confect, Conserve, Cremocarp, Crop, Dessert, Drupe, Eater, Encarpus, Etaerio, First, Follicle, Forbidden, Fritter, Harvest, Issue, Multiple, Orchard, Poof, Primeur, Primitiae,

Product(ion), Pseudocarp, Regma(ta), Replum, Result, Return, Rich, Ripe, Schizocarp, Seed, Silicle, Silicula, Siliqua, Silique, Soft, Sorosis, Stoneless, Succade, Sweetie, Sweety, Syconium, Syncarp, Utricle, Valve, Wall, Xylocarp, Yield

FRUIT

3 letters:
Fig
Haw
Hep
Hip
Hop
Jak
Key
Nut

4 letters:
Akee
Bael
Bito
Date
Gage
Gean
Jack
Kaki
Kiwi
Lime
Pear
Pepo
Plum
Pome
Sloe
Sorb
Star
Tuna
Ugli®
Yuzu

5 letters:
Ackee
Anana
Anona
Apple
Assai
Berry
Bread
Choko
Genip
Gourd
Grape
Guava

Jaffa
Lemon
Lotus
Mango
Melon
Nancy
Naras
Nashi
Nelis
Olive
Papaw
Prune
Rowan
Whort

6 letters:
Almond
Ananas
Babaco
Banana
Banian
Banyan
Carica
Cherry
Chocho
Citron
Citrus
Comice
Damson
Durian
Durion
Emblic
Feijoa
Lichee
Litchi
Longan
Lychee
Mammee
Medlar
Narras
Nelies
Oilnut
Orange
Papaya
Pawpaw

Pepino
Pomace
Pomelo
Pruine
Quince
Raisin
Rennet
Russet
Samara
Sapota
Sharon
Squash
Tomato
Wampee

7 letters:
Apricot
Avocado
Bullace
Chayote
Crab-nut
Cypsela
Geebung
Genipap
Gherkin
Kumquat
Leechee
Litchee
Manjack
Morello
Passion
Pimento
Pinguin
Poperin
Pumpkin
Pupunha
Ruddock
Satsuma
Soursop
Tangelo
Winesap

8 letters:
Abricock
Apricock

Bergamot
Bilberry
Blimbing
Calabash
Dewberry
Fraughan
Goosegog
Hagberry
Hastings
Hedgehog
Kalumpit
Minneola
Mulberry
Physalis
Plantain
Prunello
Rambutan
Rathripe
Sebesten
Shaddock
Sunberry
Tamarind
Tayberry
Teaberry
Waxberry

9 letters:
Algarroba
Apple-john
Aubergine
Bakeapple
Blueberry
Butternut
Canteloup
Carambola
Caryopsis
Cherimoya
Cranberry
Freestone
Haanepoot
Hackberry
Mirabelle
Myrobalan
Naseberry
Nectarine

Neesberry	**10 letters:**	Youngberry	**12 letters:**
Ortanique	Blackberry		Blackcurrant
Persimmon	Canteloupe	**11 letters:**	Checkerberry
Plumdamas	Cherimoyer	Boysenberry	Custard-apple
Poppering	Clementine	Hesperidium	Service-berry
Ratheripe	Clingstone	Huckleberry	Whortleberry
Sapodilla	Elderberry	Lingonberry	
Saskatoon	Granadilla	Marionberry	**13 letters:**
Shadberry	Grenadilla	Pampelmoose	Bullock's heart
Sorb-apple	Jargonelle	Pampelmouse	Sapodilla plum
Star-apple	Mangosteen	Pomegranate	
Tangerine	Paddymelon	Pompelmoose	**14 letters:**
Tomatillo	Pick-cheese	Pompelmouse	Worcesterberry
Victorine	Punicaceae	Salmonberry	
Whimberry	Scaldberry		
Whinberry	Watermelon		

Fruitful(ness) Calathus, Ephraim, Fat, Fecund, Feracious, Fertile, Productive, Prolific, Uberty, Worthwhile

Fruitless Bare, Futile, Sisyphean, Sterile, Useless, Vain

Frump(ish) Dowdy, Judy, Shabby, Unkempt

Frustrate(d) Baffle, Ba(u)lk, Beat, Blight, Bugger, Check, Cheesed off, Confound, Countermine, Dash, Disappoint, Discomfit, Dish, Foil, Hogtie, Outwit, Scotch, Stymie, Tantalise, Thwart

Fry, Fried Blot, Brit, Christopher, Elizabeth, Fricassee, Fritter, Frizzle, Parr, Sauté, Sizzle, Small, Spawn, Whippersnapper, Whitebait

Fuddle(d) Drunk, Fluster, Fuzzle, Maudlin, Ta(i)vert, Tosticated, Woozy

▷ **Fuddle(d)** *may indicate* an anagram

Fudge Cook, Doctor, Dodge, Drivel, Evade, Fiddlesticks, Nonsense, Rot, Stop-press

Fuel Anthracite, Argol, Astatki, Atomic, Avgas, Biodiesel, Biogas, Borane, Briquet(te), Bunker, Butane, Candle-coal, Cannel, Carbonette, Charcoal, Coal, Coalite®, Coke, Derv, Diesel, Eilding, Eldin(g), Ethane, Faggot, Fire(wood), Fossil, Gasohol, Gasoline, Go-juice, Haxamine, Hydrazine, Hydyne, Jud, Kerosene, Kerosine, Kindling, Knitch, Lignite, Mox, Napalm, Naphtha, Nuclear, Orimulsion, Outage, Paraffin, Peat, Propane, Propellant, Smokeless, Solid, Sterno®, Stoke, Tan balls, Triptane, Unleaded, Yealdon

Fug Frowst

Fugitive Absconder, Ephemeral, Escapee, Fleeting, Hideaway, Lot, Outlaw, Refugee, Runagate, Runaway, Runner, Transient, Vagabond

Fugue Ricercar(e), Ricercata

Fulcrum Key-pin, Pivot

Fulfil(ment) Accomplish, Complete, Consummate, Fruition, Honour, Implementation, Meet, Pass, Realise, → **SATISFY**, Steed, Subrogation

Fulgent Bright, Shining

Full(ness), Fully Abrim, Ample, Arrant, Bouffant, Capacity, Chock-a-block, Chocker, Complete, Copious, Embonpoint, Engorged, Entire, Fat, Fed, Flush, Fou, Frontal, German, High, Hoatching, Hotch, Mill, Plein, Plenary, Plenitude, Pleroma, Plethora, Replete, Rich, Sated, Satiated, Thorough, Torose, Torous, Toss, Turgid, Turgor, Ullage, Up, Wau(l)k, Wholly

Full-faced Caboched, Caboshed

Full-throated Goitred

Fulminate, Fulmination Detonate, Explode, Levin, Lightning, Rail, Renounce, Thunder

Fumarole Hornito, Mofette

Fumble Blunder, Faff, Grope, Misfield, Muff

Fume(s) Bluster, Gas, Halitus, Nidor, Rage, Reech, Reek, Settle, Smoke, Stum, Vapours

Fumigate, Fumigator Disinfect, Pastil(le), Smoke, Smudge

Fun(ny), Funny bone Amusing, Antic, Boat, Buffo, Caper, Clownery, Comedy, Comic(al), Crack, Craic, Delight, Droll, Frolic, Gammock, Gas, Gig, Giocoso, Glaik, Guy, Hilarity, Humerus, Humorous, Hysterical, Ill, Jest, Jouisance, Jouysaunce, Killing, Kinky, Lark, Music, Play, Pleasure, Priceless, Rag, Rib-tickling, Rich, Rummy, Scream, Sidesplitting, Skylark, Sport, Uproarious, Weird(o), Wit, Yell

Funambulist Blondin, Equilibrist, Tight-rope

Function(al) Act, Algebraic, Antilog, Apparatchik, Arccos, Arcsine, Arctan, Assignment, Bodily, Bunfight, Ceremony, Characteristic, Circular, Cosec, Cosh, Cot(h), Cotangent, Dance, Density, Discriminant, Distribution, Dynamic, Exponential, Gamma, Gibbs, Hamilton(ian), Helmholtz, Hyperbolic, Integral, Integrand, Inverse, Jacobian, Job, Logarithm, Map(ping), → OPERATE, Periodic, Polymorphic, Probability, Propositional, Quadric, Quantical, Reception, Recursive, Role, Run, Secant, Sech, Sentential, Service, Sine, Sinh, State, Ste(a)d, Step, Surjection, Tan(h), Tangent, Tick, Transcendental, Trigonometric, Truth, Use, Utensil, Utility, Versin, Vital, Wave, → WORK

Functionless Otiose

Fund(s), Funding, Fundraising Bank, Bankroll, Barrel, Capital, Chest, Consolidated, Emendals, Endow, Evergreen, Finance, Fisc, Fisk, Gild, Green, Hedge, Imprest, Index, Jackpot, Kitty, Managed, Mutual, Nest-egg, Pension, Pool, Pork-barrel, Prebend, Private, Public, Purse, Revolving, Roll-up, Sinking, Slush, Social, Sou-sou, Stabilisation, Stock, Store, Subsidise, Sustentation, Susu, Telethon, Tracker, Treasury, Trust, Vulture, Wage(s), War chest, Wherewithal

Fundamental(ist) Basic(s), Bedrock, Cardinal, Essence, Grass-roots, Hamas, Integral, Missing, Nitty-gritty, Organic, Prime, Principle, Radical, Rudimentary, Taleban, Taliba(a)n, Ultimate

Fund-holder Rentier

Funeral, Funereal Charnel, Cortege, Dismal, Exequy, Feral, Hearse, Obit, Obsequy, Sad-coloured, Solemn, Tangi

Fungicide Benomyl, Biphenyl, Bordeaux mixture, Burgundy mixture, Captan, Diphenyl, Ferbam, Menadione, PCP, Resveratrol, Thiram, Zineb

Fungoid, Fungus Agaric, Amadou, Amanita, Ambrosia, Anthersmut, Anthracnose, Apothecium, Armillaria, Asci(us), Ascomycete, Aspergillus, Barm, Basidium, Beefsteak, Bird's nest, Black, Blackknot, Blewits, Blue-mould, Blue-rot, Boletus, Bootlace, Botrytis, Bracket, Brand, Bread-mould, Bunt, Candida, Ceps, Chantarelle, Chanterelle, Claudosporium, Clubroot, Conk, Coral spot, Corn smut, Cramp-ball, Craterellus, Cryptococcus, Cup, Death-cap, Death-cup, Dermatophytosis, Destroying angel, Discomycetes, Dutch elm, Earth-star, Elf-cup, Empusa, Endophyte, Ergot, Eumycetes, Fairy butter, Favus, Flowers of tan, Funnel-cap, Fuss-ball, Fuzz-ball, Gall, Gibberella, Gill, Honey, Horsehair, Hypersarcoma, Hypha, Imperfect, Ink-cap, Ithyphallus, Jelly, Jew's ear, Jupiter's beard, Lawyer's wig, Liberty cap, Lichen, Magic mushroom, Merulius, Mildew, Milk cap, Monilia, Morel, Mould, Mucor(ales), Mushroom, Mycelium, Mycetes, Mycology, Noble rot, Oak-leather, Oak-wilt, Oidium, Oomycete, Orange-peel, Penicillium, Pest, Peziza, Phallus, Phycomycete, Pileum, Plica Polonica, Polyporus, Porcino,

Pore, Prototroph, Puccinia, Puckfist, Puffball, Pythium, Rhizomorph, Rhizopus, Rhytisma, Russula, Rust, Saccharomyces, Saprolegnia, Saprophyte, Sariodes, Scab, Shaggy cap, Shaggy mane, Shoestring, Slime, Smut, Sooty mould, Spunk, Stinkhorn, Stipe, Stromata, Sulphur tuft, Tarspot, Thalline, Thallophyte, Toadstool, Torula, Tremella, Trichophyton, Truffle, Tuckahoe, Uredine, Ustilago, Velvet shank, Wax cap, Wheat rust, Witches' meat, Wood hedgehog, Wood woollyfoot, Yeast, Yellow brain, Yellow rust, Yellows, Zygomycete, Zygospore

Fungus-eater Mycophagist

Funicular Cable-car

Funk(y) Blue, Dodge, Dread, Fear, Scared, Stylish

Funnel Buchner, Chimney, Choana, Drogue, Flue, Hopper, Infundibulum, Separating, Smokestack, Stack, Stovepipe, Tun-dish, Tunnel, Wine

Fur Astrakhan, Astrex, Beaver(skin), Boa, Broadtail, Budge, Calabre, Caracul, Castor, Chinchilla, Coonskin, Crimmer, Ermelin, Ermine, Fitchew, Flix, Flue, Fun, Galyac, Galyak, Genet, Kolinsky, Krimmer, Lettice, Marten, Minever, Miniver, Mink, Mouton, Musquash, Ocelot, Otter, Palatine, Pane, Pashm, Pean, Pekan, Rac(c)oon, Roskyn, Sable, Sealskin, Sea-otter, Stole, Tincture, Tippet, Vair(e), Victorine, Wolverine, Zibeline, Zorino

Furbish Polish, Renovate, Spruce, Vamp

Furl Clew up, Fold, Roll, Stow, Wrap

Furlough Congé, Leave

Furnace Arc, Athanor, Blast, Bloomery, Bosh, Breeze, Calcar, Cockle, Cremator, Cupola, Destructor, Devil, Electric, Finery, Firebox, Forge, Glory-hole, Incinerator, Kiln, Lear, Lehr, Lime-kiln, Oast, Oon, Open-hearth, Oven, Pot, Producer, Reverberatory, Scaldino, Solar, Stokehold, Stokehole, Tank, Wind

Furnish(ing) Appoint, Array, Deck, Decorate, Endow, Endue, Equip, Feed, Fledge, Gird, Lend, Produce, Provision, Soft, Stock, Supply, Tabaret, Upholster

Furniture, Furniture designer Biedermeier, Chattels, Chippendale, Duncan Phyfe, Encoignure, Escritoire, Etagère, Flatpack, Fyfe, Hepplewhite, Insight, Lumber, Moveable, Queen Anne, Sheraton, Sideboard, Sticks, Stoutherie, Street, Tire, Unit, Washstand, Whatnot

Furore Brouhaha, Commotion, Outburst, Stink, Storm, Uproar

Furrier Trapper

Furrow(ed) Crease, Feer, Feerin(g), Furr, Groove, Gutter, Plough, Pucker, Rill(e), Rugose, Rut, Stria, Sulcus, Vallecula, Wrinkle

Fur-seal Seecatch(ie)

Further(more), Furthest Additional, Advance, Again, Aid, Also, Besides, Deeper, Else, Expedite, Extend, Extra, Extreme, Fresh, Infra, Longer, Mo(e), Mow, Other, Promote, Serve, Speed, Subserve, Then

Furtive(ly) Clandestine, Cunning, Hole and corner, Secret, Shifty, Sly, Sneaky, Stealthy, Stowlins, Stownlins

Fury, Furies, Furious Acharné, Agitato, Alecto, → **ANGER**, Apoplexy, Atropos, Avenger, Eriny(e)s, Eumenides, Exasperation, Frantic, Frenzied, Furor, Hectic, Incensed, → **IRE**, Livid, Maenad, Megaera, Paddy, Rabid, Rage, Red, Savage, Seething, Tisiphone, Virago, Wood, Wrath, Yond

Furze Gorse, Whin

Fuse(d), Fusion Anchylosis, Ankylosis, Blend, Coalesce, Cohere, Colliquate, Conflate, Encaustic, Endosmosis, Flow, Flux, Igniter, Knit, Match, Merge, Merit, Nuclear, Percussion, Portfire, Proximity, Rigelation, Run, Sacralization, Safety, Saucisse, Saucisson, Short, Slow-match, Symphytic, Syncretism, Syngamy, Time, Tokamak, Unite

Fuselage Body, Monocoque, Structure

Fuss(y) Ado, Agitation, Anile, Ballyho, Bobsie-die, Bother, Br(o)uhaha, Bustle, Carfuffle, Carry on, Chichi, Coil, Commotion, Complain, Cosset, Create, Cu(r)fuffle, Dust, Faff, Fantad, Fantod, Fiddle-faddle, Finical, Finikin, Hairsplitter, Hoohah, Hoopla, Mither, Mother, Niggle, Nit-pick, Noise, Old-womanish, Overexact, Overnice, Overwrought, Palaver, Particular, Perjink, Pernickety, Picky, Pother, Precise, Prejink, Primp, Prissy, Pudder, Racket, Razzmatazz, Rout, Song, Song and dance, Spoffish, Spoffy, Spruce, Stashie, Stickler, Stink, → **STIR**, Stishie, Stooshie, Stushie, Tamasha, To-do, Tracasserie

Fustian Bombast, Gas, Pompous, Rant

Futile Empty, Feckless, Idle, Inept, No-go, Nugatory, Null, Otiose, Pointless, Sleeveless, Stultified, Trivial, Useless, → **VAIN**

Future(s), Futurist Again, Be-all, Coming, Demain, Financial, Hence, Horoscope, Index, Interest-rate, Later, Long-range, Offing, Ovist, Paragogic, Posterity, Prospect, To-be, Tomorrow

Fuzz(y) Blur, Crepe, Down, Fluff, Foggy, Lint, Pig, Policeman

Gg

G George, Golf, Gravity

Gab(ble), Gabbler Chatter, Dovercourt, Jabber, Pie, Prattle, Talkative, Yabber

Gable Clark, Corbie, Jerkinhead, Pediment, Pine end

Gabriel Angel, Walter

Gad(about), Gadzooks Gallivant, Lud, Rover, Sbuddikins, Sdeath, Traipse, Trape(s), Viretot

Gadfly Breese, Breeze, Brize

Gadget Adaptor, Appliance, Artifice, Device, Dingbat, Dingus, Doodad, Doodah, Doofer, Doohickey, Gismo, Gizmo, Gubbins, Hickey, Jiggumbob, Jimjam, Notion, Possum, Tool, Utility, Waldo, Widget

Gadolinium Gd

Gadzooks Odsbobs

Gaekwar Baroda

Gael(ic) Celt, Erse, Goidel, Scottish, Teague

Gaff(e), Gaffer Bêtise, Blague, Bloomer, Error, Floater, Foreman, Gamble, Game, Solecism, Spar, Throat, Trysail, Yokel

Gag Brank, Choke, Estoppel, Joke, Pong, Prank, Retch, Silence(r), Smother, Wheeze

Gage Challenge, Pawn, Pledge, Plum

▶ **Gaiety** *see* **GAY**

Gain(s), Gained Acquire, Appreciate, Attain, Avail, Boodle, Boot, Bunce, Capital, Carry, Catch, Chevisance, Clean-up, Derive, Earn, Edge, Fruit, → **GET**, Good, Gravy, Land, Lucre, Obtain, Plus, Profit, Purchase, Rake-off, Reap, Thrift, Use, Velvet, Wan, Win, Windfall, Winnings

Gainsay Contradict, Deny

Gait Bearing, Canter, Pace, Piaffer, Rack, Trot

Gaiter(s) Cootikin, Cu(i)tikin, Gambado, Hogger, Legging(s), Puttee, Spat(s), Spattee, Spatterdash, Vamp

Gala Banquet, Festival

Galaxy, Galaxies Active, Andromeda, Blazar, Great Attractor, Heaven, Irregular, Magellanic cloud, Milky Way, Radio, Regular, Seyfert, Spiral, Stars

Galbanum Ferula

Gale(s) Backfielder, Equinoctial, Fresh, Moderate, Near, Peal, Ripsnorter, Sea turn, Snorter, Squall, Storm, Strong, Tempest, Whole, Winder

Gall, Gall bladder Aleppo, Bedeguar, Bile, Bitterness, Canker, Cholecyst, Ellagic, Enrage, Fell, Irritate, Mad-apple, Maugre, Maulgre, Oak(nut), Oak apple, Saddle, Sage-apple, Sandiver, → **SAUCE**, Tacahout, Vine

Gallant(ry) Admirer, Amorist, Beau, Blade, Buck, Cavalier, Chevalier, Cicisbeo, Courtliness, Lover, Prow, Romeo, Sigisbeo, Spark, Valiance

Galleon Galloon, Ghostly, Ship

Gallery Accademia, Alure, Amphitheatre, Arcade, Assommoir, Belvedere, Brattice, Bretasche, Bretesse, Brettice, Brow, Burrell (Collection), Catacomb,

Pam

Celestials, Cupola, Dedans, Fly, Gods, Hayward, Hermitage, Jube, Ladies', Loft, Loggia, Louvre, Machicolation, Mine, Minstrel, National, Organ, Pawn, Picture, Pinacotheca, Pinakothek, Pitti, Prado, Press, Public, Rogues', Scaffolding, Serpentine, Shooting, Strangers', Tate, Terrace, Traverse, Tribune, Triforium, Uffizi, Veranda(h), Whispering, Whitechapel, Winning

Galley Bireme, Bucentaur, Caboose, Drake, Galliot, Kitchen, Lymphad, Penteconter, Proof

Gallimaufry Macedoine, Mishmash, Stew

Gallium Ga

Gallon(s) Bushel, Cong(ius), Cran, Hin, Imperial, Pottle, Tierce

Galloon Lace, Osiris

Gallop(er) Aide, Canter, Canterbury, Career, Lope, Trot, Wallop

Gallows Bough, Cheat, Drop, Dule-tree, Forks, Gibbet, Nub, Nubbing-cheat, Patibulary, Three-legged mare, Tree, Tyburn, Tyburn-tree, Widow, Woodie

Gallows-bird Crack-halter, Crack-hemp, Crack-rope

Gall-stone Cholelith

Galore Abundance, À gogo, Plenty, Whisky

Galosh Overshoe, Rubber

Galvanise Activate, Buck up, Ginger, Rouse, Zinc

Galvanometer Tangent

Gam Pod

Gambit Manoeuvre, Ploy, Stratagem

Gamble(r), Gambling (place) Adventure, Amber, Ante, Back, Bet, Casino, Chance, Dice(-play), Flutter, Gaff, Hold, Jeff, Martingale, Mise, Pari-mutuel, Parlay, Partingale, Piker, Plunge, Policy, Punt(er), Raffle, Reno, Risk, Roulette, School, Spec, Speculate, Speculator, Sweep(stake), Throw(ster), Tinhorn, Tombola, Tontine, Treble chance, Two-up, → **WAGER**

Gambol Frisk, Frolic

Game(s) Away, Closed, Commonwealth, Computer, Console, Decider, Electronic, Fair, Frame, Gallant, Gammy, Ground, Gutsy, High-jinks, Highland, Home, Intrepid, Isthmian, Jeu, → **LAME**, Match, Middle, Mind, MUD, Nemean, Numbers, Olympic, On, Open, Panel, Paralympic, Parlour, Perfect, Platform, Play, Plaything, Preference, Pythian, Raffle, Ready, Road, Role-playing, Round, Rubber, Saving, Scholar's, Secular, Spoof, Sport, Square, String, Table, Tie-break, Vie, Waiting, Willing, Zero-sum

---

GAMES

2 letters:	Pam	Crap	Main
Eo	Pit	Dibs	Mora
Go	Put	Fa-fi	Palm
PE	Sim	Faro	Polo
RU	Swy	Goff	Pool
	Tag	Golf	Putt
3 letters:	Tig	Grab	Ruff
Cat	War	I-spy	Scat
Hob		Keno	Skat
Loo	*4 letters:*	Kino	Slam
Maw	Base	Laik	Snap
Nap	Brag	Loto	Solo
Nim	Bull	Ludo	Taws

Vint
Wall
Word

5 letters:
Bingo
Bocce
Bowls
Cards
Catch
Chess
Cinch
Craps
Darts
Fives
Gleek
Goose
Halma
House
Jacks
Keeno
Lotto
Lurch
Merel
Meril
Monte
Morra
Noddy
Novum
Omber
Ombre
Poker
Quino
Roque
Rummy
Shogi
Stops
Tarok
Tarot
Trugo
Trump
Two-up
Ulama
Video
Whisk
Whist

6 letters:
Basset
Beetle
Bo-peep

Boston
Boules
Bounce
Casino
Chemmy
Clumps
Crambo
Ecarté
Euchre
Fantan
Footer
Gammon
Gobang
Gomoku
Hockey
Hoopla
Hurley
Kitcat
Merell
Peepbo
Pelota
Piquet
Quinze
Quoits
Shinny
Shinty
Soccer
Socker
Squash
Tenpin
Tipcat
Uckers
Vigoro

7 letters:
Ba'spiel
Bezique
Braemar
Camogie
Canasta
Cassino
Charade
Chicken
Codille
Conkers
Coon-can
Croquet
Curling
Diabolo
Doubles
Hangman

Hurling
In-and-in
Jai alai
Jukskei
Kabaddi
Kalooki
Lottery
Mahjong
Mancala
Marbles
Matador
Muggins
Murphy's
Netball
Old maid
Pachisi
Pallone
Passage
Patball
Peekabo
Peevers
Pharaoh
Pinball
Plafond
Pontoon
Primero
Push-pin
Pyramid
Rackets
Reversi
Ring-taw
Seven-up
Singles
Snooker
Squails
Tag ends
Tenpins
Vingt-un
Zero sum

8 letters:
All-fives
All-fours
Baccarat
Baseball
Bob-apple
Bumpball
Buzkashi
Canfield
Charades
Chequers

Chouette
Conquian
Cottabus
Cribbage
Dominoes
Draughts
Fivepins
Football
Forfeits
Four-ball
Foursome
Gin rummy
Goalball
Handball
Handicap
Hardball
Kalookie
Kickball
Klondike
Klondyke
Korfball
Lacrosse
Leapfrog
Mahjongg
Michigan
Monopoly®
Napoleon
Ninepins
Nintendo®
Octopush
Pachinko
Pall-mall
Pastance
Patience
Peekaboo
Pegboard
Penneech
Penneeck
Penuchle
Petanque
Ping-pong
Pinochle
Pintable
Pope Joan
Push-ball
Pyramids
Reversis
Rolypoly
Roulette
Rounders
Sardines

Scrabble®
Skittles
Slapjack
Softball
Sphairee
Subbuteo®
Teetotum
Trap-ball
Tray-trip
Tredille
Tric-trac
Verquere
Verquire

9 letters:
Acey-deucy
Aunt Sally
Badminton
Bagatelle
Billiards
Black-cock
Black-jack
Bob-cherry
Broomball
Crokinole
Cutthroat
Dodgeball
Duplicate
Fillipeen
Hacky Sack®
Hopscotch
Jingo-ring
Lanterloo
Level-coil
Matrimony
Mistigris
Mournival
Mumchance
Newmarket
Paintball
Parcheesi®
Pelmanism
Punchball
Quadrille
Quidditch®
Shell game

Shoot'em-up
Solitaire
Solo whist
Spoilfive
Stoolball
Strap-game
Tip-and-run
Tredrille
Twenty-one
Vingt-et-un
Water polo

10 letters:
Angel-beast
Backgammon
Basketball
Battledore
Bouillotte
Candlepins
Cat's cradle
Deck tennis
Dumb crambo
Five-stones
Flapdragon
Geocaching
Handy-dandy
Horseshoes
Hot cockles
Jackstones
Jackstraws
Knurr-spell
Lansquenet
Paddleball
Paper chase
Phillipina
Phillipine
Philopoena
Pooh sticks
Punto-banco
Put and take
Shuffle-cap
Snapdragon
Spillikins
Strip poker
Tablanette
Tchoukball

Thimblerig
Trick-track
Troll-madam
Trou-madame
Volley-ball

11 letters:
Barley-brake
Barley-break
Bumble-puppy
Catch-the-ten
Chemin de fer
Fox and geese
General post
Gerrymander
Hide and seek
Mumbletypeg
Post and pair
Puncto-banco
Racquetball
Rouge et noir
Sancho-pedro
Shovelboard
Speculation
Tick-tack-toe
Tiddlywinks
Troll-my-dame

12 letters:
Bar billiards
Consequences
Fast and loose
Hoodman-blind
Knucklebones
Minister's cat
One-and-thirty
Pitch and putt
Pitch and toss
Shuffleboard
Span-farthing
Troll-my-dames

13 letters:
Blind man's buff
Chicken-hazard
Double or quits

French cricket
Jingling match
Musical chairs
Postman's knock
Prisoner's base
Scavenger hunt
Space Invaders®
Spin-the-bottle
Tenpin bowling
Tickly-benders

14 letters:
British bulldog
Crown and anchor
Ducks and drakes
Fives and threes
Follow-my-leader
Hunt-the-slipper
Pig-in-the-middle
Prick-the-garter
Shove-halfpenny
Snip-snap-snorum
Tenpins bowling
Three-card monte

15 letters:
Chinese whispers
Puss-in-the-corner

16 letters:
Piggy-in-the-
  middle
Snakes and ladders
Trente-et-quarante

17 letters:
Noughts and
  crosses

20 letters:
Kiss-me-quick-in-
  the-ring

Game, Game birds Bag, Fowl, Grouse, Guan, Hare, Meat, Partridge, Pheasant,
  Prairie chicken, Ptarmigan, Quail, → **QUARRY**, Rype(r), Snipe, Spatchcock,
  Woodcock
Gamekeeper Mellors, Velveteen, Venerer, Warrener

Gamete Ootid
Gaming place Bucket-shop, Casino, Saloon, Table
Gammerstang Taupie, Tawpie
Gammon Baloney, Bilge, Tosh
Gamut Compass, Range
Gander Airport, Look-see
Gandhi Mahatma
Gang Baader-Meinhof, Band(itti), Bikers, Bing, Bunch, Canaille, Chain, Coffle, Core, Crew, Crue, Droog, Elk, Go, Group, Hell's Angels, Horde, Mob, Mods, Nest, Outfit, Pack, Posse, Press, Push, Ratpack, Ring, Rockers, Shearing, Triad, Tribulation, Troop, Yardie
Ganglia Basal
Gangrene Canker, Gas, Noma, Phaged(a)ena, Sphacelate, Thanatosis
Gangster Al, Bandit, Capone, Crook, Dacoit, Dakoit, Hatchet-man, Highbinder, Hood, Mafioso, Mobster, Ochlocrat, Scarface, Skollie, Skolly, Tsotsi, Yakuza, Yardie
Gangway Brow, Catwalk, Road
Gannet Alcatras, Booby, Guga, Solan(d)
Gantry Elmer
Ganymede Cupper
▸ **Gaol(er)** *see* JAIL(ER)
Gap Aperture, Belfort, Breach, Chasm, Chink, Credibility, Day, Deflationary, Diastema, Dollar, Embrasure, Energy, F-hole, Financing, Flaw, Fontanel(le), Gender, Generation, Gulf, Gulph, Hair-space, Hiatus, Hole, Inflationary, Interlude, Interstice, Kirkwood, Lacunae, Leaf, Lin(n), Loophole, M(e)use, Mews, Muset, Musit, Node of Ranvier, Opening, Ostiole, Pass, Rest, Rift, Rima, Shard, Sherd, Skills, Slap, → SPACE, Spark, Street, Synapse, Trade, Truth-value, Vacancy, Vent, Water, Wind, Window
Gape(r), Gaping Comber, Dehisce, Fatiscent, Gant, Ga(u)p, Gerne, Hiant, Mya, Outstare, Rictal, Rictus, Ringent, Rubberneck, Stare, Yawn, Yawp
Garage Barn, Carport, Chopshop, Hangar, Lock-up, Muffler shop
Garb Apparel, Costume, Gear, Gere, Guise, Ihram, Invest, Leotard, Raiment, Toilet
Garbage Bunkum, Junk, Refuse, Rubbish, Trash
Garble Edit, Jumble, Muddle
▷ **Garble** *may indicate* an anagram
Garden(ing), Gardens Arbour, Area, Babylon(ian), Bagh, Bear, Beer, Botanic, Chinampa, Colegarth, Container, Cottage, Covent, Cremorne, Dig, Eden, Erf, Floriculture, Garth, Gethsemane, Hanging, Hesperides, Hoe, Horticulture, Italian, Japanese, Kailyard, Kew, Kitchen, Knot, Landscape, Lyceum, Market, Monastery, NJ, Olitory, Paradise, Parterre, Physic, Plantie-cruive, Pleasance, Plot, Potager, Ranelagh, Rockery, Roji, Roof, Rosarium, Rosary, Rosery, Tea, Tilth, Topiary, Tuileries, Vauxhall, Walled, Welwyn, Window, Winter, Yard, Zoological
Gardener Adam, Capability Brown, Fuchs, Hoy, Jekyll, Landscape, Mali, Mallee, Mary, Nurseryman, Topiarist, Tradescant, Trucker
Gargantuan Enormous, Huge, Pantagruel, Vast
Gargle Gargarism, Mouthwash
Gargoyle Waterspout
Garish Criant, Flashy, Gaudy, Glitzy, Jazzy, Painty, Roary, Rorie, Rory, Technicolour
Garland Anadem, Anthology, Chaplet, Coronal, Crants, Festoon, Lei, Stemma, Toran(a), Vallar(y), Wreath
Garlic Clove, Elephant, Hedge, Rams(on), Rocambole
Garment Aba(ya), Abba, Alb, Ao dai, Barrow, Blouse, Blouson, Bodice, Body

warmer, Bolero, B(o)ub(o)u, B(o)urk(h)a, Brassière, Breeks, Burnous, Burqa, Busuuti, Caftan, Catsuit, Cerements, Chador, Chasuble, Chausses, Chimer, Cilice, Cimar, Clout, Cote-hardie, Cotta, Cover-slut, Crop top, Dalmatic, Dashiki, Dirndl, Dishdasha, Djibbah, Doublet, Dreadnought, → DRESS, Ephod, Exomion, Exomis, Fanon, Foundation, Gambeson, Gilet, Gipon, Gown, G-suit, Habiliment, Habit, Hand-me-down, Himation, Hug-me-tight, Ihram, Izar, Jeistiecor, Jibbah, Jubbah, Jumpsuit, Jupon, Kaftan, K(h)anga, Kanzu, Kaross, Kilt, Kittel, Leotard, Levis, Lingerie, Mandilion, Mandylion, Mantle, Mantua, Negligée, One-piece, Pallium, Pannicle, Pantihose, Pantyhose, Partlet, Pelerine, Pelisse, Penitential, Peplos, Pilch, Polonaise, Polonce, Polony, Poncho, Popover, Rail, Ramée, Rami(e), Reach-me-down, Rochet, Rompers, Ruana, Sackcloth, Salopettes, Sanbenito, Sari, Sarong, Scapular, Shroud, Singlet, Skirt, Skivvy, Slop, Soutane, Step-in, Stola, Stole, Sulu, Surcoat, Surplice, Swimsuit, Tabard, Tankini, Tank-top, Thong, Toga, Togs, Trunks, Tunic(le), Two-piece, Unitard, Vestment, Vesture, Waistcoat, Weed, Woolly, Wrapper, Yukata, Zephyr

Garnet Alabandine, Almandine, Andradite, Carbuncle, Demantoid, Essonite, Grossular(ite), Hessonite, Melanite, Pyrenite, Pyrope, Rhodolite, Spessartite, Topazine, Topazolite, Uvarovite

Garnish Adorn, Attach, Crouton, Decorate, Gremolata, Lard, Parsley, Sippet, Staffage

Garret Attic, Loft, Sol(l)ar, Sol(l)er

Garrison Fort, Man, Presidial

Garrulity, Garrulous Babbling, Gas, Gushy, Sweetiewife, Windbag

Garter Bowyang, Crewel, Flash, G(r)amash, Gramosh, Nicky-tam

Gary Glitter, Player

Gas(sy) Acetylene, Afterdamp, Air, Ammonia, Argon, Argonon, Arsine, Azote, Blah(-blah), Blather, Blether, Bloat, Blue water, Bottle(d), Butadiene, Butane, Butene, BZ, Calor®, Carbonic acid, Carburetted, Carrier, Chat, Chlorine, Chokedamp, Chrom(at)osphere, CN, Coal(-oil), Crypton, CS, Cyanogen, Damp, Diphosgene, Dispersant, Electrolytic, Emanation, Ethane, Ethene, Ether(ion), Ethine, Ethylene, Euchlorine, Firedamp, Fizz, Flatulence, Flatus, Flocculus, Flue, Fluorin(e), Formaldehyde, Fugacity, Gabnash, Greenhouse, H, Halitus, He, Helium, Hot-air, Hydrogen, Ideal, Inert, Jaw, Ketene, Kr(ypton), Laughing, Lewisite, Lurgi, Mace®, Marsh, Methane, Methylamine, Mofette, Mustard, Napalm, Natural, Ne, Neon, Nerve, Nitrogen, Noble, North Sea, Nox, O, Oil, Olefin(e), Orotund, Oxyacetylene, Oxygen, Ozone, Perfect, Petrol, Phosgene, Phosphine, Plasma, Poep, Poison, Prate, Producer, Propane, Propellant, Propene, Propylene, Protogalaxy, Protostar, Radon, Rare, RN, Sarin, Semiwater, Sewage, Sewer, Silane, Solfatara, Soman, Sour, Stibine, Sulphur dioxide, Swamp, Sweet, Synthesis, Tabun, → TALK, Taraniki wind, Tear, Tetrafluoroethene, Tetrafluoroethylene, Therm, Thoron, Town, Utility, V-agent, Vapour, VX, Waffle, War, Water, Whitedamp, → WIND, Xenon, Yackety-yak

Gasbag Blimp, Envelope, Prattler

Gascon(ade) Boast, Braggart, Skite

Gash Incise, Rift, Score, Scotch, → SLASH

Gas-mask Inhaler

Gasp(ing) Anhelation, Apn(o)ea, Chink, Exhale, Kink, Oh, Pant, Puff, Singult, Sob

Gast(e)ropod Ataata, Conch, Cowrie, Cowry, Dog-whelk, Dorididae, Euthyneura, Fusus, Glaucus, Haliotis, Harp-shell, Limpet, Mitre, Mollusc, Money cowry, Murex, Nerita, Nerite, Nudibranch, Opisthobranch, Ormer, Pelican's foot, Pennywinkle, Periwinkle, Pteropod, Purpura, Sea-ear, Sea-hare, Slug, Snail, Spindle-shell,

Streptoneura, Stromb, Top, Triton, Turbo, Turritella, Unicorn, Wentletrap, Whelk, Winkle

Gate(s), Gateway Alley, Attendance, Bill, Brandenburg, Caisson, Cilician, Crowd, Decuman, Entry, Erpingham, Golden, Head, Iron, Ivory, Kissing, Lock, Lych, Mallee, Menin, Moon, Moravian, Nor, Pearly, Portal, Portcullis, Postern, Praetorian, Propylaeum, Propylon, Pylon, Sallyport, Starting, Tail, Taranaki, Toran(a), Torii, Traitor's, Turnout, Turnstile, Waste, Water, Wicket, Yate, Yet(t)

Gatecrash(er) Interloper, Intrude, Ligger, Sorn, Unasked

Gatepost Sconcheon, Scontion, Scuncheon

▷ **Gateshead** *may indicate* 'g'

Gather(ed), Gathering Accrue, Amass, Assemble, Bee, Braemar, Cluster, Collate, → COLLECT, Colloquium, Concourse, Conglomerate, Congregate, Conventicle, Conversazione, Corral, Corroboree, Crop, Crowd, Cull, Derive, Eve, Fest, Frill, Function, Gabfest, Galaxy, Get together, Glean, Glomerate, Hangi, Harvest, Hear, Hootenanny, Hotchpot, Hui, Husking, In, Infer, Jamboree, Kommers, Learn, Lek, Lirk, Love-in, Meinie, Menyie, Multitude, Pleat, Plica, Plissé, Pucker, Purse, Raft, Raising-bee, Rake, Rally, Rave, Reef, Reunion, Round-up, Rout, Ruche, Ruff(le), Salon, Shindig, Shir(r), Shoal, Shovel, Singsong, Social, Spree, Swapmeet, Take, Tuck, Vindemiate, Vintage, Wappensc(h)aw, Witches' sabbath

Gauche Awkward, Clumsy, Farouche, Graceless

Gaudy Classy, Criant, Fantoosh, Flash, Garish, Glitz(y), Meretricious, Tacky, Tinsel

Gauge Absolute, Alidad(e), Anemometer, → ASSESS, Block, Bourdon, Broad, Calibre, Denier, Depth, Dial, Estimate, Etalon, Evaluate, Feeler, Judge, Lee, Limit, Loading, Manometer, Marigraph, Measure, Meter, Narrow, Nilometer, Oil, Ombrometer, Oncometer, Perforation, Plug, Pressure, Rain, Rate, Ring, Scantle, Size, Slip, Standard, Steam, Strain, Tape, Template, Tonometer, Tram, Tread, Tyre, Udometer, Vacuum, Water, Weather, Wind, Wire

Gauguin Paul

Gaul Asterix, Cisalpine, Transalpine, Vercingetorix

Gaunt Haggard, Lancaster, Lean, Randletree, Ranneltree, Rannletree, Rantletree, Rawbone, → THIN, Wasted

Gauntlet C(a)estus, Gantlope

Gauss G

Gautama Buddha

Gauze, Gauzy Gas mantle, Gossamer, Muslin, Sheer, Tiffany, Wire

Gawky Clumsy, Cow, Gammerstang, Sloucher

Gawp Rubberneck

Gay, Gaiety Blithe, Bonny, Boon, Buxom, Camp, Canty, Daffing, Debonair, Festal, Frolic, Gallant, Gladsome, Glee, Gordon, Grisette, Inverted, Jolly, Lightsome, May, Merry, Nitid, Out, Rackety, Riant, Rorty, Tit(t)upy, Volatile

Gaze Moon, Pore, Regard, Stare

Gazelle Ariel, Gerenuk, Goa, Mhorr, Mohr, Tabitha, Thomson's

Gazette London, Paper

Gear(ing), Gearbox Alighting, Angel, Arrester, Attire, Bags, Bevel, Capital, Clobber, Dérailleur, Differential, Draw, Duds, Engrenage, Epicyclic, Fab, Finery, Granny, Harness, Helical, Herringbone, High, Hypoid, Idle wheel, Involute, Kit, Landing, Lay-shaft, Low, Mesh, Mess, Mitre, Neutral, Notchy, Overdrive, Planetary, Ratio, Reverse, Rig, Riot, Rudder, Running, Spur, Steering, Straight, Sun and planet, Switch, Synchromesh, → TACKLE, Timing, Tiptronic®, Top, Trim, Tumbler, Valve, Variable, Worm(-wheel)

Gecko Tokay

Gee Horse, Hump, My, Reist, Sulk, Tout, Towt, Urge
Geiger-counter Scintillator
Geisha Maiko
Gel Hair, Pectin, Pectise, Silica
Gelatine, Gelatinous Blasting, Calipash, Collagen, Glutinous, Isinglass, Size, Tunicin
Geld(ing) Castrate, Lib, Neuter, Sort, Spado
Gelignite Jelly
Geller Uri
Gem Abraxas, Agate, Alexandrite, Almandine, Amazonite, Andradite, Asteria, Baguette, Birthstone, Bloodstone, Boule, Brilliant, Briolette, Cabochon, Cacholong, Cairngorm, Callais, Carbuncle, Carnelian, Cat's eye, Chrysoberyl, Chrysolite, Chrysoprase, Cornelian, Cymophane, Demantoid, Diamante, Diamond, Dumortierite, Emerald, Girasol(e), Girosol, Grossular(ite), Hawk's eye, Heliodor, Heliotrope, Hessonite, Hiddenite, Hyacinth, ID, Idaho, Indicolite, Iolite, Jacinth, Jargo(o)n, Jasper, Jaspis, → **JEWEL**, Kunzite, Lapis lazuli, Ligure, Marcasite, Marquise, Melanite, Menilite, Mocha stone, Moonstone, Morganite, Onyx, Opal, Pearl, Peridot(e), Plasma, Prase, Pyrope, Rhinestone, Rhodolite, Rose-cut, Rubellite, Ruby, Sapphire, Sard, Sardius, Sardonyx, Scarab, Scarabaeoid, Smaragd, Solitaire, Sparkler, Spessartite, Starstone, Stone, Sunstone, Tiger's eye, Topazolite, Tourmaline, Turquoise, Uvarovite, Verd antique, Zircon
Gemination, Gemini Diplogenesis, Twins
Gemma Bud, Knosp
Gen Info
Gendarme Flic
Gender Form, Natural, Sex
Gene(tics) Allel(e), Allelomorph, Anticodon, Codon, Complementary, Creation, Designer, Disomic, Dysbindin, Episome, Exon, Factor, Gay, Genome, Hereditary, Heterogamy, Holandric, Hologynic, Intron, Jumping, Lysenkoism, Mendel, Michurinism, Molecular, Muton, Oncogene, Operon, Regulatory, Reporter, Reverse, Selfish, Structural, Synteny, Telegony, Terminator, Transposon, Weismannism
Genealogist, Genealogy Armory, Family, Heraldry, Line, Pedigree, Seannachie, Seannachy, Sennachie, Whakapapa
General Agamemnon, Agricola, Agrippa, Alcibiades, Allenby, Antigonus, Antipater, Antony, Ataman, At large, Banquo, Barca, Blucher, Booth, Botha, Boulanger, Broad, C in C, Clive, Common, Communal, Conde, Cornwallis, Crassus, Current, Custer, De Gaulle, De Wet, Diadochi, Eclectic, Ecumenical, Election, Fairfax, Franco, Gamelin, Gen, GOC, Gordon, Grant, Hadrian, Hannibal, Holofernes, Ike, Inspector, Joshua, Kitchener, Lafayette, Lee, Leslie, Macarthur, Main, Marius, Marshall, Massena, Montcalm, Napier, Napoleon, Omnify, Overall, Overhead, Patton, Pershing, Pompey, Prevailing, Raglan, Regulus, Rife, Rommel, Scipio, Sherman, Shrapnel, Smuts, Stilwell, Strategist, Structural, Sulla, Tom Thumb, Turenne, → **UNIVERSAL**, Usual, Vague, Wide, Wolfe
Generate, Generation, Generator Abiogenetic, Age, Beat, Beget, Boomerang, Breeder, Charger, Cottonwool, Create, Dynamo, Electrostatic, Epigon, Father, Fuel-cell, House, Kipp, Loin, Lost, Magneto, Motor, Noise, Olds, Powerhouse, Signal, Sire, Spawn, Spontaneous, Stallion, Van de Graaff, Windmill, X, Yield
Generosity, Generous Bounty, Charitable, Free-handed, Free-hearted, Handsome, Kind, Largess(e), → **LAVISH**, Liberal, Magnanimous, Munificent, Noble(-minded), Open, Open-handed, Open-hearted, Philanthropic, Plump, Profuse, Selfless, Sporting, Unstinting
▸ **Genetic** *see* **GENE**

Geneva(n) Calvinist, Gin, Hollands
Genial(ity) Affable, Amiable, Benign, Bluff, Bonhomie, Chin, Convivial, Cordial, Human, Kindly, Mellow
Genie Djinn, Mazikeen, Shedeem
Genipap Lana
Genital(s) Ballocks, Bol(l)ix, Bollocks, Box, Cooze, Crack, Crotch, Cunt, Fanny, Front bottom, Labia, Lunchbox, Minge, Muff, Naff, Nympha, Private parts, Privates, Pubes, Pudendum, Pun(a)ani, Pun(a)any, Pussy, Quim, Secrets, Tackle, Tail, Twat, Vagina, Vulva, Wedding tackle, Yoni
Genitive Ethical
Genius Agathodaimon, Brain, Daemon, Einstein, Engine, Flash, Ingine, Inspiration, Ka, Mastermind, Michaelangelo, Numen, Prodigy
Genome Prophage
Genre Splatterpunk, Tragedy
Gent(leman), Gentlemen, Gentlemanly Amateur, Baboo, Babu, Beau, Caballero, Cavalier, Dandy, Duni(e)wassal, Dunniewassal, Esq(uire), Gemman, Gemmen, Ja(u)nty, Knight, Messrs, Milord, Mister, Mr, Nob, Proteus, Ritter, Runner, Rye, Sahib, Senor, Signor, Sir, Sirra(h), Smuggler, Squire, Sri, Stalko, Stir(rah), Swell, Tea, Toff, Tuan, Von, Yeoman
Genteel Conish, Polite, Proper, Refined
Gentian European, Felwort, Violet, Yellow
Gentile(s) Aryan, Ethnic, Goy, Nations, Shi(c)ksa, Uncircumcised
Gentle Amenable, Amenage, Bland, Clement, Delicate, Gradual, Grub, Light, Maggot, Mansuete, Mild, Tame, Tender
Gentry County, Landed, Quality, Squir(e)age
Gents Bog, John, Lav, Loo, WC
Genuflexion Bend, Curts(e)y, Kowtow, Salaam
Genuine Authentic, Bona-fide, Dinkum, Dinky-di, Echt, Frank, Heartfelt, Honest, Intrinsic, Jannock, Jonnock, Kosher, Legit(imate), McCoy, Nain, Proper, Pucka, Pukka, Pure, Pusser, → REAL, Real McCoy, Right, Simon-pure, Sincere, Square, Sterling, True, Unsophisticated, Veritable
Genus Class, Form, -ia, Mustela
Geode Druse
Geographer, Geography Chorography, Dialect, Economic, Hakluyt, Linguistic, Mercator, Pausanias, Physical, Political, Strabo
Geology, Geologist Economic, Geodynamics, Historical, Hutton, Isotope, Mineralogy, Phanerozoic, Seismology, Self-rock, Tectonics, Werner
Geometry, Geometrician, Geometer Affine, Analytical, Conics, Coordinate, Descriptive, Differential, Elliptic, Euclid(ean), Hyperbolic, Moth, Non-Euclidean, Parabolic, Plane, Porism, Projective, Riemannian, Solid, Spherics, Topologist
Geordie Guinea, Tynesider
George(s) Autopilot, Best, Borrow, Eliot, Farmer, Lloyd, Orwell, Pilot, Sand
Georgia(n) Abkhaz, Ga, Hanover, Iberian, Mingrel(ian)
Geraint Knight
Geranium Dove's foot, Rose, Stork's bill, Yellow
Gerbil Jird
Germ(s) Bacteria, Bug, Culture, Klebsiella, Seed, Spirilla, Strep, Virus, Wheat, Zyme
German(y) Al(e)main(e), Alemannic, Angle, Anglo-Saxon, Bavarian, Berliner, Blood-brother, Boche, Cimbri, Composer, Cousin, Denglish, Franconian, Frank, Fritz, G, Goth, Habsburg, Hans, Hapsburg, Herr, Hessian, High, Hun, Jerry, Jute, Kaiser, Kraut, Landgrave, Low, Lusatian, Neanderthal, Ossi, Ostrogoth, Otto,

Palsgrave, Pennsylvania, Plattdeutsch, Pruce, Prussian, Salic, Saxon, Squarehead, Tedesco, Teuton(ic), Vandal, Visigoth, Wessi, Wolfgang

Germane Apt, → **PERTINENT**, Relevant

Germanium Ge

Germ-free Aseptic

Germinate Grow, Pullulate, Sprout

Gesticulate, Gesticulation, Gesture(s) Ameslan, Beck(on), Ch(e)ironomy, Fico, Gest(e), Harvey Smith, Mannerism, Mime, Motion, Mudra, Salute, → **SIGN**, Signal, Snook, Token

Get(ting), Get(ting) by, Get(ting) on Acquire, Advance, Aggravate, Annoy, Attain, Bag, Become, Becoming, Brat, Bring, Capture, Cop, Cope, Derive, Fet(ch), Fette, Gain, Gee, Land, Learn, Make, Manage, Milk, Net, Noy, → **OBTAIN**, Pass, Peeve, Procure, Progress, Reach, Realise, Rile, Roil, Secure, See, Sire, Twig, Understand, Win

Getaway Disappearance, Escape, Vamoose

▷ **Getting** *may indicate* an anagram

Getting better Convalescing, Improving, Lysis

Get-up Tog(s)

Geum Avens

Gewgaw Bagatelle, Bauble, Doit, Tat, Trifle

Geyser Soffioni, Therm

Ghanaian Ashanti, Fantee, Fanti, Tshi, Twi

Ghastly Charnel, Gash, Grim, Hideous, Lurid, Macabre, Pallid, Spectral, Ugsome, Welladay, White

Gherkin Cornichon

Ghetto Barrio, Slum

Ghost(ly) Acheri, Apparition, Apport, Banquo, Caddy, Chthonic, Duende, Duppy, Eerie, Eery, Fantasm, Fetch, Gytrash, Haunt, Hint, Holy, Jumbie, Jumby, Larva(e), Lemur, Malmag, No'canny, Paraclete, Pepper's, Phantasm(agoria), Phantom, Revenant, Sampford, Shade, Shadow, Spectre, Spectrology, → **SPIRIT**, Spook, Trace, Truepenny, Umbra, Vision, Visitant, Waff, Wraith

Ghoul Fiend

GI Joe, Yankee

Giant(ess) Alcyoneus, Alifanfaron, Anak, Antaeus, Archiloro, Argus, Ascapart, Atlas, Balan, Balor, Bellerus, Blunderbore, Bran, Briareus, Brobdingnagian, Cacus, Colbrand, Colbronde, Colossus, Coltys, Cormoran, Cottus, Cyclop(e)s, Despair, Enceladus, Ephialtes, Eten, Ettin, Ferragus, Gabbara, Galligantus, Gargantua, Géant, Gefion, Geirred, Gigantic, Gog, Goliath, Grim, Harapha, Hrungnir, Hymir, Idris, Irus, Jotun(n), Jumbo, Krasir, Lestrigon, Leviathan, Magog, Mammoth, Mimir, Monster, Oak, Og, Ogre, Orion, Otus, Pallas, Pantagruel, Patagonian, Polyphemus, Pope, Red, Rounceval, Skrymir, Slaygood, Talos, Talus, Thrym, Titan, Tityus, Tregeagle, Triton, Troll, Tryphoeus, Typhon, Urizen, Utgard, Ymir, Yowie

Gibberish Claptrap, Double Dutch, Greek, Jargon

Gibbet Gallows, Patibulary, Potence, Ravenstone, Tree

Gibbon(s) Hoolock, Hylobate, Orlando, Siamang, Stanley, Wou-wou, Wow-wow

Gibe Barb, Brocard, Chaff, Fleer, Glike, Jeer, Jibe, Quip, Shy, Slant, Wisecrack

Gibraltar Calpe

Giddy (girl), Giddiness Capernoitie, Cap(p)ernoity, Dizzy, Fisgig, Fishgig, Fizgig, Giglot, Glaikit, Glaky, Haverel, Hellicat, Hoity-toity, Jillet, Light, Light-headed, Skipping, Staggers, Sturdy, Turn, Vertigo, Volage(ous), Wheel, Woozy

Gift(s), Gifted Ability, Alms, Aptitude, Bef(f)ana, Bequest, Blessing, Blest, Bonbon,

Bonsel(l)a, Boon, Bounty, Charism(a), Congiary, Corban, Covermount, Cumshaw, Dash, Deodate, → **DONATION**, Etrenne, Fairing, Fidecommissum, Flair, Foy, Free, Freebie, Gab, Garnish, Godsend, Grant, Greek, Handout, Han(d)sel, Hogmanay, Indian, Knack, Koha, Kula, Lagniappe, Largesse, Legacy, Manna, Ne'erday, Nuzzer, Offering, Parting, Peace-offering, PET, Potlatch, → **PRESENT**, Presentation, Prezzie, Propine, Reward, Sop, Talent, Tongues, Treat, Tribute, Wakf, Waqf, Windfall, Xenium

Gig Cart, Dennet, Moze, Whisk(e)y

Gigantic Atlantean, Briarean, Colossal, Goliath, → **HUGE**, Immense, Mammoth, Monster, Patagonian, Rounceval, Titan, Vast

Giggle, Giggling Cackle, Fou rire, Ha, Keckle, Simper, Snicker, Snigger, Tehee, Titter

Gigolo Gallant, Ladykiller, Pimp

Gilbert Bab, Gb, White, WS

Gild(ed), Gilding Checklaton, Embellish, Enhance, Inaurate, Ormolu, S(c)hecklaton, Vermeil

Gill(s) Beard, Branchia, Cart, Ctenidium, Jill, Noggin, Spiracle, Trematic

Gillman's Aqualung

Gilpin Draper, John, Renowned

Gilt Elt, Parcel, Sow

Gimcrack Gewgaw, Tawdry, Trangam

Gimmick Doodad, Doodah, Hype, Ploy, Ruse, Stunt

Gin Bathtub, Geneva, Genever, Hollands, Juniper, Lubra, Max, Mother's ruin, Noose, Old Tom, Pink, Ruin, Schiedam, Schnapp(s), Sloe, Snare, Springe, Toil, Trap, Trepan, Twankay

Ginger Activist, Amomum, Asarum, Cassumunar, Costus, Curcuma, Galanga(l), Galengale, Galingale, Gari, Malaguetta, Nut, Pachak, Pep, Pop, Putchock, Putchuk, Race, Rase, Red(head), Root, Spice, Stem, Turmeric, Zedoary, Zingiber

Gingerbread D(o)um-palm, Lebkuchen, Parkin, Parliament(-cake), Pepper-cake

Gingivitis Ulitis

▶ **Gipsy** see **GYPSY**

Giraffe Camelopard, Okapi

Gird Accinge, Belt, Equip, Gibe, Jibe, Quip

Girder Beam, Binder, H-beam, I-beam, Lattice, Loincloth, Spar

Girdle Baldric, Center, Cestus, Chastity, Cincture, Cingulum, Corset, Enzone, Equator, Hippolyte, Hoop, Mitre, Panty, Pectoral, Pelvic, Sash, Shoulder, Surcingle, Surround, Zona, Zone, Zonulet

Girl(s) Backfisch, Ball, Bimbo, Bint, Bird, Bit, Bobby-dazzler, Bobby-soxer, Bohemian, Broad, Burd, Call, Charlie, Chit, Chorus, Coed, Colleen, Cover, Crumpet, Cummer, Cutey, Cutie, Cutty, Dam(o)sel, Deb, Dell, Demoiselle, Dish, Doll, Dollybird, Essex, Filly, Fisgig, Fizgig, Flapper, Flower, Fluff, Fraulein, Frippet, Gaiety, Gal, Gammerstang, Geisha, Gibson, Gill(et), Gilp(e)y, Gouge, Gretel, Grisette, Hen, Hoiden, Hoyden, Hussy, It, Italian, Judy, Kimmer, Kinchinmort, Ladette, Land, Lass(ock), Lorette, Maid(en), Mauther, Mawr, Mawther, May, Miss(y), Moppet, Mor, Mot, Mousmé, Mousmee, Mystery, Nautch, Number, Nymph(et), Oanshagh, Peach, Peacherino, Petticoat, Piece, Pigeon, Popsy, Poster, Principal, Puss, Quean, Queyn, Quin(i)e, Randy, Señorita, Sheila, Shi(c)ksa, Sis(s), Smock, Sweater, Tabby, Taupie, Tawpie, Teddy, Tiller, Tit, Tootsie, Trull, Weeny-bopper, Wench, Widgie, Wimp

▷ **Girl** *may indicate* a female name

Girl friend Baby, Chérie, Confidante, Date, Flame, Hinny, Leman, Moll, Peat

Girth Cinch, Compass, Exploitable, Size, Surcingle

Gist Drift, Essence, Kernel, → **NUB**, Pith, Substance

Give(r), Give up, Giving Abandon, Abstain, Accord, Administer, Afford, Award, Bend, Bestow, Buckle, Cede, Confiscate, Consign, Contribute, Dative, Dispense, Dole, → **DONATE**, Duck, Elasticity, Enable, Endow, Enfeoff, Forswear, Gie, Grant, Hand, Impart, Indian, Jack, Largition, Present, Provide, Render, Resign, Sacrifice, Sag, Spring, Stop, Tip, Vacate, Vouchsafe, Yeve, Yield

Give-away Freebie, Gift-horse

Given If

Give out Bestow, Dispense, Emit, Exude, Peter

Give over Cease, Lin

Glacial, Glaciation Gunz, Mindel, Riss, Wurm

Glacier Aletsch, Crevasse, Drumline, Fox, Franz-Josef, Hanging, Iceberg, Ice-cap, Icefall, Moraine, Moulin, Muir, Rhône, Riss, Serac, Stadial, Stoss, Tasman

Glad(ly), Gladden, Gladness Cheer, Fain, → **HAPPY**, Lettice, Lief, Willing

Glade La(u)nd

Gladiator Retiarius, Spartacus

Glamour(ise), Glamorous Charm, Glitter(ati), Glitz, Halo, It, Prestige, SA, Sexy, Spell

Glamour girl Cheesecake, Odalisk, Odalisque, Pin-up

Glance Allusion, Amoret, Argentite, Blink, Browse, Carom(bole), Copper-head, Coup d'oeil, Dekko, Draw, Eld, Eliad, Eye-beam, Galena, Glad eye, Glimpse, Illiad, Inwick, Lustre, Oeillade, Once-over, Peek, → **PEEP**, Ray, Redruthite, Ricochet, Scan, Sheep's eyes, Shufti, Shufty, Side, Silver, Skellie, Skelly, Slant, Snick, Squint, Squiz, Twire, Vision, Waff

Gland Acinus, Adenoid, Adenoma, Adrenal, Apocrine, Bartholin's, Bulbourethral, Colleterial, Conarium, Cowper's, Crypt, Digestive, Ductless, Duodenal, Eccrine, Endocrine, Epiphysis, Exocrine, Goitre, Green, Holocrine, Hypophysis, Hypothalamus, Ink-sac, Lachrymal, Lacrimal, Liver, Lymph, Mammary, Meibomian, Musk-sac, Nectary, Oil, Osmeterium, Ovary, Pancreas, Paranephros, Parathyroid, Parotid, Parotis, Parotoid, Perineal, Pineal, Pituitary, Pope's eye, Preen, Prostate, Prothoracic, Salivary, Scent, Sebaceous, Sericterium, Shell, Silk, Sublingual, Submaxillary, Suprarenal, Sweat, Sweetbread, Tarsel, Tear, Testicle, Testis, Third eye, Thymus, Thyroid, Tonsil, Uropygial, Vesicle, Vulvovaginal, Zeiss

Glanders Farcy

Glandular (trouble) Adenitis

Glare, Glaring Astare, Blare, Dazzle, Flagrant, Garish, Gleam, Glower, Holophotal, Iceblink, Lour, Low(e), Naked, Shine, Vivid, Whally

Glass(es), Glassware, Glassy Amen, Ampul(la), Aneroid, Avanturine, Aventurine, Baccara(t), Barometer, Bell, Bifocals, Bins, Borosilicate, Bottle, Brimmer, Bumper, Burmese, Burning, Calcedonio, Case, Cheval, Cloche, Cocktail, Cooler, Copita, Cordial, Coupe, Cover, Crookes, Crown, Crystal, Cullet, Cupping, Cut, Dark, Delmonico, Diminishing, Eden, Euphon, Favrile, Fibre, Field, Flint, Float, Flute, Foam, Frigger, Frit, Fulgurite, Gauge, Glare, Goblet, Goggles, Granny, Green, Ground, Hand, Highball, Horn-rims, Humpen, Hyaline, Iceland agate, Jar, Jena, Jigger, Keltie, Kelty, Lace, Lalique, Laminated, Lanthanum, Latticinio, Lead, Lens, Liqueur, Liquid, Log, Lorgnette, Loupe, Lozen(ge), Lunette, Magma, Magnifying, Metal, Mica, Middy, Milk, Millefiori, Minimizing, Mirror, Moldavite, Monocle, Mousseline, Multiplying, Murr(h)ine, Muscovy, Musical, Nitreous, Object, Obsidian, One-way, Opal, Opal(ine), Opera, Optical, Pane, Parison, Paste, Pearlite, Pebble, Peeper, Pele, Pele's hair, Perlite, Perspective, Pier, Pince-nez,

Pinhole, Pitchstone, Plate, Pocket, Pon(e)y, Pressed, Prospective, Prunt, Psyche, Pyrex®, Quarrel-pane, Quarry, Quartz, Reducing, Roemer, Ruby, Rummer, Safety, Schmelz, Schooner, Seam, Seidel, Sheet, Silex, Silica, Sleever, Slide, Smalt(o), Snifter, Soluble, Specs, → **SPECTACLES**, Spun, Stained, Stein, Stem, Stemware, Stone, Storm, Strass, Straw, Sun, Supernaculum, Tachilite, Tachylite, Tachylyte, Tektite, Telescope, Tiffany, Tiring, Toilet, Trifocals, Triplex®, Tumbler, Uranium, Varifocals, Venetian, Venice, Vernal, Vita, Vitrail, Vitreous, Vitrescent, Vitro-di-trina, Volcanic, Watch, Water, Waterford, Weather, Window (pane), Wine, Wire

Glass-gall Sandiver

Glass-house Conservatory, Orangery

Glassite Sandemania

Glass-maker Annealer, Blower, Glazier, Lalique, Pontie, Pontil, Ponty, Puntee, Punty

Glaze(d), Glazing Aspic, Ciré, Coat, Double, Eggwash, Film, Flambé, Frit, Glost, Ice, Majolica, Peach-blow, Salt, Sancai, Slip, Tammy, Temmoku, Velatura

Gleam(ing) Blink, Flash, Glint, Glisten, Glitter, Gloss, Leme, Light, Lustre, Ray, Relucent, Sheen, Shimmer, → **SHINE**

Glean(er) Gather, Harvest, Lease, Stibbler

Glee Exuberance, Joy, Mirth, Song

Glen Affric, Ghyll, Gill, Rushy, Silicon, Vale

Glib Flip, Pat, Slick, Smooth

Glide(r), Glideaway, Gliding Aquaplane, Aviette, Chassé, Coast, Elapse, Float, Illapse, Lapse, Luge, Microlight, Off, On, Portamento, Rogallo, Sail, Sailplane, Sashay, Scorrendo, Scrieve, Skate, Ski, Skim, Sleek, Slide, Slip, Slur, Swim, Volplane

Glimmer(ing) Gleam, Glent, Glint, Glow, Inkling, Light, Stime, Styme, Twinkle, Wink

Glimpse Aperçu, Flash, Glance, Gledge, Glisk, Stime, Styme, Waff, Whiff

Glint Flash, Shimmer, → **SPARKLE**, Trace, Twinkle

Glisten(ing) Ganoid, Glint, Sheen, Shimmer, → **SHINE**, Sparkle

Glitter(ing) Clinquant, Garish, Gemmeous, Glee, Paillon, Sequin, Spang(le), Sparkle, Tinsel

Gloat(ing) Crow, Drool, Enjoy, Exult, Schadenfreude

Globe, Globule Artichoke, Ball, Bead, Celestial, Drop, Earth, Orb, Pearl, Shot, Sphear, Sphere

Globulin Legumin, Protein

Gloom(y) Atrabilious, Benight, Blues, Cheerless, Cimmerian, Cloud, Crepuscular, Damp, Dark, → **DESPAIR**, Dingy, Disconsolate, Dismal, Dool(e), Downbeat, Drab, Drear, Drumly, Dump(s), Dyspeptic, Feral, Funereal, Glum, Grey, Grim, Louring, Mirk, Misery, Mopish, Morne, Morose, Mumps, Murk, Obscurity, Overcast, Sable, Sad, Saturnine, Sepulchral, Solein, Solemn, → **SOMBRE**, Sourpuss, Stygian, Sullen, Tenebrious, Tenebrose, Tenebrous, Unlit, Wan

Glorification, Glorify Aggrandise, Apotheosis, Avatar, Bless, → **EXALT**, Extol, Halo, Laud, Lionise, Praise, Radiance, Splendour

Glorious, Gloria, Glory Chorale, Grand, Halo, Hosanna, Ichabod, Knickerbocker, Kudos, Lustre, Magnificent, Nimbus, Strut, Sublime, Twelfth

Glory-pea Kaka-beak, Kaka-bill, Kowhai

Gloss(y) Ciré, Enamel, Gild, Glacé, Interpret, Japan, Lip, Lustre, Patina, → **POLISH**, Postillate, Sheen, Sleek, Slick, Slide, Slur, Supercalendered, Veneer, Wetlook, Whitewash

Glossary Catalogue, Clavis, Index, K'thibh

Gloucester Cheese

Glove Boxing, Cestus, Dannock, Gage, Gauntlet, Kid, Mermaid's, Mitten, Mousquetaire, Muffle, Oven, Velvet

Glow(er), Glowing, Glowworm Aflame, Ashine, Aura, Bloom, Burn, Calescence, Candent, Candescence, Firefly, Flush, Foxfire, Gegenschein, Gleam, Halation, Iceblink, Incandescence, Lambent, Lamp-fly, Leam, Leme, Luculent, Luminesce, Lustre, Perspire, Phosphorescence, Radiant, Reflet, Rushlight, Shine, Snowblink, Translucent, → **WARMTH**

Glucin(i)um Gl

Glucose, Glucoside Aesculin, Amygdalin, Dextrose, Digitalin, Indican, Maltose, Salicin(e), Saponin, Solanine

Glue(y) Alkyd, Araldite®, Bee, Cement, Colloidal, Gelatin(e), Gunk, Hot-melt, Ichthyocolla, Isinglass, Marine, Paste, Propolis, Rice, Size, Spetch

Glum Dour, Livery, Lugubrious, Moody, Morose, Ron, Sombre

Glut Choke, Gorge, Sate, Satiate, Saturate, Surfeit

Gluten, Glutinous Goo, Ropy, Seiten, Sticky, Tar, Viscid, Zymome

Glutton(ous), Gluttony Bellygod, Carcajou, Cormorant, Edacity, Feaster, Free-liver, Gannet, Gorb, Gourmand, Greedyguts, Gulosity, Gutser, Gutsy, Gutzer, Hog, Lurcher, Pig, Ratel, Scoffer, Sin, Trencherman, Trimalchio, Wolverine

Glyceride, Glycerine Ester, Olein, Palmitin

Glycoside Hesperidin

Gnarl(ed) Knot, Knuckly, Knur, Nob

Gnash(ing) Bruxism, Champ, Grate

Gnat Culex, Culicidae, Midge, Mosquito

Gnaw(ing) Corrode, Erode, Fret, Lagomorph, Rodent

Gnome Adage, Bank-man, Chad, Cobalt, Financier, Kobold, Maxim, Motto, Proverb, Saw, Sprite

Gnostic(ism) (A)eon, Archontic, Cainite, Mand(a)ean, Marcionism, Ophite, Sabian, Tsabian, Zabian

Gnu Brindled, Horned horse, White-tailed, Wildebeest

Go, Going (after, for, off, on, up, etc) Advance, Afoot, Anabasis, Animation, Assail, Attempt, Bash, Betake, Bing, Brio, Choof, Clamber, Continuance, Crack, Depart, Die, Do, Energy, Fare, Gae, Gang, Gee, Gonna, Green, Hamba, Hark, Heavy, Hence, Hie, Imshi, Imshy, Ish, → **LEAVE**, March, Match, Off, Path, Pep, Perpetual, Ply, Quit, Raik, Repair, Resort, Resume, Run, Scat, Scram, Segue, Shoo, Shot, Skedaddle, Snick-up, Sour, Spank, Square, Stab, Success, Transitory, Trine, Try, Turn, Vam(o)ose, Verve, Via, Viable, Wend, Work, Yead, Yede, Yeed, Zap, Zing, Zip

Goad Ankus, Brod, Gad, Impel, Incite, → **NEEDLE**, Prod, Rowel, Spur, Stimulate, Stimulus, Taunt

Goal(posts) Ambition, Basket, Bourn(e), Cage, Destination, Dool, Dream, Drop, Dule, End, Ettle, Field, Golden, Grail, Hail, Home, Horme, Hunk, Limit, Mission, Moksha, Own, Score, Silver, Tap-in, Target, Touch-in, Ultima Thule, Uprights

Goat(-like) Alpine, Amalthea, Angora, Antelope, Antilope, Billy, Bok, Bucardo, Buck, Caprine, Cashmere, Cilician, Gait, Gate, Giddy, Goral, Hircine, Ibex, Izard, Kashmir, Kid, Libido, Markhor, Mountain, Nan(ny), Nubian, Rocky Mountain, Saanen, Sassaby, Serow, Serpent-eater, Steenbok, Steinbock, Tahr, Takin, Tehr, Thar, Toggenburg

Goatsucker Fern-owl, Nightjar

Gob(bet) Clot, Dollop, Mouth, Yap

Gobble Bolt, Devour, Gorge, Gulp, Slubber, Wolf

Gobelin Tapestry

Go-between Broker, Factor, Intermediate, Link, Mediate, Middleman, Pandarus, Pander, Shuttle

Goblet Chalice, Hanap

Goblin Banshee, Bargaist, Barg(h)est, Bodach, Bogey, Bogle, Bogy, Brownie, Bucca, Croquemitaine, Empusa, Erl-king, Esprit follet, Genie, Gnome, Gremlin, Knocker, Kobold, Lob-lie-by-the-fire, Lubberfiend, Lutin, Nis(se), Phooka, Phynnodderree, Pooka, Pouke, Puca, Pug, Red-cap, Red-cowl, Shellycoat, → **SPRITE**, Troll, Trow

Goby Dragonet

God(s) All-seer, Amen, Ancient of Days, → **DEITY**, Deus, Di, Divine, Gallery, Gracious, Holy One, Household, Immortals, Inner Light, Light, Maker, Od(d), Olympian, Prime Mover, Principle, Providence, Serpent, The Creator, Tin, Trinity, Truth, Unknown, Vanir, War, Water

---

GODS

1 letter:	Asur	Ammon	Yahwe
D	Aten	Bragi	
	Atum	Comus	*6 letters:*
2 letters:	Baal	Cupid	Adonai
An	Brag	Dagan	Aeolus
As	Bran	Dagon	Amen-ra
Ra	Cama	Donar	Amon-ra
Re	Deva	Freyr	Anubis
	Dieu	Haoma	Apollo
3 letters:	Eros	Horus	Ashtar
Anu	Faun	Hymen	Asshur
Bel	Frey	Indra	Avatar
Bes	Joss	Janus	Balder
Dis	Kama	Khnum	Boreas
Gad	Kami	Liber	Brahma
Geb	Llyr	Lludd	Cabiri
Jah	Loki	Mimir	Chemos
Lar	Lugh	Momus	Cronus
Lir	Mars	Njord	Delian
Lug	Mors	Numen	Elohim
Mot	Nebo	Orcus	Faunus
Pan	Odin	Orixa	Ganesa
Set	Ptah	Pales	Garuda
Sol	Rama	Picus	HaShem
Tiu	Seth	Pluto	Helios
Tiw	Siva	Rudra	Hermes
Tum	Soma	Satyr	Hughie
Tyr	Thor	Sebek	Hypnos
	Tyrr	Shiva	Kronos
4 letters:	Yama	Sinis	Mammon
Abba	Zeus	Surya	Marduk
Agni		Thoth	Mexitl
Aitu	*5 letters:*	Titan	Mextli
Amun	Aegir	Woden	Mithra
Apis	Aesir	Wotan	Molech
Ares	Allah	Yahve	Moloch

Nereus
Njorth
Oannes
Orisha
Ormazd
Ormuzd
Osiris
Panisc
Panisk
Plutus
Rimmon
Saturn
Somnus
Tammuz
Teraph
Teshup
Thamiz
Thunor
Triton
Uranus
Varuna
Vishnu
Vulcan
Yahweh
Zombie

7 letters:
Alastor
Alpheus
Angus Og

Anteros
Bacchus
Bhagwan
Chemosh
Daikoku
Ganesha
Hanuman
Heimdal
Jehovah
Jupiter
Krishna
Kuan Yin
Kwan Yin
Mercury
Mithras
Neptune
Nisroch
Oceanus
Penates
Phoebus
Priapus
Proteus
Rameses
Sarapis
Sat Guru
Serapis
Setebos
Shamash
Silenus
Thammuz

Zagreus

8 letters:
Achelous
Dionysus
Heimdall
Hyperion
Kamadeva
Mahadeva
Morpheus
Mulciber
Nataraja
Pantheon
Poseidon
Quirinus
Silvanus
Sylvanus
Terminus
Trimurti
Wahiguru
Zephyrus

9 letters:
All-father
Asclepius
Fabulinus
Heimdallr
Jagganath
Promachos
Tetragram

Thunderer
Vertumnus
Zernebock

10 letters:
Ahura Mazda
Demogorgon
Elegabalus
Hephaestus
Hephaistos
Juggernaut
Karttikaya
Mumbo-jumbo
Prometheus
Trophonius

11 letters:
Adrammelech
Aesculapius
Bodhisattva

12 letters:
Quetzalcoati
Supreme Being
Trismegistus

14 letters:
Tetragrammaton

God-bearing Deiparous
Goddess(es) Divine, Green, Muse

GODDESSES

2 letters:
Ge

3 letters:
Ate
Eos
Hel
Mut
Nox
Nut
Nyx
Ops
Pax

4 letters:
Dian
Eris
Gaea
Gaia
Hera
Idun
Iris
Isis
Juno
Kali
Leda
Leto
Luna

Maat
Maut
Nike
Norn
Pele
Rhea
Sita
Thea

5 letters:
Aruru
Ceres
Diana
Dione

Durga
Erato
Flora
Freya
Grace
Horae
Houri
Hulda
Iduna
Irene
Kotys
Moera
Moira
Pales

		7 *letters:*	8 *letters:*
Tanit	Hecate	Artemis	Cloacina
Terra	Hertha	Astarte	Cytherea
Tyche	Hestia	Astraea	Libitina
Ushas	Huldar	Bellona	Rhiannon
Venus	Hyaeia	Cotytto	Valkyrie
Vesta	Idalia	Cynthia	Victoria
	Ishtar	Demeter	Walkyrie
6 *letters:*	Ithunn	Fortuna	
Aglaia	Lucina	Kotytto	9 *letters:*
Ashnan	Pallas	Lakshmi	Aphrodite
Athene	Parcae	Megaera	Ashtaroth
Aurora	Phoebe	Minerva	Ashtoreth
Bastet	Pomona	Nemesis	Eumenides
Cybele	Satyra	Nepthys	Mnemosyne
Cyrene	Selene	Parvati	Sarasvati
Eastre	Semele	Sabrina	
Freyja	Tellus	Strenia	10 *letters:*
Frigga	Tethys	Victory	Amphitrite
Graeae	Themis		Proserpina
Graiae	Thetis		Proserpine
Hathor			

Godfather, Godmother Capo, Cummer, Fairy, Gossip, Kimmer, Rama, Sponsor, Woden

Godless Agnostic, Atheistic, Atheous, Impious, Profane

Godly Deist, Devout, Holy, Pious

Godown Hong

God-willing Deo volente, DV, Inshallah, Mashallah

Go-getter Arriviste, Hustler

Goggle(s) Snow-eyes, Stare

Going wrong Aglee, Agley, Misfiring

▷ **Going wrong** *may indicate* an anagram

Goitre Derbyshire neck, Exophthalmic, Graves' disease, Struma

Gold(en) Age, Amber, Apple, Ass, Au, Aureate, Auriferous, Bendigo, Bough, Bull, Bullion, California, Chryselephantine, Doubloon, Dutch, Eagle, Electron, Electrum, Emerods, Filigree, Filled, Fleece, Fool's, Free, Fulminating, Gate, Gule, Handshake, Hind, Horde, Horn, Ingot, Kolar, Leaf, Lingot, Moidore, Mosaic, Muck, Nugget, Oaker, Obang, Ochre, Ophir, Or, Oreide, Ormolu, Oroide, Pistole, Placer, Pyrites, Red, Reef, Rolled, Silence, Silver-gilt, Sol, Standard, Stream, Stubborn, Talmi, Thrimsa, Tolosa, Treasury, Venice, Virgin, White, Witwatersrand, Yellow

Gold-digger Forty-niner, Prospector

Golden fleece Phrixus

Goldfield Rand

Goldfinch Charm, Chirm, Redcap

Gold leaf Ormolu

Gold rush Kalgoorlie, Klondike

Goldsmith Cellini, Fabergé, Oliver

Golf (ball) Better-ball, Clock, Crazy, Foursome, Gutta, Matchplay, Medal play, Repaint, Round, Stableford

Golfer Alliss, Braid, Cotton, Els, Faldo, Hogan, Lyle, Pivoter, Rees, Roundsman, Seve, Snead, Teer, Texas scramble, Tiger Woods, Trevino, Wolstenholme, Yipper

Golly Crumbs, Gosh
Gondolier Balloonist, Bargee
Gone Ago, Dead, Defunct, Napoo, Out, Past, Ygo(e), Yod
▷ **Gone off** *may indicate* an anagram
Gone west Had it
Gong Bell, DSO, → **MEDAL**, Tam-tam, VC
Gonorrhoea Clap
Goo Gleet, Gloop, Gunge, Poise, Ulmin
Goober Monkey nut
Good(ness), Goody-goody Agatha, Agathodaimon, Altruism, Angelic, Bad, Bein, Benefit, Blesses, Bon, Bonzer, Bosker, Bounty, Brod, Budgeree, Canny, Castor, Civil, Clinker, Common, Coo, Cool, Crack(ing), Credit, Dab, Dandy, Def, Dow, Enid, Estimable, Fantabulous, Finger lickin', First-class, G, Gear, Giffen, Glenda, Gosh, Guid, Humdinger, Lois, Lor, Ma foi, Neat, Nobility, → **NO GOOD**, Pi, Plum, Prime, Proper, Purler, Rattling, Rectitude, Riddance, Right, Rum, Sake, Salutary, Samaritan, Sanctity, Slap-up, Smashing, Spiffing, St, Suitable, Super, Taut, Tollol, Topping, Valid, Virtue, Virtuous, Weal, Welfare, Whacko, Wholesome, Worthy
Goodbye Addio, Adieu, Adios, Aloha, Apopemptic, Arrivederci, Cheerio, Ciao, Congé, Farewell, Haere ra, Hamba kahle, Hooray, Hooroo, Sayonara, See-you, Tata, Toodle-oo, Toodle-pip, Vale
Good evening Den
Goodfellow Brick, Puck, Robin, Samaritan, Worthy
Good-for-nothing Bum, Donnat, Donnot, Dud, Idler, Layabout, Lorel, Lorrell, Losel, Napoo, Sca(l)lawag, Scallywag, Scant o'grace, Sculpin, Shot-clog, Useless, Vaurien, Waff, Waster, Wastrel
Good Friday Parasceve, Pasch of the Cross
Good-humour(ed), Good-natured Amiable, Bonhomie, Gruntled, Kind
Good-looking Bon(n)ie, Bonny, Bonwie, Comely, Fair, Handsome, Personable, Pretty, Wally
Good news Evangel
Good number Thr(e)ave
Good order Eutaxy, Shipshape
Goods Bona, Brown, Cargo, Consumer, Disposable, Durable, Durables, Fancy, Flotsam, Freight, Futures, Gear, Hardware, Insight, Ironware, Lagan, Lay-away, Line, Piece, Products, Property, Schlock, Soft, Sparterie, Truck, Wares, White
Goodwill Amity, Bonhom(m)ie, Favour, Gree
Goody Wrong'un
Goon Bentine, Milligan, Secombe, Sellers
Goose, Geese Anserine, Barnacle, Bernicle, Blue, Brent, Canada, Cape Barren, Colonial, Daftie, Ember, Gaggle, Gander, Gannet, Golden, Greylag, Grope, Harvest, Hawaiian, Idiot, Juggins, MacFarlane's, Magpie, Michaelmas, Mother, Nana, Nene, Pink-footed, Quink, Roger, Saddleback, Silly, Simpleton, Skein, Snow, Solan, Strasbourg, Stubble, → **STUPID PERSON**, Swan, Team, Wav(e)y, Wawa, Whitehead
Gooseberry Cape, Chaperon(e), Chinese, Coromandel, Detrop, Fool, Gog, Groser(t), Groset, Grossart, Grozer, Honey blob, Kiwi, Physalis, Tomato
Gooseflesh Horripilation
Goosefoot Allgood, Amarantaceae, Beet, Blite, Fat-hen, Mercury, Orache, Saltbush
Gooseherd Quill-driver
Gopher Camass-rat, Minnesota, Pocket
Gordian Knot

Gordon Chinese, Flash, Rioter

Gore Blood, Cloy, Gair, Horn, Inset, Toss

Gorge(s) Abyss, Arroyo, Barranca, Barranco, Canyon, Chasm, Cheddar, Cleft, Couloir, Cram, Defile, Donga, Flume, Gap, Ghyll, Glut, Grand Canyon, Grand Coulee, Gulch, Iron Gate, Khor, Kloof, Lin(n), Nala, Nalla(h), Nulla(h), Olduvai, Overeat, Overfeed, Pass, Ravine, Snarf, Staw, → STUFF, Throat, Tire, Tums, Valley, Yosemite

Gorgeous Delectable, Dreamboat, Grand, Splendid, Superb

Gorgon Euryale, Medusa, Ogress, Stheno

▸ **Gorilla** *see* MONKEY

Gorse Broom, Furze, Gosse, Ulex, Whin

Gosh Begad, Begorra, Blimey, Coo, Cor, Gadzooks, Gee, Gracious, Gum, Heavens, Lor, My, Och, Odsbobs, Odso

Gospel(s), Gospeller Apocryphal, Creed, Diatessaron, Evangel, Fact, John, Kerygma, Luke, Mark, Matthew, Nicodemus, Prosperity, Protevangelium, Synoptic, Truth, Waldensian

Gossamer(y) Araneous, Byssoid, Cobwebby, Gauzy

Gossip Ana(s), Aunt, Backbite, Blether, Cackle, Cat, Causerie, Chat, Chin, Chitchat, Clash, Claver, Cleck, Clish-clash, Clishmaclaver, Confab, Coze, Crack, Cummer, Dirt, Flibbertigibbet, Gab(nash), Gabfest, Gas, Gash, Goster, Gup, Hearsay, Hen, Jaw, Loose-tongued, Maundrel, Nashgab, Natter, Noise, On dit, Pal, Personalist, Prattle, Prose, Quidnunc, Reportage, Rumour, Scandal(monger), Schmooze, Scuttlebutt, Shmoose, Shmooze, Sweetie-wife, Tabby(cat), Talk(er), Tattle, Tattletale, Tibby, Tittle(-tattle), Twattle, Yatter, Yenta

Got Gat, Obtained

Goth(ic) Alaric, Lurid, Moesia

Gothamite Abderian, New Yorker

Gouge Chisel, Groove, Scoop

Gourd Bottle, Calabash, Courgette, Dishcloth, Guiro, Hercules' club, Loofa, Melon, Monkeybread, Pumpkin, Squash, Zucchini

Gourmand, Gourmet Apicius, → EPICURE, Gastronome, Gastrosopher, Lickerish, Table, Trencherman, Ventripotent

Gout Chiragra, Hamarthritis, Podagra, Taste, Tophus

Govern(or), Government Adelantado, Administer, Ag(h)a, Agricola, Alderman, Amban, Amman, Amtman, ANC, Andocracy, Archology, Aristocracy, Autarchy, Autocrat, Autonomy, Bahram, Ban, Bashaw, Beehive, Beg, Beglerbeg, Bencher, Bey, Bridler, Bureaucracy, Burgrave, Cabinet, Caciquism, Caretaker, Castellan, Catapan, Cham, Circar, Classis, Coalition, Command, Commonwealth, Condominium, Congress, Constable, Constitution, Consulate, Cybernetic, Darogha, Democracy, Dergue, Despotism, Dey, Diarchy, Dictatorship, Dinarchy, Directoire, Directory, Dominate, Downing St, Duarchy, Dulocracy, Duumvirate, Dyarchy, Dynast, Earl, Ecclesiarchy, Empery, Eparch, Ergatocracy, Escapement, Ethnarch, Exarch, Fascism, Federal, G, Gauleiter, Gerontocracy, Gov, Grieve, Gubernator, Guv, Gynarchy, Hagiarchy, Hagiocracy, Hague, Hajjaz, Hakim, Haptarchy, Harmost, HE, Helm, Hexarchy, Hierocracy, Honcho, Hospodar, Imperialism, Ins, Inspector, Isocracy, Junta, Kaimakam, Kakistocracy, Kawanatanga, Kebele, Kemalism, Khalifate, Khan, Kremlin, Legate, Local, Majlis, Majorism, Monarchy, Monocracy, Mudir, Nabob, Naik, Nomarch, Nomocracy, Ochlocracy, Oireachtas, Oligarchy, Optic®, Pa, Pacha, Padishah, Pasha, Pater, Pentarch, Père, Petticoat, Physiocracy, Pilate, Placemen, Plutocracy, Podesta, Polity, Polyarchy, Porte, Power, Priest-king, Proconsul, Propraetor, Proveditor, Provedor(e), Providor,

Ptochocracy, Quadrumvirate, Quirinal, Raj, Realpolitik, Rection, Rector, Rectrix, Regency, Regié, Regime(n), Reign, Rein, Ride, → **RULE**, Satrap, Senate, Serkali, Shogun, Signoria, Sircar, Sirkar, Stad(t)holder, Stakhanovism, Statecraft, Steer, Stratocracy, Subadar, Sway, Technocracy, Tetrarchy, Thalassocracy, Thalattocracy, Thatcherism, Thearchy, Theocracy, Theonomy, Timocracy, Totalitarianism, Triarchy, Triumvirate, Tuchun, Tyranny, Vali, Viceregal, Viceroy, Vichy, Wali, Warden, Wealsman, Whitehall, White House, Witan

Governess Duenna, Eyre, Fraulein, Griffin, Mademoiselle, Prism, Vicereine

Government revenue Jaghir(e), Jagir

Gown Banian, Banyan, Dressing, Empire, Geneva, Green, Johnny, Kirtle, Manteau, Manto, Mantua, Manty, Morning, Mother Hubbard, Peignoir, Polonaise, Robe, Sack, Silk, Slammakin, Slammerkin, Slop, Stola, Stuff, Tea, Wrap(per)

Grab Annexe, Bag, Clutch, Cly, Collar, Glaum, Grapnel, Hold, Holt, Rap, Seise, Seize, → **SNATCH**, Steal, Swipe

Gracchi Jewels

Grace(s), Graceful Aglaia, Airy, Amnesty, Anna, Bad, Beauty, Become, Benediction, Bethankit, Blessing, Charis(ma), Charites, Charity, Cooperating, Darling, Dr, Elegance, Euphrosyne, Fluent, Gainly, Genteel, Genty, Godliness, Grazioso, Handsome, Light, Mense, Mercy, Molinism, Mordent, Omnium, Ornament, Polish, Pralltriller, Prayer, Sacrament, Saving, Spirituelle, Streamlined, Style, Thalia, Thanks, Thanksgiving, WG, Willowy

Gracious Benign, By George, Charismatic, Generous, Good, Handsome, Hend, Merciful, Polite

Gradation Ablaut, Cline, Degree, Nuance, Stage

Grade, Gradient Alpha, Analyse, Angle, Assort, Beta, Bubs, Class(ify), Conservation, Dan, Degree, Delta, Echelon, Gamma, Geothermal, Gon, Gride, Hierarchy, Inclination, Kyu, Lapse, Measure, Order, Ordinary, Pressure, Rank, Reserve, Score, Seed, Slope, Stage, Standard, Status, Temperature, Thermocline

Gradual Gentle, Grail, Imperceptible, Inchmeal, Piecemeal, Slow

Graduate, Graduation Alumnus, BA, Bachelor, Calibrate, Capping, Classman, Incept, Laureateship, Licentiate, LlB, MA, Master, Nuance, Optime, Ovate

Graffiti Bomb, Doodle, Tag, Tagger

Graft Anaplasty, Autoplasty, Boodle, Bribery, Bud, Bypass, Cion, Cluster, Crown, Dishonesty, Dub, Enarch, Enrace, Flap, Hard, Heteroplasty, Imp, Implant, Inarch, Inoculate, Payola, Pomato, Racket, Scion, Shoot, Sien(t), Skin, Slip, Syen, Transplant, Whip, Ympe

Grail Chalice, Cup, Sangraal, Sangrail, Sangreal

Grain(y) Bajra, Bajree, Bajri, Bear, Bere, Boll, Bran, Cereal, Corn, Couscous, Crop, Curn, Curn(e)y, Cuscus, Distillers', D(o)urra, Extine, Frumentation, Gr, Graddan, Granule, Groats, Grumose, Intine, Kaoliang, Knaveship, Malt, Mashlam, Mashlin, Mashloch, Mashlum, Maslin, Mealie, Millet, Milo, Minim, Mongcorn, Oats, Panic(k), Pannick, Pickle, Pinole, Pollen, Polynology, Popcorn, Proso, Psyllium, Puckle, Quarter, Quinoa, Rabi, Raggee, Raggy, Ragi, Rhy, Rye, Sand, Scruple, Seed, Semsem, Sorghum, Thirlage, Tola, Touch, Wheat, Wholemeal

Gram Black, Chich, Chick-pea, Green, Teen, Tene, Urd

Grammar(ian), Grammatical Ablative absolute, Accidence, Amphibology, Anacoluthia, Anacoluthon, Anaphora, Anastrophe, Case, Cataphora, Categorical, Donat, Donet, Generative, Gr, Linguistics, Montague, Paradigm, Paucal, Pivot, Primer, Priscianist, Priscianus, Protasis, Scholiast, Stratificational, Syndetic, Syndeton, Synectics, Synesis, Syntax, Systemics, Tagmeme, Transformational, Trivium, Typto, Universal, Valency

Gramophone Record player, Victrolla®
Grampus Orc, Thresher-whale, Whale
Granary Barn, Girnel, Silo
Grand(eur), Grandiose Big, Canyon, Epical, Flugel, G, Gorgeous, Guignol, High-faluting, Hotel, Imposing, La(h)-di-da(h), Long, Lordly, Magnificent, Majestic, Megalomania, Palatial, Piano(forte), Pompous, Regal, Splendid, Stately, Stoor, Stour, Stowre, Sture, Sublime, Swell, Tour
Grandchild Mokopuna, Niece, Oe, Oy(e)
Grandee Adelantado, Don, Magnifico
Grandfather Ancient, Avital, Clock, Goodsire, Gramps, Gudesire, Gutcher, Luckie-dad, Oldster, Old-timer, Oupa
Grandmother Babushka, Beldam, Gran(nie), Granny, Moses, Nan(a), Ouma
Grandparent(al) Aval, Avital
Grand Prix Race(-cup)
Grandsire Peal
Grange Moated
Granite Aberdeen, Chinastone, Graphic, Greisen, Luxul(l)ianite, Luxulyanite, NH, Pegmatite, Protogine
Grannie Forebear, Knot, Nan(a)
Grant(ed) Accord, Aid, Award, Bestow, Beteem(e), Block, Bounty, Bursary, Carta, Cary, Cede, Charta, Charter, Concession, → CONFER, Cy, Datum, Endow, Exhibition, Feoff, Give, Hugh, Land, Lend, Let, Munich, Obreption, Patent, President, Regium donum, Send, Sop, Subsidy, Subvention, Supply, Teene, Ulysses, Vouchsafe, Yeven, Yield
Granule, Granulate(d) Kern, Otolith, Pearl, Plastid, Pound, Prill
Grape(s) Aligoté, Botros, Botryoid, Bullace, Cabernet, Cabernet Sauvignon, Catawba, Chardonnay, Chenin blanc, Colombard, Concord, Delaware, Diamond, Fox, Gamay, Gewurztraminer, Grenache, Haanepoot, Hamburg(h), Hanepoot, Honeypot, Hyacinth, Lambrusco, Malbec, Malmsey, Malvasia, Malvesie, Malvoisie, Marsanne, Merlot, Muscadel, Muscadine, Muscat(el), Noble rot, Oregon, Petite Syrah, Pinot, Pinot blanc, Pinot Chardonnay, Primitivo, Ptisan, Racemose, Raisin, Rape, Riesling, Sauvignon, Scuppernong, Sémillon, Sercial, Shiraz, Sour, Staphyline, Steen, Sultana, Sweet-water, Sylvaner, Syrah, Tokay, Uva, Verdelho, Véronique, Vino, Wineberry, Zinfandel
Grapefruit Pampelmoose, Pomelo, Pompelmouse, Pompelo, Pumple-nose, Shaddock, Ugli®
Grapeshot Mitraille
Grape-sugar Glucose
Grapevine Hearsay, Mocassin telegraph, Moccasin telegraph
Graph, Graphic(s) Bar, Chart, Computer, Contour, Diagram, Histogram, Learning curve, Nomograph, Ogive, Picturesque, Pie (chart), Profile, Sonogram, Table, Turtle, Vivid, Waveform, Waveshape
Graphite Kish, Plumbago
Grapple Clinch, Close, Hook, Lock, Struggle, Wrestle
Grasp(ing) Apprehend, Catch, Clat, Claut, Clinch, → CLUTCH, Compass, Comprehend, Fathom, Get, Grab, Grapple, Greedy, Grip(e), Hent, Hug, Prehend, Prehensile, Raptorial, Realise, Rumble, Sense, Snap, Snatch, Twig, Uptak(e)
Grass(land), Grass roots, Grassy Agrostology, Alang, Alfa(lfa), Arrow, Avena, Bahia, Bamboo, Bang, Barbed wire, Barley, Barnyard, Beard, Bennet, Bent, Bermuda, Bhang, Blade, Blady, Blue(-eyed), Blue moor, Bristle, Brome-grass, Bromus, Buffalo, Buffel, Bunch, Bush, Canary, Cane, Canna, Cannach, Carpet,

Cat's tail, Chess, China, Citronella, Cleavers, Clivers, Clover, Cochlearia, Cocksfoot, Cockspur, Cogon, Cord, Cortaderia, Cotton, Couch, Cow, Crab, Culm, Cuscus, Cutty, Dactylis, Danthonia, Dari, Darnel, Deergrass, Dhur(r)a, Diss, Divot, Dogstail, Dog's tooth, Dogwheat, Doob, Doura, Dura, Durra, Eddish, Eel, Eelwrack, Elephant, Emmer, Esparto, Feather, Fescue, Finger, Fiorin, Flinders, Floating, Flote, Fog, Foggage, Foxtail, Gage, Gama-grass, Ganja, Gardener's garters, Glume, Glumella, Goose, Grama, Green(sward), Hair, Halfa, Harestail, Hassock, Haulm, Hay, Haycock, Heath(er), Hemp, Herbage, High veld, Holy, → **INFORM**, Jawar(i), Job's tears, Johnson, Jowar(i), Kangaroo, Kans, Kentucky blue, Khuskhus, Kikuyu, Knoll, Knot, Lalang, Laund, Lawn, Lay, Lea, Lee, Lemon, Locusta, Lolium, Lop, Lucern(e), Lyme, Mabela, Machair, Manna, Marram, Marrum, Mary Jane, Mat, Materass, Matweed, Mead, Meadow(-fescue), Meadow foxtail, Melic, Melick, Millet, Milo, Miscanthus, Monkey, Moor, Nark, Nassella tussock, Nature strip, Nose, Nut, Oat, Orange, Orchard, Oryza, Painted, Palet, Pamir, Pampas, Panic, Paspalum, Pasturage, Peach, Pennisetum, Pepper, Persicaria, Phleum, Plume, Poa, Porcupine, Pot, Purple moor, Puszta, Quack, Quaking, Quick, Quitch, Ramee, Rami(e), Rat, Rat on, Redtop, Reed, Rescue, Rhodes, Rib, Ribbon, Rice, Rips, Roosa, Rough, Rumble(r), Rusa, Rush, Rye(-brome), Sacaton, Sago, Salt, Sand, Savanna(h), Saw, Scorpion, Scraw, Scurvy, Scutch, Sea-reed, Sedge, Seg, Sesame, Shave, Sheep's fescue, Shop, Sing, Sinsemilla, Sisal, Sneak(er), Snitch, Snout, Snow, Sorghum, Sour-gourd, Sourveld, Spanish, Spear, Spelt, Spike, Spinifex, Splay, Split, Squeal, Squirrel-tail, Squitch, Stag, Star(r), Stipa, Stool-pigeon, Storm, Sudan, Sugar, Sward, Swath(e), Sword, Tape, Taramea, Tath, Tea, Tef(f), Tell, Teosinte, Timothy, Toad, Toetoe, Toitoi, Triticale, Triticum, True-love, Tuffet, Turf, Tussac, Tussock, Twitch, Veld(t), Vernal, Vetiver, Viper's, Whangee, Wheat, Wheatgrass, Whitlow, Windlestraw, Wire, Witch, Wood melick, Worm, Yard, Yellow-eyed, Yorkshire fog, Zizania, Zostera, Zoysia

Grasshopper Cicada, Cricket, Grig, Katydid, Locust, Long-horned, Meadow, Tettix, Wart-biter, Weta

Grate(r), Grating Abrade, Burr, Cancelli, Chain, Chirk, Crepitus, Diffraction, → **FRET**, Graticule, Gravelly, Grid, Grill, Guichet, Guttural, Hack, Haik, Hake, Hearth, Heck, Hoarse, Ingle, Jar, Mort-safe, Portcullis, Rasp, Risp, Rub, Ruling, Scrannel, → **SCRAPE**, Scrat, Shred, Siver, Strident, Syver

Grateful Beholden, Cinders, Indebted, Obliged

Gratification, Gratify(ing) Aggrate, Indulge, Kick, Masochism, Narcissism, Oblige, Pleasure, Regale, Reward, Sadism

Gratitude God 'a mercy, Ta, Thanks

Gratuitous, Gratuity Baksheesh, Beer-money, Bonsella, Bonus, Bounty, Cumshaw, Free, Glove-money, Gratis, Mag(g)s, Tip

Grave(yard) Accent, Arlington, Bass, Bier, Burial, Charnel, Chase, Critical, Darga, Demure, Dust, God's acre, Heavy, Heinous, Important, Ingroove, Kistvaen, Kurgan, Long home, Mool, Mould, Mound, Passage, Pit, Sad, Saturnine, Serious, Sober, Sombre, Speos, Staid, Stern, Tomb, Watery

Grave-digger Bederal, Fossor, Sexton

Gravel(ly) Calculus, Channel, Chesil, Chisel, Eskar, Esker, Glareous, Grail(e), Grit, Hoggin(g), Murram, Nonplus, Pay, Pea, Pingo, Shingle

Gravity Barycentric, G, Geotaxis, Geotropism, Great Attraction, Magnitude, Mascon, Quantum, Specific, Weight, Zero

Gravy Baster, Bisto®, Browning, Coin, Jus, Sauce

Gravy-boat Argyle, Argyll

▶ **Gray** *see* **GREY**

Grayling Umber

Graze, Grazing, Grazier Abrade, Agist, Bark, Brush, Crease, Crop, Feed, Gride, Gryde, Heft, Herdwick, Leasow(e), Machair, Moorburn, Muirburn, Pascual, Pastoralist, Pasture, Rake, Rangeland, Scrape, Scrawn, Shave, Sheepwalk, Shieling, Zero

Grease, Greasy Bribe, Creesh, Dope, Dubbing, Elaeolite, Elbow, Enseam, Glit, Lanolin, Lard, Lubricate, Ointment, Pinguid, Seam(e), Shearer, Sheep-shearer, Smarm, Smear, Suint, Unctuous

Great(ly), Greater, Greatest, Greats Alfred, Ali, Astronomical, Bully, Capital, Colossus, Extreme, Gargantuan, Gatsby, Gay, Gey, Gran(d), Grit, Gt, Guns, Hellova, Helluva, Immortal, Important, Lion, Macro, Magnus, Main, Major, Massive, Mega, Mickle, Mochell, Modern, Much, Muchel(l), Muckle, No end, OS, Profound, Rousing, Stoor, Stour, Stupendous, Sture, Sublime, Super, Superb, Swingeing, Synergy, Tall, Titan(ic), Top notch, Tremendous, Unco, Untold, Utmost, Vast, Voluminous, Zenith

Great deal Mort

Grebe Cargoose

Grecian Bend, Nose

Greed(y) Avarice, Avid, Bulimia, Bulimy, Cupidity, Edacious, Esurient, Gannet, Gare, Grabby, Grip(ple), Gulosity, Harpy, Insatiable, Killcrop, Lickerish, Liquorish, Mercenary, Money-grubbing, Piggery, Pleonexia, Rapacity, Selfish, Shark's manners, Solan, Voracity, Wolfish

Greek(s) Achaean, Achaian, Achilles, Aeolic, Agamemnon, Ajax, Ancient, Aonian, Arcadia, Archimedes, Argive, Aristides, Athenian, Attic, Boeotian, Byzantine, Cadmean, Cleruch, Corinthian, Cretan, Cumae, Cyzicus, Delphian, Demotic, Ding, Diomedes, Dorian, Doric, Elea, Eoka, Eolic, Epaminondas, Ephebe, Epirus, Euclid, Evzone, Fanariot, Gr, Helladic, Hellene, Hellenic, Homer, Hoplite, Ionian, Isocrates, Italiot(e), Javan, Katharev(o)usa, Klepht, Koine, Laconian, Lapith, Late, Leonidas, Linear B, Locrian, Lucian, Lysander, Macedonia, Medieval, Middle, Modern, Molossian, Momus, Nestor, Nike, Nostos, Orestes, Paestum, Patroclus, Pelasgic, Pelopid, Perseus, Phanariot, Pythagoras, Romaic, Samiot, Seminole, Spartacus, Spartan, Stagirite, Strabo, Sybarite, Tean, Teian, Theban, Thersites, Theseus, Thessal(on)ian, Thracian, Timon, Typto, Uniat, Xenophon, Zorba

Green(ery) Almond, Apple, Avocado, Baggy, Bice, Biliverdin, Bleaching, Bottle, Bowling, Caesious, Callow, Celadon, Cerulein, Chard, Chartreuse, Chlorophyll, Chrome, Citron, Cole, Collard, Common, Copper, Corbeau, Crown, Cyan, Dioptase, Eau de nil, Eco-, Ecofriendly, Emerald, Emerande, Envious, Erin, Fingers, Foliage, Forest, Fundie, Fundy, Gaudy, Glaucous, Go, Goddess, Grass, Gretna, Gull, Immature, Inexpert, Jade, Jungle, Kendal, Kensal, Khaki, Lawn, Leafage, Lime, Lincoln, Loden, Lovat, Mead, Monastral®, Moss, Moulding, Naive, New, Nile, Oasis, Olive, Paris, Pea, Peridot, Pistachio, Porraceous, Putting, Raw, Realo, Reseda, Rifle, Rink, Sage, Sap, Scheele's, Sea, Sludge, Smaragdine, Sward, Teal, Tender, Terre-vert, Turacoverdin, Tyro, Unfledged, Uninitiated, Unripe, Untrained, Uranite, Verdant, Verd antique, Verdigris, Verdure, Vert, Virent, Virid, Vir(id)escent, Young

Greenheart Bebeeru

Greenhorn Baby, Dupe, Put(t), Rookie, Sucker

Greenhouse Conservatory, Orangery, Phytotron, Polytunnel

Greens Broccoli, Cabbage, Calabrese, Cash, Money, Sprout, Vegetable(s)

Greet, Greeting(s) Abrazo, Accost, All hail, Arvo, Banzai, Benedicite, Bid, Blubber, Bonsoir, Chimo, Ciao, Gorillagram, Hail, Hallo, Halse, Handclasp, Handshake,

Haway, Heil, Heita, Hello, Herald, Hi, High-five, Hiya, Hongi, How, How d'ye do, Howsit, Jai Hind, Jambo, Kia ora, Kiss, Kissagram, Mihi, Namaskar, Namaste, Respects, Salaam, Salam alaikum, Salute, Salve, Sd, Shalom, Shalom aleichem, Sorry, Strippagram, Strippergram, Tena koe, Tena korua, Tena koutou, Wave, → WELCOME, Wotcher, Yo

Gregarious Social

Gregorian Chant, NS, Plagal

▸ **Gremlin** *see* GOBLIN

Grenade, Grenadier Bomb, Egg, Hand, Pineapple, Rat-tail, Rifle, Stun

Greta Garbo

Grey(ing), Gray Age, Agnes, Argent, Ashen, Ashy, Battleship, Beige, Bloncket, C(a)esius, Charcoal, Cinereous, Dapple, Dorian, Dove, Drab, Ecru, Feldgrau, Field, Glaucous, Gloomy, Gr, Gridelin, Griesie, Gries(l)y, Grise, Grisy, Grizzled, Gunmetal, Gy, Hoary, Hodden, Hore, Inn, Iron, Leaden, Liard, Livid, Lloyd, Lucia, Lyart, Mouse-coloured, Neutral, Olive drab, Oyster, Pearl, Perse, Pewter, Poliosis, Putty, Sclate, Slaty, Steel, Taupe, Zane

Greyfriars Bunter, Magnet

Greyhound Grew, Italian, Lapdog, Longtail, Ocean, Persian, Saluki, Sapling, Whippet

Grey matter Cinerea

Grid(dle), Gridiron Bar, Barbecue, Brandreth, Cattle, Control, Dot matrix, Grate, Graticule, Grating, National, Network, Reseau, Reticle, Roo-bar, Screen, Starting, Suppressor, Tava(h), Tawa, Windscale

Gride Creak, Grate

Grief, Grievance, Grieve, Grievous Axe, Bemoan, Bitter, Complaint, Condole, Cry, Dear(e), Deere, Distress, Dole, Dolour, Gram(e), Gravamen, Grudge, Heartbreak, Hone, Illy, Io, → MISERY, Monody, Noyous, O(c)hone, Overset, Pain, Pathetic, Plaint, Rue, Score, Sore, Sorrow, Teen, Tene, Tragic, Wayment, Weeping, Woe, Wrong

Griffin Gripe, Grype, Novice, Pony

Grill(er), Grilling Braai, Brander, Broil, Carbonado, Crisp, Devil, Gridiron, Inquisition, Interrogate, Kebab, Mixed, Pump, Question, Rack, Radiator, Reja, Yakimona

Grim Dire, Dour, Forbidding, Gaunt, Glum, Gurly, Hard, Macabre, Stern

▹ **Grim** *may indicate* an anagram

Grimace Face, Girn, Moe, Mop, Moue, Mouth, Mow, Murgeon, Pout, Wince

Grime(s), Grimy Colly, Dirt, Peter, Rechie, Reechie, Reechy, Soil, Sweep

Grin Fleer, Girn, Risus, Simper, Smirk, Sneer

Grind(ing), Grinder Bray, Bruxism, Chew, Crunch, → CRUSH, Droil, Drudgery, Gnash, Grate, Graunch, Grit, Home, Kern, Kibble, Labour, Levigate, Mano, Metate, Mill, Mince, Molar, Muller, Offhand, Pug, Pulverise, Slog, Stamp, Triturate

Grip(ping), Gripper Ascendeur, Bite, Chuck, Clam, Clamp, Clip, Clutch, Craple, Embrace, Engrasp, Enthral, Get, Grapple, → GRASP, Haft, Hair, Hairpin, Hand(fast), Handhold, Hend, Hold, Hug, Key, Kirby®, Lewis, Obsess, Pincer, Pinion, Pistol, Prehensile, Purchase, Raven, Rhine, Sally, Setscrew, Sipe, Strain, Streigne, Traction, Twist, Valise, Vice, Walise, Wrestle

Gripe(s) Colic, Complain, Ditch, Grasp, Griffin, Ileus, Pain, Tormina

Grisly Gory, Macabre

Grist Burden

Gristle, Gristly Cartilage, Chondroid, Lytta, Raven's bone

Grit(s), Gritty Blinding, Clench, Gnash, Granular, Grate, Guts, Hominy, Mattress,

Millstone, Nerve, Pluck, Resolution, Sabulose, Sand, Shingle, Swarf, Valour, Yorkshire

Grizzle(d) Grey

Groan(er) Bewail, Bing, Moan, Titus

Grocer Grasshopper, Jorrocks, Pepperer, Symbol

Groggy Dazed, Shaky

Groin Gnarr, Inguinal, Lisk

Groom(ed) Brush, Coistrel, Coistril, Comb, Curry, Dress, Fettler, Kempt, Ostler, Palfrenier, Paranymph, Preen, Primp, Prink, S(a)ice, Smarten, Spouse, Strapper, Syce, Tiger, Tracer, Train, Wrangler

▷ **Groom** *may indicate* an anagram

Groove(s), Grooved, Groovy Bezel, Canal, Cannelure, Chamfer, Channel, Chase, Clevis, Coulisse, Croze, Dièdre, Exarate, Fissure, Flute, Fuller, Furr, Furrow, Glyph, Gouge, Hill and dale, Kerf, Key-seat, Keyway, Lead-in, Lead-out, Oche, Pod, Rabbet, Race(way), Raggle, Raphe, Rare, Rebate, Rif(f)le, Rifling, Rigol(l), Rout, → **RUT**, Scrobe, Sipe, Slot, Sulcus, Throat, Track, Trough, Vallecula

Grope(r) Feel, Fumble, Grabble, Hapuka, Ripe, Scrabble

Gross All-up, Coarse, Complete, Crass, Dense, Earn, Earthy, Flagrant, Frankish, Fustilugs, Giant, Gr, Loathsome, Material, Obese, Outsize, Overweight, Pre-tax, Rank, Ribald, Rough, Stupid, Sum, Whole

▷ **Gross** *may indicate* an anagram

Grotesque Antic, Bizarre, Fantastic, Fright, Gargoyle, Magot, Outlandish, Rabelaisian, Rococo, Teras

Grotto Cave, Lupercal

Ground(s) Abthane, Arena, Astroturf, Basis, Bottom, Breeding, Campus, Cause, Common, Criterion, Crushed, Deck, Dregs, Eard, Earth, Edgbaston, Epig(a)eal, Epig(a)ean, Epig(a)eous, Floor, Footing, Gathering, Grated, Grist, Grouts, Happy hunting, Headingley, High, Hunting, Justification, Lees, Leeway, Lek, Lords, Lot, Marl, Meadow, Mealed, Middle, Occasion, Oval, Parade, Piste, Pitch, Plat, Pleasure, Plot, Policy, Proving, Quad, → **REASON**, Rec(reation), Réseau, Ring, Sandlot, Sediment, Slade, Soil, Solum, Sports, Stadium, Stamping, Strand, Terra, Terrain, Tom Tiddler's, Touch, Tract, Turf, Udal, Vantage, Venue, Waste(land), Yard, Yird

▷ **Ground** *may indicate* an anagram

Groundbait Chum

Ground-crew Erk

Ground-rent Crevasse

Groundsheet Hutchie

Groundsman Greenkeeper

Group Abelian, Acyl, Affinity, 'A'list, Band, Batch, Battle, Beatles, Bee, Bevy, Bloc(k), Blood, Bloomsbury, Body, Bracket, Bratpack, Break-out, Bruges, Caboodle, Cadre, Camarilla, Camp, Cartel, Category, Caucus, Cave, Cell, Chain, Chordata, Circle, Clade, Clan, Class(is), Clique, Cluster, Clutch, Cohort, Colony, Combo, Commune, Community, Concertina, Confraternity, Congregation, Consort(ium), Contact, Contingent, Control, Convoy, Coterie, Covey, Crew, Deme, Demi-monde, Denomination, Department, Detail, Enclave, Encounter, Ensemble, Faction, Family, Fascio, Focus, Fold, Fraternity, Front, Galère, Gang, Gemeinschaft, Gender, Generation, Genotype, Genus, Gesellschaft, Ginger, Globe, Guild, Hapu, Heading, Hexad, Hirsel, House, Income, In-crowd, Ketone, Kit, Knot, League, Lichfield, Local, Lumpenproletariat, Marathon, Marshal, Minority, Minyan, Nexus, Order, Outfit, Oxford, Pack(et), Panel, Parti, Party, Passel, Peer, Phalange, Phratry, Phylum, Platoon, Pleiad, Plump, Pocket, Pod, Point, Pool, Pop, Pressure,

Prosthetic, Push, Quincunx, Raceme, Racemose, Rap, Reading, Ring, Rush, School, Sector, Seminar, Series, Set, Several, Sex, Shower, Society, Sort, Sorus, Splinter, Strain, Stream, String, Study, Subfamily, Sub-general, Sub-order, Support, Symbol, Syndicate, T, Tales, Taxon, Tetrad, Tithing, Topological, Trainband, T-Rex, Tribe, Tribune, Trilogy, Trio, Troop, Troupe, TU, Umbrella, Unit, User, Vigilante, Workshop, Zaibatsu, Zupa

Grouse Black, Blackcock, Bleat, Blue, Caper(caillie), Capercailzie, Covey, Gorcock, Greyhen, Gripe, Growl, Grumble, Hazel-hen, Heath-cock, Heathfowl, Heath-hen, Jeremiad, Moan, Moorcock, Moorfowl, Moor-pout, Muir-poot, Muir-pout, Mutter, Natter, Peeve, Pintail, Prairie-hen, Ptarmigan, Red, Red game, Resent, Ruffed, Rype(r), Sage, Sharp-tailed, Snarl, Spruce, Twelfth, Wheenge, W(h)inge, Willow

Grove Academy, Arboretum, Bosk, Bosquet, Copse, Glade, Hurst, Lyceum, Motte, Nemoral, Orchard, Orchat, Silva, Tope

Grovel Cheese, Crawl, Creep, Fawn, Ko(w)tow, Worm

Grow(ing), Grow out, Growth Accrete, Accrue, Acromegaly, Adenoma, Aggrandisement, Angioma, Apophysis, Arborescence, Auxesis, Bedeguar, Boom, Braird, Breer, Burgeon, Car(b)uncle, Chancre, Cholelith, Chondroma, Compensatory, Condyloma, Corn, Crescendo, Crop, Culture, Cyst, Down, Ectopia, Edema, Ellagic, Enate, Enchondroma, Enlarge, Epinasty, Epitaxy, Excrescence, Exostosis, Expansion, Fibroid, Flor, Flourish, Flush, Gain, Gall, Germinate, Get, Goitre, Hepatocele, Hummie, Hyperostosis, Hyponasty, Increase, Keratosis, Knur(r), Lichen, Lipoma, Mole, Monopodial, Mushroom, Myoma, Nur(r), Oedema, Oncology, Osselet, Osteoma, Osteophyte, Pharming, Polyp, Proleg, Proliferate, Rampant, Rank, Scirrhus, Septal, Snowball, Spavin, → **SPROUT**, Stalagmite, Stand, Stipule, Sympodial, Tariff, Thigmotropism, Thrive, Trichome, → **TUMOUR**, Tylosis, Vegetable, Wart, Wax, Weed, Wox

▷ **Grow(n)** *may indicate* an anagram

Growl(ing) Fremescent, Gnar, Groin, Grr, Gurl, Roar(e), Roin, Royne, Snar(l)

Grown up Adult, Mature, Risen

Grub(by) Assart, Aweto, Bardie, Bardy, Bookworm, Caddis, Caterpillar, Cheer, Chow, Chrysalis, Deracinate, Dig, Eats, Fare, Fodder, → **FOOD**, Gentle, Groo-groo, Gru-gru, Larva, Leatherjacket, Mawk, Mess, Nosh, Palmerworm, Peck, Pupa, Root(le), Rout, Rowt, Sap, Slave, Stub, Tired, Wireworm, Witchetty, Wog, Worm

Grudge, Grudging Chip, Derry, Envy, Grievance, Grutch, Resent, Score, Sparse, Spite, Spleen

Gruel Brochan, Bross, Loblolly, Skilligalee, Skilligolee, Skilly

Gruesome Ghastly, Grisly, Grooly, Horror, Livid, Macaberesque, Macabre, → **MORBID**, Sick

Gruff Guttural, Hoarse, Surly

Grumble Beef, Bellyache, Bitch, Bleat, Chunter, Crab, Croak, Girn, Gripe, Grizzle, Groin, Growl, Moan, Murmur, Mutter, Nark, Natter, Repine, Rumble, Whinge, Yammer

Grump(y) Attercop, Bearish, Cross, Ettercap, Grouchy, Moody, Sore-headed, Surly

Grunt Groin, Grumph, Humph, Oink, Pigfish, Spanish, Ugh, Wheugh

Guano Dung, Sombrerite

Guanoco Llama

Guarantee Accredit, Assure, Avouch, Certify, Ensure, Gage, Hallmark, Insure, Mainprise, Money-back, Pignerate, Pignorate, → **PLEDGE**, Plight, Seal, Secure, Sponsion, Surety, Underwrite, → **VOUCHSAFE**, Warn, Warrandice, Warrant(y)

Guard(ed), Guards Acolouthos, Advance, Apron, Beefeaters, Blues, Bostangi, Bouncer, Bracer, Cabiri, Cage, Cag(e)y, Cerberus, Chaperon(e), Chary,

Cheesemongers, Cherry-pickers, Coast, Coldstream, Colour, Cordon, Crinoline, Curator, Custodian, Custos, Diehards, Dragoons, Duenna, Equerry, Escort, Eunuch, Excubant, Exon, Fence, Fender, Gaoler, Gauntlet, Grenadiers, Greys, Hedge, Home, Horse, INS, Iron, Jaga, Jailer, Keep, Lancers, Life, Lilywhites, Look out, Mask, Mort-safe, National, Nightwatch(man), Nutcrackers, Out-rider, Out-sentry, Pad, Palace, Patrol, Picket, Point, Praetorian, → **PROTECT**, Provost, Quillon, Rail, Red, Ride, Roof, Screw, Secure, Security, Sentinel, Sentry, Shadow, Shield, Shin, Shopping, Shotgun, SS, Strelitz, Streltzi, Swiss, Switzer, Tapadera, Tapadero, Tile, Toecap, Tsuba, Turnkey, Vambrace, Vamplate, Varangian, Vigilante, Visor, Wage, Wait(e), Ward, Wary, Watch (and ward), Watchdog, Watchman, Wear, Weir, Wire, Yeoman

Guardian Altair, Argus, Curator, Custodian, Custos, Dragon, Gemini, Granthi, Hafiz, Janus, Julius, Miminger, Templar, Trustee, Tutelar(y), Tutor, Warder, Watchdog, Xerxes

Gudgeon Fish, Pin, Trunnion

Guenon Grivet, Vervet

Gue(r)rilla Bushwhacker, Chetnik, Contra, ETA, Fedayee, Gook, Haiduk, Heyduck, Irregular, Khmer Rouge, Komitaji, Maquis, Mujahadeen, Mujahed(d)in, Mujahedeen, Mujahideen, Partisan, Phalanx, Red Brigade, Tamil Tiger, Terrorist, Tupamaro, Urban, Viet Cong, Zapata, Zapatista

Guess Aim, Aread, Arede, Arreede, Conjecture, Divine, Estimate, Harp, Hazard, Hunch, Imagine, Infer, Level, Mor(r)a, Mull, Psych out, Shot, Speculate, Suppose, Surmise, Theorise, Venture

Guessing game Handy-dandy, Mor(r)a, Quiz

Guest(s) Caller, Company, House-party, Inquiline, Invitee, Parasite, Paying, PG, Symbion(t), Symphile, Synoecete, Umbra, Visitant, → **VISITOR**, Xenial

Guesthouse B & B, Minshuku, Taverna, Xenodochium

Guff Bosh, Gas

Guianian S(a)ouari

Guidance, Guide, Guideline, Guiding Advice, Antibarbus, Auspice, Baedeker, Bradshaw, Cicerone, Clue, Command, Concordance, Conduct, Counsel, Courier, Curb, Cursor, Director(y), Docent, Dragoman, Drive, → **ESCORT**, Field, Gillie, Graticule, Helm, Heuristic, Homing, Index, Inertial, Inspire, Itinerary, Jig, Key, Lad, Landmark, Lead, Lodestar, Map, Mark, Marriage, Mentor, Michelin, Missile, Model, Navaid, Navigate, Nose, Pelorus, Pilot, Pointer, Postil(l)ion, Principle, Queen's, Rainbow, Range, Ranger, Reference, Rein, Relate, Rudder, Sabot, Shepherd, Sherpa, Shikaree, Shikari, Sight, Sign, Sixer, Stear, Steer, Stire, Template, Templet, Terminal, Terrestrial, Tiller, Train, Travelogue, Tutelage, Vocational, Voyageur, Waymark, Weise, Weize, Wise

Guild Artel, Basoche, Company, Freemason, Gyeld, Hanse, Hoastman, League, Mistery, Mystery, Society, Tong, Union

Guile Art, Cunning, Deceit, Dole, Malengine

Guillotine Closure, Louisiette, Maiden, Marianne

Guilt(y) Affluenza, Angst, Blame, Cognovit, Flagitious, Mea culpa, Nocent, Peccavi, Remorse, Wicked

Guinea(s) Canary, Geordie, Gns, Job, Ls, Meg, Spade

Guinea-fowl Pintado

Guinea-pig Abyssinian, Agoute, Agouti, Cavie, Cavy, Paca

Guinea-worm Dracunculus

Guise Form, Manner, Shape

Guitar(ist) Acoustic, Axe(man), Bass, Bottleneck, Cithern, Cittern, Dobro®, Electric,

Fender®, Gittarone, Gittern, Hawaiian, Humbucker, Lute, Lyre, Pedal steel, Plankspanker, Samisen, Sancho, Sanko, Shamisen, Sitar, Slide, Spanish, Steel, Uke, Ukulele

Gulf Aden, Anadyr, Aqaba, Bay, Bothnia, California, Cambay, Campeche, Carpentaria, Chasm, Chihli, Corinth, Cutch, Darien, Dvina, Exmouth, Fonseca, Genoa, Gonaives, Hauraki, Honduras, Iskenderun, Isthmus, Izmit, Joseph Bonaparte, Kutch, Lepanto, Leyte, Lingayen, Lions, Mannar, Martaban, Maw, Mexico, Ob, Patras, Persian, Pozzuoli, Queen Maud, Rapallo, Riga, St Lawrence, St Vincent, Salerno, Salonika, Saronic, Saros, Siam, Sidra, Spencer, Taganrog, Taranto, Tongking, Tonkin, Trieste, Tunis, Van Diemen, Venice, Vorago

Gull(s) Black-backed, Bonxie, Cheat, Cob(b), Cod, Cony, Cozen, Dupe, Fool, Geck, Glaucous, Have, Hoodwink, Ivory, Kittiwake, Laridae, Larus, Maw, Mew, Mollyhawk, Pickmaw, Pigeon, Queer, Rook, Sabine's, Saddleback, Scaury, Scourie, Scowrie, Sea-cob, Sea-mew, Sell, Simp, Skua, Sucker, Swart-back, Tern, Tystie, Xema

Gullet Crop, Enterate, Maw, Oesophagus, Throat, Weasand-pipe

Gullible Green, Mug punter, Naive, Sucker

Gulliver Lemuel

Gully Couloir, Donga, Fielder, Geo, Gio, Goe, Grough, Gulch, Infielder, Pit, Rake, Ravine, Sloot, Sluit, Wadi

Gulp Bolt, Draught, Gollop, Quaff, Slug, Sob, → SWALLOW, Swig, Swipe, Wolf

Gum (tree) Acacia, Acajou, Acaroid, Agar, Algin, Angico, Arabic, Arabin, Arar, Arctic, Asafoetida, Bablah, Balata, Balm, Bandoline, Bdellium, Benjamin, Benzoin, Bloodwood, Blue, Boot, Bubble, Cerasin, Chicle, Chuddy, Chutty, Coolabah, Courbaril, Cow®, Dextrin(e), Dragon's-blood, Ee-by, Eucalyptus, Euphorbium, Flooded, Frankincense, Galbanum, Gamboge, Ghost, Gingival, → GLUE, Goat's-thorn, Gosh, Grey, Guar, Ironbark, Karri, Kauri, La(b)danum, Lac, Lentisk, Mastic(h), Mucilage, Myrrh, Nicotine, Olibanum, Opopanax, Oshac, Red, River red, Sagapenum, Sarcocolla, Scribbly, Size, Sleep, Snow, Spearmint, Spirit, Starch, Sterculia, Stringybark, Sugar, Sweet, Tacamahac, Tragacanth, Tupelo, Ulmin, Water, White, Xanthan

Gumbo Okra

Gumboil Parulis

Gumption Nous, Spirit

Gun(fire), Guns, Gunfight Amusette, Archibald, Archie, Arquebus, Automatic, Barker, Baton, Bazooka, Beanbag, Beretta, Big Bertha, Biscayan, Blunderbuss, Bofors, Bombard, Breech(-loader), Bren, Broadside, Brown Bess, Browning, Bulldog, Bullpup, Bundook, Burp, Caliver, Cannonade, Carbine, Carronade, Cement, Chokebore, Coehorn, Colt®, Dag, Derringer, Electron, Elephant, Escopette, Falcon(et), Field, Fieldpiece, Firearm, Fire lock, Flame, Flash, Flintlock, Four-pounder, Fowler, Fowlingpiece, Garand, Gas, Gat(ling), Gingal(l), Grease, HA, Hackbut, Half-cock, Harquebus, Heater, Hired, Howitzer, Jezail, Jingal, Kalashnikov, Lewis, Long Tom, Luger®, Machine, Magazine, Magnum, Maroon, Martini-Henry®, Matchlock, Mauser®, Maxim, Metal, Minnie, Minute, Mitrailleuse, Morris Meg, Mortar, Musket(oon), Muzzle-loader, Nail, Needle, Neutron, Noonday, Oerlikon, Ordnance, Over and under, Owen, Paderero, Paterero, Ped(e)rero, Pelican, Perrier, Petronel, Piece, Pistol(et), Pompom, Pump (action), Punt, Purdey®, Quaker, Radar, Ray, Repeater, Rev, Revolver, Riot, Rod, Roscoe, Saker, Sarbacane, Scatter, Self-cocker, Shooter, Shooting iron, Shoot-out, Sidearm, Siege, Smoothbore, Snapha(u)nce, Spear, Speed, Spray, Squirt, Staple, Starting, Sten, Sterculia, Sterling, Stern-cannon, Stern-chaser, Stun, Swivel, Taser®, Tea,

Thirty eight, Thompson, Tier, Time, Tommy, Tool, Tupelo, Turret, Uzi, Walther, Wesson, Young, Zip

Gunge Gowl, Paste

Gunman Ace, Assassin, Bandit, Earp, Greaser, Pistoleer, Sniper, Starter

Gunner, Gunner's assistant Arquebusier, Arsenal, Artillerist, Cannoneer, Cannonier, Culverineer, Gr, Matross, RA

Gunpowder Charcoal, Pebble-powder, Saucisse, Saucisson

Gunwale Gunnel, Portland, Portlast, Portoise

Guppy Million

Gurgle Burble, Clunk, Glug, Gobble, Gollar, Goller, Guggle, Ruckle, Squelch

Gurnard Tubfish

Guru Lifestyle, Sadhu, Teacher

Gush(ing) Blether, Effusive, → **FLOOD**, Flow, Jet, Outpour, Rail, Raile, Regurgitate, Rhapsodize, Scaturient, Spirt, Spout, Spurt, Too-too

Gusset Godet, Gore, Insert, Inset, Mitre

Gust Blast, Blore, Flaught, Flaw, Flurry, Puff, Sar, Waff

Gusto Élan, Relish, Verve, Zest

Gut(s), Gutty Archenteron, Balls, Beer, Bowel(s), Chitterlings, Cloaca, Disembowel, Draw, Duodenum, Enteral, Enteron, Entrails, Fore, Gill, Hind, Ileum, Insides, Kyle, Mesenteron, Mid, Minikin, Omental, Omentum, Purtenance, Remake, Sack, Sand, Snell, Stamina, Staying-power, Strip, Thairm, Tripe, Ventriculus, Viscera

Gutta-percha Jelutong, Pontianac, Pontianak

Gutter(ing) Arris, Channel, Conduit, Coulisse, Cullis, Grip, Gully, Kennel, Rhone, Rigol(l), Roan, Rone, Sough, Spout, Strand, Swale, Swayl, Sweal, Sweel

Guttersnipe Arab, Gamin, Thief

Guttural Faucal, Throaty

Guy Backstay, Bo, Burgess, Cat, Chaff, Clewline, Decamp, Deride, Effigy, Fall, Fawkes, Fellow, Gink, Josh, Mannering, Parody, Rib, Rope, Scarecrow, Stay, Tease, Vang, Wise

Guzzle(d) Gannet, Gorge, Go(u)rmandize, Overeat, Snarf

Gwyn Nell

Gym(nasium), Gymnast(ic) Acrobat, Akhara, Arena, Contortionist, Dojo, Jungle, Lyceum, Palaestra, PE, PT, Rhythmic, Sokol, Tumbler, Turner

Gymnosophist Yogi

Gypsum Alabaster, Gesso, Plaster, Satin-stone, Selenite, Terra alba

Gypsy, Gipsy Bohemian, Cagot, Caird, Caqueux, Chai, Chal, Chi, Collibert, Egyptian, Esmeralda, Faw, Gipsen, Gitano, Hayraddin, Lavengro, Meg, Pikey, Rom(any), Rye, Scholar, Tinker, Traveller, Tsigane, Tzigane, Tzigany, Vagabond, Vlach, Walach, Wanderer, Zigan, Zigeuner, Zincala, Zincalo, Zingaro

Gyrate Revolve, Rotate, → **SPIN**, Twirl

Hh

H Ache, Aitch, Aspirate, Height, Hospital, Hotel, Hydrant, Hydrogen

Haberdasher(y) Clothier, Ferret, Hosier, Notions

Habit(s), Habitual, Habituate, Habitué Accustom, Addiction, Apparel, Assuefaction, Assuetude, Bent, Cacoethes, Chronic, Clothes, Coat, Consuetude, Crystal, Custom, Diathesis, Dress, Ephod, Frequenter, Garb, Inure, Inveterate, Motley, Mufti, Nature, Outfit, Pathological, Practice, Raiment, Regular, Riding, Robe, Rochet, Routine, Scapular, Schema, Season, Second nature, Set, Soutane, Suit, Surplice, Toge, Trait, Trick, Tway, Usual, Way, Won, Wont, Xerotes

Habitat Element, Environment, Haunt, Home, Locality, Station

Hacienda Ranch

Hack(er) Blackhat, Chip, Chop, Cough, Cut, Drudge, Garble, Gash, Ghost, Grub-Street, Hag, Hash, Hedge-writer, Heel, Hew, Horse, Journo, Mangle, Mutilate, Nag, Notch, Pad, Paper-strainer, Penny-a-liner, Phreak, Pick, Pot-boiler, Rosinante, Script kiddie, Spurn, Steed, Tadpole, Taper, Tussis, Unseam, White hat

Hackle(s) Comb, Rough

Hackney(ed) Banal, Cab, Cliché, Corny, Percoct, Stale, Threadbare, Tired, Trite, Worn

Haddock Arbroath smokie, Findram, Finnan, Fish, Norway, Rizzered, Smoky, Speldin(g), Speldrin(g), Whitefish

Hades Dis, Hell, Orcus, Pit, Tartarus

Had (to) Moten, Must, Obliged, Threw

Haematite Oligist

Haemoglobin Chelate

Haemorrhoids Farmer Giles, Piles

Hafnium Hf

Hag(-like) Anile, Beldame, Besom, Carlin(e), Crone, Harpy, Harridan, Hell-cat, Hex, Moss, Nickneven, Occasion, Rudas, Runnion, Trot, Underwood, Witch

Haggard Drawn, → GAUNT, Pale, Rider

Haggis Kishke

Haggle Argue, Badger, → BARGAIN, Barter, Chaffer, Dicker, Horse-trade, Niffer, Palter, Prig

Ha-ha Dike, So there, Sunk-fence

Hahnium Hn

Hail(er) Acclaim, Ahoy, Ave, Bull-horn, Cheer, Fusillade, Graupel, Greet, Hi, Ho, Megaphone, Salue, Salute, Shower, Signal, Skoal, Skol, Sola, Stentor, Storm, Trumpet, Whoa-ho-ho

Hair(y), Haircut, Hairlike, Hair problem/condition, Hair style Afro, Ailes de pigeon, Ainu, Alopecia, Backcomb, Baldy, Bang, Barnet, Beard, Beehive, Bezoar, Bingle, Bob, Bouffant, Braid, Brede, Bristle, Brutus, Bumfluff, Bun, Bunches, Butch, Cadogan, Camel, Capillary, Catogan, Chignon, Cilia, Cleopatra, Coat, Cockernony, Coif, Coiffure, Comal, Comate, Comb-over, Cornrow, Corymbus, Cowlick, Crepe,

Crew-cut, Crinal, Cronet, Crop, Cue, Curlicue, DA, Dangerous, Dreadlocks, Dubbing, Duck's arse, Ducktail, Earmuffs, Elf locks, En brosse, Esau, Excrement, Eyelash, Feather, Feather-cut, Fetlock, Filament, Flat-top, Floccus, Forelock, French pleat, French roll, Frenulum, Fringe, Fur, Garconne, Glib(s), Glochidium, Guard, Hackles, Heard, Heer(i)e, Hispid, Hog, Indumentum, Kemp, Kesh, Lanugo, Lash, List, Lock, Lovelock, Lowlights, Madarosis, Mane, Marcel, Mohican, Mop, Mullet, Muttonchops, Not(t), Number two, Pageboy, Pappus, Pashm, Pele(s), Pelt, Perm(anent), Pigtail, Pika, Pile, Pilus, Pincurl, Plait, Plica, Plica Polonica, Pompadour, Ponytail, Poodle cut, Porcupine, Pouf(fe), Pow, Psilosis, Puberulent, Pubescent, Pudding basin, Punk, Queue, Quiff, Radicle, Rat-tail, Red mullet, Rhizoid, Roach, Root, Scaldhead, Scalp lock, Scopate, Scopula, Sericeous, Set, Shag, Shingle, Shock, Sideburns, Sidelock, Snell, Spikes, Stinging, Strammel, Strand, Strigose, Strummel, Switch, Sycosis, Tête, Thatch, Tomentose, Tonsure, Toorie, Topknot, Tour(ie), Tragus, Tress, Trichoid, Trichology, Trichome, Trichosis, Trim, Velutinous, Vibrissi, Villi, Villosity, Villus, Wedge, Widow's peak, Wig, Wisp, → **WOOL**, Xerasia

Hair-cream, Hair-oil Conditioner, Pomade

Hairdresser Barber, Coiffeur, Comb, Crimper, Friseur, Marcel, Salon, Stylist, Trichologist

Hairless Bald, Callow, Glabrate, Glabrescent, Glabrous, Irate

Hairline Brow, Nape

Hairnet Kell, Snood

Hairpiece Frisette, Merkin, Postiche, Strand, Toupee, → **WIG**

Hairpin Barrette, Bodkin, Slide, U, U-turn

Hair-shirt Ab(b)a, Cilice

Haiti RH

Hal Prince

Halberd Spontoon

Halcyon Calm, Kingfisher, Mild

Hale(r) Drag, Healthy, Koruna, Raucle, Robust, Well

Half, Halved Bifid, Demi, Dimidiate, Dirempt, Divide, Hemi, Moiety, Semi, Share, Split, Stand-off, Term

Half-a-dozen Six, VI

Half-asleep, Half-conscious Dove, Dozy

Half-baked Foolish, Mediocre, Samel, Slack-bake

Half-breed, Half-caste Bastard, Baster, Creole, Eurasian, Mameluco, Mestee, Mestiza, Mestizo, Metif, Métis(se), Miscegen, Mongrel, Mulatto, Mustee, Octaroon, Quadroon, Quarteroon, Quintero, Quintroon, Sambo, Yellow-boy, Yellow-girl, Zambo

Half-guinea Smelt

Half-hearted Reluctant, Tepid

Half-hour Bell

Half-pence, Half-penny Mag, Maik, Mail(e), Make, Obolus, Patrick, Portcullis, Posh, Rap, Wood's

Half-turn Caracol(e), Demivolt

Half-wit Changeling, Mome, Simpleton, → **STUPID**

Hall Anteroom, Apadana, Atrium, Auditorium, Aula, Basilica, Carnegie, Casino, Chamber, Citadel, City, Concert, Concourse, Corridor, Dance, Divinity, Dojo, Domdaniel, Dome, Dotheboys, Ex(h)edra, Festival, Foyer, Gallen, Hardwick, Holkham, Judgement, Kedleston, Liberty, Lobby, Locksley, Megaron, Mess, Moot, Music, Narthex, Newby, Odeon, Palais, Palais de danse, Passage, Prytaneum, Rathaus, Rideau, Salle, Saloon, Stationer's, Tammany, Tara, Tolsel, Town, Trullen,

Valhalla, Vestibule, Walhall(a), Wildfell

Hallmark(ed) Brand, Contrôlé, Logo, Seal, Stamp

▸ **Hallo** *see* **HELLO**

Hallow Revere, Worship

Hallucinate, Hallucination, Hallucinogen Autoscopy, DT's, Fantasy, Formication, Freak, Freak out, Illusion, Image, Mirage, Negative, Photism, Psilocin, Psilocybin, Psychedelic, Trip

Halo Antheolion, Areola, Aura, Aureola, Corona, Galactic, Gloria, Gloriole, Mandorla, Nimbus, Rim, Vesica, Vesica piscis

Halogen Iodine

Halt(er) Abort, Arrest, Block, Brake, Bridle, Cavesson, Cease, Check, Full stop, Game, Hackamore, Heave-to, Hilch, Lame(d), Limp, Noose, Prorogue, Rope, Stall, Standstill, Staw, → **STOP**, Stopover, Toho, Tyburn-tippet, Whoa

Ham(s) Amateur, Barnstormer, Flitch, Gammon, Haunch, Hock, Hoke, Hough, Hunker, Jambon, Jay, Mutton, Nates, Overact, Overplay, Parma, Pigmeat, Prat, Prosciutto, Radio, Serrano, Tiro, Westphalian, York

Hamfisted Maladroit, Unheppen

Hamite Berber, Nilot(e)

Hamlet Aldea, Auburn, Cigar, Clachan, Dane, Dorp, Hero, Kraal, Stead, Thorp(e), Vill(age), Wick

Hammer(ed), Hammerhead About-sledge, Ballpeen, Ballpein, Beetle, Bully, Bush, Celt, Claw, Drop, Excudit, Flatten, Fore, Fuller, Gavel, Hack, Incuse, Jack, Kevel, Knap, Knapping, Kusarigama, Lump, Madge, Mall(et), Malleate, Martel, Maul, Mjol(l)nir, Monkey, Nevel, Oliver, Pane, Pean, Peen, Pein, Pene, Percussion, Piledriver, Planish, Plessor, Plexor, Pneumatic, Rawhide, Repoussé, Rip, Sheep's-foot, Shingle, Sledge, Steam, Stone, Strike, Tack, Tenderizer, Tendon, Tilt, Trip, Umbre, Water, Wippen

▹ **Hammered** *may indicate* an anagram

Hammerthrower Thor

Hammock Cott

▹ **Hammy** *may indicate* an anagram

Hamper Basket, Cabin, Ceroon, Cramp, Cumber, Delay, Encumber, Entrammel, Hamstring, Handicap, Hobble, Hog-tie, Obstruct, Pad, Pannier, Ped, Pinch, Restrict, Rub, Sero(o)n, Shackle, Tangle, Trammel, Tuck

Hamster Cricetus, Idea

Hamstring Cramp, Hock, Hox, Lame, Popliteal, Thwart

Hand(s), Hand over, Hand down, Hand-like, Handwriting Assist(ance), Bananas, Bequeath, Cacography, Calligraphy, Charge, Chicane, Chirography, Clap(ping), Claque, Club, Clutch, Copperplate, Court, Crew, Cursive, Dab, Daddle, Danny, Dawk, Dead, Deal, Deck, Deliver, Devolve, Donny, Dukes, Dummy, Famble, Fin, Fist, Flipper, Flush, Free, Glad, Graphology, Help, Helping, Hidden, Hond, Hour, Impart, Iron, Israel, Italian, Jambone, Jamboree, Jemmy, Kana, L, Lone, Man, Manual, Manus, Maulers, Medieval, Minute, Mitt(en), Nes(h)ki, Niggle, Operative, Orthography, Pad, Palaeography, Palm(atifid), Part, Pass, Paw, Podium, Post, Pud, R, Referral, Rein (arm), Round, Running, Script, Second, Secretary, Signature, Span, Spencerian, Stage, Station, Straight, Sweep, Text, Tiger, Uncial, Upper, Whip, Widow, Worker, Yarborough

Handbag Caba(s), Grip, Indispensable, Pochette, Purse, Reticule, Valise

Handbook Baedeker, Companion, Enchiridion, Guide, Manual, Vade-mecum

Handcuff(s) Bracelet, Darbies, Golden, Irons, Manacle, Mittens, Nippers, Snaps, Wristlet

Handful Few, Gowpen, Grip, Problem, Pugil, Rip(p), V

Handicap Bisque, Burden, Cambridgeshire, Ebor, Encumber, Hamper, Impede, Impost, Lame, Liability, Lincolnshire, Mental, → **OBSTACLE**, Off, Physical, Restrict, Weigh(t), Welter-race

Handicraft Marquetry

Handkerchief, Hanky Bandan(n)a, Belcher, Billy, Buffon, Clout, Fogle, Foulard, Kleenex®, Madam, Madras, Monteith, Mouchoir, Muckender, Napkin, Nose-rag, Orarium, Romal, Rumal, Sudary, Tissue, Wipe(r)

Handle(d) Ansate, Bail, Bale, Behave, Bitstock, Brake, Broomstick, Cope, Crank, Dead man's, Deal, Doorknob, Dudgeon, Ear, Feel, Finger, Forename, Gaum, Gorm, Grab, Grip, Gunstock, Haft, Helve, Hilt, Hold, Knob, Knub, Lug, → **MANAGE**, Manipulate, Manubrium, Maul, Moniker, Name, Nib, Palp, Paw, Pistol-grip, Pommel, Process, Rounce, Shaft, Snath, Snead, Sneath, Sned, Staff, Staghorn, Stale, Starting, Steal(e), Steel, Steil, Stele, Stilt, Stock, Tiller, Title, To-name, Touch, Transact, Treat, Use, Whipstock, Wield, Withe

Handmaid(en) Iras, Manicurist, Valkyrie

Hand-out Alms, Charity, Dole, Gift, Release, Sample

Handshake Golden

Hand-signal Beck(on), Point, Wave

Handsome Adonis, Apollo, Attractive, Bonny, Brave, Comely, Dashing, Dishy, Featuous, Fine, Gracious, Kenneth, Liberal

Handspring, Handstand Cartwheel, Diamodov

Hand-warmer Muff, Pome

Hand-washer Pilate

▶ **Handwriting** *see* **HAND**

Handy(man) Accessible, Close, Convenient, Deft, Dext(e)rous, Digit, Factotum, Get-at-able, Jack(-of-all-trades), Near, Nigh, Palmate, Palmist, Ready, Skilful, Spartan, Useful

Hang, Hanger, Hanging(s) Append, Arras, Aweigh, Chick, Chik, Coat, Dangle, Darn, Depend, Dewitt, Dossal, Dossel, Dosser, Drape, Droop, Execute, Frontal, Gobelin, Hinge, Hoove, Hove(r), Kakemono, Kilt, Lime, Lobed, Loll, Lop, Lynch, Mooch, Noose, Nub, Pend(ant), Sag, Scenery, Scrag, Set, Sit, Sling, Suspend, Suspercollate, Swing, Tapestry, Tapet, Tapis, The rope, Toran(a)

Hanger-on Bur, Lackey, Leech, Limpet, Liripoop, Parasite, Satellite, Sycophant, Tassel, Toady

Hangman, Hangmen Bull, Calcraft, Dennis, Derrick, Gregory, Ketch, Marwood, Nubbing-cove, Pierrepoint, Topsman

Hangnail Agnail

Hangover Canopy, Cornice, Crapulence, Drape, DT's, Head, Hot coppers, Katzenjammer, Mistletoe, Remnant, Tester

Hank Bobbin, Coil, Fake, Lock, Skein

Hanker(ing) Desire, Envy, Hunger, Itch, Long, Yearn, Yen

Hannibal Punic

Hansard Minutes

Haphazard Casual, Chance, Helter-skelter, Higgledy-piggledy, Hit and miss, Hitty-missy, Promiscuous, → **RANDOM**, Rough and tumble, Scattershot, Slapdash, Willy-nilly

Happen(ing), Happen to Afoot, Be, Befall, Befortune, Betide, Come, Crop up, Event(uate), Fall-out, Materialise, → **OCCUR**, Pan, Pass, Prove, Subvene, Thing, Tide, Transpire, Worth

Happiness, Happy Apposite, Ave, Beatific, Beatitude, Blessed, Bliss, Bluebird,

Bonny, Carefree, Cheery, Chuffed, Cock-a-hoop, Dwarf, Ecstatic, Elated, Eud(a)emony, Exhilarated, Felicity, Felix, Fool's paradise, Fortunate, Glad(some), Gleeful, Golden, Goshen, Gruntled, Halcyon, Half-cut, Hedonism, High-feather, Jovial, Joy, Kvell, Larry, Light-hearted, Merry, Opportune, Radiant, Rapture, Sandboy, Seal, Seel, Sele, Serene, Sunny, Tipsy, Trigger, Warrior

Hara-kiri Eventration, Seppuku, Suicide

Harangue Declaim, Diatribe, Earwigging, Lecture, Oration, Perorate, Philippic, Sermon, Speech, Spruik, Tirade

Harass(ed) Afflict, Annoy, Badger, Bait, Beleaguer, Beset, Bother, Chivvy, Distract, Dun, Gall, Grill, Grind, Grounden, Hassle, Haze, Heckle, Hector, Henpeck, Hound, Irritate, Needle, Persecute, Pester, Plague, Press, Tailgate, Thwart, Trash, Vex

Harbinger Herald, Omen, Precursor, Usher

Harbour(ed) Alee, Anchorage, Basin, Brest, Cherish, Dock, Entertain, Foster, Herd, Hide, Hythe, Incubate, Lodge, Manukau, Marina, Mulberry, Pearl, PLA, Poole, Port, Quay, Reset, Scapa Flow, → **SHELTER**, Watemata, Wellington

Hard(en), Hardness Abstruse, Adamant(ine), Adularia, Augean, Austere, Bony, Brindell, Brinell, Brittle, Bronze, Cake, Calcify, Callous, Caramel, Cast-iron, Chitin, Concrete, Cornute, Crusty, Dentin(e), Difficult, Dour, Draconian, Ebonite, Endure, Enure, Exacting, Firm, Flint(y), Geal, Granite, Gruelling, H, Hawkish, Hellish, Herculean, HH, Horny, Indurate, Inure, Iron(y), Jasper, Knotty, Liparite, Lithoid, Metallic, Metally, Moh, Moh's scale, Murder, Nails, Obdurate, Obdure, Osseous, Ossify, Permafrost, Permanent, Petrify, Picrite, Raw, Rugged, Ruthless, Scirrhus, Schist, Scleral, Set, Severe, Solid, Sore, Steel(y), Steep, Stereo, Stern, Sticky, Stiff, Stoic, Stony, Teak, Temper, Temporary, Tough, Wooden

Hardback Case-bound

Hard-core Riprap, Scalpins

Hard-headed Stegochepalian

Harding Warden

Hardliner Hawk

Hardly Borderline, Ill, Just, Scarcely, Uneath(es), Unnethes

Hard-pressed Strait, Taxed

Hardship Affliction, Grief, Mill, Mishap, Penance, Privation, Rigour, Trial, Trouble

Hardware → **COMPUTER HARDWARE**, Gear, Ironmongery

Hardy Brave, Dour, Durable, Gritty, Manful, Oliver, Ollie, Rugged, Spartan, Sturdy, Thomas

Hare Arctic, Baud(rons), Bawd, Belgian, Doe, Dolicholis, Down, Electric, Husk, Jack-rabbit, Jugged, Jumping, Lam, Leporine, Malkin, Mara, March, Mawkin, Mountain, Mouse, Ochotona, Pika, Piping, Puss, Scut, Snowshoe, Spring, Wat

Hare-brained Giddy, Madcap, Scatty

Harem Gynaeceum, Gynoecium, Seraglio, Serai(l), Zenana

Hark(en) Ear, Hear, List(en)

Harlequin Chequered, Columbine, Pantaloon

Harlot Blue gown, Drab, Hussy, Loon, Loose, Paramour, Plover, Pusle, Pussel, Quail, Rahab, Scrubber, Slut, Strumpet, Whore

Harm(ed), Harmful Aggrieve, Bane, Blight, Damage, Deleterious, Detriment, Endamage, Evil, Hurt, Inimical, Injury, Insidious, Maleficent, Malignant, Maltreat, Mischief, Nocuous, Noxious, Pernicious, Sinister, Spoil, Wroken, Wrong

Harmless Benign, Canny, Drudge, Informidable, Innocent, Innocuous, Innoxious, Inoffensive

Harmonica Harp, Orpheus

Harmonious, Harmonise, Harmonist, Harmony Agree(ment), Alan, Allan, Allen, Alternation, Assort, Atone, Attune, Balanced, Barbershop, Blend, Chord, Close, Concent, Concentus, Concert, Concinnity, Concord, Congruous, Consonant, Consort, Coordinate, Correspondence, Counterpoint, Descant, Diapason, Diatessaron, Doo-wop, Euphony, Eur(h)ythmy, Faburden, Feng-shui, Go, Jibe, Keeping, Match, Melody, Mesh, Musical, Overblow, Overtone, Rappite, Solidarity, Symmetry, Sympathy, Symphonious, Sync, Thorough-bass, Tone, Tune, Unanimity, Unison, Unity

Harmotome Cross-stone

Harness(maker) Breeching, Bridle, Cinch, D-ring, Equipage, Frenum, Gear, Girth, Hitch, Inspan, Lorimer, Loriner, Pad-tree, Partnership, Swingletree, Tack(le), Throat-stop, Tie, Trace, Trappings, Whippletree, Yoke

Harp(sichord) Aeolian, Cembalo, Clairschach, Clarsach, Clavier, Drone, Dwell, Irish, Jew's, Lyre, Nebel, Trigon, Triple, Virginal, Welsh, Wind, Zither

Harpagon L'avare, Miser

Harpoon(er) Bart, Fis(h)gig, Fizgig, Grain, Iron, Lily iron, Peg, Spear, Specktioneer, Toggler, Tow-iron, Trident

Harpy Aello, Celeno, Eagle, Ocypete

Harridan Hag, Harpy, Shrew, Termagant, Xantippe, Zantippe, Zentippe

Harrier Hen, Montagu's

Harriet Hetty, Martineau

Harris Boatman, Isle, Rolf

Harrow(ing) Alas, Appal, Brake, Disc, Drag, Frighten, Herse, Lacerant, Pitch-pole, Plough, Rake, Rend, Shock

Harry Aggravate, Badger, Bother, Champion, Chase, Chivvy, Coppernose, Dragoon, Flash, Fret, Hal, Harass, Hassle, Hector, Herry, Houdini, Hound, Lauder, Lime, Maraud, Molest, Nag, Pester, Plague, Rag, Reave, Reive, Rieve, Rile, Tate, Tchick, Torment

▷ **Harry** *may indicate* an anagram

Harsh(ness) Abrasive, Acerbic, Austere, Barbaric, Brassy, Cacophonous, Cruel, Desolate, Discordant, Draconian, Extreme, Glary, Grating, Gravelly, Grim, Gruff, Guttural, Hard, Inclement, Oppressive, Raucle, Raucous, Raw, Rigour, Rude, Ruthless, Scabrid, Scrannel, Screechy, → SEVERE, Sharp, Spartan, Stark, Stern, Stoor, Stour, Stowre, Strict, Strident, Unkind

Hart Deer, Spade, Spay, Spay(a)d, Venison

Harte Bret

Hartebeest Bubal, Kaama, Kongoni

Harum-scarum Bayard, Chaotic, Madcap, Rantipole

Harvest(er), Harvest home Combine, Crop, Cull, Fruit, → GATHER, Hairst, Hawkey, Hay(sel), Hockey, Horkey, In(ning), Ingather, Kirn, Lease, Nutting, Pick, Produce, Rabi, Random, Reap, Shock, Spatlese, Spider, Tattie-howking, Thresh, Vendage, Vendange

Has Habet, Hath, Owns, 's

Has-been Effete, Ex, Outmoded

Hash(ish) Bungle, Charas, Discuss, Garble, Garboil, Hachis, Lobscouse, Mince, Pi(e), Ragout

▷ **Hashed** *may indicate* an anagram

Hasn't Hant, Nas

Hassle Aggro, Bother, Moider, M(o)ither

Hassock Kneeler, Pouf(fe), Stool, Tuffet

Haste(n), Hastening, Hastily, Hasty Cursory, Despatch, Expedite, Express,

Festinately, Fly, Hare, Headlong, Hie, Hotfoot, → **HURRY**, Hurry-scurry, Impetuous, Precipitant, Race, Ramstam, Rash, Rush, Scuttle, Speed, Spur, Stringendo, Subitaneous, Sudden, Tear, Tilt, Urge

Hastings Banda, Bustles, Senlac, Warren

Hat Akubra®, Ascot, Astrakhan, Balibuntal, Balmoral, Basher, Beanie, Beany, Bearskin, Beaver, Beret, Bicorn, Billycock, Biretta, Bluebonnet, Boater, Bobble, Bollinger, Bonnet, Bowler, Boxer, Brass, Breton, Broad-brim, Bronx, Busby, Cabbage tree, Cap, Capotain, Cartwheel, Castor, Chaco, Chapeau, Cheese-cutter, Chimneypot, Christie, Christy, Claque, Cloche, Cocked, Cockle-hat, Coolie, Cossack, Cowboy, Crusher, Curch, Deerstalker, Derby, Dolly Varden, Dunstable, Envoy, Fedora, Fez, Flat-cap, Fore-and-after, Gaucho, Gibus, Gimme, Glengarry, Hard, Hattock, Headdress, Head-rig, Hennin, Homburg, Kamelaukion, Kepi, Lamington, Leghorn, Lid, Lum, Matador, Mitre, Mob-cap, Mountie's, Mushroom, Nab, Opera, Pagri, Panama, Petasus, Picture, Pilion, Pill-box, Pilleus, Pilos, Pith, Pixie, Planter's, Plateau, Plug, Poke(-bonnet), Pork-pie, Potae, Profile, Puggaree, Puritan, Ramil(l)ies, Red, Runcible, Safari, Sailor, Scarlet, Shako, Shovel, Silk, Skimmer, Skull-cap, Slouch, Snap-brim, Snood, Sola(-helmet), Solah, Sola-topi, Sombrero, Songkok, Souwester, Steeple-crown, Stetson®, Stovepipe, Straw, Sugarloaf, Sunbonnet, Sundown, Sunhat, Tam (o' Shanter), Tarboosh, Tarb(o)ush, Tarpaulin, Ten-gallon, Terai, Thrummed, Tile, Tin, Tit(fer), Toorie, Top(per), Topee, Topi, Toque, Tricorn(e), Trilby, Turban, Tyrolean, Ugly, Wide-awake, Witch's

Hat-band Weeper

Hatch(ment), Hatching Achievement, Altricial, Booby, Breed, Brew, Brood, Cleck, Clutch, Companion, Concoct, Cover, Devise, Eclosion, Emerge, Escape, Incubate, Service, Set, Trap-door

Hatchet(-shaped) Axe, Bill, Chopper, Claw, Cleaver, Dolabriform, Tomahawk

▷ **Hatching** *may indicate* an anagram

Hatchway (surround) Companionway, Fiddley, Guichet, Porthole, Scuttle, Service

Hate(ful), Hatred Abhor, Abominable, Abominate, Anims, Aversion, Bugbear, Detest, Enmity, Haterent, Loathe, Misogyny, Odium, Pet, Phobia, Racism, Resent, Spite, Ug(h), Vitriol

Hatless Bareheaded, Unbeavered

Hat-plant S(h)ola

Hatter Mad

Hatty Etta

Haughty, Haughtiness Aloof, Aristocratic, Arrogant, Bashaw, Cavalier, Disdainful, Dorty, Fastuous, High, Hogen-mogen, Hoity-toity, Hye, Imperious, Lofty, Morgue, Orgillous, Orgulous, Paughty, → **PROUD**, Scornful, Sdeignful, Sniffy, Stiff-necked, Toplofty, Upstage

Haul(age), Haulier Bag, Bouse, Bowse, Brail, Carry, Cart, Catch, Drag, Heave, Hove, Kedge, Long, Loot, Plunder, Pull, Rug, Sally, Scoop, Snake, Snig, TIR, Touse, Touze, Tow(se), Towze, Transporter, Trice, Winch, Yank

Haunch Hance, Hip, Huckle, Hunkers, Quarter

Haunt(s) Catchy, Den, Dive, Frequent, Ghost, Hang-out, Honky-tonk, Houf(f), Howff(f), Infest, Obsess, Purlieu, Resort, Spot, Spright

Hauteur Bashawism, Height, Morgue, Vanity

Havana Cigar

Have, Having Bear, Ha(e), Han, Hoax, Hold, Of, → **OWN**, Possess, Sell

Haven Asylum, Harbour, Hithe, Hythe, Oasis, Port, Refuge, Refugium, Retreat, Safe, Shelter, Tax

Haver(s) Blether, Clanjamfray, Dither, Gibber, Nigel

▶ **Haversack** *see* RUCKSACK

Havoc Desolation, Devastation, Hell, Ravage, Waste

▷ **Havoc** *may indicate* an anagram

Haw Drawl, Hip, Sloe

Hawaiian Kanaka

Hawk(er), Hawkish Accipitrine, Auceps, Badger, Bastard, Buzzard, Cadger, Camelot, Caracara, Cast, Cheapjack, Cooper's, Cry, Duck, Eagle, Elanet, Eyas, Falcon, Fish, Gerfalcon, Goshawk, Haggard, Hardliner, Harrier, Harrumph, Hobby, Honey-buzzard, Keelie, Kestrel, Kite, Lammergeier, Lanner(et), Marsh, Merlin, Molla(h), Monger, Moolah, Mosquito, Mullah, Musket, Night, Nyas, Osprey, Ossifrage, Passager, Pearlie, Pearly, Peddle, Pedlar, Peregrine, Pigeon, Privet, Ringtail, Sacre(t), Sell, Slab, Slanger, Soar(e), Sorage, Sore(-eagle), Sparrow, Spiv, Staniel, Stone, Sutler, Tallyman, Tarsal, Tarsel(l), Tassel, Tercel(et), Tiersel, Trant(er), Trucker, Warlike

Hawkeye IA, Iowa

Hawk-keeper Austringer, Ostreger

Hawser Line, Rope

Hawthorn Albespine, Albespyne, May(flower), Quickset

Hay(cock), Hey Antic, Cock, Contra-dance, Fodder, Goaf, Hi, Kemple, Math, Mow, Pleach, Pook, Salt, Stack, Straw, Truss, Windrow

Hayfever Pollenosis, Pollinosis

Haymaker Blow, Slog

Hayseed Chaw-bacon, Hodge, Joskin, Rustic

Hazard(ous) Bet, Breakneck, Bunker, Chance, Danger, Dare, Die, Dye, Game, Gremlin, Guess, Imperil, In-off, Jeopardy, Losing, Main, Minefield, Moral, Nice, Niffer, Occupational, Perdu(e), Peril, Pitfall, Play, Pothole, Queasy, → RISK, Stake, Trap, Venture, Vigia, Wage, Winning

Haze, Hazy Blear, Cloud, Filmy, Fog, → MIST, Mock, Muzzy, Nebulous, Smaze, Smog, Tease

▷ **Haze** *may indicate* an anagram

Hazel(wort) Amenta, Asarabacca, Catkin, Cob, Corylus, Filbert

HC Encomia, Encomium

He, HE A, Helium, Tag, Tig, → TNT, Tom

Head(s), Heading, Headman, Head shaped, Heady Aim, Apex, Ard-ri(gh), Beachy, Bean, Behead, Bill, Block, Bonce, Boss, Bound, Brain, Brainpan, Bregma, Brow, But(t), Caboceer, Cape, Capitani, Capitate, Capitulum, Capo, Captain, Caption, Caput, Caudillo, Cephalic, Chaton, Chief, Chump, Coarb, Coconut, Coma, Commander, Conk, Cop, Coppin, Costard, Cranium, Crest, Crisis, Crown, Crumpet, Cylinder, Dateline, Director, Dome, Dummy, Each, Ear, Exarch, Figure, Flamborough, Foam, Foreland, Froth, General, Glomerate, Grand Mufti, Hegumen(os), Herm(a), Hoe, Hogh, Huff-cap, Inion, Jowl, Karmapa, Keyword, Knob, Knowledge-box, Lead(er), Lid, Lizard, Loaf, Loave, Loo, Lore, Malik, Manager, Mayor, Maz(z)ard, Melik, Mocuddum, Mogul, Mokaddam, Mr Big, Mull, Muqaddam, Nab, Nana, Napper, Nappy, Ness, Nob, Noddle, Noggin, Noll, Noup, Nowl, Nut, Obverse, Occiput, Onion, Panicle, Panorama, Parietal, Pash, Pate, Pater(familias), Patriarch, Pick-up, Point, Poll, Pow, Prefect, President, Pressure, Principal, Promontory, Provost, Ras, Read-write, Ream, Rector, Rubric, Sarpanch, Scalp, Scaup, Scaw, Scholarch, Scolex, Sconce, Short, Sinciput, Skaw, Skull, Sound, Source, Spume, Squeers, Starosta, Strapline, Subject, Superior, Taipan, Talking, Tanadar, Tete, Thanadar, Throne, Tight, Tintagel, Title, Toilet, Top, Topic, Tsantsa, Twopenny, Upperworks, Vaivode, Velocity, Voivode, Yorick, Zupan

▷ **Head** *may indicate* the first letter of a word

Headache Cephalalgia, Encephalalgia, Hangover, Megrim, Migraine, Neuralgia, Red out, Scotodinia, Splitter

Headband Fillet, Garland, Infula, Sphendone, T(a)enia

Headdress, Headcover Ampyx, Balaclava, Bandeau, Bas(i)net, Bonnet, Burnous(e), Busby, Calotte, Caul, Chaplet, Circlet, Comb, Commode, Cor(o)net, Cowl, Coxcomb, Crownet, Curch, Doek, Dopatta, Dupatta, Fascinator, Fontange, Fool's cap, Frontlet, Hat(tock), Helm(et), Joncanoe, Juliet cap, Kaffiyeh, Kell, Kerchief, Kuffiyeh, Kufiah, Kufiya(h), Mantilla, Mitre, Mobcap, Modius, Mortarboard, Nubia, Periwig, Pill-box, Plug-hat, Porrenger, Porringer, Romal, Sakkos, Ship-tire, Silly-how, Skullcap, Sphendome, Stephane, Taj, Tarbush, Tiara, Tire-vallant, Tower, Tulban, Turban, War bonnet, Wig, Wimple

Header Bonder, Dive, Fall, Rowlock

Headhunter Naga

Headland Beachy Head, Bill, Cape, Cape Horn, Dungeness, Finisterre, Foreland, Head-rig, Hoe, Hogh, Land's End, Morro, Naze, Ness, Noup, → **PROMONTORY**, Ras, Ross, St Vincent, Scaw, Skaw

Headless Acephalous

Headlight(s) Beam, Brights, Dip, Halo

Headline Banner, Caption, Drophead, Frown, Kicker, Ribbon, Scare-head, Screamer, Streamer, Title

Headlock Chancery

Headlong Breakneck, Pell-mell, Precipitate, Ramstam, Reckless, Steep, Sudden, Tantivy, Tearaway

▸ **Headman** *see* **HEAD**

Headmaster Principal, Squeers

Headphone(s) Cans, Earpiece, Walkman®

Headquarters Base, Command, Depot, Guardhouse, Guildhall, Pentagon, SHAEF, SHAPE, Station

▷ **Heads** *may indicate* a lavatory

Headstrong Obstinate, Rash, Stubborn, Unruly, Wayward, Wilful

Head-to-tail Tête-bêche

Headway Advancement, Headroom, Progress

Head-word Lemma

Heal(ing) Aesculapian, Ayurveda, Balsam, Chiropractic, Cicatrise, Cleanse, Curative, Cure, Esculapian, G(u)arish, Hele, Hippocratise, Intention, Knit, Mend, Mental, New Thought, Olosis, Osteopathy, Restore, Sain, Salve, Sanitory, Spiritual, Therapeutic, Vulnerary

Healer Althea, Asa, Doctor, Homeopath, Naturopath, Osteopath, Sangoma, Shaman, Time

Health(y) Bouncing, Bracing, Chin-chin, Constitution, Doer, Fit, Flourishing, Gesundheit, Hail, Hale, Hartie-hale, Heart, Holism, Kia-ora, L'chaim, Lustique, Lusty, Medicaid, Medicare, Pink, Prosit, Public, Robust, Rosy, Salubrious, Sane, Slainte, Sound, Toast, Tope, Valentine, Valetudinarian, Vigour, Well, WHO, Wholesome

Heap(ed) Acervate, Agglomerate, Amass, Bing, Boneshaker, Bulk, Car, Clamp, Coacervate, Cock, Congeries, Cumulus, Drift, Hog, Jalopy, Lot, Pile, Raff, Raft, Rick(le), Ruck, Scrap, Shell, Slag, Stash, Tass, Toorie, Up-piled

Hear(ing) Acoustic, Attend, Audience, Audile, Avizandum, Captain's mast, Catch, Clairaudience, Dirdum, Ear, Harken, Learn, List(en), Oyer, Oyez, Panel, Paracusis, Pick up, Session, Subpoena, Try

▷ **Hear(say)** *may indicate* a word sounding like one given
Hearsay Account, Gossip, Report, Rumour, Surmise
Hearse Bier, Catafalco, Catafalque, Meat wagon, Shillibeer
Heart(en), Heartily, Hearty, Heart-shaped AB, Agood, Auricle, Backslapping, Beater, Bleeding, Bluff, Bosom, Bradycardia, Cant, Cardiac, Centre, Cheer, Cockles, Columella, Cordate, Cordial, Core, Courage, Crossed, Daddock, Embolden, Encourage, Essence, Floating, Gist, H, Hale, Herz, Inmost, Jarta, Kernel, Lepid, Lonely, Memoriter, Mesial, Mid(st), Middle, Nub, Nucleus, Obcordate, Purple, Robust, Root, Sacred, Sailor, Seafarer, Seaman, Sinoatrial, Staunch, Tachycardia, Tar, Ticker, Yarta, Yarto
Heart-break Crève-coeur, Grief, Sorrow
Heartburn Brash, Cardialgia, Pyrosis
Heartfelt Deep, Genuine, Real, Sincere, Soulful
Hearth Cupel, Finery, Fireside, Home, Ingle, Killogie
Heartless Callous, Cored, Cruel, Three-suited
Heart's ease Pansy
Heart trouble Bradycardia, Fallot's tetralogy, Fibrillation, Murmur, Tachycardia
Heat(ed), Heater, Heating Anneal, Ardour, Arousal, Atomic, Barrage, Beath, Blood, Brazier, Calcine, Califont, Caloric, Calorifier, Central, Chafe, Convector, Dead, Decay, Dielectric, Dudgeon, Eccaleobion, Element, Eliminator, Endothermic, Enthalpy, Estrus, Etna, Excite, Exothermic, Fan, Ferment, Fever, Fire, Fluster, Fug, Furnace, Het, Hibachi, Hyperthermia, Hypocaust, Immersion, Incalescence, Induction, J, Kindle, Latent, Liquate, Lust, Moxibustion, Normalise, Oestrus, Panel, Prelim, Prickly, Q, Radiant, Radiator, Rankine, Recalescence, Red, Render, Repechage, Rut, Salt, Scald, Sinter, Sizzle, Solar, Space, Specific, Spice, Stew, Storage, Stove, Swelter, Teend, Temperature, Tind, Tine, Torrefy, Total, Tynd(e), Underfloor, Warming-pan, Warmth, White, Zip®
Heath(land) Bearberry, Bent, Briar, Brier, Egdon, Epacrid, Erica, Geest, Lande, Manoao, Manzanita, Moor, Muir, Stead, Ted
Heathen(s) Ethnic, Gentile, Infidel, Litholatrous, Nations, Pagan, Pa(i)nim, Paynim, Philistine, Primitive, Profane, Proselyte of the gate
Heather Bell, Broom, Calluna, Epacrid, Erica, Foxberry, Ling, Rhodora, Sprig
▷ **Heating** *may indicate* an anagram
Heave(d) Cast, Fling, Frost, Heeze, Hoise, Hoist, Hump, Hurl, Popple, Retch, Shy, Sigh, Vomit
▷ **Heave** *may indicate* 'discard'
Heaven(s), Heavenly Air, Aloft, Ama, Ambrosial, Arcady, Asgard, Bliss, Celestial, Celia, Divine, Ecstasy, Elysian, Elysium, Empyrean, Ethereal, Fiddler's Green, Firmament, Hereafter, Himmel, Holy, Hookey Walker, Land o' the Leaf, Leal, Lift, Mackerel, New Jerusalem, Olympus, Paradise, Pole, Rapture, Seventh, Shangri-la, Sion, Sky, Supernal, Svarga, Swarga, Swerga, Tir na n'Og, Uranian, Welkin, Zion
Heavy(weight), Heavily, Heaviness Ali, Clumpy, Dutch, Elephantine, Embonpoint, Endomorph, Grave, Hefty, Last, Leaden, Lumpish, Onerous, Osmium, Pesante, Ponderous, Sad, Scelerate, Stodgy, Stout, Top, Upsee, Ups(e)y, Weighty, Wicked
Hebe Barmaid
Hebrew Aramaic, Eli, Heb, Jesse, Karaism, Levi, Mishnayoth, Modern, Rabbinical, Yid
Hebridean Harris
Heckle Badger, Gibe, Harass, Hatchel, Jeer, Needle, Spruik
Hectic Ding-dong, Feverish, Frenetic

Hector Badger, Bluster, Browbeat, Bully, → **HARASS**, Nag

Hedge, Hedging Box, Bullfinch, Enclosure, Equivocate, Evade, Haw, Hay, Lay off, Meuse, Mews, Muse, Pleach, Privet, Quickset, Raddle, Sepiment, Shield, Stonewall, Texas, Thicket, Waffle

Hedgehog Gymnure, Hérisson, Tenrec, Tiggywinkle, Urchin

Hedge-parson Bucklebeggar, Patercove

Hedge-sparrow Accentor

Hedonist Cyreniac, Epicurean, Playboy, Sybarite

Heed(ed), Heedful Attend, Listen, → **MIND**, Notice, Obey, Observe, Rear, Reck, Regard(ant), Reke, Respect, Rought, Tent, Tinker's cuss

Heedless Careless, Inattentive, Incautious, Rash, Scapegrace, Scatterbrain

Heel Achilles, Cad, Calcaneum, Cant, Careen, Cuban, Dogbolt, Foot, French, Kitten, List, Louse, Rogue, Seel, Spike, Stacked, Stiletto, Tilt, Wedge

Heel-tap Snuff

Hefty Brawny, Heavy, Solid, Weighty

Heifer Io, Quey, Stirk

Height(en), Heights Abraham, Altitude, Cairngorm, Ceiling, Dimension, Elevation, Embroider, Eminence, Enhance, Golan, H, Hill, Hypsometry, Level, Might, Peak, Procerity, Spot, Stature, Stud, Sum, → **SUMMIT**, Tor, X

Heinous Abominable, Atrocious, Flagrant

Heir Alienee, Claimant, Coparcener, Dauphin, Devisee, Distributee, Eigne, H(a)eres, Institute, Intitule, Legatee, Parcener, Scion, Sprig, Tanist

Heirless Escheat, Intestate

Held Captive, Hostage, Sostenuto, Ten(uto)

▷ **Held by** *may indicate* a hidden word

Helen Elaine, Nell(y)

Helicopter, Heliport Airstop, Chopper, Egg-beater, Gunship, Hover, Iroquois, Medevac, Rotodyne, Sea Cobra, Sea King, Sea Knight, Sea Sprite, Sea Stallion, Sikorsky, Sky-hook, Whirlybird

Helios Hyperion

Heliotrope Cherry-pie

Helium He

Helix Alpha, Double, Parastichy

Hell(ish) Abaddon, Abyss, Ades, Agony, Amenthes, Annw(yf)n, Avernus, Below, Blazes, Chthonic, Dis, Erebus, Furnace, Gehenna, Hades, Heck, Inferno, Jahannam, Lower regions, Malebolge, Naraka, Netherworld, Orcus, Pandemonium, Perditious, Pit, Ruin, Sheol, Stygian, Tartar(ean), Tartarus, Tophet, Torment

Hellbender Menopome, Mud-puppy

Hellebore Itchweed, Setterwort

Hellenic Dorian

Hellespont Dardanelles

Hello, Hallo, Hullo Aloha, Chin-chin, Ciao, Dumela, Golden, Hi, Ho(a), Hoh, Howdy, Howzit, Yoo-hoo

Helm(sman) Cox, Navigator, Pilot, Steer, Tiller, Timon(eer)

Helmet Armet, Balaclava, Basinet, Beaver, Burganet, Burgonet, Cask, Casque, Comb, Crash, Galea, Heaume, Knapscal, Knapscull, Knapskull, Montero, Mor(r)ion, Nasal, Pickelhaube, Pith, Plumed, Pot, Pressure, Salade, Sal(l)et, Shako, Skid-lid, Smoke, Topee, Topi

Helot Esne, Slave

Help(er), Helping, Helpful Abet, Accomplice, Adjuvant, Advantage, Aid(ance), Aidant, Aide, Alexis, Alleviate, Ally, Asset, → **ASSIST**, Avail, Back, Beet-master,

Beet-mister, Befriend, Benefit, Bestead, Boon, Brownie, Char(woman), Coadjutor, Complice, Conducive, Daily, Dollop, Dose, Ezra, Forward, Further(some), Go, Hand, Henchman, Hint, Home, Hyphen, Instrumental, Leg-up, Life-saver, Maid, Mayday, Monitor, Obliging, Ophelia, Order, Patronage, Ration, Recourse, Relieve, Servant, Serve, Slice, SOS, Stead, Sted, Subserve, Subvention, Succour, Taste, Therapeutic, Use

Helpless(ness) Adynamia, Anomie, Downa-do, Feeble, Impotent, Paralytic, Useless

Helpmate Consort

Hem Border, Fringe, Hoop, List

He-man Adonis, Hunk, Jock, Macho

Hemisphere, Hemispherical Dominant, Magdeburg, Rose-cut, Western

Hemlock Conia, Cowbane, Insane root, Tsuga

Hemp Abaca, Bhang, Boneset, Bowstring, Carl(ot), Choke-weed, Codilla, Dagga, Fimble, Ganja, Hards, Henequen, Hiniquin, Indian, K(a)if, Kef, Love-drug, Manil(l)a, Mauritius, Moorva, Murva, Neckweed, Pita, Sida, Sunn, Tat, Tow

Hen(s) Ancona, Andalusian, Australorp, Biddy, Buff Orpington, Chock, Cochin, Dorking, Eirack, Fowl, Grig, Houdan, Langshan, Layer, Leghorn, Maori, Marsh, Mother, Mud, Orpington, Partlet, Pertelote, Plymouth Rock, Poulard, Poultry, Pullet, Ree(ve), Rhode Island red, Sitter, Spanish fowl, Sultan, Tappit, Welsummer, Wyandotte

Hence Apage, Avaunt, Ergo, Go, Hinc, So, Therefore, Thus

Henchman Attendant, Follower, Myrmidon, Satellite

Hen-house Battery, Eggery

Henna Camphire

Hennery Run

Hen-pecked Pussy-whipped, Spineless, Woman-tired

Henry Eighth, H, Hal, Hank, Hooray, Hy, James, Navigator, O

Hep Bacca, Berry, Hip

Hepatic Scale-moss

Hepatitis Favism, Jaundice

Herald(ic), Heraldry Abatement, Al(l)erion, Argent, Armory, Azure, Bagwyn, Bars, Baton sinister, Bearing, Bend, Bendwise, Blazonry, Bloody Hand, Blue Mantle, Bordure, Caboched, Cabré, Calygreyhound, Checky, Chevron, Chief, Cicerone, Cinquefoil, Clarenc(i)eux, Cleché, Compone, Compony, Couchant, Coue, Counter-passant, Coupee, Coward, Crest, Crier, Debruised, Degraded, Difference, Displayed, Dormant, Endorse, Enfiled, Erased, Fecial, Fess(e), Fetial, File, Flory, Forerunner, Gardant, Garter, Gironny, Golp(e), Gules, Gyronny, Hauriant, Hermes, Honour-point, Issuant, King-of-arms, Lionel, Lis, Lodged, Lyon, Lyon King of Arms, Manchet, Martlet, Messenger, Minocaine, Morne, Mullet, Naiant, Naissant, Nascent, Nombril, Norroy, Nowed, Nowy, Opinicus, Or, Ordinary, Pale, Pallet, Paly, Passant, Pile, Portcullis, Portend, Potent, Precursor, Proclaim, Purpure, Pursuivant, Quartering, Rampant, Red Hand, Regardant, Rouge Croix, Rouge Dragon, Roundel, Roundle, Sable, Salient, Scarp, Sea lion, Segreant, Sejant, Statant, Stentor, Subordinary, Tenné, Trangle, Tressure, Trick, Trippant, Trundle, Umbrated, Undifferenced, Urinant, Usher, Vaunt-courier, Verdoy, Vert, Vol(ant), Vorant, Wivern, Woodhouse, Woodwose, Wyvern, Yale

Herb(s) Aconite, Agrimony, Ajowan, Alecost, Allspice, Angelica, Anise, Aristolochia, Arugula, Avens, Basil, Bay, Bennet, Bergamot, Borage, Capers, Caraway, Cardamom, Centaury, Chamomile, Chervil, C(h)ive, Cilanto, Cohosh, Comfrey, Coriander, Costmary, Cum(m)in, Dill, Dittany, Echinacea, Eruca, Estragon,

Exacum, Eyebright, Felicia, Fennel, Fenugreek, Ferula, Feverfew, Fireweed, Fitch, Fluellin, Forb, Garlic, Garnish, Gentian, Germander, Good-King-Henry, Gunnera, Haworthia, Hyssop, Inula, Kalanchoe, Knapweed, Lamb's ears, Laserpicium, Laserwort, Lewisia, Lovage, Madder, Madwort, Mandrake, Marjoram, Maror, Medic, Mint, Moly, Mustard, Oca, Oleraceous, Oregano, Origan(e), Origanum, Ornithogalum, Orval, Paprika, Parakeelya, Parakelia, Parsley, Paterson's curse, Phlomis, Pia, Pipsissewa, Plantain, Purpie, Purslane, Pussytoes, Reed-mace, Rest-harrow, Rhizocarp, Rodgersia, Rosemary, Rue, Rupturewort, Saffron, Sage, Salad, Saloop, Salsify, Savory, Senna, Sesame, Soapwort, Sorrel, Southernwood, Spearmint, Staragen, Sweet cicely, Tacca, Tansy, Tarragon, Thyme, Tormentil, Turmeric, Typha, Valerian, Veronica, Vervain, Vetch, Weed, Willow, Wormwood, Wort, Yarrow, Yerba

Herbert Alan, AP(H), Lom, Spencer

Herbicide Agent Orange, Atrazine, Defoliant, Diquat, Picloram, Simazine

Herbivore Iguanodon, Sauropod

Hercules Alcides, Huge, Rustam, Rustem

Herd(er), Herdsman Band, Corral, Drive, Drover, Flock, Gang, Marshal, Meinie, Mein(e)y, Menyie, Mob, Pod, Raggle-taggle, Round-up, Shepherd, Tinchel, Vaquero

Here Adsum, Hi, Hic, Hither, Local, Now, Present

Hereditary, Heredity Ancestry, Blood, Breeding, Codon, Dynastic, Eugenics, Exon, Genetics, Id(ant), Idioplasm, Mendelism, Panagenesis

▷ **Herein** *may indicate* a hidden word

Here is laid HS

Heresiarch Nestor

Heresy, Heretic(al) Agnoitae, Albi, Albigensian, Apollinaris, Apostasy, Arian, Bab, Bogomil, Bugger, Cathar, Cerinthus, Docete, Donatist, Dulcinist, Encratite, Eudoxian, Giaour, Gnosticism, Heresearch, Heterodoxy, Lollard, Manichaean, Montanism, Nestorian, Nonconformist, Origen, Patarin(e), Pelagius, Phrygian, Racovian, Rebel, Unitarian, Zendik

Heritage Birthright, Due, NT, Ottilie, Patrimony

Hermaphrodite Androgynous, Gynandromorph, Monochinous, Monoecious, Prot(er)andry

Hermes (rod) Caduceus, Mercury

Hermetic Alchemist, Sealed

Hermit(age), Hermit-like Anchoret, Anchorite, Ascetic, Ashram(a), Augustinian, Austin, Cell, Cloister, Crab, Eremite, Grandmontine, Loner, Marabout, Monk, Museum, Nitrian, Pagurid, Peter, Recluse, Retreat, Robber-crab, Sannyasi, Soldier-crab, Solitary, Troglodyte

Hernia Bubonocele, Cystocoele, Diverticulum, Enterocele, Hiatus, Inguinal, Rectocele, Rupture

Hero(ic) Achilles, Aeneas, Agamemnon, Aitu, Ajax, Alcides, Amadis, Asterix, Bader, Balarama, Bellerophon, Beowulf, Brave, Bunyan, Champ(ion), Cid, Couplet, Crockett, Cuchulain, Cuchullain, Cyrano, Dambuster, Dan Dare, Demigod, Drake, Epic, Eponym, Eric, Everyman, Faust, Fingal, Finn, Finn MacCool, Folk, Garibaldi, Glooscap, Gluscap, Gluskap, God, Goody, Great, Hector, Heracles, Hercules, Hiawatha, Howleglass, Hudibrastic, Icon, Ideal, Idol, Ivanhoe, Jason, Kaleva, Kami, Leonidas, Lion, Lochinvar, Lothair, Marmion, Meleager, Nestor, Noble, Odysseus, Oliver, Onegin, Orion, Owl(e)glass, Ow(l)spiegle, Paladin, Parashurama, Parsifal, Pericles, Perseus, Philoctetes, Priestess, Principal, Ramachandra, Rambo, Raven, Resolute, Revere, Rinaldo, Roderego, Roderick, Roland, Rustem, Rustum, Saladin, Sheik, Siegfried, Sigurd, Superman, Tam o' Shanter, Tancred, Tarzan, Tell,

Theseus, Tragic, Triptolemus, Tristan, Trist(r)am, Ulysses, Valiant, Vercingetorix, Virago, Volsung, White knight, Zorro

Herod Agrippa, Antipas

Heroin Dogfood, Doojie, Dynamite, Gumball, H, Harry, Henry, Horse, Jack, Junk, Scag, Shit, Skag, Smack, Snow, Snowball, Speedball, Sugar

Heroine Andromeda, Ariadne, Candida, Darling, Demigoddess, Hedda, Imogen, Isolde, Judith, Juliet, Leda, Leonora, Manon, Mimi, Nana, Norma, Pamela, Star, Tess, Una

Heron(s) Ardea, Bird, Bittern, Boat-billed, Butter-bump, Egret, Green, Handsaw, Kotuko, Screamer, Sedge, Siege, Squacco, Winnard

Herpes Cold sore, Dartre, Shingles, Shiver

Herring Bismarck, Bloater, Brisling, Brit, Buckling, Caller, Cisco, Clupea, Digby chick(en), Gaspereau, Glasgow magistrate, Kipper, Lake, Ma(a)tjes, Maise, Maize, Mattie, Maze, Mease, Menhaden, Norfolk capon, Ox eye, Rabbitfish, Red, Rollmop, Sea-stick, Shotten, Sild, Silt, Sparling, Teleost, Whitebait

Herringbone Sloping

Hesitant, Hesitate, Hesitation Balance, Boggle, Cunctation, Delay, Demur, Dicker, Dither, Doubtful, Dubitate, Er, Falter, Halting, Haver, Haw, Irresolute, Mammer, Mealy-mouthed, → **PAUSE**, Qualm, Scruple, Shillyshally, Shrink, Stagger, Stammer, Swither, Tarrow, Teeter, Tentative, Think twice, Um, Ur, Vacillate, Wait, Waver

Hesperus Vesper

Hessian Burlap, Hireling

Heterodoxy Heresy

Heterogeneous Diverse, Motley, Piebald

Heterosexual Hasbian, Straight

Hew(er) Ax, Chop, Cut, Gideon, Hack, Sever

Hex Bewitch, Jinx, Voodoo

Hexameter Dolichurus

▶ **Hey** *see* **HAY**

Heyday Prime, Summer

Hi Cooee, Hello, Howdie

Hiatus Caesura, Entr'acte, Gap, Hernia, Interact, Interregnum, Interval, Lacuna, Lull

Hibernal, Hibernate, Hibernating Estivate, Hiemal, Hole up, Latitant, Sleep, Winter

Hibernian Irish

Hibiscus Okra, Roselle, Rozelle

Hiccup Glitch, Singultus, Snag, Spasm, Yex

Hick Jake, Oaf, Podunk, Rube, Yokel

Hickory Black, Jackson, Mockernut, Pecan, Scaly-bark, Shagbark

Hidden Buried, Cabalistic, Covert, De(a)rn, Doggo, Hooded, Latent, Obscure, Occult, Pentimento, Recondite, Screened, Secret, Shuttered, Sly, Ulterior, Unseen, Veiled, Wrapped

▷ **Hidden** *may indicate* a concealed word

Hide, Hiding (place) Abscond, Basan, Befog, Bield(y), Blind, Box-calf, Burrow, Bury, Butt, Cache, Camouflage, Ceroon, Coat, → **CONCEAL**, Cootch, Cordwain, Couch, Cour, Crop, Curtain, Cwtch, Deerskin, Doggo, Earth, Eclipse, Encave, Ensconce, Enshroud, Envelop, Epidermis, Fell, Flaught, Flay, Gloss over, Harbour, Heal, Heel, Hele, Hell, Hole-up, Hoodwink, Incave, Inter, Kip, Kipskin, Lair, Leather, Mai-mai, Mask, Mobble, Nebris, → **OBSCURE**, Parfleche, Pell, Pelt, Plank, Plant, Priest's hole, Repress, Robe, Saffian, Screen, Secrete, Shadow, Shellac(k), Shroud, Skin,

Spetch, Stash, Strap-oil, Tappice, Thong, Thrashing, Trove, Veil, Wallop, Whang, Wrap

Hideous(ness) Deform(ed), Enormity, Gash, Grotesque, Horrible, Monstrous, Odious, Ugly, Ugsome

Hierarchic, Hierarchy Byzantine, Elite, Theocracy

Hieroglyph Cipher, Pictogram

Higgledy-piggledy Mixtie-maxtie

High(er), Highly, Highness Alt(a), Altesse, Altissimo, Apogee, Atop, Brent, Climax, Doped, Drugged, E-la, Elation, Elevated, Eminent, Exalted, Excelsior, Frequency, Gamy, Haut(e), Intoxicated, Lofty, Maggotty, Mind-blowing, Orthian, Prime, Rancid, Ripe, School, Senior, Sent, Shrill, So, Steep, Stenchy, Stoned, String-out, Strong, Superior, Swollen, Tall, Tension, Tipsy, Top-lofty, Topmost, Treble, Ultrasonic, Up(per), Very, Wired, Zonked

▷ **High** *may indicate* an anagram

High and mighty Haughty, Hogen-mogen

Highball Drink, Lob, Loft

Highbrow Brain, Egghead, Intelligentsia, Long-hair

High-class Best, Superior, U

High-crowned Copataine

Highest Best, Climax, Mostwhat, Ne plus ultra, Progressive, Supreme

Highest note E-la

High-flown Bombastic, Euphuism

Highland(er), Highlands Blue-bonnet, Blue-cap, Cameron, Cat(h)eran, Down, Duniwassal, Dun(n)iewassal, Gael, Irish Scot, Karoo, Kiltie, Masai, Nainsel(l), Plaid(man), Redshank, Riff, Scot, Seaforth, Shire, Teuchter

Highlight Feature, Focus, Heighten, Stress

▸ **High-pitched** *see* HIGH

High-spirited Extravert, Extrovert

High tension HT

Highway Alaska, Alcan, Autobahn, Autopista, Autostrada, Camino Real, Divided, Flyover, Freeway, Information, Interstate, King's, Motorway, Overpass, Pass, Queen's, Road, Rode, Tarseal, Thoroughfare, Tightrope

Highwayman, Highway robber(y) Bandit, Bandolero, Duval, Footpad, Fraternity, Gilderoy, Jack Sheppard, Land-pirate, Land-rat, Latrocinium, MacHeath, Motorist, Rank-rider, Road-agent, Scamp, Skyjacker, Toby, Tobyman, Turpin, Twitcher, Wheel

Hijack(er) Abduct, Pirate

Hike(r) Backpack, Bushbash, Bushwalk, Raise, Rambler, Ramp, Rise, Traipse, Tramp, Trape(s), Upraise

Hilarious, Hilarity Hysterical, Jollity, Mirth, Riot

Hilary Term

Hill(s), Hillock, Hillside Ant, Antidine, Arafar, Areopagus, Aventine, Barrow, Beacon, Ben, Bent, Berg, Beverly, Black, Bluff, Bombay, Brae, Breed's, Brew, Broken, Bunker, Butte, Caelian, Calvan, Capitol(ine), Cheviots, Chiltern, Chin, Cleve, Cone, Coteau, Crag-and-tail, Crest, Damon, Djebel, Drumlin, Dun(e), Dunsinane, Eminence, Esquiline, Fell, Flodden, Gebel, Golan Heights, Golgotha, Gradient, Grampians, Hammock, Height, Helvellyn, Highgate, Holt, Horst, How, Howe, Hummock, Incline, Inselberg, Janiculum, Jebel, Kip(p), Knap, Knoll, Knot, Kop(je), Koppie, Lammermuir, Lavender, Law, Loma, Low, Ludgate, Malvern, Mamelon, Man, Matopo, Mendip, Merrick, Mesa, Monadnock, Monte Cassino, Monticule, Morro, Mound, Mount Lofty Ranges, Nab, Naga, Nanatak, Nilgiri(s), North Downs,

Otway Ranges, Palatine, Pap, Pennines, Pike, Pingo, Pnyx, Quantocks, Quirinal, Rand, Range, Saddleback, Savoy, Scaur, Seven, Silbury, Sion, Stoss, Tara, Tel(l), Toft, Toot, Tor, Tump, Tweedsmuir, Valdai, Viminal, Wolds, Wrekin, Zion

Hillbilly Yap

Hill-dweller Ant

Hillman Areopagite, Nepalese

Hilltop Crest, Knoll, Nab

Hilt Basket, Coquille, Haft, Handle, Hasp, Shaft

Him(self) He, Ipse, Un

Himalaya(n) Nepali, Panda, Sherpa, Tibetan

Hind(most) Back, Deer, Lag, Rear, Starn, Stern

Hinder, Hindrance Back, Bar, Block, Check, Counteract, Cramp, Crimp, Cumber, Debar, → **DELAY**, Deter, Encumber, Estop, Hamper, Handicap, Harass, Holdback, Impeach, Impede, Inconvenience, Obstacle, Overslaugh, Porlock, Posterior, Pull-back, Rear, Rein, Remora, Rump, Set back, Shackle, Slow, Stop, Stunt, Taigle, Thwart, Trammel

Hindi, Hindu(ism) Arya Samaj, Babu, Bania(n), Banyan, Brahman, Brahmin, Dalit, Gentoo, Gurkha, Harijan, Jaina, Kshatriya, Maharishi, Nagari, Pundit, Rajpoot, Rajput, Rama, Sad(d)hu, Saiva, S(h)akta, Saktas, Sanatana Dharma, Sankhya, Shaiva, Sheik(h), Shudra, Smriti, Sudra, Swami, Swinger, Trimurti, Untouchable, Urdu, Vaishnava, Vais(h)ya, Varna, Vedanta

Hindquarters Backside, Crupper, Haunches

Hinge(d) Butt, Cardinal, Cross-garnet, Drop-leaf, Garnet, Gemel, Gimmer, Ginglymus, Joint, Knee, Mount, Parliament, Pivot, Stamp, Strap

▷ **Hinge(s)** *may indicate* a word reversal

Hingeless Ecardinate

Hinny Ass, Donkey, Joe

Hint Allude, Clew, Clue, Cue, Element, Gleam, Hunch, Idea, Imply, Inkle, Inkling, Innuendo, Insinuate, Intimate, Key, Mint, Nuance, Office, Overtone, Pointer, Preview, Scintilla, Shadow, Soupçon, → **SUGGEST**, Tang, Tip, Touch, Trace, Trick, Wind, Wink, Wisp, Word, Wrinkle

▷ **Hint** *may indicate* a first letter

Hip(pie), Hippy, Hips Cafard, Cheer, Coxa(l), Drop-out, Huck(le), Hucklebone, Hunkers, Ilium, Informed, Ischium, Pubis, Sciatic, Tonish

Hippopotamus Behemoth, River-horse, Sea-cow, Sea horse

Hire(d), Hiring Affreightment, Charter, Employ, Engage, Fee, Freightage, Job, Lease, Merc(enary), Never-never, Pensionary, Rent, Shape-up, Ticca, Wage

Hirsute Hairy, Pilose, Shaggy

▷ **His** *may indicate* greetings

Hispanic Latino

Hiss(ing) Boo, Fizzle, Goose, Hish, Sibilant, Siffle, Sizzle, Static, Swish

Historian Acton, Adams, Antiquary, Archivist, Arrian, Asellio, Bede, Biographer, Bryant, Buckle, Camden, Carlyle, Centuriator, Chronicler, Etain, Froude, Gibbon, Gildas, Green, Griot, Herodotus, Knickerbocker, Livy, Macaulay, Oman, Paris, Pliny, Plutarch, Ponsonby, Renan, Roper, Sallust, Spengler, Starkey, Strachey, Suetonius, Tacitus, Taylor, Thiers, Thucydides, Toynbee, Trevelyan, Wells, Xenophon

History, Historic(al) Account, Anamnesis, Ancient, Annal, Bunk, Case, Chronicle, Clio, Diachronic, Epoch(a), Ere-now, Ever, Heritage, Legend, Life, Living, Mesolithic, Modern, Natural, Ontogency, Oral, Past, Record, Renaissance

Histrionic Operatic, Theatrical

Hit Bang, Bash, Baste, Bat, Bean, Belt, Bepat, Blip, Blockbuster, Bloop, Blow,

Bludgeon, Boast, Bolo, Bonk, Bunt, Catch, Clobber, Clock, Clout, Club, Collide, Cuff, Dot, Flail, Flick, Flip, Foul, Fourpenny-one, Fungo, Fustigate, Get, Hay, Head-butt, Home(-thrust), Impact, Knock, Lam, Lob, Magpie, Mug, Pandy, Paste, Pepper, Pistol-whip, Polt, Prang, Punto dritto, Ram, Roundhouse, Sacrifice, Score, Sensation, Six, Skier, Sky, Slam, Slap, Slosh, Smash(eroo), Smit(e), Sock, Spank, Spike, Stoush, Straik, Stricken, Strike, Strook, Struck, → **SUCCESS**, Swat, Switch, Thwack, Tip, Tonk, Touché, Undercut, Venewe, Venue, Volley, Wallop, Wham, Wing, Ythundered, Zap, Zonk

Hitch(ed) Catch, Contretemps, Edge, Espouse, Harness, Hike, Hirsle, Hoi(c)k, Hotch, Jerk, Lorry-hop, Rub, Setback, Sheepshank, Sheet bend, Shrug, Snag, Technical, Thumb, Wed

Hitherto Before, Yet

Hittite Uriah

Hive(s) Nettlerash, Skep, Spread, Swarm, Wheal

Hoar(y) Ashen(-grey), Canescent, Froren, Frost, Gaudy-day, Grizzled, Rime

Hoard(ing) Accumulate, Amass, Bill, Billboard, Cache, Coffer, Eke, Heap, Hoord, Husband, Hutch, Mucker, Plant, Pose, Salt away, Save, Sciurine, Snudge, Squirrel, Stash, Stock, Store, Stow, Treasure

Hoarse(ness) Croupy, Frog, Grating, Gruff, Husky, Raucous, Roar(er), Roopit, Roopy, Roup, Throaty

Hoax April-fish, Bam, Canard, Cod, Do, Doff, Fub, Fun, Gag, Gammon, Gowk, Gull, Hum, Huntie-gowk, Kid, Leg-pull, Piltdown, Put-on, Quiz, Sell, Sham, Skit, Spoof, String, Stuff, Supercherie, → **TRICK**

Hob Ceramic, Cooktop, Ferret, Goblin, Lout

Hobble, Hobbling Game, Hamshackle, Hilch, Hitch, Lame, Limp, Pastern, Picket, Spancel, Stagger, Tether

Hobby Avocation, Fad, Falcon, Interest, Pastance, → **PASTIME**, Predator, Pursuit, Recreation, Scrimshaw

Hobby-horse Dada, Obsession, Play-mare

Hobgoblin Bog(e)y, Puck

Hobnail Clinker, Tacket

Hobnob Chat, Mingle

Hobo Bum, → **TRAMP**, Vagrant

Hock Cambrel, Dip, Gambrel, Gambril, Gammon, Ham, Heel, Hough, Hypothecate, Pawn, Pledge, Rhenish, Wine

Hockey Field, Grass, Hurling, Ice, Pond, Shinny, Shinty, Street

Hod Carrier, Tray

Hodge Peasant, Rustic, Yokel

Hoe Claut, Dutch, Grub, Grubbing, Jembe, Nab, Pecker, Prong, Rake, Scuffle, Thrust, Weed

Hog Babiroussa, Babirussa, Boar, Glutton, Guttle, Peccary, Pig, Porker, Puck, Road, Shoat, Shott, Whole

Hogmanay Ne'erday

Hog-rat Hutia

Hogshead Butt, Cask, Muid

Hogwash Bull, Nonsense, Swill, Twaddle

Hoi-polloi Prole(tariat), Rabble

Hoist Boom, Bouse, Crane, Davit, Derrick, Garnet, Gin, Heft, Hills, Jack, Lewis, Lift, Raise, Shearlegs, Shears, Sheerlegs, Sheers, Sway, Teagle, Trice, Whip-and-derry, Wince, Winch, Windas, Windlass

Hold(er), Holding, Hold back, out, up, etc Absorb, Anchor, Backbreaker, Belay,

Believe, Boston crab, Canister, Cease, Cement, Cinch, Clamp, Clasp, Cling, Clutch, Contain, Cotland, Defer, Delay, Detain, Display, Dog, Embrace, Engross, Er, Facebar, Farm, Fast, Fief, Fistful, Frog, Full nelson, Garter, → **GRASP**, Grip, Grovet, Half-nelson, Hammerlock, Handle, Haud, Have, Headlock, Heft, Heist, Hiccup, Hinder, Hitch, Ho(a), Hoh, Hoy, Hug, Impedance, Impede, Impediment, Impound, Incumbent, Intern, Intray, Japanese stranglehold, Keep, Keepnet, Lease, Maintain, Manure, Nelson, Nurse, Occupant, Own, Port, Proffer, Rack, Reach, Reluct, Reserve, Restrain, Rivet, Rob, Rundale, Runrig, Save, Scissors, Shelve, Shore, Sleeve, Sostenuto, Stand, Suplex, Suspend, Tenancy, Tenement, Tenure, Toehold, Toft, Tray, Tripod, Wristlock, Zarf, Zurf

Hole(s), Holed, Holey Ace, Agloo, Aglu, Albatross, Antrum, Aubrey, Beam, Birdie, Black, Bogey, Bolt, Cat, Cave, Cavity, Cenote, Cissing, Coal, Coalsack, Collapsar, Crater, Cubby, Cup, Dell, Den, Dene, Dog-leg, Dolina, Doline, Dormie, Dormy, Dreamhole, Dry, Dugout, Eagle, Earth, Ethmoid, Eye(let), Faveolate, Finger, Foramen, Funk, Gap, Geat, Glory, Gnamma, Gutta, Hag(g), Hideout, Kettle, Knot, Lenticel, Lill, Limber, Loop, Loup, Lubber's, Lumina, Maar, Mortise, Moulin, Namma, Nineteenth, Oillet, → **OPENING**, Orifex, Orifice, Ozone, Perforate, Pierce, Pigeon, Pinprick, Pit, Pocket, Pore, Port, Pot, Potato, Priest's, Punctuate, Punctum, Puncture, Rabbet, Rivet, Rowport, Sallyport, Scupper, Scuttle, Scye, Situation, Slot, Snag, Snow, Soakaway, Socket, Sound, Spandrel, Spider, Spiraculum, Starting, Stead, Stew, Stop, Stove, Swallow, Tear, Thirl, Thumb, Touch, Trema, Vent, Ventage, Ventige, Voided, Vug, Watering, Well, White, Wookey

Holiday(s) Bank, Benjo, Break, Busman's, Childermas, Days of Awe, Ferial, Festa, → **FESTIVAL**, Fête, Fiesta, Furlough, Gala, Half(term), High, Honeymoon, Kwanzaa, Lag b'Omer, Laik, Leasure, Leave, Legal, Leisure, Long, Minibreak, Off-day, Off-time, Outing, Packaged, Pink-eye, Play-day, Playtime, Public, Purim, Recess, Repose, Rest, Roman, Schoolie, Seaside, Shabuoth, Shavuot, Sojourn, Statutory, Stay, Sunday, Tax, Trip, → **VACATION**, Villegiatura, Wake(s), Whitsun

Holinshed Chronicler

Holland(s) Batavia, Genevese, Gin, Hogen-mogen, Netherlands, NL

Hollow Acetabulum, Alveary, Antar, Antre, Antrum, Armpit, Axilla, Blastula, Boss, Bowl, Cave(rn), Cavity, Chasm, Chott, Cirque, Cleché, Comb(e), Concave, Coomb, Corrie, Crater, Cup(mark), Cwm, Deaf, Dean, Dell, Delve, Den(e), Dent, Dimple, Dingle, Dip, Dish(ing), Dolina, Doline, Empty, Fossette, Frost, Gilgai, Glenoid, Gnamma-hole, Gowpen, Grot(to), Hole, How, Howe, Igloo, Incavo, Insincere, Keck(sy), Kettle(hole), Kex, Khud, Lip-deep, Mortise, Namma-hole, Niche, Omphaloid, Orbita, Pan, Philtrum, Pit, Punt, Redd, Rout, Rut, Scoop, Shott, Sinus, Slade, Sleepy, Slot, Slough, Socket, Swire, Thank-you-ma'am, Trematic, Trough, Vlei, Vola, Wame, Wem

Holly Aquifoliaceae, Eryngo, Ilex, Mate, Yaupon

Hollyhock Althaea, Malva, Rose mallow

Hollywood Bowl, Tinseltown

Holm Isle

Holmes Sherlock, Wendell

Holmium Ho

Holocaust Churban, Shoah

Hologram, Holograph Laser, MS

Holothurian Trepang

Holster Sheath

Holy(man), Holiness Adytum, Alliance, Ariadne, Blessed, → **DIVINE**, Godly, Grail, Halidom, Helga, Hery, Khalif, Loch, Mountain, Olga, Orders, Pan(h)agia, Pious,

Sacred, Sacrosanct, Sad(d)hu, Saintly, Sanctitude, Sannayasi(n), Santon, Sekos, Sepulchre, Shrine, Starets, Staretz, SV, Tirthankara, War

Holy books, Holy writing Adigranth, Atharvaveda, Bible, Gemara, Granth, Hadith, Koran, Mishnah, NT, OT, Pia, Purana, Rigveda, Sama-Veda, → **SCRIPTURE**, Shaster, Shastra, Smriti, Sura(h), Tanach, Writ, Yajur-Veda

Holy building, Holy city, Holy place Chapel, Church, Kaaba, Mashhad, Mecca, Medina, Meshed, Najaf, Penetralia, Sanctum, Synagogue, Temenos, Temple

Holy Ghost Paraclete

Holy water Amrit

Homage Bow, Cense, Honour, Kneel, Manred, Obeisance, Tribute, Vail

Home(land), Homeward Abode, Apartment, Base, Blighty, Burrow, Cheshire, Chez, Clinic, Community, Convalescent, Domal, Domicile, Earth, Eventide, Family, Fireside, Flat, Funeral, Gaff, Goal, Habitat, Harvest, Heame, Hearth, Heme, Hospice, House, In, Lair, Libken, Lockwood, Lodge, Maisonette, Mental, Mobile, Montacute, Nest, Nursing, Old sod, Pad, Penny-gaff, Plas Newydd, Remand, Res(idence), Rest, Starter, Stately, Tepee, Turangawaewae, Up-along, Villa

Homecoming Nostos

Home counties SE

Homeless Outler, Rootless, Skell

Homer(ic) Comatose, Cor, Epic(ist), Nod, Pigeon, Somnolent

Home-rule Parnellism, Swaraj

Homesick(ness) Heimweh, Mal du pays

Homespun Cracker-barrel, Plain, Raploch, Russet, Simple

Homestead Ranch, Toft

Homework → **DIY**, Prep, Preparation

Homicidal, Homicide Chance-medley, Justifiable, Killing, Manslaughter

Homily Lecture, Midrash, Pi, Postil, Prone, Sermon, Tract

▷ **Homing** *may indicate* coming back

Hominid Oreopitheous

Homogeneous Indiscrete

Homogram, Homograph Abac, Heteronym

Homosexual(ity) Auntie man, Bardash, Batty boy, Bender, Bent, Buftie, Bufty, Camp, Cat, Catamite, Closet queen, Cocksucker, Cottaging, Dike, Dyke, Fag(got), Fairy, Friend of Dorothy, Fruit, Gay, Gaydar, Ginger, Homophile, Invert, Lesbian, Moffie, Muscle Mary, Pederast, Ponce, Poof(tah), Poofter, Poove, Pouf(fe), Poufter, Puff, Punk, Quean, Queer, Quiff, Rough trade, Shirt-lifter, Swish(y), Tonk, Tribade, Uranism, Urning, Woofter

Hone Grind, → **SHARPEN**, Whet

Honest(y), Honestly Aboveboard, Afauld, Afawld, Amin, Candour, Clean, Fair dinkum, Genuine, Incorruptible, Injun, Jake, Jannock, Jonnock, Legitimate, Lunaria, Lunary, Mensch, Open-faced, Penny, Probity, Rectitude, Reputable, Righteous, Round, Sincere, Square, Squareshooter, Straight, Straight-arrow, Straight-out, Trojan, → **TRUE**, Upfront, Upright, Upstanding

Honey Comb, Flattery, Hybdean, Hybla, Hymettus, Mel, Melliferous, Nectar, Oenomel, Oxymel, Palm, Peach, Popsy-wopsy, Sis, Sugar, Sweetheart, Sweetie, Virgin, Wild, Wood

Honeycomb(ed) Cellular, Faveolate, Favose, Waxwork

Honey-eater Bear, Blue-eye, Pooh

Honeypot Haanepoot

Honeysuckle Abelia, Anthemion, Caprifoil, Caprifole, Lonicera, Rewa rewa, Suckling, Woodbind, Woodbine

Honour(s), Honourable, Honoured, Honorary, Honorific A, Accolade, Ace, Adore, Birthday, Blue, Bow, CBE, Commemorate, Credit, Curtsey, Dan, Elate, Emeritus, Ennoble, → **ESTEEM**, Ethic, Face-card, Fame, Fête, Gloire, Glory, Grace, Greats, Homage, Insignia, Invest, Izzat, J, Jack, K, King, Knave, Knight, Kudos, Laudation, Laureate, Laurels, MBE, Mention, Military, OBE, Optime, Pundonor, Q, Queen, Remember, Repute, Respect, Revere, Reward, Ten, Tenace, Titular, Tripos, Venerate, Worship, Wranglers

Honourable companion CH

Honourless Yarborough

Hooch Hogan, Hogen, Moonshine

Hood(ed) Almuce, Amaut, Amice, Amowt, Apache, Balaclava, Bashlik, Biggin, Blindfold, Calash, Calèche, Calyptra, Capeline, Capuccio, Capuche, Chaperon(e), Coif, Cope, Cowl, Cucullate(d), Fume, Gangster, Jacobin, Kennel, Lens, Liripipe, Liripoop, Mantle, Mazarine, Nithsdale, Pixie, Robin, Rowdy, Snood, Trot-cosey, Trot-cozy, Visor

Hoodlum Gangster, Roughneck, Thug, Wanksta

Hoodoo Moz(z)

Hoodwink(ed) Blear, Bluff, Cheat, → **DECEIVE**, Gull, Nose-led, Seel

Hoof(ed) Artiodactyla, Cloot, Coffin, Frog, Trotter, Ungula

Hoohah Humdudgeon

Hook(er), Hooked, Hooks Addict, Adunc, Aduncous, Arrester, Barb(icel), Becket, Butcher's, Cant(dog), Catch, Chape, Claw, Cleek, Clip, Cocotte, Corvus, Crampon, Cromb, Crome, Crook, Crotchet, Cup, Drail, Fifi, Fish, Floozy, Fluke, Fly, Gab, Gaff, Gig, Grapnel, Grappling, Hamate, Hamose, Hamulus, Heel, Hitch, Inveigle, Kype, Meat, Pot, Prostitute, Pruning, Retinaculum, Sister, Snell, Sniggle, Swivel, Tala(u)nt, Tart, Tenaculum, Tenter, Tie, Trip, Uncus, Wanton, Welsh

Hookah Bong, Chillum, Hubble-bubble, Kalian, Narg(h)ile, Narghil(l)y, Nargileh, Nargil(l)y, Pipe

Hooligan Apache, Bogan, Casual, Desperado, Droog, Hobbledehoy, Hoon, Keelie, Larrikin, Lout, Ned, Rough(neck), Ruffian, Skollie, Skolly, Tearaway, Ted, Tityre-tu, Tough, Tsotsi, Yahoo, Yob(bo)

Hoop Bail, Band, Circle, Farthingale, Garth, Gird, Girr, Hula®, O, → **RING**, Tire, Trochus, Trundle

Hooray Whoopee, Yippee

Hoot(er) Conk, Deride, Honk, Madge, Nose, Owl, Riot, Screech-owl, Siren, Ululate

Hoover Dam

Hop(per) An(o)ura, Ball, Bin, Cuscus, Dance, Flight, Jeté, Jump, Kangaroo, Leap, Lilt, Long, Opium, Pogo, Roo, Saltate, Scotch, Skip, Spring, Tremié, Vine

Hope(ful) Anticipate, Aspirant, Comer, Contender, Daydream, Desire, Dream, Esperance, Evelyn, Expectancy, Forlorn, Gleam, Good, Pipe-dream, Promising, Roseate, Rosy, Sanguine, Trust, Valley, White, Wish

Hopeless(ness), Hopeless quest Abattu, Anomie, Anomy, Black, Buckley's chance, Despair, Despondent, Forlorn, Goner, Non-starter, Perdu, Pessimist

Hopscotch Peevers

Horace Flaccus, Ode, Satirist

Horatio Nelson

Horatius Cocles

Horde Crowd, Golden, Many, Mass, Mob, Swarm

Horizon A, Apparent, Artificial, B, C, Celestial, Event, Gyro, Rational, Scope, Sea-line, Sensible, Skyline, Visible

Horizontal Advection, Flat, Level, Prone, Supine, Tabular

Hormone ACTH, Adrenalin®, Adrenaline, Aldosterone, Androgen, Androsterone, Angiotensin, Antidiuretic, Autacoid, Auxin, Biosynthesis, Bursicon, Calcitonin, Catecholamine, Cholecystokinin, Corticoid, Corticosteroid, Corticosterone, Cortisone, Cytokinin, Ecdysone, Endocrine, Erythropoietin, Estrogen, Florigen, Folliculin, Gastrin, Gibberellin, Glucagon, Gonadotrophic, Gonadotrop(h)in, Growth, Hydrocortisone, IAA, Inhibin, Insulin, Intermedin, Juvenile, Kinin, Leuteotropic, Lipotropin, Luteinizing, Melanotropine, Melatonin, Mineralo corticord, Noradrenalin(e), Norepinephrine, Oestradiol, Oestriol, Oestrogen, Oestrone, Oxytocin, Pancreozymin, Parathyroid, Progesterone, Progestin, Progestogen, Prolactin, Prostaglandin, Relaxin, Secretagogue, Secretin, Secretion, Serotonin, Sex, Somatomedin, Somatostatin, Somatotrop(h)in, Steroid, Stilboestrol, Testosterone, Thymosin, Thyroid, Thyrotrop(h)in, Thyroxine, Triiodothyronine, TSH, Vasopressin

Horn(y) Acoustic, Advancer, Amalthea, Antenna(e), Antler, Baleen, Basset, Bez, Brass, Buck, Bugle, Cape, Ceratoid, Cor, Cornet, Cornett, Cornopean, Cornu(a), Cornucopia, Cromorna, Cromorne, Cusp, Dilemma, English, Exponential, Flugel-horn, French, Frog, Golden, Gore, Hooter, → **HORNBLOWER**, Hunting, Ivory, Keratin, Klaxon, Lur, Morsing, Mot, Oliphant, Periostracum, Plenty, Post, Powder, Pryse, Ram's, Scur, Shofar, Shophor, Spongin, Tenderling, Trey, Trez, Trumpet, Tusk, Waldhorn

Hornblende Syntagmatite

Hornblower Brain, Horatio, Peel, Triton, Trumpeter

Hornbook Battledoor, Battledore

Horned (sheep) Cabrié, Cabrit, Cornute, Hamate, Lunate, Mouflon, Muflon

Hornless Doddy, Humbel, Humlie, Hummel, Mooly, Mul(l)ey, Poley, Polled

Hornpipe Matelote

Horoscope Figure, Future, Prophecy, Star-map

Horrible, Horror Aw(e)some, Brat, Dire, Dread(ful), Execrable, Ghastly, Grisly, Gruesome, Grysie, Hideous, Loathsome, Minging, Odious, Shock, Terror, Ugh, Vile

Horrid, Horrific, Horrify(ing) Dire, Dismay, Dreadful, Frightful, Ghastly, Gothic, Grim, Grisly, H, Loathy, Odious, Spine chilling, Spiteful, Ugly

Hors d'oeuvres Antipasto, Canapé, Carpaccio, Ceviche, Hoummos, Houmus, Hummus, Mez(z)e, Pâté, Smorgasbord, Smor(re)brod, Smør(re)brød, Zak(o)uski

Horse Airer, Bidet, Bloodstock, Carriage, Cut, Cutting, Dark, Doer, Dray, Drier, Drug, Equine, Form, H, → **HEROIN**, High, Hobby, Iron, Knight, Kt, Light, Malt, Outsider, Pack, Pantomime, Plug, Ride, Rocking, Sawbuck, Screen, Selling-plate, Sense, Stalking, Standard-bred, Stayer, Steeplechaser, Stiff, Stock, Teaser, Trestle, Vaulting, Willing, Wooden

---

HORSES

2 letters:	Nag	Barb	Jade
GG	Pad	Buck	Mare
	Pot	Cert	Pole
3 letters:	Rip	Colt	Pony
Ass	Tit	Crib	Post
Bay		Dale	Prad
Cob	*4 letters:*	Fell	Roan
Dun	Arab	Foal	Scag
Gee	Aver	Hack	Snow

Span
Stud
Taki
Trot
Yale
Yaud

5 letters:
Arion
Arkle
Bevis
Borer
Caple
Capul
Favel
Filly
Genet
Morel
Mount
Neddy
Pacer
Pinto
Poler
Punch
Rogue
Screw
Seian
Shire
Stage
Steed
Tacky
Takhi
Troop
Waler
Wheel
White

6 letters:
Ambler
Bayard
Bronco
Brumby
Calico
Canuck
Cayuse
Chaser
Cooser
Crollo
Curtal
Cusser
Dobbin

Entire
Exmoor
Favell
Ganger
Garran
Garron
Gennet
Hogget
Hunter
Jennet
Kanuck
Keffel
Lampos
Livery
Morgan
Mudder
Novice
Pad-nag
Plater
Pommel
Poster
Quagga
Random
Remuda
Roarer
Rouncy
Runner
Sabino
Saddle
Shoo-in
Sorrel
String
Stumer
Summer
Tandem
Tarpan
Tracer
Trojan
Vanner

7 letters:
Bobtail
Breaker
Cavalry
Centaur
Charger
Clipper
Coacher
Courser
Cuisser
Dappled

Draught
Eclipse
Eventer
Gelding
Hackney
Hobbler
Liberty
Marengo
Marocco
Morocco
Mustang
Palfrey
Pegasus
Piebald
Pointer
Quarter
Remount
Saddler
Sheltie
Spanker
Starter
Sumpter
Swallow
Swinger
Trigger
Trotter
Walking
Wheeler
Xanthos
Xanthus

8 letters:
Aquiline
Bangtail
Bathorse
Boerperd
Buckskin
Camargue
Chestnut
Clay-bank
Cocktail
Dartmoor
Destrier
Eohippus
Friesian
Galloway
Highland
Holstein
Hyperion
Kochlani
Lusitano

Palomino
Schimmel
Shetland
Skewbald
Sleipnir
Springer
Stallion
Stibbler
Warragal
Warragle
Warragul
Warrigal
Welsh cob
Whistler
Yarraman
Yearling

9 letters:
Appaloosa
Black Bess
Caballine
Clavileno
Coldblood
Connemara
Gringolet
Houyhnhnm
Icelandic
Incitatus
Knabstrup
Percheron
Rosinante
Rozinante
Warmblood

10 letters:
Andalusian
Bucephalus
Buckjumper
Buttermilk
Clydesdale
Copenhagen
Lipizzaner
Lippizaner
Pliohippus
Przewalski
Showjumper
Stagecoach
Svadilfari

11 letters:
Daisy-cutter

	12 letters:	Thoroughbred	16 letters:
High-stepper	Cleveland Bay		Tennessee Walking
Przewalski's	Hambletonian	13 letters:	
	Suffolk Punch	Perissodactyl	

Horseback Croup
Horse-box Stable, Stall
Horse-chestnut Aesculus, Conker
Horse collar Brecham, Hame
Horse complaint, Horse disease, Horse problem, Horse trouble Blind staggers, Blood spavin, Bogspavin, Bot(t)s, Broken wind, Capel(l)et, Cracked heels, Curb, Dourine, Equinia, Eweneck, Farcy, Fives, Founder, Frush, Glanders, Gourdy, Head staggers, Heaves, Hippiatric, Knee spavin, Laminitis, Lampas, Lampers, Malander, Mallander, Mallender, Megrims, Miller's disease, Mooneye, Mud fever, N(a)gana, Poll-evil, Quartercrack, Quitter, Quittor, Ringbone, Sallenders, Sand crack, Scratches, Seedy-toe, Spavie, Spavin, Springhalt, Staggers, Strangles, Stringhalt, Summer sores, Surra, Sway-back, Sween(e)y, Thorough-pin, Thrush, Toe-crack, Tread, Vives, Weed, Weid, Whistling, Windgall, Wind-sucking, Wire-heel, Yellows
Horse-dealer Buster, Coper
Horse-lover Philip
Horseman Ataman, Caballero, Cavalry, Centaur, Conquest, Cossack, Cowboy, Death, Dragman, Famine, Farrier, Hobbler, Hussar, Knight, Lancer, Nessus, Ostler, Parthian, Picador, Pricker, Quadrille, Revere, → **RIDER**, Slaughter, Spahi, Stradiot, Tracer
Horsemanship Manège
Horseplay Caper, Chukka, Knockabout, Polo, Rag, Rant, Romp
Horsepower Hp, Indicated, Ps
Horseradish Ben, Moringa
Horseshoe(-shaped) Henge, Hippocrepian, King-crab, Lunette, Manilla, Oxbow, Plate
Horsetail Equisetum
Horse thief Blanco, Rustler
Horticultural, Horticulture, Horticulturist Grower, Pomology, RHS
Hose Chausses, Fishnet, Galligaskins, Gaskins, Lisle, Netherstock(ing), Nylons, Panty, Sock, Stockings, Tabi, Tights, Trunk, Tube
Hospitable, Hospitality Cadgy, Convivial, Entertainment, Euxine, Kidgie, Lucullan, Open house, Philoxenia, Social, Xenial
Hospital Ambulance, Asylum, Barts, Base, Bedlam, Clinic, Cottage, Day, Dressing station, ENT, Field, General, Guys, H, Home, Hospice, Imaret, Isolation, Karitane, Lambarene, Lazaretto, Leprosarium, Leprosery, Lock, Loony bin, Lying-in, MASH, Mental, Nosocomial, Ozzie, Pest-house, Polyclinic, Rathouse, San, Scutari, Sick bay, Snake-pit, Special, Spital, Spittle, Teaching, Trust, UCH
Host(s), Hostess Amphitryon, Army, Barmecide, Bunny girl, Chatelaine, Compere, Crowd, Definitive, Emcee, Entertainer, Eucharist, Heavenly, Hirsel, Hotelier, Innkeeper, Intermediate, Inviter, Laban, Landlady, Landlord, Legend, Legion, Lion-hunter, Lot, Mass, Mavin, MC, Publican, Quickly, Sabaoth, Swarm, Taverner, Throng, Trimalchio
Hostage Gherao, Pawn, Pledge, POW
Hostel Asylum, Dharms(h)ala, Dorm, Entry, Halfway house, Inn, YHA, Youth
Hostile, Hostility Adverse, Aggressive, Alien, Animus, Aversion, Bellicose, Bitter,

Chilly, Currish, Diatribe, Feud, Forbidding, Hating, Icy, Ill, Ill-will, Inimical, Inveterate, Oppugnant, Unfriendly, Vitriolic, War

Hot (tempered) Ardent, Big, Blistering, Breem, Breme, Cajun, Calid, Candent, Dog days, Enthusiastic, Facula, Fervid, Feverish, Fiery, Fuggy, Gospeller, Het, In, Incandescent, Irascible, Lewd, Live, Mafted, Mirchi, Mustard, Pepper, Piping, Potato, Quick, Randy, Red, Roaster, Scorcher, Sexpot, Sizzling, Spicy, Stewy, Stifling, Stolen, Sultry, Sweaty, Sweltering, Sweltry, Tabasco®, Thermidor, Torrid, Toustie, Tropical, Zealful

Hotchpotch Bricolage, Farrago, Mish-mash, Powsowdy, Welter

Hotel, Hotelkeeper Bo(a)tel, Boutique, Commercial, Fleabag, Flophouse, Gasthaus, Gasthof, H, Hilton, Host, Hydro, Inn, Motel, Parador, Patron(ne), Posada, Private, Ritz, Roadhouse, Savoy, Tavern, Temperance, Trust, Watergate

Hothead(ed) Impetuous, Rash, Spitfire, Volcano

Hot-house Conservatory, Nursery, Orangery, Vinery

Hot plate Salamander

Hot rod Dragster

Hotspur Harry, Hothead, Rantipole

Hottentot Griqua, Khoikhoi, Strandloper

Hot water Soup, Therm

Hound(s) Afghan, Basset, Beagle, Bellman, Brach, Cad, Canine, Cry, → **DOG**, Entry, Gabriel's, Hamiltonstovare, Harass, Harrier, Hen-harrier, Ibizan, Javel, Kennet, Lyam, Lym(e), Mute, Otter, Pack, Pharaoh, Pursue, Rache, Ranter, Reporter, Saluki, Talbot, True, Tufter

Hound's bane Palay

Hour(s) Canonical, Complin(e), Elders', Eleventh, Golden, H, Happy, Holy, Hr, Literacy, Little, Lunch, None(s), Office, Orthros, Peak, Prime, Rush, Sext, Sidereal, Small, Staggered, Terce, Tide, Time, Undern, Unsocial, Vespers, Visiting, Witching, Working, Zero

House(s), Housing, Household(er) Abode, Accepting, Adobe, Astrology, Audience, Auditorium, B, Bach, Bastide, Beehive, Beth, Bhavan, Bhawan, Biggin, Bingo, Black, Block, Boarding, Bondage, Brick veneer, Broadcasting, Broiler, Brownstone, Bundestag, Casa, Chalet, Chamber, Chapter, Charnel, Château, Chattel, Chez, Clapboard, Clearing, Coffee, Commercial, Concern, Convent, Cote, Cottage (orné), Council, Counting, Country, Crankcase, Crib, Custom(s), Dacha, Dail, Demain, Demesne, Derry, Des res, Discount, Disorderly, Domal, Domestic, Domicile, Donga, Door, Dower, Drostdy, Drum, Duplex, Dwelling, Dynasty, Edifice, Entertain, Establishment, Este, Eyrie, Familial, Fashion, Fibro(cement), Finance, Firm, Forcing, Frame, Fraternity, Free, Frontager, Full, Gaff, Gambling, Garage, Gite, Government, Grace and favour, Habitat, Habitation, Hacienda, Halfway, Hall, Harbour, Hearth, HK, Ho, Home, Homestead, Ice, Igloo, Inn, Insula, Issuing, Joss, Ken, Lodge, Lofted, Loose, Lot(t)o, Maison(ette), Malting, Manor, Manse, Mansion, Mas, Meeting, Meiney, Meinie, Meiny, Ménage, Menyie, Messuage, Mobility, Monastery, Montagne, Nacelle, Node, Open(-plan), Opera, Pad, Parliament, Pent, Picture, Pilot, Pleasure, Pole, Pondokkie, Post, Prefab, Printing, Public, Quinta, Radome, Ranch, Ratepayer, Register, Residence, Rooming, Rough, Sacrament, Safe, Satis, Schloss, School, Seat, Semi, Shanty, Sheltered, Show, Sign, Social, Software, Spec-built, Sporting, Stable, Station, Steeple, Storey, Succession, Tavern, Tea, Tenement, Terrace, Theatre, Third, Tied, Toft, Tombola, Tower, Town, Tract, Treasure, Tree, Trust, Vaulting, Vicarage, Villa, Villa(-home), Wash, Watch, Weather, Weatherboard, Weigh, Wendy, Whare, Wheel, White, Work, Zero, Zodiac

HOUSES

3 letters:
Leo

4 letters:
Bush
Keys
Syon
York

5 letters:
Lords
Scala
Tudor
Upper
Usher

6 letters:
Orange
Queen's

Seanad
Stuart
Wilton

7 letters:
Althing
Althorp
Bourbon
Commons
Hanover
Kenwood
Knesset
Lodging
Osborne
Stewart
Trinity
Windsor

8 letters:
Burghley
Chequers
Harewood
Hatfield
Holyrood
Lagthing
Longleat
Petworth
Somerset

9 letters:
Admiralty
Chartwell
Knebworth
Lancaster
Odelsting

10 letters:
Chatsworth
Heartbreak
Kirribilli
Odelsthing

11 letters:
Plantagenet
Russborough
Sandringham

12 letters:
Lockwood Home

13 letters:
Seanad Eireann

15 letters:
Representatives

House-boat Wangun, Wan(i)gan
House-builder Jack
House-keeper Chatelaine, Matron, Publican
House-leek Sengreen
Housemaid's knee Bursa
Houseman Betty, Doctor, Intern, Peer
House-warming Infare
Housewife Etui, Needlecase, WI
Housework Chore, DIY
Housing Case, Crankcase, Shabrack, Shelter, Slum, Tenement
Hova Malagash
Hove Plim, Swell
Hovel Cru(i)ve, Den, Pigsty, Shack, Shanty
Hover Hang, Levitate, Lurk, Poise
How Hill, Hollow
How'dyedo, How d'ye do Hallo, Pass, Salve
However As, But, Even-so, Leastwise, Sed, Still, Though, Yet
Howitzer Gun
Howl(er) Banshee, Bawl, Bay, Bloop, Clanger, Hue, Mycetes, Slip up, Squawk, Ululate, War whoop, Wow, Yawl, Yowl
How much The
Hoy Bilander, Ship
HP Never-never
HQ Centre, Headquarters, SHAPE
Hub Boss, Centre, Focus, Hob, Nave, Pivot, Tee
Hubbub Charivari, Chirm, Coil, Din, Level-coil, Palaver, Racket, Row, Stir
Hubris Pride
Huckster Hawker, Kidd(i)er, Pedlar
Huddle Cringe, Gather, Hunch, Ruck, Shrink

Hudson River, Rock
Hue Colour, Dye, Outcry, Proscription, Steven, Tincture, Tinge, Utis
Huff Dudgeon, Hector, Pant, Pet, Pique, Snuff, Strunt, Umbrage, Vex
Hug Bear, Coll, Cuddle, → EMBRACE, Squeeze
Huge (number) Astronomical, Brobdingnag, Colossal, Enorm(ous), Gargantuan,
    Giant, → GIGANTIC, Gillion, Ginormous, Humongous, Humungous, Immane,
    Immense, Leviathan, Lulu, Mega-, Milliard, Monolithic, Monster, Octillion,
    Prodigious, Socking, Tall, Titanian, Tremendous, Vast, Whacking
Hugo Victor
Huguenot Camisard
Hulk Lout, Ruin, Shale, Shell, Ship
Hull Bottom, Framework, Husk, Inboard, Monocoque, Pod, Sheal, Sheel, Shell,
    Shiel, Shill, Shiplap
Hullabaloo Outcry, Razzamatazz, Raz(z)mataz(z)
▶ **Hullo** *see* HELLO
Hum(ming) Bombilate, Bombinate, Bum, Chirm, Chirr, Drone, Lilt, Moan, Murmur,
    Nos(e)y, Pong, Ponk, Rank, Reek, Sowf(f), Sowth, Stench, Stink, Stir, Whir(r), Zing
Human(e), Humanist, Humanity Anthropoid, Bang, Colet, Earthling, Erasmus,
    Incarnate, Kindness, Mandom, Merciful, Mortal, Philanthropic, Species, Sympathy,
    Ubuntu, Virtual, Wight
Humble Abase, Abash, Afflict, Baseborn, Chasten, Cow, Degrade, Demean,
    Demiss(ly), Lower, Lowly, Mean, → MEEK, Modest, Morigerate, Obscure, Poor,
    Rude, Small, Truckle
Humbug Berley, Blague, Blarney, Buncombe, Bunk(um), Burley, Cant, Claptrap,
    Con, Delude, Flam, Flummery, Fraud, Fudge, Gaff, Gammon, Gas, Guff, Gum,
    Hoax, Hoodwink, Hookey-walker, Kibosh, Liar, Maw-worm, Nonsense, Prig,
    Shenanigan, Wind
Humdinger Cracker, Lulu
Humdrum Banal, Boredom, Bourgeois, Monotonous, Mundane, Ordinary, Prosaic,
    Tedious
Humid(ity) Clammy, Damp, Dank, Machie, Machy, Muggy, Saturation, Steam,
    Sticky, Sultry
Humiliate(d), Humiliation, Humility Abase, Abash, Baseness, Degrade,
    Disbench, Eating crow, Fast, Indignity, Laughing stock, Lose face, Mortify,
    Put-down, → SHAME, Skeleton, Take-down, Wither
Humming-bird Colibri, Hermit, Rainbow, Sabre-wing, Sapphire-wing, Sappho,
    Sylph, Thornbill, Topaz, Trochilus
Hummock Tump
Humorist Cartoonist, Comedian, Jester, Leacock, Lear, Punster, Twain, Wodehouse
Humour, Humorous Aqueous, Bile, Blood, Caprice, Cardinal, Chaff, Choler, Coax,
    Cocker, Coddle, Cosher, Cuiter, Cuittle, Daut, Dawt, Dry, Facetious, Fun, Gallows,
    Ichor, Indulge, Irony, Jocose, Jocular, Juice, Kidney, Levity, Light, Melancholy,
    → MOOD, Observe, One-liner, Pamper, Phlegm, Pun, Pythonesque, Ribaldry, Salt,
    Serum, Temper, Trim, Vein, Vitreous, Vitreum, Wetness, Whim, Whimsy, Wit
Humourless Dry, Po(-faced)
Hump(ed) Boy, Bulge, Dorts, Dowager's, Gibbose, Gibbous, Hog, Huff, Hummock,
    Hunch, Middelmannetjie, Pip, Ramp, Road, Speed bump, Tussock
▶ **Humpback** *see* HUNCHBACK
Humphrey Bogart
Humus Compost, Leafmould, Moder, Mor, Mull
Hun Alaric, Atli, Attila, Fritz, German

Hunch, Hunchback Camel, Chum, Crookback, Gobbo, Intuition, Kyphosis, Premonition, Quasimodo, Roundback, Sense, Urchin

Hundred(s), Hundredth Burnham, C, Cantred, Cantref, Cent, Centesimal, Centum, Century, Chiltern, Commot, Days, Desborough, Great, Host, → IN A HUNDRED, Long, Northstead, Old, Shire, Stoke, Ton, Wapentake

Hundred and fifty CL, Y

Hundred and sixty T

Hundredweight Centner, Long, Metric, Quintal, Short

Hung Displayed, Executed, Framed, High

Hungarian, Hungary Bohunk, Cheremis(s), Csardas, Magyar, Nagy, Szekely, Tzigane, Ugric, Vogul

Hunger, Hungry Appestat, Appetite, Bulimia, Bulimy, Clem, → CRAVE, Desire, Edacity, Empty, Esurient, Famine, Famish, Fast, Hanker, Hunter, Pant, Peckish, Rapacious, Raven, Ravin, Sharp-set, Unfed, Unfuelled, Yaup, Yearn

▷ **Hungry** *may indicate* an 'o' in another word

Hunk(s) Beefcake, Chunk, Dry-fist, Miser(ly), Slab, Wedge

Hunker Squat

Hunt(er), Hunting, Huntress, Huntsman Actaeon, Alew, Archer, Artemis, Atalanta, Battue, Beagle, Bellman, Bounty, Calydon, Chace, Chase(r), Chasseur, Chevy, Cool, Coursing, Crockett, Cynegetic, Dog, Drag(net), Esau, Ferret, Fox, Free-shot, Gun, Halloo, Herne, Hound, Jager, Lamping, Leigh, Letterbox, Lurcher, Montero, National, Nimrod, Orion, Peel, Pig-sticking, Poacher, Poot, Pout, Predator, Pursue, Quest, Quorn, Rabbit, Rach(e), Rake, Ran, Rancel, Ranzel, Ride, Rummage, Run, Scavenge(r), Scorse, Scout, → SEARCH, Seek, Shikar(ee), Shikari, Skirter, Slipper, Stag, Stalk, Sticker, Still, Swiler, Terrier, Thimble, Ticker, Tinchel, Tower, Trail, Trap, Treasure, Venatic, Venator, Venerer, Venery, → WATCH, Whip, Whipper-in, Witch, Wolfer, Woodman, Woodsman, Yager

Hunting-call Rechate, Recheat, Tally-ho, View-halloo

Hunting-ground Forestation, Walk

Hurdle(r) Barrier, Doll, Fence, Flake, Gate, Hemery, Obstacle, Raddle, Sticks, Wattle

Hurdy (gurdy) Barrel-organ, Hainch, Haunch, Vielle

Hurl(ing) Camogie, Cast, Dash, → FLING, Heave, Put(t), Throw, → TOSS

Hurly-burly Furore, Noise

Hurrah Cheers, Huzza, Io, Whee

Hurricane Baguio, Tornade, Tornado, Typhoon, → WIND

Hurry Belt, Bustle, Chivvy, Chop-chop, Dart, Dash, Drive, Festinate, Fisk, Frisk, Gad, Gallop, Giddap, Giddup, Giddy-up, Hadaway, Hare, Haste, Hie, Hightail, Induce, Mosey, Post-haste, Press, Push, Race, Railroad, → RUSH, Scamper, Scoot, Scramble, Scur(ry), Scutter, Scuttle, Skelter, Skurry, Spank, Speed, Streak, Tear, Whirr

Hurt(ful) Abuse, Ache, Aggrieve, Ake, Bruise, Cutting, Damage, De(a)re, Disservice, Harm, Harrow, Hit, → INJURE, Lesion, Maim, Nocent, Nocuous, Noisome, Noxious, Noyous, Pain, Pang, Prick(le), Scaith, Wound, Wring

Hurtle Rush, Spin, Streak, Streek

Husband(ry), Husbands Add, Baron, Breadwinner, Consort, Darby, Ear, Eche, Economy, Eke, Ere, Farm, Gander-mooner, Georgic, Goodman, Groom, H, Hoddy-doddy, Hodmandod, Hubby, Ideal, Man, Manage, Mate, Partner, Polyandry, Retrench, Save, Scrape, Scrimp, Spouse, Squirrel, → STORE, Tillage

Hush(-hush) Bestill, Gag, Sh, Silent, Smug, St, Tace, Wheesh(t), Whisht

Husk(s), Husky Acerose, Bran, Draff, Eskimo, Hoarse, Hull, Malemute, Seed, Sheal, Shuck

Hussar Cherry-picker, Cherubim
Hussite Calixtin(e), Taborite
Hussy Besom, Hen, Limmer, Loose, Minx, Vamp
Hustle(r) Fast talk, Frogmarch, Jostle, Pro, Push, Railroad, Shoulder, Shove, Skelp
Hut(s) Banda, Booth, Bothie, Bothy, Bustee, Cabin, Caboose, Chalet, Choltry,
Gunyah, Hogan, Humpy, Igloo, Mia-mia, Nissen, Pondok(kie), Quonset®,
Rancheria, Rancho, Rondavel, Shack, Shanty, Sheal(ing), Shebang, Shed, Shiel(ing),
Skeo, Skio, Succah, Sukkah, Tilt, Tolsel, Tolsey, Tolzey, Tramping, Wan(n)igan,
Whare, Wi(c)kiup, Wigwam, Wil(t)ja, Wurley, Wurlie
Hutch Buddle, Crate, Pen, Rabbit
Hyacinth Cape, Grape, Starch, Wild
Hybrid Bigener, Bois-brûlé, Cama, Catalo, Centaur, Chamois, Chichi, Chimera,
Citrange, Cockatrice, Cross, Dso, Funnel, Geep, Graft, Hippogriff, Hircocervus,
Interbred, Jersian, Jomo, Jumart, Lurcher, Mameluco, Mermaid, Merman, Metif,
Métis, Mongrel, Mule, Mutation, Noisette, Opinicus, Ortanique, Ox(s)lip, Percolin,
Plumcot, Pomato, Ringed, Tangelo, Tiglon, Tigon, Topaz, Ugli, Zho(mo)
▷ **Hybrid** *may indicate* an anagram
Hydra Polyp
Hydrant Fireplug, H
Hydrocarbon Acetylene, Aldrin, Alkane, Alkene, Alkyl, Alkyne, Amylene,
Arene, Asphaltite, Benzene, Butadiene, Butane, Butene, Camphane, Camphene,
Carotene, Cetane, Cubane, Cycloalkane, Cyclohexane, Cyclopropane, Cymogene,
Decane, Diene, Dioxin, Diphenyl, Ethane, Gutta, Halon, Hatchettite, Heavy oil,
Hemiterpene, Heptane, Hexane, Hexene, Hexyl(ene), Indene, Isobutane, Isoprene,
Ligroin, Limonene, Mesitylene, Naphtha, Naphthalene, Naphthalin(e), Nonane,
Octane, Olefin(e), Paraffin, Pentane, Pentene, Pentylene, Phenanthrene, Phene,
Pinene, Polyene, Propane, Pyrene, Pyridine, Retene, Squalene, Stilbene, Styrene,
Terpene, Toluene, Triptane, Wax, Xylene, Xylol
Hydrogen Deut(er)on, Diplon, Ethene, H, Muonium, Protium, Replaceable, Tritium
Hydrometer Salinometer
Hydrophobic Rabid
Hydroplane Skid
Hydroponic Soil
Hydrozoa(n) Campanularia, Millepore, Portuguese man-of-war, Siphonophore
Hyena Aard-wolf, Earthwolf, Laughing, Nandi bear, Spotted, Strand-wolf,
Tiger-wolf
Hygiene, Hygienic Aseptic, Dental, Oral, Sanitary, Sepsis, Sleep
Hymen Maidenhead
Hymn(s) Anthem, Benedictine, Bhajan, Canticle, Carol, Cathisma, Choral(e),
Coronach, Dies Irae, Dithyramb, Doxology, Gloria, Hallel, Introit(us), Ithyphallic,
Lay, Magnificat, Mantra, Marseillaise, Nunc Dimittis, Ode, P(a)ean, Psalm,
Recessional, Rigveda, Sanctus, Secular, Sequence, Stabat Mater, Sticheron,
Tantum Ergo, Te Deum, Trisagion, Troparion, Veda
Hymnographer, Hymnologist David, Faber, Heber, Moody, Neale, Parry, Sankey,
Watts
Hype(d) Aflutter
Hyperbole, Hyperbolic Auxesis, Exaggeration, Sech
Hypercritical Captious
Hyperion Titan
Hypersensitive Allergic, Idiosyncratic
Hypha(e) Conidiophore, Stroma

Hyphen(ated) Dash, Parasyntheton, Soft
Hypnosis, Hypnotise, Hypnotic, Hypnotism, Hypnotist Braidism, Chloral,
Codeine, Enthral, Entrance, Hypotonia, Magnetic, Meprobamate, Mesmerism,
Psychognosis, Svengali
Hypochondria(c) Atrabilious, Hyp, Nosophobia, Phrenesiac, Valetudinarian
Hypocrisy, Hypocrite, Hypocritical Archimago, Bigot, Byends, Cant, Carper,
Chadband, Creeping Jesus, Deceit, Dissembler, False-faced, Heep, Holy Willie,
Humbug, Insincere, Janus-faced, Mucker, Nitouche, Pecksniff, Pharisaic, Pharisee,
Piety, Prig, Sanctimony, Self-pious, Sepulchre, Tartuf(f)e, Two-faced, Whited
sepulchre
Hypothesis, Hypothetical Avogadro, Biophor, Conditional, Continuum, Gluon,
Graviton, Nebular, Notional, Null, Planetesimal, Sapir-Whorf, Suppositious,
Virtual, Working
Hyrax Cony, Daman, Dassie, Klipdas, Rock rabbit
Hysteria, Hysteric(al) Achiria, Astasia, Conniption, Delirium, Frenzy, Meemie,
Mother

Ii

I A, Ch, Cham, Che, Dotted, Ego, Ich, Indeed, India, Iodine, Italy, J, Je, Me, Muggins, One, Self, Yours truly

Ian Scot

Iberian Celtiberean

Ibex Izard

Ibis Hadedah, Sacred, Waldrapp

Ice(d), Ice-cream, Icing, Icy Alcorza, Anchor, Arctic, Ballicatter, Banana split, Berg, Black, Brash, Camphor, Cassata, Coconut, Cone, Cool, Cornet, Coupe, Cream, Crystal, Diamonds, Drift, Dry, Floe, Frappé, Frazil, Freeze, Frigid, Frore, Frosting, Frosty, Gelato, Gelid, Gems, Glacé, Glacial, Glacier, Glare, Glaze, Glib, Granita, Graupel, Ground, Growler, Hailstone, Hok(e)y-pok(e)y, Hommock, Hummock, Kitty-benders, Knickerbocker glory, Kulfi, Lolly, Macallum, Marzipan, Neapolitan, Oaky, Pack, Pancake, Pingo, Polar, Popsicle®, Rime, Rink, Ross, Royal, Sconce, Serac, Shelf, Sherbet, Slay, Slider, Slob, Sludge, Sorbet, Spumone, Spumoni, Stream, Sugar, Tickly-benders, Topping, Tortoni, Tutti-frutti, Verglas, Virga, Wafer, Water, Wintry

Ice-axe Piolet

Iceberg Calf, Floe, Growler

Ice-box Cooler, Freezer, Fridge, Frig, Yakhdan

▸ **Ice-cream** *see* **ICE**

Iceland IS

Ice-skating Choctaw, Figure, Glide

Icicle Tangle

Icon Fashion, Idol, Image, Madonna, Sprite

Icterus Jaundice

ID PIN

Id(e) Ego, Fish, Orfe

Idea(s) Archetype, Brainchild, Brainwave, Clou, Clue, Conceit, Concept, Fancy, Figment, Fixed, Germ, Hunch, Idée fixe, Idolum, Image, Inkling, Inspiration, Interpretation, Keynote, Light, → **NOTION**, Obsession, Plan, Plank, Rationale, Recept, Theory, Thought, Whimsy, Zeitgeist

Ideal(ise) A1, Abstract, Apotheosis, Bee's knees, Cat's whiskers, Dream, Eden, Ego, Goal, Halo, Hero, Model, Monist, Nirvana, Notional, Paragon, Pattern, → **PERFECT**, Romantic, Siddhi, Sidha, Sublimate, Transcendental, Utopian, Vision

Idealism, Idealist(ic) Dreamer, More, Perfectionist, Quixotic, Romantic, Transcendental, Visionary

Identical Alike, Clone, Congruent, Equal, Menechmian, One, Same, Selfsame, Verbatim, Very

Identification, Identify Bertillonage, Codeword, Credentials, Designate, Diagnosis, Differentiate, Discern, Document, Dog-tag, Earmark, Empathy, Espy, Finger(print), ID, Identikit®, Label, Mark, Monomark, Name, Name-tape, Password, Photofit®,

Pin, Pinpoint, Place, Point up, Recognise, Reg(g)o, Secern, Spot, Swan-hopping, Swan-upping, Verify

Identikit® E-fit

Identity Alias, Appearance, Corporate, Credentials, Equalness, Likeness, Mistaken, Numerical, Oneness, Personal, Qualitative, Seity, Self, Selfhood

Ideology, Ideologue Credo, Hard-liner, Ism

Idiom Americanism, Argot, Britishism, Cant, Expression, Idioticon, Jargon, Language, Pahlavi, Parlance, Pehlevi, Persism, Scotticism, Syri(a)cism, Syrism

Idiosyncrasy, Idiosyncratic Foible, Mannerism, Nature, Quirk, Way, Zany

Idiot(ic), Idiocy Congenital, Dingbat, Dolt, Eejit, Fatuity, Fool, Goose, Half-wit, Imbecile, Inane, Maniac, Moron, Natural, Nerk, Nidget, Noncom, Numpty, Oaf, Ouph(e), → **STUPID**, Tony, Twit, Village, Whacko, Zany

Idle(ness), Idler Beachcomber, Bludger, Boondoggle, Bum, Bumble, Bummle, Cockaigne, Dally, Deadbeat, Diddle, Dilly-dally, Dole-bludger, Donnat, Donnot, Do-nothingism, Drone, Fainéant, Fallow, Farnarkel, Fester, Flaneur, Flim-flam, Footle, Frivolous, Gold brick, Groundless, Hawm, Inaction, Indolent, Inert, Lackadaisical, Laesie, Lallygag, Layabout, Laze, Lazy, Lead-swinger, Lie, Lig, Light, Limer, Loaf, Lollop, Lollygag, Lotophagus, Lounge, Lusk, Micawber, Mike, Mollusc, Mooch, Mouch, Otiose, Otium, Patagonian, Piddle, Ride, Scapegrace, Shiftless, Skive, Sloth, Sluggard, Spiv, Stalko, Stock-still, Stooge, Stroam, Tarry, Transcendental, Trock, Troke, Truant, Truck, Twiddle, Unbusy, Unoccupied, Vain, Vegetate, Veg out, Waste

Idol(ise) Adore, Adulate, Baal(im), Baphomet, Bel, Crush, E(i)luned, Fetich(e), Fetish, God, Heartthrob, Hero, Icon, Image, Joss, Juggernaut, Lion, Mammet, Manito, Manitou, Matinee, Maumet, Mawmet, Molech, Moloch, Mommet, Moorish, Mumbo-jumbo, Stotter, Swami, Teraph(im), Termagant, Vision, Wood, Worship

Idyll(ic) Arcady, Eclogue, Eden, Pastoral, Peneian

Ie Sc

If, If it All-be, An('t), Condition, Gif, Gin, In case, Pot, Provided, Sobeit, Whether

Igloo Snowden

Igneous Pyrogenic

Ignis-fatuus Elf-fire, Fire-dragon, Fire-drake, Friar's lanthorn, Wildfire

Ignite, Ignition Coil, Electronic, Flare, Kindle, Lightning, Spark, Starter

Ignoble Base, Inferior, Mean, Vile

Ignominious, Ignominy Base, Dishonour, Fiasco, Infamous, Scandal, → **SHAME**

Ignorance, Ignorant Agnoiology, Analphabet, Anan, Artless, Benighted, Blind, Clueless, Darkness, Green, Hick, Illiterate, Inerudite, Ingram, Ingrum, Inscient, Know-nothing, Lewd, Lumpen, Misken, Nescience, Night, Oblivious, Oik, Philistine, Purblind, Red-neck, Unaware, Uneducated, Unlettered, Unread, Unschooled, Untold, Unversed, Unwist

Ignore Alienate, Ba(u)lk, Blink, Bypass, Connive, Cut, Discount, Disregard, Forget, Neglect, Omit, Overlook, Override, Overslaugh, Pass, Pass-up, Rump, Scrub round, Slight, Snub

Igor Prince

Iguana Chuckwalla

I know Iwis, Ywis

Iliad Homeric

Ill Adverse, All-overish, Bad, Bilious, Cronk, Crook, Evil, Inauspicious, Income, Off-colour, Poorly, Queer, Sea-sick, → **SICK**, Unweal, Unwell, Valetudinarian, Wog, Wrong

▷ **Ill** *may indicate* an anagram

Ill-adjusted Sad sack
Ill-balanced Lop-sided
Ill-bred Churlish, Plebeian, Uncouth, Unmannerly
▷ **Ill-composed** *may indicate* an anagram
Ill-defined Diagnosis, Hazy, Unclear, Vague
Ill-dressed Frumpish
Illegal, Illicit Adulterine, Black, Bootleg, Breach, Furtive, Ill-gotten, Malfeasance, Misbegotten, Pirated, Shonky, Unlawful
Illegitimate Baseborn, Bastard, By-blow, Come-o'-will, Fitz, Irregular, Love-child, Lucky-piece, Mamzer, Misbegotten, Misborn, Misfortunate, Momzer, Natural, Scarp, Slink, Spurious, Unlineal
Ill-favoured Lean, Offensive, Thin, Ugly
Ill-feeling, Ill-humour Bad blood, Bile, Curt, Dudgeon, Glum, Hate, Miff, Peevish, Pique, Rheumatic
Illiberal Insular, Skinflint, Strict
▶ **Illicit** *see* ILLEGAL
Illiterate Ignoramus, Unlettered, Unread
Ill-looking Peaky, Poorly
Ill-luck Ambs-ace, Ames-ace, Bad trot, Deuce-ace, Misfortune
Ill-mannered, Ill-natured Attercop, Bitchy, Coarse, Crabby, Ethercap, Ettercap, Goop, Gurrier, Guttersnipe, Huffy, Stingy, Sullen, Ugly, Uncouth, Unkind
Illness Aids, Ailment, Attack, Autism, Brucellosis, Complaint, Croup, Death-bed, Diabetes, Disease, DS, Dwalm, Dwaum, Dyscrasia, Eale, Eclampsia, Grippe, Hangover, Hypochondria, Lockjaw, Malady, ME, SAD, Scarlatina, Sickness, Terminal, Toxaemia, Urosis, Weed, Weid, Wog
Ill-nourished Emaciated
Illogical Inconsequent, Non-sequitur
Ill-sighted Owl, Purblind
Ill-smelling F(o)etid, High, Hing, Miasmic, Stinking
▶ **Ill-tempered** *see* ILL-MANNERED
Ill-timed Inopportune, Unseasonable
Illuminate(d), Illumination, Illuminating Aperçu, Brighten, Clarify, Cul-de-lampe, Decorate, Enlighten, Floodlit, Lamplight, Langley, Light, Limn, Miniate, Nernst, Pixel, Radiate, Rushlight
Illusion, Illusory, Illusive Air, Apparition, Barmecide, Deception, Déjà vu, Fallacy, Fancy, Fantasy, Hallucination, Ignis-fatuus, Mare's-nest, Maya, Mirage, Muller-Lyer, Optical, Phantom, Phi-phenomenon, Size-weight, Specious, Transcendental, Trompe l'oeil, Unreality, Will o'the wisp
Illustrate(d), Illustration, Illustrator Artwork, Case, Centrefold, Collotype, Demonstrate, Drawing, Eg, Elucidate, Epitomise, Exemplify, Explain, Figure, Frontispiece, Grangerize, Graphic, Half-tone, Illume, Illumin(at)e, Instance, Instantiate, Keyline, Limner, Lithograph, Pictorial, Plate, Show, Sidelight, Spotlight, Tenniel, Vignette, Visual
Illustrious Bright, Celebrated, Famous, Legendary, Renowned
Ill-will Animosity, Enmity, Grudge, Hostility, Malice, Maltalent, Mau(l)gre, Spite
I'm I'se
Image(s) Atman, Blip, Brand, Corporate, Discus, Effigy, Eidetic, Eidolon, Eikon, Eiluned, Emotion, Enantiomorph, Fine-grain, Graphic, Graven, Hologram, Hypnagogic, Icon, Iconograph, Ident, Idol, Invultuation, Joss, Latent, Likeness, Matte, Mirror, Morph, Murti, Paranthelium, Paraselene, Pentimento, Phantasmagoria, Photogram, Photograph, Pic(ture), Pixel(l)ated, Pixil(l)ated,

Poetic, Profile, Public, Real, Recept, Reflectogram, Reflectograph, Representation, Scintigram, Search, Shadowgraph, Simulacrum, Spectrum, Spitting, Split, Stereotype, Symbol, Teraph(im), Thumbnail, Tiki, Tomogram, Totem, Venogram, Video, Virtual, Xoanon

Imagine(d), Imaginary (land), Imagination, Imaginative Assume, Bandywallop, Believe, Boojum, Bullamakanka, Cloud-cuckoo-land, Cockaigne, Cockayne, Conceive, Conjure, Cyborg, Dystopia, Envisage, Esemplasy, Faery, Faine, Fancy, Feign, Fictional, Fictitious, Fictor, Figment, Figure, Hallucinate, Hobbit, Ideate, Invent, Mind's eye, Moral, Oz, Picture, Poetical, Prefigure, Pretend, Recapture, Replicant, Scotch mist, Snark, Straw, → **SUPPOSE**, Surmise, Think, Tulpa, Vicarious, Visualise, Whangam

Imbecile Anile, Fool, Idiot, → **STUPID**

▷ **Imbecile** *may indicate* an anagram

Imbibe Absorb, Drink, Lap, Quaff, Suck, Swallow

Imbricate Overlie

Imbroglio Complication, Maze

Imbrue, Imbue Colour, Impregnate, Indoctrinate, Infuse, Inoculate, Permeate, Soak, Steep

Imitate, Imitation, Imitator Act, Ape, Burlesque, Copy(cat), Counterfeit, Dud, Echo, Echopraxia, Emulate, Epigon(e), Ersatz, Fake, False, Faux, Follow, Marinist, Me-too, Mime, Mimetic, Mimic(ry), Mini-me, Mockery, Monkey, Onomatopoeia, Parody, Parrot, Paste, Pastiche, Pinchbeck, Potichomania, Rip-off, Sham, Simulate, Stumer, Take-off, Travesty

Immaculate Conception, Flawless, Lily-white, Perfect, Pristine, Spotless, Virgin

Immanentist Pantheist

Immaterial Insignificant, Spiritual, Trifling

Immature(ly), Immaturity Callow, Crude, Embryo, Ergate(s), Green, Inchoate, Larval, Neotenic, Non-age, Puberal, Puberulent, Pupa, Raw, Sophomoric, Tender, Unbaked, Underage, Unformed, Unripe, Young

▷ **Immature** *may indicate* a word incompleted

Immediate(ly) Alsoon, At once, B(e)live, Direct, Eftsoons, Ekdum, First-time, Forthwith, Imminent, Incontinent, Instantaneous, Instanter, Lickety-split, Near, Next, → **NOW**, Now-now, On the knocker, Outright, Present, Pronto, Right-off, Short-term, Slapbang, Spontaneous, Stat, Statim, Straight, Straight off, Sudden, Then, Tout de suite

Immense Astronomical, Brobdingnag, Cosmic, Enormous, → **GIGANTIC**, Huge, Vast, Wide

Immerse Baptise, Demerge, Demerse, Drench, Embathe, Emplonge, Enew, Engage, Imbathe, Plunge, Soak, Steep

Immigrant, Immigration, Immigrate Aliya(h), Aussiedler, Brain gain, Carpet-bagger, Cayun, Chalutz, Freshie, Greener, Greenhorn, Halutz, Illegal, Incomer, Issei, Merino, Metic, New chum, Nisei, Non-quota, Olim, Outsider, Overstayer, Pilgrim, Pommy, Quota, Redemption(er), Reffo, Sanei, Sansei, Settler, Wetback, Whenwe

Imminent Approaching, Close, Immediate, Pending

Immobility, Immobile, Immobilise(r) Akinesia, Cataplexy, Catatonia, Hog-tie, Inertia, Pinion, Rigidity, Taser, Tether

Immoderate Excessive, Extreme, Inordinate, Intemperate, Lavish, Undue, Unreasonable

Immodest(y) Brash, Brazen, Forward, Impudicity, Indelicate, Unchaste

Immolation Sacrifice, Sati, Suttee

Immoral(ity) Corrupt, Degenerate, Dissolute, Evil, Lax, Libertine, Licentious, Loose, Nefarious, Peccable, Reprobate, Scarlet, Turpitude, Unholy, Unsavoury, Vice, Vicious, Wanton

Immortal(ity) Agelong, Amarant(h), Amarantin, Amritattva, Athanasy, Deathless, → **DIVINE**, Enoch, Eternal, Ever-living, Famous, Godlike, Memory, Sin, Struldbrug, Timeless, Undying

Immovable Fast, Firm, Obdurate, Rigid, Stable, Stubborn

Immune, Immunisation, Immunise(r), Immunity Acquired, Active, Amboceptor, Anamnestic, Anergy, Bar, Cree, Diplomatic, Free, Humoral, Inoculate, Klendusic, Natural, Non-specific, Passive, Pasteurism, Pax, Premunition, Properdin, Serum, Tachyphylaxis, Vaccine

Immure Confine, Encloister, Imprison

Imp(ish) Devilet, Elf, Flibbertigibbet, Gamin(e), Hobgoblin, Limb, Lincoln, Litherly, Nickum, Nis(se), Puck, Ralph, Rascal, Spright, Sprite

Impact Bearing, Bump, Clash, Collision, Feeze, High, Impinge, Jar, Jolt, Pack, Percuss, Pow, Slam, Souse, Strike home, Wham

Impair(ed), Impairment Appair, Cripple, Damage, Disease, Enfeeble, → **HARM**, Injure, Lame, Mar, Mental, Odd, Pair(e), Paralogia, Stale, Vitiate

Impala Pallah

Impale Elance, Ga(u)nch, Skewer, Spike, Transfix

Impart Bestow, Convey, Divulge, Impute, Infect, Shed, Tell

Impartial Candid, Detached, Equitable, Even-handed, Fair, Just, Neutral, Unbiased

Impasse, Impassable Deadlock, Dilemma, Invious, Jam, Mexican standoff, Snooker, Stalemate, Zugzwang

Impassioned Emotional, Fervid, Fiery, Heated, Zealous

Impassive Apathetic, Deadpan, Stoical, Stolid

Impatience, Impatient Chafing, Chut, Dysphoria, Fiddle-de-dee, Fiddlesticks, Fidgety, Fretful, Hasty, Hoot(s), Irritable, Och, Peevish, Peremptory, Petulant, Pish, Restless, Tilly-fally, Till(e)y-vall(e)y, Tut

Impeach Accuse, Challenge, Charge, Delate, Indict

Impeccable Faultless, Novice

Impecunious Penniless, Poor, Short

Impedance, Impede, Impediment Burr, Clog, Dam, Diriment, Encumber, Halt, Hamstring, Handicap, → **HINDER**, Hog-tie, Let, Log, Obstacle, Obstruct, Reactance, Rub, Shackle, Snag, Stammer, Stymie, Tongue-tie, Trammel, Veto, Z

Impel(led) Actuate, Coerce, Drave, Drive, Drove, Goad, Inspire, → **URGE**

Impend(ing) Imminent, Looming, Toward

Impenetrable Adamantine, Air-tight, Dense, Hard, Impervious, Proof, Watertight

Imperative Categorical, Dire, Hypothetical, Jussive, Mood, Need-be, Pressing, Vital

Imperceptible, Imperceptive Blind Freddie, Intangible, Invisible, Latent, Minimal, Subtle

Imperfect(ion) Aplasia, Aplastic, Blotch, Defect, Deficient, Faulty, Feathering, Flawed, Half-pie, Kink, Kinkle, Lame, Poor, Rough, Second, Unideal

Imperial(ist), Imperious Beard, C(a)esarian, Commanding, Haughty, Majestic, Masterful, Mint, Peremptory, Regal, Rhodes, Royal, Tuft

Imperil Endanger, Risk

Imperishable Eternal, Immortal, Indestructible

Impermeable Airtight, Athermanous, Proof, Resistant

Impersonal Abstract, Cold, Detached, Inhuman, Institutional

Impersonate, Impersonation, Impersonator Amphitryon, Ape, As, Double, Imitate, Impression, Mimic, Pose, Spoof

Impertinence, Impertinent Crust, Flip(pant), Fresh, Impudent, Irrelevant, Rude, Sass, Sauce

Imperturbable Cool, Placid, Stoic, Tranquil

Impervious(ness) Athermancy, Callous, Hardened, Obdurate, Proof, Tight

Impetigo Scrumpox

Impetuous, Impetuosity Birr, Brash, Bullheaded, Élan, → HASTY, Headstrong, Heady, Hothead, Impulsive, Rash, Rhys, Tearaway, Vehement, Violent, Young Turk

Impetus Birr, Drift, Incentive, MacGuffin, Momentum, Propulsion, Slancio, Steam, Swing

Impious Blasphemous, Godless, Irreverent, Unholy

Implant(ation) AID, Cochlear, Embed, Engraft, Enroot, Graft, Inset, Instil, Nidation, Silicone, Sow

Implausible Lame, Off-the-wall

Implement Agent, Backscratcher, Biffer, Celt, Cultivator, Disgorger, Eolith, Execute, Flail, Follow out, Fork, Fulfil, Hacksaw, Harrow, Hayfork, Mop, Muller, Pin, Pitchfork, Plectrum, Plough, Pusher, Rest, Ripple, Scarifier, Scythe, Seed drill, Shoehorn, Sickle, Snuffer, Spatula, Splayd®, Squeegee, Strickle, Tongs, → TOOL, Toothpick, Tribrach, Utensil

Implicate, Implication Accuse, Concern, Connotation, Embroil, Incriminate, Innuendo, → INVOLVE, Material, Overtone

Implore Beg, Beseech, Crave, → ENTREAT, Obsecrate, Petition, Plead, Pray

Imply, Implied Hint, Insinuate, Involve, Predicate, Signify, → SUGGEST, Tacit

Impolite Ill-bred, Rude, Uncivil

Import(s) Convey, Denote, Drift, Invisible, Mean, Parallel, Sense, Signify, Spell, Visible

Importance, Important (person) Big, Big cheese, Big wheel, Billing, Calibre, Cardinal, Central, Cheese, Cob, Coming, Consequence, Considerable, Core, Cornerstone, Count, Critical, Crucial, Crux, Earth-shaking, Earth-shattering, Eminent, Epochal, Grave, Gravitas, Gravity, Greatness, Heavy, High, High-muck-a-muck, His nibs, Historic, Honcho, Hotshot, Huzoor, Key, Keystone, Macher, Magnitude, Main, Major, Material, Matters, Megastar, Mighty, Milestone, Moment(ous), Nabob, Nawab, Nib, Note, Numero uno, Obbligato, Overriding, Personage, Pivotal, Pot, Preponderate, Prime, Principal, Red-carpet, Salient, Seminal, Serious, Significant, Something, Special, Stature, Status, Stress, Substantive, Tuft, Urgent, VIP, Weight, Weighty, Worth

Importune, Importunate Beg, Coax, Flagitate, Press(ing), Prig, Solicit, Urgent

Impose(r), Imposing, Imposition Allocate, Assess, August, Burden, Charge, Cheat, Diktat, Dread, Enforce, Enjoin, Epic, Fine, Flam, Foist, Fraud, Grand(iose), Hidage, Homeric, Hum, Impot, Inflict, Kid, Lay, Levy, Lumber, Majestic, Obtrude, Pensum, Pole, Scot, Sponge, Stately, Statuesque, Stonehand, Sublime, Whillywhaw

Impossible Hopeless, Incorrigible, Insoluble, Insurmountable, No-go, No-no, Unacceptable

Impost Excise, Levy, Tax, Toll

Imposter, Impostor Bunyip, Charlatan, Disaster, Faitor, Faitour, → FAKE, Fraud, Idol, Pretender, Sham, Triumph, Warbeck

Impotent Barren, Helpless, Spado, Sterile, Weak

Impound(er) Appropriate, Bond, Confiscate, Intern, Pen, Pinder, Poind

Impoverish(ed) Bankrupt, Bare, Beggar, Exhaust, Indigent, Straiten

Impractical Absurd, Academic, Blue-sky, Chim(a)era, Idealist, Inoperable, Laputan, Not on, Other-worldly, Quixotic, Useless

Imprecation Oath, Pize, 'Slife

Imprecise Approximate, Inaccurate, Indeterminate, Intangible, Loose, Nebulous, Rough, Sloppy, Vague

Impregnate Conceive, Enwomb, Imbue, Inseminate, Milt, Permeate, Resinate

Impresario Maestro, Manager, Producer, Showman

Impress(ive), Impression(able) Air, Astonish, Awe, Blur, Blurb, Bowl over, Brand, Cliché, Commanding, Conscript, Crimp, Deboss, Dent, Dramatic, Edition, Effect, Engram(ma), Engrave, Enstamp, Epic, Feel(ing), Fingerprint, Fossil, Frank, Gas, Glorious, Grab, Grandiose, Heroic, Homeric, Idea, Idée, Imitation, Impinge, Imprint, Incuse, Intaglio, Kick ass, Knock, Let, Majestic, Name-drop, Niello, Noble, Note, Palimpsest, Plastic, Plate, Pliable, Powerful, Prent, Presence, Press(gang), Print, Proof, Recruit, Register, Repute, Resplendent, Responsive, Ripsnorter, Rotund, Seal, Seize, Sense, Shanghai, Slay, Smite, Soft, Spectacular, Stamp, Stereotype, Strike, Stunning, Susceptible, Sway, Tableau, Touch, Type, Vibrant, Watermark, Weal, Weighty, Woodcut, Wow

Impressionist Caxton, Cézanne, Impersonator, Liebermann, Lumin(ar)ist, Manet, Matisse, Monet, Morisot, Renoir

Imprint Edition, Engrave, Etch, Stamp

Imprison(ment) Cape, Committal, Confine, Constrain, Custody, Durance, False, Immure, Incarcerate, Intern, Jail, Penal servitude, Quad, Quod, Time

Improbable Buckley's chance, Buckley's hope, Dubious, Far-fetched, Unlikely

Impromptu Ad lib(itum), Extempore, Improvised, Offhand, Spontaneous, Sudden, Unrehearsed

Improper, Impropriety Abnormal, Blue, Demirep, False, Illegitimate, Indecent, Indecorum, Naughty, Outré, Prurient, Solecism, Undue, Unmeet, Unseemly, Untoward

▷ **Improperly** *may indicate* an anagram

Improve(ment), Improver, Improving Advance, Ameliorate, Beat, Benefit, Bete, Break, Buck, Cap, Chasten, Conditioner, Convalesce, Cultivate, Détente, Didactic, Ease, Edify, Edutainment, Embellish, Emend, Enhance, Enrich, Eugenic, Euthenics, File, Gentrify, Kaizen, Meliorate, Mend, Potentiate, Promote, Rally, Refine, Reform, Resipiscence, Retouch, Revamp, Sarvodaya, Slim, Streamline, Surpass, Tart, Tatt, Titivate, Top, Touch-up, Turn round, Tweak, Uptrend, Upturn

Improvident Feckless, Micawber

Improvise(d), Improvisation Adlib, Break, Devise, Drumhead, Extemporise, Invent, Knock-up, Lash-up, Noodle, Ride, Scratch, Sudden, Vamp, Wing

Imprudent Foolhardy, Foolish, Impetuous, Impolitic, Indiscreet, Injudicious, Rash, Reckless, Unwary, Unwise

Impudence, Impudent Audacious, Backchat, Bardy, Bold, Brash, Brassy, Brazen, Cheeky, Cool, Crust, Effrontery, Forward, Gall, Gallus, Hussy, Impertinent, Insolent, Jackanapes, Lip, Malapert, Neck, → **NERVE**, Pert, Sass(y), Sauce, Saucebox, Saucy, Slack-jaw, Temerity, Whippersnapper, Yankie

Impugn Censure, Challenge, Defame, Impeach, Malign

Impulse, Impulsive Beat, Compelling, Conatus, Dictate, Drive, Efferent, Headlong, Horme, Ideopraxist, Impetus, Instigation, → **INSTINCT**, Libido, Madcap, Nerve, Nisus, Premature, Premotion, Send, Signal, Snap, Specific, Spontaneous, Tendency, Thrust, Tic, Urge, Whim

Impure, Impurity Adulterated, Contaminated, Donor, Faints, Feints, Indecent, Lees, Lewd, Regulus, Scum, Unclean

Imputation, Impute Ascribe, Attribute, Charge, Scandal, Slander, Slur

In A, Amid, At, Batting, Chic, Current, Home, Hostel, I', Inn, Intil, Occupying, On, Pop(ular), Pub, Trendy, Within

Inability Anosmia, Aphagia, Aphasia, Apraxia

Inaccessible Abaton, Impervious, Remote, Unattainable, Uncom(e)atable

Inaccurate Distorted, Erroneous, Faulty, Imprecise, Inexact, Out, Rough, Slipshod, Unfaithful

Inactive, Inaction, Inactivity Acedia, Cabbage, Comatose, Dead, Dormant, Extinct, Fallow, Hibernate, Idle, Inert, Languor, Moratorium, Passive, Quiescent, Racemic, Rusty, Sedentary, Sluggish, Stagnation, Torpid, Veg(etate)

In addition Eke, Else, Further, Moreover, Plus, To boot, Too

Inadequate Derisory, Feeble, Inapt, Inferior, Pathetic, Poor, Ropy, Scanty, Slight, Thin, Unequal

Inadvertent(ly) Accidental, Careless, Chance, Unwitting

▷ **In a flap** *may indicate* an anagram

In a high degree So

In a hundred Percent

Inane Empty, Fatuous, Foolish, Imbecile, Silly, Vacant

Inanimate Abiotic, Lifeless

Inappropriate Amiss, Incongrous, Infelicitous, Malapropos, Off-key, Pretentious, Unapt, Unbecoming, Undue, Unmeet, Unsuitable, Untoward

Inapt Maladroit, Unsuitable

Inarticulate(ness) Indistinct, Mumbling, Psellism

Inartistic Artless, Crude

Inattentive, Inattention Absent, Asleep, Deaf, Distrait, Dwaal, Dwa(l)m, Dwaum, Heedless, Loose, Slack, Unheeding, Unobservant

Inaudible Silent, Superhet

Inaugurate Han(d)sel, Initiate, Install, Introduce

Inauspicious Adverse, Ominous, Sinister

▷ **In a whirl** *may indicate* an anagram

▷ **In a word** *may indicate* two clue words linked to form one

Inborn, Inbred Homogamy, Inherent, Innate, Native, Selfed, Sib

Inca Quechua, Quichua

Incalculable Endless, Unpredictable, Untold

Incandescent Alight, Bright, Brilliant, Excited, Radiant

Incantation Charm, Magic, Mantra, Spell

Incapable Can't, Downa-do, Powerless, Unable, Useless

Incarnation Advent, Avatar, Embodiment, Fleshing, Krishna, Rama, Ramachandra

In case Lest, So

Incautious Foolhardy, Rash, Reckless, Unwary

Incendiary Arsonist, Combustible, Firebug, Fire-lighter, Fireship, Napalm, Thermite

Incense(d), Incenser Anger, Aroma, Elemi, Enfelon, Enrage, Homage, Hot, → **INFLAME**, Joss-stick, Navicula, Onycha, Outrage, Pastil(le), Provoke, Thurible, Thus, Vex, Wrathful

Incentive Carrot, Carrot and stick, Feather-bed, Fillip, Impetus, Motive, Premium, Spur, Stakhanovism, Stimulus, Wage

Incessant Constant, Endless, Unremitting

Incest Backcross, Spiritual

Inch(es) Ait, Column, Edge, Isle, Mil, Miner's, Sidle, Tenpenny, Uncial

Inchoate Formless, Immature, Incipient

Incident(al) Affair, Baur, Bawr, Carry-on, Chance, Circumstance, Episode, Event, Facultative, Handbags, Negligible, Occasion, Occurrent, Page, Peripheral, Scene, Throwaway

Incinerate, Incinerator Burn, Combust, Cremate, Destructor

Incipient Beginning, Germinal, Inchoate

Incise, Incision, Incisive(ness) Bite, Cut, Engrave, Incavo, Lobotomy, McBurney's, Mordant, Notch, Phlebotomy, Punchy, Rhizotamy, Scarf, Scribe, Slit, Surgical, Thoracotomy, Tracheotomy, Trenchant

Incisor Foretooth

Incite(ment) Abet, Drive, Egg, Fillip, Good, Hortative, Hoy, Impassion, Inflame, Instigate, Kindle, Motivate, Prod, Prompt, Provoke, Put, Rouse, Sa sa, Sedition, Set, Sic(k), Sool, → **SPUR**, Sting, Suborn, Suggest, Tar, Urge

Incline(d), Inclination Acclivity, Angle, Aslant, Aslope, Atilt, Bank, Batter, Bent, Bias, Bow, Camber, Clinamen, Cock, Crossfall, Declivity, Dip, Disposed, Drift, Enclitic, Glacis, → **GRADIENT**, Grain, Habitus, Hade, Heel, Hill, Italic, Kant, Kip, Lean, Liking, List, Maw, Minded, Nod, On, Partial, Peck, Penchant, Proclivity, Prone, Propensity, Rake, Ramp, Ready, Rollway, Set, Shelve, Slant, → **SLOPE**, Steep, Steeve, Stomach, Supine, Tend, Tilt, Tip, Trend, Upgrade, Velleity, Verge, Weathering, Will

Include(d), Inclusion, Inclusive Add, All-told, Bracket, Compass, Comprise, Connotate, Contain, Cover, Embody, Embrace, Enclose, Involve, Short-list, Social, Subsume, Therein

Incognito Anonymous, Disguised, Faceless, Secret, Unnamed

Incoherent Confused, Disconnected, Disjointed, Gabbling, Inarticulate, Rambling, Spluttering

Incombustible Clinker

Income Annuity, Benefice, Disposable, Dividend, Earned, Entry, Fixed, Franked, Livelihood, Living, Meal-ticket, Milch cow, National, OTE, Penny-rent, Prebend, Primitiae, Private, Proceeds, Rent, Rente, Rent-roll, Returns, Revenue, Salary, Stipend, Unearned, Unfranked, Wages

Incommunicado Isolated, Silent

Incomparable Supreme, Unequalled, Unique, Unmatched

Incompatible, Incompatibility Contradictory, Dyspathy, Incongruous, Inconsistent, Mismatched, Unsuited

Incompetent Bungler, Deadhead, Helpless, Hopeless, Ill, Inefficient, Inept, Palooka, Slouch, Unable, Unfit

Incomplete Broadbrush, Cagmag, Catalectic, Deficient, Inchoate, Lacking, Partial, Pendent, Rough, Unfinished

Incomprehensible, Incomprehension Acatamathesia, Double Dutch, Hard, Unbelievable

Inconceivable Impossible, Incredible

▷ **In confusion** *may indicate an anagram*

Incongruous, Incongruity Absurd, Discordant, Heterogenous, Irish, Ironic, Sharawadgi, Sharawaggi

In connection with Re

Inconsiderable Light, Slight

Inconsiderate High-handed, Hog, Petty, Presumptuous, Roughshod, Thoughtless, Unkind

Inconsistency, Inconsistent Alien, Anacoluthon, Anomaly, Contradictory, Discrepant, Oxymoronic, Paradoxical, Unequal, Unsteady, Variance

Inconsolable Heartbroken, Niobe

Inconspicuous Unobtrusive

Inconstant Chameleon, Desultory, Fickle, Light, Mutable, → **VARIABLE**

Inconvenience, Inconvenient Awkward, Bother, Discommode, Fleabite,

Incommodious, → **TROUBLE**, Unseemly, Untoward
Incorporate(d), Incorporation Absorb, Embody, Inc, Integrate, Introgression, Introject, Join, Merge, Subsume
Incorporeal Aery, Airy, Spiritual
Incorrect Catachresis, False, Improper, Invalid, Naughty, Wrong
Incorrigible Hopeless, Obstinate
Incorruptible Copper-bottomed, Honest, Immortal, Pure, Robespierre, Sea-green
Increase(s), Increasing Accelerando, Accelerate, Accession, Accrue, Add, Additur, Aggrandise, Amplify, Amp up, Appreciate, Approve, Augment, Auxetic, Bolster, Boost, Bulge, Crank up, Crescendo, Crescent, Crescive, Deepen, Dilate, Double, Ech(e), Eech, Eik, Eke, Enhance, Enlarge, Escalate, → **EXPAND**, Explosion, Greaten, → **GROW**, Heighten, Ich, Increment, Interbreed, Jack, Jack up, Joseph, Lift, Magnify, Mark up, Mount, Multiply, Plus, Proliferate, Propagate, Ramp up, Redshift, Reflation, Regrate, Rise, Snowball, Swell, Thrive, Up, Upsize, Upswell, Upswing, Wax
Incredible Amazing, Cockamamie, Extraordinary, Fantastic, Steep, Stey, Tall, Unreal
Incredulity, Incredulous Distrust, Infidel, Suspicion, Thunderstruck, Unbelief
Increment Accrual, Augment, Growth, Increase
Incriminate Accuse, Implicate, Inculpate
Incubate, Incubator Brooder, Develop, Eccaleobion, Hatch
Incubus Demon, Load, Nightmare
Inculcate Implant, Infuse
Incumbent Lying, Obligatory, Occupier, Official
Incur Assume, Earn, Involve
Incursion Foray, Inroad, Invasion, Raid, Razzia
Indecent Bare, Blue, Fescennine, Free, Immodest, Immoral, Improper, Lewd, Obscene, Rabelaisian, Racy, Scurril(e), Sotadic, Spicy, Sultry, Unnatural, Unproper, Unseem(ly), X-rated
Indecision, Indecisive Demur, Dithery, Doubt, Hamlet, Havering, Hesitation, Hung jury, Inconclusive, Shilly-shally, Suspense, Swither, Weakkneed
Indeclinable Aptote
Indecorous Graceless, Immodest, Outré, Unbecoming
Indeed Atweel, Ay, Aye, Da, Een, Even, Faith, Haith, I, Insooth, Ja wohl, La, Marry, Quotha, Truly, Verily, Yah, Yea
Indefensible Implausible, Inexcusable, Vincible
Indefinite(ly) A, An, Any, Evermore, Hazy, Nth, Some, Undecided, Vague
Indelible Fast, Permanent
Indelicate Broad, Coarse, Improper, Vulgar, Warm
Indemnify, Indemnification, Indemnity Assythement, Compensation, Double, Insurance
Indent(ed), Indentation Apprentice, Contract, Crenellate, Dancetty, Dimple, Impress, Niche, Notch, Order, Philtrum, Subentire
Independence, Independent Apart, Autocephalous, Autogenous, Autonomy, Crossbencher, Detached, Extraneous, Free(dom), Free-lance, Free spirit, Freethinker, I, Liberty, Mana motuhake, Maverick, Mugwump, Perseity, Self-sufficient, Separate, Separatist, Sui juris, Swaraj, Udal, UDI, Uhuru
Indescribable Incredible, Ineffable
Indestructible Enduring, Impenetrable, Inextirpable
Indeterminate Borderline, Formless, Incalculable, Open-ended, Unknown
Index Alidad(e), All-Ordinaries, Catalogue, Cephalic, Colour, Cranial, Dial,

Dow Jones, Exponent, Facial, Finger, Fist, Fog, Footsie, Forefinger, Gazetteer, Glycaemic, Hang Seng, Kwic, Librorum Prohibitorum, Margin, Misery, Nasal, Nikkei, Opsonic, Power, Price, Refractive, → **REGISTER**, Rotary, Share, Stroke, Table, Thumb, TPI, UV, Verborum

India(n) Adivisi, Asian, Assamese, Ayah, Baboo, Babu, Bharat(i), Bihari, Canarese, Carib, Chin, Dard, Dravidian, East, File, Goanese, Gond(wanaland), Gujarati, Harijan, Harsha, Hindu, Indic, Ink, Jain, Jat, Jemadar, Kafir, Kanarese, Kannada, Khalsa, Kisan, Kolarian, Kshatriyas, Lepcha, Ma(h)ratta, Maratha, Mazhbi, → **MEXICAN**, Mission, Mofussil, Mogul, Mulki, Munda, Munshi, Naga, Nagari, Nair, Nasik, Nation, Nayar, → **NORTH AMERICAN**, Nuri, Ocean, Oriya, Pali, Panjabi, Pargana, Parsee, Parsi, Peshwa, Plains, Prakrit, Punja(u)bee, Punjabi, Red, Sanskrit, Sepoy, Shri, Sikh, Sind(h), → **SOUTH AMERICAN**, Sowar, Summer, Swadeshi, Taino, Tamil, Telegu, Vakeel, Vakil, West

Indiaman Clive

Indiana, Indianian Hoosier

Indicate, Indication, Indicative, Indicator Adumbrate, Allude, Argue, Bespeak, Blinker, Cite, Clue, Cursor, → **DENOTE**, Design, Desine, Dial, Dial gauge, Endeixis, Evidence, Evince, Fluorescein, Gesture, Gnomon, Litmus, Manifest, Mean, Mood, Nod, Notation, Performance, Pinpoint, Plan-position, Point, Portend, Proof, Ray, Register, Remarque, Representative, Reveal, Show, → **SIGN**, Signify, Specify, Symptom, Tip, Token, Trace, Trafficator, Trait, Winker

Indictment Accusation, Arraign, Caption, Charge, Dittay, Reproach, Trounce

Indifference, Indifferent Adiaphoron, Aloof, Apathetic, Apathy, Blasé, Blithe, Callous, Cavalier, Cold, Cool(th), Dead, Detached, Disdain, Easy-osy, Empty, Incurious, Insouciant, Jack easy, Mediocre, Neutral, Nonchalant, Perfunctory, Phlegm, Pococurante, Sangfroid, So-so, Stoical, Supercilious, Supine, Tepid, Unconcerned

Indigence, Indigent Need, Pauper, Penury, Poverty, Want

Indigenous Aboriginal, Endemic, Native

▷ **Indi-gent** *may indicate* Baboo or Babu

Indigestion Apepsia, Apepsy, Dyspepsia, Heartburn

Indignant, Indignation Anger, Annoyed, Incensed, Irate, Outrage, Pique, Resentful, Steamed up, Wrathful

Indignity Affront, Outrage

Indigo Anil, Blue, Bunting, Carmine, Indole, Isatin(e), Wild

Indirect Back-handed, By(e), Devious, Implicit, Mediate, Oblique, Remote, Roundabout, Sidelong, Zig-zag

Indiscreet, Indiscretion Blabbermouth, Folly, Gaffe, Imprudence, Indelicate, Injudicious, Loose cannon, Rash, Unguarded, Wild oats

Indiscriminate Haphazard, Random, Scattershot, Sweeping

Indispensable Basic, Essential, King-pin, Necessary, Sine qua non, Vital

Indispose(d), Indisposition Adverse, Disincline, Ill, Incapacitate, Sick, Unwell

Indisputable Evident

Indistinct Ambiguous, Bleary, Blur, Bumble, Bummle, Faint, Fuzzy, Hazy, Misty, Nebulous, Neutral, Nondescript, Pale, S(c)hwa, Sfumato, → **VAGUE**

▷ **In distress** *may indicate* an anagram

Indite Compose, Pen, Write

Indium In

Individual(ist), Individuality Apiece, Being, Discrete, Exclusive, Free spirit, Gemma, Haecceity, Identity, Ka, Libertarian, Loner, Man, Man-jack, Morph, One-to-one, Own, Particular, Person, Poll, Respective, Separate, Single, Singular,

Solo, Soul, Special, Unit, Zoon

Indoctrinate Brainwash, Discipline, Instruct

Indo-European Aryan, Jat(s)

Indolence, Indolent Bone idle, Fainéance, Inactive, Languid, Lazy, Otiose, Sloth, Sluggish, Supine

Indomitable Brave, Dauntless, Invincible

Indonesia(n) Batavian, Nesiot, RI

Indoor(s) Within

Indubitably Certainly, Certes, Manifestly, Surely

Induce(ment) Bribe, Carrot, Cause, Coax, Draw, Encourage, Get, Inveigle, Lead, Motivate, → **PERSUADE**, Prevail, Suasion, Suborn, Tempt

Induct(ion), Inductance Epagoge, Henry, Inaugurate, Initiate, Install, L, Logic, Mutual, Prelude, Remanence

Indulge(nce), Indulgent Absolution, Binge, Coddle, Drink, Favour, Gratify, Humour, Law, Luxuriate, Oblige, Orgy, Pamper, Pander, Pardon, Permissive, Pet, Pettle, Please, → **SATISFY**, Splurge, Spoil, Spoonfeed, Surfeit, Tolerant, Venery, Voluptuous, Wallow

Industrial, Industrious, Industry Appliance, Application, Basic, Business, Busy, Cottage, Deedy, Diligence, Eident, Energetic, Growth, Labour, Millicent, Ocnus, Operose, Ruhr, Service, Smokestack, Sunrise, Technical, Technics, Tourism, Zaibatsu

▶ **Inebriate** *see* **INTOXICATE**

Inedible Inesculent, Noisome, Rotten

Ineffective, Ineffectual Clumsy, Deadhead, Drippy, Droob, Dud, Empty, Fainéant, Fruitless, Futile, Idle, Ill, Impotent, Mickey Mouse, Neutralised, Null, Powerless, Resty, Sterile, Toothless, → **USELESS**, Void, Weak, Wet

Inefficient Clumsy, Incompetent, Lame, Shiftless, Slack

Inelegant Awkward, Inconcinnity, Stiff, Turgid, Unneat

Ineligible Unqualified

Inept Absurd, Anorak, Cack-handed, Farouche, Nerd, Otaku, Plonker, Sad sack, Schlimazel, Schmo, Unskilled, Wet

Inequality Anomaly, Chebyshev's, Disparity, Injustice, Odds, Tchebyshev's

Inert(ia) Catatonia, Comatose, Dead, Dull, Excipient, Inactive, Languid, Leaden, Mollusc, Neon, Oblomovism, Potato, Rigor, Sluggish, Stagnant, Stagnation, Thowless, Torpid

Inestimable Incalculable, Invaluable, Priceless

Inevitable, Inevitably Automatic, Certain, Fateful, Inescapable, Inexorable, Needs, Perforce, TINA, Unavoidable

Inexact(itude) Cretism, Incorrect, Terminological, Wrong

Inexorable Relentless

Inexpedient Impolitic, Imprudent, Unwise

Inexpensive Bargain, Cheap, Dirt-cheap, Economic

Inexperience(d), Inexpert Amateur, Callow, Colt, Crude, Fresh, → **GREEN**, Greenhorn, Ham, Ingénue, Jejune, Put(t), Raw, Rookie, Rude, Tender, Unconversant, Unseasoned, Unseen, Unversed, Yardbird, Youthful

Inexplicable Magical, Mysterious, Paranormal, Unaccountable

Infallible Foolproof, Right, Sure-fire, Unerring

Infamous, Infamy Base, Ignominious, Notorious, Opprobrium, Shameful, Villainy

Infant Babe, Baby, Innocent, Lamb, Minor, Oral, Rug rat

Infantry(man) Buff, Foot, Grunt, Jaeger, Phalanx, Pultan, Pulto(o)n, Pultun, → **SOLDIER**, Tercio, Turco, Voetganger, Zouave

▷ **Infantry** *may refer to* babies

Infatuate(d), Infatuating, Infatuation Assot, Besot, Circean, Crush, Enamoured, Engou(e)ment, Entêté, Fanatic, Foolish, Lovesick, Mash, → **OBSESSION**, Pash, Rave, Turn

Infect(ed), Infecting, Infection, Infectious Angina, Anthrax, Babesiasis, Babesiosis, Candidiasis, Carrier, Catching, Catchy, Cholera, Communicable, Contagious, Contaminate, Corrupt, Cowpox, Cryptococcosis, Diseased, Fascioliasis, Fester, Focal, Fomes, Giardiasis, Gonorrhoea, Herpes, Impetigo, Leishmaniasis, Listeria, Lockjaw, Mycetoma, NSU, Opportunistic, Orf, Overrun, Poison, Polio(myelitis), → **POLLUTE**, Py(a)emia, Quittor, Ringworm, Roup, Salmonella, Sarcoid, Scabies, Septic, Shingles, Smit(tle), Strongylosis, Taint, Tetanus, Thrush, Tinea, Toxocariasis, Trichuriasis, Typhoid, Typhus, Virion, Virulent, Whitlow, Wog, Yersiniosis, Zoonosis, Zymosis

Infeftment Sasine, Seisin

Infer(ence), Inferred Conclude, Conjecture, Deduce, Divine, Educe, Extrapolate, Generalise, Guess, Illation, Imply, Judge, Obversion, Putative, Surmise, Syllogism

▷ **Infer** *may indicate* 'fer' around another word

Inferior Base, Bodgier, Cheap-jack, Cheesy, Coarse, Crummy, Degenerate, Dog, Ersatz, Gimcrack, Grody, Grub-Street, Indifferent, Infra, Jerkwater, Less, Lo-fi, Lower, Low-grade, Minor, Naff, Nether, One-horse, Ornery, Paravail, Petty, Poor, Rop(e)y, Schlock, Second, Second-best, Shlock, Shoddy, Sprew, Sprue, Subjacent, Subordinate, Substandard, Surat, Tatty, Tinpot, Trashy, Under(man), Underneath, Understrapper, Untermensch, Waste, Worse

Infernal Cotton-picking, Demogorgon, Diabolic, Hellish, Phitonian, Tartarean, Unholy

Infertile Barren, Farrow, Sterile

Infest(ed), Infestation Acariasis, Acrawl, Beset, Blight, Dog, Hoatching, Overrun, Pediculosis, Phthiriasis, → **PLAGUE**, Stylopised, Swamp, Swarm, Torment, Trombiculiasis, Trombidiasis, Uncinariasis

Infidel Atheist, Caffre, Giaour, Heathen, Heretic, Kafir, Pagan, Paynim, Saracen

Infield Intown

Infiltrate Encroach, Enter, Instil, Intrude, Pervade

Infinite, Infinity Cosmic, Endless, Eternal, N

Infinitive Split

Infirm Decrepit, Doddery, Feeble, Lame, Shaky, Sick

▷ **Infirm** *may indicate* 'co' around another word

Infirmary Hospital, Sick bay

Inflame(d), Inflammable, Inflammation Afire, Anger, → **AROUSE**, Bloodshot, Enamoured, Enchafe, Enfire, Enkindle, Fever, Fire, Founder, Gleet, Ignite, Impassion, Incense, Infection, Ire, Methane, Napalm, Naphtha, → **RED**, Stimulate, Swelling, Touchwood

INFLAMMATIONS

3 letters:	*5 letters:*	*6 letters:*	
Stye	Croup	Ancome	Iritis
Sty	Felon	Angina	Otitis
		Bunion	Quinsy
4 letters:		Coryza	Thrush
Acne		Eczema	Ulitis
Gout		Garget	
Noma			

7 letters:
Bubonic
Catarrh
Colitis
Ecthyma
Ignatis
Ileitis
Onychia
Pinkeye
Prurigo
Rosacea
Sunburn
Sycosis
Tylosis
Uveitis
Whitlow

8 letters:
Adenitis
Aortisis
Bursitis
Carditis
Colpitis
Cystisis
Fibrosis
Hyalitis
Mastitis
Metritis
Mycetoma
Myelitis
Myositis
Neuritis
Orchitis
Osteitis
Ovaritis
Phlegmon
Pleurisy
Pyelitis
Rachitis
Rhinitis
Uvulitis
Vulvitis
Windburn

9 letters:
Arteritis
Arthritis
Balanitis

Barotitis
Cheilitis
Chilblain
Cloacitis
Enteritis
Fasciitis
Frostbite
Gastritis
Glossitis
Keratitis
Laminitis
Nephritis
Onychitis
Parotitis
Phlebitis
Phrenitis
Pneumonia
Proctitis
Pyorrhoea
Retinitis
Scleritis
Sinusitis
Splenitis
Strumitis
Synovitis
Typhlitis
Vaginitis
Vent gleet

10 letters:
Asbestosis
Bronchitis
Cellulitis
Cephalitis
Cerebritis
Cervicitis
Dermatitis
Duodenitis
Erysipelas
Fibrositis
Gingivitis
Hepatitis A
Hepatitis B
Intertrigo
Laryngitis
Meningitis
Oophoritis
Ophthalmia

Papillitis
Paronychia
Phlegmasia
Phlogistic
Stomatitis
Tendinitis
Thrombosis
Tracheitis
Tympanitis
Urethritis
Valvulitis
Vasculitis

11 letters:
Blepharitis
Farmer's lung
Mad staggers
Mastoiditis
Myocarditis
Parotiditis
Peritonitis
Pharyngitis
Pneumonitis
Prostatitis
Salpingitis
Sandy blight
Sclerotitis
Shin splints
Spondylitis
Tennis elbow
Thoroughpin
Thyroiditis
Tonsillitis
Utriculitis
Woody-tongue

12 letters:
Appendicitis
Encephalitis
Endocarditis
Endometritis
Folliculitis
Golfer's elbow
Lymphangitis
Lympodenitis
Mesenteritis
Osteoporosis
Panarthritis

Pancreatitis
Pericarditis
Polymyositis
Polyneuritis
Sacroillitis
Swimmer's itch
Vestibulitis

13 letters:
Cholecystitis
Enterocolitis
Jogger's nipple
Labyrinthitis
Lymphadenitis
Osteomyelitis
Perihepatitis
Perinephritis
Periodontisis
Perityphlitis
Tenosynovitis
Tenovaginitis
Thrombophilia

14 letters:
Conjunctivitis
Diverticulitis
Osteoarthritis
Pyelonephritis
Sleepy staggers
Trichomoniasis
Vincent's angina

15 letters:
Gastroenteritis
Pachymeningitis

16 letters:
Bronchopneumonia

17 letters:
Encephalomyelitis
Meningocephalitis

Inflate(d), Inflation Aerate, Aggrandise, Bloat, Bombastic, Cost-push, Dilate, Distend, Distent, Exaggerate, Grade, Increase, Pneumatic, Pump, Remonetise, RPI,

Spiral, Stagflation, Stagnation, Swell

Inflect(ion) Accidence, Conjugation, Tone

Inflexible, Inflexibility Adamant(ine), Byzantine, Doctrinaire, Hard-ass, Hard-liner, Iron, Obstinate, Ossified, Relentless, Resolute, Rigid, Rigour, Set, Staid, Stubborn, Unbending

Inflict(ion) Deal, Force, Give, Impose, Subject, Trouble, Visit, Wreak

Inflorescence Bostryx, Catkin, Ci(n)cinnus, Drepanium, Glomerule, Panicle, Pleiochasium, Polychasium, Raceme, Umbel, Verticillaster

Inflow Affluence, Influx

Influence(d), Influential Act, Affect, After, Backstairs, Charm, Clamour, Clout, Credit, Determine, Drag, Earwig, Eclectic, Embracery, Éminence grise, Factor, Force, Get at, Govern, Hold, Hypnotise, Impact, Impinge, Impress, Incubus, Inspire, Interfere, Lead, Leverage, Lobby, Macher, Mastery, Militate, Mogul, Octopus, Operation, Outreach, Power, Preponderant, Pressure, Prestige, → **PULL**, Push, Reach, Rust, Say, Seminal, Significant, Star, Star-blasting, Stimulus, Suggest, Svengali, Sway, Swing, Telegony, Undue, Weigh with, Will, Work, Wull

Influenza Asian, Equine, Flu, Gastric, Grippe, Lurgi, Wog, Yuppie

Influx Inbreak

Inform(ation), Informant, Informed, Informer Acquaint, Advise, Agitprop, Apprise, Au fait, Aware, Beagle, Bit, Burst, Canary, Ceefax®, Clype, Contact, Cookie, Datum, Deep throat, Delate, Dob(ber), Dobber-in, Dope, Education, Exposition, Facts, Fact sheet, Feedback, Fink, Fisgig, Fiz(z)gig, Gen, Genome, Good oil, Grapevine, Grass, Griff, Gunsel, Hep, Immersive, Input, Inside, Instruct, Izvesti(y)a, Light, Lowdown, Media, Moiser, Nark, Nepit, Nit, Nose, Notify, Occasion, Oracle®, Peach, Pem(m)ican, Pentito, Pimp, Poop, Prestel®, Prime, Printout, Propaganda, Prospectus, Rat, Read-out, Revelation, Rheme, Rumble, Shelf, Shop, Sidelight, Sing, Sneak, Snitch, Squeak, Squeal, Stag, Stoolie, Stool-pigeon, Supergrass, Sycophant, Teletext®, Tell, Tidings, Tip-off, Up, Videotext®, Viewdata®, Whistle(-blower), Wire

Informal Casual, Intimate, Irregular, Outgoing, Rough and ready, Unofficial

Infra Under

Infra dig Ignominious

Infrequent Casual, Occasional, Rare, Scant, Seldom, Sparse

Infringe Contravene, Violate

Infuriate Anger, Bemad, Bepester, Enrage, Exasperate, Incense, Madden, Pester, Provoke

Infuse(r), Infusion Brew, Distill, Gallise, Instil, Mash, Ooze, Saloop, Saturate, Steep, Tea, Tea-ball, Tea-egg, Tisane, Toddy, Uva-ursi

Ingenious, Ingenuity Adept, Adroit, Art, Artificial, Clever, Cunning, Cute, Inventive, Natty, Neat, Resourceful, Smart, Subtle, Trick(s)y, Wit

Ingenuous Artless, Candid, Green, Innocent, Naive, Open, Transparent

Ingest Eat, Endue, Incept, Indue, Swallow

In good condition Fit, Shipshape, Taut, Trim

Ingot Bar, Billet, Bullion, Lingot, Sycee, Wedge

Ingrain Fix, Impregnate, Train

Ingrate Thankless, Viper

Ingratiate, Ingratiating Bootlick, Butter, Court, Flatter, Greasy, Silken, Smarm(y)

Ingredient(s) Additive, Admixture, Basis, Content, Element, Factor, Formula, Makings, Staple

Ingrowing, Ingrowth Onychocryptosis, T(h)ylosis

Inhabit(ants) Affect, Children, Denizen, Dweller, Inholder, Inmate, Live, Native, Occupant, People, Resident

Inhale(r), Inhalation Aspirate, Breath(e), Draw, Gas, Inspire, Intal, Sniff, Snort, Snuff, Take, Toot, Tout

Inharmonious Out, Patchy

Inherent Characteristic, Essential, Immanent, Inbred, Innate, Native

Inherit(ance), Inherited, Inheritor Accede, Birthright, Borough-English, Congenital, Feoffee, Gene, Genom, Heirloom, Inborn, Legacy, Legitim, Meek, Mendelism, Particulate, Patrimony, Portion, Reversion, Succeed, Tichborne, Ultimogenitive

Inhibit(ing), Inhibition, Inhibitor ACE, Captopril, Chalone, Chalonic, Deter, Enalapril, Forbid, Hang-up, Protease, Restrain, Retard, Retroactive, Stunt, Suppress, Tightass

Inhuman Barbarous, Brutal, Merciless

Inimical Adverse, Harmful, Hostile

Iniquity, Iniquitous Diabolical, Evil, Offence, Sin, Vice

Initial Acronym, First, Letter, Monogram, Paraph, Prelim(inary), Primary, Rubric

▷ **Initially** *may indicate* first letters

Initiate(d), Initiating, Initiation, Initiative Baptism, Begin, Bejesuit, Blood, Bora, Bring, Ceremony, Debut, Démarche, Enter, Enterprise, Epopt, Esoteric, Gumption, Induct, Instigate, Instruct, → **LAUNCH**, Nous, Onset, Proactive, Spark, → **START**

Inject(or), Injection Antiserum, Bang, Blast, Booster, Collagen, Enema, Epidural, Fuel, Hypo, Implant, Innerve, Inoculation, Instil, Introduce, Jab, Jack up, Jag, Mainline, Pop, Reheat, Serum, Shoot, Shoot up, Skin-pop, Solid, Syringe, Transfuse, Venipuncture

Injunction Command, Embargo, Freezing, Mandate, Mareva, Quia timet, Swear, Writ

Injure(d), Injury, Injurious, Injustice ABH, Abuse, Aggrieve, Bale, Bled, Bruise, Concuss, Contrecoup, Contuse, Damage, De(a)re, Disservice, Forslack, Frostbite, Gash, GBH, Harm, → **HURT**, Ill-turn, Impair, Industrial, Iniquity, Lesion, Malign, Mar, Mayhem, Mistreat, Mutilate, NAI, Needlestick, Nobble, Nocuous, Non-accidental, Noxal, Nuisance, Occupational, Oppression, Outrage, Packet, Paire, Prejudice, Rifle, RSI, Scaith, Scald, Scath(e), Scotch, Sore, Sprain, Teen(e), Tene, Tort, Trauma, Umbrage, Whiplash, Wound, Wrong

▶ **Injury** *see* **AFTER INJURY**

Ink(y) Atramental, Black, Bray, China, Chinese, Copying, Cyan, Gall, Gold, Indian, Invisible, Magnetic, Marking, Monk, Printer's, Printing, Sepia, Stained, Sympathetic, Tusche

Inkling Clue, Glimpse, Hint, Idea

Inkpot Standish

Inlaid, Inlay(er) Boulle, Buhl, Damascene, Emblemata, Empaestic, Enamel, Enchase, Incrust, Intarsia, Intarsio, Koftgar(i), Marquetrie, Marquetry, Pietra-dura, Piqué, Set, Tarsia, Veneer

Inland Hinterland, Interior, Up

Inlet Arm, Bay, Bohai, Cook, Cove, Creek, Entry, Estuary, Fiord, Firth, Fjord, Fleet, Flow, Geo, Gio, Golden Horn, Gusset, Hope, Infall, Ingate, Jervis Bay, McMurdo Sound, Moray Firth, Pamlico Sound, Pearl Harbor, Plymouth Sound, Pohai, Port Jackson, Puget Sound, Solway Firth, Strait, Sullom Voe, Table Bay, The Wash, Tor Bay, Zuyder Zee

▷ **Inlet** *may indicate* 'let' around another word

Inmate Intern(e), Lodger, Patient, Prisoner, Resident

Inn(s), Innkeeper Albergo, Alehouse, Auberge, Barnard's, Boniface, Caravanserai, Chancery, Change-house, Coaching, Court, Gray's, Halfway-house, Host, Hostelry, Hotel, House, Imaret, In, Inner Temple, Jamaica, Khan, Ladin(ity), Law, Licensee, Lincoln's, Lodging, Luckie, Lucky, Middle Temple, Motel, Padrone, Parador, Patron, Porterhouse, Posada, Posthouse, Pothouse, Publican, Roadhouse, Ryokan, Serai, Tabard, Taphouse, Tavern(er), Victualler

▷ **Inn** *may refer to* the law

Innards Entrails, Giblets, Gizzard, Guts, Harigals, Harslet, Haslet, Omasa, Rein, Viscera

Innate Congenital, Essential, Inborn, Inbred, Inbuilt, Ingenerate, Instinctive, Natural

Inner(most) Bencher, Esoteric, Internal, Intima, Intimate, Lining, Man, Marrow, Medulla, Private, Red, Woman

Innings Chance, Knock, Turn

▶ **Innkeeper** *see* **INN**

Innocent Absolved, Angelic, Arcadian, Babe, Blameless, Canny, Chaste, Cherub, Childlike, Clean, Dewy-eyed, Doddypoll, Dodipoll, Dove, Encyclical, Green, Guileless, Idyllic, Ingenue, Lamb, Lily-white, Maiden, Naive, Opsimath, Pope, → **PURE**, Sackless, Seely, Simple, St, Unwitting, White

Innocuous Harmless, Innocent

Innovate, Innovative, Innovation, Innovator Alteration, Cutting edge, Departure, Ground-breaking, Newell, Novelty, Pioneer, Promethean, Radical

Inn-sign Bush

Innu Naskapi

Innumerable Countless, Infinite, Myriad, N

Inoculate, Inoculation Engraft, Immunise, Jab, Protect, Vaccine, Variolate

Inoffensive Mild, Pleasant

Inoperative Futile, Nugatory, Silent, Void

Inopportune Disadvantageous, Inconvenient, Intempestive, Untimely

Inordinate Excessive, Irregular, Undue

▷ **Inordinately** *may indicate* an anagram

In place of For, Qua, Vice, With

Input Direct, OCR

Inquest Debriefing, Hearing, Inquiry, Investigation

Inquire, Inquiring, Inquiry Ask, Demand, Investigation, Maieutic, Nose, Organon, Probe, Query, Question, See, Speer, Speir

Inquisition, Inquisitive, Inquisitor Curious, Interrogation, Meddlesome, Nosy, Prying, Rubberneck, Snooper, Spanish, Stickybeak, Torquemada

▷ **In revolt, In revolution** *may indicate* an anagram

Inroad(s) Breach, Encroachment, Honeycomb, Infall, Invasion

Insane, Insanity Absurd, Batty, Crack-brained, Crazy, Deranged, Headcase, Hebephrenia, Loco, Lune, Mad, Manic, Mattoid, Nutso, Paranoia, Pellagra, Psycho, Schizo, Troppo, Yarra

Insatiable Greedy, Ravenous, Voracious

Insatiate child Killcrop

Inscribe(d), Inscription Chisel, Chronogram, Colophon, Dedicate, Emblazon, Endoss, Engrave, Enter, Epigraph, Epitaph, Exergue, Graffiti, Hic jacet, Hierograph, Lapidary, Legend, Lettering, Neum(e), Posy, Writ

Inscrutable Deadpan, Esoteric, Mysterious, Sphinx

Insect(s) Entomic, Nonentity, Non-person

INSECTS

3 letters:
Ant
Bee
Bot
Bug
Fly
Ked
Lac
Nit
Wax
Wog

4 letters:
Flea
Gnat
Grig
Lice
Mite
Moth
Pium
Pupa
Tick
Wasp
Weta
Zimb

5 letters:
Aphis
Borer
Brise
Cimex
Emmet
Gogga
Louse
Midge
Nymph
Ox-bot
Scale
Stick
Zebub

6 letters:
Acarid
Breese
Breeze
Capsid
Chigoe
Cicada
Cicala

Coccid
Day-fly
Earwig
Elater
Gadfly
Hopper
Hornet
Instar
Locust
Maggot
Mantid
Mantis
Mayfly
Noctua
Psocid
Psylla
Punkie
Redbug
Sawfly
Scarab
Slater
Spider
Tettix
Thrips
Vespid
Walker
Weevil

7 letters:
Antlion
Bristle
Buzzard
Carabid
Chalcid
Chigger
Corixid
Cornfly
Cricket
Culicid
Cutworm
Daphnid
Ergates
Firefly
Gallfly
Girdler
Gordius
Goutfly
Grayfly
Hexapod

Hive-bee
Humbuzz
Katydid
Ladybug
Odonata
Oestrus
Oniscus
Phasmid
Pill-bug
Pyralis
Sandfly
Spectre
Spittle
Stylops
Tabanus
Termite

8 letters:
Alderfly
Bookworm
Circutio
Coccidae
Crane-fly
Dipteras
Firebrat
Fruit fly
Gall-wasp
Glossina
Goatmoth
Greenfly
Horntail
Horsefly
Itchmite
Lacewing
Ladybird
Lygus bug
Mealybug
Metabola
Milliped
Mosquito
Myriapod
Pauropod
Pillworm
Puss-moth
Reduviid
Ruby-tail
Scarabee
Silkworm
Snowflea

Stinkbug
Stonefly
Symphile
Waterbug
Wheelbug
Whitefly
Wireworm
Woodworm

9 letters:
Ametabola
Booklouse
Butterfly
Caddis-fly
Campodeid
Centipede
Cochineal
Cockroach
Damselfly
Dobsonfly
Dor-beetle
Dragonfly
Ephemerid
Hemiptera
Homoptera
Leaf-miner
Mecoptera
Millepede
Millipede
Rearhorse
Robber-fly
Songololo
Synoekete
Tabanidae
Tiger-moth
Woodlouse
Xylophage

10 letters:
Apterygota
Bark mantis
Bluebottle
Casebearer
Chironomid
Cockchafer
Coleoptera
Collembola
Fan-cricket
Fen-cricket

Froghopper
Greendrake
Harvestman
Leaf-cutter
Leafhopper
Mallophaga
Orthoptera
Phylloxera
Plant-louse
Pond-skater
Psocoptera
Rhipiptera
Silverfish
Springtail
Thysanuran

Treehopper
Waterstick
Web spinner

11 letters:
Bristletail
Collembolan
Dermapteran
Grasshopper
Greenbottle
Hymenoptera
Mole-cricket
Neuropteran
Rhopalocera
Tiger-beetle

Trichoptera

12 letters:
Bishop's mitre
Creepy-crawly
Dictyopteran
Heteropteran
Neuropterous
Orthopterous
Rhipidoptera
San Jose scale
Strepsiptera
Thousand-legs
Thysanoptera
Water boatman

13 letters:
Cotton stainer
Daddy-long-legs
Jenny-longlegs
Leatherjacket
Praying mantis
Staphylinidae
Water scorpion

14 letters:
Strepsipterous

Insecticide Allethrin, Aphicide, Carbaryl, Chromene, Cube, DDT, Deet, Derris, Dieldrin, Endosulfan, Endrin, Flycatcher, Gammexane®, Ivermectin, Lindane®, Malathion®, Menazon, Methoxychlor, Miticide, Naphthalene, Parathion, Paris green, Piperazine, Pyrethrin, Pyrethrum, Rotenone, Spray, Timbo, Toxaphene, Zineb

Insectivore Agoura, Desman, Donaea, Drosera, Hedgehog, Jacamar, Nepenthaceae, Otter-shrew, Sarracenia, Tanrec, Tenrec(idae), Venus flytrap, Zalambdodont

Insecure Infirm, → **LOOSE**, Precarious, Shaky, Unsafe, Unstable, Unsteady, Vulnerable

Insensitive, Insensitivity Analgesia, Blunt, Callous, Dead, Log, Numb, Obtuse, Pachyderm, Stolid, Tactless, Thick-skinned

Inseparable Indiscrete, One, United

Insert(ed), Insertion, Inset Anaptyxis, Cue, Empiecement, Enchase, Enter, Entry, Foist, Fudge, Godet, Gore, Graft, Gusset, Immit, Imp, Implant, Inchase, Inject, Inlay, Input, Intercalar, Interject, Interpolate, Interpose, Intersperse, Introduce, Intromit, Lexical, Mitre, Pin, Punctuate, Sandwich

Inside(r) Content, Core, Entrails, Gaol, Heart, Indoors, Interior, Internal, Interne, Inward, Inwith, Mole, Tum, → **WITHIN**

Insidious Artful, Crafty, Sly

Insight Acumen, Anagoge, Aperçu, Enlightenment, Hunch, Inkling, Intuition, → **PERCEPTION**, Tais(c)h

Insignia Armour, Arms, Badger, Charge, Chevron, Mark, Regalia, Ribbon, Roundel, Tab

Insignificant (person) Dandiprat, Fico, Fiddling, Flea-bite, Fractional, Gnat, Inconsiderable, Insect, Jerkwater, Mickey Mouse, Minimus, Miniscule, Minnow, Nebbich, Nobody, Nominal, Nondescript, Nonentity, One-eyed, Petit, Petty, Pipsqueak, Pissant, Quat, Scoot, Scout, Scrub, Shrimp, Slight, Small potatoes, Small-time, Squirt, Squit, Tenuous, Trifling, Trivial, Two-bit, Unimportant, Venial, Warb, Whiffet, Whippersnapper

Insincere Affected, Artificial, Barmecide, Cant, Double, Double-faced, Empty, Factitious, Faithless, False, Glib, Greenwash, Hollow, Janus-faced, Lip service, Mealy-mouthed, Meretricious, Mouth-made, Pseudo, Shallow, Synthetic, Two-faced

Insinuate, Insinuating, Insinuation Allude, Foist, Hint, Imply, Innuendo, Intimate, Sleek, Slur, Sneck-draw

Insipid Banal, Blab, Bland, Drippy, Fade, Flat, Insulse, Jejune, Lash, Mawkish, Milk and water, Shilpit, Tame, Tasteless, Vapid, Weak, Wearish, Wersh

Insist(ent) Adamant, Assert, Demand, Dogmatic, Exact, Stickler, → **STIPULATE**, Stress, Swear, Threap, Threep, Urge

Insolence, Insolent Audacity, Bardy, Brassy, Cheek, Contumely, Cub, Effrontery, Gum, Hubris, Hybris, Impudence, Lip, Rude, Snash, Stroppy, Wanton

Insoluble Cerasin, Hard, Irresolvable, Mysterious

Insolvent Bankrupt, Broke, Destitute, Penniless

Insomnia Agrypnotic, Sleeplessness, Wakefulness, White night

Insouciant Carefree, Careless, Cavalier

Inspect(ion), Inspector Alnage(r), Auditor, Case, Comb, Conner, Darogha, Examine, Go-over, Government, Investigator, Jerque, Keeker, Lestrade, Look-see, Morse, Muster, Once-over, Peep, Perlustrate, Proveditor, Rag-fair, Recce, Review, Sanitary, School, Scrutinise, Spot check, Survey, Test, Vet, Vidimus, Visitation

Inspire(d), Inspiration, Inspiring Actuate, Aerate, Afflatus, Aganippe, Animate, Brainstorm, Brainwave, Breath(e), Castalian, Draw, Duende, Elate, Exalt, Fire, Flash, Geist, Hearten, Hunch, Hwyl, Idea, Illuminate, Impress, Impulse, Induce, Inflatus, Infuse, Kindle, Motivate, Move, Muse, Pegasus, Prompt, Prophetic, Satori, Sniff(le), Stimulus, Taghairm, Theopnautic, Theopneust(y), Uplift, Vatic, Verbal

In spite of Augre

Instability Anomie, Anomy

Install(ation) Elect, Enchase, Enthrone, Inaugurate, Induction, Infrastructure, Insert, Invest, Put (in)

Instalment Episode, Fascicle, Fascicule, Heft, Insert, Livraison, Never-never, Part, Serial, Tranche

Instance, Instant As, Case, Chronon, Example, Flash, Jiffy, Moment, Present, Say, Shake, Spur, Tick, Trice, Twinkling, Urgent

Instead (of) Deputy, For, Lieu, Locum, Vice

Instigate Arouse, Foment, Impel, Incite, Prompt, Spur

Instil(l) Implant, Inculcate, Infuse, Inspire, Teach, Transfuse

Instinct(ive) Automatic, Flair, Gut, Herd, Id, Impulse, Inbred, Innate, Intuition, Life, Nature, Nose, Pleasure principle, Prim(a)eval, Talent, Tendency, Visceral

Institute, Institution Academy, Activate, Asylum, Bank, Begin, Bring, Broadmoor, Charity, College, Collegiate, Erect, Found(ation), I, Inaugurate, Mechanical, MORI, Orphanage, Poorhouse, Protectory, Raise, Redbrick, Retraict, Retrait(e), Retreat, Royal, Smithsonian, Start, Technical, University, Women's, Workhouse

Instruct(ed), Instruction, Instructor ADI, Advice, Algorithm, Apprenticeship, Brief, CAI, Catechism, Chautauquan, Clinic, Coach, Course, Didactic, Direct(ive), Document, Edify, Educate, Enjoin, Ground(ing), Guide, How-to, Inform, Lesson, Loop, Macro, Manual, Mystagogue, Mystagogus, Notify, Order, Precept, Prescription, Program, Recipe, Rubric, Script, Swami, → **TEACH**, Train, Tutelage, Tutorial, Up

Instrument(al) Ablative, Act, Agent, Dash(board), Helpful, Kit, Mean(s), Mechanical, → **MUSICAL INSTRUMENT**, Negotiable, → **RESPONSIBLE**, → **TOOL**, Transit, Transposing, → **UTENSIL**, Weapon

---

INSTRUMENTS

3 letters:	*4 letters:*		*5 letters:*
Fan	Celt	Mike	Brake
Gad	Clam	Prog	Curet
	Dupe	Rasp	Fleam
	Fork	Rote	Float
		Tram	

Gadge
Groma
Meter
Miser
Organ
Probe
Sonde
Wecht

6 letters:
Bougie
Broach
Etalon
Megger®
Opener
Pallet
Pestle
Scythe
Sector
Speedo
Strobe
Trocar
Wimble

7 letters:
Alidade
Cadrans
Caliper
Caltrop
Cautery
Compass
Curette
Dilator
Diopter
Flesher
Forceps
Grapple
Monitor
Organic
Pelican
Plotter
Pointel
Pricker
Probang
Scriber
Sextant
Shuttle
Spatula
Stapler
Strigil
Swazzle

Swingle
Swozzle
Syringe
Trammel
Vocoder

8 letters:
Barnacle
Burdizzo
Diagraph
Dividers
Ecraseur
Enlarger
Iriscope
Luxmeter
Myograph
Odometer
Ohmmeter
Otoscope
Oximeter
Quadrant
Repeater
Scalprum
Scissors
Snuffler
Speculum
Strickle
Trephine
Tweezers
Vuvuzela
Waywiser

9 letters:
Algometer
Alphonsin
Arcograph
Areometer
Astrolabe
Atmometer
Auriscope
Auxometer
Barometer
Baryscope
Bolometer
Cauterant
Coelostat
Crows-bill
Cryoprobe
Cryoscope
Cymograph
Depressor

Dermatome
Dip-circle
Dosemeter
Dosimeter
Dropsonde
Endoscope
Ergograph
Eriometer
Extractor
Fadometer
Fetoscope
Flowmeter
Fluxmeter
Focimeter
Graduator
Haemostat
Heliostat
Hodometer
Hourglass
Konimeter
Kymograph
Lysimeter
Machmeter
Manometer
Marigraph
Megaphone
Megascope
Metronome
Microtome
Milometer
Monochord
Nocturnal
Nut-wrench
Oedometer
Oncometer
Ondograph
Optometer
Optophone
Osmometer
Osteotome
Pedometer
Periscope
Pintadera
Polygraph
Potometer
Pyrometer
Pyroscope
Raspatory
Retractor
Rheometer
Skiascope

Somascope
Sonograph
Tasimeter
Telemeter
Telescope
Tellurian
Tellurion
Tenaculum
Tonometer
Toothpick
Tripmeter
Voltmeter
Volumeter
Wavemeter
Xylometer
Zymometer

10 letters:
Acidimeter
Almacantar
Almucantar
Altazimuth
Anemometer
Araeometer
Buttonhook
Ceilometer
Clinometer
Colposcope
Comparator
Cryophorus
Cyclograph
Cystoscope
Densimeter
Drosometer
Fibrescope
Gaussmeter
Geodimeter®
Goniometer
Gonioscope
Gravimeter
Heliograph
Hydrometer
Hydroscope
Hygrograph
Hygrometer
Hypsometer
Iconometer
Integrator
Lactoscope
Micrograph
Micrometer

Microphone
Microscope
Mileometer
Multimeter
Nephograph
Nephoscope
Nitrometer
Opisometer
Orthoscope
Oscillator
Osteoclast
Pantograph
Photometer
Piezometer
Pilliwinks
Planimeter
Protractor
Pulsimeter
Pulsometer
Pycnometer
Radiometer
Radiophone
Radioscope
Radiosonde
Rhinoscope
Scotometer
Siderostat
Spirograph®
Spirometer
Tachograph
Tachometer
Telewriter
Tensimeter
Theodolite
Thermopile
Thorascope
Tribometer
Tromometer
Urinometer
Variometer
Voltameter

11 letters:
Actinometer
Auxanometer
Cardiograph
Chronograph

Chronometer
Chronoscope
Coercimeter
Colonoscope
Coronagraph
Craniometer
Crescograph
Dilatometer
Fluorometer
Fugitometer
Gastroscope
Gradiometer
Helicograph
Intoximeter
Jacob's staff
Laparoscope
Nephroscope
Odontograph
Opeidoscope
Pinnywinkle
Pitchometer
Planetarium
Plastometer
Polarimeter
Polariscope
Proctoscope
Psychograph
Pyranometer
Pyrgeometer
Quantometer
Rangefinder
Rocketsonde
Sclerometer
Screwdriver
Seismograph
Seismoscope
Solarimeter
Spherometer
Stactometer
Stadiometer
Stauroscope
Stereometer
Stereoscope
Stethoscope
Stroboscope
Synthesizer
Tacheometer

Thermometer
Thermoscope
Vaporimeter
Vectorscope
Velocimeter
Voltammeter

12 letters:
Aethrioscope
Bronchoscope
Camera lucide
Cephalometer
Densitometer
Electrometer
Galactometer
Galvanometer
Galvanoscope
Harmonograph
Harmonometer
Inclinometer
Isoteniscope
Kaleidoscope
Katharometer
Keraunograph
Laryngoscope
Meteorograph
Myringoscope
Nephelometer
Oscilloscope
Penetrometer
Pinniewinkle
Psychrometer
Respirometer
Scarificator
Sensitometer
Snooperscope
Spectrometer
Spectroscope
Sphygmograph
Sphygmophone
Synchroscope
Tellurometer
Turbidimeter
Urethroscope
Zenith-sector

13 letters:
Accelerometer
Alcoholometer
Dipleidoscope
Opthalmometer
Pharyngoscope
Phonendoscope
Pneumatograph
Pneumatometer
Potentiometer
Pyrheliometer
Reflectometer
Refractometer
Saccharometer
Sigmoidoscope
Stalagmometer
Tachistoscope
Weatherometer

14 letters:
Diffractometer
Interferometer
Oesophagoscope
Ophthalmometer
Ophthalmoscope
Phosphoroscope
Pyrophotometer
Scintillascope
Scintilloscope
Spinthariscope
Synchronoscope

15 letters:
Phenakestoscope
Radiogoniometer
Telestereoscope

16 letters:
Sphygmoma-
nometer
Telespectroscope

17 letters:
Spectrophotometer

Insubordinate Contumacious, Faction, Mutinous, Rebel, Refractory
Insubstantial Airy, Brief, Flimsy, Frothy, Illusory, Jackstraw, Slight, Syllabub, Thin,
Wispy, Ye(a)sty

Insufferable Egregious
Insufficient Exiguous, Inadequate, Poor, Scant, Shortfall
Insular Isolated, Moated, Narrow, Xenophobe
Insulate, Insulation, Insulator Biotite, Corkboard, Dielectric, Electret, Enwind, Grommet, Haybox, Inwind, Lagging, Mica, Non-conductor, Padding, Pugging, Sleeving, Tog
Insult(ing) Abuse, Affront, Aspersion, Barb, Becall, Charientism, Contumely, Cut, Dyslogistic, Embarrass, Facer, Fig, Injurious, Lese-majesty, Mud, Mud-pie, Offend, Opprobrious, Rip on, Skit, Slagging, Sledge, Slight, Slur, Snub, Trauma, Uncomplimentary, Verbal, Yenta, Yente
Insure(r), Insurance Abandonee, Accident, Cover, Endowment, Fidelity, Fire, Group, Guarantee, Hedge, Indemnity, Knock-for-knock, Life, Lloyds, Marine, Medibank, Medicare, Mutual, National, Participating, Pluvius, Policy, Public liability, Reversion, Security, Social, Term, Underwrite, Whole-life
Insurgent, Insurrection Cade, Jacquerie, Mutiny, Outbreak, Pandy, Rebel, Revolt, Sedition, Uprising, Whisky
▷ **Insurgent** *may indicate* 'reversed'
Intact Complete, Entire, Inviolate, Unused, Whole
Intaglio, Intagliate Diaglyph, Incavo
Intake Absorption, Entry, Fuel
Integer, Integral Component, Definite, Entire, Improper, Inbuilt, Indefinite, Needful, Number, Organic, Unitary
Integrate(d), Integration Amalgamate, Assimilate, Combine, Coordinate, Fuse, Harmonious, Holistic, Large-scale, Mainstream, Merge, Postural, Tightknit
Integrity Honesty, Principle, Probity, Rectitude, Strength, Uprightness, Whole
Integument Coat, Primine, Secundine, Sheath, Skin, Velum
Intellect, Intellectual(s) Academic, Aptitude, Belligerati, Brain, Cerebral, Cultural, Dianoetic, Egghead, Eggmass, Far-out, Genius, Grey matter, Highbrow, Intelligent, Intelligentsia, -ist, Learned, Literati, Luminary, Mastermind, Mental(ity), Mind, Noesis, Noetic, Noology, Nous, Profound, Reason, Sublime, Titan
Intelligence, Intelligent Advice, Artificial, Boss, Brainiac, Brains, Bright, CIA, Discerning, Dope, Eggmass, Emotional, Esprit, G, Grey matter, GRU, Humint, Info, Ingenious, IQ, Knowledgeable, Machiavellian, Machine, MI, Mossad, Mother wit, News, Pate, Pointy-headed, Rational, Sconce, Sense, Sharp, Shrewd, Smart, Spetsnaz, Spetznaz, Tidings, Wit
Intelligible Exoteric
Intemperance Acrasia, Crapulent, Excess, Gluttony, Immoderation
Intend(ed), Intending Allot, Betrothed, Contemplate, Design, Destine, Ettle, Fiancé(e), Going, → MEAN, Meditate, Planned, Propose, Purpose
Intense, Intensify, Intensity Acute, Aggravate, Ardent, Compound, Crash, Crescendo, Deep, Depth, Earnest, Earthquake, Emotional, Enhance, Escalate, Estro, Excess, Extreme, Fervent, Keen, Luminous, Might, Profound, Radiant, Redouble, Sharpen, Vehement, Vivid
Intent, Intention(al) À dessein, Animus, Deliberate, Dole, Earnest, Ettle, Hellbent, Manifesto, Mens rea, Mind, Paradoxical, Prepense, Purpose, Rapt, Resolute, Set, Studious, Systematic, Thought, Tire, Witting, Yrapt
Inter Bury, Entomb
Interaction Chemistry, Enantiodromia, Solvation
Interbreed(ing) Miscegenation
Intercalation Embolism
Intercede, Intercession Mediate, Negotiate, Plead, Prayer

Intercept Absciss(a), Abscisse, Check, Hack, Meet, Waylay

Interchange(d) Altercation, Alternate, Clover-leaf, Crossing, Equivalent, Junction, Mutual, Permute, Reciprocate, Substitute, Transpose

Intercom Entryphone®

Intercourse Arse, Ball, Bang, Bed, Blow job, Boff, Bone, Bonk, Buggery, Bukkake, Bump, Coition, Coitus, Commerce, Commixture, Congress, Connection, Consummation, Converse, Copulation, Cottaging, Coupling, Cover, Cunnilingus, Deflowering, Enjoy, Fluff, Fornication, Gam, Gamahuche, Gamaruche, Gangbang, Greens, Hochmagandy, Houghmagandie, Jass, Jazz, Jig(-a)-jig, Jiggy, Jiggy-jiggy, Jump, Knee-trembler, Knock, Know(ledge), Koap, Laying, Leg-over, Lie with, Make, Marriage bed, Nail, Naughty, Necrophilia, Nookie, Nooky, Poke, Poontang, Pussy, Quickie, Ride, Rim, Roger, Root, Rump, Rumpy(-pumpy), Satyriasis, Screw, Sexual, Shaft, Shag, Shtup, Sixty-nine, Sociality, Sodomy, Soixante-neuf, Stuff, Swive, Tail, Teledildonics, The other, Tie, Trade, Tribadism, Trock, Troilism, Truck, Whoredom

Interdict Ban, Forbid, Prohibit, Taboo

Interest(ed), Interesting Amusive, APR, Attention, Behalf, Benefit, Clou, Compound, Concern, Contango, Controlling, Coupon, Dividend, Ear-grabbing, Engage, Engross, Enthusiasm, Fad, Fascinate, Fee-simple, Fee-tail, Grab, Hot, Human, Import, Income, Insurable, Int(o), Intrigue, Landed, Life, Line, Negative, Part, Partisan, Percentage, Readable, Rente, Respect, Revenue, Reversion, Riba, Scene, Sepid, Share, Side, Sideline, Simple, Spice, Stake, Tickle, Topical, Usage, Usance, Use, Usure, Usury, Vested, Vig(orish), Warm

Interfere(r), Interference Busybody, Clutter, Disrupt, Hamper, Hinder, Intrude, Mar, → **MEDDLE**, Molest, Nose, Officious, Pry, Radio, Shash, Shot noise, Static, Tamper, Teratogen

Interferometer Etalon

Intergrowth Perthite

Interim Break, Meantime, Meanwhile, Temporary

Interior Backblocks, Cyclorama, Domestic, Innards, Innate, Inner, Inside, Outback, Plain, Up-country, Vitals

Interject(ion) Ahem, Begorra(h), Chime-in, Gertcha, Haith, Hoo-oo, Interpolate, Lackaday, Lumme, Nation, Sese(y), Sessa, 'Sheart, 'Slid, Tarnation, Tush

Interlace Mingle, Pleach, Weave, Wreathe

Interlock Dovetail, Engage, Knit, Tangle

Interlocutor Elihu, MC, Questioner

Interloper Gate-crasher, Intruder, Trespasser

Interlude Antimask, Antimasque, Divertimento, Entr'acte, Interruption, Kyogen, Lunch-hour, Meantime, Pause, Verset

Intermediary, Intermediate Agent, Bardo, Comprador(e), Contact man, Go-between, In-between, Instar, Mean, Medial, Mesne, Mezzanine, Middleman, Middle-of-the-road, Thirdsman, Transitional

Interminable Endless, Infinite, Unending

Intermission Apyrexia, Break, Interval, Pause, Recess

Intermittent Broken, Fitful, Off-on, Periodic, Random, Spasmic, Spasmodic, Sporadic

Intern(e) Confine, Doctor, Impound, Restrict, Trainee

Internal Domestic, Inner, Internecine, Inward, Within

International Cap, Cosmopolitan, Fourth, Lion, Second, Test, Trotskyist, UN, Universal

Internet Dotcom, Infobahn, URL, Web, WWW

Interpolate(r), Interpolation Diaskeuast, Insert, Intercalate, Interrupt,

Spatchcock, Tmesis

Interpose Butt in, Horn in, Interject, Interlay, Interprone, Intervene, Spatchcock, Stickle

Interpret(er) Aread, Ar(r)e(e)de, Conster, Construe, Decipher, Decode, Dobhash, Dragoman, Exegete, Explain, Exponent, Expositor, Expound, Glossator, Hermeneutist, Hierophant, Jehovist, Latiner, Lingster, Linguistic, Linkster, Medium, Moonshee, Moonshi, Moralise, Munshi, Oneirocritic, Oneiroscopist, Origenist, Prophet, Read, Rede, Reed(e), Render, Represent, Spokesman, Textualist, → **TRANSLATE**, Truchman, Ulema

Interpretation Anagoge, Anagogy, Construction, Copenhagen, Eisegesis, Euhemerism, Exegesis, Exegete, Gematria, Gloss(ary), Gospel, Halacha(h), Halakah, Hermeneutics, Midrash, Oneirocriticism, Portray, Reading, Rede, Rendition, Spin, Targum, Translation, Tropology

Interrogate, Interrogation Catechism, Debrief(ing), Enquire, Examine, Grill, Maieutic, Pump, → **QUESTION**, Quiz

Interrupt(ion), Interrupter Ahem, Aposiopesis, Blip, Break, Butt, Chequer, Chip in, Disturb, Entr'acte, Heckle, Hiatus, Intercept, Interfere, Interpellate, Interpolate, Interpose, Interregnum, Intrusion, Overtalk, Pause, Portage, Rheotome, Stop, Suspend, Time-out

Intersect(ion) Carfax, Carfox, Carrefour, Chiasm(a), Cross, Crunode, Cut, Decussate, Divide, Groin, Metacentre, Orthocentre, Trace

Intersperse Dot, Interlard, Interpose, Scatter, Sprinkle

Interstice Areole, Interlude, Pore, Space

Intertwine Braid, Impleach, Knit, Lace, Plait, Splice, Twist, Writhe

Interval Between, Break, Breather, Class, Closed, Comma, Confidence, Contour, Diapente, Diastaltic, Diatesseron, Diesis, Distance, Ditone, Duodecimo, Entr'acte, Fifth, Gap, Half-time, Harmonic, Hiatus, Hourly, Interim, Interlude, Interregnum, Interruption, Interspace, Interstice, Limma, Lunitidal, Meantime, Meantone, Meanwhile, Melodic, Microtone, Minor third, Ninth, Octave, Open, Ottava, Perfect, Pycnon, Respite, Rest, Schisma, Semitone, Seventh, Sixth, Space, Span, Spell, Tritone, Twelfth, Unison, Wait

Intervene, Intervention Agency, Arbitrate, Expromission, Interfere, Interjacent, Interrupt, Mediate, Mesne, Theurgy, Up

Interview Audience, Audition, Beeper, Conference, Doorstep, Examine, Hearing, Oral, Press conference, See, Vox pop

Interweave, Interwoven, Interwove Entwine, Interlace, Monogram, Pirnit, Plait, Plash, Pleach, Raddle, Wreathed

Intestate Heirless, Unwilling

Intestinal, Intestine(s) Bowel, Chit(ter)lings, Derma, Duodenum, Enteric, Entrails, Guts, Harigals, Innards, Jejunum, Kishke, Large, Mesenteron, Omenta, Rectum, Small, Splanchnic, Thairm, Tripes, Viscera

Intimacy, Intimate(ly) Achates, À deux, Boon, Bosom, Close, Communion, Connote, Familiar, Friend, Heart-to-heart, Inmost, Innuendo, Intrigue, Nearness, Opine, Pack, Private, Signal, Special, Thick, Throng, Warm, Well

Intimation Clue, Hint, Implication, Inkling, Innuendo, Si quis

Intimidate, Intimidating Awe, Browbeat, Bulldoze, Bully, Cow, Daunt, Dragon, Hector, Niramiai, Psych, Threaten, Tyrannise, Unnerve

Into At, Intil, Within

Intolerant, Intolerable Allergic, Bigotry, Egregious, Excessive, Illiberal, Impatient, Impossible, Ombrophobe, Self-righteous

Intone, Intonation Cadence, Just, Twang

In touch Au fait

Intoxicate(d), Intoxicant, Intoxicating, Intoxication Alcoholic, Areca-nut, Benj, Bhang, Coca, Corn, Cup, Disguise, Fuddle, Ganja, Half-cut, Heady, → **HIGH**, Hocus, Hou high, Inebriate, Jag, Merry, Mescal, Peyote, Pixil(l)ated, Rumbullion, Shroom, Slewed, Soma, Sozzle, Spirituous, Swacked, Temulent, Whiskeyfied, Whiskified, Zonked

Intractable Disobedient, Kittle, Mulish, Obdurate, Perverse, Surly, Unruly, Wilful

Intransigent Adamant, Inflexible, Rigid, Uncompromising

Intransitive Neuter, Objectless

Intrepid Aweless, Bold, Brave, Dauntless, Doughty, Firm, Gallant, → **RESOLUTE**, Valiant

Intricate Complex, Daedal(ian), Daedale, Dedal, Gordian, Intrince, Involute, Knotty, Pernickety, Sinuous, Tirlie-wirlie, Tricky, Vitruvian

Intrigue(r), Intriguing Affaire, Artifice, Brigue, Cabal, Camarilla, Cloak and dagger, Collogue, Conspiracy, Fascinate, Hotbed, Ignatian, Interest, Jesuit, Jobbery, Liaison, Machinate, Plot, Politic, Rat, → **SCHEME**, Stairwork, Strategy, Traffic, Trinketer

Intrinsic(ally) Basically, Genuine, Inherent, Innate, Inner, Per se

▷ **Intrinsically** *may indicate* something within a word

Introduce(r), Introduction, Introductory Acquaint, Anacrusis, Curtain-raiser, Debut, Emcee, Enseam, Exordial, Foreword, Immit, Import, Induct, Initiate, Inject, Insert, Instil(l), Institutes, Intercalate, Interpolate, Intrada, Introit, Isagogic, Lead-in, Opening, Phase in, Plant, Preamble, Preface, Preliminary, Prelude, Prelusory, Preparatory, Present, Presentment, Proem, Prolegomena, Prolegomenon, Prologue, Proponent, Referral, Standfirst, Start, Usher

▷ **Introduction** *may indicate* a first letter

Intromission Vicious

Introspective Musing, Reflex, Ruminant

▷ **In trouble** *may indicate* an anagram

Introvert(ed) Cerebrotonic, Ingrow, In-toed, Invaginate, Reserved, Shy

Intrude(r), Intrusion, Intrusive Abate, Aggress, Annoy, Bother, Burglar, Derby dog, Disturb, → **ENCROACH**, Gatecrash, Hacker, Interloper, Invade, Meddle, Nosey, Personal, Porlocking, Presume, Raid, Sorn, Trespass

Intuition, Intuitive Belief, ESP, Hunch, Insight, Instinct, Inwit, Noumenon, Premonition, Presentiment, Seat-of-the-pants, Telepathy, Theosophy, Visceral

▷ **In two words** *may indicate* a word to be split

Inuit Caribou, Eskimo, Inuk, Yupik

Inundate, Inundation Flood, Overflow, Overwhelm, Submerge, Swamp

Inure Acclimatise, Accustom, Harden, Season, Steel

Invade(r), Invasion Angle, Attack, Attila, Dane, Descent, Encroach, Goth, Hacker, Hengist, Horsa, Hun, Infest, Inroad, Intruder, Irrupt, Jute, Lombard, Martian, Norman, Norsemen, Ostrogoth, Overlord, Overrun, Permeate, Raid, Trespass, Vandal, Viking, Visigoth

Invalid(ate), Invalidation Bad, Bogus, Bunbury, Cancel, Chronic, Clinic, Defunct, Diriment, Erroneous, Expired, False, Inauthentic, Inform, Inoperative, Irritate, Lapsed, Nugatory, Null, Nullify, Overturn, Quash, Refute, Shut-in, Terminate, Valetudinarian, Vitiate, Void

Invaluable Essential, Excellent, Precious, Useful

Invariable, Invariably Always, Constant, Eternal, Habitual, Perpetual, Steady, Uniform

Invective Abuse, Billingsgate, Diatribe, Philippic, Reproach, Ribaldry, Tirade

Inveigh Declaim, Denounce, Protest, Rail

Invent(ion), Inventive Adroit, Babe, Baby, Brainchild, Chimera, Coin, Contrive, Cook up, → CREATE, Daedal, Design, Device, Excogitate, Fabricate, Fain, Fantasia, Feign, Figment, Imaginary, Improvise, Ingenuity, Mint, Myth, Originate, Patent, Plateau, Pretence, Resourceful, Synectics, Whittle, Wit

Inventor Archimedes, Arkwright, Artificer, Author, Babbage, Baird, Bell, Biro, Boys, Bramah, Brix, Cartwright, Celsius, Coiner, Creator, Crompton, Daedalus, Edison, Engineer, Galileo, Geiger, Hansom, Jubal, Marconi, Maxim, Mercator, Mills, Minié, Mint-master, Morse, Nernst, Newcomen, Nobel, Patentee, Savery, Schmidt, Siemens, Solvay, Tesla, Torricelli, Tull, Watt, Wheatstone, Whitney

Inventory Account, Index, Itemise, List, Perpetual, Personality, Register, Steelbow, Stock, Terrier

Inverse, Inversion, Invert(ed) Anastrophe, Antimetabole, Antimetathesis, Capsize, Chiasmus, Entropion, Entropium, First, Homosexuality, Opposite, Overset, Reciprocal, Resupinate, Reverse, Second, Tête-bêche, Turn, Upset

Invertebrate Acanthocephalan, Annelida, Anthozoan, Arrowworm, Arthropod, Brachiopod, Cnidarian, Coelenterate, Crinoid, Ctenophore, Decapod, Echinoderm, Echinoid, Euripterid, Feather star, Gast(e)ropod, Globigerina, Hydrozoan, Mollusc, Onychophoran, Parazoan, Pauropod, Peritrich, Platyhelminth, Polyp, Poriferan, Protostome, Rotifer, Roundworm, Scyphozoan, Sea-cucumber, Sea-lily, → SHELLFISH, Slug, Spineless, Spoonworm, Starfish, Tardigrade, Trepang, Trochelminth, Unio, Water bear, Worm, Zoophyte

Invest(or), Investment Agamemnon, Ambient, Angel, Bate, Beleaguer, Besiege, Bet, Blockade, Blue-chip, Capitalist, Collins Street farmer, Contrarian, Dignify, Dub, Embark, Empanoply, Enclothe, Endow, Enrobe, Ethical, Financier, Flutter, Gilt, Girt, Holding, Infeft, Install, Inward, On, Pannicle, Panniculus, Parlay, Place, Portfolio, Put, Ring, Robe, Saver, Share, Siege, Sink, Spec, Speculation, Stag, Stake, Stock, Surround, Tessa, Tie up, Trust, Trustee, Venture, Zaitech

▷ **Invest** *may indicate* one word surrounding another

Investigate, Investigator, Investigation Canvass, Case, Chart, CID, Delve, Examine, Explore, Fed, Ferret, Fieldwork, Go into, Gumshoe, Hunt, Inquest, Inquirendo, Inquiry, Inquisition, McCarthyism, Nose, Organon, Organum, Probe, Pry, Quester, Rapporteur, Research, Scan, Scout, Screen, Scrutinise, Search, Sleuth, Snoop, Study, Suss, Tec, Test, T-man, Track, Try, Zetetic

Investiture Award, Inauguration

Inveterate Chronic, Double-dyed, Dyed-in-the-wool, Engrained, Habitual, Hardened

Invidious Harmful, Hostile, Malign

Invigilator Proctor

Invigorate, Invigorating, Invigoration Analeptic, Brace, Brisk, Cheer, Elixir, Energise, Enliven, Fortify, Insinew, Pep, Refresh, Renew, Stimulate, Tonic, Vital

Invincible Almighty, Brave, Stalwart, Valiant

Inviolatable, Inviolate, Inviolable Intemerate, Sacred, Sacrosanct

Invisible Blind, Hidden, Imageless, Infra-red, Secret, Tusche, Unseen

Invite, Invitation, Inviting Ask, Attract, Bid, Call, Card, Overture, → REQUEST, Solicit, Stiffie, Summons, Tempt, Toothsome, Woo

Invocation, Invoke Appeal, Call, Conjure, Curse, Entreat, Epiclesis, Solicit, White rabbits

Invoice Account, Bill, Docket, Itemise, Manifest, Pro forma

Involuntary Automatic, Instinctive, Unwitting

Involve(d), Involvement Active, Commitment, Complicate, Complicit, Concern,

Embroil, Engage, Entail, Envelop, Imbroglio, Immerse, → **IMPLICATE**, Include, Intricate, Meet, Necessitate, Participate, Tangle

▷ **Involved** *may indicate* an anagram

Inward(s) Afferent, Centripuntal, Homefelt, Introrse, Mental, Private, Varus, Within

Iodine I, Kelp, Thyroxin(e)

Iolanthe Peri

Ion Ammonium, Anion, Carbanion, Carborium, Hydrogen, Hydronium, Hydroxyl, Isomer, Onium, Zwitterion

Ionian Iastic, Te(i)an

Iota Atom, Jot, Subscript, Whit

IOU Cedula, Market, PN, Shinplaster, Vowels

IOW Vectis

IRA Provisional, Provo

Iran(ian) Babist, Kurd, Mede, Osset, Pahlavi, Parsee, Pehlevi, Ta(d)jik, Tadzhik

Irascible Choleric, Crusty, Fiery, Peevish, Snappy, Tetchy, Toustie

Irate Angry, Cross, Infuriated, Wrathful

Ire Anger, Bait, Cholera, Fury, Rage, Wrath

Ireland Composer, Deirdre, Gaeltacht, Hibernia, Innisfail, Irena, IRL, Iverna, Twenty-six counties

Irenic Peaceful

Iridescence, Iridescent Chatoyant, Flambé, Opaline, Reflet, Shimmering, Shot, Water-gall

Iridium Ir

Iris Areola, Eye, Flag, Fleur-de-lis, Gladdon, Ixia, Lily, Lis, Orris, Rainbow, Roast-beef plant, Sedge, Seg, Stinking, Sunbow

Irish(man) Bark, Bog-trotter, Boy, Celt(ic), Clan-na-gael, Defender, Dermot, Dubliner, Eamon(n), Eirann, Erse, Fenian, Gael, Gaeltacht, Goidel, Greek, Keltic, Kern(e), Mick(e)(y), Middle, Milesian, Mulligan, Ogamic, Orange(man), Ostmen, Paddy(-whack), Partholon, Pat(rick), Rapparee, Redshank, Reilly, Riley, Rory, Ryan, Sean, Shoneen, Teague, Temper, Ultonian, Whiteboy, Wildgeese

Irk(some) Annoy, Bother, Irritate, Needle, Tedious

Iron(s), Ironwork(s) Airn, Alpha, Angle, Beta, Carron, Cast, Cautery, Chains, Chalybeate, Chancellor, Channel, Climbing, Coquimbite, Corrugated, Cramp(on), Crimp, Cross, Curling, Curtain, Delta, Derringer, Dogs, Eagle-stone, Fayalite, Fe, Ferredoxin, Ferrite, Fetter, Fiddley, Flip-dog, Galvanised, Gamma, Gem, Golfclub, Goose, Grappling, Grim, Grozing, → **GUN**, Gyve, Horse, Ingot, Italian, Kamacite, Laterite, Lily, Lofty, Long, Maiden, Malleable, Marcasite, Mars, Martensite, Mashie, Mashy, Merchant, Meteoric, Mitis (metal), Pea, Pig, Pinking, → **PRESS**, Pro-metal, Rabble, Rations, Rod, Sad, Scrap, Shooting, Short, Smoother, Soft, Soldering, Specular, Spiegeleisen, Steam, Stirrup, Stretching, Strong, Taconite, Taggers, Terne, Tin terne, Toggle, Tow, Wafer, Waffle, Wear, Wedge, White, Wrought

Iron age Latene, Villanovan

Ironic, Irony Antiphrasis, Asteism, Dramatic, Meiosis, Metal, Ridicule, Sarcasm, Satire, Socratic, Tongue-in-cheek, Tragic, Trope, Wry

Ironside Edmund

Ironwood Pyengadu

▶ **Ironwork(s)** *see* **IRON**

Irrational Absurd, Brute, Delirious, Foolish, Illogical, Number, Superstitious, Surd, Wild

Irreconcilable Poles apart

Irrefutable Evident, Positive, Undeniable
Irregular(ity) Abnormal, Alloiostrophus, Anomaly, Aperiodic, A salti, Asymmetric,
  Atypical, Bashi-bazouk, Blotchy, Crazy, Episodic, Erratic, Evection, Fitful, Flawed,
  Formless, Free-form, Guerilla, Heteroclitic, Incondite, Inordinate, Jitter, Kink,
  Occasional, Orthotone, Para-military, Partisan, Patchy, Rambling, Random, Rough,
  Scalene, Scrawl, Sebundy, Sharawadgi, Sharawaggi, Snatchy, Solecism, Sporadic,
  TA, Uneven, Unsteady, Unwonted, Variable, Wayward, Zigzag
▷ **Irregular** *may indicate* an anagram
Irrelevant Academic, Digression, Extraneous, Gratuitous, Immaterial, Inept,
  Non sequitur, Ungermane, Unrelated
Irreligious Heathen, Impious, Pagan, Profane
Irremedial Hopeless, Incurable, Laches
Irrepressible Resilient
Irreproachable Blameless, Spotless, Stainless
Irresistible Almighty, Endearing, Inevitable, Mesmeric, Overwhelming
Irresolute, Irresolution Aboulia, Doubtful, Hesitant, Timid, Unsure, Wavery,
  Weak-willed
Irresponsible Capricious, Feckless, Flighty, Fly-by-night, Slap-happy, Strawen,
  Trigger-happy, Wanton, Wildcat
Irreverent Blasphemous, Disrespectful, Godless, Impious, Profane
Irrigate, Irrigation Canalise, Colonic, Douche, Enema, Flood, Get, Water
Irritable, Irritability, Irritant, Irritate(d), Irritation Acerbate, Anger, Annoy,
  Bête noire, Blister, Bother, Bug, Chafe, Chauff, Chippy, Chocker, Crabbit, Crabby,
  Cross-grained, Crosspatch, Crotchety, Crusty, Dod, Dyspeptic, Eat, Eczema, Edgy,
  Emboil, Enchafe, Erethism, Ewk, Exasperate, Fantod, Feverish, Fiery, Fleabite,
  Frabbit, Fractious, Fraught, Fretful, Gall, Get, Goad, Grate, Gravel, Hasty, Heck,
  Humpy, Intertrigo, Irk, Itch, Jangle, Livery, Mardy, Narky, Needle, Nettle, Niggly,
  Ornery, Peckish, Peevish, Peppery, Pesky, Pestilent(ial), Pet, Petulance, Pinprick,
  Pique, Prickly, Provoke, Rag'd, Ragde, Rankle, Rasp, Rattle, Ratty, Rile, Roil, Rub,
  Ruffle, Savin(e), Scratchy, Shirty, Snappy, Snit, Snitchy, Splenetic, Sting, Tease,
  Techy, Testy, Tetchy, Thorn, Tickle, Tiresome, Toey, Touchy, Uptight, → **VEX**, Waxy,
  Windburn, Yuke
▷ **Irritated** *may indicate* an anagram
Irving Actor, Berlin
Is Est, Ist
Isaiah Is
Isinglass Carlock, Fish-glue, Mica, Sturgeon
Islam(ic) Al Queda, Crescent, Druse, Druz(e), Hamas, Kurd(ish), Senus(si), Sheriat,
  Shia(h), Shiite, Sunni(te), Taleban, Taliban, Wah(h)abi
Island, Isle(t) Ait, Archipelago, Atoll, Cay, Char, Desert, Eyot, Floating, Holm, I,
  Inch, Is, Key, Lagoon, Mainland, Motu, Refuge, Traffic

ISLANDS

2 letters:	Fyn	Sea	Attu
TT	Hoy	Yap	Bali
	Kos		Biak
3 letters:	Man	*4 letters:*	Bute
Aru	May	Amoy	Calf
Cos	Rat	Aran	Cebu
Diu	Rum	Arru	Coll

Cook
Cuba
Dogs
Eigg
Elba
Erin
Fair
Fiji
Guam
Heat
Herm
Holy
Hova
Idse
Iona
Java
Jolo
Jura
Keos
King
Line
Long
Mahe
Maui
Mazu
Mona
Muck
Mull
Niue
Oahu
Rona
Ross
Saba
Sark
Skye
Spud
Truk
Uist
Unst
Wake
Yell

5 letters:
Aland
Apple
Arran
Aruba
Banka
Banks
Barra
Batan

Belle
Bioko
Bohol
Bonin
Canna
Capri
Ceram
Cheju
Chios
Clare
Cocos
Coney
Coral
Corfu
Crete
Delos
Disko
Ellis
Faial
Farne
Faroe
Fayal
Funen
Haiti
Hondo
Ibiza
Islay
Isola
Iviza
Jerba
Kiska
Kuril
Lanai
Lewis
Leyte
Lundy
Luzon
Maewo
Malta
Matsu
Melos
Nauru
Naxos
Nevis
North
Oland
Ormuz
Palau
Panay
Papua
Paros

Pelew
Pemba
Pines
Qeshm
Qishm
Reil's
Rhode
Samar
Samoa
Samos
Saria
Seram
South
Spice
Sumba
Sunda
Thera
Thule
Timor
Tiree
Tonga
Upolu
Whale
White
Wight
Youth
Zante

6 letters:
Achill
Aegean
Aegina
Amager
Andros
Aurora
Avalon
Azores
Baffin
Banaba
Bangka
Barrow
Bedloe
Bikini
Borneo
Bounty
Butung
Caicos
Canvey
Cayman
Ceylon
Chiloe

Cyprus
Devil's
Diomed
Djerba
Easter
Eelpie
Ellice
Euboea
Flores
Fraser
Hainan
Harris
Hawaii
Hobart
Honshu
Hormuz
Icaria
Imbros
Indies
Insula
Ionian
Ischia
Ithaca
Jersey
Kodiak
Kurile
Kvaley
Kyushu
Labuan
Laputa
Lemnos
Lesbos
Leucas
Leukas
Levkas
Lipari
Lizard
Lombok
Madura
Majuro
Marajo
Mercer
Midway
Negros
Ogygia
Paphos
Patmos
Penang
Pharos
Philae
Phuket

Pladdy	Celebes	Palmyra	Barbados
Quemoy	Channel	Paracel	Bathurst
Ramsey	Chatham	Phoenix	Billiton
Rhodes	Cipango	Purbeck	Blefuscu
Rialto	Corsica	Rathlin	Bora-Bora
Robben	Crannog	Reunion	Bornholm
Royale	Curacao	Roanoke	Canaries
Ryukyu	Cythera	Rockall	Caroline
Safety	Diomede	Salamis	Catalina
Saipan	Elvissa	San Juan	Choiseul
Savage	Emerald	Sheppey	Colonsay
Savaii	Eriskay	Shikoku	Cyclades
Scilly	Falster	Society	Dominica
Sicily	Frisian	Socotra	Falkland
Skerry	Fur Seal	Sokotra	Farquhar
Skyros	Gambier	Solomon	Flinders
Snares	Gilbert	Spratly	Foulness
Soemba	Gotland	St Croix	Friendly
Soenda	Grenada	Stewart	Gothland
Staffa	Hawaiki	St Kilda	Gottland
Staten	Howland	St Kitts	Guernsey
Tahiti	Ireland	St Lucia	Hamilton
Taiwan	Iwo Jima	Sumatra	Hatteras
Thanet	Jamaica	Sumbawa	Hebrides
Thasos	Keeling	Suqutra	Hokkaido
Tobago	Laaland	Surtsey	Hong Kong
Tresco	Ladrone	Tenedos	Jan Mayen
Tubuai	La Palma	Tokelau	Kangaroo
Tuvalu	Leeward	Tortola	Kermadec
Unimak	Liberty	Tortuga	Kiribati
Ushant	Lofoten	Tutuila	Ladrones
Veneti	Lolland	Visayan	Lilliput
Virgin	Madeira	Volcano	Lord Howe
	Majorca	Waihake	Luggnagg
7 letters:	Mariana	Watling	Mackinac
Aeolian	Masbate	Western	Maldives
Aldabra	Mayotte	Wrangel	Mallorca
Amboina	Mindoro	Zealand	Malvinas
Andaman	Minicoy	Zetland	Marianas
Antigua	Minorca		Marquesa
Austral	Molokai	*8 letters:*	Marshall
Bahamas	Moreton	Alcatraz	Mauna Loa
Baranof	Mykonos	Alderney	Melville
Barbuda	Nicobar	Aleutian	Mindanao
Basilan	Norfolk	Amindiva	Miquelon
Batavia	Oceania	Anglesey	Moluccas
Battery	Okinawa	Anguilla	Mustique
Bedloe's	Orcades	Antilles	Njazidja
Bermuda	Orkneys	Atlantis	Northern
Bonaire	Pacific	Auckland	Pelagian
Cartier	Palawan	Balearic	Pitcairn

Pleasant
Portland
Pribilof
Principe
Sakhalin
Sandwich
Sardinia
Schouten
Shetland
Soembawa
Somerset
South Sea
Sporades
Sri Lanka
St Helena
St Helier
St Martin
St Thomas
Sulawesi
Svalbard
Sverdrup
Tasmania
Tenerife
Terceira
Thousand
Thursday
Trinidad
Tsushima
Unalaska
Venetian
Victoria
Viti Levu
Windward
Zanzibar

9 letters:

Admiralty
Alexander
Andreanof
Anticosti
Antipodes
Ascension
Barataria
Belle Isle
Benbecula
Chichagof
Christmas
Elephanta
Ellesmere
Falklands

Fortunate
Galapagos
Governors
Greenland
Hainan Tao
Halmahera
Innisfree
Jamestown
Kerguelen
Laccadive
Lampedusa
Lanzarote
Macquarie
Manhattan
Margarita
Marquesas
Mascarene
Mauritius
Melanesia
Nantucket
New Guinea
Polynesia
Rangitoto
Rarotonga
Runnymede
Saghalien
Santorini
Sao Miguel
Shetlands
Sjaelland
Stromboli
St Vincent
Teneriffe
Trobriand
Vancouver
Vanua Levu
Walcheren

10 letters:

Basse-Terre
Bermoothes
Campobello
Cape Barren
Cape Breton
Cephalonia
Corregidor
Dodecanese
Formentera
Grand Manan
Grenadines

Guadeloupe
Heligoland
Hispaniola
Isle Royale
Kiritimati
Langerhans
Madagascar
Manitoulin
Marinduque
Martinique
Micronesia
Montserrat
New Britain
New Georgia
New Ireland
Pescadores
Poor Knight
Puerto Rico
Sahghalien
Samothrace
Sandalwood
Seychelles
Three Kings
Vesteralen
West Indies
Whitsunday

11 letters:

Austronesia
Dry Tortugas
Glubdubdrib
Grand Bahama
Grand Canary
Grande-Terre
Guadalcanal
Lakshadweep
Lesser Sunda
Lindisfarne
Mount Desert
New Siberian
Pantelleria
Philippines
San Salvador
Southampton
South Orkney
Spitsbergen

12 letters:

Bougainville
Cassiterides

Glubbdubdrib
Greater Sunda
Marie Galante
New Caledonia
Newfoundland
Nusa Tenggara
Prince Edward
San Cristobal
Santa Barbara
Seringapatam
South Georgia
Torres Strait

13 letters:

Espiritu Santo
Forneaux Group
Fuerteventura
Juan Fernandez
New Providence
Prince of Wales
Santa Catalina
South Shetland

14 letters:

Amboina oceanic
D'Entrecasteaux
Lesser Antilles
Papua New
 Guinea
Queen Charlotte
Queen Elizabeth
Tristan da Cunha
Turks and Caicos
Vestmannaeyjar

15 letters:

Greater Antilles
Mont-Saint-Michel
Wallis and Futuna

16 letters:

Heard and
 McDonald

17 letters:

Fernando de
 Noronha

Islander Chian, Cretan, D(a)yak, Filipino, Kanaka, Kelper, Laputan, Madeiran, Maltese, Mauritian, Native, Nesiot, Newfie, Orcadian, Parian, Rhodian, Samiot, Sican, Singalese, Taiwanese
Isle of Wight Vectis
Isn't Aint, Nis, Nys
Isolate(d) Ancress, Apart, Backwater, Cleidoic, Cut off, Desolate, Enclave, Enisle, Incommunicado, Inisle, In vacuo, Island, Lone, Maroon, Pocket, Quarantine, Sea-girt, Seclude, Secret, Segregate, Separate, Sequester, Six-finger country, Solitary, Sporadic, Stray
Isomer Carotene, Carotin, Carvacrol, Geranial, Neral, Pinene, Theophylline
Isopod Gribble
Isosceles Triangle
Isotope Actinon, Cobalt-60, Deuterium, Iodine-131, Muonium, Protium, Strontium-90, Thoron, Tritium
Israel(i) Beulah, IL, Meir, Sabra
Issue(s) Bonus, Capitalization, Children, Come, Crux, Debouch, Denouement, Derive, Disclose, Dispense, Edition, Effluence, Egress, → **EMANATE**, Emerge, Emit, Escape, Exit, Exodus, Family, Feigned, Fiduciary, Flotation, Fungible, General, Government, Gush, Immaterial, Ish, Litter, Material, Matter, Mise, Number, Offspring, Outflow, Part, Privatization, Proof, Publish, Result, Rights, Sally, Seed, Side, Son, Spawn, Special, Spring, Stream, Subject, Topic, Turn, Utter
Istanbul Byzantium, Constantinople
Isthmus Darien, Karelian, Kra, Neck, Panama, San Blas, Suez, Tehuantepec
It A, Chic, Hep, Id, Italian, Oomph, SA, 't, Vermouth
Italian, Italy Alpini, Ausonia, Bolognese, Calabrian, Chian, Dago, Ding, Este, Etnean, Etrurian, Etruscan, Eyeti(e), Eytie, Faliscan, Florentine, Genoese, Ghibelline, Guelf, Guelph, Hesperia, Irredentist, It, Latian, Latin, Lombard, Medici, Mezzogiorno, Moro, Oscan, Paduan, Patarin(e), Rocco, Roman, Sabine, Samnite, Sicel, Sienese, Signor(i), Sikel, Spag, Tuscan, Umbrian, Venetian, Vermouth, Volscian, Wop
Italic Swash
Itch(ing), Itchiness Acariasis, Annoy, Cacoethes, Dhobi, Euk, Ewk, Hanker, Heat rash, Jock, Miliaria, Photopsy, Prickle, Prickly heat, Prurience, Prurigo, Pruritis, Psora, Scabies, Scrapie, Seven-year, Tickle, → **URGE**, Urtication, Yeuk, Youk, Yuck, Yuke
Item(ise) Also, Article, Bulletin, Detail, Entry, Flash, Line, List, Number, Piece, Point, Spot, Too, Topic
Iterate Repeat
Itinerant, Itinerary Ambulant, Didakai, Didakei, Did(d)icoy, Dusty Feet, Gipsy, Gypsy, Hobo, Journey, Log, Pedlar, Peripatetic, Pie-powder, Roadman, Roamer, Romany, Rootless, Route, Stroller, Traveller, Vagrom
Itself Per se
Ivan Russian, Terrible
Ivory (tower) Black, Bone, Chryselephantine, Dentine, Distant, Eburnean, Impractical, Incisor, Key, Solitude, Teeth, Tower, Tusk, Vegetable, Whale's bone
Ivy Ale-hoof, Angelica-tree, Aralia, Boston, Bush, Cat's-foot, Climber, Creeper, Evergreen, Gill, Grape, Ground, Hedera, Helix, Japanese, Panax, Poison, Shield, Sweetheart, Udo, Weeping
Izzard Z

Jj

J Curve, Juliet, Pen

Jab(ber) Chatter, Foin, Gabble, Immunologist, Inject, Jaw, Jook, Nudge, One-two, Peck, Poke, Prattle, Prod, Proke, Punch, Puncture, Sook, Sputter, Stab, Stick, Venepuncture, Yak

Jack(s) AB, Apple, Artocarpus, Ass, Ball, Boot, Bower, Bowl(s), Boy, Card, Cheap, Coatcard, Crevalle, Deckhand, Dibs(tones), Five stones, Flag, Frost, Hoist, Honour, Hopper, Horner, Hydraulic, Idle, J, Jock, Jumping, Ketch, Kitty, Knave, Knucklebones, Lazy, London, Loord, Lout, Lumber, Mark, Matlow, Mistress, Nob, Noddy, Pilot, Point, Pot, Pur, Rabbit, Raise, Rating, Ripper, Roasting, Robinson, Russell, Sailor, Salt, Screw, Seafarer, Shaun, Sprat, Spring-heeled, Springtail, Steeple, Sticker, Straw, Tar, Tee, Tradesman, Turnspit, Union, Uplift, Wood, Yellow

Jackal Anubis, Dieb, Hack, Stooge

Jackass Aliboron, Goburra, Kookaburra, Stupid

Jackdaw Bird, Chawk, Chough, Daw, Kae, Raven, Rheims, Thief

Jacket Acton, Afghanistan, Air, Amauti(k), Anorak, Atigi, Bainin, Baju, Bania(n), Banyan, Barbour®, Basque, Battle, Bawneen, Bed, Bellhop, Biker, Blazer, Blouse, Blouson, Body-warmer, Bolero, Bomber, Brigandine, Bumfreezer, Bush, Cagoul(e), Camisole, Can, Caraco, Cardigan, Carmagnole, Casing, → **COAT**, Dinner, Dolman, Donkey, Drape, Dressing, Dressing-sack, Duffel coat, Duffle coat, Dust-cover, Dustwrapper, Duvet, Fearnought, Flak, Fleece, Gambeson, Gendarme, Grego, Habergeon, Hacking, Ha(c)queton, Half-kirtle, Hug-me-tight, Jerkin, Jupon, Kagool, Kaross, Life, Life preserver, Lumber, Mackinaw, Mae West, Mandarin, Mandilion, Mao, Matinée, Mess, Monkey, Nehru, Newmarket, Norfolk, Parka, Pea, Petenlair, Pierrot, Pilot, Polka, Potato, Pyjama, Railly, Reefer, Safari, Sayon, Shearling, Shell, Shooting, Shortgown, Simar(re), Sleeve, Slip-cover, Smoking, Spencer, Sports, Steam, Strait, Tabard, Tailcoat, Toreador, Tunic, Tux(edo), Tweed, Vareuse, Waistcoat, Wam(m)us, Wampus, Water, Windbreaker®, Windcheater, Windjammer, Wrapper, Zouave

Jackknife Dive, Fold, Jockteleg, Pike

Jackpot Cornucopia, Kitty, Pool

Jackson Stonewall

Jackstraw Spellican, Spil(l)ikin

Jacobite(s) Non-compounder, Non juror, Wild Geese

Jacquard Matelasse

Ja(c)ques Melancholy, Tati

Jade(d) Axe-stone, Bidet, Cloy, Crock, Disjaskit, Exhaust, Fatigue, Greenstone, Hack, Hag, Horse, Hussy, Limmer, Minx, Nag, Nephrite, Pounamu, Rip, Rosinante, Sate, Screw, Slut, Spleenstone, Stale, Tired, Trite, Weary, Yaud, Yu(-stone)

Jaeger Skua

Jag(ged) Barbed, Cart, Drinking, Erose, Gimp, Injection, Laciniate, Ragde, Ragged, Serrate, Snag, Spree, Spur, Tooth

Jagger Mick, Pedlar
Jaguar American tiger, Car, Caracal, Cat, E-type, Ounce, Tiger
Jail(er) Adam, Alcaide, Alcatraz, Bedford, Bin, Bridewell, Can, Clink, Commit, Cooler, Gaol, Hoosegow, Imprison, Incarcerate, Jug, Keeper, Kitty, Limbo, Lockup, Marshalsea, Newgate, Nick, Pen, Pokey, → PRISON, Screw, Shop, Slammer, Spandau, Strangeways, Tronk, Turnkey, Warder
Jailbird Con, Lag, Lifer, Trusty
Jain(ism) Mahavira
Jakarta Batavia
Jake Honest, Hunkydory, OK, Rube
Jalopy Banger, Boneshaker, Buggy, Car, Crate, Heap, Shandry(dan), Stock-car
Jam(my) Apple butter, Block, Choke, Clog, Confiture, Crush, Cushy, Dilemma, Gridlock, Hold-up, How d'ye do, Jeelie, Jeely, Lock, Log, Plight, → PREDICAMENT, Preserve, Press, Quince, Seize, Snarl-up, Spot, Squeeze, Stall, Stick, Tailback, Tangle, Traffic, Vice, Vise, Wedge
Jamaica(n) Rasta(farian), Rastaman, Yardie
Jamb Doorpost, Durn, Sconcheon, Scontion, Scuncheon, Upright
James Agee, Bond, Bothwell, Henry, Jacobite, Jemmy, Jesse, Jim, Joyce, Screw, Seamus, Seumas, Sid, Watt
Jane Austen, Calamity, Eyre, Seymour, Shore, Sian
Jangle Clank, Clapperclaw, Clash, Rattle, Wrangle
Janitor Doorman, Porter, Servitor, Sweeper, Tiler
Jankers KP
Jansky Jy
Janus Two-faced
Japan(ese), Japanese drama Ainu, Burakumin, Daimio, Eta, Geisha, Genro, Gloss, Haiku, Heian, Hondo, Honshu, Issei, Kabuki, Kami, Kana, Kirimon, Lacquer, Mandarin, Meiji, Mikado, Mousmé, Mousmee, Nihon, Nip, Nippon, Nisei, No(h), Resin, Sansei, Satsuma, Shinto, Shogun, Taisho, Togo, Tycoon, Yamato, Yellow peril
Jape Jeer, Joke, Prank, Trick
Jar(ring) Albarello, Amphora, Bell, Canopus, Churr, Clash, Crock, Cruet, Din, Dissonant, Distune, Dolium, Enrough, Gallipot, Gas, Grate, Greybeard, Gride, Grind, Gryde, Humidor, Hydria, → JOLT, Kalpis, Kang, Kilner®, Leyden, Mason, Monkey, Off-key, Olla, Pint, Pithos, Pot(iche), Quarrel, Rasp, Rock, Screwtop, Shelta, Shock, Stamnos, Start, Stave, Stean, Steen, Stein, Tankard, Tinaja, Turn, Vessel, Water-monkey
Jargon Argot, Baragouin, Beach-la-mar, Buzzword, Cant, Chinese, Chinook, Eurobabble, Eurospeak, Geekspeak, Gobbledegook, Gobbledygook, Jive, Kennick, Legalese, Lingo, Lingoa geral, Lingua franca, Mumbo-jumbo, Netspeak, Newspeak, Officialese, Parlance, Patois, Patter, Patter-flash, Psychobabble, Shelta, Shoptalk, → SLANG, Technobabble, Technospeak, Vernacular
Jasmine Cape, Frangipani, Gelsemine, Gelsemium, Gessamine, Jessamy, Madagascar, Olea
Jasper Basanite, Bloodstone, Egyptian, Porcelain, Touchstone
Jaundice(d) Cynical, Icterus, Prejudiced, Sallow, Yellow
Jaunt Journey, Outing, Sally, Stroll, Swan, Trip
Jaunty Airy, Akimbo, Chipper, Debonair, Perky, Rakish
▷ **Jaunty** *may indicate* an anagram
Java man Pithecanthropus
Javelin Dart, Gavelock, Harpoon, Jereed, Jerid, Pile, Pilum, Spear

Jaw(s), Jawbone Blab, Chaft, Chap, Chat, Chaw, Cheek, Chide, Chin, Entry, Glass, Gnathic, Gnathite, Gonion, Hypognathous, Jabber, Jobe, Kype, Lantern, Lumpy, Mandible, Masseter, Maxilla, Mesial, Muzzle, Mylohyoid, Natter, Opisthognathous, Overbite, Overshot, Phossy, Pi, Premaxillary, Prognathous, Ramus, Rubber, Shark, Stylet, Underhung, Undershot, Wapper-jaw, Ya(c)kety-Ya(c)k

Jay Bird, J, Sirgang, Whisky-jack, Whisky-john

Jazz(er), Jazzman Acid, Afro-Cuban, Barber, Barrelhouse, Basie, Bebop, Blues, Boogie, Boogie-woogie, Bop, Cat, Cool, Dixieland, Enliven, Gig, Gutbucket, Hardbop, Hipster, Jive, Latin, Lick, Mainstream, Modern, New Orleans, Progressive, Ragtime, Riff, Scat, Skiffle, Slap base, Stomp, Swinger, Tailgate, Trad, Traditional, West Coast

Jealous(y) Envious, Green(-eyed), Green-eyed monster, Grudging, Zelotypia

Jean(s) Chinos, Denims, Levis®, Pants, Trousers, Wranglers®

Jeer(ing) Ballyrag, Barrack, Belittle, Birl, Boo, Burl, Digs, Fleer, Flout, Gird, Heckle, Hoot, Jape, Jibe, → **MOCK**, Rail, Razz, Ridicule, Scoff, Sling off, Sneer, Taunt, Twit, Yah

Jeeves Valet

Jehovah God, Lord, Yahve(h), Yahwe(h)

Jehovah's Witness Russellite

Jehu Charioteer, Driver

Jejune Arid, Barren, Dry, Insipid, Juvenile

Jelly Acaleph(a), Acalephe, Agar(-agar), Aspic, Brawn, Calf's foot, Chaudfroid, Comb, Cow-heel, → **EXPLOSIVE**, Flummery, Gel, Isinglass, Jam, Kanten, K-Y®, Liquid paraffin, Macedoine, Meat, Medusa, Mineral, Mould, Napalm, Neat's foot, Petroleum, Quiddany, Royal, Shape, Tunicin, Vaseline®, Vitreous humour

▷ **Jelly** *may indicate* an anagram

Jellyfish Acaleph(a), Acalephe, Aurelia, Blubber, Box, Cnidaria, Discomedusae, Discophora, Hydromedusa, Hydrozoa, Irukandji, Medusa, Mesogloea, Physalia, Planoblast, Portuguese man-of-war, Quarl, Scyphistoma, Scyphozoan, Sea-blubber, Sea-nettle, Sea-wasp, Strobila

Jemmy Betty, Crowbar, Lever

Jenkins Ear, Roy, Up

Jenny Ass, Lind, Long, Mule, Short, Spinner, Spinning, Spinster, Wren

Jeopardise, Jeopardy Danger, Double, Expose, Hazard, Peril, Risk

Jerboa Desert rat

Jeremiad Lament, Tragedy, Woe

Jeremy Fisher, Jerry

Jerk(y), Jerkily, Jerking, Jerks Aerobics, A salti, Bob, Braid, Cant, Diddle, Ebrillade, Flirt, Flounce, Gym(nastics), Hike, Hitch, Hoi(c)k, Idiot, Jut, Kant, Knee, PE, Peck, Physical, Saccade, Shove, Spasm, Start, Strobe, Surge, Switch, Sydenham's chorea, Tic, Toss(en), Tweak, → **TWITCH**, Wrench, Yank

Jerkin Body warmer, Jacket, Tabard

Jerome Kern, Vulgate

Jerry, Jerry-built Boche, Flimsy, Fritz, Hun, Kraut, Lego, Mouse, Po(t)

Jersey(s) Bailiwick, CI, Cow, Frock, Gansey, Guernsey, Kine, Lily, Maillot, Polo, Roll-neck, Singlet, → **SWEATER**, Sweatshirt, Yellow, Zephyr

Jerusalem Ariel, Hierosolymitan, Sion, Zion

Jess(e) James, Strap

Jest(er), Jesting Badinage, Barm, Baur, Bawr, Bourd(er), Buffoon, Clown, Cod, Comic, Droll, Gleek, Goliard, Inficete, Jape, Jig, Joker, Josh, Merryman, Miller, Motley, Patch, Quip, Raillery, Ribaldry, Rigoletto, Scogan, Scoggin, Sport, Toy,

Trinculo, Wag, Wit, Yorick

Jesuit Bollandist, Ignatius, Loyola, SJ

Jesus → CHRIST, Emmanuel, IHS, Immanuel, INRI, Isa, Jabers, Lord

Jet, Jet lag Airbus®, Aircraft, Beadblast, Black, Burner, Chirt, Douche, Fountain, Geat, Harrier, Ink, Jumbo, Plane, Pump, Soffione, Spirt, Spout, Spray, Spurt, Squirt, Stream, Time-zone disease, Time-zone fatigue, Turbine, Turbo, Vapour, Water

Jettison Discard, Dump, Flotsam, Jetsam, Lagan, Ligan

Jetty Groin, Mole, Pier, Wharf

Jew(ish), Jews Ashkenazi, Chas(s)id, Diaspora, Essene, Falasha, Grecian, Greek, Has(s)id, Hebrew, Hellenist, Kahal, Karaite, Kike, Landsman, Levite, Lubavitch, Maccabee, Marrano, Misnaged, Mitnag(g)ed, Nazarite, Neturei Karta, Nicodemus, Peculiar People, Pharisee, Refusenik, Sabra, Sadducee, Semite, Sephardim, Sheeny, Shemite, Shtetl, Smouch, Smouse, Tobit, Wandering, Yid(dish), Zealot

Jewel(s), Jeweller(y) Agate, Aigrette, Almandine, Artwear, Beryl, Bijouterie, Bling(-bling), Brilliant, Chrysoprase, Cloisonné, Cornelian, Costume, Crown, Diamond, Earbob, Ear-drop, Emerald, Ewe-lamb, Fabergé, Fashion, Ferron(n)ière, Finery, Garnet, → GEM, Girandole, Gracchi, Jade, Junk, Lherzolite, Marcasite, Navette, Olivine, Opal, Parure, Paste, Pavé, Pearl, Pendant, Peridot, Rivière, Rock, Rubin(e), Ruby, Sapphire, Sard, Scarab, Smaragd, Solitaire, Stone, Sunburst, Tom, Tomfoolery, Topaz, Torc, Treasure, Trinket

Jezebel Harlot, Loose, Whore

Jib Ba(u)lk, Boggle, Boom, → DEMUR, Face, Flying, Foresail, Genoa, Milk, Reest, Reist, Stay-sail, Storm

Jibe Barb, Bob, Correspond, Crack, Dig, Fling, Gleek, → JEER, Mock, Quip, Sarcasm, Slant, Taunt

Jiffy Mo, Pronto, Twinkling, Whiff

Jig(gle) Bob, Bounce, Dance, Fling, Frisk, Hornpipe, Jog, Juggle, Morris

Jigger(ed) Beat, Chigoe, Jolley, Ruin

Jill Ferret

Jilt Discard, Reject, Shed, Throw-over

Jim(my) Diamond, Dismal, Jas, Lucky, Pee, Piddle, Riddle

Jingle(r) Clerihew, Clink, Ditty, Doggerel, Rhyme, Tambourine, Tinkle

Jingo(ism) Odzooks, Patriot, War-rant

Jink Elude

Jinn(i) Afreet, Eblis, Genie, Marid, Spirit

Jinx Curse, Hex, Jonah, Kibosh, Moz(z), Spoil, Voodoo, Whammy

Jitter(s), Jittery Coggly, DT, Fidgets, Funk, Jumpy, Nervous, Willies

▷ **Jitter(s)** *may indicate* an anagram

Jo → LOVER, Sweetheart

Job(bing) Agiotage, Appointment, Berth, Career, Chore, Comforter, Crib, Darg, Errand, Gig, Hatchet, Homer, Inside, Métier, Mission, Nixer, Oratorio, Paint, Patient, Pensum, Place(ment), Plum, Position, Post, Problem, Pursuit, Put-up, Sinecure, Snow, Spot, Steady, → TASK, Ticket, Trotter, Truck, Undertaking, Work

▷ **Job** *may indicate* the biblical character

Jock Deejay, DJ, Mac, Sawn(e)y, Scot

Jockey Carr, Cheat, Diddle, Disc, Jostle, Jump, Lester, Manoeuvre, Mouse, Rider, Steve, Suicide, Swindle, Trick, Video, Winter

▷ **Jockey** *may indicate* an anagram

Jocose, Jocular, Jocund Cheerful, Debonair, Facete, Facetious, Jesting, Lepid, Scurril(e), Waggish

Joe(y), Joseph Addison, Dogsbody, GI, Kangaroo, Pal, Roo, Sloppy, Stalin, Surface, Trey

Jog(ger), Joggle, Jog-trot Arouse, Canter, Dog-trot, Dunch, Dunsh, Heich-how, Heigh-ho, Hod, Jiggle, Jolt, Jostle, Memo, Mosey, Nudge, Piaffe, Prompt, Ranke, Remind, Run, Shake, Shog, Tickle, Trot, Whig

Johannesburg Jozi

John(ny) Ajax, Augustus, Barleycorn, Bog, Bright, Brown, Bull, Bunyan, Cloaca, Collins, Doree, Dory, Elton, Evan, Gaunt, Gents, Gilpin, Groats, Halifax, Ia(i)n, Ivan, Lackland, Latecomer, Lav, Little, Loo, Peel, Prester, Stage-door, Throne, Toot, Tout, WC

Johnny-come-lately Upstart

Johnson Cham, Doctor, Idler

Join(er), Joined, Joining Abut, Accede, Accompany, Add, Affix, Alligate, Ally, Amalgamate, And, Annex, Associate, Attach, Braze, Butt-end, Cement, Cleave, Combine, Conflate, Conglutinate, Conjugate, Conjunct, Connect, Cope, → **COUPLE**, Dovetail, Engraft, Enlist, Enrol, Enter, Federate, Fuse, Glue, Graft, Hasp, Hitch, Hyphen, Include, Inosculate, Interconnect, Jugate, Knit, Link, Marry, Meet, Member, Menuisier, Merge, Mix, Mortar, Mortise, Oop, Oup, Overlaunch, Piece, Piecen, Rebate, Regelation, Rivet, Scarf, Seam, Se-tenant, Sew, Siamize, Snug, Solder, Splice, Spot-weld, Squirrel, Staple, Stylolite, Tenon, Unite, Wed, Weld, Yoke

Joint(ed) Ancon, Ankle, Arthrosis, Articular, Ball and socket, Bar, Baron, Butt, Capillary, Cardan, Carpus, Chine, Clip, Co, Cogging, Collar, Colonial goose, Commissure, Compression, Conjunction, Cuit, Cup and ball, Cut, Dive, Dovetail, Drumstick, Elbow, Enarthrosis, Entrecôte, Expansion, False, Fish, Gambrel, Genu, Gimmal, Gimmer, Ginglymus, Hainch, Haunch, Heel, Hinge, Hip, Hough, Huck, Hunker, J, Joggle, Jolly, Junction, Knee, Knuckle, Lap(ped), Lith, Loin, Marijuana, Meat, Mitre, Mortise, Mouse (buttock), Mouse-piece, Mutton, Mutual, Phalange, Phalanx, Pin, Popliteal, Psoas, Push-fit, Rabbet, Rack, Raphe, Reducer, Reefer, Rhaphe, Ribroast, Roast, Saddle, Scarf, Schindylesis, Seam, Shoulder, Silverside, Sirloin, Splice, Spliff, Stifle, Straight, Strip, Symphysis, Syndesmosis, T, Tarsus, T-bone, Tenon, Together, Toggle, Tongue and groove, Topside, Trochanter, Trochite, Undercut, Universal, Vertebra, Water, Wedging, Weld, Wrist

Joist Accouplement, Bar, Beam, Dormant, Ground plate, Groundsill, H-beam, I-beam, Rib, Rolled-steel, Sleeper, Solive, String, Trimmer

Joke(r), Joke-book, Joking Banter, Bar, Baur, Bawr, Booby-trap, Bourdon, Card, Chaff, Chestnut, → **CLOWN**, Cod, Comedian, Comic, Crack, Cut-up, Farceur, Farceuse, Fool, Fun, Funster, Gab, Gag, Glike, Guy, Have-on, Hazer, Hoax, Hum, Humorist, In fun, Jape, Jest, Jig, Jocular, Josh, Lark, Legpull, Merry-andrew, Merryman, Mistigris, One, One-liner, Pleasantry, Practical, Prank(ster), Pun, Punchline, Pundigrion, Quip, Rag, Rib-tickler, Rot, Sally, Scherzo, Scogan, Scoggin, Sick, Skylark, Sottisier, Squib, Standing, Wag, Wheeze, Wild, Wisecrack, Wit

Jollity, Jolly 'Arryish, Bally, Cheerful, Convivial, Cordial, Do, Festive, Galoot, Gaucie, Gaucy, Gawcy, Gawsy, Gay, Hilarious, Jocose, Jovial, Marine, Mirth, Rag, RM, Roger, Sandboy, Tar, Very

Jolt Bump, Jar, Jig-a jig, Jog(gle), Jostle, Jounce, Shake, Shog, Start

Jonah Hoodoo, Jinx, Moz(z)

Jones Davy, Emperor, Inigo

Jordan Pot, Urinal

Joris Horseman

▶ **Joseph** see **JOE**

Josh Chaff, Kid, Rib, Tease

Josiah Stamp, Wedgewood

Joss Incense, Luck, Stick

Jostle Barge, Bump, Compete, Elbow, Hog-shouther, Hustle, Push, Shoulder, → SHOVE, Throng

Jot(ter), Jotting(s) Ace, Fig, Iota, Memo, Mite, Note, Pad, Stime, Styme, Tittle, Whit

Journal Band(e), Blog, Chronicle, Daily, Daybook, Diary, Ephemeris, Gazette, Hansard, Lancet, Log, Noctuary, Organ, Paper, Periodical, Pictorial, Punch, Rag, Record, TES, TLS, Trade, Weblog

Journalism, Journalist Cheque-book, Columnist, Commentariat, Contributor, Diarist, Diurnalist, Ed, Fleet St, Freelance, (GA) Sala, Gonzo, Hack, Hackery, Hackette, Hatchetman, Inkslinger, Interviewer, Investigative, Keyhole, Lobby, Muckraker, Newshound, Northcliffe, NUJ, Penny-a-liner, Pepys, Press(man), Reporter, Reviewer, Scribe, Sob sister, Stead, Stringer, Wireman, → WRITER, Yellow

Journey Circuit, Cruise, Errand, Expedition, Eyre, Foray, Grand Tour, Hadj, Hop, Jaunce, Jaunse, Jaunt, Long haul, Mush, Odyssey, Passage, Periegesis, Ply, Raik, Rake, Red-eye, Ride, Run, Sabbath-day's, Sentimental, Soup run, Tour, Travel, Trek, Viatical, Walkabout

Journeyman Artisan, Commuter, Craftsman, Sterne, Yeoman

Joust Giust, Tilt, Tournament, Tourney

Jove Egad, Gad, Igad, Jupiter, Thunderer

Jovial Bacchic, Boon, Convivial, Cordial, Festive, Genial, Jolly

Jowl(s) Cheek, Chollers, Chops, Jaw

Joy(ful), Joyous Ah, Bliss, Blithe, Charmian, → DELIGHT, Dream, Ecstasy, Elation, Exulting, Fain, Felicity, Festal, Frabjous, Glad, Glee, Gloat, Groove, Hah, Hey, Jubilant, Nirvana, Rapture, Schadenfreude, Sele, Tra-la, Transport, Treat, Yippee

Joyce Haw Haw, Traitor

JP Beak, Queer cuffin, Quorum

Jubilant, Jubilation, Jubilee Celebration, Cock-a-hoop, Diamond, Ecstatic, Elated, Exultant, Holiday, Joy, Triumphant

Judaism Semitism

Judas Double-crosser, Iscariot, Traitor, Tree

Judder Put-put, Shake, Vibrate

Jude Obscure

Judge(ment), Judges Absolute, Addoom, Adjudicator, Agonothetes, Alacus, Alcalde, Arbiter, Areopagite, Aret(t), Arrêt, Assess, Assize, Auto-da-fé, Avizandum, Banc, Brehon, Cadi, Calculate, Censure, Centumvirus, Circuit(eer), Common Serjeant, Comparative, Connoisseur, Consider, Coroner, Court, Critic(ise), Daniel, Dayan, Daysman, Deborah, Decern(e), Decide, Decision, Decreet, Deem(ster), Dempster, Dicast, Dies non, Differential, Dikast, Discern(ment), District, Ephor, Ermined, Estimate, Evaluate, Faisal, Faysal, Gauge, Gesse, Gideon, Good-sense, Guess, Hakeem, Hakim, Hearing, Hold, Honour, Inky-smudge, Interlocutor, J, Jeffreys, Jephthah, Justice, Justicier, Last, Line, Lud, Lynch, Minos, Mufti, Non prosequitur, Nonsuit, Official Referee, Old Fury, Opine, Opinion, Ordinary, Outfangthief, Panel, Paris, Podesta, Providence, Provisional, Puisne, Puny, Reckon(ing), Recorder, Ref(eree), Regard, Rhadamanthus, Ruler, Samson, Samuel, Sapience, Scan, Second guess, See, Sentence, Sentiment, Shallow, Sheriff, Sober, Solomon, Sound, Suppose, Surrogate, Syndic, Tact, Think, Touch, Trior, Try, Umpire, Value, Verdict, Ween, Weigh up, Wig, Wik, Wisdom, Worship

Judicious Critical, Discreet, Politic, Rational, Sage, Sensible, Shrewd, Sound

Judo, Judo costume Dojo, Gi(e), Kyu, Shiai

Jug(s) Amphora, Aquamanale, Aquamanile, Bellarmine, Bird, Blackjack, Bombard, Breasts, Can, Cooler, Cream(er), Crock, Enghalskrug, Ewer, Flagon, Gaol, Gotch,

Greybeard, Growler, John Roberts, Malling, Measuring, Olpe, Pitcher, Pound, Pourer, Pourie, → **PRISON**, Quad, Quod, Shop, Stir, Tits, Toby, Urceolus

Juggle(r) Conjuror, Cook, Escamotage, Fake, Fire-eater

Juice, Juicy Aloe vera, Bacca, Cassareep, Cassaripe, Cremor, Current, Fluid, Fruity, Gastric, Hypocist, Ichor, Jungle, La(b)danum, Laser, Latex, Lush, Moist, Must, Oil, Pancreatic, Perry, Petrol, Ptisan, Rare, Sap, Snake, Soma, Spanish, Succ(o)us, Succulent, Tarantula, Thridace, Vril, Walnut, Zest

Juju Charm, Fetish

Jujube Christ's thorn, Lotus, Nabk, Padma, Sweet

Jukebox Nickelodeon

Julian Apostate

July Dogdays

Jumble Cast offs, Chaos, Conglomeration, Farrago, Garble, Huddle, Jabble, Lumber, Mass, Medley, Mingle-mangle, Mish-mash, Mixter-maxter, Mixtie-maxtie, Mixture, Mix(t)y-max(t)y, Pastiche, Praiseach, Printer's pie, Raffle, Ragbag, Scramble, Shuffle, Wuzzle

▷ **Jumbled** *may indicate* an anagram

Jumbo Aircraft, Elephant, Jet, Large-scale, Mammoth, OS, Plane

Jump(er), Jumping, Jumpy Aran, Assemble, Axel, Bate, Batterie, Boomer, Bound, Bungee, Bungy, Bunny-hop, Caper, Capriole, Cicada, Cicata, Crew-neck, Cricket, Croupade, Daffy, Desultory, Entrechat, Euro, Eventer, Flea, Fosbury flop, Gansey, Gazump, Gelande(sprung), Guernsey, Halma, Helicopter, High, Hurdle, Impala, Itchy, Jersey, Joey, Jolly, Kangaroo, Katydid, Knight, Lammie, Lammy, Leap(frog), Lep, Long, Lope, Lutz, Nervous, Nervy, Ollie, Parachute, Pig, Pogo, Polo-neck, Pounce, Prance, Prank, Pronking, Puissance, Quantum, Quersprung, Rap, Salchow, Saltatory, Saltigrade, Saltus, Scissors, Scoup, Scowp, Shy, Skip, Skipjack, Skydiver, → **SPRING**, Star, Start, Straddle, Sweater, Toe(-loop), Trampoline, Triple, Turtle-neck, Vau(l)t, V-neck, Water, Western roll

Jumping jack Pantine

Junction Abutment, Alloyed, Angle, Box, Bregma, Carfax, Close, Clover-leaf, Connection, Crewe, Crossroads, Diffused, Gap, Intersection, Joint, Josephson, Knitting, Meeting, Node, P-n, Point, Raphe, Spaghetti, Stage, Suture, T, Tight, Union

Juneberry Saskatoon, Shadbush

Jungle Asphalt, Blackboard, Boondocks, Bush, Concrete, Forest, Shola, Tangle

Junior Cadet, Chota, Cion, Dogsbody, Fils, Minor, Name-son, Office, Petty, Puisne, Scion, Sub(ordinate), Underling, Understrapper, Younger

Juniper Cade, Pencil-cedar, Red-cedar, Savin(e)

Junk(shop), Junkie Bric-à-brac, Chuck in, Jettison, Litter, Lorcha, Lumber, Refuse, Ship, Tagareen, Tatt, Trash, User

▷ **Junk** *may indicate* an anagram

Junker Prussian

Junket(ing) Beano, Creel, Custard, Feast, Picnic, Rennet, Spree

Juno Lucina

Junta Cabal, Council

Jupiter Jove, Newspaper

Jurassic Bajocian, Lias, R(h)aetic

Jurisdiction Authority, Bailiwick, Domain, Province, Soke(n)

Juror(s), Jury Array, Assize, Blue-ribbon, Dicast, Grand, Hung, Inquest, Judges, Mickleton, Old Fury, Pais, Panel, Party, Petit, Petty, Sail, Special, Strike, Tales, Tribunal, Venire, Venireman, Venue

Just(ice) Adeel, Adil, Alcalde, All, Aristides, Astraea, Balanced, Barely, Condign, Cupar, Deserved, Equal, Equity, E(v)en, Fair, Fair-minded, Forensic, Honest, Impartial, J, Jasper, Jeddart, Jethart, Jurat, Kangaroo, Mere, Moral, Natural, Nemesis, Newly, Nice, Only, Palm-tree, Piso, Poetic, Provost, Puisne, Pure and simple, Quorum, Recent, Restorative, Right(ful), Righteous, Rightness, Rough, Shallow, Silence, Simply, Solely, Sommer, Street, Themis, Tilt, Upright

Justifiable, Justification, Justify Apology, Autotelic, Avenge, Aver, Avowry, Clear, Darraign(e), Darrain(e), Darrayn, Defend, Deraign, Excusable, Explain, Grounds, Rationale, Reason, Vindicate, Warrant

Just so Exactly, Sic, Stories

Jut Beetle, Bulge, Overhang, Project, Protrude, Sail

Jute Burlap, Corchorus, Gunny, Hengist, Hessian, Horsa, Jew's mallow, Urena, Wool bale

Juvenile Childish, Teenage(r), Yonkers, Young, Younkers, Youth

Juxtaposition Parataxis

Kk

K Kelvin, Kilo, King, Kirkpatrick
K2 Dapsang, Godwin Austen
Kaffir Shares, Xosa
Kail, Kale Borecole, Cabbage, Cole, Curly-greens, Ninepins
Kaiser Doorn
Kaleidoscope Dappled, Motley, Myrioscope, Various
Kangaroo Bettong, Boodie-rat, Boomer, Boongary, Bounder, Brush, Cus-cus, Diprotodont, Euro, Forester, Joey, Macropodidae, Nototherium, Old man, Potoroo, Rat, Red, Steamer, Tree, Troop, Wallaby, Wallaroo
Kansas Sunflower
Kaolin Lithomarge
Karate Kung Fu, Shotokan, Wushu
Karma Destiny, Fate, Predestination
Kate Greenaway, Shrew
Kayak Bidarka
Kebab Cevapcici, Doner, Gyro, Satay, Sate, Shashli(c)k, Sosatie, Souvlakia
Keel Bilge, Bottom, Carina, Centreboard, Even, Faint, False, Fin, List, Overturn, Skeg(g), Sliding
Keen(ness), Keener Acid, Acute, Agog, Ardent, Argute, Aspiring, Astute, Athirst, Avid, Aygre, Bemoan, Bewail, Breem, Breme, Cheap, Coronach, Dash, Devotee, Dirge, Eager, Elegy, Enthusiastic, Fanatical, Fell, Greet, Grieve, Hone, Hot, Howl, Into, Lament, Mourn, Mustard, Mute, Narrow, Ochone, Ohone, Overfond, Partial, Peachy, Perceant, Persant, Pie, Raring, Razor, Ready, Red-hot, Rhapsodic, Sharp, Shrewd, Shrill, Snell, Thirsting, Threnodic, Thrillant, Trenchant, Ululate, Wail, Whet, Zeal(ous)
Keep(er), Keeping Ames, Armature, Austringer, Castellan, Castle, Celebrate, Chatelain(e), Citadel, Conceal, Conserve, Curator, Custodian, Custody, Depositary, Depository, Detain, Donjon, Escot, Fastness, Finder, Fort, Gaoler, Goalie, Guardian, Have, Hoard, → **HOLD**, Maintain, Nab, Net, Observe, Ostreger, Own, Park, Pickle, Preserve, Retain, Safe, Safeguard, Save, Stay, Stet, Stock, Store, Stow, Stumper, Support, Sustain, Tower, Warden, Withhold
Keep back Detain, Recoup, Reserve, Retard, Stave
Keepsake Memento, Souvenir, Token
Keep under Cow, Subdue, Submerge
Keg Barrel, Cask, Powder, Tub, Tun, Vat
Kelly('s) Eye, Gene, Ned
Kelvin Absolute, K
Ken Eyeshot, Know(ledge), Purview, Range
Kennel(s) Guard, Home, House, Shelter
Kent Lathe, SE, Superman
Kentuckian, Kentucky Chicken, Corn-cracker, Derby, KY

Kenya(n) Luo, Masai, Mau Mau
Kerala Nair, Nayar
Kerb Edge, Gutter, Roadside
Kerchief Babushka, Bandan(n)a, Headcloth, Romal, Scarf
Kernel Copra, Core, Corn, Grain, Nucleus, Pine, Praline, Prawlin
Kestrel Bird, Hawk, Keelie, Stallion, Staniel, Stannel, Stanyel, Windhover
Ket Carrion, Wool
Ketch Jack
Ketchup Relish, Sauce, Tomato
Kettle Boiler, Cauldron, Dixie, Dixy, Drum, Fanny, Pot, Tea, Turpin, War, Whistling
Key(s), Keyhole A, Ait, Allen, Alt, Ash, B, Backspace, Basic, C, Cay, Central,
    Chip, Church, Cipher, Claver, Clavis, Clew, Clink, Clue, Control, Crib, D, Del(ete),
    Dichotomous, Digital, Dital, Dominant, E, Enter, Esc(ape), Essential, F, Flat,
    Florida, Fruit, Function, G, Greek, High, Holm, Hot, Ignition, Important, Inch,
    Index, INS, Instrumental, Islet, Ivory, Kaie, King-pin, Latch, Legend, Linchpin,
    Locker, Low, Main, Major, Master, Minor, Note, Nut, Octachord, Opener,
    Oustiti, Outsiders, Pass(word), Passe-partout, Piano, Pipe, Pivot, Pony, Prong,
    Reef, Return, Semibreve, Shift, Signature, Skeleton, Spanner, Spline, Stimulate,
    Subdominant, Supertonic, Tab, Table, Tipsy, Tonal, Turning, USB, Vital, Watch,
    Water, Wedge, Woodruff, Yale®
Keyboard, Keypad Azerty, Console, Digitorium, Dvorak, Electronic, Manual,
    Martenot, Numeric(al), Piano, Pianola®, Qwerty, Spinet
Keyholder Occupant, Resident, Tenant, Warder
Key man Islander, Kingpin
Keynote Line, Mese, Theme, Tonic
Keystone Cops, Crux, PA, Pennsylvania, Quoin, Sagitta, Voussoir
Keyword Kwic, Sesame
Khan Aga, Chagan, Cham, Serai, Shere
Kick(ing) Back-heel, Bicycle, Boot, Buzz, Corner, Dribble, Drop, Fling, Flutter, Fly,
    Free, Frog, Garryowen, Goal, Grub, Hack, Heel, High, Hitch, Hoof, Lash, Nutmeg,
    Pause, Penalty, Pile, Place, Punce, Punt, Recalcitrate, Recoil, Recoyle, Savate,
    Scissors, Sixpence, Speculator, Spot, Spur, Spurn, Squib, Stab, Tanner, Tap, Thrill,
    Toe, Up and under, Vigour, Volley, Wince, Yerk, Zip
Kid(s) Arab, Befool, Billy, Brood, Cheverel, Chevrette, Child, Chit, Cisco, Con,
    Delude, Giles, Goat, Hircosity, Hoax, Hocus, Hoodwink, Hum, Joke, Leather, Mag,
    Minor, Misguide, Nipper, Offspring, Outwit, Pretend, Rag, Rib, Spoof, Suede,
    Sundance, → TEASE, Tot, Trick, Whiz(z), Wiz
Kidnap Abduct, Hijack, Plagium, Shanghai, Snatch, Spirit, Steal
Kidney(-shaped) Character, Mettle, Nature, Reins, Renal, Reniform, Sort, Type
Kildare Dr
Kill(ed), Killer, Killing Assassin, Attrit, Axeman, Battue, Behead, Biocidal,
    Boojum, Booth, Bump off, Butcher, Carnage, Carnifex, Category, Chance-medley,
    Choke, Comical, Croak, Crucify, Cull, Deep six, Despatch, Destroy, Electrocute,
    Euthanasia, Execute, Exhibition, Exterminate, Extirpate, For(e)do, Frag, Garotte,
    Germicide, Gun, Handsel, Hatchet man, Hilarious, Homicide, Honour, Humane,
    Ice, Immolate, Infanticide, Jugulate, K, Knacker, Knock off, Liquidate, Lynch,
    Mactation, Matador(e), Mercy, Misadventure, Mortify, Murder, Napoo, Necklace,
    Ninja, NK, Off, Orc(a), Penalty, Pesticide, -phage, Pick off, Pip, Predator, Prolicide,
    Quell, Quietus, Regrate, Sacrifice, Serial, Settle, Shochet, Shoot up, Slaughter,
    Slay(er), Slew, Smite, Snuff, Spike, Stifle, Stonker, Strangle, Swat, Tailor, Thagi,
    Thug(gee), Top, Toreador, Total, Vaticide, Veto, Waste, Zap

Killjoy Crab, Puritan, Sourpuss, Spoilsport, Trouble-mirth, Wowser
Kiln Lime, Oast, Oven
Kilometre Km, Verst
Kilt Drape, Filabeg, Fil(l)ibeg, Fustanella, Phil(l)abeg, Phil(l)ibeg, Plaid, Tartan
Kimono Yukata
Kin(sman) Ally, Family, Kith, Like, Nearest, Relation, Sib(b), Sybbe
Kind(ly) Akin, Amiable, Avuncular, Benefic, Benevolent, Benign, Boon, Breed, Brood, Brotherly, Category, Class, Clement, Considerate, Favourable, Gender, Generic, Generous, Genre, Gentle, Genus, Good, Gracious, Humane, Ilk, Kidney, Kin, Lenient, Manner, Modal, Nature, Nice, Sisterly, → SORT, Species, Strain, Strene, Thoughtful, Trine, Type, Understanding, Variety, Well-disposed, Ylke
Kindle, Kindling Accend, Fire, Ignite, Incense, Incite, Inflame, → LIGHT, Litter, Lunt, Stimulate, Teend, Tind, Tine, Touchwood, Tynd(e)
Kindness Aloha, Benevolence, Clemency, Favour, Humanity, Mitzvah, Ubuntu
Kindred Allied, Blood, Like, Related
King(s), Kingly Ard-ri(gh), Butcher, Coatcard, Cobra, Csar, Elvis, English, ER, Evil, Highness, Kong, Ksar, Majesty, Monarch, Negus, Pearly, Peishwa(h), Penguin, Peshwa, Pharaoh, Philosopher, Potentate, R, Ransom, Reigner, Rex, Rial, Roi, Royalet, Ruler, Ryal, Sailor, Seven, Shah, Shepherd, Shilling, Sovereign, Stork, Tsar, Tzar

KINGS

2 letters:	Lear	Lludd	Darius
GR	Loki	Louis	Duncan
Og	Nudd	Midas	Edmund
Re	Numa	Minos	Egbert
	Offa	Mpret	Farouk
3 letters:	Olaf	Ninus	Fergus
Asa	Otto	Osric	Harold
Erl	Saul	Penda	Hellen
Ine	Zeus	Priam	Hyksos
Lir		Rufus	Josiah
Log	*5 letters:*	Uther	Lucomo
Lud	Apple		Ludwig
Zog	Balak	*6 letters:*	Lycaon
	Basil	Acetes	Memnon
4 letters:	Brute	Aegeus	Miledh
Agag	Creon	Alaric	Nestor
Agis	Cyrus	Alfred	Oberon
Ahab	David	Alonso	Ogyges
Atli	Edgar	Amasis	Paphos
Brut	Edwin	Arthur	Peleus
Ceyx	Etzel	Atreus	Philip
Cnut	Gyges	Attila	Ramses
Cole	Herod	Baliol	Rhesus
Edwy	Hiram	Brutus	Utgard
Fahd	Idris	Canute	Xerxes
Inca	Ixion	Cheops	
Jehu	James	Clovis	*7 letters:*
Knut	Laius	Daneus	Acestes

Admetus
Athamas
Baldwin
Balliol
Beowulf
Busiris
Caradoc
Cecrops
Cepheus
Croesus
Danaiis
Diomede
Elidure
Evander
Gentius
Gordius
Gunther
Jupiter
Kenneth
Macbeth
Malcolm
Oedipus
Porsena
Ptolemy
Pyrrhus
Rameses
Regulus
Servius
Sigmund
Solomon

Stephen
Tarquin
Umberto

8 letters:
Adrastus
Aegyptus
Alberich
Alcinous
Cambyses
Cophetua
Diomedes
Endymion
Ethelred
Hezekiah
Jereboam
Jonathan
Leonidas
Menander
Menelaus
Milesius
Nehemiah
Odysseus
Pentheus
Porsenna
Rehoboam
Sarpedon
Siegmund
Sisyphus
Tantalus

Thutmose
Thyestes
Tigranes
Zedekiah

9 letters:
Agamemnon
Ahasuerus
Alexander
Athelstan
Bretwalda
Brian Boru
Conchobar
Cunobelin
Cymbeline
Ethelbert
Florestan
Frederick
Gambrinus
Gargantua
Gilgamesh
Idomeneus
Lionheart
Lobengula
Nabonidus
Pygmalion
Ras Tafari
Rodomonte
Sigismund
Tarquinus

Tyndareus
Vortigern
Wenceslas

10 letters:
Belshazzar
Cadwaladar
Caractacus
Erechtheus
Ozymandias
Wenceslaus

11 letters:
Charlemagne
Hardicanute
Jehoshaphat
Melchizedek
Prester John
Sennacherib
Tutenkhamen

12 letters:
Wayland Smith

14 letters:
Harold Harefoot
Nebuchadnezzar
Sweyn Forkbeard
Uther Pendragon

Kingdom, Kingship Animal, An(n)am, Aragon, Arles, Armenia, Ashanti, Assyria, Austrasia, Babylonia, Barataria, Belgium, Bhutan, Bohemia, Brandenburg, Brunel, Burgundy, Castile, Cilicia, Connacht, Connaught, Dahomey, Dalriada, Darfur, Denmark, Dominion, Edom, Elam, Fes, Fez, Fife, Granada, He(d)jaz, Heptarchy, Hijaz, Jordan, Latin, Leon, Lesotho, Lydia, Macedon(ia), Mercia, Meroe, Middle, Mineral, Moab, Morocco, Murcia, Naples, Navarre, Nepal, Netherlands, Neustria, Noricum, Northumbria, Norway, Parthia, Plant, Pontic, Realm, Reame, Reign, Royalty, Ruritania, Saba, Samaria, Sardinia, Saudi Arabia, Sennar, Sheba, Siam, Spain, Sphere, Swaziland, Sweden, Thailand, Throne, Tonga, Two Sicilies, Ulster, Vegetable, Wessex, Westphalia, World
Kingfisher Alcyone, Halcyon
Kingmaker Neville, Warwick
King-of-arms Clarenc(i)eux, Garter, Lyon, Norroy (and Ulster)
King's evil Crewels, Cruels, Scrofula
Kingsley Amis, Charles
King's son Dauphin, Delphin, P, Prince
Kink(y) Bent, Buckle, Crapy, Curl, Enmeshed, Flaw, Gasp, Knurl, Null, Nurl, Odd, Perm, Perverted, Quirk, Twist, Wavy
▷ **Kink(y)** *may indicate* an anagram
Kinkajou Honey-bear, Potto

Kip(per) Cure, Dosser, Doze, Limey, Nap, → SLEEPER, Smoke
Kipling Beetle
Kirkpatrick K
Kismet Destiny, Fate, Karma, Predestination
Kiss(er), Kissing Air, Baisemain, Buss, Butterfly, Caress, Contrecoup, Cross, Deep,
    French, Lip, Mouth, Neck, Osculate, Pax(-board), Pax-brede, Peck, Pet, Plonker, Pree,
    Salue, Salute, Smack(er), Smooch, Smouch, Snog, Spoon, Suck face, Thimble, X, Yap
Kit Accoutrement, Christopher, Clobber, Clothes, Dress, Housewife, Jack, Layette,
    Marlowe, Mess, → OUTFIT, Rig, Set, Slops, Sportswear, Strip, Tackle, Uniform
Kitchen Caboose, Cookhouse, Cuisine, Galley, Scullery, Soup, Thieves
Kite Belly, Bird, Box, Chil, Crate, Dragon, Elanet, Forktail, Gled(e), Hawk, Milvus,
    Paunch, Puttock, Rokkaku
Kitten(ish) Cute, Kindle, Sexy
Kittiwake Bird, Gull, Hacklet, Haglet
Kitty Ante, Cat, Fisher, Float, Fund, Jackpot, Pool, Pot, Tronc
Kiwi Apteryx, Chinese gooseberry, NZ, Ratitae
Klu-Klux-Klan Nightrider
Knack Art, Faculty, Flair, Forte, Gift, Hang, Instinct, → TALENT, Technique, Trick
Knacker Castanet, Exhaust
Knapsack Musette
Knapweed Matfelon
Knave(ry) Bezonian, Bower, Boy, Cad, Card, Coatcard, Coistril, Coystril, Custrel,
    Dog, Drôle, Fripon, Jack(-a-napes), Jock, Loon, Makar, Maker, Nob, Noddy, Pam,
    Pur, Rapscallion, → RASCAL, Recreant, Ropery, Scoundrel, Skelm, Taroc, Tarot,
    Tom, Treachery, Varlet, Villain
Knead Conche, Malax(ate), Massage, Mould, Pug, Pummel, Work
Knee(s), Knee-cap, Knee-pan Genicular, Genu, Hock, Housemaid's, Lap,
    Marrowbones, Patella, Poleyn, Popliteal, Punch, Rotula, Whirl bone
Kneel(er) Defer, Genuflect, Hassock, Kowtow, Prie-dieu, Truckle
Knell Bell, Curfew, Dirge, Peal, Ring, Toll
Knicker(bocker), Knickers Bloomers, Culottes, Directoire, Irving, Panties,
    Plus-fours, Shorts, Trousers
Knick-knack Bagatelle, Bibelot, Bric-à-brac, Gewgaw, Pretty(-pretty), Quip, Smytrie,
    Toy, Trangam, Trifle, Victoriana
Knife Anelace, Athame, Barlow, Barong, Bistoury, Blade, Boline, Bolo, Bolster,
    Bowie, Bush, Butterfly, Carver, Carving, Case, Catling, Chakra, Chiv, Clasp, Cleaver,
    Couteau, Cradle, Cuttle, Cutto(e), Da(h), Dagger, Dirk, Fleam, Flick, Fruit, Gamma,
    Gully, Hay, Hunting, Jockteleg, Kard, Keratome, Kukri, Lance(t), Machete, Matchet,
    Moon, Oyster, Palette, Pallet, Panga, Paper, Parang, Peeler, Pen, Pigsticker, Pocket,
    Putty, Scalpel, Scalping, Sgian-dhu, Sgian-dubh, Sheath, Shiv, Simi, Skean-dhu,
    Slash, Snee, Snickersnee, Spade, Stab, Stanley, Steak, Sticker, Stiletto, Switchblade,
    Table, Toothpick, Tranchet, Trench
Knight(hood) Accolon, Aguecheek, Alphagus, Amfortas, Artegal, Balan, Banneret,
    Bayard, Bedivere, Black, Bliant, Bors, Britomart, Caballero, Calidore, Cambel,
    Caradoc, Carpet, Cavalier, Chevalier, Companion, Crusader, Douceper, Douzeper,
    Dub, Equites, Errant, Galahad, Gallant, Gareth, Garter, Gawain, Geraint, Giltspurs,
    Grey, Guyon, Hospitaller, Kay, KB, KBE, Kemper, KG, Lamorack, La(u)ncelot,
    Launfal, Lionel, Lochinvar, Lohengrin, Maecenas, Malta, Mark, Medjidie, Melius,
    Modred, Mordred, N, Noble, Orlando, Paladin, Palmerin, Palomides, Papal,
    Paper, Parsifal, Perceforest, Perceval, Percival, Pharamond, Pinel, Precaptory,
    Preux chevalier, Red Cross, Ritter, Round Table, St Columba, Samurai, Sir,

Tannhauser, Templar, Teutonic, Tor, Trencher, Tristan, Tristram, Valvassor, Vavasour, White

Knit(ting), Knitwear Aran, Contract, Crochet, Double, Entwine, Fair Isle, Hosiery, Intarsia, Interlock, Intertwine, K, Mesh, Porosis, Purl, Seam, Set, Stockinet, Weave, Wrinkle

Knob(by) Berry, Boll, Boss, Botoné, Bottony, Bouton, Bur(r), Cam, Caput, Cascabel, Croche, Gear, Handle, Hill, Inion, Knub, Knur(r), Node, Noop, Pellet, Pommel, Protuberance, Pulvinar, Push-button, Snib, Snub, Snuff, Stud, Torose, Tuber, Tuner

Knobless Enodal

Knock(er), Knock down, off, out, Knockout Bang, Beaut, Biff, Blow, Bonk, Bump, Ca(a), Chap, Clash, Clour, Collide, Con, Criticise, Dad, Daud, Dawd, Degrade, Denigrate, Deride, Dev(v)el, Ding, Dinnyhauser, Dod, Etherise, Eyeful, Floor, Grace-stroke, → **HIT**, Innings, King-hit, KO, Lowse, Lowsit, Mickey Finn, Opportunity, Pan, Pink, Quietus, Rap, Rat-tat, Six, Skittle, Spat, Steal, Stop, Strike, Stun(ner), Tap, Technical, Thump, Tonk, Wow

Knock-kneed Valgus

Knot(ted), Knotty Apollo, Baff, Bend, Bind, Blackwall hitch, Bow, Bowline, Bur(r), Burl, Carrick-bend, Cat's paw, Clinch, Clove hitch, Cluster, Crochet, Diamond hitch, Englishman's, Entangle, Figure of eight, Fisherman's (bend), Flat, French, Gnar, → **GNARL**, Gordian, Granny, Half-hitch, Harness hitch, Hawser-bend, Herculean, Hitch, Interlace, Knag, Knap, Knar, Knur(r), Loop, Love(r's), Macramé, Macrami, Magnus hitch, Marriage-favour, Matthew Walker, Mouse, Nirl, Node, Nowed, Nub, Nur(r), Overhand, Peppercorn, Picot, Porter's, Problem, Prusik, Quipu, Reef, Rolling hitch, Root, Rosette, Running, Seizing, Sheepshank, Sheetbend, Shoulder, Shroud, Sleave, Slip, Slub, Spurr(e)y, Square, Stevedore's, Surgeon's, Sword, Tangle, Tat, Thumb, Tie, Timberhitch, Torose, Truelove, Tubercle, Turk's head, Virgin, Wale, Wall, Weaver's (hitch), Windsor, Witch

Know(how), Knowing(ly), Knowledge(able), Known Acquaintance, Autodidactic, Aware, Carnal, Cognition, Common, Compleat, Comprehend, Cred, Epistemics, Erudite, Expertise, Famous, Fly, Gnosis, Gnostic, Have, Hep, Hip, Info, Information, Insight, Intentional, Intuition, Jnana, Ken, Kith, Kydst, Lare, Light, Lore, Mindful, Omniscience, On, On to, Pansophy, Paragnosis, Party, Polymath, Positivism, Privity, Realise, Recherché, → **RECOGNISE**, Sapient, Savvy, Science, Scienter, Scilicet, Sciolism, Sciosophy, Shrewd, Smattering, Suss, Technology, Telegnosis, Understand(ing), Up, Versed, Wat(e), Weet(e), Well-informed, Well-read, Wis, Wise, Wist, Wit, Wonk, Wot

Know-all Arrogant, Besserwisser, Bumptious, Cognoscenti, Pansophist, Polymath, Poseur, Smart alec(k), Smart-arse, Smart-ass, Wiseacre

Knuckle (bone) Apply, Dolos, Fist, Joint, Ossein, Submit

Koko List

Kookaburra Laughing jackass, Settler's clock

Kop Spion

Koran Scripture, Sura(h)

Korea(n) Chosen, ROK

Kosher Approved, Genuine, Legitimate, Real

Kremlin Fortress

Kri Masora

Krypton Kr

Kudos Credit, Glory, Praise

Kurd Yezidi

Kyanite Disthene

Ll

L Latitude, League, Learner, Left, Length, Liberal, Lima, Litre, Long, Luxembourg, Pound

La Indeed, My

Label Badge, Band, Book-plate, Brand, Crowner, Designer, Docket, File, Identifier, Indie, Mark, Own, Seal, Sticker, Style, Tab, Tag, Tally, Ticket, Trace

Labiate Catmint, Hoarhound, Horehound

Laboratory Lab, Language, Skylab, Space-lab, Studio, Workshop

Labour(er), Laboured, Laborious Aesthetic, Agonise, Arduous, Begar, Birth, Carl, Casual, Chore, Churl, Coolie, Corvée, Cottager, Cottar, Culchie, Dataller, Day, Direct, Docker, Dwell, Emotional, Forced, Gandy-dancer, Ganger, Gibeonite, Grecian, Grind, Grunt, Hard, Hercules, Hod carrier, Hodge, Hodman, Ida, Indirect, Job, Journeyman, Kanaka, Katorga, Leaden, Manpower, Militant tendency, Moil, Navvy, New, Okie, Operose, Opposition, Pain, Peon, Pioneer, Prole, Redneck, Roll, Rouseabout, Roustabout, Rouster, Sisyphean, Slave, Spalpeen, Statute, Stertorous, Stint, Strive, Sudra, Swagman, Sweated, Task, Tedious, The grip, The lump, → **TOIL(S)**, Toss, Travail, Uphill, Vineyard, Wetback, → **WORK(ER)**, Workmen, Yakka

Labrador Innu, Retriever, Tea

Labyrinth Daedalus, Maze, Mizmaze, Warren, Web

▷ **Labyrinthine** *may indicate* an anagram

Lac Lacquer, Lakh, Resin, Shellac, Tomans

Lace, Lacy Alençon, Babiche, Beat, Blonde, Bobbin, Bone, Bourdon, Brussels, Chantilly, Cluny, Colbertine, Dash, Dentelle, Duchesse, Filet, Galloon, Guipure, Honiton, Inweave, Irish, Jabot, Lash, Macramé, Malines, Mechlin, Mignonette, Mode, Net, Orris, Pearlin, Picot, Pillow, Point, Queen Anne's, Reseau, Reticella, Ricrac, Rosaline, Seaming, Shoestring, Shoe-tie, Spiderwork, Spike, Stay, Tat(ting), Tawdry, Thrash, Thread, Torchon, Trim, Trol(le)y, Truss, Tucker, Valenciennes, Venise, Weave, Welt, Window-bar

Lacerate(d) Ganch, Gash, Gaunch, Maul, Rent, Rip, Slash, Tear

Lachrymose Maudlin, Niobe, Tearful, Water-standing, → **WEEPY**

Lack(ing), Lacks Absence, Aplasia, Bereft, Dearth, Famine, Ha'n't, Insufficiency, Manqué, Minus, → **NEED**, Poverty, Privation, Remiss, Sans, Shortfall, Shy, Void, Want

Lackadaisical Languid, Listless, Torpid

Lackaday Haro

Lackey Boots, Flunkey, Moth, Page, Poodle, Satellite, Skip-kennel

Lacklustre Dull, Insipid, Matt

Lack of confidence Doubt, Scepsis

Laconic Blunt, Close-mouthed, Curt, Spartan, Succinct, Terse

Lacquer Coromandel, Enamel, Hair(spray), Japan, Shellac, → **VARNISH**

Lad Boy(o), Bucko, Callan(t), Chiel(d), Child, Geit, Gyte, Knight, Loonie, Master,

Nipper, Shaver, Stableman, Stripling, Tad, Whipper-snapper

Ladder(y) Accommodation, Aerial, Bucket, Companion, Companionway, Etrier, Extension, Fish, Jack, Jacob's, Pompier, Potence, Rope, Run, Salmon, Scalado, Scalar, Scaling, Sea, Squash, Step, Stie, Sty, Stye, Trap, Turntable

▶ **Lade** *see* **LOAD**

Ladle Bail, Dipper, Punch, Scoop, Shank, Toddy

Lady, Ladies Baroness, Bevy, Bountiful, Burd, Dame, Dark, Dinner, Don(n)a, Duenna, Female, First, Frau, Frow, Gemma, Godiva, Hen, Khanum, Leading, Luck, Maam, Madam(e), Martha, Memsahib, Muck, Nicotine, Peeress, Señora, Shopping bag, Signora, Tea, WC, White, Windermere

▷ **Lady** *may indicate* an '-ess' ending

Ladybird Cushcow, Hen, Vedalia

▷ **Ladybird** *may indicate* a female of a bird family

Ladykiller Bluebeard, Lothario, Masher, Wolf

Lady of the Lake Vivian

Lady's fingers Gumbo, Okra

Lady's maid Abigail

Lag(gard) Culture, Dawdle, Delay, Drag, Flag, Hysteresis, Inmate, Jailbird, Jet, Leng, → **LINGER**, Loiter, Prisoner, Retard, Slowcoach, Slowpoke, Time, Tortoise, Trail

Lager Pils(e)ner

Lagoon Aveiro, Barachois, Haff, Pontchartrain, Pool, Salina, Saline, Vistula

▶ **Laic, Laid** *see* **LAY**

Lair Couch, Den, Earth, Haunt, Hideaway, Kennel, Lodge, Warren

Lake(s) Alkali, Basin, Bayou, Carmine, Cirque, Cowal, Crater, Crimson, Cut off, Finger, L, Lacustrine, Lagoon, Lagune, → **LOCH**, Lochan, Lough, Madder, Mead, Mere, Nyanza, Ox-bow, Poets, Pool, Red, Reservoir, Salina, Salt, Shott, Soda, Tank, Tarn, Turlough, Vlei, Wine

LAKES

2 letters:	Taal	Myall	Barlee
No	Tana	Nam Co	Bienne
	Thun	Neagh	Bitter
3 letters:		Nyasa	Broads
Ewe	5 letters:	Onega	Cayuga
Van	Atlin	Pitch	Corrib
	Chott	Playa	Edward
4 letters:	Cowan	Poopo	Geneva
Amin	Frome	Pskov	Kariba
Bala	Garda	Sevan	Kittle
Biel	Gatun	Tahoe	Ladoga
Bled	Great	Taupo	Lugano
Chad	Huron	Tsana	Malawi
Como	Ilmen	Urmia	Miveru
Erie	Leman	Volta	Mobutu
Erne	Leven		Monona
Eyre	Lower	6 letters:	Nakuru
Kivu	Malar	Albert	Nam Tso
Mead	Morar	Argyle	Nyassa
Nyos	Mungo	Averno	Oneida
Pink	Mweru	Baikal	Peipus

Poyang
Rudolf
Saimaa
St John
Te Anau
Tekapo
Vanern
Varese
Zurich

7 letters:
Amadeus
Aral Sea
Avernus
Axolotl
Balaton
Bizerte
Dead Sea
Iliamna
Katrine
Koko Nor
Lucerne
Managua
Mendota
Nipigon
Ontario
Red Deer
Rotorua
Sempach
Shkoder
St Clair
Toronto
Torrens
Turkana

Vattern

8 letters:
Balkhash
Bodensee
Carnegie
Dongting
Gairdner
Grasmere
Issyk-kul
Kinneret
Maggiore
Manitoba
Masurian
Menindee
Michigan
Naumachy
Okanagan
Onondaga
Regillus
Reindeer
Schwerin
Superior
Tiberias
Titicaca
Tonle Sap
Tungting
Veronica
Victoria
Wakatipu
Wanawaka
Winnipeg

9 letters:
Athabasca
Bangweulu
Champlain
Constance
Ennerdale
Everglade
Genfersee
Great Bear
Great Salt
Innisfree
Killarney
Macquarie
Manapouri
Maracaibo
Naumachia
Neuchatel
Nicaragua
Nipissing
Serbonian
Thirlmere
Trasimene
Trasimono
Ullswater
Wairarapa
Wast Water
Winnebago
Ysselmeer

10 letters:
Buttermere
Chautawqua
Clearwater
Great Slave

Hawes Water
Ijsselmeer
Miraflores
Mistassini
Of the Woods
Okeechobee
Okefenokee
Serpentine
Tanganyika
Washington
Windermere

11 letters:
Lesser Slave
Paralimnion
Stanley Pool

12 letters:
Derwentwater
Memphremagog
Waikaremoana
Winnipegosis

13 letters:
Bassenthwaite
Coniston Water
Crummock Water
Pontchartrain

14 letters:
Chiputneticook
Disappointment
Ennerdale Water

Lake-dwelling Crannog
Lakeland Cumbria
Lam Flee, Scram
Lama Dalai, Karmapa, Panchen, Tashi
Lamb(skin) Baa, Barometz, Beaver, Budge, Bummer, Cade, Canterbury, Caracul, Cosset, Ean(ling), Elia, Fat, Fell, Grit, Innocent, Keb, Larry, Noisette, Paschal, Persian, Poddy, Rack, Shearling, Target, Yean(ling)
Lambent Flickering, Glowing, Licking
Lambert Constant
Lame(ness) Accloy, Claude, Cripple, Crock, Game, Gammy, Gimp(y), Halt, Hamstring, Hirple, Hors de combat, Maim, Main, Spavined, Springhalt, Stringhalt, Weak
Lament(able), Lamentation, Lamenter Bemoan, Bewail, Beweep, Complain, Croon, Cry, Dirge, Dumka, Dump, Elegy, Funest, Jeremiad, Jeremiah, Keen, Meane, Mein, Mene, Moon, Mourn, Ochone, Paltry, Piteous, Plain, Repine, Sigh, Sorry, Threne, Threnody, Ululate, → **WAIL**, Welladay, Wel(l)away, Yammer

Lamia Deadnettle
Lamina(te) Film, Flake, Folium, Formica®, Lamella, Layer, Plate, Scale, Table, Veneer
Lamp(s) Aladdin's, Aldis, Anglepoise, Arc, Argand, Bowat, Bowet, Buat, Cru(i)sie, Cru(i)zie, Crusy, Davy, Daylight, Eye, Eyne, Flame, Fluorescent, Fog, Geordie, Glow, Head, Hurricane, Incandescent, Induction, Kudlik, Lampion, Lantern, Lava, Lucigen, Mercury vapour, Miner's, Moderator, Neon, Nernst, Nightlight, Padella, Photoflood, Pilot, Platinum, Quartz, Reading, Riding, Safety, Sanctuary, Scamper, Searchlight, Signal, Sodium, Sodium-vapour, Spirit, Standard, Street, Stride, Stroboscope, Sun, Tail, Tantalum, Tiffany, Tilley, Torchier(e), Tungsten, Uplight(er), Veilleuse, Xenon
Lamplighter Leerie, Spill
Lampoon Caricature, Parody, Pasquil, Pasquin(ade), Satire, Skit, Squib
Lamprey Hag, Lampern, Sandpride
Lancaster Burt, Osbert
Lance Dart, Harpoon, Morne, Pesade, Pike, Prisade, Prisado, Rejôn, Spear, Speisade, Thermic, White arm
Lancelet Amphioxus
Lancer Bengal, Picador, Uhlan
Lancet Fleam
Land(s), Landed Acreage, Aina, Alight, Alluvion, Arpent, Bag, Beach, Bigha, Bovate, Byrd, Carse, Carucate, Cavel, Conacre, Corridor, Country, Croft, Crown, Curtilage, Debatable, Demain, Demesne, Disbark, Disembark, Ditch, Doab, Dock, Earth, Edom, Enderby, Estate, Fallow, Farren, Farthingland, Fee, Feod, Feoff, Feud, Fief, Freeboard, Gair, Glebe, Gondwanaland, Gore, Graham, Ground, Hide, Holding, Holm, Holy, Horst, Ind, Innings, Isthmus, Kingdom, La-la, Laurasia, Lea, Leal, Ley, Light, Link, Machair, Maidan, Manor, Marginal, Marie Byrd, Mesnalty, Métairie, Moose pasture, Morgen, Mortmain, Nation, Never-never, Nod, No man's, Odal, Onshore, Oxgang, Oxgate, Pakahi, Palmer, Pangaea, Panhandle, Parcel, Pasture, Peneplain, Peneplane, Peninsula, Piste, Plot, Ploughgate, Point, Polder, Pr(a)edial, Premises, Private, Promised, Property, Public, Purlieu, Queen Maud, Real estate, Realm, Realty, Reservation, Roman candle, Rundale, Runrig, Rupert's, Savanna(h), Set-aside, Settle, Spit, Swidden, Tack, Taluk, Terra(e), Terra-firma, Terrain, Territory, Thwaite, Tie, Tir na n'Og, Touchdown, Turbary, Tye, Udal, Unship, Ure, Van Diemen's, Veld(t), Victoria, Wainage, Waste, Whenua, Wilkes, Yird
▶ **Landfall** see LANDSLIDE
Landing (craft, stair, system) Autoflare, Crash, Forced, Gallipoli, Gha(u)t, Half, Halfpace, Hard, Instrument, LEM, Module, Pancake, Pier, Quay, Quayside, Soft, Solar, Sollar, Sol(l)er, Splashdown, Three-point, Three-pricker, Touchdown, Undercarriage
Landlock Embay
Landlord, Land owner Absentee, Balt, Boniface, Bonnet laird, Copyholder, Eupatrid, Fiar, Franklin, Herself, Host, Innkeeper, Junker, Laird, Lessor, Letter, Licensee, Patron, Patroon, Proprietor, Publican, Rachman, Rentier, Squattocracy, Squire, Squirearchy, Squireen, Thane, Zamindar(i), Zemindar
Landmark Meith, Watershed
Landmass Laurasia
Land right Emphyteusis
Landscape Karst, Paysage, Picture, Saikei, Scene, Vista
Landslide, Landfall Avalanche, Earthfall, Éboulement, Lahar, Scree, Slip
Landsman Lubber

Land tenure Frankalmoign, Raiyatwari, Rundale, Runrig, Ryotwari

Lane Boreen, Bus, Corridor, Crawler, Drangway, Drury, Express, Fast, Fetter, Gut, Inside, Loan, Lois, Loke, Memory, Middle, Mincing, Nearside, Offside, Outside, Overtaking, Passage, Petticoat, Pudding, Ruelle, Sea-road, Slow, Twitten, Twitting, Vennel, Wynd

Langerhans Insulin, Islets

Language(s) Argot, Artificial, Assembly, Auxiliary, Basic, Body, Cant, Centum, Command, Community, Computer, → **COMPUTER LANGUAGE**, Dead, Dialect, Formal, Georgian, High-level, Hobson-Jobson, Humanities, Idioglossia, Idiolect, Idiom, Inclusive, Jargon, Langue, Ledden, Lingo, Lingua franca, Macaroni, Machine code, Mellowspeak, Meta-, Mixed, Modern, Mother tongue, Native, Natural, Newspeak, Novelese, Object, Officialese, Page description, Parlance, Philology, Pidgin, Plain, Polysynthetic, Pragmatics, Private, Procedural, Programming, Prose, Query, Register, Relay, Rhetoric, Sea-speak, Second, Sign, Sociolect, → **SPEECH**, Strong, Style, Symbolic, Synthetic, Target, Technobabble, Telegraphese, Tone, → **TONGUE**, Tropology, Tushery, Union, Vedic, Verbiage, Vernacular, Vocabulary, Wawa, Words, World

LANGUAGES

3 letters:
Ada
Bat
Edo
Fur
Giz
Gur
Ibo
Ido
Kwa
Luo
Mam
Mon
Neo
San
Tai
Tiv
Twi

4 letters:
Ainu
Avar
Cham
Dani
Erse
Geez
Igbo
Inca
Innu
Komi
Krio

Lozi
Manx
Mari
Maya
Motu
Naga
Nuba
Nupe
Pali
Pedi
Pict
Shan
Susu
Taal
Thai
Tshi
Tupi
Urdu
Xosa
Zulu
Zuni

5 letters:
Aleut
Aryan
Azeri
Balti
Bantu
Batak
Cajun
Carib

Chewa
Cobol
Dogon
Doric
Fanti
Farsi
Galla
Ganda
Gondi
Hausa
Hindi
Hokan
Indic
Joual
Kafri
Koine
Kriol
Kuo-yu
Ladin
Lamba
Lamut
Latin
Lubon
Lunda
Lyele
Malay
Mande
Maori
Mayan
Munda
Nguni

Norse
Oriya
Oscan
Papua
P-Celt
Sakai
Sango
Satem
Saxon
Shona
Shono
Shuar
Sinha
Sioux
Sotho
Suomi
Swazi
Taino
Tajik
Tamil
Temne
Te reo
Tigre
Tonga
Turki
Ugric
Venda
Vogul
Welsh
Wolof
Xhosa

Yakut
Yuman
Yupik

6 letters:
Adyahe
Adygei
Adyghe
Altaic
Arabic
Aranda
Aymara
Basque
Basutu
Berber
Bihari
Bokmal
Brahui
Breton
Celtic
Chadic
Coptic
Creole
Cymric
Dardic
Divehi
Eskimo
Evenki
Fantee
Fijian
Finnic
Fulani
Gaelic
Gagauz
German
Gullah
Hebrew
Herero
Italic
Ladino
Lahnda
Lakota
Lepcha
Lu-wian
Lycian
Lydian
Manchu
Micmac
Mishmi
Na-Dene
Nepali

Novial
Nubian
Ostyak
Pahari
Paiute
Pakhti
Papuan
Pashto
Pashtu
Polish
Pushto
Pushtu
Romany
Rwanda
Salish
Shelta
Sindhi
Siouan
Slovak
Somali
Strine
Tanoan
Tartar
Telegu
Telugu
Tigray
Tongan
Tsonga
Tswana
Tuareg
Tungus
Turkic
Udmurt
Ugrian
Uralic
Yoruba
Zyrian

7 letters:
Adamawa
Amerind
Amharic
Aramaic
Ashanti
Austric
Bengali
Bislama
Cabiric
Caddoan
Catalan
Chaldee

Chinook
Chuvash
Cushite
Dzongka
Elamite
Flemish
Frisian
Gagauzi
Gaulish
Hamitic
Hin Motu
Hittite
Janlish
Japlish
Kannada
Khoisan
Kirundi
Kurdish
Kushite
Lallans
Laotian
Lingala
Luganda
Malinke
Marathi
Miao-Yao
Mingrel
Miskito
Mordvin
Nahuatl
Nauruan
Ndebele
Nilotic
Nyungar
Oceanic
Ossetic
Ottoman
Pahlavi
Pehlevi
Pictish
Prakrit
Punjabi
Pushtoo
Quechua
Romance
Romanes
Romansh
Saharan
Samnite
Samoyed
Semitic

Serbian
Servian
Sesotho
Sinhala
Sinitic
Slovene
Sogdian
Sorbian
Spanish
Sudanic
Swahili
Swedish
Tagalog
Tahitan
Tibetan
Tlingit
Turkish
Turkmen
Umbrian
Uralian
Venetic
Volapuk
Voltaic
Walloon
Wendish
Yerkish
Yiddish

8 letters:
Akkadian
Albanian
Arawakan
Assamese
Bulgaric
Cheremis
Cherkess
Chibchan
Chichewa
Croatian
Cushitic
Dzongkha
Ethiopic
Etrurian
Etruscan
Faliscan
Fanagalo
Filipino
Frankish
Friesian
Goidelic
Gujarati

Gujerati
Gurkhali
Hiri-Motu
Illyrian
Japhetic
Javanese
Judezono
Jugoslav
Kashmiri
Kingwana
Kolarian
Kwakiutl
Landsmal
Lusatian
Malagasy
Mandarin
Mongolic
Mon-Khmer
Netspeak
Nez Perce
Ossetian
Penutian
Pilipino
Polabian
Rhaetian
Romanian
Romansch
Rumansch
Rumonsch
Salishan
Sanscrit
Sanskrit
Scythian
Setswana
Shemitic
Shoshone
Slavonic
Sumerian
Tahitian
Teutonic
Thracian
Tigrinya
Tshiluba
Tungusic

Turanian
Turkoman
Tuvaluan
Ugaritic
Volscian
Wakashan
Warlpiri
Yugoslav

9 letters:
Abkhazian
Afrikaans
Algonkian
Algonquin
Anatolian
Brythonic
Cantonese
Chari-Nile
Cheremiss
Cingalese
Diglossia
Dravidian
Esperanto
Esthonian
Euskarian
Franglais
Goidhelic
Gujarathi
Gujerathi
Hottentot
Inuktitut
Iroquoian
Kamilaroi
Kiswahili
Landsmaal
Langue d'oc
Leizghian
Malayalam
Marquesan
Messapian
Mongolian
Muskogean
Nostratic
Onondagan

Provençal
Putonghua
Roumanian
Roumansch
Sabellian
Semi-Bantu
Sinhalese
Tocharian
Tokharian
Tokharish
Tungurian
Ukrainian
Ursprache
Winnebago

10 letters:
Algonquian
Araucanian
Athabascan
Azerbayani
Beach-la-Mar
Bêche-la-Mar
Caprolalia
Circassian
Diachronic
Eteocretan
Finno-Ugric
Gallo-Roman
Himyaritic
Hindustani
Langue d'oil
Macedonian
Malayalaam
Melanesian
Mingrelian
Muskhogean
Niger-Congo
Papiamento
Police Motu
Proto-Norse
Rajasthani
Serbo-Croat
Singhalese
Synchronic

Ural-Altaic
Uto-Aztecan
Vietnamese

11 letters:
Belarussian
Celtiberean
Dagestanian
Interglossa
Interlingua
Kordofanian
Langobardic
Micronesian
Nilo-Saharan
Old Paissian
Osco-Umbrian
Pama-Nyungan
Sino-Tibetan
Sranantongo
Tessaraglot
Tupi-Guarani

12 letters:
Billingsgate
Gallo-Romance
Idiom neutral
Indo-European
Platt-deutsch
Tibeto-Burman
Volga-Baltaic

13 letters:
Neo-Melanesian
Semito-Hamitic
Serbo-Croatian

14 letters:
Thraco-Phrygian

16 letters:
Malayo-Polynesian

Languid, Languish Die, Divine, Droop, Feeble, Flagging, Listless, Lukewarm, Lydia, Melancholy, Quail, Torpid, Wilt
Languor Lassitude
Lanky Beanpole, Gangly, Gawky, Spindleshanks, Windlestraw
Lanolin Woolfat, Yolk
Lantern Aristotle's, Bowat, Bowet, Buat, Bull's eye, Chinese, Dark(e)y, Epidiascope,

Episcope, Friar's, Glim, Japanese, Jaw, Lanthorn, Magic, Sconce, Stereopticon, Storm, Turnip

Lanthanum La

Laodicean Lukewarm

Lap Circuit, Drink, Gremial, Leg, Lick, Lip, Luxury, Override, Pace, Sypher

Lapdog Messan, Shough, Showghe

▷ **Lapdog** *may indicate* 'greyhound'

Lapel Revers

Laplander, Lapp Saam(e), Sabme, Sabmi, Sami

Lappet Infula

Lapse Backslide, Drop, Error, Expire, Fa', Fall, Nod, Sliding, Trip

Lapwing Hornywink, Teru-tero

Larceny Compound, Grand, Petty, Simple

Larch Hackmatack, Tamarack

Lard Enarm, Leaf, Saim, Seam(e)

Larder Buttery, Pantry, Spence, Springhouse

Large(ness), Largest Ample, Astronomical, Big, Boomer, Bulky, Buster, Colossus, Commodious, Decuman, Enormous, Epical, Extensive, Gargantuan, → **GIGANTIC**, Ginormous, Great, Grit, Gross, Hefty, Helluva, Huge, Hulking, Humdinger, Humongous, Humungous, Kingsize, L, Lunker, Macrocephaly, Massive, Maximin, Maximum, Outsize, Plethora, Prodigious, Rounceval, Rouncival, Skookum, Slew, Slue, Sollicker, Spacious, Spanking, Stonker, Stout, Swingeing, Tidy, Titanic, Vast, Voluminous, Whopping

Large number Centillion, Fermi, Giga, Gillion, Googol, Googolplex, Grillion, Infinitude, Jillion, Lac, Lakh, Legion, Mille, Nation, Nonillion, Quadrillion, Quintillion, Raft, Regiment, Ruck, Scads, Sea, Septillion, Sextillion, Shitload, Slather, Slew, Slue, Squillion, Toman, Trillion, Zillion

Largess Alms, Charity, Frumentation, Generosity

Lariat Lasso, Reata, Riata

Lark Adventure, Aunter, Caper, Dido, Dunstable, Exaltation, Fool, Giggle, Guy, Laverock, Magpie, Mud, Pipit, Prank

Larkspur Stavesacre

Larva Ammacoete, Amphibiotic, Amphiblastule, Aphid lion, Army-worm, Augerworm, Axolotl, Bagworm, Bipinnaria, Bloodworm, Bookworm, Bot(t), Budworm, Cabbage worm, Caddice, Caddis(-worm), Cankerworm, Caterpillar, Cercaria, Chigger, Chigoe, Coenurus, Corn borer, Corn earworm, Cysticercoid, Doodlebug, Grub, Hellgram(m)ite, Hydatid, Indusium, Instar, Jigger, Jointworm, Leather-jacket, Leptocephalus, Maggot, Mealworm, Measle, Microfilaria, Miracidium, Muckworm, Mudeye, Naiad, Nauplius, Neoteny, Nigger, Nymph, Ox-bot, Planula, Pluteus, Porina, Redia, Screwworm, Shade, Silkworm, Strawworm, Tadpole, Trochophore, Trochosphere, Veliger, Water penny, Wireworm, Witchetty, Witchetty grub, Woodworm, Zoea

Laryngitis Croup, Hives

Lascar Seacunny, Tindal

Lascivious(ness) Crude, Goaty, Horny, Lewd, Lubric, Paphian, Satyric, Sotadic, Tentigo, Wanton

Lash(ed), Lashing(s) Cat, Cilium, Firk, Flagellum, Frap, Gammon, Knout, Mastigophora, Mousing, Oodles, Oup, Quirt, Riem, Rope's end, Scourge, Secure, Sjambok, Stripe, Swinge, Tether, Thong, Trice, Whang, → **WHIP**, Wire

Lass(ie) Damsel, Maid, Quean, Queyn, Quin(i)e

Lassitude Accidie, Acedie, Languor, Lethargy

Lasso Lariat, Reata, Rope

Last(ing) Abide, Abye, Aftermost, → **AT LAST**, Boot-tree, Bottom, Cargo, Chronic, Coda, Dernier, Dure, Endmost, Endurance, Endure, Extend, Extreme, → **FINAL**, Hinder, Hindmost, Latest, Latter, Linger, Live, Load, Long-life, Model, Nightcap, Outstay, Perdure, Permanent, Perpetuate, Persist, Rearmost, Spin, Stable, Stand, Stay, Supper, Survive, Swan-song, Thiller, Thule, Tree, Trump, Ult(imate), Ultimo, Utmost, Wear, Weight, Whipper-in, Yester, Z

Last drop Supernaculum

Last resort Pis aller

Last syllable Ultima

Last word(s) Amen, Envoi, Farewell, Ultimatum, Zythum

Latch Bar, Clicket, Clink, Espagnolette, Lock, Night, Sneck, Thumb, Tirling-pin

Late(r), Latest After(wards), Afterthought, Behindhand, Chit-chat, Dead, Deid, Ex, Former, Gen, Infra, Lag, Lamented, New(s), Overdue, Overrunning, Past, Recent, Serotine, Sine, Slow, State-of-the-art, Stop-press, Syne, Tardive, Tardy, Top shelf, Trendy, Umquhile

Late-learner Opsimath

Latent Concealed, Delitescent, Dormant, Maieutic, Potential

Lateral Askant, Edgeways, Sideways

Latex Antiar, Gutta-percha, Jelutong, Ule

Lath Lag, Splat

Lathe Capstan, Mandrel, Mandril, Turret

Lather Flap, Foam, Froth, Sapples, Suds, Tan

Latin(ist) Biblical, Classical, Criollo, Dago, Dog, Erasmus, Eyeti, Greaseball, High, Humanity, Italiot, L, Late, Law, Low, Medieval, Middle, Modern, Neapolitan, New, Pig, Quarter, Rogues', Romanic, Romish, Scattermouch, Silver, Spic, Thieves', Vulgar, Wop

Latin-American Criollo, Tico

Latitude Breadth, Celestial, Ecliptic, Free hand, Horse, L, Leeway, Liberty, Licence, Meridian, Parallel, Play, Roaring forties, Scope, Tropic, Width

Latrine Ablutions, Bog, Cloaca, Furphy, Garderobe, Loo, Privy, Rear

Latter Last, Previous

Latter-day Recent, Saints, Young

Lattice Bravais, Clathrate, Espalier, Grille, Space, Treillage, Trellis

Lattice-leaf Ouvirandra

Latvian Lett

Laud(able), Lauder Commend, Eulogist, Extol, Harry, Praise, Worthily

Lauderdale Caballer

Laugh(ing), Laughable, Laughter Belly, Cachinnate, Cackle, Chortle, Chuckle, Cod, Corpse, Democritus, Deride, Derision, Fit, Fou rire, Gelastic, Giggle, Goster, Guffaw, Ha, He-he, Ho-ho, Homeric, Hoot, Horse, Hout, Howl, Irrision, Isaac, Last, Lauch, Leuch, Levity, Ludicrous, → **MIRTH**, Mock, Nicker, Peal, Present, Riancy, Riant, Rich, Rident, Ridicule, Risus, Scream, Snigger, Snirt(le), Snort, Tehee, Titter, Yo(c)k

Laughing-stock Outspeckle, Sport

Launcelot Gobbo

Launch(ing), Launch pad Begin, Blast-off, Catapult, Chuck, Cosmodrome, ELV, Fire, Float, Hurl, Initiate, Lift-off, Moonshot, Motoscalp, Opening, Pioneer, Presentation, Release, Rolling, Roll out, Send, Shipway, Slipway, Start, Steam, Unstock, Upsend, VTO

Launder, Laund(e)rette, Laundry Bagwash, Clean, Coin-op, Lav, Steamie, Tramp,

Transfer, Wash, Washhouse, Whites

Laurel(s) Aucuba, Bay, Camphor, Cherry, Daphne, Japan, Kalmia, Kudos, Mountain, Pichurim, Rose (bay), Sassafras, Spicebush, Spotted, Spurge, Stan, Sweet-bay, True

Laurence Sterne

Lava Aa, Block, Bomb, Coulée, Cysticercus, Dacite, Flood basalt, Lahar, Lapilli, Magma, Mud, Nuée ardente, Pahoehoe, Palagonite, Pillow, Pitchstone, Plug, Pumice, Pyroclast, Scoria, Tephra, Toadstone

Lavatory Ajax, Bogger, Brasco, Can, Carsey, Carzey, Cludgie, Comfort station, Convenience, Cottage, Dike, Dunnakin, Dunny, Dyke, Earth closet, Elsan®, Facilities, Forica, Furphey, Gents, Heads, Jakes, Jane, John, Kars(e)y, Karzy, K(h)azi, Kleinhuisie, Kybo, Ladies, Lat(rine), Loo, Necessary, Netty, Office, Outhouse, Portaloo®, Privy, Rear(s), Reredorter, Shithouse, Shouse, Siege, Smallest room, Superloo, Throne, Thunderbox, Toilet, Toot, Tout, Urinal, Washroom, WC

Lave Lip, Wash

Lavender Aspic, Sea, Spike

Lavengro Borrow

Laver Moabite, Nori, Ore-weed

Lavish Barmecidal, Copious, Excessive, Exuberant, Flush, Free, Fulsome, Generous, Liberal, Lucullan, Lush, Prodigal, Shower, Slap-up, Sumptuous, Wanton, Waste

Law(s) Abingdon, Act, Agrarian, Anti-trust, Ass, Association, Avogadro's, Babo's, Bar, Barratry, Bernoulli's, → **BILL**, Biogenetic, Blue-sky, Bode's, Bonar, Boyle's, Bragg's, Brehon, Brewster's, Brocard, Buys Ballot's, Byelaw, Cain, Canon, Capitulary, Case, Chancery, Charles's, Civil, Code, Common, Constitution, Corn, Coulomb's, Criminal, Cupar, Curie's, Curie-Weiss, Cy pres, Dalton's, Dead-letter, Decree, Decretals, Decretum, De Morgan's, Deodand, Dharma, Dictate, Digest, Din, Distributive, Dry, Edict, Einstein's, Enact, Excise, Forensic, Forest, Fuero, Fundamental, Fuzz, Game, Gas, Gay-Lussac's, Graham's, Gresham's, Grimm's, Grotian, Haeckel's, Halifax, Hardy-Weinberg, Henry's, Homestead, Hooke's, Hubble's, Hudud, Hume's, International, Irade, Iure, Joule's, Jura, Jure, Jus, Kain, Kashrut(h), Kepler's, Kirchhoff's, Labour, Land, Lay, Leibniz's, Lemon, Lenz's, Lien, Liquor, Lor(d), Losh, Lydford, Lynch, Magdeburg, Mariotte's, Martial, May, Mendel's, Mercantile, Military, Mishna(h), Mishnic, Moral, Mosaic, Murphy's, Natural, Newton's, Noahide, Nomistic, Nomothetic, Octave, Ohm's, Oral, Ordinance, Pandect, Parity, Parkinson's, Pass, Penal, Periodic, Planck's, Plebiscite, Poor, Principle, Private, Public, Regulation, Roman, Rubric, Rule, Salic, Salique, Scout, Sharia(h), Sheria(t), Shield, Shulchan Aruch, Snell's, Sod's, → **STATUTE**, Stefan's, Stokes, Sumptuary, Sunna, Sus(s), Sword, Table, Talmud, Tenet, Thorah, Thorndike's, Torah, Tort, Tradition, Twelve Tables, Ulema, Unwritten, Use, Verner's, Vigilante, Written

Lawless(ness) Anarchy, Anomie, Anomy, Antinomian, Bushranger, Piratical, Rowdy

Lawmaker, Lawman, Lawyer Alfaqui, Ambulance chaser, Attorney, AV, Avocat, Barrack room, Barrister, Bencher, BL, Bluebottle, Bramble, Bush, Canon, Coke, Counsel, DA, Decemvir, Deemster, Defence, Dempster, Doge, Draco, Earp, Enactor, Fiscal, Greenbag, Grotius, Hammurabi, Jurisconsult, Jurist, Legal eagle, Legist, Mooktar, Moses, MP, Mufti, Mukhtar, Nomothete, Notary, Penang, Pettifoggers, Philadelphia, Proctor, Procurator fiscal, Prosecutor, Rabbi, Shirra, Shyster, Silk, Solicitor, Spenlow, Stratopause, Talmudist, Templar, Thesmothete, Vakil, WS

Lawn Cloth, Grass, Green, Linen, Sward, Turf

Lawrence DH, Ross, Shaw, TE

Lawrencium Lr

Lawsuit Case, Cause, Plea, Trover

▶ **Lawyer(s), Lawman** *see* **LAWMAKER**

▷ **Lax** *may indicate* an anagram

Lax(ity) Freedom, Inexact, Laissez-aller, Latitude, Lenience, Loose, Remiss, → **SLACK**, Wide, Wide-open

Laxative Aloin, Aperitive, Cascara, Cassia, Cathartic, Eccoprotic, Elaterin, Elaterium, Glauber's salt, Gregory (powder), Loosener, Physic, Purgative, → **PURGE**, Saline, Senna-pod, Taraxacum

Lay(ing), Layman, Laic, Laid, Laity Air, Amateur, Antepost, Aria, Ballad, Bed, Bet, Blow, Chant, Civil, Ditty, Drop, Earthly, Egg, Embed, Fit, Impose, Lied, Lodge, Man, Minstrel, Oat, Oblate, Ode, Ordinary, Outsider, Oviparous, Oviposit, Parabolanus, Pose, Secular, Set, Sirvente, → **SONG**, Sypher, Temporalty, Tertiary, Tribal, Wager, Warp

Layabout Idler, Loafer, Lotophagus, Ne'er-do-well, Slob

Lay-by Rest stop

Layer(s) Abscission, Aeuron(e), Ancona, Appleton, Battery, Boundary, Cake, Caliche, Cladding, Coating, Crust, D, Depletion, E, Ectoplasm, Ectosarc, Ekman, Epiblast, Epilimnion, Epitaxial, Epitheca, Epithelium, Erathem, E-region, Exine, Exocarp, Film, Flake, Friction, Ganoin, Germ, Gossan, Gozzan, Granum, Ground, Heaviside, → **HEN**, Herb, Hypotheca, Intima, Inversion, Kennelly(-Heaviside), Kerf, Lamella, Lamina, Lap, Leghorn, Lenticle, Lie, Malpighian, Media, Miocene, Ozone, Pan, Patina, Paviour, Photosphere, Ply, Retina, Reversing, Rind, Scale, Sclerite, Screed, Shrub, Skim, Skin, Skiver, Sliver, Spathic, Stratify, Stratopause, Stratum, Substratum, Tabular, Tapetum, Tier, Tremie, Trophoblast, Trophoderm, Uvea, Varve, Vein, Velamen, Veneer

Lay-off Dismiss, Hedge, Redundance

Lay-out Ante, Design, Fell, Format, Map, Mise, Pattern, Spend, Straucht, Straught, Streak, Streek, Stretch

Laze, Laziness, Lazy (person) Bed-presser, Bummer, Cabbage, Couch potato, Faineant, Hallian, Hallion, Hallyon, Indolent, Inert, Lackadaisical, Laesie, Languid, Layabout, Lie-abed, Lig(ger), Lime, Lither, Loaf, Lotus-eater, Lusk, Mollusc, Ne'er-do-well, Oblomovism, Resty, Sloth, Slouch, Slug(-a-bed), Sluggard, Susan, Sweer, Sweir, Veg, Workshy

▷ **Lazily** *may indicate* an anagram

Lea Grass, Meadow

Leach(ing) Cheluviation, Lixivial, Ooze

Lead(er), Leading, Leadership Ag(h)a, Ahead, Akela, Amakosi, Anglesite, Article, Atabeg, Atabek, Ayatollah, Bab, Bellwether, Black, Bluey, Brand, Cable, Cade, Calif, Caliph, Came, Capitano, Capo, Captain, Castro, Caudillo, Causal, Centre, Ceruse, Cheer, Chieftain, Chiliarch, Chin, China white, Choragus, Choregus, CO, Codder, Condottiere, Conducive, Conduct, Coryphaeus, Coryphee, Demagogue, Dictator, Duce, Dux, Editorial, Escort, Ethnarch, Extension, Figurehead, Floor, Foreman, Foremost, Frontrunner, Fu(e)hrer, Fugleman, Gaffer, Gandhi, Garibaldi, Gerent, Go, Graphite, Guide(r), Halter, Hand, Headman, Headmost, Headnote, Hegemony, Heresiarch, Hero, Hetman, Honcho, Idi, Imam, Imaum, Ink(h)osi, Inveigle, Jason, Jefe, Jump, Juve(nile), Kabir, Kame, King, Ksar, Leam, Litharge, Livid, Loss, Lost, Lyam, Lyme, Mahatma, Mahdi, Main, Market, Marshal, Massicot, Masticot, Mayor, Meer, Mehdi, Minium, Mir, Nanak, No 1, Nomarch, Nose, Numero uno, Omrah, Open, Pacemaker, Pacesetter, Padishah, Panchen Lama, Pb, Pilot, Pioneer, Pit, Plumb(um), Plummet, PM, Precentor, Premier(e), President, Price, Rangitara, Ratoo, Rebbe, Rebecca, Red, Role, Ruler, Sachem, Sagamore, Saturn,

Saturn's tree, Scotlandite, Scout, Scuddaler, Scudler, Sharif, Sheik(h), Sixer, Skipper, Skudler, Soaker, Soul, Sounding, Spearhead, Staple, Star, Sultan, Supremo, Taoiseach, Tecumseh, Tetraethyl, Top banana, Top dog, Trail(blazer), Tribune, Tsaddik, Tsaddiq, Tzaddik, Up, Usher, Vaivode, Van(guard), Vanadinite, Va(u)nt, Vaunt-courier, Voivode, Vozhd, Waivode, Wali, Warlord, White, Whitechapel, Wulfenite, Youth, Zaddik, Zia

▷ **Lead(s), Leaders** *may indicate* first letters of words

Leaden Flat, Plumbeous, Saturnine

Lead-glance Galena

Leading to Pre

Leaf(y), Leaves Acanthus, Acrospire, Amphigastrium, Amplexicaul, Ascidia, At(t)ap, Baccy, Betel, Blade, Bract, Carpel, Cataphyll, Cladode, Coca, Compound, Consent, Corolla, Costate, Cotyledon, Dolma, Drop, Duff, Fig, Finial, Foil, Foliage, Foliar, Folio(se), Folium, Frond, Glume, Gold, Green, Holiday, Induviae, Jugum, K(h)at, Maple, Megaphyll, Microphyll, Needle, Nervate, Out, P, Pad, Page, Pan, Phyllid, Phyllome, Qat, Repair, Riffle, Rosula, Salad, Scale, Sclerophyll, Secede, Sepal, Sheet, Siri(h), Skip, Spathe, Sporophyll, Stipule, Tea, Title, Tobacco, TTL, Valve, Vert, Vine, Withdraw

Leafhopper Thrip

Leafless Ebracteate, Scape

Leaflet At(t)ap, Bill, Bracteole, Circular, Dodger, Fly-sheet, Foliolose, Handbill, Pinna, Pinnula, Prophyll, Stipel, → TRACT

League Achaean, Alliance, Arab, Band, Bund, Compact, Decapolis, Delian, Entente, Federation, Gueux, Guild, Hanse(atic), Holy, Ivy, Land, Major, Minor, Nations, Parasang, Primrose, Redheaded, Rugby, Solemn, Super, Union, Ypres, Zollverein, Zupa

Leak(y) Bilge, Drip, Escape, Extravasate, Gizzen, Holed, Holey, Ooze, Pee, Porous, Seepage, Sype, Trickle, Wee, Weep, Wee-wee

Leak-proof Airtight

Leamington Spa

Lean(ing) Abut, Barren, Batter, Bend, Careen, Carneous, Carnose, Griskin, Heel, Hike out, → INCLINE, Lie, Lig(ge), Minceur, Prop, Propend, Rake, Rely, Rest, Scraggy, Scrawny, Skinny, Spare, Stoop, Taste, Tend, Tilt, Tip, Walty, Wiry

Leander Abydos

Lean-to Skillion

Leap(ing), Leapt Assemblé, Bound, Brisé, Cabriole, Caper, Capriole, Cavort, Clear, Croupade, Curvet, Echappé, Entrechat, Falcade, Fishdive, Frisk, Galumph, Gambade, Gambado, Gambol, Jeté, Jump, Loup, Luppen, Ollie, Over, Pigeon-wing, Pounce, Pronk, Quantum, Sally, Salto, Somersa(u)lt, Somerset, → SPRING, Stag, Transilient, Vault, Volte

Leap year Bissextile, Penteteric

Lear Edward, King, Nonsense

Learn(ed), Learner Beginner, Blue, Bluestocking, Chela, Classical, Con, Discover, Distance, Doctor, Don, Erudite, Gather, Get, Glean, Hear, Kond, L, Lear(e), Leir, Lere, Literate, Literati, Literato, Lucubrate, Master, Memorise, Mirza, Mug up, → NOVICE, Opsimath, Pandit, Polymath, Programmed, Pundit, Pupil, Rookie, Savant, Scan, Scholar, Scient, See, Starter, Student, → STUDY, Tiro, Trainee, Tutee, Tyro, Wise

Learning Blended, Culture, Discipline, Discrimination, Distance, Erudition, Index, Insight, Instrumental, Latent, Lifelong, Lore, Machine, New, Open, Opsimathy, Rep, Sleep, Wit

Lease(-holder) Charter, Farm, Feu, Gavel, Hire, Let, Long, Novated, → **RENT**, Set(t), Tack, Tacksman

Leash Lead, Lune, Lyam, Lym(e), Slip, Three, Trash, Triplet

Least Minimum, Rap

Leather(s), Leathery Artificial, Bouilli, Bouilly, Box-calf, Buckskin, Buff, Cabretta, Calf, Capeskin, Chammy, Chamois, Chaps, Checklaton, Cheverel, Chevrette, Cordovan, Cordwain, Corium, Counter, Cowhide, Crispin, Cuir(-bouilli), Deacon, Deerskin, Diphthera, Doeskin, Dogskin, Durant, Fair, Foxing, Goatskin, Grain, Hide, Hog-skin, Horsehide, Japanned, Kid, Kip(-skin), Lacquered, Lamp, Levant, Marocain, Maroquin, Mocha, Morocco, Mountain, Nap(p)a, Neat, Nubuck®, Oak, Ooze, Oxhide, Paste-grain, Patent, Pigskin, Plate, Rand, Rawhide, Rexine®, Riem(pie), Roan, Rock, Rough-out, Russia, Saffian, Shagreen, Shammy, Sharkskin, Shecklaton, Sheepskin, Shoe, Skiver, Slinkskin, Snakeskin, Spetch, Split, Spur, Stirrup, Strand, Strap, Suede, Tan, Taw, Thong, Upper, Wallop, Wash, Waxed, White, Whitleather, Yuft

Leatherneck Marine, RM

Leave(r), Leavings, Leave off Abandon, Abiturient, Abscond, Absit, Absquatulate, Acquittal, Adieu, Avoid, Bequeath, Blessing, Bug, Compassionate, Congé, Congee, Decamp, Depart, Desert, Desist, Devisal, Devise, Ditch, Evacuate, Exeat, Exit, Exodus, Extrude, Forego, Forgo, Forsake, French, Furlough, Gardening, Garlandage, → **GO**, Inspan, Ish, Legate, Liberty, Licence, Maroon, Mass, Maternity, Mizzle, Omit, Orts, Pace, Parental, Park, Part, Paternity, → **PERMISSION**, Permit, → **QUIT**, Residue, Resign, Sabbatical, Scapa, Scat, Scram, Shore, Sick, Skedaddle, Skidoo®, Stick, Strand, Vacate, Vade, Vamo(o)se, Will, Withdraw

Leaven Barm, Ferment, Yeast

Lebanese, Lebanon Druse, RL

Lecher(ous), Lechery Gate, Goaty, Lascivious, Libertine, Lickerish, Lustful, Profligate, Rake, Roué, Salaciousness, Satirisk, Satyr, Silen, Whoremonger, Wolf

Lectern Ambo, Desk, Eagle, Oratory

Lecture(r), Lectures, Lecturing Address, Aristotelian, Chalktalk, Creed, Curtain, Docent, Dissert(ator), Don, Earful, Erasmus, Expound, Homily, Hulsean, Jaw, Jawbation, Jobe, L, Lector, Pi-jaw, Prelect, Privatdocent, Prone, Rate, Read(er), Rede, Reith, Rubber chicken circuit, Scold, Sententious, → **SERMON**, Spout, Talk, Teacher, Teach-in, Wigging, Yaff

Ledge Altar, Berm, Buttery-bar, Channel, Fillet, Gradin(e), Linch, Misericord(e), Nut, Rake, Scarcement, Settle, → **SHELF**, Window (sill)

Ledger Book, Purchase, Register

Lee(s) Dregs, Dunder, Heeltaps, Sediment, Shelter, Ullage

Leech Bleeder, Gnathobdellida, Horse, Medicinal, Parasite, Rhynchobdellida

Leek Allium, Fouat, Fouet, Porraceous, Rocambole, Sengreen

Leer Eliad, Fleer, Oeillade, Ogle, Perv

Leeway Drift

Left (hand), Left-handed, Left-hander, Left-winger Abandoned, Adrift, Balance, Bolshy, Corrie-fisted, Dolly-push, Gallock, Hie, High, Inherited, L, Laeotropic, Laevorotation, Larboard, Links, Loony, Lorn, Near, New, Other, Over, Pink, Port, Portsider, Quit, Rad, Red, Relic, Residuum, Resigned, Secondo, Sinister, Soc(ialist), Southpaw, Thin, Titoism, Trot, Verso, Vo, Went, West, Wind, Yet

Left-over Astatki, Dregs, End, Gone, Lave, Oddment, Offcut, Orra, Remains, Remanet, → **REMNANT**, Residue, Waste

Leg(s), Leggings, Leggy, Leg-wear Antigropelo(e)s, Bandy, Barbados, Barley-sugar, Bow, Breeches, Cabriole, Cannon, Chaparajos, Chaparejos, Chaps,

Crural, Crus, Dib, Drumstick, Fine, Fly-sail, Gaiter, Galligaskins, Gam(b), Gamash, Gambado, Garter, Gaskin, Giambeux, Gigot, Gramash, Gramosh, Ham, Haunch, Hest, Hock, Jamb, Jambeau, Jambeaux, Knock-knee(d), Limb, Long, Member, Milk, Myriapod, Oleo, On(side), Peg, Peraeopod, Periopod, Peroneal, Pestle, Pin, Podite, Proleg, Puttees, Pylon, Relay, Section, Shanks, Shanks's pony, Shaps, Shin, Short, Spats, Spatterdash, Spider, Spindleshanks, Square, Stage, Stump, Thigh, Tights, White

Legacy Bequest, Cumulative, Demonstrative, Dowry, Entail, General, Heirloom, Residuary, Specific, Substitutional

Legal(ism), Legally, Legitimate Bencher, Decriminalised, Forensic, Halacha, Halaka(h), Halakha, Lawful, Licit, Nomism, Scienter, Statutory

Legal book Halacha, Halaka(h), Halakha, Talmud

Leg-armour, Leg-covering Cootikin, Cu(i)tikin, Gambado, Jamb(e), Pad

Legate, Legator Ambassador, Consul, Devisor, Emissary, Envoy, Nuncio

▷ **Legend** *may indicate* leg-end (e.g. foot, talus)

Legend(ary) Arthurian, Caption, Edda, Fable, Folklore, Hadith, Motto, Myth, Saga, Story, Urban, Yowie

Leger Swindler

Leghorn Livorno

Legible Clear, Lucid, Plain

Legion(ary), Legionnaire Alauda, American, Army, British, Cohort, Countless, Deserter, Foreign, Geste, Honour, → **HOST**, Maniple, Many, Throng, Thundering, Zillions

Legislate, Legislator, Legislature Assemblyman, Congress, Decemvir, Decree, MP, Nomothete, Oireachtas, → **PARLIAMENT**, Persian, Senator, Solon, Zemstvo

Legitimate Kosher, Loyal

Legless Amelia, Blotto, Boozy, Caecilia, Drunk, Mermaid, Psyche

Leg-pull Chaff, Joke, Rise, Rot

Legume, Leguminous Bean, Guar, Lentil, Lomentum, Pea, Pipi, Pod, Pulse

Leibniz Monadism

Leigh Amyas

Leisure(ly) Adagio, Ease, Lento, Liberty, Moderato, Otium, Respite, Rest, Vacation

Lemming Morkin

Lemon Answer, Cedrate, Citron, Citrus, Smear-dab, Sole, Yellow

Lemur Angwantibo, Aye-aye, Babacoote, Bush-baby, Colugo, Galago, Half-ape, Indri(s), Loris, Macaco, Malmag, Mongoose, → **MONKEY**, Nagapie, Potto, Ringtail, Sifaka, Spectre, Tana, Tarsier

Lend Advance, Loan, Prest, Sub, Vaunce

Length(y), Lengthen(ing), Lengthwise Archine, Arsheen, Arshin(e), Aune, Barleycorn, Braccio, Cable, Chain, Cubit, Distance, Eke, Ell, → **ELONGATE**, Endways, Ennage, Epenthetic, Expand, Extensive, Focal, Foot, Furlong, Inch, Ley, Mile, Nail, Passus, Perch, Piece, Plethron, Pole, Prolate, Prolix, Prolong, Protract, Reach, Remen, Rod, Rope, Slow, Span, Stadium, Toise, Vara, Verbose, Yard

Lenient Clement, Exurable, Lax, Mild, Permissive, Soft, Tolerant

Lens Achromatic, Acoustic, Anamorphic, Anastigmat, Aplanatic, Apochromat(ic), Bifocal, Bull's eye, Compound, Contact, Corneal, Crookes, Crown, Crystalline, Dielectric, Diopter, Dioptre, Diverging, Electron, Electrostatic, Eye, Eyeglass, Eye-piece, Facet, Fish-eye, Fresnel, Gas-permeable, Gravitational, Hard, Immersion, Lentil, Macro, Magnetic, Metallic, Mirror, Object-glass, Optic, Pantoscope, Phacoid, Piano-concave, Piano-convex, Soft, Soft-focus, Stanhope, Sunglass, Telephoto, Toric, Trifocal, Varifocal, Water, Wide-angle, Zoom

Lent Carême, Fast, Laetare, Out, Quadragesimal, Term
Lentil(s) D(h)al, Dholl, Ervalenta, Lens, Phacoid, Pulse, Puy, Revalenta
Leonora Overture
Leopard Clouded, Hunting, Leap, Libbard, Ounce, Panther, Pard, Snow, Spots
Leopold Bloom
Leotard Maillot
Leper, Leprosy, Leprous Gehazi, Hansen's disease, Lazar, Leontiasis, Lionism, Meazel, Mesel, Outcast, Pariah
Lepidopterist Aurelian, Moth-er, Pendleton, Treacler
Leprechaun Elf, Gremlin, Imp
Lepton Muon
Lesbian Boi, Bull dyke, Crunchie, Diesel, Dike, Dyke, Homophile, Lipstick, Sapphist, Tribade
Lese-majesty Treason
Lesion Cut, Gash, Pannus, Scar, Serpiginous, Sore, Wheal, Whelk
Less(en), Lesser, Lessening Abate, Alaiment, Bate, Contract, Deaden, Decline, Deplete, Derogate, Dilute, → **DWINDLE**, Extenuate, Fewer, Junior, Littler, Meno, Minus, Play down, Reduce, Relax, Remission, Subordinate, Subsidiary, Tail, Under
Lesson Example, Lear(e), Lection, Leir, Lere, Life, Masterclass, Moral, Object, Parashah, Period, Sermon, Shiur, Tutorial
Let (go, off, out), Letting Allow, Cap, Charter, Conacre, Displode, Divulge, Enable, Entitle, Explode, Hire, Impediment, Indulge, Lease, Litten, Loot(en), Luit(en), Lutten, Net, Obstacle, Obstruct, → **PERMIT**, Rent, Reprieve, Sett, Tenancy, Unhand, Warrant
Let down Abseil, Betray, Lower, Sell, Vail
Let-down Disappointment, Non-event
Lethal Deadly, Fatal, Fell, Mortal
Lethargic, Lethargy Accidie, Apathy, Coma, Drowsy, Ennui, Hebetude, Inertia, Lassitude, Listless, Passive, Sleepy, Sluggish, Stupor, Supine, Torpid, Turgid
Letter(s) Ache, Aerogam, Aesc, Airgraph, Aleph, Alif, Alpha, Ascender, A(y)in, Bayer, Begging, Beta, Beth, Block, Breve, Cadmean, Canine, Caph, Capital, Capon, Casket, Chain, Cheth, Chi, Chitty, Circular, Col, Collins, Consonant, Covering, Cue, Cuneiform, Daled, Daleth, Dead, Dear John, Delta, Digamma, Digraph, Dominical, Edh, Ef(f), Emma, Encyclical, Ep(isemon), Epistle, Epsilon, Eta, Eth, Fan, Favour, Form, Fraktur, French, Gamma, Gimel, Grapheme, He, Heth, Initial, Iota, Izzard, Jerusalem, Kaph, Kappa, Koppa, Kufic, Labda, Lambda, Lamed(h), Landlady, Landlord, Lessee, Lessor, Literal, Love, Mail, Mail-shot, Majuscule, Mem, Memo, Miniscule, Minuscule, Missive, Monogram, Mu, Nasal, Night, Note, Notelet, Nu, Nun, Og(h)am, Omega, Omicron, Open, Pahlavi, Paston, Pastoral, Patent, Pe, Pehlevi, Phi, Pi, Plosive, Poison-pen, Polyphone, Postbag, Psi, Pythagorean, Qoph, Resh, Rho, Rhyme, Rom, Runestave, Sad(h)e, Samekh, Samian, Sampi, San, Scarlet, Screed, Screeve, Screwtape, Script, See, Shin, Ship, Siglum, Sigma, Sign, Signal, Sin, Sort, Stiff, Swash, Tau, Tav, Taw, Teth, Theta, Thorn, Toc, Tsade, Typo, Uncial, Upsilon, Vau, Vav, Versal, Vowel, Waw, Wen, Wyn, Wynn, Xi, Yod(h), Yogh, Ypsilon, Zayin, Zed, Zeta
Lettering Cufic, Kufic
Lettuce Batavia, Butterhead, Cabbage, Chicon, Corn-salad, Cos, Frog's, Iceberg, Lactuca, Lamb's, Lollo rosso, Mizuna, Romaine, Salad, Sea, Thridace
Leucoma Albugo
Levant(ine) Coptic, Go, Israelite, Jew, Ottamite, Ottomite
Levee Bank, Dyke, Embankment, Party

Level(ler) A, Abney, Abreast, Aclinic, Ad eundum, Aim, Awash, Bargaining, Base, Break even, Bulldoze, Champaign, Confidence, Countersink, Degree, Dumpy, Echelon, Energy, Equal, → **EVEN**, Extent, Flat, Flight, Flush, Fog, Grade, Logic, O, Occupational, Ordinary, Par, Plane, Plat(eau), Point, Price, Race, Rank, Rase, Raze, Reduced, Savanna, Sea, Spirit, Split, Springing, → **SQUARE**, Status, Stratum, Street, Strew, Strickle, Subsistence, Support, Surveyor's, Tier, Top, Trophic, True, Water, Y

Lever(age) Backfall, Bell-crank, Brake, Cock, Crampon, Crowbar, Dues, Gear, Handspike, Jaw, Jemmy, Joystick, Key, Knee-stop, Landsturm, Pawl, Peav(e)y, Pedal, Prise, Prize, Pry, Purchase, Stick, Sweep, Swipe, Tappet, Throttle, Tiller, Treadle, Treddle, Tremolo arm, Trigger, Tumbler, Typebar

Leviathan Whale

Levitate Float, Hover, Rise

Levity Flippancy, Glee, Humour, Jollity

Levy Capital, Estreat, Impose, Imposition, Leave, Militia, Octroi, Raise, Scutage, Stent, Talliate, Tax, Tithe, Toll

Lewd(ness) Bawdy, Blue, Debauchee, Impure, Libidinous, Lubricity, Obscene, Priapism, Prurient, Silen(us), Unclean

Lewis Carroll, Tenon

Lexicographer, Lexicon Compiler, Craigie, Drudge, Etymologist, Florio, Fowler, Glossarist, Grove, Johnson(ian), Larousse, Liddell, Mental, Murray, OED, Thesaurus, Vocabulist, Webster, Words-man

Liability, Liable Anme, Apt, Current, Debt, Employer's, Incur, Limited, Open, Product, Prone, Subject, Susceptible, White elephant

Liaison Affair, Amour, Contact, Link

Liana Guarana

Libel(lous) Defamatory, Malign, Sclaunder, Slander, Smear, Sully, Vilify

Liberal(ity) Abundant, Adullamites, Ample, Besant, Bounteous, Bountiful, Breadth, Bright, Broad, Catholic, Enlightened, Free(hander), Free-hearted, → **GENEROUS**, Giver, Grey, Grimond, Grit, Handsome, Indulgent, L, Largesse, Lavish, Limousine, Octobrist, Open, → **PROFUSE**, Rad(ical), Samuelite, Simonite, Steel, Tolerant, Trivium, Unstinted, Verlig, Verligte, Whig

Liberate(d), Liberation, Liberator Bolivar, Deliver, Emancipate, Fatah, → **FREE**, Gay, Inkatha, Intolerant, Messiah, PLO, Release, Save, Sucre, Unfetter, UNITA, Women's

Liberian Kroo, Kru

Libertarian, Libertine Chartered, Corinthian, Debauchee, Don Juan, Laxist, Lecher, Lothario, Lovelace, Playboy, Rake, Rip, Roué, Wencher, Wolf

Liberty Bail, Civil, Discretion, Franchise, Freedom, Hall, Mill, Sauce

Library, Librarian Bibliothecary, BL, Bodleian, Bookmobile, British, Chartered, Circulating, Copyright, Cottonian, Film, Gene, Genomic, Harleian, Laurentian, Lending, Mazarin, Mobile, Morgue, PL, Public, Radcliffe, Reference, Rental, Subscription, Tauchnitz

Librettist Boito, Gilbert, Hammerstein, Lyricist

▶ **Lice** *see* **LOUSE**

Licence, License Abandon, Allow, Authorisation, Carnet, Charter, Dispensation, Driving, Enable, Exequatur, Fling, Franchise, Free(dom), Gale, Imprimatur, Indult, → **LATITUDE**, Let, Marriage, Occasional, Passport, → **PERMIT**, Poetic, Pratique, Provisional, Road-fund, Rope, Slang, Special, Table

Licentious Artistic, Corinthian, Debauchee, Hot, Immoral, Large, Lax, Liberal, Loose, Prurient, Ribald, Sensual, Wanton

Lichen Apothecia, Archil, Corkir, Crotal, Crottle, Cup, Epiphyte, Epiphytic, Graphis,

Korkir, Lecanora, Litmus, Orchel, Orchil(la), Orcine, Orseille, Parella, Parelle, Roccella, Rock tripe, Sea-ivory, Stone-rag, Stone-raw, Tree-moss, Usnea, Wartwort

Lick(ing) Bat, Beat, Deer, Lambent, Lap, Leather, Rate, Salt, Slake, Speed, Tongue, Whip

▸ **Licorice** *see* **LIQUORICE**

Lid Cover, Hat, Kid, Maximum, Opercula, Screwtop, Twist-off

Liddell Alice

Lido Beach, Pool

Lie(s), Liar, Lying Abed, Accubation, Accumbent, Ananias, Bam, Bare-faced, Bask, Billy, Bounce(r), Braide, Cau(l)ker, Cellier, Clipe, Clype, Concoction, Contour, Couchant, Cracker, Cram(mer), Cretism, Cumbent, Deception, Decubitous, Decumbent, Direct, Doggo, Fable, False(r), Falsehood, Falsify, Falsity, Fib, Fiction, Figment, Flam, Gag, Gonk, Hori, Incumbent, Invention, Inveracity, Kip, Lair, Leasing, Lee(ar), Lig(ge), Lurk, Mythomania, Obreption, Oner, Perjury, Plumper, Porky (pie), Procumbent, Prone, Prostrate, Pseudologia, Recline, Recumbent, Repent, Repose, Reptant, Ride, Romance(r), Sham, Sleep, Strapper, Stretcher, Supine, Swinger, Tale, Tappice, Tar(r)adiddle, Thumper, Tissue, Try, Untruth, Whacker, Whid, White, Whopper, Yanker

Lied Art-song, Song

Lie-detector Polygraph

Lien Mortgage, Title

Lieu Locus, Place

Lieutenant Cassio, Flag, Loot, Lt, No 1, Sub(altern)

Life Age, Animation, Being, Bio, Biog(raphy), Brian, Brio, C'est la vie, Chaim, Clerihew, CV, Esse, Eva, Eve, Existence, Good, Heart, High, Mean, Memoir, Nelly, Night, Pep, Plasma, Private, Real, Shelf, Span, Spirit, Still, Subsistence, Time, True, Useful, Vita, Zoe

Life-blood Essence, Lethee

Lifeboat Ark

Life-cell Energid

Life-cycle Redia

Life-force, Life-style Chi, Mana, Port, Qi

Lifeguard Cheesemonger

Lifeless(ness) Abiosis, Algidity, Amort, Arid, Azoic, Barren, Catatonic, Cauldrife, → **DEAD**, Dull, Flat, Inanimate, Inert, Log, Mineral, Possum, Sterile, Stonen, Wooden

Lifelike Breathing, Speaking

Lifeline Umbilicus

Life-rent Usufruct

Life-saver Lineman, Preserver, Raft, Reelman

Lift(ed), Lifter, Lifting Arayse, Arsis, Attollent, Bone, Cable-car, Camel, Chair, Cly, Copy, Crane, Davit, Dead, Dumb waiter, Elate, Elevator, Enhance, Extol, Filch, Fillip, Fireman's, Heave, Heeze, Heezie, Heft, Heist, Hitch, Hoise, Hoist, Hove, Jack, Jigger, Kleptomania, Leaven, Lefte, Lever, Lewis, Nab, Nap, Otis®, Paternoster, Pilfer, Press, Pulley, → **RAISE**, Ride, Scoop, Ski, Sky, Snatch, Spout, Stair, Steal, T-bar, Teagle, Theft, Thumb, Topping, Up, Winch, Windlass

Ligament Annular, Cruciate, Fr(a)enum, Paxwax, Peacock-stone, Spring, Suspensory, Tendon, Urachus

Ligation, Ligature Aesc, Bandage, Bind, Tubal

Light(en), Lighting, Lighter, Lights Aerate, Afterglow, Airy, Albedo, Ale, Alow, Alpenglow, Amber, Ancient, Ans(wer), Arc, Aurora, Back-up, Barge, Batement,

Batswing, Beacon, Beam, Bengal, Beshine, Bezel, Birlinn, Bleach, Brake, Breezy, Bude, Bulb, Calcium, Candle, Cannel, Casco, Casement, Chiaroscuro, Cierge, Clue, Courtesy, Day, Dewali, Diffused, Direct, Diwali, Dream-hole, Drop, Drummond, Earth-shine, Eddystone, Electrolier, Ethereal, Fairy, Fall, Fan, Fantastic, Fastnet, Fetch-candle, Fidibus, Fill, Fire, First, Fixed, Flambeau, Flame, Flare, Flax(y), Flicker, Flippant, Flit(t), Floating, Flood, Fluorescent, Fog (lamp), Frothy, Fuffy, Gas-poker, Gegenschein, Gleam, Glim(mer), Glow, Gossamer, Green, Guiding, Gurney, Haggis, Hazard, Head, House, Idiot, Ignite, Illum(in)e, Incandescence, Indirect, Induction, Inner, Irradiate, Junior, Keel, Key, Kindle, Kiran, Klieg, Lamp, Land, Lantern, Lanthorn, Laser, Leading, LED, Leerie, Leggiero, Levigate, Lime, Link, Linstock, Loadstar, Lobuli, Lodestar, Lozen, Lucarne, Lucigen, Luminaire, Lumine, Luminescence, Luminous, Lunt, Lustre, Lux, Mandorla, Match, Mercurial, Merry-dancers, Mithra(s), Moon, Naphtha, Navigate, Navigation, Neon, New, Nit, Northern, Obstruction, Od(yl), Offal, Optics, Pale, Pane, Parhelion, Pavement, Pennyweight, Phosphene, Phosphorescence, Phot, Photon, Pilot, Pipe, Polar, Pontoon, Portable, Pra(a)m, Producer-gas, Range, Rear, Red, Reflex, Relume, Rembrandt, Reversing, Riding, Rocket, Running, Rush, Safe(ty), Satori, Scoop, Sea-dog, Search, Shine, Shy, Southern, Southern-vigil, Spill, Spot, Spry, Steaming, Strip, Strobe, Stroboscope, Subtle, Sun, Sunshine, Suttle, Svelte, Tail, Tally, Taper, Taps, Tead, Threshold, Tind, Tine, Torch, Torchère, Touchpaper, Traffic, Trivial, Ultraviolet, Unchaste, Unoppressive, UV, Ver(e)y, Vesica, Vesta, Vigil, Watch, Wax, Welsbach burner, White, Windock, Window, Winnock, Zippo, Zodiacal

▷ **Light** *may indicate* an anagram

Lighthouse Beacon, Caisson, Eddystone, Fanal, Fastnet, Phare, Pharos, Sea-mark, Signal

Lightless Aphotic, Dark, Obscure, Unlit

Lightness Buoyancy, Galant, Levity, Pallor

Lightning Ball, Catequil, Chain, Dry, Éclair, Enfouldered, Fireball, Fire flag, Forked, Fulmination, Heat, Levin, Sheet, Thunderbolt, Wildfire, Zigzag

Lightship Nore

Lightweight Nobody, Oz, Trivial

Lignite Jet, Surtarbrand, Surturbrand

Like(ness), Liking À la, As, Broo, Care, Corpse, Dig, Duplicate, Effigy, Eg, Egal, Enjoy, Equal, Fancy, Fellow, Guise, Lich, Palate, Parallel, Peas, Penchant, Please, Predilection, Semblant, Shine, Similar, Simile, Smaak, Sort, Speaking, Taste, Tiki, Uniformity

Likely, Likelihood Apt, Fair, Maximum, Odds-on, Offchance, On, Plausible, Possible, Probable, Probit, Prone, Prospective

Likewise Also, Ditto, Do, Eke, Item, So, Too, Tu quoque

Lilac French, Laylock, Mauve, Pipe-tree, Syringa

Lilliputian Minute

Lilt Swing

Lily African, Agapanthus, Aloe, Amaryllis, Annunciation, Arum, Asphodel, Aspidistra, Belladonna, Blackberry, Calla, Camas(h), Camass, Canada, Candock, Chincherinchee, Colchicum, Colocasia, Convallaria, Corn, Crinum, Dale, Day, Easter, Elaine, Fawn, Fleur de lys, Fritillary, Galtonia, Guernsey, Haemanthus, Hemerocallis, Herb-Paris, Jacobean, Jacob's, Jersey, Kniphofia, Laguna, Lent, Leopard, Lote, Lotos, Lotus, Madonna, Mariposa, Martagon, Meadow, Moorva, Mount Cook, Nelumbo, Nenuphar, Nerine, Nuphar, Orange, Padma, Phormium, Pig, Plantain, Pond, Quamash, Regal, Richardia, Sabadilla, Sansevieria, Sarsa, Scilla, Sego, Skunk cabbage, Smilax, Solomon's seal, Spider, Star of Bethlehem,

Stone, Sword, Tiger, Trillium, Tritoma, Tuberose, Turk's cap, Vellozia, Victoria, Water, Water maize, Yucca, Zephyr

Lily-maid Elaine

Lima Sugar bean

Limb Arm, Bough, Branch, Crural, Exapod, Flipper, Hindleg, Imp, Leg, Leg-end, Member, Phantom, Proleg, Pterygium, Ramus, Scion, Shin, Spald, Spall, Spaul(d), Wing

Limbless Amelia

Limbo Bardo, Isolation

Lime Bass(wood), Beton, Calc, Calcicolous, Caustic, Lind(en), Malm, Mortar, Slaked, Soda, Teil, Tilia, Trap, Unslaked, Viscum, Whitewash

Limerick Doggerel, Twiner, Verse

Limestone Burren, Calc-sinter, Calm, Calp, Ca(u)m, Clint, Coquina, Coral Rag, Cornbrash, Cornstone, Forest Marble, Grike, Karst, Kentish rag, Kunkar, Kunkur, Magnesian, Muschelkalk, Oolite, Pisolite, Rottenstone, Scaglia, Stinkstone, Travertin(e)

Limey Rooinek

Limit(ation), Limited, Limiting Ambit, Bind, Border, Borné, Bound, Bourn(e), Brink, Cap, Cash, Ceiling, Chandrasekhar, Circumscribe, Climax, Compass, Confine, Curb, Deadline, Define, Demark, Determine, Earshot, Eddington, Edge, End, Entail, Esoteric, → **EXTENT**, Extreme, Finite, Frontier, Gate, Goal, Gole, Impound, Induciae, Insular, Limes, Lite, Lynchet, March, Maximum, Meare, Mete, Minimum, Nth, Outedge, Pale, Parameter, Perimeter, Periphery, Predetermine, Qualify, Range, Rate-cap, Ration, Reservation, Restrict, Rim, Roche, Roof, Scant, Shoestring, Sky, Speed, Stint, String, Sumptuary, Tail(lie), Tailye, Tailzie, Term(inus), Tether, Three-mile, Threshold, Thule, Tie, Time, Tropic, Twelve-mile, Utmost, Utter, Verge

▷ **Limit** *may indicate* 'surrounding'

Limner RA

Limousine Daimler, Rolls, Stretch, Zil

Limp Claudication, Dot, Droopy, Flabby, Flaccid, Flaggy, Flimsy, Floppy, Hilch, Hirple, Hitch, Hobble, Hop, Lank, Lifeless, Spancel, Tangle

Limpet Keyhole, Patella, Slipper, Streptoneura

Limpid Clear, Lucid, Pure

Linch Terrace

Lincoln(shire) Abe, Poacher, Yellow-belly

Linden Baucis, Lime, Tilia

Line(d), Lines, Lining Abreast, Aclinic, Agate, Agonic, Allan, Anacreontic, → **ANCESTRY**, Anent, Angle, Apothem, Arew, Asclepiadean, Assembly, Asymptote, Axis, Babbitt, Bakerloo, Bar, Barcode, Baton, Battle, Baulk, Becket, Bikini, Bluebell, Bob, Body, Bombast, Bottom, Boundary, BR, Brail, Branch, Bread, Building, Bush, By, Canal, Carolingian, Carriage, Casing, Cathetus, Cell, Ceriph, Chord, Ciel, Clew, Club, Coach, Coffle, Colour, Column, Contour, Cord(on), Coseismal, Course, Crease, Credit, Crib, Crocodile, Crowfoot, Crow's feet, Curve, Cushion, Dancette, Date, Datum, Dead-ball, Delay, Descent, DEW, Diagonal, Diameter, Diffusion, Directrix, Distaff, Dochmiachal, Dotted, Doublure, Downhaul, Downrigger, Dress, Dynasty, Earing, El, E-la-mi, Encase, Equator, Equinoctial, Equinox, Faint, Fall(s), Fault, Feint, Fess(e), Fettle, File, Finishing, Firing, Firn, Flex, Flight, Frame, Fraunhofer, Front, Frontier, Frost, Furr(ow), Geodesic, Geotherm, Germ, Gimp, Giron, Goal, Graph, Grass, Green, Gridiron, Gymp, Gyron, Hachure, Halyard, Hard, Hatching, Hawser, Header, Hemistich, Heptameter, Hexameter, Hexapody,

High-watermark, Hindenburg, Hockey, Hogscore, Hot, House, Impot, Inbounds, Inbred, Incase, Insole, Interfluve, Intima, Isallobar, Isentrope, Isobar, Isobath, Isobront, Isocheim, Isochime, Isochron(e), Isoclude, Isocryme, Isogloss, Isogonal, Isogram, Isohel, Isohyet, Isolex, Isomagnetic, Isonome, Isopach(yte), Isophone, Isophote, Isopiestic, Isopleth, Isopyenal, Isotach, Isothere, Isotherm, Kill, Knittle, L, Land, Lane, Lansker, Lap, Lariat, Lateral, Latitude, Lead, Leash, Le(d)ger, Ley, Lie, Ling, LMS, Load, Log, Longitude, Lossy, Loxodrome, Lubber, Lugger, Lye, Macron, Maginot, Main, Mainsheet, Mark, Marriage, Mason-Dixon, Median, Meridian, Mesal, Miurus, Monorail, Multiplet, Naman, Nazca, Nidation, Noose, Norsel, Northern, Number, Oche, Octastichon, Ode, Oder-Neisse, Og(h)am, Omentum, Onedin, Ordinate, Orphan, Orthostichy, Painter, Panty, Parallel, Parameter, Parastichy, Party, Paternoster, Path, Penalty, Pencil, Phalanx, Picket, Pinstripe, Plimsoll, Plumb, Poetastery, Police, Policy, Popping-crease, Poverty, Power, Product(ion), Profession, Punch, Pure, Queue, Race, Radial, Radius, Rail, Rank, Raster, Ratlin(e), Ratling, Rattlin, Ray, Receiving, Red, Reticle, Retinue, Rew, Rhumb, Ripcord, Rope, Route, Row, Rugose, Rugous, Rule, Ry, Sarking, Scazon, Score, Script, Secant, Seperatrix, Serif, Seriph, Service, Set, Shielded, Shore, Shout, Shroud, Siding, Siegfried, Sield, Sight, Silver, Six-yard, Slur, Snood, Snow, Soft, Solidus, Sounding, Spectral, Spider, Spilling, Spring, Spunyarn, Squall, SR, Staff, Stance, Stanza, Starting, Static, Stave, Stean, Steen, Stein, Stem, Stich(os), Stock, Story, Strap, Streak, Striate, String, Stripe, Stuff, Subtense, Swap, Swifter, Symphysis, Syzygy, Tag, Tailback, Talweg, Tangent, Teagle, Tea lead, Terminator, Tetrameter, Thalweg, Thin blue, Thin red, Thread, Throwaway, Tidemark, Tie, Timber, Touch, Trade, Transmission, Transoceanic, Transversal, Tree, Trimeter, Tropic, Trot, Trunk, Try, Tudor, Upstroke, Variety, Verse, Vinculum, Virgule, Wad, Wallace's, Washing, Water(shed), White, Widow, Wire, World, Wrinkle, Yellow, Zag, Zip, Zollner's

Lineage Ancestry, Descent, Extraction, Filiation, Parage, Pedigree

Linen Amice, Amis, Barb, Bed, Byssus, Cambric, Crash, Damask, Dornick, Dowlas, Ecru, Flax, Harn, Huckaback, Inkle, Lawn, Lint, Lockram, Moygashel, Napery, Percale, Seersucker, Sendal, Silesia, Table, Toile, Undies

Liner Artist, Bin-bag, Eye, Ocean greyhound, RMS, Ship, Sleeve, Steamer, Steen, Titanic

Linesman Parodist, → **POET**, Touch-judge

Linger(ing) Chronic, Dawdle, Dwell, Hang, Hove(r), Lag, → **LOITER**, Straggle, Tarry, Tie

Lingerie Bra, Drawers, Undies

Lingo Argot, Bat, Cant, Jargon, Polglish, Speech

Linguist(ic), Linguistics Glottic, Historical, Philological, Phonemics, Polyglot, Semantics, Structural, Stylistics, Syntax, Tagmemics, Taxeme

Liniment Balm, Carron-oil, Embrocation, Ointment, Opodeldoc, Salve

Link(ed), Linking, Links Associate, Between, Bond, Bridge, Chain, Cleek, Colligate, Concatenation, Connect, Copula, Couple, Cross-reference, Cuff, Desmid, Drag, Ess, Flambeau, Golf, Hookup, Hot, Hotline, Incatenation, Index, Interconnect, Interface, Internet, Intertwine, Karabiner, Krab, Liaise, Machair, Missing, Nexus, On-line, Pons, Preposition, Relate, Tead(e), → **TIE**, Tie-in, Tie-line, Torch, Unite, Weakest, Yoke

Linkman Lamplighter, Mediator

Linnet Finch, Lintie, Lintwhite, Twite

Linoleum Waxcloth

Lint Charpie, Dossil

Lintel Summer, Transom

Lion(ess) Androcles, Aphid, Chindit, Elsa, Glitterati, Hero, Leo, Maned, Mountain, Nemean, Opinicus, Personage, Pride, Simba

Lionel Trilling

Lion-tamer Dan(iel)

Lip(py), Lips Beestung, Cheek, Fat, Fipple, Flews, Hare, Helmet, Jib, Labellum, Labiate, Labret, Labrum, Ligula, Muffle, Philtrum, → **RIM**, Rubies, Sass, Sauce, Slack-jaw, Submentum

Lipase Steapsin

Lipstick Chapstick

Liquefy Dissolve, Fuse, Melt

Liqueur, Liquor Abisante, Absinthe, Advokaat, Ale, Almondrado, Amaretto, Anise, Anisette, Apry, Benedictine, Bree, Brew, Broo, Broth, Calvados, Cassis, Cerise, Chartreuse, Chasse, Cherry Marnier®, Cher-suisse, Chicha, Choclair, Chococo, Cocoribe, Cointreau®, Creature, Crème, Crème de cacao, Crème de menthe, Curaçao, Drambuie®, Eau des creoles, Elixir, Enzian, Feni, Fenny, Fraises, Framboise, Fumet, Fustian, Galliano, Geropiga, Grand Marnier®, Hogan, Hogan-mogen, Hogen, Hooch, John Barleycorn, Jungle juice, Kahlua®, Kaoliang, Kir, Kirschwasser, Kirsh(wasser), Kummel, Lager, Lap, Malt, Maraschino, Mastic, Metheglin, Mickey Finn, Midori®, Mirabelle, Mobbie, Mobby, Noyau, Oedema, Ooze, Ouzo, Parfait d'amour, Pasha, Pastis, Pernod®, Persico, Pot, Potation, Pousse-café, Prunelle, Rakee, Raki, Ratafia, Roiano, Roncoco, Rose, Rotgut, Rum, Rum shrub, Sabra, Sambuca, Samshoo, Schnapps, Sciarada, Shypoo, Skink, Stingo, Stock, Stout, Strega®, Strunt, Stuff, Supernaculum, Tape, Taplash, Tequila, Tia Maria®, Tickle-brain, Tiff, Triple sec, Van der Hum®, White lightning, Wine, Witblits, Wort

Liquid(ate), Liquidity, Liquids, Liquefaction Acetal, Amortise, Annihilate, Apprize, Aqua-regia, Azeotrope, Bittern, Bouillon, Bromine, Butanal, Butanol, Butyraldehyde, Butyrin, Cacodyl, Cadaverine, Cash, Cash flow, Chloramine, Cinerin, Clyster, Court-bouillon, Creosol, Creosote, Decoction, Dispersant, Dope, Eluate, Erase, Ethanol, Ether, Eucalyptol, Eugenol, Flow, Fluid, Fural, Furfural, Furol, Halothene, Isoprene, Jaw, Kakodyl, Lewisite, Limonene, Linalool, Lye, Massacre, Mess, Minim, Mouillé, Nebula, Picamar, Pipe, Potion, Protoplasm, Ptisan, Pyrrole, Pyrrolidine, Quinoline, Raffinate, Rhigolene, Safrole, Serum, Solution, Solvent, Syrup, Terebene, Thixotropy, Titer, Titre, Tuberculin, Tusche, Ullage, Verjuice, Whey, Wind up, Wort

Liquorice Indian, Jequirity, Nail, Nail-rod, Pomfret, Pontefract-cake, Spanish juice, Sugarallie, Sugarally

Lis Iris, Lily

Lisa Mona

Lisp(er) Ephraimite, Sibilance

Lissom(e) Agile, Lithe, Nimble, Svelte

▷ **List** *may indicate* 'listen'

List(s), Listing A, Active, Agenda, Antibarbarus, Appendix, Army, Atilt, B, Barocco, Barrace, Bead-roll, Bibliography, British, Canon, Cant, Catalog(ue), Categorise, Catelog, Cause, Check, Choice, Civil, Class, Compile, Credits, Danger, Debrett, Docket, Entry, Enumerate, Front, Glossary, Hark, Hearken, Heel, Hit, Hit-parade, Honours, Index, Indian, Interdiction, Inventory, Itemise, Laundry, Lean, Leet, Line-up, Linked, Lloyds, Mailing, Manifest, Menu, Navy, Notitia, Official, Panel, Paradigm, Party, Price, Prize, Register, Repertoire, Reserved, Retired, Roin, Roll, Roon, Roster, Rota, Rund, Schedule, Short, Sick, Slate, Slope, Strip, Syllabus (of Errors), Table, Tariff, Tick, Ticket, Tilt, Timetable, Tip, Transfer, Union, Waiting,

Waybill, White, Wine, Wish

Listen(er) Attend, Auditor, Auscultate, Ear, Eavesdropper, Gobemouche, Hark,
→ **HEED**, Lithe, Lug, Monitor, Oyez, Simon, Sithee, Wire-tap, Yo-ho(-ho)

▷ **Listen to** *may indicate* a word sounding like another

Listless(ness) Abulia, Accidie, Acedia, Apathetic, Atony, Dawney, Draggy, Inanition,
Indolent, Lackadaisical, Languor, Mooning, Mope, Mopus, Sloth, Thowless,
Torpor, Upsitting, Waff

Lit Alight, Landed

▷ **Lit** *may indicate* an anagram

Litany Eirenicon

Literacy Emotional

Literal(ly), Literal sense Etymon, Misprint, Simply, Typo, Verbatim

Literary Academic, Bas bleu, Booksie, Erudite, Lettered

Literary girls Althea, Jenny, Maud, Pippa

Literature Belles lettres, Corpus, Fiction, Gongorism, Hagiology, Midrash, Musar,
Page, Picaresque, Polite, Prose, Responsa, Samizdat, Splatterpunk, Wisdom

Lithe Flexible, Limber, Pliant, Souple, → **SUPPLE**, Svelte, Willowy

Lithium Li

Litigant Barrator, John-a-Nokes, John-a-Stiles, John Doe, Party, Richard Roe, Suer,
Suitor

Litmus Indicator, Lacmus, Lichen, Turnsole

Litre L

Litter Bed, Brancard, Brood, Cacolet, Cat, Cubs, Debris, Deep, Doolie, Duff,
Emu-bob, Farrow, Jampan, Kago, Kajawah, Kindle, Mahmal, Mor, Nest, Norimon,
Palankeen, Palanquin, Palkee, Palki, Pup, → **REFUSE**, Scrap, Sedan, Stretcher,
Sweepings, Team

Little Bagatelle, Billee, Brief, Chota, Curn, Dorrit, Drib, Drop, Fewtrils, Ickle, Insect,
Iota, John, Jot, Leet, Lilliputian, Limited, Lite, Lyte, Mini, Miniscule, Minnow,
Minuscule, → **MINUTE**, Modicum, Morceau, Nell, Paltry, Paucity, Paul, Petite,
Pink, Pittance, Ronte, Runt, Scant, Scut, Shade, Shoestring, Shred, Shrimp, Slight,
Sma', → **SMALL**, Smattering, Smidge(o)n, Smidgin, Some, Soupçon, Spot, Tad,
Teensy, Tich, Tiddly, Tine, Titch, Touch, Tyne, Vestige, Wee, Weedy, Whit, Women

Littoral Coast(al)

Liturgical, Liturgy Divine, Doxology, Hallel, Rite, Versicle

Live(d), Livelihood, Living, Liveliness, Lively, Lives Active, Alert, Allegretto,
Allegro, Am, Animated, Animation, Animato, Are, AV, Awake, Be, Birkie, Bouncy,
Breezy, Brio, Brisk, Cant(y), Capriccio(so), Cheery, Chipper, Chirpy, Cohabit, Con
moto, Con spirito, Crouse, Durante vita, → **DWELL**, Dynamic, Ebullient, Entrain,
Exist, Exuberant, Feisty, Frisky, Galliard, Gamy, Gay, Giocoso, Gracious, Grig,
Hang-out, Hard, High jinks, Hijinks, Hot, Is, Jazz, Kedge, Lad, Lead, Mercurial,
Merry, Outgo, Pacey, Peart, Pep, Piert, Quicksilver, Rackety, Racy, Reside, Rousing,
Salt, Saut, Scherzo, Skittish, Smacking, Spiritoso, Spirituel(le), Sprack, Spry,
Spunky, Sustenance, Swinging, Vibrant, Vigoroso, Vital, Vitality, Vivace, Vive, Vivo,
→ **VOLATILE**, Vyvyan, Wick, Zappy, Zingy, Zippy, Zoe

▶ **Livelihood** *see* **LIVE(D)**

Liver(ish) Foie gras, Hepar, Hepatic(al), Porta, Puce, Resident, Tomalley

Liverpool, Liverpudlian Scouse

Liverwort Gemma-cup, Hepatica, Riccia

Livery(man) Ermine, Flunkeydom, Goldsmith, Skinner, Tiger, Uniform

Livid Blae, Bruised, Cross, → **FURIOUS**, Pale

Living Advowson, Benefice, Biont, Bread, Canonry, Crust, Glebe, Inquiline, Lodging,

Quick, Resident, Simony, Subsistence, Symbiotic, Vicarage, Vital

Livingstone Doctor, Ken

Liza, Lizzie Bess, Betty, Flivver, Hexam, Tin

Lizard Abas, Agama, American chameleon, Amphisbaena, Anguis, Anole, Basilisk, Bearded, Bearded-dragon, Blindworm, Blue-tongued, Brontosaurus, Chameleon, Chuckwalla, Dinosaur, Draco, Dragon, Eft, Evet, Fence, Flying, Frilled, Frill-necked, Galliwasp, Gecko(ne), Gila, Gila monster, Glass snake, Goanna, Gotcha, Guana, Hatteria, Hellbender, Horned, Iguana, Jew, Kabaragoya, Komodo (dragon), Lacerta, Legua(a)n, Lounge, Malayan monitor, Mastigure, Menopome, Mokomoko, Moloch, Monitor, Mosasaur(us), Mountain devil, Newt, Ngarara, Perentie, Perenty, Reptile, Rock, Sand, Sauria, Scincoid, Seps, Skink, Slow-worm, Snake, Sphenodon, Stellio(n), Sungazer, Swift, Tegu(exin), Thorny devil, Tokay, Tuatara, Tuatera, Varan, Wall, Whiptail, Worm, Worral, Worrel, Zandoli, Zonure

Llama Alpaca, Alpaco, Guanaco, Huanaco, Paco, Vicuña

Load(ed), Loader, Loading, Loads Accommodation, Affluent, Back-end, Ballast, Base, Boot-strap, Boozy, Burden, Cargo, Charge, Cobblers, Dead weight, Disc, Dope, Drunk, Dummy, Fardel, Fother, Freight, Front-end, Fulham, Full, Gestant, Glyc(a)emic, Heap, Input, Jag, Lade, Lard, Last, Live, Onus, Pack, Packet, Pay, Peak, Power, Prime, Rich, Seam, Shipment, Shoal, Some, Span, Super, Surcharge, → **TIGHT**, Tod, Traction, Ultimate, Useful, Wealthy, Weight, Wharfinger, Wing

Loaf(er), Loaves Baguette, Barmbrack, Batch, Baton, Beachbum, Beachcomber, Bloomer, Bludge, Bonce, Boule, Brick, Bum, Bu(r)ster, Cad, Cob, Coburg, Cottage, Currant, Danish, Farmhouse, French stick, Hawm, Hoe-cake, Idle, → **LAZE**, Long tin, Lusk, Manchet, Miche, Milk, Mouch, Pan, Pan(h)agia, Plait, Quartern, Roll, Roti, Shewbread, Showbread, Slosh, Split tin, Square tin, Sugar, Tin, Vantage, Vienna, Yob

Loam Clay, Loess, Loss, Malm

Loan(s) Advance, Balloon, Benevolence, Bottomry, Bridging, Call, Consolidation, Debenture, Demand, Droplock, Imprest, Lane, Mutuum, Omnium, Out, Prest, Respondentia, Roll-over, Soft, Start-up, Sub, Time, Top-up, War

Loathe, Loathing, Loathsome Abhor(rent), Abominate, Carrion, Detest, Hate, Nauseate, Odious, Scunner, Ug(h)

Lob Loft, Sky, Underarm

Lobby Demo, Division, Entry, Foyer, Gun, Hall, Press, Urge

Lobe(d) Anisocercal, Fluke, Frontal, Insula, Jugum, Lacinia, Lap, Occipital, Optic, Palmate, Parietal, Pinnule, Prostomium, Runcinate, Segment, Temporal, Uvula, Vermis

Lobster Cock, Crawfish, Crayfish, Crustacean, Decapoda, Langouste, Newburg, Norway, Pot, Rock, Scampo, Spiny, Squat, Thermidor, Tomalley

Local(ity) Area, Bro, Des(h)i, Endemic, Home, Inn, Insider, Landlord, Native, Near, Nearby, Neighbourhood, Number, Parochial, Pub, Regional, Resident, Swadishi, Tavern, Topical, Vernacular, Vicinal

▷ **Local** *may indicate* a dialect word

Locale Scene, Site

Locate, Location Address, Connect, Find, Fix, Lay, Milieu, Node, Pinpoint, Place, Plant, Recess, Site, Situate, Situation, Sofar, Spot, Trace, Ubiety, Website, Where, Zone

Loch, Lough Allen, Ashie, Awe, Derg, Earn, Eil, Erne, Etive, Fine, Gare, Garten, Holy, Hourn, Katrine, → **LAKE**, Larne, Leven, Linnhe, Lomond, Long, Moidart, Morar, More, Nakeel, Neagh, Ness, Rannoch, Ryan, Shiel, Strangford, Tay, Torridon

Lock(ing), Locker, Locks, Lock up Bar, Barnet, Bolt, Canal, Central, Chubb®,

Clinch, Combination, Cowlick, Curlicue, Davy Jones, Deadbolt, Detent, Drop, Fastener, Fermentation, Foretop, Gate, Haffet, Haffit, Handcuff, Hasp, Hold, Intern, Key, Latch, Lazaretto, Man, Mortise, Percussion, Prison, Quiff, Ragbolt, Rim, Ringlet, Safety, Sasse, Scalp, Scissors, → **SECURE**, Sluice, Snap, Spring, Sta(u)nch, Stock, Strand, Tag, Talon, Time, Trap, Tress, Tuft, Tumbler, Vapour, Villus, Ward, Wheel, Wrestle, Yale®

Locket Lucy

Lockjaw Tetanus, Trismus

Locksmith Garret-master, Hairdresser

Locomotive Banker, Bogie, Bul(l)gine, Engine, Iron horse, Mobile, Rocket, Steam, Steamer, Train

Locum Deputy, Relief, Stand-in, Stopgap

Locus Centrode, Horopter, Lemniscate, Place, Spot

Locust, Locust tree Anime, Carob, Cicada, Hopper, Nymph, Robinia, Seventeen-year, Voetganger

Lode Comstock, Lodge, Mother, Reef, Vein

Lodestone Magnes, Magnet

Lodge(r) Billet, Board(er), Box, Cosher, Deposit, Dig, Doss, Encamp, Entertain, Freemason, Grange, Grove, Guest, Harbour, Host, Inmate, Layer, Lie, Masonic, Nest, Orange, Parasite, PG, Porter's, Put up, Quarter, Rancho, Resident, Room(er), Roomie, Stay, Storehouse, Stow, Sweat, Tenant, Tepee, Wigwam

Lodging(s) Abode, B and B, Chummage, Dharms(h)ala, Diggings, Digs, Dosshouse, Ferm, Grange, Grove, Hostel, Inquiline, Kip, Minshuku, Pad, Padding-ken, Pension, Pied-à-terre, Quarters, Resiant, Rooms, Singleen, Sponging-house, Spunging-house, YHA

Loft(iness), Lofty Aerial, Airy, Arrogant, Attic, Celsitude, Chip, Choir, Exalted, Garret, Grand, Haymow, High, Jube, Lordly, Magniloquent, Noble, Olympian, Pulpitum, Rarefied, Rigging, Rood, Roost, Sky, Sublime, Tallat, Tallet, Tallot

Log Billet, Black box, Cabin, Chip, Chock, Deadhead, Diarise, Diary, Hack, Ln, Mantissa, Nap(i)erian, Neper, Patent, → **RECORD**, Stock, Yule

Logarithm Common, Lod, Mantissa, Nap(i)erian, Natural

Logic(al) Alethic, Analytical, Aristotelian, Boolean, Chop, Deontic, Dialectic(s), Distributed, Doxastic, Epistemics, Formal, Fuzzy, Heuristics, Iff, Mathematical, Modal, Organon, Philosophical, Premise, Pusser's, Ramism, Rational(e), Reason, Sane, Sequacious, Shared, Sorites, Syllogism, Symbolic, Tense, Trivium

Logo Colophon

Loin(s) Flank, Inguinal, Lungie, Lunyie, Reins

Loincloth Dhoti, Lungi, Pareu, Waist-cloth

Loiter(ing) Dally, Dare, Dawdle, Dilatory, Dilly-dally, Idle, Lag, Lallygag, Leng, Lime, → **LINGER**, Lollygag, Mike, Mooch, Mouch, Potter, Saunter, Scamp, Suss, Tarry

Lola Dolores

Loll Hawm, Lounge, Sprawl

Lollipop, Lolly Ice pole, Lulibub

Lolly Money, Popsicle®, Sweetmeat

London(er) 'Arry, Big Smoke, Cockaigne, Cockney, Co(c)kayne, East-ender, Flat-cap, Jack, Roseland, Smoke, Town, Troynovant, Wen

London pride None-so-pretty

Lone(r), Lonely Remote, Rogue, Saddo, Secluded, Sole, Solitary, Unked, Unket, Unkid

Long(er), Longing, Longs Ache, Aitch, Ake, Appetent, Aspire, Brame, Covet, Desire, Die, Earn, Erne, Far, Greed, Green, Grein, → **HANKER**, Huey, Hunger,

Inveterate, Island, Itch, L, Lanky, Large, Lengthy, Longa, Lust, Macron, Miss, More, → **NO LONGER**, Nostalgia, Option, Pant, Parsec, → **PINE**, Prolix, Sesquipedalian, Side, Sigh, Tall, Thirst, Trews, Weary, Wish, Wist, Yearn, Yen

Long-eared Spicate

Longitude Celestial, Ecliptic, Meridian

Long-lashed Mastigophora(n)

Long live(d) Banzai, Macrobian, Viva, Vive, Zindabad

Longshoreman Hobbler, Hoveller, Wharfinger

Long-suffering Job, Patient, Stoical

Long-tailed Macrural

Long-winded Prolix, Verbose, Wordy

Loo Ajax, Bog, Can, Chapel, Dike, Game, Gents, Jakes, John, Privy, Toilet

Loofah Towel gourd

Look(s), Look at After-eye, Air, Aspect, Behold, Belgard, Bonne-mine, Busk, Butcher's, Butcher's hook, Clock, Close-up, Crane, Daggers, Decko, Deek, Dekko, Ecce, Ecco, Expression, Eye, Eye-glance, Face, Facies, Gander, Gawp, Gaze, Geek, Glance, Glare, Gleam, Gledge, Glimpse, Glom, Glower, Goggle, Good, Grin, Hallo, Hangdog, Hey, Iliad, Inspect, Keek, La, Leer, Lo, Mien, New, Ogle, Old-fashioned, Peek, Peep, Prospect, Ray, Recce, Refer, → **REGARD**, Scan, Scrutinise, Search, See, Seek, Shade, Sheep's eyes, Shufti, Shufty, Spy, Squint, Squiz, Stare, Survey, Toot, V, Vista, Wet

Look-out (man) Cockatoo, Crow's nest, Dixie, Huer, Mirador, Nit, Sangar, Sentinel, Sentry, Sungar, Tentie, Toot(er), Watch, Watchtower

▷ **Look silly** *may indicate* an anagram

Loom Beamer, Dobby, Emerge, Impend, Jacquard, Lathe, Menace, Picker, Temple, Threaten, Tower

Loon Diver

Loop(ed), Loophole, Loopy Articulatory, Becket, Bight, Billabong, Bouclé, Carriage, Chink, Closed, Coil, Eyelet, Eyesplice, Fake, Frog, Frontlet, Grom(m)et, Ground, Grummet, Hank, Henie's, Hysteresis, Infinite, Kink, Knop, Lasket, Lippes, Local, Lug, Noose, Oillet, Parral, Parrel, Pearl(-edge), Picot, Prusik, Purl, Scrunchie, Staple, Stirrup, Tab, Terry, Toe, Twist

Loos Anita

Loose(n), Loose woman Absolve, Abstrict, Afloat, Anonyma, Baggage, Bail, Besom, Bike, Bunter, Chippie, Chippy, Cocotte, Cutty, Demi-mondaine, Demirep, Demivierge, Desultory, Dissolute, Dissolve, Doxy, Draggletail, Dratchell, Drazel, Ease, Emit, Flipperty-flopperty, Flirt-gill, Floosie, Floozie, Floozy, Floppy, Franion, Free, Gangling, Gay, Hussy, Insecure, Jade, Jezebel, Lax, Light-heeled, Loast, Mob, Mort, Naughty pack, Painted, Pinnace, Profligate, Promiscuous, Quail, Ramp, → **RELAX**, Sandy, Scrubber, Skanky-ho, Slag, Slapper, Slut, Streel, Tart, Tramp, Trull, Ungyve, Unhasp, Unhitch, Unknit, Unknot, Unlace, Unpin, Unreined, Unscrew, Unthread, Untie, Vague, Waistcoateer, Wappend, Whore

Loot Boodle, Booty, Cragh, Creach, Foray, Haul, Mainour, Peel, Pluck, → **PLUNDER**, Ransack, Rape, Reave, Rieve, Rob, Sack, Smug, Spoils, Spoliate, Swag, Treasure, Waif

Lop Behead, Clop, Curtail, Detruncate, Droop, Shroud, Sned, Trash

Lope Stride

Loquacious Chatty, Gabby, Garrulous, Rambling

Lord(s), Lordship, Lordly Adonai, Ahura Mazda, Anaxandron, Arrogant, Boss, Byron, Cyril, Dieu, Domineer, Dominical, Duc, Earl, Elgin, Gad, Gilded Chamber, God, Haw-haw, Herr, Idris, Imperious, Jim, Justice, Kami, Kitchener, Landgrave,

Law, Ld, Liege, Lonsdale, Losh, Lud, Mesne, Misrule, Mynheer, Naik, Oda Nobunaga, Omrah, Ordinary, Ormazd, Ormuzd, Peer, Sea, Seigneur, Seignior, Shaftesbury, Sire, Spiritual, Taverner, Temporal, Tuan, Ullin

Lords and ladies Wake-robin

Lore Cab(b)ala, Edda, Lair, Lare, Riem, Upanis(h)ad

Lorelei Siren

Lorgnette Starers

Lorna Doone

Lorry Artic(ulated), Camion, Crummy, Drag, Flatbed, Juggernaut, Low-loader, Rig, Tipper, Tonner, → **TRUCK**, Wagon

Lose(r) Also-ran, Decrease, Drop, Elude, Forfeit, Hesitater, Leese, Misère, Mislay, Misplace, Nowhere, Spread, Tank, Throw, Tine(r), Tyne, Underdog, Unsuccessful, Waste, Weeper

Loss, Lost Anosmia, Aphesis, Aphonia, Apocope, Apraxia, Astray, Attainder, Boohai, Chord, Cost, Dead, Decrease, Depreciation, Detriment, Disadvantage, Elision, Extinction, Foredamned, Forfeited, Forgotten, Forlorn, Gone, Lore, Lorn, Lurch, Missing, Omission, Outage, Pentimento, Perdition, Perdu, Perished, Preoccupied, Privation, Psilosis, Reliance, Tine, Tinsel, Tint, Toll, Traik, Tribes, Tyne(d), Ullage, Unredeemed, Wastage, Wasted, Will, Write-off, Wull

Loss of memory Amnesia, Black-out, Fugue, Infonesia, Paramnesia

▷ **Lost** *may indicate* an anagram or an obsolete word

Lot(s) Abundant, Amount, Aret(t), Badly, Batch, Boatload, Caboodle, Cavel, Chance, Deal, Dole, Doom, Drove, Due, → **FATE**, Fortune, Group, Hantle, Hap, Heaps, Horde, Host, Item, Job, Kevel, Kismet, Lank, Lashings, Legion, Loads, Luck, Manifold, Many, Mass, Moh, Moira, Mony, Mort, Myriad, Oceans, Omnibus, Oodles, Oodlins, Pack, Parcel, Parking, Plenitude, Plenty, Portion, Power, Purim, Raft, Rich, Scads, Set, Sight, Slather, Slew, Slue, Sortilege, Sortition, Stack, Sum, Tall order, The works, Tons, Vole, Wagonload, Weird

Loth Averse, Circumspect, Sweer(t), Sweir(t), Unwilling

Lothario Lady-killer, Libertine, Poodle-faker, Rake, Womaniser

Lotion After-shave, Blackwash, Calamine, Collyrium, Cream, Eye-wash, Humectant, Setting, Suntan, Unguent, Wash, Yellow wash

Lottery, Lotto Art union, Ballot, Bingo, Cavel, Draw, Gamble, National, Pakapoo, Pools, Postcode, Punchboard, Raffle, Rollover, Scratchcard, Sweepstake, Tattersall's, Tombola

Lotus (eater), Lotus land Asana, Djerba, Lotophagus, Padmasana, White

Loud(ness), Loudly Bel, Big, Blaring, Booming, Brassy, Decibel, F, FF, Flashy, Forte, Fracas, Full-mouthed, Garish, Gaudy, Glaring, Hammerklavier, High, Lumpkin, Noisy, Orotund, Plangent, Raucous, Roarie, Siren, Sone, Stentor(ian), Strident, Tarty, Vocal, Vociferous, Vulgar

Loudspeaker Action, Boanerges, Bullhorn, Hailer, Megaphone, Stentor, Subwoofer, Tannoy®, Tweeter, Woofer

▶ **Lough** *see* **LOCH**

Louis Baker, Roi

Louisianian Cajun

Lounge(r) Cocktail, Da(c)ker, Daiker, Departure, Hawm, Idle, Laze, Lizard, Loll, Lollop, Parlour, Paul's man, Sitkamer, Slouch, Sun, Transit

Louse (up), Lousy, Lice Acrawl, Argulus, Bolix, Bollocks, Chat, Chicken, Cootie, Crab, Crummy, Fish, Head, Isopod(a), Kutu, Nit, Oniscus, Pedicular, Phthiriasis, Plant, Psocoptera, Psylla, Slater, Snot, Sowbug, Sucking, Vermin, Whale

Lout Clod(hopper), Coof, Cuif, Hallian, Hallion, Hallyon, Hick, Hob, Hobbledehoy,

Hooligan, Hoon, Jack, Jake, Keelie, Lager, Larrikin, Litter, Lob(lolly), Loord, Lubber, Lumpkin, Lycra, Oaf, Oik, Rube, Swad, Tout, Tripper, Yahoo, Yob(bo)

Louvre Shutter

Love(d), Lovable, Lover Abelard, Admire, Adore, Adulator, Affection, Agape, Alma, Amabel, Amanda, Amant, Amateur, Ami(e), Amoret, Amoroso, Amour, Angharad, Antony, Ardour, Ariadne, Aroha, Aucassin, Beau, Bidie-in, Blob, Calf, Care, Casanova, Chamberer, Cicisbeo, Concubine, Coquet, Court, Courtly, Cupboard, Cupid, Dona(h), Dotard, Dote, Doxy, Duck(s), Ducky, Dulcinea, Eloise, Eloper, Emotion, Enamorado, Eros, Esme, Fan, Fancy man, Flame, Frauendienst, Free, Goose-egg, Greek, Idolise, Inamorata, Inamorato, Iseult, Isolde, Item, Jo, Kama, Lad, Leander, Leman, Like, Lochinvar, Loe, Loo, Lurve, Man, Nihility, Nil, Nothing, Nought, O, Pairs, Paramour, Pash, Passion, Philander, -phile, Platonic, Precious, Protestant, Psychodelic, Puppy, Revere, Rhanja, Romance, Romeo, Sapphism, Spooner, Stale, Storge, Suitor, Swain, Thisbe, Touch, Toyboy, Troilus, True, Turtle(-dove), Valentine, Venus, Virtu, Woman, Worship, Zeal, Zero

Love-apple Tomato, Wolf's-peach

Love-bite Hickey

Love-child By-blow, Come-by-chance

Love-in-a-mist Nigella

Love letter Capon

Lovely Adorable, Belle, Dishy, Dreamy, Exquisite, Nasty

Love-making → **INTERCOURSE**, Kama Sutra, Sex, Snog

Love-sick Smit(ten), Strephon

Loving(ly) Amoroso, Amorous, Fond, Tender

Low(est), Low-cut, Lower(ing) Abase, Abate, Abysmal, Amort, Area, Avail(e), Avale, B, Basal, Base(-born), Bass(o), Beneath, Blue, Caddish, Cartoonist, Cheap, Church, Condescend, Contralto, Cow, Croon, Crude, Darken, Debase, Décolleté, Deepmost, Degrade, Demean, Demit, Demote, Depress, Devalue, Dim, Dip, Dispirited, Doldrums, Drawdown, Drop, Early, Embase, Flat, Foot, Frown, Gazunder, Glare, Guernsey, Gurly, Hedge, Humble, Ignoble, Imbase, Inferior, Jersey, Laigh, Lallan, Law, Light, Lite, Mass, Mean, Menial, Moo, Mopus, Morose, Nadir, Net, Nether, Nett, Non-U, Ostinato, Paravail, Plebeianise, Profound, Prole, Relegate, Ribald, Rock-bottom, Sad, Scoundrel, Scowl, Secondo, Settle, Shabby, Short, Soft, Stoop, Subordinate, Sudra, Undermost, Unnoble, Vail, Vulgar, Weak, Wretched

Lowbrow Philistine

Lowdown Gen, Info

▷ **Lower** *may refer to* cattle

Lowland(er) Carse, Gallovidian, Glen, Laigh, Lallans, Merse, Mudflat, Plain, Polder, Sassenach, Vlei

Low-lying Callow, Epigeous, Fens, Inferior, Sump

Low person Boor, Bunter, Cad, Caitiff, Cocktail, Demirep, Ratfink, Snot

Loyal(ty) Adherence, Allegiant, Brick, Dependable, Esprit de corps, Faithful, Fast, Fidelity, Gungho, Leal, Patriotic, Pia, Stalwart, Staunch, → **TRUE**, True blue, Trusty

Loyalist Hard core, Paisley, Patriot, Tory

Lozenge Cachou, Catechu, Fusil, Jujube, Mascle, Pastille, Pill, Rhomb, Rustre, Tablet, Troche, Voided

LSD Acid, Money

Lubber(ly), Lubbers Booby, Clod, Clumsy, Gawky, Hulk, Lob, Looby, Oaf, Slowback, Swab, Swads

Lubricant, Lubricate, Lubrication Carap-oil, Coolant, Derv, Fluid, Force-feed,

Grease, Oil, Petrolatum, Sebum, Unguent, Vaseline®, Wool-oil

Luce Ged

Lucerne Alfalfa, Medick, Nonsuch

Lucia Mimi

Lucid Bright, Clear, Perspicuous, Sane

Lucifer Devil, Match, Proud

Luck(y) Amulet, Auspicious, Beginner's, Bonanza, Break, Caduac, Canny, Cess, Chance, Charmed, Chaunce, Daikoku, Dip, Fate, Fluke, → **FORTUNE**, Godsend, Hap, Heather, Hit, Jam(my), Joss, Lady, Lot, Mascot, Mozzle, Pot, Prosit, Providential, Pudding-bag, Purple patch, Seal, Seel, Sele, Serendipity, Sess, Sonsie, Sonsy, Star(s), Streak, Success, Talisman, Tinny, Tough, Turn-up, Windfall, Worse

Luckless Hapless, Wight

Lucre Money, Pelf, Tin

Lucy Locket

Lud Gad

Luddite Saboteur, Wrecker

Ludicrous Absurd, Bathetic, Bathos, Farcical, Fiasco, Inane, Irish, Jest, Laughable, Risible

Ludo Uckers

Luff Derrick

Lug Ear, Earflap, Sea-worm, Sowle, Tote, Tow

Luggage Bags, Carryon, Cases, Dunnage, Excess, Grip, Hand, Kit, Petara, Suiter, Traps, Trunk

Luggage-carrier Grid

Lugubrious Dismal, Drear

Luke-warm Laodicean, Lew, Tepid

Lull, Lullaby Berceuse, Calm, Cradlesong, Hushaby, Respite, Rock, Sitzkreig, Soothe, Sopite

Lulu Stunner

Lumber(ing) Clump, Galumph, Jumble, Pawn, Ponderous, Raffle, Saddle, Scamble, Timber

Lumberjack Bushwhacker, Feller, Logger, Logman

Luminance, Luminous, Luminosity, Luminescence Aglow, Arc, Foxfire, Glow, Ignis-fatuus, L, Light, Nit, Phosphorescent, Scintillon, Sea-dog, Wildfire, Will o' the wisp

Lumme Coo, Lor

Lump(y) Aggregate, Bubo, Bud, Bulge, Bur(r), Caruncle, Chuck, Chunk, Clat, Claut, Clod, Clot, Cob, Combine, Dallop, Da(u)d, Dollop, Enhydros, Epulis, Flocculate, Ganglion, Geode, Gnarl, Gob(bet), Goiter, Goitre, Grape, Grip, Hunch, Hunk, Inium, Knarl, Knob, Knub, Knur(r), Knurl, Lob, Lunch, Malleolus, Mass, Mote, Mott, Myxoma, Neuroma, Nibble, Nirl, Node, Nodule, Nodulus, Nub, Nubble, Nugget, Nur(r), Nurl, Osteophyte, Plook, Plouk, Quinsy, Raguly, Sarcoma, Scybalum, Sitfast, Slub, Strophiole, Tragus, Tuber(cle), Wart, Wodge

Lumpsucker Sea-owl

Lunacy, Lunatic Bedlam, Dementia, Demonomania, Folly, Insanity, Mad(ness), Psychosis

Lunar Evection, Mascon

▷ **Lunatic** *may indicate* an anagram

Lunch(time) Bait, Crib, Dejeune, Déjeuner, L, Nacket, Nocket, Nuncheon, Packed, Piece, Ploughman, Pm, Power, Tiff(in), Working

Lung(s) Alveoli, Bellows, Coalminer's, Farmer's, Green, Iron, Lights, Pulmo, Pulmonary, Soul

Lung disease Anthracosis, Byssinosis, Emphysema, Farmer's lung, Pneumoconiosis, Siderosis, Silicosis, Tuberculosis

Lunge Breenge, Breinge, Dive, Stab, Thrust, Venue

Lungfish Dipnoi(an)

Lupin Arsene

Lurch Reel, Stoit, Stumble, Swee

Lure Bait, Bribe, Carrot, Decoy, Devon minnow, Entice, Horn, Inveigle, Jig, Judas, Plug, Roper, Spinner, Spoon, Spoonbait, Spoonhook, Squid, Stale, Temptation, Tice, Tole, Toll, Train, Trepan, Wormfly

Lurgi Illness

Lurid Gruesome, Purple

Lurk(ing) Dare, Latitant, Skulk, Slink, Snoke, Snook, Snowk

Lusatia(n) Wend(ic), Wendish

Luscious Succulent

Lush Alcoholic, Alkie, Alky, Dipso(maniac), Drunk, Fertile, Green, Juicy, Lydian, Sot, Tosspot, Verdant

Lust(ful), Lusty Cama, Concupiscence, Corflambo, Desire, Eros, Frack, Greed, Kama, Lech(ery), Lewd, Megalomania, Obidicut, Randy, Rank, Raunchy, Salacious, Venereous

Lustre, Lustrous Brilliance, Census, Chatoyant, Galena, Gaum, Gilt, Gloss, Gorm, Inaurate, Lead-glance, Pentad, Reflet, Satiny, Schiller, → **SHEEN**, Water

Lute, Lutist Amphion, Chitarrone, Cither, Dichord, Orpharion, Pandora, Pandore, Theorbo, Vielle

Lutetium Lu

Lutheran Adiaphorist, Calixtin(e), Pietist, Ubiquitarian

Lux Lx

Luxemburg L

Luxuriant, Luxuriate, Luxurious, Luxury (lover) Bask, Clover, Cockaigne, Cockayne, Copious, Deluxe, Dolce vita, Extravagant, Fleshpots, Lavish, Lucullan, Lush, Mollitious, Ornate, Pie, Plush, Posh, Rank, → **RICH**, Ritzy, Sumptuous, Sybarite, Wallow

Lycanthropist Werewolf

Lydia Languish

Lye Buck

▶ **Lying** *see* **LIE**

Lymph Chyle

Lymphoma Burkett's

Lynch(ing), Lyncher Dewitt, Hang, Necktie party, Nightrider

Lynx Bay, Bobcat, Caracal, Desert, Rooikat

Lyre Cithern, Harp, Psaltery, Testudo, Trigon

Lyric(s), Lyrical, Lyricist, Lyrist Cavalier, Dit(t), Epode, Gilbert, Hammerstein, Melic, Ode, Orphean, Paean, Pean, Poem, Rhapsodic, Song, Words

Mm

M Married, Member, Metre, Mike, Mile, Thousand

Mac Mino, Scot, Waterproof

Macabre Gothic, Grotesque, Sick

Macaroni Beau, Blood, Cat, Dandy, Elbow, Exquisite, Fop, Jack-a-dandy, Olio, Pasta, Petitmaitre

Macaroon Biscuit, Signal

Macaulay Layman

Mace Club, Nutmeg, Sceptre, Spice

Mace-bearer Beadle, Bedel, Poker

Macedonian Philip, Stagirite, Stagyrite

Machine(ry) Air-engine, Answering, Apparat(us), Appliance, Automaton, Bathing, Bulldozer, Calender, Centrifuge, Clobbering, Cycle, → **DEVICE**, Dialyser, Dredge(r), Drum, Dynamotor, Engine, Enginery, Facsimile, Fax, Fourdrinier, Fruit, Gin, Hawk-Eye®, Heck, Hopper, Hot-press, Infernal, Instrument, Jawbreaker, Jukebox, Lathe, Life-support, Linotype®, Linter, Lithotripter, Loom, Ludlow, Milling, Moulinet, Moviola®, Mule, Nintendo®, Party, Pile-driver, Planer, Plant, Pokie, Press, Processor, Propaganda, Pulsator, Robot, Rotavator®, Rototiller, Rowing, Sausage, Sewing, Slicer, Slot, Spin, Spinning jenny, Stenotype®, Symatron, Tape, Teaching, Tedder, Throstle, Time, Transfer, Treadmill, Tumbler, Turbine, Turing, Twin tub, Typewriter, Vending, Virtual, War, Washing, Weighing, Willow, Wimshurst, Wind(mill), Wringer

Macho Jock, Laddish

Mackerel Albacore, Brack, Dory, Fish, Horse, Pacific, Pimp, Scad, Scomber, Sky, Spanish, Spotted, Trevally

Mackintosh Burberry®, Mac, Mino, Oilskin, Slicker, Waterproof

Macropus Euro, Wallaroo

Mad(den), Madman, Madness Angry, Balmy, Bananas, Barking, Barmy, Bedlam, Besotted, Bonkers, Crackbrained, Crackpot, Crazy, Cuckoo, Cupcake, Daffy, Delirious, Dement, Distract, Dotty, Enrage, Fay, Fey, Folie, Folly, Frantic, Frenetic(al), Fruitcake, Furioso, Fury, Gelt, Gyte, Harpic, Hatter, Idiotic, Incense, Insane, Insanie, Insanity, Into, Ireful, Irritate, Kook, Loco, Lunatic, Lycanthropy, Madbrained, Maenad, Mango, Mania, Mattoid, Mental, Meshug(g)a, Metric, Midsummer, Moonstruck, Motorway, Mullah, Nuts, Porangi, Psycho, Rabid, Rasputin, Raving, Redwood, Redwud, Scatty, Screwy, Short-witted, Starkers, Tonto, Touched, Troppo, Unhinged, Wacko, Wood, Wowf, Wrath, Wud, Xenomania, Yond, Zany

▷ **Mad(den)** *may indicate* an anagram

Madagascan, Madagascar Aye-aye, Hova, Indri, Lemur, Malagasy, RM

Madam(e) Baggage, Lady, M, Proprietress

Madcap Impulsive, Tearaway

Madder Alizari, Alyari, Chay(a), Gardenia, Genipap, Rose, Rubia, Shaya

Made (it) Built, Did, Fec(it), Ff, Gart, Invented
Madge Pie
▷ **Madly** *may indicate* an anagram
Madonna Lady, Lily, Mary, Pietà, Sistine, Virgin
Madras Chennai
Madrigal Ballet, Fala, Song
Maelstrom Voraginous, Vortex, Whirlpool
Maenad Devotee, Fan
Maestro Artist, Toscanini, Virtuoso
Mafia Camorra, Capo, Cosa nostra, Godfather, Goombah, Mob, Ndrangheta,
  Omerta, The Mob
Mag Mail
Magazine Arsenal, Clip, Colliers, Contact, Cornhill, Cosmopolitan, Digizine,
  Economist, E-zine, Field, Girlie, Glossy, Granta, Jazz mag, Lady, Lancet, Life,
  Listener, Little, Magnet, Organ, Part work, Periodical, Pictorial, Playboy, Powder,
  Private Eye, Pulp, Punch, She, Skin, Slick, Spectator, Store, Strand, Tatler, Time,
  Vogue, Warehouse, Weekly, Yoof, Zine
Magdalene St Mary
Maggie Rita
Maggot Bot, Flyblow, Gentiles, Gentle, Grub, Larva, Mawk, Myiasis, Whim, Worm
Magi Balthazar, Gaspar, Melchior
Magic(al), Magician, Magic square Archimage, Art, Baetyl, Black, Black art,
  Charm, Circle, Conjury, Diablerie, Diablery, Enchanting, Faust, Faustus, Fetish,
  Genie, Goetic, Goety, Gramary(e), Grimoire, Hermetic, Houdini, Illusionist,
  Incantation, Makuto, Math, Medea, Merlin, Mojo, Moly, Morgan le Fay, Myal,
  Nasik, Natural, Necromancer, Obeah, Pawaw, Powwow, Prospero, Reim-kenner,
  Rhombus, Shamanism, Sorcery, Sortilege, Spell, Speller, Supernatural,
  Sympathetic, Talisman, Thaumaturgics, Theurgy, Voodoo, Warlock, White,
  Wizard, Zendik
Magistracy, Magistrate Aedile, Amman, Amtman, Archon, Avoyer, Bailie,
  Bailiff, Bailli(e), Bench, Burgess, Burgomaster, Cadi, Censor, Consul, Corregidor,
  Demiurge, Doge(ate), Draco, Edile, Effendi, Ephor, Field cornet, Finer, Foud,
  Gonfalonier, JP, Judiciary, Jurat, Kotwal, Landamman(n), Landdrost, Lord Provost,
  Maire, Mayor, Mittimus, Novus homo, Podesta, Portreeve, Pr(a)efect, Pr(a)etor,
  Prior, Proconsul, Propraetor, Provost, Qadi, Quaestor, Recorder, Reeve, Shereef,
  Sherif, Stad(t)holder, Stipendiary, Syndic, Tribune, Worship
Magnanimity, Magnanimous Big, Charitable, → **GENEROUS**, Largeness, Lofty,
  Noble
Magnate Baron, Bigwig, Industrialist, Mogul, Onassis, Randlord, Tycoon,
  Vanderbilt, VIP
Magnesia, Magnesium Humite, Kainite, Mg, Periclase
Magnet(ic), Magnetism Animal, Artificial, Attraction, Bar, Charisma, Field, Gauss,
  Horseshoe, It, Loadstone, Lodestone, Maxwell, Od, Oersted, Permanent, Personal,
  Polar, Pole, Pole piece, Poloidal, Pull, Remanence, Retentivity, Slug, Solenoid,
  Terrella, Terrestrial, Tesla, Tole
Magnificence, Magnificent Fine, Gorgeous, Grandeur, Imperial, Laurentian,
  Lordly, Noble, Pride, Regal, Royal, Splendid, Splendo(u)r, State, Sumptuous,
  Superb
Magnifier, Magnify(ing) Aggrandise, Augment, Binocle, → **ENLARGE**, Exaggerate,
  Increase, Loupe, Megaphone, Microscope, Teinoscope, Telescope
Magniloquent Bombastic, Orotund

Magnitude Absolute, Abundance, Amplitude, Apparent, Earthquake, Extent, Muchness, Photoelectric, Scalar, Size, Visual

Magnolia An(n)ona, Beaver-tree, Champac, Champak, Mississippi, Sweet bay, Umbrella-tree, Yulan

Magpie Bell, Bird, Bishop, Chatterer, Madge, Mag, Margaret, Outer, Pica, Piet, Pyat, Pyet, Pyot

Magus Artist

Magyar Hungarian, Szekel(y), Szekler, Ugrian, Ugric

Mahogany Acajou, African, Carapa, Cedrela, Philippine, Wood

Mahommedan Dervish, Shiah

Maid(en) Abigail, Aia, Amah, Biddy, Bonibell, Bonne, Bonnibell, Burd, Chamber, Chloe, Clothes-horse, Damosel, Dell, Dey, Dresser, Femme de chambre, First, Girl, Guillotine, Ignis-fatuus, Imago, Inaugural, Io, Iras, Iron, Lorelei, M, Marian, May, Miss, Nymph, Opening, Over, Parlour, Pucelle, Rhian, Rhine, Skivvy, Soubrette, Suivante, Table, Thestylis, Tirewoman, Tweeny, Valkyrie, Virgin, Walkyrie, Wench, Wicket

Maidenhair Fern, Ginkgo

Mail Air, → **ARMOUR**, Byrnie, Cataphract, Chain, Da(w)k, Direct, E(lectronic), Express, Fan, Habergeon, Hate, Hauberk, Helm, Junk, Letter, Media, Metered, Panoply, Pony express, Post, Ring, Send, Snail, Spam, Surface, Tuille(tte), Voice

Mailbag Pouch

Mailboat Packet

Maim Cripple, Impair, Lame, Main, Mayhem, Mutilate, Vuln

Main(s) Atlantic, Brine, Briny, → **CENTRAL**, Chief, Cockfight, Conduit, Essential, Foremost, Gas, Generally, Grid, Gross, Head, → **KEY**, Lead(ing), Major, Pacific, Palmary, Predominant, Prime, Principal, Ring, → **SEA**, Sheer, Spanish, Staple, Water

Mainland Continent, Pomona

Mainstay Backbone, Bastion, Pillar, Support

Maintain(er), Maintenance Alimony, Allege, Ap(p)anage, Argue, Assert, Aver, Avouch, Avoure, Avow, Claim, Contend, Continue, Defend, Escot, Insist, Keep (up), Lengthman, Preserve, Run, Sustain, Upbear, Uphold, Upkeep

Maize Corn, Hominy, Indian, Indian corn, Mealie, Popcorn, Samp, Silk, Stamp, Zea

Majestic, Majesty August, Britannic, Dignity, Eagle, Grandeur, Imperial, Maestoso, Olympian, Regal, SM, Sovereign, Stately, Sublime, Tuanku

Major (domo) Barbara, Drum, → **IMPORTANT**, Pipe, PM, Seneschal, Senior, Sergeant, Star, Trumpet, Wig

Majority Absolute, Age, Body, Eighteen, Landslide, Latchkey, Maturity, Moral, Most, Preponderance, Relative, Silent, Working

Make(r), Make do, Making Amass, Brand, Build, Clear, Coerce, Coin, Compel, Compulse, Concoct, Creant, Create, Devise, Earn, Execute, Fabricate, Factive, Fashion, Faute de mieux, Fet(t), Forge, Form, Gar(re), God, Halfpenny, Mail(e), Manage, Marque, Prepare, Production, Reach, Render, Shape, Sort, Temporise, Wright

▷ **Make** *may indicate an anagram*

Make believe Fantasy, Fictitious, Pretend, Pseudo

Make good Abet, Compensate, Remedy, Succeed, Ulling

Make hay Ted

Make off Bolt, Leg it, Mosey, Run, Scarper

Makeshift Bandaid, Crude, Cutcha, Expedient, Jury-rigged, Kacha, Kachcha, Kludge, Kutcha, Lash-up, Mackle, Pis-aller, Rude, Stopgap, Timenoguy

Make up Ad lib, Compensate, Compose, Concealer, Constitution, Cosmetics, Fucus, Gaud, Gawd, Gene, Greasepaint, Identikit®, Kohl, Liner, Lipstick, Maquillage, Mascara, Metabolism, Paint, Pancake, Panstick, Powder, Reconcile, Rouge, Slap, Tidivate, Titivate, Toiletry, Visagiste, War paint, White-face

Maladroit Awkward, Clumsy, Graceless, Inelegant, Unperfect

Malady Disease, Illness

Malagas(e)y Hova, RM

Malaise Affluenza

Malapropism Catachresis, Slipslop

Malaria Ague, Falciparum, Marsh-fever, Paludism, Tap, Vivax

Malawi Nyasa

Malay(an), Malaysian Austronesian, Bahasa, Bajou, Datin, Datuk, D(a)yak, Jawi, Madurese, Moro, Sakai, Tokay, Tuan

Male Alpha, Arrhenotoky, Buck, Bull, Butch, Dog, Ephebe, Ephebus, Gent, Hob, John Doe, Macho, Mansize, Masculine, Ram, Rogue, Spear(side), Stag, Stamened, Telamon, Tom

Malediction Curse, Cuss, Oath, Slander

Malefactor Criminal, Felon, Villain

Malevolent, Malevolence Evil, Fell, Malign, Pernicious, Venomous

Malformation Teratogenesis

Malfunction Glitch, Hiccup

Mali RMM

Malice, Malicious Bitchy, Catty, Cruel, Despiteous, Envy, Hatchet job, Malevolent, Malign, Narquois, Prepense, Schadenfreude, Serpent, Snide, Spite, Spleen, Venom, Virulent, Vitriol

Malign(ant), Malignity Asperse, Backbite, Baleful, Defame, Denigrate, Evil, Gall, Harm, Hate-rent, Hatred, Libel, Poor-mouth, Sinister, Slander, Spiteful, Swart(h)y, Toxin, Vicious, Vilify, Vilipend, Viperous, Virulent

Malinger(er) Dodge, Leadswinger, Scrimshank, Shirk, Skrimshank, Truant

Mall Parade

Mallard Duck, Sord

Malleable Clay, Ductile, Fictile, Pliable

▷ **Malleable** *may indicate* an anagram

Mallet Beetle, Club, Hammer, Mace, Maul, Serving, Stick

Mallow Abutilon, Dwarf, Musk, Sida, Urena

Malodorous Mephitic, Stenchy

Malpractice(s) Sculduggery, Skulduggery

Malt Brewer's grain, Diastase, Grains, Grist, Single, Straik, Wort

Maltese (cross) Falcon, GC

Maltreat Abuse, Harm, Maul, Mishandle, Misuse

Mammal Animal, Anta, Armadillo, Artiodactyl, Binturong, Bobcat, Cacomistle, Cacomixle, Caracal, Cervid, Cetacean, Chalicothere, Charronia, Chevrotain, Chiropteran, Ciscus, Colugo, Creodont, Dhole, Dinothere, Dolphin, Dugong, Eutheria, Fisher, Glires, Glutton, Glyptodon, Grison, Guanaco, Hydrax, Hyrax, Indri, Jaguarondi, Jaguarundi, Kinkajou, Lagomorph, Leporid, Linsang, Loris, Lynx, Manatee, Margay, Marten, Meerkat, Metatherian, Mongoose, Monodelphia, Monotreme, Musteline, Notocingulate, Numbat, Olungo, Otter, Pachyderm, Pangolin, Peccary, Pekan, Perissodactyl, Pika, Pine marten, Pinniped, Platypus, Polecat, Porpoise, Primate, Pronghorn, Prototherian, Pudu, Raccoon, Rasse, Ratel, Rhytina, Sable, Serval, Shrew, Sirenian, Skunk, Sloth, Solenodon, Springhaas, Stegodon(t), Taguan, Tahr, Takin, Tamandu(a), Tanrec, Tapir, Tayra, Teledu,

Tenrec, Theria(n), Titanothere, Tylopod, Uintathere, Vicuña, Viverrid, Weasel, Whale, Wolverine, Zorilla

Mammon Money, Riches, Wealth

Mammoth Epic, Gigantic, Huge, Jumbo, Mastodon, Whopping, Woolly

Man(kind), Manly Adam, Advance, Andrew, Ask(r), Belt, Best, Betty, Bimana(l), Biped, Bloke, Bo, Boxgrove, Boy, Boyo, Bozo, Cad, Cairn, Calf, Castle, Cat, Chal, Chap, Checker, Chequer, Chiel, Cockey, Cod, Contact, Continuity, Crew, Cro-Magnon, Cuffin, Cully, Dog, Don, Draught, Dude, Emmanuel, Essex, Everyman, Family, Fancy, Fella, Feller, Fellow, Folsom, Friday, Front, G, Gayomart, Geezer, Gent, Grimaldi, Guy, He, Heidelberg, Himbo, Hombre, Hominid, Homme, Homo, Homo sapiens, Inner, IOM, Iron, Isle, It, Jack, Java, Joe (Bloggs), Joe Blow, Joe Sixpack, Joe Soap, John(nie), John Doe, Josser, Limit, Link, Lollipop, M, Male, Medicine, Microcosm, Mister, Mon, Mondeo, Mr, Muffin, Mun, Neanderthal, Numbers, Nutcracker, Oreopithecus, Organisation, Ou, Paleolithic, Party, Pawn, Peking, Person, Piece, Piltdown, Pin, Pithecanthropus, Property, Raff, Ray, Remittance, Renaissance, Resurrection, Rhodesian, Right-hand, Rook, Sandwich, Servant, Servitor, Ship, Sinanthropus, Sodor, Soldier, Solo, Spear, Staff, Stag, Standover, Straw, Third, Thursday, Trinil, Twelfth, Tyke, Type, Utility, Valet, Vir, White van, Wight

Man-about-town Boulevardier

Manacle Fetter, Handcuff, Iron, Shackle

Manage(r), Manageable, Management, Managing Adhocracy, Administer, Agent, Amildar, Attain, Aumil, Behave, Boss, Chief, Come by, Conduct, Contrive, Control, Cope, Darogha, Direct, Docile, Exec(utive), Fare, Fend, Find, Floor, Fund, Gerent, Get by, Govern, Grieve, Handle, Head bummer, Honcho, IC, Impresario, Intendant, Line, Logistical, MacReady, Maître d('hotel), Manipulate, Manoeuvre, Middle, Nomenklatura, Organise, Proctor, Procurator, Régisseur, Rig, Roadie, → RUN, Scrape, Shift, Steward, Strategy, Subsist, Succeed, Suit, Superintend, Supervisor, Swing, Tawie, Top, Tractable, Transact, Treatment, Trustee, Wangle, Wield(y), Yare

Manatee Lamantum, Mermaid, Sea-ape

Manchu Fu

Mandarin Bureaucrat, Chinaman, Kuo-Yu, Nodding, Satsuma, Yamen

Mandate Authority, Decree, Fiat, Order

Mandela Madiba, Nelson

Mandrake Springwort

Mandrel Triblet

Mane(d), Manes Crest, Encolure, Jubate, Larva(e), Shades

Manège Horseplay, Train

Manganese Diagolite, Mn, Synadelphite, Wadd

Manger Cratch, Crib, Hack, Stall

Mangle Agrise, Butcher, Distort, Garble, Hack, Hackle, Haggle, Wring(er)

▷ **Mangle** *may indicate* an anagram

Mango Dika

Manhandle Frogmarch, Maul, Rough

Manhater Misanthrope

Manhattan Bowery

Mania Cacoethes, Craze, Frenzy, Paranoia, Passion, Rage

Manichaean Albi

Manifest(ation), Manifestly Apparent, Attest, Avatar, Epiphany, Evident, Evince, Exhibit, Extravert, Extrovert, Feat, List, Marked, Mode, Notably, Obvious,

Open, Show, Undisguised

Manifesto Communist, Plank, Platform, Policy, Pronunciamento

Manifold(ness) Many, Multeity, Multiple

Manila Abaca, Cheroot

Manioc Cassava

Maniple Fannel, Fanon

Manipulate, Manipulative, Manipulator, Manipulation Bend, Chiropractor, Cog, Control, Cook, Demagogic, Diddle, Fashion, Finagle, Finesse, Gerrymander, Handle, Jerrymander, Juggle, Legerdemain, Logodaedalus, Masseuse, Milk, Osteopath, Play off, Ply, Rig, Tweeze, Use, Wangle, → **WIELD**

▷ **Manipulate** *may indicate* an anagram

Manna Alhagi, Food, Trehala, Turkish

Manner(ism), Mannerly, Manners Accent, Airs, À la, Appearance, Attitude, Bedside, Behaved, Behaviour, Bon ton, Breeding, Carriage, Conduct, Couth, Crew, Custom, Deportment, Ethos, Etiquette, Farand, Farrand, Farrant, Guise, Habit, How, Mien, Mister, Mode, Morality, Mores, Of, Ostent, Panache, Politesse, Presentation, P's & Q's, Quirk, Rate, Sort, Style, Table, Thew(s), Thewe(s), Trick, Upsee, Upsey, Upsy, Urbanity, Way, Wise

Manoeuvre(s) Alley-oop, Campaign, Castle, Christie, Christy, Démarche, Engineer, Exercise, Faena, Fianchetto, Fork, Gambit, Half-board, Heimlich, Hot-dog, Jink(s), Jockey, Manipulate, Op(eration), Pendule, Pesade, Ploy, Pull out, Renversement, Ruse, Skewer, Stickhandle, Tactic, Takeover, Use, U-turn, Valsalva, Wear, Wheelie, Whipstall, Wile, Wingover, Zigzag

▷ **Manoeuvre** *may indicate* an anagram

Man-of-war Armada, Bluebottle, Destroyer, Ironclad, Portuguese

Manor (house) Area, Demain, Demesne, Estate, Hall, Kelmscott, Schloss, Vill(a), Waddesdon

Mansion Broadlands, Burghley House, Casa, Castle Howard, Chatworth House, Cliveden, Knole, Luton Hoo, Mentmore, Penshurst Place, Queen's House, Seat, Stourhead, Stowe, Waddesdon Manor, Woburn Abbey

Mantle Asthenosphere, Authority, Burnous(e), Capote, Caracalla, Chlamydate, Dolman, Elijah, Gas, Pall, Pallium, Paludament, Pelisse, Rochet, Sima, Toga, Tunic, Vakas, Veil

Mantuan Maro, Virgil

Manual Blue collar, Bradshaw, Cambist, Console, Enchiridion, Great (organ), Guide, Hand, Handbook, How-to, Portolan(o), Positif, Sign

Manufacture, Manufacturing Fabricate, Industrial, Kanban, Make, Produce

Manure Compost, Dressing, Dung, → **FERTILISER**, Green, Guano, Hen-pen, Lime, Muck, Sha(i)rn, Tath

Manuscript(s) Book of Kells, Codex, Codicology, Folio, Hand, Holograph, Longhand, Miniscule, MS, Opisthograph, Palimpsest, Papyrus, Parchment, Script, Scroll, Scrowl(e), Uncial, Vellum

Manx(man) Cat, IOM, Kelly, Kelt

▷ **Manx** *may indicate* a last letter missing

Many C, CD, Countless, D, Hantle, Herd, Horde, Host, L, Lot, M, Manifold, Mony, Multi(tude), Myriad, Scad, Sight, Stacks, Tons, Umpteen, Untold

▷ **Many** *may indicate* the use of a Roman numeral letter

Maoist Naxalite, Red Guard

Maori (house) Hauhau, Hori, Jikanga, Mallowpuff, Moa hunter, Tangata whenua, Te reo, Wahine, Whare

Map(s), Mapping Atlas, A-Z, Card, Cartogram, Chart, Chorography, Choropleth,

Chromosome, Cognitive, Contour, Digital, Face, Genetic, Inset, Key, Loxodromic, Mappemond, Mental, Mosaic, Moving, Mud, OS, Perceptual, Plan, Plot, Portolano, Relief, Road, Sea-card, Sea-chart, Site, Star, Strip, Topography, Weather

Maple Acer, Flowering, Japanese, Manitoba, Mazer, Norway, Plane, Silver, Sugar, Sycamore, Syrup

Map-maker Cartographer, OS, Speed

Maquis Queach, Underground

Mar Blight, Denature, Dere, Impair, Soil, Spoil, Taint

Marabout Sofi, Sufi

Marathon Comrades, Huge, London, Race, Two Oceans

Maraud(er) Amalekite, Attacker, Bandit, Pillager, Pirate, Predator, Prowler, Raid

Marble(s), Marbling Aeginetan, Agate, All(e)y, Arch, Arundelian, Bonce, Bonduc, Bool, Boondoggle, Bowl, Carrara, Chequer, Cipollino, Commoney, Devil's, Dump, Elgin, Humite, Hymettus, Knicker, Languedoc, Lucullite, Marl, Marmarosis, Marmoreal, Marver, Mottle, Nero-antico, Nickar, Nicker, Onychite, Onyx, Paragon, Parian, Pavonazzo, Pentelic(an), Petworth, Phigalian, Plonker, Plunker, Purbeck, Rance, Ringer, Ring-taw, Ruin, Sanity, Scagliola, Spangcockle, Taw, Variegate, Xanthian

Marcel Proust

March(ing) Abut, Adjoin, Advance, Anabasis, Border(er), Borderland, Dead, Defile, Demo, Étape, File, Footslog, Forced, Freedom, Fringe, Galumph, Go, Goosestep, Hikoi, Hunger, Ides, Jarrow, Lide, Limes, Lockstep, Long, Meare, Music, → **PARADE**, Paso doble, Procession, Progress, Protest, Quick, Rogue's, Route, Slow time, Step, Strunt, Strut, Trio, Tromp, Troop, Wedding, Yomp

▷ **March** *may indicate* 'Little Women' character, Amy, Beth, Jo, Meg

Marco Il Milione, Polo

Mare Dam, Flanders, Horse, M, MacCurdle's, Shanks's, Spanish, Yaud

Margaret Anjou, Meg, Peg, Rita

Margarine Oleo

Marge, Margin(al) Annotate, Bank, Border, Brim, Brink, Curb, Edge, Fimbria, Hair's breadth, Kerb, Lean, Leeway, Limit, Lip, Littoral, Neck, Nose, Peristome, Profit, Rand, Repand, → **RIM**, Selvedge, Sideline, Spread, Tail, Term

Marginal note Apostil(le), K'ri

Margosa Melia, Nim

Maria(nne) France, Tia

Marie Dressler, Tempest

Marigold Calendula, Kingcup, Tagetes

Marijuana Alfalfa, Camberwell carrot, Dagga, Gage, Ganja, Grass, Greens, Gungeon, Ha-ha, Hay, Herb, J, Jive, Joint, Kaif, Kef, Kif, Leaf, Lid, Locoweed, Mary-Jane, Pot, Roach, Rope, Shit, Sinsemilla, Splay, Spliff, Tea, Toke, Weed

Marina Wharf

Marinade Chermoula, Escabeche

Marine (animal) Aquatic, Bootie, Bootneck, Cephalopod, Chaetognath, Cnidarian, Coelenterate, Comatulid, Ctenophora, Cunjevoi, Enteropneusta, Flustra, Foram(inifer), Galoot, Graptolite, Harumfrodite, Hemichorda, Holothurian, Horse, Hydrocoral, Hydroid, Hydromedusa, Jarhead, Jolly, Lancelet, Leatherneck, Lobster, Mercantile, Mere-swine, Mistress Roper, Oceanic, Physalia, Pollywag, Pollywog, Salpa, Sea-soldier, Seston, Thalassian, Ultra

Mariner AB, Ancient, MN, Noah, RM, Sailor, Salt, Seafarer, Spacecraft, Tar

Marionette(s) Fantoccini, Puppet

Marjoram Amaracus, Origan, Pot, Sweet, Wild, Winter-sweet

Mark(ing), Marked, Marks Accent, Antony, Apostrophe, Asterisk, Astrobleme, Badge, Banker, Bethumb, Birth, Blaze, Blot, Blotch, Brand, Bruise, Bull, Butt, Cachet, Caract, Caret, Caste, CE, Cedilla, Chatter, Chequer, Cicatrix, Class, Clout, Colon, Comma, Coronis, Crease, Criss-cross, Cross, Cup (and ring), Dash, Denote, Dent, Diacritic, Diaeresis, Dieresis, Distinction, DM, Duckfoot quote, Dupe, Emblem, Ensign, Enstamp, Exclamation, Expression, Feer, Fleck, Freckle, Genetic, Glyph, Gospel, Grade, Guillemet, Gybe, Haček, Haemangioma, Hair-line, Hash, Hatch, Heed, High water, Hyphen, Impress(ion), Indicium, Ink, Inscribe, Insignia, Interrogation, Keel, Kite, Kumkum, Lentigo, Line, Ling, Livedo, Logo, Lovebite, Low water, M, Macron, Matchmark, MB, Medical, Merk, Mint, Minute, Mottle, NB, Nota bene, Notal, Note, Notice, Obelisk, Observe, Oche, Paginate, Paraph, Period, Pilcrow, Pit, Plage, Pling, Pock, Point, Popinjay, Port wine, Post, Presa, Printer's, Proof, Punctuation, Question, Quotation, Record, Reference, Register, Regulo, Remarque, Ripple, Roundel, Sanction, Scar, Score, Scratch, Section, See, Service, Shadow, Shilling, Shoal, Sigil, Sign, Smit, Smut, Smutch, Soft touch, Speck, Splodge, Splotch, Stain, Stencil, Stigma(ta), Strawberry, Stress, Stretch, Stroke, Sucker, Swan-upping, Symbol, Tag, Target, Tarnish, Tatow, Tattoo, Tee, Theta, Thread, Tick, Tide, Tika, Tikka, Tilak, Tilde, Tittle, Token, Touchmark, Trace, Track, Trout, Tug(h)ra, Twain, Umlaut, Ure, Victim, Wand, Warchalking, Watch, Weal, Welt

Marker Biological, Bollard, Buck, Cairn, Cross(let), Fanion, Flag, Gnomon, Infinitive, Ink, Inukshuk, Label, Medical, Scorer, Tie

Market(ing), Market day, Market place Advergaming, Agora, Alcaiceria, Available, Baltic, Bazaar, Bear, Billingsgate, Black, Black stump, Borgo, Bull, Buyers', Capital, Captive, Cattle, Change, Chowk, Cinema, Circular, Cluster, Common, Demo, Denet, Direct, Discount, Dragon, EC, Emerging, Emporium, Errand, Exchange, Exhibition, Fair, Farmers', Feeing, Flea, Forum, Forward, Free, Grey, Growth, Insert, Internal, Kerb, Lloyds, Main, Mandi, Mart, Meat, Mercat, Money, Niche, Nundine, Obigosony, Oligopoly, Open, Order-driven, Outlet, Overt, Pamphlet, Perfect, Piazza, Poster, Press, Radio, Reach, Relationship, Sale, Sellers', Servqual, Share, Shop, Single, Social, Societal, Sook, Souk, Spot, Stance, Staple, Stock, Stock Exchange, Tattersall's, Terminal, Test, Third, Tiger, Trade, Tron, Tryst, USP, Vent, Viral, Wall Street

Market garden Truck-farm

Marksman Sharpshooter, Shootist, Shot, Sniper, Tell

Marlborough Blenheim

Marlene Lilli

Marmalade Cat, Mammee-sapota, Preserve, Squish

Marmoset Jacchus, Mico, Midas, Monkey, Wistiti

Marmot Bobac, Bobak, Dassie, Groundhog, Hoary, Hyrax, Rodent, Whistler, Woodchuck

Maroon Brown, Castaway, Enisle, Firework, Inisle, Isolate, Strand

Marquee Pavilion, Tent, Top

Marquess, Marquis Granby, Lorne, Sade

Marquetry Boul(l)e, Buhl, Inlay

Marriage → ALLIANCE, Bed, Beenah, Bigamy, Bridal, Buckle-beggar, Civil, Coemption, Common law, Commuter, Confarreation, Conjugal, Connubial, Coverture, Digamy, Endogamy, Espousal, Exogamy, Gandharva, Genial, Group, Hedge, Hetaerism, Hetairism, Hymen(eal), Jugal, Ketubah, Knot, Lavender, Levirate, Match, Mating, Matrilocal, Matrimony, Mésalliance, Mixed, Monandry, Monogamy, Morganatic, Noose, Nuptial, Open, Pantagamy, Patrilocal, Polygamy,

Punalua, Putative, Sacrament, Shidduch, Shotgun, Tie, Trial, → UNION, Wedding, Wedlock

Marriageable Marrow, Nubile, Parti

Marriage-broker Shadchan

Marrow Courgette, Friend, Gist, Kamokamo, Medulla, Myeloid, Pith, Pumpkin, Squash, Vegetable

Marry, Married Ally, Amate, Buckle, Cleek(it), Confarreate, Couple, Coverture, Espouse, Feme covert, Forsooth, Fuse, Goody, Hitch, Join, Knit, M, Mate, Matron, Memsahib, Missis, Missus, Pair, Pardie, Quotha, Sannup, Splice, Tie, Tie the knot, Troggs, Troth, Umfazi, Unite, W, Wed, Wive

Mars Areography, Ares, Red (planet)

Marsh(y) Bayou, Bog, Chott, Corcass, Emys, Everglades, Fen, Hackney, Maremma, Merse, Mire, Morass, Ngaio, Paludal, Plashy, Pontine, Pripet, Quagmire, Romney, Salina, Salt, Shott, Slade, Slough, Sog, Spew, Spue, Swale, Swamp, Taiga, Terai, Vlei, Wetlands

Marshal Arrange, Array, Commander, Earp, Foch, French, Hickok, MacMahon, Muster, Neil, Ney, Order, Pétain, Provost, Shepherd, Steward, Tedder, Usher, Yardman

Marshmallow Althaea, Mallowpuff

Marsupial Bandicoot, Bilby, Cuscus, Dasyure, Dibbler, Didelphia, Diprotodon(t), Dunnart, Honey mouse, Honey possum, Kangaroo, Koala, Macropod, Metatheria, Notoryctes, Nototherium, Numbat, Opossum, Pademelon, Pad(d)ymelon, Petaurist, Phalanger, Polyprodont, Possum, Potoroo, Pouched mouse, Pygmy glider, Quokka, Quoll, Roo, Tammar, Tasmanian devil, Theria, Thylacine, Tuan, Wallaby, Wambenger, Wombat, Yapo(c)k

Marten Fisher, Mustela, Pekan, Pine, Sable, Woodshock

Martha Vineyard

Martial (arts) Bellicose, Budo, Capoeira, Capuera, Chopsocky, Dojo, Iai-do, Judo, Ju-jitsu, Karate, Kendo, Kick boxing, Kumite, Kung fu, Militant, Muay thai, Ninjitsu, Ninjutsu, Shintaido, Tae Bo®, Tae kwon do, T'ai chi (chuan), Warlike, Wushu

Martin Bird, Luther, Swallow

Martinet Captious, Ramrod, Stickler, Tyrant

Martini® Cocktail, Henry

Martyr(dom), Martyrs Alban, Alphege, Colosseum, Donatist, Justin, Latimer, Metric, MM, Passional, Persecute, Sebastian, Stephen, Suffer, Tolpuddle, Wishart

Marvel(lous) Bodacious, Bully, Épatant, Fab, Fantabulous, Lulu, Magic, Marl, Miracle, Mirific, Phenomenon, Prodigious, Selcouth, Superb, Super-duper, Swell, Terrific, Wonder

Marx(ism), Marxist Aspheterism, Chico, Comintern, Commie, Groucho, Gummo, Harpo, Karl, Lenin, Mao, Menshevik, Revisionism, Tanky, Tipamaro, Zeppo

Mary Bloody, Celeste, Madonna, Moll, Morison, Our Lady, Tum(my), Typhoid, Virgin

Marylebone Station

Marzipan Marchpane

Mascara Eye-black

Mascot Charm, → TALISMAN, Telesm, Token

Masculine, Masculinity He, He-man, Linga(m), M, Machismo, Macho, Male, Manly, Virile

Maser Laser

Mash(er) Beat, Beau, Beetle, Brew, Lady-killer, Pap, Pestle, Pound, Sour, Squash

Mask(ed) Bird cage, Camouflage, Cloak, Cokuloris, Death, Disguise, Dissemble,

Domino, Face pack, False face, Front, Gas, Hide, Larvated, Life, Loo, Loup, Mascaron, Matte, Oxygen, Persona, Respirator, Screen, Semblance, Shadow, Stalking-horse, Stocking, Stop out, Template, Visor, Vizard

Mason(ry) Ashlar, Ashler, Brother, Builder, Cowan, Emplecton, Isodoma, Isodomon, Isodomum, Lodge, Moellon, Nogging, Opus, Perry, Random, Squinch, Stylobate

Masque(rade), Masquerader Comus, Domino, Guisard, Mum(m), Pose, Pretend

Mass(es) Aggregate, Agnus Dei, Anniversary, Atomic, Banket, Bezoar, Bike, Body, Bulk, Cake, Chaos, Clot, Congeries, Conglomeration, Consecration, Core, Crith, Critical, Crowd, Demos, Density, Flake, Flysch, Folk, Geepound, Gramme, Gravitational, Great, Herd, High, Horde, Hulk, Inertial, Jud, Kermesse, Kermis, Kilo(gram), Kirmess, Low, Lump, M, Majority, Missa, Mob, Month's mind, Mop, Nest, Phalanx, Pile, Plebs, Plumb, Pontifical, Populace, Proper, Raft, Requiem, Rest, Ruck, Salamon, Salmon, Scrum, Sea, Serac, Service, Shock, Sicilian, Size, Slub, Slug, Solar, Solemn, Solid, Stack, Stroma, Sursum Corda, Te Igitur, Tektite, Trental, Vesper, Vigil, Volume, Wad, Weight, Welter

Massacre Amritsar, Beziers, Blood-bath, Butcher, Carnage, Glencoe, Havock, Kanpur, Manchester, Peterloo, Pogrom, Purge, St Bartholomew's Day, Scullabogue, Scupper, September, Sicilian vespers, Slaughter, Slay, Wounded Knee

Massage, Masseur An mo, Chafer, Chavutti thirumal, Do-in, Effleurage, Hellerwork, → **KNEAD**, Malax, Palp, Petrissage, Physio, Rolf(ing), Rubber, Shampoo, Shiatsu, Stone, Stroke, Swedish, Tapotement, Thai, Tripsis, Tui na

Massif Makalu

Massive Big, Bull, Colossal, Gargantuan, Heavy, Herculean, Huge, Monumental, Strong, Titan

Mast(ed), Masthead Acorn, Banner, Captain's, Crosstree, Flag, Foretop, High top, Hounds, Jigger, Jury, M, Mizzen, Mooring, Pannage, Pole, Racahout, Royal, Ship-rigged, Spar, Top-gallant, Truck, Venetian

Master(ly) Artful, Baalebos, Baas, Beak, Beat, Boss, Buddha, Bwana, Careers, Checkmate, Conquer, Control, Dan, Dominate, Dominie, Employer, Enslave, Exarch, Expert, Gov, Grand, Harbour, Herr, Himself, International, Learn, Lord, MA, Maestro, Mas(s), Massa, Mes(s), Nkosi, Old, Ollamh, Ollav, Oner, Oppress, Original, Overcome, Overlord, Overpower, Overseer, Passed, Past, Pedant, Question, Rabboni, Schoolman, Seigneur, Seignior, Signorino, Sir(e), Skipper, → **SUBDUE**, Subjugate, Superate, Surmount, Swami, Tame, Task, Thakin, Towkay, Tuan, Usher, Vanquish, Virtuoso

Mastermind Brain, Conceive, Direct

Masterpiece Chef d'oeuvre, Creation

Mastersinger Sachs

Master-stroke Coup, Triumph

Masturbate, Masturbation Abuse, Blow, Frig, Gratify, Jerk off, Jock, Onanism, Toss off, Wank, Whack off

Mat(ted), Matting Bast, Capillary, Coaster, Doily, Dojo, Doyley, Dutch mattress, Felt, Inlace, Pad, Paunch, Place, Plat, Prayer, Rug, Surf, Table, Taggy, → **TANGLE**, Tat(ami), Tatty, Taut, Tautit, Tawt, Tomentose, Welcome, Zarf

Matador Card, Espada, Ordonez, Theseus, Torero

Match(ed) Agree, Alliance, Amate, Balance, Besort, Bonspiel, Bout, Carousel, Compare, Compeer, Congreve, Contest, Cope, Correlate, Correspond, Counterpane, Doubles, Emulate, Engagement, Equal(ise), Equate, Even, Exhibition, Fellow, Fit, Fixture, Four-ball, Friction, Friendly, Fusee, Fuzee, Game, Go, Greensome, Grudge, International, Joust, Light, Locofoco, Love, Lucifer, Main, Marrow, Marry, Meet,

Mouse, Needle, Pair(s), Paragon, Parti, Pit, Prizefight, Promethean, Reproduce, Return, Rival, Roland, Rubber, Safety, Semifinal, Sevens, Shield, Shoo-in, Shooting, Shouting, Singles, Slanging, Slow, Spunk, Striker, Suit, Sync, → **TALLY**, Team, Test, Tie, Twin, Union, Venue, Vesta, Vesuvian, Wedding

Matchbox label (collecting) Phillumeny

Match girl Bride

Match-holder Lin(t)stock

Matchless Non(e)such, Orinda

Matchmaker Blackfoot, Broker, Pairer, Promoter, Shadchan

Mate, Mating Achates, Adam, Amigo, Amplexus, Bedfellow, Bo, Breed, Buddy, Buffer, Butty, Check, Chess, China, Chum, Cobber, Cock, Comrade, Consort, Crony, Cully, Digger, Eve, Feare, Feer, Fellow, Fere, Fiere, First, Fool's, Helper, Husband, Ilex, Maik, Make, Marrow, Marry, Match, Mister, Mucker, Nick, Oldster, Oppo, → **PAIR**, Pal, Panmixia, Panmixis, Paragon, Partner, Pheer(e), Pirrauru, Running, Scholar's, Second, Serve, Sex, Skaines, Smothered, Soul, → **SPOUSE**, Tea, Tup, Wack, Wacker, Wife, Wus(s)

Material(ism) Agalmatolite, Aggregate, Agitprop, Apt, Armure, Ballast, Blastema, Bole, Borsic, Byssus, Celluloid, Cellulose, Ceramic, Cermet, → **CLOTH**, Cob, Compo, Concrete, Copy, Corfam®, Corporeal, Data, Documentation, Earthy, Fablon®, → **FABRIC**, Factual, Fallout, Fertile, Fettling, Fibrefill, Fibreglass, Fines, Flong, Fomes, Frit(t), Fuel, Gang(ue), Germane, Gypsum, Historical, Hylic, Illusion, Illuvium, Interfacing, Lambskin, Leading, Macintosh, Matter, Metal, Moxa, Oasis®, Oilcloth, Oilskin, Papier-maché, Pertinent, Phantom, Physical, Pina-cloth, Plasterboard, Polystyrene, Polythene, Positive, Protoplasm, Protore, Pug(ging), Raw, Regolith, Relevant, Sackcloth, Sagathy, Samsonite®, Silicone, Skirting, Staff, Stuff, Substance, Swish, Tangible, Tape, Textile, Thermolite®, Thingy, Towelling, Tusser, Wattle and daub, Worldly

Materialise Appear, Apport, Click, Reify

Materialist(ic) Banausian, Hylist, Hyloist, Philistine, Somatist

Mathematician Agnesi, Apollonius, Archimedes, Archytas, Bernoulli, Bessel, Boole, Bourbaki, Briggs, Cantor, Cocker, De Morgan, Descartes, Diophantos, Dunstable, Eratosthenes, Euclid, Euler, Fermat, Fibonacci, Fourier, Friedmann, Gauss, Godel, Goldbach, Gunter, Hawking, Lagrange, Laplace, Leibniz, Lie, Mandelbrot, Mercator, Minkowski, Napier, Newton, Optime, Pascal, Penrose, Playfair, Poisson, Ptolemy, Pythagoras, Pytheas, Riemann, Statistician, Torricelli, Turing, Von Leibnitz, Walker, Wrangler, Zeno

Mathematics, Mathematical, Maths Algebra, Applied, Arithmetic, Arsmetrick, Calculus, Geometry, Higher, Logarithms, Mechanics, New, Numbers, Porism, Pure, Topology, Trig, Trigonometry

Matilda Liar, Swag, Untruthful, Waltzing

Matinee Coat, Idol, Show

Mating Pangamy

Matins Nocturn

Matricide Orestes

Matrimony Bed, Conjugal, Marriage, Sacrament, Spousal, Wedlock

Matrix Active, Array, Boston, Hermitian, Jacobian, Mould, Orthogonal, Pattern, Scattering, Square, Uterus

Matron Dame, Hausfrau, Lucretia, Nurse, Warden

Matt(e) Dense, Dingy, Dull

Matter Alluvium, Bioblast, Biogen, Body, Concern, Condensed, Consequence, Dark, Degenerate, Empyema, Epithelium, Gear, Gluon, Go, Grey, Hyle, Impost(h)ume,

Issue, Mass, Material, Molecule, Multiverse, Phlegm, Pith, Point, Positron, Protoplasm, Pulp, Pus, Quark, Reading, Reck, Reke, Scum, Shebang, Signify, Solid, Stuff, Subject, → SUBSTANCE, Thing, Topic, Tousle, Touzle, White, Ylem

Matthew Arnold

Mattress Bed(ding), Biscuit, Dutch, Featherbed, Foam, Futon, Lilo®, Pa(i)lliasse, Pallet, Spring, Tick

Mature, Maturity Adult, Age, Blossom, Bold, Concoct, Develop, Mellow, Metaplasis, Old, Puberty, Ripe(n), Rounded, Seasoned, Upgrow(n)

Maudlin Fuddled, Mawkish, Sentimental, Slip-slop, Sloppy, Too-too

Maul Hammer, Manhandle, Paw, Rough, Savage

Maundy Money, Nipter, Thursday

Mauretanian, Mauritania(n) Moor, RIM

Mausoleum Helicarnassus, Mole, Sepulchre, Taj Mahal, Tomb

Mauve Lilac, Mallow, Perkin's

Maverick Misfit, Nonconformist, Rogue

Mavis Throstle

Maw Crop, Gorge, Gull(et), Mouth, Oesophagus

Mawkish Sentimental, Sickly

Maxim Adage, Aphorism, Apo(ph)thegm, Axiom, Byword, Gnome, Gorki, Gun, Hiram, Moral, Motto, Proverb, Restaurateur, → RULE, Saw, Saying, Sentence, Sentiment, Watchword

Maximum All-out, Full, Highest, Most, Peak, Utmost

May Blossom, Can, Hawthorn, Merry, Might, Month, Mote, Quickthorn, Shall, Whitethorn

Maybe Happen, Mebbe, Peradventure, Percase, Perchance, Perhaps, Possibly

▷ **May become** *may indicate* an anagram

May day Beltane, SOS

Mayfair WI

Mayfly Ephemera, Ephemeroptera, Green-drake, Sedge

Mayhem Chaos, Crime, Damage, Havoc, Pandemonium

Mayonnaise Aioli, Rémoulade

Mayor Alcaide, Burgomaster, Casterbridge, Charter, Councilman, Portreeve, Provost, Whittington

Maze Honeycomb, Labyrinth, Meander, Theseus, Warren, Wilderness

MC Compere, Host, Ringmaster

MD Doctor, Healer

ME Yuppie flu

Me I, Mi

Mead(ow) Flood, Grass, Haugh, Hydromel, Inch, Ing, Lea(se), Ley, Meath(e), Metheglin, → PASTURE, Runnymede, Saeter, Salting, Water

Meadowsweet Dropwort

Meagre Bare, Exiguous, Measly, Paltry, Pittance, Scant, Scrannel, Scranny, Scrawny, Skimpy, Skinny, Spare, Sparse, Stingy, Thin

Meal(s), Mealie, Mealy Banquet, Barbecue, Barium, Beanfeast, Blow-out, Board, Breakfast, Brunch, Buffet, Cassava, Cereal, Cholent, Chota-hazri, Collation, Corn, Cornflour, Cottoncake, Cottonseed, Cou-cou, Cribble, Dejeune(r), Deskfast, Dinner, Drammock, Ear, Ervalenta, Fare, Farina, Feast, Flour, Food, Grits, Grout, Hangi, High tea, Iftar, Indian, Italian, Kai, Lock, Lunch, Mandioc, Mandioc(c)a, Mani(h)oc, Matzo, Melder, Meltith, Mensal, Mess, Mush, No-cake, Nosh, Nuncheon, Obento, Ordinary, Picnic, Piece, Plate, Poi, Polenta, Porridge, Prandial, Prix fixe, Rac(c)ahout, Refection, Repast, Revalenta, Rijst(t)afel, Salep, Scambling, Scoff,

Seder, Smorgasbord, Snack, Spread, Square, Supper, Table d'hôte, Takeaway, Tea, Thali, Tiffin, Tightener, Twalhours, Undern

Meal-ticket LV

Mean(ing), Meant Aim, Arithmetic(al), Average, Base, Betoken, Bowsie, Caitiff, Connotation, Curmudgeon, Definition, Denotate, Denote, Design, Dirty, Drift, Essence, Ettle, Feck, Footy, Foul, Geometric(al), Gist, Golden, Hang, Harmonic, Humble, Hunks, Ignoble, Illiberal, Imply, Import, Inferior, Insect, Intend, Intermediate, Kunjoos, Lexical, Low, Mang(e)y, Marrow, Medium, Mesquin, Method, Mid, Miserly, Narrow, Near, Norm, Nothing, One-horse, Ornery, Paltry, Par, Penny-pinching, Petty, Piker, Pinch-penny, Pith, Point, Purport, → **PURPOSE**, Quadratic, Ratfink, Revenue, Roinish, Roynish, Scall, Scrub, Scurvy, Semanteme, Semantic(s), Sememe, Sense, Shabby, Signify, Slight, Small, Sneaky, Snoep, Snot, Sordid, Sparing, Spell, Stingy, Stink(ard), Stinty, Substance, Symbol, Thin, Threepenny, Tightwad, Two-bit, Value, Vile, Whoreson

Meander Fret, Ring, Sinuate, Stray, Wander, Weave, Wind

Meaningless Ducdame, Empty, Hollow, Hot air, Insignificant, Nonny, Rumbelow

Means Agency, Dint, Income, Instrumental, Media, Method, Mode, Opulence, Organ, Private, Resources, Staple, Substance, Tactics, Visible, Ways, Wherewithal

Meantime, Meanwhile Among, Emong, Greenwich, Interim

Measles Morbilli, Roseola, Rose-rash, Rubella, Rubeola, Sheep

Measure(d), Measuring, Measurement By(e)law, Calibre, Circular, Crackdown, → **DANCE**, Démarche, → **DIMENSION**, Distance, Dose, Dry, Gavotte, Gross, Imperial, Limit, Linear, Moratorium, Of, Offset, Precaution, Prophylactic, Quickstep, Ration, Share, Short, → **SIZE**, Standard, Statute, Step, Strike, Struck, Survey, Token, Wine

---

MEASURING INSTRUMENTS

2 letters:	Wey	Line	Thou
As		Link	Unit
Em	4 letters:	Maze	Vara
En	Acre	Mete	Volt
Mu	Aune	Mile	Warp
	Bath	Mole	Yard
3 letters:	Boll	Mott	
Are	Bolt	Muid	5 letters:
Bel	Comb	Nail	Anker
Cab	Cord	Omer	Ardeb
Cor	Coss	Pace	Barye
Ell	Cran	Peck	Bekah
Erg	Culm	Pint	Bigha
Fat	Dram	Pipe	Caneh
Hin	Epha	Pole	Carat
Lay	Foot	Pood	Chain
Lea	Gage	Ream	Clove
Ley	Gill	Reau	Combe
Log	Hank	Rood	Coomb
Lug	Hide	Rope	Crore
Mil	Inch	Shot	Cubit
Rod	Koss	Span	Cumec
Tot	Last	Tape	Cusec

Depth
Ephah
Fermi
Float
Gauge
Grain
Groma
Hanap
Homer
Joule
Kaneh
Lento
Liang
Ligne
Lippy
Loure
Mease
Meter
Metre
Middy
Optic®
Perch
Plumb
Quart
Romer
Ruler
Scale
Skein
Sound
Stade
Stere
Tesla
Therm
Toise
Verst
Wecht
Yojan

6 letters:
Albedo
Alnage
Arpent
Arshin
Barrel
Barren
Beegah
Bovate
Bushel
Chenix
Chopin
Cicero

Cubage
Denier
Double
Etalon
Exergy
Fathom
Firkin
Firlot
Gallon
Height
Hemina
Jigger
Kelvin
Kilerg
League
Lippie
Liquid
Metage
Modius
Morgan
Mutton
Noggin
Oxgang
Parsec
Pascal
Pottle
Radius
Runlet
Sazhen
Stadia
Thread
Tierce
Yojana

7 letters:
Aneroid
Arshine
Breadth
Burette
Caliper
Candela
Chalder
Choenix
Conguis
Coulomb
Cyathus
Decibel
Drastic
Entropy
Furlong
Geodesy

Lambert
Leaguer
Pelorus
Quarter
Refract
Rundlet
Sleever
Spindle
Spondee
Venturi
Virgate

8 letters:
Angstrom
Calliper
Carucate
Chaldron
Crannock
Desyatin
Diameter
Exitance
Fistmele
Foot rule
Hogshead
Kilogray
Luxmeter
Mutchkin
Odometer
Oximeter
Parasang
Poulter's
Puncheon
Tape-line
Teraflop
Viameter
Waywiser

9 letters:
Astrolabe
Atmometer
Bolometer
Cryometer
Decalitre
Decastere
Dosimeter
Ergometer
Eriometer
Kilometre
Konimeter
Lysimeter
Manometer

Mekometer
Nipperkin
Octameter
Oenometer
Pentapody
Potometer
Steradian
Tappet-hen
Telemeter
Titration
Tonometer
Yardstick

10 letters:
Acidometer
Amphimacer
Anemometer
Barleycorn
Bathometer
Centimetre
Coulometer
Cyclometer
Densimeter
Dessiatine
Dessyatine
Drosometer
Eudiometer
Goniometer
Gravimeter
Humidistat
Hydrometer
Hygrometer
Lactometer
Micrometer
Millimetre
Opisometer
Photometer
Piezometer
Resistance
Touchstone
Tromometer
Winchester

11 letters:
Actinometer
Auxanometer
Calorimeter
Dioptometer
Dynamometer
Intoximeter
Jacob's staff

Stereometer	*12 letters:*	Extensimeter	Viscosimeter
Tacheometry	Cathetometer	Extensometer	
Venturi tube	Coulombmeter	Galactometer	*13 letters:*
Weighbridge	Densitometer	Nephelometer	Saccharometer
	Electrometer	Permittivity	
	Electronvolt	Tellurometer	

Meat(s) Aitchbone, Bacon, Bard, Beef, Biltong, Brawn, Brisket, Brown, Burger, Cabob, Carbonado, Carrion, Charcuterie, Chop, Collop, Confit, Croquette, Cut, Dark, Devon, Dog-roll, Easy, Edgebone, Entrecôte, Escalope, Essence, Fanny Adams, Fleishig, Fleishik, Flesh, Flitch, Force, Galantine, Gigot, Gobbet, Gosht, Griskin, Ham, Haslet, Jerky, Joint, Junk, Kabab, Kabob, Kebab, Kebob, Lamb, Loin, Luncheon, Mart, Mince, Mutton, Noisette, Offal, Olive, Oyster, Pastrami, Paupiette, Pem(m)ican, Piccata, Pith, Pope's eye, Pork, Processed, Prosciutto, Rack, Red, Rillettes, Roast, Saddle, Sasatie, Satay, Scaloppino, Schnitzel, Scran, Scrapple, Sey, Shashlik, Shishkebab, Side, Sirloin, Sosatie, Spam®, Spare rib, Spatchcock, Spaul(d), Steak, Strong, Tenderloin, Tiring, Tongue, Variety, Veal, Venison, Vifda, Virgate, Vivda, Weiner schnitzel, White, Wurst

Meatball(s) Cecils, Croquette, Faggot, Falafel, Felafel, Fricadel, Frikkadell, Goujon, Knish, Kofta, Kromesky, Quenelle, Rissole

Meat extract Brawn, Gravy, Juice, Stock

Meatless Banian, Lent, Maigre, Vegetarian

Mecca Centre, Kaaba, Keblah, Kibla(h), Qibla

Mechanic(s) Apron-man, Artificer, Artisan, Banausic, Bottom, Celestial, Classical, Dynamics, Engineer, Fitter, Fluid, Fundi, Grease monkey, Greaser, Hand, Journeyman, Kinematics, Kinesiology, Kinetics, Newtonian, Operative, Quantum, Rock, Soil, Statics, Statistical, Technician, Wave

▷ **Mechanic(al)** *may indicate* characters from 'A Midsummer Night's Dream'

Mechanical, Mechanism Action, Apparatus, Auto, Banausic, Clockwork, Defence, Dérailleur, Escape, Escapement, Gimmal, Instrument, Machinery, Movement, Organical, Pulley, Pushback, Regulator, Robotic, Servo, Synchroflash, Synchromesh, Trippet, Works

Medal(lion)(s) Award, Bar, Bronze, Congressional, Croix de guerre, Decoration, Dickin, DSM, GC, George, Gold, Gong, Gorget, Military, MM, Numismatic, Pan(h)agia, Purple Heart, Putty, Roundel, Silver, Tony, Touchpiece, VC, Vernicle

Meddle(r), Meddlesome Busybody, Dabble, Finger, Hen-hussy, → **INTERFERE**, Interloper, Marplot, Mell, Monkey, Officious, Potter, Pragmatic, Pry, Snooper, Spoilsport, Tamper, Tinker, Trifle

Media Mass, Mixed, New, PR

Mediate, Mediator ACAS, Arbitrate, Intercede, Interpose, Intervene, Liaison, Muti, Referee, Thirdsman, Trouble-shooter

Medical, Medicine (chest), Medicament, Medication Aesculapian, Algology, Allopathy, Aloetic, Alternative, Andrology, Anodyne, Antacid, Antibiotic, Antidote, Antisepsis, Antiseptic, Arnica, Asafetida, Aviation, Ayurveda, Bi, Bismuth, Blister, Brunonian, Buchu, Bucku, Calumba, Carminative, Charm, Chinese, Chiropody, Chlorodyne, Chrysarobin, Clinician, Complementary, Cordial, Corpsman, Cubeb, Curative, Defensive, Diapente, Diascordium, Diatessaron, Dose, Draught, Drops, → **DRUG**, Dutch drops, Electuary, Elixir, Emmenagogue, Empirics, Enema, Epulotic, Excipient, Expectorant, Fall-trank, Febrifuge, Feldsher, Folk, Forensic, Fringe, Galen, Galenism, Gelcap, Genitourinary, Gripe water®, Gutta, Haematinic, Herb, Herbal, Hesperidin, Holistic, Hom(o)eopathy, Horse-drench,

Iatric(al), Imhotep, Industrial, Inhalant, Inro, Internal, Iodine, Ipecac(uanha), Iron, Ko cycle, Lariam®, Laxative, Leechcraft, Legal, Loblolly, Lotion, Magnesia, Menthol, Microbubbles, Mishmi, Mixture, Moxar, Muti, Nephritic, Nervine, Nosology, Nostrum, Nuclear, Nux vomica, Ob-gyn, Officinal, Oncology, Oporice, Orthopoedics, Osteopath, Palliative, Panacea, Paregoric, Patent, Pathology, Pharmacy, Physic, Physical, Pill, Placebo, Polychrest, Polypill, Posology, Potion, Poultice, Preparation, Preventive, Proctology, Psionic, Psychiatry, Quinacrine, Quinine, Quin(quin)a, Radiology, Red Crescent, Red Cross, Relaxative, → REMEDY, Salve, Sanative, Sanguinaria, Senna, Serology, Simple, Space, Specific, Sports, Steel, Stomachic, Stomatology, Stramonium, Stupe, Suppository, Synergast, Syrup, Tabasheer, Tabashir, Tablet, Tar-water, Tetracycline, Therapeutics, TIM, Tisane, Tocology, Tonic, Totaquine, Trade, Traditional Chinese, Traumatology, Treatment, Trichology, Troche, Valerian, Veronal, Veterinary, Virology

Medicine man, Medico Bone-setter, Koradji

Medic(k) Lucern(e), Snail

Medieval Archaic, Feudal, Gothic, Med, Old, Trecento

Mediocre Fair, Indifferent, Middle-of-the-road, Middling, Ordinary, Pap, Respectable, Run-of-the-mill, So-So, Undistinguished

Meditate, Meditation, Meditator, Meditative Brood, Chew, Cogitate, Gymnosophy, Hesychast, Muse, Mystic, Pensive, Ponder, Reflect, Reverie, Revery, Ruminate, Thanatopsis, Transcendental, Vipassana, Weigh, Yoga, Zazen

Mediterranean Levant, Midi, Scattermouch

Medium (A)ether, Agency, Average, Channel, Clairvoyant, Contrast, Culture, Dispersive, Element, Ether, Even, Happy, Home, Intermediary, Interstellar, M, Magilp, Mean, Megilp, Midsize, Midway, Milieu, Oils, Organ, Ouija, Planchette, Press, Radio, Regular, Shaman, Spiritist, Spiritualist, Television, Telly, TV, Vehicle

Medley Charivari, Collection, Gallimaufry, Jumble, Macedoine, Melange, Mishmash, Mix, Pastiche, Patchwork, Pi(e), Pot-pourri, Quodlibet, Ragbag, Salad, Salmagundi, Series, Tat

▷ **Medley** *may indicate* an anagram

Medusa Planoblast

Meek Docile, Griselda, Humble, Milquetoast, Patient, Tame

Meerkat Suricate

Meerschaum Sepiolite

Meet(ing), Meeting place Abide, Abutment, AGM, Appointment, Apropos, Assemble, Assembly, Assignation, Audience, Baraza, Bosberaad, Briefing, Camporee, Caucus, Chapterhouse, Chautauqua, Clash, Conclave, Concourse, Concur, Confluence, Confrontation, Congress, Connivance, Consistory, Consulta, Contact, Conterminous, Convene, Convent(icle), Convention, Converge, Conversazione, Convocation, Correspond, Cybercafé, Defray, Demo, EGM, Encounter, Ends, Experience, Face, Find, Fit, For(e)gather, Forum, Fulfil, Gemot, Giron, Gorsedd, Guild, Gyeld, Gymkhana, Gyron, Howf(f), Hunt, Hustings, Imbizo, Indaba, Infall, Interface, Interview, Join, Junction, Kgotla, Korero, Lekgotla, Liaise, Marae, Moot, Mother's, Obviate, Occlusion, Occur, Oppose, Overflow, Pay, Plenary, Plenum, Pnyx, Pow-wow, Prayer, Prosper, Quadrivial, Quaker, Quorate, Quorum, Race, Races, Rally, Rencontre, Rencounter, Rendezvous, Reunion, Sabbat(h), Satisfy, Séance, See, Seminar, Session, Sit, Social, Sports, Suitable, Summit, Symposium, Synastry, Synaxis, Synod, Tackle, Talkfest, Think-in, Town, Track, Tryst, Venue, Vestry, Wapinshaw, Wardmote, Wharenui, Wharepuni, Workshop

Megalith(ic) Sarsen, Skara Brae, Stonehenge

Megalomaniac Monarcho

Megaphone Bull-horn, Loudhailer
Megapode Mound-bird, Talegalla
Meiosis Understatement
Melancholy, Melancholic Adust, Allicholy, Allycholly, Anatomy, Atrabilious, Cafard, Despond(ency), Dreary, Dump(s), Gloom, Heart-sore, Hipped, Hump, Hyp, Hypochondria, Jaques, Lienal, Panophobia, Pensieroso, Pensive, Saturnine, Sombre, Spleen, Splenetic, Triste, Tristesse, Weltschmerz
Melanesian Kanak
Mêlée Brawl, Commotion, Fracas, Rally, Salmagundi, Scrum
Melia Margosa, Neem, Nim
Mellifluent, Mellifluous Cantabile, Melodic
Mellow Fruity, Genial, Mature, Ripe, Smooth
Melodrama(tic) Bathos, Histrionic, Sensation, Transpontine
Melody, Melodious Air, Arioso, Cabaletta, Canorous, Cantabile, Cantilena, Canto (fermo), Cantus, Chopsticks, Conductus, Counterpoint, Descant, Dulcet, Euphonic, Fading, Musical, Orphean, Plainsong, Ranz-des-vaches, Refrain, Songful, Strain, Theme, Tunable, → **TUNE(S)**
Melon(like) Cantaloup(e), Cas(s)aba, Charentais, Galia, Gourd, Honeydew, Mango, Musk, Nar(r)as, Ogen, Pepo, Persian, Rock, Spanspek, Winter
Melt(ed), Melting Ablate, Colliquate, → **DISSOLVE**, Eutectic, Eutexia, Flux, Found, Fuse, Fusil(e), Liquescent, Liquid, Run, Smectic, Syntexis, Thaw, Touch
Member Adherent, Arm, Branch, Bro(ther), Charter, Chin, Confrère, Cornice, Coulisse, Crossbeam, Crypto, Direction, Felibre, Fellow, Forearm, Forelimb, Founder, Gremial, Harpin(g)s, Insider, Keel, Leg, Limb, Lintel, Longeron, M, MBE, Montant, MP, Organ, Part, Partisan, Peer, Politicaster, Politician, Private, Rood-beam, Soroptomist, Stile, Stringer, Strut, Syndic, Toe
Membrane, Membranous Amnion, Arachnoid, Axilemma, Caul, Cell, Chorioallantois, Chorion, Choroid (plexus), Chromoplast, Conjunctiva, Cornea, Cyst, Decidua, Dissepiment, Dura (mater), Endocardium, Endometrium, Endosteum, Ependyma, Exine, Extine, Film, Frenulum, Fr(a)enum, Haw, Head, Hyaloid, Hymen, Indusium, Intima, Intine, Involucre, Mater, Mediastinum, Meninx, Mesentery, Mucosa, Mucous, Neurolemma, Nictitating, Patagium, Pellicle, Pericardium, Pericarp, Perichondrium, Pericranium, Periost(eum), Periton(a)eum, Pia mater, Plasma, Pleura, Putamen, Retina, Rim, Sarcolemma, Scarious, Schneiderian, Sclera, Serosa, Serous, Skin, Synovial, Tectorial, Tela, Third eyelid, Tissue, Tonoplast, Trophoblast, Tympan(ic), Vacuolar, Velamen, Velum, Vitelline, Web, Yolk-sac
Memento, Memoir Keepsake, Locket, Relic, Remembrancer, Souvenir, Token, Trophy
Memo(randum) Bordereau, Cahier, Chit, IOU, Jot, Jurat, Minute, Note, Notepad, → **REMINDER**
Memoirist Casanova
Memorable, Memorise, Memory Associative, ATLAS, Bubble, Cache, Catchy, Collective, → **COMPUTER MEMORY**, Con, Core, DRAM, Echoic, Engram(ma), Extended, Flash (bulb), Folk, Get, Highlight, Historic, Hypermnesia, Iconic, Immortal, Immunological, Learn, Living, Long-term, Main, Mainstore, Memoriter, Mind, Mneme, Mnemonic, Mnemosyne, Non-volatile, Noosphere, Notable, Pelmanism, Photographic, Race, Read-write, Recall, Recovered, → **REMEMBER**, Retention, Retrospection, Ro(a)te, Samskara, Screen, Semantic, Short-term, Souvenir, Sovenance, Static, Video, Virtual, Volatile, Word, Working
Memorial Altar tomb, Cenotaph, Cromlech, Ebenezer, Gravestone, Hatchment,

Headstone, Marker, Monument, Mount Rushmore, Obelisk, Plaque, Relic, Statue, Tomb, Trophy, War

▶ **Memory loss** *see* **LOSS OF MEMORY**

Men(folk) Amadoda, Chaps, Chess, Cuffins, Male, Messrs, Mortals, OR, People, Race, Troops

Menace, Menacing Danger, Dennis, Endanger, Foreboding, Minatory, Peril, Pest, Threat(en)

Menagerie Ark, Circus, Zoo

Mend Beet, Bete, Bushel, Cobble, Correct, Darn, Fix, Heal, Improved, Mackle, Patch, Piece, Recover, Remedy, → **REPAIR**, Set, Sew, Solder, Trouble-shoot

Mendelevium Md

Mendicant Beggar, Calender, Fakir, Franciscan, Servite

Menial Bottlewasher, Drudge, Drug, Eta, Fag, Flunkey, Lowly, Scullion, Servile, Toady, Underling, Wood-and-water joey

Meninx (D)jerba

Menopause Andropause, Climacteric

Menstruation Menarche, Menses

Mental (condition), Mental disorder Alienism, Doolally, Eject, Hallucinosis, Insane, Noetic, Paranoia, Psychic

▷ **Mental** *may indicate* the chin

Mention(ed) Allusion, Bename, Benempt, Broach, Bynempt, Citation, Hint, Honourable, Name, Notice, Quote, Refer, Speech, State, Suggest, Touch

Mentor Guru, Rebbe, Tutor

Menu Agenda, Card, Carte, Carte du jour, Cascading, Drop-down, Fare, List, Table d'hôte, Tariff

Mercantile Commercial, Trade

Mercator Cartographer

Mercenary Arnaout, Condottiere, Freelance, Greedy, Hack, Hessian, Hired gun, Hireling, Landsknecht, Legionnaire, Pindaree, Pindari, Rutter, Sordid, Spoilsman, Swiss Guard, Venal, Wildgeese

Merchandise Cargo, Goods, Line, Produce, Ware(s)

Merchant(man) Abudah, Antonio, Broker, Bun(n)ia, Burgher, Chandler, Chap, Crare, Crayer, Dealer, Factor, Flota, Gossip, Hoastman, Importer, Jobber, Law, Magnate, Marcantant, Mercer, Monger, Négociant, Pedlar, Polo, Provision, Retailer, Seller, Shipper, Speed, Squeegee, Stapler, Sutler, Trader, Vintner, Wholesaler

Mercia Offa

Merciful, Mercy Amnesty, Charity, Clement, Compassionate, Corporal, Grace, Humane, Kind, Kyrie, Lenient, Lenity, Miserere, Misericord(e), Pacable, Pity, Quarter, Ruth, Sparing, Spiritual

Merciless Cruel, Hard, Hard-hearted, Inclement, Pitiless

Mercurial, Mercuric sulphide, Mercury Azoth, Cyllenius, Dog's, Fulminating, Herald, Hermes, Hg, Horn, Hydrargyrum, Messenger, Quicksilver, Red, Red-man, Spurge, Tiemannite, Volatile

Mere(ly) Allenarly, Bare, Common, Lake, Pond, Pool, Pure, Sheer, Tarn, Very

Merge(r), Merging Amalgamate, Blend, Coalesce, Composite, Conflate, Consolidate, Die, Elide, Fusion, Incorporate, Interflow, Interpenetrate, Liquesce, Meld, Melt, Mingle, Syncretism, Synergy, Unify, Unite

Meridian Magnetic, Noonday, Prime

Meringue Pavlova

Merit(ed) CL, Condign, Deserve, Due, Earn, Found, Rate, Virtue, Worth(iness)

Mermaid Dugong, Halicore, Merrow, Siren, Tavern, Undine

Merriment, Merry Andrew, Blithe(some), Bonny, Boon, Cant, Cherry, Chirpy, Crank, Elated, Full, Gaudy, Gay, Gean, Gleesome, Greek, Jocose, Jocular, Jocund, Jolly, Joyous, L'allegro, Lively, Nitid, On, Page, Riant, Sportive, Sunny, Vogie, Waggery, Wassail

Merry-andrew Clown, Jack-pudding, Pickle-herring

Merry-go-round Carousel, Galloper, Whirligig

Merry-making Cakes and ale, Carnival, Festivity, Gaiety, Gaud, Gawd, Revel

Merrythought Clavicle, Collarbone, Wishbone

Mesh Cancellate, Chain, Entangle, Mantle, Net, Reseau, Screen

Mess(y) Balls-up, Bedraggled, Boss, Botch, Canteen, Caudle, Chaos, Clamper, Clutter, Cock-up, Failure, Farrago, Fiasco, Flub, Garboil, G(l)oop, Glop, Gory, Guddle, Gunge, Gunk, Gun-room, Hash, Horlicks, Hotch-potch, Hugger-mugger, Imbroglio, Lash-up, Louse, Mash, Meal, Mismanage, Mix, Mixter-maxter, Modge, Muck, Muff, Mullock, Muss, Mux, Pi(e), Piss-up, Plight, Pollute, Pottage, Screw-up, Scungy, Shambles, Shambolic, Shemozzle, Sight, Slaister, Smudge, Snafu, Soss, Sty, Sully, Untidy, Wardroom, Whoopsie, Yuck(y)

Message(s) Aerogram, Bull, Bulletin, Cable, Contraplex, Dépêche, Despatch, Dispatch, Email, Errand, Error, Flame, Kissagram, Kissogram, Missive, News, Note, Pager, Ping, Posting, Postscript, Radiogram, Rumour, Signal, Slogan, SOS, Stripagram, Strippergram, Subtext, Telegram, Telephone, Teletype®, Telex, Text, Tidings, Toothing, Wire, → **WORD**

Messenger Angel, Angela, Apostle, Azrael, Beadle, Caddie, Caddy, Chaprassi, Chuprassy, Courier, Culver, Despatch-rider, Emissary, Envoy, Forerunner, Gaga, Gillie-wetfoot, Gillie whitefoot, Hatta, Herald, Hermes, Internuncio, Iris, Ladas, Mercury, Nuncio, Page, Peon, Post, Pursuivant, Runner, Send, Shellycoat, Valkyrie

Messiah Christ, Emmanuel, Immanuel, Mahdi, Mashiach, Saviour, Son of man

Met Old Bill, Weather, Weatherman

Metabolism Basal

Metal(s), Metallic, Metalware, Metalwork Ag, Aglet, Aiglet, Aiguillette, Al, Alkali, Aluminium, Antifriction, Antimony, Babbitt, Base, Bell, Billon, Brassy, Britannia, Cadmium, Chrome, Chromium, Cobalt, Copper, Death, Dutch, Dysprosium, Er(bium), Europium, Expanded, Filler, Foil, Fusible, Gallium, Germanium, Gib, Gold, Heavy, Hot, Ingot, Invar®, Iridium, Iron, Jangling, Leaf, Magnolia, Manganese, Mineral, Misch, Mitis, Monel(l), Muntz, Natrium, Nickel, Noble, Nonferrous, Ore, Ormolu, Osmium, Parent, Perfect, Planchet, Platinum, Precious, Prince's, Protore, Regulus, Rhenium, Road, Ruthenium, Samarium, Scrap, Sheet(-iron), Silver, Slug, Sm, Sn, Sodium, Speculum, Speiss, Sprue, Steel, Strontium, Taggers, Tantalum, Terbic, Terbium, Terne, Thallium, Thorium, Thrash, Tin, Tole, Toreutics, Tramp, Transition, Tutania, Tutenag, Type, White, Wolfram, Yellow, Zinc

Metal-worker Founder, Lorimer, Smith, Spurrier, Tubal Cain

Metamorphose Transmogrify

▷ **Metamorphosing** *may indicate* an anagram

Metaphor Conceit, Figure, Image, Kenning, Malonym, Mixed, Symbol, Trope, Tropical

Metaphysics Ontology, Scotism

Mete Inflict

Meteor(ic), Meteorite Achondrite, Aerolite, Aerosiderite, Bolide, Chondrite, Comet, Drake, Falling star, Fireball, Geminid, Iron, Leonid, Perseid, Quadrantid, Siderite, Siderolite, Star(dust), Stony, Tektite

Meter Alidad(e), Electric, Exposure, Flow, Gas, Light, Orifice, Parking, Postage, Postal, Torque, Torsion, Water, White
Methamphetamine Ice
Methane Alkane
Methedrine® Speed
Method(ology), Methodical Art, Billings, Buteyko, Direct, Feldenkrais, Formula, Gram's, Historical, Hi-tec(h), Kenny, Kumon, Line, Manner, Mode, Modus, Modus operandi, Monte Carlo, Montessori, Neat, Orderly, Ovulation, Painstaking, Plan, Ploy, Procedure, Process, Q, Rhythm, Schafer's, Scientific, Socratic, Stanislavski, → SYSTEM, Tactics, Technique, Way, Withdrawal
Methodism, Methodist Huntingdonian, Jumper, Methody, Primitive, Ranter, Scientism, Southcottian, Swaddler, Wesley
Methuselah Bottle, Macrobiote
Meticulous Careful, → EXACT, Finicky, Minute, Precise, Punctilious, Quiddler, Scrupulous, Thorough
Métier Line, Trade, Vocation
Metre Alexandrine, Amphibrach, Amphimacer, Anapaest, Antispast, Arsis, Ballad, Cadence, Choliamb, Choree, Choriamb, Common, Dipody, Galliambic, Iambic, Ithyphallic, Long, M, Prosody, Pyrrhic, Rhythm, Sapphic, Scansion, Scazon, Service, Short, Spondee, Strophe, Tripody, Trochee
Metric (system) MKS
Metroland Subtopia
Metropolitan Eparch
Mettle Ardour, Bravery, Courage, Ginger, Guts, Pith, → PLUCK, Pride, Smeddum, Spirit, Spunk, Steel
Mew Caterwaul, Miaou, Miaow, Pen, Purr, Seagull, Waul, Wrawl
Mews Meuse, Muse(t), Musit, Stables
Mexican (Indian) Atlalt, Aztec, Carib, Chicano, Chichibec, Diaz, Greaser, Gringo, Hairless, Hispanic, Maya, Mixe-Zoque, Mixtec, Montezuma, Nahuatl, Norténo, Olmec, Otomi, Pachuco, Spic, Spik, Taino, Toltec, Wetback, Zapotec, Zuni
Mezzanine Entresol
Mezzo-soprano Tessa
Mica Biotite, Daze, Fuchsite, Glimmer, Isinglass, Lepidolite, Lepidomelane, Muscovite, Paragonite, Phlogopite, Rubellan, Sericite, Talc, Verdite, Vermiculite
Micawber Wilkins
Mick(ey) Greek, Mouse
Micro Mu
Microbe, Microorganism Extremophile, Germ, Lactobacillus, Nanobe, Organism
Microphone Bug, Carbon, Crystal, Lavaliere, Lip, Mike, Phonic Ear®, Radio, Ribbon, Throat
Microscope Compound, Confocal, Darkfield, Dissecting, Electron, Engyscope, Lens, Optical, Phase-contrast, Proton, Reflecting, SEM, Simple, Solar, TEM, Ultraviolet
Microwave Nuke
Mid(st) Amongst, Mongst
Midas Goldinger, Tamarin
Midday Meridian, N, Noon, Noon-tide, Noon-time
Middle, Middling Active, Basion, Centre, Core, Crown, Enteron, Excluded, Eye, Girth, Heart, Innermost, Loins, Median, Mediocre, Meridian, Meseraic, Mesial, Mesne, Meso, Midriff, Moderate, Noon, Passive, Turn, Twixt, Via media, Wa(i)st
Middle age Menopause
Middle-Cambrian Menevian

Middle class Bourgeois, Hova, Mondeo Man
Middle Eastern Arab, Iraqi, Omani
Middleman Broker, Comprador(e), Diaphragm, Interlocutor, Intermediary, Jobber,
   Median, Navel, Regrater, Regrator
Middlesex Hermaphrodite
Midge Gall, Gnat
Midget Dwarf, Homunculus, Lilliputian, Pygmy, Shrimp
Midianite Prowler
Midlander Brummie
Midlands Mercia
Midnight G, O Am
▸ **Midnight** *see* **PAST MIDNIGHT**
Midriff Phrenic, Skirt, Waist
Midshipman Brass-bounder, Easy, Middy, Oldster, Reefer, Snottie, Snotty
▸ **Midst** *see* **MID**
Midwife Accoucheur, Doula, Gran(nie), Granny, Howdie, Howdy, Lucina, Mab,
   Obstetric
Mien Air, Bearing, Demean, Manner
Might(iness), Mighty Force, Main, Mote, Nibs, Potence, → **POWER**, Prowess,
   Puissant, Should, Strength
Mignon(ette) Dyer's rocket, Fillet, Reseda, Weld
Migraine Megrim, Scotodinia, Teichopsia
Migrant Economic, Externe, Gastarbeiter, Lemming, Traveller
Migrate, Migration, Migratory Colonise, Diapedesis, Diaspora, Drift, Eelfare,
   Exodus, Fleet, Great Trek, Run, Tre(c)k, Volkwanderung
Mikado Emperor, Kami
Mike Bug, Stentorphone
Milanese Patarine
Mild(ly) Balmy, Benign, Bland, Clement, Euphemism, Genial, Gentle, Lenient,
   Litotes, Mansuete, Meek, → **MODERATE**, Pacific, Patient, Sarcenet, Sars(e)net,
   Temperate
Mildew Downy, Foxing, Fungus, Mould, Oidium, Powdery, Vine
Mile(s) Admiralty, Coss, Coverdale, Food, Geographical, Irish, Knot, Kos, Li,
   Milliary, Nautical, Passenger, Roman, Royal, Scots, Sea, Soldier, Square, Standish,
   Statute, Swedish, Train
Milesian Teague
Milestone Milliary, MS
Milfoil Yarrow
Militant, Military Activist, Aggressive, Battailous, Black Panther, Black Power,
   Commando, Fortinbras, Hawkish, Hezbollah, Hizbollah, Hizbullah, Hostile,
   Ireton, Janjaweed, Janjawid, Kshatriya, Landsturm, Landwehr, Lumper, Mameluke,
   Martial, Presidio, Provisional, Provo, Soldatesque, Stratocracy, West Point
Militia(-man) Fyrd, Guard, Haganah, Minuteman, Reserve, Tanzim, Trainband,
   Yeomanry
Milk(er), Milky Acidophilus, Beestings, Bland, Bleed, Bonny-clabber, Bristol,
   Casein, Certified, Colostrum, Condensed, Creamer, Crud, Curd, Dairy, Emulge,
   Evaporated, Exploit, Galactic, Glacier, Goat's, Homogenised, Jib, Kefir, Kephir,
   K(o)umiss, Lactation, Lacteal, Latex, Maas, Madafu, Madzoon, Magnesia, Malted,
   Mamma, Matzoon, Mess, Moo-juice, Opaline, Pasteurised, Pigeon's, Pinta, Posset,
   Raw, Rice, Sap, Semi-skimmed, Shedder, Skim(med), Soya, Squeeze, Strippings,
   Stroke, Suckle, Town, UHT, Whig, Whole, Yaourt, Yogh(o)urt

Milking-machine, Milking parlour Loan, Tapper
Milking-pail Leglan, Leglen, Leglin
Milkless Agalactic, Dry, Eild
Milkmaid, Milkman Chalker, Dey, Emulge, Kefir, Kephir, Radha, Rounder, Roundsman, Skimmed
Milksop Coward, Meacock, Namby-pamby, Nance, Pance, Weakling
Milk-vetch Loco
Milkweed Asclepias
Milkwort Senega
Milky Way Via Lactea
Mill(ing), Mills Aswarm, Ball, Barker's, Boxing, Coffee, Crazing, Economist, Gang, Gastric, Grind(er), Hayley, Kibble, Knurl, Malt, Mano, Melder, Molar, Nurl, Oil, Paper, Pepper, Post, Powder, Press, Pug, Quartz, Quern, Reave, Rob, Rolling, Rumour, Satanic, Scutcher, Smock, Spinning, Stamp, Stamping, Strip, Sugar, Surge, Thou, Tide, Tower, Tuck, Water, Wool(len), Works
Miller Dusty, Glen, Grinder, Jester, Joe, Molendinar, Multurer
Millet Bajra, Bajree, Bajrii, Couscous, Dari, Dhurra, Doura, Dur(r)a, Grain, Miliary, Negro-corn, Pearl, Proso, Ragee, Raggee, Ragi, Whisk
Millionaire Astor, Carnegie, Rockefeller, Rothschild, Vanderbilt
Millions, Millionth Crore, Femto-, Milliard, Muckle, Pico-
Millipede Songololo
Millstone Ligger, Rind, Rynd
Mim Perjink
Mime, Mimic(ry) Ape, Batesian, Copycat, Farce, Imitate, Impersonate, Lipsync, Mina, Mullerian, Mummer, Parody, Sturnine
Mimosa Cacoon, Saman
Mince Cecils, Chop, Dice, Grate, Grind, Keema, Prance, Rice
Mind(er) Aide, Beware, Brain, Genius, Handler, Head, → HEED, Herd, Id, Intellect, Noology, Noosphere, Nous, One-track, Open, Phrenic, Psyche, Psychogenic, Resent, Sensorium, Tabula rasa, Tend, Thinker, View, Wit, Woundwort
Mine, Mining Acoustic, Antenna, Bomb, Bonanza, Bottom, Bouquet, Burrow, Camouflet, Chemical, Claymore, Colliery, Contact, Creeping, Dane-hole, Data, Dig(gings), Drifting, Egg, Eldorado, Excavate, Explosive, Floating, Flooder, Fougade, Fougasse, Gallery, Gob, Golconda, Gold, Gopher, Grass, Homing, Land, Limpet, Magnetic, Naked-light, Nostromo, Open-cast, Open-cut, Ophir, Pit, Placer, Pressure, Prospect, Rising, Sap, Set(t), Show, Sonic, Stannary, Stope, Strike, Strip, Undercut, Wheal, Win, Workings
Mine-deflector Otter, Paravane
Mine-owner Operator
Miner, Mine-worker, Mine-working Bevin boy, Butty-gang, Collier, Continuous, Corporal, Cutter, Digger, Forty-niner, Geordie, Leaf, Molly Maguire, Noisy, NUM, Oncost(man), Pitman, Shot-firer, Stall, Tippler, Tributer, UDM
Mineral(s) Accessory, Essential, Index

MINERALS

3 letters:	4 letters:		
YAG	Clay	Mica	Trap
	Foid	Sard	Urao
	Gang	Spar	
		Talc	

5 letters:
Balas
Borax
Chert
Emery
Flint
Fluor
Macle
Mafic
Nitre
Prase
Topaz
Trona
Umber

6 letters:
Acmite
Albite
Augite
Blende
Galena
Gangue
Garnet
Glance
Gypsum
Hauyne
Illite
Jargon
Lithia
Natron
Nosean
Pinite
Pyrite
Quartz
Rutile
Schorl
Silica
Sphene
Spinel
Tincal
Zircon

7 letters:
Alunite
Anatase
Apatite
Axinite
Azurite
Barytes
Biotite
Bornite

Brucite
Calcite
Calomel
Catseye
Cuprite
Cyanite
Diamond
Dysodil
Epidote
Euclase
Eucrite
Fahlore
Felspar
Gahnite
Göthite
Gummite
Hessite
Ice spar
Jadeite
Jargoon
Kainite
Kernite
Kyanite
Leucite
Mellite
Mullite
Nacrite
Olivine
Pennine
Peridot
Pyrites
Realgar
Rosaker
Sylvine
Sylvite
Thorite
Thulite
Tripoli
Turgite
Ulexite
Uralite
Uranite
Uranium
Zeolite
Zeuxite
Zincite
Zoisite
Zorgite

8 letters:
Adularia

Allanite
Analcime
Analcite
Andesine
Ankerite
Antimony
Aphanite
Asbestos
Autunite
Blue john
Boehmite
Boracite
Braunite
Bronzite
Brookite
Calamine
Cerusite
Chlorite
Chromite
Cinnabar
Cleveite
Corundum
Crocoite
Cryolite
Datolite
Dendrite
Diallage
Diaspore
Disthene
Dolomite
Dysodile
Dysodyle
Epsomite
Erionite
Euxenite
Fayalite
Feldspar
Flinkite
Fluorite
Galinite
Gibbsite
Goethite
Gyrolite
Hematite
Idocrase
Ilmenite
Iodyrite
Jarosite
Lazulite
Lazurite
Lewisite

Limonite
Massicot
Meionite
Melilite
Mimetite
Monazite
Nephrite
Noselite
Orpiment
Petuntse
Picotite
Prehnite
Pyroxene
Resalgar
Rock-salt
Sanidine
Saponite
Siderite
Smectite
Sodalite
Stannite
Stibnite
Stilbite
Taconite
Tenorite
Titanite
Troilite
Vesuvian
Xenotime
Zaratite

9 letters:
Alabaster
Allophane
Amazonite
Amphibole
Anglesite
Anhydrite
Anorthite
Aragonite
Argentite
Atacamite
Blackjack
Blacklead
Carnelian
Carnotite
Celestine
Celestite
Cerussite
Chabazite
Chalybite

Cheralite
Chondrule
Cobaltine
Cobaltite
Coccolite
Columbate
Columbite
Covellite
Cystolith
Dolomitic
Elaeolite
Endomorph
Enhydrite
Enstatite
Erythrite
Fibrolite®
Fluorspar
Gehlenite
Germanite
Geyserite
Gmelinite
Goslarite
Haematite
Harmotome
Hercynite
Hiddenite
Hornstone
Kaolinite
Kermesite
Kieserite
Magnesite
Magnetite
Malachite
Manganite
Marcasite
Margarite
Marialite
Microlite
Microlith
Millerite
Mispickel
Mizzonite
Moonstone
Muscovite
Natrolite
Nepheline
Nephelite
Niccolite
Nitratine
Olivenite
Ottrelite

Paramorph
Pargasite
Pectolite
Periclase
Pericline
Perimorph
Phenacite
Pleonaste
Polianite
Pollucite
Powellite
Proustite
Rhodonite
Rubellite
Scapolite
Scheelite
Scolecite
Septarium
Spodumene
Sylvanite
Tantalite
Tremolite
Troostite
Tungstite
Uraninite
Uvarovite
Variscite
Vulpinite
Wavellite
Wernerite
Willemite
Witherite
Wulfenite
Zinkenite

10 letters:
Actinolite
Alabandine
Alabandite
Andalusite
Bastnasite
Calaverite
Carnallite
Chalcocite
Chessylite
Chrysolite
Colemanite
Cordierite
Crocoisite
Dyscrasite
Forsterite

Gadolinite
Garnierite
Glauconite
Halloysite
Heulandite
Honey-stone
Hornblende
Indicolite
Indigolite
Jamesonite
Laurdalite
Meerschaum
Microcline
Oligoclase
Orthoclase
Paragonite
Perovskite
Phosgenite
Piemontite
Polybasite
Polyhalite
Pyrolusite
Pyrrhotine
Pyrrhotite
Redruthite
Riebeckite
Ripidolite
Samarskite
Saphir d'eau
Sapphirine
Saussurite
Serpentine
Smaragdite
Sperrylite
Sphalerite
Staurolite
Tennantite
Thaumasite
Thenardite
Thorianite
Tiemannite
Torbernite
Tourmaline
Triphylite
Vanadinite
Wolframite

11 letters:
Alexandrite
Amblygonite
Annabergite

Apophyllite
Baddeleyite
Bastnaesite
Cassiterite
Chiastolite
Chrysoberyl
Clinochlore
Crocidolite
Dendrachate
Franklinite
Greenockite
Hypersthene
Idiomorphic
Josephinite
Labradorite
Molybdenite
Pentlandite
Phosphorite
Piedmontite
Pitchblende
Plagioclase
Pseudomorph
Psilomelane
Pyrargyrite
Pyrrhotiner
Sal ammoniac
Sillimanite
Smithsonite
Tabular spar
Tetradymite
Vermiculite
Vesuvianite
Ythro-cerite

12 letters:
Adularescent
Arfvedsonite
Arsenopyrite
Babingtonite
Chalcanthite
Chalcopyrite
Cristobalite
Dumortierite
Feldspathoid
Fluorapatite
Hemimorphite
Pyromorphite
Pyrophyllite
Senarmontite
Skutterudite
Strontianite

Synadelphite	*13 letters:*	*15 letters:*
Tetrahedrite	Cummingtonite	Gooseberry-stone
Wollastonite	Rhodochrosite	Montmorillonite

Mineral water Apollinaris, Tonic
Minesweeper Oropesa, Unity
Mingle, Mingling Blend, Circulate, Consort, Interfuse, Mell, Merge, → **MIX**, Participate, Socialise, Theocrasy, Unite
Mini Cab, Car, Skirt, Teen(s)y
Miniature, Miniaturist Cosway, Microcosm, Midget, Model, Toy, Young
Minimise, Minimum (range) Bare, Downplay, Fewest, Least, Neap, Shoestring, Stime, Styme, Threshold, Undervalue
▷ **Minimum of** *may indicate* the first letter
Minion Flunkey, Lackey, Pet, Subordinate, Tool, Vassal
Minister Ambassador, Attend, Buckle-beggar, Cabinet, Chancellor, Chaplain, Cleric, Coarb, Commissar, Deacon, Dewan, Diplomat, Divine, D(i)wan, Dominee, Dominie, Envoy, First, Foreign, Holy Joe, Mas(s)john, Mes(s)john, Moderator, Nurse, Officiant, Padre, Parson, Pastor, Peshwa, Preacher, Predikant, Presbyter, Prime, Rector, Secretary, Seraskier, → **SERVE**, Stick, Stickit, Subdeacon, Tend, Visier, Vizier, Wazir, Wizier
Ministry Defence, Department, Dept, DoE, MOD, MOT, Orders, Service
▷ **Ministry** *may indicate* some government department
Mink Kolinsky, Mutation, Vison
Minnow Devon, Penk, Pink, Tiddler
Minoan Knossus
Minor(ity) Child, Comprimario, Ethnic, Faction, Few, Infant, Junior, Less, Minutia, Nonage, One-horse, Peripheral, Petty, Pupillage, Signed, Slight, Small-time, Trivial, Ward
Minotaur Bull-headed
Minstrel Allan-a-Dale, Bard, Blondel, Bones, Busker, Cantabank, Christy, Cornerman, Gleeman, Hamfatter, Joculator, Jongleur, Minnesinger, Nigger, Pierrot, Scop, Singer, Taillefer
Mint Aim, Bugle-weed, Catnip, Coin, Ettle, Fortune, Herb, Horse, Humbug, Labiate, Monarda, Monetise, Nep, New, Penny-royal, Pepper, Pile, Polo®, Poly, Royal, Selfheal, Spear, Stamp, Stone, Strike, Unused, Utter, Water
Minute(s), Minutiae Acta, Alto, Degree, Detailed, Diatom, Entry, Infinitesimal, Little, Micron, Mo, Mu, Nano-, New York, Pinpoint, Resume, Small, Teen(t)sy, Teeny, Tine, Tiny, Trivia, Tyne, Wee
Minx Hellion
Miracle(s), Miraculous Cana, Marvel, Merel(l), Meril, Morris, Mystery, Phenomenon, Supernatural, Thaumatology, Thaumaturgic, Theurgy, Wirtschaftswunder, Wonder, Wonderwork
Mirage Fata morgana, Illusion, Loom, Northern lights
Mire Bog, Glaur, Lair(y), Latch, Lerna, Lerne, Loblolly, Marsh, Mud, Quag, Sludge, Soil
Mirky Dark, Dirk(e)
Mirror(s), Mirrored Alasnam, Antidazzle, Busybody, Cambuscan, Catoptric, Cheval, Claude Lorraine glass, Coelostat, Conde, Conjugate, Dare, Enantiomorph, Glass, Image, Imitate, Keeking-glass, Lao, Magnetic, Merlin, One-way, Pierglass, Primary, Psyche, Rearview, → **REFLECT**, Reynard, Shisha, Siderostat, Sign, Specular, Speculum, Stone, Tiring-glass, Two-way, Vulcan, Wing

Mirror-image Perversion

Mirth(ful) Cheer, Dream, Festive, Hilarity, Joy, Laughter, Spleen

▷ **Misalliance** *may indicate* an anagram

Misanthrope Cynic, Timon

Misapplication Catachresis, Misuse

Misappropriate, Misappropriation Asport, Detinue, Purloin, Steal

Miscarry Abort, Backfire, Fail, Slink, Warp

Miscegenation Allocarpy

Miscellaneous, Miscellany Assortment, Chow, Collectanea, Diverse, Etceteras, Misc, Odds and ends, Odds and sods, Olio, Omnium-gatherum, Potpourri, Raft, Ragbag, Sundry, Varia, Variety, Various

Mischance Misfare

Mischief(-maker), Mischievous Ate, Bale, Bane, Cantrip, Cloots, Devilment, Diablerie, Dido, Disservice, Gallus, Gremlin, Harm, Hellery, Hellion, Hob, Imp, Injury, Jinks, Larrikin, Limb, Litherly, Make-bate, Malicho, Mallecho, Monkey-tricks, Nickum, Owl-spiegle, Pestilent, Pickle, Prank, Puckish, Rascal, Scally(wag), Scamp, Scapegrace, Shenanigans, Spriteful, Tricksy, Wag, Wicked, Widgie

Misconception Delusion, Idol(on), Idolum, Misunderstanding

Misconduct Impropriety, Malfeasance, Malversation

Miscreant Reprobate, Sinner

Misdeed Offence, Peccadillo, Trespass, Wrong

▷ **Misdelivered** *may indicate* an anagram

Misdemeanour Delict, Offence, Peccadillo, Tort, Wrongdoing

Miser(ly) Carl, Cheapskate, Cheese-parer, Close, Curmudgeon, Gare, Grasping, Harpagon, Hunks, Marner, Meanie, Mingy, Niggard, Nipcheese, Nipcurn, Nipfarthing, Pennyfather, Pinch-commons, Puckfist, Runt, Scrape-good, Scrape-penny, Screw, Scrimping, Scrooge, Skinflint, Snudge, Storer, Tightwad, Timon

Miserable, Misery, Miserably Abject, Angashore, Bale, Cat-lap, Crummy, Distress, Dole, Forlorn, Gloom, Grief, Heartache, Hell, Joyless, Lousy, Perdition, Punk, Sad, Scungy, Sorry, Sourpuss, Tragic, Triste, → **UNHAPPY**, Woe(begone), Wretched

Misfire Dud

Misfit Drop-out, Geek, Loner, Maverick, Sad sack

Misfortune Accident, Affliction, Bale, Calamity, Curse, Disaster, Distress, Dole, Hex, Ill, Reverse, Rewth, Ruth, Wroath

Misgiving(s) Anxiety, Doubt, Dubiety, Qualms, Scruples

Misguide(d) Impolitic, Off-beam

▷ **Misguided** *may indicate* an anagram

Mishandle Abuse

Mishap Accident, Contretemps, Misaunter, Misfortune, Pile-up, Wroath

Misheard Mondegreen

Mishit, Misstroke Crab, Draw, Edge, Fluff, Muff, Sclaff, Shank, Slice, Thin, Toe, Top

Misinterpret(ation) Mondegreen, Wrest

Mislay Leese, Lose

Mislead(ing) Blind, Bum steer, Cover-up, Deceive, Delude, Dupe, Equivocate, Fallacious, False, Gag, Red herring, Runaround, Smoke and mirrors

▷ **Misled** *may indicate* an anagram

Mismanage Blunder, Bungle, Muddle

Mismatch Kludge

Misplace(ment) Anachorism, Ectopia
Misplay Fluff, Whitechapel
Misprint Error, Literal, Literal error, Slip, Typo
Mispronunciation Cacoepy, Lallation, Lambdacism
Misrepresent(ation) Abuse, Belie, Calumny, Caricature, Colour, Distort, Falsify, Garble, Lie, Slander, Subreption, Traduce, Travesty
Miss(ing) Abord, Air, Avoid, AWOL, Colleen, Desiderate, Dodge, Drib, Err(or), Fail, Forego, Gal, → GIRL, Kumari, Lack, Lass, Link, Lose, Mademoiselle, Maid, Maiden, Mile, Muff(et), Near, Neglect, Negligence, Omit, Otis, Overlook, Señorita, Shy, Skip, Spinster, Stoke, Unmeet, Wanting, Whiff
▷ **Miss** *may refer to* Missouri
Missal Breviary, Te igitur, Triodion
Misshapen Crooked, Deformed, Dysmelia, Gnarled
Missile Air-to-air, ALCM, Ammo, Anti-ballistic, Arrow, Artillery, Atlas, Ball, Ballistic, Beam Rider, Blue streak, Bolas, Bolt, Bomb, Boomerang, Brickbat, Bullet, Condor, Cruise, Dart, Dingbat, Doodlebug, Dum-dum, Exocet®, Falcon, Fléchette, Genie, Grenade, Guided, HARM, Harpoon, Hawk, Hellfire, Hound Dog, ICBM, Interceptor, Jired, Kiley, Kyley, Kylie, Lance, Mace, MARV, Maverick, Minuteman, MIRV, Missive, Mx, Onion, Patriot, Pellet, Pershing, Phoenix, Polaris, Poseidon, Qual, Quarrel, Rocket, SAM, Scud, Sea Skimmer, Sergeant, Shell, Shillelagh, Shot, Shrike, Side-winder, Smart bomb, Snowball, Sparrow, Spartan, Spear, Sprint, SSM, Standard Arm, Standoff, Styx, Subroc, Surface to air, Surface to surface, Talos, Tartar, Terrier, Thor, Titan, Tomahawk, Torpedo, Tracer, Trident, UAM, Warhead
Mission(ary) Aidan, Alamo, Antioch, Apostle, Assignment, Augustine, Barnabas, Bethel, Caravan, Charge, Delegation, Embassage, Embassy, Errand, Evangelist, Foreign, Iona, Legation, Livingstone, LMS, Message, NASA, Neurolab, Ninian, Op, Paul, Pr(a)efect, Quest, Reclaimer, Redemptorist, Schweitzer, Task, Vocation, Xavier
Missis, Missus, Mrs Devi, Maam, Mrs, Wife
Missive Letter, Message, Note
Missouri Mo
▶ **Misstroke** *see* MISHIT
Mist(y) Australian, Blur, Brume, Cloud, Dew, Drow, Dry-ice, Film, Fog, Haar, Haze, Hoar, Miasma, Moch, Nebular, Niflheim, Rack, Red, Roke, Scotch, Sea-fret, Sfumato, Smir(r), Smog, Smur, Spotted, Vapour
Mistake(n) Barry (Crocker), Bish, Bloomer, Blooper, Blunder, Boner, Boob, Booboo, Boss, Botch, Category, Clanger, Clinker, Confound, Deluded, Domino, Erratum, Error, Fault, Floater, Flub, Fluff, Folly, Gaffe, Goof, Horlicks, Howler, Identity, Incorrect, Lapse, Malapropism, Miss, Muff, Mutual, Nod, Off-beam, Oversight, Plonker, Pratfall, Ricket, Screw-up, → SLIP, Slip-up, Solecism, Stumer, Trip, Typo
▷ **Mistake(n)** *may indicate* an anagram
Mister Babu, Effendi, Mr, Sahib, Señor, Shri, Sir, Sri
Mistletoe Album, Missel, Parasite, Viscum
Mistreat Abuse, Attrite, Manhandle, Violate
Mistress Amie, Aspasia, Canary-bird, Chatelaine, Concubine, Courtesan, Demimondaine, Devi, Doxy, Goodwife, Herself, Hussif, Inamorata, Instructress, Kept woman, Lady, Leman, Maintenon, Martha, Montespan, Mrs, Natural, Paramour, Stepney, Teacher, Wardrobe, Wife
Mistrust(ful) Askant, Doubt, Gaingiving, Suspect, Suspicion
Misunderstand(ing) Disagreement, Discord, Mistake
Misuse Abuse, Catachresis, Defalcate, Malappropriate, Malapropism, Maltreat,

Perversion, Torment

Mite Acaridian, Acarus, Berry bug, Bit, Bulb, Cheese, Child, Dust, Flour, Forage, Fowl, Gall, Harvest, Itch, Lepton, Little, (Red) spider, Rust, Sarcoptes, Speck, Sugar, Trombiculid, Tyroglyphid, Varroa, Widow's

Mitigate, Mitigating Abate, Allay, Allieve, Ameliorate, Assuage, Extenuating, Lenitive, Lessen, Mease, Palliate, Quell, Relief, Relieve

Mitosis Anaphase

Mitre Hat, Tiar(a)

Mitt(en), Mittens Fist, Glove, Hand, Paw, Pockies

Mix(ed), Mixer, Mixture, Mix-up Alloy, Amalgam, Associate, Assortment, Attemper, Balderdash, Bigener, Bland, Blend, Blunge, Bordeaux, Brew, Carburet, Card, Caudle, Chichi, Chow, Cocktail, Co-meddle, Compo, Compound, Conglomerate, Consort, Cross, Cut, Disperse, Diversity, Dolly, Drammock, Embroil, Emulsion, Eutectic, Farrago, Fold-in, Freezing, Garble, Grill, Griqua, Half-breed, Heather, Hobnob, Hotchpotch, Hybrid, Imbroglio, Interlace, Intermingle, Isomorphous, Jumble, Lace, Lard, Lignin, Linctus, Load, Macedoine, Marketing, Matissé, Meddle, Medley, Melange, Mell, Meng(e), Ment, Mess, Mestizo, Métis, Ming(le), Miscellaneous, Miscellany, Mishmash, Mong, Motley, Muddle, Muss(e), Neapolitan, Octaroon, Octoroon, Olio, Olla, Pi(e), Potin, Pousowdie, Powsowdy, Praiseach, Promiscuous, Raggle-taggle, Ragtag, Salad, Scramble, Shuffle, Soda, Spatula, Stew, Stir, Temper, Through-other, Trail, Vision, Yblent

▷ **Mixed** *may indicate* an anagram

Mizzle Decamp, Scapa, Scarper

Mnemonic(s) Fleming's rules, Memoria technica, Quipo, Quipu, Reminder

Moab(ite) Balak, Ruth, Wash-pot

Moan(ing) Beef, Bewail, Bleat, Complain, Groan, Hone, Keen, → **LAMENT**, Meane, Plangent, Sigh, Snivel, Sough, Wail, W(h)inge

Moat Dike, Ditch, Foss(e)

Mob(ster) Army, Assail, Canaille, Crew, Crowd, Doggery, Faex populi, Flash, Gaggle, Gang, Herd, Hoi-polloi, Hoodlum, Horde, Lynch, Many-headed beast, Ochlocrat, Press, Rabble, Rabble rout, Raft, Ragtag, Ribble-rabble, Riff-raff, Rout, Scar-face

Mobile, Mobilise, Mobility Donna, Downward, Fluid, Horizontal, Intergenerational, Movable, Plastic, Rally, Thin, Upward(ly), Vagile, Vertical

Mob-rule Ochlocracy

Mocassin Larrigan, Shoe, Snake

Mock(ery), Mocking Ape, Banter, Chaff, Chyack, Cod, Cynical, Deride, Derisory, Dor, Ersatz, False, Farce, Fleer, Flout, Gab, Geck, Gibe, Gird, Guy, Imitation, Irony, Irrisory, Jape, → **JEER**, Jibe, Lampoon, Laugh, Mimic, Narquois, Parody, Paste, Pillorise, Rail(lery), Rally, Ridicule, Sacrilege, Sardonic, Satirise, Scorn, Scout, Sham, Simulate, Slag, Sneer, Travesty, Wry

Mocking-bird Mimus, Sage-thrasher

Mode Aeolian, Church, Convention, Dorian, Ecclesiastical, Fashion, Form, Formal, Greek, Gregorian, Hyperdorian, Hypo(dorian), Hypolydian, Iastic, Ionian, Locrian, Lydian, Major, Manner, Material, Medieval, Minor, Mixolydian, Phrygian, Plagal, Rate, Real-time, Sleep, Step, Style, Ton

Model(ler), Modelling Archetype, Bozzeto, Cast, Copy, Demonstration, Diorama, Doll, Dummy, Ecorché, Effigy, Epitome, Example, Exemplar, Exemplary, Fictor, Figure, Figurine, Icon, Ideal, Image, Instar, Jig, Last, Lay-figure, Layman, Madame Tussaud, Manakin, Manikin, Mannequin, Maquette, Mark, Mirror, Mock-up, → **MOULD**, Norm, Original, Orrery, Papier-mâché, Parade, Paragon, Pattern, Phelloplastic, Pilot, Plasticine, Play-Doh®, Pose(r), Posture-maker, Prototype,

Replica, Role, Scale, Sedulous, Sitter, Specimen, Standard, Superwaif, T, Template, Templet, Terrella, Toy, Trilby, Twiggy, Type, Typify, Waif, Waxwork, Working
▷ **Model(s)** *may indicate* an anagram
Modem Subset
Moderate(ly), Moderation Abate, Allay, Alleviate, Assuage, Attemper, Average, Ca'canny, Centre, Chasten, Continent, Diminish, Discretion, Ease, Gentle, Girondist, Ho, Lessen, Lukewarm, Measure, Mediocre, Medium, Menshevik, Mezzo, Middling, Mild, Mitigate, OK, Politique, Reason(able), Restraint, RR, Slake, So-so, Sumptuary, Temper(ate), Temperance, Tolerant, Tone, Via media, Wet
Modern(ise) AD, Aggiornamento, Contemporary, Fresh, Latter(-day), Milly, Neonomian, Neoterical, → **NEW**, Present-day, Progressive, Recent, Retrofit, Swinger, Trendy, Update, Up-to-date
Modest(y) Aidos, Blaise, Chaste, Coy, Decent, Demure, Discreet, Fair, Humble, Humility, Ladylike, Low-key, Maidenly, Mim, Mussorgsky, Propriety, Prudish, Pudency, Pure, Reserved, Shame, Shy, Unassuming, Unpretending, Unpretentious, Verecund
Modicum Dash
Modifiable, Modification, Modifier, Modify Adapt, Adverb, Alter, Backpedal, Change, Enhance, Extenuate, H, Leaven, Misplaced, Plastic, Qualify, Retrofit, Sandhi, Scumble, Soup, Streamline, Temper, Top, Trim, Vary
Modulation, Module, Modulus Accent, Amplitude, Bulk, Cadence, Command, Distance, Excursion, Frequency, Habitat, Inflexion, Lem, Lunar, Mitigate, Phase, Pulse, Service, Tune, Unit, Vary, Velocity, Young's
Mogul Bigwig, Magnate, Nawab, Padishah, Plutocrat, Potentate, Taipan, VIP
Mohair Moire
Mohammed, Mohammedan (era) Hadith, Hegira, Hejira, Hejra, Hijra, Islamite, Mahdi, Mahoun(d), Moslem, Muezzin, Mussulman, Prophet, Said, Shiite, Sunna(h)
Moist(en), Moisture Baste, Bedew, Damp, Dank, De(a)w, Humect, Latch, Love-in-a-mist, Madefy, Mesarch, Moil, Nigella, Oozy, Slake, Slocken, Soggy, Sponge, Wet
▷ **Moither** *may indicate* an anagram
Molar Grinder, Mill-tooth, Secodont, Tooth, Wang
Molasses Blackstrap, Sorghum, Treacle
Mole(hill) Breakwater, Fen-cricket, Golden, Hydatidiform, Jetty, Marsupial, Miner, Mo(u)diewart, Moudi(e)wart, Mouldiwarp, Naeve, Notoryctes, Orology, Pier, Sea-wall, Shrew, Sleeper, Spot, Spy, Star-nose(d), Talpa, Want(hill), Want knap, Warp
Molecule, Molecular Acceptor, Atom, Buckyball, Carbene, Cavitand, Chiral, Chromophore, Closed chain, Cobalamin, Codon, Coenzyme, Cofactor, Dimer, DNA, Electrogen, Enantiomorph, Footballene, Fullerene, Gram, Hapten, Iota, Isomer, Kinin, Kisspeptin, Ligand, Long-chain, Metabolite, Metameric, Monomer, Nanotube, Peptide, Polymer, Polysaccharide, Quark, Replicon, Ribozyme, Semantide, Stereoisomer, Trimer, Uridine, Vector
Molendinar Mill
Molest(er) Annoy, Bother, Disturb, Harass, Nonce, Scour
Moll(y), Mollie Bloom, Bonnie, Carousal, Cutpurse, Flanders, Girl, Maguire, Malone, May, Sissy
Mollify Appease, Fob, Mease, Mitigate, Pacify, Placate, Relax, Soften, Temper
Mollusc(s) Ammonite, Amphineura, Arca, Argonaut, Ark-shell, Belemnite, Bivalve, Bulla, Capiz, Cephalopod, Chiton, Clam, Cockle, Conch, Cone-shell, Cowrie, Cowry, Cuttle(fish), Dentalium, Doris, Gaper, Gast(e)ropod, Goniatite,

Heart-cockler, Heart-shell, Helix, Horse mussel, Idler, Lamellibranch, Limpet, Malacology, Marine boxer, Money cowry, Monoplacophora, Murex, Mussel, Mya, Nautiloid, Nautilus, Neopilina, Octopod, Octopus, Olive, Opisthobranch, Oyster, Pandora, Paper nautilus, Paper-sailor, Pearly nautilus, Pecten, Pelican's-foot, Pholas, Piddock, Pinna, Polyp, Poulpe, Protostome, Pteropod, Quahaug, Quahog, Razor-clam, Razor-fish, Razorshell, Saxicava, Scallop, Scaphopoda, Sea-hare, Sea-lemon, Sea-slug, Sepia, → **SHELLFISH**, Shipworm, Slipper limpet, Slug, Snail, Solen, Spat, Spirula, Spoot, Squid, Strombus, Tectibranch, Tellen, Tellin, Teredo, Toheroa, Top-shell, Triton, Trochophore, Trochus, Trough-shell, Turbo, Tusk-shell, Unio, Univalve, Veliger, Venus, Venus shell, Vitrina, Wentletrap, Whelk, Wing-shell, Winkle

Mollycoddle Indulge, Nanny, Pamper

Moloch Thorn-devil

Molten Dissolved, Fusil, Melted

Molybdenum Mo

Moment(s), Momentous Aha, Bending, Bit, Dipole, Electromagnetic, Eureka, Flash, Hogging, Import, Instant, Jiffy, Magnetic, → **MINUTE**, Mo, Nonce, Point, Psychological, Pun(c)to, Sagging, Sands, Sec, Senior, Shake, Stound, Stownd, Tick, Time, Trice, Twinkling, Weighty, Wink

Momentum Angular, Impetus, L, Speed, Thrust

Mona(s) I, IOM

Monaco Grimaldi

Mona Lisa La Gioconda

Monarch(y) Absolute, Autocrat, Butterfly, Caesar, Constitutional, Crown, Dual, Emperor, HM, K, Karling, King, Limited, Merry, Potentate, Q, Queen, R, Raine, Reign, Ruler, Tonga, Tsar

Monarchist Cavalier

Monastery Abbey, Abthane, Charterhouse, Chartreuse, Cloister, Community, Gompa, Hospice, Lamaserai, Lamasery, La Trappe, Laura, Priory, Vihara, Wat

Monastic Abthane, Celibate, Holy, Monkish, Oblate, Secluded

Monday Black, Collop, Handsel, J'ouvert, Meal, Oatmeal, Plough, Whit

Mondrian Piet

Money, Monetary Ackers, Akkas, Allowance, Annat, Ante, Appearance, Archer, Assignat, Banco, Batta, Blood, Blue, Blunt, Boodle, Bottle, Brass, Bread, Bread and honey, Broad, Bull's eye, Cabbage, Capital, Cash, Caution, Century, Change, Chink, Cob, Cock, → **COIN**, Collateral, Confetti, Conscience, Crackle, Cranborne, Crinkly, Currency, Danger, Dib(s), Dingbat, Dollar, Dosh, Dust, Earnest, Easy, Even, Fat, Fee, Fiat, Float, Folding, Fonds, Found, Fund, Funny, Gate, Gelt, Gilt, Godiva, Gold, Grand, Grant, Gravy, Greens, Hard, Head, Hello, Hoot, Hot, Housekeeping, Hush, Husk, Idle, Ingots, Investment, Jack, Kale, Kembla, Key, Knife, L, Legal tender, Lolly, Loot, Lucre, M, Mammon, Maundy, Mazuma, Means, Mint, Monkey, Monopoly, Moola(h), Narrow, Near, Necessary, Needful, Nest-egg, Note, Nugger, Numismatic, Nummary, Oaker, Ochre, Offertory, Oof, Option, Outlay, P, Packet, Paper, Passage, Pavarotti, Payroll, Peanuts, Pecuniary, Pelf, Pin, Pine-tree, Pittance, Plastic, Plum, Pocket, Pony, Posh, Press, Prize, Proceeds, Profit, Protection, Purse, Push, Quid, Ration, Ready, Rebate, Resources, Revenue, Rhino, Ring, Risk, Rogue, Rowdy, Salt(s), Score, Scratch, Scrip, Seed, Shell, Shin-plaster, Ship, Short, Siller, Silly, Silver, Slush, Smart, Soap, Soft, Spondulicks, Stake, Sterling, Stipend, Stuff, Subsistence, Sugar, Sum, Table, Takings, Tender, Tin, Toea, Token, Tranche, Treaty, Tribute, Turnover, Viaticum, Wad, Wealth, Wonga

Money-box Penny-pig, Piggy bank

Moneylender Gombeen, Shroff, Shylock, Usurer

Moneymaking Earner, Profitable, Quaestuary

Mongol(ian) Bashkir, Buriat, Buryat, Calmuck, Chuvash, Evenski, Golden Horde, Kalmuck, Kara-Kalpak, Kazak(h), Khalkha, Kubla(i) Khan, Kyrgyz, Lapp, Lepcha, Manchoo, Manchu, Mishmi, Mogul, Pareoean, Samoyed, Shan, Sherpa, Tamerlane, Tatar, Tungus(ic), Uig(h)ur, Ural-altaic, Uzbek

Mongoose Herpestes, Ichneumon, Mangouste, Meerkat, Suricate, Urva

Mongrel Bitser, Cross(bred), → **DOG**, Goorie, Goory, Hybrid, Kuri, Lurcher, Mutt, Quadroon, Tyke, Underbred, Zo

Monitor(ing) Dataveillance, Detect, Goanna, Iguana, Lizard, Observe, Offer, Ofgas, Ofgem, Oflot, Ofsted, Oftel, Ofwat, Prefect, Preview, Record, Screen, Ship, Track, Warship, Watchdog, Whole-body, Worral, Worrel

Monk(s) Abbey-lubber, Abbot, Acoemeti, Angelico, Archimandrite, Arhat, Asser, Augustinian, Austin, Basilian, Bede, Beghard, Benedictine, Bernardine, Bethlehemite, Bhikhu, Black, Bonaventura, Bonze, Bro, Brother, Bruno, Caedmon, Caloyer, Carthusian, Celestine, Cellarist, Cenobite, Cistercian, Cluniac, Coenobite, Cowl, Crutched Friar, Culdee, Dan, Dervish, Dom, Dominican, Félibre, Feuillant, Fraticelli, Friar, General, Gyrovague, Hegumen, Hermit, Hesychast, Hildebrand, Ignorantine, Jacobin, Jacobite, Jerome, Lama, Maurist, Mechitharist, Mekhitarist, Mendel, Norbertine, Obedientiary, Oblate, Olivetan, Order, Pelagian, Prior, Rakehell, Rasputin, Recluse, Recollect, Religieux, Roshi, Salesian, Sangha, Savonarola, Simeon Stylites, Sub-prior, Talapoin, Theatine, Thelemite, Thelonious, Thomas à Kempis, Tironensian, Trappist, Votary

Monkey Anger, Ape, Aye-aye, Baboon, Bandar, Bobbejaan, Bonnet, Bushbaby, Capuchin, Catar(r)hine, Cebidae, Cebus, Chacma, Coaita, Colobus, Cynomolgus, Diana, Douc, Douroucouli, Drill, Durukuli, Entellus, Galago, Gelada, Gibbon, Gorilla, Grease, Green, Grison, Grivet, Guenon, Guereza, Hanuman, Hoolock, Howler, Hylobates, Indri, Jacchus, Jackey, Jocko, Kippage, Langur, Leaf, Lemur, Loris, Macaco, Macaque, Magot, Malmag, Mandrill, Mangabey, Marmoset, Meddle, Meerkat, Mico, Midas, Mona, Mycetes, Nala, Nasalis, New World, Old World, Orang-utang, Ouakari, Ouistiti, Phalanger, Platyrrhine, Powder, → **PRIMATE**, Proboscis, Pug, Puzzle, Rage, Ram, Rapscallion, Rascal, Rhesus, Sago(u)in, Saguin, Sai(miri), Sajou, Saki, Sapajou, Satan, Semnopithecus, Siamang, Sifaka, Silen(us), Silverback, Simian, Simpai, Slender loris, Spider, Squirrel, Talapoin, Tamarin, Tamper, Tana, Tarsier, Tee-tee, Titi, Toque, Trip-hammer, Troop, Tup, Uakari, Vervet, Wanderoo, White-eyelid, Wistiti, Wou-wou, Wow-wow, Wrath, Zati

Monkey-nut Earth-pea

Monkey-puzzle Araucaria, Bunya-bunya

Monkshood Aconite

Monocle Eye-glass, Gig-lamp, Lorgnon, Quiz(zing-glass)

Monocot(yledon) Araceae, Endogen, Tradescantia

Monodon Narwhal

Monogram, Monograph Chi-rho, Cipher, Study, Treatise, Tug(h)ra

Monolith Ayers Rock, Cenotaph, Chambers Pillar, Uluru

Monologue Interior, Patter, Rap, Recitation, Soliloquy, Speech

Monopolise, Monopoly Appalto, Bloc, Bogart, Cartel, Corner, Engross, Octroi, Régie, Trust

Monorail Aerobus

Monosyllable Proclitic

Monotonous, Monotony Boring, Dull, → **FLAT**, Grey, Humdrum, Same(y), Sing-song, Tedious

Monsoon Dry, Hurricane, Typhoon, Wet, → **WIND**
▷ **Monsoon** *may indicate* weekend (Mon soon)
Monster, Monstrous Alecto, Apollyon, Asmodeus, Bandersnatch, Behemoth, Bunyip, Caliban, Cerberus, Cete, Charybdis, Chichevache, Chim(a)era, Cockatrice, Colossal, Cyclops, Dabbat, Deform, Dinoceras, Dismayd, Div, Dragon, Echidna, Enormous, Erebus, Erinys, Erl-king, Eten, Ettin, Evil-one, Fiend, Fire-drake, Frankenstein, Freak, Geryon, Ghost, Giant, Gila, Golem, Gorgon, Green-eyed, Grendel, Harpy, Hippocampus, Hippogriff, Hippogryph, Huge, Hydra, Jabberwock, Kraken, Lamia, Leviathan, Lilith, Lusus naturae, Mastodon, Medusa, Minotaur, Misbegotten, Moloch, Mooncalf, Mylodont, Nessie, Nicker, Nightmare, Ogopogo, Ogre, Ogr(e)ish, Opinicus, Orc, Outrageous, Pongo, Sasquatch, Satyral, Scylla, Serra, Shadow, Simorg, Simurg(h), Siren, Skull, Snark, Spectre, Sphinx, Spook, Stegodon, Stegosaur, Succubus, Taniwha, Teras, Teratism, Teratoid, Triceratops, Troll, Typhoeus, Typhon, Unnatural, Vampire, Vast, Wasserman, Wendego, Wendigo, Wer(e)wolf, Wyvern, Xiphopagus, Yowie, Ziffius
Monstrance Ostensory
Month(ly) Ab, Abib, Adar, Anomalistic, April, Asadha, Asvina, August, Bhadrapada, Brumaire, Bul, Calendar, Cheshvan, Chislev, December, Dhu-al-Hijjah, Dhu-al-Qadah, Draconic, Elul, February, Floréal, Frimaire, Fructidor, Germinal, Hes(h)van, Iy(y)ar, January, July, Jumada, June, Jysaitha, Kartuka, Kisleu, Kislev, Lide, Lunar, Lunation, Magha, March, Margasirsa, May, Messidor, Mo, Moharram, Moon, Muharram, Muharrem, Nisan, Nivôse, Nodical, November, October, Periodical, Phalguna, Pluviôse, Prairial, Rabia, Rajab, Ramadan, Ramazon, Rhamadhan, Safar, Saphar, September, Sha(a)ban, Shawwal, S(h)ebat, Sidereal, Sivan, Solar, Stellar, Synodic, Tammuz, Tebeth, Thermidor, Tishri, Tisri, Tropical, Vaisakha, Veadar, Vendémiaire, Ventôse
Monument Ancient, Arch, Archive, Cenotaph, Charminar, Column, Cromlech, Dolmen, Henge, Megalith, Memorial, Menhir, Monolith, National, Pantheon, Pyramid, Sacellum, Stele(ne), Stone, Stonehenge, Stupa, Talayot, Tombstone, Trilith, Trilithon, Urn
Mood(y) Active, Anger, Atmosphere, Attitude, Capricious, Conjunctive, Dudgeon, Emoticon, Enallage, Fettle, Fit, Foulie, Glum, Grammar, Humour, Hump, Imperative, Indicative, Infinitive, Mercurial, Morale, Optative, Passive, Peat, Pet, Revivalist, Sankey, Spleen, Subjunctive, Temper, Tid, Tone, Tune, Vein, Vinegar, Whim
Moon(light), Moony Aah, Alignak, Aningan, Apogee, Artemis, Astarte, Blue, Callisto, Calypso, Chandra, Cheese, Cynthia, Diana, Epact, Eye, Flit, Full, Gander, Ganymede, Gibbous, Glimmer, Grimaldi, Harvest, Hecate, Hunter's, Hyperion, Inconstant, Juliet, Leda, Lucina, Luna(r), Mani, Mascon, McFarlane's Buat, Midsummer, Mock, Month, Mope, New, Nimbus, Nocturne, Octant, Oliver, Paddy's lantern, Paraselene, Paschal, Pasiphaë, Phoebe, Plenilune, Proteus, Raker, Satellite, Selene, Set, Shepherd, Shot, Sickle, Sideline, Silvery, Sonata, Stargaze, Stone, Syzygy, Thebe, Thoth, Titan, Triton, Umbriel, Wander
Moonraker Astrogeologist, Gothamite
Moonshine(r) Hootch, Poteen, Rot, Shebeener
Moor(ing), Moorish, Moorland Berth, Bodmin, Culloden, Dock, Fen, Flow country, Grouse, Heath, Iago, Ilkley, Makefast, Marina, Marston, Moresque, Moroccan, Mudéjar, Othello, Palustrine, Roadstead, Ryepeck, Saracen, Sternfast, Tether, → **TIE**, Wharf, Wold
Mop(ping) Dwile, Flibbertigibbet, Girn, Glib, Shag, Squeegee, Squilgee, Swab, Swob, Thatch, → **WIPE**

Mope Boody, Brood, Peak, Sulk

Mor Humus

Moral(ity), Morals Apologue, Austere, Deontic, Ethic(al), Ethos, Everyman, Fable, High-minded, Integrity, Precept, Principled, Puritanic, Righteous, Sittlichkeit, Tag, Upright, Virtuous, Well-thewed

Morale Ego, Mood, Spirit, Zeal

Moralise, Moralising Preach, Sententious

Moralist Prig, Prude, Puritan, Whitecap

Morass Bog, Fen, Flow, Marsh, Moss, Quagmire, Slough

Morbid(ity) Anasarca, Ascites, Cachaemia, Dropsy, Ectopia, Ghoul(ish), Gruesome, Pathological, Plethora, Prurient, Religiose, Sick, Sombre, Unhealthy

Mordant Biting, Caustic, Critic(al), Sarcastic, Tooth

Mordent Inverted, Pralltriller, Upper

More Added, Additional, Else, Extra, Increase, Less, Mae, Merrier, Mo(e), → NO MORE, Over, Piu, Plus, Stump, Utopia

Moreover Also, Besides, Eft, Either, Eke, Further, Too, Yet

Morgan Buccaneer, Pirate

Moribund Dying, Stagnant, Withered

Mormon Danite, Latter-day Saint, Salt Lake City, Utah, Young

Morning Ack-emma, Am, Antemeridian, Dawn, Daybreak, Early, Forenoon, Levée, Matin(al), Morrow, Sparrowfart

Morning-glory Bindweed, Ipomoea, Turbith, Turpeth

Morning-star Morgenstern, Phosphor(us), Threshel, Venus

Moroccan, Morocco Agadir, French, Leather, Levant, MA, Mo(o)r, Persian, Riff, Tangerine, Venus

Moron Fool, Idiot, Schmuck, → STUPID

Morose Acid, Boody, Churlish, Crabby, Cynical, Disgruntled, Gloomy, Glum, Grum, Moody, Sour-eyed, Sullen, Surly

Morph Phase

Morris Car, Dance, Fivepenny, Merel(l), Meril, Nine Men's, Ninepenny

Morrow Future

Morse Code, Endeavour, Iddy-umpty, Walrus

Morsel Bit, Bite, Bouche, Canape, Crumb, Dainty, Morceau, Ort, Scrap, Sippet, Sop, Tidbit, Titbit

Mortal(ity) Averr(h)oism, Being, Deathly, → FATAL, Grave, Human, Lethal, Yama

Mortar, Mortar-board Bowl, Cannon, Cement, Co(e)horn, Compo, Grout, Gunite, Hawk, Life, Metate, Mine-thrower, Minnie, Moaning (Minnie), Parget, Plaster, Pot gun, Screed, Square, Squid, Toc emma, Trench(er)

Mortgage(e) Balloon, Bond, Cedula, Chattel, Debt, Dip, Encumbrance, Endowment, First, Hypothecator, Loan, Pension, Pledge, Wadset(t)

Mortification, Mortified, Mortify Abash, Ashame, Chagrin, Crucify, Crush, Gangrene, Humble, Humiliate, Infarct, Necrose, Penance, Sick, Sphacelus, Wormwood

Mosaic Buhl, Cosmati, Inlay, Intarsia, Musive, Opus musivum, Pietra dura, Screen, Tarsia, Terrazzo, Tessella(te), Tessera, Tobacco, Venetian

Moscow Dynamo

Moses Grandma

▸ **Moslem** *see* MUSLIM

Mosque Dome of the Rock, El Aqsa, Jami, Masjid, Medina, Musjid

Mosquito Aedes, Anopheles, Culex, Culicine, Gnat, Parasite, Stegomyia

Moss(y) Acrogen, Agate, Bryology, Bur(r), Carrag(h)een, Ceylon, Club, Fog,

Fontinalis, Hag(g), Hypnum, Iceland, Irish, Lecanoram, Lichen, Litmus, Liverwort, Long, Lycopod, Marsh, Musci, Muscoid, Parella, Peat, Polytrichum, Reindeer, Rose, Scale, Selaginella, Spanish, Sphagnum, Staghorn, Tree, Usnea, Wall, Wolf's claw

Most Largest, Major, Maxi(mum), Optimum

Mot Quip, Saying

Mote Atom, Particle, Speck

Moth(s) Abraxas, Antler, Arch, Arctiidae, Atlas, Bag, Bee, Bell, Bobowler, Bogong, Bombycid, Brown-tail, Buff-tip, Bugong, Burnet, Cabbage, Cactoblastis, Carpenter, Carpet, Cecropia, Cinnabar, Clearwing, Clifden nonpareil, Clothes, Codlin(g), Corn (-borer), Dagger, Dart-moth, Death's head, Diamondback, Drepanid, Drinker, Eggar, Egger, Emerald, Emperor, Ermine, Flour, Fox, Geometer, Geometrid, Ghost, Giant peacock, Gipsy, Goat, Goldtail, Gooseberry, Grass, Gypsy, Hawk, Herald, Honeycomb, Hook-tip, House, Hummingbird, Imago, Io, Kentish glory, Kitten, Lackey, Lappet, Large emerald, Lasiocampidae, Leafroller, Leopard, Lepidoptera, Lichen, Lobster, Luna, Lymantriidae, Macrolepidoptera, Magpie, Meal, Microlepidoptera, Mother of pearl, Mother Shipton, Muslin, Noctua, Noctuid, Notodonta, Nun, Oak-egger, Owl, Owlet, Peppercorn, Peppered, Pine-beauty, Pine-carpet, Plane, Plume, Polyphemus, Privet hawk, Processionary, Prominent, Psyche, Pug-moth, Purple emperor, Puss, Pyralidae, Red underwing, Sallow-kitten, Saturnia, Saturniid, Scavenger, Silkworm, Silver-Y, Snout, Sphingid, Sphinx, Swift, Tapestry, Thorn, Tiger, Tinea, Tineidae, Tortrix, Turnip, Tussock, Umber, Underwing, Unicorn, Vapourer, Veneer, Wainscot, Wave, Wax, Wheat, Winter, Woodborer, Yellow underwing, Y-moth, Zygaena

Mothball(s) Abeyance, Camphor, Naphtha, Preserver

Mother Bearer, Church, Cognate, Cosset, Courage, Dam(e), Dregs, Ean, Earth, Eve, Foster, Generatrix, Genetrix, Genitrix, Goose, Hubbard, Lees, Ma, Machree, Madre, Mam(a), Mamma, Mater, Maya, Minnie, Mom, Multipara, Mum, Native, Nature, Nourish, Nursing, Parity, Pourer, Primipara, Reverend, Shipton, Superior, Surrogate, Theotokos, Wit

▷ **Mother** *may indicate* a lepidopterist (moth-er)

Motherless Adam, Orphan

Motif Anthemion, Design, Gist, Idée, Theme

Motion Angular, Contrary, Diurnal, Early day, Fast, Gesture, Harmonic, Impulse, Kepler, Kinematics, Kinetic, Link, Move, Oblique, Offer, Parallactic, Parallel, Peculiar, Perpetual, PL, Proper, Proposal, Rack and pinion, Rider, Similar, Slow, Spasm, Wave

Motionless Doggo, Frozen, Immobile, Quiescent, Stagnant, Stasis, Still, Stock-still

Motive, Motivate, Motivation Actuate, Cause, Ideal, Impel, Incentive, Intention, Mainspring, Mobile, Object, → PURPOSE, Spur, Ulterior

Motley Jaspé, Medley, Piebald, Pied

Motor(boat) Auto, Car, Dynamo, Electric, Engine, Hot rod, Inboard, Induction, Jato, Linear, Outboard, Rocket, Scooter, Series-wound, Stator, Synchronous, Thruster, Turbine, Universal, Water

Motorcycle, Motorcyclist Bambi, Bikie, Chookchaser, Chopper, Farm-bike, Harley Davidson, Hell's Angel, Minimoto, Moped, Pipsqueak, Scooter, Scramble, Trail bike, Yamaha®

Motorist(s) AA, Driver, Petrolhead, RAC, Tripper

Motorman Austin, Benz, Ford, Morris

Motor race Rally, Scramble, TT

Motorway Autobahn, Autopista, Autoput, Autoroute, Autostrada, Expressway, M(1), Orbital, Superhighway, Throughway, Thruway

Mottle(d) Brindled, Chiné, Jaspé, Marbled, Marly, Mirly, Pinto, Poikilitic, Tabby
Motto Device, Epigraph, Excelsior, Gnome, Impresa, Imprese, Impress(e), Legend, Maxim, Mot, Poesy, Posy, Saw
Mou(e) Grimace, Mim
Mould(ed), Moulder, Mouldable, Moulding, Mouldy Accolade, Architrave, Archivolt, Astragal, Baguette, Balection, Bandelet, Beading, Bend, Black, Blow, Blue, Bolection, Bread, Briquet(te), Cabling, Casement, Cast(ing), Cavetto, Chessel, Chill, Cold, Cornice, Coving, Cyma, Cymatium, Dancette, Dariole, Die, Die-cast, Dogtooth, Doucine, Dripstone, Ductile, Echinus, Egg and dart, Emboss, Flong, → **FORM**, Foughty, Fousty, Fungose, Fungus, Fusarol(e), Fust, Gadroon, Godroon, Gorgerin, Green, Hood-mould, Hore, Humus, Injection, Iron, Jelly, Leaf, Machine, Matrix, Mildew, Model, Mool, Moulage, Mucid, Mucor, Must, Mycetozoan, Myxomycete, Nebule, Necking, Noble rot, Ogee, Ovolo, Palmette, Papier-mâché, Penicillin, Phycomycete, Picture, Pig, Plasm(a), Plastic, Plastisol, Plat, Platband, Plate, Prototype, Prunt, Quarter-round, Reeding, Reglet, Rhizopus, Rot, Rust, Sandbox, Scotia, Shape, Slime, Smut, Soil, Soot(y), Spindle, Storiated, Stringcourse, Stucco, Surbase, Tailor, Talon, Template, Templet, Timbale, Tondino, Torus, Trochilus, Vinew, Water table
Moult(ing) Cast, Metecdysis, Mew, Shed
Mound Agger, Bank, Barp, Barrow, Berm, Cahokia, Cone, Dike, Dun, Embankment, Heap, Hog, Kurgan, Mogul, Molehill, Monticule, Mote, Motte, Orb, Pile, Pingo, Pome, Rampart, Rampire, Remblai, Tel(l), Teocalli, Teopan, Tuffet, Tumulus, Tussock
Mound-bird Megapode
Mount(ed), Mounting, Mountain (peak), Mountains Air, → **ALPINE**, Ascend, Aspiring, Back, Barp, Ben, Berg, Board, Breast, Butter, Chain, Charger, → **CLIMB**, Colt, Cordillera, Cradle, Dew, Display, Djebel, Dolly, Escalade, Frame, Hinge, Horse, Inselberg, Jebel, Massif, Monture, Mt, Nunatak, Orography, Orology, Passe-partout, Pike, Pile, Pin, Pownie, Quad, Ride, Saddlehorse, Saddle up, Scalado, Scale, Sclim, Set, Soar, Stage, → **STEED**, Stie, Strideways, Tel, Tier, Topo, Tor, Turret, Upgo, Volcano

MOUNTAINS

2 letters:	Hoss	Andes	Idris
K2	Jaya	Aneto	Kamet
	Jura	Athos	Kenya
3 letters:	Meru	Atlas	Logan
Apo	Nebo	Badon	Munro
Ida	Oeta	Black	Ozark
Kaf	Ossa	Blanc	Pelée
Ore	Rigi	Coast	Rocky
	Ubac	Djaja	Rydal
4 letters:	Zeil	Eiger	Sayan
Alai		Ellis	Serra
Blue	*5 letters:*	Er Rif	Sinai
Bona	Abora	Ghats	Siple
Cook	Adams	Green	Smoky
Etna	Aldan	Guyot	Snowy
Fuji	Altai	Hekla	Table
Harz	Amara	Horeb	Tabor

Tatra
Tirol
Tyree
Tyrol
Uinta
Urals
Welsh
White

6 letters:
Ala Dag
Alaska
Amhara
Anadyr
Arafat
Ararat
Averno
Balkan
Bogong
Carmel
Cho Oyu
Dragon
Egmont
Elbert
Elberz
Elbrus
Erebus
Gilead
Hermon
Hoggar
Hoosac
Katmai
Kazbek
Kunlun
Lhotse
Makalu
Mourne
Olives
Ortles
Pamirs
Pelion
Pindus
Pisgah
Pocono
Robson
Scopus
Sintra
Sorata
Steele
Tasman
Taunus

Taurus
Umbria
Vernon
Vosges
Zagros

7 letters:
Aetolia
Ala Dagh
Aorangi
Aragats
Arcadia
Bernina
Brocken
Buffalo
Calvary
Cariboo
Cascade
Chianti
Corbett
Dapsang
Estreia
Everest
Helicon
Kennedy
Khingan
Kuenlun
Lebanon
Lucania
Manaslu
Markham
Nan Shan
Olympic
Olympus
Palomar
Perdido
Pilatus
Rainier
Rhodope
San Juan
Scafell
Selkirk
Skiddaw
Snowdon
Sperrin
Stanley
St Elias
Sudeten
Tibesti
Travers
Troglav

Whitney
Wicklow

8 letters:
Anapurna
Ben Nevis
Cambrian
Carstenz
Catskill
Caucasus
Cevennes
Cumbrian
Demavend
Grampian
Guerrero
Hymettus
Illimani
Jungfrau
Kinabalu
King Peak
Leibnitz
McKinley
Mulhacen
Ngaliema
Ouachita
Pennines
Pyrenees
Rushmore
Seamount
St Helen's
Taraniki
Tian Shan
Tien Shan
Vesuvius
Victoria
Wrangell

9 letters:
Aconcagua
Allegheny
Annapurna
Apennines
Ben Lomond
Blackburn
Blue Ridge
Cairngorm
Carstensz
Catskills
Caucasian
Connemara
Demavrand

Dolomites
El Capitan
Grampians
Guadalupe
Helvellyn
Highlands
High Tatra
Himalayas
Hindu Kush
Jebel Musa
Karakoram
Lenin Peak
Longs Peak
Marmolada
Mont Blanc
Monte Rosa
Nanda Devi
Parnassus
Pikes Peak
Ruwenzori
Shivering
Sugar Loaf
Tirich Mir
Trans Alai
Tupungato
Vancouver
Venusberg
Voralberg
Weisshorn
Woodroffe
Yablonovy
Zugspitze

10 letters:
Altazimuth
Arakan Yoma
Armageddon
Black Hills
Cantabrian
Carpathian
Delectable
Dhaulagiri
Equatorial
Erymanthus
Erzgebirge
Great Gable
Great Smoky
Harney Peak
Horselberg
Kongur Shan
Koscuiszko

Laurentian
Masharbrum
Masherbrum
Matterhorn
Monte Corno
Montserrat
Pentelicus
Pentelikon
Puncak Jaya
Puy de Sancy
Qomolangma
Sagarmatha
St Michael's
Tengri Khan
Teton Range
Vorarlberg
Washington
Waziristan
Wellington
Wetterhorn

11 letters:
Adirondacks
Alaska Range
Anti-Lebanon
Appalachian
Bartle Frere
Bimberi Peak
Brooks Range
Drakensberg
Fairweather

Gerlachovka
Kilimanjaro
Kirkpatrick
Kolyma Range
Nanga Parbat
Picode Anito
Salmon River
Scafell Pike
Sierra Madre

12 letters:
Albert Edward
Cascade Range
Eastern Ghats
Godwin Austen
Gran Paradiso
Ingleborough
Kanchenjunga
Monte Perdido
Ruahine Range
Sierra Morena
Sierra Nevada
Slieve Donard
Southern Alps
Tararua Range
Victoria Peak
Vindhya Range
Vinson Massif
Wasatch Range
Western Ghats

13 letters:
Carrantuohill
Croagh Patrick
Flinders Range
Great Dividing
Grossglockner
Humphrey's Peak
Kangchenjunga
Massif Central
Mount Klinovec
Petermann Peak
San Bernardino
Stanovoi Range
Tibesti Massif

14 letters:
Admiralty Range
Bohemian Forest
Carnarvon Range
Finsteraarhorn
Hamersley Range
Kaikoura Ranges
Kommunizma Peak
Liverpool Range
Musgrove Ranges
Queen Maud Range
Ruwenzori Range
Sangre de Cristo
Stirling Ranges
Thadentsonyane
Wind River Range

15 letters:
New England Range
Teutoburger Wald

16 letters:
Emperor
  Seamounts
Macdonnell Ranges
Owen Stanley
  Range
Thabana-Ntlenyana

17 letters:
Continental Divide
Transylvanian Alps

18 letters:
Great Dividing
  Range

19 letters:
Macgillicuddy's
  Reeks

20 letters:
Salmon River
  Mountains

Mountain-building Orogenesis

Mountaineer(ing) Aaron, Abseil, Alpinist, Arnaut, Climber, Hunt, Sherpa, Smythe, Upleader

Mountebank Antic(ke), Baladin(e), Charlatan, Jongleur, Quack, Saltimbanco

Mourn(er), Mournful, Mourning Adonia, Black, Dirge, Dole, Elegiac, Grieve, Grone, Half-mast, Hatchment, Jamie Duff, Keen, Lament, Mute, Niobe, Omer, Ovel, Plangent, Saulie, Shibah, Shivah, Shloshim, Sorrow, Tangi, Threnetic, Threnodial, Weeds, Weep, Willow

Mouse(like), Mousy Black eye, Church, Deer, Dun(nart), Fat, Field, Flitter, Harvest, Honey, House, Icon, Jumping, Kangaroo, Marsupial, Meadow, Muridae, Murine, Optical, Pocket, Pouched, Rodent, Shiner, Shrew, Vermin, Waltzer, White-footed

Mousetrap Samson's post

Mousse Styling

Moustache(d) Algernon, Boxcar, Burnside, Charley, Charlie, Chevron, Excrement, Fu Manchu, Handlebar, Hindenburg, Horseshoe, Kaiser, Mistletoe, Pencil, Pyramid, Regent, Roman T, Ronnie, Soupstrainer, Toothbrush, Walrus, Waxed, Wings, Zapata

Mouth(piece) Aboral, Bazoo, Bocca, Brag, Buccal, Cakehole, Chapper, Check, Crater, Debouchure, Delta, Embouchure, Estuary, Fauces, Fipple, Gab, Gam,

Geggie, Gills, Gob, Gum, Hard, Kisser, Labret, Laughing gear, Lawyer, Lip, Manubrium, Maw, Neb, Orifex, Orifice, Os, Oscule, Ostium, Outfall, Outlet, Port, Potato trap, Rattle-trap, Speaker, Spokesman, Spout, Stoma, Swazzle, Swozzle, Teat, Trap, Trench, Uvula

Mouthful Bite, Gob, Gobbet, Morceau, Morsel, Sip, Sup, Taste

Mouthless Astomatous

Mouth-organ Harmonica, Harp, Palp, Sang

Move(d), Mover, Movable, Moving Act, Actuate, Affect, Andante, Astir, Budge, Carry, Catapult, Chattel, Claw off, Coast, Counter-measure, Coup, Decant, Démarche, Displace, Disturb, Ease, Eddy, Edge, Evoke, Extrapose, False, Flit, Flounce, Fluctuate, Forge, Fork, Frogmarch, Gambit, Gee, Go, Gravitate, Haulier, Hustle, Inch, Inspire, Instigate, Jee, Jink, Kedge, Kinetic, Knight's progress, Link, Mill, Mobile, Mosey, Motivate, Nip, Opening, Overcome, Pan, People, Poignant, Prime, Proceed, Progress, Prompt, Propel, Quicken, Qui(t)ch, Rearrange, Redeploy, Relocate, Remuage, Retrocede, Roll, Rollaway, Rouse, Roust, Sashay, Scoot, Scramble, Scroll, Scuttle, Sealed, Sell, Shift, Shog, Shoo, Shunt, Sidle, Skelp, Slide, Soulful, Spank, Steal, Steer, Step, Stir, Styre, Surf, Sway, Swish, Tack, Tactic, Taxi, Transfer, Translate, Translocate, Transplant, Transport, Travel, Troll, Trundle, Turn, Unstep, Up, Upsticks, Vacillate, Vagile, Veronica, Vire, Volt(e), Waft, Wag, Wapper, Whirry, Whish, Whisk, Whiz, Wuther, Yank, Zoom, Zwischenzug

Movement(s) Action, Advection, Aerotaxis, Akathisia, Al Fatah, Allegro, Allemande, Almain, Andantino, Antic, Antistrophe, Arts and crafts, Azapo, Badinerie, Bandwagon, Brownian, Cadence, Capoeira, Cell, Charismatic, Chartism, Chemonasty, Constructivism, Course, Crusade, Dadaism, Diaspora, Diastole, Ecumenical, Enlightenment, Eoka, Eurhythmics, Expressionism, Faction, Feint, Fianchetto, Fris(ka), Gait, Gallicanism, Geneva, Gesture, Groundswell, Hip-hop, Honde, Imagism, Indraught, Inkatha, Intermezzo, Jhala, Jor, Kata, Keplarian, Kinesis, Kin(a)esthetic, Kinetic, Larghetto, Largo, Lassu, Ligne, Logistics, Manoeuvre, Motion, Mudra, Nastic, Naturalism, Naziism, New Urbanism, New Wave, Nihilism, Official, Operation, Orchesis, Oxford, Pantalon, Parallax, Pase, Passade, Pedesis, Photokinesis, Photonasty, Piaffer, Pincer, Plastique, Play, Populist, Poule, Poulette, Procession, Progress, Provisional, Punk, Puseyism, Reformation, Regression, REM, Renaissance, Resistance, Revivalism, Ribbonism, Risorgimento, Romantic, Rondo, Saccade, Scherzo, Seiche, Sinn Fein, Solifluction, Solifluxion, Spuddle, Stir(e), Sturm und Drang, Swadeshi, Swing, Symbolist, Tachism, Tamil Tigers, Tantrism, Taxis, Tectonic, Telekinesis, Thigmotaxis, Tic, Tide, Tractarianism, Transhumance, Trend, Trenise, Ultramontanism, UNITA, Verismo, Veronica, Wave, Wheel, Women's, Zionism

Movie Bioscope, Buddy, Cine(ma), Disaster, Film, Flick, Nudie, Popcorn, Road, Slasher, Snuff, Splatter, Talkie

Mow(er), Mowing Aftermath, Cut, Grimace, Lattermath, Lawn, Math, Rawing, Rawn, Rowan, Rowen, Rowing, Scytheman, Shear, Sickle, Strimmer®, Tass, Trim

MP Backbencher, Commoner, Gendarme, Knight of the Shire, Member, Politico, Provost, Redcap, Retread, Snowdrop, Stannator, Statist, TD

▶ **Mr** *see* MISTER

▶ **Mrs** *see* MISSIS

Mrs Copperfield Agnes, Dora

Mrs Siddons Tragic muse

Much Abundant, Far, Glut, Great, Lots, Mickle, Scad, Sore, Viel

Mucilage Gum, → MUCUS, Putty, Resin

Muck (up), Mucky Bungle, Dirt, Dung, Island, Leep, Manure, Midden, Mire, Rot,

Sludge, Soil, Sordid, Spoil, Stercoral

Mucker Fall, Pal, Purler

Mucus Blennorrhoea, Catarrh, Phlegm, Pituate, Pituita, Snivel, Snot, Snotter, Sputum

Mud(dy) Adobe, Clabber, Clart, Clay, Cutcha, Dirt, Drilling, Dubs, Fango, Glaur, Glob, Gutter, Kacha, Lahar, Lairy, Limous, → MIRE, Moya, Ooze, Peloid, Pise, Red, Riley, Roily, Salse, Slab, Slake, Sleech, Slime, Slob, Slough, Sludge, Slur(ry), Slush, Slutch, Tocky, Trouble, Turbid, Volcanic

Muddle(d) Befog, Bemuse, Botch, Cock up, Confuse, Disorder, Embrangle, Fluster, Gump, Higgledy-piggledy, Mash, Mêlée, Mess, Mix, Mull, Pickle, Puddle, Shemozzle, Snarl-up, Stupefy, Ta(i)vert, Tangle

▷ **Muddled** *may indicate* an anagram

Mudfish Lepidosiren

Mudguard Splashboard, Wing

Mudlark Ragamuffin, Urchin

Muesli Granola

Muff Boob, Botch, Bungle, Drop, Snoskyn

Muffin Bun, Mule, Popover

Muffle(d), Muffler Baffle, Damp, Envelop, Hollow, Mob(b)le, Mute, Scarf, Silencer, Sourdine, Stifle

Mug(ger), Muggy Assault, Attack, Bash, Beaker, Bock, Can, Club, Con, Croc(odile), Cup, Dial, Dupe, Enghalskrug, Face, Fool, Footpad, Gob, Humid, Idiot, Latron, Learn, Mou, Noggin, Pan, Pot, Puss, Rob, Roll, Sandbag, Sap, Sconce, Simpleton, Steamer, Stein, Sucker, Swot, Tankard, Tax, Thief, Thug(gee), Tinnie, Tinny, Toby, Trap, Ugly, Visage, Yap

Mulatto Griff(e)

Mulberry Artocarpus, Breadfruit, Cecropia, Contrayerva, Cow-tree, Indian, Jack, Morat, Morus, Murrey, Overlord, Sycamine

Mulch Compost

Mulct Fine

Mule Ass, Bab(o)uche, Barren, Donkey, Funnel, Hemionus, Hybrid, Mocassin, Moccasin, Moyl(e), Muffin, Muil, Pack, Rake, Shoe, Slipper, Spinning, Sumpter

Muleteer Arriero

Mull Brood, Chew, Kintyre, Ponder, Promontory, Study

Mullein Aaron's rod

Mullet Goatfish

Mullion Monial

Multi-coloured Scroddled

Multiform Allotropic, Diverse, Manifold

Multiple, Multiplication, Multiplied, Multiplier, Multiply Augment, Breed, Common, Double, → INCREASE, Manifold, Modulus, Populate, Product, Proliferate, Propagate, Scalar, Severalfold

Multi-purpose Polychrest

Multitude Army, Crowd, Hirsel, Horde, Host, Legion, Populace, Shoal, Sight, Throng, Zillion

Mum(my) Boutonné, Carton(n)age, Corpse, Egyptian, Embalm, Mamma, Mine, Mute, Quiet, Sh, Silent, Tacit, Whisht, Wordless

Mumble Grumble, Moop, Moup, Mouth, Mump, Mushmouth, Mutter, Royne, Slur

Mumbo jumbo Hocus pocus, Mammet, Maumet, Mawmet, Mommet

Mummer Actor, Mime, Scuddaler, Scudler, Skudler

Mumps Parotitis

Munch Champ, Chew, Chomp, Expressionist, Moop, Moup, Scranch

Mundane Banal, Common, Earthly, Nondescript, Ordinary, Prosaic, Quotidian, Secular, Subcelestial, Trite, Workaday, Worldly

Municipal Civic

Munificent Bounteous, Generous, Liberal, Profuse

Munition(s) Arms, Artillery, Matériel, Ordnance

Munro Saki

Mural(s) Fresco, Graffiti

Murder(er), Murderess, Murderous Aram, Assassin, Blue, Bluebeard, Bravo, Burke, Butcher, Butler, Cain, Cathedral, Crackhalter, Crippen, Crows, Cutthroat, Do in, Eliminate, Filicide, First degree, Fratricide, Genocide, Hare, Hatchet man, Hit, Hitman, Homicide, Internecine, Judicial, → **KILL**, Liquidate, Locusta, Made man, Massacre, Matricide, Modo, Parricide, Patricide, Petty treason, Poison, Red, Regicide, Ripper, Ritual, Ritz, Rub out, Second degree, Sikes, Slaughter, Slay, Strangle(r), Take out, Thagi, Throttle, Thug(gee), Ugly man, Vaticide, Whodun(n)it

Murk(y) Black, Dirk(e), Gloom, Obscure, Rookish, Stygian

Murmur(ing) Brool, Bruit, Bur(r), Burble, Coo, Croodle, Croon, Grudge, Heart, Hum, → **MUTTER**, Purr, Repine, Rhubarb, Rumble, Rumour, Souffle, Sowf(f), Sowth, Sturnoid, Undertone, Whisper

Murphy Chat, Potato, Pratie, Spud, Tater

Muscle, Muscular Abductor, Abs, Accelerator, Accessorius, Adductor, Agonist, Anconeus, Aristotle's lantern, Aryepiglottic, Arytaenoid, Athletic, Attollens, Beef(y), Beefcake, Biceps, Bowr, Brachialus, Brawn, Buccinator, Cardiac, Ciliary, Clout, Complexus, Corrugator, Creature, Cremaster, Delt(oid), Depressor, Diaphragm, Digastric, Dilat(at)or, Duvaricator, Écorché, Effector, Elevator, Erecter, Erector, Evertor, Extensor, Eye-string, Flexor, Force, Gastrocnemius, Gemellus, Glut(a)eus, Gluteus maximus, Gracilis, Hamstring, Hiacus, Iliacus, Intrinsic, Involuntary, Kreatine, Lat, Latissimus dorsi, Laxator, Levator, Lumbricalis, Masseter, Mesomorph, Might, Motor, Mouse, Myalgia, Mylohyoid, Myology, Myotome, Nasalis, Oblique, Occlusor, Omohyoid, Orbicularis, Pathos, Pec(s), Pectoral, Perforans, Perforatus, Peroneus, Plantaris, Platysma, Popliteus, → **POWER**, Pronator, Protractor, Psoas, Pylorus, Quad(riceps), Quadratus, Rambo, Rectus, Retractor, Rhomboid, Rhomboideus, Ripped, Risorius, Rotator, Sarcolemma, Sarcous, Sartorius, Scalene, Scalenus, Serratus, Sinew, Six-pack, Smooth, Soleus, Sphincter, Spinalis, Splenial, Sthenic, Striated, Striped, Supinator, Suspensory, Temporal, Tenaculum, Tendon, Tensor, Teres, Thenar, Thew, Tibialis, Tonus, Trapezius, Triceps, Vastus, Voluntary, Zygomatic

Muscovite Mica, Talc

Muse(s), Muse's home, Musing Aglaia, Aonia(n), Attic, Calliope, Clio, Cogitate, Consider, Erato, Euphrosyne, Euterpe, Goddess, Helicon, Inspiration, IX, Melpomene, Mull, Nine, Nonet, Pensée, Pierides, Poly(hy)mnia, Ponder, → **REFLECT**, Ruminate, Study, Teian, Terpsichore, Thalia, Tragic, Urania, Wonder

Museum Alte-Pinakothek, Ashmolean, BM, British, Fitzwilliam, Gallery, Getty, Guggenheim, Heritage centre, Hermitage, Hunterian, Louvre, Metropolitan, Parnassus, Prado, Repository, Rijksmuseum, Science, Smithsonian, Tate, Uffizi, VA, V and A, Waxworks

Mush Cree, Glop, Goo, Mess, Porridge, Puree, Schmaltz, Slop

Mushroom Agaric, Blewits, Boletus, Burgeon, Button, Cep, Champignon, Chanterelle, Darning, Enoki, Escalate, Expand, Fly agaric, → **FUNGUS**, Girolle, Grisette, Gyromitra, Honey fungus, Horse, Hypha(l), Ink-cap, Liberty cap, Magic, Matsutake, Meadow, Morel, Oyster, Parasol, Penny-bun, Pixy-stool, Porcino,

Russula, Sacred, St George's, Scotch bonnet, Shaggymane, Shiitake, Sickener, Spread, Start-up, Straw, Truffle, Upstart, Velvet shank, Waxcap
Music Absolute, Light, Lounge, Medieval, Minstrelsy, Mood, → MUSICAL INSTRUMENTS, Passage work, Phase, Piece, Pop(ular), Programme, Score, Sound, Table

MUSIC

2 letters:
Oi

3 letters:
Air
AOR
Art
Dub
Emo
Gat
Jor
Mas
Pop
Rag
Rai
Rap
Rug
Ska
Son

4 letters:
Alap
Chin
Duet
Folk
Funk
Go-go
Jazz
Loco
Meno
Note
Opus
Prom
Raga
Rave
Riff
Rock
Romo
Soca
Soul
Surf
Tala
Trad

Trio
Tune
Zouk

5 letters:
Alaap
Alapa
Bebop
Benga
Canon
Chant
Cliff
Cu-bop
Disco
Dream
Early
Fugue
Funky
Gabba
House
Indie
Jhala
Kwela
Largo
March
Motet
Muzak®
Neume
Nonet
Outro
Piped
Ragga
Rondo
Roots
Rough
Salon
Salsa
Salve
Sheet
Sokah
Staff
Suite
Swing

Thema
Tonal
Trash
Truth
Vocal
World

6 letters:
Arioso
Aubade
Bebung
Bouree
Decani
Doo-wop
Enigma
Equali
Façade
Fugato
Fusion
Gagaku
Galant
Garage
Gospel
Gothic
Grunge
Hip-hop
Jungle
Khayal
Kirtan
Kwaito
Lydian
Mantra
Marabi
Mashup
Melody
Motown®
New Age
Popera
Pycnon
Ragini
Redowa
Reggae
Rhythm

Rootsy
Sextet
Sonata
Strain
Techno
Tenuto
Thrash
Trance
Verset
Zydeco

7 letters:
Allegro
Andante
Ars nova
Ballade
Baroque
Bhangra
Bluette
Bourree
Britpop
Cadenza
Calypso
Cantata
Ceilidh
Chamber
Chorale
Country
Dad rock
Euterpe
Fanfare
Gangsta
Hardbag
Introit
Klezmer
Landler
Marcato
Melisma
Messiah
Morceau
New Wave
Numbers
Nu-metal

Organum
Orphean
Partita
Passion
Pecking
Pibroch
Prelude
Qawwali
Quartet
Quintet
Ragtime
Rastrum
Requiem
Reverse
Romanza
Rondeau
Rondino
Rosalia
Roulade
Sanctus
Scherzo
Secondo
Setting
Skiffle
Soukous
Toccata
Trip hop
Ziganka

8 letters:
Acid rock
Aleatory
Berceuse
Blue beat
Chaconne
Cock rock
Concerto
Concrete
Continuo
Coranach
Coronach
Entracte
Fantasia
Flamenco
Folk rock

Glam rock
Hard core
Hard rock
High life
In nomine
Janizary
Karnatak
Lollipop
Madrigal
Maggiore
Mariachi
Mbaqanga
Modality
Nocturne
Notation
Old-skool
Oratorio
Parlando
Partitur
Pastiche
Postlude
Post-rock
Preludio
Psalmody
Punk rock
Rhapsody
Ricercar
Saraband
Serenade
Serenata
Symphony
Synth-pop
Waltzian

9 letters:
Acid-house
Allemande
Antiphony
Arabesque
Bagatelle
Bluegrass
Breakbeat
Cantilena
Capriccio
Dixieland

Drum'n'bass
Fioritura
Grandioso
Hillbilly
Honky-tonk
Interlude
Klezmorim
Obbligato
Partitura
Pastorale
Plainsong
Polyphony
Prick-song
Quodlibet
Reggaeton
Ricercare
Rock'n'roll
Septimole
Spiritual
Swingbeat
Tambourin
Technopop
Toccatina
Voluntary
Warehouse

10 letters:
Albumblatt
Anacrustic
Chopsticks
Coloratura
Death metal
Desert rock
Electronic
Gangsta rap
Gothic rock
Heavy metal
Hindustani
Humoresque
Incidental
Intermezzo
Jam session
Martellato
Mersey beat
New Country

Percussion
Polyhymnia
Ragamuffin
Rare groove
Ritornello
Rockabilly
Rocksteady
Seguidilla
Toccatella
Twelve-tone
Urban blues

11 letters:
Motor rhythm
Passacaglia
Psychobilly
Raggamuffin
Renaissance
Sinfonietta
Solmisation
Stadium rock
Third stream
Thrash metal

12 letters:
Blue-eyed soul
Boogie-woogie
Concertstück
Contrapuntal
Divertimento
Electroclash
Nunc Dimittis
Pralltriller

13 letters:
Detroit techno
Progressional

14 letters:
Rhythm and blues

15 letters:
Musique concrete
Progressive rock

Musical Arcadian, Azione, Brigadoon, Cats, Chess, Euphonic, Evergreen, Evita, Gigi, Grease, Hair, Harmonious, Kabuki, Kismet, Lyric, Mame, Melodic, Oliver, Opera, Operetta, Orphean, Revue, Showboat
Musical box Juke-box, Polyphon(e)
Musical chairs Level-coil

MUSICAL INSTRUMENTS

2 letters:
Ax
Gu

3 letters:
Axe
Gue
Kit
Oud
Saz
Uke
Zel

4 letters:
Buva
Chyn
Crwd
Drum
Erhu
Fife
Gong
Harp
Horn
Kora
Koto
Lure
Lute
Lyre
Moog®
Oboe
Pipa
Rate
Reed
Rote
Sang
Tuba
Vina
Viol
Zeze

5 letters:
Aulos
Banjo
Bugle
Cello
Clave
Cobza
Corno
Crowd

Crwth
Esraj
Flute
Gazog
Guiro
Gusla
Gusle
Gusli
Kazoo
Mbira
Naker
Nebel
Organ
Piano
Quena
Rebec
Regal
Sanko
Sansa
Sarod
Shalm
Shawm
Sitar
Stick
Tabla
Tabor
Tenor
Tibia
Veena
Viola
Zanze
Zinke

6 letters:
Antara
Biniou
Bisser
Bongos
Citole
Cornet
Cymbal
Euphon
Flugel
Guitar
Kanoon
Maraca
Poogye
Racket
Rebeck

Ribibe
Sancho
Santir
Santur
Shalme
Shofar
Sittar
Spinet
Syrinx
Tom-tom
Trigon
Vielle
Violin
Yidaki
Zither
Zufolo

7 letters:
Alphorn
Anklong
Bagpipe
Bandore
Bandura
Baryton
Bassoon
Bazooka
Celesta
Celeste
Cembalo
Chikara
Cithara
Cittern
Clarino
Clarion
Clavier
Clogbox
Console
Cornett
Dichord
Dulcian
Fagotto
Flutina
Gamelan
Gazogka
Gittern
Hautboy
Helicon
High-hat
Kalimba

Kantela
Kantele
Kithara
Klavier
Lyricon
Mandola
Marimba
Musette
Ocarina
Pandora
Pandore
Pandura
Pianola®
Piccolo
Poogyee
Posaune
Rackett
Ribible
Sackbut
Sambuca
Samisen
Santour
Sarangi
Saxhorn
Saxtuba
Serpent
Tambour
Tambura
Theorbo
Timbrel
Timpano
Trumpet
Tympany
Ukelele
Ukulele
Vihuela
Violone
Whistle
Zuffolo

8 letters:
Angklung
Archlute
Autoharp®
Barytone
Berimbau
Bombarde
Bouzouki
Calliope

Canorous
Carillon
Charango
Cimbalom
Clarinet
Clarsach
Clavecin
Cornetto
Cornpipe
Cromorna
Cromorne
Crumhorn
Dulcimer
Gemshorn
Guarneri
Guimbard
Handbell
Hautbois
Humstrum
Jew's harp
Key-bugle
Langspel
Lyra-viol
Mandolin
Manzello
Martenot
Melodeon
Melodica
Melodion
Mirliton
Oliphant
Ottavino
Pan pipes
Phorminx
Polyphon
Psaltery
Recorder
Reco-reco
Slughorn
Spinette
Sticcado
Sticcato
Surbahar
Tamboura
Tamburin

Tenoroon
Theremin
Triangle
Trichord
Trombone
Virginal
Vocalion
Zambomba
Zampogna

9 letters:
Accordion
Aerophone
Alpenhorn
Balalaika
Bandoneon
Bandurria
Banjulele
Bombardon
Chalumeau
Clarionet
Cornemuse
Decachord
Dulcitone®
Euphonium
Flageolet
Flexatone
Flute-à-bec
Gittarone
Gutbucket
Harmonica
Harmonium
Idiophone
Kent-bugle
Krummhorn
Langspiel
Mandoline
Mellotron®
Monochord
Mouth-harp
Nose flute
Orpharion
Pantaleon
Pastorale
Polyphone

Saxophone
Seraphine
Slughorne
Snare-drum
Sonometer
Sopranino
Stockhorn
Trompette
Vibraharp
Washboard
Xylophone
Xylorimba

10 letters:
Bullroarer
Chitarrone
Clavichord
Colascione
Concertina
Cor anglais
Didgeridoo
Flugelhorn
French horn
Gramophone
Hurdy-gurdy
Kettledrum
Lagerphone
Light organ
Mellophone
Nun's fiddle
Ophicleide
Orpheoreon
Pentachord
Shakuhachi
Squeeze-box
Stylophone®
Symphonium
Tambourine
Thumb piano
Vibraphone
Wokka board

11 letters:
Chordophone
Clairschach

Contrabasso
Harmoniphon
Harpsichord
Heckelphone
Nickelodeon
Octave flute
Orchestrina
Orchestrion
Phonofiddle
Straduarius
Synthesizer
Trump-marine
Violoncello
Wobble-board

12 letters:
Chapman stick®
Chinese block
Clavicembalo
Glockenspiel
Harmoniphone
Metallophone
Penny-whistle
Sarrusophone
Stock and horn
Stradivarius
Tromba-marina
Tubular bells

13 letters:
Contrabassoon
Ondes Martenot
Panharmonicon
Physharmonica

14 letters:
Glass harmonica
Jingling Johnny
Ondes musicales
Piano accordion

18 letters:
Chinese temple
  block

Music-hall Alhambra, Disco, Empire, Odeon
Musician(s), Musicologist Accompanist, Arion, Arist, Beiderbecke, Brain,
   Buononcini, Casals, Chanter, Clapton, Combo, → **COMPOSER**, Conductor, Crowder,
   Duet, Ensemble, Executant, Flautist, Gate, Grove, Guido d'Arezzo, Guslar, Handel,
   Jazzer, Jazzman, Joplin, Mahler, Mariachi, Menuhin, Minstrel, Muso, Noisenik,

Nonet, Octet, Orphean, Pianist, Quartet, Quintet, Rapper, Reed(s)man, Répétiteur, Rubinstein, Septet, Session, Sextet, Sideman, Spohr, String, Techno, Tortelier, Troubador, Trouvère, Violinist, Waits

Musk Civet, Mimulus, Must

Musket Brown Bess, Caliver, Carabine, Eyas, Flintlock, Fusil, Hawk, Jezail, Nyas, Queen's-arm, Weapon

Musketeer Aramis, Athos, D'Artagnan, Fusilier, Ja(e)ger, Porthos, Rifleman, Sam

Muslim (ritual), Moslem Alaouite, Alawite, Ali, Almohad(e), Balochi, Baluchi, Berber, Black, Caliph, Dato, Dervish, Druse, Fatimid, Ghazi, Hadji, Hafiz, Hajji, He'zbolah, Iranian, Islamic, Ismaili, Karmathian, Khotbah, Khotbeh, Khutbah, Mahometan, Mawlawi, Meivievi, Mogul, Mohammedan, Moor, Morisco, Moro, Mufti, Mus(s)ulman, Mutazilite, Nawab, Panislam, Paynim, Pomak, Said, Saracen, Say(y)id, Senus(s)i, Shafiite, Shia(h), Shiite, Sofi, Sonnite, Sufi, Sulu, Sunna, Sunni(te), Tajik, Turk, Ummah, Wahabee, Wahabi(te), Wahhabi

Muslin Butter, Cloth, Coteline, Gurrah, Jamdani, Leno, Mousseline, Mull, Nainsook, Organdie, Tarlatan, Tiffany

Musquash Ondatra

Mussel(s) Bearded, Bivalve, Clabby-doo, Clam, Clappy-doo, Deerhorn, Edible, Horse, Moules marinières, Mytilus, Naiad, Niggerhead, Pearl, Swan, Unio, Zebra

Mussorgsky Modest

Must(y) Amok, Essential, Foughty, Froughy, Frowsty, Frowy, Funky, Fust, Gotta, Man, Maun(na), Mote, Mould, Mucid, Mun, Need(s)-be, Shall, Should, Stum, Wine

▷ **Must** *may indicate* an anagram

Mustard Black, Brown, Charlock, Cress, English, Erysimum, French, Garlic, Gas, Nitrogen, Praiseach, Quinacrine, Runch, Sarepta, Sauce-alone, Senvy, Treacle, Wall, White, Wild, Wintercress

Mustard plaster Sinapism

Musteline Skunk

Muster Array, Assemble, Bangtail, Call up, Mass, Raise, Rally, Really, Recruit, Round-up, Wappenshaw

Mutability Wheel

Mutate, Mutant, Mutation Auxotroph(ic), Change, Saltation, Somatic, Sport, Suppressor, Terata, Transform, Vowel

▷ **Mutation** *may indicate* an anagram

Mute(d) Deaden, Dumb, Harpo, Noiseless, Silent, Sordino, Sordo, Sourdine, Stifle

Mutilate(d), Mutilation Castrate, Concise, Deface, Dismember, Distort, Garble, Hamble, Injure, Maim, Mangle, Mayhem, Obtruncate, Riglin, Tear

▷ **Mutilate(d)** *may indicate* an anagram

Mutineer, Mutiny Bounty, Caine, Christian, Curragh, Indian, Insurrection, Jhansi, Meerut, Nore, Pandy, → **REVOLT**, Rising, Sepoy

Mutter(ing) Chunter, Fremescent, Grumble, Maunder, Mumble, Mump, Murmur, Mussitate, Rhubarb, Roin, Royne, Rumble, Whittie-whattie, Witter

Mutton Braxy, Colonial goose, Em, Ewes, Fanny Adams, Gigot, Macon, Rack, Saddle, Sheep, Theave, Traik

Mutual (aid) Common, Log-roll, Reciprocal, Symbiosis

Muzzle Decorticate, Gag, Jaw, Mouth, Restrain, Snout

My Christ, Coo, Gemini, Golly, Gosh, Ha, Lor, Lumme, M, Musha, Odso, Oh, Our, Tush

Mynah Stare, Starling

Mynheer Stadholder

Myopia, Myopic Hidebound, Mouse-sight, Narrow, Short-sighted, Thick-eyed

Myriad Host, Zillion
Myristic Nutmeg
Myrrh Stacte
Myrtle Bog, Callistemon, Crape, Creeping, Crepe, Eucalyptus, Gale, Jambolana, Tasmanian, Tooart, Trailing, Tuart
Mysterious, Mystery Abdabs, Abdals, Acroamatic, Arcane, Arcanum, Cabbala, Closed book, Craft, Creepy, Cryptic, Dark, Deep, Delphic, Eleusinian, Enigma, Esoteric, Grocer, G(u)ild, Incarnation, Inscrutable, Miracle, Mystagogue, Numinous, Occult, Original sin, Orphic, Penetralia, Riddle, → SECRET, Telestic, Trinity, UFO, Uncanny, Whodunit
▷ **Mysterious(ly)** *may indicate* an anagram
Mystic (word), Mystical Abraxas, Agnostic, Cab(e)iri, Eckhart, Epopt, Fakir, Familist, Gnostic, Hesychast, Mahatma, Occultist, Quietism, Rasputin, Secret, Seer, Sofi, Sufi, Swami, Tantrist, Theosophy, Transcendental, Zohar
Mystify Baffle, Bamboozle, Bewilder, Metagrabolise, Metagrobolise, Perplex, Puzzle
Myth(ology), Mythical (beast) Allegory, Behemoth, Bunyip, Centaur, Cockatrice, Dragon, Euhemerism, Fable, Fantasy, Fictitious, Folklore, Garuda, Geryon, Griffin, Hippocampus, Impundulu, Kelpie, Kylin, Legend, Leviathan, Lore, Lyonnesse, Otnit, Pantheon, Pegasus, Phoenix, Sea horse, Selkie, Solar, Speewah, Sphinx, Sun, Thunderbird, Tokoloshe, Tragelaph, Unicorn, Urban, Wivern, Wyvern, Yale, Yeti

Nn

N Name, Nitrogen, Noon, North, November
Nab Arrest, Capture, Collar, Confiscate, Grab, Seize
Nabob Deputy, Nawab, Wealthy
Nadir Bottom, Depths, Dregs, Minimum
Nag(ging) Badger, Bidet, Brimstone, Callet, Cap, Captious, Complain, Fret, Fuss, Harangue, Harp, Henpeck, Horse, Jade, Jaw, Keffel, Peck, Pester, Plague, Rosinante, Rouncy, → **SCOLD**, Tit, Xant(h)ippe, Yaff
Nail(ed) Brad, Brod, Catch, Clinker, Clout, Coffin, Fasten, Hob, Keratin, Onyx, Pin, Rivet, Screw, Secure, Shoe, Sisera, Sixpenny, Sparable, Sparrow-bill, Spick, Spike, Sprig, Staple, Stub, Stud, Tack(et), Talon, Tenpenny, Tenterhook, Thumb, Tingle, Toe, Unguis, Wire
Naive(té) Artless, Green, Guileless, Gullible, Ingenuous, Innocence, Open, Pollyanna, Simpliste, Simplistic, Unsophisticated, Wide-eyed
Naked Adamical, Artless, Bare, Blunt, Buff, Clear, Cuerpo, Defenceless, Encuerpo, Exposed, Gymno-, Kaal gat, Nuddy, Nude, Querpo, Raw, Scud, Simple, Skyclad, Stark(ers), Uncovered
Namby-pamby Milksop, Nance, Sissy, Weak, Weakling, White-shoe
Name(d), Names Agnomen, Alias, Allonym, Anonym, Appellation, Appoint, Attribute, Baptise, Behight, Byline, Call, Celeb(rity), Christen, Cite, Cleep, Clepe, Cognomen, Day, Designate, Dinges, Dingus, Dit, Domain, Dub, Entitle, Epithet, Eponym, Exonym, Family, First, Generic, Given, Handle, Hete, Hight, Hypocorism, Identify, Identity, Label, Maiden, Marque, Masthead, Mention, Metronymic, Middle, Moni(c)ker, Mud, N, Nap, Nemn, Nempt, Nom, Nomen(clature), Noun, Onomastics, Onymous, Patronymic, Pennant, Personage, Pet, Place, Praenomen, Proper, Proprietary, Pseudonym, Quote, Red(d), Repute, Scilicet, Sign, Signature, Sir, Specify, Stage, Street, Substantive, Tag, Teknonymy, Term, → **TITLE**, Titular, Titule, Toponymy, Trade, Trivial
Name-dropper Eponym
Nameless Anon, Unchrisom
Namely Ie, Sc, Scilicet, To-wit, Videlicet, Viz
Namesake Homonym
Name unknown Anon, A N Other, NU
Nancy Coddle, Effeminate, Milksop
Nanny Ayah, Foster, Goat, Nurse
Naos Cell(a)
Nap(py) Ale, Bonaparte, Diaper, Doze, Drowse, Fluff, Frieze(d), Fuzz, Happen, Hippin(g), Kip, Moze, Oose, Ooze, Oozy, Power, Put(t), Shag, Siesta, → **SLEEP**, Slumber, Snooze, Tease, Teasel, Teaze, Tipsy, Tuft
Nape Niddick, Noddle, Nucha, Scrag, Scruff, Scuff, Scuft
Napier Logarithm
Napkin Cloth, Diaper, Doily, Doyley, Linen, Muckender, Paper, Sanitary,

Serviette, Table

Napless Threadbare

Napoleon Badinguet, Bonaparte, Boustrapa, Cognac, Coin, Consul, Corporal Violet, Corsican, December, Little Corporal, Nantz, Nap, Pig, Rantipole

▷ **Napoleon** *may indicate* a pig

Napper Bonce, Shearman

Narcissus Echo, Egocentric, Jonquil

Narcotic Ava, Benj, B(h)ang, Charas, Churrus, Coca, Codeine, Datura, Dope, → **DRUG**, Heroin, Hop, Kava, Laudanum, Mandrake, Marijuana, Meconium, Methadone, Morphia, Narceen, Narceine, Opiate, Pituri, Sedative, Tea, Trional

Nark Grass, Inform, Irritate, Nose, Pique, Roil, Squealer, Stag

Narrate, Narration, Narrative, Narrator Allegory, Anecdote, Cantata, Describe, Diegesis, Fable, History, Oblique, Periplus, Plot, Raconteur, Récit, Recite, Recount, Saga, Scheherazade, Splatterpunk, Story, Tell, Voice-over

Narrow(ing), Narrow-minded Alf, Bigoted, Borné, Bottleneck, Constringe, Cramp, Ensiform, Grundy(ism), Hidebound, Illiberal, Insular, Kyle, Limited, Meagre, Nary, One-idead, Parochial, Phimosis, Pinch, Pinch-point, Provincial, Prudish, Puritan, Scant, Sectarian, Shrink, Slender, Slit, Specialise, Squeak, Stenosed, Strait, Straiten, Strait-laced, Strict, Suburban, Verkramp, Wafer-thin, Waist

Narwhal Monodon

Nasal Adenoidal, Sonorant, Twang

Nash Beau

Nashville Bath

Nastiness, Nasty Disagreeable, Drevill, Filth, Fink, Ghastly, Lemon, Lo(a)th, Malign(ant), Noisome, Noxious, Obscene, Odious, Offensive, Ribby, Scummy, Sif, Sordid, Vile

Nat(haniel) Hawthorne, Winkle

Natal Inborn, Native, Patrial

Natant Afloat, Swimming

Nation(s), National(ist), Nationalism Anthem, Baathist, Broederbond, Casement, Chetnik, Country, Cuban, Debt, Eta, Federal, Five, Folk, Grand, Hindutva, Indian, IRA, Israeli, Jingoist, Kuomintang, Land, Mexican, Oman, Pamyat, Parnell, Patriot, → **PEOPLE**, Plaid Cymru, Polonia, Race, Rainbow, Risorgimento, Scottish, Shivsena, Six, SNP, Subject, Swadeshi, United, Verkrampte, Vietminh, Wafd, Yemini, Young Ireland, Zionist

Native(s) Abo(rigin), Aborigine, African, Amerind, Annamese, Arab, Ascian, Australian, Autochthon, Aztec, Basuto, Belonging, Bengali, Boy, Bushman, Cairene, Carib, Carioca, Chaldean, Citizen, Colchester, Conch, Creole, Criollo, Domestic, Dyak, Edo, Enchorial, Eskimo, Fleming, Fuzzy-wuzzy, Genuine, Habitual, Home-bred, Inborn, Inca, Indigene, Indigenous, Inhabitant, Intuitive, John Chinaman, Kaffir, Libyan, Local, Malay, Maori, Mary, Micronesian, Moroccan, Norwegian, Oyster, Polack, Portuguese, Scythian, Son, Spaniard, Te(i)an, Thai, Tibetan, Uzbeg, Uzbek, Whitstable, Yugoslav

Nativity Birth, Jataka, Putz

Natron Urao

Natter Chat, Gossip, Jack, Prate

Natty Bumppo, Chic, Dapper, Leatherstocking, Smart, Spruce

Natural(ly), Naturalised, Naturalism Artless, Ass, Denizen, Easy, Genuine, Homely, Idiot, Illegitimate, Inborn, Inbred, Indigenous, Ingenerate, Inherent, Innate, Moron, Native, Nidget, Nitwit, Nude, Ordinary, Organic, Prat, Real, Simpleton, Simpliciter, Sincere, True, Undyed, Untaught, Verism

Naturalist Bates, Buffon, Darwin, Wallace, White
Nature Adam, Akin, Character, Disposition, Esse(nce), Ethos, Haecceity, Human, Hypostasis, Inscape, Manhood, Mould, Quiddity, Quintessence, Second, SN, Temperament
Naught Cypher, Failure, Nil, Nothing, Zero
Naughty Bad, Disobedient, Girly, Improper, Indecorous, Light, Marietta, Nonny, Rascal, Remiss, Spright, Sprite, Wayward
Nausea, Nauseous Disgust, Fulsome, Malaise, Queasy, Sickness, Squeamish, Wamble, Wambly
Nave Aisle, Apse, Centre, Hub, Modiolus, Nef
Navel Belly-button, Jaffa, Naff, Nave, Omphalos, Orange, Tummy button, Umbilicus
Navigate, Navigator Albuquerque, Bougainville, Cabot, Cartier, Columbus, Control, Da Gama, Dias, Direct, Franklin, Frobisher, Gilbert, Hartog, Haul, Henry, Hudson, Keel, Magellan, Navvy, Orienteer, Pilot, Raleigh, Sail, Star-read, → STEER, Tasman, Traverse, Vancouver, Vespucci
Navigation (aid, system) Asdic, Cabotage, Celestial, Decca, Dectra, Echosounder, Fido, Gee, Inertial, Inland, Loran, Loxodromics, Navarho, Omnirange, Portolan(o), Portulan, Radar, Satnav, Seamark, Shoran, Tacan, Teleran®, Vor
Navvy Workhorse
Navy, Naval AB, Armada, Blue, Fleet, French, Maritime, Merchant, N, Red, RN, Senior Service, Wavy, Wren
Nawab Huzoor, Nabob, Viceroy
Nazi Brownshirt, Gauleiter, Hess, Hitler, Jackboot, SS, Stormtrooper, Wer(e)wolf
NB Niobium, Nota bene
NCO Bombardier, Corp(oral), Havildar, Noncom, Orderly, Sergeant, SM
Neanderthal Mousterian
Neap Low, Tide
Neapolitan Ice
Near(er), Nearest, Nearby, Nearly, Nearness About, Adjacent, All-but, Almost, Anigh, Approach, Approximate, Beside, By, Close, Cy pres, Degree, Even, Ewest, Feckly, Forby, Gain, Handy, Hither, Imminent, Inby(e), Mean, Miserly, Narre, Neist, Next, Nie, Niggardly, Nigh, Oncoming, Outby, Propinquity, Proximity, Short-range, Stingy, Thereabout(s), To, Upon, Warm, Well-nigh
Neat(ly) Bandbox, Cattle, Clean-cut, Clever, Dainty, Dapper, Deft, Dink(y), Doddy, Donsie, Elegant, Feat(e)ous, Featly, Featuous, Gayal, Genty, Gyal, Intact, Jemmy, Jimpy, Lower, Nett, Ninepence, Orderly, Ox(en), Preppy, Pretty, Rother, Shipshape, Short, Smug, Snod, Spruce, Straight, → TIDY, Trig, Trim, Unwatered, Well-groomed
Neb Beak, Bill, Nose, Snout
Nebula, Nebulous Aeriform, Celestial, Cloudy, Dark, Emission, Gum, Hazy, Horsehead, Obscure, Planetary, Reflection, Shadowy, Vague
Necessary, Necessarily Bog, Cash, De rigueur, → ESSENTIAL, Estovers, Important, Indispensable, Intrinsic, Money, Needful, Ought, Perforce, Prerequisite, Requisite, Vital, Wherewithal
Necessitate, Necessity Ananke, Compel, Constrain, Cost, Emergency, Entail, Exigent, Fate, Indigence, Logical, Mathematical, Moral, Must, Natural, Need, Need-be, Oblige, Perforce, Require, Requisite
Neck(ed) Bottle, Brass, Canoodle, Cervical, Cervix, Channel, Col, Crag, Craig, Crop, Cuff, Embrace, Ewe, Gall, Gorgerin, Halse, Hawse, Inarm, Inclip, Isthmus, Kiss, Mash, Nape, Pet, Polo, Rack, Rubber, Scoop, Scrag, Scruff, Smooch, Snog, Stiff, Strait, Surgical, Swan, Swire, Theorbo, Torticollis, Trachelate, Vee

▷ **Necking** *may indicate* one word around another

Necklace Afro-chain, Anodyne, Brisingamen, Chain, Choker, Collar, Corals, Lava(l)lière, Lunula, Mangalsutra, Negligee, Pearls, Rope, Sautoir, String, Torc, Torque

Neckline Boat, Collar, Cowl, Crew, Décolletage, Lanyard, Palter, Plunging, Sweetheart, Turtle, Vee

Neckwear Ascot, Barcelona, Boa, Bow, Collar, Cravat, Fur, Rail, Steenkirk, Stock, Tie

Necromancer Goetic, Magician, Ormandine, Osmand, Witch, Wizard

Necrosis Infarct, Sphacelus

Nectar Ambrosia, Amrita, Honey, Mead

Ned(dy) Donkey, Kelly, Ludd

Need(ed), Needy Beggarly, Call, Demand, Desiderata, Egence, Egency, Exigency, Gap, Gerundive, Impecunious, Indigent, → **LACK**, Mister, Pressing, PRN, Require, Strait, Strapped, Want

Needle(s) Acerose, Acicular, Aciform, Between, Bodkin, Cleopatra's, Darning, Dip, Dry-point, Electric, Etching, Goad, Gramophone, Hagedorn, Hype, Hypodermic, Ice, Icicle, Inoculate, Knitting, Leucotome, Magnetic, Miff, Monolith, Neeld, Neele, Netting, Obelisk, Packing, Pine, Pinnacle, Pique, Pointer, Prick, R(h)aphis, Sew, Sharp, Spanish, Spicule, Spike, Spine, Stylus, Tattoo, Tease, Thorn, Wire

Needlewoman Cleopatra, Seamstress

Needlework Baste, Crewel, Drawn(-thread), Embroidery, Fag(g)oting, Fancy work, Gros point, Mola, Patchwork, Petit point, Piqué, Plainwork, Rivière, Sampler, Smocking, Spanish, Tapestry, Tattoo, White-seam, Woolwork, Worsted-work

Ne'er-do-well Badmash, Budmash, Bum, Good-for-nothing, Scullion, Shiftless, Skellum, Wastrel

Negation, Negative Ambrotype, Anion, Apophatic, Cathode, Denial, Double, Enantiosis, False, Ne, No, Non, Nope, Nullify, Pejorative, Photograph, Refusal, Resinous, Unresponsive, Veto, Yin

Neglect(ed), Neglectful, Negligence, Negligent Careless, Casual, Cinderella, Contributory, Cuff, Default, Dereliction, Disregard, Disuse, Failure, Forget, Forlorn, Heedless, Inadvertence, Inattention, Incivism, Laches, Malpractice, Misprision, Omission, Oversight, Pass, Pass-up, Rack and ruin, → **REMISS**, Scamp, Shirk, Slight, Slipshod, Undone, Unilateral, Waif, Wanton

▷ **Neglected** *may indicate* an anagram

Negligee Déshabillé, Manteau, Mob, Nightgown, Peignoir, Robe

Negligible Fig, Minimal

Negotiate, Negotiator Arbitrate, Arrange, Bargain, Clear, Confer, Deal, Diplomat, Haggle, Intercede, Interdeal, Intermediary, Liaise, Manoeuvre, Mediator, Parley, Trade, Transact, Treat(y), Weather

Negro(id) → **AFRICAN**, Baganda, Bambara, Barotse, Bemba, Bergdama, Bini, Black, Blackamoor, Buck, Chewa, Creole, Cuffee, Cuffy, Damara, Dinge, Duala, Dyula, Ebon(y), Edo, Efik, Ethiop, Ewe, Fang, Ga, Ganda, Gullah, Hausa, Hottentot, Hutu, Ibibio, Ibo, Igbo, Igorot, Jim Crow, Kikuyu, Kongo, Luba, Luganda, Malinke, Maninke, Mestee, Moke, Moor, Mossi, Mustee, Ndebele, Nilote, Nupe, Nyanja, Nyoro, Ovambo, Pondo, Quashee, Quashie, Sambo, Snowball, Sotho, Spade, Susu, Temne, Thick-lips, Tiv, Tonga, Tsonga, Tswana, Twi, Uncle Tom, Venda, Watu(t)si, Wolof, Xhosa, Yoruba, Zambo, Zulu

Negus Emperor, Rumfruction, Selassie

Nehru Pandit

Neigh Bray, Hinny, Nicker, Whicker, Whinny

Neighbour(ly), Neighbouring, Neighbours Abut(ter), Adjoin, Alongside,

Amicable, Bor, Border, But, Friendly, Joneses, Nearby, Next-door, Vicinal

Neighbourhood(s) Acorn®, Area, Community, District, Environs, Locality, Precinct, Vicinage, Vicinity

Neither Nor

Nell(ie), Nelly Bly, Dean, Trent

Nelson Columnist, Eddy, Horatio

Nemesis Alastor, Avenger, Deserts, Downfall, Fate, Retribution, Revenge

Neodymium Nd

Neolithic Avebury, Halafian, Skara Brae, Stonehenge

Neon Ne

Nepalese Gurkha

Neper N

Nephrite Yu

Nepotism Kin, Partisan, Patronage

Neptune God, Planet, Poseidon

Neptunium Np

Nerd Anorak, Otaku

Nereid Cymodoce, Nymph, Panope

Nerve(s), Nervous(ness), Nervure, Nerve centre, Nervy Abdabs, Abducens, Accessory, Acoustic, Afferent, Aflutter, Afraid, Alveolar, Appestat, Auditory, Axon, Baroreceptor, Bottle, Bouton, Brass neck, Buccal, Chord, Chutzpah, Collywobbles, Column, Commissure, Cones, Courage, Cranial, Cyton, Depressor, Edgy, Effector, Efferent, Electrotonus, Epicritic, Excitor, Facial, Fearful, Gall, Ganglion, Glossopharyngeal, Grit, Guts, Habdabs, Heart-string, High, Highly-strung, Hyp, Hypoglossal, Impudence, Jitters, Jittery, Jumpy, Median, Mid-rib, Motor, Moxie, Myelon, Nappy, Neck, Neurological, Nidus, Oculomotor, Olfactory, On edge, Optic, Pavid, Perikaryon, Proprioceptor, Rad, Radial, Receptor, Restiform, Restless, Sacral, Sangfroid, Sauce, Sciatic, Screaming abdabs, Screaming meemies, Sensory, Shaky, Shpilkes, Solar plexus, Splanchnic, Spunk, Squirrel(l)y, Steel, Strung-up, Synapse, Tense, Tizzy, Toey, Tongue-tied, Trembler, Tremulous, Trigeminal, Trochlear, Twitchy, Ulnar, Uptight, Vagus, Vapours, Vestibulocochlear, Wandering, Willies, Windy, Wired, Yips

Nervous disease, Nervous disorder Chorea, Epilepsy, Neuritis, Tetany

▷ **Nervously** *may indicate* an anagram

Ness Cape, Headland, Ras

Nessus Centaur

Nest Aerie, Aery, Aiery, Ayrie, Bike, Bink, Brood, Byke, Cabinet, Cage, Caliology, Clutch, Dray, Drey, Eyrie, Eyry, Lodge, Love, Nid, Nide, Nidify, Nidus, Norwegian, Sett, Termitarium, Turkey, Wurley

Nestle Burrow, Coorie, Cose, Courie, Cuddle, Nuzzle, Snug(gle)

Nestor Counsellor, Kea, King, Parrot, Sage

Net(ting), Nets, Network(ing) Anastomosis, Bamboo, BR, Bunt, Butterfly, Cast, Casting, Catch, Caul, Clap, Clathrate, Clear, Cobweb, → **COMPUTER NETWORK**, Crinoline, Criss-cross, Crossover, Drift, Earn, Eel-set, Enmesh, Equaliser, Fetch, File server, Filet, Final, Fish, Flew, Flue, Fyke, Gill, → **GRID**, Hammock, Heliscoop, Honeycomb, Insect, Kiddle, Lace, Land, Landing, Lattice, Leap, Line, Linin, Mains, Malines, Mattress, Maze, → **MESH**, Mist, Mosquito, Neuropil, Old boys', PCN, Plexus, Portal system, Pound, Pout, Purse-seine, Quadripole, Reseau, Rete, Retiary, Reticle, Reticulate, Reticulum, Ring, Safety, Sagene, Scoop, Screen, Sean, Seine, Senior, Set(t), Shark, Snood, Speed, Stake, Sweep-seine, Symplast, System, Tangle, Tela, Telex, Toil, Torpedo, Trammel,

Trap, Trawl, Trepan, Tulle, Tunnel, Wire

Netball Let

Nether Below, Inferior, Infernal, Lower, Under

Nettle(rash) Anger, Annoy, Day, Dead, Hemp, Hives, Horse, Irritate, Labiate, Nark, Ongaonga, Pellitory, Pique, Ramee, Rami, Ramie, Rhea, Rile, Roman, Ruffle, Sting, Urtica(ceae), Urticaria

Neuralgia, Neuritis Migraine, Sciatica, Tic

Neurosis Combat, Compulsion, Obsessive-compulsive, Shellshock

Neuter Castrate, Gib, Impartial, Neutral, Sexless, Spay

Neutral(ise) Alkalify, Angel gear, Buffer zone, Counteract, Degauss, Grey, Impartial, Inactive, Schwa, Sheva, Shiva, Unbiased

Neutron(s) Delayed, Fast, Nucleon, Prompt, Slow, Thermal, Virgin

Never(more) Nary, Nathemo(re), No more, Nowise, St Tibb's Eve

Never-ending Age-long

Nevertheless Algate, Anyhow, But, Even, However, Quand même, Still, Tout de même, Yet

▷ **New** *may indicate* an anagram

New(s), Newborn, News agency Bulletin, Copy, Coranto, Dope, Euphobia, Evangel, Flash, Forest, Fresh, Fudge, Gen, Green, Griff, Info, Innovation, Intelligence, Itar Tass, Item, Kerygma, Latest, Mint, Modern, N, Novel, Oil(s), Original, PA, Paragraph, Pastures, Pristine, Propaganda, Raw, Recent, Report, Reuter, Scoop, Span, Split, Stranger, Tass, Teletext®, Tidings, Ultramodern, Unco, Usenet, Wire service, Word

New boy Gyte

Newcomer Dog, Freshman, Griffin, Immigrant, Jackaroo, Jackeroo, Jillaroo, Johnny-come-lately, Newbie, Novice, Parvenu, Pilgrim, Settler, Tenderfoot, Upstart

Newfoundland Dog, Nana, Vinland

Newgate Calendar

Newly wed Benedick, Benedict, Bride, Groom, Honeymooner, Neogamist

Newman Cardinal, Noggs

New moon Rosh Chodesh

Newsman, News-reader Announcer, Editor, Journalist, Legman, Press, Reporter, Sub, Sysop

Newsmonger, News-vendor Butcher, Gossip, Quidnunc

Newspaper Blat(t), Broadsheet, Courier, Daily, Express, Fanzine, Feuilleton, Freesheet, Gazette, Guardian, Heavy, Herald, Journal, Jupiter, Le Monde, Mercury, National, Organ, Patent inside, Patent outside, Post, Pravda, Press, Print, Rag, Red-top, Scandal sheet, Sheet, Spoiler, Squeak, Sun, Tabloid, Today

Newsreel Actualities

Newt(s) Ask(er), Eft, Evet, Swift, Triton, Urodela

Newton N

New World USA

New Year Hogmanay, Ne'er-day, Rosh Hashana(h), Tet

New York(er) Big Apple, Gotham, Knickerbocker

New Zealand(er) Aotearoa, Enzed, Jafa, Kiwi, Maori, Mooloo, Moriori, Pakeha, Pig Island, Ronz(er), Shagroon, Zelanian

Next Adjacent, Adjoining, After, Alongside, Beside, Following, Immediate, Later, Nearest, Neist, Proximate, Proximo, Sine, Subsequent, Syne

Nib(s) Cocoa, J, Pen, Point, Tip

Nibble Bite, Brouse, Browse, Byte, Crop, Eat, Gnaw, Knap(ple), Moop, Moup, Munch, Nag, Nepit, Nosh, Peck, Pick, Snack

Nice(ty) Accurate, Amene, Appealing, Cool, Dainty, Fastidious, Fine, Finical, Genteel, Lepid, Mooi, Ninepence, Pat, Pleasant, Precise, Quaint, Rare, Refined, Subtil(e), Subtle, Sweet, T

Niche Alcove, Almehrahb, Almery, Ambry, Apse, Aumbry, Awmrie, Awmry, Columbarium, Cranny, Exedra, Fenestella, Mihrab, Recess, Slot

Nicholas Santa

Nick(ed) Appropriate, Arrest, Bin, Blag, Can, Chip, Cly, Colin, Copshop, Cut, Denay, Dent, Deny, → **DEVIL**, Erose, Groove, Hoosegow, Kitty, Knock, Nab, Nap, Nim, Nock, Notch, Pinch, Pook, Pouk, Prison, Scratch, Sneak, → **STEAL**, Steek, Swan-upping, Swipe, Thieve, Whip, Wirricow, Worricow, Worrycow

Nickel (silver) Coin, Garnierite, Jitney, Millerite, Ni, Packfong, Paktong, Zaratite

Nicker Bonduc, Neigh, Whinny

Nickname Alias, Byname, Byword, Cognomen, So(u)briquet, To-name

Nicotine Tobacco, Weed

Nifty Smart, Stylish

Nigeria(n) Biafran, Cross River, Efik, Hausa, Ibibio, Ibo, Igbo, Nupe, WAN, Yoruba

Niggard(ly) Dry-fist, Illiberal, Mean, Miser, Near-(be)gaun, Nippy, Nirlit, Parsimonious, Pinchcommons, Pinchgut, Pinchpenny, Scrunt, Skinflint, Tightwad

Niggle Carp, Gripe, Nag, Potter, Trifle

Night(s), Nightfall Acronical, Acronychal, Arabian, Burns, Darkling, Darkmans, First, Gaudy, Guest, Guy Fawkes, Hen, Leila, Nacht, Nicka-nan, Nutcrack, Nyx, School, Stag, Twelfth, Twilight, Walpurgis, Watch, White

Night-blindness Day-sight, Nyctalopia

Night-cap Biggin, Cocoa, Kilmarnock cowl, Nip, Pirnie, Sundowner

Nightclub Clip joint, Dive, Honkytonk

Night-dew Serein, Serene

Nightdress Wylie-coat

Nightingale Bulbul, Florence, Jugger, Lind, Philomel, Scutari, Swedish, Watch

Nightjar Chuck-will's-widow, Churn-owl, Evejar, Fern-owl, Goatsucker, Poorwill, Potoo

Night-light Moonbeam

Nightmare, Nightmarish Cacod(a)emon, Ephialtes, Incubus, Kafkaesque, Oneirodynia, Phantasmagoria

Night-rider Revere

Nightshade Atropin(e), Belladonna, Bittersweet, Black, Circaea, Deadly, Dwale, Enchanter's, Henbane, Morel, Solanum, Woody

Nightwatchman Charley, Charlie, Rug-gown

Nightwork Lucubrate

Nihilist Anarchist, Red, Sceptic

Nil Nothing, Nought, Zero

Nile Albert, Blue, Luvironza, Victoria, White

Nimble(ness), Nimbly Active, → **AGILE**, Alert, Deft, Deliver, Fleet, Legerity, Light, Light-footed, Lissom(e), Lithe, Quiver, Sciolto, Springe, Spry, Supple, Swack, Wan(d)le, Wannel, Wight, Ya(u)ld

Nimbus Aura, Aureole, Cloud, Gloriole, Halo

Nimrod Hunter

Nincompoop Ass, Imbecile, Ninny, Stupid

Nine, Ninth Choral, Ennead, Muses, Nonary, Nonet, Novenary, Pins, Sancho, Skittles, Tailors, Worthies

Nine hundred Sampi

Nine of diamonds Curse of Scotland

Nineteen(th) Bar, Decennoval
Ninetieth, Ninety N, Nonagesimal
Ninevite Assyrian
Ninny (hammer) Fool, Goose, Idiot, Stupid, Tony
Ninon Nan
Niobium Nb
Nip(per) Bite, Check, Chela, Chill, Claw, Cutpurse, Dip, Dram, Fang, Gook, Jap, Lad, Lop, Nep, Nirl, Peck, Pickpocket, Pincers, Pinch, Pook, Pop, Scotch, Sneap, Susan, Tad, Taste, Tot, Tweak, Urchin, Vice, Vise
Nipa At(t)ap, Palm
Nipple Dug, Grease, Jogger's, Mastoid, Pap, Teat
Nis Brownie, Goblin, Kobold, Sprite
Nit Egg, Insect, Louse
Nitre Saltpetre
Nitric, Nitrogen Azote, Azotic, Gas, N, Quinoline
Nitroglycerine Glonoin
Nitwit Ass, Flat, Fool, Simpleton, → STUPID
No Aikona, Denial, Na(e), Nah, Naw, Negative, Nix, Nope, Nyet, O, Refusal
Noah Arkite, Beery, Utnapishtim
Nob(by) Grandee, Parage, Prince, Swell, Toff
Nobble Dope, Hilch, Injure, Interfere
▷ **Nobbled** *may indicate* an anagram
Nobelium No
Noble(man), Noblewoman, Nobility Adela, Adele, Adeline, Aneurin, Aristocrat, Atheling, Baron(et), Baronne, Bart, Blue blood, Boyar, Brave, Bt, Burgrave, Childe, Contessa, Count, County, Daimio, Dom, Don, Doucepere, Douzeper(s), Duc, Duke, Duniwassal, Earl, Empress, Eorl, Ethel, Eupatrid, Fine, Galahad, Gent, Glorious, Graf, Grandee, Grandeur, Great, Heroic, Hidalgo, Highborn, Infant, Jarl, Junker, King, Landgrave, Lord, Magnate, Magnifico, Manly, Margrave, Marquis, Mona, Nair, Nayar, Palatine, Patrician, Patrick, Peer, Rank, Rose, Seigneur, Seignior, Sheik(h), Stately, Sublime, Thane, Thegn, Titled, Toiseach, Toisech, Vavasour, Vicomte, Vidame, Viscount
Noble gas(es) Argon, Helium, Krypton, Neon, Radon, Xenon
Nobody Diarist, Gnatling, Jack-straw, Nebbish, Nemo, None, Nonentity, Nyaff, Pipsqueak, Pooter, Quat, Schlepp, Scoot, Shlep, Zero
Nocturnal (creature) Bat, Galago, Moth, Night, Owl
Nod(ding) Agree, Assent, Beck(on), Bob, Browse, Catnap, Cernuous, Dip, Doze, Drowsy, Headbang, Mandarin, Nutant, Somnolent
Node, Nodular, Nodule Ascending, Boss, Descending, Enhydros, Geode, Knot, Lump, Lymph, Milium, Pea-iron, Ranvier, Root, Septarium, Swelling, Thorn, Tophus, Tubercle
No doubt Iwis, Ywis
Noel Christmas, Coward, Yule
Nog(gin) Ale, Cup, → DRINK, Peg
No good Dud, NG, Ropy
No-hoper Gone goose, Goner
Noise, Noisy Ambient, Babel, Bedlam, Big, Blare, Bleep, Blip, Blue murder, Bobbery, Boing, Boink, Bruit, Cangle, Charm, Chellup, Clamant, Clamour, Clangour, Clash, Clatter, Clitter, Clutter, Coil, Crackle, Creak, Deen, Din, Dirdum, Euphonia, Euphony, F, Flicker, Fuss, Hewgh, Howlround, Hubbub, Hue, Hullabaloo, Hum, Hurly-burly, Knocking, Loud, Mush, Obstreperous, Ping, Pink, Plangent, Quonk,

Racket, Report, Roar, Robustious, Rorie, Rort, Rory, Row(dow-dow), Rowdedow, Rowdy(dow)(dy), Rucous, Schottky, Schottky-Utis, Scream, Screech, Shindig, Shindy, Shot, Shreek, Shreik, Shriech, Shriek, Solar, Sone, Sonorous, Sound, Strepent, Strepitation, Strepitoso, Stridor, Surface, Thermal, Thunder, Tinnitus, Top, Tumult, → **UPROAR**, VIP, Vociferous, White, Zoom

Noisome Fetid, Invidious, Noxious, Offensive, Rank

No longer Ex, Past

Nomad(ic) Amalekite, Ammonites, Bedawin, Bed(o)uin, Bedu, Berber, Chal, Edom(ite), Fula(h), Gypsy, Hottentot, Hun, Hunter-gatherer, Hyksos, Itinerant, Kurd, Kyrgyz, Lapp, Rom, Rootless, Rover, Saracen, Sarmatian, Strayer, Tsigane, Tsigany, Tuareg, Turk(o)man, Unsettled, Vagabond, Vagrant, Zigan

Noman Ta(r)tar

No man's land Tom Tiddler's ground

Nome Province

Nomenclature Term

Nominal Formal, Onomastic, Titular, Trifling

Nominate, Nomination Appoint, Baptism, Designate, Elect, Postulate, Present, → **PROPOSE**, Slate, Specify, Term

Nomogram Abac

No more Gone, Napoo

Nomothete Enactor, Legislator

Non-Aboriginal Wudjula

Non-attender Absentee, Recusant

Non-believer Atheist, Cynic, Infidel, Sceptic

Non-catalyst Zymogen

Nonchalance, Nonchalant Blasé, Casual, Cool, Debonair, Insouciant, Jaunty, Poco

Non-Christian Saracen

Noncommittal Trimmer

Non-communist West

Non-conformist, Non-conformity Beatnik, Bohemian, Chapel, Deviant, Dissent(er), Dissident, Drop-out, Ebenezer, Heresiarch, Heretic, Maverick, Odd-ball, Outlaw, Pantile, Patarine, Rebel, Recusant, Renegade, Renegate, Sectarian, Wesleyan

Nondescript Dull, Grey, Insipid, Neutral, Nyaff

Non-drip Thixotropic

None Nada, Nary, Nil, Nought, Zero

Nonentity Cipher, Nebbich, Nebbish(er), Nebish, Nobody, Pipsqueak, Quat

Non-essential Adiaphoron, Extrinsic, Incidental

Nonesuch Model, Nonpareil, Paradigm, Paragon, Rarity

Nonetheless Mind you

▷ **Nonetheless** *may indicate* an 'o' to be omitted

Non-existent Unbeing, Virtual

Non-finite Verbid

Non-Gypsy Gajo, Gorgio

Non-interference Laissez faire

Non-Jewish Goy, Shi(c)ksa, Shkitzim, Sho(y)getz

Non-juror Usager

Non-Maori Tangata tiriti, Tauiwi

Non-Muslim Raia, Rayah

No-nonsense Hardball

Nonpareil Nonesuch, Pearl, Peerless, Type, Unequal, Unique

Nonplus(sed) Baffle, Bewilder, Blank, Perplex, Stump
Non-professional Amateur, Laic
Non-radiative Auger
Non-resident Extern, Outlier
Non-runner Scratched, Solid
Nonsense Absurdity, Amphigon, Amphigory, Balderdash, Baloney, Bilge,
Bizzo, Blague, Blah, Blarney, Blat(her), Blatherskite, Blether, Bollocks, Boloney,
Bora(c)k, Borax, Bosh, Bull, Bulldust, Bullshit, Bull's wool, Buncombe, Bunkum,
Clamjamfr(a)y, Clamjamphrie, Claptrap, Cobblers, Cock, Cockamamie, Cod,
Codswallop, Crap, Crapola, Drivel, Dust, Eyewash, Faddle, Falderal, Fandangle,
Fiddlededee, Fiddle-faddle, Fiddlesticks, Flannel, Flapdoodle, Flim-flam,
Folderol, Footling, Fudge, Gaff, Galimatias, Gammon, Gas and gaiters, Get away,
Gibberish, Guff, Gum, Hanky-panky, Haver, Hogwash, Hokum, Hooey, Hoop-la,
Horsefeathers, Humbug, Jabberwocky, Jive, Kibosh, Kidstakes, Malark(e)y,
Moonshine, Mouthwash, My eye, Niaiserie, Phooey, Piffle, Pishogue, Pshaw,
Pulp, Ratbaggery, Rats, Rawmaish, Rhubarb, Rigmarole, Rot, Rubbish, Scat,
Shenanigans, Shit(e), Squit, Stuff, Tom(foolery), Tommy-rot, Tosh, Trash, Tripe,
Tush, Twaddle, Unreason, Waffle
Non-sequitur Anacoluthia, Irrelevant
Non-stick PTFE, Teflon®, Tusche
Non-stop Through
Non-U Naff
Non-violence Ahimsa, Pacificism, Satyagraha
Non-white Coloured, Yolk
Noodle(s) Capellini, Crispy, Daw, Fool, Head, Laksa, Lokshen, Manicotti, Mee,
Moony, Ninny, Pasta, Sammy, Simpleton, Soba, Udon
Nook Alcove, Angle, Corner, Cranny, Niche, Recess, Rookery
Noon Am end, M, Midday, N, Narrowdale
No one Nemo, None
Noose Fank, Halter, Lanyard, Loop, Necktie, Rope, Rope's end, Snare, Twitch
▶ **Nor** *see* **NOT**
Nordic, Norse(man) Icelander, Norn, Scandinavian, Viking
▶ **Nordic** *see* **NORWAY, NORWEGIAN**
Norm Canon, Criterion, Rule, Standard
Normal Average, Conventional, Customary, Everyday, General, Natural, Norm,
Ordinary, Orthodox, Par, Perpendicular, Regular, Standard, Unexceptional, Usu(al)
Normal eyes Emmetropia
Norman French, Rufus
▶ **Norse** *see* **NORWAY, NORWEGIAN**
North(ern), Northerner Arctic, Boreal, Cispontine, Copperhead, Dalesman,
Doughface, Eskimo, Geographic, Hyperborean, Magnetic, N, Norland, Runic,
Septentrion, True, Up
North American (Indian) Ab(e)naki, Algonki(a)n, Algonqui(a)n, Apache, Arapaho,
Assiniboine, Basket Maker, Blackfoot, Brave, Caddoan, Cajun, Cayuga, Cherokee,
Cheyenne, Chibcha, Chickasaw, Chinook, Chipewyan, Choctaw, Comanche,
Copperskin, Creek, Crow, Delaware, Dene, Erie, Five Nations, Fox, Galibi,
Geronimo, Gwich'in, Haida, Hiawatha, Hopi, Huron, Injun, Innu, Iroquois, Kiowa
Apache, Kloo(t)ch, Kootenai, Kootenay, Kutenai, Kwakiutl, Lakota, Mahican,
Malecite, Mandan, Manhattan, Massachuset(ts), Melungeon, Menominee,
Menomini, Mescalero, Micmac, Mikasuki, Miniconjou, Minneconjou, Mission,
Mogollon, Mohave, Mohawk, Mohegan, Mohican, Montagnais, Montagnard,

Mound Builder, Mugwump, Musk(h)ogean, Muskogee, Narraganset, Natchez, Navaho, Nez Percé, Nootka, Northern P(a)iute, Oglala, Ojibwa(y), Okanagon, Okinagan, Omaha, Oneida, Onondaga, Osage, P(a)iute, Palouse, Papago, Papoose, Pawnee, Pequot, Pima, Plains, Pocahontas, Pomo, Ponca, Pontiac, Potawatom, Pueblo, Quapaw, Red(skin), Sachem, Sagamore, Sahaptan, Sahapti(a)n, Salish, Sannup, Sauk, Scalper, Seminole, Senecan, Serrano, Shahaptin, Shawnee, Shoshone, Sioux, Sitting Bull, Siwash, Six Nations, Southern P(a)iute, Status, Suquamash, Susquehannock, Tahitan, Taino, Tarahumara, Teton, Tewa, Tiwa, Tlingit, Totemist, Tribe, Tsimshian, Tuscarora, Ute, Uto-Aztecan, Wampanoag, Wichita, Winnebago, Wyandot(te), Yalkama, Yanqui, Yuman, Zuni
Northern Ireland NI, Six Counties
Northwestern Aeolis
Norway, Norwegian Bokmal, Fortinbras, Landsma(a)l, N, Nordic, Norweyan, Nynorsk, Rollo, Scandinavian
Nose, Nosy A(d)jutage, Aquiline, Beak, Bergerac, Boko, Bouquet, Breather, Catarrhine, Conk, Cromwell, Curious, Desman, Droop, Fink, Flair, Gnomon, Grass, Grecian, Greek, Grog-blossom, Honker, Hooter, Index, Informer, Leptorrhine, Meddle, Muffle, Muzzle, Nark, Neb, Nozzle, Nuzzle, Parker, Platyrrhine, Proboscis, Prying, Pug, Rhinal, Roman, Schnozzle, Shove, Smelly, Sneb, Sniff, Snoot, Snout, Snub, Squeal, Stag, Stickybeak, Toffee
Noseband Barnacle, Cavesson, Musrol
Nose-bleed Epistaxis
Nosh Eat, Food, Nibble, Snack
Nostalgia Longing, Retrophilia, Yearning
Nostril(s) Blowhole, Cere, Choana, Nare
Nostrum Elixir, Medicine, Remede, Remedy
Not, Nor Dis-, Na(e), Narrow A, Ne, Neither, Never, No, Pas, Polled, Taint
Notable, Notability Conspicuous, Distinguished, Eminent, Especial, Landmark, Large, Lion, Memorable, Personage, Signal, Striking, Unco, VIP, Worthy
Not allowed NL
▷ **Not allowed** *may indicate* a word to be omitted
Notary Apostolical, Ecclesiastical, Escribano, Scrivener
Notation(al) Benesh, Cantillation, Descriptive, Entry, Formalism, Hexadecimal, Memo, Octal, Polish, Positional, Postfix, Romic, Staff, Tablature
Notch(ed) Crena(l), Crenel, Cut, Dent, Erode, Erose, Gain, Gap, Gimp, Indent, Insection, Jag, Kerf, Mush, Nick, Nock, Raffle, Score, Serrate, Serrulation, Sinus, Snick, Tally, Vandyke
Not clear Blocked, NL, Obscure, Opaque, Pearl
Note(s), Notebook A, Acciaccatura, Accidental, Advance, Adversaria, Advice, Agogic, Apostil(le), Apparatus, Appoggiatura, Arpeggio, Auxiliary, B, Bill(et), Bradbury, Breve, C, Cedula, Chit(ty), Chord, Cob, Comment, Conceit, Continental, Cover, Credit, Crotchet, Currency, D, Debit, Delivery, Demand, Dig, Do(h), Dominant, Double-dotted, E, E-la, F, Fa(h), False, Fame, Fiver, Flat, Flim, G, Gamut, Gloss(ary), Gold, Grace, Greenback, Heed, Hemiole, Identic, Index rerum, IOU, Item(ise), Jot(tings), Jug(-jug), Key, Kudos, La, Large, Leading, Lichanos, Line, Liner, Log, Long, Longa, Lower mordent, Marginalia, Masora(h), Me, Melisma, Melody, Memo(randum), Mese, Mi, Minim, Minute, → **MONEY**, Mordent, Nachschlag, Natural, NB, Nete, Neum(e), Oblong, Observe, Octave, Oncer, Open, Ostmark, Outline, Parhypate, Passing, Postal, Post-it®, Pound, Promissory, Prompt, Prosiambanomenos, Protocol, PS, Quarter, Quaver, Rag-money, Re, Record, Remark, Renown, Request, Right, Root, Scholion, Scholium, Semibreve,

Semiquaver, Semitone, Sensible, Sextolet, Sharp, Shinplaster, Shoulder, Si, Sick, Sixteenth, Sixty-fourth, Sleeve, Smacker, So(h), Sol, Stem, Strike, Subdominant, Submediant, Subtonic, Supertonic, Te, Ten(ner), Third, Thirty-second, Tierce, Tonic, Treasury, Treble, Undecimole, Ut, Variorum, Verbal, Wad, Warison, Whole, Wolf, Wood

Note-case Pochette, Purse, Wallet

▷ **Notes** *may indicate* the use of letters A-G

Noteworthy Eminent, Extraordinary, Memorable, Particular, Signal, Special

Nothing, Nought Cipher, Devoid, Diddlysquat, Emptiness, FA, Gratis, Jack, Love, Nada, Napoo, Naught, Nihil, Niks-nie, Nil, Nix(-nie), Noumenon, Nowt, Nuffin, Nullity, O, Rap, Rien, Sweet FA, Void, Zero, Zilch, Zip(po)

Notice(able) Ad(vertisement), Advance, Advice, Affiche, Apprise, Attention, Avis(o), Banns, Bill, Blurb, Bold, Caveat, Circular, Clock, Cognisance, Crit, D, Descry, Detect, Discern, Dismissal, Enforcement, Gaum, Get, Gorm, Handbill, → **HEED**, Intimation, Marked, Mensh, Mention, NB, No(t)chel, Obit, Observe, Oyez, Perceptible, Placard, Plaque, Playbill, Poster, Press, Proclamation, Prominent, Pronounced, → **REMARK**, Review, See, Short, Si quis, Spot, Spy, Sticker, Tent, Whip

Notify Acquaint, Advise, Apprise, Awarn, Inform, → **TELL**, Warn

Notion(al) Academic, Conceit, → **CONCEPT**, Crotchet, Fancy, Hunch, Idea, Idée, Idolum, Inkling, Opinion, Reverie, Vapour, Whim

Notoriety, Notorious Arrant, Byword, Crying, Egregious, Esclandre, Fame, Flagrant, Infamous, Infamy, Notour, Proverbial, Réclame, → **RENOWN**, Repute

No trump Laical, Lay, NT

Notwithstanding Although, Despite, Even, For, Howbeit, However, Mau(l)gre, Nath(e)less, Natheless(e), Naythles, Nevertheless, Spite

Nougat Montelimar, Sundae

▶ **Nought** *see* **NOTHING**

Noughts and crosses Tic(k)-tac(k)-to(e)

Noumenon Thing-in-itself

Noun Abstract, Agent, Agentive, Aptote, Collective, Common, Concrete, Count, Gerund, Mass, N, Proper, Substantive, Tetraptote, Verbal, Vocative

Nourish(ing), Nourishment Aliment, Battill, Cherish, Cultivate, Feed, Ingesta, Meat, Nurse, Nurture, Nutrient, Promote, Replenish, Sustenance, Trophic

Nous Intellect, Intelligence, Reason

Nova Scotia(n) Acadia, Blue-nose

Novel(ty) Aga-saga, Bildungsroman, Bonkbuster, Book, Campus, Change, Clarissa, Different, Dime, Dissimilar, Emma, Epistolary, Fad, Fiction, Fresh, Gimmick, Gothic, Graphic, Historical, Horror, Idiot, Innovation, Ivanhoe, Kenilworth, Kidnapped, Kim, Middlemarch, → **NEW**, Newfangled, Original, Outside, Page-turner, Pamela, Paperback, Pendennis, Penny dreadful, Persuasion, Picaresque, Pot-boiler, Primeur, Pulp, Rebecca, River, Roman-à-clef, Romance, Roman fleuve, Scoop, Sex and shopping, Shilling-dreadful, Shilling-shocker, Terror, Thesis, Ulysses, Unusual, Whodun(n)it, Yellowback

▷ **Novel** *may indicate* an anagram

▶ **Novelist** *see* **WRITER**

Novice Acolyte, Apprentice, Beginner, Cadet, Chela, Colt, Cub, Greenhorn, Griffin, Jackaroo, Jillaroo, Johnny-raw, Kyu, L, Learner, Neophyte, New chum, Patzer, Postulant, Prentice, Rabbit, Rookie, Tenderfoot, Tyro(ne), Unweaned

Now(adays) AD, Alate, Anymore, Current, Here, Immediate, Instanter, Interim, Nonce, Nunc, Present, Pro tem, This

Nowhere Limbo
Nowt Cattle, Cows, Ky(e), Neat, Nothing
Noxious Harmful, Offensive, Poisonous, Toxic, Toxin, Venomous
Nozzle A(d)jutage, Aerospike, Fishtail, Nose, Nose-piece, Rose, Spout, Stroup, Syringe, Tewel, Tuyere, Tweer, Twier, Twire, Twyer(e)
Nuance Gradation, Nicety, Overtone, Shade
Nub Crux, Gist, Knob, Lump, Point
Nubile Beddable, Marriageable, Parti
Nuclear, Nucl(e)ide, Nucleus Cadre, Calandria, Centre, Core, Crux, Daughter, Deuteron, Eukaryon, Euratom, Even-even, Even-odd, Heartlet, Hub, Isomer, Isotone, Karyon, Kernel, Linin, Mushroom, Nuke, Pith, Prokaryon, Recoil, Synkaryon, Triton
▷ **Nucleus** *may indicate* the heart of a word
Nude, Nudism, Nudist, Nudity Adamite, Altogether, Aphylly, Bare, Buff, Eve, Exposed, Full-frontal, Gymnosophy, → **NAKED**, Nuddy, Scud, Stark, Stripped, Undress
Nudge Dunch, Dunsh, Elbow, Jostle, Poke, Prod
Nudibranch Sea-slug
Nugget Chunk, Cob, Gold, Lump
Nuisance Bore, Bot, Bugbear, Chiz(z), Drag, Impediment, Inconvenience, Mischief, Pest, Plague, Public, Terror, Trial
Null(ification), Nullify Abate, Cancel, Counteract, Defeasance, Destroy, Diriment, Disarm, Invalid(ate), Negate, Neutralise, Overturn, Recant, Terminate, Undo, Veto, Void
Numb(ness) Asleep, Blunt, Dead(en), Stun, Stupor, Torpefy, Torpescent, Torpid, Unfeeling
Number(s) Abscissa, Abundant, Accession, Air, Aleph-null, Aleph-zero, Algebraic, Algorithm, Aliquant, Aliquot, Amicable, Anaesthetic, Analgesic, Antilog, Apocalyptic, Apostrophus, Army, Atomic, Augend, Avogadro, Babylonian, Binary, Box, Brinell, Calculate, Cardinal, Cetane, Chromosome, Class, Cocaine, Coefficient, Cofactor, Complex, Composite, Concrete, Constant, Coordination, Count, Cyclic, Decillion, Deficient, Deficit, Diapason, Digit, Drove, E, Edition, Epidural, Ether, Eucaine, Ex-directory, F, Feck, Fraction, Friendly, Frost(bite), Froude, Gas, Gobar, Golden, Googol, Handful, Hantle, Hash(mark), Hemlock, Host, Hyperreal, Imaginary, Include, Incomposite, Index, Infimum, Integer, Irrational, Isospin, Isotopic, Item, Lac, Lakh, Legion(s), Lepton, Livraison, Local, Mach, Magazine, Magic, Mass, Melodic, Milliard, Minuend, Minyan, Mixed, Mort, Muckle, Multiple, Multiplex, Multiplicity, Multitude, Myriadth, Nasik, Natural, Neutron, No(s), Nonillion, Nth, Nuclear, Nucleon, Num, Numerator, Numerical, Octane, Octillion, Opiate, Opium, Opposite, Opus, Ordinal, OT, Paginate, Par, Paucal, Peck, Perfect, Pile, PIN, Plural, Polygonal, Prime, Production, Proton, Quantum, Quarternion, Quorum, Quotient, Radix, Raft, Random, Rational, Real, Reckon, Registration, Regulo®, Repunit, Reynolds, Sampi, Scads, Serial, Sight, Slew, Slue, Some, Square, Strangeness, Strength, Subtrahend, Summand, Surd, T, Tale, Telephone, Tell, Thr(e)ave, Totient, Totitive, Transcendental, Transfinite, Troop, Turn-out, Umpteen, Umpty, Urethan(e), Verse, Wave, Whole, Wrong, Zeroth
▷ **Number** *may indicate* a drug
Numeral(s) Arabic, Chapter, Figure, Ghubar, Gobar, Integer, Number, Roman, Sheep-scoring
Numerous(ness) Divers, Galore, Legion, Lots, Many, Multeity, Myriad, Teeming
Numskull Blockhead, Booby, Dunce, Stupid

Nun Beguine, Bhikkhuni, Clare, Cluniac, Conceptionist, Dame, Minim, Minoress, Mother Superior, Outsister, Pigeon, Poor Clare, Prioress, Religeuse, Sister, Sister of Mercy, Top, Ursuline, Vestal, Vowess, Zelator, Zelatrice, Zelatrix
▷ **Nun** *may indicate* a biblical character, father of Joshua
Nuptial (chamber) Bridal, Marital, Marriage, Thalamus
Nurse(ry) Aia, Alice, Amah, Ayah, Bonne, Caledonia, Care(r), Cavell, Charge, Cherish, Consultant, Crèche, Day, Deborah, District, Dry, EN, Flo(rence), Foster, Gamp, Glumdalclitch, Harbour, Health visitor, Karitane, Mammy, Midwife, Minister, Mother, Mrs Gamp, Nan(n)a, Nanny, Night, Nightingale, Nourice, Nourish, Parabolanus, Phytotron, Playroom, Playschool, Plunket, Probationer, RN, School, Seminary, SEN, Sister, Staff, Suckle, Tend, VAD, Visiting, Wet
Nursery(man) Conservatory, Crèche, Garden, Hothouse, Rhyme, Seedsman, Slope
▷ **Nursing** *may indicate* one word within another
Nurture Cultivate, Educate, Feed, Foster, Suckle, Tend
Nut(s), Nutcase, Nutshell, Nut tree, Nutty Acajou, Acorn, Almond, Amygdalus, Anacardium, Aphorism, Arachis, Areca, Arnut, Babassu, Barcelona, Barking, Barmy, Bats, Beech-mast, Bertholletia, Betel, Brazil, Briefly, Buffalo, Butterfly, Butternut, Cashew, Castle, Chock, Cob, Coffee, Cola, Conker, Coquilla, Coquina, Core, Cranium, Cream, Cuckoo, Dukka(h), En, Filberd, Filbert, Frog, Gelt, Gilbert, Gland, Glans, Goober, Gum, Hard, Hazel, Head, Hickory, Illipe, Ivory, Kachang puteh, Kernel, Kola, Lichee, Li(t)chi, Litchi, Loaf, Lug, Lunatic, Lychee, Macadamia, Macahuba, Macaw-palm, Macoya, Manic, Marking, Mast, Mockernut, Monkey, Noisette, Noodle, Nucule, Oak, Oil, Pakan, Palmyra, Para, Pate, Pecan, Pekan, Philippina, Philippine, Philopoena, Physic, Pili, Pine, Pistachio, Poison, Praline, Prawlin, Quandang, Quantong, Queensland, Rhus, Sapucaia, Sassafras, Shell, Skull, Slack, Sleeve, Stuffing, Supari, Thumb, Tiger, Tough, Walnut, Weirdo, Wing, Zany, Zealot
▷ **Nut** *may refer to* Egyptian god, father of Osiris
▶ **Nutcase, Nutshell** *see* **NUT**
Nutcracker Cosh
Nutmeg Calabash, Connecticut, CT, Mace, Myristica
Nutrient, Nutriment, Nutrition Eutrophy, Food, Ingesta, Protein, Sustenance, Trace element, Trophic
▷ **Nuts** *may indicate* an anagram
Nuzzle Snoozle
Nyasaland Malawi
Nymph(et) Aegina, Aegle, Amalthea, Arethusa, Callisto, Calypso, Camenae, Carme, Clytie, Constant, Cymodoce, Daphne, Doris, Dryad, Echo, Egeria, Eurydice, Galatea, Hamadryad, Hesperides, Houri, Hyades, Ida, Insect, Larva, Liberty, Lolita, Maelid, Maia, Maiden, Mermaid, Naiad, Nereid, Oceanid, Oenone, Oread, Pupa, Rusalka, Sabrina, Scylla, Siren, Sylph, Syrinx, Tessa, Tethys, Thetis, Water, Wood

Oo

O Blob, Duck, Nought, Omega, Omicron, Oscar, Oxygen, Spangle, Tan, Zero

Oaf Auf, Changeling, Dolt, Fool, Mou, Ocker, Ouph(e), Stupid, Twit, Yahoo

Oak(s) Bog, Bur, Cerris, Classic, Cork, Desert, Dumbarton, Durmast, Flittern, Fumed, Gabriel, Herne, Holly, Holm, Honour, Ilex, Jerusalem, Kermes, Live, Major, Native, Parliament, Pedunculate, Philemon, Poison, Quercus, Red, Roble, Royal, Sessile, Silky, Swamp, Swilcar, → **TREE**, Turkey, Valonia, Watch, White

Oakley Annie

Oar(s), Oarsmen Blade, Ctene, Eight, Leander, Organ, Paddle, Palm, Propel, Rower, Scull, Spoon, Stroke, Sweep

Oasis Biskra, Buraimi, Haven, Hotan, Hotien, Refuge, Spring, Tafilalet, Tafilelt

Oat(meal), Oats Ait, Athole brose, Avena, Brome-grass, Fodder, Grain, Grits, Groats, Gruel, Haver, Loblolly, Parritch, Pilcorn, Pipe, Porridge, Quaker®, Rolled, Wild

Oatcake Bannock, Clapbread, Farle, Flapjack, Jannock

Oath Affidavit, Begorrah, Blast, Burgess, Curse, Dang, Demme, Doggone, Drat, Ecod, Egad, Expletive, God-so, Gospel, Halidom, Hippocratic, Igad, Imprecation, Jabers, Lumme, Lummy, Nouns, Oons, Promise, Sacrament, Sal(a)mon, Sapperment, Saucer, Sdeath, Sfoot, Sheart, Slid, Strewth, Stygian, Swear, Tarnation, Tennis-court, Voir dire, Vow, Zbud, Zounds

Obdurate Adamant, Cruel, Flinty, Hard, Intransigent, Stony, Stubborn, Tenacious

Obedient, Obedience, Obey Bent, Bridlewise, Canonical, Comply, Dutiful, Follow, Hear, Mindful, Obsequious, Observe, Obtemper, Passive, Perform, Pliant, Servant, Yielding

Obeisance → **BOW**, Salaam

Obelisk, Obelus Aguilla, Column, Dagger, Monument, Needle, Pillar

Oberon King, Merle

Obese, Obesity Bariatrics, Corpulent, Fat, Stout

Object(s), Objection(able), Objective(ness), Objector Ah, Aim, Ambition, Argue, Article, Bar, Beef, Case, Cavil, Challenge, Clinical, Cognate, Complain(t), Conchy, Conscientious, Cow, Demur, Detached, Direct, End, Exception, Fuss, → **GOAL**, Her, Him, Impersonal, Improper, Indifferent, Indirect, Intensional, Intention, It, Item, Jib, Loathe, Mind, Moral, Niggle, Non-ego, Noumenon, Ob, Obnoxious, Offensive, Oppose, Outness, Perspective, Plan, Plot, Point, Protest, Proximate, Question, Quibble, Quasi-stellar, Quiddity, Rank, Rebarbative, Recuse, Refuse, Relation, Resist, Retained, Sake, Scruple, Sex, Subject, Sublime, Target, Thing, Transitive, Tut, Ultimate, Unbiased, Virtu, Wart

▷ **Object** *may indicate* a grammatical variant

Objectless Intransitive

Oblate, Oblation Gift, Monk, Offering, Offertory, Prothesis, Sacrifice

Oblige, Obliging, Obligation, Obligatory Accommodate, Affable, Behold, Binding, Burden, Charge, Compel, Complaisant, Compliant, Contract, Corvée,

Debt, De rigueur, Duty, Easy, Encumbent, Force, Giri, Gratify, Impel, Incumbent, IOU, Mandatory, Must, Necessitate, Novation, Obruk, Obstriction, Peremptory, Promise, Recognisance, Sonties, Synallagmatic, Tie, Wattle

Oblique(ly) Askance, Askew, Asklent, Asquint, Athwart, Awry, Cross, Diagonal, Indirect, Perverse, Plagio-, Separatrix, Sidelong, Skew, Skewwhiff, Slanting, Solidus, Squint, Virgule

▷ **Oblique** *may indicate* an anagram

Obliterate(d) Annul, Black out, Blot, Dele(te), Efface, Expunge, Exterminate, Rase, Rast, Raze, Wash away, Wipe

Oblivion, Oblivious Forgetful, Lethe, Limbo, Nirvana, Obscurity

Oblong Rectangular

Obloquy Opprobrium

Obnoxious Eyesore, Foul, Horrid, Offensive, Pestilent, Repugnant, Septic, Sod

Obscene(ly), Obscenity Bawdy, Blue, Fescennine, Gross, Hard-core, Indecent, Lewd, Lubricious, Paw(paw), Porn(o), Salacious, Smut, Vulgar

Obscure, Obscurity Abstruse, Anheires, Becloud, Befog, Blend, Blot out, Cloud, Cobweb, Conceal, Cover, Cryptic, Darken, Deep, Dim, Disguise, Eclipse, Encrypt, Envelop, Esoteric, Filmy, Fog, Hermetic, Hide, Indistinct, Jude, Mantle, Mist, Murk, Nebular, Night, Nubecula, Obfuscate, Obnubilate, Opaque, Oracular, Overcloud, Overshade, Overshadow, Recherché, Recondite, Shadowy, Tenebrific, Twilit, Unclear, → **VAGUE**, Veil, Vele, Wrap

▷ **Obscure(d)** *may indicate* an anagram

Obsequious(ness) Bootlicker, Brown nose, Creeping Jesus, Fawn, Fulsome, Grovelling, Kowtowing, Menial, Parasitic, Pig, Servile, Slavish, Sleeveen, Slimy, Subservient, Suck-hole, Sycophantic, Tantony, Toady

Observance, Observant, Observation Adherence, Alert, Attention, Comment, Custom, Empirical, Espial, Eyeful, Holy, Honour, Lectisternium, Mass, → **NOTICE**, Obiter dicta, Perceptive, Percipient, Recce, Remark, Right, Rite, Ritual, Vising

Observatory Arecibo, Atalaya, Greenwich, Herstmonceux, Hurstmonceux, Jodrell Bank, Lookout, Mount Palomar, Tower

Observe(d), Observer Behold, Bystander, Celebrate, Commentator, Detect, Espy, Eye, Fly-on-the-wall, Heed, Keep, Mark, NB, Note, Notice, Obey, Onlooker, Optic, Regard(er), Remark, Rite, Scry, See, Seer, Sight, Spectator, Spial, Spot, Spy, Study, Take, Twig, View, Voyeur, Watch, Witness

Obsess(ed), Obsession, Obsessive Anal, Besot, Bug, Bugbear, Craze, Dominate, Fetish, Fixation, Hang-up, Haunt, Hobbyhorse, Hooked, Idée fixe, Infatuation, Mania, Monomania, Necrophilia, Neurotic, One-track, Preoccupy, Thing, Wonk

Obsidian Pe(a)rlite

Obsolete, Obsolescence, Obsolescent Abandoned, Antique, Archaic, Dated, Dead, Defunct, Disused, Extinct, Latescent, Obs, Outdated, Outworn, Passé, Planned

Obstacle Barrage, Barrier, Boyg, Cheval de frise, Chicane, Dam, Drag, Dragon's teeth, Drawback, Gate, Handicap, Hindrance, Hitch, Hurdle, Node, Oxer, Remora, Rock, Sandbank, Snag, Stimie, Stumbling-block, Stymie, Tank-trap

Obstetrics Gynaecology, Midwifery, Tocology, Tokology

Obstinacy, Obstinate Asinine, Bigoted, Buckie, Bullish, Contrarian, Contumacious, Cussed, Die-hard, Dour, Entêté, Froward, Headstrong, Inflexible, Intractable, Intransigent, Mule, Persistent, Perverse, Pervicacious, Piggish, Pig-headed, Recalcitrant, Refractory, Restive, Rusty, Self-will, Stiff(-necked), Stubborn, Thraward, Thrawart, Wilful

Obstreperous Noisy, Stroppy, Truculent, Unruly

Obstruct(ion) Bar, Block, Bottleneck, Chicane, Clog, Crab, Cross, Cumber, Dam, Embolus, Fil(l)ibuster, Gridlock, Hamper, Hand-off, Hedge, Hinder, Hurdle, Ileus, Impede, Let, Obstacle, Occlude, Sab(otage), Sandbag, Snarl-up, Snooker, Stall, Stap, Stonewall, Stop, Stymie, Sudd, Thwart, Trammel, Trump

Obtain Achieve, Acquire, Cop, Exist, Gain, Get, Land, Pan, Prevail, Procure, Realise, Secure, Succeed, Wangle, Win

Obtrude, Obtrusive Expel, Impose, Loud, Prominent, Push, Sorn, Thrust

Obtuse Blunt, Dense, Dull, Purblind, Stupid, Thick

Obverse Complement, Cross, Face, Front, Head

Obviate Forestall, Preclude, Prevent

Obvious Apparent, Axiom, Blatant, Brobdingnag, Clear, Distinct, Evident, Flagrant, Frank, Inescapable, Kenspeck(le), Manifest, Marked, Open(ness), Open and shut, Overt, Palpable, Patent, Pikestaff, Plain, Pronounced, Salient, Self-evident, Stark, Transparent, Truism, Visible

Occasion Call, Cause, Ceremony, Encheason, Event, Fête, Field day, Nonce, → OPPORTUNITY, Reason, Ride, Sometime, Tide, Time

Occasional(ly) Casual, Chance, Daimen, Intermittent, Irregular, Motive, Orra, Periodic, Sometimes, Sporadic, While

Occident(al) West, Western(er)

Occlude, Occlusion Absorb, Clog, Coronary, Embolism, Obstruct

Occult(ist) Angekkok, Arcane, Art, Esoteric, I-Ching, Magic, Mysterious

Occupant, Occupation, Occupy(ing) Absorb, Activity, Avocation, Beset, Business, Busy, Denizen, Embusy, Employ, Engage, Engross, Fill, Hold, In, Incumbent, Indwell, Inhabitant, Inmate, Involve, Line, Métier, People, Profession, Pursuit, Reserved, Resident, Runrig, Sideline, Squat, Stay, Tenancy, Tenant, Tenure, Thrift, Trade, Upon, Use, Vocation, Walk of life

Occur(rence) Arise, Be, Betide, Betime, Case, Contingency, Crop up, Event, Fall, Happen, Incident, Instance, Outbreak, Outcrop, Pass, Phenomenon

Ocean(ic), Oceania Abundance, Abyssal, Antarctic, Arctic, Atlantic, Blue, Deep, German, Hadal, Herring-pond, Indian, Melanesia, Micronesia, Pacific, Panthalassa, Pelagic, Polynesia, Sea(way), Southern, Thalassic, Waves, Western

Och aye Troggs

Ochre Burnt, Keel, Lemnian ruddle, Rubric, Ruddle, Sienna

Octave Diapason, Diminished, Eight, Great, Ottava, Perfect, Small, Utas

Octopus Blue-ringed, Cephalopod, Cuero, Devilfish, Paper nautilus, Polyp, Poulp(e), Scuttle, Squid

Octoroon Mestee, Mestizo, Mustee

Od Energy, Force

Odd (person), Oddity Abnormal, Anomaly, Bizarre, Card, Cure, Curio, Droll, Eccentric, Eery, Erratic, Gink, Impair, Imparity, Jimjam, Offbeat, Original, Orra, Outré, Paradox, Parity, Peculiar, Queer, Quiz, Random, Rare, Remote, Rum, Screwball, Singular, → STRANGE, Unequal, Uneven, Unmatched, Unusual, Weird, Whims(e)y

▷ **Odd(s)** *may indicate* an anagram or the odd letters in words

Oddfellow OF

Odd job man Joey, Loppy, Orraman, Rouster, Smoot, Thronner

Odds, Oddments Bits, Carpet, Chance, Gubbins, Handicap, Line, Long, Price, Short, SP, Tails, Variance

Ode Awdl, Dit, Epicede, Epicedium, Epinicion, Epinikion, Genethliacon, Horatian, Hymn, Lay, Lyric, Monody, Paeon, Pindaric, Poem, Sapphic, Song, Stasimon, Strophe, Threnody, Verse

Odin One-eyed, Woden

Odium, Odious Comparison, Disestimation, Disgrace, Foul, Hatred, Heinous, Invidious, Ponce, Repugnant, Stigma

Odorous, Odour Air, Bad, BO, Flavour, Funk, Good, Hum, Opopanax, Perfume, Quality, Redolence, Sanctity, Scent, Smell, Whiff

Odourless Silent

Odyssey Epic, Journey, Wandering

Oedipus Complex, Parricide

Oeillade Glance, Leer, Ogle, Wink

Oesophagus Crop

Oestrogen, Oestrus Frenzy, Heat, Isoflavone, Mestranol, Must, Rut, Stilb(o)estrol

Of (me) About, Among, Aus, By, De, From, In, My, Re

▷ **Of** *may indicate* an anagram

Of course Certainly, Natch, Yes

Off Absent, Agee, Ajee, Away, Discount, Distance, Far, From, High, Inexact, Licence, Odd, Reasty, Reesty, Relâche, Start

▷ **Off** *may indicate* an anagram

Offal Cagmag, Carrion, Chidlings, Chitterling, Entrails, Fry, Giblets, Gralloch, Gurry, Haggis, Ha(r)slet, Heart, Innards, Kidney, Lamb's fry, Lights, Liver, Numbles, Pig's fry, Pluck, Sweetbread, Tripe, Variety meat

Off-beat Zoppo

Off-colour Pale, Seedy, Wan

▷ **Off-colour** *may indicate* an anagram

Offence Attack, Crime, Delict, Delinquency, Distaste, Fault, Huff, Hurt, Lapse, Lese majesty, Miff, Misdemeanour, Misprision, Outrage, Peccadillo, Pip, Pique, Piracy, Regrate, Sedition, → **SIN**, Summary, Trespass, Umbrage, Violation

Offend(ed), Offender Affront, Anger, Annoy, Boobhead, Bridles, Culprit, Default, Disoblige, Displease, Distaste, Hip, Huff, Hurt, Hyp, Infringe, Inveigh, Miffy, Miscreant, Nettle, Nonce, Nuisance, Peeve, Perp, Provoke, Sin(ner), Stray, Transgress, Twoccer, Violate, Wrongdoer

Offensive Affront, Aggressive, Alien, Attack, Bombardment, Campaign, Cruel, Derisatory, Embracery, Euphemism, Execrable, Eyesore, Foul, Gobby, Hedgehog, Hedgepig, Indelicate, Invidious, Miasmic, Nasty, Noisome, Obnoxious, Obscene, Peccant, Personal, Push, Putrid, Rank, Repugnant, → **RUDE**, Scandalous, Scurrilous, Sortie, Storm, Ugly, Unbecoming, Unsavoury, War

Offer(ing) Alms, Altarage, Anaphora, Bargain, Bid, Bode, Bouchée, Cadeau, Corban, Deodate, Dolly, Epanophora, Extend, Ex voto, Gift, Godfather, Hold, Inferiae, Introduce, Invitation, Oblation, Overture, Peace, Peddle, Plead, Pose, Potla(t)ch, Present, Propine, → **PROPOSE**, Propound, Sacrifice, Shewbread, Shore, S(h)raddha, Special, Stamp, Stand, Submit, Suggestion, Tender, Utter, Volunteer, Votive, Wave, Xenium

Offhand Airy, Banana, Brusque, Casual, Cavalier, Curt, Extempore, Impromptu, Indifferent, Snappy

Office(s) Agency, Bedelship, Booking, Box, Branch, Broo, Bucket shop, Bureau, Buroo, Caliphate, Chair, Chancery, Clerical, Colonial, Complin(e), Consulate, Crown, Cube farm, Cutcher(r)y, Daftar, Dataria, Dead-letter, Deanery, Den, Divine, Dogate, Employment, Evensong, Foreign, Function, Holy, Home, Job, Land, Last, Left luggage, Lieutenancy, Little, Little hours, Loan, Lost property, Mayoralty, Met(eorological), Ministry, Missa, Mistery, Mudiria, Mutessarifat, Mystery, Nocturn, Nones, Obit, Oval, Palatinate, Papacy, Patent, Penitentiary, Personnel, Petty Bag, Pipe, Place, Plum, Portfolio, Position, Post, Prefecture, Prelacy, Press,

Prime, Printing, Provosty, Record, Regency, Register, Registry, Rite, Scottish, Secretarial, See, Seraskierate, Shogunate, Sinecure, Situation, Sorting, Stationery, Tariff, Tenebrae, Terce, Ticket, Tierce, Tol(l)booth, Tribunate, Vespers, War, Yamen

Officer(s) Acater, Adjutant, Admiral, Ag(h)a, Agistor, Aide, Apparitor, Bailiff, Beatty, Bimbashi, Black Rod, Blimp, Blue Rod, Bombardier, Bos(u)n, Branch, Brass-hat, Brigadier, Bumbailiff, Capt(ain), Catchpole, Catchpoll, Cater, Cellarist, Centurion, Chamberlain, Chancellor, CIGS, Colonel, Commander, Commissioned, Commissioner, Commodore, Compliance, Constable, Cop(per), Co-pilot, Cornet, Coroner, Counter-round, Cursitor, Customs, Darogha, Datary, Deacon, Decurion, Duty, Earl Marshal, Engineer, Ensign, Equerry, Exciseman, Executive, Exon, Field Marshal, Filacer, Filazer, First, First mate, Flag, Flying, Gallant, Ga(u)ger, Gazetted, Gen(eral), GOC, Grand Vizier, Group, Group captain, Gunner, Havildar, Hayward, Hetman, Ima(u)m, Incumbent, Infirmarian, Intendant, Jamadar, Janty, Jauntie, Jaunty, Jemadar, Jemidar, Jonty, Jurat, Justiciar, Lance-sergeant, Liaison, Lictor, Lord High Steward, Lt, Major, Marshal, Mate, Moderator, NCO, Non-commissioned, Number one, Nursing, Official Solicitor, Orderly, Oxon, Pantler, Peace, Petty, Pilot, Pipe major, PO, Police, Posse, Prefect, President, Prison, Probation, Proctor, Procurator fiscal, Provost, Provost-marshal, Purser, Pursuivant, Quartermaster, Quartermaster-sergeant, Radio, Relieving, Remembrancer, Returning, Rodent, Rupert, Safety, Samurai, Sbirro, Scene-of-crime, Schout, Sea Lord, Second mate, Securocrat, Select-man, Serang, Sergeant-major, Sewer, Sexton, Sheriff, Silver-stick, Skipper, SL, SM, Speaker, Staff, Striper, Sub(altern), Suba(h)dar, Subchanter, Sublieutenant, Supercargo, Superintendent, Tahsildar, Tidewaiter, Tindal, Tipstaff, Treasurer, Tribune, Usher, Varlet, Waldgrave, Warden, Wardroom, Warrant, Watch, Woodward, Yeoman

Official(s), Officiate, Officious Aga, Agent, Aleconner, Amban, Amtman, Atabeg, Atabek, Attaché, Authorised, Beadle, Bossy, Bureaucrat, Catchpole, Censor, Chamberlain, Chancellor, Chinovnik, Claviger, Commissar, Commissioner, Consul, Count, Count palatine, Dean, Diplomat, Dockmaster, Dogberry, Ealdorman, Ephor, Equerry, Escheater, Eurocrat, Executive, Fonctionnaire, → **FORMAL**, Functionary, Gauleiter, Gymnasiarch, Handicapper, Hayward, Incumbent, Inspector, Intendant, Jack-in-office, Jobsworth, Keeper, Landdrost, Lictor, Linesman, Mandarin, Marplot, Marshal, Mayor, MC, Meddlesome, Mirza, Mueddin, Mukhtar, Nazir, Notary, Notary public, Ombudsman, Omlah, Overbusy, Palatine, Paymaster, Placeman, Pleaseman, Plenipotentiary, Polemarch, Pontificate, Poohbah, Postmaster, Praefect, Pragmatic, Prefect, Proctor, Procurator, Prog, Proveditor, Provedor(e), Providor, Reeve, Régisseur, Registrar, Remembrancer, Shammash, Shammes, Sherpa, Silentiary, Souldan, Staff, Steward, Suffete, Suit, Syndic, Timekeeper, Tipstaff, Tribune, Trier, Trior, Triumvir, Turncock, Valid, Valuer General, Veep, Verderer, Verger, Vizier, Walla(h), Whiffler, Whip, Woodward, Yamen, Yeoman

Offprint Separate

Off-putting Dehortative, Discouraging, Mañana, Negative, Procrastination, Rebarbative, Repellent, Yips

Offset Balance, Cancel, Compensate, Counter(act), Counterbalance

Offshoot Bough, Branch, Cion, Limb, Lye, Member, Outgrowth, Plant, Scion, Sien, Sient, Swarm, Syen

Offspring Boy, Burd, Chick, Children, Daughter, Descendant, Family, Fry, Get, Girl, Heir, Procreation, Product, Progeny, Seed, Sient, Son, Spawn

Offstage Wings

Often Frequent, Habitual, Repeated

▷ **Often** *may indicate* 'of ten'

Ogee Cyma, Moulding, Talon
Ogle Drake, Eliad, Eye, Glance, Leer, Oeillade, Wodewose
Ogre(ss) Baba Yaga, Boyg, Brute, Eten, Etten, Fiend, Giant, Monster, Orc
Ohio Buckeye
Oil(s), Oily, Oil producer Anele, Anoint, Balm, Black gold, Bribe, Crude, Derv, Diesel, Drying, Essence, Essential, Ethereal, Fatty, Fish, Fixed, Frying, Fuel, Good, Grease, Heavy, Lamp, Lipid, Long, Lubricant, Midnight, Mineral, Monounsaturated, Multigrade, Oint, Oleaginous, Pellitory, Polyunsaturated, Pomade, Seed, Short, Sleek, Slick, Smalmy, Smarmy, Smeary, Sweet, Topped crude, Unction

---

OILS

2 letters:
BP®

3 letters:
Ben
Emu
Gas
Nim
Nut

4 letters:
Baby
Bath
Bone
Coal
Corn
Musk
Neem
Nimb
Oleo
Otto
Palm
Poon
Rape
Rock
Rose
Rusa
Slum
Tall
Tolu
Tung
Wool
Yolk

5 letters:
Ajwan
Argan
Attar

Benne
Benni
Clove
Colza
Copra
Fusel
Grass
Niger
Olive
Ottar
Poppy
Pulza
Rosin
Savin
Sebum
Shale
Shark
Snake
Sperm
Spike
Stand
Thyme
Train
Ulyie
Ulzie
Whale

6 letters:
Ajowan
Almond
Balsam
Banana
Butter
Canola
Carapa
Carron
Castor
Chrism

Cineol
Cohune
Croton
Elaeis
Jojoba
Magilp
Megilp
Monola®
Neroli
Peanut
Ramtil
Savine
Semsem
Sesame
Shamoy
Tallow
Virgin
Walnut

7 letters:
Apiezon®
Bittern
Cajeput
Cajuput
Camphor
Cineole
Coconut
Dittany
Eugenol
Gingili
Linalol
Linseed
Lumbang
Menthol
Mirbane
Moringa
Mustard
Myrbane

Myrrhol
Naphtha
Picamar
Pyrrole
Retinol
Ricinus
Saffron
Safrole
Spindle
Verbena
Vitriol
Wallaba

8 letters:
Bergamot
Camphire
Cod-liver
Creasote
Creosote
Gingelli
Gingelly
Hazelnut
Kerosene
Kerosine
Lavender
Linalool
Macassar
North Sea
Oiticica
Pachouli
Paraffin
Photogen
Pristane
Rapeseed
Rosewood
Volatile

9 letters:
Aleuritis
Beech-mast
Candlenut
Carvacrol
Eleoptene
Golomynka
Grapeseed
Groundnut
Neat's-foot
Parathion
Patchouli
Patchouly
Petroleum

Photogene
Safflower
Sassafras
Spearmint
Spikenard
Star-anise
Sunflower
Vanaspati
Vegetable

10 letters:
Chaulmugra
Citronella
Cotton-seed

Elaeoptene
Eucalyptus
Guttiferae
Petit grain
Sandalwood
Turpentine
Ylang-ylang

11 letters:
Camphorated
Chaulmoogra
Chinese wood
Extra virgin
Stearoptene

Wintergreen

12 letters:
Benzaldehyde
Brilliantine

14 letters:
Glutaraldehyde
Parnassus grass

15 letters:
Evening primrose

Oilcake Poonac
Oilcan Pourie
Oilcloth American, Lino
Oilman Driller, Prospector, Rigger, Texan
Oil painting Master, Titian
Ointment Balm, Basilicon, Boracic, Boric, Cerate, Collyrium, Cream, Liniment, Lipsalve, Nard, Pomade, Pomatum, Salve, Spikenard, Theriac, Unguent, Vaseline®, Zinc
OK Agree(d), Approve, Authorise, Clearance, Copacetic, Copesettic, Go-head, Green light, Hunky-dory, Initial, Kosher, Mooi, Right(o), Sanction, Sound, U, Vet
Okra Bhindi, Gumbo, Lady's fingers
Old(er), Oldie Ae(t), Aged, Aine(e), Ancient, Antique, Auld, Bean, Decrepit, Dutch, Fogram, Former, Gaffer, Geriatric, Glory, Golden, Gray, Grey, Hills, Hoary, Immemorial, Major, Mature, Methusaleh, Moore, Nestor, Nick, O, OAP, Obsolete, Off, Ogygian, One-time, Outworn, Palae-, Passé, Primeval, Ripe, Rugose, Sen(escent), Senile, Senior, Shot, Signeur, Stale, Trite, Venerable, Veteran, Victorian(a), Worn
Old boy, Old girl Alumnae, Alumnus, Fossil, OB
Old days Once, Past, Yore
Old English OE
Old-fashioned Aging, Ancient, Antediluvian, Antwackie, Arch(aic), Arriéré, Bygone, Corn(y), Dated, Dowdy, Fogey, Fuddy-duddy, Medieval, Museum piece, Neanderthal, No tech, Obsolete, Ogygian, Oldfangled, Outdated, Outmoded, Passé, Podunk, Primeval, Quaint, Relic, Retro, Rinky-dink, Schmaltzy, Shot, Square, Square-toes, Steam, Stick-in-the-mud, Traditional, Uncool, Vieux jeu, Worm-eaten
Old hat Clichéd
Old maid Biddy, Spinster
Old man, Old woman Anile, Aunty, Bodach, Buda, Budi, Burd, Cailleach, Carlin(e), Codger, Crow, Crumbly, Faggot, Fantad, Fantod, Fogey, Fogramite, Fogy, Fussy, Gammer, Geezer, Grandam, Grannam, Greybeard, Greyhen, Husband, Kangaroo, Koro, Kuia, Luckie, Lucky, Matriarch, Methuselah, Mort, Mzee, OAP, Oom, Pantaloon, Patriarch, Presbyte, Rudas, Trot, Trout, Wife, Wight, Woopie, Wrinkly
Old-timer Hourglass, Sundial, Veteran
Oleander Nerium
Olid Fetid, Foul, High, Rancid, Rank

Olio Hash, Medley, Mess, Potpourri, Stew
Olive (grove), Olivine Calamata, Cerulein, Drupe, Dunite, Gethsemane, Kalamata, Lilac, Olea(ster), Peridot, Queen
Oliver Bath, Cromwell, Goldsmith, Hardy, Noll, Protector, Twist
Olympian, Olympus Asgard, Athlete, Celestial, Elis, Pantheon, Quadrennium, Zeus
Omelette Crêpe, Foo yong, Foo yung, Frittata, Fu yung, Pancake, Spanish, Tortilla
Omen Abodement, Absit, Augury, Auspice, Foreboding, Forewarning, Freet, Freit, Portent, Presage, Prodrome, Sign, Token, Warning
Omentum Caul, Epiploon
Ominous Alarming, Baleful, Bodeful, Dire, Dour, Forbidding, Grim, Inauspicious, Oracular, Sinister, Threatening
Omission, Omit Aph(a)eresis, Apocope, Apospory, Apostrophe, Asyndeton, Caret, Disregard, Drop, Elide, Elision, Ellipse, Ellipsis, Failure, Haplography, Haplology, Lipography, Loophole, Miss, Neglect, Nonfeasance, Oversight, Paral(e)ipomenon, Pass, Senza, Skip
Omnibus Anthology, Coach, Collection
Omniscient Encyclopedia
Omnivorous Pantophagous
On (it) Aboard, About, Agreed, An, An't, At, Atop, By, Game, Half-cut, In, Leg, O', Of, Oiled, Over, Pon, Re, Tipsy, Up(on)
▷ **On** *may indicate* an anagram
On account of Over
▷ **On board** *may indicate* chess, draughts, or 'SS' around another word
Once(r) Ance, As was, → **AT ONCE**, Bradbury, Earst, Erst(while), Ever, Ex, Fore, Former, Jadis, Oner, Onst, Secular, Sole, Sometime, Whilom
One(self) A, Ace, Ae, Alike, An(e), Any, Body, Chosen, Eeny, Ego, Ein, Formula, I, Individual, Integer, Me, Monad, Per se, Single(ton), Singular, Solo, Tane, Un, Unify, Unit(y), Unitary, United, Us, We, Yin, You
One-act-er Playlet
One-eared Monaural
One-eyed Arimasp(ian), Cyclops
One-man band Moke
One o'clock 1 am, NNE
One-off Ad hoc
One-rayed Monact
Onerous Arduous, Exacting, Taxing, Tedious, Weighty
Onion(s) Allium, Bengi, Bonce, Bulb, Chibol, Chive, Cibol, Cive, Eschalot, Green, Head, Ingan, Jibbons, Leek, Lyonnaise, Moly, Pearl, Ramp, Ramson, Rocambole, Ropes, Scallion, Scilla, Shal(l)ot, Soubise, Spanish, Spring, Squill, Sybo(e), Sybow, Tree, Welsh
Onlooker Bystander, Kibitzer, Rubberneck, Spectator, Witness
Only Allenarly, Anerly, But, Except, Just, Meer, Merely, Nobbut, Seul, Singly, Sole
Onset Affret, Attack, Beginning, Charge, Dash, Ending, Rush, → **START**, Thrust
Onslaught Attack, Dead-set, Onset, Raid, Spreagh, Storm, Swoop
On time Pat, Prompt, Punctual
Onus Burden, Charge, → **DUTY**, Responsibility
Onward Advance, Ahead, Away, Forth, Forward, Progress
Oodles Heaps, Lashings, Lots, Slather
Oolite Pisolite, Roestone
Oomph Energy, It, SA, Verve
Ooze Drip, Exhale, Exude, Gleet, Mud, Percolate, Pteropod(a), Seep, Sew, Sipe,

Slime, Slob, Spew, Spue, Sweat, Sype, Transude

Opal(escent) Black, Cymophanous, Fire, Gem, Girasol, Girosol, Hyalite, Hydrophane, Liver, Menilite, Noble, Potch, Wood

Opaque, Opacity Dense, Dull, Intense, Leucoma, Obscure, Obtuse, Onycha, Roil, Thick, Turbid

Open(er), Opening, Openness Adit, Aedicule, Ajar, Antithesis, Anus, Apert(ure), Apparent, Apse, Autopsy, Bald, Bare, Bat, Bay, Bole, Breach, Break, Broach, Buttonhole, Candid, Cardia, Cavity, Champaign, Chance, Chasm, Chink, Circumscissile, Clear, Crevasse, Dehisce, Deploy, Dispark, Door, Dup, Embrasure, Exordium, Expansive, Eyelet, Fair, Fenestra, Fissure, Fistula, Flue, Fontanel(le), Foramen, Frank, Free, Gambit, Gap, Gaping, Gat, Gate, Give, Glasnost, Glottis, Guichet, Gullwing, Hagioscope, Hatch, Hatchback, Hatchway, Hiatus, Hilus, → **HOLE**, Inaugural, Intake, Interstice, Intro, Key, Lacy, Lance, Lead, Loid, Loophole, Loose, Machicolation, Manhole, Meatus, Micropyle, Mofette, Moongate, Mouth, Nare, Oillet, Orifice, Oscule, Osculum, Ostiole, Ostium, Overture, Patent, Peephole, Pert, Pervious, Pick(lock), Placket, Plughole, Pore, Port(age), Porta, Porthole, Preliminary, Premiere, Prise, Pro-am, Public, Pylorus, Receptive, Rent, Riva, Room, Scuttle, Scye, Sesame, Sicilian, Sincere, Slit, Spare, Spirant, Squint, Start, Stenopaic, Stoma, Syrinx, Thereout, Thirl, Touchhole, Transparent, Trapdoor, Trema, Trou, Truthful, Unbar, Unbolt, Unbutton, Uncork, Undo, Unfurl, Unhasp, Unlatch, Unscrew, Unstop, Unsubtle, Untie, Unzip, Upfront, Vent, Vulnerable, Wide, Window

Open air Alfresco, Sub divo, Sub Jove

Opera, Opera house Aida, Ariadne, Ballad, Bouffe, Buffo, Burletta, Carmen, Comic, Comique, Dramma giocoso, Electra, ENO, Ernani, Falstaff, Faust, Fedora, Fidelio, Glyndebourne, Grand, Hansel and Gretel, Horse, Idomeneo, Iolanthe, I Puritani, La Bohème, La Scala, Light, Lohengrin, Lulu, Macbeth, Met, Musical, Nabucco, Norma, Oater, Oberon, Onegin, Open Wingrave, Orfeo, Otello, Parsifal, Pastorale, Patience, Peter Grimes, Pinafore, Rienzi, Rigoletto, Ruddigore, Savoy, Seria, Singspiel, Soap, Space, Tell, The Met, Threepenny, Tosca, Turandot, Verismo, Werther, Work, Zarzuela

Opera-glasses Jumelle

Opera-lover Wagnerite

Opera-singer Baritone, Bass, Contralto, Diva, Savoyard, Soprano

Operate, Operation(s), Operative Act(ion), Activate, Actuate, Agent, Artisan, Attuition, Barbarossa, Bypass, Caesarean, Campaign, Conduct, Couching, Current, Desert Storm, Detective, Exercise, Function, Game, Hobday, Holding, Keystroke, Laparotomy, Leucotomy, Liposuction, Lithotomy, Lobotomy, Logical, Manipulate, Mechanic, Mules, Nose job, Oner, Overlord, Plastic, Practice, Run, Sealion, Shirodkar's, Sortie, Strabotomy, Titration, Ure, Valid, Wertheim, Work

Operator Agent, Conductor, Dealer, Laplace, Manipulator, Nabla, Sawbones, Sparks, Surgeon

Opiate, Opium Buprenorphine, Dope, Drug, Hop, Laudanum, Meconin, Meconium, Morphine, Narcotic, Religion, Soporific, Thebaine

Opinion, Opinionative Attitude, Belief, Bet, Consensus, Cri, Dictum, Dogma, Doxy, Entêté, Esteem, Feeling, Groundswell, Guess, Judgement, Mind, Mumpsimus, Parti pris, Pious, Prejudice, Private, Public, Pulse, Say, Second, Sense, Sentence, Sentiment, SO, Stand, Take, Tenet, Utterance, View, Viewpoint, Voice, Vox pop, Vox populi

Opossum Lie, Marmose, Phalanger, Tarsipes, Vulpine, Water, Yapo(c)k

Oppidan Cit, Townsman, Urban

Opponent(s) Adversary, Antagonist, Anti, E-N, Enemy, E-S, Foe, Gainsayer, Mitnaged, N-E, N-W, S-E, Straw-man, S-W, W-N, W-S

Opportune, Opportunist, Opportunity Appropriate, Apropos, Break, Carpetbagger, → CHANCE, Day, Equal, Facility, Favourable, Ganef, Ganev, Ganof, Godsend, Go-go, Golden, Gonif, Gonof, Heaven-sent, Occasion, Opening, Pat, Photo, Room, Seal, Seel, Sele, Snatcher, Tabula rasa, Tide, Timely, Timous, Well-timed, Window

Oppose(d), Opposer, Opposing, Opposite, Opposition Against, Agin, Anti, Antipathy, Antipodes, Antiscian, Antithesis, Antithetic, Antitype, Antonym, Argue, At, Au contraire, Averse, Battle, Black, Breast, Colluctation, Combat, Confront, Contradict, Contrary, Converse, Counter, Diametric, Dis(en)courage, Disfavour, Dissent, Distance, E contrario, Face, Foreanent, Fornen(s)t, Hinder, Hostile, Impugn, Inimical, Inverse, Militate, Mugwump, Noes, Object, Obscurant, Overthwart, Polar, Reactance, Reaction, Reluct, Repugn, Resist, Retroact, Reverse, Rival, Shadow, Subtend, Syzygy, Teeth, Terr, Thereagainst, Thwart, Toto caelo, Traverse, V, Versus, Vis-à-vis, Withstand

Oppress(ion), Oppressive Airless, Bind, Burden, Close, Crush, Despotic, Incubus, Jackboot, Onerous, Overpower, Persecute, Ride, Snool, Stifling, Sultry, Tyrannise

Opprobrium Disgrace, Envy, Odium, Scandal

Oppugn Attack, Criticise

Opt, Option(al) Alternative, → CHOICE, Choose, Crown-jewel, Decide, Default, Double zero, Elect, Facultative, Fine, Leipzig, Local, Menu, Omissible, Pick, Plump, Select, Share, Soft, Swap, Trade(d), Traditional, Voluntary, Votive, Wale, Zero(-zero)

Optic(al), Optics Active, Adaptive, Electron, Fibre, Fire, Lens, Prism, Reticle, Visual

Optimism, Optimist(ic) Bull, Chiliast, Elated, Expectant, Feelgood, Hopeful, Micawber, Morale, Pangloss, Pollyanna, Rosy, Sanguine, Starry-eyed, Upbeat, Utopiast, Yea-sayer

Opulent Abundant, Affluent, Moneyed, Rich, Wealthy

Opus Piece, Study, Work

Or Au, Either, Ere, Gold, Ossia, Otherwise, Sol

Oracle(s), Oracular Delphi, Dodonian, Mirror, Prophet, Pythian, Pythoness, Sage, Seer, Sibyl(line), Thummim, Urim, Vatic

Oral Acroamatic, Sonant, Spoken, Verbal, Viva, Viva voce, Vocal

Orange An(n)atta, An(n)atto, Arnotto, Aurora, Bergamot, Bigarade, Bilirubin, Bitter, Blood, Blossom, Calamondin, Chica, Claybank, Clockwork, Croceate, Flame, Flamingo, Fulvous, Genip(ap), Jaffa, Kamala, Kamela, Kamila, Karaka, Kumquat, Mandarin, Mock, Naartje, Nacarat, Nartjie, Navel, Ochre, Osage, Pig, Roucou, Ruta, Satsuma, Seville, Shaddock, Sour, Sweet, Tangerine, Tenné, Ugli®, Ulsterman

Orang-utan Ape, Monkey, Satyr

Orate, Oration Address, Declaim, Eloge, Elogium, Elogy, Eulogy, Harangue, Panegyric, Philippics, Speech

Oratorio, Orator(y) Boanerges, Brompton, Brougham, Cantata, Cicero, Creation, Demosthenes, Diction, Elijah, Hwyl, Isocrates, Lectern, Morin, Nestor, Prevaricator, Proseucha, Proseuche, Rhetor, Samson, Spellbinder, Stump, Tub-thumper, Windbag, Yarra-banker

Orb Ball, Eyeball, Firmament, Globe, Mound, Ocellus, Pome, Sphere

Orbit Apse, Apsis, Circuit, Dump, Eccentric, Ellipse, Eye, Graveyard, Osculating, Parking, Path, Periastron, Perigee, Perihelion, Perilune, Periselenium, Polar, Revolution, Stationary, Synchronous

Orcadian Hoy

Orchard Arbour, Grove, Holt

Orchestra(te), Orchestration Chamber, Charanga, Concertgebouw, Concerto, ECO, Ensemble, Gamelan, Hallé, Instrumentation, LPO, LSO, Palm-Court, Pit, Ripieno, Score, SNO, String, Symphony

Orchid Adam and Eve, Adder's mouth, Arethusa, Babe-in-a-cradle, Bee, Bee-orchis, Bird's nest, Bog, Burnt-tip, Butterfly, Calanthe, Calypso, Cattleya, Cooktown, Coralroot, Cymbidium, Cypripedium, Disa, Epidendrum, Fly, Fly orchis, Fragrant, Fringed orchis, Frog, Helleborine, Lady, Lady's slipper, Lady's tresses, Lizard, Man, Marsh, Military, Moccasin-flower, Monkey, Musk, Naked lady, Odontoglossum, Oncidium, Pogonia, Purple-fringed, Puttyroot, Pyramidal, Rattlesnake plantain, Salep, Scented, Slipper, Snakemouth, Soldier, Spider, Spotted, Swamp pink, Swan, Twayblade, Vanda, Vanilla

Ord Beginning, Point

Ordain Arrange, Command, Decree, Destine, Enact, Induct, Japan, Priest

Ordeal Corsned, Disaster, Preeve, Test, → TRIAL, Via Dolorosa

Order(ed), Orderly, Orders Acoemeti, Adjust, Administration, Affiliation, Alphabetical, Anton Piller, Apollonian, Apple-pie, Arrange, Array, Attendant, Attention, Attic, Avast, Bade, Banker's, Bankruptcy, Bath, Batman, Battalia, Bed, Behest, Benedictine, Bespoke, Bid, Book, Call, Camaldolite, Canon, Category, Caveat, CB, Chaprassi, Charter, Cheque, Chit, Chuprassy, Class, Coherent, Command(ment), Committal, Compensation, Composite, Corinthian, Cosmo, Cosmos, Court, Decorum, Decree, Demand, Dictate, Diktat, Direct(ion), Directive, Dispone, Distringas, Dominican, Doric, DSO, Edict, Embargo, Enclosed, Enjoin, En règle, Established, Establishment, Eutaxy, Eviction, Exclusion, Feldsher, Fiat, Fiaunt, Firing, Firman, Form(ation), Franciscan, Fraternity, Freemason, Gagging, Garnishee, Garter, Gilbertine, Ginkgo, Good, Grade, Habeas corpus, Heast(e), Hecht, Hest, Holy, Indent, Injunction, Instruct, Interdict, Ionic, Irade, Khalsa, Kilter, Knights Hospitallers, Kosmos, Language, Large, Lexical, Loblolly boy, Loblolly man, Loose, Mail, Major, Mandamus, Mandate, Marching, Marist, Market, Marshal, Masonic, Medjidie, Merit, Methodical, Minor, Mittimus, Monastic, Money, Monitor, Natural, Neatness, Nunnery, OBE, Oddfellows, Official, OM, Open, Orange, Ord, Ordain, Organic, Pecking, Possession, Postal, Precedence, Precept, Premonstrant, Prescribe, Preservation, Provisional, Pyragyrite, Rank, Receiving, Reception, Règle, Regular, Religious, Restraining, Return, Right, Rule, Ruly, Sailing, Sealed, Search, Seraphic, Series, Settle, Shipshape, Short, Side, Standing, Starter's, State, Statutory, Stop(-loss), Straight, Subpoena, Summons, Supersedere, Supervision, System, Tabulate, Tall, Taxis, Tell, Templar, Teutonic, Third, Thistle, Tidy, Trim, Tuscan, Ukase, Uniformity, Warison, Warrant, Word, Writ

▷ **Ordering** *may indicate* an anagram

Ordinal Book, Number, Second, Sequence

Ordinance Byelaw, Capitulary, Decree, Edict, Law, Prescript, Rescript, Rite, Statute

Ordinary Average, Banal, Bog standard, Canton, Chevron, Comely, Common (or garden), Commonplace, Cot(t)ise, Everyday, Fess(e), Flanch, Flange, Folksy, Grassroots, Hackneyed, Mass, Mediocre, Middling, Mundane, → NORMAL, O, OR, Pedestrian, Plain, Prosy, Pub, Rank and file, Run-of-the-mill, Saltier, Saltire, Simple, Tressure, Trivial, Unexceptional, Uninspired, Usual, Workaday, Your

Ordnance Artillery, Cannon, Guns, Pelican, Supply

Ordure Cess, Dung, Fertiliser, Manure

Ore Alga, Babingtonite, Bauxite, Bornite, Breunnerite, Calamine, Calaverite, Cerusite, Chalcocite, Chalcopyrite, Chloanthite, Coffinite, Coin, Coltan, Copper, Crocoite, Element, Galenite, Glance, Haematite, Hedyphane, Horseflesh, Ilmenite,

Iridosmine, Ironstone, Kidney, Limonite, Mat, Melaconite, Middlings, Millhead, Milling grade, Mineral, Minestone, Morass, Niobite, Oligist, Peacock, Pencil, Phacolite, Pipe, Pitchblende, Proustite, Psilomelane, Pyrargyrite, Pyromorphite, Realgar, Red-lead, Ruby silver, Schlich, Seaweed, Siderite, Sinoptite, Slime, Slug, Smaltite, Speiss, Sphalerite, Stephanite, Stilpnosiderite, Stockwork, Stream-tin, Taconite, Tailing, Tenorite, Tetrahedrite, Tin, Wad(d), White-lead, Yellow cake

Organ(s), Organic Adnexa, American, Anlage, Antimere, Apollonicon, Appendix, Archegonium, Barrel, Biogenic, Calliope, Carpel, Carpogonium, Cercus, Chamber, Chemoreceptor, Choir, Chord, Claspers, Clave, Colour, Conch(a), Console, Corti's, Cribellum, Ctene, Ear, Echo, Electric, Electronic, Electroreceptor, End, Essential, Exteroceptor, Feeler, Fin, Flabellum, Fundus, Gametangium, Gill, Glairin, Gonad, Hammond®, Hand, Hapteron, Harmonica, Harmonium, Haustorium, House, Hydathode, Hydraulos, Imine, Isomere, Kerogen, Kidney, Lien, Light, Liver, Lung-book, Lyriform, Means, Mechanoreceptor, Media, Medulla, Melodion, Ministry, Nasal, Natural, Nectary, Nematocyst, Nephridium, Newspaper, Oogonia, Ovary, Ovipositor, Ovotestis, Palp, Pancreas, Parapodium, Part, Pedal, Photogen, Photophore, Photoreceptor, Physharmonics, Pipe, Pipeless, Placenta, Plastid, Portative, Positive, Procarp, Prothallus, Pulmones, Purtenance, Pyrophone, Radula, Receptor, Recit, Reed, Regal, Relict, Sang, Saprobe, Scent, Sense, Sensillum, Serinette, Serra, Siphon, Spinneret, Spleen, Sporangium, Sporophore, Stamen, Statocyst, Steam, Swell, Syrinx, Tentacle, Textual, Theatre, Theca, Thymus, Tongue, Tonsil, Tool, Tympanum, Uterus, Vegetative, Velum, Verset, Viscera, Viscus, Vitals, Voice, Voluntary, Womb, Wurlitzer®

Organelle Peroxisome

Organise(d), Organisation, Organiser Activate, Aggregator, Anatomy, → ARRANGE, Association, Brigade, Caucus, Class(ify), Collect, Comecon, Company, Constitution, Coordinate, Design, Embody, Entrepreneur, Fascio, Firm, Impresario, Infrastructure, Jaycee, Ku Klux Klan, Logistics, Machine, Mafia, Marshal, Mobilise, Octopus, Opus Dei, Orchestrate, Outfit, Personal, PLO, Promotor, Quango, Rally, Regiment, Resistance, Rosicrucian, Run, Setup, Sharpbender, Social, Soroptimist, Sort, Stage, Stahlhelm, Steward, System, Tidy, Together, UN, Viet Minh

▷ **Organise(d)** *may indicate* an anagram

Organism Aerobe, Agamic, Auxotroph, Being, Biont, Biotic, Cell, Chimeric, Chlamydia, Ciliate, Clade, Coral, Diplont, Ecad, Endogenous, Entity, Epibenthos, Epizoite, Epizoon, Eucaryote, Euglena, Eukaryote, Eurytherm, Germ, Halobiont, Halophile, Haplont, Hemiparasite, Holophyte, Holoplankton, Homeotherm, Incross, Infauna, Infusoria(n), Lichen, Macrobiote, Medusa, Meroplankton, Metamale, Microbe, Moneron, Morphology, Nekton, Neuston, Paramecium, Pathogen, Periphyton, Phenetics, Plankter, Plankton, Pleuston, Protist, Protista, Protozoan, Radiolarian, Saprobe, Saprotroph, Schizomycete, Streptococcus, Symbion(t), Teratogen, Thermophile, Torula, Virino, Volvox, Vorticella

Organ-part, Organ-stop Bourdon, Clarabella, Diapason, Gamba, Montre, Nasard, Principal, Pyramidon, Quint, Salicet, Stop

Organ-tuner Reed-knife

Orgy Bacchanalia(n), Binge, Blinder, Bust, Carousal, Dionysian, Feast, Revel, Saturnalia, Spree, Wassail

Orient(al) Adjust, Annamite, Chinoiserie, Dawn, Dayak, E, East(ern), Fu Manchu, Hindu, Levant, Leyton, Malay, Mongol, Mongolian, Pareoean, Shan, Sunrise, Tatar, Thai, Tibetan, Turk(o)man

Orifice Aperture, Blastosphere, Gap, Hole, Micropyle, Nare, Opening, Pore, Spiracle, Trema, Vent

Origen's work Tetrapla
Origin(al), Originate, Originating Abo, Adam, Arise, Beginning, Birth, Come, Cradle, Creation, Derive, Editio princeps, Elemental, Emanate, Epicentre, Etymon, Extraction, First, Firsthand, Focus, Found, Generic, Genesis, Genetical, Germ, Grow, Hatch, Incunabula, Initial, Innovate, Invent, Master, Mother, Nascence, Natality, New, Novel, Ord, Primal, Primary, Primigenial, Primordial, Pristine, Prototype, Provenance, Provenience, Rise, Root, Seminal, Source, Spring, Start, Ur, Ylem, Zoism
Oriole Firebird, Hangbird
Orison Blessing, Prayer
Ormer Abalone, Haliotis
Ornament(al), Ornamentation Acroter(ia), Additament, Adorn, Aglet, Aiguillette, Anaglyph, Antefix, Anthemion, Aplustre, Arabesque, Bahuti, Ball-flower, Barbola, Baroque, Barrette, Bead, Bedeck, Bez(z)ant, Billet, Blister, Boss, Bracelet, Breloque, Broider, Brooch, Bugle, Bulla, Cartouche, Chase, Clock, Cockade, Conceit, Corbeil(le), Cornice, Crocket, Cross-quarters, Curin, Curlicue, Decorate, Decoration, Diamanté, Die-work, Diglyph, Dog's-tooth, Doodad, Dreamcatcher, Embellish, Emblem(a), Enrich, Epaulet(te), Epergne, Fallal, Fandangle, Fiddlehead, Figuration, Figurine, Filagree, Filigrain, Filigree, Fillagree, Fleuret, Fleurette, Fleuron, Florid, Fret, Fretwork, Frill, Frounce, Furbelow, Furnish, Gadroon, Gaud, Gingerbread, Gorget, Griff(e), Guilloche, Gutta, Headwork, Heitiki, Helix, Honeysuckle, Illustrate, Inlay, Knotwork, Labret, Lambrequin, Leglet, Lotus, Macramé, Mantling, Mense, Millefleurs, Mordent, Moresque, Motif, Nail-head, Necklet, Netsuke, Nicknackery, Niello, O, Okimono, Ouch, Ovolo, Palmette, Parure, Paternoster, Paua, Pawa, Pectoral, Pendant, Picot, Pipe, Pompom, Pompo(o)n, Poppyhead, Pounce, Pralltriller, Prettify, Prunt, Purfle, Quatrefoil, Rel(l)ish, Rocaille, Rococo, Scalework, Scrollwork, Spangle, Spar, Tassel, Tettix, Tiki, Tool, Torque, Torsade, Tracery, Trappings, Trill, Trimming, Trinket, Triquetra, Turn, Versal, Wally, Water-leaf, Whigmaleerie, Whigmaleery
Ornate Baroque, Churrigueresque, Dressy, Elaborate, Fancy, Florid, Flowery
▷ **Ornate** *may indicate* an anagram
Ornithologist Audubon, Birdman
Orotund Bombastic, Grandiose, Pompous, Rhetorical, Sonant
Orphan Annie, Foundling, Topsy, Ward
Orpiment Arsenic, Zarnich
Orpington Buff, Hen
Ort Bit, Crumb, Morsel, Remnant
Orthodox Bien-pensant, Cocker, Conventional, Hardshell, Proper, Sound, Standard
Orthorhombic Enstatite
Ortolan Bird, Bunting, Rail
Oscar Award, O, Wilde
Oscillate, Oscillation, Oscillator Dynatron, Excitor, Fluctuate, Librate, Local, Parasitic, Relaxation, Ripple, Rock, Seesaw, Seiche, Squeg, Surge, Swing, Vibrate, Waver
Osier Red, Reed, Sallow, Willow
Osmium Os
Osmosis Reverse
Osprey Fish-hawk, Lammergeier, Ossifrage, Pandion
Osseous Bony, Hard, Skeletal, Spiny
Ostensibly Apparent, External, Seeming
Ostentation, Ostentatious Camp, Display, Dog, Éclat, Epideictical, Extravagant,

Fantoosh, Flamboyant, Flash(y), Flaunt, Florid, Flourish, Garish, Gaudy, Highfalutin(g), Parade, Pomp, Ponc(e)y, Pretence, Puff, → **SHOW(ING)**, Side, Splash, Swank, Tacky, Tulip

Ostler Stabler

Ostracise, Ostracism Banish, Blackball, Boycott, Cut, Exclude, Exile, Petalism, Potsherd, Snub, Taboo, Tabu

Ostrich Em(e)u, Estrich, Estridge, Nandoo, Nandu, Ratite, Rhea, Struthio(nes), Titanis

Othello Moor, Morisco

Other(s), Otherwise Additional, Aka, Alia, Alias, Allo-, Alternative, Besides, Different, Distinct, Else, Et al, Et alli, Etc, Excluding, Former, Further, Rest, Significant

Other things Alia

▷ **Otherwise** *may indicate* an anagram

Otiose Idle, Indolent, Ineffective, Lazy, Needless, Superfluous

Otis Bustard

Otter Edal, Paravane, Sea, Tarka

Otto Attar, Chypre, Mahratta

Ottoman Osmanli, Porte, Rumelia, Turk

Oubliette Dungeon, Pit, Prison

Ouch Brooch, Ornament, Ow

Ought All, Should

Ouida Ramée

Ounce Cat, Fluid, Liang, Oz, Panther, Tael, Uncial

Our(selves) Us, We

▶ **Ousel** *see* **OUZEL**

Oust Depose, Dislodge, Eject, Evict, Expel, Fire, Supplant, Unnest, Unseat

Out Absent, Aglee, Agley, Asleep, Aus, Away, Begone, Bowl, Dated, En ville, Exposed, External, Forth, Furth, Haro, Harrow, Hence, Hors, Oust, Skittle, Striking, Stump, Taboo, Uit, Unfashionable, Up, York

▷ **Out** *may indicate* an anagram

Out and out Absolute, Arrant, Rank, Sheer, Stark, Teetotal, Thorough, Totally, Utter

Outback Backblocks, Bundu, The mulga

Outbreak Epidemic, Eruption, Explosion, Flare-up, Plague, Putsch, Rash, Recrudescence

Outburst Access, Blurt, Bluster, Boutade, Evoe, Explosion, Fit, Flaw, Furore, Fusillade, Gush, Gust, Paroxysm, Passion, Philippic, Salvo, Storm, Tantrum, Tumult, Volley

Outcast Cagot, Discard, Eta, Exile, Exul, Ishmael, Leper, Mesel, Pariah, Rogue

Outcome Aftermath, Consequence, Dénouement, Effect, Emergence, End, Event, Issue, → **RESULT**, Sequel, Upshot, Wash-up

Outcrop Basset, Blossom, Crag, Creston, Inlier, Mesa, Rognon, Spur, Tarpit

Outcry Alew, Bray, → **CLAMOUR**, Halloo, Howl, Hue, Humdudgeon, Protest, Racket, Shright, Steven, Uproar, Utas

Outdated, Out of date Archaic, Dinosaur, Effete, Feudal, Fossil, Horse and buggy, Obsolete, Old hat, Outmoded, Passé, Square

Outdo Beat, Best, Cap, Picnic, Surpass, Top, Trump, Worst

Outdoor(s) Alfresco, External, Garden, Open air, Plein-air

Outer External, Extrogenous, Magpie, Superficial, Top

Outfit(ter) Accoutrement, Catsuit, Ensemble, Equipage, Fitout, Furnish, Get-up, Haberdasher, Habit, Kit, Rig, Samfoo, Samfu, Strip, Suit, Team, Trousseau,

Weed(s), Whites

Outflank Overlap

Outflow Anticyclone, Discharge, Effluence, Eruption, Gorge, Issue, Surge

Outgoing Egression, Exiting, Extrovert, Open, Retiring

Outgrowth Ala(te), Aril, Bud, Caruncle, Enation, Epiphenomenon, Exostosis, Flagellum, Ligule, Offshoot, Osteophyte, Propagulum, Root-hair, Sequel, Strophiole, Trichome

Outhouse Lean to, Privy, Shed, Skilling, Skillion, Skipper, Stable

Outing Excursion, Jaunt, Junket, Picnic, Sortie, Spin, Spree, Treat, Trip, Wayzgoose

Outlandish Barbarous, Bizarre, Exotic, Foreign, Peregrine, Rum

Outlaw Allan-a-Dale, Attaint, Badman, Ban, Bandit(ti), Banish, Exile, Fugitive, Hereward, Horn, Jesse James, Proscribe, Put to the horn, Robin Hood, Rob Roy, Ronin, Tory, Waive

Outlay Cost, Expense, Mise

Outlet Débouché, Egress, Escape, Estuary, Exit, Femerall, Market, Opening, Orifice, Outfall, Overflow, Sluice, Socket, Spout, Tuyere, Tweer, Twier, Twire, Twyer(e), Vent

Outline Adumbration, Aperçu, Circumscribe, Configuration, Contorno, Contour, Delineate, Digest, → **DRAFT**, Esquisse, Footprint, Layout, Note, Perimeter, Plan, Profile, Prospectus, Relief, Scenario, Schematic, Shape, Silhouette, Skeletal, Skeleton, Sketch, Summary, Syllabus, Synopsis, T(h)alweg, Trace

Outlook Casement, Perspective, Prospect, View, Vista, Weltanschauung

Outmoded Wasm

▷ **Out of** *may indicate* an anagram

Out of date Corny, Obs, Passé, Scrap, Square, Worn

Out of form Amorphous, Awry

Out of order Fritz

Out of sorts Cachectic, Nohow, Peevish, Poorly

▷ **Out of sorts** *may indicate* an anagram

Out of tune Discordant, Flat, Scordato, Scordatura

Outpost Colony, Picquet

Outpour(ing) Effuse, Flood, Flow, Gush, Libation, Stream, Torrent

Output Data, Emanation, Get, Produce, Production, Turnout, Yield

▷ **Output** *may indicate* an anagram

Outrage(ous) Affront, Appal, Atrocity, Desecrate, Disgust, Egregious, Enorm(ity), Flagitious, Flagrant, Insult, OTT, Rich, Sacrilege, Scandal, Shocking, Ungodly, Unholy, Violate

▷ **Outrageously** *may indicate* an anagram

Outright Clean, Complete, Entire, Point-blank, Utter

Outset Beginning, Start

Outshine Eclipse, Excel, Overshadow, Surpass, Upstage

Outside Ab extra, Crust, Exterior, External, Extramural, Front, Furth, Hors, Periphery, Plein-air, Rim, Rind, Rine, Surface

Outsider Alien, Bolter, Bounder, Cad, Extern, Extremist, Foreigner, Incomer, Oustiti, Palagi, Pariah, Ring-in, Roughie, Stranger, Stumer, Unseeded, Upstart

Outsize Capacious, Giant, Gigantic, Huge, OS

Outskirts Edge, Fringe, Periphery, Purlieu

Outspoken Bluff, Blunt, Broad, Candid, Explicit, Forthright, Frank, Plain, Rabelaisian, Round, Vocal

Outstand(ing) Ace, Beaut(y), Belter, Billowing, Bulge, Chief, Egregious, Eminent, Especial, Exceptional, Extant, First, Fugleman, Highlight, Humdinger, Impasto, Jut,

Lulu, Marked, Matchless, Oner, Overdue, Owing, Paragon, Phenom(enal), Pièce de résistance, Prince, Prize, Prominent, Promontory, Prosilient, Protrude, Proud, Purler, Relief, Relievo, Salient, Signal, Special, Squarrose, Star, Stellar, Strout, Superb, Tour de force, Unpaid, Unsettled

Outstrip Best, Cap, Cote, Distance, Exceed, Overtake

Outward Efferent, Extern(e), External, Extrinsic, Extrorse, Extrovert, Posticous, Postliminary, Superficial

Outweigh Preponderate

Outwit Baffle, Best, Circumvent, Crossbite, Dish, Euchre, Fox, Outthink, Over-reach, → **THWART**, Trick

Outwork Demilune, Jetty, Moon, Tenail(le), Tenaillon

Outworn Decrepit, Obsolete, Used

Ouzel Ring, Water

Oval(s) Cartouche, Cassini, Ellipse, Henge, Navette, Obovate, Ooidal

Ovary Oophoron

Ovation Applause, Cheer, Standing

Oven(-like) Aga®, Calcar, Camp, Combination, Convection, Cul-de-four, Dutch, Electric, Furnace, Gas, Hangi, Haybox, Horn(it)o, Kiln, Lear, Leer, Lehr, Lime kiln, Maori, Microwave, Muffle, Norwegian, Oast, Oon, Stove, Umu

Over Above, Across, Again, Atop, C, Clear, Done, Finished, Hexad, Left, Maiden, Of, On, Ore, Ort, Owre, Sopra, Spare, Superior, Surplus, Through, Uber, Wicket maiden, Yon

Overact Burlesque, Emote, Ham, Hell, Hoke

Overactive Hyper

Overall(s) Boiler suit, Chaps, Denims, Dungarees, Dust-coat, Fatigues, Jumper, Smicket, Smock, Tablier, Workwear

Overbearing Arrogant, Dogmatic, Domineering, High-muck-a-muck, Imperious, Insolent, Lordly

Overbid Gazump

Overcast Cloudy, Lowering, Sew, Sombre

Overcharge Clip, Extort, Fleece, Gyp, OC, Rack-rent, Rook, Rush, Soak, Sting

Overcoat Balmacaan, Benjamin, Benny, British warm, Chesterfield, → **COAT**, Crombie, Dolman, Grego, Inverness, Joseph, Paletot, Petersham, Pos(h)teen, Prince Albert, Raglan, Redingote, Spencer, Surtout, Tabard, Taglioni, Ulster, Warm, Wooden, Wrap-rascal

Overcome Beat, Bested, Conquer, Convince, Defeat, Hit for six, Kill, Master, Mither, Moider, Moither, Prevail, Quell, Speechless, Stun, Subdue, Subjugate, Superate, Surmount, Vanquish, Win

Overcrowd Congest, Jam, Pack

Overdo(ne) Exceed, Ham, Hokey, Hokum, OTT, Percoct, Tire

Overdose OD

Overdraft Red

▷ **Overdrawn** *may indicate* 'red' outside another word

Overdress(ing) Dudism, Flossy, Overall

Overdue Behindhand, Belated, Excessive, Late

Overeat(ing) Binge, Gorge, Hypertrophy, Pig out, Satiate

Overemphasize Rub in, Stress

Overfeed Gorge, Sate, Stuff

Overflow(ing) Abrim, Lip, Nappe, Ooze, Ream, Redound, Spillage, Surfeit, Teem

Overfull Brimming, Hept

Overgrow(n) Ivy'd, Jungle, Ramp(ant), Rank, Rhinophyma

Overhang(ing) Beetle, Bulge, Cornice, → JUT, Project, Shelvy
Overhaul Bump, Catch, Overtake, Recondition, Revision, Service, Strip
Overhead(s) Above, Aloft, Ceiling, Cost, Exes, Hair(s), Headgear, Oncost, Rafter, Upkeep, Zenith
Overhear Catch, Eavesdrop, Tap
Overheat Enrage
Overindulge(nt) Crapulent, Crass, Dissipated, Dissolute, Pig
Overjoy Elate, Thrill
Overland Portage
Overlap(ping) Correspond, Equitant, Imbricate, Incubous, Kern(e), Limbous, Obvolute, Stretto, Tace, Tasse
Overlay Ceil, Smother, Stucco, Superimpose, Veneer
Overlearned Pedantic
Overload Burden, Plaster, Strain, Surcharge, Tax
Overlook Condone, Disregard, Excuse, Forget, Miss, Pretermit, Superintend, Waive
Overlord Edwin, Excess, Invasion
Overlying Incumbent, Jessant, Pressing
Overmuch Excessive, Surplus, Too, Undue
Overplay Ham, Hoke
Overpower(ing) Crush, Evince, Mighty, Onerous, Oppress, Overwhelm, Subdue, Surmount, Swelter, Whelm
Overpraise Adulate
Over-refined Dainty, Nice, Pernickety, Precious
Override, Overrule Abrogate, Disallow, Outweigh, Reverse, Talk down, Veto
Overrun Exceed, Extra, Infest, Inundate, Invade, Swarm, Teem
Overseas Abroad, Colonial, Outremer, Transmarine, Ultramarine
Oversee(r) Baas, Boss, Captain, Care, Deputy, Direct, Eyebrow, Foreman, Forewoman, Grieve, Handle, Induna, Moderator, Periscope, Steward, Supercargo, Survey(or)
Oversentimental Byronic, Slushy
Overshadow(ed) Cloud, Dominate, Eclipse, Obscure, Outclass, Umbraculate
Overshoe Arctic, Galosh, Sandal, Snowboot
Oversight Blunder, Care, Error, Gaffe, Lapse, Neglect, Parablepsis
Overstate(ment) Embroider, Exaggerate, Hyperbole
Overstrained Epitonic
Overt Manifest, Patent, Plain, Public
Overtake Catch, For(e)hent, Lap, Leapfrog, Overget, Overhaul, → PASS, Supersede, Usurp
Overthrow Dash, Defeat, Demolish, Depose, Down, Labefact(at)ion, Ruin, Smite, Stonker, Subvert, Supplant, Topple, Unhorse, Usurp, Vanquish, Whemmle, Whommle, Whummle, Worst
Overture Advance, Carnival, Concert, Egmont, French, Hebrides, Intro, Italian, Leonora, Offer, → OPENING, Prelude, Propose, Sinfonia, Toccata, Toccatella, Toccatina
Overturn(ing) Catastrophe, Coup, Cowp, Engulf, Quash, Reverse, Tip, Topple, Up(set), Upend, Whemmle
Overvalue Exaggerate, Salt
Overweening Bashaw, Cocky, Excessive, Imperious, Presumptuous
Overweight Sunk
Overwhelm(ed), Overwhelming Accablé, Assail, → CRUSH, Defeat, Deluge, Engulf, Flabbergast, Foudroyant, Inundate, KO, Mind-boggling, Oppress,

Overcome, Scupper, Smother, Submerge, Swamp, Whup

Overwork(ed) Fag, Hackneyed, Ornament, Slog, Stale, Supererogation, Tax, Tire, Toil

Overwrought Frantic, Hysterical, Ore-rested, Ornate, Rococo

Ovid Naso

Ovum Egg, Oosphere, Seed

Owe(d), Owing Attribute, Due, OD

Owen Glendower

Owl(s) African, Barn, Barred, Blinker, Boobook, Brown, Bubo, Bunter, Chinese, Eagle, Elegant, English, Fish, Glimmergowk, Hawk, Hoo(ter), Horned, Howlet, Jenny, Little, Long-eared, Longhorn, Madge, Moper, Mopoke, Mopus, Night, Ogle, Parliament, Ruru, Saw-whet, Scops, Screech, Sea, Snowy, Strich, Striges, Strigiformes, Tawny, Wood

Own(er), Owning, Ownership Admit, Agnise, Confess, Domain, Dominium, Fess, Have, Hold, Mortmain, Nain, Of, Personal, Possess, Proper, Proprietor, Recognise, Reputed, Title, Use

Ox(en) Anoa, Aquinas, Aurochs, Banteng, Banting, Bison, Bonas(s)us, Buffalo, Bugle, Bullock, Cat(t)alo, Fee, Gaur, Gayal, Gyal, Kouprey, Mart, Musk, Musk-sheep, Neat, Ovibos, Rother, Saola, Sapi-utan, S(e)ladang, Steare, Steer, Stirk, Taurus, Ure, Urus, Water, Water buffalo, Yak, Yoke, Zebu, Z(h)o

Oxford (group) Buchmanism, OU, Puseyism, Shoe

Oxhead Aleph

Oxidation, Oxide Alumina, Anatase, Ceria, Erbium, Eremacausis, Gothite, Gummite, Holmia, Kernite, Lithia, Magnesia, Nitrous, Psilomelane, Quicklime, Red lead, Rutile, Samarskite, Strontia, Thoria, Zaffer, Zaffre

▷ **Oxtail** *may indicate* 'x'

Oxygen (and lack of) Anoxia, Epoxy, Liquid, Lox, Loxygen, O, Vital air

Oyer Hearing, Trial

Oyster (bed), Oyster disease, Oyster-eater Avicula, Bivalve, Bonamia, Bush, Cul(t)ch, Kentish, Lay, Mollusc, Native, Ostrea, Ostreophage, Pandore, Pearl, Plant, Prairie, Salsify, Scalp, Scaup, Seed(ling), Spat, Spondyl, Stew, Vegetable

Oyster-catcher Sea-pie

Oyster-plant Gromwell, Salsify

Oz Amos, Australia

Ozone Air, Atmosphere, Oxygen

Pp

P Papa, Parking, Penny, Piano, Prince

PA Aide, Tannoy

Pabulum Aliment, Cheer, Food, Fuel, Nourishment

Pace, Pacemaker Canter, Clip, Cracking, Dog-trot, Easter, Gait, Geometric, Heel and toe, Jog-trot, Lope, Measure, Military, Pari passu, Pioneer, → **RATE**, Roman, Scout's, Snail's, Spank, Speed, Step, Stride, Stroll, Tempo, Tramp, Tread, Trot

Pachyderm Armadillo, Elephant, Hippo, Mastodon, Rhino

Pacific, Pacify Appease, Bromide, Conciliate, Dove, Ease, Irenic, Lull, Mild, Moderate, Ocean, Placate, Placid, Quiet, Serene, Soothe, Subdue, Sweeten, Tranquil

Pacifist CO, Conciliator, D(o)ukhobor, Dove, Peacenik

Pack(age), Packed, Packing Back, Bale, Blister, Bobbery, Box, Bubble, Bundle, Cards, Cold, Compress, Congest, Cram, Crate, Crowd, Cry, Deck, Dense, Dunnage, Embox, Entity, Everest, Excelsior, Face, Fardel, Floe, Gasket, Gaskin, Glut, Hamper, Hunt, Ice, Jam, Kennel, Knapsack, Load, Matilda, Naughty, Pair, → **PARCEL**, Pikau, Power, Pun, Rout, Rucksack, Set, Shiralee, Shrink-wrap, Steeve, Stow, Suits, Sumpter, Tamp, Tread, Troop, Truss, Wad, Wet, Wolf, Wrap

Packet Boat, Bundle, Deck, Liner, Mailboat, Mint, Parcel, Pay, Red, Roll, Sachet, Steam, Steamboat, Wage

Pack-horse Sumpter

Packman Chapman, Hawker, Hiker, Pedlar, Tinker

Pact Agreement, Alliance, Bargain, Bilateral, Cartel, Contract, Covenant, Locarno, Munich, Stability, Suicide, → **TREATY**, Warsaw

Pad(ding) Batting, Bombast, Brake, Bustle, Compress, Condo, Crash, Cushion, Dabber, Damper, Dossil, Enswathe, Expand, Falsies, Filler, Flat, Frog, Gumshield, Hard, Hassock, Horse, Ink, Launch, Leg-guard, Lily, Nag, Note, Numnah, Patch, Paw, Ped, Pillow, Pincushion, Plastron, Pledget, Plumper, Pouf(fe), Protract, Pudding, Puff, Pulvillus, Pulvinar, Scratch, Shoulder, Stamp, Stuff, Sunk, Swab, Tablet, Thief, Touch, Tournure, Tylopod, Tympan, Velour(s), Velure, Wad, Wase, Writing

Paddington Bear, Station

Paddle, Paddle boat, Paddle-foot Canoe, Dabble, Doggy, Oar, Pinniped, Row, Seal, Side-wheel, Spank, Splash, Stern-wheeler, Wade

Paddock Field, Frog, Holding, Meadow, Park, Sacrifice

Paddy, Paddy field Fury, Ire, Irishman, Mick, Pat(rick), Pet, Rag, Rage, Sawah, Tantrum, Temper, Wax

Padre Chaplain, Cleric, Father, Monk, Priest

Paean Hymn, Ode, Praise, Psalm

Paedophile Nonce

Pagan Animist, Atheist, Gentile, Gentoo, Godless, Heathen, Idolater, Infidel, Odinist, Paynim, Saracen

Page(s), Pageboy Back, Bellboy, Bellhop, Bleep, Boy, Buttons, Callboy, Centrefold, Flyleaf, Folio, Foolscap, Front, Gate-fold, Groom, Haircut, Hairdo, Home, Hornbook, Leaf, Master, Messenger, Moth, Octavo, Op-ed, P, Pane, PP, Problem, Quarto, Ream, Recto, Ro, Servant, Sheet, Side, Splash, Squire, Tear sheet, Tiger, Title, Varlet, Verso, Web, Yellow

Pageant Antique, Cavalcade, Pomp, Spectacle, Tattoo, Triumph

Pagoda Anking, Anqing, Temple, To

Pah Pish, Tush, Umph

▶ **Paid** *see* **PAY**

Pail Bucket, Kettle, Leglan, Leglen, Leglin, Piggin, Slop

Pain(ful), Pains Ache, Aggrieve, Agony, Ake, Algesis, Angina, Anguish, Arthralgia, Bad, Bale, Bedsore, Bitter, Bore, Bot(t), Bother, Burn, Causalgia, Colic, Cramp, Crick, Distress, Dole, Doleur, Dolour, Dool(e), Dysmenorhoea, Dysury, Eina, Excruciating, Fibrositis, Gastralgia, Gip, Grief, Gripe, Growing, Gyp, Harrow, Heartburn, Hemialgia, → **HURT**, Ill, Kink, Laborious, Lumbago, Mal, Mastalgia, Mastodynia, Metralgia, Migraine, Misery, Mulligrubs, Myalgia, Neuralgia, Nociceptive, Pang, Persuant, Pest, Phantom, Pleurodynia, Prick, Pungent, Rack, Raw, Referred, Sair, Sciatica, Smart, Sore, Sorrow, Splitting, Sten(d), Sting, Stitch, Strangury, Stung, Teen(e), Tene, Throe, Topalgia, Torment, Tormina, Torture, Travail, Twinge, Wo(e), Wrench, Wring

▷ **Pain** *may indicate* bread (French)

Painkiller Aminobutene, Analgesic, Bute, Cocaine, Distalgesic, Endorphin, Enkephalin, Jadeite, Meperidine, Metopon, Morphine, Number, Pethidine

Painless(ness) Analgesia, Easy

Painstaking Assiduous, Careful, Diligent, Elaborate, Exacting, Meticulous, Sedulous, Studious, Thorough

Paint(ed), Painting Abstract, Abstract expressionism, Acrylic, Action, Airbrush, Alla prima, Aquarelle, Arcimboldo, Art autre, Art deco, Artificial, Art nouveau, Ash Can School, Barbizon, Battlepiece, Bice, Blottesque, Camaieu, Canvas, Cellulose, Chiaroscuro, Clair-obscure, Clobber, Coat, Colour, Cubism, Dadaism, Daub, Dayglo, Decorate, Depict, Describe, Diptych, Distemper, Duco, Eggshell, Emulsion, Enamel, Encaustic, Fard, Fauvism, Finery, Finger, Flatting, Flemish, Fore-edge, Fresco, Fucus, Genre, Gild, Gloss, Gouache, Gravure, Grease, Grisaille, Hard-edge, Historical, Icon, Impasto, Impressionism, Intimism(e), Intonaco, Intumescent, Lead, Limn, Luminous, Magilp, Matt, Megilp, Mehndi, Miniate, Miniature, Modello, Mona Lisa, Monotint, Mural, Naive, Neo-Impressionism, Neo-Plasticism, Nightpiece, Nihonga, Nocturne, Non-drip, Oaker, Ochre, Oil, Old Master, Oleo(graph), Op art, Orphism, Paysage, Pentimento, Pict, Picture, Pigment, Pinxit, Plein air, Pointillism(e), Portray, Poster, Post-Impressionism, Predella, Primitive, Quadratura, Raddle, Rag-rolling, Rosemaling, Roughstuff, Sand, Scenography, Scumble, Secco, Sfumato, Sien(n)ese, Skyscape, Spray, Stencil, Stereochrome, Still life, Stipple, Suprematism, Tablature, Tachism(e), Tag, Tall-oil, Tanka, Tempera, Tenebrism, Thangka, Tondo, Ukiyo-e, Umber, Umbrian, Undercoat, Underglaze, Vanitas, Veduta, Vorticism, War, Wax

Painted woman Courtesan, Harlot, Pict, Tart

Painter(s) Animalier, → **ARTIST**, Ash Can School, Colourist, Cubist, Decorator, Gilder, Illusionist, Impressionist, Limner, Little Master, Miniaturist, Old Master, Paysagist, Plein-airist, Primitive, Sien(n)ese, Soutine, Sunday

Pair(ing) Brace, Cooper, Couple(t), Duad, Duo, Dyad(ic), Exciton, Fellows, Geminate, Item, Jugate, Jumelle, Link, Lone, Match, Mate, Minimal, Ocrea, Pigeon, Pr, Span, Spouses, Synapsis, Syndyasmian, Syzygy, Tandem, Thummim,

Twa(e), Tway, Two, Urim, Yoke

Paisley Ian, Orange, Shawl

Pakistan(i) Pathan

Pal Ally, Amigo, Bud(dy), China, Chum, Comrade, Crony, Cully, Friend, Mate, Wus(s)

Palace Alcazar, Alhambra, Basilica, Blenheim, Buckingham, Court, Crystal, Edo, Élysée, Escorial, Escurial, Fontainebleau, Forbidden City, Fulham, Gin, Goslar, Holyrood, Holyroodhouse, Hotel, Istana, Lambeth, Lateran, Linlithgow, Louvre, Mansion, Nonsuch, Palatine, Picture, Pitti, Pushkin, Quirinal, St James's, Sans Souci, Schloss, Seraglio, Serail, Shushan, Topkapi, Trianon, Tuileries, Valhalla, Vatican, Versailles

Paladin Champion, Charlemagne, Defender, Douzeper, Fièrabras, Ganelon, → **KNIGHT**, Ogier, Oliver, Orlando, Rinaldo, Roland

Palanquin Doolie, Kago, Litter, Palkee, Palki, Sedan

Palatable, Palatalized, Palate Cleft, Dainty, Hard, Mouille, Relish, Roof, Sapid, Savoury, Soft, Taste, Toothsome, Uranic, Uraniscus, Uvula, Velum

Palatial Ornate, Splendid

Palatinate, Palatine Officer, Pfalz

Palaver Chatter, Debate, Parley, Powwow, → **TALK**

Pale, Paling Ashen, Blanch, Bleach, Cere, Dim, English, Etiolate(d), Fade, → **FAINT**, Fence, Ghostly, Haggard, Insipid, Jewish, Lily (white), Livid, Mealy, Ox-fence, Pallescent, Pastel, Peaky, Peelie-wally, Picket, Sallow, Shilpit, Stang, Verge, Wan, Whey-faced, White, Wishy-washy

Paleography Diplomatics

Pal(a)eolithic Acheulean, Acheulian, Azilian, Chellean, Gravettian, Levallois(ian), Lower, Madelenian, Magdalenian, Middle, Neanderthal, Perigordian, Solutrean, Strepyan, Upper

Paleozoic Permian, Silurian

Palestine, Palestinian Amorite, Fatah, Gadarene, Intifada, Israel, Pal, Per(a)ea, PLO, Samaria

Palette Board, Cokuloris

Palindrome, Palindromic Cancrine, Sotadic

Palisade Barrier, Fence, Fraise, Stacket, Stockade

Pall Bore, Cloy, Curtain, Damper, Glut, Mantle, Mortcloth, Satiate, Shroud

Palladium Defence, Pd, Safeguard

Pallas Athene

Pallet Bed, Cot, Couch, Mattress, Tick

Palliate, Palliative Alleviate, Anetic, Ease, Extenuate, Lessen, Mitigate, Reduce, Relieve, Sedative

Pallid Anaemic, Ashen, Insipid, Pale, Wan, Waxy

Palm Accolade, Areca, Assai, Atap, Babassu, Bangalow, Betel, Buriti, Burrawang, Bussu, Cabbage, Calamus, Carna(h)uba, Chamaerops, Chiqui-chiqui, Coco, Cohune, Conceal, Coquito, Corozo, Corypha, Cycad, Date (tree), Doom, Doum, Elaeis, Euterpe, Fan, Feather, Fob, Foist, Gomuti, Gomuto, Groo-groo, Gru-gru, Hand, Ita, Itching, Ivory, Jip(p)i-Jap(p)a, Jipyapa, Jupati, Kentia, Kittul, Laurels, Loof, Looves, Macahuba, Macaw, Macoya, Moriche, Nikau, Nipa, Oil, Palmyra, Paxiuba, Peach, Pupunha, Raffia, Raphia, Rat(t)an, Royal, Sabal, Sago, Saw palmetto, Sugar, Talipat, Talipot, Thatch, Thenar, Toddy, Triumph, Troelie, Troolie, Trooly, Trophy, Vola, Washingtonia, Wax, Wine, Zamia

Palmer Lilli, Pilgrim

Palmerston Pam

Palmistry Ch(e)irognomy

Palm-leaf Frond
Palpable Evident, Gross, Manifest, Patent, Plain, Tangible
Palpitate, Palpitation Flutter, Pitpat, Pulsate, Throb, Twitter, Vibrate
Palsy Bell's, Cerebral, Paralysis, Shakes
Paltry Bald, Cheap, Exiguous, Mean, Measly, Peanuts, Pelting, Petty, Poor, Puny, Scald, Scalled, Shoestring, Sorry, Tin(-pot), Tinny, Trashy, Trifling, Two-bit, Vile, Waff, Whiffet
Pamper(ed) Cocker, Coddle, Cosher, Cosset, Cuiter, Feather-bed, Gratify, High-fed, → **INDULGE**, Mollycoddle, Overfeed, Pet, Pompey, Spoon-fed
Pamphlet Brochure, Catalogue, Chapbook, Leaflet, Notice, Sheet, Tract
Pan Agree, Auld Hornie, Bainmarie, Balit, Basin, Betel(-pepper), Braincase, Chafer, Dent, Dial, Drip, Dripping, Goat-god, Goblet, God, Hard, Ice-floe, Iron, Karahi, Ladle, Lavatory, Muffin, Nature-god, Oil, Pancheon, Panchion, Patella, Patina, Peter, Poacher, Preserving, Prospect, Roast, Salt, Search, Skid, Skillet, Slag, Slate, Spider, Vessel, Warming, Wo(c)k, Work
Panacea All-heal, Azoth, Catholicon, Cure(-all), Elixir, Ginseng, Parkleaves, Remedy, Tutsan
Panache Bravura, Crest, Dash, Flair, Paz(z)azz, Piz(z)azz, Plume, Pzazz, Show, Talent
Pancake Blin(i), Blintz(e), Burrito, Crêpe (suzette), Crumpet, Drop(ped)-scone, Flam(m), Flapjack, Flaune, Flawn, Fraise, Fritter, Froise, Latke, Pikelet, Poppadum, Potato, Quesadilla, Scotch, Slapjack, Spring roll, Suzette, Taco, Tortilla, Tostada, Waffle
Pancreas Isles of Langerhans, Sweetbread
Panda Bear-cat, Chi-chi, Chitwah, Common, Giant, Lesser, Red
Pandarus Go-between
Pandemonium Inferno, Uproar
Pander Broker, Indulge, Pimp, Procurer, Toady
Pane Glass, Light, Panel, Quarrel, Quarry, Sheet
Panegyric Encomium, Eulogy, Laudation, Praise, Tribute
Panel(ling) Adoption, Array, Board, Cartouche, Children's, Control, Dashboard, Fa(s)cia, Gore, Hatchment, Inset, Instrument, Jury, Lacunar, Mandorla, Mimic, Mola, Orb, Patch(board), People's, Reredorse, Reredos(se), Rocker, Screen, Skreen, Solar, Stile, Stomacher, Table, Tablet, Valance, Volet, Wainscot
Pang Achage, Ache, Crick, Qualm, Spasm, Stab, Stound, Twinge, Wrench
Pangloss Optimist
Pangolin Ant-eater, Manis
Panhandle(r) Beggar, W. Virginia
Panic Alar(u)m, Amaze, Consternation, Fear, Flap, Flat-spin, Flip, Fright, Funk, Guinea-grass, Lather, Millet, Raggee, Raggy, Ragi, Sauve qui peut, → **SCARE**, Scarre, Stampede, Stampedo, State, Stew, Tailspin, → **TERROR**
Panicle Thyrse
Panjandrum Bashaw
Pannier Basket, Cacolet, Corbeil, Dosser, Saddlebag, Skip, Whisket
Panoply Armour, Array, Pomp
Panorama, Panoramic Cyclorama, Range, Scenery, Veduta, View, Vista
Pansy Gay, Heart's-ease, Herb-trinity, Kiss-me-quick, Nance, Powder-puff, Queer, Viola
Pant(s) Bags, Breeches, Capri, Cargo, Chaps, Chinos, Culottes, Deck, Dhoti, Drawers, Fatigues, Flaff, Gasp, Gaucho, Harem, Hot, Long johns, Longs, Parachute, Pech, Pedal-pushers, Pegh, Puff, Ski, Slacks, Smalls, Stovepipe, Sweat, Throb,

Toreador, Training, Trews, Trousers, Wheeze, Yearn

Pantaloon Columbine, Dupe, Pants

Pantheism Idolatry, Immanency

Panther Bagheera, Black, Cat, Cougar, Grey, Jaguar, Leopard, Pink

Panties Briefs, Knickers, Scanties, Step-ins, Undies

Pantomime, Pantomime character Aladdin, Charade, Cheironomy, Dumb-show, Farce, Galanty, Harlequinade, Pierrot, Play

Pantry Buttery, Closet, Larder, Spence, Stillroom

Pap Dug, Mealie, Mush, Nipple, Teat, Udder

Papal, Papist Catholic, Clementine, Concordat, Guelf, Guelph, Legation, Pontifical, RC, Roman, Vatican

Paper(s), Paperwork, Papery Allonge, Antiquarian, Art, Atlas, Ballot, Baryta, Bible, Blotting, Bond, Brief, Broadsheet, Broadside, Bromide, Brown, Building, Bumf, Bumph, Butter, Cap, Carbon, Cartridge, Cellophane®, Chad, Chinese, Chiyogami, Cigarette, Colombier, Command, Commercial, Confetti, Corrugated, Cream-laid, Cream-wove, Credentials, Crêpe, Crown, Cutch, Daily, Decorate, Demy, Document, Dossier, Eggshell, Elephant, Emery, Emperor, Essay, Exam, File, Filter, Final, Flock, Folio, Foolscap, Fourdrinier, FT, Funny, Galley, Garnet, Gazette, Gem, Glass(ine), Glumaceous, Government, Grand eagle, Grand Jesus, Graph, Greaseproof, Green, Guardian, Hieratica, Imperial, India, Japanese, Jesus, Journal, Kent cap, Kraft, Kutch, Lace, Laid, Lavatory, Legal cap, Linen, Litmus, Manifold, Manil(l)a, Marble, Mercantile, Mirror, MS, Munimenti, Music(-demy), Needle, News(print), Note, Notelet, Oil, Onion-skin, Order, Packing, Pad, Page, Papillote, Papyrus, Parchment, Pickwick, Plotting, Position, Post, Pot(t), Pravda, Press, Print, Printing, Quair, Quarto, Quire, Rag, Ramee, Rami(e), Ream, Retree, Rhea, Rice, Rolled, Rolling, Royal, Safety, Satin, Saxe, Scent, Scotsman, Scrip, Scroll, Scrowl, Sheaf, Sheet, Ship's, Silver, Skin, Slipsheet, Spoilt, Stamp, Starch, State, Sugar, Sun, Tabloid, Taffeta, Tap(p)a, Tar, TES, Test, Thesis, Thread, Tiger, Tissue, Today, Toilet, Torchon, Touch, Tracing, Trade, Transfer, Treatise, Treeware, Turmeric, Two-name, Vellum, Velvet, Voucher, Walking, Wall, Waste, Watch, Wax(ed), Web, Whatman®, White, Willesden, Wood(chip), Woodfree, Worksheet, Wove, Wrapping, Writing, Zine

Paperback Limp(back)

Paper-cutting, Paper-folding Decoupage, Kirigami, Origami, Psaligraphy

Papier-mâché Carton-pierre, Flong

Paprika Spanish

Par Average, Equate, Equivalent, → NORMAL, Scratch

Parable Allegory, Fable, Proverb

Parabola Arc, Curve, Hyperbola

Parachute, Parachutist Aeroshell, Aigrette, Brake, Drag, Drogue, Extraction, Float, Golden, Jump, Pack, Pappus, Para, Parabrake, Parapente, Red Devil, Ribbon, Silk, Sky-diving, Skyman, Thistledown, Umbrella

Parade (ground) Air, Arcade, Cavalcade, Church, Concours d'élégance, Display, Dress, Drill, Easter, Emu, Flaunt, Gala, Hit, Identification, Identity, Line-up, Maidan, March-past, Monkey-run, Pageantry, Passing-out, Pomp, Procession, Prom(enade), Sashay, Show, Sick, Stand-to, Ticker tape, Troop

Paradise Arcadia, Avalon, Bliss, Eden, Elysium, Fool's, Garden, Happy-hunting-ground, Heaven, Lost, Malaguetta, Nirvana, Park, Regained, Shangri-la, Svarga, Swarga, Swerga, → UTOPIA

Paradox(ical) Absurdity, Cantor's, Contradiction, Dilemma, Electra, French, Gilbertian, Hydrostatic, Koan, Liar, Olber's, Puzzle, Russell's, Sorites, Twin, Zeno's

Paraffin Earthwax, Kerosene, Kerosine, Liquid, Ozocerite, Ozokerite, Photogen(e), Propane

Paragon Model, Non(e)such, Pattern, Pearl, Phoenix, Role model, Rose

Paragraph (mark) Balaam, Causerie, Note, Passage, Piece, Pilcrow

Parakeet Parrot, Popinjay, Rosella

Parallax Annual, Daily, Diurnal, Geocentric, Heliocentric

Parallel Analog, Collimate, Corresponding, Equal, Even, Forty-ninth, Like

Parallelogram Rhomb

Paralysis, Paralyse Apoplexy, Cataplexy, Catatonia, Cramp, Curarise, Cycloplegia, Diplegia, Halt, Hemiplegia, Infantile, Lithyrism, Monoplegia, Numbness, Palsy, Paraplegia, Paresis, Polio, Quadriplegia, Radial, Scram, Shock, Shut, Spastic, Spina bifida, Stun, Torpefy

Paramedic Ambulance-man

Paramilitary Phalangist, SAS, Sena, UDA

Paramount Chief, Dominant, Greatest, Overall, Premier, → SUPREME, Topless, Utmost

Paramour Beau, Franion, Gallant, Leman, Lover, Mistress, Thais

Paranormal Clairvoyant, ESP, Spiritual, Telekinesis

Parapet (space) Barbette, Bartisan, Bartizan, Battlement, Breastwork, Brisure, Bulwark, Crenel, Flèche, Machicolation, Merlon, Rampart, Redan, Surtout, Terreplein, Top, Wall

Paraphernalia Belongings, Equipment, Gear, Trappings

Parasite, Parasitic Ascarid, Autoecious, Aweto, Babesiasis, Bilharzia, Biogenous, Biotroph, Bladder-worm, Bloodsucker, Bonamia, Bot, Candida, Chalcid, Coccus, Conk, Copepod, Crab-louse, Cryptosporidium, Cryptozoite, Dodder, Ectophyte, Endamoeba, Endophyte, Entophyte, Entozoon, Epiphyte, Epizoon, Facultative, Filarium, Flatworm, Flea, Gapeworm, Giardia, Gregarinida, Haematozoon, Hair-eel, Heartworm, Heteroecious, Hook-worm, Ichneumon, Inquiline, Isopod, Kade, Ked, Lackey, Lamprey, Leech, Leishmania, Licktrencher, Liverfluke, Louse, Lungworm, Macdonald, Mallophagous, Measle, Mistletoe, Monogenean, Necrotroph, Nematode, Nit, Obligate, Orobanche, Pinworm, Plasmodium, Puccinia, Pulix, Rafflesia, Redia, Rhipidoptera, Rickettsia, Root, Roundworm, Schistosoma, Scrounger, Shark, Smut-fungus, Sponge(r), Sporozoa(n), Strepsiptera, Strongyle, Strongyloid, Stylops, Sucker, Symphile, Tapeworm, Tick, Toady, Toxoplasma, Trematode, Trencher-friend, Trencher-knight, Trichina, Trichomonad, Tryp(anosoma), Vampire, Viscum, Wheatworm, Whipworm, Worms

Parasol Awning, Brolly, En tout cas, Sunshade, Umbrella

Paratrooper Skyman

Parcel Allocate, Allot, Aret, Bale, Bundle, Holding, Lot, Package, Packet, Sort, Wrap

Parch(ed) Arid, Bake, Dry, Graddan, Hot coppers, Roast, Scorched, Sere, Thirsty, Toast, Torrid

Parchment Diploma, Forel, Mezuzah, Panel, Papyrus, Pell, Pergameneous, Roll, Roule, Scroll, Sheepskin, Vegetable, Vellum, Virgin

Pard Leopard, Pal, Partner

Pardon(able), Pardoner Absolve, Amnesty, Anan, Assoil, Clear, Condone, Eh, Excuse, → FORGIVE, Grace, Mercy, Quaestionary, Qu(a)estor, Release, Remission, Remit, Reprieve, Venial, What

Pare Flaught, Flay, Peel, Shave, Skive, Sliver, Strip, Whittle

Parent(al) Ancestral, Father, Forebear, Genitor, Maternal, Mother, Paternal, Single, Storge

Parenthesis Aside, Brackets, Innuendo
Parhelion Sun-dog
Pariah Ishmael, Leper, Outcast, Pi(e)dog, Pyedog
Paris(ian), Parisienne Abductor, Athene, Elle, Gai, Gay, Grisette, Lutetia (Parisiorum), Lutetian, Maillotin, Midinette, Trojan
Parish Charge, District, Flock, Kirkto(w)n, Parischan(e), Parishen, Parochin(e), Peculiar, Province, Title
Parity Smithsonian
Park(ing) Algonquin, Alton Towers, Amusement, Banff National, Battery, Brecon Beacons, Business, Car, Caravan, Common, Country, Daintree, Dales, Dartmoor, Death Valley, Disneyland, Egmont National, Enclosure, Etosha, Everglades, Exmoor, Fiordland, Forest, Fun, Game, Garage, Gardens, Grand Canyon, Green, Green lung, Grounds, Hwange, Hyde, Industrial, Jasper, Jasper National, Jurassic, Kakadu, Kalahari Gemsbok, Katmai, Kejionkujik, Kobuk Valley, Kruger, Lake District, Lamington, Lassen Volcanic, Lung, Mammoth Cave, Mansfield, Mesa Verde, Motor, Mount Aspiring, Mount Kenya National, Mount McKinley, Mount Rainier, Mungo, Nahanni National, Nairobi, National, Northumberland, Osterley, Oyster, P, Paradise, Peak District, Phoenix, Pitch, Pittie-ward, Prater, Preserve, Rec, Regent's, Riding Mountain, Safari, Sanctuary, Sandown, Science, Sequoia, Sequoia National, Serengeti, Shenandoah National, Siding, Snowdonia, Stand, Stop, Technology, Theme, Trailer, Tsavo, Valet, Wildlife, Wind, Wood Buffalo, Yard, Yellowstone, Yosemite
Parka Atigi
Parker Dorothy, Nos(e)y
Parkleaves Tutsan
Parley Confer, Discourse, Palaver, Speak, Tret
Parliament Addled, Althing, Barebones, Black, Boule, Bundestag, Commons, Congress, Cortes, Council, Cross-bench, Dail, Diet, D(o)uma, Drunken, Eduskunta, European, Folketing, House, Imperial, Knesset, Lack-learning, Lagt(h)ing, Landst(h)ing, Lawless, Legislature, Lok Sabha, Long, Lords, Majlis, Merciless, Mongrel, Odelst(h)ing, Political, Rajya Sabha, Reichsrat, Reichstag, Riksdag, Rump, St Stephens, Sanhedrin, Seanad, Seanad Éireann, Sejm, Short, Stannary, States-general, Stirthing, Stormont, Stort(h)ing, The Beehive, Thing, Tynwald, Tynwald (Court), Unicameral, Unlearned, Useless, Vidhan Sabha, Volkskammer, Volksraad, Westminster
Parliamentarian Cabinet, Fairfax, Ireton, Leveller, Member, MP, Roundhead, Whip
Parlour Beauty, Funeral, Ice-cream, Lounge, Massage, Milking, Salon, Snug, Spence
Parnassus Museum, Verse
Parochial Insular
Parody Burlesque, Cod, Lampoon, Mock, Piss-take, Satire, Send-up, Skit, Spoof, Travesty
Parole Pledge, Promise, Trust, Word
Paronychia Agnail, Felon, Whitlow
Paroxysm Fit, Frenzy, Rapture, Spasm, Subintrant, Throe
Parricide Cenci
Parrot Amazon, Cockatoo, Conure, Copy, Flint, Green leek, Grey, Imitate, Kaka(po), Kea, Lorikeet, Lory, Lovebird, Macaw, Mimic, Nestor, Owl, Parakeet, Paroquet, Poll(y), Popinjay, Psittacine, Quarrion, Repeat, Rosella, Rote, Shell, Stri(n)gops, T(o)uraco
Parrot-bill Glory-pea
Parry Block, Counter, Defend, Dodge, Forestall, Parade, Riposte, Sixte,

Tac-au-tac, Thwart, Ward

Parsee Zoroastrian

Parsimonious, Parsimony Aberdonian, Cheese-paring, Mean, Narrow, Near(ness), Niggardly, Stingy, Tight

Parsley Apiol, Cicely, Dog, Kecks, Kex, Persillade, Pot-herb

Parsnip Buttered, Buttery, Dill, Masterwort, Sium, Skirret

Parson Clergyman, Cleric, Minister, Non juror, Pastor, Priest, Rector, Rev, Sky-pilot, Soul-curer, Yorick

Parsonage Glebe, Manse, Rectory, Vicarage

Part(s), Parting Accession, Aliquot, Antimere, Area, Aught, Bulk, Bye, Cameo, Character, Chunk, Cog, Component, Constituent, Crack, Cue, Dislink, Diverge, Dole, Element, Episode, Escapement, Farewell, Fascicle, Fork, Fraction, Goodbye, Half, Imaginary, Instalment, Into, Lathe, Lead, Leave, Leg, Lill, Lilt, Lines, List, Livraison, Member, Meronym, Parcel, Passus, → **PIECE**, Portion, Primo, Principal, Private, Proportion, Pt, Quota, Rape, Ratio, Region, Rive, Role, Scena, Scene, Secondo, Section, Sector, Segment, Separate, Serial, Sever, Shade, Share, Shed, Sleave, Sle(i)ded, → **SOME**, Spare, Split, Stator, Sunder, Synthon, Tithe, Tranche, Unit, Vaunt, Voice, Walking, Walk on, Wrench

Partake(r) Allottee, Eat, Participate, Share

Parthenogenesis Deuterotoky, Thelytoky

Partial(ity), Partially Biased, Ex-parte, Fan, Favour, Halflins, Imbalance, Incomplete, One-sided, Predilection, Slightly, Unequal, Weakness

Participate, Participant Engage, Join, Partake, Share, Traceur

Participle Dangling, Misrelated, Past, Perfect, Present

Particle(s) Alpha, Anion, Antineutron, Antiproton, Atom, Baryon, Beta, Bit, Boson, Charmonium, Corpuscle, Curn, Dander, Delta, Deuteron, Effluvium, Elementary, Episome, Fermion, Fleck, Fragment, Fundamental, Gauge boson, Gemmule, Globule, Gluon, Grain, Granule, Graviton, Hadron, Heavy, Higgs, Hyperon, Ion, J, Jot, J/psi, Kaon, Lambda, Lemail, Lemel, Lepton, Lipoplast, Liposome, Meson, Micelle, Microsome, Mite, Molecule, Monopole, Mote, Muon, Negatron, Neutralino, Neutrino, Neutron, Nibs, Nobiliary, Omega-minus, Parton, Pentaquark, Photon, Pion, Plasmagene, Platelet, Positon, Positron, Preon, Proton, Psi(on), Quark, Radioactivity, Shives, Shower, Sigma, Singlet, Sinter, Smithereen, Spark, Speck, Strange, Subatom, Submicron, Tachyon, Tardyon, Tau neutrino, Tauon, Thermion, Tittle, Virion, W, Whit, WIMP, X-hyperon, Z

Parti-coloured Fancy, Motley, Piebald, Pied, Variegated

Particular Choosy, Dainty, → **DETAIL**, Endemic, Especial, Essential, Express, Fiky, Fog, Fussy, Item, Itself, London fog, Nice, Niffy-naffy, Own, Pea-souper, Peculiar, Pernickety, Pet, Point, Prim, Proper, → **RESPECT**, Special, Specific, Stickler, Strict, Stripe

Partisan Adherent, Axe, Biased, Carlist, Champion, Devotee, Factional, Fan, Irregular, Partial, Provo, Queenite, Sider, Spear, Supporter, Yorkist

Partition(ed) Abjoint, Bail, Barrier, Brattice, Bretasche, Bulkhead, Cloison, Cubicle, Diaphragm, Dissepiment, Division, Hallan, Mediastinum, Parpane, Parpen(d), Parpent, Parpoint, Perpend, Perpent, Replum, → **SCREEN**, Scriene, Septum, Tabula, Wall, With

Partlet Hen, Overlaid

Partner(ship) Accomplice, Ally, Associate, Bidie-in, Butty, Cahoot(s), Coachfellow, Cohab(itee), Cohabitor, Colleague, Comrade, Confederate, Consort, Copemate, Couple, Dutch, Escort, E-W, Firm, Gigolo, Limited, Mate, N-S, Oppo, Pair, Pal, Pard, Rival, Sidekick, Significant other, Silent, Sleeping, Sparring, Spouse,

Stablemate, Stand, Symbiosis

▷ **Part of** *may indicate* a hidden word

Partridge Bird, Chik(h)or, Chukar, Chukor, Covey, Quail, Red-legged, Tinamou, Ynambu

Party Acid house, Aftershow, Alliance, Apparat, Assembly, At-home, Ba'ath, Ball, Band, Barbecue, Bash, Beano, Bee, Bloc, Blowout, Body, Bottle, Buck's, Bunfight, Bust, Caboodle, Camp, Carousal, Carouse, Caucus, Celebration, Clambake, Cocktail, Commando, Communist, Concert, Congress, Conservative, Contingent, Cookie-shine, Cooperative, Coterie, Cult, Democratic, Detail, Ding, Discotheque, Do, Drum, Faction, Falange, Federalist, Fest, Fête champêtre, Fête Galante, Fianna Fáil, Fine Gael, Firing, Foy, Function, Funfest, Gala, Galravage, Gang, Garden, Ghibel(l)ine, Green, Greenback, Grumbletonian, Guelf, Guelph, Guilty, Hen, High heels, Hoedown, Hooley, Hootenannie, Hootenanny, Hoot(a)nannie, Hoot(a)nanny, House, Housewarming, Hurricane, Irredentist, Jana Sangh, Jol(lities), Junket, Junto, Kettledrum, Kitchen tea, Klat(s)ch, Knees-up, Kuomintang, L, Labour, Launch, Lib, Liberal, Love-in, Low heels, Luau, Mallemaroking, Mollie, Movement, Musicale, National, Necking, Neck-tie, Octobrist, Opposition, Orgy, People's, Person, Petting, Plaid, Posse, Progressive, Prohibition, Pyjama, Rage, Rave, Rave-up, Razzle(-dazzle), Reception, Republican, Reunion, Revel, Ridotto, Rocking, Roister, Rort, Rout, SDP, Search, Sect, Set, Shindig, Shine, Shivoo, Shower, Shower tea, Side, Slumber, Smoker, SNP, Soc(ialist), Social, Social Credit, Social Democratic, Socialise, Soirée, Spree, Squad(rone), Squadrone volante, Stag, Symposium, Tailgate, Tea, Teafight, Third, Thrash, Tory, Treat, Ultramontane, Unionist, United, Wafd, Warehouse, Whig, Whoop-de-do(o), Wine, Wingding, Working

Partygoer Raver, Reveller, Socialite

Party-piece Solo

Parvenu Arriviste, Upstart

Pascal Blaise, Pa, Pressure

Pash Crush, Devotion

Pasha Achmed, Dey, Emir, Ismet

Pass(ed), Passing, Pass on, Past Ago, Agon, Annie Oakley, Aorist, Approve, Arise, Arlberg, Before, Behind, Bernina, Beyond, Boarding, Bolan, Botte, Brenner, Brief, Burgess, By, Bygone, Caudine Forks, Centre, Cerro Gordo, Chal(l)an, Chilkoot, Chine, Chit(ty), Cicilian Gates, Clear, Col, Cote, Cross, Cursory, Death, Defile, Delate, Demise, Diadron, Die, Disappear, Double, Elapse, Emit, Enact, End, Ensue, Ephemeral, Exceed, Exeat, Faena, Flashback, Fleeting, Foist, Forby, Forgone, Former, Forward, Gap, Gate, Gha(u)t, Glencoe, Glide, Go, Go by, Gorge, Great St Bernard, Gulch, Halse, Hand, Happen, Hause, Hospital, Impart, Impermanent, Interval, In transit, Jark, Khyber, Killiecrankie, Kloof, La Cumbre, Lap, Late, Lead, Long syne, Mesmerism, Migrate, Mont Cenis, Moravian Gate, Nek, Nod through, Notch, Nutmeg, Nye, Occur, Oer, OK, Okay, Oke, Omit, One-time, Overhaul, Overshoot, Overslaugh, Overtake, Pa, Palm, Parade, Participle, Perish, Permeate, Permit, Perpetuate, Poll, Poort, Predicament, Preterit(e), Pretty, Proceed, Propagate, Pun(c)to, Qualify, Railcard, Reach, Reeve, Refer, Relay, Retro, Retroactive, Retrospect, Reverse, Roncesvalles, Safe conduct, St Bernard, St Gotthard, San Bernardino, Sanitation, Scissors, Senile, Serve, Shipka, Simplon, Since, Skim, Skip, Skirt, Slap, Sling, Snap, Spend, Stab, State, Thermopylae, Thread, Through, Ticket, Tip, Transient, Transilient, Transitory, Transmit, Transude, Travel, Triptyque, Troop, Uspallata, Veronica, Vet, Visa, Visé, Wall, Wayleave, Weather, While, Wrynose, Yesterday, Yesteryear, Ygoe

Passable Adequate, Fair, Navigable, Tolerable

Passage Adit, Airway, Aisle, Alley(way), Alure, Apostrophe, Arcade, Archway, Areaway, Arterial, Atresia, Bank, Breezeway, Bridge, Bylane, Cadenza, Caponier(e), Career, Channel, Chute, Citation, Clarino, Clause, Close, Coda, Conduit, Corridor, Creep, Crossing, Crush, Cundy, Dead-end, Deambulatory, Defile, Drake, Drift, Duct, Eel-fare, Episode, Excerpt, Extract, Fare, Fat, Fistula, Flat, Flight, Flue, Gallery, Gangway, Gap, Gat, Gate, Ghat, Ginnel, Gut, Hall, Head, Inlet, Journey, Kyle, Labyrinth, Lane, Lapse, Larynx, Lick, Lientery, Loan, Lobby, Locus, Meatus, Melisma, Meridian, Middle, Mona, Moto perpetuo, Movement, Northeast, Northwest, Para(graph), Path, Pend, Pericope, Phrase, Pore, Portion, Prelude, Prose, Purple, Race, Retournelle, Ride, Ripieno, Rite, Ritornell(o), Road, Rough, Route, Sailing, Screed, Shaft, Shunt, Slap, Slype, Snicket, Sprue, Strait, Street, Stretta, Stretto, Subway, Sump, Text, Thirl, Thorough(fare), Throat, Tour, Trachea, Trance, Transe, Transit(ion), Travel, Tunnel, Tutti, Undercast, Unseen, Ureter, Voyage, Walkway, Way, Windpipe

▷ **Passage of arms** *may indicate* 'sleeve'

Passé Corny, Dated, Ex, Obsolete

Passenger(s) Cad, Commuter, Fare, Payload, Pillion, Rider, Slacker, Steerage, Straphanger, Transit, Traveller, Voyager, Way, Wayfarer

Passion(ate), Passionately Anger, Appetite, Ardour, Con fuoco, Duende, Fervour, Fire, Flame, Frampold, Fury, Gust, Gutsy, Hate, Heat, Hot, Hunger, Hwyl, Ileac, Iliac, Intense, Ire, Irish, Kama, Love, Lust, Mania, Obsession, Oestrus, Rage, Reverent, Sizzling, Stormy, Sultry, Torrid, Vehement, Violent, Warm, Wax, Wrath, Yen, Zeal

Passion-fruit Water-lemon

Passion play Oberammergau

Passive (stage) Apathetic, Dormant, Inert, Pathic, Patient, Pupa, Stolid, Supine, Yielding

Pass out Faint, Graduate, Swarf, Swarve, Swoon

Passover Agadah, Haggada, Omer, Pesach

Passport Access, Clearance, Congé(e), E, ID, Key, Laissez-passer, Nansen, Navicert, Sea-letter, Visa, Visitor's

Password Code, Countersign, Logon, Nayword, Parole, Sesame, Shibboleth, Sign, Tessera, Watchword

▸ **Past** *see* **PASS**

Pasta Agnolotti, Angel hair, Cannelloni, Cappelletti, Cellentani, Conchiglie, Durum, Eliche, Farfal, Farfel, Fedelini, Fettuc(c)ine, Fusilli, Gnocch(ett)i, Lasagna, Lasagne, Linguini, Macaroni, Maccheroncini, Manicotti, Noodles, Orecchietti, Orzo, Penne, Perciatelli, Ravioli, Rigatoni, Ruote, Spaghetti, Spaghettina, Tagliarini, Tagliatelle, Tortelli(ni), Vermicelli, Ziti

Paste, Pasty Almond, Ashen, Batter, Beat, Berbere, Botargo, Boule, Bridie, Cerate, Clobber, Cornish, Dentifrice, Dough, Electuary, Fake, Filler, Fondant, Frangipane, Gentleman's Relish®, Glue, Guarana, Hard, Harissa, Knish, Lute, Magma, Marchpane, Marzipan, Masala, Mastic, Meat, Miso, Mountant, Pale, Pallid, Pâté, Patty, Pearl-essence, Pie, Piroshki, Pirozhki, Poonac, Punch, Putty, Rhinestone, Rout, Samosa, Slip, Slurry, Soft, Spread, Strass, Tahina, Tahini, Tapenade, Taramasalata, Wan, Wasabi

Pastern Hobble, Knee, Tether

Pastiche Cento, Collage, Medley, Patchwork, Potpourri

Pastille Jujube, Lozenge

Pastime Diversion, Game, Hobby, Recreation, Seesaw, Sport

Past master Champion, Expert, Historian, Pro

Past midnight 1 am

Pastor(al) Arcadia, Bucolic, Curé, Eclogue, Endymion, Idyl(l), Minister, Priest, Rector, Rural, Shepherd, Simple

Pastry Apfelstrudel, Baclava, Bakemeat, Baklava, Beignet, Bouchée, Brik, Calzone, Chausson, Cheese straw, Choux, Clafoutis, Coquile, Creamhorn, Cream puff, Croustade, Cruller, Crust, Danish, Dariole, Dough, Eclair, Empanada, Feuilleté, Filo, Flaky, Flan, Frangipane, French, Gougère, Hamantasch, Millefeuille, Phyllo, Pie, Pie-crust, Pirog, Piroshki, Pirozhki, Profiterole, Puff, Quiche, Rough-puff, Rug(g)elach, Samosa, Shortcrust, Strudel, Tart, Turnover, Vol-au-vent

Pasture Alp, Eadish, Eddish, Feed, Fell, Fodder, Grassland, Graze, Herbage, Kar(r)oo, Lair, Lare, Lay, Lea, Lease, Leasow(e), Leaze, Lee, Ley, Machair, Mead(ow), Moose, Pannage, Potrero, Raik, Rake, Soum, Sowm, Tie, Transhume, Tye

▶ **Pasty** *see* PASTE

Pat Apt, Bog-trotter, Butter, Chuck, Clap, Dab, Glib, Lump, On cue, Postman, Print, Prompt, Rap, Slap, Tap

Patch(y) Bed, Bit, Cabbage, Chloasma, Clout, Coalsack, Cobble, Cooper, Court plaster, Cover, Friar, Fudge, → MEND, Mosaic, Nicotine, Pasty, Piebald, Piece, Plage, Plaque, Plaster, Pot, Purple, Shinplaster, Shoulder, Solder, Tingle, Tinker, Vamp, Variegated

Patchwork Cento, Miscellany, Mosaic, Piecing

Pate, Pâté Crown, Paste, Rillettes, Taramasalata, Terrine

Patent(ed) Breveté, Clear, Copyright, Evident, Letters, Licence, License, Obvious, Overt, Plain, Rolls

Pater(nity) Father, Filiation, Walter

Paterfamilias Coarb, Master

Path(way) Aisle, Allée, Alley, Arc, Berm, Berme, Boreen, Borstal(l), Bridle, Byroad, Causeway, Causey, Clickstream, Corridor, Course, Eclipse, Embden-Meyerhof, Flare, Flight, Garden, Gate, Gennel, Ginnel, Glide, Lane, Ley, Lichwake, Lichway, Locus, Lykewake, Mean-free, Metabolic, Orbit, Pad, Parabola, Peritrack, Primrose, Ride, Ridgeway, Route, Run, Runway, Sidewalk, Spurway, Stie, Sty(e), Swath(e), Taxiway, Tow, Track, Trail, Trajectory, Trod, Walkway, → WAY, Xystus

Pathan Pakhto, Pakhtu, Pashto, Pashtu, Pushto(o), Pushtu

Pathetic(ally) Doloroso, Drip, Forlorn, Piss-poor, Piteous, Poignant, Sad, Saddo, Schnook, Touching

Pathfinder Compass, Explorer, Guide, Pioneer, Scout

Pathological Diseased, Gangrene, Morbid, Septic

Pathos Bathos, Pity, Sadness, Sob-stuff

Patience Calm, Endurance, Forbearance, Fortitude, Indulgence, Longanimity, Monument, Operetta, Solitaire, Stoicism, Virtue

Patient(s) Calm, Case, Clinic, Forbearing, Grisel(da), Grisilda, Invalid, Job, Long-suffering, Passive, Private, Resigned, Stoic, Subject, Ward

Patois Argot, Cant, Dialect, Gumbo, Jargon, Jive, Lingo, Scouse

Patriarch Aaron, Abraham, Abuna, Asher, Catholicos, Ecumenical, Elder, Enoch, Isaac, Job, Levi, Maron, Methuselah, Nestor, Noah, Pope, Simeon, Venerable

Patrician Aristocrat, Noble, Senator

Patrick Mick, Paddy, Pat, Spens

Patrimony Ancestry, Estate, Heritage

Patriot(ic), Patriotism Cavour, Chauvinist, DAR, Emmet, Flag-waving, Flamingant, Garibaldi, Hereward, Irredentist, Jingoism, Loyalist, Maquis, Nationalist, Revere, Tell

Patrol Armilla, Guard, Outguard, Picket, Piquet, Prowl-car, Reconnaissance, Round, Scout, Sentinel, Sentry-go, Shark, Shore, Turm

Patron(age), Patroness, Patronise(d), Patronising Advowson, Aegis, Auspices, Benefactor, Business, Champion, Client, Customer, Donator, Egis, Fautor, Lady Bountiful, Maecenas, Nepotic, Protector, Protégé, Provider, Shopper, → **SPONSOR**, Stoop, Stoup

Patsy Dupe, Hendren, Scapegoat, Stooge

Patter Backchat, Cant, Jargon, Lingo, Mag, Pitch, Rap, S(c)htick, Schtik, Spiel

Pattern(ed) Agouti, Agouty, Aguti, Argyle, Bird's eye, Blueprint, Branchwork, Broché, Candy stripe, Check, Chequer, Chiné, Chladni figure, Clock, Design, Dévoré, Diaper, Diffraction, Dog's tooth, Draft, Egg and dart, Epitome, Example, Exemplar, Fiddle, Figuration, Format, Fractal, Fret, Gestalt, Grain, Grammadion, Greek key, Greque, Herringbone, Holding, Hound's tooth, Intarsia, Intonation, Koru, Kowhaiwhai, Matel(l)asse, Matrix, Meander, → **MODEL**, Moire, Moko, Mosaic, Norm, Paisley, Paradigm, Paragon, Pinstripe, Plan, Polka-dot, Pompadour, Precedent, Prototype, Queenstitch, Quincunx, Radiation, Raster, Scansion, Shawl, Stencil, Symmetry, Syndrome, Tala, Talea, Tangram, Tarsia, Tattersall, Template, Tessella, Tessera, Tracery, Traffic, Tread, Type, Willow

Patty Bouchée, Fishcake, Pie

Paul Jones, Oom, Pry, Revere, Robeson, S, St

Pauline Day-boy, Perils

Paunch Belly, Corporation, Gut, Kite, Kyte, Pod, Rumen, Tripe, Tum

Pauper Bankrupt, Beggar, Have-not, Mendicant, Penniless

Pause Break, Breakpoint, Breather, Caesura, Cessation, Cesura, Comma, Desist, Er, Fermata, Hesitate, Interkinesis, Interregnum, Interval, Limma, Lull, Pitstop, Pregnant, → **RESPITE**, Rest, Selah, Stop, Tacet, Time out

Pave(ment), Paving Causeway, Clint, Cobble, Corsey, Crazy, Diaper, Granolith, Limestone, Moving, Path, Plainstanes, Plainstones, Roadside, Set(t), Sidewalk, Tessellate, Travolator, Trottoir

Pavilion Ear, Gazebo, Jingling Johnny, Kiosk, Marquee, Tent

Paw Kangaroo, Maul, Mitt, Pad, Pat, Pud, Pug

Pawky Dry, Humorous, Shrewd, Sly

Pawn(shop), Pawnbroker, Pawnee Agent, Betel, Chessman, Counter, Derby, Dip, Gage, Gallery, Hanging, Hock, Hockshop, Hostage, Isolated, Leaving-shop, Lumber, Lumberer, Moneylender, Monte-de-piété, Monti di pietà, Nunky, Pan, Passed, Peacock, Piece, Pignerate, Pignorate, Pledge, Pledgee, Pop, Security, Sheeny, Siri, Spout, Stalking horse, Tiddleywink, Tool, Uncle, Usurer, Wadset, Weed

Pax Peace, Truce

Pay(master), Payment, Paid, Pay off, Pay out Aby, Advertise, Agterskot, Amortise, Annat, Annuity, Ante, Arles, Atone, Balloon, Basic, Batta, Blench, Bonus, Bukshee, Bukshi, Cain, Cashier, Cens, Cheque, COD, Commute, Compensate, Consideration, Damage, Defray, Disburse, Discharge, Dividend, Down, Dub, E, Emolument, Endow, Equalisation, Eric, Escot, Farm, Fee, Feu-duty, Finance, Foot, Fork out, Fund, Gale, Gate, Give, Grassum, Grave, Greenmail, Han(d)sel, Hazard, Hire, Hoot(oo), HP, Imburse, Kain, Kickback, Leads and lags, Lobola, Lobolo, Mail, Meet, Merchet, Métayage, Mise, Modus, Overtime, Payola, Pension, Pittance, Pony, Posho, Prebendal, Premium, Primage, Pro, Pro forma, Progress, Purser, Quarterage, Quit(-rent), Ransom, Reap-silver, Redundancy, Refund, Remittance, Remuneration, Rent, Requite, Residual, Respects, Royalty, Salary, Satisfaction, Scot, Screw, Scutage, Settle, Severance, Shell, Shell out, Shot, Sick, Sink, Sold(e),

Soul-scat, Soul-scot, → **SPEND**, Square, Stipend, Strike, Stump, Sub, Subscribe, Sweetener, Table, Take-home, Tar, Tender, Token, Tommy, Transfer, Treasure, Treat, Tribute, Truck, Unpurse, Usance, Veer, Wage, Wardcorn, X-factor

PE Aerobics, Gym

Pea(s) Carling, Chaparral, Chickling, Desert, D(h)al, Dholl, Egyptian, Garbanzo, Goober, Hastings, Legume, Mangetout, Marrow, Marrowfat, Passiform, Petit pois, Pigeon, Pulse, Rounceval, Split, String, Sturt's desert, Sugar

Peace(ful), Peaceable, Peace-keeper, Peace organisation, Peace symbol Ahimsa, Antiwar, Ataraxy, Calm, Ease, Frieda, Frith, Halcyon, Hush, Interceder, Irenic(on), King's, Lee, Lull, Nirvana, Olive, Order, Pacific, Pax, Pbuh, Queen's, Quiet, Repose, Rest, Roskilde, Salem, Serene, Sh, Shalom, Siegfried, Siesta, Silence, Solomon, Still, Tranquil, Truce, UN

Peacemaker ACAS, Arbitrator, Conciliator, Mediator, Trouble-shooter, Wilfred

Peach Blab, Cling, Clingstone, Dish, Dob, Freestone, Inform, Laetrile, Malakatoone, Melba, Melocoto(o)n, Nectarine, Oner, Quandang, Shop, Sneak, Split, Squeak, Stunner, Tattle, Tell, Victorine

Peachum Polly

Peacock Coxcomb, Dandy, Fop, Junonian, Muster, Paiock(e), Pajock(e), Pavo(ne), Pawn, Payock(e), Pown, Sashay

Peak(y) Acme, Aiguille, Alp, Ancohuma, Apex, Ben, Cap, Climax, Comble, Communism, Cone, Crag, Crest, Darien, Drawn, Eiger, Flower, Gable, Gannett, Horn, Matterhorn, Mons, → **MOUNTAIN**, Nevis, Nib, Nunatak, Optimum, Pale, Petermann, Pikes, Pin, Pinnacle, Piton, Pyramidal, Rainier, Sallow, Snowdon, Spire, Stalin, Sukarno, Top, Tor, Visor, Widow's, Zenith

Peal Carillon, Chime, Clap, Toll, Triple

Peanut(s) Arnut, Chickenfeed, Goober, Groundnut, Monkey-nut, Pittance

Pear Aguacate, Alligator, Anchovy, Anjou, Asian, Asparagus, Avocado, Bartlett, Bergamot, Beurré, Blanquet, Carmelite, Catherine, Colmar, Comice, Conference, Cuisse-madame, Dutch admiral, Jargonelle, Muscadel, Muscatel, Musk, Nashi, Neli(e)s, Nelis, Perry, Poperin, Poppering, Poprin, Prickly, Pyrus, Queez-maddam, Seckel, Seckle, Taylor's Gold, Warden, William

Pearl(s), Pearly Barocco, Barock, Baroque, Cultured, False, Gem, Imitated, Jewel, Mabe, Margaret, Margaric, Nacrous, Olivet, Orient, Prize, Rope, Seed, Simulated, String, Sulphur, Unio(n)

Pear-shaped Obconic, Pyriform

Peasant Bogtrotter, Bonhomme, Boor, Bumpkin, Chouan, Churl, Clodhopper, Contadino, Cossack, Cottar, Cott(i)er, Fellah(s), Fellahin, Hick, Jungli, Kern(e), Kisan, Kulak, M(o)ujik, Muzhik, Quashi(e), Raiyat, Roturier, Rustic, Ryot, Swain, Tyrolean, Volost, Whiteboy, Yokel

Pea-shaped Pisiform

Peat(y) Moss-litter, Sod, Turbary, Turbinacious, Turf, Yarfa, Yarpha

Pebble(s), Pebbly Banket, Bibble, Calculus, Cobblestone, Dornick, Dreikanter, Gallet, Gooley, Gravel, Psephism, Pumie, Pumy, Scotch, Scree, Shingle, Ventifact

Peccadillo Mischief, Misdemeanour, Offence

Peccary Mexican hog, Tayassuid

Peck Bill, Bushel, Dab, Forpet, Forpit, Gregory, Kiss, Lip, Lippie, Nibble, Pickle, Tap

Pecksniff Charity

Peculiar(ity) Appropriate, Characteristic, Distinct, Eccentric, Especial, Exclusive, Ferly, Funny, Idiosyncratic, Kink, Kooky, Odd, Own, Proper, Queer, Quirk, Royal, Singular, → **SPECIAL**, Specific, Strange, Unusual

▷ **Peculiar** *may indicate* an anagram

Pedagogue Academic, B.Ed, Teacher
Pedal Bike, Chorus, Clutch, Cycle, Damper, Lever, P, Rat-trap, Soft, Sostenuto,
  Sustaining, Treadle, Treddle
Pedal-coupler Tirasse
Pedant(ic) Casaubon, Chop logic, Dogmatic, Don, Dryasdust, Elucubrate, Inkhorn,
  Intellectual, Jobsworth, Lucubrate, Nit-picking, Pedagogue, Pernickety, Pompous,
  Precisian, Quibbler, Scholastic, Sesquipedalian
Peddle, Pedlar Bodger, Boxwallah, Camelot, Chapman, Cheapjack, Colporteur,
  Drummer, Duffer, Hawk, Huckster, Jagger, Packman, Pedder, Pether, Sell, Smouch,
  Smouse(r), Sutler, Tallyman, Tink(er), Yagger
▷ **Peddling** *may indicate* an anagram
Pedestal Acroter(ion), Dado, Footstool, Pillar, Support
Pedestrian Banal, Commonplace, Dull, Earth-bound, Ganger, Hack, Hike, Itinerant,
  Jaywalker, Laborious, Mundane, Trite, Voetganger, Walker
Pedigree(s) Ancestry, Blood, Breeding, Descent, Genealogy, House, Lineage,
  Phylogeny, Stemma(ta), Stirp(s), Studbook, Thoroughbred, Whakapapa
Pediment Fronton
Peduncle Scape, Stalk
Peek Eye, Glance, Glimpse, Peep
Peel(er) Bark, Bobby, Candied, Decorticate, Desquamate, Exfoliate, Flype, Orange,
  Pare, PC, Pill, Rind, Rine, Scale, Shell, Skin, → **STRIP**, Tirr, Zest
▷ **Peeled** *may indicate* outside letter(s) to be removed from a word
Peep(er), Peephole Cheep, Cook, Crow, Glance, Gledge, Judas, Keek, Kook, Lamp,
  Nose, Peek, Pink, Pry, Spy, Squeak, Squint, Stime, Styme, Voyeur
Peer(age), Peers Archduke, Aristocrat, Backwoodsman, Baron(et), Burke, Coeval,
  Daimio, Doucepere, Douzeper(s), Duke, Earl, Egal, Elevation, Equal, Eyeball,
  Gynt, Life, Lord, Match, Noble, Paladin, Peregal, Pink, Rank, Representative, Scry,
  Spiritual, Squint, Stare, Stime, Styme, Temporal, Toot, Tweer, Twire
Peerless Matchless, Nonpareil, Supreme
Peevish(ness) Capernoited, Captious, Crabby, Cross, Doddy, Frabbit, Frampal,
  Frampold, Franzy, Fretful, Lienal, Meldrew, Moody, Nattered, Pet, Petulant,
  Pindling, Protervity, Querulous, Shirty, Sour, Spleen, Teachie, Testy, Te(t)chy
Peewit Lapwing, Peewee
Peg Cheville, Cleat, Clothespin, Cotter-pin, Crawling, Die, Fix, Freeze, Knag, Leg,
  Margaret, Nail, Nog, Odontoid, Pin, Piton, Snort, Spigot, Spile, Square, Stengah,
  Stinger, Support, Tap, Tee, Thole, Tholepin, Thowel, Toggle, Tot, Tuning, Vent,
  Woffington
Pegboard Solitaire
Pelagic Deep-sea, Marine, Oceanic
Pelf Lucre, Mammon, Money, Notes, Riches
Pelican Alcatras, Bird, Crossing, Golden Hind, LA, Louisiana, Steganopode
Pellagra Maidism
Pellet Birdshot, Bolus, Buckshot, Bullet, Pill, Pithball, Prill, Slug
Pelmet Valance
Pelt Assail, Clod, Fleece, Fur, Hail, Hide, Hie, Lam, Pepper, Random, Sealskin,
  Shower, Skin, Squail, Stone
Peltast Soldier, Targeteer
Pelvis Ilium, Pubis, Renal
Pen Author, Ballpoint, Bamboo, Bic®, Biro®, Cage, Calamus, Cartridge, Catching,
  Confine, Coop, Corral, Crawl, Crow-quill, Cru(i)ve, Cub, Cyclostyle, Dabber,
  Data, Enclosure, Fank, Farm, Felt(-tipped), Fold, Fountain, Gaol, Gladius, Hen,

Highlighter, Hoosegow, J, → JAIL, Keddah, Kraal, Lair, Laser, Light, Marker, Mew, Mure, Music, Piggery, Poison, Pound, Quill(-nib), Ree, Reed, Ring, Rollerball, Scribe, Stell, Stie, Stir, Sty(e), Stylet, Stylo, Stylograph, Stylus, Submarine, Swan, Sweatbox, Tank, Write, → WRITER

▷ **Pen** *may indicate* a writer

Penal(ize) Cost, Fine, Gate, Handicap, Huff, Mulct, Punitive, Servitude

Penalty Abye, Amende, Card, Cost, Death, Eric, Fine, Fixed, Forfeit, Han(d)sel, Huff, Keltie, Kelty, Pain, Price, Punishment, Rubicon, Sanction, Ticket, Wide

Penance Atonement, Shrift

Penates Lares

Pence D, P, Peter's

Penchant Predilection

Pencil Beam, Ca(l)m, Caum, Charcoal, Chinagraph®, Crayon, Draft, Draw, Eyebrow, Fusain, Grease, Harmonic, Ink, Keelivine, Keelyvine, Lead, Outline, Propelling, Slate, Stump, Styptic, Tortillon

Pendant Albert, Chandelier, Drop, Girandole, Laval(l)ière, Necklace, Poffle, Stalactite

Pending Imminent, In fieri, Unresolved, Until

Pendragon Uther

Pendulous, Pendulum Compensation, Dewlap, Foucault's, Metronome, Noddy, One-way, Swing, Wavering

Penetrate, Penetrating, Penetration Acumen, Acuminate, Bite, Bore, Bridgehead, Cut, Enpierce, Enter, Imbue, Impale, Incisive, Indent, Indepth, Infiltrate, Insight, Into, Intrant, Lance, Permeate, Pierce, Probe, Sagacious, Shear, Thrust, Touch, X-ray

Penguin Adélie, Aeroplane, Anana, Auk, Blue, Emperor, Fairy, Gentoo, King, Korora, Little, Macaroni, Rock-hopper

Penicillin Cloxacillon, Fleming

Peninsula Alaska, Alte, Antarctic, Arabian, Ards, Arm, Avalon, Baja California, Balkan, Banks, Bataan, Black Isle, Boothia, Brittany, Cape, Cape Blanco, Cape Bon, Cape Cod, Cape Verde, Chalcidice, Chersonese, Chukchi, Coromandel, Cowal, Crimea, Deccan, Delmarva, East Cape, Eyre, Florida, Freycinet, Furness, Fylde, Gallipoli, Galloway, Gaspé, Gower, Graham Land, Hispania, Iberia(n), Indo-China, Istria, Jutland, Kamchatka, Kathiawar, Kerch, Kintyre, Kola, Korea, Kowloon, Labrador, Leizhou, Liaodong, Liaotung, Lleyn, Luichow, Malay, Malaysia, Melville, Neck, Northland, Nova Scotia, Olympic, Otago, Palmer, Peloponnese, Portland, Promontory, Quiberon, Rhinns of Galloway, Scandinavian, Seward, Sinai, Spit, Spur, S.W. Malay, Taimyr, Tasman, Taymyr, The Lizard, Upper, Wilson's Promontory, Wirral, Yorke, Yucatan

Penis Archie, Chopper, Cor(e)y, Dick, Dildo(e), Dipstick, Dong, Ferret, Giggle(stick), Horn, Jack, John Thomas, Knob, Langer, Membrum virile, Mojo, Organ, Pecker, Peezle, Percy, Phallus, Pillicock, Pintle, Pisser, Pizzle, Plonker, Prick, Putz, Rod, Roger, Schlong, Shaft, Stiffy, Tallywhacker, Tockley, Todger, Tonk, Tool, W(h)ang, Willie, Willy, Winkle, Yard, Zeppelin

Penitent(iary) Calaboose, Cilice, Clink, Contrite, Gaol, Jail, Jug, Prison, Repenter, Rosary, Stir

Pennant, Pennon Banner, Broad, Bunting, Fane, Flag, Guidon, Streamer

Penniless Bankrupt, Boracic, Broke, Bust, Impecunious, Poor, Skint, Strapped

Penny Bean, Cartwheel, Cent, Copper, D, Dreadful, Gild, Honest, New, P, Pretty, Sen, Sou, Sterling, Stiver, Win(n), Wing

Penny-farthing Bicycle, Ordinary

Pension(er) Allowance, Ann(at), Annuitant, Board, Chelsea, Cod, Cor(r)ody, Gasthaus, Gratuity, Guest-house, Half-board, Hotel, Non-contributory, Occupational, Payment, Personal, Retire(e), Serps, SIPP, Stakeholder, Stipend, Superannuation

Pensive Dreamy, Moody, Musing, Thoughtful, Triste, Wistful

Pentateuch T(h)orah

Pentecost Whit(sun)

Penthouse Cat, Lean-to, Roof, Skyhome

Peon Peasant, Serf, Slave, Ticca

Peony Moutan

People Beings, Bods, Body, Chosen, Commonalty, Commons, Demos, Ecology, Enchorial, Flower, Folk, Fraim, Gens, Grass roots, Guild, Human, Inca, Inhabit, Janata, Kin, Land, Lapith, Lay, Man(kind), Men, Mob, Nair, Nation(s), Nayar, One, Peculiar, Personalities, Phalange, Populace, Proletariat(e), Public, Punters, Quorum, Race, September, Settle, Society, Souls, They, Tribe, Tuath, Volk

Pep Buck, Dash, Enliven, Gism, Go, Jism, Jissom, Stamina, Verve, Vim

Pepper Alligator, All-spice, Ava, Betel, Bird, Black, Caper, Capsicum, Cayenne, Cherry, Chilli, Chipotle, Condiment, Cubeb, Devil, Dittander, Dittany, Ethiopian, Green, Guinea, Habanero, Jalapeno, Jamaica, Kava, Long, Malaguetta, Matico, Negro, Paprika, Pelt, Pim(i)ento, Piper, Piperine, Piquillo, Red, Riddle, Sambal, Spice, Sprinkle, Sweet, Szechwan, Tabasco®, Wall, Water, White, Yaqona, Yellow

Peppercorn Nominal, → PAYMENT, → RENT

Peppermint Bull's Eye, Humbug, Pandrop

Peptide Substance P

Per By, Each, Through

Perambulate, Perambulator Buggy, Expatiate, Pedestrian, Pram, Stroller, Wagon, Walker

Perceive, Perception, Perceptive Acumen, Alert, Anschauung, Apprehend, Astute, Clairvoyance, Clear-eyed, Cryptaesthetic, Descry, Dianoia, Discern, Divine, ESP, Extrasensory, Feel, Insight, Intelligence, Intuit(ion), Kinaesthesia, Notice, Observe, Pan(a)esthesia, Remark, → SEE, Sense, Sensitive, Sentience, Shrewd, Sixth sense, Subliminal, Tact, Taste, Tel(a)esthesia, Telegnosis, Understanding

Percentage Agio, Commission, Contango, Cut, Mark-up, Proportion, Royalty, Scalage, Share, Vigorish

Perch(ing) Aerie, Alight, Anabis, Bass, Comber, Eyrie, Fish, Fogash, Gaper, Insessorial, Lug, Miserere, Ocean, Perca, Pole, Roost, Ruff(e), Seat, Serranid, → SIT, Wall-eye, Zingel

Percolate, Percolation Filter, Infiltrate, Leach, Lixiviate, Ooze, Osmosis, Permeate, Seep, Sipe, Soak, Strain, Sype

Percussion (cap) Amorce, Chinese temple block, Idiophone, Impact, Knee, Knock, Thump, Timbrel

Percy Hotspur, Shelley

Perdition Ades, Hades

Peremptory Absolute, Decisive, Haughty, Imperative, Imperious

Perennial Continual, Enduring, Flower, Livelong, Perpetual, Recurrent

Perfect(ly), Perfection(ist) Absolute, Accomplish, Accurate, Acme, Apple-pie, Bloom, Complete, Consummation, Cross-question, Dead, Develop, Fare-thee-well, Finish, Flawless, Fulfil, Full, Holy, Ideal(ist), Impeccable, Intact, It, Mint, Par, Paragon, Past, Pat, Peace, Pedant, Point-device, Practice, Present, Pure, Quintessential, Refine, Salome, Siddha, Soma, Sound, Spot-on, Stainless, Sublime, The nines, Thorough, Three-pricker, Unblemished, Unqualified, Utopian,

Utter, Whole, Witeless

Perfidy Betrayal, Falsehood, Treachery, Treason

Perforate(d), Perforation, Perforator Cribrate, Cribrose, Drill, Eyelet, Hole, → **PIERCE**, Prick, Punch, Puncture, Riddle, Trephine, Trocar

Perforce Necessarily, Needs

Perform(ed), Performer, Performing Achieve, Act(or), Appear, Artist(e), Basoche, Busk, Carry out, Chansonnier, Comedian, Contortionist, Discharge, Do, Enact, Entertainer, Execute, Exert, Exhibit, Fancy Dan, Fire-eater, Fulfil, Function, Geek, Hand, Headliner, Hersall, Hot dog, Houdini, Implement, Interlocutor, Majorette, Make, Moke, On, Perpetrate, Player, Praxis, Recite, Render, Ripieno, Strongman, Supererogate, Sword-swallower, Throw, Vaudevillian, Virtuoso, Wire-dancer

Performance Accomplishment, Achievement, Act, Auto, Blinder, Bravura, Broadcast, Command, Concert, Dare, Deed, Demonstration, Discharge, Entr'acte, Execution, Gas, Gig, Hierurgy, Holdover, Hootenanny, House, Masterstroke, Matinee, One-night stand, Operation, Perpetration, Practice, Première, Production, Programme, Recital, Rehearsal, Rendering, Rendition, Repeat, Repertoire, Rigmarole, Scene, Show, Showing, Sneak preview, Solo, Specific, Spectacle, Stunt, Theatricals, Track record, Turn

Perfume (box) Abir, Angel water, Aroma, Attar, Bergamot, Cassolette, Chypre, Civet, Cologne, C(o)umarin, Eau de toilette, Enfleurage, Essence, Fragrance, Frangipani, Incense, Ionone, Lavender (water), Linalool, Millefleurs, Muscone, Muskone, Myrrh, Opopanax, Orris, Orrisroot, Otto, Patchouli, Patchouly, Pomander, Potpourri, Redolence, → **SCENT**, Smellies, Terpineol, Toilet water

Perfunctory Apathetic, Careless, Cursory, Indifferent, Token

Perhaps A(i)blins, Belike, Haply, Happen, May(be), Peradventure, Percase, Perchance, Possibly, Relative, Say, Yibbles

▷ **Perhaps** *may indicate an anagram*

Perigee Apsis, Epigeum

Peril(ous) → **DANGER**, Hazard, Jeopardy, Precarious, Risk, Threat, Yellow

Perimeter Boundary, Circuit, Circumference, Limits

Period(ic) Abbevillian, Acheulian, AD, Age, Alcher(ing)a, Andropause, Annual, Archaean, Aurignacian, Azilian, Base, Cal(l)ippic, Cambrian, Carboniferous, Chalcolithic, Chukka, Chukker, Climacteric, Cooling off, Cretaceous, Critical, Curse, Cycle, Day, Decad(e), Devonian, Diapause, Dot, Dreamtime, → **DURATION**, Eocene, Epoch, Excerpt, Floruit, Full-stop, Glacial, Grace, Hercynian, Holocene, Horal, Incubation, Innings, Interregnum, Jurassic, Kalpa, Latency, Latent, Lesson, Liassic, Limit, Meantime, Meanwhile, Menopause, Mesolithic, Mesozoic, Middle Kingdom, Miocene, Monthly, Neocomian, Neolithic, Neozoic, Octave, Olde-worlde, Oligocene, Ordovician, Paleolithic, Permian, Phanerozoic, Phase, Phoenix, Pleistocene, Pliocene, Pre-Cambrian, Proterozoic, Protohistory, Quarter, Quarternary, Reformation, Refractory, Regency, Rent, Riss, Romantic, Safe, Season, Session, Sidereal, Silurian, Span, Spell, Stage, Stop, Stretch, Synodic, Term, Tertiary, Trecento, Triassic, Trimester, Usance, Window

Periodic(al) Catamenia, Comic, Digest, Economist, Etesian, Journal, Liassic, Listener, Mag, New Yorker, Organ, Paper, Phase, Publication, Punch, Rambler, Regency, Review, Solutrean, Solutrian, Spectator, Strand, Stretch, Tatter, Tract

Peripatetic Gadabout, Itinerant, Promenader, Travelling

Periphery Ambit, Bounds, Fringe, Outskirts, Surface

Periscope Eye(-stalk)

Perish(able), Perished, Perishing Brittle, → **DIE**, End, Ephemeral, Expire, Fade, Forfair, Fungibles, Icy, Tine, Tint, Transitory, Tyne, Vanish

Periwinkle Apocynum, Blue, Myrtle
Perjure(d) Forswear, Lie, Mansworn
Perk(s), Perky Brighten, Chipper, Freebie, Freshen, Jaunty, LV, Perquisite
Perm(anent) Abiding, Durable, Enduring, Eternal, Everlasting, Fixed, For keeps, Full-time, Indelible, → **LASTING**, Marcel, Stable, Standing, Stative, Wave
Permeable, Permeability, Permeate Infiltrate, Leaven, Magnetic, Osmosis, Penetrate, Pervade, Poromeric, Porous, Seep, Transfuse
Permission, Permit(ted) Allow, Authorise, By-your-leave, Carnet, Chop, Clearance, Congé(e), Consent, Copyright, Enable, Give, Grant, Lacet, Laisser-passer, Latitude, Leave, Legal, Let, Liberty, Licence, License, Lief, Luit, Nihil obstat, Ok(e), Pace, Pass, Placet, Planning, Power, Pratique, Privilege, Safe-conduct, Sanction, Stamp-note, Suffer, Ticket, Triptyque, Visa, Vouchsafe, Way-leave, Wear
Pernicious Damnable, Evil, Harmful, Lethal, Noisome, Pestilent, Wicked
Pernickety Fikish, Niggly
Peroration Pirlicue, Purlicue
Peroxide Bleach, Blonde, Colcothar
Perpendicular Aplomb, Apothem, Atrip, Cathetus, Erect, Normal, Orthogonal, Plumb, Sheer, Sine, → **UPRIGHT**, Vertical
Perpetrate Commit, Effect, Execute
Perpetual Constant, Eternal, Incessant, Sempiternal
Perplex(ed), Perplexity Anan, Baffle, Bamboozle, Beset, Bewilder, Bother, Buffalo, Bumbaze, Cap, Confound, Confuse, Embarrass, Feague, Floor, Flummox, Knotty, Meander, Mystify, Nonplus, Out, Pother, Pudder, Puzzle, Quizzical, Stump, Tangle, Tickle, Tostication
Perquisite Ap(p)anage, Emolument, Extra, Gratuity, → **PERK**, Tip
Perrier Stoner
Perry Mason
Persecute, Persecution Afflict, Annoy, Badger, Crucify, Dragon(n)ades, Harass, Haze, Intolerant, McCarthyism, Oppress, Pogrom, Ride, Torment, Torture, Witch hunt
Persevere, Perseverance Assiduity, Continue, Fortitude, Insist, Patience, Persist, Plug, Stamina, Steadfastness, Stick, Stickability, Tenacity
Persia(n) Achaemenid, Babee, Babi, Bahai, Cyrus, Dari, Farsi, Iran(ian), Mazdean, Mede, Middle, Pahlavi, Parasang, Parsee, Pehlevi, Pushtu, Samanid, Sassanid, Sohrab, Xerxes, Zoroaster
Persimmon Kaki, Sharon fruit
Persist(ence), Persistent Adhere, Assiduity, Chronic, Continual, Diligent, Doggedness, Endure, Importunate, Labour, Longeval, Lusting, Nag, Persevere, Press, Sedulous, Sneaking, Stick, Tenacity, Urgent
Person(s), Personal(ly) Alter, Artificial, Aymaran, Being, Bird, Bod(y), Chai, Chal, Character, Chav, Chi, Cookie, Displaced, Entity, Everyman, Figure, First, Fish, Flesh, Head, Human, Individual, In propria persona, Natural, One, Own, Party, Passer-by, Pod, Private, Quidam, Second, Selfhood, Skate, Sod, Soul, Specimen, Tales, Third, Walla(h)
Personage, Personality Anima, Celeb(rity), Character, Charisma, Dignitary, Ego, Grandee, Identity, Jekyll and Hyde, Megastar, Multiple, Noble, Notability, Panjandrum, Presence, Psychopath, Sama, Schizoid, Seity, Sel, Self, Sell, Somatotonia, Split, Star, Tycoon, Viscerotonia
Personified, Personification, Personify Embody, Incarnate, Prosopop(o)eia, Represent
Personnel Employees, Hands, Liveware, Manpower, Staff
Perspective Aerial, Attitude, Distance, Linear, Point of view, Proportion, Slant,

View, Vista

Perspicacious Astute, Clear-sighted, Discerning, Keen, Shrewd

Perspiration, Perspire, Perspiring Aglow, Forswatt, Glow, Hidrosis, Sudor, Suint, Sweat, Swelter

Persuade(d), Persuasion, Persuasive Cajole, Coax, Cogent, Conviction, Convince, Disarm, Eloquent, Faith, Feel, Forcible, Geed, Get, Induce, Inveigle, Lead on, Move, Plausible, → **PREVAIL**, Religion, Smooth-talking, Soft sell, Suborn, Truckled, Wheedle, Winning

Pert(ness) Bold, Brisk, Cocky, Dicacity, Flippant, Forward, Fresh, Impertinent, Insolent, Jackanapes, Minx, Quean, Saucy, Tossy

Pertain Apply, Belong, Concern, Effeir, Effere, Relate, Touch

Pertinacious Dogged, Obstinate, Persistent, Stickler, Stubborn

Pertinent Ad rem, Apropos, Apt, Fit, Germane, Relevant, Timely

Perturb(ation) Aerate, Confuse, Dismay, Disturb, Dither, State, Trouble, Upset, Worry

Peru(vian) Inca, PE, Quechua(n), Quichua(n)

Peruse, Perusal Examine, Inspect, Read, Scan, Scrutiny, → **STUDY**

Pervade, Pervasion, Pervasive(ness) Diffuse, Drench, Immanence, Permeate, Saturate

Perverse, Perversion, Pervert(ed), Perversity Aberrant, Abnormal, Algolagnia, Awkward, Awry, Balky, Cam(stairy), Camsteary, Camsteerie, Cantankerous, → **CONTRARY**, Corrupt, Crabbed, Cussed, Deviate, Distort, Donsie, False, Froward, Gee, Kam(me), Kinky, Licentious, Misinterpret, Misuse, Nonce, Paraphilia, Protervity, Refractory, Sadist, Sicko, Stubborn, Thrawn, Traduce, Unnatural, Untoward, Uranism, Warp(ed), Wayward, Wilful, Wrest, Wry

▷ **Perverted** *may indicate* an anagram

Pessimism, Pessimist(ic) Alarmist, Bear, Crapehanger, Crepehanger, Cynic, Defeatist, Dismal Jimmy, Doomwatch, Doomy, Doubter, Downbeat, Fatalist, Glumbum, Jeremiah, Killjoy, Negative

Pest(er) Aggravate, Badger, Bedbug, Blight, Bot, → **BOTHER**, Brat, Breese, Bug, Dim, Disagreeable, Earbash, Fly, Fowl, Greenfly, Harass, Irritate, Mither, Mouse, Nag, Nudnik, Nuisance, Nun, Pize, Plague, Rotter, Scourge, Tease, Terror, Thysanoptera, Vermin, Weevil

Pesticide Botanic(al), DDT, Derris, Heplachlor, Mouser, Permethrin, Synergist, Warfarin

Pestilence, Pestilent Curse, Epidemic, Evil, Lues, Murrain, Murren, Noxious, Outbreak, Pernicious, Plague

Pet Aversion, Cade, Canoodle, Caress, Chou, Coax, Coddle, Cosset, Dandle, Daut(ie), Dawt(ie), Dod, Dort, Ducky, Favourite, Fondle, Glumps, Hamster, Huff, Hump, Ire, Jarta, Jo, Lallygag, Lapdog, Miff, Mouse, Neck, Pique, Rabbit, Smooch, Snog, Spat, Strum, Sulk(s), Tantrum, Teacher's, Tiff, Tout, Towt, Umbrage, Virtual, Yarta

Petal Ala, Keels, Labellum, Leaf, Standard, Vexillum

Petard Firework, Squib

Peter Aumbry, Bell, Dwindle, Grimes, Pan, Principle, Quince, Quint, Rabbit, Safe, Saint, Sellers, Simon, Simple, Wane, Weaken

Petite Dainty, Mignon, Small

Petition(er) Appeal, Beg, Boon, Crave, Entreaty, Litany, Millenary, Orison, Plaintiff, Postulant, Prayer, Representation, Request, Round robin, Solicit, Sue, Suit(or), Suppli(c)ant, Vesper

Pet-name Hypocorisma, Nickname, So(u)briquet

Petrel Bird, Mother Carey's chicken, Nelly, Prion, Procellaria, Stormbird, Stormy, Wilton's

Petrify(ing) Fossilise, Frighten, Lapidescent, Niobe, Numb, Ossify, Scare, Terrify

Petrol(eum) Cetane, Cutting, Diesel, Esso®, Ethyl, Fuel, Gas, High-octane, High-test, Ligroin, Maz(o)ut, Octane, Oilstone, Olein, Refinery, Rock oil, Rock-tar, STP, Unleaded, Vaseline

Petticoat Balmoral, Basquine, Crinoline, Female, Filabeg, Fil(l)ibeg, Jupon, Kilt, Kirtle, Phil(l)abeg, Phil(l)ibeg, Placket, Sarong, Shift, Underskirt, Wylie-coat

Pettifogger Lawmonger

Petty, Pettiness Baubling, Bumbledom, Childish, Little, Mean, Minor, Narrow, Niggling, Nyaff, One-horse, Parvanimity, Picayunish, Pimping, Puisne, Shoestring, Small, Small-minded, Stingy, Tin, Trivial, Two-bit

Petulance, Petulant Fretful, Huff, Moody, Peevish, Perverse, Procacity, Querulous, Sullen, Toutie, Waspish

Pew Box, Carrel, Chair, Seat, Stall

Pewter Trifle, Tutenag

Phaeton Spider

Phalanger Cus-cus, Honey-mouse, Opossum, Petaurist, Phascogale, Possum, Sugar glider, Tait, Tarsipes, Tuan, Wambenger

Phalanx Cohort, Coterie, Legion

Phalarope Lobe-foot

Phallus Linga(m), Penis, Priapus

Phantasist, Phantasm Apparition, Chimera, Spectre, Werewolf

Phantom Apparition, Bogey, Bugbear, Eidolon, Idol, Incubus, Maya, Pepper's ghost, Shade, Spectre, Tut, Wraith

Pharaoh Akhenaton, Amenhotep, Cheops, Egyptian, Rameses, River-dragon, Thutmose, Tut, Tutankhamen, Tutankhamun, Tyrant

Pharisee Formalist, Humbug, Hypocrite, Nicodemus

Pharmacist, Pharmacologist → CHEMIST, Dispenser, MPS, Officinal, Preparator

Phase Coacervate, Colour, Cycle, Form, Period, Post-boost, Primary, Quarter, REM, Stage, State, Synchronise, Transition

Pheasant Argus, Bird, Fireback, Junglefowl, Mona(u)l, Nide, Nye, Peacock, Ring-necked, Tragopan

Phenol Orcine, Orcinol, Resorcinol, Xylenol

Phenomenon Autokinetic, Blip, Effect, Event, Figure ground, Flying saucer, Flysch, Heterography, Marvel, Miracle, Mirage, Paranormal, Phenology, Phi, Psi, Rankshift, Reynaud's, Synergy

Phial Bologna, Bottle, Flask

Phil, Philip Fluter, Macedonia, Pip

Philander(er) Flirt, Lothario, Playboy, Toyer, → TRIFLE, Wolf, Womaniser

Philanthropist, Philanthropy Altruist, Benefactor, Carnegie, Charity, Coram, Donor, Freemason, Humanist, Humanitarian, Nobel, Rockefeller, Samaritan, Shaftesbury, Tate, Wilberforce

Philately Timbromania

Phileas Fogg

▶ **Philip** *see* PHIL

Philippic Diatribe, Invective, Tirade

Philippine(s) Bisayan, Igorot, Moro, PI, RP, Tagalog, Visayan

Philistine, Philistinism Artless, Ashdod, Barbarian, Foe, Gath, Gaza, Gigman, Goliath, Goth, Lowbrow, Podsnappery, Vandal

Philology Linguistics, Semantics, Speechcraft

Philosopher, Philosophy Academist, Activism, Ahimsa, Analytical, Animism,

Anthrosophy, Antinomianism, Antiochian, Atomist, Attitude, Averr(h)oism, Cartesian, Casuist, Comtism, Conceptualism, Conservatism, Cracker-barrel, Critical, Cynic, Deipnosophist, Deontology, Eclectic, Eleatic, Empiricism, Enlightenment, Epistemology, Ethics, Existentialism, Fatalism, Gymnosophist, Hedonism, Hobbism, Holist, Humanism, I Ching, Idealism, Ideology, Instrumentalism, -ism, Kaizen, Linguistic, Logical atomism, Logicism, Logos, Maieutic, Marxism, Materialism, Megarian, Metaphysician, Metaphysics, Metempiricism, Monism, Moral(ist), Natural, Neoplatonism, Neoteric, Nihilism, Nominalism, Occamist, Occam's razor, Opinion, Peripatetic, Phenomenology, Platonism, Populism, Positivism, Rationalism, Realism, Rosminian, Sage, Sankhya, Sceptic, Schoolman, Scientology, Sensist, Shankara(-charya), Sophist, Stoic, Synthetic, Taoism, Theism, Theosophy, Thomist, Transcendentalism, Ultraism, Utilitarianism, Utopianism, Voluntarism, Weltanschauung, Yoga, Yogi

PHILOSOPHERS

4 letters:
Ayer
Hume
Jedi
Kant
Mach
Mill
Ryle
Weil
Wolf
Zeno

5 letters:
Amiel
Bacon
Comte
Croce
Dewey
Hegel
Locke
Paine
Plato
Quine
Renan
Smith
Sorel
Taine

6 letters:
Agnesi
Cicero
Engels
Godwin
Herder
Hobbes

Olbers
Ortega
Pascal
Popper
Pyrrho
Sartre
Scotus
Seneca
Thales

7 letters:
Abelard
Aquinas
Bentham
Bergson
Diderot
Emerson
Erasmus
Erigena
Herbart
Hypatia
Leibniz
Malthus
Marcion
Marcuse
Mencius
Meng-tse
Ptolemy
Russell
Schlick
Sheffer
Spencer
Spinoza
Steiner
Vedanta

8 letters:
Avicenna
Berkeley
Boethius
Cyreniac
Diogenes
Epicurus
Foucault
Hamilton
Harrison
Menippus
Old Moore
Plotinus
Plutarch
Rousseau
Socrates
Xenophon

9 letters:
Aristotle
Bosanquet
Cleanthes
Confucius
Descartes
Euhemerus
Heidegger
Leucippus
Lucretius
Nietzsche
Santayana
Schelling
Whitehead

10 letters:
Anacharsis

Anaxagoras
Anaximenes
Antiochene
Apemanthus
Apollonius
Aristippus
Campanella
Chrysippus
Democritus
Empedocles
Heraclitus
Hutchinson
Paracelsus
Parmenides
Protagoras
Pythagoras
Saint Simon
Swedenborg
Von Leibniz
Xenocrates
Xenophanes

11 letters:
Anaximander
Antisthenes
Kierkegaard
Montesquieu

12 letters:
Callisthenes
Schopenhauer
Wittgenstein

Philosophic(al) Rational, Resigned, Thoughtful, Tranquil
Philtre Aphrodisiac, Charm, Drug, Hippomanes, Potion
Phlegm(atic) Calm, Composed, Pituita(ry), Pituite, Stolid, Unperturbed, Unruffled
Phloem Leptome, Liber
Phobia Aversion, Dread, Fear, Thing
Phoebe, Phoebus Apollo, Artemis, Day-star, Deaconess, Moon, Selene, Sol, Sun
Phoenician Tripolitania
Phoenix Bird-of-wonder, Fum, Fung, Paragon, Self-begotten
Phone Bell, Blower, Call, Cellular, Dial, Intercom, Mob(i)e, Mobile, Moby, Pay,
  Picture, Ring, Smart, Talkback, → TELEPHONE, Text
Phonetic(s) Acoustic, Articulatory, Auditory, Mouille, Oral, Palaeotype, Palatal,
  Plosion, Spoken, Symbol, Synaeresis
▷ **Phonetically** *may indicate* a word sounding like another
Phon(e)y Bogus, Charlatan, Counterfeit, Fake, Hokey, Impostor, Poseur, Quack,
  → SHAM, Specious, Spurious
▷ **Phony** *may indicate* an anagram
Phosphate Monazite, Torbernite, Vivianite, Wavellite, Xenotime
Phosphor(escent), Phosphorescence, Phosphorus Bologna, Briming, Foxfire,
  Friar's lantern, Ignis fatuus, Jack o'lantern, Luminescent, Malathion®, Noctilucent,
  P, Pyrosome, Sarin, Sea-fire, Tabun, Will o' the wisp
Photo(copy), Photograph(y), Photographic, Photo finish Ambrotype,
  Anaglyph, Angiogram, Beefcake, Black and white, Blow-up, Cabinet, Calotype,
  Clog, Close-up, Composite, Contre-jour, Daguerrotype, Diazo, Duplicate, Enprint,
  Exposure, Ferroprint, Ferrotype, Film, Flash, Half-tone, Headshot, Heliochrome®,
  Heliotype, Hologram, Infra-red, Kallitype, Kirlian, Kodak®, Microdot, Microfilm,
  Microgram, Micrograph, Microprint, Monochrome, Montage, Mugshot, Negative,
  Nephogram, Opaline, Panel, Picture, Pinhole, Platinotype, Polaroid®, Positive,
  Print, Resorcin, Rotograph, Rotogravure, Schlieren, Sepia, Shoot, Shot, Shutterbug,
  Slide, Snap, Spirit, Still, Take, Talbotype, Time-lapse, Tintype, Tomography, Topo,
  Trimetrogon, Vignette, Wire, Woodburytype, Xerography, X-ray
Photographer Beaton, Brandt, Cameraman, Cameron, Cartier-Bresson, Daguerre,
  Fox Talbot, Paparazzo, Schlierin, Shutterbug
Phrase Abject, Actant, Asyndeton, Buzzword, Catch(word), Catchcry, Cliché,
  Climacteric, Comma, Expression, Heroic, Hook, Laconism, Leitmotiv, Locution,
  Mantra, Noun, Phr, Refrain, Riff, Slogan, Soundbite, Tag, Term, Trope
Phrygian Midas
Phthisis Decay, TB
Phylactery Amulet, Talisman, Tefillin, Tephillin
Phyllopod Brine-shrimp
Physic(s) Cluster, Cryogenics, Culver's, Cure, Dose, Electrostatics, Geostatics,
  Health, High-energy, Kinematics, Medicine, Nuclear, Nucleonics, Particle,
  Photometry, Purge, Remedy, Rheology, Science, Solid-state, Sonics,
  Thermodynamics, Ultrasonics
Physical Bodily, Carnal, Corpor(e)al, Material, Natural, Tangible
Physician Allopath, Buteyko, Doctor, Galen, Hakim, Hansen, Harvey, Hippocrates,
  Internist, Leech, Linacre, Lister, Medic(o), Menière, Mesmer, Mindererus, Paean,
  Paracelsus, Practitioner, Preceptor, Quack, Roget, Sézary, Stahl, Therapist, Time
Physicist Alfren, Ampère, Angstrom, Appleton, Archimedes, Avogadro, Becquerel,
  Bohr, Bondi, Born, Bose, Bragg, Brewster, Carnot, Cockcroft, Coulomb, Crookes,
  Curie, Dalton, Davisson, Debye, Dicke, Dirac, Einstein, Faraday, Fermi, Friedmann,
  Galileo, Gamow, Gauss, Geiger, Giorgi, Gold, Hahn, Hawking, Heaviside,

Heisenberg, Henry, Hertz, Hooke, Hoyle, Huygens, Joliot-Curie, Josephson, Joule, Kerv, Kirchhoff, Landau, Lawe, Lodge, Lorentz, Mach, Marconi, Maxwell, Meitner, Michelson, Morley, Newton, Oersted, Ohm, Oppenheimer, Pauli, Peebles, Penzias, Pic(c)ard, Planck, Popov, Rankine, Rayleigh, Reaumur, Robertson, Ro(e)ntgen, Rutherford, Schottky, Schrödinger, Scientist, Sievert, Stark, Torricelli, Tyndall, Van Allen, Van der Waals, Volta, Watson-Watt, Weber, Wheeler, Wilson, Young

Physiognomist, Physiognomy Face, Features, Lavater

Physiology, Physiologist Malpighi, Pavlov, Wagner, Zoonomia

Physiotherapist Masseur

Physique Body, Build, Figure, Pyknic, Somatotype

Pi, Pious Breast-beater, Craw-thumper, Devotional, Devout, Fraud, Gallio, God-fearing, Godly, Holy, Holy Willie, Mid-Victorian, Religiose, Sanctimonious, Savoury, Smug, Wise, Zaddik

Piaffe Spanish-walk

Pianist Anda, Arrau, Hambourg, Hess, Hofmann, Liszt, Mingus, Morton, Pachmann, Paderewski, Répétiteur, Schnabel, Tatum, Vamper, Virtuoso

Piano Baby grand, Bechstein, Boudoir grand, Celesta, Celeste, Concert grand, Cottage, Flugel, Forte, Grand, Honkytonk, Keyboard, Mbira, Overstrung, P, Player, Prepared, Semi-grand, Softly, Steinway, Stride, Thumb, Upright

Piano-maker Erard

Picaresque Roman à tiroirs

Picaroon Brigand, Corsair, Pirate, Rogue

Piccadilly Whist

Piccolo Ottavino

Pick(er), Pickaxe, Picking, Pick up Break, Choice, → CHOOSE, Cream, Cull, Elite, Flower, Gather, Glean, Gurlet, Hack, Holing, Hopper, Mattock, Nap, Nibble, Oakum, Plectrum, Pluck, Plum, Select, Single, Sort, Steal, Strum, Tong, Wale

▷ **Picked** *may indicate* an anagram

Picket Demonstrate, Flying, Pale, Palisade, Protester, Stake, Tether, Tie

Pickings Harvest, Profits, Scrounging, Spoils

Pickle(r) Achar, Brine, Cabbage, Caper, Chow-chow, Chutney, Corn, Cucumber, Cure, Dilemma, Dill, Eisel, Esile, Gherkin, Girkin, Jam, Kimchi, Marinade, Marinate, Mess, Mull, Olive, Onion, Peculate, Peregrine, Piccalilli, → PLIGHT, Relish, Samp(h)ire, Scrape, Souse, Trouble, Vinegar, Wolly

Picklock Oustiti, Peterman

Pick-me-up Bracer, Drink, Restorer, Reviver, Tonic

Pickpocket(s) Adept, Bung, Cly-faker, Cutpurse, Dip, Diver, Fagin, File, Nipper, Swell mob, Wire

Pick-up Arrest, Light o'love, Truck, Ute

Picnic Alfresco, Braaivleis, Burgoo, Clambake, Fun, Outing, Push-over, Spread, Tailgate, Wase-goose, Wayzgoose

Picture(s) Anaglyph, Arpillera, Art, Bambocciades, Bitmap, Canvas, Collage, Cutaway, Cyclorama, Decoupage, Depict, Describe, Diptych, Drawing, Drypoint, Emblem, Envisage, Epitome, Etching, Film, Flick, Fresco, Gouache, Graphic, Histogram, Icon, Identikit®, Imagery, Inset, Kakemono, Landscape, Likeness, Lithograph, Montage, Motion, Movie, Moving, Movy, Mugshot, Myriorama, Oil, Photo, Photofit®, Photogram, Photomontage, Photomosaic, Photomural, Pin-up, Pix, Plate, Polyptych, Portrait, Predella, Prent, Presentment, Print, Retraitt, Retrate, Rhyparography, Scene, Shadowgraph, Shot, Slide, Snapshot, Stereochrome, Stereogram, Stereograph, Stevengraph, Still-life, Table(au), Talkie, Thermogram, Tone, Topo, Transfer, Transparency, Vanitas, Vectograph, Vision,

Votive, Vraisemblance, Word, Zincograph

Picturesque Idyllic, Scenic

Pidgin Chinook jargon, Creole, Fanagalo, Fanakalo, Japlish, New Guinea, Police Motu, Solomon Islands, Tok Pisin

Pie(s) Anna, Banoffee, Battalia, Bridie, Camp, Chewet, Cobbler, Cottage, Coulibiac, Curry puff, Custard, Deep-dish, Easy, Flan, Floater, Florentine, Hash, Humble, Koulibiaca, Madge, Meat, Mess, Mince, Mud, Mystery bag, Pandowdy, Pastry, Pasty, Patty, Périgord, Pica, Piet, Pirog, Pizza, Printer's, Pyat, Pyet, Pyot, Quiche, Rappe, Resurrection, Shepherd's, Shoofly, Spoil, Squab, Stargaz(e)y, Star(ry)-gazy, Sugar, Tart, Tarte tatin, Torte, Tourtière, Turnover, Tyropitta, Umble, Vol-au-vent, Warden

▷ **Pie** *may indicate* an anagram

Piebald Calico, Dappled, Motley, Pied, Pinto, Skewbald

Piece(s) Add, Bishop, Bit, Blot, Cameo, Cannon, Cent, Charm, → **CHESSMAN**, Chip, Chunk, Coin, Companion, Component, Concerto, Conversation, Crumb, Domino, End, Episode, Extract, Firearm, Flitters, Fragment, Frust, Gat, Goring, → **GUN**, Haet, Hait, Hunk, Item, Join, Mammock, Médaillons, Mite, Money, Morceau, Morsel, Museum, Nip, Novelette, Oddment, Off-cut, Ort, Part, Party, Pastiche, Patch, Pawn, Period, Peso, Pin, Pistareen, Pole, → **PORTION**, Recital, Scliff, Scrap, Section, Set, Shard, Sherd, Skliff, Slice, Sliver, Sou, Speck, String, Stub, Swatch, Tait, Tate, Tile, Toccata, Truncheon, Wedge

Pièce de résistance Star-turn

Piecemeal, Piecework Gradually, Intermittent, Jigsaw, Serial, Tut

Pie-crust Coffin, Lid, Pastry

Pied-à-terre Nest, Pad

Pieman Pastrycook, Shepherd

Pier(s) Anta, Groyne, Jetty, Jutty, Landing, Mole, Plowman, Quay, Slipway, Swiss roll, Wharf

Pierce(d), Piercer, Piercing Accloy, Awl, Broach, Cleave, Cribrose, Dart, Drill, Endart, Fenestrate(d), Fulminant, Gimlet, Gore, Gride, Gryde, Hull, Impale, Jag, Keen, Lance, Lancinate, Lobe, Move, Needle, Penetrate, Perforate, Pike, Pink, Poignant, Punch, Puncture, Riddle, Rive, Shrill, Skewer, Slap, Sleeper, Spear, Spike, Spit, Stab, Steek, Stiletto, Sting, Thirl, Thrill(ant)

Piety Devotion, Purity, Sanctity

Piffle Bilge, Codswallop, Hogwash, Poppycock, Tommy-rot, Twaddle

Pig(s), Piggy, Pigskin Anthony, Babe, Babirusa, Baconer, Barrow, Bartholomew, Bessemer, Bland, Boar, Bonham, British Lop, Bush, Captain Cooker, Doll, Duroc, Elt, Farrow, Fastback, Football, Gadarene, Gilt, Gloucester, Gloucester Old Spot, Glutton, Grice, Grumphie, Gryce, Guffie, Guinea, Gus, Ham, Hog, Ingot, Iron, Javelina, Kentledge, Kintledge, Kunekune, Lacombe, Landrace, Lard, Large Black, Large white, Lingot, Long, Middle White, Napoleon, Old Spot, Peccary, Policeman, Pork(er), Razorback, Rosser, Runt, Saddleback, Shoat, Shot(e), Shott, Slip, Snowball, Sounder, Sow, Squealer, Sucking, Suid(ae), Tamworth, Tayassuid, Tithe, Toe, Tootsie, Truffle, Vietnamese Pot-bellied, Warthog, Welsh, Yelt

Pig-disease Bullnose

Pigeon Archangel, Barb, Bird, Bronze-winged, Cape, Capuchin, Carrier, Clay, Cropper, Culver, Cumulet, Danzig, Dove, Fairy Swallow, Fantail, Goura, Ground, Gull, Homer, Homing, Horseman, Jacobin, Kereru, Kuku, Manumea, New Zealand, Nun, Owl, Passenger, Peristeronic, Piwakawaka, Pouter, Ringdove, Rock(er), Roller, Ront(e), Ruff, Runt, Scandaroon, Solitaire, Spot, Squab, Squealer, Stock-dove, Stool, Stork, Swift, Talkie-talkee, Tippler, Tooth-billed, Tumbler,

Turbit, Wonga(-wonga), Zoozoo

Pigeonhole Classify, Compartment, File, Label, Postpone, Shelve, Slot, Stereotype

Pigeon-house Columbary, Cote, Dovecot(e)

Pig-food Mast, Swill

Pig-headed Self-willed

Pig-iron Kentledge, Kintledge

Pigment(s), Pigmentation Accessory, Anthoclore, Anthocyan(in), Argyria, Betacyanin, Bilirubin, Biliverdin, Bister, Bistre, Bronzing, Cappagh-brown, Carmine, Carotene, Carotenoid, Carotin, Carotinoid, Chloasma, Chlorophyll, Chrome, Chromogen, Cobalt, Colcothar, Colour, Crocus, Curcumin, Dye, Etiolin, Eumelanin, Flake-white, Flavin(e), Fucoxanthin, Gamboge, Gossypol, Haem, Hem(e), H(a)ematin, H(a)emocyanin, H(a)emoglobin, Iodopsin, Lake, Lamp-black, Lithopone, Liverspot, Lutein, Luteolin, Lycopene, Madder, Melanin, Monastral®, Naevus, Naples yellow, Nigrosine, Ochre, Opsin, Orpiment, Paris-green, Phthalocyanine, Phycobilin, Phycoerythrin, Phycophaein, Phycoxanthin, Phytochrome, Porphyrin, Porphyropsin, Pterin, Quercetin, Realgar, Red lead, Respiratory, Retinene, Rhiboflavin, Rhodophane, Rhodopsin, Saffron, Scheele's green, Sepia, Sienna, Sinopia, Sinopsis, Smalt, Tapetum, Tempera, Terre-verte, Tincture, Toner, Ultramarine, Umber, Urobilin, Urochrome, Verditer, Vermilion, Viridian, Whitewash, Xanthophyll, Xanthopterin(e), Zinc white

Pigtail Braid, Cue, Plait, Queue

Pi jaw Cant

Pike Assegai, Crag, Dory, Fogash, Gar(fish), Ged, Gisarme, Glaive, Hie, Holostei, Javelin, Lance, Luce, Partisan, Pickerel, Ravensbill, Scafell, Snoek, Spear, Speed, Spontoon, Vouge, Walleyed

▸ **Pilaster** *see* PILLAR

Pile(d), Piles, Piling Agger, Amass, Atomic, Bing, Bomb, Camp-sheathing, Camp-shedding, Camp-sheeting, Camp-shot, Clamp, Cock, Column, Crowd, Deal, Down, Emerods, Farmers, Fender, Fig, Floccus, Fortune, Galvanic, Hair, Haycock, Heap, Hept, Historic, Hoard, Load, Lot, Marleys, Mass, Moquette, Nap, Pier, Post, Pyre, Raft, Reactor, Ream(s), Rouleau, Screw, Shag, Sheet, Slush, → STACK, Starling, Stilt, Trichome, Upheap, Velvet, Voltaic, Wealth, Windrow, Wodge

Pile-driver Tup

Pilfer(ing) Crib, Filch, Finger, Maraud, Miche, Nick, Peculate, Pickery, Pickle, Pinch, Plagiarise, Plunder, Purloin, Snitch, → STEAL

Pilgrim(age) Aske, Childe Harold, Expedition, Fatima, Gaya, Hadj(i), Haji, Hajj(i), Karbala, Kerbela, Kum, Loreto, Lourdes, Mathura, Mecca, Nasik, Nikko, Palmer, Pardoner, Qom, Qum, Reeve, Scallop-shell, Shrine, Voyage, Yatra

Pill(s) Abortion, Ball, Beverley, Bitter, Bolus, Caplet, Capsule, Chill, Dex, Doll, Dose, Globule, Golfball, Goofball, Lob, Medication, Medicine, Number nine, Peace, Peel, Pellet, Pep, Pilula, Pilule, Placebo, Poison, Protoplasmal, Radio, Sleeping, Spansule, Tablet, Troche, Trochisk, Upper

Pillage Booty, Devastate, Plunder, Ransack, Rapine, Ravage, Razzia, Robbery, Sack, Spoil

Pillar(ed), Pillars Anta, Apostle, Atlantes, Baluster, Balustrade, Boaz, Canton, Caryatides, Cippus, Columel, Column, Earth, Eustyle, Gendarme, Hercules, Herm, Impost, Islam, Jachin, Lat, Man, Modiolus, Monolith, Newel, Nilometer, Obelisk, Pedestal, Peristyle, Pier, Post, Respond, Saddle, Serac, Stalactite, Stalagmite, Stoop, Telamon, Tetrastyle, Trumeau

Pill-box Hat, Inro

Pillion Cushion, Pad, Rear

Pillory Cang(ue), Cippus, Crucify, Jougs, Little-ease, Pelt, Satirise, Slam

Pillow(case) Bear, Beer, Bere, Bolster, Cod, Cow, Cushion, Headrest, Hop, Lace, Pad, Pulvinar

Pilot Ace, Airman, Auto(matic), Aviator, Captain, → **CONDUCT**, Experimental, Flier, George, Govern, Guide, Hobbler, Lead, Lodesman, Lodestar, Palinure, Palinurus, Pitt, Prune, Shipman, Steer, Test, Tiphys, Trial, Usher, Wingman

Pimento Allspice

Pimp Apple-squire, Bludger, Fancyman, Fleshmonger, Hoon, Lecher, Mack, Pandarus, Pander, Ponce, Procurer, Solicit, Souteneur

Pimpernel Bastard, Bog, Scarlet, Water, Wincopipe, Wink-a-peep, Yellow

Pimple, Pimply Blackhead, Botch, Bubukle, Button, Gooseflesh, Grog-blossom, Hickey, Horripilation, Milium, Papilla, Papula, Papule, Plook, Plouk, Pock, Pustule, Quat, Rumblossom, Rum-bud, Spot, Tetter, Uredinial, Wen, Whelk, Whitehead, Zit

Pin Bayonet, Belaying, Bolt, Brooch, Candle, Cask, Cotter, Curling, Dowel, Drawing, Drift, End, Fasten, Fid, Firing, Fix, Gam, Gudgeon, Hair, Hairgrip, Hob, Joggle, Kevel, King, Leg, Nail, Needle, Nog, Panel, Peg, Pintle, Pivot, Preen, Rivet, Rolling, Saddle, Safety, Scarf, SCART, Scatter, Shear, Shirt, Skewer, Skittle, Skiver, Spike, Spindle, Split, Staple, Stick, Stump, Swivel, Taper, Thole, Thumbtack, Tie, Tre(e)nail, U-bolt, Woolder, Wrest, Wrist

Pinafore Apron, Brat, HMS, Overall, Pinny, Save-all, Tire

Pinball Pachinko

Pince-nez Nose-nippers

Pincers Chela, Claw, Forceps, Forfex, Nipper, Tweezers

Pinch(ed) Arrest, Bit, Bone, Chack, Constrict, Cramp, Crimp, Crisis, Emergency, Gaunt, Misappropriate, Nab, Nick, Nim, Nip, Peculate, Peel, Pilfer, Pocket, Pook(it), Prig, Pugil, Raft, Rob, Scrimp, Scrounge, Skimp, Smatch, Snabble, Snaffle, Sneak, Sneap, Sneeshing, Snuff, Squeeze, → **STEAL**, Swipe, Tate, Tweak, Twinge

Pine(s), Pining Arolla, Bristlecone, Celery, Cembra, Chile, Cluster, Cone, Conifer, Cypress, Droop, Dwine, Earn, Erne, Fret, Green, Ground, Hone, Hoop, Huon, Jack, Japanese umbrella, Jeffrey, Kauri, Languish, Languor, Loblolly, Lodgepole, Long, Longleaf, Monkey-puzzle, Moon, Norfolk Island, Norway, Nut, Oregon, Parana, Picea, Pinaster, Pitch, Radiata, Red, Scotch, Scots, Screw, Softwood, Spruce, Starve, Stone, Sugar, Tree, Umbrella, Urman, Waste, White, Yearn

Pineapple Anana, Bomb, Bromelia, Grenade, Piña, Poll, Sorosis, Tillandsia

Ping Knock, Whir(r)

Pinguin Anana(s)

Pinion Fetter, Penne, Pinnoed, Secure, Shackle, Wing

Pink Blush, Carolina, Castory, Cheddar, Clove, Colour, Coral, Dianthus, Dutch, Emperce, FT, Fuchsia, Gillyflower, Indian, Knock, Lake, Lily, Lychnis, Maiden, Moss, Mushroom, Oyster, Peach-blow, Peak, Perce, Pierce, Pompadour, Pounce, Rose(ate), Ruddy, Salmon, Scallop, Sea, Shell, Shocking, Shrimp, Spigelia, Spit, Stab, Tiny

Pinnacle Acme, Apex, Crest, Crown, Gendarme, Height, Needle, Pinnet, Summit

Pinniped Seal

Pin-point Focus, Highlight, Identify, Isolate, Localise

Pint(s) Cab, Jar, Log, Reputed

Pintail Duck, Smeath, Smee(th)

Pin-up Cheesecake, Dish, Star

Pioneer Baird, Bandeirante, Blaze, Boone, Colonist, Emigrant, Explore, Fargo, Fleming, Frontiersman, Harbinger, Innovator, Lead, Marconi, Oecist, Pathfinder,

Planter, Rochdale, Sandgroper, Settler, Spearhead, Trail-blazer, Trekker, Voortrekker, Waymaker, Wells

▶ **Pious** *see* PI

Pip Ace, Acinus, Blackball, Bleep, Hip, Hump, Phil, Pyrene, Seed, Star

Pipe(s), Piper, Pipeline, Piping Antara, Aorta, Aulos, Balance, Barrel, Blub, Boatswain's, Bong, Briar, Briarroot, Broseley, Bubble, Calabash, Call, Calumet, Chanter, Cheep, Cherrywood, Chibouk, Chibouque, Chillum, Churchwarden, Clay, Cob, Conduit, Corncob, Crane, Cutty, Down, Downcomer, Drain, Drill, Drillstring, Dry riser, Duct, Dudeen, Dudheen, Ell, Escape, Exhaust, Faucet, Feed, Fistula, Flue, Flute, Gage, Gas main, Gedact, Gedeckt, Hawse, Hod, Hogger, Hooka(h), Hose, Hubble-bubble, Hydrant, Indian, Irish, Jet, Kalian, Kelly, Mains, Manifold, Marsyas, Meerschaum, Mirliton, Montre, Narghile, Narg(h)il(l)y, Nargile(h), Oat(en), Oboe, Organ, Ottavino, Pan, Peace, Pepper, Pibroch, Piccolo, Pied, Pifferaro, Pitch, Poverty, Pule, Qanat, Quill, Rainwater, Recorder, Ree(d), Rise, Riser, Sack-doudling, Salicional, Sennit, Serpent, Service, Sewer, Shalm, Shawm, Shisha, Shrike, Sing, Siphon, Skirl, Sluice, Soil, Squeak, Stack, Standpipe, Stopcock, Stummel, Sucker, Syrinx, Tail, Tee, Throttle, Tibia, Tootle, Trachea, Tremie, Tube, Tubule, Tweet, U-bend, Uillean(n), Union, Uptake, U-trap, U-tube, Vent, Ventiduct, Volcanic, Waste, Water(-spout), Watermain, Weasand, Whistle, Woodcock's head, Woodnote

Pipefish Sea-adder

Pipe-laying Graft

Pipit Bird, Skylark, Titlark

Pippin Apple, Orange, Ribston

Pipsqueak Nobody

Piquancy, Piquant Pungent, Racy, Relish, Salt, Sharp, Spicy, Tangy

Pique Dod, Huff, Resentment, Titillate

Piranha Caribe, Characinoid, Piraya

Pirate(s), Piratical, Piracy Algerine, Barbarossa, Blackbeard, Boarder, Bootleg, Brigand, Buccaneer, Buccanier, Cateran, Condottier, Conrad, Corsair, Crib, Dampier, Fil(l)ibuster, Flint, Gunn, Hijack, Hook, Kidd, Lift, Loot, Morgan, Penzance, Picaro(on), Pickaroon, Plagiarise, Plunder, Rakish, Rover, Sallee-man, Sallee-rover, Sea-dog, Sea-king, Sea-rat, Sea-robber, Sea-wolf, Silver, Skull and crossbones, Smee, Steal, Teach, Thief, Viking, Water-rat, Water-thief

Pistillate Female

Pistol Air, Ancient, Automatic, Barker, Barking-iron, Colt®, Dag, Derringer, Gat, → GUN, Hackbut, Horse, Iron, Luger®, Pepperbox, Petronel, Pocket, Puffer, Revolver, Rod, Saloon, Shooter, Starter, Starting, Very, Water, Weapon

Piston Four-stroke, Plunger, Ram, Trunk

Pit(ted), Pitting Abyss, Alveolus, Antrum, Bottomless, Catch, Cave, Cesspool, Chasm, Cissing, Cloaca, Colliery, Crater, Den, Depression, Depth, Dungmere, Ensile, Fossa, Fovea, Foxhole, Gehenna, Hangi, Heapstead, Hell, Hole, Hollow, Inferno, Inspection, Khud, Lacunose, Lime, Mark, Match, Measure, → MINE, Mosh, Orchestra, Parterre, Pip, Plague, Play, Pock-mark, Potato, Punctate, Putamen, Pyrene, Ravine, Rifle, Salt, Scrobicule, Silo, Slime, Soakaway, Solar plexus, Stone, Sump, Tar, Tear, Trap, Trous-de-loup, Underarm

Pitch(ed) Absolute, Asphalt, Atilt, Attune, Bitumen, Burgundy, Coal-tar, Concert, Crease, Diamond, Dive, Ela, Elect, Elevator, Encamp, Erect, Establish, Fever, Fling, Fork, Ground, International, Intonation, Key, Knuckleball, Labour, Length, Level, Lurch, Maltha, Mineral, Nets, Neume, Patter, Peck, Perfect, Philosophical, Piceous, Pight, Pin, Plong(e), Plunge, Pop, Purl, Resin, Rock, Ruff(e), Sales, Scend,

Seel, Send, Shape, Sling, Slope, Soprarino, Spiel, Stoit, Tar, Tessitura, Tilt, Tone, Tonemic, Tonus, Tremolo, Tune, Vibrato, Wicket, Wood

Pitchblende Cleveite

Pitcher(-shaped) Aryt(a)enoid, Ascidium, Bowler, Cruse, Ewer, Jug, Steen, Urceolus

Pitchfork Hurl, Toss

Pitfall Ambush, Danger, Hazard, Snare, Trap

Pith(y) Ambatch, Aphorism, Apo(ph)thegm, Core, Down, Essence, Gnomic, Hat-plant, Heart, Marrow, Medulla, Moxa, Nucleus, Rag, Succinct, Terse

Pithead Broo, Brow, Minehead

Pithless Thowless

Pitiless Flint-hearted, Hard, Ruthless

Piton Rurp

Pitt Chatham

Pity, Piteous, Pitiful, Pitiable Ah, Alack, Alas, Commiseration, → COMPASSION, Hapless, Mercy, Pathos, Pilgarlic, Red-leg, Rue, Ruth(ful), Seely, Shame, Sin, Sympathy

Pivot(al) Ax(i)le, Central, Focal, Fulcrum, Gooseneck, Gudgeon, Kingbolt, Revolve, Rotate, Slue, → SWIVEL, Trunnion, Turn, Wheel

Pixie Brownie, Elf, Fairy, Gremlin, Sprite

Pizza Calzone, Pepperoni

Placard Affiche, Bill, Playbill, Poster

Placate Appease, Conciliate, Pacify, Propitiate, Soothe

Place(ment) Ad loc, Aim, Allocate, Area, Berth, Bro, Decimal, Deploy, Deposit, Fix, Habitat, Hither, Howf, Identify, Impose, → IN PLACE OF, Install, Job, Joint, Juxtapose, Lay, Lieu, Locality, Locate, Locus, Parking, Pitch, Plat, Plaza, Point, Posit, → POSITION, Product, Put, Realm, Region, Repose, Resting, Scene, Second, Set, Site, Situate, Situation, Slot, Spot, Stead, Sted(e), Stedd(e), Stratify, Town, Vendôme

Placid Cool, Easy, Easy-osy, Quiet, Tame, Tranquil

Plagiarise, Plagiarist Copy, Crib, Lift, Pirate, Steal

Plague (spot) Annoy, Bane, Bedevil, Black death, Boil, Bubonic, Burden, Cattle, Curse, Dog, Dun, Frogs, Goodyear, Goujeers, Harry, Infestation, Locusts, Lues, Murrain, Murran, Murrin, Murrion, Nag, Pest, Pester, Pox, Press, Scourge, Tease, Token, Torture, Try, Vex

Plaid Maud, Roon, Shepherd's, Tartan, Wales

Plain(s) Abraham, Archimedes, Artless, Ascetic, Au naturel, Bald, Banat, Bare, Blatant, Broad, Campagna, Campo, Candid, Carse, Ceará, Chryse, Clavius, Clear, Cook, Dowdy, Downright, Dry, Esdraelon, Evident, Explicit, Flat, Flood, Girondist, Gran Chaco, Great, Homely, Homespun, Inornate, Jezreel, Kar(r)oo, Lande, Langrenus, Llano, Lombardy, Lowland, Maidan, Manifest, Marathon, Mare, Monochrome, Nullarbor, Obvious, Ocean of Storms, Oceanus Procellarum, Olympia, → ORDINARY, Outspoken, Overt, Packstaff, Pampa(s), Paramo, Patent, Pikestaff, Plateau, Playa, Polje, Prairie, Prose, Ptolemaeus, Purbach, Sabkha(h), Sabkha(t), Sailing, Salisbury, Savanna(h), Secco, Serengeti, Sharon, Simple, Sodom, Spoken, Staked, Steppe, Tableland, Thessaly, Tundra, Vega, Veldt, Visible, Walled

Plainchant Canto fermo

Plainsman Llanero

Plainsong Ambrosian, Chant

Plaint(ive) Complaint, Dirge, Lagrimoso, Lament, Melancholy, Sad, Whiny

Plaintiff Doe, Impeacher, Litigant, Suer

Plait Braid, Crimp, Cue, Frounce, Furbelow, Goffer, Intertwine, Pigtail, Plica, Plight, Queue, Ruche, Sennit, Sinnet, Splice

Plan(ned), Planner, Planning Aim, American, Angle, Architect, Arrange, Axonometric, Blueprint, Brew, Budget, Care, Chart, Commission, Complot, Contingency, Contrive, Dalton, Dart, Deep-laid, Deliberate, Delors, Design, Desyne, Device, Devise, Diagram, Draft, Drawing, Elevation, Engineer, European, Family, Five-Year, Floor, Format, Galveston, Game, Ground, Hang, Ichnography, Idea, Idée, Instal(l)ment, Intent, Lay(out), Leicester, Leicestershire, Map, Marshall, Master, Mastermind, Mean, Nominal, Open, Outline, Pattern, Pipe-dream, Plat, Plot, Ploy, Policy, Premeditate, Prepense, Procedure, Programme, Project, Projet, Proposal, Prospectus, Protraction, Rapacki, Road map, Scenario, Schedule, Scheme, Schlieffen, Shape, Spec(ification), Stratagem, Strategy, Subterfuge, System, Tactician, Town, Wheeze

Plane(s) Aero(dyne), Air, → **AIRCRAFT**, Airliner, Airship, Bandit, Block, Boeing, Bomber, Bus, Buttock, Camel, Canard, Cartesian, Chenar, Chinar, Comet, Concorde, Crate, Dakota, Datum, Delta-wing, Even, Facet, Fault, Fillister, Flat, Focal, Galactic, Glider, Gliding, Gotha, Homaloid, Hurricane, Icosahedron, Icosohedra, Inclined, Jack, Jet, Jointer, Jumbo, Level, London, Main, MIG, Mirage, Mosquito, Moth, Octagon, Perspective, Platan(us), Polygon, Pursuit, Rocket, Router, Shackleton, Shave, Smooth, Sole, Spitfire, Spokeshave, Spy, Stealth (bomber), STOL, Surface, Sycamore, Tail, Taube, Thrust, Tow, Trainer, Tree, Trident, Tropopause, Trying, Viscount

Plane figure Endecagon, Hendecagon

Planet(s), Planetary Alphonsine, Ariel, Asteroid, Body, Cabiri, Ceres, Chiron, Constellation, Earth, Eros, Extrasolar, Gas giant, Georgian, Giant, House, Hyleg, Inferior, Inner, Jovian, Jupiter, Lucifer, Major, Mars, Mercury, Minor, Moon, Neptune, Outer, Pallas, Pluto, Primary, Psyche, Quartile, Red, Satellitium, Saturn, Sedna, Sphere, Starry, Sun, Superior, Terrestrial, Uranus, Venus, Vista, Vulcan, World, Zog

Plangent Mournful

Plank Board, Chess, Deal, Duckboard, Garboard, Plonk, Sarking, Slab, Spirketting, Straik, Strake, Stringer, Weatherboard, Wood, Wrest

Plankton Nekton, Neuston, Pelagic, Red tide, Seston, Spatfall

Plant(s), Plant part Acrogen, Amphidiploid, Anemochore, Annual, Anther, Aphotoic, Autophyte, Bed, Biennial, Biota, Bloomer, Bryophyte, CAM, Catchfly, Chamaephyte, Chomophyte, Cotyledon, Cultigen, Cultivar, Dayflower, Dibble, Ecad, Eccremocarpus, Embed, Endogen, Enrace, Epilithic, Epiphyllous, Epiphyte, Equisetum, Establish, Factory, Fix, Forb, Geophyte, G(u)ild, Growth, Gymnosperm, Halophyte, Halosere, Helophyte, Herbage, Herbarium, House, Humicole, Hydrastus, Hydrophyte, Hygrophyte, Hylophyte, Incross, Insert, Instil, Inter, Labiate, Land, Lathe, Lithophyte, Livelong, Longday, Machinery, Mill, Monocotyledon, Ornamental, Phanerogam, Phloem, Pilot, Pitcher, Power, Protophyte, Ramet, Resurrection, Root, Rosin, Saprophyte, Schizophyte, Sciophyte, Sclerophyll, Scrambler, Sensitive, Sere, Shortday, Shrub, Simple, Soma, Sow, Steelworks, Stickseed, Sticktight, Stickweed, Strangler, Streptocarpus, Succulent, Superweed, Thallophyte, Therophyte, Thickleaf, → **TREE**, Trifolium, Tropophyte, Vegetal, Vegetation, Wasabi, Washery, Wilding, Works, Zoophyte

---

PLANTS

3 letters:	Hop	Meu	Set
Dal	Ivy	Pia	Til
Hom	Kex	Rue	Udo

Urd
Yam

4 letters:
Alga
Aloe
Anil
Arum
Beet
Bixa
Chay
Cube
Daal
Dahl
Deme
Dhal
Dill
Fern
Flag
Flax
Geum
Grex
Guar
Herb
Hioi
Homa
Hoya
Ixia
Kali
Loco
More
Musk
Nard
Ombu
Pita
Rape
Reed
Rhus
Rush
Sage
Sego
Sida
Snow
Sola
Sunn
Tare
Taro
Thea
Vine
Weld
Woad

Wort
Yarr

5 letters:
Agave
Ajwan
Anise
Anona
Aroid
Aster
Basil
Benni
Betel
Blite
Bluet
Boree
Broom
Buchu
Bucku
Bugle
Calla
Camas
Canna
Carex
Chara
Chaya
Chufa
Clary
Clote
Cress
Cubeb
Cumin
Daisy
Erica
Ficus
Fouat
Fouet
Gemma
Glaux
Gorse
Guaco
Hosta
Hovea
Inula
Jalap
Kenaf
Kudzu
Laser
Ledum
Liana
Linum

Loofa
Lotus
Luffa
Lupin
Lurgi
Medic
Morel
Murva
Musci
Orach
Orpin
Orris
Oshac
Oxeye
Oxlip
Panax
Pansy
Peony
Phlox
Pilea
Sedge
Sedum
Senna
Shaya
Spink
Stock
Tansy
Tetra
Timbo
Tulip
Urena
Vetch
Vinca
Viola
Vitex
Vitis
Xyris
Yucca
Yulan
Zamia

6 letters:
Acacia
Acorus
Ajowan
Alisma
Allium
Alpine
Althea
Ambari
Ambary

Annona
Arabis
Aralia
Arnica
Azalea
Bablah
Balsam
Bamboo
Bauera
Betony
Borage
Briony
Bryony
Burnet
Cactus
Caltha
Camash
Camass
Cassia
Catnep
Catnip
Celery
Cicuta
Cissus
Cistus
Cleome
Clivia
Clover
Clusia
Cnicus
Cockle
Cohage
Cohash
Coleus
Conium
Coonty
Cornel
Cosmea
Cosmos
Cotton
Cowpea
Crinum
Crocus
Croton
Cummin
Dahlia
Daphne
Darnel
Datura
Derris
Dodder

Echium	Protea	Begonia	Freesia
Endive	Radish	Boneset	Frogbit
Erinus	Ramtil	Brinjal	Fuchsia
Exacum	Rattle	Bugbane	Gazania
Exogen	Reseda	Bugloss	Genista
Fat hen	Retama	Burdock	Gentian
Fennel	Rubber	Burweed	Gerbera
Ferula	Ruscus	Calluna	Ginseng
Funkia	Salvia	Caltrap	Godetia
Garlic	Savory	Caltrop	Gunnera
Gnetum	Scilla	Campion	Haemony
Henbit	Senega	Caraway	Hawkbit
Hoodia	Sesame	Cardoon	Hemlock
Hyssop	Seseli	Carduus	Henbane
Iberis	Silene	Carline	Hogweed
Jojoba	Smilax	Cassava	Ipomoea
Juncus	Sorbus	Catechu	Isoetes
Kentia	Sorrel	Catmint	Jasmine
Kerria	Spider	Cat's ear	Jonquil
Knawel	Spirea	Chayote	Kingcup
Kochia	Spurge	Chelone	Lantana
Korari	Spurry	Chervil	Lettuce
Kumara	Squill	Chicory	Liatris
Kumera	Styrax	Clarkia	Lobelia
Lichen	Sundew	Cocoyam	Logania
Lolium	Teasel	Comfrey	Lucerne
Loofah	Thrift	Compass	Lychnis
Lovage	Tomato	Coontie	Lythrum
Lupine	Tulipa	Cowbane	Madwort
Madder	Turnip	Cowbird	Mahonia
Maguey	Tutsan	Cowhage	Manihot
Mallow	Violet	Cowherb	Maranta
Manioc	Viscum	Cowitch	Mayweed
Medick	Yarrow	Cowslip	Melilot
Mimosa	Yautia	Cudweed	Mercury
Monoao	Zinnia	Curcuma	Milfoil
Moorva		Cushion	Mimulus
Nerine	***7 letters:***	Dasheen	Monarda
Nerium	Absinth	Deutzia	Mugwort
Nettle	Aconite	Diascia	Mullein
Nuphar	Alkanet	Dioecia	Mustard
Orache	All-good	Dittany	Nelumbo
Orchid	Allheal	Dogbane	Nemesia
Orchis	Allseed	Drosera	Nigella
Orpine	Alyssum	Epacris	Nonsuch
Oxalis	Anchusa	Ephedra	Olearia
Oyster	Arachis	Erodium	Opuntia
Pachak	Astilbe	Eugenia	Palmiet
Paeony	Awlwort	Felwort	Pareira
Peanut	Barilla	Filaree	Parsley
Pieris	Bartsia	Fly-trap	Parsnip

Penthia
Petunia
Pigface
Pinguin
Potherb
Primula
Puccoon
Pumpkin
Ragwort
Rampion
Raoulia
Redroot
Rhatany
Rhodora
Rhubarb
Ricinus
Robinia
Romneya
Rosebay
Ruellia
Saffron
Salfern
Salsify
Salsola
Sampire
Sanicle
Sawwort
Scandix
Seakale
Senecio
Setwall
Skirret
Solanum
Spignel
Spinach
Spiraea
Spurrey
Squilla
Stachys
Stapela
Statice
Syringa
Tagetes
Thallus
Trefoil
Triffid
Tritoma
Turbith
Turpeth
Vanilla
Verbena

Vervain
Weigela
Zebrina
Zedoary

8 letters:
Abelmosk
Absinthe
Abutilon
Acanthus
Achillea
Ageratum
Agrimony
Agueweed
Alocasia
Alumroot
Angelica
Apocynum
Arenaria
Argemone
Asphodel
Barometz
Bauhinia
Bedstraw
Bellwort
Bergamot
Bergenia
Bignonia
Bindi-eye
Bindweed
Bluebell
Bottonia
Boxberry
Brassica
Buckbean
Buddleia
Buplever
Caladium
Calamint
Calathea
Calthrop
Camomile
Canaigre
Cannabis
Capsicum
Cardamom
Cardamum
Cat's foot
Centaury
Chenopod
Chickpea

Cilantro
Cleavers
Clematis
Costmary
Crowfoot
Crucifer
Cucurbit
Cumbungi
Cunjevoi
Cyclamen
Daffodil
Damewort
Diandria
Dianthus
Dicentra
Dielytra
Dogberry
Dracaena
Dropwort
Duckweed
Dumbcane
Eelgrass
Erigeron
Eucharis
Euonymus
Feverfew
Fireweed
Fleabane
Fleawort
Fluellin
Foxglove
Fumitory
Furcraea
Galangol
Galtonia
Geranium
Gesneria
Gladioli
Gloriosa
Gloxinia
Glyceria
Gnetales
Goutweed
Gromwell
Hag-taper
Harakeke
Hardhack
Hawkweed
Helenium
Henequen
Hepatica

Heuchera
Hibiscus
Honewort
Hornwort
Horokaka
Hyacinth
Hydrilla
Hyperium
Japonica
Knotweed
Kohlrabi
Krameria
Larkspur
Lathyris
Lavatera
Lavender
Lungwort
Macleaya
Mandrake
Marigold
Mariposa
Marjoram
Milkweed
Milkwort
Miltonia
Monstera
Moonseed
Mosspink
Myosotis
Navicula
Oleander
Opopanax
Origanum
Oxtongue
Pandanus
Paspalum
Phacelia
Phormium
Physalis
Pinkroot
Pipewort
Plantain
Plumbago
Pokeroot
Pokeweed
Polygata
Pondweed
Primrose
Prunella
Psilotum
Psoralea

Psyllium	Withwind	Claytonia	Horehound
Purslane	Woodroof	Clianthus	Horsemint
Putchock	Woodruff	Clintonia	Horse-tail
Ratsbane	Woodrush	Colchicum	Houstonia
Roly-poly	Wormseed	Colicroot	Hydrangea
Sainfoin		Colicweed	Hypericum
Saltwort	**9 letters:**	Collinsia	Impatiens
Salvinia	Achimenes	Colocasia	Kalanchoe
Samphire	Adderwort	Colocynth	Kniphofia
Sandwort	Alfilaria	Coltsfoot	Laserwort
Scabious	Alfileria	Columbine	Liver-wort
Scammony	Amaryllis	Cordaites	Lousewort
Sea-blite	Anacharis	Coreopsis	Mare's-tail
Self-heal	Andromeda	Coriander	Marshwort
Sept-foil	Anthurium	Corydalis	Mitrewort
Shamrock	Aquilegia	Creamcups	Monandria
Sidalcea	Arracacha	Crocosnia	Moneywort
Silkweed	Arrowhead	Dandelion	Monkshood
Silphium	Arrowroot	Digitalis	Monogynia
Snowdrop	Artemisia	Dittander	Monotropa
Soapwort	Artichoke	Dog fennel	Moschatel
Solidago	Artillery	Doronicum	Mousetail
Sowbread	Asclepias	Dulcamara	Muscadine
Sparaxis	Asparagus	Echeveria	Narcissus
Spergula	Astrantia	Echinacea	Navelwort
Stapelia	Aubrietia	Edelweiss	Nemophila
Staragen	Ayabuasca	Eglantine	Nicotiana
Starwort	Bald-money	Erythrina	Oenothera
Sweet pea	Baneberry	Euphorbia	Ouviranda
Tamarisk	Birthroot	Eyebright	Patchouli
Tarragon	Birthwort	Fenugreek	Pearlwort
Tayberry	Breadroot	Feverwort	Pellitory
Tigridia	Bromeliad	Forsythia	Pennywort
Trigynia	Brooklime	Fourcroya	Penstemon
Trillium	Brookweed	Galingale	Peperomia
Tritonia	Broom-rape	Germander	Pimpernel
Trollius	Buckwheat	Gladiolus	Pineapple
Tuberose	Burrawang	Glasswort	Pokeberry
Tuckahoe	Butterbur	Goldenrod	Polygonum
Turmeric	Buttercup	Goosefoot	Portulaca
Turnsole	Calcicole	Grindelia	Quillwort
Valerian	Calcifuge	Groundnut	Rafflesia
Venidium	Calendula	Groundsel	Rattlebox
Veratrum	Campanula	Gypsywort	Rocambole
Veronica	Candytuft	Hardheads	Rosinweed
Viburnum	Cardamine	Hellebore	Rudbeckia
Viscaria	Carnation	Helophyte	Sabadilla
Wait-a-bit	Celandine	Herb-Paris	Safflower
Wallwort	Centaurea	Hieracium	Sagebrush
Wistaria	Chamomile	Hoarhound	Santoline
Wisteria	Cineraria	Hollyhock	Santonica

Saponaria
Saxifrage
Screwpine
Shoreweed
Sinningia
Snakeroot
Spearmint
Spearwort
Speedwell
Spikenard
Spikerush
Sprekalia
Stinkweed
Stone-crop
Strapwort
Sweet-gale
Taraxacum
Tomatillo
Toothwort
Tormentil
Twinberry
Vaccinium
Verbascum
Vetchling
Wake-robin
Wincopipe
Witchweed
Withywind
Wolf's bane
Woundwort

10 letters:
Agapanthus
Alexanders
Ampelopsis
Anacardium
Angiosperm
Artocarpus
Asarabacca
Aspidistra
Astralagus
Barrenwort
Beggarweed
Biddy-biddy
Bitterweed
Brugmansia
Butterwort
Candelilla
Catananche
Chionodoxa
Cinquefoil

Cloudberry
Commiphora
Coneflower
Corncockle
Cornflower
Cottonweed
Cow parsley
Cow parsnip
Cranesbill
Deadnettle
Delphinium
Dragonhead
Dragonroot
Dyer's-broom
Earth-smoke
Elecampane
Escallonia
Eupatorium
Five-finger
Foamflower
Four o'clock
Fraxinella
Fritillary
Gaillardia
Gaultheria
Glycophate
Gnaphalium
Goat-sallow
Goatsbeard
Goat's-thorn
Goat-willow
Goldenseal
Goldilocks
Goldthread
Gypsophila
Hawksbeard
Heathberry
Helianthus
Heliotrope
Hyoscyamus
Icosandria
Illecebrum
Immortelle
Jew's mallow
Jimsonweed
Loganberry
Maidenhair
Marguerite
Masterwort
Meconopsis
Mignonette

Montbretia
Moonflower
Motherwort
Nasturtium
Nightshade
Nipplewort
Parkleaves
Passiflora
Pennycress
Pennyroyal
Pentagynia
Pentandria
Pentstemon
Peppermint
Periwinkle
Pimpinella
Pipsissewa
Poinsettia
Polemonium
Polianthes
Polyanthus
Potentilla
Ranunculus
Rest-harrow
Rhoicissus
Salicornia
Sarracenia
Scindapsus
Scorzonera
Silverweed
Snapdragon
Sneezewort
Spiderwort
Stavesacre
Stitchwort
Storksbill
Strelitzia
Thalictrum
Thunbergia
Tibouchina
Tillandsia
Touch-me-not
Tragacanth
Tropaeolum
Tropaesium
Tumbleweed
Wallflower
Watercress
Yellowroot
Yellowweed
Yellowwort

11 letters:
Acidanthera
Antirrhinum
Bear's-breech
Bittercress
Bittersweet
Bristle-fern
Calceolaria
Callitriche
Convolvulus
Cotoneaster
Dusty-miller
Erythronium
Forget-me-not
Fothergilla
Gentianella
Gillyflower
Helichrysum
Hippeastrum
Horseradish
Hurtleberry
Incarvillea
Lithotripsy
Loosestrife
Marsh mallow
Meadowsweet
Monadelphia
Nancy-pretty
Pachysandra
Paritaniwha
Pelargonium
Potamogeton
Saintpaulia
Sansevieria
Schizanthus
Selaginella
Sempervivum
Slipperwort
Sparaganium
Steeplebush
Stephanotis
Strawflower
Swiss cheese
Thimbleweed
Thoroughwax
Tous-les-mois
Trumpetweed
Vallisneria
Welwitschia
Wintergreen
Xeranthemum

12 letters:	Pasqueflower	Wandering Jew	*14 letters:*
Adam's flannel	Philodendron	Water-soldier	Bougainvillaea
Alstroemeria	Phytobenthos	Zantedeschia	Chincherinchee
Aristolochia	Pickerelweed		Lords and ladies
Checkerbloom	Pterydophyte	*13 letters:*	Partridgeberry
Darlingtonia	Salpiglossis	Bougainvillea	Shepherd's purse
Epacridaceae	Sarsaparilla	Carrion-flower	
Eschscholzia	Scrophularia	Dieffenbachia	*16 letters:*
Fennelflower	Sempervivium	Eschscholtzia	Mesembrian-
Helianthemum	Southernwood	Passionflower	themum
Lithospermum	Strophanthus	Spathyphyllum	
Midsummermen	Sweet William	Sweet woodruff	*17 letters:*
Morning glory	Tradescantia	Townhall clock	Mother-of-
None-so-pretty	Venus flytrap	Traveller's joy	thousands
Parsley-piert	Virgin's bower		

Plantagenet Angevin, Broom

Plantain Mato(o)ke, Ribwort, Waybread

Plantation Arboretum, Bosket, Bosquet, Estate, Grove, Hacienda, Pen, Pinetum, Ranch, Tara, Veticetum, Vineyard

Plant disease Anthracnose, Bunt, Club-root, Curlytop, Eyespot, Frogeye, Psillid yellows, Rosette, Smut, Sooty mould

Planted In, Under

Planter Dibber, Farmer, Settler, Trowel

Plaque Calculus, Dental, Plateau, Scale

Plasm Germ

Plasma Dextran, Sigmond

Plaster(ed), Plaster board Bandage, Blister, Blotto, Butterfly clip, Cake, Cataplasm, Clam, Clatch, Compo, Court, Daub, Diachylon, Diachylum, Drunk, Emplastrum, Fresco, Gesso, Grout, Gyprock®, Gypsum, Intonaco, Laying, Leep, Lit, Mud, Mustard, Oiled, Parge(t), Polyfilla®, Porous, Poultice, Render, Roughcast, Scratch-coat, Screed, Secco, Shellac, Sinapism, Smalm, Smarm, Smear, Sowsed, Staff, Sticking, Stookie, Stucco, Teer

Plastic Bakelite®, Cel(luloid), Cling film, Ductile, Fablon®, Fictile, Fluon, Formica®, Ionomer, Laminate, Loid, Lucite®, Melamine, Mylar®, Perspex®, Plexiglass®, Pliant, Polyethylene, Polystyrene, Polythene, Polyvinyl, PVC, Reinforced, Styrene, Styrofoam®, Teflon®, Urea-formaldehyde, Vinyl, Wet-look, Yielding

▷ **Plastic** *may indicate* an anagram

Plastic surgeon McIndoe

Plastic surgery Neoplasty, Nose job, Otoplasty, Rhinoplasty

Plate(s), Plated, Platelet, Plating Acierage, Ailette, Angle, Anode, Armadillo, Armour, Ashet, Baffle, Bakestone, Baleen, Batten, Brass, Butt, Chamfrain, Chape, Charger, Chrome, Coat, Coccolith, Communion, Copper, Cramper, Cribellum, Ctene, Dasypus, Deadman, Denture, Diaphragm, Dinner, Disc, Dish, Echo, Electro, Electrotype, Elytron, Elytrum, Enamel, Entoplastron, Escutcheon, Face, Fashion, Feet, Fine, Fish, Flatware, Foil, Frog, Frons, Futtock, Glacis, Gold, Graal, Ground, Gula, Half, Hasp, Home, Horseshoe, Hot, Illustration, L, Lame, Lamella, Lamina, Lanx, Latten, Licence, Madreporic, Mascle, Mazarine, Nail, Nef, Neural, Nickel, Notum, Number, Ortho, Osteoderm, Paten, Patina, Patine, Pauldron, Peba, Petri, Phototype, Planometer, Plaque, Plastron, Platter, Pleximeter, Poitrel, Prescutum, Print, Quarter, Race, Registration, Riza, Roof, Rove, Salamander, Scale, Screw,

Scrim, Scutcheon, Scute, Scutum, Seg, Selling, Sheffield, Shield, Side, Sieve, Silver, Slab, Soup, Spacer, Spoiler, Squama, Steel, Stencil, Stereo(type), Sternite, Strake, Surface, Swash, T, Tablet, Tace, Tasse(l), Tea, Tectonic, Tergite, Terne, Thali, Theoretical, Tin(ware), Torsel, Touch, Trade, Tramp, Trencher, Trivet, Trophy, Tsuba, Tuill(ett)e, Tymp, Urostegite, Vane, Vanity, Vassail, Vessail, Vessel, Wall, Water, Web, Wet, Whirtle, Whole, Wobble, Workload, Wortle, Wrap(a)round, Zincograph

Plateau Altiplano, Central Karoo, Chota Nagpur, Darling Downs, Dartmoor, Deccan, Durango, Eifel, Field, Fjeld, Had(h)ramaut, Highland, Highveld, Horst, Kalahari, Kar(r)oo, Kurdestan, Kurdistan, La Mancha, Langres, Laurentian, Mat(t)o Grosso, Mesa Verde, Meseta, Nilgiris, Ozark, Paramo, Piedmont, Puna, Shan, Shillong, Tableland, The Kimberleys, Ust Urt, Ustyurt

Platform Accommodation, Almemar, Bandstand, Barbette, Base, Bema, Bier, Catafalque, Catwalk, Crane, Crow's nest, Dais, Deck, Dolly, Drilling, Emplacement, Entablement, Estrade, Exedra, Exhedra, Fighting top, Flake, Footpace, Footplate, Foretop, Gangplank, Gantry, Gauntree, Gauntry, Gravity, Hustings, Kang, Landing stage, Launch-pad, Machan, Oil, Oil-rig, Pad, Paint-bridge, Pallet, Perron, Plank, Podium, Predella, Production, Programme, Pulpit, Raft, Rig, Rostrum, Round-top, Scaffold, Shoe, Skidway, Soapbox, Space, Sponson, → **STAGE**, Stand, Stereobate, Stoep, Stylobate, Tee, Terminal, Thrall, Ticket, Top, Traverser, Tribunal, Tribune, Turntable, Wave-cut, Wharf

Platinum Pt, Ruthenium, Sperrylite

Platitude Bromide, Cliché, Commonplace, Truism

Platocephalus Flat-headed

Platonic, Platonist Academician, Ideal, Spiritual

Platoon Company, Squad, Team

Platter Dish, EP, Graal, Grail, Lanx, LP, Plate, Record, Salver, Trencher

Platypus Duckbill, Duck-mole, Water mole

Plausible, Plausibility Cogent, Credible, Fair, Glib, Logical, Oil, Probable, Proball, Sleek, Smooth, Specious

Play(s), Playing Accompany, Active, Amusement, Antic, Antigone, Brand, Bust, Candida, Caper, Charm, Chronicle, Clearance, Crucible, Curtain-raiser, Daff, Dandle, Docudrama, Doodle, Drama, Echo, Endgame, Epitasis, Equus, Escapade, Everyman, Extended, Fair, Finesse, Foul, Freedom, Frisk, Frolic, Fun, Gamble, Gambol, Game, Ghosts, Grand Guignol, Hamlet, Harp, History, Holiday, Inside, Interlude, Jam, Jape, Jest, Jeu, Kinderspiel, Kitchen-sink, Laik, Lake, Lark, Latitude, Lear, Leeway, Licence, Lilt, Long, Loot, Macbeth, Mask, Masque, Match, Medal, Melodrama, Miracle, Monodrama, Morality, Mousetrap, Mummers, Mysteries, Nativity, Nurse, Oberammergau, On, One-acter, Orestaia, Othello, Parallel, Passion, Pastorale, Perform, Personate, Peter, Portray, Prank, Pretend, Puppet, Recreation, Represent, Riff, Role, Rollick, Romp, Room, Rope, RUR, Satyr, Saw, Screen, Shadow, Shoot, Shuffle, Sketch, Sport, Squeeze, Stage, Straight, Strain, Strike up, Stroke, Strum, Summerstock, Tolerance, Tonguing, Touchback, Toy, Tragedy, Tragicomedy, Trifle, Triple, Tweedle, Twiddle, Two-hander, Vamp, Vent, Whitechapel, Word

▷ **Play** *may indicate* an anagram

Playback Echo, Repeat, Replay

Playboy Casanova, Don Juan, Hedonist, Rake, Roué

Player(s) Actor, Athlete, Back, Backstop, Black, Brass, Bugler, Busker, Cast, CD, Centre, Colt, Contestant, Cornerback, Defenceman, Disc, DVD, E, East, ENSA, Equity, Fetcher, Fiddle, Flanker, Flying wing, Franchise, Fullback, Gary,

Ghetto-blaster, Goalie, Half, Half-back, Half-forward, Harlequin, Hooker, Infielder, It, Juke-box, Keg(e)ler, Kest, Kicker, Linebacker, Lineman, Lion, Lock, Long-leg, Longstop, Lutanist, Lutenist, Man, Marquee, Midfield, Mid-on, Mime, Musician(er), N, Nero, Nickelback, Nightwatchman, North, Ombre, Onside, Orpheus, Outfielder, Out(side)-half, Pagliacci, Participant, Pianola®, Pitcher, Pocket, Pone, Pro, Prop, Quarterback, Receiver, Record, Reliever, Rover, S, Safetyman, Scrape, Scratch, Scrum half, Seagull, Secondo, Seed, Shamateur, Short-leg, Shortstop, Side, South, Split end, Stand-off, Stand-off half, Stereo, Striker, Strings, Strolling, Substitute, Super, Sweeper, Target man, Team, Thespian, Tight end, Troubador, Troupe, Upright, Utility, Virtuosi, W, Walkman®, West, White, Wing, Winger, Wingman

Playfair Code

Playfellow Actor, Chum, Companion

Playful Arch, Coy, Frisky, Humorous, Jocose, Kittenish, Ludic, Merry, Piacevole, Scherzo, Skittish, Sportive

Playgirl Actress, Electra

Playgoer Groundling

Playground Adventure, Close, Garden, Park, Rec(reational), Rectangle, Theatre, Tot lot, Yard

Playhouse Amphitheatre, Cinema, Theatre, Wendy

Playsuit Rompers

Playwright Aeschylus, Albee, Anouilh, Arden, Ayckbourn, Barrie, Barry, Beaumarchais, Beaumont, Beckett, Behan, Bellow, Bennett, Besier, Bolt, Brecht, Chekhov, Congreve, Corneille, Coward, Dekker, Delaney, → **DRAMATIST**, Dramaturge, Dramaturgist, Drinkwater, Dryden, Euripides, Feydeau, Fletcher, Frayn, Fry, Gems, Genet, Goldoni, Gorky, Hare, Harwood, Hay, Ibsen, Ionesco, Jonson, Marlowe, Massinger, Menander, Miller, Molière, Mortimer, O'Casey, Odets, O'Neill, Orton, Osborne, Pinero, Pinter, Pirandello, Priestley, Racine, Rattigan, Rostard, Scriptwriter, Shaw, Sheridan, Sherry, Simpson, Sophocles, Stoppard, Storey, Strindberg, Synge, Tate, Terence, Thespis, Travers, Vanbrugh, Webster, Wesker, Wilde

Plea(s) Appeal, Claim, Common, Defence, Entreaty, Excuse, Exoration, Nolo contendere, Orison, Placit(um), Prayer, Rebuttal, Rebutter, Rogation, Suit

Plead(er) Answer, Argue, Beg, Entreat, → **IMPLORE**, Intercede, Litigate, Moot, Special, Supplicant, Vakeel, Vakil

Please(d), Pleasant, Pleasing, Pleasure(-seeker) Aggrate, Agreeable, Alcina, Algolagnia, Amene, Amiable, Amuse, Arride, Benign, Bitte, Braw, Cheerful, Chuffed, Comely, Comfort, Content, Cordial, Cute, Delectation, Delice, Delight, Do, Euphonic, Fair, Felicitous, Fit, Flatter, Fun, Genial, Glad, Gladness, Gratify, Hedonism, Jammy, Joy, Kama, Kindly, Lekker, Lepid, List, Naomi, Oblige, Piacevole, Primrose path, Prithee, Prythee, Purr, Queme, Satisfy, Suit, Tasty, Tickle, Tickle pink, Treat, Vanity, Voluptuary, Wally, Will, Winsome, Wrapped, Xanadu List

Pleasure-garden, Pleasure-ground Lung, Oasis, Park, Policy, Ranelagh, Tivoli

Pleat Accordion, Box, Crimp, Fold, French, Frill, Goffer, Gusset, Inverted, Kick, Knife, Plait, Pranck(e), Prank, Sunburst, Sunray

Pleb(eian) Common, Essex Man, Homely, Laic, Ordinary, Roturier

Pledge Affidavit, Arlene, Arles, Band, Betroth, Bond, Borrow, Bottomry, Dedicate, Deposit, Earnest(-penny), Engage, Fine, Gage, Gilbert, Giselle, Guarantee, Hock, Hypothecate, Impignorate, Mortgage, Oath, Pass, Pawn, Pignerate, Pignorate, Plight, Promise, Propine, Sacrament, Security, Sponsorship, Stake, Surety, Teetotal, Toast, Troth, Undertake, Vow, Wad, Wage(r), Wed

Pleiades Alcyone, Celaeno, Electra, Maia, Merope, Sterope, Taygete

Plenitude Stouth and routh

Plentiful, Plenty Abounding, Abundance, Abundant, Ample, Bags, Copious, Copy, Easy, Excess, Foison, Fouth, Ful(l)ness, Fushion, Galore, Goshen, Lashings, Lots, Oodles, Pleroma, Profusion, Quantity, Riches, Rife, Routh, Rowth, Scouth, Scowth, Slue, Sonce, Sonse, Umpteen

Plenum Spaceless

Pliable, Pliant Amenable, Flexible, Limber, Limp, Lithe, Malleable, Plastic, Sequacious, Supple, Swack, Swank, Wanle

▶ **Pliers** *see* **PLY**

Plight Betrothal, Case, Misdight, Peril, Pickle, Pledge, State, Troth

Plimsoll(s) Dap, Gutty, Gym-shoe, Line, Mutton-dummies, Sandshoe, Tacky

Plinth Acroter, Base, Block, Socle, Stand, Zocco

Plod(der) Drudge, Ploughman, Traipse, Tramp, Trog, Trudge

Plonk Rotgut, Wine

Plop Cloop, Drop, Fall, Plap, Plump

Plot(s) Allotment, Babington, Bed, Brew, Carpet, Chart, Cliché, Collude, Connive, Conspiracy, Conspire, Covin, Covyne, Engineer, Erf, Erven, Frame-up, Graden, Graph, Gunpowder, Imbroglio, Intrigue, Locus, Lot, Machination, Map, Meal-tub, Odograph, Pack, Patch, Plan, Plat, Popish, Rye-house, Scenario, → **SCHEME**, Sect(ion), Seedbed, Shot, Site, Story, Storyline, Taluk, Terf, Turf, Web

Plotter Artist, Brutus, Cabal, Camarilla, Casca, Catesby, Conspirator, Engineer, Incremental, Microfilm, Oates, Schemer

Plough(man), Ploughed, Ploughing Arable, Ard, Arval, Big Dipper, Breaker, Bull tongue, Chamfer, Charles's Wain, Contour, Dipper, Disc, Drail, Drill, Ear, Earth-board, Ere, Fail, Fallow, Farmer, Feer, Flunk, Gadsman, Gang, Great bear, Harrow, Lister, Middlebreaker, Middlebuster, Mouldboard, Piers, Pip, Pleuch, Pleugh, Push, Rafter, Rib, Ridger, Rive, Rotary, Rove, Sand, Scooter, Septentrion(e)s, Sill, Sow, Stump-jump, Swing, Till(er), Trench, Triones, Wheel

Plough-cleaner Pattle, Pettle

Ploughshare Co(u)lter, Sock

Ploughwise Boustrophedon

Plover Bud, Dott(e)rel, Lapwing, Pratincole, Prostitute, Stand, Tewit, Wing

Plowman Piers

Ploy Brinkmanship, Dodge, Gambit, Manoeuvre, M(a)cGuffin, Stratagem, Strike, Tactic, Wile

Pluck(ing), Plucky Avulse, Bare, Carphology, Cock, Courage, Deplume, Epilate, Evulse, Floccillation, Gallus, Game, → **GRIT**, Guts, Loot, Mettle, Pick, Pinch, Pip, Pizzicato, Plectron, Plectrum, Ploat, Plot, Plunk, Pook(it), Pouk(it), Pull, Race, Scrappy, Snatch, Spin, Spirit, Spunk, Summon, Tug, Twang, Tweak, Tweeze, Vellicate, Yank

Plug Access eye, Ad, Banana, Block, Bung, Caulk, Chew, Commercial, Dam, DIN, Dook, Dossil, Dottle, Douk, Fipple, Fother, Gang, Glow, Go-devil, Heater, Hype, Jack, Lam, Operculum, Pessary, Phono, Prod, Promote, Publicity, Ram, Rawlplug®, Recommendation, Safety, Salt, Scart, Spark(ing), Spile, Spiling, Stop(per), Stopple, Strobili, Suppository, Tampion, Tap, Tent, Tompion, Vent, Volcanic, Wage, Wander, Wedge

Plum Bullace, Cherry, Choice, Damask, Damson, Gage, Greengage, Ground, Jamaica, Japanese, Java, Kaki, Mammee-sapota, Marmalade, Maroon, Mirabelle, Musk, Mussel, Myrobalan, Naseberry, Persimmon, Proin(e), Pruin(e), Prune, Quetsch, Raisin, Sapodilla, Sebesten, Victoria

Plumage, Plume Aigrette, Crest, Eclipse, Egret, Feather, Hackle, Mantle, Panache, Preen, Ptilosis, Quill

Plumb(er) Bullet, Dredge, Fathom, Lead(sman), Perpendicular, Plummet, Sheer, Sound, Test, True, Vertical

Plumbago Graphite, Wad(d), Wadt

Plummet Dive, Drop, Lead, → **PLUNGE**

Plump(er) Bold, Bonnie, Bonny, Buxom, Choose, Chubbed, Chubby, Cubby, Dumpy, Embonpoint, Endomorph, Fat, Fleshy, Flop, Fubsy, Full, Lie, Matronly, Opt, Plank, Plonk, Plop, Podgy, Portly, Pudgy, Roll-about, Rolypoly, Rotund, Round, Rubenesque, Sonsie, Sonsy, Soss, Souse, Squab, Squat, Stout, Swap, Swop, Tidy, Well-fed

Plunder(er) Berob, Booty, Depredate, Despoil, Devastate, Escheat, Fleece, Forage, Freebooter, Gut, Harry, Haul, Herriment, Herryment, Hership, Loot, Maraud, Peel, Pill(age), Prey, Privateer, → **RANSACK**, Rape, Rapparee, Raven, Ravin, Ravine, Reave, Reif, Reive, Rieve, Rifle, Rob, Sack, Scoff, Shave, Skoff, Spoil(s), Spoliate, Sprechery, Spuilzie, Spuly(i)e, Spulzie, Swag

Plunge(r) Dasher, Demerge, Dive, Douse, Dowse, Duck, Enew, Immerge, Immerse, La(u)nch, Nose-dive, Plummet, Plump, Raker, Send, Sink, Souse, Swoop, Thrust

Plural Multiply, Pl

Plus Addition, And, Gain, More, Positive

Plush(ed) Die, Luxurious, Rich, Smart, Tint, Velour, Velvet

Pluto(crat), Plutonic Abyssal, Dis, Dog, Hades, Hypogene, Magnate, Nob, Pipeline, Underground

Plutonium Pu

Ply, Plier(s) Bend, Birl, Cab, Exercise, Exert, Gondoliers, Importune, Layer, Practise, Run, Trade, Wield

▷ **Plying** *may indicate* an anagram

Plymouth Brethren Darbyite

PM Addington, Afternoon, Arvo, Asquith, Attlee, Autopsy, Bute, Cabinet-maker, Chatham, De Valera, Disraeli, Gladstone, Major, Melbourne, Peel, Pitt, Portland, Premier, → **PRIME MINISTER**, Salisbury, Taoiseach

Pneumonia Lobar, Lobular, Visna

Poach Cook, Encroach, Filch, Lag, Steal, Trespass

Pochard Duck, Scaup

Pocket Air, Appropriate, Bag, Bin, Breast, Cavity, Cly, Cup, Enclave, Fob, Glom, Hideaway, Hip, Jenny, Misappropriate, Patch, Placket, Plaid-neuk, Pot, Pouch, Purloin, Purse, Sac, Sky, Slash, Sling, Slit, Steal, Take, Trouser, Watch

Pod(s) Babul, Bean, Belly, Carob, Chilli, Dividivi, Engine, Gumbo, Lablab, Lomentum, Neb-neb, Okra, Pipi, Pregnant, Pudding-pipe, Siliqua, Tamarind, Vanilla

Podgy Roly-poly

Poem(s), Poetry Acmeism, Acrostic, Aeneid, Alcaic, Anthology, Awdl, Ballad(e), Beowulf, Bestiary, Byliny, Caccia, Canzone, Cargoes, Cento, Choliamb, Choriamb, Cicada, Cinquain, Complaint, Concrete, Decastich, Dit(t), Dithyramb, Divan, Dizain, Doggerel, Duan, Dub, Dunciad, Eclogue, Elegy, Elene, Epic(ede), Epigram, Epilogue, Epithalamium, Epode, Epopee, Epopoeia, Epos, Epyllion, Erotic, Fifteener, Finlandia, Gauchesco, Georgic, Ghazal, Graveyard, Haikai, Haiku, Heptastich, Heroic, Hexastich, Hokku, Hull, Hypermeter, Idyll, If, Iliad, Imagism, Inferno, Jazz, Lay, Limerick, Logaoedic, London, Mahabharata(m), Mahabharatum, Meliboean, Melic, Metaphysical, Metre, Mock-heroic, Monostich, Monostrophe, Nostos, Ode, Odyssey, Palinode, Paracrostic, Parnassus, Pastoral, Penill(ion), Pentastich, Performance, Poesy, Prelude, Prose, Prothalamion, Punk, Purana,

Qasida, Quatorzain, Quatrain, Quire, Ramayana, Rat-rhyme, Renga, Rhapsody, Rig-Veda, Rime, Rime riche, Rondeau, Rondel, Rubai(yat), Rune, Scazon (iambus), Senryu, Sestina, Sijo, Sirvente, Song, Sonnet, Sound, Spondee, Stanza, Stornello, Symphonic, Tanka, Telestich, Temora, Tercet, Tetrastich, Thebaid, Title, Tone, Triolet, Tristich, Vers(e), Versicle, Villanelle, Völuspá, Voluspe, Waka

Poet(s), Poetic Amorist, Bard(ling), Beatnik, Cavalier, Cumberland, Cyclic, Elegist, Georgian, Iambist, Imagist, Lake, Laureate, Layman, Lyrist, Maker, Meistersinger, Metaphysical, Metrist, Minnesinger, Minor, Minstrel, Mistral, Monodist, Odist, Parnassian, Performance, PL, Pleiad(e), Poetaster, Rhymer, Rhymester, Rhymist, Rymer, Scald, Scop, Skald, Smart, Sonneteer, Spasmodic, Spasmodic School, Thespis, Tragic, Trench, Troubadour, Trouvère, Trouveur, Vers librist(e), Water

POETS

2 letters:
AE

3 letters:
Gay
Poe

4 letters:
Abse
Blok
Cory
Dyer
Gray
Gunn
Hogg
Hood
Hugo
Hunt
Lang
Omar
Ovid
Owen
Pope
Rowe
Rumi
Tate
Vega

5 letters:
Arion
Auden
Blair
Blake
Burns
Byron
Cadou
Carew

Cinna
Clare
Dante
Donne
Eliot
Frost
Gower
Griot
Heine
Hesse
Homer
Horne
Hulme
Iqbal
Keats
Keyes
Lewis
Logue
Lorca
Lucan
Makar
Marot
Meyer
Moore
Nashe
Noyes
Plath
Pound
Prior
Rilke
Rishi
Sachs
Tasso
Theon
Wyatt
Yeats
Young

6 letters:
Alonso
Arnold
Austin
Barham
Barnes
Belloc
Borges
Brecht
Brooke
Butler
Clough
Cowper
Crabbe
Dowson
Dryden
Dunbar
Ennius
George
Glycon
Goethe
Graves
Hesiod
Horace
Hughes
Landor
Larkin
Lawman
Lowell
Marini
Milton
Morris
Motion
Ossian
Pindar
Racine
Sappho

Seaman
Shanks
Sidney
Tagore
Thomas
Villon
Virgil
Waller

7 letters:
Addison
Alcaeus
Aretino
Ariosto
Beddoes
Belleau
Bridges
Bunting
Caedmon
Campion
Chapman
Chaucer
Collins
Corinna
Cynwulf
Emerson
Flaccus
Flecker
Heredia
Herrick
Hopkins
Housman
Juvenal
Layamon
Martial
Marvell
Montale

Newbolt
Orpheus
Pushkin
Ronsard
Russell
Sassoon
Service
Shelley
Sitwell
Skelton
Sotades
Southey
Spender
Spenser
Statius
Terence
Thomson
Vaughan
Whitman

8 letters:
Anacreon
Betjeman
Brentano
Browning
Campbell

Catullus
Cummings
Cynewulf
Davenant
Day Lewis
De la Mare
Ginsberg
Hamilton
Kynewulf
Laforgue
Langland
Leopardi
Lovelace
Macaulay
Mallarmé
Menander
Petrarch
Rossetti
Schiller
Shadwell
Stephens
Suckling
Taliesin
Tennyson
Thompson
Traherne

Tyrtaeus
Verlaine
Whittier

9 letters:
Aeschylus
Bunthorne
Coleridge
Euripides
Goldsmith
Henderson
Lamartine
Lucretius
Marinetti
Masefield
Quasimodo
Shenstone
Simonides
Sophocles
Stevenson
Swinburne

10 letters:
Baudelaire
Chatterton
Drinkwater

Fitzgerald
Longfellow
Propertius
Tannhauser
Theocritus
Wordsworth

11 letters:
Apollinaire
Archilochus
Asclepiades
Bildermeier
Maeterlinck
Pherecrates

12 letters:
Archilochian
Aristophanes

14 letters:
Dante Alighieri

15 letters:
Ettrick Shepherd

Poetaster Della-Cruscan
Poetess Ingelow, Orinda
Poet laureate Motion, PL
▶ **Poetry** *see* POEM
Po-faced Stolid
Poignant Acute, Biting, Haunting, Keen, Pungent, Stirring, Touching
Point(ed), Pointer, Points Accumulation, Ace, Acerose, Acnode, Acro-, Aculeate,
    Aim, Antinode, Antler, Apex, Aphelion, Apogee, Appui, Apse, Apsis, Ascendant,
    Bar, Barb, Barrow, Basis, Bisque, Boiling, Break(ing), Brownie, Calk, Cape, Cardinal,
    Cash, Catch, Centre, Choke, Clou, Clovis, Clue, Colon, Comma, Compass,
    Compensation, Cone, Conic, Corner, Cover, Crisis, Critical, Crux, Culmination,
    Cultrate, Curie, Cursor, Cusp, Cuss, Cutting, Dead, Decimal, Degree, Descendant,
    Detail, Dew, Diamond, Direct, Dot, Dry, E, Ear, End, Entry, Epanodos, Épée,
    Equant, Equinoctial, Eutectic, Exclamation, Fang, Fastigiate, Feature, Fesse,
    Fielder, Firing, Fitch(e), Five, Fixed, Flash, Focal, Focus, Foreland, Fourteen,
    Freezing, Fulcrum, Gallinas, Game, Germane, Gist, Gnomon, Gold, Hastate,
    Head, High, Hinge, Hint, Home-thrust, Ideal, Index, Indicate, Indicator, Intercept,
    Ippon, Isoelectric, Jag, Jester, Jog, Juncture, Keblah, Kiblah, Kip(p), Knub, Lace,
    Lagrangian, Lance, Lead, Limit, Lizard, Locate, Locus, Low, Mandelbrot set, Mark,
    Match, Melting, Metacentre, Microdot, Moot, Mucro, Muricate, N, Nail, Nasion,
    Near, Neb, Needle, Neel, Ness, Nib, Nocking, Node, Nodus, Nombril, Now, Nub,
    Obconic, Obelion, Obelisk, Objective, Opinion, Ord, Organ, Oscillation, Particle,
    Peak, Pedal, Penalty, Perigee, Perihelion, Perilune, Pin, Pinch, Pinnacle, Place,
    Pour, Power, Pressure, Promontory, Prong, Prow, Punctilio, Punctual, Punctum,

Purpose, Radix, Rallying, Ras, Reef, Respect, Rhumb, Rhumbline, S, Sample, Saturation, Scribe, Seg(h)ol, Set, Shaft, Sheva, Show, Shy, Silly, Socket, Sore, Spearhead, Specie, Spicate, Spick, Spike, Spinode, Spinulose, Stage, Stagnation, Starting, Stationary, Steam, Sticking, Stigme, Stiletto, Sting, Stipule, Strong, Sum, Suspension, Synapse, Tacnode, Talking, Tang, Taper, Tax, Technicality, Tine, → **TIP**, Tongue, Trafficator, Train, Transition, Trig, Trigger, Triple, Turning, Urde(e), Urdy, Use, Vane, Vanishing, Vantage, Verge, Verse, Vertex, Vowel, Voxel, W, Weak, Yad, Yield, Yuko

Pointless Blunt, Curtana, Flat, Futile, Idle, Inane, Inutile, Muticous, Otiose, Stupid, Vain

Point of honour Pundonor

Poise Aplomb, Balance, Composure, P, Serenity

Poison(er), Poisoning, Poisonous Abron, Aconite, Acrolein, Adamsite, Aflatoxin, Aldrin, Amanita, Antiar, Apocynum, Aqua-tofana, Arsenic, Aspic, Atropia, Atropin(e), Bane, Barbasco, Belladonna, Benzidine, Boletus, Borgia, Botulism, Brom(in)ism, Brucine, Bufotalin, Bufotenine, Cacodyl, Cadaverine, Calabar-bean, Cannabin, Cicuta, Colchicine, Coniine, Contact, Cowbane, Coyotillo, Cube, Curare, Curari, Cyanide, Cyanuret, Datura, Daturine, Deadly nightshade, Deleterious, Digitalin, Dioxin, Dumbcane, Durban, Echidnine, Embolism, Emetin(e), Envenom, Ergotise, Exotoxin, Fluorosis, Flybane, Flypaper, Food, Fool's parsley, Formaldehyde, Gelsemin(in)e, Gila, Gila monster, Gossypol, Hebenon, Hebona, Hemlock, Henbane, Hydrargyrism, Hydrastine, Hyoscyamine, Iodism, Jimson weed, Lead, Lewisite, Limberneck, Lindane, Listeriosis, Lobeline, Loco, Locoweed, Malevolent, Manchineal, Mandragora, Mephitic, Methanol, Mezereon, Miasma, Mineral, Monkshood, Muscarine, Mycotoxin, Nerve gas, Neurine, Neurotoxin, Neutron, Nicotine, Noogoora burr, Noxious, Obeism, Ouabain, Ourali, Ourari, Paraquat®, Paris green, Phallin, Phalloidin, Phosphorism, Picrotoxin, Pilocarpine, Plumbism, Ptomaine, Py(a)emia, Raphania, Ratsbane, Rot, Safrole, Salicylism, Salmonella, Samnitis, Santonin, Sapraemia, Sarin, Sassy wood, Saturnism, Saxitoxin, Septic(aemia), Solanine, Solpuga, Soman, Stibine, Stibium, Stonefish, Strophanthus, Strychnine, Sugar of lead, Surinam, Systemic, Tanghin, Tanghinin, Tetro(do)toxin, Thebaine, Thorn-apple, Timbo, Toxaphene, Toxic, Toxicology, Toxicosis, Toxin, Toxoid, Trembles, Tropine, Tutu, Upas, Urali, Urushiol, V-agent, Venefic, Venin, Venom(ous), Veratridine, Veratrin(e), Viperous, Virose, Virous, Virulent, Wabain, Warfarin, Wolfsbane, Woorali, Woorara, Wourali, Yohimbine

Poke, Poky Bonnet, Broddle, Chook, Garget, Itchweed, Jab, Jook, Meddle, Mock, Nousle, Nudge, Nuzzle, Ombu, Peg, Pick, Poach, Pote, Pouch, Powter, → **PRISON**, → **PROD**, Prog, Proke, Punch, Root(le), Rout, Rowt, Sporran, Stab, Thrust

Poker (work) Bugbear, Curate, Draw, Game, High-low, Lowball, Mistigris, Penny ante, Pyrography, Red-hot, Salamander, Strip, Stud(-horse), Texas hold'em, Tickler, Tine

Poland PL, Sarmatia

Polar, Pole(s), Poler Animal, Anode, Antarctic, Arctic, Boathook, Boom, Bowsprit, Bum(p)kin, Caber, Celestial, Clothes, Copernicus, Cowl-staff, Cracovian, Crossbar, Extremity, Fishgig, Fizgy, Flagstaff, Flagstick, Galactic, Gas, Geomagnetic, Icy, Janker, Kent, Liberty, Lug, Magnetic, Mast, May, N, Nadir, Negative, Nib, North, Periscian, Po, Polack, Positive, Punt, Quant, Quarterstaff, Racovian, Range, Ricker, Ripeck, Rood, Ry(e)peck, S, Shaft, Slav, South, Spar, Spindle, Sprit, Staff, Stake, Stanchion, Stang, Starosta, Stilt, Sting, Stobie, Telegraph, Terrestrial, Thyrsos, Thyrsus, Tongue, Topmast, Totem, Utility, Vegetal, Zenith

▷ **Polar** *may indicate* with a pole

Polaris Rhodanic, Rocket, Star

Polecat Ferret, Fitch, Fitchet, Foulmart, Foumart, Weasel

Polemic(al) Argument, Controversy, Debate, Eristic(al)

Police(man), Policewoman Babylon, Bear, Beast, Bizzy, Black and Tans, Blue, Bluebottle, Bobby, Bog(e)y, Boss, Boys in blue, Bull, Busy, Carabinero, Carabiniere, Catchpole, Centenier, Cheka, Chekist, CID, Constable, Cop(per), Cotwal, Crusher, Detective, Dibble, Druzhinnik, Europol, Filth, Flatfoot, Flattie, Flic, Flying Squad, Force, Fuzz, Garda, Garda Siochana, Gendarme, Gestapo, Gill, G-man, Guard, Gumshoe, Harmanbeck, Heat, Hermandad, Inspector, Interpol, Jamadar, Jemadar, John Hop, Keystone, Kitchen, Kotwal, Limb, Mata-mata, Met(ropolitan), Military, Morse, Mountie, MP, Mulligan, Nabman, Nark, Ochrana, Officer, OGPU, Ovra, Patrolman, PC, Peeler, Peon, Pig, Pointsman, Polis, Polizei, Porn squad, Posse (comitatus), Prefect, Provincial, Provost, Puppy-walker, Ranger, Redbreast, Redcap, Regulate, RIC, Riot, Robert, Rosser, Roundsman, Rozzer, RUC, Sbirro, SC, Secret, Securitate, Securocrat, Sepoy, Shamus, Sleeping, Slop, Smokey, Sowar(ry), Special, Special Branch, Stasi, State Trooper, Super, Superintendent, Sureté, Sweeney, Texas Rangers, T(h)anadar, The Bill, The Law, Thirdborough, Thought, Trap, Vice squad, Vigilante, Walloper, Wolly, Woodentop, Zabtieh, Zaptiah, Zaptieh, Zomo

Police car Black Maria, Panda, Patrol, Prowl

Police station Copshop, Lock-up, Tana, Tanna(h), Thana(h), Thanna(h), Watchhouse

Policy Assurance, Ballon d'essai, CAP, Comprehensive, Course, Demesne, Endowment, Expedience, First-loss, Floating, Good neighbour, Gradualism, Insurance, Knock for knock, Laisser-faire, Lend-lease, Line, Method, Open(-sky), Open door, Perestroika, Plank, Platform, Pork-barrel, Practice, Programme, Reaganism, Revanchism, Scorched earth, Stop-go, Tack, Tactics, Ticket, Traditional, Valued, White Australia

Polish(ed), Polisher Beeswax, Black, Blacklead, Bob, Bruter, Buff, Bull, Burnish, Chamois, Complaisant, Edit, Elaborate, Elegant, Emery, Enamel, Finish, French, Furbish, Gentlemanly, Glass, Gloss, Heelball, Hone, Inland, Lap, Lustre, Nail, Perfect, Planish, Polite, Polverine, Pumice, Refinement, Refurbish, Rottenstone, Rub, Sand, Sandblast, Sandpaper, Sejm, Sheen, Shellac, Shine, Slick, Slickenside, Sophistication, Supercalender, Svelte, Tutty, Urbane, Veneer, Wax

Polite Civil, Courteous, Genteel, Grandisonian, Mannered, Suave, Urbane, Well-bred

Politic(al), Politics Apparat, Body, Chartism, Civic, Diplomacy, Discreet, Dog-whistle, Expedient, Falange, Fascism, Gesture, Leftism, Party, Poujadism, Power, Practical, Public, Radicalism, Rightism, State, Statecraft, Tactful, Wise, Yuppie, Yuppy

Politician(s) Bright, Carpet-bagger, Catiline, Chesterfield, Congressman, Coningsby, Demagogue, Demo(crat), Diehard, Disraeli, Eden, Euro-MP, Evita, Green, Incumbent, Independent, Ins, Isolationist, Laski, Left, Legislator, Liberal, Log-roller, MEP, Minister, Moderate, MP, Octobrist, Parliamentarian, Parnell, Politico, Polly, Poujade, Puppet, Rad, Rep, Senator, Socialist, Statesman, Statist, Tadpole, Taper, TD, Tory, Trotsky, Unionist, Veep, Warhorse, Whig, Wilberforce

Poll(ing) Advance, Ballot, Bean, Canvass, Count, Cut, Deed, Dod, Election, Exit, Gallup, Head, Humlie, Hummel, Lory, MORI, Nestor, Not(t), Opinion, Parrot, Pineapple, Pow, Push, Referendum, Scrutiny, Straw, Votes

▷ **Poll** *may indicate* a first letter

Pollack Fish, Lob, Lythe

Pollard Doddered

Pollen, Pollinate(d), Pollination Anemophilous, Beebread, Dust, Errhine, Farina, Fertilised, Geitonogamy, Intine, My(i)ophily, Sternotribe, Witch-meal, Xenia

Pollenbrush Scopa

Pollex Thumb

Pollster Psephologist

Pollute(d), Pollutant, Pollution Adulterate, Contaminate, Defile, Dirty, File, Foul, Impure, Infect, Light, Miasma, Noise, Nox, Oil slick, Rainout, Smog, Soil, Soilure, Stain, Sully, Taint, Violate, Waldsterben

Polly Flinders, Parrot, Peachum

Polo Bicycle, Chukka, Marco, Mint, Navigator, Rink, Water

Polonium Po

Poltergeist Apport, Ghost, Spirit, Trouble-house

Poltroon Coward, Craven, Dastard, Scald, Scaramouch

Polyandry Nair

Polygraph Lie-detector

Polymath Knowall, Toynbee

Polymer Elastomer, Isotactic, Lignin, Oligomer, Resin, Seloxane, Silicone, Tetramer, Trimer

Polymorphic Multiform, Proteus, Variform

Polynesian Moriori, Tahitian, Tongan

Polyp(s) Alcyonaria, Gonophore, Hydra, Hydranth, Nematophore, Obelia, Sea-anemone, Tumour

Polyphony Counterpoint

Polystyrene Expanded

Polyzoan Sea-mat

Pom Choom

Pomander Pounce(t)-box

Pomegranate Punica, Punic apple

Pommel Beat, Knob, Pound, Pummel

Pomp(ous) Big, Bombastic, Budge, Ceremonial, Display, Dogberry, Euphuistic, Fustian, Grandiloquent, Grandiose, Heavy, Highfalutin(g), High-flown, High-muck-a-muck, High-sounding, Hogen-mogen, Inflated, Orotund, Ostentatious, Pageantry, Parade, Pretentious, Sententious, Solemn, Splendour, Starchy, State, Stilted, Stuffed shirt, Stuffy, Turgid

Pom-pom Ball, Tassel

Ponce Pander, Solicit, Souteneur

Poncho Ruana

Pond(s) Curling, Dew, Dub, Flash, Hampstead, Lakelet, Lentic, Mill, Pool, Pound, Puddle, Settling, Shield(ing), Slough, Stank, Stew, Tank, Turlough, Vivarium, Viver

Ponder(ous) Brood, Cogitate, Contemplate, Deliberate, Heavy, Laboured, Mull, Muse, Perpend, Poise, Pore, Reflect, Ruminate, → **THINK**, Vise, Volve, Weight(y), Wonder

Poniard Bodkin, → **DAGGER**, Dirk, Stiletto

Pontiff, Pontifical, Pontificate Aaron, Aaronic, Antipope, Dogmatise, Papal

Pontoon Blackjack, Bridge, Caisson, Chess, Game, Twenty one, Vingt-et-un

Pony Bidet, Canuck, Cayuse, Cow, Dales, Dartmoor, Eriskay, Exmoor, Fell, Garran, Garron, Gen(n)et, GG, Griffin, Griffon, Gryfon, Gryphon, Jennet, Jerusalem, Mustang, New Forest, One-trick, Pit, Polo, Pownie, Sable Island, Shanks', Sheltie, Shetland, Show, Tangun, Tat(too), Timor, Welsh, Welsh Mountain, Western Isles

Poodle Barbet, Swan

Pooh Bah, Bear, Pugh, Winnie, Yah

Pool Backwater, Bank, Bethesda, Billabong, Birthing, Bogey hole, Cenote, Cess, Collect, Combine, Dub, Dump, Flash, Flow, Gene, Hag, Hot, Jackpot, Jacuzzi®, Kitty, Lido, Lin(n), Meer, Mere, Mickery, Mikvah, Mikveh, Millpond, Moon, Natatorium, Piscina, Piscine, Plash, Plesh, Plunge, → **POND**, Reserve, Share, Siloam, Snooker, Spa, Stank, Stanley, Sump, Tank, Tarn, Water(ing) hole, Wave

Poor(ly) Bad, Bare, Base, Bijwoner, Breadline, Buckeen, Bywoner, Catchpenny, Cheapo, Churchmouse, Conch, Cronk, Destitute, Gritty, Half-pie, Hard-up, Have-nots, Hopeless, Humble, Hungry, Ill(-off), Impecunious, Indigent, Lazarus, Lean, Lo-fi, Lousy, Low, Low-downer, Low-fi, Meagre, Mean, Needy, Obolary, One-horse, Pauper, Peaky, Poxy, Redleg, Roinish, Rop(e)y, Roynish, Sad, Scrub, Shabby, Shitty, Sober, Sorry, Sub, Thin, Third-rate, Trashy, Undeserving, Unwell, Wattle, Wishy-washy

▷ **Poor** *may indicate* an anagram

Poorhouse Union, Workhouse

Pooter Nobody, Nonentity

Pop (off), Popper, Popping Bang, Brit, Burst, Cloop, Crease, Die, → **DRUG**, Father, Fr, Gingerbeer, Hip-hop, Hock, Insert, Lumber, Mineral, Nip, Party, Pater, Pawn, Pledge, Population, Press-stud, Punk, Sherbet, Soda, Splutter, Weasel

▷ **Pop** *may indicate* an anagram

Pope(s) Adrian, Alexander, Atticus, Benedict, Black, Boniface, Borgia, Clement, Dunciad, Eminence, Fish, Great Schism, Gregory, Hildebrand, Holiness, Innocent, Joan, Leo, Papa, Pius, Pontiff, Ruff(e), Schism, Sixtius, Theocrat, Tiara, Urban, Vatican, Vicar-general of Christ, Vicar of Christ

Pop-gun Bourtree-gun

Popinjay Barbermonger, Coxcomb, Dandy, Fop, Macaroni, Parrot, Prig, Skipjack

Poplar Abele, Aspen, Balsam, Cottonwood, Lombardy, Trembling, Tulip, White, Yellow

Poppet Cutie pie, Valve

Poppy Argemone, Bloodroot, Blue, California, Chicalote, Coquelicot, Corn, Diacodin, Eschscholtzia, Field, Flanders, Horned, Iceland, Matilija, Mawseed, Opium, Papaver, Plume, Ponceau, Prickly, Puccoon, Rhoeadales, Shirley, Tall, Welsh

Poppycock Bosh, Nonsense, Rubbish

Popular(ity) Common, Crowd-pleaser, Cult, Demotic, Enchorial, General, Grass roots, Heyday, Hit, In, Laic, Lay, Mass, Plebeian, Prevalent, Public, Successful, Tipped, Trendy, Vogue

Population, Populace Catchment, Census, Closed, Demography, Inhabitants, Malthusian, Mass, Mob, Optimum, → **PEOPLE**, Public, Universe

Porcelain Arita, Artificial, Bamboo, Belleek®, Blanc-de-chine, Celadon, Chantilly, Chelsea, China, Coalport, Crackle(ware), Crown Derby, Derby, Dresden, Eggshell, Famille, Famille jaune, Famille noir, Famille rose, Famille verte, Goss, Hard-paste, Hizen, Imari, Ivory, Jasp(er), Jasper(ware), Kakiemon, Limoges, Lithophane, Meissen, Minton, Parian, Sèvres, Softpaste, Spode, Sung, Yuan

Porch Galilee, Lanai, Stoa, Stoep, Veranda(h)

Porcupine Hedgehog, Urson

Pore Browse, Hole, Hydrathode, Lenticel, Muse, Ostium, Outlet, Ponder, Stoma, Study

Porgy Braise, Scup(paug)

Pork(y) Bacon, Boar, Brawn, Chap, Char sui, Crackling, Flitch, Griskin, Ham, Lie, Pancetta, Salt, Scrapple, Scruncheon, Scrunchion, Spare-rib, Spek, Tenderloin

Porn(ography), Pornographic Curiosa, Erotica, Hard, Hard-core, Jazz mag,

Rhyparography, Snuff-film, Soft, Soft-core

Porous Cellular, Permeable, Pumice, Sponge

Porpoise Bucker, Dolphin, Mereswine, Pellach, Pellack, Pellock, Phocaena, Sea pig, Sea swine

Porridge Berry, Bird, Brochan, Brose, Burgoo, Busera, Crowdie, Drammach, Drammock, Gaol, Grits, Grouts, Gruel, Hominy, Kasha, Mabela, Mahewu, Mealie pap, Mielie pap, Oaten, Oatmeal, Parritch, Pease-brose, Polenta, Pottage, Praiseach, Sadza, Samp, Sentence, Skilly, Stirabout, Stretch, Sup(p)awn, Time, Ugali

Porridge stick Thible, Thivel

Port(s) Beeswing, Carry, Cinque, Container (terminal), Entrepot, Free, Gate, Gateway, Geropiga, → **HARBOUR**, Haven, Hinterland, Hithe, Induction, Larboard, Left, Manner, Mien, Outport, Parallel, Serial, Tawny, Treaty, USB, Wine

---

PORTS

3 letters:	Lima	Arica	Horta
Abo	Linz	Aulis	Hythe
Ayr	Lomé	Bahia	Izmir
Gao	Luda	Bahru	Jaffa
Hué	Naha	Barry	Jedda
Rio	Oban	Basra	Jembi
Rye	Omsk	Batum	Jidda
Tyr	Oran	Beira	Joppa
	Oslo	Belem	Kerch
4 letters:	Oulu	Bharu	Kochi
Acre	Perm	Blyth	Larne
Aden	Pori	Brest	Leith
Akko	Pula	Cadiz	Lulea
Amoy	Puri	Cairo	Mainz
Apia	Ruse	Canea	Malmo
Baku	Safi	Colon	Masan
Bari	Said	Dakar	Merca
Boma	Salé	Davao	Miami
Cobh	Sfax	Derry	Mocha
Cork	Suez	Dilli	Mokpo
Deal	Susa	Dover	Narva
Dill	Suva	Duala	Newry
Doha	Tang	Dubai	Omaha
Eisk	Tema	Eilat	Osaka
Elat	Tvev	Elath	Ostia
Faro	Tyre	Emden	Palos
Gary	Vigo	Gabes	Ponce
Hilo	Wick	Galle	Poole
Hull	Wuhu	Gavie	Pusan
Icel		Genoa	Pylos
I-pin	*5 letters:*	Ghent	Rabat
Kiel	Akaba	Gijon	Rouen
Kiev	Anzio	Goole	Saida
Kobe	Aqaba	Haifa	Sakai
Kure	Arhus	Hania	Salto

Selby
Sidon
Skien
Split
Surat
Susah
Tajik
Tampa
Tanga
Tunis
Turku
Vaasa
Varna
Visby
Vlore
Volos
Yalta
Yeisk
Yeysk
Yibin

6 letters:
Aarhus
Abadan
Agadir
Albany
Alborg
Amalfi
Ancona
Andong
Annaba
Aveiro
Balboa
Bastia
Batumi
Bergen
Bilbao
Bissao
Bissau
Blanca
Bombay
Bootle
Boston
Braila
Bremen
Bukavu
Burgas
Cairns
Calais
Callao
Candia

Cannes
Canton
Cavite
Chania
Chi-lin
Cochin
Cuiaba
Cuyaba
Da Nang
Danzig
Darwin
Dieppe
Djambi
Douala
Duluth
Dunbar
Dundee
Durban
Durres
Elblag
Galata
Galati
Gdansk
Gdynia
Harbin
Havana
Hobart
Ichang
Iligan
Iloilo
Inchon
Jaffna
Jarrow
Juneau
Kalmar
Kisumu
Lepaya
Lisbon
Lobito
Lubeck
Lushun
Macelo
Mackay
Madras
Malabo
Malaga
Manado
Manama
Manaos
Manaus
Manila

Maputo
Matadi
Menado
Mersin
Mobile
Mumbai
Muscat
Namibe
Nantes
Napier
Naples
Narvik
Nassau
Nelson
Newark
Ningbo
Ningpo
Nizhni
Odense
Odessa
Oporto
Ostend
Padang
Patras
Peoria
Pesaro
Quebec
Quincy
Rabaul
Ragusa
Recife
Rijeka
Rimini
Romney
Roseau
Rostov
Samara
Samsun
Santos
Sarnia
Sasebo
Savona
Skikda
Smyrna
Sousse
Speyer
Spires
St John
St Malo
St Paul
Suakin

Sydney
Syzran
Tacoma
Tajiki
Timaru
Tobruk
Toledo
Toulon
Tromso
Tyumen
Velsen
Venice
Vyborg
Weihai
Whitby
Wismar
Wonsan
Yangon
Yantai

7 letters:
Aalborg
Abidjan
Ajaccio
Alesund
Almeria
Antalya
Antibes
Antwerp
Aracaju
Astoria
Augusta
Averiro
Bangkok
Bayonne
Bengasi
Berbera
Bizerta
Bizerte
Bristol
Buffalo
Bushire
Calabar
Cam Ranh
Canopus
Cantala
Cardiff
Catania
Changde
Changte
Chicago

Chilung	Masbate	Tampico	Chongjin
Cologne	Massaua	Tangier	Cuxhaven
Colombo	Massawa	Taranto	Drogheda
Conakry	Maulman	Trabzon	Duisburg
Corinth	Memphis	Trapani	Dunleary
Corunna	Messina	Trieste	El Ferrol
Cotonou	Milazzo	Tripoli	Elsinore
Derbent	Mombasa	Ushuaia	Falmouth
Detroit	Moulman	Vitebsk	Flushing
Drammen	Munster	Vitoria	Freetown
Dunedin	Nanjing	Wanxian	Gisborne
Dunkirk	Nanking	Wenchou	Gonaives
El Minya	Nanning	Wenchow	Goteborg
Ephesus	Neusatz	Wenzhou	Greenock
Esbjerg	Newport	Whyalla	Haiphong
Foochow	Niigata	Yakutsk	Hakodate
Fukuoka	Niteroi	Yichang	Halmstad
Funchal	Novi Sad	Yingkou	Hamilton
Geelong	Oakland	Yingkow	Hangchow
Grimsby	Okayama		Hangzhou
Halifax	Onitsha	**8 letters:**	Harfleur
Hamburg	Otranto	Aalesund	Hartford
Harwich	Pahsien	Aberdeen	Hastings
Heysham	Palermo	Acapulco	Helsinki
Hodeida	Pelotas	Alicante	Holyhead
Horsens	Phocaea	Alleppey	Honolulu
Houston	Piraeus	Arbroath	Iraklion
Hungnam	Qingdao	Auckland	Istanbul
Incheon	Randers	Badalona	Jayapura
Iquique	Rangoon	Barletta	Jinjiang
Iquitos	Rapallo	Batangas	Kanazawa
Kaolack	Ravenna	Bathurst	Kawasaki
Karachi	Rosario	Benghazi	Keflavik
Kavalla	Rostock	Benguela	Kingston
Kenitra	Runcorn	Bobruisk	Klaipeda
Kherson	Salerno	Bobryusk	La Coruna
Kinsale	San Remo	Bordeaux	La Guaira
Kolding	Sao Luis	Boulogne	La Guyara
Konakri	Seattle	Brindisi	La Spezia
Kowloon	Sekondi	Brisbane	Lattakia
Kuching	Setubal	Bromberg	Les Cayes
La Plata	Seville	Caesarea	Limassol
Latakia	Shantou	Cagliari	Limerick
Legaspi	Shantow	Calcutta	Luderitz
Le Havre	Sinuiju	Castries	Mariupol
Lepanto	Stettin	Changsha	Matanzas
Liepaja	St John's	Changteh	Maulmain
Livorno	St Louis	Chaochow	Mayaguez
Lorient	Sukhumi	Cheribon	Mazatlan
Makurdi	Swansea	Chimbote	Monrovia
Marsala	Tadzhik	Chingtao	Montreal

Moulmein
Murmansk
Mytilene
Nagasaki
Nan-ching
Newhaven
Nha Trang
Novgorod
Nykøbing
Pago Pago
Paramibo
Pavlodar
Paysandu
Peiraeus
Penzance
Pevensey
Plymouth
Pnom Penh
Port Said
Pozzuoli
Qui Nhong
Ramsgate
Rio Bravo
Salvador
Samarang
Sanarang
Sandakan
San Diego
Sandwich
Santarem
Santiago
Savannah
Schiedam
Selencia
Semarang
Shanghai
Sorrento
Stockton
Surabaja
Surabaya
Syracuse
Szczecin
Tadzhiki
Taganrog
Takoradi
Tangiers
Tarshish
Tauranga
Teresina
Tjirebon
Tsingtao

Valdivia
Valencia
Veracruz
Victoria
Wanganui
Weymouth
Yarmouth
Yokohama
Yokosuka
Zaanstad

9 letters:
Anchorage
Angostura
Annapolis
Antserana
Archangel
Balaclava
Balaklava
Baltimore
Barcelona
Bass-Terre
Bhavnagar
Bujumbura
Bydgoszcz
Carnarvon
Cartagena
Cherbourg
Chisimaio
Chongqing
Chungking
Cleveland
Constanta
Dartmouth
Den Helder
Djajapura
Dordrecht
Dubrovnik
Ellesmere
Epidaurus
Esperance
Essaouira
Europoort
Famagusta
Fishguard
Fleetwood
Flensburg
Fortaleza
Fremantle
Gallipoli
Gateshead

Gravesend
Guayaquil
Hangchoio
Helsinger
Heraklion
Hiroshima
Immingham
Inhambane
Jasselton
Kagoshima
Kaohsiung
King's Lynn
Kingstown
Kirkcaldy
Kota Bahru
Kozhikode
Kronstadt
Las Palmas
Lowestoft
Magdeburg
Mahajanga
Mangalore
Maracaibo
Mariehamn
Marseille
Matamoros
Matsuyama
Melbourne
Milwaukee
Morecambe
Newcastle
Nuku'alofa
Palembang
Phnom Penh
Pontianak
Port Blair
Port Louis
Port Sudan
Reykjavik
Rotterdam
Santa Cruz
Santander
Schleswig
Sheerness
Singapore
Soerabaja
Stavanger
St George's
St Nazaire
Stornoway
Stralsund

Stranraer
Sundsvall
Takamatsu
Tarragona
Toamasina
Trebizond
Trondheim
Tynemouth
Volgograd
Walvis Bay
Weihaiwei
Whangarei
Zamboanga
Zeebrugge

10 letters:
Alexandria
Belize City
Birkenhead
Bratislava
Bridgeport
Bridgetown
Caernarvon
Cap-Haitien
Casablanca
Charleston
Cheboksary
Chittagong
Cienfuegos
Copenhagen
Corrientes
Dzerzhinsk
East London
Felixstowe
Folkestone
Fray Bentos
Fredericia
Georgetown
Gothenburg
Hammerfest
Hartlepool
Herakleion
Iskenderun
Joao Pessoa
Karlskrona
Khabarovsk
Khota Bharu
Kitakyushu
La Rochelle
Launceston
Los Angelos

Louisville
Matozinhos
Montevideo
Mostaganem
New Bedford
New Orleans
Norrkoping
Paramaribo
Pittsburgh
Pontevedra
Port Gentil
Portobello
Portsmouth
Port Talbot
Providence
Queenstown
Sacramento
Santa Marta
Sebastopol
Sevastopol
Strasbourg
Sunderland
Talcahuano
Thunder Bay
Townsville
Valparaiso
Willemstad
Wilmington
Winchelsea

11 letters:
Antofagusta
Antseranana

Banjarmasin
Banjermasin
Baranquilla
Bremerhaven
Cheng-chiang
Dares Salaam
Fredrikstad
Grangemouth
Helsingborg
Hermoupolis
Kaliningrad
Makhachkala
New Plymouth
Newport News
Nuevo Laredo
Pointe-Noire
Port Moresby
Porto Alegre
Port of Spain
Punta Arenas
Rockhampton
San Fernando
Scarborough
Shimonoseki
Southampton
Telukbetong
Trincomalee
Vizagapatam
Vlaardingen
Vladivostok

12 letters:
Angtofagasta

Bandjarmasin
Bandjermasin
Barranquilla
Buenaventura
Chandemagore
Dun Laoghaire
Ho Chi Min City
Jacksonville
Kota Kinabalu
Kristiansand
Milford Haven
Philadelphia
Pointe-à-Pitre
Ponta Delgada
Port Adelaide
Port-au-Prince
Port Harcourt
Prince Rupert
Rio de Janeiro
San Francisco
San Sebastian
Santo Domingo
South Shields
St Petersburg
Tanjungpriok
Thessaloniki
Ujung Pandang
Usti nad Labem

13 letters:
Chandernagore
Charlottetown
Ciudad Bolivar

Corpus Christi
Florianopolis
Great Yarmouth
Ho Chi Minh City
Port Elizabeth
Tandjungpriok
Teloekbetoeng
Trois Rivières
Visakhapatnam
Wilhelmshaven

14 letters:
Mina Hassen Tani
Nizhni Novgorod
Santiago de Cuba
Vishakhapatnam

15 letters:
Alexandroupolis
Angra-de-Heroismo
Blagoveshchensk
Sault Saint Marie

16 letters:
Reggio di Calabria
Sault Sainte Marie

18 letters:
Castellon de la
  Plana

Portable Lapheld, Laptop, Palmtop
Portend, Portent(ous) Augur, Awesome, Bode, Dire, Omen, Ostent, Phenomenon,
  Presage, → **WARN(ING)**
Porter Ale, Bearer, Bellboy, Bellhop, Bummaree, Caddie, Caddy, Cole, Concierge,
  Coolie, Door-keeper, Doorman, Dvornik, Entire, Gatekeeper, Hamaul, Ham(m)al,
  Humper, Janitor, October, Ostiary, Plain, Red-cap, Stout
Portfolio Holding
Portico Colonnade, Decastyle, Distyle, Dodecastyle, Exedra, Loggia, Narthex,
  Parvis(e), Porch, Propylaeum, Prostyle, Stoa, Veranda(h), Xyst(us)
Portion Aliquot, Ann(at), Bit, Deal, Distribute, Dole, Dose, Dotation, Fraction,
  Fragment, Helping, Heritage, Hunk, Instalment, Jointure, Lot, Measure, Meed,
  Mess, Modicum, Nutlet, Ounce, → **PART**, Piece, Ratio, Scantle, Scantling, Section,
  Segment, Serving, Share, Size, Slice, Something, Spoonful, Tait, Taste, Tate, Tittle,
  Tranche, Wodge
Portland Bill, Cement, Stone
Portly Ample, Corpulent, Gaucie, Gaucy, Gawcy, Gawsy, Stout
Portmanteau Bag, Combination, Holdall, Valise

Portrait(ist) Carte de visite, Depiction, Drawing, Eikon, Icon, Identikit®, Ikon, Image, Kit-cat, Lely, Likeness, Painting, Retraitt, Retrate, Sketch, Vignette
Portray(al) Caricature, Depict, Describe, Feature, Image, Limn, Paint, Personate, Render, Represent, → SHOW
Portsmouth Pompey
Portugal, Portuguese Lusitania(n), Luso-, Macanese, Senhor
Pose(r), Poseur Aesthete, Affect(ation), Arabesque, Asana, Ask, Contrapposto, Drape, Lotus, Mannequin, Man(n)ikin, Masquerade, Model, Place, Plastique, Posture, Pretend, Problem, Propound, Pseud, Puzzle, Sit, Stance, Sticker, Tickler
Poseidon Earthshaker
Posh Chic, Classy, Grand, Lah-di-dah, Ornate, Ritzy, Swanky, Swish, U
Position Asana, Attitude, Bearing(s), Close, Codille, Delta, Emplacement, Enfilade, False, Fixure, F(o)etal, Foothold, Fowler's, Grade, Instal, Lay, Lie, Location, Locus, Lodg(e)ment, Lotus, Missionary, Mudra, Office, Open, Pass, Peak, Place, Plant, Point, Pole, Possie, Post, Pozzy, Put, Recumbent, Root, Seat, Set(ting), Sextile, Sims, Site, Situ, Situs, Stance, Standing, Standpoint, Station, Status, Strategic, Syzygy, Tagmeme, Thesis, Tierce, Trendelenburg's, Tuck, Viewpoint
Positive, Positivist Absolute, Anode, Assertive, Categorical, → CERTAIN, Comte, Definite, Emphatic, False, Plus, Print, Sure, Thetic, Upbeat, Veritable, Yang, Yes
Posse Band, Mob, Vigilantes
Possess(ed), Possession(s), Possessive Adverse, Apostrophe, Asset, Aver, Bedevil, Belonging(s), Demonic, Driven, Energumen, Estate, Have, Haveour, Haviour, Heirloom, His, Hogging, Know, Lares (et) penates, Mad, Obsessed, Occupation, → OWN, Sasine, Seisin, Sprechery, Substance, Tenancy, Usucap(t)ion, Vacant, Worth
Possible, Possibility, Possibly Able, Contingency, Feasible, Likely, Maybe, Mayhap, Off-chance, Peradventure, Perchance, Perhaps, Posse, Potential, Prospect, Resort, Viable, Will
▷ **Possibly** *may indicate* an anagram
Possum Burramys, Cataplexy, Opossum, Pygmy, Ringtail, Sugar glider, Sugar squirrel, Tait
Post(s), Postage Affix, After, Assign, Bitt, Bollard, Carrick bitt, Command, Correspondence, Dak, Dawk, Delivery, Dragon's teeth, Emily, Excess, Finger, First, Flagpole, Graded, Gradient, Guardhose, Heel, Hitching, Hovel, Hurter, Jamb, Joggle, King, Last, Listening, Log, Mail, Mast, Newel, Observation, Outstation, Pale, Paling, Parcel, Pendant, Penny, Picket, Pigeon, Pile, Piling, Piquet, Placard, Place, Plant, Plum, Pole, Position, Presidio, Puncheon, Pylon, Queen, Quintain, Quoin, Registered, Remit, Residency, RM, Rubbing, Samson's, Seat, Send, Sheriff's, Snubbing, Sound, Spile, Staff, Staging, Stake, Starting, Station, Stell, Stoop, Stoup, Stud, Studdle, Term(inal), Tom, Tool, Trading, Upright, Vacancy, Waymark, Winning
Postcard(s) Deltiology, Picture
Poster Advertisement, Affiche, Bill, Broadsheet, Placard, Playbill, Sender
Posterior Behind, Bottom, Jacksie, Jacksy, Later, Lumbar, Pygal, Rear, Tail
Post-free Franco
Postman, Postmaster, Postwoman Carrier, Courier, Emily, Hill, Messenger, Nasby, Pat, Portionist, Sorter
Postmark Frank
Post-modern Po-mo
Post mortem Autopsy, Enquiry, Necropsy
Postpone(ment) Adjourn, Backburner, Contango, Defer, Delay, Frist, Hold over,

Lay over, Long-finger, Moratorium, Mothball, Pigeon-hole, Postdate, Prorogue, Put over, Reprieve, Respite, Shelve, Stay, Suspend, Withhold

Postulant Candidate, Noumenon, Novice

Postulate(s) Assert, Assume, Claim, Koch's, Propound

Posture(r), Posturing Affectation, Asana, Attitude, Birkie, Camp, Carriage, Counter-view, Decubitus, Deportment, Mudra, Pose, Pretence, Site, Stance, Vorlage

Posy Bouquet, Buttonhole, Corsage, Nosegay, Tussiemussie, Tuzzi-muzzy

Pot(s), Potting, Potty Abridge, Aludel, Ante, Bankroll, Basil, Belly, Billycan, Cafetière, Ca(u)ldron, Cannabis, Casserole, Ceramic, Chamber, Chanty, Chatti, Chatty, Chimney, Coal, Cocotte, Crewe, Crock(ery), Crucible, Cruse(t), Cupel, Delf(t), Dixie, Ewer, Flesh, Gage, Gallipot, Ganja, Gazunder, Grass, Hash(ish), Helmet, Hemp, In off, Inurn, Jardinière, Jordan, Kettle, Kitty, Livery, Lobster, Lota(h), Maiolica, Majolica, Marijuana, Marmite, Melting, Ming, Monkey, Olla, Olpe, Pan, Papper, Pat, Piñata, Pint, Pipkin, Planter, Po, Pocket, Poot, Posnet, → **POTTERY**, Pottle, Pounce, Pout, Prize, Quart, Samovar, Shoot, Skeet, Skillet, Smudge, Steamer, Stomach, Tajine, Tea, Test, Throw, Togine, Trivet, Tureen, Urn, Vial, Ware, Wash, Wok

Potash Kalinite, Polverine, Sylvine, Sylvite

Potassium K, Kalium, Pearl ash, Saleratus, Saltpetre

Potation Dram, Drink

Potato(es) African, Aloo, Alu, Batata, Chat, Clean, Couch, Datura, Duchesse, Early, Fluke, Hashbrowns, Hog, Hole, Hot, Irish, Jacket, Jersey, Kidney, Kumara, Lyonnaise, Mash, Murphy, Parmentier, Peel-and-eat, Pratie, Praty, Roesti, Rumbledethump(s), Seed, Small, Solanum, Stovies, Sweet, Tatie, Tattie, Teddy, Tuber, Ware, White, Yam

Pot-bearer Trivet

Pot-bellied Kedge, Kedgy, Kidge, Paunchy, Portly, Stout

Potboiler Hob

Pot-boy Basil, Ganymede, Scullion

Potent(ate) Dynamic, Emeer, Emir, Emperor, Huzoor, Influential, Kinglet, Mogul, Nawab, Panjandrum, Powerful, Ras, Ruler, Satrap, Squirearch, Sultan, Virile

Potential(ly) Action, Capacity, Chemical, Electric, Electrode, In posse, Ionization, Making(s), Manqué, Possible, Promise, Resting, Scope, Viable

▷ **Potentially** *may indicate* an anagram

Pothole(r) Chuckhole, Giant's kettle, Spelunker

Pot-house Shebeen, Tavern

Potion Dose, Draught, Drink, Dwale, Love, Mixture, Philtre, Tincture

Pot-pourri Hotchpotch, Medley, Miscellany, Pasticcio, Salmi

Potsherd Ostracon, Ostrakon

Pottage Berry

Potter Cue, Dabbity, Dabble, Dacker, Daidle, Daiker, Daker, Dibble, Dilly-dally, Dodder, Etruscan, Fettle, Fiddle, Footer, Footle, Fouter, Gamesmanship, Harry, Idle, Mess, Minton, Muck, Niggle, One-upmanship, Plouter, Plowter, Poke, Spode, Thrower, Tiddle, Tink(er), Troke, Truck, Wedgewood, Wedgwood

▷ **Potter** *may indicate* a snooker-player

Pottery Agatewear, Bank, Basalt, Bisque, Cameo ware, Celadon, Ceramet, Ceramic, China, Creamware, Crock, Crouch-ware, Dabbity, Delf(t), Earthenware, Encaustic, Etruria(n), Faience, Flatback, Gombroon, Granitewear, Hollowware, Ironstone, Jomon, Lustreware, Maiolica, Majolica, Ming, Minton, Pebbleware, Raku, Red-figured, Satsuma, Scroddled, Sgraffito, Slab, Slipware, Smalto, Spode, Spongeware, Stoneware, Studio, Sung, Terra sigillata, Ware,

Wedgwood®, Wemyss, Whieldon

Pouch(ed) Bag, Brood, Bum-bag, Bursa, Caecum, Cheek, Cisterna, Codpiece, Diverticulum, Fanny pack, Gill, Jockstrap, Marsupial, Marsupium, Poke, Posing, Purse, Sac, Scrip, Scrotum, Spleuchan, Sporran, Tobacco

Poultice Application, Cataplasm, Embrocation, Epithem(a), Lenient, Plaster

Poultry Dorking, Fowl, Gallinaceous, Plymouth Rock, Poot, Pout, Welsummer

Poultry disease Keel, Scaly-leg, Vent gleet

Pounce Claw, Jump, Lunge, Powder, Sere, Souse, Sprinkle, Swoop, Talon

Pound(er) Ache, As, Bar, Bash, Batter, Beat, Bombard, Bradbury, Bray, Broadpiece, Bruise, Catty, Contund, Coop, Drub, Embale, Enclosure, Ezra, Fold, Green, Hammer, Hatter, Imagist, Intern, Iron man, Jail, Jimmy o'goblin, Kiddle, Kidel, Kin, Knevell, L, Lam, Lb, Lock, Mash, Nevel, Nicker, Oncer, One-er, Oner, Pale, Pen, Penfold, Pestle, Pin, Pindar, Pinfold, Powder, Pulverise, Pun, Quid, Quop, Rint, Scots, Smacker, Sov(ereign), Squid, Stamp, Sterling, Strum, Tenderise, Thump, Tower, Troy, Weight

Pour Be mother, Birl(e), Bucket, Cascade, Circumfuse, Decant, Diffuse, Flood, Flow, Jaw, Jirble, Libate, Rain, Seil, Shed, Sile, Skink, Spew, Stream, Teem, Trill, Turn, Vent, Weep, Well

Pout Bib, Blain, Brassy, Eel, Fish, Horn(ed), Mope, Mou(e), Scowl, Sulk, Tout, Towt, Whiting

Poverty Beggary, Dearth, Deprivation, Illth, Indigence, → LACK, Locust years, Need, Paucity, Penury, Poortith, Puirtith, Squalor, Want

Powder(ed), Powdery Alumina, Amberite, Araroba, Baking, Ballistite, Bleaching, Boracic, Calamine, Chalk, Chilli, Cosmetic, Crocus, Culm, Curry, Custard, Cuttlefish, Dentifrice, Dover's, Dust, Dusting, Eupad, Explosive, Face, Floury, Fulminating, Giant, Glaucous, Goa, Gregory, Grind, Gun, Hair, Insect, Itching, Kohl, Levigate, Lithia, Litmus, Lupulin, Meal, Mould-facing, Moust, Mu(i)st, Pearl, Pemoline, Percussion, Persian, Plaster of Paris, Plate, Polishing, Pollen, Pounce, Priming, Prismatic, Projecting, Pruinose, Pulver, Pulvil, Putty, Rachel, Rochelle, Rottenstone, Rouge, Saleratus, Seidlitz, Seme(e), Sherbet, Silver iodide, Sitosterol, Smeddum, Smokeless, Snuff, Soap, Spode, Spodium, Talc(um), Talcose, Thimerosal, Toner, Tooth, Triturate, Tutty, Washing, Zein

Power(ful), Powers Ability, Able, Aeon, Aggrandisement, Almighty, Amandla, Arm, Arnold, Atomic, Attorney, Audrey, Autarchy, Authority, Axis, Beef, Big, Chakra, Cham, Charisma, Clairvoyance, Clout, Cogency, Colossus, Command, Corridor, Cube, Danger, Despotic, Diadem, Dioptre, Dominion, Effective, Eminence, Éminence grise, Empathy, Empery, Energy, Eon, Exponent, Facility, Faculty, Fire, Flower, Force, Force majeure, Geothermal, Grey, Gutty, Hands, Hefty, Hegemony, High, Hildebrandic, Horse, Hot, Hp, Hydroelectric, Imperium, Influence, Kami, Kilowatt, Log, Logarithm, Lusty, Mana, Mastery, Megalomania, Might, Mogul, Motive, Motor, Movers and shakers, Muscle, Nature, Nth, Nuclear, Od-force, Omnificent, Omnipotent, Option, P, Panjandrum, People, Pester, Plenipotency, Posse, Potency, Prepollence, Prepotent, Puissant, Punch, Purchasing, Regime, Resolving, Say-so, Siddhi, Sinew, Solar, Soup, Stamina, Staying, Steam, Stiff, Stopping, Strength, → STRONG, Supercharge, Supreme, Suzerain, Teeth, Telling, Throne, Tidal, Tycoon, Tyrone, Ulric, Valency, Vertu(e), Vigour, Vis, Volt, Vroom, Water, Watt, Wattage, Wave, Weight, Wind, World, Yeast

Powerless Diriment, Downa-do, Failing, Freewheel, Hamstrung, Helpless, Impotent, Impuissant, Incapable, Inert, Unable, Unarmed, Weak

Powwow Confab, Conference, Council, Meeting

Pox Orf, Pize

Practical, Practicable, Practicalities Active, Applied, Brass tacks, Doable, Easy-care, Hard-boiled, Joker, Logistics, No-nonsense, Nuts and bolts, On, Pragmatic, Realist(ic), Realpolitik, Rule of thumb, Sensible, Shrewd, Useful, Utilitarian, Viable, Virtual

Practice, Practise, Practitioner, Practised Abuse, Adept, Custom, Distributed, Do, Drill, Enure, Exercise, General, Group, Habit, Inure, Ism, Keep, Knock-up, Massed, Meme, Nets, Operate, Order, Ply, Policy, Praxis, Private, Prosecution, Pursuit, Rehearsal, Rehearse, Restrictive, Rite, Rule, Rut, Sadhana, Sharp, Spanish, Target, Teaching, Test-run, Trade, Tradition, Train, Trial, Ure, Usage, Use

Pragmatic, Pragmatist Ad hoc, Busy, Dogmatic, Humanist, Meddling, Officious, Realist

Prairie IL, Illinois, Llano, Plain, Savanna, Steppe, Tundra, Veldt

Prairie dog Whippoorwill, Wishtonwish

Praise(worthy) Acclaim, Adulation, Alleluia, Allow, Anthem, Applause, Belaud, Bless, Blurb, Bouquet, Butter, Carol, Citation, CL, Commend(ation), Compliment, Cry up, Dulia, Ego boost, Encomium, Envy, Eulogise, Eulogium, Eulogy, Exalt, Extol, Gloria, Glory, Hero-worship, Herry, Hery(e), Hosanna, Hymn, Hype, Incense, Kudos, Laud, Lip service, Lo(o)s, Meritorious, Palmary, Panegyric, Puff(ery), Rap, Roose, Tribute

Pram Carriage, Cart, Scow

Prance Brank, Canary, Caper, Cavort, Galumph, Gambol, Jaunce, Jaunse, Prank(le), Swagger, Tittup, Trounce

Prang Accident, Crash, Smash, Whale

Prank(s) Attrap, Bedeck, Bedizen, Caper, Dido, Escapade, Fredaine, Frolic, Gaud, Jape, Lark, Mischief, Pliskie, Rag, Reak, Reik, Rex, Rig, Spoof, Trick, Vagary, Wedgie

Praseodymium Pr

Prat Bottom, → STUPID PERSON

Prate Babble, Boast, Haver, Talk

Prattle Babble, Blat(her), Chatter, Gab(nash), Gas, Gibber, Gossip, Gup, Lalage, Patter, Smatter, Yap

Prawn Banana, Dublin Bay, King, Scampi, School, Shrimp

Pray(ing) Appeal, Bed, Beg, Beseech, Bid, Daven, → ENTREAT, Impetrate, Intone, Invoke, Kneel, Mantis, Solicit, Wrestle

Prayer(s), Prayer book Acoemeti, Act, Amidah, Angelus, Ardas, Ave (Maria), Bead, Beadswoman, Bede, Bene, Bidding, Breviary, Collect, Commination, Common, Confiteor, Cry, Cursus, Daven, Deus det, Devotion, Eleison, Embolism, Entreaty, Epiclesis, Euchologion, Evensong, Geullah, Grace, Habdalah, Hail Mary, Hallan-shaker, Imam, Intercession, Invocation, Kaddish, Khotbah, Khotbeh, Khutbah, Kol Nidre, Kyrie, Kyrie eleison, Lauds, Litany, Lord's, Loulat-ul-qadr, Lychnapsia, Ma(c)hzor, Mantis, Mat(t)ins, Mincha(h), Missal, Morning, Musaf, Novena, Orant, Orarium, Orison, Our Father, Paternoster, Patter, Petition, Phylactery, Placebo, Plea, Preces, Proseucha, Proseuche, Puja, Requiem, Requiescat, Rogation, Rosary, Salat, Secret, Shema, Siddur, State, Stations of the Cross, Suffrage, Te igitur, Tenebrae, Triduum, Venite, Yajur-Veda, Yizkor

▷ **Prayer** *may indicate* one who begs

Preach(er) Ainger, Boanerges, Circuit rider, Dawah, Devil-dodger, Dominican, Donne, Ecclesiastes, Evangelist, Exhort, Gospeller, Graham, Holy Roller, Itinerant, Knox, Lecture, Local, Mar-text, Minister, Moody, → MORALISE, Patercove, Pontificate, Postillate, Predicant, Predicate, Predikant, Priest, Prophet, Pulpiteer,

Rant, Revivalist, Spintext, Spurgeon, Teach, Televangelist
Preamble Introduction, Preface, Proem, Prologue
Prearrange(d) Stitch up
Pre-Cambrian Torridonian
Precarious Dangerous, Parlous, Perilous, Risky, Touch and go, Trickle, Uncertain, Unsteady
Precaution Care, Fail-safe, Guard, In case, Prophylaxis, Safeguard
Precede(nce), Precedent Antedate, Example, Forego, Forerun, Head, Herald, Pas, Predate, Preface, Priority, Protocol
Precept(s) Adage, Canon, Commandment, Maxim, Mishna, Motto, Saw
Precession Larmor
Precinct(s) Ambit, Area, Banlieue, Close, Courtyard, District, Environs, Pedestrian, Peribolos, Region, Shopping, Temenos, Verge, Vihara
Precious Adored, Chary, Chichi, Costly, Dear, Dearbought, Ewe-lamb, La-di-da, Murr(h)a, Nice, Owre, Precise, Prissy, Rare, Valuable
Precipice Bluff, Cliff, Crag, Krans, Kran(t)z, Sheer
Precipitate, Precipitation, Precipitous Abrupt, Accelerate, Cause, Deposit, Hailstone, Headlong, Impetuous, Launch, Lees, Pellmell, Pitchfork, Rash, Sca(u)r, Sheer, Shoot, Sleet, Snowflake, Start, → **STEEP**, White
Précis Abstract, Aperçu, Epitome, Résumé, Summary
Precise(ly), Precisian, Precision Absolute, Accurate, Dry, Exact, Explicit, Fine-drawn, Literal, Minute, Nice(ty), Overnice, Particular, Perfect, Plumb, Point-device, Prig, Prim, Punctilious, Sharpness, Spang, Specific, Starchy, Stringent, Succinct, Surgical, Tight, Very
Preclude Bar, Debar, Estop, Foreclose, Hinder, Impede, Prevent
Precocious(ness) Advanced, Bratpack, Forward, Premature, Protogyny
Preconception Ideating
Precursor Avant-courier, Forerunner, Harbinger
Predator(y) Carnivore, Eagle, Fox, Glede, Harpy-eagle, Jackal, Kestrel, Kite, Lycosa, Marauder, Predacious, Puma, Tanrec, Tarantula, Tenrec
Pre-dawn Antelucan, Ante lucem
Predecessor Ancestor, Forebear, Foregoer
Predestined Doomed, Fated, Tramway
Predicament Box, Dilemma, Embarrassment, Embroglio, Hobble, Hole, Jam, Pass, Peril, Pickle, Plight, Quandary, Scrape, Spot
Predict(ion), Predictable, Predictor Augur, Belomancy, Bet, Damn, Divination, Far-seeing, Forecast, Foreordain, Foresay, Foreshadow, Foreshow, Forespeak, Foretell, Forsay, Horoscope, Nap, Necromancy, Portend, Presage, Previse, Prognosis, Prophecy, Prophesy, Regular, Second-guess, Soothsayer, Spae
Predilection Fancy, Liking, Prejudice, Taste, Tendency
Predisposition Aptitude, Inclination, Parti-pris, Tendency
Predominate Abound, Govern, Overshadow, Prevail, Reign
Pre-eminence, Pre-eminent Arch, Foremost, Palm, Paramount, Primacy, Supreme, Topnotch, Unique
Pre-empt Enter
Preen Perk, Primp, Prink, Prune, Titivate
Prefab(ricated) Quonset, Terrapin®
Preface Foreword, Herald, Intro, Preamble, Precede, Proem, Prolegomenon, Usher
Prefect Prepositor, Pr(a)eposter
Prefer(ence), Preferred Advance, Better, Choose, Discriminate, Elect, Faard, Faurd, Favour, Imperial, Incline, Lean, Liquidity, Predilect(ion), Prefard, Priority,

Proclivity, Promote, Rather, Sooner, Stocks, Taste, Will
Prefix Eka, Introduce, Name
Pregnancy, Pregnant Big, Clucky, Cyesis, Ectopic, Enceinte, Fertile, F(o)etation,
   Gestation, Gravid(a), Great, Heavy, In foal, In pig, In pup, Knocked-up, Phantom,
   Pseudocyesis, Pudding-club, Stomack, Up the spout, Up the stick, With child
Prehistoric Ancient, Azilian, Beaker Folk, Boskop, Brontosaurus, Cambrian, Clovis,
   Cro-Magnon, Eocene, Folsom, Mound Builder, Ogygian, Primeval, Primitive,
   Pteranodon, Pterodactyl(e), Pterosaur, Saurian, Sinanthropus, Stonehenge,
   Titanosaurus, Trilith(on)
Prejudice(d) Bias, Bigotry, Derry, Discrimination, Down, Illiberal, Impede, Inequity,
   Injure, Insular, Intolerance, Partiality, Parti pris, Preoccupy, Prepossession, Racism
Prelate Archiepiscopal, Cardinal, Churchman, Exarch, Monsignor, Odo, Priest
Preliminary Draft, Exploration, Heat, Initial, Introductory, Precursory, Preparatory,
   Previous, Prodrome, Prolusion, Propaedeutic, Rough, Title-sheet
Prelude Entrée, Forerunner, Intrada, Overture, Proem(ial), Ritornell(e), Ritornello
Premature Early, Precocious, Pre(e)mie, Premy, Previous, Slink, Untimely,
   Untimeous
Premedication Atropia
Premeditate Anticipate, Foresee, Plan
Premier Chief, Leader, Main, PM, → PRIME MINISTER, Tojo
Premise(s) Assumption, Datum, Epicheirema, Ground, Hypothesis, Inference,
   Lemma, Major, Postulate, Property, Proposition, Reason
Premium Ap, Bond, Bonus, Discount, Grassum, Pm, Reward, Scarce, Share
Premonition Hunch, Omen, Presentiment, Prodromal, Warning
Preoccupation, Preoccupied, Preoccupy Absorb, Abstracted, Distrait, Engross,
   Hang-up, Intent, Obsess, Self-centred, Thing
Prepaid Pro-forma, Sae
Prepare(d), Preparation Address, À la, Arrange, Attire, Boun, Bowne, Busk, Calver,
   Cock, Concoct, Cooper, Countdown, Decoct, Did, Do, Dress, Edit, Forearm, Game,
   Groom, Ground, Inspan, Key, Lay, Legwork, Lotion, Measure, Mobilise, Parasceve,
   Pomade, Preliminary, Prime, Procinct, Prothesis, Provide, Psych, → READY,
   Rehearsal, Ripe, Rustle up, Set, Spadework, Stand-to, Suborn, Train, Truss,
   Warm-up, Whip up, Yare
▷ **Prepare(d)** *may indicate* an anagram
Preponderance, Preponderant, Preponderate Important, Majority, Outweigh,
   Paramount, Prevalence, Sway
Preposition Premise
Prepossessing, Prepossession Attractive, Fetching, Predilection, Winsome
Preposterous Absurd, Chimeric, Foolish, Grotesque, Unreasonable
▷ **Preposterous** *may indicate* a word reversed
Pre-Raphaelite Rossetti, Waterhouse
Prerequisite Condition, Essential, Necessity, Sine qua non
Prerogative Faculty, Franchise, Liberty, Privilege, Right, Royal
Presage Abode, Foresight, Omen, Portend, Presentiment, Prophesy
Presbyter(ian) Berean, Blue, Cameronian, Covenanter, Elder, Knox, Macmillanite,
   Moderator, Sacrarium, Seceder, Secesher, Secession Church, Whig(gamore)
Prescient Clairvoyant, Fly
Prescribe, Prescription Appoint, Assign, Dictate, Enjoin, Impose, Negative,
   Ordain, Positive, Rule, Scrip, Set
Prescription Cipher, Decree, Direction, Formula, Medicine, R, Rec, Receipt, Ritual,
   Specific

Presence Aspect, Bearing, Closeness, Company, Debut, Face, Hereness, Real, Shechinah, Shekinah, Spirit

Present(ation), Presented, Presenter, Presently Ad sum, Anchorman, Anon, Assists, Autocutie, Award, Bestow, Bonsela, Boon, Bounty, Box, Breech, By, By and by, Cadeau, Congiary, Coram, Current, Debut, Dee-jay, Deodate, DJ, Donate, Dotal, Douceur, Dower, Emcee, Endew, Endow, Endue, Enow, Étrenne, Existent, Fairing, Feature, Format, Front-man, Gie, → **GIFT**, Give, Going, Grant, Gratuity, Hand, Here, Historical, Hodiernal, Inst, Introduce, Jock(ey), Largess(e), Linkman, MC, Mod, Nonce, Now, Nuzzer, Offering, On hand, Porrect, Potlach, Pr, Prevailing, Produce, Proffer, Pro-tem, Put, Render, Show, Slice, The now, Tip, Today, Vee-jay, Xenium, Yeven

Preserve(d), Preservative, Preserver Bottle, Burnettize, Can, Chill, Chow-chow, Confect, Confiture, Corn, Creosote, Cure, Dehydrate, Dry, Eisel, Embalm, Fixative, Formaldehyde, Formalin, Freeze, Guard, Hain, Hesperides, Jam, Jerk, Keep, Kinin, Kipper, Konfyt, Kyanise, Life, Lifebelt, → **MAINTAIN**, Marmalade, Mummify, On ice, Pectin, Peculiar, Piccalilli, Pickle, Pot, Powellise, Salt, Salve, Saut, Season, Souse, Store, Stratify, Stuff, Tanalith, Tanalized, Tar, Tin, Vinegar, Waterglass

Preshrunk Sanforized®

Preside(nt) Abe, Adams, Banda, Bush, Carter, Chair, Childers, Cleveland, Coolidge, Coty, Dean, De Gaulle, Director, Eisenhower, Ford, Garfield, Grand Pensionary, Grant, Harding, Harrison, Hayes, Hoover, Ike, Johnson, Kennedy, Kruger, Lead, Lincoln, Madison, Mitterand, Moderator, Nixon, Old Hickory, P, Peron, Polk, Pompidou, Pr(a)eses, Prexy, Reagan, Roosevelt, Sa(a)dat, Speaker, Superintendent, Supervisor, Taft, Tito, Truman, Tyler, Veep, Washington, Wilson

Press(ed), Pressing, Pressure Acute, Aldine, Armoire, Atmospheric, Bar, Bench, Blackmail, Blood, Bramah, Button, Cabinet, Chivvy, Clarendon, Closet, Clothes, Coerce, Cram, Crease, Crimp, Critical, Crowd, Crush, Cupboard, Cylinder, Dragoon, Drill, Dun, Durable, Duress, Duresse, Enforcement, Enslave, Exigent, Filter, Flat-bed, Fluid, Fly, Folding, Force, Fourth estate, Full-court, Goad, Greenmail, Gutter, Hasten, Head, Heat, Herd, Hie, High, Hug, Hustle, Hydraulic, Hydrostatic, Impact, Important, Importune, Inarm, Intense, Iron, Isobar, Jam, Jostle, Knead, Leverage, Lie, Lobby, Low, Mangle, Megabar, Microbar, Mill, Minerva, Newspapers, Obligate, Oil, Onus, Osmotic, PA, Partial, Pascal, Peer, Permanent, Persist, Piezo-, Ply, Prease, Printing, Private, Psi, Pump, → **PUSH**, Racket, Ram, Ratpack, Record, Recruit, Reporter, Ridge, Roll, Root, Rotary, Rounce, Rush, Samizdat, Screw, Scrooge, Scrouge, Scrowdge, Scrum, Serr(e), Sit, Speed, Spur, Squash, Squeeze, Stanhope, Static, Stop, Strain(t), Stress, Tension, Thlipsis, Threap, Threep, Throng, Throttle, Thrutch, Torr, Tourniquet, Turgor, → **URGE**, Urgence, Urgency, Vanity, Vapour, Vice, Waid(e), Wardrobe, Weight, Wine, Wring, Yellow

Press agent Flack, Spin doctor

Press-gang Crimp, Force, Impress, Shanghai

Pressman Ed, Journalist, Journo, PRO, Reporter, Twicer

Prestidigitate(r) Conjure, Juggle, Legerdemain, Magician, Palm

Prestige, Prestigious Asma, Cachet, Credit, Distinguished, Fame, Influence, Izzat, Kudos, Notable, Status

Presume, Presumably, Presumption, Presumptuous Allege, Arrogant, Audacity, Believe, Bold, Brass, Cocksure, Cocky, Doubtless, → **EXPECT**, Familiar, Forward, Gall, Impertinent, Insolent, Liberty, Outrecuidance, Pert, Probably, Put upon, Suppose, Uppish, Whipper-snapper

Pretence, Pretend(er), Pretext Act, Affect(ation), Afflict, Assume, Blind, Bluff, Charade, Charlatan, Claim, Claimant, Cover, Cram, Dissemble, Dissimulate,

Dive, Excuse, False, Feign, Feint, Gondolier, Guise, Hokum, Humbug, Hypocrisy, Impostor, Jactitation, Kid(stakes), Lambert Simnel, Let-on, Make-believe, Malinger, Masquerade, Obreption, Old, Parolles, Perkin Warbeck, Pose, Profess, Pseud(o), Quack, Sham, Simulate, Stale, Stalking-horse, Subterfuge, Suppose, Warbeck, Young

Pretentious(ness), Pretension Arty, Bombast, Chi-chi, Fantoosh, Fustian, Gaudy, Grandiose, High-falutin(g), Kitsch, La-di-da, Orotund, Ostentatious, Overblown, Paraf(f)le, Pompous, Ponc(e)y, Pseud(o), Sciolism, Showy, Snob, Snobbish, Squirt, Tat, Tattie-peelin, Tinhorn, Toffee-nosed, Uppity, Wanky, Whippersnapper

Pretty Attractive, Becoming, Chocolate-box, Comely, Cute, Dear, Decorate, Dish, Elegant, Fair(ish), Fairway, Inconie, Incony, Keepsaky, Looker, Moderately, Pass, Peach, Picturesque, Primp, Quite, Sweet, Twee, Winsome

Prevail(ing) Dominate, Endure, Go, Induce, Outweigh, Persist, Persuade, Predominant, Preponderate, Reign, Ring, Triumph, Victor, Win

Prevalent Catholic, Common, Dominant, Endemic, Epidemic, Obtaining, Rife, Set in, Widespread

Prevaricate, Prevarication Equivocate, Hedge, Lie, Runaround, Stall, Whittie-whattie

Prevent(ive) Avert, Bar, Debar, Deter, Disenable, Embar, Estop, Foreclose, Forfend, Help, Impound, Inhibit, Keep, Let, Obstruct, Obviate, Preclude, Prophylactic, Sideline, Stop, Theriac, Trammel

Preview Sneak, Trailer, Vernissage

Previous(ly) Afore, Already, Before, Earlier, Ere(-now), Fore, Foreran, Former, Hitherto, Once, Prior

Prey Booty, Currie, Curry, Feed, Kill, Pelt, Plunder, Predate, Proul, Prowl, Quarry, Raven, Ravin(e), Soyle, Spreagh, Victim

Price(d), Pricing, Price-raising Appraise, Assess, Bride, Charge, Consequence, Contango, → cost, Dearth, Due, Evens, Exercise, Expense, Fee, Fiars, Hammer, Hire, Intervention, Issue, Limit, List, Loco, Market, Offer, Packet, Perverse, Predatory, Prestige, Quotation, Quote, Rack, Rate, Regrate, Reserve, Sale, Selling, Shadow, Song, Spot, Starting, Street value, Striking, Subscription, Toll, Trade, Unit, Upset, Value, Vincent, Weregild, Wergeld, Wergild, Worth, Yardage

Prick(ed), Prickle, Prickly Acanaceous, Accloy, Argemone, Arrect, Bearded, Brakier, Bramble, Brog, Bunya, Cactus, Cloy, Cnicus, Echinate, Goad, Gore, Hedgehog, Hedgepig, Impel, Inject, Jab, Jook, Juk, Kali, Penis, Perse, Pierce, Prod, Prog, Puncture, Rowel, Rubus, Ruellia, Seta, Setose, Smart, Spicula, Spinate, Stab, Star-thistle, Stimulus, Sting, Tattoo, Tatu, Teasel, Thistle, Thorn, Tingle, Urge

Prickly heat Miliaria

Prickly-pear Opuntia, Tuna

Pride Bombast, Brag, Conceit, Elation, Esprit de corps, Glory, Hauteur, Hubris, Inordinate, Lions, London, Machismo, Plume, Preen, Purge, Triumphalism, Vainglory, Vanity

Priest(ess), Priests Aaron, Abaris, Abbess, Abbot, Ananias, Annas, Archimandrite, Bacchae, Bacchantes, Baptes, Becket, Bonze, Brahmin, Caiaphas, Cardinal, Clergyman, Cleric, Cohen, Concelebrant, Corybant(es), Curé, Dalai Lama, Druid, Eli, Elisha, Father, Fetial, Flamen, Fr, Habacuc, Habakkuk, Hero, Hieratic, Hierophant, High, H(o)ungan, Io, Jethro, Kohen, Lack-Latin, Lama, Laocoon, Levite, Lucumo, Mage, Magus, Mallet, Mambo, Marabout, Metropolitan, Minister, Missionary, Monsignor, Mufti, Norma, Oratorian, P, Padre, Papa, Parish, Parson, Pastor, Patercove, Patrico, Pawaw, Père, Pontifex, Pontiff, Pope, Pope's knight, Powwow, Pr, Preacher, Prelate, Presbyter, Prior(ess), Pythia, Pythoness,

Rabbi, Rebbe, Rector, Rev, Sacerdotal, Salian, Savonarola, Seminarian, Shaman, Shaveling, Sky pilot, Spoiled, Tohunga, Vicar, Vivaldi, Worker, Zadok

Prig Dandy, Fop, Humbug, Nimmer, Pilfer, Prude, Puritan

Prim Demure, Mun, Neat, Old-maidish, Perjink, Preceese, Precise, Proper, Starchy

Primacy, Primate Angwantibo, Ape, Aye-aye, Bandar, Bigfoot, Biped, Bishop, Bush baby, Cardinal, Ebor, Gibbon, Hanuman, Hominid, Jackanapes, King Kong, Lemur, Loris, Macaque, Magot, Mammal, Marmoset, → **MONKEY**, Orang, Pongid, Potto, Prosimian, Protohuman, Quadruman, Ramapithecus, Rhesus, Sifaka, Tarsier, Zinjanthropus

Prima donna Diva, Patti, Star

Prime(r), Primary, Priming Arm, Basic, Bloom, Cardinal, Charging, Chief, Choice, Claircolle, Clearcole, Clerecole, Closed, Detonator, Direct, Donat, Donet, Election, Enarm, First, Flower, Heyday, Mature, Open, Original, Paramount, Peak, Radical, Remex, Sell-by-date, Supreme, Thirteen, Tip-top, Totient, Totitive, Valuable, Windac, Windas, Ylem

Prime Minister Asquith, Attlee, Baldwin, Balfour, Begin, Bute, Canning, Chamberlain, Chatham, Dewan, Diefenbaker, Disraeli, Diwan, Eden, Grand Vizier, Grey, Home, Leaderene, Liverpool, North, Number Ten, Peel, Pitt, PM, Premier, Shastri, Tanaiste, Taoiseach, Thatcher, Trudeau, Walpole

Prim(a)eval Ancient, Prehistoric, Primitive

Primitive Aborigine, Amoeba, Antediluvian, Arabic, Archaic, Atavistic, Barbaric, Caveman, Crude, Early, Evolué, Fundamental, Naive, Neanderthal, Neolithic, Old, Persian, Prim(a)eval, Primordial, Pro, Prothyl(e), Protomorphic, Protyl(e), Radical, Rudimentary, Savage, Subman, Turkish, Uncivilised, Ur

Primordial Blastema, Fundamental, Original

Primrose, Primula Auricula, Bear's ear, Cape, Evening, League, Oenothera, Onagra, Ox-lip, Pa(i)gle, Rosebery, Vicar, Yellow

Prince(ly) Ahmed, Albert, Ameer, Amir, Amphitryon, Anchises, Arjuna, Atheling, Barmecide, Black, Cadmus, Caliph, Chagan, Charming, Crown, Czarevich, Elector, Equerry, Eugene, Florizel, Fortinbras, Gaekwar, Gospodar, Guicowar, Hal, Highness, Hospodar, Huzoor, Igor, Inca, Infante, Khan, Ksar, Lavish, Lucumo, Maharaja, Margrave, Meleager, Merchant, Mir, Mirza, Nawab, Nizam, Noble, Otto, P, Pantagruel, Pendragon, Pirithous, Porphyrogenite, Potentate, Rainier, Rajah, Rana, Ras, Rasselas, Ratoo, Ratu, Regal, RH, Rudolph, Rupert, Serene, Sharif, Shereef, Sherif, Siegfried, Student, Tengku, Tereus, Tsar(evich), Tunku, Upper Roger

Princess Andromache, Andromeda, Anne, Ariadne, Begum, Creusa, Czarevna, Czarista, Danae, Di(ana), Electra, Electress, Eudocia, Europa, Helle, Hermione, Hesione, Ida, Imogen, Infanta, Iseult, Isolde, Jezebel, Maharanee, Maharani, Medea, Philomela, Pocahontas, Procne, Rani, Regan, Sara(h), Tou Wan, Tsarevna, Tsarista, Turandot, Yseult

Principal Arch, Capital, Central, → **CHIEF**, Decuman, Especial, First, Foremost, Head, Leading, Main(stay), Major, Mass, Protagonist, Ringleader, Staple, Star

Principality Andorra, Flanders, Liechtenstein, Moldavia, Moldova, Monaco, Muscovy, Orange, Wales, Wal(l)achia

Principle(s), Principled Accelerator, Animistic, Anthropic, Archimedes, Axiom, Basis, Bernouilli, Brocard, Canon, Carnot, Code, Cosmological, Criterion, Cui bono, Cy pres, D'Alembert's, Doctrine, Dogma, Element, Entelechy, Essential, Exclusion, Fermat's, First, Fourier, Gause's, Generale, Germ, Greatest happiness, Ground rule, Guideline, Heisenberg uncertainty, Honourable, Huygen's, Ideal, Interdeterminacy, Key, Law, Least time, Le Chatelier's, Logos, Methodology, Modus, Object soul,

Occam's razor, Organon, Ormazd, Ormuzd, Pauli-exclusion, Peter, Plank, Platform, Pleasure, Precautionary, Precept, Prescript, Psyche, Purseyism, Rationale, Reality, Reason, Reciprocity, Relativity, Remonstrance, Rudiment, Rule, Sakti, Seed, Shakti, Spirit, Summum bonum, Tenet, Theorem, Ticket, Verification, Vital, Yang, Yin

Prink Beautify, Bedeck, Dress

Print(er), Printing Baskerville, Batik, Benday, Bromide, Calotype, Caveman, Caxton, Chain, Chapel, Chromo, Cibachrome, Cicero, Collotype, Contact, Copperplate, Cyclostyle, Dab, Dot matrix, Electrothermal, Electrotint, Electrotype, Elzevir, Engrave, Etching, Ferrotype, Fine, Flexography, Font, Gravure, Gurmukhi, Gutenberg, Half-tone, Hectograph, Heliotype, Image, Impact, Impress, Incunabula, India, Ink-jet, Intaglio, Italic, Jobbing, Laser, Letterpress, Letterset, Line, Line-engraving, Lino-cut, Lithograph, Logotype, Lower-case, Matrix, Mimeograph®, Monotype®, Moon, Non-impact, Off-line, Offset, Old-face, Oleo, Oleograph, Opaline, Perfector, Phototype, Plate, Platinotype, Positive, Press, Process, Publish, Remarque, Report, Reproduction, Retroussage, Reverse, Rotogravure, Samizdat, Screen, Serigraph, Ship, Silk-screen, Small, Smoot, Splash, Spore, Stamp, Stenochrome, Stereotype, Stonehand, Strike, Thermal, Three-colour, Thumb, Trichromatic, Typesetter, Typography, Typothetae, Whorl, Woodburytype, Woodcut, Xerography, Xylograph, Zincograph

Printing-press Rounce

Prior(ity) Abbot, Afore, Antecedent, Anterior, Aperture, Earlier, Former, Grand, Hitherto, Monk, Overslaugh, Pre-, Precedence, Prefard, Preference, Previous, Privilege, Shutter, Triage, Until

▶ **Prise** *see* **PRIZE**

Prism(s), Prismatic Catadioptric, Iriscope, Nicol, Periaktos, Rhombohedron, Spectrum, Teinoscope, Wollaston

Prison Albany, Alcatraz, Bagnio, Barracoon, Bastille, Bin, Bird, Boob, Bridewell, Brig, Brixton, Bullpen, Cage, Can, Cell, Chillon, Chok(e)y, Clink, Club, College, Confine, Cooler, Coop, Counter, Dartmoor, Dispersal, Dungeon, Durance, Fleet, Fotheringhay, Gaol, Glass-house, Guardhouse, Guardroom, Gulag, Hokey, Holloway, Hoos(e)gow, Hulk(s), Internment, → **JAIL**, Jug, Kitty, Labour camp, Limbo, Lob's pound, Lock-up, Logs, Lumber, Marshalsea, Massymore, Mattamore, Maze, Newgate, Nick, Oflag, Open, Panopticon, Pen, Penitentiary, Pentonville, Pit, Pok(e)y, Porridge, Pound, Princetown, Quad, Quod, Rasp-house, Reformatory, Roundhouse, Scrubs, Shop, Sing-Sing, Slammer, Spandau, Stalag, State, Stir, Strangeways, The Leads, Tol(l)booth, Tower, Tronk, Wandsworth, Wormwood Scrubs

Prisoner Canary-bird, Captive, Collegian, Collegiate, Con(vict), Detainee, Detenu, Hostage, Inmate, Internee, Jailbird, Lag, Lifer, Political, POW, Trustee, Trusty, Yardbird, Zek

Pristine Fire-new, Fresh, New, Original, Unmarked, Unspoiled

Private(ly) Ain, Aside, Atkins, Auricular, Buccaneer, Byroom, Clandestine, Close, Closet, Conclave, Confidential, Enisle(d), Esoteric, Homefelt, Hush-hush, In camera, Individual, Inner, Intimate, Non-com, Own, Personal, Piou-piou, Poilu, Postern, Proprietary, Pte, Rank(er), Retired, Sanction, Sapper, Secret, Several, Single soldier, → **SOLDIER**, Squaddie, Sub rosa, Tommy, Under the rose

Privateer(s) Buccaneer, Corsair, Freebooter, Marque(s), Pirate

Privation Hardship, Penury, Want

Privilege(d) Birthright, Blest, Charter, Curule, Enviable, Exempt, Favour, Franchise, Freedom, Indulgence, Insider, Liberty, Mozarab, Nomenklatura, Octroi,

Parliamentary, Patent, Prerogative, Pryse, Regale, Regalia, Right, Sac

Privy Apprised, Can, Closet, Intimate, Jakes, John, Loo, Necessary, Reredorter, Secret, Sedge, Siege

Prize(s), Prizewinner, Prized Acquest, Apple, Archibald, Assess, Award, Best, Booby, Booker, Bravie, Capture, Champion, Consolation, Creach, Cup, Dux, Efforce, → **ESTEEM**, Force, Garland, Goncourt, Grice, Honour, Jackpot, Jemmy, Lever, Lot, Man Booker, Money, Nobel, Palm, Pearl, Pewter, Pie, Plum, Plunder, Pot, Premium, Prix Goncourt, Pulitzer, Purse, Ram, Reprisal, → **REWARD**, Rollover, Scalp, Ship, Spreaghery, Sprechery, Stakes, Taonga, Tern, Treasure, Trophy, Turner, Value

Pro Aye, Coach, For, Harlot, Moll, Paid, Tramp, Yea, Yes

▶ **Pro** *see* **PROSTITUTE**

Probable, Probability Apparent, Belike, Classical, Conditional, Ergodic, Feasible, Likely, Marginal, Mathematical, Possible, Posterior, Prior, Verisimilar

Probation(er) Cadet, Novice, Novitiate, Stibbler, Test, Trainee, Trial

Probe Antenna, Bore, Bougie, Canopus, Cassini, Corot, Delve, Dredge, Explore, Fathom, Feeler, Fossick, Galileo, Giotto, Inquire, Investigate, Magellan, Mariner, Mars Surveyor, Pelican, Pioneer, Poke, Pump, Ranger, → **SEARCH**, Seeker, Sonde, Sound, Space, Stardust, Stylet, Tent, Thrust, Tracer, Venera

Probity Honour, Integrity, Justice

Problem(s) Acrostic, BO, Boyg, Brainteaser, Business, Crisis, Crux, Dilemma, Egma, Enigma, Facer, Glitch, Handful, Hang-up, Headache, Hiccup, Hitch, Hurdle, Indaba, Knot(ty), Koan, Mind-body, Miniature, Musive, Net, Nuisance, Obstacle, Pons asinorum, Poser, Quandary, Question, Re, Rebus, Riddle, Rider, Snag, Sorites, Sum, Teaser, Teething, Thing, Tickler, Toughie, Trouble, Tsuris, Yips

Problem-solving Synectics

Proboscis Haustellum, Promuscis, Snout, Trunk

Proceed(s), Proceeding, Procedure Acta, Afoot, Algorithm, Continue, Course, Do, Drill, Emanate, Fand, Flow, Fond, Goes, Haul, Issue, Machinery, March, Mechanics, Method, Mine, MO, Modal, Move, On, Pass, Practice, Praxis, Process, Profit, Protocol, Punctilio, Pursue, Put, Rake, Return, Rigmarole, Rite, Ritual, Routine, Sap, Steps, Subroutine, System, Take, Use, Yead(s), Yede, Yeed

Process(ing), Procession, Processor Acromion, Action, Additive, Ala, Ambarvalia, Axon, Ben Day, Bessemer, Bosch, Castner, Catalysis, Cavalcade, Cibation, Cortège, Cyanide, Demo, Diagonal, Front-end, Haber, Handle, Managing, Markov, Method, Moharram, Mond, Motorcade, Muharram, Multiple pounding, Odontoid, Open hearth, -osis, Pageant, Parade, Parallel, Paseo, Photosynthesis, Pipeline, Planar, Pomp, Primary, Pterygoid, Puddling, Pultrusion, Purex, Recycle, Screen, Secondary, Series, Silkscreen, Skimmington, Solvay, Speciation, Sterygoid, String, Subtractive, Thermite, Thought, Torchlight, Train, Transverse, Treat, Trial, Turn(a)round, Unit, Vermiform, Xiphoid, Zygomatic

Proclaim, Proclamation Announce, Annunciate, Ban, Blaze, Blazon, Boast, Broadsheet, Cry, Edict, Enounce, Enunciate, Herald, Indiction, Kerygma, Oyez, Preconise, Predicate, Profess, Publish, Ring, Shout, Trumpet, Ukase

Procrastinate, Procrastinating, Procrastinator Cunctator, Defer, Delay, Dilatory, Dilly-dally, Linger, Pettifog, Postpone, Shelve, Temporise, Vacillate

Procreate Beget, Engender, Generate, Initiate

Procrustean Conformity

Proctor Agent, King's, Monitor, Prog, Proxy, Queen's

Procurator, Procure(r) Achieve, Aunt, Crimp, Earn, Get, Induce, Naunt, Obtain, Pander, Pilate, Pimp, Sort, Suborn

Prod Cattle, Egg, Goad, Impel, Jab, Job, Jog, Nudge, Poke, Pote
Prodigal Costly, Lavish, Profligate, Spendall, Unthrift, Wanton, Wasteful, Waster
Prodigious, Prodigy Abnormal, Amazing, Huge, Immense, Infant, Monster, Monument, Mozart, Phenomenal, Portentous, Tremendous, Wonder, Wonderwork, Wunderkind
Produce(r), Producing Afford, Bear, Beget, Breed, Cause, Create, Crop, Disney, Ean, Edit, Effect, Engender, Evoke, Exhibit, Extend, Fruit, Generate, Get, Grow, Home-grown, Impresario, Ingenerate, Issue, Kind, Make, Offspring, Onstream, Originate, Output, Propage, Propound, Raise, Son, Spawn, Stage, Supply, Teem, Throw, Trot out, Wares, Whelp, Yield
▷ **Produces** *may indicate* an anagram
Product(ion), Productive(ness), Productivity Actualities, Apport, Artefact, Ashtareth, Ashtaroth, Astarte, Bore, Cartesian, Coefficient, Commodity, Cross, Dot, Drama, End, Factorial, Fecund, Fertile, Fruit, Genesis, Global, Handiwork, Harvest, Net domestic, Net national, Output, Outturn, Pair, Partial, Primary, Profilic, Result, Rich, Scalar, Secondary, Set, Show, Speiss, Substitution, Uberous, Uberty, Vector, Waste, Work, Yield
▷ **Production** *may indicate* an anagram
Proem Foreword, Overture, Pre, Preface
Profane, Profanation, Profanity Coarse, Coprolalia, Desecrate, Impious, Irreverent, Sacrilege, Unholy, Violate
Profess(ed), Professor Absent-minded, Academic, Adjoint, Admit, Artist, Aspro, Asset, Assistant, Associate, Avow, Challenger, Claim, Declare, Disney, Emeritus, Full, Higgins, Hodja, Kho(d)ja, Know-all, Ostensible, Own, Practise, Pundit, Regent, Regius, RP, STP, Visiting
Profession(al) Admission, Assurance, Avowal, Buppy, Business, Career, Creed, Expert, Métier, Practitioner, Pretence, Pursuit, Regular, Salaried, Skilled, Trade, Vocation, Yuppie
Proffer Give, Present, Proposition, Tender
Proficiency, Proficient Able, Adept, Alert, Dan, Expert, Forte, Past master, Practised, Skill, Technique
Profile Analysis, Contour, Cross, Half-cheek, Half-face, Long, Loral, Low, Outline, Silhouette, Sketch, Statant, T(h)alweg, Vignette
Profit(able), Profiteer, Profits Advantage, Arbitrage, Asset, Avail, Benefit, Boot, Bunce, Cere, Clear, Divi(dend), Earn, Economic, Edge, Emblements, Emoluments, Exploit, Fat, Gain, Gelt, Graft, Gravy, Grist, Gross, Income, Increment, Issue, Jobbery, Juicy, Landshark, Leech, Lucrative, Makings, Margin, Melon, Mesne, Milch cow, Mileage, Moneymaker, Negative, Net, Pay(ing), Perk, Pickings, Preacquisition, Productive, Rake-off, Return, Reward, Royalty, Scalp, Spoils, Use, Usufruct, Utile, Utility, Vail
Profligate Corinthian, Corrupt, Degenerate, Dissolute, Extravagant, Lech(er), Libertine, Lorel, Losel(l), Oatmeal, Rakehell, Reprobate, Roué, Spend-all, Wastrel
Profound Altum, Bottomless, Complete, Deep, Intense, Recondite
Profuse, Profusion Abounding, Abundant, Copious, Excess, Free, Galore, Lavish, Liberal, Lush, Quantity, Rank, Rich, Two-a-penny
Progenitor, Progenitrix Ancestor, Ma, Predecessor, Sire, Stock
Progeny Burd, Children, Descendants, Fruit, Issue, Offspring, Seed
Prognosis Forecast, Prediction
Prognosticate, Prognostication Augur, Foretell, Omen, Predict, Presage, Prophesy
▶ **Program(ming), Programming language, Programmer**
  see **COMPUTER PROGRAMS**

Programme Agenda, Broadcast, Card, Chat show, Code, Community, Docudrama, Documentary, Docusoap, Dramedy, Est, Event, Faction, Fly-on-the-wall, Infotainment, Linear, Mockumentary, PDL, Phone-in, Pilot, Plan, Playbill, Prank, Radiothon, RECHAR, Regimen, Report, Schedule, Scheme, Sepmag, Shockumentary, Show, Simulcast, Sitcom, Sked, Soap, Software, Sustaining, Syllabus, System, Telecast, Teleplay, Telethon, Timetable

Progress(ive), Progression → **ADVANCE**, Afoot, Arithmetic, Avant garde, Course, Fabian, Flow, Forge, Forward, Forward-looking, Gain, Geometric, Get along, Go, Growth, Harmonic, Headway, Incede, Knight's, Liberal, Move, Onwards, Paraphonia, Pilgrim's, Prosper, Rack, Radical, Rake's, Reformer, Roll, Run, Sequence, Series, Step, Vaunce, Way, Yead, Yede, Yeed

Prohibit(ed), Prohibition(ist) Ban, Block, Debar, Dry, Embargo, Estop, Forbid, Hinder, Index, Injunct, Interdict, Noli-me-tangere, Off-limits, Prevent, Pussyfoot, Rahui, Suppress, Taboo, Tabu, Verboten, Veto

Project(ile), Projecting, Projection, Projector Aim, Ammo, Antitragus, Assignment, Astral, Astrut, Axonometric, Azimuthal, Ball, Ballistic, Beetle, Bullet, Butt, Buttress, Cam, Cast, Catapult, Channel, Cinerama®, Cog, Conceive, Condyle, Conic, Conical, Console, Corbel, Coving, Crossette, Cutwater, Denticle, Diascope, Discus, Eaves, Echinus, Elance, Enterprise, Episcope, Excrescence, Exsert, Extrapolate, Fet(ter)lock, Flange, Gair, Gore, Guess, Halter(e), Hangover, Helicity, Hoe, Homolosine, Housing, Hurtle, Inion, Jut, Kern, Kinetoscope, Knob, Ledge, Lobe, Lug, Magic lantern, Malleolus, Manhattan, Map, Mercator, Mitraille, Mohole, Mollweide, Mucro, Mutule, Nab, Nose, Nunatak(er), Olecranon, Opaque, Orillion, Orthogonal, Orthographic, Outcrop, Outjet, Outjut, Outshot, Overhang, Overhead, Oversail, Palmation, Peter's, Pitch, Planetarium, Planisphere, Polyconic, Pork barrel, Prickle, Promontory, → **PROTRUDE**, Proud(er), Pseudopod, Quillon, Raguly, Roach, Rocket, Sail, Salient, Sally, Sanson-Flamsteed, Scaw, Scheme, Screen, Shelf, Shrapnel, Sinusoidal, Skaw, Skeg, Slide, Snag, Snout, Spline, Sponson, Sprocket, Spur, Squarrose, Stand out, Stereopticon, Stick out, Stud, Tang, Tappet, Tenon, Throw, Toe, Tongue, Tracer, Trimetric, Trippet, Trunnion, Turnkey, Turtleback, Tusk, Umbo, Underhung, Undertaking, Villus, Vitascope, Whizzbang, Zenithal

Prolapse Procidence

Proletarian, Proletariat Jamahiriya, People, Plebeian, Popular

Proliferate Expand, Increase, Multiply, Propagate, Snowball

Prolific Abounding, Fecund, Fertile, Fruitful, Profuse, Teeming

Prolix(ity) Lengthy, Prosaic, Rambling, Rigmarole, Verbose, Wire-draw, Wordy

Prologue Introduce, Preface

Prolong(ed) Continue, Extend, Lengthen, Protract, Sostenuto, Spin, Sustain

Prom(enade) Alameda, Boulevard, Cakewalk, Catwalk, Crush-room, Esplanade, Front, Mall, Parade, Paseo, Pier, Sea-front, Stroll, → **WALK**

Prometheus Fire

Promethium Pm

Prominence, Prominent Antitragus, Blatant, Bold, Colliculus, Condyle, Conspicuous, Egregious, Emphasis, Featured, Gonion, High profile, Important, Insistent, Luminary, Manifest, Marked, Obtrusive, Outstanding, Salient, Signal, Solar, Tall poppy, Teat, Toot, Tragus

Promiscuous, Promiscuity Casual, Chippie, Chippy, Demivierge, Fast, Free, Goer, Hornbag, Horny, Indiscriminate, Licentious, Light, Loslyf, Mixed, Motley, Pell-mell, Skanky(-ho), Slapper, Trollop, Whoredom

Promise, Promising Accept, Assure, Augur, Auspicious, Avoure, Behest, Behight,

Behote, Bode, Coming, Compact, Covenant, Earnest, Engagement, Foretaste, Gratuitous, Guarantee, Hecht, Hest, Hete, Hight, IOU, Likely, Manifest, Parole, Pledge, Plight, Pollicitation, Potential, Pregnant, Recognisance, Recognizance, Rosy, Sign, Sponsor, Swear, Tile, Undertake, Vow, Warranty, Word

Promised land Beulah, Canaan, Israel

Promissory note IOU, PN

Promontory Bill, Cape Sable, Cliff, Flamborough Head, Foreland, Giant's Causeway, Hatteras, → **HEADLAND**, Hoe, Hogh, Mull, Mull of Galloway, Naze, Ness, Nose, Peak, Pillars of Hercules, Ras, Spit, The Lizard, Tintagel Head

Promote(r), Promotion Adman, Advance, → **ADVERTISE**, Advocate, Aggrandise, Aid, Assist, Blurb, Boost, Campaign, Churn, Dog and pony show, Elevate, Encourage, Exponent, Foment, Foster, Further, Help, Hype, Increase, Kick upstairs, Make, Pracharak, Prefer, Prelation, Promulgate, Provoke, Push, Queen, Raise, Rear, Remove, Roadshow, Run, Salutary, Sell, Sponsor, Spruik, Stage, Step, Subserve, Tendencious, Tendentious, Upgrade, Upload, Uprate

Prompt(er), Promptly, Promptness Actuate, Alacrity, Autocue®, Believe, Celerity, Chop-chop, Cue, Egg, Expeditious, Frack, Idiot-board, Immediate, Incite, Inspire, Instigate, Move, On-the-nail, Opposite, Pernicious, Premove, Punctual, Quick, Ready, Speed(y), Spur, Stage right, Stimulate, Sudden, Tight, Tit(e), Titely, Tyte, Urgent

Promulgate Preach, Proclaim, Publish, Spread

Prone Apt, Groof, Grouf, Grovel, Liable, Lying, Prostrate, Recumbent, Subject, Susceptible

Prong Fang, Fork, Grain, Peg, Tang, Tine

Pronghorn Cabrie, Cabrit

Pronoun Oneself, Personal, Reciprocal, Relative

Pronounce(d), Pronouncement Adjudicate, Affirm, Agrapha, Articulate, Assert, Asseveration, Clear, Conspicuous, Declare, Definite, Dictum, Emphatic, Enunciate, Fiat, Indefinite, Marked, Opinion, Palatalise, Pontificate, Predication, Recite, Utter, Velarise, Vocal, Voice, Vote

Pronto PDQ

Pronunciation Betacism, Cacoepy, Delivery, Diction, Etacism, Itacism, Lallation, Localism, Orthoepy, Phonetics, Plateasm, Proclitic, Received, Rhotacism, Sound, Tense

Proof Apagoge, Argument, Artist's, Assay, Bona fides, Confirmation, Direct, Evidence, Firm, Foundry, Galley, Godel's, Indirect, Justification, Lemma, Positive, Preif(e), Probate, Pull, Quality, Refutation, Remarque, Reproduction, Resistant, Revision, Secure, Slip, Strength, Test, Tight, Token, Trial, Upmake, Validity

Prop Airscrew, Bolster, Buttress, Clothes, Crutch, Dog-shore, Fulcrum, Leg, Loosehead, Misericord(e), Pit, Point d'appui, Punch(eon), Rance, Rest, Scotch, Shore, Sprag, Spur, Staff, Stay, Stempel, Stemple, Stilt, Stoop, Stoup, Studdle, Stull, → **SUPPORT**, Tighthead, Trig, Underpin

Propaganda, Propagandist Agitprop, Ballyhoo, Black, Brainwashing, Chevalier, Doctrine, Exponent, Goebbels, Grey, Promotion, Psyop, Psywar, Publicity, Slogan, Spin doctor, White

Propagate, Propagator, Propagation Breed, Dispread, Generate, Graft, Hatch, Hotbed, Hothouse, Increase, Layering, Produce, Promulgate, Provine, Spread, Tan-bed

Propel(ler) Airscrew, Ca', Drive, Fin, Frogmarch, Launch, Leg, Lox, → **MOVE**, Oar, Paddle, Pedal, Pole, Project, Push, Rotor, Row, Screw, Send, Tail rotor, Throw, Thruster, Vane

Propensity Aptness, Bent, Inclination, Penchant, Tendency

Proper(ly) Ain, Convenance, Correct, Decent, Decorous, Due, Eigen, En règle, Ethical, → **FIT**, Genteel, Governessy, Kosher, Noun, Ought, Own, Pakka, Pathan, Prim, Pucka, Pukka, Puritanic, Real, Rightful, Seemly, Suitable, Tao, Trew, True, Veritable, Well

Property, Properties Assets, Attribute, Aver, Belongings, Capacitance, Chattel, Chose, Contenement, Dead-hand, Demesne, Des res, Dowry, Effects, Enclave, Escheat, Escrow, Estate, Fee, Feu, Flavour, Fonds, Freehold, Goods, Haecceity, Hereditament, Hot, Hotchpot, Immoveable, Inertia, Intellectual, Jointure, Leasehold, Living, Means, Mortmain, Paraphernalia, Peculium, Personal, Personalty, Predicate, Premises, Private, Projective, Public, Quale, Quality, Real, Stock, Stolen, Theft, Thixotropy, Time-share, Timocracy, Trait, Usucapion, Usucaption

Prophesy, Prophecy, Prophet(s), Prophetess, Prophetic Amos, Augur, Bab, Balaam, Calchas, Cassandra, Daniel, Deborah, Divine, Druid, Elias, Elijah, Elisha, Ezekiel, Ezra, Fatal, Fatidical, Forecast, Foretell, Former, Geomancer, Habakkuk, Haggai, Hosea, Is, Isa, Is(a)iah, Jeremiah, Joel, Jonah, Latter, Mahdi, Mahound, Major, Malachi, Mani, Mantic, Micah, Minor, Mohammed, Mopsus, Mormon, Moses, Nahum, Nathan, Nostradamus, Obadiah, Old Mother Shipton, Ominous, Oracle, Portend, Predictor, Prognosticate, Pythoness, Samuel, Second sight, Seer, Sibyl, Tipster, Tiresias, Vatic, Vaticinate, Völuspá, Zachariah, Zarathustra, Zechariah, Zephaniah, Zoroaster, Zwickau

Prophylactic, Prophylaxis Inoculation, Preventive, Serum, Vaccine, Variolation

Propitiate Appease, Atone, Pacify, Reconcile, Sop

Propitious Benign, Favourable, Lucky

Proponent Advocate, Backer, Partisan

Proportion(ate) Commensurable, Dimension, Harmonic, Inverse, Portion, Pro rata, Quantity, Quota, Ratio, Reason, Regulate, Relation, Sine, Size, Soum, Sowm

Propose(r), Proposal Advance, Bid, Bill, Canvass, Eirenicon, Feeler, Fiancé, Irenicon, Mean, Motion, Move, Nominate, Offer, Overture, Plan, Pop, Premise, Proffer, Propound, Recommend, Resolution, Scheme, Slate, Submission, → **SUGGEST**, Table, Tender, Volunteer, Woot, Would

Proposition Asses' bridge, Axiom, Convertend, Corollary, Deal, Disjunction, Ergo, Hypothesis, Identical, Implicature, Lemma, Overture, Pons asinorum, Porism, Premise, Premiss, Rider, Sorites, Spec, Superaltern, Theorem, Thesis

Propound Advocate, Purpose, State

Proprietor, Propriety Convenance, Correctitude, Decorum, Etiquette, Grundy, Keeper, Lord, Master, Owner, Patron, Rectitude

Prosaic Common, Drab, Flat, Humdrum, Tedious, Workaday

Proscenium Forestage

Proscribe Exile, Forbid, Outlaw, Prohibit

Prose, Prosy Euphuism, Haikai, Polyphonic, Purple, Purple patch, Saga, Stich, Verbose, Version, Writing

Prosecute, Prosecutor, Prosecution Allege, Avvogadore, Charge, Crown, Fiscal, Furtherance, Impeach, Indict, Lord Advocate, Practise, Public, Sue, Wage

Proselytise(r), Proselytism Indoctrination, Propagandism, Souper

Prospect(or) Bellevue, Dowser, Explore, Forty-niner, Fossick, Look-out, Mine, Opportunity, → **OUTLOOK**, Panorama, Perspective, Pleases, Possibility, Reefer, Scenery, Search, Sourdough, View, Vista, Visto, Wildcatter

Prospectus Menu, Pathfinder

Prosper(ity), Prospering, Prosperous Aisha, Ay(e)sha, Blessed, Blossom, Boom,

Fair, Fat cat, Flourish, Get ahead, Heyday, Mérimée, Palmy, → SUCCEED, Thee, Thrift, Thrive, Up, Warison, Wealth, Welfare, Well-heeled, Well-to-do

Prostitute, Prostitution Brass, Broad, Bulker, Callet, Catamite, Chippie, Cockatrice, Cocotte, Debase, Dell, Demi-mondaine, Dolly-mop, Doxy, Fancy woman, Fille de joie, Harlot, Hetaera, Hetaira, Hierodule, Ho, Hooker, Jailbait, Lady of the night, Loon, Loose-fish, Loose woman, Lowne, Madam, Magdalen(e), Moll, Mutton, Night-walker, Pict, Plover, Pole-cat, Pro, Punk, Quail, Quiff, Rent-boy, Road, Rough trade, Scrubber, Shippie, Slap, Social evil, Stew, Streetwalker, Strumpet, Tart, Tramp, Trull, Venture, Wench, Whore

Prostrate, Prostration Collapse, Exhausted, Fell, Flat, Flatling, Ko(w)tow, Laid, Obeisance, Overcome, Procumbent, Prone, Repent, Throw

Protactinium Pa

Protean Amoebic, Fusible, Variable

Protect(ed), Protection, Protector Adonise, Aegis, Alexin, Arm, Armour, Asylum, Auspice, Bastion, Bestride, Bield, Buckler, Bullet-proof, Chaffron, Chain mail, Chamfrain, Chamfron, Charm, Cherish, Cloche, Coat, Cocoon, Coleor(r)hiza, Conserve, Copyright, Cosset, Cover, Covert, Cromwell, Cushion, Danegeld, Data, Defend, Defilade, Degauss, Egis, Enamel, Entrenchment, Escort, Estacade, Faun, Fence, Flank, Gobo, Groundsheet, Guard(ian), Gumshield, Hedge, House, Hurter, Immune, Inalienable, Indemnify, Insure, Integument, Keckle, Keep, Kickback, Klendusic, Lee, Mac(k)intosh, Mail, Male, Mollycoddle, Mother, Mouthpiece, Mudguard, Muniment, Noll, Nosey, Oliver, Ombrella, Orillion, Overall, Parados, Patent, Patron, Penthouse, Police, Pomander, Preserve, Rabbit's foot, Raymond, Redome, Revetment, Ride shotgun, Safeguard, Sandbag, Save, Schanse, Schan(t)ze, Screen, Scug, Shadow, Sheathing, Sheeting, Shelter, → SHIELD, Skug, Souteneur, Splashback, Splashboard, Splasher, Starling, Sunscreen, Talisman, Testa, Tribute, Tutelar, Twilled, Umbrella, Underlay, Underseal, Vaccine, Ward(ship), Warhead, Warrant, Weatherboard, Weatherstrip, Windbreaker, Windshield, Wing, Write

Protég(é) Pupil, Tutee, Ward

Protein Abrin, Actin, Actomyosin, Adipsin, Alanine, Albumen, Albumin, Aleuron(e), Allergen, Amandine, Analogon, Angiostatin, Angiotensin, Antibody, Apoenzyme, Aquaporin, Avidin, Bradykinin, Calmodulin, Capsid, Capsomere, Caseinogen, Ceruloplasmin, Collagen, Complement, Conchiolin, Conjugated, Copaxone®, CREB, Cyclin, Cytokine, Dystrophin, Elastin, Enzyme, Factor VIII, Ferritin, Ferrodoxin, Fibrin, Fibrinogen, Fibroin, Flagellin, Gelatin, Gliadin(e), Glob(ul)in, Glutelin, Gluten, Haemoglobin, Haptoglobin, Histone, Hordein, Huntingtin, Immunoglobulin, Incaparina, Integrin, Interferon, Interleukin, Lactalbumin, Lactoglobulin, Lectin, Legumin, Leptin, Leucin(e), Lewy bodies, Luciferin, Lymphokine, Lysin, Meat, Mucin, Myogen, Myoglobin, Myosin, Nuclein, Opsin, Opsonin, Ossein, Ovalbumin, Pepsin(e), Peptide, Phaseolin, Prion, Prolamin(e), Properdin, Protamine, Proteose, Prothrombin, Pyrenoid, Quorn®, Renin, Repressor, Ribosome, Sclerotin, Sericin, Serum albumin, Serum globulin, Single-cell, Soya, Spectrin, Spongin, Tempeh, Thrombogen, Toxalbumin, Transferrin, Tropomyosin, Troponin, TSP, Tubulin, TVP, Ubiquitin, Vitellin, Zein

Protest(er) Abhor, Andolan, Aver, Avouch, Black Bloc(k), Clamour, Come, Démarche, Demo, Demonstrate, Demur, Deprecate, Dharna, Dissent, Expostulate, Gherao, Go-slow, Hartal, Inveigh, Lock-out, Luddite, March, Moonlighter, Nimby, Object, Outcry, Picket, Plea, Refus(e)nik, Remonstrate, Sit-in, Squawk, Squeak, Squeal, Stand, Suffragette, Work-to-rule

Protestant Amish, Anabaptist, Anglo, Arminian, Calvin, Congregationalism, Covenanter, Cranmer, Dissenter, Evangelic, Gospeller, Huguenot, Independent,

Lady, Loyalist, Lutheran, Mennonite, Methodist, Moravian, Neo-Orthodoxy, Nonconformist, Oak-boy, Orangeman, Peep o' day Boys, Pentecostal, Pietism, Prod, Puritan, Religioner, Right-footer, Sacramentarian, Stundist, Swaddler, Wasp, Wesleyan

Protocol Agreement, Code, Convention, Etiquette, Geneva, Kyoto, Point-to-Point

Proton Nucleon, Quark

Protoplasm(ic) Coenocyte, Coenosarc, Cytode, Sarcode

Prototype Blueprint, Exemplar, Model, Original, Pattern

Protozoa(n) Am(o)eba, Foraminifer, Giardia, Globigerina, Gregarine, Heliozoan, Infusoria, Leishmania, Mastigophoran, Moner(a), Moneron, Paramecium, Peritricha, Phagocyte, Radiolaria, Rhizopod, Thrichomonad, Trophozoite, Trypanosome, Volvox, Vorticella

Protract(ed) Delay, → EXTEND, Lengthen, Livelong, Long, Prolong

Protrude, Protrusion Bulge, Eventration, Exsert, Hernia, Jut, Pop, Pout, Project, Pseudopodium, Rectocele, Strout, Tel

Protuberance, Protuberant Apophysis, Bulge, Bump, Burl, Condyle, Crankle, Gibbous, Hump, Knap, Knob, Malleolus, Node, Papillose, Papule, Spadix, Swelling, Tragus, Tuber, Tubersity, Venter

Proud Arrogant, Boaster, Cocky, Conceited, Dic(k)ty, Elated, Flush, Haughty, Haut, Level, Lordly, Orgulous, Protruding, Superb, Vain

Prove(d), Proving Apod(e)ictic, Argue, Ascertain, Assay, Attest, Authenticate, Aver, Confirm, Convince, Deictic, Establish, Evince, Justify, → PROOF, Quote, → SHOW, Substantiate, Test, Trie

Proverb Adage, Axiom, Byword, Gnome, Maxim, Paroemia, Saw

▷ **Proverbial** *may refer to* the biblical Proverbs

Provide(d), Provident(ial) Afford, Allow, Arrange, Besee, Bring, Cater, Compare, Conditional, Endow, Equip, Far-seeing, Feed, Fend, Find, Furnish, Generate, Give, Grubstake, Heaven sent, If, Lay on, Maintain, Plenish, Proviso, Purvey, Quote, Serve, So, Sobeit, → SUPPLY, Suttle

Province, Provincial(ism) Area, Circar, District, Eparchy, Exclave, Eyalet, Forte, Insular, Land, Mofussil, Narrow, Nomarchy, Nome, Nomos, Oblast, Palatinate, Pale, Petrographic, Realm, Regional, Rural, Sircar, Sirkar, Subah, Suburban, Territory, Vilayet

---

PROVINCES

2 letters:	Hebei	Tirol	Quebec
NI	Henan	Tyrol	Raetia
	Honan		Sanjak
4 letters:	Hopeh	*6 letters:*	Shansi
Gaul	Hopei	Acadia	Shanxi
Ifni	Hubei	Artois	Shensi
Shoa	Hunan	Basque	Sikang
Sind	Jehol	Bengal	Ulster
	Jilin	Fujian	Yunnan
5 letters:	Kansu	Fukien	
Anhui	Kirin	Hainan	*7 letters:*
Anjou	Liege	Kosovo	Alberta
Anwei	Namur	Marche	Almeria
Coorg	Natal	Poitou	Antwerp
Gansu	Otago	Punjab	Brabant

Drenthe
Eritrea
Gascony
Gauteng
Granada
Guienne
Guizhou
Guyenne
Hainaut
Jiangsu
Jiangxi
Jiazhou
Kiangsi
Kiangsu
Kwazulu
Limpopo
Livonia
Munster
Ningsia
Ontario
Picardy
Prairie
Qinghai
Rhaetia
Satrapy
Shaanxi
Sichuan
Suiyuan
Utrecht
Western
Zeeland

8 letters:
Atlantic
Chekiang
Chinghai
Connacht
Dauphine
Hainault
Helvetia
Kiaochow
Leinster
Liaoning
Limousin
Lorraine
Lyonnais
Manitoba
Maritime
Ninghsia
Normandy
Northern
Pashalic
Pashalik
Provence
Shandong
Shantung
Szechuan
Szechwan
Touraine
Tsinghai
Zhejiang

9 letters:
Apeldoorn

Aquitaine
Connaught
Flevoland
Free State
Friesland
Groningen
Guangdong
Hainan Tao
Illyricum
Kurdistan
Languedoc
Lusitania
Nivernais
North West
Orleanais
Santa Cruz
Sungkiang
Transvaal

10 letters:
Gelderland
Mpumalanga
New Castile
Overijssel
Patavinity
Roussillon
Wellington

11 letters:
Balochistan
Baluchistan
Guelderland

Hesse-Nassau
Kaliningrad
Paphlagonia
West Prussia

12 letters:
Heilongjiang
New Brunswick
North Brabant
North Holland
Saskatchewan
South Holland

13 letters:
Syrophoenicia

14 letters:
Eastern Rumelia
Flemish Brabant
Walloon Brabant

15 letters:
British Columbia
Orange Free State

17 letters:
North West Frontier

23 letters:
Newfoundland and
Labrador

Provision(s), Provisional Acates, A(p)panage, Board, Fodder, Foresight, Insolvency, Jointure, Larder, Lend-lease, Proggins, Scran, Skran, Stock, Supply, Suttle, Viands, Viaticum, Victuals

Proviso, Provisional Caution, Caveat, Clause, Condition, Interim, IRA, Makeshift, Nisi, On trial, Reservation, Salvo, Stipulation, Temporary, Tentative

Provocation, Provocative, Provoke Agacant, Alluring, Egg, Elicit, Erotic, Exacerbate, Excite, Flirty, Gar, Harass, Incense, Induce, Inflame, Instigate, Irk, Irritate, Needle, Nettle, Occasion, Pique, Prompt, Raise, Red rag, Sedition, Spark, Stimulate, Stir, Tar, Tease, Urge, Vex, Wind up

Provost Dean, Keeper, Marshal, Warden

Prow Bow, Cutwater, Fore, Nose, Prore, Stem

Pro-war Hawk

Prowess Ability, Bravery, Forte, Fortitude

Prowl(er) Hunt, Lurch, Lurk, Mooch, Prog, Prole, Rache, Ramble, Ratch, Roam, Rove, Snoke, Snook, Snowk, Tenebrio, Tom

Proxime accessit Next best

Proximity Handiness

Proxy Agent, Attorn, Deputy, PP, Regent, Sub, Surrogate, Vicar, Vice

Prude(nce), Prudent, Prudery Bluenose, Canny, Caution, Circumspect, Comstocker, Conservative, Discreet, Discretion, Far-sighted, Foresight, Frugal, Grundyism, Judicious, Metis, Mrs Grundy, Politic, Prig, Prissy, Provident, Sage, Sensible, Sparing, Strait-laced, Strait-lacer, Thrifty, Tight-laced, Vice-nelly, Victorian, Ware, Wary, Well-advised, Wise

Prune(r) Bill-hook, Clip, Dehorn, Lop, Plum, Proign, Proin(e), Reduce, Reform, Secateur, Shred, Sned, Thin, Trim

Prunella Hedge-sparrow, Self-heal

Prurient Avaricious, Itchy, Lewd, Obscene

Prussia(n) Blue, Junker, Pruce, Spruce, Westphalian

Pry Ferret, Force, Lever, Meddle, Nose, Paul, Peep, Question, Search, Snoop, Stickyback, Toot

Psalm Anthem, Cantate, Chant, Chorale, Hallel, Hymn, Introit, Jubilate, Metrical, Miserere, Neck-verse, Paean, Penitential, Proper, Ps, Song, Tone, Tract, Venite

Pseud(o) Bogus, Mock, Posy, Sham, Spurious

Pseudonym Aka, Alias, Allonym, Anonym, Pen-name, Stage-name

Pshaw Chut, Pooh, Tilley-valley, Tilly-fally, Tilly-vally

Psyche Ego, Self, Soul, Spirit, Superego

Psychiatrist, Psychologist Adler, Alienist, Clare, Coué, Ellis, Freud, Headshrinker, Jung, Laing, Müller-Lyer, Rat-tamer, Reich, Shrink, Trick-cyclist

Psychic, Psychosis ESP, Korsakoff's, Lodge, Medium, Seer, Telekinesis, Telepathic

Psychological, Psychology, Psychologist Analytical, Behaviourism, Clinical, Comparative, Constitutional, Depth, Dynamic, Educational, Experimental, Eysenck, Gestalt, Hedonics, Humanistic, Industrial, James, Latah, Occupational, Organisational, Piaget, Social, Structural

Psychosis, Psychotic Korsakoff's, Manic-depressive, Organic, Schizophrenia

Psychotherapy Rebirthing

Ptarmigan Rype

Ptomaine Neurine

Pub Bar, Beerhall, Beverage room, Boozer, Chequers, Free-house, Gin-palace, Houf(f), House, Howf(f), Inn, Jerry-shop, Joint, Local, Mughouse, Pothouse, Potshop, Rubbidy, Rubbity, Shanty, Tavern, Tiddlywink

Puberty Adolescence, Hebetic, Teens

Pubescence Tomentum

Public Apert, Bar, Civil, Common, Demos, General, Great unwashed, Inn, Janata, Lay, Limelight, National, Open, Out, Overt, Populace, State, Vulgar, World

Publican Ale-keeper, Bung, Host, Landlord, Licensee, Tapster, Taverner

Publication Announcement, Bluebook, Book, Broadsheet, Edition, Ephemera, Exposé, Festschrift, Issue, → JOURNAL, Lady, Mag, Magazine, Organ, Pictorial, Samizdat, Tabloid, Tatler, Tract, Tribune, Yearbook

Publicist, Publicity Ad(vert), Airing, Ballyhoo, Billing, Build up, Coverage, Exposure, Flack, Glare, Headline, Hype, Leakage, Limelight, Notoriety, Plug, PR(O), Promotion, Propaganda, Réclame, Spin-doctor, Splash

Publish(er), Published, Publishing, Publicise Air, Blaze, Cape, Delator, Desktop, Disclose, Edit, Electronic, Evulgate, Gollancz, Issue, Noise, OUP, Out, Pirate, Plug, Post, Print(er), Proclaim, Propagate, Put about, Release, Run, Stationer, Vanity, Vent, Ventilate

Puck Disc, Elf, Lob, Sprite, Squid

Pucker(ed) Bullate, Cockle, Contract, Gather, Plissé, Purse, Ruck, Shir(r), Wrinkle

Pud Fin, Paw

Pudding Afters, Baked Alaska, Bakewell, Black, Blancmange, Blood, Bread (and butter), Brown Betty, Cabinet, Charlotte, Christmas, Clootie dumpling, College, Crumble, Custard, → **DESSERT**, Drisheen, Duff, Dumpling, Eve's, Flummery, Fritter, Fromenty, Frumenty, Furme(n)ty, Furmity, Haggis, Hasty, Hodge, Hog's, Kugel, Lokshen, Mealie, Milk, Nesselrode, Panada, Pandowdy, Parfait, Pease, Plum, Plum-duff, Popover, Queen's, Rice, Roly-poly, Sago, Savarin, Semolina, Sowens, Sponge, Spotted dick, Stickjaw, Stodge, Suet, Summer, Sundae, Sweet, Tansy, Tapioca, Umbles, White, White hass, White hause, White hawse, Yorkshire, Zabaglione

Puddle Collect, Dub, Flush, Pant, Plash, Plouter, Plowter, Pool, Sop

Puff(ed), Puffer, Puffy Advertise, Blouse, Blow, Blowfish, Blurb, Bouffant, Breath, Chuff, Chug, Cream, Drag, Encomist, Eulogy, Exsufflicate, Fag, Flaff, Flatus, Fluffy, Fuff, Globe-fish, Grampus, Gust, Hype, Lunt, Pech, Pegh, Pluffy, Plug, Powder, Quilt, Recommend, Skiff, Slogan, Smoke, Steam, Swell, Toke, Twilt, Waff, Waft, Waif, Whiff, Whiffle

Puffin Fratercula, Rockbird, Sea-parrot, Tammie Norie, Tam Noddy

Pug(ilist), Pugilism Belcher, Boxer, Bruiser, Carlin, Fancy, Fistic, Monkey, Ring

Pugnacious Aggressive, Belligerent, Combative, Scrappy

Puke Retch, Sick, Vomit

Pukka Authentic, Genuine, Real, True, Valid

Pulchritude Beauty, Cheese-cake, Grace

Pull (up) Adduce, Attraction, Crane, Drag, Draw, Earn, Force, Haul, Heave, Heeze, Hook, → **INFLUENCE**, Lug, Mousle, Pluck, Rein, Ring, Rove, Rug, Saccade, Sally, Sole, Sool(e), Sowl(e), Stop, Tit, Touse, Touze, Tow, Towse, Towze, Trice, Tug, Undertow, Wrest, Yank

Pulley Block, Capstan, Idle(r), Jack-block, Swig, Trice, Trochlea, Truckle

Pullover Jersey, Jumper, Sweater, Sweatshirt, Tank-top, Windcheater

Pullulate Teem

▶ **Pull up** *see* **PULL**

Pulp Cellulose, Chyme, Chymify, Crush, Flong, Gloop, Kenaf, Marrow, Mash, Mush, Pap, Paste, Pomace, Pound, Puree, Rot, Rubbish, Squeeze, Squidge, Wood

Pulpit(e) Ambo(nes), Lectern, Mimbar, Minbar, Pew, Rostrum, Tent, Tub, Wood

Pulsar Geminga

Pulsate Beat, Palpitate, Quiver, Throb, Vibrate

Pulse Adsuki, Adzuki, Alfalfa, → **BEAN**, Beat, Calavance, Caravance, Chickpea, D(h)al, Dholl, Dicrotic, Fava (bean), Flageolet, Garbanzo, Gram, Groundnut, Ictus, Lentil, Lucerne, Pea, Rhythm, Sain(t)foin, Soy beans, Sphygmic, Sync, Systaltic, Systole, Throb

Pulverise Calcine, Comminute, Contriturate, Demolish, Grind, → **POUND**, Powder

Puma Catamount, Cougar, Mountain lion, Panther

Pummel(ling) Beat, Drub, Fib, Knead, Nevel, Pound, Tapotement, Thump

▷ **Pummelled** *may indicate* an anagram

Pump Air, Bellows, Bicycle, Bowser, Breast, Centrifugal, Chain, Compressor, Cross-question, Diaphragm, Donkey, Drive, Electromagnetic, Elicit, Feed, Filter, Force, Geissler, Grease-gun, Grill, Heart, Heat, Hydropult, Inflate, Interrogate, Knee-swell, Lift, Monkey, Mud, Nodding-donkey, Parish, Petrol, Piston, Pulsometer, Question, Rotary, Scavenge, Shoe, Sodium, Stirrup, Stomach, Suction, Turbine, Vacuum, Water, Wind

Pumpernickel Rye (bread)

Pumphandle Sweep

Pumpkin Butternut, Cashaw, Gourd, Pampoen, Quash, Queensland blue

Pun Calembour, Clinch, Equivoque, Paragram, Paronomasia, Quibble, Quip, Ram, Wordplay

Punch(ed) Antic, Bell, Biff, Blow, Boff, Bolo, Box, Bradawl, Bumbo, Card, Centre, Chad, Check, Chop, Clip, Cobbler's, Conk, Dry-beat, Fib, Fid, Fist(ic), Gang, Glogg, Haymaker, Hit, Hook, Horse, Jab, Key, Kidney, Knevell, Knobble, Knubble, KO, Lander, Mat, Milk, Nail set, Nevel, Nubble, One-er, Overhand, Perforate, Pertuse, Planter's, Plug, Poke, Polt, Pommel, Pounce, Prod, Pummel, Rabbit, Roundhouse, Rum, Rumbo, Slosh, Sock, Steed, Sting(o), Stoush, Sucker, Suffolk, Sunday, Swop, Tape, Upper-cut, Wap, Wind, Zest

Punctilious Exact, Formal, Nice, Particular, Picked, Precise, Prim, Stickler

Punctual(ity) Politesse, Prompt, Regular

Punctuate, Punctuation (mark) Apostrophe, Bracket, Close, Colon, Comma, Duckfoot quote, Emphasize, Guillemet, Interabang, Interrobang, Interrupt, Mark, Semicolon

Puncture(d) Bore, Centesis, Criblé, Cribrate, Deflate, Drill, Flat, Hole, Lumbar, Perforate, Pierce, Pounce, Prick, Scarify, Thoracocentesis

Pundit Egghead, Expert, Guru, Maven, Oracle, Sage, Savant, Swami, Teacher

Pungency, Pungent Acid, Acrid, Acrolein, Alum, Ammonia, Bite, Bitter, Caustic, Hot, Mordant, Nidorous, Piquant, Poignant, Point, Racy, Sair, Salt, Spice, Sting, Tangy, Witty

Punish(ment), Punished, Punishing Algates, Amerce, Attainder, Baffle, Bastinado, Beat, Birch, Brasero, Bum rap, Cane, Capital, Cart, Castigate, Chasten, Chastise, Come-uppance, Commination, Corporal, Correct, Cucking-stool, Dam(nation), Defrock, Desert(s), Detention, → DISCIPLINE, Fatigue, Fine, Flog, Gantlope, Gate, Gauntlet, Gruel, Hellfire, Hiding, Horsing, Hot seat, Imposition, Impot, Interdict, Jankers, Jougs, Keelhaul, Knout, Laldie, Laldy, Lambast(e), Lines, Log, Marmalise, Necklace, Nemesis, Pack-drill, Padre Pio, Pandy, Peine forte et dure, Penalise, Penance, Penology, Pensum, Perdition, Picket, Pillory, Pine, Rap, Reprisal, Retribution, Ruler, Scaffold, Scath, Scourge, Sentence, Serve out, Six of the best, Smack, Smite, Spank, Spif(f)licate, Stocks, Strafe, Straff, Strap, Strappado, Swinge(ing), Talion, Tar and feather, Toco, Toko, Tophet, Treadmill, Trim, Tron, Trounce, Tumbrel, Tumbril, Vice anglais, Visit, War(r)ison, What for, Whip, Wild mare, Ywrake, Ywroke

▷ **Punish** *may indicate* an anagram

Punk Goop, Inferior, Ne'er-do-well, Nobody, Touchwood, Worthless

Punnet Basket, Thug

Punt(er), Punting Antepost, Back, Bet, Gamble, Kent, Kick, Pound, Quant, Turfite, Wager

Puny Frail, Inferior, Petty, Reckling, Runtish, Scram, Shilpit, Sickly, Small, Weak

Pup(py) Cub, Whelp

Pupa Chrysalis, Exarate, Neanic, Nymph, Obtect

Pupil Abiturient, Apple, Apprentice, Boarder, Cadet, Catechumen, Dayboy, Daygirl, Disciple, Etonian, Exit, Eyeball, Follower, Gyte, Junior, L, Monitor, Prefect, Preppy, Protégé(e), Scholar, Senior, Student, Tutee, Ward

▷ **Pupil** *may refer to* an eye

Puppet(s), Puppeteer Bunraku, Creature, Doll, Dummy, Fainéant, Fantoccini, Galanty show, Glove, Guignol, Jack-a-lent, Judy, Mammet, Marionette, Mawmet, Mommet, Motion(-man), Pageant, Pawn, Pinocchio, Promotion, Punch(inello), Quisling, Rod, Tool

Purchase(r), Purchasing Acquisition, Bargain, Buy, Coff, Compulsory, Earn, Emption, Gadsden, Get, Grip, Halliard, Halyard, Hold, Layaway, → LEVERAGE,

Louisiana, Money, Offshore, Oligopsony, Parbuckle, Perquisitor, Secure, Shop, Toehold

Pure, Purity Absolute, Cando(u)r, Cathy, Chaste, Chiarezza, Clean(ly), Cleanness, Cosher, Fine, Glenys, Good, Holy, Immaculate, Incorrupt, Innocent, Intemerate, Inviolate, Kathy, Kosher, Lily, Lilywhite, Maidenhood, Me(a)re, Meer, Net(t), Pristine, Quintessence, Sanctity, Sheer, Simon, Simple, Sincere, Snow-white, Stainless, True, Unalloyed, Undrossy, Vertue, Virgin, Virtue, White

Puree Baba ghanoush, Coulis, Dahl, Dal, Dhal, Fool

Purgative, Purge Aloes, Aloetic, Araroba, Aryanise, Cacoon, Calomel, Cascara, Cassia, Castor-oil, Catharsis, Cholagogue, Colquintida, Croton, Delete, Diacatholicon, Diarrh(o)ea, Drastic, Elaterin, Elaterium, Eliminate, Eluant, Emetic, Enos®, Erase, Evacuant, Exonerate, Expiate, Flux, Gleichschaltung, Hiera-picra, Hydragogue, Ipecacuanha, Ipomoea, Jalap, Jalop, Laxative, McCarthyism, Physic, Picra, Pride's, Relaxant, Scour, Scur, Senna, Soil, Turbith, Turpeth, Wahoo

Purification, Purifier, Purify(ing) Absolve, Bowdlerise, Catharsis, Clay, Clean(se), Depurate, Despumate, Dialysis, Distil, Edulcorate, Elution, Exalt, Expurgate, Filter, Fine, Gas-lime, Green vitriol, Lustre, Lustrum, Niyama, Refine, Retort, Samskara, Sanctify, Scorify, Scrub, Smudging, Try

Puritan(ical) Bible belt, Bluenose, Browne, Digger(s), Ireton, Ironsides, Killjoy, Pi, Pilgrim, Plymouth Colony, Precisian, Prig, Prude, Prynne, Roundhead, Seeker, Strait-laced, Traskite, Waldenses, Wowser, Zealot

Purl(er) Cropper, Eddy, Fall, Knit, Ripple, Stream

Purloin Abstract, Annex, Appropriate, Lift, Nab, Pilfer, Snaffle, Sneak, Steal

Purple Amarantin(e), Amethyst, Assai, Aubergine, Burgundy, Cassius, Chlamys, Claret, Corkir, Cudbear, Dubonnet, Eminence, Golp(e), Heather, Heliotrope, Hyacinthine, Imperial, Indigo, Korkir, Lavender, Lilac, Magenta, Mallow, Mauvin(e), Mulberry, Murrey, Orcein, Orcin(e), Orcinol, Pance, Pansy, Plum, Pompadour, Pontiff, Porporate, Proin(e), Prune, Puce, Puke, Punic, Purpure, Rhodopsin, Royal, Solferino, Tyrian, Violet, Visual

Purport Bear, Claim, Drift, Feck, Mean, Tenor

Purpose(ful) Advertent, Aim, Avail, Calculated, Cautel, Design, Errand, Ettle, Goal, Here-to, Idea, → **INTENT**, Marrow, Mean(ing), Meant, Mint, Motive, Object, Plan, Point, Raison d'être, → **REASON**, Resolution, Resolve, Sake, Telic, Telos, Tenor, Use

Purposeless Dysteleology, Futile, Indiscriminate, Otiose

Purr Curr, Rumble

Purse Ad crumenam, Bag, Bung, Caba, Clutch, Crease, Crumenal, Fisc, Fisk, Long Melford, Mermaid's, Pocket, Prim, Privy, Prize, Public, Pucker, Spleuchan, Sporran, Wallet, Whistle

▷ **Pursed** *may indicate* one word within another

Purslane Sea, Water

Pursue(r), Pursuit Alecto, Business, Chase, Chivvy, Course, Dog, Follow, Follow up, Hobby, Hot-trod, Hound, Hunt, Line, Practice, Practise, Proceed, Prosecute, Quest, Scouring, Stalk, Trivial

Pursuivant Blue Mantle

Purulent Mattery

Purvey(or) Cater, Provide, Provisor, Sell, Supply

Pus Empyema, Matter, Purulence, Quitter, Quittor

Push(er), Push in Airscrew, Barge, Birr, Boost, Bunt, Butt, Detrude, Drive, Edge, Effort, Elbow, Fire, Horn, Hustle, Impulse, Invaginate, Jostle, Motivation, Nose, Nudge, Nurdle, Obtrude, Pitchfork, Plod, Ply, Press, Promote, Propel, Railroad,

Ram, Rush, Sell, Shoulder, → SHOVE, Snoozle, Subtrude, Thrust, Urge

Pushchair Baby Buggy®, Buggy, Stroller, Trundler

Pushover Doddle, Soda

Pusillanimous Coward, Timid, Weak, Weak-kneed, Yellow

Puss(y) Amentum, → CAT, Catkins, Face, Galore, Hare, Malkin, Mouth, Rabbit, Septic

Pussyfoot Dry, Equivocate, Inch, Paw, Steal, TT

Pustule Blotch, Pimple, Pock

Put (off; on; out; up) Accommodate, Add, Alienate, Bet, Cup, Daff, Defer, Dish, Do, Don, Douse, Implant, Impose, Incommode, Inn, Lade, Lay, Locate, Lodge, Lump, Oust, Pit, Place, Plonk, Set, Smore, Snuff, Station, Stow

Put away, Put by Distance, Save, Sheathe, Store, Stow

Put down Abase, Degrade, Demean, Disparage, Floor, Humiliate, Land, Repress, Reprime, Snuff, Write

▷ **Put off** *may indicate* an anagram

Putrefaction, Putrefy(ing), Putrid Addle, Bitter, Corrupt, Decay, Fester, Mephitic, Olid, Rot, Sepsis, Septic

Putter Chug, Club

Putt(ing) Gimme, Gobble, Green, Hash, Pigeon, Sink, → STUPID PERSON

Put together Assemble, Compile, Synthesize

Putty Glaziers', Jewellers', Painters', Plasterers', Polishers'

Puzzle(r) Acrostic, Baffle, Bemuse, Bewilder, Brainteaser, Chinese, Confuse, Conundrum, Crossword, Crux, Egma, Elude, Enigma, Fox, Glaik, Gravel, Intrigue, Jigsaw, Kittle, Logogriph, Magic pyramid, Mind-bender, Monkey, Mystify, Nonplus, Perplex, Ponder, Pose(r), Rebus, Riddle, Rubik's Cube®, Sorites, Sphinx, Stick(l)er, Stump, Tangram, Teaser, Tickler, Wordsearch, Wordsquare

Pygmy Atomy, Dwarf, Negrillo, Negrito, Pyknic, Thumbling

Pyjamas Baby-doll, Churidars, Jimjams

Pyramid Cheops, Chephren, Frustum, Magic, Population, Stack, Teocalli

Pyre Bale(-fire), Bonfire, Brasero, Darga, Gha(u)t

Pyrenean Basque

Pyrites Arsenical, Cockscomb, Copper, Fool's gold, Iron, Magnetic, Mispickel, Mundic, Spear, White

Pyrotechnics Arson, Fireworks

Pyroxene Aegirine, Aegirite, Diopside

Pyrus Service-tree

Pythagoras Samian

Pythian (seat) Delphic, Tripod

Python Anaconda, Diamond, Kaa, Monty, → SNAKE, Zombi(e)

Qq

Q Koppa, Quebec, Question
QC Silk
Qua As
Quack Charlatan, Crocus, Dulcamara, Empiric, Fake, Homeopath, → **IMPOSTOR**, Katerfelto, Mountebank, Pretender, Saltimbanco
Quad(rangle) Close, Complete, Compluvium, Court, Em, En, Horse, Pane
Quadrilateral Lambeth, Tetragon, Trapezium, Trapezoid
Quadrille Dance, Lancers, Matador(e), Pantalon
Quaff Carouse, Drink, Imbibe
Quagmire Bog, Fen, Imbroglio, Marsh, Morass, Swamp, Wagmoire
Quahog Clam
Quail Asteria, Bevy, Bird, Blench, Bob-white, Button, Caille, Colin, Flinch, Harlot, Hen, Quake, Shrink, Tremble
Quaint Cute, Naive, Odd, Old-world, Picturesque, Strange, Twee, Wham, Whim(sy)
Quake(r), Quaking Aminadab, Broad-brim, Dither, Dodder, Fox, Friend, Fry, Hicksite, Obadiah, Penn, Quail, Seism, Shake(r), Shiver, → **TREMBLE**, Tremor, Trepid
Qualification, Qualified, Qualify Able, Adapt, Adverb, Capacitate, Caveat, Competent, Condition, Credential, Degree, Diplomatic, Entitle, Fit, Graduate, Habilitate, Higher Still, Meet, Modifier, Nisi, Pass, Past-master, Proviso, Restrict, Temper, Versed
Quality Aroma, Attribute, Body, Calibre, Cast, Charisma, Esse, Essence, Fabric, Fame, First water, Five-star, Flavour, Grade, Inscape, It, Kite-mark, Letter, Long suit, Mystique, Nature, Pitch, Plus, Premium, Primary, Property, Q, Quale, Reception, Savour, Sort, Standard, Stature, Style, Substance, Suchness, Thew, Thisness, Timbre, Tone, Total, Up-market, Vinosity, Virgin, Virtu(e), Water, Worth
Qualm Compunction, Misgiving, Scruple
Quandary Dilemma, Fix, Predicament, Trilemma
Quantity → **AMOUNT**, Analog(ue), Batch, Bundle, Capacity, Deal, Dose, Feck, Fother, Hank, Hundredweight, Idempotent, Intake, Jag, Lock, Lot, Mass, Measure, Melder, Myriad, Nonillion, Number, Ocean(s), Operand, Parameter, Parcel, Peck, Plenty, Posology, Pottle, Qs, Qt, Quire, Quota, Quotient, Ream, Scalar, Slather, Slew, Slue, Sum, Surd, Tret, Unknown, Vector, Warp, Whips
Quantum Graviton, Isospin, Phonon, Photon, Roton
Quarantine Isolate, Lazarette
Quark Flavo(u)r, Strange
Quarrel(some) Affray, Aggress, Altercate, Arrow, Barney, Barratry, Barretry, Bate, Bicker, Brabble, Brattle, Brawl, Breach, Breeze, Broil, Brulyie, Brulzie, Bust-up, Cagmag, Cantankerous, Carraptious, Cat and dog, Caterwaul, Chance-medley, Chide, Clash, Combative, Contretemps, Difference, Disagree, Dispute, Domestic, Dust-up, Eristic, Estrangement, Exchange, Fall out, Feisty, Fracas, Fractious,

Fratch(et)y, Fray, Hassle, Issue, Jar, Loggerheads, Outcast, Outfall, Pugnacious, Ragbolt, Row, Spat, Squabble, Tiff, Tile, Tink, Vendetta, Wap, Whid, Wrangle

Quarry, Quarry face Chalkpit, Chase, Currie, Curry, Game, Heuch, Mine, Pit, Prey, Scabble, Scent, Stone pit, Victim

Quart Winchester

Quarter(ing), Quarters Airt, Barrio, Billet, Canton(ment), Casbah, Casern(e), Chinatown, Clemency, Close, Coshery, District, Dorm, E, Empty, Enclave, Fardel, Farl, First, Fo'c'sle, Forecastle, Forpet, Forpit, Fourth, Ghetto, Ham(s), Harbour, Haunch, Last, Latin, Medina, → **MERCY**, N, Note, Oda, Pity, Point, Principium, Quadrant, Region, S, Season, Sector, Tail, Trimester, W, Wardroom, Warp, Winter

Quarter-day LD

▷ **Quarterdeck** *may indicate* a suit of cards

Quartet Foursome, Mess, String, Tetrad

Quarto Crown, Demy, Foolscap, Imperial, Medium, Royal, Small

Quartz Agate, Amethyst, Bristol diamond, Buhrstone, Cacholong, Cairngorm, Chalcedony, Chert, Citrine, Flint, Granophyre, Itacolumite, Jasp(er), Morion, Onyx, Plasma, Prase, Rainbow, Rose, Rubasse, Sapphire, Silex, Silica, Smoky, Spanish topaz, Stishovite, Tiger-eye, Tonalite, Whin Sill

Quash Abrogate, Annul, Nullify, Quell, Rebut, Recant, Scotch, Subdue, Suppress, Terminate, Void

Quaver(ing) Shake, Tremulous, Trill, Vibrate, Warble

Quay Bund, Levee, Wharf

Queasy Delicate, Nauseous, Squeamish

Quebec Q

Queen(ly) Adelaide, African, Alcestis, Alexandra, Anna, Anne, Artemesia, Atossa, Balkis, Beauty, Bee, Begum, Bess, Boadicea, Boudicca, Brunhild(e), Camilla, Candace, Card, Caroline, Cleopatra, Closet, Clytemnestra, Coatcard, Dido, Drag, Drama, Eleanor(a), Ellery, Ena, ER, Esther, FD, Gertrude, Guinevere, Hatshepset, Hatshepsut, Hecuba, Helen, Hera, Here, Hermione, Hippolyta, HM, Isabel, Isabella, Ishtar, Isolde, Jocasta, Juno, King, Leda, Maam, Mab, Maeve, Marie Antoinette, Mary, Matilda, May, Medb, Mobled, Monarch, Nance, Nefertiti, Omphale, Pance, Pansy, Parr, Paunce, Pawnce, Pearly, Penelope, Persephone, Phaedra, Prince, Prom, Proserpina, Qu, R, Ranee, Rani, Regal, Regina(l), Sara, Semiramis, Sheba, Sultana, Titania, Vashti, Victoria, Virgin, Warrior

Queen Anne Mrs Morley

Queer(ness) Abnormal, Berdash, Bizarre, Crazy, Cure, Curious, Fey, Fie, Fifish, Gay, Nance, Nancy, → **ODD**, Outlandish, Peculiar, Pervert, Poorly, Quaint, Rum, Spoil, Uranism, Vert

Quell Alegge, Allay, Calm, Quiet, Repress, Subdue, Suppress

Quench Assuage, Cool, Extinguish, Satisfy, Slake, Slo(c)ken, Sta(u)nch, Yslake

▶ **Query** *see* **QUESTION**

Quest Goal, Graal, Grail, Hunt, Pursuit, Search, Venture

Question(ing), Questionnaire Appose, Ask, Bi-lateral, Burning, Catechise, Chin, Contest, Conundrum, Cross-examine, Debrief, Dichotomous, Direct, Dispute, Dorothy Dixer, Doubt, Erotema, Eroteme, Erotesis, Examine, Fiscal, Good, Grill, Heckle, Homeric, Impeach, Impugn, Indirect, Information, Innit, Interpellation, Interrogate, Interview, Koan, Leading, Loaded, Maieutic, Matter, Open, Oppugn, Peradventure, Pop, Pose, Previous, Probe, Problem, Pump, Q, Qu, Quaere, Quiz, Rapid-fire, Refute, Rhetorical, Riddle, Speer, Speir, Survey, Suspect, Tag, Teaser, Tickler, Vexed, West Lothian, WH, What, Worksheet

Questionable Ambiguous, Dubious, Fishy, Socratic

Question-master Interrogator, Socrates, Torquemada, Ximenes

Queue Braid, Breadline, Cercus, Crocodile, Cue, Dog, File, Kale, → **LINE**, Pigtail, Plait, Plat, Stack, Tail(back), Track

Quibble(r), Quibbling Balk, Carp, Carriwitchet, Casuist, Cavil, Chicaner, Dodge, Elenchus, Equivocate, Hairsplitting, Nitpick, Pedantry, Pettifoggery, Prevaricate, Pun, Quiddity, Quillet, Quirk, Sophist

Quiche Flan, Tart

Quick(en), Quickening, Quicker, Quickie, Quickly, Quickness Accelerate, Acumen, Adroit, Agile, Alive, Allegr(ett)o, Animate, Apace, Breakneck, Breathing, Brisk, Celerity, Chop-chop, Citigrade, Cito, Con moto, Core, Cracking, Cuticle, Dapper, Deft, Enliven, Existent, Expeditious, Express, Fastness, Festination, Foothot, Gleg, Hasten, Hie, High-speed, Hotfoot, Impulsive, Jiffy, Keen, Lickety-split, Living, Mercurial, Meteoric, Mistress, Mosso, Nailbed, Nimble, Nippy, Nooner, Pdq, Piercing, Piu mosso, Post-haste, Prestissimo, Presto, Prompt, Pronto, Rapid, Rath(e), Ready, Rough and ready, Schnell, Sharp, Skin, Slippy, Smart, Snappy, Snort, Sodain(e), Soon, Spry, Streamline, Stretta, Stretto, Sudden, Swift, Swith, Tout de suite, Trice, Up tempo, Veloce, Vital, Vite, Vivify, Wikiwiki, Yare

Quicksand Flow, Syrtis

Quicksilver Mercury

Quid Chaw, Chew, L, Nicker, Oner, Plug, Pound, Quo, Sov, Tertium, Tobacco

Quid pro quo Mutuum, Tit-for-tat

Quiescence, Quiescent Calm, Di(o)estrus, Inactive, Inert, Latent, Still

Quiet(en), Quietly Accoy, Allay, Appease, Barnacle, Calm, Compose, Conticent, Doggo, Ease, Easeful, Easy, Encalm, Entame, Gag, Grave, Kail, Laconic, Loun(d), Low, Lown(d), Low-profile, Lull, Meek, Mezzo voce, Mp, Muffle, Mute, P, Pacify, Pauciloquent, Pause, Peace, Piano, Pipe down, Plateau, QT, Reserved, Reticent, Sedate, Settle, Sh, Shtoom, Shtum, Silence, Sitzkrieg, Sly, Sober, Soothe, Sotto voce, Still, Stum(m), Subact, Subdued, Tace, Taciturn, Tranquil, Wheesht, Whish, Whisht, Whist

Quill Calamus, Feather, Float, Plectre, Plectron, Plectrum, Plume, Remex

Quillwort Isoetes

Quilt(ed), Quilting Comfort(er), Continental, Counterpane, Cover, Crazy, Doona®, Duvet, Echo, Eiderdown, Futon, Kantha, Matel(l)asse, Patch(work), Puff, Trapunto

Quince Bael, Bel, Bengal, Bhel, Flowering, Japanese, Japonica

Quinine China, Crown-bark, Kina, Quina, Tonic

Quinsy Angina, Cynanche, Garget, Squinancy

Quintessence, Quintessential Classic, Heart, Pith

Quintet Pentad, Trout

Quip Carriwitchet, Crack, Epigram, Gibe, Jest, Jibe, Joke, Taunt, Zinger

Quirk Concert, Foible, Idiosyncrasy, Irony, Kink, Mannerism, Twist

Quisling Collaborator, Traitor

Quit(s) Abandon, Absolve, Ap(p)ay, Cease, Desert, Even(s), Go, Leave, Meet, Resign, → **STOP**

Quite Actually, All, Ap(p)ay, Clean, Dead, Enough, Enow, Fairly, Fully, Mezzo, Precisely, Real, Right, Sheer, Very

Quiver(ing) Aspen, Quake, Shake, Sheath, The yips, Tremble, Tremolo, Tremor, Tremulate, Trepid, Vibrant, Vibrate, Wobble

Qui vive Go-go

Quixote, Quixotic Don, Errant, Impractical

Quiz Bandalore, Bee, Catechism, Examine, Interrogate, I-spy, Mastermind, Oddity,

Probe, Pump, Question, Smoke, Trail, Yo-yo

Quizzical Askance, Curious, Derisive, Odd, Queer, Socratic

Quod Can, Clink, Jail, Prison

Quoit Disc(us), Disk, Ring

Quondam Once, Sometime, Whilom

Quorum Minyan

Quota Numerus clausus, Proportion, Ration, Share

Quotation, Quote(d), Quote Adduce, Citation, Cite, Co(a)te, Duckfoot, Epigraph, Evens, Extract, Forward, Instance, Name, Price, Recite, Reference, Say, Scare, Soundbite, Tag, Verbatim, Wordbite

Quoth Co, Said

Quotient Achievement, Intelligence, Kerma, Quaternion, Ratio, Respiratory

Rr

R Arithmetic, Dog letter, King, Queen, Reading, Recipe, Right, Romeo, Run, Writing

Rabbi Dayan, Mashgiah, Rav, Rebbe

Rabbit Angora, Astrex, Brer, British Lop, Buck, Bun(ny), Chat, Con(e)y, Cottontail, Daman, Dassie, Doe, Earbash, Harp, Haver, Hyrax, Jabber, Jack, Jaw, Klipdas, Long White, Lop-eared, Marmot, Muff, Nest, Novice, Oarlap, Palaver, Patzer, Prate, Rattle, Rex, Rock, Sage, Snowshoe, Tapeti, Terricole, Waffle, Welsh, White, Witter, Yak, Yap, Yatter

Rabble, Rabble-rousing Canaille, Clamjamphrie, Clanjamfray, Colluvies, Crowd, Demagoguery, Doggery, Galère, Herd, Hoi-polloi, Horde, Legge, Meinie, Mein(e)y, Menyie, Mob, Raffle, Rag-tag, Rascaille, Rascal, Riff-raff, Rout, Scaff-raff, Shower, Tag, Tagrag

Rabelaisian Pantagruel, Panurge

Rabid, Rabies Extreme, Frenzied, Hydrophobia, Lyssa, Mad, Raging, Virulent

Raccoon Coati, Panda, Procyon

Race(course), Racing, Race meeting Aintree, Alpine, Ancestry, Arms, Ascot, Autocross, Bathtub, Belt, Boat, Boskop, Breed, Broose, Brouze, Bumping, Cambridgeshire, Career, Catadrome, Catterick, Caucus, Cesarewitch, Chantilly, Chase, Claiming, Classic, Comrades, Cone, Contest, Corso, Country, Course, Current, Cursus, Cyclo-cross, Dash, Derby, Doggett's Coat and Badge, Dogs, Doncaster, Drag, Dromos, Egg and spoon, Enduro, Epsom, Event, F1, Fastnet, Flapping, Flat, Flow, Formula One, Fun-run, Generation, Ginger, Goodwood, Grand National, Grand Prix, Guineas, Handicap, Hare and hounds, Harness, Herrenvolk, Hialeah, High hurdles, Hippodrome, Human(kind), Hurdles, Hurry, Inca, Indy, Indy car, Kermesse, Kind, Lampadedromy, Lampadephoria, Leat, Leet, Leger, Le Mans, Lick, Lignage, Line(age), Longchamps, Madison, Man, Marathon, Master, Meets, Mile, Motocross, Nascar, → NATIONAL, Newmarket, Nursery, Nursery stakes, Oaks, Obstacle, One-horse, Paceway, Palio, Paper chase, Pattern, Picnic, Plate, Pluck, Point-to-point, Potato, Pre-Dravidian, Prep, Pursuit, Rallycross, Rallying, Rapids, Rat, Redcar, Regatta, Relay, Rill, Rod, Ronne, Roost, Run-off, Sack, St Leger, Scramble, Scratch, Scud, Scurry, Seed, Selling, Shan, Sheep, Slalom, Slipstream, Sloot, Slot-car, Sluit, Smock, Speedway, Sprint, Stakes, Steeplechase, Stem, Stirp(s), Stirpes, Stock, Strain, Streak, Strene, Supermoto, Sweepstake, Tail, Taste, Tear, Thousand Guineas, Three-legged, Tide, Torch, Torpids, Towcester, Tribe, Trotting, TT, Turf, Two-horse, Two Thousand Guineas, Velodrome, Volsungs, Walking, Walk-over, Waterway, Welter, Wetherby, Whid, White, Wincanton

Racehorse, Racer Eclipse, Filly, Go-kart, Hare, Maiden, Novice, Plater, Red Rum, Steeplechaser, Trotter

Raceme Corymb, Panicle

Racial (area), Racialist Apartheid, Colour, Ethnic, Ghetto, National Front, Quarter

Rack Agonise, Bin, Cloud, Cratch, Drier, Flake, Frame, Hack, Hake, Heck, Pipe,

Plate, Pulley, Roof, Stretcher, Toast, Torment, Torture, Touse, Towse

Racket(eer) Bassoon, → **BAT**, Battledore, Bloop, Brattle, Caterwaul, Chirm, Clamour, Crime, Deen, Din, Discord, Earner, → **FIDDLE**, Gyp, Hubbub, Hustle, → **NOISE**, Noisiness, Protection, Ramp, Rort, Sokaiya, Stridor, Swindle, Tumult, Uproar, Utis

Racy Ethnic, Piquant, Pungent, Ribald, Salty, Spicy, Spirited

Rad Rem

Radar Acronym, Angel, AWACS, Beacon, DEW line, Doppler, Gadget, Gee, Gull, Lidar, Loran, Monopulse, Navar, Rebecca-eureka, Shoran, Surveillance, Teleran®, Tracking

Raddle Hurdle, Ochre, Red

Radial Osteal, Quadrant, Rotula, Spoke, Tire, Tyre

Radiance, Radiant Actinic, Aglow, Aureola, Beamish, Brilliant, Gleam(y), Glory, Glow, Happy, Lustre, Refulgent, Shechina, Sheen, Shekinah

Radiate, Radiating, Radiation, Radiator Actinal, Adaptive, Air-colour, Beam, Bremsstrahlung, Cavity, Characteristic, C(h)erenkov, Disseminate, Dosimetry, Effuse, Emanate, Emit, Exitance, Fluorescence, Gamma, Glow, Hawking, Heater, Infrared, Insolation, Ionizing, Isohel, Laser, Millirem, Non-ionizing, Pentact, Photon, Pulsar, Quasar, Rem(s), Rep, Roentgen, → **SHINE**, Sievert, Soft, Spherics, Spoke, Stellate, Stray, SU, Sun, Synchrotron, Terrestrial, Ultra violet, UVA, UVB, Van Allen, Visible

Radical Acetyl, Allyl, Amide, Ammonium, Amyl, Aryl, Benzil, Benzoyl, Bolshevist, Bolshie, Butyl, Calumba, Carbene, Cetyl, Drastic, Dyad, Ester, Extreme, Free, Fundamental, Gauchist, Genre-busting, Glyceryl, Glycosyl, Hydroxy, Innate, Isopropyl, Jacobin, Leftist, Leveller, Ligand, Maximalist, Methyl, Montagnard, Nitryl, Oxonium, Parsnip, Phenyl, Phosphonium, Pink, Propyl, Red, Revolutionary, Rhizocaul, Root, Rudiment, Sulfone, Sulphone, Trot(sky), Uranyl, Vinyl, Whig, Xylyl

Radio Bluetooth, Boom-box, Cat's whisker, CB, Cellular, Citizen's band, Cognitive, Community, Crystal set, Digital, Ether, Gee, Ghetto-blaster, Local, Loudspeaker, Marconigraph, Receiver, Rediffusion®, Reflex, Rig, Set, Simplex, Sound, Steam, Talk, Talkback, Tranny, Transceiver, Transistor, Transmitter, Transponder, Walkie-talkie, Walkman®, Walky-talky, Wireless

Radioactive, Radioactivity Actinide, Americium, Astatine, Autinite, Bohrium, Cobalt 60, Emanation, Fall-out, Hot, Nucleonics, Plutonium, Radon, Steam, Thorium, Torbernite, Uranite

Radiogram, Radiograph(y) Cable, Telegram, Venography, Ventriculography, Wire

Radiology Interventional

Radish Charlock, Mooli, Runch

Radium Ra

Radius Bone, Long, Schwarzschild, Short

Radon Rn

Raffia Rabanna

Raffle(s) Burglar, Draw, Lottery, Sweepstake

Raft(ing) Balsa, Carley float, Catamaran, Float, Kon-Tiki, Life, Mohiki, Pontoon, Whitewater

Rafter Barge-couple, Beam, Chevron, Jack, Joist, Principal, Ridge, Spar, Timber

Rag(ged), Rags Bait, Bate, Clout, Coral, Daily, Deckle, Dud(s), Duddery, Duddie, Duster, Fent, Figleaf, Glad, Gutter press, Guyed, Haze, Kid, Lap(pie), Lapje, Mop, → **NEWSPAPER**, Nose, Paper, Red, Remnant, Revel, Rivlins, Roast, Rot, Scabrous, S(c)hmatte, Scold, Scrap, → **SHRED**, Slate, Slut, Splore, Tack, Tat(t),

Tatter(demalion), Tatty, Taunt, → **TEASE**, Tiger, Tongue, Uneven
▷ **Rag(ged)** *may indicate* an anagram
Rage, Raging → **ANGER**, Ardour, Bait, Bate, Bayt, Chafe, Conniption, Explode, Fashion, Fierce, Fit, Fiz(z), Fume, Furibund, Furore, Fury, Gibber, Go, Ire, Mode, Monkey, Paddy(-whack), Passion, Pelt, Pet, Pique, Rabid, Rail, Ramp, Rant, Road, See red, Snit, Storm, Tear, Temper, Ton, Trolley, Utis, Wax, Wrath
Raglan Sleeve
Ragout Compot, Goulash, Haricot, Stew
Rag-picker Bunter
Raid(er) Assault, Attack, Baedeker, Bear, Bodrag, Bust, Camisado, Chappow, Commando, Corporate, Dawn, Do, For(r)ay, Imburst, Incursion, Inroad, Inrush, Invade, Jameson, Maraud, March-treason, Mosstrooper, Pict, Pillage, Plunder, Ram, Ransel, Razzia, Reive, Sack, Scrump, Skrimp, Skrump, Smash-and-grab, Sortie, Spreagh, Storm, Viking
Rail(er), Railing Abuse, Amtrack, Arm, Arris, Balustrade, Ban, Banister, → **BAR**, Barre, Barrier, Bird, Bullhead, Cloak, Communion, Conductor, Coot, Corncrake, Crake, Criticise, Dado, Fender, Fiddle, Fife, Flanged, Flat-bottomed, Flow, Gush, Insult, Inveigh, Light, Live, Metal, Monkey, Neckerchief, Notornis, Parclose, Picture, Pin, Plate, Post, Pulpit, Pushpit, Rack, Rag, Rate, Rave, Rung, Scold, Slang-whang, Slate, Slip, Snash, Sneer, Sora, Soree, Spar, T, Taffrail, Takahe, Taunt, Thersites, Third, Towel, Train, Vituperation, Weka
Raillery Badinage, Banter, Chaff, Persiflage, Sport
Railroad, Railway Aerial, Amtrak, BR, Bulldoze, Cable, Cash, Coerce, Cog, Crémaillère, Dragoon, El, Elevated, Funicular, Gantlet, GWR, Inclined, L, Light, Lines, LMS, LNER, Loop-line, Maglev, Marine, Metro, Monorail, Mountain, Narrow-gauge, Rack, Rack and pinion, Rly, Road, Rollercoaster, Ropeway, ROSCO, Ry, Scenic, Ship, Siding, SR, Stockton-Darlington, Switchback, Telpher-line, Track, Train, Tramline, Tramway, Trans-Siberian, Tube, Underground
Railwayman Driver, Fettler, Gandy dancer, Guard, Locoman, NUR, Stephenson, Stoker, Tracklayer
Raiment Apparel, Clothes, Garb, Ihram
Rain(y), Rainstorm Acid, Brash, Deluge, Drizzle, Flood, Hyad(e)s, Hyetal, Mistle, Mizzle, Oncome, Onding, Onfall, Pelt, Pelter, Piss, Pluviose, Pluvious, Pour, Precipitation, Right, Roke, Scat, Seil, Serein, Serene, Shell, Shower, Sile, Silver thaw, Skiffle, Skit, Smir(r), Smur, Soft, Spat, Spet, Spit, Storm, Thunder-plump, Virga, Weep, Wet, Yellow
Rainbow(-maker) Arc, Arc-en-ciel, Bifrost, Bruise, Dew-bow, Indescence, Iris, Moon-bow, Spectroscope, Sunbow, Sundog, Water-gall, Weather-gall, White
Raincoat Burberry®, Gaberdine, Mac, Mino, Oils(kins), Slicker, Waterproof
Raingauge Ombrometer, Udometer
Rain-maker Indra
Rain tree Saman
Raise(d), Raising Advance, Aggrade, Attollent, Boost, Bouse, Bowse, Build, Cat, Coaming, Cock, Collect, Elate, → **ELEVATE**, Emboss, Enhance, Ennoble, Erect, Escalate, Exalt, Extol, Fledge, Grow, Heave, Heezie, Heft, High, Hike, Hoick, Hoist, Increase, Jack, Key, Leaven, Lift, Mention, Overcall, Perk, Rear, Regrate, Repoussé, Revie, Rouse, Saleratus, Siege, Sky, Snarl, Step-up, Sublimate, Upgrade, Weigh
Rake, Raker, Rakish Casanova, Comb, Corinthian, Croupier, Dapper, Dissolute, Don Juan, Enfilade, Gay dog, Jaunty, Lecher, Libertine, Lothario, Raff, Reprobate, Rip, Roué, Scan, Scour, Scowerer, Scratch, Strafe, Stubble, Swash-buckler, Swinge-buckler, Wagons

Rale Crepitus, Rattle

Rally, Rallying-point Autocross, Autopoint, Badinage, Banter, Demo, Gather, Jamboree, Meeting, Mobilise, Monte Carlo, Muster, Oriflamme, Persiflage, Recover, Rely, Rest, Revive, Risorgimento, Roast, Rouse, Scramble, Spirit

Ralph Imp, Nader, Rackstraw

Ram Aries, Battering, Buck, Bunt, Butt, Butter, Corvus, Crash, Drive, Hidder, Hydraulic, Mendes, Pun, Sheep, Stem, Tamp, Thrust, Tup, Wether

Ramble(r), Rambling Aberrant, Aimless, Digress, Incoherent, Liana, Liane, Rigmarole, Roam, Rose, Rove, Skimble-skamble, Sprawl, Stray, Stroll, Vagabond, Wander

Rameses Pharaoh

Ramp Bank, Gradient, Helicline, Incline, Runway, Slipway, Slope, Speed

Rampage Fury, Spree, Storm, Warpath

Rampant Lionel, Predominant, Profuse, Rearing, Rife

▷ **Rampant** *may indicate* an anagram or a reversed word

Rampart Abat(t)is, Brisure, Butt, Defence, Fortification, Parapet, Terreplein, Vallum, Wall

Ramrod Gunstick

Ramshackle Decrepit, Heath Robinson, Rickety, Rickle

Ranch Bowery, Corral, Dude, Estancia, Farm, Hacienda, Spread, Stump

Rancid Frowy, Reast(y), Reest(y), Reist(y), Sour, Turned

Rancour Gall, Hate, Malice, Resentment, Spite

Rand Border, R, Roon

Random Accidental, Aleatoric, Arbitrary, → **AT RANDOM**, Blind, Casual, Desultory, Fitful, → **HAPHAZARD**, Harvest, Hit-or-miss, Hobnob, Indiscriminate, Scattershot, Sporadic, Stochastic, Stray

▷ **Random(ly)** *may indicate* an anagram

Range(r), Rangy Admiralty, Align, Ambit, Andes, Atlas, AZ, Ballpark, Band, Bowshot, Bushwhack, Capsule, Carry, Cascade, Chain, Cheviot, Compass, Cotswolds, Course, Darling, Diapason, Dispace, Dolomites, Dynamic, Err, → **EXTENT**, Eye-shot, Flinders, Forest, Gamut, Glasgow, Gunshot, Hamersley, Harmonic, Helicon, Himalayas, Home, Interquartile, Ken(ning), Kolyma, Ladakh, Leggy, Limit, Line, Long, Massif, Middleback, → **MOUNT**, Orbit, Oven, Owen Stanley, Palette, Point-blank, Prairie, Purview, Rake, Reach, Register, Repertoire, Rifle, Roam, Rocket, Scale, Scope, Sc(o)ur, Selection, Serra, Shooting, Short, Sierra, Sloane, Spectrum, Sphere, Stanovoi, Stanovoy, Stove, Strzelecki, Tape, Tessitura, Teton, Texas, The Wolds, Tier, Urals, Waldgrave, Wasatch, Waveband, Woomera

Rank(s) Arrant, Assort, Ayatollah, Begum, Brevet, Caste, Category, Cense, Classify, Cornet, Curule, Degree, Dignity, Downright, Earldom, Estate, État(s), Flight sergeant, Grade, Graveolent, Gree, Gross, High, Hojatoleslam, Hojatolislam, Majority, Olid, Parage, Percentile, Place, Range, Rate, Rooty, Row, Seed, Seigniorage, Sergeant, Serried, Shoulder-strap, Sort, Standing, → **STATION**, Status, Substantive, Taxi, Tier, → **TITLE**, Titule, Utter, Viscount

Rankle Chafe, Fester, Gall, Irritate, Nag

Ransack Fish, Loot, Pillage, Plunder, Rifle, Ripe, Rob, Rummage

Ransom King's, Redeem, Release, Rescue

Rant(er), Ranting Bombast, Declaim, Fustian, Ham, Harangue, Rail, Rodomontade, Scold, Slang-whang, Spout, Spruik, Stump, Thunder, Tub-thump

Rap(ped) Blame, Censure, Chat, Clour, Gangsta, Halfpenny, Knock, Ratatat, Shand, Strike, Swapt, Tack, Tap

Rapacious Accipitrine, Esurient, Exorbitant, Greedy, Harpy, Kite, Predatory,

Ravenous, Ravine

Rape Abuse, Assault, Belinda, Cole-seed, Colza, Creach, Creagh, Date, Deflower, Despoil, Gangbang, Grass(line), Hundred, Lock, Lucretia, Navew, Oilseed, Plunder, Ravish, Statutory, Stuprate, Thack, Tow, Violate

Rapid(ity), Rapidly Chute, Dalle, Double-quick, Express, Fast, Meteoric, Mosso, Presto, Pronto, Quick-fire, Riffle, Sault, Shoot, Skyrocket, Speedy, Stickle, Swift, Tantivy, Veloce, Vibrato, Wildfire

Rapier Sword, Tuck

Rappel Abseil

Rapport Accord, Affinity, Agreement, Harmony

Rapprochement Détente, Reconciliation

Rapt Riveted

Raptor Eagle, Kestrel, Osprey, Standgale, Staniel, Stannel, Stanyel, Stooper

Rapture, Rapturous Bliss, → DELIGHT, Ecstasy, Elation, Joy, Trance

Rare, Rarity Blue moon, Curio, Earth, Geason, Infrequent, Intemerate, One-off, Rear, Recherché, Scarce, Seeld, Seld(om), Singular, Thin, → UNCOMMON, Uncooked, Underdone, Unusual

Rarefied Thin

Rascal(ly) Arrant, Bad hat, Cad, Cullion, Cur, Deer, Devil, Gamin, Hallian, Hallion, Hallyon, → KNAVE, Limner, Loon, Losel, Low, Nointer, Rip, Rogue, Scallywag, Scamp, Scapegrace, Schelm, Skeesicks, Skellum, Skelm, Smaik, Spalpeen, Tinker, Toe-rag, Varlet, Varmint, Villain

Rash(ness), Rasher Acne, Bacon, Barber's, Brash, Collop, Daredevil, Eruption, Erysipelas, Exanthem(a), Fast, Foolhardy, Harum-scarum, → HASTY, Headlong, Heat, Hives, Hotspur, Ill-advised, Impetigo, Impetuous, Imprudent, Impulsive, Lardo(o)n, Lichen, Madbrain, Madcap, Miliaria, Morphew, Nappy, Nettle, Outbreak, Overhasty, Pox, Precipitate, Purpura, Reckless, Road, Roseola, Rubella, Sapego, Scarlatina, Serpigo, Spots, Temerity, Tetter, Thoughtless, Unheeding, Unthinking, Unwise, Urticaria

Rasp(er) File, Grate, Odontophore, Radula, Risp, Rub, Scrape, Scroop, Xyster

Raspberry Berate, Black(cap), Boo, Bronx-cheer, Etaerio, Hindberry, Razz

Rastafarian Dread

Rat(s), Ratty Agouta, Bandicoot, Blackleg, Blackneb, Boodie, Brown, Bug-out, Camass, Cane, Cur, Defect, Desert, Fink, Footra, Foutra, Geomyoid, Gym, Heck, Hood, Hydromys, Informer, Kangaroo, Malabar, Mall, Maori, Mole, Moon, Norway, Pack, Pig, Poppycock, Potoroo, Pouched, Pshaw, Pup(py), Renegade, Renegate, Rice, Rink, Rodent, Roland, Rot(ten), Scab, Sewer, Shirty, Squeal, Stinker, Turncoat, Vole, Water, Wharf, Whiskers, White, Wood

Rat-catcher Cat, Ichneumon, Mongoose, Pied Piper

Rate(s), Rating A, Able, Able-bodied, Apgar, Appreciate, Assess, Base, Basic, Birth, Bit, Carpet, Castigate, Cess, Classify, Conception, Cost, Count, Credit, Deserve, Erk, Estimate, Evaluate, Exchange, Grade, Headline, Hearty, Hurdle, Incidence, Interest, ISO, Lapse, Leading, Mate's, Mortality, Mortgage, MPH, Octane, Ordinary, OS, Pace, Penalty, Percentage, PG, Piece, Poor, Prime (lending), Rag, Rebuke, Red, Refresh, Reproof, Rocket, Row, Sailor, Scold, → SET, Slew, → SPEED, Standing, Starting, Surtax, Take-up, TAM, Tariff, Tax, Tempo, Tog, U, Upbraid, Value, Water, Wig, World-scale, X

Rather Assez, Degree, Fairly, Gey, Instead, Lief, Liever, Loor, More, Prefer, Pretty, Some(what), Sooner, Yes

Ratify Amen, Approve, Confirm, Homologate, Pass, Sanction, Validate

Ratio Advance, Albedo, Aspect, Bypass, Cash, Compound, Compression, Cosine,

Distinctiveness, Duplicate, Focal, Fraction, Gear, Golden, Gyromagnetic, Inverse, Liquidity, Loss, Mass, Neper, PE, Pi, Pogson, Poisson's, Position, Price-dividend, Prise-earnings, Proportion, Protection, Quotient, Reserve, Savings, Signal-to-noise, Sin(e), Slip, Space, Tensor, Trigonometric
Ration(s) Allocate, Apportion, Compo, Dole, Étape, Iron, K, Quota, Restrict, Scran, Share, Short commons, Size
Rational(ism), Rationalisation A posteriori, Descartes, Dianoetic, Level-headed, Logical, Lucid, Matter-of-fact, Sane, Sensible, Sine, Sober, Tenable, Wice
Rationale Motive
Rattle (box), Rattling Chatter, Clack, Clank, Clap, Clatter, Clitter, Conductor, Crescelle, Crotalaria, Death, Demoralise, Disconcert, Gas-bag, Hurtle, Jabber, Jangle, Jar, Maraca, Natter, Nonplus, Rale, Rap, Red, Reel, Rhonchus, Ruckle, Sabre, Shake, Sistrum, Sunn, Tirl, Upset, Yellow
Raucous Guttural, Hoarse, Loud, Strident
Ravage Depredation, Desecrate, Despoil, Havoc, Pillage, Prey, Ruin, Sack, Waste
Rave, Raving Boil, Enthuse, Praise, Redwood, Redwud, Storm, Ta(i)ver, Tear
Ravel Disentangle, Explain, Fray, Involve, Snarl, Tangle
Raven(ous) Black, Corbel, Corbie, Corvine, Croaker, Daw, Grip, Hugin, Munin, Unkindness, Wolfish
Ravine Arroyo, Barranca, Barranco, Canada, Canyon, Chasm, Chine, Clough, Coulée, Couloir, Dip, Flume, Ghyll, Gorge, Goyle, Grike, Gulch, Gully, Kedron, Khor, Khud, Kidron, Kloof, Lin(n), Nal(l)a, Nallah, Nulla(h), Pit
Ravish Constuprate, Debauch, Defile, Devour, Rape, Stuprate, Transport, Violate
Raw Brut, Chill, Coarse, Crude, Crudy, Damp, Fresh, Greenhorn, Natural, Recruit, Rude, Uncooked, Wersh
Raw-boned Gaunt, Lanky, Lean, Randle-tree
Ray(s), Rayed Actinic, Alpha, Beam, Beta, Canal, Cathode, Cosmic, Cramp-fish, Death, Delta, Devil, Diactine, Dun-cow, Eagle, Electric, Extraordinary, Fish, Gamma, Grenz, Guitarfish, Homelyn, Manta, Medullary, Monactine, Numbfish, Ordinary, Polyact, Positive, R, Radius, Re, Roentgen, Roker, Röntgen, Sawfish, Sea-devil, Sea-vampire, Sephen, Shaft, Skate, Starburst, Stick, Sting, Stingaree, Tetract, Thornback, Torpedo, Vascular
Rayon Acetate, Faille, Viscose
Raze Annihilate, Bulldoze, Demolish, Destroy, Level
Razor(-maker) Cut-throat, Occam, Safety, Straight
Razorbill Murre
Razor-fish Solen
Razz Raspberry
RE Sappers
Re About, Rhenium, Touching
Reach(ed) Ar(rive), Attain, Boak, Boke, Carry, Come, Get out, Hent, Hit, Key-bugle, Lode, Octave, Peak, Raught, Rax, Retch, Ryke, Seize, Stretch, Touch, Win
Reach-me-downs Slop-clothing
React(or), Reaction(ary) Addition, Allergy, Anaphylaxis, Answer, Backlash, Backwash, Behave, Blimp, Blowback, Bourbon, Breeder, Bristle, Bummer, CANDU, Catalysis, Chain, Chemical, Converter, Convertor, Core, Counterblast, Dark, Dibasic, Diehard, Diels-Adler, Dinosaur, Double-take, Dounreay, Exoergic, Falange, Fast(-breeder), Feedback, Fission, Flareback, Flehmen, Furnace, Fusion, Gas-cooled, Graphite, Gut, Heavy-water, Hydrolysis, Imine, Incomplete, Insulin, Interplay, Junker, Kickback, Knee-jerk, Light, Magnox, Neanderthal, Nuclear, Outcry, Oxidation, Pebble-bed, Photolysis, Pile, Poujade,

Pressure-tube, Pressurized water, Reciprocate, Recoil, Redox, Repercussion, Respond, Reversible, Rigid, Sensitive, Solvolysis, Spallation, Sprocket, Swing-back, Thermal, Thermonuclear, Tokamak, Topochemistry, Ultraconservative, Vaccinia, Wassermann, Water

▷ **Reactionary** *may indicate* reversed or an anagram

Read(ing) Bearing, Browse, Decipher, Decode, Exegesis, First, Grind, Grounden, Haftarah, Haphtarah, Haphtorah, Interpret, Learn, Lection, Lesson, Lu, Maftir, Maw, Paired, Pericope, Peruse, Pore, Rad, Rennet-bag, Scan, Second, See, Skim, Solve, Speed, Stomach, → **STUDY**, Third, Vell, Ycond

Reader(s) ABC, Academic, Alidad(e), Bookworm, Document, Editor, Epistoler, Homeridae, Lay, Lector, Primer, Silas Wegg, Tape, Taster

Readiest, Readily, Readiness, Ready Alacrity, Alamain, Alert, Amber, Apt, Atrip, Available, Boun, Bound, Brass, Cash, Conditional, Dough, Eager, Early, Eftest, Fettle, Fit, Forward, Game, Geared-up, Gelt, Go, Keyed, Latent, Lolly, Masterman, Money, On, Predy, Prepared, Present, Prest, Primed, Prompt, Promptitude, Reckoner, Ripe, Running costs, Set, Soon, Spot, Turnkey, Usable, Wherewithal, Willing, Yare, Yark

Readjust Mend, Regulate, Retrue

Readymade Bought, Precast, Prepared, Prêt-à-porter, Slops, Stock, Store

Reagent Analytical, Grignard, Ninhydrin, Reactor, Schiff's, Titrant

Real, Reality, Realities, Really Actual, Augmented, Bona-fide, Brass tacks, Coin, Deed, De facto, Dinkum, Dinky-di(e), Earnest, Echt, Ens, Entia, Entity, Essence, → **GENUINE**, Honest, Indeed, Mackay, McCoy, McKoy, Naive, Ontic, Positive, Quite, Royal, Simon Pure, Sooth, Sterling, Straight up, Substantial, Tangible, Tennis, Thingliness, True, Verismo, Verity, Very, Virtual

Realgar Rosaker, Zarnec, Zarnich

Realise, Realisation, Realism, Realistic Achieve, Attain, Attuite, Cash, Dirty, Down-to-earth, Embody, Encash, Fetch, Fruition, Fulfil, Learn, Lifelike, Magic, Naive, Practical, Pragmatism, Sell, Sense, Socialist, Suss, Understand, Verité

▶ **Realities, Reality** *see* **REAL**

Realm Domain, Dominion, Field, Kingdom, Land, Notogaea, Region, Special(i)ty, UK

Ream Bore, Foam, Froth, Paper, Printer's, Rime, Screed

Reap(er) Binder, Crop, Death, Earn, Gather, Glean, Harvest, Scythe, Shear, Sickleman, Solitary, Stibbler

Reappear(ance) Emersion, Materialise, Recrudesce

Rear(ing) Aft, Back(side), Background, Baft, Behind, Breeches, Bring-up, Bunt, Cabré, Catastrophe, Derrière, Empennage, Foster, Haunch, Hind, Hindquarters, Loo, Natch, Nousell, Nurture, Prat, → **RAISE**, Serafile, Serrefile, Stern, Tonneau

Rearmament Moral

Rearrange(ment) Adjust, Anagram, Ectopia, Permute, Reorder

Reason(able), Reasoning A fortiori, Analytical, Apagoge, A priori, Argue, Argument, Basis, Call, Casuistry, Cause, Colour, Consideration, Deduce, Economical, Expostulate, Fair, Ground(s), Hypophora, Ijtihad, Inductive, Intelligent, Ipso facto, Justification, Logic, Logical, Logistics, Logos, Metamathematics, Mind, Moderate, Motive, Noesis, Petitio principii, Plausible, Point, Practical, Pretext, Pro, Proof, Pure, Purpose, Ratiocinate, Rational(e), Sanity, Sense, Sensible, Settler, Syllogism, Synthesis, Temperate, Think, Why, Wit

Reave Despoil, Reif, Rob, Spoil

Rebate Diminish, Lessen, Refund, Repayment

Rebecca Sharp

Rebel(s), Rebellion, Rebellious Aginner, Apostate, Arian, Beatnik, Bolshy, Boxer, Cade, Contra, Croppy, Danton, Defiance, Diehard, Disobedient, Emeute, Fifteen, Forty-five, Frondeur, Glendower, Green Mountain Boys, Hampden, Hereward the Wake, Iconoclast, Insurgent, Insurrection, IRA, Jacobite, Jacquerie, Kick, Luddite, Mutine(er), Mutiny, Oates, Pilgrimage of Grace, Putsch, Rebecca, Recalcitrant, Recusant, Reluct, Resist, → REVOLT, Rise, Rum, Scofflaw, Sedition, Sepoy, Spartacus, Steelboy, Straw, Taiping, Ted, Titanism, Tyler, Venner, Warbeck, Wat Tyler, Whiteboy, Zealot
▷ **Rebellious** *may indicate* a word reversed
Rebirth Palingenesis, Reincarnation, Renaissance, Revival, Samsara
Rebound Backfire, Bounce, Cannon, Elastic, Recoil, Repercussion, Ricochet, Snapback
Rebuff Check, Cold-shoulder, Noser, Quelch, Repulse, Retort, Rubber, Setdown, Sneb, Snib, Snub
Rebuke Admonish, Berate, Check, Chide, Earful, Lecture, Neb, Objurgate, Rap, Rate, Razz, Reprimand, Reproof, Reprove, Rollick, Scold, Score, Slap, Slate, Snib, Snub, Strop, Threap, Threep, Tick off, Trim, Tut, Upbraid, Wig
Rebut Disprove, Refute, Repulse, Retreat
Recalcitrant Mulish, Obstinate, Renitent, Unruly, Wilful
Recall(ing) Annul, Echo, Eidetic, Encore, Evocative, Partial, Reclaim, Recollect, Redolent, Remember, Remind, Reminisce, Repeal, Retrace, Revoke, Total, Unsay, Withdraw
Recant(ation) Disclaim, Palinode, Retract, Revoke
Recap(itulate), Recapitulation Epanodos, Summarise
Recapture Rescue
▷ **Recast** *may indicate* an anagram
▶ **Recce** *see* RECONNAISSANCE
Recede Decline, Ebb, Lessen, Regress, Retrograde, Shrink, Withdraw
Receipt(s) Acknowledge, Chit, Docket, Quittance, Recipe, Revenue, Take, Voucher
Receive(d), Receiver Accept, Accoil, Admit, Aerial, Antenna, Assignee, Bailee, Bleeper, Dipole, Dish, Donee, Ear, Fence, Get, Grantee, Greet, Hydrophone, Inherit, Intercom, Official, Pernancy, Phone, Pocket, Radio, Reset, Responser, Responsor, Roger, Set, Sounder, Take, Tap, Transistor, Transponder, Wide
Recent(ly) Alate, Current, Fresh, Hot, Just, Late, Low, Modern, New, Yesterday, Yestereve, Yesterweek
Receptacle Ash-tray, Basket, Bin, Bowl, Box, Chrismatory, Ciborium, Container, Cyst, Hell-box, Locket, Loom, Monstrance, Receiver, Reliquary, Relique, Reservatory, Sacculus, Spermatheca, Tank, Thalamus, Tidy, Tore, Torus, Trash can
Reception, Receptive Accoil, At home, Bel-accoyle, Couchée, Court, Durbar, Entertainment, Greeting, Helpdesk, Infare, Kursaal, Levée, Open, Ovation, Pervious, Ruelle, Saloon, Sensory, Soirée, Superheterodyne, Teleasthetic, Warm, Welcome
Receptor(s) Metabotropic, Steroid
Recess(ion) Alcove, Antrum, Apse, Apsidal, Apsis, Bay, Bole, Bower, Break, Closet, Columbarium, Corner, Corrie, Cove, Croze, Dinette, Ebb, Embrasure, Exedra, Fireplace, Grotto, Hitch, Inglenook, Interval, Loculus, Mortise, → NICHE, Nook, Oriel, Outshot, Rabbet, Rebate, Respite, Rest, Slump, Withdrawal
▷ **Recess** *may indicate* 'reversed'
Rechabite TT
Réchauffé Hachis, Hash, Salmi
Recidivist Relapser

▷ **Recidivist** *may indicate* 'reversed'

Recipe Dish, Formula, Prescription, R, Receipt, Take

Recipient Assignee, Beneficiary, Disponee, Grantee, Heir, Legatee, Receiver, Suscipient

Reciprocal, Reciprocate Corresponding, Elastance, Exchange, Inter(act), Mutual, Repay, Return

Recite(r), Recital, Recitation(ist) Ave, Concert, Declaim, Diseuse, Enumerate, Incantation, Litany, Monologue, Mystic, Parlando, Quote, Reading, Reel, Relate, Rhapsode, Say, Sing, Tell

Reckless(ness) Blindfold, Careless, Catiline, Desperado, Desperate, Devil-may-care, Gadarene, Harum-scarum, Hasty, Headfirst, Headlong, Hell-bent, Irresponsible, Madcap, Perdu(e), Ramstam, Rantipole, → **RASH**, Slapdash, Temerity, Ton-up, Wanton, Wildcat

▷ **Reckless** *may indicate* an anagram

Reckon(ing) Assess, Bet, Calculate, Cast, Census, Computer, Consider, Count, Date, Doomsday, Estimate, Fancy, Figure, Guess, Number, Rate, Settlement, Shot, Tab

Reclaim(ed), Reclamation Assart, Empolder, Impolder, Innings, Novalia, Polder, Recover, Redeem, Restore, Swidden, Tame, Thwaite

Recline, Reclining Accubation, Accumbent, Lean, Lie, Lounge, Rest

Recluse Anchor(et), Anchorite, Ancress, Eremite, Hermit, Solitaire

Recognise(d), Recognition Accept, Acknow(ledge), Admit, Anagnorisis, Appreciate, Ascetic, Character, Cit(ation), Exequatur, Gaydar, Identify, Isolated, Ken, → **KNOW**, Nod, Notice, Oust, Own, Reward, Salute, Scent, Standard, Sung, Voice, Weet, Wot

Recoil Backlash, Bounce, Kick(back), Quail, Rebound, Redound, Repercussion, Resile, Reverberate, Shrink, Shy, Spring, Start, Whiplash

Recollect(ion) Anamnesis, Memory, Pelmanism, Recall, → **REMEMBER**, Reminisce

▷ **Recollection** *may indicate* an anagram

Recommend(ation) Advise, Advocate, Counsel, Direct, Endorse, Exhort, Nap, Praise, Promote, Rider, Suggest, Testimonial, Tip, Tout

Recompense Cognisance, Deodand, Deserts, Expiate, Guerdon, Pay, Remunerate, Repayment, Requite, Restitution, Reward

Reconcile(d) Adapt, Adjust, Affrended, Atone, Harmonise, Henotic, Make up, Mend

Recondite Difficult, Esoteric, Mystic, Obscure, Occult, Profound

Reconnaissance, Reconnoitre Case, Investigate, Recce, Scout, Survey

Reconstitute, Reconstitution Diagenesis

Reconstruction Perestroika

Record(er), Record company, Recording Album, Ampex, Analogue, Annal(ist), Archive, Archivist, Audit trail, Aulos, Bench-mark, Black box, Blue Riband, Book, Campbell-Stokes, Can, Cardiograph, Cartulary, Casebook, CD, Chart, Chronicle, Clickstream, Clock, Clog-almanac, Coat(e), Congressional, Daybook, Diary, Dictaphone®, Dictograph®, Digital, Disc, Document, Dossier, Eloge, Elpee, EMI, Endorsement, English flute, Enter, Entry, EP, Ephemeris, Estreat, Ever, Filater, File, Film, Flight, Flute, Form, Forty-five, Ghetto blaster, Gram, Gramophone, Hansard, Helical scan, Hierogrammat, History, Hologram, Incremental, Indie, Journal, Lap-chart, Ledger, List, Log, Logbook, LP, Marigram, Mark, Maxi-single, Memento, Memo(randum), Memoir, Memorial, Memorise, Meter, Mind, Minute, Mono, Noctuary, Notate, Notch, Note, Odometer, Oscillogram, Pass book, Platter, Playback, Practic(k), Pratique, Pressing, Previous, Protocol, Public, Quadrophonics, Quipo, Quipu, Quote, Rapsheet, Rec, Reel-to-reel, Regest, Register, Release,

Remembrancer, Roll, Score(board), Set down, Seven-inch, Seventy-eight, Shellac, Single, Spectogram, Sphygmogram, Spirogram, Stenotype®, Studbook, Sunshine, Tachograph, Tally, Tallyman, Tape, Thirty-three, TiVo®, Toast, Trace, Track, Transcript, Travelog, Trip, Twelve-inch, VERA, Vid(eo), Videotape, Vote, Wax, Wire, Wisden, Worksheet, Write

Record-holder Champion, Sleeve

Record-player DJ, Stereo

Recount Describe, Enumerate, → **NARRATE**, Relate, Tell

Recourse Access, Resort

Recover(y) Amend, Clawback, Comeback, Common, Convalescence, Cure, Dead cat bounce, Get over, Lysis, Over, Perk, Pull through, Rally, Rebound, Reclaim, Recoup, Redeem, Regain, Rehab, Repaint, Replevin, Replevy, Repo(ssess), Rescript, Rescue, Resile, → **RETRIEVE**, Revanche, Salvage, Salve, Second-wind, Spontaneous, Upswing, Upturn

Recreate, Recreation Diversion, Hobby, Palingenesia, Pastime, Play, Revive, Sport

Recriminate, Recrimination Ruction

Recruit(s) Attestor, Bezonian, Choco, Conscript, Crimp, Draft, Employ, Engage, Enlist, Enrol, Headhunt, Intake, Muster, Nignog, Nozzer, Press, Rookie, Sprog, Volunteer, Wart, Yardbird, Yobbo

Rectangle, Rectangular Golden, Matrix, Oblong, Quad, Quadrate, Square

Rectifier, Rectify Adjust, Amend, Dephlegmate, Redress, Regulate, → **REMEDY**, Right, Silicon

Recto Ro

Rector R

Rectum Tewel

Recuperate Convalesce, Rally, Recover

Recur(rent), Recurring Chronic, Quartan, Quintan, Recrudesce, Repeated, Repetend, Return

▷ **Recurrent** *may indicate* 'reversed'

Recycler, Recycling Freegan

Red(den), Redness Admiral, Alizarin, Angry, Archil, Arun, Ashamed, Auburn, Beet, Bilirubin, Blush, Bolshevik, Brick, Burgundy, C, Cain-coloured, Carmine, Carroty, Castory, Cent, Cerise, Cherry, Chica, Chinese, Choy-root, Chrome, Cinnabar, Claret, Coccineous, Commo, Communist, Congo, Copper, Coquelicot, Coral, Corallin(e), Corkir, Cramesy, Cremosin, Crimson, Crocoite, Cuprite, Cyanin, Damask, Debit, Dubonnet, Duster, Embarrassed, Eosin, Eric, Erik, Erythema, Ffion, Flame, Flaming, Florid, Flush, Foxy, Garnet, Geranium, Ginger, Gory, Grog-blossom, Gule(s), Guly, Hat, Henna, Herring, Incarnadine, Indian, Indigo, Inflamed, Infra, Inner, Intertrigo, Iron, Jacqueminot, Keel, Kermes, Korkir, Lac-lake, Lake, Lateritious, Left(y), Lenin, Letter, Magenta, Maoist, Maroon, Marxist, McIntosh, Menshevik, Miniate, Minium, Modena, Mulberry, Murrey, Neaten, Orchel, Orchilla-weed, Orseille, Oxblood, Phenol, Pillar-box, Pinko, Plethoric, Plum, Pompeian, Ponceau, Poppy, Pyrrhous, Raddle, Radical, Raspberry, Raw, Realgar, Rhodamine, Rhodopsin, Ridinghood, Roan, Rosaker, Rose, Rot, Rouge, Roy, Rubefy, Rubella, Rubescent, Rubicund, Rubric, Ruby, Ruddle, Ruddy, Rufescent, Rufus, Russ(e), Russet, Russian, Rust(y), Rutilant, Sang-de-boeuf, Sanguine, Santalin, Sard, Scarlet, Sericon, Setter, Solferino, Stammel, Tape, Tidy, Tile, Titian, Trot, Trotsky, Turacin, Turkey, Tyrian, Venetian, Vermeil, Vermilion, Vermily, Vinaceous, Wallflower, Wine

▷ **Red** *may indicate* an anagram

Redcoat Rust, Soldier

Redeem(er), Redemption Cross, Liberate, Mathurin, Messiah, Ransom, Retrieve, Salvation, Save

Red-faced Coaita, Florid, Flushed

Red-head Auburn, Blue(y), Carroty, Commissar, Mao, Rufus

Red herring Soldier

▶ **Red Indian** *see* **NORTH AMERICAN INDIAN**

Redirect Sublimate

▷ **Rediscovered** *may indicate* an anagram

Redolent Aromatic, Fragrant, Reeking, Suggestive

Redoubtable Stalwart

Redress Amends, Offset, Recompense, Rectify, Regrate, Remedy, Right

Redshank Gambet, Totanus

Redskin Indian, Tomato

Red spot Tika

Reduce(r), Reduced, Reduction Abatement, Allay, Alleviate, Amortize, Attenuate, Bate, Beggar, Beneficiate, Clip, Commute, Condense, Contract, Cut, Cutback, Damping, Debase, Decimate, Decrease, Decrement, Demote, Deoxidate, Deplete, Depreciation, Detract, Devalue, Diminish, Diminuendo, Discount, Downgrade, Downsize, Draw-down, Epitomise, Foreshorten, Grind, Hatchet job, Jeff, Kinone, → **LESSEN**, Lite, Markdown, Mitigate, Moderate, Palliate, Pot, Pulp, Put, Quinol, Razee, Remission, Retrench, Rundown, Scant, Shade, Shorten, Shrinkage, Slash, Strain, Taper, Telescope, Thin, Weaken, Write-off

Redundancy, Redundant Frill, Futile, Needless, Otiose, Pink slip, Pleonasm, Superfluous, Surplus

Redwood Amboyna, Mahogany, Sanders, Wellingtonia

Reed Arundinaceous, Broken, Calamus, Free, Oboe, Papyrus, Pipe, Quill, Raupo, Rush, Sedge, Seg, Sley, Spear, Sudd, Syrinx, Thatch, Twill, Whistle

Reef Atoll, Barrier, Bioherm, Bombora, Bommie, Cay, Coral, Fringing, Great Barrier, Key, Knot, Lido, Motu, Saddle, Sca(u)r, Skerry, Witwatersrand

Reefer Cigarette, Jacket, Joint

Reek Emit, Exude, Stink

Reel Bobbin, Dance, Eightsome, Hoolachan, Hoolican, Lurch, Multiplier, News, Pirn, Spin, Spool, Stagger, Strathspey, Sway, Swift, Swim, Totter, Virgina, Wheel, Whirl, Wintle

Refectory Frater

Refer Advert, Allude, Assign, Cite, Direct, Mention, Pertain, Relate, Remit, Renvoi, Renvoy, See, Submit, Touch, Trade

Referee Arbiter, Commissaire, Mediate, Oddsman, Official, Ref, Umpire, Voucher, Whistler, Zebra

Reference Allusion, Apropos, Biaxal, Character, Coat, Grid, Index, Innuendo, Mention, Passion, Quote, Regard, Renvoi, Respect, Retrospect, Testimonial, Vide

Referendum Mandate, Plebiscite, Vox populi

Refill Replenish

Refine(d), Refinement, Refiner(y) Alembicated, Attic, Catcracker, Couth, Cultivate, Culture, Distinction, Elaborate, Elegance, Exility, Exquisite, Genteel, Grace, Nice, Nicety, Polish(ed), Polite, Précieuse, Pure, Rare(fy), Recherché, Saltern, Sieve, Sift, Smelt, Sophisticated, Spirituel, Sublimate, Subtilise, Tasteful, Try, U, Urbane, Veneer

Reflect(ing), Reflection, Reflective, Reflector Albedo, Blame, Catoptric, Cat's eye®, Chaff, Chew, Cogitate, → **CONSIDER**, Echo, Glass, Glint, Image, Meditate, Mirror, Muse, Nonspecular, Ponder, Redound, Repercuss, Ricochet, Ruminate,

Spectacular, Speculum, Symmetrical, Tapetum, Thought

Reflex Achilles, Babinski, Bent, Cancrizans, Knee-jerk, Patellar, Pavlovian, Re-entrant, Single-lens, Tic, Twin-lens

Reform(er) Amend, Apostle, Beveridge, Bloomer, Calvin, Chartism, Chastise, Correct, Enrage, Fourier, Fry, Gandhi, Gradualism, Howard, Hussite, Improve, Knox, Land, Lollard, Luther, Meiji, Melanchthon, Mend, Mucker, New Deal, Owenite, Pietism, PR, Progressionist, Protestant, Proudhon, Puritan, Rad(ical), Really, Recast, Reclaim, Reconstruction, Rectify, Regenerate, Resipiscence, Ruskin, Satyagraha, Savonarola, Syncretise, Tariff, Transmute, Tyndale, Wycliffe, Young Turk, Zwingli

▷ **Reform(ed)** *may indicate* an anagram

Reformatory Borstal, Magdalen(e)

Refract(ion), Refractive, Refractor(y) Anaclastic, Double, Firestone, Obstinate, Perverse, Prism, Recalcitrant, Refringe, Restive, Stubborn, Sullen, Wayward

Refrain Abstain, Alay, Avoid, Bob, Burden, Chorus, Desist, Epistrophe, Fa-la, Forbear, Hemistich, Mantra, O(v)erword, Repetend, Ritornello, Rumbelow, Rum(p)ti-iddity, Rum-ti-tum, Spare, Tag, Tirra-lirra, Tirra-lyra, Turn again, Undersong, Waive, Wheel

Refresh(ment), Refresher Air, Bait, Be(a)vers, Buffet, Cheer, Elevenses, Enliven, Food, Four-hours, Nap, New, Nourishment, Purvey, Refection, Reflect, Refocillate, Reinvigorate, Renew, Repast, Restore, Revive, Seltzer, Shire, Slake, Water

Refrigerator Chill, Chiller, Cooler, Deep freeze, Esky®, Freezer, Freon, Fridge, Ice-box, Minibar, Reefer

Refuge Abri, Ark, Asylum, Bolthole, Burrow, Dive, Fastness, Funkhole, Girth, Grith, Harbour, Haven, Hideaway, Hole, Holt, Home, Hospice, Oasis, Port, Reefer, Resort, Retreat, Sanctuary, Sheet-anchor, → **SHELTER**, Soil, Stronghold, Women's

Refugee(s) Boat people, DP, Economic, Escapist, Fugitive, Grenzganger, Huguenot, Reffo

Refund Clawback, Repayment

▷ **Refurbished** *may indicate* an anagram

Refusal, Refuse Attle, Bagasse, Ba(u)lk, Bilge, Bin, Black, Blackball, Boycott, Bran, Brash, Breeze, Brock, Bull, Bunkum, Cane-trash, Chaff, Clap-trap, Crane, Crap, Cul(t)ch, Debris, Decline, Denay, Deny, Disown, Draff, Drivel, Dross, Dunder, Dung, Eighty-six, Fag-end, Fenks, Fiddlesticks, Finks, First, Flock, Frass, Garbage, Gob, Guff, Hards, Hogwash, Hold-out, Hurds, Husk, Interdict, Jews' houses, Jews' leavings, Jib, Junk, Knickknackery, Knub, Lay-stall, Leavings, Litter, Lumber, Mahmal, Marc, Megass(e), Midden, Mullock, Mush, Nay(-say), Nill, No, Noser, Nould, Nub, Offal, Off-scum, Orts, Pellet, Pigwash, Potale, Punk, Radwaste, Raffle, Rape(cake), Rat(s), Rebuff, Recrement, Recusance, Red(d), Redargue, Redline, Reest, Regret, Reneg(u)e, Renig, Rot, → **RUBBISH**, Ruderal, Scaff, Scrap, Scree, Screenings, Scum, Sewage, Shant, Shell heap, Slag, Sordes, Spurn, Sullage, Sweepings, Swill, Tinpot, Tip, Toom, Tosh, Trade, Trash, Tripe, Trock, Troke, Trumpery, Turndown, Twaddle, Unsay, Utter, Wash, Waste, Wastrel

▷ **Re-fused** *may indicate* an anagram

Refutation, Refute Deny, Disprove, Elench(us), Rebut, Redargue, Refel

Regain Recoup, Recover, Revanche

▶ **Regal** *see* **ROYAL**

Regalia → **CIGAR**, Mound, Orb, Sceptre

Regard(ing) Anent, As to, Attention, Care, Consider, → **ESTEEM**, Eye, Gaum, Look, Observe, Odour, Pace, Rate, Re, Repute, Respect, Revere, Sake, Steem, Value, Vis-à-vis

Regardless Despite, Heedless, Irrespective, Notwithstanding, Rash, Though, Uncaring, Unmindful, Willy-nilly

Regatta Head of the river, Henley

Regenerate Restore

Regent Interrex, Ruler, Viceroy

Regent's Park Zoo

Reggae Ska

Regicide Ireton, Macbeth

Regime(n) Administration, Control, Diet(etics), Method, Reich

Regiment Black Watch, Buffs, Colour(s), Discipline, Greys, Ironsides, Lifeguard, Marching, Monstrous, Nutcrackers, Organise, RA, RE, REME, Rifle, Royals, → **SAS**, Tercio, Tertia

▷ **Regiment** *may indicate* an anagram

Region Aceh, Alsace, Alsatia, Amhara, Arctogaea, → **AREA**, Asir, Asturias, Belt, Borders, Brie, Brittany, Bundu, Calabria, Camargue, Cappadocia, Caria, Cariboo, Carniola, Carnnatic, Catalonia, Caucasia, Central, Chald(a)ea, Champagne-Ardenne, Chiasma, Cilicia, Circassia, Climate, Clime, Constantia, Critical, D, Dacia, District, E, Ecosphere, End, F, Guiana, Hinterland, Holarctic, Hundred, Illyria, Ionia, Kashmir, Katanga, Lacustrine, Lothian, Low Countries, Lusitania, Lycia, Lydia, Macao, Macedonia, Maghreb, Manchuria, Mascon, Masuria, Matabeleland, Mauretania, Mecklenburg, Mesopotamia, Midi, Molise, Moravia, Murcia, Mysia, Namaqualand, Negeb, Negev, Nejd, Neogaea, New Castile, New Quebec, Nubia, Nuristan, Offing, Ogaden, Old Castile, Opher, Oriental, Ossetia, Oudh, Pannonia, Pargana, Part, Pergunnah, Persis, Piedmont, Province, Quart(er), Realm, Refugium, Rhizosphere, Ruthenia, Sarmatia, Scythia, Sector, Sogdiana, Stannery, Strathclyde, Subtopia, Sumer, Tagma, Tayside, Territory, Tetrarchate, Thessaly, Thrace, Thule, Tibet, Tigray, Tigré, Tract, Transcaucasia, Transdniestria, Transylvania, Troas, Tundra, Turkestan, Turkistan, Tuscany, Ultima Thule, Umbria, Ungava, Val d'Aosta, Valois, Variable, Vaud, Veneto, Vojvodina, Vuelta Abajo, Weald, Zone, Zululand

Register(ing), Registration, Registry Actuarial, Almanac, Annal, Cadastral, Cadastre, Calendar, Cartulary, Cash, Census, Check-in, Child abuse, Dawn, Diptych, Docket, Enlist, Enrol, Enter, Flag out, Gross, Handicap, Index, Indicate, Inscribe, Inventory, Land, Ledger, List, Lloyd's, Log, Matricula, Menology, NAI, Net, Note, Notitia, Obituary, Parish, Park, Patent, Poll, Quotation, Read, Record, Reg(g)o, Rent-roll, Roll, Roule, Score, Shift(ing), Ship's, Sink in, Soprano, Terrier, Voice

Registrar Actuary, Greffier, Medical, Protocolist, Recorder, Specialist, Surgical

Regress(ion) Backslide, Recidivism, Revert

Regret(ful), Regrettable Alack, Alas, Apologise, Bemoan, Deplore, Deprecate, Ewhow, Forthwink, Ichabod, Lackaday, Lament, Mourn, Otis, Pity, Remorse, Repentance, Repine, Resent, Rew, → **RUE**, Ruth, Sorrow, Tragic

Regular(ity), Regularly Clockwork, Constant, Custom, Episodic, Even, Giusto, Goer, Habitual, Habitué, Hourly, Insider, Methodic, Nine-to-five, Normal, Often, Orderly, Orthodox, Patron, Peloria, Periodic, Rhythmic, Routine, Set, Smooth, → **STANDARD**, Stated, Statutory, Steady, Strict, Symmetric, Uniform, Usual, Yearly

Regulate, Regulation, Regulator Adjust, Appestat, Bye-law, Code, Control, Correction, Curfew, Customary, Direct, Gibberellin, Governor, Guide, King's, Logistics, Metrostyle, Order, Ordinance, Police, Queen's, Rule, Snail, Square, Standard, Statute, Stickle, Stopcock, Sumptuary, Thermostat, Valve

Regulus Matte

Regurgitation Trophallaxis
Rehab(ilitate), Rehabilitation AA, Cure, Orthotics, Physio(therapy), Repone
Rehearsal, Rehearse Band-call, Dress, Drill, Dry-block, Dry-run, Dummy-run, Practice, Practise, Preview, Recite, Repeat, Run through, Trial, Walk through
Reichenbach Falls, Od
Reign Era, Govern, Meiji, Prevail, Raine, Realm, Restoration, → **RULE**
Reimburse(ment) Indemnity, Recoup, Redress, Repay
Rein(s) Bearing, Check, Control, Curb, Free, Gag, Leading strings, Long, Lumbar, Restrain, Safety, Tame, Tight
Reindeer Blitzen, Caribou, Comet, Cupid, Dancer, Dasher, Donner, Moss, Prancer, Rudolf, Tarand, Vixen
Reinforce(ment) Aid, Augment, Beef up, Bolster, Boost, Brace, Buttress, Cleat, Counterfort, Line, Negative, Partial, Plash, Pleach, Positive, Recruit, Reserve, → **STRENGTHEN**, Support, Tetrapod, Underline
Reinstate Repone
Reinvigorate Recruit
Reiterate(d), Reiteration Battology, Emphasize, Ostinato, Plug, → **REPEAT**
Reject(ion) Abhor, Abjure, Athetise, Bin, Blackball, Brush off, Cast, Cast off, Deny, Dice, Disallow, Discard, Disclaim, Discount, Disdain, Disown, Diss, Elbow, Eliminate, Export, Flout, Frass, Iconoclasm, Jettison, Jilt, Kest, Kill, Knock-back, Ostracise, Oust, Outcast, Outtake, Pip, Plough, Rebuff, Recuse, Refuse, Reny, Repel, Reprobate, Repudiate, Repulse, Scout, Scrub, Spet, Spike, Spin, Spit, → **SPURN**, Sputum, Thumbs-down, Turndown, Veto
Rejoice, Rejoicing Celebrate, Exult, Festivity, Gaude, Glory, Joy, Maffick, Sing
Rejoin(der), Rejoined Answer, Counter, Relide, Reply, Response, Retort, Reunite
Rejuvenation Shunamitism
Relapse Backslide, Deteriorate, Hypostrophe, Recidivism, Regress, Revert, Sink
Relate(d), Relation(ship), Relative Account, Affair, Affine, Affinity, Agnate, Akin, Allied, Antibiosis, Appertain, Associate, Blood, Brer, Brisure, Causality, Cognate, Commensal, Concern, Connection, Connexion, Consanguinity, Coosen, Cousin, Coz, Deixis, Dependent, Dispersion, Eme, Enate, Equivalence, External, False, Formula, German(e), Granny, Guanxi, Heterogeneous, Homologous, Impart, Industrial, In-law, Internal, Item, Kin, Kinsman, Labour, Liaison, Link, Love-hate, Mater, Material, Matrix, Mutualism, Narrative, Nooky, One-to-one, Osculant, Pertain, Phratry, Pi, Plutonic, Poor, Predation, Privity, → **PROPORTION**, Proxemics, Public, Race, Rapport, Rapprochement, Ratio, Reciprocity, Recite, Recount, Rede, Refer(ence), Relevant, Respect(s), Saga, Sib(b), Sibbe, Sibling, Sine, Sybbe, Symbiosis, Syntax, Tale, Tell, Who
Relating to Of
Relax(ation), Relaxant, Relaxed Abate, Atony, Autogenics, Calm, Chalone, Chill out, Com(m)odo, Contrapposto, Dégagé, Détente, Diversion, Downbeat, Ease, Easy-going, Flaccid, Gallamine, Icebreaker, Informal, Laid-back, Leisured, Lesh states, Lighten, → **LOOSEN**, Mellow out, Mitigate, Outspan, Peace, Relent, Relief, Remit, Rest, Settle, Slacken, Sleep, Slump, Toneless, Unbend, Unknit, Unrein, Untie, Unwind, Veg out
▷ **Relaxed** *may indicate* an anagram
Relay(er) Convey, Medley, Race, Shift, Tell, Telstar, Torch-race, Webcast
▷ **Relay(ing)** *may indicate* an anagram
Release Abreact, Abrogation, Announcement, Bail, Block, Cable, Catharsis, Clear, Day, Death, Deliver(y), Desorb, Disburden, Discharge, Disclose, Disengage, Disimprison, Dismiss, Disorb, Emancipate, Enfree, Excuse, Exeem, Exeme,

Extricate, Exude, Free, Handout, Happy, → **LIBERATE**, Manumit, Merciful, Moksa, Nirvana, Parole, Press, Quietus, Quittance, Relinquish, Ripcord, Soft, Spring, Tre corde, Unconfine, Uncouple, Undo, Unhand, Unleash, Unloose, Unpen, Unshackle, Unsnap, Unteam, Untie

Relegate Banish, Consign, Demote, Exile, Marginalise, Sideline, Stellenbosch

Relent Bend, Mollify, Soften, Weaken, Yield

Relentless Cruel, Hard, Hardface, Indefatigable, Inexorable, Pitiless, Rigorous, Stern

Relevance, Relevant Ad rem, Applicable, Apposite, Apropos, Apt, Bearing, Germane, Material, Pertinent, Point, Valid

▸ **Reliable, Reliance** *see* **RELY**

Relic Antique, Ark, Artefact, Fly-in-amber, Fossil, Leftover, Memento, Neolith, Remains, Sangraal, Sangrail, Sangreal, Souvenir, Survival

Relict Survivor, Widow

Relief, Relieve(d) Aid, Air-lift, Allay, Allegeance, Alleviate, Alms, Anaglyph, Anastatic, Anodyne, Assistance, Assuage, Bas, Beet, Beste(a)d, Bete, Cameo, Cavo-relievo, Comfort, Cure, Détente, Ease(ment), Emboss, Emollient, Free, Grisaille, High, Indoor, Let-up, Lighten, Linocut, Low, Lucknow, Mafeking, On the parish, Outdoor, Palliate, Phew, Photo, Pog(e)y, Reassure, Redress, Remedy, Replacement, Repoussé, Reprieve, → **RESCUE**, Respite, Retirement, Rid, Spare, Spell, Stand-in, Stiacciato, Succour, Taper, Tax, Thermoform, Tondo, Toreutics, Wheugh, Whew, Woodcut

Religion, Religious (sect) Animism, Baha'i, Biblist, Bogomil, Brahmanism, Buddhism, Camaldolite, Cargo cult, Carthusian, Celestine, Christadelphian, Christianity, Cistercian, Coenobite, Confucianism, Congregant, Creed, Culdee, Denomination, Devout, Din, Doctrine, Druse, Druz(e), Faith, Falun Gong, Familist, Gilbertine, Gnosticism, God-squad, Gueber, Guebre, Hadith, Hare Krishna, Has(s)id, Hieratic, Hospital(l)er, Ignorantine, Islam, Ismaili, Jain(a), Jansenism, Jehovah's Witness, Jesuit, Jewry, Judaism, Khalsa, Lamaism, Loyola, Lutheran, Macumba, Mahatma, Manichee, Maoism, Mazdaism, Mazdeism, Missionary, Missioner, Mithraism, Moony, Mormonism, New Light, Nun, Oblate, Opium, Orphism, Pagan, Pantheist, Parseeism, Parsism, Pi, Piarist, Pietà, Postulant, Premonstratensian, Progressive, Rastafarian, Reformation, Resurrectionist, Revealed, Revivalism, Ryobu Shinto, Sabbatarian, Sabian, Sacramentarian, Santeria, Scientology®, Serious, Shaker, Shamanism, Shango, Shiism, Shinto(ism), Sikhism, Sodality, Solifidian, Sons of Freedom, Spike, State, Sunna, Swedenborgian, Taoism, Theatine, Theology, Tractarianism, Tsabian, Utraquist, Voodooism, Whore, Wicca, Zabian, Zarathustric, Zealous, Zend-Avesta, Zoroaster, Zwinglian

Religious book Bible, Koran, Missal, NT, OT, Sefer, Tantra, Targum, T(h)orah

Relinquish Abdicate, Cede, Demit, Discard, Drop, Forlend, Remise, Waive(r), Yield

Reliquary Chef, Encolpion, Encolpium, Simonious, Tope

Relish(ing) Aspic, Botargo, Catsup, Chakalaka, Chow-chow, Condiment, Enjoy, Flavour, Gentleman's, Gout, Gust(o), Ketchup, Lap(-up), Lust, Opsonium, Palate, Pesto, Piccalilli, Pickle, Sapid, Sar, Sauce, Savour, Seasoning, Tang, Tooth, Worcester sauce, Zest

Reluctant Averse, Backward, Chary, Circumspect, Cockshy, Grudging, Half-hearted, Laith, Loath, Loth, Nolition, Renitent, Shy, Under protest, Unwilling

Rely, Reliance, Reliant, Reliable Addiction, Authentic, Bank, Confidence, Constant, Copper-bottomed, → **COUNT**, Dependent, Found, Hope, Jeeves, Leal, Lean, Loyal, Mensch, Presume, Pukka, Rest, Robin, Safe, Secure, Solid, Sound,

Sponge, Stalwart , Stand-by, Staunch, Trustworthy, Trusty, Unfailing

Remain(s), Remainder, Remaining Abide, Ash(es), Balance, Bide, Continue, Corse, Dreg(s), Dwell, Embers, Estate, Exuviae, Fag-end, Fossils, Kreng, Last, Late, Lave, Left, Lie, Locorestive, Manet, Nose, Oddment, Orts, Other, Outstand, Persist, Relic(ts), Reliquae, → **REMNANT**, Residue, Rest, Ruins, Scourings, Scraps, Stay, Stick, Stub, Surplus, Survive, Tag-end, Talon, Tarry, Wait, Wreck(age)

Remark Aside, Barb, Bromide, Comment(ary), Descry, Dig, Epigram, Generalise, Mention, Noise, → **NOTE**, Notice, Obiter dictum, Observe, Platitude, Pleasantry, Reason, Sally, Shot, State

Remarkable, Remarkably Amazing, Arresting, Beauty, Bodacious, Come-on, Conspicuous, Dilly, Egregious, Extraordinary, Heliozoan, Legendary, Lulu, Mirable, Notable, Notendum, Noteworthy, Personal, Phenomenal, Rattling, → **SIGNAL**, Singular, Some, Striking, Tall, Unco, Uncommon, Visible

Remedial, Remedy Adaptogen, Aid, An mo, Antacid, Antibiotic, Antidote, Antiodontalgic, Antispasmodic, Arcanum, Arnica, Azoth, Bach®, Bach Flower®, Basilicon, Calomel, Catholicon, Corrective, Cortisone, → **CURE**, Dinic, Drug, Elixir, Febrifuge, Femiter, Feverfew, Fumitory, Ginseng, Heal, Ipecac, Leechdom, Medicate, Medicine, Moxa, Nosode, Nostrum, Palliative, Panacea, Panpharmacon, Paregoric, Poultice, Provisional, Rectify, Redress, Repair, Rescue®, Salutory, Salve, Simillimum, Simple, Specific, Taraxacum, Therapeutic, Tonga, Treatment, Tutsan

Remember(ing), Remembrance Bethink, Commemorate, Con, Mem, Memorial, Memorise, Mention, Mneme, Recall, Recollect, Remind, Reminisce, Retain, Rosemary, Souvenir

▷ **Remember** *may indicate* RE-member, viz. Sapper

Remind(er) Aftertaste, Aide-memoire, Bookmark, Evocatory, Evoke, Jog, Keepsake, Mark, Memento, Memo, Mnemonic, Mnemotechnic, Monition, Nudge, Phylactery, Prod, Prompt, Shades of, Souvenir, Token

Reminiscence(s), Reminiscent Ana, Evocative, Memory, Recall, Recollect, Remember, Retrospect

Remiss Careless, Derelict, Lax, Lazy, Negligent, Tardy

Remission Abatement, Absolution, Acceptilation, Indulgence, Pardon, Pause, Spontaneous

Remit Excuse, Forward, Pardon, Postpone

Remnant Butt, End, Fent, Heeltap, Leavings, Left-over, Odd-come-short, Offcut, Relic, Relict, → **REMAINDER**, Rump, Trace, Vestige, Witness

Remonstrate Argue, Complain, Expostulate, Protest, Reproach

Remorse Angst, Ayenbite, Breast-beating, Compunction, Contrition, Had-i-wist, Pity, → **REGRET**, Repentance, Rue, Ruing, Ruth, Sorrow, Worm

Remote Aloof, Aphelion, Back blocks, Backveld, Backwater, Backwood, Boondocks, Bullamakanka, Bundu, → **DISTANT**, Far flung, Forane, Inapproachable, Insular, Irrelevant, Jericho, Long(inquity), Out(part), Outback, Scrub, Secluded, Shut-out, Slightest, Surrealistic, Unlikely, Withdrawn, Woop Woop, Wop-wops

Remount(s) Remuda

Removal, Remove(d) Abduct, Ablation, Abstract, Airbrush, Apocope, Asport, Banish, Blot, Circumcision, Clear, Couch, Declassify, Dele(te), Depilate, Depose, Deracinate, Detach, Detract, Dishelm, Dislodge, Disloign, Dispel, Doff, Efface, Eject, Eloi(g)n, Emend, Eradicate, Erase, Esloyne, Estrange, Evacuate, Evict, Exalt, Excise, Extirpate, Extradite, Extricate, Far, Flit, Huff, Nick, Raise, Raze, Razee, Recuse, Redline, Remble, Rid, Scratch, Sequester, Shift, Spirit, Sublate, Subtract, Supplant, Transfer, Transport, Unbelt, Unperson, Unseat, Uproot

Remuneration Pay, Return, Reward, Salary, Solde
Remus Uncle
Renaissance Awakening, Cinquecento, Early, High, Quattrocento, Revival
Rend Cleave, Harrow, Lacerate, Rip, Rive, Rupture, Tear
Render(ing) Construe, Deliver, Do, Gie, Give, Interpretation, Make, Melt,
Pebble-dash, Plaster, Provide, Recite, Represent, Restore, Setting, Tallow, Try, Yeve
Rendezvous Date, Meeting, Philippi, Tryst, Venue
Rendition Account, Delivery, Interpretation, Translation, Version
René Descartes
Renegade, Renege, Renegue Apostate, Default, Defector, Deserter, Rat(ton),
Recreant, Traitor, Turncoat, Weasel out
▷ **Renegade** *may indicate* a word reversal
Renew(al) Instauration, Neogenesis, Palingenesis, Refresh, Replace, Resumption,
Retrace, Revival, Urban
Rennet Steep, Vell
Renounce, Renunciation Abandon, Abdicate, Abjure, Abnegate, Disclaim,
Disown, For(e)go, For(e)say, Forfeit, Forisfamiliate, Forsake, Forswear, Kenosis,
Outclaim, Quitclaim, Recede, Relinquish, Renay, Retract, Sacrifice
Renovate(d), Renovation Duff, Face-lift, Instauration, Makeover, Refurbish,
Renew, Repair, Restore, Revamp, Touch up
Renown(ed) Fame, Glory, Illustrious, Kudos, Lustre, Notoriety, Prestige, Stardom
Rent(er), Renting Broken, Charge, Cornage, Cost, Crack, Cranny, Cuddeehih,
Cuddy, Division, Economic, Fair, Farm, Fee, Fissure, Gale, Gavel, Ground, → **HIRE**,
Lease, Let, List, Mail, Market, Occupy, Penny(-mail), Peppercorn, Quit-rent, Rack,
Rip, Rived, Riven, Screed, Seat, Slit, Split, Stallage, Subtenant, Tare, Tenant, Tithe,
Tore, Torn, Tythe, White
Reorganise Rationalise
▷ **Reorganised** *may indicate* an anagram
Reorientate Rabat
Repair(s), Repairer, Reparation Amend(s), Anaplasty, Assythment, Botch,
Cobble, Damages, Darn, Doctor, Excision, Expiation, Fettle, Fitter, Fix, Go, Haro,
Harrow, Jury rig, → **MEND**, Overhaul, Patch, Piece, Recompense, Redress, Refit,
Reheel, Remedy, Renew, Renovate, Repoint, Resort, Restore, Retouch, Revamp,
Roadworks, Running, Satisfaction, Stitch, Tenorrhaphy, Ulling, Vamp, Volery
Repartee Backchat, Badinage, Banter, Persiflage, Rejoinder, Retort, Riposte, Wit
Repast Bever, Collection, Food, Meal, Tea, Treat
Repay(ment) Avenge, Compensate, Quit, Refund, Requite, Retaliate, Reward,
Satisfaction
Repeal Abrogate, Annul, Cancel, Rescind, Revoke
Repeat(ed), Repeatedly, Repetition, Repetitive Again, Alliteration, Anadiplosis,
Anaphora, Ancora, Battology, Belch, Bis, Burden, Burp, Copy, Ditto(graphy), Do,
Duplicate, → **ECHO**, Echolalia, Encore, Epanalepsis, Epistrophe, Epizeuxis, Eruct,
Facsimile, Habitual, Harp, Image, Imitate, Ingeminate, Iterate, Iterum, Leit-motiv,
Merism, Ostinato, Palillogy, Parrot, Parrot-fashion, Passion, Perpetuate, Playback,
Polysyndeton, Recite(r), Redo, Refrain, Regurgitate, Reiterate, Renew, Rep,
Repetend, Reprise, Rerun, Retail, Rondo, Rosalia, Rote, Same(y), Screed, Segno,
Symploce, Tautology, Tautophony, Thrum, Trite, Verbigerate
Repel(lent) Estrange, Harsh, Offensive, Rebarbative, Reject, Repulse, Revolt,
Squalid, Turn-off, Ug(h), Ward
Repent(ant), Repentance Metanoia, Penitent, Regret, Rue, Sackcloth, Yamim
Nora'im

Repercussion Backlash, Backwash, Echo, Effect, Impact, Recoil

Repertoire, Repertory Company, Depot, Rep, Store

▶ **Repetition** *see* REPEAT

Replace(ment), Replaceable, Replacing Change, Deputise, Diadochy, For, Pre-empt, Prosthesis, Raincheck, Refill, Relief, Replenish, Restore, Stand-in, Substitute, Supersede, Supplant, Surrogate, Taxis, Transform, Transliterate, Understudy, Usurp

Replay Action, Instant, Iso(lated), Segno

Replenish Refill, Refresh, Revictual, Stock, Supply, Top

Replete, Repletion Awash, Full, Gorged, Plenitude, Plethora, Sated, Satiation

Replica Clone, Copy, Duplicate, Facsimile, Image, Repetition, Spit

Reply Accept, Answer, Churlish, Duply, Over, Rejoinder, Replication, Rescript, Response, Retort, Roger, Surrebut, Surrebutter, Surrejoin, Triply

Report(er) Account, Announce, Annual, Auricular, Bang, Beveridge, Blacksmith, Bruit, Bulletin, Cahier, Clap, Columnist, Comment, Commentator, Correspondent, Court, Cover, Crack, Crump, Cub, Debrief, Disclose, Dispatch, Dissertation, Explosion, Fame, Fireman, Grapevine, Hansard, Hearsay, Informant, Item, Jenkins, Journalist, Legman, Libel, News, Newshawk, Newshound, Newsman, Noise, Pop, Powwow, Pressman, Protocol, Rapporteur, Relate, Relay, Representation, Repute, Return, Roorback, Rumour, Sitrep, Sound(bite), Staffer, State(ment), Stringer, Tale, → TELL, Thesis, Transcribe, Tripehound, Troop, Update, Weather, Whang, Wolfenden, Write up

▷ **Reported** *may indicate* the sound of a letter or word

Repose Ease, Kaif, Kef, Kif, Lie, Lig, Peace, Relax, → REST, Serenity

Repository Archive, Ark, Cabinet, Container, Genizah, Reservoir, Sepulchre, Vault

Reprehend Blame, Censure, Criticise, Rebuke, Warn

Represent(ation), Representative, Represented Agent, Ambassador, Anaconic, Caricature, Client, Commercial, Cross-section, Delegate, Depict, Deputation, Describe, Display, Drawing, Drummer, Effigy, Elchee, Eltchi, Emblem, Embody, Emissary, Epitomise, Example, Figurative, Image, Instantiate, John Bull, Legate, Lobby, Map, Mimesis, Mouthpiece, MP, Personate, Personify, Portray, Proportional, Quintessence, Rep, Resemble, Salesman, Senator, Shop steward, Simulacrum, Spokesman, Stand-in, Status, Steward, Symbolic, Syndic, Tableau, Tiki, Transcription, Typical, Vakeel, Vakil, Vernicle

▷ **Represented** *may indicate* an anagram

Repress(ed) Check, Curb, Pent, Quell, Reprime, Sneap, Stifle, Stultify, Subjugate, Withhold

Reprieve Delay, Postpone, Relief, Respite

Reprimand Admonish, Bounce, Carpet, → CENSURE, Chew out, Chide, Dressing-down, Earful, Jobe, Lace, Lambast, Lecture, Rark up, Rating, Rebuke, Reproof, Rocket, Rollicking, Slate, Strafe, Targe, Tick off, Tongue-lashing, Wig

Reprint Copy, Paperback, Replica

Reprisal(s) Marque, Recaption, Retaliation, Revenge

Reproach Blame, Braid, Byword, Chide, Discredit, Dispraise, Exprobate, Gib, Mispraise, Odium, Opprobrium, Rebuke, Ronyon, Runnion, Scold, Shend, Sloan, Stigma, Taunt, Truant, Upbraid, Upcast, Yshend

Reprobate Cur, Lost soul, Outcast, Rascal, Scallywag, Scamp

Reprocess Re-make

Reproduce(r), Reproduction, Reproductive (organ) Amphimixis, Ape, Apomixis, Archegonium, Carpel, Clone, Copy, Counterfeit, Depict, Ectype, Edition, Etch, Eugenics, Gamogenesis, Gemmate, Homogenesis, Isospory, Loins,

Megaspore, Meristematic, Mono, Monogenesis, Monogony, Multiply, Oogamy, Ozalid®, Parthenogenesis, Phon(e)y, Pirate, Playback, Proliferate, Propagate, Pullulation, Refer, Replica, Roneo®, S(h)akti, Schizogony, Seminal, Simulate, Spermatia, Stereo, Strobilation, Syngamy, Syngenesis, Vegetative

▷ **Reproduce** *may indicate* an anagram

Reproof, Reprove Admonish, Berate, Chide, Correction, Correption, Lecture, Rate, Rebuff, Rebuke, Scold, Sloan, Take to task, Tut, Upbraid

Reptile, Reptilian Agamid, Alligarta, Alligator, Base, Basilisk, Caiman, Cayman, Chameleon, Chelonian, Creeper, Crocodile, Cynodont, Diapsid, Dicynodont, Dinosaur, Galliwasp, Goanna, Herpetology, Lacertine, Lizard, Mamba, Pelycosaur, Pteranodon, Pterodactyl, Rhynchocephalian, Sauroid, → **SNAKE**, Sphenodon, Squamata, Synapsid, Tegu(exin), Thecodont, Therapsid, Theriodontia, Tortoise, Tuatara, Tuatera, Turtle, Worm

Republic(s) Banana, Federal, Fifth, First, Fourth, People's, Second, State, Third, Weimar

---

REPUBLICS

1 letter:
R

3 letters:
RMM
UAR
USA

4 letters:
Chad
Cuba
Eire
Fiji
Iran
Iraq
Komi
Laos
Mali
Peru
Togo
Tuva

5 letters:
Adhar
Altai
Belau
Benin
Chile
China
Congo
Czech
Egypt
Gabon

Ghana
Haiti
India
Italy
Kenya
Khmer
Libya
Malta
Nauru
Niger
Palau
Sakha
Sudan
Syria
Tatar
Yakut
Yemen
Zaire

6 letters:
Adygai
Adygei
Angola
Bharat
Biafra
Brazil
Bukavu
Buryat
France
Gambia
Greece
Guinea
Guyana

Ingush
Israel
Kalmyk
Latvia
Malawi
Mari-El
Mexico
Myanma
Panama
Poland
Rwanda
Serbia
Turkey
Udmurt
Uganda
Venice
Zambia

7 letters:
Adharca
Albania
Algeria
Andorra
Armenia
Austria
Bashkir
Belarus
Bolivia
Burundi
Chechen
Chuvash
Comoros
Croatia

Ecuador
Estonia
Finland
Georgia
Germany
Hungary
Iceland
Ireland
Jibouti
Kalmuck
Kalmyck
Khakass
Lebanon
Liberia
Moldova
Myanmar
Namibia
Nigeria
Romania
Senegal
Somalia
Surinam
Tunisia
Ukraine
Uruguay
Vanuatu
Vietnam
Yakutia

8 letters:
Botswana
Bulgaria
Buryatia

Cambodia
Cameroon
Chechnya
Colombia
Dagestan
Djibouti
Dominica
Esthonia
Honduras
Karelian
Kiribati
Malagasy
Maldives
Moldavia
Mongolia
Pakistan
Paraguay
Portugal
Roumania
Sinn Fein
Slovakia
Slovenia
Sri Lanka
Suriname
Tanzania
Zimbabwe

9 letters:
Argentina
Badakshan
Cape Verde
Costa Rica
Dominican
Guatemala
Indonesia
Kazakstan
Lithuania
Macedonia
Mauritius
Nicaragua
San Marino
Singapore
Venezuela

10 letters:
Azerbaijan
Bangladesh
Belarussia
El Salvador
Gorno-Altai
Kara-Kalpak
Kazakhstan
Kyrgyzstan
Madagascar
Mauritania

Montenegro
Mordvinian
Mozambique
North Korea
North Yemen
South Korea
South Yemen
Tajikistan
Ubang-Shari
Uzbekistan
Yugoslavia

11 letters:
Afghanistan
Burkina-Faso
Byelorussia
Cote d'Ivoire
Nakhichevan
Philippines
Sierra Leone
South Africa
Soviet Union
Switzerland
Tadjikistan
West Germany

12 letters:
Guinea-Bissau

South Vietnam
Turkmenistan

13 letters:
Bashkortostan
North Ossetian

14 letters:
Czechoslovakia

15 letters:
Gorno-Badakhshan
Kabardino-Balkar
Marshall Islands
United Provinces

16 letters:
Congo-Brazzaville
Equatorial Guinea
Karachai-Cherkess
São Tomé e Príncipe

17 letters:
Bosnia-Herzegovina
Mari El-
Nakhichevan
Trinidad and
Tobago

Republican Antimonarchist, Democrat, Fenian, Fianna Fáil, Girondist, GOP, International Brigade, IRA, Iraqi, Leveller, Montagnard, Mugwump, Plato, Red, Sansculotte, Sansculottic, Sinn Fein, Whig

Repudiate Abjure, Deny, Discard, Disclaim, Disown, Ignore, Recant, Reject, Renounce, Repel, Retract

Repugnance, Repugnant Abhorrent, Alien, Disgust, Distaste, Fulsome, Horror, Loathing, Nastiness, Revulsion

Repulsive, Repulse Creepy, Grooly, Lo(a)th, Off-putting, Rebuff, Rebut, Refel, Refuse, Repel, Repugnant, Slimy, Squalid, Ugly, Vile

Reputable, Reputation, Repute(d) Bubble, Dit, Estimate, Fame, Good, Izzat, Loos, Los, Name, Note, Notoriety, Odour, Opinion, Prestige, Putative, Regard, Renown, Said, Sar, → STANDING, Status, Stink, Stock, Trustworthy

Request Adjure, Appeal, Apply, Ask, Beg, Desire, D-notice, Entreaty, Invite, Petition, Plea, Prayer, Precatory, Solicit, Supplication

Requiem Agnus Dei, Mass

Require(d), Requirement Charge, Crave, De rigueur, Desire, Enjoin, Entail, Exact, Expect, Incumbent, Lack, Necessity, Need, Prerequisite, Sine qua non, Stipulate

Requisite, Requisition Commandeer, Due, Embargo, Essential, Indent, Necessary, Needful, Order, Press, Simplement

Rescind Abrogate, Annul, Recant, Remove, Repeal

Rescue Aid, Air-sea, Deliver, Free, Liberate, Ransom, Recover, Recower, Redeem, Regain, Relieve, Reprieve, Retrieve, Salvage, Salvation, → SAVE

Research(er) Audience, Boffin, Delve, Dig, Enquiry, Explore, Fieldwork, Investigate, Legwork, Market, MORI, Motivation(al), Near-market, Operational, Pioneer, Psychical, Sus(s), Think-tank

Resell Scalp

Resemblance, Resemble, Resembling Affinity, Apatetic, Approach, Assonant, Dead ringer, Homophyly, Likeness, -oid, -opsis, Replica, Similitude, Simulate

Resent(ful), Resentment Anger, Bridle, Chippy, Choler, Cross, Derry, Dudgeon, Grudge, Indignation, Ire, Jaundiced, Malign, Miff, Mind, Pique, Rankle, Smart, Spite, Umbrage

Reservation, Reserve(d), Reservist(s) Aloof, Arrière-pensée, Backlog, Bashful, Book, By, Capital, Caveat, Central, Cold, Demiss, Detachment, Distant, Earmark, Engage, Ersatz, Except, Fall-back, Federal, Fort Knox, General, Gold, Hold, Husband, Ice, Indian, Introvert, Landwehr, Layby, Locum, Mental, Militiaman, Modesty, Nature, Nest-egg, Nineteenth man, Proviso, Qualification, Reddendum, Res, Rest, Restraint, Retain, Reticence, Retiring, Rez, Salvo, Sanctuary, Save, Scenic, Scruple, Set aside, Special, Spoken for, Stand-by, Stand-offishness, Starch, Stash, Stock(pile), Substitute, TA (men), Twelfth man, Uncommunicate, Understudy, Warren, Waves, Withhold

Reservoir Basin, Cistern, Font, G(h)ilgai, Gilgie, Header tank, Oilcup, Repository, Rybinsk, Service, Stock, Sump, Tank, Water tower

Reset Taxis

Reside(nce), Resident(s), Residential Abode, Address, Amban, Chequers, Commorant, Consulate, Denizen, Domicile, Dwell, Embassy, Establishment, Expatriate, Exurb(anite), Gremial, Guest, Home, In, Indweller, Inholder, Inmate, Intern, Ledger, Lei(d)ger, Lieger, Liveyer(e), Lodger, Metic, Occupant, Pad, Parietal, Permanent, Resiant, Settle, Sojourn, Stay, Tenant, Tenement, Up, Vicinage, Villager, Yamen

Residual, Residue Ash, Astatki, Boneblack, Calx, Caput, Chaff, Cinders, Coke, Crud, Dottle, Draff, Dregs, Expellers, Greaves, Heeltap, Leavings, Mazout, Mortuum, Prefecture, Remainder, Remanent, Remnant, Scourings, Slag, Slurry, Snuff, Vinasse

Resign(ed), Resignation Abandon, Abdicate, Demit, Fatalism, Heigh-ho, Leave, Meek, → QUIT, Reconcile, Stoic, Submit

Resilience, Resilient Bounce, Buoyant, Elastic, Flexible, Recoil, Springy

Resin Acaroid, Acrylic, Agila, Alkyd, Amber, Amine, Amino, Anime, Arar, Asaf(o)etida, Bakelite®, Bal(sa)m of Gilead, Balsam, Benjamin, Benzoin, Burgundy pitch, Bursera, Cachou, Cannabin, Cannabis, Caranna, Carauna, Catechu, Charas, Cholestyramine, Churrus, Colophony, Conima, Copai(ba), Copaiva, Copal(m), Coumarone, Courbaril, Cutch, Cymene, Dam(m)ar, Dammer, Dragon's blood, Elaterite, Elemi, Epoxy, Frankincense, Galbanum, Galipot, Gambi(e)r, Gamboge, Glyptal, Guaiacum, Gum, Hasheesh, Hashish, Hing, Jalapic, Jalapin, Kino, Labdanum, Lac, Ladanum, Lignaloes, Limonene, Lupulin, Mastic, Melamine, Methacrylate, Myrrh, Natural, Olibanum, Opopanax, Perspex®, Phenolic, Phenoxy, Plastisol, Podophyl(l)in, Polycarbonate, Polyester, Polymer, Polysterene, Polyvinyl, Propolis, Retinite, Roset, Rosin, Rosit, Rozet, Rozit, Sagapenum, Sandarac(h), Saran®, Scammony, Shellac, Silicone, Storax, Styrene, Synthetic, Tacamahac, Tacmahack, Takamaka, Taxin, Thus, Urea, Vinyl, Xylenol

Resist Bristle, Buck, Combat, Contest, Defy, Face, Fend, Gainstrive, Impede, Oppose, Redound, Reluct, Stand (pat), Toughen, → WITHSTAND

Resistance, Resistant, Resistor Barretter, Bleeder, Ceramal, Cermet, Chetnik, Coccidiostat, Combat, Drag, Element, Friction, Hostile, Immunity, Impediment,

Internal, Intifada, Invar, Klendusic, Klepht, Maquis, Maraging, Market, Megohm, Microhm, Negative, Obstacle, Ohm, Passive, Pat, Pull, R, Radiation, Reluctance, Renitent, Resilient, Rheostat, Sales, Satyagraha, Shockproof, Soul-force, Specific, Stability, Stand, Stonde, Stubborn, Tough

Resolute, Resolution Analysis, Bold, Cast-iron, Casuistry, Courage, Decided, Decision, Denouement, Determined, Doughty, → FIRM, Fortitude, Granite, Grim, Grit, Hardiness, Insist, Joint, Pertinacity, Promotion, Rede, Reed(e), Resolve, Stable, Stalwart, Staunch, Stout, Strength, Sturdy, Telic, Tenacity, Unbending, Valiant, Willpower

Resolve(d), Resolver Analyse, Calculate, Decide, Declare, → DETERMINE, Deus ex machina, Factorise, Fix, Hellbent, Intent, Nerve, → PURPOSE, Settle, Steadfast, Tenacity, Vow, Will

▷ **Resolved** *may indicate* an anagram

Resonance, Resonant, Resonator Canorous, Cavity, Electromer, Morphic, Orotund, Parallel, Rhumbatron, Ringing, Sonorous, Timbre, Vibrant

Resort Biarritz, Centre, Dive, Étaples, Expedient, Frame, Frequent, Haunt, Health, Hove, Hydro, Invoke, Lair, Last, Las Vegas, Lowestoft, Malibu, Morecambe, Nassau, Paignton, Pau, Pis aller, Rapallo, Recourse, Repair, Riviera, Southend, Spa(w), Stand by, Use, Watering place, Worthing, Zermatt

▷ **Resort(ing)** *may indicate* an anagram

Resound(ing) Echo, Plangent, Reboant, Reboation, Reverberate, Ring

Resource(s), Resourceful Assets, Beans, Bottom, Chevisance, Clever, Enterprise, Faculty, Funds, Gumption, Human, Ingenious, Input, Inventive, Means, Natural, Renewable, Shared, Sharp, Stock-in-trade, → VERSATILE, Wealth

Respect(ed), Respectable, Respectful Admire, Ahimsa, Aspect, Behalf, Consider, Decent, Deference, Devoir, Duty, Eminent, Esteem, Gigman, Homage, → HONOUR, Intent, Kempt, Kowtowing, Latria, Obeisant, Officious, Pace, Particular, Preppy, Prestige, Proper, Reference, Regard, Relation, Reputable, Revere, Sir, S(t)irrah, U, Venerate, Wellborn, Well-thought-of, Wise, Worthy

Respirator, Respire, Respiration Artificial, Blow, Breathe, Exhale, External, Gasmask, Inhale, Iron lung, Mouth-to-mouth, Pant, Snorkel

Respite Break, Breather, Frist, Interval, Leisure, Let up, Pause, Reprieve, Rest, Stay, Truce

Respond, Response, Responsive Amenable, Answer, Antiphon, Backlash, Bi, Comeback, Conditioned, Counteroffer, Duh, Echo, Feedback, Flechman, Grunt, Immune, Kneejerk, Kyrie, Litany, Nastic, Pavlovian, Photonasty, Prebuttal, Psychogalvanic, React(ion), Reflex, Reply, Repost, Retort, Rheotaxis, Rheotropism, Rise, Stayman, Synapte, Syntonic, Tender, Thigmotropic, Tic, Tropism, Unconditioned, Voice, Warm, Wilco

Responsibility, Responsible Accountable, Anchor, Answerable, Baby, Blame, Buck, Charge, Culpable, Dependable, Diminished, Duty, Frankpledge, Guilty, Hot seat, Incumbent, Instrumental, Liable, Mea culpa, Onus, Pigeon, Sane, Solid, Stayman, Trust

Rest(ing), Rest day Alt, Anchor, Avocation, Balance, Bed, Beulah, Break, Breather, Calm, Catnap, Cetera, Comma, Depend, Dwell, Ease, Easel, Etc, Fermata, Feutre, Fewter, Gite, Half-time, Halt, Inaction, Jigger, Lance, Lave, Lean, Lie, Lie-in, Light, Lodge, Loll, Lound, Lyte, Minim, Nap, Noah, Nooning, Others, Outspan, Overlie, Pause, Quiescence, Quiet, Relâche, Relax, Rely, Remainder, Repose, Requiem, Reserve, Residue, Respite, Sabbath, Siesta, → SLEEP, Slide, Sloom, Slumber, Spell, Spider, Static, Stopover, Support, Surplus, Teabreak, Time out, Y-level

Re-start Da capo, Reboot

Restaurant, Restaurateur Automat, Beanery, Bistro, Brasserie, British, Cabaret, Café, Canteen, Chew'n'spew, Chip-shop, Chophouse, Commissary, Cook shop, Creperie, Diner, Eatery, Eating-house, Estaminet, Greasy spoon, Grill, Grillroom, Grub shop, Luncheonette, Maxim's, Noshery, Padrone, Porter-house, Rathskeller, Ratskeller, Roadhouse, Rotisserie, Slap-bang, Steakhouse, Takeaway, Taqueria, Taverna, Teahouse, Tearoom, Teashop, Trattoria

Rest-home Aggie, Hospice

Resting-place Bed, Couch, Dharmsala, Gite, Grave, Inn, Khan, Serai, She'ol, Stage

Restitute, Restitution Amends, Apocatastasis, Reparation, Restore, Return

Restive, Restless(ness) Chafing, Chorea, Fidgety, Fikish, Free-arm, Itchy, Jactitation, Toey, Unsettled

▷ **Restless** *may indicate* an anagram

Restoration, Restorative, Restore(d) Bring to, Cure, Descramble, Heal, Mend, Pentimento, Pick-me-up, Postliminy, Rally, Recondition, Redeem, Redintegrate, Redux, Refurbish, Regenerate, Rehabilitate, Rejuvenate, Remedial, Renew, Renovate, Replevy, Repone, Restitute, Resuscitate, Retouch, Revamp, Revive, Stet, Tonic, Whole

Restrain(ed), Restraint Abstinence, Ban, Bate, Bit, Bottle, Branks, Bridle, Cage, Chain, Chasten, → **CHECK**, Checks and balances, Coerce, Cohibit, Compesce, Confinement, Contain, Control, Cramp, Curb, Dam, Decorum, Detent, Dry, Duress, Embargo, Enfetter, Estoppel, Freeze, Halt, Hamshackle, Handcuffs, Harness, Heft, Hinder, Hopple, Impound, Inhibit, Jess, Leg-iron, Lid, Low-key, Manacle, Measure, Mince, Moderation, Muzzle, Patient, Quiet, Rein, Repress, Restrict, Ritenuto, Shackle, Sober, Sobriety, Squeeze, Stay, Stent, Stint, Straitjacket, Temper, Tether, Tie, Trash

Restrict(ed), Restriction Band, Bar, Bind, Bit, Burden, Cage, Catch, Censorship, Chain, Circumscribe, Closet, Condition, Cord, Corset, Cramp, Curb, Curfew, DORA, Fence, Fold, Gate, Ground, Guard, Hamper, Hidebound, Hobble, Inhibit, Intern, Kennel, Let, → **LIMIT**, Localise, Lock, Mere, Narrow, Net, Nick, No-go, Pale, Parochial, Pen, Pent, Pier, Pin, Pot-bound, Private, Proscribed, Qualify, Regulate, Rein, Rent, Repression, Rope, Safety belt, Scant, Seal, Section, Selected, Shackle, Snare, Squeeze, Stenopaic, Stent, Stint, Stop, Straiten, Stunt, Tether, Tie

Restructure, Restructuring Perestroika

Result(s) After-effect, Aftermath, Ans(wer), Bring, Causal, Consequence, Effect, Emanate, End, Ensue, Entail, Event, Eventuate, Finding, Fruict, Fruits, Issue, Karmic, Knock-on, Lattermath, → **OUTCOME**, Outturn, Pan, Proceeds, Quotient, Sequel, Side-effect, Sum, Upshot, Wale

Resume, Résumé Continue, Pirlicue, Purlicue, Summary

Resurrect(ion) Anabiosis, Anastasia, Rebirth, Revive, Zomb(ie)

Resuscitate(d), Resuscitation Mouth-to-mouth, Quicken, Redivivus, Restore, Revive

Retail(er) Chandler, Dealer, → **NARRATE**, Regrate, Sell, Shopkeeper, Symbol, Tell

Retain(er), Retains Brief, Contain, Deposit, Fee, Hold, Hold-all, Keep, Panter, Pantler, Reserve, Retinue, Servant

Retaliate, Retaliation Avenge, Counter, Lex talionis, Quid pro quo, Quit(e), Redress, Repay, Reprisal, Requite, Retort, Talion

Retard(ed) Arrest, Belate, Brake, Cretin, Encumber, Hinder, Slow, Stunt

Retch Boak, Bock, Boke, Cowk, Gap, Heave, Keck, Reach, Vomit

Reticence, Reticent Clam, Coy, Dark, Reserve, Restraint, Secretive, Shy, Taciturn

Reticule, Reticulum Bag, Carryall, Dragnet, Lattice, Net

Retina Detached, Fovea, Macula lutea

Retinue Comitatus, Company, Cortège, Equipage, Following, Meiney, Meinie, Meiny, Menyie, Sowarry, Suite

Retire(d), Retiree, Retirement, Retiring Abed, Aloof, Baccare, Backare, Backpedal, Blate, Bowler-hat, Bow out, Cede, Coy, Depart, Ebb, Emeritus, Essene, Former, Leave, Lonely, Modest, Mothball, Nun, Outgoing, Pension, Perfing, Private, Quit, Recede, Recluse, Reserved, Resign, Retract, Retread, Retreat, Retrocedent, Roost, Rusticate, Scratch, Sequester, Shy, Superannuate, Unassertive, Withdraw

▷ **Retirement** *may indicate* 'bed' around another word, or word reversed

Retort Alembic, Comeback, Courteous, Quip, Repartee, → **REPLY**, Retaliate, Riposte, Still, Tu quoque

Retract(ion) Backpedal, Backtrack, Disavow, Epanorthosis, Palinode, Recall, Recant, Renounce, Revoke

Retreat Abbey, Arbour, Ashram(a), Asylum, Backpedal, Backwater, Bower, Bug, Camp David, Cell, Cloister, Convent, Crawfish, Dacha, Departure, Donjon, Girth, Grith, Hermitage, Hideaway, Hide-out, Hole, Interstadial, Ivory-tower, Katabasis, Lair, Lama(sery), Mew, Monastery, Nest, Neuk, Nook, Recede, Recoil, Recu(i)le, Redoubt, Reduit, Refuge, Retire, Retraite, Right-about, Rout, Shangri-La, Shelter, Skedaddle, Stronghold, Withdraw

Retribution Come-uppance, Deserts, Nemesis, Revenge, Reward, Utu, Vengeance

Retrieve(r), Retrieval Access, Bird-dog, Chesapeake Bay, Field, Gundog, Labrador, Read-out, Recall, Recoup, Recover, Redeem, Rescue, Salvage

Retroflex Cacuminal

Retrograde Backward, Deasi(u)l, Deasoil, Decadent, Decline, Hindward, Rearward, Regrede

Retrospect(ive) Contemplative, Ex post facto, Hindsight, Regardant

Return(s) Agen, Answer, Bricole, Census, Comeback, Day, Diminishing, Dividend, Elect, Er, Extradite, Gain, Nil, Pay, Proceeds, Profit, Rebate, Rebound, Recur, Redound, Regress, Reject, Render, Rent, Repay, Replace, Reply, Requital, Respond, Rest, Restitution, Restore, Retour, Revenue, Reverse, Revert, Riposte, Takings, Tax, Traffic, → **YIELD**

Rev Gun, Minister

Reveal(ing), Revelation Acute, Advertise, Air, Apocalyptic, Bare, Betray, Bewray, Confess, Descry, Disclose, Discover, Discure, → **DIVULGE**, Epiphany, Exhibit, Explain, Expose, Eye-opener, Giveaway, Hierophantic, Impart, Indicate, Ingo, Kythe, Leak, Let on, Manifest, Open, Out, Pentimento, Satori, → **SHOW**, Spill, Tell-tale, Unclose, Uncover, Unfold, Unheal, Unmask, Unveil

Revel(ling), Revelry Ariot, Bacchanalia, Bend, Carnival, Carouse, Comus, Dionysian, Feast, Gloat, Glory, Joy, Merriment, Orgy, Rant, Rejoice, Riot, Roister, Rollicks, Rout, Royst, Saturnalia, Splore, Swig, Upsee, Ups(e)y, Wallow, Wassail, Whoopee

Reveller Bacchant, Birler, Corybant, Guisard, Guiser, Maenad, Merrymaker, Orgiast, Silenus

Revenant Fetch, Ghost, Spectre

Revenge(r), Revengeful Aftergame, Avenge, Commination, Goel, Grenville, Montezuma's, Nightrider, Payback, Reprise, Requite, Retaliation, Revanche, Ultion, Utu, Vindictive

Revenue Capital, Finance, Fisc(al), Fisk, Income, Inland, Internal, Jaghire, Jag(h)ir, Prebend, Primitiae, Rent, Taille, Tax, Turnover, Zamindar, Zemindar

Reverberate Echo, Recoil, Reflect, Repercuss, Resound

Revere(nce) Admire, Awe, Bostonian, Dread, Dulia, Esteem, Fear, Hallow, Hery,

Homage, → **HONOUR**, Hyperdulia, Idolise, Latria, Obeisance, Paul, Respect, Venerate

Reverie Brown study, Daydream, Dream(iness), Fantasy, Memento

Revers Lap(p)el

Reversal, Reverse, Reversing, Reversion, Reversible Antithesis, Antonym, Arsy-versy, Atavism, Back(slide), Change-over, Chiasmus, Commutate, Counter(mand), Escheat, Evaginate, Exergue, Flip, Inversion, Misfortune, → **OPPOSITE**, Overturn, Palindrome, Pile, Regress, Revoke, Rheotropic, Setback, Switchback, Tails, Throwback, Transit, Turn, Turnabout, Two-faced, Un-, Undo, U-turn, Verso, Vice versa, Volte-face, Woman

Revert Annul, Backslide, Regress, Relapse, Resort, Retrogress, Return

Review(er) Appeal, Censor, Credit, Critic, Critique, Editor, Encomium, Feuilleton, Footlights, Inspect, Judicial, Magazine, March-past, Notice, Pan, Peer, Recapitulate, Repeat, Revise, Rundown, Spithead, Summary, Summing-up, Survey, Write-up

▷ **Review** *may indicate* an anagram or a reversed word

Revile, Reviling Abuse, Execrate, Inveigh, Rail, Rayle, Vilify, Vituperate

Revise(r), Revision Alter, Amend, Correct, Diaskeuast, Edit, Peruse, Reappraise, Reassess, Recense, Reform, Rev, Update

▷ **Revise(d)** *may indicate* an anagram

Revive, Revival, Revivify, Reviving Araise, Classical, Enliven, Gothic, Greek, Rake up, Rally, Reanimate, Reawake(n), Rebirth, Redintegrate, Redux, Refresh, Rekindle, Relive, Renaissance, Renascent, Renew, Renovate, Restore, Resurrect, Resuscitate, Risorgimento, Romantic, Rouse, Wake

Revoke Abrogate, Cancel, Countermand, Negate, → **RECALL**, Repeal, Rescind

Revolt(ing), Revolution(ary) Agitator, Agitprop, American, Anarchist, Apostasy, Appal, Bloodless, Bolivar, Bolshevik, Bolshevist, Boxer, Bulldog, Cade, Castro, Chartist, Che, Chinese, Circle, Commune, Coup d'état, Cultural, Cycle, Danton, Defection, Dervish, Desmoulins, Disgust, Emeute, Emmet, Engels, Enrage, February, Fenian, Foul, French, Girondin, Girondist, Glorious, Green, Grody, Guevara, Gyration, Industrial, Inqilab, → **IN REVOLT**, Insurgent, Insurrection, Intifada, IRA, Jacobin, Jacquerie, Komitaji, Lap, Lenin, Marat, Marx, Maximalist, Maypole, Minimalist, Montagnard, Mutiny, Nauseating, Nihilist, October, Orbit, Outbreak, Palace, Paris Commune, Peasants, Poujadist, Putsch, Radical, → **REBEL**, Red, Red Guard, Red Shirt, Reformation, Riot, Rise, Robespierre, Roll, Rotation, Round, Run, Russian, Sandinista, Sansculotte(rie), Sedition, Sicilian Vespers, Spartacus, Syndicalism, The Mountain, Thermidor, Titanomachy, Trot(sky), Twist, Up(rise), → **UPRISING**, Velvet, Villa, Wat Tyler, Weatherman, Whirl, Wolfe Tone, Young Turk, Zapata

▷ **Revolutionary** *may indicate* 'reversed'

Revolve(r), Revolving Carrier, Catherine wheel, Centrifuge, Colt®, Gat, Girandole, Grindstone, → **GUN**, Gyrate, Iron, Klinostat, Lathe, Maelstrom, Peristrephic, Pistol, Pivot, Planet, Roller, Rotate, Rotifer, Rotor, Roundabout, Run, Six-shooter, Spin, Tone, Turn(stile), Turntable, Turret, Wheel, Whirl(igig), Whirlpool

Revue Follies

Reward(ing) Albricias, Bonus, Bounty, Compensate, Consideration, Desert, Emolument, Fee, Guerdon, Head money, Medal, Meed, Payment, Premium, Price, Prize, Profit, Purse, Recompense, Reguerdon, Remuneration, Requital, Requite, S, Shilling, Tanti, Tribute, Wage, War(r)ison

Reword Edit, Paraphrase

Reworking Rifacimento

Rex Priam, R
Reynolds Joshua, PRA
Rhapsodic, Rhapsody Ecstasy, Epic, Music, Unconnected
Rhea Em(e)u, Nandoo, Nandu, Nhandu, Ostrich, Rami
Rhenium Re
Rhesus Bandar, Macaque, Monkey
Rhetoric(al) Alliteration, Anaphora, Antimetabole, Antithesis, Antostrophe,
  Apophasis, Aposiopesis, Assonance, Aureate, Bombast, Brachylogia, Cacophony,
  Catachresis, Chiasmus, Ecbole, Eloquence, Enantiosis, Epanorthosis, Epexegesis,
  Epistrophe, Epizeuxis, Erotema, Eroteme, Erotesis, Euphemism, Hendiadys,
  Hypallage, Hyperbole, Litotes, Metonymy, Oratory, Oxymoron, Paradox,
  Paral(e)ipsis, Periphrasis, Peroration, Platform, Pleonasm, Scesisonomaton,
  Syllepsis, Synoeciosis, Trivium, Zeugma
Rhino Blunt, Bread, Cash, Lolly, Loot, → MONEY, Tin
Rhinoceros Baluchitherium, Keitloa, Square-lipped, Sumatran, White
Rhodes, Rhodesia(n) Cecil, Colossus, Ridgeback, Scholar, Zimbabwe
Rhodium Rh
Rhubarb Pie-plant, Rhapontic, Rheum, Rot, Spat
Rhyme(s), Rhymer, Rhyming Assonance, Clerihew, Closed couplet, Counting out,
  Couplet, Crambo, Cynghanedd, Doggerel, Eye, Feminine, Head, Identical, Internal,
  Jingle, Male, Masculine, Measure, Near, Nursery, Pararhyme, Perfect, Poetry,
  Rich, Riding, Rime riche, Rondel, Royal, Runic, Sight, Slang, Slant, Tail(ed), Tercet,
  Terza-rima, Thomas, Triple, → VERSE, Virelay, Vowel
Rhythm(ic) Agoge, Alpha, Asynartete, Backbeat, Beat, Beta, Bo Diddley beat,
  Breakbeat, Cadence, Circadian, Duple, Hemiol(i)a, In-step, Meter, Movement,
  Oompah, Pulse, Pyrrhic, Rove-over, Rubato, Scotch catch, Scotch snap, Sdrucciola,
  ·Sesqualtera, Singsong, Sprung, Swing, Syncopation, Tala, Talea, → TEMPO, Time,
  Voltinism
Rib(bed), Ribbing, Rib-joint Bar, Chaff, Chiack, Chip, Chyack, Cod, Costa,
  Cross-springer, Dutch, Eve, False, Fin, Floating, Futtock, Groin, Intercostal, Lierne,
  Nervate, Nervular, Nervure, Ogive, Persiflage, Rack, Rag, Rally, Short, Spare,
  Springer, Subcosta, Taunt, Tease, Tierceron, Tracery, True, Wife
Ribald(ry) Balderdash, Bawdy, Coarse, Scurrilous, Smut, Sotadic, Vulgar
Ribbon Band, Bandeau, Blue, Bow, Braid, Caddis, Caddyss, Cordon, Fattrels, Ferret,
  Fillet, Grosgrain, Hatband, Infula, Multistrike, Pad, Petersham, Radina, Red, Rein,
  Riband, Soutache, Taenia, Tape, Teniate, Tie, Torsade, Yellow
Ribless Ecostate
Rice Arborio, Basmati, Bir(i)yani, Brown, Canada, Carnaroli, Elmer, Entertainer,
  Indian, Kedgeree, Miracle, Paddy, Patna, Pilaf, Pilau, Pilaw, Pillau, Reis, Risotto,
  Spanish, Sushi, Twigs, Water, Wild
Rich(es) Abounding, Abundant, Affluent, Amusing, Bonanza, Buttery, Comic,
  Copious, Croesus, Dives, Edmund, Edwin, Fat, Feast, Fertile, Flamboyant, Flush,
  Fruity, Full, Golconda, Haves, Heeled, High, Larney, Loaded, Luscious, Lush,
  Luxurious, Mammon, Moneybags, Moneyed, Nabob, New, Oberous, → OPULENT,
  Plenteous, Plush, Plutocrat, Resonant, Rolling, Silvertail, Sumptuous, Toff,
  Vulgarian, → WEALTHY, Well-heeled, Well off, Well-to-do
Richard Angevin, Burbage, Dick(y), Lionheart, Rick, Roe
Richthofen Red Baron
Rick (burning) Goaf, Sprain, Swingism, Wrench
Rickets, Rickety Dilapidated, Rachitis, Ramshackle, Rattletrap, Shaky, Unsound
▷ **Rickety** *may indicate* an anagram

Rickshaw Pedicab, Tuktuk

Ricochet Boomerang, Glance, Rebound

Rid Clear, Deliver, Ditch, Eliminate, Eradicate, Expunge, Free, Obviate, Offload, Purge, Scrap, Scrub, Shot

Riddle Boulter, Charade, Colander, Dilemma, Enigma, Koan, Logogriph, Pepper, Perforate, Permeate, Puzzle, Screen, Searce, Search, Seil, Sieve, Sift, Sile, Siler, Sorites, Strain, Tems(e), Trommel

Ride, Riding Annoy, Aquaplane, Bareback, Bestride, Big dipper, Bruise, Canter, Coast, Crog(gy), Cycle, District, Division, Drive, Equitation, Field, Hack, Harass, Haute école, Hitchhike, Merry-go-round, Mount, Pick(-a-)back, Pickpack, Piggyback, Postil(l)ion, Rape, Revere's, Roadstead, Rollercoaster, Sit, Spin, Stang, Switchback, Third, Trot, Weather, Welter, Wheelie, Whip, White-knuckle

Rider(s) Addendum, Adjunct, Appendage, Attachment, Boundary, Bucket, Cavalier, Charioteer, Circuit, Codicil, Condition, Corollary, Dispatch, Equestrian, Eventer, Freedom, Gaucho, Godiva, Guidon, Haggard, Horseman, Jockey, Lochinvar, Messenger, Peloton, Postil(l)ion, Proviso, PS, Revere, Scrub, Spurrer, Transport, Walkyrie

Ridge(pole) Alveolar, Anthelix, Antihelix, Arête, Arris, As(ar), Balk, Bank, Baulk, Berm, Bur(r), Carina, Chine, Clint, Costa, Crease, Crest, Crista, Cuesta, Culmen, Darling Range, Drill, Drum(lin), Dune, Eskar, Esker, Fret, Gonys, Gyrus, Hammock, Hoe, Hogback, Horst, Hummock, Interfluve, Kaim, Kame, Keel, Knur(l), Ledge, Linch, List(er), Lynchet, Mid-Atlantic, Mid-ocean, Missionary, Nek, Nut, Oceanic, Offset, Pressure, Promontory, Ramp, Rand, Raphe, Razor-back, Reef, Rib, Riblet, Rig, Rim, Roof-tree, Sastruga, Screw-thread, Serac, Serpentine, Shoulder, Sowback, Torus, Varix, Verumontanum, Vimy, Wale, Weal, Whelp, Whorl, Windrow, Withers, Witwatersrand, Wrinkle, Yardang, Zastruga

Ridicule, Ridiculous Absurd, Badinage, Bathos, Chaff, Cockamamie, Deride, Derisory, Egregious, Foolish, Gibbet, Gibe, Gird, Guy, Haze, Jibe, Josh, Laughable, Ludicrous, Mimic, Mock, Paradox, Pasquin, Pillory, Pish, Pooh-pooh, Raillery, Rally, Rich, Roast, Satire, Scoff, Scout, Screwy, Send up, Sight, Silly, Skimmington, Taunt, Travesty

Ridinghood Nithsdale, Red

Riding-master RM

Riding-school Manège

Rife Abundant, Manifest, Numerous, Prevalent

Riffle Rapid

Riff-raff Canaille, Hoi polloi, Mob, Populace, Rag-tag, Scaff, Scum, Trash

Rifle Air, Armalite®, Assault, Bone, Browning, Bundook, Burgle, Calic, Carbine, Chassepot, Enfield, Enfield musket, Express, Garand, → **GUN**, Kalashnikov, Lee Enfield, Loot, Martini®, Martini-Henry, Mauser®, MI, Minié, Pea, Petronel, Pick, Pilfer, Pillage, Ransack, Remington, Repeater, Rob, Ruger, Saloon, Shiloh, Springfield, Winchester®

Rift Altercation, Canyon, Chasm, Chink, Cleft, Crevasse, Fault, Fissure, Gap, Gulf, Split

Rig(ging) Accoutre, Attire, Bermuda, Drilling, Equip, Feer, Gaff, Get-up, Gunter, Hoax, Jack-up, Mainbrace, Manipulate, Marconi, Martingale, Oil, Outfit, Panoply, Ratline, Ropes, Schooner, Semisubmersible, Slant, Sport, Stack, Standing, Strip, Swindle, Tackle, Togs, Top hamper, Trull, Wanton

▷ **Rigged** *may indicate* an anagram

Right(s), Righten, Rightness Accurate, Advowson, Affirmative, Ancient lights, Angary, Animal, Appropriate, Appurtenance, Ay, Befit, Blue-pencil, BNP,

Bote, Cabotage, Champart, Civil, Claim, Competence, Conjugal, Conservative, Copyhold, → **CORRECT**, Cor(r)ody, Coshery, Cuddy, Cure, Curtesy, Customer, Dead on, De jure, Dexter, Direct, Divine, Doctor, Droit, Due, Easement, Eminent domain, Emphyteusis, Equity, Esnecy, Estover, Ethical, Exactly, Faldage, Farren, Fascist, Feu, Fire-bote, Fitting, Forestage, Franchise, Free-bench, Freedom, Gay, Germane, Gunter, Haybote, Hedge-bote, Human, Infangthief, Interest, Isonomy, Iure, Junior, Jural, Jure, Jus (mariti), Leet, Legit, Letters patent, Liberty, Lien, Maritage, Maternity, Meet, Miner's, Moral, Naam, New, Ninepence, Off, Offhand, Offside, OK, Okay, Oke, Okey-dokey, Option, Ortho-, Oughtness, Paine, Passant, Pasturage, Pat, Patent, Paternity, Performing, Pit and gallows, Ploughbote, Pose, Postliminy, Pre-emption, Prerogative, Primogeniture, Priority, Prisage, Privilege, Proper, Property, Pukka, R, Rain, Reason, Recourse, Rectify, Rectitude, Redress, Remainder, Remedy, Repair, Rt, Sac, Sake, Side, So, Soc, Squatter's, Stage, Starboard, Stillicide, Suo jure, Suo loco, Tao, Tenants', Terce, Ticket, Tickety-boo, Title, Trivet, Trover, True, Turbary, User, Usucap(t)ion, Usufruct, Venville, Vert, Warren, Water, Women's

Right-angle(d) Orthogonal

Righteous(ness) Devout, Good, Just, Moral, Pharisee, Prig, Rectitude, Sanctimonious, Tzaddik, Virtuous

Right-hand Dexter, E, Far, Recto, RH, Ro

Right-winger Falangist, Neo-fascist

Rigid(ity) Acierated, Catalepsy, Craton, Extreme, Fixed, Formal, Hard and fast, Hard-set, Hard-shell, Hidebound, Inflexible, Renitent, Rigor, Set, Slavish, Starch(y), Stern, Stiff, Stretchless, Strict, Stringent, Tense, Turgor

Rigmarole Nonsense, Palaver, Paraphernalia, Protocol, Ragman, Ragment, Riddlemeree, Screed

Rigorous, Rigour Accurate, Austere, Cruel, Exact, Firm, Hard, Inclement, Iron-bound, Stern, Strait, Strict, Stringent

Rile Anger, Annoy, Harry, Irritate, → **NETTLE**, Vex

▷ **Rile(y)** *may indicate* an anagram

Rill Purl, Sike

Rim Atlantic, Border, Chimb, Chime, Edge, Felloe, Felly, Flange, Kelyphitic, → **LIP**, Margin, Pacific, Strake, Verge

Rime Crust, Frost, Hoar, Rhyme, Rhythm

Rind Bark, Crackling, Peel, Skin

Ring(ed), Ringer, Ringing, Rings Anchor, Angelus, Annual, Annulus, Anthelion, Arcus, Arena, Band, Bangle, Bayreuth, Bell, Benzine, Boom-iron, Broch, Brogh, Call, Cambridge, Carabiner, Cartel, Cartouche, Change, Chime, Circinate, Circle, Circlet, Circlip, Circus, Claddagh, Clam, Clang, Clink, Coil, Collet, Cordon, Corona, Corral, Corrida, Cramp, Crawl, Cricoid, Cringle, Cromlech, Cycle, Cyclic, Dead, Death's head, Dial, Dicyclic, Ding, Disc, Dohyo, Dong, D(o)uar, Draupnir, Echo, Encircle, Encompass, Engagement, Enhalo, Enlace, Environ, Enzone, Eternity, Extension, Eyelet, Fainne, Fairlead(er), Fairy, Ferrule, Fisherman, Fistic(uffs), Gas, Gimmal, Gird(le), Girr, Gloriole, Groin, Grom(m)et, Growth, Grummet, Guard, Gyges, Gymmal, Gyre, Halo, Hob, → **HOOP**, Hoop-la, Hula-hoop, Ideal, Inner, Inorb, Involucre, Jougs, Jow, Karabiner, Kartell, Keeper, Key, Knell, Knock-out, Kraal, Lifebelt, Link, Loop, Luned, Lute, Magpie, Manacle, Manilla, Marquise, Mourning, Napkin, Newton's, Nibelung, Nimbus, Nose, O, Orb, Outer, Pappus, Parral, Parrel, Peal, Pele, Pen, Phone, Ping, Piston, Potato, Price, Prize, Puteal, Quoit, Resonant, Resound, Retaining, Round, Rove, Rowel, Rundle, Runner, Sale, Scarf, Scraper, Scrunchy, Seal, Signet, Slinger, Slip, Snap-link, Solomon, Sound,

Spell, Split, Stemma, Stemme, Stonehenge, Surround, Swivel, Syndicate, Tang, Tattersall, Teething, Terret, Territ, Thimble, Thumb, Timbre, Ting, Tingle, Tink, Tinnitius, Tintinnabulate, Toe, Token, Toll, Toplady, Tore, Torquate, Torques, Torret, Torus, Travelling, Tree, Trochus, Turret, Tweed, Varvel, Vervel, Vice, Vortex, Wagnerian, Washer, Wedding, Welkin, Withe, Woggle, Zero

Ring-dance Carol

Ring-leader Bell-wether, Fugleman, Instigator

Ringlet Curl(icue), Lock, Tendril, Tress

Ringmaster Wagner

Ringworm Serpigo, Tinea

Rinse Bathe, Blue, Cleanse, Douche, Sind, Sine, Swill, Synd, Syne, Tint, Wash

Riot(er), Riotous(ly), Riots Anarchy, Brawl, Clamour, Demo, Deray, Gordon, Hilarious, Hubbub, Luddite, Medley, Mêlée, Nicker, Orgy, Pandemonium, Peterloo, Petroleur, Porteous, Profusion, Quorum, Race, Rag, Rebecca, Rebel, Roaring, Roister, Rout, Rowdy, Ruction, Ruffianly, Scream, Swing, Tumult

▷ **Rioters, Riotous** *may indicate* an anagram

Rip(per), Ripping Basket, Buller, Cur, Grand, Handful, Horse, Jack, Lacerate, Rent, Rep, Roué, Splendid, Tear, Tide, Topnotch, To-rend, Unseam

Ripe, Ripen(ing) Auspicious, Full, Geocarpy, Mature, Mellow, Rathe, Ready

Riposte Repartee, Retaliate, Retort

Ripple Bradyseism, Fret, Overlap, Popple, Purl, Undulation, Wave, Wavelet, Wrinkle

▷ **Rippling** *may indicate* an anagram

Rise(r), Rising Advance, Appreciate, Ascend, Assurgent, Bull, Butte, Cause, Dutch, Easter, Eger, Elevation, Emerge, Émeute, Eminence, Erect, Escalate, Get up, Hance, Hauriant, Haurient, Heave, Heliacal, Hike, Hill, Hummock, Hunt's up, Improve, Increase, Incremental, Insurgent, Intumesce, Jibe, Knap, Knoll, Lark, Levee, Levitate, Lift, Mount, Mutiny, Orient, Origin, Peripety, Point, Prove, Putsch, Rear, Resurgent, Resurrection, → **REVOLT**, Saleratus, Scarp, Sklim, Soar, Stand, Stie, Sty, Stye, Surface, Surge, The Fifteen, Tor, Tower, Transcend, Up, Upbrast, Upburst, Upgo, Uprest, Upsurge, Upswarm, Upturn, Well

Risk(y) Actuarial, Adventure, Back, Calculated, Chance, Compromise, Counterparty, → **DANGER**, Daring, Dice, Dicy, Emprise, Endanger, Fear, Gamble, Game, Hairy, Hazard, Imperil, Jeopardy, Liability, Peril, Precarious, Security, Shoot the works, Spec, Throw, Touch and go, Touchy, Unsafe, Venture

Risorgimento Renaissance

Risqué Blue, Racy, Salty, Scabrous, Spicy

Rissole(s) Cecils, Croquette, Faggot, Quennelle, Veggieburger

Rite(s) Asperges, Bora, Ceremony, Eastern, Exequies, Initiation, Liturgy, Mystery, Nagmaal, Obsequies, Powwow, Ritual, Sacrament, Sarum use, Superstition, York

Ritual Agadah, Arti, Ceremony, Chanoyu, Customary, Formality, Haggada, Lavabo, Liturgy, Mumbo-jumbo, Puja, Rite, Sacring, Seder, Social, Use

Rival(ry), Rivals Absolute, Acres, Aemule, Binocular, Compete, Contender, Emulate, Emule, Envy, Fo(n)e, → **MATCH**, Needle, Opponent, Retinal, Touch, Vie

River Dalles, Ea, Estuary, Flood, Flower, Fluvial, Potamic, Potamology, R, Riverain, Runner, Stream, Tide, Tributary, Waterway

RIVERS

2 letters:		3 letters:	
Ay	Po	Aar	Axe
Ob	Si	Aln	Ayr
	Xi		Bug

Cam	Deva	Saar	Culbá
Dee	Doon	Sava	Dasht
Don	Dove	Soar	Desna
Ems	Drin	Spey	Doubs
Esk	Earn	Styx	Douro
Exe	East	Swan	Drava
Fal	Ebbw	Swat	Drave
Fly	Ebro	Taff	Duero
Fox	Eden	Tana	Dvina
Han	Eder	Tarn	Eblis
Hsi	Elbe	Tees	Firth
Hué	Erne	Teme	Fleet
Inn	Esla	Test	Forth
Lee	Eure	Tone	Gogra
Lot	Gila	Tyne	Green
Luo	Gota	Uele	Havel
Lys	Huon	Ural	Hotan
Mur	Idle	Uvod	Indre
Nar	Isar	Vaal	Indus
Oil	Iser	Waal	Isere
Oka	Isis	Wear	Ishim
Ord	Jiul	Xero	James
Red	Juba	Yalu	Jumna
San	Kama	Yare	Juruá
Tay	Kill	Yate	Kasai
Tet	Kura	Yser	Kaven
Ure	Kwai	Yuan	Kenga
Usk	Lahn	Yuen	Kuban
Wye	Lech		Lethe
Yeo	Lena	***5 letters:***	Liard
	Liao	Abana	Limay
	Luan	Acton	Loire
4 letters:	Lune	Adige	Marne
Abus	Maas	Afton	Mbomu
Abzu	Main	Agate	Meuse
Acis	Meta	Aisne	Minho
Adur	Milk	Aldan	Mosel
Aire	Mino	Apure	Mulla
Alma	Mole	Argun	Mures
Alph	Nene	Avoca	Namoi
Amur	Neva	Benue	Negro
Aran	Nile	Boyne	Neman
Aras	Nith	Broad	Niger
Arno	Oder	Cauca	Ogowe
Aude	Ohio	Chari	Onega
Avon	Oise	Clyde	Oreti
Back	Ouse	Clyst	Peace
Beni	Oxus	Colne	Pearl
Bomu	Prut	Congo	Pecos
Cher	Rock	Conwy	Pelly
Culm	Ruhr	Cross	Piave
Dart			

Pison
Plate
Purus
Rainy
Rance
Rhine
Rhône
Rogue
Saône
Seine
Shari
Shire
Siang
Siret
Skien
Slave
Snake
Snowy
Somme
Spree
Staff
Stour
Swale
Tagus
Tamar
Tapti
Tarim
Teign
Terek
Tiber
Tisza
Tobol
Trent
Tweed
Volga
Volta
Warta
Weser
Xiang
Xingu
Yaqui
Yarra
Yonne
Yssel
Yukon

6 letters:
Allier
Amazon
Anadyr
Angara

Arzina
Atbara
Barcoo
Barrow
Bio-Bio
Broads
Calder
Canton
Chenab
Clutha
Colima
Croton
Crouch
Cydnus
Danube
Dawson
Donets
Duddon
Durack
Escaut
Finlay
Fraser
Gambia
Ganges
Glomma
Granta
Harlem
Hodder
Hsiang
Hudson
Humber
Iguacu
Ijssel
Irtish
Irtysh
Irwell
Isonzo
Itchen
Japura
Javari
Javary
Jhelum
Jordan
Kaduna
Kagera
Kennet
Kistna
Kolyma
Komati
Liffey
Mamoré

Medway
Mekong
Mersey
Mohawk
Molopo
Morava
Moskva
Murray
Neckar
Neisse
Nelson
Nyeman
Ogooue
Orange
Orwell
Ottawa
Pahang
Parana
Peneus
Platte
Pripet
Prosna
Rakaia
Ribble
Riffle
Rother
Sabine
Salado
Sambre
Santee
Seneca
Severn
St John
Struma
Sutlej
Swanee
Tanana
Tarsus
Tevere
Teviot
Thames
Ticino
Tigris
Tugela
Tyburn
Ubangi
Ussuri
Vardar
Vienne
Vitava
Vyatka

Wabash
Wairau
Wensum
Wharfe
Wupper
Yarrow
Yellow

7 letters:
Acheron
Aruwimi
Bassein
Berbice
Berezua
Bermejo
Buffalo
Burnett
Caqueta
Cauvery
Chagres
Cocytus
Damodar
Darling
Derwent
Detroit
Dnieper
Dubglas
Durance
Ettrick
Fitzroy
Garonne
Genesee
Gironde
Guapore
Hari Rud
Helmand
Hooghly
Huang He
Hwangho
Iguassu
Irawadi
Kanawha
Krishna
Lachlan
Limpopo
Lualaba
Madeira
Manning
Maranon
Maritsa
Mataura

Meander
Moselle
Narbada
Narmada
Neuquén
Niagara
Nipigon
Orinoco
Orontes
Parrett
Pechora
Pharpar
Potomac
Red Deer
Rubicon
Sabrina
Salinas
Salween
Salzach
Sanders
Scheldt
Senegal
Shannon
Songhua
St Clair
St Croix
St Mary's
Swannee
Tapajos
Thomson
Tugaloo
Ucayali
Uruguay
Vistula
Waikato
Washita
Wateree
Welland
Yangtse
Yenisei
Yenisey
Zambese
Zambezi

8 letters:
Amu Darya
Anderson
Apurimac

Araguaia
Araguaya
Arkansas
Berezina
Blue Nile
Canadian
Charente
Cherwell
Chindwin
Chu Kiang
Clarence
Colorado
Columbia
Congaree
Daintree
Demerara
Dneister
Dordogne
Flinders
Franklin
Gascoyne
Godavari
Granicus
Guadiana
Hamilton
Illinois
Kentucky
Klondike
Kootenay
Maeander
Mahanadi
Manawatu
Menderes
Missouri
Mitchell
Ocmulgee
Okanagan
Okavango
Okovango
Ouachita
Pactolus
Paraguay
Parnaiba
Putumayo
Rio Negro
Safid Rud
Saguenay
Savannah

Suwannee
Syr Darya
Tonle Sap
Torridge
Toulouse
Tunguska
Van Hades
Veronezh
Victoria
Volturno
Wanganui
Windrush
Zhu Jiang

9 letters:
Allegheny
Ashburton
Billabong
Churchill
Crocodile
Des Moines
Essequibo
Euphrates
Irrawaddy
Kuskokwim
Mackenzie
Magdalena
Murchison
Parnahiba
Perihonca
Pilcomayo
Porcupine
Qu'Appelle
Rangitata
Richelieu
Rio Branco
Rio Grande
Salambria
Santa Cruz
St George's
White Nile
Wisconsin

10 letters:
Black Volta
Blackwater
Chao Phraya
Courantyne

Cumberland
Great Slave
Housatonic
Kizil Irmak
Phlegethon
Rangitaiki
Rangitikei
Sacramento
San Joaquin
Schuylkill
St Lawrence
White Volta
Yesil Irmak

11 letters:
Aegospotami
Assiniboine
Brahmaputra
Connecticut
Cooper Creek
Delaguadero
Guadalentin
Lesser Slave
Madre de Dios
Mississauga
Mississippi
Monongahela
Shatt-al-Arab
Susquehanna
Yellowstone

12 letters:
Guadalquivir
Murrumbidgee
Saõ Francisco
Saskatchewan

13 letters:
Little Bighorn

17 letters:
North
  Saskatchewan
South
  Saskatchewan

River-bank, Riverside Brim, Carse, Riparian
River-bed T(h)alweg

River-mouth Firth, Frith

Rivet(ing) Bolt, Clinch, Clink, Concentrate, Explosive, Fasten, Fix, Pean, Peen, Stud, Transfix, Unputdownable

Rivulet Beck, Brook, Burn, Gill, Rill, Runnel, Strand

RNA Antisense, → DNA, Messenger, Molecule, Retrotransposon, Ribosomal, Ribosome, Ribozyme, Soluble, Transcribe, Transfer, Uracil

Roach Fish, Red-eye

Road(s), Roadside, Road surface A, A1, Access, Anchorage, Arterial, Asphalt, Autobahn, Autopista, Autostrada, Ave(nue), B, Beltway, Blacktop, Boulevard, Burma, Carriageway, Causeway, Clay, Clearway, Close, Cloverleaf, Coach, Concession, Corduroy, Corniche, Course, Cul-de-sac, Dirt, Drift-way, Driveway, Dunstable, Escape, Exit, Expressway, Fairway, Feeder, Fly-over, Fly-under, Foss(e) Way, Freeway, Grid, Hampton, Highway, Horseway, Kerb, Lane, Loan, Loke, Mall, Metal, M1, Motorway, Orbital, Overpass, Parkway, Path, Pike, Post, Private, Rat-run, Rd, Relief, Ride, Ridgeway, Ring, → ROUTE, Royal, Service, Shoulder, Shunpike, Side, Skid, Slip, Speedway, Spur(way), St(reet), Superhighway, Switchback, Tarmac, Tar-seal, Thoroughfare, Tobacco, Toby, Track(way), Trunk, Turning, Turnpike, Unadopted, Underpass, Unmade, Verge, Via, Viaduct, Way

Road-block Barrier, Cone, Jam, Toll

Road-keeper Way-warden

Road-maker Drunkard, Macadam, Navigator, Telford, Wade

Roadstead La Hogue

Roam Extravagate, Peregrinate, Rake, Ramble, Rove, Stray, Wander, Wheel

Roan Barbary, Bay, Horse, Leather, Schimmel, Strawberry

Roar(ing) Bawl, Bell(ow), Bluster, Boom, Boys, Cry, Forties, Guffaw, Laugh, Roin, Rote, Rout, Royne, Thunder, Tumult, Vroom, Wuther, Zoom

Roast Bake, Barbecue, Baste, Birsle, Brent, Cabob, Cook, Crab, Crown, Decrepitate, Grill, Kabob, Pan, Pot, Ridicule, Scald, Scathe, Sear, Slate, Tan, Torrefy

Rob(bed), Robber(y) Abduct, Bandalero, Bandit, Barabbas, Bereave, Blag, Brigand, Burgle, Bust, Cabbage, Cacus, Cateran, Clyde, Dacoit, Dakoit, Daylight, Depredation, Despoil, Do, Drawlatch, Fake, Filch, Fleece, Flimp, Footpad, Gilderoy, Heist, Hership, Highjack, High toby, Highwayman, Hijack, Hold-up, Hustle, Job, Kondo, Ladrone, Land-pirate, Larceny, Latrocinium, Latron, Loot, Mill, Moskonfyt, Mosstrooper, Pad, Pandoor, Pandour, Pillage, Pinch, Piracy, Pluck, Plunder, Procrustes, Ramraid, Rapine, Reave, Reft, Reive, Rieve, Rifle, Roberdsman, Robertsman, Roll, Rover, Roy, Rubbet, Rustler, Sack, Sciron, Screw, Short change, Sinis, Skinner, Smash and grab, Snaphaunch, Spoiler, Spoliation, → STEAL, Steaming, Stick-up, Sting, Swindle, Thief, Toby, Turn-over, Turpin

Robe(s) Alb, Amice, Amis, Attrap, Buffalo, Camis, Camus, Cassock, Chimer, Chrisom(-cloth), Christom, Dalmatic, Dolman, → DRESS, Gown, Ihram, Jilbab, Kanzu, Khalat, Khilat, Kill(a)ut, Kimono, Mantle, Night, Parament, Parliament, Pedro, Peplos, Pontificals, Purple, Regalia, Rochet, Saccos, Sanbenito, Soutane, Sticharion, Stola, Stole, Talar, Tire, Vestment, Yukata

Robert Bob(by), Bridges, Browning, Burns, Cop, Flic, Peel, Rab, Rob

Robin Adair, American, Bird, Cock, Day, Goodfellow, Hob, Hood, Puck(-hairy), Ragged, Redbreast, Reliant, Round, Ruddock, Starveling, Wake

Robot Android, Automaton, Cyborg, Dalek, Golem, Nanobot, Puppet, RUR, Telechir

Robust Hale, Hardy, Healthy, Hearty, Iron, Lusty, Muscular, Sound, Stalwart, Sthenic, Stout, Strapping, Sturdy, Vigorous

Roc Bird, Ruc, Rukh

Rock(s), Rocker, Rocking, Rocky Acid, Ages, Agitate, Astound, Ayers, Cap, Cock,

Country, Cradle, Destabilise, Edinburgh, Erratic, Garage, Gib(raltar), Heavy metal, Hybrid, Mantle, Marciano, Matrix, Native, Nunatak(kr), Permafrost, Petrology, Platform, Plymouth, Punk, Quake, Reel, Reggae, Reservoir, Rip-rap, Rudaceous, Sally, Scare, → SHAKE, Shoogle, Showd, Soft, Stonehenge, Stun, Sway, Swee, Swing, Ted, Teeter, Totter, Tremble, Uluru, Unstable, Unsteady, Weeping, Wind, Windsor

ROCKS

2 letters:
Aa

3 letters:
Gem
Ice
Jow
Tor

4 letters:
Bell
Coal
Crag
Gang
Glam
Jura
Lava
Lias
Noup
Reef
Sill
Sima
Trap
Tufa
Tuff
Wall
Zoic

5 letters:
Arête
Brash
Calpe
Chair
Chalk
Chert
Cliff
Craig
Elvan
Emery
Flint
Geode
Glass
Krans

Loess
Magma
Nappe
Peter
Scalp
Scrae
Scree
Shale
Slate
Solid
Stone
Trass
Wacke

6 letters:
Albite
Aplite
Arkose
Banket
Basalt
Dacite
Desert
Diapir
Dogger
Dunite
Flaser
Flysch
Fossil
Gabbro
Gangue
Garnet
Gibber
Gneiss
Gossan
Gozzan
Inlier
Kingle
Living
Marble
Masada
Norite
Oolite
Oolith

Ophite
Pelite
Pluton
Pumice
Rognon
Sarsen
Schist
Sinter
Skerry
Sklate
S. Peter
Stonen
Synroc
Tephra

7 letters:
Aquifer
Archean
Arenite
Boulder
Breccia
Clastic
Cuprite
Cyanean
Diamond
Diorite
Erathem
Eucrite
Fastnet
Felsite
Geofact
Granite
Greisen
Haplite
Igneous
Lignite
Lorelei
Marlite
Minette
Molasse
Moraine
Needles
Olivine

Ophites
Outcrop
Outlier
Peridot
Picrite
Remanie
Rhaetic
Sinking
Spilite
Stadium
Syenite
Terrane
Thulite
Tripoli
Wenlock

8 letters:
Adularia
Aegirine
Aiguille
Andesite
Aphanite
Archaean
Asbestos
Basanite
Brockram
Burstone
Calcrete
Calc-tufa
Calc-tuff
Ciminite
Diabasic
Dolerite
Dolomite
Eclogite
Eklogite
Elvanite
Eutaxite
Fahlband
Felstone
Footwall
Ganister
Hepatite

Hornfels
Idocrase
Inchcape
Isocline
Laterite
Lenticle
Lopolith
Mesolite
Mudstone
Mylonite
Obsidian
Peperino
Petuntse
Phyllite
Pisolite
Plutonic
Porphyry
Psammite
Psephite
Ragstone
Regolith
Rhyolite
Rocaille
Roe-stone
Saxatile
Saxonite
Scorpion
Sunstone
Taconite
Tarpeian
Tephrite
The Olgas
Tonalite
Trachyte
Trappean
Volcanic
Xenolith

9 letters:
Anticline
Argillite
Batholite
Batholith
Bentonite
Bluestone
Buhrstone
Claystone
Cockhorse

Colluvium
Cornstone
Dalradian
Diatomite
Dolostone
Eddystone
Evaporite
Firestone
Flagstone
Flowstone
Gannister
Goslarite
Granulite
Greensand
Greystone
Greywacke
Gritstone
Hornstone
Impactite
Intrusion
Ironstone
Laccolite
Laccolith
Lardalite
Larvikite
Limestone
Meteorite
Mica-slate
Migmatite
Monadnock
Monocline
Monzonite
Mortstone
Mugearite
Natrolite
Neocomian
Ophiolite
Ottrelite
Pegmatite
Phonolite
Phosphate
Pleonaste
Propylite
Protogine
Quartzite
Sandstone
Saprolite
Scablands

Schistose
Siltstone
Soapstone
Tachylyte
Theralite
Tinguaite
Toadstone
Travertin
Underclay
Variolite
Veinstone
Veinstuff
Ventifact
Vulcanite
Whinstone
White Lias
Whunstane
Zechstein

10 letters:
Ailsa Craig
Amygdaloid
Camptonite
Epidiorite
Foundation
Granophyre
Greenstone
Grey-wether
Hypabyssal
Ignimbrite
Kersantite
Kimberlite
Laurdalite
Laurvikite
Lherzolite
Limburgite
Mica-schist
Novaculite
Orthophyre
Palagonite
Peridotite
Phenocryst
Pitchstone
Pyroxenite
Rupestrian
Schalstein
Serpentine
Sparagmite

Stinkstone
Stonebrash
Syntagmata
Teschenite
Touchstone
Travertine
Troctolite

11 letters:
Agglomerate
Amphibolite
Annabergite
Anorthosite
Carbonatite
Geanticline
Halleflinta
Lamprophyre
Metamorphic
Monchiquite
Napoleonite
Nephelinite
Phillipsite
Pyroclastic
Sedimentary
Symplegades

12 letters:
Babingtonite
Baltic Shield
Coal Measures
Granodiorite
Grossularite
Slickenslide
Straticulate
Stromatolite
Syntagmatite
Thunderstone

13 letters:
Hypersthenite

14 letters:
Roche moutonnée

18 letters:
Scandinavian Shield

Rock-boring Pholas
Rock-cress Arabis

Rocket Arugula, Blue, Booster, Capsule, Carpet, Carrier, Congreve, Dame's, Delta, Drake, Dressing down, Dyer's, Engine, Eruca, Flare, Ion, Jato, Life, London, Missile, Multistage, Onion, Posigrade, Reprimand, Reproof, Retro, Rockoon, Salad, SAM, Sea, Skylark, Soar, Sonde, Sounding, Step, Stephenson, Take-off, Thruster, Tourbillion, Ullage, Upshoot, V1, Vernier, Von Braun, Wall, Warhead, Weld, Yellow, Zero stage

Rock-living Rupicoline, Saxatile, Saxicoline, Saxicolous

Rock-pipit Sea-lark

▷ **Rocky** *may indicate* an anagram

Rococo Baroque, Fancy, Ornate, Quaint

Rod(-shaped), Rodlike, Rods Aaron's, Axle, Baculiform, Bar, Barbe(l)l, Barre, Birch, Caduceus, Caim, Came, Can, Cane, Centre, Connecting, Control, Cue, Cuisenaire®, Dipstick, Divining, Dowser, Drain, Ellwand, Fasces, Filler, Fin-ray, Firearm, Fisher, Fishing, Fly, Fuel, Gold stick, Gun, Handspike, Jacob's staff, Kame, King, Laver, Lightning, Linchpin, Lug, Mapstick, Mopstick, Moses, Napier's bones, Nervure, Newel, Notochord, Perch, Pin, Pistol, Piston, Pitman, Pointer, Poker, Poking-stick, Pole, Pontie, Pontil, Ponty, Probang, Puntee, Punty, Push, Raddle, Regulating, Rhabdoid, Rhabdus, Riding, Rood, Scollop, Shaft, Sounding, Spindle, Spit, Stadia, Stair, Stanchion, Staple, Stave, Stay-bolt, Stick, Strickle, Switch, Tension, Tie, Track, Triblet, Tringle, Trocar, Twig, Urochord, Ventifact, Verge, Virgate, Virgulate, Wand, Welding, Withe

Rod-bearer Lictor

Rode Raid

Rodent Acouchi, Acouchy, Ag(o)uti, Agouty, Bandicoot, Bangsring, Banxring, Beaver, Biscacha, Bizcacha, Bobac, Bobak, Boomer, Capybara, Cavy, Chickaree, Chincha, Chinchilla, Chipmunk, Civet, Coypu, Cricetus, Dassie, Deer-mouse, Delundung, Dormouse, Fieldmouse, Gerbil(le), Glires, Glutton, Gnawer, Gopher, Groundhog, Guinea pig, Ham(p)ster, Hedgehog, Hog-rat, Hutia, Hyrax, Hystricomorph, Jerboa, Jird, Lemming, Marmot, Mole rat, Mouse, Murid, Mus, Musk-rat, Musquash, Ochotona, Ondatra, Paca, Porcupine, Potoroo, Prairie dog, Rat, Ratel, Ratton, Renegade, Runagate, Sciurine, Sewellel, Shrew, Simplicidentate, S(o)uslik, Spermophile, Springhaas, Springhase, Squirrel, Taguan, Taira, Tuco-tuco, Tucu-tuco, Vermin, Viscacha, Vole, Woodchuck, Woodmouse

Roderick Random, Usher

Rodomontade Bluster, Boast, Bombast, Brag, Gas

Roe Avruga, Caviar(e), Coral, Fry, Hard, Melt, Milt(z), Pea, Raun, Rawn, Soft

Roger Ascham, Bacon, Jolly, OK, Rights

Rogue, Roguish(ness) Arch, Bounder, Charlatan, Chiseller, Drole, Dummerer, Elephant, Espiègle(rie), Ganef, Ganev, Ganof, Gonif, Gonof, Greek, Gypsy, Hedge-creeper, Hempy, Herries, Imp, Knave, Latin, Limmer, Monkey, Panurge, Picaresque, Picaroon, Pollard, Poniard, Rapparee, Ra(p)scal(l)ion, Riderhood, Savage, Scamp, Schellum, Schelm, Scoundrel, Skellum, Sleeveen, Slip-string, Sly, Swindler, Varlet, Villain, Wrong' un

Roil Agitate, Annoy, Churn, Provoke, Vex

Roister(er) Blister, Carouse, Ephesian, Revel, Rollick, Scourer, Scowrer, Swashbuckler, Swinge-buckler

Role Bit, Cameo, Capacity, Function, Gender, Métier, → **PART**, Prima-donna, Stead, Title, Travesty

Roll(ed), Roller, Roll-call, Rolling, Rolls Absence, Bagel, Bap, Barrel, Beigel, Billow, Birmingham, Bolt, Bridge, Brioche, Butterie, Calender, Cambridge, Chamade, Comber, Convolv(ut)e, Cop, Couch, Court, Croissant, Cylinder, Dandy,

Drum, Dutch, Electoral, Enswathe, Eskimo, Even, Fardel, Fardle, Flatten, Forward, Furl, Go, Goggle, Hotdog, Inker, Involute, Labour, List, Loaded, Lurch, Makimono, Mangle, Mano, Matricula, Motmot, Moving, Music, Muster, Notitia, Opulent, Paradiddle, Patent, Paupiette, Pay, Petit-pain, Piano, Pigeon, Pipe, Platen, Rafale, Ragman, Record, Reef, Reel, Register, Ren, Rent, Revolute, Revolve, Rhotacism, Ring, Road, Rob, Rolag, Roster, Rota, Rotate, Rotifer, Roul(e), Roulade, Rouleau, RR, Rub-a-dub, Rumble, Run, Sausage, Schnecke(n), Skin up, Snap, Somersault, Spool, Spring, Sway, Swell, Swiss, Table, Tandem, Taxi, Temple, Tent, Terrier, Thread, Toilet, Tommy, Trill, Trindle, Trundle, Valuation, Victory, Volume, Volutation, Wad, Wallow, Wamble, Waul, Wave, Wawl, Web, Welter, Western, Wince, Wrap, Yaw, Zorbing

Rollick(ing) Frolic, Gambol, Romp, Sport

▷ **Rollicking** *may indicate* an anagram

Roly-poly Chubby

Roman Agricola, Agrippa, Aurelius, Calpurnia, Candle, Catholic, Cato, Consul, CR, Crassus, Decemviri, Decurion, Empire, Flavian, Galba, Holiday, Italian, Jebusite, Latin, Maecenas, Papist, Patrician, PR, Quirites, Raetic, RC, Retarius, Rhaetia, Road, Scipio, Seneca, Sulla, Tarquin, Tiberius, Trebonius, Type, Uriconian, Veneti, Volsci

Romance, Romantic (talk) Affair, Amorous, Byronic, Casanova, Catalan, Dreamy, Fancy, Fantasise, Fib, Fiction, Gest(e), Gothic, Historical, Invention, Ladin(o), Ladinity, Langue d'oc(ian), Langue d'oil, Langue d'oui, Liaison, Lie, Neo-Latin, New, Novelette, Poetic, Quixotic, R(o)uman, Stardust, Tale

▸ **Romanian** *see* RO(U)MANIAN

Romanov Nicholas

▸ **Romany** *see* GYPSY

Rome Holy See, Imperial City

Romeo Casanova, Montagu, R, Swain

Romp(ing) Carouse, Escapade, Fisgig, Fizgig, Frisk, Frolic, Hoyden, Jaunce, Randy, Rig, Rollick, Skylark, Sport, Spree

Ron Glum, Moody

Rondo Rota

Ronnie Biggs

Röntgen R, X-ray

Roo Joey

Roof (edge), Roofing Belfast, Bell, Broach, Ceil, Cl(e)ithral, Cover, Curb, Divot, Dome, Drip, Eaves, French, Gable, Gambrel, Hardtop, Hip(ped), Home, Hypostyle, Imperial, Jerkin-head, Leads, Mansard, Monopitch, Palate, Pavilion, Pent, Pitched, Pop-top, Porte-cochère, Rag top, Rigging, Saddle, Saddleback, Shingle, Skillion, Skirt, Span, Sun(shine), Targa top, Tectiform, Tectum, Tegula, Thatch, Thetch, Tiling, Top, Uraniscus

Roof-climber Stegopholist

Roofless Hypaethral, Upaithric

Rook Bird, Castle, Cheat, Crow, Fleece, Fool, Overcharge, R, Swindle

Rookie Beginner, Colt, Galoot, Greenhorn, Nignog, Novice, Recruit, Tenderfoot, Tyro

Room(s), Roomy Antechamber, Anteroom, Apadana, Apartment, Assembly, Attic, Ben, Berth, Bibby, Boardroom, Boiler, Boudoir, Bower, But, Cabin(et), Camarilla, Camera, Capacity, Casemate, CC, Ceiling, Cell, Cellar, Cenacle, Chamber, Chancellery, Changing, Chat, Chaumer, Closet, Cockloft, Combination, Commodious, Compartment, Composing, Conclave, Consulting, Control, Cubicle,

Cuddy, Cutting, Dark, Day, Delivery, Digs, Dissecting, Divan, Dojo, Drawing, Dressing, Durbar, Elbow, End, Engine, Ex(h)edra, Extension, Foyer, Gap, Garret, Genizah, Green, Grill, Gun, Herbarium, Incident, Kiva, Kursaal, Lab, Latitude, Laura, Lavra, Lebensraum, Leeway, Leg, Library, Living, Locker, Lodge, Loft, Long, Loo, Lounge, Margin, Megaron, Misericord(e), Mould-loft, Music, Oda, Operations, Oratory, Orderly, Oriel, Pad, Palm Court, Panic, Parlour, Parvis, Penetralia, Pentice, Pentise, Powder, Press, Priesthole, Private, Projection, Property, Public, Pump, Reading, Receiving, Reception, Recitation, Recovery, Recreation, Rest, Rm, Robing, Rubber, Rumpus, Sacristy, Sale(s), Salle, Salon, Sanctum, School, Scope, Scriptorium, Scullery, Serdab, Servery, Service, Shebang, Single, Single-end, Sitkamer, Sitting, Smoking, Snug, Solar, Solarium, → **SPACE**, Spacious, Spare, Spence, Spheristerion, Staff, Standing, Steam, Still, Stock, Stowage, Street, Strong, Studio, Study, Suite, Sun, Tap, Tea, Throne, Tiring, Tool, Twin, Two-pair, Ullage, Utility, Vestiary, Vestry, Voorkamer, Waiting, Ward, Wash, Wiggle, Work, Zeta

Roost(er) Cock, Perch, Siskin, Sit

Root(s), Rooted, Rooting Aruhe, Asarum, Beet, Buttress, Calamus, Calumba, Cassava, Cheer, Contrayerva, Costus, Cube, Culver's, Cuscus, Dasheen, Delve, Deracinate, Derivation, Derris, Dig, Eddo, Elecampane, Eradicate, Eringo, Eryngo, Etymic, Etymon, Extirpate, Fern, Fibrous, Foundation, Gelseminine, Ginseng, Grass, Grout, Grub, Heritage, Horseradish, Hurrah, Immobile, Implant, Incorrigible, Insane, Irradicate, Jalap, Jicama, Knee, Lateral, Licorice, Mallee, Mandrake, Mangold, Mishmee, Mishmi, Mooli, More, Myall, Navew, Nousle, Nuzzle, Origins, Orris, Pachak, Pleurisy, Pneumatophore, Poke, Prop, Pry, Putchock, Putchuk, Race, Radical, Radish, Radix, Repent, Rhatany, Rhizic, Rhizoid, Rhizome, Scorzonera, Senega, Sessile, Setwall, Snuzzle, Source, Square, Stilt, Stock, Tap, Taro, Tuber, Tuberous, Tulip, Turbith, Turnip, Turpeth, Vetiver, Yam, Zedoary

Rootless Psilotum

Rope(s) Abaca, Backstay, Ba(u)lk, Becket, Bind, Bobstay, Boltrope, Bracer, Brail, Breeching, Bunt-line, Cable, Cablet, Colt, Cord, Cordage, Cordon, Cringle, Downhaul, Drag, Earing, Fake, Fall, Flemish coil, Fore-brace, Foresheet, Forestay, Funicular, Futtock-shroud, Gantline, Grist, Guest, Guide, Guy, Halliard, Halser, Halter, Halyard, Hawser, Hawser-laid, Headfast, Inhaul, Jack-stay, Jeff, Jib-sheet, Jump, Kernmantel, Knittle, Ladder, Lanyard, Lasher, Lashing, Lasso, Lazo, Leg, Line, Longe, Lunge, Mainbrace, Mainsheet, Manil(l)a, Marlin(e), Match-cord, Messenger, Monkey, Mooring, Nettle, Nip, Noose, Oakum, Outhaul, Painter, Parbuckle, Pastern, Prolonge, Prusik, Pudding, Rawhide, Reef point, Riata, Ridge, Ringstopper, Roband, Robbin, Rode, Runner, St Johnston's ribbon, St Johnston's tippet, Sally, Seal, Selvagee, Sennit, Sheet, Shroud, Sinnet, Span, Spancel, Spun-yarn, Stay, Sternfast, Stirrup, String, Sugan, Swifter, Tackle, Tail, Tether, Tie, Timenoguy, Tippet, Tow(line), Trace, Trail, Triatic, Triatic stay, Vang, Wanty, Warp, Widdy, Wire

Rosalind Ganymede

Rosary Beads, Mala, Paternoster

Rose(-red), Rosie, Rosy Albertine, Amelanchier, Aurorean, Avens, Bear's-foot, Blooming, Bourbon, Breare, Briar, Brier, Burnet, Cabbage, Canker, Ceiling, Cherokee, China, Christmas, Compass, Corn, Damask, Dog, Eglantine, Eglatère, England, Floribunda, Geum, Golden, G(u)elder, Hellebore, Hybrid, Jack, Jacque, Jacqueminot, Lal(age), Lancaster, Lee, Monthling, Moss, Multiflora, Musk, Noisette, Opulus, Peace, Petra, Pink, Potentilla, Promising, Provence, Province, Provincial, Provine, Pyrus, Quillaia, Quillaja, Rambler, Red(dish), Remontant,

Rhoda, Rhodo-, Rock, Rugosa, Scotch, Snowball, Sprinkler, Standard, Sweetbrier, Tea, Tokyo, Tudor, White, Whitethorn, York

Rose-apple Jamboo, Jambu

Rose-bay Oleander

Rosemary Rosmarine

Rosette Buttonhole, Chou, Cockade, Favour, Patera, Rosula

Rosin Colophony, Resin, Roset, Rosit, Rozet, Rozit

Rosinante Jade

Roster List, Register, Scroll, Table

Rostrum Ambo, Bema, Lectern, Podium, Pulpit, Tribune

Rot(ten), Rotting Addle, Baloney, Boo, Bosh, Botrytis, Bull, Caries, Carious, Corrode, Corrupt, Crown, Daddock, Decadent, → **DECAY**, Decompose, Decrepitude, Degradable, Dotage, Dry, Eat, Erode, Fester, Foot, Foul, Gangrene, Kibosh, Manky, Mildew, Noble, Nonsense, Poppycock, Poxy, Punk, Putid, Putrefy, Putrid, Rail, Rancid, Rank, Rat, Red, Ret, Rhubarb, Ring, Rust, Sapropel, Septic, Soft, Sour, Squish, Twaddle, Vrot, Wet

Rotate, Rotating, Rotation, Rotator Crop, Feather, Gyrate, Laevorotation, Lay-farming, Optical, Pivot, Pronate, Rabat(te), Reamer, Revolve, Roll, Selsyn, Teres, Trundle, Turn, Turntable, Twiddle, Vorticose, Wheel, Windmill

Rote Heart, Memory, Recite, Routine

Rotor Auxiliary, Flywheel, Impeller, Tilt

▶ **Rotten** see **ROT**

▷ **Rotten** may indicate an anagram

Rotter Cad, Knave, Stinker, Swine

Rotund Chubby, Corpulent, Plump, Round, Stout, Tubby

Rotunda Pantheon

Roué Debauchee, Decadent, Libertine, Profligate, Rake(-shame), Rip

Rouge Blush, Gild, Jeweller's, Raddle, Redden, Reddle, Ruddy

Rough(en), Roughly, Roughness About, Abrasive, Approximate, Asper(ate), Burr, C, Ca, Choppy, Circa, Coarse, Craggy, Crude, Exasperate, Frampler, Grained, Gross, Gruff, Gurly, Gusty, Hard, Harsh, Hispid, Hoodlum, Hooligan, Impolite, Imprecise, Incondite, Inexact, Irregular, Jagged, Karst, Keelie, Kokobeh, Muricate, Obstreperous, Or so, Push, Ragged, Ramgunshoch, Raspy, Raucle, Rip, Risp, Robust, Row, Rude, Rugged, Rusticate, Rusty, Sandblast, Scabrid, Scabrous, Sea, Shaggy, Sketchy, Some, Spray, Spreathe, Squarrose, Stab, Strong-arm, Stubbly, Swab, Tartar, Tearaway, Ted, Textured, Tousy, Touzy, Towsy, Towzy, Uncut, Violent, Yahoo

Roughage Ballast, Bran, Fodder

Rough breathing Asper, Rale, Wheeze

Roughcast Harl

▷ **Roughly** may indicate an anagram

Roulette Russian

Ro(u)manian, Rumanian Ro, R(o)uman, Vlach, Wal(l)achian

Round(ness) About, Ammo, Ball, Beat, Bombe, Bout, Cartridge, Catch, Circle, Complete, Cycle, Dome, Doorstep, Fat, Figure, Full, Global, Globate, Hand, Heat, Jump-off, Lap, Leg, Milk, O, Oblate, Orb, Orbicular, Orbit, Orby, Ought, Patrol, Peri-, Pirouette, Plump, Qualifying, Quarter, Quarter-final, Rev, Ring, Robin, Roly-poly, Ronde, Rondure, Rota, Rotund, Route, Routine, Rundle, Rung, Salvo, Sandwich, Sarnie, Sellinger's, Semi-final, Shot, Skirt, Slice, Sphaer, Sphere, Spherical, Spiral, Step, Table, Tour, Tubby, U-turn

▷ **Round** may indicate a word reversed

Roundabout Ambages, Approximately, Bypass, Carousel, Circle, Circuit, Circumambient, Circumbendibus, Circus, Devious, Eddy, → INDIRECT, Merry-go-round, Peripheral, Rotary, Tortuous, Traffic circle, Turntable, Waltzer, Whirligig, Windlass

Round building Tholos, Tholus

Rounders Patball

Round-mouth Hag

Round-up Bang-tail muster, Collate, Corner, Corral, Gather, Herd, Rodeo, Spiral

Roup Auction, Croak, Pip, Roop

Rouse, Rousing Abrade, Abraid, Abray, Amo(o)ve, Animate, Beat, Bestir, Emotive, Enkindle, Firk, Flush, Hearten, Heat, Innate, Kindle, Knock up, Rear, Send, Stimulate, Suscitate, Unbed, Waken, Whip

Rousseau Émile

Rout Clamour, Debacle, Defeat, Drub, Fleme, Flight, Hubbub, Hurricane, Rabble, Retreat, Rhonchal, Snore, Thiasus, Upsee, Upsey, Upsy, Vanquish, Whoobub

Route Arterial, Avenue, Byroad, Causeway, Course, Direction, Itinerary, I-way, Line, Ling, M-way, Path, Red, Road, Stock, Track, Trade, Via, Way

Routine Automatic, Day-to-day, Drill, Everyday, Grind, Groove, Habitual, Heich-how, Heigh-ho, Ho-hum, Jogtrot, Journeywork, Monotony, Pattern, Perfunctory, Pipe-clay, Red tape, Rota, Rote, Round, Rut, S(c)htick, Schtik, Treadmill, Workaday

Rove(r), Roving Car, Discursive, Enrange, Errant, Freebooter, Gad, Globetrotter, Marauder, Nomad, Proler, Prowl, Ralph, Range, → ROAM, Slub(b), Stray, Vagabond, Varangarian, Viking, Wander

Row(er) Align, Altercation, Arew, Argue, Argument, Bank, Barney, Bedlam, Bobbery, Bow, Brattle, Cannery, Colonnade, Death, Debate, Deen, Din, Dispute, Dust-up, Feud, File, Fireworks, Food, Fyle, Hoo-ha, Hullabaloo, Leander, Line(-up), Noise, Note, Oar, Octastich, Paddle, Parade, Peripteral, Pluriserial, Pull, Quarrel, Rammy, Range, Rank, Raunge, Remigate, Reproach, Rew, Rhubarb, Rotten, Ruction, Rumpus, Scene, Scull, Series, Set, Shindig, Shindy, Shine, Skid, Spat, Splore, Stern, Stound, Street, Stridor, Stroke, Stushie, Sweep, Terrace, Tier, Tiff, Tone, Torpid, Wetbob, Wherryman

Rowan Ash, Quicken

Rowdy, Rowdiness Cougan, Hoo, Hooligan, Loud, Noisy, Rorty, Rough, Roughhouse, Ruffian, Scourer, Scozza, Skinhead, Stroppy, Unruly, Uproarious

Roy Rob

Royal(ty), Royalist Academy, Angevin, Basilical, Battle, Bourbon, Emigré, Exchange, Fee, Hanoverian, Imperial, Imposing, Inca, Kingly, King's man, Majestic, Malignant, Palatine, Payment, Pharaoh, Plantagenet, Prince, Princess, Purple, Queenly, Real, Regal, Regis, Regius, Regnal, Sail, Sceptred, Society

Rub(bing), Rubber(y), Rub out Abrade, Attrition, Balata, Buff, Buna®, Bungie, Bungy, Bunje(e), Bunjie, Bunjy, Butyl, Calk, Calque, Camelback, Caoutchouc, Chafe, Cold, Condom, Corrade, Corrode, Cow gum®, Crepe, Cul(t)ch, Destroy, Dunlop®, Ebonite, Efface, Elastic, Elastomer, Embrocate, Emery, Erase, Factice, Factis, Fawn, Foam, Fray, Fret, Friction, Fridge, Frottage, Fudge, Funtumia, Gall, Galoch, Goodyear®, Grate, Graze, Grind, Guayule, Gum elastic, Gutta-percha, Hale, Hard, Hevea, Hule, India, Inunction, Irritate, Isoprene, Jelutong, Lagos, Latex, Leather, Masseur, Negrohead, Neoprene, Nuzzle, Obstacle, Para, Polish, Pontianac, Pontianak, Root, Safe, Sandpaper, Scour, Scrub, Scuff, Seringa, Silastic®, Smoked, Sorbo®, Sponge, Stroke, Synthetic, Towel, Trace, Ule, Vulcanite, Wild, Wipe, Xerotripsis

▷ **Rubbed** *may indicate* an anagram

Rubbish Balls, Brash, Brock, Bull, Bunkum, Cack, Clap-trap, Cobblers, Codswallop, Culch, Debris, Dre(c)k, Drivel, Fiddlesticks, Garbage, Grot, Grunge, Hogwash, Kack, Kak, Landfill, Leavings, Litter, Mullock, Nonsense, Phooey, Piffle, Pish, Raff, Raffle, → **REFUSE**, Scrap, Sewage, Stuff, Tinpot, Tip, Tom(fool), Tosh, Totting, Trade, Tripe, Trouch, Truck, Trumpery, Twaddle

Rubbish heap Dump, Lay-stall, Sweepings, Toom

Rubble Brash, Debris, Detritus, Moellon, Random, Remains, Riprap, Talus

Rubidium Rb

Ruby Agate, Balas, Brazilian, Colorado, Cuprite, Oriental, Pigeon's blood, Port, Red, Spinel, Star

Ruck Furrow, Scrum, Wrinkle

Rucksack Backpack, Bergen, Pikau

Ruction Ado, Fuss, Quarrel

Rudder Budget, Helm, Steerer

Ruddle Lemnian

Ruddy Bally, Bloody, Flashy, Florid, Red, Roseate, Rubicund, Rufous, Sanguine

Rude Abusive, Barbaric, Bear, Bestial, Bumpkin, Callow, Churlish, Coarse, Discourteous, Elemental, Goustrous, Green, Ill-bred, Impolite, Indecorous, Inficete, Ingram, Ingrum, Insolent, Ocker, Offensive, Peasant, Raw, Risqué, Rough, Simple, Surly, Unbred, Uncomplimentary, Uncourtly, Unlettered, Unmannered, Vulgar

Rudiment(ary), Rudiments ABC, Absey, Anlage, Beginning, Element, Embryo, Foundation, Germ(en), Germinal, Inchoate, Seminal, Vestige

Rudolph Hess, Reindeer

Rue(ful) Boulevard, Dittany, Goat's, Harmala, Harmel, Herb of grace, Meadow, Mourn, Regret, Repent, Rew, Ruta, Sorry, Wall

Ruff Collar, Crest, Fraise, Frill, Mane, Partlet, Pope, Rabato, Rebato, Ree, Trump

Ruffian Apache, Bashi-bazouk, Brute, Bully, Cut-throat, Desperado, Goon(da), Highbinder, Hoodlum, Hooligan, Keelie, Larrikin, Lout, Miscreant, Mohock, Myrmidon, Phansigar, Plug-ugly, Raff, Rowdy, Skinhead, Sweater, Tearaway, Thug, Toe-ragger, Trailbaston, Tumbler

Ruffle(d) Bait, Dishevel, Falbala, Flounce, Fluster, Fret, → **FRILL**, Gather, Irritate, Jabot, Peplum, Rouse, Ruche, Rumple, Shirty, Tousle

▷ **Ruffle** *may indicate* an anagram

Rug Afghan, Bearskin, Buffalo-robe, Carpet, Drugget, Ensi, Flokati, Gabbeh, Hearth, Herez, Heriz, Kelim, K(h)ilim, Kirman, Lap robe, Mat, Maud, Numdah, Oriental, Prayer, Runner, Rya, Scatter, Tatami, Throw, Travelling

Rugby (player) Back, Fifteen, Forward, Harlequin, Lion, Pack, Quin, RU, Scrum, Sevens, Threequarter, Touch, Wing

Rugged Craggy, Harsh, Knaggy, Rough, Strong

Ruin(ed), Ruins Annihilate, Blast, Blight, Blue, Carcase, Collapse, Corrupt, Crash, Crock, Damn, Decay, Defeat, Demolish, Despoil, Destroy, Devastate, Disfigure, Dish, Disrepair, Dogs, Doom, Downcome, Downfall, End, Fordo, Hamstring, Heap, Hell, Insolvent, Inure, Kaput(t), Kibosh, Loss, Mar, Mocers, Mockers, Mother's, Overthrow, Perdition, Petra, Pigs and whistles, Pot, Puckerood, Ravage, Reck, Relic, Scotch, Scupper, Scuttle, Shatter, Sink, Smash, Spill, → **SPOIL**, Stramash, Subvert, Undo, Unmade, Ur, Violate, Vitiate, Whelm, Woe, Wrack

▷ **Ruined** *may indicate* an anagram

Rule(r), Rules, Ruling Algorithm, Align, Aristocrat, Arrêt, Article, Bylaw, Caesar, Calliper, Canon, Chain, Club-law, Code, Condominium, Constitution, Control,

Criterion, Decree, Domineer, Dominion, Empire, Establishment, Estoppel, Etiquette, Fatwa, Feint, Fetwa, Fleming's, Formation, Formula, Gag, Global, Golden, Govern, Govern-all, Ground, Home, In, Jackboot, Law, Leibniz's, Lesbian, Lex, Lindley, Liner, Majority, Matriarchy, Maxim, McNa(u)ghten, Mede, Meteyard, Method, Ministrate, Mistress, Mobocracy, Motto, Naismith's, Netiquette, Norm(a), Oppress, Ordinal, Organon, Organum, Parallel, Parallelogram, Phase, Phrase-structure, Pie, Placitum, Plumb, Precedent, Precept, Prescript, Prevail, Principle, Protocol, Pye, Rafferty's, Raine, Realm, Reciprocity, Rector, Regal, Regnant, Regula, Reign, Rewrite, Ring, Rubric, Scammozzi's, Setting, Slide, Standard, Statute, Stylebook, Sutra, Sway, Ten-minute, Ten-yard, Three, Thumb, Transformation(al), Trapezoid, T-square, Tycoon, Tyrant, Uti possidetis, Wield

---

RULERS

1 letter:
K
R

3 letters:
Ban
Bey
Dey
Mir
Oba
Raj
Rex

4 letters:
Amir
Cham
Czar
Doge
Duce
Emir
Imam
Inca
Khan
King
Nero
Pope
Rana
Shah
Tsar
Vali
Wali

5 letters:
Ameer
Ardri
Dewan
Diwan
Henry
Herod
Hoyle
Hyleg
Mogul
Mpret
Mudir
Nawab
Negus
Nizam
Pasha
Queen
Rajah
Shaka
Sheik
Sophi
Sophy
Tenno

6 letters:
Atabeg
Atabek
Bosman
Caliph
Castro
Chagan
Cheops
Dergue
Despot
Dynast
Exarch
Franco
Führer
Gerent
Harold
Hitler
Judges

Kabaka
Kaiser
Mamluk
Manchu
Mikado
Peshwa
Prince
Regent
Ronald
Sachem
Satrap
Sherif
Shogun
Sirdar
Squier
Squire
Stalin
Sultan
Swaraj
Walter

7 letters:
Abbasid
Ardrigh
Bajayet
Bajazet
Bodicea
Catapan
Chogyal
Elector
Emperor
Gaekwar
Gaikwar
Jamshid
Jamshyd
Khedive
Miranda

Monarch
Omayyad
Pharaoh
Podesta
Richard
Saladin
Serkali
Souldan
Toparch
Umayyad
Viceroy
Zamorin

8 letters:
Archduke
Autocrat
Bismarck
Boudicca
Burgrave
Caligula
Caudillo
Cromwell
Dictator
Ethnarch
Frederic
Heptarch
Hespodar
Hierarch
Maharaja
Mamaluke
Mameluke
Napoleon
Oligarch
Overlord
Padishah
Pericles
Reginald

Roderick	Bretwalda	Tamerlane	Prester John
Sagamore	Britannia		Queensberry
Sassanid	Cleopatra	**10 letters:**	Stadtholder
Suleiman	Cosmocrat	Caractacus	Tutankhamun
Suzerain	Frederick	Plantocrat	
Synarchy	Montezuma	Principate	**12 letters:**
Tetrarch	Ochlocrat	Rajpramukh	Chandragupta
Thearchy	Pendragon	Stratocrat	
	Plutocrat		**13 letters:**
9 letters:	Potentate	**11 letters:**	Haile Selassie
Alexander	President	Charlemagne	
Amenhotep	Sovereign	Genghis Khan	

Rule-book Code, Pie, Pye

Rum(mer) Abnormal, Bacardi, Bay, Cachaca, Curious, Daiquiri, Demerara, Eerie, Eery, Glass, Grog, Island, Jamaica, Odd(er), Peculiar, Quaint, Queer, Screech, Strange, Tafia, Weird

▶ **Rumanian** *see* RO(U)MANIAN

Rumble, Rumbling Borborygmus, Brool, Curmurring, Drum-roll, Groan, Growl, Guess, Lumber, Mutter, Rumour, Thunder, Tonneau, Twig

Ruminant, Ruminate Antelope, Cabrie, Camel, Cavicornia, Cervid, Champ, Chew, Contemplate, Cow, Gemsbok, Gnu, Goat, Meditate, Merycism, Nilgai, Nyala, Okapi, Oorial, Palebuck, Pecora

Rummage Delve, Fish, Foray, Jumble, Powter, Ransack, Rifle, Root, Rootle, Scavenge, Search, Tot

Rummy Canasta, Cooncan, Game, Gin, Queer

Rumour Breeze, Bruit, Buzz, Canard, Cry, Fame, Furphy, → GOSSIP, Grapevine, Hearsay, Kite, Kite-flying, Mail, Noise, On-dit, Pig's-whisper, Report, Repute, Say-so, Smear, Tale, Talk, Underbreath, Unfounded, Vine, Voice, Whisper, Word

Rump Arse, Bottom, Buttocks, Croup(e), Croupon, Crupper, Curpel, Derrière, Nates, Parliament, Podex, Pygal, Steak, Uropygium

Rumple Corrugate, Crease, Mess, Muss, Touse, Tousle, Touze, Towse, Towze, Wrinkle

Rumpus Bagarre, Commotion, Noise, Riot, Row, Ruction, Shindig, Shindy, Shine, Stushie, Tirrivee, Uproar

Run(ning), Run away, Run into, Run off, Runny, Runs Admin(ister), Arpeggio, Black, Bleed, Blue, Bolt, Break, Bunk, Bye, Career, Chase, Coop, Corso, Course, Cresta, Cross-country, Current, Cursive, Cut, Dart, Dash, Decamp, Direct, Double, Drive, Dry, Dummy, Enter, Escape, Extra, Fartlek, Flee, Flit, Flow, Fly, Follow, Fun, Fuse, Gad, Gallop, Gauntlet, Go, Green, Ground, Hare, Haste(n), Hennery, Hie, Hightail, Home, Idle, Jog, Jump bail, Ladder, Lauf, Leg, Leg bye, Lienteric, Liquid, Lope, Manage, Marathon, Melt, Milk, Mizzle, Mole, Molt, Monkey, Neume, Now, On, On-line, Operate, Pace, Pacific, Paper chase, Parkour, Pelt, Ply, Pour, Print, Purulent, R, Race, Range, Red, Renne, Rin, Romp, Roulade, Rounder, Ruck, Scamper, Scapa, Scarper, School, Schuss, Scud, Scutter, Scuttle, See, Sequence, Shoot, Single, Skate, Skedaddle, Ski, Skid, Skirr, Skitter, Slalom, Slide, Smuggle, Spew, Split, Spread, Sprint, Sprue, Squitters, Stampede, Straight, Streak, Stream, Taxi, Tear, Tenor, Tie-breaker, Trial, Trickle, Trill, Trot

Runaway Drain, Easy, Escapee, Fugitive, Fugue, Refugee

Run down Asperse, Belie, Belittle, Calumniate, Denigrate, Derelict, Dilapidated, Infame, Knock, Low, Obsolesce(nt), Poorly, Rack, Résumé, Scud, Seedy, Tirade, Traduce

Rune, Runic Ash, Futhark, Futhorc, Futhork, Kri, Ogham, Spell, Thorn, Wen, Wyn(n)

Rung Crossbar, Roundel, Rundle, Stave, Step, Tolled, Tread

Runner(s) Atalanta, Bean, Blade, Bow Street, Carpet, Coe, Courser, Deserter, Emu, Field, Geat, Gentleman, Gillie-wetfoot, Harrier, Hatta, Hencourt, Internuncio, Lampadist, Leg bye, Legman, Messenger, Miler, Milk, Mohr, Mousetrap, Nurmi, Owler, Rug, → **RUN(NING)**, Sarmentum, Scarlet, Series, Slipe, Smuggler, Stolon, Stream, Tailskid, Trial

▷ **Running, Runny** *may indicate* an anagram

Runt Dilling, Oobit, Oubit, Reckling, Scalawag, Scrog, Smallest, Titman, Woobut, Woubit

Run through Impale, Pierce, Rehearsal

Runway Airstrip, Drive, Slipway, Strip, Tarmac®

Run wild Lamp, Rampage

Rupee(s) Lac, Lakh, Re

Rupert Bear

Rupture Breach, Burst, Crack, Hernia, Rend, Rhexis, Rift, Split

Rural Agrarian, Agrestic, Boo(h)ai, Booay, Boondocks, Bucolic, Country, Cracker-barrel, Forane, Georgic, Hick, Mofussil, Platteland, Praedial, Predial, Redneck, Rustic, Sticks, The Shires, Wop-wops

Ruse Artifice, Decoy, Dodge, Engine, Hoax, Pawk, Stratagem, → **TRICK**

Rush(ed) Accelerate, Barge, Bolt, Bustle, Career, Charge, Dart, Dash, Eriocaulon, Expedite, Faze, Feese, Feeze, Feze, Fly, Frail, Friar, Gad, Gold, Gust, Hare, Hasten, High-tail, → **HURRY**, Hurtle, Jet, Juncus, Lance, Lash, Leap, Luzula, Moses, Odd-man, Onset, Palmiet, Pellmell, Phase, Pheese, Pheeze, Phese, Plunge, Precipitate, Railroad, Rampa(u)ge, Rash, Rayle, Reed, Rip, Scamp(er), Scirpus, Scour, Scud, Scurry, Sedge, Spate, Speed, Stampede, Star(r), Streak, Streek, Surge, Swoop, Swoosh, Tear, Thrash, Thresh, Tilt, Torrent, Tule, Viretot, Zap, Zoom

Rusk Zwieback

Russell AE, Bertrand, Jack

Russet Rutile

Russia(n), Russian headman, Russian villagers Apparatchik, Ataman, Belorussian, Beria, Bolshevik, Boris, Boyar, Byelorussian, Chechen, Chukchee, Chukchi, Circassian, Cossack, Dressing, D(o)ukhobor, Esth, Igor, Ingush, Ivan, Kabardian, Kalmuk, Kalmyck, Leather, Lett, Mari, Menshevik, Mingrel(ian), Minimalist, Mir, Misha, Muscovy, Octobrist, Osset(e), Red, Romanov, Rus, Russ(niak), Russki, Ruthene, Salad, Serge, Slav, Stakhanovite, SU, Thistle, Udmurt, Uzbeg, Uzbek, Vladimir, Vogul, White, Yakut, Yuri, Zyrian

Rust(y) Aeci(di)um, Blister, Brown, Corrode, Cor(ro)sive, Erode, Etch, Ferrugo, Iron oxide, Iron-stick, Maderise, Oxidise, Puccinia, Rubiginous, Soare, Stem, Teleutospore, Telium, Uredine, Uredo, Verdigris, Yellow

Rust-fungus Aecidiospore

Rustic Arcady, Bacon, Bor(r)el(l), Bucolic, Bumpkin, Chawbacon, Churl, Clodhopper, Clown, Corydon, Cracker-barrel, Culchie, Damon, Doric, Forest, Georgic, Hayseed, Hick, Hillbilly, Hind, Hob, Hobbinoll, Hodge, Homespun, Idyl(l), Pastorale, Peasant, Pr(a)edial, Put(t), Rube, Rural, Strephon, Swain, Sylvan, Uplandish, Villager, Villatic, Yokel

▷ **Rustic** *may indicate* an anagram

Rusticate Banish, Seclude

Rustle(r), Rustling Abactor, Crinkle, Duff, Fissle, Frou-frou, Gully-raker, Poach,

Speagh(ery), Sprechery, Steal, Stir, Susurration, Swish, Thief, Whig
Rust-proof Zinced
Rut Channel, Furrow, Groove, Heat, Routine, Sulcus, Track
Ruth Babe, Compassion, Mercy, Pity, Remorse
Ruthenium Ru
Rutherfordium Rf
Ruthless Brutal, Cruel, Dog eat dog, Fell, Hard, Hardball, Hard-bitten
Rwanda(n) Tutsi
Rye Gentleman, Grain, Grass, Spelt, Whisky

Ss

S Ogee, Saint, Second, Sierra, Society, South, Square

SA It, Lure

Sabbatarian Wee Free

Sabbath Juma, Lord's Day, Rest-day, Shabbat, Sunday, Witches'

Sabbatical Leave

Sabine Horace, Women

Sable American, Black, Jet, Negro, Pean, Zibel(l)ine

Sabotage, Saboteur Cripple, Destroy, Frame-breaker, Hacktivism, Ratten, Spoil, Treachery, Undermine, Vandalise, Worm, Wrecker

Sabre, Sabre rattler Jingo, Sword, Tulwar

Sabrina Severn

Sac Air, Allantois, Amnion, Aneurism, Aneurysm, Bag, Bladder, Bursa, Caecum, Cisterna, Cyst, Diverticulum, Embryo, Follicle, Pericardium, Peritoneum, Pod, Scrotum, Spermatheca, Tylose, Tylosis, Vesica, Vocal, Yolk

Saccharine Dulcite, Dulcose

Sack(cloth), Sacking Bag, Bed, Boot, Bounce, Budget, Burlap, Can, Cashier, Chasse, Chop, Coal, Congé, Congee, Dash, Depredate, Despoil, Discharge, Doss, Fire, Gunny, Havoc, Hessian, Hop-pocket, Jute, Knap, Lay waste, Loot, Mailbag, Maraud, Mitten, Pillage, Plunder, Poke, Push, Rapine, Reave, Replace, Rieve, Road, Rob, Sad, Sanbenito, Sherris, Sherry, Spoliate, Vandalise

▷ **Sacks** *may indicate* an anagram

Sacrament Baptism, Christening, Communion, Confirmation, Eucharist, Extreme unction, Housel, Lord's Supper, Matrimony, Nagmaal, Orders, Penance, Promise, Reconciliation, Ritual, Unction, Viaticum

Sacred (object), Sacred place Adytum, Churinga, Hallowed, Harim, Heart, Hierurgy, → HOLY, Ineffable, Manito(u), Nine, Omphalos, Padma, Pietà, Sacrosanct, Sanctum, Taboo, Tapu, Temenos

Sacrifice Alcestic, Cenote, Forego, Gambit, Gehenna, Hecatomb, Holocaust, Immolate, Iphigenia, Isaac, Lay down, Molech, Moloch, Oblation, → OFFERING, Peace offering, Relinquish, Sati, Suovetaurilia, Supreme, Surrender, Suttee, Taurobolium, Tophet, Vicarious, Victim

Sacrilege, Sacrilegious Blaspheme, Impiety, Profane, Violation

Sacristan, Sacristy Diaconicon, Sceuophylax, Sexton

Sacrosanct Inviolable

Sad(den), Sadly, Sadness Alas, Attrist, Blue, Con dolore, Dejected, Depressed, Desolate, Disconsolate, Dismal, Doleful, Dolour, Downcast, Drear, Dull, Dumpy, Fadeur, Heartache, Lovelorn, Low, Lugubrious, Mesto, Mournful, Oh, Plangent, Sorrowful, Sorry, Tabanca, Tearful, Tear-jerker, Threnody, Tragic, Triste, Tristesse, Unhappy, Wan, Wo(e)begone

Saddle (bag, cloth, girth, pad) Alforja, Aparejo, Arson, Burden, Cantle, Cinch, Col, Crupper, Demipique, Kajawah, Lumber, Numnah, Oppress, Pack, Pad, Panel,

Pigskin, Pilch, Pillion, Seat, Sell(e), Shabrack, Shabracque, Side, Stock, Tree, Western

Saddle-bow Arson

Saddler Whittaw(er)

Sadie Thompson

Sadism, Sadistic Algolagnia, Cruel

▷ **Sadly** *may indicate* an anagram

Safari Expedition, Hunt

Safe(ty) Active, Allright, Almery, Ambry, Coolgardie, Copper-bottomed, Delouse, Deposit, GRAS, Harmless, Immunity, Impunity, Inviolate, Keister, Meat, Night, Passive, Peter, Reliable, Roadworthy, Sanctuary, Secure, Sound, Strong-box, Strongroom, Sure, Whole-skinned, Worthy

Safeguard Bulwark, Caution, Ensure, Fail-safe, Frithborh, Fuse, Hedge, Palladium, Protection, Register, Ward

Saffron Bastard, Crocus, False, Meadow, Mock, Yellow

Sag(gy) Decline, Dip, Droop, Hang, Hogged, Lop, Slump, Swayback, Wilt

Saga Aga, Chronicle, Edda, Epic, Icelandic, Laxdale, Legend, Odyssey, Volsunga

Sagacity, Sagacious Astute, Commonsense, Depth, Elephant, Judgement, Sapience, Wisdom

Sage(s) Abaris, Aquinian, Bactrian, Bias, Carlyle, Cheronian, Chilo(n), Clary, Cleobulus, Confucius, Counsellor, Egghead, Greybeard, Hakam, Herb, Imhotep, Jerusalem, Maharishi, Mahatma, Malmesbury, Manu, Mirza, Orval, Pandit, Periander, Philosopher, Pittacus, Rishi, Salvia, Savant, Seer, Seven, Solon, Tagore, Thales, Wiseacre, Wood

Sage-brush Nevada

Sago Portland

Sahib Pukka

Said Co, Emir, Port, Quo(th), Related, Reputed, Spoken, Stated

▷ **Said** *may indicate* 'sounding like'

Sail(s), Sailing Balloon, Bunt, Canvas, Circumnavigate, Cloth, Coast, Course, Cross-jack, Cruise, Drag, Drift, Fan, Fore(course), Fore-and-aft, Full, Gaff(-topsail), Genoa, Goose-wing, Head, Jib, Jigger, Jut, Land, Lateen, Leech, Luff, Lug, Moon, Moonraker, Muslin, Navigate, Orthodromy, Parachute spinnaker, Peak, Plain, Plane, Ply, Rag, Reef, Rig, Ring-tail, Royal, Sheet, Shoulder-of-mutton, Solar, Spanker, Spencer, Spinnaker, Spritsail, Square, Staysail, Steer, Studding, Stun, Suit, Top(-gallant), Top-hamper, Van, Vela, Wardrobe, Water, Yard

Sailor(s) AB, Admiral, Anson, Argonaut, Blue-jacket, Boatman, Boatswain, Bos'n, Bos(u)n, Budd, Commodore, Crew, Deckhand, Drake, Evans, Foremastman, Freshwater, Galiongee, Gob, Greenhand, Grommet, Hat, Hearties, Helmsman, Hornblower, Hydronaut, Jack, Janty, Jauntie, Jaunty, Jonty, Khalasi, Killick, Killock, Kroo(boy), Krooman, Kru(boy), Kruman, Lascar, Leadsman, Limey, Loblolly boy, Lt, Lubber, Mariner, Matelot, Matlo(w), Middy, MN, Nelson, Noah, NUS, Oceaner, OS, Polliwog, Pollywog, Popeye, Powder monkey, Privateer, Rating, RN, Salt, Seabee, Seacunny, Sea-dog, Sea-lord, → **SEAMAN**, Serang, Shellback, Sin(d)bad, Stowaway, Submariner, Tar, Tarp(aulin), Tarry-breeks, Tindal, Topman, Triton, Waister, Wandering, Water-dog, Yachtsman

Saint(ly), Saints Agatha, Agnes, Aidan, Alban, Alexis, Aloysius, Alvis, Ambrose, Andrew, Anselm, Anthony, Asaph, Audrey, Augustine, Barbara, Barnabas, Bartholomew, Basil, Bees, Benedict, Bernard, Bernardette, Boniface, Brandan, Brendan, Bridget, Brigid, Canonise, Canonize, Catharine, Cecilia, Chad, Christopher, Clement, Columba(n), Crispian, Crispin(ian), Cuthbert, Cyr, David,

Denis, Denys, Diego, Dominic, Dorothea, Dunstan, Dymphna, Elmo, Eloi, Elvis, Eulalie, Francis, Genevieve, George, Gertrude, Giles, Hagiology, Hallowed, Helena, Hilary, Hilda, Holy, Hugh, Ignatius, Isidor, James, Jerome, John, Joseph, Jude, Just, Kentigern, Kevin, Kilda, Latterday, Lawrence, Leger, Leonard, Linus, Loyola, Lucy, Luke, Malo, Margaret, Mark, Martha, Martin, Matthew, Michael, Monica, Mungo, Nicholas, Ninian, Odyl, Olaf, Oswald, Pancras, Patrick, Patron, Paul(inus), Peter, Pi, Pillar, Plaster, Polycarp, Quentin, Regulus, Ride, Rishi, Roch, Ronan, Roque, Rosalie, Rule, S, Sebastian, Severus, Simeon, Simon, Simon Zelotes, SS, St, Stanislaus, Stephen, Sunday, Swithin, Templar, Teresa, Thecia, Theresa, Thomas, Tobias, Ursula, Valentine, Veronica, Vincent, Vitus, Walstan, Wilfred, William, Winifred

St Anthony's fire Ergotism, Erysipelas
St Elmo's fire Corona discharge, Corposant
St James Scallop-shell
St Jerome Hieronymic
St John's bread Carob
St Lucia WL
St Paul's Wren-ch
St Vincent WV
Sake Account, Behalf, Cause, Drink
Sal Volatile
Salacious, Salacity Fruity, Lewd, Lust, Obscene, Scabrous
Salad Burnet, Caesar, Calaloo, Calalu, Chef's, Chicon, Corn, Cos, Cress, Cucumber, Days, Endive, Escarole, Fennel, Finnochio, Finoc(c)hio, Frisée, Fruit, Greek, Guacamole, Horiatiki, Lactuca, Lamb's lettuce, Lettuce, Lovage, Mesclum, Mesclun, Mixture, Niçoise, Purslane, Radicchio, Radish, Rampion, Rocket, Rojak, Roquette, Russian, Salmagundi, Salmagundy, Slaw, Tabbouleh, Tabbouli, Tomato, Waldorf, Word
▷ **Salad** *may indicate* an anagram
Salamander Axolotl, Congo eel, Ewt, Hellbender, Lizard, Menopome, Mole, Mudpuppy, Olm, Proteus, Siren, Snake, Spring-keeper
Salami, Salami technique Fraud, Peperoni
Salary Emolument, Fee, Hire, Pay, Prebend, Screw, Stipend, → **WAGE**
Sale(s) Auction, Breeze up, Cant, Car-boot, Clearance, Farm-gate, Fire, Garage, Jumble, Market, Outroop, Outrope, Pitch, Raffle, Retail, Roup, Rummage, Subhastation, Trade, Turnover, Upmarket, Venal, Vend, Vendue, Vent, Voetstoets, Voetstoots, Warrant, Wash, White, Wholesale, Yard
Saleroom Pantechnicon
Salesman Agent, Assistant, Bagman, Broker, Buccaneer, Bummaree, Counterhand, Counter jumper, Drummer, Huckster, Loman, Pedlar, Rep, Retailer, Tallyman, Tout, Traveller
Salient Coign, Jut, Projection, Prominent, Redan, Spur
Salisbury Cecil, Sarum
Saliva Drool, Parotid, Ptyalism, Sial(oid), Slobber, Spawl, Spit(tle), Sputum
Sallow Adust, Pallid, Pasty, Sale, Sauch, Saugh, Wan
Sally Aunt, Boutade, Charge, Dash, Escape, Excursion, Flight, Foray, Issue, Jest, Mot, Pleasantry, Quip, Ride, Sarah, Sortie, Wisecrack, Witticism
Salmagundi Mess
Salmon Alevin, Atlantic, Australian, Baggit, Blueback, Blue-cap, Boaz, Burnett, Chinook, Chum, Cock, Coho(e), Dog, Dorado, Grav(ad)lax, Grilse, Humpback, Kelt, Keta, King, Kipper, Kokanee, Lax, Ligger, Lox, Masu, Mort, Nerka, Oncorhynchus,

Ouananiche, Par(r), Peal, Pink, Quinnat, Red, Redfish, Rock, Samlet, Shedder, Silver, Skegger, Slat, Smelt, Smolt, Smout, Smowt, Sockeye, Sparling, Spirling, Sprod

Salon, Saloon Barrel-house, Car, Hall, Honkytonk, Last chance, Lounge, Nail bar, Pullman, Sedan, Shebang, Tavern

Salt(s), Salty AB, Acid, Alginate, Aluminate, Andalusite, Antimonite, Arsenite, Aspartite, Attic, Aurate, Azide, Base, Bath, Bicarbonate, Bichromate, Borate, Borax, Brackish, Brine, Bromate, Bromide, Capr(o)ate, Caprylate, Carbamate, Carbonate, Carboxylate, Celery, Cerusite, Chlorate, Chlorite, Chromate, Citrate, Complex, Corn, Cure(d), Cyanate, Cyclamate, Datolite, Deer lick, Diazonium, Dichromate, Dioptase, Dithionate, Double, Enos, Epsom, Ferricyanide, Formate, Glauber, Glutamate, Halite, Halo-, Health, Hydrochloride, Hygroscopic, Iodide, Ioduret, Isocyanide, Kosher, Lactate, Lake-basin, Lithate, Liver, Magnesium, Malate, Malonate, Manganate, Mariner, Matelot, Microcosmic, Monohydrate, Mucate, Muriate, NaCl, Nitrate, Nitrite, Oleate, Orthosilicate, Osm(i)ate, Oxalate, Palmitate, Pandermite, Perborate, Perchlorate, Periodate, Phosphate, Phosphite, Phthalate, Picrate, Piquancy, Plumbate, Plumbite, Potassium, Powder, Propionate, Pyruvate, Rating, Reh, Resinate, Rochelle, Rock, Rosinate, Sailor, Sal ammoniac, Salify, Sal volatile, Saut, Sea-dog, Seafarer, Seasoned, Sebate, Selenate, Smelling, Soap, Sodium, Solar, Sorrel, Stannate, Stearate, Suberate, Succinate, Sulfite, Sulphate, Sulphite, Sulphonate, Table, Tannate, Tantalate, Tartrate, Tellurate, Tellurite, Thiocyanate, Thiosulphate, Titanate, Tungstate, Uranin, Urao, Urate, Vanadate, Volatile, Water-dog, White, Wit(ty), Xanthate

Salt meat Mart

Saltpetre Caliche, Chile, Cubic, Nitre, Norway

Salt-water Sea

Salubrious Healthy, Sanitary, Wholesome

Salutary Beneficial, Good, Wholesome

Salutation, Salute Address, Asalam-wa-leikum, Australian, Ave, Banzai, Barcoo, Bid, Cap, Cheer, Command, Coupé(e), Curtsey, Embrace, Feu de joie, Fly-past, Genuflect, Greet, Hail, Hallo, Halse, Homage, Honour, Jambo, Kiss, Middle finger, Namas kar, Namaste, Present, Salaam, Salvo, Sieg Heil, Toast, Tribute, Wassail

Salvador Dali

Salvage Dredge, Lagan, Ligan, Reclaim, Recover, Recycle, Rescue, Retrieve, Tot

Salvation(ist) Booth, Redemption, Rescue, Socinian, Soterial, Yeo

Salve Anele, Anoint, Assuage, Ave, Lanolin(e), Lotion, Ointment, Remedy, Saw, Tolu, Unguent, Weapon

Salver Tray, Waiter

Salvo Fusillade, Salute, Volley

Sal volatile Hartshorn

Sam Browse, Soapy, Uncle, Weller

Samara Ash-key

Samaritan Good

Samarium Sm

Same(ness) Ae, Agnatic, Contemporaneous, Do, Egal, Ejusd(en), Equal, Ib(id), Ibidem, Id, Idem, Identical, Identity, Ilk, Iq, Like, One, Thick(y), Thilk, Uniform, Ylke

Samovar Urn

Samoyed Dog, Uralian, Uralic

Sample, Sampling Amniocentesis, Biopsy, Blad, Browse, Example, Fare, Foretaste, Handout, Matched, Muster, Pattern, Pree, Prospect, Quadrat, Quota, Scantling,

Smear, Specimen, Spread, Stratified, Swatch, Switch, → **TASTE**, Taster, Transect, Try

Samuel Pepys, Smiles

Samurai Ronin

▷ **Sam Weller** *may indicate* the use of 'v' for 'w' or vice versa

Sanctify Consecrate, Purify, Saint

Sanctimonious Banbury, Creeping Jesus, Devout, Goody-goody, Pi, Religiose, Righteous, Saintly

Sanction(s), Sanctioned Allow, Appro, Approbate, Approof, Approve, Authorise, Bar, Countenance, Economic, Endorse, Green light, Imprimatur, Legitimate, Mandate, OK, Pass, Pragmatic, Ratify, Smart, Sustain, Upstay, Warrant

Sanctities, Sanctity Halidom, Holiness, Hollidam, Sonties

Sanctuary, Sanctum Adytum, Asylum, By-room, Cella, Ch, Church, Frithsoken, Frithstool, Girth, Grith, Holy, Kaaba, Lair, Naos, Oracle, Penetralia, Preserve, Refuge, Sacellum, Sacrarium, → **SHELTER**, Shrine, Tabernacle, Temple

Sand(s), Sandbank, Sandbar, Sandy Alec, Alex, Alexander, Areg, Arena(ceous), Arenose, Arkose, As, Atoll, Bar, Barchan(e), Bark(h)an, Beach, Caliche, Dene, Desert, Dogger Bank, Down, Dudevant, Dune, Dupin, Eremic, Erg, Esker, Foundry, Gat, George, Ginger, Goodwin, Grain, Granulose, Hazard, Hurst, Light, Loess, Machair, Nore, Oil, Overslaugh, Podsol, Podzol, Portlandian, Psammite, Ridge, River, Sabulous, Sawney, Seif dune, Shelf, Shoal, Shore, Singing, Tar, Tee, Time, Tombolo

Sandal(s) Alpargata, Buskin, Calceamentum, Chappal, Espadrille, Flip-flop, Ganymede, Geta, Huarache, Jelly, Patten, Pump, Slip-slop, Talaria, Thong, Zori

Sandalwood Algum, Almug, Chypre, Pride, Santal

Sandarac Arar

Sander Pike-perch

Sandhopper Amphipod

Sandhurst RMA

Sand-loving Ammophilous, Psammophil

Sandpiper Bird, Dunlin, Knot, Oxbird, Ree, Ruff, Sandpeep, Stint, Terek

Sandstone Arkose, Calciferous, Cat's brains, Dogger, Fa(i)kes, Flysch, Grit, Hassock, Holystone, Itacolumite, Kingle, Molasse, New Red, Old Red, Psammite, Quartzite, Red, Silica

Sandstorm Haboob, Tebbad

Sandwich(es) Bruschetta, Butty, Club, Clubhouse, Croque-monsieur, Cuban, Doorstep, Earl, Hamburger, Hoagie, Island, Jeely piece, Open, Panini, Piece, Roti, Round, Sanger, Sango, Sarmie, Sarney, Sarnie, Smørbrød, Smörgåsbord, Smørrebrød, Stottie, Sub, Submarine, Tartine, Thumber, Toastie, Toebie, Triple-decker, Twitcher, Victoria, Wad, Zak(o)uski

▷ **Sandwich(es)** *may indicate* a hidden word

Sane, Sanity Compos mentis, Formal, Healthy, Judgement, Rational, Reason, Sensible, Wice

Sangfroid Aplomb, Cool, Poise

Sanguine Confident, Hopeful, Optimistic, Roseate, Ruddy

Sanitary Hygienic, Salubrious, Sterile

Sanskrit Bhagavad-Gita, Panchatantra, Purana, Ramayana, Sutra, Upanishad, Vedic

Santa (Claus) Abonde, Kriss Kringle, Secret

Sap Benzoin, Bleed, Cremor, Drain, Enervate, Entrench, Ichor, Juice, Laser, Latex, Lymph, Mine, Mug, Pulque, Ratten, Resin, Roset, Rosin, Rozet, Rozit, Secretion, Soma, Sura, Swot, Undermine, Weaken

Sapid Flavoursome, Savoury, Tasty
Sapience, Sapient Discernment, Sage, Wisdom
Sapling Ash-plant, Ground-ash, Plant, Tellar, Teller, Tiller, Youth
Sapper(s) Miner, RE
Sapphire Star, Water, White
Sappho Lesbian
Sapwood Alburnum
Sarah Battle, Gamp, Sal
Sarcasm, Sarcastic Acidity, Antiphrasis, Biting, Cutting, Cynical, Derision, Irony, Mordacious, Mordant, Pungent, Quip, Quotha, Sarky, Satire, Sharp, Smartmouth, Snide, Sting, Wisecrack
Sardine Fish, Sard
Sardonic Cutting, Cynical, Ironical, Scornful, Wry
Sargasso Ore, Sea(weed)
Sark Chemise, CI, Shirt
Sarong Sulu
SAS Red Devils
Sash Baldric(k), Band, Belt, Burdash, Cummerbund, Fillister, Obi, Scarf, Window
Sassaby Tsessebe
Sassenach English, Lowlander, Pock-pudding
Satan Adversary, Apollyon, Arch-enemy, Cram, → **DEVIL**, Eblis, Evil One, Lucifer, Prince of darkness, Shaitan, Tempter
Satchel Bag, Scrip
Sate(d), Satiate Cloy, Glut, Replete, Sad, Surfeit
Satellite Adrastea, Ananke, Ariel, Artificial, Astra, Atlas, Attendant, Aussat, Belinda, Bianca, Bird, Callisto, Calypso, Camenae, Carme, Charon, Communications, Comsat®, Cordelia, Cosmos, Cressida, Deimos, Desdemona, Despina, Dione, Disciple, Early bird, Earth, Echo, Elara, Enceladus, Europa, Explorer, Fixed, Follower, Galatea, Galilean, Ganymede, Geostationary, Helene, Henchman, Himalia, Hipparchus, Hyperion, Iapetus, Intelsat, Io, Janus, Lackey, Larissa, Leda, Lysithea, Meteorological, Metis, Mimas, Miranda, Moon, Mouse, Nereid, Oberon, Ophelia, Orbiter, Pan, Pandora, Pasiphae, Phobos, Phoebe, Portia, Prometheus, Puck, Rhea, Rosalind, Sinope, SPOT, Sputnik, Syncom, Telesto, Telstar, Tethys, Thalassa, Thebe, Tiros, Titan, Titania, Triton, Umbriel, Weather
▶ **Satin** *see* **SILK**
Satire, Satirical, Satirist Arbuthnot, Archilochus, Burlesque, Butler, Candide, Chaldee, Dryden, Horace, Iambographer, Juvenal, Lampoon, Lash, Lucian, Mazarinade, Menippean, Mockery, Pantagruel, Parody, Pasquil, Pasquin(ade), Pope, Raillery, Sarky, Sotadic, Spoof, Squib, Swift, Travesty
Satisfaction, Satisfactory, Satisfy(ing), Satisfied, Satisfactorily Agree, Ah, Ap(p)ay, Appease, Assuage, Atone, Change, Compensation, Complacent, → **CONTENT**, Defrayment, Enough, Feed, Fill, Fulfil, Glut, Gratify, Happy camper, Indulge, Jake, Job, Liking, Meet, OK, Okey-dokey, Pacation, Palatable, Pay, Please, Propitiate, Qualify, Redress, Repay, Replete, Sate, Satiate, Serve, Settlement, Slake, Square, Suffice, Supply, Tickety-boo, Well
Saturate(d) Drench, Glut, Imbue, Impregnate, Infuse, Permeate, → **SOAK**, Sodden, Steep, Waterlog
Saturday Holy, Sabbatine
Saturn God, Kronos, Lead, Planet, Rocket
Satyr Faun, Leshy, Lesiy, Libertine, Marsyas, Pan, Silen(us), Woodhouse, Woodwose
Sauce, Saucy Agrodolce, Alfredo, Allemanse, Apple, Arch, Baggage, Barbecue,

Béarnaise, Béchamel, Bigarade, Bold(-faced), Bolognese, Bordelaise,
Bourguignonne, Bread, Brown, Caper, Carbonara, Catchup, Catsup, Chasseur,
Chaudfroid, Cheek, Chilli, Chutney, Condiment, Coulis, Cranberry, Cream,
Cumberland, Custard, Dapper, Dip, Dressing, Enchilada, Espagnole, Fenberry,
Fondue, Fu yong, Fu yung, Gall, Garum, Gravy, Hard, Hoisin, Hollandaise,
Horseradish, HP®, Impudence, Jus, Ketchup, Lip, Malapert, Marinade, Marinara,
Matelote, Mayonnaise, Melba, Meunière, Mint, Mirepoix, Mole, Monkeygland,
Mornay, Mousseline, Nam pla, Nerve, Newburg, Nuoc mam, Oxymal, Oyster,
Panada, Parsley, Passata, Peart, Peking, Pert, Pesto, Piert, Piri-piri, Pistou, Ponzu,
Portugaise, Ravigote, Relish, Remoulade, Rouille, Roux, Sabayon, Sal, Salpicon,
Salsa, Salsa verde, Sambal, Sass, Satay, Shoyu, Soja, Soubise, Soy, Soya, Stroganoff,
Sue, Supreme, Sweet and sour, Tabasco®, Tamari, Tartar(e), Tomato, Topping,
Tossy, Velouté, Vinaigrette, White, Wine, Worcester, Worcestershire
Sauceboat-shaped Scaphocephalate
Saucepan Chafer, Goblet, Skillet, Steamer, Stockpot
Saucer Ashtray, Discobolus, Pannikin, UFO
Sauna Bath, Sudatorium, Sudorific
Saunter Amble, Dacker, Da(i)ker, Dander, Lag, Mosey, Promenade, Roam, Shool,
Stroll, Toddle
Sausage(s) Andouille, Andouillette, Banger, Black pudding, Blood, Boerewors,
Bologna, Boudin, Bratwurst, Cervelat, Cheerio, Chipolata, Chorizo, Cumberland,
Devon, Drisheen, Frankfurter, Hot dog, Kishke, Knackwurst, Knockwurst,
Liver(wurst), Mortadella, Mystery bag, Pep(p)eroni, Polony, Pudding, Salami,
Sav(eloy), Snag(s), Snarler, String, Weenie, Weeny, White pudding, Wiener(wurst),
Wienie, Wurst, Zampone
Sausage-shaped Allantoid
Savage Ape, Barbarian, Boor, Brute, Cannibal, Cruel, Feral, Fierce, Frightful, Grim,
Gubbins, Immane, Inhuman, Maul, Noble, Sadistic, Truculent, Vitriolic, Wild
Savanna Plain, Sahel
Savant Expert, Mahatma, Sage, Scholar
Save, Saving(s) Bank, Bar, Besides, But, Capital, Conserve, Cut-rate, Deposit,
Economy, Except, Hain, Hoard, Husband, ISA, Keep, Layby, National, Nest egg,
Nirlie, Nirly, Not, PEPS, Post office, Preserve, Put by, Reclaim, Redeem, Relieve,
Reprieve, → **RESCUE**, Reskew, Sa', Salt, Salvage, Scrape, Scrimp, Shortcut, Slate
club, Soak away, Sock away, Spare, Stokvel, Succour, TESSA, Unless
Saviour Deliverer, Jesu(s), Messiah, Redeemer
Savour(ed), Savoury Aigrette, Bouchée, Canapé, Devils-on-horseback, Essence,
Fag(g)ot, Flavour, Olent, Ramekin, Relish, Resent, Sair, Sapid, Sar, Smack, Starter,
Tang, → **TASTE**, Vol au vent
Savoy Cabbage, Opera
Saw Adage, Aphorism, Apothegm, Azebiki, Back, Band, Beheld, Bucksaw, Buzz,
Chain, Circular, Cliché, Compass, Coping, Cross-cut, Crown, Cut, Dictum, Dovetail,
Dozuki, Flooring, Frame, Fret, Gang, Glimpsed, Gnome, Grooving, Hack, Hand, Jig,
Keyhole, Legend, Log, Maxim, Met, Motto, Pad, Panel, Paroemia, Pitsaw, Proverb,
Pruning, Quarter, Rabbeting, Rack, Ribbon, Rip, Ryoba, Sash, Saying, Scroll, Serra,
Skil®, Skip-tooth, Slogan, Span, Spied, Stadda, Stone, Sweep, Tenon, Trepan,
Trephine, Whip, Witnessed
Sawbones Surgeon
Saw-toothed Runcinate
Saxifrage Astilbe, Bishop's cap, Burnet, Golden, Heuchera, London pride,
Mitre-wort, St Patrick's cabbage

Saxon Cedric, Hengist, Wend

Say, Saying(s) Adage, Agrapha, Allege, Aphorism, Apophthegm, Apostrophise, Articulate, Axiom, Beatitude, Bon mot, Bromide, Byword, Cant, Catchphrase, Cliché, Declare, Dict(um), Eg, Enunciate, Epigram, Express, Fadaise, Gnome, Impute, Logia, Logion, → MAXIM, Mean, Mot, Mouth, Observe, Predicate, Pronounce, Proverb, Put, Quip, Recite, Rede, Relate, Remark, Report, Saine, Saw, Sc, Sententia, → SPEAK, Suppose, Sutra, Utter, Voice, Word

▷ **Say, Saying(s)** *may indicate* a word sounding like another

Scab(by) Blackleg, Crust, Eschar, Leggism, Leprose, Mangy, Rat, Scald, Scall, Sore, Strike-breaker

Scabbard Frog, Pitcher, Sheath, Tsuba

Scabies Itch, Psora, Scotch fiddle

Scabrous Harsh, Rough, Thersites

Scaffold(ing), Scaffolder Gallows, Gantry, Hoarding, Putlock, Putlog, Rig, Spiderman, Stage

Scald Blanch, Burn, Leep, Ploat, Plot

Scale(s), Scaly Analemma, API gravity, Ascend, Balance, Baumé, Beaufort, Binet-Simon, Bismar, Brix, Bud, Burnham, Celsius, Centigrade, Ceterach, Chromatic, → CLIMB, Cottony-cushion, Dandruff, Desquamate, Diagonal, Diatonic, Douglas, Elo, Escalade, Fahrenheit, Flake, Full, Furfur, Gamme, Gamut, Ganoid, Gapped, Gauge, Gravity, Gunter's, Hexachord, Humidex, Indusium, Interval, Kelvin, Ladder, Lamina, Layer, Leaf, Lepid, Lepidote, Leprose, Libra, Ligule, Likert, Lodicule, Loricate, Magnitude, Major, Mercalli, Mesel, Minor, Mohs, Munsell, Natural, Nominal, Octad, Ordinal, Palea, Palet, Patagium, Peel, Pentatonic, Pholidosis, Placoid, Plate, Platform, Ramentum, → RANGE, Rankine, Ratio, Réaumur, Regulo, Richter, San Jose, Scan, Scarious, Scent, Scincoid, Scurf, Scutellate, Shin, Skink, Sliding, Speel, Spring, Squama, Squame(lla), Submediant, Tegmentum, Tegula, Tonal, Tridymite, Tron(e), Unified, Vernier, Wage, Weighbridge, Wentworth, Wind

Scallop(ed) Bivalve, Clam, Coquille, Crenate, Escalop, Frill, Gimp, Mush, Pecten, Queenie, Vandyke

Scallywag Rascal, Scamp, Skeesicks, Whippersnapper

Scalp Cut, Scrape, Skin, Trophy

Scalpel Bistoury, Knife

Scam Ramp

Scamp Fripon, Imp, Limb, Lorel, Lorrell, Losel, Lozell, Neglect, → RASCAL, Reprobate, Rip, Rogue, Scallywag, Skeesicks, Toerag

Scamper Gambol, Lamp, Run, Scurry, Skedaddle, Skelter, Skitter

Scan(ning), Scanner CAT, CT, Examine, Flat-bed, Helical, Interlaced, OCR, Optical, Oversee, Peruse, PET, Rake, Raster, Scrutinise, Sector, SEM, Sequential, SPET, Survey, Tomography, Ultrasound, Vertical, Vet

Scandal(ous), Scandalise Belie, Canard, Commesse, Disgrace, Exposé, Gamy, Hearsay, Muck-raking, Opprobrium, Outrage, Shame, Slander, Stigma, Stink, Watergate

Scandinavian Dane, Finn, Laplander, Lapp, Nordic, Norman, Norseland, Northman, Olaf, Runic, Squarehead, Swede, Varangian, Viking

Scandium Sc

Scant(y) Bare, Brief, Exiguous, Ihram, Jejune, Jimp, Meagre, Poor, Scrimpy, Short, Shy, Skimpy, Slender, Spare, Sparse, Stingy

Scapegoat Butt, Fall-guy, Hazazel, Joe Soap, Patsy, Stooge, Target, Victim, Whipping-boy

Scapula Blade, Omoplate

Scar(face) Al, Blemish, Cheloid, Cicatrix, Cliff, Craig, Epulotic, Hilum, Keloid, Leucoma, Leukoma, Mark, Pockmark, Stigma, Ulosis, Wipe

Scarab Beetle, Gem

Scarce(ly), Scarcity Barely, Dear, Dearth, Famine, Few, Hardly, Ill, Lack, Paucity, Rare, Scanty, Seldom, Short, Strap, Uncommon, Want

Scare(mongering), Scaring Alarmist, Alert, Amaze, Fleg, Fright, Gally, Gliff, Glift, Hairy, Panic, Petrify, Skeer, Spook, Startle

Scarecrow Bogle, Bugaboo, Dudder, Dudsman, Gallibagger, Gallibeggar, Gallicrow, Gallybagger, Gallybeggar, Gallycrow, Malkin, Mawkin, Potato-bogle, Ragman, S(h)ewel, Tattie-bogle

Scarf Babushka, Belcher, Cataract, Comforter, Cravat, Curch, Doek, Dupatta, Fichu, Hai(c)k, Haique, Headsquare, Hyke, Lambrequin, Madras, Mantilla, Muffettee, Muffler, Neckatee, Neckcloth, Neckerchief, Neckgear, Neckpiece, Neckwear, Nightingale, Orarium, Pagri, Palatine, Pashmina, Pugg(a)ree, Rail, Rebozo, Sash, Screen, Stock, Stole, Tallith, Tippet, Trot-cosy, Trot-cozy, Vexillum

Scarifier Scuffler

Scarlet Cinnabar, Cochineal, Crimson, Pimpernel, Pink, Ponceau, Red, Vermilion

Scarper Abscond, Bunk, Run, Shoo, Welsh

Scat Aroint, Dropping

Scathe, Scathing Mordant, Sarcastic, Savage, Severe, Vitriolic

Scatter(ed), Scattering Bestrew, Broadcast, Diaspora, Disject, Dispel, → DISPERSE, Dissipate, Flurr, Inelastic, Interspace, Litter, Rayleigh, Rout, Scail, Skail, Sow, Sparge, Splutter, Sporadic, Spread, Sprinkle, Squander, Straw, Strew

Scatterbrain(ed) Dippy, Ditsy, Tête folie

Scavenge(r) Ant, Dieb, Forage, Hunt, Hy(a)ena, Jackal, Rake, Ratton, Rotten, Scaffie, Sweeper, Totter

Scenario Outline, Plot, Script, Worst case

Scene(ry) Arena, Boscage, Cameo, Coulisse, Decor, Flat(s), Landscape, Locale, Prop, Prospect, Set, Set piece, Sight, Site, Sketch, Stage, Tableau, Tormenter, Tormentor, Transformation, Venue, View

Scent Aroma, Attar, Chypre, Cologne, Eau de cologne, Essence, Fragrance, Frangipani, Fumet(te), Gale, Moschatel, Nose, Odour, Orris, Ottar, Otto, Perfume, Sachet, Smell, Spoor, Vent, Waft, Wind

Scentless Anosmia

Sceptic, Sceptical(ly), Scepticism Agnostic, Askant, Cynic, Doubter, Incredulous, Infidel, Jaundiced, Nihilistic, Nullifidian, Pyrrho(nic), Sadducee, Solipsism

Schedule Agenda, Calendar, Classification, Itinerary, Prioritise, Programme, Register, Slot, Table, Timescale, Timetable

Scheme(r), Scheming CATS, Colour, Concoct, Conspire, Crafty, Cunning, Dare, Darien, Dart, Decoct, Design, Devisal, Diagram, Dodge, Draft, Gin, Honeytrap, Housing, Intrigue, Jezebel, Machiavellian, Machinate, Manoeuvre, Nostrum, Pilot, → PLAN, Plat, Plot, Project, Proposition, Purpose, Put-up job, Racket, Rhyme, Ruse, Set-aside, Stratagem, System, Table, Top-hat, Wangle, Wheeze

Schism(atic) Disunion, Division, Eastern, Great, Greek, Heterodox, Rent, Secession, Split, Western

Schizo(phrenia) Catatonic, Dementia praecox, Hebephrenia

Schmaltz(y) Goo, Slush, Tear-jerker

Schmieder S

Schmuck Gunsel

Schnapps Enzian

Scholar, Scholiast Abelard, Academic, Alcuin, Alumni, Atticus, BA, Bookman,

Boursier, Catachumen, Clergy, Clerisy, Clerk, Commoner, Demy, Disciple, Erasmus, Erudite, Etonian, Exhibitioner, Extern(e), Externat, Goliard, Graduate, Grecian, Hafiz, Inkhorn, Jowett, Literate, Littérateur, MA, Mal(l)am, Masorete, Maulana, Noter, Occam Ulama, Ollamh, Ollav, Pauline, Plutarch, Polymath, Pupil, Rhodes, Sap, Savant, Schoolboy, Sizar, Soph, → **STUDENT**, Tabardar, Taberdar, Taberder, Tom Brown

Scholarship Bursary, Closed, Education, Erudition, Exhibition, Grant, Grant-in-aid, Learning, Lore, Mass, Rhodes

School Academy, Ampleforth, Approved, Ash Can, Barbizon, Bauhaus, Beacon, Benenden, Bluecoat, Board, Boarding, Charm, Charterhouse, Chartreux, Chautauqua, Cheder, Choir, Church, Classical, Coed, Community, Composite, Comprehensive, Conservative, Conservatoire, Conservatory, Cool, Correspondence, Council, Crammer, Cult, Dada, Dame, Day, Direct grant, Dojo, Downside, Drama, Drill, Driving, Dual, Educate, Elementary, Essenes, Eton, Exercise, Externat, Faith, Fettes, Finishing, First, Flemish, Foundation, Frankfurt, Free, Gam, Giggleswick, Gordonstoun, Grade, Graduate, Grammar, Grant-aided, Grant-maintained, Group, Gymnasien, Gymnasium, Harrow, Heder, Hedge, High, Historical, Home, Honour, Hospital, Hostel, Hypermodern, Independent, Industrial, Infant, Institute, Integrated, Intermediate, Ionic, Jim Crow, Junior, Kailyard, Kaleyard, Kant, Kindergarten, Lake, Lancing, Language, Life, List D, Loretto, Lower, LSE, Lycée, Lyceum, Madrassah, Magnet, Mahayana, Maintained, Maintaining, Manchester, Mannheim, Marlborough, Middle, National, Night, Normal, Nursery, Old, Oundle, Palaestra, Parnassian, Parochial, Pensionnat, Perse, Piano, Play, Pod, Poly, Porpoises, Prep, Preparatory, Primary, Private, Progymnasium, Provided, Public, RADA, Ragged, RAM, Ramean, Real, Reformatory, Repton, Residential, Rhodian, Roedean, Rossall, Rydal, Sabbath, Sadducee, St Trinian's, Satanic, Scandalous, Sciences, Scul, Scull(e), Secondary(-modern), Sect, Seminary, Separate, Shoal, Single-sex, Sink, Ski, Slade, Sole charge, Song, Spasmodic, Special, State, Stonyhurst, Stowe, Style, Summer, Sunday, Teach, Tonbridge, Trade, → **TRAIN**, Tutor, Upper, Voluntary(-aided), Voluntary-controlled, Wellington, Whales, Winchester, Writing, Yeshiva

Schoolboy, Schoolgirl Carthusian, Coed, Colleger, East, Etonian, Fag, Gait, Geit, Gyte, Miss, Monitor, Oppidan, Petty, Stalky, Wykehamist

School-leaver Abiturient

Schoolma'am, Schoolman, Schoolmaster, Schoolmistress Aram, Beak, Dominie, Duns, Holofernes, Miss, Occam, Orbilius, Pedagogue, Pedant, Sir, Squeers, Teacher, Tutress, Ursuline

Schooner Glass, Hesperus, Prairie, Ship, Tern

Sciatica Hip-gout

Science Anatomy, Anthropology, Applied, Art, Astrodynamics, Astrophysics, Atmology, Axiology, Biology, Botany, Chemistry, Christian, Cognitive, Computer, Cybernetics, Dismal, Domestic, Earth, Electrodynamics, Entomology, Eth(n)ology, Euphenics, Exact, Geodesy, Geology, Information, Life, Materia medica, Mechanics, Metallurgy, Natural, Noble, Nomology, Occult, Ology, Ontology, Optics, Optometry, Pedagogy, Penology, Physical, Physics, Policy, Political, Pure, Rocket, Rural, Serology, Skill, Social, Soft, Soil, Sonics, Stinks, Stylistics, Tactics, Technics, Technology, Telematics, Thremmatology, Toxicology, Typhlology, Zootechnics

Science fiction Cyberpunk

Scientist Alchemist, Anatomist, Archimedes, Aston, Astronomer, Atomist, Boffin, BSc, Cavendish, Climatologist, Copernicus, Curie, Dalton, Davy, Dopper, Egghead, Einstein, Experimenter, Expert, Faraday, Fourier, FRS, Galileo, Geodesist, Harvey,

Heaviside, Kennelly, Lodge, Lovell, Mendeleev, Newton, Oersted, Pascal, Pasteur, Pauli, Piccard, Potamologist, Réaumur, Researcher, Theremin, Volta

Scimitar Acinaciform, Sword

Scintillate Dazzle, Emicate, Gleam, Glitter, → **SPARKLE**

Scion Cion, Graft, Imp, Offspring, Sien(t), Sprig, Sprout, Syen

Scissors Clippers, Criss-cross, Cutters, Forfex, Nail, Probe, Shears

Scoff Belittle, Boo, Chaff, Deride, Dor, Eat, Feast, Flout, Food, Gall, Gibe, Gird, Gobble, → **JEER**, Mock, Rail, Rib, Ridicule, Roast, Scaff, Scorn, Sneer, Taunt

Scold(ing) Admonish, Berate, Callet, Catamaran, Chastise, Chide, Clapperclaw, Cotquean, Do, Earful, Earwig, Flite, Flyte, Fuss, Jaw(bation), Jobation, Lecture, Nag, Objurgate, Philippic, Rant, Rate, → **REBUKE**, Reprimand, Reprove, Revile, Rouse on, Row, Sas(s)arara, Sis(s)erary, Slang, Slate, Termagant, Threap, Threep, Through-going, Tick-off, Tongue-lash, Trimmer, Upbraid, Virago, Wig, Xant(h)ippe, Yaff, Yankie, Yap

Sconce Candlestick, Crown, Forfeit, Head, Ice, Nole

Scone Drop, Girdle

Scoop Bale, Dipper, Exclusive, Gouge, Grab, Hollow, Ladle, Lap, Pale, Rout, Shovel, Trowel

Scooter Vespa®

Scope Ambit, Bargaining, Diapason, Domain, Elbow-room, Extent, Freedom, Gamut, Ken, Latitude, Leeway, Play, Purview, Range, Remit, Room, Rope, Scouth, Scowth, Size, Sphere

Scorch(er) Adust, Blister, Brasero, → **BURN**, Char, Destroy, Frizzle, Fry, Parch, Scouther, Scowder, Scowther, Sear, Singe, Soar, Speed, Swale, Swayl, Sweal, Sweel, Torrefy, Torrid, Wither

Score(s), Scoring Apgar, Behind, Bill, Birdie, Bradford, Bye, Capot, Chalk up, Chase, Conversion, Count, Crena, Debt, Eagle, Etch, Full, Groove, Hail, Honours, Ingroove, Ippon, Koka, Law, Lots, Magpie, Make, Music, Net, Nick, Notation, Notch, Nurdle, Open, Partitur(a), Peg, Pique, Point, Record, Repique, Rit(t), Rouge, Run, Rut, Scotch, Scratch, Scribe, Scrive, Set, Single, Spare, Stableford, Stria, String, Sum, Tablature, → **TALLY**, TE, Twenty, Vocal, Waza-ari, Win

Score-board, Score-sheet Card, Telegraph

▷ **Scorer** *may indicate* a composer

▷ **Scoring** *may indicate* an anagram

Scorn(ful) Arrogant, Bah, Contemn, Contempt, Contumely, Deride, Despise, Dis(s), Disdain, Dislike, Disparagement, Flout, Geck, Haughty, Insult, Meprise, Mock, Opprobrium, Phooey, Putdown, Rebuff, Ridicule, Sarcastic, Sardonic, Sarky, Scoff, Scout, Sdaine, Sdeigne, Sneer, Sniffy, Spurn, Wither

Scorpion Book, Chelifer, False, Father-lasher, Pedipalp(us), Vinegarroon, Water, Whip

Scot(sman), Scots(woman), Scottish Angus, Antenati, Berean, Blue-bonnet, Bluecap, Caledonian, Celt, Clansman, Covenanter, Duni(e)wassal, Dunniewassal, Erse, Fingal, Gael, Highland, Ian, Jock, Kelt, Kiltie, Kitty, Knox, Laird, Lallan(s), Lot, Lowland, Luckie, Lucky, Mac, Mon, Peght, Pict, Ross, Sandy, Sawn(e)y, Shetlander, Stuart, Tartan, Tax, Teuchter, Torridonian

Scotch(man) Censor, Dish, Distiller, Glenlivet®, Notch, Score, Scratch, Thwart, Usquebaugh, Whisky

Scot-free Wreakless

Scotland Alban(y), Albion, Caledonia, Gaeltacht, Gaidhealtachd, Lallans, Lothian, NB, Norland, Scotia

Scoundrel Cad, Cur, Dog, Fink, Heel, Knave, Rat, Reprobate, Scab, Smaik, Varlet, → **VILLAIN**

Scour Beat, Depurate, Full, Holystone, Purge, Quarter, Scrub
▷ **Scour** *may indicate* an anagram
Scourge Bible-thumper, Cat, Discipline, Flagellate, Knout, Lash, Pest, → **PLAGUE**, Scorpion, Whip, Wire
Scout Akela, Beaver, Bedmaker, Bird dog, Colony, Disdain, Explorer, Flout, Guide, King's, Outrider, Pathfinder, Pickeer, Pioneer, Queen's, Reconnoitre, Rover, Runner, Scoff, Scorn, Scourer, Scurrier, Scurriour, Sea, Sixer, Spial, Spyal, Talent, Tenderfoot, Tonto, Track, Vedette, Venture
Scowl(ing) Frown, Glower, Gnar, Lour, Lower, Sullen
Scrabble Paw
Scrag(gy) Bony, Dewitt, Ewe-necked, Neck, Scrawny
Scram Begone, Hence, Scat, Shoo
Scramble Addle, Clamber, Encode, Grubble, Hurry, Mêlée, Mix, Motocross, Muss(e), Scamble, Sprattle, Sprawl, Swerve, Texas
Scrap(s), Scrappy Abandon, Abrogate, → **BIT**, Cancel, Conflict, Cutting, Discard, Dump, → **FIGHT**, Fisticuffs, Fragment, Fray, Iota, Jot, Junk, Mêlée, Mellay, Morceau, Morsel, Odd, Off-cut, Ort, Ounce, Papier collé, Patch, Piece, Pig's-wash, Rag, Rase, Raze, Remnant, Scarmoge, Scissel, Scissil, Scrub, Set-to, Shard, Sherd, Shred, Skerrick, Skirmish, Snap, Snippet, Spall, Tait, Tate, Tatter, Titbit, Trash, Truculent, Whit
Scrap book Album, Grangerism
Scrap box Tidy
Scrape(r) Abrade, Agar, Bark, Clat, Claw, Comb, Curette, D and C, Erase, Escapade, Grate, Graze, Gride, Harl, Hoe, Hole, Jar, Kowtow, Lesion, Lute, Predicament, Racloir, Rake, Rasorial, Rasp, Rasure, Raze, Razure, Saw, Scalp, Scart, Scrat(ch), Scroop, Scuff, Shave, Skimp, Skive, Squeegee, Strake, Stridulate, Strigil, Xyster
Scraping noise Curr, Scroop
Scrap merchant Didakai, Didakei, Diddicoi, Diddicoy, Didicoi, Didicoy, Gold-end-man, Totter
Scratch(es), Scratched, Scratching Annul, Cancel, Cla(u)t, Claw, Cracked heels, Curry, Devil, Efface, Eradicate, Erase, Grabble, Graze, Mar, Nick, Par, Periwig, Pork, Quit, Race, Rase, Rasp, Rast, Root, Satan, Scarify, Scart, Score, Scrab(ble), Scram(b), Scrape, Scrattle, Scrawm, Scrawp, Scrooch, Scrorp, Scrub, Spag, Streak, Striation, Tease, Teaze, Wig, Withdraw
▷ **Scratch(ed)** *may indicate* an anagram
Scrawl Doodle, Scribble, Squiggle
Scream(er) Bellow, Cariama, Caterwaul, Comedian, Comic, Cry, Eek, Headline, Hern, Kamichi, Laugh, Priceless, Primal, Riot, Scare-line, Screech, Seriema, Shriek, Skirl, Squall, Sutch, Yell
Scree Bahada, Bajada, Eluvium, Talus
Screech(ing) Cry, Screak, Screich, Screigh, Scriech, Scritch, Skreigh, Skriech, Skriegh, Ululant, Whoot
Screed Megillah, Ms, Plastered, Rat-rhyme, Tirade
Screen(s) Abat-jour, Arras, Back projection, Backstop, Blind(age), Block, Blue, Boss, Brise-soleil, Camouflage, Chancel, Check, Chick, Cinerama®, Cloak, Cornea, Coromandel, Cover, Cribble, Curtain, Divider, Dodger, Eyelid, Festoon-blind, Fire, Fluorescent, Glib, Gobo, Grille, Hallan, Help, Hide, Hoard, Hoarding, Iconostas(is), Intensifying, Jube, Lattice, Mantelet, Mask, Net, Nintendo®, Nonny, Obscure, Organ, Over-cover, Parclose, Partition, Part-off, Pella, Plasma, Pulpitum, Purdah, Radar, Reardos, Reredorse, Reredos(se), Retable, Riddle, Rood, Scog, Sconce, Scope, → **SHADE**, Shelter, Shield, Shoji, Show, Sift, Sight, Silver, Skug, Small,

Smoke, Split, Sunblock, Televise, Tems, Test, TFT, Touch, Transenna, Traverse, Umbrella, VDU, Vet, Wide, Windbreak, Window, Windshield, Winnow

Screw Adam, Allen, Archimedes, Butterfly, Cap, Coach, Countersunk, Double-threaded, Dungeoner, Extort, Female, Grub, Ice, Interrupted, Jailer, Jailor, Lag, Lead, Levelling, Lug, Machine, Male, Micrometer, Miser, Monkey-wrench, Niggard, Perpetual, Phillips®, Prop(ellor), Robertson, Salary, Skinflint, Spiral, Swiz(zle), Thumb(i)kins, Twin, Twist, Vice, Whitworth, Worm

Screwdriver Pozidriv®, Ratchet, Stubby, Tweaker

Scribble Doodle, Pen, Scrawl

Scribe Clerk, Ezra, Mallam, Scrivener, Sopherim, Tabellion, Writer, WS

Scrimmage Bully, Maul, Mêlée, Rouge, Scrap, Skirmish, Struggle

Scrimp Economise, Pinch, Save, Scrape, Skrimp

Script Book, Calligraphy, Devanagari, Gurmukhi, Hand, Hiragana, Italic, Jawi, Kana, Libretto, Linear A, Linear B, Lines, Lombardic, Miniscule, Nagari, Nastalik, Nastaliq, Ogam, Prompt book, Ronde, Scenario, Screenplay, Shooting, Writing

Scripture(s), Scriptural version Adi Granth, Agadah, Antilegomena, Avesta, Bible, Gemara, Gematria, Gospel, Granth (Sahib), Guru Granth, Haggada(h), Hermeneutics, Hexapla, Holy book, Holy writ, Koran, K'thibh, Lesson, Lotus Sutra, Mishna(h), OT, Rig-veda, Smriti, Tantra, Targum, Testament, Upanishad, Veda, Vedic, Verse, Vulgate

Scrofula Crewels, Cruel(l)s, King's evil, Struma

Scroll(-work) Cartouche, Dead Sea, Gohonzon, Makimono, Megillah, Mezuza(h), Monkeytail, Parchment, Pell, Roll, Roul(e), Scrow, Sefer Torah, Stemma, Torah, Turbinate, Upcurl, Vitruvian, Volume, Volute

Scrooge Blagueur, Miser

Scrotum Oscheal

Scrounge(r) Blag, Bludge(r), Borrow, Bot, Cadge, Forage, Freeload, Layabout, Ligger, Scunge, Sponge

Scrub(s), Scrubber Cancel, Chaparral, Cleanse, Dele(te), Gar(r)igue, Hog, Holystone, Loofa(h), Luffa, Mallee, Masseur, Negate, Pro, Rub, Scour, Sticks, Tart, Wormwood

▷ **Scrub** *may indicate* 'delete'

Scruff(y) Dog-eared, Grubby, Nape, Raddled, Tatty, Uncombed, Untidy

Scrum(mage) Bajada, Maul, Melée, Mob, Rouge, Ruck

Scrummy, Scrumptious Delectable, Delicious, Toothy, Yum-yum

Scrunt Carl

Scruple(s), Scrupulous Compunction, Conscience, Doubt, Meticulous, Nicety, Precise, Punctilious, Qualm, Queasy, Righteous, Stickle

Scrutinize, Scrutiny Check, Docimasy, Examine, Inspect, Observe, Peruse, Pore, Pry, → **SCAN**, Size up, Study

Scud East, Scoot, Spark, Spindrift, Spoom, Spoon, Spray

Scuff Brush, Shuffle

Scuffle Bagarre, Brawl, Scarmage, Skirmish, Struggle, Tussle

▷ **Scuffle** *may indicate* an anagram

Scull Oar, Row

Sculpt(ure) Acrolith, Aeginetan, Bas-relief, Boast, Bronze, Calvary, Canephor(a), Canephore, Canephorus, Carve, Chryselephantine, Della-robbia, Figure, Kore, Kouros, Mobile, Nude, Pergamene, Pietà, Relief, Relievo, Sc, Scabble, Scapple, Shape, Stabile, → **STATUARY**, Topiary

Sculptor Arp, Artist, Bartholdi, Bernini, Brancusi, Canova, Cellini, Daedalus, Della Robbia, Donatello, Giacometti, Gibbons, Gill, Hepworth, Klippel, Landseer,

Michelangelo, Myron, Nollekens, Paclozzi, Phidias, Pisano, Praxiteles, Pygmalion, Rodin, Scopas, Stevens, Wheeler

Scum Confervoid, Dregs, Dross, Epistasis, Glass-gall, Kish, Legge, Mantle, Mother, Pond, Rabble, Sandiver, Scorious, Scruff, Slag, Slime, Spume, Sullage, Vermin

Scupper Drain, Ruin, Scuttle, Sink

Scurf, Scurvy Dander, Dandriff, Dandruff, Furfur, Horson, Lepidote, Lepra, Leprose, Scabrous, Scall, Scorbutic, Whoreson, Yaw(e)y, Yaws

Scurrilous Fescennine, Profane, Ribald, Sotadic, Thersites, Vulgar

Scurry Beetle, Hurry, Scamper, Scutter, Skedaddle, Skelter

Scut Fud, Tail

Scute Plate

Scuttle Abandon, Dan, Hod, Purdonium, Scoop, Scrattle, Scupper, Scurry, Sink, Wreck

Scythe Bushwhacker, Cut, Hook, Sickle, Sieth, Snath(e), Snead, Sneath, Sned

Sea(s) Adriatic, Aegean, Amundsen, Andaman, Arabian, Arafura, Aral, Azov, Baltic, Banda, Barents, Beam, Beaufort, Bellingshausen, Benthos, Bering, Billow, Biscay, Bismarck, Black, Blue, Bosp(h)orus, Brine, Briny, Caribbean, Caspian, Celebes, Celtic, Ceram, Channel, China, Chukchi, Coral, Dead, Ditch, Drink, East China, Euphotic, Euripus, Euxine, Flores, Foam, Four, Galilee, Great, Greenland, Head, Herring-pond, High, Hudson Bay, Icarian, Inland, Ionian, Irish, Japan, Java, Kara, Kattegat, Labrador, Laptev, Ler, Ligurian, Main, Mare, Mare clausum, Mare liberum, Marmara, Marmora, Med, Mediterranean, Narrow, Nordenskjold, North, Norwegian, → OCEAN, Offing, Offshore, Oggin, Okhotsk, Pelagic, Philippine, Polynya, Quantity, Red, Ross, Sargasso, Seven, Short, Skagerrak, South, South China, Spanish Main, Strand, Sulu, Tasman, Tethys, Thalassic, Tiberias, Tide, Tide-rip, Timor, Tyrrhenian, Waddenzee, Water, Weddell, White, Yellow, Zee

Sea-anemone Actinia, Zoantharia

Sea-bear Fur-seal, Otary, Seal, Seecatchie

Sea-beast Ellops, Manatee

Sea-bream Carp, Fish, Porgie, Porgy, Tai

Sea-cow Dugong, Lamantin, Manatee, Rhytina, Sirenian

Sea-cucumber Bêche-de-mer, Trepang

Sea-dog Salt, Tar

Sea-ear Abalone, Paua

Sea-fight Naumachy

Seafood Crab, Crevette, → FISH, Lobster, Prawn, Shrimp, Zooplankton

Sea-front, Seashore, Seaside Beach, Coast(line), Esplanade, Littoral, Orarian, Prom(enade), Seaboard

Sea-god Neptune, Nereus, Triton

Sea-green Glaucous, Incorruptible, Robespierre

Sea-horse Hippocampus, Hippodame, Lophobranchiate, Morse, Pipefish, Tangie

Seal(s), Sealant, Seal box Airtight, Appose, Atlantic, Bachelor, Bladdernose, Block(ade), Bull(a), Cachet, Cap, Caulk, Chesterfield, Chop, Clinch, Close, Cocket, Common, Consign, Crab-eater, Cylinder, Eared, Earless, Elephant, Emblem, Fob, Fur, Gasket, Great, Greenland, Hair, Harbour, Harp, Hermetic, Hooded, Hudson, Impress, Jark, Lemnian, Lute, Monk, Obsign, O-ring, Otary, Phoca, Pinnipedia, Pintadera, Pod, Privy, Proof, Putty, Quarter, Ribbon, Ringed, Ronan, Rookery, Saddleback, Sea-bear, Sealch, Sea-leopard, Sealgh, Seecatch(ie), Selkie, Sigil, Signet, Silkie, Silky, Size, Skippet, Solomon's, Sphragistics, Stamp, Tar, Wafer, Washer, Water, Weddell, Whitecoat, Womb, Zalophus, Ziplock

Sea-legs Balance, Pleons

Sea-level Geoid
Sea-lily Crinoid, Palmatozoa
Seam Channel, Commissure, Fell, French, Furrow, Join, Layer, Middle-stitching, Monk's, Sew, Suture, Thread, Welt
Seaman, Seamen AB, Crew, Jack, Lascar, Lubber, Mariner, OD, Ordinary, PO, RN, → SAILOR, Salt, Swabby, Tar
Sea-mat Flustra, Hornwrack
Sea-matiness Gam
Sea-monster Kraken, Merman, Wasserman
Sea-mouse Bristle-worm
Séance Communication, Session, Sitting
Sea-parrot Puffin
Sear Brand, Burn, Catch, Cauterise, Frizzle, Parch, Scath(e), Scorch, Singe, Wither
Search(ing) Beat, Body, Comb, Dragnet, Examine, Ferret, Fingertip, → FORAGE, Fossick, Frisk, Global, Google(-whack), Grope, Home, Hunt, Indagate, Inquire, Jerk, Jerque, Kemb, Manhunt, Perquisition, Perscrutation, Probe, Proll, Prospect, Proul, Prowl, Quest, Rake, Rancel, Ransack, Ransel, Ranzel, Ravel, Ripe, Root, Rootle, Rummage, Scan, Scour, Scur, Sker, Skirr, Snoop, Strip, Thumb, Trace, Trawl, Zotetic
Sea-rover Norseman, Viking
Sea-serpent, Sea-snake Ellops, Hydrophidae, Phoca
▶ **Seaside** *see* SEA-FRONT
Sea-slug Bêche-de-mer, Trepang
Sea-snail Neritidae
Season(able), Seasonal, Seasoned, Seasoning Accustom, Age, Aggrace, Autumn, Betimes, Christmas, Close, Condiment, Devil, Dress, Duxelles, Easter, Enure, Etesian, Fall, Fennel, Festive, Flavour, Garlic, G(h)omasco, Growing, Hiems, High, In, Inure, Lent, Marjoram, Master, Mature, Nutmeg, Open, Paprika, Pepper, Powellise, Practised, Ripen, Salt, Sar, Seal, Seel, Seil, Sele, Silly, Solstice, Spice, Spring, Summer(y), Tahini, Ticket, Tide, Time, Whit, Winter, Xmas
Sea-squirt Ascidian, Cunjevoi
Seat Backside, Banc, Banquette, Beanbag, Bench, Bleachers, Booster, Borne, Bosun's chair, Bottom, Box, Bucket, Bum, Bunker, Buttocks, Canapé, Centre, Chair, Chaise longue, Coit, Couch, Country, Creepie, Croup(e), Croupon, Cushion, Davenport, Deckchair, Derrière, Dick(e)y, Dicky, Divan, Ejector, Epicentre, Faldistory, Faldstool, Foundation, Fud, Fundament, Gradin, Hall, Home, Hot, Houdah, Howdah, Humpty, Hurdies, Judgement, Jump, Knifeboard, Love, Marginal, Marquise, Mercy, Misericord, Natch, Nates, Ottoman, Palanquin, Palfrey, Perch, Pew, Pillion, Pit, Pouffe, Ringside, Rumble, Rumble-tumble, Rump, Saddle, Safe, Sagbag, Sedes, Sedile, Sedilium, See, Sell, Selle, Settee, Settle, Siege, Siege Perilous, Sliding, Sofa, Squab, Stool, Strapontin, Subsellium, Sunk(ie), Sunlounger, Synthronus, Throne, Tonneau, Window, Woolsack
Sea-urchin Asteria, Echinus, Pluteus, Whore's egg
Sea-vampire Manta
Sea-wall Bulwark, Dyke, Groyne
Sea-weed Agar, Alga(e), Arame, Badderlock, Bladderwort, Bladderwrack, Carrag(h)een, Ceylon moss, Chondrus, Conferva, Coralline, Cystocarp, Desmid, Diatom, Driftweed, Dulse, Enteromorpha, Fucus, Gulfweed, Heterocontae, Hornwrack, Karengo, Kelp, Kilp, Kombu, Konbu, Laminaria, Laver, Lemon-weed, Nori, Nullipore, Oarweed, Ore, Peacock's tail, Phyco-, Porphyra, Redware, Rockweed, Sargasso, Seabottle, Sea-furbelow, Sea-girdle, Sea-lace, Sea-lettuce,

Sea-mat, Sea-moss, Sea-tangle, Seaware, Sea-whistle, Sea-wrack, Tang, Tetraspore, Ulva, Varec(h), Vraic, Wakame, Wakane, Ware, Wrack

Sea-wolf Pirate

Sea-worm Palolo, Spunculid

Sebastian Coe

Secede, Secession(ist) Adullamite, Antiburgher, Defy, Desert, Dissident, Flamingant, Separatist, Sever, Splinter

Seclude, Seclusion Cloister, Incommunicado, Isolate, Ivory tower, Maroon, Nook, Privacy, Purdah, Quarantine, Retiracy, Retreat, Secret, Sequester, Shyness, Solitude

Second(s), Secondary Abet, Alternative, Another (guess), Appurtenance, Assist, Atomic, Back(er), Beta, Coming, Comprimario, Deuteragonist, Ephemeris, Flash, Friend, Handler, Imperfect, Indirect, Inferior, Instant, Jiffy, Latter, Leap, Lesser, Minor, Mo(ment), Nature, Other, Pig's-whisper, Redwood, Runner-up, Saybolt-Universal, Sec, Shake, Share, Side(r), Sight, Silver, Split, Subsidiary, Support, Tick, Trice, Twinkling, Universal, Wind

Second-best Worsted

▸ **Second-class** *see* SECOND-RATE

Second coming Parousia

Second earth Antichthon

Second-hand Hand-me-down, Hearsay, Preloved, Reach-me-down, Re-paint, Tralatitious, Used, Vicarious

Second-rate, Second-class B, Inferior, Mediocre

Second-sight Deuteroscopy, Divination, Tais(c)h

Second tine Bay, Bez

Second-year student Semi(e)(-bajan), Sophomore

Secrecy, Secret(s), Secretive Apocrypha, Arcana, Arcane, Arcanum, Backstairs, Cabbalistic, Cagey, Clam, Clandestine, Closet, Code, Conventicle, Covert, Cranny, Cryptadia, Cryptic, Crypto, Dark, Dearn, Deep, Deep-laid, Dern, Devious, Esoteric, Hidden, Hidling, Hidlin(g)s, Hole and corner, Hugger-mugger, Hush-hush, Hushy, Inly, Inmost, Latent, Mysterious, Mystical, Mystique, Open, Oyster, Password, Penetralia, Petto, → PRIVATE, Privity, Privy, QT, Rune, Scytale, Shelta, Silent, Slee, Sly, State, Stealth, Sub rosa, Tight-lipped, Top, Trade, Unbeknown, Undercover, Underhand, Undescried, Unknown, Unre(a)d, Unrevealed, Untold

Secretary Aide, Amanuensis, Chancellor, Chronicler, CIS, Desk, Desse, Famulus, Home, Minuteman, Moonshee, Munshi, Notary, Parliamentary, Permanent, Private, Prot(h)onotary, Scrive, Social, Steno(grapher), Stenotyper, Temp

Secretary-bird Messenger, Serpent-eater

Secrete, Secretion Aequorin, Aldosterone, Allomone, Apocrine, Autacoid, Cache, Castor, Chalone, Colostrum, Cuckoo-spit, Discharge, Emanation, Exude, Hide, Honeydew, Hormone, Juice, Lac, Lactate, Lerp, Melatonin, Mucus, Musk, Osmidrosis, Pruina, Ptyalin, Recrement, Renin, Resin, Rheum, Saliva, Sebum, Secern, Smegma, Spit(tle), Succus, Trypsin

Sect(arian), Secret society Abelite, Adamite, Ahmadiy(y)ah, Albigenses, Amish, Anabaptist, Assassin, Babee, Babi, Bahai, Bigendian, Brahmin, Cabal, Cainite, Calixtine, Camorra, Campbellite, Cathar, Clan, Clapham, Covenantes, Crypto, Cult, Cynic, Danite, Darbyite, Dissenter, Docate(s), Donatist, Druse, Druze, Dunkard, Dunker, Ebionite, Encratite, Essene, Familist, Gabar, Gheber, Ghebre, Giaour, Glassite, Gnostic, Group, Gueber, Guebre, Gymnosophist, Harmonist, Harmonite, Hassid, Hauhau, Hemerobaptist, Hesychast, Hillmen, Holy Roller, Hutterite, Illuminati, Ismaili, Jacobite, Jansenist, Jodo, Karaite, Karmathian, Little-endian,

Lollard, Macedonian, Macmillanite, Mandaean, Marcionite, Maronite, Mendaites, Monothelite, Montanist, Moonie, Mormon, Mucker, Muggletonian, Nasorean, Nazarine, Noetian, Ophites, Order, Partisan, Patripassian, Paulician, Perfectionist, Pharisee, Philadelphian, Phrygian, Picard, Pietist, Plymouth Brethren, Plymouthite, Porch, Pure Land, Rappist, Ribbonism, Sabbatian, Sabian, Sadducee, Saktas, Sandeman, School, Schwenkfelder, Seekers, Senus(s)i, Seventh Day Adventist, Sex, Shafiite, S(h)aiva, Shaker, Shembe, Shia(h), Soka Gakkai, Sons of Freedom, Taliban, Therapeutae, Tunker, Unitarian, Utraquist, Vaishnava, Valdenses, Vaudois, Wahabee, Wahabi(i)te, Waldenses, Yezdi, Yezidee, Yezidi, Zealot, Zen, Zezidee

Section, Sector Area, Balkanize, Caesarian, Chapter, Classify, Conic, Cross, Cut, Division, Ellipse, Empennage, Eyalet, Gan, Golden, Gore, Hyperbola, Lith, Lune, Meridian, Metamere, Mortice, Movement, Octant, Outlier, Panel, Passus, → PIECE, Platoon, Private, Public, Pull-out, Quarter, Rhythm, Rib, Segment, Severy, Slice, Stage, Ungula, Unit, Warm, Zenith, Zone

Secular(ise) Earthly, Laic, Non-CE, Profane, Temporal, Ungod, Worldly

Secure, Security Anchor, Assurance, Bag, Bail, Band, Bar, Batten, Belay, Bellwether, Belt and braces, Bolt, Bond, Bottomry, Buck Rogers, Calm, Catch, Cement, Chain, Cheka, Cinch, Clamp, Clasp, Clench, Clinch, Close, Cocoon, Collateral, Collective, Come by, Consolidate, Consols, Cosy, Cushy, Debenture, Dunnage, Engage, Enlock, Ensure, Equity, Establishment, Fasten, Fastness, Fortify, Frap, Fungibles, Gilt, Grith, Guarantee, Guy, Hypothec, Immune, Impregnable, Indemnity, Inlock, Invest(ment), Knot, Lace, Land, Lash, Latch, Lien, Listed, Lock, Lockaway, Lockdown, Lockfast, Long-dated, Longs, Medium-dated, Mortgage, Nail, National, Obtain, Padlock, Patte, Pin, Pledge, Pot, Pre-empt, Preference, Procure, Protect, Quad, Rope, Rug, → SAFE, Safety, Settle, Snell, Snug, Social, Sound, Stable, Stanchion, Staple, Staylace, Stock, Strap, Sure(ty), Tack, Take, Tie, Tight, Trap, Trice, Warrant, Watertight, Wedge, Win

Sedan Battle, Brougham, Chair, Jampan(i), Jampanee, Litter, Palanquin, Palkee, Palki, Saloon

Sedate Calm, Cool, Decorous, Demure, Dope, Douce, Drug, Sad, Serene, Sober(sides), Staid, Stand

Sedative Amytal®, Anodyne, Aspirin, Barbitone, Bromal, Bromide, Chloral, Depressant, Deserpidine, Hypnic, Laurel water, Lenitive, Lupulin, Meprobamate, Metopryl, Miltown, Morphia, Narcotic, Nembutal®, Opiate, Paraldehyde, Pethidine, Phenobarbitone, Premed(ication), Roofie, Scopolamine, Seconal®, Soothing, Temazepam, Thridace, Valerian, Veronal®

Sedentary Inactive, Sessile, Stationary

Sedge Carex, Chufa, Cinnamon, Clubrush, Grey, Seg, Xyris

Sediment Alluvium, Chalk, Deposit, Dregs, F(a)eces, Fecula, Flysch, Foots, Grounds, Grouts, Lees, Molasse, Placer, Residue, Salt, Sapropel, Silt, Sludge, Terrigenous, Till, Turbidite, Varve, Warp

Sedition, Seditious Incitement, Insurrection, Revolt, Riot, Treason

Seduce(r), Seductive Allure, Bed, Betray, Bewitch, Bribe, Cuckold-maker, Debauch, Dishonour, Entice, Honeyed, Honied, Jape, Lothario, Luring, Mislead, Pull, Siren, Slinky, Tempt, Trepan, Undo, Vamp, Wrong

▷ **Seduce** *may indicate* one word inside another

See(ing) Acknow, Apostolic, Barchester, Behold, Bishopric, C, Consider, Deek, Descry, Diocesan, Discern, Durham, Ebor, Ecce, Ely, Episcopal, Eye, Get, Glimpse, Holy, La, Lo, Meet, Norwich, Notice, Observe, Papal, Perceive, Realise, Remark, Ripon, Rumble, Since, Sodor and Man, Spae, Spot, Spy, Truro, Twig, Understand,

V, Vatican, Vid(e), View, Vision, Visit, Voilà, Witness, York

Seed(s), Seedy Achene, Argan, Arilli, Arillode, Ash-key, Bean, Ben, Best, Blue, Bonduc, Cacoon, Caraway, Carvy, Cebadilla, Cevadilla, Chickpea, Cocoa, Colza, Coriander, Corn, Crabstone, Cum(m)in, Dragon's teeth, Embryo, Endosperm, Ergot, Favourite, Fern, Germ, Grain, Gritty, Issue, Ivory-nut, Kernel, Lima, Lomentum, Mangy, Mawseed, Miliary, Nickar, Nicker, Niger, Nucellous, Nut, Offspring, Ovule, Pea, Pinon, Pip, Poorly, Poppy, Sabadilla, Scuzz, Semen, Seminal, Sesame, Shabby, Shea-nut, Silique, Sorus, Sow, Sperm, Spore, Stone, Terminator, Zoosperm

Seed-case Aril, Bur(r), Endopleura, Husk, Pea(s)cod, Pod, Testa, Theca

Seed-leaf Cotyledon

Seedsman Driller, Nurseryman, Sower

Seek(er) Ask, Beg, Busk, Chase, Court, Endeavour, Ferret out, Gun for, Pursue, Quest, Scur, Search, Skirr, Solicit, Suitor

Seem(ingly) Appear, Look, Ostensible, Purport, Quasi, Think

Seemly Comely, Decent, Decorous, Fit, Suitable

Seep Dribble, Exude, Leak, Ooze, Osmose, Percolate, Permeate

Seer Augur, Auspex, Eye, Melampus, Nahum, Observer, Oculiform, Onlooker, Oracle, Prescience, Prophet, Sage, Sibyl, Soothsayer, T(e)iresias, Witness, Zoroaster

Seesaw Bascule, Teeter(-totter), Teeter-board, Tilt, Vacillate, Wild mare

Seethe(d) Boil, Bubble, Churn, Ferment, Simmer, Smoulder, Sod

Segment Antimere, Arthromere, Cut, Division, Gironny, Gyronny, Intron, Lacinate, Lith, Lobe, Merome, Merosome, Metamere, Part, Piece, Pig, Proglottis, Propodeon, Prothorax, Scliff, Section, Share, Shie, Skliff, Somite, Split, Sternite, Syllable, Tagma, Telson, Trochanter, Urite, Uromere

Segregate, Segregation Apartheid, Exile, Insulate, Intern, → **ISOLATE**, Jim Crow, Seclude, Separate

Seidlitz Powder, Rochelle

Seismic Terremotive

Seismograph Tromometer

Seize, Seizure Angary, Apprehend, Areach, Arrest, Assume, Attach(ment), Bag, Bone, Capture, Claw, Cleek, Cly, Collar, Commandeer, Confiscate, Distrain, Distress, Extent, For(e)hent, → **GRAB**, Grip, Hend, Impound, Impress, Maverick, Na(a)m, Nab, Nap, Nim, Point, Possess, Pot, Raid, Replevy, Rifle, Sease, Sequestrate, Smug, Snag, Tackle, Trover, Usurp, Wingding

Seldom Infrequent, Rare, Unoften

Select(ion), Selecting, Selector Artificial, Assortment, Bla(u)d, Cap, Casting, Choice, Choose, Classy, Cull, Darwinism, Discriminate, Draft, Draw, Eclectic, Edit, Elite, Excerpt, Exclusive, Extract, Favour, Garble, Inside, K, Kin, Nap, Natural, Pericope, → **PICK**, Pot-pourri, Prefer, Recherché, Sample, Seed, Sex, Single, Sort, Stream, Tipster, Triage, UCCA

Selenium Se, Zorgite

Self Atman, Auto, Character, Ego, Person, Psyche, Seity, Sel, Soul

Self-confident, Self-confidence, Self-willed Aplomb, Ego, Headstrong

Self-conscious Guilty

Self-contained Absolute, Reticent, SC, Taciturn

Self-contradictory Absurd, Irish

Self-control, Self-discipline Ascesis, Encraty, Modesty, Patience, Restraint, Temper(ance)

▶ **Self-defence** *see* **MARTIAL (ARTS)**

Self-esteem Amour-propre, Conceit, Confidence, Egoism, Pride, Vainglory
Self-evident Axiom, Manifest, Obvious, Patent, Truism, Truth
Self-existence Solipsism
Self-fertilisation, Self-origination Aseity, Autogamy
Self-governing Autonomy, Idior(r)hythmic, Kabele, Kebel, Puritanism, Swaraj
Self-help Smiles
Self-important, Self-indulgent, Self-interested Aristippus, Arrogant, Chesty, Cocky, Conceited, Immoderate, Jack-in-office, Licentious, Narcissistic, Pompous, Pragmatic, Profligate, Solipsist, Sybarite
Selfish(ness) Avaricious, Egocentric, Egoist, Grabby, Greedy, Hedonist, Mean, Solipsism
Selfless(ness) Non-ego, Tuism
Self-limiting Kenotic
▶ **Self-origination** *see* SELF-FERTILISATION
Self-pollinating Cl(e)istogamic
Self-possession Aplomb, Composure, Cool, Nonchalant
Self-satisfied, Self-satisfaction Complacent, Narcissism, Smug, Tranquil
Self-service Automat, Buffet, Cafeteria, Supermarket
Self-sufficient, Self-sufficiency Absolute, Autarky, Complete, Hunter-gatherer
Self-taught Autodidact
Sell(er), Selling Apprize, Auction, Barter, Bear, Betray, Catch, Chant, Chaunt, Cold-call, Cope, Costermonger, Direct, Dispose, Divest, Do, Fancier, Flog, Go, Hard, Have, Hawk, Huckster, Hustle, Inertia, Knock down, Market, Marketeer, Ménage, Merchant, Missionary, Oligopoly, Pardoner, Party, Peddle, Peddler, Pick-your-own, Purvey, Push, Pyramid, Rabbito(h), Realise, Rep, Retail, Ruse, Short, Simony, Soft, Stall-man, Sugging, Switch, → TRADE, Vend
Selvage Border, Edge, Roon, Rund
Semantics General, Generative, Interpretive, Notional, Onomasiology, Semasiology, Sematology
Semaphore Signal, Tic-tac, Wigwag
Semblance Aspect, Guise, Likeness, Sign, Verisimilitude
Semen Jis(so)m, Milt, Spunk
Semi-circular D, Hemicycle
Semi-conductor Germanium, LED, Thryristor
Seminar(y) Class, Colloquium, Group, Theologate, Tutorial, Workshop
Semiotics Syntactics
Semi-paralysis Dyaesthesia
Semitic Accadian, Akkadian, Ammonite, Amorite, Arab, Aramaic, Canaanite, Chaldean, Geez, Jewish, Phoenician
Semitone Pycnon
Senate Council, Curia, Seanad (Eireann)
Senator Antiani, Cicero, Elder, Legislator, Solon
Send, Sent Consign, → DESPATCH, Disperse, Emit, Entrance, Issue, Launch, Mail, Order, Post, Rapt, Ship, Transmit, Transport
Send back Refer, Remand, Remit, Return
Send down Demit, Lower, Refer, Rusticate
Send up Chal(l)an, Lampoon, Promote
Senegal SN
Senescence Age
Senile, Senility Caducity, Dementia, Disoriented, Doddery, Doitit, Dotage, Eild, Eld, Gaga, Nostology, Twichild

Senior Aîné, Doyen, Elder, Father, Grecian, Mayor, Oubaas, Père, Primus, Superior, Upper

Senna Bladder

Señor(a) Caballero, Don(a), Hidalga, Hidalgo

Sensation(al) Acolouthite, Anoesis, Aura, Blood, Commotion, Drop-dead, Emotion, Empfindung, Feeling, Gas, Impression, Lurid, Melodrama, Organic, Par(a)esthesia, Phosphene, Pyrotechnic, Shocker, Shock-horror, Showstopper, Splash, Stir, Styre, Synaesthesia, Thrill, Tingle, Vibes, Wow, Yellow

Sense, Sensual, Sensing Acumen, Aura, Carnal, Coherence, Common, Dress, ESP, Faculty, Feel, Gross, Gumption, Gustation, Hearing, Horse, Idea, Import, Instinct, Intelligence, Intuition, Lewd, Meaning, Moral, Nous, Olfactory, Palate, Perceptual, Rational, Receptor, Remote, Rumble-gumption, Rumgumption, Rum(m)el-gumption, Rum(m)le-gumption, Sight, Sixth, Slinky, Smell, Spirituality, Sybarite, Synesis, Taste, Touch, Voluptuary, Voluptuous, Wisdom, Wit

Senseless Absurd, Anosmia, Illogical, Inane, Mad, Numb, Stupid, Stupor, Unconscious, Unwise, Vegetal

Sensible Aware, Clear-headed, Dianoetic, Down to earth, No-nonsense, Prudent, Raisonné, Rational, Sane, Solid, Well-balanced

Sensitive, Sensitivity Algesia, Alive, Allergic, Atopy, Dainty, Delicate, Erethism, Erogenous, Hypaesthesia, Keen, Nesh, Nociceptive, Orthochromatic, Passible, Radiesthesia, Sympathetic, Tactful, Tender, Thermaesthesia, Thin-skinned, Ticklish, Touchy(-feely), Vulnerable

Sensor(y) Detector, Exteroceptor, Interoceptor, Palpi, Proprioceptor, Remote

Sentence(s) Assize, Bird, Carpet, Clause, Closed, Commit, Complex, Compound, Condemn, Custodial, Death, Decree(t), Deferred, Doom, Fatwah, Indeterminate, Judgement, Life, Matrix, Open, Pangram, Paragraph, Period(ic), Porridge, Predicate, Rap, Rheme, Rune, Simple, Stretch, Suspended, Swy, Tagmene, Time, Topic, Verdict, Versicle, Weigh off

Sententious Concise, Gnomic, Laconic, Pithy, Pompous, Terse

Sentiment(al), Sentimentality Byronism, Corn, Cornball, Drip, Feeling, Goo, Govey, Gucky, Gush, Hokey, Icky, Maudlin, Mawkish, Mind, Mush, Namby-pamby, Nationalism, Nostalgia, Opinion, Romantic, Rose-pink, Rosewater, Saccharin, Schmaltzy, Sloppy, Smoochy, Soppy, Spoony, Sugary, Tear-jerker, Traveller, Treacly, Twee, View, Weepy, Yucky

Sentry Custodian, Guard, Jaga, Picket, Sentinel, Vedette, Vidette, Watch

Separate(d), Separation, Separately Abstract, Asunder, Atmolysis, Avulsion, Comma, Compartmentalise, Cull, Cut, Decollate, Decompose, Decouple, Deduct, Deglutinate, Demarcate, Demerge, Detach, Dialyse, Diastasis, Diazeuxis, Diremption, Disally, Discerp, Disconnect, Discrete, Disjunction, Dissociate, Distance, Distinct, Disunite, Divide, Division, Divorce, Eloi(g)n, Elute, Elutriate, Esloin, Estrange, Filter, Grade, Gulf, Heckle, Hive, Hyphenate, Insulate, Intervene, Isolate, Judicial, Laminate, Lease, Legal, Monosy, Part, Particle, Peel off, Piece, Prescind, Ramify, Red(d), Rift, Scatter, Schism, Screen, Scutch, Secern, Segregate, Sequester, Sever, Several, Shear, Shed, Shore, Shorn, Sift, Sleave, Sle(i)ded, Solitary, Sort, → **SPLIT**, Steam-trap, Stream, Sunder, Sundry, Tems(e), Tmesis, Try, Twin(e), Unclasp, Unravel, Winnow, Wrench, Yandy

Sepia Cuttle, Ink

Seppuku Hara-kiri, Hari-kari

Septic Poisonous, Rotting

Septimus Small

Septum Mediastinum

Sepulchral, Sepulchre Bier, Cenotaph, Charnel, Crypt, Easter, Funeral, Monument, Pyramid, Tomb, Vault, Whited

Sequel After-clap, Consequence, Effect, Outcome, Suite

Sequence Agoge, Algorithm, Byte, Chronological, Consecution, Consensus, Continuity, Continuum, Escape, Fibonacci, Intervening, Intron, Line, Main, Montage, Order, Peptide, Polar, Program(me), Routine, Run, Seriatim, Series, Shot, Signal, Succession, Suit, Suite, Train, Vector

Sequester, Sequestrate Confiscate, Esloin, Esloyne, Impound, Isolate, Retire, Seclude, Separate

Sequin Paillette, Zecchino

Sequoia Redwood

Seraph Abdiel, → ANGEL

Serb(ian) Chetnik

Sere Arid, → DRY, Scorch, Wither

Serenade(r) Aubade, Charivari, Horning, Love song, Minstrel, Nocturne, Shivaree, Sing-song, Wait, Wake

Serene, Serenity Calm, Composed, Impassive, Placid, Repose, Sangfroid, Sedate, Seraphic, Smooth, → TRANQUIL

Serf(dom) Adscript, Bondman, Ceorl, Churl, Helot, Manred, → SLAVE, Thete, Thrall, Vassal, Velle(i)nage, Villein

Serge Russian, Say

Sergeant Buzfuz, Colour, Cuff, Drill, Flight, Havildar, Kite, Lance, Master, → NCO, Platoon, RSM, Sarge, SL, SM, Staff, Technical, Troy

Serial(ism) Episode, Feuilleton, Heft, Livraison, Total

Series Actinide, Actinium, Arithmetical, Balmer, Catena, Chain, Concatenation, Continuum, Course, Cycle, Cyclus, Electromotive, Enfilade, Engrenage, En suite, Episode, Epos, Ethylene, Fibonacci, Fourier, Geometric, Gradation, Harmonic, Homologous, Lanthanide, Line, Links, Loop, Maclaurin's, Methane, Neptunium, Partwork, Pedigree, Power, Process, → PROGRESSION, Radioactive, Rest, Routine, Rubber, Run, Sequence, Ser, Sitcom, String, Succession, Suit, Taylor's, Thorium, Time, Tone, Train, Uranium, World

Serious(ly) Critical, Earnest, Grave, Gravitas, Heavy, Important, Intense, Major, Momentous, Pensive, Sad, Serpentine, Sober, Solemn, Sombre, Staid, Straight(-faced), Very

Sermon Address, Discourse, Gatha, Homily, Khutbah, Lecture, Preachment, Prone, Spital

Serow Goral, Thar

Serpent(ine) Adder, Amphisbaena, Anguine, Apepi, Apophis, Asp, Aspic(k), Basilisk, Boa, Caduceus, Cockatrice, Dipsas, Firedrake, Midgard, Nagas, Ophiolite, Ouroboros, Peridotite, Pharaoh's, Retinalite, Sea-snake, Shesha, → SNAKE, Traitor, Uraeus, Verd-antique, Verde-antico, Viper, Wyvern

Serrate(d) Diprionidian, Saw, Scallop, Serried

Serum Albumin, Antiglobulin, Antilymphocyte, Antitoxin, ATS, Fluid, Globulin, Humoral, Opsonin, Senega

Serval Bush-cat

Servant, Server Aide, Attendant, Ayah, Batman, Bearer, Bedder, Bedmaker, Between-maid, Boot-catcher, Boots, Boy, Butler, Caddie, Chaprassi, Chuprassy, Civil, Columbine, Cook, Daily, Domestic, Dromio, Drudge, Employee, Factotum, Famulus, File, Flunkey, Footboy, Footman, Friday, Gehazi, G(h)illie, Gip, Gully, Gyp, Haiduk, Handmaid, Helot, Henchman, Heyduck, Hind, Hireling, Iras, Jack, Jack-slave, Jeames, Khansama(h), Khidmutgar, Khitmutgar, Kitchen-knave,

Lackey, Lady's maid, Lazy Susan, Maid, Major-domo, Man, Man Friday, Menial, Minion, Mixologist, Muchacha, Muchacho, Myrmidon, Nethinim, Obedient, Page, Pantler, Person, Postman, Public, Retainer, Retinue, Scout, Scrub, Scullion, Servitor, Sewer, Skip, Slavey, Soubrette, Steward, Tablespoon, Tapsman, Tendance, Theow, Thete, Tiger, Tweeny, Underling, Vails, Vales, Valet, Valkyrie, Varlet, Vassal, Waiter, Wash-rag, Weller

Serve, Service(s) Ace, Act, Active, Amenity, Answer, Arriage, Asperges, Assist, ATS, Attendance, Avail, Benediction, Breakfast, Candlemas, Cannonball, Ceefax®, China, Christingle, Civil, Communion, Community, Complin(e), Conscription, Corvée, Credo, Devotional, Dien, Dinnerset, Diplomatic, Dish, Divine, Do, Dow, Drumhead, Duty, Ecosystem, Employ, Evensong, Facility, Fault, Fee, Feudal, Fish, Foreign, Forensic, Forward, → **FUNCTION**, Further, Go, Help, Helpline, Hour, Ibadat, Ka(e), Kol Nidre, Let, Line, Ling, Lip, Litany, Liturgy, Ma'ariv, Mass, Mat(t)ins, Memorial, Mincha, Minister, Ministry, Missa, National, Nocturn, Nones, Oblige, Office, Oracle, Overarm, Overhaul, Pass, Pay, Personal, Pit stop, Possum, Pottery, Prime, Proper, Public, RAF, Requiem, Rite, RN, Room, Sacrament, Secret, Selective, Senior, Sext, Shacharis, Shaharith, Shuttle, Silver, Social, Sorb, Stead, Sted, Sue, Tableware, Tea, Tenebrae, Tierce, Trental, Uncork, Under-arm, Use, Utility, Vespers, Wait, Waiterage, Watch-night, Wild, Worship, Yeoman('s)

Service-book Hymnal, Hymnary, Missal, Triodion

▷ **Serviceman** *may indicate* a churchman

Servile, Servility Abasement, Base, Crawling, Knee, Kowtowing, Lickspittle, Menial, Obsequious, Slavish, Slimy, Submissive, Suck-hole, Sycophantic, Tintookie, Truckle

Serving Helping, Heuristic, Portion

Servitude Bondage, Domination, Peonism, Slavery, Thirlage, Thrall, Vassalry, Yoke

Sesame Gingelly, Gingili, Grapple-plant, Jinjilli, Semsem, Tahini, Til

Session(s) Bout, Executive, Galah, Jam, Kirk, Meeting, Nightshift, Petty, Poster, Quarter, Rap, Round, Séance, Sederunt, Settle, Sitting, Term

Set(ting) (aside; down; in; off; out; up) Activate, Adjust, Appoint, Arrange, Batch, Bent, Bezel, Boun, Brooch, Cabal, Cake, Case, Cast, Chaton, Class, Claw, Clique, Cliveden, Closed, Coagulate, Cock, Cockshy, Codomain, Collection, Collet, Comp(ositor), Companion, Compose, Congeal, Context, Coterie, Couvert, Crew, Crystal, Cyclorama, Data, Dead, Decline, Decor, Detonate, Diorama, Dispose, Earmark, Earnest, Earth, Enchase, Ensky, Environment, Establish, Explode, Film, Fit, Flagstone, Flash, Flat(s), Found, Garniture, Geal, Gel, Genome, Group, Harden, Ilk, Inchase, Incut, Infinite, Inlay, Jee, Jeel, Jell(y), Jet, Julia, Kit, Laid, Land, Lay, Leg, Locale, Locate, Lot, Mandelbrot, Milieu, Mise en scène, Monture, Mournival, Nail, Nest, Occident, Open, Ordered, Ordinate, Ouch, Pair, Parure, Pavé, Permanent, Physique, Pitch, Place(ment), Plant, Plaste, Ply, Point, Posed, Posit, Power, Put, Radio, Ready, Receiver, Relay, Rigid, Rooted, Rubber, Saw, Scenery, Series, Showcase, Sink, Smart, Solidify, Solution, Squad, Stand, Stationed, Stede, Stell, Stick, Stiffen, Still, Stream, Subscriber, Suit, Suite, Surround, Synchronize, Tar, Tea, Team, Teeth, Televisor, Telly, The four hundred, Tiffany, Till, Toilet, Trannie, Transistor, Trigger, Truth, Tube, Union, Universal, Venn (diagram), Weather, Wide-screen, Yplast

Setback Bodyblow, Checkmate, Hiccup, Jolt, Relapse, Retard, Retreat, Reversal, Scarcement, Sickener, Tes, Vicissitude

Setter Cement, Comp, Dog, English, Gelatin(e), Gordon, Gundog, Irish, Pectin, Red, Smoot, Sphinx, Trend

Settle(d), Settler, Settlement Adjust, Agree, Alight, Appoint, Arrange, Ascertain,

Ausgleich, Avenge, Balance, Bandobast, Bed, Bench, Boer, Borghetto, Botany Bay, Bundobust, Bustee, Camp, Clear, Clench, Clinch, Colonial, Colonise, Colony, Compose, Compound, Compromise, Crannog, Decide, Defray, Determine, Diktat, Discharge, Dispose, Dorp, Dowry, Ekistics, Encamp, Endow, Ensconce, Entail, Establish, Expat, Faze, Feeze, Finalise, Fix, Foot, Foreclose, Gravitate, Gridironer, Guilder, Habitant, Hama, Illegitimate, Informal, Jamestown, Jointure, Kibbutz, Land, Ledge, Light, Lyte, Manyat(t)a, Merino, Mise, Mission, Moreton Bay, Moshav, Nahal, Nest, Nestle, New Amsterdam, Oecist, Oikist, Opt, Outpost, Over, Pa(h), Pakka, Pale, Patroon, Pay, Peise, Penal, Perch, Pheazar, Pheese, Pheeze, Phese, Pilgrim, Pioneer, Placate, Planter, Populate, Port Arthur, Port Nicholson, Presidio, Pucka, Pueblo, Pukka, Rancheria, Rancherie, Readjust, Reduction, Reimburse, Remit, Reside, Resolve, Rest, Sate, Satisfaction, Seat, Secure, Sedimentary, Set fair, Shagroon, Shtetl, Silt, Smoot, Sofa, Soldier, Solve, Soweto, Square, Square up, State, Still, Straits, Subside, Taurus, Township, Ujamaa, Utu, Vest(ed), Viatical, Voortrekker

▷ **Settlement** *may indicate* an anagram

▷ **Settler** *may indicate* a coin

Set upon Assail, Attack, Sick

Seven(th), Seven-sided Ages, Days, Dials, Great Bear, Hebdomad, Hepta-, Hills, Magnificent, Nones, Pleiad(es), S, Sages, Seas, Septenary, Septilateral, Septimal, Sins, Sisters, Sleepers, Stars, Wonders, Zeta

Seventy S

Seven-week Omer

Sever Amputate, Cut, Detach, Divide, Sunder

Several Divers, Many, Multiple, Some, Sundry

Severe(ly), Severity Acute, Bad, Caustic, Chronic, Cruel, Dour, Draconian, Drastic, Eager, Extreme, Grave, Grievous, Gruel(ling), Hard, → **HARSH**, Ill, Inclement, Morose, Penal, Rhadamanthine, Rigo(u)r, Roarming, Roundly, Serious, Sharp, Snell(y), Sore, Spartan, Stern, Strict, Swingeing

Sew(ing), Sew up Baste, Clinch, Cope, Embroider, Fell, Fine-draw, Machine, Mitre, Overcast, Overlock, Run, Seam, Seel, Stitch, Tack, Whip

Sewage, Sewer Cesspool, Cloaca, Culvert, Dorcas, → **DRAIN**, Effluence, Jaw-box, Jaw-hole, Mimi, Needle, Privy, Shore, Soil, Sough, Soughing-tile, Waste

Sex(y), Sexist Bed-hopping, Coupling, Cunnilingus, Erotic, Fair, Favours, Fellatio, Female, Foreplay, Fornication, French, Gam(ic), Gamahuche, Gamaruche, Gender, Hanky-panky, Hump, Incest, Intercourse, Kind, Libidinous, Libido, Lingam, Lumber, Male, Mate, Nookie, Oomph, Opposite, Oral, Outercourse, Paedophilia, Pederasty, Phallocratic, Phat, Priapean, Race, Randy, Raunchy, Rut(ish), Safe, Salacious, Screw, Sect, Steamy, Sultry, Teledildonics, Troilism, Unprotected, Venereal, Venery, VI, Voluptuous, Weaker

Sex appeal It, Oomph, SA

Sexcentenarian Shem

Sexless Agamogenetic, Atoke, N, Neuter

Sextet Over, Six

Sexton Blake, Fossor, Sacristan, Shammes, Warden

Seychelles SY

Sh P, Quiet

Shabby Base, Buckeen, Dog-eared, Down-at-heel, Fusc(ous), Grotty, Mangy, Mean, Moth-eaten, Old hat, Oobit, Oorie, Oubit, Ourie, Outworn, Owrie, Raunch, Scaly, Scruffy, Seedy, Shoddy, Squalid, Tacky, Tatty, Worn, Woubit

Shack Fibro, Heap, Hideout, Hovel, Hut

Shackle(s) Bilboes, Bind, Bracelet, Chain, Darbies, Entrammel, Fetter(lock), Gyve, Hamper, Irons, Manacle, Restrict, Tie, Trammel, Yoke

Shad Allice, Allis, Fish, Twait(e)

Shaddock Grapefruit, Pomelo

Shade(d), Shades, Shading, Shadow, Shady Adumbrate, Arbour, Arcade, Awning, Blend, Blind, Bongrace, Bowery, Brise-soleil, Brocken spectre, Buff, Cast, Chiaroscuro, Chroma, Cloche, Cloud, Cross-hatch, Degree, Dis, Dog, Dubious, Eclipse, Eye, Five o'clock, Galanty, Gamp, Ghost, Gradate, Gray, Hachure, Hell, Herbar, Hint, Hue, Inumbrate, Larva, Lee, Melt, Mezzotint, Nuance, Opaque, Overtone, Parasol, Pastel, Phantom, Presence, Rain, Ray-Bans®, Satellite, Screen, Shroud, Sienna, Silhouette, Silvan, Skia-, Soften, Sound, Spectre, Spirit, Stag, Sunglasses, Swale, Swaly, Tail, Tenebrious, Tinge, Tint, Tone, Ugly, Umbra(tile), Umbrage(ous), Underhand, Velamen, Velar(ium), Velum, Visor

Shadowless Ascian

Shaft(ed), Shafting Arbor, Arrow, Axle tree, Barb, Barrow-train, Beam, Capstan, Cardan, Chimney, Column, Crank, Cue, Diaphysis, Disselboom, Dolly, Drive, Escape, Fil(l), Fust, Gleam, Idler, Incline, Journal, Lamphole, Limber, Loom, Mandrel, Mandril, Manhole, Moon pool, Moulin, Parthian, Passage, Pile, Pit, Pitbrow, Pitch, Pole, Propeller, Quill (drive), Ray, Rib, Scape, Scapus, Shank, Snead, Spindle, Staff, Stairwell, Stale, Steal(e), Steel, Stele, Stem, Stulm, Sunbeam, Telescopic, Thill, Tige, Tomo, Trave, Truncheon, Upcast, Well, Winning, Winze

Shag Cronet, Hair, Intercourse, Nap, Pile, Scart(h), Skart(h), Tire, Tobacco

Shaggy Ainu, Comate, Hairy, Hearie, Hirsute, Horrid, Horror, Nappy, Rough, Rugged, Shock, Shough, Tatty, Tousy, Touzy, Towsy, Towzy, Untidy

Shah Ruler, Sophi, Sophy

Shake(n), Shakes, Shaky Agitate, Ague(-fit), Astonish, Bebung, Brandish, Coggle, Concuss, Dabble, Dick(e)y, Didder, Diddle, Dither, Dodder, → **DT'S**, Feeble, Groggy, Hod, Hotch, Jar, Jiggle, Joggle, Jolt, Jounce, Judder, Jumble, Milk, Mo, Nid-nod, Press flesh, Quake, Quiver, Quooke, Rattle, Rickety, Rickle, → **ROCK**, Rouse, Shimmer, Shiver, Shock, Shog, Shoogle, Shudder, Succuss(ation), Sweat, Tremble, Tremolo, Tremor, Tremulous, Trill(o), Tumbledown, Undulate, Vibrate, Vibrato, Wag, Waggle, Wind, Wobble, Wonky

▷ **Shake** *may indicate* an anagram

Shakedown Blackmail, Chantage, Pallet

Shakespeare Bard, Will, WS

Shale Blaes, Fa(i)kes, Kerogen, Oil, Rock, Till, Torbanite

Shall Sal

Shallot C(h)ibol, Onion, Scallion, Sybo(e), Sybow

Shallow(s) Ebb, Flat, Fleet, Flew, Flue, Justice, Neritic, Sandbar, Shoal, Slight, Superficial

Sham Apocryphal, Bluff, Bogus, Braide, Charade, Counterfeit, Deceit, Fake, → **FALSE**, Hoax, Idol, Impostor, Mimic, Mock, Phony, Pinchbeck, Postiche, Potemkin, Pretence, Pseudo, Repro, Simulated, Snide, Spurious, Straw man

Shamble(s) Abattoir, Bauchle, Butchery, Mess, Shuffle, Totter, Tripple

Shame(ful), Shame-faced Abash, Aidos, Chagrin, Contempt, Crying, Degrade, Discredit, Disgrace, Dishonour, Embarrass, Fi donc, Fie, Gross, Hangdog, Honi, Humiliate, Ignominy, Infamy, Inglorious, Modesty, Mortify, Pity, Pudency, Pudor, Pugh, Shend, Sin, Slander, Stain, Stigma, Yshend

Shameless Audacious, Brash, Brazen, Flagrant, Immodest, Ithyphallic

Shampoo(ing) Massage, Tripsis, Wash

Shandy Drink, Sterne, Tristram

Shanghai Abduct, Kidnap, Trick

Shank Leg, Shaft, Steal(e), Steel, Steil, Stele, Strike

Shanty, Shanty town Boatsong, Bothy, Bustee, Cabin, Dog-hole, Favela, Forebitter, Hutment, Lean-to, Pondok, Sea, Shack, Shypoo, Song

Shape(d), Shapely, Shaping Blancmange, Boast, Bruting, Cast, Contour, Face, Fashion, Figure, Form, Format, Geoid, Gnomon, Headquarters, Hew, Holohedron, Jello, Model, Morph, → **MOULD**, Net, Pendentive, Polyomine, Ream, Rhomb(us), Scabble, Sculpt, Spile, Step-cut, Tromino, Turn, Whittle, Wrought, Zaftig, Zoftig

Shapeless Amorphous, Chaos, Dumpy, Indigest, Vague

Shard Fragment, Sliver, Splinter

Share(d), Shares, Sharing Allocation, Allotment, Apportion, Blue-chip, Bovate, Cahoots, Chop, Co, Cohabit, Coho(e), Common, Communal, Contango, Culter, Cut, Deferred, Divi(dend), Divide, Divvy, Dole, Dutch, Equity, Finger, Founders, Golden, Grubstake, Impart, Interest, Job, Kaffer, Kaf(f)ir, Kangaroo, Lion's, Market, Moiety, Odd lot, Ordinary, Oxgang, Oxgate, Oxland, Parcener, → **PART**, Partake, Participate, Penny, PIBS, Plough, Plough-iron, Portion, Prebend, Pref(erred), Preference, Pro rata, Prorate, Quarter, Quota, Rake off, Ration, Rug, Rundale, Scrip, Security, Shr, Slice, Snack, Snap, Sock, Split, Stock, Taurus, Teene, Time, Tranche, Two-way, Whack

Shareholder Stag

Shark Angel, Basking, Beagle, Blue, Bluepointer, Bonnethead, Bronze-whaler, Bull, Carpet, Cestracion, Cow, Demoiselle, Dog(fish), Flake, Fox, Great white, Gummy, Hammerhead, Houndfish, Huss, Lemonfish, Leopard catshark, Loan, Mackerel, Mako, Miller's dog, Monkfish, Noah, Nurse, Penny-dog, Plagiostomi, Porbeagle, Requiem, Reremai, Rhin(e)odon, Rigg, Sail-fish, Saw, School, Sea-ape, Sea-lawyer, Sevengill, Sharp, Shortfin mako, Shovelhead, Smoothhound, Soupfin, Spotted ragged-tooth, Squaloid, Swindler, Thrasher, Thresher, Tiger, Tope, Usurer, Whale, Whaler, Wobbegong, Zygaena

Sharkskin Shagreen

Sharp(er), Sharpen(er), Sharpness Abrupt, Accidental, Acerose, Acidulous, Acrid, Aculeus, Acumen, Acuminate, Acute, Alert, Angular, Arris, Bateless, Becky, Benchstone, Bitter, Brisk, Cacuminous, Cheat, Clear, Coticular, Cutting, Dital, Edge(r), Fine, Fly, Gleg, Grind, Hone, Hot, Keen, Kurtosis, Massé, Oilstone, Penetrant, Peracute, Piquant, Poignant, Pronto, Pungent, Quick-witted, Razor, Rogue, Rook, Set, Shrewd, Snap, Snell, Sour, Spicate, Strop, Swindler, Tart, Testy, Tomium, Twenty-twenty, Vivid, Volable, Whet

Sharpshooter Bersaglier, Franc-tireur, Sniper, Tirailleur, Voltigeur

Shatter(ing) Astone, Astound, Break, Brisance, Craze, Dash, Explode, Shiver, Smash, Smithereen, Splinter, Unnerve

Shave(r), Shaving(s) Barb(er), Electric, Excelsior, Filings, Flake, Grain, Moslings, Pare, Plane, Pogonotomy, Poll, Raze, Scrape, Skive, Sliver, Splinter, Swarf, Todd, Tonsure, Whittle

Shaw Artie, Green, Spinn(e)y, Wood

Shawl Afghan, Buibui, Cashmere, Chuddah, Chuddar, Dopatta, Dupatta, Fichu, India, Kaffiyeh, Kashmir, Manta, Mantilla, Maud, Paisley, Partlet, Prayer, Serape, Stole, Tallis, Tallit(ot), Tallith, Tonnag, Tozie, Tribon, Whittle, Wrap(per), Zephyr

She A, Hoo

Sheaf Aplustre, Bundle, Folder, Gait, Garb(e), Gerbe, Mow, Shock, Thr(e)ave

Shear(s), Shearer Clip, Cut, Fleece, Greasy, Jaws of life, Pinking, Poll, Pruning, Ring(er), Shave, Snips, Trim, Wind

Sheath Axolemma, Capsule, Case, Cocoon, Coleoptile, Coleorhiza, Condom,

Cover, Extine, Fingerstall, Glume, Medullary, Myelin, Neurilemma, Neurolemma, Oc(h)rea, Perineurium, Periosteum, Quiver, Rhinotheca, Root, Scabbard, Spathe, Thecal, Thumbstall, Urceolus, Vagina, Volva, Wing

Sheave Bee, Clevis

Shed(ding), Shedder Autotomy, Barn, Cast, Cho(u)ltry, Coducity, Cootch, Cwtch, Depot, Discard, Doff, Drop, Ecdysis, Effuse, Emit, Exuviate, Hangar, Hovel, Hut, Infuse, Lair, Lean-to, Linhay, Linn(e)y, Mew, Milking, Moult, Outhouse, Pent, Potting, Salmon, Shearing, Shippen, Shippon, Shuck, Skeo, Skillion, Skio, Slough, Sow, Spend, Spent, Spill, Tilt, Tool

Sheen Glaze, Gloss, Luminance, Lustre, Patina, Schiller, Shine

Sheep(ish) Ammon, Ancon(es), Aoudad, Argali, Barbary, Bell(wether), Bharal, Bident, Bighorn, Black, Blackface, Blate, Border Leicester, Broadtail, Burhel, Burrel(l), Caracul, Charollais, Cheviots, Coopworth, Corriedale, Cotswold, Coy, Crone, Dinmont, Domestic, Dorset Down, Dorset Horn, Down, Drysdale, Embarrassed, Ewe, Exmoor, Fank, Fat-tailed, Flock, Fold, Hair, Hampshire, Hampshire Down, Hangdog, Herdwick, Hidder, Hirsel, Hog(g), Hogget, Jacob, Jemmy, Jumbuck, Karakul, Kent, Kerry Hill, Lamb, Lanigerous, Leicester, Lincoln, Lo(a)ghtan, Loghtyn, Long, Lonk, Marco Polo, Masham, Merino, Mor(t)ling, Mouf(f)lon, Mountain, Muflon, Mug, Mus(i)mon, Mutton, Oorial, Ovine, Oxford Down, Perendale, Portland, Ram, Rambouillet, Romeldale, Romney Marsh, Rosella, Ryeland, Scottish Blackface, Shearling, Shetland, Short, Shorthorn, → **SHY**, Soay, Southdown, Spanish, Stone('s), Suffolk, Sumph, Swaledale, Teeswater, Teg(g), Texel, Theave, Trip, Tup, Two-tooth, Udad, Urial, Vegetable, Welsh Mountain, Wensleydale, Wether, Wiltshire Horn, Woollyback, Yow(e), Yowie

Sheep disease, Sheep problem Black, Blue tongue, Braxy, Dunt, Gid, Hoove, Louping-ill, Orf, Ringwomb, Rubbers, Scabby mouth, Scrapie, Sturdy, Swayback, Variola, Water-brain, Wildfire, Wind

Sheepdog Collie, Huntaway, Maremma, Polish Lowland, Puli

Sheepfold Fank, Pen

Sheepskin Basan, Caracul, Karakul, Mouton, Roan, Wool

Sheeptrack Terracette

Sheer Absolute, Clear, Main, Mere, Peekaboo, Plumb, Precipitous, Pure, Simple, Stark, Steep, Swerve, Thin, Utter

Sheet(s), Sheeting Balance, Cellophane, Cere-cloth, Cerement, Charge, Chart, Clean, Crime, Cutch, Dope, Expanse, Film, Flow, Fly, Folio, Foolscap, Heft, Ice, Inset, Intrusive, Lasagne, Leaf, Membrane, Nappe, Out-hauler, Page, Pane, Pot(t), Pour, Proof, Prospectus, Rap, Ream, Rope, Sail, Scandal, Scratch, Shroud, Stern, Stratus, Taggers, Tarpaulin(g), Tear, Tentorium, Terne, Thunder, Time, Title, Web, White, Winding

Sheet-anchor Letter-weight, Paperweight

Sheet-iron Taggers, Terne(plate)

Sheik(dom) Abu Dhabi, Bahrein, Dubai

Shekel Mina, Sickle

Sheldrake Bergander

Shelf, Shelve(s) Bank, Bar, Bracket, Continental, Counter, Credence, Delay, Dresser, Étagère, Grand Banks, Hob, Ice, Ledge, Leeboard, Mantle, Overmantel, Parcel, Postpone, Rack, Retable, Ross Ice, Shunt, Sidetrack, Sill, Spinsterhood, Whatnot, Windowsill

Shell(ed), Shellfish, Shellwork Abalone, Acorn-shell, Admiral, Ambulacrum, Ammo, Argonaut, Balamnite, Balanus, Balmain bug, Bivalve, Blitz, Boat, Bodywork, Bombard, Buckie, Camera, Capiz, Capsid, Carapace, Cartridge, Casing, Chank,

Chelonia, Chitin, Clam, Clio, Coat-of-mail, Cochlea, Cockle, Cohog, Conch, Cone,
Copepoda, Cover, Cowrie, Cowry, Crab, Crustacea, Cuttlebone, Dariole, Deerhorn,
Dentalium, Dop, Drill, Electron, Escallop, Eugarie, Foraminifer, Framework,
Frustule, Geoduck, Globigerina, Haliotis, Hull, Husk, Hyoplastron, Isopoda, Lamp,
Langouste, Limacel, Limpet, Live, Lobster, Lorica, Lyre, Malacostraca, Midas's ear,
Mitre, Mollusc, Monocoque, Moreton Bay bug, Mother-of-pearl, Murex, Music,
Mussel, Nacre, Nautilus, Olive, Ormer, Ostracod, Ostrea, Otter, Oyster, Paua,
Pawa, Pea(s)cod, Peag, Peak, Pecten, Pereia, Periostracum, Periwinkle, Pilgrim's,
Pipi, Pipsqueak, Plastron, Pod, Prawn, Projectile, Purple, Putamen, Quahaug,
Quahog, Razor, Rocaille, Sal, Scalarium, Scallop, Scollop, Sea-ear, Sea-pen, Shale,
Shard, Sheal, Sheel, Shiel, Shill, Shock, Shot, Shrapnel, Shrimp, Shuck, Sial,
Smoke-ball, Spend, Spindle, Star, Stomatopod, Stonk, Straddle, Strafe, Stromb(us),
Swan-mussel, Tear, Test(a), Thermidor, Toheroa, Tooth, Top, Torpedo, Tracer,
Trivalve, Trough, Turbo, Turritella, Tusk, Univalve, Valency, Venus, Wakiki,
Wampum, Whelk, Whiz(z)bang, Winkle, Xenophya, Yabbie, Yabby, Zimbi
Shelled Cracked, Kernel
▷ **Shelled** *may indicate* an anagram
Shell money Wakiki, Wampum, Zimbi
Shelter Abri, Anderson, Asylum, Awn, Awning, Belee, Bender, Bield, Billet, Blind,
Blockhouse, Booth, Bunker, Burladero, Butt, Cab, Carport, Casemate, Cot(e),
Cove, Covert, Coverture, Defence, Dodger, Donga, Dovecote, Dripstone, Dug-out,
Fall-out, Garage, Gunyah, Harbour, Haven, Hithe, Hospice, Hostel, House, Hovel,
Humpy, Hut, Hutchie, Kipsie, Lee, Lee-gage, Loun, Lound, Lown, Lownd, Mai mai,
Mission, Morrison, Nodehouse, Pilothouse, → **REFUGE**, Retreat, Roof, Sanctuary,
Scog, Sconce, Scoog, Scoug, Screen, Scug, Shed, Shiel(ing), Shroud, Skug,
Snowshed, Stell, Storm-cellar, Succah, Sukkah, Summerhouse, Tax, Tent, Testudo,
Tortoise, Tupik, Twigloo, Umbrage, Weather, Wheelhouse, Wickyup, Wi(c)kiup,
Wil(t)ja, Windbreak
Shemozzle Debacle
Shenanigan Antic
Shepherd(ess) Abel, Acis, Amaryllis, Amos, Bergère, Bo-peep, Bucolic, Chloe,
Clorin, Conduct, Corin, Corydon, Cuddy, Daphnis, Dorcas, Drover, Endymion,
Escort, Ettrick, German, Good, Grubbinol, Gyges, Herdsman, Hobbinol, Lindor,
Marshal, Menalcas, Padre, Pastor(al), Pastorella, Phebe, Sheepo, Strephon,
Tar-box, Thenot, Thyrsis, Tityrus
Sheriff Bailiff, Deputy, Earp, Grieve, Land-dros(t), Lawman, Process-server,
Shireman, Shirra, Shrievalty, Viscount
Sherry Amoroso, Bristol milk, Cobbler, Cream, Cyprus, Doctor, Dry, Fino, Gladstone,
Jerez, Manzanilla, Oloroso, Palo cortado, Sack, Solera, Sweet, Whitewash, Xeres
Sherwood Anderson, Forest
Shiah Ismaili
Shibboleth Password
Shield(s), Shield-shaped Ablator, Achievement, Aegis, Ancile, Armour, Arms,
Baltic, Biological, Bodyguard, Box, Buckler, Canadian, Cartouche, Clypeus, Defend,
Dress, Escutcheon, Fence, Gobo, Guard, Gyron, Hatchment, Heat, Hielaman,
Human, Insulate, Laurentian, Lozenge, Mant(e)let, Mask, Pavis(e), Pelta, Plastron,
Protect, Randolph, Ranfurly, Riot, Rondache, Scandinavian, Screen, Scute, Scutum,
Sheffield, Splashboard, Sternite, Targe(t), Thyroid, Vair, Visor, Water
Shift(er), Shifty Amove, Astatic, Back, Blue, Budge, Change, Chemise, Core,
Cymar, Day, Devious, Displace, Dogwatch, Doppler, Einstein, Evasive, Expedient,
Fend, Function, Graveyard, Great Vowel, Hedging, Lamb, Landslide, Lateral,

Linen, Louche, Move, Night, Nighty, Paradigm, Red, Relay, Remove, Rota, Ruse,
Scorch, Sell, Shirt, Shovel, Shunt, Simar(re), Slicker, Slip(pery), Sound, Spell, Split,
Stagehand, Stick, Stint, Swing, Tour, Transfer, Tunic, Turn, Vary, Veer, Warp
▷ **Shift(ing)** *may indicate* an anagram
Shilling Bob, Deaner, Falkiner, Hog, King's, Queen's, S, Teston
Shilly-shally Whittie-whattie
Shimmer(ing) Avanturine, Aventurine, Chatoyant, Glint, Glitter, Iridescence, Shine
▷ **Shimmering** *may indicate* an anagram
Shin Clamber, Climb, Cnemial, Leg, Shank, Skink, Swarm
Shindig, Shindy Bobbery, Row, Rumpus, Shivoo, Uproar
Shine(r), Shining, Shiny Aglitter, Aglow, Beam, Bright, Buff, Burnish, Deneb,
Effulge, Excel, Flash, Gleam, Glimmer, Glisten, Glitzy, Gloss, → **GLOW**, Irradiant,
Japan, → **LAMP**, Leam, Leme, Lucent, Luminous, Lustre, Mouse, Nitid, Nugget,
Phoebe, Phosphoresce, Polish, Radiator, Refulgent, Relucent, Resplend, Rutilant,
Skyre, Sleek, Twinkle, Varnish
Shingle(s), Shingly Beach, Chesil, Cut, Dartre, Dartrous, Gravel, Herpes, Herpes
Zoster, Herpetic, Loose metal, Shake, Shale, Stone, Zona, Zoster
Shinpad Greave
Shinty Caman, Camanachd
▷ **Shiny** *may indicate* a star
Ship(s), Shipping Boat, Container, Convoy, Cruiser, → **DISPATCH**, Embark, Export,
Flagship, Flatboat, Her, Hulk, Jolly, Keel, Man, Marine, MV, Post, Privateer,
Prize, Prow, Raft, Ram, Sail, Saique, She, Smack, SS, Tall, Transport, Tub, Vessel,
Victualling, Weather

SHIPS

1 letter:	*4 letters:*	*5 letters:*	
Q	Dory	Prahu	
	Duck	Aviso	Prore
2 letters:	Fire	Barge	Pucan
PT	Flat	Broke	Razee
	Grab	Camel	Rover
3 letters:	Isis	Canoe	Sabot
Ark	Koff	Coble	Saick
Cat	Long	Coper	Scoot
Cog	Nina	Crare	Screw
Dow	Pink	Dandy	Scull
Fly	Pont	Dingy	Shell
Hoy	Pram	Drake	Skiff
Kit	Prau	Ferry	Slave
Red	Proa	Funny	Sloop
	Ro-ro	Ketch	Tramp
4 letters:	Saic	Jolly	Troop
Argo	Scow	Laker	U-boat
Bark	Snow	Liner	Umiak
Brig	Tern	Moses	Wager
Buss	Trow	Oiler	Whiff
Cock	Yawl	Pinky	Xebec
Cott	Zulu	Pinto	Yacht
Dhow		Plate	Zabra
		Praam	Zebec

6 letters:
Argosy
Banker
Barque
Bateau
Bawley
Beagle
Bethel
Bireme
Borley
Bottom
Bounty
Caique
Carack
Carvel
Castle
Coaler
Cobble
Codder
Cooper
Crayer
Curagh
Cutter
Decker
Dingey
Dinghy
Dogger
Droger
Dromon
Drover
Dugout
Escort
Flying
Frigot
Galiot
Galley
Gay-you
Goldie
Hooker
Howker
Jigger
Launch
Lorcha
Lugger
Masula
Monkey
Mother
Nuggar
Packet
Pedalo
Pequod

Pinkie
Pirate
Pitpan
Pulwar
Puteli
Randan
Reefer
Sampan
Sandal
School
Schuit
Schuyt
Settee
Slaver
Tanker
Tartan
Tender
Tonner
Torpid
Trader
Trek-ox
Turret
Whaler
Wherry
Zebeck

7 letters:
Belfast
Bidarka
Bumboat
Capital
Caravel
Carrack
Carract
Carrect
Catboat
Clipper
Coaster
Collier
Consort
Coracle
Counter
Currach
Curragh
Dredger
Drifter
Drogher
Dromond
Factory
Felucca
Flattop

Flyboat
Frigate
Gabbard
Gabbart
Galleon
Galliot
Galloon
Geordie
Gondola
Gunboat
Jetfoil
Kontiki
Liberty
Lymphad
Masoola
Mistico
Monitor
Mudscow
Mystery
Oomiack
Patamar
Pelican
Pinnace
Piragua
Pirogue
Polacca
Polacre
Pontoon
Revenge
Sculler
Shallop
Sharpie
Steamer
Stew-can
Tartane
Titanic
Trawler
Trireme
Tugboat
Vedette
Victory
Vidette

8 letters:
Acapulco
Bilander
Billyboy
Bylander
Cabotage
Corocore
Corocoro

Corvette
Dahabieh
Faldboat
Foldboat
Galleass
Galliass
Gallivat
Hospital
Hoveller
Indiaman
Ironclad
Longboat
Longship
Mackinaw
Mary Rose
Masoolah
Merchant
Monohull
Mosquito
Pinafore
Sallyman
Savannah
Schooner
Shanghai
Showboat
Training

9 letters:
Bucentaur
Catamaran
Cutty Sark
Dahabeeah
Dahabiyah
Dahabiyeh
Discovery
Dromedary
First-rate
Freighter
Frigatoon
Hydrofoil
Klondiker
Klondyker
Lapstrake
Lapstreak
Leviathan
Lightship
Mayflower
Minelayer
Monoxylon
Multihull
Outrigger

Peter-boat
Sallee-man
Shear-hulk
Sheer-hulk
Steamboat
Submarine
Vaporetto
Whale-back
Whaleboat

10 letters:
Brigantine
Golden Hind
Hydroplane

Icebreaker
Knockabout
Mine-hunter
Paddleboat
Quadrireme
Santa Maria
Trekschuit
Triaconter
Windjammer

11 letters:
Barquentine
Bellerophon
Berthon-boat

Cockleshell
Dreadnought
Merchantman
Minesweeper
Penteconter
Quinquereme
Side-wheeler
Skidbladnir
Submersible
Supertanker
Three-decker
Three-master
Torpedo boat

12 letters:
East Indiaman
Fore-and-after
Great Eastern
Marie Celeste
Stern-wheeler
Tangle-netter

13 letters:
Paddle steamer

14 letters:
Flying Dutchman
Ocean greyhound

Shipmate Crew, Hearty, Sailor
Shipping line P and O
Ship's biscuit Dandyfunk, Dunderfunk
Shipshape Apple-pie, Neat, Orderly, Tidy, Trim
Shipwreck Split
Shire County
Shirk(er) Cuthbert, Dodge, Embusqué, Evade, Funk, Malinger, Mike, Pike, Poler, Scrimshank, Skive, Skrimshank, Slack, Soldier
Shirt Black, Boiled, Brown, Bush, Calypso, Camese, Camise, Chemise, Choli, Cilice, Dasheki, Dashiki, Dick(e)y, Dress, Fiesta, Garibaldi, Grandad, Hair, Hawaiian, Hoodie, Jacky Howe, Kaftan, Kaross, K(h)urta, Nessus, Non-iron, Parka, Partlet, Polo, Rash, Red, Rugby, Safari, Sark, Serk, Shift, Smock, Sports, Stuffed, Subucula, Swan(n)dri®, Sweat, T
Shiva Destroyer
Shiver(ing), Shivers, Shivery Aguish, Atingle, Break, Chitter, Crumble, Dash, Dither, Fragile, Frisson, Grew, Grue, Malaria, Nither, Oorie, Ourie, Owrie, Quake, Quiver, → **SHAKE**, Shatter, Shrug, Shudder, Smash, Smither, Smithereens, Splinter, Timbers, Tremble
▷ **Shiver(ed)** *may indicate* an anagram
Shoal Bar, Fish, Quantity, Reef, Run, School, Shallows, Shelf, Tail
Shock(ed), Shocker, Shocking Acoustic, Aghast, Agitate, Anaphylactic, Appal, Astound, Astun, Awhape, Bombshell, Brunt, Bunch, Consternate, Criminal, Culture, Defibrillate, Disgust, Dorlach, Dreadful, Drop, Earthquake, ECT, Egregious, Electric, Electrocute, Épatant, Epiphenomenon, Fleg, Floccus, Forelock, Gait, Galvanism, Gobsmack, Hair, Horrify, Impact, Infamous, Insulin, Jar, Jolt, Live, Mane, Mop, Outrage, Poleaxe, Putrid, Recoil, Return, Revolt, Rick(er), Scandal(ise), Seismic, Shaghaired, Shake, Sheaf, Shell, Shilling, Shog, Shook, Stagger, Start(le), Stitch, Stook, Stound, Stun, Tangle, Thermal, Trauma, Turn
Shock-absorber Buffer, Oleo, Snubber
▷ **Shocked** *may indicate* an anagram
Shod Calced
Shoddy Cagmag, Catchpenny, Cheap, Cheapjack, Cheapo, Cloth, Cowboy, Drecky, Gimcrack, Imitation, Oorie, Ourie, Owrie, Rag-wool, Ropy, Schlock, → **SHABBY**, Slopwork, Tatty, Tawdry, Tinny
Shoe(s) Accessory, Arctic, Athletic, Ballet, Balmoral, Bauchle, Blocked, Boat, Boot, Bootee, Brake, Brogan, Brogue, Brothel creepers, Buskin, Calceate, Calk(er), Calkin,

Casuals, Caulker, Cawker, Charlier, Chaussures, Chopin(e), Clodhopper, Clog, Co-respondent, Court, Creeper, Dap, Deck, Espadrille, Flattie, Galoche, Galosh, Gatty, Geta, Ghillie, Golosh, Gumboot, Gumshoe, Gym, High-low, High tops, Hot, Hush-puppies®, Jandal®, Jellies, Kletterschue, Kurdaitcha, Launch(ing), Loafer, Mary-Janes®, Mocassin, Moccasin, Muil, Mule, Open-toe, Oxford, Oxonian, Panton, Patten, Peeptoe, Pennyloafer, Pile, Plate, Plimsole, Plimsoll, Poulaine, Pump, Rivlin, Rope-soled, Rubbers, Rullion, Sabaton, Sabot, Saddle, Safety, Sandal, Sandshoe, Sannie, Scarpetto, Shauchle, Skid, Skimmer, Slingback, Slip-on, Slipper, Slip-slop, Sneaker, Snow, Sock, Soft, Solleret, Spike, Stoga, Stogy, Suede, Tackies, Takkies, Tennis, Tie, Topboot, Track, Trainer, Upper, Vamp(er), Veld-schoen, Veldskoen, Velskoen, Vibram®, Vibs, Wagon lock, Wedgie, Welt, Winkle-picker, Zori

Shoeless Barefoot, Discalced

Shoemaker Blacksmith, Clogger, Cobbler, Cordiner, Cordwainer, Cosier, Cozier, Crispi(a)n, Farrier, Gentle craft, Leprechaun, Sachs, Smith, Snob, Soutar, Souter, Sowter, Sutor

Shoe-string Cheap, Lace, Pittance

Shoe-toe Poulaine

Shoo Away, Begone, Hoosh, Off, Scat(ter), Voetsek

Shoot(er), Shooting Ack-ack, Airgun, Arrow, Bine, Bostryx, Braird, Breer, Bud, Bulbil, Catapult, Chit, Cion, Cyme, Dart(le), Delope, Discharge, Drib, Elance, Enate, Eradiate, Film, Fire, Flagellum, Germ, Germain(e), Germen, Germin(ate), Glorious Twelfth, → **GUN**, Gunsel, Head-reach, Hurl, Imp, Layer, Limb, Loose, Offset, Photocall, Photograph, Pluff, Plug, Poot, Pop, Pot, Pout, Ramulus, Rapids, Ratoon, Riddle, Rod, Rove, Runner, Scion, Septembriser, Sien(t), Skeet, Snap, Snipe, Spire, Spirt, Spout, Spray, Sprout, Spurt, Spyre, Start, Stole, Stolon, Strafe, Sucker, Syen, Tellar, Teller, Tendril, Tiller, Trap, Turion, Twelfth, Twig, Udo, Vimen, Wand, Weapon, Whiz(z), Wildfowler, Zap

Shop(s), Shopper Agency, Arcade, Assembly, Atelier, Betray, Body, Boutique, Bucket, Buy, Chain, Charity, Chippy, Closed, Coffee, Commissary, Cook, Co-op, Cop, Corner, Cut-price, Dairy, Delicatessen, Denounce, Dobbin, Dolly, Duddery, Duka, Duty-free, Emporium, Factory, Galleria, Gift, Grass, In bond, Inform, Junk, Luckenbooth, Machine, Mall, Mall-rat, Market, Megastore, Mercat, Muffler, Officinal, Off-licence, Off-sales, Open, Opportunity, Outlet, Parlour, Patisserie, Personal, Precinct, Print, PX, Rat on, Retail, RMA, Salon, Sex, Shambles, Share, Shebang, Spaza, Squat, → **STORE**, Studio, Sundry, Superette, Supermarket, Superstore, Swap, Talking, Tally, Tea, Thrift, Tick, Tommy, Trade, Truck, Tuck, Union, Vintry, Warehouse, Works

Shopkeeper British, Butcher, Chemist, Clothier, Gombeen-man, Greengrocer, Grocer, Haberdasher, Hosier, Ironmonger, Merchant, Newsagent, Provisioner, Retailer, Stationer, Tradesman

Shoplift(er) Boost, Heist

Shore Bank, Beach, Buttress, Coast, Coastline, Coste, Eustatic, Foreside, Landfall, Littoral, Machair, Offing, Prop, Rance, Rivage, Saxon, Seaboard, Strand, Strandline, Support

Short(en), Shortly Abbreviate, Abridge, Abrupt, Anon, Apocope, Brief, Brusque, Close-in, Commons, Compendious, Concise, Contract, Crisp, Cross, Curt, Curtail, Curtal, Diminish, Drink, Eftsoons, Epitomise, Ere-long, Fubsy, Fuse, Inadequate, Lacking, Laconical, Light, Limited, Low, Mini, Near, Nip, Nutshell, Pudsey, Punch, Pyknic, Reduce, Reef, Retrench, Scanty, Scarce, Shrift, Shy, Soon, Sparse, Spirit, Squab, Squat, Squat(ty), Staccato, Stint, Stocky, Strapped, Stubby, Succinct, Syncopate, Systole, Taciturn, Teen(s)y, Temporal, Temporaneous, Terse, Tight, Tot,

Towards, Transient, Wee

Shortage Dearth, Deficit, Drought, Famine, Lack, Need, Paucity, Scarcity, Sparsity, Wantage

Short circuit Varistor

Shortcoming Weakness

Shorthand Gregg, Outline, Phonographic, Pitman, Speedwriting®, Stenography, Stenotypy, Tachygraphy, Tironian, Tironian notes, Triphone, Weblish

Short-headed Brachycephal

Short-lived Ephemeral, Fragile, Meson, Transitory

Shorts Bermuda, Board, Boxer, Briefs, Culottes, Cycling, Hot pants, Kaccha, Lederhosen, Plus-fours, Skort, Stubbies®, Trunks

Short-sight Myopia, Myosis

Short-winded Breathless, Concise, Puffed, Purfled, Pursy, Succinct

Shot(s) Aim, All-in, Ammo, Approach, Attempt, Backhand, Ball, Bank, Barrage, Bisque, Blank, Blast, Bricole, Bull, Bullet, Burl, Canna, Cannonball, Cartridge, Case, Chain, Chatoyant, Chip, Corner, Cover, Crab, Crack, Daisy cutter, Dink, Dolly, Dram, Draw, Drop, Duckhook, Dum dum, Dunk, Elt, Essay, Exhausted, Forehand, Gesse, Get, Glance, Go, Grape, Guess, Gun-stone, Hook, Jump, Langrage, Langrel, Langridge, Lay-up, Longjenny, Magpie, Marksman, Massé, Matte, Money, Moon-ball, Mulligan, Multi-coloured, Musket, Noddy, Pack, Parthian, Parting, Passing, Pelican, Pellet, Penalty, Photo, Plant, Pluff, Pop, Pot, Puff, Push, Rid, Round, Safety, Salvo, Scratch, Shy, Sighter, Silk, Six, Slam-dunk, Slap, Slice, Slug, Slung, Sped, Spell, Spent, Square cut, Stab, Still, Streaked, Tap in, Throw, Tonic, Tracking, Trial, Try, Turn, Volley, Warning, Wrist

Should Ought

Shoulder(-blade) Carry, Cold, Crossette, Epaule, Frozen, Hard, Hump, Joggle, Omohyoid, Omoplate, Pick-a-back, Roadside, Scapula, Shouther, Soft, Spald, Spall, Spaul(d), Speal, Spule, Tote, Withers

Shout(er), Shouting Barrack, Bawl, Bellock, Bellow, Boanerges, Call, Claim, Clamour, Conclamation, Cry, Din, Exclaim, Geronimo, Heckle, Hey, Hoi(cks), Holla, Holla-ho(a), Holler, Hollo, Holloa, Hooch, Hosanna, Howzat, Hue, Oi, Oy, Parnell, Rah, Rant, Root, Round, Sa sa, Treat, Trumpet, Vociferate, Whoop, Yell(och), Yippee, Yoohoo, Yorp

Shove Barge, Birr, Elbow, Jostle, Push, Ram, Spoon, Thrust

Shovel Backhoe, Dustpan, Hat, Loy, Main, Peel, Power, Scoop, Shool, Spade, Steam, Trowel, Van

Show(ing), Shown, Showy Anonyma, Appearance, Aquacade, Bad, Bench, Betray, Branky, Broadcast, Brummagem, Burlesque, Cabaret, Chat, Circus, Come, Con, Cruft's, Demo(nstrate), Depict, Diorama, Display, Do, Dramedy, Dressy, Dumb, Effeir, Effere, Endeictic, Entertainment, Epideictic, Establish, Evince, → **EXHIBIT**, Expo, Extravaganza, Exude, Facade, Fair, Fangled, Farce, Flamboyant, Flash, Flaunt, Floor, Galanty, Game, Garish, Gaudy, Gay, Give, Glitter, Glitz(y), Gloss, Good, Horse, Indicate, Jazzy, Kismet, Light, Loud, Manifest, Matinée, Meritricious, Minstrel, Musical, Naumachy, One-man, Ostensible, Ostentatious, Pageant, Panel game, Pantomime, Parade, Patience, Performance, Phen(o), Point, Pomp, Portray, Presentation, Pretence, Pride, Procession, Prog(ramme), Project, Prominence, Prove, Pseudery, Puff, Puppet, Quiz, Raree, Razzmatazz, Reality, Represent, Reveal, Revue, Road, Roll-out, Ruddigore, Rushes, Screen, Shaw, Sight, Sitcom, Slang, Soap, Son et lumière, Specious, Spectacle, Splash, Splay, Stage, Stunt, Talk, Tamasha, Tattoo, Tawdry, Telecast, Telethon, Theatrical, Three-man, Tinhorn, Tulip, Unbare, Uncover, Usher, Vain,

Variety, Vaudeville, Veneer, Viewy, Wear, Wild west, Zarzuela

Showdown Confrontation, Crunch

Shower Douche, Exhibitor, Flurry, Hail, Indicant, Indicator, Kitchen tea, Meteor, Party, Pelt, Pepper, Precipitation, Rain, Scat, Scouther, Scowther, Skatt, Skit, Snow, Spat, Spet, Spit, Splatter, Spray, Sprinkle, Ticker tape

▷ **Showers** *may indicate* an anagram

Showgirl Evita, Nanette

▷ **Showing, Shown in** *may indicate* a hidden word

Showman Bailey, Barnum, Entertainer, Goon, Impresario, Lord Mayor, MC, Ringmaster

Show-off Coxcomb, Exhibitionist, Extrovert, Jack the lad, Peacock, Poseur, Sport, Swagger, Swank

Showpiece Flagship

Show-place Exhibition, Olympia, Pavilion, Theatre

Shrapnel Fragment, Shell, Splinter

Shred Clout, Filament, Grate, Julienne, Mammock, Mince, Mummock, Rag, Screed, Swarf, Tag, Ta(i)ver, Tatter, Thread, To-tear, Wisp

Shrew Bangsring, Banxring, Callet, Catamaran, Elephant, Fury, Hellcat, Kate, Marabunta, Musk, Nag, Otter, Pygmy, Show, Solenodon, Sondeli, Sorex, Spitfire, Squirrel, Tana, Termagant, Tree, Trull, Tupaia, Virago, Vixen, Water, Xant(h)ippe, Yankie, Yenta

Shrewd Acute, Arch, Argute, Artful, Astucious, Astute, Callid, Canny, Clued-up, Cute, File, Gnostic, Gumptious, Hard-nosed, Judicious, Knowing, Pawky, Politic, Sagacious, Sapient(al), Wily, Wise

Shriek Cry, Scream, Scrike, Shright, Shrike, Shrill, Shritch, Skirl, Yell

Shrift Attention, Penance, Short

Shrike Bird, Butcher-bird

Shrill Argute, High, Keen, Piping, Reedy, Screech, Sharp, Skirl, Treble

Shrimp(s) Brine, Fairy, Freshwater, Krill, Mantis, Midge, Opossum, Potted, Prawn, Runt, Sand, Skeleton, Small, Spectre, Squill(a), Stomatopod

Shrine Adytum, Altar, Dagaba, Dagoba, Dargah, Delphi, Fatima, Feretory, Harem, Holy, Joss house, Kaaba, Marabout, Martyry, Naos, Pagoda, Reliquary, Scrine, Scryne, Stupa, Tabernacle, Temple, Tope, Vimana, Walsingham

Shrink(age), Shrinking, Shrunk Alienist, Analyst, Blanch, Blench, Boggle, Cling, Compress, Constringe, Contract, Cour, Cower, Creep, Crine, Cringe, Dare, Decrew, Depreciate, Dread, Dwindle, Flinch, Funk, Gizzen, Less, Nirl, → **PSYCHIATRIST**, Pycnosis, Quail, Recoil, Reduce, Retract, Sanforised, Shrivel, Shrug, Shy, Sphacelate, Timid, Violet, Wane, Waste, Wince, Wizened

Shrivel(led) Cling, Crine, Desiccate, Dry, Nirl, Parch, Scorch, Scrump, Sear, Shrink, Skrimp, Skrump, Tabid, Welk, Wither, Wizened, Writhled

Shropshire Salop

Shroud(s) Chadri, Chuddah, Chuddar, Cloak, Cloud, Conceal, Cover, Futtock, Grave-cloth, Pall, Rigging, Screen, Sheet, Sindon, Turin, Veil, Winding-sheet, Wrap

Shrub(bery) Arboret, Brush, → **BUSH**, Dead-finish, Horizontal, Plant, Undergrowth, Wintergreen

---

SHRUBS

3 letters:		*4 letters:*	
Kat	Qat	Coca	Dita
	Rue	Cola	Grex
			Hebe

Kava
Nabk
Olea
Rhus
Ruta
Titi
Tutu
Ulex

5 letters:
Aalii
Bosky
Brere
Buaze
Buazi
Buchu
Caper
Gorse
Hakea
Hazel
Henna
Ledum
Maqui
Monte
Mulga
Nebek
Peony
Pyxie
Ramee
Ramie
Salal
Savin
Senna
Thyme
Toyon
Wahoo
Yapon
Yupon
Zamia

6 letters:
Acacia
Alhagi
Ambach
Aucuba
Azalea
Bauera
Cobaea
Correa
Croton
Crowea

Daphne
Fatsia
Feijoa
Frutex
Fynbos
Garrya
Jojoba
Kalmia
Lignum
Manoao
Maquis
Matico
Mimosa
Myrica
Myrtle
Nebbuk
Nebeck
Neinei
Paeony
Pituri
Privet
Protea
Prunus
Savine
Smilax
Storax
Sumach
Tutsan
Yaupon

7 letters:
Acerola
Akiharo
Ambatch
Arbutus
Bauhini
Boronia
Bullace
Cascara
Cytisus
Deutzia
Dogwood
Emubush
Epacris
Ephedra
Filbert
Fuchsia
Guayule
Hop-tree
Jasmine
Juniper

Lantana
Mahonia
Mesquit
Muntrie
Oleacea
Rhatany
Romneya
Rosebay
Savanna
Shallon
Skimmia
Syringa
Tea-tree
Waratah
Weigela

8 letters:
Abutilon
Allspice
Barberry
Bayberry
Berberis
Bignonia
Bilberry
Bluebush
Buddleia
Camellia
Coprosma
Cowberry
Danewort
Euonymus
Gardenia
Hardhack
Heketara
Hibiscus
Horopito
Inkberry
Japonica
Jetbread
Koromiko
Krameria
Lavender
Leadwort
Magnolia
Mairehau
Mezereon
Ninebark
Ocotillo
Oleander
Oleaster
Photinia

Rangiora
Rock rose
Rosemary
Saltbush
Savannah
Shadbush
Sorbaria
Spekboom
Sweetsop
Tamarisk
Viburnum
Waxplant

9 letters:
Andromeda
Bearberry
Buckthorn
Ceanothus
Clianthus
Cordyline
Coreopsis
Coyotillo
Crowberry
Eucryphia
Firethorn
Forsythia
Gelsemium
Grevillia
Hamamelis
Hydrangea
Jaborandi
Jessamine
Kumarahou
Manzanita
Melaleuca
Mistletoe
Patchouli
Pernettya
Perovskia
Rauwolfia
Snowberry
Spicebush
Sterculia

10 letters:
Aphelandra
Cascarilla
Crossandra
Embothrium
Eriostemon
Escallonia

Fatshedera	Poinsettia	Cotoneaster	*12 letters:*
Frangipani	Potentilla	Honeysuckle	Phanerophyte
Gaultheria	Pyracantha	Huckleberry	Philadelphus
Gooseberry	Schefflera	Leatherwood	Rhododendron
Greasewood	Supplejack	Pittosporum	Serviceberry
Holodiscus	Twinflower	Staggerbush	Southernwood
Joshua tree		Steeplebush	Streptosolen
Laurustine	*11 letters:*	Stephanotis	Strophanthus
Parkleaves	Beautybrush	Wortleberry	
Pilocarpus	Bottlebrush		

Shrug Discard, Toss

Shudder(ing) Abhor, Ashake, Frisson, Grew, Grise, Grue, Horror, Jerk, Quake, Shake, Spasm, Tremble, Tremor

Shuffle(d) Dodge, Drag, Hedge, Make, Mix, Palter, Permute, Redeployment, Riffle, Scuff, Shamble, Shauchle, Soft-shoe, Stack

▷ **Shuffle(d)** *may indicate* an anagram

Shun Attention, Avoid, Eschew, Evade, Forbear, Ignore, Ostracise, Secede, → **SPURN**

Shunt Move, Shelve, Shuttle, Side-track

Shut (down; in; out; up), Shut(s) Bar, Cage, Close, Confined, Coop, Debar, Embar, Emure, Fasten, Fend, Impale, Impound, Latch, Lay-off, Lock, Occlude, Rid, Scram, Seal, Shet, Slam, Spar, Steek, Telescope, Tine, To

Shutter(s) Blind, B-setting, Dead-lights, Douser, Jalousie, Louvre, Persiennes, Shade

Shuttle Alternate, Commute, Drawer, Flute, Go-between, Navette, Orbiter, Shoot, Shunt, Space, Tat(t), Weave

Shy Bashful, Blate, Blench, Cast, Catapult, Chary, Coy, Deficient, Demure, Farouche, Flinch, Funk, Heave, Jerk, Jib, Laithfu', Leery, Lob, Mim, Mims(e)y, Mousy, Rear, Recoil, Reserved, Reticent, Retiring, Sheepish, Shrinking, Skeigh, Start, Thraw, Throw, Timid, Tongue-tied, Toss, Try, Verecund, Violet, Willyard, Willyart, Withdrawn

Shyster Ambulance chaser

Siamese, Siamese twins Chang, Eng, Parabiosis, Seal-point, T(h)ai

Siberia(n) Chukchi, Evenki, Ostiak, Ostyak, Samo(y)ed, Tungus, Vogul, Yakut, Yupik

Sibilant Hissing, Whistling

Sibling Brother, German, Kin, Sister

Sibyl Oracle, Prophetess, Seer, Soothsayer, Witch

Sicilian Sicanian, Trinacrian

Sick(en), Sickening, Sickliness, Sickly, Sickness Aegrotat, Affection, Ague, Ail, Altitude, Bad, Bends, Cat, Chalky, Chunder, Colic, Crapulence, Crook, Decompression, Delicate, Disorder, Donsie, Gag, Green, Hangover, Icky, Ill, Infection, Leisure, Maid-pale, Mal, Mawkish, Milk, Morbid, Morning, Motion, Mountain, Nauseous, Pale, Peaky, Peelie-wallie, Peely-wally, Pestilent, Pindling, Plague, Puly, Puna, Queachy, Queasy, Queechy, Radiation, Regorge, Repulsive, Retch, Serum, Shilpit, Sleeping, Soroche, Space, Spue, Squeamish, Sweating, Travel, Twee, Uncle Dick, Valetudinarian, Virus, Vomit, Wamble-cropped, Wan

Sick bay San

Sickle(-shaped) Falcate, Falx, Grasshook, Hook, Scythe

Side Abeam, Airs, Ally, B, Beam, Blind, Border, Branch, Camp, Cis-, Distaff, Division, Edge, Effect, Eleven, English, Epistle, Ex intraque parte, Facet, Flank, Flip, Gospel, Gunnel, Hand, Heavy, Hypotenuse, Iliac, Lateral, Lee(ward), Left, Long, Obverse,

Off, On, OP, Pane, Part, Partisan, Party, Port, Pretension, Profile, Prompt, Rave, Reveal, Reverse, Right, Rink, Short, Silver, Slip, Spear, Starboard, Swank, → **TEAM**, Tight, Weak, West, Wind, Windward, Wing, XI

Sideboard(s) Beauf(f)et, Buffet, Cellaret, Commode, Credence, Credenza, Dresser, Whiskers

Side-effect, Side-issue Fall-out, Logograph, Logogriph, Offshoot, Secondary, Spin-off

Sidekick Right-hand man, Satellite

Side-line Hobby, Lye, Siding, Spur

Side-step Crab, Dodge, Evade, Hedge, Maori, Volt

Side-track Distract, Divert, Shunt

Sidewalk Crab, Footpath, Pavement

Sideways Askance, Indirect, Laterally, Laterigrade, Oblique

Siding Alliance, Byway, Lie, Lye, Spur, Turnout

Sidle Edge, Passage

Siege (work) Alamo, Antioch, Antwerp, Beleaguer, Beset, Blockade, Charleston, Gherao, Investment, Khartoum, Ladysmith, Leaguer, Mafeking, Masada, Metz, Obsidional, Perilous, Pleven, Plevna, Poliorcetic, Ravelin, Sarajevo, Surround, Verdun, Vicksburg, Warsaw

Sienese Tuscan

Sienna Burnt, Raw

Siesta Nap, Noonday, Nooning

Sieve, Sift(ing) Analyse, Bolt(er), Boult(er), Bunting, Colander, Coliform, Cribble, Cribrate, Cribrose, Cullender, Eratosthenes, Ethmoid, Filter, Molecular, Riddle, Screen, Searce, Search, Separate, Siler, Strain, Sye, Tamis, Tammy, Tems(e), Trommel, Try, Winnow

Sigh Exhale, Heave, Lackaday, Long, Moan, Sough, Suspire, Welladay

Sight(ed) Aim, Barleycorn, Bead, Conspectuity, Eye(ful), Eyesore, Glimpse, Ken, Long, Oculated, Panoramic, Peep, Prospect, Range, Rear, Riflescope, Scene, Scotopia, Second, See, Short, Spectacle, Taish, Telescopic, Vane, → **VIEW**, Visie, Vision, Vista, Vizy, Vizzie

Sight-screen Eyelid

Sightseer, Sightseeing Lionise, Observer, Rubberneck, Tourist, Tripper, Viewer

Sign(s), Signing, Signpost Accidental, Ache, Addition, Ale-stake, Ampassy, Ampersand, Aquarius, Archer, Aries, Arrow, Auspice, Autograph, Badge, Balance, Beck, Beckon, Board, Brand, Bull, Bush, Call, Cancer, Capricorn, Caract, Caret, Chevron, Clue, Coronis, Crab, Cross, Cue, Dactylology, Dele, Diacritic, Di(a)eresis, Diphone, Division, Dollar, DS, Earmark, Emblem, Endeixis, Endorse, Endoss, Enlist, Evidence, Exit, Fascia, Fish, Gemini, Gesture, Goat, Grammalogue, Hallmark, Hamza(h), Harbinger, Harvey Smith, Hex, Hieroglyphic, Hint, Ideogram, Indian, Indicate, Indication, Indicium, Initial, INRI, Inscribe, Ivy-bush, Leo, Lexigram, Libra, Local, Logogram, Milepost, Milestone, Minus, Mudra, Multiplication, Negative, Neume, Nod, Notice, Obelisk, Obelus, Omen, Peace, Phraseogram, Pisces, Plus, Positive, Pound, Presa, Presage, Prodrome, Prodromus, Radical, Ram, Ratify, Rest, Rune, Sacrament, Sagittarius, Sain, Scorpio, Segno, Semeion, Semiotics, Shingle, Show, Sigil, Sigla, Signal, Star, Subscribe, Subtraction, Superscribe, Symbol, Symptom, Syndrome, Tag, Taurus, Tic(k)tac(k), Tilde, Titulus, Token, Trace, Triphone, Twins, Umlaut, V, Vestige, Virgo, Vital, Warning, Waymark, Word, Zodiac

Signal(ler) Alarm, Aldis lamp, Alert, Amber, Assemble, Baud, Beacon, Bell, Bleep, Bugle, Busy, Buzz, Chamade, Code, Compander, Compandor, Cone, Cue,

Detonator, Diaphone, Distress, Duplex, Earcon, Flag, Flagman, Flare, Flash, Fog, Gantry, Gesticulate, Gong, Griffin, Gun, Harmonic, Heliograph, Heliostat, Herald, Heterodyne, High sign, Hooter, Horse and hattock, Icon, Important, Interrupt, Interval, Luminance, Mark, Mase, Megafog, Message, Modem, Morse, Navar, NICAM, Notation, Noted, Output, Password, Peter, Pinger, Pip, Pollice verso, Prod, Pulsar, Radio, Renowned, Reveille, Robot, Salient, Semaphore, Semiology, Simplex, Singular, Smoke, Sonogram, SOS, Spoiler, Squawk, Taps, Target, Tchick, Telegraph, Teles(e)me, Thumb, Tic(k)-tac(k), Time, Traffic, Troop, Very, Video, V-sign, Waff, Waft, Wave, Wave-off, Wigwag

Signature Alla breve, Allograph, Autograph, By-line, Digital, Hand, John Hancock, John Henry, Key, Mark, Onomastic, Specimen, Subscription, Time

Signet Ring, Seal, Sigil, Sphragistics

Significance, Significant Cardinal, Consequence, Cosmic, Emblem, Great, Impact, Important, Indicative, Key, Magnitude, Major, Material, Matter, Meaningful, Milestone, Moment(ous), Noted, Noteworthy, Other, Paramount, Pith, Pregnant, Salient, Special, Telling

Signify Bemean, Denote, Imply, Indicate, Intimate, Matter, → **MEAN**, Represent

Sign language Ameslan, Semaphore, Tic(k)tac(k)

Sikh(ism) Granth, Kaccha, Kangha, Kara, Kesh, Khalsa, Kirpan, Mazhbi, Mechanised, Nanak, (Ranjit) Singh

Silas Uncle, Wegg

Silence(r), Silent Amyclaean, Choke-pear, Clam, Clamour, Conticent, Creepmouse, Dumbstruck, Earplug, Gag, Hesychastic, Hist, Hush, Hushkit, Mim(budget), Muffler, Mum(p), Mumchance, Mute, Obmutescent, Omertà, Quench, Quiesce, → **QUIET**, Reticence, Shtoom, Shush, Speechless, Still, Sulky, Tace(t), Tacit(urn), Throttle, Tight-lipped, Unvoiced, Wheesh(t), Whis(h)t

Silhouette Contour, Outline, Planform, Profile, Shadow figure, Shadowgraph, Shape, Skyline

Silica(te) Albite, Analcite, Andalusite, Chabazite, Chert, Cristobalite, Datolite, Diopside, Dioptase, Fayalite, Float-stone, Gadolinite, Harmotome, Hiddenite, Humite, Iolite, Kieselguhr, Kyanite, Monticellite, Montmorillonite, Olivine, Opal, Pectolite, Penninite, Phillipsite, Pinite, Rhodonite, Riebeckite, Saponite, Scapolite, Silex, Spodumene, Staurolite, Stishovite, Tridymite, Tripoli, Ultrabasic, Vermiculite, Vitreous, Zeolite

Silicon Chip, Si

Silk(y), Silk screen Alamode, Atlas, Barathea, Blonde-lace, Brocade, Bur(r), Charmeuse®, Chenille, Chiffon, Cocoon, Corn, Crape, Crepe, Duchesse, Dupion, Faille, Fibroin, Filature, Filoselle, Florence, Florentine, Flosh, Floss, Flox, Foulard, Gazar, Gazzatum, Georgette, Gimp, Glossy, Grosgrain, KC, Kincob, Lustrine, Lustring, Lutestring, Makimono, Malines, Marabou(t), Matelasse, Mercery, Moiré, Ninon, Oiled, Organza, Ottoman, Paduasoy, Parachute, Peau de soie, Pongee, Prunella, Prunelle, Prunello, Pulu, QC, Raw, Samite, Sars(e)net, Satin, Schappe, Seal(ch), Sendal, Seric, Sericeous, Sericite, Serigraph, Shalli, Shantung, Sien-tsan, Sleave, Sleek, Sle(i)ded, Slipper satin, Smooth, Spun, Surah, Tabaret, Tabby, Taffeta, Tasar, Thistledown, Tiffany, Tram, Tulle, Tussah, Tusseh, Tusser, Tussore, Vegetable, Velvet, Wild

Silkworm (eggs), Silkworm disease Bombyx, Eria, Graine, Multivoltine, Muscardine, Sericulture, Tussore

Sill Ledge, Straining, Threshold

Silly, Silliness Absurd, Anserine, Apish, Brainless, Buffer, Crass, Cuckoo, Daft, Dandy, Ditsy, Divvy, Drippy, Dumb, Dunce, Fatuous, Folly, Fool, Footling, Frivolous,

Goopy, Goosey, Gormless, Hen-witted, Idiotic, Imbecile, Inane, Inept, Infield(er), Liminal, Mid-off, Mid-on, Mopoke, Puerile, Season, Simple, Soft(y), Spoony, → **STUPID**, Tripe, Wacky

▷ **Silly** *may indicate* relating to a sill

Silt Alluvium, Deposit, Dregs, Land, Lees, Loess, Residue, Sullage, Varve

Silver(skin) Ag, Albata, Alpac(c)a, Arg(ent), Argyria, British plate, Cardecue, Cerargyrite, Diana's tree, Electroplate, Free, Fulminating, German, Grey, Horn, Luna, Nickel, One-legged, Pakt(h)ong, Parcel-gilt, Pegleg, Piastre, Plate, Plateresque, Ruby, Stephanite, Sterling, Sycee, Thaler

▷ **Silver** *may indicate* a coin

Silversmith Demetrius, Lamerie, Plater

Simian Apelike, Catar(r)hine

Similar(ity) Analog(ue), Analogical, Corresponding, Equivalent, Etc, Homoeoneric, Homogeneous, Homoiousian, Homologous, Homonym, Isomorphism, Kindred, → **LIKE**, Parallel, Patristic, Resemblance, Samey, Suchlike

Simile Epic

Similitude Parable

Simmer Bubble, Poach, Seethe, Stew

Simon Bolivar, Cellarer, Magus, Peter, Pure, Simple

Simper Bridle, Giggle, Smirk

Simple(r), Simplicity, Simplify, Simply Aefa(u)ld, Afa(w)ld, Arcadian, Artless, Austere, Bald, Bare, Basic, Crude, Daw, Doddle, Doric, → **EASY**, Eath(e), Elegant, ESN, Ethe, Facile, Fee, Folksy, Gomeral, Gotham, Green, Herb(alist), Herborist, Homespun, Idyllic, Incomposite, Inornate, Jaap, Japie, Mere, Moner(on), Naive(té), Naked, Niaiserie, Noddy, One-fold, Open and shut, Ordinary, Paraphrase, Pastoral, Peter, Plain, Pleon, Provincial, Pure, Reduce, Rustic, Saikless, Sapid, Semplice, Sheer, Silly, Simon, Spartan, Stupid, Tout court, Understated, Woollen

Simpleton Abderite, Airhead, Cokes, Cuckoo, Daw, Duffer, Flat, Fool, Gaby, Galah, Gomeral, Gomeril, Greenhorn, Juggins, Spoon, → **STUPID PERSON**, Wiseacre, Zany

Simulate, Simulating Affect, Anti, Feign, Pretend

Simultaneous Coinstantaneous, Contemporaneous, Synchronous, Together

Sin(ful) Aberrant, Accidie, Acedia, Actual, Anger, Avarice, Besetting, Bigamy, Capital, Cardinal, Covetousness, Crime, Deadly, Debt, Depravity, Envy, Err, Evil, Folly, Gluttony, Hamartiology, Harm, Hate, Impious, Lapse, Lust, Misdeed, Misdoing, Mortal, → **OFFENCE**, Original, Peccadillo, Piacular, Pride, Scape, Scarlet, Shirk, Sine, Sloth, Transgress, Trespass, Unrighteous, Venial, Vice, Wicked, Wrath, Wrong

Sinai Horeb, Mount

Since Ago, As, Meantime, Seeing, Sens, Sine, Sinsyne, Sith(en), Syne, Whereas, Ygo(e)

Sincere(ly), Sincerity Bona-fide, Candour, Earnest, Entire, Frank, Genuine, Heartfelt, Honest, Open, Real(ly), True, Verity, Whole-hearted

Sinclair Lewis, Upton

Sine Versed

Sinecure Bludge, Commendam

Sinew(y) Fibre, Ligament, Nerve, String, Tendinous, Tendon

▶ **Sinful** *see* **SIN**

Sing(ing) Antiphony, Barbershop, Bel canto, Belt out, Bhajan, Carol, Chant, Cheep, Chorus, Coloratura, Community, Cough, Croon, Crow, Diaphony, Diddle, Doo-wop, Glee club, Gorgia, Hum, Inform, Intone, Karaoke, Kirtan, La-la, Lilt, Melic,

Parlando, Peach, Pen(n)illion, Pipe, Plainchant, Rand, Rant, Rap, Record, Render, Scat, Second(o), Solmization, Sprechgesang, Sprechstimme, Squeal, Tell, Thrum, Trill, Troll, Vocalise, Warble, Yodel

Singe Burn, Char, Scorch, Swale, Swayl, Sweal, Sweel

Singer(s) Alto, Balladeer, Bard, Baritone, Bass, Beatle, Bing, Bird, Blondel, Buffo, Callas, Canary, Cantabank, Cantatrice, Cantor, Car, Carreras, Caruso, Castrato, Chaliapin, Chanteuse, Chantor, Chazan, Cher, Chorister, Coloratura, Comprimario, Countertenor, Crooner, Dawson, Diva, Dylan, Ella, Falsetto, Folk, Glee club, Gleemaiden, Gleeman, Grass, Haz(z)an, Heldentenor, Isaac, Kettle, Lark, Lauder, Lay clerk, Lead, Lind, Lorelei, Lulu, Mathis, Melba, Minstrel, Opera, Oscine, Patti, Piaf, Pitti, Precentor, Prima donna, Qawwal, Robeson, Semi-chorus, Session, Sinatra, Siren, Snitch, Songstress, Soprano, Soubrette, Stoolie, Succentor, Swan, Tatiana, Tenor, Tenure, Torch, Treble, Troubador, Vocalist, Voice, Wait, Warbler

Single, Singly Ace, Aefa(u)ld, Aefawld, Alone, Azygous, Bachelor, Celibate, Discriminate, EP, Exclusive, Feme sole, Individual, Matchless, Monact, Mono, Odd, One-off, Only, Pick, Run, Sole, Solitary, Spinster, Unary, Unattached, Uncoupled, Uniparous, Unique, Unwed, Versal, Yin

Single-cell Protista

Single-chambered Monothalamous

Singlestick Sword

Singlet Tunic, Vest

Singular(ity) Curious, Especial, Exceptional, Extraordinary, Ferly, Naked, Odd, Once, One, Peculiar, Queer(er), Rare, → **UNIQUE**, Unusual

Singultus Hiccup

Sinister Bend, Dark, Dirke, Evil, L, Left, Lh, Louche, → **OMINOUS**

Sink(ing), Sunken Basin, Bog, Cadence, Carbon, Cower, Delapse, Depress, Descend, Devall, Dip, Down, Drain, Draught-house, Drink, Drop, Drown, Ebb, Flag, Founder, Gravitate, Heat, Hole, Immerse, Invest, Jawbox, Kitchen, Lagan, Laigh, Lapse, Ligan, Merger, Pad, Poach, Pot, Prolapse, Put(t), Relapse, Sag, Scupper, Scuttle, Set, Settle, Shipwreck, Slump, Steep-to, Sty, Submerge, Subside, Swag, Swamp

Sinner Evildoer, Malefactor, Offender, Reprobate, Trespasser

Sinuous Curvy, Ogee, Slinky, Snaky, Wavy, Winding

Sinus Cavity, Recess

Sip(ping) Delibate, Hap'orth, Libant, Sample, Sowp, Sup, Taste, Tiff(ing)

Siphon Draw, Rack, Soda, Suck, Transfer

Sir Dan, Dom, K, Knight, Kt, Lord(ing), Sahib, Signor, Sirrah, Stir, Stirra(h), Towkay, Tuan

Sire Beget, Father, Get

Siren Alarm, Alert, Diaphone, Enchanter, Femme fatale, Hooter, Houri, Leucosia, Ligea, Lorelei, Mermaid, Oceanides, Parthenope, Salamander, Shark, Teaser, Temptress, Vamp

Sirenian Dugong, Lamantin, Manatee, Manati, Sea-cow

Sirloin Backsey

Sirree Bo

Sisal Agave

Siskin Aberdevine, Bird, Finch

Sister(s) Anne, Beguine, Lay, Minim, → **NUN**, Nurse, Out, Religeuse, Sib, Sibling, Sis, Sob, Soul, Swallow, Theatre, Titty, Ugly, Ursuline, Verse, Ward, Weird

Sisyphean Uphill

Sit(ter), Sitting Bestride, Clutch, Dharna, Duck, Gaper, Lime, Lit de justice, Model,

MP, Perch, Pose, Reign, Represent, Roost, Séance, Sederunt, Sejeant, Session, Squat

Site, Siting Area, Arpa, Brownfield, Building, Camp, Caravan, Feng shui, Greenfield, Home-page, Location, Lot, Mirror, Pad, Place, Plot, Ramsar, Rogue, Sacred, Silo, Spot, Stance

Situation Ballpark, Berth, Cart, Case, Catch, Catch-22, Cliff-hanger, Contretemps, Cow, Dilemma, Galère, Hole, Job, Lie, Location, Lurch, Matrix, Nail-biter, Niche, No-win, Office, Plight, Position, Post, Scenario, Schmear, Schmeer, Set-up, Shebang, Showdown, Status quo, Sticky wicket, Strait, Where, Worst case

Six(th) Digamma, French, German, Half(-a)dozen, Hexad, Italian, Neapolitan, Prime, Sax, Senary, Sestette, Sextet, Sice, Size, Vau, VI

Six counties NI

Six days Hexa(e)meron

Six feet Fathom

Sixpence Bender, Kick, Slipper, Tanner, Tester(n), Testril(l), Tizzy, VID, VIP, Zack

Sixteen Sweet

Sixty Degree, Threescore

Size(able) Amplitude, Area, Bulk, Calibre, Clearcole, Countess, Demy, Displacement, → **EXTENT**, Format, Girth, Glair, Glue, Gum, Imperial, Measure, Particle, Physique, Plus, Pot(t), Princess, Proportion, Tempera, Tidy, Trim

Sizzle Fry, Hiss, Scorch

Skate(r), Skateboard(er), Skating Blade, Bob, Cheap, Choctaw, Cousins, Curry, Dean, Fakie, Figure, Fish, Free, Grommet, In-line, Maid, Mohawk, Rink, Rock(er), Roller, Rollerblade®, Runner, Speed

Skedaddle Scarper, Shoo, Vamoose

Skein Hank, Hasp

Skeleton, Skeletal Anatomy, Atomy, Axial, Bones, Cadaverous, Cadre, Cage, Coenosteum, Corallite, Corallum, Family, Framework, Key, Ossify, Outline, Scenario, Sclere, Tentorium

Sketch(y) Cameo, Character, Charade, Croquis, Delineate, Diagram, Doodle, Draft, → **DRAW**, Ébauche, Esquisse, Illustration, Limn, Line, Maquette, Modello, Outline, Pencilling, Playlet, Pochade, Précis, Profile, Skit, Summary, Tenuous, Thumbnail, Trick, Vignette, Visual

Skew Agee, Ajee, Oblique, Sheer, Squint, Swerve, Veer

Skewer Brochette, En brochette, Prong, Spit, Transfix

Ski(ing) Aquaplane, Glide, Glissade, Hot-dog, Langlauf, Mogul, Nordic, Schuss, Super G, Telemark, Vorlage, Wedeln

Skid Aquaplane, Drift, Jackknife, Side-slip, Slew, Slide, Slip, Slither, Spinout

▷ **Skidding** *may indicate* an anagram

Skiff Canoe, Dinghy, Outrigger

Skill(ed), Skilful Ability, Able, Ace, Address, Adept, Adroit, Art, Bravura, Canny, Chic, Competence, Craft, Deacon, Deft, Dextrous, Enoch, Expertise, Facility, Feat, Finesse, Flair, Gleg, Habile, Hand, Handicraft, Handy, Hend, Hot, Ingenious, Knack, Know-how, Knowing, Lear(e), Leir, Lere, Masterly, Masterpiece, Mastery, Mean, Métier, Mistery, Mystery, Mystique, Practised, Proficient, Prowess, Quant, Resource, Savvy, Science, Skeely, Sleight, Soft, Speciality, Tactics, Talent, Technic, Technique, Touch, Trade, Trick, Versed, Virtuoso

Skim Cream, Despumate, Flit, Glide, Graze, Plane, Ream, Scan, Scud, Scum, Skiff, Skitter

Skimp Restrict, Scamp, Scrimp, Stint

Skin(s) Agnail, Armour, Bark, Basan, Basil, Box-calf, Bronzed, Calf, Callus, Case,

Cere, Chevrette, Coat, Corium, Cortex, Crackling, Cutaneous, Cuticle, Cutis, Deacon, Deer, Derm(a), Dermatome, Dermis, Dewlap, Disbark, Ectoderm, Enderon, Epicanthus, Epicarp, Epidermis, Eschar, Excoriate, Exterior, Fell, Film, Flaught, Flay, Flench, Flense, Flinch, Forel, Fourchette, Goldbeater's, Hangnail, Hide, Integra®, Jacket, Kip, Kirbeh, Leather, Membrane, Muktuk, Nebris, Pachyderm, Parfleche, Peau, Peel, Pell, Pellicle, Pelt, Perinychium, Plew, Plu(e), Prepuce, Pteryla, Rack, Rape, Rind, Scalp, Scarfskin, Serosa, Shell, Shoder, Spetch, Strip, Swindle, Tegument, Tulchan, Veneer, Water-bouget, Wattle, Woolfell

Skin disease, Skin trouble Boba, Boil, Buba, Causalgia, Chloasma, Chloracne, Cowpox, Cradle cap, Cyanosis, Dartre, Dermatitis, Dermatosis, Dyschroa, EB, Ecthyma, Eczema, Erysipelas, Exanthem(a), Favus, Flay, Framboesia, Gum rash, Herpes, Hives, Ichthyosis, Impetigo, Leishmaniasis, Leucoderma, Lichen, Livedo, Lupus vulgaris, Maidism, Mal del pinto, Mange, Miliaria, Morphew, Morula, Patagium, Pellagra, Pemphigus, Pinta, Pityriasis, Prurigo, Psoriasis, Pyoderma, Rash, Red-gum, Ringworm, Rosacea, Rose-rash, St Anthony's fire, Sapego, Scabies, Sclerodermia, Scurvy, Seborrhoea, Serpigo, Strophulus, Telangiectasis, Tetter, Tinea, Vaccinia, Verruca, Verruga, Vitiligo, Xanthoma, Xerodermia, Yaws, Yawy

Skinflint Cheapo, Dryfist, Miser, Niggard, Pinch-gut, Scrooge, Tightwad

Skinful Drunk, Sausage

Skinhead Not, Punk, Scalp

Skink Seps

Skinless Ecorché

Skinny Barebone, Bony, Dermal, Emaciate, Lean, Scraggy, Thin, Weed

Skint Broke, Ghat, Penniless, Stony

Skip(ped), Skipper Boss, Caper, Captain, Cavort, Drakestone, Dumpster, Elater, Frisk, Hesperian, Jump, Jumping-mouse, Lamb, Luppen, Miss, Omit, Patroon, Ricochet, Saury, Scombresox, Spring, Tittup, Trounce(r)

Skirl Humdudgeon, Pibroch, Pipe, Screigh

Skirmish(er) Brush, Dispute, Escarmouche, Fray, Pickeer, Spar, Tirailleur, Velitation

Skirt(ing) Bases, Bell, Border, Bouffant, Cheongsam, Circle, Coat, Crinoline, Culotte(s), Dado, Dirndl, Edge, Fil(l)ibeg, Fringe, Fustanella, Fustanelle, Girl, Gore, Grass, Harem, Hobble, Hoop, Hug, Hula, Kilt, Lamboys, Lava-lava, Marge, Mini, Mopboard, Pareo, Pareu, Pencil, Peplum, Petticoat, Philibeg, Pinafore, Piu-piu, Plinth, Puffball, Ra-ra, Rim, Sarong, Sidestep, Stringboard, Tace, Tail, Taslet, Tasse(t), Tonlet, Tutu, Washboard, Wrap(a)round, Wrapover

Skit Lampoon, Parody, Sketch

Skittish Coy, Curvetting, Frisky, Restless

Skittle(s) Bayle, Bowl, Kail(s), Kayle, Kingpin, Ninepin, Pin, Spare

Skive(r) Absentee, Scrimshank, Shirk

Skivvy Drudge, Slave

Skrimshank Bludge, Skive

Skulk Lurk, Mooch, Shool

Skull Brainpan, Bregma(ta), Calvaria, Cranium, Fontanel, Harnpan, Head, Malar, Maz(z)ard, Obelion, Occiput, Pannikell, Phrenology, Scalp, Sinciput

Skullcap Ya(r)mulka, Yarmulke, Zucchetto

Skunk Atoc, Atok, Hognosed, Polecat, Pot, Teledu, Zoril(lo)

Sky(-high), Skywards Air, Azure, Blue, Canopy, Carry, El Al, E-layer, Element, Empyrean, Ether, Firmament, Heaven, Lift, Loft, Mackerel, Occident, Octa, Rangi, Uranus, Welkin

Sky-diver Para
Skylark Aerobatics, Bird
Skylight Abat-jour, Aurora, Comet, Lunette, Star
Skyline Horizon, Rooftops
Sky-pilot Chaplain, Vicar
Slab(s) Briquette, Bunk, Bunk(er), Cake, Cap(e)stone, Chunk, Dalle, Hawk, Ledger, Marver, Metope, Mihrab, Mud, Paving-stone, Planch, Plank, Sclate, Sheave, Slate, Slice, Stela, Stelene, Tab, Tile, Wood-wool
Slack(en), Slackness Abate, Careless, Crank, Dilatory, Dross, Ease, Easy-going, Glen, Idle, Lax(ity), Let-up, Loose, Malinger, Nerveless, Relax, Release, Remiss, Shirk, Skive, Slatch, Slow, Surge, Unscrew, Unwind, Veer
Slag Basic, Calx, Cinder, Dross, Scoria, Scum, Sinter, Tap cinder, Tart
Slake Abate, Cool, Quench, Refresh, Satisfy
Slalom Super-G
Slam Crash, Criticise, Dad, Grand, Little, Pan(dy), Small, Sock, Swap, Swop, Vole, Wap
Slander(ous) Asperse, Backbite, Calumny, Defame, Derogatory, Detraction, Disparage, Libel, Malediction, Malign, Missay, Mud, Mudslinging, Obloquy, Sclaunder, Smear, Traduce, Vilify, Vilipend
Slang Abuse, Argot, Back, Berate, Blinglish, Cant, Colloquial, Ebonics, Flash, Jargon, Lingo, Nadsat, Parlyaree, Polari, Rhyming, Slate, Tsotsitaal, Verlan, Zowie
Slant(ed), Slanting Angle, Asklent, Atilt, Bevel, Bias, Brae, Cant, Careen, Chamfer, Clinamen, Diagonal, Escarp, Oblique, Prejudice, Slew, → **SLOPE**, Splay, Squint, Talus, Tilt, Virgule
Slap Clatch, Clout, Cuff, Make-up, Pandy, Piston, Sclaff, Scud, Skelp, Smack, Spat, Tape, Twank
Slapdash Careless, Hurried, Random
Slash(ed) Chive, Cut, Diagonal, Gash, Hack, Jag, Lacerate, Laciniate, Leak, Oblique, Rash, Rast, Reduce, Scorch, Scotch, Separatrix, Slice, Slit, Solidus, Stroke, Virgule, Wee
Slat(s) Fish, Jalousie, Louvre
Slate, Slaty, Slating Alum, Berate, Calm, Cam, Caum, Countess, Credit, Criticise, Decry, Diatribe, Double, Duchess, Duchy, Enter, Griseous, Imperial, Killas, Knotenschiefer, Lady, Marchioness, Ottrelite, Pan, Peggy, Polishing, Princess, Queen, Rag(g), Roof, Schalstein, Shingle, Slat, Small, Tomahawk, Viscountess
Slater Hellier, Insect
Slattern Bag, Besom, Drab, Drazel, Frump, Mopsy, Sloven, Slummock, Sozzle, Traipse, Trapes, Trollop
Slaughter(house), Slaughterer Abattoir, Behead, Bleed, Bloodshed, Butcher, Carnage, Decimate, Hal(l)al, Holocaust, Jhatka, Kill, Mactation, → **MASSACRE**, S(c)hechita(h), Scupper, Shambles, Shochet, Smite
Slav Bohunk, Croat, Czech, Kulak, Lusatia, Polabian, Serb, Sorb, Wend(ic)
Slave(ry), Slaves Addict, Aesop, Aida, Androcles, Barracoon, Blackbird, Bond, Bond(s)man, Bondwoman, Bordar, Boy, Caliban, Coffle, Contraband, Dogsbody, Drudge, Drug, Dulocracy, Dulosis, Esne, Galley, Gibeonite, Helot, Hierodule, Mameluke, Mamluk, Marmaluke, Maroon, Minion, Odalisk, Odali(s)que, Peasant, Pr(a)edial, Rhodope, Serf, Servitude, Spartacus, Terence, Theow, Thersites, Thete, Thrall, Topsy, Vassal, Villein, Wage, White, Yoke
Slave-driver, Slave-owner Assam, Task-master
Slaver Bespit, Dribble, Drivel, Drool, Slabber, Slobber, Spawl
Slay(er), Slaying Destroy, Execute, Ghazi, → **KILL**, Mactation, Murder, Quell, Saul, Slaughter

Sleazy Flimsy, Red-light, Scuzzy, Seamy, Sordid, Squalid, Thin

Sled(ge), Sleigh(-ride) Bob, Dog train, Dray, Hurdle, Hurly-hacket, Kibitka, Komatik, Lauf, Luge, Mud-boat, Mush, Polack, Pulk(h)(a), Pung, Skeleton bob(sleigh), Skidoo®, Slipe, Stoneboat, Tarboggin, Toboggan, Train, Travois

Sleek Bright, Shine, Silky, Smarm, Smooth, Smug

Sleep, Sleeper(s), Sleepiness, Sleeping, Sleepy Beauty, Bed, Bivouac, Blet, Bundle, Bye-byes, Car, Catnap, Coma, Couchette, Crash, Cross-sill, Cross-tie, Dormant, Dormient, Doss, Doze, Drop off, Drowse, Earring, Endymion, Epimenides, Gowl, Gum, Hibernate, Hypnology, Hypnos, Kip, Lethargic, Lie, Morpheus, Nap, Narcolepsy, Narcosis, Nod, Over, Paradoxical, Petal, Pop off, Psychopannychism, REM, Repast, Repose, Rest, Rip Van Winkle, Rough, Sandman, Seven, Shuteye, Skipper, Sloom, Slumber, Snooz(l)e, Somnolent, Sopor(ose), Sownd, Swone, Tie, Torpid, Twilight, Wink, Zeds, Zizz

Sleeping place Bed, Cot, Dormitory, Kang

Sleeping sickness Trypanosomiasis

Sleepless Wake-rife, Wauk-rife

Sleep-walking Noctambulation

Sleet Graupel, Hail

Sleeve (opening) Arm(hole), Balloon, Batwing, Bishop's, Bush, Cap, Collet, Cover, Dolman, Gatefold, Gigot, Gland, Kimono, Lawn, Leg-o'-mutton, Liner, Magyar, Manche, Pagoda, Pudding, Querpo, Raglan, Record, Sabot, Scye, Slashed, Trunk, Turnbuckle, Wind

▸ **Sleigh** *see* SLED

Sleight Artifice, Conjury, Cunning, Dodge, Legerdemain, Trick

Slender(ness) Asthenic, Ectomorph, Elongate, Exiguity, Exility, Fine, Flagelliform, Flimsy, Gracile, Jimp, Leptosome, Loris, Narrow, Skinny, Slight, Slim, Small, Spindly, Stalky, Styloid, Svelte, Swank, Sylph, Tenuous, Trim, Waif

Sleuth Bloodhound, Detective, Dick, Eye, Lime-hound, Lyam(-hound), Lyme(-hound)

Slew Number, Skid, Slide, Twist

Slice Cantle, Chip, Collop, Cut, Doorstep, Fade, Frustrum, Lop, Piece, Rasure, Round, Sector, Segment, Share, Sheave, Shive, Slab, Sliver, Spoon, Tranche, Wafer, Whang

▷ **Slice of** *may indicate* a hidden word

Slick Adroit, Glim, Oil, Sleeveen, Smooth, Suave

Slide Barrette, Chute, Cursor, Diapositive, Drift, Ease, Glissando, Hair, Hirsle, Ice-run, Illapse, Lantern, Mount, Pulka, Schuss, Skid, Skite, Slip, Slippery dip, Slither, Snowboard, Transparency

Slight(ly) Affront, Belittle, Cold shoulder, Cut, Detract, Disparage, Disregard, Facer, Flimsy, Halfway, Insult, Minor, Misprise, Neglect, Nominal, Pet, Petty, Rebuff, Remote, → SLENDER, Slim, Slimsy, Slur, Small, Smattering, Sneaking, Snub, Subtle, Superficial, Sylphine, Tenuous, Thin, Tiny, Wee, Wispy

Slim Bant, Jimp, Macerate, Reduce, Slender, Slight, Sylph, Tenuous, Thin

Slime, Slimy Glair, Glit, Gorydew, Guck, Gunk, Mother, Muc(o)us, Myxomycete, Oily, Ooze, Sapropel, Slake, Sludge, Uliginous

Sling Balista, Catapult, Drink, Fling, Hang, Parbuckle, Prusik, Support, Toss, Trebuchet

Slink Lurk, Skulk, Slope

Slip(ped), Slipping, Slips Boner, Cover, Cutting, Disc, Docket, Drift, EE, Elapse, Elt, Engobe, Error, Faux pas, Fielder, Form, Freudian, Glide, Glissade, Infielder, Label, Landslide, Lapse, Lapsus linguae, Lath, Lauwine, Lingual, Mistake, Muff,

Nod, Oversight, Parapraxis, Petticoat, Pink, Prolapse, Ptosis, Quickset, Rejection, Relapse, Run, Scape, Sc(h)edule, Scoot, Set, Shim, Sin, Ski, Skid, Skin, Skite, Slade, Slidder, Slide, Slither, Slive, Spillican, Stumble, Surge, Ticket, Trip, Tunicle, Underskirt, Unleash, Wage(s)

Slipper(s) Baboosh, Babouche, Babuche, Baffies, Calceolate, Carpet, Eel, Japanese, Mocassin, Moccasin, Moyl, Muil, Mule, Pabouche, Pampootie, Pantable, Pantof(f)le, Panton, Pantoufle, Pump, Rullion, Runner, Ski, Sledge, Sneaker, Sock

Slippery Eely, Foxy, Glid, Icy, Lubric, Shady, Shifty, Skidpan, Slick

Slipshod Careless, Hurried, Jerry, Lax, Slapdash, Slatternly, Sloppy, Slovenly, Toboggan

▷ **Slipshod** *may indicate* an anagram

Slit Buttonhole, Cranny, Cut, Fent, Fissure, Fitchet, Gash, Gill, Loop, Pertus(at)e, Placket, Placket-hole, Race, Rit, Scissure, Spare, Speld(er), Vent

Slithy Tove

Sliver Flake, Fragment, Moslings, Rove, Shaving, Slice, Splinter, Trace

Slob(ber) Drool, Lout, Slaver, Smarm, Wet

Sloe Blackthorn, Slae

Slog(ger) Drag, Strike, Swink, Swot, Traipse, Tramp, Trape, Trauchle, Trudge, Yacker, Yakka, Yakker

Slogan Amandla, Byword, Catchword, Chant, Jai Hind, Masakhane, Mot(to), Murdabad, Phrase, Rallying-cry, Slughorn(e), Tapline, Warcry, Watchword

Sloop Cutter, Hoy, Ship

Slop(s) Cop(per), Gardyloo, Jordeloo, Muck, Policeman, Rossers, Rozzers, Schmaltz, Sop, Spill, Swill

Slope(s), Sloping Acclivity, Angle, Anticline, Bahada, Bajada, Bank, Batter, Bevel, Borrow, Borstal(l), Brae, Breast, Camber, Chamfer, Cuesta, Declivity, Delve, Diagonal, Dip, Dry, Escarp, Fastigate, Fla(u)nch, Foothill, Geanticline, Glacis, Grade, Gradient, Heel, Hill, Incline, Isoclinical, Kant, Lean, Natural, Nursery, Oblique, Pent, Periclinal, Pitch, Rake, Ramp, Rollway, Scarp, Schuss, Scrae, Scree, Shelve, Sideling, Skewback, Slant, Slippery, Slipway, Splay, Steep, Stoss, Talus, Tilt, Verge, Versant, Weather

Sloppily, Sloppy Lagrimoso, Lowse, Madid, Mushy, Remiss, Schmaltzy, Slapdash, Slipshod, Sloven, Slushy, Untidy, Weepie

▷ **Sloppy** *may indicate* an anagram

Slosh(y) Dowse, Fist, Splash, Wet

Slot(ted) Expansion, Graveyard, Groove, Hasp, Hesp, Hole, Key, Keyway, Mortice, Mortise, Seat, Slit, Swanmark, Time

Sloth(ful) Accidie, Acedia, Ai, Bradypus, Edentate, Ground, Idle, Inaction, Indolent, Inertia, Lazy, Lie-abed, Megatherium, Mylodon, Slugabed, Sweer(t), Sweered, Sweir(t), Three-toed, Unau

Slot machine One-armed bandit, Pokey, Pokie

Slouch Lop, Mooch, Mope, Slump

Slough(ing) Cast, Despond, Ecdysis, Eschar, Exuviae, Lerna, Marish, Marsh, Mire, Morass, Paludine, Shed, Shuck, Swamp

Sloven(ly) Careless, Dag(gy), Down-at-heel, D(r)aggle-tail, Frowsy, Grobian, Jack-hasty, Mawkin, Rag-doll, Ratbag, Slaister, Slammakin, Slammerkin, Slattern, Sleazy, Slipshod, Slubberdegullion, Slubberingly, Slummock, Slut, Streel, Untidy

Slow(ing), Slower, Slowly Adagio, Allargando, Andante, Brady, Brake, Broad, Calando, Crawl, Dawdle, Deliberate, Dilatory, Dull, Dumka, ESN, Flag, Gradual, Inchmeal, Lag, Langram, Larghetto, Largo, Lash, Lassu, Late, Lean-witted,

Leisurely, Lentando, Lento, Lifeless, Loiter, Losing, Meno mosso, Obtuse, Pedetentous, Rall(entando), Rein, Reluctant, Retard, Ribattuta, Ritardando, Ritenuto, Slack, Slug, Sluggish, Snaily, Solid, Stem, Tardigrade, Tardive, Tardy, Tardy-gaited

Slowcoach Slowpoke, Slug

Slow-match Portfire

Sludge Activated, Gunge, Mire, Muck, Sapropel, Slob

Slug(s) Ammo, Bêche-de-mer, Blow, Bullet, Cosh, Drink, Limaces, Limax, Linotype®, Mollusc, Nerita, Pellet, Shot, Snail, Trepang

Sluggard Drone, Lazy, Lie-abed, Lusk, Unau

Sluggish Dilatory, Drumble, Idler, Inactive, Inert, Jacent, Lacklustre, Laesie, Languid, Lazy, Lentor, Lethargic, Lug, Phlegmatic, Saturnine, Sleepy, → **SLOW**, Stagnant, Tardy, Torpid, Unalive

Sluice Aboideau, Aboiteau, Drain, Gutter, Koker, Penstock, Rinse, Sasse

Slum Basti, Bustee, Busti, Cabbagetown, Cardboard city, Ghetto, Pavela, Rookery, Shanty, Slurb, Warren

Slumber Doze, Drowse, Nap, Nod, Sleep, Sloom, Snooze

Slump Decrease, Depression, Deteriorate, Dip, Flop, Recession, Sink, Slouch, Sprawl

Slur(ring) Defame, Drawl, Innuendo, Libel, Opprobrium, Slight, Smear, Synaeresis, Tie

Slush Bathos, Boodle, Bribe, Drip, Money, Mush, Pap, Slop, Sposh, Swash

Slut Candle, Dollymop, Draggle-tail, Dratchell, Drazel, Floosie, Harlot, Slattern, Sow, Tart, Traipse, Trapes, Trollop

Sly Christopher, Clandestine, Coon, Covert, Cunning, Foxy, Furtive, Leery, Peery, Reynard, Secretive, Shifty, Slee, Sleekit, Sleeveen, Slicker, Sneaky, Stallone, Stealthy, Subtle, Surreptitious, Tinker, Tod, Tricky, Weasel, Wily

▷ **Slyly** *may indicate* an anagram

Smack(er) Buss, Cuff, Flavour, Foretaste, Fragrance, Hooker, Kiss, Klap, Lander, Lips, Pra(h)u, Relish, Salt, Saut, Skelp, Slap, Slat, Smatch, Smouch, Soupçon, Spank, Spice, Splat, Tack, → **TANG**, Taste, Thwack, Tincture, Trace, Twang, X, Yawl

Small (thing) Ateleiosis, Atom, Bantam, Beer, Bijou, Bittie, Bitty, Centesimal, Chotta, Curn, Denier, Diminutive, Dinky, Drib, Elfin, Few, Fry, Grain, Haet, Ha'it, Half-pint, Handful, Hobbit, Holding, Hole-in-the-wall, Hyperosmia, Insect, Ion, Leet, Lilliputian, Limited, Lite, → **LITTLE**, Lock, Low, Meagre, Mean, Measly, Microscopic, Midget, Mignon, Miniature, Minikin, Minority, Minute, Mite, Modest, Modicum, Peerie, Peewee, Petit(e), Petty, Pigmean, Pigmy, Pink(ie), Pinky, Pint-size, Pittance, Pocket, Poky, Poujadist, Rap, Reduction, Runt, S, Santilla, Scattering, Scrump, Scrunt, Scut, Shrimp, Single, Skerrick, Slight, Slim, Smattering, Smidge(o)n, Smidgin, Smithereen, Smout, Soupçon, Sprinkling, Spud, Stim, Stunted, Tad, Teenty, Thin, Tidd(l)y, Tiny, Titch(y), Tittle, Tot(tie), Totty, Trace, Trivial, Unheroic, Wee, Weedy, Whit

Smallest Least, Minimal, Runt

Smallholder, Smallholding Croft, Nursery, Rundale, Share-cropper, Stead

Small-minded(ness) Parvanimity, Petty

Smallness Exiguity, Exility, Paucity

Smallpox Alastrim, Variola

Smarm(y) Oil, Smoothie, Unctuous

Smart(en), Smartest Ache, Acute, Alec, Astute, Best, Bite, Chic, Classy, Clever, Cute, Dandy, Dapper, Dressy, Elegant, Flash, Flip, Fly, Groom, Gussy up, Kookie, Kooky, Natty, Neat, Nifty, Nip, Nobby, Pac(e)y, Pacy, Posh, Preen, Primp, Prink,

Pusser, Raffish, Rattling, Ritzy, Saucy, Slick, Sly, Smoke, Smug, Snappy, Soigné(e), Spiff, Sprauncy, Sprightly, Spruce, Sprush, Spry, Sting, Stylish, Swagger, Sweat, Swish, Tiddley, Tippy, Titivate, Toff, U, Well-groomed, Wiseacre

Smash(ed), Smasher, Smashing Atom, Bingle, Brain, Break, Corker, Crush, Demolish, Devastate, Dish, Forearm, High, Jarp, Jaup, Kaput, Kill, Lulu, Shatter, Shiver, Slam, Squabash, Stave, Super, Terrific, Tight, To-brake, → **WRECK**

▷ **Smash(ed)** *may indicate* an anagram

Smear Assoil, Bedaub, Besmirch, Blur, Borm, Cervical, Clam, Daub, Defile, Denigrate, Discredit, Drabble, Enarm, Gaum, Gild, Gorm, Lick, Oil, Pap(anicolaou), Pay, Plaster, Slairg, Slaister, Slake, Slander, Slather, Slime, Slubber, Slur, Smalm, Smarm, Smudge, Sully, Teer, Traduce, Wax

Smell(ing), Smelly Aroma, Asafoetida, BO, Caproate, Effluvium, Empyreuma, Fetor, F(o)etid, Fug, Gale, Gamy, Graveolent, Guff, Hing, Honk, Hum, Mephitis, Miasm(a), Ming, Musk, Nidor, Niff, Nose, Odour, Olent, Olfact(ory), Osmatic, Perfume, Pong, Ponk, Pooh, Rank, Redolent, Reech, Reek, Sar, Savour, → **SCENT**, Sniff, Snifty, Snook, Snuff, Steam, Stench, Stifle, Stink, Tang, Whiff

Smelling salts Sal volatile

Smelt(ing) Atherinidae, Melt, Salmon, Scoria, Sparling, Speiss, Spirling

Smile(s), Smiling Agrin, Beam, Cheese, Favour, Gioconda, Grin, Rictus, Samuel, Self-help, Simper, Smirk

Smirk Grimace, Simper

Smite, Smitten Assail, Enamoured, Hit, Strike, Strook

Smith Adam, Farrier, FE, Forger, Hammerman, Mighty, Stan, Vulcan, Wayland

Smithy Forge, Smiddy, Stithy

Smock Blouse, Chemise, Drabbet, Gather, Shift, Slop, Smicket

Smoke(r), Smoking, Smoky Blast, Bloat, Censer, Chain, Chillum, → **CIGAR(ETTE)**, Cure, Drag, Fog, Fuliginous, Fume, Funk, Gasper, Hemp, Incense, Indian hemp, Inhale, Kipper, Latakia, Lum, Lunt, Mainstream, Manil(l)a, Nicotian, Passive, Peat reek, Peaty, Pother, Pudder, Puff, Reech, Reek, Reest, Roke, Smeech, Smeek, Smirting, Smoor, Smoulder, Smudge, Snout, Tear, Toke, Vapour, Viper, Water, Whiff, Wreath

Smoke-hating Misocapnic

Smoking-room Divan

Smollett Tobias

▶ **Smooch** *see* **SMOUCH**

Smooth(e), Smoother, Smoothly Alabaster, Bald, Bland, Brent, Buff, Chamfer, Clean, Clockwork, Dress, Dub, Easy, Even, Fettle, File, Flat, Fluent, Glabrous, Glare, Glassy, Glib, Goose, Iron, Legato, Level, Levigate, Linish, Mealy-mouthed, Mellifluous, Oil, Plane, Plaster, Rake, Roll, Rub, Sand(er), Satiny, Scrape, Shiny, Sleek, Slick, Slickenslide, Slur, Smug, Snod, Sostenuto, Streamlined, Suave, Swimmingly, Terete, Terse, Trim, Urbane

Smooth-haired Lissotrichous

Smother Burke, Choke, Muffle, Oppress, Overlie, Smoor, Smore, Smoulder, Stifle, Suppress

Smouch Cheat, Kiss, Lallygag, Lollygag, Neck

Smoulder Burn, Seethe

Smudge Blur, Dab, Offset, Slur, Smear, Smooch, Stain

Smug Complacent, Conceited, Goody-goody, Goody-two-shoes, Neat, Oily, Pi, Sanctimonious, Self-satisfied, Trim

Smuggle(d), Smuggler, Smuggling Body-packer, Bootleg, Contraband, Contrabandist, Donkey, Fair trade, Gunrunning, Moonshine, Mule, Owler,

Rum-runner, Run, Secrete, Steal, Traffic

Smut(ty) Bawdy, Blight, Blue, Brand, Burnt-ear, Coom, Filth, Grime, Racy, Soot, Speck, Stinking

Smut-fungus Basidia, Ustilago

Snack Bever, Bhelpuri, Bite, Blintz, Breadstick, Brunch, Butty, Canapé, Chack, Crudités, Elevenses, Entremets, Four-by-two, Gorp, Meze, Nacket, Nibble, Nigiri, Nocket, Nooning, Nuncheon, Padkos, Pie, Popcorn, Rarebit, Refreshment, Samo(o)sa, Sandwich, Sarnie, Savoury, Scroggin, Small chop, Tapa, Taste, Toast(y), Trail mix, Vada, Voidee, Wada, Wrap, Zakuska

Snaffle Bit, Bridoon, Grab, Purloin

Snag Catch, Contretemps, Drawback, Hindrance, Hitch, Impediment, Knob, Nog, Obstacle, Remora, Rub, Snubbe, Stub, Tear

Snail Brian, Cowrie, Cowry, Dew, Dodman, Escargot, Garden, Gasteropod, Giant African, Helix, Hodmandod, Limnaea, Lymnaea, Nautilus, Nerite, Planorbis, Pond, Ramshorn, Roman, Slow, Slug, Strombus, Unicorn-shell, Univalve, Wallfish, Whelk, Wing

Snake Adder, Aesculapian, Amphisbaena, Anaconda, Anguine, Anguis, Apod(e), Asp, Bandy-bandy, Berg-adder, Blacksnake, Blind, Blue-racer, Boa, Boma, Boomslang, Brown, Bull, Bush-master, Camoodi, Carpet, Cerastes, Clotho, Coachwhip, Cobra, Coluber, Congo, Constrictor, Copperhead, Coral, Corn, Cottonmouth, Cribo, Crotalidae, Daboia, Death-adder, Dendrophis, Diamond(-back), Dipsas, Drag, Dugite, Elaeis, Elaps, Ellops, Fer-de-lance, Garter, Glass, Gopher, Grass, Habu, Hamadryad, Hognose, Homorelaps, Hoop, Horned viper, Horsewhip, Hydra, Indigo, Jararaca, Jararaka, Joe Blake, Kaa, K(a)rait, King (cobra), Lachesis, Langaha, Mamba, Massasauga, Massasauger, Meander, Milk, Mocassin, Moccasin, Mulga, Naga, Naia, Naja, Ophidian, Pipe, Pit-viper, Plumber's, Puff-adder, Python, Racer, Rat, Rattler, Reptile, Ribbon, Ringhals, Ringneck, Rinkhals, River jack, Rock, Sand viper, Sea, Seps, → **SERPENT**, Sidewinder, Slowworm, Smooth, Spitting, Squamata, Sucurujú, Surucucu, Taipan, Takshaka, Thirst, Thread, Tiger, Timber rattlesnake, Tree, Uraeus, Vasuki, Viper, Water (moccasin), Whip, Wind, Worm

Snake-charmer Lamia

Snake-in-the-grass Peacher, Rat, Traitor

Snake-root Bistort, Senega, Snakeweed, Virginia, White

Snap(per), Snappy, Snap up Alligator, Autolycus, Bite, Break, Brittle, Camera, Click, Cold, Crack, Crocodile, Cross, Curt, Edgy, Fillip, Girnie, Glom, Gnash, Hanch, Knacker, Knap, Livery, Mugshot, Photo, Photogene, Scotch, Snack, Snatch, Spell, Still, Tetchy, Vigour

Snare Bait, Benet, Engine, Enmesh, Entrap, Gin, Grin, Hook, Illaqueate, Inveigle, Net, Noose, Rat-trap, Springe, Springle, Toil, → **TRAP**, Trapen, Trepan, Web, Weel, Wire

Snarl(ing) Chide, Complicate, Cynic, Enmesh, Girn, Gnar(l), Gnarr, Growl, Grumble, Knar, Knot, Snap, Tangle, Yirr

Snatch Claucht, Claught, Excerpt, Fragment, Glom, Grab, Kidnap, Nip, Pluck, Race, Ramp, Rap, Rase, Raunch, Refrain, Snippet, Song, Spell, Steal, Strain, Take, Tweak, Wrap, Wrest

▷ **Snatch** *may indicate* the first letter of a word

Snazzy Cat

Snead Snath

Sneak(y) Area, Carry-tale, Clipe, Clype, Furtive, Inform, Lurk, Mumblenews, Nim, Peak, Scunge, Skulk, Slink, Slip, Slyboots, Snitch, Snoop, Split, Steal, Stoolie,

Surreptitious, Tell(-tale), Underhand
Sneer(ing) Barb, Critic, Cynical, Fleer, Gibe, Jeer, Scoff, Smirk, Snide, Twitch
Sneeze (at), Sneezing Atishoo, Neese, Neeze, Ptarmic, Scorn, Sternutation
Snick Click, Cut, Edge, Glance
Snicker Snigger, Titter, Whinny
Snide Bitchy, Shand
Sniff Inhale, Nose, Nursle, Nuzzle, Scent, Smell, Snivel, Snort, Snuffle, Vent, Whiff
Snigger Giggle, Laugh, Snicker, Snirtle, Titter, Whicker
Snip(pet) Bargain, Cert, Clip, Cut, Doddle, Piece, Sartor, Snatch, Snick, Tailor
Snipe(r) Bird, Bushwhacker, Criticise, Franc-tireur, Gutter, Heather-bleat(er), Heather-bluiter, Heather-blutter, Pick off, Scape, Shoot, Walk, Wisp
Snitch Conk, Konk, Nose
Snivel Blubber, Snotter, Snuffle, Weep, Whine
Snob(bery), Snobbish Cobbler, Crachach, Crispin, High-hat, Inverted, Scab, Side, Snooty, Soutar, Souter, Sowter, Toffee-nose, Vain, Vamp
Snooker Pool, Stimie, Stimy, Stym(i)e
Snoop(er) Meddle, Nose, Pry, Tec
Snooty Bashaw, Snob(bish)
Snooze Calk, Caulk, Dove, Doze, Nap, Nod, Siesta, Sleep
Snore, Snoring Rhonchus, Rout, Snort, Snuffle, Stertorous, Zz
Snort(er) Dram, Drink, Grunt, Nare, Nasal, Roncador, Snore, Toot
Snot(ty) Mucoid
Snout Bill, Boko, Cigar, Gasper, Gruntie, Informer, Muzzle, Nose, Nozzle, Proboscis, Schnozzle, Tinker, Tobacco, Wall
Snow(y), Snowstorm Brig, Buran, Cocaine, Coke, Corn, Cornice, Crud, Firn, Flake, Flurry, Graupel, Half-pipe, Heroin, Marine, Mogul, Neve, Nival, Niveous, Nivose, Oncome, Onding, Powder, Red, Sastruga, Sleet, Spotless, Stall, Virga, White-out, Wintry, Wreath, Yellow, Zastruga
Snowball Accelerate, Cramp-bark, Cumulative, Guelder-rose, Increase, Magnify, Opulus, Pelt, Rose
Snowdrop Avalanche, Eirlys
Snowflake Leucojum, St Agnes' flower
Snow-goose Wav(e)y
Snowman Abominable, Eskimo, Junkie, Sherpa, Yeti
Snowmobile Sno-cat
Snowshoe Bear paw, Racket, Racquet
Snub Cut, Diss, Go-by, Lop, Pug, Put-down, Quelch, Rebuff, Reproof, Retroussé, Set-down, Short, Slap, Slight, Sloan, Sneap, Snool, Wither
Snuff(le) Asarabacca, Dout, Errhine, Extinguish, Maccabaw, Maccaboy, Maccoboy, Ptarmic, Pulvil, Rappee, Smother, Snaste, Sneesh(an), Sniff, Snift, Snush, Tobacco, Vent
Snuffbox Anatomical, Mill, Mull
Snug(gle) Burrow, Cose, → **cosy**, Couthie, Couthy, Croodle, Cubby, Cuddle, Embrace, Lion, Neat, Nestle, Nuzzle, Rug, Snod, Tight, Trim
So Argal, Ergo, Forthy, Hence, Sae, Sic(h), Sol, Therefore, This, Thus, True, Very, Yes
Soak(ed) Bate, Bath(e), Beath, Bewet, Bloat, Blot, Buck, Cree, Deluge, Drench, Drink, Drook, Drouk, Drown, Drunk, Duck, Dunk, Embay, Embrue, Fleece, Grog, Imbrue, Impregnate, Infuse, Lush, Macerate, Marinate, Mop, Oncome, Permeate, Plastered, Rait, Rate, Ret(t), Rinse, Rob, Saturate, Seep, Sipe, Sog, Sop, Souce, Souse, Sows(s)e, Steep, Sype, Thwaite, Toper, Wet
Soap(y), Soap opera Cake, Carbolic, Castile, Eluate, Flake, Flannel, Flattery, Green,

Hard, Joe, Lather, Marine, Metallic, Moody, Mountain, Pears®, Pinguid, Saddle, Safrole, Saponaceous, Saponin, Sawder, Shaving, Slime, Soft, Spanish, Suds, Sudser, Sugar, Syndet, Tablet, Tall-oil, Toheroa, Toilet, Washball, Windsor, Yellow

Soapstone French chalk, Spanish chalk, Steatite, Talc

Soar(ing) Ascend, Essorant, Fly, Glide, Hilum, Plane, Rise, Tower, Zoom

Sob (stuff) Blub(ber), Boohoo, Goo, Gulp, Lament, Singult, Singultus, Snotter, Wail, Weep, Yoop

Sober(sides) Abstemious, Calm, Demure, Pensive, Sedate, Staid, Steady, TT

Sobriquet Byname, Cognomen, Nickname, To-name

So-called Alleged, Nominal, Soi-disant

Sociable, Sociability Affable, Camaraderie, Chummy, Clubby, Cosy, Extravert, Extrovert, Folksy, Friendly, Genial, Gregarious, Phatic

Social(ise) Convivial, Hobnob, Hui, Mingle, Mix, Musicale, Phatic, Tea-dance, Yancha

Socialism, Socialist Ba'(a)th, Champagne, Chartist, Dergue, Engels, Fabian, Fourierism, Guild, ILP, International, Karmathian, Lansbury, Left(y), Marxism, Menchevik, Menchevist, National, Nihilism, Owen(ist), Owenite, Parlour pink, Pinko, Red, Revisionist, St Simonist, Sandinista, Spartacist, Utopian, Webb

Socialite Deb, Sloane

Society Affluent, Association, Band of Hope, Beau monde, Benefit, Body, Broederbond, Building, Camorra, Carbonari, Class, Club, College, Company, Conger, Co-op, Cooperative, Culture, Danite, Defenders, Dorcas, Eleutheri, Elite, Elks, Fabian, Fashion, Foresters, Freemans, Freemasons, Friendly, Friends, Glee club, Grand monde, Grotian, Group, Guarantee, Guilds, Haut monde, Hetairia, High, Humane, Illuminati, Institute, Invincibles, John Birch, Ku-Klux-Klan, Kyrle, Law, Linnean, Lodge, Mafia, Malone, Masonic, Mau-Mau, Ménage, Molly Maguire, National, Oddfellows, Oral, Orangemen, Oratory, Order, Permissive, Phi Beta Kappa, Plunket, Plural, Pop, Provident, Repertory, Ribbonism, Rosicrucian, Rotary, Royal, S, School, Secret, Soc, Soroptomist, Sorority, Stakeholder, Surveillance, Tammany, Theosophical, Toc H, Ton, Tong, Triad, U, Whiteboy, World

Sociologist Weber

Sock(s) Argyle, Argyll, Biff, Bobby, Bootee, Digital, Hose(n), Lam, Leg warmer, Punch, Rock, Slipper, Slosh, Strike, Tabi, Trainer, Walk, Wind

Socket Acetabulum, Alveole, Budget, Gudgeon, Hollow, Hosel, Hot shoe, Jack, Nave, Nozzle, Ouch, Outlet, Pod, Point, Port, Power-point, Shoe, Strike, Torulus, Whip

Sock-eye Nerka, Salmon

Socrates, Socratic Ironist, Maieutics, Sage

Sod Clump, Delf, Delph, Divot, Fail, Gazo(o)n, Mool, Mould, Mouls, Scraw, Sward, Turf

Soda, Sodium Acmite, Arfvedsonite, Baking, Barilla, Bicarb, Caustic, Club, Cream, La(u)rvikite, Na, Natrium, Natron, Reh, Saleratus, Splash, Trona, Washing

Sofa Canapé, Chesterfield, Couch, Daybed, Divan, Dos-à-dos, Dosi-do, Ottoman, Settee, Squab, Tête-à-tête

So far (as) As, As yet, Quoad, Until, Yonder

Soft(en), Softener, Softening, Softly Amalgam, Anneal, B, BB, Blet, Boodle, Calm, Casefy, Cedilla, Cree, Dim, Dolcemente, Doughy, Ease, Emolliate, Emollient, Flabby, Gentle, Hooly, Humanise, Intenerate, Lash, Lax, Lenient, Lenition, Limp, Low, Macerate, Malacia, Malax(ate), Malleable, Mardarse, Mardie, Mease, Mellow, Melt, Mild, Milksop, Mitigate, Modulate, Mollify, Mollities, Morendo, Mulch, Mush(y), Mute, Neale, Nesh, Option, P, Palliate, Pastel, Piano, Plushy, Porous, Propitiate, Rait, Rate, Relent, Scumble, Sentimental, Silly, Slack, Squashy, Squidgy,

Squishy, Sumph, Talcose, Temper, → **TENDER**, Tone, Velvet, Weak

Softness Lenity

▶ **Software** *see* **COMPUTER SOFTWARE**

Sog(gy) Goop, Sodden

Soil(ed), Soily Acid, Adscript, Agrology, Agronomy, Alkali(ne), Alluvium, Azonal, Backfill, Bedraggle, Chemozem, Clay, Cohesive, Defile, Desecrate, Desert, Dinge, Dirt(y), Discolour, Earth, Edaphic, Frictional, Gault, Glebe, Grey, Grimy, Ground, Gumbo, Hotbed, Humus, Illuvium, Intrazonal, Lair, Land, Latosol, Lithosol, Loam, Loess, Lome, Loss, Mire, Mool, Mo(u)ld, Mud, Mulch, Mull, Night, Peat, Ped, Pedalfer, Pedocal, Pedology, Phreatic, Planosol, Podsol, Podzol, Prairie, Pure, Regar, Regolith, Regosol, Regur, Rendzina, Rhizosphere, Root-ball, Sal, Sedentary, Smudge, Smut, Solonchak, Solonetz, Solum, Soot, Stain, Stonebrash, Sub, Sully, Tarnish, Tash, Terrain, Terricolous, Tilth, Top, Tschernosem, Udal, Umber, Virgin, Yarfa, Yarpha, Zonal

Soirée Drum, Levee, Musicale

Sojourn Abide, Respite, Stay, Tarry

Sol G, Soh, Sun

Solace Cheer, Comfort

Solar(ium) Heliacal, Tannery

Sold Had

Solder Braze, Join, Spelter, Tin, Weld

Soldier(s) Achilles, Alpini, Amazon, Ant, Anzac, Army, Arna(o)ut, Askari, Atkins, ATS, Banner, Bashi-Bazouk, Battalion, Bersaglier(e), Blue beret, Bluecoat, Bluff, Bod, Bombardier, Borderer, Botha, Brave, Brigade, Buff-coat, Buff-jerkin, Butter-nut, Cadet, Caimac(am), Campaigner, Cannoneer, Cannon-fodder, Car(a)bineer, Car(a)binier, Cataphract, Centinel(l), Centonel(l), Centurion, Chasseur, Chindit, Chocko, Choco, Chocolate, Cohort, Colonel, Colours, Commando, Confederate, Contingent, Cornet, Corp(s), Cossack, Crusader, Cuirassier, Ded, Desert rat, Detail, Digger, Dog-face, Doughboy, Draftee, Dragoon, Dugout, Emmet, Engineer, Enomoty, Evzone, Fag(g)ot, Federal, Fencibles, Fighter, Flanker, Foederatus, Foot, Forlorn-hope, Fugleman, Fusilier, Fuzzy-wuzzy, Fyrd, Gallo(w)glass, Galoot, General, GI, GI Joe, Gippo, Goorkha, Grenadier, Greycoat, Grim dig, Grunt, Guardee, Guardsman, Guerilla, Gurkha, Gyppo, Hackbuteer, Hobbler, Hoplite, Hussar, Immortal, Impi, Inf(antry), Iron Duke, Ironside, Irregular, Jackman, Janissary, Janizary, Jawan, Joe, Johnny Reb(el), Kaimakam, Kern(e), Kitchener, Knight, Lancer, Landsknecht, Lansquenet, Lashkar, Leatherneck, Legionary, Legionnaire, Levy, Line, Linesman, Lobster, Maniple, Martinet, Men-at-arms, Miles (gloriosus), Militiaman, Miner, Minuteman, Missileer, Musketeer, Nahal, Naik, Nasute, Nizam, Non-com, Old Bill, Old Contemptibles, Old moustache, OR, Orderly, Palatine, Palikar, Pandoor, Pandour, Pandy, Paratroop, Partisan, Peltast, Peon, Perdu(e), Persevere, Phalanx, Pikeman, Piou-piou, Pistoleer, Platoon, Poilu, Point man, Pongo, Post, POW, Private, Rajput, Ranger, Rank(er), Rank and file, Rapparree, Rat-tail, Reb, Redcoat, Reformado, Regiment, Regular, Reiter, Reservist, Retread, Rifleman, Rutter, Sabre, Saddler, Sammy, Samurai, SAS, Sebundy, Sentinel, Sepoy, Serviceman, Signaller, Silladar, Snarler, So(d)ger, Soldado, Sowar(ee), Sowarry, Spearman, Squaddie, Squaddy, Stalhelm(er), Stormtrooper, Strelitz, Subaltern, Swad(dy), Sweat, Targeteer, Tarheel, Templar, Terrier, Territorial, Timariot, Tin, Tommy, Toy, Train-band, Trencher, Trooper, Troops, Turco(pole), Uhlan, Unknown, Velites, Vet(eran), Voltigeur, Volunteer, Wagon, Warhorse, Warmonger, Warrior, Whitecoat, Wild Geese, Woodbind, Woodbine, Yardbird, Yeoman, Zouave

▷ **Soldiers** *may indicate* bread for boiled eggs

Sole, Solitaire Alone, Anchoret, Anchorite, Clump, Convex, Dover, Dropped, Fish, Incommunicado, Lemon, Lonesome, Megrim, Merl, Meunière, Monastical, Monkish, Only, Pad, Palm, Patience, Pelma, Planta(r), Plantigrade, Platform, Recluse, Scaldfish, Single(ton), Skate, Slip, Smear-dab, Tap, Thenar, Tread, Unique, Vibram®, Vola

Solemn Agelast, Austere, Devout, Earnest, Grave, Gravitas, Impressive, Majestic, Owlish, Po-faced, Sacred, Sedate, Serious, Sober, Sobersides, Sombre

Solent Lee

Solicit Accost, Approach, Ask, Attract, Bash, → **BEG**, Canvass, Commission, Cottage, Drum up, Importun(at)e, Plead, Ply, Proposition, Speer, Speir, Tout, Woo

Solicitor(s) Advocate, Attorney, Avoué, Beggar, Canvasser, Hallanshaker, Law-agent, Lawyer, Notary, Official, Side-bar, SL, Tout, Trull, Writer to the Signet, WS

Solid(arity), Solidify Cake, Chunky, Clot, Clunky, Compact, Comradeship, Concrete, Cone, Congeal, Consolidate, Cube, Cylinder, Dense, Enneahedron, Esprit de corps, Ethan, Firm, Foursquare, Freeze, Frustrum, Fuchsin(e), Gel, Hard, Holosteric, Impervious, Kotahitanga, Masakhane, Merbromin, Octahedron, Pakka, Petrarchan, Platonic, Polyhedron, Prism, Pucka, Pukka, Purin(e), Robust, Set, Skatole, Stilbene, Sublimate, Substantial, Tetrahedron, Thick, Unanimous

Solipsism Egotism, Panegoism

Solitary Antisocial, Friendless

▶ **Solitary** *see* **SOLE**

Solitude Privacy, Seclusion

Solo Aria, Cadenza, Cavatine, Concertante, Lone, Monodrama, Monody, Ombre, One-man, Scena, Variation

Solon Sage

So long Cheerio, Ciao, Goodbye, Tata

Solstice Summer, Tropic, Winter

Soluble Alkaline, Consolute, Surfactant

Solution Acetone, Alkali, Ammonia, Amrit, → **ANSWER**, Austenite, Benedict's, Collodion, Colloidal, Dakin's, Dobell's, Éclaircissement, Electrolyte, Elixir, Emulsion, Eusol, Fehling's, Final, Key, Leachate, Limewater, Lixivium, Lye, Normal, Oleoresin, Rationale, Reducer, Ringer's, Rinse, Rubber, Saline, Solid, Solvent, Soup, Standard, Suspensoid, Tincture, Titrate, Viscose

▷ **Solution** *may indicate* an anagram

Solve(d), Solver Absolve, Assoil, Calculate, Casuist, Clear, Crack, Decode, Holmes, Loast, Loose, Read(er), Suss out, Troubleshoot, Unclew, Undo, Unriddle, Work

Solvent Acetaldehyde, Acetone, Afloat, Alcahest, Aldol, Alkahest, Anisole, Aqua-regia, Banana oil, Chloroform, Cleanser, Cyclohexane, Cyclopentane, Cymene, Decalin, Diluent, Dioxan(e), Eleunt, Eluant, Ether, Funded, Furan, Hexane, Ligroin, Megilp, Menstruum, Methanol, Methylal, Naphtha, Paraldehyde, Picoline, Protomic, Pyridine, Sound, Stripper, Terebene, Terpineol, Tetrachloromethane, Thinner, Thiophen, Toluene, Toluol, Trike, Trilene, Turpentine

Sombre Dark, Drab, Drear, Dull, Gloomy, Grave, Morne, Morose, Subfusc, Subfusk, Sullen, Triste

Some Any, Arrow, Ary, Certain, Divers, Few, One, Part, Portion, Quota, These, They, Wheen

▷ **Some** *may indicate* a hidden word

Somebody Dignitary, Name, Notable, One, Person, Quidam, Someone, → **VIP**

Somehow Somegate

▷ **Somehow** *may indicate* an anagram

Somersault Back-flip, Barani, Deltcher, Flip(-flap), Flip-flop, Handspring, Pitchpole, Pitchpoll

Something Aliquid, Chattel, Matter, Object, Summat, What, Whatnot

Sometime(s) Erstwhile, Ex, Former, Occasional, Off and on, Quondam

Somewhat Bit, -ish, Mite, Partly, Quasi, Quite, Rather, Relatively

Somewhere Somegate

Son Boy, Descendant, Disciple, Epigon(e), Fils, Fitz, Lad, Lewis, M(a)c, Native, Offspring, Prodigal, Progeny, Scion

Song Air, Amoret, Anthem, Antistrophe, Aria, Art, Aubade, Ayre, Ballad, Ballant, Ballata, Barcarol(l)e, Belter, Berceuse, Bhajan, Blues, Brindisi, Burden, Burthen, Cabaletta, Calypso, Cancionero, Canticle, Cantilena, Cantion, Canzona, Canzone, Canzonet(ta), Carmagnole, Carol, Catch, Cavatina, Chanson, Cha(u)nt, Come-all-ye, Conductus, Corn-kister, Corroboree, Cycle, Descant, Dirge, Dithyramb, Ditty, Epithalamion, Epithalamium, Fado, Fit, Flamenco, Folk, Forebitter, Gita, Glee, Gorgia, Gradual, Hillbilly, Hum, Hymeneal, Hymn, Internationale, Jug(-jug), Lament, Lay, Lied(er), Lilt, Lullaby, Lyric, Madrigal, Magnificat, Marseillaise, Matin, Melic, Melisma, Melody, Mento, Negro spiritual, Noel, Number, Nunc dimittis, Oat, Paean, Pane, Part, Patter, Pennillion, Plain, Plaint, Plantation, Pop, Prick, Prothalamion, Prothalamium, Psalm, Qawwali, Rap, Recitativo, Relish, Rhapsody, Rispetto, Roulade, Roundelay, Rune, Scat, Scolion, Sea-shanty, Secular, Serenade, Shanty, Shosholoza, Siren, Sirvente, Skolion, Sososholoza, Spiritual, Stave, Stomper, Strain, Strophe, Swan, Taps, Tenebrae, Theme, Torch, Trill, Tune, Tyrolienne, Villanella, Volkslied, Waiata, War, Warble, Wassail, Waulking, Yodel, Yodle

Songbook Cancionero, Hymnal, Kommersbuch, Libretto, Psalter

Songsmith, Songwriter Carmichael, Dowland, Espla, Foster, Kern, Minot, Waitz, Zappa

Sonnet Amoret, Elizabethan, English, Italian, Miltonic, Petrarch(i)an, Shakespearean, Shakespearian, Spenserian

Sonometer Monochord

Soon(er) Anon, Directly, Erelong, Lief, OK, Oklahoma, Presently, Shortly, Tight, Timely, Tit(ely), Tite, Tyte

Soot(y) Colly, Coom, Crock, Fuliginous, Gas black, Grime, Lampblack, Smut, Speck

Soothe, Soothing Accoy, Allay, Anetic, Anodyne, Appease, Assuage, Bucku, Calm, Compose, Demulcent, Dulcet, Emollient, Irenic, Lenitive, Lull, Mellifluous, Mollify, Pacific, Paregoric, Poultice, Quell, Rock

Soothsayer Astrologer, Augur, Calchas, Chaldee, Divine, Forecaster, Haruspex, Melampus, Oracle, Picus, Prophet, Pythoness, → **SEER**, Shipton, Tiresias

Sop Appease, Berry, Douceur, Rait, Ret, Sponge

Sophist(ic) Casuist, Elenchic, Quibbler

Sophisticate(d) Blasé, Boulevardier, City slicker, Civilised, Cosmopolitan, Couth, Doctor, High-end, Patrician, Polished, Sative, Slicker, Svelte, Urbane, Worldly

▷ **Sophoclean** *may indicate* Greek (alphabet, etc)

Sophomore Semie

Soporific Barbiturate, Bromide, Drowsy, Halothane, Hypnotic, Lullaby, Narcotic, Opiate, Sedative, Tedious

Soppiness, Soppy Maudlin, Schwärmerei, Sloppy, Slushy

Soprano Caballé, Castrato, Crespin, Descant, Lind, Patti, Treble

Sorb Wend

Sorbet Water ice

Sorcerer, Sorceress, Sorcery Angakok, Ashipu, Circe, Conjury, Diablerie, Hoodoo, Kadaitcha, Kurdaitcha, Lamia, Mage, Magian, Magic(ian), Magus, Medea, Merlin, Morgan le Fay, Mother Shipton, Necromancer, Obi, Pishogue, Shaman, Sortilege, Venefic(ious), Voodoo, Warlock, Witch, Witch knot, Wizard

Sordid Base, Low-life, Miserable, Scungy, Seamy, Sleazy, Squalid, Vile

Sore(ly), Sores Abrasion, Anthrax, Bitter, Blain, Boil, Canker, Chancre, Chap, Chilblain, Cold, Dearnly, Felon, Gall, Impost(h)ume, Ireful, Kibe, Nasty, Pressure, Quitter, Quittor, Raw, Running, Rupia(s), Saddle, Sair, Shiver, Sitfast, Surbate, Ulcer(s), Whitlow, Wound

Sore throat Garget, Prunella, Quinsy, Tonsillitis

Sorghum Kaoliang, Milo

Sorrel Common, French, Hetty, Mountain, Oca, Roman, Sheep, Soar(e), Sore, Sourock

Sorrow(ful) Affliction, Distress, Dole, Dolente, Dolour, Emotion, Fee-grief, → GRIEF, Lament, Misery, Nepenthe, Ochone, Penance, Pietà, Remorse, Rue, Triste, Wae, Waugh, Wirra, Woe, Yoop

Sorry Ashamed, Contrite, Miserable, Oops, Penitent, Pitiful, Poor, Regretful, Relent, Wretched

▷ **Sorry** *may indicate* an anagram

Sort(ing) Arrange, Brand, Breed, Category, Character, Classify, Collate, Drive, Grade, → KIND, Nature, Pranck(e), Prank, Sift, Species, Stamp, Tidy, Triage, Type, Variety

Sortie Attack, Foray, Mission, Outfall, Raid, Sally

▶ **Sorts** *see* OUT OF SORTS

So-so Average, Indifferent, Mediocre, Middling

So to speak Quasi

▷ **So to speak** *may indicate* 'sound of'

Sotto voce Murmur, Whisper

▶ **Soubriquet** *see* SOBRIQUET

Sough Rustle, Sigh

Soul(ful) Alma, Ame, Anima, Animist, Atman, Ba, Bardo, Brevity, Deep, Entelechy, Eschatology, Expressive, Heart, Inscape, Ka, Larvae, Lost, Manes, Object, Person, Pneuma, Psyche, Saul, Shade, Spirit, Universal

Sound(ed), Soundness, Sound system Accurate, Ach-laut, Acoustic, Affricate, Albemarle, Allophone, Alveolar, Amphoric, Audio, Bay, Bleep, Blip, Blow, Boing, Bong, Breathed, Cacophony, Chime, Chirr(e), Chord, Chug, Clam, Clang, Clink, Clop, Clunk, Consistent, Continuant, Dah, Dental, Dit, Dive, Dolby®, Dream, Echo, Euphony, Fast, Fathom, Fere, Fettle, Fit, Foley, Glide, Good, Hale, Harmonics, Healthy, Hearty, Hi-fi, Ich-laut, Inlet, Islay, Jura, Kalmar, Knell, Kyle, Labiodental, Lo-fi, Long Island, Lucid, Mach, Madrilene, McMurdo, Mersey, Milford, Mouillé, Musak, Music, Narrow, → NOISE, Onomatopaeia, Oompah, Optical, Orate, Orthodox, Palatal, Palato-alveolar, Pamlico, Paragog(u)e, Peal, Pectoriloquy, Phone(me), Phonetic, Phonic, Phonology, Pitter(-patter), Plap, Plink, Plonk, Plop, Plosion, Plumb, Plummet, Plunk, Plymouth, Probe, Puget, Put-put, Quadraphonic(s), Quadrophonic(s), Rale, Rational, Real, Reliable, Ring, Roach, Robust, Rong, Rumble, Rustle, Sabin, Safe, Sandhi, Sane, S(c)hwa, Scoresby, Sensurround®, Skirl, Solid, Sonance, Sone, Souffle, Sough, Sowne, Splat, Stereo, Stereophony, Strait, Surround, Swish, Tamber, Tannoy®, Thorough, Timbre, Ting, Tone, Toneme, Trig, Triphthong, Trumpet, Twang, Ultrasonic(s), Unharmed, Uvular, Valid, Viable, Voice, Vowel, Wah-wah, Watertight, Well, Whine, Whistle, Whole(some), Whump, Wolf

Sounder Echo, Lead
Sounding board Abat-voix
Soundproof Deaden
Sound-track Dubbing, Movietone®, Stripe
Soup Alphabet, Avgolemono, Bird's nest, Bisk, Bisque, Borsch, Bouillabaisse,
  Bouillon, Brewis, Broth, Burgoo, Chowder, Cock-a-leekie, Cockieleekie,
  Cockyleeky, Consommé, Duck, Garbure, Gazpacho, Gomb(r)o, Gruel, Gumbo,
  Harira, Hoosh, Julienne, Kail, Kale, Madrilene, Marmite, Mess, Minestrone, Mock
  turtle, Mulligatawny, Oxtail, Palestine, Pea(se), Pot-au-feu, Pot(t)age, Primordial,
  Puree, Ramen, Rice, Rubaboo, Sancoche, Scotch broth, Shchi, Shtchi, Skilligalee,
  Skilligolee, Skilly, Skink, Stock, Tattie-claw, Toheroa, Turtle, Vichyssoise
▷ **Soup** *may indicate* an anagram
Soupçon Thought, Touch
Sour(puss) Acerb, Acescent, Acid, Acidulate, Alegar, Bitter, Citric, Crab, Eager,
  Esile, Ferment, Moody, Stingy, Subacid, → TART, Turn, Unamiable, Verjuice,
  Vinegarish
Source Authority, Basis, Bottom, Centre, Closed, Database, Derivation, Egg, Fons,
  Font, Fount, Fountain-head, Germ, Head-stream, Literary, Mine, Mother, Neutron,
  Origin, Parent, Pi, Pion, Point, Provenance, Quarry, Reference, Rise, Riverhead,
  Root, Seat, Seed, Spring, Springhead, Stock, Supply, Urn, Well, Wellhead,
  Wellspring, Widow's cruse, Ylem
Sour milk Curds, Smetana, Whey, Whig, Yogh(o)urt
Souse Beath, Duck, Immerse, Pickle, Plunge, Soak, Spree, Steep
South(ern), Southerner Austral, Confederacy, Dago, Decanal, Decani, Deep,
  Dixieland, Meridian, Meridional, S
South Africa(n) Azania, Bantu, Caper, Ciskei, Grikwa, Griqua, Hottentot, Kaf(f)ir,
  Qwaqwa, SA, Soutie, Soutpiel, Springbok, Swahili, Xhosa, ZA, Zulu
South American Araucanian, Arawak, Argentino, Aymara, Bolivian, Carib, Chibcha,
  Chilean, Galibi, Guarani, Inca, Jivaro, Kechua, Latin, Llanero, Mam, Mapuchi,
  Mayan, Mixe-Zogue, Mixtac, Mochica, Quechua, SA, Shuar, Tapuyan, Tupi
Southwark Boro'
Souvenir Keepsake, Memento, Relic, Remembrance, Scalp, Token, Trophy
Sovereign(ty), Sovereign remedy Anne, Autocrat, Bar, Condominium, Couter,
  Dominant, ER, Goblin, Haemony, Harlequin, Imperial, Imperium, James, King,
  L, Liege, Nizam, Pound, Quid, Rangatiratanga, Royalty, Ruler, Shiner, Supreme,
  Swaraj, Synarchy, Thick' un, Thin' un
Soviet Circassian, Council, Estonian, Russian, Stalin, Supreme, Volost
Sow(ing) Catchcrop, Elt, Foment, Gilt, Inseminate, Plant, Scatter, Seed, Sprue,
  Strew, Yelt
Soya Sitosterol, Tempe(h)
Spa Baden, Baden-Baden, Bath, Buxton, Evian, Godesberg, Harrogate, Hydro,
  Kurhaus, Kursaal, Leamington, Vichy
Space(d), Spacing, Spacious, Spaceman Abyss, Acre, Area, Areola, Bay,
  Bracket, Breathing, Cellule, Cislunar, Clearing, C(o)elom, Coelome, Compluvium,
  Concourse, Contline, Crookes, Cubbyhole, Deep, Diastema, Distal, Distance,
  Elbow-room, Esplanade, Ether, Exergue, Expanse, Extent, Flies, Footprint,
  Forecourt, Freeband, Gagarin, Gap, Glade, Glenn, Goaf, Gob, Gutter, Hair,
  Hash(mark), Headroom, Homaloid, Indention, Inner, Intergalactic, Interim,
  Interlinear, Interplanetary, Interstellar, Interstice, Invader, Kerning, Killogie,
  Kneehole, Lacuna, Lair, Leading, Lebensraum, Legroom, Life, Logie, Lumen,
  Lunar, Lung, Machicolation, Maidan, Metope, Mihrab, Minkowski, Muset,

Musit, Orbit, Outer, Palatial, Parvis(e), Peridrome, Personal, Plenum, Polemics, Pomoerium, Priest hole, Proportional, Quad, Retrochoir, Riemannian, → **ROOM**, Ruelle, Sample, Sheets, Shelf room, Slot, Spandrel, Spandril, Step, Storage, Third, Topological, Tympanum, Ullage, Uncluttered, Vacuole, Vacuum, Vast, Vector, Void

Spacecraft, Space agency, Space object, Spaceship, Space station Apollo, Capsule, Columbia, Deep Space, Explorer, Galileo, Genesis, Giotto, Lander, LEM, Luna, Lunik, Mariner, MIR, Module, NASA, Orbiter, Pioneer, Probe, Quasar, Ranger, Salyut, Shuttle, Skylab, Soyuz, Sputnik, Starship, Tardis, Viking, Vostok, Voyager, Zond

Space walk EVA

Spade Breastplough, Caschrom, Cas crom, Castrato, Detective, Flaughter, Graft, Loy, Negro, Paddle, Pattle, Peat, Pettle, Pick, S, Shovel, Slane, Spit, Suit, Turf, Tus(h)kar, Tus(h)ker, Twiscar

Spain E, Hesperia, Iberia

Spalpeen Sinner

Span Age, Arch, Attention, Bestride, Bridge, Chip, Ctesiphon, Extent, Life, Memory, Range, Timescale

Spangle(d) Avanturine, Aventurine, Glitter, Instar, O, Paillette, Sequin

Spaniard, Spanish Alguacil, Alguazil, Andalusian, Barrio, Basque, Cab, Caballero, Carlist, Castilian, Catalan, Chicano, Dago, Don, Fly, Grandee, Hidalgo, Hispanic, José, Main, Mestizo, Mozarab, Pablo, Papiamento, Señor, Spic(k), Spik

Spaniel Blenheim, Cavalier, Clumber, Cocker, Crawler, Creep, Dog, Fawner, Field, Irish water, King Charles, Maltese, Papillon, Placebo, Skip-kennel, Springer, Sussex, Tibetan, Toad-eater, Toady, Toy, Water, Welsh springer

Spank(ing) Cob, Paddywhack, Rapid, Scud, Slap, Slipper, Sprack

Spanner Arc, Box, Bridge, Clapper, Key, Ring, Shifter, Shifting, Socket, Torque, Wrench

Spar Barite, Barytes, Blue John, Boom, Bowsprit, Box, Cauk, Cawk, Fight, Gaff, Iceland, Jib-boom, Mainyard, Manganese, Martingale, Mast, Nail-head, Outrigger, Rafter, Rail, Ricker, Schiller, Shearleg, Sheerleg, Snotter, Spathic, Sprit, Steeve, Stile, Tabular, Triatic, Whiskerboom, Whiskerpole, Yard

Spare, Sparing Angular, Cast-off, Dup(licate), Economical, Free, Frugal, Gash, Gaunt, Hain, Lean, Lenten, Other, Pardon, Reserve, Rib, Save, Scant, Skimp, Slender, Stint, Subsecive, Thin

Spark Animate, Arc, Beau, Blade, Bluette, Dandy, Flash, Flaught, Funk, Ignescent, Kindle, Life, Muriel, Quenched, Scintilla, Smoulder, Spunk, Trigger, Vital, Zest

Sparkle(r), Sparkling Aerated, Aventurine, Bling, Coruscate, Crémant, Diamanté, Effervesce, Élan, Emicate, Fire, Fizz, Flicker, Frizzante, Glamour, Glint, Glisten, Glitter, Life, Pétillant, Scintillate, Seltzer, Seltzogene, Spangle, Spritzig, Spumante, Twinkle, Verve, Witty, Zap

Sparrow Bird, Cape, Chipping, Hedge, Isaac, Java, Junco, Mah-jong(g), Mossie, Passerine, Piaf, Prunella, Song, Spadger, Speug, Sprug(gy), Titling, Tree

Sparrow-grass Asparagus, Sprue

Sparse Meagre, Rare, Scant, Thin

Spartan(s) Austere, Basic, Enomoty, Hardy, Helot, Heraclid, Lacedaemonian, Laconian, Lysander, Menelaus, Severe, Valiant

Spasm(s), Spasmodic Blepharism, Chorea, Clonus, Convulsive, Cramp, Crick, Fit(ful), Hiccup, Hippus, Hyperkinesis, Intermittent, Irregular, → **JERK**, Kink, Laryngismus, Nystagmus, Paroxysm, Periodical, Start, Strangury, Tetany, Throe, Tonic, Tonus, Trismus, Twinge, Twitch, Vaginismus, Writer's cramp

▷ **Spasmodic** *may indicate* an anagram

Spastic Athetoid, Clonic, Jerky

Spat(s) Bicker, Brattle, Gaiters, Legging, Quarrel, Shower, Tiff

Spate Flood, Sluice, Torrent

Spatter Disject, Ja(u)p, Scatter, Splash, Splosh, Spot, Sprinkle

▷ **Spattered** *may indicate* an anagram

Spawn(ing), Spawning place Anadromous, Blot, Fry, Progeny, Propagate, Redd, Roud, Seed, Spat, Spet, Spit

Speak(er), Speaking Address, Articulate, Broach, Chat, Cicero, Collocuter, Communicate, Converse, Coo, Declaim, Dilate, Discourse, Diseur, Dwell, Effable, Elocution, Eloquent, Expatiate, Express, Extemporise, Filibuster, Intercom, Intone, Inveigh, Jabber, Jaw, Lip, Loq, Mang, Mention, Mike, Mina, Mouth, Mouthpiece, Nark, Native, Open, Orate, Orator, Palaver, Parlance, Parley, Perorate, Pontificate, Prate, Preach, Prelector, Rhetor, → **SAY**, Sayne, Spout, Spruik, Squawk box, Stump, Talk, Tannoy®, Tongue, Trap, Tub-thumper, Tweeter, Utter, Voice, Waffle, Witter, Word

Speakeasy Fluent, Shebeen

Spear Ash, Asparagus, Assagai, Assegai, Barry, Dart, Fishgig, Fizgig, Gad, Gavelock, Gig, Glaive, Gleave, Gum digger's, Gungnir, Hastate, Impale, Javelin, Lance(gay), Launcegaye, Leister, Morris-pike, Partisan, Pierce, Pike, Pilum, Prong, Skewer, Spike, Trident, Trisul(a), Waster

Spear-rest Feutre, Fewter

Special Ad hoc, Constable, Designer, Distinctive, Extra, Important, Notable, Notanda, Particular, Peculiar, S, Specific

Specialise, Specialist(s) Authority, Concentrate, Connoisseur, Consultant, ENT, Expert, Illuminati, Maestro, Major, Quant, Recondite, Technician

Species Class, Genre, Genus, Indicator, Infirma, Kind, Pioneer, Strain, Taxa

Specific(ally), Specified, Specify, Specification Adduce, As, Ascribe, Assign, Concretize, Cure, Define, Detail, Explicit, Full-blown, Itemise, Medicine, Namely, Precise, Quantify, Remedy, Sp, Special, State, Stipulate, Stylesheet, The, Trivial

Specimen(s) Example, Exemplar, Imago, Model, Museum piece, Sample, Slide, Swab, Topotype, Type

Specious False, Glib, Hollow, Pageant, Plausible, Spurious

Speck(led) Atom, Bit, Dot, Fleck, Floater, Freckle, Gay, Muscae volitantes, Particle, Peep(e), Pip, Spot, Spreckle, Stud

Spectacle(s), Spectacled, Spectacular Arresting, Barnacles, Bifocals, Blazers, Blinks, Bossers, Cheaters, Colourful, Epic, Escolar, Giglamps, → **GLASSES**, Goggles, Horn-rims, Lorgnette, Lorgnon, Nose-nippers, Oo, Optical, Outspeckle, Pageant, Pince-nez, Pomp, Preserves, Raree-show, Scene, Show, Sight, Son et lumière, Sunglasses, Tamasha, Tattoo, Trifocal, Varifocals

Spectator(s) Audience, Bystander, Dedans, Etagère, Eyer, Gallery, Gate, Groundling, Kibitzer, Observer, Onlooker, Standerby, Witness

Spectograph, Spectometer Aston, Calutron

Spectral, Spectre Apparition, Boggle, Bogy, Brocken, Eidolon, Empusa, Ghost, Idola, Iridal, Larva, Malmag, Phantasm, Phantom, Phasma, Spirit, Spook, Tarsier, Walking-straw, Wraith

Spectrum Absorption, Band, Continuous, Emission, Iris, Optical, Radio, Rainbow, Sunbow, Sundog, Visible, X-ray

Speculate, Speculative, Speculator, Speculation Agiotage, Arbitrage, Bear, Better, Bull, Conjecture, Flier, Flyer, Gamble, Guess, Ideology, If, Imagine, Meditate, Notional, Operate, Pinhooker, Shark, Stag, Theoretical, Theorise, Theory, Thought, Trade, Wonder

Speech, Speech element Accents, Address, Argot, Articulation, Bunkum, Burr, Curtain, Delivery, Dialect, Diatribe, Diction, Direct, Discourse, Dithyramb, Drawl, Éloge, English, Epilogue, Eulogy, Filibuster, Free, Gab, Glossolalia, Grandiloquence, Harangue, Helium, Idiolect, Idiom, Inaugural, Indirect, Jargon, Keynote, King's, Lallation, → **LANGUAGE**, Lingua franca, Litany, Maiden, Monologue, Morph(eme), Motherese, Musar, Oblique, Occlusive, Oral, Oration, Parabasis, Parle, Peroration, Phasis, Philippic, Phonetics, Prolocution, Prolog(ue), Queen's, Reported, Rhetoric, Sandhi, Scanning, Screed, Sermon, Set, Side, Slang, Soliloquy, Stemwinder, Stump, Tagmeme, Talk, Taxeme, Tirade, Tongue, Uptalk, Vach, Visible, Voice, Wawa, Whaikorero, Whistle-stop, Xenoglossia

Speech defect, Speech disease Alogia, Dysarthria, Dysphasia, Dysphoria, Echolalia, Idioglossia, Lallation, Lisp, Palilalia, Paralalia, Paraphasia, Pararthria, Psellism, Rhinolalia, Stammer, Stutter

Speechless Alogia, Dumb, Dumbstruck, Inarticulate, Mute, Silent, Tongue-tied

Speed(ily), Speedy Accelerate, Alacrity, Amain, Amphetamine, Apace, Average, Bat, Belive, Belt, Breakneck, Burn, Cast, Celerity, Clip, Dart, Despatch, DIN, Dispatch, Expedite, Fang, Fast, Film, Fleet, Further, Gait, Gallop, Goer, Group, Gun, Haste, Hie, Hotfoot, Hypersonic, Induce, Instantaneous, Knot, Landing, Lick, Mach, Merchant, MPH, → **PACE**, Phase, Pike, Post-haste, Pronto, Race, Rapidity, Rate, RPS, Rush, Scorch, Scud, Scurr, Skirr, Soon, Spank, Split, Stringendo, Supersonic, Swift, Tach, Tear, Tempo, Ton up, V, Velocity, Ventre à terre, Vroom, Wave, Whid, Wing

Speedwell Brooklime, Fluellin, Germander, Veronica

Spelaean Troglodyte

Spelk Skelf, Splinter

Spell(ing) Abracadabra, Bewitch, Bout, Cantrip, Charm, Conjuration, Do, Elf-shoot, Enchantment, Entrance, Fit, Go, Gri(s)-gri(s), Hex, Incantation, Innings, Jettatura, Juju, Knock, Knur, → **MAGIC**, Mojo, Need-fire, Nomic, Open sesame, Orthography, Period, Philter, Philtre, Phonetic, Pinyin, Relieve, Ride, Romaji, Run, Rune, Scat, Shot, Signify, Sitting, Snap, Snatch, Sorcery, Sp, Span, Spasm, Splinter, Stint, Stretch, Tack, Tour, Trick, Turn, Weird, Whammy, Witchcraft

Spelling-book ABC, Grimoire

Spencer Topcoat, Tracy, Vest

Spend(er), Spending Anticipate, Birl, Blue, Boondoggling, Consume, Deplete, Disburse, Exhaust, Fritter, Lash out, Lay out, Live, Outlay, Pass, Pay, Shopaholic, Splash, Splash out, Splurge, Ware

Spendthrift Essex Man, High-roller, Prodigal, Profligate, Profuser, Scattergood, Wastrel

Spent Consumed, Dead, Done, Expended, Stale, Tired, Used, Weak, Weary

Sperm Seed, Semen

Spew Eject, Emit, Gush, Spit, Vomit

Sphagnum Moss, Peat

Sphere, Spherical Armillary, Attraction, Celestial, Discipline, Earth, Element, Field, Firmament, Globe, Magic, Mound, Orb(it), Planet, Primum mobile, Prolate, Province, Realm, Schwarzschild, Theatre, Wheel

Sphinx Hawk-moth, Oracle, Riddler

Spice, Spicy Amomum, Anise, Aniseed, Aryl, Caraway, Cardamom, Cardamon, Cardamum, Cassareep, Cassaripe, Cinnamon, Clove, Clow, Coriander, Cubeb, Cum(m)in, Dash, Devil, Garam masala, Ginger, Mace, Malaguetta, Marjoram, Masala, Myrrh, Nutmeg, Oregano, Paprika, Peppercorn, Picante, Pimento, Piperic, Piquant, Salsa verde, Season, Stacte, Staragen, Tamal(e), Tamara, Tansy, Tarragon,

Taste, Turmeric, Vanilla, Variety

Spick Dink, Neat, Spike, Tidy

Spicule Sclere, Tetract

Spider(s) Anancy, Ananse, Arachnid, Aranea, Araneida, Arthrapodal, Attercop, Bird, Black widow, Bobbejaan, Cardinal, Cheesemite, Chelicerate, Citigrade, Diadem, Epeira, Epeirid, Ethercap, Ettercap, Funnel-web, Harvester, Harvestman, House, Hunting, Huntsman, Jumping, Katipo, Lycosa, Mite, Money, Mygale, Orb-weaver, Pan, Phalangid, Podogona, Pycnogonid, Red, Redback, Rest, Ricinulei, Saltigrade, Scorpion, Solifugae, Solpuga, Spinner, Strap, Tarantula, Telary, Trapdoor, Violin, Water, Wolf, Zebra

Spiderwort Tradescantia

Spiel Spruik

Spignel Baldmoney, Meu

Spigot Bung, Plug, Tap

Spike(d) Barb, Brod, Calk, Calt(h)rop, Chape, Cloy, Crampon, Ear, Fid, Foil, Gad, Gadling, Goad, Grama, Herissé, Icicle, Impale, Lace, Locusta, Marlin(e), Nail, Needle, → **PIERCE**, Point, Pricket, Prong, Puseyite, Rod, Sharp, Shod, Skewer, Spadix, Spear, Spicate, Spicule, Spire, Strobiloid, Tang, Thorn, Tine

Spill(age) Divulge, Drop, Fidibus, Jackstraw, Lamplighter, Leakage, Let, Overflow, Overset, Reveal, Scail, Scale, Shed, Skail, Slart, Slop, Stillicide, Taper, Tumble

Spin(ner), Spinning Aeroplane, Arabian, Arachne, Bielmann, Birl, Camel, Centrifuge, Cribellum, Cut, Day trip, Dextrorse, DJ, Flat, Flip, Gimp, Googly, Gymp, Gyrate, Gyre, Gyroscope, Hurl, Isobaric, Isotopic, Lachesis, Mole, Nun, Peg-top, Piecener, Piecer, Pirouette, Pivot, PR, Precess, Prolong, Purl, Reel, Rev(olve), Ride, Rotate, Royal, Screw, Side, Sinistrorse, Slide, Spider, Stator, Strobic, Swirl, Swivel, Throstle, Tirl, Toss, Trill, Trundle, Twirl, Twist, Wheel, Whirl, Whirligig, Work

Spinach Florentine, Orach(e), Popeye, Sa(a)g

Spinal (chord), Spine(d), Spiny Acanthoid, Acerose, Acromion, Aculeus, Areole, Arête, Backbone, Barb, Chine, Coccyx, Column, Doorn, Dorsal, Epidural, Muricate, Myelon, Notochord, Ocotillo, Prickle, Quill, Rachial, R(h)achis, Ray, Thorn, Torso, Tragacanth

Spindle(-shanks), Spindly Arbor, Axle, Bobbin, Capstan, Fusee, Fusiform, Fusil, Mandrel, Mandril, Pin, Scrag, Staff, Triblet

▶ **Spine** see **SPINAL**

Spinel Balas, Picotite

Spineless Inerm, Muticous, Timid, Weak

Spinn(e)y Coppice, Shaw, Thicket

Spinning-wheel Chark(h)a

Spinster Discovert, Feme sole, Old maid, Tabby

Spiral Archimedes, Caracol, Chalaza, Cochlea, Coil, Dexiotropic, Dextrorse, Ekman, Gyrate, Helical, Helix, Hyperbolic, Inflationary, Logarithmic, Loxodromical, Parastichy, Screw, Scroll, Sinistrorse, Spin, Tailspin, Turbinate, Vibrio, Volute, Whorl, Wind

Spire(-shaped) Broach, Flèche, Peak, Shaft, Steeple, Thyrsoid

Spirit(s), Spirited Ahriman, Akvavit, Alcohol, Ammonia, Angel, Animal, Animation, Apathodaimon, Applejack, Apsaral, Aquavit, Aqua vitae, Arak, Arch(a)eus, Ardent, Ariel, Arrack, Asmoday, Astral, Bitters, Blithe, Boggart, Bogle, Brandy, Bravura, Brio, Brollachan, Buggan(e), Buggin, Cant, Cherub, Cognac, Courage, Creature, Crouse, Daemon, Dash, Deev, Deva, Distillation, Div, Djinn(i), Domdaniel, → **DRINK**, Dryad, Duende, Duppy, Dybbuk, Eblis, Eidolon, Élan, Element(al), Emit, Empusa, Entrain, Erdgeist, Erl king, Esprit, Essence, Etheric,

Ethos, Eudemon, Fachan, Faints, Familiar, Feints, Feisty, Feni, Fenny, Fetich(e), Fetish, Fettle, Fight, Firewater, Free, Fuath, Gamy, Geist, Geneva, Genie, Genius, → **GHOST**, Ghoul, Ginger, Ginn, Gism, Glastig, Glendoveer, Go, Grappa, Gremlin, Grit, Grog, Gumption, Gytrash, Hartshorn, Heart, Hollands, Holy, Huaca, Hugh, Imp, Incubus, Indwelt, Jann, Jinn(i), Jinnee, Jism, Ka, Kachina, Kehua, Kelpie, Kindred, Kirsch, Kobold, Larva, Lemur(e), → **LIQUOR**, Lively, Loki, Manes, Manito(u), Manitu, Mare, Marid, Metal, Meths, Methyl(ated), Mettle, Mindererus, Mineral, Mobbie, Mobby, Morale, Mystique, Nain rouge, Neutral, Nis, Nix, Nobody, Numen, Ondine, Orenda, Panache, Paraclete, Party, Peart, Pecker, Pep, Peri, Pernod®, Petrol, Phantom, Pluck(y), Pneuma, Poltergeist, Pooka, Potato, Poteen, Presence, Pride, Proof, Psyche, Puck, Python, Racy, Rakee, Raki, Rakshas(a), Rectified, Rosicrucian, Ruin, Rum(bullion), Rye, Salt, Samshoo, Samshu, Saul, Schnapps, Seraph, Shade, Shadow, Shaitan, She'ol, Short, Smeddum, Soul, Spectre, Spright, Sprite, Spunk, Steam, Strunt, Surgical, Sylph, Tafia, Tangie, Taniwha, Team, Tequila, Tokoloshe, Ton, Turpentine, Turps, Undine, Verve, Vigour, Vim, Vodka, Voodoo, Wairua, Water horse, Weltgeist, White, Wili, Wine, Witblits, Wood, Wraith, Zeitgeist, Zephon, Zing, Zombie

Spiritless Craven, Dowf, Insipid, Languid, Meek, Milksop, Poor, Tame, Vapid

Spirit-level Vial

Spiritual(ism), Spiritualist Aerie, Aery, Coon-song, Ecclesiastic, Ethereous, Eyrie, Eyry, Incorporeal, Negro, Planchette, Platonic, Psychic, Swedenborg, Table-rapping, Table-turning

Spirt Gush, Jet, Rush

Spit(ting), Spittle Barbecue, Broach, Brochette, Chersonese, Dead ringer, Dribble, Drool, Emptysis, Eructate, Expectorate, Fuff, Gob, Golly, Gooby, Goss, Grill, Hawk, Hockle, Impale, Jack, Lookalike, Peninsula, Ras, Ringer, Rotisserie, Saliva, Skewer, Slag, Spade(ful), Spawl, Spear, Sputter, Sputum, Tombolo, Yesk, Yex

Spite(ful) Backbite, Bitchy, Catty, Grimalkin, Harridan, Irrespective, Malevolent, Malgrado, Malgré, Malice, Mau(l)gre, Mean, Nasty, Petty, Pique, Rancour, Spleen, Venom, Viperish, Waspish

Spitfire Cacafogo, Cacafuego, Wildcat

Spittoon Cuspidor(e)

Spiv Lair, Rorter

Splash Blash, Blue, Dabble, Dash, Dog, Drip, Feature, Flouse, Fl(o)ush, Gardyloo, Jabble, Ja(u)p, Jirble, Paddle, Plap, Plop, Plowter, Sket, Slosh, Slush, Soda, Soss, Sozzle, Spairge, Spat(ter), Spectacle, Splat(ch), Splatter, Splodge, Splosh, Splotch, Spray, Spree, Squatter, Swash, Swatter, Water, Wet

Splay(ed) Curl, Flew, Flue, Patté(e), Spread

Spleen Acrimony, Bite, Lien, Melt, Milt(z), Pip, Stomach, Vitriol, Wrath

Splendid, Splendour Ah, Braw, Brilliant, Bully, Capital, Champion, Clinker, Dandy, Éclat, Effulgent, Excellent, Fine, Finery, Fulgor, Gallant, Garish, Glitterand, Glittering, Glorious, Glory, Gorgeous, Grand(eur), Grandiose, Ha, Heroic, Lustrous, Majestic, Mooi, Noble, Palatial, Panache, Pomp, Proud, Radiant, Rich, Ripping, Royal, Stunning, Super(b), Wally, Zia

Splice(d) Braid, Eye, Join, Knit, Mainbrace, Wed

▷ **Spliced** *may indicate* an anagram

Splint Airplane, Banjo, Brace, Cal(l)iper, Splenial, T

Splinter(s) Bone-setter, Breakaway, Flinder, Fragment, Matchwood, Shatter, Shiver, Skelf, Sliver, Spale, Spall, Speel, Spelk, Spell, Spicula, Spill

Split Areolate, Axe, Banana, Bifid, Bifurcate, Bisect, Break, Broach, Burst, Chasm, Chine, Chop, Clint, Clove(n), Crack, Crevasse, Cut, Decamp, Departmentalise,

Disjoin, Distrix, → **DIVIDE**, Division, Divorce, End, Fissile, Fissure, Flake, Fork(ed), Fragment, Grass, Lacerate, Partition, Red(d), Rift(e), Rip, Rive, Russian, Ryve, Schism, Scissor, Segregate, Separate, Septemfid, Sever, Share, Skive, Slit, Sliver, Spall, Spalt, Speld, Tattle, Tmesis, Told, To-rend, To-tear, Wedge

▷ **Split** *may indicate* a word to become two; one word inside another; or a connection with Yugoslavia

Splodge, Splotch Blot, Drop, Splash

Splurge Binge, Indulge, Lavish, Spend, Splash, Spree

Splutter Chug, Expectorate, Fizz, Gutter, Spray, Stammer

Spoil(s), Spoilt Addle, Agrise, Agrize, Agryze, Blight, Blunk, Booty, Botch, Bribe, Coddle, Corrupt, Crool, → **DAMAGE**, Dampen, Deface, Defect, Deform, Dish, Foul, Gum, Hames, Harm, Impair(ed), Indulge, Loot, Maderise, Maltreat, Mar, Mardy, Mollycoddle, Muck, Mutilate, Mux, Pamper, Pet, Pickings, Pie, Plunder, Prejudicate, Prize, Queer, Rait, Rate, Ravage, Ret, Rot, Ruin, Scupper, Spuly(i)e, Swag, Taint, Tarnish, Vitiate, Wanton, Winnings

▷ **Spoil(ed), Spoilt** *may indicate* an anagram

Spoilsport Damper, Killjoy, Meddler, Party pooper, Wet blanket, Wowser

Spoke(s) Concentric, Radius, Ray, Rung, Said, Sed, Strut

▷ **Spoken** *may indicate* the sound of a word or letter

Spokesman Foreman, Mouthpiece, Orator, Prophet, Representative

Spoliation, Spoliative Devastation, Pillage, Plunder, Predatory, Reif

Sponge(r), Spongy Alcoholic, Ambatch, Argentine, Battenburg, Bum, Cadge, Cake, Cleanse, Diact, Diploe, Fozy, Free-loader, Glass-rope, Hexact, Hyalonema, Leech, Lig, Lithistid(a), Loofa(h), Madeira, Madeleine, Mermaid's glove, Mooch, Mop, Mouch, Mump, Parasite, Parazoa, Pentact, Poachy, Porifera(n), Quandong, Rhabdus, Sarcenchyme, Scambler, Schnorrer, Scrounge, Shark, Shool, Shule, Siphonophora, Smell-feast, Sooner, Sop, Sucker, Swab, Sycophant, Tectratine, Tetract, Tetraxon, Tiramisu, Tylote, Vegetable, Velamen, Venus's flowerbasket, Wangle, Wipe, Zimocca, Zoophyte

Spongewood Sola

Sponsor(ship) Aegis, Angel, Auspice, Backer, Egis, Finance, Godfather, Godparent, Gossip, Guarantor, Lyceum, Patron, Surety

Spontaneous Aleatoric, Autonomic, Gratuitous, Immediate, Impromptu, Improvised, Impulsive, Instant, Intuitive, Natural, Ultroneus, Unasked, Unpremeditated, Unprompted, Unrehearsed

Spoof Chouse, Cozenage, Deception, Delusion, Fallacy, → **HOAX**, Imposture, Ramp, Swindle, Trick

Spook(s), Spooky CIA, Eerie, Fantom, Frightening, Ghost, Phantom, Shade

Spool Bobbin, Capstan, Pirn, Reel, Trundle

Spoon(ful), Spoon-shaped Apostle, Canoodle, Cochlear, Deflagrating, Dollop, Dose, Eucharistic, Gibby, Greasy, Horn, Labis, Ladle, Mote, Neck, Rat-tail, Runcible, Salt, Scoop, Scud, Server, Snuff, Spatula, Sucket, Trolling, Trout, Woo, Wooden

Spoonerism Marrowsky, Metathesis

Spoor Trace, Track, Trail

Sporadic Fitful, Isolated, Occasional, Patchy

Spore(s), Spore case Asexual, Conidium, Ex(t)ine, Fungus, Glomerule, Lenticel, Palynology, Seed, Sexual, Sorus, Spreathed, Telium, Uredinium

Sporran Pock

Sport(s), Sporting, Sportive Amusement, Blood, Breakaway, Brick, By-form, Contact, Daff, Dalliance, Dally, Deviant, Extreme, Field, Freak, Frisky, Frolic, Fun,

→ **GAME**, Gent, In, Joke, Laik, Lake, Lark, Merimake, Merry, Morph, Mutagen, Pal, Recreate, Rogue, Rules, Spectator, Tournament, Tourney, Toy, Wear, Winter

SPORTS

2 letters:
RU

3 letters:
Gig

4 letters:
Polo
Sumo

5 letters:
Basho
Fives
Kendo

6 letters:
Aikido
Hockey
Karate
Shinny
Shinty
Squash
Tennis

7 letters:
Angling
Archery
Camogie

Curling
Fencing
Hurling
Netball
Parkour
Skating
Snooker
Surfing
Tailing

8 letters:
Aquatics
Ballgame
Bonspiel
Eventing
Korfball
Lacrosse
Langlauf
Natation
Octopush
Softball
Speedway
Swoffing

9 letters:
Abseiling
Autocross
Autopoint

Canyoning
Potholing
Skijoring
Skydiving
Speedball
Twitching
Water polo
Wrestling

10 letters:
Cyclo-cross
Drag-racing
Kickboxing
Monoskiing
Pancratium
Parakiting
Paraskiing
Rallycross
Street luge

11 letters:
Coasteering
Fell walking
Hang-gliding
Paragliding
Paralympics
Parapenting
Parasailing

Table tennis
Truck racing
Water-skiing
Windsurfing

12 letters:
Bar billiards
Boardsailing
Cross country
Heli-boarding
Orienteering
Parascending
River bugging
Sailboarding
Snowboarding
Speed-skating
Steeplechase
Trampolining
Trapshooting
Wakeboarding

13 letters:
Bungee-jumping
Prizefighting
Weightlifting

17 letters:
Whitewater rafting

▷ **Sport(s)** *may indicate* an anagram

Sportsman, Sportsmen All-rounder, Athlete, Blue, Corinthian, Half-blue, Hunter, Nimrod, Pentathlete, Pitcher, Shamateur, Shikaree, Shikari, Showjumper

Spot(s), Spotted, Spotting, Spotty Ace, Acne, Area, Areola, Areole, Baily's beads, Bausond, Bead, Beauty, Befoul, Blackhead, Blain, Blemish, Blind, Blip, Blister, Blob, Blot, Blotch(ed), Blur, Brind(l)ed, Café-au-lait, Carbuncle, Caruncle, Cash, Check, Cloud, Colon, Comedo, Corner, Curn, Cyst, Dance, Dapple(-bay), Defect, Dick, Dilemma, Discern, Discover, Dot, Drop, Eruption, Espy, Eye, Facula, Flat, Flaw, Fleck, Floater, Fogdog, Foxed, Freak, Freckle, Furuncle, G, Gay, Glimpse, Gout, Gräfenberg, Gricer, Guttate, High, Hot, Identify, Jam, Leaf, Lentago, Light, Little, Liver, Location, Loran, Mackle, Macle, Macul(at)e, Mail, Meal, Measly, Microdot, Milium, Moil, Mole, Morbilli, Mote, Motty, Muscae volitantes, Naevoid, Naevus, Note, Notice, Ocellar, Ocellus, Paca, Papule, Paraselene, Pardal, Parhelion, Patch, Peep(e), Penalty, Perceive, Performance, Petechia, Pied, Pimple, Pin, Pip, Place, Plague, Plight, Plook, Plot, Plouk, Pock, Point, Predicament, Punctuate, Pupil, Pustule, Quat, Radar, Rash, Recognise, Red, Rose-drop, Scene, Scotoma, Situation, Skewbald, Smut, Soft, Speck(le), Speculum, Splodge, Spy, Stigma, Sully, Sun, Sweet,

Taint, Tar, Tight, Touch, Trace, Trouble, Weak, Whelk, Whitehead, Witness, X, Yellow, Zit

Spotless Clean, Immaculate, Pristine, Virginal

Spotlight Ace, Baby, Bon-bon, Brute, Maxi-brute

Spot on To a t

Spouse Companion, Consort, Dutch, Feare, Feer, F(i)ere, Hubby, Husband, Mate, Oppo, Partner, Pheer, Pirrauru, Significant other, Wife, Xant(h)ippe

Spout(er) Adjutage, Erupt, Gargoyle, Geyser, Grampus, Gush, Impawn, Jet, Mouth, Nozzle, Orate, Pawn, Pourer, Raile, Rote, Spurt, Stream, Stroup, Talk, Tap, Vent

Sprain(ed) Crick, Rax, Reckan, Rick, Stave, Strain, Wrench, Wrick

Sprat Brit, Fish, Garvie, Garvock

Sprawl Grabble, Loll, Scramble, Sprangle, Spread, Stretch, Urban

Spray Aerosol, Aigrette, Antiperspirant, Atomiser, Bespatter, Buttonhole, Corsage, Cyme, Egret, Fly, Hair, Mace®, Nasal, Nebuliser, Posy, Rose, Rosula, Shower, Sparge, Spindrift, Splash, Spoondrift, Sprent, Sprig, Sprinkle, Spritz, Strinkle, Syringe, Twig, Wet

▷ **Spray** *may indicate* an anagram

Spread(ing), Spreader Air, Apply, Banquet, Bestrew, Beurre, Blow-out, Branch, Bush, Butter, Carpet, Centre, Circumfuse, Contagious, Couch, Coverlet, Coverlid, Deploy, Diffract, Diffuse, Dilate, Disperse, Dissemination, Distribute, Divulge, Double, Drape, Dripping, Elongate, Emanate, Expand, Extend, Fan, Feast, Flare, Guac(h)amole, Honeycomb, Jam, Lay, Mantle, Marge, Marmite®, Metastasis, Middle-age(d), Multiply, Mushroom, Nutter, Oleo, Open, Overgrow, Paste, Pâté, Patent, Patté, Patulous, Perfuse, Pervade, Picnic, Pour, Propagate, Radiate, Rampant, Ran, Run, Scale, Scatter, Sea-floor, Set, Sheet, Slather, Smear, Smörgåsbord, Sow, Span, Speld, Spelder, Spillover, Splay, Sprawl, Spray, Straddle, Straw, Stretch, Strew, Strow, Suffuse, Systemic, Tath, Teer, Unfold, Unfurl, Unguent, Vegemite®, Widen, Wildfire

▷ **Spread** *may indicate* an anagram

Spree Bat, Batter, Beano, Bender, Binge, Bum, Bust, Buster, Carousal, Frolic, Jag, Jamboree, Juncate, Junket, Lark, Loose, Randan, Rantan, Razzle(-dazzle), Revel, Rouse, Splore, Tear, Ups(e)y

Sprig Brad, Branch, Cion, Cyme, Nail, Scion, Sien, Sient, Spray, Syen, Twig, Youth

Sprightly Agile, Airy, Chipper, Jaunty, Mercurial

Spring(s), Springtime, Springy Aganippe, Air, Alice, Arise, Bolt, Bounce, Bound, Box, Bunt, Cabriole, Caper, Capriole, Castalian, Cavort, Cee, Coil, Dance, Elastic, Eye, Fount(ain), Gambado, Germinate, Geyser, Grass, Hair, Helix, Hippocrene, Hop, Hot, Jump, Leaf, Leap, Lent, Lep, Litt, Low-water, May, Mineral, Originate, Persephone, Pierian, Pounce, Prance, Primavera, Prime, Resilient, Ribbon, Rise, Saddle, Season, Skip, Snap, Source, Spa, Spang, Spaw, Stem, Stot, Submarine, Sulphur, Summer, Thermae, Thermal, Trampoline, Valve, Vault, Vaute, Vawte, Vernal, Voar, Ware, Watch, Waterhole, Weeping, Well(-head), Whip, Winterbourne

▷ **Spring(y)** *may indicate* an anagram

Springbok Amabokoboko

Springless Telega

Springtail Apterygota

Sprinkle(r), Sprinkling Asperge, Aspergill(um), Bedash, Bedrop, Bescatter, Caster, Dredge, Dust, Hyssop, Lard, Pouncet, Powder, Rose, Scatter, Scouthering, Shower, Sow, Spa(i)rge, Spatter, Splash, Spray, Spritz, Strinkle

Sprint(er) Burst, Dash, Race, Rash, Run, Rush, Wells

Sprite Apsaras, Banshee, Croquemitaine, Dobbie, Dobby, Echo, Elf, Fairy, Fiend, Genie, Goblin, Gremlin, Hobgoblin, Icon, Nickel, Ondine, Puck, Spirit, Troll, Trow, Umbriel, Undine

Sprout Braird, Breer, Brussels, Bud, Burgeon, Chit, Crop, Eye, Germ(inate), Grow, Pullulate, Shoot, Spire, Tendron, Vegetate

Spruce Balsam, Dapper, Engelmann, Hemlock, Natty, Neat, Norway, Picea, Pitch-tree, Prink, Shipshape, Sitka, Smart, Spiff, Tidy, Tree, Trim, Tsuga, White

Spry Active, Agile, Constance, Dapper, Nimble, Volable

Spud Murphy, Potato, Spade, Tater, Tatie

Spume Eject, Foam, Froth, Lather, Spet, Spit

Spunk Courage, Grit, Pluck, Tinder

Spur(s) Accourage, Activate, Calcar(ate), Encourage, Fame, Fire, Galvanise, Gee, Gilded, Goad, Groyne, Heel, Incite, Limb, Lye, Needle, Offset, Prick, Rippon, Rowel, Shoot, Spica, Stimulus, Strut, Stud, Tar, Urge

Spurge (tree) Candelilla, Croton, Euphorbia, Kamala, Poinsettia, Ricinus

Spurious Adulterine, Apocryphal, Bogus, Counterfeit, Dog, False, Phoney, Pseudo, Sciolism

▷ **Spurious** *may indicate* an anagram

Spurn Despise, Disdain, Ignore, Jilt, Reject, → SCORN, Sdayn, Shun

Spurt Burst, Forge, Geyser, Jet, Outburst, Pump, Spout, Start

Sputter Fizzle, Spit, Splutter, Stutter

Spy(ing), Spies Agent, Beagle, Caleb, CIA, Cicero, Curtain-twitcher, Descry, Dicker, Double agent, Eavesdrop, Emissary, Espionage, Fink, Fuchs, Informer, Keeker, Mata Hari, MI, Mole, Mouchard, Nark, Ninja, Nose, Operative, Pimp, Plant, Pry, Recce, Scout, See, Setter, Shadow, Sinon, Sleeper, Spetsnaz, Spook, Tout, Wait

Spyhole Eyelet, Judas-hole, Oillet, Peephole

Squab Chubby, Cushion, Obese

Squabble Argue, Bicker, Brabble, Quarrel, Rhubarb, Row, Scrap

Squad(ron) Band, Blue, Company, Crew, Death, Drugs, Escadrille, Fifteen, Firing, Flying, Fraud, Hit, Nahal, Platoon, Porn, Red, Snatch, Vice, White, Wing

Squalid, Squalor Abject, Colluvies, Dickensian, Dinge, Dingy, Filth, Frowsy, Grungy, Mean, Poverty, Scuzzy, Seedy, Skid Row, Sleazy, Slum(my), Slurb, Sordid

Squall Blast, Blow, Chubasco, Commotion, Cry, Drow, Flaw, Flurry, Gust, Line, Sumatra, Wail, White, Yell, Yowl

Squander Blow, Blue, Fritter, Frivol, Lash, Mucker, Slather, Splash, Splurge, Ware, → WASTE

Square(d), Squares Agree, Anta, Arrière, Ashlar, Ashler, Bang, Barrack, Belgrave, Berkeley, Bevel, Block, Bribe, Chequer, Compone, Compony, Corny, Deal, Dinkum, Even(s), Fair, Fog(e)y, Forty-nine, Fossil, Four, Gobony, Grey, Grosvenor, Latin, Least, Leicester, Level, Magic, Market, Meal, Mitre, Nasik, Neandert(h)aler, Nine, Norma, Old-fashioned, Palm, Passé, Pay, Perfect, Piazza, Place, Platz, Plaza, Quad(rangle), Quadrate, Quarry, Quits, Red, Rood, S, Set(t), Sloane, Solid, Squier, Squire, Straight, T, Tee, Times, Traditionalist, Trafalgar, Try, Unhip

Squash(y) Adpress, Butternut, Conglomerate, Crush, Gourd, Kia-ora®, Knead, Marrow, Mash, Obcompress, Oblate, Pattypan, Press, Pulp, Shoehorn, Silence, Slay, Slew, Slue, Soft, Squeeze, Squidge, Squidgy, Suppress, Torpedo

Squat(ter), Squatting Bywoner, Caganer, Crouch, Croup(e), Cubby, Dumpy, Fubby, Fubsy, Hunker, Occupy, Pudsey, Pyknic, Rook, Ruck, Sit, Spud, Stubby, Stumpy, Swatter, Usucaption

Squaw Kloo(t)chman

Squawk Cackle, Complain, Cry, Scrauch, Scraugh

Squeak(er) Cheep, Creak, Narrow, Near, Peep, Pip, Scroop, Shoat, Squeal
Squeal(er) Blow, Eek, Howl, Inform, Pig, Screech, Sing, Sneak, Tell, Wee, Yelp
Squeamish(ness) Delicate, Disgust, Missish, Nervous, Prudish, Queasy, Reluctant
Squeeze(r) Bleed, Chirt, Coll, Compress, Concertina, Constrict, Cram, Credit,
     Crowd, Crush, Dispunge, Exact, Express, Extort, Extrude, Hug, Jam, Mangle, Milk,
     Preace, Press, Sandwich, Sap, Scrooge, Scrouge, Scrowdge, Scruze, Shoehorn,
     Squash, Squish, Sweat, Thrutch, Thumbscrew, Vice, Wring
Squelch Gurgle, Squash, Squish, Subdue
Squib Banger, Damp, Firework, Lampoon
Squid Calamari, Calamary, Cephalopod, Cuttlefish, Ink-fish, Loligo, Mortar,
     Nautilus, Octopus, Sleeve fish
Squiffy Drunk, Tiddley
▷ **Squiggle** *may indicate* an anagram
Squill Sea, Spring
Squint(ing) Boss-eyed, Cast, Cock-eye, Cross-eye, Glance, Gledge, Glee, Gley,
     Hagioscope, Heterophoria, Louche, Opening, Proptosis, Skellie, Skelly, Sken,
     Squin(n)y, Strabism, Swivel-eye, Vergence, Wall-eye
Squire Armiger(o), Beau, Donzel, Escort, Hardcastle, Headlong, Land-owner,
     Scutiger, Swain, Western, White
Squirm(ing) Fidget, Reptation, Twist, Worm, Wriggle, Writhe
Squirrel, Squirrel's nest Aye-aye, Boomer, Bun, Cage, Chickaree, Chipmuck,
     Chipmunk, Dray, Drey, Flickertail, Flying, Fox, Gopher, Grey, Ground, Hackee,
     Hoard(er), Meerkat, Petaurist, Phalanger, Red, Sciuroid, Sewellel, Skug, S(o)uslik,
     Spermophile, Taguan, Vair, Zizel
Squirt(er) Chirt, Cockalorum, Douche, Jet, Scoosh, Scoot, Skoosh, Spirt, Spout,
     Spritz, Urochorda, Wet, Whiffet, Whippersnapper
Sri Lanka(n) Ceylon, Cingalese, CL, Serendip, Sinhalese, Tamil, Vedda
St Saint, Street
Stab Bayonet, Chib, Crease, Creese, Dag, Effort, Go, Gore, Guess, Jab, Knife, Kreese,
     Kris, Lancinate, Pang, Pierce, Pink, Poniard, Prick, Prong, Stick, Stiletto, Turk,
     Wound
Stabilise(r), Stability Aileron, Balance, Balloonet, Emulsifier, Even, Fin, Maintain,
     Pax Romana, Peg, Permanence, Plateau, Poise, Steady, Tail panel
Stable(s) Augean, Balanced, Barn, Byre, Certain, Constant, Durable, Equerry,
     Equilibrium, Firm, Livery, Loose box, Manger, Mews, Poise, Secure, Solid, Sound,
     Stall, Static(al), Steadfast, Steady, Stud, Sure, Together
Stableman Groom, Lad, Ostler
Stachys Betony
Stack(s) Accumulate, À gogo, Chimney, Clamp, Cock, End, Funnel, Heap, Lum,
     → **PILE**, Rick, Shock, Smoke, Staddle
Stadium Arena, Ballpark, Bowl, Circus, Circus Maximus, Coliseum, Hippodrome,
     Speedway, Velodrome
Staff Aesculapius, Alpenstock, Ash-plant, Bato(o)n, Bourdon, Burden, Caduceus,
     Cane, Crook, Crosier, Cross(e), Crozier, Crutch, Cudgel, Entourage, Equerry,
     État-major, Faculty, Ferula, Ferule, Flagpole, General, Jacob's, Jeddart, Linstock,
     Lituus, Mace, Omlah, Pastoral, Personnel, Pike, Pole, Ragged, Rod, Rung,
     Runic, Sceptre, Seniority, Skeleton, Stave, Stick, Taiaha, Tapsmen, Tau, Thyrsus,
     Truncheon, Verge, Wand, Workers, Workforce, Wring
Stag Actaeon, Brocket, Buck, Deer, For men, Hummel, Imperial, Line, Male, Party,
     Royal, Rutter, Ten-pointer, Wapiti
Stage Act, Anaphase, Apron, Arena, Bardo, Bema, Boards, Catasta, Centre,

Chrysalis, Committee, Diligence, Dog-leg, Estrade, Fare, Fargo, Fit-up, Grade, Hop, Juncture, Key, Landing, Leg, Level, Metaphase, Milestone, Moment, Mount, Oidium, Perform, Phase, Phasis, Pier, Pin, Platform, Podium, Point, Postscenium, Prophase, Proscenium, PS, Puberty, Report, Resting, Rostrum, Scene, Sensorimeter, Sound, Stadium, Step, Stor(e)y, Subimago, Theatre, Thrust, Transition, Trek, Yuga, Zoea

Stage-coach Diligence, Thoroughbrace

Stagecraft Pinafore

Stagehand Flyman, Grip

Stagger(ed) Alternate, Amaze, Astichous, Astonish, Awhape, Daidle, Falter, Floor, Lurch, Recoil, Reel, Rock, Shock, Stoiter, Stot(ter), Stumble, Sway, Teeter, Thunderstricken, Thunderstruck, Titubate, Tolter, Totter, Wamble, Wintle

▷ **Staggered** *may indicate* an anagram

Stagirite, Stagyrite Aristotle

Stagnant, Stagnation Cholestasis, Foul, Inert, Scummy, Stasis, Static

Staid Decorous, Demure, Formal, Grave, Matronly, Prim, Prudish, Sad, Seemly, Sober, Stick-in-the-mud

Stain(er) Aniline, Bedye, Besmirch, Blemish, Blob, Blot, Blotch, Discolour, Dishonour, Dye, Embrue, Ensanguine, Eosin, Fox, Gram's, Grime, Imbrue, Iodophile, Keel, Maculate, Mail, Meal, Mote, Portwine, Slur, Smirch, Smit, Soil, Splodge, Splotch, Stigma, Sully, Taint, Tarnish, Tinge, Tint, Vital, Woad

Stair(case), Stairs Apples, Apples and pears, Caracol(e), Cochlea, Companionway, Escalator, Flight, Moving, Perron, Rung, Scale (and platt), Spiral, Step, Tread, Turnpike, Vice, Wapping, Winding

Stake(s) Ante, Bet, Claim, Deposit, Gage, Go, Holding, Impale, Impone, Interest, Lay, Loggat, Mark, Mise, Nursery, Paal, Pale, Paliform, Paling, Palisade, Peel, Peg, Pele, Picket, Pile, Play, Post, Pot, Punt, Put, Rest, Revie, Risk, Septleva, Spike, Spile, Stang, Stob, Straddle, Sweep, Tether, Vie, Wager, Welter

Stalactite Dripstone, Dropstone, Helictite, Lansfordite, Soda straw

Stale Aged, Banal, Flat, Fozy, Frowsty, Fusty, Hackneyed, Handle, Hoary, Mouldy, Musty, Old, Pretext, Rancid, Urine, Worn

▷ **Stale** *may indicate* an obsolete word

Stalemate Deadlock, Dilemma, Hindrance, Impasse, Mexican standoff, Saw-off, Standoff, Tie, Zugswang

Stalk(s), Stalker Anthophore, Bun, Cane, Caulicle, Follow, Funicle, Garb(e), Gynophore, Ha(u)lm, Keck(s), Kecksey, Keksye, Kex, Ommatophore, Pedicel, Pedicle, Peduncle, Petiole, Petiolule, Phyllode, Pursue, Rush, Scape, Seta, Shaw, Spear, Spire, Stem, Sterigma, Still-hunter, Stipe(s), Stride, Strig, Strut, Stubble, Stump, Trail, Yolk

Stalking-horse Stale

Stall(s) Arrest, Bay, Booth, Box, Bulk, Crib, → **DELAY**, Floor, Flypitch, Hedge, Kiosk, Loose-box, Orchestra, Pen, Pew, Prebendal, Seat, Shamble, Sideshow, Stand, Starting, Stasidion, Temporise, Trap, Traverse, Travis, Trevis(s), Whip, Whipstall

Stallion Cooser, Cuisser, Cusser, Entire, → **HORSE**, Stag, Staig, Stonehorse, Stud

Stalwart Anchor-man, Buirdly, Firm, Manful, Robust, Sturdy, Trusty, Valiant

Stamen(ed) Androecium, Octandria, Polyandria

Stamina Endurance, Fibre, Fortitude, Guts, Last, Stamen, Stay, Steel

Stammer(ing) Balbutient, Er, Hesitate, Hum, Psellism, Sputter, Stumble, → **STUTTER**, Waffle

Stamp(s), Stamped Albino, Appel, Cast, Character, Date(r), Die, Dry print, Enface, Fiscal, Frank, Health, Imperforate, Impress, Imprint, Incuse, Label, Matchmark,

Mint, Pane, Penny black, Perfin, Philately, Pintadera, Postage, Press(ion), Rubber, Seal, Seebeck, Se-tenant, Signet, Spif, Strike, Swage, Tête-bêche, Touch, Touchmark, Trading, Trample, Tread, Tromp, Type

Stamp-collecting Philately, Timbrology, Timbrophily

Stampede Debacle, Flight, Panic, Rampage, → **RUSH**

Stance Attitude, Ecarté, Pose, Position, Posture, Quinte

Stand(ing), Stand for, Stand up Apron, Arraign, Attitude, Base, Be, Bear, Bide, Binnacle, Bipod, Bristle, Brook, Canterbury, Caste, Confrontation, Cradle, Crease, Dais, Degree, Desk, Dock, Dree, Dumb-waiter, Easel, Epergne, Étagère, Face, Foothold, Freeze, Gantry, Gueridon, Hard, Hob, Importance, Insulator, Klinostat, Last, Lazy Susan, Lectern, Leg, Lime, Music, Nef, Odour, One-night, Ovation, Pedestal, Place, Plant, Podium, Pose, Position, Pou sto, Prestige, Promenade, Protest, Qua, Rack, Rank, Regent, Remain, Represent, Repute, Rise, Stall, Statant, Station, → **STATUS**, Stay, Stillage, Stock, Stool, Straddle, Straphang, Stroddle, Strut, Table, Tantalus, Taxi, Teapoy, Terrace, Toe, → **TREAT**, Tree, Tripod, Trivet, Umbrella, Upright, Whatnot, Witness

Standard(s) Banner, Base, Baseline, Basic, Benchmark, Bogey, British, Canon, CAT, Classic(al), Cocker, Colour(s), Criterion, Double, Eagle, English, Ethics, Etiquette, Examplar, Example, Exemplar, Fiducial, Flag, Ga(u)ge, Gold, Gonfalon, Grade, Guidon, Ideal, Labarum, Level, Living, Model, Netiquette, Norm(a), Normal, Numeraire, Old Glory, Oriflamme, Par, Parker Morris, Pennon, Principle, Rate, Regular, Rod, Rose, Routine, Royal, → **RULE**, Silver, Spec(ification), Staple, Sterling, Stock, Time, Touchstone, Tricolour, Troy, Two-power, Usual, Valuta, Vexillum, Yardstick

Standard-bearer Alferez, Cornet, Ensign, Vexillary

Stand-by Adminicle, Reserve, Substitute, Support, Understudy

Stand-in Double, Locum, Stunt man, Sub(stitute), Surrogate, Temp, Understudy

Standish Miles

Stand-off(ish) Aloof, Remote, Reserved, Stalemate, Upstage

Standpoint Angle, Slant, View

Standstill Deadset, Halt, Jam

Stanley Baldwin, Knife, Rupert

Stannic Tin

Stanza Ballad, Elegiac, Envoi, Envoy, Heroic, Ottava, Ottava rima, Poem, Sixaine, Spenserian, Staff, Stave, Tetrastich, Verse

Staple Basic, Bread, Chief, Maize, Oats, Pin, Rice, Stock, Wool

Star(s) Aster(isk), Binary, Body, Celebrity, Companion, Constant, Constellation, Cynosure, Dark, Double, Esther, Exploding, Falling, Feather, Feature, Film, Fixed, Flare, Giant, Headline, Hero, Hester, Hexagram, Idol, Late type, Lead, Lion, Mogen David, Movie, Multiple, Pentacle, Personality, Phad, Pip, Plerion, Pointer, Principal, Pulsating, Seven, Shell, Shine, Shooting, Sidereal, Solomon's seal, Spangle, Starn(ie), Stellar, Stern, Swart, (The) Pointers, Top banana, Top-liner, Ultraviolet, Valentine, Variable, Vedette

---

STARS

3 letters:	4 letters:		
Dog	Argo	Lyra	Ursa
Sol	Beta	Mira	Vega
	Grus	Nova	Vela
	Lode	Pavo	Zeta
		Pole	

5 letters:
Acrux
Agena
Algol
Alpha
Ceres
Comet
Delta
Deneb
Draco
Dubhe
Dwarf
Gamma
Hyads
Indus
Lupus
Mensa
Merak
Mizar
Norma
North
Polar
Radio
Rigel
Rigil
Spica
Theta
Venus
Virgo
Wagon
Whale

6 letters:
Alioth
Alkaid
Altair
Aquila
Auriga
Bootes
Carbon

Carina
Castor
Cygnus
Dorado
Étoile
Fornax
Galaxy
Hyades
Lizard
Megrez
Merope
Meteor
Mullet
Octans
Phecda
Plough
Pollux
Psyche
Pulsar
Puppis
Quasar
Saturn
Sirius
Sothis
Uranus
Vesper
Volans

7 letters:
Antares
Calaeno
Canopus
Capella
Cepheus
Chamber
Columba
Dolphin
Epsilon
Estoile
Evening

Gemingo
Lucifer
Morning
Neutron
Perseus
Phoenix
Polaris
Procyon
Proxima
Regulus
Sabaism
Serpens
Sterope
Triones
Wagoner

8 letters:
Achernar
Arcturus
Barnard's
Circinus
Denebola
Equuleus
Hesperus
Magnetar
Mira Ceti
Pegasean
Phosphor
Pleiades
Praesepe
Red dwarf
Red giant
Scorpius
Synastry
Waggoner

9 letters:
Aldebaran
Andromeda
Bellatrix

Big Dipper
Black hole
Centaurus
Collapsar
Delphinus
Fire-drake
Fomalhaut
Meteorite
Ophiuchus
Pentagram
Rigil-Kent
Supernova
Wolf-Rayet

10 letters:
Betacrucis
Betelgeuse
Betelgeuze
Brown dwarf
Cassiopeia
Orion's Belt
Phosphorus
Supergiant
White dwarf

11 letters:
Circumpolar

12 letters:
Little Dipper

13 letters:
Southern Cross

15 letters:
Proxima Centauri

Starboard Right
Starch(y), Starch producer Amyloid, Animal, Arrowroot, Cassava, Ceremony, Congee, Conjee, Coontie, Coonty, Cycad, Farina, Fecula, Formal, Glycogen, Manioc, Maranta, Pentosan, Sago, Stamina, Statolith, Stiff, Tapioca, Tous-les-mois
Stare Eyeball, Fisheye, Gape, Gapeseed, Gawp, Gaze, Geek, Glare, Goggle, Gorp, Look, Ogle, Outface, Peer, Rubberneck, Scowl
Starfish Asterid, Asteroid(ea), Bipinnaria, Brittlestar, Ophiurid, Radiata
Star-gaze(r), Star-gazing Astrodome, Astronomy, Copernicus
Stark Apparent, Austere, Bald, Bare, Gaunt, Harsh, Naked, Nude, Sheer, Stiff, Utterly

Starling Bird, Gippy, Hill mynah, Murmuration, Pastor, Rosy pastor, Stare
Star of Bethlehem Chincherinchee, Chinkerinchee
Start(ed), Starter Ab ovo, Abrade, Abraid, Abray, Activate, Actuate, Begin, Boggle, Boot-up, Bot, Broach, Bug, Bump, Chance, Commence, Crank, Create, Crudités, Dart, Ean, Embryo, Face-off, False, Fire, Flinch, Float, Flush, Flying, Found, Gambit, Gan, Genesis, Getaway, Gun, Handicap, Head, Hot-wire, Impetus, Imprimis, Incept(ion), Initiate, Instigate, Institute, Intro, Jerk, Judder, Jump, Jump lead, Jump-off, Kick-off, L, Lag, Launch, Lead, Off, Offset, Onset, Ope(n), Ord, Origin, Outset, Preliminary, Prelude, Proband, Push, Put-up, Reboot, Resume, Roll, Roul, Rouse, Scare, Set off, Shy, Slip, Snail, Spring, Spud, String, Tee-off, Wince
▷ **Start** *may indicate* an anagram or first letter(s)
Startle, Startling Alarm, Bewilder, Disturb, Eye-opener, Flush, Frighten, Magical, Rock, Scare
Starvation, Starve(d), Starving Anorexia, Anoxic, Bant, Clem, Cold, Deprive, Diet, Famish, Inanition, Macerate, Perish, Pine, Undernourished
▷ **Starving** *may indicate* an 'o' in the middle of a word
Stash Secrete
State(s), Stateside Affirm, Alle(d)ge, Aread, Arrede, Assert, Assever, Attest, Aver, Avow, Buffer, Case, Circar, Cite, Client, Commonwealth, Condition, Confederate, Country, Critical, Cutch, Declare, Dependency, Emirate, Empire, État, Federal, Fettle, Flap, Free, Habitus, Humour, Kingdom, Land, Lesh, Mess, Name, Nanny, Nation, Native, Palatinate, Papal, Para, Plateau, Plight, Police, Posit, Predicament, Predicate, Premise, Pronounce, Protectorate, Puppet, Quantum, Realm, Republic, Rogue, Samadhi, Satellite, Say, Sircar, Sirkar, Slave, Sorry, Standing, Steady, Succession, Threeness, Uncle Sam, Union, United, Welfare

---

STATES

2 letters:	4 letters:	5 letters:	
Ga	Abia	Amapa	Nepal
Ia	Acre	Assam	Oshun
Md	Chad	Bahar	Perak
Me	Conn	Benin	Piaui
Mi	Gulf	Benue	Qatar
NC	Iowa	Ceará	Reich
NY	Kano	Dixie	Sabah
Pa	Kogi	Dubai	Samoa
RI	Mass	Gabon	Texas
UK	Ogun	Ghana	
US	Ohio	Hesse	6 letters:
Ut	Oman	Idaho	Alaska
Va	Ondo	Kalat	Balkan
	Osun	Kedah	Baltic
	Shan	Kutch	Baroda
3 letters:	Swat	Kwara	Bauchi
Ark	Togo	Lippe	Belize
Del	Utah	Maine	Bremen
Fla		Malay	Brunei
Oyo		Mewar	Cochin
Wis			Colima

Dakota
Hawaii
Jigawa
Johore
Kaduna
Kansas
Kerala
Khelat
Kuwait
Madras
Malawi
Mysore
Nevada
Oaxaca
Oregon
Orissa
Pahang
Parana
Penang
Perlis
Puebla
Punjab
Rivers
Saxony
Sikkim
Sokoto
Sonora
Sparta
Styria
Tonkin

7 letters:
Alabama
Alagoas
Anambra
Andorra
Arizona
Barbary
Bavaria
Buffalo
Chiapos
Durango
Florida
Georgia
Gujarat
Gujerat
Haryana
Hidalgo
Indiana
Ireland
Jalisco

Jamaica
Jodhpur
Kashmir
Malacca
Manipur
Mizoram
Montana
Morelos
Nayarit
New York
Nirvana
Paraiba
Pradesh
Prussia
Roraima
Sarawak
Sergipe
Sinaloa
Tabasco
Tongkin
Tonking
Tripura
Trucial
Udaipur
Vermont
Vietnam
Wyoming
Yucatan

8 letters:
Abu Dhabi
Amazonas
Arkansas
Campeche
Carolina
Coahuila
Colorado
Delaware
Ethiopia
Honduras
Illinois
Jharkand
Kelantan
Kentucky
Maranhao
Maryland
Michigan
Missouri
Nagaland
Nebraska
Oklahoma

Rondonia
Saarland
Sao Paulo
Selangor
Tanzania
Tasmania
Tiaxcala
Tongking
Veracruz
Victoria
Virginia

9 letters:
Chihuahua
Dixieland
Guatemala
Karnataka
Louisiana
Manchukuo
Meghalaya
Michoacán
Minnesota
Nassarawa
New Jersey
New Mexico
Nuevo Léon
Queretaro
Rajasthan
Rajputana
St Vincent
Tamil Nadu
Tennessee
Thuringia
Tocantins
Trengganu
Venezuela
Wisconsin
Zacatecas

10 letters:
California
Guanajuato
Jamahiriya
Jumhouriya
Manchoukuo
Orange Free
Pernambuco
Queensland
Tamaulipas
Tanganyika
Terengganu

Travancore
Washington

11 letters:
Brandenberg
Connecticut
Maharashtra
Mecklenburg
Minas Gerais
Mississippi
North Dakota
Quintana Roo
South Dakota
Uttaranchal
Vatican City

12 letters:
Chhattisgarh
Madhya Bharat
New Hampshire
Pennsylvania
Saxony-Anholt
Uttar Pradesh
West Virginia

13 letters:
Andhra Pradesh
Madhya Pradesh
Massachusetts
Negri Sembilan
New South Wales
San Luis Potosi
Santa Catarina
South Carolina

14 letters:
Rio Grande do Sul
South Australia
Vindhya Pradesh

15 letters:
Himachal Pradesh
Schaumburg-Lippe
St Kitts and Nevis

16 letters:
Rio Grande do
  Norte

17 letters:
Schleswig-Holstein

19 letters:	*20 letters:*

Rhineland-
  Palatinate
	North Rhine-
	  Westphalia

▷ **Stated** *may indicate* a similar sounding word

Stately, Stately home August, Dome, Grand, Imposing, Junoesque, Majestic, Mansion, Noble, Regal

Statement Accompt, Account, Affidavit, Aphorism, Assertion, Asseveration, Attestation, Avowal, Bill, Bulletin, Case, Communiqué, Deposition, Dictum, Diktat, Encyclical, Evidence, Expose, Factoid, Generalisation, Grand Remonstrance, Indictment, Invoice, Jurat, Manifesto, Mission, Outline, Paraphrase, Pleading, Press release, Profession, Pronouncement, Proposition, Protocol, Quotation, Release, Report, Sentence, Shema, Soundbite, Sweeping, Testimony, Theologoumenon, Truism, Utterance, Verb

Stateroom Bibby, Cabin

Statesman American, Attlee, Augustus, Botha, Briand, Bright, Canning, Cato, Clarendon, Diplomat, Disraeli, Draco, Elder, Flaminius, Franklin, Genro, Georgian, Gladstone, Gracchi, Grotius, Guy, Kissinger, Kruger, Lafayette, Lie, Mitterand, Nasser, North, Politician, Politico, Seneca, Smuts, Stein, Talleyrand, Tasmanian, Thiers, Tito, Walpole, Walsingham, Wealsman, Yankee

Static Atmospherics, Becalmed, Electricity, Inert, Maginot-minded, Motionless, Sferics, Stagnant, Stationary

Station(s) Action, Base, Berth, Birth, Camp, Caste, CCS, Coaling, Comfort, Crewe, Deploy, Depot, Docking, Dressing, Euston, Filling, Fire, Garrison, Gas, Generation, Halt, Head, Hill, Hilversum, Ice, Lay, Location, Marylebone, Nick, Outpost, Paddington, Panic, Pay, Petrol, Pitch, Place, Plant, Point, Police, Polling, Post, Power, Powerhouse, Quarter, Radio, Rank, Relay, Rowme, Seat, Service, Sheep, Sit, Space, Stance, Stand, Status, Stond, Subscriber, Tana, Tanna(h), Terminus, Testing, Thana(h), Thanna(h), Tracking, Transfer, Triangulation, Victoria, Waterloo, Waverley, Way, Weather, Work

Stationary Fasten, Fixed, Immobile, Parked, Sessile, Stable, Static

Stationer(y), Stationery-case Continuous, Multi-part, Papeterie

Statistic(ian), Statistics Actuary, Descriptive, Fermi-Dirac, Figure, Gradgrind, Graph, Inferential, Isotype, Lod, Nonparametric, Number, Parametric, Percentage, Quantum, Sampling, Student's t, Vital

Statuary, Statue(tte) Acrolith, Bronze, Bust, Colossus (of Rhodes), Discobolus, Effigy, Figure, Figurine, Galatea, Idol, Image, Kore, Kouros, Liberty, Memnon, Monolith, Monument, Oscar, Palladium, Pietà, Sculpture, Sphinx, Stonework, Stookie, Tanagra, Torso, Xoanon

Stature Growth, Height, Inches, Rank

Status Beacon, Caste, Class, Political, → **POSITION**, Prestige, Quo, Rank, Standing

Statute Act, Capitular, Chapter 11, Chapter 7, Decree, Edict, Law, Novels, Westminster

Staunch Amadou, Leal, Resolute, Steady, Stem, Stout, Styptic, Watertight

Stave Break, Dali, Forestall, Lag, Slat, Stanza, Ward

Stay(s) Alt, Avast, Bide, Board, Bolster, Cohab(it), Corselet, Corset, Embar, Endure, Fulcrum, Gest, Guy, Hawser, Indwell, Jump, Lie, Lig, Linger, Lodge, Manet, Moratorium, Piers, Prop, → **REMAIN**, Reprieve, Restrain, Settle, Sist, Sleepover, Sojourn, Stem, Stop off, Stop-over, Strut, Sustain, Tarry, Triatic, Villeggiatura

Stay-at-home Indoor, Tortoise
STD Aids, Herpes, Telephone, VD
Steadfast Changeless, Constance, Constant, Dilwyn, Firm, Implacable, Resolute, Sad, Stable
Steady Andantino, Ballast, Beau, Boyfriend, Changeless, Composer, Constant, Even, Faithful, Firm, Girlfriend, Measured, Regular, Rock, Stabilise, Stable, Unswerving
Steak Carpet-bag, Chateaubriand, Chuck, Diane, Fillet, Flitch, Garni, Mignon, Minute, Pope's eye, Porterhouse, Rump, Slice, Tartare, T-bone, Tenderloin, Tournedos, Vienna
Steal(ing) Abstract, Bag, Bandicoot, Bone, Boost, Cabbage, Cly, Condiddle, Convey, Creep, Crib, Duff, Edge, Embezzle, Filch, Glom, Grab, Half-inch, Heist, Hotting, Joyride, Kidnap, Knap, Knock down, Knock off, Lag, Liberate, Lift, Loot, Mag(g), Mahu, Mill, Naam, Nam, Nap, Nick, Nim, Nip, Nobble, Nym, Peculate, Phone-jack, Pilfer, Pillage, Pinch, Piracy, Plagiarise, Plunder, Poach, Pocket, Prig, Proll, Purloin, Ram-raid, Remove, Rifle, Rip-off, Rob, Rustle, Scrump, Skrimp, Smug, Snaffle, Snatch, Sneak, Snitch, Souvenir, Swipe, Take, Theft, Thieve, Tiptoe, TWOC, Whip
Stealth(y) Art, Catlike, Covert, Cunning, Furtive, Obreption, Surreptitious, Tiptoe
Steam(ed), Steaming, Steamy Boil, Condensation, Cushion, Dry, Fume, Gaseous, Het, Humid, Live, Livid, Mist, Porn, Radio, Roke, Sauna, Spout, Vapor, Vapour, Wet
Steamer, Steamboat Kettle, Showboat, Side-wheeler, SS, Str, Tramp, Turbine
Steam-hammer Ram
Steed Charger, Horse, Mount
Steel(y) Acierate, Adamant, Bethlehem, Blade, Blister, Bloom, Brace, Carbon, Cast, Chrome, Chromium, Cold, Concrete, Crucible, Damascus, Damask, High-carbon, High-speed, Low-carbon, Magnet, Manganese, Maraging, Martensite, Metal, Mild, Nickel, Pearlite, Ripon, Rolled, Shear, Silver, Sorbite, Spray, Stainless, Structural, Sword, Toledo, Tool, Tungsten, Vanadium, Wootz
Steelyard Bismar
Steep(ening) Abrupt, Arduous, Bold, Brent, Costly, Embay, Expensive, High-pitched, Hilly, Krans, Krantz, Kranz, Macerate, Marinade, Marinate, Mask, Monocline, Precipice, Precipitous, Rait, Rapid, Rate, Ret, Saturate, Scarp, → **SHEER**, Soak, Sog, Sop, Souse, Stey, Stickle, Tan
Steeple(jack) Spiderman, Spire, Turret
Steer(er), Steering Ackerman, Airt, Buffalo, Bullock, Bum, Cann, Castor, Con(n), Cox, Direct, → **GUIDE**, Helm, Navaid, Navigate, Ox, Pilot, Ply, Power, Rudder, Stot, Whipstaff, Zebu
Stem Alexanders, Arrow, Axial, Biller, Bine, Bole, Caudex, Caulicle, Caulome, Check, Cladode, Cladophyll, Confront, Corm, Culm, Dam, Epicotyl, Floricane, Ha(u)lm, Kex, Pedicle, Peduncle, Pin, Pseudaxis, Rachis, R(h)achilla, Rhachis, Rhizome, Rise, Rod, Sarment, Scapus, Seta, Shaft, Shank, Sobole(s), Spring, Stalk, Staunch, Stipe, Stolon, Stopple, Straw, Sympodium, Tail
Stench F(o)etor, Funk, Miasma, Odour, Smell, Stink, Whiff
Stencil Copy, Duplicate, Mimeograph®, Pochoir
Stenographer, Stenography Amanuensis, Secretary, Shorthand, Typist
Step(s) Act, Balancé, Chassé, Choctaw, Corbel, Corbie, Curtail, Dance, Degree, Démarche, Echelon, Escalate, False, Flight, Fouetté, Gain, Gait, Glissade, Goose, Grade, Grecian, Greece, Grees(e), Greesing, Grese, Gressing, Grice, Griece, Grise, Grize, Halfpace, Lavolt, Lock, Measure, Move, Notch, Pace, Pas, Pas de souris, Phase, Pigeon('s) wing, Quantal, Raiser, Ratlin(e), Rattlin(e), Rattling, Roundel,

Roundle, Rung, Sashay, Shuffle, Slip, Stage, Stair, Stalk, Stile, Stope, Stride, Toddle, Trap, Tread, Trip, Unison, Waddle, Walk, Whole, Winder

Stephen Martyr, Stainless

Stepmother Novercal

Stepney Spare

Steppe Kyrgyz, Llano, Plain

Stereo IPod®, Personal

Stereotype(d) Hackney, Ritual

Sterile, Sterilise(r), Sterilisation, Sterility Acarpous, Aseptic, Atocia, Autoclave, Barren, Clean, Dead, Fruitless, Impotent, Infertile, Neuter, Pasteurise, Spay, Tubal ligation, Vasectomy

Sterling Excellent, Genuine, Pound, Silver, Sound

Stern Aft, Austere, Back, Counter, Dour, Flinty, Grim, Hard, Implacable, Iron, Isaac, Nates, Poop, Rear, Relentless, Rugged, Stark, Strict, Tailpiece, Transom

Steroid Anabolic, Androsterone, Calciferol, Cortisone, Dexamethasone, Ergosterol, Fusidic, Lipid, Lumisterol, Mifepristone, Nandrolone, Predniso(lo)ne, Spironolactone, Stanozolol, Testosterone, Tetrahydrogestrinone

Sterol Stigmasterol

Stertorous Snore

Stet Restore

Stevedore Docker, Dockhand, Longshoreman, Stower, Wharfinger

Stevenson RLS, Tusitala

Stew(ed), Stews Bagnio, Bath, Blanquette, Boil, Bordel(lo), Bouillabaisse, Bouilli, Braise, Bredie, Brothel, Burgoo, Carbonade, Carbonnade, Casserole, Cassoulet, Cholent, Chowder, Coddle, Colcannon, Compot(e), Daube, Flap, Fuss, Goulash, Haricot, Hash, Hell, Hot(ch)pot(ch), Irish, Jug, Lather, Lobscouse, Maconochie, Matapan, Matelote, Mulligan, Navarin, Olla podrida, Osso bucco, Oyster, Paddy, Paella, Pepperpot, Pot-au-feu, Pot-pourri, Ragout, Ratatouille, Rubaboo, Salmi, Sass, Scouse, Seethe, Simmer, Slumgullion, Squiffy, Stie, Stove, Stovies, Sty, Succotash, Sweat, Swelter, Tajine, Tatahash, Tzimmes, Zamzawed, Zarzuela

Steward Butler, Cellarer, Chamberlain, Chiltern Hundreds, Dewan, Factor, Hind, Malvolio, Manciple, Maormor, Mormaor, Official, Oswald, Panter, Purser, Reeve, Seneschal, Sewer, Shop, Smallboy, Sommelier, Waiter

▷ **Stewed** *may indicate* an anagram

Stibnite Antimony, Kohl

Stick(ing) (out), Sticks, Sticky, Stuck Adhere, Affix, Agglutinant, Aground, Ash, Ashplant, Atlatl, Attach, Bamboo, Bastinado, Bat, Baton, Bauble, Bayonet, Blackthorn, Bludgeon, Bond, Boondocks, Caman, Cambrel, Cammock, Cane, Celery, Cement, Chalk, Chapman, Clag, Clam(my), Clarty, Clave, Cleave, Cleft, Cling, Clog, Club, Cocktail, Cohere, Coinhere, Composing, Control, Crab, Crosier, Cross(e), Crotch, Crozier, Crummack, Crummock, Cue, Distaff, Divining-rod, Dog, Dure, Endure, Fag(g)ot, Firewood, Fix, Flak, Founder, Fuse, Gad(e), Gaid, Gambrel, Gelatine, Glair, Gliadin, Glit, Glue, Goad, Gold, Goo, Gore, Ground-ash, Gum, Gunge, Gunk, Harpoon, Hob, Hurley, Immobile, Impale, Inhere, Isinglass, Jab, Jam, Joss, Jut, Kebbie, Kid, Kierie, Kindling, Kip, Kiri, Knife, Knitch, Knobkerrie, Ko, Lance, Lath(i), Lathee, Lentisk, Limy, Lug, Message, Minder, Molinet, Needle, Orange, Parasitic, Paste, Penang-lawyer, Persist, Phasmid, Piceous, Pierce, Piolet, Plaster, Pogo, Pole, Posser, Pot, Protrude, Protuberant, Pugol, Q-tip, Quarterstaff, Rash, Ratten, Rhubarb, Rhythm, Rod, Ropy, Scouring, Seat, Shillela(g)h, Shooting, Size, Ski, Smudge, Spanish windlass, Spear, Spurtle, Squail(er), Staff, Stand, Stang, Stob, Stodgy, Supplejack, Swagger, Switch, Swizzle, Swordstick, Tacamahac,

Tack(y), Tally, Tar, Thick, Throwing, Toddy, Tokotoko, Truncheon, Trunnion, Twig, Vare, Viscid, Viscous, Waddy, Wait, Walking, Wand, White, Woolder, Woomera(ng), Yardwand

Sticker Araldite®, Barnacle, Bumper, Bur, Glue, Label, Limpet, Partisan, Poster, Slogan

Stickler Pedant, Poser, Problem, Purist, Rigid, Rigorist, Tapist

Stiff, Stiffen(er), Stiffening, Stiffness Anchylosis, Angular, Ankylosis, Baleen, Bandoline, Brace, Buckram, Budge, Corpse, Corpus, Dear, Defunct, Expensive, Formal, Frore(n), Frorn(e), Gammy, Goner, Grommet, Gut, Hard, Lignin, Mort, Myotonia, Petrify, Pokerish, Prim, Ramrod, Rigid, Rigor, Rigor mortis, Sad, Set, Shank-iron, Size, Solid, Starch, Stark, Stay, Steeve, Stieve, Stilted, Stoor, Stour, Stowre, Sture, Trubenize®, Unbending, Unyielding, Whalebone, Wigan, Wooden

Stifle Crush, Dampen, Depress, Funk, Muffle, Scomfish, Smore, Smother, Stive, Strangle

Stigma(tise) Blemish, Brand, Carpel, Discredit, Note, Slur, Smear, Spot, → STAIN, Wound

Stile Gate, Slamming, Steps, Sty

Stiletto Bodkin, Heel, Knife

Still Accoy, Airless, Alembic, Assuage, Becalm, Calm, Check, Current, Doggo, Ene, Even(ness), Freeze-frame, Higher, Howbe, However, Hush, Illicit, Inactive, Inanimate, Inert, Kill, Languid, Limbec(k), Lull, Motionless, Nevertheless, Nonetheless, Patent, Peaceful, Photograph, Placate, Placid, Posé, Pot, Quiescent, Quiet, Resting, Silent, Snapshot, Soothe, Stagnant, Static, Stationary, Though, Yet

Stilt Avocet, Bird, Poaka, Prop, Scatch

Stilted Formal, Pedantic, Stiff, Unruffled, Wooden

Stimulate, Stimulus, Stimulant, Stimulation Activate, Adrenaline, Anilingus, Ankus, Antigen, Aperitif, Arak, Arouse, Auxin, Benny, Caffeine, Cinder, Clomiphene, Coca, Conditioned, Coramine, Cue, Dart, Dex(edrine)®, Digitalin, Digoxin, Egg, Energise, Erotogenic, Evoke, Excitant, Fillip, Foreplay, Fuel, Galvanize, Ginger, Goad, Grains of Paradise, G-spot, Guinea grains, Hormone, Incentive, Incite, Innerve, Inspire, Irritate, Jog, Key, K(h)at, Kick, L-dopa, Mneme, Motivate, Nikethamide, Oestrus, Oxytocin, Paraphilia, Pemoline, Pep, Peyote, Philtre, Pick-me-up, Piquant, Pituitrin, Potentiate, Prod, Promote, Provoke, Psych, Qat, Rim, Roborant, → ROUSE, Rowel, Rub, Sassafras, Sensuous, Spur, Sting, Stir, Tannin, Tar, Theine, Tickle, Tik-tik, Titillate, Tone, Tonic, Tropism, Unconditioned, Upper, Whet(stone), Wintergreen, Winter's bark

Sting(ing) Aculeate, Barb, Bite, Cheat, Cnida, Goad, Nematocyst, Nettle(tree), Overcharge, Perceant, Piercer, Poignant, Prick, Provoke, Pungent, Rile, Scorpion, Sephen, Smart, Spice, Stang, Stimulus, Surcharge, Tang, Tingle, Trichocyst, Urent, Urtica

Sting-ray Sephen, Trygon

Stingy Cheeseparing, Chintzy, Close, Costive, Hard, Illiberal, Mean, Miserly, Narrow, Near, Niggardly, Nippy, Parsimonious, Skimpy, Snippy, Snudge, Tight(wad), Tight-arse

▷ **Stingy** *may indicate* something that stings

Stink(er), Stinking, Stinks Abroma, Atoc, Atok, Brock, Cacodyl, Crepitate, Desman, Fetor, Foumart, Guff, Heel, Hellebore, Malodour, Mephitis, Miasma, Ming, Niff, Noisome, Pong, Ponk, Rasse, Reek, Rich, Science, → SMELL, Sondeli, Stench, Teledu

Stinkbird Hoa(c)tzin

Stint Chore, Economise, Limit, Scamp, Scantle, Scrimp, Share, Skimp

Stipend Ann(at), Annexure, Pay, Prebend, Remuneration, Salary, Wages

Stipulate, Stipulation Clause, Condition, Covenant, Insist, Provision, Proviso, Rider, Specify

Stipule Ocrea

Stir(red), Stirring Accite, Admix, Ado, Afoot, Agitate, Amo(o)ve, Animate, Annoy, Arouse, Awaken, Bird, Bother, Bustle, Buzz, Can, Churn, Cooler, Excite, Foment, Furore, Fuss, Gaol, Hectic, Impassion, Incense, Incite, Inflame, Instigate, Insurrection, Intermix, Jee, Jog, Kitty, Limbo, Live, → **MIX**, Move, Noy, Paddle, Penitentiary, Poach, Poss, Pother, → **PRISON**, Prod, Provoke, Quad, Quatch, Quetch, Quinche, Qui(t)ch, Quod, Rabble, Rear, Roil, Rouse, Roust, Rummage, Rustle, Sod, Steer, Styre, Swizzle, To-do, Upstart, Wake

▷ **Stir(red), Stirring** *may indicate* an anagram

Stirrup (guard) Bone, Footrest, Footstall, Gambado, Iron, Stapes, Tapadera, Tapadero

Stitch(ing), Stitch up Bargello, Basket, Baste, Blanket, Blind, Box, Buttonhole, Cable, Chain, Couching, Crewel, Crochet, Cross, Daisy, Embroider, Fancy, Feather, Fell, Flemish, Florentine, Garter, Gathering, Grospoint, Hem, Herringbone, Honeycomb, Insertion, Kettle, Knit, Lazy daisy, Lock, Middle, Monk's seam, Moss, Needle, Open, Overcast, Overlock, Pearl, Petit point, Pinwork, Plain, Purl, Queen, Rag, Railway, Rib, Rope, Running, Saddle, Satin, Screw, Sew, Slip, Smocking, Spider, Stab, Stay, Steek, Stem, Stockinette, Stocking, Straight, Sutile, Suture, Tack, Tailor's tack, Tent, Topstitch, Vandyke, Wheat-ear, Whip, Whole, Zigzag

Stock(ed), Stocks, Stocky Aerie, Aery, Alpha, Ambulance, Amplosome, Barometer, Blue-chip, Bouillon, Bree, Breech, Brompton, Buffer, But(t), Capital, Cards, Carry, Cattle, Choker, Cippus, Common, Congee, Conjee, Court-bouillon, Cravat, Dashi, Debenture, Delta, Die, Endomorph, Equip, Evening, Fumet, Fund, Gamma, Gear(e), Government, Graft, Gun, Handpiece, He(a)rd, Hilt, Hoosh, Industrial, Intervention, Inventory, Joint, Just-in-time, Kin, Larder, Laughing, Line, Little-ease, Locuplete, Night-scented, Omnium, Pigeonhole, Preferred, Pycnic, Race, Ranch, Recovery, Rep(ertory), Replenish, Reserve, Rolling, Root, Scrip, Seed, Shorts, Soup, Squat, Staple, Steale, Steelbow, Stirp(e)s, → **STORE**, Strain, Stubby, Supply, Surplus, Talon, Tap, Taurus, Team, Tie, Trite, Trust(ee), Utility, Virginian, Water

Stockade Barrier, Eureka, Zare(e)ba, Zereba, Zeriba

Stocking(s) Bas, Body, Boot-hose, Fishnet, Hogger, Hose, Leather, Legwarmer, Moggan, Netherlings, Netherstocking, Nylons, Popsock, Seamless, Sheer, Sock, Spattee, Support, Surgical, Tights

Stockman, Stockbroker Broker, Jobber, Neatherd

Stodge, Stodgy Dull, Filling, Heavy

Stoic(al) Impassive, Job, Logos, Patient, Philosophical, Plato, Porch, Seneca(n), Spartan, Stolid, Zeno

Stoke(r), Stokes Bram, Coal-trimmer, Fire(man), Fuel, S, Shovel

Stole(n) Bent, Epitrachelion, Hot, Maino(u)r, Manner, Manor, Nam, Orarion, Orarium, Reft, Scarf, Soup, Staw, Tippet, Tweedle, Waif, Wrap

Stolid Beefy, Deadpan, Dull, Impassive, Phlegmatic, Po(-faced), Thickset, Wooden

Stomach(ic) Abdomen, Abomasum, Accept, Appetite, Belly, Bible, Bingy, Bonnet, Bread-basket, Brook, C(o)eliac, Corporation, Epigastrium, Epiploon, Fardel-bag, Gaster, Gizzard, Gut, Heart, Jejunum, King's-hood, Kite, Kyte, Little Mary, Manyplies, Mary, Maw, Mesaraic, Midriff, Omasum, Opisthosoma, Paunch, Potbelly, Propodon, Proventriculus, Psalterium, Puku, Pylorus, Read, Rennet, Reticulum, Rumen, Stand, Stick, Swagbelly, → **SWALLOW**, Tripe, Tum, Tun-belly, Urite, Vell, Venter, Wame, Washboard, Wem, Zingiber

Stomach-ache Colic, Colitis, Collywobbles, Gastralgia, Giardiasis, Gripe, Gutrot, Mulligrubs

Stone(s), Stone age, Stoned, Stony Blotto, Cast, Drunk, Henge, Imposing, Ink, Inukshuk, Lucky, Lydian, Mort, Niobe(an), Pelt, Precious, Putting, Rolling, Seeing, Sermon, Standing, Step(ping), Through, Touch, Tusking

STONES

2 letters:
St

3 letters:
Gem
Hog
Pit
Rag
Tin

4 letters:
Bath
Blue
Celt
Door
Flag
Hone
Horn
Iron
Jasp
Kerb
Lias
Lime
Lode
Onyx
Opal
Plum
Ragg
Sard
Skew
Slab
Soap
Tile
Trap

5 letters:
Agate
Amber
Balas
Beryl
Black
Chalk
Chert
Coade

Culch
Drupe
Flint
Gooly
Grape
Jewel
Kenne
Lapis
Logan
Menah
Metal
Mocha
Paste
Prase
Pumie
Quern
Quoin
Quoit
Rubin
Rufus
Rybat
Satin
Scone
Scree
Slate
Slick
Sneck
Stela
Stele
Topaz
Wacke
Wyman

6 letters:
Amazon
Arthur
Ashlar
Ashler
Baetyl
Bezoar
Brinny
Chesil
Chisel
Cobble

Coping
Cultch
Dolmen
Flusch
Fossil
Gibber
Gooley
Goolie
Gravel
Humite
Iolite
Jargon
Jasper
Kidney
Kingle
Ligure
Lithic
Menhir
Metate
Mihrab
Mosaic
Muller
Nutlet
Oamaru
Paving
Pebble
Pot-lid
Pumice
Pyrene
Rip-rap
Samian
Sarsen
Scarab
Summer
Tanist
Yonnie

7 letters:
Asteria
Avebury
Blarney
Bologna
Boulder
Breccia

Callais
Cat's eye
Chuckie
Clinker
Curling
Girasol
Granite
Hyacine
Hyalite
Jargoon
Lia-fail
Lithoid
Moabite
Olivine
Parpane
Parpend
Parpent
Pennant
Peridot
Perpend
Perpent
Petrous
Pudding
Purbeck
Putamen
Rocking
Rosetta
Rubbing
Sardine
Sardius
Sarsden
Scaglia
Schanse
Schanze
Smaragd
Staddle
Tektite
Telamon
Thunder
Trilith
Tripoli
Urolith

8 letters:
Aerolite
Aerolith
Amethyst
Asteroid
Baguette
Cabochon
Calculus
Cinnamon
Cromlech
Cryolite
Ebenezer
Elf-arrow
Endocarp
Essonite
Ganister
Girasole
Lapidate
Megalith
Menamber
Monolith
Nephrite
Omphalos

Onychite
Parpoint
Peastone
Petrosal
Phengite
Pisolite
Portland
Potstone
Rollrich
Sapphire
Sardonyx
Scalpins
Schantze
Specular
Tonalite
Voussoir

9 letters:
Alabaster
Asparagus
Cairngorm
Carnelian
Cholelith

Chondrite
Cornelian
Crossette
Dichroite
Firestone
Gannister
Greensand
Hessonite
Hoarstone
Lithiasis
Meteorite
Paleolith
Pipestone
Rubicelle
Scagliola
Trilithon
Turquoise
Ventifact

10 letters:
Adamantine
Alectorian
Aragonites

Chalcedony
Draconites
Enhydritic
Foundation
Gastrolith
Grey-wether
Kimberlite
Lherzolite
Lithophyte
Pearlstone
Penny-stone
Rhinestone
Sleekstone
Slickstone

11 letters:
Pencil-stone
Peristalith

12 letters:
Carton-pierre
Philosopher's

Stone-crop Orpin(e), Sedum, Succulent

Stone-pusher Sisyphus

Stone-thrower Bal(lista), Catapult, David, Mangonel, Onager, Perrier, Sling, Trebuchet

Stone-wall(er) Block, Jackson, Mule, Revet

Stoneware Crouch-ware

Stone-worker Jeweller, Knapper, Sculptor

Stooge Butt, Cat's-paw, Feed, Straight man

Stook(s) Sheaf, Stack, Thr(e)ave

Stool Buffet, Coppy, Cracket, Creepie, Cricket, Cucking, Curule, Cutty, Ducking, Faeces, Hassock, Litany, Milking, Music, Piano, Pouf(fe), Repentance, Ruckseat, Seat, Sir-reverence, Step, Stercoral, Sunkie, Taboret, Tripod, Tripos, Turd

Stoop Bend, Condescend, C(o)urb, Crouch, Daine, Deign, Incline, Porch, Slouch

Stop(page), Stopcock, Stopper, Stopping Abort, Adeem, An(n)icut, Arrest, Avast, Bait, Ba(u)lk, Bide, Blin, Block, Brake, Buffer, Bung, Canting-coin, → CEASE, Cessation, Chapter, Check, Checkpoint, Cheese, Cholestasis, Clarabella, Clarino, Clarion, Clog, Close, Colon, Comfort, Comma, Conclude, Cork, Coupler, Cremo(r)na, Cremorne, Cromorna, Cut, Deactivate, Debar, Demurral, Desist, Deter, Devall, Diapason, Diaphone, Discontinue, Discourage, Dit, Dolce, Dot, Dulciana, Echo, Embargo, End, Fare stage, Field, Fifteenth, Flag, Flue, Flute, Foreclose, Foundation, Fr(a)enum, Freeze, Full, Full point, Gag, Gamba, Gemshorn, Glottal, Gong, Halt, Hamza(h), Hartal, Heave to, Hinder, Hitch, Ho, Hoa, Hoh, Hold, Hoy, Inhibit, Intermit, Ischuria, Jam, Kibosh, Let-up, Lill, Lin, Lute, Media, Mutation, Nasard, Oboe, Obstruent, Obturate, Occlude, Oppilate, Organ, Outage, Outspan, Pause, Period, Piccolo, Pit, Plug, Point, Poop, Preclude, Prevent, Principal, Prorogue, Pull-in, Pull over, Pull-up, Punctuate, Pyramidon, Quash, Quint, Quit, Racket, Red, Reed, Refrain, Register, Rein, Remain, Request, Rest, Salicet,

Salicional, Scotch, Screw-top, Semi-colon, Sese, Sesquialtera, Sext, Sist, Snub, Solo, Spigot, Stall, Stanch, Standstill, Stash, Stasis, Station, Staunch, Stay, Stent, Stive, Strike, Subbase, Subbass, Suction, Supersede, Suppress, Suspend, T, Tab, Tamp(ion), Tap, Tenuis, Terminate, Toby, Toho, Truck, Twelfth, Voix celeste, Vox angelica, Vox humana, Waldflute, Waldhorn, Waypoint, When, Whistle, Whoa

Stopgap Caretaker, Gasket, Gaskin, Interim, Makeshift, Pis aller, Temporary

Storage, Store(house) Accumulate, Archive, Armoury, Arsenal, Associative, Backing, Barn, Bin, Bottle, Bottom drawer, Boxroom, Bunker, Buttery, Cache, Capacitance, Cell, Cellar, Chain, Clamp, Clipboard, Convenience, Co-op(erative), Co-operative, Cootch, Core, Cupboard, Cutch, Database, Deli, Dene-hole, Dépanneur, Department(al), Depository, Depot, Dime, Discount, Dolia, Dolly-shop, Elevator, Emporium, Ensile, Entrepot, Étape, Fund, Galleria, Garner, Genizah, Girnal, Glory hole, Go-down, Granary, Groceteria, Hive, → HOARD, Hog, Hold, Hope chest, House, Houseroom, Humidor, Husband, Hypermarket, Imbarn, Larder, Lastage, Lazaretto, Liquor, Locker, Lumber room, Magazine, Main, Mart, Mattamore, Memory, Mine, Morgue, Mothball, Mow, Multiple, Nest-egg, Off-licence, One-step, Package, Pantechnicon, Pantry, Pithos, Provision, Pumped, Rack(ing), RAM, Repertory, Reposit, ROM, Root house, Sector, Shed, → SHOP, Silage, Silo, Spence, Spooling, Springhouse, Squirrel, Stack, Stash, Stock, Stockpile, Stockroom, Stow, Superbaza(a)r, Superette, Supermarket, Supply, Tack-room, Tank, Thesaurus, Tithe-barn, Tommy-shop, Virtual, Volutin, Warehouse, Woodshed, Woodyard, Wool (shed)

▶ **Storey** *see* STORY

Stork Adjutant, Antigone, Argala, Bird, Jabiru, Marabou(t), Marg, Saddlebill, Shoebill, Wader, Whale-headed, Wood, Wood ibis

Stork's bill Erodium

Storm(y) Ablow, Adad, Assail, Attack, Baguio, Blizzard, Bluster, Bourasque, Brouhaha, Buran, Calima, Charge, Cockeye(d) bob, Cyclone, Devil, Dirty, Dust, Electric, Enlil, Expugn, Furore, Gale, Gusty, Haboob, Hurricane, Ice, Line, Magnetic, Monsoon, Onset, Oragious, Pelter, Rage(ful), Raid, Rain, Rampage, Rant, Rave, Red spot, Rugged, Rush, Shaitan, Snorter, Squall, Sumatra, Tea-cup, Tebbad, Tempest, Tornade, Tornado, Tropical, Unruly, Violent, Weather, Willy-willy, Wroth, Zu

▷ **Stormy** *may indicate* an anagram

Story, Storyline, Storey, Stories Account, Allegory, Anecdote, Apocrypha, Arthuriana, Attic, Bar, Basement, Baur, Bawr, Biog, Blood and thunder, Chestnut, Clearstory, Clerestory, Cock and bull, Conte, Cover, Decameron, Edda, Epic, Episode, Étage, Exclusive, Exemplum, Fable, Fabliau, Feature, Fib, Fiction, Flat, Floor, Folk-tale, Gag, Geste, Ghost, Glurge, Hard-luck, Heptameron, Hitopadesa, Horror, Idyll, Iliad, Jataka, Lee, Legend, Lie, Mabinogion, Märchen, Mezzanine, Myth(os), Mythus, Narrative, Nouvelle, Novel(la), Oratorio, Parable, Passus, Pentameron, Photo, Plot, Rede, Report, Romance, Rumour, Saga, Scoop, Script, Serial, SF, Shaggy dog, Shocker, Short, Smoke-room, Sob, Spiel, Spine-chiller, Splash, Stage, Success, Tale, Tall, Thread, Thriller, Tier, Triforium, Upper, Version, Yarn

Story-teller Aesop, Fibber, Griot, Liar, Munchausen, Narrator, Raconteur, Shannachie, Tusitala, Uncle Remus

Stoup Benitier, Bucket, Vessel

Stout(ness) Ale, Beer, Black velvet, Burly, Chopping, Chubby, Embonpoint, Endomorph, Entire, Fat, Fubsy, Hardy, Humpty-dumpty, Lusty, Manful, Milk, Obese, Overweight, Porter, Portly, Potbelly, Robust, Stalwart, Stalworth, Sta(u)nch,

Strong, Stuggy, Sturdy, Substantial, Tall, Velvet

Stove Baseburner, Break, Calefactor, Chauf(f)er, Cockle, Cooker, Cooktop, Furnace, Gasfire, Oven, Potbelly, Primus®, Range, Salamander

Stow Cram, Flemish (down), Load, Pack, Rummage, Stack, Stash, Steeve

Strabismus Squint

Straddle, Straddling Bestride, Enjamb(e)ment, Strodle

Strafe Bombard, Shell, Shoot

Straggle(r), Straggly Estray, Gad, Meander, Ramble, Rat-tail, Spidery, Sprawl, Stray, Wander

Straight(en), Straightness Align, Bald, Beeline, Correct, Die, Direct, Downright, Dress, Frank, Gain, Het(ero), Home, Honest, Lank, Legit, Level, Neat, Normal, Ortho-, Orthotropous, Rectilineal, Rectitude, Righten, Sheer, Slap, Tidy, True, Unbowed, Uncurl, Unlay, Upright, Veracious, Virgate

Straight edge Lute, Ruler

Straightfaced Agelast

Straightforward Candid, Direct, Downright, Easy, Even, Forthright, Honest, Jannock, Level, Plain sailing, Pointblank, Simple

Straight-haired Leiotrichous

Strain(ed), Strainer, Straining Agonistic, Ancestry, Aria, Breed, Bulk, Carol, Clarify, Colander, Distend, Drawn, Effort, Exert, Filter, Filtrate, Fit, Fitt(e), Force, Fray, Fytt(e), Intense, Kind, Melody, Milsey, Minus, Molimen, Music, Note, Overtask, Passus, Percolate, Plus, Pressure, Pull, Purebred, Rack, Raring, Reck(an), Repetitive, Retch, Rick, Seep, Seil(e), Set, Shear, Sieve, Sift, Sile, Stape, Start, Stirps, Stock, Streak, Stress, Stretch, Sye, Tamis, Tammy, Tax, Tems(e), Tenesmus, Tense, Tension, Threnody, Try, Tune, Unease, Vein, Vice, Work, Wrick

Strait(s) Bab el Mandeb, Basilan, Bass, Bering, Bosp(h)orus, Canso, Channel, Condition, Cook, Crisis, Cut, Dardanelles, Davis, Denmark, Desperate, Dover, Drake Passage, Euripus, Florida, Formosa, Foveaux, Gat, Gibraltar, Golden Gate, Great Belt, Gut, Hainan, Hormuz, Hudson, Johore, Juan de Fuca, Kattegat, Kerch, Korea, Kyle, Little Belt, Lombok, Mackinac, Magellan, Malacca, Menai, Messina, Mona Passage, Narrow, North Channel, Otranto, Palk, Predicament, Soenda, Solent, Sound, St, Sumba, Sunda, Taiwan, Tatar, Tiran, Torres, Tsugaru, Windward Passage

Straiten(ed) Impecunious, Impoverish, Poor, Restrict

Strait-laced Blue-nosed, Narrow, Prig, Primsie, Prudish, Puritan, Stuffy

Strand(ed) Abandon, Aground, Bank, Beach, Desert, Fibre, Haugh, Hexarch, Isolate, Lock, Maroon, Neaped, Ply, Rice, Rope, Shore, Sliver, Thread, Three-ply, Tress, Twist, Wisp

Strange(ness), Stranger Alien, Aloof, Amphitryon, Curious, Dougal, Eerie, Exotic, Ferly, Foreign, Fraim, Frem(d), Fremit, Frenne, Funny, Guest, Jimmy, Malihini, New, Novel, Odd(ball), Outlandish, Outsider, Quare, Queer, Rum, S, Screwy, Selcouth, Singular, Surreal, Tea-leaf, Uncanny, Unco, Uncommon, Unfamiliar, Unked, Unket, Unkid, Unused, Unusual, Wacky, Weird, Wondrous

▷ **Strange** *may indicate* an anagram

Strangle(r) Choke, Garotte, Jugulate, Suppress, Throttle, Thug(gee)

Strap(ping) Able-bodied, Band, Barber, Beat, Bowyangs, Braces, Brail, Braw, Breeching, Browband, Cheekpiece, Crownpiece, Crupper, Cuir-bouilli, Curb, Deckle, Girth, Halter, Harness, Holdback, Jess, Jock(ey), Kicking, Larrup, Lash, Ligule, Lorate, Lore, Manly, Martingale, Nicky-tam, Octopus, Overcheck, Pandy, Rand, Rein, Robust, Shoulder, Sling, Spaghetti, Spider, Strop, Surcingle, Suspender, T, Tab, Taws(e), T-bar, Thong, Throatlash, Throatlatch, Trace,

Tump-line, Wallop, Watch, Watchband

Stratagem, Strategist, Strategy Artifice, Clausewitz, Contrivance, Coup, Deceit, Device, Dodge, Exit, Fetch, Finesse, Fraud, Heresthetic, Kaupapa, Lady Macbeth, Maskirovka, Masterstroke, Maximum, Minimax, Plan, Rope-a-dope, → **RUSE**, Salami, Scheme, Scorched earth, Sleight, Subterfuge, Tack, Tactic(s), Tactician, Trick, Wile

Stratum, Strata Bed, Coal Measures, Kar(r)oo, Layer, Neogene, Permian, Schlieren, Seam, Syncline

Straw(s), Strawy Balibuntal, Boater, Buntal, Chaff, Cheese, Halm, Hat, Haulm, Hay, Insubstantial, Last, Leghorn, Monkey-pump, Nugae, Oaten, Panama, Parabuntal, Pea(se), Pedal, Rush, Short, Sipper, Stalk, Stramineous, Strammel, Strummel, Stubble, Trifles, Truss, Wisp, Ye(a)lm

Strawberry Alpine, Barren, Birthmark, Fragaria, Fraise, Garden, Hautbois, Hautboy, Potentilla, Wild

Stray Abandoned, Chance, Depart, Deviate, Digress, Err, Forwander, Foundling, Gamin, Maverick, Meander, Misgo, Pye-dog, Ramble, Roam, Sin, Straggle, Streel, Traik, Unowned, Waff, Waif, Wander

Streak(ed), Streaker, Streaky Archimedes, Bended, Blue, Brindle, Comet, Flaser, Flash, Fleck, Freak, Hawked, Highlights, Lace, Layer, Leonid, Lowlight, Marble, Mark, Merle, Mottle, Primitive, Race, Run, Schlieren, Seam, Shot, Striate, Striga, Strip(e), Vein, Venose, Vibex, Waif, Wake, Wale, Yellow

Stream Acheron, Anabranch, Arroyo, Beam, Beck, Bogan, Bourne, Brook, Burn, Consequent, Course, Current, Driblet, Fast, Flow, Flower, Freshet, Gulf, Gush, Headwater, Influent, Jet, Kill, Lade, Lane, Leet, Logan, Meteor, Nala, Nalla(h), Nulla(h), Obsequent, Pokelogan, Pour, Pow, Riffle, Rill, River, Rivulet, Rubicon, Run, Runnel, Sike, Slough, Spill, Spruit, Star, Strand, Streel, Subsequent, Syke, The Fleet, Third, Thrutch, Tide-race, Torrent, Tributary, Trickle, Trout, Watercourse, Water-splash, Winterbourne

Streamer Banderol(e), Bandrol, Banner(all), Bannerol, Pennon, Pinnet, Ribbon, Tape, Tippet, Vane

Streamline(d), Streamliner Clean, Fair, Fairing, Simplify, Sleek, Slim

Street Alley, Ave(nue), Bay, Bowery, Broad, Carey, Carnaby, Cato, Causey, Champs Elysées, Cheapside, Civvy, Close, Corso, Court, Crescent, Downing, Drive, Easy, Fleet, Gate, Grub, Harley, High(way), Kármán vortex, Lane, Lombard, Main, Meuse, Mews, One-way, Parade, Paseo, Queer, Road, Sesame, Side, Sinister, St, Strand, Terrace, Thoroughfare, Threadneedle, Throgmorton, Two-way, Vortex, Wall, Wardour, Watling, Way, Whitehall

Street arab Mudlark

Streetcar Desire, Tram

Strength(en), Strengthened, Strengthening Afforce, Anneal, Asset, Ausforming, Bant, Beef, Brace, Brawn, Build, Confirm, Consolidate, Enable, Energy, Field, Fish, Foison, Force, Forte, Fortify, Freshen, Grit, Heart, Herculean, Horn, Intensity, Iron, Line, Main, Man, Might, Munite, Muscle, Nerve, → **POWER**, Prepotence, Pre-stress, Proof, Reinforce, Roborant, Shear, Sinew, Spike, Stamina, Steel, Sthenia, Stoutness, → **STRONG**, Tensile, Thews, Titration, Ultimate, Unity, Vim, Yield

Strenuous Arduous, Effort, Exhausting, Hard, Laborious, Vehement

Strephon Rustic, Wooer

Stress(ed) Accent, Arsis, Birr, Brunt, Careworn, Emphasis, Ictus, Impress, Italicise, Marcato, Orthotonesis, Oxytone, Paroxytone, Post-traumatic, Primary, Proof, PTSD, Rack, Ram, Rhythm, RSI, Secondary, Sentence, Sforzando, Shear, Strain,

Taut, Tense, → TENSION, Try, Underline, Underscore, Urge, Wind shear, Word, Yield (point)

Stretch(able), Stretched, Stretcher, Stretching Belt, Brick, Crane, Distend, Draw, Ectasis, Eke, Elastic, Elongate, Exaggerate, Expanse, Extend, Extensile, Farthingale, Fib, Frame, Give, Gurney, Home, Lengthen, Litter, Narrows, Outreach, Pallet, Pandiculation, Porrect, Procrustes, Prolong, Protend, Pull, Rack, Rax, → REACH, Sentence, Shiner, Span, Spell, Spread, Spreadeagle, Strain, Streak, Taut, Tend, Tense, Tensile, Tenter, Term, Time, Tract, Tractile, Tree, Trolley

Stretcher-bearer Fuzzy-wuzzy angel

Striate Lineolate, Vein

Stricken Beset, Hurt, Overcome, Shattered

Strict Dour, Exacting, Harsh, Literal, Medic, Narrow, Orthodox, Penal, Proper, Puritanical, Rigid, Rigorous, Severe, Spartan, Stern, Strait(-laced), Stringent

Stride Gal(l)umph, Leg, Lope, March, Pace, Piano, Stalk, Sten, Stend, Straddle, Stroam, Strut, Stump

Strident Brassy, Grinding, Harsh, Raucous, Screech

Strife Bargain, Barrat, Bate(-breeding), Colluctation, Conflict, Conteck, Contest, Discord, Disharmony, Dissension, Feud, Food, Friction, Ignoble, Scrap(ping), Sturt

Strike(s), Striker, Striking, Strike out Affrap, Air, Alight, Annul, Appulse, Arresting, Attitude, Backhander, Baff, Band, Bandh, Bang, Bash, Bat, Baton, Batsman, Batter, Beat, Belabour, Better, Biff, Black, Bla(u)d, Bonanza, Bop, British disease, Buff, Buffet, Bund(h), Butt, Cane, Catch, Chime, Chip, Clap, Clash, Clatch, Clip, Clock, Clout, Club, Cob, Collide, Conk, Constitutional, Coup, Cue, Cuff, Dad, Dent, Dev(v)el, Ding, Dint, Dismantle, Distingué, Douse, Dowse, Dramatic, Drive, Dush, Éclat, Événement, Fet(ch), Fillip, Firk, Fist, Flail, Flog, Frap, General, Get, Gnash, Go-slow, Gowf, Hail, Handsome, Hartal, Head-butt, → HIT, Horn, Hour, Hunger, Ictus, Illision, Impact, Impinge, Impress, Jarp, Jaup, Jole, Joll, Joule, Jowl, Knock, Lam, Lambast, Laser, Lay(-off), Lightning, Match, Middle, Mint, Notable, Noticeable, Official, Out, Pash, Pat(ter), Pat, Pean, Peen, Pein, Pene, Percuss, Picket, Pize, Plectrum, Pronounced, Pummel, Punch, Ram, Rap, Remarkable, Rolling, Roquet, Salient, Scrub, Scutch, Shank, Sick out, Sideswipe, Signal, Sitdown, Sit-in, Slam, Slap, Slat, Slog, Slosh, Smack, Smash, Smite, Sock, Souse, Sowce, Sowse, Spank, Stayaway, Stop(page), Stub, Swap, Swat, Swinge, Swipe, Swop, Sympathy, Tan, Tapotement, Tat, Thump, Thwack, Tip, Token, Tonk, Tripper, Twat, Unconstitutional, Unofficial, Walk-out, Wallop, Wap, Whack, Whale, Whang, Whap, Wherret, Who does what, Whomp, Whop, Wick, Wildcat, Wipe, Wondrous, Zap

Strike-breaker Blackleg, Fink, Rat, Scab

String(s), Stringy Band, Bant, Beads, Bootlace, Bow, Bowyang, Cello, Chalaza, Chanterelle, Cord, Cosmic, Creance, Cremaster, Drill, Enfilade, Fiddle, Fillis, First, G, Glass, Gut, Henequin, Heniquin, Hypate, Idiot, Injection, Keyed, Kill, Lace, Lag, Leading, Lichanos, Macramé, Mese, Necklace, Nete, Nicky-tam, Oil, Paramese, Pledget, Production, Proviso, Purse, Quint, Ripcord, Rope, Rough, Second, Series, Shoe(-tie), Sinewy, Snare, Spit, Stable, Straggle, Strand, Sympathetic, Team, Tendon, Thairm, Tie, Tough, Train, Trite, Viola, Violin, Wreathed

String-course Moulding, Table

Stringent Extreme, Rigid, Severe, Strict, Urgent

Strip(ped), Stripper, Striptease Airfield, Armband, Band, Bare, Bark, Batten, Belt, Bereave, Bimetallic, Blowtorch, Casparian, Chippendale, Comic, Cote, Defoliate, Denude, Deprive, Derobe, Despoil, Devest, Disbark, Dismantle, Dismask, Disrobe, Divest, Dosing, Drag, Ecdysiast, Ecdysis, Écorché, Fannel(l), Fiche, Film, Flashing,

Flaught, Flay, Fleece, Flench, Flense, Flight, Flinch, Flounce, Flype, Furring, Gaza, Goujon, Hatband, Infula, Jib, Label, Landing, Lap-dancer, Lardon, Lath, Ledge, Linter, List, Littoral, Loading, Locust, Maniple, Median, Möbius, Panhandle, Parting, Peel, Pillage, Pluck, Pull, Puttee, Puttie, Rand, Raunch, Raw, Ribbon, Ring-bark, Roon, Royne, Rumble, Rund, Runway, Screed, Scrow, Shear, Shed, Shim, Shuck, Skin, Slat, Slit, Sliver, Spellican, Spilikin, Spill(ikin), Splat, Splent, Spline, Splint, Splinter, Spoil, Straik, Strake, Strap, Streak, Strop, Sugar soap, Swath, Sweatband, Tack, Tear, Tee, Thong, Tirl, Tirr, Tongue, Uncase, Unclothe, Undeck, Undress, Unfrock, Unrig, Unrip, Unrobe, Unvaile, Valance, Weather, Widow, Zone

Stripe(d) Band, Bausond, Candy, Chevron, Cingulum, Cove, Endorse, Go-faster, Lance-jack, Laticlave, Line, List, Magnetic, → **NCO**, Ombré, Pale, Paly, Pin, Pirnie, Pirnit, Slash, Snip, Straik, Strake, Streak, Stroke, Tabaret, Tabby, Tiger, Tragelaph(us), Vitta, Weal

Strive, Striving Aim, Aspire, → **ATTEMPT**, Contend, Endeavour, Enter, Kemp, Labour, Nisus, Pingle, Press, Strain, Struggle, Toil, Try, Vie

Stroke Apoplex(y), Backhander, Bat, Bisque, Blow, Boast, Breast, Butterfly, Caress, Carom, Chip, Chop, Counterbuff, Coup, Coy, Crawl, Dash, Dint, Dog(gy)-paddle, Down-bow, Drear(e), Drere, Dropshot, Effleurage, Estrarnazone, Exhaust, Feat, Flick, Fondle, Foozle, Forehand, Glance, Ground, Hairline, Hand(er), Ictus, Inwick, Jenny, Jole, Joll, Joule, Jowl, Knell, Knock, Lash, Lightning, Like, Line, Loft, Long jenny, Loser, Massé, Oarsman, Oblique, Odd, Off-drive, Outlash, Palp, Paw, Pot-hook, Pull, Punto reverso, Put(t), Reverso, Ridding straik, Roquet, Rub, Scart, Scavenge, Sclaff, Scoop, Seizure, Sheffer's, Short Jenny, Sider, Sixte, Slash, Smooth, Solidus, Spot, Strike, Stripe, Sweep, Swipe, Tact, Tittle, Touch, Touk, Trait, Trudgen, Trudgeon, Tuck, Upbow, Virgule, Wale, Whang

Stroll(er), Strolling Ambulate, Bummel, Dander, Daun(d)er, Dawner, Flânerie, Flâneur, Idle, Lounge, Ramble, Saunter, Stravaig, Stray, Toddle, Walk, Walkabout, Wander

Strong(est) Able, Boofy, Brawny, Cast-iron, Doughty, Durable, F, Firm, Fit, Forceful, Forcible, Forte, Full-blown, Hale, Heady, Hercules, High-powered, Humming, Husky, Intense, Mighty, Nappy, Pithy, Pollent, Potent, Powerful, Pungent, Racy, Rank, Robust, Samson, Solid, Stalwart, Stark, Steely, Sthenic, Stiff, Stout, Str, Strapping, → **STRENGTH**, Sturdy, Substantial, Suit, Tarzan, Tenable, Thesis, Thickset, Trusty, Vegete, Vehement, Vigorous, Violent, Virile, Well-built, Well-set, Ya(u)ld

Stronghold Acropolis, Aerie, Bastion, Castle, Citadel, Eyrie, Eyry, Fastness, Fortalice, Fortress, Keep, Kremlin, Redoubt, Tower

Strontium Sr

Strop Leather, Sharpen, Strap

Struck Aghast, Raught, Smitten

Structural, Structure Allotrope, Analysis, Anatomy, Armature, Atomic, Building, Catafalque, Cold frame, Compage(s), Conus, Data, Deep, Edifice, Erection, Fabric, Fairing, Format(ion), Formwork, Frame, Galea, Heterarchy, Hyperbolic, Hyperfine, Ice-apron, Kekulé, Lantern, Macrocosm, Mole, Organic, Palmation, Pediment, Pergola, Phloem, Physique, Pod, Power, Protein, Retinaculum, Set-up, Shape, Skeleton, Sponson, Sporocarp, Squinch, Staging, Stand, Starling, Stylobate, Surface, Syntax, System, Tectonic, Telomere, Texas, Texture, Trabecula, Trochlea, Undercarriage

Struggle, Struggling Agon(ise), Agonistes, Amelia, Buckle, Camp, Chore, Class, Conflict, Contend, Contest, Cope, Debatement, Effort, Encounter, Endeavour,

Fight, Flounder, Grabble, Grapple, Jockey, Kampf, Labour, Luctation, Mill, Pingle, Rat-race, Reluct, Scrabble, Scrape, Scrimmage, Scrum, Scrummage, Scuffle, Slugfest, Sprangle, → **STRIVE**, Toil, Tug, Tussle, Uphill, Vie, War(sle), Wrestle

▷ **Struggle** *may indicate* an anagram

Strum Thrum, Twang, Tweedle, Vamp

Strumpet Cocotte, Harlot, Hiren, Lorette, Paramour, Succubus, Wench

Strut(ter), Strutting Bracket, Brank, Bridging, Cock, Dolphin striker, Flounce, Haught(y), Jet, Kingrod, Longeron, Martingale boom, Member, Nervure, Peacock, Pown, Prance, Prop, Scotch, Shore, Spur, Stalk, Stretcher, Strunt, Swagger, Swank, Tail-boom, Tie-beam

Stuart Anne, James, Pretender

Stub(by) Butt, Counterfoil, Dout, Dowt, Dumpy, Squat, Stob, Stocky

Stubble Ar(r)ish, Bristle, Designer, Hair, Ill-shaven, Stump

Stubborn(ness) Adamant, Bigoted, Bull-headed, Contumacious, Cross-grained, Cussed, Diehard, Dogged, Entêté, Hard(-nosed), Hidebound, Intransigent, Inveterate, Moyl(e), Mulish, Mumpsimus, Obdurate, Obstinate, Opinionated, Ornery, Ortus, Pertinacious, Perverse, Recalcitrant, Reesty, Refractory, Rigwiddie, Rigwoodie, Self-willed, Stiff, Stout, Tenacious, Thrawn, Wrong-headed

Stuck Fast, Glued, Jammed, Set, Stopped, Wedged

Stuck-up Chesty, Highty-tighty, Hoity-toity, La(h)-di-da(h), Proud, Sealed, Vain

Stud(ded) Boss, Cooser, Cripple, Cu(i)sser, Doornail, Farm, Frost, He-man, Knob, Nail, Press, Race, Rivet, Seg, Set, Shear, Sire, Stop

Student(s) Abiturient, Alphabetarian, Alumnus, Apprentice, Bajan, Bejant, Bursar, Bursch(en), Cadet, Catechumen, Class, Coed, Commoner, Dan, Dig, Disciple, Dresser, Dux, Exchange, Exhibitioner, Extensionist, External, Form, Fresher, Freshman, Gownsman, Graduand, Green welly, Gyte, Ikey, Internal, Junior, Kommers, Kyu, → **LEARNER**, Magistrand, Matie, Mature, Medical, Nomologist, NUS, Opsimath, Ordinand, Oxonian, Peking duck, Pennal, Plebe, Poll, Postgraduate, Preppy, Pupil, Reader, Rushee, Sap, → **SCHOLAR**, Self-taught, Semi, Seminar, Seminarian, Shark, Sizar, Sizer, Smug, Softa, Soph(omore), Sophister, Spod, Subsizar, Swot, Templar, Tiro, Tosher, Trainee, Tuft, Tukkie, Tutee, Wedge, Witsie, Wonk, Wooden wedge, Wrangler, Year

Studio(s) Atelier, Bottega, Elstree, Gallery, Pinewood, Workshop

Study, Studies, Studied, Studious, Studying Analyse, Bone, Brown, Carol, Case, Classics, Comparability, Con(ne), Conscious, Consider, Course, Cram, Den, Dig, Étude, Eye, Feasibility, Field, Gen up, Isagogics, Learn, Liberal, Lucubrate, Media, Motion, Mug up, Mull, Muse, Nature, Perusal, Peruse, Pilot, Pore, Post-doctoral, Probe, Read, Recce, Reconnoitre, Research, Reverie, Revise, Sanctum, Sap, Scan, Scrutinise, Shiur, Specialize, Stew, Swot, Take, Time and motion, Trade-off, Tutorial, Typto, Voulu, Work

Stuff(iness), Stuffing, Stuffy Airless, Bombast, Canvas, Close, Cloth, Codswallop, Cram, Crap, Dimity, Farce, Feast, Fiddlesticks, Fill, Force, Forcemeat, Frows(t)y, Frowzy, Fug, Gear, Gobble, Gorge, Guff, Havers, Hooey, Horsehair, Hot, Lard, Line, Linen, → **MATERIAL**, Matter, Musty, No-meaning, Nonsense, Overeat, Pad, Pang, Panne, Pompous, Ram, Replete, Rot, Salpicon, Sate, Satiate, Scrap, Sob, Stap, Steeve, Stew, Stifling, Taxidermy, Trig, Upholster, Wad, Youth

Stultify Repress, Ridicule, Smother

Stumble Blunder, Bobble, Daddle, Err, Falter, Flounder, Founder, Lurch, Peck, Snapper, Stoit, Titubate, Trip

Stump(ed), Stumps, Stumpy Black, Butt, Clump, Fag-end, Floor, More, Nog, Nonplus, Orate, Runt, Scrag, Snag, Snooker, Squab, St, Staddle, Stob, Stock, Stool,

Stub(ble), Stud, Tortillon, Tramp, Truncate, Wicket

Stun(ning), Stunned Astonish, Astound, Awhape, Bludgeon, Concuss, Cosh, Daze, Dazzle, Deafen, Donnard, Donnert, Dove, Drop-dead, Glam, KO, Shell-shocked, Shock, Stoun, Stupefy, Taser®

Stunner Belle, Bobby-dazzler, Cheese, Cosh, Doozy, KO, Peach, Taser®

Stunt(ed) Aerobatics, Confine, Droichy, Dwarf, Escapade, Feat, Gimmick, Hot-dog, Hype, Jehad, Jihad, Loop, Nirl, Puny, Ront(e), Runt, Ruse, Scroggy, Scrub(by), Scrunt(y), Stub, Trick, Wanthriven, Wheelie

Stupefaction, Stupefy(ing), Stupefied Amaze(ment), Assot, Benumb, Catatonic, Dozen, Dumbfound, Etherise, Fuddle, Hocus, Moider, Moither, Narcoses, Numb, Stonne, Stun

Stupid, Stupid person Anserine, Asinine, Besotted, Blockish, Braindead, Crass, Daft, Datal, Dense, Desipient, Dim(wit), Donner(e)d, Dozy, Dull(ard), Fatuous, Flat, Foolish, Gormless, Gross, Half-baked, Hammerheaded, Hare-brained, Inane, Insensate, Insipient, Mindless, Natural, Obtuse, Silly, Thick, Thick-witted, Torpid, Vacuous, Wooden(head)

STUPID PERSON

3 letters:	Clot	Meff	Bumbo
Ass	Cony	Mome	Chick
Auf	Coof	Mong	Chump
Bev	Coot	Mook	Clunk
Bob	Dill	Mutt	Cokes
Cod	Ditz	Nana	Cuddy
Daw	Doat	Nerd	Cully
Div	Does	Nerk	Dicky
Fon	Dolt	Nong	Divvy
Git	Dorb	Nurd	Dorba
Jay	Dork	Ouph	Dubbo
Lob	Dote	Poon	Dumbo
Log	Fogy	Poop	Dummy
Nit	Fool	Prat	Dunce
Oaf	Fozy	Putt	Dweeb
Owl	Gaby	Putz	Eejit
Put	Gaga	Rook	Fogey
Sap	Geck	Simp	Galah
Sot	Gelt	Slow	Golem
Twp	Goat	Stot	Goofy
Wof	Goof	Tony	Goose
Yap	Goon	Twit	Hoser
	Goop	Warb	Idiot
4 letters:	Gorm	Yo-yo	Kerky
Berk	Gouk	Zany	Klutz
Bete	Gowk		Looby
Bobb	Gull	5 letters:	Loony
Bozo	Gump	Bevan	Lowne
Burk	Hash	Blent	Moron
Cake	Jaap	Bobby	Neddy
Calf	Jerk	Booby	Ninny
Clod	Lown	Brute	Nitty

Noddy
Ocker
Ouphe
Patch
Plank
Prune
Quo-he
Schmo
Simon
Snipe
Spoon
Stock
Stupe
Sumph
Twerp
Waldo
Wally
Yampy

6 letters:
Bampot
Boodle
Buffer
Cretin
Cuckoo
Cuddie
Dawney
Dickey
Dodkin
Donkey
Doofus
Dottle
Drongo
Gander
Gaupus
Gunsel
Ignaro
Ingram
Ingrum
Josser
Lummox
Lurden
Nidget
Nig-nog
Nincum
Nitwit
Noodle
Nudnik
Numpty

Oxhead
Schlep
Schmoe
Scogan
Sucker
Tavert
Thicko
Tosser
Tumphy
Turkey
Turnip
Wommit
Zombie

7 letters:
Airhead
Asinico
Barmpot
Becasse
Buffoon
Charlie
Damfool
Dawbake
Dim bulb
Dizzard
Donnard
Donnart
Donnert
Fuckwit
Gomeral
Gomeril
Gubbins
Half-wit
Haverel
Insulse
Jackass
Juggins
Jughead
Lurdane
Mafflin
Mampara
Muggins
Palooka
Pampven
Pillock
Pinhead
Plonker
Pot-head
Saphead

Schmock
Schmuck
Schnook
Scoggin
Taivert
Thickie
Tosspot
Want-wit
Wazzock

8 letters:
Abderian
Abderite
Baeotian
Boeotian
Bonehead
Boofhead
Clodpole
Clodpoll
Crackpot
Deadhead
Dickhead
Dipstick
Dodipoll
Dotterel
Dottrell
Dumbbell
Flathead
Gobshite
Goofball
Goose-cap
Gormless
Imbecile
Knobhead
Liripipe
Liripoop
Lunkhead
Maffling
Meathead
Moon-calf
Omadhaun
Pea-brain
Shithead
Shot-clog
Softhead
Tom-noddy
Wiseacre
Woodcock

9 letters:
Beccaccia
Blockhead
Capocchia
Chipochia
Clarthead
Doddipoll
Doddypoll
Dottipoll
Dumb-cluck
Gothamite
Ignoramus
Jobernowl
Lamebrain
Malt-horse
Schlemiel
Schlemihl
Simpleton
Thickhead
Woodentop

10 letters:
Analphabet
Changeling
Dummelhead
Dunderhead
Dunderpate
Headbanger
Loggerhead
Muttonhead
Nincompoop
Sheepshead
Thickskull
Thimblewit
Touchstone

11 letters:
Chowderhead
Featherhead
Knucklehead
Leather-head
Ninny-hammer
Simple Simon
Van der Merwe

12 letters:
Featherbrain
Shatterbrain

Stupidity Goosery, Hebetude, Thickness, Torpor

Stupor Catatony, Coma, Daze, Dwa(u)m, Fog, Lethargy, Narcosis, Trance

Sturdy Burly, Dunt, Gid, Hardy, Hefty, Lubbard, Lubber, Lusty, Robust, Stalwart, Staunch, Steeve, Stieve, Strapping, Strong, Stuffy, Thickset, Turnsick, Vigorous

Sturgeon Beluga, Ellops, Fish, Huso, Osseter, Sevruga, Sterlet

Stutter Hesitate, Stammer

Sty Frank, Hogpen, Hovel, Pen

Stye Eyesore, Hordeolum

Style(s), Stylish, Stylist Adam, À la, A-line, Band, Barocco, Barock, Baroque, Biedermeier, Blow-dry, Brachylogy, Burin, Call, Cantilena, Carry-on, Chic, Chinoiserie, Chippendale, Class, Cultism, Cut, Dapper, Dash, Decor, Decorated, Demotic, Diction, Directoire, Dub, Élan, Elegance, Empire, Entitle, Euphuism, Execution, Face, Farand, → **FASHION**, Finesse, Flamboyant, Flossy, Form(at), Free, Genre, Gnomon, Gongorism, Gothic, Grace, Gr(a)ecism, Grand, Groovy, Hair-do, Hand, Hepplewhite, Heuristic, Hip, Homeric, House, International (Gothic), Intitule, Katharev(o)usa, Lapidary, Locution, Manner, Marivaudage, Mod(e), Modernism, Modish, Natty, New, Nib, Nifty, Old, Panache, Pattern, Pen, Perm, Perpendicular, Personal, Phrase, Pistil, Pointel, Port, Post-modernism, Preponderant, Probe, Queen Anne, Rakish, Rank, Regency, Rococo, Romanesque, Sheraton, Silk, Snazzy, Spiffy, Sporty, Street, Swish, Taste, Term, Title, Ton, Tone, Touch, Traditional, Tuscan, Uncial, Vogue, Way

Stymie Baulk, Frustrate, Thwart

Styptic Alum, Amadou, Matico, Sta(u)nch

Suave Bland, Debonair, Oily, Smooth, Unctuous, Urbane

Sub Advance, Due, Submarine, Subordinate, U-boat, Under

Sub-atomic Mesic

Subconscious Inner, Instinctive, Not-I, Subliminal, Suppressed

Sub-continent India(n)

Subcontract Outsource

Subdivision Arm, Branch, Oblast, Sanjak, Senonian, Sheading, Tepal, Wapentake

Subdominant Fah

Subdue(d) Abate, Adaw, Allay, Chasten, Conquer, Cow, Crush, Dant(on), Daunt(on), Dominate, Entame, Lick, Low-key, Master, Mate, Mute, Overpower, Quail, → **QUELL**, Quieten, Reduce, Refrain, Repress, Slow, Sober, Soft pedal, Subact, Suppress, Tame, Under

Subfusc, Subfusk Dim, Dressy, Dusky, Evening, Sombre

Subhuman Apeman, Bestial

Subject(s), Subjection, Subject to Amenable, Art, Bethrall, Caitive, Case, Citizen, Contingent, Core, Cow, Donné(e), Enthrall, Foundation, Gist, Hobby, Hobby-horse, Inflict, Liable, Liege(man), Matter, National, On, Overpower, PE, People, Poser, Rayah, RE, RI, Serf, Servient, Servitude, Sitter, Slavery, Snool, Submit, Suit, Syllabus, → **THEME**, Thirl, Thrall, Topic, Under, Vassal, Villein

Subjugate Enslave, Master, Oppress, Overcome, Reduce, Repress, Suppress

Sublieutenant Cornet

Sublimate(r) Aludel, Cleanse, Suppress, Transfer

Sublime Ali, Alice, August, Empyreal, Grand, Great, Lofty, Majestic, Outstanding, Perfect, Porte, Splendid

Submarine Diver, Innerspace, Nautilus, Pig-boat, Polaris, Sub, U-boat, Undersea, X-craft

▷ **Submarine** *may indicate* a fish

Submerge(d) Dip, Dive, Drown, Embathe, Engulf, Imbathe, Lemuria, Overwhelm, Ria, Sink, Take, Whelm

Submissive, Submit Acquiesce, Bow, Capitulate, Comply, Defer, Docile, File, Knuckle, Meek, Obedient, Obtemperate, Passive, Pathetic, Refer, Render, Resign, Snool, Stepford, Stoop, Succumb, Truckle, → **YIELD**

Subordinate Adjunct, Dependent, Flunky, Inferior, Junior, Minion, Myrmidon, Offsider, Postpone, Secondary, Second banana, Servient, Stooge, Subject, Subservient, Subsidiary, Surrender, Under(ling), Underman, Under-strapper, Vassal

Subscribe(r), Subscription Abonnement, Approve, Assent, Conform, Due, Pay, Sign(atory), Signature, Undersign, Underwrite

Subsequent(ly) Anon, Consequential, Future, Later, Next, Postliminary, Since, Then, Ulterior

Subservient Kneel, Obedient, Obsequious

Subside, Subsidence, Subsidy Abate, Adaw, Aid, Assuage, Bonus, Diminish, Ebb, Grant, Sink, Sit, Swag

Subsidiary, Subsidise Auxiliar(y), By(e), Feather-bed, Junior, Secondary, Side, Spin-off, Succursal

Subsist(ence) Batta, Bread-line, Dole, Keep, Live, Maintain, Rely, Survive

Substance, Substantial Ambergris, Anethole, Antithrombin, Antitoxin, Blocky, Body, Calyx, Cermet, Chalone, Chemzyne, Chitin, Chromatin, Colloid, Considerable, Content, Cosmin(e), Creatine, Ectocrine, Ectoplasm, Elemi, Enzyme, Essential, Excipient, Extender, Exudate, Fabric, Fixative, Getter, Gist, Gluten, Gossypol, Gravamen, Growth, Guanazolo, Hearty, Hefty, Indol, Inhibitor, Iodoform, Iodophor, Isatin(e), Isomer, Lase, Lecithin, Leucotriene, Linin, Luciferin, Material, Matter, Meaning, Meat(y), Metabolite, Metol, Mineral, Mole, Morphogen, Mucigen, Murr(h)ine, Mutagen, Naloxone, Neurotoxin, Orgone, Papier mâché, Particulate, Phlogiston, Polymer, Protyl(e), Purin(e), Queen (bee), Quid, Reality, Resin, Secretagogue, Sense, Sequestrant, Smeclic, Solid, Sorbitol, Stuff, Suint, Sum, Surfactant, Sympathin, Tabasheer, Tabashir, Tangible, Thiouracil, Thiourea, Tusche, Viricide, Volutin, Weighty, Ylem

Substandard Infra dig, Off, Poor, Schlo(c)k, Second, Small

▸ **Substantial** see **SUBSTANCE**

Substantiate Confirm, Flesh, Prove, Strengthen, Support

Substantive Direct, Noun

Substitute, Substitution Acting, Carborundum®, Change, Changeling, Commute, Creamer, Deputy, Dextran, Double, Dub, Emergency, Ersatz, -ette, Euphemism, Eusystolism, Exchange, Fill-in, Improvise, Instead, Lieu(tenant), Locum, Makeshift, Metonymy, Pinch-hit, Proxy, Regent, Relieve, Replace, Represent, Reserve, Resolution, Ringer, Sentence, Seth, Simulacrum, Stalking-horse, Stand-in, Stead, Stopgap, Subrogate, Succedaneum, Supernumerary, Surrogate, Switch, Swop, Synthetic, Understudy, Vicar(ial), Vicarious

Substructure Base, Foundation, Keelson, Platform, Podium

Subterfuge Artifice, Chicane, Evasion, Hole, Manoeuvre, Off-come, Ruse, Strategy, Trick

Subterranean Concealed, Mattamore, Sunken, Underground, Weem

Subtle(ty) Abstruse, Alchemist, Crafty, Fine(spun), Finesse, Ingenious, Nice, Nice(ty), Refinement, Sly, Suttle, Thin, Wily

Subtle difference Nuance

Subtract(ion) Commission, Deduct, Discount, Sum, Take, Tithe, Withdraw

Suburb(s) Banlieue, Dormitory, Environs, Exurbia, Faubourg, Garden, Metroland, Outskirts, Purlieu, Subtopia

Subversion, Subvert Fifth column, Overthrow, Reverse, Sabotage, Sedition,

Treasonous, Undermine, Upset

Subway Metro, Passage, Tube, Underground

Succeed, Success(ful) Accomplish, Achieve, Arrive, Blockbuster, Boffo, Breakthrough, Chartbuster, Contrive, Coup, Éclat, Effective, Efficacious, Fadge, Felicity, Flourish, Follow, Fortune, Gangbuster, Get, Go, Hit, Hotshot, Inherit, Killing, Landslide, Luck, Made, Manage, Masterstroke, Mega, Midas touch, Offcome, Pass, Prevail, Procure, Prosper, Purple patch, Reach, Replace, Riot, Score, Seal, Seel, Sele, Sell out, Soaraway, Socko, Speed, Stardom, Superstar, Sure thing, Tanistry, Triumph, Up, Up and coming, Upstart, Vault, Weather, W(h)iz(z)kid, Win, Wow, Wunderkind

Succession Apostolic, Chain, Cognate, Dead men's shoes, Line, Order, Reversion, Sequence, Seriatim, Series, Suite

Successor Co(m)arb, Deluge, Descendant, Ensuite, Epigon(e), Heir, Incomer, Inheritor, Khalifa, Next, Syen

Succinct Brief, Cereus, Compact, Concise, Houseleek, Laconic, Pithy, Short

Succour Aid, Assist, Help, Minister, Relieve, Rescue, Sustain

Succulent Agave, Cactus, Echeveria, Juicy, Lush, Rich, Saguaro, Sappy, Spekboom, Tender, Toothy

Succumb Capitulate, Fall, Go under, Surrender, Yield

Such Like, Sae, Sike, Similar, That

Suck(er), Sucking Absorb, Acetabular, Acetabulum, Amphistomous, Antlia, Aphis, Aspirator, Ass, Bull's eye, Culicidae, Dracula, Drink, Dupe, Fawn, Fellatio, Gnat, Graff, Graft, Gull, Haustellum, Haustorium, Hoove, Lamia, Lamprey, Leech, Liquorice, Lollipop, Mammal, Monotremata, Mouth, Mug, Muggins, Osculum, Patsy, Plunger, Remora, Rook, Shoot, Siphon, Slurp, Smarm, Spire, Spyre, Straw, Surculus, Swig, Sycophant, Tellar, Teller, Tick, Tiller, Toad-eater, Turion, Vampire

Suckle Feed, Mother, Nourish, Nurse, Nurture

Suction Adhere, Pump, Siphon

Sud(s) Foam, Lather, Sapples

Sudanese Dinka, Mahdi, Nuba

Sudden(ly) Abrupt, Astart, Astert, Extempore, Ferly, Fleeting, Foudroyant, Fulminant, Hasty, Headlong, Impulsive, Overnight, Precipitate, Rapid, Slap, Sodain, Subitaneous, Subito, Swap, Swop, Unexpected

Sue Ask, Beseech, Dun, Entreat, Implead, Implore, Litigate, Petition, Pray, Process, Prosecute, Woo

Suede Split

Suffer(er), Suffering Abide, Aby(e), Ache, Affliction, Agonise, Auto, Be, → **BEAR**, Brook, Calvary, Cop, Die, Distress, Dree, Dukkha, Endurance, Endure, Feel, Gethsemane, Golgotha, Grief, Hardship, Have, Incur, Let, Luit, Mafted, Martyr, Pain, Passible, Passion, Passive, Patible, Patience, Pellagrin, Permit, Pine, Plague, Purgatory, Stand, Stomach, Sustain, Thole, Tolerate, Toll, Torment, Trial, Tribulation, Undergo, Use, Victim

Suffering remnant Macmillanite

Suffice, Sufficient Adequate, Ample, Basta, Do, Due, Enough, Enow, Experimental, Run to, Satisfy, Serve

Suffix Enclitic

Suffocate Asphyxiate, Choke, Smoor, Smore, Smother, Stifle, Stive, Strangle, Throttle

Suffrage(tte) Ballot, Feminist, Franchise, Manhood, Vote

Suffuse Colour, Glow, Imbue, Saturate, Spread

Sugar(y), Sugar cane Aldohexose, Aldose, Amygdalin, Arabinose, Barley, Beet,

Blood, Brown, Candy, Cane, Caramel, Carn(e), Cassonade, Caster, Cellobiose, Cellose, Chaptalise, Confectioner's, Daddy, Demerara, Deoxyribose, Dextrose, Disaccharide, Flattery, Fructose, Fucose, Furanose, Galactose, Gallise, Glucose, Glucosoric, Glycosuria, Goo(r), Granulated, Grape, Gur, Heroin, Hexose, Honeydew, Hundreds and thousands, Iced, Icing, Inulin, Invert, Jaggary, Jaggery, Jagghery, Lactose, Laevulose, Loaf, Lump, Maltose, Manna, Mannose, Maple, Milk, Money, Monosaccharide, Muscovado, Nectar, Nucleoside, Palm, Panocha, Pentose, Penuche, Raffinose, Rhamnose, Ribose, Saccharine, Saccharoid, Simple, Sis, Sorbose, Sorg(h)o, Sorghum, Sparrow, Spun, Sweet, Trehalose, Triose, White, Wood, Xylose

Sugar-daddy Lyle, Tate

Suggest(ion), Suggestive Advance, Advice, Advise, Connote, Counter-proposal, Cue, Hint, Idea, Imply, Innuendo, Insinuate, Intimate, Mention, Modicum, Moot, Posit, Posthypnotic, Prompt, Proposal, Propound, Provocative, Racy, Raise, Recommend, Redolent, Reminiscent, Risqué, Savour, Smacks, Soft core, Suspicion, Touch, Trace, Twang, Undertone, Vote, Wind, Wrinkle

Suicide Felo-de-se, Hara-kiri, Hari-kari, Kamikaze, Lemming, Lethal, Sati, Seppuku, Shinju, Suttee

Suit Action, Adapt, Adjust, Agree, Answer, Anti-G, Apply, Appropriate, Become, Befit, Beho(o)ve, Bequest, Beseem, Besit, Birthday, Boiler, Cards, Case, Cat, Clubs, Conform, Courtship, Demob, Diamonds, Dittos, Diving, Do, Drapes, Dress, Effeir, Effere, Etons, Fadge, Fashion, Fit, G, Garb, Gee, Gree, Hearts, Hit, Jump, Lis pendens, Long, Lounge, Major, Mao, Match, Minor, Monkey, NBC, Noddy, Orison, Outcome, Paternity, Petition, Plaint, Play, Plea, Please, Point, Prayer, Pressure, Process, Pyjama, Quarterdeck, Queme, Romper(s), Safari, Sailor, Salopettes, Samfoo, Samfu, Satisfy, Serve, Shell, Siren, Skeleton, Slack, Space, Spades, Strong, Sun, Sunday, Supplicat, Sweat, Swim, Tailleur, Three-piece, Track, Trouser, Trumps, Tsotsi, Twin, Two-piece, Uniform, Union, Wet, Wingsuit, Zoot

Suitable Apposite, Appropriate, Apropos, Apt, Becoming, Capable, Congenial, Consonant, Convenance, Convenient, Due, Expedient, → **FIT**, Giusto, Habile, Keeping, Meet, Opportune, Relevant, Seasonal, Seemly, Sittlichkeit, Very, Worthy

Suite Allemande, Apartment, Chambers, Court, Edit, Ensemble, Entourage, Hospitality, Lounge, Nutcracker, Partita, Retinue, Rooms, Serenade, Set, Skybox, Tail, Three-piece, Train, Two-piece

Suitor Beau, Gallant, John Doe, Lover, Petitioner, Pretender, Suppli(c)ant, Swain, Wooer

Sulk(y), Sulkiness B(r)oody, Disgruntled, Dod, Dort, Gee, Glout(s), Glower, Glum, Grouchy, Grouty, Grumps, Huff, Hump, Jinker, Mardy, Maungy, Mope, Mulligrubs, Mump, Pet, Pique, Pout, Spider, Strunt, Stuffy, Stunkard, Sullen, Tout(ie), Towt, Umbrage

Sullen Dorty, Dour, Farouche, Glum(pish), Grim, Moody, Peevish, Stunkard, Sulky, Surly, Truculent

Sully Assoil, Bedye, Besmirch, Blot, Defile, Glaur(y), Smear, Smirch, Smutch, Soil(ure), Tarnish, Tar-wash

Sulphate, Sulphide Alum, Alunite, Blende, Bluestone, Bornite, Copperas, Coquimbite, Glance, Melanterite, Pyrites, Zarnec, Zarnich

Sulphur Baregine, Brimstone, Cysteine, Hepar, Oleum, S, Stannite, Thionic

Sultan(a), Sultanate Brunei, Caliph, Emir, Grand Seignoir, Grand Turk, Hen, Kalif, Nejd, Oman, Osman, Padishah, Roxane, Saladin, Soldan, Suleiman, Tippoo, Tipu, Wadai

Sultry Humid, Sexy, Smouldering, Steamy, Tropical

Sum(s), Sum up Add(end), Aggregate, All, Amount, Arsmetric, Bomb, Connumerate, Encapsulate, Foot, Logical, Lump, Number, Perorate, Plumule, → **QUANTITY**, Re-cap, Refund, Remittance, Reversion, Solidum, Total, Vector

Summarize, Summary Abridge, Abstract, Aperçu, Bird's eye, Brief, Compendium, Condense, Conspectus, Digest, Docket, Epanodos, Epitome, Gist, Instant, Memo, Minute, Offhand, Outline, Overview, Précis, Recap, Resume, Résumé, Round-up, Syllabus, Synopsis, Tabloid, Tabulate, Tabulation, Wrap-up

Summer(time) Aestival, August, BST, Computer, Estival, Heyday, Indian, Lintel, Luke, Prime, St Luke's, St Martin's, Season, Solstice, Totter

Summerhouse Belvedere, Chalet, Conservatory, Folly, Gazebo

Summit Acme, Acri-, Apex, Braeheid, Brow, Climax, Conference, → **CREST**, Crown, Height, Hillcrest, Jole, Peak, Pike, Pinnacle, Spire, Vertex, Vertical, Yalta

Summon(s) Accite, Arrière-ban, Azan, Beck(on), Call, Call in, Cist, Cital, Citation, Command, Conjure, Convene, Convent, Drum, Evoke, Garnishment, Gong, Hail, Invocation, Muster, Order, Page, Post, Preconise, Rechate, Recheat, Reveille, Signal, Sist, Ticket, Warn, Warrant, Whoop, Writ

Sumo Makunouchi, Yokozuna

Sump Bilge, Drain, Pool, Sink

Sumpter Led horse, Pack-horse

Sumptuous Expensive, Lavish, Palatial, Rich(ly), Superb

Sun(-god), Sunlight, Sunny, Sunshine Albedo, Amen-Ra, Amon-Ra, Apollo, Ashine, Aten, Bright, Cheer, Combust, Daily, Day(star), Dry, Earthshine, Eye of the day, Glory, Heater, Helio(s), Helius, Horus, Mean, Midnight, New Mexico, Paranthelion, Parhelion, Pet-day, Phoebean, Photosphere, Ra, Radiant, Rays, Re, Rising, Shamash, Sol(ar), Soleil, Sonne, Surya, Svastika, Swastika, Tabloid, Tan, Titan, UV

Sunbathe Apricate, Bask, Brown, Tan

Sunbeam Car, Ray

Sunblock Parasol

Sunburn Bronze, Combust, Peeling, Tan

Sunday Advent, Best, Cantate, Care, Carle, Carling, Dominical, Easter, Fig, Jubilate, Judica, Laetare, Lord's Day, Lost, Low, Mid-Lent, Mothering, Orthodox, Palm, Passion, Quadragesima, Quasimodo, Quinquagesima, Refection, Refreshment, Remembrance, Rogation, Rose, Rush-bearing, S, Septuagesima, Sexagesima, Stir-up, Tap-up, Trinity, Whit

Sunday school SS

Sunder Divide, Divorce, Part, Separate, Sever, Split

Sundew Drosera, Eyebright

Sundial Analemma, Gnomon, Solarium

Sundry Divers, Several, Various

Sunflower Kansas, KS

Sunglasses Ray-Bans®, Shades

▶ **Sun-god** *see* **SUN**

▶ **Sunken** *see* **SINK**

Sunrise, Sun-up Aurora, Cosmical, Dawn, East

Sunset Acronical, Evening

Sunshade Awning, Brise-soleil, Canopy, Chi(c)k, Cloud, Parasol, Umbrella

Sunspot Facula, Freckle, Macula

Sunstroke Heliosis, Siriasis

Sunwise Deasi(u)l, Deasoil, Deis(h)eal, Eutropic

Sun-worshipper Heliolater

Sup Dine, Eat, Feast, Sample, Sip, Swallow
Super A1, Actor, Arch, Extra, Fab(ulous), Great, Grouse, Ideal, Lulu, Paramount, Superb, Terrific, Tip-top, Tops, Walker-on, Wizard
Superadded Advene
Superb A1, Concours, Fine, Grand, Great, Majestic, Peerless, Phat, Splendid, Top-notch
Supercilious Aloof, Arrogant, Bashaw, Cavalier, Haughty, Lordly, Snide, Sniffy, Snooty, Snotty, Snouty, Superior, Toffee-nosed, Upstage
Superficial Cosmetic, Cursenary, Cursory, Dilettante, Exterior, Facile, Glib, Outside, Outward, Overlying, Perfunctory, Shallow, Sketchy, Skindeep, Smattering, Veneer
▷ **Superficial(ly)** *may indicate* a word outside another
Superfluous, Superfluity Cheville, De trop, Extra, Lake, Mountain, Needless, Otiose, Pleonastic, Plethora, Redundant, Spare, Unnecessary
Superhuman Bionic, Herculean, Heroic, Supernatural
Superintend(ent) Boss, Director, Foreman, Guide, Janitor, Oversee(r), Preside, Provost, Sewer, Supercargo, Surveillant, Warden, Zanjero
Superior(ity) Abbess, Abeigh, Above, Advantage, Aloof, Atop, Better, Brahmin, Choice, Condescending, Custos, De luxe, Dinger, Elite, Eminent, Excellent, Exceptional, Finer, Forinsec, Gree, Herrenvolk, High-class, High-grade, Jethro, Lake, Liege, Mastery, Morgue, Mother, Nob, Outstanding, Over, Paramount, Pooh-Bah, Posh, Predominance, Prestige, Pretentious, Prior, Smug, Superordinate, Supremacy, Swell, Top(-loftical), Transcendent(al), U, Udal, Upper(most), Uppish, Upstage
Superlative Best, Exaggerated, Peerless, Smasheroo, Supreme, Utmost
Superman Batman, Bionic, Titan, Übermensch
Supermarket Co-op, Fund, GUM, Self service, Store
Supernatural Divine, Eerie, Fay, Fey, Fie, Fly, Gothic, Kachina, Mana, Metaphysical, Paranormal, Sharp, Siddhi, Uncanny, Unearthly, Wight
Supernova Plerion
Supernumerary Additional, Corollary, Extra, Mute, Orra
Supersede Replace, Stellenbosch, Supplant
Superstition Aberglaube, Abessa, Fable, Folk-lore, Freet, Myth, Pisheog, Pishogue, Uncertainty
Superstructure Mastaba(h)
Supertonic Ray
Supervise(d), Supervision, Supervisor Administer, Chaperone, Check, Direct, Engineer, Floorwalker, Foreman, Grieve, Handle, Honcho, Invigilate, Manager, Monitor, Officiate, Overman, Oversee(r), Probation, Proctor, Shopwalker, Stage-manage, Targe, Under, Walla(h)
Supine Inactive, Inert, Lying, Passive, Protract
Supper Burns, Dinner, → **DRINK(ER)**, Hawkey, Hockey, Horkey, Last, Meal, Nagmaal, Repast, Soirée
Supplant Displace, Exchange, Oust, Overthrow, Pre-empt, Replace, Substitute, Supersede
Supple Compliant, Leish, Limber, Lissom(e), → **LITHE**, Loose, Loose-limbed, Pliable, Souple, Wan(d)le, Wannel, Whippy
Supplement(ary) Addend(um), Addition, And, Annex(e), Appendix, Augment, Auxiliary, Bolt-on, Codicil, Colour, Eche, Eik, Eke, Extra, Incaparina, Paralipomena, Postscript, Relay, Ripienist, Ripieno, Rutin, Weighting
Supplicant, Supplicate Beg, Entreat, Importune, Invoke, Petition, Plead, Request, Schnorr, Sue

Supply, Supplies, Supplier Accommodate, Advance, Afford, Cache, Cater, Commissariat, Contribute, Crop, Endue, Equip, Excess, Exempt, Feed, Fill, Find, Fit, Foison, Fund, Furnish, Give, Grist, Grubstake, Heel, Holp(en), Indue, Issue, Lay on, Lend, Lithely, Mains, Matériel, Pipeline, Plenish, Ply, → **PROVIDE**, Provision, Purvey, RASC, Replenishment, Reservoir, Retailer, Serve, Source, Stake, Stock, → **STORE**, Viands, Vintner, Water, Widow's cruse, Yield

Support(er), Supporting Abacus, Abet, Abutment, Adherent, Adminicle, Advocate, Affirm, Aficionado, Aftercare, Aid, Aidance, Aliment(ative), Ally, Ammunition, Anchor, Ancillary, Andiron, Anta, Appui, Arch, Arm, Assistant, Athletic, Axle, Back(bone), Back-up, Baculum, Baluster, Banister, Bankroll, Barrack, Barre, Base, Batten, Beam, Bear, Befriend, Belt, Bibb, Bier, Bolster, Boom, Bouclée, Bra, Brace, Bracket, Brassiere, Breadwinner, Breast-summer, Bridge, Bridgeboard, Buttress, C(ee)-spring, Chair, Champion, Chaptrel, Circumstantiate, Clientele, Column, Confirm, Console, Corbel, Corbel-table, Cornerstone, Countenance, Cradle, Cross-beam, Crutch, Dado, Diagrid, Dog-shore, Doula, Easel, Encourage, Endorse, Endow, Engager, Enthusiast, Espouse, Family, Fan, Favour, Fid, Finance, Flying buttress, Fly-rail, Footrest, Footstool, For, Friend, Gamb, Gantry, Garter, Girder, Glia, Grass roots, Groundswell, Handrail, Hanger, Harpin(g)s, Headrest, Help, Henchman, Hold with, Horse, Hound, I-beam, Idealogue, Impost, Income, Instantiate, Ite, Jack, Jackstay, Jockstrap, Joist, Keep, Kingpost, Knee, Knighthead, Learning, Lectern, Leg, Lierne, Lifebelt, Lifebuoy, Lobby, Loper, Loyalist, Mahlstick, Mainstay, Maintain, Makefast, Mill-rind, Miserere, Misericord(e), Monial, Moral, Mortsafe, Nervure, Neuroglia, -nik, Nourish, Pack, Paranymph, Parawalker, Partisan, Partizan, Partners, Patronage, Pedestal, Pessary, Phalanx, Pier, Pillar, Pin, Plinth, Poppet, Post, Potent, Price, Prop, Proponent, Prop-root, PTA, Pull-for, Purlin(e), Purlins, Pylon, Raft, Rally round, Reinforce, Relieve, Respond, Rest, Rind, Rod, Roof-plate, Root, Royalist, Rynd, Samaritan, Sanction, Sawhorse, Scaffolding, Second, Shoetree, Shore, Skeg, Skeleton, Skewput, Skid, Sleeper, Sling, Snotter, Socle, Solidarity, Spectator, Splat, Splint, Sponson, Sprag, Spud, Staddle, Staddlestone, Staff, Staging, Stake, Stalwart, Stanchion, Stand(-by), Stay, Steady, Stem(pel), Step, Stick, Stirrup, Stool, Stringer, Strut, Stylobate, Subscribe, Subsidy, Succour, Suffragist, Summer, Suppedaneum, Suspender, Sustain, Tailskid, Technical, Tee, Telamon, Tendril, Third, Tie, Tige, Torsel, Trabecula, Tress(el), Trestle, Tripod, Trivet, Truss, Underlay, Underpin, Understand, Unipod, Uphold, Upkeep, Viva, Walker, Waterwings, Well-wisher, Y-level, Zealot

Suppose(d), Supposition An, Assume, Believe, Daresay, Expect, Guess, Hypothetical, Idea, If, Imagine, Imply, Infer, Opine, Presume, Putative, Said, Sepad, Theory, What if

Suppository Pessary

Suppress(ion) Abolish, Adaw, Burke, Cancel, Censor, Clampdown, Conditioned, Crush, Cushion, Ecthlipsis, Elide, Elision, Gleichschaltung, Hush-up, Mob(b)le, Quash, Quell, Quench, Restrain, Silence, Smother, Squash, Stifle, Submerge, Subreption, Throttle

Suppurate, Suppuration Diapyesis, Discharge, Exude, Fester, Maturate, Ooze, Pus, Pyorrhoea, Rankle

Supreme, Supremacy, Supremo Apical, Baaskap, Caudillo, Consummate, Kronos, Leader, Napoleon, Overlord, Paramount, Peerless, Pre-eminent, Regnant, Sovereign, Sublime, Sudder, Superlative, Top, Utmost, White

Surcharge Addition, Extra, Tax

Surd Voiceless

Sure(ly) Assured, Ay, Bound, Cert(ain), Confident, Definite, Doubtless, Firm, Indeed,

Infallible, Know, Pardi(e), Pardy, Perdie, Positive, Poz, Safe, Secure, Shoo-in, Sicker, Syker, Uh-huh, Yep, Yes

Surety Bail, Frithborth, Guarantee, Mainprise, Security, Sponsional

Surf(er), Surfing Breach, Breaker, Grommet, Internet, Lurk, Rollers, Rote, Sea, Waxhead

Surface Aerofoil, Appear, Area, Arise, Camber, Carpet, Caustic, Control, Day, Dermal, Dermis, Emerge, Epigene, Exterior, External, Face, Facet, Flock, Interface, Macadam, Meniscus, Nanograss, Notaeum, Out, Outcrop, Outward, Paintwork, Patina, Pave, Plane, Reveal, Rise, Salband, Side, Skin, Soffit, Spandrel, Superficial, Superficies, Tarmac®, Tar-seal, Texture, Top, Topping, Toroid, Wearing course, Worktop

Surf-boat, Surfboard(ing) Goofy-footer, Masoola(h), Masula

Surfeit(ed) Blasé, Cloy, Excess, Glut, Overcloy, Plethora, Satiate, Stall, Staw

▷ **Surfer** *may indicate* programming

Surge Billow, Boom, Drive, Gush, Onrush, Seethe, S(c)end, Storm, Sway, Swell, Wind

Surgeon Abernethy, BCh, BS, CHB, CM, Doctor, House, Hunter, Lister, Medic, Operator, Orthopod, Plastic, Sawbones, Staff, Tang, Vet(erinary)

Surgery Anaplasty, Bypass, Cosmetic, Facelift, Keyhole, Knife, Laparotomy, Laser, LASIK, Medicine, Nip and tuck, Nose job, Op, Open-heart, Orthop(a)edics, Osteoplasty, Plastic, Prosthetics, Reconstructive, Repair, Spare-part, Ta(g)liacotian, Thoracoplasty, Zolatrics

Surly Bluff, Cantankerous, Chough, Chuffy, Churl(ish), Crabby, Crusty, Cynic, Glum, Gruff, Grum, Grumpy, Rough, Snarling, Sullen, Truculent

Surmise Extrapolate, Guess, Imagine, Infer, Presume, Suppose

Surmount Beat, Climb, Conquer, Crest, Master, Overcome, Scan, Superate, Tide, Transcend

Surname Cognomen, Patronymic

Surpass Bang, Beat, Best, Cap, Cote, Ding, Eclipse, Efface, Exceed, Excel, Outdo, Outgun, Out-Herod, Outman, Outreach, Outshine, Outstrip, Overshadow, Overtop, Transcend

Surplice Cotta, Ephod, Rochet, Sark, Serk, Vakass

Surplus Excess, Extra, Glut, Lake, Mountain, Out-over, Over, Overabundance, Overage, Overcome, Remainder, Rest, Spare, Surfeit

Surprise(d), Surprising Ag, Alert, Amaze, Ambush, Arrah, Astonish, Aykhona wena, Bewilder, Blimey, Boilover, Bombshell, By Jove, Caramba, Catch, Confound, Coo, Cor, Crick(e)y, Crikey, Criminé, Cripes, Criv(v)ens, Dear, Eye-opener, Gadso, Gee, Geewhiz, Gemini, Geminy, Gemony, Gobsmacked, Golly, Good-lack, Gorblimey, Gordon Bennett, Gosh, Ha, Hah, Hallo, Heavens, Hech, Heck, Heh, Hello, Hey, Ho, Jeepers, Jeepers creepers, Jeez(e), Jinne, Jirre, Law, Lawks, Lor, Lordy, Lumme, Lummy, Man alive, Marry, Musha, My, Nooit, Obreption, Och, Odso, Omigod, Oops, Open-mouthed, Overtake, Phew, Pop-eyed, Really, Sheesh, Shock, Singular, Sjoe, Spot, Stagger, Startle, Strewth, Struth, Stun, Sudden, Treat, Turn-up, Uh, Whew, Whoops, Wonderment, Wow, Wrongfoot, Yikes, Yipes, Yow, Zinger, Zowie

Surrealist Bizarre, Dali, Ernst, Grotesque, Magritte, Man Ray, Miró

Surrender Capitulate, Cave-in, Cession, Enfeoff, Extradite, Fall, Forego, Forfeit, Handover, Hulled, Kamerad, Naam, Recreant, Release, Relinquish, Remise, Rendition, Roll over, Submit, Succumb, Waive, → **YIELD**, Yorktown

Surreptitious Clandestine, Covert, Fly, Furtive, Secret, Slee, Sly, Stealthy, Underhand

Surrey Carriage, Sy

Surrogate Agent, Depute, Deputy, Locum, Proxy

Surround(ed), Surrounding(s) Ambient, Amongst, Architrave, Background, Bathe, Bego, Beset, Bundwall, Circumvallate, Circumvent, Compass, Doughnutting, Ecology, Embail, Encase, → **ENCIRCLE**, Enclave, Enclose, Encompass, Enfold, Entomb, Envelop, Environ, Enwrap, Fence, Gherao, Gird, Hedge, Hem in, Impale, Inorb, Invest, Mid, Orb, Orle, Outflank, Outside, Perimeter, Setting, Wall

Surtees Jorrocks, Sponge

Surveillance, Survey(ing), Surveyor Behold, Cadastre, Case, Census, Chartered, Conspectus, Dialler, Domesday, Doomwatch, Espial, Examination, Eye, Geodesy, Geological, Groma, Look-see, Once-over, Ordnance, Patrol, Poll, Prospect, Quantity, Recce, Reconnaissance, Regard, Review, Scan, Scrutiny, Stakeout, Straw poll, Supervision, Terrier, Theodolite, Triangulate, Trilateration, Vigil, Watch

Survival, Survive, Surviving, Survivor Cope, Die hard, Endure, Extant, Finalist, Hibakusha, Last, Leftover, Live, Outdure, Outlast, Outlive, Outwear, Overlive, Persist, Relic(t), Ride, Street-wise, Viability, Warhorse, Weather

Susan Lazy

Susceptible, Susceptibility Anaphylaxis, Electrical, Impressionable, Liable, Receptive, Vulnerable

Suspect, Suspicion, Suspicious Askance, Assume, Breath, Dodgy, Doubt, Dubious, Fishy, Grain, Grey list, Guess, Hint, Hunch, Jalouse, Jealous, Leery, Misdeem, Misdoubt, Misgiving, Mislippen, Mistrust, Modicum, Notion, Paranoia, Queer, Scent, Smatch, Soupçon, Thought, Tinge, Whiff

▷ **Suspect, Suspicious** *may indicate* an anagram

Suspend(ed), Suspense, Suspension Abate, Abeyance, Adjourn, Anabiosis, Anti-shock, Cliffhanger, Colloid, Dangle, Defer, Delay, Dormant, Freeze, Ground, → **HANG**, Hydraulic, Independent, Intermit, Lay off, Mist, Moratorium, Nailbiter, Pensile, Poise, Prorogue, Put on ice, Reprieve, Respite, Rub out, Rusticate, Sideline, Sol, Stand off, Swing, Tension, Tenterhooks, Truce, Withhold

▷ **Suspended** *may indicate* 'ice' (on ice) at the end of a down light

Sussex Rape

Sustain(ed), Sustaining, Sustenance Abide, Afford, Aliment, Bear, Constant, Depend, Endure, Food, Keep, Last, Maintain, Nutrient, Nutriment, Pedal, Prolong, Sostenuto, Succour, Support, Ten(uto), Upbear

Sutler Vivandière

Suture Button, Catgut, Cobbler, Lambda, Pterion, Purse-string, Sagittal, Stitch

Suzanne, Suzie Lenglen, Wong

Svelte Lithe, Slender, Slim

Swab Dossil, Dry, Mop, Pledget, Scour, Sponge, Squeegee, Stupe, Tampon, Tompon, Wipe

Swaddle, Swaddling Bind, Envelop, Incunabula, Swathe, Wrap

Swag Booty, Encarpus, Festoon, Haul, Loot, Maino(u)r, Manner, Matilda, Shiralee, Toran(a)

Swagger(er), Swaggering Birkie, Bluster, Boast, Brag, Bragadisme, Bravado, Bucko, Cock, Crow, Jaunty, Matamore, Nounce, Panache, Pra(u)nce, Roist, Roll, Rollick, Roul, Royster, Ruffle, Side, Strive, Swank, Swash(-buckler), Tigerism

Swain Amoretti, Beau, Churl, Corin, Damon, Hind, Lover, Rustic, Shepherd, Strephon, Wooer

Swallow(able), Swallowing Accept, Aerophagia, Ariel, Barn, Bird, Bolt, Cliff, Consume, Deglutition, Devour, Down, Drink, Eat, Endue, Englut, Engulf, Engulph, Esculent, Glug, Gobble, Gula, Gulp, Hirundine, Incept, Ingest, Ingulf, Ingurgitate,

Itys, Lap, Martin, Martlet, Progne, Quaff, Shift, Sister, Slug, Stomach, Swig, Take, Take off

Swamp(y) Bog, Bunyip, Cowal, Cypress, Deluge, Dismal, Drown, Engulf, Everglade, Flood, Great Dismal, Inundate, Lentic, Lerna, Lerne, Loblolly, Mar(i)sh, Morass, Muskeg, Okavango, Okefenokee, Overrun, Overwhelm, Pakihi, Paludal, Quagmire, Slash, Slough, Sudd, Uliginous, Urman, Vlei, Vly, Wetland

Swan(s) Avon, Bewick's, Bird, Black, Cob, Cygnet, Cygnus, Game, Leda, Lindor, Mute, Pen, Seven, Seward, Song, Stroll, Trumpeter, Whistling, Whooper, Whooping

Swank(y) Boast, Lugs, Pretentious, Side, Style

Swan-song Finale, Last air

Swap, Swop → BARTER, Chop, Commute, Exchange, Scorse, Switch, Trade, Truck

▷ **Swap(ped)** *may indicate* an anagram

Sward Grass, Green, Lawn, Sod, Turf

Swarm(ing) Abound, Alive, Bike, Bink, Byke, Cast, Clamber, Cloud, Crowd, Flood, Geminid, Hoatching, Host, Hotter, Infest, Meteor, Overrun, Pullulate, Rife, Shin, Shoal, Throng

Swarthy Dark, Dusky, Melanotic

Swash Swig, Swill

Swash-buckler Adventurer, Boaster, Braggart, Gascon, Swordsman

Swastika Filfot, Fylfot, Gamma(dion), Hakenkreuz

▶ **Swat** *see* SWOT

Swathe Bind, Enfold, Enroll, Swaddle, Wrap

Sway(ing) Careen, Carry, Command, Diadrom, Domain, Dominion, Flap, Fluctuate, Govern, Hegemony, Influence, Lilt, Oscillate, Prevail, Reel, Reign, Rock, Roll, Rule, Shog, Shoogle, Swag, Swale, Swee, Swing(e), Teeter, Titter, Totter, Vacillate

Swear(ing), Swear word Attest, Avow, Billingsgate, Coprolalia, Curse, Cuss, Depose, Execrate, Expletive, Invective, Jurant, Juratory, Oath, Pledge, Plight, Rail, Sessa, Tarnal, Tarnation, Verify, Vow

Sweat(ing), Sweaty Apocrine, Beads, Clammy, Cold, Dank, Diaphoresis, Excrete, Exude, Flop, Forswatt, Glow, Hidrosis, Lather, Ooze, Osmidrosis, → PERSPIRE, Secretion, Slave, Stew, Sudament, Sudamina, Sudate, Swelter

Sweater Aran, Argyle, Circassian, Circassienne, Cowichan, Fair Isle, Gansey, Guernsey, Indian, Jersey, Polo, Pullover, Roll-neck, Siwash, Skinny-rib, Skivvy, Slip-on, Slop-pouch, Sloppy Joe, Turtleneck, Woolly

Swede Nordic, Rutabaga, Scandinavian, Sven, Turnip

Sweeney Police, Todd

Sweep(er), Sweeping(s) Besom, Broad, Broom, Brush, Chimney, Chummy, Clean, Curve, Debris, Detritus, Expanse, Extensive, Lash, Libero, Lottery, Net, Oars, Pan, Phasing, Police-manure, Range, Scavenger, Scud, Sling, Snowball, Soop, Sooterkin, Street, Stroke, Surge, Swathe, Sway, Vacuum, Waft, Well, Wide

Sweepstake Draw, Gamble, Lottery, Raffle, Tattersall's, Tombola

Sweet(s), Sweeten(er), Sweetmeat, Sweetness Acesulflame-K, Acid drop, Adeline, Afters, Alcorza, Aldose, Amabile, Aspartame, Barley sugar, Bombe, Bonbon, Bonus, Brandyball, Bribe, Bull's eye, Burnt-almonds, Butterscotch, Candy, Candyfloss, Caramel, Chaptalise, Charity, Charming, Cherubic, Choc(olate), Choccy, Cloying, Coconut ice, Comfit, Confect(ion), Confetti, Confiserie, Confit, Conserve, Crème, Cute, Cyclamate, → DESSERT, Dolce, Dolly, Dolly mixture, Douce(t), Dowset, Dragée, Dulcet, Dulcie, Dulcitude, Elecampane, Fairy floss, Flummery, Fondant, Fool, Fragrant, Fresh, Fudge, Glucose, Glycerin, Gob-stopper, Goody, Gum(drop), Gundy, Hal(a)vah, Halva, Honey(ed), Humbug, Hundreds and thousands, Ice, Icky, Indican, Jelly baby, Jelly bean, Jube, Jujube, Kiss, Lavender, Lemon drop, Licorice, Liquorice, Lollipop, Lolly, Lozenge, Luscious, Marchpane, Marshmallow, Marzipan, Melodious, Mint, Mousse, Muscavado, Nanaimo Bar, Nectared, Noisette, Nonpareil, Nougat, Pandrop, Pastille, Pea, Peardrop, Peppermint cream, Peppermint drop, Pet, Pick'n'mix, Pie, Praline, Pud(ding), Redolent, Rock, Romic, Saccharin(e), Scroggin, Seventeen, Sillabub, Sixteen, Solanine, Soot(e), Sop, Sorbet, Spice, Split, Stickjaw, Sucker, Sucrose, Sugar, Sugarplum, Swedger, Syllabub, Syrupy, Tablet, Taffy, Tart, Thaumatin, Toffee, Torte, Trifle, Truffle, Turkish delight, Twee, Uses, William, Wine-gum, Winsome, Xylitol, Zabaglione

Sweetbread Bur(r), Inchpin, Pancreas

Sweetheart Amoret, Amour, Beau, Darling, Dona(h), Dowsabel(l), Doxy, Dulcinea, Flame, Follower, Honey(bunch), Honeybun, Jarta, Jo(e), Lass, Leman, Lover, Masher, Neaera, Peat, Romeo, Steady, Toots(y), True-love, Valentine, Yarta, Yarto

Sweet-seller Butcher, Confectioner

Swell(ing) Adenomata, Ague-cake, Anasarca, Aneurysm, Apophysis, Bag, Balloon, Bellying, Berry, Billow, Blab, Blister, Bloat, Blow, Boil, Boll, Bolster, Botch, Braw, Bubo, Bulb, Bulge, Bump, Bunion, Capellet, Carnosity, Cat, Chancre, Chilblain, Clour, Cratches, Curb, Cyst, Dandy, Desmoid, Diapason, Dilate, → **DISTEND**, Dom, Don, Eche, Ectasia, Eger, Elephantiasis, Encanthis, Enhance, Entasis, Epulis, Excellent, Farcy-bud, Frog, Gall, Gathering, Gent, Goiter, Goitre, Gout, Grandee, Ground, H(a)ematoma, Heave, Heighten, Hove, Hydrocele, Hydroma, Hygroma, Increase, Inflate, Intumesce, Kibe, L, Lampas(se), Lampers, Louden, Lump, Macaroni, Mouse, Nodule, Odontoma, Oedema, OK, Onco-, Ox-warble, Parotitis, Plim, Plump, Protrude, Protuberance, Proud, Pulvinus, Rise, Roil, Scirrhus, Scleriasis, Sea, Shinsplints, Splenomegaly, Strout, Struma, Stye, Stylopodium, Surge, Teratoma, Toff, Torose, Torulose, Tragus, Tuber(cle), Tumefaction, Tumescence, Tumour, Tympany, Upsurge, Varicocele, Venter, Wallow, Warble, Wen, Whelk, Windgall, Xanthoma

▷ **Swelling** *may indicate* a word reversed

Swelter(ing) Perspire, Stew, Sweat, Tropical

Swerve, Swerving Bias, Broach, Careen, Deflect, Deviate, Lean, Sheer, Shy, Stray, Sway, Swee, Swing, Warp, Wheel

Swift(ly) Apace, Bird, Dean, Dromond, Fleet, Flock, Hasty, Martlet, Newt, Nimble, Presto, Prompt, Pronto, Quick, → **RAPID**, Reel, Slick, Spanking, Velocipede, Wight

Swig Drink, Gulp, Nip, Scour, Swill, Tighten

Swill Guzzle, Leavings, Rubbish, Slosh, Swash

▷ **Swilling** *may indicate* an anagram

Swim(ming) Bathe, Bogey, Bogie, Crawl, Dip, Float, Freestyle, Naiant, Natatorial, Paddle, Reel, Run, Skinny-dip, Soom, Synchro(nized), Trudgen, Whim, Whirl

▷ **Swim** *may indicate* an anagram

Swimmer Bather, Cichlid, Copepod(a), Duckbill, Duckmole, Dugong, Frogman, Leander, Pad(d)le, Paidle, Planula, Pleopod, Pobble, Terrapin, Trudgen, Webb

▷ **Swimmer** *may indicate* a fish

Swimming costume Bathers, Bikini, Cossie, Maillot, Monokini, One-piece, Tanga, Tankini, Tog, Trunks

Swindle(r) Beat, Bite, Bucket-shop, Bunco, Bunkosteerer, Cajole, Champerty, → **CHEAT**, Chouse, Con, Crimp, Defraud, Diddle, Do, Escroc, Fake, Fiddle, Finagle, Fineer, Fleece, Fraud, Gazump, Gip, Goose-trap, Graft, Grifter, Gyp, Hocus, Hoser, Hustler, Leg, Leger, Long-firm, Magsman, Mountebank, Mulct, Nobble, Peter Funk, Plant, Racket, Ramp, Rig, Rogue, Scam, Sell, Shakedown, Shark, Sharper,

Shicer, Shyster, Skelder, Skin, Skin game, Slicker, Sting, Stitch-up, Stumer, Suck, Swiz(z), Trick, Twist, Two-time

Swine(herd) Boar, Brute, Cad, Eumaeus, Gadarene, Heel, Hog, Peccary, Pig, Porcine, Pork, Rotter, Sounder, Sow, Sybotic

Swing(er), Swinging Colt, Dangle, Flail, Hang, Hep, Kip(p), Lilt, Metronome, Mod, Music, Oscillate, Pendulate, Pendulum, Reverse, Rock, Rope, Shog, Shoogie, Shuggy, Slew, Swale, Sway, Swee, Swerve, Swey, Swipe, Trapeze, Vibratile, Voop, Wave, Western, Wheel, Whirl, Yaw

Swipe(s) Backhander, Beer, Haymaker, Steal, Strike, Tap-lash

Swirl Eddy, Purl, Swoosh, Tourbill(i)on, Twist, Whirl

▷ **Swirling** *may indicate* an anagram

Swish Cane, Frou-frou, Rustle, Smart, Whir, Whisper

Swiss Genevese, Ladin, Roll, Tell, Vaudois

Switch(ed), Switches, Switching Birch, Change, Convert, Crossbar, Cryotron, Dimmer, Dip, Exchange, Gang, Hairpiece, Knife, Legerdemain, Mercury, Message, Pear, Point, Replace, Retama, Rocker, Rod, Scutch, Thyristor, Time, Toggle, Tress, Trip, Tumbler, Twig, Wave, Zap

▷ **Switched** *may indicate* an anagram

Switzerland CH, Helvetia

Swivel Caster, Pivot, Root, Rotate, Spin, Terret, Territ, Torret, Turret, Wedein

Swiz Chiz(z)

Swollen Blown, Bollen, Bombe, Bulbous, Full, Gourdy, Gouty, Incrassate, Nodose, Puffy, Tumid, Turgescent, Turgid, Varicose, Ventricose, Vesiculate

Swoon Blackout, Collapse, Deliquium, Dover, Dwa(l)m, Dwaum, Faint

Swoop Descend, Dive, Glide, Plummet, Souse

▶ **Swop** *see* **SWAP**

Sword(-like), Swordplay Andrew Ferrara, Anelace, Angurvadel, Anlace, Arondight, Assegai, Balisarda, Balmunc, Balmung, Bilbo, Blade, Brand, Brandiron, Broad(sword), Brondyron, Caliburn, Cemitare, Claymore, Colada, Court, Curtal-ax, Curtana, Curtax, Cutlass, Daisho, Damascene, Damaskin, Damocles, Dance, Dirk, Duranda(l), Durindana, Ensate, Ensiform, Epée, Espada, Estoc, Excalibur, Falchion, Faulchi(o)n, Firangi, Foil, Forte, Fox, Gladius, Glaive, Gleave, Glorious, Hanger, Iai-do, Jacob's staff, Joyeuse, Katana, Kendo, Khanda, Kirpan, Kreese, Kris, Kukri, Kusanagi, Machete, Mandau, Merveilleuse, Mimming, Montanto, Morglay, Nothung, Parang, Philippan, Rapier, Rosse, Sabre, Samurai, Schiavone, Schläger, Scimitar, Semita(u)r, Shabble, Shamshir, Sharp, Sigh, Simi, Skene-dhu, Smallsword, Spadroon, Spirtle, Spit, Spurtle(blade), Steel, Toasting-iron, Toledo, Tuck, Tulwar, Two-edged, Waster, Whinger, Whiniard, Whinyard, White-arm, Xiphoid, Yatag(h)an

Sword-bearer, Swordsman(ship), Swordswoman Aramis, Athos, Blade, Brenda(n), D'Artagnan, Fencer, Frog, Gladiator, Matador, Porthos, Sai-do, Selictar, Spadassin, Spadroon, Spartacus, Swashbuckler, Zorro

Sword-dancer Matachin

Swordfish Espada, Istiophorus, Xiphias

Sword-swallower Samite

Swot Dig, Grind, Kill, Mug, Read up, Smug, Stew, Strike, Swat

Sybarite Aristippus, Epicure, Hedonist, Voluptuary

Sycamore Acer, Maple, Plane, Tree

Sycophant(ic) Apple polisher, Brown-nose, Claqueur, Crawler, Creeper, Damocles, Fawner, Gnathonic, Lickspittle, Parasite, Pickthank, Placebo, Toad-eater, Toady, Yesman

Syllabary Hiragana, Kana, Katakana

Syllable(s) Acatalectic, Anacrusis, Aretinian, Nonsense, Om, Outride, Tonic

Syllabus Program(me), Prospectus, Résumé, Summary, Table, Timetable

Syllogism Argument, Conclusion, Deduction, Enthymeme, Epicheirema, Sorites

Sylph Ariel, Nymph

Symbol(s), Symbolic, Symbolism, Symbolist Acrophony, Agma, Algebra, Allegory, Ampersand, Aniconic, Ankh, Apostrophus, Aramanth, Asterisk, Badge, Cachet, Caret, Cedilla, Character, Charactery, Chord, Choropleth, Christogram, Cipher, Clef, Colon, Crest, Daffodil, Decadent, Del, Descriptor, Diesis, Dingbat, Double-axe, Eagle, Emblem, Emoticon, Eng, Equal, Fertility, Grammalogue, Grapheme, Hash, Heitiki, Hieroglyph, Hierogram, Hiragana, Ichthus, Icon, Iconography, Ideogram, Index, Kalachakra, Kanji, Length mark, Lexigram, Logo(gram), Logograph, Mandala, Mark, Menorah, Metaphor, Mezuzah, Minus, Mogen David, Moral, Motif, Mystical, Nabla, Neum(e), Nominal, Notation, Obelus, Om, One, Operator, Ouroborus, Paragraph, Pentacle, Phonetic, Phonogram, Phraseogram, Pi, Pictogram, Pictograph, Plus, Presa, Punctuation, Quantifier, Redon, Rose, Rune, Sacrament, Segno, Semicolon, Semiotic, Sex, Shamrock, Sigla, Sign, Slur, Smiley, Star of David, Status, Svastika, Swastika, Syllabary, Syllabogram, Synthetism, Tag, Talisman, Tetragrammaton, Thistle, Tiki, Tilde, Token, Totem, Trademark, Triskele, Triskelion, Type, Uraeus, Waymark, Wild card, Yoni

Symmetric(al), Symmetry Balance, Bilateral, Digonal, Diphycercal, Even, Harmony, Isobilateral, Mirror, Pseudocubic, Radial, Regular, Skew

Sympathetic, Sympathise(r), Sympathy Approval, Commiserate, Commiseration, Compassion, Condole(nce), Condone, Congenial, Crypto, Dear-dear, Empathy, Fellow-traveller, Humane, Mediagenic, Par, Pathos, Pity, Rapport, Ruth, Side, Vicarious, Well-disposed

Symphony Concert, Eroica, Farewell, Fifth, Jupiter, Manfred, Music, New World, Opus, Pastoral, Sinfonia, Sinfonietta, Unfinished

Symposium Assembly, Conference, Synod

Symptom(s) Epiphenomenon, Feature, Indicia, Merycism, Mimesis, Prodrome, Semiotic, Sign, Syndrome, Token, Trait, Withdrawal

Synagogue Beit Knesset, Beth Knesseth, Shul, Temple

Synchronise(r) Coincide, Genlock, Tune

Syncopated, Syncopation, Syncope Abridged, Breakbeat, Revamp, Vasovagal, Zoppa, Zoppo

Syndicate Associate, Cartel, Combine, Mafioso, Pool, Ring, Stokvel

Syndrome Adams-Stokes, Asperger's, Carpal tunnel, Cerebellar, Characteristic, China, Chinese restaurant, Chronic fatigue, Compartment, Couvade, Cri du chat, Crush, Cushing's, De Clerambault's, Down's, Economy-class, Empty nest, Fetal alcohol, Fragile X, Goldenhar's, Gorlin, Guillain-Barré, Gulf War, Hughes, Hutchinson-Gilford, Irritable-bowel, Jerusalem, Klinefelter's, Korsakoff's, Locked-in, Marfan, ME, Menières, Metabolic, Munch(h)ausen's, Nonne's, Overuse, Parkinson's, Pattern, POS, Postviral, Prader-Willi, Premenstrual, Proteus, Reiter's, Rett's, Reye's, SADS, SARS, Savant, Sezary, Sick building, SIDS, Sjogren's, Stevens-Johnson, Stockholm, Stokes-Adams, Sturge-Weber, Tall-poppy, Temperomandibular, TMJ, Total allergy, Tourette's, Toxic shock, Turner's, Wag the dog, Wernicke-Korsakoff, Williams, Wobbler, XYY

Synod Assembly, Conference, Convocation, General, Whitby

Synonym(ous) Comparison, Reciprocal

Synopsis Abstract, Blurb, Conspectus, Digest, Outline, Résumé, Schema,
→ SUMMARY

Syntax Grammar
Synthesis Amalgam, Aperture, Fusion, Merger
Synthesizer Moog®, Vocoder, Wind
Synthetic Empirical, Ersatz, Fake, False, Mock, Plastic, Polyamide, Silicone, Spencerian
Syphilis Chancre, Lues, Pip
Syrian Aramaean, Aramaic, Druse, Druz(e), Hittite, Hurrian, Levantine, Phoenician
Syringe(s) Douche, Flutes, Harpoon, Hypo, Hypodermic, Needle, Reeds, Spray, Squirt, Wash, Works
Syrphid Hoverfly
Syrup Capillaire, Cassareep, Cassis, Cocky's joy, Coquito, Corn, Diacodion, Diacodium, Flattery, Glycerol, Golden, Grenadine, Linctus, Maple, Molasses, Moskonfyt, Orgeat, Quiddany, Rob, Sorghum, Sugar, Treacle
System(s), Systematic ABO, Alpha, An mo, Bertillon, Binary, Bordereau, Braille, Carboniferous, Centauri, Circulatory, Code, Colonial, Compander, → **COMPUTER SYSTEMS**, Continental, Copernican, Cosmos, Course, Crystal, Decimal, Delsarte, Dewey (Decimal), Distributed, Early warning, Economy, Eocene, Ergodic, Establishment, Expert, Feudal, Fixed, Formal, Fourierism, Froebel, Giorgi, Grading, Harvard, HLA, Honour, Hub and spoke, Iastic, Immune, Imprest, Imputation, Induction loop, Inertial, ISA, Kalamazoo, Kanban, Life-support, Limbic, Lobby, Loop, Lymphatic, Madras, Mercantile, Merit, → **METHOD**, Metric, Microcosm, Midi, Miocene, Movable, Muschelkalk, Natural, Navigational, Nervous, Network, Nicam, Notation, Number, Octal, Operating, Order, Organon, Panel, Periodic, Permian, Pleiocene, Plenum, Points, Process, Ptolemaic, Public address, Purchase, Quota, Quote-driven, Raisonné, Regime, Regular, Respiratory, Root, Run-time, Scheme, Scientific, Servo, Sexual, SI, Sofar, Solar, Solmisation, Sonar, Sound, Spoils, Sprinkler, Squish lip, Stack(ing), Staff, Stanislavski, Star, Stakhanovism, Structure, Studio, Sweating, Tactic, Talk-down, Tally, Ternary, Theory, Third-rail, Tommy, Touch, Trias(sic), Truck, Turnkey, Tutorial, Two-party, Universe, Unix, Urogenital, Vestibular, VOIP, Warehousing, Water, Water vascular, Weapon

Tt

T Bone, Junction, Potence, Tango, Tau-cross, Tee, Time, Toc(k)

Tab Bill, Check, Decimal, → **LABEL**, Ring-pull, Stay-on, Tally, Trim, Trimming

Tabby Blabbermouth, Brindled, → **CAT**, Gossip, Mottled, Spinster, Striped, Trout

Tabitha Gazelle

Table(-like) Alphonsine, Altar, Board, Bradshaw, Breakfast, Calendar, → **CHART**, Coffee, Communion, Console, Contingency, Corbel, Counter, Credence, Credenza, Decision, Desk, Diagram, Dinner, Dolmen, Draw-leaf, Draw-top, Dressing, Drop-leaf, Drum, Ephemeris, Experience, Food, Gateleg, Gate-legged, Glacier, Graph, Green-cloth, Gueridon, High, Imposing, Index, Key, League, Life, Light, → **LIST**, Lord's, Lowboy, Mahogany, Matrix, Mensa(l), Mesa, Monopode, Mortality, Multiplication, Occasional, Operating, Orientation, Pembroke, Periodic, Piecrust, Pier, Plane, Platen, Pool, Prothesis, Pythagoras, Ready-reckoner, Reckoner, Refectory, Roll, Round, Rudolphine, Sand, Schedule, Scheme, Slab, Sofa, Spoon, Stall, Statistical, Stone, Taboret, Tabular, Tea, Te(a)poy, Throwing, Tide, Times, Toilet, Toning, Top, Traymobile, Trestle, Trolley, Truth, Twelve, Washstand, Water, Whirling, Wool, Workbench, Writing

Tableau Semantic

Tablecloth Damask, Linen

Table-land Barkly, Kar(r)oo, Mesa, Plateau, Puna

Table-list Memo, Menu

Tablet Abacus, Album, Aspirin, Caplet, Eugebine, Graphics, Hatch, Medallion, Opisthograph, Osculatory, Ostracon, Ostrakon, → **PAD**, → **PILL**, Pilule, Plaque, Slate, Stele, Stone, Tombstone, Torah, Triglyph, Triptych, Troche, Trochisk, Ugarit, Votive

Table-talker Deipnosophist

Table-turner Tartar

Table-ware China, Cutlery, Silver

Taboo, Tabu Ban(ned), Bar, Blackball, Forbidden, Incest, Non dit, No-no, Unclean

Tachograph Spy-in-the-cab

Tacit, Taciturn(ity) Implicit, Laconic, Mumps, Oyster, Reticent, Silent, Understood

Tack(y) Bar, Baste, Beat, Boxhaul, Brass, Cheesy, Cinch, Clubhaul, Cobble, Gybe, Leg, Martingale, Nail, Saddlery, Salt-horse, → **SEW**, Sprig, Stirrup, Tailor's, Veer, Wear, White-seam, Yaw, Zigzag

Tackle Accost, Approach, Attempt, Beard, Bobstay, Burton, Cat, Claucht, Claught, Clevis, Clew-garnet, Collar, Dead-eye, Fishing, Garnet, Gear, Haliard, Halyard, Harness, Jury-rig, Nose, Rig, Rigging, Scrag, Straight-arm, Topping-lift, Undertake

Tact, Tactful Delicacy, Diplomacy, Diplomatic, Discreet, Discretion, Politic, Savoir-faire

Tactic(s) Audible, Finesse, Hardball, Manoeuvre, Masterstroke, Plan, Ploy, Ruse, Salami, Scare, Shock, Smear, → **STRATEGY**, Strong-arm, Zwischenzug

Tactless(ness) Blundering, Brash, Crass, Gaffe, Gauche, Indelicate, Maladroit

Tadpole Ascidian, Polliwig, Polliwog, Pollywig, Pollywog, Porwiggle

Taffy Thief, Toffee, Welshman

Tag Aglet, Aiguillette, Cliché, Dog, Electronic, End, Epithet, → **FOLLOW**, Kabaddi, Kimball, Label, Meta, Price, Question, Quote, Remnant, Tab, → **TICKET**, Treasury

Tail, Tailpiece, Tailboard All-flying, Amentum, Apocopate, → **APPENDAGE**, Bob, Brush, Caudal, Cercal, Cercus, Coda, Codetta, Colophon, Cue, Dock, Empennage, Endgate, Fan, Fee, Flag, Floccus, → **FOLLOW**, Fud, Liripoop, Parson's nose, Pole, Pope's nose, PS, Queue, Rumple-bane, Scut, Seat, Shirt, Stag, Stern, Telson, → **TIP**, Train, Uro(some), Uropygium, Women

Tailless Acaudal, An(o)urous, Fee-simple

Tail-lobes Anisocercal

Tailor(ed) Adapt, Bespoke, Bushel, Cabbager, Couturier, Cutter, Darzi, Draper, Durzi, Epicene, Feeble, Flint, Merchant, Nine, Outfitter, Pick-the-louse, Pricklouse, Sartor, Seamster, Snip, Starveling, Style, Whipcat, Whipstitch

▷ **Tailor** *may indicate* an anagram

Taint(ed) Besmirch, Blemish, Fly-blown, High, Infect, Leper, Off, Poison, → **SPOIL**, Stain, Stale, Stigma, Tinge, Trace, Unwholesome

Taiwan RC

Take(n), Take in, Taking(s), Take over, Takeover Absorb, → **ACCEPT**, Adopt, Assume, Attract, Bag, Beg, Bite, Bone, Borrow, Bottle, → **CAPTURE**, Catch, Charming, Claim, Cop, Coup, Detract, Dishy, Distrain, Entr(y)ism, Exact, Expropriate, Film, Get, Grab, Greenmail, Handle, Haul, Hent, House, Howe, Huff, Incept, Ingest, Leveraged buy out, Mess, Misappropriate, Nick, Occupy, Pocket, Quote, R, Rec, Receipt, Receive, Recipe, Reverse, Rob, Seise, Sequester, Ship, Smitten, Snatch, Sneak, → **STEAL**, Stomach, Subsume, Swallow, Sweet, Swipe, Toll, Trump, Turnover, Usher, Usurp, Wan, Winsome, Wrest

Take away, Take-away, Take off Aph(a)eresis, Asport, Carry-out, Deduct, Dock, Doff, Esloin, Exenterate, Expropriate, Indian, Jato, Minus, Parody, Parrot, Press-gang, Shanghai, Skit, Subtract, Vertical, VTO(L)

Take care Guard, See, Tend, Watch

▷ **Taken up** *may indicate* reversed

Take part Act, Engage, Side

Talbot House Toc H

Talc Potstone, Rensselaerite, Soapstone, Steatite, Venice

Tale(s) Aga-saga, Allegory, Anecdote, Blood, Boccaccio, Conte, Decameron, Edda, Fable, Fabliau, Fairy, Fairy story, Fiction, Folk, Gag, Geste, Hadith, Iliad, Jataka, Jeremiad, Legend, Lie, Mabinogion, Maise, Ma(i)ze, Märchen, Mease, Milesian, Narrative, Odyssey, Old wives', Pentameron, Rede, Saga, Sandabar, Score, Sinbad, Sind(a)bad, Sob-story, Spiel, → **STORY**, Tradition, Traveller's, Weird

Tale-bearer, Tale-teller Gossip, Grass, Informer, Sneak, Tattler, Tusitala

Talent(ed) Ability, Accomplishment, Aptitude, Bent, Dower, Faculty, Flair, Forte, Genius, Gift, Ingenium, Knack, Long suit, Nous, Prodigy, Schtick, Strong point, Versatile, Virtuoso, W(h)iz(z), Whiz-kid

Talion Reprisal

Talisman Amulet, Charm, Mascot, Saladin, Sampo, Scarab, Telesm

Talk(ing), Talking point, Talker, Talks Address, Ana, Articulate, Babble, Bibble-babble, Blab, Blague, Blat, Blather, Blether-skate, Cant, Chalk, Chat, Chinwag, Chirp, Circumlocution, Colloquy, Commune, Confabulate, Confer, Converse, Coo, Cross, Descant, Dialog(ue), Diatribe, Dilate, Discourse, Diseur, Dissert, Double, Earbash, Earful, Express, Fast, Filibuster, Froth, Gab, Gabble, Gabnash, Gas, Gibber, Gossip, Grandiloquence, Guff, Harp, High-level, Imparl,

Jabber, Jargon, Jaw, Jazz, Korero, Lalage, Lip, Logorrhoea, Macrology, Mang, Maunder, Mince, Monologue, Motormouth, Nashgab, Natter, Noise, Omniana, Palabra, Palaver, Parlance, Parley, Patter, Pawaw, Pep, Perorate, Phraser, Pidgin, Pillow, Pitch, Potter, Powwow, Prate, Prattle, Presentation, Prose, Proximity, Ramble, Rap, Rigmarole, Rote, Sales, SALT, Shop, Slang(-whang), Small, Soliloquy, → **SPEAK**, Spiel, Spout, Straight, Sweet, Table, Tachylogia, Topic, Turkey, Twaddle, Twitter, Unbosom, Up(s), Utter, Vocal, Waffle, Wibble, Witter, Wongi, Wrangle, Yabber, Yack, Yad(d)a-yad(d)a-yad(d)a, Yak, Yalta, Yammer, Yap, Yatter

Talkative Chatty, Fluent, Gabby, Garrulous, Gash, Glib, Loquacious, Vocular, Voluble

Tall Etiolated, Exaggerated, Far-fetched, Hie, High, Hye, Lanky, Lathy, Leggy, Lofty, Long, Order, Procerity, Randle-tree, Rantle-tree, Tangle, Taunt, Tower, Towery

Tallboy Chest, Dresser

Tallow Greaves, Hatchettite, Lead-arming, Mineral, Vegetable, Wax

Tally Accord, → **AGREE**, Census, Correspond, Count, Match, Nickstick, Notch, Record, → **SCORE**, Stick, Stock, Tab, Tag

Talmud Gemara, Mishna

Talon Claw, Ogee, Single

Talus Scree

Tamarind Assam

Tamasha Fuss, To-do

Tame Amenage, Break, Docile, Domesticate, Lapdog, Mail, Mansuete, Meek, Mild, Safe, Snool, Subdue

Tammany Hall, Sachem

Tamp, Tampon Plug

Tamper(ing) Bishop, Cook, Doctor, Fake, Fiddle, Meddle, Medicate, Monkey, Nobble, Phreaking

Tam-tam Gong

Tan(ned), Tanned skin, Tanning Adust, Bablah, Babul, Bark, Basil, Beige, Bisque, Boarding, Bronze, → **BROWN**, Canaigre, Catechu, Furan, Furfuran(e), Insolate, Lambast, Leather, Neb-neb, Paste, Pipi, Puer, Pure, Spank, Sun, Sunbathe, Tenné, Umber, Val(l)onia, Valonea, Ybet

Tandem Duo, Randem

Tang Relish, Smack, Taste

Tangent Ratio, Slope, Touching

Tangible Concrete, Palpable, Plain, Solid, Tactual

Tangle Alga, Badderlock, Burble, Dulse, Embroil, Entwine, Fank, Fankle, Heap, Implication, Ket, → **KNOT**, Labyrinth, Laminaria, Lutin, Mat, Mix, Nest, Oarweed, Ore, Perplex, Pleach, → **RAVEL**, Sea-girdle, Seaweed, Skean, Skein, Snarl, Taigle, Taut(it), Tawt, Thicket, Tousle, Varec

▷ **Tangled** *may indicate* an anagram

Tank(ed) Abrams, Alligator, Amphibian, Aquarium, Back boiler, Belly, Bosh, Casspir, Centurion, Cesspool, Challenger, Chieftain, Cistern, Drop, Drunk, Feedhead, Float, Flotation, Gasholder, Header, Keir, Kier, Mouse, Panzer, Pod, Quiescent, → **RESERVOIR**, Ripple, Sedimentation, Septic, Sherman, Shield pond, Sponson, Sump, Surge, Think, Tiger, Valentine, Vat, Ventral, Vivarium, Whippet

Tankard Blackjack, Peg, Pewter, Pot, Stein, Tappit-hen

Tanker Bowser, Lorry, Oiler

Tanner(y) Bender, Currier, Kick, Solarium, Sunbather, Sunshine, Tawery, Tester(n), 'Vld', Zack

Tannin Catechu

Tantalise Entice, Tease, Tempt, Torture
Tantalum Ta
Tantivy Alew, Halloo
Tantrum Hissyfit, Paddy, Pet, Rage, Scene, Snit, Tirrivee, Tirrivie
Tanzania EAT
Tap(ping), Taps Accolade, Bibcock, Blip, Bob, Broach, Bug, Cock, Col legno, Drum, Faucet, Fillip, Flick, Hack, Mag, Milk, Mixer, Monitor, Paracentesis, Pat, Patter, Percuss, Petcock, → **RAP**, Screw, Spigot, Spinal, Stopcock, Stroup, Tack, Tat, Tit, Touk, Tuck, Water
Tape Chrome, DAT, → **DRINK**, Duct, Ferret, Finish, Friction, Gaffer, Grip, Idiot, Incle, Inkle, Insulating, Magnetic, Masking, Measure, Metal, Narrowcast, Paper, Passe-partout, Perforated, Punched, Record, Red, Scotch, Sellotape®, Shape, Stay, Sticky, Ticker, Video, Welding
Taper(ed), Tapering Diminish, Fastigiate, Featheredge, Flagelliform, Fusiform, Lanceolate, Morse, Narrow, Nose, Subulate, Tail
Tapestry Alentous, Arras(ene), Aubusson, Bayeux, Bergamot, Crewel-work, Dosser, Gobelin, Hanging, Oudenarde, Petit point, Tapet, Weaving
Tapeworm Echinococcus, Hydatid, Measle, Scolex, Strobila, Taenia, Teniasis
Tapioca Cassava, Pearl, Yuca, Yucca
Tapir Anta, S(e)ladang
Tar, Tar product AB, Bitumen, Carbazole, Coal, Creosote, Egg, Furan, Gladwellise, Gob, Indene, Maltha, Matelot, Matlo, Mineral, Naphtha, Needle, OS, Parcel, Pay, Picamar, Picene, Pine, Pitch, Rating, Retene, Sailor, Salt, Uintahite, Uintaite, Wood, Wood pitch, Xylol
Tardy Behindhand, Dilatory, Late, → **SLOW**
Tare Tine, Vetch
Target → **AIM**, Attainment, Blank, Butt, Clout, Cockshy, Dart, Drogue, End, Hit, Home, Hub, Inner, Magpie, Mark, Motty, → **OBJECT**, Outer, Pelta, Pin, Prey, Prick, Quintain, Sitter, Sitting, Tee, Victim, Wand
Tariff List, Menu, Preferential, Protective, Rate, Revenue, Zabeta
Tarnish Defile, Discolour, Soil, Stain, Sully, Taint
Taro Arum, Coc(c)o, Dasheen, Eddo
Tarot Arcana
Tarpaulin Weathercloth
Tarragon Staragen
Tarry Bide, Dally, Leng, → **LINGER**, Stay, Sticky
Tarsier Malmag
Tarsus Saul
Tart Acetic, Acid, Bakewell, Broad, Charlotte, Cheesecake, Cocotte, Croquante, Cupid, Custard, Dariole, Doxy, Duff, Flam(m), Flan, Flawn, Frock, Harlot, Hussy, Jade, Lemony, Mirliton, Moll, Mort, Nana, Painted woman, → **PIE**, Pinnace, Piquant, Pro, Quean, Quiche, Quine, → **SHARP**, Slapper, Slut, Snappy, Sour, Stew, Strumpet, Tatin, Tramp, Treacle, Trull, Unsweet
Tartan Argyle, Argyll, Maud, Plaid, Set(t), Trews
Tartar Argal, Argol, Beeswing, Calculus, Crust, Hell, Plaque, Rough, Scale, Tam(b)erlane, Zenocrate
Tashkent Uzbek
Task Assignment, Aufgabe, → **CHORE**, Clat, Duty, Errand, Exercise, Fag, Imposition, Mission, Ordeal, Pensum, Stint, Thankless, Vulgus
Tasmania Apple Isle, Van Diemen's Land
Tassel Pompom, Toorie, Tourie, Tsutsith, Tuft

Taste(ful), Taster, Tasty Acquired, Aesthetic, Appetite, Degust, Delibate, Delicious, Discrimination, → **EAT**, Elegant, Fashion, Flavour, Form, Gout, Gust, Gustatory, Hint, Lekker, Lick, Palate, Penchant, Pica, Pree, Refinement, Relish, → **SAMPLE**, Sapor, Sar, Savour, S(c)hme(c)k, Sip, Smack, Smatch, Smattering, Snack, Soupçon, Stomach, Succulent, Tang, Titbit, Toothsome, → **TRY**, Umami, Vertu, Virtu, Waft, Wine

Tasteless Appal, Brassy, Fade, Flat, Insipid, Insulse, Kitsch, Stale, Tacky, Vapid, Vulgar, Watery, Wearish, Wersh

Tat, Tatter, Tatty Rag, Ribbon, Roon, Scrap, Shred, Tag, Ta(i)ver, Tan, Untidy

Tattie-bogle Scarecrow

Tattle(r) Blab, Chatter, Gash, → **GOSSIP**, Prate, Rumour, Sneak, Snitch, Totanus, Willet

Tattoo Devil's, Drum, Edinburgh, Moko, Rataplan, Row-dow, Tat

Tatum Art

Taught Up

Taunt Dig, Fling, Gibe, Gird, → **JEER**, Rag, Ridicule, Twight, Twit

Taut Stiff, Tense

Tavern Bar, Bodega, Bousing-ken, Bush, Fonda, → **INN**, Kiddleywink, Kneipe, Mermaid, Mitre, Mughouse, Pothouse, Shebeen, Taphouse

Taw Alley, Ally, Marble

Tawdry Catchpenny, → **CHEAP**, Flashy, Gaudy, Raffish, Sleazy, Tatty, Tinsey

Tawny Brindle, Dusky, Fawn, Fulvous, Mulatto, Port, Tan

Tawse Cat, Lash, Thong, Whip

Tax(ing), Taxation ACT, Agist, Aid, Alms-fee, Assess, Capitation, Carbon, Carucage, Cense, Cess, → **CHARGE**, Corporation, Council, Custom, Danegeld, Direct, Duty, Energy, EPT, Escot, Escuage, Eurotax, Exact, Excise, Exercise, EZT, Fat, Gabelle, Geld, Gift, Head, Head money, Hearth money, Hidage, Impose, Imposition, Impost, Impute, Indirect, Inheritance, IR, Jaghir(e), Jagir, Land, Levy, Likin, Lot, Murage, Negative, Octroi, Operose, Overwork, Pavage, PAYE, Peter-pence, Poll, Poundage, Precept, Primage, Property, Proportional, PT, Punish, Purchase, Rate, Regressive, Road, Rome-pence, Sales, Scat(t), Scot (and lot), Scutage, Sess, SET, Sin, Single, Skat, Stealth, Stent, Streetage, Stumpage, Super, Taille, Tallage, Talliate, Tariff, Task, Teind, Tithe, Tobin, Toilsome, Toll, Tonnage, Tribute, Try, Turnover, Unitary, Value-added, VAT, Wattle, Wealth, Weary, White rent, Windfall, Window, Withholding, Zakat

Tax area Tahsil, Talooka, Taluk(a)

Tax-collector, Taxman Amildar, Cheater, Exciseman, Farmer, Gabeller, Inspector, IR(S), Publican, Stento(u)r, Tithe-proctor, Tollman, Undertaker, Zemindar

Taxi Cab, Gharri, Gharry, Hackney, Joe baxi, Samlor, Zola Budd

Taxidermist Venus

▶ **Taxman** *see* **TAX-COLLECTOR**

TB Scrofula

TE Lawrence, Ross, Shaw

Tea Afternoon, Assam, Beef, Black, Bohea, Brew, Brew-up, Brick, Bubble, Bush, Cambric, Camomile, Caper, Ceylon, Cha, Chamomile, Chanoyu, China, Chirping-cup, Congo(u), Cream, Cuppa, Darjeeling, Earl Grey, Grass, Green, Gunfire, Gunpowder, Herb(al), High, Hyson, Indian, Jasmine, K(h)at, Kitchen, Labrador, Lapsang, Lapsang Souchong, Leaves, Ledum, Lemon, Malt, Manuka, Marijuana, Maté, Mexican, Mint, Morning, Mountain, New Jersey, Oolong, Orange pekoe, Oulong, Paraguay, Pekoe, Post and rail, Pot, Qat, Red-root, Rooibos, Rosie Lee, Russian, Sage, Senna, Souchong, Stroupach, Stroupan, Switchel, Tay, Thea,

Theophylline, Tousy, Twankay, Yerba (de Maté)

Teach(er), Teaching (material), Teachings Acharya, Adjoint, Advisory, Agrege, AMMA, Anthroposophy, Apostle, Aristotle, Barbe, Beale, BEd, Bhagwan, Buss, Catechist, Chalk and talk, Chalkface, → **COACH**, Con(ne), Didactic, Didascalic, Docent, Doctrine, Dogma, Dominie, Dressage, Edify, → **EDUCATE**, Educationalist, Edutainment, EIS, ELT, Explain, Faculty, Froebel, Gerund-grinder, Gooroo, Gospel, Governess, Guru, Head, Heuristic, Hodja, Inculcate, Indoctrinate, Inform, Instil, Instruct, Ism, Kho(d)ja, Kumon (Method), Lair, Lancasterian, Larn, Lear(e), Lecturer, Leir, Lere, Maam, Maggid, Magister, Maharishi, Mahavira, Mallam, Marker, Marm, Master, Maulvi, Mentor, Miss, Mistress, Molla(h), Monitor, Montessorian, Moola(h), Moolvi(e), Mufti, Mullah, Munshi, Mwalimu, Mystagogue, Nuffield, Paedotribe, Pedagogue, Pedant, Peripatetic, Phonic method, Posture-master, Pr(a)efect, Preceptor, Privat-docent, Proctor, Prof, Prog, PT, Pupil, Rabbetzin, Rabbi, Rav, Realia, Rebbe, Remedial, Rhetor, Scholastic, Schoolie, Schoolman, Scribe, Sensei, Show, Sir, Smriti, Socrates, Sophist, Staff, Starets, Staretz, Sunna, Supply, Swami, Tantra, Team, Tonic sol-fa, Train(er), Tutelage, Tutor, Tutress, Tutrix, Usher

Teach-in Seminar

Teahouse Sukiya

Teak African, Bastard, White

Team Bafana Bafana, Colts, Crew, Dream, Écurie, Eleven, Équipe, Farm, Fifteen, Outfit, Oxen, Panel, Possibles, Probables, Proto, Relay, Scrub, → **SIDE**, Span, Special, Spurs, Squad, Squadron, Staff, Tiger, Troupe, Turnout, Unicorn, United, XI

Tea-party Boston, Bunfight, Cookie-shine, Drum, Kettledrum, Shine

Teapot Billycan, Cadogan, Samovar

Tear(s), Tearable, Tearful, Tearing Beano, Claw, Crocodile, Divulsion, Drop, Eye-drop, Eye-water, Greeting, Hurry, Lacerate, Laniary, Mammock, Pelt, Ranch, Rash, Reave, → **REND**, Rheum, Rip, Rive, Rume, Scag, Screed, Shred, Snag, Split, Spree, Tire, Waterworks, Wet, Worry, Wrench, Wrest

Tearaway Get, Hothead, Ned

Tear-jerker Melodrama, Onion

Tear-pit Crumen, Larmier

Tease, Teaser, Teasing Arch, Backcomb, Badinage, Bait, Banter, Card, Chaff, Chap, Chiack, Chip, Chyack, Cod, Coquet, Enigma, Grig, Guy, Hank, Imp, Ironic, Itch, Josh, Kemb, Kid, Mag, Mamaguy, Nark, Persiflage, → **RAG**, Raillery, Rally, Razz, Rib, Rip on, Rot, Strip, → **TANTALISE**, Toaze, Torment(or), Touse, Touze, Towse, Towze, Twilly, Twit, Worrit

Teasel Dipsacus, Valerian

Teat Dug, Dummy, Mamilla, Mastoid, Nipple, Pap, Soother, Tit

Tea-time Chat

Teaze Gig, Moze

Technetium Tc

Technical, Technician, Technique Adept, Alexander, Artisan, Brushwork, College, Cusum, Delphi, Execution, Foley artist, Footsteps editor, Harmolodics, Honey-trap, Junior, Kiwi, Know-how, Layback, Manner, → **METHOD**, Operative, Phasing, Pixil(l)ation, Salami, Sandwich, Science, Senior, Serial, Split-screen, Stop-motion, Toe and heel

Technology, Technological High, Information, Intermediate, State of the art, Stealth

Ted(dy) Bodgie, Dexter, Ducktail, Moult, Widgie, Yob

Tedium, Tedious Boring, Chore, Deadly, Doldrums, Drag, Dreich, Dull, Ennui,

Foozle, Heaviness, Long, Longspun, Longueur, Monotony, Operose, Prosy, Soul-destroying, Tiresome, → **TIRING**, Twaddle, Wearisome, Yawn

Tee Hub, Umbrella, Wind

Teem(ing) Abound, Bustling, Empty, Great, Pullulate, Swarm

Teenager Adolescent, Bobbysoxer, Junior, Juvenile, Minor, Mod, Rocker, Sharpie, Skinhead, Youth

▶ **Teeth** *see* **TOOTH**

Teething ring Coral

Teetotal(ler) Abdar, Blue Ribbon, Nephalist, Rechabite, Temperate, TT, Water-drinker, Wowser

Tegument Seed coat

Telecommunications Cellnet®, Vodafone®

Telegram, Telegraph Bush, Cable, Ems, Facsimile, Fax, Grapevine, Greetings, International, Message, Moccasin, Mulga wire, Overseas, Singing, Telex, Wire

Telepathy, Telepathic Clairvoyance, ESP, Seer

Telephone Ameche, ATLAS, Bell, Blower, BT, Call, Cellphone, Centrex, Cordless, Dial, Dog and bone, Freephone®, GRACE, Handset, Horn, Hotline, Intercom, Line, Lo-call®, Mercury, Mobile, Noki, Pay-station, Pdq, → **PHONE**, POTS, Ring, Snitch line, Squawk box, STD, Textphone, Tie line, Touch-tone, Utility, Vodafone®, Wire

Teleprinter Creed

Telescope Altazimuth, Astronomical, Binocle, Cassegrain(ian), Collimator, Coudé, Electron, Equatorial, Finder, Galilean, Gemini, Glass, Gregorian, Heliometer, Hubble, Intussuscept, Meniscus, Newtonian, Night-glass, Optical, Palomar, Perspective, Radio, Reflecting, Reflector, Refractor, Schmidt, Shorten, Sniperscope, Snooperscope, Spyglass, Stadia, Terrestrial, Tube, X-ray, Zenith

Teletext® Ceefax®, Oracle®

Television, Telly Appointment, Box, Cable, Closed-circuit, Confessional, Digital, Diorama, Docu-soap, Event, Flatscreen, Goggle box, Image orthicon, Interactive, ITV, MAC, Narrowcast, PAL, Pay, Plumbicon®, Projection, RTE, Satellite, SECAM, Set, Small screen, Subscription, Tree and branch, Tube, → **TV**, Video

Tell(ing) Acquaint, Announce, Apprise, Archer, Beads, Blab, Break, Clipe, Clype, Compt, Direct, → **DISCLOSE**, Divulge, Effective, Grass, Impart, Influential, Inform, → **NARRATE**, Noise, Notify, Number, Recite, Recount, Relate, Report, Retail, Rumour, Sneak, Snitch, Spin, Teach, Unbosom, William

Tellurium Te

Temerity Cheek, Gall, Impertinence, Imprudence, Impudence, Incaution, Rashness, Recklessness

Temper, Temperate Abstemious, Abstinent, Allay, Anneal, Assuage, Attune, Balmy, Bile, Blood, Calm, Cantankerous, Choler, Comeddle, Continent, Dander, Delay, Ease, Fireworks, Flaky, Inure, Irish, Leaven, → **MILD**, Mitigate, Moderate, Modify, → **MOOD**, Neal, Paddy, Paddywhack, Pet, Radge, Rage, Season, Short fuse, Snit, Sober, Soften, Spitfire, Spleen, Strop, Swage, Tantrum, Techy, Teen, Teetotal, Tetchy, Tiff, Tone, Trim, Tune

Temperament(al) Bent, Blood, Choleric, Crasis, Disposition, Equal, Just, Kidney, Mean-tone, Melancholy, Mettle, Moody, → **NATURE**, Neel, Over-sensitive, Phlegmatic, Prima donna, Sanguine, Unstable, Viscerotonia

Temperance Good Templar, Moderation, Pledge, Rechabite

Temperature Absolute, Celsius, Centigrade, Chambré, Colour, Critical, Curie, Dew point, Eutectic, Fahrenheit, Fever, Flashpoint, Heat, Heterothermal, Hyperthermia, Kelvin, Néel, Permissive, Regulo, Restrictive, Room, Supercritical, T, Thermodynamic, Transition, Weed, Weid

Tempest(uous) Bourasque, Euraquilo, Euroclydon, Gale, High, Marie,
→ **STORM(Y)**, Wrathy

Temple, Temple gate Abu Simbal, Abydos, Adytum, Amphiprostyle, Artemis,
Capitol, Cella, Chapel, Church, Delphi, Delubrum, Ephesus, Erechtheum,
Erechthion, Fane, Gompa, Gurdwara, Haffet, Haffit, Heroon, Inner, Mandir(a),
Masjid, Middle, Monopteron, Monopteros, Mosque, Museum, Naos, Nymphaeum,
Pagod(a), Pantheon, Parthenon, Serapeum, → **SHRINE**, Shul(n), Teocalli, Teopan,
Torii, Vihara, Wat

Tempo Agoge, Lento, Rate, → **RHYTHM**, Rubato

Temporal Petrosal, Petrous

Temporary Acting, Caretaker, Cutcha, Ephemeral, Hobjob, Impermanent, Interim,
Kutcha, Locum, Makeshift, Pro tem, Provisional, Quick-fix, Short-term, Stopgap,
Temp, Transient, Transitional

Temporise(r) Politique

Tempt(ation), Tempting, Tempter, Temptress Allure, Apple, Bait, Beguile,
Beset, Circe, Dalilah, Decoy, Delilah, → **ENTICE**, Eve, Groundbait, Impulse, Lure,
Peccable, Providence, Satan, Seduce, Siren, Snare, Tantalise, Test, Tice, Trial

Ten Commandments, Decad, Dectet, Decury, Denary, Googol, 10, Iota, Long, Tera-,
Tribes, X

Tenacious, Tenacity Clayey, Determined, Dogged, Fast, Guts, Hold, Intransigent,
Persevering, Persistent, Resolute, Retentive, Sticky

Tenancy, Tenant(s) Censuarius, Cosherer, Cottar, Cotter, Cottier, Dreng, Feuar,
Feudatory, Gravelman, Homage, Ingo, Inhabit, Kindly, Leaseholder, Lessee,
→ **LODGER**, Metayer, Occupier, Periodic, Regulated, Rentaller, Renter, Secure,
Shorthold, Sitting, Socager, Socman, Sokeman, Suckener, Tacksman, Valvassor,
Vassal, Vavasour, Visit

Tend Care, Dress, Herd, Incline, Lean, Liable, Mind, Nurse, Prone, Run, Shepherd,
Verge

Tendency Apt, Bent, Bias, Central, Conatus, Drift, Genius, Idiosyncrasy, Import,
Militant, Penchant, Proclivity, Propensity, Trend

Tender(iser), Tenderly, Tenderness Affettuoso, Amoroso, Bid, Bill, Coin, Con
amore, Crank, Dingey, Ding(h)y, Fond, Frail, Gentle, Green, Humane, Jolly-boat,
Legal, Nesh, Nurse, → **OFFER**, Painful, Papain, Pinnace, Pra(a)m, Prefer, Present,
Proffer, Proposal, Quotation, Red Cross, Sair, Shepherd, → **SOFT**, Sore, SRN,
Submit, Sweet, Sympathy, Tendre

Tenderfoot Babe, Chechacho, Chechako, Cub, Greenhorn, Innocent

Tenderloin Psoas, Undercut

Tendon Achilles, Aponeurosis, Hamstring, Kangaroo, Leader, Paxwax, Sinew,
String, Vinculum, Whitleather

Tendril(led) Capreolate, Cirrose, Cirrus, Tentacle

Tenement(s) Dominant, Land, Rook, Tack

Tenet Adiaphoron, Creed, → **DOCTRINE**, Dogma

Tenfold Decuple

Tennis Close, Court, Deck, Lawn, LTA, Real, Royal, Set, Short, Sphairistike, Squash,
Table, Wimbledon

Tenon Cog, Dovetail, Lewis, Tusk

Tenor Course, Domingo, → **DRIFT**, Effect, Ferreras, Gigli, Gist, Heroic, Pavarotti,
Purport, Singer, T, Tide, Timbre, Trial, Vein

Tense Aor, Aorist, Case, Clench, Drawn, Edgy, Electric, Essive, Flex, Imperfect,
Keyed up, Mood(y), Nervy, Overstrung, Past, Perfect, Pluperfect, Preterit, Preterite,
Rigid, Simple, Stiff, Strained, Stressed(-out), Strict, T, → **TAUT**, Tighten, Uptight

Tensing Sherpa

Tension Creative, High, Isometrics, Isotonic, Meniscus, Nerviness, Premenstrual, → **STRAIN**, Stress, Stretch, Surface, Tone, Tonicity, Tonus, Yips

Tent Bell, Bivvy, Cabana, Douar, Dowar, Duar, Ger, Gur, Kedar, Kibitka, Marquee, Oxygen, Pavilion, Probe, Pup, Red wine, Ridge, Shamiana(h), Shamiyanah, Shelter, Tabernacle, Teepee, Tepee, Tilt, Tipi, Top, Topek, Trailer, Tupek, Tupik, Wigwam, Wine, Y(o)urt

Tentacle Actinal, Cirrate, Feeler, Hectocotylus, Horn, Lophophore

Tentative Empirical, Experimental, Gingerly, Peirastic

Tent-dweller, Tent-maker Camper, Indian, Kedar, Omar, St Paul

Tenth Disme, Teind, Tithe

Ten Thousand Toman

Tenuous Frail, Slender, Slight, Thin, Vague

Tenure Blench, Burgage, Copyhold, Cottier(ism), Drengage, Fee, Fee-farm, Feu, Frankalmoi(g)n(e), Frank-fee, Gavelkind, Leasehold, Manorial, Occupation, Raiyatwari, Rundale, Runrig, Ryotwari, Socage, → **TERM**, Vavasory, Venville, Zemindar

Tepid Laodicean, Lew, Lukewarm

Terbium Tb

Terete Centric(al)

Term(s), Terminal, Termly Air, Anode, Buffer, Cathode, Coast, Container, Coste, Designate, Desinant, Distal, Distributed, Dumb, → **EPITHET**, Euphemism, Expression, Final, Gnomon, Goal, Half, Hilary, Inkhorn, Intelligent, Law, Lent, Major, Michaelmas, Middle, Minor, → **PERIOD**, Point-of-sale, Rail(head), Real, Removal, Sabbatical, School, Semester, Session, Stint, Stretch, Trimester, Trimestrial, Trinity, Ultimatum, Waterloo, → **WORD**, Work station, Zeroth

Termagant Jade, Shrew, Shrow, Spitfire, Vixen

Terminate, Termination, Terminus Abort, Axe, Cease, Conclude, Depot, Desinent, Earth, → **END**, Expiry, → **FINISH**, Goal, Liquidate, Naricorn, Railhead, Suffix

Termite Duck-ant

Tern Egg-bird, Scray, Three

Terpene Squalene

Terrace Barbette, Beach, Bench, Kop, Linch, Lynchet, Offset, Perron, River, Row house, Shelf, Stoep, Tarras, Undercliff, Veranda(h)

Terra-cotta Tanagra

Terrain Area, Landscape, Scablands, Tract

Terrapin Diamondback, Emydes, Emys, Slider, Turtle

Terrible, Terribly Appalling, Awful, Deadly, Fell, Frightful, Ghastly, Hellacious, Horrible, Ivan, Much, Odious, Very

Terrible person Humgruffi(a)n, Ivan, Ogre

Terrier Aberdeen, Airedale, Apsos, Australian, Australian silky, Bedlington, Black and tan, Border, Boston, Bull, Catalogue, Cesky, Dandie Dinmont, Fox, Glen of Imaal, Griffon, Irish, Jack Russell, Kerry blue, Lakeland, Maltese, Manchester, Norfolk, Norwich, Pinscher, Pit bull, Ratter, Register, Schauzer, Scotch, Scottie, Scottish, Sealyham, Silky, Skye, Soft-coated wheaten, Staffordshire bull, Sydney silky, TA, Tibetan, Welsh, West Highland, West Highland white, Westie, Wire-haired, Yorkshire

Terrific, Terrified, Terrify(ing) Affright, Aghast, Agrise, Agrize, Agryze, Appal, Awe, Blood-curdling, Enorm, Fear, Fine, Fley, Gast, Helluva, Huge, Overawe, → **PETRIFY**, Scare, Superb, Unman, Yippee

Territory Abthane, Ap(p)anage, Colony, Domain, Dominion, Duchy, Emirate, Enclave, Exclave, Goa, Indian, Latium, Lebensraum, Manor, Margravate, No-man's-land, Northern, Northwest, Nunavut, Palatinate, Panhandle, Papua, Petsamo, Principate, Protectorate, Province, Realm, → **REGION**, Rupert's Land, Scheduled, Sphere, Sultanate, Swazi, Ter(r), Trieste, Trust, Tuath, Union, Yukon

Terror(s) Blue funk, Bugaboo, Bugbear, Eek, → **FEAR**, Fright, Holy, Imp, Night, Panic, Skrik

Terrorism, Terrorist Alarmist, Al Fatah, Anarchist, Black Hand, Bogeyman, Bomber, Bully, Cagoulard, Consumer, Desperado, Dynamitard, Eta, Grapo, Hijacker, Ku Klux Klan, Mau-mau, Maximalist, Mountain, Nightrider, Nihilist, OAS, Pirate, PLO, Provo, Red Brigade, Robespierre, Ustashi

Terry Ellen, Towel

Terse Abrupt, Brusque, Curt, Laconic, Pithy, Precise, Succinct

Tertiary Cainozoic, Eocene, Miocene, Oligocene, Palaeogene, Pliocene

Tessellation Mosaic

Test(er), Testing Achievement, Acid, Alpha, Ames, Amniocentesis, Apgar, Appro, Aptitude, Assay, Audition, Barany, Bench, Bender, Benedict, Beta, Blood, Breath, Breathalyser®, Brinell, Burn-in, Candle, Canopy, Check, Chi-square, Cis-trans, Cloze, Conn(er), Coomb's, Crash, Criterion, Crucial, Crucible, Crunch, Dick, Docimastic, Driving, Drop, Dummy-run, Éprouvette, Examine, Exercise, Experiment, Field, Flame, Frog, Hagberg, Ink-blot, Intelligence, International, Litmus, Mann-Whitney, Mantoux, Match, Mazzin, Means, Medical, Mom, MOT, Mug, Neckverse, Needs, Objective, Oral, Ordalian, → **ORDEAL**, Pale, Pap, Papanicolaou, Paraffin, Patch, Paternity, Performance, Personality, PH, Pilot, Pons asinorum, Pree, Preeve, Preif, Preve, Probative, Probe, Projective, Proof, Prove, Proving-ground, Pyx, Q-sort, Qualification, Quiz, Rally, Reagent, Reliability, Road, Rorschach, SAT, Scalogram, Scan, Schick's, Schilling, Schutz-Charlton, Scratch, Screen, Shadow, Shibboleth, Showdown, Shroff, Sign, Signed-ranks, Significance, Sixpence, Skin, Slump, Smear, Smoke, Snellen, Soap, Sound, Sounding, Spinal, Stanford-Binet, Stress, Tempt, Tensile, Touch, Touchstone, Trial, Trier, Trior, Try, Turing, Ultrasonic, Viva, Wassermann's, Weigh, Wilcoxon, Zack

Testament Bible, Covenant, Hagographa, Heptateuch, Hexateuch, Hornolog(o)umena, Midrash, New, Old, Pentateuch, Scripture, Septuagint, Tanach, Targum, Will

Testicle(s) Ballocks, Balls, Bollix, Bollocks, Bush oyster, Cobblers, Cojones, Cruet, Family jewels, Gool(e)y, Goolie, Knackers, Monkey-gland, Monorchid, Nads, Nuts, Orchis, Pills, Ridgel, Ridgil, Rig(gald), Rocks, Stone

Testify, Testimonial, Testimony Character, Chit, Declare, Depone, Deposition, → **EVIDENCE**, Rap, Scroll, Tribute, Viva voce, Vouch, Witness

Testy, Tetchy Cross, Narky, Peevish, Ratty

Tetanus Lockjaw

Tête-à-tête A quattr' occhi, Collogue, Confab, Hobnob, Twosome

Tether Cord, Endurance, Hitch, Noose, Picket, Seal, Stringhalt, → **TIE**

Tetrahedrite Fahlerz, Fahlore

Tetrarchy Iturea

Tetrasyllabic Paeon

Tetrode Resnatron

Teuton(ic) Erl-king, German, Goth, Herren, Vandal

Texas Ranger

Text(s), Textbook, Texting ABC, Body, Brahmana, Church, Codex, Donat, Ennage, Greeked, Harmony, Libretto, Mandaean, Mantra, Mezuzah, Minitel, Octapla,

Op-cit, Philology, Plain, Proof, Pyramid, Quran, Responsa, Rubric, Script, S(h)astra, Shema, SMS, → **SUBJECT**, Sura, Sutra, Tefillin, Tephillin, Tetrapla, Thesis, Topic, Tripitaka, Typography, Upanis(h)ad, Urtext, Variorum, Viewdata, Vulgate, Zohar

Textile Cloth, Fabric, Mercy

Texture Constitution, Feel, Fiber, Fibre, Grain, Open, Set(t), Wale, Weave, Woof

Thai(land) Karen, Lao(s), Mon, Shan, Siam

Thalamus Optic

Thallium Tl

Thames Father, Tamesis

Than And

Thane Banquo, Ross

Thank(s), Thankful, Thanksgiving Appreciate, Collins, Deo gratias, Gloria, Grace, Gramercy, Grateful, Gratitude, Kaddish, Mercy, Roofer

Thankless Ingrate, Vain

That (is), That one As, Cestui, Das heisst, Dh, Exists, How, Id est, Ie, Ille, Namely, Que, Sc, Such, Thence, Thon(der), What, Which, Yon, Yonder, Yt

Thatch(er), Thatching At(t)ap, Daych, Hair, Heard, Hear(i)e, Hele, Hell, Mane, PM, Reed, Straw, Thack, Theek, Wig

Thaw Debacle, Defreeze, Defrost, → **MELT**, Melt-water, Relax

▷ **Thaw** *may indicate* 'ice' to be removed from a word

The Der, Die, El, Il, La, Le, Los, T', That, Ye, Ze

Theatre(s), Theatrical(ity) Abbey, Absurd, Adelphi, Arena, Balcony, Broadway, Camp, Cinema, Circle, Coliseum, Criterion, Crucible, Drama, Event, Everyman, Field, Fringe, Gaff, Gaiety, Globe, Grand Guignol, Great White Way, Hall, Haymarket, Hippodrome, Histrionic, House, Kabuki, La Scala, Legitimate, Little, Lyceum, Melodramatic, Mermaid, Music-hall, National, News, Nickelodeon, Noh, Odeon, Odeum, Off-Broadway, Off-off-Broadway, Operating, OUDS, Palladium, Panache, Pennygaff, Pit, Playhouse, Political, Rep(ertory), Sadler's Wells, Shaftesbury, Sheldonian, Shop, Stage, Stalls, Stoll, Straw-hat, Street, Summer stock, Total, Touring, Vic, Windmill, Zarzuela

Theatregoer Circle, Gallery, Gods, Pit, Pittite, Stalls

Theft, Thieving Appropriation, Bluesnarfing, Burglary, Heist, Identity, Kinchinlay, Larceny, Maino(u)r, Manner, Petty larceny, Pilfery, Plagiarism, Plunder, Pugging, Ram-raid, Robbery, Stealth, Stouth(rief), → **THIEF**, Touch, TWOC, Walk-in

Their Her

Theist Believer, Unitarian

Them 'Em, Hem, Tho

Theme Burden, Crab canon, Donnée, Fugue, Idea, Leitmotiv, Lemma, Lemmata, → **MELODY**, Motif, Peg, Question, → **SUBJECT**, Text, Topic, Topos

Then(ce) Already, Away, Next, Since, Sine, So, Syne, Thereupon, Tho

▷ **The northern** *may indicate* t'

Theodolite Diopter, Dioptre, Groma, Tacheometer, Tachymeter, Transit

Theologian, Theologist, Theology Abelard, Aquinas, Barth, Calvin, Christology, Colet, DD, Divine, Eckhart, Erastus, Eschatology, Eusebius, Exegetics, Fideism, Genevan, Hase, Infralapsarian, Irenics, Jansen, Kierkegaard, Knox, Liberation, Luther, Moral, Mullah, Natural, Newman, Niebuhr, Origen, Paley, Pastoral, Pectoral, Pelagius, Pusey, Rabbi, Religious, Sacramentarian, Schoolman, Schwenkfeld, Scotus, Softa, STP, Supralapsarian, Swedenborg, Tertullian, Ulema, Universalist

Theory, Theorem, Theoretical, Theorist Academic, Atomic, Attachment, Attribution, Automata, Band, Bayes(ian), Bernouilli's, Big bang, Binomial, Bohr,

Boo-hurrah, Catastrophe, Chaos, Complexity, Connectionism, Conspiracy, Corpuscular, Darwinian, Decision, Deduction, Dependency, Dictum, Doctrinaire, Domino, Double aspect, Dow, Einstein, Emboîtement, Empiricism, Epigenesist, Exponential, Fermat's (last), Gaia, Galois, Game, Gauge, Germ, Gödel's, Grand Unified, Grotian, Group, Guess, Holism, Hormic, Hypothesis, Ideal, Identity, Ideology, Information, Ism(y), James-Lange, Kinetic, Laingian, Lamarckism, Lemma, Lunar, MAD, Milankovitch, Model, Monism, Mythical, Nernst heat, Notion, Number, Object relations, Perturbation, Petrinism, Pluralism, Poynting, Probability, Proof, Pure, Pythagoras, Quantity, Quantum, Queueing, Random walk, Reception, Relativism, Relativity, Satisfaction, Set, Solipsism, Speculative, Steady state, String, Superdense, Superstring, Supersymmetry, System, Tachyon, TOE, Traducianism, Twistor, Tychism, Utilitarianism, Voluntarism, Vortex, Vulcanist, Wasm, Wave, Wholism, Wolfian

Therapy, Therapeutic Acupressure, Acupuncture, Aura-Soma, Auricular, Aversion, Behaviour, Bowen, Brachytherapy, Cellular, Chavuttithirumal, Chelation, Client-centred, Cognitive, Cognitive-behavioural, Colour, Combination, Craniosacral, Crystal (healing), CST, Curative, Curietherapy, Deep, Dianetics, Drama, ECT, Electric shock, Electroconvulsive, Electroshock, Family, Faradism, Fever, Flotation, Gemstone, Gene, Germ(-line), Gestalt, Group, Heliotherapy, Hellerwork, HRT, Hypnosis, Immunotherapy, Implosive, Insight, Larval, Light, Live cell, Logop(a)edics, Looyenwork, Magnetic, Metamorphic technique, Minimal invasive, MLD, Movement, Music, Narco, Narcotherapy, Natal, Natural, Non directive, Occupational, ORT, Osteopathy, Past life, Pattern, Physical, Phytotherapy, Polarity, Pressure, Primal, Primal (scream), Psychodrama, Psychosynthesis, Radiation, Radio, Radium, Rainbow, Reflexology, Regression, Reichian, Reiki, Relaxation, Retail, Rogerian, Rolfing, Röntgenotherapy, Root-canal, Sanatory, Scientology®, Scream, Serum, Sex, SHEN, Shiatsu, Shiatzu, Shock, Sitz-bath, Sound, Speech, Speleotherapy, Supportive, TENS, Thalassotherapy, Theriacal, Thermotherapy, Touch, → TREATMENT, Water cure, X-ray, Zone

There(after), Thereby, Thereupon Attending, Holla, Ipso facto, Present, Thither, Thon, Upon, With that, Y, Yonder

Therefore Argal, Ergo, Forthy, Hence, So, Why

Thermodynamic Enthalpy, Entropy

Thermometer Aethrioscope, Centesimal, Clinical, Gas, Glass, Katathermometer, Maximum and minimum, Psychrometer, Pyrometer, Resistance, Thermograph, Water, Wet and dry bulb, Wet bulb

Thermoplastic Cel(luloid), Resin

Thesaurus Dictionary, Lexicon, Roget, Treasury, Word-finder

These Thir

Theseus Champion

Thesis Argument, Dissertation, Doctorial, Theme

Thespian → ACTOR, Ham, Performer

Thessalonian Lapith

They A

Thick(en), Thickening, Thickener, Thickness, Thickset Abundant, Algin, Burly, Bushy, Callosity, Callus, Clavate, Cloddy, Cruddle, Curdle, Dense, Dextrin(e), Dumose, Engross, Grist, Grouty, Grume, Guar, Gum, Hyperostosis, Incrassate, Inspissate, Kuzu, Liaison, Lush, Nuggety, Pally, Panada, Reduce, Roux, Sclerosis, → SOLID, Soupy, Squat, Stumpy, → STUPID, Thieves, This, Thixotropic, Waulk, Wooden, Xantham

Thick-coated Atheromatous

Thicket Bosk, Brake, Brush, Cane-brake, Chamisal, Chapparal, Coppice, Copse, Dead-finish, Greve, Grove, Macchie, Maquis, Queach, Reedrand, Reedrond, Salicetum, Shola

Thick-lipped Labrose

Thick-skinned Armadillo, Callous, Pachyderm, Tough

Thief, Thieves, Thievish Abactor, Autolycus, Blood, Chummy, Coon, Corsair, Cutpurse, Dismas, Dysmas, Filcher, Flood, Footpad, Freebooter, Furacious, Ganef, Gestas, Gully-raker, Heist, Hotter, Huaquero, Ice-man, Jackdaw, Kiddy, Kondo, Larcener, Light-fingered, Limmer, Looter, Mag, Montith, Nip(per), Nuthook, Pad, Peculator, Pilferer, Pirate, Plagiarist, Poacher, Poddy-dodger, Prig, Raffles, River-rat, → **ROBBER**, Rustler, St Nicholas's clerks, Shark, Shop-lifter, Sneak, Sticky fingers, Taffy, Taker, Tea-leaf, Thick, Twoccer

Thigh Femoral, Gaskin, Ham, Haunch, Hock, Meros

Thin(ner), Thinness Acetone, Atomy, Attenuate, Bald, Beanpole, Bony, Cornstalk, Cull, Diluent, Dilute, Ectomorph, Emaciated, Enseam, Fine, Fine-drawn, Flimsy, Gaunt, Hairline, Hair('s-)breadth, Inseam, Lanky, Lean, Matchstick, Mawger, Puny, Rackabones, Rangy, Rare, Rarefied, Reedy, Scant, Scraggy, Scrannel, Scrawny, Sheer, Sieve, Skeletal, Skimpy, Skinking, Slender, Slim, Slimline, Slink, → **SPARE**, Sparse, Spindly, Stilty, Stringy, Subtle, Taper, Tenuous, Turps, Wafer, Washy, Waste, Watch, Water(y), → **WEAK**, Weedy, Whirtle, Wiry, Wispy, Wortle, Wraith

Thing(s) Alia, Article, Chattel, Chose, Craze, Doodah, Doofer, Entia, Fetish, Fixation, It, Item, Jingbang, Job, Last, Material, Matter, Near, Noumenon, → **OBJECT**, Obsession, Paraphernalia, Phobia, Res, Tool, Vision, Whatnot

Thingummy Dingbat, Dinges, Doodad, Doodah, Doofer, Doohickey, Gubbins, Hoot(a)nanny, Hootenanny, Whatsit, Yoke

Think(er), Thinking Associate, Believe, Brain, Brood, Casuistry, Cogitate, Conjecture, Consider, Contemplant, → **CONTEMPLATE**, Deem, Deliberate, Descartes, Dianoetic, Divergent, Esteem, Fancy, Fear, Feel, Fogramite, Ghesse, Gnostic, Guess, Hegel, Hold, → **IMAGINE**, Judge, Lateral, Meditate, Mentation, Mindset, Mull, Muse, Opine, Pensive, Philosopher, Phrontistery, Ponder, Pore, Presume, Ratiocinate, Rational, Reckon, Reflect, Reminisce, Ruminate, Synectics, Trow, Vertical, Ween, Wishful

Thin-skinned Sensitive

Third, Third rate Bronze, C, Eroica, Gamma, Gooseberry, Interval, Mediant, Minor, Picardy, Quartan, Tertiary, Tertius, Tierce, Trisect

Third man Abel, Lime

Thirst(y) Adry, → **CRAVE**, Dives, Drought, Drouth, Dry, Hydropic, Nadors, Pant, Polydipsia, Thrist

Thirteen Baker's dozen, Devil's dozen, Long dozen, Riddle, Triskaidekaphobia, Unlucky

Thirty Lambda

Thirty nine books All-OT, OT

This Hic, Hoc, The, Thick, Thilk, Thir

Thistle Canada, Carduus, Carline, Cnicus, Creeping, Dayshell, Echinops, Milk, Musk, Rauriki, Russian, Safflower, Scotch, Sow, Spear, Star, Thrissel, Thristle

This year Ha

Thomas Aquinas, Arnold, Christadelphian, De Quincey, Didymus, Doubting, Dylan, Erastus, Hardy, Loco, Parr, Rhymer, Tompion, True, Turbulent

Thomas Aquinas Angelic Doctor

Thong Babiche, Jandal®, Lash, Latchet, Leather, Lore, Riem, Riempie, Shoe-latchet, → **STRAP**, Strop, Taws(e), Whang, Whip

Thor Thunderer
Thorax Chest, Peraeon, Pereion, Scutellum, Throat
Thorium Th
Thorn(y) Acantha, Bael, Bel, Bhel, Bramble, Briar, Coyotillo, Doom, Edh, Eth, Irritation, Jerusalem, Jew's, Mahonia, Mayflower, Nabk, Nebbuk, Nebe(c)k, → **NEEDLE**, Paloverde, Pricker, Prickle, Slae, Spine, Spinescent, Spinulate, Trial, Wagn'bietjie, Y, Ye, Zare(e)ba, Zariba, Zeriba
Thorn-apple Jimpson-weed
Thornless Inerm
Thorough(ly) À fond, Complete, Deep, Even-down, Firm, Fully, Ingrained, Inly, Out, Out and out, Painstaking, Pakka, Pucka, Pukka, Radical, Ripe, Root and branch, Searching, Sound, Strict, Total, Tout à fait, Up
Thoroughbred Arab, Bloodstock, Pedigree
Thoroughfare Avenue, Broadway, Causeway, Freeway, Highway, Parkway, → **ROAD**, Street
Those Thae, Thaim, Them, Tho, Yon
Thou M, Mil
Though Albe, Albeit, All-be, Ever, Tho, Whenas
Thought(s), Thoughtful(ness) Avisandum, Broody, Censed, Cerebration, Cogitation, Concept, Considerate, Contemplation, Dianoetic, Felt, Idea, Indrawn, Innate, Kind, Maieutic, Mind, Musing, Notion, Opinion, Pansy, Pensée, Pensive, Philosophy, Reflection, Rumination, Second
Thoughtless Blindfold, Careless, Heedless, Improvident, Incogitant, Inconsiderate, Pillock, → **RASH**, Reckless, Remiss, Scatter-brained, Vacant, Vain
Thousand(s) Chiliad, Gorilla, K, Lac, Lakh, M, Millenary, Millennium, Myriad, Octillion, Plum, Toman
Thracian Spartacus
Thrall Captive, Esne, Serf, Slave
Thrash(ing) → **BEAT**, Belabour, Belt, Bepelt, Binge, Bless, Cane, Dress, Drub, Flail, Flog, Jole, Joll, Joule, Jowl, Lace, Laidie, Laidy, Lambast, Larrup, Lather, Leather, Lick, Marmelise, Paste, Ploat, Quilt, Slog, Smoke, Strap-oil, Swat, Tank, Targe, Thraiping, Towel, Trim, Trounce, Wallop, Whale, Whap, Writhe
Thread, Threadlike Acme screw, Ariadne, Bar, Bottom, Bride, Buttress, Chalaza, Chromatid, Chromatin, Chromosome, Clew, Clue, Cop(pin), Cord, Coventry blue, Eel-worm, End, Female, Fibre, Filament, File, Filiform, Filose, Filoselle, Float, Flourishing, Gist, Gold, Gossamer, Heddle, Ixtle, Lace, Lap, Lingel, Lingle, Link, Lisle, Lurex®, Male, Meander, Mycellum, Nematode, Nematoid, Organzine, Pack, Pearlin(g), Pick, Plasmodesm, Ravel, Reeve, Sacred, Screw, Sellers screw, Seton, Silver, Single, Spireme, → **STRAND**, Stroma, Suture, Tassel, Tendril, Theme, Thrid, Thrum, Trace, Tram, Trundle, Tussore, Twine, Warp, Watap, Wax(ed), Weft, Whitworth, Whitworth screw, Wick, → **WIND**, Wisp, Worm
Threadbare Hackneyed, Napless, Shabby, Worn
Threadworm Nemathelminth, Strongyl, Vinegar-eel
Threat(en), Threatened, Threatening Baleful, Blackmail, Bluster, Brutum fulmen, Coerce, Comminate, Face, Fatwa, Fraught, Greenmail, Greymail, Hazard, Impend, Imperil, Loom, → **MENACE**, Minacious, Minatory, Mint, Omen, Ominous, Overcast, Overhang, Parlous, Peril, Portent, Ramp, Sabre-rattling, Shore, Strongarm, Ugly, Veiled, Warning
Three, Threefold, Three-wheeler, Thrice Graces, Har, Harpies, Jafenhar, Leash, Muses, Musketeers, Pairial, Pair-royal, Parial, Prial, Ter, Tern, Terzetta, Thrice, Thridi, Tid, T.i.d, Tierce, Tray, Trey, Triad, Tricar, Triennial, Trifid, Trigon, Trilogy,

Trinal, Trine, Trinity, Trio, Triple, Triptote, Troika
Three-D(imensional) Lenticular, Stereopsis
Three-day Triduan, Triduum
Threehalfpence Dandiprat, Dandyprat
Three-handed Cutthroat
Three-headed Cerberus, Geryon
Three hundred B, Carpet
Three-legged IOM, Triskele, Triskelion
Threepence, Threepenny bit Tickey, Tray, Trey, Treybit
Three-quarter Wing
Three-year old Staggard
Threnody Dirge, Epicede, → LAMENT
Thresh Beat, Flail, Separate
Threshold Absolute, Brink, Cill, Difference, Doorstep, Limen, Liminal, Nuclear, Sill, Tax, Verge
▶ **Thrice** see THREE
Thrift(y) Economy, Frugal, Husbandry, Oeconomy, Sea-grass, Sea-pink, Virtue, Wary
Thrill(er), Thrilling Atingle, Buzz, Delight, Dindle, Dinnle, Dirl, Dread, Dynamite, Emotive, → ENCHANT, Enliven, Excite, Film noir, Frisson, Gas, Jag, Kick, Page-turner, Perceant, Plangent, Pulsate, Pulse, Quiver, Sensation, Thirl, Tinglish, Tremor, Vibrant, Whodunit
Thrive Batten, Blossom, Boom, Do, Fl, → FLOURISH, Flower, Grow, Mushroom, → PROSPER, Succeed, Thee
Throat(y) Craw, Crop, Deep, Dewlap, Fauces, Gorge, Gular, Gullet, Guttural, Hot coppers, Jugular, Laryngeal, Maw, Pereion, Pharynx, Prunella, Quailpipe, Red lane, Roopit, Roopy, Strep, Swallet, Thrapple, Thropple, Throttle, Weasand, Wesand, Whistle, Windpipe
Throb(bing) Beat, Palpitate, Pant, Pit-a-pat, Pound, Pulsate, Quop, Stang, Tingle, Vibrato
▷ **Throbbing** *may indicate* an anagram
Throe(s) Agony, Pang, Paroxysm
Thrombosis Deep-vein
Throne Bed-of-justice, Cathedra, Episcopal, Gadi, → LAVATORY, Mercy-seat, Peacock, Rule, Seat, See, Siege, Tribune
Throng(ing) Crowd, Flock, Host, Press, Resort, Swarm
Throttle → CHOKE, Gar(r)otte, Gun, Mug, Regulator, Scrag, Silence, Stifle, Strangle, Strangulate, Thrapple, We(a)sand
Through, Throughout Along, Ana, By, Dia-, During, Everywhere, Over, Passim, Per, Pr, Sempre, Sic passim, To, Trans, Via, Yont
▶ **Throw(n)** see TOSS
Throw (up), Thrower, Throw-out Bin, Cast-off, Chunder, Discobolus, Egesta, Emesis, Flying mare, Go, Jettison, Pash, Puke, Spew, Squirt, Squit, → TOSS
Throwback Atavism, Echo
Thrush Ant, Aphtha, Bird, Chat, Fieldfare, Hermit, Homescreetch, Mavis, Missel, Mistle, Olive-back, Pitta, Prunella, Redwing, Sprue, Turdine, Veery
Thrust, Thruster Abdominal, Aventre, Bear, Boost, Botte, Burn, Burpee, Detrude, Dig, Drive, Elbow, Exert, Extrude, Flanconade, Foin, → FORCE, Gist, Hay, Imbroc(c)ata, Impulse, Job, Lunge, Montant(o), Obtrude, Oust, Pass, Passado, Peg, Perk, Pitchfork, Poach, Poke, Potch(e), Pote, Probe, Prog, Propel, Pun, Punto, → PUSH, Put, Ram, Remise, Repost, Run, Shoulder, Shove, Single-stock, Sock,

Sorn, Squat, Stap, Stick, Stoccado, Stoccata, Stock, Stuck, Thrutch, Tilt, Tuck, Venue

Thud Drum, Dump, Flump, Phut, Plod, Thump, Whump

Thug(s) Brute, Gangster, Goon(da), Gorilla, Gurrier, Hoodlum, Loord, Ninja, Ockers, Phansigar, Plug-ugly, Roughneck, SS, Strangler, Ted, Tityre-tu, Tsotsi

Thule Ultima

Thulium Tm

Thumb Bally, Green, Hitch, Midget, Ovolo, Pollex, Scan, Sore, Tom

Thump(ing) Blow, Bonk, Clobber, Cob, Crump, Da(u)d, Dawd, Ding, Dod, Drub, Dub, Hammer, Knevell, Knock, Nevel, Oner, Paik, → **POUND**, Pummel, Slam, Slosh, Souse, Swat, Swingeing, Thud, Trounce, Tund, Whud

Thunder(ing), Thunderstorm Bolt, Boom, Clap, Coup de foudre, Donnerwetter, Foudroyant, Foulder, Fulminate, Intonate, Lei-king, Pil(l)an, Raiden, → **ROAR**, Rumble, Summanus, Tempest, Thor, Tonant

Thursday Chare, Holy, Maundy, Sheer, Shere

Thus Ergo, Sic, So, Therefore

Thwart Baffle, Balk, → **CROSS**, Dash, Dish, Foil, Frustrate, Hamstring, Hogtie, Obstruct, Outwit, Pip, Prevent, Scotch, Snooker, Spike, Spite, Stonker, Stymie, Transverse

Thy Yourn

Thyme Basil, Lemon, Water

Thyroid Goitre, Myxodema

Tiara Cidaris, Crownet, Triple crown

Tiberius Gracchus

Tibetan Lamaist, Naga, Sherpa, Sitsang

Tic Vocal

Tick, Tick off Acarida, Acarus, Beat, Bloodsucker, Check, → **CHIDE**, Click, Cr, → **CREDIT**, Deer, HP, Idle, Instant, Jar, Ked, Mattress, Mile, Mo, Moment, Ricinulei, Second, Sheep, Soft, Strap, Worm

Ticket(s) Billet, Bone, Brief, Carnet, Commutation, Complimentary, Coupon, Day, Docket, Dream, Excursion, Kangaroo, Label, Meal, One-day, One-way, Open-jaw, Parking, Pass, Pass-out, Pawn, Platform, Raffle, Raincheck, Return, Round-trip, Rover, Saver, Scratchcard, Season, Single, Soup, Split, Straight, Stub, Supersaver, → **TAG**, Tempest, Tessera(l), Through, Tix, Transfer, Tyburn, Unity, Voucher, Walking, Zone

Ticket-seller Scalper

Tickle, Ticklish Amuse, Delicate, Divert, Excite, Gratify, Gump, → **ITCH**, Kittle, Queasy, Thrill, Titillate

Tiddler Brit, Tom

Tide, Tidal Current, Drift, Eagre, Easter, Eger, Estuary, Flood, High, High water, Lee, Low, Marigram, Neap, Red, Rising, River, Roost, Sea, Seiche, Slack water, Spring, Surge, Trend, Wave

Tide-gate Aboideau, Aboiteau, Weir

Tidings Gospel, → **NEWS**, Rumour, Word

Tidy Big, Comb, Considerable, Curry, Do, Fair, Fettle, Groom, Kempt, Large, Neat, Neaten, → **ORDER**, Pachyderm, Predy, Preen, Primp, Red(d), Slick, Snug, Sort, Spruce, Trim, Valet

Tie, Tied, Tying Ascot, Attach, Barcelona, Berth, Bind, Black, Bolo, → **BOND**, Bootlace, Bow, Bowyang, Cable, Cope, Cravat, Cup, Dead-heat, Drag, Draw, Four-in-hand, Frap, Halter, Handicap, Harness, Hitch, Holdfast, Kipper, → **KNOT**, Lace, Lash, Level, Ligament, Ligate, Ligature, Link, Marry, Match, Moor, Neck and neck, Oblige, Obstriction, Old School, Oop, Oup, Overlay, Raffia, Restrain, Rod, Scarf, School, Score draw, Scrunchie, Semifinal, Shackle, Shoelace, Shoestring, Sleeper, Slur, Solitaire, Soubise, Splice, Stake, Strap, String, Tawdry-lace, Tether, Together, Trice, Truss, Unite, White, Windsor

Tier Apron, Bank, Gradin(e), Knotter, Layer, Range, Rank, Stage, Storey

Tierce Leash, Tc

Tiff Bicker, Contretemps, Difference, Dispute, Feed, Feud, Huff, Miff, Skirmish, Spat, Squabble

Tiffany Gauze

Tiger Bengal, → **CAT**, Clemenceau, Demoiselle, Lily, Machairodont, Machairodus, Man-eater, Margay, Paper, Sabre-tooth, Smilodon, Tamil, Tasmanian, Woods

Tight(en), Tightness, Tights Boozy, Bosky, Brace, Cinch, Close(-hauled), Constriction, Cote-hardie, → **DRUNK**, Fishnet, Fleshings, High, Hose, Jam, Leggings, Leotards, Lit, Loaded, Maillot, Mean, Merry, Niggardly, Oiled, Pang, Pantihose, Phimosis, Pickled, Pinch(penny), Plastered, Prompt, Proof, Rigour, Snug, Squiffy, Stenosis, → **STINGY**, Stinko, Strict, Stringent, Swift, Swig, Taut, Tense, Tipsy, Trig, Woozy

Tightrope(-walker) Aerialist, Blondin, Equilibrist, Funambulist, Petauriste

Tightwad Cheapskate, → **MISER**, Scrooge

Tile(s), Tiled Antefix, Arris, Azulejo, Carpet, Chapeau, Dalle, Derby, Dutch, Encaustic, Field, → **HAT**, Imbrex, Imbricate, Lid, Lino, Mahjong(g), Ostracon, Ostrakon, Peever, Quarrel, Quarry, Rag(g), Ridge, Rooftop, Sclate, Shingle, Slat, → **SLATE**, Tegular, Tessella, Tessera, Titfer, Topper, Wall, Wally

Till Cashbox, Checkout, Coffer, Ear, Eulenspiegel, Farm, Hasta, Hoe, Husband, Lob, Peter, → **PLOUGH**, Set, Unto

Tiller Gardener, Helm, Ploughman, Rotavator, Wheel

Tilt Awning, Bank, Camber, Cant, Cock, Dip, Heel, Hut, Joust, Just, → **LIST**, Quintain, Rock, Tip, Unbalance

Timber Apron, Balk, Batten, Beam, Bolster, Bond, Bridging, Cant-rail, Carapa, Chess, Clapboard, Compass, Coulisse, Cross-tree, Cruck, Dogshores, Dwang, Elmwood, Flitch, Float, Four-by-two, Futchel, Futtock, Greenheart, Groundsell, Hardwood, Harewood, Intertie, Iroko, Ironwood, Joist, Knee, Knighthead, Lauan, Ligger, Lintel, Log, Lumber, Nogging, Nothofagus, Plank-sheer, Purlin(e), Putlock, Putlog, Pyengadu, Radiata, Ramin, Rib, Ridgepole, Roundwood, Rung, Sandalwood, Sapele, Sapodilla, Satinwood, Scantling, Shook, Shorts, Sissoo, Skeg, Sneezewood, Softwood, Souari, Stemson, Stere, Sternpost, Sternson, Straddle, Stud, Stull, Stumpage, Summer, Swing-stock, Tilting fillet, Towing-bitts, Transom, Trestletree, Two-by-four, Wale, Wall plate, Weatherboard, Whitewood, → **WOOD**, Yang

Timbre Clang, Klang(farbe), Register, → **TENOR**, Tone

Time(s), Timer Access, African, Agoge, Apparent, Assymetric, Astronomical, Autumn, Awhile, Bird, BST, Central, Chronaxy, Chronic, Chronometer, Chronon, Clock, Closing, Common, Compound, Connect, Core, Counter, Cryptozoic, Date, Day, Dead, Decade, Dimension, Double, Duple, Duration, Early, Eastern, Eastern Standard, Egg-glass, Enemy, Eon, Ephemeris, Epoch, Equinox, Era, European, Eve(ning), Extra, Father, Flexitime, Forelock, Four-four, Free, Full, Gest, Glide, Half, Healer, High, Horologe, Hour, Hourglass, Hr, Idle, Imprisonment, Injury, Innings, Instant, Interlude, Jiff, Juncture, Kalpa, Latent, Lay-day, Lead, Lean, Leisure, Life, Lighting-up, Lilac, Local, Lowsing, Mean, Menopause, Metronome, Mountain standard, Multiple, Needle, Nonce, Nones, Normal, Occasion, Oft, → **ON TIME**, Opening, Pacific, Paralysis, Part, Period, Phanerozoic, Pinger, Porridge, Post,

Prelapsarian, Prime, Proper, Quadruple, Quality, Question, Quick, Reaction, Real, Reaper, Recovery, Response, Responsum, Reverberation, Rhythm, Run(ning), Sandglass, Seal, → **SEASON**, Seel, Seil, Semeion, Serial, Session, Shelf-life, Sidereal, Sight, Simple, Sith(e), Slow, Solar, Solstice, Space, Span, Spare, Spell, Spin, Split, Spring, Squeaky-bum, Standard, Stoppage, Stopwatch, Stound, Stownd, Stretch, Summer, Sundial, Sundown, Sythe, T, Tem, Tempo, Tempore, Tense, Thief, Three-four, Thunderer, Tick, Tid, Tide, Trice, Triple, True, Turnaround, Two-four, Universal, Usance, What, While, Winter, X, Yonks, Zero

Timebomb Demographic

Time-keeper, Timepiece Ben, Chronometer, Clock, Hourglass, Ref, Sand-glass, Sundial, Ticker, Tompion, Watch

Timeless Eternal, Nd, Undying

Timely Appropriate, Apropos, Happy, Opportune, Pat, Prompt, Punctual

Timescale Geological

Time-server Prisoner, Trimmer

Timetable Bradshaw, → **CHART**, Schedule

Timid, Timorous Afraid, Aspen, Bashful, Blate, Chicken, Cowardly, Eerie, Eery, Faint-hearted, Fearful, Hare, Hen-hearted, Milquetoast, Mouse, Mous(e)y, Pavid, Pigeon-hearted, Pusillanimous, Pussy, Quaking, Schnok, Shrinking, → **SHY**, Skeary, Sook, Yellow

Timothy Cat's-tail, Grass, Phleum

Tin(ned), Tinfoil, Tinny Argentine, Block, Britannia metal, Can, Cash, Debe, Dixie, Maconochie, Mess, → **MONEY**, Moola(h), Ochre, Plate, Rhino, Sn, Stannary, Stannic, Stream, Tain, Tole

Tincture Arnica, Bufo, Chroma, Elixir, Fur, Infusion, Laudanum, Metal, Or, Sericon, Sol, Spice, Taint, Tenné, Vert

Tinder Amadou, Faggot, Fuel, Funk, Punk, Spark, Spunk, Touchwood

Tine Antler, Bay, Cusp, Grain, Prong, Snag, Surroyal, Trey

Tinge(d) Dye, Eye, Flavour, Gild, → **HUE**, Infuscate, Taint, Tincture, Tone, Touch

Tingle, Tingling Dinnle, Dirl, Paraesthesia, Pins and needles, Prickle, Thrill, Throb, Tinkle

Tinker Bell, Caird, Coster, Didakai, Didakei, Diddicoy, Didicoy, Didikoi, → **FIDDLE**, Gypsy, Mender, Pedlar, Potter, Prig, Putter, Repair, Sly, Snout, Tamper, Tramp, Traveller

Tinkle Pink

Tinsel(ly) Clinquant, Gaudy, Glitter, O, Spangle, Turkey

Tint Colour, Henna, Hue, Pigment, → **STAIN**, Tinct, Tinge, Woad

Tiny Atto-, Baby, Diddy, Dwarf, Ha'it, Infinitesimal, Itsy-bitsy, Lilliputian, Minikin, Minim, Mite, Negligible, Petite, Small, Smidgeon, Stime, Teeny, Tiddl(e)y, Tiddy, Tim, Tine, Tottie, Totty, Toy, Wee

Tip (off), Tipping Apex, Arrowhead, Ash-heap, Asparagus, Backshish, Baksheesh, Batta, Beer-money, Bonsel(l)a, Bonus, B(u)onamono, Cant, Cert, Chape, Counsel, Coup, Cowp, Crown, Cue, Cumshaw, Douceur, Dump, Extremity, Fee, Felt, Ferrule, Filter, Forecast, Glans, Gratillity, Gratuity, Heel, → **HINT**, Hunch, Inkle, Iridise, Lagniappe, Largess(e), List, Mess, Middenstead, Nap, Nib, Noop, Ord, Perk, Perquisite, Point, Pointer, Pour, Pourboire, Previse, Prong, Straight, Suggestion, Summit, Tag, Tail, Tilt, Toom, Touch, Tronc, Upset, Vail, Vales, Warn, Whisper, Wink, Wrinkle

Tippet Cape, Fur, Scarf

Tipple Bib, Booze, → **DRINK**, Paint, Pot, Poteen

Tipster Prophet, Tout

Tipsy Bleary, Boozy, Bosky, → **DRUNK**, Elevated, Moony, Nappy, Oiled, On, Rocky, Screwed, Slewed, Slued, Squiffy, Wet

▷ **Tipsy** *may indicate* an anagram

Tiptoe Digitigrade, Spanish, Walk

Tirade Diatribe, Invective, Jobation, Laisse, Philippic, Rand, Rant, Screed, Slang

Tire(d), Tiredness, Tiring All-in, Aweary, Beat, Bore, Bushed, Caparison, Deadbeat, Dress, Drowsy, → **EXHAUST**, Fag, Fagged out, Fatigue, Flag, Fordid, Fordod, Forjeskit, Frazzle, Gruel, Irk, Jack, Jade, Lassitude, Limp, ME, Overspent, Pall, Poop, Puggled, → **ROBE**, Rubber, Sap, Shagged, Sicken, Sleepry, Sleepy, Spent, Swinkt, Tax, Tedious, Tucker, Wabbit, Wappend, Weary, Wrecked

Tiresome Boring, Exhausting, Humdrum, Pill, Tedious, Vexing

Tirl Rattle, Risp, Strip, Turn

▶ **Tiro** *see* **TYRO**

Tissue Adenoid, Adhesion, Adipose, Aerenchyma, Aponeurosis, Archesporium, Callus, Carbon, Cartilage, Cementum, Chalaza, Cheloid, Chlorenchyma, Coenosarc, Collagen, Collenchyma, Commissure, Conducting, Connective, Cortex, Dentine, Diploe, Elastin, Epimysium, Epineurium, Epithelium, Eschar, Evocator, Fabric, Fascia, Flesh, Gamgee, Gauze, Gleba, Glia, Granulation, Gum, Heteroplasia, Histogen, Histoid, Infarct, Keloid, Kleenex®, Lamina, Liber, Lies, Ligament, Luteal, Lymphate, Lymphoid, Macroglia, Marrow, Matrix, Mechanical, Medulla, → **MEMBRANE**, Meristem, Mesenchyme, Mesophyll, Mestom(e), Mole, Muscle, Myelin(e), Myocardium, Neoplasm, Neuroglia, Nucellus, Olivary, Pack, Palisade, Pannus, Paper, Papilla, Parenchyma, Periblem, Perichylous, Pericycle, Peridesmium, Perimysium, Perinephrium, Perineurium, Perisperm, Phellogen, Phloem, Pith, Placenta, Plerome, Polyarch, Pons, Primordium, Procambium, Prosenchyma, Prothallis, Pterygium, Pulp, Radula, Sarcenet, Sars(e)net, Scar, Sclerenchyma, Scleroma, Sequestrum, Sinew, Soft, Somatopleure, Stereome, Stroma, Submucosa, Suet, Tarsus, Tela, Tendon, Tonsil, Tunica, Vascular, Velum, Web, Wound, Xylem, Zoograft

Tit, Tit-bit(s) Analecta, Canapé, Crested, Currie, Curry, Delicacy, Dug, Nag, Nipple, Nun, Pap, Quarry, Sample, Scrap, Snack, Teat, Tug, Twitch, Willow, Wren, Zakuska

Titan(ic), Titaness Atlas, Colossus, Cronos, Cronus, Drone, Enormous, Giant, Huge, Hyperion, Kronos, Large, Leviathan, Liner, Oceanus, Phoebe, Prometheus, Rhea, Themis, Vast

Titanium, Titanite Rutin, Sagenite, Sphene, Ti

Tit for tat Deserts, Revenge, Talion

Tithe Disme, Dyzemas, Frankpledge, Teind, Tenth

Titian Abram, Auburn

Titillate(r) Delight, Excite, Fluffer, Tickle

Titivate Preen, Primp

Title Abbé, → **ADDRESS**, Ag(h)a, Antonomasia, Appellative, Bahadur, Baroness, Baronet, Bart, Bastard, Bhai, Bretwalda, Calif, Caliph, Caption, Charta, Chogyal, Claim, Conveyance, Count(ess), Courtesy, Credit, Dan, Datin, Datuk, Dauphin, Dayan, Deeds, Devi, Dom, Don, Don(n)a, Dowager, Dub, Duchess, Duke, Earl, Effendi, Eminence, Epithet, Esquire, Excellency, Fra, Frau(lein), Gospodin, Grand Master, Gyani, Hafiz, Handle, Header, Heading, Headline, Hojatoleslam, Hon, Honour, Imperator, Interest, Kabaka, Kalif, Kaliph, Kaur, King, Kumari, Lady, Lala, Lemma, → **LIEN**, Lord, Mal(l)am, Marchesa, Marchese, Marquess, Marquis, Master, Masthead, Maulana, Memsahib, Meneer, Mevrou, Miladi, Milady, Milord, Mirza, Mr(s), Name, Native, Negus, Nizam, Nomen, Padishah, Pasha, Peerage, Pir, Polemarch, Prefix, Prince(ss), Queen, → **RANK**, Reb, Reverence, Reverend,

→ **RIGHT**, Rubric, Running, Sahib, Sama, San, Sardar, Sayid, Senhor(a), Señor(a), Shri, Singh, Sir, Sirdar, Son, Sowbhagyawati, Sri, Stratum, Tannie, Tenno, Titule, Torrens, Tycoon, U, Worship

Title-holder Cartouche, Champion, Landlord, Noble

Titmouse Bird, Hickymal, Mag, Reedling, Tit

Titter Giggle, Snigger, Tehee

Tittle Jot

Titus Oates

Tizz(y) Pother, Spin, Tanner, Testril, VId

TNT Explosive, Trotyl

To(wards) At, Beside, Inby, Onto, Prone, Shet, Shut, Till

Toad(y) Bootlicker, Bufo, Bumsucker, Cane, Clawback, Cocksucker, Crapaud, Crawler, Fawn, Frog, Horned, Jackal, Jenkins, Knot, Lackey, Lick-platter, Lickspittle, Midwife, Minion, Natterjack, Nototrema, Paddock, Parasite, Pick-thank, Pipa, Placebo, Platanna, Puddock, Queensland cane, Sook, Spade-foot, Surinam, Sycophant, Tree, Tuft-hunter, Walking, Warty, Xenopus, Yesman

Toadstool Amanita, Death-cap, Death-cup, Destroying angel, Fly agaric, → **FUNGUS**, Grisette, Horsehair, Paddock-stool, Parrot, Saffron milk cap, Sickener, Sulphur tuft, Verdigris, Wax cap

Toast(er) Bacchus, Bell, Birsle, Brindisi, → **BROWN**, Bruschetta, Bumper, Cheers, Chin-chin, Crostini, Crouton, Drink-hail, French, Gesundheit, Grace-cup, Grill, Health, Iechyd da, Kia-ora, L'chaim, Lechayim, Loyal, Melba, Pledge, Pop up, Propose, Prosit, Round, Scouther, Scowder, Scowther, Sentiment, Sippet, Skoal, Slainte, Slainte mha(i)th, Soldier, Sunbathe, Wassail, Zwieback

Toastmaster MC, Symposiarch

Tobacco, Tobacco-field Alfalfa, Bacchi, Baccy, Bird's eye, Broadleaf, Burley, Canaster, Capa, Caporal, Cavendish, Chew, Dottle, Filler, Honeydew, Indian, Killikinnick, Kinnikinick, Latakia, Mundungus, Nailrod, Navy-cut, Negro-head, Nicotian, Nicotine, Niggerhead, Perique, Pigtail, Plug, Quid, Rapper, Régie, Returns, Shag, Sneesh, Snout, Snuff, Straight cut, Stripleaf, Turkish, Twist, Vega, Virginia, Weed

Toboggan Sled(ge), Sleigh

Toby Dog, High, Highwayman, Jug, Low

Tocsin Alarm, Siren

Today Hodiernal, Now, Present

Toddle(r) Baim, Gangrel, Mite, Tot, Totter, Trot, Waddle

Toddy Arrack, → **DRINK**, Sura, Whisky

To-do Sensation, Stir

Toe(s) Dactyl, Digit, Fissiped, Hallux, Hammer, Piggy, Pinky, Pointe, Poulaine, Prehallux, Tootsie

Toff Nob, Nut, Swell

Toffee Banket, Butterscotch, Caramel, Cracknel, Gundy, Hard-bake, Hokey-pokey, Humbug, Tom-trot

Toga Palla

Together Among, At-one, Atone, Attone, En bloc, En masse, Gathered, Infere, → **JOINT**, Pari-passu, Sam, Unison, Wed, Y, Yfere, Ysame

Toggle Fastener, Netsuke

Togs Clothes, Gear, Rig, Strip

Toil(s) Drudge, Fag, Industry, → **LABOUR**, Mesh, Net, Seine, Sisyphus, Slog, Sweat, Swink, Tela, Tew, Trap, Trauchle, Travail, Tug, Web, → **WORK**, Wrest, Yacker, Yakka, Yakker

Toilet Can, Chemical, Coiffure, John, Lat(rine), Lavabo, → **LAVATORY**, Loo, Necessary house, Necessary place, Pot, Powder room, Toot, WC

Token Abbey-piece, Buck, Check, Counter, Coupon, Disc, Double-axe, Emblem, Gift, Indication, Mark, → **MEMENTO**, Monument, Nominal, Portend, Seal, Sign, Signal, Slug, Symbol, Symptom, Tessella, Tessera, Valentine

Tolerable Acceptable, Bearable, Mediocre, Passable, So-so

Tolerance, Tolerant, Tolerate(d) Abear, Abide, → **ALLOW**, Bear, Broadminded, Brook, Endure, Enlightened, Good-natured, Hack, Had, Immunological, Latitude, → **LENIENT**, Lump, Mercy, Permit, Stand, Stick, Stomach, Studden, Suffer, Support, Thole, Wear, Zero

Toll Chime, Customs, Due, Duty, Excise, Jole, Joll, Joule, Jowl, Light-dues, Octroi, Pierage, Pike, Pontage, Rates, → **RING**, Scavage, Streetage, Tariff, Tax

Tom(my) Atkins, Bell, Bowling, Bread, Brown, → **CAT**, Collins, Edgar, Gib, Grub, Gun, He-cat, Jerry, Jones, Mog(gy), Nosh, Peeping, Private, Pte, Puss, Ram-cat, Sawyer, Snout, Soldier, Stout, Thos, Thumb, Tiddler, Tucker

Tomato Beef(steak), Cherry, Gooseberry, Husk, Love-apple, Plum, Portuguese, Strawberry, Tamarillo, Tree, Wolf's peach

Tomb(stone) Burial, Catacomb, Catafalque, Cenotaph, Cist, Coffin, Dargah, Durgah, Grave, Hypogeum, Inurn, Kistvaen, Marmoreal, Mastaba, Mausoleum, Megalithic, Monument, Pyramid, Repository, → **SEPULCHRE**, Sepulture, Serdab, Shrine, Speos, Tell el Amarna, Tholos, Tholus, Through-stone, Treasury, Vault

Tombola Draw, Lottery, Raffle

Tomboy Gamine, Gilpey, Gilpy, Hoyden, Ladette, Ramp, Romp

Tome → **BOOK**, Volume

Tomfoolery Caper, Fandangle, Shenanigan

Tomorrow Future, Manana, Morrow

Tompion Watchman

Tom Snout Tinker

Ton(nage) C, Chic, Displacement, Freight, Gross, Hundred, Long, Measurement, Metric, Net register, Register, Shipping, Short, T

Tone, Tonality Aeolian, Brace, Combination, Compound, Dialling, Differential, Engaged, Fifth, Gregorian, Harmonic, Hum, Inflection, Key, Klang, Minor, Ninth, Partial, Passing, Pure, Qualify, Quarter, Resultant, Ringing, Side, → **SOUND**, Strain, Summational, Temper, Tenor, Timbre, Touch, Trite, Whole

Tong(s) Curling, Lazy, Sugar, Wafer

Tongue Brogue, Burr, Chape, Clack, Clapper, Doab, Double, Final, Forked, Glossa, Glossolalia, Glottal, Jinglet, → **LANGUAGE**, Languet(te), Lap, Ligula, Lill, Lingo, Lingual, Lingulate, Mother, Organ, Radula, Ranine, Rasp, Red rag, Single, Spit, Tab, Triple, Voice, Vulgar

Tongue-tied Mush-mouthed

Tongue-twister Jaw-breaker, Shibboleth

Tonic Booster, Bracer, C(h)amomile, Doh, Key, Mease, Medicinal, Mishmee, Mishmi, Myrica, Oporice, Pareira brava, Pick-me-up, Quassia, Refresher, Roborant, Sage tea, Sarsaparilla, Solfa

▷ **Tonic** *may indicate* a musical note

Tonsil, Tonsillitis Amygdala, Antiaditis, Pharyngeal, Quinsy

Tonsure(d) Epilate, Haircut, Peel, Pield

Tony Bête, Chic, Fool, Smart

Too Als(o), As well, Besides, Eke, Excessive, Item, Likewise, Moreover, Oer, Over, Overly, Plus, Troppo

Took Naam, Nam, Set, Stole, Wan, Won

Tool(s) Adze, Aiguille, Airbrush, Auger, Awl, Ax(e), Beetle, Bevel, Billhook, Bit, Broach, Brog, Bur(r), Burin, Calipers, Catspaw, Chaser, Chisel, Chopper, Clippers, Come-along, Croze, Dibber, Dibble, Die, Dolly, Drawknife, Drawshave, Drift(pin), Drill, Eatche, Edge, Elsin, Eolith, Facer, Fid, File, Firmer, Flatter, Float, Float-stone, Former, Fraise, Fretsaw, Froe, Frow, Fuller, Gad, Gimlet, Go-devil, Gouger, Grapnel, Grattoir, Graver, Hammer, Hardware, Hardy, Hob, Hoe, Husker, → **IMPLEMENT**, Insculp, → **INSTRUMENT**, Iron, Jackal, Jackhammer, Jemmy, Jim Crow, Jointer, Jumper, Laster, Loggerhead, Loom, Lute, Machine, Mallet, Marlin(e)spike, Microlith, Mitre square, Moon-knife, Muller, Nippers, Oustiti, Outsiders, Palaeolith, Pattle, Pawn, Penis, Percussion, Pestle, Pick, Pickaxe, Picklock, Pitchfork, Piton, Plane, Pliers, Plunger, Power, Pricker, Property, Prunt, Punch, Puncheon, Rabble, Rasp, Reamer, Ripple, Rocking, Roll(er), Rounder, Router, Sander, Saw, Saw set, Scalpel, Scauper, Scissors, Scorper, Scraper, Screwdriver, Scriber, Scutch, Scythe, Seamset, Secateurs, Set, Shoder, Shooting stick, Sickle, Slasher, Slater, Sleeker, Snake, Spade, Spanner, Spirit-level, Spitsticker, Spokeshave, Spudder, Strickle, Strike, Strimmer®, Swage, Swingle, Swipple, Tint, Tjanting, Toothpick, Tranchet, Triblet, Trowel, Try square, Tweezers, Twibill, Upright, Vibrator, Vice, Wimble, Wire-stripper, Wrench

Toot(er) Blow, Horn, Parp, Trumpet

Tooth(ed), Toothy, Teeth Baby, Bicuspid, Bit, Buck, Bunodont, Cadmean, Canine, Carnassial, Chactodon, Cheek tooth, Cog, Comb, Cott's, Crena(te), Ctenoid, Cusp, Denticle, Dentin(e), Dentures, Egg, Eye, False, Fang, Gam, Gat, Gnashers, Grinder, Heterodont, Impacted, Incisor, Ivory, Joggle, Laniary, Milk, Mill, Molar, Nipper, Odontoid, Orthodontics, Overbite, Pawl, Pearly gates, Pectinate, Periodontics, Peristome, Permanent, Phang, Plate, Poison-fang, Pre-molar, Prong, Ratch, Scissor, Secodont, Sectorial, Serration, Set, Snaggle, Sprocket, Store, Sweet, Trophi, Tush, Tusk, Uncinus, Upper, Wallies, Wang, Wiper, Wisdom, Wolf, Zalambdodont

Toothache, Tooth troubles Caries, Odontalgia

Toothless(ness) Anodontia, Edentate, Gummy, Pangolin

Toothpaste Dentifrice

Top (drawer; hole; line; notcher), Topmost, Topper Ace, Acme, Altissimo, A1, Apex, Apical, Behead, Best, Better, Big, Blouse, Blouson, Boob tube, Brow, Bustier, Cacumen, Cap, Capstone, Ceiling, Coma, Cop, Coping, Corking, Cream, → **CREST**, Crista, Crop, Crown, Culmen, De capo, Decollate, Diabolo, Dog, Dome, Double, Drawer, Dreid(e)l, Dux, Elite, Execute, Fighting, Finial, Flip, Gentry, Gyroscope, Halterneck, Hard, Hat, → **HEAD**, Height, Hummer, Humming, Imperial, Jumper, Lid, Maillot, Nun, One-er, Optimate, Orb, Parish, → **PEAK**, Peerie, Peery, Peg, Peplos, Peplus, Pinnacle, Pitch, Replenish, Ridge, Roof, Sawyer, Screw, Secret, Shaw, Shirt, Skim, Slay, Soft, Spinning, Star, Summit, Superate, Superb, Supernal, Supreme, Supremo, Surface, Sweater, Table, Tambour, Targa, Teetotum, Texas, Tile, Trash, T-shirt, Turbinate, Up(most), Uppermost, V, Vertex, Whipping, Whirligig

▷ **Top** *may indicate* first letter

Topaz Citrine, Colorado, Occidental, Oriental, Pycnite, Rose, Scottish, Spanish

Topcoat Finish, Overcoat, Ulster

Tope(r) Boozer, Bouser, Dagaba, Dagoba, → **DRUNK**, Sot, Tosspot

Topic(al) Head, Hobbyhorse, Item, Local, Motion, Shop, Subject, Text, → **THEME**

Top-knot Tuft

Topping Grand, Icing, Meringue, Pepperoni, Piecrust, Streusel

Topple Oust, Overbalance, Overturn, Tip, Upend, → **UPSET**

Topsy Parentless
Topsy-turvy Careen, Cockeyed, Inverted, Summerset, Tapsalteerie, Tapsleteerie
Torah Maftir
Torch Brand, Cresset, Flambeau, Hards, Hurds, Lamp, Lampad, Link, Olympic, Plasma, Roughie, Tead(e), Wisp
Torch-bearer Usherette
Toreador Escamillo, Matador, Picador, Torero
Torment(ed), Tormentor Agony, Anguish, Bait, Ballyrag, Bedevil, Butt, Cruciate, Crucify, Curse, Distress, Excruciate, Frab, Gehenna, Grill, Hag-ridden, Harass, Hell, Martyrdom, Molest, Nag, Nettle, Pang, Pine, Plague, → **RACK**, Sadist, Tantalise, Tease
Tornado Cyclone, Twister, Waterspout
Toronto Hogtown
Torpedo Bangalore, Bomb, Fish, Missile, Ray, Subroc, Tin fish, Weapon
Torpedo-guard Crinoline
Torpid, Torpor Accidie, Acedia, Comatose, Dormant, Inertia, Languid, Lethargic, Sluggish, Slumbering
Torrent Flood, Spate
Torrid Amphiscian, Fiery, Hot, Sultry, Tropical
Torsk Cusk
Torso Body, Midriff, Trunk
Tortilla Pancake, Taco, Tostada
Tortoise Chelonia, Emydes, Emys, Galapagos, Giant, Hic(c)atee, Kurma, Pancake, Snapping-turtle, Terrapin, Testudo, Timothy, Turtle, Water
Tortoiseshell Epiplastra, Hawksbill, Testudo
Tortuous Ambagious, Twisty, Winding
▷ **Tortuous** *may indicate* an anagram
Torture, Torture chamber, Torture instrument Agonise, Auto-da-fé, Bastinade, Bastinado, Boot, Bootikin, Catasta, Chinese burn, Chinese water, Crucify, Engine, Excruciate, Flageolet, Fry, Gadge, Gauntlet, Gyp, Hell, Iron maiden, Knee-cap, Naraka, Persecute, Pilliwinks, Pine, Pinniewinkle, Pinnywinkle, → **RACK**, Sadism, Scaphism, Scarpines, Scavenger, Scavenger's daughter, Scourge, Strappado, Tantalise, Third degree, Thumbscrew, Torment, Tumbrel, Tumbril, Water, Wheel, Wrack
▷ **Tortured** *may indicate* an anagram
Torturer Torquemada
Torus Disc, Stellarator
Tory Abhorrer, Blimp, Blue, C, Opposition, Right, Tantivy, Unionist
Toss(ing), Throw(n) Abject, Bandy, Bounce, Buck, Bung, Buttock, Cant, Canvass, Cast, Catapult, → **CHUCK**, Cottabus, Crabs, Crap, Cross-buttock, Dad, Daud, Dawd, Deal, Disconcert, Dod, Elance, Estrapade, Falcade, → **FLING**, Flip, Flump, Flutter, Flying (head)-mare, Free, Full, Gollum, Haunch, Heave, Hipt, Hoy, → **HURL**, Jack, Jact(it)ation, Jaculation, Jeff, Juggle, Jump, Lance, Lob, Loft, Nick, Pash, Pick, Pitch, Purl, Put(t), Round-arm, Seamer, Shy, Slat, Sling, Squail, Unhorse, Unseat, Upcast
Toss-up Cross and pile, Heads or tails
Tot Add, Babe, Bairn, → **CHILD**, Dop, Dram, Infant, Mite, Nightcap, Nip(per), Nipperkin, Slug, Snifter, Snort, Tad
Total, Toto Absolute, Aggregate, All(-out), All told, Amount, Balance, Be-all, → **COMPLETE**, Entire, Gross, Lot, Mass, Sum, Tale, Tally, Unqualified, Utter, Whole
Totalitarian Autocrat, Despot, Étatiste, Fascist

Tote Bear, → **CARRY**, Yomp

Totem Fetish, Icon, Image, Pole

Tottenham Hotspur

Totter Abacus, Daddle, Daidle, Didakai, Didakei, Did(d)icoy, Didicoi, Halt, Ragman, Reel, Rock, → **STAGGER**, Swag, Sway, Topple, Waver

Touch(ed), Touching, Touchy Accolade, Adjoin, Affect, Anent, Badass, Barmy, Cadge, Captious, Carambole, Caress, Carom, Common, Concern, Connivent, Contact, Contiguous, Dash, Emove, → **FEEL**, Finger, Finishing, Flick, Fondle, Haptic, Heart-warming, Huffy, → **IN TOUCH**, Iracund, Irascible, J'adoube, Liaison, Libant, Loan, Loco, Midas, Miffy, Near, Nie, Nigh, Nudge, Palp, Pathetic, Paw, Potty, Re, Sense, Shade, Skiff, Soft, Sore, Spice, → **SPOT**, Tactile, Tactual, Tag, Tangible, Tap, Taste, Tat, Tetchy, Tickle, Tig, Tinderbox, Tinge, Titivate, Trace, Trait, Tuck, Vestige

Touchline Tangent

Touchstone Basanite, Criterion, Norm, Standard

Touchwood Absit omen, Monk, Punk, Spunk, Tinder

Tough(en) Adamantine, Anneal, Apache, Arduous, Ballsy, Burly, → **HARD**, Hard-boiled, Hard-nosed, Hardy, Heavy duty, He-man, Hood, Hoodlum, Husky, Indurate, Knotty, Leathern, Leathery, Nut, Pesky, Rambo, Rigwiddie, Rigwoodie, Roughneck, Sinewy, Spartan, Steely, Stiff, Strict, String, Sturdy, Teuch, Thewed, Tityre-tu, Virile

Toupee Hairpiece, Rug, Tour, → **WIG**

Tour(er), Tourism, Tourist Adventure, Barnstorm, Circuit, Cook's, Emmet, Excursion, Gig, Grand, Grockle, GT, Holiday-maker, Itinerate, → **JOURNEY**, Lionise, Mystery, Outing, Parra, Posting, Roadie, Rubberneck, Safari, Sightsee, Swing, Tiki, → **TRAVEL**, Trip(per), Viator, Whistle-stop

Tourmaline Indicolite, Indigolite, Schorl, Zeuxite

Tournament American, Basho, Bonspiel, Carousel, Drive, Event, Jereed, Jerid, Joust, Just, Ladder, Plate, Pro-am, Round robin, Royal, Super Twelve, Swiss, Tilt, Tourney, Wimbledon

Tourniquet Garrot, Throttle, Torcular

Tousle Dishevel, Rumple

Tout Barker, Laud, Ply, Praise, Runner, Solicit, Toot, Work-watcher

Tow(ing) Aquaplane, Button, Fibre, → **HAUL**, Pull, → **ROPE**, Ski, Skijoring, Stupe, Track

▶ **Towards** see **TO**

Towel Dry, Jack, Nappy, Roller, Rub, Sanitary, Tea, Tea-cloth, Terry, Turkish

Tower AA, Aspire, Atalaya, Babel, Barbican, Bastille, Bastion, Belfry, Bell, Bloody, Brattice, Brettice, Brogh, Campanile, Clock, Conning, Control, Cooling, Donjon, Dungeon, Edifice, Eiffel, Fly, Fortress, Gantry, Garret, Gate, Giralda, Gopura(m), Guérite, Horologium, Ivory, Keep, Leaning, Loom, Maiden, Martello, Minar(et), Monument, Mooring, Mouse, Nuraghe, Nurhag, Overtop, Peel, Pinnacle, Pisa, Pound, Pylon, Rear, Rise, Rolandseck, Rood, Round, Sail, Sears, Shot, Sikhara, Silo, Ski-lift, Space Needle, Specula, Spire, Stealth, Steeple, Swiss Re, Tête-de-pont, Texas, Tractor, Tugboat, → **TURRET**, Victoria, Watch, Water, Yagura, Ziggurat, Zikkurat

Town, Township Boom, Borgo, Borough, Bourg, Burg(h), City, Conurbation, County, Deme, Dormitory, Dorp, Favella, Garrison, Ghost, Ham(let), Intraurban, Market, Municipal, Nasik, One-horse, Open, Podunk, Pueblo, Satellite, Shanty, Soweto, Staple, Tinsel, Tp, Twin, Urban, Whistle stop, Wick

Townee, Townsman Cad, Cit(izen), Dude, Freeman, Oppidan, Philister, Resident

Town hall Prytaneum

Toxaemia Eclampsia

Toxic(ity), Toxin Abrin, Aflatoxin, Antigen, Botox®, Botulin, Cadaverine, Cadmium, Chlorin(e), Coumarin, Curare, Deadly, Dioxan, Dioxin, Eclampsia, Fluorin(e), Lethal, Melittin, Muscarine, Phalloidin, Phenol, Phenothiazine, Pre-eclampsia, Psoralen, Ricin, Sepsis, Serology, Venin, Venomous, Virulence, Zootoxin

Toy Bauble, Bull-roarer, Cockhorse, Cyberpet, Dally, Dandle, Dinky®, Doll, Executive, Faddle, Finger, Flirt, Frisbee®, Gewgaw, Golly, Gonk, Jack-in-the-box, Jumping-jack, Kaleidoscope, Kickshaw, Knack, Lego®, Meccano®, Noah's ark, Novelty, Paddle, Pantine, Peashooter, Pinwheel, Plaything, Praxinoscope, Rattle, Russian doll, Scooter, Shoofly, Skipjack, Taste, Teddy, Thaumatrope, Top, → **TRIFLE**, Trinket, Tu(r)ndun, Whirligig, Windmill, Yoyo, Zoetrope

Trace Atom, Cast, Derive, Describe, Draft, Draw, Dreg, Echo, Footprint, Ghost, → **HINT**, Leaf, Limn, Mark, Memory, Outline, Relic, Relict, Remnant, Scintilla, Semblance, Sign, Smack, Soupçon, Strap, Tinge, → **TOUCH**, Track, Vestige, Whiff, Whit

Tracery Filigree

Track(s), Tracker, Tracking, Trackman Aintree, Band, B-road, Caterpillar®, Cinder, Circuit, Course, Crawler, Cycleway, Dog, DOVAP, Drift, Ecliptic, El, Fast, Fettler, Footing, Gandy dancer, Hunt, Ichnite, Ichnolite, Icknield Way, Inside, Lane, Ley, Line, Loipe, Loopline, Mommy, Monitor, Monza, → **PATH**, Persue, Piste, Pug, Pursue, Race, Raceway, Rail, Railway, Rake, Ridgeway, Riding, Route, Run, Rut, Siding, Sign, Skidway, Sleuth, Slot, Sonar, Speedway, Spoor, Tan, Tan-ride, Taxi, Tenure, Tideway, Title, → **TRAIL**, Trajectory, Tram, Tramline, Tramroad, Tramway, Tread, Trode, Tug(boat), Twin, Wake, Wallaby, Way, Y

Tract(able), Tracts Area, Belt, Bench, Clime, Colporteur, Common, Dene, Digestive, Enclave, Flysheet, Lande, Leaflet, Monte, Moor, Olfactory, → **PAMPHLET**, Park, Prairie, Province, Purlieu, Pusey, Region, Screed, Taluk, Tawie, Terrain, Wold

Tractarian(ism) Newman, Oxford movement, Pusey(ism)

Tractor Bombardier®, Bulldozer, Cat, Caterpillar®, Chelsea, Fendalton, Pedrail, Remuera, Skidder, Tower

Trade(r), Tradesman, Trading Arb(itrageur), Art, Banian, Banyan, Bargain, Barter, Bilateral, Bricks and clicks, Bun(n)ia, Burgher, Business, Cabotage, Calling, Carriage, Chaffer, Chandler, Chapman, Cheapjack, Clicks and mortar, Coaster, Comanchero, → **COMMERCE**, Coster, Costermonger, Crare, Crayer, Deal(er), Dicker, Easterling, Errand, Exchange, Factor, Fair, Floor, Free, Handle, Horse, Hosier, Hot, Importer, Indiaman, Industry, Insider, Ironmonger, Jobber, Logrolling, Line, Merchant, Mercosur, Métier, Middleman, Mister, Monger, Mystery, Occupy, Outfitter, Paralleling, Pitchman, Ply, Program(me), Rag, Retailer, Roaring, Rough, Roundtripping, Scalp, Screen, Sell, Simony, Slave, Stallenger, Stallinger, Stationer, Sutler, Suttle, → **SWAP**, Traffic, Transit, Trant, Truck, Union, Vaisya, Vend, Wholesaler, Wind

Trademark Brand, Chop, Idiograph, Label, Logo, Tm

Trade union ASLEF, COHSE, Local, Solidarity, Syndicalism, UNISON, USDAW

Trading money, Trading post Cabotage, Fort, Wampum

Tradition(s), Traditional(ist) Ancestral, Classical, Convention, Custom(ary), Eastern, Folksy, Folkway, Hadith, Heritage, Legend, Lore, Mahayana, Misoneist, Old guard, Old-school, Orthodox, Pharisee, Pompier, Practice, Purist, Suburban, Time-honoured, Trad, Tralaticious, Tralatitious, Unwritten

Traduce Abuse, Asperse, Defame, Impugn, Malign, Smear, Vilify

Traffic, Traffic pattern Air, Barter, Broke, Cabotage, Clover-leaf, Commerce, Contraflow, Deal, Negotiate, Passage, Run, Slave trade, Smuggle, Tailback, Through, Trade, Truck, Vehicular

Tragedian, Tragedy, Tragic Aeschylus, Buskin, Calamity, Cenci, Corneille, Dire, → **DRAMA**, Euripides, Macready, Melpomene, Oedipean, Oresteia, Otway, Pathetic, Seneca, Sophoclean, Thespian, Thespis

Trail(er), Trailing Abature, Advert, Audit, Bedraggle, Caravan, Condensation, Creep, Dissipation, Drag, Draggle, Follow, Ipomaea, Ivy, Lag, Liana, Liane, Nature, Oregon, Paper, Path, Persue, Preview, Promo(tion), Pursue, Repent, Runway, Santa Fe, Scent, Shadow, Sign, Sleuth, Slot, Spoor, Straggle, Stream, Streel, Tag, Trace, → **TRACK**, Trade, Traipse, Trape, Trauchle, Trayne, Troad, Vapour, Vine, Virga, Wake

Train(er), Training Accommodation, Advanced, APT, Autogenic, BR, Breed, Bullet, Caravan, Cat, Cavalcade, Choo-choo, Circuit, Coach, Commuter, Condition, Cortège, Diesel, Direct, Discipline, Dog, Double-header, Dressage, Drill, Drive, Educate, Entourage, Enure, Epicyclic, Eurostar®, Excursion, Exercise, Express, Fartlek, Field, Flier, Flight simulator, Freightliner®, Fuse, Gear, Ghan, Ghost, Gravy, Grounding, GWR, Handle(r), → **INSET**, Instruct, Intercity®, Interval, Jerkwater, Journey, Liner, Link, LMS, LNER, Loco, Longe, Lunge, Maglev, Mailcar, Manège, Manrider, Meinie, Mein(e)y, Mentor, Milk, Nopo, Nurture, Nuzzle, Omnibus, Orient Express, Owl, Pack, Paddy, Parliamentary, PE, Pendolino, Personal, Potty, Practise, → **PREPARE**, Procession, PT, Puffer, Puff-puff, Push-pull, Q, Queue, Rattler, Rehearse, Retinue, Road, Roadwork, Rocket, Ry, Sack, → **SCHOOL**, Series, Shoe, Shuttle service, Siege, Sinkansen, Skill centre, Sloid, Sloyd, Sowarree, Sowarry, Special, SR, Steer, String, Suite, Tail, Tame, → **TEACH**, Through, Tire, Tirocinium, Track shoe, Trail, Tube, Twin bill, Wage, Wagon, Wave, Way

▷ **Train(ed)** *may indicate* an anagram

Trainee → **APPRENTICE**, Cadet, Cub, Intern, Jackaroo, Jackeroo, Learner, Ordinand, Rookie, Rooky

Train-spotter Gricer

Trait Characteristic, Feature, Knack, Ph(a)enotype, Sickle-cell, Strain, Thew, Trick, Vein

Traitor Benedict Arnold, Betrayer, Casement, Dobber-in, Joyce, Judas, Judas Maccabaeus, Nid(d)ering, Nid(d)erling, Nithing, Proditor, Quisling, Renegade, Reptile, Tarpeian, Traditor, Treachetour, Turncoat, Viper, Wallydraigle, Weasel

Trajectory Parabola, Track

▷ **Trammel** *may indicate* an anagram

Tramp, Trample Bog-trotter, Bum, Caird, Clochard, Clump, Crush, Deadbeat, Derelict, Derro, Dingbat, Dosser, Down and out, Estragon, Footslog, Freighter, Gadling, Gangrel, Gook, Hike, Hobo, Knight of the road, Meff, Override, Overrun, Pad, Piker, Plod, Poach, Potch(e), Rover, Scorn, Ship, Splodge, Sundowner, Swagman, → **TINKER**, Toe-rag(ger), Track, Traipse, Tread, Trek, Trog, Tromp, Truant, Trudge, Tub, Vagabond, Vagrant, Weary Willie

Trampoline Trampet(te)

Trance Catalepsy, Cataplexy, Goa, Narcolepsy

Tranche Gold, Reserve

Tranquil(lity) Ataraxy, Calm, Composure, Easy, Halcyon, Lee, Peaceful, Placid, Quietude, Sedate, → **SERENE**

Tranquillise(r) Appease, Ataractic, Ataraxic, → **CALM**, Diazepam, Downer, Hypnone, Hypnotic, Largactil®, Librium®, Nervine, Nitrazepam, Oxazepam,

Placate, Satisfy, Soothe, Still, Valium®

Transaction(s) Affair, Agio, Brokerage, Deal, Escrow, Fasti, Leaseback, Tr

Transcend(ent), Transcendental(ist) Excel, Mystic, Overtop, Surpass, Thoreau

Transcribe, Transcript(ion) Copy, Inclusive, Rescore, Tenor, → **TRANSLATE**, Transume

Transfer(ence) Alien, Alienate, → **ASSIGN**, Attorn, Calk, Calque, Cede, Chargeable, Communize, Consign, Convey(ance), Credit, Crosstalk, Decal, Demise, Devolve, Download, Exchange, Explant, Hive off, Make over, Mancipation, Metathesis, Mortmain, Nuclear, On-lend, Pass, Photomechanical, Print through, Provection, Reassign, Redeploy, Remit, Remove, Repot, Second, Settlement, Thought, Transduction, Transfection, Uproot, Vire, Virement

▷ **Transferred** *may indicate* an anagram

Transfix Impale, Rivet, → **SKEWER**, Spear, Spit

Transform(ation), Transformer Alter, Apotheosis, Balun, Change, Fourier, Lorentz, Metamorphism, Metamorphose, Metamorphosis, Metaplasia, Metastasis, Morphallaxis, Morphing, Permute, Rectifier, Sea change, Tinct, Toupee, Transmogrify, Wig

▷ **Transform(ed)** *may indicate* an anagram

Transfusion Apheresis

Transgress(ion) Encroach, Err, Infringe, Offend, Overstep, Peccancy, → **SIN**, Violate

Transient, Transit(ion), Transitory Brief, Ephemeral, Fleeting, Fly-by-night, Forbidden, Fugacious, Hobo, Metabasis, Passage, Passing, Provisional, Seque, Sfumato, T, Temporary

Transistor Drift, Epitaxial, Field-effect, Junction

Translate, Translation, Translator Calque, Construe, Convert, Coverdale, Crib, Explain, Free, Horse, Interpret, In vitro, Jerome, Key, Linguist, Loan, Machine, Metaphrase, Nick, Paraphrase, Pinyin, Polyglot, Pony, Reduce, Render, Rendition, Rhemist, Simultaneous, Targum, Tr, Transcribe, Transform, Trot, Unseen, Version(al), Vulgate, Wycliffe

▷ **Translate(d)** *may indicate* an anagram

Transmigrate, Transmigration Exodus, Metempsychosis, Passage, Trek

Transmit(ter), Transmitted, Transmission Air, Allele, Analogue, Automatic, Band, Baseband, Beacon, Broadband, → **BROADCAST**, Cable, Carry, CB, Communicate, Conduct, Consign, Contagion, Convection, Convey, Digital, Facsimile, Filler, Forward, Gearbox, Gene, Heredity, Impart, Intelsat, Manual, Mast, Microphone, Modem, Nicol, Permittivity, Pipe, Propagate, Racon, Radiate, Radio, Receiver, Responser, Simplex, Simulcast, Sonabuoy, Spark, Synchronous, Tappet, Telautograph®, Telecast, Telegony, Telematics, Telemetry, Teleprinter, Teletex, Televise, Telex, Tiros, Traduce, Traject, Tralaticious, Tralatitious, UART, Ultrawideband, Uplink, Upload, Walkie-talkie

Transom Reverse, Traverse

Transparent, Transparency Adularia, Clear, Crystal(line), Diaphanous, Dioptric, Glassy, Glazed, Hyaloid, Iolite, Leno, Limpid, Lucid, Luminous, Patent, Pellucid, Sheer, Slide, Tiffany

Transpire Happen, Occur

Transplant Allograft, Anaplasty, Graft, Repot, Reset, Shift

Transport(ed), Transporter, Transportation Active, Aerotrain, Argo, Bear, Bike, Broomstick, BRS, Bus, Cargo, Carract, → **CARRY**, Cart, Cat-train, Charm, Convey, Cycle, Delight, Ecstasy, Electron, Eloin, Enrapt, Enravish, Entrain, Esloin, Estro, Fishyback, Freight, Haul(age), Helicopter, Jerrican, Joy, Kurvey, Lift, Lug, Maglev, Mambrane, Matatu, Monorail, Pack animal, Palanquin, Pantechnicon, Public,

Put, Rape, Rapine, Rapture, Roadster, Ship, Shuttle, Sidecar, Sledge, Supersonic, Tandem, Tanker, Tape, Tote, Train, Trap, Tuktuk, Waft, Wheels, Wireway

Transpose, Transposition Anagram, Commute, Convert, Invert, Metathesis, Shift, Spoonerism, Switch, Tr

▷ **Transposed** *may indicate* an anagram

Transsexual Invert

Transubstantiate, Transubstantiation Capernaite

Transverse Across, Crosscut, Diagonal, Obliquid, Thwart

Transvest(it)ism, Transvestite Berdache, Berdash, Cross-dressing, Eonist

Tranter Dolly

Trap(s), Trapdoor, Trapped, Trappings Ambush, → **BAGGAGE**, Bags, Belongings, Booby, Buckboard, Bunker, Carriage, Catch, Catch-pit, Clapnet, Corner, Cru(i)ve, Deadfall, Death, Decoy, Dogcart, Downfall, Eelset, Emergent, Ensnare, Entrain, Fall, Fit-up, Fly, Flypaper, Frame-up, Fyke, Gig, Gin, Gob, Grin, Hatch, Housings, Ice-bound, Jinri(c)ksha(w), Keddah, Kettle, Kheda, Kiddle, Kidel, Kipe, Kisser, Knur(r), Light, Lime, Live, → **LUGGAGE**, Lure, Mesh, Mouth, Net, Nur(r), Paraphernalia, Pitfall, Plant, Police, Pot, Poverty, Putcheon, Putcher, Quicksand, Radar, Regalia, Sand, Scruto, → **SNARE**, Speed, Spell, Spider, Springe, Stake-net, Star, Steam, Stench, Sting, Stink, Sun, Tangle, Tank, Teagle, Toil, Tonga, Trojan horse, Trou-de-loup, Two-wheeler, U, U-bend, Vampire, Web, Weel, Weir, Wire

Trapezist Leotard

Trapper Carson, Voyageur

Trash(y) Bosh, Deface, Dre(c)k, Garbage, Junk, Kitsch, Pulp, → **RUBBISH**, Schlock, Scum, Tinpot, Trailer, Vandalise, White, Worthless

Trauma Insult, Shock

Travel(ler), Travelling Aeneas, Backpack, Bagman, Bushwhacker, Commercial, Commute, Crustie, Crusty, Drive, Drummer, Fare, Fellow, Fly, Fogg, Geoffrey, Gipsen, Gipsy, Gitano, Globe-trotter, Go, Gulliver, Gypsy, Hike, Interrail, Itinerant, Journey, Long-haul, Marco Polo, Meve, Migrant, Motor, Move, Mush, New Age, Nomad, Passenger, Passepartout, Peregrination, Peripatetic, Pilgrim, Ply, Polo, Pootle, Range, Rep, Ride, Rom(any), Rove, Safari, Sail, Salesman, Samaritan, Space, → **TOUR**, Trek, Tripper, Tsigane, Viator, Voyage, Wanderjahr, Wayfarer, Wend, Wildfire, Zigan

Traverse Cross, Girdle, Measure, Quest, Trace

Travesty Burlesque, Charade, Distortion, Parody, Show, Skit

Trawl Drag-net, Hose-net, Net

Tray Antler, Bottle-slide, Carrier, Case, Charger, Coaster, Gallery, Joe, Lazy Susan, Plateau, → **SALVER**, Shower, Tea, Trencher, Typecase, Voider, Waiter

Treacherous, Treachery Bad faith, Deceit, Delilah, Fickle, Ganelon, Guile, Insidious, Judas-kiss, Knife, Mala fide, Medism, Perfidious, Punic, Punic faith, Quicksands, Serpentine, Sleeky, Snaky, Trahison, Traitor, → **TREASON**, Two-faced, Viper

Treacle Black(jack), Butter, Molasses, Venice

Tread Clamp, Clump, Dance, Pad, Step, Stramp, Track, Trample

Treadle Footboard

Treason Betrayal, Constructive, High, Insurrection, Lèse-majesté, Lese-majesty, Perduellion, Petty, Sedition, → **TREACHERY**

Treasure(r), Treasury Banker, Bursar, Cache, Camerlengo, Camerlingo, Cherish, Chest, Cimelia, Coffer, Ewe-lamb, Exchequer, Fisc(al), Fisk, Godolphin, Golden, Heritage, Hoard, Montana, Palgrave, Pork barrel, → **PRIZE**, Procurator, Purser, Relic, Riches, Steward, Taonga, Thesaurus, Trove

Treat, Treatment Action, Acupuncture, Allopathy, Antidote, Archilowe, Arenation, Aromatherapy, Balneotherapy, Beano, Besee, Body wrap, Botox®, Capitulate, Care, Chemotherapy, Chiropractic, Condition, Course, Crymotherapy, Cryotherapy, Cupping, Cure, Deal, Detox(ification), Dialysis, Do, → **DOCTOR**, Dose, Dress, Dutch, Enantiopathy, Entertain, Est, Facial, Faith-healing, Fango, Figuration, Foment, Frawzey, Handle, Holistic, Homeopathy, HRT, Hydrotherapy, Hypnotherapy, Immunotherapy, Intermediate, Jin shin do, Kenny, Laser, Manage, Massotherapy, Mechanotherapy, Medicate, Moxibustion, Naturopathy, Negotiate, Opotherapy, Organotherapy, Osteopathy, → **OUTING**, Pasteur, Pedicure, Pelotherapy, Physic, Physiotherapy, Pie, Poultice, Probiotics, Process, Prophylaxis, Psychoanalysis, Psychodrama, Psychotherapy, Radiotherapy, Regale, Rehab(ilitation), Rest cure, Root, Secretage, Serotherapy, Setter, Shout, Shrift, Sironise, Smile, Speleotherapy, → **STAND**, Tablet, Tebilise®, Thalassotherapy, Themotherapy, Therapy, Titbit, Traction, Twelve-step, Usance, Use, Vet

▷ **Treated** *may indicate* an anagram

Treatise Almagest, Commentary, Didache, Discourse, Dissertation, Essay, Monograph, Pandect, Prodrome, Profound, Summa, Tract(ate), Upanishad, Vedanta

Treaty Agreement, Alliance, Assiento, Concordat, Covenant, Entente, Jay's, Lateran, Locarno, Lunéville, Maastricht, Nijmegen, North Atlantic, → **PACT**, Paris, Private, Protocol, Rapallo, Rijswijk, Ryswick, San Stefano, Sovetsk, Test-ban, Utrecht, Verdun, Versailles, Yorktown

Treble Castrato, Choirboy, Chorist(er), Pairial, Soprano, → **TRIPLE**, Triune, Voice

Tree(s) Actor, → **ANCESTRY**, Axle, Beam, Bluff, Boom, Bosk, Clump, Conifer, Coppice, Corner, Cross, Daddock, Deciduous, Decision, Dendrology, Descent, Family, Fault, Fringe, Gallows, Genealogical, Grove, Hang, Hardwood, Jesse, Nurse, Pedigree, Pole, Rood, Roof, Sawyer, Shoe, Softwood, Staddle, Stemma, Summer, Timber, Tyburn, Vista, Wicopy, → **WOOD**

TREES

2 letters:	Nim	Cade	Ming
Bo	Oak	Coco	Mira
Ti	Oil	Cola	Mott
	Sal	Dali	Mowa
3 letters:	Tea	Dhak	Neem
Ake	Til	Dika	Nipa
Ash	Ule	Dita	Noni
Asp	Wax	Eugh	Olea
Bay	Yew	Gean	Ombu
Bel		Hule	Palm
Ben	*4 letters:*	Jack	Pine
Box	Acer	Kaki	Pipe
Cow	Akee	Karo	Pith
Elm	Aloe	Kiri	Plum
Fir	Amla	Kola	Poon
Gum	Arar	Lime	Puka
Ita	Atap	Lote	Rain
Jak	Bael	Mako	Rata
Koa	Bhel	Meal	Rhus
Mot	Bito	Milk	Rimu

Sack
Shea
Silk
Sloe
Soap
Sorb
Tawa
Teak
Teil
Titi
Toon
Tung
Tutu
Upas
Yang

5 letters:
Abele
Abies
Ackee
Afara
Agila
Alamo
Alder
Alnus
Anona
Areca
Argan
Aspen
Banak
Beech
Belah
Birch
Bodhi
Boree
Butea
Cacao
Carap
Cedar
Ceiba
China
Cocoa
Cocus
Coral
Ebony
Elder
Fagus
Fever
Flame
Fruit
Genip

Grass
Guava
Hakea
Hazel
Hevea
Holly
Iroko
Ivory
Jambu
Jarul
Judas
Kapok
Karri
Kauri
Khaya
Kiaat
Kokum
Larch
Lemon
Lilac
Lotus
Mahoe
Mahua
Mahwa
Maire
Mamey
Mango
Mapau
Maple
Marri
Matai
Melia
Motte
Mowra
Mugga
Mulga
Mvule
Myall
Ngaio
Nikau
Nyssa
Olive
Opepe
Osier
Palas
Palay
Panax
Peach
Pecan
Pinon
Pipal

Pipul
Pitch
Plane
Quina
Ramin
Roble
Rowan
Sabal
Saman
Sassy
Scrog
Silva
Smoke
Sumac
Tawai
Taxus
Thorn
Thuja
Thuya
Tilia
Tsuga
Tuart
Tulip
Vitex
Wahoo
Wenge
Wilga
Withy
Xylem
Yacca
Yulan
Zaman
Zamia

6 letters:
Abroma
Acacia
Akeake
Alerce
Angico
Annona
Antiar
Arbute
Arolla
Babaco
Balsam
Banyan
Baobab
Bilian
Bombax
Bonsai

Bo-tree
Bottle
Buriti
Cadaga
Cadagi
Carapa
Carica
Cashew
Cembra
Cercis
Cerris
Chaste
Chenar
Cherry
Chinar
Citron
Coffee
Cordon
Cornel
Cornus
Damson
Deodar
Diana's
Dragon
Durian
Durion
Emblic
Eumong
Eumung
Feijoa
Fustet
Fustic
Gallus
Garjan
Gidgee
Gidjee
Gingko
Ginkgo
Glinap
Gnetum
Gopher
Guango
Gurjun
Gympie
Hupiro
Illipe
Illipi
Illupi
Jarool
Jarrah
Joshua

Jujube
Kamahi
Kamala
Kamela
Kapuka
Karaka
Karamu
Karite
Kowhai
Laurel
Lebbek
Linden
Locust
Longan
Loquat
Lucuma
Lungah
Macoya
Mallee
Manuka
Mastic
Mazard
Medlar
Mimosa
Missel
Mopane
Mopani
Myrtle
Nutmeg
Obeche
Orange
Orihou
Padauk
Padouk
Pagoda
Papaya
Pawpaw
Peepul
Pepper
Platan
Pomelo
Poplar
Popple
Protea
Puriri
Quince
Red-bud
Red gum
Ricker
Roucou
Rubber

Sabicu
Sallow
Samaan
Sapele
Sapium
Sapota
Saxaul
She-oak
Sinder
Sorrel
Souari
Spruce
Styrax
Sumach
Sunder
Sundra
Sundri
Tallow
Tamanu
Tawhai
Tewart
Thyine
Titoki
Tooart
Totara
Tupelo
Waboom
Wandoo
Wicken
Willow
Witgat
Yarran
Zamang

7 letters:
Ailanto
Amboina
Apricot
Arbutus
Avodire
Bebeeru
Bilimbi
Bilsted
Bubinga
Buck-eye
Bursera
Cajeput
Cajuput
Calamus
Camphor
Camwood

Canella
Carbeen
Cascara
Cassava
Catalpa
Champac
Champak
Chayote
Coquito
Corylus
Corypha
Cumquat
Dagwood
Dogwood
Dryades
Durmast
Geebung
Genipap
Gluinap
Gumtree
Hickory
Hog-plum
Holm-oak
Houhere
Jipyapa
Kumquat
Lacquer
Lagetto
Lentisk
Logwood
Lumbang
Madrono
Mahaleb
Manjack
Marasca
Margosa
Mazzard
Mesquit
Moringa
Morrell
Mustard
Papauma
Pereira
Pimento
Platane
Pollard
Populus
Pukatea
Quassia
Quicken
Quillai

Quinain
Radiata
Rampick
Rampike
Redwood
Rock elm
Saksaul
Sandbox
Saouari
Sapling
Sausage
Sequoia
Seringa
Service
Shittah
Sourgum
Soursop
Spindle
Sundari
Taraire
Taupata
Tawhiri
Trumpet
Varnish
Wallaba
Wirilda
Witchen
Wych-elm
Xylopia
Zelkova

8 letters:
Aguacate
Algaroba
Aquillia
Bangalay
Bangalow
Basswood
Benjamin
Bergamot
Berrigan
Blackboy
Blimbing
Bountree
Bourtree
Breadnut
Brigalow
Calabash
Cinchona
Cinnamon
Cocoplum

Coolabah
Coolibah
Corkwood
Crabwood
Cucumber
Cudgerie
Dendroid
Dracaena
Espalier
Flittern
Fraxinus
Garcinia
Ghost-gum
Gnetales
Guaiacum
Hagberry
Hawthorn
Hinahina
Hornbeam
Huon-pine
Igdrasil
Inkberry
Ironbark
Ironwood
Jelutong
Kawakawa
Kingwood
Laburnum
Lacebark
Lecythis
Loblolly
Magnolia
Mahogany
Makomako
Mangrove
Manna-ash
Mesquite
Mulberry
Ocotillo
Oiticica
Oleaceae
Oleaster
Pachouli
Palmetto
Pandanus
Parapara
Pichurim
Pinaster
Pithtree
Pyinkado
Quandang

Quandong
Quantong
Quillaia
Quillaja
Raintree
Rambutan
Rangiora
Rewa-rewa
Sago-palm
Sandarac
Santalum
Sapindus
Sapucaia
Sasswood
Sea grape
Shagbark
Simaruba
Snowball
Snowdrop
Soapbark
Sourwood
Standard
Stinging
Sweet gum
Sweetsop
Sycamine
Sycamore
Sycomore
Tamarack
Tamarind
Tamarisk
Taxodium
Umbrella
Whitegum
Wine-palm
Ygdrasil

9 letters:
Agila-wood
Ailantous
Albespine
Angophora
Azedarach
Bilimbing
Bitternut
Blackbutt
Blackjack
Blackwood
Bloodwood
Bolletrie
Boobialla

Broadleaf
Bully-tree
Bulwaddee
Burrawary
Butternut
Caliatour
Caliature
Candlenut
Canoewood
Carambola
Casuarina
Chempaduk
Cherimoya
Chincapin
Chinkapin
Coachwood
Cordyline
Courbaril
Cupressus
Eaglewood
Evergreen
Firewheel
Flame-leaf
Greenwood
Grevillea
Hackberry
Ivory palm
Jacaranda
Kahikatea
Krummholz
Kurrajong
Lancewood
Lemonwood
Leylandii
Macadamia
Marmalade
Mirabelle
Mockernut
Monkeypot
Naseberry
Nectarine
Nux vomica
Paloverde
Paperbark
Patchouli
Patchouly
Paulownia
Persimmon
Pistachio
Pitch-pine
Poinciana

Ponderosa
Pontianac
Quebracho
Rauwolfia
Rose-apple
Sapodilla
Saskatoon
Sassafras
Satinwood
Shellbark
Simarouba
Soapberry
Star-anise
Star-apple
Stinkwood
Sweetwood
Tacamahac
Tamarillo
Terebinth
Toothache
Torchwood
Wagenboom
Wayfaring
Whitebeam
Whitewood
Wineberry
Wych-hazel
Yggdrasil
Zebrawood

10 letters:
Arbor Vitae
Axe-breaker
Bitterbark
Blackbully
Breadfruit
Bulletwood
Buttonball
Buttonwood
Calamondin
Calliature
Candle-wood
Cannonball
Chamaerops
Chaulmugra
Cheesewood
Chinaberry
Chinquapin
Cottonwood
Cowrie-pine
Eucalyptus

Fiddlewood	Pohutukawa	Bladderwort	Sitka spruce
Flamboyant	Quercitron	Cabbage-palm	Stringybark
Flindersia	Ribbonwood	Chaulmoogra	
Frangipani	Sandalwood	Chokecherry	**12 letters:**
Green-heart	Sappanwood	Copperbeech	African tulip
Hackmatack	Silk-cotton	Cryptomeria	Haemotoxylon
Ilang-ilang	Silverbell	Dipterocarp	Hercules' club
Jaboticaba	Sneezewood	Eriodendron	Liriodendron
Jippi-jappa	Spotted gum	Flamboyante	Mammee-sapota
Kaffirboom	Strawberry	Fothergilla	Masseranduba
Kotokutuku	Tawheowheo	Gingerbread	Monkey-puzzle
Letter-wood	Traveller's	Honey locust	Washingtonia
Lilly-pilly	Turpentine	Jesuit's bark	Wellingtonia
Macrocarpa	Witch-hazel	Leatherwood	
Manchineel	Witgatboom	Lignum vitae	**13 letters:**
Mangabeira	Woollybutt	Liquidambar	Paper-mulberry
Mangosteen	Yellowwood	Maceranduba	
Marblewood	Ylang-ylang	Metasequoia	**14 letters:**
Nithofagus		Pomegranate	Western hemlock
Palisander	**11 letters:**	Purpleheart	
Paper birch	Appleringie	Shittimwood	

Tree-climber, Tree-dweller Monkey, Opossum, Sciurus, Squirrel, Unau
Tree disease Dutch elm, Waldsterben
Tree-man Ent
Tree-moss Usnea
Tree-paeony Moutan
Tree-pecker Picus
Tree-shrew Tana
Trefoil Bird's foot, Clover, Hop, Lotos, Lotus
Trek Hike, Journey, Leg, Odyssey, Safari, Yomp
Trellis Espalier, Lattice, Pergola, Treillage, Treille
Tremble, Trembling, Tremor Aftershock, Ashake, Butterfly, Dither, Dodder, Foreshock, Hotter, Intention, Judder, Marsquake, Moonquake, Palpitate, Quail, Quake, Quaver, Quiver, Seismal, → **SHAKE**, Shiver, Shock, Shudder, Stound, Temblor, Titubation, Trepid, Twitchy, Vibrant, Vibrate, Vibration, Vibratiuncle, Vibrato, Wobble, Wuther, Yips
Tremendous Big, Enormous, Howling, Immense, Marvellous
Tremolo Bebung, Trillo
▶ **Tremor** see **TREMBLE**
Tremulous Dithering, Hirrient, Quaking, Shaky, Timorous
Trench(er) Boyau, Cunette, Cuvette, Delf, Delph, Dike(r), → **DITCH**, Dyke(r), Encroach, Fleet, Foss(e), Foxhole, Fur(r), Furrow, Grip, Gullet, Gutter, Leat, Line, Mariana, Moat, Oceanic, Outwork, Rill, Rille, Ring-dyke, Robber, Salient, Sap, Shott, Slit, Sod, Sondage
Trenchant Acid, Cutting
Trend(y), Trendsetter Bent, Bias, Chic, Climate, Drift, Fashion, Hep, In, Mainstream, New Age(r), Newfangled, Pacemaker, Pop, Poserish, Posey, Rage, Right-on, Style, Swim, Tendency, Tendenz, Tenor, Tide, Tonnish
Trespass(ing) Aggravated, Encroach, Errant, Hack, Impinge, Infringe, Offend, Peccancy, Sin, Trench, Wrong

Tress(es) Curl, Lock, Ringlet, Switch, Tallent
Trestle Sawhorse
Triad Chord, Ternion, Trimurti
Trial Adversity, Affliction, Appro, Approbation, Approval, Assize, Attempt, Bane,
   Bernoulli, Bout, Clinical, Compurgation, Corsned, Court-martial, Cow, Cross, Dock,
   Essay, → **EXPERIMENT**, Field, Fitting, Hearing, Nuremberg, Ordeal, Pilot, Pree,
   Probation, Proof, Rehearsal, Salem, Scramble, Sheepdog, Show, State, Taste, Time
Triangle(d), Triangular Acute, Bermuda, Circular, Cosec, Deltoid, Equilateral,
   Eternal, Gair, Golden, Gore, Gyronny, Isosceles, Obtuse, Pascal's, Pedimental,
   Pendentive, Pyramid, Rack, Right-angled, Scalene, Similar, Spherical, Trigon,
   Triquetral, Tromino, Warning
Trias(sic) Bunter, Keuper, Muschelkalk, Rhaetic
Tribe(s), Tribal, Tribesmen Amalekite, Ammonites, Ashanti, Asher, Benjamin,
   Celt, Cherokee, Clan(nish), Cree, Creek, Dan, D(a)yak, Dinka, Dynasty, Edomites,
   Ephraim, Family, Gad, Gens, Gentes, Gentilic, Gond, Goth, Guarani, Hapu, Helvetii,
   Hittite, Horde, Hottentot, Ibo, Iceni, Israelite, Issachar, Iwi, Jat, Judah, Kaffir,
   Kenite, Kurd, Lashkar, Levi, Levite, Longobardi, Lost, Manasseh, Masai, Moabite,
   Mongol, Moro, Naga, Naphtali, Nation, Nervii, Ngati, Ordovices, Ostrogoths,
   Pathan, Phyle, Picts, → **RACE**, Reuben, Riff, Rod, Sakai, Salian, Schedule,
   Senones, Senussi, Sept, Shawnee, Silures, Simeon, Strandloper, Tasaday, Teuton,
   Trinobantes, Vandals, Wolof, Wyandot(te), X(h)osa, Zebulun
Tribune, Tribunal Aeropagus, Bema, Bench, → **COURT**, Divan, Employment,
   Forum, Hague, Industrial, Leader, Platform, Rienzi, Rota, Star-chamber, Waitangi
Tributary Affluent, Bogan, Branch, Creek, Fork
Tribute Cain, Capelline, Citation, Commemoration, Compliment, Dedication,
   Deodate, → **DUE**, Epitaph, Festschrift, Gavel, Heriot, Homage, Kain, Memento,
   Ode, Panegyric, Peter's pence, → **PRAISE**, Rome-penny, Rome-scot, Scat(t), Tax,
   Testimonial, Toast, Wreath, Wroth
Trice Flash, Instant
Trichosanthin Q
Trick(ed), Trickery, Tricks(ter), Tricky Antic, Art, Artifice, Attrap, Awkward,
   Bamboozle, Begunk, Book, Bunco, Bunko, Cantrip, Capot, Catch, Cheat,
   Chicane(ry), Chouse, Claptrap, Cod(-act), Cog, Con(fidence), Coyote, Crook,
   Davenport, Deception, Deck, Delicate, Delude, Device, Dirty, → **DO**, → **DODGE**,
   Dupe, Elf, Elfin, Elvan, Fard, Feat, Fetch, Fiddle, Finesse, Flam, Flim-flam, Fob,
   Fox, Fraud, Fun, Game, Gaud, Gleek, Glike, Guile, Had, Hanky-panky, Hey
   presto, Hoax, Hocus(-pocus), Hoodwink, Hornswoggle, Hum, Illude, Illusion,
   Illywhacker, Jadery, Jockey, John, Kittle, Knack, Lark, Magsman, Mislead, Monkey,
   Monkey-shine, Murphy's game, Nap, Nasruddin, Palter, Parlour, Pass, Pawk,
   Pleasantry, Pliskie, Prank, Prestige, Put-on, Quick, Ramp, Raven, Reak, Reik,
   Rex, Rig, Rope, Ropery, Roughie, Ruse, Scam, Sell, Set-up, Shanghai, Shavie,
   Shenanigan, Shifty, Shill, Skin-game, Skite, Skul(l)duggery, Skylark, Slam, Sleight,
   Slight, Slinter, Sophism, Spoof, Stall, Stint, Subterfuge, Sug, Swiftie, Thimble-rig,
   Three-card, Ticklish, Tip, Trap, Tregetour, Trump, Turn, Tweedler, Undercraft,
   Underplot, Vole, Wangle, Wheeze, Wile, Wrinkle
▷ **Trick** *may indicate* an anagram
Trickle Drib(ble), Driblet, Dropple, Leak, Rill, Seep
Trickless Misère
Triclinic Anorthic
Trident Fork, Plane, Trisul(a)
Trifle(s), Trifling Bagatelle, Banal, Baubee, Bauble, Bibelot, Birdseed, Bit, Bubkas,

Cent, Chickenfeed, Coquette, Dabble, Dalliance, → **DALLY**, Denier, Desipient, Dessert, Do, Doit, Faddle, Falderal, Falderol, Fallal, Fattrell, Feather, Fewtril, Fiddle, Fiddle-faddle, Fig, Fingle-fangle, Flamfew, Fleabite, Flirt, Folderol, Fool, Footle, Fribble, Frippery, Fritter, Frivol, Gewgaw, Idle, Iota, Kickshaw, Knick-knack, Luck-penny, Mess, Mite, Nick-nacket, Niff-naff, Nothing, Nugae, Nugatory, Nyaff, Old song, Palter, Paltry, Peanuts, Peddle, Peppercorn, Petty, Philander, Picayune, Piddle, Piffle, Pin, Pingle, Pittance, Play, Potty, Quelquechose, Quiddity, Quiddle, Slight, Small beer, Smatter, Song, Sport, Stiver, Strae, Straw, Sundry, Sweet Fanny Adams, Tiddle, Tom, Toy, Trinket, Trivia, Whifflery, Whim-wham, Whit

Trig(onometry) Neat, Sech, Spherical, Tosh, Trim

Trigger Activate, Detent, Hair, Instigate, Krytron, Pawl, Precipitate, Schmitt, Start, Touch off

Trill(ed), Triller, Trilling Burr, Churr, Hirrient, Quaver, Ribattuta, Roll, Staphyle, Trim, Twitter, Warble

Trilobite Olenellus, Olenus, Paradoxide

Trim(med), Trimmer, Trimming Ballast, Barb, Bleed, Braid, Bray, Chipper, Clip, Dapper, Dinky, Dress, Ermine, Face, Falbala, Fettle, File, Froufrou, Garni, Garnish, Garniture, Gimp, Guimpe, Macramé, Macrami, Marabou, Neat, Net(t), Ornament, Pare, Passament, Passement(erie), Pipe, Plight, Posh, Preen, Proign, Proyn(e), Pruin(e), Prune, Roach, Robin, Ruche, Sax, Sett, Shipshape, Smirk, Smug, Sned, Snod, → **SPRUCE**, Straddle, Stroddle, Strodle, Stylist, Svelte, Tiddley, → **TIDY**, Time-server, Top, Torsade, Trick, Whippersnipper, Wig

Trinidadian Carib

Trinity, Trinitarian Mathurin(e), Prosopon, Triad, Trimurti, Triune, Word

Trinket(s) Bauble, Bibelot, Bijou(terie), Charm, Fallal, Nicknack, Toy, Trankum, Trumpery

Trio Catch, Graces, Skat, Terzetto, Threesome

Trip(per) Awayday, Cruise, Dance, Day, Ego, Errand, → **FALL**, Field, Flight, Flip, Guilt, Head, High, Jolly, Journey, Junket, Kilt, Link, Outing, Passage, Pleasure, Power, Ride, Round, Run, Sail, Sashay, Spin, Spurn, → **STUMBLE**, Tour, Trek, Trial, Voyage

▷ **Trip** *may indicate* an anagram

Tripe Abracadabra, Bosh, Caen, Entrails, Honeycomb, Offal, Plain, Rot

Triple, Triplet Codon, Hemiol(i)a, Sdrucciola, Ternal, Tiercet, Treble, Trifecta, Trilling, Trin(e), Tripling

Tripod Cat, Cortina, Highhat, Oracle, Triangle, Trippet, Trivet

Triptych Volet

Trishaw Cycle

Trite Banal, Boilerplate, Cornball, Corny, Hackneyed, Hoary, Laughable, Novelettish, Platitude, Rinky-dink, Stale, Stock, Time-worn, Worn

Triton Eft, Evet, Ewt, Trumpet-shell

Triumph(ant) Cock-a-hoop, Codille, Cowabunga, Crow, Eureka, Exult, Glory, Impostor, Killing, Oho, Olé, Ovation, Palm, Prevail, Victorious, → **WIN**

Triumvir Caesar, Crassus, Pompey

Trivet Tripod, Trippet

Trivia(l), Triviality Adiaphoron, Bagatelle, Balaam, Bald, → **BANAL**, Footling, Frippery, Frothy, Futile, Idle, Inconsequential, Light, Minutiae, Nitpicking, Nothingism, Paltry, Pap, Peppercorn, Pettifoggery, Petty, Picayune, Piddling, Piffling, Puerile, Shallow, Small, Small beer, Small fry, Snippety, Squirt, Squit, Toy(s), Vegie

Trochee Choree

Troglodyte Ape, Caveman, Hermit, Spelean, Wren
Trojan Aeneas, Agamemnon, Dardan, Iliac, Priam, Teucrian, Troic
Troll → FISH, Gnome, Rove, Spoon, Trawl, Warble
Trolley Brute, Cart, Crane, Dolly, Gurney, Hostess, Shopping, Tea, Teacart, Traymobile, Truck, Trundler
▶ **Trollop** *see* LOOSE WOMAN
Trombone Bass, Posaune, Sackbut, Tenor
Trompe l'oeil Quadratura, Quadrature
Troop(s), Trooper Alpini, Band, BEF, Brigade, Company, Depot, Detachment, Guard, Horde, Household, Logistics, Midianite, Militia, Pultan, Pulton, Pultoon, Pultun, SAS, School, Shock, → SOLDIER, Sowar, State, Storm, Subsidiary, Tp, Turm(e), Velites
Troopship Transport
Trophy Adward, Ashes, → AWARD, Bag, Belt, Cup, Emmy, Memento, Palm, Plate, → PRIZE, Scalp, Schneider, Spoils, Tourist, TT
Tropic(al) Cancer, Capricorn, Derris, Jungle, Neogaea, Sultry
Trot(ter), Trot out Air, Clip, Crib, Crubeen, Hag, Job, Jog, Passage, Pettitoes, Piaffe, Pony, Ranke, Red(-shirt), Rising, Tootsie, Trotskyist
Troth Perfay, Troggs
Trotsky(ist) Entr(y)ism, Leon, Militant Tendency
Troubador Blondel, Griot, Manrico, Minstrel, Singer, Sordello
Trouble(s), Troublemaker, Troublesome Ache, Ado, Affliction, Aggro, Agitate, Ail, Alarm, Annoy, Bale, Barrat, Beset, → BOTHER, Bovver, Brickle, Burden, Care, Coil, Concern, Debate, Disaster, Disquiet, Distress, Disturb, Dog, Dolour, Eat, Esclandre, Exercise, Fash, Fashious, Finger, Firebrand, Fossick, Frondeur, Gram(e), Grief, Hag-ride, Harass, Harry, Hassle, Hatter, Heat, Heist, Hellion, Hot water, Howdyedo, Hydra, Inconvenience, Infest, → IN TROUBLE, Jam, Kiaugh, Mess, Mixer, Moil, Molest, Noy, Perturb, Pester, Pestiferous, Picnic, Plague, Play up, Poke, Reck, Rub, Scamp, Scrape, Shake, Shtuck, Soup, Spiny, Stir, Storm, Sturt, Tartar, Teen, Teething, Thorny, Tine, Toil, Trial, Tsouris, Tsuris, Turn-up, Tyne, Unsettle, Vex, → WORRY
Trouble-free Gallio
Trouble-shooter Ombudsman
▷ **Troublesome** *may indicate* an anagram
Trough Back, Bed, Bucket, Buddle, Channel, Chute, Culvert, Graben, Hod, Hutch, Langmuir, Launder, Leachtub, Manger, Pneumatic, Puerto Rico, Stock, Straik, Strake, Syncline, Troffer, Tundish, Tye, Watering
Trounce → BEAT, Hammer, Thump
Trouser(s) Bags, Bell-bottoms, Bloomers, Breeches, Bumsters, Capri pants, Cargo pants, Churidars, Clam-diggers, Combat, Continuations, Cords, Corduroys, Cossacks, Culottes, Daks, Denims, Drainpipe, Drawers, Ducks, Dungarees, Eel-skins, Flannels, Flares, Galligaskins, Gaskins, Gauchos, Hip-huggers, Hipsters, Inexpressibles, Innominables, Jeans, Jodhpurs, Jog-pants, Kaccha, Ke(c)ks, Knee cords, Lederhosen, Levis, Longs, Loons, Moleskins, Overalls, Oxford bags, Palazzo (pants), Palazzos, Pantaloons, Pants, Pedal pushers, Pegtops, Plus-fours, Plus-twos, Pyjamas, Reach-me-downs, Salopettes, Shalwar, Ski pants, Slacks, Stirrup pants, Stovepipes, Strides, Strossers, Sweatpants, Thornproofs, Trews, Trouse, Unmentionables, Unutterables, Utterless
Trout Aurora, Brook, Brown, Bull, Coral, Finnac(k), Finnock, Fish, Gillaroo, Hag(fish), Herling, Hirling, Kamloops, Peal, Peel, Phinnock, Pogies, Quintet, Rainbow, Salmon, Sewen, Sewin, Speckled, Splake, Steelhead, Togue, Whitling

Trow Faith, Meseems

Trowel Float, Slicker

Troy Ilium, Laomedon, Sergeant, T, Weight

Truant Absentee, AWOL, Bunk off, Dodge, Hooky, Kip, Mich(e), Mitch, Mooch, Mouch, Wag

Truce Armistice, Barley, Ceasefire, Fainites, Fains, Hudna, Interlude, Keys, Pax, Stillstand, Treague, Treaty

Truck Bakkie, Bogie, Breakdown, Business, Cabover, Cattle, Cocopan, Dealings, Dolly, Dumper, Flatbed, Forklift, Haul, Hopper, Journey, → **LORRY**, Low-loader, Monster, Pallet, Panel, Pick-up, Semi, Sound, Stacking, Tipper, Tommy, Tow(ie), Traffic, Trolley, Trundle, Ute, Utility, Van, Wrecker

Trudge Footslog, Jog, Lumber, Pad, Plod, Stodge, Stramp, Taigle, Traipse, Trash, Trauchle, Trog, Vamp

True Accurate, Actual, Apodictic, Axiomatic, Candid, Constant, Correct, Exact, Factual, Faithful, Genuine, Honest, Indubitable, Leal, Literal, Loyal, Platitude, Plumb, Pure, Real, Realistic, Richt, Right, Sooth, Very

Truffle Tartuffe, Tuber, Tuberaceae

Trug Basket, Wisket

Truly Certainly, Certes, Fegs, Forsooth, Honestly, Indeed, Insooth, Surely, Verily, Yea

Trump(s), Trumpet(er) Agami, Alchemy, Alchymy, Armstrong, Bach, Blare, Blast, Bray, Buccina, Bugle(r), Call, Card, Clang, Clarion, Conch, Cornet, Corona, Crossruff, Crow, Daffodil, Ear, Elephant, Fanfare, Hallali, Honours, → **HORN**, Invent, Jew's, Last, Lituus, Long ten, Lur(e), Lurist, Manille, Marine, Megaphone, → **NO TRUMP**, Overruff, Proclaim, Ram's-horn, Rant, Resurrect, Ruff, Salpingian, Salpinx, Satchmo, Sennet, Shofar, Shophar, Slug-horn, Speaking, Splash, Surpass, Tantara, Tantarara, Tar(at)antara, Theodomas, Tiddy, Triton, Triumph

Trumpery Fattrels, Jimcrack, Paltry, Trashy

Truncate(d) Abrupt, Cut, Dock, Shorten

Truncheon Billie, Billy, Blackjack, Cosh, Night-stick, Warder

Trundle Hump, Roll, Trill, Troll, Wheel

Trunk(s) Aorta(l), A-road, Body, Bole, Box, Bulk, Bus, But(t), Cabin, Carcase, Chest, Coffer, Hose, Imperial, Log, Peduncle, Pollard, Portmanteau, Portmantle, Proboscis, Ricker, Road, Saratoga, Shorts, STD, Stock, Stud, Synangium, Torso, Valise, Wardrobe

Truss → **BIND**, Ligate, Oop, Oup, Sheaf, Tie, Upbind

Trust(y), Trusting, Trustworthy Active, Affy, Apex, Authentic, Belief, Blind, Care, Cartel, Charge, Charitable, Combine, Confide, Credit, Dependable, Discretionary, → **FAITH**, Fiduciary, Gullible, Honest, Hope, Hospital, Investment, Leal, Lippen, Loyal, National, NT, Reliable, Reliance, Rely, Repose, Reputable, Sound, Special, Split, Staunch, Tick, Trojan, Trow, True, Trump, Unit

Trustee Agent, Executor, Fiduciary, Judicial, Pensioneer, Tr

Truth(ful), Truism Accuracy, Alethic, Axiom, Bromide, Cliché, Cold turkey, Dharma, Dialectic, → **FACT**, Facticity, Forsooth, Gospel, Griff, Home, Honesty, Idea(l), Logical, Maxim, Naked, Necessary, Pravda, Principle, Reality, Sooth, Soothfast, Troggs, Veracity, Veridical, Verisimilitude, Verity, Vraisemblance

Try(ing) Aim, Approof, Assay, Attempt, Audition, Bash, Bate, Bid, Birl, Burden, Burl, Conative, Contend, Crack, Effort, Empiric(utic), → **ENDEAVOUR**, Essay, Examine, Experiment, Fand, Fish, Fling, Foretaste, Go, Gun for, Harass, Hard, Hear, Impeach, Importunate, Irk, Noy, Offer, Ordalium, Penalty, Pop, Practise, Pree, Prieve, Prove, Push-over, → **SAMPLE**, Seek, Shot, Sip, Stab, Strain, Strive, Taste, Tax, Tempt, Test, Touchdown, Whirl

Tryst Date, Rendezvous

Tsar(ist) Alexis, Emperor, Godunov, Octobrist, Romanov, Ruler

TT Rechabite

Tub(by), Tubbiness, Tub-thumper Ash-leach, Back, Bath, Boanerges, Bran, Corf, Cowl, Dan, Diogenes, Dolly, Endomorph, Firkin, Keeve, Kid, Kieve, Kit, Luckydip, Mashing, Meat, Pin, Podge, Pot-bellied, Pudge, Pulpit, Seasoning, Stand, Swill, Tun, Twin, Vat, Wash, Whey

Tuba Bombardon, Euphonium, Helicon

Tube, Tubing, Tubular Acorn, Arteriole, Artery, Barrel, Blowpipe, Bronchus, Buckytube, Burette, Calamus, Camera, Canaliculus, Cannula, Capillary, Casing, Catheter, Cathode-ray, Cave, Conduit, Crookes, Digitron, Diode, Discharge, Drain, Draw, Drift, Dropper, Duct, Electron, Endiometer, Epididymis, Eustachian, Extension, Fallopian, Fistula, Flash, Fluorescent, Fulgurite, Geissler, Germ, Glowstick, Grommet, Hose, Iconoscope, Image (orthicon), Inner, Kinescope, Klystron, Macaroni, Malpighian, Matrass, Metro, Morris, Nasogastric, Neural, Nixie, Optic, Orthicon, Oval, Oviduct, Pastille, Pentode, Picture, Pilot-static, → **PIPE**, Pipette, Pitot, Pitot(-static), Pneumatic, Pollen, Postal, Promethean, Salpinx, Saticon®, Saucisse, Saucisson, Schnorkel, Shadow-mask, Shock, Sieve, Siphon, Siphonet, Siphonostele, Siphuncle, Skelp, Skiatron, Sleeve, Slide, Snorkel, Spaghetti, Speaking, Spout, Staple, Static, Stent, Stone canal, Storage, Strae, Straw, Strobotron, Subway, Sucker, Swallet, Telescope, Teletron, Television, Terete, Test, Tetrode, Thermionic, Thyratron, Tile, Torpedo, Torricellian, Trachea, Travelling-wave, Triniscope, Trocar, Trochotron, Trunk, Tunnel, Tuppenny, U, Underground, Ureter, Urethra, Vacuum, Vas, VDU, Vein, Vena, Venturi, Video, Vidicon®, Worm, X-ray

Tuber(s) Arnut, Arracacha, Bulb, Chufa, Coc(c)o, Dahlia, Dasheen, Earth-nut, Eddoes, Jicama, Mashua, Oca, Potato, Salep, Taproot, Taro, Tuckahoe, Yam

Tuberculosis Consumption, Crewels, Cruel(l)s, Decline, King's evil, Lupus, Lupus vulgaris, Phthisis, Scrofula, White plague

Tuck Dart, Friar, Gather, Grub, Hospital corner, Kilt, Pin, Pleat, Scran, Truss, Tummy

Tudor Stockbrokers'

Tuesday Hock, Pancake, Shrove, Super

Tuff Schalstein

Tuft(ed) Aigrette, Amentum, Beard, Candlewick, Catkin, C(a)espitose, Cluster, Coma, Comb, Cowlick, Crest, Dollop, Flaught, Floccus, Flock, Goatee, Hassock, Knop, Lock, Pappus, Penicillate, Quiff, Scopate, Shola, Tait, Tassel, Tate, Toorie, Topknot, Toupee, Tourie, Tussock, Tuzz, Whisk

Tug Drag, Haul, Jerk, Lug, Pug, → **PULL**, Rive, Saccade, Ship, Sole, Soole, Sowl(e), Tit, Tow, Towboat, Yank

Tui Poebird

Tuition Masterclass, Seminal

Tully Cicero

Tumble, Tumbler Acrobat, Cartwheel, Drier, Fall, → **GLASS**, Header, Pitch, Popple, Purl, Realise, Spill, Stumble, Tailer, Topple, Touser, Towser, Trip, Twig, Voltigeur, Welter

▷ **Tumble** *may indicate* an anagram

Tumbledown Decrepit, Dilapidated, Ramshackle, Rickle, Ruinous

Tumbril Caisson

Tummy Belly, Colon, Mary, Paunch, Pod

Tummy-ache Colic, Gripe, Tormina

Tumour Adenoma, Anbury, Angioma, Angiosarcoma, Astroblastoma, Astrocytoma, Burkitt('s) lymphoma, Cancer, Carcinoid, Carcinoma, Carcinosarcoma, Chondroma, Condyloma, Crab(-yaws), Dermoid, Encanthis, Encephaloma, Enchondroma, Endothelioma, Epulis, Exostosis, Fibroid, Fibroma, Ganglion, Germinoma, Gioblastoma, Glioma, Granuloma, Grape, → **GROWTH**, Gumma, Haemangioma, Haematoma, Hepatoma, Lipoma, Lymphoma, Medullablastoma, Melanoma, Meningioma, Mesothelioma, Metastasis, Mole, Myeloma, Myoma, Myxoma, Neoplasm, Nephroblastoma, Neuroblastoma, Neuroma, Odontoma, -oma, Oncology, Osteoclastoma, Osteoma, Osteosarcoma, Papilloma, Polypus, Retinoblastoma, Rhabdomyoma, Sarcoma, Scirrhous, Secondary, Seminoma, Steatoma, Struma, Syphiloma, Talpa, Teratoma, Thymoma, Wart, Warthin's, Wen, Wilm's, Windgall, Wolf, Xanthoma, Yaw

Tumult Brattle, Brawl, Coil, Deray, Ferment, Fracas, Hirdy-girdy, Hubbub, Hurly-burly, Reird, Riot, → **ROAR**, Romage, Rore, Stoor, Stour, Stowre, Stramash, Tew, Tristan, Tristram, → **UPROAR**

Tumulus Barrow, How(e), Mote, Motte

Tun Cask, Keg

Tuna Pear, Yellowfin

Tundra Barren Grounds, Barren Lands

Tune(s), Tuneful, Tuner, Tuning Adjust, Air, Aria, Canorous, Carillon, Catch, Choral, Dump, Earworm, Étude, Fine, Fork, Harmony, Hornpipe, Jingle, Key, Maggot, Measure, Melisma, → **MELODY**, Old Hundred, → **OUT OF TUNE**, Peg, Planxty, Port, Potpourri, Raga, Rant, Ranz-des-vaches, Signature, Snatch, Song, Spring, Strain, Sweet, Syntonise, Temper, Temperament, Theme, Tone, Toy, Tweak

Tungstate, Tungsten Scheelite, W, Wolfram

Tunic Ao dai, Caftan, Chiton, Choroid, Cote-hardie, Dalmatic, Dashiki, Gymslip, Hauberk, Kabaya, Kaftan, Kameez, K(h)urta, Salwar kameez, → **SINGLET**, Surcoat, Tabard, Toga

Tunicate Salpa

Tunnel(ler) Blackwall, Bore, Channel, Chunnel, Condie, Countermine, Culvert, Cundy, Earthworm, Euro, Gallery, Head, Mine, Mole, Qanat, Rotherhithe, Simplon, Smoke, Stope, Subway, Syrinx, Tube, Underpass, Water, Wind, Wormhole

Tunny Bonito, Tuna

Turban Bandanna, Hat, Mitral, Pagri, Puggaree, Puggery, Puggree, Sash, Scarf, Tulipant

Turbid Cloudy, Dense, Drumly, Roily

Turbine Francis, Gas, Impulse, Ram air, Reaction, Steam, Water, Wind

Turbulence, Turbulent Atmospheric, Becket, Bellicose, Buller, Factious, Fierce, Overfall, Rapids, Roil, Stormy, Unruly

▷ **Turbulent, Turbulence** *may indicate* an anagram

Turf Caespitose, Clod, Divot, Earth, Fail, Feal, Flaught, Gazo(o)n, → **GRASS**, Greensward, Peat, Screw, → **SOD**, Sward

Turk(ish) Anatolian, Bashaw, Bashkir, Bey, Bimbashi, Bostangi, Byzantine, Caimac(am), Crescent, Effendi, Golden Horde, Grand, Gregory, Horse(tail), Irade, Kaimakam, Kazak(h), Kurd, Mameluke, Mutessarif(at), Omar, Osman(li), Ottamite, Ottoman, Ottomite, Rayah, Scanderbeg, Selim, Seljuk(ian), Seraskier, Spahi, Tartar, Tatar, Timariot, Usak, Uzbeg, Uzbek, Yakut, Young

Turkey, Turkey-like Anatolia, Antioch, Brush, Bubbly(-jock), Cold, Curassow, Eyalet, Flop, Gobbler, Norfolk, Plain, Scrub, Sultanate, Talegalla, Talk, TR, Trabzon, Vulturn

Turkish delight Rahat lacoum, Trehala

Turmeric Curcumine
Turmoil Chaos, Din, Ferment, Mess, Pother, Pudder, Stoor, Stour, Tornado, Tracasserie, Tumult, → **UPROAR**, Welter
▷ **Turn(ing)** *may indicate* an anagram
Turn(ing), Turned away, Turned up, Turns Acescent, Act, Adapt, Addle, Advert, Antrorse, Apostrophe, Apotropaic, Avert, Bad, Bank, Become, Bend, Buggins, Bump, Canceleer, Cancelier, Caracol(e), Careen, Cartwheel, Cast, Chainé, Chandelle, Change, Char(e), Chore, Christiana, Christie, Christy, Churn, Cock, Coil, Crank(le), Cuff, Curd(le), Curve, Defect, Deflect, Demi-volt(e), Detour, Deviate, Dig, Digress, Divert, Ear, Earn, Elbow, Evert, Fadge, Flip, Forfend, Go, Good, Gruppetto, Hairpin, Handbrake, Head-off, Hie, High, Hinge, Hup, Immelmann, Influence, Innings, Intussuscept, Invert, Jar, Jink, Jump, Keel, Kick, Laeotropic, Lodging, Lot, Luff, Mohawk, Number, Obvert, Parallel, Parry, Penchant, Pivot, Plough, Pronate, Prove, PTO, Quarter, Quersprung, Rebut, Refer, Refract, Remuage, Retroflex, Retroussé, Retrovert, Rev, Revolt, Ride, Riffle, Rocker, Roll, Root, → **ROTATE**, Rote, Roulade, Rout, Routine, Screw, Secund, Sheer, → **SHOT**, Shout, Sicken, Skit, Slew, Slue, Solstice, Sour, → **SPELL**, Spin, Spot, Sprain, Star, Start, Stem, Step, Swash, Swing, Swivel, Telemark, Thigmotropism, Three-point, Throw, Tiptilt, Tirl, Torque, Transpose, Trend, Trick, Trie, Trochilic, Turtle, Twiddle, Twist, U, Uey, Up, Veer, Versed, Version, Vertigo, Volta, Volte-face, Volutation, Wap, Warp, Wedeln, Wend, Went, → **WHEEL**, Whelm, Whirl, Whorl, Wimple, Wind, Wrast, Wrest, Wriggle, Zigzag
Turn-coat Apostate, Cato, Defector, Quisling, Rat, Renegade, Tergiversate, Traitor
Turner Axle, Lana, Lathe, Painter, Pivot, Rose-engine, Spanner, Tina, Worm, Wrench
Turning point Crisis, Crossroads, Landmark, Watershed
Turnip(-shaped) Baggy, Bagie, Hunter, Jicama, Napiform, Navew, Neep, Prairie, Rutabaga, Shaw, → **STUPID PERSON**, Swede, Tumshie
Turnkey Gaoler, Jailer
Turn-out Eventuate, Gathering, Product, Rig, Splay, Style
Turn over Capsize, Careen, Flip, Inversion, Production, PTO, Somersault, TO, Up-end
Turnpike Highway, Toll
Turnstile Tourniquet
Turntable Racer, Rota, Rotator
Turpentine Galipot, Rosin, Thinner, Turps, Venice
Turquoise Bone, Fossil, Ligure, Occidental, Odontolite, Oriental, Turkey stone
Turret(ed) Barmkin, Bartisan, Garret, Louver, Louvre, Mirador, Pepperbox, Sponson, → **TOWER**, Turriculate
Turtle, Turtle head Bale, Calipash, Calipee, Chelone, Diamondback, Emys, Floor, Green, Hawk(s)bill, Inverted, Leatherback, Loggerhead, Matamata, Mossback, Mud, Musk, Ridley, Screen, Snapper, Snapping, Soft-shelled, Stinkpot, Terrapin, Thalassian
Tuscany Chiantishire
Tusk Gam, Horn, Ivory, Tooth, Tush
Tusker Dicynodont, Elephant, Mastodon
Tussle Giust, Joust, Mêlée, Scrimmage, Scrum, Scuffle, Skirmish, Touse, Touze, Towse, Towze, Tuilyie, Wrestle
Tussock Hassock, Niggerhead, Tuft
Tut(-tut) Och, Pooh
Tutelary Guardian, Protector

Tutor Abbé, Aristotle, Ascham, Bear, → **COACH**, Crammer, Don, Instruct, Leader, Mentor, Preceptor, Répétiteur, Supervisor, Teacher

Tuxedo DJ

TV Baird, Box, Cable, Digital, Docusoap, Idiot-box, Lime Grove, Monitor, PAL, Pay, Reality, SECAM, Sky, Tele, → **TELEVISION**, Telly, Tube, Video

Twaddle Blether, Drivel, Rot, Slipslop, Tripe

Twang Nasal, Pluck, Plunk, Rhinolalia

Tweak Pluck, Primp, Twiddle, Twist, Twitch

Tweed(y) Donegal, Harris®, Homespun, Lovat, Raploch

Tweet Chirrup

Twelfth, Twelve Apostles, Dozen, Epiphany, Glorious, Grouse, Midday, Midnight, N, Night, Noon, Ternion, Twal

Twenty, Twenty-sided Icosahedron, Score, Vicenary, Vicennial, Vicesimal, Vigesimal

Twenty-five, Twentyfifth Pony, Quartern, Semi-jubilee

Twenty-four Thr(e)ave

Twerp Pipsqueak

▶ **Twice** *see* **TWO**

Twice-yearly Biennial, Equinox

Twiddle Fidget, Twirl

Twig(s) Besom, Birch, Cotton, Cow, Dig, Grasp, Kow, Osier, Realise, Reis, Rice, Rumble, Sarment, See, Sprig, Sticklac, Switch, Understand, Walking, Wand, Wattle, Whip, Wicker, Withe

Twilight Astronomical, Civil, Cockshut, Crepuscular, Demi-jour, Dimpsy, Dusk, Gloam(ing), Götterdämmerung, Nautical, Summerdim

Twill Cavalry, Chino

Twin(s) Asvins, Castor, Coetaneous, Conjoined, Didymous, Dioscuri, Ditokous, Dizygotic, Double, Fraternal, Gemel, Hemitrope, Identical, Isogeny, Juxtaposition, Kindred, Macle, Monozygotic, Parabiotic, Pigeon-pair, Pollux, Siamese, Thomas, Tweedledee, Tweedledum

Twine Binder, Braid, Coil, Cord, Inosculate, Packthread, Sisal, Snake, String, Twist, Wreathe

Twinge Pang, Scruple, Stab, Twang

Twinkle, Twinkling Glimmer, Glint, Mo(ment), → **SPARKLE**, Starnie, Trice

Twirl Spin, Swivel, Tirl, Tirlie-wirlie, Trill, Trundle, Twiddle, Twizzle, Whirl

▷ **Twirling** *may indicate* an anagram

Twist(ed), Twister, Twisting, Twisty Anfractuous, Askant, Askew, Baccy, Becurl, Bought, Braid, Buckle, Card-sharper, Chisel, Coil, Contort, Convolution, Crinkle, Crinkum-crankum, Crisp, Cue, Curl(icue), Cyclone, Deform, Detort, Distort, → **DODGE**, Entwine, Garrot, Helix, Imposture, Kink, Mangulate, Mat, Möbius strip, Oliver, Pandanaceous, Plait, Quirk, Raddle, Ravel, Rick, Rogue, Rotate, Rove, Serpent, Skew, Slew, Slub(b), Slue, Snake, Snarl, Spin, Spiral, Sprain, Squiggle, Squirm, Swivel, Tendril, Thrawn, Torc, Tornado, Torque, Torsade, Torsion, Torticollis, Tortile, Turn, Tweak, Twiddle, Twine, Twirl, Typhoon, Valgus, Volvulus, Wamble, Warp, Welkt, Wigwag, Wind, Wound-wrap, Wrast, Wreathe, Wrench, Wrest, Wrethe, Wrick, Wriggle, Wring, Writhe, Wry, Zigzag

▷ **Twisted, Twisting** *may indicate* an anagram

Twit, Twitter Chaff, Cherup, Chirrup, Dotterel, Gear(e), Giber, → **JEER**, Stupid, Taunt, Tweet, Warble

Twitch(ing), Twitchy Athetosis, Clonic, Fibrillation, Grass, Jerk, Life-blood, Start, Subsultive, Tic, Tig, Tit, Tweak, Twinge, Vellicate, Yips

Two(some), Twofold, Twice Bice, Bis, Bisp, Both, Brace, Couple(t), Deuce, Double, Duad, Dual, Duet, Duo, Duple, Dyad, → **PAIR**, Swy, Tête-à-tête, Twain, Twins, Twister

Two-edged Ancipitous

Two-faced Dihedral, Dorsiventral, Hypocritical, Janus, Redan

Two-gallon Peck

Two-headed Amphisbaenic, Dicephalous, Orthos

Two hundred H

Two hundred and fifty E, K

Two-master Brig

Two-rayed Diactinal

Two-sided Bilateral, Equivocatory

Two thousand Z

Two-up Kip, Swy

Two-wheeler Bicycle, Scooter

Tycoon Baron, Empire-builder, Magnate, Mogul, Nabob, Plutocrat, Shogun

Type(s), Typing A, Agate, Aldine, Antimony, Antique, B, Balaam, Baskerville, Bastard, Beard, Bembo, Black-letter, Block, Blood, Bodoni, Body, Bold face, Bourgeois, Braille, Brand, Brevier, Brilliant, Canon, Caslon, Category, Character, Chase, Cicero, Clarendon, Class, Columbian, Condensed, Cut, Egyptian, Elite, Elzevir, Em, Emblem, Emerald, En(nage), English, Face, Font, Form(e), Founder's, Fount, Fraktur, Fudge, Garamond, Gem, Genre, Gent, Gothic, Great primer, Gutenberg, Hair, Ilk, Image, Kern(e), Key, Kidney, Kind, Late-star, Ligature, Light-faced, Logotype, Longprimer, Ludlow, Mating, Melanochroi, Minion, Modern, Monospaced, Moon, Mould, Non-pareil, Norm, Old English, Old-face, Old Style, Paragon, Pattern, Pearl, Peculiar, Personality, Pi, Pica, Pie, Plantin, Point, Primer, Print, Quad(rat), Roman, Ronde, Ruby, Sanserif, Secretary, Semibold, Serif, Serological, Slug, → **SORT**, Sp, Species, Spectral, Stanhope, Style, Times, Tissue, Touch, Version

▷ **Type of** *may indicate* an anagram

Typewriter Golfball, Portable, Stenograph, Stenotype®, Varityper®

Typhoid, Typhus Camp-fever, Scrub, Tick-borne

Typhoon Cyclone, Hurricane, Monsoon, Tornado, Wind

Typical Average, Characteristic, Classic, Echt, Normal, Representative, Standard, Symbolic, True-bred, Usual

Typist Audio, Copy, Printer, Steno(grapher), Temp

Tyrannise(d) Domineer, Lord, Under

Tyrant, Tyranny, Tyrannical Absolutism, Autocrat, Caligula, Czar, Despot, Dictator, Drawcansir, Gelon, Herod, Lordly, Nero, Oppressor, Pharaoh, Sardanapalus, Satrap, Stalin, Totalitarian, Tsar, Yoke

Tyre(s) Balloon, Cross-ply, Cushion, Earthing, Michelin®, Pericles, Pneumatic, Radial, Radial(-ply), Recap, Remould, Retread, Shoe, Sidewall, Slick, Snow, Spare, Stepney, Tread, Tubeless, Whitewall

Tyro Beginner, Ham, → **NOVICE**, Rabbit, Rookie, Rooky, Starter

Tyrolese R(h)aetian

Uu

U, U-type Gent, Unicorn, Universal, Uranium
Ubiquitous Everywhere, Omnipresent
Udder Bag, Dug
Ugandan Obote
Ugly Butters, Cow, Customer, Eyesore, Foul, Gorgon, Gruesome, Hideous, Homely, Huckery, Loath, Loth, Mean, Ominous, Plain
Ugrian Ostiak, Ostyak, Samo(y)ed, Vogul
UK GB
Ukase Decree
Ukraine Ruthene, UA
Ulcer(ous) Abscess, Aphtha, Bedsore, Canker, Chancre, Chancroid, Decubitus, Duodenal, Enanthema, Gastric, Helcoid, Noli-me-tangere, Noma, Peptic, Phagedaena, Rodent, Rupia, Sore, Varicose, Wolf
Ulster NI, Overcoat, Raincoat, Ulad
Ulterior External, Hidden
Ultimate Absolute, Basic, Deterrent, Eventual, Final, Furthest, Last, Maximum, So, Supreme, Thule
Ultra Drastic, Extreme, Radical
Ultra-modern Space age
Ultra-republican Leveller
Ultrasound Lithotripsy
Ulysses Bloom, Grant, Odysseus
Umbellifer(ous) Angelica, Arnut, Car(r)away, Dill, Honewort, Narthex, Pig-nut, Seseli
Umber Burnt, Mottled, Raw, Waved
Umbrage Offence, Pique, Resentment, Shade
Umbrella(-shaped) Bubble, Bumbershoot, Chatta, Gamp, Gingham, Gloria, Mush(room), Nuclear, Parasol, Sunshade, Tee
Umbria Eugubine, Iguvine
Umpire Arb(iter), Byrlawman, Daysman, Decider, Judge, Oddjobman, Odd(s)man, Overseer, Oversman, Referee, Rule, Stickler, Thirdsman
Unabashed Bare-faced, Brazen, Shameless
Unable Can't, Downa-do, Incapable
Unaccented Atonic, Proclitic
Unacceptable Non-U, Not on, Out, Stigmatic
Unaccompanied A cappella, Alone, High-lone, Secco, Single, Solo, Solus
Unaccustomed Desuetude, New
Unadorned Bald, Plain, Stark
Unadulterated Sincere
Unaffected Artless, Genuine, Homely, Insusceptible, Natural, Plain, Sincere, Unattached
Unaided Single-handed, Solo

Unaltered Constant, Same
Unambiguous Categorical, Univocal
Unanimous Accord, Nem con
Unanswerable Erotema, Irrefragable, Irrefutable
Unappreciated Thankless
Unarguable Erotema
Unarmed Inerm, Naked, Vulnerable
Unashamed Blatant, Brazen, Open
Unassigned Adespota, Anonymous
Unassuming Lowly, Modest
Unattached Freelance, Loose
Unattractive Drac(k), Lemon, Minger, Plain, Plug-ugly, Rebarbative, Seamy, Ugly
Unattributable Anon
Unauthentic Plagal
▷ **Unauthentic** *may indicate* an anagram
Unavail(able), Unavailing Bootless, Futile, Ineluctable, Lost, No use, Off, Useless, Vain
Unavoidable Inevitable, Necessary, Perforce
Unaware Heedless, Ignorant, Incognisant, Innocent, Oblivious
Unbalanced Asymmetric, Deranged, Doolalli, Doolally, Loco, Lopsided, Out to lunch, Uneven
Unbearable Bassington, Intolerable
Unbeaten, Unbeatable All-time, Perfect
Unbecoming, Unbefitting Improper, Infra dig, Shabby, Unfitting, Unseemly, Unsuitable, Unworthy
Unbelievable, Unbeliever Agnostic, Atheist, Cassandra, Doubter, Giaour, Heathen, Incredible, Infidel, Pagan, Painim, Paynim, Sceptic, Tall, Zendik
Unbent Relaxed
Unbiased Fair, Impartial, Just, Neutral, Objective, Unattainted
Unblemished Spotless, Vestal
Unblinking Alert, Astare, Fearless
Unborn Future, Unbred
Unbowed In-kneed, Resolute
Unbreakable Infrangible, Inviolate
Unbridled Fancy free, Footloose, Lawless, Uncurbed, Unrestricted, Unshackled, Untramelled
Unburden Confide, Offload, Relieve, Unload
Uncanny Eerie, Eldritch, Extraordinary, Geason, Rum, Spooky, Weird
Uncastrated Stone
Unceasing Continuous
Uncertain(ty) Acatalepsy, Agnostic, Blate, Broken, Chancy, Chary, Contingent, Delicate, Dicey, Dither, Doubtful, Dubiety, Grey, Heisenberg, Hesitant, Iffy, Indeterminate, Indistinct, Irresolute, Peradventure, Precarious, Queasy, Risky, Slippery, Tentative, Vor, Wide open
▷ **Uncertain** *may indicate* an anagram
Unchallengeable, Unchallenge(d) Irrecusable, Sackless
Unchangeable, Unchanged, Unchanging As is, Enduring, Eternal, Idempotent, Immutable, Monotonous, Pristine, Stable, Standpat
Uncharacteristic Atypical
Uncharged Neutral, Neutron
Unchaste Corrupt, Immodest, Immoral, Impure, Lewd, Wanton

Unchecked Rampant
Uncivil(ised) Barbaric, Benighted, Boondocks, Discourteous, Disrespectful, Giant-rude, Goth, Heathen, Impolite, Liberty, Military, Rude, Rudesby
Uncle Abbas, Afrikaner, Arly, Bob, Dutch, Eme, Nunky, Oom, Pawnbroker, Pop-shop, Remus, Sam, Tio, Tom, Usurer, Vanya
Unclean Defiled, Dirty, Impure, Obscene, Ordure, Squalid, Tabu, T(e)refa(h)
Unclear Ambitty, Hazy, Nebulous, Obscure
Unclothed Bald, Nude
Uncloven Soliped
Uncommitted Evasive, Laodicean
Uncommon Rara avis, Rare, Sparse, Strange, Unusual
▷ **Uncommon(ly)** *may indicate* an anagram
Uncommunicative Reserved, Tight-lipped
Uncompanionable Threesome
Uncomplimentary Blunt
Uncomprehending Anan, Ignorant
Uncompromising Cutthroat, Hardline, Hardshell, Intransigent, Rigid, Strict, Ultra
Unconcealed Open, Pert
Unconcerned Bland, Careless, Casual, Cold, Indifferent, Insouciant, Nonchalant, Strange
Unconditional Absolute, Free, Pure
Unconnected Asyndetic, Detached, Disjointed, Off-line
Unconscious(ness) Asleep, Catalepsy, Cold, Comatose, Instinctive, Non-ego, Not-I, Subliminal, Syncope, Trance, Under
Unconsidered Impetuous, Rash
Unconsummated Mariage blanc
Uncontrolled Adrift, Atactic, Free, Incontinent, Loose, Loose cannon, Wild
Unconventional Beatnik, Bohemian, Drop-out, Eccentric, Gonzo, Heretic, Heterodox, Hippy, Informal, Irregular, Offbeat, Off-the-wall, Original, Outlandish, Outré, Raffish, Spac(e)y, Unorthodox
▷ **Unconventional** *may indicate* an anagram
Unconverted Neat
Unconvincing Farfet(ched), Lame, Thin
Uncoordinated Asynergia, Ataxic, Awkward, Clumsy
Uncorrect Stet
Uncouth(ness) Backwoodsman, Bear, Churlish, Crude, Gothic, Inelegant, Rough, Rube, Rude, Rugged, Uncivil
Uncover(ed) Bare, Disclose, Dismask, Expose, Inoperculate, Open, Overt, Peel, Reveal, Shave, Shill, Shuck, Uncap, Unveil
Unction, Unctuous(ness) Anele, Balm, Chrism, Extreme, Oil(y), Ointment, Oleaginous, Ooze, Smarm, Soapy
Uncultivated, Uncultured Artless, Bundu, Fallow, Ignorant, Incult, Philistine, Rude, Tramontane, Wild
Undamaged Intact, Sound, Whole
Undated Sine die
Undecided Doubtful, Moot, Non-committal, Open-ended, Pending, Pendulous, Uncertain, Wavering
Undefiled Chaste, Clean, Pure, Virgin
Undeniable Fact, Incontestable, Irrefutable
Under Aneath, Below, Beneath, Hypnotized, Hypo-, Sotto, Sub-, Unconscious, Unneath

Underarm Axilla, Lob
Underburnt Samel
Under-butler Bread-chipper
Undercarriage Bogie, Chassis
Undercoat Base, Primer
Undercooked Rare, Raw, Samel
Undercover Espionage, Secret, Veiled
Undercurrent Acheron, Undertone, Undertow
Underdeveloped, Underdevelopment Ateleiosis, Retarded
Underdog Cerberus, Loser, Victim
▸ **Undergarment** *see* UNDERWEAR
Undergo Bear, Dree, Endure, Solvate, Sustain
Undergraduate Fresher, L, Pup, Sizar, Sophomore, Student, Subsizar, Tuft
Underground (group) Basement, Catacomb, Cellar, Fogou, Hell, Hypogaeous, Irgun, Kiva, Macchie, Maquis, Mattamore, Metro, Phreatic, Pict, Plutonia, Pothole, Secret, Souterrain, Subsoil, Subterranean, Subway, Tube
Undergrowth Brush, Chaparral, Firth, Frith, Scrub
Underhand Backstair, Dirty, Haunch, Insidious, Lob, Oblique, Secret, Sinister, Sly, Sneaky, Surreptitious
Underlease Subtack
Underlie, Underlying Subjacent, Subtend
Underline Emphasise, Insist
Underling Bottle-washer, Cog, Inferior, Jack, Menial, Minion, Munchkin, Subordinate
Undermine Erode, Fossick, Sap, Subvert, Tunnel, Weaken
Undernourished Puny, Starveling
Underpass Simplon, Subway
Underside Bed, Soffit
Understand(able), Understanding Accept, Acumen, Agreement, Apprehend, Capeesh, Clear, Cognisable, Comprehend, Conceive, Concept, Cotton-on, Deal, Dig, Enlighten, Entente, Exoteric, Fathom, Follow, Gather, Gauge, Gaum, Geddit, Gorm, Grasp, Have, Head, Heels, Insight, Intuit, Ken, Kind, Knowhow, Learn, Light(s), Omniscient, Pact, Plumb, Prajna, Rapport, Rapprochement, Realise, Savey, Savvy, See, Sense, Sole, Substance, Tolerance, Treaty, Tumble, Twig, Uptak(e), Wisdom, Wit
Understate(d), Understatement Litotes, M(e)iosis, Subtle
Understood Implicit, OK, Perspicuous, Roger, Tacit, Unspoken
Understudy Deputy, Double, Stand-in, Sub
Undertake, Undertaking Attempt, Contract, Covenant, Emprise, Enterprise, Essay, Feat, Guarantee, Pledge, Promise, Scheme, Shoulder, Venture, Warranty
Undertaker Entrepreneur, Mortician, Obligor, Sponsor, Upholder
Under-ten Unit, Yarborough
Undertone Murmur, Rhubarb, Sotto voce
Underwater Demersal
Underwear Balbriggan, Balconette, Bloomers, Bodice, Body, Body stocking, Body suit, Bra(ssiere), Briefs, Broekies, Butt bra, Camiknickers, Camisole, Chemise, Chemisette, Chuddies, Combinations, Combs, Corset, Dainties, Drawers, (French) knickers, Frillies, Girdle, Grundies, Innerwear, Jump, Linen, Lingerie, Linings, Long johns, Pantalets, Pantaloons, Panties, Pantihose, Panty girdle, Petticoat, Scanties, Semmit, Shift, Shorts, Singlet, Skivvy, Slip, Smalls, Stays, Step-ins, Subucula, Suspenders, Tanga, Teddy, Thermal, Trunks, Underdaks, Undergarments,

Underpants, Undershirt, Underthings, Undies, Unmentionables, Vest, Wyliecoat, Y-fronts®

Underworld Chthonic, Criminal, Hades, Hell, Lowlife, Mafia, Shades, Tartar(e), Tartarus, Tartary

Underwrite, Underwritten Assure, Endorse, Guarantee, Insure, Lloyds, PS

Undeserving Immeritous

Undesirable Kibitzer

Undeveloped Backward, Depauperate, Green, Inchoate, Latent, Nubbin, Ridgel, Ridgil, Ridgling, Rig, Riggald, Riglin(g), Rudimentary, Seminal

Undifferentiated Thalliform, Thallus

Undigested Crude

Undignified (end) Disaster, Foot, Improper, Infra dig, Unseemly

Undiluted Neat, Pure, Sheer, Straight

Undiminished Entire, Intact, Whole

Undiplomatic Brusque, Tactless

Undisciplined Hothead, Rule-less, Rulesse, Sloppy, Unruly, Wanton

Undisclosed Hidden, In petto

Undisguised Apert, Clear, Plain

Undistinguished Plebeian

Undivided Aseptate, Complete, Entire, Indiscrete, One

Undo(ing) Annul, Defeat, Destroy, Disconnect, Downfall, Dup, Poop, Poupe, Release, Rescind, Ruin, Unravel

Undoctored Neat

Undone Arrears, Left, Postponed, Ran, Ruined

Undoubtedly Certes, Ipso facto, Positively, Sure

Undress(ed) Bare, Disarray, Disrobe, En cuerpo, Expose, Négligé, Nude, Nue, Peel, Querpo, Raw, Rough, Self-faced, Spar, Strip, Unapparelled

Undulate, Undulating Billow, Nebule, Ripple, Roll, Wave

▷ **Unduly** *may indicate* an anagram

Undyed Greige

Undying Amaranthine, Eternal

Unearth(ly) Astral, Dig, Discover, Disentomb, Exhumate, Indagate

Unease, Uneasiness, Uneasy Angst, Anxious, Creeps, Disquiet, Inquietude, Itchy, Malaise, Queasy, Restive, Shy, Tense, The willies, Uptight, Windy, Womble-cropped

Unedifying Idle

Unembarrassed Blasé, Dégagé

Unemotional Bland, Cool, Iceberg, Matter-of-fact, Sober, Stolid

Unemployed, Unemployment Drone, Idle, Laik, Lake, Latent, Lay-off, Redundant, Residual, Stalko, Surfie

Unending Chronic, Eternal, Lasting, Sempiternal

Unenlightened Ignorant, Nighted

Unenthusiastic Cool, Damp, Tepid

Unenveloped Achlamydeous

Unequal(led) Aniso-, Disparate, Non(e)such, Scalene, Unjust

Unerring Dead, Exact, Precise

Unestablished Free

Unethical Amoral, Corrupt, Immoral

Uneven(ness) Accident, Blotchy, Bumpy, Erose, Irregular, Jaggy, Patchy, Ragged, Scratchy

▷ **Unevenly** *may indicate* an anagram

Unexceptional Ordinary, Workaday
Unexpected(ly) Abrupt, Accidental, Adventitious, Fortuitous, Inopinate, Ironic, Snap, Sodain(e), Sudden, Turn-up, Unawares, Unwary
Unexperienced Strange
Unexplained Obscure
Unexploded Live
Unfading Evergreen, Immarcescible
Unfailing Sure
Unfair Bias(s)ed, Crook, Dirty, Inclement, Invidious, Mean, Partial
Unfaithful Disloyal, Godless, Infidel, Traitor, Two-timing
Unfamiliar New, Quaint, Strange
Unfashionable Cube, Dowdy, Out(moded), Out-of-date, Passé, Square
▷ **Unfashionable** *may indicate* 'in' to be removed
Unfasten Undo, Untie, Untruss
Unfathomable Bottomless
Unfavourable Adverse, Ill, Inimical, Poor, Untoward
Unfeeling Adamant, Callous, Cold, Cruel, Dead, Hard, Inhuman(e), Insensate, Iron-witted, Robotic
Unfinished Crude, Inchoate, Raw, Scabble, Scapple, Stickit
Unfit(ting) Cronk, Disabled, Faulty, Ill, Impair, Inept, Outré, Trefa, Tre(i)f, Unable
▷ **Unfit** *may indicate* an anagram
Unfixed Isotropic, Loose
Unfledged Gull
Unflinching Fast, Staunch
Unfold Deploy, Display, Divulge, Evolve, Interpret, Open, Relate, Spread
Unforced Voluntary
Unforeseen Accident, Sudden
Unfortunate(ly) Accursed, Alack, Alas, Hapless, Ill-starred, Luckless, Shameless, Sorry, Star-crossed, Unlucky, Worse luck
Unfounded Groundless
Unfriendly Aloof, Antagonistic, Asocial, Chill(y), Cold, Fraim, Fremd, Fremit, Hostile, Icy, Remote, Surly
Unfruitful Abortive, Barren, Sterile
Unfulfilled Manqué
Ungainly Awkward, Gawkish, Uncouth, Weedy
Ungenerous Small
Ungodliness, Ungodly Impiety, Pagan, Perfidious, Profane
Ungracious Cold, Mesquin(e), Offhand, Rough, Rude
Ungrammatical Anacoluthia
Ungrateful Ingrate, Snaky
Unguent Nard, Pomade, Salve
Ungulate Antelope, Dinoceras, Eland, Equidae, Hoofed, Moose, Rhino, Ruminantia, Takin, Tapir, Tylopoda
Unhappily, Unhappy, Unhappiness Blue, Depressed, Disconsolate, Dismal, Distress, Doleful, Downcast, Down-hearted, Dysphoria, Glumpish, Love-lorn, Lovesick, Miserable, Sad, Sore, Tearful, Unlief, Upset
▷ **Unhappily** *may indicate* an anagram
Unharmed Safe, Scatheless
Unharness Outspan
Unhealthy Bad, Clinic, Diseased, Epinosic, Insalubrious, Morbid, Noxious, Peaky, Prurient, Sickly

Unholy Profane, Wicked
Unhurried Gradual, Patient
Uniat Maronite, Melchite
Unicorn Ch'i-lin, Coin, Monoceros, Moth, Myth, Narwhal
Unidentified Anon, Anonym(ous), Incognito, Ligure
Unification, Unify(ing) Esemplastic, Henotic, Integrate, Risorgimento, Unite
Uniform Abolla, Alike, Battledress, Consistent, Dress, Equable, Equal, Even, Flat, Forage-cap, Homogeneous, Homomorphic, Identical, Khaki, Kit, Livery, Regimentals, Regular, Rig, Robe, Same, Sole, Standard, Steady, Strip, Unvaried
Unimaginative Banausic, Literalistic, Pedestrian, Pooter
Unimpaired Entire, Intact, Sound
Unimportant Cog, Down-the-line, Expendable, Fiddling, Footling, Frivolous, Idle, Immaterial, Inconsequent, Inconsiderable, Insignificant, MacGuffin, Makeweight, Minnow, Minutiae, Negligible, Nugatory, Peripheral, Petty, Small-time, Trifling, Trivia(l)
Unimpressible Cynical
Uninformed Ingram
Uninhabited Bundu, Deserted, Lonely
Uninhibited Bold, Raunchy
Uninspired Humdrum, Pedestrian, Pompier, Tame
Unintelligent Dumb, Obtuse, Stupid, Witless
Unintelligible Arcane, Code, Greek, Inarticulate
Unintentional Inadvertent, Unwitting
Uninterested, Uninteresting Apathetic, Bland, Dreary, Dry, Dull, Grey, Incurious, Nondescript
Uninterrupted Constant, Continuous, Incessant, Running, Steady
Uninvited Gatecrasher, Interloper, Intruder, Sorner, Trespasser, Umbra
Union(ist) Affiance, African, Allegiance, Alliance, Anschluss, Art, Association, Bed, Benelux, Bond, Close, Combination, Company, Concert, Confederacy, Covalency, Craft, Credit, Customs, Diphthong, Economic, Enosis, Ensemble, Equity, EU, European, Fasciation, Federal, Federation, French, Frithgild, Fusion, Group, Guild, Heterogamy, Horizontal, Impanation, Industrial, Integration, Knight of labour, Latin, Liaison, Liberal, Link-up, Management, Marriage, Match, Merger, NUM, Nuptials, NUR, NUS, NUT, Pan-American, Parabiosis, Pearl, Postal, Print, RU, Rugby, Samiti, Sex, Sherman, Solidarity, Soviet, Splice, Sponsal, Student, Symphysis, Syngamy, Synizesis, Synostosis, Synthesis, Syssarcosis, Teamsters, Tenorrhaphy, → **TRADE UNION**, TU, U, UNISON, USDAW, Uxorial, Verein, Vertical, Vienna, Wedding, Wedlock, Wield, ZANU, Zollverein, Zygosis
Unique(ness) Alone, A-per-se, Hacceity, Inimitable, Irreplaceable, Lone, Matchless, Nonesuch, Nonpareil, Nonsuch, One-off, One(-to)-one, Only, Peerless, Rare, Singular, Sole, Sui generis
Unisex(ual) Epicene, Hermaphrodite
Unison Chorus, Harmony, One, Sync
Unit Abampere, Absolute, Ace, Amp, Angstrom, Archine, Archiphoneme, Astronomical, Bar, Bargaining, Barn, Base, Baud, Becquerel, Bioblast, Biogen, Biophor(e), Bit, Bohr magneton, Brigade, BTU, Byte, Cadre, Calory, Candela, Cell, Cent(i)are, Centimorgan, Centipoise, Chaldron, Chronon, Codon, Cohort, Commune, Congius, Control, Corps, Coulomb, Crith, Cusec, Dalton, Daraf, Darcy, Debye, Degree, Denier, Derived, Dessiatine, Detachment, DIN, Dioptre, Division, Dobson, Dol, Dyne, Echelon, Ecosystem, Electromagnetic, Electron, Electrostatic,

Element, Em, EMU, En, Energid, Ensuite, Episome, Erg, Erlang, Farad, Feedlot, Fermi, Field, Flight, Foot-candle, Foot-lambert, Foot-pound, Foot-ton, Fps, Fresnel, Fundamental, Gal, Gauss, Gestalt, GeV, Gigabit, Gigaflop, Gigahertz, Gigawatt, Gilbert, Glosseme, Gram, Grav, Gray, Hank, Hapu, Hartree, Henry, Hertz, Hide, Hogshead, Holon, Home, Hub, Income, Ion, Item, Jansky, Joule, K, Katal, Kelvin, Kilderkin, Kilerg, Kilowatt, Lambert, Langley, Last, League, Lexeme, Lumen, Lux, Maceral, Magneton, Man-hour, Maxwell, Measure, Megabyte, Megahertz, Megaton, Megawatt, Megohm, Message, Metre, Mho, Micella, Micelle, Microcurie, Microinch, Micron, Mil, Module, Mole, Monad, Monetary, Mongo(e), Morgen, Morpheme, Mutchkin, Neper, Nepit, Nest, Newton, Nit, Octa, Oersted, Ohm, Okta, Organelle, Panzer, Parasang, Pascal, Ped, Peninsular, Pennyweight, Period, Peripheral, Phoneme, Phot, Phyton, Pica, Pixel, Ploughgate, Point, Poise, Pond, Poundal, Power, Practical, Probit, Protoplast, Qubit, RA, Radian, Rem, Remen, Rep, Ro(e)ntgen, Rood, Rutherford, Sabin, Sealed, Second, Secure, Semeion, Sememe, Shed, SI, Siemens, Sievert, Singleton, Sink, Slug, Sone, Steradian, Stere, Stilb, Stock, Stoke(s), Strontium, Syllable, Syntagm(a), TA, Tagmeme, Terabyte, Teraflop, Terminal, Tesla, Tetrapody, Tex, Theme, Therblig, Therm, Timocracy, Tog, Token, Torr, Tower, Tripody, Vanitory, Vanity, Var, Vara, Volt, Wall, Watt, Watt-hour, Weber, Wing, X, Yrneh

Unitarian Arian, Paulian, Racovian, Socinian

Unite(d), Unity Accrete, Bind, Coalesce, Combine, Concordant, Connate, Connect, Consolidate, Consubstantiate, Covalent, Ecumenical, Fay, Federal, Federalise, Federate, Fuse, Gene, Graft, Injoint, Inosculate, Join, Kingdom, Knit, Lap, Link, Marry, Meint, Meng, Ment, Merge, Meynt, Ming, Nations, Oop, Oup, Siamese, Solid, States, Tie, Unify, → **WED**, Weld, Yoke

United Ireland Fine Gael

United Kingdom Old Dart, UK

Unity Harmony, One, Solidarity, Sympathy, Togetherness

Univalent Monatomic

Universal, Universe All, Catholic, Cosmos, Creation, Ecumenic(al), Emma, Expanding, General, Global, Infinite, Inflationary, Island, Macrocosm, Mandala, Microcosm, Oscillating, Sphere, U, Via Lactea, World(wide)

University Academe, Academy, Alma mater, Aston, Berkeley, Bonn, Brown, Campus, Civic, College, Columbia, Cornell, Dartmouth, Exeter, Gown, Harvard, Ivy League, Open, OU, Oxbridge, Pennsylvania, Princeton, Reading, Redbrick, St Andrews, Sorbonne, Stamford, Varsity, Whare wanaga, Wittenberg, Yale

Unjust(ified) Groundless, Inequity, Iniquitous, Invalid, Tyrannical

Unkempt Dishevelled, Greebo, Mal soigné, Raddled, Ragged, Raggle-taggle, Scody, Scraggy, Scuzzy, Shaggy, Tousy, Touzy, Towsy, Towzy

Unknown Agnostic, Anon, A.N. Other, Hidden, Ign, Incog(nito), Inconnu, N, Nobody, Noumenon, Occult, Quantity, Secret, Soldier, Strange, Symbolic, Tertium quid, Unchartered, Untold, Warrior, X, Y

Unleavened Azymous

Unless Nisi, Save, Without

Unliable Exempt

Unlicensed Illicit

Unlike(ly) Difform, Disparate, Dubious, Far-fetched, Improbable, Inauspicious, Long shot, Outsider, Remote, Tall, Unlich

Unlimited Almighty, Boundless, Indefinite, Measureless, Nth, Universal, Vast

Unlisted Ex-directory

Unload Disburden, Discharge, Drop, Dump, Jettison, Land, Strip

Unlock(ed) Bald

Unlucky Donsie, Hapless, Ill(-starred), Inauspicious, Infaust, Jonah, Misadventure, Misfallen, S(c)hlimazel, Sinister, Stiff, Thirteen, Untoward, Wanchancie, Wanchancy

Unman Castrate

Unmannerly Crude, Discourteous, Impolite, Low bred, Rude

Unmarried Bachelor, Common-law, Single, Spinster

Unmask Expose, Rumble

Unmatched Bye, Champion, Orra, Unique

Unmentionable(s) Bra, Foul, No-no, Secret, → UNDERWEAR, Undies

Unmindful Heedless, Oblivious

Unmistakable Clear, Manifest, Plain

Unmitigated Absolute, Arrant, Sheer, Ultra

Unmixed Me(a)re, Meer, Neat, Nett, Pure, Raw, Straight

Unmoved, Unmoving Adamant, Doggo, Firm, Serene, Static, Stolid

Unnamed Anon

Unnatural Abnormal, Affected, Cataphysical, Contrived, Eerie, Flat, Geep, Irregular, Strange

▷ **Unnaturally** *may indicate* an anagram

Unnecessary De trop, Extra, Gash, Gratuitous, Needless, Otiose, Redundant, Superfluous

Unnerve, Unnerving Discouraging, Eerie, Rattle

Unobserved Backstage, Sly, Unseen

Unobtainable Nemesis

Unobtrusive Low profile

Unoccupied Empty, Idle, Otiose, Vacant, Void

Unofficial Disestablish, Fringe, Wildcat

Unoriginal Banal, Copy, Derivative, Imitation, Plagiarised, Slavish

Unorthodox Heretic, Heterodox, Maverick, Off-beat, Off-the-wall, Unconventional

▷ **Unorthodox** *may indicate* an anagram

Unpaid Amateur, Brevet, Hon(orary), Outstanding, Voluntary

Unpaired Azygous, Bye

Unpalatable Acid, Bitter, Unsavoury

Unparalleled Supreme, Unique

Unpartitioned Aseptate

Unperturbed Bland, Calm, Serene

Unplanned Impromptu, Improvised, Spontaneous

Unpleasant, Unpleasant person Cow, Creep, Fink, God-awful, Grim, Grotty, Gruesome, Harsh, Hoor, Horrible, Icky, Insalubrious, Invidious, Nasty, Obnoxious, Odious, Offensive, Painful, Pejorative, Rank, Rebarbative, Shady, Shitty, Shocker, Snarky, Sticky, Thorny, Toerag, Wart

Unploughed Lea-rig

Unpolluted Sterile

Unpopular Detested, Hat(e)able

Unpractical Futile, Orra

Unpredictable Aleatory, Dicy, Erratic, Maverick, Wild card

Unprepared Ad lib, Extempore, Impromptu, Last minute, Unready

Unpretentious Quiet

Unprincipled Amoral, Dishonest, Irregular, Reprobate, Unscrupulous

Unproductive Arid, Atokal, Atokous, Barren, Dead-head, Eild, Fallow, Futile, Lean, Poor, Shy, Sterile, Yeld, Yell

Unprofitable Bootless, Fruitless, Lean, Thankless, Wasted
Unprogressive Inert, Square
Unprotected Exposed, Nude, Vulnerable
Unpublished Inedited
Unpunctual Tardy
Unqualified Absolute, Entire, Outright, Perfect, Profound, Pure, Quack, Sheer, Straight, Thorough, Total, Utter
Unquestionably, Unquestioning Absolute, Certain, Doubtless, Implicit
Unravel(ling) Construe, Denouement, Disentangle, Feaze, Fray, Solve
Unreadable Poker-faced
Unready Unripe
Unreal(istic) Eidetic, En l'air, Escapist, Fake, Fancied, Illusory, Insubstantial, Mirage, Oneiric, Phantom, Phon(e)y, Planet Zog, Pseudo, Romantic, Sham, Spurious
Unreasonable, Unreasoning Absurd, Bigot, Extreme, Illogical, Irrational, Misguided, Perverse, Rabid, Steep
Unrecognised Incognito, Inconnu, Invalid, Thankless, Unsung
Unrefined Coarse, Common, Crude, Earthy, Gur, Impure, Rude, Vul(g), Vulgar
Unrehearsed Extempore, Impromptu
Unrelenting Implacable, Remorseless, Severe, Stern
Unreliable Dodgy, Dubious, Erratic, Fair-weather, Fickle, Flighty, Fly-by-night, Shonky, Unstable, Wankle, Weak sister, Wonky
Unremarkable Nondescript
Unremitting Dogged, Intensive
Unresponsive Aloof, Cold, Frigid, Nastic, Rigor
Unrest Discontent, Ferment
Unrestrained Effusive, Extravagant, Free, Hearty, Homeric, Immoderate, Incontinent, Lax, Lowsit, Rampant, Wanton, Wild
Unreturnable Ace
Unrighteousness Adharma
Unrivalled Nonesuch
Unromantic Classic(al), Mundane
Unruffled Calm, Placid, Serene, Smooth, Tranquil
Unruly Anarchic, Bodgie, Buckie, Camstairy, Camsteary, Camsteerie, Coltish, Exception, Fractious, Lawless, Obstreperous, Obstropalous, Ragd(e), Raged, Ragged, Rambunctious, Rampageous, Rattlebag, Riotous, Tartar, Turbulent, Turk, Wanton, Wayward, Zoo
▷ **Unruly** *may indicate* an anagram
Unsafe Deathtrap, Fishy, Insecure, Perilous, Precarious, Vulnerable
Unsatisfactory, Unsatisfying Bad, Lame, Lousy, Meagre, Rocky, Thin, Wanting
Unsavoury Epinosic
Unscramble Decode, Decrypt
Unscripted Ad lib
Unscrupulous Chancer, Rascally, Slippery
Unseasonable, Unseasoned Green, Murken, Raw, Untimely
Unseat Depose, Dethrone, Oust, Overset, Overthrow, Throw
Unseemly Coarse, Improper, Incivil, Indecent, Indecorous, Indign, Seedy, Untoward
Unselfish Altruist, Generous
Unsent Square
Unsettle(d) Faze, Homeless, Hunky, Indecisive, Nervous, Outstanding, Queasy, Restive, Restless, Troublous

▷ **Unsettled** *may indicate* an anagram

Unsexy N, Neuter

Unsheltered Bleak, Exposed, Homeless

Unsight(ed), Unsightly Eyeless, Hideous, Repulsive, Ugly

Unsinning Impeccable, Pure

Unskilled Awkward, Dilutee, Gauche, Green, Inexpert, Raw, Rude

Unsmiling Agelastic

Unsociable Anchoretic, Grouchy, Solitary, Stay-at-home

Unsophisticated Alf, Boondocks, Boonies, Bushie, Cornball, Corny, Cracker-barrel, Direct, Down-home, Faux-naïf, Hillbilly, Homebred, Homespun, Inurbane, Jaap, Jay, Naive, Provincial, Rube, Rustic, Verdant

Unsound Barmy, Infirm, Invalid, Shaky, Wildcat, Wonky

▷ **Unsound** *may indicate* an anagram

Unsparing Severe

Unspeakable Dreadful, Ineffable, Nefandous

Unspecific, Unspecified General, Generic, Somehow, Such, Vague

Unspoiled, Unspoilt Innocent, Natural, Perfect, Pristine, Pure

Unspoken Silent, Tacit

Unstable, Unsteady Anomic, Astatic, Bockedy, Casual, Crank, Crank(y), Dicky, Erratic, Flexuose, Flexuous, Fluidal, Giddy, Groggy, Infirm, Insecure, Labile, Rickety, Shaky, Shifty, Slippy, Tickle, Top-heavy, Tottery, Totty, Variable, Volatile, Walty, Wambling, Wankle, Warby, Wobbly

Unstated Concordat, Tacit, Unknown

▸ **Unsteady** *see* **UNSTABLE**

Unstressed Enclitic

▷ **Unstuck** *may indicate* an anagram

Unsubstantial Aeriform, Airy, Flimsy, Paltry, Shadowy, Slight, Thin, Yeasty

Unsuccessful Abortive, Futile, Joyless, Manqué, Vain

Unsuitable Ill-timed, Impair, Improper, Inapt, Incongruous, Inexpedient, Malapropos, Unbecoming, Unfit

Unsupported, Unsupportable Astylar, Floating, Stroppy, Unfounded

Unsure Hesitant, Tentative

Unsurpassed All-time, Best, Supreme

Unsuspecting Credulous, Innocent, Naive

Unsweetened Brut, Natural

Unsymmetrical Heterauxesis(m), Irregular, Lopsided

Unsympathetic Short shrift

Unthinking Mechanical

Untidy Daggy, Dishevelled, Dowd(y), Frowzy, Litterbug, Ragged, Raunchy, Scruff(y), Slipshod, Slovenly, Tatty

▷ **Untidy** *may indicate* an anagram

Untie Free, Undo, Unlace

Until Hasta

Untilled Fallow

Untiring Assiduous

Untold Secret, Umpteen, Unread, Unred, Vast

Untouchable Burakumin, Dalit, Harijan, Immune, Sacrosanct, Sealed

Untouched Intact, Inviolate, Pristine, Virgin

▷ **Untrained** *may indicate* 'BR' to be removed

Untried New, Virgin

Untroubled Insouciant

Untrue, Untruth Apocryphal, Eccentric, Fabrication, Faithless, False(hood), Lie, Prefabrication, Unleal

Untrustworthy Dishonest, Fickle, Fly-by-night, Mamzer, Momzer, Shifty, Sleeky, Tricky

Untypical Anomalous, Etypic(al), Isolated, Unusual

Unused, Unusable Impracticable, New, Over, Wasted

Unusual(ly) Abnormal, Atypical, Exceptional, Extra(ordinary), Freak, New, Novel, Odd, Offbeat, Out-of-the-way, Outré, Particular, Queer, Rare, Remarkable, Singular, Special, → **STRANGE**, Unco, Unique, Untypical, Unwonted

▷ **Unusual** *may indicate* an anagram

Unutterable Ineffable

Unvarying Constant, Eternal, Monotonous, Stable, Static, Uniform

Unveil Expose, Honour

Unvoiced Surd

Unwanted De trop, Exile, Gooseberry, Nimby, Outcast, Sorn

Unwashed Grubby

Unwavering Steadfast

Unwed Celibate, Single

Unwelcome, Unwelcoming Frosty, Icy, Lulu, Obtrusive, (Persona) Non grata

Unwell Ailing, Crook, Dicky, Ill, Impure, Poorly, Quazzy, Queasy, Seedy, Shouse, Toxic

Unwholesome Insalutary, Miasmous, Morbid, Noxious

Unwieldy Cumbersome, Elephantine

Unwilling(ness) Averse, Disinclined, Intestate, Loath, Loth, Nolition, Nolo, Obdurate, Perforce, Reluctant

Unwind Relax, Straighten, Unclew, Unreave, Unreeve

▷ **Unwind** *may indicate* an anagram

Unwinnable Catch 22

Unwise Foolish, Ill-advised, Ill-judged, Impolitic, Imprudent, Inexpedient, Injudicious, Rash

Unwitting Accidental, Nescient

Unwonted Inusitate

Unworkable Impossible, Inoperable

Unworried Carefree

Unworthy Below, Beneath, Indign, Inferior, Infra dig

Unwritten Verbal

Unyielding Adamant, Eild, Firm, Hardline, Inexorable, Inextensible, Intransigent, Obdurate, Rigid, Steely, Stubborn, Tough, Unalterable

Unyoke Outspan

Up(on), Upturned, Upper, Uppish A, Acockbill, Afoot, Antidepressant, Arrogant, Astir, Astray, Astride, Cloud-kissing, Erect, Euphoric, Heavenward, Hep, Horsed, Incitant, Off, On, Overhead, Primo, Range, Ride, Riding, Risen, Skyward, Speed, → **UPPER CLASS**, Vamp, Ventral

Up-anchor Atrip, Weigh

Upbeat Anacrusis, Arsis

Upbraid Abuse, Rebuke, Reproach, Reprove, Scold, Storm, Twit

Upcountry Anabasis, Inland

Update Brief, Renew, Report, Sitrep

Upfront Open

Upheaval Cataclysm, Chaos, Eruption, Rummage, Seismic, Shake out, Stir

▷ **Upheld** *may indicate* 'up' in another word

Uphill Arduous, Borstal, Sisyphean

Uphold Assert, Defend, Maintain

Upholstery Lampas, Moquette, Trim

Upkeep Support

Upland(s) Alps, Downs, Hilly, Wold

Uplift Boost, Edify, Elate, Elevation, Exalt, Hoist, Levitation, Sky

Upper class, Upper crust Aristocrat, County, Crachach, Nobility, Patrician, Posh, Sial, Top-hat, Tweedy, U

Upright(s), Uprightness Aclinic, Anend, Apeak, Apeek, Aplomb, Arrect, Atrip, Erect, Goalpost, Honest, Incorrupt, Jamb, Joanna, Merlon, Moral, Mullion, Orthograde, Perpendicular, Piano, Pilaster(s), Post, Rectitude, Roman, Splat, Stanchion, Stares, Stile, Stud, Vertical, Virtuous

Uprising Incline, Intifada, Meerut, Rebellion, Revolt, Tumulus

Uproar(ious) Ballyhoo, Bedlam, Blatancy, Brouhaha, Charivari, Clamour, Clangour, Collieshangie, Commotion, Cry, Din, Dirdam, Dirdum, Durdum, Emeute, Ferment, Flaw, Fracas, Furore, Garboil, Hell, Hoopla, Hubbub(oo), Hullabaloo, Hurly(-burly), Imbroglio, Katzenjammer, Madhouse, Noise, Noyes, Outcry, Pandemonium, Racket, Raird, Randan, Reird, Riotous, Roister, Romage, Rowdedow, Rowdydow(dy), Ruckus, Ruction, Rumpus, Shemozzle, Stramash, Turmoil, Utis, Whoobub

Uproot Deracinate, Eradicate, Evict, Outweed, Supplant, Weed

Upset(ting) Aggrieve, Alarm, Applecart, Bother, Capsize, Catastrophe, Choked, Coup, Cowp, Crank, Derange, Dip, Discomboberate, Discombobulate, Discomfit, Discomfort, Discommode, Disconcert, Dismay, Disquiet, Distraught, Disturb, Dod, Eat, Fuss, Heart-rending, Inversion, Keel, Miff, Nauseative, Offend, Overthrow, Overturn, Peeve, Perturb, Pip, Pother, Purl, Rattle, Rile, Ruffle, Rumple, Sad, Seel, Shake, Sore, Spill, Tapsalteerie, Tip, Topple, Trauma, Undo, Unsettled

▷ **Upset** *may indicate* an anagram; a word upside down; or 'tes'

Upshot Outcome, Result, Sequel

Upside down Inverted, Resupinate, Tapsie-teerie, Topsy-turvy

Upstart Buckeen, Jumped-up, Mushroom, Parvenu, Vulgarian

▷ **Upstart** *may indicate* 'u'

Upstream Thermal

Upsurge Thrust, Waste

Uptake Shrewdness, Understanding, Wit

Up to Till, Until

Up-to-date Abreast, Contemporary, Current, Mod, New-fashioned, Right-on, State-of-the-art, Swinging, Topical, Trendy

Upwards Acclivious, Aloft, Antrorse, Cabré

Uranium Depleted, Pitchblende, U, Yellowcake

Urban Civic, Megalopolis, Municipal, Town

Urbane Civil, Debonair, Refined, Townly

Urchin Arab, Brat, Crinoid, Crossfish, Cystoid, Echinoderm, Echinoidea, Echinus, Gamin, Guttersnipe, Gutty, Heart, Mudlark, Nipper, Pluteus, Ragamuffin, Sand-dollar, Sea, Sea-egg, Spatangoidea, Spatangus, Street-arab, Townskip

Urge, Urgent Admonish, Ca, Coax, Constrain, Crying, Dire, Drive, Egg, Enjoin, Exhort, Exigent, Goad, Hard, Hie, Hoick, Hunger, Hurry, Id, Immediate, Impel, Impulse, Incense, Incite, Insist(ent), Instance, Instigate, Itch, Kick, Libido, Nag, Peremptory, Persuade, Press(ing), Prod, Push, Scrub, Set on, Spur, Strenuous, Strident, Strong, Threapit, Threepit, Wanderlust, Whig, Yen

▷ **Urgent** *may indicate* 'Ur-gent', viz. Iraqi

Uriah Hittite, Humble, Umble

Urinal Bog, John, Jordan, → LAVATORY, Loo, Pissoir

Urinate, Urine Chamber-lye, Emiction, Enuresis, Lant, Leak, Micturition, Number one, Oliguria, Pee, Piddle, Piss, Planuria, Relieve, Slash, Stale, Strangury, Tiddle, Werris (Creek), Widdle

Urn(s), Urn-shaped Canopic, Cinerarium, Ewer, Grecian, Lachrymal, Olla, Ossuary, Samovar, Storied, Tea, Urceolate, Vase

Us 's, UK, Uns, We

Usage, Use(r), Used, Utilise Application, Apply, Avail, Boot, Consume, Custom, Deploy, Dow, → EMPLOY, End, Ex, Exercise, Exert, Expend, Exploit, Flesh, Habit, Hand-me-down, Inured, Manner, Ply, Practice, Sarum, Spare, Spent, Sport, Take, Tradition, Treat, Try, Ure, Wield, With, Wont

Useful Asset, Availing, Commodity, Dow, Expedient, Invaluable

Useless Base, Bung, Cumber, Cumber-ground, Dead-wood, Dud, Empty, Futile, Gewgaw, Grotty, Ground, Idle, Inane, Ineffective, Lame, Lemon, Nonstarter, Otiose, Plug, Sculpin, Sterile, Swap, US, Vain, Void, Wet

Usher Black Rod, Blue Rod, Chobdar, Commissionaire, Conduct(or), Doorman, Escort, Guide, Herald, Huissier, Macer, Rod, Show, Steward

Usual Common, Customary, Habit(ual), Natural, Normal, Ordinary, Routine, Rule, Solito, Standard, Stock, Typical, Wont

Usurer, Usury Gombeen, Lender, Loanshark, Moneylender, Note-shaver, Shark, Uncle

Usurp(er) Abator, Arrogate, Encroach, Invade

Ut As, Doh, Utah

Utah Ut

Utensil(s) Batterie, Battery, Canteen, Chopsticks, Colander, Cookware, Corer, Double boiler, Fish-kettle, Fork, Funnel, Gadget, Grater, Gridiron, Holloware, Implement, Instrument, Jagger, Knife, Mandolin(e), Ricer, Scoop, Skillet, Spatula, Spoon, Things, Tool, Whisk, Zester

▶ **Utilise** *see* USE

Utilitarian Benthamite, Mill, Practical, Useful

Utility Elec(tricity), Expected, Gas, Public, Water

Utmost Best, Extreme, Farthest, Maximum, Nth

Utopia(n) Adland, Cloud-cuckoo-land, Ideal, Pantisocracy, Paradise, Perfect, Shangri-la

Utter(ance), Uttered, Utterly Absolute, Accent, Agrapha, Agraphon, Aread, Arrant, Cry, Dead, Deliver, Dictum, Dog, Downright, Ejaculate, Emit, Enunciate, Express, Extreme, Glossolalia, Issue, Judgement, Lenes, Lenis, Locution, Mint, Most, Oracle, Pass, Phonate, Pronounce, Pure, Quo(th), Rank, Rap, Rattle, Remark, Saw, → SAY, Sheer, Speak, Spout, Stark, State, Syllable, Tell, Vend, Vent, Very, Voice

Uvula Staphyle

Vv

V Anti, Bomb, Del, Five, Nabla, See, Sign, Verb, Verse, Versus, Victor(y), Volt, Volume

Vacancy, Vacant Blank, Empty, Glassy, Hole, Hollow, Inane, Place, Space, Vacuum

Vacation Holiday, Leave, Long, Non-term, Outing, Recess, Trip, Voidance

Vaccination, Vaccine Antigen, Antiserum, Bacterin, Cure, HIB, Jenner, MMR, Sabin, Salk, Serum, Subunit

Vacillate, Vacillating Chop, Dither, Feeble, Hesitate, Shilly-shally, Trimmer, Wabble, Wave(r), Whiffle

Vacuous Blank, Empty, Toom, Vacant

Vacuum Blank, Cleaner, Dewar, Emptiness, Magnetron, Nothing, Plenum, Thermos®, Torricellian, Ultra-high, Void

Vade-mecum Ench(e)iridion, Notebook

Vagabond Bergie, Gadling, → **GYPSY**, Hobo, Landlo(u)per, Outcast, Rapparee, Romany, Rover, Runabout, Runagate, Tramp

Vagrant Beachcomber, Bum, Bummer, Caird, Crusty, Derro, Dosser, Drifter, Gangrel, Gang-there-out, Goliard, Gypsy, Hobo, Landlo(u)per, Lazzarone, Nomad, Patercove, Pikey, Rinthereout, Rogue, Romany, Scatterling, Strag, Straggle, Stroller, Swagman, Tinker, → **TRAMP**, Truant, Walker

Vague(ness) Amorphous, Bleary, Blur, Confused, Dim, Equivocal, Hazy, Ill-defined, Ill-headed, Indeterminate, Indistinct, Loose, Mist, Nebulous, Shadowy, Woolly-minded

▷ **Vaguely** *may indicate* an anagram

Vain Bootless, Coxcomb, Coxcomical, Egoistic, Empty, Fruitless, → **FUTILE**, Hollow, Idle, Peacock, Pompous, Profitless, Proud, Strutting, Unuseful, Useless, Vogie

Vainglory Panache

Valance Pand, Pelmet

Vale Addio, Adieu, Cheerio, Coomb, Dean, Dedham, Dene, Ebbw, Enna, Evesham, Glen, Ta-ta, Tempé, Valley

Valediction, Valedictory Apopemptic, Cheerio, Farewell

Valentine Card, Sweetheart

Valerian All-heal, Cetywall, Greek, Red, Setuale, Setwale, Setwall, Spur

Valet Aid, Andrew, Gentleman's gentleman, Jeames, Jeeves, Man, Passepartout, Quint, Servant, Skip-kennel

Valetudinarian Hypochondriac, Invalid

Valiant Brave, Doughty, Heroic, Resolute, Stalwart, Stouthearted, Wight

Valid(ity), Validate Confirm, Establish, Just, Legal, Probate, Rational, Sound

Valise Bag, Case, Dorlach, Satchel

Valkyrie Brynhild

Valley Ajalon, Aosta, Baca, Barossa, Bekaa, Beqaa, Bolson, Cleavage, Clough, Comb(e), Coomb, Cwm, Dale, Dargle, Dean, Death, Defile, Dell, Den, Dene, Dingle, Dip, Drowned, Dry, Gehenna, Ghyll, Glen, Glencoe, Glyn, Graben, Great Glen,

Great Rift, Grindelwald, Hanging, Haugh, Heuch, Hollow, Hope, Humiliation, Hutt, Ladin, Lagan, Lallan, Nemea, Olympia, Ravine, Rhondda, Ria, Rift, San Fernando, Seaton, Silicon, Slack, Slade, Strath(spey), Tempe, Tophet, Trossachs, Umbria, U-shaped, Valdarno, Vale, Vallambrosa, Water, Water gap, Yosemite

Valour Bravery, Courage, Heroism, Merit, Prowess

Valuable, Valuation, Value(s) Absolute, Acid, Appraise, Appreciate, Apprize, Assess(ment), Asset, Bargain, Book, Break up, Calibrate, Carbon, Checksum, Cherish, CIF, Cop, Cost, Crossover, Datum, Denomination, Equity, Esteem, Estimate, Expected, Face, Feck, Hagberg, Intrinsic, Limit, Market, Modulus, Net present, Net realizable, Nominal, Nuisance, Omnium, Par, pH, Place, Precious, Premium, Present, Price, Prize, Prys, Q, Quartile, Rarity, Rate, Rateable, Rating, Regard, Residual, Respect, Rogue, Salt, Sentimental, Set, Snob, Steem, Stent, Store, Street, Surrender, Taonga, Time, Treasure, Tristimulus, Truth, Valuta, → **WORTH**

Valueless Bum, Fig, Mare's nest, Orra, Useless, Worthless

Valve Acorn, Air, Aortic, Ball, Bicuspid, Bleed, Blow, Butterfly, Check, Clack, Cock, Drawgate, Dynatron, Escape, Exhaust, Flip-flop, Foot, Gate, Induction, Magnetron, Mitral, Mixing, Needle, Non-return, Pallet, Pentode, Petcock, Piston, Poppet, Pulmonary, Puppet, Radio, Resnatron, Safety, Seacock, Semilunar, Shut-off, Side, Sleeve, Slide, Sluice, Sluicegate, Snifter, Snifting, Stopcock, Suction, Tap, Tetrode, Thermionic, Throttle, Thyratron, Triode, Turncock, Vacuum, Ventil, Vibroton

Vamoose Abscond, Decamp, Scat, Scram

Vamp Adlib, Charm, Rehash, Seduce, Siren, Strum, Twiddle

Vampire Bat, Dracula, False, Ghoul, Lamia, Lilith, Pontianak, Stringes

Van(guard) Advance, Box-car, Brake, Breakdown, Camper, Cart, Cube, Delivery, Dormobile®, Forefront, Foremost, Front, Furniture, Guard's, Head, Kombi®, Lead, Leader(s), Lorry, Loudspeaker, Luggage, Meat wagon, Panel, Panel-truck, Pantechnicon, Patrol-wagon, Prison, Removal, Spearhead, Truck, Ute, Wagon

Vanadium V

Vandal(ise), Vandalism Desecrate, Hooligan, Hun, Loot, Pillage, Ravage, Rough, Sab(oteur), Sack, Saracen, Skinhead, Slash, Trash

Vandyke Beard, Painter

Vane(s) Dog, Fan, Guide, Rudder, Swirl, Telltale, Vexillum, Weather(cock), Web, Wind (tee), Wing

Vanessa Butterfly

Vanilla Pinole

Vanish(ed), Vanishing Cease, Disappear, Disperse, Dissolve, Evanesce(nt), Evaporate, Extinct, Faint(ed), Mizzle, Slope, Transitory, Unbe

Vanity Amour-propre, Arrogance, Ego, Esteem, Futility, Pomp, Pretension, Pride, Self-conceit, Self-esteem

Vanquish Beat, Conquer, Floor, Master, Overcome, Rout

Vantage (point) Ascendancy, Coign(e), Height

Vaporise, Vapour Boil, Cloud, Contrail, Effluent, Fog, Fume, Halitus, Iodine, Miasma, Mist, Reek, Roke, Skywriting, → **STEAM**, Steme, Water

▸ **Variable, Variance, Variant, Variation** *see* **VARY**

Varicose Haemorrhoids

▸ **Varied, Variety** *see* **VARY**

▷ **Varied** *may indicate* an anagram

Variegate(d) Calico, Dappled, Flecked, Fretted, Motley, Mottle, Pied, Rainbow, Skewbald, Tissue

▷ **Variety of** *may indicate* an anagram

Various Divers(e), Manifold, Multifarious, Separate, Several, Sundry

Various years Vy

Varlet Cad, Knave, Rascal, Rogue

Varnish(ing) Arar, Bee-glue, Copal, Cowdie-gum, Dam(m)ar, Desert, Dope, Dragon's-blood, Glair, Japan, Lacquer, Lentisk, Nail, Nibs, Oil, Resin, Sandarac, Shellac, Spirit, Tung-oil, Tung-tree, Vernis martin, Vernissage

Vary(ing), Variable, Variance, Variant, Variation, Varied, Variety Ablaut, Aelotropy, Alter, Amphoteric, Assortment, Breed, Brew, Cepheid, Change, Chequered, Colour, Contrapuntal, Counterpoint, Daedal(e), Dedal, Dependent, Differ, Discrepancy, Diverse, Diversity, Dummy, Eclectic, Eclipsing, Enigma, Farraginous, Fickle, Fluctuating, Form, Grid, Iid, Inconsistent, Inconstant, Independent, Intervening, Isochor, Isopleth, Isotopy, Line, Local, Medley, Mix, Morph, Morphosis, Multifarious, Multiplicity, Music hall, Mutable, Nimrod, Nuance, Olio, Omniform, Orthogenesis, Parametric, Partita, Protean, Random, Remedy, Response, Smörgåsbord, Sort, Species, Spice, Sport, Stirps, Stochastic, Strain, String, Timeserver, Tolerance, Twistor, Var, Versatile, Versiform, Version, Vicissitude, Vl, Wane, Wax, X, Y, Z

Vase Bronteum, Canopus, Cornucopia, Diota, Hydria, Jardinière, Kalpis, Lachrymal, Lecythus, Lekythos, Moon flask, Murr(h)a, Portland, Pot, Potiche, Stamnos, Urn, Vessel

Vasectomy Desexing

Vassal Client, Daimio, Feoffee, Lackey, Liege, Liegeman, Man, Manred, Servant, Vavaso(u)r

Vast(ness) Big, Cosmic, Cyclopic, Enormous, Epic, Extensive, Huge(ous), Immense, Mighty, Monumental, Ocean, Prodigious

Vat Back, Barrel, Blunger, Chessel, Copper, Cowl, Cuvée, Fat, Girnel, Keir, Kier, Pressfat, Stand, Tank, Tan-pit, Tub, Tun, Winefat

Vatican Rome, V

Vaudeville Zarzuela

Vaughan Silurist

Vault(ed), Vaulting Arch, Barrel, Cavern, Cellar, Chamber, Charnel house, Clear, Cross, Crypt, Cul-de-four, Cupola, Dome, Dungeon, Fan, Firmament, Fornicate, Groin, Hypogeum, Jump, Kiva, Leap(frog), Lierne, Mausoleum, Ossuary, Palm, Pend, Pendentive, Pole, Rib, Safe, Sepulchre, Serdab, Severy, Shade, Souterrain, Tholus, Tomb, Tunnel, Underpitch, Vaut, Wagon, Weem, Wine

▷ **Vault** *may indicate* an anagram

Vaunt Boast, Brag, Crow

Veal Escalope, Fricandeau, Galantine, Scallop, Schnitzel, Wiener schnitzel

Vector, Vector operator Dyad, Nabla, Phasor, Polar, Radius

Veda Yajurveda

Veer Bag, Boxhaul, Broach, Deviate, Draw, Gybe, Splay, Swerve, Tack, Turn, Wear, Yaw

Vegan Parev(e), Parve

Vegetable(s) Alexanders, Allium, Artichoke, Asparagus, Aubergine, Beans, Beet(root), Borecole, Brassica, Broccoli, Cabbage, Calabrese, Calaloo, Calalu, Cardoon, Carrot, Castock, Cataloo, Catalu, Cauliflower, Celeriac, Celery, Chard, Chicory, Chiffonade, Chive, Choko, Chufa, Cocoyam, Colcannon, Cole, Collard, Corn-on-the-cob, Coulis, Courgette, Crout, Cucumber, Custock, Daikon, Endive, Escarole, Eschalot, Fennel, Finocchio, Flora, Garlic, Gherkin, Greens, Guar, Hastings, Inert, Ingan, Jardinière, Jerusalem artichoke, Jicama, Kale, Kohlrabi, Kumara, Kumera, Lablab, Leek, Legume(n), Lettuce, Macedoine, Mangel(-wurzel), Mangetout, Mangold, Marrow(-squash), Mato(o)ke, Mirepoix, Mooli, Navew, Neep,

Oca, Okra, Okro, Olitory, Onion, Orach(e), Parsnip, Pea(se), Pepper, Pimento, Plant, Pomato, Potato, Pottage, Pratie, Primavera, Pulse, Pumpkin, Quinoa, Radicchio, Radish, Rapini, Ratatouille, Rocambole, Root, Rutabaga, Sabji, Salad, Salsify, Samphire, Sauce, Sauerkraut, Savoy, Scorzonera, Shallot, Sibol, Sium, Skirret, Sorrel, Spinach(-beet), Spinage, Sprouts, Spud, Squash, String bean, Succotash, Swede, Sweet corn, Sweet potato, Taro, Tomato, Tonka-bean, Triffid, Truck, Turnip, Udo, Witloof, Wort, Yam, Zucchini

Vegetable extract Solanine

Vegetarian Herbivore, Maigre, Meatless, Parev(e), Parve, Pythagorean, Vegan, Veggie

Vegetate, Vegetator, Vegetation Alga, Brush, Cover, Flora, Fynbos, Gar(r)igue, Greenery, Herb, Lemna, Maquis, Quadrat, Scrub, Stagnate, Sudd, Transect

Vehemence, Vehement(ly) Amain, Ardent, Fervid, Forcible, Frenzy, Heat, Hot, Intense, Violent

Vehicle Ambulance, Amtrack, Artic, Articulated, ATV, Autocycle, Autorickshaw, Brake, Brancard, Buckboard, Buggy, Bus, Cab, Camper, Car, Caravan, Carry-all, Cart, Casspir, Channel, Chariot, Commercial, Conveyance, Crate, Curricle, Cycle, Delta, Dennet, Dog-cart, Dormobile®, Dragster, Dray, Duck, Dune buggy, Estate car, Fiacre, Float, Fly, Four-by-four, Four-seater, Gharri, Gharry, Gladstone, Go-cart, Go-kart, Go-Ped®, Gritter, Growler, Half-track, Hansom, Hatchback, Hearse, Hovercraft, Humvee, Jeep®, Jeepney, Jet-Ski, Jingle, Jinker, Jitney, Juggernaut, Kago, Kart, Koneke, Landau, Land Rover®, Launch, LEM, Limber, Litter, Load-lugger, Lorry, Machine, Mammy wagon, Means, Medium, Micro-scooter, Minibus, Minicab, Minivan, Motor, Motorhome, Multipurpose, Norimon, Offroad, Paddock-basher, Pantechnicon, Pedicab, Penny-farthing, People carrier, People-mover, Perambulator, Personnel carrier, Phaeton, Pick-up, Quad, Recreational, Re-entry, Ricksha(w), Roadroller, Runabout, Rust-bucket, Samlor, Sand-yacht, Scow, Shay, Shuttle, Sidecar, Skibob, Skidoo®, Sled(ge), Sleigh, Sno-Cat®, Snowmobile, Snowplough, Soyuz, Space, Spider, Stanhope, Station wagon, Steam-car, Sulky, Surrey, Tarantas(s), Tardis, Taxi, Tempera, Three-wheeler, Tipcart, Tip-up, Tonga, Tracked, Tractor, Trailer, Tram, Transporter, Trap, Tricar, Tricycle, Trishaw, Troika, Trolley, Trolleybus, Truck, Tuk tuk, Tumble-car(t), Tumbril, Turbo, Two-seater, Two-wheeler, Unicycle, Ute, Utility, Vahana, Velocipede, Vespa®, Volante, Wagon, Wagonette, Weasel, Wheelbarrow, Wheels, Wrecker

Veil Burk(h)a, Calyptra, Chad(d)ar, Chador, Chuddah, Chuddar, Cloud, Cover, Curtain, Envelop, Eucharistic, Hejab, Hijab, Humeral, Kalyptra, Kiss-me, Lambrequin, Mantilla, Mist, Niqab, Obscure, Purdah, Sacramental, Scene, Veale, Volet, Weeper, Wimple, Yashmak

Vein Artery, Azygas, Basilic, Coronary, Costa, Diploic, Epithermal, Fahlband, Gate, H(a)emorrhoid, Hemiazygous, Innominate, Jugular, Ledge, Lode, Mainline, Media, Midrib, Mood, Nervure, Organic, Outcrop, Percurrent, Pipe, Portal, Postcava, Precava, Pulmonary, Rake, Rib, Saphena, Sectorial, Spur, Stockwork, Stringer, Style, Thread, Varicose, Varix, Vena, Venule, Vorticose

Vellum Cutch, Japanese, Kutch, Parchment

Velocity Angular, Escape, Mustard, Muzzle, Orbital, Parabolic, Radial, Rate, Speed, Terminal, V

Velvet Bagheera, Chenille, National, Panné, Pile, Three-pile, Velour, Velure

Venal Corruptible, Mercenary, Sale

Vend(or) Hawk, Peddle, Pedlar, Rep, Sammy, Sell, Sutler

Vendetta Feud

Veneer Facade, Gloss, Varnish
Venerable Aged, August, Augustus, Bede, Guru, Hoary, Sacred, Sage, Vintage
Venerate, Veneration Adore, Awe, Douleia, Dulia, Hallow, Homage, Honour, Hyperdulia, Idolise, Latria, Revere, Worship
Venereal NSU, VD
Venery Chase
Venetian Aldine, Blind, Doge, Gobbo, Polo
Vengeance, Vengeful Commination, Erinyes, Reprisal, Ultion, Vindictive, Wannion, Wrack, Wreak
Venice La Serenissima
Venison Cervena, Deer
Venom(ous) Gall, Gila, Jamestown-weed, Jim(p)son-weed, Poison, Rancour, Solpuga, Spite, Toxic, Virus, Zootoxin
Vent Airway, Aperture, Belch, Chimney, Emit, Express, Fumarole, Hornito, Issue, Ostiole, Outlet, Smoker, Solfatara, Spiracle, Undercast, Wreak
Venter Uterus
Ventilate, Ventilator Air, Air-brick, Air-hole, Discuss, Express, Louvre, Plenum, Shaft, Voice, Windsail, Windway, Winze
Venture(d) Ante, Callet, Chance, Dare, Daur, Durst, Enterprise, Flutter, Foray, Handsel, Hazard, Jump, Opine, Presume, Promotion, Prostitute, Risk, Spec, Throw
Venue Bout, Locale, Place, Showground, Stadium, Stateroom, Tryst, Visne
Venus Cohog, Cytherean, Hesper(us), Love, Lucifer, Morning-star, Phosphorus, Primavera, Quahaug, Quahog, Rokeby, Vesper
Venus fly-trap Dionaea
Veracity, Veracious Accurate, Factual, Sincere, Truth(ful)
Veranda(h) Balcony, Gallery, Lanai, Patio, Piazza, Porch, Sleep-out, Stoep, Stoop, Terrace
Verb(al), Verbs Active, Argy-bargy, Auxiliary, Causative, Conative, Copula, Ergative, Factitive, Infinitive, Intransitive, Irregular, Modal, Passive, Perfective, Performative, Phrasal, Preterite, Stative, Transitive, Vb, Word-of-mouth
Verbascum Mullein
Verbatim Literally
Verbena Vervain
Verbose, Verbosity Padding, Prolix, Talkative, Wordy
Verdant Lush
Verdict Decision, Formal, Judg(e)ment, Majority, Open, Opinion, Pronouncement, Resolution, Ruling, Special
Verdigris Aeruginous, Patina
Verge Border, Brink, → EDGE, Hard shoulder, Incline, Long paddock, Rim
Verger Beadle, Pew-opener
Verify, Verification Affirm, Ascertain, Check, Confirm, Constatation, Control, Crosscheck, Prove, Validate
Verily Yea
Verisimilitude Artistic, Authenticity, Credibility
Verity Fact, Sooth, Truth
Vermifuge Cow(h)age, Cowitch
Vermilion Cinnabar, Minium, Red
Vermin(ous) Carrion, Catawampus, Lice, Mice, Pest, Ratty, → RODENT, Scum
Vermouth Absinthiated, French, It(alian), Martini®
Vernacular Common, Dialect, Idiom, Jargon, Lingo, Native, Patois, Vulgate
Veronica Hebe, Hen-bit, Speedwell

Verruca Wart
Versatile Adaptable, All-rounder, Flexible, Handy, Many-sided, Protean, Resourceful
Verse(s), Versed Dactyl, Free, Linked, Logaoedic, Passus, Poetry, Political, Reported, → RHYME

VERSES

1 letter:
V

3 letters:
Fit

4 letters:
Awdl
Blad
Duan
Epic
Epos
Fitt
Hymn
Neck
Poem
Rime
Sijo
Song
Vers

5 letters:
Blank
Blaud
Canto
Comus
Epode
Fitte
Fytte
Gazal
Haiku
Hokku
Ionic
Lyric
Meter
Poesy
Renga
Rubai
Spasm

Stave
Tanka
Tract
Triad

6 letters:
Adonic
Ballad
Burden
Ghazal
Ghazel
Gnomic
Haikai
Heroic
Jingle
Laisse
Miurus
Octave
Pantun
Rondel
Scazon
Stanza
Strain
Tercet

7 letters:
Alcaics
Couplet
Dimeter
Elegiac
Epigram
Fabliau
Huitain
Leonine
Pantoum
Pennill
Prosody
Pythian
Rondeau

Sapphic
Sestina
Sestine
Sixaine
Stiches
Strophe
Tiercet
Triolet
Tripody

8 letters:
Cinquain
Clerihew
Doggerel
Glyconic
Kyrielle
Madrigal
Nonsense
Pindaric
Quatrain
Rhopalic
Rove-over
Rubaiyat
Scansion
Senarius
Sirvente
Syllable
Terzetta
Trimeter
Tristich
Versicle

9 letters:
Amphigory
Asclepiad
Beatitude
Dithyramb
Ditrochee
Goliardic

Hexameter
Macaronic
Monometer
Octameter
Octastich
Saturnian
Stornello
Terza rima
Vers libre

10 letters:
Asynartete
Catalectic
Cynghanedd
Fescennine
Hypermeter
Mock-heroic
Ottava rima
Pennillion
Pentameter
Rhyme-royal
Serpentine
Tetrameter
Tetrastich
Villanelle

11 letters:
Acatalectic
Alexandrine
Hudibrastic
Riding-rhyme
Septenarius

12 letters:
Archilochian
Asclepiadean
Hudibrastics
Octosyllabic

▷ **Versed** *may indicate* reversed
Versed sine Sagitta
Versifier Lyricist, Poetaster, Rhymer, Rhymester
Version Account, Adaptation, Authorised, Cephalic, Cover, Edition, Form,

Paraphrase, Rede, Rendering, Rendition, Revised, Revision, Rhemish, Standard, Translation

Vertebra(e), Vertebrate Agnathan, Amniote, Amphioxus, Ascidian, Atlas, Axis, Bone, Centrum, Cervical, Chordae, Cyclostome, Dorsal, Gnathostome, Ichthyopsida, Lamprey, Lumbar, Placoderm, Reptile, Sacral, Sauropsida, Spondyl, Tetrapod, Tunicata, Vermis

Vertex Apex, Crest, Crown, Summit, Zenith

Vertical Apeak, Apeek, Atrip, Erect, Lapse, Montant, Ordinate, Perpendicular, Plumb, Prime, Sheer, Standing, Stemmed, Stile, Upright

Vertigo Dinic, Dizziness, Fainting, Giddiness, Megrim, Nausea, Staggers, Whirling

Verve Dash, Energy, Go, Gusto, Panache, Vigour

Very (good, well) A1, Ae, Assai, Awfully, Boffo, Bonzer, Boshta, Boshter, Dashed, Def, Ever, Extreme(ly), Fell, Frightfully, Gey, Grouse, Heap, Hellova, Helluva, Highly, Jolly, Keen, Light, Mighty, Molto, Much, OK, Opt, Precious, Precise, Purler, Real, Right, Self same, So, Sore, Stinking, Très, Unco, Utter, V, VG, Way

Vesicle Ampul, Bladder

Vespers Evensong, Lychnic, Placebo, Sicilian

Vessel → BOAT, Capillary, Container, Craft, Dish, Motor, Pressure, Receptacle, Seed, → SHIP, Utensil, Vascular, Weaker

VESSELS

3 letters:	Snow	Scoop	Dolium
Bin	Vase	Shell	Elutor
Cog	Vein	Sloop	Flagon
Cup	Vena	Stean	Frigot
Dow	Vial	Steen	Galiot
Fat	Zulu	Stoop	Galley
Obo		Stoup	Goblet
Pan	*5 letters:*	Tazza	Goglet
Pig	Aorta	Varix	Guglet
Pyx	Blood	Xebec	Humpen
Tub	Cogue	Zabra	Jet-ski
Urn	Crare		Kettle
Vas	Crewe	*6 letters:*	Lorcha
Vat	Crock	Aludel	Mortar
	Cruet	Argyle	Noggin
4 letters:	Cruse	Argyll	Retort
Bowl	Cupel	Artery	Rumkin
Buss	Dandy	Banker	Sailer
Cask	Dixie	Beaker	Sampan
Cowl	Gourd	Bicker	Sconce
Dhow	Ketch	Bouget	Shippo
Etna	Laver	Bucket	Situla
Font	Lotah	Carafe	Steane
Grab	Mazer	Carboy	Tassie
Horn	Oiler	Chatty	Trough
Lota	Phial	Copper	Tureen
Olpe	Pokal	Crayer	Venule
Raft	Quart	Dinghy	Wherry
Skin	Round	Dogger	

7 letters:
Amphora
Ampulla
Canteen
Chalice
Cistern
Costrel
Creamer
Cresset
Cuvette
Cyathus
Dredger
Drifter
Felucca
Frigate
Galleon
Galliot
Gunship
Gurglet
Jugular
Mudscow
Patamar

Pinnace
Pitcher
Polacca
Precava
Steamer
Tankard
Terreen
Vedette
Washpot

8 letters:
Calabash
Cauldron
Ciborium
Colander
Coolamon
Crucible
Cucurbit
Decanter
Figuline
Flatboat
Galleass

Galliass
Gallipot
Gallivat
Hoveller
Hydroski
Jerrican
Longboat
Monteith
Pancheon
Panchion
Pannikin
Sinusoid
Workboat

9 letters:
Alcarraza
Autoclave
Bucentaur
Calandria
Casserole
Cullender
Destroyer

Hydrofoil
Privateer
Tappit-hen

10 letters:
Bathyscaph
Deep-sinker
Jardinière
Triaconter

11 letters:
Aspersorium
Bathyscaphe
Side-wheeler

12 letters:
Fore-and-after
Lachrymatory
Stern-wheeler
Sternwheeler

Vest Beset, Confer, Crop top, Gilet, Modesty, Rash, Semmit, Singlet, Skivvy, Spencer, Sticharion, String, Undercoat, Undershirt, Waistcoat

Vestibule Anteroom, Atrium, Entry, Exedra, Foyer, Hall, Lobby, Narthex, Oeil-de-boeuf, Porch, Portico, Pronaos, Tambour

Vestige Hint, Mark, Mention, Shadow, Sign, Trace

Vestment Alb, Breastplate, Canonicals, Chasuble, Chimar, Chimer(e), Cotta, Dalmatic, Ephod, Fannel, Fanon, Garb, → **GARMENT**, Maniple, Mantelletta, Omophorion, Pallium, Parament, Ph(a)elonian, Pontificals, Raiment, Rational, Rochet, Rocquet, Sakkos, Sticharion, Stole, Surplice, Tunic(le)

Vestry Common, Sacristy, Select

Vet(ting), Veterinary, Vets Check, Doc(tor), Examine, Ex-serviceman, Inspect, OK, Positive, Screen, Veteran, Zoiatria, Zootherapy

Vetch Bitter, Ers, Fitch, Kidney, Locoweed, Milk, Tare, Tine

Veteran BL, Expert, GAR, Master, Oldster, Old sweat, Old-timer, Old 'un, Retread, Seasoned, Soldier, Stager, Stalwart, Stalworth, Vet, War-horse, Warrior

▷ **Veteran** *may indicate* 'obsolete'

Veto Ban, Bar, Blackball, Debar, Item, Local, Negative, Pocket, Reject, Taboo, Tabu

Vex(ing), Vexed Anger, Annoy, Bother, Chagrin, Debate, Fret, Gall, Grieve, Harass, Irritate, Madden, Mortify, Noy, Pester, Rankle, Rile, Sore, Spite, Tease, Torment, Trouble, Worrisome

Vexation(s) Barrator, Chagrin, Drat, Grief, Nuisance, Pique, Spite, Trouble

Vexatious Trying

Vexillum Web

Via By, Per, Through

Viable Economic, Going, Healthy, Possible

Vial Spirit-level

Viand Cate

Vibrate, Vibration(s), Vibrant Atmosphere, Chatter, Diadrom, Dinnle, Dirl,

Energetic, Flutter, Free, Fremitus, Harmonogram, Hotter, Jar, Judder, Oscillate, Plangent, Pulse, Quake, Resonance, Resonant, Rumble, Seiche, Shimmy, Shudder, Thrill, Throb, Tingle, Tremble, Tremor, Trill, Trillo, Twinkle, Uvular, Wag, Whir(r)

Viburnum Opulus

Vicar Apostolic, Bray, Choral, Elton, Forane, General, Incumbent, Lay, Pastoral, Plenarty, Primrose, Rector, Rev(erend), Trimmer

Vice Clamp, Cramp, Crime, Deputy, Eale, Evil, Foible, Greed, Iniquity, Instead, Jaws, Regent, Second (in command), → **SIN**, Stair

Vice-president Croupier, Veep

Viceroy Khedive, Nawab, Provost, Satrap, Willingdon

Vichy water Eau

Vicinity Area, Environs, Hereabouts, Locality, Neighbourhood, Region

Vicious Cruel, Flagitious, Hotbed

Victim Abel, Angel, Butt, Casualty, Currie, Curry, Dupe, Fashion, Frame, Host, Lay-down, Mark, Martyr, Nebbich, Neb(b)ish, Pathic, Patsy, Pigeon, Prey, Quarry, Sacrifice, Scapegoat, Target

Victor(y) Bangster, Banzai, Beater, Cadmean, Cannae, Captor, Champ(ion), Conqueror, Conquest, Epinicion, Epinikion, Eunice, Flagship, Fool's mate, Gree, Gris, Hallelujah, Hugo, Jai, Jai Hind, Kobe, Landslide, Lepanto, Ludorum, Mature, Moral, Nike, Palm, Philippi, Pyrrhic, Romper, Runaway, Scalp, Signal, Squeaker, Triumph, VE (day), Vee, Vic, Walk-away, Walkover, Win(ner)

Victoria(n) Aussie, Empress, Plum, Prig, Station

Victualler Caterer, Grocer, Licensed, Purveyor, Supplier, Vivandière

Video(-tape) Betacam®, Digital, Full-motion, Interactive, Laser vision, Minitel, Pixelation, Promo, Quadruplex, Reverse, Scratch, Still, Vera

Vie Compete, Contend, Emulate, Strive

Vienna Wien

Vietcong Charley, Charlie

Vietnamese Cham

View(er) Aim, Angle, Aspect, Belief, Bird's eye, Cineaste, Consensus, Consider, Cosmorama, Dekko, Dogma, Doxy, Endoscope, Exploded, Eye, Facet, Gander, Glimpse, Grandstand, Helicopter, Idea, Introspect, Kaleidoscope, Landscape, Line, Notion, Opinion, Optic®, Outlook, Pan, Panorama, Point, Private, Profile, → **PROSPECT**, Scan, Scape, Scene(ry), See, Sight, Skyscape, Slant, Specular, Standpoint, Stereoscope, Strain, Synop(sis), Tenet, Terrain, Thanatopsis, Theory, Vantage-point, Veduta, Vista, Visto, Watch, Witness, Worm's eye

Viewpoint Angle, Attitude, Belvedere, Conspectus, Eyeshot, Grandstand, Instance, Observatory, Perspective, Sight, Sightline, Voxpop

Vigil, Vigilant(e) Awake, Aware, Baseej, Basij, Deathwatch, Eve, Guardian angel, Hawk-eyed, Lyke-wake, Pernoctate, Wake, Wake-rife, Wary, Watch, Waukrife, Whitecap

Vignette Print, Profile, Sketch

Vigorous(ly), Vigour Athletic, Bant, Billy-o, Billy-oh, Birr, Blooming, Brio, Brisk, Con brio, Cracking, Drastic, Élan, Emphatic, Energetic, Flame, Forceful, Full-blooded, Furioso, Go, Green, Heart(y), Heterosis, Hybrid, Lush, Lustihood, Lustique, Lusty, P, Pep, Pith, Potency, Punchy, Pzazz, Racy, Rank, Raucle, Robust, Round, Rude, Smeddum, Spirit, Sprack, Sprag, Steam, Sthenic, Stingo, Strength, Strong, Thews, Tireless, Tone, Tooth and nail, Trenchant, Vegete, Vim, Vitality, Vivid, Vivo, Voema, Zip

▷ **Vigorously** *may indicate* an anagram

Viking Dane, Norseman, Rollo, R(y)urik, Sea king, Sea wolf, Varangian

Vile(ness) Base, Corrupt, Depraved, Dregs, Durance, Earthly, Infamy, Mean, Offensive, Scurvy, Vicious

Vilify Smear

Villa Bastide, Chalet, Dacha, House

Village Aldea, Auburn, Borghetto, Burg, Clachan, Corporate, Dorp, Endship, Global, Gram, Greenwich, Hamlet, Kaik, Kainga, Kampong, Kraal, Manyat(t)a, Mir, Outlet, Pit, Pueblo, Rancheria, Rancherie, Shtetl, Skara Brae, Thorp(e), Ujamaa, Vill, Wick

Villain(y) Baddy, Bluebeard, Bravo, Crim(inal), Crime, Dastard, Dog, Heavy, Iago, Knave, Macaire, Miscreant, Mohock, Nefarious, Ogre, Reprobate, Rogue, Scab, Scelerat, Scoundrel, Skelm, Tearaway, Traitor

Villein Bordar, Churl, Serf

Vim Go, Vigour, Vitality, Zing

Vincent Van Gogh

Vindicate, Vindication Absolve, Acquit, Apologia, Avenge, Clear, Compurgation, Darraign(e), Darrain(e), Darrayn, Defend, Deraign, Justify

Vindictive Hostile, Malevolent, Repay(ing), Spiteful, Vengeful

Vine(yard) Akatea, Ampelopsis, Ayahuasco, Balloon, Balsam apple, Bine, Bush rope, Château, Clinging, Clos, Colocynth, Cross, Cru, Cubeb, Cypress, Dodder, Domaine, Grapery, Hop, Idaean, Kangaroo, Kudzu, Lawyer, Liana, Martha's, Matrimony, Muskmelon, Naboth's, Potato, Puncture, Quinta, Russian, Sarsaparilla, Stephanotis, Supplejack, Swallowwort, Trumpet, Turpeth, Vitis, Winery, Wonga-wonga, Yam, Yquem

Vinegar Acetic, Acetum, Alegar, Balsam, Balsamic, Eisel(l), Esile, Malt, Oxymel, Tarragon, Wine, Wood

Vintage Classic, Crack, Cru, Old, Quality

Viol(a), Violet African, Alto, Amethyst, Archil, Crystal, Dame's, Dog, Dog's tooth, Gamba, Garden, Gentian, Gridelin, Heart's ease, Hesperis, Ianthine, Indole, Ionone, Kiss-me, Lyra, Mauve, Methyl, Neapolitan, Orchil, Pansy, Parma, Prater, Quint(e), Rock, Saintpaulia, Shrinking, Sweet, Tenor, Visual, Water

Violate, Violating, Violation Abuse, Breach, Contravene, Defile, Desecrate, Fract, Infraction, → **INFRINGE**, March-treason, Outrage, Peccant, Rape, Ravish, Solecism, Stuprate, Transgress, Trespass

Violence, Violent(ly) Acquaintance, Amain, Attentat, Bangster, Berserk, Brutal, Brute force, Drastic, Droog, Extreme, Fierce, Flagrant, Force, Frenzied, Furious, Heady, Het, High, Hot, Inbreak, Mighty, Onset, Rage, Rampage, Rampant, Rough, Rough stuff, Rude, Severe, Slap, Stormy, Strongarm, Ta(r)tar, Tearaway, Terrorism, Thuggery, Tinderbox, Tub-thumping, Vehement, Vie, Wrath

▸ **Violet** *see* **VIOLA**

Violin(ist), Violin-maker, Violin-shaped Alto, Amati, Cremona, Fiddle, Griddle, Gu(e), Guarneri(us), Guarnieri, Kennedy, Kit, Kubelik, Leader, Luthier, Menuhin, Nero, Oistrakh, Paganini, Pandurate, Rebeck, Rote, Stradivarius

VIP Bashaw, Bigshot, Bigwig, Brass, Cheese, Cob, Effendi, Envoy, Grandee, Imago, Kingpin, Magnate, Magnifico, Mugwump, Nabob, Nib, Nob, Pot, Snob, Someone, Swell, Tuft, Tycoon, Worthy

Viper Asp, Cerastes, Gaboon, Horned, Pit, Rattlesnake, River-jack, Russell's, Sand, Saw-scaled, → **SNAKE**, Traitor, Villain

Virago Amazon, Battle-axe, Beldam(e), Harpy, Randy, Shrew

Virgil Maro

Virgin(al), Virginity, Virgin Mary Airline, Blessed, Celibate, Chaste, Cherry, Extra, Intact, Maiden, Maidenhead, Maidenhood, May, New, Pan(h)agia, Parthenos, Pietà, Pucel(l)age, Pucelle, Pure, Queen, Snood, Tarpeia, Theotokos, Untainted, Vestal

Virginia(n) Creeper, Old Dominion, Tuckahoe, Va, Wade
Virile, Virility Energetic, Machismo, Macho, Manly, Red-blooded
Virtu Curio
Virtue(s), Virtuous, Virtual Angelic, Aret(h)a, Assay-piece, Attribute, Cardinal, Caritas, Charity, Chastity, Continent, Dharma, Efficacy, Ethical, Excellent, Faith, Fortitude, Good, Goody-goody, Grace, Hope, Justice, Moral(ity), Natural, Patience, Plaster-saint, Practical, Principal, Prudence, Qua, Say-piece, Squeaky-clean, Temperance, Theological, Upright, Worth
Virtuosity, Virtuoso Artist, Bravura, Excellence, Executant, Maestro, Paganini, Savant
Virulent Acrimonious, Deadly, Hostile, Malign, Noxious, Toxic, Vitriolic, Waspish
Virus AIDS, Antigen, Arbovirus, Bacteriophage, Boot, Capsid, Computer, Contagium, Coxsackie, Defective, EB, Ebola, Echo, Epstein-Barr, Filterable, Fowlpest, Germ, Granulosis, Hantavirus, Hendra, Herpes, HIV negative, HIV positive, Lassa, Latent, Leaf-mosaic, Lentivirus, Michelangelo, Oncogen, Parainfluenza, Parvo(virus), Pathogen, Peach-yellow, Picornavirus, Polyoma, Prophage, Reovirus, Retrovirus, Rhabdovirus, Rhinovirus, Ross River, Rotavirus, SARS, Shingles, Slow, Street, SV40, Tobacco mosaic, Varicella, Virino, Virion, Zoster
Visa Transit
Viscera Bowels, Entrails, Giblets, Guts, Harigal(d)s, Haslet, Innards, Omentum, Splanchnic, Umbles, Vitals
Viscount Vis
Viscous (liquid), Viscosity Absolute, Glaireous, Gluey, Gummy, Kinematic, Slab, Specific, Sticky, Stoke, Tacky, Tar, Thick, Thixotropic
Visible Clear, Conspicuous, Evident, Explicit, Obvious
Visigoth Asaric
Vision(ary) Aery, Aisling, Apparition, Beatific, Bourignian, Double, Dream(er), Emmetropia, Fancy, Fantast, Fey, Idealist, Illusionist, Image, Kef, Moonshine, Mouse-sight, Mystic, Ocular, Phantasm(a), Phantom, Pholism, Photism, Photopia, Rainbow-chaser, Romantic, Seeing, Seer, Sight, Stereo, Sweven, Tunnel, Twenty-twenty, Viewy
Visit(or) Affliction, Alien, Caller, Domiciliary, ET, Event, First-foot, Frequent, Gam, Guest, Habitué, Haunt, Health, Hit, Kursaal, Manuhiri, Prison, See, Sightseer, Stay, Stranger, Take
Visor, Vizor Eyeshade, Mesail, Mezail, Umbrel, Umbr(i)ere, Umbril, Vent(ayle)
Vista Enfilade, Outlook, Scene, View
Visual(ise) Envisage, Ocular, Optical, Visible
Vital(ity) Alive, Central, Critical, Crucial, Energy, Esprit, Essential, Existent, Foison, Gusto, Indispensable, Key, Kick, Life-blood, Linchpin, Lung, Mites, Momentous, Necessary, Oomph, Organ, Pizzazz, Salvation, Sap, Viable, Vigour, Zing, Zoetic
Vitals Numbles, Umbles, Viscera
Vitamin(s) A, Aneurin, Axerophthol, B, Bioflavonoid, Biotin, C, Calciferol, Calcitriol, Citrin, Cobalamin, D, E, Ergocalciferol, Folacin, H, Inositol, K, Linoleic, Menadione, Menaquinone, Niacin, P, Pan(to)thenol, Phylloquinone, Phytonadione, Pyridoxine, Retinene, Retinol, Riboflavin, Ribose, Thiamin(e), Tocopherol, Torulin, Tretinoin
Vitiate(d) Flaw(ed)
Vitreous Glassy, Hyaline
Vitriol(ic) Acid, Acrimonious, Biting, Blue, Caustic, Green, Mordant, White
Vituperate Abuse, Berate, Castigate, Censure, Defame, Inveigh, Lash, Rail, Scold
Viva Oral

Vivacity, Vivacious Animation, Brio, Esprit, Exuberant, Sparkle, Spirit, Verve
Vivid Bright, Brilliant, Dramatic, Eidetic, Fresh, Graphic, Keen, Live, Pictorial, Picturesque, Sharp, Violent
Vixen Catamaran, Harridan, Shrew, Virago
Viz Sc, Videlicet
Vizier Pheazar, Wazir
▸ **Vizor** *see* **VISOR**
Vocabulary Active, Glottochronology, Idiolect, Idioticon, Jargon, (Kata)kana, Lexicon, Lexis, Meta-language, Nomenclator, Passive, Wordbook
Vocal(isation), Vocalist Articulate, Doo-wop, Eloquent, Minstrel, Oral, Singer, Sprechgesang
Vocation Call, Career, Métier, Mission, Priesthood, Profession, Pursuit, Shop
Vociferous(ly) Clamant, Loud, Ore rotundo, Strident
Vogue Chic, Day, → **FASHION**, It, Mode, Rage, Style, Ton
Vogul Ugrian, Ugric
Voice(d) Active, Air, Alto, Ancestral, Bass, Chest, Contralto, Countertenor, Descant, Edh, Emit, Eth, Express, Falsetto, Glottis, Harp, Head, Intonate, Lyric, Mezzo-soprano, Mouth, Opinion, Passive, Phonic, Pipe, Presa, Quill, Say, Sonant, Soprano, Speak, Spinto, Sprechstimme, Steven, Syrinx, Tais(c)h, Tenor, Throat, Tone, → **TONGUE**, Treble, Utter, White
Voiceless Aphonia, Aphony, Dumb, Edh, Eth, Mute, Silent, Tacit
Void Abyss, Annul, Belch, Blank, Chasm, Counter, Defeasance, Defecate, Diriment, Empty, Evacuate, Gap, Hollow, Inane, Invalid, Irritate, Lapse, Nullify, Quash, Space, Vacuum
Volatile Excitable, Explosive, Latin, Live(ly), Mercurial, Temperamental, Terpene
Volcano(es), Volcanic Agglomerate, Black smoker, Burning mountain, Cone, Conic, Fumarole, Hornito, Ice, Idocrase, Igneous, Ignimbrite, Monticule, Mud, Obsidian, Pele, Pelée, Plinian, Pozz(u)olana, Pumice, Puzzolana, Sandblow, Shield, Soffioni, Solfatara, Stratovolcano, Tephra, Trass, Tuff

---

VOLCANOES

2 letters:	Okmok	Comoros	Krakatoa
Aa	Salse	El Misti	Mauna Kea
	Thera	Huascan	Mauna Loa
3 letters:		Iliamna	St Helena
Aso	*6 letters:*	Iwo Jima	St Helens
Puy	Ararat	Mofette	Taraniki
	Asosan	Rotorua	Unalaska
4 letters:	Azores	Ruapehu	Vesuvius
Etna	Egmont	Semeroe	
Fuji	Erebus	St Kilda	*9 letters:*
Maui	Ischia	Tambora	Aniakchak
Taal	Katmai		Corcovado
	Kazbek	*8 letters:*	Haleakala
5 letters:	Lipari	Amygdale	Helgafell
Askja	Semeru	Andesite	Huascaran
Hekla	Tolima	Antisana	Mount Fuji
Kauai		Cameroon	Nevis Peak
Mayon	*7 letters:*	Cotopaxi	Paricutin
Misti	Aragats	Jan Mayan	Stromboli

Tangariro

10 letters:
Chimborazo
Lassen Peak
Montserrat
Mount Eigon
Mount Kenya
Mount Pelée
Nyiragongo

11 letters:
Erciyas Dagi

Kilimanjaro
Mount Erebus
Mount Katmai
Mount Kazbek
Nyamuragira
Olympus Mons
Pico de Teide
Pico de Teyde

12 letters:
Citlaltépetl
Ixtaccahuatl
Iztaccahuatl

National Park
Popocatepetl

13 letters:
Mount Demavend
Mount St Helens

14 letters:
Mount Suribachi
Nevada de Colima
Nevada de Toluca
Soufrière Hills

17 letters:
Fernando de
Noronha
Warrumbungle
Range

20 letters:
D'Entrecasteau
Islands

Vole Arvicola, Meadow mouse, Muskrat, Musquash, Ondatra

Volition Velleity, Will

Volley Barrage, Boom, Broadside, Platoon, Salvo, Tirade, Tire

Volt(age) BeV, Bias, Grid bias, HT

Voltaire Arouet

Volte face U-turn

Voluble Fluent, Glib

Volume Atomic, Band, Barrel, Book, Bushel, Capacity, CC, Code(x), Content, Critical, Cubage, Gallon, Hin, Loudness, Mass, Ml, Molecular, Omnibus, Peck, Pint, Quart, Quart(o), Roll, Roul(e), Size, Space, Specific, Stere, Swept, Tidal, Tom, Tome, Ullage, Vol

Voluntary, Volunteer Docent, Enlist, Fencible, Free, Free-will, Honorary, Offer, Postlude, Reformado, Spontaneous, Tender, Tennessee, Terrier, TN, Ultroneous, Yeoman

Voluptuary, Voluptuous Carnal, Hedonist, Houri, Luscious, Sensuist, Sensuous, Sybarite

Volute Helix, Roll

Vomit(ing) Anacatharsis, Barf, Black, Boak, Boke, Cascade, Cat, Chuck up, Chunder, Disgorge, Egist, Egurgitate, Emesis, Fetch-up, Haematemesis, Honk, Keck, Kotch, Parbreak, Posset, Puke, Ralph, Regorge, Regurgitate, Retch, Rolf, Spew, Technicolour yawn, Throw up, Upchuck

Voodoo Charm, Jettatura, Kurdaitcha, Macumba, Mambo, Obeah, Sorcery, Zombi(e)

Voracious, Voracity Bulimia, Edacity, Gluttony, Greed, Ravenous, Serrasalmo

Vortex Charybdis, Eddy, Gyre, Trailing, Whirlpool

Votary Adherent, Cenobite, Devotee, Disciple, Fan, Nun, Swinger, Zealot

Vote(r), Votes, Voting Alternative, Assentor, Aye, Ballot, Block, Card, Casting, Choose, Colonist, Coopt, Cross, Crossover, Cumulative, Division, Donkey, Fag(g)ot, Floating, Franchise, Free, Grey, Informal, Mandate, Nay, Negative, No, Opt, People, Placet, Plebiscite, Plump, Plural, Poll, Postal, Pot-wabbler, Pot-waller, Pot-walloner, Pot-walloper, Pot-wobbler, PR, Preferential, Proportional representation, Qualified majority, Referendum, Return, Scrutin de liste, Scrutiny, Show of hands, Side, Single transferable, Straw(-poll), Suffrage, Swinging, Tactical, Ten-pounder, Theta, Ticket, Token, Transferable, Voice, X, Yea, Yes

Vote-catcher Pork

Vouch(er), Vouchsafe Accredit, Assure, Attest, Beteem(e), Book token, Chit, Coupon, Endorse, Gift, Guarantee, Luncheon, Meal-ticket, Receipt, Ticket, Token, Warrant

Voussoir Quoin, Wedge

Vow Baptismal, Behight, Behot(e), Earnest, Ex voto, Hecht, Hest, I do, Nuncupate, → OATH, Pledge, Plight, Promise, Simple, Solemn, Swear, Troth, Vum

Vowel(s) Ablaut, Anaptyxis, Aphesis, Breve, Cardinal, Diphthong, Gradation, Indeterminate, Monophthong, Mutation, Point, Rhyme, S(c)hwa, Seg(h)ol, Svarabhakti, Triphthong

Voyage(r) Anson, Course, Cruise, Launch, Maiden, Passage, Peregrinate, Sinbad, Travel

Voyeur Scopophiliac

VTOL Convertiplane

Vulcan(ite) Blacksmith, Ebonite, Fire, Mulciber, Spock, Wayland

Vulgar(ian) Banausic, Barbaric, Base, Blatant, Blue, Brassy, Buffoon, Canaille, Cheap, Cit, Coarse, Common, Crude, Demotic, Flash, Forward, Gaudy, General, Gent, Gross, Heel, Hussy, Ignorant, Indecent, Laddish, Lavatorial, Lewd, Low(-life), Naff, Obscene, Ostentatious, Pandemian, Plebby, Plebeian, Popular, Proletarian, Raffish, Riff-raff, Rude, Scaff, Scurrilous, Tacky, Tawdry, Threepenny, Tiger, Tink, Upstart, Vulg

Vulnerable Exposed, Open, Susceptible, Unguarded, Wide-open

Vulture Aasvogel, Bearded, Bird, Buzzard, California (condor), Condor, Culture, Falcon, Gallinazo, Gier, Griffon, Gripe, Grype, King, Lammergeier, Lammergeyer, Ossifrage, Predator, Turkey, Urubu, Zopilote

Ww

W Watt, West, Whisky, Women

Wad(ding) Batt(ing), Lump, Pad, Pledget, Roll, Swab, Wodge

Waddle Toddle, Waggle

Waddy Club, Cowboy, Stick

Wade(r), Wading Antigropelo(e)s, Curlew, Dikkop, Egret, Flamingo, Gallae, Godwit, Grallatorial, Greenshank, Gumboot, Heron, Ibis, Jacksnipe, Limpkin, Oyster-catcher, Paddle, Phalarope, Plodge, Sarus, Seriema, Shoebill, Splodge, Stilt(bird), Terek, Virginia

Waesucks Ewhow, O(c)hone

Wafer Biscuit, Cracker, Crisp, Gaufer, Gaufre, Gofer, Gopher, Host, Papad, Seal

Waff Flap, Flutter, Wave

Waffle Adlib, Blather, Equivocate, Gas, Gaufer, Gaufre, Gofer, Gopher, Hedge, Poppycock, Prate, Rabbit

Waft(ing) Airborne, Aura, Blow, Drift, Float

Wag(gish), Waggle Arch, Card, Comedian, Facetious, Joker, Lick, Niddle-noddle, Nod, Rogue, Shake, Sway, Wit(snapper), Wobble

Wage(s) Ante, Award, Fee, Hire, Income, Living, Meed, Minimum, Nominal, Pay, Portage, Practise, Prosecute, Rate, Salary, Screw, Subsistence

Wage-earner Breadwinner, Employee, Proletariat(e)

Wager Ante, Back, → **BET**, Gamble, Lay, Pascal's, Stake, Wed

Wagon(er) Ar(a)ba, Aroba, Boötes, Boxcar, Brake, Break, Buck, Buckboard, Buggy, Caisson, Carriage, Cart, Cattle truck, Chuck, Coachman, Cocopan, Conestoga, Corf, Covered, Democrat, Dray, Flatcar, Fourgon, Gambo, Go-cart, Hopper, Hutch, Low-loader, Mammy, Paddy, Palabra, Patrol, Plaustral, Police, Prairie schooner, Rave, Reefer, Rubberneck, Shandry, Station, Tank, Tartana, Telega, Tender, Trap, Trekker, Truck, Van, Victoria, Wain, Water

Waif Arab, Foundling, Jetsam, Stray, Urchin, Victoria, Wastrel, Water, Weft

Wail(er) Banshee, Bawl, Blubber, Howl, Keen, Lament, Moan, Skirl, Threnody, Threnos, Ululate, Vagitus, Wah-wah, Yammer

Wain Cart, Dray, Wagon

Waist(band) Belt, Cummerbund, Girdlestead, Girth, Hour-glass, Middle, Midship, Obi, Sash, Shash, Wasp, Zoster

Waistcoat Gilet, Jerkin, Lorica, MB, Pressure, Sayon, Shawl, Vest, Weskit

Wait(er), Waiting Abid(e), Ambush, Barista, Bide, Busboy, Butler, Buttle, Carhop, Commis, Cupbearer, Dally, Delay, Estragon, Expect, Flunkey, Frist, Garçon, Hang on, Hesitate, Hover, Interval, Khidmutgar, Lead time, Lime, Linger, Lurch, Maître d', Maître d'hôtel, Minority, Omnibus, Pannier, Pause, Pozzo, Remain, Serve(r), Sommelier, Stacking, Stay, Steward, Suspense, Taihoa, Tarry, Tend(ance), Tray, Vladimir, Wine, Won

Waitress Hebe, Miss, Mousme(e), Nippy, Server

Waive Abandon, Defer, Forgo, Overlook, Postpone, Relinquish, Renounce

Wake(n) Abrade, Abraid, Abray, Aftermath, Alert, American, Animate, Arouse, Astern, Deathwatch, Excite, Hereward, Keen, Knock-up, Like, Lyke, Prod, Rear, → ROUSE, Train, Wash

Waldo Emerson

Wale(r) Prop, Ridge, Weal

Wales Cambria, Cymru, Dyfed, Principality

Walk(er), Walking, Walkabout, Walkway Alameda, Alley, Alure, Amble, Ambulate, Arcade, Berceau, Birdcage, Charity, Cloister, Clump, Constitutional, Daddle, Dander, Dauner, Emu, Esplanade, EVA, Expatiate, Flânerie, Frescade, Gait, Gallery, Ghost, Go, Gradient, Gressorial, Heel and toe, Hike, Hookey, Hump, Lambeth, Leg, Lumber, Mainstreeting, Mall, March, Mince, Mosey, Pace, Pad, Pasear, Paseo, Passage, Path, Ped, Perambulate, Pergola, Perp, Pipe-opener, Pound, Power, Prance, Prom(enade), Rack, Ramble, Rampart, Random, Ring, Routemarch, Sashay, Shamble, Sidle, Slommock, Space, Spanish, Sponsored, Stalk, Step, Striddle, Stroll, Strut, Stump, Terrace, Toddle, Tramp, Trash, Travolator, Tread, Trog, Truck, Trudge, Turn, Wade, Wend, Widow's, Xyst

Walk-over Doddle, Pie, Scratch

Wall Antonine, Bail, Bailey, Barrier, Berlin, Berm, Cavity, Cell, Chinese, Climbing, Countermure, Crib, Curtain, Dado, Dam, Dike, Dry-stone, Enceinte, Epispore, Exine, Fail-dike, Fourth, Fronton, Frustule, Gable, Great, Hadrian's, Hanging, Hangman, Head, Immure, Intine, Mahjongg, Mani, Merlon, Myocardium, Non-bearing, Parapet, Parietal, Parie(te)s, Parpane, Parpen(d), Parpent, Parpoint, Partition, Party, Peribolos, Pericarp, Perpend, Perpent, Pleuron, Podium, Puteal, Qibla, Retaining, Revet(ment), Ring, River, Roman, Roughcast, Sea, Septum, Severus, Side, Somatopleure, Spandrel, Spandril, Street, Studding, Tambour, Tariff, Trumeau, Vallation, Vallum, Video, Wa', Wailing, Western, Withe, Zooecia

Wallaby Brusher, Dama, Kangaroo, Pad(d)ymelon, Pademelon, Quokka, Tammar, Whiptail

Wallah Competition

Wallaroo Euro

Wall-covering, Wallpaper Anaglypta®, Arras, Burlap, Flock, Lincrusta, Paper, Tapestry, Tapet

Waller Fats, Mason

Wallet Billfold, Case, Flybook, Folder, Notecase, Pochette, Pocket-book, Purse, Scrip

Wallflower Crucifer, Dowd(y), Pariah

Wall-game Eton, Mahjongg

Wallop Bash, Baste, Batter, Beat, Biff, Clout, Cob, → HIT, Lam, Lounder, Polt, Pound, Slog, Strap, Swinge, Tan, Tat, Trounce

Wallow(ing) Bask, Flounder, Luxuriate, Revel, Roll, Splash, Swelter, Tolter, Volutation, Welter

Wall-painting Fresco, Graffiti, Grisaille

▶ **Wallpaper** *see* WALL-COVERING

Wall-plate Tassel, Torsel

Wall-support Beam, Foundation, Pier, Rear-arch, Rere-arch

Wally Dipstick, Prat

Walnut Black, Butternut, Hickory, Juglans, Satin, White

Walrus Morse, Moustache, Pinniped, Rosmarine, Sea-horse, Tash

Walter Bruno, Mitty, Pater, Scott

Waltz Anniversary, Blue Danube, Boston, Concert, Dance, Hesitation, Rotate, Valse

Wampum Peag(e), Shell-money

Wan Lurid, Pale, Pallid, Pasty, Sanguine, Sorry
Wanchancy Unlucky
Wand Baton, Caduceus, Rod, Runic, Stick, Thyrse, Thyrsus, Vara, Vare
Wander(er), Wandering Aberrance, Amble, Bedouin, Berber, Bum, Caird, Daiker,
  Delirious, Desultory, Deviate, Digress, Divagate, Drift, Errant, Estray, Evagation,
  Excursive, Expatiate, Extravagate, Gad(about), Grope, Hobo, Jew, Landloper,
  Maunder, Meander, Meandrian, Mill, Mither, Moider, Moither, Moon, Nomad(e),
  Odysseus, Pedder, Peregrine, Peripatetic, Polar, Rache, Ramble, Range, Ratch,
  Roamer, Romany, Room, Rove, Solivagant, Stooge, Straggle, Stravaig, Stray,
  Strayve, Streel, Stroam, Stroll, Swan, Ta(i)ver, Tramp, Troll, Truant, Tuareg,
  Vagabond, Vagile, Vagrant, Vague, Waif, Wend, Wheel, Wilder, Wolves
▷ **Wandering** *may indicate* an anagram
Wane Decline, Decrease, Diminish, Ebb
Wangle Arrange, Finagle, Trick
Want(ing), Wants Absence, Conative, Covet, Crave, Dearth, Defect, Deficient,
  Derth, Desiderata, → **DESIRE**, Destitution, Envy, Hardship, Indigent, Itch, Lack,
  Long, Mental, Moldwarp, Mole, Need, Penury, Require, Scarceness, Scarcity,
  Shortfall, Shy, Void, Wish, Yen
Wanton(ness) Bona-roba, Cadgy, Chamber, Cocotte, Colt's tooth, Deliberate,
  Demirep, Filly, Flirt-gill, Gammerstang, Giglet, Giglot, Gillflirt, Hussy, Jay, Jezebel,
  Jillflirt, Lewd, Licentious, Loose, Nice, Protervity, Rig, Roué, Slut, Smicker,
  Sportive, Sybarite, Toyish, Twigger, Unchaste, Wayward
Wap Blow, Knock, Strike
War(fare), Wars American Civil, American Independence, Ares, Armageddon,
  Arms, Asymmetrical, Attrition, Bacteriological, Barons', Bate, Battle, Biological,
  Bishop, Chemical, Civil, Clash, Class, Cod, Cold, Combat, Conflict, Crescentade,
  Crimean, Crusade, Electronic, Emergency, Feud, → **FIGHT**, Flame, Food,
  Franco-Prussian, Fray, Germ, Gigantomachy, Great, Guer(r)illa, Gulf, Holy,
  Hostilities, Hot, Hundred Years', Information, Internecine, Jehad, Jenkins'
  ear, Jihad, Jugurthine, Korean, Krieg, Limited, Mars, Mexican, Napoleonic,
  Nuclear, Opium, Peasants', Peloponnesian, Peninsular, Phony, Price, Private,
  Psychological, Punic, Push-button, Queen Anne's, Rebellion, Revolutionary, Roses,
  Russo-Japanese, Secession, Seven against Thebes, Seven Years', Shooting, Six Day,
  Social, Spam, Spanish-American, Spanish Civil, Star, Stoush, Sword, Terrapin,
  Theomachy, Thirty Years', Total, Trench, Trojan, Turf, Vietnam, Winter, World,
  Yom Kippur
Warble(r) Carol, Cetti's, Chiff-chaff, Chirl, Fauvette, Peggy, Record, Rel(l)ish, Trill,
  Vibrate, Yodel, Yodle
War-chant, War-cry Alalagmos, Haka, Slogan
Ward (off) Artemus, Averruncate, Avert, Care, Casual, Casualty, Charge, Defend,
  District, Fend, Guard, Hand-off, Maternity, Nightingale, Oppose, Parry, Protégé,
  Pupil, Soc, Soken, Vintry, Wear, Weir
Warden Caretaker, Concierge, Constable, Crossing, Curator, Custodian, Game,
  Guardian, Keeper, Maori, Meter maid, Pear, Provost, Ranger, Septimus, Spooner,
  Steward, Traffic, Way
Warder Beefeater, Gaoler, Guardian, Keeper, Provost, Screw, Turnkey, Twirl
Wardrobe Almirah, Capsule, Closet, Clothes, Garderobe, Outfit, Vestuary
Ware(s) Arretine, Basalt, Beware, Biscuit, Cameo, Canton, Chelsea, China, Etruria,
  Faience, Goods, Jasper, Lustre, Merchandise, Palissy, Queen's, Samian, Sanitary,
  Satsuma, Shippo, Truck, Wemyss
Warehouse Bonded, Data, Depository, Entrepôt, Freight-shed, Go-down, Hong, Store

▶ **Warfare** *see* **WAR**

War-game Kriegs(s)piel

War-god Ares, Mars, Tiu, Tiw, Tyr

Warhead Atomic, Supremo

Warhorse Charger, Destrier, Fighter

Wariness, Wary Ca'canny, Cagey, Careful, Cautel, Caution, Chary, Discreet, Distrust, Guarded, Leery, Mealy-mouthed, Prudent, Sceptical, Suspicious, Tentie, Tenty, Vigilant

Warlike Battailous, Bellicose, Gung-ho, Lachlan, Martial, Militant

Warlord Haw-haw, Kitchener, Shogun

Warm(er), Warming, Warmth Abask, Admonish, Air, Ardour, Balmy, British, Calefacient, Calid(ity), Chambré, Cordial, Empressement, Enchafe, Fervour, Foment, Gemütlich, Genial, Global, Glow, → **HEAT**, Hot, Incalescent, Kang, Lew, Logic, Loving, Muff, Muggy, Mull, Radiator, Tepid, Thermal, Toast, Toasty

Warm-blooded Homothermal, Homothermic, Homothermous, Idiothermous

Warmonger Hawk

Warn(ing) Admonish, Alarum, Alert, Amber, Aposematic, Apprise, Beacon, Beware, Bleep, Buoy, Caution, Caveat, Caveat emptor, Commination, Cone, Counsel, Document, Early, En garde, Example, Foghorn, Fore, Foretoken, Gardyloo, Garnishment, Griffin, Harbinger, Hazchem, Heads up, Hoot, Horn, Klaxon, Larum, Lesson, Light, Maroon, Monition, Nix, Nota bene, Notice, Omen, Pi-jaw, Portent, Premonitory, Presage, Prodromal, Profit, Protevangelium, Riot Act, Rumble strip, Scaldings, Scarborough, Sematic, Shore, Signal, Storm, Tattler, Threat, Timber, Tip-off, Token, Vigia, Vor, Yellow card

Warner Alarm, Fore, Plum, Siren

Warp(ed) Bias, Buckle, Cast, Contort, Distort, Kam, Kedge, Pandation, Time, Twist, Weft

Warpath Rampage

▷ **Warped** *may indicate* an anagram

Warrant(y) Able, Authorise, Behight, Behote, Bench, Caption, Certificate, Death, Detainer, Distress, Fiat, Fiaunt, Fugle, General, Guarantee, Justify, Mittimus, Peace, Permit, Precept, Reprieve, Royal, Search, Sepad, Special, Swear, Transire, Vouch, Warn

Warren Burrow, Colony, Hastings, Rabbit

Warrior Achilles, Agamemnon, Ajax, Amazon, Anzac, Berserk(er), Brave, Cold, Cossack, Crusader, Eorl, Fianna, Fighter, Finlay, Finley, Geronimo, Ghazi, Heimdall, Housecarl, Impi, Lewis, Louis, Myrmidon, Nestor, Rainbow, Rajpoot, Rajput, Roger, Samurai, Soldier, Tatar, Unknown, Warhorse, Warwolf, Zulu

Warship Battleship, Castle, Cog, Corvette, Cruiser, Destroyer, Drake, Dromon(d), Frigate, Invincible, Man-o-war, Mine-layer, Monitor, Privateer, Ram, Repulse, Wooden Walls

Wart(y) Anbury, Angleberry, Blemish, Keratose, Muricate, Plantar, Tuberous, Verruca, Wen

Warwick Kingmaker

▶ **Wary** *see* **WARINESS**

Was Erat, Existed, Lived, Past

Wash(ed), Washer, Washing (up), Wash out Ablution, Affusion, Alluvion, Bath, Bay(e), Bidet, Bubble-dancing, Bur(r), Calcimine, Circlip, Clean(se), Cradle, D, Dashwheel, Dele(te), Dip, Edulcorate, Elute, Elutriate, Enema, Erode, Fen, Flush, Freshen, Gargle, Grommet, Grummet, Irrigate, Kalsomine, Lap, → **LAUNDER**,

Lavabo, Lave, Leather, Lip, Lotion, Marsh, Maundy, Mop, Nipter, Pan, Pigswill, Poss, Purify, Rinse, Sapple, Scrub, Shampoo, Shim, Sind, Sloosh, Sluice, Soogee, Soojee, Soojey, Squeegie, Stream, Sujee, Swab, Synd, Syne, Tie, Toilette, Top and tail, Twin tub, Tye, Wake, Wudu, Yellow

Washbasin, Washtub, Washhouse Copper, Lavabo, Steamie

Washerman, Washerwoman Dhobi, Laundress

Washington Wa

Wasn't Nas, Wasna

Wasp(ish) Appledrain, Bembex, Bink, Bite, Chalcid, Cuckoo-fly, Cynipidae, Cynips, Digger, European, Fig, Fretful, Gall(-fly), Gold, Hornet, Horntail, Hoverfly, Irritable, Marabunta, Mason, Miffy, Muddauber, Paper, Peevish, Pompilid, Potter, Ruby-tail, Sand, Seed, Solitary, Spider, Syrphus, Velvet ant, Vespa, Wood, Yellow jacket

▷ **Wasp** *may indicate* a rugby player

Wasp's nest Bike, Bink, Byke

Wassail Carouse, Pledge, Toast

Wast Wert

Wastage, Waste(d), Wasting, Wasteful, Wasteland Amyotrophy, Atrophy, Blow, Blue, Boondoggle(r), Cesspit, Cirrhosis, Consume, Contabescent, Coom(b), Cotton, Crud, Culm, Decay, Dejecta, Desert, Detritus, Devastate, Dilapidate, Dissipate, Dross, Dung, Dwindle, Dwine, Dystrophy, Effluent, Egesta, Emaciate, Erode, Estrepe, Excrement, Exhaust, Expend, Exudate, Faeces, Flue, Forpine, Fribble, Fritter, Garbage, Gash, Gob, Gunge, Haggard, Havoc, Hazardous, High-level, Husk, Knub, Lavish, Loose, Lose, Loss, Low-level, Marasmus, Merino, Misspent, Moor, Moulder, Muir, Mullock, Mungo, Natural, Novalia, Nub, Nuclear, Offal, Oller, Ordure, Pellagra, Phthisis, Pigswill, Pine, Prodigalise, Radioactive, Rammel, Rank and manger, Ravage, Recrement, Red mud, Red tape, → **REFUSE**, Reif, Rubble, Ruderal, Schappe, Scissel, Scoria, Scrap, Sewage, Slag, Slurry, Spend, Spill, Spoil(age), Squander, Sullage, Syntexis, Tabes, Tailing, Thin, Thwaite, Ureal, Urine, Uropoiesis, Vast, Wanze, Wear, Wilderness, Yearn

▷ **Wasted** *may indicate* an anagram

Wastrel Idler, Profligate, Scattergood, Spend-all, Spendthrift, Stalko, Vagabond

Watch(er) Accutron®, Analog(ue), Analogon, Argus, Await, Bark, Behold, Bird-dog, Black, Clock, Coastguard, Cock-crow, Digital, Dog, Eryl, Espy, Eyeball, Fob, Glom, Gregory, Guard, Half-hunter, Huer, Hunter, Kettle, Latewake, Lever, Lo, Look, Look-out, Middle, Monitor, Morning, Nark, Neighbourhood, Night, Nit, Note, Nuremberg egg, Observe, Overeye, Patrol, Pernoctation, Posse, Quartz, Regard, Repeater, Rolex®, Scout, Sentinel, Sentry, Shadow, Spectate, Spotter, Stemwinder, Suicide, Surveillance, Tend, Ticker, Timekeeper, Timepiece, Timer, Tompion, Tout, Turnip, Vedette, → **VIGIL**, Voyeur, Wait, Wake, Weather eye, Wrist(let)

Watch-chain Albert, Slang

Watch-control Escapement

Watchful(ness) Alert, Aware, Care, Dragon, Ira, Jealous, Vigilant, Wakerife, Wary, Waukrife

Watchman Argus, Bellman, Charley, Charlie, Chok(e)y, Cho(w)kidar, Guard, Sentinel, Sentry, Speculator, Tompion, Viewer

Watch-tower Atalaya, Barbican, Beacon, Mirador, Sentry-go

Watchword Cry, Password, Shibboleth, Slogan

Water(ed), Waters, Watery Adam's ale, Adam's wine, Aerated, Amrit, Apollinaris, Aq(ua), Aquatic, Aqueous, Barley, Bayou, Bedabble, Bilge, Bound, Branch, Brine, Broads, Brook, Burn, Canal, Cancer, Chresard, Chuck, Cold,

Compensation, Conductivity, Connate, Dead, Deaw, Deg, Demersal, Dew, Dill, Dilute, Dribble, Drinking, Eau, Ebb, Echard, Element, Ennerdale, Epilimnion, Euphotic, Evian®, First, Flood, Ford, Fossil, Functional, Gallise, Gallize, Ganga jal, Grey, Gripe, Ground, Hard, Heavy, Hectum, Hellespont, High, Holy, Hot, Hungary, Hydatoid, Irrigate, Javel(le), Kuroshio, Kyle, Lagoon, Lagune, Lake, Lant, Laurel, Lavender, Leachate, Lentic, Light, Limnology, Lithia, Loch(an), Lode, Lotic, Lough, Low, Lubricated, Lymph, Melt, Meteoric, Mineral, Miner's inch, Moiré, Mother, Nappe, North, Oasis®, Oedema, Overfall, Pani, Pawnee, Pee, Perrier®, Phreatic, Pisces, Polly, Polynia, Polynya, Poppy, Potash, Potass, Pump, Purest, Quick, Quinine, Rain, Rapids, Rate, Reach, Rice, Rip, Riverine, Rose, Running, Runny, Rydal, Saltchuck, Scorpio, Sea, Seltzer, Sera, Serous, Serum, Shoal, Shower, Simpson, Skinkling, Slack, Slick, Sluice, Soda, Sodden, Soft, Solent, Sound, Souse, Southampton, Stream, Surface, Tabby, Table, Tam, Tap, Tar, Territorial, Thin, Tide, Toilet, Tonic, Urine, Utility, Vadose, Vichy, Viscous, Vlei, Vly, Wai, Wash(y), Weak, Wee, Whey, White, White coal, Wild, Wishy-washy

Waterbaby Moses, Tom

Water-boa Anaconda

Water-boatman Notonecta

Water-brash Pyrosis

Water-buckets Noria

Water-carrier Aqueduct, Bheestie, Bheesty, Bhistee, Bhisti, Bucket, Carafe, Chatty, Furphy, Hose, Hydra, Hydria, Kirbeh, Pail, Pitcher, Rigol

Water-chestnut Saligot

Water-colour Aquarelle, Painting, Pastel, RI

Water-course Arroyo, Billabong, Canal, Ditch, Dyke, Falaj, Furrow, Gutter, Khor, Lead, Leat, Nala, Nalla(h), Nulla, Nullah, Rean, Rhine, Riverway, Shott, Spruit, Wadi, Whelm

Watercress Nasturtium

Water-device Shadoof, Shaduf

Water-diviner Dowser, Hydrostat

Waterfall Angel (Falls), Cataract, Churchill, Chute, Cuquenan, Force, Foss, Iguaçú, Kabiwa, Kaieteur, Kile, Lasher, Lin(n), Mardel, Mtarazi, Niagara, Overfall, Rapid, Salmon leap, Sault, Sutherland, Takakkaw, Tugela, Victoria, Yellowstone, Yosemite

Water-fern Marsilea, Salvinia

Water-gate Penstock, Sluice, Sluse

Water-god Aleion, Aleyin, Alpheus

Water-hen Gallinule

Water-hole Bore, Gilgai, Oasis

Water-lily Lotus, Nenuphar, Nuphar, Spatterdock, Victoria

Waterloo Rout

Waterman Aquarius, Bargee, Ferryman, Oarsman

Water-monster Nicker

Water-nymph Kelpie, Kelpy, Naiad, Ondine, Rusalka

Water-parsnip Sium, Skirret

Water-plant Alisma, Aquatic, Cress, Crowfoot, Elodea, Gulfweed, Lace-leaf, Lattice-leaf, Nelumbo, Nenuphar, Nuphar, Ouvirandra, Pontederia, Quillwort, Reate, Sea-mat, Sedge, Seg, Stratiotes, Urtricularia, Vallisneria

Waterproof, Water-tight Caisson, Camlet, Caulk, Cerecloth, Cofferdam, Corfam®, Dampcourse, Dubbin(g), Groundsheet, Loden, Mac, Mino, Oilers, Oilskin, Pay, Seaworthy, Stank, Sta(u)nch, Tarp, Waders

Water-rat Arvicola, Musk-rat, Ratty, Vole

Watershed Divide, Hilltop
Water-spout Gargoyle, Geyser, Hurricano
Water-sprite Kelpie, Kelpy, Nix(ie), Nixy, Tangie, Undine, Water-nymph
Water supply Dewpond, H, Hydrant, Spring, Tank, Tap
Waterway Aqueduct, Billabong, Canal, Channel, Creek, Culvert, Ditch, Igarapé, Illinois, Intracoastal, Lode, River, St Lawrence Seaway, Sny(e), Sound, Straight, Suez
Water-wheel Noria, Pelton, Sakia, Saki(y)eh
Wattle(s) Acacia, Boobialla, Boree, Dewlap, Gills, Golden, Mimosa, Mulga, Sallow, Savanna, Snot
Wave(s), Waved, Wavelength, Wavy Alfven, Alpha, Beachcomber, Beam, Beck, Beta, Billow, Bore, Bow, Brain, Brandish, Breaker, Carrier, Circular polarisation, Clapotis, Cold, Comber, Complex, Continuous, Crenulate, Crest, Crime, Crimp, Crispate, Cymotrichous, De Broglie, Decuman, Delta, Dominant, Dumper, Electromagnetic, Finger, Flap, Flaunt, Float, Flote, Flourish, Gesticulate, Gravitational, Gravity, Graybeard, Ground, Groundswell, Gyrose, Harmonic, Haystack, Head sea, Heat, Hertzian, Internal, Ionospheric, Lee, Long, Longitudinal, Marcel, Matter, Medium, Mexican, Nebule, New, Oundy, Peristalsis, Perm(anent), Plunger, Primary, Pulse, Radar, Radiation, Radio, Rayleigh, Repand, Rip, Ripple, Roller, Rooster, Sastrugi, Scrub, Sea, Secondary, Seiche, Seismic, Shake, Shock, Short, Sine, Sinuate, Sky, Snaky, Soliton, Sound, Spiller, Square, Squiggle, Standing, Stationary, Stream, Supplementary, Surf, Surge, Sway, Tabby, Theta, Third, Thought, Tidal, Tidal bore, Tide, Train, Transverse, Travelling, Tsunami, Ultrasonic, Undate, Unde, Undulate, Vermicular, Waffle, Waft, Wag, Waive, Wash, Waw, Wawe, Whitecap, White-horse, Wigwag
▷ **Wave(s)** *may indicate* an anagram
Wave-band Channel
Wave-detector Coherer
Wavelength Band, Complementary, De Broglie, Ultrashort
Waver(ing), Waverer Dither, Falter, Flag, Gutter, Halt, Hesitate, Oscillate, Stagger, Sway, Swither, Teeter, Trimmer, Vacillate, Waffle, Wet, Wow
Wax(ed), Waxing, Waxy Adipocere, Ambergris, Appal, Bate, Bees, Bone, Brazilian, Candelilla, Carna(h)uba, Cere, Ceresin, Cerumen, Chinese, Cobbler's, Cutin, Earth, Effuse, Enseam, Ethal, Geraldton, Gr(e)aves, Grow, Heelball, Honeycomb, Increase, Increscent, Inseam, Ire, Japan, Kiss, Lecithin, Lipide, Livid, Lost, Lyrical, Mineral, Montan, Mummy, Myrtle, Ozocerite, Ozokerite, Paraffin, Parmacitie, Pela, Petroleum, Propolis, Pruina, Rage, Seal, Sealing, Spermaceti, Suberin, Tallow, Tantrum, Temper, Toxaphene, Vegetable, White, Yielding
Waxwing Cedar-bird, Icarus
Way(s), Wayside Access, Agate, Appian, Autobahn, Avenue, Borstal(l), Budo, Bypass, Companion, Course, Crescent, Defile, Direction, Door, Draw, E, Each, Entrance, Family, Fashion, Flaminian, Foss(e), Gate, Habit, Hatch, Hedge, High, Hither, How, Icknield, Lane, Manner, Means, Method, Milky, MO, Mode, Modus, N, Pass, Path, Pennine, Permanent, Pilgrim's, Procedure, Railroad, Regimen, Ridge, → **ROAD**, Route, S, Sallypost, St(reet), Style, System, Taoism, Technique, Third, Thoroughfare, Thus, Trace, Trail, Troade, Turnpike, Underpass, Untrodden, Via, W, Wise
Wayfarer Commuter, Piepowder, Pilgrim, Traveller, Voyager
Waylay Accost, Ambuscade, Ambush, Beset, Bushwhack, Buttonhole, Molest, Obstruct, Stick up
Way-out Advanced, Bizarre, Egress, Esoteric, Exit, Exotic, Extreme, Offbeat, Trendy

Wayward Capricious, Disobedient, Errant, Erratic, Loup-the-dyke, Obstreperous, Perverse, Stray, Unruly, Wilful

We I and I, Oo, Royal, Us

Weak(er), Weaken(ing), Weakest, Weakness Achilles' heel, Acrasia, Antimnemonic, Aphesis, Appair, Appal, Arsis, Asthenia, Attenuate, Blot, Brickle, Brittle, Cachexia, Cataplexy, Chink, Cripple(d), Debile, Debilitate, Decrease, Delay, Delicate, Dilute, Disable, Effete, Emasculate, Enervate, Enfeeble, Entender, Fade, Faible, Failing, Faint, Fatigue, Feeble, Fissile, Flag, Flaw, Flimsy, Foible, Fragile, Frail(tee), Frailty, Give, Gone, Ham, Hamartia, Helpless, Honeycomb, Impair, Impotence, Infirm, Knock-kneed, Labefaction, Lassitude, Leptosomatic, Low, Low ebb, Meagre, Mild, Milk and water, Myasthenia, Namby-pamby, Pale, Pall, Paraparesis, Paresis, Penchant, Puny, Push-over, Pusillanimous, Reckling, Reduce, Simp, Slack, Soft spot, Tenuous, Thesis, Thin, Thready, Tottery, Unable, Underdog, Undermine, Unnerve, Unstable, Vapid, Velleity, Vessel, Vulnerability, W, Washy, Water(y), Wish(y)-wash(y), Wuss(y)

Weakling Dilling, Drip, Milksop, Nerd, Nisgul, Reed, Softie, Wuss

Weal Ridge, Stripe, Urticant, Wealth, Welfare, Welt, Whelk

Wealth(y) Abundance, Affluence, Bullion, Croesus, Digerati, Ease, Fat-cat, Fortune, Golconda, Jet-set, Klondike, Klondyke, Load(sa), Loaded, Loadsamoney, Lolly, Mammon, Means, Mine, Mint, Moneyed, Nabob, Opulence, Ore, Pelf, Plutocrat, Reich, Rich, Ritzy, Solid, Substance, Treasure, Trustafarian, Untold, Well-heeled, Well-off, Well-to-do

Wean Ablactation, Bairn, Spain, Spane, Spean

Weapon(s) Ammo, Arm, Arsenal, Assault, Binary, Deterrent, Greek fire, Hoplology, Long-range, Missile, Munition, Nuclear, Nuke, Theatre, Tool, Traditional

---

WEAPONS

2 letters:	*5 letters:*	*6 letters:*	Tomboc
V1	Arrow	Airgun	Voulge
	Baton	Cestus	
3 letters:	Blade	Cohorn	*7 letters:*
Axe	Estoc	Creese	Arblast
Dag	Flail	Cudgel	Assegai
Gad	Knife	Dagger	Ataghan
	Kukri	Dragon	Bayonet
4 letters:	Lance	Duster	Bazooka
Bill	Lathi	Gingal	Blowgun
Bolo	Maxim	Glaive	Bondook
Bomb	Orgue	Jingal	Caliver
Club	Pilum	Katana	Caltrap
Cosh	Rifle	Lathee	Caltrop
Dart	Sabre	Mauser®	Carbine
Gade	Saker	Mortar	Chopper
Gaid	Spear	Musket	Coehorn
Kris	Staff	Onager	Cutlass
Mere	Stick	Pistol	Dragoon
Pike	Sting	Rapier	Enfield
Spat	Sword	Sparke	Fougade
Sten	Taser®	Sparth	Gingall
	Vouge	Taiaha	Gisarme

Grenade
Halberd
Halbert
Harpoon
Hatchet
Javelin
Longbow
Machete
Matchet
Petrary
Poleaxe
Sandbag
Shotgun
Sidearm
Torpedo
Trident

8 letters:
Alderman
Arbalest
Armalite®
Arquebus
Ballista
Blowpipe

Bludgeon
Calthrop
Catapult
Culverin
Elf-arrow
Fougasse
Howitzer
Mangonel
Nunchaku
Partisan
Petronel
Revolver
Scimitar
Scorpion
Shuriken
Skean-dhu
Skene-dhu
Spontoon
Stiletto
Stinkpot
Tomahawk
Whirl-bat
Whorl-bat
Yataghan

9 letters:
Arquebuse
Backsword
Battleaxe
Boomerang
Catchpole
Chainshot
Derringer
Doodlebug
Excalibur
Flintlock
Forty-five
Harquebus
Sarbacane
Slingshot
Sword cane
Trebuchet
Truncheon

10 letters:
Broadsword
Knobkerrie
Pea-shooter
Shillelagh

Smallsword
Swordstick
Throw-stick

11 letters:
Morgenstern
Snickersnee

12 letters:
Flamethrower
Quarterstaff

13 letters:
Knuckleduster
Life-preserver
Manrikigusari

14 letters:
Nunchaku sticks

Wear(ing), Wear Out Abate, Ablative, Abrade, Air, Attrition, Chafe, Corrade, Corrode, Deteriorate, Detrition, Efface, Erode, Erosion, Fashion, For(e)spend, Fray, Frazzle, Fret, Garb, Impair, In, Mush, Pack, Scuff, Sport, Stand, Tedy, Tolerate, Utility

▷ **Wear** *may indicate* the NE (eg Sunderland)

Weariness, Wearisome, Weary(ing) Beat, Bejade, Blethered, Bore, Cloy, Dog-tired, Ennui, Ennuyé, Exhaust, Fag, Fatigate, Fatigue, Harass, Hech, Irk, Jade, Lacklustre, Lassitude, Pall, Puny, Ramfeezle, Sick, Sleepy, Spent, Tire, Tiresome, Trash, Try, Tucker, Wabbit, Worn

Weasel Beech-marten, Cane, Delundung, Ermine, Ferret, Glutton, Grison, Kolinsky, Marten, Mink, Mustela, Pekan, Polecat, Stoat, Taira, Tayra, Vermin, Whitterick, Whit(t)ret, Whittrick, Wolverine, Woodshock

Weather, Weather forecast Atmosphere, Climate, Cyclone, Discolour, Ecoclimate, Elements, El Niño, Endure, Met, Monkey's wedding, Sky, Stand, Survive, Tiros, Undergo, Withstand

Weatherboard Rusticating

Weathercock Barometer, Fane, Vane

Weave(r), Weaves, Weaving Arachne, Basket, Broché, Cane, Complect, Contexture, Entwine, Finch, Fishnet, Folk, Heald, Heddle, Interlace, Jacquard, Lace, Lease, Leno, Lion, Loom, Marner, Osiery, Penelope, Pick, Plain, Plait, Raddle, Ripstop, Rya, Shuttle, Sparrow, Spider, Splice, Stevengraph, Taha, Textorial, Texture, Throstle, Throwster, Tissue, Tweel, Twill, Twine, Wabster, Waggle, Webster, Zigzag

Weaver-bird Amadavat, Avadavat, Quelea, Rice-bird, Taha

Web(bed), Webbing, Web-footed, Web-site Aranea, Fissipalmate, Food, Fourchette, Infomediary, Internet, Mat, Maze, Mesh(work), Offset, Palama,

Palmate, Palmiped, Patagium, Pinnatiped, Retiary, Skein, Snare, Spider, Tear, Tela, Tissue, Toil, Totipalmate, World Wide

Webster Spider, Weaver

Wed(ding), Wedlock Alliance, Bet, Diamond, Espousal, Golden, Hymen, Join, Knobstick, Liaison, Link, Marriage, Marry, Mate, Matrimony, Meng(e), Me(i)nt, Meynt, Ming, Monkey's, Nuptials, Pair, Penny, Ruby, Shotgun, Silver, Spousal, → **UNION**, Unite, White, Y

Wedge(d) Accretionary, Canting-coin, Chock, Chunk, Cleat, Cotter, Cuneal, Doorstop, Feather, Forelock, Gagger, Gib, Impacted, Jack, Jam, Key, Niblick, Pitching, Prop, Quoin, Sand, Scotch, Shim, Sphenic, Stick, Texas, Trig, Vomerine, Voussoir, Whipstock

Wedgwood Benn, China

Wednesday Ash, Midweek, Pulver, Spy

Wee Leak, Little, Pee, Slash, Sma(ll), Tinkle, Tiny, → **URINATE**, Widdle

▷ **Weed** *may indicate* 'urinated'

Weed(y) Adderwort, Agrestal, Alga, Allseed, Anacharis, Arenaria, Bedstraw, Bell-bind, Blinks, Burdock, Buttercup, Carpetweed, Catch, Charlock, Chickweed, Chlorella, Cigar(ette), Cissy, Clotbur, Clover, Cobbler's pegs, Cockle, Cocklebur, Colonist, Coltsfoot, Corncockle, Couch, Daisy, Dallop, Dandelion, Darnel, Dock, Dollop, Dulse, Elder, Elodea, Ers, Fag, Fat hen, Femitar, Fenitar, Fluellen, Fluellin, Fucoid, Fumitory, Ground elder, Groundsel, Helodea, Hoe, Indian, Joe-pye, Knapweed, Knawel, Knot-grass, Lanky, Lemna, Mare's-tail, Marijuana, Matfelon, Mayweed, Nard, Nettle, Nipplewort, Nostoc, Onion, Oxygen, Paterson's curse, Pearlwort, Pilewort, Pineapple, Piri-piri, Plantain, Potamogeton, Purslane, Ragi, Ragwort, Reate, Rest-harrow, Ribbon, Ribwort, Ruderal, Runch, Sagittaria, Sargasso, Scal(l)awag, Scallywag, Senecio, Softy, Sorrel, Speedwell, Spurge, Spurrey, Sudd, Sun-spurge, Swine's-cress, Tansy, Tare, Thistle, Tine, Tobacco, Tormentil, Twitch, Ulotrichale, Ulva, Vetch, Viper's bugloss, Wartcress, Widow's, Winnow, Yarr

Weedkiller Arsenic, Atrazine, Dalapon, Diquat, Diuron, Herbicide, Paraquat®, Selective, Simazine

Week(s), Weekly Ember, Expectation, Great, Hebdomadary, Holy, Omer, Orientation, Ouk, Oulk, Passion, Periodical, Rag, Rogation, Schoolies, Sennight, Working

Weekday Feria

Weekend K, Sat, Sun

Weep(er), Weepy, Wept Bawl, Blubber, Cry, Grat, Greet, Lachrymose, Lament, Loser, Maudlin, Niobe, Ooze, Pipe, Screet, Seep, Sob, Wail

Weevil Anthonomous, Bean, Boll, Bug, Cornworm, Curculio, Diamond-beetle, Grain, Insect, Pea, Rice, Seed, Snout beetle

Weft Roon, Shot, Texture, Warp, Woof

Weigh(ing), Weigh down, Weight(s), Weighty All-up, Apothecaries', Arroba, Artal, As, Atomic, Avoirdupois, Balance, Bantam, Baric, Bob, Bow, Bulk, Burden, Candie, Candy, Cantar, Carat, Catty, Cental, Centner, Clout, Clove, Consider, Count, Counterpoise, Cruiser, Ct, Dead, Decagram(me), Deliberate, Derham, Dirham, Dirhem, Drachm(a), Drail, Dram, Dumbbell, Emphasis, Equivalent, Feather, Fother, G, Gerah, Grain, Gram, Grammage, Gross, Heft, Importance, Impost, Incumbent, Journey, Kandy, Kantar, Kat(i), Katti, Kerb, Khat, Kin, Kip, Last, Liang, Libra, Lisp(o)und, Live, Load, Mark, Massive, Maund, Metage, Metrology, Mina, Minimum, Mna, Molecular, Moment, Mouse, Nail, Nett, Obol, Oke, Onerous, Oppress, Ounce, Overpoise, Oz, Pease, Peaze, Peck, Peise, Peize, Perpend,

Peyse, Pikul, Plumb-bob, Plummet, Poise, Ponderal, Pood, Pound, Pregnant, Preponderance, Prey, Pud, Pudge, Quintal, Recul, Rod, Rotl, Rotolo, Sash, Scruple, Seer, Semuncia, Ser, Sinker, Sit, Slang, Slung-shot, Stone, Stress, Talent, Tare, Throw, Tical, Tod, Tola, Ton(nage), Tonne, Tophamper, Tron(e), Troy, Truss, Trutinate, Unce, Unmoor, Welter, Wey, Wt

Weighing machine Bismar, Scales, Steelyard, Tron(e)

Weightless Agravic

Weight-lifter Crane, Lewis, Windlass

Weir Cauld, Dam, Garth, Kiddle, Kidel, Lasher, Pen, Watergate

Weird Bizarre, Curious, Dree, Eerie, Eery, Eldritch, Kookie, Offbeat, Spectral, Strange, Supernatural, Taisch, Uncanny, Zany

Welch, Welsh Abscond, Cheat, Default, Embezzle, Levant, Rat, Reneg(u)e, Renig, Skedaddle, Weasel

Welcome, Welcoming Aloha, Ave, Bel-accoyle, Ciao, Embrace, Entertain, Glad-hand, Greet, Haeremai, Hallo, Halse, Hello, Hi, Hospitable, How, Hullo, Karanga, Powhiri, Receive, Reception, Salute, Yellow-ribbon

Weld(ing) Arc, Butt, Cold, Explosion, Fillet, Friction, Fuse, Gas, Join, Merge, MIG, Resistance, Seam, Sinter, Stud, Tack, TIG, Ultrasonic, Unite

Welfare Advantage, Alms, Benison, Ha(y)le, Heal, Health, Sarvodaya, Social, Weal

Welkin Firmament, Sky

Well (done) Artesian, Atweel, Aweel, Bien, Bore(hole), Bravo, Carbon, Casinghead, Cenote, Chipper, Development, Discovery, Dropping, Dry hole, Euge, Famously, Fine, Fit, Gas, Gasser, Good, Gosh, Gusher, Hale, → **HEALTHY**, Hot, Inkpot, Ka pai, Law, Mickery, My, Namma hole, Odso, Oh, Oil, Phreatic, Potential, Pump, So, Source, Spa, Spring, Sump, Surge, Teek, Um, Upflow, Wildcat, Zemzem

Wellbeing Atweel, Bien-être, Comfort, Euphoria, Euphory, Good, Health, Oomph, Welfare

Well-born Eugene

Well-bred Genteel

Well-built Sturdy, Tight

Well-covered Chubby, Padded

Well-curb Puteal

Welles Orson

Wellington, Welly Accelerate, Boot, Green, Gumboot, Iron Duke, Nosey

Well-known Famous, Illustrious, Notorious, Notour, Prominent

Well-off Affluent, Far, Rich, Wealthy

Well part Bucket, Shadoof, Shaduf

Wells Bombardier, Fargo, Sadler's

Well-wisher Friend

▶ **Welsh** *see* **WELCH**

Welsh(man) Briton, Brittonic, Brython, Cake, Cambrian, Celtic, Cog, Cym(ric), Cymry, Dai, Ebbw, Emlyn, Evan, Fluellen, Gareth, Harp, Idris, Ifor, Ivor, Keltic, P-Celtic, P-Keltic, Rabbit, Rarebit, Rees, Rhys, Sion, Taff(y), Tudor, W

Wen Cyst, Talpa, Tumour, Wart

Wench Blowze, Court, Girl, Gouge, Hussy, Maid, Ramp, Rig, Smock, Strumpet

Wend Meander, Sorb, Steer

Wendy Darling, House

Went Left, Sold, Yode

Werewolf Loup-garou, Lycanthrope, Nazi, Turnskin, Vampire

Wesleyan Epworth, Methodist

West(ern), Westerly Ang mo, Far, Favonian, Hesperian, Mae, Middle, Movie,

Oater, Occidental, Ponent, Spaghetti, Sunset, W, Wild

West African Fantee, Fanti, Kroo, Wolof

▷ **West end** *may indicate* 't' or 'W1'

West Indian Carib, Creole, Jamaican, Taino

Westminster SW1

Wet(ting) Bedabble, Bedraggled, Clammy, Daggle, Damp, Dank, Dew, Dip, Douse, Dowse, Drench, Drip(ping), Drook, Drouk, Embrue, Enuresis, Feeble, Humect, Humid, Hyetal, Imbrue, Imbue, Irrigate, Irriguous, Madefy, Madid, Marshy, Moil, Moist(en), Molly, Namby-pamby, Pee, Piddle, Pouring, Rainy, Ret(t), Roral, Roric, Runny, Saturate, Shower, Simp(leton), Sipe, Sluice, → SOAK, Sodden, Sopping, Sour, Steep, Tiddle, Tipsy, Urinate, Wat, Wee, Widdle, Wimpy, Wringing

Whack(ed) Belt, Bemaul, Biff, Deadbeat, Joll, Joule, Jowl, Lambast, Lounder, Swat, Swish, Thump

Whale(meat), Whaling Baleen, Beaked, Beluga, Black, Blower, Blubber, Blue, Bottlehead, Bottlenose, Bowhead, Bull, Cachalot, Calf, Cetacea(n), Cete, Cow, Cowfish, Dolphin, Dorado, Fall, Fin(back), Finner, Gam, Glutton, Grampus, Greenland, Grey, Greyback, Humpback, Killer, Kreng, Leviathan, Manatee, Minke, Monodon, Mysticeti, Narwhal, Odontoceti, Paste, Physeter, Pilot, Pod, Porpoise, Right, River dolphin, Rorqual, School, Scrag, Sea-canary, Sea-unicorn, Sei, Social, Sperm, Spouter, Sulphur-bottom, Thrasher, Toothed, Toothless, White, Zeuglodon(t)

▷ **Whale** *may indicate* an anagram

Whalebone Busk

Whaler Ahab, Harpooner, Ship, Specksioneer, Specktioneer, Waister

Whales' meat Clio

Wham Bang, Collide

Whang Blow, Flog, Thrash, Whack

Wharf(inger) Dock(er), Jetty, Key, Landing, Pier, Quay, Roustabout, Rouster, Staith(e)

What Anan, Eh, How, Pardon, Que, Siccan, That, Which

Whatnot, What's-its-name Dinges, Dingus, Doings, Doobrey, Doobrie, Étagère, Gismo, Jiggamaree, Jiggumbob, Thingamy, Thingumajig, Thingumbob, Thingummy, Timenoguy

Wheat Amber, Amelcorn, Bald, Beard(ed), Beardless, Blé, Bulg(h)ur, Cone, Couscous, Cracked, Durum, Einkorn, Emmer, Federation, Fromenty, Frumenty, Furme(n)ty, Furmity, Grain, Hard, Mummy, Red, Rivet, Sarrasin, Sarrazin, Seiten, Semolina, Sharps, Soft, Spelt, Spring, Triticum, White, Winter

Wheatsheaf Bale, Gerbe, Stook

Wheedle Banter, Barney, Blandish, Butter up, Cajole, Coax, Cog, Cuiter, Cuittle, Flatter, Inveigle, Tweedle, Whilly(whaw)

Wheel(er) Balance, Bedel, Bevel, Bicycle, Big, Bogy, Breast, Buff(ing), Caracol(e), Caster, Castor, Catherine, Chain, Chark(h)a, Circle, Cistern, Count, Crown, Cycle, Daisy, Disc, Driving, Emery, Epicycloidal, Escape, Fan, Felloe, Felly, Ferris, Fifth, Fortune, Gear, Grinding, Gyrate, Helm, Hurl, Idle(r), Jagger, Kick, Lantern, Magnate, Medicine, Mitre, Monkey, Mortimer, Nabob, Nose, Paddle, Pattern, Pedal, Pelton, Perambulator, Persian, Pin, Pinion, Pitch, Pivot, Planet, Potter's, Prayer, Pulley, Rag, Ratchet, Rhomb, Roll, Rotate, Roulette, Rowel, Sheave, Snail, Spider, Spinning, Sprocket, Spur, Star, Steering, Stepney, Stitch, Swing, Tail, Throwing-table, Tread, Trindle, Trochus, Trolley, Truckle, Trundle, → TURN, Tympan(um), Water, Web, Wharve, Wire, Worm, Zoetrope

Wheelbarrow Monotroch

Wheelhouse Caravan, Paddle-box

Wheel-hub Axle, Nave

Wheelman Cyclist, Ixion

Wheelwright Spokesman

Wheeze Asthma, Jape, Joke, Pant, Ploy, Rale, Reak, Reik, Rhonchus, Ruse, Stridor, Trick, Whaisle, Whaizle

Whelk Buckie, Limpet, Shellfish, Stromb, Triton

Whelm Nalla(h), Nulla(h)

Whelp Bear, Bra(t)chet, Pup

When(ever) Although, As, If, Once, Though, Time

Where(abouts) Location, Neighbourhood, Place, Site, Vicinity, Whaur, Whither

Wherefore Cause, Reason, Why

Whereupon So, When

Wherewithal Finance, Means, Money, Needful, Resources

Wherry Barge, Rowboat

Whet(stone) Coticular, Excite, Hone, Rubstone, Sharpen, Stimulate

Whether Conditional, If

Whey Plasma, Serum, Whig

Which(ever), Which is Anyway, As, QE, Whatna, Whilk, Who

Whiff Breath, Cigarette, Gust, Hum, Puff, Redolence, Smatch, Sniff, Trace, Waft

Whig Adullamite, Jig, Rascal, Tory, Whey

While Although, As, Interim, Since, Space, Span, Spell, Though, Throw, Time, When, Whenas, Whereas, Yet

Whim(s), Whimsical, Whimsy Bizarre, Caprice, Conceit, Crotchet, Fad, Fancy, Fantastic, Fay, Fey, Fie, Flisk, Impulse, Kicksy-wicksy, Kink, Notion, Quaint, Quirk, Tick, Toy, Vagary

Whimper Cry, Grizzle, Mewl, Pule, Snivel, Whine

Whin Furze, Gorse, Ulex

Whine, Whinge Cant, Carp, Complain, Cry, Grumble, Kvetch, Mewl, Moan, Peenge, Pule, Snivel, Whimper, Yammer

Whinny Neigh, Nicker, Whicker

Whip(ped), Whip out, Whipping Beat, Braid, Brede, Bullwhack, Bullwhip, Cat, Cat o' nine tails, Chabouk, Chantilly, Chastise, Chief, Cilium, Colt, Crop, Drive, Feague, Firk, Five-line, Flagellate, Flagellum, Flay, Gad, Hide, Jambok, Knout, K(o)urbash, Larrup, → **LASH**, Leather, Limber, Lunge, Quirt, Rawhide, Riem, Scourge, Sjambok, Slash, Steal, Stock, Strap-oil, Swinge, Swish, Switch, Taw, Thong, Three-line, Trounce, Welt, West Country, Whap, Whop

Whippersnapper Dandiprat, Dandyprat, Pup, Squirt

Whirl(er), Whirling Bullroarer, Circumgyrate, Dervish, Eddy, Gyrate, → **IN A WHIRL**, Pivot, Reel, Spin, Swing, Swirl, Vortex, Vortical, Vorticose, Vortiginous, Whirry

Whirlpool Eddy, Gulf, Gurge, Maelstrom, Moulin, Sea purse, Swelchie, Vorago, Vortex, Weel, Wiel

Whirlwind Cyclone, Dust devil, Eddy, Sand-devil, Tornado, Tourbillion, Typho(o)n, Vortex, Willy-willy

Whirr Birr

Whisk Balloon, Chowri, Chowry, Fly, Swish, Switch, Whid, Whip

Whisker(s) Beard, Beater, Burnsides, Cat's, Dundreary, Hackle, Hair, Moustache, Mutton-chop, Samuel, Satyric tuft, Side(-boards), Side-burns, Stibble, Stubble, Vibrissa

Whisk(e)y Alcohol, Barley-bree, Barley-broo, Barley-broth, Bond, Bourbon,

Canadian, Cape smoke, Chain lighting, Corn, Cratur, Crayther, Creature, Fife, Fire-water, Hard stuff, Hard tack, Highball, Hokonui, Hoo(t)ch, Irish, Malt, Monongahela, Moonshine, Morning, Mountain dew, Nip, Peat-reek, Pot(h)een, Ragwater, Red eye, Rye, Scotch, Sourmash, Southern Comfort®, Spunkie, Tanglefoot, Tarantula juice, Usquebaugh, Wheech, Whiss

▷ **Whisky** *may indicate* an anagram

Whisper Breath(e), Bur(r), Hark, Hint, Innuendo, Murmur, Round, Rumour, Rustle, Sigh, Stage, Susurrus, Tittle, Undertone, Whittie-whattie

Whist Dummy, Hush, Long, Progressive, Quiet, Sh, Short, Solo, Whisk and swabbers

Whistle(r) Blow, Boatswain's, Calliope, Catcall, Feedback, Flageolet, Hiss, Marmot, Penny, Ping, Pipe, Ref, Siffle(ur), Sowf(f), Sowth, Steam, Stop, Stridor, Swab(ber), Swanee, Tin, Toot, Tweedle, Tweet, Warbler, Wheeple, Wheugh, Whew, Whiffle, Wolf

Whit Atom, Doit, Figo, Haet, Hait, Hate, Iota, Jot, Particle, Pentecost, Point, Red cent, Straw

White(n), Whitener, Whiteness, White-faced Agene, Agenise, Alabaster, Albedo, Albescent, Albino, Albugineous, Albumen, Argent, Ashen, Au lit, Bakra, Blameless, Blanch, Blanche, Blanco, Bleach, Buckra, Cabbage, Calm, Cam, Camstone, Candid, Candida, Candour, Canescent, Canities, Caucasian, Caum, China, Chinese, Christmas, Cliffs, Collar, Company, Dealbate, Egg, Elephant, Ermine, European, Fang, Fard, Feather, Flag, Flake, French, Glair, Gwen(da), Gwendolen, Gwyn, Hawked, Honorary, Hore, House, Innocent, Ivory, Large, Leucoma, Lie, Lily, Livid, Man, Marbled, Mealy, Niveous, Opal, Oyster, Pakeha, Pale(face), Pallor, Paper, Paris, Pearl, Poor, Pure, Redleg, Russian, Sclerotic, Selborne, Sheep, Silver, Small, Snow(y), Spanish, Taw, Vitiligo, Wan, Wedding, Wyn, Zinc

Whitefish Menominee

Whitefriars Alsatia

Whitehall Ministry

Whitehead Milium

White horse(s) Skipper's daughters, Wave

White man Anglo, Ba(c)kra, Buckra, Caucasian, Corn-cracker, Cracka, Gora, Gub(bah), Haole, Honkie, Honky, Kabloona, Larney, Mzungu, Occidental, Ofay, Pakeha, Paleface, Redleg, Redneck, Umlungu, WASP

Whitewash Calcimine, Excuse, Kalsomine, Lime, Skunk, Trounce

Whitlow Ancome, Felon, Panaritium, Paronychia

Whitsun Pinkster, Pinxter

Whittle Carve, Pare, Sharpen

Whizz Wheech

Who As, Doctor

Whodunit Mystery

Whole, Wholehearted, Wholeness, Wholly All, Cosmos, Eager, Entire(ty), Entity, Fully, Hale, Indiscrete, Intact, Integer, Integrity, Largely, Lot, Sum, Systemic, Thoroughly, Total, Unbroken, Uncut

Wholesale(r) Cutprice, En bloc, Engrosser, Jobber, Root and branch, Stockjobber, Supplier, Sweeping

Wholesome Clean, Good, Healthy, Physical, Sound

Whoop(er), Whooping cough Alew, Celebrate, Chincough, Crane, Cry, Excite, Kink(cough), Kink-host, Pertussis, Swan, War

Whoopee Carouse, Evoe, Hey-go-mad, Roister

Whoosh Birr, Swish

Whopper, Whopping Barn, Crammer, Huge, Immense, Jumbo, Lie, Lig, Oner, Out and outer, Scrouger, Slapper, Slockdolager, Soc(k)dalager, Soc(k)dolager, Soc(k)doliger, Soc(k)dologer, Sogdolager, Sogdoliger, Sogdologer, Stonker, Tale, Taradiddle

Whore Drab, Harlot, Loose woman, Pinnace, Pro, Prostitute, Quail, Road, Strumpet, Tart

Whorl Corolla, Eucyclic, Spiral, Swirl, Verticil, Volute

Why Reason, Yogh

Wick Farm, Rush, Snaste, Snuff, Vill(age)

Wicked(ness) Adharma, Atrocity, → **BAD**, Candle, Criminal, Cru(i)sie, Crusy, Depravity, Devilish, Evil, Facinorous, Flagitious, Goaty, Godless, Heinous, High-viced, Immoral, Impious, Improbity, Iniquity, Lantern, Nefarious, Night-light, Ponerology, Pravity, Rush, Satanic, Scelerate, Sin(ful), Taper, Turpitude, Unholy, Vile

▷ **Wicked** *may indicate* containing a wick

Wicker(work) Basketry, Sale, Seal

Wicket Gate, Hatch, Infield, Pitch, Square, Sticky, Stool, Stump, Yate

Wicket-keeper Stumper

Wide, Widen(ing), Width Abroad, Ample, Bay, Broad, Dilate, Drib, Eclectic, Expand, Extend, Far, Flanch, Flange, Flare, Flaunch, Ga(u)ge, General, Latitude, Miss, Prevalent, Roomy, Set, Spacious, Span, Spread, Sundry, Sweeping, Vast

Wide-awake Alert, Fly, Hat, Wary, Watchful

Widespread Catholic, Diffuse, Epidemic, Extensive, General, Pandemic, Panoramic, Prevalent, Prolate, Rife, Routh(ie), Sweeping

Widow(ed) Bereft, Black, Dame, Dowager, Golf, Grass, Hempen, Jointress, Relict, Sati, Sneerwell, Suttee, Vidual, Viduous, Whydah-bird, Widdy

Wield Brandish, Control, Exercise, Handle, → **MANIPULATE**, Ply, Sound

Wife, Wives Bride, Concubine, Consort, Devi, Dutch, Enid, Evadne, Feme, Feme covert, Fiere, Frau, Goody, Haram, Harem, Harim, Helpmate, Helpmeet, Hen, Her indoors, Kali, Kickie-wickie, Kicksy-wicksy, Kloo(t)chman, Lakshmi, Little woman, Mate, Memsahib, Missis, Missus, Mrs, Mummer's, Partner, Penelope, Pirrauru, Potiphar's, Rib, Seraglio, Spouse, Squaw, Stepford, Trophy, Trouble and strife, Umfazi, Ux(or), Vrou, W

Wig Adonis, Bagwig, Bob(wig), Brigadier, Brutus, Buzz-wig, Cadogan, Campaign, Carpet, Cauliflower, Caxon, Chevelure, Chide, Cockernony, Dalmahoy, Fright, Full-bottomed, Gizz, Gooseberry, Gorgone, Gregorian, Hair(piece), Heare, Jas(e)y, Jazy, Jiz, Macaroni, Major, Periwig, Peruke, Postiche, Ramil(l)ie(s), Rate, Reprimand, Rug, Scold, Scratch, Sheitel, Spencer, Targe, Tie, Toupee, Toupet, Tour

Wiggle, Wiggly Jiggle, Scoleciform, Wobble, Wriggle

Wight Man, Vectis

Wigwam Te(e)pee

Wild Aberrant, Agrestal, Barbarous, Berserk, Bundu, Bush, Chimeric, Crazy, Dionysian, Earl, Errant, Erratic, Extravagant, Farouche, Feral, Frantic, Frenetic, Haggard, Hectic, Lawless, Mad(cap), Manic, Meshugge, Myall, Natural, Rampant, Raver, Riotous, → **SAVAGE**, Unmanageable, Unruly, Violent, Warrigal, West, Woolly

▷ **Wild(ly)** *may indicate* an anagram

Wild beast Eyra, Sapi-utan, Scrubber

Wildcat Lion, Manul, Ocelot, Strike, Tiger

Wilderness Bush, Desert, Ruderal, Sinai, Solitude, Waste

Wild goose Chase, Greylag

Wild oats Haver

Wile, Wily Art, Artful, Artifice, Astute, Braide, → CUNNING, Deceit, Foxy, Peery, Ruse, Shifty, Shrewd, Slee, → SLY, Spider, Stratagem, Streetwise, Subtle, Trick, Versute, Wide

Wilful Deliberate, Headstrong, Heady, Obstinate, Recalcitrant, Wayward

Will, Willing(ly) Alsoon, Amenable, Bard, Bequeath, Bewildered, Biddable, Bill(y), Complaisant, Compliant, Conation, Content, Desire, Devise, Fain, Force, Free, Game, General, Hay, Holographic, Leave, Legator, Leve, Lief, Lieve, Living, Noncupative, Obedient, On, Please, Prone, Purpose, Raring, Rather, Ready, Receptive, Scarlet, Soon, Spirit, Swan, Testament, Testate, Thelma, Volens, Volition, Voluntary, Volunteer, Way, Wimble, Woot

▷ **Will** *may indicate* an anagram

William(s) Bill(y), Conqueror, Occam, Orange, Pear, Rufus, Silent, Sweet, Tell, Tennessee

Will o' the wisp Fen-fire, Friar's lantern, Ignis-fatuus, Jack o'lantern, Min min, Nightfire, Rush, Spunkie

Willow(ing), Willowy Arctic, Crack, Diamond, Lissom(e), Lithe, Osier, Poplar, Port Jackson, Pussy, Salix, Sallow, Sauch, Saugh, Supple, Twilly, Weeping, Withy

Willpower Ab(o)uha, Determination, Strength

Willy-nilly Nolens volens, Perforce

Wilt Decline, Droop, Fade, Flag, Sap, Shalt, Wither

Wiltshireman Moonraker

▶ **Wily** *see* WILE

Wimp(ish) Namby-pamby, Pantywaist, Weed

Wimple Gorget, Meander, Ripple, Turn

▷ **Wimple** *may indicate* an anagram

Win(ner), Winning Achieve, Acquire, Ahead, Appealing, Bangster, Banker, → BEAT, Capot, Champion, Conciliate, Conquer, Cup, Cute, Decider, Disarming, Dormie, Dormy, Earn, Effect, Endearing, First, Gain, Gammon, Hit, Jackpot, Land, Laureate, Lead, Medallist, Motser, Motza, Nice, Pile, Pot, Prevail, Profit, Purler, Repique, Result, Rubicon, Scoop, Shoo-in, Slam, Snip, Success, Sweet, Take, Top dog, → TRIUMPH, Up, Vellet, Velvet, Victor(y), Vole, Walk over, Wrest

Wince Blench, Cringe, Flinch, Recoil

Winch Crab, Crane, Jack, Windlass

Winchester® Rifle

Wind(er), Winding(s), Windy Aeolian, Air, Airstream, Ambages, Anabatic, Anfractuous, Anti-trade, Aquilo(n), Argestes, Auster, Backing, Baguio, Bend, Berg, Bise, Blore, Blow, Bluster, Bora, Boreas, Bottom, Bourasque, Brass, Breeze, Brickfielder, Buran, Burp, Buster, Cape doctor, Capstan, Carminative, Caurus, Chili, Chill, Chinook, Coil, Colic, Cordonazo, Corus, Crank, Creeky, Curl, Curve, Cyclone, Downwash, Draught, Draw, Dust devil, Easterly, Etesian, Euraquilo, Euroclydon, Eurus, Evagation, Favonian, Favonius, Fearful, Firn, Flatulence, Flatus, Flaw, Fo(e)hn, Gale, Gas, G(h)ibli, Greco, Gregale, Gust, Haboob, Harmattan, Heaves, Hurricane, Hurricano, Jet stream, Kamseen, K(h)amsin, Katabatic, Knee-swell, Levant(er), Libecc(h)io, Libs, Link, Maestro, Meander, Meltemi, Mistral, Monsoon, Muzzler, Nervous, Noreast, Norther, Nor(th)wester(ly), Noser, Notus, Ostro, Pampero, Periodic, Ponent, Poop, Prevailing, Puna, Purl, Quarter, Quill, Reeds, Reel, Rip-snorter, Roll, Samiel, Sciroc, Scirocco, Screw, Sea, Second, Series, Serpentine, Shamal, Shimaal, Simoom, Simoon, Sinuous, Sirocco, Slant, Snake, Snifter, Snorter, Solano, Solar, Sough, Souther, Southerly buster, Spiral, Spool,

Squall, Stellar, Sumatra, Surface, Swirl, Tail, Taranaki, Tehuantepecer, Thread, Throw, Tornado, Tortuous, Tourbillon, Trade, Tramontana, Trend, Turn, Twaddle, Twine, Twister, Twisty, Typhon, Typhoon, Vayu, Veer, Veering, Ventose, Volturnus, Waffle, Weave, Wester, Westerly, Whirlblast, White squall, Williwaw, Willy-willy, Winch, Woold, Wrap, Wreathe, Wrest, Wuthering, Zephyr(us), Zonda

Windbag Balloon, Bore, Drogue, Prattler, Whoopee cushion, Zeppelin

Windfall Bonanza, Buckshee, Caduac, Fortune, Godsend, Manna

Windflower Anemone

Windlass Differential, Spanish, Whim, Winch

Windmill Pinwheel, Post, Smock, Whirligig

Window(s) Atmosphere, Bay, Bow, Casement, Catherine-wheel, Companion, Compass, Day, Deadlight, Dormer, Dream-hole, Eye, Eyelids, Fanlight, Fenestella, Fenestra, French, Gable, Garret, Glaze, Guichet, Jalousie, Jesse, Jet, Judas, Lancet, Lattice, Launch, Loop-light, Louver, Louvre, Lozen, Lucarne, Lunette, Luthern, Lychnoscope, Marigold, Mezzanine, Mirador, Monial, Mullion, Oculus, Oeil-de-boeuf, Ogive, Orb, Oriel, Ox-eye, Pane, Pede, Picture, Pop-under, Porthole, Quarterlight, Radio, Re-entry, Rosace, Rose, Round, Sash, Sexfoil, Shop, Shot, Spyhole, Storm, Transom, Trellis, Ventana, Weather, Wheel, Wicket, Windock, Winnock

Window-bar, Window-fastening Astragal, Espagnolette

Windpipe Bronchus, Gular, Throat, Trachea, Weasand

Windscale Beaufort

Windsock Drogue, Sleeve

Windswept Scud

Wind-up End, Fright, Liquidate, Span

Windward Ahold, Aloof, Laveer, Luff, Up

Wine Bin, Cabinet, Case, Cup, Cuvée, Doc, Essence, Fortified, Grand cru, Low, Must, Piece, Pigment, Premier cru, Prisage, Rotgut, Rouge, Sparkling, Steen, Terroir, The grape, Tirage, Varietal, Vat, Vintage, Zymurgy

WINES

2 letters:	Race	Médoc	6 letters:
It	Rosé	Mirin	Barley
	Rosy	Mosel	Barolo
3 letters:	Sack	Negus	Barsac
Dao	Sekt	Pinot	Beaune
Red	Stum	Plonk	Bishop
Sec	Tent	Rhine	Bubbly
Tun	Tutu	Rioja	Canary
Vin	Vino	Soave	Claret
		Straw	Ginger
4 letters:		Syrah	Graves
Asti	5 letters:	Table	Lisbon
Brut	Anjou	Tavel	Malaga
Cava	Anker	Toddy	Merlot
Hock	Biddy	Tokay	Muscat
Mull	Blanc	White	Piment
Palm	Bombo	Xeres	Plotty
Pipe	Comet		Red Ned
Port	Gallo		Sherry
	Macon		

Shiraz
Solera

7 letters:
Alicant
Amoroso
Auslese
Bastard
Catawba
Chablis
Château
Chianti
Cowslip
Demi-sec
Dessert
Eiswein
Fendant
Icewine
Madeira
Malmsey
Margaux
Marsala
Moselle
Oenomel
Orvieto
Pomerol
Pommard
Retsina
Rhenish
Sangria
Vouvray

8 letters:
Bordeaux
Bucellas
Buckfast®
Burgundy
Cabernet
Champers
Charneco
Dubonnet®

Espumoso
Essencia
Frascati
Glühwein
Jerepigo
Kabinett
Log-juice
Malvasia
Malvesie
Montilla
Mountain
Muscadel
Muscadet
Muscatel
Oenology
Pinotage
Pradikat
Red biddy
Resinata
Rheingau
Riesling
Sancerre
Sangaree
Sauterne
Sémillon
Spätlese
Spumante
St Julien
Sylvaner
Verdelho
Vermouth

9 letters:
Bacharach
Bardolino
Champagne
En primeur
Falernian
Gladstone
Hermitage
Hippocras

Hoccamore
Inglenook
Lambrusco
Languedoc
Loll-shrob
Malvoisie
Meersault
Minervois
Muscadine
Ordinaire
Pinot noir
Sauvignon
St Emilion
Tafelwein
Tarragona
Zinfandel

10 letters:
Beaujolais
Bull's blood
Chambertin
Chardonnay
Constantia
Elderberry
Genevrette
Hochheimer
Loll-shraub
Manzanilla
Montrachet
Muscadelle
Napa Valley
Peter-see-me
Piesporter
Sangiovese
Vinho verde

11 letters:
Amontillado
Dom Perignon
Niersteiner
Petite Sirah

Pouilly-Fumé
Rudesheimer
Scuppernong
Steinberger

12 letters:
Johannisberg
Marcobrunner
Supernaculum
Valpolicella
Vin ordinaire

13 letters:
Beerenauslese
Entre-Deux-Mers
Liebfraumilch
Montepulciano
Pouilly-Fuissé

14 letters:
Gewürztraminer
Johannisberger

15 letters:
Lachryma Christi
Liebfrauenmilch

16 letters:
London particular

17 letters:
Cabernet Sauvignon
Châteaux cardboard
Nuits Saint Georges

20 letters:
Trockenbeeren
-auslese

Wine-cellar, Wine-shop Bistro, Bodega, Vault, Vaut(e)
Wine-glass Flute
Wine-making Gallising, Remuage
Wing(s), Winged, Winger, Wing-like Aerofoil, Ala(r), Alula, Annexe, Appendage, Arm, Bastard, → **BIRD**, Branch, Buffalo, Canard, Cellar, Corium, Coulisse, Delta, Dipteral, El(l), Elevon, Elytral, Elytriform, Elytron, Elytrum, Fender, Flap, Flew, Flex, Flipper, Flying, Forward, Gull, Halteres, Hurt, Left, Limb, Parascenia, Parascenium, Patagium, Pennate, Pennon, Pinero, Pinion, Pip, Pterygoid, Putto, Right, Rogallo, Sail, Samariform, Scent-scale, Segreant,

Seraphim, Split, Standard, Sweepback, Sweptback, Sweptwing, Swift, Swingwing, Tailplane, Tectrix, Tegmen, Tormentor, Transept, Van, Vol(et), Water, Wound(ed)

Winged sandals Talaria

▷ **Winger** *may indicate* a bird

Wing-footed Aliped, Fleet, Swift

Wingless Apteral

Wink (at) Atone, Bat, Condone, Connive, Eyelid, Flicker, Ignore, Instant, Nap, Nictitate, Pink, Twinkle

Winnie Pooh

Winnow Fan, Riddle, Separate, Sift, Van, Wecht

Winsome Bonny, Engaging, Gay, Pleasant

Winter, Wintry Blackthorn, Bleak, Brumal, Cold, Dec, Fimbul, Frigid, Frore, Hibernate, Hiemal, Hiems, Hodiernal, Jack Frost, Jasmine, Nuclear, Snowy, W

Winter cherry Chinese lantern

Wintergreen Chickweed, Pyrola, Sarcodes

Winter pear Nelis

Winter-sport Ski

Wipe (out), Wiping Abolish, Abrogate, Absterge, Amortise, Cancel, Cleanse, Demolish, Destroy, Deterge, Dicht, Dight, Eradicate, Expunge, Forget, Hanky, Mop, Nose-rag, Null, Purge, Raze, Retroussage, Slorm, Sponge, Tersion, Tissue

Wire(s), Wiry Aerial, Barb(ed), Cable, Cat's whiskers, Chicken, Coil, Earth, Fencing, Filament, Filar, File, Heald, Heddle, High, Kirschner, Lean, Lecher, Live, Marconigram, Mil, Nichrome®, Nipper, Number eight, Piano, Pickpocket, Razor, Sevice, Shroud, Sinewy, Snake, Solenoid, Spit, Staple, Stilet, Strand, String, Stylet, Telegram, Telegraph, Thoth, Thread, Trace

Wireless (operator), Wireless part Baffle, Set, Sparks, Valve

Wise(acre), Wisdom Advisedly, Ancient, Astute, Athena, Athene, Canny, Depth, Ernie, Ganesa, Gothamite, Gudrun, Hep, Hindsight, Judgement, Judicious, Learned, Long-headed, Lore, Manner, Mimir, Minerva, Norman, Oracle, Owl, Penny, Philosopher, Philosophy, Politic, Polymath, Prajna, Profound, Prudence, Sagacity, Sage, Salomonic, Sapience, Savvy, Shrewd, Smartie, Solomon, Solon, Sophia, Tooth, Wice

Wisecrack Dig, One-liner, Quip

Wise man Balthazar, Caspar, Heptad, Melchior, Nestor, Sage, Sapient, Seer, Solomon, Swami, Thales, Tohunga, Worldly

Wish(es) Ache, Ake, Covet, Crave, Death, Desiderate, → **DESIRE**, Hope, List, Long, Pant, Pleasure, Precatory, Regards, Velleity, Want, Yearn

Wishbone Furcula, Marriage-bone, Merrythought, Skipjack

Wishy-washy Bland, Feeble, Insipid, Irresolute, Milksop, Weak, Wheyey

Wisp(y) Cirrate, Frail, Scrap, Shred, Virga, Wase

Wit(s), Witticism, Witty Acumen, Attic, Badinage, Banter, Brevity, Commonsense, Concetto, Cunning, Dry, Epigram, Esprit, Estimation, Eutrapelia, Eutrapely, Facetious, Fantasy, Gnome, Hartford, Humour, Imagination, Intelligence, Irony, Jest, Jeu d'esprit, Joke, Marbles, Marinism, Memory, Mind, Mot, Mother, Native, Nous, Pawky, Pun, Repartee, Rogue, Sally, Salt, Saut, Sconce, → **SENSE**, Shaft, Smart, Videlicet, Viz, Wag, Weet, Wisecrack, Word-play

Witch(craft) Broomstick, Cantrip, Carline, Circe, Coven, Craigfluke, Crone, Cutty Sark, Enchantress, Ensorcell, Galdragon, Glamour, Goety, Gramary(e), Gyre-carlin, Hag, Hecat(e), Hex, Invultuation, Lamia, Magic, Medea, Myal(ism), Necromancy, Night-hag, Obeahism, Obia, Obiism, Pishogue, Pythoness, Salem, Selim, Sibyl, Sieve, Sorceress, Speller, Sycorax, Trout, Valkyrie, Vaudoo, Vilia,

Voodoo, Water, Weird, Wicca

Witch-doctor Boyla, Medicine man, Mganga, Obi, Pawaw, Powwow, Sangoma, Shaman

Witch-hazel Fothergilla, Platan(e), Winter-bloom

Witch-hunter McCarthy

With And, By, Con, Cum, Hereby, In, Mit, Of, Plus, W

Withdraw(al), Withdrawn Abdicate, Alienate, Aloof, Back out, Breakaway, Cold turkey, Cry off, Detach, Disengage, Distrait, Enshell, Evacuate, Hive off, Inshell, Introvert, Leave, Offish, Palinode, Preserve, Recant, Recoil, Repair, Resile, Reticent, Retire, Retract(ion), Retreat, Revoke, Revulsion, Scratch, Secede, Secesh, Sequester, Shrink, Shy, Stand down, Subduce, Subduct, Unreeve, Unsay

Wither(ed), Withering, Withers Arefy, Atrophy, Blight, Burn, Corky, Die, Droop, Dry, Evanish, Fade, Forpine, Googie, Languish, Marcescent, Miff, Nose, Scram, Sere, Shrink, Shrivel, Welk, Welt

Withershins Eastlin(g)s

▷ **With gaucherie** *may indicate* an anagram

Withhold(ing), Withheld Abstain, Conceal, Curt, Deny, Detain, Detinue, Hide, Keep, → **RESERVE**, Ritenuto, Trover

Within Enclosed, Endo-, Immanent, Indoors, Inside, Interior, Intra

With it Hep, Hip, Syn, Trendy, W

Without Bar, Beyond, Ex, Lack(ing), Less, Minus, Orb, Outdoors, Outside, Sans, Save, Sen, Senza, Sine, X

▷ **Without** *may indicate* one word surrounding another

▷ **Without restraint** *may indicate* an anagram

Without stimulus Nastic

Withstand Blight, Brave, Contest, Defy, Endure, Oppose, Resist, Weather

Witless Crass, → **STUPID PERSON**

Witness Attend, Attest, Bystander, Catch, Character, Compurgator, Confirm, Crown, Deponent, Depose, Endorse, Evidence, Experience, Expert, Eye, Glimpse, Hostile, Jehovah's, Mark, Martyr, Material, Muggletonian, Note, Notice, Observe, Obtest, Onlooker, Perceive, Proof, → **SEE**, Show, Sight, Sign, Spy, Stander-by, Survey, Testament, Teste, Testify, Testimony, View, Watch

Witness-box Peter, Stand

▶ **Witticism** *see* **WIT**

Wizard (priest) Archimage, Carpathian, Conjuror, Expert, Gandalf, Hex, Magician, Merlin, Obiman, Oz, Prospero, Shaman, Sorcerer, Super, Warlock, → **WITCH-DOCTOR**

Wizen(ed) Dehydrate, Dry, Sere, Shrivel, Sphacelate, Wither

Woad Anil, Dye, Indigo, Isatis, Pastel, Pastil

Wobble, Wobbling, Wobbly Chandler's, Coggle, Precess, Quaver, Reel, Rock, Shimmy, Shoggle, Shoogle, Teeter, Totter, Tremble, Trillo, Unstable, Wag, Waggle, Walty, Waver, Wibble

Wodehouse Plum

Woe(ful) Alack, Alas, Bale, Bane, Distress, Doole, Dule, Ewhow, Execrable, Gram, Grief, Hurt, Jeremiad, Lack-a-day, Misery, Pain, Plague, → **SORROW**, Torment, Tribulation, Unhappy

Wolds Lincoln(shire), Yorkshire

Wolf(ish), Wolf-like Akela, Assyrian, Bolt, Cancer, Carcajou, Casanova, Coyote, Cram, Dangler, Earth, Engorge, Fenrir, Fenris, Gorge, Grey, Ise(n)grim, Lobo, Lone, Lothario, Lupine, Luster, Lycanthrope, MI, Michigan, Pack, Prairie, Rake, Ravenous, Red, Rip, Roué, Rout, Rudolph, Rye, Scoff, Sea, Strand, Tasmanian,

Thylacine, Tiger, Timber, Wanderer, Were, Whistler

Wolfram Tungsten

Wolf's bane Aconite, Friar's-cap

Wolseley Sir Garnet

Woman(hood), Women Anile, Bellibone, Besom, Biddy, Bimbo, Bint, Bit, Boiler, Broad, Cailleach, Callet, Chai, Chapess, Chook, Citess, Cotquean, Crone, Cummer, Dame, Daughter, Distaff, Doe, Dona(h), Dorcas, Doris, Drab, Duenna, Eve, F, Fair, Fair sex, → **FEMALE**, Feme, Flapper, Floozy, Frail, Frow, Gammer, Gimmer, Gin, Girl, Gyno-, -gyny, Harpy, Harridan, Hen, Her, Ho, Inner, It, Jade, Jane, Kloo(t)chman, Lady, Liberated, Lilith, Lorette, Madam(e), Mademoiselle, Maenad, Mary, Miladi, Milady, Millie, Minge, Mob, Mort, Ms, Muliebrity, Painted, Pandora, Peat, Pict, Piece, Piece of goods, Placket, Popsy, Quean, Queen, Ramp, Rib, Ribibe, Ronyon, Rudas, Runnion, Sabine, Sakti, Scarlet, Shakti, Shawlay, Shawlie, She, Skirt, Sloane Ranger, Sort, Squaw, Tail, Tedesca, Tib, Tiring, Tit, Tottie, Totty, Trot, Umfazi, Vahine, Wahine, Weaker sex, Wifie, Zena

Womaniser Casanova, Lady-killer, Poodle-faker, Wolf

Womb Belly, Matrix, Metritis, Side, Uterus, Ventricle

Women's club, Women's lib S(h)akti, Soroptimist

Won Chon, W

Wonder(s) Admire, Agape, Amazement, AR, Arkansas, Arrah, Awe, Chinless, Colossus, Ferly, Grape-seed, Marle, → **MARVEL**, Meteor, Mirabilia, Miracle, Muse, Nine-day, Phenomenon, Prodigy, Seven, Speculate, Stupor, Suppose, Surprise, Thaumatrope, Wheugh, Whew, Wow

Wonderful(ly) Amazing, Bees' knees, Bitchin(g), Chinless, Épatant, Fantastic, Far-out, Ferly, Geason, Gee-whiz, Glorious, Gramercy, Great, Keen, Lal(l)apalooza, Magic, Mirable, Old, Purely, Ripping, Smashing, Sublime, Superb

Wonder-worker Fakir, Thaumaturgist, Thaumaturgus

Wonky Cockeyed

Wont(ed) Accustomed, Apt, Custom, Habit, Shan't, Used, Winna

Woo(er) Address, Beau, Carve, Court, Seduce, Suitor, Swain

Wood(s), Wooden, Woodland, Woody Arboretum, Batten, Beam, Board, Boord(e), Brake, Cask, Channel, Chipboard, Chuck, Chump, Clapboard, Conductor, Dead, Deadpan, Expressionless, Fardage, Fathom, Fire, Fish, Funk, Furious, Gantry, Gauntree, Hanger, Hard, Hyle, Kindling, Knee, Lath, Lumber, Mad, Magnetic, Miombo, Nemoral, Nemorous, Offcut, Pallet, Plastic, Pulpwood, Punk, Silvan, Slat, Spinney, Splat, Spline, Splint, Stolid, Sylvan, Three-ply, Timber, Tinder, Touch, Treen, Trees, Twiggy, Vert, Xylem, Xyloid

WOODS

3 letters:			5 letters:
Ash	Bowl	Lima	Agila
Box	Carr	Lime	Algum
Cam	Cord	Pine	Almug
Elm	Cork	Rata	Balsa
Log	Deal	Rock	Bavin
Red	Eugh	Shaw	Beech
	Gapó	Soft	Cedar
	Holt	Spar	Copse
4 letters:	Iron	Wild	Drive
Beef	King	Yang	Ebony
Bent	Lana		

Elfin
Firth
Frith
Green
Grove
Heben
Hurst
Igapó
Iroko
Jarul
Joist
Kokra
Lance
Maple
Mazer
Myall
Opepe
Peach
Plane
Ramin
Rowan
Sapan
Spoon
Stink
Taiga
Thorn
Tiger
Tulip
Zante
Zebra

6 letters:
Alerce
Bamboo
Beaver
Birnam
Bocage
Brazil
Canary
Carapa
Cheese
Citron

Citrus
Dingle
Forest
Fustet
Fustic
Fustoc
Gaboon
Gopher
Herman
Jarool
Jarrah
Letter
Lignum
Loggat
Manuka
Obeche
Orache
Orange
Paddle
Poplar
Raddle
Sabele
Sabicu
Sandal
Sapele
Sappan
Sissoo
Sponge
Tallow
Waboom
Walnut
Wandoo
Yellow

7 letters:
Amboina
Barwood
Boscage
Brassie
Cambium
Coppice
Dudgeon

Dunnage
Duramen
Gambrel
Gumwood
Hadrome
Hickory
Leopard
Meranti
Palmyra
Paranym
Pimento
Sanders
Sapwood
Shawnee
Shittim
Trumpet
Wallaba

8 letters:
Agalloch
Alburnum
Basswood
Bushveld
Caatinga
Coulisse
Harewood
Hornbeam
Kingwood
Laburnum
Ligneous
Mahogany
Masonite®
Mountain
Pyengadu
Pyinkado
Rosewood
Sapucaia
Shagbark
Southern
Tamarack

9 letters:
Briarwood
Butternut
Caliature
Campeachy
Cocuswood
Eaglewood
Fruitwood
Heartwood
Ivorywood
Krummholz
Matchwood
Partridge
Porcupine
Quebracho
Satinwood
Snakewood
Torchwood

10 letters:
Afrormosia
Blockboard
Bulletwood
Calamander
Candlewood
Cheesewood
Chittagong
Coromandel
Fiddlewood
Greenheart
Hackmatack
Nettle-tree
Palisander
Sneezewood
Springwood
Summerwood

11 letters:
Lignum-vitae
Sanderswood
Slippery elm

▷ **Wood** *may indicate* an anagram (in sense of mad)
Wood-carver Bodger, Gibbons, Whittler
Woodchuck Bobac, Marmot
Woodcock Becasse, Beccaccia, Snipe
Woodlouse Isopod, Oniscus, Slater
Woodman Ali (Baba), Coureur de bois, Feller, Forester, Hewer, Logger, Lumberjack, Sawyer
Woodpecker Bird, Flicker, Hickwall, Picarian, Rainbird, Sapsucker, Saurognathae,

Witwall, Woodspite, Woodwale, Yaffle

Wood-pigeon Bird, Cushat, Que(e)st, Qu(o)ist, Torquate

Wood-sorrel Oca

Wood-tar Furan, Furfuran

Woodwind Bassoon, Clarinet, Cornet, Flute, Oboe, Piccolo, Pipe, Recorder, Reed

Woodwork(er) Ebonist, Intarsia, Marquetrie, Marquetry, Sloid, Sloyd, Tarsia, Termite

Woodworm Gribble, Termes

Wookey Stalactite

Wool(len), Woolly Alpaca, Angora, Aran, Ardil, Bainin, Barège, Beige, Berlin, Botany, Bouclé, Calamanco, Cardi(gan), Cashmere, Cas(s)imere, Clean, Clip, Cotton, Crutchings, Daglock, Delaine, Doeskin, Dog, Doily, Down, Doyley, Drugget, Duffel, Fadge, Fingering, Fleece, Flock, Frib, Frieze, Fuzz, Glass, Greasy, Guernsey, Hank, Hause-lock, Hogget, Indumentum, Jaeger, Jersey, Kashmir, Ket, Lanate, Laniferous, Lanigerous, Lanose, Lock, Loden, Merino, Mineral, Mortling, Moul, Mullein, New, Noil(s), Nun's-veiling, Offsorts, Oo, Pashm, Pelage, Persian, Pine, Qiviut, Rock, Rolag, Sagathy, Saxon, Say, Shahtoosh, Shalloon, Shamina, Shetland, Shoddy, Skein, Skin, Slag, Slipe, Slip-on, Slub, Smart, Spencer, Staple, Steel, Strouding, Swansdown, Tamise, Tammy, Telltale, Thibet, Three-ply, Tod, Tricot, Tweed, Twin set, Vicuña, Virgin, Wire, Wood, Worcester, Yarn, Zephyr, Zibel(l)ine

Wool-gather(er), Woolgathering Argo, Dreamer, Reverie

Wool-holder, Woolsack Bale, Distaff

Woolly-bear Tiger-moth, Woubit

Wool-oil Yolk

Wooster Bertie

Woozy Drunk, Faint, Vague, Woolly

Worcester Wigorn

Word(s), Wording, Wordy Appellative, Bahuvrihi, Buzz, Cheville, Claptrap, Clipped, Clitic, Code, Comment, Content, Dick, Dit(t), Echoic, Embolalia, Enclitic, Epos, Etymon, Faith, Four-letter, Function, Ghost, Grace, Hapax legomenon, Hard, Heteronym, Hint, Homograph, Homonym, Household, Hyponym, → **IN A WORD**, → **IN TWO WORDS**, Janus, Jonah, Key, Last, Lexeme, Lexicon, Lexis, Loan, Logia, Logos, Long-winded, Lyrics, Mantra, Meronym, Message, Morpheme, Mot, Neologism, News, Nonce, Nonsense, Noun, Oracle, Order, Palabra, Paragram, Paranym, Parenthesis, Parole, Paronym, Paroxytone, Particle, Perissology, Peristomenon, Phrase, Piano, Pledge, Pleonasm, Polysemen, Portmanteau, Preposition, Prolix, Promise, Pronoun, Reserved, Rhematic, Rhyme, Rumour, Saying, Selah, Semantics, Signal, Subtitle, Surtitle, Tatpurusha, Term, Tetragram, Text, Trigger, Trope, Typewriter, Verb, Verbiage, Verbose, Vocab(ulary), Vogue, Warcry, Weasel, Wort, Written

Word-blindness Alexia, Dyslexia

Word-play Charade, Paronomasia, Pun

Workable Feasible, Practical

Workaholic, Work(er), Working(-class), Workmen, Works, Workman(ship) Act(ivate), Ant, Appliqué, Apronman, Artefact, Artel, Artifact, Artificer, Artisan, At it, Barmaid, Beaver, Bee, Blue-collar, Blue-singlet, Bohunk, Boondoggle, Boon(er), Bull, Business, Careerist, Casual, Char, Chargehand, Chigga, Chippy, Chore, Claim, Clock, Colon, Community, Coolie, Corvée, Craftsman, Crew, Darg, Do, Dog, Dogsbody, Draft-mule, Droil, Drudge, Drug, Dung, Earn, Effect, Effort, Em, Erg(ataner), Ergatoid, Erg-nine, Ergon, Ergonomics, Erg-ten, Eta, Everything, Evince, Exercise, Exploit, Factotum, Facture, Fast, Fat, Fettler, Field, Flex(i)time,

Floruit, Fret, Fuller, → **FUNCTION**, Gastarbeiter, Gel, Go, Graft, Grass, Grind, Grisette, Hand, Harness, Hat, Hobo, Horse, Hot-desking, Hunky, Industry, Innards, Job, Journeyman, Key, Knead, Kolhoznik, Labour, Laid, Luddite, Lump, Machinist, Maid, Man, Manipulate, Manpower, McJob, Mechanic, Meng, Menge, Menial, Midinette, Mine, Ming, MO, Moider, Moil, Moonlight, Movement, Navvy, Neuter, Number, Oeuvre, On, Op, Opera(tion), Operative, Operator, Opus, Opusc(u)le, Outside, Ouvrier, Ox, Parergon, Part, Passage, Peasant, Peg, Pensum, Peon, Pink-collar, Ply, Poker, Portfolio, Potboiler, Practise, Production, Prole(tariat), Prud'homme, Public, Pursuit, Red-neck, Reduction, Rep, Ride, Robot, Roughneck, Rouseabout, Roustabout, Run, Salaryman, Samiti, Sandhog, Satisfactory, Scabble, Scapple, Serve, Service, Servile, Seven, Shift, Shop, Situation, Skanger, Slogger, Smithy, Social, Spide, Staff, Stakhanovite, Stevedore, Stint, Strap, Straw, Strive, Support, Surface, Swaggie, Swagman, Sweat, Swink, Take, Tamper, Task, Team, Telecommuter, Temp, Tenail(le), Tenaillon, Termite, Tew, Tick, Till, Toccata, Toil, Toreutic, Travail, Treatise, Trojan, TU, TUC, Turk, Tut, Typto, Uphill, Wage plug, Walla(h), Wark, Welfare, White-collar, Wobblies, Yacker, Yakka, Yakker, Yarco

Work-basket, Workbox Caba(s), Nécessaire

Workbench Banker, Siege

Workhouse Casual ward, Spike, Union

▷ **Working** *may indicate* an anagram

Working-party Bee, Quilting-bee, Sewing-bee, Squad

Workmate Yokefellow

Work out Deduce

Works, Workshop Atelier, Engine, Factory, Forge, Foundry, Garage, Hacienda, Hangar, Innards, Lab, Mill, Passage, Plant, Public, Shed, Shop, Skylab, Smithy, Studio, Sweatshop, Telecottage, Time, Tin, Turnery, Upper

Workshy Indolent, Lazy, Sweer(ed), Sweert, Sweir(t)

World(ly), Worldwide Adland, Carnal, Chthonic, Cosmopolitan, Cosmos, Cyberspace, Dream, Earth, First, Fleshly, Fourth, Free, Ge, Globe, Kingdom, Lay, Lower, Mappemond, Meatspace, Microcosm, Mondaine, Mondial, Mould, Mundane, Nether, New, Old, Orb, Other, Oyster, Planet, Possible, Second, Secular, Sensual, Society, Sphere, Spirit, Temporal, Terra, Terrene, Terrestrial, Third, Universe, Vale, Web, Welt

Worm(-like), Worms, Wormy Acorn, Anguillula, Annelid, Annulata, Apod(e), Apodous, Army, Arrow, Articulata, Ascarid, Bilharzia, Bladder, Blind, Blood, Bob, Bootlace, Brandling, Bristle, Caddis, Capeworm, Caseworm, Catworm, Cestode, Cestoid, Chaetopod, Clamworm, Copper, Dew, Diet, Diplozoon, Edge, Enteropneust, Fan, Filander, Filaria, Flag, Flat, Fluke, Galley, Gape, Gilt-tail, Gordius, Gourd, Gru-gru, Guinea, Hair, Hair-eel, Hairworm, Heartworm, Helminth, Hemichordata, Hookworm, Horsehair, Idle, Inchworm, Leech, Liver-fluke, Lob, Lumbricus, Lytta, Maw, Measuring, Merosome, Miner's, Mopani, Muck, Nemathelminthes, Nematoda, Nematode, Nematodirus, Nematomorpha, Nemertea, Nemertina, Nereid, Night-crawler, Oligochaete, Onychophoran, Paddle, Palmer, Palolo, Paste-eel, Peripatus, Pile, Pin, Piper, Planarian, Platyhelminth, Polychaete, Ragworm, Ribbon, Roundworm, Sabella, Sand-mason, Schistosome, Scoleciform, Scolex, Screw, Seamouse, Serpula, Servile, Ship, Sipunculacea, Sipunculoidea, Stomach, Strawworm, Strongyl(e), Taenia, Tag-tail, Taint, Tapeworm, Tenioid, Teredo, Termite, Threadworm, Tiger tail, Tongue, Toxocara, Trematode, Trichin(ell)a, Trichinosed, Triclad, Tube, Tubifex, Turbellaria, Vermiform, Vinegar, Vinegar eel, Wheat-eel, Wheatworm, Whipworm

Wormkiller Anthelmintic, Santonin

Wormwood Absinth, Appleringie, Artemisia, Moxa, Mugwort, Santonica, Southernwood

Worn (out) Attrite, Bare, Decrepit, Detrition, Effete, Épuisé, Exhausted, Forfairn, Forfoughten, Forjaskit, Forjeskit, Frazzled, Knackered, Old, On, Passé, Raddled, Rag, Seedy, Shabby, Shot, Spent, Stale, Threadbare, Tired, Traikit, Trite, Used, Weathered, Whacked

Worried, Worrier, Worry Agonise, Angst, Annoy, Anxiety, Badger, Bait, Beset, Bother, Brood, Burden, Care(worn), Cark, Chafe, Concern, Deave, Deeve, Distress, Disturb, Dog, Eat, Exercise, Faze, Feeze, Frab, Fret, Fuss, Gnaw, Harass, Harry, Headache, Hyp, Inquietude, Knag, Nag, Perturb, Pester, Pheese, Pheeze, Phese, Pingle, Pium, Preoccupy, Rile, Sool, Stew, Tew, Touse, Towse, Trouble, Unease, Unnerve, Vex, Wherrit, Worn

▷ **Worried** *may indicate* an anagram

Worse(n) Adversely, Degenerate, Deteriorate, Exacerbate, Impair, Inflame, Pejorate, Regress, Relapse, War(re), Waur

Worship(per) Adore, Adulation, Ancestor, Angelolatry, Aniconism, Autolatry, Bless, Churchgoer, Cult, Deify, Devotion, Douleia, Dulia, Epeolatry, Exercise, Fetish, Glorify, Gurdwara, Happy-clappy, Henotheism, Hero, Ibadat, Idolatry, Idolise, Latria, Lauds, Lionise, Liturgics, Lordolatry, Mariolatry, Oncer, Orant, Praise, Puja, Revere, Sabaism, Sakta, Service, Shacharis, Shakta, Sun, Synaxis, Thiasus, Vaishnava, Venerate, Votary, Wodenism

Worst Beat, Best, Defeat, Get, Nadir, Outdo, Overpower, Pessimum, Rock-bottom, Scum, Severest, The pits, Throw, Trounce

Worsted Caddis, Caddyss, Challis, Coburg, Genappe, Lea, Ley, Serge, Shalli, Tamin(e), Whipcord

▷ **Worsted** *may indicate* an anagram

Wort Hopped, Laser, Parkleaves, Plant, Sweet, Tutsan

Worth(while), Worthy, Worthies Admirable, Asset, Be, Cop, Cost, Deserving, Eligible, Estimable, Feck, → **MERIT**, Nine, Notable, Substance, Tanti, Use, Value, Venerable, Virtuous, Wealth

Worthless (person) Base, Beggarly, Bilge, Blown, Bodger, Bootless, Bum, Catchpenny, Cheapjack, Crumb, Cypher, Damn, Despicable, Docken, Dodkin, Doit, Doitkin, Draffish, Draffy, Dreck, Dross, Duff, Fallal, Footra, Fouter, Foutre, Frippery, Gimcrack, Gingerbread, Glop, Gubbins, Hilding, Javel, Jimcrack, Left, Light, Lorel, Lorrell, Losel, Lozell, Manky, Mare's nest, Mud, Nugatory, Nyaff, Obol, Orra, Otiose, Paltry, Pin, Poxy, Punk, Raca, Rag, Rap, Riffraff, Rubbishy, Scabby, Scrote, Scum, Shinkin, Shotten, Siwash, Sorry, Straw, Tinhorn, Tinpot, Tinsel, Tittle, Toerag, Trangam, Trashy, Trumpery, Tuppenny, Twat, Two-bit, Twopenny, Useless, Vain, Vile, Waff, Wanworthy, Wauff

Wotchermean Anan

Would be Assumed, Pseudo, Soi-disant

Wouldn't Nould(e)

Wound(ed) Battery, Bite, Bless, Blighty, Bruise, Chagrin, Coiled, Crepance, Cut, Dere, Engore, Entry, Exit, Flesh, Ganch, Gash, Gaunch, Gore, Harm, Hurt, Injury, Lacerate, Lesion, Maim, Maul, Molest, Mortify, Offend, Pip, Sabre-cut, Scab, Scar, Scath, Scotch, Scratch, Shoot, Snaked, Snub, Sore, Stab, Sting, Trauma, Twined, Umbrage, Vuln, Vulnerary, Walking, Wing, Wint

Woundwort Clown's, Marsh

Woven Faconne, Inwrought, Knitted, Pirnit, Textile, Wattle

Wow Amaze, Howl, Impress, My, Success

Wrack Destroy, Downfall, Kelp, Ore, Torment, Varec(h), Vengeance

Wraith Apparition, Fetch, Ghost, Phantom, Shadow, Spectre

Wrangle(r), Wrangling Altercate, Argie-bargie, → **ARGUE**, Bandy, Bicker, Brangle, Broil, Dispute, Haggle, Horse, Mathematical, Rag, Second, Senior, Vitilitigation

Wrap(per), Wrapping, Wraparound, Wrap up Amice, Amis, Bind, Body, Bubble, Bundle, Cellophane®, Cere, Clingfilm, Cloak, Clothe, Cocoon, Conclude, Emboss, Enfold, Enrol(l), Ensheath(e), Envelop(e), Enwind, Foil, Folio, Furl, Gladwrap®, Hap, Hem, Kimono, Kraft, Lag, Lap, Mail, Mob, Muffle, Negligee, Nori, Outsert, Package, Parcel, Plastic, Roll, Rug, Shawl, Sheath(e), Shroud, Stole, Swaddle, Swathe, Throw, Tinfoil, Tsutsumu, Velamen, Wap, Wimple

Wrasse Conner, Cunner, Parrot-fish, Scar

Wrath Anger, Cape, Fury, Ire, Passion, Vengeance

Wreak Avenge, Indulge, Inflict

Wreath(e) Adorn, Anadem, Bridal, Chaplet, Coronal, Crown, Entwine, Festoon, Garland, Laurel, Lei, Torse, Tortile, Twist

Wreathe(d) Hederated

Wreck(age), Wrecked, Wrecker Blotto, Crab, Debris, Demolish, Devastate, Flotsam, Founder, Goner, Hesperus, Hulk, Lagan, Ligan, Loss, Luddite, Mutilate, Nervous, Ruin(ate), Sabotage, Shambles, Shatter, Sink, Smash, Subvert, Torpedo, Trash, Wrack

▷ **Wrecked** *may indicate* an anagram

Wren Architect, Bird, Fire-crested, Golden-crested, Hannah, Heath, Jenny, Kinglet, Rifleman-bird, Sailor, Superb blue, Willow

Wrench Allen, Bobbejaan, Box, Fit, Jerk, Lug, Mole, Monkey, Nut, Pin, Pipe, Pull, Screw, Socket, Spanner, Spider, Sprain, Stillson®, Strain, Strap, T-bar, Tear, Torque, Twist, Windlass, Wrest

Wrestle(r), Wrestling All-in, Antaeus, Arm, Backbreaker, Basho, Bearhug, Bodycheck, Boston crab, Catch-as-catch-can, Catchweight, Clinch, Clothes line, Cross press, Featherweight, Flying mare, Folding-press, Freestyle, Full-nelson, Gr(a)eco-Roman, Grapple, Grovet, Half-nelson, Hammerlock, Haystacks, Headlock, Hip-lock, → **HOLD**, Indian, Judo, Knee-drop, Makunouchi, Milo, Monkey climb, Mud, Nelson, Niramiai, Ozeki, Palaestral, Pancratium, Pinfall, Posting, Rikishi, Sambo, Stable, Straight arm lift, Struggle, Sumo, Sumotori, Suplex, Tag, Tag (team), Tussle, Whip, Wraxle, Wristlock, Writhe, Yokozuna

Wretch(ed) Abject, Bally, Blackguard, Blue, Caitiff, Chap-fallen, Cullion, Donder, Forlorn, Git, Hapless, Lorn, Low, Measly, Miser, Miserable, Peelgarlic, Pilgarlick, Pipsqueak, Pitiable, Poltroon, Poor, Punk, Rat, Scoundrel, Scroyle, Seely, Snake, Unblest, Wo(e), Woeful

▷ **Wretched** *may indicate* an anagram

Wriggle Hirsle, Shimmy, Squirm, Twine, Wiggle, Writhe

Wring(er) Drain, Extort, Mangle, Screw, Squeeze, Twist

Wrinkle(d), Wrinkly Clue, Cockle, Corrugate, Crankle, Crease, Crepy, Crimple, Crimpy, Crinkle, Crow's-foot, Crumple, Fold, Frounce, Frown, Frumple, Furrow, Gen, Groove, Headline, Hint, Idea, Line, Lirk, Plissé, Plough, Pucker, Purse, Ridge, Rimple, Rivel, Rop(e)y, Ruck(le), Rugose, Rumple, Runkle, Seamy, Shrivel, Sulcus, Time-worn, Tip, Whelk, Wizened, Wrizled

Wrist Carpus, Radialia, Shackle-bone

Writ(s) Attachment, Audita querela, Capias, Certiorari, Cursitor, Dedimus, Distringas, Elegit, Fieri facias, Filacer, Habeas corpus, Holy, Injunction, Jury process, Latitat, Law-burrows, Mandamus, Mise, Mittimus, Noverint, Praemunire, Process, Quo warranto, Replevin, Scirefacias, Significat, Subpoena, Summons,

Supersedeas, Supplicavit, Tolt, Venire, Venire facias, Warrant

Write(r), Writing Allograph, Amphigory, Annotator, Apocrypha, → **AUTHOR**, Automatic, Ballpoint, Biographer, Biro®, Bloomsbury Group, Book-hand, Boustrophedon, Calligraphy, Causerie, Cento, Charactery, Clerk, Clinquant, Collectanea, Columnist, Continuity, Copperplate, Creative, Cuneiform, Cursive, Diarist, Dite, Draft, → **DRAMATIST**, Elohist, Endorse, Endoss, Engross, Epigrammatise, Epistle, → **ESSAYIST**, Expatiate, Farceur, Festschrift, Fist, Form, Formulary, Freelance, Ghost, Gongorism, Graffiti, Grammatology, Graphite, Hack, Hairline, Hand, Haplography, Hieratic, Hieroglyphics, Hiragana, Indite, Ink, Inkhorn-mate, Ink-jerker, Inkslinger, Inscribe, Join-hand, Jot(tings), Journalese, Journalist, Journo, Kalakana, Kaleyard School, Kana, Kanji, Katakana, Keelivine, Keelyvine, Leader, Lexigraphy, Lexis, Linear A, Lipogram, Littérateur, Longhand, Lucubrate, Marivaudage, Memoirist, Minoan, Mirror, Miscellany, Ms(s), Nesk(h), Nib, Notary, Notate, Novelese, → **NOVELIST**, Paragraphia, Pasigraphy, Pen, Pencil, Penmanship, Penne, Penny-a-liner, Pentel®, Phrasemonger, Picture, Pinyin, Planchette, → **POET**, Polemic, Pot-hook, Prosaist, Proser, Pseudepigrapha, Psychogram, Psychography, Purana, Purple patch, Quill, Roundhand, Samizdat, Sanskrit, Sci-fi, Scissorer, Scratch, Screed, Screeve, Scribe, Scrip(t), Scripture, Scrivener, Scrow, Scytale, Secretary, Shaster, Shastra, Sign, Sling-ink, Small-hand, Space, Spirit, Stichometry, Style, Stylography, Subscript, Superscribe, Sutra, Syllabary, Syllabic, Syllabism, Syngraph, Tantra, Text, Tractarian, Transcribe, Treatise, Tushery, Uncial, Wordsmith, Zend-Avesta

WRITERS

3 letters:
APH
Eco
Lee
Paz
Poe
RLS

4 letters:
Amis
Asch
Aymé
Bede
Behn
Bolt
Cary
Dahl
Elia
Gide
Hope
Hugo
Hunt
King
Lamb
Lang
Loos
Loti
Lyly
Mann
More
Nash
Opie
Ovid
Pope
Saki
Sand
Shaw
Snow
Ward
West
Zola

5 letters:
Acton
Albee
Auden
Ayres
Bates
Blake
Caine
Camus
Corvo
Crane
Defoe
Doyle
Dumas
Eliot
Ellis
Genet
Gogol
Gorki
Gorky
Gosse
Greer
Grimm
Hardy
Harte
Henty
Hesse
Heyer
Homer
Hoyle
Ibsen
Innes
James
Joyce
Kafka
Lewis
Lodge
Lorca
Mason
Milne
Munro
Musil
Nashe
Orczy
Ouida
Pater
Paton
Pliny
Pound
Powys
Reade
Renan
Rilke
Sagan
Scott
Seuss
Shute
Spark
Stark
Stein
Swift
Synge

Twain
Verne
Vidal
Waugh
Wells
White
Wilde
Woolf
Yates
Yonge

6 letters:
Ambler
Arnold
Artaud
Asimov
Atwood
Austen
Balzac
Baring
Barrie
Belloc
Bellow
Borges
Borrow
Braine
Bronte
Buchan
Bunyan
Butler
Capote
Cicero
Clarke
Conrad
Cowper
Cronin
Daudet
Dryden
Engels
Fowles
France
Gibbon
Goethe
Graves
Greene
Heller
Hobbes
Hughes
Huxley
Jerome
Jonson

Le Fanu
London
Lucian
Lytton
Mailer
Malory
Mannin
Masoch
Miller
Milton
Morgan
Nerval
Nesbit
Onions
Orwell
Proust
Racine
Romaji
Runyon
Ruskin
Sapper
Sappho
Sayers
Sendac
Sewell
Smiles
Steele
Sterne
Stoker
Storey
Thomas
Updike
Virgil
Walton
Wilder

7 letters:
Addison
Aldrich
Aretino
Bagehot
Bagnold
Ballard
Beckett
Bennett
Bentley
Boileau
Boswell
Burgess
Carlyle
Chaucer

Chekhov
Cobbett
Cocteau
Colette
Collins
Cookson
Coppard
Corelli
Cranmer
Deeping
Dickens
Dodgson
Drabble
Dreiser
Durrell
Emerson
Fenelon
Forster
Gissing
Golding
Haggard
Herbert
Hichens
Johnson
Kipling
Lardner
Marryat
Maugham
Mauriac
Mérimée
Mitford
Moravia
Murdoch
Nabokov
Naipaul
Peacock
Pushkin
Pynchon
Ransome
Rostand
Rushdie
Saroyan
Sassoon
Shelley
Simenon
Sitwell
Surtees
Terence
Thoreau
Tolkien
Tolstoy

Travers
Wallace
Walpole
Wharton
Whitman
Wyndham

8 letters:
Anacreon
Andersen
Beaumont
Bradbury
Browning
Caldwell
Cartland
Chandler
Childers
Christie
Constant
De la Mare
Disraeli
Faulkner
Fielding
Flaubert
Forester
Goncourt
Ishiguro
Kingsley
Langland
Lawrence
Mannheim
Meredith
Perrault
Plutarch
Proudhon
Rabelais
Rattigan
Remarque
Rousseau
Salinger
Schiller
Sillitoe
Smollett
Stendhal
Taffrail
Traherne
Trollope
Turgenev
Voltaire
Williams

9 letters:
Aeschylus
Ainsworth
Blackmore
Boccaccio
Burroughs
Cervantes
Corneille
Dos Passos
Du Maurier
Edgeworth
Goldsmith
Hawthorne
Hemingway
Isherwood
Lermontov
Linklater
Lovecraft
Mackenzie
Madariaga
Mansfield
Martineau
Oppenheim
Pasternak
Priestley
Santayana
Sholokhov
Steinbeck
Stevenson
Thackeray
Wodehouse

10 letters:
Ballantyne
Chesterton
Dostoevsky
Fitzgerald
Galsworthy
Mandeville
Maupassant
Richardson
Williamson

11 letters:
Machiavelli
Maeterlinck
Shakespeare

12 letters:
Aristophanes
Solzhenitsyn

13 letters:
Chateaubriand
Sackville-West

15 letters:
Somerset Maugham

Write-off Amortise, Annul, Cancel, Scrap
Writhe, Writhing Athetosis, Contort, Curl, Scriggle, Squirm, Thraw, Twist, Wriggle
▷ **Writhing** *may indicate* an anagram
Writing-case Kalamdan
Writing-room Scriptorium
Wrong(ful) Aggrieve, Agley, Amiss, Astray, Awry, Bad, Bum, Chout, Delict,
  Disservice, Err, Fallacious, False, Falsism, Harm, Ill, Immoral, Improper, Incorrect,
  Injury, Mischief, Misintelligence, Misled, Mistake(n), Misuse, Nocent, Offbase,
  Offend, Pear-shaped, Peccadillo, Perverse, Private, Public, Sin(ful), Tort, Tortious,
  Transgress, Unethical, Unright, Unsuitable, Withershins, Wryly, X
▷ **Wrong** *may indicate* an anagram
Wrong opinion Cacodoxy
Wrought (up) Agitated, Beaten, Carved, Created, Excited, Filigree, Freestone,
  Shaped
Wrung Twisted, Withers
Wry Askew, Contrary, Devious, Distort, Droll, Grimace, Ironic
Wryneck Iynx, Jynx, Torticollis, Yunx
Wycliffian Lollard
Wyoming Wy

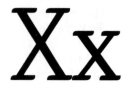

X(-shaped) Buss, By, Chi, Christ, Cross, Decussate, Drawn, Kiss, Ten, Times,
Unknown, X-ray
Xant(h)ippe Battle-axe, Dragon
Xenon Xe
Xerophyte, Xerophytic Cactus, Cereus, Mesquite, Tamaricaceae, Tamarisk
Xhosan Caffre, Kaf(f)ir
Ximenes Cardinal
▶ **Xmas** *see* **CHRISTMAS**
X-ray Angiogram, Anticathode, C(A)T-scanner, Cholangiography, Emi-Scanner,
Encephalogram, Encephalograph, Fermi, Grenz, Mammogram, Plate, Pyelogram,
Radioscopy, Rem, Roentgen, Sciagram, Screening, Skiagram, Tomography,
Venogram, Xeroradiography
Xylophone Marimba, Sticcado, Sticcato

Yy

Y Samian, Unknown, Yankee, Yard, Year, Yen, Yttrium
Yacht Britannia, Dragon, Ice, Keelboat, Ketch, Knockabout, Land, Maxi, Sailboat, Sand
Yachtsman, Yachtsmen Chichester, RYS
Yak Gup, Talk
Yale® Key, Lock
Yam Adjigo, Batata, Breadroot, Camote, Dioscorea, Diosgenin, Kumara
Yank(ee) Bet, Carpetbagger, Hitch, Jerk, Jonathan, Lug, Northerner, Pluck, Pull, Rug, Schlep(p), So(o)le, Sowl(e), → **TUG**, Tweak, Twitch, Wrench, Wrest
▷ **Yank** *may indicate* an anagram
Yap Bark, Yelp
Yard(s) Area, CID, Close, Court, Farm-toun, Garden, Hard, Haw, Hof, Junk, Kail, Knacker's, Main, Marshalling, Mast, Measure, Navy, Patio, Poultry, Prison, Ree(d), Sail, Scotland, Show, Spar, Sprit, Steel, Stick, Stride, Switch, Tilt, Timber, Victualling, Y, Yd
Yarn(s) Abb, Berlin, Bouclé, Caddice, Caddis, Chenille, Clew, Clue, Cop, Cord, Crewel, Fib, Fibroline, Fingering, Genappe, Gimp, Gingham, Guimp(e), Gymp, Homespun, Jaw, Knittle, Knot, Lay, Lea, Ley, Line, Lisle, Lurex®, Marl, Merino, Mohair, Nylon, Organzine, Orlon®, Ply, Rigmarole, Ripping, Rogue's, Rope, Saxony, Schappe, Sennit, Sinnet, Skein, Spun, Story, Strand, Tale, Taradiddle, Thread, Thrid, Thrum(my), Tram, Warp, Weft, Woof, Wool, Worsted, Zephyr
Yarrow Milfoil
Yashmak Veil
Yaw(s) Boba, Buba, Deviate, Framboesia, Lean, Morula, Tack, Veer
Yawn(ing) Boredom, Chasmy, Fissure, Gant, Gape, Gaunt, Greys, Hiant, Oscitation, Pandiculation, Rictus
Yea Certainly, Truly, Verily, Yes
Year(ly), Years A, Age, Anno, Annual, Anomalistic, Astronomical, Calendar, Canicular, Civil, Common, Cosmic, Decennium, Donkey's, Dot, Ecclesiastical, Egyptian, Embolismic, Equinoctial, Financial, Fiscal, Gap, Great, Hebrew, Holy, Indiction, Julian, Leap, Legal, Light, Lunar, Lunisolar, Natural, PA, Perfect, Platonic, Riper, Sabbatical, School, Sidereal, Solar, Sothic, Summer, Sun, Tax, Theban, Time, Towmon(d), Towmont, Tropical, Twelvemonth, Vintage, Wander
Yearbook Annual
Yearling Colt, Hogget, Stirk, Teg
Yearn(ing) Ache, Ake, Aspire, Brame, Burn, Covet, Crave, Curdle, Desire, Erne, Greed, Hanker, Hone, → **LONG**, Lust, Nostalgia, Pant, Pine, Sigh
▷ **Yearning** *may indicate* an anagram
Year's end Dec
Yeast Barm, Bees, Brewer's, Ferment, Flor, Leaven, Saccharomycete, Torula, Vegemite®

Yell Cry, Hue, Shout, Skelloch, Squall, Thunder, Tiger, Waul, Yoick

Yellow(ish) Abram, Amber, Anthoclore, Auburn, Back, Beige, Bisque, Bistre, Buff, Butternut, Cadmium, Canary, Chicken, Chrome, Citrine, Cowardly, Craven, Curcumin(e), Daffadowndilly, Daffodil, Eggshell, Etiolin, Fallow, Fever, Filemot, Flavescent, Flavin(e), Flavon, Flaxen, Fulvous, Gamboge, Gold, Icteric, Isabel(le), Isabella, Jack, Jaundiced, King's, Lammer, Lemon(y), Lupulin, Lurid, Lutein, Luteous, Lutescent, Mustard, Nankeen, Naples, Oaker, Ochery, Ochre(y), Or(eide), Oroide, Pages, Peril, Pink, Primrose, Queen's, River, Saffron, Sallow, Sand, Sear, Sherry, Spineless, Straw, Sulphur, Tawny, Topaz, Tow, Vitelline, Weld, Xanthous, Yolk

Yellowhammer Bunting, Yeldring, Yeldrock, Yite, Yoldring

Yellow-wood Gopher

Yelp Cry, Squeal, Whee, Ya(w)p

Yemeni Adeni, Saba, Sabean, Sheba

Yen Desire, Itch, Longing, Urge, Y, Yearn

Yeoman Beefeater, Exon, Goodman, Goodwife, Salvation

Yep OK, Yes

Yes Ay(e), Da, Indeed, Ja, Jokol, Nod, OK, Oke, Quite, Sure, Truly, Uh-huh, Wilco, Yea, Yokul, Yup

Yesterday Démodé, Eve, Hesternal, Pridian

Yet But, Even, How-be, Moreover, Nay, Nevertheless, Now, Still, Though

Yeti Abominable snowman, Sasquatch

Yew Podocarp(us), Taxus

Yibbles A(i)blins

Yield(ing), Yielded Abandon, Afford, Bend, Bow, Breed, Capitulate, Catch, Cede, Come, Comply, Concede, Crack, Crop, Defer, Dividend, Docile, Ductile, Easy, Elastic, Exert, Facile, Flaccid, Flexible, Give, Harvest, Interest, Knuckle, Knuckle under, Meek, Meltith, Mess, Output, Pan, Pay, Pliant, Produce, Quantum, Redemption, Relent, Render, Return, Sag, Soft, → **SUBMIT**, Succumb, Surrender, Susceptible, Sustained, Temporise, Truckle, Weak-kneed, Yold

Yodel Song, Warble

Yoga, Yogi As(h)tanga, Bear, Bhakti, Fakir, Hatha, Maha, Power, Raja, Sid(d)ha, Sivananda

Yog(h)urt Dahi, Madzoon, Matzoon, Tzatziki

Yoke Bow, Cang(ue), Collar, Couple, Harness, Inspan, Jugal, Oxbow, Pair, Span, Square, Tucker

Yokel Boor, Bumpkin, Chaw(-bacon), Clumperton, Culchie, Hayseed, Hick, Jake, Jock, Peasant, Rustic

Yolk Parablast, Vitellicle, Vitellus, Yelk, Yellow

Yon(der) Distant, Further, O'erby, Thae, There, Thether, Thither

Yore Agone, Olden, Past

Yorick Sterne

York(shire), Yorkshireman Batter, Bowl, Ebor, Pudding, Ridings, Tyke

Yorker Tice

You One, Sie, Thee, Thou, Usted, Wena, Ye

Young (person), Youngster, Youth(ful) Adolescent, Ageless, Amorino, Bev(an), Bodgie, Boy, Boyhood, Brigham, Bub, Buckie, Buppie, Calf-time, Ch, Charver, Chick, Chicken, Chiel, Child, Chile, Cion, Cockerel, Cockle, Colt, Comsomol, Cornstalk, Cub, Day-old, Dell, Dilling, DJ, Early, Ephebe, Ephebus, Esquire, Flapper, Fledgling, Foetus, Fox, Fry, Gigolo, Gilded, Gillet, Girl, Gunsel, Halfling, Hebe, Hobbledehoy, Immature, Imp, Infant, Issue, Jeunesse d'orée, Junior, Juvenal, Juvenesce, Juvenile,

Keral, Kid, Kiddo, Kiddy, Kipper, Knave-bairn, Komsomol, Lad, Lamb, Latter-day, Leaping-time, Less, Litter, Little, Loretta, Middle, Minor, Misspent, Mod, Mormon, Mot, Nance, Neanic, Ned(ette), Neophyte, Nestling, New, New Romantic, Nipper, Nurs(e)ling, Nymph, Plant, Popsy, (Pre-)pubescent, Progeny, Protégé(e), Punk, Pup, Sapling, Scent, Scion, Shaveling, Shaver, Sien(t), Skinhead, Slip, Son, Spawn, Sprig, Springal(d), Stripling, Subteen, Swain, Syen, Ted, Teenager, Teens, Teenybopper, Toyboy, Vernal, Well-preserved, Whelp, Whippersnapper, Widge, Wigga, Wigger, Yippy, Yoof, Yopper, Younker, Yumpie, Yuppie

Younger, Youngest Baby, Benjamin, Cadet, Last born, Less, Minimus, Seneca, Wallydrag, Wallydraigle, Yr

Your(s) Thee, Thine, Thy

▶ **Youth** *see* **YOUNG PERSON**

Yo-yo Bandalore

Ytterbium Yb

Yttrium Y

Yucatan Maya

Yucca Adam's needle

Yucky Gooey, Grooly, Sickly, Sticky

Yugoslav Croat(ian), Serb, Slovene, Ustashi

Yukon YT

Yuletide Advent, Dec, Noel, Xmas

Zz

Z Izzard, Izzet, Zambia, Zebra
Zamenhof Esperanto
Zander Fogash, Sander
Zany Bor(r)el, Comic, Cuckoo, Idiotic, Mad, Offbeat
Zanzibar Swahili
Zeal(ous) Ardour, Bigotry, Devotion, Eager, Enthusiasm, Evangelic, Fervour, Fire, Hamas, Perfervid, Study
Zealot Bigot, Devotee, Fan(atic), St Simon, Votary
Zebra Convict, Quagga
Zenith Acme, Apogee, Height, Pole, Summit, Vertex
Zeno Colonnade, Elea, Stoic
Zeolite Analcime, Analcite, Gmelinite
Zephyr Breeze, Wind
Zeppelin Airship, Balloon, Dirigible
Zero Absolute, Blob, Cipher, Circle, Donut, Double, Ground, Nil, Nothing, Nought, O, Status, Year, Z
Zest Condiment, Crave, Élan, Enthusiasm, Gusto, Pep, Piquancy, Relish, Spark, Spice, Tang, Zap, Zing
Ziegfeld Flo
Zigzag Crémaillère, Crinkle-crankle, Dancette, Feather-stitch, Indent, Major Mitchell, Ric-rac, Slalom, Stagger, Switchback, Tack, Traverse, Vandyke, Yaw
Zinc Blende, Gahnite, Mossy, Sherardise, Spelter, Sphalerite, Tutenag, Tutty, Willemite, Wurtzite, Zn
Zip(per) Dash, Energy, Fastener, Fly, Go, O, Oomph, Presto, Side fastener, Stingo, Vim, Vivacity, Whirry, Zero
Zircon Hyacinth, Jacinth, Jargo(o)n
Zirconium Baddeleyite, Zr
Zither Autoharp, Cithara, Kantela, Kantele, Koto
Zodiac(al) Aquarius, Archer, Aries, Bull, Cancer, Capricorn, Counter-glow, Crab, Fish, Gegenschein, Gemini, Goat, Horoscope, Leo, Libra, Lion, Ophiuchus, Pisces, Ram, Sagittarius, Scales, Scorpio(n), Taurus, Twins, Virgin, Virgo, Watercarrier
Zola Budd, Emile, Nana, Realism
Zombie Catatonic, Dolt, Robot
Zone(s) Abyssal, Anacoustic, Area, Arid, Auroral, Band, Bathyal, Belt, Benioff, Buffer, Canal, Climate, Collision, Comfort, Convergence, Crumple, Drop, Economic, Ecotone, End, Enterprise, Erogenous, Euro, Exclusion, F layer, Fracture, Free, Fresnel, Frigid, Hadal, Home, Hot, Impact, Ionopause, Krumhole, Low velocity, Neutral, No-fly, Nuclear-free, Precinct, → **REGION**, Rift, Ring, Russian, Sahel, Sector, Shear, Skip, Smokeless, Soviet, Stratopause, Strike, Subduction, T, Temperate, Time, Tolerance, Torrid, Tundra, Twilight
Zoo Bedlam, Circus, Menagerie, Vivarium, Whipsnade

Zoologist, Zoology Biologist, Botanist, Cetology, Naturalist, Primatology

Zoom Close-up, Speed

Zoroastrian Gabar, Gheber, Ghebre, Gueber, Guebre, Magus, Mazdaist, Mazdean, Ormazd, Ormuzd, Parsee, Parsi

Zulu Chaka, Impi, Inkatha, Matabele, Niger, Shaka, Warrior

Zut Crimini